Textbook of Geriatric Medicine and Gerontology

Textbook of Geriatric Medicine and Gerontology

EDITED BY

J. C. Brocklehurst
MSc MD FRCP
Professor of Geriatric Medicine,
University of Manchester

THIRD EDITION

CHURCHILL LIVINGSTONE
EDINBURGH LONDON MELBOURNE AND NEW YORK 1985

CHURCHILL LIVINGSTONE
Medical Division of Longman Group Limited

Distributed in the United States of America by Churchill
Livingstone Inc., 1560 Broadway, New York,
N.Y. 10036, and by associated companies, branches and
representatives throughout the world.

First Edition 1973
Second Edition 1978
Third Edition 1985

ISBN 0 443 02696 3

British Library Cataloguing in Publication Data
Textbook of geriatric medicine and gerontology.
— 3rd ed.
1. Geriatrics
I. Brocklehurst, J.C.
618.97   RC952

Library of Congress Cataloguing in Publication Data
Main entry under title:
Textbook of geriatric medicine and gerontology.
Includes index.
1. Geriatrics. 2. Gerontology. I. Brocklehurst,
J. C. (John C.) [DNLM; 1. Aging. 2. Geriatrics. WT
100 T355
RC952.T45   1985   618.97   83–27277

Printed in Hong Kong
by Mandarin Offset Printing Ltd

Preface

Each year the number of physicians involved in the medicine of old age increases. In part this reflects the increasing proportion of world wide population now achieving old age: in part it reflects old people's increasing awareness of the help and benefit that medicine can afford them: and in part, it reflects advances in medical knowledge and attitudes. The specialty of geriatric medicine, developing in Great Britain since 1948, now comprises 500 consultants (a similar number to paediatrics). In Commonwealth countries and in much of Europe the specialty is well founded and is gaining recognition through special qualifications and accreditation. In the United States of America it has achieved recognition as an academic discipline — to be taught to medical students and to be researched — and this is a major development in the past 5 years. On the wider fronts of medicine and surgery, specialists and family practitioners alike are becoming better informed and more adept in dealing with the complex problems of medicine in old age.

Gerontology, the application of fundamental science to the processes of aging, continues to grow in stature, particularly in the United States of America. It is as important for clinicians dealing with the elderly to understand something of the physiology of aging as it is for paediatricians to understand the physiology of growth and development.

Advances in gerontology and in geriatric medicine are reflected by structural developments in care systems for the old — social, medical and nursing. Practitioners in the medicine of old age must be aware of (and contribute towards) these developments.

This textbook therefore in its first edition in 1973 was presented in three main sections — gerontology, geriatric medicine and services for the old. These sections have been retained in this third edition and all of them further developed. This third edition has also set out to be more comprehensive — dealing as far as possible, with all the medical aspects of old age and not just with those that find no place in textbooks of medicine. The opportunity has also been taken to widen the relevance of the book to geriatric developments in the United States.

All the chapters have been revised and updated and many of them rewritten. New authors or new joint authors have been introduced as follows: Dr C. M. Cheshire, Dr K. Cumming, Dr Margaret Dobson, Dr Anne Kilvert, Dr P. Lewis, Prof M. D. W. Lye, Dr Patricia O'Connor, Dr J. W. Rowe, Dr J. Vallery-Masson and Dr B. Williams.

A number of entirely new chapters have been added in an attempt to achieve comprehensive coverage. These include the immunology of aging (Professor Roy Fox); the psychology of aging (Professor H. Thomae and Dr James Fozard); the pharmacology of aging (Dr D. Robertson); neurochemistry of the aging brain and dementia (Dr M. Rossor); the dementias (Dr L. Jarvik and Dr R. Neshkes); aging and the prostate (Professor N. J. Blacklock); care of the aged in the United States (Dr R. Butler); a psychogeriatric service (Professor T. Arie); and rehabilitation (Dr K. Andrews).

In a work of this magnitude acknowledgements and thanks are due to many people. Where illustrations have been taken from other publications acknowledgement is made in the text. Thanks are due to Medical Illustration Departments in many institutions in Great Britain and in North America and likewise manuscript preparation to many secretaries. In particular the hard task of editing has been much lightened by the excellent secretarial support of Susan Williamson and May Hudson. Churchill Livingstone have once again demonstrated their preeminence in the field of medical publishing. Finally, I must acknowledge in gratitude the ready response of the many authors involved — who have so excellently made their scholarship available to those who use this book.

Manchester, 1985   J. C. Brocklehurst

Contributors

J. N. Agate CBE MA MD FRCP
Lately, Consultant Physician,
Department of Geriatrics,
The Ipswich Hospital

K. Andrews MD MRCP
Consultant Geriatrician,
University Hospital of South Manchester;
Honorary Lecturer,
Department of Geriatric Medicine,
University of Manchester

T. H. D. Arie MA BM FRCPsych FFCM FRCP
Professor of Health Care of the Elderly,
University of Nottingham

A. Bigot PhD
Consultant in Gerontological,
Health Care, and Nutrition Services
for Older Adults
Fort Worth, Texas

N. J. Blacklock MVO OBE MSc MB FRCS
Professor of Urology,
University of Manchester

F. Bourlière MD DSc
Professor emeritus, Faculty of Medicine
University of Paris

J. C. Brocklehurst MSc MD FRCP
Professor of Geriatric Medicine,
University of Manchester

A. D. G. Brown MB ChB FRCOG
Consultant Obstetrician & Gynaecologist,
Eastern General Hospital,
Edinburgh; Honorary Senior Lecturer, Department of
Obstetrics and Gynaecology, University of Edinburgh

R. N. Butler MD
Professor and Head,
Department of Geriatrics,
Mount Sinai Medical Center,
New York

F. I. Caird DM FRCP
David Cargill Professor of Geriatric Medicine,
University of Glasgow

D. Charlesworth DSc MD FRCS
Reader in Surgery,
University of Manchester;
Consultant Surgeon,
University Hospital of South Manchester

C. M. Cheshire BSc MRCP
Consultant Physician in Geriatric Medicine,
Manchester Royal Infirmary; Honorary Associate
Lecturer in Geriatric Medicine; University of
Manchester

W. J. K. Cumming BSc MD FRCP
Consultant Neurologist,
University Hospital of South Manchester

J. L. C. Dall MD FRCP (Glas.)
Consultant Physician in Geriatric Medicine, Victoria
Infirmary, Glasgow; Honorary Clinical Lecturer in
Geriatric Medicine, University of Glasgow Visiting
Professor in Geriatric Medicine, University of Ottawa,
Canada

I. Davies PhD MIBiol
Research Fellow and Associate Director,
Geigy Unit for Research in Aging,
Department of Geriatric Medicine,
University of Manchester

W. Davison TD MA MB ChB FRCP (Edin.)

Consultant Physician in Geriatric Medicine,
Addenbrooke's Hospital, Cambridge

A. D. Dayan MD MRCP FRCPath

Adviser in Toxicology, Wellcome Research
Laboratories,
Beckenham

M. E. Dodson MD FFARCS

Consultant Anaesthetist,
Royal Liverpool Hospital,
Liverpool

J. V. G. A. Durnin MA MB ChB DSc FRCP (Glas.)
FRSE

Professor of Physiology, University of Glasgow

I. W. Dymock MB MRCP (Edin.), MRCP (Glas.)

Consultant Physician and Gastroenterologist,
Stepping Hill Hospital,
Stockport

A. N. Exton-Smith CBE MA MD FRCP

Barlow Professor of Geriatric Medicine,
University College Hospital,
London

L. Fisch MD DLO

Hon. Audiological Physician,
Royal National Throat, Nose and Ear Hospital
London

M. G. FitzGerald MD FRCP

Consultant Physician,
The General Hospital,
Birmingham;
Clinical Lecturer in Medicine,
University of Birmingham

R. A. Fox BSc MD FRCP FACP FRCP (C)

formerly Professor of Geriatric Medicine, University of
Manchester; Professor of Medicine, Dalhousie
University and Consultant Geriatrician to the Teaching
Hospitals, Halifax, Nova Scotia

J. L. Fozard PhD

Director,
Patient Treatment Service,
Office of Geriatrics & Extended Care,
Veterans Administration,
Washington

E. Freeman FRCP

Consultant Geriatrician,
University Hospital of South Manchester;
Honorary Lecturer,
Department of Geriatric Medicine,
University of Manchester

D. L. Gardner MD PhD FRCP, FRCP (Edin.)
FRCPath

Professor of Histopathology,
University of Manchester

R. Grahame MD FRCP

Consultant Rheumatologist,
Guy's Hospital,
London;
Honorary Lecturer,
Department of Medicine,
Guy's Hospital Medical School

D. A. Hall BSc PhD DSc

Life Fellow,
University of Leeds

M. R. P. Hall MA DM FRCP (Lond. & Edin.)

Professor of Geriatric Medicine,
University of Southampton

H. M. Hodkinson MA BM FRCP

Professor of Geriatric Medicine
Royal Postgraduate Medical School,
London

D. E. Hyams MB BS FRCP

Senior Director,
Medical and Scientific Affairs,
Merck, Sharp & Dohme International,
Rahway,
New Jersey

R. E. Irvine CBE MA MD FRCP

Consultant Physician,
Department of Medicine for the Elderly,
Hastings

B. Isaacs MD FRCP (Glas. & Edin)

Charles Hayward Professor of
Geriatric Medicine, University of Birmingham

L. F. Jarvik MD PhD

Professor, UCLA Neuropsychiatric Institute; Chief,
Psychogeriatric Unit, West Los Angeles VA Medical
Center, Brentwood Division, Los Angeles

M. Jefferys BSc Econ
Emeritus Professor of Medical Sociology,
University of London

A. Kilvert BSc MB BS MRCP
Medical Registrar,
The General Hospital,
Birmingham

D. A. Leighton MD FRCS
Consultant Ophthalmologist,
St Helens Hospital,
St Helens

P. D. Lewis DSc MD MRCP FRCPath
Reader in Histopathology,
Royal Postgraduate Medical School,
London

M. D. W. Lye MD MRCP
Professor of Geriatric Medicine, University of
Liverpool

A. L. Macmillan BSc MA MRCP
Consultant Dermatologist,
Southend Hospital,
Essex

J. M. A. Munnichs PhD
Professor of Psychogerontology, Department of Social
Gerontology, University of Nijmegen, Nijmegen

R. E. Neshkes MD
Assistant Professor of Psychiatry, University of
California, Los Angeles, School of Medicine; Chief,
Geropsychiatry Treatment unit, West Los Angeles VA
Medical Centre, Los Angeles

P. O'Connor PhD
Research Fellow,
Department of Histopathology,
University of Manchester

J. Parkhouse MA MD MSc FFARCS
Postgraduate Dean and Director of the Regional
Postgraduate Institute for Medicine and Dentistry,
University of Newcastle upon Tyne

M. S. J. Pathy FRCP (Lond. and Edin.)
Professor of Geriatric Medicine,
Welsh National School of Medicine, University of
Wales; Cardiff

F. Post MD FRCP FRCPsych
Consultant Psychiatrist,
London

D. Robertson MB BS FRCP (Edin.) FRCP(C) FACP
Professor and Head,
Division of Geriatric Medicine,
University of Saskatchewan,
Saskatoon,
Canada

M. N. Rossor MA MB BChir MRCP
Senior Registar, Department of Neurology King's
College Hospital, London

J. W. Rowe MD
Associate Professor of Medicine and Director,
Division of Aging,
Harvard Medical School,
Boston

L. B. Sourander MD
Assistant Chief Physician,
City Hospital of Turka,
Tuureporinkatu,
Finland

J. M. K. Spalding DM FRCP
Consulting Neurologist, Oxford

R. Storer MSc FDSRCS DRDRCS
Dean of Dentistry,
University of Newcastle-upon-Tyne

H. Thomae MD
Director, Institute of Psychology,
University of Bonn

J. Vallery-Masson MD
Epidemiologist, INSERM, Paris

K. W. Walton MD DSc PhD MRCS LRCP FRCPath
Professor of Experimental Pathology and Director,
Rheumatism Research Wing,
University of Birmingham;
Honorary Consultant Pathologist,
United Birmingham Hospitals and
Birmingham Regional Hospital Board

S. G. P. Webster MA MB MRCP
Consultant Physician in General and Geriatric Medicine,
Cambridge District Hospitals; Associate Lecturer,
Department of Medicine, University of Cambridge

B. O. Williams MB ChB FRCP (Glas.)
Senior Lecturer,
Department of Geriatric Medicine,
University of Glasgow

J. Williamson MB ChB FRCP (Edin.)
Professor of Geriatric Medicine,
University of Edinburgh

L. Wollner MB FRCP
Consultant Physician, Department of Geriatric
Medicine, Radcliffe Infirmary, Oxford

Contents

PART ONE

Human Aging

Epidemiology and ecology of aging

The prospects of a happy retirement at 60 or 65 years of age, and of a healthy old age afterwards, are still the privilege of the citizens of a small number of industrial nations. Europe is the continent in which the number of aged people is the largest. As shown in Table 1.1, there are now 22.2 per cent of people over 60 years of age in Sweden, as against 15.7 per cent in the United States and 12.5 per cent in Japan. By contrast, the percentage of people over 60 is very low in all developing countries of the Eastern and Western hemispheres. For instance, it reaches only 5.7 per cent in Egypt and 5.3 per cent in both Brazil and India. Old people are even less numerous in most of the poorer countries of the tropical and subtropical world. According to the 1982 edition of the UN World Population Data Sheet, the percentage of people aged 65 and over ranges from 6 per cent in continental China to 1.5 per cent in Mali. For about 10 countries of Africa, Asia and Central America, including Indonesia and Nigeria, this percentage varies from 2.5 to 1.5 per cent only.

Table 1.1 Percentages of the population 60 and 65 years of age and over in 19 countries (1979–1981)

	60 and over	65 and over
Sweden	22.2	16.4
Norway	20.1	14.7
United Kingdom	19.7	14.7
Denmark	19.5	14.4
Western Germany	19.2	15.6
Austria	19.2	15.5
Switzerland	18.2	13.8
Belgium	18.1	14.2
Luxemburg	17.6	13.5
France	17.4	13.9
Italy	17.4	13.5
Greece	17.4	13.0
USA	15.7	11.3
Netherlands	15.6	11.5
Spain	15.1	10.9
Ireland	14.8	10.7
Japan	12.5	8.7
Egypt	5.7	3.6
Brazil	5.3	3.3
India	5.3	3.1

THE DEMOGRAPHIC AGING OF INDUSTRALIZED COUNTRIES

The increase of the elderly segment of the population is a relatively new phenomenon in Euro-American industrial societies. For instance, Coulbert (1982) considers that no more than 6 to 7 per cent of the rural population of France was over 60 years of age in the seventeenth century as compared to 18 per cent in 1982. This percentage was probably even lower in the largest cities of the time, where the expectation of life was very low due to poor sanitary conditions. Even if we discard John Graunt's (1662) figures for the City of London, the estimates given by Halley (1693) for Breslau, Mourgue (1785) for Montpellier, Duvillard (1806) for Geneva and a number of Parisian parishes, all indicate that the prospects of reaching their sixties or seventies were very low indeed for the citizens of the above mentioned cities. The fragmentary life table for part of Philadelphia published by Barton (1793) confirms this point of view. We can therefore concur with the opinion of Dublin et al (1942) and Dupaquier (1979) according to whom the expectation of life at birth of the most technically advanced european countries at the end of the eighteenth century must have been about 35 to 40 years.

The situation remained more or less the same for the first half of the nineteenth century, as shown in Table 1.2 for three European countries for which we have an extended series of life tables. It was mostly during the second half of the century that the expectation of life at birth began to increase regularly, the gain for the most privileged countries being of the order of 10 years or slightly more. However, in the meantime, the gain of expectation of life at 60 years of age was much more modest, almost nil in England and France, and of about 3 years in Sweden. This same trend towards a regular increase in expectation of life at birth has continued during the twentieth century in industrialized countries (Table 1.2). The gain in average length of life ranging from 21.4 to 25.9 years for males, and from 24.7 to 30.0 years for females, in the three countries concerned.

Table 1.2 Expectation of life at birth and at 60 years of age in various industralized countries during the past 150 years

	Expectation of life at birth		Expectation of life at 60 years of age	
	males	females	males	females
England and Wales				
1838–1854	39.9	41.8	13.5	14.3
1891–1900	44.1	47.7	12.9	14.1
1937	60.1	64.4	14.3	16.4
1974–1978	70.0	76.2	15.8	20.4
France				
1805–1807	35.3	38.0	13.0	13.3
1840–1842	39.1	40.1	13.8	14.1
1900–1902	45.1	48.3	13.0	14.2
1947–1950	61.8	67.5	15.2	17.9
1979	70.1	78.3	17.2	22.3
Sweden				
1816–1840	39.5	43.5	12.0	13.2
1891–1900	50.9	53.6	15.4	16.5
1936–1940	64.3	66.9	16.3	17.1
1975–1979	72.3	78.3	17.6	21.7

Of course, such an increase in average life span was, for the most part, due to a drastic reduction of infantile and juvenile mortality, as shown in Figure 1.1, the reduction in adult and old age mortality being far less spectacular. Whereas the maximum life span of our own species has not changed since recorded history and remains at about 100 years, an increasingly larger number of people now survives to this genetically fixed

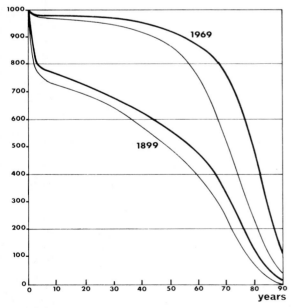

Fig. 1.1 Changes in mortality rates of the population of France between 1899 and 1969. During this 70 year period the survival curves of males (thin lines) and females (heavy lines) became more and more rectangular.

life span. The much smaller gains in life expectancy at 60 years of age shown in Table 1.2 clearly emphasize the fact that modern medicine has been far less successful in controlling the degenerative age-associated diseases than the infectious ones. This is still the case now, despite the large amount of money invested in biomedical research by many governments. In a country such as the United States, the gain in life expectation at ages 65 and 75 from 1900 to 1950 was respectively of 1.9 and 1.3 years; from 1950 to 1974 it has been of 1.8 and 1.4 years only.

It has long been established that men have on average a higher mortality rate than women in most populations, the difference varying in magnitude however from one country to another. Such a trend persists in present day industrialized societies and even becomes more marked in older age groups, as apparent in Figure 1.2 which compares the survival curves of the population of six Euro-American countries and Japan during 1977–1978. In France, for instance, the average difference in life expectation at age 60 between men and women was only 1.2 years in 1900; it now exceeds 5 years (Fig. 1.3). The cross-national comparison of trends in mortality rates among elderly people over 65 years of age, undertaken by Myers (1978) in 10 industrialized countries, also provides evidence of a continued strong mortality decline of death rates for females. In males, however, the decline is substantially smaller at each age level. In countries such as the Netherlands and Norway, the mortality rate of men has even increased between 65 and 79 years of age, between 1950 and 1975.

The causes of such an excess mortality in elderly males are far from clear. Alcoholism, psycho-social stresses, poor adaptation to new working conditions, and early compulsory retirement have all been suspected without convincing evidence; the phenomenon is quite likely multifactorial. It remains to be seen whether the increasing percentage of women at work, and the adoption of more masculine roles by professional women, will modify this new trend in differential aging during the next few decades.

Another unexpected trend in mortality changes with age has also occurred since the late 1960s, at least in the most privileged countries: the decline in mortality of the extreme aged. This was already apparent in the survival tables of four European countries published by Despoids (1973), but the magnitude of the phenomenon has recently been demonstrated in the United States by Rosenwaike et al (1980). Up to the middle of the present century the downward trend in mortality showed a close association with age: in general, the younger the age group, the greater the rate of decline. For instance, between 1933 and 1966, the death rate among the US citizens aged 85 and over declined only 10 per cent. In

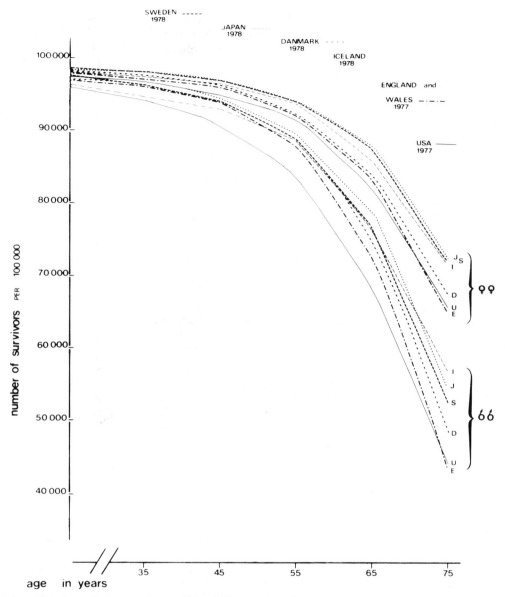

Fig. 1.2 Male and female survival curves, between 25 and 75 years of age, in six industrialized countries, 1977–1978

contrast, between 1966 and 1977 this secular pattern was reversed and a 26 per cent decline in mortality rate occured among persons 85 years and over (Table 1.3). The decline was slightly more marked in females than in males, and it occurred among non-whites as well as among whites. This sharp downturn in mortality rate of the extreme aged might be the result of a substantial reduction in the risk of dying from heart and cerebro-vascular diseases, and also of the positive developments

in emergency, acute, and long-term care for patients with coronary heart disease and stroke, according to Rosenwaike et al (1980); this is quite possible. However, it must not be forgotten that studies of death rates are but one means of appraising the conditions of life of the elderly; they tell us nothing about the quality of life of those surviving. Could not an increased number of in-capacitated and bed-ridden persons be a likely counter-part of the reduced mortality rate of the extreme aged?

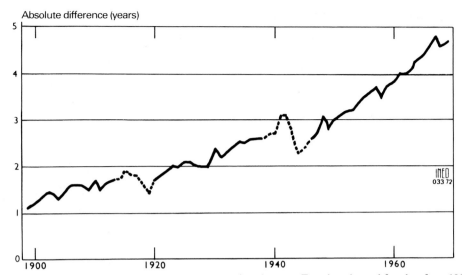

Fig. 1.3 The increasing difference of life expectancy at 60 years of age between French males and females, from 1900 to 1970 (after Vallin, 1973)

Table 1.3 Percentage change in death rates among population in age groups 25 years and over, by sex: United States, 1933 to 1966 and 1966 to 1977. (From Rosenwaike et al, 1980).

Sex and Years	25–34	35–44	45–54	Age 55–64	65–74	75–84	85+
Total							
1933–1966	−63.4	−50.0	−34.2	−27.2	−24.5	−25.0	−10.1
1966–1977	−6.7	−19.4	−17.3	−15.4	−17.3	−14.0	−26.3
Male							
1933–1966	−53.5	−42.6	−23.3	−10.8	−7.6	−14.1	−5.4
1966–1977	−5.0	−17.9	−18.2	−16.4	−14.5	−7.7	−21.4
Female							
1933–1966	−71.8	−58.2	−45.9	−44.8	−39.1	−32.4	−12.1
1966–1977	−27.3	−21.7	−17.0	−10.8	−20.4	−17.4	−28.2

EPIDEMIOLOGY OF AGING IN INDUSTRIALIZED SOCIETIES

It is not an easy matter to discover the respective roles of physiological aging and of age-associated diseases in the increase of the mortality rate which characterizes population aging in all living organisms. By physiological aging one means the progressive decline in functional performance of most bodily functions and control mechanisms, and the resulting loss of adaptation to life stresses so characteristic of old age in all human populations so far studied. By age-associated diseases, on the contrary, is meant those illnesses whose incidence generally increases regularly with age, but whose prevalence rates greatly vary from one population to another to become almost negligible in some rare instances as shown later in this chapter. Do these so-called 'degenerative' diseases represent cases of premature or accel-

erated aging in response to peculiar genetic or environmental factors (or both !), or do they represent the specific reaction of the aging organism to some particular stimulus? We still do not know the answer, but in any case it is compulsory firstly to evaluate the impact of the better known age-associated diseases in our populations, if only for public health motives.

To achieve this goal we can either use mortality or morbidity data. To begin with disease-specific mortality we can take advantage of the most reliable general estimates provided by the census bureaux or social security services of the most advanced countries. However one must remain aware of the inherent bias of mortality and morbidity estimates based on the general population, as far as elderly persons are concerned. There are two major reasons for the low reliability of many available statistics. First of all, the recording of the actual cause of death must be as accurate and complete as possible.

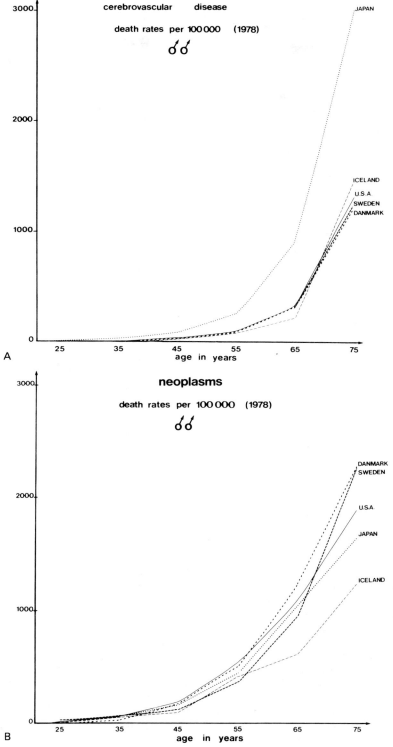

Fig. 1.4 Death rates of males from cerebrosvascular diseases (A) and cancer (B) in five industralized countries during 1978

By complete, epidemiologists mean not only that all actual deaths are recorded, but also that assigned causes are shifted from vague and ambiguous categories such as 'senility' to ones that are as explicit as possible (McMahon et al, 1960). Secondly, accuracy and completeness in death registration is made more difficult in elderly subjects than in younger ones by the frequent difficulty of distinguishing proximate (or underlying) and ultimate (or contributory) causes of death in many old patients, even during a post-mortem examination. Pathologists have emphasized, long since, the multiplicity of degenerative lesions developing silently in otherwise 'clinically healthy' old people. It is now widely recognized that multiple lesions increase in frequency with advancing age (Howell, 1963a, b; Ishii et al, 1980). In the United States, at age 75 and over, respectively 69.2 per cent of white male and 72.7 per cent of white female deaths have more than a single cause of death listed on the death certificate (Manton, 1980). Such a multiple pathology does not facilitate the task of medical statisticians. National mortality statistics must therefore be interpreted with caution.

DISEASE-SPECIFIC MORTALITY IN THE ELDERLY

In all industrialized societies the major causes of death in the elderly are presently the cardiovascular diseases (ischaemic heart disease, cerebrovascular diseases and stroke included). Cancer and infectious diseases are nowadays far less important than they were 50 years ago and earlier. There are important differences between countries, however, as exemplified by Figure 1.4a and b, which show the increase with age of the death rates of males for cerebrovascular disease and cancer, in four Euro-American countries and Japan during 1978. Of course, such cross-national comparisons are always delicate and sometimes tricky exercises, as the level and quality of medical care can differ a great deal from one country to another, misreporting can affect differentially the various age groups, and some populations may be 'racially' more heterogeneous than others. However, the major differences displayed by the graphs cannot be accounted for only by such differences and methodological biases. The entirely different approach taken by pathologists comparing the results of their post-mortem investigations (Fig. 1.5) leads to very similar conclusions: whereas the mortality rates of the major 'degenerative' diseases change everywhere with age, following a similar pattern, significant differences do occur between countries, even between those having reached a comparable level of industrial development. Some of the possible causes of these mortality differentials will be discussed later in this chapter.

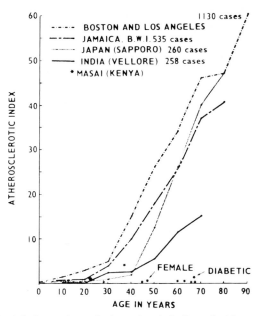

Fig. 1.5 Comparison of atherosclerotic indices of white-American, black American, Japanese, Indian and Masai populations (after Ho et al, 1971)

The study of disease-specific mortality rates can also disclose unexpected differences between the major 'racial' components of a given national population. This is the case for whites and blacks in the United States (Manton et al, 1979; Manton, 1980). Studying the five disease categories which accounted for 64 per cent of all white and black deaths in 1969, Manton describes what he calls the 'black/white mortality crossover' (Figs. 1.6 and 1.7). In other words, black mortality rates drop below white mortality rates at about age 75. Manton then convincingly demonstrates that this crossover does not result from enumeration errors or age misreporting differentially affecting whites and blacks. More likely this crossover is the result of the differential early mortality which selects the least robust persons from the disadvantaged population at relatively earlier age so that, at advanced ages, the disadvantaged population has proportionately more robust persons. In the present example, the larger population of whites survive to advanced ages because of better living conditions, better medical treatment and management of the chronic effect of disease; on the other hand, blacks are less likely to survive a disease event at earlier ages, so that they would have a *proportionately* lower prevalence of chronic conditions at advanced ages. This is, after all, only an extreme case of a very general situation: biological selection operates throughout the individual life span in all populations, those individuals who survive to an extreme age have a good chance of representing the fittest members of their cohort.

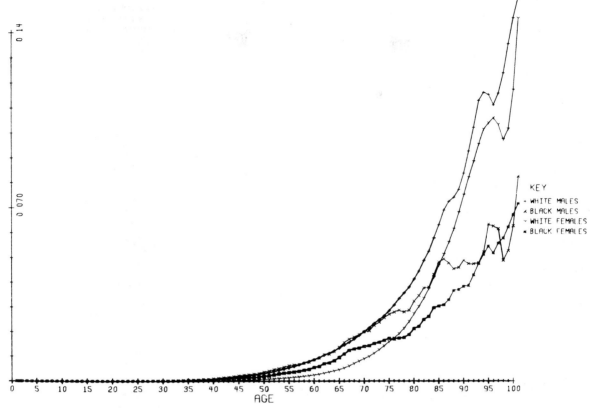

Fig. 1.6 Net probability of death from ischaemic heart disease in white and black north Americans, during 1969 (after Manton, 1980)

The evaluation of disease-specific mortality rates has moreover another practical advantage, especially for those responsible for public health policies, that of detecting short term changes in mortality rates. This has been the case for the mortality resulting from *all* cardiovascular diseases since the mid-1960s in the United States. Stern (1979) has recently reviewed the situation, focusing on ischaemic heart disease mortality. His figures show that this mortality has declined markedly from 1968 to 1976 in both sexes, all age-groups and in the three major race/ethnic categories concerned (Table 1.4). The decline for the extreme aged (85 and older) is particularly noticeable; in that case it can only be due to improved medical care and better treatment of hypertension, and not to primary prevention.

A similar time trend is also apparent for cerebrovas-

Table 1.4 Decline (%) in ischaemic heart disease mortality from 1968 to 1976 by age, sex and race in the United States. (From Stern 1969).

Age (years)	White			Non white and Spanish-surnamed persons		
	Both Sexes	Male	Female	Both Sexes	Male	Female
25–34	−25.0	−23.2	−36.4	−44.1	−39.1	−53.3
35–44	−26.6	−26.6	−28.2	−40.4	−33.1	−51.7
45–54	−20.8	−21.1	−19.6	−26.7	−22.3	−33.5
55–64	−20.4	−20.4	−20.1	−25.9	−20.4	−32.4
65–74	−22.9	−19.9	−26.8	−25.2	−22.5	−27.8
75–84	−16.2	−12.6	−17.6	−12.1	−11.2	−12.7
85 and older	−19.8	−17.1	−20.6	−30.2	−29.9	−29.5

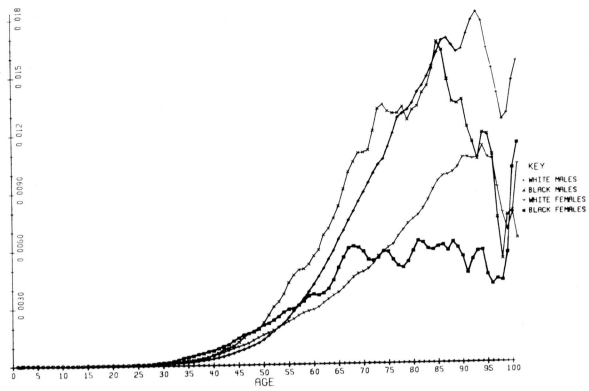

Fig. 1.7 Net probability of death from cancer in white and black north Americans, during 1969 (after Manton, 1980)

cular mortality. Sigurjonsson (1974) had already drawn attention on the decline in deaths from cerebrovascular lesions which took place from the 1950s to 1969 in a number of western countries, including the United States, England and Wales, Switzerland, the Netherlands and Iceland. That such a downward trend has continued from 1973 to 1978 is shown by the figures in Table 1.5 based on *WHO Vital Statistics and Causes of Death* report for 1980. A closer study of the death records, however, shows that all categories of cerebrovascular diseases probably do not display the same downward trend in mortality. In England and Wales, for instance, Haberman et al (1978) do find a downward trend in cerebral haemorrhage mortality rates from 1958 to 1973 correlated with a similar trend of mortality rates due to hypertensive diseases, but they also note an opposite trend in cerebral thrombosis and ischaemic heart disease mortality; they conclude that this divergence contradicts the widely held view that these diseases have all a common etiology.

Contrary to what happens for most cardiovascular diseases, cancer mortality still continues to increase with age, as apparent in Table 1.6, even though a certain dece-

Table 1.5 Cerebrovascular diseases. Death rates specific for sex and age per 100 000 population.

	1973		1978	
	M	F	M	F
United States				
55–64	125.9	90.0	92.4	67.0
65–74	425.0	301.3	310.2	221.0
75 and over	1659.2	1609.8	1330.4	1296.9
Sweden				
55–64	91.5	67.5	85.4	45.1
65–74	337.8	227.3	313.7	229.1
75 and over	1347.6	1288.5	1213.8	1245.1
Denmark				
55–64	88.9	54.5	81.3	50.1
65–74	352.0	224.1	317.6	208.9
75 and over	1448.0	1340.5	1196.6	1141.1
Iceland				
55–64	63.3	146.3	81.4	100.0
65–74	407.4	283.3	203.4	287.9
75 and over	1878.8	2162.8	1432.4	1173.1
Japan				
55–64	366.8	198.7	247.1	133.1
65–74	1254.0	781.1	890.8	553.5
75 and over	3770.8	3048.1	3008.9	2490.0

Table 1.6 Neoplasms. Death rates specific for sex and age per 100 000 population.

	1973		1978	
	M	F	M	F
United States				
55–64	519.3	360.1	525.2	372.7
65–74	1044.6	571.0	1077.0	588.7
75 and over	1745.9	955.8	1886.3	1005.0
Sweden				
55–64	365.0	319.4	365.3	327.6
65–74	958.2	631.1	948.6	604.9
75 and over	2203.0	1360.6	2246.8	1304.5
Denmark				
55–64	499.4	386.4	506.1	437.3
65–74	1187.0	693.8	1234.0	723.9
75 and over	2039.5	1382.9	2264.3	1401.4
Iceland				
55–64	354.4	317.1	418.6	433.3
65–74	777.8	783.3	610.2	621.2
75 and over	1515.2	907.0	1243.2	1173.1
Japan				
55–64	466.0	286.0	449.1	259.4
65–73	1051.0	555.4	1035.8	528.4
75 and over	1537.3	855.4	1643.6	894.6

leration is presently noticeable for subjects under the age of 45 (Fig. 1.8). However it is dangerous to generalize too quickly in this field. The incidence of the various cancer categories varies not only with age but also with countries and living conditions. In most countries, for instance, the risk for all cancers is greater in the lower socio-economic classes, except for the breast cancer in women (Cohart and Muller, 1955; Graham et al, 1972; Kitagawa and Hauser, 1973). This does not necessarily mean that the less privileged people in a given country are more exposed to various cancer risk factors than the

upper social classes. This might well be due to more limited access to medical facilities, and hence a smaller chance of cancers being detected and treated early. The changing trends in cancer mortality for a number of European countries between 1955 and 1974 have recently been documented by Campbell (1980). During these two decades, lung cancer mortality has increased for both sexes, as well as mortality from cancer of the prostate in men and breast cancer in women. Mortality from cancer of the stomach has declined in both sexes. The increase of cancer mortality in people over 45 years of age, as opposed to the decrease in younger age groups (Fig. 1.8), is at least in part due to the fact that chemotherapy tends to be less effective in older individuals. Furthermore, chemotherapy has so far been of limited benefit for some of the major forms of cancer, such as non-small-cell lung cancer, melanoma, gastro-intestinal and prostate cancer (Frei, 1982).

Morbidity studies

Modern epidemiology no longer deals only with the study of epidemics; it is increasingly concerned with the investigation of all factors relevant to the development of a disease, whether it be infectious or degenerative. As pointed out by Dawber (1980) epidemiology is presently more and more concerned with the study of the natural history of diseases, how and why they develop or regress. The major thrust of epidemiological investigations being the discovery of the factor(s) that affect the original development of a given disease, its ultimate goal is to open new avenues for the primary prevention of that disease. In this perspective it is obviously not enough to measure mortality rates in successive age categories. The development of the disease must be traced from its very beginning, long before it can cause death, and both its changes in prevalence and incidence with age must be assessed as accurately as possible. Let us remember at this stage that the word prevalence refers to the amount of disease existing at a particular time, whereas incidence refers to the number of new cases developing within a given period of time.

One of the most important objectives of morbidity studies is the discovery of predictive variables — what are often called risk factors* — which point the way to

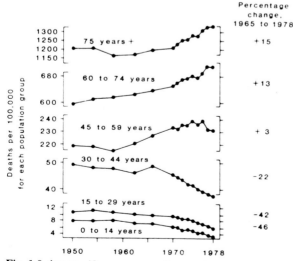

Fig. 1.8 Age-specific cancer mortality trends in the United States 1950 to 1978 (after Frei III, 1982)

* The most generally accepted risk factors for cardiovascular diseases in modern industralized societies are cigarette smoking, high cholesterol level, hypertension, diabetes and obesity. However the influence of obesity on longevity of the aged has been recently questioned (Andres, 1981). The relation of obesity to specific important diseases is undoubted, but this does not mean that the more obese you are in your mature years, the shorter your life-span. During the Framinghan study, for instance, men were found to live longest when moderately overweight; among women, mortality was highest among the very thinnest and fattest. It appears that in the absence of hypertension, overweight is not a risk factor at all.

preventive efforts. Great caution must be exerted however when dealing with causality relationships in epidemiology. Most, if not all, diseases imply the action of two categories of factors, extrinsic and intrinsic. Indeed, not all individuals exposed to an infectious agent develop the infection, and the same applies to those exposed to risk factors. This is why more and more epidemiologists nowadays prefer to speak of the causes of a disease rather than concentrating on a single one. A combination of circumstances may lead to an increased occurrence of a disease, yet no single factor must necessarily be present. The relative importance of each of the factors involved must then be assessed individually and in combination with the other factors (Dawber, 1980).

Some methodological issues

There are two ways of measuring age changes in disease prevalence or functional performances in human populations: either to compare samples of people belonging to successive age categories, say from 20–29 to 70–79 years of age and over (i.e. the cross-sectional approach), or to follow throughout their life-span, or a few decades at least, a group of people born in the same year (i.e. the longitudinal approach). These two alternative research strategies both have their own advantages and disadvantages, and they may be combined.

The cross-sectional approach is the simplest, the cheapest and that which produces results the most quickly. It has, however, a very serious drawback. When one examines, at a particular time, individuals aged 25 and 75, for instance, we are comparing subjects belonging to very different generations. The past history of each cohort has obviously not been the same, as far as its education, life-style, nutrition, etc. is concerned. Furthermore, a cross-sectional study does not allow epidemiologists to calculate incidence rates of age-associated diseases; only their changes in prevalence can be estimated.

Obviously the longitudinal approach is much more attractive. The follow-up of a same cohort of individuals enables the observer(s) to estimate both the incidence of a disease and the number of deaths occuring during the observation period; it can also be used to measure the functional change in performances of aging subjects. Unfortunately, longitudinal studies inevitably take a lot of time, sometimes decades, before bringing useful results; the same observer(s) very seldom can participate from the beginning to the end of the study, and change of observers invariably implies additional observation biases. Furthermore, extensive longitudinal studies are very expensive, as the number of subjects at the start must be large enough to end the study with enough individuals to draw meaningful conclusions, despite the inescapable 'drop-outs' by migration or other causes.

This is why so many people feel that the results obtained by long-term longitudinal studies are not commensurate with the labour and money involved. As a matter of fact longitudinal studies have not often been carried out in our field. There are however some brilliant exceptions such as the Pooling Project (1978) which included the Framingham Study (Dawber, 1980), the Seven Countries Study (Keys, 1980), the Baltimore Study (Birren et al, 1963; Granik and Patterson, 1971), the Duke Longitudinal Study (Palmore, 1970, 1974), the Paris Prospective Study (Ducimetiere et al, 1981), the Gothenburg Study (Svanborg, 1977) and a few others to which reference will be made in the following pages. Oddly enough, in most of these studies all the participants were males, although most elderly people in western societies are females.

Whatever the approach chosen, the choice of the group to be studied is a most important step in the planning of an epidemiological investigation. General population studies are sometimes undertaken, encompassing a community as a whole, such as the population of the city of Framingham, Massachusetts, or the septuagenarians of Gothenburg, Sweden. More often, however, studies are carried out on selected subgroups of the general population: occupational categories, insured persons, or medical care subgroups for instance. In all cases, random samples are taken. Finally, some 'in depth' studies, such as those at Baltimore and Duke, are carried out on volunteers. This is attractive, because of the relative ease of obtaining detailed information from such subjects; the possibility of bias resulting from self-selection, however, remains a major problem. Institutionalized persons raise problems of their own; they must not be forgotten in general population studies, but in no case they should be considered as representative of the aged population as a whole.

As for the description of the sample and its environment, it must be done very carefully, particularly as regards its ethnic, socio-cultural, professional and family characteristics.

Morbidity due to age-associated diseases in some industrialized countries

There are few reliable studies giving some indication of the prevalence of the major disease categories in middle-aged and elderly people. Among the most recent are the Health Surveys undertaken in the city of Uppsala, Sweden, by Waern (1978) for men of 50 and 60 years of age. Their most important results are summarized on Table 1.7. An increase in general morbidity between the ages of 50 and 60 is apparent. Of particular importance, however, is the increase in diseases of the circulatory system and endocrine and metabolic disorders. As for specific diagnosis, the prevalence of hypertension rose from 3.7 to 12.4 per cent, that of ischaemic heart disease

Table 1.7 Prevalence of diagnoses in health surveys of 50- and 60-year old men in Uppsala, Sweden (Waern, 1978). Groups of diagnoses according to the International Classification of Diseases (3rd. Rev. Ed.).

Group of diagnoses	50-year-old men (n = 2322) Subjects per cent	60-year-old men (n = 331) Subjects per cent
Circulatory diseases	5.9	31.3
Mental disorders	1.5	3.0
Endocrine, metabolic	1.2	12.1
Nervous diseases	0.8	3.6
Musculoskeletal disorders	0.7	7.9
Respiratory diseases	0.3	2.4
Tumours	0.2	1.5

from 0.6 to 4.2 per cent, and that of diabetes mellitus from 0.1 to 0.9 per cent. The increase in the use of drugs reflected the same tendency; in the younger age group 9.6 per cent of the men reported a daily drug intake, compared with 38.1 per cent in the older group. A similar study on the 70-year-olds of the city of Gothenburg, Sweden (Svanborg, 1977) gives complementary information on the next age category, and includes women as well as men. It shows a sharp increase in the prevalence of circulatory diseases, and in musculoskeletal and mental disorders; about 3 per cent of the 70-year-olds suffered from advanced handicaps or disease to such an extent that institutional care was necessary. In their study of a male managerial population 63–64 years old at the beginning of their 3-year longitudinal study, Vallery-Masson et al (1981) have also found high prevalence and incidence rates of musculoskeletal and cardiovascular diseases (Table 1.8). In a still unpublished study of the whole non-institutionalized Finnish population 65 years old and over, the Research Institute for Social Security in Helsinki has gathered most interesting information on the self-reported occurrence of chronic diseases in the whole of the country. Here again diseases of the circulatory system rank first, followed by musculoskeletal disorders and diabetes (T. Klaukka, personal communication).

It is hard to compare the prevalence and incidence rates obtained in studies such as those just mentioned, though an effort of standardization had been made, as far as methodology, criteria of diagnosis and classification were concerned. For example, the incidence rate per 1000 individuals of ischaemic heart disease for middle-aged people varied from 5.3 to 43.0 per 1000. The higher rates were found in the United States and the lower ones in South-Eastern Europe, middle values being reported in Western Europe (France: 29.7 per 1000; Holland: 31.1 per 1000). Such differences cannot be accounted for by differences in methodology only. Ethnic factors (race, nutrition, life-styles, culture) have to be taken into consideration, besides differences in exposure to more classic risk-factors. In the United States, for instance, hypertension is about twice as prevalent among black as among white adults (U.S. Vital and Health Statistics, 1981).

Next to the diseases of the cardiovascular system, the musculoskeletal disorders rank second. The prevalence of osteoporosis in elderly people is most difficult to assess as it depends above all upon the definition of the disorder. Diagnostic criteria vary and are commonly based on arbitrary definitions of normality. All adult men and women lose bone as they grow older, especially women after the menopause. But the borderline between such a physiological loss of bone and the senile osteoporosis syndrome is hard to delineate. No wonder then that the prevalence of osteoporosis ranged from 18 per cent in adult women to 20 and 23 per cent respectively in elderly men and women, depending upon the criteria used (Adams et al, 1970).

For the time being, it is probably wiser to restrict our assessment of the occurrence of osteoporosis to that of the most common complication of osteopenia, the fracture of the hip. Its increased prevalence with age provides a useful index of the differential incidence of osteoporosis in elderly people. The 10-year study of the population of the city of Rochester, Minnesota, yielded some of the most reliable incidence figures so far obtained in North American whites (Gallagher et al, 1980). The results show a doubling of the fracture rate

Table 1.8 Prevalence and incidence rates (percentage) of major disease categories in a sample of a French managerial population at retirement (Vallery-Masson et al, 1981).

Affected system	Non-retirees (n = 51) Prevalence rate Wave 1	Wave 2	Incidence rate	Retirees (n = 105) Prevalence rate Wave 1	Wave 2	Incidence rate
Musculoskeletal*	75	82	16	67	79	9
Cardiovascular (heart and arteries)	45	65	27	38	44	16
Digestive*	35	39	10	43	39	13

*Every subject suffering from a chronic disease of the two systems concerned was included.

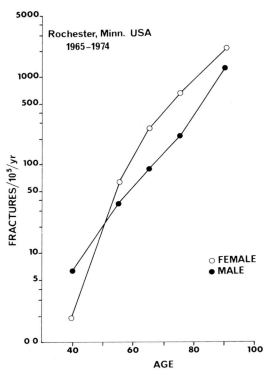

Fig. 1.9 Age-specific incidence of males and females with fracture of the proximal femur (after Gallagher et al, 1980)

Table 1.9 Prevalence (percentage) of dementia among the elderly population in six different countries (After Rinder Bollerup, 1975).

	Senile and arteriosclerotic dementia	Other types of dementia	Total
England, 65+ years old Kay et al, 1964	4.6	1.0	5.6
Scotland, 65+ years old Primrose, 1962	3.6	0.9	4.5
Iceland, 74–76 years old Helgason, 1973	3.6	1.4	5.0
Norway, 60+ years old Bentsen, 1970	5.3	—	5.3
Sweden, 60+ years old Essen-Möller, 1956	5.0	—	5.0
Denmark, 70 years old Rinder Bollerup, 1975	3.2	1.8	5.0

in each decade of life after age 50 years (Fig. 1.9). The fracture rate was much greater in women than in men, and by age 90 years, about 32 per cent of women and 17 per cent of men had suffered a fracture. Very high incidence rates were also found in Sweden, Jerusalem and Copenhagen (Steen Jensen, 1980). On the contrary, much lower rates were found in Singapore and Hong Kong, among South African Bantus and black Americans, as well as among Croatians from Zagreb (Matkovic et al, 1980). The importance of ethnic factors is, here again, quite obvious (Fig. 1.10).

The prevalence of mental diseases and abnormalities in aged populations has mostly been studied in Scandinavian countries, United Kingdom and North America. For instance Rinder Bollerup (1975) investigated a random sample of 70-year-old males and females living in nine suburbs of Copenhagen. The total psychiatric morbidity was found to be 15.5 per cent, 6.4 per cent suffering from psychoses and 7.4 per cent being classified as 'neuroses and personality disorders'. Males were more numerous among the psychotics and females among the neurotics. Only 15 per cent of the psychotic group were institutionalized. The prevalence findings of this Danish study are, on the whole, very similar to those of the few other studies concerned with population samples over 65 years of age. For instance, the preva-

lence rate of dementia ranges from 4.5 to 5.6 per cent (Table 1.9), the most severe cases representing 3 per cent. Most of the cases of 'neurosis and personality disorders' are represented by anxiety neurosis or depressive neurosis. Their percentage was low in the Danish study, as compared to the results of most other mental health surveys which generally give percentages of about 12 per cent. The discrepancy is quite likely due to difference in diagnostic definition. As for the prevalence of depressive states, it was of 1.76 per cent in Copenhagen suburbs, a figure not too dissimilar from that (3 per cent) found by Kay et al (1964) in Newcastle. The prevalence figures for 'significant depressive symptoms' in a number of North American population samples given by Gerner (1979) are much higher, however.

Prevalence of 'disability' and 'dependence'
Apart from the prevalence and incidence rates of age-associated diseases, it is important to estimate — if only for public health purposes — the prevalence of 'disability' and 'dependence' among elderly persons. Let us remember first that 'disability' is defined by epidemiologists as a state in which existence at home without help is considered impossible, the elderly being unable to perform unaided activities essential to daily life, whereas 'dependence' is defined as disability for self-care. The best studies in this field have been done in the United Kingdom, and their major results are summarized in Table 1.10. The percentages are impressive and of crucial importance for the planning of health and welfare services. Unfortunately Bennett et al (1970) did not give data for the main groups of diagnoses contributing to disability over the age of 75 years in Lambeth. Harris (1971) gave detailed information on the causes of

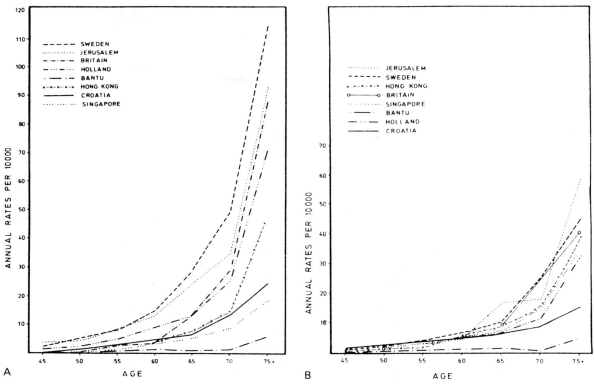

Fig. 1.10 International comparison of annual age-specific hip fractures rates in women (A) and men (B) (after Markovic et al, 1980)

impairment and handicap, as reported by the subjects themselves, but did not specify which conditions were of greatest importance at different ages. Badley et al (1978), however, re-examined the data gathered by the Government Social Survey and concluded that stroke, arthritis and circulatory disorders were the most frequent causes of severe disability in aged persons. Fortunately, the results of the study of a random sample of 200 people living in the town of Kilsyth are much more precise (Akhtar et al, 1973). In 48 per cent of the disabled subjects over the age of 65, a neurological disorder contributed to disability; 22 per cent had a

Table 1.10 Comparison of prevalence rates of disability and dependence (After Akhtar et al, 1973).

Survey	Age Sex Criterion	65–74		75+	
		M	F	M	F
Bennett et al (1970)	Unable to get into street unaided	2.2*	3.8*	13.8	25.1
Harris (1971)	Handicap appreciable or greater	6.3	11.5	9.5	18.8
Akhtar et al (1973)	Disability	10.3	18.5	36.3	51.5
Bennett et al (1970)	Unable to dress and undress unaided	0.9*	0.9*	3.2	3.3
Harris (1971)	Severe or very severe handicap	2.1	4.0	5.8	10.4
Akhtar et al (1973)	Dependence	0	3.2	4.2	6.4

*Age 55–74

functional psychiatric disorder, 38 per cent a cardiorespiratory diagnosis, 25 per cent joint disease, 16 per cent obesity and 11 per cent visual impairment. Only 3 per cent were persistently incontinent. Ninety-three per cent of the dependent subjects had a neurological disorder (77 per cent with dementia) and 33 per cent were persistently incontinent.

ECOLOGY OF HUMAN SENESCENCE

The computation of mortality rates, or of the prevalence and incidence of age-associated diseases, is but one way to evaluate the pace of aging in human populations. The progressive decline in performance, which charaterizes most of our physiological functions and mental abilities, can also be quantified. Such a functional aging is obviously a normal inescapable process; it follows a pattern specific to each major function, but its rate can be altered by a number of internal and external factors. In all societies, some individuals age more quickly, and others more slowly, than most of the other members of their own generation (cohort). This is the phenomenon presently known as differential aging. Its theoretical and practical implications are many. Some factors capable of accelerating senescence and increasing the incidence of some age-associated diseases are already identified, and the prevention of these 'risk factors' has already proved to be possible and beneficial. But if we were able to identify some other factors capable of slowing down the process of aging and postpone (if not prevent) the occurrence of most age-associated diseases, the benefit would be even larger. Thus the identification of the environmental factors and life conditions capable of influencing the rate of aging in human populations has now become one of the major goals of human ecology. To achieve this aim it is, first of all, necessary to have at one's disposal an adequate examination battery to assess functional changes quantitatively.

A number of test batteries for measuring aging rates in humans have already been used in epidemiological studies (Hollingsworth et al, 1965, 1969; Szafran, 1968; Bourlière, 1969; Comfort, 1969, 1979; Reff and Schneider, 1982). They usually include some anthropometric measurements, a number of physiological and biochemical tests, and sometimes also some psychometric tests. The use of the latter, however, should be restricted to the Euro-American and Japanese populations for which they were elaborated, as none of them is entirely 'culture free'. Among the biological tests, two categories must be distinguished: those which measure baseline performances of a given function at rest, and those which attempt to assess the progressive reduction of the reserve capacity of a given system (exercise tests, loading tests). The latter are often the most sensitive to

age changes, and they provide useful indices of adaptability for the functions concerned.

In the establishment of a test battery the criteria for selection will obviously depend much upon the objective of the study itself and of the population on which the study will be carried out. For an epidemiological survey, however, the variables chosen must:

1. Change sufficiently, and sufficiently regularly, with age for the investigator to expect significant differences over a 10-year period.

2. Be sufficiently diverse to give a balanced picture of the aging of the organism as a whole.

3. Be measurable in non-institutionalized subjects and cause minimal trauma.

The tests selected should be as simple as possible, provide highly reproducible results and have low variability. In all circumstances, the test battery must be supplemented by a routine medical examination and by basic information (using questionnaires whenever possible) on the subject's life history and social environment.

Before dealing with the role of environmental factors as major determinants of differential aging, we need to mention briefly the possible influence of heredity. Of course, no such thing as a single gene for longevity is present in humans. Length of life is the end result of the multiple interactions taking place between the genome as a whole and the environment, throughout the whole life-span of the individual. However, genetic differences in aging patterns do exist in our species. Pearl and Pearl (1934) showed that the expectation of life of the sons of short-lived fathers is less than that of the sons of moderately longevous fathers, and still less than that of the sons of extremely long-lived fathers. Later Jalavisto (1951), making use of Finnish and Swedish genealogies, confirmed these results. She was able to establish that both maternal and paternal longevity tend to increase the mean length of life of the offspring. However, the effect of maternal longevity exceeds that of paternal longevity. Yet the more convincing evidence of the role of heredity as a determinant of human developmental programme and longevity is provided by the longitudinal study of twins (Bank and Jarvis, 1978): intrapair differences in life span are significantly smaller for monozygotic twins than for dizygotic pairs. In the study reported, mean intrapair differences ranged from 36.9 months in monozygotic twins to 78.3 months in dizygotic partners of same sex (difference significant at $P < 0.05$). In the preceeding pages we have already referred to a number of differences in the prevalence rate of some age-associated diseases consistently found between white and black Americans which cannot be explained entirely by differences of living conditions or socio-economic status; some genetic predisposition seems likely. In the same way, the high prevalence of hyperuricaemia in New

Zealand Maoris (Prior et al, 1964) and micronesian islanders (Zimmet et al, 1978), as well as the frequent occurence of diabetes among the Pima Indians of North America (Bennett et al, 1971) probably have a genetic origin. Such might also be the case for the highly efficient negative feedback control of endogenous cholesterol biosynthesis discovered by Ho et al (1971) among the East African Masai.

The three categories of environmental factors which are presently known to be able to influence the rate and modalities of human senescence can be conveniently grouped under three headings, physical, biotic and psycho-social factors.

The physical factors

Whereas the speed of development and the rate of aging of cold-blooded animals very largely depend upon physical factors such as temperature, warm blooded vertebrates have become highly tolerant to them. This is especially true for man. Very early in his history this progressive primate has displayed unusual abilities to colonize a broad spectrum of environments, from the tropics to the arctic, and he has successfully adapted to them, both biologically and culturally. It is only recently that man has had to face a new situation generated by his own industrial activities: the threat of major pollution by ionizing radiations and toxic chemicals. These physico-chemical factors have now become, for man, a much more serious environmental hazard than the harshest climates have ever been.

The possible role of these two categories of physical variables of the environment on aging of the human organism will be examined in turn.

The extreme climates

The biological adaptation of man to the extremes of heat, cold and altitude has been studied by environmental physiologists for a long time, but all these studies were short-term and very little is known of the possible influence of drastic climatic conditions on aging processes.

It is often claimed that native tropical people, in the humid tropics particularly, age more quickly than people from temperate latitudes. Such opinions are generally based upon their reduced expectation of life at birth, their poor state of health and the external appearance of the oldest members of the community. However, it has never been proved that this situation was due to climatic conditions *per se*, and not to associated factors like poor nutrition, heavy parasite load and tropical diseases.

None of the tropical hunter-gatherers so far studied show any evidence of a premature decline in performance which might be interpreted as accelerated aging. The two African pygmy populations, the Mbuti of

North-eastern Zaïre surveyed by Mann et al (1961) and the Babinga of the Central African Republic studied by G. Jaeger (personal communication) were remarkably well-adjusted to the hard conditions of the rain-forest and their endurance was remarkable despite a broad spectrum of parasites. In both cases, the increase in systolic and diastolic blood pressure between 20 and 60 years of age was small, particularly in males. The serum cholesterol levels of the Mbuti were consistently low and did not increase with age; the mean levels were somewhat higher among Babingas, and rose in the older subjects. No electrocardiogram definitely diagnostic of myocardial infarction was found.

The Bushmen of the Kalahari desert studied by Truswell and Hansen (1976) age in a very similar way to that of the forest pygmies. Mean blood pressure did not rise between the ages of 20 and 83; no case of hypertension was discovered in the population, nor was any clinical evidence found of coronary heart disease. In taking histories Truswell and Hansen did not find anyone who was subject to angina pectoris or who had heard of sudden death. Serum cholesterol were found to be very low and did not show any significant variation with age or sex. The high percentage of old people (10 per cent of the population being over 60 years of age) is also worth noting (Lee, 1972). The aged hold a respected position; they are the leaders of the camps, the collective owners of the waterholes, and the repositories of traditional ritual-medical skills. All this contradicts the widely held notion that the hunter-gatherer's life is so rigorous that people rarely live beyond the age of 45 and die prematurely senile.

At the other extreme of the climate gradient, the Eskimos do not appear to age prematurely either, despite the difficult conditions under which they exert their hunting activities. Their pattern of age changes is very similar to that of many non-European populations: in Alaska, weight, skinfold thickness and blood pressure do not increase between 20 and 54 years of age in some groups (Mann, 1962) and increase slightly in others (Scott et al, 1958). Cholesterol levels do not change much with age among males in the same time-interval (Scott et al, 1958). In both sexes a normal decline in vital capacity and hand-grip has been found in Eastern Greenland between the third and the fifth decade of life (Robbe, 1976).

High altitude also does not appear to speed up the aging processes, at least in individuals born and living permanently over 3500 m. Among Peruvian Indians, blood pressure does not increase much between 20 and 60 years of age, and the values observed are uniformly lower than those reported at sea-level (Ruiz and Penaloza, 1970). Similar results have been obtained by Corone et al (1977) in their study of a large sample of Indians from the Bolivian *altiplano*; the prevalence of ischaemic heart disease was also very low in this population. That altitude is not a serious handicap for resident people is also suggested by the fact that most of the highly-publicized communities of 'centenarians' (Abkhasians or Hunzas) are to be found in mountain areas.

Ionizing radiations and pollutants
Whole body chronic irradiation has often been held responsible for an acceleration of aging processes. Recent investigations do not support this claim. That chronic exposure to ionizing radiations, at least above a certain threshold, shortens life in experimental animals is beyond question. But an increased mortality rate cannot be equated with an acceleration of the rate of aging. Such irradiated animals die without ever displaying most of the physiological changes normally associated with aging in mammals. Life expectation of radiologists does not seem to have been significantly reduced by their exposure to radiation either. Court-Brown and Doll (1958) have analyzed the records of longevity in 1377 male English radiologists from 1897 to 1957. They found no tendency to shorter life, even in the pioneer years when protection was minimal, apart from a small excess mortality from skin tumours. In their study, the performance of radiologists was, if anything, slightly better than that of comparable professional groups.

Data from atomic bomb survivors have not so far provided any evidence of premature aging among them, although the incidence of leukaemia was higher than in the non-irradiated population. In Hiroshima Hollingsworth et al (1969) were unable to detect any change definitely related to radiation when using three tests of neuromuscular function. Only for hand grip strength was there evidence that the relationship between age and test score varied significantly between exposure groups; however these differences were more likely to have resulted from socio-economic factors than from variations in the level of radiation.

People born and permanently living in areas with intense background radioactivity, like coastal Kerala in Southern India, do not appear to age more quickly than others. Nor do the native rats studied in these areas of high gamma-radiation (1.6 rad a year) differ in any way from the controls (Gruneberg, 1966).

Pollution is sometimes supposed to be a factor in premature aging. This is particularly the case with air-pollution which, as a cause of chronic pulmonary disease, might speed up the decline of ventilatory performances normally associated with aging. Even when this is the case (Lampert and Reid, 1970), it does not mean that air pollutants accelerate the aging rate of the whole organism. In any event such an extra risk factor would not be limited to industrialized societies.

Master (1974), for instance, has shown how serious air pollution may be in stone-age cultures. To keep warm during cold nights, natives from the highlands of New Guinea burn smoky fires in small closed huts, where they inhale extremely high levels of particulate matter and aldehydes. Consequently, pulmonary disease appears at an early age and is present in 78 per cent of subjects over 40 years of age. However those highlanders do not display any sign of premature aging at the organismic level.

A relationship between the hardness of drinking water and aging of the cardiovascular system has been sometimes assumed during the past two decades. Conflicting results have been published, but the study of Allwright et al (1974) on three matched communities in Los Angeles appears to rule out this hypothesis: mortality from cardiovascular diseases was not related inversely to water hardness.

The biotic factors
Like any other animal, man shares his habitat with many organisms, and interacts with them in a variety of ways. Some compete for resources with him, as 'pests' of all kinds and many parasites, whereas pathogens and predators threaten his survival. However, the most essential relationship between man and his living environment is represented by his mandatory use of some plants and animals for food. Not only do we need to find out among our community partners, wild or domestic, the amount of energy necessary for our maintenance and reproduction, but also we must find in such organic material the nutrients necessary to cover our specific nutritional needs. The quantity and quality of available foodstuff varying enormously between cultures and climatic zones, it is no wonder that nutrition so markedly influences human development and aging.

The diet
A low caloric diet does not see to much alter the basic pattern of development and aging in man. Caloric restriction during infancy neither prolongs the growth period, nor extends life span as it does in rodents (McCay et al, 1939). At most a slight retardation of the skeletal growth (up to 25 years of age in males) has been found in some populations suffering from a chronic shortage of food (Bourlière and Parot, 1962).

The most obvious charateristic of people living on a low caloric diet (i.e. ranging from 1800 to 2500 kcal/day (7560 to 10 500 kJ/day)) is the conspicuous absence of any marked increase in body weight past their third decade of life. Contrary to what is the rule in industrialized Euro-American populations the subcutaneous fat deposits do not increase with age among adults, as shown by skinfold measurements (Fig. 1.11). This is the case for the rural Kabyles of Algeria (Bourlière and

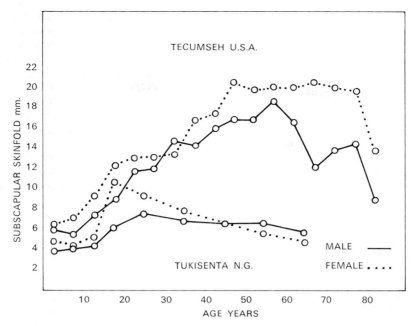

Fig. 1.11 Relationship between subscapular skinfold thickness and age for the Papuans of Tukisenta, New Guinea, as compared with white north-Americans from Tecumseh, USA (after Montoye et al, 1965)

Parot, 1962), the rural population around Delhi (Padmovati and Gupta, 1959), the pygmies of Eastern Zaïre (Mann et al, 1961) and of the Central African Republic (Jaeger, personal communication), the Saras of Central Africa (Jaeger, personal communication), the Eastern African Masai (Mann et al, 1964–65), the Papuans of New Guinea (Maddocks, 1967; Sinnett and Whyte, 1973; Sinnett et al, 1973; Boyce et al, 1978), the Solomon Islands natives (Page et al, 1977) and even some Japanese samples (Kagan et al, 1974).

A low caloric diet is also generally deficient in animal proteins, at least seasonally. For instance, the diet of the New Guinean Highlanders studied by Sinnett et al (1973) consisted almost entirely of sweet potato, this single staple supplying about 90 per cent of their total intake. As the varieties of sweet potato analysed contained from 1 to 1.9 per cent protein by weight, this dietary pattern imposed serious limitations on the protein intake: on average the adults did not consume more than 25 g of protein per day. It was therefore no wonder that the decrease of their lean body mass with age appeared to be very marked, evidenced by such simple measurements as a decrease of the muscle indices of the arm and calf after 30 years of age, and a decrease in urinary creatinine excretion of 10 933 mg/year for males. An early and sharp decrease in arm circumference with age has also been noted by Maddocks (1967) in other New Guinean tribes. However, a low caloric diet is also generally poor in fats, particularly in satu-

rated animal fats, and this has definite advantages. Such is the case of the Kalahari bushmen's diet (Truswell and Hansen, 1976). Their major source of food is mongongo nuts (*Ricinodendron rautanenii*) which do contain 57 per cent fats, but polyunsaturated ones very rich in linoleic acid (43 per cent). The other major food source for these hunter-gatherers is game, whose meat has a much lower fat content than that of farm animals, this fat being moreover less saturated and containing appreciable amounts of polyunsaturated fatty acids (Crawford, 1968).

These populations, living on low caloric diets, all share the privilege of having low blood pressures which do not rise with age (Fig. 1.12), and low serum cholesterols which show no significant variation over the years (Fig. 1.13). The Kalahari bushmen have long been known to have lower lipid values than any previously reported: total cholesterol, 77 mg/100 ml; phospholipids, 107 mg/100 ml; triglycerides, 49 mg/100 ml (Miller et al, 1968). In most cases neither clinical evidence nor ECG indication of coronary heart disease have been found in the samples studied, which can be considered to be fairly representative of a life-style which was that of our forbears during hundreds of thousands of years. This supports the now well documented view that the rise of blood pressure with age, so characteristic of western societies, is a function of life style rather than an inevitable part of man's aging process.

High caloric diets (more than 3200 kcal/day

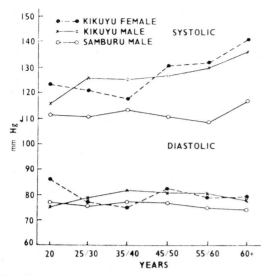

Fig. 1.12 Age changes in systolic blood pressure among two African tribes with contrasting ecologies: the Kikuyu, sedentary agriculturalists, and the Samburu, nomadic cattle herders (after Williams, 1969)

among women (Fig. 1.11). This rise in weight is due to a marked thickening of fat deposits with advancing age, as shown by an increased skinfold thickness after maturity. Such propensity to obesity among present day Euro-American populations is widespread; it has been found in Tecumseh, USA (Montoyer et al, 1965) as well as in Paris, France (Bourlière et al, 1966b). Similarly, there is a general tendency towards a higher blood pressure rising steadily with age, high serum cholesterol showing significant increase with age up to 55 years at least among males and 65 years among females (Keys et al, 1957; Bourlière et al, 1966b), and increased prevalence of atherosclerosis and of coronary heart disease (Ho et al, 1971).

Some of the so-called 'primitive' people can also have too rich a traditional diet. For instance although the daily caloric intake of the Masai, nomadic herdsmen of East Africa, averages only 3000 calories, 66 per cent of its caloric value is made of animal fat. Their estimated average daily cholesterol intake ranges from 600 to 2000 mg per adult person — an amount well in excess of that recommended for westerners. However their physical fitness is remarkable despite their heavy parasite load and the high prevalence rate of infectious diseases, especially malaria and syphilis (Mann et al, 1964–1965). Masai are about the same height as the average white Euro-American, but they appear much taller. This is due to their linear body type, their low body weight (rarely above 60 kg in adults) and the thin-

(13 440 kJ/day) for men and 2200 kcal/day (9240 kJ/day) for women) have quite opposite effects on the pattern of aging. Their most common consequence is a steady increase in weight up to 50 or even 60 years of age in most of the Euro-American populations, especially

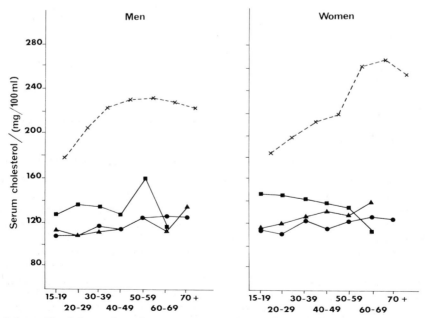

Fig. 1.13 Serum cholesterol levels by age for males and females in three Solomon Island unacculturated Melanesian populations (lower curves) and an USA population sample (upper curves). (adapted from Prior et al, 1977 and Page et al, 1974)

ness of their subcutaneous fat layer (the humeral skinfold does not exceed 3 mm, as against 11 to 14 mm in the average white Euro-American). Their main staple is milk, sometimes supplemented with blood and meat. Despite the high fat intake, no increase in body weight and skinfold thickness was noted between 25 and 55 years of age. Blood pressure, blood cholesterol and beta-lipoprotein levels were surprisingly low and did not increase with age. Clinical and autopsy examinations revealed a paucity of atherosclerosis and little evidence of coronary heart disease. A highly efficient negative feedback control mechanism of endogenous cholesterol synthesis has been found in metabolic studies (Ho et al, 1971) and appears to be the main factor protecting the Masai from developing hypercholesterolaemia. The serum lipid level of a westernized Masai, who had been living in the United States for 10 years has also been determined; it showed exactly the same pattern as that of his fellow tribesmen. This strongly suggests that the striking biological characteristics of the tribe are genetically determined, or at least definitely induced very early in life. In any case such a trait is probably not unique to the Masai; other East African cattle-tribes apparently share with them this remarkable adaptation to a high fat diet. The Somali camel herdsmen studied by Lapiccirella et al (1962) can, for example, drink up to 5 litres of camel milk per day. This represents a daily fat intake of 335 g and a maximum calory intake of 6247 cal/day (26 238 kJ/day)! Yet their serum cholesterol did not exceed 153 mg/100 ml, though the beta/alpha lipoprotein ratio was high. Furthermore, their body weight, serum cholesterol and beta-lipoprotein levels did not increase significantly with age. There was a moderate rise in blood pressure from age 21 to 70, but none of the subjects studied showed any clinical symptom suggestive of atherosclerosis.

Other cattle-tribes of Northern Kenya sharing with the Masai and Somali a similar life-style and a predominantly milk diet, have higher serum cholesterol levels than their neighbours. This is the case for the Samburu and Rendile studied by Shaper and Jones (1962) and Shaper et al (1969). The average cholesterol level of the Samburu is 190 mg/100 ml and that of the Rendile 233 mg/100 ml. Yet neither these levels, nor the body weight, the skinfold thickness or the blood pressure rise significantly with age.

The Eskimo situation is somewhat different from that of the African Nilo-Hamitic tribes. Their daily caloric intake can reach 3100 kcalories (13 020 kJ) in some tribes, of which 35 to 66 per cent is fat and 22 to 32 per cent is animal protein. However, the meat consumed is rich in polyunsaturated fatty acids. The diet is very low in carbohydrates and this low sugar and high protein content has necessitated a number of metabolic adaptations. In the more conservative samples studied in

Alaska, the weight, skinfold thickness and blood pressure do not change with age between 20 and 54 years of age (Mann, 1962). In others, there is a slight increase in blood pressure and cholesterol level with age (Scott et al, 1958). In Eastern Greenland, Robbe (1976) did not find any increase in weight after 25 years of age in the traditional village of Tileqila, and only slight rises in skinfold thickness and blood pressure in the same age group. A detailed study of the plasma lipid and lipoprotein pattern in Greenlandic west coast Eskimos has been made by Bang et al (1971). It showed that most lipids were decreased, compared with Danish controls. Pre-beta-lipoproteins were nearly absent on the electrophoretic strips. Furthermore, plasma lipids and plasma lipoproteins did not increase much between the ages of 31 and 61, in both sexes. The incidence of ischaemic heart disease was low. The fact that the blood lipid pattern of Eskimos living in Denmark resembled that of the Danes points strongly towards an environmental determinism of the low lipid levels and related age-changes of the Greenlandic Eskimos.

A further advantage of the diet of the eastern Greenland Eskimos is its high content in eicosapentaenoic acid, which is present in high concentration in certain marine fish such as mackerel. Unlike arachidonic acid, it does not induce platelet aggregation. The high levels of eicosapentaeonic acid and low levels of arachidonic acid in the Eskimos blood might protect them against thrombosis (Dyerberg et al, 1978; Dyerberg and Bang, 1978).

Predominantly vegetarian people can also have too rich a diet. Such is the case of the Polynesians studied by Prior et al (1977) in the Tokelau Island. The diet on this atoll is a traditional one of bread-fruit, taro, pulaka, fish and coconut, with chicken and pork added on special occasions. Fifty-six per cent of the calorie intake is made up of saturated fat, three-quarters of which are supplied by coconuts; pork fat also contains short chain saturated fatty acids. Cholesterol intake is very low and dairy products are rarely consumed. Correlatively the weight of Tokelauans rises with age in both sexes to age 45–54 and then declines. There is a steady increase with age of skinfold thickness in both sexes, the peak for triceps and subscapular skinfolds being reached in the 55–64 age group in the males and in the 45–54 age groups for the females. Serum cholesterol levels have mean values of 184.5 mg/100 ml and 198.2 mg/100 ml in young adult males and females respectively, and rise with age to a peak of 220.4 in males aged 45–54 and 245.4 in females aged 55–64. Triglycerides also increase with age in both sexes. Blood pressure rises slowly in males and females, the female levels exceeding the male levels from age 35–44 on. Angina pectoris and myocardial infarction are present, though their prevalence rate is smaller than that of Europeans and New Zealand

Maoris. On the contrary the prevalence of diabetes is high.

Another important dietary factor which undoubtedly influences aging in man is a high salt intake. Very wide variations of salt consumption exist between cultures. The Yanomamo Indians, an unacculturated tribe inhabiting the tropical rain forest of northern Brazil and southern Venezuela, do not use salt in their diet (Oliver et al, 1975). Their major staple consists of the plantain *Musa paradisiaca* supplemented by irregular additions of game, fish, insects and wild plants. The tribe has no access to sodium chloride except where the substance has been introduced by missionaries. Consequently the average daily sodium excretion — of about 1 mmol — is the lowest observed so far. It corresponds to a sustained sodium intake lower than any previously recorded for man. Several individuals excreted as little as 2 mg of sodium per day, a remarkable physiological feat. The average potassium excretion is 152 mmol per day and the sodium/potassium ratio is reversed. Aldosterone excretion is in excess of the upper limit of the norm obtained for Euro-Americans on a normal diet. Similarly, all plasma renin values were within or exceeded the range seen in normal ambulatory Caucasians ingesting short term 10 mmol sodium diets. Correlatively, the Yanomamo blood pressure does not increase after the third decade of life,

but even seems to decline slightly (Fig. 1.14).

The data published by Page et al (1977) on a number of Melanesian populations differing in their dietary habits also support the view that sodium intake is a major variable influencing the aging of the cardiovascular system. One of the six Solomon Islands tribes studied, the Lau, have for a long time boiled their vegetables in sea-water; this results in a daily salt intake ranging from 130 to 230 mmol per day. Other tribes, like the Baeger, Aita and Kwaio, use very little salt, and their intake ranges from 10 to 30 mmol per day. Also, the Lau were found to have the highest systolic and diastolic blood pressures for both sexes and nearly all ages. Blood pressures greater than 140 mmHg systolic and 90 mmHg diastolic were found in 7.8 per cent of the Lau men and 9.9 per cent of the women. Pressures in this range were rare in the other societies. A striking absence of most ECG abnormalities, and particularly of those commonly associated with coronary heart disease, was noted in all four tribes (Page et al, 1974). Quite unexpectedly high uric acid levels were found in the serum of the Melanesian groups. This is probably due to their use of the sweet potato as major staple food. A similar finding has been reported by Jeremy and Rhodes (1971) in New Guinea; they were also able to show that addition of salt to the sweet potato diet produced a fall in uric acid levels.

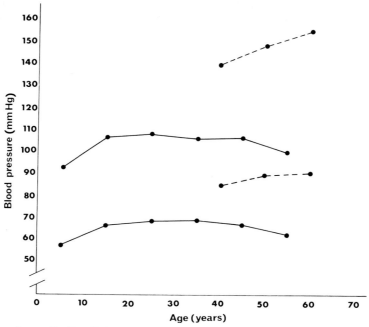

Fig. 1.14 The age changes in systolic diastolic blood pressure in males of a 'No-salt' culture, the Yanomamo Indians (the two lower curves) and Japanese from Atika with a very high salt intake (the two upper curves) (after Oliver et al, 1975 and Komachi et al, 1971)

Unlike the rain forest people, the Japanese are well known for their high salt intake. They are fond of a traditional diet of rice, salted pickles, miso and soya sauces, which are produced from fermented beans, cereals and salt. In the 1950s the average daily salt intake of a Japanese adult was 15–20 g per day (Sasaki et al, 1960) and at times as much as 50 g/day (Kimura, 1960). More recently Komachi et al (1971) reported a daily salt intake of 20 g in a rural community (Akita), and of 8–14 g/day in Osaka. This has been correlated with the much higher prevalence of stroke among the Japanese than among Euro-Americans. Recent epimiological research, however, has shown that this relationship is indeed more complex (Hatano, 1975): regional differences in blood pressure and mortality from strokes are important. Blood pressure is higher in the north-eastern part of the main island and the coastal areas of northern Japan, and is lower in the southern Pacific border, around the Kyoto and Osaka areas and on Shikoku Island. This regional difference in blood pressure distribution corresponds to a large extent to the difference in the prevalence of cerebrosvascular diseases. The death rate from stroke is higher in the north-eastern regions, decreases towards the south-west and is lower in the central part of the main island and on Shikoku. A significant correlation has also been found between the death rate from cerebrosvascular disease on a regional basis (Sasaki et al, 1960) or by villages and towns (Kojima, 1966) and the *per capita* miso consumption and total salt consumption. In their study Komachi et al (1971) also found that the incidence of cerebral stroke and the prevalence rates of hypertension and abnormal fundus oculi findings were higher in north-eastern Japan (Akita) than in Osaka, this difference being on par with a total calorie and salt intake 50 per cent higher in Akita than in Osaka. Therefore, a chronic salt overload appears to play a major role in the high prevalence of cerebrovascular diseases in Japan.

Physical exercise

Before concluding this section devoted to the influence of dietary factors on aging in man, an often neglected variable should be mentioned: exercise. Most of the populations mentioned so far display remarkable physical fitness, despite their heavy parasite load, frequent malnutrition, poor hygiene and living conditions, at least by our Western standards. Yet their endurance and environmental adjustment are often astonishing. Such is the case, for instance, of the Masai studied by Mann et al (1965). By means of an electrically driven treadmill it was possible for Mann and his co-workers to measure the Masai's running performance, the cardiovascular adjustment to effort and the maximum oxygen consumption of 53 men between 14 and 64 years of age. The most striking results of this study are shown in Figure 1.15. The fitness of these 'untrained' cattle herders is remarkable. Many of them outperformed athletes of Olympic standard. Two of the Masai exceeded the records of Don Lash the Olympic distance runner and Jernberg the Swedish skier. Sinnet et al (1973a) have also stressed the remarkable physical

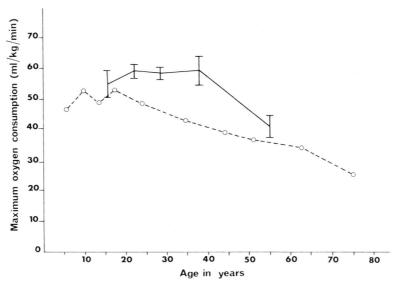

Fig. 1.15 The physical fitness of Masai cattle herders (upper curve) and Boston residents (lower curves) as shown by their maximum oxygen consumption during the treadmill test (adapted from Mann et al, 1965)

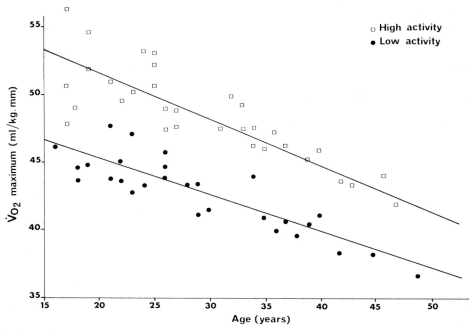

Fig. 1.16 The effect of sustained physical exercise upon physical fitness at various ages. Aerobic capacity of two samples of Nepalese sherpas, with differing activity levels (adapted from Weitz, 1963)

fitness of the Tukisenta Papuans. 'Good' or 'superior' scores to the Harvard Pack Test were gained by 76 per cent of the men and 36 per cent of the women. The score for men did not fall with age and was significantly superior to the scores obtained in Royal Australian Air Force personnel. The bicycle ergometer tests gave also an estimated maximum oxygen uptake greater than the value reported for white Australians.

Another good example of the effect of sustained training upon functional aging is shown on Figure 1.16, where the aerobic capacity of two groups of Nepalese sherpas of various ages are compared (Weitz, 1973). The 'high activity' group was made of males primarily engaged in farming and herding activities, but working occasionally as porters or guides. The 'low activity' group included traders who moved from village to village depending upon the demand for their services. Both groups were examined in the Mount Everest area at an altitude of 3440 m. The better performances of the 'highly active' sherpas are obvious in any age class. That most of the present day Euro-Americans, brought up in our sedentary, overfed 'affluent' society, actually develop and use only a fraction of their functional potential is made obvious by the extreme case of the Tarahumara (Groom, 1971). These indians live in the mountains of northern Mexico and have long been known to anthropologists for their remarkable physical performances. They were famous for their primitive way

of hunting a deer: running after it relentlessly for a couple of days until the animal dropped from exhaustion. But their most remarkable feat is their 'Kick-ball' races, during which they run continuously, day and night, along paths and trails over mountainous terrain, kicking a wooden tennis-sized ball. Races covering a length of 120 km are common. Groom (1971) was able to study eight male Tazahumara runners, aged 18 to 48 years, competing in two teams of four each, over a distance of 45.7 km. The winners covered this distance in 4 hours 55 minutes, the others finishing approximately 15 minutes later. All runners, checked both at the three-quarter point and at the end of the race showed declines of systolic as well as diastolic blood pressures! No abnormality was seen in their electrocardiograms either before or after the race. No enlargement of the heart was evident on physical examination or X-ray.

Such phenomenal feats of physical endurance are made possible by intensive training, begun early in life and progressively increased during the developmental years. As in most 'primitive' tribes natural selection also plays a role, through many generations of adjustment to such a rigorous existence, high infant mortality and lifelong elimination of the 'unfits'. This balanced and sustained physical training enables the adults to make the best use of their physical abilities. Another advantage of sustained exercise could be to prevent the accumulation of fatty deposits during adulthood and to decrease the cholesterol level.

The psycho-social factors

That the 'stress of life' accelerates the pace of aging has long been taken for granted. However, it is even more difficult to quantify a given pyscho-social stimulus in 'field' conditions than to measure functional aging in man. Consequently, much remains to be done to demonstrate that certain stimuli originating in social relationships (Levi, 1972; Henry and Stephens, 1977) are able to quicken functional aging, and/or to increase the prevalence of age-associated diseases.

So far, the most solid evidence supporting the common view that repeated stressing situations have a deleterious effect on our aging pattern comes from comparative epidemiology.

First of all, acculturation (i.e. the process of rapid cultural change taking place when two different cultures are brought into contact) very often alters the pattern of age changes, particularly those of the cardiovascular system. Some attempts have been made recently to develop scales of acculturation, to assign 'acculturation rank' to sets of populations or of individuals and to single-out cultural variables which might be particularly important in inducing biological changes. For instance, Page et al (1977), during the Harvard project in the Solomon Islands, have considered the following factors: 1. evidence of demographic change within the defined populations; 2. secular increase in adult height; 3. length and intensity of contact with western culture; 4. religious change from 'pagan' to Christian belief; 5. education; 6. availability of medical care; 7. extent of entry into cash economy; and 8. adoption of European-style dietary items (tinned meat and fish, flour, etc.). On the other hand Marmot (1975) and Marmot and Syme (1976) have used a more refined scale of acculturation to study the relationship between culture changes and prevalence of coronary heart disease in Japanese-Americans. The three acculturation indices they used were devised in order to study the influence of: 1. the culture of upbringing; 2. that of cultural assimilation, i.e. the degree to which an individual has given up cultural forms such as speaking Japanese and traditional practices (including dietary preferences); and 3. that of social assimilation, i.e. the degree to which the individual has left the ethnic group for work, for professional help from doctor or church, or for social relationships.

The results obtained by the above mentioned studies are very encouraging and should help to identify the most significant social variables. For instance, among the six Solomon Islands tribes studied, the three most acculturated, at almost all ages in both sexes, showed higher cholesterol levels than the three less acculturated tribes. In the same groups, systolic blood pressure increased significantly with age in women. Such a selective effect on females has also been noted in other partially acculturated populations belonging to very different racial stocks: Australian aborigines (Abbie and Schroder, 1960), Melanesians (Maddocks, 1967; Boyce et al, 1978), Polynesians (Prior et al, 1968) and Amerindians from Surinam (Glanville and Geerdink, 1972).

The Japanese-American study has also shown the importance of more subtle psycho-social factors as determinants of differential aging. While the most traditional group had a coronary heart disease prevalence rate as low as that observed in Japan, the group that was the most acculturated to Western culture had a three to five fold excess in coronary heart disease prevalence. Furthermore, this difference could not be accounted for by differences in the major coronary risk factors: dietary preferences, smoking habits, blood pressure level, serum cholesterol, serum triglyceride, relative weight and serum glucose. In their concluding remarks Marmot (1975) and Marmot and Syme (1976) emphasize the importance of 'a stable society whose members enjoy the support of their fellows in closely knit groups' as a way to ensure protection against the various forms of social stress.

Psycho-social factors are not only important in acculturated groups; they play a far from negligible role in more 'stable' societies. A study by Desplanques (1973), for instance, points out the importance of working conditions (and associated variables) as a major determinant of the average life-span in present-day France. Comparing the further expectations of life of the major socio-economic groups, Desplanques found a 5.3 years difference at age 35, and a 3.9 years difference at age 60, between the 'winners' and the 'losers'. The former (school teachers and professionals) had still 40.8 and 18.6 years to live respectively at ages 35 and 60, whereas the latter (unskilled city workers) had only 33.5 and 14.7 years ahead of them. That harsh working conditions are more important than income in this connection is shown by the fact that well-to-do professionals enjoyed the same advantage as poorly paid school teachers. Furthermore, the living environment as a whole does not play a major role either, since wage-earning farm workers living in the country come very close to the unskilled city workers, their further expectation of life being of only 34.9 years at age 35 and 14.9 years at age 60.

The research on variations of aging rate according to occupation and working conditions also supports the view that aging proceeds more rapidly in some occupations than in others. A survey undertaken 10 years ago on assembly-line workers with a 50 hour working week and frequent night shifts in a large automobile factory near Paris showed how poor some of their physical and mental performances were already at 50 years of age

(Clément et al, 1968). On the contrary, the random sample of Parisian school teachers studied in the same way by Clément (1961) exhibited quite a different pattern. Whereas their weight, vital capacity and blood pressure varied with age in much the same way as those of the 'average' middle-class Parisians, their muscular strength (hand grip) declined more rapidly, while most of their mental performances remained far superior at every age and for both sexes. Particularly striking was the fact that the teachers lost their memory only about half as fast as the controls. Differential aging can even occur within small rural communities. Such was the case in the traditional village of Plozevet, in Brittany (Bourlière et al, 1966). Although farmers, fishermen and shopkeepers had the same ancestry (the fathers of half the fishermen and of 44 per cent of the shop-keeper being farmers), each of these occupational groups aged in a somewhat different manner. Furthermore, these rural people were not in better physical or mental health than Parisian controls of comparable socio-economic level. Similar conclusions were drawn from the study of another rural sample (Clément et al, 1973). Bourlière (1976) has also shown that regional differences in mortality from 'social stress' diseases had little to do in France with population density, urbanization or 'environmental quality', but rather with working and housing conditions, 'life-satisfaction', and possibly also with more subtle cultural factors still to be determined. Occupational differences in the pattern of age change of the cardiovascular system have also been found in Japan (Komachi et al, 1971).

To conclude, our present knowledge of how environmental factors affect the pattern and rate of aging in man is still inadequate. There is no doubt that climatic parameters *per se* have little influence, wheras dietary and psycho-social factors are of much greater importance, both in traditional and industrialized populations. Unfortunately the role of the various environmental parameters is complex and difficult to disentangle using traditional techniques. New research strategies have to be developed, and they should imply the participation of specialists from many disciplines, including psychologists and social scientists. Great care will have to be taken to avoid oversimplification, especially when studying the role of psycho-social stimuli and cultural factors. Furthermore there will always be individual differences in the 'ability to cope' with adverse conditions. Some of them may be genetic, but many others are learned more or less early in life. In many cases therefore we cannot expect to make much progress in our understanding of the action of environment upon aging processes unless some carefully planned longitudinal studies can be initiated — however difficult and costly they may be.

REFERENCES

Abbie A L, Schroder J 1960 Blood pressures in Arnhem land aborigines. Medical Journal of Australia 2: 493–496

Adams P, Davies G T, Sweetnam P 1970 Osteoporosis and the effect of ageing on bone mass in elderly men and women. Quarterly Journal of Medicine 39: 601–615

Akhtar A J, Broe G A, Crombie A, McLean W M R, Andrews G R, Caird F I 1973 Disability and dependence in the elderly at home. Age and Ageing 2: 102–111

Allwright S P A, Coulson A, Detels R 1974 Mortality and water-hardness in three matched communities in Los Angeles. Lancet 2: 860–864

Andres R 1981 Influence of obesity on longevity in the aged. In: Danon D, Shock N W, Marois M (eds) Ageing: a challenge to science and society. Volume 1. Biology. Oxford University Press, Oxford, pp 196–203

Badley E M, Thompson R T, Wood P H N 1978 The prevalence and severity of major disabling conditions. A reappraisal of the Government Social Survey on the handicapped and impaired in Great Britain. International Journal of Epidemiology 7: 145–151

Bang J O, Dyerberg J, Nielsen A B 1971 Plasma lipid and lipoprotein pattern in Greenlandic West Coast Eskimos. Lancet i: 1143–1146

Bank L, Jarvik L F 1978 A longitudinal study of aging twins. In: Schneider E L (ed) The Genetics of Aging, Plenum Press, New York, pp 303–333

Bennett A E, Garrad J, Halil T 1970 Chronic disease and disability in the community: A prevalence study. British Medical Journal 3: 762–765

Bennett P H, Burch T A, Miller M 1971 Diabetes mellitus in American (Pima) indians. Lancet ii: 125–128

Bentsen B G 1970 Illness and general practice. Universitetsforlaget, Oslo. Quoted after Rinder Bollerup 1975

Birren J A, Butler R N, Greenhouse S W, Sokoloff L, Yarrow M R (eds) 1963 Human Aging. A Biological and Behavioral Study, NIMH, Bethesda, Md, XI, p 328

Bourlière F 1969 Les méthodes de mesure de l'âge biologique chez l'homme. Geneva, WHO, Cahiers de Santé Publique, 37, pp 1–73

Bourlière F 1976 Ageing in French rural communities. Paper presented at the symposium Society, Stress and Disease: Aging and Old Age. Stockholm, June 14–19, 1976

Bourlière F, Parot S 1962 Le vieillissement de deux populations blanches vivant dans des conditions écologiques très différentes, étude comparative. Revue Francaise d'etudes cliniques et biologiques 7: 629–635

Bourlière F, Cendron H, Clément F 1966 Le vieillissement individuel dans une population rurale francaise. Etude de la commune de Plozevet, Finistère. Bulletin et memoires de la societe d'anthropologie Paris XI 10: 41–101

Bourlière F, Clément F, Parot S 1966 'Normes' de vieillissement morphologique et physiologique d'une population de niveau socio-économique élevé de la région parisienne. Bulletin et memoires de la societe d'anthropologie Paris XI 10: 11–39

Boyce A J, Attenborough R D, Harrison G A, Hornabrook R W, Sinnett P 1978 Variation in blood pressure in a New Guinea population. Annals of Human Biology 5: 313–319

Campbell H 1980 Cancer mortality in Europe. Site specific patterns and trends 1955 to 1974. World Health Statistics 33: 241–280

Clément F 1961 Recherches sur le vieillissement d'un groupe professionnel homogène, les instituteurs des écoles publiques de la Seine. Revue française de gérontologie 7: 7–52

Clément F, Cendron H, Housset P 1968 Le vieillissement différentiel d'une population ouvrière dans la région parisienne. Bulletin INSERM 23: 889–920

Clément F, Cendron H, Olivier-Martin R, Vallery-Masson J 1973 Problèmes de vieillissement en milieu rural. Cahiers, Fondation Nationale de Gérontologie, Paris 3: 1–91

Cohart, E M, Muller C 1955 Socio-economic distribution of cancer of female sex organs in New Haven. Cancer 8: 34–41

Comfort A 1969 The Test-battery to measure ageing-rate in man Lancet ii: 1411–1415

Comfort A 1979 The Biology of Senescence. 3rd edn. Churchill Livingstone, Edinburgh and London, IX, p 414

Corone P, Drouet L, Escourrou P, Antezana G 1977 Epidémiologie cardio-vasculaire de sujets boliviens résidant en haute et basse altitude. In: Ruffié J, Quilici J C, Lacoste M C (eds) Anthropologie des populations andines. INSERM, Paris, pp 441–452

Coulbert P 1982 La vie quotidienne des paysans francais au XVIIIe siècle. Hachette, Paris, p 319

Court Brown W M, Doll R 1958 Expectation of life and mortality from cancer among British radiologists. British Medical Journal 2: 181–187

Crawford M A 1968 Fatty-acid ratios in free-living and domestic animals: possible implications for atheroma. Lancet i: 1329

Dawber T R 1980 The Framingham Study. The epidemiology of atherosclerotic disease. Harvard University Press, Cambridge Mass., VIII, p 257

Depoid F 1973 La mortalité des grands vieillards. Population 28: 755–792

Desplanques G 1973 A 35 ans les instituteurs ont encore 41 ans à vivre, les manoeuvres 34 seulement. Economie et Statistiques 49: 3–20

Dublin L L, Lotka A J, Spiegelman M 1942 Length of Life. A Study of the life table. Revised edition, Ronald Press, New York, XXV, p 379

Ducimetière P, Richard J, Claude J R, Warnet J M 1981 Les cardiopathies ischémiques. Incidence et facteurs de risque. L'étude prospective parisienne. INSERM, Paris p 149

Dupâquier J 1979 La population francaise aux XVIIe et XVIIIe siècles. Presses Universitaires de France, Paris, p 128

Duvillard E E 1806 Analyse et tableaux de l'influence de la petite vérole sur la mortalité à chaque âge, et de celle qu'un préservatif tel que la vaccine peut avoir sur la population et la longévité. Imprimerie Impériale, Paris, p 210

Dyerberg J, Bang H O 1979a Haemostatic function and platelet polyunsaturated fatty acids in Eskimos. Lancet ii: 433–435

Dyerberg J, Bang H O 1979b Lipid metabolism, atherogenesis, and haemostasis in Eskimos: the role of the prostaglandin-3 family. Haemostasis 8: 227–233

Dyerberg J, Bang H O, Stoffersen E, Moncada S, Vane J R 1978 Eicosapentaenoic acid and prevention of thrombosis and atherosclerosis. Lancet ii: 117–119

Essen-Möller E 1956 Individual traits and morbidity in a Swedish rural population Acta psychiatrica Scandinavica, suppl 100. Quoted after Rinder Bollerup, 1975

Frei III E 1982 The National Cancer Chemotherapy Program. Science 217: 600–606

Gallagher J C, Melton L J, Riggs B L, Bergstrath E 1980 Epidemiology of fractures of the proximal femur in Rochester, Minnesota. Clinical Orthopaedics and related research 150: 163–171

Gerner R H 1979 Depression in the elderly. In: Kaplan O J (ed) Psychopathology of Aging, Academic Press, New York, pp 97–148

Glanville E V, Geerdink R A 1972 Blood pressure of Amerindians from Surinam. American Journal of Physical Anthropology 37: 251–254

Graham S, Levin M, Lilienfeld A M 1960 The socio economic distribution of cancer of various sites in Buffalo, New York, 1948–1952. Cancer 13: 180–191

Granick S, Patterson R D (eds) 1971 Human Aging II. An eleven-year follow up biomedical and behavioral study. NIMH, Rockville, Md, VII, p 144

Groom D 1971 Cardiovascular observations on Tarahumara indian runners, the modern Spartans. American Heart Journal 81: 304–314

Gruneberg H 1966 A search for genetic effects of high natural radioactivity in South India. HMSO, London

Haberman S, Capildeo R, Clifford Rose F 1978 The changing mortality of cerebrovascular disease. Quarterly Journal of Medicine 47: 71–88

Halley E 1693 Degrees of mortality of mankind. Johns Hopkins Press, Baltimore, 1942, VI, p 21 (Originally published in 1693 as 'An estimate of the degrees of mortality of mankind drawn from curious tables of the births and funerals of the city of Breslaw') In:

Philosophical Transactions of the Royal Society of London 17: 596

Harris A I 1971 Handicapped and impaired in Great Britain. HMSO, London

Hatano S 1975 Hypertension in Japan: A review. In: Oglesby P (ed) Epidemiology and Control of Hypertension. Medical Books, Miami, pp 63–95

Hayflick L 1981 Prospects for human life extension by genetic manipulation. In: Danon D, Schock N W, Marois M (eds) Aging: a Challenge to Science and Society, volume 1, Biology. Oxford University Press, Oxford, p 169–179

Helgason T 1973 Epidemiology of mental disorders in Iceland: A geriatric follow-up. In: R. de la Fuente, Weisman M (eds) Proceedings of the Fifth World Congress of Psychiatry, Mexico, 1971, Sect. VIII B

Henry J P, Stephens P M 1977 Topics in environmental physiology and medicine. Stress, Health and the Social Environment. Springer Verlag, Berlin, Heidelberg and New York, p 263

Ho K J, Biss K, Mikkelson B, Lewis L A, Taylor C B 1971 The Masai of East Africa: some unique biological characteristics. Archives of Pathology 91: 387–410

Hollingsworth D R, Hollingsworth J W, Bogitch S, Keehn R J 1969 Neuro-muscular tests of ageing in Hiroshima subjects. Journal of Gerontology 24: 276–283

Hollingsworth J W, Hashizume A, Jablon S 1965 Correlations between tests of aging in Hiroshima subjects. An attempt to define 'physiologic age'. Yale Journal of Biology and Medicine 38: 11–26

Howell T 1963a Multiple pathology in nonagenarians. Geriatrics 18: 899–902

Howell T 1963b Causes of death in nonagenarians. Gerontologia Clinica 5: 139–143

Ishii T, Hosoda Y, Maeda K 1980 Cause of death in the extreme aged. A pathologic survey of 5106 elderly persons 80 years and over. Age and Ageing 9: 81–89

Jalavisto E 1951 Inheritance of longevity according to finnish and swedish genealogies. Annales medicinae internae Fenniae 40: 263–274

Jeremy R, Rhodes F A 1971 Studies of serum urate levels in New Guineans living in different environments. Medical Journal of Australia 1: 897–899

Kagan A, Harris B R, Winkelstein W, Johnson K G, Kato H, Syme S L et al 1974 Epidemiologic studies of coronary heart disease and stroke in Japanese men living in Japan, Hawaii and California: demographic, physical, dietary and biochemical characteristics. Journal of Chronic Diseases 27: 345–364

Kay D W K, Beamish P, Roth M 1964 Old age mental disorders in Newcastle upon Tyne. British Journal of Psychiatry 110: 146–158, 668–682

Keys A (ed) 1980 Seven countries. A multivariate analysis of death and coronary heart disease. Harvard University Press, Cambridge, XI, p 381

Keys A, Kimura N, Kusukawa A, Bronte-Stewart B, Larsen N P, Keys M H 1957 Diet and serum cholesterol of Japanese men in Japan, Hawaii and California. Federation Proceedings 16: 204

Kimura T 1960 Excessive salt intake and blood pressure. Nippon Serigaku Zasshi 22: 91–95

Kitagawa E M, Hauser P M 1973 Differential mortality in the United States. Harvard University Press, Cambridge Mass., p 253

Kojima S 1966 Distinctive features of cerebral apoplexy seen around the Akita district. Nippon Koshueisei Zasshi 13: 907–924

Kojima S 1975 CVA in rural areas with special reference to dietary intake. In: Asahina K, Shigiya R (eds) Physiological Adaptability and Nutritional Status of the Japanese. JIBP Synthesis. Tokyo, 4: 198–206

Komachi Y, Iida M, Shimamoto T, Chikayama Y, Takahashi H, Konishi M, Tominaga S 1971 Geographic and occupational comparisons of risk factors in cardiovascular diseases in Japan. Japanese Circulation Journal 35: 189–207

Lambert P M, Reid D D 1970 Smoking, air pollution, and bronchitis in Britain. Lancet i: 853–856

Lapiccirella V, Lapiccirella R, Abboni F, Liotta S 1962 Enquête clinique, biologique et cardiographique parmi les tribus nomades de la Somalie qui se nourissent seulement de lait. Bulletin of the World Health Organization 27: 681–697

Lee R B 1972 The Kung Bushmen of Botswana. In: Bicchieri M G (ed) Hunters and Gatherers Today, Holt, Rinehart and Winston,

New York, pp 327–368

Levi L 1972 Stress and distress in response to psychosocial stimuli. Acta Medica Scandinavica Suppl. 528: 1–166

MacCay C M, Maynard L A, Sperling G, Barnes L L 1939 Retarded growth, life-span, ultimate body size and age changes in the albino rat after feeding diets restricted in calories. Journal of Nutrition 18: 1–13

MacMahon B, Pugh T F, Ipsen J 1960 Epidemiologic Methods. Little Brown Co, Boston and Toronto, p 302

Maddocks I 1967 Blood pressures in Melanesians. Medical Journal of Australia 1: 1123–1126

Mann G V 1962 The health and nutritional status of Alaskan Eskimos. American Journal of Clinical Nutrition 11: 31–76

Mann G V, Roels O A, Price D L, Merril J M 1961 Cardiovascular disease in African pygmies. Journal of Chronic Diseases 15: 341–371

Mann G V, Shaffer R D, Anderson R S, Sandstead H H 1964 Cardiovascular disease in the Masai. Journal of Atherosclerosis Research 4: 289–312

Mann G V, Shaffer R D, Rich A 1965 Physical fitness and immunity to heart-disease in Masai. Lancet ii: 1308–1310

Manton K G 1980 Sex and race specific mortality differentials in multiple causes of death data. Gerontologist 20: 480–493

Manton K G, Sandomirsky Poss S, Wing S 1979 The black/white mortality crossover: investigation from the perspective of the components of aging. Gerontologist 19: 291–300

Marmot M G 1975 Acculturation and coronary heart disease in Japanese Americans. Ph.D. Thesis, University of California, Berkeley

Marmot M G, Syme S L 1976 Acculturation and coronary heart disease in Japanese-Americans. American Journal of Epidemiology 104: 225–247

Master K M 1974 Air pollution in New Guinea. Journal of the American Medical Association 226: 1653–1655

Matkovic V, Ciganovic M, Tominac C, Kostial K 1980 Osteoporosis and epidemiology of fractures in Croatia. An international comparison. Henry Ford Hospital Medical Journal 28: 116–126

Miller K, Rubenstein A, Astrand P O 1968 Lipid values in Kalahari Bushmen. Archives of Internal Medicine 121: 414–417

Moldawer M, Zimmerman S J, Collins L C 1965 Incidence of osteoporosis in elderly whites and elderly Negroes. Journal of the American Medical Association 194: 859–862

Montoye H J, Epstein F H, Kjelsberg M O 1965 The measurement of body fatness. A study in a total community. American Journal of Nutrition 16: 417–427

Mourgue J A 1785 Observations sur les naissances, les mariages et les morts à Montpellier. Histoire de la Société Royale de Médecine, années 1780–1781, p 378–392

Myers G C 1978 Cross-national trends in mortality rates among the elderly. Gerontologist 18: 441–448

Oliver W J, Cohen E L, Neel J V 1975 Blood pressure, sodium intake, and sodium related hormones in the Yanomamo Indians, a 'No Salt' culture. Circulation 52: 146–151.

Padmavati S, Gupta S 1959 Blood pressure in rural and urban groups in Delhi. Circulation 19: 395–405

Page L B, Damon A, Moellering R C Jr 1974 Antecedents of cardiovascular disease in six Solomon Islands societies. Circulation 49: 1132–1146

Page L, Friedlaender J, Moellering R C Jr 1977 Culture, human biology and disease in the Solomon Islands. In: Harrison G A (ed) Population Structure and Human Variation. Cambridge University Press, Cambridge, pp 143–163

Palmore E (ed) 1970 Normal aging. Reports from the Duke Longitudinal Study, 1955–1969. Duke University Press, Durham, XXIV, p 431

Palmore E (ed) 1974 Normal aging II. Reports from the Duke Longitudinal Study, 1970–1973. Duke University Press, Durham, XIX, p 316

Pearl R, Pearl R D 1934 The ancestry of the long-lived. Johns Hopkins University Press, Baltimore, p 163

Pooling Project Research Group 1978 Relationship of blood pressure, serum cholesterol, smoking habit, relative weight and ECG abnormalities to incidence of major coronary events: final report of the Pooling Project. Journal of Chronic Diseases 31: 201–306

Primrose E J R 1962 Psychological Illness. A community study.

Tavistock Publications, London. Quoted after Rinder Bollerup (1975)

Prior I A M, Hooper A, Huntsman J W, Stanhope J M, Salmond C E 1977 The Tokelau Island migrant study. In Harrison G A (ed) Population Structure and Human Variation. Cambridge University Press, Cambridge, pp 165–186

Prior I A M, Rose B S 1964 Metabolic maladies in New Zealand Maoris. British Medical Journal 1: 1065–1069

Prior I A M, Rose B S, Harvey J P B, Davidson F 1966 Hyperuricaemia, gout, and diabetic abnormality in Polynesian people. Lancet i: 333–338

Reff M E, Schneider E L 1982 Biological markers of aging. NIH Publication No 82.2221, Washington, VII, p 252

Rinder Bollerup T 1975 Prevalence of mental illness among 70-year-olds domiciled in nine Copenhagen suburbs. The Glostrup Survey. Acta psychiatrica Scandinavica 51: 327–339

Robbe B 1976 Effets biologiques des changements du mode de vie et des habitudes alimentaires sur une population eskimo de la côte est du Groenland. Anthropologie, Paris 80: 515–517

Rosenwaike M A, Yaffe N, Sagi P C 1980 The recent decline in mortality of the extreme aged: an analysis of statistical data. American Journal of Public Health 70: 1074–1080

Ruiz L, Penaloza D 1970 Research Project (Altitude and cardiovascular disease). Progress Report 1969–1970. Lima

Sasaki N, Takeda J, Fukushi S 1960 Nutritional factors related to the geographical difference in the death rate from apoplexy in Japan. Nippon Koshueisei Zasshi 7: 1137–1143

Scott E M, Griffith I V, Hoskins D D, Whaley R D 1958 Serum-cholesterol levels and blood pressure of Alaskan Eskimo men. Lancet ii: 667–668

Shaper A G, Jones K W 1962 Serum-cholesterol in camel-herding nomads. Lancet ii: 1305–1307

Shaper A G, Wright D H, Kyobe J 1969 Blood pressure and body build in three nomadic tribes of Northern Kenya. East African Journal of Medical Research 46: 273–281

Sigurjonsson J 1974 Differences in mortality patterns of coronary heart disease and cerebrosvascular lesions. Journal of the American Geriatrics Society 22: 241–245

Sinnett P, Whyte H M 1973 Epidemiological studies in a total highland-population, Tukisenta, New Guinea. Cardiovascular disease and relevant clinical, electrocardiographic, radiological and biochemical findings. Journal of Chronic Diseases 26: 265–290

Sinnett P, Keig G, Craig W 1973 Nutrition and age-related changes in the body build of adults: studies in a New Guinea highland community. Human Biology in Oceania 2: 50–62

Steen Jensen J 1980 Incidence of hip fractures. Acta orthopaedica Scandinavica 51: 511–513

Stern M P 1979 The recent decline in ischemic heart disease mortality. Annals of Internal Medicine 91: 630–640

Svanborg A 1977 Seventy-year-old people in Gothenburg. A population study in an industrialized swedish city. II. General presentation of social and medical conditions. Acta medica Scandinavica, Suppl 5: 1–37

Szafran J 1968 Psychophysiological studies of aging in pilots. In: Talland G A (ed) Human Aging and Behavior. New York Academic Press, New York

Truswell A S, Hansen J D L 1976 Medical research among the !Kung. In: Lee R B, DeVore I (eds) Kalahari Hunter-Gatherers. Harvard University Press

Vallery-Masson J, Poitrenaud J, Burnat G, Lion M R 1981 Retirement and morbidity: a three-year longitudinal study of a french managerial population. Age and Ageing 10: 271–276

Vallin J 1973 La mortalité par génération en France depuis 1899. Institut National d'Etudes Démographiques, Paris, Travaux et Documents, 63, XV, p 483

Waern U 1978 Health and disease at the age of sixty. Findings in a health survey of 60-year-old men in Uppsala and a comparison with men 10 years younger. Uppsala Journal of Medical Sciences 83: 153–162

Weitz C A 1973 The effects of aging and habitual activity pattern on exercise performance among a high altitude Nepalese population. Ph.D. Thesis, Pennsylvania State University. p 175

Zimmet P Z, Whitehouse S, Jackson L, Thorna K 1978 High prevalence of hyperuricaemia and gout in an urbanized micronesian population. British Medical Journal 1: 1237–1239

Biology of aging — general principles

It has been a major preoccupation of man to dwell on his own mortality and there have been many attempts to alleviate the problems and sufferings of the late part of the life-span by the use of potions and elixirs. Unfortunately, the early, metaphysical theories proposed to explain aging phenomena set the tone of aging research for many centuries, and the attempts to 'cure' aging led to many scientists shunning this field of research.

Several definitions of aging have been put forward, and indeed aging has many different aspects. It has social, psychological (behavioural), physiological, morphological, cellular and molecular aspects and a definition encompassing them all does not seem possible. Biologists involved in the study of aging operate on the premise *that aging is characterised by a failure to maintain homeostasis under conditions of physiological stress, and that this failure is associated with a decrease in viability and an increase in vulnerability of the individual* (Comfort, 1979). Aging is obviously a function of time, but development and maturation also involve changes which are age(time)-related. However, both of the latter processes lead to the attainment of peak physiological function, whereas the above definition implies that aging is a deteriorative process.

Most of the recognizable features of aging occur after the period of reproductive activity has ceased. The term senescence is usually applied to this part of the life-cycle and its usage is more precise when referring to the deteriorative effects associated with the passage of time.

THE AGING PROCESS

Two principal types of investigation can be used to study the aging process — cross-sectional and longitudinal — and both are subject to some drawback. A cross-sectional study involves the analysis of changes in groups of individuals at different ages. Unfortunately, this allows secular (cohort) changes in the population to contribute greatly to any differences that may be seen, particularly in human studies. On the other hand, longitudinal studies while theoretically the more inform-

ative (in that the same individual is studied at various stages of the life-span), are subject to the rapidly improving technology used in the measurement of biological and clinical variables, and in addition, to alterations in the focus of the scientific viewpoint brought about by an increase in our basic knowledge. Such changes may not be particularly great over a period of say 5 years, but over five decades may be very significant indeed.

Faced with such difficulties it is usual to employ an animal model, or to use tissue culture techniques (Schneider and Smith, 1981). The literature on aging contains references to studies on both invertebrates and vertebrates (Benhke et al, 1978; Comfort, 1979), and the reader is directed elsewhere for reviews of animal models in the study of senescence. Many of the metazoan invertebrates are useful because of their mainly post-mitotic cell population, short life-span and ease of manipulation in strictly controlled environments. Among the vertebrates, research has been concentrated on the laboratory rodent which displays many of the features associated with the aging process. Fundamental investigations of the physiology, immunology, endocrinology and biochemistry of aging have been carried out on both rats and mice.

A major problem for the gerontologist is in choosing a species and/or strain of animal to study. There are at least 200 inbred strains of mice, each with their own specific life-span and disease patterns (Gibson, 1972; Gibson et al, 1979). Detailed records must be kept of colonies of animals used in research with information on environmental conditions, growth rates, food consumption and causes of death being a minimum requirement. Old animals are particularly vulnerable to respiratory disorders and they must be continuously monitored for possible infections, so frequent bacteriological and viral screening of the colony is required. These requirements make the use of laboratory animals in aging research an extremely complex and costly process!

Tissue culture and in-vitro aging

At the turn of the century August Weismann argued

that the physiological decline seen in aged animals could be due to the evolution of a limited reproductive capacity of the somatic cells (see review by Kirkwood & Cremer, 1982). However, Carrel, and subsequently Ebeling (Kirkwood & Cremer, 1982) claimed to have isolated chick embryo tissues and maintained cultures of these cells for over 30 years. Thus, it was proposed that if cells were isolated from a metazoan they would be immortal. Later work on cell cultures derived from normal mouse tissues and human tumours (e.g. HeLa cervical tumour cells), apparently confirmed these early experiments. However, Hayflick and Moorehead (1961) described a different system when they showed that cells from a variety of normal human tissues would only proliferate in culture for a defined period before degenerating and dying out. These cultured cells are elongated and spindle-shaped, and are defined as human diploid, fibroblast-like (HDF) cells. HDF cells were clearly not immortal and the suggestion was made that this was the cellular expression of the aging process (Hayflick, 1965).

There have been several criticisms of this idea based on various shortcomings in the culture process. Thus, the limited survival of HDF may be due to deficiencies in the culture media (Hay and Strehler, 1967; Hay et al, 1968; Ryan et al 1975). Perhaps more fundamental to the study of aging is the lack of interaction between cell types in such an experimental system (Franks, 1970), but as long as these drawbacks are fully understood then the in vitro model can be an extremely powerful tool in the study of aging in mitotic cells. Indeed, the study of aging in vitro has led to the proposal of new theories to explain senescence in culture, such as the 'commitment theory' put forward by Kirkwood and Holliday (1975), and the model of 'clonal attenuation' proposed by Prothero and Gallant (1981). This area of investigation has developed rapidly and the reader is directed elsewhere for information on progress in this field (Harley and Goldstein, 1980; Holliday et al, 1977, 1981; Kirkwood & Cremer, 1982).

Accumulated population doublings are used as a measure of the culture age. The cells display different growth characteristics at different stages of the culture life-cycle. In the early stages the cells proliferate rapidly and the sub-cultivation intervals are short, but in the senescent phase of the culture the cells become larger and divide more slowly. The average number of population doublings of foetal lung and skin fibroblasts before the senescent phase is approximately 50, and the total number of doublings is 63 (Fig. 2.1) (Hayflick, 1965). If cells are isolated from adult tissues rather than fetal sources, there is a reduction in the number of population doublings achieved by the cells (Martin et al, 1970). Thus, instead of a potential of 50 doublings, only 30 can be obtained before the senescent phase. The growth potential of cells in culture decreases with the

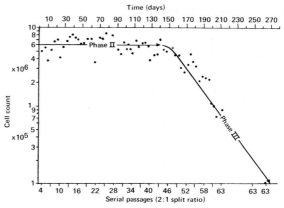

Fig. 2.1 The life-cycle of human diploid fibroblast-like cells in vitro (copied with permission from Hayflick, 1965)

age of the donor. Furthermore, there is an age-related latent period for the outgrowth of cells from human skin explants, with this period increasing linearly with age; however, this phenomenon is subject to a great deal of individual variation which is also a function of the donor's age (Waters and Walford, 1970).

There are species differences in the response of fibroblast-like cells to culture conditions. Chick fibroblast-like cells have a stable, limited life-span and never appear to give rise to 'immortal' cell lines. Similar cells from mice and rats also have a characteristic growth pattern which comprises rapid proliferation of the cells followed by a decline, and then almost always a spontaneous transformation into an immortal cell line. Human cells on the other hand can be 'transformed' to an immortal cell type by some treatment, such as exposure to the SV 40 virus (Cristofalo and Stanulis, 1978).

Hayflick (1965) proposed that in vitro senescence is due to some form of programmed control. Wright and Hayflick (1975) carried out hybridization experiments to investigate the role of cytoplasmic factors in in vitro senescence. Hybrids between anucleate cytoplasms (cytoplasts) and 'inactivated' normal HDF showed that the enzymes of untreated cytoplasts replaced inactivated enzymes of whole cells and permitted hybrid cell survival (Wright & Hayflick 1975). The hybrids formed by *old cytoplasts–old cells* and *young cytoplasts–old ·cells* had a low doubling potential, whereas those hybrids involving young cells survived similar doublings to the controls (Wright and Hayflick, 1975). Norwood et al (1974) suggested that post-mitotic, aged HDF may synthesize some specific repressor molecule(s) which inhibits the initiation of DNA synthesis. Subsequent work (Norwood et al, 1975) showed that heterokaryons of old HDF and either SV80 transformed HDF, or HeLa cells, initiated DNA synthesis in the old nuclei. These results strongly implicate some positive control of DNA synthesis by the HeLa and SV80-transformed-cells over that of the proposed repressor compound. More recently it has been shown that if young HDF are in the S-phase of the cell cycle when they are fused to senescent cells then DNA synthesis proceeds (Yanishevsky and Stein, 1980). On the other hand entry into the S-phase is inhibited because young HDF in the G1phase of the cell cycle (when fused with senescent HDF), do not synthesise DNA (Yanishevsky and Stein, 1980).These results are consistent with the hypothesis that the molecular basis for the senescent phenotype involves a block that prevents cells in the G1-phase from entering the S-phase (Stein and Yanishevsky, 1979).

It has also been shown that late passage cultures of HDF cells demonstrate less DNA repair activity than young cells after exposure to ultraviolet (UV) radiation (Mattern and Cerutti, 1975; Hart and Setlow, 1976). It was argued that these results indicated a decrease in the ability of senescent cells to integrate the various operations needed for DNA repair. However, Painter et al (1973) while showing a decline in UV-induced repair with culture age, demonstrated that this reduction occurred only in the last passage prior to cessation of cell division. Thus, they concluded that this deficiency in repair was not the basis for in vitro aging. This methodology offers the exciting prospect of being able to analyse the exact roles of the cell nucleus and cytoplasm in the in vitro model of aging. Recent publications indicate that it is possible to induce a superficial senescent phenotype in HDF cells using various manipulations, and that it is possible to analyse and 'dissect' cells from such treatments using hybridisation procedures (Norwood et al, 1979; Rabinovitch and Norwood, 1980).

Transplantation experiments
We have described the fixed number of mitotic cell population doublings that take place in vitro but is this also the case in vivo? The transplantation of tissues between immunologically compatible (histocompatible or syngeneic) animals has been used to address this question. Krohn (1962) transplanted ovaries and skin between young and old animals. He demonstrated that young fertilised ovaries, or eggs, functioned less well in old as compared to young recipients. Thus, factors outside the ovary affect reproductive ability in the aging rodent. The results of these studies however, were not easy to interpret because of the variability found in the tissues from old animals. The skin grafting results were also equivocal; in some cases the grafts from old animals grew as well as those from younger mice. During successive transplants the grafts became progressively smaller and many were lost, but this was common to samples from both young and old sources. A major problem in this study was that of cells from the host

tissue migrating into the transplant during the process of wound repair.

In an attempt to overcome the problem of the identification of 'host-tissue', transplants of bone-marrow stem-cells have been employed. However, the host has to be lethally irradiated to kill all of its intrinsic stem-cell population. Ogden and Micklem (1976) used an abnormal chromosome to identify donor stem-cells in an elegant study of the division capacity of marrow stem-cells in mice. After 12 months in the first host the marrow cells were transplanted into a second recipient and the cells checked for the presence of the abnormal chromosome to make certain that they were from the original donor. This procedure was repeated annually and after about four successive transplants the stem-cells were found to have a reduced capacity to repopulate the host's marrow. It was therefore concluded that the maximum life-span of the mouse was very close to that of the functional division capacity of the marrow cells and that they were programmed in some way to age and die at the same time.

It has been shown that successive transplantations can cause non-specific damage to the stem-cells. Also the stem-cell pool can become 'exhausted' in conditions where constant division is stimulated (a factor later confirmed by Micklem's group; Ross et al, 1982). Harrison et al (1978) proposed three criteria to avoid ambiguous results in transplant experiments; firstly, the functional ability of the cells must be investigated; secondly, the identity of the transplanted tissue must be unambiguous; and thirdly, young and old animal tissues should be treated in an identical fashion.

Harrison and his co-workers studied mice with a genetic defect which caused a hereditary anaemia due to stem-cell abnormalities. In this case the mice did not require prior lethal irradiation and if the transplant was successful then the anaemia was cured. Red cell production could be measured in the recipients after transplantation, so a direct measure of stem-cell function was obtained. Since the cure of the hereditary anaemia never occurred spontaneously the donor cells were identified unambiguously, and in addition, the experiments were controlled in that the effects of both young and old donor cells could be compared in the recipients. In these studies there was no evidence for intrinsic aging of the red-cell-producing stem-cells.

This is an area of investigation beset with technical problems, not least with the procedure of transplantation itself. The ever increasing sophistication of the experiments reflects our increased knowledge of the stem-cell population and the procedures which can damage them. It is only when such factors are adequately understood and controlled that suitable experiments can be performed to study the aging process.

Models of aging in humans

There are genetic syndromes which have relevance to the pathobiology of human aging. Several of the so-called progeroid (accelerated aging) syndromes have been proposed as models of human aging (Epstein et al, 1966; Martin, 1978), and furthermore, fibroblasts isolated from such individuals have been used to study certain age-associated changes in functional ability. There are three classical progeroid syndromes; Hutchinson-Gilford, Werner's and Cockayne syndromes (Epstein et al, 1966; Martin, 1978), which are characterised by young individuals having a senile appearance. Each of these syndromes is autosomal recessive in its mode of inheritance (Martin, 1978). Fibroblasts from individuals with these abnormalities have a shorter in vitro life-span than fibroblasts from normal adults of the same age. Fibroblasts isolated from Hutchinson-Gilford and Werner's patients only undergo 10 doublings as compared to the average of 30 doublings in cells derived from normal adults. There have also been reports of decreases in mitotic activity, DNA synthesis, DNA repair efficiency and cloning efficiency in cells isolated from individuals with these syndromes. It has been suggested that the study of fibroblasts from these subjects will give valuable insights into these conditions and may also prove to be a starting point for the genetic analysis of the aging process in humans (Martin, 1978).

Down's syndrome also shows certain features of accelerated aging (Martin, 1978). Down's syndrome is a condition of mental retardation with various associated abnormalities caused by the presence of three copies of chromosome 21 (trisomy). Brain autopsy specimens from old Down's subjects have been shown to have the neuropathological signs associated with senile dementia (Crapper, et al 1975; Ball and Nuttall, 1980, 1981). This is a very important finding and it is possible that examination of Down's syndrome subjects will give important clues as to the genetic factors predisposing towards senile dementia.

The life-table

A direct life-table is compiled in the laboratory by studying the survival of a cohort of animals. The raw data needed are time, and the numbers of surviving animals at that time (Deevey, 1947). The number of survivors (l_x) at the beginning of a time interval is recorded, and this can be transformed to a percentage figure to produce a survival curve (Figure 2.2). The number of deaths noted at the same time interval is d_x. Other variables can also be determined such as the age-specific death-rate (q_x), and the mean expectation of life (e_x) at each time interval (Comfort, 1979). *Populations said to be undergoing senescence show an increase in the age-specific death-rate with time.*

The construction of life-tables for natural populations

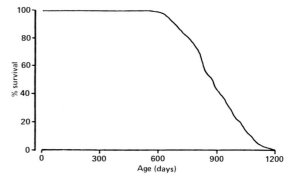

Fig. 2.2 The survival curve for female C57BL/Icrfa[t] mice

is more difficult (Deevey, 1947). It is possible to determine the age of some organisms by the study of anatomical features such as the growth rings found respectively on the shells and scales of certain molluscs and fish, and also in certain trees. In cases where these features can be linked accurately to a time-scale then indirect life-tables can be obtained, but they do require considerable care in interpretation (Comfort, 1979). Ecologists have devised procedures for constructing direct life-tables for natural populations of birds and fish and these are discussed in detail by Deevey (1947). There are many obvious problems to overcome in the construction of these life-tables, particularly the losses due to migration and predation. *In life-tables such as these the age-specific death-rate is frequently constant for each time interval and the population is defined as not undergoing senescence.* The small numbers of organisms remaining in the population late in the life-span however, makes the computation of the age-specific death-rate very inaccurate. It must also be pointed out that the individuals within such a natural population do become senescent, but the life-table does not show the necessary increase in the age-specific death-rate with time. If such species are studied in captivity, then invariably the life-table is similar to that found for man, domestic, and laboratory animals. The difference between the two types of survival pattern is the reduction of environmental interactions in the domestic population.

Life-tables for human populations are also of the indirect type, and are constructed using data collected from death certificates and population censuses. Usually the life-table parameters are calculated for a theoretical cohort of 100 000 individuals using the age-structure of the population under study at any given time. Such information is periodically updated so that a form of running commentary can be made on various survival statistics. Figure 2.3 is a 'curve of deaths' which shows a major peak at about 75 years for men and 80 years for women (Benjamin and Overton, 1981) This terminal peak can be regarded as the central value of deaths

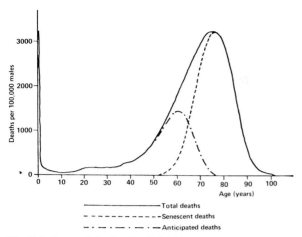

Fig. 2.3 Curve of deaths: English Life Table No. 11 1950–1952 (males) (reproduced with permission from Benjamin and Overton, 1981)

caused by senescence. The remainder of the earlier deaths can be attributed to disease or accident. These deaths are known as 'anticipated' or 'premature', and over the last 130 years there has been a proportional increase in senescent deaths from around 40 per cent to over 80 per cent for women, and to more than 70 per cent for men. However, during this period in the UK the peak age has only shifted 3 years for men and 9 years for women (Benjamin and Overton, 1981)! This subject is dealt with in detail in Chapter 1.

Variation in the length of life
This subject has been exhaustively reviewed by Comfort (1979). Much of the information available has been obtained from zoo records and in many cases must be treated with caution since the maximum longevities reported for some species have been obtained by extrapolation from growth rings or body-weight. Comfort (1979) tabulates the maximum longevities for many species and the reader is advised to consult this reference for details.

There has been considerable interest shown in the variation in the length of life of different mammals. In mammals, but not in other groups, there is a very strong correlation between life-span and body-weight, that is a high body-weight is associated with long life. Alternatively, a low basal metabolic rate is associated with a long life-span. However, man does not fit into this general pattern (Sacher, 1959). Sacher studied the relationship between various body variables and life-span in mammals. A good correlation can be obtained with brain weight, but the best relationship of all is obtained when considering both body-weight and the brain:body weight ratio (the so-called index of cephalization) in the equation. Once more caution must be exercised in the

highly inbred strains of animals, or crosses between such strains, so in carefully conducted experiments animal variation can be minimised. The bulk of the research into the aging process is performed on cross-sectional studies of such animals and most of the experiments described in Chapter 4 on the theories of aging follow this design.

Life-span manipulation
It has been claimed that the only way to study the aging process is to manipulate it. Various techniques have been used to shorten life-span such as exposure to ionizing radiation, increased oxygen concentrations and high temperatures. The relevance of life-shortening effects to the study of the aging process has been questioned — unless the agent used causes a uniform acceleration of age-related events it is not acceptable. However, it is difficult to see how this criterion can be rigorously applied since it is impossible to measure all aspects of the aging process simultaneously.

Life-span extension has been attempted using several approaches. Certain drugs such as beta-aminopropionitrile (BAPN) (LaBella, 1972, LaBella and Vivian, 1978), interpretation of these data. Although the correlations derived by Sacher and his various co-workers hold in general, they do not always hold in detail. Some hibernating mammals, and those which undergo overnight quiescent periods such as the bat, do not conform to the relationship. In this case it is argued that the lowering of the basal metabolic rate during these periods would lead to a longer expectation of life. Also within a species there is no close correlation between the various variables mentioned above and life-span. Others factors may also be important and there is a possibility that an increase in brain size may be correlated with a capability to avoid death. Thus, if natural selection favours an increase in brain size, then long-life may be a secondary feature of this selection process.

METHODS OF STUDY

There are essentially two ways of studying the aging process. Firstly, one can study some feature of interest at various stages of the life-span, and secondly, one can manipulate the life-span by attempting to shorten or extend it.

Study of particular age-stages
The method of study can be either cross-sectional or longitudinal. We have already discussed the difficulties of studies of this kind in human populations where we are faced with widely different genetic backgrounds, exposure to disease and environmental insults. Most animal studies involve research on genetically defined,

and anti-oxidants such as Vitamin E, are claimed to extend life. The effects of such treatments however, vary with the species and strain of animal used (Davies and Schofield, 1980). The hormone hydrocortisone can extend the number of population doublings of HDF cells in culture (Rosner and Cristofalo, 1979), but only if it is present throughout the life-span of the culture.

There are two reliable methods of extending the life-span of experimental animals. In poikilotherms either a reduction of temperature, or dietary manipulation, have been shown to extend both the mean- and maximum life-spans. In homeotherms dietary manipulation is the only method successful in extending life-span. Some aspects of the effects of temperature on the life-span will be dealt with later, and the remainder of this discussion will centre on the effects of dietary manipulation.

Dietary manipulation
It is possible to extend the life-span of all animals so far investigated by manipulation of the diet, usually by restricting the food intake. The early experiments on the crustacean *Daphnia* showed that life-span increased if food was restricted (Ingle et al, 1937), and later experiments by McCay et al (1939) showed that the same effect could also be demonstrated in mammals.

The effect of calorie restriction, that is, the provision of a fully balanced diet complete in all aspects of nutritional requirement, but reduced in quantity, allows the animal to attain a very significant increase in life-span. Indeed, increases in the order of 100 per cent in maximum life-span have been obtained under certain circumstances. The effect of dietary restriction is reproducible and is effective in both rats and mice and invariably the reproductive development of the animal is delayed (McCay et al, 1939; Berg, 1960; Berg and Simms, 1960; Ross, 1959, 1961). Rats which have been maintained on a restricted diet for long periods (in some cases longer than the mean life-span previously recorded for the species), can be fed on an *ad libitum* diet when growth resumes and the animals live out a much longer life-span. Experiments involving dietary restriction have been reviewed by Masoro et al (1980).

There are many beneficial side-effects to this life extension; one is that the onset of age-related diseases is significantly delayed in restricted animals; another is that they appear 'fitter' than normally fed rats (McCay et al, 1939; Berg, 1960; Berg and Simms, 1960; Ross, 1959, 1961). The development of the immune system is also delayed (Walford et al, 1974). Studies of enzyme activities in dietary restricted animals show that they differ from both normal control animals of the same age, and fully-fed rats of a much younger age (Ross, 1969).

Thus, we do not appear to be studying a slowing down of the aging process; rather that dietary restriction embarks the animal on a completely different developmental pathway.

More recently Ross et al (1976) have shown that the longevity of rats can be predicted surprisingly accurately (even when they are allowed freedom of dietary choice), solely on the basis of their dietary behaviour and growth responses early in life. In these experiments three diets were presented with the same calorific value, but differing in their protein:carbohydrate ratios. The individual rats were presented with the three diets simultaneously and records were kept of the intake of each individual diet — each rat selected a diet differing in both quantity and composition. In general dietary composition did not correlate as well with life-span as did body-weight variables. Those animals that chose, and efficiently utilised, a low-protein (but otherwise complete) diet early in life, and also completed the greater part of their growth by 100 days of age, would probably be short-lived. Conversely, rats that grew slowly, particularly between 50 and 150 days of age would be more likely to live longer. Calorie intake was not an important factor influencing the aging rate of the rats in this experiment, but according to the authors this was not necessarily at variance with earlier work. They point out the importance of the interactions between rate of growth and body weight in the determination of subsequent events. Thus, the variables such as absolute body weight changes, and the times required to attain specific weights are very important, and these seem to be related to the protein:carbohydrate ratio in the diet early in life.

Much more work is necessary before an accurate assessment can be made of the influence of diet on aging and survival. Some suggest that dietary restriction alters a fundamental biological 'clock' while others have discussed the idea of a so-called 'dietary hypophysectomy'. The two ideas are connected in that the hypothalamus is central to the control of all physiological function, and mediates much of this activity by means of the pituitary. It has also been implicated as the area controlling biological rhythms. Comfort (1979) has suggested that the hypothalamus contains a 'clock' mechanism which could control the aging process. However, there is insufficient experimental evidence to allow the critical assessment of this hypothesis. An alternative view regarding the effect of diet on life-span can be offered. The unlimited intake of food by rats and mice in captivity was probably adopted so that maximum growth could be obtained. It could be that maximum growth rate is not (as Ross's work implies), conducive to the attainment of maximum longevity, and that the *ad libitum* diet actually shortens life-span.

GENERAL CONCEPTS ABOUT THE AGING PROCESS

Any system is comprised of sub-units which act together to perform a function which cannot be performed by the individual components. In our definition of aging (p. 29) we referred to the failure of the process of homeostasis by which the organism maintained a steady-state in the face of environmental change. The changes that occur during development and maturation are integrated by the endocrine tissues. Functional decline in the endocrine system is an important factor in the aging process, and indeed, historically it was believed that the administration of suitable hormone(s) would either delay, or mitigate the effects of age (Comfort, 1979). In this section the role of the endocrine system in aging will be discussed as an illustration of the breakdown of integration between sub-units within a system. The reader is also referred to Chapter 5 for a discussion of age-related changes in the function of the immune system, which is also an excellent example of changes in the integration of function with time.

Age-related endocrine changes

The study of age-related changes in the endocrine system has been gathering momentum in the last decade and has been reviewed on several occasions (Gusseck, 1972; Gregerman and Bierman, 1974; Sartin et al, 1980). The endocrine system is complex but there are five components basic to its mode of action:

1. *Detection* of changes in the external or internal environment by a *receptor* system.
2. Stimulation of the *production or release* of hormone in response.
3. Transport of the hormone to some *target tissue*.
4. *Response* of the target tissue to the hormone, and the return of the internal environment to a *steady-state*.
5. *Feed-back* to return hormone secretion to the steady-state.

Age-related changes in endocrine cell response

Hypothalamic-pituitary system

Hypothalamo-adenohypophysial axis.   There is a well-documented decline in the reproductive system of both laboratory rodents and humans.

Females.   After about 18 months the laboratory rodent ceases to display the regular 4- to 5-day changes in the oestrus cycle, and in older rats and mice phases of constant oestrus and pseudo-pregnancy are common. The ovaries produce oestrogen which regulates, by a process of negative feedback, the secretion of the various hypothalamic and anterior pituitary hormones. Many studies have been directed at determining whether or not there is a primary age-related failure of the hypothalamic-anterior pituitary axis or the gonads (Meites et al, 1980).

An old female in the state of constant oestrus shows no cyclic surges of the gonadotrophic (GnRH)-, luteinizing (LH)-, and follicle stimulating (FSH) hormones, prolactin, oestrogens or progesterone (reviews in Finch, 1977; Meites et al, 1980). Serum prolactin however, is increased in old rats and is believed to be partly responsible for the increased incidence of spontaneous mammary cancer in some of these animals. Indeed, Steger (1981) has suggested that the elevated levels of oestrogen found in old rats may be partially responsible for the raised prolactin. In addition, even under conditions of appropriate stimulation, old, irregularly-cycling rats, show a reduced capacity to release LH and FSH from the anterior pituitary (Miller and Reigle, 1978).

The levels of hypothalamic neurotransmitters are of major importance in the regulation of hormonal surges in the oestrus cycle. It has been proposed that age-changes in these neurotransmitters may lead to disturbances in the oestrus cycle. There are age-related reductions in the levels of the hypothalamic catecholamines (noradrenalin and dopamine), and an increase in serotonin (5-hydroxytryptamine), in rats. The catecholamines (particularly noradrenalin), stimulate GnRH release whereas serotonin inhibits it (dopamine inhibits, and serotonin stimulates prolactin release). It has been shown that the neurosecretory activity of the dopaminergic neurones of the hypothalamus is impaired in old rats in a state of constant oestrous. In addition, this defect can be overcome by increasing the availability of the dopamine precursor L-DOPA, but not with L-tyrosine (Reymond and Porter, 1981). The decline in hypothalamic catecholamine levels, and the rise in serotonin levels in old rats may account for their reduced capacity to secrete GnRH and may also be responsible for the increase in serum prolactin (Meites et al, 1980).

Another facet of the hypothalamic control of the adenohypophysis is the role of the ubiquitous enkephalins. It has been shown that there is no age-related change in the hypothalamic concentration of met-enkephalin, but older rats, particularly those in a state of pseudopregnancy, do have significantly higher levels of this material in the anterior pituitary (Kumar et al, 1980).

In the human female in the years prior to the menopause the menstrual cycles tend to become irregular and shortened. There are pronounced ovarian changes during this period and the number of anovular cycles increases. There is a reduction in the secretion of hormones by the ovaries and in the post-menopausal phase there is an almost total lack of of these hormones in the serum (Meites et al, 1980). The importance of these hormone secretions in the elderly is unclear and it is difficult to determine the contribution made by the adrenal cortex to sex steroid levels in the aged (Gusseck, 1972). The secretion of the gonadotropic hormones from the anterior pituitary rises rapidly after the menopause in an apparent attempt to stimulate the ovaries and the levels remain high for many years (Meites et al, 1980).

Males. No age-related reduction in the levels of the anterior pituitary hormones can be detected in healthy male mice. If GnRH is used to stimulate the anterior pituitary to produce LH then no age-related effects can be detected. Thus, in some strains of mice certain responses to trophic hormones by both the pituitary and the testes are maintained throughout life, whereas in certain strains of rat (Wistar and Long-Evans) an age-related impairment does exist (Finch et al, 1977). In addition, coincidental pathology also plays a very important role in the expression of age-changes in laboratory rodents (Nelson et al, 1975). These findings imply species differences in the effect of age on pituitary and testes function in rodents. It is of interest that Steger et al (1980) report a possible relationship between the increased levels of the hypothalamic opiate met[5]-enkephalin and the lower serum concentrations of LH. Indeed, there may be an age-related alteration in the control of enkephalin levels in the hypothalamus because old animals seem less responsive to the stimulatory effects of the opiate agonist — naloxone (Steger et al, 1980).

Other age-related changes in this axis. Many studies are now being conducted into aging changes in this crucial region of the brain including increasingly sophisticated analyses of the structure and function of cells and molecular products. Barnea et al (1982) have investigated age-related changes in the molecular-weight profiles of corticotrophin in the aging rat. In a study of the medial basal and the preoptic anterior hypothalamus, and the pituitary gland they showed an age-related decline in the production of the precursor molecule — pro-opiocortin — in the female rat. Others (Sonntag et al, 1980), have demonstrated a decrease in the pulsatile release of growth-hormone (GH) in old male rats. The administration of L-DOPA to male animals in late maturity is followed by an increase in the amplitude of GH pulses; also the mean plasma levels of GH are raised to those found in young males (Sonntag et al, 1982).

Hypothalamo-neurohypophyseal axis. It has been suggested that many changes commonly associated with aging in man are reminiscent of neurohypophysial failure (Findley, 1949). This is supported by experimental work on rats, relating age-changes to a form of diabetes insipidus (Friedman and Friedman, 1957). This evidence has been reviewed recently (Davies, 1983;

Turkington and Everitt, 1976). The picture is extremely complicated with marked inter-species differences becoming evident.

There is no simple change in hormone production with age; for example, Helderman et al (1978), showed hypersensitivity to an osmotic load in elderly male human volunteers. They also found a disturbance in the response of plasma vasopressin to ethanol in old males. Unfortunately, the two populations investigated appeared to be of different ages making comparison difficult. An alternative explanation for the observations is that the hypersensitivity may be a 'resistance' of the kidney to the effects of elevated plasma levels of vasopressin. Raised levels of vasopressin may then be required to elicit an equivalent physiological response. In addition, the challenges administered were of only short duration and may be of litle use when attempting to interpret chronic changes.

The effect of chronic water deprivation in the Fischer 344 rat at various ages was described by Sladek et al (1981). The increases in serum vasopressin and renin concentrations seen in young rats were not observed in old animals, in spite of apparently comparable alterations in fluid volume and osmotic pressure. They showed that relative to body weight the vasopressin content of the neural lobe was significantly reduced and was more severely depleted by dehydration in aged rats. They also studied several parameters of renal function in their animals. Although none was in renal failure all showed some evidence of reduced renal function. In spite of such abnormalities the old rats did raise a significant antidiuretic response to dehydration; however, with prolonged fluid deprivation they were unable to attain serum vasopressin or renin concentrations at the level of young rats.

Changes in salt and water metabolism have been demonstrated in the aging rat by Friedman et al (1960) — with increases in the following variables:

— extracellular fluid volume
— extracellular sodium levels
— 24-hour urine volume
— 24-hour sodium excretion

— the latter even in conditions of water deprivation. Also, the adrenal glands were larger.

These observations suggest some similarity with the condition of diabetes insipidus in the rat. Additionally both the work performance and the distribution of water, sodium and potassium of the old rats could be improved by modest doses of pitressin over a short period, especially if augmented with traces of aldosterone (Friedman et al, 1960).

Prolonged treated involving a regimen of subcutaneous injections of posterior pituitary powder increased the average lifespan of the experimental groups

(Friedman and Friedman, 1964; Friedman et al, 1965). This treatment also suppressed the age-related weight increases observed in the kidney, heart, adrenals and pituitary glands of rats. Another experimental group, in which aldosterone was added to the posterior pituitary supplement showed no additional benefits in terms of survival. Bodansky and Engel (1966) confirmed these results and concluded that the 'active ingredient' was oxytocin. Friedman's experiments can be criticised because of the small numbers of animals employed, but the observations are repeatable and hence warrant more thorough examination.

Morphological studies. There have been few direct investigations of the neuroendocrine cells that produce the hormones vasopressin and oxytocin. An immuno-histochemical study of the magnocellular neurons in the rat (McNeill et al, 1980) showed that the numbers of cells and fibres immunoreactive for the neurophysin protein molecule were similar at each age studied, but there was an age-related increase in the size and number of axonal dilatations. Another study of the peptidergic target cells of the hypothalamus claims to have shown a decline in the noradrenergic innervation of the supraoptic neucleus (SON) (Sladek et al, 1980).

The response of these neuroendocrine cells to physiological stress can be followed by studying changes induced in cellular morphology. A series of quantitative ultrastructural studies of the vasopressin and oxytocin producing cells of the SON of the mouse showed no age-related changes in the production of hormone containing organelles (Figure 2.4a and b). Nor was there an age-associated decline of hormone granule production when the animals were under osmotic stress (which causes these cells to synthesise fresh hormone) (Davies and Fotheringham, 1980, 1981a, b). Further studies of the neurohypophysis of the mouse indicate that although there are subtle age-related changes in the ultrastructure, there are no gross changes with age (Wilkinson and Davies, 1981; Davies et al, 1983).

It can be concluded that there is no simple age-related change in hormone production in this axis. There may be species differences in the types of age-change seen and the large reservoir of hormone stored in the neurohypophysis adds to the difficulties. However, the understanding of hypothalamo-neurohypophyseal function in the young animal is now very advanced and studies on this unique section of the neuroendocrine system may soon lead to a much deeper understanding of the effects of age on neuronal fuction.

Thyroid
Thyroid hormes are involved in the regulation of enzyme levels, cell membrane permeability, protein synthesis and metabolic rate. There is no overall age-related decline in hormone production however, and the thyroid itself seems able to respond to various stimuli at all ages (Gregerman et al, 1962), however, tissue-utilisation of thyroid hormones declines (Gregerman et al, 1962).

A difficulty in the study of thyroid aging arises from marked developmental changes in thyroid metabolism in both man and laboratory rodents (Valueva and Verzhikovskaya, 1977; Ooka, 1979; Ducasson et al, 1980; White et al, 1980). This affects levels of serum thyroxin binding globulin, thyroid-stimulating hormone (TSH) metabolism, and the conversion of thyroxine to

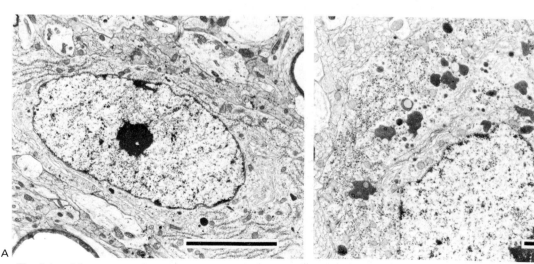

Fig. 2.4 a. A lower power electron micrograph of a neurone from the supraoptic nucleus of a 6 month old mouse. Note the well organised 'stacks' of rough endoplasmic reticulum, and the lack of lipofuscin organelles. Scale bar = 5 µm. b. A low power electron micrograph of a neuron from the supraoptic nucleus of a 28 month old mouse, compare with a. Note the large numbers of lipofuscin organelles. Scale bar = 2 µm. (Micrographs courtesy of Andrew P. Fotheringham)

triiodothyronine. In addition, an age-related accumulation of high molecular weight forms of TSH (possibly biosynthetic precursors to TSH) may inhibit the thyroid response to normal TSH (Klug and Adelman, 1977).

Pancreas

The effect of age on the function of the pancreas has been the subject of intense study (Gusseck, 1972). A reduction in glucose tolerance is thoroughly documented in both laboratory rodents (Gusseck, 1972; Gommers and Genne, 1975), and man (Gusseck, 1972). Recent studies of the kinetics of native insulin in diabetic, obese and aged men however, show differences between the changes seen in 'maturity-onset' diabetes and aging (McGuire et al, 1979). McGuire et al (1979) conclude that the changes in the metabolism of insulin are not large and it is unlikely that they are the sole cause of major alterations in glucose tolerance seen with either aging, obesity or diabetes in humans. Indeed, Ferrero et al (1980) claim to be unable to detect signs of beta-islet cell exhaustion after repeated stimulation in the elderly.

Investigations into age-related changes in the function of the Islets of Langerhans have been pursued using in vitro preparations. Kitahara and Adelman (1979) have shown that 'small' and 'large' islets can be isolated and that they have distinctly different biphasic secretory responses to glucose stimulation. The studies so far however, clearly show that the major age-related differences in the response to glucose challenge takes place during the maturation of the animal (up to 12 months of age). Reaven and Reaven (1980) have shown that Islets prepared from 12 month old animals oxidise significantly less glucose than those from 2 month old rats; this raises the possibility that age-changes in glucose-stimulated insulin secretion may be secondary to the effect of age on Islet glucose metabolism. This conclusion is partially supported by Lipson et al (1981), who showed decreases of up to 60 per cent in the activity of adenylate cyclase in the Islets of 12 month old animals when compared with 2.5 month controls. In addition, subtle alterations in the ratio of the precursor molecule pro-insulin and insulin suggest alterations in the rate of synthesis of hormone in older animals (Gold et al, 1981). The latter propose age-related alterations in the so-called 'glucose responsive pool'.

Adrenals

The function of the adrenal glands as indicated by the basal plasma cortisol levels shows no consistent alteration with age. However, knowledge of the steady-state levels of hormones in blood is not always useful in interpreting the effect of age on the rate of hormone production or tissue utilisation. In the case of most endocrine glands there appears to be a considerable reserve capacity even in the old animal (Gusseck, 1972). Recent studies of the circadian rhythm of cortisol secretion in the elderly (Dean and Felton, 1979), conclude that older individuals have normal plasma cortisol levels with similar diurnal rhythms. Parker et al (1981) confirmed that both basal- and ACTH-stimulated levels of cortisol and aldosterone were unchanged in elderly subjects. However, basal levels of the adrenal androgens were reduced in the aged, and ACTH-stimulation showed some impairment in the androgen response (Parker et al, 1981). These findings might be due to an age-related loss of adrenal enzymes (or the cell population that produced adrenal androgens), the loss or decrease of ACTH receptors specific for adrenal androgen production, or the loss of a pituitary factor necessary for adrenal androgen secretion.

Gonads

In the aging laboratory rodent the ovaries remain potentially functional throughout the life-span (Meites et al, 1980). In humans there has been much talk of a male 'menopause' but its physiological basis is uncertain. If decreased gonadal secretions were of major importance in senescence then it could be reasoned that castrated subjects would show early manifestations of old age, but this does not seem to be the case. One study (Hamilton and Mestler, 1969) showed that eunuchs live at least as long as intact males. A recent report using strictly healthy, aged volunteers shows that serum levels of male sex steroid hormones are not influenced by age even though the serum LH levels rise significantly (Harman and Tsitouras, 1980). A study of the aging rhesus macaques monkey also failed to find age-related changes in the levels of the diurnal patterns of testosterone, dihydro-testosterone or oestradiol (Chambers and Phoenix, 1981).

Several studies have determined the numbers of receptors found in endocrine cells. The Leydig cells of the testes of rats respond to increased levels of gonadotropic hormones by the synthesis and secretion of testosterone but no age-related changes in this system have been detected in vivo.

Target-tissue responsiveness

If a physiological stress is imposed on an aging animal, there is often a delay in the appearance of the response. This has been amply demonstrated in studies of enzyme induction in response to a cold stress or to other, more direct forms of endocrine challenge. It has been shown that aging animals can undergo a delay of several minutes to several hours in these induction processes (Figure 2.5).

The regulation of the hepatic enzyme, tyrosine amino transferase (TAT), during cold-stress has been studied

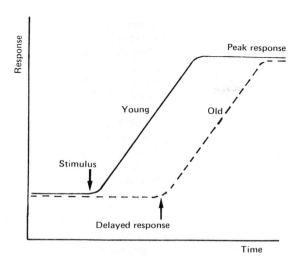

Fig. 2.5 A diagram showing the typical age-related time-lag in the initiation of cellular activity in response to a physiological stimulus

in the aging mouse (Finch et al, 1969a). The induction of TAT is dependent upon active RNA synthesis (Finch et al, 1969b), and in young animals this enzyme is induced rapidly during exposure to cold conditions; however, in old mice there is a pronounced lag period before the increased levels of TAT can be detected. After this lag however, the rate of increase of the enzyme is similar to that seen in younger animals. The application of exogenous insulin and glucocorticoids (both hormones acting directly on liver) shows that the target cells are as capable of responding rapidly to this stimulus as those in young animals (Finch et al, 1969a). In short there is some defect in the integrated response to the stimulus which may be at any of a number of points in the neuroendocrine or endocrine system. Similar experiments have been employed by Adelman et al (1972) with essentially the same results.

There have been several investigations into altered target tissue responsiveness (Roth and Adelman, 1975). The stimulation of salivary gland DNA synthesis and cell division in rats by isoproterenol (a synthetic catecholamine) is progressively reduced and delayed with age. Other experiments have been conducted on the effects of glucocorticoids on lymphoid cells isolated from animals of different ages. This treatment induces an inhibitor protein which prevents the entry of substrates into cells. In two separate studies (Makman et al, 1971; Roth, 1975) it was shown that radio-labelled uridine uptake by splenic leucocytes from the rat is inhibited by cortisol. However, older rats (24 to 26 months) showed a 60 per cent reduction in cortisol-induced inhibition of uridine uptake when compared with mature animals (12 to 14 months). Specific binding sites for glucocorticoids in senescent animals are approximately 60 per

cent those those found in young groups.

Several studies have shown a reduction in target-tissue endocrine receptors with age. One model system used has been the post-mitotic fat-cell (adipocyte). The numbers of receptors for noradrenalin on adipocytes of the same size are reduced, so that the cells from rats at 8 months of age have approximately 41 000 receptors, while at 30 months the number of receptors fall to approximately 7000. Decreases in receptor numbers for neurotransmitters, peptide and steroid hormones have been observed in diverse tissues including brain, skeletal muscle, liver and gonads, and in cells such as lymphocytes and human-diploid, fibroblast-like cells (Roth, 1979).

Roth (1979) also points out that age-related receptor loss is not universal. Losses have been detected in some tissues during development and maturation, but not during adulthood and aging. In addition, an increase in certain types of receptor has been shown in both the seminal vesicles and skin fibroblasts (Roth, 1979).

These changes are difficult to analyse, partly because of different techniques generating different results (such as in tissue culture when actively-dividing are compared with non-dividing cells). Another problem is that of differential changes in the same receptor type: thus, there is no age-related change in noradrenalin receptors in the cerebral cortex, but there are significant reductions in these receptors in the cerebellum and the corpus striatum of the brain. Another factor lies in the complexity of tissue structure — a variable frequently ignored in biochemical investigations. There are numbers of different cell types within a tissue. In brain for example, there are different neuronal types, several glial populations, the neuroendocrine cells and those cells associated with the blood-vascular system and the ventricular ependymal cells — thus, the term 'brain cell' has little meaning. A detailed study should be made of *defined* cell populations at various stages of the life-cycle, but this is obviously very difficult to do.

It is impossible to summarize all aspects of age-related changes in the endocrine system in so short a space, the account given is sparse but it does indicate the types of change that may be expected, and also the complexity of the events in this particular area. These changes are obviously fundamental to the control of homeostasis, and strenuous efforts are being made to investigate the cellular and molecular basis of these changes.

Cellular aging

Most research in this field has been conducted on mammalian cells. There are four principal cell-types within the body:

— Fixed, post-mitotic cells such as the neurones and the striated muscle cells.

— Cells that remain capable of division throughout the life-span but otherwise turn-over very slowly, such as the cells of the liver, kidney and cartilage.

— Cells that divide rapidly throughout the life-span of the organism, but have themselves a relatively short life-span ranging from days to months. The cells in this category are the lymphocytes, red blood-, skin- and gut epithelial cells.

— Stem-cells that maintain the cell populations described in the section above.

It has been argued that only the fixed post-mitotic, and the cells that turn-over slowly will show intrinsic aging changes, since these cells are present throughout the life-span of the organism. This view is not necessarily correct but the importance of fixed post-mitotic cells has focussed considerable attention on to age-related changes in their structure and function.

One concept of the aging process is that it involves the loss of irreplaceable cells, such as the neurones, and this hypothesis — the 'pacemaker' theory of aging — has been presented in a refined form by Franks (1970) and Finch (1972). These authors imply that aging may be partially controlled by alterations in small groups of critical cells. Thus, aging may be due to either an overall programmed sequence of events, or to the accumulation of accidental damage but, in either case, defects in a small group of irreplaceable cells within the hypo-thalamo-hypophysial axis (which is central to the control of homeostasis), would be lethal.

Neuronal loss. The dogma of neuronal loss is constantly reiterated but usually without critical appraisal of the data. Macroscopic observations from cross-sectional studies of the aging human brain suggest an overall shrinkage with age. Several studies over the last century have claimed an age-related neurone loss occurring in such diverse species as bees and man; equally as many studies imply that this is not the case (Hanley, 1974; Curcio et al, 1982). This argument may never be resolved for various reasons. Firstly, there are technical difficulties in sampling organs as large and as complex as the human brain (and the measurement of tissue shrinkage during processing for histological exam-ination, is also frequently ignored). Secondly, experi-ments on animals suggest that developmental conditions (including dietary balance and sufficiency) can influence neurone number and synapse formation (McConnell and Berry, 1978; Leuba and Rabinowicz, 1979a, b; Bedi et al, 1980). If this is also true for humans then it is impossible to be certain about neuronal loss. Thirdly, research on laboratory mammals indicates that neuronal loss is not a consistent feature of aging (Curcio et al, 1982). Only one recent study has claimed massive neuronal loss in old animals (Johnson and Erner, 1972), but the methods used involved the mechanical disrup-tion of tissues prior to cell counting. Techniques used in this investigation have been questioned Franks et al (1974). The reader is recommended to read the review of the literature by Curcio et al (1982), for an excellent critical appraisal of the field.

Age-related changes in cellular morphology. One of the commonest findings in aging cells is the presence of the granular age-pigment — lipofuscin (Figure 2.6, and see Chapter 4, p. 66). Other morphological changes have also been observed, ranging from fragmentation of the rough endoplasmic reticulum, degeneration of myofi-brils in muscle tissue and extensive damage to the mitochondria. The latter can be observed in almost all old cells, and it has been argued (Miquel et al, 1980) that this is to do with free-radical damage to these organelles. Review books are now becoming available on these topics and the reader is directed to these for details (Johnson, 1981; Cervos-Navarro and Sarkander, 1983).

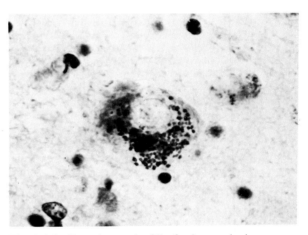

Fig. 2.6 A photomicrograph of lipofuscin granules in a neuron from the cerebral cortex of a human female, age 80 years. (Micrograph courtesy of Ann Wilkinson).

Molecular biology of aging

All molecules undergo conformational changes with time and become disordered, perhaps due to the effects of temperature or of free-radicals. How then does an organism overcome this problem? Firstly, it may have a large excess of cells or molecules in a particular organ, each capable of performing the same function — the concept of redundancy. Secondly, it may have efficient repair mechanisms. Thirdly, it may be able to remove degenerate molecules and synthesise new ones, and finally, all three forms of protection may operate simul-taneously. As complex molecules were evolved, main-tainance and self-replication processes were also developed — such processes have been termed 'life-extending' strategies (Cutler, 1976).

There have been many attempts to investigate changes in the amounts of the chief classes of molecules found in cells and tissues, such as DNA, RNA, lipids, sugars and the larger carbohydrate polymers such as glycogen, and proteins. This section will only be concerned with an introduction to the possible changes that can take place in DNA, since this is fundamental to all other cellular activities (Gensler and Bernstein, 1981).

Changes in DNA

DNA has been considered a prime target for age-changes since this macro-molecule is unique in that it has to replicate, and maintain itself, so preserving the primary genetic message of the cell through cell division and through any accidental events which may damage the DNA. In situations other than cell division DNA has to be maintained so that its function as a template for other cellular molecules is preserved for the life-span of the cell.

DNA damage

Various agents induce damage in DNA by either physical, chemical or biological actions. DNA can be broken, distorted or chemically altered, and the source

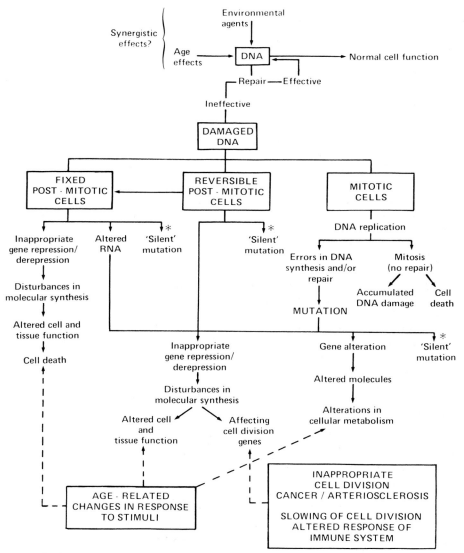

Fig. 2.7 A diagrammatic view of the possible forms of damage to DNA and subsequent cellular responses. *These changes are only of consequence during redifferentiation and/or stimulation of further mitoses. (Modified from various sources).

of the agent causing this damage can be either from within the cell or from some external source (Gensler and Bernstein, 1981). Free-radicals (see p. 69) and other reactive metabolites of normal cellular metabolism, can cause 'cross-linkage' of DNA to DNA, or DNA to intra-nuclear proteins. The fact that the DNA molecule exists at a relatively high temperature (body temperature) has been implicated as the cause of the loss of bases from the DNA polymer and the subsequent development of so-called 'single-strand' breaks. UV-radiation, gamma- and X-rays all cause specific types of damage ranging from the distortion of the helix in the case of UV, and either base removal or damage from free-radicals generated by gamma- or X-rays. Chemical mutagens and carcinogens also cause damage to DNA, as does viral-DNA which can be inserted into the genome of the host and so alter the information content of the cell. It is of interest that viral-DNA can be detected in cells from old animals when compared to young (Ono and Cutler, 1978). Mutations may also be a significant cause of age-related disfunction. They can arise either from errors in DNA-replication during the process of mitosis, by the mis-pairing of bases at the site of damage in the DNA molecule, or as a consequence of errors in the enzymic processes responsible for the synthesis of DNA.

Cellular lesions generated by DNA damage
The effect of the various lesions described above depends on several factors (Figure 2.7). Any alteration of the information content of the DNA can have substantial effects on cellular function, for example, the various physiological consequences following a mutation depend on whether the organism is a homo- or hetero-zygote, and whether or not the gene affected is dominant or recessive. Most mutations are probably not lethal, especially since in a differentiated cell much of the DNA is not expressed. It is therefore highly probable that a mutation would be in a non-transcribed (repressed) region rather than a transcribed (de-repressed) one.

A mutation in a repressed zone would be 'silent', but this could be changed if the cell had to either undergo division or respond to a hormone, and so utilise a previously unused region of the genome. Mutations in gene-control regions could cause gene repression or de-repression which may then result in synthesis of the wrong molecules at the wrong time. It has been shown, for example, that 'brain cells' from old mice contain significant quantities of RNA coding for the protein globin, when compared to similar cells from young animals (Ono and Cutler, 1978). If the mutation involves genes which control cell division, then abnormal cell proliferation may lead to tumour production, or other disease states. A mutation in the transcribed region of the DNA would be expressed immediately in terms of altered RNA and hence protein (either structural proteins or enzymes).

DNA-Repair
It is possible to repair DNA strand-breaks, remove damaged bases and insert new ones (excision repair). There is also increasing evidence that efficient repair of some forms of DNA damage is correlated with the maximum life-span potential of several mammalian species (see Chapter 4). In differentiated post-mitotic cells certain areas of the genome cannot be transcribed due to the presence of histone proteins. Certainly there seems to be a decreased ability for the chromatin from old animals to support some aspects of RNA-synthesis — the age-related reduction in chromatin template activity (see p. 68). The presence of age-related DNA inter-strand cross-links or DNA-protein cross-links, may also hinder the repair of DNA damage because access to the nucleic acid polymer by repair enzymes is restricted. Thus, it is possible that DNA damage could outstrip repair in such cells.

This discussion indicates the broad scope of the field of aging. All aspects of biological investigation are involved in the study of this phenomenon and we are only just beginning to assess the extent of age-related changes in a variety of organisms.

REFERENCES

Adelman R C, Freeman C, Cohen B S 1972 Enzyme adaptation as a biochemical probe of development and aging. Advances in Enzyme Regulation 10: 365–382

Ball M J, Nuttall K D 1980 Neurofibrillary tangles, granulovacuolar degeneration, and neuron loss in Down syndrome: quantitative comparison with Alzheimer dementia. Annals of Neurology 7: 462–465

Ball M J, Nuttall K D 1981 Topography of neurofibrillary tangles and granulovacuoles in hippocampi of patients with Downs-syndrome. Quantitative comparison with normal aging and Alzheimers-disease. Neuropathology and Applied Neurobiology 7: 13–20

Barnea A, Cho G, Porter J C 1982 Molecular weight profiles of immunoreactive corticotropin in the hypothalamus of the aging rat. Brain Research 232: 355–363

Bedi K S, Hall R, Davies C A, Dobbing J J 1980 A stereological analysis of the cerebellar granule and Purkinje cells of 30-day-old and adult rats undernourished during early postnatal life. Journal of Comparative Neurology 193: 863–870

Behnke A, Finch C E, Moment G B (eds) 1978 The Biology of Aging. Plenum Press, New York, London, p 388

Benjamin F, Overton E 1981 Prospects for mortality decline in England and Wales. Population Trends 23: 22–34

Berg B N 1960 Nutrition and longevity in the rat. 1. Food intake in relation to size, health and fertility. Journal of Nutrition 71: 242–254

Berg B N, Simms H S 1960 Nutrition and longevity in the rat. 2. Longevity and onset of disease with different levels of food intake. Journal of Nutrition 71: 255–263

Bodansky M, Engel S L 1966 Oxytocin and the life-span of male rats. Nature (London) 210: 751

Cervos-Navarro J, Sarkander H J (eds) 1983 Brain Aging: Neuropathology and Neuropharmacology. Aging vol. 21: Raven Press, New York

Chambers K C, Phoenix C H 1981 Diurnal patterns of testosterone, dihydrotestosterone, estradiol and cortisol in behaviour in aging males. Hormones and Bahaviour 15: 416–426

Comfort A 1979 The Biology of Senescence. 3rd edn. Elsevier, New York

Crapper D R, Dalton A J, Skopitz M, Scott J W, Hachinski V 1975 Alzheimer degeneration in Down syndrome. Archives of Neurology 32: 618–623

Cristofalo V J, Stanulis B M 1978 Cell aging: A model system approach. In: Behnke J A, Finch C E, Moment G B (eds) The Biology of Aging, Plenum Press, New York

Curcio C A, Buell S J, Coleman P D 1982 Morphology of the aging central nervous system: Not all downhill. In: Mortimer J A, Pirozzolo F J, Coleman P D (eds) The Aging Motor System. Advances in Neurocytology 3: Prager, New York

Cutler R G 1976 Nature of aging and life maintenance processes. In: Cutler R G (ed) Cellular Ageing: Concepts and Mechanisms. Part 1: General Concepts. Mechanisms I: Fidelity of Information Flow. Interdisciplinary Topics in Gerontology 9: Karger, Basel, p 83–133

Davies I 1983 Influence of age on the hypothalamo-neurohypophyseal system. In: Cervos-Navarro J, & Sarkander H J (eds) Brain Aging: Neuropathology and Neuropharmacology. Aging vol. 21: Raven Press, New York

Davies I, Fotheringham A P 1980 The influence of age on the hypothalamus-neurohypophyseal system of the mouse: A quantitative ultrastructural analysis of the supraoptic nucleus. Mechanisms of Ageing and Development 12: 93–105

Davies I, Fotheringham A P 1981a The influence of age on the response of the supraoptic nucleus of the hypothalamo-neurohypophyseal system to physiological stress. I. Ultrastructural aspects. Mechanisms of Ageing and Development 15: 355–366

Davies I, Fotheringham A P 1981b The influence of age on the response of the supraoptic nucleus of the hypothalamo-neurohypophyseal system to physiological stress. II. Quantitative morphology. Mechanisms of Ageing and Development 15: 367–378

Davies I, Schofield J D 1980 Connective tissue ageing: the influence of a lathyrogen (β-aminopropionitrile) on the life-span of female C57BL/Icrfa^t mice. Experimental Gerontology 15: 487–494

Davies I, Fotheringham A P, Roberts C 1983 The effect of lipofuscin on cell function. Mechanisms of Ageing and Development 23: 347–356

Dean S, Felton S P 1979 Circadian rhythm in the elderly: a study using a cortisol-specific radio-immunoassay. Age and Ageing 8: 243–245

Deevey E S 1947 Life-tables for natural populations of animals. Quarterly Review of Biology 22: 283–314

Ducasson D, Rashedi M, Breudel A, Gasparoux S 1980 Thyroxin binding globulin (TBG) radioimmunoassay. Normal patients results according to age, and sex, and in the cases of disthyroidisms. Pathologie et Biologie 28: 168–172

Epstein C J, Martin G M, Schultz A L, Motulsky A G 1966 Werner's syndrome. A review of its symptomatology, natural history, pathological features, genetics and relationship to the natural aging process. Medicine, Baltimore 45: 177–186

Ferrero E, Casale G, Ciaponi A 1980 Studies on the exhaustion of beta-cells in the aged after repeated stimuli. Minerva Medicine 71: 2489–2496

Finch C E 1972 Cellular pacemakers of ageing in mammals. In: Harris R, Allin P, Viza D (eds) Cell Differentiation, Munksgaard, Copenhagen

Finch C E 1977 Endocrine and neural factors of reproductive senescence in rodents. In: Ts'o P O P (ed) Molecular Biology of the Mammalian Genetic Apparatus. Volume 2, Elsevier/North Holland Biomedical Press, BV, Amsterdam, p 303–311

Finch C E, Foster J R, Mirsky A E 1969a Aging and the regulation of cell activities during exposure to cold. Journal of General Physiology 54: 690–712

Finch C E, Huberman H S, Mirsky A E 1969b Regulation of liver tyrosine aminotransferase by endogenous factors in the mouse. Journal of General Physiology 54: 675–689

Finch C E, Jonec V, Wisner J R, Sinha Y N, Develis J S, Swerdloff R S 1977 Hormone production by pituitary and testes of male C57BL/6J mice during aging. Endocrinology 101: 1310–1317

Findley T 1949 Role of the neurohypophysis in the pathogenesis of hypertension and some allied disorders associated with aging. American Journal of Medicine 7: 70–84

Franks L M 1970 Cellular aspects of ageing. Experimental Gerontology 5: 281–289

Franks L M, Wilson P D, Whelan R D 1974 The effect of age on total DNA and cell number in the mouse brain. Gerontologia (Basel) 20: 21–26

Friedman S M, Friedman C L 1957 Salt and water balance in ageing rats. Gerontologia (Basel) 1: 107–121

Friedman S M, Friedman C L 1964 Prolonged treatment with posterior pituitary powder in aged rats. Experimental Gerontology 1: 37–48

Friedman S M, Friedman C L, Nakashima M 1960 Effect of pitressin on old-age changes of salt and water metabolism in the rat. American Journal of Physiology 199: 35–38

Friedman S M, Nakashima M, Friedman C L 1965 Prolongation of life-span in the old rat by adrenal and neurohypophyseal hormones. Gerontologia (Basel) 11: 129–140

Gensler H L, Bernstein H 1981 DNA damage as the primary cause of aging. Quarterly Review of Biology 56: 279–303

Gibson D C 1972 Development of the Rodent as a Model System of Aging. National Institute of Child Health and Early Human Development, Bethesda, Maryland USA

Gibson D C, Adelman R C, Finch C E (eds) 1979 Development of the Rodent as a Model System of Aging. US Department of Health, Education and Welfare, Public Health Service, National Institutes of Health, USA

Gold G, Reaven G M, Reaven E P 1981 Effect of age on pro-insulin and insulin secretory patterns in isolated rat islets. Diabetes 30: 77–82

Gommers A, Genne H 1975 Effect of aging on insulin and insulin-glucose sensitivity tests in rats. Acta Diabetologica Latina 12: 303–309

Gregerman R I, Bierman E L 1974 Aging and hormones. In: Williams R I (ed) Textbook of Endocrinology, 5th edn. W B Saunders Company, Philadelphia, USA, p 1059–1070

Gregerman R I, Gaffney G W, Shock N W, Crowder S E 1962 Thyroxine turnover in euthyroid man with special reference to changes with age. Journal of Clinical Investigation 41: 2065–2074

Gusseck D J 1972 Endocrine mechanisms and aging. Advances in Gerontological Research 4: 105–166

Hamilton J B, Mestler G E 1969 Mortality and survival: comparison of eunuchs with intact men and women in a mentally retarded population. Journal of Gerontology 24: 395–411

Hanley T, 1974 'Neuronal fall-out' in the ageing brain: a critical review of the quantitative data. Age and Ageing 3: 133–151

Harley C B, Goldstein S 1980 Retesting the commitment theory of cellular ageing. Science (Washington) 207: 191–192

Harman S M, Tsitouras P D 1980 Reproductive hormones in aging man. 1. Measurement of sex steroids, basal luteinizing hormone, and Leydig cell response to human chorionic gonadotropin. Journal of Clinical Endocrinology and Metabolism 51: 35–40

Harrison D E, Astle C M, Delaittre J A 1978 Loss of proliferative capacity in immunohemopoietic stem cells caused by serial transplantation rather than aging. Journal of Experimental Medicine 147: 1526–1532

Hart R W, Setlow R B 1976 DNA repair in late-passage human cells. Mechanisms of Ageing and Development 5: 67–77

Hay R J, Menzies R A, Morgan H P, Strehler B L 1968 The division potential of cells in continuous growth as compared to cells subcultivated after maintenance in stationary phase. Experimental Gerontology 3: 35–44

Hay R J, Strehler B L 1967 The limited growth span of cell strains isolated from the chick embryo. Experimental Gerontology 2: 123–135

Hayflick L 1965 The limited in vitro lifetime of human diploid cell strains. Experimental Cell Research 37: 614–636

Hayflick L, Moorehead P S 1961 The serial cultivation of human diploid cell strains. Experimental Cell Research 25: 585–621

Helderman J H, Vestal R E, Rowe J E, Tobin J D, Andres R, Robertson J L 1978 The response of arginine vasopressin to intravenous ethanol and hypertonic saline in man: the impact of aging. Journal of Gerontology 33: 39–47

Holliday R, Huschtscha L I, Tarrant G M, Kirkwood T B 1977 Testing the commitment theory of cellular aging. Science (Washington) 198: 366–372

Holliday R, Huschtscha L I, Kirkwood T B 1981 Cellular aging — further evidence for the commitment theory. Science (Washington) 213: 1505–1508

Ingle L, Wood T R, Banta A M 1937 A study of longevity, growth, reproduction and heart rate in Daphnia longispina as influenced by limitations in quantity of food. Journal of Experimental Zoology 76: 325–352

Johnson J E Jr. (ed) 1981 Aging and Cell Structure. Vol. 1: Plenum Press, New York

Johnson H, Erner S 1972 Neuron survival in the ageing mouse. Experimental Gerontology 7: 111–117

Kirkwood T B L, Cremer T 1982 Cytogerontology since 1881 — a reappraisal of August Weismann and a review of modern progress. Human Genetics 60: 101–121

Kirkwood T B, Holliday R 1975 Commitment to senescence: A model for the finite and infinite growth of diploid and transformed human fibroblasts in culture. Journal of Theoretical Biology 53: 481–497

Kitahara A, Adelman R C 1979 Altered regulation of insulin secretion in isolated islets of different sizes in aging rats. Biochemical and Biophysical Research Communications 87: 1207–1213

Klug T L, Adelman R C 1977 Evidence for a large thyrotropin and its accumulation in rats. Biochemical and Biophysical Research Communications 77: 1431–1438

Krohn P L 1962 Review lectures on senescence II. Heterochronic transplantation in the study of aging. Proceedings of the Royal Society (London) 157: 128–147

Kumar M S A, Chen C L, Huang H H 1980 Pituitary and hypothalamic concentration of met-enkephalin in young and old rats. Neurobiology of Aging 1: 153–155

LaBella F S 1972 Pharmacolongevity; control of ageing by drugs. In: Rubin A A (ed) Search for New Drugs, Marcel Dekher Inc., New York

LaBella F S, Vivian S 1978 Beta-aminopropionitrile promotes longevity in mice. Experimental Gerontology 13: 251–154

Leuba G, Rabinowicz Th 1979a Long-term effects of postnatal undernutrition and maternal malnutrition on the mouse cerebral cortex. I. Cellular densities, cortical volume and total numbers of cells. Experimental Brain Research 37: 283–298

Leuba G, Rabinowicz Th 1979b Long-term effects of postnatal undernutrition and maternal malnutrition on the mouse cerebral cortex. II. Evolution of dendritic branchings and spines in the visual region. Experimental Brain Research 37: 299–308

Lipson L G, Bush M J, Tietjen G E, Yoon A 1981 Role of the adenylate cyclase system in altered insulin release from Islets of Langerhans of aging rats. Acta Endocrinologica 96: 222–226

Makman M H, Dvorkin B, White A 1971 Evidence for induction by cortisol in vitro by a protein inhibitor of transport and phosphorylation in rat thymocytes. Proceedings of the National Academy of Sciences (USA) 68: 1269–1273

Martin G M 1978 Genetic syndromes in man with potential relevance to the pathobiology of aging. In: Bergsma D, Harrison D E (ed) Genetic Effects on Aging. Birth Defects: Original Article Series, Vol. 14: Alan R Liss for the National Foundation — March of Dimes, p 5–40

Martin G M, Sprague C A, Epstein C J 1970 Replicative life-span of cultivated human cells. Effects of donor's age, tissue and genotype. Laboratory Investigation 23: 86–92

Masoro E J, Yu B P, Bertrand H A, Lynd F T 1980 Nutritional probe of the aging process. Federation Proceedings of the Federation of the American Societies for Experimental Biology 39: 3178–3182

Mattern M R, Cerutti P A 1975 Age-dependent excision repair of damaged thymine from γ-irradiated DNA by isolated nuclei from human fibroblasts. Nature (London) 254: 450–452

McCay C M, Maynard L A, Sperling G, Barnes L L 1939 Retarded growth, life-span, ultimate body size and age changes in the albino rat after feeding diets restricted in calories. Journal of Nutrition 18: 1–13

McConnell P, Berry M 1978 The effect of refeeding after neonatal starvation on Purkinje cell dendritic growth in the rat. Journal of Comparative Neurology 178: 759–772

McGuire E A, Tobin J D, Berman M, Andres R 1979 Kinetics of native insulin in diabetic, obese and aged men. Diabetes 28: 110–120

McNeill T H, Clayton C J, Sladek J R 1980 Immunocytochemical charaterics of hypothalamic magnocellular neurons in the aged rat. Journal of Histochemistry and Cytochemistry 28: 611–612

Meites J, Steger R W, Huang H H 1980 Relation of neuroendocrine system to the reproductive decline in aging rats and human subjects. Federation Proceedings of the Federation of the American Societies for Experimental Biology 39: 3168–3172

Miller A E, Reigle G D 1978 Hypothalamic LH-releasing activity in young and aged intact and gonadectomized rats. Experimental Aging Research 4: 145–156

Miquel J, Economos A C, Fleming J, Johnson J E Jr. 1980 Mitochondrial role in cell aging. Experimental Gerontology 15: 575–591

Nelson J F, Latham K R, Finch C E 1975 Plasma testosterone levels in C57BL/6J male mice: effects of age and disease. Acta Endocrinologica 80: 744–753

Norwood T H, Pendergrass, W R, Sprague C A, Martin G M 1974 Dominance of the senescent phenotype in heterokaryons between replicative and post-replicative human fibroblast-like cells. Proceedings of the National Academy of Sciences (USA) 71: 2231–2234

Norwood T H, Pendergrass, W R, Martin G M 1975 Reinitiation of DNA synthesis in senescent human fibroblasts upon fusion with cells of unlimited growth potential. Journal of Cell Biology 64: 551–557

Norwood T H, Pendergrass W R, Bornstein P, Martin G M 1979 DNA synthesis of sublethally injured cells in heterokaryons and its relevance to clonal senescence. Experimental Cell Research 119: 15–22

Ogden D A, Micklem H S, 1976 The fate of serially transplanted bone marrow cell populations from young and old donors. Transplantation 22: 287–298

Ooka H 1979 Changes in extrathyroidal conversion of thyroxine (T4) to 3,3,5 — triiodothyronine (T3) in vitro during development and aging of the rat. Mechanisms of Ageing and Development 10: 151–156

Ono T, Cutler R G 1978 Age-dependent relaxation of gene expression — increase of endogenous murine leukaemia virus-related and globin-related RNA in brain and liver of mice. Proceedings of the National Academy of Sciences (USA) 75: 4431–4435

Painter R B, Clarkson J M, Young B R 1973 Ultra-violet induced repair replication in aging diploid human cells (WI-38). Radiation Research 56: 560–564

Parker L, Gral T, Perrigo V, Skowsky R 1981 Decreased adrenal androgen sensitivity to ACTH during aging. Metabolism 30: 601–604

Prothero J, Gallant J A 1981 A model of clonal attenuation, Proceedings of the National Academy of Sciences (USA) 78: 333–337

Rabinovitch P S, Norwood T H 1980 Comparative heterokaryon study of cellular senescence and the serum-deprived state. Experimental Cell Research 130: 101–109

Reaven G M, Reaven P D 1980 Effect of age on glucose oxidation by isolated rat islets. Diabetologia 18: 69–72

Reymond M J, Porter J C 1981 Secretion of hypothalamic dopamine into pituitary-stalk blood of aged female rats. Brain Research Bulletin 7: 69–73

Rosner B A, Cristofalo V J 1979 Hydrocortisone: a specific modulator of in vitro cell proliferation and aging. Mechanisms of Ageing and Development 9: 485–496

Ross E A M, Anderson N, Micklem H S 1982 Serial depletion and regeneration of the murine haematopoietic system: implications for haematopoietic organisation and the study of cellular aging. Journal of Experimental Medicine 155: 432–444

Ross M H 1959 Protein, calories and life expectancy. Federation Proceedings of the Federation of the American Societies for Experimental Biology 18: 1190–1207

Ross M H 1961 Length of life and nutrition in the rat. Journal of Nutrition 75: 197–210

Ross M H 1969 Aging, nutrition, and hepatic enzyme activity patterns in the rat. Journal of Nutrition 97 (Supplement 1, part 2): 565–601

Ross M H, Lustbader E, Bras G 1976 Dietary practices and growth responses as predictors of longevity. Nature (London) 262: 548–553

Roth G S 1975 Reduced glucocorticoid responsiveness and receptor concentration in splenic leucocytes of senescent rats. Biochimica et Biophysica Acta 399: 145–157

Roth G S 1979 Hormone receptor changes during adulthood and senescence: significance for aging research. Federation Proceedings of the Federation of the American Societies for Experimental Biology 38: 1910–1914

Roth G S, Adelman R C 1975 Age related changes in hormone binding by target cells and tissues; possible role in altered adaptive responsiveness. Experimental Gerontology 10: 1–13

Ryan J M, Sharf B B, Cristofalo V J 1975 The influence of culture medium volume on cell density and life-span of human diploid fibroblasts. Experimental Cell Research 91: 389–393

Sacher G A 1959 Relationship of life-span to brain weight and body weight in mammals. In: Wolstenholme, O'Connor (eds) Ciba Foundation Colloquia on the Lifespan of Animals. Vol. 5: Churchill, London, p 115–133

Sartin J, Chaudhuri M, Obenrader M, Adelman R C 1980 The role of hormones in changing adaptive mechanisms during aging. Federation Proceedings of the Federation of the American Societies for Experimental Biology 39: 3163–3167

Schneider E L, Smith J R 1981 The relationship of in vitro studies to in vivo human aging. International Review of Cytology 69: 261–270

Sladek C D, McNeill T H, Gregg C M, Blair M L, Baggs R B 1981 Vasopressin and renin response to dehydration in aged rats. Neurobiology of Aging 2: 293–302

Sladek J R Jr, Khachaturian H, Hoffman G E, Scholer J 1980 Aging of central endocrine neurons and their aminergic afferents. Peptides 1 (Supplement 1): 141–157

Sonntag W E, Forman L J, Miki N, Trapp J M, Gotschall P E, Meites J 1982 L-DOPA restores amplitude of growth hormone pulses in old male rats to that observed in young male rats. Neuroendocrinology 34: 163–168

Sonntag W E, Steger R W, Forman L J, Meites J 1980 Decreased pulsatile release of growth-hormone in old male-rats. Endocrinology 107: 1875–1879

Steger R W 1981 Age-related changes in the control of prolactin secretion in the female rat. Neurobiology of Aging 2: 119–123

Steger R W, Sonntag W E, Vugt D A van, Forman L J, Meites J 1980 Reduced ability of naloxone to stimulate LH and testosterone release in aging male rats; possible relation to increase in hypothalamic met$_5$-enkephalin. Life Sciences 27: 747–754

Stein G H, Yanishevsky R M 1979 Entry into S-phase is inhibited in two immortal cell lines fused to senescent human diploid cells. Experimental Cell Research 120: 155–166

Turkington M R, Everitt A V 1976 The neurohypophysis and aging with special reference to the antidiuretic hormone. In: Everitt A V, Burgess J A (eds) Hypothalamus, Pituitary and Aging. C C Thomas, Springfield, Illinois.

Valueva G V, Verzhikovskaya N V 1977 Thyrotropic activity of hypophysis during aging. Experimental Gerontology 12: 97–107

Walford R L, Liu R K, Gerbase-Delima M, Mathies M, Smith G S 1974 Longterm dietary restriction and immune function in mice: Response to sheep red blood cells and to mitogenic agents. Mechanisms of Ageing and Development 2: 447–454

Waters H, Walford R L 1970 Latent period for outgrowth of human skin explants as a function of age. Journal of Gerontology 25: 381–383

White N, Griffith E C, Jeffcoat S L, Milner R D G, Preece M A 1980 Age-related changes in the degradation of thyrotropin releasing hormone by human and rat serum. Journal of Endocrinology 86: 397–402

Wilkinson A, Davies I 1981 The influence of age on the hypothalamo-neurohypophyseal system of the mouse: a quantitative ultrastructural analysis of the posterior pituitary. Mechanisms of Ageing and Development 15: 129–139

Wright W E, Hayflick L 1975 Contributions of cytoplasmic factors to in vitro cellular senescence. 34: 76–80

Yanishevsky R M, Stein G H 1980 Ongoing DNA synthesis continues in young human diploid cells (HDC) fused to senescent HDC, but entry into S phase is inhibited. Experimental Cell Research 126: 469–472

Biology of aging — structural and metabolic aspects

INTRODUCTION

General theories of aging have been propounded repeatedly throughout this century. They have ranged from concepts relating to the gradual utilization of certain unspecific irreplaceable materials with which the body is endowed at birth, through suggestions regarding the possible accumulation of what has been termed 'the debris of life', with the eventual 'clogging' of the vital processes, to highly philosophical proposals that the aging process has a role to play in evolution, by the elimination from a population of the ineffective elderly. Theories such as these have been current since the late nineteenth century, and have been resuscitated and reintroduced off and on up to the present day. As a basis for more specific theories they may have had their importance, but individually many may be regarded merely as intellectual exercises.

There has, however, been an increasing tendency to attempt the impossible of recent years; namely, to devise a unitary theory of aging (Sanders, 1972) on the basis of which all the observed aging phenomena can be explained. One such has been the error catastrophe theory propounded by Orgel (1963) which has been in part substantiated by the observations of Holliday (1972), Holliday and Tarrant (1972) and Lewis and Tarrant (1972) but later refuted by Baird et al, (1975); Finch, (1976). This theory suggests that a number of faults accumulate in certain 'permanent' macromolecules during life due to errors which occur either in their synthesis or in the synthesis of enzyme systems involved in their production.

Studies of structural changes in the aging body have provided evidence for the programmed control of the aging process on the one hand (Hall, 1981) and the involvement of random effects on the other (Hall, 1976) on the basis of which it appears likely that neither may represent the incontravertible answer to man's long-standing question: 'How and why do I age?' (Hall, 1979).

STRUCTURAL ASPECTS OF AGING

Connective tissues

General introduction

Connective tissues are widely distributed throughout the body, and are therefore very diverse in composition. However, they invariably consist of a relatively meagre cellular component imbedded in an extracellular matrix consisting essentially of ground substance and fibrous proteins. Age changes can best be observed in this matrix. It is clear, however, that such changes will depend on alterations in the cellular components which synthesize the majority of the extracellular material.

All connective tissues contain collagen in some form or other, depending on the nature and function of the organ concerned. Some contain elastin in addition and elderly tissues also contain pseudoelastin (Hall, 1968, 1976); a form of partially-degraded collagen. In addition, there are quite considerable deposits of lipid, both within the cells and either free or bound to the fibrous proteins in the matrix. The whole of the extracellular fibrous protein matrix is bathed in a semi-solid structureless gel consisting of a glycosaminoglycan-protein complex, the so-called ground substance. These various components differ quantitatively from site to site and, as will be described in detail below, their distribution also changes with age. Some of the individual components also change qualitatively with age (see below). Studies of age changes in connective tissue therefore require the assessment of alterations which can be observed in both the quantity and quality of the fibrous proteins and of the ground substance, and also of the factors which may bring about such changes.

Collagen

Structure. This protein consists basically of a rigid complex macromolecule, tropocollagen, which is 260 nm in length and 1.4 nm wide. This macromolecule consists of three separate protein chains each having a molecular weight of approximately 100 000 daltons (Ramachandran, 1967). Each chain is in the form of a helix, and all three are twisted together to form a super helix (Figs. 3.1, 3.2 and 3.3). The pitch of these helices determines the characteristic parameters measurable on X-ray diffraction plates, and in electron microscope pictures. In its newly synthesized state the individual subunits of the tropocollagen macromolecule are held together by hydrogen bonds between carbonyl and imino and amino groups in adjacent chains. In this state they are easily separable from one another either by thermal denaturation or by reagents capable of breaking hydrogen bonds, to give free polypeptide chains — the so-called α-components of collagen. As the tissue matures, these fundamental chains become cross-linked with the formation of dimers (β-components) or trimers (γ-components). Fractionation of the α-chains by a variety of physical methods (Piez et al, 1966) has shown that in many mammalian tissues there are two forms of α-collagen differing in amino acid composition (Table 3.1), but in certain tissues, notably in codfish skin (Piez, 1964) all three α-chains differ chemically from one another. Since there are only two different components

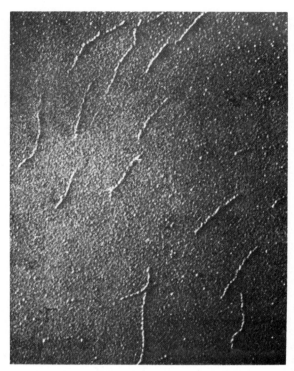

Fig. 3.2 Electron micrograph of individual tropocollagen molecules from the soluble collagen of fish swim bladder. The thickness of the molecules has been enhanced by platinum shadowing until their original 1.4 nm width has been increased to a value at which they can be resolved in the microscope (Ramachandran, 1961).

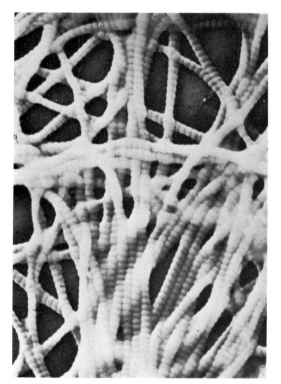

Fig. 3.1 Electron micrograph of chromium shadowed collagen microfibrils from human skin, showing cross striations at 64 nm intervals

in many collagens, twice as many of one component (α1) as of the other (α2) make up the complete tropocollagen molecule, hence the β-component can vary in composition, being composed either of 2α chains (β_{11}), or of one chain of each species (β_{12}). Higher polymers, such as trimers, may either reflect the heterogeneous structure of the individual tropocollagen triple helix (γ_{112}) or may be of such a composition as to indicate that intermolecular cross-linkages are formed (γ_{122}) since the α2 chains in such a complex could only be derived from separate tropocollagen molecules. Veis and Anesey (1965) have also demonstrated the existence of these linkages joining adjacent tropocollagen molecules by the separation and identification of a β-collagen species which is composed of two α2 chains.

Until recently it was tacitly assumed that all mammalian collagen was identical, but Chung and Miller (1974) and Adam and Deyl (1976) have demonstrated that many preparations of collagen consist of more than one species of protein. Type I and Type III collagen consisting of $\alpha1(I)_2\alpha2$ and $\alpha1(II)_3$ molecules

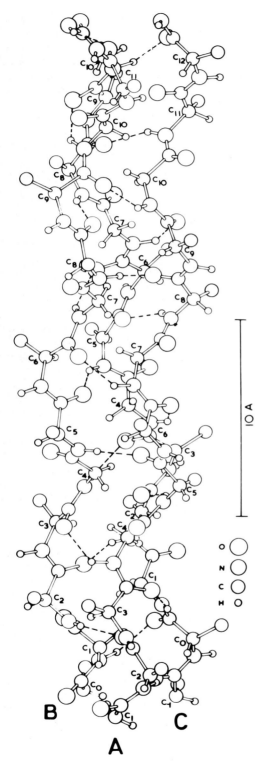

Fig. 3.3 Diagrammatic representation of the trihelical structure of the collagen molecule (Ramachandran, 1961)

Table 3.1 Amino acid composition of various connective tissue proteins (Residues/1000 total amino acid residues)

	Insoluble collagen	Elastin	Pseudo-elastin*	Pseudo-elastin†
Hydroxyproline	61.0	15.2	17.2	14.2
Aspartic acid	59.0	7.5	14.5	4.3
Threonine	29.5	8.4	6.1	5.3
Serine	28.2	9.5	8.3	3.1
Glutamic acid	83.0	20.4	27.4	19.1
Proline	115.0	113.0	184.8	114.2
Glycine	295.0	333.0	341.2	314.1
Alanine	102.5	247.0	256.2	251.0
Valine	2υ.2	136.7	77.8	135.0
Methionine	6.0	—	—	—
Isoleucine	14.5	30.5	4.8	23.1
Leucine	35.2	6.1	28.2	58.0
Tyrosine	4.8	11.0	14.5	19.7
Phenylalanine	16.5	36.3	16.6	22.1—
Hydroxylysine	8.2	—	—	—
Lysine	34.0	6.8	0.4	4.8
Histidine	3.5	tr	tr	1.3
Arginine	47.0	5.7	1.9	7.6
Desmosines etc.	—	14.4	9.1	10.4

* 4-year-old ox aorta.
† 71-year-old human skin.

respectively are present in skin tissues. The latter is present in greater concentration in embryonic and young skin (Epstein, 1973), the former in normal adult skin, indicating the repression and activation of different gene loci in the fibroblast as age proceeds (Hall, 1981). Type I is also present in tendon and bone and Type III in aortic wall where its concentration relative to Type I rises with increasing age (Layman and Titus, 1975; Rauterberg et al, 1977). Two other types (II and IV) consisting of $\alpha 1(II)_3$ and $\alpha 1(IV)_3$ molecules are present in cartilage and basement membrane respectively. As yet there is little evidence as to the types of age change which may occur in these connective tissues.

As the collagen matures the proportion of dimers and higher polymers present in any tissue increases. An assessment of the figures presented by Heikkinen and Kulonen (1964) indicates, however, that in mouse skin the decrease in the number of α-components does not result in an increase in the concentration of β-components. The polymers which are present are trimers and higher molecular weight species which are derived by the formation of larger numbers of cross linkages (Fig. 3.4). On the other hand, Bakerman (1964) has shown that there is no similar increase in the more highly polymerized collagen species with increasing age of human subjects, although this ratio does change with disease (Bakerman, 1965). Free monomers — the α-chains — are easily soluble in normal physiological saline (0.15 mol/l), but as collagen becomes increasingly more cross-linked, it requires higher concentrations of sodium chloride for its dissolution (Bakerman, 1964),

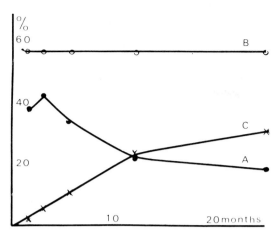

Fig. 3.4 Microdensitometric assessment of the amounts of collagen macromolecules of varying degrees of complexity extracted from mouse skins of various ages. α-chains (A) are single protein molecules, β-chains (B) dimers formed by cross linkage between pairs of chain, γ-specials (C) are trimers or larger polymeric fragments. (Calculated from figures reported by Heikkinen and Kulonen, 1964).

until a molarity of 2 is reached. Sodium chloride at this concentration removes all the soluble collagen which can be removed in solutions of neutral salt. Further amounts of collagen can be taken into solution in dilute acid. However, radioactive tracer studies have demonstrated that this material, which is not soluble in neutral salt solutions but can be dissolved by acid, is not a precursor of the mature insoluble form of the protein. It represents a proportion of the latter material which is lightly cross-linked, and bound to the mature matrix, but which is still susceptible to attack by dilute acid.

Until recently, biochemical studies on collagen have in the main been carried out on these soluble fractions and little account has been taken of the increasing proportion which, with advancing age, remains undissolved even after prolonged extraction. A variety of methods have, however, been devised over the past few years, making it possible to take this mature collagen into solution. When in solution this hitherto intractable fraction of the tissue can be fractionated and purified more easily.

Reed et al (1963) suggested that controlled alkaline hydrolysis under conditions in which the swelling of the tissue was restricted by high concentrations of sodium sulphate would permit the solution of a far larger proportion of the collagen. Nevertheless there was a considerable degree of degradation, giving a very heterogeneous distribution of molecular weights. The method derived by Steven and Jackson (1967), following the early experiments by Nishihara and Miyata (1962) in which pretreatment by relatively crude preparations of α-amylase or the chelating agent EDTA is used to separate the collagen from its non-collagenous matrix, has resulted in the production of a more homogeneous preparation of soluble collagen of very high molecular weight (Steven, 1976). They were able to demonstrate that in the mature insoluble form of collagen which increases in amount with age, tropocollagen molecules as well as being closely cross-linked to one another, are also joined to a glycoprotein containing glucose, fucose and mannose (Grant and Jackson, 1968).

Cross-linkages and their change with age. During maturation the collagen molecule becomes stabilized by the introduction of linkages between individual α-chains and between adjacent tropocollagen molecules. These linkages, based on the interaction of aldehyde groupings, formed by the deamination of lysine or hydroxlysine residues, either with one another or with the ε-amino group of intact lysine residues are located in the terminal portions of the collagen α-chains. Hydrolysis of mature collagen permits linkage molecules to be identified. Robins et al (1973), Fujii et al (1976) and Ruiz-Torres (1978) have demonstrated that of the various types of cross linkage which can be identified, some, present in high concentration in the foetus, decrease rapidly in infancy whereas others rise to peak values at maturity (Fig. 3.5). The decrease which is apparent thereafter may be due to the conversion of these linkages into other forms which have not yet been identified, or to the greater stability of the collagenous tissue prohibiting the recovery of these linkage molecules after hydrolysis.

Biosynthesis of collagen. The biosynthesis of collagen has, in the main, been studied in chick embryo preparations (Fitton-Jackson, 1975) or in granulomata induced by the implantation of sterile polyvinyl sponges (Gould, 1958; Kulonen, 1970). The former of these methods provides little evidence on which to base the effects of age. However, these can be determined by studies of the latter type of system.

The implantation of sponge into the tissues of animals of various ages results in the production of similar types of collagen in all cases. Thus it may be assumed that the organism retains within itself the capability of synthesizing collagen, as long as viable fibroblasts remain.

It would appear, therefore, that ribosomal synthesis occurs throughout life, but that newly synthesized collagen in tissues from an old animal is small. Thus Neuberger et al (1951), studying the uptake of labelled amino acids by tendon and skin, were able to demonstrate that there is little synthesis after maturity in most tissues, and that the half-life of collagen is roughly equivalent to the half-life of the animal.

Although the amino acid hydroxyproline is relatively unique to collagen, only occurring in small amounts in elastin (Bentley and Hanson, 1969) and in the C1q fraction of complement (Reid et al, 1972), it is not possible

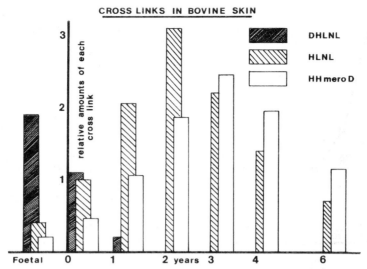

Fig. 3.5 Age changes in the relative amounts of three cross-links in bovine skin collage. DMLNL — dihydroxylysinonorleucine; HH mero D — Histidinohydroxymerodesmasine (after Robins et al, 1973)

to induce the direct incorporation of labelled hydroxyproline. It has been proved unequivocably (Gould, 1968) that hydroxyproline cannot itself be built into the collagen molecule since there is no specific codon for this imino acid in the nucleotide language. Where hydroxyproline is ultimately destined to appear in the collagen molecule, proline is built into the nascent collagen precursor and is later converted to the hydroxylated from by an enzyme system capable of catalysing this reaction (Berg and Prockop, 1973). As yet there is no evidence as to whether the level of this enzyme is affected by age, since collagen and both its precursors and degradation products are identified by their hydroxyproline content. Poorly or complete unhydroxylated collagen has been identified in tissues which are deficient in ascorbic acid, however, a condition which is often prevelent in the elderly.

Physical changes in collagen and collagenous tissue. In view of the supportive and protective nature of collagenous tissues, it is not surprising that an appreciable amount of work has been carried out on their physical properties and the changes which occur in these parameters on aging. The work of Verzar and his school (Verzar, 1955), of Banga et al (1954) and of Elsden (1964) has demonstrated that various physical properties of collagen change with age. Thus, long before the cross-linkages described above were identified, their existence could be deduced from Verzar's observations. If a tendon fibre is denatured, either by heat or by chemical reagents (Banga, 1966), it contracts. This contraction can be prevented by loading the fibre. The force required to prevent contraction increases with age, thus

demonstrating that there are progressive changes in structure. Elsden (1964) has demonstrated a similar change with age in some pf the constants required for an empirical formula which he derived to characterize the relationship between extension and load. This relationship, if linear, is known as Young's modulus and defines the Hookeian relationship between load and extension. However, in practice, no natural fibres demonstrate such a linear relationship over long ranges of extension. For instance Viidik (1967) has published an oscillograph tracing for the extension of a tendon (Fig. 3.6). From this it can be seen that the curve has a toe and a shoulder, and is roughly linear for only a short intermediate period. The slope of this line, giving a value for Young's modulus which is a measure of the 'stiffness' of the fibre, becomes steeper with increasing age, indicating a greater stiffness in the elderly tendon. In dermal preparations, however, it does not prove quite so easy to obtain even a transitory linearity. Ridge and Wright (1966) demonstrated that at least one of the constants of the empirical equation, which they derived for skin samples, $E = c + kL^b$, namely the power b to which the load is raised, increases with age, and then fails again, reaching a peak at about an age of 45 years. This is in agreement with the concept that aging, at least as characterized by physical changes in connective tissues, may be divided into two phases (Hall, 1967, 1981), one providing an increases in stiffness, the other a decrease. Since the algebraic sum of these two provides the resultant 'stiffness factor' at all ages, it is apparent that the degradative phase supersedes the maturative one at the age of 45.

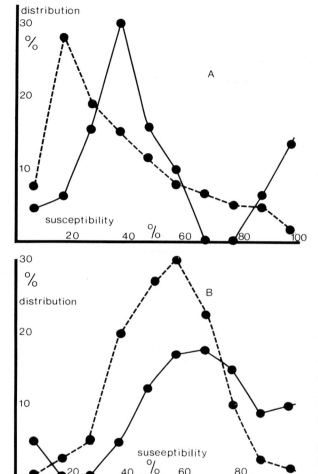

Fig. 3.6 The distribution of the percentage susceptibility (ordinate) of (A) biopsy and (B) postmortem samples of mature skin collagen (after complete removal of the neutral salt-soluble fraction) to attack by *Clostridium histolyticum* collagenase. The full line in each graph represents the distribution of susceptibility in a 0 to 55-year-old group, the broken line the susceptibility of a 35 to 100-year-old group. It can be seen that the effect if age is greater on the susceptibility of biopsy than postmortem material.

Collagenase. The question of degradation raised in the previous section introduces the concept of the existence of a collagenolytic enzyme system capable of such catabolic activity. However, the identification of collagenases in mammalian tissues has only been achieved in recent years (Lazarus and Fullmer, 1969; Eisen, 1969; Evanson et al, 1968; Harris and Cartwright, 1977; Woessner, 1978, 1980), and many of the studies that have been carried out on the effect of collagenase on collagens of different ages have been performed with bacterial enzymes derived in the main from strains of clostridia. Collagenase from *Clostridium histolyticum*

(Mandl et al, 1964) has been utilized (Reed and Hall, 1974) to determine the stability of skin, bone and disc collagen, and hence to provide an indirect assessment of the degree of cross-linkage in these tissues. If it can be assumed that the mammalian collagenases demonstrate a similar specificity to the bacterial forms, it may be deduced that the degree of degradation of the connective tissue collagen which occurs in older age groups will, under normal circumstances, be less. However, there are conditions in which excessive collagenolytic activity appears to take place. Some of these are not particularly age-oriented; such as the involution of the postparum uterus (Woessner and Brewer, 1963; Woessner, 1965) or the remodelling of wound scar tissue (Houck and Jacob, 1963; Shoshan, 1981), when rather non-typical collagenases appear to be active. Others, such as that which occurs in the degeneration of the bone matrix in osteoporosis, are more closely controlled by age and in this particular instance may well be dependent on changes in the parathormone concentration in the plasma (Harris and Sjoerdsma, 1966).

Urinary excretion of hydroxyproline. The in situ degradation of connective tissue results in the appearance of hydroxyproline in the urine. Normally, the degradation of a protein forming part of one of the tissues of the body results in an increase in the amount of amino acids available for the resynthesis of tissue proteins. This is true of the majority of the amino acids which constitute the non-imino acid fraction of collagen, and of the proline portion of the imino acid fraction.

Two acids, however, hydroxyproline and hydroxylysine, cannot be incorporated directly into collagen, but must be synthesized from proline and lysine after these acids have been incorporated into the nascent collagen polypeptides (Prockop and Kivirikko, 1967). Thus, the degradation of collagen within the body is accompanied by the secretion of hydroxyproline. Hydroxyproline constitutes some 11 per cent of the total collagenous protein, but is virtually absent from all other proteins (see, however, above). It is relatively easy to identify, being fundamentally different in chemical properties from all amino acids and from proline, and hence may be identified in the urine and used as a diagnostic sign of the degradation of collagen.

It has been shown that the hydroxyproline content of the urine of infants and young people is relatively high compared to that of mature and elderly non-pathological subjects (Table 3.2). It has also been shown by radioactive tracer studies that the majority of the hydroxyproline which appears in the urine of these young subjects is derived from poorly cross-linked collagen. Hence it may be assumed that a large proportion of the collagen which is synthesized by the fibroblasts of young subjects is never deposited in the position in which it will ultimately form part of a tissue or an organ (Lind-

Table 3.2 Changes in the urinary excretion of hydroxyproline with increasing age. Each value is the mean of more than twenty individuals in each age group. All values are expressed in terms of mg per 24 h.

Age range	Hydroxyproline
0 to 1 year	37.5
1 to 5 years	42.5
6 to 10 years	67.0
11 to 15 years	122.5
15 to 21 years	46.0
Adults (over 21)	16.5

stedt and Prockop, 1961). Where there is an increase in the rate of excretion of hydroxyproline, even in an old subject, such as occurs during the healing of a wound, this may represent an excessive production of soluble non-cross-linked collagen followed by the remodelling of the wound tissue and the disappearance of the majority of the protein. Under normal circumstances the loss of tissue which occurs in elderly subjects without any pathological involvement is so slow that the release of hydroxyproline cannot be measured by its appearance in the urine. Hence this type of slow remodelling which can occur in the tissues of aging subjects cannot be identified.

Elastin

Structure. The other major fibrous component of connective tissue, elastin, is more selectively distributed than collagen, being present only in those tissues which are destined to provide long-range elasticity under the action of the normal forces associated with bodily extension and contraction. The major sites of elastin deposition within the body are the skin, the walls of major blood vessels, the heart, the lungs and the ligaments. In all these sites elastin and collagen form a two-phase system providing spring-like elasticity, to counter the effects of the musculature, and rigidity akin to that provided by reinforcing bars to restrain excessive extension. In each tissue the topographical relationship of the two types of fibre is dependent on the type of elasticity to be provided. In a ligament, for instance, the elasticity is essentially one-dimensional along the axis of the tissue and the elastic fibres are arranged roughly parallel to this axis. Wood (1954) has shown that initially the collagen fibres are also arranged parallel to the elastin fibres, but that after repeated elongation and contraction cycles the collagen fibres which cannot be extended tend to slide over one another when the tissue is in the extended state, and then to crumple up when the load is removed. Thus in later life they do not restrict the extension of the ligament until they are themselves fully extended, but they prevent complete disruption of the ligament when excessive loads are applied.

In the aorta the elastin fibres are fused together to form lamellae which lie around the lumen of the vessel. The collagen fibres lie in between the lamellae, and when the young vessel is at rest they assume an alignment which is at an angle to the axis of the vessel. Each layer of collagen is laid down in an opposite direction to those in the interlamellar spaces to either side. Distension of the vessel results in the realignment of these reinforcing fibres until they assume a parallel circumferential pattern. Between each pair of lamellae, fibrils of elastic tissue cross the collagen-filled spaces, holding adjacent lamellae together.

It is difficult to distinguish between true aging changes in the elastin and those which can be related to pathological conditions. Thus in the skin and in the aortic wall there are marked changes whcih can be observed by histological techniques, but these may be due to degenerative diseases of the dermis or to atherosclerotic changes in the artery.

Pseudoelastin. As elastic tissue ages its true elastin content decreases, although a considerable number of workers have actually reported increases in elastin with advancing age (Scarcelli, 1961), due to the inclusion of partially degraded collagen along with the true elastin.

It has become apparent during recent years that these inconsistencies in the analysis of elastin tissue are due to variations in methods of analysis (Hall, 1967). It was first observed by Hall (1955) that elastin preparations from old tissues contain a third protein in addition to elastin and collagen which, although similar in many respects to elastin, can in fact be separated from this protein, with which the normal methods of purification separate it, by drastic treatment with reagents such as boiling 8M urea. More recent studies on ox elastin (Hall 1968a) and human elastin (Labella et al, 1966) have shown that this material, which has an amino acid analysis between that of collagen and elastin, is firmly bound to elastin especially during middle age, but thereafter becomes less closely attached to this protein. For this reason elastin, with the classical analysis of the protein from young subjects, can be isolated from the elastin tissues of very old subjects. It has been suggested that this third protein should be called pseudoelastin (Hall, 1964, 1976). It stains very similarly to elastin, it is insoluble in the normal collagen solvents — dilute acid and dilute alkali — but, as mentioned above, differs from elastin in its solubility in a variety of solvents which are capable of more drastic action, such as concentrated urea or formic acid. It is this material which causes the apparent increase in elastin in tissue from more elderly subjects and those with certain pathological conditions.

Initially it was assumed that the increase in elastica-staining material in elastic tissue, which could be observed with age, reflected an overall increase in elastin. Electron microscope studies of areas of apparent elastosis, however, demonstrated (Tunbridge et al, 1952) that the material present in these areas although staining like elastin, and hence named pseudoelastin, is either a degradation product of collagen or a faulty form of that protein.

The amino acid analysis of pseudoelastin differs from site to site. It also depends on the nature of the phenomenon which produces it. Its electron microscopic appearance may also differ. For instance, although pseudoelastin is present in both senile elastotic skin and in skin from subjects with pseudoxanthoma elasticum, the two do not appear identical when viewed in the electron microscope (Fig. 3.7). In the former case the collagen fibres are bent and broken and covered with masses of amorphous material. In the latter the fibres are shorter than normal, but are not bent and broken, nor covered with amorphous substance. Consideration of the origins of pseudoelastin reopens the question of collagen degradation referred to above.

It is usually assumed that collagen molecules are stable, since there is little evidence for the incorporation of labelled proline or the excretion of hydroxyproline in the urine of adult subjects. However, it can be calculated from the rate at which age changes occur that the excretion of hydroxyproline would only be 300 mg per year. (The mean loss of skin collagen in males between 30 and 80 years of age is 15 μg per mm^2 of skin surface per decade; Slater and Hall, 1973.) It is unlikely, therefore, that the consequent appearance of between 50 and 60 μg hydroxyproline per 100 ml in the urine per day would be easily observable. Moreover the failure of adult collagenous tissues to incorporate proline only implies that total ribosomal synthesis of collagen does not occur. It is assumed that this precludes all metabolic activity on the part of the collagen, but this may not necessarily be the case. Thus tropocollagen may be laid down on templates such as the glycoproteins postulated by Snellman (1963) or the glycosaminoglycans, which have been suggested by Wood (1960) as controlling factors in fibre formation; it may be mobilized at a later stage, and redeposited on the same or similar templates. It would not be possible to identify this type of reaction by the normal technique of pulse labelling. Klein and Weiss (1966), however, have reported the appearance in the surrounding tissue of radioactively-labelled hydroxyproline derived from proline incorporated into granuloma tissue. These observations have not been confirmed, and are doubted by many workers in the field. Should they prove capable of repetition, however, they could indicate that at least partial degradation of already formed collagen occurs, with the resultant incorporation of fragments containing hydroxyproline into newly laid-down tissue. It could, therefore, be inferred that the destruction of collagen is restricted to depolymerization either into discrete tropo-collagen molecules or at most into individual α- or β-components. These may then be reconstituted on the appropriate extracellular glycoprotein or glycosaminoglycan templates to reproduce mature microfibrillar structures. In a tissue such as a granuloma, further degradation may normally ensue, with some of the tropocollagen molecules being completely disrupted and liberating hydroxyproline either free or in oligopeptide-bound form.

Pseudoelastin may represent the aggregation of partially degraded tropocollagen molecules which, although broken down to such an extent as to have become partially depleted of certain of the amino and imino acids characteristic of mature collagen, are still sufficiently similar structurally to native tropocollagen to permit their absorption on the templates which normally bring about resynthesis of collagen. Once the intact or degraded tropocollagen molecules have interacted with one another they will become separated from the template and their degree of degradation will determine the stability of the tertiary structures so formed. Those with only slight degradation will simulate the normal appearance and properties of collagen. Those with a greater degree of degradation will be incapable of retaining the ordered structure of this protein, and will collapse, producing the essentially structureless form characteristic of pseudoelastin. The pseudoelastin typical of age lies part way between these two extremes, while that present in the dermis of pseudoxanthoma elasticum lies closer to true collagen, merely appearing fragmented in the electron microscope (Hall, 1973). That which appears in the exposed aged dermis on the forearms or neck, where the effects of aging and actinic degradation are superimposed (Slater and Hall, 1973) is both fragmented and degraded to the extent that the typical 64 nm cross-striations of collagen are almost completely obliterated by an adhering amorphous coating. This may, in extreme circumstances, provide the majority of the 'fibrous' tissue in these sites (Fig. 3.7).

These differences in the degree of degradation which can be observed in the electron microscope, and which also result in changes in staining properties, are mirrored by changes in amino acid composition. Pseudoelastin cannot be defined as a single protein, of constant composition throughout all tissues, but differs in composition from site to site, from age to age and from one pathological condition to another. The fact that the more heavily degraded forms of collagen demonstrated an amino acid analysis more closely related to that of elastin may be fortuitous. Nevertheless it may indicate that true elastin is itself synthesized by the association of part of the collagen molecule which, after ribosomal synthesis, becomes available for selection and interaction under the stimulus of such mechanical

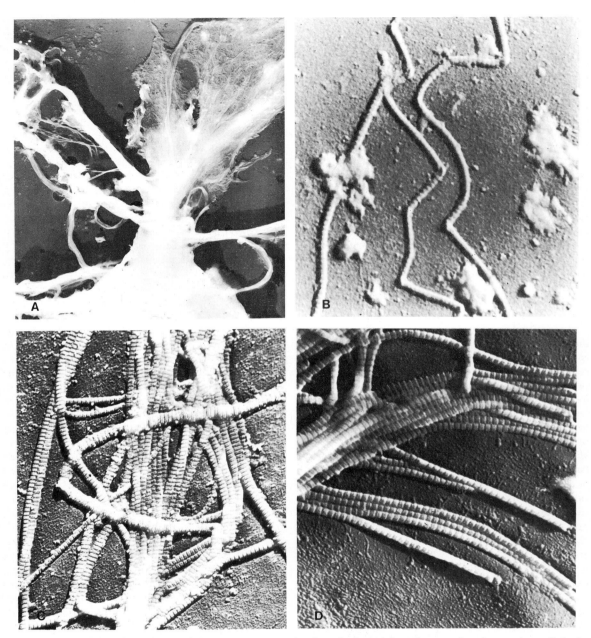

Fig. 3.7 Comparison of the electronmicroscope appearance of various elastica staining substances from human tissue. Only the pseudoelastin of actinic origin (B) shows a degree of degradation which provides appreciable amounts of amorphous material similar to that of true elastin. All the preparations demonstrate collagenous origin of the pseudoelastin with varying degrees of degradation (cf. Fig. 2.1). (A) Electronmicrograph of elastin from human aorta. A teased preparation from one of the medial elastic lamellae. Both fibrous and amorphous components are visible. Pseudoelastin from the exposed aspect of the forearm of an 81-year-old woman. (C) Pseudoelastin from the interlamella regions of an aorta from a human subject aged 84. (D) Pseudoelastin from the skin of a patient with pseudoxanthoma elasticum.

forces as are present in these tissues in which elastin is laid down.

Hall (1971) has shown that the precipitation of collagen under repeated cycles of extension and contraction results in the formation of material which is less soluble in dilute acid and under the action of collagenase than is normal collagen, and more soluble in elastase. It is not suggested that collagen is converted to elastin under these circumstances, but that its structure is in fact being altered to a state in which it resembles elastin.

The sclerotic changes which accompany aging in the walls of the great vessels are not solely confined to the deposition of lipid, although this may represent a major factor in this development (see below). Willman and Edwards (1950) showed that the aorta increases in circumference from below 30 mm to above 60 mm between the first and tenth decades, the rate of increase being rapid during growth, but remaining constant thereafter. The initial change in diameter can be attributed to growth and to an increase in the number of elastic lamellae (Berry et al, 1972). The thickness of the individual lamellae also increases with age, but neither of these two factors can account for the lifelong progressive increase in diameter. In youth the elastic lamellae, after the removal of the aorta from the body, are typically convoluted, although under normal intraluminal pressure they may be relatively circular in section. With increasing age, however, even the relaxation resulting from removal from the body is insufficient to return the lamellae to their youthful convoluted state. It is apparent that the tensile properties of the tissue will also change with age, the lag which precedes elongation of an elastic lamellar segment under tension disappearing as the age of the subject increases. Roach and Burton (1957) have calculated, by double differentiation of the load extension curves for rings of excised aorta, that the same proportion of the collagen fibres, which provide relatively inextensible 'reinforcing bars' in the aortic wall, are extended when young tissue is stretched by 60 per cent as when old tissue is stretched by 25 per cent. The failure of the wall to relax to a convoluted state and hence the reason for this greater involvement of the collagen fibres even at low extension would appear to be due to the changes which take place in the elastic lamellae. Saxl and Hall (1967) have demonstrated in chickens that under conditions in which the elastic lamellae can suffer degradation, i.e. following the intravenous administration of elastase, dietary lipid reacts with elastin in the aortic wall with the production of elastolipoprotein complexes. This may, therefore, explain the degeneration of elastic lamellae and the localization of lipid in the artery wall.

The varied degradation of collagen may be due to alterations in the availability of specific proteolytic enzymes in the cellular components of the tissues concerned. The development of these adaptive systems could be due to alterations in the enzymic make up of fibroblasts under the action of mutated lymphocytes which are specific for them. Again, however, this conjecture remains at present purely hypothetical.

Elastase

The control of the elastin content of connective tissues can be ascribed to the pancreatic enzyme elastase. Since its discovery by Balo and Banga (1949) this enzyme has been implicated on a number of occasions in arterial elastolysis, but until recently the deduction that it may, under the action of certain stimuli, appear in the circulation has not been proved unequivocally.

The exocrine secretion of elastase by the pancreas mirrors that of other pancreatic enzymes, being controlled by the presence of factors which affect the volume and nature of the pancreatic juice. Bartos and Groh (1969) have shown that stimulation of the pancreas by single doses of pancreozymin and secretin induces the secretion of similar volumes of pancreatic juice having similar composition with respect to bicarbonate and amylase content, from both young and old subjects. If, however, the gland is repeatedly stimulated, the mean values for these parameters fall with increasing age. The fall in bicarbonate secretion virtually mirrors the reduction in volume, thus maintaining the pH of the secretion at a constant level.

Similar evidence for a reduction in response to glandular stimulation has resulted from the observations of Hall (1968b) and Loeven (1967) on the elastase content of the plasma and the pancreas respectively. The level of this enzyme falls with age in both the pancreas, where it originates, and in the plasma where it appears transiently before becoming associated with the elastic tissues of the body. This is true of male subjects only after they have reached about 20 to 30 years of age (Tesal and Hall, 1972), and although true for females from early youth and also in extreme old age, the continuous fall is interrupted during the period between 40 and 60 years of age by an appreciable increase in the amount of enzyme present in the plasma.

Loeven (1967) has observed similar inconsistencies in the decreasing levels of elastase in the pancreas. Here, however, the elastase levels are appreciably below the mean value over the same period of 40 to 60 years of age calculated from the slope of the rest of the line relating pancreatic enzyme levels to age. On the basis of these observations both authors have suggested that the release of elastase into the plasma, rather than into the pancreatic duct, is under hormonal control. The rising concentration of androgenic hormones which are secreted by the male subject in adolescence and early

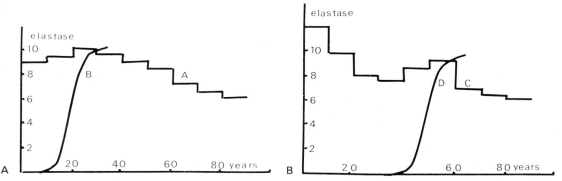

Fig. 3.8 A comparison of the elastase content of human plasma, with conditions which are directly under hormonal control. (A) The histogram represents a series of mean values for the elastase content of plasma (arbitrary values based on the release of Congo Red from dyed elastin) from male subjects grouped by decades. The curve B represents the age distribution of the attainment of full sexual maturity in a male population. (B) C is similar histogram to A but for female subjects, and the curve D represents the age distribution of the occurrence of the menopause.

adulthood is able to bring about the secretion of increasing levels of elastase into the plasma, without depleting the pancreas (Fig. 3.8). The hormonal imbalance which occurs about the period of the menopause results in a similar increased liberation of elastase from the pancreas. However, in this later age group it may be deduced that this happens at a rate which is both greater than that at which the enzyme can be synthesized by the α-cells of the gland, and also at a rate which is too great for the utilization of the enzyme in sites of potential elastic tissue degradation throughout the body. The net result of these two phenomena is a depletion of the pancreatic enzyme and an increase in the levels observed in the plasma. Elastase can also be caused to appear in the plasma in preference to the pancreatic duct by feeding lipid-rich meals (Slater, 1966). It has been shown that repeated administration of lipid to rats by stomach tube results in a lowered response — less elastase appearing in the plasma following each successive lipid meal. There is no direct evidence on the basis of which elastase secretion by the pancreas can be correlated with lipase secretion, but both enzymes do originate in similar regions in the pancreas. It may be, therefore, that similar changes in the lipase content of plasma exist in elderly subjects. Reduction in lipase levels could explain the alterations in lipid tolerance observed in elderly subjects (see below) with the consequent retention of lipid in the plasma for excessively long periods following a lipid-rich meal.

Recently El-Ridi and Hall (1976) have isolated elastase from human plasma thus demonstrating that the earlier concept (Balo and Banga, 1949) that the enzyme is involved in in vivo elastolysis is most probably correct. The increasing amount of elastolysis which occurs in old age, even in the presence of lowered concentrations of elastase (Fig. 3.8), can be explained by a concomitant fall in the level of plasma elastase inhibitor (Hall, 1968c).

Hall et al (1980, a, b) have reported that the elastase level of the plasma of patients who have suffered a cerebrovascular accident of thrombotic origin, rises appreciably above the normal level for their age group, reaching a peak value between 2 and 12 days after the stroke and returning to normal over the next 3 weeks. Moreover the speed which the peak elevation of the elastase content is reached is proportional to the age of the patient whereas the actual height of the peak is inversely proportional to age. It would appear that this enhancement of the elastase content of the plasma is directly related to the level of lipid present in the circulation.

METABOLIC ASPECTS OF AGING

Tissue lipids

Age changes in the metabolism of the lipid components of the body to a certain extent bridge the gap between those aspects of aging which can definitely be ascribed to tissue changes, and those which represent more closely such metabolic alterations as are age-determined. Lipids are present in normal young tissues as structural entities in all cell wall membranes, especially in the myelin sheaths of nerve fibres, and in storage cells in the liver and other fat depots throughout the body.

In elderly subjects alterations can be observed in the quantity, quality and distribution of the lipids and, as will be apparent from the following pages, these three aspects of lipid metabolism are intimately interconnected.

Lipid contents of aging tissues

The amount of lipid in male tissues increases up to the

sixth decade and thereafter decreases slowly, whereas fat accumulates continuously in female tissue. This is also true of the plasma, the 'tissue' of the body for which data are most easily obtainable. One of the major difficulties in assessing lipid changes, which can truly be ascribed to age, is the separation of these changes on the one hand from those essentially short-term variations that can be brought about by diet and on the other from those which are determined by purely pathological conditions. It is usually only possible to ensure that dietary regimes of a given type are adhered to when the subject is in hospital or when the regimes are imposed by religious or social habits. Unfortunately, in many cases such ritualistic dietary differences are often also associated with genetic considerations, since racial identity and social habits are often closely correlated. For this reason much of the work relating dietary intake to the levels of lipid in the body has had to be carried out on animals, where much stricter control is possible. There is however, no direct justification for the extrapolation of results obtained from such experiments to the human situation.

Moreover, it is unlikely that omnivorous animals such as the rat (or indeed the human subject) will have similar dietary requirements to herbivores such as the rabbit. Within these limitations, hwever, it has proved possible to study the relationship of age to the distribution of lipid throughout the body and, from it, to derive some evidence which may of use in a consideration of obesity and the other lipid dyscrasias observed in elderly human subjects.

The lipids in the body consist of a number of distinct classes, namely free fatty acids, triglycerides, cholesterol and cholesterol esters, phospholipids and non-cholesterol steroids. Triglycerides form the major portion of the fat deposits throughout the body and during transfer from one site to another, or immediately after ingestion, they represent a major portion of the lipid droplets, the chylomicrons, which are in suspension in the plasma. Metabolism of these triglycerides necessitates fission of the linkages between the glycerol moiety of the triglyceride and the three individual fatty acids with which its hydroxyl groups are esterified. This is accomplished by lipases either located in tissues or circulating in the plasma. Free fatty acids thus appear which are themselves insoluble, but which combine with albumin to provide soluble complexes. Under normal circumstances the level of free fatty acid in tissues other than the plasma is negligible. However, in the plasma they may reach measurable levels before they are removed by further metabolism. The plasma also contains appreciable levels of cholesterol esters and phospholipids — fractions which also appear significantly, but at a far lower level, in the liver and in the heart tissue.

Much lipid is stored in endothelial cells of artery

walls, and also extracellularly between the elastic lamellae and the collagen fibres. Even in infant tissue the fine streaks indicating fat deposition have been observed (Lev and Sullivan, 1951), but as will be shown later there is still considerable discussion as to whether these deposits represent the beginning of changes which can be associated directly with age or are the first developmental stages of atherosclerotic lesions.

Cholesterol levels in plasma increase slightly during later adolescence and early adulthood (Lopez et al, 1967) from the low levels present in infancy (68 mg per cent at birth according to Russ et al, 1954). This rise then proceeds steadily with increasing age to a normal adult range of 120 to 330 mg per cent. The composition of the cholesterol esters also changes with age; the proportion of the total cholesterol which is esterified by linoleic acid increases until it is the major fatty acid of this lipid fraction (Nichaman et al, 1967). The relevance of the relationship of linoleic acid and its metabolic products to aging has been studied in detail for total lipids of the liver and the testis (Burdett et al, 1972) and it has been shown that for one particular strain of rat at least, there is little significant difference between the linoleic acid content of liver or testis lipids between $2\frac{1}{2}$ and 20 months of age; nor is there much change in the levels of the ultimate metabolic product of linoleic acid, the more unsaturated, longer chain arachidonic acid. However, if animals are fed diets restricted in lipid content, the intake of linoleic acid, which cannot be synthesized in the body, is cut off. The normal conversion of linoleic acid to arachidonic acid by processes of chain elongation and desaturation is then superseded by similar changes taking place in another series of fatty acids, derived from oleic acid, which can be synthesized from acetate taken in with the diet or resulting from β-oxidation of other lipids. Lipid deficiency, therefore, results in a change in the ratio of the arachidonic acid content to that of the product of oleic acid metabolism, eicosotrienoic acid. This ratio, which is high in normal animals of all ages and can assume very low levels in deficient young animals, remains at medium levels in the case of animals of older ages (Table 3.3). It appears, therefore, either that the enzyme systems capable of elongating and desaturating oleic acid are rendered defective with increasing age or that the lipids of the linoleic acid series which accumulate in the aging animal are not as easily metabolized and destroyed when older animals are placed on a fat free diet. Whichever proves to be the case, these observations indicate that some of the enzyme systems controlling lipid metabolism are altered by age (Hall and Burdett, 1975).

Such age changes can also be seen in those enzyme systems which control the transport of lipid in the plasma. The metabolism of postprandial lipids is dependent on the availability of an enzyme — lipopro-

Table 3.3 The ratio of the arachidonic acid content (percentage) of total liver lipids of rats of various ages to the eicosotrienoic acid levels, for animals maintained on normal and essential fatty acid deficient diets for six months prior to death. (The 2.5-month-old animals were suckled by deficient mothers).

Age (months)	Ratio=20 : 4ω 6/20 : 3ω 9*	
	Normal diet	Deficient diet
2.5	177	0.24
7.5	127	0.40
17.5	105	4.00

* 20 : 4ω 6 = arachidonic acid.
  20 : 3ω 9 = eicosotrienoic acid.

tein lipase — specific for the hydrolysis of triglyceride in combination with protein. It has been shown that the clearing of postabsorptive lipaemia is either slowed down significantly, or virtually stopped in elderly subjects (Engelberg, 1958; Hall et al, 1982) apparently because of a marked reduction in the level of circulating lipoprotein lipase (Nikkila and Niemi, 1957).

Age pigments and polyunsaturated fatty acids
The involvement of polyunsaturated fatty acids in age mediated lipid changes introduces the whole question of the so-called lipofuscin granules and the problem of autoxidation. Lipofuscin granules and intracellular bodies are characterized by their appearance, staining and physical properties at the light microscope level. They are insoluble in lipid solvents, but stain black with Sudan Black, and give a positive performic acid–Schiff reaction. However, the degree to which the granules manifest such properties differs from site to site and individual to individual.

These bodies can be identified in a great variety of cells, such as those of nervous tissue, muscle, liver, spleen, kidney and adrenal cortex, often showing marked increases with age. It was shown as early as 1886 (Koneff, 1886) that the number of pigment granules in nerve cells was directly related to the age of the individual. This has since been verified for other tissues (Tomanek and Karlson, 1973; Blackett and Hall, 1981). The granules consist of a complex of protein and lipid in proportions which various workers have reported as being between 2 : 5 and 5 : 3 (Strehler, 1964; Pearse, 1968) In addition a number of enzyme systems have also been identified histochemically in these tissue components and, on the basis of these observations and the general results of analytical studies, it has been deduced that they represent degraded mitochrondia. However, other extracellular organelles, namely lysosomes and the reticular endothelium, have also been suggested as representing the origin of the granules, whereas another suggestion has been that they represent accumulations of secretory products from the Golgi apparatus, near which they are often located. These four hypotheses each have much to recommend them, and the true source of the granules has not yet been elucidated.

Age changes in polysaccharides
In the body, polysaccharides assume a number of forms, dependent on the one hand on their function in the tissue, and on the other on their chemical structure. Thus glycogen, present in muscle and liver as a storage polysaccharide, consists of a polymer of glucose to which it can be converted as required through the mediation of the necessary glycogenolytic enzymes. A reduction in the amount of any one of these enzymes may result in a slowing down of this essentially rapid process, leading to the accumulation of glycogen at the points of storage. Since vigorous exercise results in the conversion of all the glycogen in the muscle into energy or lactic acid, and may also drain the stores in the liver, the inability of the elderly to carry out prolonged vigorous exercise may be due to a failure of glycogen storage, a failure to degrade glycogen to glucose on demand, or, of course, to a reduced oxygen tension leading to the conversion of the normal oxidative, energy-releasing glycolytic pathway to an anaerobic one from which less energy can be derived.

The control of carbohydrate in the plasma is determined by the insulin secretion of the pancreas. The effective level of insulin may itself be reduced either by a failure on the part of the β-cells of the islets of Langerhans to synthesize the hormone, or to a failure in the release of the hormone from the cells. Fisher and Scott (1934) have shown that the insulin concentration in the pancreas increases with age in the case of cattle, and Griffiths (1941) has shown the same in the case of the rat. Conversely, in the human there appears to be no change (Scott and Fisher, 1938). The relatively constant values for the insulin content of the plasma observed in the human subject do not imply that the effectiveness of insulin remains at a constant level throughout life. Schneeberg and Finestone (1952), for instance, have demonstrated that the mean plasma glucose level one hour after ingestion of the test dose of glucose is only 7 per cent above the fasting level in the case of subjects up to the age of 39, whereas at ages above 41 it remains 43 per cent above the resting level. Silverstone et al (1957) have reported that not only are there marked reductions in the rates at which glucose disappears from the plasma in elderly subjects, thus indicating a potentially diabetic state in a high proportion of elderly subjects, but that a given dose of insulin is only about one-third as effective in clearing glucose from the blood of a 78-year-old as in a 31-year-old. It is therefore possible that the apparent diabetes of elderly subjects may be due to either or both of two phenomena; namely a reduction in the effective availability of insulin or to a reduction in the sensitivity of the receptor sites throughout the body, resulting in a lowered rate of cellular incorporation of glucose (Andres and Tobin, 1975; Davidson, 1979).

The structural polysaccharides in the body are essentially polymers of various glycosamines and uronic acids either free or in a sulphated form, and less is known about the age changes of these polysaccharides. It is, however, possible to assert that one of the major age changes in these structural entities lies in their association with protein. This can best be illustrated by reference to certain specific protein–polysaccharide complexes such as those which are present in cartilage and synovial fluid and in skin and other soft connective tissues. Unfortunately there is as yet little evidence on which to base the distinction between pure aging phenomena and pathological changes in these tissues. Sobel and Marmorsten (1956) first suggested that there was a reciprocal relationship between collagen and mucopolysaccharide, following their studies of the age changes in the relative amounts of hexosamine and hydroxyproline in connective tissues. The former is characteristic of the glycosaminoglycan content of the tissue, the latter of the collagen. They demonstrated that, whereas the former decreased with age, the latter increased. Wood (1960) showed that various glycosaminoglycans initiated the formation of collagen fibres. Hence it may be suggested that the initially high concentration of these polysaccharides provides the stimulus for the production of new collagen fibres. Wood reported the results of in vitro experiments in which soluble collagen molecules were caused to aggregate and precipitate. His observations are therefore not directly applicable to in vivo situations such as those observed by Sobel, since in his systems the overall collagen concentrations remained the same. It may, however, be assumed that the removal of soluble collagen by precipitation under the influence of the glycosaminoglycans will induce the synthesis of more collagen.

The intercellular matrix of cartilage contains chondroitin sulphuric acid, at least part of which is combined with collagen. Matthews (1953) has suggested that the load-bearing regions have a higher concentration of glycosaminoglycan, possibly due to a greater synthetic activity of the cells which produce this component. Reduction of activity of these cells may result in a lowering of the polysaccharide content (Sylven and Malmgren, 1952) with a consequent reduction in stability of the tissue as a whole (Hall, 1975, 1976).

REFERENCES

Adam M, Deyl Z 1976 Preparation of insoluble collagen In: Hall D A (ed) Methodology of Connective Tissue Research, Joynson-Bruvvers, Oxford, p 1–9

Andres R, Tobin J D 1975 Aging and the deposition of glucose in explorations in aging. Advances in Experimental Biology and Medicine 61: 239–249

Balo J, Banga I 1949 The destruction of the elastic fibres of vessel walls. Schweizerische Zeitschrift für Pathologie und Bakteriologie 12: 350–362

Baird M B, Samis H V, Massie H R, Zimmerman J A 1975 A brief argument in opposition to the Orgel hypothesis. Gerontologia 21: 57–59

Bakerman S 1964 Distribution of the α and β components in human skin collagen with age. Biochimica et Biophysica Acta, 90: 621–623

Bakerman S 1965 Distribution of the alpha and beta components in human skin collagen with age. Nature (London), 206: 634–636

Banga I 1966 Structure and function of elastin and collagen. Budapest: Akademiai Kiado

Banga I, Balo J, Szabo D 1954 Contraction and relaxation of collagen fibres. Nature (London), 174: 788–789

Bartos V, Groh J 1969 The effect of repeated stimulation of the pancreas on the pancreatic secretion in young and old men. Gerontologia Clinica, 17: 56–62

Bentley J P, Hanson A N 1969 The hydroxyproline of elastin. Biochimica et Biophysica Acta, 175: 339–344

Berg R A, Prockop D J 1973 The thermal transition of a non-hydroxylated form of collagen. Evidence for a role for hydroxyproline in stabilizing the triple helix of collagen. Biochemical and Biophysical Research Communications, 52: 115–120

Berry C L, Looker T, Germain J 1972 The growth and development of the rat aorta. I. morphological aspects. Journal of Anatomy, 113: 1–16

Blackett A D, Hall D A 1981 Tissue vitamin E levels and lipofuscin accumulation with age in the mouse. Journal of Gerontology, 36: 529–533

Burdett P E, Davies T, Griffin H, Hall D A 1972 The effect of age on the metabolism of polyunsaturated fatty acids. Symposia of the Swedish Nutrition Foundation, vol. 10: 69–76

Chung E, Miller E J 1974 Collagen polymorphism: characterization of molecules with the chain composition $(\alpha 1(III))_3$ in human tissues. Science, 183, 1200

Davidson M B 1979 The effect of aging on carbohydrate metabolism: a review of the English literature and a practical approach to the diagnosis of diabetes mellitus in the elderly. Metabolism, 28: 288–705

Eisen A Z 1969 Human skin collagenase. i) localisation and distribution in human skin. ii) relationship to the pathogenesis of epidermolysis bullosa dystrophica. Journal of Investigative Dermatology, 52: 442–454

El-Ridi S S, Hall D A 1976 Isolation of elastase from human serum. Biochemical Society Transactions, 4: 336–337

Elsden H R 1964 Aging of rat tail tendons Journal of Gerontology, 19: 173–178

Engleberg H 1958 Human endogenous plasma lipemia clearing activity: observations in 482 individuals. Journal of Applied Physiology: Respiratory, Environmental and Exercise Physiology, 13: 375–380

Epstein E H 1974 α1(III)₃ Human skin collagen. Journal of Biological Chemistry, 249: 3325–3231

Evanson J M, Jeffrey J J, Krane S M 1968 Studies on collagenase from rheumatoid synovium in tissue culture. Journal of Clinical Investigation, 47: 2639–2651

Finch C E 1976 The regulation of physiological changes during mammalian aging. Quarterly Review of Biology, 51: 49–61

Fisher A M, Scott D A 1934 The insulin content of the pancreas in cattle of various ages. Journal of Biological Chemistry, 106: 305–310

Fitton-Jackson S 1957 Structural problems associated with the formation of collagen fibrils in vivo. In Connective Tissues, ed. Tunbridge R E, pp 77–85. Oxford: Blackwell

Fujii K, Kaboki Y, Sasaki S 1976 Aging of human bone and articular cartilage collagen: changes in the reducible cross-links and their precursors. Gerontology, 22: 363–370

Gould, B S 1958 Biosynthesis of collagen II. Journal of Biological Chemistry, 232: 637–645

Gould B S 1968 In International Reviews of Connective Tissue Research, ed. Hall D A, vol. 4, pp 35–67. New York: Academic press

Grant M E, Jackson D S 1968 Carbohydrate content of bovine collagen preparations. Biochemical Journal, 108: 587–591

Griffiths M 1941 The influence of anterior pituitary extracts on the insulin content of the pancreas of the hypophysectomized rat. Journal of Physiology, 100: 104–111

Hall D A 1955 The reaction between elastase and elastic tissue. I. The substrate. Biochemical Journal, 59: 459–465

Hall D A 1964 Elastolysis and Ageing Springfield: Charles C. Thomas

Hall D A 1967 Elastic tissue alterations in vascular disease. In Cowdry's Arteriosclerosis, ed. Blumenthal H T, 2nd edn., pp. 121–140. Springfield: C. Thomas

Hall D A 1968a The aging of connective tissues. Experimental Gerontology, 3: 77–89

Hall D A 1968b Age changes in the levels of elastase and its inhibitor in human plasma. Gerontologia, 14: 97–108

Hall D A 1971 Changes in the properties of reconstricted collagen brought about by mechanical treatment. Nature, 228, 1314

Hall D A 1972 The use of stress as a tool in gerontological research. Age and Ageing, 1: 141–145

Hall D A 1973 Ageing or disease? Modern Geriatrics, 3: 26–32

Hall D A 1975 Mucopolysaccharides and aging. In Inborn Errors of Skin, Hair and Connective Tissues, ed. Holton J B, Ireland I T, pp. 139–146. Lancaster: Medical and Technical Publishing Co.

Hall D A 1976 In Ageing of Connective Tissue, London: Academic Press.

Hall D A 1979 the biochemical background to current theories of Ageing. In "Drugs and the Elderly", Crooks J, Stevenson I H Macmillan, London pp 3–14

Hall D A 1981 Gerontology: collagen disease. Clinics in Endocrinology and Metabolism, 10: 23–56

Hall D A, Burdett P E 1975 Age changes in the metabolism of essential fatty acids. Biochemical Society Transactions, 3: 42–46

Hall D A, Reed F B 1973 Protein/polysaccharide relationships in tissues subjected to repeated stress throughout life. II. The intervertebral disc. Age and Ageing, 2: 218–224

Hall D A, Elridi S S, Zajac A, Middleton R S W 1980a Related changes in the elastase and lipid contents of normal and hemiplegic subjects of various ages. Mechanisms of Ageing and Development, 14: 293–304

Hall D A, Middleton R S W, Elridi S S, Zajac A 1980b Serum elastase levels following a stroke in elderly subjects. Gerontology, 26: 167–173

Hall D A, Zajac A R, Cox R, Spanswick J 1982 The effect of enzyme therapy on plasma lipid levels in the elderly. Atherosclerosis (in press)

Harris E D J, Sjoerdsma A 1966 Effect of parathyroid extract on collagen metabolism. Journal of Clinical Endocrinology, 26: 359–359

Harris E D jr, Cartwright E C 1977 Mammalian collagenases. In Proteinases in Mammalian Cells and Tissues, A J Barrett ed., pp. 249–283, Elsevier, Amsterdam

Heikkinen E, Kulonen E 1964 Age factor in the maturation of collagen. Intramolecular linkages in mildly denatured collagen. Experientia, 20: 310–312

Holliday R 1972 Aging of human fibroblasts in culture: studies on enzymes and mutation. Humangenetik, 16: 83–86

Holliday R, Tarrant G M 1972 Altered enzyme in aging human fibroblasts. Nature (London), 238: 26–30

Houck, J C, Jacob R A 1963 Connective tissue. VIII. Effect of rickets on chemistry of inflammation. Proccedings of the Society for Experimental Biology and Medicine, 112: 446–448

Klein L R, Weiss P H 1966 Reutilisation of mature collagen in vivo. Biochemical and Biophysical Research Communications, 21: 311–317

Koneff H 1886 Beitrage zur Kenntniss der Nervenzellen in den peripheren Ganglien. Mitt Naturforsch Ges Bern, 44–45, 13–44

Kulonen E 1970 Studies on experimental granuloma. In Chemistry and Molecular Biology of the Intracellular Matrix, ed. Balazs E A,

vol. 3, pp. 1811–1820. London and New York: Academic Press

Labella F S, Vivian S, Thornhill D P 1966 Amino acid composition of human aortic elastin as influenced by age. Journal of Gerontology, 21: 550–555

Layman D L, Titus J L 1976 Synthesis of type I collagen by human smooth muscle cells in vitro. Laboratory Investigation, 33: 103–107

Lazarus G S, Fullman H M 1969 Collagenase production by human dermis in vitro. Journal of Investigative Dermatology, 52: 545–547

Lev M, Sullivan C 1951 The relationship of aging changes to the development of arteriosclerosis in the human aorta. American Journal of Pathology, 27: 684–686

Lewis C M, Tarrant G M 1972 Error theory and aging in human diploid fibroblasts. Nature (London), 239: 316–318

Lindstedt S, Prockop D J 1961 Isotopic studies on urinary hydroxyproline as evidence for rapidly catabolized forms of collagen in the young rat. Journal of Biological Chemistry, 236: 1309–1403

Loeven W A 1967 Elastoproteinase and elastomucases: the effect of age on the enzyme content in human pancreas. Gerontologia, 13: 200–210

Lopez S A, Krehl W A, Hodges R E 1967 Relationship between total cholesterol and cholesterylesters with age in human blood plasma. American Journal of Clinical Nutrition, 20: 808–815

Mandl I, Keller S, Manahan J 1964 Multiplicity of Clostridium histolyticum collagenases. Biochemistry, 3: 1737–1741

Matthews B F 1953 Collagen/chondroitin sulphate ratio of human articular cartilage related to function. British Medical Journal, ii, 1296

Neuberger A, Perrone J C, Slack H G B 1951 Relative metabolic inertia of tendon collagen in the rat. Biochemical Journal, 49: 199–204

Nichaman M Z, Sweeley C C, Olsen R E 1967 Plasma fatty acids in normolipaemic and hyperlipaemic subjects during fasting and after linoleate feeding. American Journal of Clinical Nutrition, 20: 1057

Nikkila E A, Niemi T 1957 Serum lipids and lipoproteins in old age. Scandinavian Journal of Clinical and Laboratory Investigation, 9: 109–115

Nishihara T, Miyata T 1962 The effects of proteases on the soluble and insoluble collagens and the structure of the insoluble collagen. Collagen Symposium, 3: 66–69

Orgel L E 1963 The maintenance of the accuracy of protein synthesis and its relevance to aging. Proccedings of the National Academy of Sciences of the United States of America, 49: 517–521

Pearse A G E 1968 Histochemistry. Theoretical and Applied Vol. 1. Churchill, London.

Piez K A 1964 Non-identity of the three α-chains in codfish skin collagen. Journal of Biological Chemistry, 239: PC 4315–4316

Piez K A, Martin G R, Kang A H, Bornstein P 1966 Heterogeneity of the α-chains of rat skin collagen and its relation to the biosynthesis of cross links. Biochemistry, 3: 3813–3820

Prockop D J, Kivirikko K I 1967 Enzymatic hydroxylation of proline and lysine in protocollagen. Proceedings of the National Academy of Sciencies of the United States of America, 57: 782–789

Ramachandran G N ed. 1967 In Treatise on Collagen. London: Academic Press

Rauterberg J, Allan G, Brehmer U, Wirtz W, Hanso W H 1977 Characterisation of the collagen synthesised by cultured human smooth muscle cells from foetal and adult aorta. Hoppe Seylers Zeitschrift fur Physiologische Chemie, 358: 401–408

Reed F B, Hall D A 1974 Changes in skin collagen in osteoporosis. In Connective Tissues: Biochemistry and Pathophysiology, ed. Fricke R, Hartman F pp. 290–299. Berlin: Springer Verlag

Reed R, Stainsby G, Ward A G 1963 The development of fibrils from solutions of eucollagen. Journal of the Society of Leather Trades Chemists, 47: 312–321

Reid K B, Lowe D M, Porter R R 1972 Isolation and characterization of $C1_q$, a sub-component of the first component of complement from human and rabbit sera. Biochemical Journal, 130: 749–763

Ridge M D, Wright V 1966 The aging of skin. Gerontologia, 12: 174–192

Roach M R, Burton A C 1957 The reason for the shape of the distensibility curves of arteries. Canadian Journal of Biochemistry and Physiology, 35: 681–713

Robins S P, Shimokamaki M, Bailey A J 1973 The chemistry of the collagen cross-links. Age related changes in the reducible components of intact bovine collagen fibre. Biochemical Journal, 131: 771–780

Ruiz-Torres A 1978 Zur frage des Umsatzes und der Polymerisation des Kollagens in Beisiehung zum Alter. Aktuelle Gerontologie, 7: 549–553

Russ E M, Eder H A, Barr D P 1954 Protein-lipid relationships in human plasma. Journal of Clinical Investigation, 33: 1662–1669

Sanders H J 1972 Human aging: the enigma persists. Chemical Engineering News, July, 13–16

Saxl H, Hall D A 1967 Elastic tissue in relation to arterial lipids. In Cowdry's Arteriosclerosis, 2nd edn, ed. Blumenthal H T, pp 141–169. Springfield: Charles C. Thomas

Scarcelli V 1961 Increase in elastin content of the human aorta during growth. Nature, 191: 710–711

Schneeberg N G, Finestone I 1952 The effect of age on the intravenous glucose tolerance test. Journal of Gerontology, 7: 54–60

Scott D A, Fisher A M 1938 The insulin and zinc content of normal and diabetic pancreas. Journal of Clinical Investigation, 17: 725–728

Shoshan S 1981 Wound healing. International Review of Connective Tissue Research, 9: 1–26

Silverstone F A, Brandfonbrenner M, Shock N W, Yiengst M J 1957 Age differences in the intravenous glucose tolerance tests and the response to insulin. Journal of Clinical Investigation, 36: 504–514

Slater R S, Hall D A 1973 Actinic and aging changes in dermal proteins. In Connective Tissue and Ageing, ed. Vogel H G, pp. 241–245. Amsterdam: Excerpta Medica

Snellman O 1963 A glycoprotein from reticulin tissue. Acta Chemica Scandinavica, 17: 11049–1056

Sobel H, Marmorsten J 1956 The possible role of the gel-fiber ratio of connective tissue in the aging process. Journal of Gerontology, 11: 2–7

Steven F S 1964 The Nishihara technique for the solubilization of collagen. Annals of the Rheumatic Diseases, 23: 300

Steven F S 1976 Preparation of macromolecular collagens. In Methodology of Connective Tissue Research, ed. Hall D A, pp. 19–28. Oxford: Joynson-Bruvvers

Steven F S, Jackson D S 1967 Purification and amino acid composition of monomeric and polymeric collagens. Biochemical Journal, 104: 534–536

Strehler B L 1964 On the histochemistry and ultrastructure of the age pigment. Advances in Gerontological Research, 1: 343–384

Sylven B, Malmgren H 1952 On alleged metachromasia of hyaluronic acid. Laboratory Investigation, 1: 413–431

Tesal S, Hall D A 1972 The hormonal control of enzymes involved in the age-mediated degradation of connective tissue. Report of 9th International Association Gerontology Kiev., 2: 58–60

Tomanek R J, Karlson U L 1973 Myocardial ultrastructure of young and senescent rats. Journal of Ultrastructure Research, 42: 201–220

Tunbridge R E, Tattersall R N, Hall S A, Astbury W T, Reed R 1952 The fibrous structure of normal and abnormal skin. Clinical Science, 11: 315–323

Veis A, Anesey J 1965 Modes of intermolecular cross-linking in mature insoluble collagen. Journal of Biological chemistry, 240: 3899–3908

Verzar F 1955 Veranderungen der thermoelastischen Kontraktion von Sehnenfasern im Alter. Helvetica Physiologica et Pharmacologica Acta, 13: 64–67

Verzar F 1963 Lectures on experimental gerontology. Springfield: Charles C. Thomas

Viidik A 1967 Experimental evaluation of the tensile strength of isolated rabbit tendons. Biological and Medical Engineering, 2: 64–67

Wellman W E, Edwards J E 1950 Thickness of the media of thoracic aorta in relation to age. Archives of Pathology, 50: 183–188

Woessner F Jr 1965 Acid hydrolases of connective tissue. In International Reviews of Connective Tissue, ed. Hall D A, pp. 201–260

Woessner F J 1978 Collagenolytic cathepsin of the involuting rat uterus. Federation Proceedings, Federation of the American Societies for Experimental Biology, 37: 1530

Woessner F Jr, Brewer T H 1963 Formation and breakdown of collagen and elastin in the human uterus during pregnancy and postpartum involution. Biochemical Journal, 89: 76–82

Woessner F Jr 1980 Collagenase in uterine resorption. In Collagenase in Normal and Pathological Connective Tissues. Woolley D E, Evanson J M eds. pp. 223–239, Wiley, New York

Wood G C 1954 Some properties of elastin tissue. Biochimica et Biophysica Acta 15: 311–324

Wood G C 1960 The formation of fibrils from collagen solutions. Biochemical Journal, 75: 598–605.

Biology of aging — theories of aging

THE EVOLUTION OF AGING

Life-table statistics show that lifespan is species specific (Deevey, 1947; Comfort, 1979). Survival curves are more or less constant for each species, and it is partly from such uniformity that the idea of a genetic influence on the life-span has been formulated. Survival statistics suggest various important concepts about aging. While it is acknowledged that in general females live longer than males, no correlation between longevity and the different types of genes associated with the X-chromosome in humans has been demonstrated so far. Sex-linked longevity in animals may depend on the particular strain. The situation is further complicated because we know that sexual activity can influence life-span in females. Thus, in both the mouse and *Drosophila*, there is evidence for a shorter life-span in mated as compared to virgin females.

Much information has been assembled from studies of inbred strains of animals. Inbred animals are homozygous for many characters and are more genetically uniform than outbred stocks. Each inbred line has its own characteristic length of life which is generally shorter than the species specific life-span — a manifestation of 'inbreeding depression'. Two inbred lines can be crossed and the first generation (F1) hybrid so derived invariably has a longer life-span than the parent stocks (Comfort, 1979). This increase in life-span, along with other improvements is termed 'hybrid vigour'. Thus, while genotype can affect the length of life of a particular strain, there have been no systematic studies of differences in the expression of the rate of aging in animals of different genotype. Goodrick (1975) measured the life-span of four inbred strains of mice and six hybrid combinations, and found that the mode of inheritance of longevity tended to be dominant for two of the strains, together with their F1 and F2 hybrids but only one genetic locus seemed to be associated with life-span. Goodrick suggested that in the case of mice this single factor acted on a set of secondary factors which were responsible for the animal's death. In insects the inheritance of lifespan for inbred lines within the species

Drosophila melanogaster is well described (Pearl and Parker, 1922), and that even within a moderately inbred line genetic differences in life-span remain constant over many generations.

Philosophical background to the evolutionary theories

Several genetic mechanisms have been proposed to account for aging phenomena, all intimately connected with ideas concerning the evolution of the aging process. Sacher (1982) gives a critical historical account of the problems associated with the development of a satisfactory evolutionary theory of aging. He draws attention to the 19th century theory of Weismann, which stated that aging was an adaptive characteristic which contributed to the 'fitness of the species' by removing reproductively inactive individuals from the population. Weismann suggested that the genetic control of senescence operates by limiting the proliferative capacity of somatic cells.

Weismann's theory has been criticized (Kirkwood and Cremer, 1982; Kirkwood and Holliday, 1979; Sacher, 1982) on the basis of circular argument (i.e. the need for somatic senescence arises because of a need to remove reproductively senescent individuals from the population), and other more general philosophical differences. Kirkwood and Holliday (1979) argue that aging is not adaptive since it reduces reproductive potential, and that the case for the removal of older organisms from the population is hard to sustain for many species. Medawar (1952) and Williams (1957) also rejected the Weismann theory, although Sacher (1982) claims this rejection was not a scientific statement but a philosophical objection. Both Medawar and Williams could not accept Weismann's central assumption that senescence is adaptive, or its implication that senescence therefore evolved by natural selection. Medawar and Williams claimed that senescence has no adaptive value and that natural selection is least effective in manipulating the characters expressed late in life.

The senescent phase of the life-span was previously defined as being the post-reproductive decline in viability and survival which accompanies chronological age (Chapter 2, p. 29). According to Mertz (1975) reproduction, and particularly births, are the central issues in this evolutionary argument. The main reason for this (in the context of reproduction) is that births which occur at different ages have different 'values' in terms of their contribution to future generations. Thus, births taking place early in the life-span of the parent are more likely to be of benefit to the population because the parent has a longer expectation of life and therefore, more opportunity to reproduce (Mertz, 1975).

The evolutionary theories
There are four separate proposals that attempt to explain the evolution of senescent processes.

Age-of-onset modifier genes. Medawar (1952) proposed that certain 'modifier' genes would suppress degenerative, age-accelerating gene effects (mutations?) for as long as possible. Sooner or later however, these 'modifier' genes would become ineffective and senescence would occur. Thus, the modifier genes would act beneficially until the organism had achieved full reproductive potential, but it is not clear why these genes would not be selected for and so extend the reproductive period indefinitely, that is, actually defer senescence.

Pleiotropic genes. The concept of pleiotropic genes was invoked by Williams (1957). He implied that certain genes would be expressed beneficially early in life, but at a later stage in the life-span they would have different, degenerative effects. The period in the life-cycle over which the various effects would be expressed would be determined by the period of maximum reproductive potential.

Reproductive energy. Other hypotheses have been put forward to explain the evolution of the aging process. Guthrie (1969) postulated that genes exist with the direct effect of shifting the age at which 'energy' for reproduction is expended. In this case senescence would result from the exhaustion of the materials or 'energy' (a poorly defined term) needed for reproduction and various life-maintenance processes. Referring back to the argument for the beneficial effects of early births, then senescence would be the by-product of a pattern of energy expenditure with a positive adaptive value — the early birth.

Genetic loading. Edney and Gill (1968), and later Sokal (1970), suggested that aging was the result of the expression, late in the life-span, of accumulated unfavourable mutations and recombinations. The degenerative effects of such a genetic load would have minimum impact on the early fitness of the organism, but would lead to inefficiency and a decline in function late in the life-span.

Both Kirkwood and Holliday (1979) and Sacher (1982), criticize the Medawar and Williams proposals because of yet another circular argument, that the concept of 'late expression' itself implies the prior existence of age-related physiological processes. Sacher (1982) further considers that there are no clear cut pre- and post-reproductive phases in the life-cycle. This is true of most biochemical and physiological functions that have been measured, and is also true of all age-related diseases. Sacher therefore rejects the hypothesis that there are genes with expression deferred to the post-reproductive phase of the life-span. He also rejects the idea of a gene being serially pleiotropic, since in order to change its expression within a single cell, with time, would require a prior environmental change to initiate that change. Thus, a pleiotropic switch could only be the result of a prior aging event, not a primary cause.

Disposable soma theory. Kirkwood (1977) and Kirkwood and Holliday (1979) propose the disposable soma theory of the evolution of aging. They argue that aging is mainly due to the accumulation of defects in macromolecules. The accuracy of synthesis of macromolecules relies on the specificity of the transcription and translation system, and also on other protective processes which degrade defective products. These mechanisms are themselves mediated by proteins, the structures of which are genetically determined. The overall accuracy of macromolecular synthesis would therefore be dependent upon the genotype of the organism.

Therefore each organism evolves to an optimum level of accuracy, and so the error frequency is not high enough to jeopardize the organization of the organism and not low enough to prevent the possibility of further evolutionary change. Kirkwood and Holliday (1979) assume (and indeed, there is indirect evidence for this) that since organisms occupy very different environments they might be expected to evolve different optimal error levels. These would be directly related to the time a species must survive in the natural environment in order to reproduce successfully.

Kirkwood and Holliday (1979) suggest that organisms that do not age (e.g. some prokaryotic cells) are in a steady-state whereby the chronologically young and old are physiologically identical. In these circumstances the synthesis of macromolecules must be sufficiently accurate to prevent the development of 'error catastrophes' (see below). This will involve energy expenditure at a high level, with the cell using sophisticated 'proofreading' and other systems to enable the production of accurate macromolecules. However, higher organisms may have found it selectively advantageous to reduce the high energy output associated with such mechanisms in somatic cells to accelerate development and reproductive processes; the inevitable consequence would be degeneration and death. However, this 'disposable soma' theory would require a high level of accuracy to be maintained in the immortal germ cell line, or else defective germ cells would have to be effectively eliminated from the gamete population.

Sacher suggests that both Weismann and his opponents failed to define the various senses of the term aging. There are several facets to consider — degenerative aging processes, age-associated disease, and death — and these have to be reconciled with the evolutionary concepts of adaptation and selection for increased fitness. Sacher introduces two concepts, the first being *obligate aging*, the second, *instrumental aging* processes.

Obligate aging is the time-related degeneration of structure and function that a given species fails to overcome, presumably because of limitations in its ability to repair such damage. In the absence of repair these degenerative processes become irreversibly fixed in the tissues. Sacher (1982) suggests that the most important category of obligate aging in the mammalian species is the rate of recessive mutation in the germ cells. The number of deleterious mutations per gamete is termed the genetic load and the tolerable load per gamete is extremely small. Sacher argues that the only way in which fitness can be maintained in a repetitively reproducing species such as man (given the existence of a finite rate of obligate aging in the germ line), is by evolving a determinate somatic life-span. The genetic mechanisms that assure a finite and determinate life-span make up the class of *instrumental aging processes*.

Sacher proposes that the evolution of instrumental somatic aging, in response to a finite rate of obligate reproductive aging, is formally equivalent to Weismann's original theory — he calls it the neo-Weismannian theory of the evolution of aging. The difference however, is that according to the revised theory senescence does not occur because of reproductive ineffectiveness, but rather because the individual is reproductively vigorous despite the accumulation of an intolerable burden of deleterious mutations in the gametes. This reformulation effectively disposes of the criticism of circular reasoning.

The disposal soma theory is attractive, and does lend itself to experimental testing. However, the foundation of this theory has been criticized previously. When the somatic mutation theory of aging was first proposed (see below), Maynard-Smith (1962) argued that if the rate of somatic mutation equalled the rate of mutation in the germ line it would be insufficient to explain the aging process. He regarded the proposal that there may be different mutation levels in the gamete population as compared to the soma as untenable. Kirkwood and Holliday's hypothesis does not consider mutations *per se* but does state that there may be differential levels of accuracy employed in the synthesis of macromolecules between the two cell populations. Their alternative

proposal is that error containing germ cells are more rigorously removed from the gamete population. Presumably in this case the sorting mechanism would only remove those gametes containing a relatively high level of errors; otherwise the possibility of further evolution would be affected adversely. A more serious problem with the 'disposable soma' theory is the central assumption that there is the likelihood of an 'error catastrophe' because of inaccuracies in the synthesis of macromolecules. This will be discussed in more detail below.

Experimental basis of evolutionary theories

There have been no exhaustive tests of these proposals. Mertz (1975) designed an experiment to test whether or not aging was due to 'age of onset' modifier or pleiotropic genes in the flour-beetle *Tribolium castaneum*. He showed that it was possible to select for improved reproductive performance during early adult life and also to induce higher mortality and lower fecundity in mid- and later-life by such selection. However, these mortality changes were *independent* of the selection pressures for early fecundity in this insect. He concluded that these observations were not consistent with the phenomenon of pleiotropy put forward by Williams (1957), but did not contradict the predictations of other evolutionary theories. These findings supported those made on *T. castaneum* by Mertz et al (1965), and Sokal (1970), and to some extent from observations made on *Drosophila* by Wattiaux (1968a,b). As stated above Sokal (1970) interpreted his results in terms of a genetic load, but Wattiaux invoked possible, non-genetic, parental effects.

Rose and Charlesworth (1980) also sought evidence for the evolutionary theories. The egg-laying performance of female *Drosophila* was studied at different ages as a way of testing the so-called mutation-accumulation theory (this incorporates both Medawar's and Edney and Gill's hypotheses). They reasoned that the daily egg-laying rate was an easily measured 'fitness component' of reproductive function. Under constant environmental conditions (and if there were no effects exerted by either accumulated, or other deleterious genetic damage), then the insect's egg-laying performance should be constant. However, if effects from either of these sources were present then there would be an increase in the variation of the egg-laying performance with time. No increase in genetic variation could be detected with age and the authors concluded that their data did not fit the 'mutation-accumulation' theory.

To test the pleiotropy theory Rose and Charlesworth selected for increased reproductive output late in the life-span and predicted a decrease in the fertility of the resulting young females and a real increase in life-span.

Their results coincided with the predictions of the pleiotropy theory. These authors concluded that senescence in *Drosophila* was due to the late-acting, deleterious effects of genes favoured by natural selection because of their beneficial effects early in the life-span.

So, there is disagreement among the investigators in this field of aging research. Mertz, using the beetle *Tribolium* argues against pleiotropic effects while Rose and Charlesworth, using *Drosophila* conclude that pleiotropy explains their observations. The controversy may be due to differences between the insect orders studied, and only more experimental data will help to clarify the situation.

The codon-restriction theory of development and aging

Strehler and his colleagues (Strehler and Barrows, 1970; Strehler et al, 1971) proposed the codon-restriction theory of development and aging. They saw the life-span as a continuum of change from development, through maturation to aging, each 'stage' being determined by its predecessor. The theory states that aging is due to the degeneration of various long-lived components which are formed during early development. During the process of differentiation the synthesis of these long-lived materials is repressed. The central assumption in this thesis is that the replacement of stable components in an organism imposes a selective disadvantage when compared with organisms in which such replacement is repressed.

Cellular specialisation is achieved by a process of differentiation usually involving a limitation of the types of protein synthesised by the cell. The types of protein produced are determined by the genes available for translation at any given time — the cell-type specific codon sets. In a metazoan the various genes of the cells are de-repressed, or repressed, so that suitable proteins can be produced in response to functional demands upon the cell. The possibility cannot be excluded that during this process some genes (which previously coded for essential proteins), would be repressed but could still be essential for the continued functioning of the cell after differentiation had ceased. Any accidental event which leads to the damage or loss of cell components, whose particular proteins are coded by these now repressed codon sets, could be expected to lead to the death of the cell.

As a test of this hypothesis the genes available for transcription at any given time in the life-cycle can be characterized by changes in the specific types of transfer RNA(tRNA), and the equivalent tRNA synthetases. Changes in the complements of such molecules have been recorded during developmental processes (Smith and Forrest, 1972), cell differentiation (Ilan et al, 1970),

and hormone stimulation (Altman et al, 1972). Wust and Rosen (1972) claim to have shown age-related changes in the tRNA molecules of the rat, but the part of the life-span they investigated probably reflected maturational changes only. Hoffman and McCoy (1974) could not demonstrate changes in the nucleotide composition of tRNA from mature and old mice, nor from mature and old mosquitoes. These workers and Gusseck (1974), have warned against the uncritical interpretation of experiments which appear to indicate differences in tRNA complements in various physiological states. Nevertheless, changes in tRNA complements if they occur, and also the complex changes observed in the overall patterns of enzymes in cells of different ages (Wilson, 1973), may be consistent with the codon restriction theory (Strehler and North, 1982).

Gene redundancy

There is considerable repetition of DNA nucleotide sequences in the genome of a eukaryotic organism (Britten and Kohne, 1968). The presence of this so-called redundant DNA is thought to be a reserve of evolution, and a method for increasing the functional expression of genetic information. However, it may also serve as a way of protecting these genes from random molecular damage. Medvedev (1966, 1972) and Cutler (1972), proposed that multiple copies of essential genes, while acting as a protective mechanism for the conservation of information, may also play a role in the determination of the aging rate for a particular species. An alternative proposal by Vilenchik (1970) was that the observed decrease in the proportion of DNA that can hybridize with denatured DNA during embryogenesis and morphogenesis may be causally related to the aging process. Vilenchik reasoned that in the de-repressed sectors of the genome of differentiated cells, the transcription from unique DNA sequences is increased compared with embryonic cells, and if this continues into post-embryonic stages, then aging may be due to the general inaccessibility of the repeated sequences. Medvedev (1972) has criticized this idea of 'over-repression' arguing that it is the repression of the unique DNA sequences of the genome that is the real initiator of aging.

Cutler (1974) determined the overall percentage of redundant DNA coding for ribosomal RNA(rRNA), but failed to correlate this with the aging rate (based on the maximum life-span potential). However, he did show that a large number of the genes coding the messenger RNA(mRNA) were to some degree redundant in mammals with a potentially long life-span. Subsequently, Cutler (1975) demonstrated a steady, age-related decline in the numbers of different types of reiterated and unique DNA sequences being transcribed in mouse liver. In brain tissue however, the sequences transcribed increased in early adulthood and gradually declined with age. The increase in transcription in maturing animals could be interpreted as an activation (i.e. de-repression) of the genome, and the gradual decrease later as repression. Accordingly, Cutler (1975) postulated that the progressive reduction in the number of different types of genes being expressed after the reproductive phase of the life-span may be a characteristic of mammalian senescence. It must be realised however, that these experiments are extremely crude when applied to such complex and heterogeneous tissues as the brain (cf. p. 39). Thus, the evidence for protection of the genome by means of redundant DNA is poor. Medvedev's prediction that a large increase in redundant DNA leads to a great increase in species longevity is not supported by Cutler's work.

Gene dosage

Various investigators have studied the hypothesis that the numbers of genes coding for ribosomal RNA(rRNA) available for transcription at any time (the gene dosage), might correlate with longevity. The number of rRNA genes in the genome available for transcription has been found to vary in certain species at different stages of the life-cycle, particularly during oogenesis (Gaubatz et al, 1976). However, estimations of the numbers of rRNA genes that can be transcribed late in the life-span as compared to early on have been inconclusive. Age-dependent losses of rRNA genes have been described in mammals (Johnson and Strehler, 1972; Johnson et al, 1975). Medvedev (1972) has noted that variation from the normal number of rRNA genes can affect the 'vigour' of a species. Gaubatz et al (1976) showed that the rRNA gene dosage was lower in the liver than in the brain of young mice, but after 12 months of age the liver rRNA gene dosage increased to the levels found in brain. No difference in rRNA gene dosage for both the liver and brain, expressed as a function of either sex, or age, could be detected in humans.

DNA repair

Efficient DNA repair would be one strategy whereby an organism could maintain the integrity of the genome for long periods (Hart et al, 1979). It has been suggested that animals with a long life-span potential have a more efficient DNA repair system (Hart and Setlow, 1974). Evidence for this has been obtained from studies on fibroblast cultures exposed to high doses of UV-radiation. Both the initial rate, and maximum incorporation, of radioactively labelled DNA precursors into DNA increased with the life-span potential of the species as shown in Figure 4.1. Subsequent work on this phenomenon has shown a strong correlation between DNA repair and longevity among mice (Sacher and Hart,

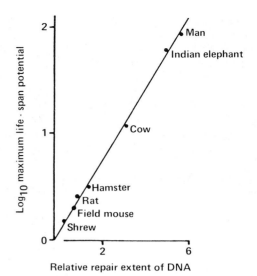

Fig. 4.1 A diagrammatic representation of the correlation between the logarithm of the maximum life-span potential of several species and the efficiency of repair of UV-damaged DNA in fibroblast cultures (redrawn with permission from Hart and Setlow 1974)

1978; Hart et al, 1979), and primates (Hart and Daniel, 1980).

ACCIDENTAL EVENTS AS A CAUSE OF AGING

Waste product theory

The cells of most aging organisms show increased levels of pigmentation. These pigments (termed lipofuscin), are particularly prominent in the fixed, post-mitotic cells of the heart and the brain. This topic has been thoroughly reviewed by Sohal (1981).

Lipofuscin is an irregular granular inclusion within cells. This pigment can emit a yellow-green to orange fluoresence when excited by UV-light (Fig. 4.2). The lipofuscin granule is extremely heterogeneous, it contains proteins, carbohydrates and lipids, and various enzymes associated with lysosomal activity and oxidative metabolism. In the electron microscope lipofuscin is highly irregular in shape and there is a certain variation in structure which is dependent on the cell type (Figure 4.3a, b). There have been several hypotheses put forward concerning the intracellular origin of this material; the main organelles implicated have been the mitochondria, endoplasmic reticulum and the lysosomes but there is now general agreement that lipofuscin is associated with the process of intracellular autophagy. Studies on post-mortem brain tissue from old humans have demonstrated that neurones are packed with lipofuscin which may influence cell function by lowering the levels of RNA within these cells (Mann and Yates, 1974).

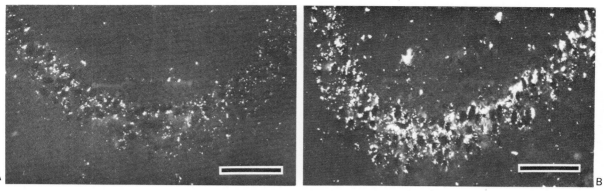

Fig. 4.2 Photomicrographs showing the increase in the levels of the autofluorescent, age-pigment — lipofuscin — in hippocampal neurons of mice. (a) is a preparation from a 6 month old animal, and (b) one from a 28 month old mouse. Scale bar = 100μm.

There is now some evidence however, for the turnover of this material. A study of the neuroendocrine cells responsible for the production of the peptide hormones vasopressin and oxytocin, shows that in old mice approximately 2 per cent of the intracellular volume is occupied by lipofuscin, as compared to 1 per cent in the cells from young ones (Davies and Fotheringham, 1980, 1981a,b). However, under conditions of osmotic challenge (when there is a massive release of vasopressin from the posterior pituitary and the initiation of hormone synthesis in the neuroendocrine cells) there is also a reduction in the volume of lipofuscin in the cells. Rehydration leads to a progressive increase in the volume of lipofuscin in these cells back to the levels seen in old control animals. The implication is that lipofuscin undergoes some form of turnover, in other words it does not necessarily accumulate with age; it is found in higher concentrations in the cells of older animals (Davies and Fotheringham, 1981b). Several workers in this field of research now suggest that lipofuscin is an *indication* of cell damage with age, and that it probably reflects an increase in the rate of cellular autophagy, perhaps due to damage caused by free-radical reactions (Sohal, 1981). It is clear from this discussion that we know very little about lipofuscin or its effect on cell function, however, it seems that the idea that this material physically disrupts cellular activity is somewhat naive.

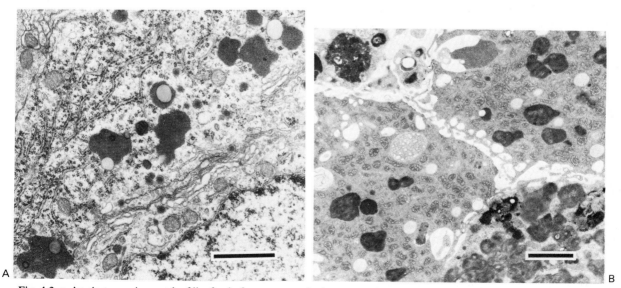

Fig. 4.3 a. An electron micrograph of lipofuscin from a neuron in the supraoptic nucleus of a 28 month old male mouse. Note the granular, electron dense matrix, with electron lucent inclusions. Scale bar = 1μm. b. An electron micrograph of lipofuscin from an adrenal cortical cell of a 28 month old mouse. Note the differences in the appearance of the electron dense granules, and the lack of electron lucent inclusions. Scale bar = 2μm.

Cross-linkage theory

The abnormal cross-linkage of macromolecules has long been regarded as a factor in the aging process. In the 1950's cross-linkage of the connective tissue proteins collagen and elastin was considered to be a major factor in the aging process (see Chapter 3), but this theory has now been extended to cover the cross-linkage of strands of DNA, and DNA-protein within the chromosome (Bjorksten, 1974).

There seems to be little direct evidence to support the concept that cross-linkage of the DNA polymer is of importance in aging. Studies using the bifunctional alkylating agents such as nitrogen mustard, myleran and chlorambucil, which cause cross-links to be formed between the strands of the DNA double helix, do shorten the life-span of treated animals in a similar way to the life-shortening induced by radiation (Alexander, 1969). Whether or not this life-shortening is a real acceleration of the aging process is disputed however (Alexander 1969, and see p. 71). There is experimental evidence for the presence of interstrand cross-links in the DNA from bacteria, insects, and cultured mammalian fibroblast-like cells (Deyl, 1968; Massie et al, 1975); however, their role in the aging process is uncertain. Direct estimates of inter-strand cross-links in *Drosophila* reveal that between 6 per cent and 9 per cent of the DNA is cross-linked in this way, and that this level does not alter with age (Massie et al, 1975).

Several investigations of chromatin-template activity have shown age-related reductions in function (von Hahn, 1963; Pyhtila and Sherman, 1968; Zhelabovskya and Berdyshev, 1972; Ryan and Cristofalo, 1975; Hill, 1976; Hill et al, 1978), although others failed to detect any differences in chromatin-template activity from dogs of different ages (Shirey and Sobel, 1972). Typically the isolated DNA-protein complexes display a reduced template activity towards DNA-dependent RNA-polymerases. However, if the DNA is purified from the DNA-protein complex then the age-related changes in activity can be abolished. It is proposed that these changes are due to interactions between the chromatin sub-units, although their exact nature is unknown.

The structural organization of mouse chromatin has been studied as a function of age (Gaubatz et al, 1979). For the variables examined for each tissue, chromatin contained essentially the same features of nucleosomal organization regardless of age. Studies of the rate and extent of nuclease digestion, and the size of the DNA repeat unit and nucleosome core are not significantly different as a function of age. However, the accessibility of internucleosomal DNA to enzyme digestion may be partially limited in the chromatin of the brain (but not the liver or heart) of older mice. According to Gaubatz et al (1979), there are no gross age-related changes in the conformational state or the organization of chromatin in these tissues.

On the other hand it has been shown that in cultured human diploid fibroblasts (HDF) qualitative changes in chromatin have been found in terms of alterations in circular dichroic properties (Maizel et al, 1975), the accumulation of alkali-sensitive (Icard et al, 1979; Suzuki et al, 1980) and endonuclease-sensitive (Dell'Orco and Whittle 1981) sites and the ultrastructural organization of chromatin fibres (Puvion-Dutilleul and Macieira-Coelho, 1982).

In two quantitative studies (Shmookler Reis and Goldstein, 1979; Macieira-Coelho et al, 1982) there is evidence of DNA loss during serial passage in culture. Shmookler Reis and Goldstein (1979) have shown a loss of reiterated DNA sequences with age in culture. Macieira-Coelho et al (1982) have analysed the segregation of DNA at the time of cell division and claim that the range in values found for the 2C and 4C DNA contents are due to quantitative differences originating during semi-conservative DNA synthesis, chromosome assembly and segregation. Ultimately this continuous rearrangement of the genome could lead either to a degerative process or to some programme of differentiation of the cell.

Medvedev and his colleagues (Medvedev and Medvedeva, 1977; Medvedev et al, 1977; Medvedev et al, 1978), have made an intensive study of age changes in the turnover rates and sub-fractional composition of rat liver and spleen histones. There is a relative increase in certain histone fractions in older animals ($F1^0$ and $F1^{0 \, met}$), and the presence of the $F1^0$ fraction in non-dividing cells only suggests that this may be an age-specific type of chromatin condensation.

Buchanan and Stevens (1978) studied the fidelity of histone protein synthesis in cultured HDF, and revealed variation in the complexity of H1 polypeptide changes, the complexity of which increased with the age of the cultured cells. A later study by Medvedev et al (1979) examined age-related changes in the pattern of non-histone chromatin (NHC) proteins from both rat and mouse liver. Aging is associated with an increase in the number and quantities of certain high molecular weight NHC proteins.

Whatever the interactions within the chromatin structure they are not irreversible. Simple, in vitro procedures can reverse these changes, but whether or not this is also true in vivo is unknown. There have been claims that free-radical reactions could cause these supposed cross-links, so presumably the inhibition of such reactions could have beneficial effects on cell function. These findings are extremely important, since it seems clear that aging in animals is to a great extent governed by alterations in gene expression.

Recent studies on the activity and fidelity of chromatin-associated DNA-polymerase-beta from aging mice of different life-spans showed that the DNA synthetic activity of liver chromatin remained constant in both species throughout their life-span (Fry et al, 1981), and that chromatin-directed and non-chromatin directed copying of a di-nucleotide polymer was similar in both *Mus musculus* (relatively short-lived) and *Peromyscus leucopus* (relatively long-lived) and remained unaltered in older animals (Fry et al, 1981). However, the fidelity of DNA polymerase enzymes are reduced in extracts from aged HDF cells maintained in tissue culture, with error frequencies between 2 and 3.4 times greater than enzymes prepared from young cultures. The main mispairing that seemed to take place was between guanine and thymine, but great care must be taken in the interpretation of these results, because the error frequency of DNA polymerase in vitro is much greater than when DNA is synthesised in vivo (Murray and Holliday, 1981).

Rate of living theory

Several eminent biologists at the turn of the century argued that life-span was related to the metabolic rate of the organism, and in the case of the poikilotherms this could be manipulated by alterations in temperature. The theory proposed was termed the rate of living theory (Economos, 1981). Many interesting experiments were performed, showing that in general high temperatures shortened life-span and low temperatures extended it.

However, one study complicates the issue. When *Drosophila subobscura* adults were transferred from a temperature of 20°C to 26°C they lived the same length of time as flies maintained at 26°C for their complete life-time. Clarke and Maynard-Smith (1961) argued that if aging was temperature-dependent then the flies should have lived longer than those kept permanently at 26°C. It was proposed that there were two stages to the life-cycle; a temperature independent aging-phase and a temperature dependent dying-phase. This is the *threshold theory of aging* and it was proposed that a balance existed between the production and consumption of essential cellular constituents (loosely termed 'vitality'), the use of which was related to the metabolic rate of the insect. Young flies were able to maintain the balance between production and use of 'vitality', even at high temperatures but, as they grew older this balance could only be maintained at lower temperatures.

These experiments have been criticized by Sohal (1981) because it was assumed that temperature influenced the metabolic rate in a directly proportional manner but this was not confirmed by measurement. Subsequent studies have investigated the effects of both temperature and metabolic rate on life-span. For example, the 'shaker' mutant of *D. melanogaster* has nervous system defects and the animals are abnormally active. The metabolic rate of the mutant is higher than for normal *D. melanogaster* and the length of life of the 'shaker' is proportional to its metabolic rate. Other experiments have shown that ambient temperature, physical activity and aging are closely interrelated in the house-fly *Musca domestica*. The life-span of the house-fly is inversely proportional to physical activity, and the effect of temperature on the life-span is very much dependent on the temperature associated variation in physical activity (Sohal, 1981).

Free-radical theory

Free-radicals are formed by the splitting of a covalent bond in a molecule so that each atom joined by the bond retains an electron from the shared pair. These reactions are comon in normal cell physiology (Halliwell, 1981). Harman (1956) proposed that uncontrolled free-radical reactions could be an important source of cellular damage in a variety of pathological processes, and that they could initiate aging, and this hypothesis has subsequently been put forward by others (Barber and Bernheim, 1967; Demopoulos, 1973; Packer et al, 1967; Tappel, 1973). Free-radical damage was thought to take place throughout the life-span causing a progressive deterioration of both nuclear and cytoplasmic components.

The free-radical hypothesis has been linked with the idea of oxygen toxicity. The respiring organism is in a difficult dilemma, it respires and obtains energy from the metabolism of oxygen, but oxygen itself can be extremely toxic; to overcome these problems several defence mechanisms have been evolved to protect the organism. Halliwell (1981) discusses the phenomenon of oxygen toxicity in a recent review.

Free-radicals

Most of the oxygen in an aerobic organism is reduced to water by the cytochrome oxidase enzyme complex of the inner mitochondrial membrane. However, some oxidases within the cell can generate hydrogen peroxide which is extremely toxic, and in the presence of transition metal ions such as iron, can decompose to form the hydroxyl radical $\cdot OH$.

$$Fe^{2+} + H_2O_2 = \cdot OH + Fe^{3+} + H_2O$$

Other enzymes catalyse oxidation reactions in which a single electron is transferred from a substrate onto each oxygen molecule; this produces the oxygen free-radical known as the superoxide.

$$O_2 + e^- = O_2^-$$

This radical is a by-product of various enzyme reactions, (particularly in the mitochondrial and chloroplast electron transport systems), and can also be caused by environmental agents such as UV-light, ultrasound, X- and gamma-rays, toxic chemicals and metal ions.

Free-radicals can cause lipid peroxidation. Membrane lipids usually contain numbers of polyunsaturated fatty-acid side-chains which undergo lipid peroxidation involving the generation of carbon radicals and finally lipid hydroperoxides. These lipid hydroperoxides decompose into cytotoxic aldehydes (e.g. malondialdehyde) and other products, causing damage to both enzymes and membranes.

These various radicals react with and damage all molecules found within cells, but the lipid and protein components of membranes seem especially vulnerable. In addition, DNA can be altered causing 'strand-breaks' and mutations.

Protection against free-radicals.   Protection of the cell against free-radical damage is effected by several mechanisms. For example, glutathione is a tripeptide which contains 'free' sulphydryl groups, and is thought to protect against the toxic effects of oxygen:

$$2GSH + \tfrac{1}{2}O_2 = GSSG + H_2O \qquad (1)$$
$$GSSG + NADPH + H^+ = 2GSH + NADP^+ \qquad (2)$$

where, GSH is glutathione; GSSG is reduced glutathione; and reaction 2 is catalysed by glutathione reductase. Hydrogen peroxide on the other hand can be removed by two types of enzyme, the catalases and the peroxidases. Another enzyme, superoxide dismutase, acts specifically in the removal of the superoxide radical:

$$O_2^{\cdot -} + O_2^{\cdot -} + 2H^+ = H_2O_2 + O_2$$

'Scavenging' systems are also present to protect the cell from lipid peroxides. For example, vitamin E (α-tocopherol) is incorporated into the membrane structure and is thought to trap free-radicals.

There are age-related changes in glutathione, glutathione reductase and superoxide dismutase from blood cells (Glass and Gershon, 1981), liver (Reiss and Gershon, 1976; Stohs et al, 1982), and the eyes (Dovart and Gershon, 1981). However, no correlation has been found between the maximum life-span potential and levels of superoxide dismutase in primates (Tolmasoff et al, 1980).

The fact that an increase in the oxygen:nitrogen ratio shortens the lifespan of *Drosophila*, and leads to an increase in the concentration of lipofuscin (Miquel et al, 1975) has been used as evidence of the toxic effects of oxygen. However, attempts to extend animal survival by feeding anti-oxidants such as cysteine hydrochloride, ethoxyquin, 2-mercaptoethylamine hydrochloride, 2,2'-diaminodiethyldisulphide dihydroxide and vitamin E through the life-span have been inconclusive (Harman, 1961; Comfort et al, 1971). There is usually a beneficial effect of 10–15 per cent on the mean life-span depending on the strain of animal, but the maximum life-span remains unaltered.

These experiments are difficult to interpret for various reasons (Comfort et al, 1971; Comfort, 1974). Firstly, the experiments should be conducted with large numbers of animals in order to provide statistically reliable results. Secondly, no assessments have been made of the physiological ages of the control and treated animals to ensure that increased survival is in fact due to delayed aging and not to an effect on a particular pathological process. Thirdly, most of these treatments result in a decrease in body-weight (Harman, 1961; Comfort et al, 1971; Kohn, 1971), so that these animals may be restricting their food intake, which can in itself lead to an extension of life. In spite of these reservations we have to accept that anti-oxidants can influence the life-span of some species. In addition, the feeding of anti-oxidants has been shown to reduce the levels of fluorescent pigments in animal tissues (Epstein and Gershon, 1972; Freund, 1979). Conversely, diets inadequate in vitamin E are generally successful in accelerating the deposition of lipofuscin in both the nervous system and the adrenal glands of rats and mice (Tappel et al, 1973). Hence, the intracellular appearance of lipofuscin may be associated with free-radical damage within cells.

The impressive list of potentially damaging free-radicals suggests that they may be instrumental in causing serious damage to cells, and this may predispose the cell to aging changes. There is little doubt that free-radical reactions can occur in vitro in isolated pure lipids and in cell-free preparations of subcellular organelles and cellular membranes (Tappel, 1972, 1973), but the contention of Green (1972) seems to remain unanswered that there is little proof of peroxidation of lipids occurring in tissues in vivo (Donato, 1981). Indeed, experiments designed to find evidence for the presence of lipid peroxides, or their breakdown products in cells in vivo have failed (Green, 1972; Schwarz, 1972; Donato, 1981). In addition, the effects of anti-oxidant supplements in the diet are equivocal and more direct evidence is required before accepting that free-radicals do have a central role in the cause of aging.

Somatic mutation theory

It is known that mutations in somatic cells can cause changes in function (see p. 42). Failla (1958, 1960) and Szilard (1959), independently proposed a theory of aging based on somatic mutations. Failla, assumed that dominant mutations were the cause of cell damage or death, while Szilard considered that aging in diploid cells was due to recessive mutational events. Thus, if one of a pair of homologous genes was damaged or 'hit' and subsequently inactivated, the other member of the pair would continue normal functioning, whereas, if both of the homologous genes were damaged, either through a previous 'hit' or some hereditary fault, then both members of the pair would be inactive and cell damage would ensue. Eventually large numbers of cells would become inefficient and the organism would die.

Both versions of this theory have been severely criticised (Maynard-Smith, 1959, 1962; Sacher, 1968). Maynard-Smith (1962) argued that recessive mutations could have little effect on the survival of somatic cells since the calculated rate of mutation in germ cells could not account for the life-span of most species. The only way around this problem would be to postulate differential mutation rates for gametes and somatic cells but according to Maynard-Smith there is no evidence for this. One prediction of the theory is that inbred organisms should live longer than outbred ones (Maynard-Smith, 1962). The inbred is homozygous at most loci, whereas outbreds are heterozygous at many positions. Inbred organisms cannot be homozygous for genetic defects because this is often a lethal combination. Since the inbreds will be heterozygous for very few 'faults' then it follows that they will express close to the species specific life-span. However, all the evidence obtained on inbreeding effects point to a reduction in life-span (Maynard-Smith, 1962).

Other observations are also consistent with Szilard's theory. One prediction is that diploid organisms should have a longer life-span than haploids, and that the haploids should be more susceptible to life-shortening effects such as ionizing radiation. Studies on the wasp *Habrobracon* have shown that such predictions are not fulfilled (Clark and Rubin, 1961). The female wasps are diploid, but the males can be obtained with both haploid and diploid gene compliments. The haploid males have the same life-span as their diploid counterparts which is inconsistent with the theory, but they are more susceptible to the effects of ionizing radiation.

Maynard-Smith (1959) showed that the survival of *Drosophila* kept at different temperatures was also inconsistent with the somatic mutation theory. *Drosophila* kept at 20°C lived longer than those kept at 30.5°C. However, if the flies were kept at 30.5°C for periods up to half their life expectation, and then maintained for the rest of lives at 20°C, then the expectation of life for males was the same as that for controls living at 20°C for the whole life-span. In the case of females under identical experimental conditions, the expectation of life was actually higher than for females kept continuously at 20°C. These results apparently contradict Szilard's theory since if somatic mutations accumulate in a temperature-dependent fashion then flies kept first at 30.5°C, then at 20°C, should have a life expectation that was shorter than those maintained continuously at 20°C,

but longer than those kept throughout the life-span at 30.5°C. These arguments are complicated and hinge on the premise that somatic mutations are directly temperature-dependent. However, to the author's knowledge there has been no direct experimental proof of this, and indeed, Sohal (1981) has previously shown that temperature and metabolic rate for example, are not simply inter-related in other insect species.

Ionizing radiation

The results of several studies on the life-shortening effects of ionizing radiation have been claimed as evidence in support of the somatic mutation theory of aging. This has been described as accelerated aging. These findings are disputed on the basis that the types of pathological changes generated are not identical to those seen in aging (Alexander, 1969; Yuhas, 1971; Price and Makinodan, 1973). Superficially, irradiated animals do show changes similar to those seen in senile animals (Lindop and Rotblat, 1962). Mice irradiated with a single dose of X-rays showed a shortening of the life-span proportional to dose. At post-mortem it was shown that these rodents died as a result of the acceleration of both malignant and non-malignant causes of death. Alexander (1969) disputed these conclusions, demonstrating differences in the times of onset of a variety of age-associated conditions (both benign and malignant neoplasms, senile cataract) between normal aging and radiation induced life-shortening.

The situation is not made any simpler by the fact that different doses of radiation affect survival in different ways. Thus, low level radiation can increase the life-span of some insects and mice (Sacher and Trucco, 1962; Sacher, 1963; Lamb, 1964), but high levels of radiation usually shorten it. At certain dosage levels the irradiation of old animals is less effective at shortening the life-span, and in some very old age-groups there is an increase in life expectancy (Yuhas, 1971). It would seem that any radiation that caused somatic mutations should also cause life-shortening at all ages. Indeed, it could be argued that such radiations should be more effective against older animals who have already sustained some degree of genetic damage. The explanation for the observed increase in life-span may be related to the removal of potentially malignant, actively dividing cells in the older age groups.

Thus, Alexander (1969) argues that aging is not due to somatic mutations since radiation causes mutations but does not clearly accelerate aging. Furthermore, mutagenic agents, such as the bifunctional alkylating agents myleran and chlorambucil, while shortening life, do not appear to hasten the aging process (Alexander, 1969). Early experiments with the potent mutagens, ethylmethane sulphate and nitrogen mustard, failed to show even a life-shortening effect in mice (Stevenson and Curtis, 1961). Perhaps the biggest problem in interpreting these experiments is that of knowing whether or not the mutational events induced either by radiation, or chemical agents, are similar to those found in the aging process. Until satisfactory explanations are available concerning the types of mutational event that take place during aging then the interpretation of the radiation and chemical mutagen experiments will remain ambiguous.

Chromosomal aberrations

Some connection has been claimed between the events of somatic mutation and the presence of chromosomal aberrations in aging cells (Curtis, 1963, 1966, 1971). The aberrations consist of chromosomal bridges and fragments which can be seen in dividing cells, particularly those in the liver. In long-lived strains of mouse the aberrations increase from an incidence of approximately 10 per cent in 2 month old animals to about 35 per cent in 24 month old mice. In short-lived mice they develop much more rapidly, from 20 per cent at 2 months to 80 per cent at 20 months (Crowley and Curtis, 1963) (Fig. 4.4). Strains with intermediate life-spans have an intermediate rate of accumulation of aberrations. Thus, at first sight it seems that life-span and the rate of development of chromosome aberrations are related, and Curtis (1966, 1971) interpreted these findings as lending strong support for the somatic mutation theory of aging.

However, there are also exceptions to this finding. Some mice with very short life-spans have a rate of accumulation of aberrations which is similar to that found in mice with long life-spans (Curtis, 1971). This

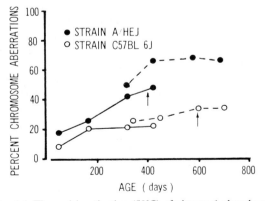

Fig. 4.4 Thermal inactivation (59°C) of glucose-6-phosphate dehydrogenase obtained from young, middle-aged and senescent cultured MRC-5 fibroblasts. ● — young cells (passage 22); ▲ — middle-aged cells (passage 48); ○ — old cells (passage 61). (Redrawn and reproduced with permission from Holliday and Tarrant 1972).

is probably because these animals develop severe pathological lesions, such as leukaemia or mammary carcinoma, and hence are not senescent in the strict sense of the term. Perhaps a more serious problem is that F1 hybrids derived from parents with different life-spans develop chromosomal aberrations at a rate intermediate between that of the parents but actually live significantly longer!

Moreover it is not clear whether or not changes in the incidence of chromosomal aberrations during the adult phase of the life-span are of physiological significance! The data presented by Curtis and Crowley (1963) suggest no change in the aberration frequency after about 10 months of age in the CD1 mouse strain (median life expectancy of 16 months). Similarly, the chromosome aberration frequency for the C57BL/6J strain is about 26 per cent at 10 to 15 months of age, and approximately 37 per cent at 20 months of age (Crowley and Curtis, 1963). However, since no statistical evaluation of these results is presented the significance of the change of aberration frequency with age is not clear (despite Curtis's suggestion of a continual increase in aberration frequency with age — Curtis 1963, 1966, 1971). Indeed, Curtis himself refers to the difficulty of measuring aberration frequencies (Curtis, 1966).

Ionizing radiation and chromosome aberrations

Curtis (1966, 1971) has suggested that ionizing radiation induces chromosomal aberrations, perhaps as a consequence of somatic mutations. Aberrations increase in frequency up to about 12 months of age in control animals, but in control mice irradiated at 2 months of age there was a dramatic increase in the frequency of such observed faults. The level of these faults returned slowly to normal levels only after many months. Subsequent experiments confirmed this finding and suggested that the decrease in incidence was due to a repair process not to the removal of aberrant cells (Curtis, 1966). However, this repair of X-ray-induced damage occured over a period when such faults in control animals actually increased — which events are supposedly related to the somatic mutation events causing aging. Curtis (1966, 1971) showed that both chronic gamma radiation and low-level neutron radiation also resulted in an increased incidence of chromosome aberrations. In addition, large single doses of neutron radiation induced a dramatic increase in chromosome faults and were equally effective in shortening life at both high and low doses. The fact that aberrations induced by X-rays decreased in frequency following irradiation, whereas those induced by neutron damage did not, suggests that the damage induced by the two types of radiation was different (Curtis, 1966). There is also the paradox that just sublethal doses of the chemical mutagen, nitrogen mustard, affects neither life-span nor the incidence of aberrations when administered over a period of many months (Stevenson and Curtis, 1961). Therefore while certain treatments, which are known to induce mutations and cause life-shortening, also induce chromosome aberrations, other treatments which induce mutations without any appreciable life-shortening do not have any effect on the incidence of chromosome aberrations.

These observations have been interpreted as supporting the argument relating somatic mutations to chromosome aberrations, and hence to the importance of somatic mutations in the aging process (Curtis, 1963, 1966, 1971). However, the data presented are difficult to reconcile with this view. The apparent repair of X-ray faults during a period of natural increase in aberration frequency suggests a fundamental difference between the two phenomena and throws doubt on the validity of Curtis's interpretation. Curtis and Crowley (1963) also observe that neutron irradiation, like X-rays, causes an immediate increase in the incidence of aberrations, but that the neutron-induced damage, unlike that produced by X-rays, persists at an undiminished level subsequent to irradiation. If aberrations are related to somatic mutations, and these in turn are the cause of aging, then the accumulation of high levels of aberrations might reasonably be expected to be quickly followed by the aging and death of the animal. This is not the case! Curtis (1971) reports that following neutron irradiation about 80 to 90 per cent of the mitotic cells observed had aberrations, yet there is no evidence for a decline in the physiological performance, e.g. of the liver (Curtis, 1971). It is also surprising that chronic administration of chemical mutagens should have no effect on lifespan if mutations are important as a mechanism of aging (Stevenson and Curtis, 1961).

Overall the evidence implies that artificial induction of somatic mutations as reflected by the incidence of chromosome aberrations, is relatively unimportant as far as the functional properties of cells containing them are concerned. This, in turn, throws doubt on the relevance of somatic mutations in aging, or alternatively, of the incidence of chromosome aberrations to somatic mutation frequency.

Thus, we have little experimental evidence available to support or deny the somatic mutation theory, and it would appear, as Price and Makinodan (1973) suggest, that somatic mutations are largely ignored as an important mechanism in aging. Nevertheless, somatic mutations have been claimed as a 'trigger-event' for age-related changes in the immune system (see Chapter 5).

Errors in protein synthesis

This theory was first proposed by Orgel in 1963 and modified in 1970. He argued that there was a small, but finite possibility that errors could take place in protein synthesis. He suggested that incorrect amino-acid insertions into proteins could take place with age, but that the actual error frequency was uncertain. His preliminary estimates were that a possible low value would be 3 in 10^8 correct insertions, and that a high one would be 1 in 10^4 insertions. Incorrect amino-acid insertions could have various effects depending on where they occured within a protein. If the 'errors' were at the catalytically active site of the enzyme for example, this could alter its activity or its specificity for a substrate. An alteration at a site responsible for control of enzyme activity (an allosteric site) may result in a loosening of control over its activity, while a change at an amino acid residue involved in the maintenance of the three dimensional structure of a protein might affect its physical characteristics.

In many proteins these changes may have little effect — for example, in the case of proteins undergoing rapid turnover. However, errors in the enzymes (the various DNA and RNA polymerases) involved in the processing of genetic information could be potentially more damaging. These polymerases have relatively long half-lives and catalyse a large number of reactions before they are degraded. Any alteration in their function could lead to the introduction of a large number of error-containing proteins which would accumulate within the cell. Orgel suggested that a critical level of such proteins in the cell could occur, and this would be followed by an 'error catastrophe' and cell death. The theoretical argument concerning the possibilities and effectiveness of 'errors in protein synthesis' on cellular function, particularly with respect to the aging process, continues unabated with the alternate cases ably argued by Goel and Islam (1977) and Kirkwood (1980).

This theory was seized upon by many biochemists and a period of intense activity followed as experiments were conducted to detect 'error containing' proteins. Technically this is very difficult to do since it is impossible to detect the error frequencies proposed using conventional techniques. Indirect approaches have therefore been employed and these will be discussed below.

Amino-acid analogues

Experiments in which amino-acid analogues were fed to animals to determine their effect on life-span were the first designed specifically to test Orgel's hypothesis (Harrison and Holliday, 1967). The rationale behind these experiments was that the analogues used were sufficiently similar to the naturally occurring amino-acids to be substituted during protein synthesis, and that the differences are sufficient to confer altered properties on proteins into which they are incorporated. The artificial introduction of altered enzymes should therefore induce a premature 'error catastrophe' resulting in life shortening.

The results of such experiments are ambiguous. Harrison and Holliday (1967) fed a mixture of amino-acids to the larvae of *D. melanogaster* and showed that the mean life-span of the adult was reduced; others however, showed that feeding analogues to young adult *Drosophila* had no effect on the longevity, even though the analogues were shown to be incorporated into proteins (Dingley and Maynard-Smith, 1969; Bozcuk, 1976). These observations suggest that an 'error catas-trophe' has not been induced by feeding such analogues, and that other explanations must be sought for the reduction in the mean life-span of *Drosophila* fed analogues during the larval stage (Harrison and Holliday, 1967; Dingley and Maynard-Smith, 1969). Furthermore, the survival curves presented by Harrison and Holliday (1967) show that the maximum life-span of the analogue-treated animals was not greatly affected, suggesting that the reduction in mean life-span was not connected with an interference with the primary aging process.

Bozcuk (1976) also showed that the proteins, which are continually being synthesized and degraded in adult *Drosophila*, and which constitute about 20 per cent of the total protein, turn-over at an increased rate in analogue-fed animals. Similar observations have been made on prokaryotes where abnormal proteins have been found to turn-over at a greater rate than normal protein (Goldberg and Dice, 1974), suggesting the rapid removal of aberrant molecules. These experiments raise the real possibility that proteins which do turn-over rapidly may be relatively unimportant in the aging process since abnormal molecules could have a short life-span. The important protein fraction may be that which does not turn-over and in which abnormal proteins may be retained.

The effects of amino-acid analogues on cultured HDF have been studied by Ryan et al (1974), who showed no difference between the life-spans of control and treated cells and, in addition, the effects of the treatment were reversible. A further difficulty in explaining senescence in normal HDF cultures in terms of the error theory is the fact that transformed, permanent cell lines do not show in vitro senescence and appear to be immortal. Clearly some mechanism would have to exist to enable the permanent cell lines to avoid an accumulation of altered proteins. Thus, permanent cell lines would be expected to show less sensitivity to the presence of amnio-acid analogues in the medium as compared to normal cells. However, Ryan et al (1974), found that the proliferative capacity of transformed cell lines, and of normal HDF were identical.

Amino-acid analogues have also been used to deter-mine the ability of protein synthesizing systems to discriminate between natural amino-acids and their analogues. Lewis and Tarrant (1972) measured the ability of HDF cultures to discriminate between methi-onine and its analogue, ethionine, during protein synthesis, and discovered that senescent cultures were not as efficient as young cultures at this task. They concluded that errors in translation were more likely to occur in senescent cultures, but Rothstein (1975) argued that technical difficulties with such experiments may invalidate such a conclusion. In vivo experiments by Ogrodnik et al (1975) suggested that the ability to discriminate between methionine and ethionine during protein synthesis decreased with increasing age; there was also a decreased discrimination between the two analogues in terms of their ability to serve as donors of alkyl groups in the transmethylation of RNA bases.

The accuracy of the translation mechanism has been examined in a cell-free protein-synthesizing system. Kurtz (1975) used polyuridylic acid (an artificial mRNA) to stimulate mouse liver microsomes to synthesize polyphenylalanine, and determined the rela-tive error rates during translation by measuring the extent of misincorporation of leucine. Kurtz showed that microsomes isolated from the livers of senescent mice have a reduced capacity to translate this artificial messenger. The rate of misincorporation of leucine for phenylalanine decreased between the ages of 1, 2 and 14 months, but not between 14, 27 and 31 months — results inconsistent with Orgel's hypothesis. However, although there is no significant age-related change in the accuracy of this particular step in protein synthesis there still remains the possibility that errors could occur with increasing frequency at other steps.

One of the predictions of the 'error catastrophe' theory of aging is that the fidelity of DNA polymerase enzymes would be reduced in extracts from aged cells. Recently, studies using HDF cells in tissue culture demonstrated a reduction in the fidelity of cytoplasmic DNA polymerases from senescent cells, with error frequencies between 2 and 3.4 times greater than enzymes prepared from young cultures. The main mispairing that seemed to take place was between guanine and thymine in these preparations. Great care must be taken in the interpretation of these results, however, because, as the authors point out (Murray and Holliday, 1981), the error frequency of DNA poly-merase in vitro is much greater than when DNA is synthesized in vivo.

Abnormally heat-labile proteins

Many experiments have been conducted on the assump-tion that the thermal inactivation kinetics of an enzyme will be altered if it contains errors. It had previously been shown that mutant proteins, containing specific amino-acid replacements, were abnormally sensitive to heat denaturation.

Holliday and Tarrant (1972) studied the thermal inactivation kinetics of proteins to determine whether or not abnormal enzymes accumulated during in vitro senescence of cultured HDF. They showed that glucose-6-phosphate dehydrogenase (G6PD) in crude extracts from young fibroblast cultures lost activity in a linear manner when heated. On extrapolation of the regression line drawn through the data to zero time they obtained an intercept value close to 100 per cent activity (Fig. 4.5). They concluded that there was very little abnormally heat-labile enzyme in the extract from young HDF cultures. On the other hand the thermal denaturation characteristics of G6PD in senescent cultures showed a biphasic decay in enzyme activity. There was an initial, rapid inactivation during the first phase, indicating the presence of abnormally heat-labile enzyme molecules, and in the second phase there was a slower decay of activity, in which the rate of inactivation was the same as that observed for young cultures (Fig. 4.5). It was estimated that the error frequency was at least 1 in 10^3 on senescent HDF cultures meaning that on average about half of the G6PD molecules in senescent cells contained a misincorporated amino-acid.

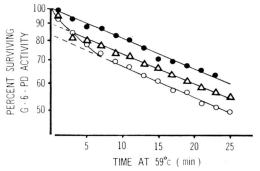

Fig. 4.5 Incidence of chromosome aberrations in regenerating liver cells of two inbred strains of female mice plotted as a function of age. The median lifespan of each strain is indicated by the arrows. (Redrawn and reproduced with permission from Crowley and Curtis, 1963).

This study has been followed by a multitude of others all examining the thermal inactivation kinetics of enzyme proteins both in vitro and in vivo, but their results have been contradictory in relation to Orgel's error hypothesis (Rothstein, 1975; Gershon and Gershon, 1976). The reader is referred to the various reviews of this topic for historical detail. One study of interest was that carried out by Schofield and Hadfield (1978) who showed an increase in the amount of abnormally heat-labile enzyme in the liver of the C57BL mouse. In this case it was shown that the amount of

heat-labile enzyme rose from about 2 per cent at 3 months to a value of 12 per cent at 12 months of age. However, there was no significant increase in the levels of heat-labile protein from this time onwards in the life-span. Thus, the levels of heat labile enzyme were 15 per cent at 18 months, and 18 per cent at 32 months of age. Similar results were reported by Harding (1973) who observed an abrupt increase in the amount of abnormally heat-labile glutathione reductase in the human lens at about 32 years of age, and no change in these levels thereafter. These results are not consistent with Orgel's hypothesis since an exponential increase in error-containing molecules would be predicted, with a sharp rise towards the end of the life-span.

Immunoprecipitation techniques

Other methods have been used to search for error-containing molecules. Gershon and Gershon (1970) presented evidence for an accumulation of inactive isocitrate lyase molecules in cultures of old nematodes. In this study an antiserum was prepared against centrifuged homogenates of *Turbatrix aceti*. Homogenates of worms ranging from 5 to 35 days were prepared and the activities of these extracts were adjusted to the same value with respect to the enzyme isocitrate lyase. The antiserum (which caused either an inactivation, or precipitation, of the enzyme extracts) was then added to the extracts and the activity of the isocitrate lyase was determined once more. The homogenates from old worms required the addition of more antiserum to precipitate the same amount of enzyme activity as the homogenates of young nematodes. This was interpreted as showing the presence of a mixture of active and inactive molecules in the old nematode cultures. This work has been confirmed by Reiss and Rothstein (1975) who purified the same enzyme from 6- and 27-day-old worms and showed that inactive forms of each of the isoenzymes occurred during aging. Several subsequent studies have reported the occurrence and accumulation of inactive enzyme molecules in senescent organisms using this technique, but once more the results are contradictory. Thus, inactive molecules of aldolase have been recorded in the muscle (Gershon and Gershon, 1973a) and livers (Gershon and Gershon, 1973b) of old mice, and in rabbit muscle (Anderson, 1974). However, in Gershon and Gershon's (1973a, 1973b) experiments only very young mice (2–3 months old) and senescent animals (31–32 months) were used. It is now becoming increasingly obvious that knowledge of intermediate age stages is necessary in order to interpret age changes correctly. The same criticism can be levelled at several other studies in which only two animal ages have been investigated. Other studies however, have not shown any accumulation of inactive enzyme molecules in senescent cells either in vivo or in vitro (Oliveira and Pfuderer, 1973; Danot et al, 1975; Rothstein, 1975; Pendergrass et al, 1975; Yagil, 1976).

The presence of inactive molecules has been taken, by some, as evidence for the presence of molecules containing incorrect amino-acid insertions. If inactive molecules are the result of such substitutions, then clearly the molecules should be permanently inactive. Yet there are examples of enzymes which occur in cells in an inactive form, e.g. prolyl hydroxylase, which can be activated under appropriate conditions (Cardinale and Udenfriend, 1974; Cardinale et al, 1975; Risteli et al, 1976).

Factors such as these raise important questions with regard to alterations in enzymes as a function of age. Do other enzymes exist as inactive and active forms, and can the inactive form become active without a change in the amount of immunoreactive protein? Situations of this kind would increase the difficulties involved in assessing Orgel's hypothesis. However, if it can be shown that there are active and inactive forms of each enzyme, and if the ratio of these two entities could be controlled by the cell, this would be of great importance in understanding the cellular control of metabolism. Such factors may be of relevance to the decline in cellular function observed during senescence.

Changes in the molecular form of an enzyme have been observed for elongation factor 1 (EF1, an enzyme involved in protein synthesis) (Bolla and Brot, 1975). A decline in the specific activity of EF1, and an accumulation of either inactive or partially active molecules during aging was observed in the nematode *T. aceti*. The molecular form of the enzyme also changed in that in young animals most of the enzyme is present in aggregate form, whereas in old animals most of it is present in a dis-aggregated state. The decrease in the specific activity of EF1 with age may be related to the change in the degree of aggregation. It would be interesting to see whether the loss of specific activity or the increase in the amount of inactive enzyme (which both occur with age) can be shown to be due to changes in the molecular form of the enzyme, and whether or not it is possible to alter the course of this age-related phenomenon.

Viruses as probes of inaccurate protein synthesis
One rather ingenious and elegant test of Orgel's hypothesis utilised the ability of viruses to use the protein-synthesizing machinery of the host cell to make new viral protein. Using the in vitro HDF system the capability of the protein-synthesizing machinery of these cells to support viral growth was tested. If senescent cells contained a transcription and translation apparatus that was prone to errors then this should result in either a reduction in the numbers of viruses produced, or abnormalities in the viral proteins. This in turn may

make the assembly of the new viral particle less efficient and such changes could alter the infectivity of the new virus.

Holland et al (1973) showed that old cultures of HDF supported infections by three different viruses as well as young cultures, and the yields of new virus were equal in each case. The infectivity of the viruses was also identical, and in addition, there was no evidence of an increased mutation rate. Similar results were reported by Tomkins et al (1974), Pitha et al (1974) and Pitha et al (1975).

Protein turnover studies
Some investigators have studied the rates of turnover of proteins as a test of the error hypothesis. The rationale for studies of this kind is based on the observation that abnormal proteins are turned over at increased rates when compared with normal proteins (Goldberg and Dice, 1974). Thus, Beauchene et al (1967) studied protein synthesis during in vitro incubation of liver slices from adult rats fed the amino-acid analogue ethionine, and observed an increase in the rate of protein synthesis compared to controls. This increase in the rate of protein synthesis was claimed as compensation for the presence of abnormal, error-containing protein molecules, which would be subject to more rapid degradation. However, when the livers from adult and old rats were compared, there was no significant difference in the rate of protein synthesis. This is rather indirect evidence, but it suggests that errors in protein synthesis do not occur to any great extent in rat liver during aging in vivo. Similarly, Menzies and Gold (1971) failed to detect an increase in the rate of turnover of mitochondria between young and old rats. Work with the nematode *T. aceti* (Zeelon et al, 1973; Rothstein, 1975) showed that there was a decrease in protein turnover in old worms, which is further indirect evidence against the error hypothesis.

Tissue culture experiments suggest that proteins produced by terminal senescent cultures have an increased susceptibility to proteolytic degradation (Bradley et al, 1975). The conclusion drawn was that if this increased degradation was due to mistranslation, then it was an effect of in vitro senescence rather than a cause of it. The rates of degradation of proteins in intact cells in vitro have also been determined and the half-life of protein in young cultures was found to be significantly shorter than in senescent cultures (Shakespeare and Buchanan, 1976). The increased degradation rate observed in cells from senescent cultures was considered to be due to the synthesis of abnormal error-containing proteins and the results were consistent with Orgel's hypothesis. Conclusions however, about the half-life of a protein pool will depend to some extent on whether or not the same proteins are produced in senescent and in young cultures, and whether they are produced in the same proportions since different proteins turn-over at different rates. This does not appear to have been fully investigated in either the study of Shakespeare and Buchanan (1976) or that of Bradley et al (1975). Goldstein et al (1976) also measured the rate of protein turnover in young and old HDF cultures and obtained evidence at variance with that described above. Once more, their results, although indirect, are not consistent with the error hypothesis.

This discussion shows that there is considerable doubt about whether or not errors in protein synthesis can be regarded as a primary mechanism in aging (although, as yet, such a mechanism cannot be completely discounted). Some predictions of the hypothesis have been confirmed. For example, some enzyme proteins do accumulate in the cell tissues of aging organisms in forms which are enzymically inactive. This is not true for all enzymes however, and although mechanisms have been suggested by which some proteins might accumulate in altered forms while others might not (Gershon and Gershon, 1976) the fact that not all proteins are affected appears to be inconsistent with an error hypothesis. There are of course, alternative ways of interpreting the data.

Post-translational protein modifications
One factor consistently ignored by many of the investigators is the possibility of *post-synthetic* modifications in protein structure (Gershon, 1979; McKerrow, 1979; Sharma and Rothstein, 1980). During aging in vivo of human and rabbit erythrocytes several enzymes have been shown to accumulate in inactive or abnormally heat-labile forms (Forniani et al, 1969). Since protein synthesis does not occur in erythrocytes at the time of this accumulation, the production of these altered proteins must be due to post-synthetic modifications. Altered proteins also accumulate in the fibre cells of the lens during aging even though protein synthesis has ceased at this site also, again indicating that post-synthetic modifications must be occurring (Kleef et al, 1975). Various post-synthetic modifications to proteins have been recorded including deamidation at asparagine or glutamine residues (Robinson and Rudd, 1974; Kleef et al, 1975), cleavage of peptide bonds (Kleef et al, 1975), acetylation of amino-terminal residues (Hoenders et al, 1968), and glycosylation of free amino groups (Bailey and Robins, 1973). Other possible reactions include phosphorylation at serine residues, sulphydryl-disulphide bond interchange or other types of changes involving cross-linking.

The detailed studies carried out by Rothstein and his co-workers (Rothstein, 1979; Sharma et al, 1979; Sharma and Rothstein, 1980; Sharma et al, 1980), show clear conformational changes in certain enzymes from aged animals. Studies on enolase in the free-living nematode *Turbatrix aceti* show that in old animals the enzyme has a lower specific activity and altered physical characteristics, including differences in secondary structure. These differences disappear when the respective proteins are 'unfolded', suggesting that there are alterations in the conformation of the enzyme (Sharma and Rothstein, 1980). Furthermore, this change is not a result of the oxidation or reduction of sulphydryl groups as these are equal in number and they all exist in the reduced form. Nor do the altered properties appear to involve deamidation, phosphorylation, or partial proteolysis. 'Old' enolase is relatively unstable to chromatography; during this treatment the enzyme is partly converted to a denatured — 'inactive' — form, which can also be found in homogenates of old *Turbatrix aceti*. This inactive material cross-reacts with the anti-serum prepared against 'young' or 'old' enzyme. 'Young' enolase, although it is more stable than 'old', can be converted to a product similar to the latter by repeated chromatography. Studies on enolase turnover in the free-living nematode *Turbatrix aceti* show that the rate of synthesis and degradation of this enzyme, and the total soluble protein fraction slow with age (Sharma et al, 1979). A later paper from this group (Sharma and Rothstein, 1980), shows that the 'young' and 'old' forms of the enzyme enolase are conformational isomers and that an in vivo transformation from young to old enzymes takes place by conformational changes without covalent modifications. The authors conclude that this process may be related to the previously discussed reduction in turnover of enolase in *T. aceti*. In addition, they state emphatically that such changes could not be due to errors in sequence as proposed by Orgel. A further paper from this laboratory (Sharma et al, 1980) suggest that a similar mechanism is in operation with regard to the enzyme phosphoglycerate kinase in the aging rat.

Conclusion
It must be emphasized that there is no single theory about aging that explains all the known facts concerning the aging process. From the above discussion it is clear that none of the proposed mechanisms of aging can be completely excluded. Thus, although some of the evolutionary and genetic mechanisms may be instrumental in determining the maximum life-span potential, and to a certain extent the aging rate, the various unprogrammed events (which may be partially modulated by external circumstances), can also play a significant role.

REFERENCES

Alexander P 1969 The relationship between aging and cancer: somatic mutations or breakdown of host defence mechanisms. Bulletin der Schweizerischen Akademie der Medizinischen Wissenschaften 24: 258–271

Altman K, Southern A L, Uretsky S C, Zabos P, Acs G 1972 Hydrocortisone induction of rat liver leucyl-transfer RNA and its synthetases. Proceedings of the National Acadamy of Sciences (USA) 69: 3567–3569

Anderson P J 1974 Aging effects on the liver aldolase of rabbits. Biochemical Journal 140: 341–343

Bailey A J, Robins S P 1973 Developments and maturation of the crosslinks in the collagen fibres of skin. Frontiers of Matrix Biology 1: 130–156

Barber A A, Bernheim F 1967 Lipid peroxidation; its measurement, occurrence and significance in animal tissues. Advances in Gerontological Research 2: 77–120

Beauchene R E, Roeder L M, Barrows Jr C H 1967 The effect of age and of ethionine feeding on the ribonucleic acid and protein synthesis of rats. Journal of Gerontology 22: 318–324

Bjorksten J 1974 Crosslinkage and the aging process. In: Rockstein M (ed) Theoretical Aspects of Aging, New York, Academic Press, p 43–59

Bolla R, Brot N 1975 Age dependent changes in enzymes involved in macromolecular synthesis in Turbatrix aceti. Archives of Biochemistry and Biophysics 169: 227–324

Bozcuk A N 1976 Testing the protein error hypothesis of ageing in Drosophila. Experimental Gerontology 11: 103–112

Bradley M O, Dice J F, Hayflick L, Schimke R T 1975 Protein alterations in aging W138 cells as determined by proteolytic susceptibility. Experimental Cell Research 96: 96–103

Britten R J, Kohne D E 1968 Repeated sequences in DNA. Science (Washington) 161: 529–540

Buchanan J H, Stevens A 1978 Fidelity of histone synthesis in cultured human fibroblasts. Mechanisms of Ageing and Development 7: 321–334

Cardinale G, Udenfriend S 1974 Prolyl hydroxylase. Advances in Enzymology 41: 245–300

Cardinale G, Stassen F L H, Kuttan R, Udenfriend S 1975 Activation of prolyl hydroxylase in fibroblasts by ascorbic acid. Annals of the New York Acadamy of Sciences 258: 278–287

Clark A M, Rubin M A 1961 The modification by X-irradiation of the life-span of haploids and diploids of the wasp Habrobracon spp. Radiation Research 15: 244–253

Clarke J M, Maynard-Smith J 1963 Two phases of ageing in Drosophila subobscura. Journal of Experimental Biology 38: 679–684

Comfort A 1974 The position of aging studies. Mechanisms of Ageing and Development 3: 1–32

Comfort A, 1979 The Biology of Senescence. 3rd edn. Elsevier, New York

Comfort A, Youhotsky-Gore I, Pathmanathan K 1971 Effect of ethoxyquin on the longevity of C3H mice. Nature (London) 229: 254–255

Crowley C, Curtis H J 1963 The development of somatic mutations in mice with age. Proceedings of the National Academy of Sciences (USA) 49: 626–628

Curtis H J 1963 Biological mechanisms underlying the aging process. Science (Washington) 141: 686–694

Curtis H J 1966 Biological Mechanisms of Aging. Charles C Thomas, Springfield, Illinois, USA

Curtis H J 1971 Genetic factors in aging. Advances in Genetics 16: 305–324

Curtis H J, Crowley C 1963 Chromosome aberrations in liver cells in relation to the somatic mutation theory of aging. Radiation Research 19: 337–344

Cutler R G 1972 Transcription of reiterated DNA sequence classes throughout the lifespan of the mouse. Advances in Gerontological Research 4: 219–321

Cutler R G 1974 Redundancy of information content in the genome of mammalian species as a protective mechanism determining aging rate. Mechanisms of Ageing and Development 2: 381–408

Cutler R G 1975 Transcription of unique and reiterated DNA sequences in mouse liver and brain tissues as a function of age. Experimental Gerontology 10: 37–61

Danot M, Gershon H, Gershon D 1975 The lack of altered enzyme molecules in 'senescent' mouse embryo fibroblasts in culture. Mechanisms of Ageing and Development 4: 289–301

Davies I, Fotheringham A P 1980 The influence of age on the hypothalamus-neurohypophyseal system of the mouse: a quantitative ultrastructural analysis of the supraoptic nucleus. Mechanisms of Ageing and Development 12: 93–105

Davies I, Fotheringham A P 1981a The influence of age on the response of the supraoptic nucleus of the hypothalamo-neurohypophyseal system to physiological stress. II. Quantitative morphology. Mechanisms of Ageing and Development 15: 367–378

Davies I, Fotheringham A P 1981b Lipofuscin — does it affect cellular performance? Experimental Gerontology 16: 119–125

Deevey E S 1947 Life-tables for natural populations of animals. Quarterly Review of Biology 22: 283–314

Dell'Orco R T, Whittle W L 1981 Evidence for an increased level of DNA damage in high doubling level human diploid cells in culture. Mechanisms of Ageing and Development 15: 141–150

Demopoulos H B 1973 The basis of free-radical pathology. Federation Proceedings of the Federation of the American Societies for Experimental Biology 32: 1859–1861

Deyl Z 1968 Macromolecular aspects of aging. Experimental Gerontology 3: 91–112

Dingley F, Maynard-Smith J 1969 Absence of life-shortening effect of amino-acid analogues in adult Drosophila. Experimental Gerontology 4: 145–149

Donato H 1981 Lipid peroxidation, cross-linking reactions, and aging. In Sohal R S (ed) Age Pigments. Elsevier/North Holland Biomedical Press, Amsterdam, New York, Oxford, p 63–82

Dovart A, Gershon D 1981 Rat lens superoxide-dismutase and glucose-6-phosphate-dehydrogenase — studies on the catalytic activity and the fate of enzyme antigen as a function of age. Experimental Eye Research 33: 651–661

Economos A C 1981 Beyond rate of living. Gerontology 27: 258–265

Edney E, Gill R 1968 Evolution of senescence and specific longevity. Nature (London) 220: 281–282

Epstein J, Gershon D 1972 Studies on ageing in nematodes IV. The effect of anti-oxidants on cellular damage and life-span. Mechanisms of Ageing and Developing 1: 257–264

Failla G 1958 The aging process and carcinogenesis. Annals of the New York Academy of Sciences 71: 1124–1135

Failla G 1960 The aging process and somatic mutations. In: Strehler B (ed) The Biology of Aging, American Institute of Biological Sciences, Washington DC, p 170–175

Fornaini G, Leoncini G, Segni P, Calabria G A, Dacha M 1969 Relationship between age and properties of human and rabbit glucose-6-phosphate dehydrogenase. European Journal of Biochemistry 7: 214–232

Freund G 1979 Effects of chronic alcohol and vitamin-E consumption on aging pigments and learning performance in mice. Life Sciences 24: 145–152

Fry M, Loeb L A, Martin G M 1981 On the activity and fidelity of chromatin-associated hepatic DNA polymerase-beta in aging murine species of different life-spans. Journal of Cellular Physiology 106: 435–444

Gaubatz J, Prashad N, Cutler R G 1976 Ribosomal RNA gene dosage as a function of tissue and age for mouse and human. Biochimica et Biophysica Acta 418: 358–376

Gaubatz J, Ellis M, Chalkley R 1979 Nuclease digestion studies of mouse chromatin as a function of age. Journal of Gerontology 34: 672–679

Gershon D 1979 Current status of age altered enzymes: alternative mechanisms. Mechanisms of Ageing and Development 9: 189–196

Gershon H, Gershon D 1970 Detection of inactive enzyme molecules in aging organisms. Nature (London) 227: 1214–1217

Gershon H, Gershon D 1973a Altered enzyme molecules in senescent organisms: muscle aldolase. Mechanisms of Ageing and Development 2: 33–41

Gershon H, Gershon D 1973b Inactive enzyme molecules in aging mice. Proceedings of the National Academy of Sciences (USA) 70: 909–913

Gershon D, Gershon H 1976 An evaluation of the 'error catastrophe' theory of aging in the light of recent experimental results. Gerontology 22: 212–219

Glass G A, Gershon D 1981 Enzymatic changes in rat erythrocytes with increasing cell and donor age — loss of superoxide-dismutase activity associated with increases in catalytically defective forms. Biochemical and Biophysical Research Communications 103: 1245–1253

Goel N S, Islam S 1977 Error catastrophe in and the evolution of the protein synthesising machinery. Journal of Theoretical Biology 68: 167–183

Goldberg A L, Dice J F 1974 Intracellular protein degradation in mammalian and bacterial cells. Annual Review of Biochemistry 43: 835–869

Goldstein S, Srotland D, Cordeiro R A J 1976 Decreased proteolysis and increased amino-acid efflux in aging human fibroblasts. Mechanisms of Ageing and Development 5: 221–233

Goodrick C L 1975 Life-span and the inheritance of longevity of inbred mice. Journal of Gerontology 30: 257–264

Green J 1972 Vitamin E and the biological antioxidant theory. Annals of the New York Academy of Sciences 203: 29–44

Gusseck D J 1974 Anomalies of tRNA-aminoacylation reaction which could lead to misinterpretation of evidence for tRNA changes during development and ageing. Mechanisms of Ageing and Development 3: 301–311

Guthrie R D 1969 Senescence as an adaptive trait. Perspectives in Biology and Medicine 12: 313–324

Hahn H P von 1963 Age-dependent thermal denaturation and viscosity of crude and purified DNA prepared from bovine thymus. Gerontologia (Basel) 8: 123–131

Halliwell B 1981 Free radicals, oxygen toxicity and aging. In: Sohal R S (ed) Age Pigments. Elsevier/North Holland Biomedical Press, p 1–62

Harding J J 1973 Altered heat-lability of a fraction of glutathione reductase in aging human lens. Biochemical Journal 134: 995–1000

Harman D 1956 Aging: a theory based on free radical and radiation chemistry. Journal of Gerontology 11: 298–300

Harman D 1961 Prolongation of the normal life-span and inhibition of spontaneous cancer by antioxidants. Journal of Gerontology 16: 247–255

Harrison B J, Holliday R 1967 Senescence and the fidelity of protein synthesis in Drosophila. Nature (London) 213: 990

Hart R W, D'Ambrosio S M, Ng K G, Modak S P 1979 Longevity, stability and DNA repair. Mechanisms of Ageing and Development 9: 203–224

Hart R W, Daniel F B 1980 Genetic stability in vitro and in vivo. In: Fenoglio C, Borek C, King D W (eds) Advances in Pathobiology, Vol. 7: Stratton, New York

Hart R B, Sacher G A, Hoskins T L 1979 DNA repair in a short- and long-lived species. Journal of Gerontology 34: 808–817

Hart R W, Setlow R B 1974 Correlation between deoxyribonucleic acid excision repair and life-span in a number of mammalian species. Proceedings of the National Academy of Sciences (USA) 71: 2169–2173

Hill B T 1976 Influence of age on chromatin transcription in murine tissues using an heterologous and an homologous RNA polymerase. Gerontology 22: 111–124

Hill B T, Whelan R D H, Whatley S 1978 Evidence that transcription changes in ageing cultures are terminal events occurring after the expression of a reduced replicative potential. Mechanisms of Ageing and Development 8: 85–96

Hoenders H J, Schoenmakers J G G, Garding J J J, Tesser G I, Bloemendal H 1968 The N-terminus of lens protein α-crystallin. Experimental Eye Research 5: 291–297

Hoffman J L, McCoy M T 1974 Stability of the nucleoside composition of tRNA during biological ageing of mice and mosquitoes. Nature (London) 247: 558–559

Holland J J, Kohne D, Doyle M V 1973 Analysis of virus replication in ageing human fibroblast cultures. Nature (London) 245: 316–319

Holliday R, Tarrant G M 1972 Altered enzymes in ageing human fibroblasts. Nature (London) 238: 26

Icard C, Beaupain R, Diatloff C, Macieira-Coelho A 1979 Effect of low dose irradiation on the division potential of cells in vitro. VI. Changes in DNA and in radiosensitivity during ageing of human fibroblasts. Mechanisms of Ageing and Development 11: 269–278

Ilan J, Ilan J, Patel N 1970 Mechanism of gene expression in Tenebrio molitor. Journal of Biological Chemistry 245: 1275–1281

Johnson L, Johnson R W, Strehler B L 1975 Cardiac hypertrophy, aging and changes in cardiac ribosomal RNA gene dosage in man. Journal of Molecular and Cellular Cardiology 7: 125–135

Johnson R, Strehler B L 1972 Loss of genes coding for ribosomal RNA in ageing brain cells. Nature (London) 240: 412–414

Kirkwood T B L 1977 Evolution of ageing. Nature (London) 270: 301–303

Kirkwood T B L 1980 Error propagation in intracellular information transfer. Journal of Theoretical Biology 82: 363–382

Kirkwood T B L, Cremer T 1982 Cytogerontology since 1881 — a reappraisal of August Weismann and a review of modern progress. Human Genetics 60: 101–121

Kirkwood T B L, Holliday R, 1979 The evolution of ageing and longevity. Proceedings of the Royal Society (London) 205: 531–546

Kleef F S M van, Jong W W de, Hoenders H J 1975 Stepwise degradations and deamidation of the eye lens protein crystallin in ageing. Nature (London) 258: 264–267

Kohn R R 1971 Effect of antioxidants on life-span of C57BL mice. Journal of Gerontology 26: 378–380

Kurtz D I 1975 The effect of ageing on in vitro fidelity of translation in mouse liver. Biochimica et Biophysica Acta 407: 479–484

Lamb M J 1964 The effects of radiation on the longevity of female Drosophila subobscura. Journal of Insect Physiology 10: 487–492

Lewis C M, Tarrant G M 1972 Error theory and aging in human diploid fibroblasts. Nature (London) 239: 316–318

Lindop P J, Rotblat J 1962 Induction of aging by radiation. In: Shock N W (ed) Biological Aspects of Aging. Columbia University Press, New York, p 216–221

Macieira-Coelho A, Bengtsson A, Van der Ploeg M 1982 Distribution of DNA between sister cells during serial subcultivation of human-fibroblasts. Histochemistry 75: 11–24

Maizel A, Nicolini C, Baserga R 1975 Structural alterations of chromatin in phase III WI-38 human diploid fibroblasts. Experimental Cell Research 96: 351–360

Mann D M A, Yates P O 1974 Lipoprotein pigments; their relationship to aging in the human nervous system. I. The lipofuscin content of nerve cells. Brain 97: 481–488

Massie H R, Baird M B, Williams T R 1975 Lack of increase in DNA crosslinking in Drosophila melanogaster with age. Gerontologia (Basel) 21: 73–81

Maynard-Smith J 1959 A theory of ageing. Nature (London) 184: 956

Maynard-Smith J 1962 Review lectures on senescence. I. The causes of ageing. Proceedings of the Royal Society (London) 157: 115

McKerrow J H 1979 Non-enzymatic, post-translational, amino acid modifications in aging. A brief review. Mechanisms of Ageing and Development 10: 371–377

Medawar P B 1952 An Unsolved Problem in Biology. Lewis, London.

Medvedev Zh A 1966 In: Shock N W (ed) Perspectives in Experimental Gerontology. Thomas, Springfield, Illinois.

Medvedev Zh A 1972 Possible role of repeated nucleotide sequences in DNA in the evolution of life spans of differentiated cells. Nature (London) 237: 453–454

Medvedev Zh A, Medvedeva M N 1977 Age changes of turnover rates and subfraction composition of rat liver and spleen histones. Aktuelle Gerontologie 7: 35–41

Medvedev Zh A, Medvedeva M N. Huschtscha L I 1977 Age-changes of the pattern of F1 histone subfractions in rat liver and spleen chromatin. Gerontology 23: 334–342

Medvedev Zh A, Medvedeva M N, Robson L 1978 Tissue specificity and age-changes of the pattern of the H1 group of histones in chromatin from mouse tissues. Gerontology 24: 286–292

Medvedev Zh A, Medvedeva M N, Robson L 1979 Age-related changes of the pattern of non-histone chromatin proteins from rat and mouse liver chromatin. Gerontology 25: 219–227

Menzies R A, Gold P H 1971 The turnover of mitochondria in a variety of tissues of young adult and aged rats. Journal of Biological Chemistry 246: 2425–2429

Mertz D B 1975 Senescent decline in flour beetle strains selected for early adult fitness. Physiological Zoology 48: 1–24

Mertz D B, Park T, Youden W J 1965 Mortality patterns in eight strains of flour beetles. Biometrics 21: 99–114

Miquel J, Lundgren P R, Bensch K G 1975 Effects of oxygen-nitrogen (1:1) at 760torr on the life-span and fine-structure of Drosophila melanogaster. Mechanisms of Ageing and Development 4: 41–59

Murray V, Holliday R 1981 Increased error frequency of DNA-polymerases from senescent human-fibroblasts. Journal of Molecular Biology 146: 55–76

Ogrodnik J P, Wulf J H, Cutler R G 1975 Altered protein hypothesis of mammalian ageing processes — II. Discrimination ration of methionine vs. ethionine in the synthesis of ribosomal protein and RNA of C57BL/6J mouse liver. Experimental Gerontology 10: 119–137

Oliveira R J, Pfuderer P 1973 Test for missynthesis of lactate dehydrogenase in aging mice by use of a monospecific antibody. Experimental Gerontology 8: 193–198

Orgel L E 1963 The maintenance of the accuracy of protein synthesis and its relevance to ageing. Proceedings of the National Academy of Sciences (USA) 49: 517–521

Orgel L E 1970 The maintenance of the accuracy of protein synthesis and its relevance to ageing. Proceedings of the National Academy of Sciences (USA) 67: 1476

Packer L, Deamer D W, Heath R L 1967 Regulation and detection of structure in membranes. Advances in Gerontological Research 2: 77–120

Pearl R, Parker S L 1922 Experimental studies on the duration of life. II — Hereditary differences in duration of life in line-bred strains of Drosophila. American Naturalist 56: 174–187

Pendergrass W R, Martin G M, Bornstein P 1975 Evidence contrary to the protein error hypothesis for in vitro senescence. Journal of Cellular Physiology 87: 3–14

Pitha J, Adams R, Pitha P M 1974 Viral probe into the events of cellular (in vitro) aging. Journal of Cellular Physiology 83: 211–218

Pitha J, Stork E, Wimmer E 1975 Protein synthesis during aging of human cells in culture. Direction by polio virus. Experimental Cell Research 94: 310–315

Price G B, Makinodan T 1973 Aging: Alteration of DNA-protein information. Gerontologia (Basel) 19: 58–70

Puvion-Dutilleul F, Macieira-Coelho A 1982 Ultrastructural organisation of nucleoproteins during aging of cultured human-embryonic fibroblasts. Experimental Cell Research 138: 423–429

Pyhtila M J, Sherman F G 1968 Age-associated studies on thermal stability and template effectiveness of DNA and nucleoproteins from beef thymus. Biochemical and Biophysical Research Communications 31: 340–344

Reiss U, Gershon D 1976 Rat-liver superoxide dismutase. Purification and age-related modifications. European Journal of Biochemistry 63: 617–625

Reiss U, Rothstein M 1975 Age-related changes in isocitrate hyase from the free-living nematode Turbatrix aceti. Journal of Biological Chemistry 250: 826–830

Ristelli J, Tuderman L, Kivirikko K I 1976 Intracellular enzymes of collagen biosynthesis in rat liver as a function of age in hepatic injury induced by dimethylnitrosamine. Biochemical Journal 158: 369–376

Robinson J, Rudd C J 1974 Deamidation of glutamyl and asparaginyl residues in peptides and proteins. In: Horecker B L, Stadtman E R, (eds) Current Topics in Cellular Regulation. Vol. 8: Academic Press, New York, p 247–295

Rose M, Charlesworth B 1980 A test of evolutionary theories of senescence. Nature (London) 287: 141–143

Rothstein M 1975 Aging and the alteration of enzymes: a review. Mechanisms of Ageing and Development 4: 325–339

Rothstein M 1979 The formation of altered enzymes in aging animals. Mechanisms of Ageing and Development 9: 197–202

Ryan J M, Cristofalo V J 1975 Chromatin template activity during aging in W1-38 cells. Experimental Cell Research 90: 456–458

Ryan J M, Duda G, Cristofalo V J 1974 Error accumulation and aging in human diploid cells. Journal of Gerontology 29: 616–622

Sacher E A 1963 Effects of X-rays on the survival of Drosophilia imagoes. Physiological Zoology 36: 295–311

Sacher G A 1968 Molecular versus systematic theories on the genesis of ageing. Experimental Gerontology 3: 265–271

Sacher G A 1982 Evolutionary theory in gerontology. Perspectives in Biology and Medicine 25: 339–353

Sacher G A, Hart R W 1978 Longevity, aging and comparative cellular and molecular biology of the house mouse, Mus musculus, and the white-footed mouse, Peromyscus leucopus. In: Bergsma D, Harrison D E (ed) Genetic Effects on Aging. Birth Defects: Original Article Series, Vol. 14: Alan R Liss for the National Foundation — March of Dimes, p 71–96

Sacher G A, Trucco E 1962 A theory of the improved performance and survival produced by small doses of radiations and other poisons. In: Shock N W, (ed) Biological Aspects of Aging. Columbia University Press, New York, p 244–251

Schofield J D, Hadfield J M 1978 Age-related alterations in the heat-lability of mouse liver glucose-6-phosphate dehydrogenase. Experimental Gerontology 13: 147–158

Schwarz K 1972 The cellular mechanisms of vitamin-E action; direct and indirect effects of α-tocopherol on mitochondrial respiration. Annals of the New York Academy of Sciences 203: 12–28

Shakespeare V, Buchanan J H 1976 Increased degradation rates of protein in aging human fibroblasts and in cells treated with an amino-acid analogue. Experimental Cell Research 100: 1–9

Sharma H K, Prasanna H R, Lane R S, Rothstein M J 1979 The effect of age on enolase turnover in the free-living nematode, Turbatrix aceti. Archives of Biochemistry and Biophysics 194: 275–291

Sharma H K, Prasanna H R, Rothstein M J 1980 Altered phosphoglycerate kinase in aging rats. Journal of Biological Chemistry 255: 5043–5050

Sharma H K, Rothstein M J 1980 Altered enolase in aged Turbatrix aceti results from conformational changes in the enzyme. Proceedings of the National Academy of Sciences (USA) 77: 5865–5968

Shirey T L, Sobel H 1972 Compositional and transcriptional properties of chromatins isolated from young, mature and old dogs. Experimental Gerontology 7: 15–29

Shmookler Reis R J, Goldstein S 1980 Loss of reiterated DNA sequences during serial passage of human diploid fibroblasts. Cell 21: 739–749

Smith R L, Forrest H S 1972 Variations in iso-accepting species of transfer RNA during embryogenesis of Oncopeltus fasciatus (Dallas). Developmental Biology 33: 123–129

Sohal R S (ed) 1981 Age Pigments. Elsevier/North-Holland Biomedical Press, Amsterdam, New York, Oxford, p 394

Sokal R R 1970 Senescence and genetic load: Evidence from Tribolium. Science (Washington) 167: 1733–1734

Stevenson K G, Curtis H J 1961 Chromosomal aberrations in irradiated and nitrogen mustard treated mice. Radiation 15: 774–785

Stohs S J, Alturk W A, Angle C R 1982 Glutathione s-transferase and glutathione-reductase activities in hepatic and extra-hepatic tissues of female mice as a function of age. Biochemical Pharmacology 31: 2113–2116

Strehler B L, Barrows C 1970 Senescence: Cell biological aspects of aging. In: Schjeide O E, (ed) Cell Differentiation. Van Nostrand-Reinhold, New York, p 266–283

Strehler B, Hirsch G, Gusseck D, Johnson R, Bick M 1971 Codon restriction theory of aging and development. Journal of Theoretical Biology 33: 429–474

Strehler B L, North D 1982 Cell-type specific codon usage and differentiation. Mechanisms of Ageing and Development 18: 285–313

Suzuki F, Watanabe E, Horikawa M 1980 Repair of X-ray induced DNA damage in aging human diploid cells. Experimental Cell Research 127: 299–308

Szilard L 1959 On the nature of the aging process. Proceedings of the National Academy of Sciences (USA) 45: 30–42

Tappel A L 1972 Vitamin E and free-radical peroxidation of lipids. Annals of the New York Academy of Sciences 203: 12–28

Tappel A L 1973 Lipid peroxidation damage to cell components. Federation Proceedings of the Federation of the American Societies for Experimental Biology 32: 1870–1874

Tappel A L, Fletcher B, Deamer D 1973 Effect of antioxidants and nutrients on lipid peroxidation fluorescent products and aging parameters in the mouse, Journal of Gerontology 28: 415–424

Tolmasoff J M, Ono T, Cutler R G 1980 Superoxide dismutase —

correlation with life-span and specific metabolic rate in primate species. Proceedings of the National Academy of Sciences (USA) 77: 2777–2781

Tomkins G A, Stanbridge E J, Hayflick L 1974 Viral probes of aging in the human diploid cell strain WI-38. Proceedings of the Society for Experimental Biology and Medicine 146: 385–390

Vilenchik M M 1970 Molecularny Mechanismy Starenija (Molecular Mechanisms of Aging) Nanka, Moscow.

Wattiaux J M 1968a Cumulative parental age effects in Drosophila subobscura. Evolution 22: 406–421

Wattiaux J M 1968b Parental age effects in Drosophila pseudoobscura. Experimental Gerontology 3: 55–61

Williams G 1957 Pleiotropy, natural selection, and the evolution of senescence. Evolution 11: 398–411

Wilson P D 1973 Enzyme changes in aging mammals. Gerontologia (Basel) 19: 79–125

Wust C J, Rosen L 1972 Aminoacylation and methylation of tRNA as a function of age in the rat. Experimental Gerontology 7: 331–343

Yagil G 1976 Are altered glucose-6-phosphate dehydrogenase molecules present in aged liver cells? Experimental Gerontology 11: 73–79

Yuhas J M 1971 Age and susceptibility to reduction in life expectancy; an analysis of proposed mechanisms. Experimental Gerontology 6: 335–344

Zeelon P, Gershon H, Gershon D 1973 Inactive enzyme molecules in aging organisms. Nematode fructose-1,6-diphosphate aldolase. Biochemistry (New York) 12: 1743–1750

Zhelabovskya S M, Berdyshev G D 1972 Composition, template activity and thermostability of the liver chromatin in rats of various ages. Experimental Gerontology 7: 313–320

Immunology of aging

INTRODUCTION

Early observations on the immune system stemmed from the knowledge that individuals recovering from infectious illnesses were protected from repeat infections. This was successfully used by Edward Jenner to vaccinate people against smallpox, by the use of antigenic material from cowpox lesions. This led to an inquiry into the nature of the immune response which conferred such protection.

Towards the end of the 19th century, it became clear that both cells and soluble substances were involved. The immune response is now known to be a series of protective reactions by the body in response to stimulation by foreign substances such as bacteria or viruses. The substances which invoke an immune response are known as immunogens, or antigens. The body responds by the production of antibody molecules and sensitized cells which combine with the antigens. The result is inactivation or eradication of the infectious agent.

THE IMMUNE RESPONSE

Antigens

Foreign substances are constantly coming into contact with and gaining access to the body. Large molecules such as proteins and polysaccharides are usually immunogenic; they contain small regions — antigenic determinants — that stimulate specific immune responses. Immunogens are found as structural components or soluble products of microorganisms.

Such material may come into contact with the body's immune system in a number of ways, such as deposition on the nasal or bronchial mucosa; on the skin; by ingestion and their absorption from the gastrointestinal tract; by inoculation subcutaneously; or by transplantation or transfusion. Once the foreign substance, immunogen, has gained access to the body it interacts with various cells but the initial interaction is usually with cells of the monocyte/macrophage lineage. These cells, together with the immunogen, then interact with lymphoid cells, either in lymph nodes or within organs such as the spleen.

The lymphoid cells arise from bone marrow stem cells and migrate through primary organs to undergo maturational change. They are divided into two main groups. One type passes through the thymus and matures as the T (thymic) lymphocyte. The other passes through the Bursa of Fabricius in chickens or its equivalent in man which is thought to be gut-associated lymphoid tissue, and matures as the B lymphocyte (Fig. 5.1). The responding unit consists of immunologically competent B and T lymphocytes and macrophages (Fig. 5.2). The immune response is recognised by its products, antibodies or sensitized cells.

Antibody response

An immune response which results from first contact with an antigen is known as a primary response. Ten to twenty days after the contact, antibody appears in the serum; this antibody is immunoglobulin M (IgM). Antibody disappears after a few weeks, but memory of the event is retained by sensitised B lymphocytes. Subsequent exposure to the same antigen results in a secondary immune response, with antibody production (IgG) after a shorter latent period of 5 to 7 days. Antibody levels are higher than in primary responses, and remain detectable in the blood for much longer periods.

The nature of the antigen or immunogen determines the type of immune response, although many are mixed. All antigens appear to be taken up by macrophages which then interact with lymphocytes (Fig. 5.2). The macrophage processes the antigen and presents it to the lymphocyte. For certain antigens such as pneumococcal polysaccharide the only other cells necessary in the immune response are B lymphocytes. B lymphocytes possess antigenic specific cell surface receptors of the IgM class. The B lymphocytes respond and divide. They go on to form plasma cells which produce specific antibody of the IgM class.

The antigens that evoke a pure B cell response are characterized by being large, polyvalent molecules with multiple repeating subunits. The majority of antigens

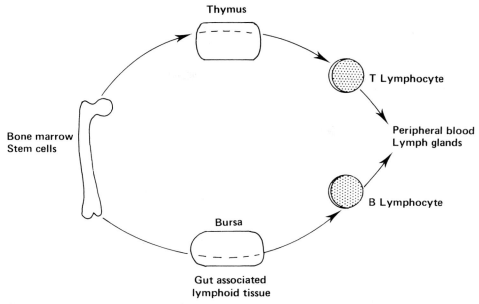

Fig. 5.1 The immune system showing the development of mature lymphocytes

are T dependent and evoke an antibody response from B and helper T cells. The B and T lymphocytes react to different determinants on the antigenic molecules, but both react specifically. The antigen binds to both B and T lymphocytes, or to T lymphocytes exclusively with release of a specific helper factor. The B lymphocyte is activated and divides and differentiates to the antibody producing plasma cell (Fig. 5.3). Cell division appears to be an essential part of antibody production which is prevented by mitotic inhibitors.

The stimulus for cell division comes from perturbation of the cell membrane. Membrane receptors are cross linked and first form clusters and then caps, prior to internalization. This process results in calcium influx and changes in intracellular cyclic AMP which triggers proliferation. This process stimulates proliferation of T cells (helper) and B cells, and thus expansion of specific clones.

The end product of this series of events is antibody which interacts with the provoking antigen. Antibodies belong to a clan of serum proteins known as immunoglobulins. All immunoglobulin molecules are made up of two polypeptides chains (50 000 daltons molecular weight) known as heavy chains and two polypeptides

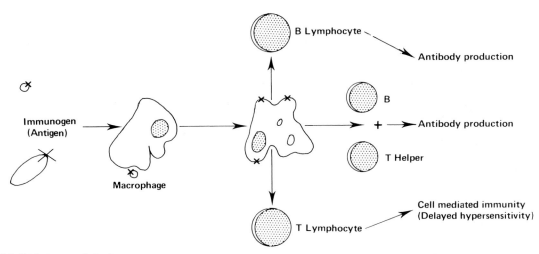

Fig. 5.2 Early stages of the immune response

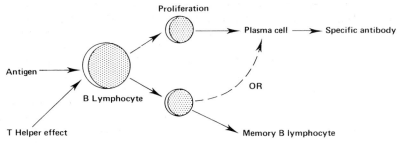

Fig. 5.3 The production of specific antibody from B lymphocytes

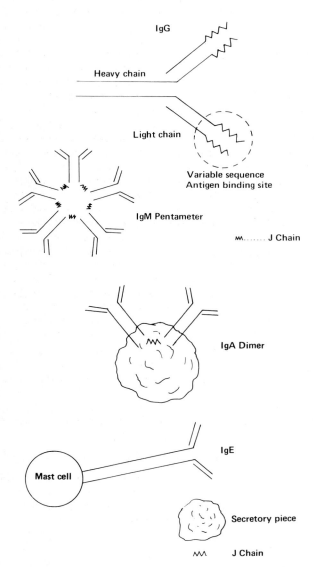

Fig. 5.4 Schematic representation of major immunoglobulins

(25 000 daltons molecular weight) known as light chains (Fig. 5.4). The carboxy terminal portions of the heavy and light chains contain invariable sequences of amino acids known as the constant region. The amino terminal ends contain highly variable sequences of amino acids — variable regions — and it is this part that contains the antigen binding site. The variability is responsible for the great diversity seen amongst immunoglobulin molecules. A single molecule, of course, has a fixed sequence and is antigen specific.

There are several classes of immunoglobulins which subserve different functions. IgG is the major immunoglobulin in serum and exists as a monomer. It is also found in interstitial fluid and can cross the placental barrier. IgA is also found in serum, but is the major immunoglobulin found in mucosal secretions such as within the respiratory or gastrointestinal tracts. It exists as a dimer, two molecules bound together by a J chain, with an additional protein known as the secretory component which allows transport across the epithelium and aids in resisting enzymic degradation. IgM is largely confined to the blood and exists in the serum as a pentamer — the individual molecules being bound together by J chains. IgE is found in low concentrations in the serum and in secretions. It binds by its heavy chain to mast cells and is involved in immediate hypersensitivity reactions. There is a fifth class of immunoglobulin molecule, IgD, which is found in small amounts in the serum. Its function is unknown, but it is thought to be important in preventing the development of tolerance.

Antibody molecules bind to antigens. They protect the host in a number of ways. IgG and IgM antibodies cause agglutination, opsonisation with promotion of phagocytosis, and activation of complement. IgA is found predominantly in secretions and does not activate complement, but does produce agglutination. IgE interacts with antigen and then activates mast cells to release vasoactive substances.

The type of antibody produced depends upon a

number of factors. For example, the location — contact within the mucosa of the respiratory tract promotes a secretory IgA response. The antigen also influences the cells which respond, although the factors that control this are poorly understood. The immune response is also under genetic control. Certain strains of experimental animals will characteristically produce a vigorous response to some antigens, and a less marked response to others. In the mouse, responder states have been found to be under genetic control and localised in the I region of the major histocompatibility complex. Similar immune response genes are undoubtedly present in man.

Certain antibody molecules are important in controlling the immune response by feedback inhibition. The IgG molecules form bridges across the surface of B lymphocytes between different membrane receptors (Sinclair, 1979). The antibody molecules may also form across links with membrane receptors on suppressor T cells. The nature and function of these suppressor T cells will be discussed later. The cross linking on B lymphocytes or between B and T lymphocytes is between antigen receptors and Fc receptors. The latter are receptors to the constant region of the heavy chains and are important in suppression.

Antibodies can also control immune responses in other ways. When the number of B lymphocytes proliferate in response to an antigen, there is a rapid expansion in specific antigen receptors. These new receptors with the unique sequence of amino acids constitute a new antigen and may involve production of an antibody, known as anti-idiotype antibody. This is concerned with suppression or control of the immune response.

Cell mediated immunity

The initial interaction with immunogen is with the macrophage. Immunogen is processed by the macro-

phage which then presents it to the T lymphocyte (Fig. 5.2). The T lymphocyte is stimulated to transform into a large lymphoblast and then to divide. The resulting lymphocyte progeny consists of memory cells and cytotoxic cells. During the transformation and proliferation the lymphocytes release substances known as lymphokines which contribute to the inflammatory response (Fig. 5.5). The delayed hypersensitivity response to tuberculosis, which is well known and demonstrated in vivo, is an example of such a reaction. T lymphocytes possess specific receptors on their cell surface which react with antibody. The specificity is thought to rest with IgM molecules which are inserted into the cell membrane, leaving the variable region to bind to the antigen.

Modulators

All immune reactions need to be controlled or modulated and this is a function of subsets of T lymphocytes. It has already been shown that the antibody response to certain antigens requires T as well as B lymphocytes. These are T helper lymphocytes which are thought to be operative in both humoral and cellular immune responses, and provide a positive amplification feedback loop.

The opposite type of control is also necessary and feedback suppressor mechanisms are thought to be important in all immune responses. Suppression is achieved in a number of ways and the ways that antibody might achieve this have been discussed. Suppression is also a property of at least two types of cells — T lymphocytes and monocytes. If these cells are added to certain immune reactions in sufficient numbers, the cellular proliferation is inhibited. Suppression appears to be specific for the antigen and also non-specific, affecting all immune reactions. Suppressor T lymphocytes can be stimulated by agents

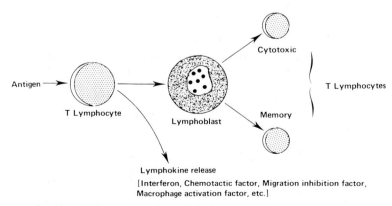

Fig. 5.5 The development of sensitised T lymphocytes in a cellular immune reaction

such as Concanavalin A, and release factors which non-specifically suppress antibody synthesis or T lymphocyte proliferation (Green et al, 1981; Fleisher et al, 1981). Specific suppressor T lymphocytes are generated during immune reactions.

Cell markers

Subsets of T lymphocytes have been defined operationally, but have also been shown to carry distinctive markers on their cell surface. In man T lymphocytes are identified as typical small lymphocytes which lack surface immunoglobulin and possess receptors for sheep red blood cells. This latter property allows identification and separation by rosetting with sheep erythrocytes.

Various tests have been used to identify the T subsets but a technique is now available which uses monoclonal antibody. Each functional subset appears to contain distinctive antigenic markers, although there is a degree of overlap. Suppressor T cells are best defined by OKT_8 antisera and helper lymphocytes by OKT_4.

Clinical consequences of immune response

The immune response is designed to protect the host. Immunity to infectious disease is specific for the particular microorganism and a competent immune system is essential for survival of the host. Certain microorganisms provoke a predominantly humoral response, others cellular. For the most part the immune system functions well, the host is protected and usually unaware that anything has taken place. However, immune responses can also produce disease in the host. During the course of a defence against infection host tissue may be damaged. This happens in many diseases, viral hepatitis is one example. The infected hepatocyte expresses viral antigen on its cell surface. For successful eradication of disease the cell needs to be destroyed. Tissue damage occurs in most infectious diseases in this way, and the damage results from the immune reaction rather than the microorganism.

The host may become sensitized to foreign antigens such as pollen or drugs. Repeat exposure may then result in an allergic reaction. Occasionally foreign materials or cells are introduced into the body and a reaction is provoked. Serum sickness or transfusion reactions are examples of this. In the same way, the host may become sensitized to its own tissues. This is protective if it is a cancer that is developing, and the immune response may successfully eradicate it. Indeed, this is the basis of the theory of immune surveillance (see below). On the other hand, the reaction may be against normal tissue. In this situation, autoimmune disease may result and hemolytic anaemia is an example.

NON-SPECIFIC DEFENCE (NON-IMMUNE MECHANISMS)

Defence against microbial invasion is dependent upon many things. There are a number of factors that influence defence and ensure successful eradication which are not truly immunological. For example the gastrointestinal tract is repeatedly exposed to a wide range of organisms, yet usually successfully prevents entry of microbes, and disease. This will be described to exemplify the non-immunological defence mechanisms.

Ingested material travels to the stomach, and this is a very important first line of defence. Gastric acidity is effective in killing microorganisms. The normal motility of the gastrointestinal tract discourages colonisation and promotes expulsion. Invasion is prevented by an intact mucosal layer and by preventing adherence to it. This is achieved by the protective layer of mucus which contains glycoproteins and other substances which block attachment (Fox, 1979). Secretory IgA is also present which promotes agglutination and expulsion.

Similar mechanisms exist on other mucosal surfaces but some microbes bypass and get through. Microbes which enter the blood then come in contact with various non-specific but highly effective defence mechanisms. The most important is the phagocytic system. White cells were first recognized in the blood in the 18th century and in the 19th century, phagocytosis, the polymorphonuclear neutrophil and the macrophage were all described.

Neutrophil

The prime function of the neutrophil is phagocytosis and destruction of microorganisms. Neutrophils are attracted to infection or injury by chemotactic factors. Bacteria activate the complement system directly and chemotactic factor is one product of this activation. Other products of this complement activation include opsonins. Preformed antibodies also act as opsonins, which coat bacteria and promote phagocytosis. The neutrophil cytoplasm contains granules of various sorts which are stimulated to migrate to the plasma membrane. Enzymes, the contents of the granules, are discharged into the membrane vacuole which contains the microbe (phagosome) or into the immediate extra-cellular environment. The enzymes include lysozyme, myeloperoxidase and hydrolases as well as substances like lactoferrin which chelates iron and is therefore bactericidal.

Macrophage

Macrophages are important in defence against certain pathogens such as viruses and fungi. These cells have their origin in the bone marrow from stem cells.

Monoblasts divide to form promonocytes and enter the blood stream as monocytes where they remain for up to 3 days. They migrate into tissues to become macrophages which are large cells (10–30 μm in diameter) with abundant cytoplasmic granules and indented or multiple nuclei.

Monocytes migrate from blood to sites of inflammation (Spector et al, 1965) and at this time their production increases (van de Meer et al, 1979). Thus, inflammatory exudates contain large numbers of young cells — more strongly positive for peroxidase (van de Meer et al, 1979). These young, peroxidase-positive cells are known to be more phagocytic (Bursaker and Goldman, 1979), more immunostimulatory (Lee and Berry, 1977), and more responsive to lymphokines (Ruco and Meltzer, 1978): exactly what is required at the site of inflammation.

The macrophage has several functions. It is actively phagocytic and this is enhanced if particles are opsonised — coated with antibody and complement. This form of defence is essentially non-immunological. However, macrophages can be activated by various microorganisms or their components like endotoxin and muramyl dipeptide. In this state the macrophage is more efficient at phagocytosis and intracellular killing. This state can be induced during an immune reaction by the production and release of a lymphokine from T lymphocytes — macrophage activation factor. Other lymphocytes may control the production and migration of monocytes/macrophages.

Macrophages are capable of lysing tumour cells which they achieve when maximally activated. A further important function of macrophages is in the immune response in priming lymphocytes. Macrophages appear to be involved in all immune responses, in the initial contact with the antigen, in processing it and in some way passing that information on to the lymphocytes (Fig. 5.2). Macrophage function can be bypassed by using certain substances like mercaptoethanol or by using much larger doses of antigen.

Another function of adherent cells, presumably that of the monocyte/macrophage series, is control of the immune response later in its development. These cells may act as suppressor cells, thus modulating immune responses.

The various functions of macrophages are summarized in Table 5.1. For all these reactions macrophages

Table 5.1 Macrophage function

Phagocytosis and intracellular killing
Tumour cell lysis
Initiation of immune response (Priming lymphocytes)
Suppression of immune response
Production of factors (complement, monokines)

synthesize and release biologically active factors, such as monokines or complement which are important in various ways in immune responses.

AGING AND IMMUNITY

In old age there is a waning of immunological vigour, and old age might be considered by some to be the most common form of immune deficiency.

Thymus and lymphoid organs

The central role of the thymus has been discussed. The thymus gland is at maximal size in later childhood and early adolescence, and begins to involute in the late teens. By middle age it is a vestigial remnant (Boyd, 1932). There is atrophy of both cortex (Andrew, 1952; Santisteban, 1960) and epithelial cells (Hirokawa, 1977). However, in old age there are small remnants of thymus tissue which are presumably functional (Goldstein and Mackay, 1969). The thymus influences maturation of T lymphocytes by the production of thymic hormone; the levels of these hormones decline with age in parallel with thymic atrophy (Bach et al, 1975).

The reasons for thymic atrophy are not understood. There is some evidence that the thymus is influenced by the hypothalamus and pituitary. Hypophysectomy influences aging and lesions in the anterior hypothalamus depress delayed hypersensitivity (Bilder and Denckla, 1977). The thymus also appears to be important in controlling hormone levels (Fabris et al, 1972; Besedovsky et al, 1975). In certain experimental situations life can be prolonged and aging delayed, for example by calorie restriction of rodents early in life. In this situation thymic involution is also delayed (Jose and Good, 1973; Gerbase-Delima et al, 1975; Weindruch et al, 1979). Thus, decline in size and function of the thymus parallels aging. The control appears to be within the thymic epithelial cells (Hays, 1967; Bellamy and Hinsull, 1975). This is the site of the clock which regulates the running of the immune system and possibly aging.

The changes in other lymphoid organs are minor in comparison. Gut-associated lymphoid tissues change in a similar way; the appendix and the tonsils decline in size throughout life. Lymph nodes and spleen decline slightly in size, lymph nodes early in life, and spleen from middle age. Lymphoid tissue of the spleen (white pulp) declines rapidly up to 30 years of age and little thereafter. Germinal centres in other cervical lymph nodes decline after maturity (Walford, 1967).

Stem cells

Stem cells are the earliest cells found in bone marrow

and are precursors to all classes of lymphocytes. Stem cells are capable of replication throughout normal life span (Harrison, 1975). However, function is impaired in old age, being less able to home to the thymus (Tyan, 1977) and less able to repair damaged DNA (Chen, 1971). B cells are produced more slowly (Farrar et al, 1974; Kishimoto et al, 1976) and their potential after transplantation deteriorates (Ogden and Mickliem, 1976).

The total number of nucleated cells in bone marrow appears to increase in old age, but their colonising capabilities actually decrease (Kay et al, 1979).

Most of these changes are intrinsic to the cells, and transplantation of old cells into a young environment does not influence behaviour (Albright and Makinodan, 1976). These changes probably result from the accumulation of genetic damage.

Humoral immunity

Serum immunoglobulin levels increase with age (Walford, 1967) and some mice strains have higher levels of IgG with advancing age (Haaijman et al, 1977). The incidence of monoclonal gammopathies increases with age (Waldenström, 1973; Buckley et al, 1974). Circulating levels of natural antibody and isoantibodies decline with age (Paul and Bunnell, 1932; Somers and Kuhn, 1972). These changes point to changes in antibody production and the B cell system.

B lymphocytes

The numbers of cells in the bone marrow appear to increase with age but the numbers of B lymphocytes in the peripheral blood do not change (Callard et al, 1977; Becker et al, 1979). However, the number of colony-forming B cells in human peripheral blood drops with advancing age (Kay, 1979) and there is a marked deficiency in maturation of B cells to antibody producing cells (Hollingsworth and Gailotte, 1981). The way in which B cells are triggered by membrane perturbation has been discussed. The rate of capping and shedding of cross linked surface immunoglobulin is slower in old rats (Woda and Feldman, 1979). In B lymphocytes from aged human, the density of surface immunoglobulin decreases (Tada et al, 1978) and there is an increase in the numbers of altered mitochondria (Biro and Berégi, 1979).

One can conclude from these observations that there are adequate numbers of B cells in old age, but there are subtle qualitative changes which might contribute to impaired efficiency. However, the situation is far from clear, as B lymphocyte responses in vitro appear to increase in old age. In vitro lymphocyte proliferation in response to pokeweed (a B cell mitogen) also increases in aged humans (Powell and Fernandez, 1980).

Antibody production

The reduction in levels of natural antibody with advancing age has been commented upon. The primary antibody response also suffers a decline in old mice (Makinodan and Peterson, 1962; Kishimoto et al, 1976), but the secondary response remains unimpaired (Makinodan and Peterson, 1962; Segre and Segre, 1976). There have been few studies in man, but information is available from studying immunization. The elderly are capable of producing adequate amounts of antibody to tetanus toxoid (Solomonova and Vizev, 1973). However, careful study of the response reveals a slower rise to lower maximal levels of antibody and an earlier decline (Kishimoto et al, 1980). These defects also result in slight impairment of the secondary responses. With influenza vaccination, the antibody response has been reported to be impaired with low antibody levels (Marine and Thomas, 1973; Howells et al, 1975) or normal with higher antibody levels in the elderly (Ferry et al, 1976; Mackenzie, 1977).

The response to certain pneumococcal antigens is less in old age, the peak levels are lower and the decline is earlier and faster than in middle aged or young adults (Amman et al, 1980; Bentley et al, 1981).

The impairment of antibody production cannot be accounted for by the changes in B lymphocytes which have been described. The reduced response is to T dependent antigens; the response to T independent antigens such as Type III pneumococcal polysaccharide does not decline (Smith, 1976). Furthermore, T helper activity for in vitro antibody production to tetanus toxoid was found to be significantly depressed in the elderly age groups (Kishimoto et al, 1980). It is concluded that the impairment of antibody production is secondary to thymic involution and the reduction of T helper lymphocyte function.

Cellular immunity

Circulating lymphocyte numbers do not change with age (Zacharski et al, 1971; Carosella et al, 1974). The observation of thymic involution suggests the T lymphocyte function might well deteriorate in old age.

T lymphocytes

T lymphocyte numbers do not change in mice (Kay et al, 1979) and probably not in man (Weksler and Hutteroth, 1974; Fernandez et al, 1976; Kay, 1979). There are some reports of a decline in numbers with age in man (Carosella et al, 1974; Foad et al, 1974; Smith et al, 1974) and a decline in colony forming T cells (Kay, 1979). There are qualitative changes in T lymphocytes with aging, such as within the mitochondria (Berégi et al, 1980) and changes in cyclic nucleotides (Tam and Walford, 1978). The surface density of theta receptors on mouse T lymphocytes declines with age (Brennan and Jaroslow, 1975). If lymphocytes from old mice are injected into syngeneic young mice a graft versus host reaction is instituted (Gozes et al, 1978) and cytotoxic antibodies can also be induced (Callard et al, 1979). This leads to the hypothesis that new antigens appear within the T lymphocyte membrane in old age.

There appear to be quantitative changes within the T lymphocyte subsets and these will be discussed in a later section.

There are functional changes within the T lymphocytes and in vitro transformation in response to T cell mitogens declines with age (Pisciotta et al, 1967; Hallgren et al, 1973; Fernandez et al, 1976). This functional decline is obvious and cannot be accounted for by the minor qualitative and quantitative changes so far described. Older individuals have fewer circulating mitogen responsive cells (Inkeles et al, 1977) and cells that do respond have a more limited reproductive capacity (Weksler, 1978). The situation is not clear cut; some studies have failed to demonstrate any decline in function with age (Portaro et al, 1978; Kay, 1979).The mixed lymphocyte reaction has been shown by some to decline with age (Adler et al, 1971; Hori et al, 1973) but not by others (Walters and Claman, 1975). The in vitro response of lymphocytes to tuberculin antigen does decline with age (Nilsson, 1971).

There is little doubt that T lymphocytes change with advancing age. and that the functional decline can be demonstrated in vitro. These changes are confirmed by studies in man and the intact experimental animal.

In vivo
The ability to induce contact sensitivity to dinitrochlorobenzene decreases in old age in man (Baer and Bowser, 1963; Gross, 1965; Waldorf et al, 1968; Grossman et al, 1975). The expression of previously acquired delayed hypersensitivity also declines with age (Forbes, 1971; Roberts-Thompson et al, 1974). This is assessed by skin testing with various antigens such as tuberculin, mumps, candida, varidase and trichophyton.

These changes appear to be a true phenomenon of aging and not due to malnutrition or associated disease. This was the conclusion from a study of healthy ambulant individuals in Albuquerque, New Mexico (Goodwin et al, 1982). The impaired skin testing correlates with impaired in vitro lymphocyte transformation to T cell mitogens.

In experimental animals skin testing reveals a similar decline with age (Stutman et al, 1968; Walters and Claman, 1975). The changes are not restricted to the skin; when tumour cells are injected intraperitoneally or intravenously into aging mice they are rejected less

efficiently than in younger mice (Goodman and Makinodan, 1975; Perkins and Cacheiro, 1977).

The anergy undoubtedly has clinical consequences. In a small series of octogenarians the majority of patients who were anergic on skin testing died within 2 years, in direct contrast to the majority of reactors who survived beyond this time (Roberts-Thompson et al, 1974). The anergy may well contribute to the reactivation of disease such as tuberculosis and varicella zoster (shingles). It seems likely to be of clinical significance in many of the infections and other diseases of old age and this will be discussed later.

Macrophage function
The number of circulating monocytes in the peripheral blood does not appear to change with increasing age. In the experimental animal the number of peritoneal macrophages increases with age (Perkins, 1971). Macrophages from old animals appear to be as good as those from young animals in initiating primary or secondary antibody responses (Valenti, 1978). Work in vitro has revealed that 'old' macrophages can adequately support mitogen or antigen induced responses (Callard, 1978).

It appears that macrophages from old animals may be activated (Heidrick, 1972; Platt and Pauli, 1972), certainly phagocytic capacity is increased (Perkins, 1971). This increased phagocytosis probably accounts for other age-related changes. High doses of antigen are required in aged mice to initiate immune responses (Price and Makinodan, 1972). Antigens in old mice may fail to localize in lymphoid follicles (Metcalf et al, 1966; Legge and Austin, 1968). Presumably the antigen is phagocytozed and destroyed efficiently. The same is found in species such as the rat (Garvey et al, 1980).Studies of monocyte function in aging humans have shown no change in phagocytosis or in chemotaxis (Gardner et al, 1981).

It is not known if there are any clinical consequences of these changes. It has been suggested that weak antigens would be less likely to initiate an immune response with advancing age, and this could be a contributing factor to the increased incidence of cancer (Makinodan and Kay, 1980). Tumour antigens are usually 'weak' antigens.

Because the aging macrophages usually function adequately it is unlikely that the production of any factors is impaired. It has been mentioned that adherent cells may suppress immune responses and there is a report of increased suppression of the primary antibody response in old age. Removal of monocytes from the peripheral blood enhanced this in vitro antibody response (Delfraissy et al, 1981). However, monocyte suppression of cellular immunity decreases with age in man (Becker et al, 1981).

The macrophage was the focus of attention for much early work on the immune response in aging because of its pivotal role. However, this cell appears to avoid the ravages of aging although many areas have yet to be studied.

Neutrophil function

Neutrophils have one major function — phagocytosis and killing. Neutrophil adherence is reported to increase with age (Silverman and Silverman, 1977; Corberand et al, 1981). Chemotaxis is impaired in a minority of healthy elderly individuals, it is normal in the vast majority (Corberand et al, 1981). The situation with phagocytosis is not as clear cut as with macrophages. There are some reports of reduced phagocyte function with age (Moroni et al, 1976; Ivanova, 1978), but others have detected no change (Corberand et al, 1981).

Intracellular killing appears to remain intact in old age (Moroni et al, 1976; Palmblad and Haak, 1978). The metabolic function of neutrophils is measured in various ways, one example is chemiluminescence. This has been reported to be reduced in individuals over 70 years of age (Van Epps et al, 1978). In our experience chemiluminescence of neutrophils remains intact in the majority of fit elderly (Puxty et al, 1983).

The Nitroblue Tetrazolium test also becomes less positive with advancing age (Moroni et al, 1976; Corberand et al, 1981). These changes point to a defect of neutrophil function with advancing age. These might well be responsible for the increased problem of staphylococcal infection in old age (Phair, 1978) since neutrophil phagocytosis is most important in defence against these organisms (Grieco, 1980).

Modulators

Suppressor cells can be identified functionally by a number of tests in both man and experimental animals. The results of such investigations are variable and somewhat confusing. Some tests show increases in suppressor cell function, others a decrease.

In man suppressor cell function has been identified with certain T lymphocyte subpopulations. One way of identifying these subpopulations has been by means of membrane receptors for the heavy chain of immunoglobulins (Fc). Suppressor cells carry Fc receptors for IgG and these can be identified with ox erythrocytes coated with IgG antibody. Using these rosetting techniques two studies revealed an increase in suppressor cells with age (Kishimoto et al, 1978; Gupta and Good, 1979) and a third, no significant change (Cobleigh et al, 1980).

These techniques have been superceded by the use of monoclonal antibodies. The percentage of peripheral blood lymphocytes falls in old age because of a decrease in the percentage and absolute number of T lymphocytes bearing the T8[+] marker, suppressor or cytotoxic lymphocytes (Nagel et al, 1981). There is no change in helper populations (T4[+]).

Is there evidence of a functional decline in suppressor cell activity? The autologous mixed lymphocyte reaction, AMLR, decreases in old age in man (Fernandez and MacSween, 1980a). The AMLR is probably an in vitro correlate of the in vivo T cell suppression of B cell proliferation. Lymphocytes produce lymphokines, and the suppressor cell population is thought to produce the lymphokine macrophage migration stimulation factor (MStF) (Fox et al, 1981). MStF production declines with age in man (Fox and Rajaraman, 1979). This subpopulation can be stimulated by the mitogen Concanavalin A and this response declines with age (Abe et al, 1981). These findings support the conclusion that in man, suppressor cell function declines with age.

One test that has been reported to measure suppressor function is the use of Concavalin A to generate suppressor cell populations in vitro. However, this does not appear to be true (Fernandez and MacSween, 1980b) and therefore the reports of increased suppressor cell activity in old age need to be interpreted with caution (Antel et al, 1978; Barrett et al, 1980).

Experimental animal work supports the conclusion of suppressor cell decline with age (Chused et al, 1973; Folch and Waksman, 1974; Gerber et al, 1974; Talal and Pillarisetty, 1975).Again, there are some reports of increased suppressor cell activity (Goidl et al, 1976; Segre and Segre, 1976). There appear to be genuine differences in animal strains.

Autoantibody production

The decline of antibody production has been discussed. It is paradoxical that as this occurs there is an increased propensity to produce antibodies to self, autoantibodies (Fig. 5.6). Antibodies to nuclear antigens, immunoglobulin (rheumatoid factor), gastric parietal cell and thyroid increase in frequency with advancing age (Rowley et al, 1968; Hooper et al, 1972; Chused et al, 1973; Diaz-Jouanen et al, 1975; Goodwin et al, 1982; Ockhuizen et al, 1982). These autoantibodies have not been implicated in any pathogenic role, and autoimmune disease does not increase in frequency with age (Kay. and Makinodan, 1978). These autoantibodies appear to be markers of reduced survival and increase in frequency as death approaches (Hooper et al, 1972). There are various degenerative diseases which increase in frequency with old age, and it is possible that autoantibody production could be linked to these or to diseases such as pernicious anaemia or idiopathic hypothyroidism which are also more common (Cammarata et al, 1967).

It has been postulated that autoantibody production and autoimmunity are responsible for normal aging (Walford, 1969). Walford postulates that with aging

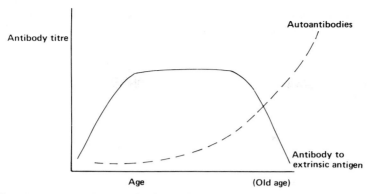

Fig. 5.6 The paradox of autoimmunity: antibody production declines in old age, autoantibody production rises

there is loss of tolerance which is due to somatic mutation of the cells of the immune system. Pantelouris (1972) suggests that the autoimmunity is linked to thymic involution. The experimental evidence reviewed so far indicates that the increased autoantibody production is secondary to thymic involution and most specifically to the decrease in numbers and function of the suppressor cells.

The experimental evidence presented is by no means clear cut and there appear to be some genuine differences. It has been postulated that there are two subpopulations of suppressor cells (Meredith et al, 1979); one which regulates the B cell response to extrinsic or foreign antigens and the other the response to intrinsic or self antigens. Only the cells controlling response to self decrease in old age, and others have produced evidence to support this concept (Goidl et al, 1981). This hypothesis does not explain why the B cells are stimulated to produce autoantibodies in the first place. It appears likely that it is due to the accumulation of substances within the body that non-specifically stimulate B lymphocytes. These substances are known as polyclonal activators and are substances like endotoxin from the cell walls of gram negative bacteria (Cohen and Ziff, 1977; Goidl et al, 1981).

Mucosal immunity

The respiratory and gastrointestinal tracts and other mucous membranes are defended against microbial invasion in different ways. The importance of non-immunological mechanisms cannot be over-emphasized. Defence can also be immunological and is two-fold. First of all, the body's immune system produces sensitized cells and specific antibody which are involved in defence of mucous membranes as well as elsewhere. Thus, changes that take place in the body's immune system with age will be detected in the mucous membranes, the same as elsewhere. The second form of immunological defence is local immunity which is due

to a separate immune system. The immune system, lymphocytes and macrophages, contact antigen within the mucosa. This induces the formation of specific antibody which is synthesized locally as secretory IgA. The effects of aging on secretory IgA production has been little studied. Alford (1968) has reported a drop in IgA concentration of nasal washings with advancing age. Intestinal SIgA drops slightly but significantly with advancing age in BALB/c mice (Lim et al, 1981). Antibody responses in nasal secretions in response to influenza virus vaccine appear to be adequate in old age (Kasel et al, 1969; Kluge and Waldman, 1979).

A recent study on intestinal cell-mediated immunity, antibody-dependent cell-mediated cytotoxicity, shows a significant decline with age in BALB/c mice (Lim et al, 1981). This decline is much more marked than that of SIgA. Furthermore, a low protein diet has no additional effect on the intestinal cellular immunity but does cause a drop in SIgA. It seems likely that mucosal immunity declines with age, and that this might be exagerrated by protein malnutrition. The clinical significance of the experimental evidence is not clear.

IMMUNE THEORY OF AGING

It has been shown that normal immune functions can begin to decline quite early in life, in fact soon after sexual maturity. The changes that take place are due to changes in the immune cells themselves and in their milieu. The changes are complex because of the many cell types that are involved in a single immune response and the varied types of immune responses. Over recent years the situation has become more difficult to interpret because of the identification of increasing numbers of subpopulations of certain cell types such as T cells.

It would seem reasonable to conclude that the thymus bears the brunt of the age changes. Indeed, changes in the thymus seem to be the most important and lead to the decline in cell mediated and humoral immunity. Understanding these age-associated changes in the thymus is essential to understanding the aging of the immune system.

There is considerable research activity in this area at present. If the reason for thymic aging can be determined then aging might be delayed or even reversed. Some research is focused upon the hypothalamus-pituitary-thymus axis, and evidence has been forthcoming that aging can be manipulated through hypophysectomy (Bilder and Denckla, 1977). Furthermore, stress can effect the immune response and this is thought to be mediated through the hypothalamus (Stein et al, 1976). Lesions in the anterior hypothalamus will depress delayed hypersensitivity (Bilder and Denckla, 1977) and growth hormone and insulin act preferentially on cell mediated immune function (Fabris et al, 1972). On the other hand, the thymus itself appears to play a role in controlling hormone levels (Fabris et al, 1972; Besedovsky et al, 1975).

Dietary manipulation in the form of calorie restriction will delay immunological maturation in rodents and this in turn will delay thymic involution and loss of immunological vigour (José and Good, 1973; Gerbase-DeLima et al, 1975; Weindruch et al, 1979). Is the thymus the site of the 'clock' that controls aging within the immune system? Or are the changes in the thymus secondary to changes elsewhere?

There is a great deal of experimental evidence to support the hypothesis of a control system intrinsic to the thymus. A number of thymic transplants can be established in the same individual and there is no diminution in the individual growth rates (Hinsull and Bellamy, 1974). The site of this control appears to be within the reticular epithelial cells. These cells appear very early in embryonic development (Auerbach, 1961). Furthermore, if a thymus is transplanted inside a millipore chamber only the epithelial cells survive (Hays, 1967). Physical contact between these cortical epithelial cells and lymphocytes is essential in regeneration and normal development (Bellamy and Hinsull, 1975).

It therefore seems safe to conclude at the present state of our knowledge, that the reticular-epithelial cell complex of the thymus is the site of the clock that controls aging of the thymus. This in turn determines the rate of running down of the immune system. The factors that control this clock are not clear.

The immune theory of aging states that immunological aging is the essential change and aging of other organs follows on from this; the basis of aging in the other organs being autoimmune (Walford, 1969; Burnet, 1970). The evidence to implicate autoimmunity in pathogenesis has not been forthcoming and has been discussed. It seems that the waning immunity is a direct result of the thymic involution, and thus the cause of various diseases.

A recent study supports the hypothesis that aging itself is responsible for the waning immunity (Goodwin et al, 1982). Cell mediated immunity declined and auto-antibodies were higher in healthy elderly volunteers compared with younger controls. The subjects had been carefully examined and were apparently healthy and fully independent, living within the community.

Cancer itself, causes a decline in cell mediated immunity. Infection also may impair immunity. Anergy occurs as a result of disseminated tuberculosis and phagocytic function declines in the presence of infection. In the debilitated, ill elderly person, the immunodeficiency of old age secondary to thymic involution may well be exaggerated by other diseases or conditions.

INFECTION IN OLD AGE

Infection is a common problem in the elderly population, indeed bronchopneumonia is still listed as the most common cause of death in extreme old age (Ishii et al, 1980). Many elderly patients who develop an infection present a typical clinical picture with the usual symptoms and signs. This is not always so, however, and in geriatric practice less typical presentations are increasingly common with advancing age.

Geriatric presentation of infection

With increasing age there is an increased chance of a 'silent' presentation. Silence is really the dampening down of various responses. For example, the inflammatory reaction is much less florid as shown in the development of peritonitis with minimal physical signs in old age (Burston and Moore-Smith, 1970). Aging affects different systems at different rates and in different ways and while the function of organs or systems may be impaired they remain compensated until additional insult results in decompensation. This may present to the physician as incontinence of urine or faeces, immobility, instability or falling and confusion; these are known as the Geriatric Giants (Isaacs, 1981). Infection in various sites may present in this way (Fig. 5.7).

Immobility may manifest itself by retirement to bed. In the setting of a rehabilitation or assessment ward, it may simply appear as an unwillingness to cooperate in rehabilitation. Stroke patients may decompensate to a lower level of functional capacity in the presence of an infection. Chest infection may present in patients with ischaemic heart disease as an exacerbation of the ischaemic symptoms.

With increasing age there is deterioration in the various homeostatic control systems within the body.

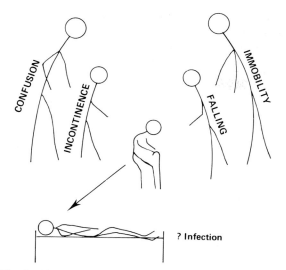

CONFUSION

INCONTINENCE

FALLING

IMMOBILITY

? Infection

Fig. 5.7 The 'Giants of Geriatrics' and the geriatric presentation of infection

These are dealt with elsewhere in this book. The degeneration in the autonomic nervous system undoubtedly contributes to various aspects of the atypical presentation. The inflammatory reaction has not been well studied but there appears to be slight deterioration in the neutrophil response. It can be seen that the paucity of typical symptoms and signs of infection is not well explained. There are several possible contributory factors.

Diagnosis of infection

In order to diagnose infection in geriatric practice one needs to have a high index of suspicion. The history may not be helpful, though careful examination may reveal the system(s) involved. Many features suggesting a diagnosis of infection in other age groups are absent in the aged. Infection in old age may occur without fever and the absence of fever or presence of a low body temperature do not make infection less likely. Part of the explanation for an absent fever response lies in aging of the autonomic nervous system (see p. 458).

An elevated white blood cell (WBC) count suggests infection. The WBC tends to drop with advancing age, so a high normal of 10, 000 or more needs to be regarded with suspicion. An elevated WBC is not an inevitable consequence of infection in old age. A leucocytosis below 15, 000 in pneumonia is common in old age and is associated with increased mortality (Chatard, 1910). Nonetheless, an elevated WBC with a raised ESR is good objective evidence for the presence of infection.

Outcome

Infections carry a high morbidity and high mortality in

old age. Some of the reasons and contributory factors are self evident such as the other pathologies and pathophysiological changes of aging that affect different organs and tissues. Because of the less florid and less characteristic physical signs, appropriate diagnostic manoeuvres are not undertaken early enough; diagnosis is delayed and outcome worsened.

Major infections in old age

There are certain infections which become increasingly common with advancing age or are of major importance in old age (Table 5.2). Pneumonia, tuberculosis and urinary tract infections are dealt with elsewhere in this book and will not be considered here. Hospital acquired infections and septicaemia need to be discussed.

Table 5.2 Common infections in the elderly

Chest infections
Tuberculosis
Hospital acquired infections
Urinary tract infections
Septicaemia and infective endocarditis

Hospital acquired infections

Hospital acquired infections increase in frequency with age (Haley et al, 1981) the most common type being those of the urinary tract, of surgical wounds, pneumonia and bacteraemia (Stamm, 1978). Bacteraemia is five times more frequent in the eighth decade than in the third.

Obviously, urinary tract infections follow urological manipulation and the use of catheters, and wound infections occur in patients undergoing bowel or rectal surgery. *Escherichia coli* and proteus are common organisms. Infections are most frequent in patients whose resistance is lowered for one reason or another (Table 5.3).

Table 5.3 Risk factors in hospital acquired infection

Age
Malignant disease
Diabetes
Malnutrition
Drugs
Immobility

The presence of underlying disease significantly increases the risk of hospital acquired infection, and also affects the prognosis of that infection. Infections are a significant problem in patients with malignancy (Inagaki et al, 1974) because of associated malnutrition and impaired immunity (Twomey et al, 1979; Phair et al, 1980). Metabolic problems such as uraemia (Perillie et al, 1962) and diabetic ketoacidosis (Bagdade et al, 1974) give rise to impaired defence mechanisms, and particularly affects polymophonuclear phagocytic function. Such defects may increase susceptibility to infection and certainly adversely influence the outcome of infections once acquired (Thornton, 1971).

Multiple pathologies and the aging process also underlie increased rate, secondary to the changes in the immune response which have been discussed previously.

Malnutrition is not uncommon in the hospitalized elderly (Gambert and Guansing, 1980) and infection rate is undoubtedly high in the malnourished (Müller et al, 1979). It is well recognized that cell mediated immunity is depressed in the presence of malnutrition. Protein calorie malnutrition, iron deficiency and deficiency of vitamin C have all been associated with depressed delayed hypersensitivity (Good et al, 1980).

A final important factor is drug administration, especially the cytotoxic drugs. Any immunosuppressant drug, including corticosteroids, will increase susceptibility to infection. The antibiotics are also important — not only interfering with normal flora but also selecting out resistant organisms.

One of the most important aspects is to prevent infection from occurring in the first place. For the elderly, hospital admissions presents a risk and therefore cannot be undertaken lightly. Hygiene presents a great challenge to confused old people and their carers. Hand carriage of organisms is common in hospital acquired infection (Fisher, 1976; Schaberg et al, 1978). Hand washing is of great importance, between patients, as well as when handling infected material which is associated with a high rate of carriage of the organisms (Steere and Mollison, 1975).

Antibiotic therapy should be kept to the essential and not used freely without serious thought. Modern technological medicine brings its own hazards and dangers. Intravascular devices need very careful monitoring and this should be part of an overall infection surveillance programme.

Infection in the long-term care setting

Various outbreaks have been reported from long-term care facilities. For example, tuberculosis (Stead, 1981), influenza (Mather et al, 1980) and diarrhoea (Cubitt and Holzel, 1980; Garibaldi et al, 1981). It would appear that individuals who reside in these institutions are more susceptible, and that once an outbreak starts it is likely to spread. Containment presents a challenge particularly in the overcrowded long-stay ward with a high percentage of confused patients. The immobile patients are reservoirs of infection due to a high rate of oropharyngeal colonisation (Valenti et al, 1978) and an increased rate of urinary tract infection (Brocklehurst et al, 1977).

Treatment needs special consideration in this setting not only of the affected patient, but also of the environment and other patients. The overriding principle needs to be consideration of the quality of life of the individual with infection.

Septicaemia and bacteraemia

The terms used to describe the presence of bacteria in the blood stream are often used loosely. Bacteraemia describes the temporary presence of bacteria in the blood, without the establishment of a general infection and with no response from the host. When bacteria persist, multiply and produce illness, the term septicaemia is used.

The incidence of septicaemia appears to be increasing, and is presumably related to modern technological medicine. Gram negative bacteria (Kreger et al, 1980a) and staphylococci (McGowan et al, 1975) contribute to this increase. The mortality rate is high and is significantly higher in the elderly (Svänbom, 1980; Wilson et al, 1981). The presence of infection anywhere in the body will predispose to septicaemia and any investigative or therapeutic procedures may then carry the risk of septicaemia — especially in old people and those with impaired defence mechanisms due to malignancy or drug therapy.

A frequently fatal complication of septicaemia is shock. With gram negative organisms this is due to endotoxin; with gram positive organisms such as pneumococci, the toxins are released — exotoxins. Such toxins are released in small amounts in most infections but are removed by the reticuloendothelial system — specifically the Kupffer cells of the liver. If this mechanism is insufficient then free toxins are present and shock results.

Endotoxin has many effects including the release of vasoactive substances like bradykinin, histamine and prostaglandins; activation of the autonomic nervous system with release of noradrenaline; activation of coagulation and fibrinolysis and interaction with leucocytes to stimulate release of endogenous pyrogen. Initial vasodilation is followed by vasoconstriction and reduced blood flow to viscera. There is pooling of blood with hypovolaemia. Subsequent anoxia and ischaemia may lead to irreversible circulatory failure and all the sequelae of shock. Treatment at this stage is difficult, and successful treatment requires early diagnosis.

In old age septicaemia may present quite typically as in any other age group, with abrupt onset of fever and later shock. The onset may be less typical with absence of the usual signs and symptoms as already discussed. Confusion may be more prominent and fever often absent (Maddern et al, 1981). Diagnosis is difficult in the elderly (Denham and Goodwin, 1977) and may only be reached at autopsy (Svänbom, 1980).

The important diagnostic test is blood culture and two or three need to be obtained from different sites at different times. Most of the positive results will be obtained from these early cultures, large numbers of repeated venesections are not necessary (Cates and Christie, 1951; Crowley, 1970; Robinson et al, 1980). Other tests may alert the clinician as to the advisability of a blood culture. The erythrocyte sedimentation rate and white blood cell count should be raised, although this is not always an early finding (Denham and Goodwin, 1977). Other tests such as those of liver function may, if abnormal, give a lead to the site of sepsis — such as cholangitis.

What are the indications for blood culture? A difficult question to answer but one which obviously needs to be considered frequently in geriatric practice. Any elderly person with unexplained confusion, general deterioration in health with immobility or unexplained hypotension needs blood culture. If infection (by examination and raised WBC and ESR) is defined as a problem then blood cultures are mandatory. If one adopts this policy then approximately 10 per cent of blood cultures will yield positive and meaningful results (Denham and Goodwin, 1977).

Treatment depends on recognition. The site of original sepsis, if identified, needs appropriate treatment. The choice of antibiotic depends on the findings, but should be potent, appropriate and usually parenteral. In the fragile environment of old age, monitoring must be close. The patient's shock needs appropriate treatment and some authorities still advise systemic administration of high dose corticosteroids (Schümer, 1976) but others do not (Kreger et al, 1980b).

The reasons for the increased incidence with advancing age are not clear but are presumably related to the impaired defence mechanisms already discussed. Because of other pathophysiological changes of aging, diagnosis is often late. For these reasons, the morbidity and mortality is high. A high index of suspicion and early definitive treatment should improve the outlook.

Treatment of infection

Successful treatment is dependent upon accurate diagnosis and the difficulties of this have been discussed. There is no place for a therapeutic trial of antibiotics when the problem definition is simply infection. Obviously when the infection is more accurately defined, so that at least the system involved is known, then therapeutic trial is a possibility. Indeed it is often the reality in clinical practice, for example with chest infection. In this case it is often difficult to obtain appropriate specimens to make an aetiological diagnosis. Nevertheless, it should be remembered that administration of antibiotics does render microbiological investigation useless. Early and appropriate investigation with culture of specimens needs to be encouraged.

There are changes with specific antibiotics which need to be considered. The oral absorption of the penicillins may be enhanced in old age with increasing achlorhydria, and there is certainly greater variability in absorption of ampicillin amongst the elderly (Triggs et al, 1980). Renal excretion of penicillin and its derivatives is prolonged in old age (Kampmann et al, 1972). There is lowered glomerular filtration rate and reduced tubular secretory capacity in old age which prolongs the half life of ampicillin (Triggs et al, 1980). The penicillins may contain large amounts of sodium which could precipitate pulmonary oedema, or of potassium which might precipitate hyperkalaemia. There are other rare side effects which are more likely in the elderly such as hypokalaemic alkalosis with penicillin G (Appel and Neü, 1977), neurotoxicity with carbenicillin, ticarcillin or penicillin G (Weinstein and Dalton, 1968; Kurtzman et al, 1970) and interference with coagulation by carbenicillin (Brown et al, 1974).

The cephalosporins are all excreted by the kidney and, because of its nephrotoxicity, cephaloridine is not recommended for use in old age. The aminoglycosides are excreted by the kidneys and clearance is similar to that for creatinine. Because of changes in creatinine clearance with age, these drugs need to be carefully monitored in the elderly. Aminoglycosides are administered parenterally and when prescribed for gram negative infection in old age, should be monitored with 'peak' (30 minutes after i.v. dose) and 'trough' (30 minutes before next dose) levels. This is important because of the ototoxicity. These toxic effects are common to all drugs of this type and are made worse by the concurrent administration of potent loop diuretics such as frusemide or ethacrynic acid (Lerner and Matz, 1980).

The tetracyclines are fairly widely used. Biliary excretion is important, but there is reabsorption and excretion by the kidney. As creatinine clearance declines with aging, so does tetracycline elimination (Vartia and Leikola, 1960). The tetracyclines aggravate renal failure (Orr et al, 1978) and are hepato-toxic. For these reasons tetracyclines need to be used with care in old age. Doxycycline is the only drug of this type that is completely excreted in the bile.

Sulphonamides are rarely indicated in old age. They can induce skin rashes and renal damage, both of which are made worse by renal impairment (Shouval et al, 1978). Sulphamethoxazole is used in combination with trimethoprim, but the latter is as effective alone.

Erythromycin is safe in the elderly and dosage does not need modification. However, this drug may cause significant gastrointestinal disorders. If erythromycin is administered with theophylline-containing drugs, there is an increased risk of theophylline toxicity (Renton et al, 1981) and this needs to be remembered if used in the patient with chronic obstructive lung disease.

Choice of antibiotics

The elderly patient with infection is often extremely ill, and the infection very advanced. The whole patient needs to be treated and certain physical aspects of therapy may be more important than antibiotics; for example, physiotherapy in chest infections and clearing the respiratory tract and mobilising the patient are of paramount importance. There is no doubt that immobility predisposes to certain infections, particularly in the respiratory tract (Valenti et al, 1978).

If antibiotics are to be used they should be both pertinent and potent. This means accurate diagnosis. If a potent antibiotic with broad spectrum is chosen whilst cultures are awaited, there is a greater risk of toxic side effects. Accurate diagnosis should allow choice of less toxic and highly specific antibiotics. There needs to be a clear establishment of goals of treatment and defining of objectives so that adequate treatment is determined. Knowledge of all other drugs concurrently administered is essential and administration needs careful monitoring.

The severely ill usually require intravenous administration. The antibiotic concentration achieved in blood or elsewhere can be measured if necessary and is often helpful. Dosages or frequency of dosage often need modification in old age. Treatment needs to be reviewed if cultures become available. After 5 days, consideration should be given to stopping the drug. Serious infections like septicaemia usually require 10 days of therapy; endocarditis will require 6 weeks; urinary tract infection can be successfully treated with very short courses. The duration in all situations needs to be decided from the clinical response.

Toxic reactions increase with age (Grieco, 1980) and the problems with the various antibiotics have been discussed. It is important to minimize the risks of selection of resistant flora.

Prophylaxis against infection

Antibiotic prophylaxis

There are only a few conditions where prophylactic antibiotics are required. As prophylaxis against endocarditis, individuals with valvular lesions of the heart should receive antibiotics before surgery. If the procedure is dental surgery, penicillin is indicated; if it is surgery of the bowel or colonoscopy, a cephalosporin such as cephradine is recommended one hour before and for 48 hours after.

Prophylactic antibiotics are given to reduce wound infection following bowel surgery. Gentamicin and metronidazole are given one hour before and 6 hours after surgery. Catheterization or other operative procedures on the genitourinary tract in patients with bacteriuria are potentially hazardous. It is wise to give a drug such as amoxycillin one hour before and 6 hours after the procedure.

Immunization

The deterioration in humoral immunity has been discussed. This is reflected in the response of elderly patients to immunization. In most studies that have been carried out the peak of antibody production is reduced in old age and it takes longer to be attained. The serum antibody levels tend to drop faster in old age. However, immunization can still successfully protect against infection and this is the crucial issue. Thus the waning humoral immunity does not appear to be of great practical significance in the majority of the elderly.

Influenza. This is an important communicable disease and carries a significant morbidity and mortality in old age. Although the over 65's account for only 10 per cent of the cases of influenza, they account for 80 per cent of the deaths (Schoenbaum et al, 1980).

The influenza viruses are classified into various subtypes, and there is no cross reactivity between subtypes. Indeed within the same subtype there may be antigenic drift with no cross reactivity between strains. This presents a formidable challenge in immunization and leads to the necessity for annual vaccination.

The virus antigens in the vaccine induce the production of hemagglutinating, inhibiting and complement fixing IgG antibodies. The antibody response in the serum begins in the second week and peaks in the fourth after initial exposure. Maximal protection results if there is a concurrent secretory antibody response. Serum and secretory responses occur in both the natural infection and as a result of immunization.

Some studies have shown that influenza immunization is not protective in the elderly (D'Allessio et al, 1969) but this resulted from use of a vaccine of poor potency. Other studies have failed to take into account the antigenic drift and the poor matching and this resulted in no protection (Ruben et al, 1974; Van Der Veen, 1977). However, there have been other studies with potent vaccines and good matching which have shown that the elderly can be adequately protected (Stuart et al, 1969; Serie, 1977; Aymard et al, 1979). The vaccine reduces hospitalisation rates amongst elderly patients (Barker and Mulody, 1980).

The antibody responses do vary but are generally similar in the elderly to younger adults (Ferry et al, 1976; Mackenzie, 1977). Some studies demonstrated reduced antibody levels (Marine and Thomas, 1973; Howells et al, 1975). These differences are age related but might not be an aging phenomenon. They might well reflect past exposure to influenza virus antigens and the maturity of the immune system at that time. Secretory antibody response to influenza virus antigens remains intact in old age (Kasel et al, 1969; Kluge and Waldman, 1979).

Overall immunization against influenza infection does appear to be effective in the elderly and aging of the immune system does not appear to reduce its efficacy. Thus immunization can be recommended for the elderly. There is no doubt that sick and disabled old people will benefit from this immunization, and it should be recommended on an annual basis. The elderly as a group are at increased risk from influenza and it is logical to recommend annual immunization for all those over 65 years of age. However, the total production of vaccine has been inadequate to meet the needs of the high risk elderly (Kavett, 1977).

Pneumococcus. Streptococcus pneumoniae is an important cause of pneumonia in the elderly and the prevalence increases dramatically with age. Successful protection for the host is dependent upon the production of opsonising antibodies and phagocytosis by polymorphonuclear phagocytes. The organism is successful in its invasion of the host because of its capsule, the polysaccharide inhibiting phagocytosis. The basis of immunization is to produce adequate levels of antibody to capsular antigens, and currently available vaccines contain 14 of the approximately 83 capsular antigens which have been defined.

The normal response to the vaccine is marked by the development of antibody with a two-fold rise in 2–3 weeks. Protective levels of antibody persist for 5–8 years (Vella et al, 1980). Thus re-vaccination is not required for at least 5 years. There is an increasing incidence of side effects with advancing age in up to 60 per cent of older people (Bentley, 1981) which consist of local erythema, induration and soreness at the injection site.

Pneumococcal vaccine has been known to be protective for a long time, and Kaufman (1947) demonstrated a significant reduction in incidence and mortality in the elderly. More recently controlled trials in a large number of individuals residing in the community or in a psychiatric institution have shown no reduction in incidence, morbidity or mortality in the vaccinated groups (Hirschmann and Lipsky, 1981). In a non-randomised trial it was found that the vaccine was not protective in the institutional setting (Bentley et al, 1981).

The antibody responses to the different capsular antigens are variable in the elderly. To some antigens the antibody response in the elderly is unimpaired and comparable to younger individuals (Amman et al, 1980). However, careful study of 15 individuals of 80 years of age compared to 20 young adults and 20 middle aged (50–80 years) has revealed that the antibody levels are lower in the old. Fewer old people experience a significant rise in titre of antibody with fewer having protective levels one month after immunization. The antibody levels also dropped more in the elderly (Bentley, 1983). These results support the evidence previously reviewed that humoral immunity wanes in old age. It would appear that this deterioration is important and might contribute to the increasing incidence of pneumococcal disease. Undoubtedly, it also contributes to increasing morbidity and mortality.

Pneumococcal vaccine is not of proven value in the elderly. The major impact of this vaccine would be within institutions where pneumococcal pneumonia is common. Use of the vaccine which is active for a few serotypes, selects the non-vaccine serotypes which then account for the bulk of disease. In the present state of knowledge the vaccine is not recommended for the institutionalized elderly. It may be of value for the at risk elderly in the community, but this has not been proven. Further study is required before its use can be advocated.

Other immunogens. There have been few studies done on immunizing the elderly. Antibody responses decline with age in both animals and man. The defects that occur in old age appear to result primarily from T cell defects, although there are changes in B cells. Information on the immune response to tetanus toxoid showed the prevalence of protective serum antibody levels to be significantly lower in the over 60s compared to younger age groups (Crossley et al, 1979). This has confirmed other studies; elderly people within nursing homes (Ruben et al, 1978) or at home (Levin and Wyman, 1965; Chapman and Davie, 1973; Trinka, 1974) have a low incidence of protective antibodies and are therefore at risk to tetanus. This information does not tell us of the immune competence of the elderly. The lack of protection is presumably related to lack of exposure to vaccine.

It would appear that exposure of the elderly to tetanus toxoid usually results in protective antibody levels (Solomonova and Vizev, 1973; Ruben et al, 1978). However, the magnitude of the response is less, with reduced peaks and earlier declines (Kishimoto et al, 1980). This defect is related to a waning of T helper cell activity. It adds to the experimental evidence already discussed. The deterioration does not appear to be of practical significance. Tetanus has an increased incidence in the elderly and they have a higher mortality from the disease. Thus tetanus immunization should be considered in old age in the same way as any other age group and in view of the low prevalence of antibodies should be a priority.

With the increasing number of elderly the question of immunization is likely to be more frequently asked. There are no biological reasons for excluding the old from immunization against disease; if they are at risk and a vaccine that has been shown to reduce the risk in young adults is or becomes available, then it is likely to reduce the risk for the elderly also. Having made this statement, which is aimed to counteract the illogical rejection of the procedure on the basis of age, it must be said that any new vaccine requires careful study in the aged as a separate group. Studies to determine capability to protect are essential.

INFECTION AND IMMUNITY

The various aspects of infection in old age have been discussed from diagnosis to treatment and back to prevention. Infection in old age presents many challenges, perhaps an understanding of the reasons for the increased prevalence, morbidity and mortality is of paramount importance. The defence against infection is complex, and the different parts of the immune system are important at different times. Because of the random nature of the aging process it is likely that changes in defence against infection with age are likely to be both complex and variable from patient to patient.

Decreased cell mediated immunity undoubtedly contributes to the reactivation of latent infection. It is very easy to postulate that infections which have been held in check, 'break out' as cell mediated immune responses decline. Thus recrudescence of tuberculosis might be due to this. This is the long-held interpretation of the development of shingles in old age and has been supported by laboratory investigations. Cell mediated immunity to *Varicella zoster* antigen, measured in a group of elderly individuals by in vitro lymphocyte transformation, is less than that found in young individuals (Miller, 1981).

The same mechanism probably accounts for the increasing inability to wall off or limit infection in old

age. There is a higher incidence of bacteraemia complicating pneumonia with advancing age (Heffron, 1979). Impaired immunity is likely to account for this and will therefore also contribute to the increased mortality associated with bacteraemic pneumonia (Dowling and Lepper, 1951). The waning humoral immunity is probably of most importance and a result of this will be reduced opsonisation and thus reduced phagocytosis. Phagocytic function may decline in old age and it is impaired in diabetes or in the presence of infection elsewhere (Copeland, 1971). These changes would contribute to the increased mortality from pneumonia.

There is little objective evidence for waning inflammatory response, but a great deal of clinical observation and anecdotal evidence supports the concept of a decline. The waning immunity and inflammatory response no doubt contribute to the increasing prevalence, morbidity and mortality from bacteraemia, septicaemia and endocarditis.

There are important changes in defence against infection with advancing age that are not understood. Mucosal immunity appears to remain intact in most elderly individuals, yet there is increasing colonization of mucosal surfaces. The increased incidence of oropharyngeal colonization by gram negative bacteria has been discussed. This appears to be linked to immobility. One suspects that there are many changes in the non-immunological systems of the body which contribute to the deteriorating defence against infection. As a result of this it is possible that the increasing prevalence of colonization and sepsis actually contributes to further changes in the immune system (Fig. 5.8).

The increased prevalence of autoantibodies has been discussed and the continued production has been linked to the waning function of suppressor T lymphocytes. No explanation has been put forward for the initial

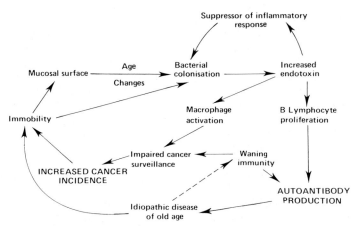

Fig. 5.8 Schematic representation of interaction of immunity and infection.

production of these autoantibodies. What is the stimulus for production in the first place?

It is of interest that the technique used to demonstrate autoantibodies to self antigens in experimental animals involves incubation with bacterial endotoxin. Incubation of cell mixtures with endotoxin allows the detection of cells which contain naturally occurring or spontaneously arising antibodies to self antigens. Cohen and Ziff (1977) suggest that the development of autoantibodies is due to the accumulation within the body of these materials that non-specifically stimulate B cells. The substances are known as polyclonal activators and include the endotoxins. This hypothesis has been put forward by others (Goidl et al, 1981).

The result of such accumulation would be the development of clones of B cells committed to the production of antibodies to self antigens. This would lead to a decline in the number of B cell clones available for production of antibodies to new, foreign antigens (Leech, 1980). There is a great deal of evidence that polyclonal activators induce autoantibody production. In the mouse they stimulate production of antibodies to serum albumin (Primi et al, 1977a), to erythrocytes and spleen cells (Primi et al, 1977b) and to DNA (Fournié et al, 1974). In man, endotoxin stimulation will give rise to antibodies cytotoxic to tonsillar cells (Primi et al, 1977c). There is also evidence to support the hypothesis of decline in numbers of available B cell clones with age. The responsiveness to polyclonal activators in vitro declines with age (Gronowicz and Coutinko, 1974; Cohen and Ziff, 1977).

This is a most interesting hypothesis. The source of polyclonal activators has not been suggested, but they are presumably derived from bacterial cell walls. Gram negative bacterial cell walls are rich sources of endotoxin. It is not known if endotoxin accumulates in old age, but the rate of oropharyngeal colonization does increase. One might speculate that this is a potential source of polyclonal activators. This hypothesis is made more interesting by the knowledge that bacterial endotoxin has anti-inflammatory effects (Verghese and Snyderman, 1981) and dampened inflammatory response in old age has not been explained.

The hypothesis presented here suggests that bacterial colonization itself, which becomes increasingly common in old age, results in stimulation of a deteriorating immune system with poorly controlled production of autoantibodies. The evidence for this has been summarized. The hypothesis has been tested in another situation. In bronchiectasis there is long-standing colonization of the bronchial tree. This condition is associated with raised serum immunoglobulin levels and an increased incidence of autoantibodies (Hilton and Doyle, 1978). In a recent study we have found that all bronchiectasis patients with raised immunoglobulin and autoantibodies

have detectable endotoxin in the serum (Horan et al, 1983). This observation supports the hypothesis that bacterial endotoxin is stimulating the production of autoantibodies; the same might be true in old age.

The interaction between immunity and infection in old age is of great interest for very practical reasons as well as academically. Although old age appears to be a time of loss, research has revealed that potential remains untapped in old age. Prevention remains an important principle, and the evidence so far supports the conclusion that immunization is possible and desirable.

CANCER

With advancing age there is an increasing incidence of many cancers including stomach, prostate, skin, large bowel, pancreas and oesophagus. Neoplastic change is a phenomenon that is closely linked to aging. Cancer ranks as the third leading cause of death in old age and two-thirds of the deaths are due to cancer of the lungs, colon, rectum, prostate, stomach and breast. It should also be made clear that multiple pathology strikes in old age and many old people die with cancer but not as a result of it. Thus death rates do not give a picture of the true incidence.

Role of immunity

The increased incidence of cancer is thought to be directly related to the waning immunity with age (Walford, 1974; Kay, 1979). In other situations where there is impaired cell mediated immunity, for instance due to immunosuppressive drug therapy, there is an increased incidence of certain tumours.

The immune system is thought to be involved in the control of cancer development in a number of ways. It has long been known that as tumour cells develop they acquire new antigens (Old and Boyce, 1964; Klein, 1968). These new antigens, usually weak immunogens, are detected by the immune system; this theory is known as immune surveillance. The immune system is induced to respond by lysing and eradicating the tumour cells. The early detection of tumour antigens is a function of macrophages and the ability of these cells to detect weak antigens becomes impaired in old age. It has been postulated that this is related to increased phagocytosis (Kay, 1979). The overactive cells phagocytize and digest weak tumour antigens and the information is not passed on to T lymphocytes. Higher doses of antigen are required to invoke an immune response (Garvey et al, 1980). Thus a higher tumour load would be present before an immune response is invoked.

Resistance to challenge with low doses of allogeneic tumours declines with age in mice and resistance can decline with age up to one hundred-fold, yet T cell immunity only declines four-fold (Goodman and Maki-nodan, 1975). The difference here is accounted for by the changing phagocytic capacity of the macrophages.

Once detected the tumour cells are lysed, and an intact cell-mediated immune system is required for this. This aspect has been shown to deteriorate in old age as a direct result of thymic involution.

If thymic involution and impaired cell mediated immunity decline with advancing age, then prevention of this decline and restoration of function to previous levels should reduce tumour incidence. The prolonged administration of bovine thymic factor to female C3H/Sn mice reduces the spontaneous tumour incidence (Anisinov et al, 1982). This reduced tumour incidence was linked to a lengthened survival time. Calorie restriction in young rats prolongs life span and delays thymic involution and the waning of cell mediated immunity. In these experiments the tumour incidence falls (Tannenbaum and Silverston, 1953; Cohen, 1979; Good et al, 1980). It seems likely that the increased cancer incidence is directly linked to the impaired cell-mediated immunity.

Immunity in diagnosis
Immunological techniques are increasingly used to aid in diagnosis. Radioimmunoassay is a widely applied technique now used for measurements of various hormones. In the field of cancer new antigens have been detected on certain cancers and advocated as aids in diagnosis. Carcinoembryonic antigen, CEA, was described in cancer of the colon (Gold and Freedman, 1965) but because of the many false positives (in other cancers, in smokers and in cirrhosis) it has a very limited role in diagnosis. It is of some benefit in following CEA-positive patients after surgery to determine if resection is adequate or whether there is recurrence. Alpha$_1$ feto-protein is found in primary liver cell cancer and is discussed elsewhere in this book.

Immunotherapy
The role of the body's own immune system in eradication of cancer has been discussed. There has been a great deal of research into the possibility of boosting the immune system and thus helping in cancer eradication. Various agents including BCG and Pertussis vaccines have been extensively tried in the various cancers. Attempts have also been made to immunize individuals against their own cancers. At the present time, immunotherapy has no accepted role in the management of cancer of the elderly.

REFERENCES

Abe T, Morimoto C, Toguchi M, Kiyotaki M, Homma M 1981 Evidence of aberrations of T cell subsets in aged individuals. Scandinavian Journal of Immunology 13: 151–157

Adler W H, Takiguchi T, Smith R T 1971 Effect of age upon primary alloantigen recognition by mouse spleen cells. Journal of Immunology 107: 1357–1367

Albright J W, Makinodan T 1976 Decline in the growth potential of spleen-colonizing bone marrow stem cells of long lived aging mice. Journal of Experimental Medicine 144: 1204–1213

Alford R H 1968 Effects of chronic broncho-pulmonary disease and aging on human nasal secretion IgA concentration. Journal of Immunology 101: 984–988

Amman A J, Schiffman G, Austrian R 1980 The antibody responses to pneumococcal capsular polysaccharides in aged individuals. Proceedings for the Society of Biology and Medicine 164: 312–316

Andrew W 1952 Cellular Changes with Age. Thomas, Springfield, Illinois, U.S.A.

Anisimov V N, Khavinson V K H, Morozov V G 1982 Carcinogenesis and aging. Mechanisms of Aging & Development 19: 245–258

Antel J P, Weinruch M, Arnason B G 1978 Circulating suppressor cells in man as a function of age. Clinical Immunology and Immunopathology 9: 134–141

Appel G B, Neü H C 1977 The nephrotoxicity of antimicrobial agents. New England Journal of Medicine 296: 663–670, 722–728, 784–786

Aüerbach R 1961 Experimental analysis of the origin of cell types in the development of the mouse thymus. Developmental Biology 3: 366–354

Aymard M, Bentejac M C, Larbaight G, Michaut D, Triau R 1979 Efficacy of the antiinfluenza A vaccination during epidemics due to A/Vic/3/75 and A/Texas/1/77 viruses. Developments in Biological Standardization 43: 231–239

Bach J F, Dardenne M, Pleu J M, Bach M A 1975 Isolation, biochemical characteristics and biological activity of the circulating thymic hormone in the mouse and the human. Annals of New York Academy of Science 249: 186–210

Baer H, Bowser R T 1963 Antibody production and development of contact skin sensitivity in guinea pigs of various ages. Science 140: 1211–1212

Bagdade J D, Root R K, Bulger R J 1974 Impaired leukocyte function in patients with poorly controlled diabetes. Diabetes 23: 9–15

Barker W H, Mullooly J P 1980 Influenza vaccination of elderly persons. Journal of the American Medical Association 244(22): 2547–2549

Barrett D J, Stenmark, Wara, D W, Ammann A J 1980 Immunoregulation in aged humans. Clinical Immunology and Immunopathology 17: 203–211

Becker M J, Farkas R, Schneider M, Drucker I, Klajman A 1979 Cell mediated cytotoxicity in humans: age-related decline as measured by a xenogenic assay. Clinical Immunology and Immunopathology 14: 204–210

Bellamy D, Hinsull S M 1975 On the role of the reticulo-epithelial complex in transplantation of the thymus. Differentiation 3: 115–121

Bentley D W 1981 Pneumococcal vaccine in the institutionalized elderly: review of past and recent studies. Reviews of Infectious Diseases 3 (suppl.): S61–70

Bentley D W 1984 Immunization. In: Fox, R A (ed) Immunology and Infection in Old Age, Churchill Livingstone, Edinburgh

Bentley D W et al 1981 Pneumococcal vaccine in the institutionalized elderly: design of a nonrandomized trial and preliminary results. Reviews of Infectious Diseases 3 (suppl.): S71–81

Berégi E, Biro J, Regius O 1980 Age related morphological changes in lymphocytes as a model of aging. Mechanisms of Aging and Development 14: 173–180

Besedorsky H, Sorkin E, Keller M, Muller J 1975 Changes in blood hormone levels during the immune response. Proceedings of the Society for Experimental Biology and Medicine 150: 466–470

Bilder G E, Denckla W D 1977 Restoration of ability to reject xenografts and clear carbon after hypophysectomy of adult rats. Mechanisms of Aging and Development 6: 153–163

Biro J, Berégi E 1979 Electronmicroscopical and immunoelectronmicroscopical examination of the lymphocytes of young and old people after influenza vaccination. Aktuel Gerontologica 9: 235–239

Boyd E 1932 The weight of the thymus gland in health and disease. American Journal of Diseases of Children 43: 1162–1214

Brennan P C, Jaroslaw B N 1975 Age associated decline in theta antigen on spleen thymus-derived lymphocytes of B6CF$_1$ mice. Cellular Immunology 15: 51–56

Brocklehurst J C, Bee P, Jones D, Palmer M 1977 Bacteriuria in geriatric hospital patients. Its correlates and management. Age & Ageing 6: 240–245

Brown C H, Natelson E A, Bradshaw M W, Williams T W, Alfrey C P 1974 The hemostatic defeat produced by carbenicillin. New England Journal of Medicine 291: 265–270

Buckley C E, Buckley E G, Dorsey F C 1974 Longitudinal changes in serum immunoglobulin levels in older humans. Federation Proceedings, Federation of the American Societies for Experimental Biology 33: 2036–2039

Burnet F M 1970 An immunological approach to aging. Lancet ii: 358–360

Bursaker I, Goldman R 1979 Derivation of resident and inflammatory peritoneal macrophages from precursor cells different in 5'-nucleotidase activity. Journal of Reticuloendothelial Society 26: 533–544

Burston G R, Moore-Smith B 1970 Occult surgical and emergencies in the elderly. British Journal of Clinical Practice 24: 239–243

Callard R E 1978 Immune function in aged mice. III Role of macrophages and effect of 2-mercaptoethanol in the response of spleen cells from old mice to phytohemagglutinin, lipopolysaccharide and allogeneic cells. European Journal of Immunology 8: 697–705

Callard R E, Basten A, Waters L K 1977 Immune function in aged mice. II. B-cell function. Cellular Immunology 31: 26–36

Callard R E, Basten A, Blanden R V 1979 Loss of immune competence with age may be due to a qualitative abnormality in lymphocyte membranes. Nature (London) 281: 218–220

Cammarata R J, Rodnan G P, Fennell R H 1967 Serum anti-gamma-globulin and antinuclear factors in the aged. Journal of the American Medical Association 199: 455–458

Carosella E D, Monchanko K, Braun M 1974 Rosette forming T cells in human peripheral blood at different ages. Cellular Immunology 12: 323–325

Cates J E, Christie R V 1951 Subacute bacterial endocarditis. Quarterly Journal of Medicine 20: 93–130

Chapman W G, Davey M G 1963 Tetanus immunity in Busselton, Western Australia, 1969. Medical Journal of Australia 2: 316–318

Chatard J A 1910 The leucocytes in acute lobar pneumonia. John Hopkins Hospital Review 15: 89

Chen M G 1971 Age related changes in hematopoietic stem cell populations of a long-lived hybrid mouse. Journal of Cellular Physiology 78: 225–232

Chused T M, Steinberg A D, Parker L M 1973 Enhanced antibody response to miceto-polyinosinic polycytidylic acid by antithymocyte serum and age-dependent loss in NZB/W mice. Journal of Immunology 111: 52–57

Cobleigh M A, Braun D P, Harris J E 1980 Age dependent changes in human peripheral blood B cells and T cell subsets. Correlation with mitogen responsiveness. Clinical Immunology and Immunopathology 15: 162–174

Cohen B J 1979 Dietary factors affecting rats used in aging research. Journal of Gerontology 34: 803–807

Cohen B J, Ziff M 1977 Abnormal polyclonal B cell activators in NAB/NZW F$_1$ mice. Journal of Immunology 119: 1534–1537

Copeland J L, Karrh L R, McCoy J, Guckman J C 1971 Bactericidal activity of polymorphonuclear leukocytes from patients with severe bacterial infections. Texas Reports on Biology and Medicine 29: 555–562

Corberand J, Ngyen F, Laharrague P et al 1981 Polymorphonuclear functions and aging in humans. Journal of the American Geriatrics Society 29: 391–397

Crossley K, Irvine P, Warren J B, Lee B K, Mead K 1979 Tetanus and diphtheria immunity in urban Minnesota adults. Journal of the American Medical Association 242: 2298–2300

Crowley N 1970 Some bacteraemia encountered in hospital practice. Journal of Clinical Pathology 23: 166–171

Cubitt W D, Holzel H 1980 An outbreak of rotavirus infection in a long stay ward of a geriatric hospital. Journal of Clinical Pathology 33: 306–308

D'Allessio D J, Cox P M Jr, Dick E C 1969 Failure of inactivated influenza vaccine to protect an aged population. Journal of the American Medical Association 210: 485–489

Delfraisey J F, Galanaud P, Dormont J, Wallon C 1981 Deficit immunitaire lie au vieillissement. Role des monocytes. Comptes Rendus de L'Academie des Sciences, Paris t 292(16): 919–922

Denham M J, Goodwin C S 1977 The value of blood cultures in geriatric practice. Age and Ageing 6: 85–88

Diaz-Jouanen E, Williams R C, Strickland R G 1975 Letter: age related changes in T and B cells. Lancet i: 688–689

Dowling H F, Lepper M H 1951 The effect of antibiotics on the fatality rate and incidence of complications in pneumococci pneumonia. American Journal of Medical Science 222: 396–403

Fabris N, Pierpaoli W, Sorkin E 1972 Lymphocytes, hormones and aging. Nature (London) 240: 557–559

Farrar J J, Lougham B E, Nordin A A 1974 Lymphopoietic potential of bone marrow cells from aged mice. Comparison of the cellular constituents of bone marrow from young and aged mice. Journal of Immunology 112: 1244–1249

Fernandez L A, MacSween J M, Langley G R 1976 Lymphocyte responses to PHA: age-related effects. Immunology 31: 583–587

Fernandez L A, MacSween M 1980a Decreased autologous mixed lymphocyte reaction with aging. Mechanisms of Aging and Development 12: 245–248

Fernandez L A, MacSween M 1980b Generation of suppressor cells by Concanavalin A. A new perspective. Journal of Immunology 125: 267–269

Ferry B J, Cheyne I M, Hampson A W, Atkinson M I E 1976 Antibody response to one and two doses of influenza virus subunit vaccine. Medical Journal of Australia 1: 186–189

Fisher E J 1976 Surveillance and management of hospital-acquired infections. Heart-Lung 5: 784–787

Fleisher T A, Greene W C, Blaese R M, Waldman T A 1981 Soluble suppressor supernatants elaborated by concanavalin A — activated human mononuclear cells II. Characterisation of a soluble suppressor of B cell immunoglobulin production. Journal of Immunology 126: 1192–1197

Foad B, Adams Y, Yamaguchi Y, Litwin A 1974 Phytomitogen responses of peripheral blood lymphocytes in young and older subjects. Clinical and Experimental Immunology 17: 657–664

Folch H, Waksman, B H 1974 The splenic suppressor cell. I Activity of thymus-derived adherent cells: changes with age and stress. Journal of Immunology 113: 140–144

Forbes I J 1971 Measurement of immunological function in clinical medicine. Australian and New Zealand Journal of Medicine 1: 160–170

Foster K G, Ellis F P, Dore C, Exton-Smith A N, Weiner J S 1976 Sweat responses in the aged. Age & Ageing 5: 91–101

Fournié G J, Lambert P H, Miescher P A 1974 Release of DNA in circulating blood and induction of anti-DNA antibodies after infection of bacterial lipopolysaccharides. Journal of Experimental Medicine 140: 1189–1206

Fox R A 1979 Membrane glycoproteins shed in defence of the cells of the gastrointestinal tract. Medical Hypotheses 5: 669–682

Fox R A, Rajaraman K 1979 Macrophage migration inhibition factor, migration stimulation factor and the role of the suppressor cells in their production. Cellular Immunology 47: 69–78

Fox R A, Rajaraman K, MacSween M 1981 Migration stimulation factor. A review. Scandinavian Journal of Immunology 14: 327–334

Gambert S R, Guansing A R 1980 Protein-calorie malnutrition in the elderly. Journal American Geriatrics Society 28: 272–275

Gardner I D, Lun S T K, Lawton J M W 1981 Monocyte function in aging humans. Mechanisms of Aging and Development 16: 233–239

Garibaldi R A, Brodine S, Matsumiya S 1981 Infections among patients in nursing homes. New England Journal Medicine 305: 731–733

Garvey J S, Shafer J W, Caperna T J 1980 Antigen handling in relation to aging. Mechanisms of Aging and Development 12: 287–303

Gerbase DeLima M, Kiu R K, Cheney K E, Mickey R K, Walford

R L 1975 Immune function and survival in a long-lived mouse strain subjected to undernutrition. Gerontologia 21: 184–202

Gerber N L, Hardin J A, Steinberg A D, Chused T M, Steinberg A D 1974 Loss with age in NZB/W mice of thymic suppressor cells in the graft vs host reaction. Journal of Immunology 113: 1618–1625

Goidl E A, Innes J B, Weksler M E 1976 Immunological studies of aging. II. Loss of IgG and high avidity plaque-forming cells and increased suppressor cell activity in aging mice. Journal of Experimental Medicine 144: 1037–1048

Goidl E A, Michelis M A, Siskind G W, Weksler M E 1981 Effect of age on the induction of autoantibodies. Clinical and Experimental Immunology 44: 24–33

Gold P, Freedman S O 1965 Demonstration of tumour specific antigens in human colonic carcinomas by immunological tolerance and absorption techniques. Journal of Experimental Medicine 121: 439–443

Goldstein G, Mackay I R 1969 The Human Thymus. Heinemann, London

Good R A, West A, Fernandez G 1980 Nutritional modulation of immune responses. Federation Proceedings 39: 3098–3104

Goodman S A, Makinodan T 1975 Effect of age on cell-mediated immunity in long-lived mice. Clinical and Experimental Immunology 19: 533–542

Goodwin J S, Searles R P, Tring A S K 1982 Immunological responses of a healthy elderly population. Clinical and Experimental Immunology 48: 403–410

Gozes Y, Umiel T, Meshover A, Trainin N 1978 Syngeneic GvH induced in popliteal lymph nodes by spleen cells of old C57 BL/6 mice. Journal of Immunology 121: 2199–2204

Greene W C, Fleisher T A, Waldmann T A 1981 Soluble suppressor supernatants elaborated by Concanavalin A-activated human mononuclear cells. I Characterisation of soluble suppressor of T cell proliferation. Journal of Immunology 126: 1185–1191

Grieco M H 1980 Infections in the Abnormal Host. York Medical Books

Gronowicz E, Coutinko A 1974 Selective triggering of B cell subpopulations by mitogens. European Journal of Immunology 4: 771–776

Gross L 1965 Immunological defect in aged populations and its relationship to cancer. Cancer 18: 201–204

Grossman J, Baum J, Fusner J, Condemi J, GLuckman J 1975 The effect of aging and acute illness on delayed hypersensitivity. Journal of Allergy and Clinical Immunology 55: 268–275

Gupta S, Good R A 1979 Subpopulations of human T lymphocytes. X. Alterations in T, B, third population cells and T cells with receptors for IgM (Tmu) or G (T gamma) in aging humans. Journal of Immunology 122: 1214–1219

Haäijman J J, Van der Berg P, Brinkhof J 1977 Immunoglobulin class and subclass levels in murine serum. Immunology 32: 923–927

Haley R W, Hooton T M, Culver D H et al 1981 Nosocomial infection in U.S. Hospitals, 1975–1976. Estimated frequency by selected characteristics of patients. American Journal of Medicine 70: 947–959

Hallgren H M, Buckley E C, Gilbertsen V A, Yunis E J 1973 Lymphocyte PHA responsiveness, immunoglobulins and autoantibodies in aging humans. Journal of Immunology 111: 1101–1107

Harrison D E 1975 Normal function of transplanted marrow cell lines from aged mice. Journal of Gerontology 30: 279–285

Hays E F 1967 The effects of allografts of thymic epithelial reticular cells on the lymphoid tissues of neonatally thymectomised mice. Blood 29: 29–40

Heffron R 1979 Pneumonia with Special Reference to Pneumococcus Lobar Pneumonia. Harvard University Press

Heidrick M L 1972 Age related changes in hydrolase activity of peritoneal macrophages. Gerontology 12: 28

Hinsull S M, Bellamy D 1974 Development and involution of thymus grafts in rats with reference to age and sex determination. Differentiation 2: 299–305

Hirokawa T 1977 In: Makinodan T, Yunis E (eds) Immunology and Aging, Plenum, New York, p 51

Hirschmann J V, Lipsky B A 1981 Pneumococcal vaccine in the United States: a critical analysis. Journal of the American Medical Association 246: 1428–1232

Hollingsworth J W, Gailotte R 1981 B lymphocyte maturation in cultures from blood of elderly men: A comparison of plaque forming cells, cells containing intracytoplasmic immunoglobulin and cell proliferation. Mechanisms of Aging and Development 15: 9–18

Hooper B, Whittingham S, Mathews J D, Mackay I R, Curnow D H 1972 Autoimmunity in a rural community. Clinical and Experimental Immunology 12: 79–87

Horan M A, Leahy B, Fox R A, Stretton T B, Haeney M 1984 Immunological abnormalities in patients with chronic bronchial sepsis; a possible relationship with endotoxaemia. British Journal of Diseases of the Chest 78: 66–74

Hori Y, Perkins E H, Halsall M K 1973 Decline in PHA responsiveness of spleen cells from aging mice. Proceedings of the Society for Experimental and Biological Medicine 144: 48–53

Howells C H L, Vesselinova-Jenkins C K, Evans A D, James J 1975 Influenza vaccination and mortality from bronchopneumonia in the elderly. Lancet i: 381–388

Inagaki J, Rodrigez V, Bodey G P 1974 Cause of death in cancer patients. Cancer 33: 568–573

Inkeles B, Innes J B, Kuntz M M, Kadish A S, Weksler M E 1977 Immunological studies of aging III: Cytokinetic basis for the impaired responses of lymphocytes from aged humans to plant lectins. Journal of Experimental Medicine 145: 1176–1187

Isaacs B 1981 'Is geriatrics a speciality?' In: Arie A (ed) Health Care of the Elderly, Croom Helm Ltd., London, ch. 14, p 224

Ishii T, Hosada Y, Maeda K 1980 Cause of death in the extreme aged — a pathologic survey of 5106 elderly persons 80 years old and over. Age and Ageing 9: 81–89

Ivanova N I 1978 Age characteristics of the phagocytic reaction of neutrophils. Vrachebnoe Delo 5: 49

José D G, Good R A 1973 Quantitative effects of nutritional protein and calorie deficiency upon immune responses to tumours in mice. Cancer Research 33: 807–812

Kampmann J, Molholm Hansen J, Siersbock-Nielsen K, Laursen H 1972 Effect of some drugs on penicillin half-life in blood. Clinical Pharmacology and Therapeutics 13: 516–519

Kasel J A, Hume E B, Fulk R V, Togo Y, Huber M, Hornick R B 1969 Antibody responses in nasal secretions and serum of elderly persons following local or parenteral administration of influenza virus vaccine. Journal of Immunology 102: 555–562

Kaufmann P 1947 Pneumonia in old age. Active immunization against pneumonia with pneumococcus polysaccharide; results of a six year study. Archives of Internal Medicine 79: 518–531

Kavett J 1977 A perspective on the significance of pandemic influenza. American Journal of Public Health 67(11): 1063–1070

Kay M M B 1979 In: Orimo K, Shimada K, Iriki M, Maeda D (eds) Recent Advances in Gerontology, Excerpta Medica, Amsterdam, p 442

Kay M M B, Makinodan T 1978 In: Natelson S, Pesce A J, Dietz A A (eds). Clinical Immunochemistry, Chemical and Cellular Bases and Applications in Disease, American Association for Clinical Chemistry, Washington DC, p 192

Kay M M B, Mendoza, J, Diven J, Denton T, Union N, Lajiness M 1979 Age related changes in the immune system of mice of medium and long-lived strains and hybrids. I. Organ, cellular and activity changes. Mechanisms of Aging and Development 11: 295–346

Kishimoto, S, Takahama T, Mizumachi H 1976 In vitro immune response to the 2,4,6 trinitrophenyl determinant in aged C57BL/6J mice: changes in the humoral immune response to avidity for the TNP determinant and responsiveness to LPS effect with aging. Journal of Immunology 116: 294–300

Kishimoto S, Tomino S, Inomata K et al 1978 Age related changes in the subsets and functions of human T lymphocytes. Journal of Immunology 121: 1773–1780

Kishimoto S, Tomino S, Mitsuya H, Fujiwaa H, Tsuda H 1980 Age related decline in the in vitro and in vivo syntheses of anti-tetanus toxoid antibody in humans. The Journal of Immunology 125(5): 2347–2352

Klein G 1968 Tumour specific transplantation antigens. A Clowes Memorial Lecture. Cancer Research 28: 625–635

Kluge R M, Waldman R H 1979 Antibody to swine influenza virus in serum and nasal secretions of volunteers over the age of 55 years. The Journal of Infectious Diseases 140: 635–636

Kreger B E, Craven D E, Car'ing P C, McCabe W R 1980a Gram negative bacteraemia III. Reassessment of aetiology, epidemiology and ecology in 612 patients. American Journal of Medicine 68: 332–343

Kreger B E, Craven D E, McCabe W R 1980b Gram negative bacteraemia IV Re-evaluation of clinical features and treatment in 612 patients. American Journal of Medicine 68: 316–335

Kurtzman N A, Rogers P W, Harter H R 1970 Neurotoxic reaction to penicillin and carbenicillin. Journal of American Medical Association 214: 1320–1321

Lee K, Berry D 1977 Functional heterogeneity in macrophages activated by Corynebacterium parvum Journal of Immunology 118: 1530–1540

Leech S H 1980 Cellular immunosenescence. Gerontology 26: 330–345

Legge J S, Austin C M 1968 Antigen localisation and the immune response as a function of age. Australian Journal of Experimental Biology and Medical Science 46: 361–365

Lerner S A, Matz G J 1980 Aminoglycoside ototoxicity. American Journal of Otolaryngology 1: 169–179

Levine L, Wyman L 1965 Survey of immunity by serologic methods. The New England Journal of Medicine 272: 23–26

McGowan J E, Barnes M W, Finland M 1975 Bacteraemia at Boston General Hospital. Journal of Infectious Diseases 132: 316–335

Mackenzie J S 1977 Influenza subunit vaccine: antibody responses to one and two doses of vaccine and length of response with particular reference to the elderly. British Medical Journal 1: 200–202

Maddern J W, Croker J R, Beynon G P J 1981 Septicaemia in the elderly. Postgraduate Medical Journal 57: 502–506

Marine W M, Thomas J E 1973 Age related response to 1000 CCA unit zonally purified, inactivated influenza vaccines in volunteers in the U.S.A. Postgraduate Medical Journal 49: 164–168

Makinodan T, Peterson W J 1962 Relative antibody-forming capacity of spleen cells as function of age. Proceedings of the National Academy of Sciences of the United States of America 48: 234–238

Makinodan T, Kay M M B 1980 Age influence on the immune system. Advances in Immunology 29: 287–330

Mather V, Bentley D W, Hall 1980 Concurrent respiratory syncytial virus and influenza A infections in the institutionalized elderly and chronically ill. Annals of Internal Medicine 93: 49–52

Meredith P J, Kristie J A, Walford R L 1979 Aging increases expression of LPS induced autoantibody-secreting B cells. Journal of Immunology 123: 87–91

Metcalf D, Moulds R, Pike B 1967 Influence of spleen and thymus on immune responses in aging mice. Clinical and Experimental Immunology 2: 109–120

Moroni M, Capsoni F, Caredda F, Lazzarin A, Besana C 1976 Dimostrazione di un diffetto granulocitario in soggetti anziani e correlazione con la presenza di auto-anticorpi. Bulletin First Sieroter Milan 55: 317–322

Miller A E 1980 Selective decline in cellular immune response to varicella zoster in the elderly. Neurology 30: 582–587

Müller J L, Gertner M H Buzby G P, Goodhart G L, Rosato B 1979 Implications of malnutrition in the surgical patient. Archives of Surgery 114: 121–125

Nagel J E, Chrest F J, Adler W H 1981 Enumeration of T lymphocyte subsets by monclonal antibodies in young and aged humans. Journal of Immunology 127: 2086–2088

Nilsson B S 1971 In vitro lymphocyte reactivity to PPD and phytohaemagglutinin in relation to PPD skin reactivity and age. Scandinavian Journal of Respiration 52: 39–47

Ockhuizen T, Pandey J P, Galbraith G M P, Fudenberg H H, Haines C G 1982 Autoantibodies and immunoglobulin allotypes in healthy North American blacks of different age groups. Mechanisms of Aging and Development 19: 103–111

Ogden D A, Mickliem H S 1976 The fate of serially transplanted bone marrow cell populations from young and old donors. Transplantation 22: 287–293

Old L J, Boyce S E A 1964 Immunology of experimental tumours. Annual Review of Medicine 15: 167–186

Orr L H, Rudisill E, Brodkin R, Hamilton R W 1978 Exacerbation of renal failure associated with doxycycline. Archives of Internal Medicine 138: 793–794

Palmblad J, Haak A 1978 Aging does not change blood granulocyte bactericidal capacity and levels of complement factors 3 and 4. Gerontology 24: 381–385

Pantelouris E M M 1972 Thymic involution and aging: an hypothesis.

Experimental Gerontology 7: 73–81

Pathy M S 1967 Clinical Presentation of myocardial infarction in the elderly. British Heart Journal 29: 190–199

Paul J R, Bunnell W W 1932 The presence of heterophilic antibodies in infectious mononucleosis. American Journal of Medical Science 183: 90–104

Perillie P E, Nolan J D, Finch S D 1962 Studies of the resistance to infection in diabetes mellitus: local exudative cellular response. Journal of Laboratory and Clinical Medicine 59: 1008–1015

Perkins E H 1971 Phagocytic activity of aged mice. Journal of the Reticuloendothelial Society 9: 642–643

Perkins E H, Cacheiro L H 1977 A multiple parameter comparison of immunocompetence and tumour resistance in aged BALB/c mice. Mechanisms of Aging and Development 6: 15–24

Phair J P 1979 Aging and infection: a review. Journal of Chronic Diseases 32: 535–540

Phair J P, Reising M S, Metzger E 1980 Bacteraemia infection and malnutrition in patients with solid tumours: investigation of host defence mechanism. Cancer 45: 2702–2706

Pisciotta A V, Westring D W, De Prey C, Walsh B 1967 Mitogenic effect of PHA at different ages. Nature, London 215: 193–194

Platt D, Pauli H 1972 Age dependent determination of lysosomal enzymes in the liver of spironolactone and aldosterone pretreated rats. Experimental Gerontology 7: 1–7

Portaro J K, Glick G I, Zighelboim J 1978 Population immunology: age and immune cell parameters. Clinical Immunology and Immunopathology 11: 339–345

Powell R, Fernandez L A 1980 Proliferative responses of peripheral blood lymphocytes to polyclonal activation. A comparison of young and elderly individuals. Mechanisms of Aging and Development 13: 241–246

Price G B, Makinodan T 1972 Immunologic deficiencies in senescence. I. Characterisation of extrinsic deficiencies. Journal of Immunology 108: 403–412

Primi D, Hammarstrom L, Smith C I E, Moller G 1977a characterisation of self reactive B cells by polyclonal B cell activators. Journal of Experimental Medicine 145: 21–30

Primi D, Smith C I E, Hämmarstom L, Lündquist P G, Moller G 1977b Evidence for the existence of self reactive human B lymphocytes. Clinical Experimental Immunology 29: 316–319

Primi D, Smith C I E, Hammarstrom L, Moller G 1977c Polyclonal B cell activators induce immunological response to autologous serum proteins. Cellular Immunology 34: 367–375

Puxty J A, Lenton J, Fox R A 1983 Unpublished results

Renton K W, Gray J D, Hung O R 1981 Depression of theophylline elimination by erythromycin. Clinical Pharmacology and Therapeutics 30: 422–426

Roberts-Thompson I C, Whittingham S, Youngchaiyud U, Mackay I R 1974 Aging, immune response and mortality. Lancet ii: 368–370

Robinson M R G, Cross R J, Shetty M B, Kittal B 1980 Bacteraemia and bacterogenic shock in district hospital urological practice. British Journal of Urology 52: 10–14

Rowley J J, Buchanan H, Mackay I R 1968 Reciprocal change with age in antibody to extrinsic and intrinsic antigens. Lancet ii: 24–26

Ruben F L, Johnston F, Streiff E J 1974 Influenza in a partially immunized aged population. Journal of the American Medical Association 230: 863–866

Ruben F L, Nagel J, Fireman P 1978 Antitoxin responses in the elderly to tetanus-diptheria (td) immunization. American Journal of Epidemiology 108(2): 145–149

Ruco L P, Meltzer M S 1978 Macrophage activation for tumor cytotoxicity: Increased lymphokine responsiveness of peritoneal macrophages during acute inflammation. Journal of Immunology 120: 1054–1062

Santisteban G A 1960 The growth and involution of lymphatic tissue and its interrelationships to aging and to the growth of the adrenal glands and sex organs in CBA mice. Anatomical Record 136: 117–126

Schaberg D R, Weinstein R A, Stamm W E 1978 Epidemics of nosocomial urinary tract infection caused by resistant gram negative bacilli: epidemiology and control. Journal of Infectious Disease 133: 363–366

Schoenbaum S C, McNeil B J, Kavet J 1976 The swine-influenza decision. The New England Journal of Medicine 295: 759–765

Schümer W 1976 Steroids in the treatment of clinical septic shock. Annals of Surgery 184: 333–341

Sègre D, Sègre M 1976 Humoral immunity in aged mice. II Increased suppressor T cell activity in immunologically deficient old mice. Journal of Immunology 116: 735–738

Serie C, Barme M, Hannoun C, Thibon M, Beck H, Aquino J P 1977 Effects of vaccination on an influenza epidemic in a geriatric hospital. Developments in Biological Standardization 39: 317–321

Shouval D, Ligumsky M, Ben-Ishay D 1978 Effect of co-trimazole on normal creatinine clearance. Lancet ii: 244–245

Silverman E M, Silverman A G 1977 Granulocyte adherence in the elderly. American Journal of Clinical Pathology 67: 49–52

Sinclair N R St C 1979 Modulation of immunity by antibody, antigen-antibody complexes and antigen. Pharmacology and Therapeutics 4: 355–432

Smith A M 1976 The effects of age on the immune response to type III pneumococcal polysaccharide and bacterial lipopolysaccharide in BALB/c, SJL/J and C3H mice. Journal of Immunology 116: 469–474

Smith S M, Evans J, Steel C M 1974 Age related variation in proportion of circulated T cells. Lancet ii: 922–924

Solomonova K, Vizev S 1973 Immunological reactivity of senescent and old people actively immunized with tetanus toxoid. Zeitschrift fuer Immunitaetsforschung 146: 81–90

Somers H, Kuhn W J 1972 Blood group antibodies in old age. Proceedings of the Society for Experimental and Biological Medicine 141: 1104–1107

Spector W G, Walters M N, Willoughby D A 1965 The origins of mononuclear cells in the inflammatory exudates induced by fibrinogen. Journal of Pathology and Bacteriology 90: 181–182

Stamm W E 1978 Infections related to medical devices. Annals of Internal Medicine 89: 764–769

Stead W W 1981 Tuberculosis among elderly persons. An outbreak in a nursing home. Annals of Internal Medicine 94: 606–610

Steere A C, Mallison G F 1975 Handwashing practices for the prevention of nosocomial infections. Annals of Internal Medicine 83: 683–690

Stein M, Schiavi R C, Camerino M 1976 Influence of brain and behaviour on the immune system. Science 191: 435–440

Stuart W H, Dull H B, Newton L H, McQueen J L, Schiff E R 1969 Evaluation of monovalent influenza vaccine in a retirement community during the epidemic of 1965–1966. Journal of the American Medical Association 209: 232–238

Stutman O, Yunis E J, Good R A 1968 Deficient immunological function of NZB mice. Proceedings of the Society for Experimental and Biological Medicine 127: 1204–1207

Svänbom M 1980 A prospective study of septicaemia II. Clinical manifestations and complications. Results of antimicrobial treatment and reports of a follow up study. Scandinavian Journal of Infectious Diseases 12: 189–206

Tada T, Takemori T, Okumura K, Nonaka T, Tokuhisa T 1978 Two distinct types of helper T cells involved in the secondary antibody response. Independent and synergistic effects of Ia$^-$$^+$ and Ia$^-$ helper T cells. Journal of Experimental Medicine 147: 446–458

Talal N, Pillarisetty R 1975 IgM and IgG antibodies to DNA, RNA and DNA:RNA in systemic lupus erythematosus. Clinical Immunology and Immunopathology 4: 24–31

Tam C F, Walford R L 1978 Cyclic nucleotide levels in resting and mitogen-stimulated spleen cell suspensions from young and old mice. Mechanisms of Aging and Development 7: 309–320

Tannenbaum A, Silverston H 1953 Nutrition in relation to cancer. Advances in Cancer Research 1: 451–501

Thornton G F 1971 Infections and Diabetes. Medical Clinics of North America 55: 931–938

Tinker G M 1981 Clinical presentation of myocardial infarction in the elderly. Age and Ageing 10: 237–240

Triggs E J, Johnson J M, Learoyd B 1980 Absorption and disposition of ampicillin in the elderly. European Journal of Clinical Pharmacology 18: 195–198

Trinca J C 1974 Immunity to tetanus in Victoria, 1973. Medical Journal of Australia 2: 595–598

Twomey P L, Catalona W J, Chretien P B 1974 Cellular immunity in cured cancer patients. Cancer 33: 435–440

Tyan M L 1977 Age related decrease in mouse T cell progenitors. Journal of Immunology 118: 846–851

Valenti W M, Trudell R, Bentley D W 1978 Factors predisposing to oropharyngeal colonization with gram negative bacilli in the aged. New England Journal of Medicine 298: 1108–1111

Van de Meer J W, Beelen R H, Fluitsma D M, van Furth R 1979 Ultrastructure of mononuclear phagocytes in liquid bone marrow cultures. A study of peroxidatic activity. Experimental Medicine 149: 17–26

Van der Veen J, Van der Werf P A M, Masurel N, Polak M F 1977 Influenza in een gedeelteliijk gevaccineerde gemeenschap van bejarrden. Nederlands Tijdschrift vcoor Geneeskunde 121: 1259–1262

Van Epps D E, Goodwin J S, Murphy S 1978 Age-dependent variations in polymorphonuclear leukocyte chemiluminescence. Infections and Immunity 22: 57–61

Vartia K O, Leikola E 1960 Serum levels of antibiotics in young and old subjects following administration of dihydrostreptomycin and tetracycline. Journal of Gerontology 15: 392–394

Vella P P, McLean A A, Woodhour A F, Weibel R E, Hilleman M R 1980 Persistence of pneumococcal antibodies in human subjects following vaccination (40891). Proceedings of the Society for Experimental Biology and Medicine 164: 435–438

Verghese M W, Snyderman R 1981 Differential anti-inflammatory effects of LPS in susceptible and resistant mouse strains. Journal of Immunology 127: 288–293

Waldenstrom J G 1973 In: Azar M A, Potter M (eds) Multiple Myeloma and Related Disorders, Harper, New York, p 247

Waldorf D S, Willkens R F, Decker J L 1968 Impaired delayed hypersensitivity in an aging population. Journal of the American Medical Association 203: 831–834

Walford R L 1967 The immunologic theory of aging. Advances in Gerontological Research 2: 159–204

Walford R L 1969 The Immunologic Theory of Aging. Munksgaard, Copenhagen

Walford R L 1974 Immunologic theory of aging: current status. Federation Proceedings 33: 2020–2027

Walters C S, Claman H N 1975 Age related changes in cell mediated immunity of BALB/c mice. Journal of Immunology 115: 1438–1443

Weindruch R H, Kristie J A, Cheney L, Kay E, Walford R L 1979 Influence of controlled dietary restriction on immunologic function and aging. Federation Proceedings 38: 2007–2015

Weinstein L, Dalton A C 1968 Host determinants of response to antimicrobial agents. New England Journal of Medicine 279: 467–473

Weksler M E 1978 The influence of immune function on lifespan. Bulletin of the New York Academy of Medicine 54: 964–969

Weksler M E, Hutteroth T H 1974 Impaired lymphocyte function in aged humans. Journal of Clinical Investigation 53: 99–104

Wilson C B, Jones T, Shave L 1981 Bacteraemia in a small non-urban community hospital. Journal of Family Practice 12: 37–41

Woda B A, Feldman J D 1979 Density of surface immunoglobulin and capping on rat B lymphocytes. Journal of Experimental Medicine 149: 416–423

Zacharski L R, Elveback L R, Kinman J W, 1971 Lymphocyte counts in healthy adults. American Journal of Clinical Pathology 56: 148–150

Psychology of aging — personality and its attributes

INTRODUCTION

The psychology of aging has changed during the last 25 years not only regarding the quantity of research but also regarding methodology, theoretical orientation, and definition of aims. The change in quantity can be illustrated by the fact that at the end of the fifties only the 'Journal of Gerontology' regularly published studies on behavioural and social aspects of aging (about 20 articles per year) whereas at the beginning of the eighties there exist about 14 journals around the world which publish exclusively, or at least regularly, findings from studies on psychological and social gerontology. As far as content is concerned, there is another decisive difference: whereas at the end of the fifties the issue of mental decline was the dominating theme, today behavioural studies on aging deal with a very broad range of topics such as cognitive and psychomotor functioning, emotional as well as social adjustment, physical and social correlates of stability and change of different attributes of personality (see Birren, 1960; Birren and Schaie, 1977; Birren and Sloane, 1980; Riegel, 1977).

The issue of cross-sectional vs longitudinal approach

The most important change in methodology is concerned with the role of cross-sectional vs. longitudinal research. At the end of the fifties only data from cross-sectional research on aging could be referred to (see Jones, 1960), whereas data from longitudinal studies on aging were not available until the end of the sixties and even most of these were cross-sectional descriptions of the samples at the first measurement point (see Stone and Norris, 1964: Eisdorfer and Cohen, 1961; Cohen et al, 1961).

The first analyses of longitudinal data did not confirm findings from cross-sectional studies regarding a universal decline in physiological functioning (Damon, 1965), mental abilities (Jarvik, 1962; Riegel et al, 1967; Schaie, 1978) or other personality dimensions (Maddox, 1965). These findings were taken as an argument against

the validity of cross-sectional studies which confound age-related changes with changes due to different socio-cultural influences as existing in different cohorts (Schaie, 1965; Baltes, 1968). Longitudinal research pointed also to a significant difference between survivors and non-survivors of the sample at the first measurement point, with survivors always scoring higher in intellectual performance (Jarvik and Falek, 1963; Riegel et al, 1967; Schaie, 1965), activity (Lehr and Schmitz-Scherzer, 1976) and other personality variables (Palmore, 1981). From these findings longitudinal studies were considered non-representative because of a selective drop-out (Riegel et al, 1967; Schaie, 1972).

As an alternative the cross-sequential analysis was recommended by which samples from different cohorts are followed through a longer period of time. Comparing two successive 7-year cohorts over each 7-year age range from 25 to 81 years Schaie and Parham (1977) showed that reliable age decrements for most of the primary mental abilities such as space, reasoning, number, education and aptitude are not found before the age of 75 years. The two exceptions are a very speed-dependent test, namely word-fluency (53 years) and intellectual aptitude (67 years). A high degree of consistency of mental test performance up to the age of 75 years was found also in the Goteborg Longitudinal Study (Svanborg et al, 1982). Discussion between the possible contributions of cross-sectional, longitudinal, and cross-sequential approaches will certainly continue.

The issue of age and interindividual variability

A second trend in the psychology of aging is related to the issue of interindividual differences. As part of a life span psychology (Baltes and Willis, 1977), psychology of aging will put the main emphasis on normative data which certainly cannot be provided by longitudinal research due to the drop-out effect. However, if aspects of personality such as the universe of interindividual differences (Cattell and Kline, 1977; Guilford, 1959) are taken account of also, in studies on infancy, adolescence, early and late adulthood (Thomae, 1979), the search for individual and for group differences in consistency and change during the life span will be of increasing interest to life span psychology.

In gerontology the issue of interindividual variability has been raised increasingly during the last decade; differences in longevity and problems of progeria have attracted attention in the biology of aging for many years (see Viidik, 1982, p. 55). Longitudinal studies on renal function (Shock et al, 1979) point to very variable patterns of change in these functions with increasing age. Koller (1972) pointed to the extended variation of parameter for blood pressure or glucose in old age. Landahl et al (1981) and Svanborg (1982) pointed to an increasing interindividual variability of other components of blood or of tolerance to drugs in old age. In biological gerontology the whole approach to the development of a 'functional age' index (Borkan and Norris, 1980; Furukawa, 1976; Shock, 1981) is based on findings of an increasing interindividual variability of parameters like metabolism, blood pressure, haemoglobin, vision, hearing, etc. A large amount of interindividual differences was found in longitudinal EEG studies (Busse, 1979).

In psychological gerontology a very significant increase with age in the standard deviation of scores of a psychomotor test was found by Mathey (1976) by two cross-sectional analyses of data from the Bonn Longitudinal Study on Aging. The standard deviation of the WAIS scores of the same sample increased from 15.1 at the first measurement point (1965) to 17.7 at the sixth measurement (1977). In the psychomotor test requiring very fast information processing the standard deviation in the time needed to meet a 50 per cent success criterion increased from 32 sec at measurement point (m.p.) I to 53 sec at m.p. V (Mathey, 1976). From an interdisciplinary study on community aged Bocher et al (1973) questioned whether it is possible to trace a 'normal process of aging' at all because of the large amount of interindividual differences.

This kind of doubt in any generalisations about the psychology of aging was raised even more in studies focussing on *cultural and societal impacts of aging*. The great changes in the age structures of industrialized societies during the last century and in developing countries in the forthcoming half century (UN World Assembly, 1982) are the outcome of progress in treatment, prevention and medical care as part of a sociocultural change. The same is true for many behavioural aspects which are influenced by changes in the whole socio-cultural system (de Beauvoir, 1970; Neugarten, 1982).

Other sources for group differences in aging are related to social class (Rosenberg, 1970), education (Rudinger, 1974), sex, ecology, and the home environment. The information gathered from this differential research has various important aspects for the design of studies on aging: for instance, there is a need for multidimensional approaches which go beyond using the age variable as the independent one and behavioural variable as the dependent one. Information on many aspects of the 'life space' of the aged person has to be gathered and so allows a multivariate analysis of the dependent variable.

In longitudinal research these variables then develop new relevance as they no longer compete with other 'normative' approaches to the study of aging. Their use is the only effective way to study different patterns of aging (Birren et al, 1963; Thomae, 1976) and the correlates of these different patterns.

Following this discussion of trends in the development of psycho-gerontology we shall now consider the possible sources of interindividual differences in consistency and change of personality in old age, and then the issue of the most relevant dimensions of these differences and finally the problem of 'patterns' of aging.

ORIGINS AND/OR CORRELATES OF INTERINDIVIDUAL VARIABILITY IN PSYCHOLOGICAL AGING

Biological and health determinants

Apart from the extreme variations of aging such as progeria on the one hand and great longevity on the other, there are important indications for a major role of heredity in the determination of differences in psychological aging. Jarvik (1975) summarized the findings of the Kallmann-Jarvik study on senescent twins by stating that mono-zygote twins were more alike than fraternal twins in mental test performance through a period of more than 20 years. The finding certainly will have to be discussed in terms of the whole nature-nurture issue regarding intelligence (see p. 107). But even allowing for the full impact of environment the hereditary components of interindividual variation must not be neglected.

The relationship between physical health and behaviour of the aged is a major research area. Simon (1965) found lower scores in different mental tests in aged persons with cardiovascular disease compared to normals. According to Birren (1963), Spieth (1965), Botwinick and Storand (1974) old people with hypertension and related cerebrovascular disease have slower reaction times in a multiple-choice reaction-test. Hypertension in middle-aged persons is associated with cognitive deficits such as found in cases with minor brain damage (Goldman et al, 1974). Decreases in WAIS scores were observed only in subjects of the Duke Longitudinal Study who suffered from high blood pressure (Wilkie and Eisdorfer, 1971). In the Bonn

Longitudinal Study on Aging (Thomae, 1976) we correlated an overall rating of the health of the subjects by our medical staff with different behavioural variables and found significantly poorer performances by the less healthy in the WAIS-test (Grombach, 1976), a psychomotor test (Mathey, 1976), and also in personality variables such as 'degree of activity', 'morale' and responsiveness.

'Health' is defined by WHO as physical, psychological and social well-being. Some studies correlate subjectively perceived health and behavioural measures. For instance, health (as measured this way) is related to life satisfaction (Adams, 1971; Lehr, 1982a) and to different ways of coping with problems (Thomae, 1983).

The relationship between the status of health care and well-being and other behavioural variables is important. No systematic studies exist so far but it is evident that the later behaviour of a stroke patient having access to a rehabilitation center will differ from one with no chance for rehabilitation. Psychology of aging is thus dependent on the progress of studies on the effectiveness of certain forms of health care. Since the availability of rehabilitation is dependent on the development of the general health care system within society, this health-behaviour relationship must take account of social factors involved in shaping health as well as behaviour.

Cultural determinants of aging

Sociologists and historians have stressed the impact of culture on the status and the behaviour of the aged. According to the modernization theory (Cowgill and Holmes, 1972; Palmore and Manton, 1974) old people in non-Western societies more often have the same social status as the young whereas in Western, industrialized societies the old have a lower status. In a cross-national study, carried out in Argentina, Chile, India, Israel, Nigeria and Bangladesh by Bengtson et al (1975) the hypothesis that the aged in non-Western societies were generally accorded a higher degree of prestige was confirmed. There were intracultural differences, however, since those subcultures in non-Western societies most exposed to Western influences, namely workers in industry, had more positive attitudes toward the aged than people in rural areas.

In a cross cultural study in 57 non-industrialized societies it was shown that 'supporting behaviour' toward the frail elderly was the most frequently observed way of interaction with the aged in most of the countries (Glascock and Feinman, 1981). However, even if these favourable behavioural patterns were present they could be replaced or supplemented by non-intervention practices or even by death-accelerating practices. Of course even the act of killing an aged person can be perceived as friendly behaviour both by the victim and the aggressor — dependent on the cultural context.

A major impact of culture on the situation of the aged results from migration of the young productive population from remote rural areas to the metropolitan centres as occurs in many African, Asian or Latin American countries. This results in a considerable deprivation of the aged with all its detrimental behavioural effects (Schade, 1982).

Education and aging

The intervening role of education in the relationship between age and cognitive functioning has been demonstrated in many, mainly cross-sectional, studies (Birren and Morrison, 1961; Granick and Friedman, 1967; Blum and Jarvik, 1974; Nehrke, 1972). In some of these studies age differences in intelligence-scores disappeared completely or decreased to insignificant levels when the cross-sectional samples were controlled for education. Since the differences between cohorts (e.g. of 1890–95 compared with 1950–55) are mainly defined by differences in educational opportunities this is a major argument for cohort-specific interpretations of cross-sectional aging data.

Rudinger (1974) used multivariate analysis of a cross-sectional study of a large sample of men and women (age 20–90 years). He showed that the huge age differences contributed to the explanation of WAIS-test scores just as much as the vastly smaller differences in degree of education — namely by 23 per cent. Occupational status explained another 20 per cent, health only 8 per cent. The same finding was confirmed by another study on community aged (Schmitz-Scherzer et al, 1974).

The (cross-sectional) sample of the first round of the second Duke Gerontological Study on Aging was divided into a group with 0–11 years of education and a group with 16 years of education. The average IQ of the first group was 81, and that of the second 127 (Palmore, 1981).

From an analysis of the data of the first (1965) and the sixth measurement point (1977) of the Bonn Longitudinal Study on Aging, Rudinger showed that the differences in the WAIS global scores between aged persons with up to 8 years education on the one hand and 9–12 years on the other hand remained consistent over a 12 year span. In the verbal scores the gaps between these groups even widened, since the scores of the group with fewer years of education decreased whereas those with more education increased by 1977.

The same study also dealt with personality differences between aged from different educational backgrounds. Activity, responsiveness and emotional stability were higher with more education at measurement point I and these differences remained consistent up to measurement point IV (Grombach, 1976).

The Duke Longitudinal Study on Aging provided evidence for differences between old people with different educational backgrounds regarding extra-familial social activities, perceived health and positive affect (Palmore, 1981). While all these findings favoured the better educated, Shanan (1975) found Israeli middle-aged men and women were more affected by the political events of their country between 1965–1972 if they had more education. Those with less education proved to be more emotionally stable.

Thus the effect of education on the behaviour and well-being of the aged will differ from situation to situation. For normal aging in the community the better educated seem to be better prepared. They are also more likely to participate in pre-retirement programmes (Lehr et al, 1981) and are less sensitive to the impact of hospitalization (Rudinger, 1974b).

Socio-economic status (SES), behaviour and well-being in the aged

The impact of socio-economic status (as defined by occupation and income) on health has been the subject of a number of studies (Riley and Foner, 1968; Harris, 1975; Hauss and Blume, 1974). Cross-sectional analysis of the first round of both Duke Longitudinal studies have clear evidence of better health and fewer psychosomatic symptoms in the upper SES group (Palmore, 1981). Eitner (1978) stressed that these SES-differences may be explained also by different life styles.

Table 6.1 Correlates of income and longitudinal patterns of consistency and change in psychological variables in community aged during 12 years (from Thomae, 1983)

Variable	r
Perceived stress regarding income	−.43‡
Satisfaction with situation in family	.3†
Satisfaction with situation in spouse role	.3†
Feeling of being needed in family	.24*
Satisfaction with situation in kin role	
Achievement-related behaviour as response to family problems	.27†
Satisfaction with situation regarding housing	.2*
Feeling of general disappointment	−.3†
Belief in unchangeability of unfavourable conditions	−.3†
Feeling of being restricted and of lacking any chances	−.5†
WAIS Global score	.2*
WAIS Performance score	.3†
Raven Progressive Matrices	.2*
Positive attitude toward future	.3†
Activity	.2*
Ego control	.3†

* significant at the .05 level
† significant at the .01 level
‡ significant at the .001 level

Another major area of research is the relationship between SES and life satisfaction. Edwards and Klemmack (1973), Chatfield (1977) and others concluded from different cross-sectional studies that income was the most important factor in the variance in life satisfaction. Palmore (1981) however found that differences in life satisfaction between SES groups required a classification system more complex than that of income. Bengston et al (1977) pointed to the relationship between the social networks for the aged which may influence life satisfaction. In analysing the correlates between income on the one hand and the longitudinal patterns of consistency and change over 12 years of quite an array of behavioural variables (as measured in the Bonn Longitudinal Study on Aging) on the other, we found 18 significant relationships (Thomae, 1933) (see Table 6.1). Apart from cognitive measures and personality variables like activity and ego control, five variables were related to the situation in and the behaviour towards the family, three to economic stress or satisfaction with housing, and three for certain systems of beliefs and motivations. These findings stress the importance of economic aspects in relation to life satisfaction in old age.

The influence of the cohort

Anastasi (1958) was the first to point to the confounding effects of cohorts in explaining the effects of the different cultural-educational influences on two cross-sectional samples of persons respectively 20 and 40 years of age. As these influences improved during the last century, Baltes (1968, 1977) predicted an acceleration of development with each later cohort and a decisive decrease in the age-differences in cognitive functioning and adjustment in the aged around the year 2030 compared to that of today (Baltes and Wiley, 1977).

Cohort effects are demonstrated also in the sex differences — which favour men — in intelligence and personality measures of pre-1930 cohorts (Rudinger, 1970; Savage et al, 1977). Studies comparing boys and girls from cohorts of 1940 and later either did not provide evidence for sex differences or show better scores for girls. These changes in sex differences between early-century and mid-century cohorts can be explained only by reference to the different social histories of boys and girls between the different generations (Maccoby and Jaklin, 1974; Lehr, 1969). A major support for the effects of cohort on mental health comes from the Midtown Manhattan Study (Srole and Fisher, 1980) in which cohorts defined by ages from 20–59 years in 1954 on the one hand and in 1974 on the other hand were compared. The dependent variable, the rate of 'mental health impairment', increased with increasing age in each of the two samples. Comparing the groups with identical age in 1954 and 1974 there was a decrease in the rate of impairment foom 22 per cent in 1954 to 10 per cent in 1974. This difference was mainly due to changes in the female group. While in the year 1954, 26 per cent of the women (age group 50–59 years) indicated some kind of mental impairment, this percentage dropped for women of the same age group 20 years later to 11 per cent. The mental impairment rate of age groups 40–49 years in men did not differ in 1954 and 1974, while in women of the same ages it dropped from 21 per cent to 8 per cent. This certainly points to the influence of social change, especially that relating to the woman's role.

Findings like these emphasize the interrelationship between the cohort-centered approach in life span psychology on the one hand and the relationships between political, social and economic history or the other. Elder (1974, 1982) and others were able to trace sex-specific effects of the great economic depression in 1930 in the Berkeley study.

Gender differences in aging

The higher life expectancy of women compared to men is observed in this century across cultures and continents (Hauser, 1976; Imhof, 1981). Palmore (1977/82) points to the same kind of gender differences in animals and hypothesizes that it may be explained by genetic influences. In many countries such as Russia the sex differences in the demographic structure of the aged population are to be explained by the heavy losses of men during two World Wars.

Contrary to this biological advantage to women there exist cumulative disadvantages in their social situations which go back to early childhood (Atchley, 1976; Lehr, 1978).

From an analysis of books for children and text books for grammar schools Lehr (1978) showed that the image of elderly women in society is worse than that of men. S. de Beauvoir (1970) brought evidence for the same thesis from historical sources, and Neugarten and Gutmann (1968) from studies on American students. Associated with poorer educational opportunities for women of the cohorts up to 1950 in most countries there is also evidence for economic disadvantages (Wedderburn, 1968; Hildemann, 1978). Apart from the differences in WAIS scores as mentioned before (see p. 108) late middle-aged women also feel much more 'overwhelmed' by severe stress than men (Fiske, 1980).

Classifying 81 survivors of the Bonn Longitudinal Study on Aging into six groups with different degrees of social competence (see p. 115) the two groups which had mainly sub-average scores for competence consisted of two men and 16 women (Thomae, 1983). It should be stressed, however, that cognitive measures, personality variables, and extra-familial activities were used as indicators for social competence. Had competence in the

home-maker role been included, the findings would have been different since women generally adapt to aging fairly well until widowhood (Wigdor, 1980). Even after widowhood they are often better prepared for an independent life than are widowers who have lost their homemaker or even care-taker. It should also be emphasized that middle-aged women are expected to take care of frail parents at the same time as they are exposed to the demands and expectations of their children and husband (Lehr, 1961; Brody, 1981). This may have unfavourable effects for their own adjustment to aging (Brody, 1981; Bruder, 1981). Finally, it should be stressed that as old people in general differ from each other, so even older women with the same 'fate' (such as widows) vary largely in any kind of personality measures (Fooken, 1981).

The impact of ecology

Ecological influences are studied mainly in terms of urban–rural differences in aging and in correlates of living in different types of neighbourhoods or institutions. Rural–urban differences in living conditions, well-being, and behaviour of the aged reflect the impact of environments which can be ordered along an urbanization continuum. High degrees of urbanization may be defined by high loadings on a small-distance-to-facilities factor, on a quality-of-dwelling-unit factor and a convenience factor. Access to services and goods which the elderly need and to activities and people they enjoy are easier in cities. Even in cities like New York the aged residents do not complain about crime and living costs, 'they talk about the ease and availability of desired activities and services'. 'Thus, the spread of activities appears to be of great benefit as they retire and age' (Cantor, 1973).

Positive aspects for the aged of life in cities were found also in the Bonn Longitudinal Study of Aging. From analysis of relevant variables Lehr and Olbrich (1976) stated that those living in central parts of cities were more ready to become involved, were more positive in their attitudes toward others, and in their mood. In the psychological interview and testing procedure they showed more confidence and they expressed more satisfaction than those coming from towns or suburban areas. Whereas the aged from rural and suburban areas cultivated more intra-family contacts, urban old people were active also in social roles like that of friend or acquaintance.

Persons of pre-retirement age living in inner city areas are more informed about problems of old age and services for the aged than persons of the same age living in suburbs or villages (Schmitz-Scherzer et al, 1976). A more passive and restricted life style in rural areas was found also in other studies (Langford, 1972; Institut, 1967; Boetticher, 1973). Even coffee hours and other entertainments offered by charity organisations were not accepted by aged people living in very remote areas whereas they were accepted by the majority of elderly people in cities. Only 48 per cent of residents of small villages read newspapers compared to 85 per cent in most urbanized areas. Interest in politics was expressed by 53 per cent of the urban aged, but only by 35 per cent of one rural area and 17 per cent of another (Institut, 1967). There is some evidence also about poorer health of the rural compared to city aged (Eitner et al, 1975; Rosenmayr, 1976).

But there are also negative aspects of life in inner cities and urban areas. Population density, disintegrated and anonymous life style (Carp, 1975; Lawton et al, 1978), and exposure to noise, pollution and to heavy traffic; also increased fear of becoming a victim of crime (Clements and Kleinman, 1976) are some of the most often mentioned problems. Such influences may explain the lower life satisfaction score for inner city old people reported in some studies (Bild and Havighurst, 1976).

A major problem, at least for many European cities, is that of elderly pedestrians. Fatal accidents are disproportionately high among the over 65's and these accidents take place mainly in cities. Difficulties in transportation which arise in suburban areas especially of large US cities are not yet as critical in many cities of Europe (Carp, 1973; Cutler, 1975).

In general, the social and ecological structure of urban life seems to offer more benefits than problems for elderly people. It offers opportunities for activity and social participation, from which the elderly are not excluded. However, these are generalizations which are subject to considerable regional as well as group variation.

In city dwellings smaller groupings and fewer storeys are preferred by elderly tenants (Lawton et al, 1975). In homes for the aged an active environment provides greater life satisfaction (Kahana et al, 1980). The sensory deprivation and isolation which exist in some institutional settings may increase deterioration and depressive states (Ernst et al, 1978). Even the translocation of elderly people from an unfavourable environment to a more favourable one can increase well-being and adjustment (Carp, 1977; Lawton, Brody et al, 1978). On the other hand housing problems are sources of great concern for the elderly (see p. 114).

Family structure and the aged

The dispersion of the three generation family is a much discussed problem of later life. Although it is likely that the traditional integrated family of the nineteenth century represents only a minority of cases, the general public still blames modernization and urbanization for their detrimental effects on intergenerational relationships. This is particularly surprising since it has been proven for almost 20 years that close relationships between the generations exist even if (and perhaps because) the aged do not share the household of their adult children. Rosenmayr (1977) and others confirm Tartler's (1960) finding that modern inter-generational structures tend toward an optimal mixture of intimacy and distance.

The impact of familial integration on the well-being of the aged has been well demonstrated. In 1956 Kutner et al showed that high interpersonal relations with children, relatives and friends was correlated to life satisfaction. The relevance of interaction with family for the well-being of the elderly was confirmed in studies by Butler and Lewis (1976), Havighurst et al (1970) and Troll et al (1979). According to Kivnick (1982) grandparenthood is instrumental in improving mental health of the elderly.

From the Bonn Longitudinal Study of Aging, Olbrich (1976) demonstrated significant and highly significant correlations between a high degree of participation in the life of the adult children and grandchildren on the one hand and mood (morale), positive attitude toward others, feeling of being needed etc on the other hand. Long-term widows and unmarried aged women demonstrate the potential for non-familial group influences on well-being and adjustment. This is also true for women of lower social status who formerly were regarded as completely dependent on family ties (Thomae and Kranzhoff, 1978).

DIMENSIONS OF VARIABILITY

As was shown in our overview most research into the origins of interindividual variability in the aged focuses on life satisfaction, morale, and activity as the dependent variable. These variables have been developed in the context of gerontological studies although they may apply to other age groups as well. More recently trait-centred approaches to personality have been applied to the psychology of aging (see also Shanan and Jacobowitz, 1983). Costa and McCrae (1976, 1980) tried to demonstrate the value of this approach by showing structural consistency across age groups ranging from 25 to 82 years both for personality dimensions of anxiety versus admustment and also for introversion versus extraversion. In a 9-year longitudinal study they showed that anxiety and extraversion remain consistent over them. Whereas this approach is oriented on Eysenck's dimensional model, Siegler et al (1979) used Cattell's 16-personality factors test to demonstrate the stability of traits over time. Others point to stability of certain 'types' from young to late adulthood (Maas and Kuypers, 1974). As Shanan and Jacobowitz (1983) point out the issue of the stability of all decisive personality traits from early to late adulthood is very controversial. Other researchers have found age as well as cohort differences regarding personality factors such as extraversion (Cameron, 1967), neuroticism, adjustment and, especially, rigidity (Schaie et al, 1977) or locus of control.

The main problem with these applications of trait theories to the study of the aged personality relates to objections to the trait approach such as those raised by Mischel (1968, 1973) and many others. They have initiated an interactionist approach taking into account person-situation relationships in the prediction of behaviour. It is unreasonable to expect complete continuity from middle into old age considering the great number of 'events' to be coped with. These arise out of the careers of parents and their children and grandchildren; in illness and loss of significant others, in changing social norms and conditions. Thus an account of stability of personality across the whole life span has to be supplemented by the study of the different adjustment processes and their outcomes needed to meet the challenges of these different situations. Therefore the trait-centred approach has to be replaced by a process-centred appooach (Thomae, 1980).

Process-centred approaches to aging personality always consider the economic, health, family and housing conditions of the elderly. One process-centred approach which has already been referred to in the context of correlates of some social conditions of the aged is *life satisfaction*. It was the central construct on one of the most influential social-psychological theories on aging, the Disengagement Theory (Cumming and Henry, 1960). Another construct developed in the context of this theory is that of *activity*. Approaches to the study of 'life events' and *stress and coping* led to the need for new methods of assessing the abilities of elderly people to meet the challenges of every day life. This directed attention to the relevance of the construct of *social competence*.

Successful aging

'Life satisfaction' was introduced by Havighurst (1962) as a measure for 'successful aging'. Implicitly and explicitly the construct is based on the hypothesis that aging is associated with some disequilibrium of the physical and especially the psychological state of the individual, the eliciting of processes to restore equilibrium. Edwards and Klemmack (1973) therefore defined 'life satisfaction' — as measured by one of the scales developed by Havighurst and his associates — as an 'equilibrium state'. Savage et al (1977) used the inventories developed by Havighurst and associates as measures of adjustment to aging. They did not find differences between the satisfaction scores of men and women or between those of the 'young-old' and 'old-old' in their sample.

The relationship between the construct 'life satisfaction' and the homeostatic model of the organism becomes even more evident in Morivaki's (1974) construct of 'affect balance' as a measure of successful aging. This is based on a model in which two independent conceptual dimensions, namely positive and negative affect, are included. Contrary to the life satisfaction approach it expects unbalanced relationships between these two affective systems to occur at any stage in life. Like the life-satisfaction scale the affect-balance scale measures the outcome of an hypothesized adjustment process which by itself is not conceptualized. Both approaches, however, point to a series of correlates some of which have been summarized already (see p. 108). An alternative way to operationalize 'life satisfaction' in those growing old consists of semistructured interviews which systematically cover different aspects of the life situation of old people in the community. These include housing, income, family and health — rating the degree of satisfaction with each of these aspects. This kind of approach avoids the interference of response sets which can result in very high life satisfaction scores even in deprived groups. Subjects of the Duke Study rated as happy and satisfied from such interviews and having survived up to 75 years were labelled as 'successful agers' by Palmore (1981). 'Successful aging' as defined in this way was predicted by mood, extra-familial activities, physical activities, and satisfaction with job as assessed at the first measurement point. From these data the 'activity theory of aging' — linking the availability of an active life style and life satisfaction — was confirmed.

Data from the Bonn Longitudinal Study on Aging dealing with satisfaction in health, housing, family and income were analysed in terms of the prevailing patterns of consistency and change during 12 years. Computing the associations of these longitudinal patterns with those of a selection of behavioural variables pointed to a complex network of interrelationships (Thomae, 1983). These can be demonstrated here by referring to satisfaction with the family situation for example (see Table 6.2).

Correlation coefficients shows that satisfaction with the family situation was generally higher over 12 years if there were fewer problems in the relationships with spouse or children and with other members of the extended family; also if the prevailing scores for reported stress regarding housing, income and health were low. Of the other satisfaction indices those for parental role had the closest relationship with the overall family satisfaction. As regards coping with stress, those with high family satisfaction were less likely to respond in depressive ways to problems in the family or in their

Table 6.2 Correlates of longitudinal patterns of consistency and change in 'congruence between desired and achieved goals' in family for a 12-year period (from Thomae 1983)

Variable	r (Pearson)
Satisfaction with situation in parent role	.5‡
Perceived problems regarding housing	−.4‡
Perceived stress regarding income	−.2★
Perceived health problems	−.2★
Perceived stress in family	−.4‡
Depressive reaction to stress in family	−.4‡
Depressive reaction to health problems	−.3†
Active resistance as response to health problems	−.2★
Mood, morale	.4‡
Adjustment	.2★
General satisfaction with daily life	.4‡
Feeling of general disappointment	−.5‡

★ significant at the .05 level
† significant at the .01 level
‡ significant at the .001 level

own health. Among the personality variables assessed from behaviour ratings, 'mood' was generally better in those more satisfied with their family situation and feelings of general disappointment were absent in these cases.

Four measures for satisfaction regarding health, income, housing and family were computed — the behavioural measure of 'mood', a scale rating the appraisal of everyday life as more positive or negative and two other measures. The sample could be classified into three groups: those with predominantly above average scores for these measures; a medium group; and those with mainly below average scores. The last group more often included women that men. Contrary to expectations the 'younger' group (born 1900–05) included more 'unhappy' persons than the older one. The main finding was related to the degee of perceived life stress. In men, those high in general life satisfaction belonged to the low stress group. In women the trend was the same but some women with low stress could report or react in an unhappy way.

Activity
The disengagement theory of aging hypothesized that decreasing activity in social roles after the age of 70 would result in higher life satisfaction — both as a reaction to the severing of ties between the aged and their social environment and also due to intrinsic disengagement (Henry, 1963). Most of the studies initiated by the disengagement theory did not confirm this thesis. They point to a positive correlation between 'life satisfaction' and 'activity' in terms of a high degree of intrafamilial and extrafamilial social participation. From these data the 'activity theory' of aging was derived. More detailed analyses of these activities-satisfaction

relationships introduced personality or social class variables in order to explain the different findings which related to these alternative theories. For example: life satisfaction was higher with a high degree of family-related social activity in old people from 'lower' classes whereas those from higher social backgrounds showed more satisfaction if extra-family social participation was high. Other cues to the relevance of the activity dimension are coming from clinical studies which point to a positive relationship between physical activity and health (Jokl, 1981; Heikkinen, 1979) or cognitive competence (Naylor, 1976; Robertson-Tschabo, 1979; Willis et al; 1981). Activation and its control is a major principle in intervention with states of deterioration (Baltes, 1973; Baroni and Kelly, 1980). The neurophysiological interpretation of the Introversion-Extraversion Personality Dimension by Eysenck (1969) suggests that intra-individual differences in this dimension are identical with differences in neural activity. From this point of view 'activity' is a very complex construct which includes physical activity, cognitive activity and social activity. These were measured in some studies by the Activity Inventory (Caven et al, 1949). Participants in the Baltimore Longitudinal Study (age range 20–89 years) did not show age differences in activity as defined by this inventory, which was administered to them at *one* of the measurement points. The Activity Inventory as presented to the Community Aged Studies in Newcastle-upon-Tyne (Savage et al, 1977) found no age and sex differences in the activity scores in the age groups 70 to 85. There were great differences in these scores between different personality styles as distinguished by the authors of the study. A 'Mature Tempered Group' showed the highest activity scores, a 'Perturbed Group' the lowest.

In the Duke Study mainly social activity was assessed. Primary group contacts as measured at the second round of the First Longitudinal Study were predicted by the data from the first round which related to size of household, secondary group contacts, by SES and mental functioning (Palmore, 1981). In general women in this study reported more secondary group activity and men more primary group activity — because fewer men were living alone. The higher degree of social activity in women was found also in the Second Duke Longitudinal Study. Those higher in leisure activity and secondary group contacts at the first round were healthier and had higher happiness ratings at the second round.

In the Bonn Longitudinal Study the following scores were combined to classify the 12 years' survivors into a high-active, medium-active and low-active group: secondary group activities; active coping with problem areas; and one measure rating the participant's activity during one week at each of the measurement points. Of

Table 6.3 Differences in the longitudinal patterns of consistency and change of social and psychological variables between high-active, medium active and low-active survivors of the Bonn Longitudinal Study

Variable	X^2
Acquaintance role	6.31*
Neighbour role	12.7‡
Citizen role	9.7*
Active coping with housing problems	18.9‡
Economic stress	7.8*
Problems in family	13.00†
Health problems	5.9*
Rating score for activity	16.6‡
Activity as club member	18.2‡
Cultivating social contacts in coping with housing problems	7.03*
Achievement related behavior in coping with economic problems	6.96*
Subjectively perceived health	5.9*
Tendency to maintain the range of interests	9.9†
Tendency to expand range of social contacts	10.96†
Responsiveness	6.6*
Dogmatism	6.8*
WAIS Performance Score	8.5†
WAIS Global Score	11.6†
Raven Progressive Matrices	6.8*
Mierke Psychomotor-test	7.4*

* significant at the .05 level
† significant at the .01 level
‡ significant at the 0.001 level

the criteria used for the classification of these groups, active coping with housing problems discriminated most significantly between these groups (Table 6.3); next came the rating score for observed activity. Of variables which were not used as criteria for classification, activity in the club-member role; coping forms of 'cultivating social contacts'; and 'achievement related behaviour' differentiated significantly between the activity groups. Of all the scores for perceived stress, only perceived health discriminated as expected: that is none of those with poorer subjective health belonged to the low-activity group. Two other motivational variables discriminate very significantly in the expected direction between the high and low activity groups — the tendency to maintain the range of one's own interests and the tendency to expand the range of social contacts. Different cognitive measures, especially the WAIS-score discriminate in a similar way. This supports the expectation that the maintenance of cognitive competence is associated with a higher degree of overall activity.

Comparing those groups defined by different levels of life satisfaction on the one hand and of activity on the other no significant relationship was shown. By the criteria used here life satisfaction and activity are shown as indepedent dimensions in the interindividual variability

of aged persons. It will be shown, however, that activity and social competence are closely related.

Exposure to stress and coping with stress
Research on critical life events gave some insight into relationships between psycho-social stress and several forms of somatic disease (Holmes and Rahe, 1967; Holmes et al, 1974; Hurst et al, 1976), although these relationships have not yet been solved (Eisdorfer and Wilkie, 1977). Renner and Birren (1980) point to the low frequency of such critical life events as death of spouse, death of a friend, divorce, loss of job as important in the initiation of disease. They may be less important than the 'chronic daily hassles' especially among the elderly. Lazarus and Cohen (1977) who introduced the term 'daily hassles' believe that an adequate description of stress and coping in the aging requires the assessment of the kind, frequency, duration, and severity of these daily hassles' and the ways in which old people cope with them. According to the cognitive model of perception of stress and reaction to stress (as developed by Lazarus and associates 1966, 1978) it is important also to assess the way in which stressors or 'daily hassles' are cognitively appraised. They may be perceived as threats or as challenges: as harm and loss — depending on the coping resources of the individual.

One of the few adaptations of this model to the study of aging was made by McCrea (1982). He administered the 'Ways of Coping Questionnaire' of Folkman and Lazarus to the sample of the Baltimore Longitudinal Study (age range 24–91 years). Contrary to some stereotypes or beliefs of experts dealing with disturbed patients (Pfeiffer, 1977) he found a decrease with age in 'immature' or 'emotional' response and an increase or 'consistency' or more 'mature' reactions. Studies like these question the validity of a 'defect' model (Albee, 1980) predicting a complete decline in the coping resources of the elderly or of the equivalence of 'old age' and 'learned helplessness' (Seligman, 1975).

McRea's findings are supported by several studies on young, middle-aged and aged persons and on patients, using structured interviews: they are also supplemented by the construct of multiple-stress-experience and its behavioural correlates (Thomae and Lehr, 1982). The 1965–1977 survivors of the Bonn Longitudinal Study of Aging were classified by objective and subjective assessments with high-stress group and average or sub-average stress group. This was on the basis of perceived stress in different aspects of family life (conflicts or worries about spouse, children, grandchildren, problems regarding housing, income and health). Women of the cohort 1900–1905 were represented significantly more often in the multiple-stress group than in any other subgroup. Contrary to expectation the 'younger' cohort

(1900–1905) belonged more often to the high-stress group than to the medium or low-stress group. This may be due to the attrition or selective drop-out effects of longitudinal studies. However it may also be explained by the different stages in which the two cohorts were exposed to the stresses of two World Wars and the economic stresses between these wars.

The differences in the longitudinal patterns of consistency and change in different experiential and behavioural aspects of personality during the 12-year observation period as presented in Table 6.4 are ambivalent when compared with the associations between the prevailing patterns in specific stress areas and behavioural aspects (see Thomae, 1983). Since, according to general beliefs and scientific evidence family problems interfere heavily with the well-being of the elderly, three of the criteria variables were related to this area. It might be expected that this global score for family stress and stress in parent-role would differentiate in the most significant way between the two stress-exposure groups. However it is surprising that 'health', as subjectively perceived, discriminated between the high and low stress groups in a highly significant way since the differentiating chances for this variable were very much lower. Objectively assessed health problems did not contribute to the stress-exposure classification of the sample. This may be due to the 'healthy' composition

of the original sample and also to the selective drop-out effect of longitudinal studies.

The low stress perceivers showed significantly lower preferences for non-criterion variables like 'active resistance' and 'depression' as responses to health problems. 'Active resistance' means that the doctor's advice or even prescriptions are rejected. Most of these responses refer to advice regarding smoking, alcohol and physical activity. The label 'depressive reaction' is used here in a non-clinical way and includes any kind of mood change or increase of worry in the range of normal psychological responses. Since the high and low groups are defined mainly by psychosocial criteria, it can be concluded from these data that the relationships between stress and health may best be studied in terms of associations between high stress and problem behaviour regarding health problems. This offers a more rational explanation of stress-health relationships than any theory relating psychosocial stress to the onset of somatic disease.

No other sociological or cognitive measures of non-criterion variables discriminated between the stress groups. However all satisfaction measures for different aspects of family life discriminate in the expected way. Psychosocially the high stress perceivers are more active in coping with housing problems. The activity as rated for the week of observation was not different in the group of high stress perceivers whereas those low in stress scores received mainly average or lower scores in this variable. From these data it seems that high-stress perception does not interfere with activity in everyday life and indeed enhances the ability to cope with problems. This points to the fact that stress as perceived by our subjects was not equivalent to distress (Selye, 1978) although it lowered satisfaction scores. It also increased (in a highly significant way) the feeling of disappointment about the whole life situation. High stress perceivers felt their whole 'life situation' as restricted and lacking any chances and opportunities.

The relationships between degree of perceived stress during 12 years on the one hand, and overall satisfaction such as defined above (see p. 112) on the other is different in men and women. Whereas low stress perceivers in the male group belong significantly more often to the more satisfied group, women low in stress awareness are distributed almost equally between the high and low satisfaction groups. In the high stress group both men and women belong significantly more often to the low satisfaction group. The relationship between degree of stress awareness and the dimensions of activity and competence will be discussed later.

It seems unlikely that the difference between 'high' and 'low' stress perceivers relates mainly to the personality variables which were defined by Renner and Birren (1980) as 'stress amplifiers' and 'stress dampeners'. The

Table 6.4 Differences in the longitudinal patterns of consistency and change of social and psychological variables between multiple-stress perceivers and low stress perceivers during a 12-year period

Criterion variables	X^2
Housing problems	7.7[†]
Economic problems	9.2[†]
Stress in parent-role	14.4[‡]
Stress in spouse-role	9.7[‡]
Stress in whole family	18.7[‡]
Perceived health problems	13.4[‡]
Objectively assessed health problems	9.6[*]
Non-criterion-variables	
Satisfaction with spouse	9.1[†]
Satisfaction in parent-role	14.4[‡]
Satisfaction in grandparent-role	4.8[*]
Satisfaction in kin-role	8.9[†]
Congruence between achieved and desired goals regarding family	8.9[†]
Active coping with housing problems	5.4[*]
Activity	6.2[*]
Feeling of general disappointment	10.5[‡]
Feeling of being restricted and without any chances	4.9[*]
Active resistance as response to health problems	8.13[†]
Depressive reaction as response to health problems	8.99[†]

[*] significant at the .05 level
[†] significant at the .01 level
[‡] significant at the .001 level

perception of 'high' versus 'low' stress is a *reflection* of the social world rather than a *construction* of this world by personality-specific perceptual-styles.

The comparison of the information given by these respondents with other available data confirms the validity of their stress perceptions. Furthermore, comparing the correlations between the longitudinal patterns of stress awareness in the different areas, significant relationships were found between perception of housing and of economic problems and these are very real, not only in the minds of the aged.

Social competence

The extent to which intelligence and other measures of cognitive functioning change wthh aging is debated (Donaldson and Horn, 1976; Baltes and Schaie, 1976; Barton et al, 1975). Indeed the relevance of intelligence to coping with daily problems has been questioned, e.g. from an ecological perspective (Lawton and Brody, 1969). Particularly in the treatment and care of the frail elderly the need for alternative measures of self-maintenance and/or procedures for clinical and nursing home populations have been developed (Pfeiffer, 1975; Fisher, 1973). The lack of measures of competence for those elderly living independently has been stressed and several criteria such as the ability to communicate proposed (North and Ulatowska, 1981). In theories on motivation a fundamental need for the experience of competence was postulated (White, 1959; Deci, 1975; Wigdor, 1980). Sociologists like Kuypers and Bengtson (1973) brought evidence for a prevalence of negative attitudes in society toward the aged resulting in an internalization of the labels of incompetence and negative values assigned by others to them. 'Normal aging' according to this theory is very often identified with an ineffectual approach to everyday life. This process can be contradicted only by making people aware that even the very old retain the three basic competencies of successful social-role performance — capacity to adapt to environmental change, and personal feelings of mastery and of internal controls.

However this theory may be evaluated from clinical experience together with the other approaches it stresses the importance of the competence dimension both for a practical as well as a theoretical perspective. A central role of this dimension is to be observed also in studies on mental health and aging (Birren and Renner, 1980).

Degrees of social competence may range from the life styles of centenarians still working or enjoying an independent life (Sachuk, 1965; Franke, 1979) to the living conditions of a chronically disabled nursing home resident needing 24 hours attendance (age 51 years). According to epidemiological findings competence will decrease beyond the age of 75 years (Svanborg et al,

1982) but interindividual variability persists. The degree of interindividual variability in social competence in 'normal aging' can only be assessed by measures which cover a broad range of adaptations and coping devices. Birren identified 19 coping patterns in middle aged men and women of professional or executive status. One of the most effective ways in career promotion and maintenance consists of the reduction of information-load by bulking information.

For lower middle class people after retirement problems of housing, income, family and health are more important than that of information overload. Therefore it is to be expected that strategies to meet the 'daily hassles' should be different from those as found in Birren's sample. They are also different for each of the problem areas, like health, housing, etc. This can be shown by comparing the response hierarchies of a sample of old people at a given measurement point (see Fig. 6.1). Contrary to expectation, as formulated within the context of the Lazarus approach to the classification of coping styles, the response hierarchies of men and women (age 70–86 years) to health and family problems diverge from each other much more than those related to family problems on the one hand and housing problems on the other hand (see Fig. 6.1). Comparing the response hierarchies at different measurement points as far apart as 12 years does not yield any significant changes. From this point of view it can be concluded that the selection of coping patterns by a sample of independent old people is reality-oriented and stable over time (Thomae, 1983).

Table 6.5 Correlates of longitudinal patterns of achievement related responses to housing, economic, family, and health problems (1966–77)

Varable	Housing	Income	Family	Health
Degree of active coping with problem	.2*	.54‡		.30†
	.2*			
Adjustment to institutional aspects of situation	—	.315†	—	.3†
Accepting/positive appraisal of situation	—	—	.4‡	—
Depressive reaction	—	—	—	-.4‡
Social activity	.3†	—	—	.2*
Activity	—	—	.28†	—
Mood, morale	—	—	.24*	—
Attitude toward future	—	-.22*	.30†	—
Range of Future time perspective	—	—	—	.27†
WAIS-score	—	—	.27†	—

* significant at the .05 level
† significant at the .01 level
‡ significant at the .001 level

Rank	Health	Family	Housing
1	Achievement related behaviour	Achievement related behaviour	Achievement related behaviour
2	Adjustment I	Identification	Adjustment II
3	Depressive reaction	Cultivation of social contacts	Cultivating social contacts
4	Accepting or positive appraisal	Adjustment II	Relying on significant others
5	Active resistance	Depressive reaction	Identification
6	Relying on significant others	Relying on significant others	Adjustment I
7	Call for help	Delay of gratification	Call for help
8	Revision of expectancies	Accepting/positive appraisal	Using chances
9	Using chances	Revision of expectancies	Accepting/positive approach
10	Identification	Call for help	Revision of expectancies
11	Hope for change	Evasive reaction	Active resistance
12	Adjustment II	Hope for change	Delay of gratification
13	Relying on external control	Using chances	Evasive reaction
14	Evasive reaction	Adjustment I	Depressive reaction
15	Delay of gratification	Active resistance	Hope for change
16	Cultivation of social contacts	Relying on external control	Relying on external control
17	Aggressive behaviour	Aggressive reaction	Aggressive behaviour

Fig. 6.1 Response hierarchies to problems regarding health, family, and housing 1977

Table 6.6 Correlates of longitudinal patterns of consistency and change in WAIS Global Scores in community aged for a twelve year observation period.

Variable	r
Education	.5‡
Income	.2*
Subjectively perceived health problems	−.23*
Objectively assessed health problems	−.22*
Raven Progressive Matrices	.6‡
Dogmatism	−.3†
Rigidity	−.3†
Responsiveness	.5‡
Range of future time perspective	.3*
Activity in citizen role	.3†
Satisfaction with situation in parent role	−.25†
Satisfaction in grandparent role	−.3†
Satisfaction with daily activities	−.3†

* significant at the .05 level
† significant at the .01 level
‡ significant at the .001 level

The degree and nature of coping can be considered therefore as valid indicators of social competence. Of the different ways of coping only achievement-related behaviour ranks highly in all problem areas. Therefore in the Bonn Longitudinal Study on Aging the degree of coping and choice of achievement-related behaviour were taken as indicators of social competence. The correlates of the longitudinal patterns of achievement related behaviour are shown in Table 6.5 and are closely connected with other indicators of social competence — especially in the area of family and health problems. Whilst WAIS-scores correlate with achievement-related behaviour only referring to family problems, the range of future time perspective as an indicator of planning and control over one's own life (Schonfield, 1972) is related to the selection of achievement-related behaviour in a very significant way. According to North and Ulatowska (1981) and many others, cognitive measures are still the most valid indicators of competence. This can be demonstrated, for example, by the correlates of the longitudinal patterns of the WAIS Global Scores (see Table 6.6) which point to social status and health as influencing the constancy or otherwise of cognitive competence. Those with more years of education and more income usually score higher in the intelligence test than those from lower status. Those of poorer health (as objectively assessed as well as subjectively perceived) have mainly subaverage/average scores. Rigidity is inversely related to intelligence. Apart from other cognitive measures, personal variables like (higher) 'responsiveness' and (higher) 'assertiveness' and an extended future time perspective are closely related to better cognitive functioning. The negative correlation between intelligence and satisfaction in parent and grandparent role may be explained by a more critical attitude of those scoring higher in intelligence. This is shown also in satisfaction with daily activities. On the other hand, the activity of the high intelligence scorers in the kin role is lower than that of the less competent.

Another group of indicators of social competence (according to the criteria mentioned above) refers to social activity. Since family contacts depend on the behaviour of both the old and the younger generations they will be less valid in demonstrating social competence than extra familial roles (such as those of acquaintance, neighbour, club-member, or citizen — see Havighurst et al, 1970). Finally, personality variables like activity, responsiveness, adjustment, or ego control contribute to social competence in a more or less decisive way.

Six patterns of competence

By distributing the longitudinal patterns of 30 indicators for competence in the Bonn Study to mainly above-average, average and sub-average scores, six groups were distinguished (Thomae, 1983):

Group 1 Above average scores in more than 15 indicators.

Group 2 Above average and average scores for 12 indicators each, below-average scores for 6 indicators.

Group 3 Above average and below average scores for 12 indicators each and average scores for 6.

Group 4 12 above-average, average, and below average scores each.

Group 5 Mainly below-average and average scores.

Group 6 Mainly below-average scores.

The last two groups consisted of 17 women and 2 men, the first two groups of 14 women and 19 men. This confirms the unfavourable effects of the socialization of women in the cohorts covered by our study. The majority of the 'younger' cohort belonged to groups 1 and 2. The older cohort was distributed almost equally to group 1/2 and 5/6.

Groups 1–6 differed from each other most significantly in the WAIS scores and the behavioural measure for activity, responsiveness and the tendency to maintain the range of one's own interests (see Table 6.7). While severity of perceived health problems did not differentiate between the competence groups, health problems as objectively assessed did, so subjects from groups 1/2 were assessed mainly as healthier whereas those from group 6 were rated as least healthy. In this way the great impact of health on social competence and adjustment

Table 6.7 Differences in longitudinal measures of the behaviour of aged belonging to different social competence groups.

Variable	p
WAIS Global Score	.0001
Raven Progressive Matrices	.05
Mierke Psychomotor Test	.003
Activity	.00005
Mood	.01
Responsiveness	.01
Adjustment	.00002
Range of future time perspective	.006
Tendency to maintain range of interests	.001
Tendency to expand range of social contacts	.01
Activity in citizen role	.03
Activity as club-member	.03
Active coping with housing problems	.007
Achievement related behaviour as response to housing problems	.05
Achievement related behaviour as response to family problems	.03
Achievement related behaviour as response to economic problems	.04
Subjective perceived health problems	.02
objectively assessed health problems	.009
active resistance as response to health problems	.03
depressive reactions as response to health problems	.03

was clearly shown. The less competent groups significantly maintained active resistance and depressive reactions to health problems. Many studies have shown that depressive reactions affect mental as well as physical health problems. Active resistance as related to health problems consists of behaviour in disagreement with the doctor's advice regarding diet, physical activity, and smoking. From this point of view a low degree of social competence goes along wtih poor compliance and therefore has a detrimental effect for health. The relevance of 'social competence' for health behaviour and health education should therefore be stressed.

Another variable discriminating in a significant way between the competence groups is belief in the unchangeability of unfavourable conditions: the less competent scoring higher in this belief. A close relationship between this belief (as measured by a scale) and the frequency of 'active resistance' and depressive reactions regarding health problems has been shown also in a cross-sectional study of more than 200 subjects (Thomae, 1981). Since belief in the unchangeability of unfavourable life conditions is an effect of a learning process (like the state of 'learned helplessness' according to Seligman, 1975), it should be possible to trace the factors influencing this learning process in which opinion leaders like doctors have a great influence. It may be concluded therefore that information about the potential for intervention in rehabilitation of the disorder should be much more widespread.

INTERRELATIONSHIPS BETWEEN THE MAIN DIMENSIONS OF INTERINDIVIDUAL VARIABILITY AMONG THE OLD

More socially competent subjects also show a higher general satisfaction with their situation. Less competent subjects show no polarization of distribution as far as life satisfaction is concerned.

The more competent subjects distribute to patterns of high-stress perceivers and low-stress perceivers almost equally. In group 4 mainly low-stress perceivers are represented. The closest relationships exist however, between competence and activity. The more competent groups consist of mainly highly active aged persons whereas the less competent groups contain no highly active individuals. This close relationship between activity and competence confirms the disuse-hypothesis of aging. This postulates that deterioration and decline are consequences of inactivity and recommends the maintenance of social, mental, and physical activities as an instrument for 'successful aging' such as is defined by social competence.

Neither the conceptualization of 'successful aging' by overall life satisfaction nor the hypothesis of a stress-induced decline of competence can be confirmed from these longitudinal data, although there are some cues pointing in this direction. Furthermore it must be pointed out that the 'medium' group of social competence consisted of mainly 'non-active' as well as of low-stress perceiving subjects. From this point of view the dimensions of satisfaction, stress-perception, activity, and competence can be regarded as more or less dependent/independent from each other in an effort to define 'patterns of aging'.

The problem of defining these patterns has been solved so far from very divergent points of view (see Table 6.8). This may be because the dimensions included for the definition of these patterns were mainly derived either from no theory of aging at all (as that of Maas and Kuypers, 1974) or by one or two of these theories.

In the Bonn Longitudinal Study of Aging patterns found during a 12-year transition from 'young-old' status were analysed. From the combination of measures for well-being such as the perception of the 'own life' situations as high stress versus low stress on the one hand and as satisfying versus non-satisfying on the other, four patterns could be differentiated:

A High stress / high/medium satisfaction	14
B High stress / low satisfaction	26
C Low stress / high/medium satisfaction	31
D Low stress / low satisfaction	10

The majority of the cases belong to groups B and C which are defined by the expected relationships between

Table 6.8 Overview of some approaches to the definition of patterns of aging

Authors	Number and labels of aging patterns	principles of classification
Reichard et al (1962)	Four adjusted patterns: 'mature', 'rocking chair men.' Two unadjusted patterns: 'angry men', self haters'	Degree and kind of adjustment to disengagement
Williams and Wirths (1965)	Autonomous vs. dependent aged persons	Degree of attaining or restoring balance between person and environment
Havighurst (1975)	Six successful patterns (e.g. re-organizers, integrated-focused, successful disengaged, holding-on-pattern) Two non-successful patterns (apathetic, disorganized)	Combining different degrees of social role activity and life-satisfaction
Maas and Kuypers (1974)	Six life styles for women (eg. 'husband-centered uncentered wives', 'visiting mothers'). Four life styles for men (eg. family centered hobbyist, unwell disengaged fathers). Four personality types for women (person-oriented, autonomous, anxious-asserting, fearful ordering mothers). Three personality types for men (person oriented, conservative-ordering, active-competent fathers).	Cluster analysis of Q-sorts
Savage et al (1977)	Four personality types 'normal', 'introverted', 'perturbed', 'mature' aged	Cluster-analysis of data from clinical personality inventories
Renner and Birren (1980)	Stress amplifiers vs. dampeners	Appraisal of stressors

high stress perception and low life satisfaction or low stress perception and high life satisfaction. The other two 'fates' point to the intervening role of personality variables which make it possible to attain high life satisfaction in high stress (group A) and prevent members of group D from attaining life satisfaction even in a situation of low stress perception. As perception of stress in our subjects had its basis in some physical or social conditions and as life satisfaction is closely correlated with many social-environmental factors these four patterns can be labelled as different 'fates of aging'.

From the analyses of the correlations of activity and

social competence with personality measures we can conclude that the variability within these two dimensions is more internally controlled and less related to external determinants. Therefore it is suggested that the different combinations of the four 'fates' with activity and social competence should be labelled as 'styles' of aging (Thomae, 1983). We found at least 12 of these 'styles of aging' in our sample the majority of which is centered around style B_3 (high stress, low satisfaction, low activity, low competence), C_1 (low stress, medium/high life satisfaction, high/medium activity, high competence) and C_2 (low stress, medium/high life satisfaction, low/medium activity, medium competence). This points to the regulating influence which stress perception and coping with stress have on activity and social competence.

Checking the case histories of the men and women assigned to these different styles as included in Thomae, 1983) great interindividual differences are seen. The practicability of this classification system may be doubted. An alternative way, focussing on the uniqueness of each of the cases would coincide with modern 'humanistic' approaches to the study of personality.

To understand the interaction between the elderly person and his situation as perceived and coped with, it would be helpful to know how he attained a balance — at whatever degree of activity and whichever level of competence. Therefore, the individual will be comprehended even more completely if studied within the framework of the dimensions as derived from recent social-gerontological research.

REFERENCES

Adams D L 1971 Correlates of life satisfaction. The Gerontologist 11, 4 Part II: 64–68

Anastasi A 1958 Differential Psychology. McMillan, New York

Atchley R 1976 Selected social and psychological differences between men & women in later life. Journal of Gerontology 31: 204–211

Baltes P B 1968 Longitudinal and crosssectional sequences in the study of age and generation effects. Human Development 11: 145–151

Baltes P B, Willis S L 1977 Toward psychological theories of aging and development. In: Birren J E, Schaie K W (eds) Handbook of Psychology of Aging. van Nostrand, New York, p 128–154

Baroni A, Kelly P 1980 Neuromuscular rehabilitation in aged hemiplegic patients. In: Barbagallo-Sangiorgi G, Exton-Smith A N (eds) The aging brain, Plenum Press, New York, p 355

Beauvoir S de 1970 La Vieillesse. Editions Gallimard, Paris

Bengtson V L, Dowd J J, Ragan P K 1977 The impact of social structures on aging individuals. In: Birren J E, Schaie K W (eds) The psychology of Aging, Van Nostrand, New York, p 327–354

Berner P, Naske R, Zapotoczky H G 1973 Zur Klinik depressiver Symptome im Alter. Zeitschrift für Getrontologie 6: 420

Birren J E 1963 Psychophysical relations. In: Birren J E, Butler R, Greenhouse S W, Sakoloff L, Yarrow M R Human aging: a biological and behavioral study. National Institute of Health, Maryland, p 289–293

Birren J E, Butler R N, Greenhouse S W, Sokoloff L, Yarrow M R 1963 Human aging: a biological and behavioral study. National Institute of Health, Bethesda, Maryland

Birren J E, Morrison D F 1961 Analysis of the WAIS subtests in relation to age & education. Journal of Gerontology 16: 363–369

Birren J E, Renner M 1977 Health, behavior, and aging. Paper presented at World Conference on: Aging, a Challenge to Science & Policy, Oxford Univ. Press

Blum J W, Jarvik L F 1974 Intellectual performance of octogenarians as a function of education and intial ability. Human Development 17: 364–375

Blume O, Hauss W H, Kuhlmeyer E, Oberwittler W 1974 Abschlussbericht der interdisziplinären Untersuchung über den Gesundheitszustand älterer Menschen. MAGS Altenhilfe 2, Dortmund Westfalendruck

Böcher W, Heemskerk J J, Marx M W 1973 Rehabilitationsmöglichkeiten alternder Menschen. Schriftenreihe des Bundesministers für Jugend, Familie und Gesundheit Bonn

Bötticher K W 1973 Geront 73, Selbstverlag, GieBen

Borkan G A, Norris A H 1980 Assessment of biological age using a profile of physiological parameters. Journal of Gerontology 35: 177–184

Botwinick J, Birren J E 1963 Mental abilities & Psychomotor response in healthy aged men. In: Birren J E, Butler R et al, Human

aging: a biological and behavioral study, p 97–110; National Institute of Health, Bethesda, Maryland

Botwinick J, Storandt M 1974 Cardiovascular status, depressive affect, and other factors in reaction time. Journal of Gerontology 29: 543–548

Brody E 1981 The women in the middle. The Gerontologist: 21

Busse E W 1979 The Duke Study: the electroencephalogram in senescence and senility. In: Orimo H, Shimada K, Iriki M, Maeda D, Recent advances in gerontology, Experta Medica, Amsterdam

Butler R M, Lewis M 1976 Aging and Mental Health. Mosby Company, St. Louis

Cameron P 1967 Introversion and egocentricity among the aged. Journal of Gerontology 22: 465–468

Cantor M H 1975 Life space and the social support system of the inner city elderly of New York. The Gerontologist 15, 1: 23–26

Carp F M 1975 Ego-defense or cognitive consistency effects on environmental evaluations. Journal of Gerontology 30: 707–711

Carp F M 1977 Impact of improved living environment on health and life expectancy. Gerontologist 17: 242–249

Carp F M 1979 Life style and location within the city. In: Byerts T O, Howell S C, Pastalan L A (eds). Environmental Context of Aging, New York & London, p 16–32

Cattell R B, Kline P 1977 The Scientific Analysis of Personality & Motivation. Academic Press, New York

Cávan R S, Burgess E W, Havighurst R J, Goldhamer H 1949 Personal adjustment in old age. Science Research Association, Chicago

Clemente F, Kleinman M B 1976 Fear of crime in the aged. The Gerontologist 16: 201–216

Costa P T, McCrae R R, Norris A H 1981 Personal adjustment toaging: longitudinal prediction from neuroticism and extraversion. Journal of Gerontology 36: 78–85

Costa P T, McCrae R R 1976 Age differences in personality structure: a cluster analysis approach. Journal of Gerontology 31: 564–570

Cowgill D O, Holmes L D 1972 Aging and modernization. Appleton-Century Crofts, New York

Cumming E, Henry W E 1961 Growing old. The process of disengagement. Basic Books, New York

Cutler S J 1972 The availability of personal transportaion, residential location and life satisfaction of the elderly. Journal of Gerontology 27: 383–389

Cutler S J 1973 Voluntary association and life satisfaction: a cautionary research note. Journal of Gerontology 28: 96–100

Damon A 1965 Discrepancies between findings of longitudinal and cross-sectional studies in adult life: physique and physiology. Human Development 8: 16–22

Desabie J 1978 Facteures économiques: l'exemple francais. In: Flesch J (ed) Ecologie et Vieillissement. Centre Internationale de

Gerontologie Sociale Paris, p 31–84

Dowd J J 1981 Age and inequality: a critique of the age stratification model. Human Development 24: 157–171

Eisdorfer C, Cohen L D 1961 The generality of the WAIS standardization for the aged. Journal of abnormal & Social Psychology 62, 520–527

Eisdorfer C, Wilkie F 1977 Stress, Disease, Aging, and Behavior. In: Birren J E, Schaie K W (eds). Handbook of the psychology of aging, Van Nostrand, New York, p 251–275

Eitner S, Eitner A 1978 Geropsychohygiene. In: Chebotarev D F, Brüschke G, Schmidt U J, Schulz F H (eds) Handbuch der Gerontologie, VEB G, Fischer, Jena, p 198

Elder G H 1974 Children of the great depression. University of Chicago Press, Chicago

Elder G H, Liker J K, Jaworski B A 1982 Economic crisis and health: historical influences from the thirties to old age in postwar America. Paper presented at Eighth Biennial West Virginia University. Conference on Life span Developmental Psychology. Morgantown, West Virginia

Enzer N, Simonson E, Blankstein S 1941 The state of sensory and motor centers in patients with hyperthyroidism. Annuals of Internal Medicine 15: 659

Ernst P, Beran B, Badosh D, Kosovsky R, Kleinhauz M 1977 Treatment of the aged mentally ill: Further unmasking of the effects of a diaprosis of chronic brain syndrome. Journal of American Geriatrics Society 25: 466–469

Ernst P, Beran B, Safford F, Kleinhauz M 1978 Isolation and the symptoms of chronic brain syndrome. The Gerontologist 18: 468–474

Eysenck H J, Eysenck S B G 1969 Personality: Structure and Measurement. Routledge & Kegan, London

Fiske M 1980 Tasks and crises of the second half of life. In: Birren J E, Sloane R B (eds) Mental Health & Adaptation. Englewood Cliffs, Prentice Hall, p 337–373

Fooken I 1980 Frauen im Alter. Lang, Frankfurt

Franke H 1979 Theorien der Langlebigkeit. actuelle gerontologie 9: 167–177

Furukawa T, Inoue M I, Kajiya F, Inada H, Takasugi S

Fukui S et al 1975 Assessment of biological age by multiple regression analysis. Journal of Gerontology 30: 422–434

George L K 1978 The impact of personality and social status factors upon level of activity and psychological wellbeing. Journal of Gerontology 33: 840–847

Glascock A P, Feinman S L 1981 Social asset or social burden: treatment of the aged in non-industrialized societies. In: Fry C L (ed) Dimensions. Aging, Culture, and Health, Praeger, New York, p 13–31

Goldman H, Kleinman K M, Snow M Y, Bidus D R, Korol B 1974 Correlation of diastolic blood pressure and signs of cognitive dysfunction in essential dysfunction. Diseases of the Nervous System 23, p 571–572

Granick S, Friedman A S 1967 The effect of education in the decline of test performance with age. Journal of Gerontology 22: 191–195

Grombach H H 1976 Consistency and change of personality variables in late life. In: Thomae H (ed) Patterns of Aging, Karger, Basel-New York, p 51–67

Guilford J B 1959 Personality. McGraw-Hill, New York

Harris L 1975 The Myth and Reality of Aging in America. National Council on the Aging, Washington, D.C.

Havighurst R J 1962 The measurement of successful aging. In: Tibbitts C, Donahue W (eds) Social and Psychological Aspects of Aging (Proc. V International Congress of Gerontology) Columbia University Press, New York, p 664

Havighurst R J, Munnichs J M A, Neugarten B, Thomae H 1970 Adjustment to retirement. Van Gorcum, Assen

Hauser P M 1976 Aging and world-wide population change. In: Binstock R, Shanas E (eds) Handbook of Aging & the Social Sciences, Van Nostrand, New York

Heikinnen E 1979 Normal aging definition, problems, and relation to physical activity. In: Orimo H, Shimada K, Iriki M, Maeda D (eds) Recent Advances in Gerontology, Excerpta Medica, Amsterdam, p 500–503

Henry E 1963 Intrinsic disengagement. Paper presented at 6th International Congress of Gerontology, Copenhagen

Hildemann K D 1978 Einige Gegelenheiten der Situation alter,

insbesondere alleinstehender Frauen in den USA, in Frankreich und in der Bundesrepublik Deutschland. In: Lehr U (ed) Seniorinnen. Steinkopff, Darmstadt, p 27–38

Holmes T H, Masuda M 1974 Life change and illness susceptibility. In: Dohrenwend B S, Dohrenwend P B (eds) Stressful Life Events: their Nature and Effects, Wiley, New York, p 45–72

Holmes T H, Rahe R M 1967 The social re-adjustment rating scale. Journal of Psychosomatic Medicine II: 213–218

Hurst T W, Jenkins C D, Rose R M 1976 The relation of psychological stress to onset of medical illness. Annual Review Medicine 27: 301–312

Imhof A 1981 Die gewonnenen Jahre. Pick, München

Institut für Selbsthilfe und Sozialforschung 1967 Daten zur Lebenslage älterer Menschen auf dem Land. Institut, Köln

Jokl E 1981 Physical activity & aging. XIII. Internationaler Kongress für Gerontologie (Hamburg), Abstr. Vol 2, p 298

Kahana E, Liang J, Felton B J 1980 Alternative models of person-environment fit: prediction of morale in three homes for the aged. Journal of Gerontology 35: 584–595

Kivnick H Q 1982 Grandparenthood: an overview of meaning and mental health. The Gerontologist 22: 59–66

Langford M 1962 Community aspects of housing for the aged. Cornell University, New York

Lawton M P, Brody E M, Turner-Massey P 1978 The relationships of environmental factors to changes in well-being. The Gerontologist 18: 133–137

Lazarus R S 1966 Stress and the Coping Process. McGraw-Hill, New York

Lazarus R S 1978 The self regulation of emotions. In: Levi L (ed) Emotions — their Parameters & Measurement. Raven Press, New York, p 47–67

Lazarus R S, Cohen J B 1977 The Hassles Scale. Stress &Coping Project. Berkeley, Ca., Universtty of California

Lehr U 1969 Frau im Beruf. Athenäum, Frankfurt

Lehr U (ed) 1978 Seniorinnen. Zur Situation der älteren Frau. Steinkopff, Darmstadt

Lehr U 1982a Depression und Lebensqualität im Alter — Korrelate negativer und positiver Gestimmtheit. Zeitschrift für Gerontologie 15: 241–249

Lehr U 1982b Patterns of aging — biographical determinants. Paper presented at 10th World Congress of Sociology, Mexico City

Lehr U 1982c Social psychological correlates longevity. Annual Review of Gerontology 3.

Lehr U, Olbrich E 1976 Ecological correlates of adjustment to aging. In: Thomae H (ed) Patterns of Aging. Karger, Basel, p 81–92

Lehr U, Quadt E, Schmitz-Scherzer R 1974 Weiterbildung im Alter. Kohlhammer, Stuttgart

Maas H S, Kuypers J A 1974 From Thirty to Seventy. Bass, San Francisco

Maccoby E E, Jaklin C N 1974 The Psychology of Sex Differences. Stanford University Press, Stanford

Maddox G L 1965 Fact and Artifact: evidence bearing on Disengagement theory from the Duke Geriatrics Project. Human Development 8: 117–130

Mathey F J 1976 Psychomotor performance and reaction speed in old age. In: Thomae H (ed) Patterns of Aging. Karger, Basel, p 36–50

Mc Crae R R 1982 Age differences in the use of coping mechanisms. Journal of Gerontology 37: 454–460

Mischel P 1968 The Assessment of Personality. Wiley, New York

Mischel P 1973 Toward a cognitive social learning reconceptualization of personality. Psychological Review 80: 252–283

Morivaki S Y 1974 The affect-balance-scale: a validity study with aged samples. Journal of Gerontology 29: 73–78

Naylor G F K 1974 Theoretical and practical application of 'educability' in the elderly. In: Proceedings of the Auckland Conference on Aging.

Nehrke F M 1972 Age, sex, and educational dffferences in syllogistic reasoning. Journal of Gerontology 27: 466–470

Neugarten B 1982 Aging: Policy issues for the developing countries of the world. In: Thomae H, Maddox G (eds) New Perspectives on Old Age. Springer, New York, p 115–120

Neugarten B, Gutmann D 1968 Age-sex-roles and Personality in Middle Age: a Thematic Apperception Study. Chicago University Press, Chicago, p 66–78

North A J, Ulatowska H K 1982 Competence in independently living older adults: assessment of older adults. Journal of Gerontology 36: 576–582

Olbrich E 1976 Der ältere Mensch in der Interaktion mit seiner sozialen Umwelt. Doctoral Dissertation Bonn

Palmore E 1977 Sex differences in longevity. Paper presented at world conference. Aging: a challenge to science and policy. Vichy, France

Palmore E 1981 Social Patterns in Normal Aging: Findings from the Duke Study. Duke University Press, Durham, N.C.

Palmore E, Manton K 1974 Modernization and the status of the aged: a correlational analysis. Journal of Gerontology 29: 205–210

Pfeiffer E 1975 Multidimensional functional assessment: The UARS methodology. Duke University Center for the Aging, Durham, N.C.

Pfeiffer E 1977 Psychopathology and social pathology. In: Birren J E, Schaie K W (eds) Handbook of the Psychology of Aging. Van Nostrand, New York, p 650–671

Renner V J, Birren J E 1980 Stress: physiological and psychological mechanisms. In: Birren J E, Sloane R B (eds) Handbook of Mental Health & Aging. Prentice Hall, Englewood Cliffs, N.Y., p 310–336

Riley M W, Foner A 1968 Aging and Society. Russell Sage Foundation, New York

Robertson-Tchabo E A, Arenberg D, Costa P T jr 1979 Temperamental predictors of longitudinal change in performance on the Benton Revised Visual Retention Test among seventy year old men — an exploratory study. In: Bayer-Symposion VII. Brain function in old age, Springer, Heidelberg, New York, p 151–159

Rosenberg G S 1970 The Worker Grows Old. Jossey-Bass, San Francisco

Rudinger G 1974a Eine Querschnittuntersuchung zur Intelligenzleistung im Altersbereich 20–90 Jahre. Zeitschrift für Gerontologie 7: 323–333

Rudinger G 1974b Psychologische Auswirkungen von Dauer des Heimaufenthaltes und sozialer Schicht. Actuelle gerontologie 4: 33–38

Rudinger G 1980 Intelligenzentwicklung unterschiedlichen sozialen Bedingungen. Proceedings XXII. International Congress of Psychology, Leipzig

Sachuk N 1965 The geography of longevity in Russia. Geriatrics 20: 606–606

Savage R D, Garber L B, Britton P G, Bolton N, Cooper A 1977 Personality and Adjustment in the Aged. Academic Press, London

Schade B 1982 Aging & old age in developing countries. In: Thomae H & Maddox G (eds) New perspectives on old age. Springer, New York, p 98–114

Schaie K W 1965 A general model for the study of developmental problems. Psychological Bulletin 64: 92

Schaie K W 1972 Can the longitudinal method be applied to psychological studies of human development? In: Mönks F J, Hartup W W, de Wit J (eds) Determinants of Behavioral Development. Academic Press, New York, p 3–22

Schaie K W 1980 Intelligence and problem solving. In: Birren J E, Sloane R B (eds) Handbook of Mental Health & Aging. Prentice Hall, Englewood Cliffs, p 262–284

Schaie K W, Parham I A 1976 Stability of adult personality traits: Facts or fable? Journal of Personality & Social Psychology 34: 146–158

Schmitz-Scherzer R, Thomae H, Angleitner A, Bierhoff H W, Grombach H, Rudinger G, Steffens K H 1974 Abschlussberichte der interdisziplinären Untersuchung über den Gesundheitszustand älterer Menschen. Altenhilfe 2. Berichte der Landesregierung von Nordrhein-Westfalen. Ministerium für Arbeit, Gesundheit und Soziales, Düsseldorf, p 81–105

Seligman M E P 1975 Helplessness: On depression, development, and death. Freeman, San Francisco

Selye H 1978 The Stress of Life. Rev.ed. McGraw-Hill, New York

Shanan J 1975 Zeitgeschichtliche Faktoren als Determinanten von Auseinandersetzungsbereitschaft und Moral während der mittleren Lebensjahre. Zeitschrift für Gerontologie 8: 87–95

Shanan J, Jacobowitz J 1983 Personality & aging. Annual Review of Gerontology & Geriatrics: 3

Shock N W 1981 Indices of functional age. In: Danon D, Shock N W, Marois M (eds)Aging: a Challenge to Science and Society Vol I, Oxford University Press, Oxford, p 270–286

Shock N W, Andres R, Norris A H, Tobin I D 1979 Patterns of longitudinal changes in renal function. In: Orimo H, Shimada K, Iriki M, Maeda D (eds) Recent Advances in Gerontology. Excerpta Medica, Amsterdam, p 525–527

Siegler I L, George L K, Okun M A 1979 cross-sequential analysis of adult personality. Developmental Psychology 15: 350–521

Simonson E 1965 Performance as a function of age and cardiovascular disease. In: Welford A T, Birren J E (eds) Aging and the Nervous System. Thomas, Springfield, p 401–434

Spieth W 1965 Slowness and cardiovascular diseases. In: Welford A T, Birren J E (eds) Behavior, Aging, and the Nervous System. Thomas, Springfield, p 366–400

Srole L, Fischer A K 1980 The Midtown Manhattan Longitudinal Study vs the 'mental paradise lost' doctrine. Archives General Psychiatry 37: 209–221

Stone J L, Norris A H 1966 Activities and attitudes of participants in the Baltimore Longitudinal Study. Journal of Gerontology 21: 575–580

Svanborg A 1979 The prospective population study of 70-years-olds in Gothenburg, Sweden. In: Orimo H, Shimada K, Iriki M, Maeda D (eds) Recent Advantages in Gerontology. Excerpta Medica, Amsterdam, p 552–553

Svanborg A, Landahl S, Mellström D 1982 Basic issues of health care. In: Thomae H, Maddox G (eds) New Perspective on Old Age. Springer, New York, p 31–52

Thomae H (ed) 1976 Patterns of Aging. Karger, Basel-New York

Thomae H 1979 The concept of development and life span developmental psychology. In: Baltes P B, Brim jr. O G B (eds) Life Span Developmental Psychology Vol 2. Academic Press, New York, p 282–312

Thomae H 1980 Personality and adjustment to aging. In: Birren J E, Sloane R B (eds) Handbook of mental health and aging. Prentice Hall, Englewood Cliffs, p 285–309

Thomae H 1981 Expected unchangeability of life stress in old age. Human Development 24a: 229–239

Thomae H 1981a The Bonn longitudinal Study of aging (BLSA): an approach to differential gerontology. In: Mednick S M, Baert A E (eds) Prospective Longitudinal Research. Oxford University Press, Oxford, p 165–191

Thomae H 1983 Alternsstile und Alternsschicksale. Huber, Bern

Thomae H, Kranzhoff E U 1979 Erlebte Unveränderlichkeit von gesundheitlicher und ökonomischer Belastung. Zeitschrift für Gerontologie 12: 439–459

Thomae H, Lehr U 1982 Conflict and stress — organizers of the life course? Paper presented at Social Science Research Council International Symposion Max Planck Institut, Berlin

Troll L E, Miller S J, Atchley R C 1979 Families in Later Life. Wadsworth Publishing Company, Belmont, CA

UN-World Assembly on Aging 1982 Draft International Plan of Action. A Conference Report of the Secretary General

Viidik A 1982 Biological aging — searching for the mechanisms of aging. In: Thomae H, Maddox G (eds), New Data on Old Age, Springer, New York

Wedderburn D 1968 The characteristics of low income receivers and the role of government. In: Shanas E, Townsend P, Wedderburn D, Friis H, Milhj P, Stehouwer J (eds) Old People in Three Industrial Societies. Atherton Press, New York, p 388–423

Wigdor B T 1980 Drives and motivations with aging. In: Birren J E, Sloane R B (eds) Handbook of Mental Health and Aging. Prentice Hall, Englewood Cliffs, p 245–261

Wilkie F, Eisdorfer C 1971 Intelligence & blood pressure in the aged. Science 172: 959–962

Willis S L, Blieszner, R, Baltes P B 1981 Intelligence training research in aging: modification of performance on the fluid ability of figural relations. Journal of Educational Psychology 73: 41–50

Psychology of aging — normal and pathological age differences in memory

INTRODUCTION

In a current review of the psychological literature on normal age-related differences in memory, Poon (in press) identified over a dozen authoritative reviews between 1980 and 1982, including some in which the present writer was involved (Fozard, 1980, 1981; Hines and Fozard, 1980; Poon and Fozard, 1980b; Poon et al, 1980). At the same time, research reports relative to pathological deficits in memory function in older adults have increased dramatically since the recent authoritative reviews of Miller (1977b, 1980, 1981b). Given these parallel developments, the present discussion will focus selectively first on the contrasts and similarities between normal and pathological age-related differences in the capacity of memory and the speed of access to information in memory. For this purpose, a psychological information processing model will be employed. Second, the present review will relate data based on subjective and psychometric clinical assessments of memory function to the major findings relative to identified normal and pathological age differences in memory. The pathological age differences in memory will be restricted largely to the dementias and depression. References are cited throughout to guide the interested reader to more detailed reviews and original sources. Because of the intentional constraint to the research literature that compares normal and pathological age differences in memory, much current research on normal aging and memory will not be addressed in detail.

The present selective view of the literature should facilitate the exchange of research and clinical information among psychologists, physicians, and others interested in memory, aging, and disease. While the author does not expect all psychologists to agree with the conceptual approach adopted for the review, it is believed that psychologists can use the ideas and vocabulary to interact effectively with non-psychologist colleagues as well as among themselves. Because of space limitations the present review does not discuss the complex literature that relates neuropathology or physiopathology of dementia to the psychological description of symptoms, nor will pharmacological interventions be reviewed (See, for example, Mohs et al, 1982). An excellent overview of dementia is provided by Reisberg (1981).

In general, the term 'dementia' in the following pages will be a shorthand phrase for the clinical syndrome defined by the American Psychiatric Association (1980) Diagnostic and Statistical Manual as primary degenerative dementia which includes Alzheimer's disease and multi-infarct dementia. As will be seen, the operational definitions for dementia and depression will vary from study to study.

INFORMATION PROCESSING VIEW OF MEMORY

The bulk of research in the past decade has employed a psychological concept of information processing involving the capacities of various hypothetical memory stores and the transfer of information among them. Age differences in the speed of retrieval of information from these stores are also of interest in the following discussion. A non-technical example of each of the memory stores is illustrated in Table 7.1, which employs the example of remembering names at a party.

Recalling one's own name from long-term or tertiary memory in Table 7.1 exemplifies the retrieval of well learned information. At the other extreme, sensory or iconic memory is defined by the minimum time necessary to identify letters of an unfamiliar name.

Table 7.1 Retrieving information from different hypothetical memory stores: examples of names at a party

Sensory	Primary	Secondary	Tertiary
Shortest time required to identify letters of new name	Recall new name just after hearing it	Recall new name after meeting 10 other people	Recall own name

Primary and secondary memory go together (Waugh and Norman, 1965). Primary memory is an ephemeral, short-term store from which information is lost if it is not rehearsed. As suggested by the example in Table 7.1, it is experienced by us as the psychological present. Secondary memory is the repository of newly learned verbal information. In the laboratory, newly learned information is defined by arbitrary lists of unrelated words or word pairs in which, after memorization, the first word of the pair serves as a cue or trigger for the recall of the second. Table 7.1 illustrates the differences between the two stores by the recall of an unfamiliar person's name immediately after the person was introduced and after the intervening introductions of a few other persons. In contrast to primary memory, the problem in secondary memory is not a lack of capacity but rather the difficulty of rehearsing the information to be remembered after hearing it (as in a receiving line). In the following discussion, it is important to remember that retrieval of information from secondary memory always involves a question of the degree of memorization or learning of the information to be recalled. This is in contrast to primary memory in which long-term retention is not involved. Such terms as 'short-term' memory frequently blur the distinctions between the two and, as will be seen, it is useful to distinguish the two for research purposes (Waugh and Norman, 1965).

Overview of research on memory capacity

The major results of research and clinical experience with respect to aging and dementia that will be discussed are summarized in Table 7.2 in which YN, EN and EI refer to young normal, elderly normal and elderly impaired adults, respectively.

With respect to age, Table 7.2 indicates that capacity of sensory and secondary memory is diminished in EN as compared to YN and that EI, in comparison to EN, is further impaired in both. The capacity of primary memory is largely unaffected by age or dementia. In contrast to the lack of differences between YN and EN in tertiary memory, EI are poorer in performance. The

following sections will present the research basis for these observations and will also review the normal and pathological age differences in speed of retrieval of memorized information. The clinical neuropsychological literature provides alternative ways of interpreting the same basic findings, e.g., chapters in Pirozzolo and Maletta (1981) and Kaplan and Alpert (1980).

Most of the comparisons to be made between normal age related and pathological memory changes in dementia are valid only for early and middle stages of dementia. At advanced stages, victims of this disease are so impaired with respect to memory and speech functions that the formal comparisons of the sort to be described are meaningless. At the earliest stages of the disease it is equally difficult to distinguish between normal and pathological changes. An example of the narrow range to which results can be generalized is given by Levy et al (1983) who found that about one in 12 potential research volunteers were acceptable for their research.

Primary and secondary memory

The study of relationships between normal and pathological age differences in memory funciton include approaches which increase interference effects in primary and secondary memory and those which enhance the retrieval of information from secondary memory. In a word the results of the studies to be discussed show that the capacity of primary memory is unimpaired in both normal and most often spared in pathological aging. In pathological aging the effects of interference on recall from secondary memory are relatively greater and the effects of improving retrieval through memory enhancement techniques (Poon et al, 1980) or other means are less.

Assessments of primary and secondary memory without experimental manipulations are available by means of standardized tests such as the Wechsler Memory Scale (Wechsler, 1945). Several studies have been reported since the early work of Inglis (1968). Kaszniak et al (1979) administered the Wechsler

Table 7.2 Memory capacity of normal young (NY) normal elderly (NE) and memory impaired elderly (IE) in four hypothetical memory stores

Level of performance	Memory store			
	Sensory	Primary	Secondary	Tertiary
Better	NY	NY, NE, IE	NY	NY, NE
to	NE		NE	IE
Worse	IE		IE	
Source of evidence:				
Laboratory research	Yes	Yes	Yes	Yes
Psychometric tests	No	Yes	Yes	Yes
Clinical observations	No	No	Yes	Yes

Memory Scale to four groups of adults; two with ages 50–59 years with normal brain or questionable atrophy or with moderate to severe atrophy, and two similar groups with ages ranging from 70–89 years. Cerebral atrophy was defined by measuring the widths of ventricles and cortical sulci using computerized tomography. Cases of stroke and focal neurological leisons or psychiatric disorders were identified by clinical evaluation.

The measure of primary memory, the forward digit span, revealed no difference in the two normal age groups while the older normal group performed more poorly on the measure of secondary memory, paired associate learning. Relative to normal age peers, the younger age groups with greater cerebral atrophy performed at 86 per cent, 77 per cent and 62 per cent, respectively, on the digits forward, digits backward and paired associates subtests. The figures for the older group were 94 per cent, 71 per cent, and 54 per cent.

The effects of pathology appeared to be additive with respect to age, in as much as none of the interactions between age and atrophy were statistically significant. The loss of a half a digit capacity in forward digit span with dementia is not always found, e.g, data of Randt et al, (1980) shown in Figure 7.9.

A study by Crook et al (1980b) provides an example of how interference effects differentiate performance between normal and pathological aging. It included two groups of normal subjects with an average age of 21 and 69 years, and a 70-year-old group with memory impairment. Memory impairment was defined by scores at least one standard deviation below the mean of age peers on 3 of the 5 sub-tests of the Guild Memory Scale (Gilbert et al, 1968), to be described later in the text and a psychiatric diagnosis of mild to moderate dementia of the Alzheimer's type, multi-infarct type, or mixed. Subjects recalled the items in lists of three, seven, or 10 visually presented digits under three interference conditions: (1) to name the one digit that was missing from the list that had just been presented; (2) to recall in order all digits in the list; and (3) to dial in order the digits on a telephone apparatus. The presentation time for each list was that required by the subjects to read all digits on the list. Recall was required immediately afterwards.

The data are summarized in Figure 7.1 which displays the fraction of correct identifications of the items in lists of three, seven or 10 digits. As would be expected from other studies of the forward digit span (Craik, 1977), there were no differences with age or memory impairment when the lists of three items were presented under any of the recall conditions. When the number of items was near or exceeded the span of immediate attention (seven items) the differences between the memory impaired elderly and the two normal groups became evident and still more pronounced at supraspan levels of 10 digits. The differential effects of normal and pathological aging were evident in all interference conditions.

In the study by Crook et al (1980b) partial credit was given for transposed digits, so even verbal and motor response interference reduce the performance for elderly

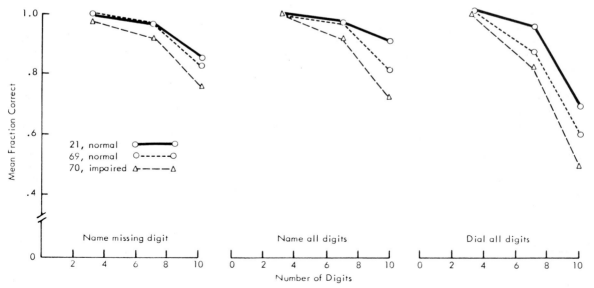

Fig. 7.1 Mean fraction of correct recalls of items in lists of 3, 7 or 10 digits presented once under three conditions of recall. The numbers in the legend designate average age of groups of normal or impaired adults. Data from Crook et al (1980b).

impaired subjects to a level where using the telephone is impractical because ordered recall of seven or 10 digits is required. The present results for the unimpaired groups extend previously reported data on the effects of stimulus and response interference on free recall of short lists of words (Talland, 1965; Fozard et al, 1972).

There has been some recent progress in the area of differential diagnosis of senile dementia. Work by Fuld et al (1982) indicates that verbal intrusion errors may be used to differentiate demented patients with Alzheimer's disease from those with multi-infarct dementia or mixed dementias. They define an intrusion as an 'inappropriate recurrence of a response (or type of response) from a preceding test item, test, or procedure' (op. cit. p. 156). Studying elderly demented patients, differentiated first on the basis of the Hachinski et al (1974) ischaemia score, Fuld et al (1982), found that 90 per cent of the patients diagnosed with Alzheimer's disease made intrusion errors during recall testing, whereas only 35 per cent of those demented patients without the disease did so. In two related experiments with nursing home residents, Fuld and colleagues discovered that, upon autopsy, those subjects who had shown verbal intrusion errors tended to have low levels of choline acetyltransferase and large numbers of cortical senile plaques. Their findings confirm earlier neuropathological studies which identify these two neurological changes as responsible, in part, for the mental deterioration associated with Alzheimer's disease.

McCarthy et al (1981) also studied the relationship between normal and pathological aging on the memorization of lists of 10 words. The lists contained items found on a shopping list, such as milk, eggs, apples, etc. As many as five presentations of the 10 list items alternated with tests for recall. After 15 minutes of other tests, a delayed recall test was given, as well as a forced choice recognition test. If subjects required fewer than five trials, the criteria for learning was two successive trials. Memory impairment was defined, as in the study of Crook et al (1980b).

Results summarized in Figure 7.2 show that the cumulative fraction of subjects in the three groups who mastered the list after 1–5 trials differed radically, as did the number achieving criterion at all: 97, 84 and 33 per cent of the young normal, elderly impaired groups, respectively, reached the criterion. The memorization deficit seen in the normal elderly by Arenberg and Robertson-Tchabo (1977) and Fozard and Popkin (1978), is much exaggerated in the impaired elderly. In particular, acquisition and storage in secondary memory is greatly deficient. Of the subjects who reached criterion, delayed recall was 98, 94 and 93 per cent, respectively, for the 21-year-old normal, 69-year-old normal, and 70-year-old memory impaired groups. Results from a subsequent recognition test showed that all subjects

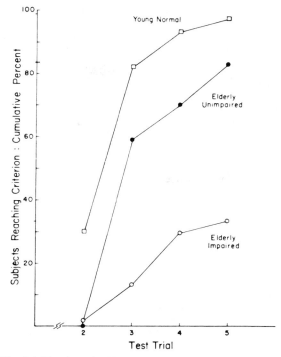

Fig. 7.2 Fraction of subjects in three groups who successfully memorized a list of 10 words on a hypothetical shopping list in five or fewer trials (reproduced with permission from McCarthy et al, 1981)

correctly identified the 10 items in the shopping list. The authors report that the corresponding figures for the percentage correct on the delayed recall test were 98, 90, and 74 for the three groups when other subjects not reaching criterion were included. The figures, although difficult to interpret because the probability of immediate recall of the item is not specified clearly, identify the existence of a retrieval difficulty in addition to a storage difficulty for the older impaired subjects.

Crook et al (1979) devised a practical variation of a memorization task which demonstrates the pervasiveness of the impairment in memorization. The same subjects described in earlier studies were required to place 10 vinyl representations of keys, billfold, umbrella, etc. on a board that represented a seven room house. The constraints were that the subjects be able to name the objects and not place more than two in a room. After 5–30 minutes the subject was to place the objects in the same room on the board he had earlier. The mean number of objects correctly placed was 9.9, 8.9 and 6.0 for the young, elderly unimpaired and elderly impaired groups, respectively. Only three of the 63 young subjects failed to make a perfect score.

Because the items are overlearned and frequently used, the authors argue that the source of interference is from the association of the target items with other items. Most of the intrusion errors on the recall test were names of items related to the target objects. A similar analysis is offered by Wilson et al (1982) who argue from other data that the difficulty in memorizing results from failure to mentally segregate the well known items in an arbitrary grouping.

The studies just cited show clearly that acquisition and storage of new verbal associations suffer relatively more with patients with dementia than in normal aging. These persons have greater retrieval deficits as well. The next studies to be described look more carefully at the question of the retrieval deficit and the conditions which alleviate it. The experimental procedure usually involves having the subject recall items in the presence of contextual cues which vary in their usefulness. One example of a powerful context was the minimal interference condition of the study of digit recall by Crook et al (1980b) in which the subject had to supply the one designated missing digit from each list. Forced choice procedures, or judgements of new and old in which subjects are presented with the target stimuli themselves amongst a group of distractors, provide the least complicated recognition test procedures.

Miller (1975) presented lists of 10 common words for memorization to a group of patients with an average age of 59 years, half of whom had a presumptive diagnosis of Alzheimer's disease. In comparison to non-demented patients, the Alzheimer's patients recalled 60 per cent as many of the words in free recall, 84 per cent as many when the first letter of the word was presented as a recall cue, recognized 59 per cent as many when each word was paired with a distractor, and recognized 31 per cent as many when the 10 target words were distributed haphazardly in an array of 10 distractors. Because the only condition in which the dementia patients did not differ significantly from controls was the cued recall, Miller suggested that a retrieval difficulty was a core problem of the dementia patients. As in the case of Spillich and Voss (1982) to be (see below), the most

powerful cue, the word itself, was not sufficient to minimize the difference in performance between normal and pathological groups. As in the earlier studies reviewed, mentally segregating familiar words into arbitrary groupings is at the core of the dementia patients' deficit in secondary memory.

Spillich and Voss (1982) studied the effects of context on free and cued recall of simple declarative sentences such as, 'John went to a restaurant', and the recognition of such sentences. Strong context for target sentences such as the example was provided by argument repetition and clearly defined thematic structure, e.g., 'It was five o'clock', 'John was downtown', 'He was hungry', followed by the target sentence. Weak context had less of these rated qualities, e.g. 'John was downtown', 'He looked in his wallet', 'There was some money there', followed by the target sentence. In the no context condition, target sentences were presented alone. In the experiment all the target sentences had strong or weak contexts, and each was presented equally often to different subjects in all three context conditions.

The younger subjects were college students, the older were residents of nursing homes or community volunteers. The nursing home subjects were divided into normal and impaired memory groups, defined by the latter having poorer scores on the Wechsler Memory Scale (<50), but not on the vocabulary test from the Scale.

The results summarized in Table 7.3 indicate that in recognition, providing strong context was sufficient to eliminate differences among the three groups. The context manipulation was most evidently a retrieval aid to the memory impaired groups. In this forced choice task the threshold for chance discrimination would be .75. The effect of providing either strong or weak contexts by employing cued recall was very strong in all groups, the fraction correct in cued recall being over double that of free recall for all groups. While the overall beneficial effects of type of cue on recall was statistically significant, the effects were small in comparison to those of cuing itself. The data on the bottom line of Table 7.3 show that stronger context

Table 7.3 Mean fraction correct recall or recognition in three age/impairement groups. Sentences presented with either strong, weak or no recall context. (Data from Table 1 of Spillach and Voss, 1982).

	Measure								
	Recognition			Cued recall					
Age/Condition				Context					
Group	Strong	Weak	None	Strong	Weak	None	Strong	Weak	None
19, Normal	1.00	.99	.99	.50	.42	—	.22	.23	.14
76, Normal	.98	.98	.96	.22	.24	—	.09	.28	.02
81, Impaired	.92	.69	.79	.14	.04	—	.08	.00	.03

helped the elderly impaired relatively more than the other groups.

With respect to normal age differences, the data suggest that as the degree of aid for retrieval increases from providing contextual cues to providing the target word itself, age differences disappear. The same trend is evident in the memory impaired group even though their recall scores are much lower. The fact that the memory impaired group performed slightly better with no context rather than a weak one suggests that the memorization process may be made more difficult where the supporting cues are ambiguous. As in the studies described earlier, this group is more susceptible to interference effects.

It should be recognized that the overall levels of performance in free recall tasks such as this are low indeed. Considering recall of the 24 sentences, the number recalled by the young normal, elderly normal and elderly impaired was 4.6, 1.5 and .83 words, respectively, so the best average performance was within or below the memory span (Miller, 1956).

The preceding studies indicate that when retrieval difficulties are minimized by use of a recognition task, differences in performance between memory impaired

and normal elderly are reduced. By how much? Ferris et al (1980b) studied the question using a continuous recognition paradigm (Shepard and Teghtsoonian, 1961) and pictures of faces as stimuli. The subject was presented with a long sequence of stimuli, each of which was presented twice in the sequence and he/she was required to decide if the item was 'new' (first presentation) or 'old' (second presentation). The number of items intervening between the two presentations of a particular face was six, 12, 24 or 48 corresponding to .5, 1, 2, or 4 min at the rate of presentation employed.

The major results summarized in Figure 7.3 were that the overall percentage of hits (0–100) did not differ among the three groups, but that the number of false alarms, i.e. identifying first presentation of an item as the second, was greater for both elderly normal and impaired groups. Application of a signal detection analysis indicated that d' or the discriminability of new and old items after adjustment for false alarm was lower in both elderly groups than in the younger one. However, the two elderly groups did not differ in the d' measure. For all groups the fraction of hits, as well as the d measures, declined with increasing separation of items in keeping with other findings (Wickelgren, 1975; Poon and

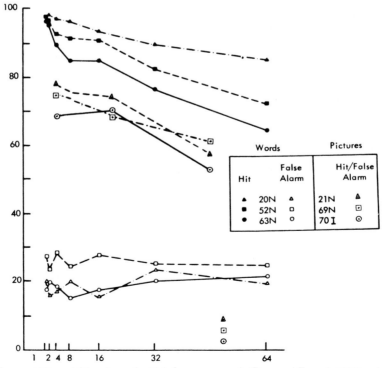

Fig. 7.3 Percentage of correct hits and false alarms for high frequency words (Poon and Fozard, 1980) and pictures of faces (Ferris et al, 1980b). The horizontal axis indicates the number of other items separating the first and second presentation of a particular item. The numbers in the legends designate the average ages of groups of normal (N) or impaired (I) adults.

Fozard, 1980). For comparison, the data of Poon and Fozard (1980a) for high frequency words are shown in Figure 7.3. Older subjects were no less likely than younger ones to guess. Accordingly, the poorer performance of the older subjects must have been due to poorer ability to discriminate between old and new faces.

Wilson et al (1983) administered two recognition memory tasks, one for faces and one for words, to patients with dementia and to normal age peers (average age 69 years) as described in the study group used by those writers. In addition, the Benton facial recognition test was given (Benton et al, 1975). In comparison to controls, dementia patients recognized both fewer words, 62 per cent versus 79 per cent, and faces, 61 per cent versus 72 per cent. The poorer facial recognition memory could not be attributed to perceptual problems measured by the Benton test and there was no difference between groups in response time. Performance on the facial recognition task was not correlated with that for the words nor with scores on the Boston Diagnostic Aphasia Examination (Goodglass and Kaplan, 1972). Thus, the memory problem in dementia patients is not limited to verbal material. These findings are consistent with those of Whitehead (1975).

Miller and Lewis (1977) studied recognition memory for simple geometric designs in three groups with average ages of 77 years, community dwelling volunteers, and two groups of patients clinically diagnosed as having either dementia or depression. The sequence of 160 stimuli involved an initial block of 20 new designs and seven subsequent blocks of 20 each with 12 new designs and eight that were repeats of the 20 designs presented first in the sequence. The unusual procedure apparently combined a learning experiment and a recognition experiment in which the probabilities of an old item being repeated increased over the course of the experiment.

The results indicated that the average d' scores for the normal, depressed and demented groups were 2.36, 2.06 and .85 respectively. While the interpretation of the absolute values is unclear from the results as described, it is clear that performance by the demented group was much poorer than the other two, a finding at variance with results of Ferris et al (1980b). The *beta* scores were 3.51, 2.94 and 1.74 for the depressed, demented and normal groups, respectively, indicating that the depressed persons were less willing to guess than normal or demented age peers.

Finally Clark (1980) studied recognition memory for words that occurred an estimated ≥ 100/million or ≤ 1/million (Kucera and Francis, 1967). In contrast to the previous experiments described in which the target words were simply presented to the subject, Clark's original presentation of the target words involved a task in which the subject was required to decide whether the

word presented was, in fact, an English word or a nonword. In her study two subgroups of demented subjects, mild and moderate, were distinguished on the basis of scores on the Guild Memory Test (Gilbert et al, 1968) and the Global Deterioration Scale (Reisberg et al, 1983).

The results were that the elderly moderately impaired group performed much more poorly on low frequency than on high frequency words. The traditional finding of better recognition on low frequency words was found in all but the moderately impaired groups. No estimates of *beta* were reported by Clark.

Although the variations among the experiments on recognition memory are considerable, they all point to poorer retrieval in demented groups when the task is appropriately difficult or the level of severity great enough. The experiments are too heterogeneous to permit a specification of the necessary and sufficient condition to produce retrieval deficits in cognitively impaired subjects. The role of response bias remains problematical as in the case of normal age research, e.g. Harkins et al (1979).

Sensory memory

The capacity of visual sensory memory may be measured by the number of letters correctly identified in a briefly presented visual display. Because the time available to identify items in a display is the sum of time of presentation of the items and the time the information is available as a positive visual after-image, it is necessary to use a visual noise display immediately after presenting the list in order to specify accurately the amount of time the information was available. Two studies using the appropriate procedure (Sperling, 1963) compared the number of items that could be identified in displays presented from 20–200 ms.

The upper two functions in Figure 7.4 summarize data of Cerella et al (1982), who used seven letter displays. The two phase function relating number of letters identified and time for the group with a mean age of 21 years is typical of the published findings for this procedure. The older normal adults in both the Cerella et al, study and the study by Miller (1977a), identified about 0.5 to 1.0 fewer letters than the younger adults. Miller used a similiar procedure with a six letter display. The elderly impaired subjects in Miller's (1977a) study performed much more poorly at all presentation times and there was no evidence for a two phase function relating performance to duration of presentation. Miller's (1977a) data were the only available for dementia in which a backward masking procedure was employed although other studies of perceptual thresholds using tachistoscopic presentations have been reported (see Miller, 1977 for a review, and Neville and Folstein, 1979).

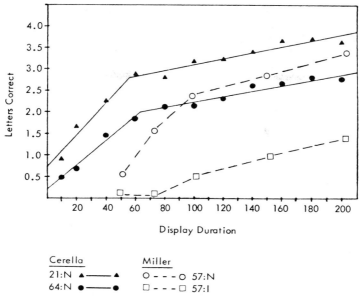

Fig. 7.4 Number of letters correctly identified in briefly presented seven letter displays (solid lines, data from Cerella et al, 1982) and six letter displays (dotted lines, data from Miller, 1978). The numbers in the legend indicate the average age of groups of normal (N) and impaired (I) groups.

Tertiary memory

There are several lines of research which indicate that the capacity of tertiary or long-term memory does not decline with age in normal adults despite the common complaints of elderly persons that they do not remember familiar information as well as they had in the past. A recent review of the literature (Fozard, 1980) identified four lines of evidence for this conclusion: (1) the rate of forgetting for pictorial material learned in the laboratory does not vary with age over a 2½ year retention interval (Fozard and Poon, 1975; Fozard et al, 1975); (2) material of idiosyncratic significance learned under natural conditions 10 to 30 years earlier is well recalled by adults (e.g. Bahrick et al, 1975; Schonfield, 1972); (3) older persons recall colloquial expressions and names of well known personalities or events available directly to the experience of young and elderly adults as well as do young persons (see Baddeley, 1981; Poon et al, 1979; and Squire, 1980, for reviews of several studies); and (4) while total knowledge increases with age, efficiency of remembering remained constant across age (Lachman and Lachman, 1980). The Lachmans (1980) measured the time taken by adults to search memory for names of events and people in relation to confidence judgements of how well they believed they knew the items. Subjects in three adult age groups all spent about 5 seconds trying to recall items they 'definitely did not know' and about 9 seconds searching for items they believed they 'could recall if given more time and a few hints'.

Wilson et al (1981) compared secondary and tertiary memory functions using the dementia patients described earlier. They found that performance tests of semantic or tertiary memory that required naming objects and word finding was largely independent of tests requiring memorization, e.g. paired associate learning. The relationship between recall for well known names of places, persons and events is illustrated in Figure 7.5 in the normal elderly and patients with dementia. The material to be recalled was itself dated according to the decades indicated on the horizontal axis. As in other studies with normal adults the recall of dated material is as good as that for more recent information. In the case of the demented patients, performance was much poorer for information regardless of the datedness of the material and whether it was hard (left) or easy (right) material.

Also in contrast to normal elderly persons, patients with dementia exhibit considerable difficulty in finding words in the early stages of the disease. Results of the controlled study by Barker and Lawson (1968) showed that 100 patients with 'organic dementia' failed 40 per cent of the time to name objects with words which had about one occurrence/150 000 words presented for 50 seconds, and failed about 5 per cent of the time to name words occuring about 100/million. The corresponding figures for normal elderly controls were 10 per cent and 1 per cent. A significant feature of the Barker and Lawson procedure was that some of the objects had their use demonstrated to the subject if they were not correctly named. Use of this procedure helped

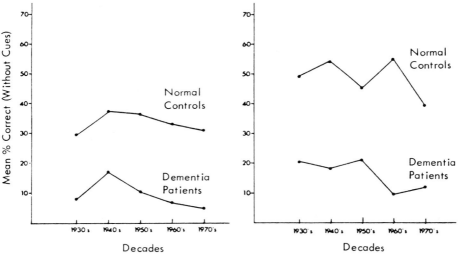

Fig. 7.5 Percentage of hard (a, left panel) or easy (b, right panel) dated names of people and events recalled by dementia patients and normal age peers (reproduced with permission from Wilson et al 1982)

patients name objects with high and low frequency names equally well, indicating that the demonstration facilitated object identification rather than simply the word finding process. The difficulty associated with memory deficit of demented persons in the studies cited above illustrates a problem in word finding which is similar to that exhibited in the studies of interference effects in secondary memory. In the latter the typical finding was that recognition was markedly superior to recall; also that other prompts which facilitated word finding assisted recall.

Long-term memory problems are less evident in elderly persons in the early stages of dementia when conventional tests of vocabulary or information are used. In later stages of the disease, however, information items tapping long-term memory such as those regarding birthdate, etc., found in the Mental Status Questionnaire are too difficult for many patients. Research by Rosen (1981) has shown that aged subjects with senile dementia of the Alzheimer's type, determined by medical records and ratings on the Hachinski et al (1974) Scale perform worse on verbal fluency tasks than normal elderly subjects. Aphasia associated with senile dementia worsens with the increasing severity of the disease. In Rosen's work, subjects were asked to name animals and to provide words beginning with the letters 'C', 'F', and 'L'. Those with moderate-to-severe dementia, as determined by scores on a mental status examinaton, exhibited significantly more impairment on both tasks than those categorized with mild dementia.

A clinical description of how aphasia progresses in cases of senile dementia has been outlined by de Ajuri-aguerra and Tissot (1975). In the early stages of the disease, they point out that speech function remains normal. Yet speech content is affected by the dementia patient's memory difficulties. As the patient begins to deteriorate, egocentric speech (normally evident in children) becomes prevalent. De Ajuriaguerra and Tissot (1975) note that patients still can communicate at this stage, 'but only in connection with practical tasks' (op cit p. 328).

Soon after, though, it becomes quite difficult to understand what the dementia patient is trying to say. His comments grow elliptical and require extralingual information to comprehend. At the most severe stages of impairment, a patient's utterings hardly can be described as speech. He is frequently unable to express wants and needs, and those verbalizations he does make generally lack motivation — apparently set off by chance or body movement.

Between-person variability in aphasia associated with dementia is substantial. Horner et al (1983) tested a group of Alzheimer's patients on two occasions using the Boston Diagnostic Aphasic Exam (Goodglass and Kaplan, 1972). About half of the patients showed some change and those who did experienced a decrease in fluency, an increase in repetitions and an increase in intrusions.

Speed of retrieval from memory

In addition to capacity changes associated with impairment, the speed of response declines in persons with dementia beyond that expected with aging. This is evident at at least three stages of information processing.

Pirozzolo and Hansch (1981) measured the time required for an individual to change fixation from a standard central point to a three letter display located 2–15 degrees from the fixation point. Right and left fields were tested. The major finding was that subjects with presumed diagnoses of Alzheimer's disease had much longer latencies than normal age controls. The 12 patients divided into three categories of severity of the disease, mild, moderate and severe, had overall latencies of 310, 380 and 455 ms respectively, compared to 225 ms for normal age peers.

The range of acceptable latencies included in the analyses was 100–400 ms for the normal 69 year old group and 100–1000 msec for the patients whose average age was also 69. Eight per cent of the values for the patients fell outside of this range, twice that of the normal age peers. While the reason for the relationship between the slowing and the disease process is unclear at present, the fact that the most severely impaired patients required twice as long to achieve a fixation than normal age peers may partially explain some of the difficulties encountered by these patients' when employing motor skills involving visual control such as walking and tasks involving shifting attention. It would be instructive to obtain estimates of the time required to name the trigrams utilized by Pirozzolo and Hansch (1981) in a condition not requiring a change of fixation. Data by Cerella et al (1982) show that normal elderly adults are slower in extracting information from trigrams presented in a backward masking experiment. In their study, the fixation point was at the same place as the display of letters.

The relation between simple and two choice reaction time for manual responses has been studied by Ferris et al (1976) and by Pirozzolo et al (1981). In the Ferris et al study, patients were selected on the basis of a clinical interview and psychometric tests. Simple reaction time was measured by a key release to a red light with a fixed 2 second warning period triggered by the word 'ready'. The choice reaction time was to presentations of a red light that were interspersed among presentations of a green or yellow light.

The average response times for Ferris et al (1976) summarized in the left half of Figure 7.6 were based on the mean of 10 observations per subject. The results were that the disjunctive reaction times rise disproportionately in the older patients. Auxiliary analysis indicated that the apparent difference in the groups in simple reaction time could be entirely accounted for by that component of simple reaction time that is also occurring in disjunctive reaction time, i.e. the central cognitive involvement. Disjunctive reaction time can differentiate between normal and elderly patients with 82 per cent accuracy. Other analyses showed that reaction times of the patients correlated more with measurements of 'confusion disorientation and the degree of dependence on others' (op cit p. 532) than with meas-

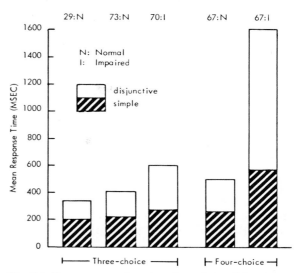

Fig. 7.6 Mean response times in a three choice disjunctive reaction task (Ferris et al, 1976) and four choice task (Pirozzolo et al, 1981). Numbers in legends above each bar graph represent average age of groups of normal (N) and impaired (I) adults.

ures of memory impairment as such. This observation is similar to those of Williams et al (1982) who found that the time required to perform 27 manual skills differentiated three groups of elderly women who differed in their degree of dependency better than a dozen other potential factors assessed by them.

The data of Pirozzolo et al (1981) summarized on the right panel of Figure 7.6, also suggest that slowness of reaction time in persons with dementia reflects great trial to trial variation in reaction time. An analysis of the role of within subject variability on age differences in reaction time is provided by Fozard (1981) that appears applicable to the findings of Pirozzolo and his colleagues.

Miller (1979) evaluated the time required to evaluate the time required to scan primary memory. Two seconds after each presentation of an array of 1–6 digits, a probe digit was presented and the subject was required to decide if the probe was in the string of digits just preceding it. As with other studies, e.g. Anders and Fozard (1973), the time required to decide increased with the number of items. In comparison to normal elderly, patients with depression required more time to make a decision and patients with a presumptive diagnosis of Alzheimer's disease required much more time. Accuracy was poorer in the two patient groups as well.

Cerella et al (1980) analyzed age differences between young and normal elderly subjects on dozens of published studies in which the simple and decision making components were both assessed. The ratio between the differences of complex and simple reaction time for young and old subjects was about 1.31, similar to that of 1.34 for Ferris et al (1976). The corresponding ratio for patients and young normal adults is about 2.5, a much larger figure.

Finally, Clark (1980) compared mildly and moderately impaired elderly patients to young and elderly controls on a lexical decision task which measured the length of time it took a subject to decide whether a string of letters was a word. As with most studies of this type, responses were faster to high frequency than to low frequency words, and somewhat slower to nonwords. The results shown in Table 7.4 indicate that moderately impaired patients are considerably slower than normal or mildly impaired age peers. The mean reaction times for a simple 'go–no go' task shown in Table 7.4 indicate that the difference between memory impaired and normal elderly in the time to access a word cannot be accounted for by the differences in simple reaction times. Mild and moderate impairment for Clark's subjects were defined as described earlier.

The results for young and normal elderly were quite similar to those of Cerella et al (in press) as seen in Table 7.4 The major difference was that the average age difference in response times to words were larger in Clark's study, while the age difference in simple reaction times were larger in the study of Cerella et al.

The difference in results, which could be due to stimuli or differences in procedures used to define simple reaction time, needs to be resolved because the bulk of evidence currently favours the hypothesis that once the perceptual motor component of the reaction time is factored out, the time required to access lexical memory is unchanged in young and old normal adults (Fozard, 1980). Nevertheless the longer times required by the moderately impaired elderly over that of normal controls are quite evident. The reader will recall that the words in the semantic memory task were the same as those used in the recognition task described earlier. Clark points out that where access to semantic memory is slower, the process of memorizing arbitrary lists of words drawn from semantic memory (Tulving, 1972) is made even more difficult.

To conclude, all available evidence indicates that the response times of demented patients are very much slower than in those of normal age peers. Studies of the sensory evoked responses, particularly the P-3 component, shows a similar slowing (Squires et al, 1980) and Kaszniak et al (1978) find that slowing of the EEG is one of the best predicators of mortality in their vast array of measures.

SELF-REPORTED AND CLINICAL ASSESSMENTS OF MEMORY COMPLAINTS IN NORMAL AND PATHOLOGICAL AGING

Complaints about declining memory with advancing age are so common that they appear normal to layman and professional alike. The reflections of this phenomenon in popular humour are indicative of the commonness of the complaint. One elderly person says to another, 'I'd like to live in the past, but I can't remember any of it'. 'The three most important things in life are love, happiness, . . . but I can't remember the third'. In the survey of psychological functioning of the mentally ill elderly in San Francisco (Lowenthal et al, 1967), positive responses to the survey item on memory problems were so ubiquitous that it failed to distinguish among otherwise clinically differentiated subgroups of persons surveyed. As seen in the review of the research literature provided earlier, there is little objective support for complaints about age-related declines in memory function except in the areas of ability to memorize arbitrary collections of verbal information (secondary memory) and greater slowness in retrieval for familiar and unfamiliar material.

In recent years there have been a number of efforts to obtain subjective assessments of memory function, and in some cases to relate those to objective or clinical assessments of psychological functioning including cognitive, personality, and affective aspects. The sections that follow will examine: (1) the emerging literature on efforts to identify self assessments of memory functioning in relation to age and with Alzheimer's disease; (2) the role of memory and cogni-

Table 7.4 Mean response times (ms) by various groups in a Lexical Decision Task for two studies (Clark, 1980; Cerella et al 1982)

Stimulus	Group					
	Young normal		Old normal		Mildly impaired (Clark)	Moderately impaired (Clark)
	(Clark)	(Cerella)	(Clark)	(Cerella)		
Nonword	700	664	1050	995	1000	1250
LF Word	680	—	975	—	910	1250
HF Word	500	—	740	—	675	920
Average	590	609	858	781	792	1085
Control	333	353	395	487	411	476

tive impairment in psychopathology of the elderly; and (3) the development of specialized assessments of memory function for persons with dementia.

Formal surveys of self-assessments of memory function

The practical significance of self-assessments in memory function is important for epidemiological research as well as diagnosis and treatment of psychopathology because epidemiological data on the prevalence of dementia often depend on subjectively reported memory complaints (Mortimer et al, 1981). As will be shown in the following sections, there is considerable overlap between normal age-related complaints of memory and those associated with depression or dementia. One implication of this fact for epidemiological studies of dementia is that reliable information that can be gathered with a simple examination will not pick up many early cases of dementia. Indeed, most research criteria for dementia are quite conservative in the sense that the disease must be fairly well developed before a positive clinical diagnosis is made. With respect to depression, subjective memory complaints are typically not borne out by objective testing. When a definitive distinction between dementia and depression is hard to make, many clinicians recommend treating depression with hope that the complaints about poor memory will disappear with successful use of anti-depressant medication. Because complaints about poor memory are only part of the symptoms of depression, it is not clear that successful treatment of depression will specifically relieve symptoms of memory complaints.

One recent study gives an example of the pervasiveness of memory complaints among the normal elderly. Sluss et al (unpublished) surveyed 135 community dwelling men (over age 60) about self-reported memory declines. The men who were volunteer subjects in a longitudinal study of aging were also administered the Mini-Mental Status Examination (Folstein et al, 1975) and a depression scale developed by the National Institute of Mental Health Center for Epidemiological Studies. Nine per cent had either a mood or cognitive disorder on the basis of the screening but, of the remaining 91 per cent of the sample, 76 per cent reported memory changes. The figures increased with age: for the six half-decades from 60–64 to 85–89, the percentages reporting memory changes were 64, 84, 79, 82, 80, and 86. Complaints of memory change were relatively more frequent with higher education and retirement status.

Because of the pervasiveness of complaints about memory in old age it has been suggested by this writer and others (Fozard, 1980; Fozard and Popkin, 1978; Treat et al, 1978; Zarit, 1980) that older persons or any person should have available a memory evaluation and,

if desired or professionally indicated, treatment of memory complaints through training and counseling either independently or as part of a treatment regimen including pharmacological intervention. Examples of efforts in this area include self-help books, individual and group counseling programs in clinics, and adult education courses. The Mini-White House Conference on Mental Health and the Elderly included such an evaluation of cognitive functioning as part of a routine mental health check as one of its conference recommendations (Santos and Vanderbos, 1982).

The success of memory intervention programs and epidemiological research in detecting early stages of psychopathology of memory depend in large part on the availability of self-assessments of memory function and a basis for relating such self-assessments to formal evaluations of memory function. There have been a number of recent efforts to develop such instruments and Herrmann (1983), and Baddely et al (1982) review several of them. Herrmann concludes that peoples' beliefs about their memory performance are stable, but not very accurate. While memory questionnaires are only moderately successful indicators of memory performance they may, nevertheless, indicate the properties of beliefs that underlie performance. Thus a person who incorrectly believes that he or she is good at remembering directions may pay less attention when receiving them or choose not to take notes that could be consulted later. Sehulster (1981) and Rabbitt (1982) provide examples of research which illustrate the importance of how personal beliefs about memory ability influence performance on tests of memory.

Perlmutter and her colleagues (Perlmutter, 1978; Perlmutter et al, 1981), as well as Zelenski et al (1980), found that older adults rated themselves more poorly than young adults on a number of memory functions, strategies and abilities. Zelenski et al (1980) elicited information on a number of memory problems and required persons to identify the degree to which these problems affected everyday functioning and what, if anything, they did about the problem. Perlmutter et al (1981) found that lower self reports correlated with poorer scores on a word recall test, and Zelenski et al (1980) found that there were significant correlations between performance on a memory test and self assessments of memory in elderly but not young adults. Zelinski and Gilewski (1982) later found that their conclusions had several qualifications.

Using a short version of the Inventory of Memory Experiences (Herrmann and Neisser, 1978), Chaffin and Herrmann (1983) assessed self descriptions of forgetting of: information learned by rote, names, people, conversations, errands, absent mindedness and difficulties in word finding; and remembering of: childhood experiences, remote experiences, and recent experiences based on conversations with friends. Results from three experiments indicated that the profile of the 10 factors differed with age although the overall level of ability did not. The age-related differences in the profile were that older adults reported greater problems with rote memory, names, and recent memory. Chaffin and Herrmann did not relate their information to objective assessments of memory. The value of their findings are the development of a profile better to describe the pattern of similarities and differences in self-reported memory problems across age.

The developments summarized in the previous paragraphs provide a basis for greater optimism about the possibilities for specifying the relationships between objective and subjective assessment of memory function than that reported by Kahn et al (1975). Yet, the relationship between the two is not straightforward as indicated by Baddeley et al (1982). In the study by Zelenski et al for example, old subjects who rated their memory performance well did much more poorly on the objective tests than the young adults who rated their memory poorly. Possible explanations for this finding are that there is greater variability in the older group than in the young, or that individuals whose memories are not as good as they were, compare present and earlier performance differently than those who do not experience changes in memory.

Baddeley et al (1982), asked adults with head injuries to keep a diary of memory problems, fill out a subjective rating scale of memory problems, and perform nine objective cognition assessments including memorization, short-term memory and reaction time. All of the objective tests distinguished between performance of the brain-injured and normal controls. For the brain-injured the diary entries, but not the questionnaire ratings, were related to poorer performance on the objective tests. Baddeley and associates (1982) conclude that because of memory impairment the patient's overall subjective ratings of their memory did not correlate with performance on memory tests. Because the diary was more specific, it imposed less of a memory load for the patients.

The relationship between subjective memory complaints and severity of dementia was studied by Reisberg et al (1981) who asked patients and their spouses to rate problems of memory, as well as emotional problems, at various stages of the disease. In Figure 7.7, increasing stages of severity were indicated by the Global Deterioration Scale from left to right on the horizontal axis and rated severity of problem on the vertical axis. The left panel shows that with greater severity of the disease the rated memory problems of the patients', as judged by the spouse, increases steadily. In contrast, the patients' own ratings increase, then decrease. On the right hand

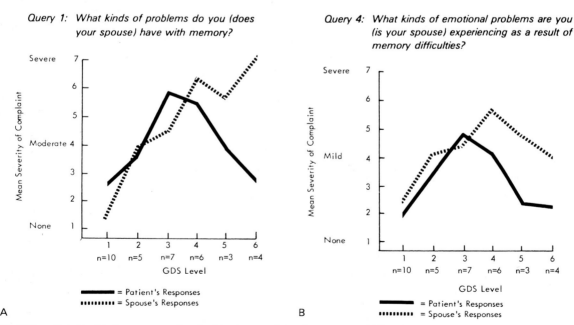

Fig. 7.7 a. Relationship between severity of subjective complaint about memory difficulties and clinically determined level of cognitive deterioration as clinically defined by the Global Deterioration Scale level. Patients' estimates indicated by solid lines, spouses' by dotted lines. b. Rated severity of emotional problems associated with memory difficulties for same respondents (reproduced with permission from Reisberg et al, 1981).

of the figure, the ratings of the emotional problems associated with memory loss first increase with severity, then decrease, for both patient and spouse.

Role of memory impairment in psychopathology

The basic literature on cognitive impairment and psychopathology has been reviewed ably by Miller (1977b, 1980, 1981a). One major effort in recent research is to distinguish better among the role of memory complaints in functional disorders, particularly depression as opposed to 'organic brain disorders.'

A cross-national study of mental disorders of the elderly (Copeland et al, 1976) was carried out in Great Britain and the U.S.A. using a standardized psychiatric interview for assessing psychopathology in persons over 65 years of age. The instrument, called the Geriatric Mental State Schedule (GMS), identified three factors related to cognitive dysfunction: (1) impaired memory defined as an error of one or more years in the patient's self-reported year of birth, failure to recall interviewer's name, and clinical impression of impaired orientation and recall; (2) cortical dysfunction defined by failures in the face hand test and clinical assessments of body

and object recognition and 'clear consciousness'; and (3) disorientation defined as errors in self-report of age, month, year, hospital, etc.

The writers, after relating results of the interview and patient's self reports of symptoms, stress the importance of objective testing to identify dementia in the elderly because the '. . . patients' report of his own symptoms does not reflect clinical understanding which enables a distinction between thought deficiencies due to organicity and depression' (op cit p. 456).

Some 10 factors identified on the basis of clinical and statistical operations distinguished between depression (all subcategories) and organic disorder (all dementias and acute brain reactions). In the profile of scores shown in Figure 7.8, the values on the ordinate are standard scores with a mean of 50 for each scale shown. As expected, poor performance on the three cognitive factors most clearly characterizes the patients with organic disorders although lack of insight and non-social speech also differentiate the groups.

One of the most widely cited studies of the role of self reported memory complaints in depression and in organic brain syndrome was reported by Kahn et al

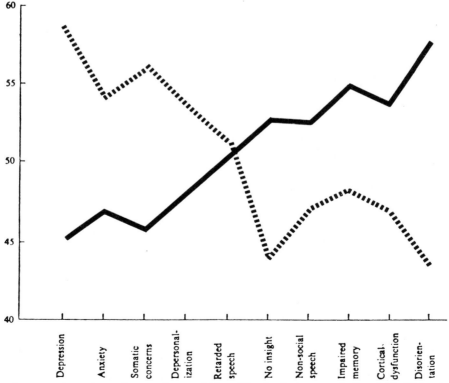

Fig. 7.8 Profile of responses by patients who were depressed (dotted lines) or had an organic disorder (solid lines) on 10 measures of psychological functioning. The vertical axis represents standard scores with a mean of 50 (reproduced with permission from Gurland et al, 1976).

(1975). They asked 153 subjects, ranging in age from 50 to 91, if he/she had any problem with memory, memory problems for recent and remote events, and had experienced any change in memory from when he/she was younger. Responses were rated on a 5 point scale. Only 24 per cent had no memory problem and in about half the complaint was more than minimal. Depression was assessed with the Hamilton Rating Scale for Depression (Hamilton, 1967); mental status was assessed with the Mental Status Questionnaire (Kahn et al, 1968); the Babcock scale (Babcock, 1930) and assessments of primary, secondary, and tertiary memory, as recommended by Fozard and Thomas (1975). The results indicated that the severity of memory complaints were more highly correlated with greater depression than with poor cognitive functioning. In particular, persons with normal cognition and high depression complained as much about memory as non-depressed persons with poor cognitive functioning who indeed performed poorly on the memory tests. The authors suggest that the the reporting of memory problems by depressed adults '. . . may be related to an underlying personality factor characterized by general exaggeration of stress and the use of stereotypes in communication' (Kahn et al 1975, p. 1573).

Clinical wisdom suggests that depression is common in dementia (e.g., Folstein and McHugh (1978). Kaszniak et al (1981) compared the severity and characteristics of depression in participants in a longitudinal study of dementia with normal controls. Depression was assessed with the aid of the Hamilton Rating Scale (Hamilton, 1967). In comparison to the controls, persons with dementia showed less interest in hobbies, work and social life, more motor retardation and greater suspiciousness, but they were not more depressed in mood than controls. No evidence was found that the patients with dementia were less depressed if they had greater severity of dementia.

Neville and Folstein (1979) used assessments of perception, attention and recall to differentiate normal controls from patients with dementia, depression or Korsakov's Syndrome. Perception was measured by the accumulated time required for a person to identify six briefly presented pictures, while attention was indexed by the number of correctly crossed out target letters in 60 seconds. After the attention task, the subject attempted to recall the six pictures. In addition, the Mini Mental State Exam (Folstein et al, 1975) was administered. In comparison to normal controls, dementia patients' median scores were 240 per cent, 37 per cent, 33 per cent, and 59 per cent, respectively, for perception, attention, recall and the Mini Mental State Exam. The 240 per cent reflects slower time to identify pictures, a finding consonant with that of Miller (1977a) described earlier in the chapter. The corresponding figures for depression, were 13 per cent, 72 per cent, 100 per cent, 100 per cent, and for Korsakov's Syndrome 10 per cent, 61 per cent, 67 per cent and 70 per cent, respectively.

In comparison to controls, then, dementia patients were less able to perceive, attend or recall; depressed patients were less able to attend; and patients with Korsakov's Syndrome less able to attend or recall. These findings amplify the results of other studies which indicate that dementia patients have more difficulty with sensory and secondary memory, while depressed patients have greater difficulty than normals in attending to task requirements. Studies by Fuld (1978) dealing with the differences between Alzheimer's disease and multi-infarct dementia along with others, summarized by Miller (1981a), show that the patterns of cognitive decline are not the same across functional and organic psychopathology. (See also Muller et al, 1975 for additional reviews.)

One would expect that poorer cognitive functioning would be related to shortened life expectancy, particularly in cases of senile dementia. The evidence for a terminal drop or decline in cognitive function is unclear (Kleemeier, 1962; Palmore and Cleveland, 1976; see Kausler, 1982, pp 600–601 for a review).

Several studies have shown that the mortality rate of subjects with senile dementia exceeds the expected rate and that their survival time is significantly shorter than that of normal age peers (e.g. Jarvik et al, 1980). One such study by Wang (1978) summarized the data of two earlier neuropathological investigations in which the initial diagnosis of brain disorder was confirmed by histopathological examination after the patient's death. Patients with senile dementia and an average age of 71.3 years lived 6 years in contrast to an actuarial expectation of 11 years.

Kral (1978) divided elderly subjects (mean age 80.5 years) with memory dysfunction into two types after clinical psychiatric examination. The first type, which he termed 'malignant', included cases of severe memory disorders, characterized by loss or recent memory, disorientation, and retrogressive loss of remote memory. The second or 'benign' type consisted of minimally impaired subjects, who were unable to recall relatively unimportant data or past experiences. He also included an aged group with clinically preserved memory. The malignant type had a significantly higher death rate than those without memory impairment. Also, the length of time between psychological testing and death was shorter for the malignant type (15.2 months) than for the benign and normal groups (25 and 23.5 months, respectively).

On the other hand, Peck et al (1978) found physical health a greater determinant of increased mortality than organic brain disorder. They examined the effect of chronic brain syndrome on life expectancy among aged patients at the Jewish Hospital and Home for the Aged in New York City. Upon entry into the hospital, patients were tested for brain syndrome following procedures described in the second edition of the *Diagnostic and Statistical Manual* (American Psychiatric Association, 1968). Five years after the entrance diagnosis, there was no significant difference between the mortality rates of males with and without chronic brain syndrome. Yet, among females the mortality rate rose sharply for those patients with chronic brain syndrome. The most drastic increase occurred in those patients who were classified in poor health upon entrance. The severity of chronic brain syndrome did not significantly affect mortality, except for those subjects in poor health. Peck et al (1978) thus suggest that 'general physical condition affects mortality somewhat more than chronic brain syndrome does' (op cit p. 306).

Surprisingly, very little work has been done on changes over time in the duration of senile dementia. There are no recent data. The most recent information was compiled by Gruenberg (1978) and Hagnell (1966) and showed that the average survival time for individuals with senile dementia increased from less than 3 years before 1949, to around 5 years in 1957. Mortimer et al (1981), note that persons with senile dementia now can be expected to live longer, given the improvements in medical care.

There is clearly a relationship between senile dementia and increased mortality, but the disease itself is rarely the direct cause of death. Research is needed to determine how senile dementia affects mortality. Kay (1962) has made a classic investigation into this area. In nearly all the senile dementia cases he studied, death was due to what he described as 'non-specific causes', which include bronchopneumonia and those somewhat vague conditions associated with death in the elderly and chronically ill. In the Peck et al (1978) study, bronchopneumonia was found to be the leading cause of death in males and females with chronic brain syndrome. They suggest that since most such patients are sedated (sometimes excessively) and often tube fed, they are particularly susceptible to respiratory problems.

In a longitudinal study of patients with dementia Kazniak et al (1978) found that dementia patients who died in a 12 month period did not differ from survivors in age, education, length of history of dementia, sex, race or degree cerebral atrophy as measured by computerized tomography. The major differences were found in terms of encepholographic abnormalities and in a variety of tests of cognitive performance, particularly tests of expressive language.

In summary, the evidence for life-shortening affects of pathological memory problems is not conclusive. At present the prospective study by Kaszniak et al (1978) provides the clearest evidence for the existence of such a relationship.

Specialized tests of cognitive functioning for dementia

At present there is no single set of assessment procedures that cover the full range of variation in memory functioning and other significant cognitive aspects of dementia. Standard tests, such as the Wechsler Memory Scale (Wechsler, 1945) are too difficult for most patients with dementia and, as shown by Kleban et al (1976) and Hersh et al (1978) there are clinically distinguishable stages in cognitive functioning below the range covered by the several variations of the Mental Status Questionnaire (Kahn et al, 1960). Most of the recent developments in the field since Miller's (1977b, 1980) definitive reviews attempt to extend the range and scope of testing. The following review will focus largely on those efforts.

Rating scales that attempt to cover cognitive impairment mood and behaviour disorders in one instrument, such as the Sandoz Clinical Assessment Geriatric (Shader et al, 1974), tend to do less well on the cognitive assessment largely because such tests require considerable time, cooperation from the patient and a degree of expertise by the rater. Rosen et al (1982) are in the process of developing a rating scale which covers all three areas and takes less than half-an-hour. The still excellent review of Salzman et al (1972) covers the characteristics of many published scales.

In addition refinements have been made in the scope of the mental status questionnaire itself, e.g. Folstein et al (1975). Most of the items in the mental status questionnaire assess awareness of current time and place and inactness of long-term memory. The 10 questions in the Pfeiffer (1975) version are typical: orientation items include today's date, day of the week, name of place, telephone number or address; memory items include age, date of birth, current and past president (prime minister, etc.), and mother's maiden name. The last question is a test of attention and arithmetic skill — counting backwards by serial threes. The Blessed et al (1968) version is similar in scope. The Memory Information Test (Rosen et al, unpublished) is based on the Blessed work because it was validated on patients with Alzheimer's disease. Later tests add additional items of a similar sort. In order to assess functioning at a level between normal elderly and dementia, assessment procedures add measures of memorization of word lists and often tests word finding or naming (early aphasia). There are several recent developments along these lines in the United States (Rosen et al, unpublished; Eisdorfer and Cohen, 1979, 1980). At the other end, a notable example is Gurel et al (1972). Gurland's (1981) excellent review about the variability in mental status scores associated with social class and education point to the need for caution in interpreting results from such instruments.

Reisberg et al (1982) have attempted to provide a clinical description of the course of dementia which provides a framework for relating stages of the disease to results of psychological tests of memory as well as clinical descriptions of other psychological characteristics. The stages are based on a synthesis of clinical and psychometric experiences rather than a prospective study, but for present purposes, their description is useful because it places the patient who makes three or more errors on the mental status questionnaire at the midpoint of a seven point scale called by Reisberg et al (1983), the Global Deterioration Scale.

Reisberg and colleagues have proposed a threefold classification of the stages of dementia — forgetfulness, confusion and dementia — which they further classify into seven stages. Three or more errors on the mental status questionnaire are only evident in the middle level of the seven. A Global Deterioration Scale proposes criteria for psychometric test scores and clinical ratings in terms of this overall scale.

Stages 1 and 2, no cognitive decline or very mild cognitive decline, define the forgetfulness phase in which there is either no psychometric evidence (Stage 1) or below average performance on fewer than three of five subtests of the Guild Memory test. Although there is no objective evidence for deterioration, subjective concern about forgetfulness is evident.

Stages 3 and 4, corresponding to the confusion phase, are associated with memory declines evident to others in work and social situations. In Stage 4, three or more errors are typically made on the Mental Status Questionnaire. Persons remain well oriented with respect to time and person, although memory problems and concentration powers are increased.

Stages 5 to 7, dementia, are characterized by 6–10 errors on the Mental Status Questionnaire, and profound changes in ability to carry out the activities of daily living. In stage 7, for example, speech and the ability to walk is often lost.

The Guild Test referred to above was developed by Gilbert et al (1968) and additional data, including those of persons with dementia, were added by Crook et al (1980a). The Guild Memory Test consists of five subtests: immediate recall for paragraphs and paired associates; recall for designs; and delayed recall of the paragraphs and paired associates. Correlations between performance on the five tests and the Memory Quotient of the Wechsler Memory Scale range from .55 to 67. Norms for the cognitively impaired elderly were developed separately according to the vocabulary scale score of the Wechsler Adult Intelligence Scale. Cutoff scores for each test were defined as one standard deviation below the mean for normal age peers, representing four

levels of performance on the vocabulary test. Patients were classified as having dementia if they scored below the cutoff score on any three of the five tests. The limitations in sampling as a basis for the norms were acknowledged by Crook et al (1980a). Their results have the advantage of relating scores of patients who meet the current American Psychiatric Association Diagnostic and Statistic Manual (1980) criteria for organic brain syndrome to the Wechsler Memory Scale for different levels of verbal intelligence as measured by the Wechsler Adult Intelligence Scale. One possible disadvantage is that the criteria for memory impairment can be achieved in several different ways.

The Fuld Object-Memory Evaluation (Fuld, 1980, 1981) is specially designed to alleviate some of the problems such as sensory handicaps and attentional difficulties, experienced in assessing the memory capabilities of elderly subjects. Subjects are first asked to identify, by touch, 10 common objects placed in a bag. Once the person names an object, he is then allowed to pull it out of the bag so that a correct naming is confirmed and any error can be corrected. The person is periodically distracted from this task by a rapid semantic retrieval test, which also screens the subjects for depression by the proportion of 'sad' or 'happy' words they retrieve. After each distraction, subjects are asked to recall the names of the 10 items in the bag. This procedure of naming, distraction, and recall is repeated five times.

The results of Fuld's own study utilizing this method of assessment differentiate impaired elderly from the normal aged (designated according to scores on the Blessed et al (1968) mental status test) by their diminished ability to store and recall information over this series of test trials. Her findings also show that, in cases of dementia, storage impairment is more significant than retrieval impairment which can also occur in normal aging.

Another test battery under development which emphasizes memorization processes is the Randt Memory Test (Randt et al, 1980). The authors give as one justification for the test the fact that the Guild Memory Test is too complex for use with any but persons with mild memory deficits or as an adjunct to the Wechsler Memory Scale.

Many subtests of the Randt Memory Test assess storage and retrieval from secondary and primary memory. For example, the first of the seven tests requires memorization of five unrelated names, and assesses retention of them shortly after or 24 hours after initial memorization, and it illustrates the philosophy of the test. The five items are spoken once each, and after the subject has counted backwards by threes for 10 seconds he/she attempts to recall the words in any order. The process is repeated except that only the unlearned words are presented until the subject has all five words correct, or has received three presentations of the list. After an intervening test the free recall of the words is measured followed by reacquisition if necessary. The procedure just described is repeated again about 24 hours later.

As indicated by the authors the procedures provide for separation of acquisition and retention, but the scoring protocol does not reflect unambiguously the intent because the recorded score on the recall tests is not linked to the actual memorization of the particular items presented. Where scores are near perfect this is not important, but when recall scores are low the relationship between acquisition and recall is relatively more difficult to interpret.

The left panel of Figure 7.9 displays the mean fraction of correct recalls of the five words under the three conditions of the test. As is typically found, delayed retention declines more sharply with age than does short-term recall. The patients' (single points) score about half as well as any other group in each condition.

The right panel of Figure 7.9 displays the data from one test that does not differ with age or disease, repeating digits forward and backwards. Because there was no difference with age or clinical condition on either version, the scores from both are combined. The scores

on the 10 mental status questionnaire items show clearly that the test items distinguish between demented and normal persons of any age. The recall of the names of the five tests shows both an age and disease effect.

The Randt Test has five alternate forms and can be administered in less than half-an-hour. Patients who are severely demented are spared the ordeal of taking the test because the mental status questionnaire is used as a screening device.

Multivariate analyses were applied to subgroups of the subjects (Osborne et al, 1982) showed that the test scores in combination discriminate young normals with 91 per cent accuracy, while old normals with 84 per cent accuracy, and the patient group with 84 per cent accuracy. The patient group excluded patients with a history of depression requiring treatment, or current evidence or depression.

CONCLUSIONS

The material reviewed in the present chapter has implications for three areas: (1) sharpening the boundaries between normal and pathological age differences in memory; (2) forcing the realization that a focus on

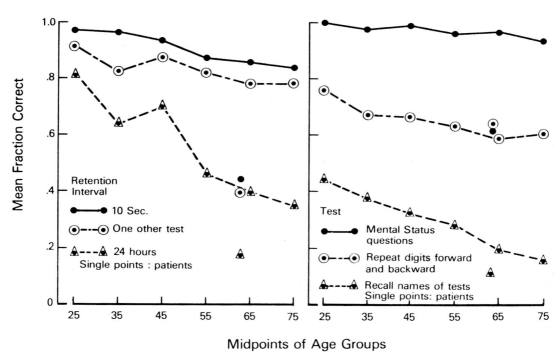

Fig. 7.9 Left panel: Mean fraction correct and recalls of lists of five words by six age groups and a group of patients with dementia with an average of 63 years (single points). Recall was measured after 20 seconds of counting backwards after 1–3 presentations of the five items, or after administration of one other test or 24 hours after the testing session. Right panel: mean fraction correct on three other subtests of the Randt Memory Test by the same subjects (data from Randt et al, 1980).

specific assessment of memory functions per se yields a critical but yet limited psychological understanding of memory in relationship to either normal or pathological aging; and (3) identifying implications for treatment of senile dementia. The following paragraphs elaborate on these three issues.

The new boundaries between normal and pathological memory

Gerontologists are accustomed to clinical speculations that a particular problem represents an example of 'accelerated aging'. Analogies are made between the effects of alcohol on cognitive functioning and aging, slow response times, 'premature graying' of the hair, and other indices correlated with aging. In fact, there is little evidence that such measures of functional aging (Fozard and Thomas, 1975) correlate well with each other or with chronological age. In the area of memory, the literature reviewed demonstrates that the 'functional' effects of dementia are, for the stages of the disease for which meaningful comparisons can be made, a radical exaggeration of normal age differences in secondary memory. Moreover, the apparently greater susceptibility of dementia patients to interference effects in memorization tasks and the relationship of that phenomenon to cholinergic deficits and the relevant pharmacological interventions provide an exciting insight into what the author considers the most significant scientific problem in memory and normal aging — memorization and the retrieval of information from secondary memory.

The other area for which dementia represents an exaggeration of normal age differences includes sensory memory and the slowness of response time. Several situations in which slowness of response speed has obviously deleterious effects on voluntary behaviour were identified. Slowness of behaviour in dementia may provide an explanation of many of the problems of attention and confusion observed in such patients (a hypothesis in need of evaluation).

The deterioration of tertiary memory function with dementia in contrast to normal aging, is a major theme emerging from current research. The effect of difficulties with long-term memory are of particular concern to elderly persons because the effects are the most evident subjectively.

The implications of these findings for research and clinical assessments of normal and pathological age differences in memory are that in addition to measuring secondary and sensory memory functions, assessments should include evaluation of tertiary memory and speed of retrieval from various memory stores.

A more comprehensive psychological description of memory

Earlier, Fozard (1980) argued that a satisfactory understanding of normal age changes in memory would not be complete unless it included a description of the relationship of personality and interests on memory and included a clear analysis of the motivational and affective aspects of behaviour as these related to memory. The literature on dementia and aging reinforces the need for such research in dementia as well. In particular, Fozard (1982) identified three major areas where psychological analyses of behaviour are needed to complement assessments of cognitive functioning in dementia, such as those described in the present chapter: (1) the relation of affective personality-motivational characteristics of behaviour to memory dysfunction; (2) the relation of abilities to carry out instrumental and basic activities of daily living to memory limitations associated with dementia; (3) a human factors analysis of the way that a person uses the memory props provided by his environment (Fozard and Thomas, 1975); and (4) an improved analysis of the changed relationships between patient and family and friends. At a practical level there is a growing tendency to provide more comprehensive psychological descriptions of dementia as exemplified in many papers in *Alzheimer's disease: A report of progress in research* (Corkin et al, 1982). Rabbitt's (1982) proposals in this regard are of particular interest to psychologists.

Implications for treatment of senile dementia

The current research reviewed in the present chapter has implications for treatment only for a relatively narrow range of the symptoms of cognitive decline observed in dementia. Many of the therapeutic approaches to patients with dementia in institutional settings including reality orientation and reminiscence are reviewed by Eisdorfer et al (1981) and Merriam (1980). Approaches to helping the patient and family as a unit are emphasized in all contemporary works, e.g. Miller (1977c), Reisberg (1981, in press), and above all, Mace and Rabins' (1981) *The Thirty-Six Hour Day*. The type of psychological and pharmacological interventions appropriate for memory problems of normal depressed and demented elderly persons are now much more sharply delineated than a few years ago (See, Ferris et al, 1980a; and Mohs et al, 1980, for lucid reviews). However, a comprehensive approach to memory problems that involve medical and psychological intervention is still best, whatever the cause of the problem (Fozard and Popkin, 1978). All in all, the very rapid developments at both practical and scientific levels provide a basis for optimism about improved management of dementia.

ACKNOWLEDGEMENT

I am very appreciative of the excellent assistance I

received in assembling, organizing and reviewing the literature for the chapter from Mr Thomas Tillman, I also appreciate the staunch encouragement throughout this endeavour by my supervisors, Dr Paul A. L. Haber and Dr John H. Mather, and to the numerous colleagues including Drs Thomas Croak, Stephen Ferris, Patricia Fuld, Lissy Jarvik and Richard Mohs, who generously shared information and insights. The opinions expressed do not necessarily reflect those of the Veterans Administration.

REFERENCES

de Ajuriaguerra J, and Tissot R 1975 Some aspects of language in various forms of senile dementia. In: Lennebert E, Lennebert E (eds) Foundations of Language Development, Vol: 1, Academic Press, New York

Albert M S Kaplan E 1980 Organic implications of neuropsychological deficits in the elderly. In: Poon L W, Fozard J L, Cermak L S, Avenberg D, Thompson L W (eds) New Directions in Memory and Aging: Proceedings of the George A. Talland Memorial Conference, Lawrence Erlbaum Associates, Hillsdale, N J.

American Psychiatric Association 1968 Diagnostic and Statistical Manual of Mental Disorders, 2 edn. American Psychiatric Association, Washington, D.C.

American Psychiatric Association 1980 Diagnostic and Statistical Manual of Mental Disorders, 3rd edn. American Psychiatric Association, Washington, D.C., p 124

Anders T R and Fozard J L 1973 The effects of age upon retrieval from primary and secondary memory. Developmental Psychology 3: 411–415

Arenberg D and Robertson-Tschabo E A 1977 Learning and aging. In: Birren J E and Schaie K W (eds), Handbook of the Psychology of Aging. New York: Van Nostrand Reinhold

Babcock H 1930 An experiment in the measurement of mental deterioration. Archives of Psychology 117: 106

Baddeley A 1981 The cognitive psychology of everyday life. British Journal of Psychology 72: 257–269

Baddeley A, Sunderland A and Harris J 1982 How well do laboratory-based psychological tests predict patients' performance outside the laboratory? In: Corkin S, Davis K L, Growden J H, Usdin E, Wurtzman R J (eds) Alzheimer's Disease: A Report of Progress in Research. New York: Raven Press, p 141–148

Bahrick H B, Bahrick P O and Wittlinger R P 1975 Fifty years of memory for names and faces: A cross sectional approach. Journal of Experimental Psychology: General 104: 54–75

Barker M G and Lawson J S 1968 Nominal asphasia in dementia. British Journal of Psychiatry 114: 1351–1356

Benton A L, Van Allan M W, Hamsher K and Levin H S 1975 Test of Facial Recognition, Form SL: Revised Manual. Iowa City, IA: University of Iowa, Neurosensory Center Publication No. 338

Blessed G, Tomlinson B E and Roth M 1968 The association between quantitative measures of dementia and of senile change in the cerebral gray matter of elderly subjects. Journal of Psychiatry 114: 797–811

Cerella J, Poon L W, Fozard J L 1982 Age and iconic read-out. Journal of Gerontology 37: 197–202

Cerella J, Fozard J L 1984 Lexical access and age. Developmental Psychology (In press)

Cerella J, Poon L W and Williams D 1980 Age and the complexity hypothesis. In Poon L W (ed) Aging in the 1980s: Psychological Issues. Washington, D.C.: American Psychological Association

Chaffin R and Herrmann D J 1983 Self-reports of memory ability by old and young adults. Human Learning.

Clark E O 1980 Semantic and episodic memory impairment in normal and cognitively impaired elderly adults. In: L K Obler and M L Albert (eds) Language and Communication with the Elderly. Lexington, MA: D C Heath and Company

Corkin S, Davis K L, Growdon J H, Usdin E, Wurtman R J (eds) 1982 Alzheimer's Disease: A Report of Progress in Research. New York: Raven Press

Craik F I M 1977 Age differences in human memory. In: Birren J E and Schaie K W (eds) Handbook of the Psychology of Aging. New York: Van Nostrand Reinhold

Crook T, Ferris S and McCarthy M 1979 The misplaced objects task: A brief test for memory dysfunction in the aged. Journal of the American Geriatrics Society 27: 284–287

Crook T, Gilbert J G and Ferris S 1980a Operationalizing memory impairment for elderly persons: The Guild Memory Test. Psychological Reports 47: 1315–1318

Crook T, Ferris S, McCarthy M and Rae D 1980b Utility of digit recall tasks for assessing memory in the aged. Journal of Consulting and Clinical Psychology 48: 228–233

Eisdorfer C and Cohen D 1979 Diagnostic criteria for primary neuronal degeneration of the Alzheimer's type. Paper presented at the Gerontological Society Meeting, Washington, D.C.

Eisdorfer C and Cohen D 1980 Workshop on Aging II: Dementia in Middle and Later Years (videotape). Sandoz Pharmaceuticals Educational Services, Rt. 10, East Hanover, N.J. 07936

Eisdorfer C, Cohen D and Preston C 1981 Behavioral and psychological therapies for the older patient with cognitive impairment. In: Miller N E and Cohen G D (eds) Clinical Aspects of Alzheimer's Disease and Senile Dementia. New York: Raven Press, 209–226

Ferris S H Reisberg B and Gershon S 1980a Neuropeptide modulation of cognition and memory in humans. In: Poon L W (ed) Aging in the 1980s: Psychological Issues. Washington, D.C.: American Psychological Association, pp 212–230

Ferris S, Crook T, Sathananthan G and Gershon S 1976 Reaction time as a diagnostic measure in senility. Journal of the American Geriatrics Society 24: 529–533

Ferris S H Crook T, Clark E, McCarthy M and Rae D 1980b Facial recognition memory deficits in normal aging and senile dementia. Journal of Gerontology 35: 707–714

Folstein M F and McHugh P R 1978 Dementia syndrome of depression. In: Katzman R, Terry R D and Bick K L (eds) Alzheimer's Disease: Senile Dementia and Related Disorders. New York: Raven Press

Folstein M F, Folstein S E and McHugh P R 1975 'Minimental state': A practical method for grading the cognitive state of patients for the clinician. Journal of Psychiatric Research 12: 189–192

Fozard J L 1980 The time for remembering. In: L W Poon (ed) Aging in the 1980s: Selected Contemporary Issues in the Psychology of Aging. Washington, D.C.: American Psychological Association

Fozard J L 1981 Speed of mental performance and aging: Costs of age and benefits of wisdom. In: Pirozzolo F and Maletta G (eds) Behavioral Assessment and Psychopharmacology, (Vol. 2): Advances in Neurogerontology. New York: Praeger

Fozard J L 1982 Psychological and public policy issues in dementia. Invited address at the American Psychological Association, Washington, D.C. August 24

Fozard J L and Poon L W 1975 Age related differences in long-term memory for pictures. Presented at the Gerontological Society Meeting, New York, October

Fozard J L and Popkin S J 1978 Optimizing adult development: Ends and means of an applied psychology of aging. American Psychologist 33: 975–989

Fozard J L and Thomas J C 1975 Psychology of aging: Basic findings and their psychiatric application. In: Howells J G (ed) Modern Perspectives in the Psychiatry of Old Age. New York: Brunner-Mazel

Fozard J L Nuttall R L and Waugh N C 1972 Age-related differences in mental performance. Aging and Human Development 3: 19–43

Fozard J L, Waugh N C and Thomas J C 1975 Effects of age on long-term retention of pictures. Proceedings of the Tenth International Congress of Gerontology (Jerusalem) 2: 137 (Abstract)

Fuld P A 1978 Psychological testing in the differential diagnosis of the dementias. In: Katzman R, Terry R D and Bick K L (eds)

Alzheimer's Disease: Senile Dementia and Related Disorders. New York: Raven Press, pp 185–193

Fuld P A 1980 Guaranteed stimulus processing in the evaluation of memory and learning. Cortex 1: 255–272

Fuld P A 1981 Fuld object-memory evaluation. Chicago, IL, Stoelting Company

Fuld P A, Katzman R, Davies P and Terry R D 1982 Intrusions as a sign of Alzheimer's Dementia: Chemical and Pathological verification. Annals of Neurology 11: 155–159

Gilbert J G, Levee R F and Catalano F L 1968 A preliminary report on a new memory scale. Perceptual and Motor Skills 27: 277–278

Goodglass H and Kaplan E 1972 The Assessment of Aphasia and Related Disorders. Philadelphia: Lea and Febiger

Gruenberg E M 1978 Epidemiology of senile dementia. In: Schonberg B S (ed) Epidemiology: Principles and Clinical Applications. New York: Raven Press

Gurel L, Linn M W and Linn B S 1972 Physical and mental impairment of function in the aged: The PAMIE scale. Journal of Gerontology 27: 83–90

Gurland B J 1981 The borderland of dementia: The infulence of socio-cultural characteristics on rates of dementia occurring in the senium. In: Miller N E and Cohen G D (eds) Clinical Aspects of Alzheimer's Disease and Senile Dementia. New York: Raven Press

Gurland B J, Fleiss J L, Goldberg K, Sharpe L, Copeland J R, Kelleher M J and Kelleff J M 1976 A semistructural clinical interview for the assessment of diagnosis and menta; state in the elderly: The geriatric mental states schedule. Psychological Medicine 63: 451–459

Hachinski V C, Lassen N A and Marshall J 1974 Multi-infarct dementia: A cause of mental deterioration in the elderly. Lancet ii: 207–210

Hagnell O 1966 A prospective study of the incidence of mental disorder. Stockholm: Svenska Bokforlaget

Hamilton M 1967 Development of a rating scale for primary depressive illness. British Journal of Social and Clinical Psychiatry 6: 276–296

Harkins S W, Chapman C R and Eisdorfer C 1979 Memory loss and response bias in senescence. Journal of Gerontology 34: 66–72

Herrmann D and Neisser U 1978 An inventory of everyday memory experiences. In: Gruneberg M M, Morris R E and Sykes R N (eds) Practical Aspects of Memory. New York: Academic Press

Herrmann D J 1983 Know thy memory: The use of questionnaires to assess and study memory. Psychological Bulletin.

Hersch E L Kral V A and Palmer R B 1978 Clinical value of the London psychogeriatric rating scale. Journal of the American Geriatrics Society 26: 348–354

Hines T M and Fozard J L 1980 Memory and aging: Relevance of recent developments for research and application. In: Eisdorfer C (ed) Annual Review of Gerontology and Geriatrics. New York: Springer Publishing

Horner J, Heyman A, Kanter J, Royall J B and Randall A 1983 Longitudinal changes in spoken discourse in Alzheimer's dementia. Presented at the International Neuropsychological Society, Mexico City, February

Inglis J 1958 Psychological investigations of cognitive deficit in elderly psychiatric patients. Psychological Bulletin 55: 197–214

Jarvik L F, Ruth V and Matsuyama S S 1980 Organic brain syndrome and aging. Archives of General Psychiatry 37: 280–866

Kahn R L, Goldfarb A I, Pollac M and Pack A 1961 Brief objective measures for the determination of mental status in the aged. American Journal of Psychiatry 117: 326–328

Kahn R L, Zarit S H, Hilbert H M, Niederehe G 1975 Memory complaint and impairment in the aged: The effect of depression and altered brain function. Archives of General Psychiatry 32: 1569–1573

Kaszniak A W, Garron D C and Fox J 1979 Differential effects of age and cerebral atrophy upon span of immediate recall and paired associate learning in older patients suspected of dementia. Cortex 15: 285–296

Kaszniak A W, Wilson R S, Lazarus L, Lessor J and Fox J H 1981 Memory and depression in dementia. Presented at the Ninth Annual Meeting of the Neuropsychological Society, February 4–7, Atlanta, GA

Kasznia A W, Fox J, Gandell D L, Garron D C, Huckman M S and

Ramsey R G 1978 Predictors of mortality in presenile and senile dementia. Annals of Neurology 3: 246–252

Kausler D H 1982 Experimental Psychology and Human Aging. New York: Wiley, pp 600–601

Kay D W K 1962 Outcome and cause of death in mental disorders of old age: A long-term follow-up of functional and organic psychoses. Acta Psychiatry Scandanavia 38: 249–276

Kleban M H, Lawton B P, Brody E M and Moss M 1976 Behavioral observations of mentally-impaired aged: Those who decline and those who do not. Journal of Gerontology 31: 333–339

Kleemeir R W 1962 Intellectual changes in the senium. In American Statistical Association, Proceedings of the Social Statistics Section 1: 290–295

Kral V A 1978 Benign senescent forgetfulness. In: Katzman R, Terry R D and Bick K L (eds) Alzheimer's Disease: Senile Dementia and Related Disorders. New York: Raven Press

Kucera H and Francis W N 1967 Computational Analysis of Present Day American English. Providence, R.I.: Brown University Press

Lachman J L and Lachman R 1980 Age and the actualization of world knowledge. In: Poon L W, Fozard J L, Cermak L S, Avenberg D and Thompson L W (eds) New Directions in Memory and Aging: Proceedings of the George A. Tellard Memorial Conference. Hillsdale, N.J.: Lawrence Erlbaum

Levy M I, Mohs R C, Rosen W G and Davis K L 1983 Research subject recruitment for gerontological studies of pharmacological agents. Neurobiology of Aging.

Lowenthal M F, Berkman P and Associates 1967 Aging and Mental Disorder in San Francisco. San Francisco: Jossey Bass

Mace N L and Rabins P V (1981) The 36-Hour Day. Baltimore: The Johns Hopkins University Press

McCarthy M, Ferris S H, Clark E and Crook T 1981 Acquisition and retention of categorized material in normal aging and senile dementia. Experimental Aging Research 7: 127–135

Merriam S 1980 The concept and function of reminiscence: A review of the research. The Gerontologist 20: 604–609

Miller E 1975 Impaired recall and the memory disturbance in presenile dementia. British Journal of Social and Clinical Psychology 14: 73–79

Miller E 1977a A note on visual information processing in presenile dementia: A preliminary report. British Journal of Social and Clinical Psychology 16: 99–100

Miller E 1977b Abnormal Aging. Chichester: Wiley

Miller E 1977c The management of dementia: a review of some possibilities. British Journal of Social and Clinical Psychology 16: 77–83

Miller E 1980 Cognitive assessment of the older adult. In: Birren J E and Sloane R B (eds) Handbook of Mental Health and Aging. Englewood Cliffs, New Jersey: Prentice Hall

Miller E 1981a The differential psychology evaluation. In: Miller N E and Cohen G D (eds) Clinical Aspects of Alzheimer's Disease and Senile Dementia. New York: Raven Press

Miller E 1981b The nature of the cognitive deficit in dementia. In: Miller N E and Cohen G D (eds) Clinical Aspects of Alzheimer's Disease and Senile Dementia. New York: Raven Press

Miller E and Lewis P 1977 Recognition memory in elderly patients with depression and dementia: A signal detection analysis. Journal of Abnormal Psychology 86: 84–86

Miller G A 1956 The magical number seven plus or minus two: Some limits on our capacity for processing information. Psychological Review 63: 81–97

Miller N E 1979 Primary Memory in Depressed, Demented and in Normal Aged. University of Chicago, Chicago, IL: Unpublished doctoral dissertation

Mohs R C, Davis K L and Darley C 1980 Cholinergic drug effects on memory and cognition in humans. In: Poon L W (ed) Aging in the 1980s: Psychological Issues. Washington, D.C.: American Psychological Association

Mohs R C Rosen W G and Davis K C 1982 Defining treatment efficacy in patients with Alzheimer's disease. In: Corkin S, Growdon J, Usdin E, Davis K L and Wurtman R (eds) Alzheimer's Disease: A Report of Progress in Research. New York: Raven Press

Mortimer J A, Schuman L M and French L R 1981 Epidemiology of dementing illness. In: Mortimer J A and Schuman L M (eds) The Epidemiology of Dementia. New York: Oxford University Press

Muller H F, Grad B and Engelsmann F 1975 Biological and psychological predictors of survival in a psychogeriatric population. Journal of Gerontology 30: 47–52

Neville H J and Folstein M F 1979 Performance on three cognitive tasks by patients with dementia, depression or Korsakov's syndrome. Gerontology 25: 285–290

Osborne D P, Brown E R and Randt C T 1982 Qualitative changes in memory function: Aging and dementia. In Corkin S, Davis K L, Growdon J H, Usdin E and Wurtman R J (eds) Alzheimer's Disease: A Report of Progress in Research. New York: Raven Press

Palmore E and Cleveland W 1976 Aging, terminal decline and terminal drop. Journal of Gerontology 31: 76–81

Peck A, Wolloch L and Rodstein M 1978 Mortality of the aged with chronic brain syndrome, II. In: Katzman R, Terry R D and Bick K L (eds) Alzheimer's Disease: Senile Dementia and Related Disorders. New York: Raven Press

Pirozzolo F J and Hansch E C 1981 Oculomotor reaction time in dementia reflects degree of cerebral dysfunction. Science 214: 349–350

Pirozzolo F J and Maletta G (eds) 1981 Behavioural Assessment and Psychopharmacology. New York: Preager

Pirozzolo F J, Christensen K J, Ogle K M, Hansch E C and Thompson W G 1981 Simple and choice reaction time in dementia: Clinical implications. Neurobiology of Aging 2: 113–117

Poon L W 1984 Theoretical and clinical aspects for memory and aging. In: Birren J E and Schaie K W (eds) Handbook of the Psychology of Aging (2nd Edition). New York: Van Nostrand Reinhold

Poon L W and Fozard J L 1980a Age and word frequency effects in continuous recognition memory. Journal of Gerontology 35: 77–86

Poon L W and Fozard J L 1980b Epilogue: New directions in memory and aging research. In: Poon L W, Fozard J L, Cermak, L S, Arenberg D and Thompson L W (eds) New Directions in Memory and Aging: Proceedings of the George A Talland Memorial Conference. Hillsdale, N.J.: Lawrence Erlbaum Associates

Poon L W, Fozard J L, Paulschock D R and Thomas J C 1979 Questionnaire assessments of age differences in retention of recent and remote events. Experimental Aging Research 5: 401–411

Poon L W, Fozard J L, Cermak L S, Arenberg D and Thompson L W (eds) 1980 New Directions in Memory and Aging: Proceedings of the George A. Talland Memorial Conference. Hillsdale, N.J.: Lawrence Erlbaum Associates

Poon L W, Walsh-Sweeny L and Fozard J L 1980 Memory skill training for the elderly: Salient issues on the use of imagery/mnemonics. In: Poon L W, Fozard J L, Cermak L S, Arenberg D and Thompson L W (eds) New Directions in Memory and Aging: Proceedings of the George A. Talland Memorial Conference. Hillsdale, N.J.: Lawrence Erlbaum Associates

Perlmutter M 1978 What is memory aging the aging of? Developmental Psychology 14: 330–345

Perlmutter M, Metzger R, Nezworski T and Miller K 1981 Spatial and temporal memory in 20 and 60 year olds. Journal of Gerontology 36: 59–65

Pfeiffer E 1975 A short portable mental status questionnaire for the assessment of organic brain deficit in elderly patients. Journal of the American Geriatrics Society 13: 433–441

Rabbitt P 1982 Development of methods to measure changes in activities of daily living in the eldery. In: Corkin S, Davis K L, Growdon J H, Usdin E and Wurtman R J (eds) Alzheimer's Disease: A Report of Progress in Research. New York: Raven Press

Randt C T, Brown E R and Osborne D P Jr. 1980 A memory test for longitudinal measurement of mild to moderate deficits. Clinical Neuropsychology 2: 184–194

Reisberg B 1981 Brain Failure: An Introduction to Current Concepts of Senility. New York: Free Press

Reisberg B 1983 Office management and treatment of primary degenerative dementia. Psychiatric Annals 12

Reisberg B, Ferris S H and Crook T 1982 Signs, symptoms, and course of age-associated cognitive decline. In: Corkin S, Davis K L, Growdon J H, Usdin E and Wurtman R J (eds) Alzheimer's Disease: A Report of Progress in Research. New York: Raven Press

Reisberg B, Ferris S H, DeLeon M J and Crook T 1983 The global deterioration scale (GDS): An instrument for the assessment of

primary degenerative dementia (PDD). American Journal of Psychiatry.

Reisberg B, Gordon B, McCarthy M and Ferris S H 1981 Insight and denial accompanying progressive cognitive decline in the aged. Presented at the National Institute on Aging Symposium, Senile Dementia of the Alzheimer's Type and Related Diseases: Ethical and Legal Issues Related to Informed Consent. Bethesda, MD, National Institutes of Health, November 23–24

Rosen W G 1981 Effects of senile dementia of the Alzheimer's type on verbal fluency. International Journal of Neuroscience 12: 245–246

Rosen W G, Mohs R C and Davis K L 1982 A new rating scale for Alzheimer's disease. Presented at the American College of Neuropsychopharmacology, San Juan, Puerto Rico, December

Salzman C, Kochansky G E and Shader R I 1972 Rating scales for geriatric psychopharmacology — a review. Psychopharmacology Bulletin 8: 3–50

Santos J F and Vandenbos G R (eds) 1982 Psychology and Older Adults: Challenges for Training in the 1980s. Washington, D.C.: American Psychological Association. Appendix B

Schonfield D 1972 Theoretical nuances and practical old questions: The psychology of aging. Canadian Psychologist 13: 252–266

Sehulster J R 1981 Structure and pragmatics of a self-theory of memory. Memory and Cognition 9: 263–276

Shader R I, Harmatz J S and Salzman C 1974 A new scale for clinical assessment in geriatric populations: Sandoz Clinical Assessment-Geriatric (SCAG). Journal of the American Geriatrics Society 12: 107–113

Shepard R N and Teghtsoonian M 1961 Retention of information under conditions approaching a steady state. Journal of Experimental Psychology 62: 302–309

Sluss T K, Rabins P, Gruenberg E M and Reedman G (unpublished) Memory changes in community residing men. Paper available from Dr. T.K. Sluss, School of Hygiene and Public Health, the Johns Hopkins University, Baltimore, MD 21205

Sperling G 1963 A model for visual memory tasks. Human Factors 5: 19–31

Spillich G J and Voss J F 1982 Contextual effects upon text memory for young, aged-normal and aged memory-impaired individuals. Experimental Aging Research 8: 147–151

Squire L R 1980 The neuropsychology of amnesia: An approach to the study of memory and aging. In: Poon L W, Fozard J L, Cermak L S, Arenberg D and Thompson L W (eds) New Directions in Memory and Aging: Proceedings of the George A. Talland Memorial Conference. Hillsdale, N.J.: Lawrence Erlbaum Associates

Squires K C, Chippendale T J, Wrege K S, Goodin D S and Starr A Electrophysiological assessment of mental function in aging and dementia. In: Poon L W (ed) Aging in the 1980s: Psychological Issues. Washington, D.C.: American Psychological Association

Storandt M, Wittels I and Botwinick J 1975 Predictors of a dimension of well-being in the relocated healthy aged. Journal of Gerontology 30: 97–102

Talland G A 1965 Three estimates of the word span and their stability over the adult years. Quarterly Journal of Psychology 17: 301–307

Treat N J, Poon L W and Fozard J L 1978 From clinical and research findings on memory to intervention programs. Experimental Aging Research 4: 235–253

Tulving E 1972 Episodic and semantic memory. In: Tulving E and Donaldson W (eds) Organization of Memory. New York: Academic Press

Wang H S 1978 Prognosis in dementia and related disorders in the aged. In: Katzman R, Terry R D and Bick K L (eds) Alzheimer's Disease: Senile Dementia and Related Disorders. New York: Raven Press

Waugh N C and Norman D A 1965 Primary memory. Psychological Review 72: 89–104

Wechsler D 1945 A standardized memory scale for clinical use. Journal of Psychology 19: 87–95

Whitehead A 1975 Recognition memory in dementia. British Journal of Social and Clinical Psychology 14: 191–194

Wickelgren W A 1975 Age and storage dynamics in continuous recognition memory. Developmental Psychology 11: 165–169

Williams M E, Hadler N M and Earp J A L 1982 Manual ability as a marker of dependency in geriatric women. Journal of Chronic Disorders 35: 115–122

Wilson R S, Kaszniak A W and Fox J H 1981 Remote memory in senile dementia. Cortex 17: 41–48

Wilson R S, Bacon L D, Kaszniak A W and Fox J H 1982 The episodic-semantic memory distinction and paired associate learning. Journal of Consulting and Clinical Psychology 50: 154–155

Wilson R S, Kaszniak A W, Bacon L D, Fox J H and Kelly M P 1983 Facial recognition memory in dementia. Cortex

Zarit S H 1980 Aging and mental disorders: Psychological approaches to assessment and treatment. New York: Free Press

Zelenski E M and Gilewski M J 1982 Memory complaint and mood in the elderly: A new wrinkle. Presented at the American Psychological Assn. Meeting, Washington, D.C., August

Zelenski E M, Gilewski M J and Thompson L W 1980 Do laboratory memory tests relate to everyday remembering and forgetting? In: Poon L W, Fozard J L, Cormak L S, Arenberg D and Thompson L W (eds) New Directions in Memory and Aging: Proceedings of the George A. Talland Memorial Conference. Hillsdale, N.J.: Lawrence Erlbaum.

Pharmacology and aging — pharmacokinetics and pharmacodynamics

INTRODUCTION

In Europe and in North America the elderly make greater use of prescription and non-prescription drugs than the young. In a comprehensive prescription drug survey, Skoll et al (1979) reported on all drugs prescribed in one year, 1976, to the elderly population of the province of Saskatchewan (Canada). The number and types of drugs prescribed for the elderly were compared with those prescribed for the middle-aged: 77.3 per cent of the elderly (age 65 and over) and 64.2 per cent of 'middle-aged' (age 35–54) received a prescription; on average, 12.8 prescriptions were filled for each older person and 6.7 prescriptions for each middle-aged person during the year; the total number of different drugs received during the study period was greater in the elderly and in each successive age group within the elderly population; an age-related increase in the number of prescriptions was found for drugs of all classes except hormones; the greatest increase in prescription rate with advancing age was found for antibiotics, cardiovascular drugs, diuretics and sedatives and tranquillizers.

Studies of drug compliance in the elderly have conflicting results no doubt due to the inclusion of different groups of patients. While drug compliance of many older persons is probably no worse than that of the young, some elderly patients living in the community encounter difficulty in using drugs appropriately. Intellectual impairment, visual impairment and inability to open drug containers have been identified as major problems (Atkinson et al, 1977) and when such problems are present, non-compliance should be expected. Supervision of prescribed and non-prescribed medications will be required if the hazards of non-compliance are to be avoided.

Since successful drug therapy of disorders which threaten life or the quality of life is achieved at the risk of adverse drug reaction, the prescribing physician must be convinced that the expected benefits of therapy outweigh potential risks. Risk-benefit evaluation requires thorough diagnostic assessment, knowledge of the course of a disease untreated, knowledge of the therapeutic and adverse effects of the proposed drug, and knowledge of the way in which aging, disease and concurrent therapy affect drug response.

DRUG HANDLING IN OLD AGE

The intensity and duration of drug action depends upon the concentration of free drug at the site of cellular action and on the sensitivity of the target organ. Pharmacokinetics describes the time course of drug action in the body and includes quantitative study of drug absorption, distribution and elimination. Normal aging and many diseases encountered in the elderly generally affect drug kinetics in such a way as to cause an increased concentration of free drug at the sites of cellular action. Pharmacodynamics describes the biological and therapeutic effect of drugs. While this aspect of pharmacology has been studied less intensively than kinetic changes, there is some evidence of increased tissue sensitivity in old age.

Pharmacokinetics

Most drugs used in human therapeutics are administered orally, absorbed into the blood, distributed throughout the body by the circulation and eliminated by biotransformation in the liver and by excretion in the urine and bile. Drugs which are administered topically usually exert a local effect, although absorption into the blood stream may lead to an intended distant action, as with nitroglycerin, or an unintended action, as with systemic absorption of atropine-like ophthalmic preparations. Parenteral administration bypasses gastrointestinal absorption but in the case of all parenteral routes except intravascular injection absorption from a parenteral site into the circulation must occur.

Drug absorption

Most drugs are absorbed from the gastrointestinal tract by passive diffusion. In this respect they differ from xylose which is absorbed by a specialized transport

process and from substances such as glucose and galactose which are actively transported through the intestinal mucosa. Since most drugs are given in the form of
tablets or capsules and can be absorbed only in solution,
drug solubility and the rate of dissolution will affect
absorption. Other factors which influence gastrointestinal absorption include the structure of the absorptive
surface and the metabolic activity of the absorptive cells
(Levine, 1970).

Age changes in gastrointestinal function might be
expected to influence the rate and completeness of drug
absorption. Diminished gastric secretion may retard
dissolution of tablets, and the higher intragastric pH
which results from reduced parietal cell function may
reduce the solubility and absorption of some drugs such
as tetracycline and reduce inactivation of acid-labile
drugs such as penicillin. Those age-related changes
which might be expected to impair drug absorption
include delayed gastric emptying, reduced gastrointestinal blood flow, and a reduction in the small bowel
absorptive surface due to blunting and thickening of
intestinal villi (Bender, 1968).

Despite these theoretical considerations, drug absorption appears to be little influenced by aging. In studies
comparing young and old subjects no difference was
found in the absorption of paracetamol, sulphamethiazole, phenylbutazone (Triggs et al, 1975), acetylsalicylic acid and practolol (Castleden et al, 1977a),
paracetamol (acetaminophen) (Divoll, 1982b), and
lorazepam (Greenblatt et al, 1979).

While healthy aged individuals appear to absorb most
drugs normally and the reported effects of aging on
gastric emptying time are conflicting (Van Liere and
Northup, 1941; Evans et al, 1981), absorption is
affected by drugs which alter the rate of gastric
emptying. Since many drugs prescribed for the elderly
either accelerate or retard gastric emptying, the consequences are more likely to be seen in older patients.

Anticholinergic agents, such as propantheline, retard
gastric emptying and thus the delivery of drugs to the
upper small intestine where most absorption occurs.
Retarded gastric emptying has been shown to delay the
absorption of paracetamol (Nimmo et al, 1973) and
sulfamethiazole and riboflavin (Parsons, 1976).
Conversely, metoclopramide, which stimulates upper
gastrointestinal motility, accelerates the absorption of
paracetamol (Nimmo et al, 1973) and tetracycline,
lithium carbonate and levodopa (Parsons, 1976).

The effect of gastric emptying and upper gastrointestinal motility on digoxin absorption depends upon the
form in which digoxin is administered. When digoxin
is given in liquid form (Manninen et al, 1973a) or when
rapidly dissolving digoxin tablets are given (Manninen
et al, 1973b) together with drugs which accelerate or
retard gastric emptying no change in absorption occurs.

Paradoxically, some oral preparations are better
absorbed when given together with drugs which reduce
gastrointestinal motility, allowing longer contact with
the absorptive surface, and less well absorbed when
given with metoclopramide, which causes the incompletely dissolved tablet to pass through the intestine.

Absorption studies of single agents administered in
the fasting state do not accurately reflect the clinical
situation where several drugs may be taken together,
often with food. When multiple drugs are in use, the
possibility of reduced absorption due to binding or
inactivation must be considered: antacids decrease
absorption of digoxin, isoniazid, indomethacin, salicylates and tetracycline; cholestyramine binds oral anticoagulants, cardiac glycosides and thyroid preparations.
When drugs are administered with or after food, the
possibility of drug–food and drug–nutrient interactions
exists: tea and orange juice respectively decrease and
increase the absorption of iron; acidic fruit juices and
carbonated beverages inactivate many acid-labile drugs
such as penicillin; and mineral oil containing laxatives
cause malabsorption of fat-soluble vitamins.

Drug distribution

From the gastrointestinal tract the absorbed drug passes
into the portal vein and, before entering the systemic
circulation, is partly metabolized during the first pass
through the liver. Upon reaching the systemic circulation, drug administered orally or parenterally distrib-
utes initially within the intravascular compartment and
subsequently in other body compartments. The pattern
of distribution of a particular drug is dependent upon
its aqueous and lipid solubility, upon the degree of
binding to plasma and tissue components, and upon the
drug delivery to various tissues of the body.

Drugs in the circulation may exist in a free state or
may be bound to blood components, principally
albumin, in the form of a reversible complex. Only the
unbound drug, which may account for as little as 1 per
cent of the total plasma concentration, is available for
diffusion into the tissues. A state of equilibrium exists
between free drug and protein-bound drug and, as free
drug enters the tissue, drug is released from binding
sites thus preventing large fluctuations in the level of
free drug in the plasma.

Drug binding to plasma albumin has been the subject
of an extensive review by Koch-Weser and Sellers
(1976a,b). Decreased plasma protein binding of warfarin
(Hayes et al, 1975a) phenytoin (Hayes et al, 1975b) and
salicylate and phenylbutazone (Wallace et al, 1976) has
been shown in the elderly. There does not appear to be
any reduction in the affinity between drugs and
albumin, and reduced binding is due to lower serum
albumin levels. Woodford-Williams (1964) first drew
attention to lower serum albumin levels in institution-

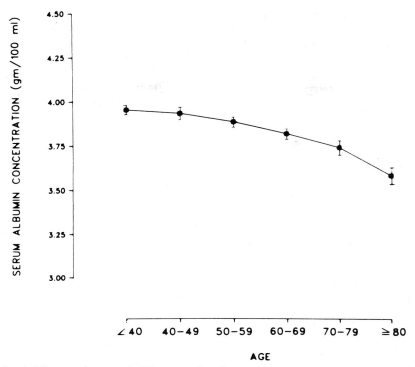

Fig. 8.1 Cross-sectional differences in mean (±SE) serum albumin concentrations with age. (Reprinted by permission of the editor Journal of the American Geriatrics Society and the author).

alized elderly patients; however some reduction in serum albumin is found even in healthy older persons. Figure 8.1 illustrates the serum albumin values of a large group of older individuals, not known to be suffering from diseases associated with altered serum proteins (Greenblatt et al, 1979). The decline in serum albumin level reduces the total number of available protein binding sites. Reduced albumin binding capacity results in a higher plasma level of free drug and enhanced therapeutic and adverse effects.

Interactions between highly protein-bound drugs may occur as a result of competition for binding sites. When sulphonamides or salicylates are administered with oral hypoglycaemic agents, drug displacement of the latter may result in profound hypoglycaemia. Drug displacement from protein-binding sites also occurs when chloral hydrate, clofibrate, nalidixic acid, or phenylbutazone are administered to patients receiving oral anticoagulants. The increased risk of haemorrhagic complications when acetylsalicylic acid and oral anticoagulants are taken together results not from competition for binding sites but from the effect of acetylsalicylic acid on platelet function and on gastric mucosa (Koch-Weser and Sellers, 1971a, b).

While most drug binding is to serum albumin, binding to other blood constituents notably erythrocytes

does occur. Age-related changes in erythrocyte-binding have been observed for two drugs: pethidine and chlormethiazole. When standard weight-related doses of pethidine (Meperidine) are given intravenously, older subjects show higher free plasma levels immediately after administration (Mather et al, 1975). This may be related to decreased pethidine erythrocyte binding, which is presumably representative of other tissue binding (Chan et al, 1975). Although reduced erythrocyte binding of chlormethiazole has been shown in older subjects (Nation et al, 1977), age changes in erythrocyte binding of other drugs have yet to be shown and erythrocyte binding of diazepam (Klotz, 1976) and pentazocine (Ehrnebo et al, 1974) is not influenced by aging.

After the initial phase of intravascular distribution and binding to blood components, drugs are distributed throughout the body. The speed with which equilibration is achieved depends on the cardiac output and on the blood flow to various tissues, so that highly perfused organs such as brain, heart and muscles receive drugs within a few moments after absorption whereas equilibration in less well perfused tissues, such as adipose tissue, may take several hours.

Apparent volume of distribution. The concentration of drug in body compartments other than plasma is reflected in the apparent volume of distribution (V_d), which is the volume of fluid into which a drug appears to distribute with a concentration equal to that in plasma. The V_d is calculated from the plasma concentration, after equilibrium, following the intravenous injection of a known quantity of drug. In the case of the dye Evans Blue, the injected material remains within the plasma and does not enter the tissues to any appreciable extent. Thus the V_d is the same as plasma volume — around 3 litres. The V_d of drugs which are taken up avidly by body tissues may greatly exceed actual body fluid. For digoxin, the V_d in a 70 kg man is around 700 litres.

The patterns of drug distribution to the various tissues of the body vary considerably. Highly lipid-soluble drugs such as diazepam and lidocaine accumulate in adipose tissue whereas acetaminophen, antipyrine and ethyl alcohol distribute almost exclusively in body water. With advancing age the V_d for more lipid-soluble

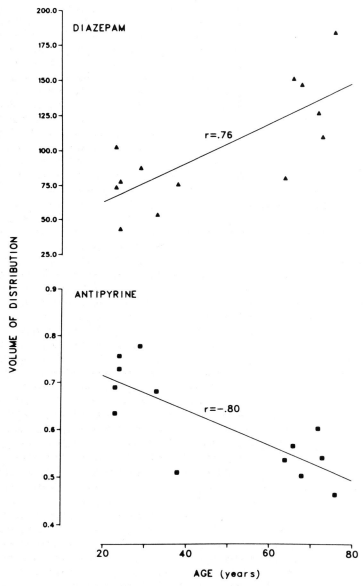

Fig. 8.2 Apparent volume of distribution for diazepam and antipyrine in 13 health male volunteers of different ages. (Reprinted from New England Journal of Medicine 306: 1084, 1982, by permission of the editor of the New England Journal of Medicine and the author).

drugs tends to increase and that for relatively water-soluble drugs to decrease. The mean volume of distribution of diazepam nearly doubles between the ages of 20 and 80 and that of antipyrine decreases by nearly 50 per cent (Greenblatt et al, 1982) (Fig. 8.2).

Age-related changes in V_d of drugs result from differences in body composition between individuals of different ages. Studies of healthy volunteers have yielded several findings: a proportional reduction of total body water and intracellular water in older males (Shock et al, 1963); a decrease in total body potassium and lean body mass (Novak, 1972; Forbes and Reina, 1970); and an increase in body fat (Novak, 1972) in older subjects. With the exception of a few subjects who were followed longitudinally (Forbes and Reina, 1970) these data are based on cross-sectional comparisons. While considerable individual variation occurs, aging is, on average, accompanied by reduced total and lean body mass, by reduced total body water, and by relatively increased adipose tissue mass.

The effect of a proportional increase in adipose tissue mass is to increase the volume of distribution for lipid soluble drugs. The V_d of lignocaine is almost twice as great in the elderly as in the middle-aged (Nation et al, 1977), and the V_d at steady rate for diazepam increases from 0.5 l/kg at age 20 to approximately 2 l/kg at age 80 (Klotz et al, 1975).

Similarly, the reduction in total body water and lean body mass per unit of total body weight affects the V_d of drugs which are relatively water soluble such as ethanol (Vestal et al, 1977), acetaminophen (Divoll et al, 1982a) and antipyrine (Greenblatt et al, 1982). The reduction in lean body mass may also contribute to higher blood levels of digoxin seen in the elderly (Cusack et al, 1979).

Drug elimination

Drug effect may be terminated by elimination of a drug from the body unchanged, or by biotransformation into inactive or less active metabolites, which are subsequently excreted. While many tissues such as the gastrointestinal tract, the lungs and the kidneys are capable of biotransforming drugs, the liver is by far the most important. Similarly, although drug excretion in bile, sweat and expired gases may be important in certain circumstances, the kidney is the main organ of elimination of drugs and their metabolites.

The rate of elimination of a drug from the body may be expressed as the elimination half-life ($T_{\frac{1}{2}}$) or as total body clearance. Elimination half-life is the time taken for plasma concentration in the post-absorptive, post-distributive phase, to fall 50 per cent and can be calculated from two or more plasma concentration values. Many of the published studies of drug metabolism in old age have measured elimination half-life, however as

Greenblatt et al (1982) pointed out, $T_{\frac{1}{2}}$ is a hybrid measure dependent on both body clearance and V_d. Since the age-related changes in body composition already described affect V_d, and therefore $T_{\frac{1}{2}}$, clearance is a better indicator of the efficiency of drug elimination in the elderly.

Total body clearance is the sum of hepatic metabolism, net biliary and renal excretion and elimination and metabolism at other sites. It is expressed as a hypothetical volume of blood cleared of drug in unit time and is measured by dividing the intravenous bolus dose of a drug by the area under the blood (or plasma) concentration–time curve from the time of injection to the time that no drug remains in the body.

Hepatic biotransformation

Biotransformation is a major route of elimination of exogenous chemicals, both drugs and toxins. In most cases, the product of hepatic metabolism is a compound which is either inactive or less active and more polar and thus more readily cleared by the kidneys. Occasionally, biotransformation results in the production of a toxic metabolite or converts a pro-drug into the active agent.

Hepatic biotransformation reactions may be divided into two types, nonsynthetic (phase I) and synthetic (phase II). Phase I reactions — oxidation, reduction and hydrolysis — generally result in an inactive or less active compound and Phase II reactions — conjugation, methylation and acetylation — result in a more polar compound. However not all drugs undergo both phases. Drug metabolism occurs largely, but not exclusively, in the smooth endoplasmic reticulum, or microsomal fraction, of the hepatocyte. Non-microsomal biotransformation contributes to the metabolism of many drugs in common use.

Of the enzymes responsible for drug metabolism in the smooth endoplasmic reticulum, a series of haemoproteins, collectively known as the cytochrome P_{450} enzyme system, has been studied most intensively. The rate of degradation of drugs metabolized by this system gives an indication of enzyme activity. Antipyrine a drug formerly used as an antipyretic analgesic, is now no longer used therapeutically but has pharmacologic characteristics which make it suitable for research purposes.

Aged inpatients metabolize antipyrine more slowly than do younger controls (O'Malley et al, 1971). Other factors have also been found to affect antipyrine metabolism: alcohol and cigarette use (Vestal et al, 1975), thyroid disease and concurrently administered drugs (Stevenson, 1977) and influenza vaccination (Kramer and McClain, 1981).

The activity of hepatic microsomal enzymes may be either inhibited or induced by a number of concurrently administered compounds. Cimetidine delays the elimination of many drugs including antipyrine, chlordiazepoxide, diazepam, propranolol and warfarin in part by inhibiting hepatic drug metabolizing enzymes. Drugs subject to non-restrictive metabolism (see below), such as propranolol, may be affected both by the reduced hepatic blood flow caused by cimetidine as well as by enzyme inhibition.

Polycyclic hydrocarbons, such as DDT, and drugs related to phenobarbitone and the anticonvulsants induce non-specific proliferation of the smooth endoplasmic reticulum and hasten both their own metabolism and that of other drugs. While this may lead, in some cases, to suboptimal plasma drug levels, enzyme induction may afford protective benefit to patients receiving multiple drugs. This protective effect may be less in the elderly since older individuals show significantly less induction of microsomal drug metabolism when given dichlorphenazone than do younger subjects (Salem et al, 1978); they are therefore less likely to tolerate concomitant administration of drugs with a narrow therapeutic index which are eliminated by hepatic metabolism.

With advancing age, hepatic cell mass and hepatic blood flow decline. The liver weight retains its percentage relationship to body weight until age 50, then declines in proportion to body weight (Geokas and Haverback, 1969). This decline in hepatic cell mass is accompanied by reduced visceral blood flow, caused in part by a decline in cardiac output (Brandfonbrenner et al, 1955) and by a redistribution of blood flow such that hepatic blood flow may decline by up to 40 per cent between the ages of 25 and 65 (Bender, 1965). Normally, the reduced hepatic blood flow does not much affect drug uptake by hepatocytes. However, with the existence of pathological conditions such as congestive heart failure, when the decreased reserve capacity of the liver is further challenged by anoxia and by reduced cardiac output, hepatic uptake of drugs which are subject to non-restrictive metabolism is impaired. Drugs which reduce hepatic blood flow, such as cimetidine (Feely et al, 1981) or propranolol, may have a similar effect.

Hepatic uptake and metabolism of drugs such as phenytoin, phenylbutazone and warfarin is restricted to the free or unbound drug in the plasma (restrictive metabolism) and is uninfluenced by hepatic blood flow. Drugs with a high extraction ratio, such as lidocaine and propranolol, are removed from plasma so rapidly that the rate-limiting step in metabolism is the hepatic blood flow (non-restrictive metabolism).

Drugs with high hepatic extraction are also extensively metabolized during their first pass through the liver thus the drug is either ineffective orally (e.g. nitroglycerin), or there is a considerable difference between the comparably effective oral and parenteral dosage (e.g. propranolol). Age changes in first-pass extraction of propranolol have been demonstrated (Castleden and George, 1979).

Commonly used biochemical tests of hepatic function cannot be used to predict drug clearance in the elderly. The slight decline in serum albumin in the healthy elderly has been discussed (Fig. 8.1). However serum levels of most enzymes are within the normal range for younger adults and give no indication of impaired metabolism. Earlier cross-sectional studies suggested that there was a change in sulphobromophthalein (BSP) retention in the elderly but a study of healthy veterans showed no change in BSP excretion (Koff et al, 1973). In general, while there is considerable individual variation, hepatic drug metabolizing capacity in the elderly is one-half to two-thirds that in the young adult. This is of particular therapeutic relevance for many drugs including theophylline, nortriptyline and propranolol — and appropriate adjustment in dosage and frequency of administration should be made.

Renal excretion

The kidney is the organ of excretion for many drugs including several antibiotics — penicillin, aminoglycosides, tetracycline and sulphamethiazole, the cardiac glycosides, phenobarbital and lithium. In contrast with the liver, where the decline in drug metabolizing activity is not reflected in common tests of hepatic function, age changes in renal function are more predictable and are reflected in tests of renal function.

Drugs and their metabolites of low molecular weight existing unbound in the plasma are filtered at the glomerulus, however lipid-soluble drugs are passively reabsorbed in the distal convoluted tubule. Polar drugs or metabolites may be excreted by glomerular filtration. A quite distinct process, renal tubular secretion, is an important route of excretion of organic acids such as the penicillins and will be considered separately.

Age-related changes in renal function, include a reduction in the number of functioning nephrons, reduced renal plasma flow, reduced glomerular filtration rate and impaired renal tubular secretion. Davies and Shock (1950) showed an age-dependent decline in inulin clearance and Rowe et al (1976) showed in a cross-sectional study of healthy men that the mean value of creatinine clearance in 80 year old men was 97 ml/min/1.73 m^2 compared with 140 ml/min/1.73 m^2 at age 30 (Fig. 8.3). Longitudinal data suggest an accelerating decline in creatinine clearance with advancing age.

The decline in creatinine clearance results from a reduction in the number of intact functioning nephrons and from reduced renal plasma flow which occur in

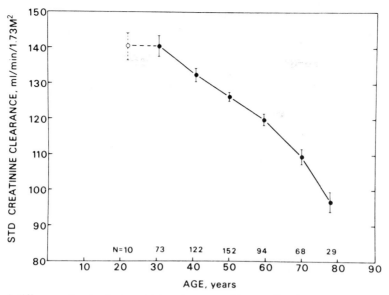

Fig. 8.3 Cross-sectional differences in standard creatinine clearance with age. (Reprinted by permission of the editor of the Journal of Gerontology and the author).

normal old age, in the absence of discernible renal disease. When dehydration or congestive heart failure are present or when drugs such as beta blockers or cimetidine are administered the glomerular filtration rate may fall to 25–50 ml/min, and fall further in chronic renal disease. In the elderly it should be assumed that some degree of renal impairment is present even when serum creatinine is within the normal range, since declining creatinine clearance is compensated, in part, by reduced endogeneous production of creatinine from the smaller muscle mass.

Endogenous creatinine clearance may be calculated from serum and urine values or may be predicted from the equation of Cockroft and Gault (1978). In men the creatinine clearance is estimated as:

$$\frac{(140 - \text{age}) \times \text{body weight (kg)}}{72 \times \text{serum creatinine level}}$$

For women the result is reduced by 15 per cent. Alternatively endogenous creatinine clearance may be calculated from the nomogram shown in Figure 8.4 (Siersbaek-Nielsen et al, 1971).

The reduction in creatinine clearance causes a 40 per cent increase in plasma half-life of digoxin in the elderly (Ewy et al, 1969). Roberts and Caird (1976) showed that renal clearance of digoxin is reduced in proportion to the reduction in creatinine clearance. When age or disease-related reduction in renal function is present the dosage or frequency of administration of drugs should be modified in accordance with published dosage guidelines

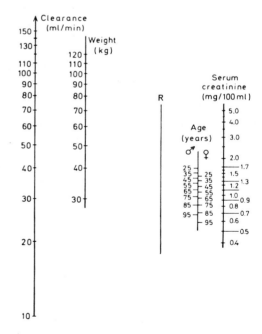

Nomogram for rapid evaluation of endogenous-creatinine clearance.

With a ruler, join weight to age. Keep ruler at crossing-point of line marked R. Then move the right-hand side of the ruler to the appropriate serum-creatinine value and read the patient's clearance from the left side of the nomogram.

Fig. 8.4 Nomogram for rapid evaluation of endogenous creatinine clearance. (Reprinted from Lancet i: 1134, 1971, by permission of the editor of The Lancet and the author).

for renal failure (Bennett et al, 1980). However, Bauer and Blouin (1982) have questioned the necessity of reducing gentamicin dosage in the aged with 'normal' renal function.

Renal tubular secretion is the major route of excretion of organic acids, particularly penicillin and the cephalosporin antibiotics. While age changes in tubular excretion have been studied less extensively than changes in glomerular filtration, tubular secretory capacity declines in parallel with the decline in GFR. The effect of decreased tubular excretion is reflected in the half-life of penicillin G which, in the elderly, is almost twice that of healthy young volunteers (Hansen et al, 1970). While this is of little relevance in oral therapy of minor infections, when high-dose intravenous therapy is given, reduced renal tubular secretion may permit drug accumulation and result in penicillin encephalopathy.

Drugs which inhibit tubular secretion, such as probenecid, may be used therapeutically to maintain serum level of penicillin. Competition between drugs which share a common transport system may occur when penicillin is administered with oral antidiabetic agents, salicylates or thiazides, competition for renal tubular secretion leads to higher plasma levels of each drug.

Pharmacodynamics

Drug activity depends not only upon the amount of agent available to bind to receptors but also upon the sensitivity of tissue receptors. Age-related changes in beta-adrenergic receptor activity are suggested by the reduced sympathetic response to exercise in old age (Conway et al, 1971) and the reduced chronotropic response of the heart to isoproterenol (London et al, 1976; Vestal et al, 1979). In experimental animals the density of beta adrenergic receptors in many areas of the brain declines with age (Weiss et al, 1979).

Evidence of alteration in pharmacodynamic response to drugs with age was first suggested by the increased frequency of adverse drug reactions to heparin in the elderly and in particular in older women (Jick et al, 1968). Subsequently the response to warfarin, measured as inhibition of synthesis of vitamin K dependent clotting factors at any particular plasma level has been shown to be greater in old than in young subjects (Hewick et al, 1975; Shepherd et al, 1977) (Fig. 8.5).

The clinical observation that the elderly tolerate central nervous system depressant drugs less well than the young has been substantiated for diazepam in epidemiological studies (Boston Collaborative Drug Surveillance Program, 1973; Reidenberg et al, 1978). Other benzodiazepine drugs such as flurazepam (Greenblatt et al, 1977) more frequently cause adverse drug reactions involving the central nervous system in the elderly. Altered sensitivity of the elderly brain to nitrazepam has been shown by Castleden et al (1977) who found that at similar plasma drug concentrations elderly subjects made significantly more mistakes than young subjects in tests of psychomotor function.

Although age-changes in pharmacodynamics are less well documented than pharmacokinetic changes they are clearly important.

Drug interactions

Drugs may interact at a number of levels: in the gastrointestinal tract, at protein binding sites or at sites of metabolism and excretion. While some drug interactions reduce the drug available for therapeutic action, the majority of interactions lead to an increased free drug and increased biological effect. Older patients are particularly susceptible to drug interactions since they more commonly receive multiple drugs. Interaction between drugs has been the subject of recent compre-

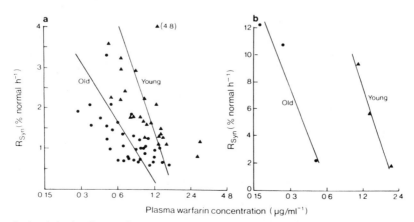

Fig. 8.5 Rate of synthesis of clotting factors (R_{syn}) plotted against logarithm of plasma warfarin concentration for old and young subjects. (Reprinted from British Journal of Clinical Pharmacology 4: 318, 1977, by permission of the editor of the British Journal of Clinical Pharmacology and the author).

hensive reviews (Dollery and Brody, 1980; Medical Letter, 1981).

Adverse drug reactions

Since adverse drug reactions (ADR) represent undesired action in a particular clinical setting, recognition of adverse reactions will depend upon the intensity with which they are sought. Hurwitz (1969a) found that the frequency of ADR in elderly patients in hospital increased with the number of drugs received. Of patients receiving one to five drugs 3.4 per cent experienced ADR compared with 24.7 per cent in those receiving six or more drugs. Adverse reactions to drugs accounted for 2.9 per cent of hospital admissions in Belfast (Hurwitz, 1969b) and adverse effect, defined as a response to medication undesired or unintended by the physician, was found in 10.2 per cent of inpatients (Hurwitz and Wade, 1969). The drugs most commonly implicated in the Belfast study, as in subject studies, are drugs affecting central nervous system function, cardiovascular drugs and antibiotics.

Drugs producing adverse effects on the central nervous system may have been given for analgesic, antidepressant, antipsychotic or sedating effect, or, as is the case with digoxin, metoclopramide and cimetidine, may have been prescribed for disorders outside the central nervous system. Age-related changes in the pharmacokinetics and the pharmacodynamic response to benzodiazepines have already been discussed and yet long-acting benzodiazepines which are metabolized into active compounds (diazepam, chlordiazepoxide, flurazepam) continue to be prescribed for the elderly even though shorter-acting drugs such as oxazepam and lorazepam would be more appropriate (Shader and Greenblatt, 1977), if indeed, benzodiazepine therapy is indicated. The adverse effects of benzodiazepines on cognitive function and balance and gait are well known (Greenblatt and Shader, 1974a, 1974b; Committee on the Review of Medicines, 1980) and while true drug dependence is not common (Editorial Lancet, 1979) withdrawal symptoms which resemble those seen after withdrawal of alcohol or other central nervous system depressants may occur. These may subside spontaneously or may symptomatically respond to propranolol (Tyrer et al, 1981).

The phenothiazine and butyrophenone drugs, in addition to their antipsychotic action are also antiemetic, hypotensive, anticholinergic, antihistaminic and hypothermic agents. Thioridazine and haloperidol are commonly used in the elderly and are potent and effective drugs with potential ADR affecting autonomic, endocrine, hepatic and cardiovascular systems. The elderly are particularly sensitive to the cardiovascular and autonomic effects, particularly hypotension and hypothermia, and to the development of extrapyramidal

reactions including drug-induced Parkinsonism, acute dystonia, akathisia, and tardive dyskinesia. While many of the extrapyramidal adverse reactions disappear on discontinuing or reducing the dosage of the drug, tardive dyskinesia often does not. Thus drugs with lesser potential for producing dyskinesia, such as thioridazine, should be used when possible, and treatment with phenothiazines and butyrophenones restricted to as short a period as necessary.

Many drugs including the antidepressant, antipsychotic and anti-Parkinsonian agents have anticholinergic effects which may present peripherally as urinary retention and constipation or centrally as confusion, disorientation and hallucinations. Withdrawal of the drug or reduction in dosage is indicated under such circumstances, however in acute poisoning intravenous administration of physostigmine will reverse the anticholinergic effects.

The cardiac and gastrointestinal effects of digitalis intoxication are well recognized; however older individuals more commonly present with non-cardiac symptoms such as listlessness, malaise, agitation and confusion, and visual symptoms (Lely and van Enter, 1972). While the serum digoxin concentration is useful in monitoring therapy it should be remembered that elderly patients may show signs of central nervous system toxicity when the serum level is in the high 'therapeutic range' and that the interaction of other drugs such as quinidine may cause a sudden rise in the serum digoxin level. Quinidine appears to displace digoxin from its tissue binding sites and reduce renal clearance and while this effect is more pronounced with continued therapy, alteration of digoxin pharmacokinetics have been shown after a single dose of quinidine (Chen and Friedman, 1980).

Since adverse reactions to digoxin are at least troublesome and may be life-threatening, the indications for continued digoxin therapy should be reviewed periodically. Many patients in sinus rhythm and some with slow atrial fibrillation may have the drug stopped without detriment (Priddle and Rose, 1966; Dall, 1970; Johnston and McDevitt, 1979).

Drugs used in the management of hypertension or congestive heart failure are associated with troublesome adverse effects in the elderly. Diuretics, particularly the rapid-acting loop diuretics, are of undoubted efficacy in congestive heart failure and sodium retaining states, however their use to treat dependent edema is to be deprecated. The metabolic effects of diuretics — glucose intolerance and azotemia — rarely limit function; however volume contraction, dehydration and postural hypotension and hypokalemia may lead to postural syncope, falls and muscle weakness. The rapid diuresis which occurs with diuretics such as frusemide may cause acute urinary retention in the individual with bladder neck or prostatic obstruction, or leakage when urinary continence is already compromised by an unstable bladder.

Older antihypertensive agents such as reserpine are now rarely used in the elderly because of their depressant effect on mood. Others are poorly tolerated, for example 25 per cent of older patients receiving alpha-methyldopa have the drug discontinued because of adverse effects (Ramsay, 1981). Beta-blockers are preferable to older antihypertensive drugs although the risk of adverse reaction to propranolol (Greenblatt and Koch-Weser, 1973), and presumably other beta-blockers, increases with age.

Drugs used in the management of gastrointestinal disorders may seriously affect central nervous system function. Antispasmodic drugs may cause the central anticholinergic syndrome and metaclopramide may cause extrapyramidal disorders including Parkinsonism, tardive dyskinesia and acute dystonia. Because of this metoclopramide appears to be contraindicated in Parkinson's disease and it should be restricted to short term use in older patients and treated with the same

respect as neuroleptics (Grimes et al, 1982). Cimetidine therapy in the elderly is often associated with mental confusion, especially where renal and hepatic function is compromised (Schentag et al, 1979). The delirium produced by cimetidine is similar to atropine-like effects commonly associated with classical antihistamine (H_1 blockers) and may be reversed by intravenous physostigmine (Mogelnicki et al, 1979).

Many adverse drug reactions may be prevented by better informed prescribing and drug taking, however, since adverse drug reactions may develop insidiously and the symptoms may be ascribed by the patient and by his physician to aging or to the disease for which the drug was prescribed, recognition may be delayed. This is particularly so when the adverse reaction is rare and does not reflect the known pharmacological action of the drug (Achong, 1978). However, since many adverse drug reactions are simply an exaggeration of the expected therapeutic effect or unavoidable pharmacological actions they should be anticipated and considered in the differential diagnosis of any unexpected decline in health or function in an older person.

REFERENCES

Achong M R 1978 When is a clinical event an adverse drug reaction? Canadian Medical Association Journal 119: 1315–1319

Atkinson L, Gibson I I J M, Andrews J 1977 The difficulties of old people taking drugs. Age & Ageing 6: 144–150

Bauer L A, Blouin R A 1982 Gentamicin pharmacokinetics: effect of aging in patients with normal renal function. Journal of the American Geriatrics Society 30: 309–31

Bender A D 1965 The effect of increasing age on the distribution of peripheral blood flow in man. Journal of the American Geriatrics Society 13: 192–198

Bender A D 1968 Effect of age on intestinal absorption: implications for drug absorption in the elderly. Journal of the American Geriatrics Society 16: 1331–1339

Bennett W M, Muther R S, Parker R A, Feig P, Morrison G, Golper T A, Singer I 1980 Drug therapy in renal failure: dosing guidelines for adults. Part II Sedatives, hypnotics, and tranquillizers; cardiovascular, antihypertensive, and diuretic agents; miscellaneous agents. Annals of Internal Medicine 93: 286–325

Boston Collaborative Drug Surveillance Program 1973 Clinical depression of the central nervous system due to diazepam and chlordiazepoxide in relation to cigarette smoking and age. New England Journal of Medicine 288: 277–280

Brandfonbrenner M, Landowne M, Shock N W 1955 Changes in cardiac output with age. Circulation 12: 557–566

Castleden C M, George C F 1979 The effect of ageing on the hepatic clearance of propranolol. British Journal of Clinical Pharmacology 7: 49–54

Castleden C M. Volans C N, Raymond K 1977a The effect of ageing on drug absorption from the gut. Age & Ageing 6: 138–143

Castleden C M, George C F, Marcer D, Hallett C 1977b Increased sensitivity to nitrazepam in old age. British Medical Journal 1: 10–12

Chan K, Kendall M J, Mitchard M, Wells W D E 1975 The effect of ageing on plasma pethidine concentration. British Journal of Clinical Pharmacology 2: 297–302

Chen T S, Friedman H S 1980 Alteration of digoxin pharmacokinetics by a single dose of quinidine. Journal of the American Medical Association 244: 669–672

Cockroft D W, Gault M H 1978 Prediction of creatinine clearance

from serum creatinine. Nephron 16: 31–41

Committee on the Review of Medicines 1980 Systematic review of the benzodiazepines. British Medical Journal 1: 910–912

Conway J, Wheeler R, Sannerstedt R 1971 Sympathetic nervous activity during exercise in relation to age. Cardiovascular Research 5: 577–581

Cusack B, Kelly J, O'Malley K, Noel J, Lavan J, Horgan J 1979 Digoxin in the elderly: pharmacokinetic consequences of old age. Clinical Pharmacology and Therapeutics 25: 772–776

Dall J L C 1970 Maintenance digoxin in elderly patients. British Medical Journal 2: 705–706

Davies D F, Shock N W 1950 Age changes in glomerular filtration rate, effective renal plasma flow, and tubular excretory capacity in adult males. Journal of Clinical Investigation 29: 496–507

Divoll M, Abernethy D R, Ameer B, Greenblatt D J 1982a Acetaminophen kinetics in the elderly. Clinical Pharmacology and Therapeutics 31: 151–156

Divoll M, Ameer B, Abernethy D R, Greenblatt D J 1982b Age does not alter acetaminophen absorption. Journal of the American Geriatrics Society 30: 240–244

Dollery C T, Brodie M J 1980 Drug interactions. Journal of the Royal College of Physicians of London 14: 190–196

Editorial 1979 Benzodiazepine withdrawal. Lancet i: 196

Ehrnebo M, Agurell S, Boreus L O, Gordon E, Lonroth U 1974 Pentazocine binding to blood cells and plasma proteins. Clinical Pharmacology and Therapeutics 16: 424–429

Evans M A, Triggs E J, Cheung M, Broe G A, Creasey H 1981 Gastric emptying rate in the elderly: implications for drug therapy. Journal of the American Geriatrics Society 29: 201–205

Ewy G A, Kapadia G G, Yao L, Lullin M, Marcus F I 1969 Digoxin metabolism in the elderly. Circulation 29: 449–453

Feely J, Wilkinson G R, Wood A J J 1981 Reduction of liver blood flow and propranolol metabolism by cimetidine. New England Journal of Medicine 304: 692–695

Forbes G B, Reina J C 1970 Adult lean body mass declines with age: some longitudinal observations. Metabolism 19: 653–663

Geokas M C, Haverback B J 1969 The aging gastrointestinal tract. American Journal of Surgery 117: 881–892

Greenblatt D J, Koch-Weser J 1973 Adverse reactions to propranolol in hospitalized medical patients: A report from the Boston Collaborative Drug Surveillance Program. American Heart Journal 86: 478–484

Greenblatt D J, Shader R I 1974a Benzodiazepines (first of two parts). New England Journal of Medicine 291: 1011–1015

Greenblatt D J, Shader R I 1974b Benzodiazepines (second of two parts). New England Journal of Medicine 291: 1239–1243

Greenblatt D J, Allen M D, Shader R I 1977 Toxicity of high dose flurazepam in the elderly. Clinical Pharmacology and Therapeutics 21: 355–361

Greenblatt D J, Sellers E M, Shader R I 1982 Drug disposition in old age. New England Journal of Medicine 306: 1081–1088

Greenblatt D J, Shader R I, Franke K 1979 Pharmacokinetics and bioavailability of intravenous, intramuscular and oral lorazepam in humans. Journal of Pharmacological Science 68: 57–63

Grimes J D, Hassan M N, Preston D N 1982 Adverse neurologic effects of metoclopramide. Canadian Medical Association Journal 126: 23–25

Hanson M J, Kampmann J, Laursen H 1970 Renal excretion of drugs in the elderly. Lancet i 1170

Hayes M J, Langman M J S, Short A H 1975a Changes in drug metabolism with age. I. Warfarin binding and plasma proteins. British Journal of Clinical Pharmacology 2: 69–72

Hayes M J, Langman M J S, Short A H 1975b Changes in drug metabolism with age. II. Phenytoin clearance and protein binding. British Journal of Clinical Pharmacology 2: 73–79

Hewick D S, Moreland T A, Shepherd A M M, Stevenson I H 1975 The effect of age on the sensitivity to warfarin sodium. British Journal of Clinical Pharmacology II: 189–190

Hurwitz N 1969a Predisposing factors in adverse reactions to drugs. British Medical Journal 1: 536–539

Hurwitz N 1969b Admission to hospital due to drugs. British Medical Journal 1: 539–540

Hurwitz N, Wade O L 1969 Intensive hospital monitoring of adverse reactions to drugs. British Medical Journal 1: 531–536

Jick H, Slone D, Borda I T, Shapiro S 1968 Efficacy and toxicity of heparin in relation to age and sex. New England Journal of Medicine 279: 284–286

Johnston G D, McDevitt D G 1979 Is maintenance digoxin necessary in patients with sinus rhythm? Lancet i: 567–570

Klotz U 1976 Pathophysiological and disease inducing changes in drug distribution volume: pharmacokinetic implications. Clinical Pharmacokinetics 1: 204–218

Klotz U, Avant G R, Hoyumpa A, Schenker S, Wilkinson G R 1975 The effects of age and liver disease on the disposition and elimination of diazepam in adult man. The Journal of Clinical Investigation 55: 347–359

Koch-Weser J, Sellers E M 1971a Drug interactions with coumarin anticoagulants (first of two parts). New England Journal of Medicine 285: 487–498

Koch-Weser J, Sellers E M 1971b Drug interactions with coumarin anticoagulants (second of two parts). New England Journal of Medicine 285: 547–558

Koch-Weser J, Sellers E M 1976a Binding of drugs to serum albumin (first of two parts). New England Journal of Medicine 294: 311–316

Koch-Weser J, Sellers E M 1976b Binding of drugs to serum albumin (second of two parts). New England Journal of Medicine 294: 526–531

Koff R S, Garvey A D J, Burney S W, Bell B 1973 Absence of an age effect on sulfobromophalein retention in healthy men. Gastroenterology 65: 300–302

Kramer P, McClain C J 1981 Depression of aminopyrine metabolism by influenza vaccination. New England Journal of Medicine 305: 1262–1264

Lely A H, van Enter C H J 1972 Non-cardiac symptoms of digitalis intoxication. American Heart Journal 83: 149–152

Levine R R 1970 Factors affecting gastro-intestinal absorption of drugs. Digestive Diseases 15: 171–188

London G M, Safar M E, Weiss Y A, Milliez P L 1976 Isoproterenal sensitivity and total body clearance of propranolol in hypertensive patients. Journal of Clinical Pharmacology 16: 174–182

Manninen V, Apajalahti A, Simonen H, Reissell P 1973a Effect of propantheline and metoclopramide on absorption of digoxin. Lancet i: 1118–1119

Manninen V, Melin J, Apajalahti A, Karesoja M 1973b Altered absorption of digoxin in patients given propantheline and metoclopramide. Lancet i: 398–400

Mather L E, Tucker G T, Pflug A E, Lindop M J, Wilkerson C 1975 Meperidine kinetics in man. Intravenous injection on surgical patients and volunteers. Clinical Pharmacology and Therapeutics 17: 21–30

Medical Letter 1981 Adverse interactions of drugs. 23: 17–28

Mogelnicki S R, Waller J L, Finlayson D C 1979 Physostigmine reversal of cimetidine-induced mental confusion. Journal of the American Medical Association 241: 826–827

Nation R L, Triggs E J, Selig M 1977a Lignocaine kinetics in cardiac patients and aged subjects. British Journal of Clinical Pharmacology 4: 439–448

Nation R L, Vine J, Triggs E J, Learoyd B 1977b Plasma levels of chlormethiazole and two metabolites after oral administration to young and aged human beings. European Journal of Clinical Pharmacology 12: 137–145

Nimmo J, Heading R C, Tothill P, Prescott L F 1973 Pharmacological modifications of gastric emptying: effects of propantheline and metoclopramide on paracetamol absorption. British Medical Journal 1: 587–589

Novak L P 1972 Aging, total body potassium, fat free mass, and cell mass in males and females between aged 18 and 85 years. Journal of Gerontology 27: 438–443

O'Malley K, Crooks J, Duke E, Stevenson I H 1971 Effect of age and sex on human drug metabolism. British Medical Journal 3: 607–609

Parsons R L 1976 The absorption of drugs in malabsorption syndromes. Hospital Update 221–230

Priddle W W, Rose M 1966 Curtailing therapy in a home for the aged, with special reference to digitalis, diuretics and low sodium diets. Journal of the American Geriatrics Society 14: 731–734

Ramsay L E 1981 The use of methyldopa in the elderly. Journal of the Royal College of Physicians of London 15: 239–244

Reidenberg M M, Levy M, Warner H, Coutinho C B, Schwartz M A, Yu G, Cheripko J 1978 The relationship between diazepam dose, plasma level, age and central nervous system depression in adults. Clinical Pharmacology and Therapeutics 23: 371–374

Roberts M A, Caird F I 1976 Steady-state kinetics of digoxin in the elderly. Age & Ageing 5: 214–223

Rowe J W, Andres R, Tobin J D, Norris A H, Shock N W 1976 The effect of age on creatinine clearance in men: a cross-sectional and longitudinal study. Journal of Gerontology 31: 155–163

Salem S A M, Rajjayabun P, Shepherd A M M, Stevenson I H 1978 Reduced induction of drug metabolism in the elderly. Age & Ageing 7: 68–73

Schentag J J, Calleri G, Rose J Q, Cerra F B, DeGlopper E, Bernhard H 1979 Pharmacokinetic and clinical studies in patients with cimetidine-associated mental confusion. Lancet i: 177–181

Shader R I, Greenblatt D J 1977 Clinical implications of benzodiazepine pharmacokinetics. American Journal of Psychiatry 134: 652–656

Shepherd A M M, Hewick D S, Moreland T A, Stevenson I H 1977 Age as a determinant of sensitivity to warfarin. British Journal of Clinical Pharmacology 4: 315–320

Shock N W, Watkin D M, Yiengst M J, Norris A H, Gaffney G W, Gregerman R I, Falzone J A 1963 Age differences in the water content of the body as related to basal oxygen consumption in males. Journal of Gerontology 18: 1–8

Siersbaek-Nielsen K, Hansen J M, Kampman J, Kristensen M 1971 Rapid evaluation of creatinine clearance. Lancet ii: 1133–1134

Skoll S L, August R J, Johnson G E 1979 Drug prescribing for the elderly in Saskatchewan during 1976. Canadian Medical Association Journal 121: 1074–1081

Stevenson I H 1977 Factors influencing antipyrine elimination. British Journal of Clinical Pharmacology 4: 261–265

Triggs E J, Nation R L, Long A, Ashley J J 1975 Pharmacokinetics in the elderly. European Journal of Pharmacology 8: 55–62

Tyrer P, Rutherford D, Huggett T 1981 Benzodiazepine withdrawal symptoms and propranolol. Lancet i: 520–524

Van Liere E J, Northup D W 1941 The emptying time of the stomach of old people. American Journal of Physiology 134: 719–722

Vestal R E, Wood A J J, Shand D G 1979 Reduced B-adrenoceptor sensitivity in the elderly. Clinical Pharmacology and Therapeutics 26: 181–186

Vestal R E, McGuire E A, Tobin J D, Andres R, Norris, A H, Mezey E 1977 Aging and ethanol metabolism. Clinical Pharmacology and Therapeutics 21: 343–354

Vestal R E, Norris A H, Tobin J D, Cohen B H, Shock N W, Andres R 1975 Antipyrine metabolism in man: influence of age, alcohol, caffeine and smoking. Clinical Pharmacology and Therapeutics 18: 425–432

Wallace S, Whiting B, Runcie J 1976 Factors affecting drug binding in plasma of elderly patients. British Journal of Clinical Pharmacology 3: 327–330

Weiss B, Greenberg L, Cantor E 1979 Age-ralted alterations in the development of adrenergic denervation supersensitivity. Federation Proceedings 38: 1915–1921

Woodford-Williams E, Alvarez A S, Webster D, Landless B, Dickson M P 1964 Serum protein patterns in 'normal' and pathological aging. Gerontologia 10: 86–99

Pharmacology of aging — prescribing and the 'treatment of aging'

Aims of treatment

In geriatric medicine the aim of treatment is usually the amelioration of disease to the extent that the elderly person can return, in reasonable comfort, to his normal way of life at home, or failing that to accept care in a residential home. In more severely ill patients, the aim might be continuing hospital care or a comfortable , dignified death. Mere prolongation of life should rarely be an aim for medical treatment, although occasional circumstances (legal or social) might demand this.

Breakdown in old age

Incurable and progressive disease constitute the major causes of morbidity and mortality in middle age and beyond. Breakdown in an elderly person may be due to an acute episode in a chronic disease already well established in middle life or to the accumulation and gradual worsening of multiple chronic disorders.

All too often in frail old people, the *coup de grâce*, is pharmacological and iatrogenic. An inappropriate prescription reduces the frail but functioning and sentient human being to a chairfast, confused, incontinent wreck. Occasionally the *coup de grâce* is intentionally self-inflicted. Psychotropic drugs recently prescribed by the attending physician are the most popular poisons used (Smith and Davison, 1971).

PRESCRIBING FOR THE ELDERLY

Principles of prescribing

The principles of prescribing are essentially the same in any age group although the doses used in older people often need to be reduced to allow for altered phamacokinetics and pharmacodynamics (Ch. 8). The patient is recognised to be ill and along with other measures, one or more drugs may be prescribed. No drug should be prescribed unless it can be expected to do good and there should be a review of the case (including the current drug schedule) before prescribing. The course of drug treatment should be as short as is practicable. Where a truly specific indication for the drug

Table 9.1 Prescribing for the elderly

1. Be clear about the indication, dose, duration and likely effects of each drug.
2. Review the whole drug schedule and keep it simple.
3. Focus on key problems; it is rarely necessary to treat everything.
4. Monitor compliance and response and remember to 'switch off'.

exists the response to treatment will usually be excellent as when vitamin B_{12} is given for pernicious anaemia or thyroxine for myxoedema and even when (though less specific) prednisolone is given for temporal arteritis. But most cases seen by the geriatrician are not so simple as this. Many of the complaints will not show a good response to drug treatment. Multimorbidity is common and it is necessary to focus on key problems. The doctor must resist the temptation to prescribe a drug for every possible target, e.g. insomnia, poor appetite, constipation, swollen feet, backache, giddy spells, generalized anxiety etc. All of these complaints may be eased to some extent by an increase in both social interaction and physical activity although an antidepressant given at night might be indicated with this symptom cluster. A chairfast old person can be expected to have swollen feet and to feel giddy on standing up. To prescribe a diuretic and a phenothiazine will almost certainly make things worse. When drugs are prescribed some attempt should be made to monitor patient compliance with the prescription as well as the response to the drug. When the drug is no longer required it should be stopped.

Diagnosis

The key to good prescribing is accurate diagnosis and a comprehensive diagnosis (physical, mental, social, functional) must always be made as a basis for rational and effective treatment. Diagnosis can be difficult in the aged because of the rather non-specific presentation of illness — e.g. increasing infirmity, postural instability, urinary incontinence, intellectual failure and immobility. Consumer demand for action can add to the difficulties. For example, the relative of an old woman who is confused, incontinent and has gone off her feet insists that: 'Something must be done'. The social pressure can be immense. The danger is that after a perfunctory examination of the problems the attending physician will prescribe a selection of medicines but have no real understanding of the underlying pathology nor a well-reasoned scientific basis for the prescription. Inevitably much of the prescribed medicine is useless and some hazardous. An astonishing amount of medical practice appears to be conducted in this way.

Regrettably the urge to prescribe often appears to be irresistable even when no rational safe effective drug is available for the purpose required. As Bourne and Lewis (1977) put it 'Physicians have a very long history as a profession with negligible genuine therapeutic power and are still disorientated by the relatively recent heritage of some treatments that work — like a sudden substantial bequest from an unknown great-uncle easily overestimated and overspent'.

Medical skills are often subverted by the great age of the patient. It is helpful to keep the patient's age out of the reckoning until the diagnosis has been made unless the proposed investigations are likely to cause great expense or great inconvenience to the patient. The patient's age assumes much more relevance when management (including drug therapy) and prognosis come under consideration.

Placebo effects

The possible beneficial response to a pharmacologically 'inert' placebo should be remembered especially for a patient who insists on drug treatment where none that is both effective and safe is available. Various symptoms can be relieved by placebos — especially anxiety, nausea, headache, cough and angina. Their pharmacology includes dose and time-related effects, side effects (drowsiness, giddiness, alteration of bowel habit etc.) and even drug dependence! However, there must be many occasions when an appropriately presented placebo would be less harmful and perhaps more beneficial than a potent but complex and incompletely understood drug.

Placebos must be used sparingly and with discretion. Everyday experience suggests that most doctors, nurses and patients do not understand placebo reactions and greatly underestimate both their frequency and intensity. Indeed a favourable response to a placebo (say for pain or insomnia) may be seen as evidence that the symptoms were not genuine. A good placebo response might thus divert the unwitting physician from the need to make a proper diagnosis. Another problem is that the difficult demanding patient is more likely to get the inert placebo and the 'good' compliant patient the 'real' drug,

viz: an injection of sterile water for the 'difficult' patient who complains of pain and 10 mg of morphia for the 'good' patient who complains of pain. The prescriptions are thereby used as a form of reward or retribution by the attending staff. As a senior resident put it: 'Placebos are used with people you hate, not to make them suffer, but to prove them wrong' (Goodwin et al 1979).

Prescribing for non-pharmacological reasons. Many prescriptions are given for reasons other than pharmacological. The prescription may be used to terminate the consultation, to validate the sick role of the patient in society or simply to 'buy' time for nature to heal or least to help clarify a diagnostic problem. There are better and safer means of 'prescribing procrastination' (Thomson, 1979); for example a mutually agreed period of observation and the education of patient, relative or neighbour in the likely course of events. It is usually much easier to manage the patient when his expectations (and those of the relatives) are roughly in accord with those of the doctor.

Overtreatment with drugs

The elderly are a major target for the prescriber, a large proportion take drugs long-term and multiple drug use is common. In one English group general practice about 50 per cent of the patients aged over 70 years were on long-term treatment especially with cardiovascular and psychotropic drugs and a sizeable minority (30 per cent) of those on drugs had made no contact with the doctor for 6 months to 6 years prior to the survey (Shaw and Opit, 1976). As many as 30 per cent of the drugs taken by elderly patients long-term are unnecessary or of doubtful value notably, tranquillizers, hypnotics, antidepressants, digoxin, diuretics, antacids and hypotensive agents (Tulloch, 1981). Unnecessary long-term drug use by elderly women in a small residential care home has recently been reported by Bruce (1982). By stopping those drugs which were not clearly beneficial he was able to reduce the drug bill by 50 per cent. Heavy long-term use of tranquillizers, sedative and hypnotic drugs is also reported to occur in the North American Nursing Home population (US Dept HEW PHS, 1976).

In a health screening programme in a retirement community in Dunedin, Florida, USA, 6.3 per cent of the elderly people reported using hypnotics and 15.6 per cent used anti-anxiety drugs. Long-term drug use was common, suggesting that for a substantial number of individuals no benefit was derived from the hypnotic and, in fact, the drugs may have been contributing to their symptoms (Stewart et al, 1982).

In a UK family practice study, drugs acting on the central nervous system (the most commonly prescribed group after antibiotics) gave the highest incidence of adverse drug reaction (ADR) even in relatively fit people of all ages (Martys, 1979). In a large group of elderly patients newly admitted to geriatric hospital wards in the UK (Williamson and Chopin, 1980) the majority (over 80 per cent) were receiving prescribed drugs and 15 per cent of these suffered from adverse drug reactions and in most of these cases the ADR had contributed to the need for admission. Adverse reactions due to hypnotics, sedatives, hypotensives and antiparkinsonian drugs seemed particularly likely to lead to hospital admission.

Details of the pharmacokinetics of drug interactions and of the more likely ADR will be found in chapter 8. Suffice it to say here that the small elderly female, with multiple chronic illnesses, with a previous adverse reaction or a history of allergic illness is particularly liable to ADR. The presence of renal or mental failure markedly increases the likelihood of ADR. The possibility that mental confusion, unstable posture, orthostatic hypotension or skin rash might be due to drugs must be kept constantly in mind.

Table 9.2 Profile of patient liable to adverse reaction to drugs

1. Small elderly female
2. History of allergic illness
3. Previous adverse reaction
4. Multiple chronic illnesses
5. Renal and mental failure

Avoidance of drug hazards. The hazards of drug treatment in old age can be minimized only by a keen awareness of the problem and by a persistent effort to hold prescribing to a practicable minimum. Regular review of the whole drug schedule will allow consideration of reducing or stopping each drug. For example, maintenance doses of digoxin and diuretics fixed shortly after the stress of an acute respiratory infection may prove to be excessive and possibly completely unnecessary in the long term. Parkinsonism due to a phenothiazine should be treated by drug withdrawal alone if at all possible. If a new drug has to be introduced some other should, whenever feasible, be stopped to make way for the newcomer. Predictable drug interactions must be looked for and their likely advantages and disadvantages considered. For example, the effects of hypnotic drugs will be potentiated by phenothiazines. This may help in management. Salicylates and phenylbutazone taken irregularly will upset anticoagulant control using drugs of the coumarin type, and could be hazardous.

Periodically the old person's house should be cleared of all medicines not on the active list. Some surprising hoards will be revealed. Once the seriousness of the situation is explained, to the patient and his relatives, agree-ment to the clear-out will usually be given. A careful watch should be kept for patients (usually women) who privately and unknown to the family doctor abuse drugs to their own detriment. The misuse of analgesics causing fatal nephropathy and of purgatives producing generalized weakness and the cathartic colon are examples. It is important to realize that many patients treat themselves with drugs readily available as 'over the counter medicines'.

With elderly patients in hospital, the avoidance of adverse drug effects is difficult enough but with the patient at home other problems arise. Can the patient manage the drug schedule prescribed for him or will he get things muddled? Often a relative or neighbour will be able to help and possibly keep complete control of the drugs. Unfit old people with poor supervision are liable to omit drugs; fitter old people are more likely to prescribe for themselves.

Three or four different preparations are about as many as most sensible old people (or young people for that matter) can reasonably manage for themselves. With these difficulties in mind, it is important that hospital doctors reduce the patient's drug burden to a minimum and make some attempt to train the patient and his relatives in the management of the drug schedule prior to discharge. It must be made quite clear which drugs are to be taken and when (see below).

The prescription

The prescription for a hospital in-patient is an instruction both to the pharmacy and to the nurses attending the patient. There is no transcription and the prescription becomes an integral part of the patient's medical record. In family practice the situation is quite different. The prescription is an instruction to the pharmacist to dispense the medicine and to label it. This transcribed information is then available to the patient and his attendants. Where the patient is in a residential home there may be a further transcription to provide a drug list for the use of the attendants. There is the possibility of error (and also let it be noted the possibility of the correction of error!) at each transcription.

Confusion often exists between the prescribing of hospital and family physicians. Drugs prescribed for the patient to take out of the hospital and those prescribed (often on long-term repeats) by the family doctor may vary considerably. Contact between patient and general practitioner after discharge from hospital is often lacking (Deacon et al, 1978) so that when the drugs provided from the hospital are exhausted the patient reverts to the repeat prescription routine which was established prior to his hospital admission — drugs which may actually have caused the admission in the first place! Alternatively the two sets of drugs may be taken concurrently.

Lack of clear instruction and adequate supervision leads to special risks with respect to overdosage, especially where the therapeutic ratio is small (e.g. digoxin or tricyclic antidepressants), or loss of control because insufficient drug is taken (e.g. antidiabetic agents).

Repeat prescriptions

Much of the excess drug burden which falls on elderly patients is due to lack of proper control of repeat prescriptions. Drugs may be prescribed as routine repeats almost indefinitely and further drugs introduced without pruning the drug list to make way for the newcomers. Most prescriptions written for elderly people in general practice are for repeat medication — usually without a careful review of the total drug intake and the patient's response. There is evidence that an increasing proportion of repeat prescriptions is written by the doctors' receptionist and that these scripts contain twice the number of errors seen in scripts written by the doctor (Dajda, 1980). Where careful review of chronic repeats has been introduced the reduction in drug use has been dramatic (Tulloch, 1981; Bruce, 1982). Fortunately there is a growing awareness of these problems and the recognition that their resolution requires improved practice organisation, proper drug use policies and the meticulous use of clear medical records including a repeat prescription and drug record card (Thomson, 1981; Stuart, 1981; Drury and Sabbagh, 1982).

Many of the long-term repeats with infrequent review are fully justified; for example in the treatment of diabetes, hypothyroidism and pernicious anaemia. Those on treatment for heart failure usually require more frequent review and those on hypnotics and psychotropics should ideally have no repeat without consultation. The doctor who has put his own house in order may then reasonably consider whether the patient is taking the drugs as prescribed. However, if the prescribing and drug review policies are chaotic it might actually be better if the patient did not take the drugs as prescribed!

Compliance

Muddled use of drugs and drug hoarding are common and exacerbated if there is little or no personal contact between patient and doctor. Medicines perceived by the patient to be unpleasant or wholly irrelevant are unlikely to be taken as prescribed. A simple drug schedule, aimed at the patient's main treatable disease, using clearly labelled containers giving full information together with a clearly legible drug list will make accurate drug taking a feasible proposition for a sensible person with good vision. If the patient is mentally confused, has a gross personality disorder or is blind, full supervision by some other person is required.

The physical ability to take the drugs as prescribed does not mean that compliance is assured. Estimates vary but probably as many as 60 per cent of elderly patients make errors. Most patients fully intend to take their pills as the doctor ordered but forget or modify the regimen to suit themselves depending on how they feel and on their own perception of the relative importance of the various medicines. Those who become drug dependent (psychologically or physically) on the other hand will go to any lengths to secure further supplies of their drug. It is impossible for the doctor to be sure which patient is compliant and which not without from time to time making some positive assessment.

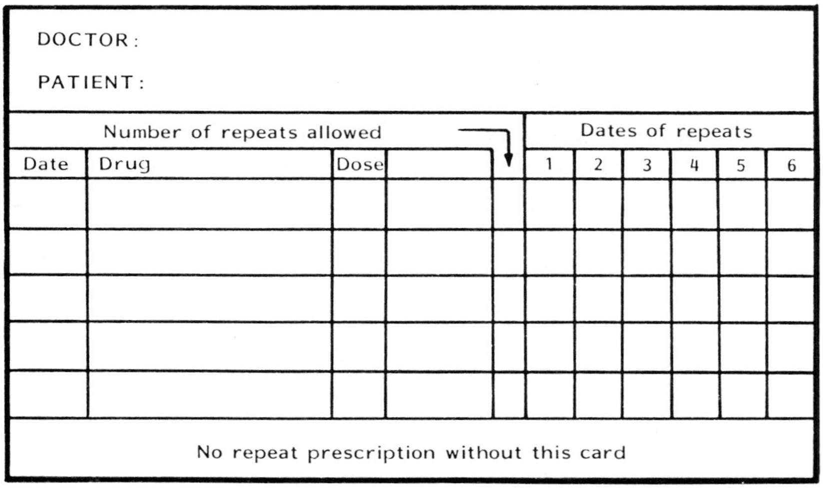

DOCTOR:										
PATIENT:										
Number of repeats allowed					Dates of repeats					
Date	Drug		Dose			1	2	3	4	5	6
No repeat prescription without this card										

Fig 9.1 Suggested layout for repeat prescription card

Assessing compliance. There are many approaches to this problem, but there are snags to most of them. Certainly tablets still in the bottle have not been consumed by the patient although regrettably the converse does not hold! (Pearson, 1982). Direct methods include tissue, body fluid or excreta sampling for the drug, its metabolites, or a marker. The more readily available indirect assessments are made by asking questions such as, 'Were you able to take all the tablets?', by assessing outcome (e.g. slowing of the pulse with digoxin or evident improvement in the hypothyroid patient on thyroxine), and by pill counts and estimates of the amount of fluid drug preparations remaining in the bottle when the patient is seen at review consultation.

No method of assessing compliance is completely effective and too much scrutiny by the doctor could upset the patient-doctor relationship. Indirect methods suffice for most purposes in clinical practice but if evaluation studies are being undertaken some blood or urine testing would probably also be needed.

Presentation of medicines
Tablets and capsules have displaced liquid preparations to a large extent because of the advantages of smaller volume and weight, more accurate dosage, easier handling, and longer shelf life. About 90 per cent of medicines consumed by old people are now in this form. Liquid oral preparations still have a place because some patients find them easier to swallow. Others however may dislike the taste and some have difficulty using the measuring spoon on account of tremor or poor visual acuity. If precise dosage is not essential a broad-based plastic measuring beaker may reduce spillage.

The standard screw-top bottle remains the favourite drug container used by most elderly patients in the UK. Increasingly the blister packs are finding acceptability but some old patients find them difficult (Gibson, 1978). Opaque or tinted containers designed to minimize the effects of sunlight on the medicines do not suit everyone. Many prefer to be able to identify the tablet or capsule by shape, size and colour before opening the bottle. The wing-top bottle can be very useful to those with weak, stiff or clumsy fingers. Child-resistant containers, although in general use for much of the population, are particularly difficult for some old people to manage. Security of the drugs, with respect to children, in these cases must be achieved in some other way.

The multidose pill box, e.g. Mediset or Dosett, may be useful to some patients. The box can be loaded with up to a week's supply of pills by the patient or a helper. Each day's pills are covered by a single transparent sliding lid with four stops to allow opening in succession the four compartments for that day labelled 9 am–11 am, 11am–1 pm and so on. The lettering on the front of the

Table 9.3 Guidelines for drug treatment in old age

1. There is no drug to combat senescence.
2. Mere prolongation of life is not a valid aim.
3. The effects of treatment must clearly be better than no treatment.
4. Multiple pathology is the rule so that a priority order regarding treatment is essential.
5. The number of drugs administered concurrently must be kept to a minimum.

box is in raised characters to provide touch reading to augment vision. On the back of the box the drug list can be displayed behind a transparent plastic window to allow a ready check on the medicines, their doses and time of administration. Alternatively a 'day' pill box is available which is about the size of a single tubular cigar container. Each day box has four compartments and a transparent sliding plastic cover. It can be used separately or as a set of seven 'day' boxes packed into a special plastic wallet to give a week's supply. For special studies the Dosett type box can be 'bugged' electronically to record the actual times of opening and an alarm system can be fitted to warn the patient that the drug is due. This of course adds bulk and weight (and cost!) to the device.

THE TREATMENT OF OLD AGE

The quest for longevity
From time immemorial man has aspired to longevity without being able to do anything rational to achieve it. History records countless devices for avoiding premature death. The mandrake root, with its frequently anthropomorphic appearance, and theriac, an ancient panacea compounded of innumerable substances such as the flesh and shell of the tortoise, and many others were widely and strongly held to possess magical healing powers and to pave the way to longevity (Mez-Mangold, 1971).

In biblical times when King David was old and advanced in years a beautiful young Shunamite maiden called Abishag was brought to minister to his needs and to lie with him to maintain vital heat. The beneficial effect of this arrangement was presumably short-lived because the scriptural account tells of his death in the very next chapter. The attractive (to older men) notion of gaining vitality from close proximity to maidens persisted. The seventeenth century German Cohausen (1749) gave an account of the revitalization of old men by the breath and spirit of young virgins entitled 'Hermippus redivivus or the Sage's triumph over old age and the grave — wherein a method is laid down for prolonging the life and vigour of man'. Cohausen's book begins with a miniature treatise on gerontology much of which remains relevant: 'Still I affirm that there are no settled periods in nature, no inevitable laws which conjoin weakness and infirmity with a certain number of years; but that it is very possible, nay and very practical too, for a man to extend the length of his life, much beyond the common date, and that without feeling the incommodities of old age, for otherwise this would rather be avoiding death than preserving life'.

Thus Cohausen affirmed that longevity without the burden of decrepitude is a practicable proposition. Yet we are still without a solution to this age old problem. Cohausen also examined the teaching of Descartes who had special ideas on diet and of Francis Bacon who held that 'preserving health and extending life are two very different things' a dictum highly germane to modern geriatrics and gerontology. Cohausen ended his book with a manifesto suitable for today's geriatrician: 'The preservation of life, the defending of the human body from decay, and rendering it a fit tenement for the soul to inhabit, in that season in which she is most capable of exerting her noblest faculties, are grave and serious subjects; with which no trivial matters ought to mingle'.

Lacassagne (1923) reviewed the literature in this field and concluded that old age is due to colloid degeneration which could be slowed down by an efficacious system of diet, sleep and exercise. Lorand (1912) had similar ideas when he laid down his 'Twelve Commandments for a green old age'. These ideas continue in much of present day philosophy regarding the preservation of health and vitality; the point being that health is not something prescribed by doctors.

The healthy lifestyle

In man there have long been claims that moderation in eating together with plentiful physical exercise is the best recipe for a long and healthy life and many of the diseases of middle and late life in Western societies are now believed to be due to a neglect of these simple rules.

Effects of physical exercise

Regular, strenuous, physical exercise has been virtually eliminated from the lives of most Western people by modern technology. However the total lifestyle of the individual may be of more importance in determining longevity than merely the amount of exercise indulged in. It is notable that endurance sports appear to be associated with longevity whereas 'heavy work' (mining, lumberjacking) is not. Presumably other factors are operating to explain the difference. For example the positive attitude towards keeping fit in the endurance sportsman will in turn affect his diet, his smoking habits and his use of alcohol. Since an increasing number of middle aged and elderly people are positively committed

to physical fitness we can anticipate lower levels of decrepitude in the next and successive generations of very old people. The beneficial and psychological effects alone should provide a worthwhile gain.

In a study of over a thousand competitors (mostly male and anglophone) in the 1975 World Masters Athletics Championships in Toronto of average age 50 years it was found that the men were 10 to 12 kilograms lighter than the average Canadian male of the same age and that body fat was less than the average sedentary male age 25 (Kavanagh and Shepherd, 1977). Generally there is a marked fall off in physical activity from age 25 to 65 but keen competitors to a large extent avoid this. The capacity for endurance work of the trained 65-year-old competitor is close to that of the sedentary student age 25! Long-term endurance exercise avoids both the premature loss of lean body mass and also the progressive build up of excess body fat which is seen in the average sedentary person.

It is impossible to be sure that regular vigorous exercise really is beneficial to health, protective against cardiovascular disease and thereby promotes longevity. At best there is much suggestive evidence rather than actual proof. More important predictors of longevity than exercise in an aging study in Boston, USA were: few illnesses, less smoking and less worry (Rose and Cohen, 1977). According to their estimates, in people with equivalent physical activity levels smokers lived on average 10 years less than non-smokers and teetotallers lived some 8 years longer than beer drinkers and about 4 years longer than spirit drinkers.

Effect of control of multiple risk factors in prevention of ischaemic heart disease.   Claims are one thing and proof is quite another. The seven year Multiple Risk Factor Intervention Trial (1982) in America has shown how difficult it can be in humans to prove that a certain course of action (in this case stopping smoking, control of raised blood pressure and reduction of hypercholesterolaemia) prevents coronary heart disease. Oliver (1982) commenting on the disappointing outcome of this phenomenally expensive trial points *inter alia* to faulty design of the study, the long incubation period of the disease and the known fact that human behaviour alters when it is studied. The fact remains that we are not yet clear how to prevent coronary heart disease although stopping smoking, a prudent diet with a reduction of fat intake as a source of energy together with the control of obesity and sloth, are sound policies for improving the public health and promoting longevity.

Chemical interference with aging

Antioxidants, lipofuscin inhibitors, crosslink inhibitors and immunoregulator drugs have all been used in animal experiments to extend life span [See Chapter 2; also

Table 9.4 Modulation of aging

Hypothesis of aging	Possible modulator
Genetic programme	Eugenics, genetic engineering
Cell debris accumulation (e.g. lipofuscin)	antioxidants, meclophenoxate
Cross linkage in collagen	Beta-aminopropionitrile (BAPN) penicillamine
Free radical excess	Antioxidants and 'scrubbers' e.g. ethanol (a free radical scavenger)
Autoimmunity	Immunosuppressants e.g. cyclophosphamide, azathioprine, corticosteroids

Kormendy and Bender (1971a, b), La Bella and Vivian (1978), Enesco and Verdone-Smith (1980), Lipman (1980), Dilman and Anisimow (1980)]. None of this has direct practical application to human aging yet but the leads are being followed up (Kormendy and Bender, 1971a, b) and more recently Sacher (1977) has reviewed the most significant attempts made to slow down the aging process by chemical intervention. The ineluctable conclusion emerges that all efficacious pharmacological therapies tested achieve their effects by a reduction of disease vulnerability and not by a decrease of the aging rate. Only calorie restriction in rats and reduction of body temperature in poikilotherms have been shown to reduce the rate of aging in an actual sense. In both these instances the likely explanation is a decreased rate of metabolism.

Disturbed homeostasis as a basis for aging

There is a tendency to make a clear distinction between the processes of aging and the diseases of aging, and to suggest that treatment of the latter can have no effect on the former. Dilman (1979) however points out that this depends on the mode of treatment or prevention. Thus early diagnosis and treatment by surgery of a variety of cancers would hardly be expected to provide a substantial gain in life expectancy. However if we can control the underlying biochemical factors this might have a more widespread effect on a number of age specific diseases and result in a substantial gain in life expectancy. As Dilman states, 85 per cent of all deaths in the developed world in middle and old age can be attributed to about seven or eight causes out of hundreds of known possibilities viz: obesity, adult onset diabetes, atherosclerosis, hypertensive disease, mental depression, decreased resistance to infection and cancer.

Dilman (1979) postulates a common thread to these specific diseases (he omitted senile dementia) in an age-associated increase in the threshold of the hypothalmus to homeostatic stimuli. Aging he suggests, is a

programmed deviation of homeostasis producing a limited range of age specific pathology and death.

Autoimmunity and immunodeficiency

The normal immune system (IS) function protects the body against invasion by bacteria, viruses and fungi and also (possibly) the body's own somatic cells. Those cells which are effete or have undergone malignant change are identified as alien and destroyed. However if the immune system behaves abnormally it may fail to recognise normal 'self' cells and proceed to destroy them as if they too were alien, (autoimmunity). The incidence of some autoimmune diseases rises with age and there has been speculation that autoimmunity is the basis for aging. See chapter 5 for detail on the immunology of aging.

Modulation of immune function. Two major possible lines of approach to the problem of failing immunocompetence have been tried experimentally to combat autoimmunity and immunodeficient states respectively. The immunosuppressive drugs have been used to suppress age-related autoimmunity. However azathioprine and cyclophosphamide which are clinically effective in the treatment of autoimmune diseases have not been successful as life extending agents presumably because they are such inherently toxic substances and because they lack specificity. An alternative approach has been to infuse immune cells from a healthy young donor into older individuals as they develop immunodeficiency. The object being to replace the host IS cells with donor IS cells. This approach throws up formidable problems of ensuring a perfect immunological match between donor and host. A possible way round this would be to store IS cells in a tissue bank during youth but in preparation for old age. Then, when the IS infusion (graft) is required autologous cells can be used.

Drugs for eternal youth

The quest for old age vitality and for longevity continues and various drugs are widely used. The value of most of them is doubtful. In the main doctors have concentrated on the treatment of known (or supposed) diseases and left natural aging to nature. This line of demarcation is becoming blurred although it still remains clear to many. Thus, by concensus, observed deficiencies of vital substances are made good in pernicious anaemia, diabetes mellitus, Addison's disease and Parkinson's disease but not generally in the menopause. The reason being that the menopause is part of normal aging and therefore should be born with fortitude like balding and greying of the hair. This view is being challenged and hormone replacement therapy (HRT) is practised on an increasing scale.

Much less attention has been given to the male

climacteric presumably because it is an insidious affair and it does not, as a general rule, cause such distress as the female menopause does. When clinical evidence of androgen deficiency exists, estimation of plasma gonadotrophin and testosterone levels will show if the deficiency is due to pituitary or hypothalamic disease or to primary testicular failure. With present knowledge only the more extreme cases of androgen deficiency should be treated.

Ginseng

Ginseng panax has been widely used for many years in Oriental Medicine and more recently it has found favour in Occidental cultures as a panacea for aging. It is readily available in health food shops and drug stores. There are an estimated five or six million users in the USA alone seeking the benefit of its tonic or stimulant action. It has been suggested that Ginseng can increase long-term resistance to stress and disease and thereby increase life span. The active principles of the root (termed ginsenosides) are incorporated into certain geriatic preparations especially in Western Europe but no British ethical pharmaceutical preparation contains ginsenosides. Solid support for the claims of increased long-term resistance to stress from ginseng in humans or increased life span is difficult to find but there is some evidence of increased arousal and adrenal response to stress in mice (Battles et al, 1979). No beneficial effects on life span were noted. Possibly the ginseng glycosides act as a steroid analogue.

A ginseng abuse syndrome has been described due to the CNS excitation and arousal. Thus some users experience a beneficial anti-fatigue and euphoriant action, others are troubled by nervousness and sleeplessness and may develop hypertension and in gross abuse the syndrome mimics corticosteroid poisoning. Overall the effects appear to be neither uniformly negative nor uniformly predictable (Siegel, 1979).

Gerovital (GH3)

Professor Ana Aslan of the Bucharest Institute of Geriatrics has studied for many years the effects of procaine hydrochloride by intra-arterial injection in various disorders including peripheral vascular disease, angina pectoris, asthma and degenerative joint disease. Favourable responses in these conditions were attributed to the vasodilating and pain-relieving properties of the drug. She also observed more general beneficial effects such as improved skin texture, improved memory and an increase in both psychomotor activity and muscle strength.

Procaine is not stable in the long term and so Gerovital H3 (GH3) was devised by the addition of benzoic acid and potassium metabisulphate to give both a longer shelf-life and an extended biological half-life. Aslan and others have found GH3 preferable to plain procaine hydrochloride solution. The metabolites of procaine, para-aminobenzoic acid (PABA) and diethylaminoethanol (DEAE) are themselves metabolically active. For a review of Aslan's work see Rockstein (1974). There she claims a dramatic difference in mortality for elderly people treated with procaine over a 15 year period compared with controls. An intermediate result was seen in the group treated with vitamin E.

There is evidence to suggest an age-related increase in monamine oxidase (MAO) levels in the human hind brain, platelets and plasma, and a related fall in noradrenalin levels in the hind brain. (Robinson et al 1972). This may have something to do with the increased incidence of mental depression in the elderly. In work on rats it has been shown that GH3 is a weak, reversible, fully competitive inhibitor of MAO, weaker than iproniazid but stronger than procaine hydrochloride (MacFarlane and Besbris, 1974). This action is in contrast with the usually prescribed powerful, irreversible MAOIs. Cohen and Ditman (1974) noted improvement with GH3 in elderly depressed patients; and Bucci (1973) found GH3 of value in schizophrenia possibly due to inhibition of monoamine oxidase.

Despite all of this, no report from Britain or the United States produces strong evidence of the clinical value of GH3. Thus Zwerling et al (1975) at the Bronx State Hospital, USA, in a double-blind study found that GH3 had no ameliorative effect on either psychological or physiological functioning. Specifically, no antidepressant effect was observed. A more recent study from the Brentwood VA Hospital in Los Angeles found that GH3 was no better than placebo in treating depressed patients (Olsen et al, 1978).

KH3 is another procaine anti-aging drug, produced in West Germany as an alternative to GH3. The basic concept of the drug is the same but the additives, including haematoporphyrin to prolong and enhance the activity of the procaine, are different. It is said to be even more widely sold than its forerunner, mostly over-the-counter and not on prescription. The main evidence for its value is in the German literature where there are claims for improvement in aged persons of many of the faculties commonly impaired by senescence viz: memory, mental concentration, sight, hearing, motor co-ordination and general emotional state (Kent, 1982).

There is no approval from the authorities in UK or USA for the use of GH3 or KH3 to make less burdensome the declining years. Double-blind trials are currently under way in the UK and Australia and it will be interesting to see if these studies provide substantial objective evidence of value other than as a mild stimulant or antidepressant. There seems little doubt that procaine in its various formulations, together with its metabolites para-aminobenzoic acid (PABA) and diethylaminoethanol (DEAE) has metabolic activity. No adverse effects are reported but the collective evidence for the clinical value of this type of treatment is not convincing.

Hormone replacement therapy

The menopause, usually around the age of 50, affects the lives of all women to a greater or lesser degree. The principal hormonal event is the cessation of ovarian secretion of 17-oestradiol. Henceforth the woman relies on oestrone (a weak oestrogen) derived from andros-tenedione produced by the adrenal and to a lesser extent the ovary under the control of the pituitary. The conversion to oestrone occurs in the liver and in fat. Overall oestrogen levels are much lower in the post-menopause than previously (Hutton et al, 1972).

One-third of the elderly female life span is postmeno-pausal and the effect of relative oestrogen deficiency on individuals varies enormously. The majority can cope without medical intervention, but for about 25 per cent of women oestrogen deprivation is a disaster. Even in those women with less severe menopausal symptoms of vasomotor and psychic disturbance, still there can be quite serious long-term effects of oestrogen deficiency: viz loss of femininity and the secondary sexual charac-teristics, urogenital atrophy, accelerated osteoporosis and vascular disease. The case for hormone replacement therapy (HRT) is strong, but indefinite duration HRT remains controversial.

Replacement therapy promptly relieves the vasomotor disturbances, many of the aches and pains, and the atrophic vaginitis and there is mounting evidence that it can give considerable protection against senile osteo-porosis when taken for several years soon after the menopause (Stevenson and Whitehead, 1982). In their review these authors stress the central role of oestrogen deficiency in postmenopausal bone resorption. Obviously many other factors must be considered (see Chapter 37) but oestrogen appears to be of undoubted effectiveness in preventing the loss of bone and so reducing the liability to fractures. It would be extremely valuable to be able to predict which women are most liable to develop serious osteoporosis so that these (rather than all) postmenopausal women could be given HRT.

The precise dose of oestrogen required to maintain bone mass and prevent genital atrophy remains conjec-tural. Preparations commonly used have included conjugated natural (equine) oestrogens 0.625 to 1.25 mg daily and ethinyl oestradiol in the range 20 to 50 μg daily. The latter is the most active oral preparation known. Recent work suggests that it is even more potent than previously believed (Mandel et al, 1982) and a daily dose of 10 μg (equivalent to 1.25 mg conjugated oestrogen in the study referred to) may be adequate for relief of vaginal atrophy and may provide protection

from the occurrence of osteoporotic fractures. The currently available oral contraceptives containing ethi-nyloestradiol provide a dose of 30 to 50 μg. In a 10 year double-blind prospective study in postmenopausal women oestrogen replacement therapy appeared to be effective in preventing bone loss especially when given within three years of the menopause (Nachtigall et al, 1979a). In a Danish study, postmenopausal HRT produced over a 3 year period considerable and continued increase in bone mass (Christiansen et al, 1981). There was no accelerated bone loss on cessation of HRT suggesting a likely lasting beneficial effect on bone mass. This accords with the reduced rate of frac-tures and spinal osteoporosis reported from a case control study of women who had received oestrogens for some years after the menopause (Hutchinson et al 1979).

Conjugated natural (equine) oestrogens have been preferred by many doctors because it is thought they are less likely to cause thrombosis. Cyclical oestrogen is used in the non-hysterectomised patient. Three weeks of oestrogen is followed by a week off treatment to allow for withdrawal bleeding. The risk of developing endom-etrial hyperplasia and carcinoma is minimised by adding a progestogen for part of the cycle. A range of pro-prietary preparations is available to give 11 days of oestrogen followed by a 7 day interval. An oestrogen-testosterone preparation is sometimes used for patients in whom libido does not improve on oestrogen alone.

Vaginal creams and pessaries containing oestrogen are already widely used in geriatrics to combat senile vagin-itis. This local treatment should be a routine if the patient wears a ring pessary for a prolapse.

Long-term adverse effects of HRT. The long-term adverse effects of systemic HRT are similar to those of long-term oral contraceptives in younger women. The incidence and severity are related both to dose and age. Similar doses of oestrogen have been used in the two groups but possibly much lower doses would be both effective and safer for HRT. Earlier anxieties with respect to hypertension, thrombo-embolic disorders and cardiovascular disease appear much less relevant with the low dose oestrogen regimens used nowadays and there is a suggestion that oestrogen replacement therapy in postmenopausal women may actually protect against ischaemic heart disease (Ross et al, 1981). The Boston Collaborative Drug Surveillance Program has suggested that postmenopausal women have no increased risk of non-fatal myocardial infarction with regular use of oestrogens in the absence of other obvious risk factors, e.g. angina, previous myocardial infarction or diabetes (Rosenberg et al, 1976).

There is speculation as to a possible increase or decrease in the risk of carcinoma of the breast in post-menopausal women on HRT. A report from Nashville, Tennessee, based on a group of 737 hysterectomy patients of different ages (mean 50 years) maintained for a collective total of 9869 years on conjugated equine oestrogens with a usual dose of 1.25 mg daily showed no increase in carcinoma of the breast (Burch et al, 1974). Indeed, a rather lower than expected fatality rate from all causes was noted as well as a lower incidence of fracture of the distal radius. A report by Hoover et al (1976) deals solely with HRT following the natural menopause in a series of women followed for an average of 12 years. Low doses (less than 1.25 mg daily) of conjugated natural oestrogens were most often used. An increase in incidence of breast cancer was observed although the numbers did not achieve more than borderline statistical significance. It was concluded that postmenopausal oestrogen therapy may increase the risk of breast cancer and this is especially so in the presence of benign breast disease.

The risk of endometrial carcinoma induced by oestrogens is a real one. Two reports where conjugated oestrogens were the commonly used preparation suggest this (Ziel and Finkle, 1975; Mack et al, 1976). The postmenopausal female appeared to be most at risk. Ziel and Finkle point to the likely role of oestrone in this context. The usual oestrogen preparation in their cases was Premarin of which some 50 per cent is oestrone — a comparatively weak oestrogen. However the endometrium converts oestrone into oestradiol with a 10-fold increase in oestrogenic activity. Furthermore, as already noted, in the postmenopausal female, the output from the adrenal of androstenedione is another source of oestrone (after conversion by body fat and liver). The use of progesterone protects the endometrium. Overall it is considered that the risk of death from fractured

neck of femur without HRT is probably a much bigger threat than that from breast and endometrial cancer if cyclic treatment with a low dose oestrogen-progestogen regimen is used.

Other adverse effects of oestrogen therapy include mental depression, loss of libido, enlargement of fibroids, cholelithiasis and thromboembolism. In a 10 year double-blind prospective study in 84 matched pairs of postmenopausal women using high dose conjugated oestrogens cyclically with progesterone, reported by Nachtigall et al (1979b), there was no statistical difference in mortality between the treated and untreated groups. There was some increase in gallstones in the treated group but no increase in malignant disease. The high incidence of thrombophlebitis (over 15 per cent) in both groups was attributed to a sedentary life. Breakthrough vaginal bleeding is avoided by cyclical oestrogen therapy or by provoking regular bleeds with progestogen. Unexpected bleeding demands diagnostic curettage to exclude serious endometrial disease. Patients who have had a hysterectomy can be managed on continuous oestrogen therapy because the hazard of endometrial carcinoma does not exist.

Contraindications to HRT include recent thromboembolic disease, oestrogen-dependent neoplasms such as carcinoma of breast, liver disease and endometriosis. Libido may be depressed by exogenous oestrogen because of reduction of ovarian androgen release via suppression of pituitary gonadotrophins. To promote libido testosterone can be included in the HRT, but this may increase facial hair and there is a remote risk of polycythaemia and cholestatic jaundice. Implants of testosterone are non-icterogenic.

REFERENCES

Battles A H, Fulder S J, Grant E C, Nicholls M R 1979. The effect of ginseng on life span and stress responses in mice. Gerontology 25: 125–131

Bourne J, Lewis E 1977. Doctors' despair: a paradox of progress. Journal of the Royal College of General Practitioners 27: 37–39

Bruce S A 1982 Regular prescribing in a residential home for elderly women. British Medical Journal 284: 1235–1237

Bucci L 1973 Procaine: a monoamine oxidase inhibitor in schizophrenia Diseases of the Nervous System 34: 389–391.

Burch J C, Byrd B F, Vaughan W K 1974 The effects of longterm estrogen on hysterectomized patients. American Journal of Obstetrics and Gynaecology 118: 778–782

Christiansen C, Christensen M S, Transbøl I 1981 Bone mass in postmenopausal women after withdrawal of oestrogen/gestagen replacement therapy. Lancet i: 459–461

Cohausen J H 1749 Hermippus redivivus: or the Sage's triumph over old age and the grave — wherein a method is laid down for prolonging the life and vigour of man, English Translation, J Campbell, J Nourse, London

Cohen J, Ditman K 1974 Gerovital H3 in the treatment of the depressed aging patient. Psychosomatics 15: 15–19

Dajda R 1980 Who prescribes? The illusion of power sharing in the surgery. In: Mapes R (ed) Prescribing and Drug Usage, Croom Helm, London

Deacon S P, Hammond L, Thompson B 1978 Drug supply

requirement for patients discharged from hospital. British Medical Journal 2: 555

Dilman V M 1979 Hypothalamic mechanisms of ageing and of specific age pathology V. A model for the mechanism of human specific age pathology and natural death. Experimental Gerontology 14: 287–300

Dilman V M, Anisimow V N 1980 Effect of treatment with phenformin , diphenylhydantoin or L-dopa on life-span and tumour incidence in C3H/Sn mice. Gerontology 26: 241–246

Drury M, Sabbagh K 1982 Four traps for the prescribing doctor. British Medical Journal 284: 634–636

Enesco H E, Verdone-Smith C 1980 Alpha-tocopherol increases the life span in the Rotifer Philodena. Experimental Gerontology 15: 335–338

Gibson I J M 1978 Are drugs in the right containers for your elderly patients? Modern Geriatrics 8/3: 39

Goodwin J S, Goodwin J M, Vogel A V 1979 Knowledge and use of placebos by house officers and nurses. Annals of Internal Medicine 91: 106–110

Hoover R, Gray L A, Cole P, MacMahon B 1976 Menopausal estrogens and breast cancer. New England Journal of Medicine 295: 401–405

Hutchinson T A, Polansky S M, Feinstein A R 1979 Postmenopausal oestrogens protect against fractures of hip and distal radius A case control study. Lancet ii: 705–09

Hutton J D, Jacobs H S, James V H T 1979 Steroid endocrinology after the menopause: a review. Journal of the Royal Society of Medicine 72: 835–841

Kavanagh T, Shephard R J 1977 Effects of continued training on the aging process. Annals of the New York Academy of Science 301: 656–70

Kent S 1982 The procaine 'youth' drugs. Geriatrics 37/4: 32–36

Kormendy C G, Bender A D 1971a Chemical interference with aging. Gerontologia 17: 52–64

Kormendy C G, Bender A D 1971b Experimental modification of the biochemistry and biology of the aging process. Journal of Pharmaceutical Sciences 60: 167–180

La Bella F, Vivian S 1978 Beta-aminopropionitrile promotes longevity in mice. Experimental Gerontology 13: 251–254

Lacassagne A 1923 A green old age, Translation: H Wilson, Bale and Sons and Danielson, London

Lipman R D 1980 Chemiluminescent measurement of free radicals and antioxidant molecular protection inside living rat mitochondria. Experimental Gerontology 15: 399–351

Lorand A 1912 Old age deferred, 3rd edn. F A Davis, Philadelphia

MacFarlane M D, Besbris H 1974 Procaine (Gerovital H3) therapy: mechanism of inhibition of monoamine oxidase. Journal of the American Geriatrics Society 22: 365–371

Mack T M, Pike M C, Henderson B E, Pfeffer R I, Gerkins V R, Arthur M, Brown S E 1976 Estrogens and endometrial cancer in a retirement community. New England Journal of Medicine 294: 1262–1267

Mandel F P, Geola F L, Lu J K H, Eggena P, Sambhi M P, Hershman J M, Judd H L 1982 Biologic effects of various doses of Ethinyl Estradiol in postmenopausal women. Obstetrics and Gynaecology 59: 673–679

Martys C R 1979 Adverse reactions to drugs in general practice. British Medical Journal 2: 1194–7

Mez-Mangold L 1971 A history of drugs, F Hofmann-La Roche, Basle, Switzerland

Multiple Risk Factor Intervention Trial 1982 Risk factor changes and mortality results. Journal of the American Medical Association 248: 1465–77

Nachtigall L E, Nachtigall R H, Nachtigall R D, Beckman E M 1979(a) Estrogen replacement therapy I: A 10-year prospective study in the relationship to osteoporosis. Obstetrics and Gynaecology 53: 277–281

Nachtigall L E, Nachtigall R H, Nachtigall R D, Beckman E M 1979(b) Estrogen replacement therapy II: a prospective study in the relationship to carcinoma and cardiovascular and metabolic problems. Obstetrics and Gynaecology 54: 74–79

Oliver M F 1982 Does control of risk factors prevent coronary heart disease? British Medical Journal 285: 1065–6

Olsen E J, Bank L, Jarvik L F 1978 Gerovital H3: a clinical trial as an antidepressant. Journal of Gerontology 33/5: 514–20

Pearson R 1982 Who is taking their tablets? British Medical Journal 285: 757–758

Robinson D S, Davis J M, Nies A, Colburn R W, Davis J N, Bourne H R, Bunney W E, Shaw D M, Coppen A J 1972 Ageing, monoamines and monoamine oxidase levels. Lancet i: 290–291

Rockstein M (ed) 1974 Theoretical Aspects of Aging, Academic Press, New York

Rose C L. Cohen M L 1977 Relative importance of physical activity for longevity. Annals of the New York Academy of Science 301: 671–702

Rosenberg L, Armstrong B, Jick H 1976 Myocardial infarction and estrogen therapy in menopausal women. New England Journal of Medicine 294: 1256–1259

Ross R K, Paganini-Hill A, Mack T M, Arthur M, Henderson B E 1981 Menopausal oestrogen therapy and protection from death from ischaemic heart disease. Lancet i: 858–860

Sacher G A 1977 Life table modification and life prolongation. In: Finch C E, Hayflick L (ed) Handbook of the Biology of Aging, Van Nostrand Reinhold, New York, p 582–638

Shaw S M, Opit L J 1976 Need for supervision in the elderly receiving long-term prescribed medication. British Medical Journal 1: 505–507

Siegel R J 1979 Ginseng abuse syndrome. Problems with the panacea. Journal of the American Medical Association 241: 1614

Smith J S, Davison K 1971 Changes in the pattern of admissions for attempted suicide in Newcastle-upon-Tyne during the 1960s. British Medical Journal 4: 412–18

Stevenson J C, Whithead J C 1982 Postmenopausal osteoporosis. British Medical Journal 285: 585–588

Stewart R B, May F E, Hale W E, Marks R G 1982 Psychotropic drug use in an ambulatory elderly population. Gerontology 28: 328–335

Stuart D 1981 Practical problems of improving records. British Medical Journal 282: 783–84

Thomson G H 1979 Prescribing procrastination Journal of the Royal College of General Practitioners 29: 550–552

Thomson P 1981 Medical Records: Middle sized group practice. British Medical Journal 282: 1432–1441

Tulloch A J 1981 Repeat prescribing for elderly patients. British Medical Journal 282: 1672–5

US Dept. HEW PHS 1976 Physicians' drug prescribing patterns in skilled nursing facilities: long-term care facility improvement campaign. Monograph No. 2 Washington USA

Williamson J, Chopin J M 1980 Adverse reactions to prescribed drugs in the elderly: a multicentre investigation. Age and Ageing 9: 73–80

Ziel H K, Finkle W D 1975 Increased risk of endometrial carcinoma among users of conjugated oestrogens. New England Journal of Medicine 293: 1167–1170

Zwerling I, Plutchik R, Hotz M, Kling R, Rubin L, Grossman J, Siegel B 1975 Effects of procaine preparation (Gerovital H3) in hospitalized geriatric patients: a double blind study. Journal of the American Geriatrics Society 23: 355–359

PART TWO

Clinical Medicine in Old Age

Atherosclerosis and aging

INTRODUCTION

It has been said that 'a man is only as old as his arteries'. In this respect, the pathology of vascular disease is an increasingly important aspect of the pathology of old age. For with the eradication or control of infectious disease, improved hygiene and social conditions, and the increased salvage of lives which has been made possible by improvements in anaesthetic, obstetrical and surgical techniques, the expectation of life has progressively lengthened during the present century in all the developed countries. But, over the same period, the relative importance of the circulatory diseases has increased correspondingly.

On a world-wide basis, figures colllected by the World Health Organization (see *Epidemiological and Vital Statistics Report, 1956*) elicited the following comment in 1957 (*Chronicle of the World Health Organization, 1957*): 'These statistics reveal that cardiovascular diseases, and in many countries, arteriosclerosis alone, cause more deaths than any other disease, cancer included. This significant fact indicates the importance of the problem which these diseases present at the present time.'

A decade later, the position had not improved. In a statistical review of the world health situation (*World Health Chronicle, 1967*) it was stated that 'Cardiovascular diseases are becoming a universal health problem. There is no doubt that the prolongation of the active lifespan of man in developed communities depends mainly on the ability to prevent and control the development of arteriosclerosis and its complications in the heart and in the brain. Moreover, rapid social and economic development and changes in the mode of living already foreshadow a similar trend in developing countries.' This trend is particularly marked in certain developing countries, such as Israel, with a high immigration rate and a policy directed at rapid assimilation into a common cultural and social pattern (see p. 174).

However, recently an encouraging and significant decline in coronary heart disease and stroke mortality has been observed in certain countries (most noticeably in the USA), the reasons for which are not fully understood (Rosenberg and Klebba, 1979; Lancet editorial, 1980). It has been suggested that this trend may be due to favourable changes in the life-styles, with alterations in various 'risk factors' (such as smoking, blood pressure, exercise habit, nature of the diet etc. — see p. 192), in individuals responding to the intensive health education programmes prevalent in the USA. But this suggestion is not universally accepted and there is still much to learn, in terms of basic understanding of how atherosclerotic vascular disease occurs and how it can be prevented.

This applies with particular force in the UK where there is less clear evidence of any similar decline in coronary heart disease and stroke mortality and morbidity (Epstein and Pisa, 1979; Wells, 1982). Broadly, therefore, the questions that arise from consideration of the world-wide prevalence of atherosclerosis are:

1. With the elimination or reduction of certain causes of mortality, it may be accepted that there has been a consequent prolongation of life. But is the relative increase in incidence of vascular disorders in many populations simply a manifestation of a natural, biological process of aging which is being uncovered, and therefore, the inevitable price of this increased longevity? Or,

2. Are these changes in the vascular tree truly a *disease*, albeit one so common as to be virtually universal? If so, are there environmental factors in the 'civilized way of life' which can be identified and thereby eliminated or circumvented so as to reduce the incidence of the disease?

Obviously, these questions cannot be answered satisfactorily until the mechanisms underlying alterations in arterial structure and function are fully understood. For as Page (1945) remarked: 'The problem of arteriosclerosis is the nub of the problem of cardiovascular disease. Notwithstanding its great importance, our knowledge is scanty regarding its aetiology, indefinite as to classification and meagre as to prevention and cure.' Fortunately, since the time when these strictures were levelled, some progress has been made with each of these aspects, which it is now proposed to review.

In the context in which the present survey is being conducted, it is perhaps necessary to begin by stressing that, while in many ways the changes consequent upon atherosclerosis give rise to geriatric problems, this form of arterial disease is not solely a senescent process. Instances of precocious or juvenile atherosclerosis are common in the children of families with essential hyper-lipidaemia, and in patients with severe diabetes of early onset. In Western countries it is also not uncommon to encounter instances of the onset of ischaemic heart disease in men in their thirties. It is therefore evident that atherosclerosis must not be regarded as an inevitable and inexorable senescence of intrinsic components of the aged artery since, in the instances quoted, evidence of atherosclerotic cardiovascular complications may occur early in life. Even in apparently healthy subjects the time scale over which atherosclerosis develops is variable in a given population. In even the countries showing a high prevalence, in most subjects the period of development extends, literally, over a life-time. In answer to the first of the questions posed above and in anticipation of the evidence to be presented, it can be stated that even when the development of atherosclerosis occurs slowly, the initial stages of the process appear to be a dynamic response by the living connective tissue gel of the arterial wall to material deposited therein. Only in the late stages of advanced plaques is there evidence of a truly degenerative process characterized by breakdown of intrinsic body components. In this sense, therefore, this form of vascular disease is not a premature nor necessarily an inevitable senescene. Instead, it can be recognized that there are, indeed, environmental and other factors which can be identified which influence the rate of progression of the process and means to eliminate or circumvent the process will be discussed.

THE DEVELOPMENT OF ATHEROSCLEROSIS AND EVOLUTION OF THE ATHEROSCLEROTIC PLAQUE

Definition
Arteriosclerosis is a generic term introduced by Lobstein (1833) for all the conditions associated with thickening and hardening of the arteries. If known infective causes (syphilis, tuberculosis) and inflammatory arteritides (granulomatous arteritis, polyarteritis, etc.) are excluded, the commonest form of arteriosclerosis is atherosclerosis.

In 1958 a Study Group was convened by the World

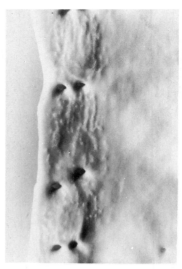

Fig. 10.1 'Fatty streaks and spots.' Early circular and linear lesions in thoracic aorta between openings of intercostal arteries. From female aged 23 in good health until killed in road accident.

Health Organization to facilitate the standardization of pathological criteria and terminology applied to vascular diseases (*WHO Technical Report No. 143*). This group defined atherosclerosis as 'a variable combination of changes of the intima of arteries (as distinguished from arterioles) consisting of a focal accumulation of lipids, complex carbohydrates, blood and blood products, fibrous tissue and calcium deposits and associated with medial changes'.

The group did not record agreement as to the histogenetical sequence in which components occur in the intima to give rise to the fully developed plaque, beyond approving the continued usage of, and redefining, the following terms:

'Fatty Streak or Spot' applied to superficial yellow or yellowish-grey intimal lesions which are stained selectively by fat stains (Fig. 10.1 and Plate 10.1).

'Fibrous Plaque' applied to a circumscribed, elevated intimal thickening which is firm and grey or pearly-white (Plate 10.2).

'Atheroma' applied to an atherosclerotic plaque in which fatty softening is predominant (Plate 10.3).

'Complicated Lesions' applied to lesions with additional changes or alterations such as thrombosis, ulceration and calcareous deposits (Plate 10.4).

These definitions have been criticized elsewhere (Walton, 1969a) because, while useful for the geographical study of atherosclerosis, they offer less guidance to those interested in the more basic problem of atherogenesis.

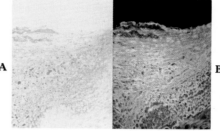

Plate 10.1 Frozen sections of 'fatty streak' from ascending aorta of boy aged 12 in good health but killed by accidental fall. (**a**) Stained with oil red 0, haematoxylin and light green to show sub-intimal infiltration by lipid droplets of varying size (red). (**b**) Adjacent section from same block treated with fluorescein-labelled anti-LDL to show bright green specific fluorescence corresponding in distribution to lipid as seen in A. (x95)

Plate 10.2 Frozen sections of 'fibrous plaque' in splenic artery of man aged 52. (**a**) Stained with oil red 0, haematoxylin and light green to show fibrous cap overlying fibro-fatty plaque and extension of lipid infiltration to media in places. (**b**) Adjacent section from same block treated with fluorescein-labelled anti-LDL to show correspondence of specific fluorescence (green) with distribution of lipid in (**a**). (x95)

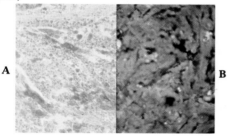

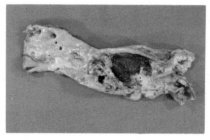

Plate 10.3 'Atheroma'. Frozen section showing mass of atheromatous gruel in advanced plaque from aorta of woman aged 73. (**a**) Stained with oil red 0, haematoxylin and light green. Note lipid as red globules of varying size and as aggregated masses—also presence of 'cholesterol clefts'. (**b**) Corresponding section treated with fluorescein-labelled anti-LDL. Note specific green fluorescence contrasting with black of 'cholesterol clefts' and also yellowish-white areas of carotenoid pigment. (x396)

Plate 10.4 'Complicated lesions'. Portion of lower abdominal aorta and iliac bifurcation from man of 85. Note numerous fibrotic lesions, some ulcerating, calcification, and early aneurysmal dilations, containing thrombus.

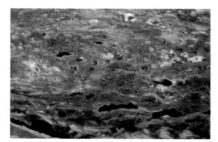

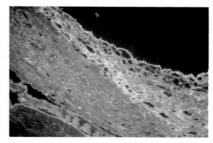

Plate 10.5 Area in lower portion of intima from large advanced plaque in aorta of man aged 53 (duplicated elastic lamina marking boundary with muscularis mucosa in lower right-hand corner). Frozen section treated with fluorescein-labelled anti-fibrinogen and photographed through yellow filter. Note irregular areas of specific fluorescence (greenish-yellow) delineating fibrin or fibrinogen lining walls of, or occluding, vascular or lymphatic channels. (x720)

Plate 10.6 Frozen section of coronary artery from area affected by previous coronary thrombosis, in man aged 48. Section treated with fluorescein-labelled anti-fibrinogen and photographed through yellow filter. Note coarse reticulated pattern of specific fluorescence (yellowish-green) in the thrombus (upper right) overlying plaque (lower left), the latter showing the presence of fibrin or fibrinogen in vascular or lymphatic channels in pattern similar to that seen in Plate 5.5.

Pathological anatomy and sequence of appearance of lesions

Many able and experienced pathologists have noted tiny mucoid elevations of the intima at sites where atherosclerotic lesions subsequently develop (e.g. Moon and Rinehart, 1952; Pollak, 1963; Lorenzen, 1963; Shimamoto, 1963; Gerö et al, 1967). The microscopical appearance presented by such lesions has been suggested to indicate sites of oedema of the endothelium and subendothelial layers, caused by local alteration of vascular permeability. The presence also, at these sites, of material giving the histochemical reactions of acid mucopolysaccharides has been suggested to be part of a generalized mesenchymal response (Hauss et al, 1969) which may be of critical importance in determining the localization of later lipid deposition (see p. 182).

The fatty streak or spot is widely accepted (despite some dissentient views, cf. Mitchell and Schwartz, 1965) as the most easily perceived next stage in the development of lesions. It seems probable that the fatty streak or spot is the most easily reversible form of atherosclerotic lesions since discrepancies have been noted between the number and distribution of these as opposed to the later lesions, at certain sites. But it seems equally unlikely that all fatty streaks disappear and are unrelated to the later lesions which appear at broadly similar sites in view of the continuity (in terms of lipoprotein infiltration-see p. 177) which has been observed between these and later uncomplicated lesions.

Lipid infiltration of subendothelial tissues evokes a cellular response which is frequently attended by fibrosis and often accompanied by calcification of varying degree. At this stage the lesion is raised above the surrounding endothelium. Necrosis or haemorrhage within the lesion, ulceration, medial involvement, aneurysmal dilatation of the vessel, etc. are later complications. The precise point at which raised lesions induce the all important complication (in human pathology) of intravascular thrombosis is still a matter of controversy and debate which will be discussed later.

Geographical incidence in man

Comparisons between populations are frequently made in terms of 'incidence' or 'prevalence'. But with a process which usually only develops over many years, like atherosclerosis, it should be realized that estimates of 'incidence' are really cross-sectional measurements of a time-dimensional process. For this reason it appears to be preferable to regard such data as point estimates of the *rate of progression* (a longitudinal parameter) in a given population.

Atherosclerotic lesions cannot be directly visualized in life, except by arteriography — a procedure which is not without hazard, and which demands specialized equipment and skilled interpretation, making it unsuitable for population screening. The rates of occurrence of lesions in a given vessel in different populations can therefore only be directly compared by compiling autopsy data from different countries. Because coronary atherosclerosis is the principal (though not the sole) factor in determining the occurrence of ischaemic heart disease, for living populations the rate of occurrence of this form of cardiovascular disease is often taken to be an indirect index of atherosclerosis. There are obvious fallacies in this assumption.

Studies on the actual prevalence of arterial lesions in certain elective sites, using the agreed and comparable criteria for the performance of autopsies, the handling, methods of examination, and grading of specimens of the International Atherosclerosis Project, have shown a world-wide distribution (McGill, 1968; Strong and Eggen, 1970). In all the populations examined, the extent of arterial involvement increases with age but the *rate of progression* varies between populations, being fastest in developed communities. The ranking of populations on this basis broadly parallels that of the mortality from atherosclerotic heart disease in the same countries and allows comparison of various environmental or ethnic factors between countries, and between given communities in any one country (Strong and Eggen, 1970).

The ranking order found between populations suggests that environmental, rather than ethnic, factors are important in determining the incidence of raised lesions. For example, on comparing Negro populations, it is seen that the occurrence of raised lesions in Negroes in New Orleans is only slightly different from that of the white population in the same area. But North American negroes show a much faster rate of involvement of their vessels than the South African Bantu (Strong and Eggen, 1970).

In developed communities in which there is a relatively rapid rate of progression with age, the arteries of males show more marked changes than those of females during the reproductive period of life. This difference between the sexes is less marked in populations in whom the overall rate of of progression of lesions is slow. Interesting but unexplained differences in the topographical distribution of lesions in the vascular tree between countries have also been observed. For instance, while the incidence of *coronary* artery disease in Japan is low as compared with Western countries, the incidence of *cerebrovascular* disease is relatively high. On the other hand the incidence of coronary artery disease among second-generation migrants of Japanese ancestry living in California approaches that of other Californians (Keys, 1963).

Countries in which there has been a rapid assimilation of immigrants from different backgrounds have provided particularly interesting data. The prevalence of myocardial infarction among hospitalized patients in Israel has been reported to be markedly higher among immigrants of European origin than among those of Yemenite or Bedouin stock (Dreyfuss, 1953; Groen et al, 1968). But with the assimilation of people from varying backgrounds into a common culture and way of life, there is evidence that a change in these morbidity patterns is already occurring (Medalie, 1970).

The interaction of environmental with other 'risk factors' (see below) has recently been examined in relation to epidemiological data on a world-wide scale (Epstein, 1971; Epstein and Pisa, 1979).

Experimental models

Many different dietary and other regimes have been used to induce arterial disease, analogous to that seen in man, in other species. The effects of these have been reviewed in detail elsewhere (Gresham and Howard, 1963; Lorenzen, 1963; Adams, 1964; Roberts and Straus, 1965; Constantinides, 1965; Thomas et al, 1970). This field will not be surveyed again, therefore, although reference will be made to experimental findings where these seem relevant to the pathogenesis of atherosclerosis in the human.

THEORIES OF ATHEROGENESIS

Classical theories

Among the numerous theories which have been propounded in the past there are, broadly speaking, two divergent views which still attract adherents and others which are no longer favoured. The two theories still current are the 'thrombogenic' and the 'insudative' hypotheses.

The thrombogenic hypothesis originated with Rokitansky (1852) who stressed the frequency with which fibrinous material occurs in association with lipid in atherosclerotic plaques and accordingly suggested the implication of thrombosis in the initiation of plaque formation. He suggested that atheromatous change was due to the repeated deposition of blood elements on the endothelium with subsequent metamorphosis and degeneration of the deposits.

The insudative hypothesis was put forward by Virchow (1862) who suggested that the lipids in atherosclerotic lesions derive from the plasma by 'imbibition' or 'insudation.' In the light of subsequent controversy as to whether mucoid change in the arterial wall precedes or influences lipid deposition, it is interesting to observe that Virchow postulated that a 'mucoid substance' in the arterial wall was implicated in atherogenesis.

It will be observed that both these hypotheses agreed in postulating that the components of the plaque originate from the blood but differed in what they proffered as the components concerned. An alternative, but now discarded, view was that propounded by Thoma (1883) who suggested that the components of the plaque arose as breakdown products (i.e. fatty and hyaline degeneration) of intrinsic elements of the arterial wall.

Later developments

Thrombogenic theory
Although the thrombogenic hypothesis was occasionally revived between 1912 and 1936 (for review, see Chandler, 1970) its strongest recent proponent has been Duguid (1946, 1948, 1955, 1960) who suggested that the material in plaques comprises the residual breakdown products of platelets or mural thrombi ('fibrin incrustations') deposited initially on the intimal surface with later endothelialization and incorporation into the wall. Duguid maintained that not only small mural thrombi but even occlusive thrombi could give rise to atherosclerotic plaques (Duguid, 1946).

The essential difficulty in accepting the thrombogenic hypothesis as the sole explanation of plaque formation has lain in the fact that thrombi serve as an inadequate source of the lipid whcich is so prominent a component of the plaque. Efforts to obtain direct experimental evidence in support of the theory by introducing emboli derived from autologous, homologous or heterologous blood clots into the pulmonary circulation of rabbits were found uniformly to give rise to fibrous lesions containing little or no lipid (Harrison, 1948; Wartman et al, 1951; Heard, 1952; Barnard, 1954; Thomas et al, 1956).

Another difficulty is that, in human pathology, one might reasonably expect, if thrombosis in fact always precedes palque formation, that patients with severe blood coagulation deficiencies would show an unusually low incidence of atherosclerosis. However, surveys of the incidence of atherosclerosis in haemophilia (Boivin, 1954), Christmas disease (Stewart and Acheson, 1957) and von Willebrand's disease (Silwer et al, 1966) have not shown this to be the case.

Observations of this kind have led to a tacit abandonment of the proposition that thrombosis, as such, always *precedes* plaque formation and instead, attention has veered to the possibility that platelet aggregates might serve as an alternative source of plaque components. This possibility was given impetus by Hellem's (1960) demonstration that systems unrelated to blood coagulation can cause platelets to aggregate and later demonstrations by others that such aggregates adhere at sites of slight damage to endothelium. However, tests of changes in platelet behaviour, as measured by the techniques hitherto devised (for review, see Hampton, 1967), seem either (1) to be non-specific in showing alterations in a wide variety of diseases in which atherosclerosis is not an especially prominent complication; or (2) to detect alterations apparently mediated by changes in the plasma rather than in the platelets themselves (Bolton, Hampton and Mitchell, 1967). Moreover, platelets also seem inadequate as the source of lipid in plaques (cf. Smith, 1970).

Insudative theory

Virchow's views were confirmed and further elaborated by Aschoff (1924, 1933). However, since little was known at the time of the various forms in which lipid is transported in the blood, the precise vehicle whereby plasma lipid is conveyed into the lesions was undefined. With the demonstration by Anitschkow (1913, 1933) that the addition of cholesterol to the diet of the rabbit induced hypercholesterolaemia and arterial lesions resembling those found in man, attention became focused on this sterol. It is only in comparatively recent years that it has been shown that cholesterol does not circulate in the free state but is bound to protein in various forms in the blood. Of these forms, the evidence that it is the plasma beta, or total low-density lipoproteins (TLDL)* which are the most important in atherogenesis, will be discussed later (p. 177).

Even among those broadly accepting the insudative theory there have been divergent views concerning the mechanism of selective localization of plasma lipid in subdendothelial tissues. It has been suggested that this occurs because plasma lipid is 'dammed-back' mechanically: (1) secondarily to medial changes such as anoxic enzymic defects (Adams et al, 1962); or (2) because of blockage of fenestrations in the elastic lamina (Gofman and Young, 1963); or (3) because of a selective 'molecular sieving' effect of the intimal gel (Adams, 1967); or (4) because the lipid in the form of low-density lipoprotein forms a selective co-acervate with the acidic mucopolysaccharides (AMPS) of the intimal gel (Amenta and Waters, 1960; Gerö et al, 1960; Walton and Williamson, 1968).

Lipid deposits occur not only in muscular arteries but also in the mitral and aortic valves which are devoid of muscle. Following the demonstration that the lipid in atherosclerotic lesions at all stages of their development from the fatty streak to the raised atheromatous plaque is in the form of TLDL (Walton, 1966, 1969c, 1970; Walton and Williamson, 1968), it was shown that the above-mentioned valvular lesions were identical in nature (Walton et al, 1970) with those in arteries,

suggesting a common mechanism of formation. Since valves lack a muscular coat and the elastica was shown to be an inefficient barrier to the ingress of lipoprotein, it was argued by these authors that no mechanical barrier 'damming back' the lipid need to postulated. Similarly since other macroglobulin components of plasma could not be demonstrated in the lesions, it was argued that retention by simple 'molecular seiving' was unlikely. On the other hand, the lipoprotein deposits were found in significant relation with material giving the histochemical reactions of AMPS, in support of postulate (4) above.

Current concepts of atherogenesis

From the foregoing discussion it will be clear that neither experimental nor clinical evidence support the concept that thrombosis is an *initiating cause* of *all* atherosclerotic plaques. This is not to deny, of course, the *some* 'pure' fibrous plaques (and especially those found in the pulmonary circulation of individuals previously suffering from peripheral venous thrombosis) might indeed be the residue of an organized embolic or thrombotic process. Similarly, it can be accepted that the organization and fibrosis of non-fatal thrombi occurring *on top of* a lipid-filled plaque may contribute to the final size and structure of a complicated plaque. However, it must be concluded that there is as yet no clear-cut evidence that either thrombosis or alteration of platelet behaviour determines the initial formation of plaques at sites where the arterial endothelium is intact and healthy. This view is supported by the failure to demonstrate platelete antigens by a sensitive immunohistological technique in *early* atherosclerotic lesions (Carstairs, 1965; Walton and Williamson, 1968).

There is, of course, no argument about the importance of intravascular thrombosis as a *secondary complication* of atherosclerosis nor about the role of platelets in this process. However, if neither thrombosis nor platelet aggregation can be accepted as mechanisms for the *initiation* of plaque formation (as opposed to accretion upon already-formed plaques) then, in the opinion of the writer, the thrombogenic hypothesis, as a general theory of the mechanism of atherogenesis, must be abandoned.

Similarly, Thoma's (1883) view of atherosclerosis as a senile degenerative process of the intrinsic components of the arterial wall, although once supported (Blumenthal et al, 1944; Lansing et al, 1950) has not been seriously entertained in recent years in view of the overwhelming evidence discussed below that the components of the plaque originate from the plasma.

In recent years some reconciliation between the apparently divergent thrombogenic and insudative hypotheses has occurred. For example, it has been suggested that blood platelets may play a role in ather-

---

* The abbreviation TLDL is used throughout the text to include all soluble lipoproteins with S_f values from 0 to 400 in a medium of density 1.063g/ml. The abbreviations LDL and VLDL are used for subfractions of TLDL, namely for the low-density (S_f 0 to 10) and very low-density (S_f 20 to 400) lipoproteins, respectively (see also p. 187).

ogenesis, not by contributing material directly to form plaques, but by way of the pharmacological effects of agents released from platelets upon arterial wall cells (Ross and Glomset, 1976; Ross and Harker, 1976). A relatively low molecular weight (ca. 30 000–35 000 daltons) cationic protein, obtained from platelets and known as platelet-derived growth factor, (Ross et al, 1980) has been shown to stimulate the growth and division in culture of some of the cell-types prevalent in arterial intima (smooth muscle cells, fibroblasts, endothelial cells). Platelets have also been shown to produce thromboxanes and leukotrienes which might in turn stimulate endothelial cells or other mesenchymal cells to synthesize prostglandins.

In theory, the balance between the activatory and inhibitory effects of these products might trigger the haemostatic mechanism or influence the permeability of the arterial wall and so influence atherogenesis. However, one of the basic characteristics of intact, normal endothelium is a lack of reactivity with circulating platelets, leucocytes or coagulation components. There is some evidence that, under certain experimental conditions, for example in arteries artificially denuded of endothelium by intra-arterial catheterization or other means (Moore et al, 1976; Minick et al, 1977, 1979; Robertson, 1980), or in animals rendered homocystinaemic and with abnormal endothelium (Harker et al, 1976), platelet factors and products may play some part in atherogenesis. But these experimental conditions cannot be extrapolated to the occurrence of human atherosclerosis in intact 'normal' arteries.

There has also been much interest recently in the nature of the mesenchymal cells proliferating in atherosclerotic lesions and in mechanisms (other than the effects of platelet product) causing such proliferation. The role of the smooth muscle cell in plaque formation has been extensively studied (for reviews, see Geer and Haust, 1972; Titus and Weilbaecher, 1980) but there is also good evidence that mononuclear cells (either blood monocytes or tissue macrophages, also play a part by accumulating lipid (lipoprotein) to form fat-filled or foam-cells in the intima (Schaffner et al, 1980).

One intrepretation of the way in which smooth muscle cells proliferate in plaques has been based on evidence of selective predominance of cells synthesizing a single isoenzyme of glucose-6-phosphate dehydrogenase in lesions from humans heterozygous for this enzyme. This has been held to be compatible with a monoclonal mutational reponse (akin to that occurring in neoplasms) possible caused by chemical mutagens or viruses (Benditt and Benditt, 1973). This interpretation has not found general acceptance (cf. Constantinides, 1978). In contrast, Hauss et al, (1979) demonstrated that in rats exposed to a wide variety of the 'risk factors' thought to influence human atherogenesis (see later section,

p. 178) arterial smooth muscle cells proliferated in a monotypic rather than a monoclonal fashion and the cells also exhibited an augmented rate of synthesis and output of their characteristic extracellular products (components of the ground substance and connective tissue fibres).

Other modern work appears to have validated the orginal insudative hypothesis of Virchow and to have extended it in two directions. Firstly, by defining among those protein components of the plasma entering the arterial wall, a family of lipoproteins (TLDL) which are positively atherogenic and another lipoprotein 'family' (HDL) which may be protective in reducing the risk of atherosclerosis. Secondly, recent research, considered in a later section (see p. 183) has been concerned with attempting to elucidate the cellular mechanisms of these opposing effects.

The relevant evidence concerning the positive atherogenic effect of TLDL will be considered first and then that relating to the apparently opposite effect of HDL.

Indirect evidence
1. It has been shown that changes in the blood levels of low-density lipoproteins (TLDL) with age and sex parallel differences in the rate of progression of atherosclerosis with age and between the sexes in developed communities.

2. In geographical comparisons between similar ethnic groups in widely different locations in the world, it has been noted that TLDL levels correlate broadly with the rate of progression of atherosclerosis in the respective locations. In particular, in population groups subsisting on severely restricted diets because of war, economic necessity, cultural convention or religious conviction, serum lipids and lipoproteins have been noted to be unusually low (by Western standards). Such populations have been noted to show a low rate of progression of atherosclerosis.

3. On the other hand, an otherwise disparate group of pathological conditions attended in common by a secondary elevation of serum TLDL levels (hypothyroidism, the nephrotic syndrome, chronic biliary cirrhosis, uncontrolled diabetes mellitus) also have in common an accelerated rate of development of atherosclerosis.

4. A group of essential (familial) hyperlipidaemias characterized by early and sustained gross elevation of serum TLDL show precocious and severe atherosclerosis, often accompanied by evidence of extravascular lipid deposits in the tissues (i.e. premature formation of corneal arcus and xanthomatosis).

5. In both secondary and primary hyperlipoproteinaemias (of the kinds referred to in paras 3 and 4 above) studies with isotopically-labelled TLDL have shown that the high serum TLDL levels reflect a greatly

increased total body pool of this lipoprotein with increase of both intra-and extravascular distribution.

Direct evidence

1. In certain instances, where autologous radio-isotopically-labelled TLDL has been administered, increased accumulation of the specific label has been demonstrated in arteries and (where xanthomatous deposits have been present) also in xanthoma tissue.

2. Confirmation of the incorporation of TLDL (but not HDL) into atherosclerotic lesions at all stages of their development has been obtained immunologically, at a histological level using the technique of immuno-fluorescence 1 (see Plates 10–10.3) and semi-quantita-tively by the elution of TLDL from aortic extracts. The immunofluorescent technique has also demonstrated the presence of fibrin or fibrinogen in lesions in the absence of platelet antigens (i.e. suggesting that this protein also gains access by 'insudation' rather than as an invariable consequence of endothelialization of thrombi). The lipid composition of early plaques has been shown to resemble chemically that of serum TLDL.

3. In the human, corneal arcus formation occurs commonly in old age ('arcus senilis') with increasing TLDL serum levels, and as a precocious phenomenon ('arcus juvenilis') in familial hyperlipoproteinaemias. Lipid deposition is histologically demonstrable in the cornea, sclera, ciliary processes, and to a lesser extent in the iris, as an accompaniment of the externally visible corneal arcus. In the lipid-fed rabbit, because of certain anatomical peculiarities of the vascular supply seen in this species, lipid deposition is more marked in the iris and ciliary body than in the cornea but the distribution otherwise resembles that seen in humans. In both species, using immunofluorescence, it has been demon-strated that the lipid is in the form of β-lipoprotein (TLDL).

4. Using similar techniques, it has been shown that rabbit β-lipoprotein is demonstrable in the arterial lesions which occur in this species on lipid-supplemented diets and in association with consequent hyperlipoprotein-aemia. Xanthomata occur spontaneously in hyperlipo-proteinaemic lipid-fed rabbits on the footpads (i.e. sites exposed to pressure and minor traumata giving rise to altered vascular permeability). It has been established that xanthomata can be induced at elective sites by the intradermal injection of histamine in lipid-fed animals and the lipid-filled cells at these sites have been shown to contain rabbit TLDL by immunofluorescence and by the injection of radioisotopically-labelled autologous TLDL.

This evidence suggests that TLDL is concerned in the formation not only of the arterial, but also of the extravascular, lesions associated with atherosclerosis. To keep this evidence in perspective, it is necessary at this point to stress that while the rate of elevation of serum TLDL levels correlates with the rate of progression of atherosclerosis (and with the formation of tissue deposits of lipids, such as xanthomata and the corneal arcus), and while TLDL is directly implicated in the transport of lipid into these lesions, yet this general mechanism does not account for the topographical distribution of the lesions. For example, the composition of the blood is uniform in relation to lipids and lipoproteins throughout the vascular tree yet atherosclerosis is absent from veins but present in arteries, and, even in the latter, lesions are distributed in a nodular and discontinuous fashion. Some of the possible factors affecting the topographical distribution of lesions are considered later.

Similarly, this general mechanism does not account, in itself, for the high and well-documented association, in human pathology, of thrombosis with atherosclerosis. For the availability of highly purified lipoproteins has allowed the unequivocal demonstration that these proteins, in their intact and native state, are quite inac-tive in relation to blood coagulation and fibrinolytic mechanisms (Howell, 1964; Walton and Wolf, unpub-lished observations). It seems unlikely, therefore, that the presence of intact TLDL in the arterial intima in the early lesion is implicated in thrombosis. However, the changes that occur when TLDL is degraded in the intima in later lesions, and the manner in which these changes may contribute to the initiation of thrombosis, are considered subsequently.

THE INSUDATIVE HYPOTHESIS CONSIDERED IN RELATION TO FACTORS PREDISPOSING TO ATHEROSCLEROSIS

Factors affecting the rate of progression of atherosclerosis

Prospective studies in certain communities have helped to define what have come to be known as 'risk factors' contributing to the development of atherosclerosis (e.g. the Framingham study, Dawber et al, 1962; the Tecumseh community study, Epstein, 1967). Although elevated serum lipids (cholesterol and triglycerides) have been recognized as risk factors in themselves, the influ-ence of other risk factors on serum lipids has not always been considered. In this context, it is necessary to state again that the plasma lipids (cholesterol, triglycerides and phospholipids) being virtually water-insoluble, do not circulate in the free state but bound to protein as lipoprotein. Since the high density lipoproteins show relatively little variation in health or disease, increase in serum lipid levels, in practice, is invariably given expression as increase of TLDL. This has two important connotations. Firstly, data from earlier studies, in which a single lipid parameter (e.g. serum

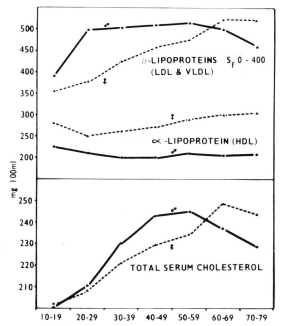

Fig. 10.2 Variation of mean serum concentration of low-density and high-density lipoproteins in relation to mean total serum cholesterol, by age and sex. Note broad parallelism between serum cholesterol and TLDL levels with age and sex.

cholesterol alone) has been measured in relation to social and environmental factors, can be reinterpreted as reflecting corresponding variation in serum TLDL levels. The association between serum cholesterol levels and serum TLDL levels for a British population is shown in Figure 10.2. A similar parallelism has been shown to hold good even for a population with relatively low serum lipid values like the South African Bantu (cf. Walker and Arvidsson, 1954; Bronte Stewart et al, 1955). Secondly, although circumstantial and direct evidence single out TLDL, and not HDL, as the component of primary importance in atherogenesis, since *both* lipoproteins act as vehicles for cholesterol, triglycerides and phospholipids, it can be inferred that *it is the nature of the vehicle for serum lipids rather than the nature of the lipids being carried* which primarily determines the retention of the lipids in the vessel wall.

In the light of these considerations, it is of interest to consider 'risk factors' in relation to serum TLDL levels.

Age and sex
Previous reference has been made to the epidemiological finding that, in developed countries, healthy males begin to form raised atherosclerotic lesions soon after puberty and that these increase in number as age advances. In healthy females the onset of these lesions is delayed but by the time of menopause the distribution and numbers of lesions increase and in later years approximate to those in males of corresponding age.

A survey by Walton and Scott (1964) suggested that similar correlations between TLDL levels and age and sex held good in apparently healthy populations in Britain and the USA, though the somewhat higher absolute serum TLDL levels for all age groups in the USA, as derived from the data reported by Glazier et al (1954), possibly reflected the greater affluence and the even higher incidence of cardiovascular disease in the USA.

It can be seen from Figure 10.2 that the most marked disparity in serum TLDL levels between the sexes occurs over the period representing the normal reproductive span — i.e. during a period when there is also the most marked disparity in the occurrence of atherosclerotic lesions between the sexes. This observation, which suggests that sex hormonal influences exert a determining effect on serum TLDL levels, and thereby on the speed of progression of atherosclerosis, is supported by clinical observations on the effects of gonadal ablation or alternatively, of hormonal therapy, on serum lipids (for references, see Walton, 1969a). Metabolic studies using radioactively-labelled TLDL by Scott et al, (1963) and by Walton et al, (1963, 1965) showed that the turnover of TLDL in healthy adults differed between the sexes, the catabolic rate being significantly higher in women. In the underdeveloped countries in which the rate of development of atherosclerotic lesions is slow, there is a corresponding slow rise with age of TLDL levels (as extrapolated from serum cholesterol values) and the disparity in both the apparent incidence of atherosclerosis and in TLDL levels between the sexes is less well marked (Mathur et al, 1961; Vakil, 1963; Subramaniam and Kulangara, 1967; Pinto et al, 1970).

In a case reported by Walton et al, (1963) in which isotopically-labelled TLDL had been administered in vivo, it was established at autopsy that material from an atheromatous lesion in the aorta had accumulated radioactivity at a higher level, per gram of tissue, than had other organs. This was confirmed in a number of other subjects by Scott and Winterbourn (1967) and by Scott and Hurley (1969, 1970). The latter authors also examined the relative distributions in artery walls and in other tissues of simultaneously administered TLDL and albumen (each labelled with a different isotope of iodine) and found differences between the gradients of permeability of these proteins in the arterial wall with higher retention of TLDL in the intimal layer. These results therefore agreed with similar studies in other species (Duncan et al, 1962; Duncan; 1963) and with identification of TLDL in the intima by chemical or immunological techniques.

Dietary factors in relation to serum lipids and atherosclerosis

Because geographic comparisons have suggested that environmental, rather than racial or ethnic, differences might determine the varying rates of progression of atherosclerosis found in different parts of the world, differences in dietary habits between populations have appeared to be an obvious matter for investigation. However, efforts to incriminate any one single dietary component have been largely unavailing. With regard to the lipids in the diet, the level of total dietary fat, the proportion of saturated to polyunsaturated fat and the dietary intake of cholesterol have all been proposed (for references, see Walton, 1969a, and Brown, 1970). The close relation between the intermediary metabolism of lipid and carbohydrate has also led to the suggestion (Yudkin, 1957, 1964; Yudkin and Roddy, 1964) that in developed countries a high sucrose intake might influence serum lipid levels and, thereby, the occurrence of atherosclerosis. This suggestion has aroused some controversy (cf. Malmros, 1969) and has not been supported by other epidemiological observations (Walker, 1971). It has been shown that there is a strong positive association between cigarette smoking and sugar intake and it has been suggested that it is the former rather than the latter which is implicated in the aetiology and manifestations of ischaemic heart disease (Burns-Cox et al, 1969; Howell and Wilson, 1969; Bennett et al, 1970).

Amongst the primitive people in some under-developed areas, it seems likely the pattern of food habits imposed by climatic conditions, i.e. irregularity of food supply on a seasonal basis as influenced by periods of drought, etc., may be of major importance in determining serum lipid levels. This is well illustrated by a study carried out among three nomadic tribes in northern Kenya by Shaper et al, (1963).

Diseases predisposing to atherosclerosis and hereditary factors

The accelerated rate of progression of atherosclerosis in primary (familial) hyperlipidaemias, occurring in association with extravascular deposits of lipids (corneal arcus and xanthoma formation), has been well documented by Khachadurian (1964). An increased incidence of atherosclerosis also occurs in secondary hyperlipidaemias such as those accompanying hypothyroidism, diabetes mellitus and the nephrotic syndrome (for references, see Walton, 1969a. Secondary hyperlipidaemias may also be accompanied by xanthomatosis (McGinley et al, 1952).

Metabolic studies in both primary and secondary hyperlipidaemias have shown that different mechanisms operate to influence the turnover of TLDL in these diseases but nevertheless produce, in common, increases in both intravascular and extravascular distribution of TLDL (Walton, 1969b). The increased incidence of vascular and extravascular lipid deposits in these diseases have been suggested to be expressions of this abnormal distribution in the form of accumulation of TLDL in arterial walls (Walton and Williamson, 1968); in the subendothelial tissue of heart valves (Walton et al, 1970); in xanthomata (Scott and Winterbourn, 1967); and in the tissues of the eye (Walton, 1973) respectively.

The influence of genetic factors is most clearly discernible in the primary hyperlipidaemias (Thannhauser, 1950; Fredrickson et al, 1967) but since some of the diseases giving rise to *secondary* hyperlipidaemia are themselves genetically mediated (viz. diabetes, some forms of nephrosis) it will be clear that genetic factors other than those determining the occurrence of essential hyperlipidaemia must be involved in atherogenesis.

Even in individuals without gross hyperlipidaemia, familial aggregation of coronary heart disease has been reported (Stamler et al, 1963) and coronary heart disease is apparently more prevalent among persons who are not of blood group O (Allan and Dawson, 1968). Significant associations between blood group, serum cholesterol and serum intestinal phosphatase activity have been noted by Langman et al, (1969) and by Oliver et al, (1969) who suggest that there may be genetically determined differences in lipid absorption from the intestine which, in turn, influence serum lipid levels.

High density lipoproteins and atherosclerosis

Despite earlier observations by Barr et al, (1951) on the inverse association between levels of alpha-lipoproteins (HDL) and the incidence of myocardial infarction and atherosclerosis, interest in this apparently protective effect of HDL only became intensifed relatively recently. It was stimulated by case-control and prospective observations by Miller and Miller (1975) and by Gordon et al (1977) of a consistent and independent negative association between HDL levels and coronary vascular events. Subsequent epidemiological studies, including the Lipid Research Clinics Program Prevalence Study (see Heiss et al, 1980) have supported the proposition that HDL 'protects' against cardiovascular disease. But the biochemical mechanism(s) producing this effect are as yet undefined. Possible mechanisms are discussed in a later section (see p. 193).

Factors affecting the distribution of lesions

Mechanical factors

Local injury to an artery has long been recognized as a localizing factor (Duff, 1935). Experimentally, it can be shown in lipid-fed hyperlipoproteinaemic animals that a variety of procedures such as direct damage by heat, freezing, X-irradiation, intra-aortic injection of enzymes, dissection of the outer coats of the vessel, etc. all localize plaques to the traumatized site (for references, see Constantinides, 1965; Adams, 1967). Since the arterial wall is living connective itssue it can be envisaged that these procedures would give rise to the liberation of vaso-active amines locally with alteration of permeability (see below) and would later interfere with drainage through the wall.

Plaques have been noted to be especially prevalent at sites of bifurcation, in bends, and in arteries which are relatively immobilized. Unusual haemodynamic stresses (Texon, 1957, 1963), eddy currents and turbulence (Mustard et al, 1963) and local variation in arterial wall shear (Caro et al, 1979) are among the mechanical factors which have been postulated, in particular by modern proponents of the thrombogenic hypothesis, as a mechanism to explain how thrombi or platelet aggregates might initiate plaque formation (e.g. Poole and French, 1961; Mustard et al, 1963; Mitchell, 1964).

It seems reasonable to accept some of the above factors as likely to determine thrombosis in *veins* where blood flow may be altered or impeded. However, venous thrombosis, although frequent in occurrence, is *not* followed by lipid-filled intimal lesions at the thrombosed sites. On the other hand, it has been established that autologous vein grafts used to replace arteries develop lipid deposits resembling atherosclerotic lesions and that the lipid is principally in the form of TLDL, as in arterial lesions. This finding suggests that arterial pressure is a more important determining factor (see below).

It has also previously been pointed out (Walton, 1969a) that in coarctation of the aorta although maximal turbulence, alteration of laminar flow, etc. occur *distal* to the point of constriction, nevertheless plaque formation is invariably sharply delimited to the segment *proximal* to the constriction. In this situation also it would seem that pressure, rather than other haemodynamic stresses, determines the site of formation of atherosclerotic lesions.

Pressure and permeability effects

Pressure. Hypertension is generally acknowledged to accelerate arterial disease in man (Gofman and Young, 1963; Giertsen, 1966) and thus to be an important 'risk factor' (Dawber et al, 1962; Morris et al, 1966). It has also been shown to accelerate the progression of arterial disease in lipid-fed animals (Heptinstall et al, 1958; McGill et al, 1961). In man, the influence of hypertension is more pronounced in diseases accompanied by hyperlipidaemia but some effect is observed even in the absence of gross elevation of serum lipids. The effect is particularly clearly seen at certain anatomical sites. For example, in addition to the two instances cited in the pre-

ceding section, TLDL infiltration is seen in the mitral and aortic valves (at arterial pressure) but not in the tricuspid and pulmonary valves which are at venous pressure (Walton et al, 1970). Similarly, atherosclerosis of the pulmonary arteries occurs only in association with pulmonary hypertension (Heath et al, 1960).

Permeability. The permeation of plasma proteins through the normal arterial wall has been established using proteins labelled with fluorescent dyes or with radioactive isotopes (Mancini et al, 1962; Duncan, 1963; Scott and Hurley, 1969, 1970). Clearly this process of plasma ultrafiltration would be influenced directly by filtration pressure and thus by hypertension to account for the observations noted above. It would also be influenced by local or generalized alterations of permeability of the wall.

Earlier reference was made to the proposition put forward by some authors that 'mucoid elevations' of the human arterial intima should be regarded as indicating intimal oedema due to localized alteration of vascular permeability. In the pig aorta, it has been demonstrated that areas in which fatty streaks and spots develop preferentially also show evidence of altered permeability in allowing the selective ingress of dyes which bind to plasma albumin (such as trypan blue) or of colloidal carbon particles (Klynstra and Bottcher, 1970).

It can reasonably be assumed that the arterial wall, like other connective tissues, is capable of reation to trauma by the *local* release of catecholamines, kinins, etc. to give rise to segregated areas of altered permeability. It has already been pointed out that this might be the physiological explanation for the localization of lesions following *externally* applied trauma to arteries.

Shimamoto (1963) has drawn attention to a more generalized (but still discontinuous) oedematous intimal reaction resulting from the intravenous injection of histamine, adrenaline and other vasoactive substances. It was suggested by Hueper (1944, 1945, 1956) that hypoxia (or 'haematic anoxaemia' as he preferred to call it) altered arterial permeability so as to allow the passage into the arterial wall of both endogenous and exogenous macromolecules from the circulation (including, of course, the plasma lipids). Experimentally, the maintenance of lipid-fed animals at lowered oxygen tension has been shown to enhance the extent and severity of arterial lesions (Myaskinov, 1958). It has also been shown that lipid-fed rabbits exposed to low concentrations of carbon monoxide develop arterial lipid-filled lesions more quickly and more intensely (Astrup et al, 1967) than animals maintained in an ordinary atmosphere. These authors postulated that hypoxia might be the primary factor and pointed out that, in cigarette smokers who inhale, levels of 10 to 15 per cent of carboxyhaemoglobin (i.e. levels found to enhance atherosclerosis in their experimental animals) are not uncommon. It is possible that this mechanism underlines the recognition of heavy smoking as yet another 'risk factor' (Rose, 1970; Kjeldsen, 1970).

In very elderly subjects (in the eighth and ninth decades of life) the thickened and pigmented intima of the aorta and larger arteries often shows diffuse lipid infiltration even in areas apparently free from discrete atherosclerotic lesions. Such areas show a diffuse reaction with anti-TLDL antisera (Kao and Wissler, 1965; Walton and Williamson, 1968; Bradly et al, 1979). This appearance suggests as overall increase in vascular permeability of arteries in advanced old age. Occasional instances have been encountered (Walton, unpublished observations) in which similar *diffuse* infiltration of the wall of the aorta, coronary, cerebral and femoral vessels by lipid (lipoprotein) has been present in much younger subjects (aged 35 to 45) who were known to be heavy cigarette-smokers. Such observations seem to support the mechanism postulated by Astrup and colleagues (1967).

Localized alteration of vascular permeability may be immunologically mediated in some circumstances. It has been shown experimentally by Minick and colleagues (1966) that the induction of serum sickness in cholesterol-fed rabbits increases the extent and severity of lipid-filled arterial injuries. It is possible that the human counterpart of this is seen in the increased severity of atherosclerosis seen in the vessels of transplanted organs undergoing rejection.

Experimentally, it has been shown that when colloidal iron is injected into lipid-fed animals in which early lipid-filled arterial lesions are forming, particles of the colloidal iron can be demonstrated microscopically in the lesions but not elsewhere in the intima suggesting a localized alteration of endothelial permeability (Veress et al, 1970). In electron microscopic studies Constantinides (1968) has shown that infused egg-yolk lipids fail to permeate the intact and normal intima of the rat aorta but enter points at which injury has occured. It has also been demonstrated by Constantinides and Robinson (1965a, b and c) that injury to endothelial cell membranes or the opening of endothelial cell junctions of the rat femoral artery follows injury caused by extreme acidosis or alkalosis, hypoxia, vasoactive amines, proteolytic (but not lipolytic) enzymes, surfactants, angiotensin and bradykinin.

Changes in the constituents of the arterial wall
Acidic mucopolysaccharides and calcium. It has been shown repeatedly both by histochemical methods and by the uptake of radioactive sulphate (for references, see Walton, 1968a) that there is a close relation between the distribution of lipid or fibrin on the one hand, and of AMPS and calcium on the other, in plaques. Sequential studies with radioactive sulphate (Buck, 1955; Curran

and Crane, 1962) have suggested a correlation between the turnover-rate, rather than the absolute amount, of AMPS, and the rate of lipid-deposition.

The calcium content of arteries increases with age and atherosclerosis, the rate of calcium accumulation being roughly parallel to the rate of atherosclerotic involvement of a given population (Anderson et al, 1955). Studies using electron probe analysis have suggested that even in the arteries of young subjects calcium may be bound to AMPS (Hale et al, 1967).

The AMPS derived from the arterial wall in vitro behave as polyanions to form precipitates (co-acervates) with fibrinogen and TLDL (Amenta and Waters, 1960; Gerö et al, 1960; Anderson, 1963) but not with other plasma proteins. At the pH and ionic strength of plasma, insoluble complex formation is favoured by the use of highly sulphated polysaccharides of large molecular size and by a critical concentration of calcium ions (Walton, 1952; Walton and Scott, 1964). Among the various sulphated mucopolysaccharides of the aortic wall, Bihari-Varga and Gerö (1966) have found heparitin sulphate to show the greatest avidity of interaction with TLDL and fibrinogen. As Walton and Williamson (1968) have pointed out, it would seem more than coincidence that their own and other immunofluorescent studies (for references, see Walton, 1969a) should show localization of TLDL and fibrinogen in plaques in close topographical relation to AMPS and calcium while other plasma proteins (including HDL) show no evidence of selective localization.

Low-density lipoprotein has also been recovered from aortic intimal extracts (Ott et al, 1968; Tracy et al, 1961; Smith and Slater, 1970) and it has been shown that the chemical composition of extracellular lipid in early lesions corresponds closely with that of plasma LDL (Smith, 1965, Smith et al, 1967).

The connective tissue AMPS are intimately concerned in the evolution of collagen and elastin, possibly allowing the orientation and steric arrangement of fibrils to allow cross-linking and aggregation (Gross, 1959; Wood, 1960). In newly-formed connective tissues, the AMPS are covalently bound to non-collagenous polypeptide. But it would seem that reactive groups of the AMPS must be available to trap calcium ions to account for the findings of Hale and colleagues (1967) already referred to, and for the perifibrous distribution of TLDL found in the early stages of formation of plaques. It has been shown by Hauss et al, (1969) that hypoxia, the injection of catecholamines and various other experimental manipulations causing localized alterations of vascular permeability (as discussed in the preceding section) also give rise to a 'mesenchymal reaction' associated with increased radiosulphate uptake, suggesting increased local production of AMPS.

If the stimuli which give rise to localized alteration of

permeability also promote local synthesis of those components of the intimal gel which are reactive with TLDL and fibrinogen, it is possible to see why these proteins become selectively entrapped. It is possible that the extent of binding by the AMPS also of calcium might determine the stability or reversibility of the co-acervates formed. From this viewpoint, calcium (and other divalent cations) might seem to play a subsidiary but important role in atherogenesis. However, epidemiological evidence suggests that there is an *inverse* relationship between water hardness and mortality from cardiovascular disease in many countries (Crawford et al, 1968), areas with a hard water supply appearing to have a *lower* death rate from all cardiovascular diseases, or from individual causes, than areas with a soft supply. Robertson (1969) has reported changes in mortality rates following changes in the hardness of water supplies in two towns in the north of England in keeping with this relation.

It should be noted that this is a statistical association with *mortality* only at the moment since no evidence is yet available concerning the effect of water hardness upon the number and nature of actual atherosclerotic lesions in subjects coming to autopsy from areas with hard and soft water supplies. In cardiovascular surveys conducted in two areas with hard water and three areas wih soft water in South Wales, Elwood et al, (1971) found no significant differences in blood pressure, serum cholesterol or certain other parameters between the populations with soft and hard water supplies.

In a comparison between areas where the hardness of the water had been respectively increased, decreased or left unchanged Crawford et al, (1971) found that the effect on mortality appeared to hold at all levels of water hardness but also observed that some towns with no change in water supply showed a larger decrease in mortality from cardiovascular disease over a 10-year period than towns in which water supplies had been softened, and also the converse.

From the pathological viewpoint, calcium may be bound not only to AMPS, but later to the fatty acids associated with TLDL to form soaps, and in grossly calcified lesions occurs as amorphous deposits or apatitic crystals. Diffuse calcification, occurring in association with diffuse lipid infiltration and fibrosis may lead to rigid but widely dilated vessels, particularly in the very elderly. This process may ensure continued, or even improved, flow through previously severely affected vessels.

In relation to coronary artery disease, water hardness appears to be related to *infarction* rather than the development of atherosclerosis (Crawford and Crawford, 1967). Since thrombosis is commoner with soft necrotic fatty plaques than with fibrous ones it would be interesting to know whether these two types of plaque differ

in calcium content and if so whether this correlates with calcium intake in water.

Arterial enzymes and cellular removal mechanisms. It can be envisaged that plasma permeating through the vessel wall is normally removed by lymphatics draining into the vasa vasorum of the adventitial coat. This mechanism is adequate for soluble plasma components, but needs reinforcement by cellular mechanisms when insoluble precipitates form in the intima. Much of the lipid in early fatty streaks is extracellular, in the interstitial spaces, or closely applied as a 'perifibrous' (Smith et al, 1967) distribution around collagen and elastic fibrils. But fat-filled or 'foam' cells rapidly appear. Many of these appear to originate from smooth muscle (Haust et al, 1962; Geer, 1965). But there is evidence that other fat-filled cells in lesions are related to macrophages, orginating from either blood monocytes or tissue histocytes (Schaffner et al, 1980; Schwartz et al, 1980). It was noted by Walton and Williamson (1968) in humans and by Walton et al, (1976) in lipid-fed rabbits that, even where lipid-filled cells are in close promixity with extracellular lipid reacting as TLDL, the cells themselves often do not show specific fluorescence for the lipoprotein. Such cells are known to contain hydrolytic enzymes and proteases (Adams, 1967) capable of digesting the protein part of the molecule (site of antigenicity) leaving a lipid residue which is immunologically unreactive.

Studies on various kinds of cells maintained in tissue culture have shown that cellular uptake and disposal of TLDL can proceed by two different pathways. Some cells (such as fibroblasts, smooth muscle cells and lymphocytes) bind, interiorise and degrade TLDL by a 'receptor mediated' mechanism which is critically dependent upon an initial step of interaction of TLDL, via its protein moiety, apolipoprotein B (apo B), with specific high-affinity surface receptors on their cell-membranes. Binding of TDTL to the receptors is considered to trigger a feed-back mechanism which, on the one hand, prevents overloading with TLDL (and hence with cholesterol and other lipids carried by the lipoproteins); and on the other hand, controls intrinsic cholesterol synthesis and esterification within the cell (Goldstein and Brown, 1974; 1977). In contrast, macrophages, liver Kupffer cells and other phagocytic cells show relatively little uptake of native LDL but exhibit great avidity for denatured or chemically altered TLDL (Mahley et al, 1979) or TLDL complexed with acidic polysaccharides (Brown et al, 1980).

Cellular uptake and catabolism of LDL by these pathways appears to serve as a removal mechanism which may be of great importance (1) in preventing the occurrence, or in effecting the regression, of lipid-filled arterial lesions; (2) in determining serum lipid and lipoprotein levels (see below).

On the other hand, foam cells have been found to show partiularly marked radiosulphate uptake (Buck, 1955; Curran and Crane , 1962) suggesting active AMPS synthesis. It can be envisaged that release of this newly synthesized AMPS into the environment might complex more TLDL and fibrinogen. The process would thus become self-perpetuating. The partial degradation of TLDL and release of cholesterol, which is known to be actively sclerogenic in connective tissue (Adams et al, 1963) would promote fibrosis — a process that is characteristically seen in raised plaques. All these processes are accompanied by a series of enzymatic changes in the vessel wall which can be demonstrated biochemically or by histochemical methods (Zemplenyi, 1962; Adams, 1967). In most instances enzymatic activity is low or absent in the normal aorta but increases in areas affected by atherosclerosis and is associated with cells infiltrating into the intima. In later lesions, enzymatic changes are also seen in the media.

Impairment of outflow from the arterial wall. The protein-rich extravascular fluids of connective tissues in general are removed by lymphatics which drain into veins. In the arterial wall this system is of particular importance since the intimal and inner medial layers of the normal artery are devoid of capillaries but lymphatic drainage occurs into the veins of the vasa vasorum in the outer coats. It has repeatedly been observed that external damage to arteries by heat, freezing, electrocoagulation or stripping of the adventitia, all of which almost certainly interfere with or abolish the normal outflow of plasma permeating through the wall by damaging lymphatics and vasa vasorum, cause localization of plaques in the intima overlying the traumatized site.

It has also been observed, in maturing or old human atherosclerotic plaques treated with fluorescein-labelled antifibrinogen, that material with the antigenic characteristics of fibrin or fibrinogen is present as aggregates in what appear to be proliferating lymphatic channels in the deeper portion of thickened intima, suggesting that some degree of distortion due to blockage of lymphatics may be a common feature of naturally-occurring old plaques (see Plates 10.5 and 10.6).

Atherosclerosis is not only superimposed upon other lesions in arteries which are *already* the seat of an inflammatory process, but actually appears to be more severe in these circumstances. For example, in an era when syphilitic arteritis was commonly seen, it was widely held that syphilitic aortitis rendered the aorta more susceptible to atherosclerosis (Turnbull, 1915; Ross and McKusick, 1953). Presumably the inflammation at a given site would render the vessel more permeable but the involvement of lymphatics, and endarteritis effecting the vasa vasorum (Nichols, 1940), would reduce drainage from that site. Similar observations have been made in other forms of granulomatous arteritis, for instance, Takayasu's disease (Ask-Upmark and Fajers, 1956; Danaraj et al, 1963; Shrire and Asherson, 1964).

THE PATHOGENESIS OF CONDITIONS ASSOCIATED WITH ATHEROSCLEROSIS

Corneal arcus formation

In the human

Corneal arcus formation is broadly correlated with atherosclerosis in man. Both corneal arcus formation and the incidence of atherosclerosis are, in turn, apparently related to TLDL levels. For example, in many populations, the incidence of corneal arcus (arcus senilis) and of atherosclerosis increase with age (Rodstein and Zeman, 1963; McAndrew and Ogston, 1965) in parallel with increase of TLDL levels (Shanoff and Little, 1964; Rifkind, 1965). On the other hand, children with familial hyperlipidaemias characterized by early and gross elevation of TLDL levels may show precocious atherosclerotic cardiovascular disease and unusually early arcus formation (arcus juvenilis) — see Khachadurian, 1964; Khachadurian and Demirjian, 1968.

When frozen sections of eyes affected by corneal arcus formation are examined, sudanophile lipid deposits are demonstrable not only in the cornea but also in the sclera, ciliary processes and, to a lesser extent, in the iris. In each of these situation the lipid is in close relation with blood vessels and is largely extracellular. Corresponding sections treated with fluorescein-labelled anti-TLDL show specific fluorescene in a distribution closely corresponding to that of the sudanophile lipid (Walton, 1971, 1972a, 1973d) suggesting that, as in the cases of arteries, the material is 'insudated' lipoprotein.

Many studies have confirmed the association of hyperlipoproteinaemia with atherosclerosis and arcus formation. But workers attempting to evaluate the significance of the arcus as a diagnostic sign or prognostic (i.e. 'risk') factor in the detection of atherosclerotic disease in a given vascular territory, as, for example, in coronary artery disease (e.g. Schettler, 1954; Beaumont et al, 1960; Pomerantz, 1962; Shanoff and Little, 1964; Rifkind, 1965; McAndrew and Ogston, 1965; Hickey et al, 1970) have, for the most part, concluded that it is of limited value.

For example, it was shown for a British population (Rifkind) and for a Canadian one (Shanoff and Little) that the corneal arcus is so frequently present in men over 55 as to be of no prognostic significance in survivors of myocardial infarction as compared with age-matched controls. The position was somewhat different in younger men in whom a significantly higher incidence of the arcus, associated with raised serum cholesterol and LDL levels, was found in subjects in the age-group 40 to 45 with histories of ischaemic heart disease than in the corresponding control subjects.

In certain populations the association between the presence of the arcus and the occurrence of atherosclerosis is even more tenuous. For instance, it has been reported that there is a high prevalence of arcus formation in American Negroes without evidence of accompanying arterial disease or raised serum lipids (Macaraeg et al, 1968). On the other hand, the arcus is rarely seen in Japanese subjects, even in the older age-groups in which cerebral atherosclerosis is common.

In a personal series based on comparison of the incidence of the arcus with the distribution and extent of atherosclerotic lesions found in a British population at autopsy, Walton (1973) concluded that, while a broad association between the overall incidence of atherosclerosis and arcus formation might exist in the British subjects examined, there was no evidence of a definite correlation with the lesions in any one particular artery. The only exception to this was confirmation of the close association between severe arcus formation and atherosclerosis of the retinal arteries which has previously been noted in the very elderly (Rodstein and Zeman, 1963).

Experimental

When hyperlipoproteinaemia is induced in rabbits on cholesterol- or lipid-supplemented diets, in addition to lipid-filled arterial lesions containing rabbit TLDL (Walton and Dunkerley, 1974), lipid deposition occurs in the eye. These eye lesions are broadly similar to those seen in the human but are modified by anatomical differences peculiar to the rabbit. In this species corneal deposits are less prominent than in man but lipid deposition is more marked in the ciliary processes and in the iris. It was suggested by Walton and Dunkerley (1974) that this greater involvement of the iris in the rabbit was associated with the extension of vascular ciliary processes along the length of the iris in this species. These authors also showed by the technique of immunofluorescence that, as in the human, the lipid was in the form of low-density lipoprotein.

Duke-Elder (1938) gave it as his opinion that 'the arcus is essentially a senile degeneration coming into the same category as atherosclerosis and presumably depending on partial and progressive obliteration of the capillary system at the limbus'. In the light of the observations discussed above one might agree that the process may be simple and in the same category as atherosclerosis. But clearly neither process is necessarily senile, nor degenerative (in the sense of being a breakdown of intrinsic components of the tissues). Moreover, far from

being dependent upon obliteration of the capillary system of the limbus, lipid (lipoprotein) infiltration of the cornea and of the other structures bounding the anterior chamber of the eye always occurs in close relation with sites of vascularity showing evidence of *increased* permeability.

Xanthomatosis

In humans

Cutaneous xanthomata are still described in some pathology textbooks as simple tumours. But they are most commonly encountered in man in association with primary (familial) hyperlipidaemias and with secondary hyperlipidaemias (Thannhauser, 1950; McGinley et al, 1952; Polano et al, 1970). Both primary and secondary hyperlipidaemias have in common a marked increase in the total body pool of TLDL with consequent increase of both intra- and extravascular distribution of this lipoprotein (Walton, 1969b). The lesions are characteristically distributed at sites subject to pressure, friction or minor traumata. Tuberous xanthomata are found on the shoulders (Fig. 10.3), buttocks (Fig. 10.4) and backs of the ankles (sites subject to pressure or friction). Planar xanthomata are observed in the creases of the palm (Fig. 10.5) or of the palmer surfaces of the metatarsophalangeal and interphalangeal joints (sites subject to pressure and constant folding of the skin). Tendinous xanthomata occur at points of constriction, pressure and friction in the tendons in the neighbourhood of small joints. This characteristic distribution has led to the suggestion that such lesions arise by leakage of LDL-

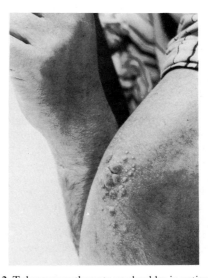

Fig. 10.3 Tuberous xanthomata on shoulder in patient with Type II hyperlipidaemia

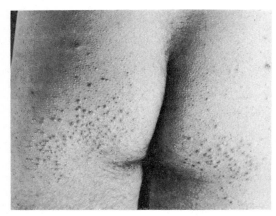

Fig. 10.4 Tubo-eruptive xanthomata on buttocks of patient with Type V hyperlipidaemia

Fig. 10.5 Planar xanthomata on palms of hands of patient with Type III hyperlipidaemia. Note distribution in skin crease at base of thenar eminence of hand on right.

rich plasma into the skin or neighbouring connective tissue because of localized increase of vascular permeability occasioned by the release of histamine and other intrinsic vasoactive agents from repeated slight trauma at the affected sites, with uptake of the lipid by tissue histocytes. This suggestion was prompted by the personal observation (Walton et al, 1972b) of the development of small xanthomata in the antecubital fossa around the sites of repeated needle-punctures in a child of 16 with a severe nephrotic syndrome and a gross secondary hyperlipidaemia.

A mechanism of this kind was strongly supported by the observations of Scott and Winterbourn (1967). These authors injected autologous radioiodinated TLDL into hyperlipidaemic subjects in whom xanthomata were appearing actively and symmetrically on both elbows. With the patient's consent and co-operation, one arm was immobilized in plaster and the patient was encouraged to move the other arm freely and to rub the xanthoma from time to time. After a suitable interval, a xanthoma from each elbow and a portion of normal skin was biopsied and the radioactivity counted. It was found that the xanthomata from both albows showed higher counts than the normal skin but that activity was consistently higher in the xanthoma from the 'active' arm (on which the xanthoma has been periodically rubbed) than in the lesion on the immobilized arm.

In lipid-fed animals

Cutaneous xanthomata may also be encountered as spontaneous lesions in the cholesterol-fed rabbit as Anitschkow (1913) first observed in his original experiments. They differ in distribution from human lesions in being most commonly encountered over the nape of the neck and the footpads. A chance observation suggested a possible reason for the localization at the first of these sites (Walton et al, 1972b). It was noticed that nodules developed in the skin of the neck in a cholesterol-fed rabbit at the point where the skin was customarily grasped in lifting the animal out of its cage. The histological structures of one of these nodules and that of a nodule from the footpad of another cholesterol-fed rabbit were similar and both resembled the appearance of human xanthomata. It was then observed that xanthomata occurred on the footpads of cholesterol-fed rabbits maintained in cages in which the floor was constructed of wire mesh but not in animals similarly fed but maintained in cages with a solid floor well padded with straw. It thus seemed possible that, once again, altered vascular permeability from trauma (in the one instance, repeated pinching of the skin and in the other, minor damage to the paws from the wire mesh of the floor) might be a localizing factor.

To put this possibility to the test, the skin of the flank was shaved in groups of normal and cholesterol-fed animals and intradermal injections of histamine were made into marked areas at two-day intervals. After 6 to 8 weeks nodules appeared at the injection-sites in the cholesterol-fed (but not in the normal) animals and these showed the characteristic histological appearance of xanthomata. By immunofluorescence, it was shown that the lipid in these areas was in the form of rabbit TLDL (Walton et al, 1972b).

This experimental induction of xanthomata at an elective site further supports the contention that altered vascular permeability is the factor determining the distribution of spontaneously-occurring lesions and that these are really granulomata of a specialized kind rather than tumours. It also has obvious implications in relation to the topography of distribution of lesions in the vascular tree because of localized alteration of permeability.

The topography of arterial and associated lesions in relation to lipoprotein disorders

The characterization of plasma lipids

Lipid is encountered in the blood in particulate form and as soluble lipoproteins. In all cases the lipid is associated with protein. The varying proportions of lipid to protein allows separation of the varying forms in terms of density, and therefore of flotation characteristics, by centrifugation or ultracentrifugation (see Fig. 10.6). In the analytical ultracentrifuge, when separation is performed in media of defined density under standardized conditions, these characteristics are expressed as sedimentation-flotation (S_f) values. Some differentiation of the protein-bound lipids in plasma on the basis of their charge and molecular size is also possible by electrophoresis on paper, cellulose acetate, in starch-gel, agar, agarose or in polyacrylamide.

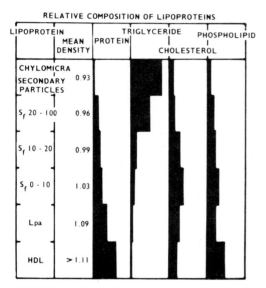

RELATIVE COMPOSITION OF LIPOPROTEINS

Fig. 10.6 Relative chemical composition of serum lipoproteins

Particulate forms of plasma lipids. The term chylomicron was originally introduced to designate the visible lipid particle transporting triglyceride from the gut *via* the chyle to the blood. The term has been widened in usage to include all visible particulate lipid in blood. However, it is now known that endogenous lipid is also transported in particulate form. These 'secondary particles' of endogenous origin can be separated from true chylomicrons and from soluble lipoproteins by the flotation characteristics and the varying tendency to aggregate in polyvinyl pyrrolidone gradients of these two classes of particle (Bierman et al, 1965). Both kinds of particle are large enough (mean molecular diameters of

about 5000 Å (500 nm)] to be visible by dark-ground illumination of plasma and both contain relatively small proportions of protein (about 1 to 2 per cent by weight). The correspondingly high lipid content results in a density of about 0.93 and very fast sedimentation-flotation characteristics (about S_f 400 + for secondary particles and S_f 1000 to 10 000 for chylomicrons, according to Cornwell, 1967). These particles adhere to the point of application on paper or cellulose acetate and fail to permeate the gels of solid media. This latter property makes their immunological analysis difficult.

In addition to the above forms, additional fine lipid-rich particles of low density (1.020 to 1.025 g per ml) occur in plasma. These particles originate from the osmiophilic granules of platelets (from which they are extruded even in the absence of coagulation) and are rich in phospholipids with active coagulant properties in blood coagulation systems (platelet factor 3). For this reason the particles have been called 'platelet dust' (Wolf, 1967).

Soluble lipoproteins. The ultracentrifugation of serum at a density of 1.063 g/ml separates a group of lipoproteins (TLDL) which float at this density. Subclasses within this group can be further differentiated according to density and flotation (S_f) characteristics as: very low density lipoproteins (VLDL) with S_f values of 20–400; intermediate lipoproteins (IDL) with S_f values of 10–20; and low density lipoproteins (LDL) with S_f values of 1–10. The lipoproteins of this group have electrophoretic mobilities of beta or pre-beta globulins.

If the residual fraction of serum from which TLDL have been removed, is re-submitted to ultracentrifugation at a density of 1.20 g/ml another group of lipoproteins (total high-density lipoproteins or THDL) can be separated by flotation. These can also be further separated into two major sub-fractions (HDL_2 and HDL_3). These lipoproteins have the electrophoretic mobility of alpha-globulins.

In some individuals, significant amounts of a lipoprotein related to the TLDL, but immunologically distinct (Berg, 1963; Walton et al, 1974) and intermediate in density between TLDL and THDL, are present. This is known as the Lp(a) lipoprotein.

Immunologically, the antigenic characteristics of the serum lipoproteins reside mainly, if not exclusively, in their protein moieties (apolipoproteins). Three major (A, B and C) and several minor apolipoproteins have been defined (Alaupovic, 1971; Osborne and Brewer, 1977) immunologically and by their separation from delipidated lipoproteins by physico-chemical techniques. The distribution of these components in ultracentrifugally separated lipoproteins is shown schematically in Fig. 10.7.

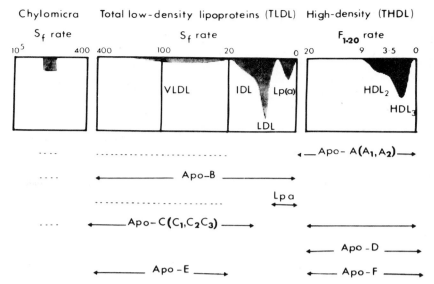

Fig. 10.7 Diagrammatic representation of distribution of some of the apolipoproteins in ultracentrifugally separated serum lipoproteins

Types of hyperlipidaemia in relation to clinical syndromes associated with atherosclerosis

In disease, increase of the serum lipids (cholesterol, triglycerides and phospholipids) is almost invariably given expression as increase of TLDL (with or without increase of chylomicra) but *not* of HDL. The *patterns* of alterations of the particulate lipids and of S_f subclasses of TLDL differ between different varieties of primary and secondary hyperlipidaemias. A provisional classification of these diseases in terms of the presenting pattern of derangement and of the associated clinical characteristics has been proposed by the World Health Organization (Beaumont et al, 1970) based on that of Fredrickson et al, (1967). It was observed by the latter authors that patients with primary hyperlipidaemias of Types II, III and IV (with preponderant increases of LDL, IDL and VLDL respectively — see Table 10.1) showed a high incidence of cardiovascular disease while patients with Type I (in which the main abnormality is increase of chylomicrons) showed little or no increased incidence of cardiovascular disease. This suggests that these very large particles are less, if at all, involved in atherogenesis. This is also borne out by earlier family studies of what would now be classified as the Type I abnormality (Ahrens et al, 1961; Kinsell et al, 1967).

The comparative risks of development of ischaemic heart disease (IHD) and of peripheral vascular disease (PVD) in different types of familial hyperlipoproteinaemic states was assessed by Slack (1969). Men with the Type II abnormality (preponderant increase of LDL), and their males relatives showed an earlier onset

Table 10.1 Risk of cardiovascular disease (CVD) in hyperlipidaemias

Type[*]	Pattern of derangement of lipoproteins	Risk of CVD[†]
I	Persistent chylomicronaemia, TLDL and THDL low	normal
IIA	Elevation of LDL only	very high
IIB	Elevation of LDL and VLDL	high
III	Increased IDL and VLDL	high
IV	Marked increase of VLDL ± increase of LDL	increased
V	Chylomicronaemia with increase of VLDL	increased

[*] Based on WHO Classification (Beaumont et al, 1970)
[†] From data of Fredrickson et al (1967) and Slack (1969)

(mean ages 42.7 and 43.8 years respectively) of IHD than men with Types III to V (preponderant increase of lipoproteins of larger molecular size). But in the latter groups the risk of PVD was increased.

It was also of interest in this study that the difference in rate of progression of atherosclerosis between males and females which obtains in random populations persisted even in this hyperlipidaemic population since women with the Type II disorder showed a later onset of ischaemic heart disease than men with the identical pattern.

It was reported by Fredrickson et al, (1967) that PVD was at least as frequent, if not more so, as IHD in patients with Type III hyperlipidaemia (see also Borrie, 1969). In a series of 116 patients presenting with peripheral arterial disease confirmed by arteriography, it was reported by Greenhalgh et al, (1971) that 44 per cent showed serum lipid abnormalities, predominantly of a pattern characterized by elevation of serum triglycerides and pre-beta lipoproteins (VLDL). The series included only two patients with the Type III abnormality. Thirty per cent of the patients also showed evidence of coexistent IHD. As an alternative to the possibility that increase of the larger lipoprotein molecules predisposes to PVD in some partially selective fashion, Greenhalgh et al, suggest that differences in the time-course and severity of atherosclerosis with the pattern of lipoprotein derangement might permit the development of the less life-threatening peripheral manifestations in those with predominant increase of the larger molecular species to give rise to this apparent association.

In a case of the Type III abnormality coming to autopsy, it was reported by Roberts et al, (1970) that, in addition to coronary artery disease and myocardial infarction, subendocardial lipid deposits were present, leading Fredrickson (1971) to speculate as to whether the vascular disease in Type III patients differed from the usual kind of atherosclerosis. In a fatal case of Type III hyperlipidaemia personally examined at autopsy (Walton, 1972c) coronary, aortic, cerebral and ileofemoral atherosclerosis were all present and severe. The lesions did not differ in any significant way from the ordinary run of atherosclerotic plaques and were shown by immunofluorescence to contain lipoproteins reacting with antiserum to apolipoprotein C as well as to antiserum to apolipoprotein B (suggesting that lipoproteins larger than LDL subclass were involved). No subendocardial deposits were seen in this case.

Xanthomatosis may occur with both primary and secondary hyperlipidaemias. The sites at which xanthomata are found, though suggested by McGinley et al, (1952) to be correlated with the pattern of alteration of S_f classes, in the experience of others (Lever et al, 1954) may be very variable in that tuberous, planar and tendinous xanthomata may be seen in any combination in Types II, III and IV primary or secondary hyperlipidaemia (see also Fredrickson et al, 1967; Poland, 1969). Indeed if the suggestion put forward for their localization (see p. 186) is correct, it would be expected that the sites in a given patient particularly subject to pressure, friction, etc. rather than the pattern of alteration of serum lipoproteins, would be the determining factor in the distribution of these kinds of xanthomata. It has been said that lipid striae or xanthochromia of the palms of the hands are seen only in Types III and IV (Polano, 1969) while eruptive xanthomatosis is commonest in Types I, IV and V.

Atherogenic potential of lipoproteins of different molecular sizes

The lipoproteins of densities less than 1.10 considerably exceed the non-lipid carrying proteins in molecular size. Electron microscopy and other measurements suggest they are globular in shape with mean molecular diameters ranging between 220 and 540 Å (22 and 54 nm). Chylomicrons, of course, are even larger, with molecular diameters up to 5000 Å or more. As noted above, persistent chylomicronaemia is not associated with the accelerated development of atherosclerosis whereas increase of VLDL, IDL and LDL is strongly so associated. A *priori* it seems likely that molecules at the bottom end of the range of molecular size (LDL) might permeate through the endothelial barrier more easily than the larger molecules (cf. Gofman and Young, 1963). This is borne out by Slack's observations referred to in the preceding section. Using fluorescein-labelled antiserum to the Lpa lipoprotein it has been shown that this lipoprotein can also be demonstrated in the atherosclerotic lesions of Lpa$^+$ subjects (Walton et al, 1974). The significance of this observation is that: (1) the Lpa lipoprotein is somewhat larger in molecular weight and molecular diameter than LDL; (2) the Lpa lipoprotein, like LDL, interacts selectively with polysaccharide sulphates (Walton et al, 1974 so the suggested mechanism (see p. 182), whereby lipoproteins are entrapped by the AMPS of the arterial wall, can also be invoked to explain the presence of this lipoprotein in lesions.

Using fluorescein-labelled anti-apolipoprotein C, strongly-reactive material with the antigenic characteristics of this apoprotein was found in the arterial lesions of a patient with Type III hyperlipidaemia coming to autopsy (Walton, 1972c) and was also present in the arterial lesions of normolipidaemic individuals. However, since apolipoprotein C is associated with both IDL and VLDL, this did not define whether only IDL, or whether VLDL lipoproteins in addition were involved in atherogenesis but did suggest that molecules larger than even the Lpa lipoprotein and LDL could be concerned in the process.

More recently, examination of atherosclerotic plaques by immuno-electron microscopy has allowed direct visualization of apolipoprotein B-containing lipoproteins in the arterial wall (Hoff and Gaubatz, 1975; 1977; Walton and Morris 1977; Morris et al, 1978). These studies reveal that particles of the size of normal LDL predominate in lesions although some spherical particles corresponding in size to IDL and even to VLDL are seen.

On the basis of statistical analysis of the S_f distributions in the sera of patients with ischaemic heart disease, Gofman et al, (1954) concluded that the concentration of S_f 12 to 20 molecules correlated most closely with the disease incidence. Attempts, on this basis, to construct an 'atherogenic index' and to use it on a predictive basis on random healthy population samples in prospective studies (as for example in the Framingham Study) gave limited success (see Dawber et al, 1962).

Despite the direct evidence from immunohistology that the particles in lesions of normolipidaemic individuals are mainly of the size of LDL, as previously stressed (see p. 188 and see Table 10.1 hyperlipidaemias of Types IIB, III, IV and V which are characterized by an increase of IDL and/or VLDL nevertheless show an (apparently paradoxical) increased incidence of atherosclerosis. An ultrastructural and chemical study of the circulating lipoproteins in such hyperlipidaemic individuals has revealed an abnormal composition of the 'core' components of the lipoproteins and an abnormal heterogeneity of size with a disproportionately high proportion of unusually small molecules in the density fractions predominating in these hyperlipidaemias Morris et al, 1983). It seems possible that such changes may account for the increased incidence of atherosclerosis in such individuals.

In some circumstances it seems likely that secondary particles and/or chylomicrons can cross the endothelial barrier. It is possible for example that the eruptive xanthomatous rashes which occur in association with 'abdominal crises' in patients with the Types I and V abnormalities are due to the escape into the skin of these particles through dilated dermal vessels. Widespread lesions of this kind are usually evanescent, as contrasted with tuberous and tendinous xanthomata which only resolve with consistent reduction of serum LDL levels.

Thrombosis and ischaemia

It is well recognized that ischaemia and infarction in an organ can arise either from progressive occlusion (stenosis) or from thrombosis of the blood vessels. There is marked disagreement about the frequency with which these alternative processes cause reduction of the blood supply in different vascular territories. For example, the proportion of cases of recent myocardial infarction showing actual coronary *thrombosis* at autopsy has been variously reported to be between 37 and 91 per cent, while in cases of cerebral infarction the proportion due to thrombosis has been reported to be 45 to 50 per cent (Jørgensen, 1970).

Many authors recognize two broadly different types of atherosclerotic plaque, the fibro-fatty and the true 'atheroma' (in which fatty softening and necrosis is predominant). Thrombosis is associated mainly, though not exclusively, with the necrotic type of plaque even when this is covered by a surface cap of fibrous tissue. Constantinides (1966) has shown convincingly, by

careful serial section of coronary arteries containing thrombi, that microscopic cracks and fissures in the plaque which communicate with the lumen, are almost invariably demonstrable. It has been suggested that disruption of the plaque may occur from haemorrhage due to the rupture of small blood vessels in the plaque. However, it has been pointed out by Haust (1970) that the intima of normal arteries is not vascularized and that the inner part of the media also lacks capillaries. Blood pressure in the arterial lumen is always high and capillaries from the vasa vasorum (supplied with blood under lower pressure) would tend to collapse if present in the inner layer of arteries. Nevertheless, an appearance resembling the formation of a limited 'dissecting aneurysm, is sometimes seen near the site of presumptive origin of a thrombus. It seems more likely in these instances that following rupture of the plaque, blood has gained ingress to the plaque from the lumen.

In the necrotic atheromatous plaque there is evidence of degradation of TLDL with the release of cholesterol and phospholipid from the original complex molecule. It is possible that there is also a lipid contribution from local synthesis (see p. 183). The availability of highly purified lipoproteins has allowed the unequivocal demonstration that these are, in their native state, quite inactive in relation to blood coagulation. It seems unlikely, therefore, that the presence of intact TLDL in the arterial intima in the early lesion is directly implicated in thrombosis. But in the later lesions, when TLDL is degraded releasing phospholipids (since these have active coagulant properties — see below) rupture of a plaque bringing this material in contact with blood can be envisaged as a process likely to be attended by local thrombosis.

In this context, altered coagulability of the blood has also been suggested as a precipitating factor in intravascular thrombosis. The report by Fullerton et al (1953) that alimentary lipaemia in man produced hypercoagulability of the blood appeared to be supported by the finding of Poole (1955) that chylomicrons showed coagulative properties like those of lipid extracts of platelets (Platelet Factor 3 activity). However, Wolf (1967) found that chylomicrons, as ordinarily prepared in vitro by low-speed centrifugation, contained 'platelet dust' and that, when this was removed, coagulant activity, as measured by thrombin generation, was reduced or abolished. On the other hand, phospholipids of the kinds that may be liberated by degradation of TLDL, and especially phosphatidylethanolamine containing unsaturated fatty acids (Maclagan and Billimoria, 1964; Billimoria et al, 1965), appear to play an important part in the early stages of blood coagulation. It is suggested that phospholipid micelles offer a large surface adsorbing Factor X and allowing its interaction with Factor V and calcium ions to form a complex which effects the conversion of prothrombin to thrombin (Jobin and Esnouf, 1967).

Thrombosis is also held to occur on plaques which show no gross evidence of necrosis or rupture (Fischer, 1964). It has been demonstrated elegantly that even discontinuities of endothelium undiscernible by light microscopy can serve as foci for the adherence of platelets (French et al, 1964). Collagen fibrils have been shown to bring about platelet aggregation and it has been suggested that endothelial discontinuity revealing the underlying collagen in fibrous plaques, might serve as the focus first for platelet adherence and aggregation and subsequently for thrombus development (Walton, 1972b).

In this connection, it has been observed experimentally by Constantinides and Robinson (1969b) that angiotensin and serotonin, both of which are known to induce platelet aggregation, also cause the contraction of arterial endothelial cells, exposing the subendothelial collagen.

In the aorta and other large arteries, necrotic plaques may progress to ulceration. The discharge of grumous material from such lesions, or the detachment of portions of thrombi formed on their surface, may result in the embolization of vessels in distant organs producing a wide variety of clinical syndromes (Retan and Miller, 1966).

Emboli arising from intracardiac mural thrombosis due to massive coronary occlusion have been reported to be a frequent cause of subsequent occlusion of the internal carotid artery and consequent cerebral infarction (Blackwood et al, 1969; Castaigne et al, 1970). Microemboli lodging in the kidney have been suggested as a possible cause of renal hypertension (Moore and Mersereau, 1968).

A discussion and analysis of the respective contributions of haemorrhage, thrombosis and embolism in acute cerebrovascular disease was presented by Yates and Hutchinson (1961). It has already been pointed out that non-fatal thromboses upon a plaque might give rise to accretion and enlargement of the plaque as proposed by Duguid (1946) and thus contribute to the rapid development of ischaemia of the territory being served.

EVIDENCE RELATING TO THE REVERSIBILITY OR PREVENTION OF ATHEROSCLEROSIS AND ASSOCIATED LESIONS

Experimental

It has been clearly established in cholesterol- or lipid-fed animals that, with restoration to a normal diet, a considerable degree of resolution of the arterial lesion occurs. In animals kept on high lipid supplements for only a short period, or given relatively low lipid supplements for a longer period, on restoration to a normal diet, the serum hyperlipoproteinaemia shows rapid reversion to normal levels. Such animals killed sequentially show progressive resolution of the lipid-filled lesions in arteries. On the other hand, animals maintained for long periods on high lipid supplements, or given frequent intermittent lipid-feeding, show lesions in which various degrees of fibrosis have occurred. These observations suggest that the severity of the disease and the nature of the lesions are functions of both the height and duration of hyperlipoproteinaemia (i.e. the exposure index, Constantinides, 1965).

In animals on low-lipid supplements, although xanthomata can be induced at elective sites by repeated injections of histamine, these lesions regress rapidly when the injections are discontinued (Walton et al, 1972b). Similarly, although lipid accumulation in the iris and other structures in the eye may be massive in cholesterol-fed animals, it was found by Walton and Dunkerley (1974) that animals restored to a normal diet and killed one and a half to two years later showed almost complete resolution of the lipid deposits in both the aorta and in the eye.

In man

From knowledge of the circumstances in which complexes between charged polysaccharides and fibrinogen or TLDL can be dissociated in vitro (Walton, 1952; Walton and Scott, 1964), and from the behaviour of the early lesions in experimental animals, it seems likely that the early stages human arterial lesions (fatty streaks) are also reversible. But if TLDL accumulation proceeds and the entrapped molecules break down it seems likely that the degradation products: (1) serve as a stimulus to cellular reaction and fibrogenesis; and (2), are a potential source of thromboplastic material which may initiate thrombosis if the plaque as a whole becomes necrotic. Fibrosis, occurring either *sui generis* as in (1), or following the organization of non-fatal superimposed thrombi on the plaque as in (2), can be looked upon as scar tissue which will resemble that formed elsewhere in the body in undergoing condensation and contraction with time but seldom, if ever, being susceptible to complete redissolution.

From the pathological standpoint, therefore, there is clearly a limit to what can be expected in the way of reversal of the later lesions of atherosclerosis. As in so many other fields in medicine, prevention would seem easier to aim for than cure, and here most attention has been paid to the question of dietary control.

Earlier reference has been made to the broad correlation between social development and affluence, on the one hand, and the rate of progression of atherosclerosis on the other (p. 174). But even in the midst of affluent societies, communities can be found subsisting habitually on frugal diets because of religious or other convictions, such as certain orders of monks (McCullagh and Lewis, 1960; Groen et al, 1962) or strict vegetarians (Kirkeby, 1966). Such communities are distinguished by low serum lipids and lipoproteins and show a low incidence of the clinical signs of atherosclersis. Even a temporary lowering of dietary standards among the population at large, such as that due to food rationing enforced by war, has been noted to exert a perceptible influence in Europe in both World War I (Zinserling, 1925; Aschoff, 1930) and World War II (Malmros, 1950; Strøm and Jensen, 1951; Yates, 1964). This suggests that with dietary limitation and consequent reduction of serum lipids either the rate of progression of lesions had decreased or possibly that some regression of lesions had occurred (see also Katz and Pick, 1963). An extreme example, but one that suggests that even the latter is possible, derives from observations on individuals who were in concentration camps (Helweg-Larsen et al, 1952). When initially interned, many of these individuals had been in relatively affluent circumstances and the nature and extent of the atherosclerotic lesion in their vessels could be taken to approximate to the average for age and sex. But after some years of extreme privation, the incidence of lipid-filled lesions was observed to be very low in those coming to autopsy, as compared with normally fed age- and sex-matched controls.

Dietary control over appreciable numbers of subjects, under peace-time conditions, is otherwise only obtained in institutions and at least two major studies of this kind have been reported. One study was conducted in Los Angeles in a Veterans Administration Hospital (Dayton et al, 1969) and the other was carried out in two mental hospitals in Helsinki (Miettinen et al, 1972). As an alternative or supplement to dietary restrictions (to which all but the most obsessive and conscientious individuals, with free access of choice to food, find it almost impossible to adhere for a lifetime) therapeutic control with serum lipid-lowering drugs has also been explored.

The largest-scale trial of this last variety was one sponsored by the World Health Organization to assess the use of clofibrate as a primary preventive of ischaemic heart disease. The study was designed to examine the effect of control of serum cholesterol levels (serum lipoproteins were not measured) alone, no advice being given to participants about modifying their way of living so as to affect other risk factors such as excessive cigarette smoking, physical inactivity etc (see Report from the Committee of Principal Investigators, 1978).

This and previous dietary trials aiming at primary prevention have been well reviewed by Oliver (1981) who noted the following similarities and differences:
— All the trials achieved a mean reduction in plasma total cholesterol of about 9–15 per cent and no more than a 10 per cent reduction outside an institution;
— A significant reduction in non-fatal myocardial infarction was obtained in two (the Helsinki Mental Hospitals and the WHO Clofibrate trials) and a similar but non-significant trend in the Los Angeles VA trial;
— No significant reduction in the incidence of fatal myocardial infarction was observed in any of the trials;
— A significant increase in mortality from non-cardiovascular causes was noted in the Los Angeles and the WHO trials and a non-significant trend in the same direction observed in the Finnish trial;
— An increase in gall stone disease was reported in the Los Angeles and WHO trials but not in the Helsinki one.

Clofibrate has also been used in secondary prevention trials, i.e. to see whether the compound reduces the incidence of myocardial infarction and sudden death in patients with already existent ischaemic heart disease (see Newcastle-upon-Tyne Physicians Group 1971; and Dewar and Oliver, 1971). These trials agreed in showing a significant reduction in mortality and especially in sudden deaths, and also in the occurrence of total cardiovascular incidents in patients with angina treated with clofibrate. In the Newcastle trial, though not in the Scottish one, there was also a favourable trend for patients with a history of myocardial infarction. This was thought possibly to reflect a difference in the selection of patients between the two trials. In both trials there was a reduction in the incidence of non-fatal infarcts. The effect of clofibrate in reducing serum lipids was maintained up to 5 years but in neither trial was it considered possible to prove that the effect on serum lipids was causally related to the improved prognosis which was obtained.

As opposed to these efforts to evaluate the effect of control of relatively modest hyperlipidaemia, there is increasing concern with the much greater risk which is associated with the gross increase of serum lipoproteins associated with primary hyperlipidaemias (Fredrickson, 1971). In these patients even more radical surgical measures, such as ileal bypass procedures have been evaluated (Buchwald et al, 1970). It has long been known that the externally visible tissue deposits of TLDL (xanthomata) in these patients resolve with control of serum lipid levels, however this is brought about (Lever et al, 1954; Walton et al, 1963; Khachadurian and Demirjian, 1968; Polano, 1969; Craig and Walton, 1972), and with some of the drugs in current use it now seems clear this is not a redistribution of the lipoprotein, i.e. removal from the tissues but increased deposition in vessels, rather it is associated with a nett reduction of the total body pool of TLDL. In a small group of patients with Type III hyperlipidaemia, which is very responsive to clofibrate therapy, it was reported by Zelis et al (1970) that objective evidence of regression of peripheral vascular disease was obtained after about one year's control of serum lipids.

Small numbers of patients with familial hypercholesterolaemia (with severe atherosclerosis and xanthomatosis) resistant to diet or drug therapy have shown a substantial reduction in hyperlipidaemia following partial ileal bypass (Buchwald and Varco, 1967), portocaval shunt (Starzl et al, 1973, 1974) or repeated plasma exchange (Thompson et al, 1975). The fall in serum LDL levels has been reported to be followed, in some of these cases, by arteriographic and functional evidence of improvement (for reviews, see Starzl et al, 1980; Buchwald et al, 1980; Stein and Glueck, 1980; Thompson et al, 1980).

The results in well-documented cases of this kind suggest that lipoprotein deposits arising from even extreme degrees of hyperlipidaemia can undergo some resolution with effective control of the blood lipids. But it would be simplistic to extrapolate from such cases to the population at large (many of whom develop their lesions despite being normolipidaemic or only minimally hyperlipidaemic) or to propose that the reduction of hyperlipidaemia is all that needs to be done in all cases to prevent or to reverse atherosclerosis. In contrast, the foregoing review of the many facets of the clinical and pathological problems associated with this form of arterial disease make it clear that this is a multifactorial problem demanding a multifactorial approach to its solution (also see below).

It must also be borne in mind that, while TLDL can be accepted as positively atherogenic, there is at least circumstantial evidence that HDL may be 'protective' in reducing the risk of CVD (Miller and Miller, 1975) and of PVD (Bradby et al, 1978). The mechanism by which such an effect might be brought about is, as yet, uncertain. Suggestions include: (1) A 'reverse cholesterol transport' role for HDL which is thought to carry cholesterol (derived from deposited LDL) from peripheral tissues back to the liver by a process involving the transformation of free cholesterol in HDL to cholesterol ester through the action of the enzyme lecithin-cholesterol acyl transferase (Glomset, 1968); (2) Alternatively HDL might exert a protective effect by reducing the cellular uptake of LDL cholesterol by interfering with LDL binding and uptake by arterial wall cells (Carew et al, 1976); or (3) HDL might act as a 'scavenger' molecule accepting lipids derived from chylomicrons and VLDL during their intravascular lipolysis (Levy and Rifkind, 1980).

Despite the absence of firm and unequivocal evidence that HDL actually fulfils any of these postulated roles there is current interest in seeking diets, drugs or other regimens which bring about an elevation of HLD levels and in seeking to evaluate the possibly beneficial effect of such a change. The results of such evaluations will be awaited with interest.

SUMMARY AND CONCLUSIONS

The foregoing review of the many facets of the clinical and pathological problems associated with atherosclerosis makes it clear that this is a condition which is multifactorial in origin. It is also evident that plaque formation, far from being a simple degenerative process brought about by an intrinsic senescence of the tissues concerned, is in fact a dynamic response by the connective tissues of the arterial wall to self-components rendered reactive by their selective combination with constituents of the intimal gel. It follows from this that the process is not necessarily an inevitable accompaniment of aging but one that may occur at any age from childhood onwards, the rate of its progression being determined by a number of identifiable factors, some of which are clearly environmental and therefore, theoretically at least, conducive to control.

In this sense, and in terms of the mechanisms concerned in its aetiology and pathogenesis, atherosclerosis cannot be considered as a single disease of universal prevalence. Instead, it must be looked upon as a form of connective tissue response which is not basically different in kind from the known responses of other connective tissues brought in contact with material of altered physicochemical characteristics.

It is suggested that atherosclerosis may have its *fons et origo* in segregated areas of altered vascular permeability. These may occasionally be recognized as mucoid elevations of the intima *before* lipid accumulation has occurred. Attention has been drawn to the experimental evidence that in areas affected by altered permeability there is a 'non-specific mesenchymal reaction' of the connective tissues attended by an increased synthesis and turnover of AMPS; and that these changes may be pharmacologically mediated by the release of intrinsic vasoactive substances. It can be envisaged that such release is usually local (to account for the nodular distribution of lesions which is characteristic). The way in which some such local stimuli might eventuate can be identified (trauma, preceding arteritis due to known causes such as syphilis) but in other instances only speculation is possible (? haemo-dynamic stresses, ? other mechanical factors, ? immune mechanisms). In some circumstances, altered vascular permeability may be mediated by a generalized stimulus but be nevertheless discontinuous in distribution, as, for example, by hypoxia of which a particular human instance may be the generalized acceleration of atherosclerosis recognized to be associated with the 'risk factor' of heavy cigarette smoking. Other factors eliciting altered permeability and the non-specific mesenchymal reaction have been listed by Hauss et al (1969).

Of course, implicit in the understanding of how the many identified 'risk factors' operate and interact in the pathogenesis of atherosclerosis, is a revision of one's fundamental concept of how an artery operates. It is necessary that one should no longer look upon arteries as rigid impermeable tubes (like the copper pipes of a central heating system) and no longer consider their thickening as being due to an accretion (like sludge formation) on a passive surface. Instead, it is essential to recognize arteries as being composed of a living gel, capable in itself of reaction, and to accept modern evidence that in these vessels, through which blood is coursing at relatively high pressure, there is normally some movement of plasma through the wall and its removal in the outer coats by lymphatics. In short, it is necessary to accept that most of the artery wall from the subendothelial tissues outwards is functionally *extravascular connective tissue* differing from other connective tissues only in being perfused at higher pressures so as to allow critical concentrations to be more readily attained between those macromolecules present in the plasma and in the connective tissue which are capable of interaction.

Current evidence indicates that the macromolecules concerned in atherogenesis are plasma total low-density lipoproteins and plasma fibrinogen on the one hand, which interact to give rise to the characteristic composition of the early atherosclerotic plaque. Once localized areas of vessels undergo changes associated with alteration of permeability and local accumulation of AMPS, in terms of the mechanism postulated, it can be appreciated that there would be a local increase in the volume of plasma transuding through the affected segment to make the macromolecular TLDL (which is normally largely confined to the vascular compartment) available for entrapment at this point, even when the overall serum concentration of TLDL is not elevated.

In the absence of a high local concentration of Ca ions, it is possible that the complex formed is reversible but with increased binding of calcium with age and simultaneous increase of TLDL serum concentration also with age, it can be conceived that some complexed material would not redissociate and so evoke a local cellular reation. It should be noted in this regard that increase of aortic AMPS alone, in the absence of elevated serum levels of TLDL, or of significant increase of calcium in arteries (as in children with Hurler's or Marfan's syndormes) is not accompanied by accelerated atherosclerosis. Possibly this merely reflects the fact that optimal concentrations of *all* the potential interactants is necessary for 'complex co-acervates' (irreversible complexes) to form.

In the light of the postulated mechanism, it is also possible to explain how another 'risk factor', hypertension operates — namely by further increase of the volume of plasma transuding through the more permeable segment of the vessel so as to make more TLDL and fibrinogen available for entrapment. Similarly, the effect of hyperlipoproteinaemia (as influenced by diet, sex and disease) is also explicable in terms of this concept, as is the combined effect of hypertension and hyperlipidaemia. Even the additive effect of three risk factors is understandable. This was clearly demonstrated in the Framingham Study (Dawber et al, 1962) in that men with low serum lipoproteins and normal blood pressures, who did not smoke were found to have one-third the standard risk of developing coronary heart disease; whereas, if all three factors were adverse, the risk increased 10 fold.

From the pathological standpoint it would seem that the escape of TLDL from the circulation, to which it is normally largely confined, actually serves as an indicator of sites of altered permeability. The presence of TLDL in the walls of arteries, at characteristic sites in the connective tissues of the eye, and in xanthomata may thus serve to indicate where vascular permeability is most frequently altered under natural circumstances.

The foregoing circumstances have all been concerned with conditions under which the flow of plasma into the wall is increased. But accumulation of TLDL and fibrinogen can also be envisaged as being affected by circumstances in which the *removal* mechanisms are impaired. It has been pointed out that external damage to arteries obliterating their lymphatic drainage or granulomatous diseases of the vessel wall, particularly those affecting the outer coats of the vessel, might act in this way. Attention has also been drawn to the distortion of lymphatics which occurs in ordinary plaques once these have become densely fibrotic.

The concept outlined above is clearly largely a restatement of the classical insudative hypothesis, validated by modern techniques and extended in the light of modern knowledge. Except in so far as the release of the breakdown products of TLDL from necrotic plaques can be held to account, it does not fully explain the association of thrombosis with atherosclerosis in man. Clearly this is an area which still demands further research.

The later lesions of atherosclerosis and their consequences have been largely dealt with in this account as though they formed a unidirectional sequence. But some attention has also been paid to the possibility of preventing or even reversing the process. At present most approaches to this problem have concentrated on control of a single factor, i.e. serum lipids or hypertension. In an earlier era, the only available means of controlling blood lipids was to prescribe a rigorous diet to which many patients found it impossible to adhere for a lifetime. Now, with the advent of at least one drug (and the promise of others to come) which effectively controls serum lipids in all but a few hyperlipidaemic states, there is the prospect of therapeutic control of serum lipids with only modest and acceptable modification of diet. Similarly, therapeutic control of disturbances of carbohydrate metabolism leading to hyperlipidaemia is now possible, as is that of hypertension (Freis, 1970).

In view of the multifactorial nature of atherosclerosis, and the evidence already referred to that where (say) three identifiable factors are adverse, their nett effect is a geometrical rather than an arithmetic summation, it would seem necessary for therapy to be directed at *all* the factors operating in a given patient rather than any single factor alone. Moreover, with improved understanding of the way in which individual factors contribute to atherogenesis, it is possible that other approaches may be possible. For example, some rectification of increased endothelial permeability from hypoxia due to smoking is probably effected by persuading patients to abandon the habit. But there has been relatively little effort directed at therapeutic measures to control this factor although it may be of fundamental importance. It would certainly seem worth evaluating if only, at first, in experimental animals. There is certainly a need for rational planning and an urgency of approach to all aspects of this problem if it is not to continue to make a progressively larger contribution to the problems of geriatric medicine.

REFERENCES

Adams C W M 1964 Arteriosclerosis in man, other mammals and birds. Biological Reviews of the Cambridge Philosophical Society 39: 372–423

Adams C W M 1967 In: Vascular Histochemistry in Relation to the Chemical and Structural Pathology of Cardiovascular Disease. Lloyd-Luke, London

Adams C W M, Bayliss O B and Ibrahim M Z M 1962 A hypothesis to explain the accumulation of cholesterol in atherosclerosis. Lancet i: 890–892

Adams C W M, Bayliss O B, Ibrahim M Z M and Webster M W 1963 Phospholipids in atherosclerosis: the modification of the cholesterol granuloma by phospholipid. Journal of Pathology and Bacteriology 86: 431–436

Ahrens E H, Hirsch J, Oette K, Farquhar J W and Stein Y 1961 Carbohydrate-induced and fat-induced lipemia. Transactions of the Association of American Physicians 74: 134–136

Alaupovic P 1971 Apolipoproteins and lipoproteins. Atherosclerosis 13: 141–146

Allan T M and Dawson A A 1968 ABO blood groups and ischaemic heart disease in men. British Heart Journal 30: 377–382

Amenta J S and Waters L L 1960 The precipitation of serum lipoproteins by mucopolysaccharides extracted from aortic tissue. Yale Journal of Biology and Medicine 33: 112–121

Anderson A J 1963 The formation of chondromucoprotein-fibrinogen and chondromucoprotein-βlipoprotein complexes. Biochemical Journal 88: 460–469

Anderson M, Walker A R P, Lutz W and Higginson J 1959 Chemical and pathological studies on aortic atherosclerosis. Archives of Pathology 68: 380–391

Anitschkow N 1913 Über die Veranderungen der Kaninchenaorta bei experimentaller cholesterinsteatose. Beitrage zur pathologischen Anatomie 56: 379–404

Anitschkow N 1933 Experimental arteriosclerosis in animals. In Arteriosclerosis, ed. Cowdry E V, p 271–322. Macmillan, New York

Aschoff L 1924 In Lectures in Pathology, p 131–135. Hoeber, New York

Aschoff L 1930 Die Arteriosklerose (Arteriopathia deformans). Ein Ernährungs—und Abmitzungsproblem. Beih. med. Klin. 26: 1–20

Aschoff L 1933 Introduction. In Arteriosclerosis, ed. Cowdery E V, p 1–18. Macmillan, New York

Ask-Upmark E and Fajers C-M 1956 Further observations on Takayasu's syndrome. Acta Medica Scandinavia 155: 275–291

Astrup P, Kjeldsen K and Wanstrup J 1967 Enhancing influence of carbon monoxide on the development of atheromatosis in cholesterol-fed rabbits. Journal of Atherosclerosis Research 7: 343–54

Barnard P J 1954 Pulmonary arteriosclerosis and cor pulmonale due to recurrent thromboembolism. Circulation 10: 343–361

Barr D P, Russ E M, Eder H A 1951 Protein-lipid relationships in human plasma. II In atherosclerosis and related conditions. American Journal of Medicine 11: 480–493

Beaumont J L, Richard J L, Anguerra G and Lenegre J 1960 The clinical significance of gerontoxon (arcus corneae). Bulletin de la societe medicale de hospitaux de Paris 76: 637–646

Beaumont J L, Carlson L A, Cooper G R, Fejfar Z, Fredrickson D S and Strasser T 1970 Classification of hyperlipidaemias and hyperlipoproteinaemias. Bulletin of the World Health Organization 43: 891–908

Benditt E P, Benditt J M 1973 Evidence for a monoclonal origin of human atherosclerotic plaques. Proceedings of the National Academy of Sciences, USA 70: 1753–1756

Bennett A E, Doll R and Howell R W 1970 Sugar consumption and cigarette smoking. Lancet i: 1011–1014

Berg K 1963 A new serum type system in man—the Lp system. Acta Pathologica et Microbiologica Scandinavica 59: 369–382

Bierman E L, Porte D, O'Hara D A, Schwartz M and Wood F C 1965 Characterization of fat particles in plasma of hyperlipemic subjects maintained on fat-free high-carbohydrate diets. Journal of Clinical Investigation 44: 261–270

Bihari-Varga M and Gero S 1966 Role of intimal mucoid substances in the pathogenesis of atherosclerosis. Investigations on the interacting components in the mucopolysaccharide-beta lipoprotein complex formation in vitro. Acta physiologica Hungarica 29: 273–281

Billimoria J D, Irani V J and Maclagan N F 1965 Phospholipid fractionation and blood clotting. Journal of Atherosclerosis Research 5: 90–101

Blackwood W, Hallspike J F, Kocen R S and Mair W G P 1969 Atheromatous disease of the carotid arterial system and embolism from the heart in cerebral infarction: A morbid anatomical study. Brain 92: 897–910

Blumenthal H T, Lansing A I and Wheeler P A 1944 Calcification of the media of the human aorta and its relation to intimal arteriosclerosis, aging and disease. American Journal Path 20: 665–679

Boivin J M 1954 Infarctus du myocarde chez un hemophile. Archives des Maladies du coeur et des Vaisseaux 47: 351–354

Bolton C H, Hampton J R and Mitchell J R A 1967 Nature of the transferable factor which causes abnormal platelet behaviour in vascular disease. Lancet ii: 1101–1105

Borrie P 1969 Type III hyperlipoproteinaemia. British Medical Journal 2: 665–667

Brady G V H, Valente A J, Walton K W 1978 Serum high-density lipoproteins in peripheral vascular disease. Lancet 2: 1271–1274

Bradby G V H, Walton K W, Watts R 1978 The binding of total low-density lipoproteins in human arterial intima affected and unaffected by atherosclerosis. Atherosclerosis 32: 403–422

Bronte-Stewart B, Keyes A, Brock J R, Moodie A D, Keyes M H, and Antonis A 1955 Serum cholesterol, diet, and coronary heart disease: An inter-racial survey in the Cape peninsula. Lancet ii: 1103–1108

Brown H B 1970 Diets that lower blood cholesterol in man. In Atherosclerosis: Proceedings of the Second International Symposium, p 426–435. Edited by R J Jones. Springer-Verlag, Berlin

Brown M S, Basu S K, Falek J R, Goldstein J L 1980 The scaveneger cell pathway for lipoprotein degradation: Specificity of the binding site that mediates the uptake of negatively-charged LDL by macrophages. Journal of Supramolecular Structure 13: 67–81

Buchwald H, Moore R B, Frantz I D and Varco R L 1970 Clinical experience with partial ileal by-pass in treatment of the hyperlipidaemias. In Atherosclerosis: Proceedings of the Second International Symposium, ed. Jones R J, p 464–468. Springer-Verlag, Berlin

Buchwald H, Moore R B, Varco R L 1980 Partial Ileal Bypass: A test of the lipid-atherosclerosis hypothesis. In: Gotto A M, Smith L C, Allen B (eds) Atherosclerosis V, Springer Verlag, New York, p 474–477

Buchwald H, Varco R L 1967 Partial ileal bypass for hypercholesterolaemia and atherosclerosis. Surgery, Gynaecology and Obstetrics, 124: 1231–1238

Buck R C 1955 Uptake of radioactive sulphate by arteries of normal and cholesterol-fed rabbits. Journal of Histochemistry and Cytochemistry 3: 435–40

Burns-Cox C J, Doll R and Ball K P 1969 Sugar intake and myocardial infarction. British Heart Journal 31: 485–490

Carew T E, Koschinsky T, Hayes S B, Steinberg D 1976 A mechanism by which high density lipoproteins may slow the atherogenic process. Lancet i: 1315–1317

Caro C G, Fitzgerald J M and Schroter R C 1969 Arterial wall shear and distribution of early atheroma in man. Nature (London) 223: 1159–1161

Carstairs K C 1965 The identification of platelets and platelet antigens in histological sections. Journal of Pathology and Bacteriology 90: 225–231

Castaigne P, Lhermitte F, Gautier J C, Escourelle R and Derouesne C 1970 Internal carotid artery occlusion. A study of 61 instances in 50 patients with postmortem data. Brain 93: 231–258

Chandler A B 1970 Thrombosis and the development of atherosclerotic lesions. In Atherosclerosis: Proceedings of the Second International Symposium, ed. Jones R J, p 88–93. Springer-Verlag, Berlin

Chronicle of the World Health Organization 1957 Mortality from arteriosclerosis, 11: 10–11

Constantinides P 1965 In Experimental Atherosclerosis. Elsevier, Amsterdam

Constantinides P 1966 Plaque fissures in human coronary thrombosis. Journal of Atherosclerosis Research 6: 1–17

Constantinides P 1968 Lipid deposition in injured arteries. Archives of Pathology 85: 280–297

Constantinides P 1978 Appraisal of the tumorigenic theory of atherosclerosis. Archives of Pathology and Laboratory Medicine 102: 490

Constantinides P and Robinson M 1969a Ultrastructural injury of arterial endothelium. I. Effects of pH, osmolarity, anoxia and temperature. Archives of Pathology 88: 99–105

Constantinides P and Robinson M 1969b Ultrastructural injury of arterial endothelium. II. Effect of vasoactive amines. Archives of Pathology 88: 106–112

Constantinides P and Robinson M 1969c Ultrastructural injury of arterial endothelium. III. Effects of enzymes and surfactants. Archives of Pathology 88: 113–117

Cornwell D G 1967 Lipoproteins. In Lipids and Lipidoses , ed. Schettler G, p 168–189. Springer-Verlag, Berlin

Craig G and Walton K W 1972 Clinical trial of methyl clofenapate (a derivative of clofibrate) in patients with essential hyperlipidaemias with special reference to Type II (primary) hyperlipidaemia. Atherosclerosis 15: 189–198

Crawford M D, Gardner M J and Morris J N 1968 Mortality and hardness of water supplies. Lancet i: 827–831

Crawford M D, Gardner M J and Morris J N 1971 Changes in water hardness and local death-rates. Lancet ii: 327–329

Crawford T and Crawford M D 1967 Prevalence and pathological changes of ischaemic heart disease in a hard water and in a soft water area. Lancet i: 229–232

Curran R C and Crane W A J 1962 Mucopolysaccharides in the atheromatous aorta. Journal of Pathology and Bacteriology 84: 405–412

Danaraj T J, Wong H O and Thomas M A 1963 Primary arteritis of aorta causing renal artery stenosis and hypertension. British Heart Journal 25: 153–165

Dawber T R, Kannel W B, Revotskie N and Kagan A 1962 The epidemiology of coronary heart disease—the Framingham enquiry. Proceedings of the Royal Society of Medicine 55: 265–271

Dayton S, Pearce M L, Hashimoto S, Dixon W J, Tomiyasu U 1969 A controlled trial of diet high in unsaturated fat in preventing complications of atherosclerosis. Circulation 40: Supplement II 1–63

Dewar H A and Oliver M F 1971 Secondary prevention trials using clofibrate: A joint commentary on the Newcastle and Scottish trials. British Medical Journal iv: 784–786

Dreyfuss F 1953 The incidence of myocardial infarctions in various communities in Israel. American Heart Journal 45: 749–755

Duff G L 1935 Experimental cholesterol arteriosclerosis and its relationship to human arteriosclerosis. Archives of Pathology 20: 81–123; 259–304

Duguid J B 1946 Thrombosis as a factor in the pathogenesis of coronary atherosclerosis. Journal of Pathology and Bacteriology 58: 207–212

Duguid J B 1948 Thrombosis as a factor in the pathogenesis of aortic atherosclerosis. Journal of Pathology and Bacteriology 60: 57–61

Duguid J B 1955 Mural thrombosis in arteries. British Medical Bulletin 11: 36–38

Duguid J B 1960 The thrombogenic hypothesis and its implications. Postgraduate Medical Journal 36: 226–229

Duke-Elder W S 1938 In Text-book of Ophthalmology, vol. 2, p 1993. Henry Kimpton, London

Duncan L E 1963 Mechanical factors in the localization of atheromata. In Evolution of the Atherosclerotic Plaque, ed. Jones R J, p 171–182. Chicago University Press, Chicago

Duncan L E, Cornfield J and Buck K 1962 The effect of blood pressure on the passage of labelled plasma albumin into canine aortic wall. Journal of Clinical Investigation 41: 1537–1545

Duncan L E, Buck K and Lynch A 1963 Lipoprotein movement through canine aortic wall. Science 142: 972–973

Elwood P C, Bainton D, Moore F, Davies D F, Wakley E J, Longman M and Sweetnam P 1971 Cardiovascular surveys in areas with different water supplies. British Medical Journal ii: 362–313

Epidemiological and Vital Statistics Report, World Health Organization 1956 9: 537–594

Epstein F H 1967 Some uses of prospective observations in the Tecumseh Community Study, Proceedings of the Royal Society of Medicine 60: 56–60

Epstein F H 1971 Epidemiologic aspects of atherosclerosis. Atherosclerosis 14: 1–11

Epstein F H, Pisa Z 1979 International comparisons in ischaemic heart disease mortality. In: Havlik R J, Feinleb M (eds) Proceedings of the Conference on the Decline in Coronary Heart Disease Mortality, National Institutes of Health Publication No 76–1610, p 11–57

Fischer S 1964 Simple and atherogenic thrombosis in the coronary vessels. Journal of Atherosclerosis Research 4: 230–238

Fredrickson D S, Levy R I and Lees R S 1967 Fat transport in lipoproteins—an integrated approach to mechanisms and disorders. New England Journal of Medicine 276: 32–44; 94–103; 148–156; 215–226; 273–281

French J E, Macfarlane R G and Sanders A G 1964 The structure of haemostatic plugs and experimental thrombi in small arteries. British Journal of Experimental Pathology 45: 467–474

Fries E D 1970 Control of mild hypertension. In Atherosclerosis: Proceedings of the Second International Symposium, ed. Jones R J, p 595–599. Springer-Verlag, Berlin

Fullerton H W, Davie W J A and Anastasopoulos G 1953

Relationship of alimentary lipaemia to blood coagulability. British Medical Journal ii: 250–2

Geer J C 1965 Fine structure of human aortic intimal thickening and fatty streaks. Laboratory Investigation 14: 1764–1783

Geer J C, Haust M D 1972 Smooth Muscle Cells in Atherosclerosis, Karger, Basel

Gerö S, Gergely J, Devenyi T, Jakab L, Szekely J and Virag S 1960 Role of mucoid substances of the aorta in the deposition of lipids. Nature (London) 187: 152–153

Gerö S, Virag S, Bihari-Varga M, Szekely J and Feher J 1967 Role of mucopolysaccharides in the deposition and metabolism of lipids. Progress in Biochemical Pharmacology 2: 290–300

Giertsen J C 1966 Atherosclerosis in an autopsy series. 7. Relation of hypertension to atherosclerosis. Acta Pathologica et Microbiologica Scandinavica 66: 331–340

Glazier F W, Tamplin A R, Strisower B, DeLalla O F, Gofman J W, Dawber T R and Phillips E 1954 Human serum lipoprotein concentrations. Journal of Gerontology 9: 395–403

Glomset J A 1968 The plasma lecithin: cholesterol acyltransferase reaction. Journal of Lipid Research 9: 155–167

Gofman J W and Young W 1963 The filtration concept of atherosclerosis and serum lipids in the diagnosis of atherosclerosis. In Atherosclerosis and its Origin, ed. Sandler M, Bourne G H, p 197–229. Academic Press, New York

Gofman J W, Tamplin A R and Strisower B 1954 Relation of fat and caloric intake to atherosclerosis. Journal of the American Dietetic Association 30: 317–326

Goldstein J L, Brown M S 1974 Binding and degradation of low density lipoproteins by cultured human fibroblasts: comparison of cells from a normal subject and from a patient with homozygous familial hypercholesterolaemia. Journal of Biological Chemistry 249: 5153–5162

Goldstein J L, Brown M S 1977 The low-density lipoprotein pathway and its relation to atherosclerosis. Annual Review of Biochemistry 46: 897–930

Gordon T, Castelli W P, Hjortland M C, Kannel W B, Dawber T R 1977 High density lipoprotein as a protective factor against coronary heart disease. American Journal of Medicine 62: 707–714

Greenhalgh R M, Lewis B, Rosengarten D S, Calnan J S, Mervart I and Martin P 1971 Serum lipids and lipoproteins in peripheral vascular disease. Lancet ii: 947–952

Gresham G A and Howard A N 1963 Comparative histopathology of the atherosclerotic lesion. Journal of Atherosclerosis Research 3: 161–177

Groen J J, Dreyfuss F and Futtman L 1968 Epidemiological, nutritional and sociological studies of atherosclerotic (coronary) heart disease among different ethnic groups in Israel. Progress in Biochemical Pharmacology 4: 20–25

Groen J J, Tijong K B, Koster A, Willebrands A F, Verdonck G and Pierloot M 1962 The influence of nutrition and ways of life on blood cholesterol and the prevalence of hypertension and coronary artery disease among Trappist and Benedictine monks. American Journal of Clinical Nutrition 10: 456–470

Gross J 1959 On the significance of the soluble collagens. In: Connective Tissue, Thrombosis and Atherosclerosis, ed. Page, I H, p 77–91. Academic Press, New York

Hale A J, Hall T and Curran R C 1967 Electronmicroprobe analysis of calcium, phosphorus and sulphur in human arteries. Journal of Pathology 93: 1–17

Hampton J R 1967 The study of platelet behaviour and its relevance to thrombosis. Journal of Atherosclerosis Research 7: 729–744

Harker L A, Ross R, Slichter S J, Scott C R 1976 Homocystine induced arteriosclerosis: The role of endothelial cell injury and platelet response in its genesis. Journal of Clinical Investigation 58: 731–741

Harrison C V 1948 Experimental pulmonary arteriosclerosis. Journal of Pathology and Bacteriology 60: 289–293

Hauss W H, Junge-Hülsing G and Hollander H J 1962 Changes in the metabolism of connective tissue associated with ageing and arterio- or atherosclerosis. Journal of Atherosclerosis Research 2: 50–61

Hauss W H, Gerlach U, Junge-Hülsing G, Themann H and Wirth W 1969 Studies on the 'nonspecific mesenchymal reaction' and the 'transit zone' in myocardial lesions and atherosclerosis. Annals of the New York Academy of Sciences 156: 207–218

Hauss W H, May J, Schulte H 1979 Effect of risk factors and antirheumatic drugs on the proliferation of aortic wall cells. Atherosclerosis 34: 119–143

Haust M D 1970 Injury and repair in the pathogenesis of atherosclerosis. In Atherosclerosis: Proceedings of the Second International Symposium, ed. Jones R J, p 12–20. Springer-Verlag, Berlin

Haust M D, Balis J U and More R H 1962 Electron microseopic study of intimal lipid accumulations in human aorta and their pathogenesis. Circulation 26: 656

Heard B E 1952 Experimental study of thickening of the pulmonary arteries of rabbits produced by the organization of fibrin. Journal of Pathology and Bacteriology 64: 13–19

Heath D, Wood E H, Dushane J W and Edwards J E 1960 The relation of age and blood pressure to atheroma in the pulmonary arteries and thoracic aorta in congenital heart disease. Laboratory Investigation 9: 259–272

Heiss G, Johnson N J, Reiland S, Davis C E, Tyroler H A 1980 The epidemiology of plasm high-density lipoprotein cholesterol levels: The Lipid Clinics Program Prevalence Study. Circulation 62: Supplement IV 116–136

Hellem H J 1960 The adhesiveness of human blood platelets in vitro. Scandinavian Journal of Clinical and Laboratory Investigation 12, suppl. 51

Helweg-Larsen P, Hofmeyer H, Kieler J, Thaysen J H, Thygsen P and Wulff M H 1952 Famine disease in German concentration camps—complications and sequels. Acta Medica Scandinavica 144, suppl. 274, p 284

Heptinstall R H, Barkley H and Porter K A 1958 Relative roles of blood cholesterol level and blood pressure level in the production of experimental aortic atheroma in rabbits. Angiology 9: 84–87

Hickey N, Maurer B and Mulcahey R 1970 Arcus senilis; its relation to certain attributes and risk factors in patients with coronary heart disease. British Heart Journal 32: 449–452

Hoff H F, Gaubatz J W 1975 Ultrastructural localisation of plasma lipoproteins in human intracranial arteries Virchow's Archives of Pathological Anatomy 369: 111–121

Hoff H F, Gaubatz J W 1977 Ultrastructural localisation of apolipoprotein B in human aortic and coronary atherosclerotic plaques. Experimental and Molecular Patholgy 26: 214–227

Howell M 1964 Lipoproteins and fibrinolysis. British Medical Bulletin 20: 200–204

Howell R W and Wilson D G 1969 Dietary sugar and ischaemic heart disease. British Medical Journal iii: 145–148

Hueper W C 1944 Arteriosclerosis. Archives of Pathology 38: 162–181; 245–285; 350–364

Hueper W C 1945 Arteriosclerosis. Archives of Pathology 39: 57–65; 117–131; 187–216

Hueper W C 1956 Pathogenesis of atherosclerosis. American Journal of Clinical Pathology 26: 559–578

Jobin F and Esnouf M P 1967 Studies on the formation of the prothrombin-converting complex. Biochemical Journal 102: 666–674

Jorgensen L 1970 Thrombosis and the complications of atherosclerosis. In Atherosclerosis: Proceedings of the Second International Symposium, ed. Jones R J, p 94–102. Springer-Verlag, Berlin

Kao V C Y and Wissler R W 1965 A study of the immunohistochemical localization of serum lipoproteins and other plasma proteins in human atherosclerotic lesions. Experimental and Molecular Pathology 4: 465–479

Katz L N and Pick R 1963 Reversibility of the atherosclerotic lesion. In Evolution of the Atherosclerotic Plaque, ed. Jones R J, p 251–264. Chicago University Press, Chicago

Keys A 1963 The role of the diet in human atherosclerosis and its complications. In Atherosclerosis and its Origin, ed. Sandler M and Bourne G H, p 263–299. Academic Press, New York

Khachadurian A K 1964 The inheritance of essential familial hypercholesterolaemia. American Journal of Medicine 27: 402–7

Khachadurian A K and Demirjian Z N 1968 Cholestyramine therapy in patients homozygous for familial hypercholesterolaemia (familial hypercholesterolaemic xanthomatosis). Journal of Atherosclerosis Research 8: 177–188

Kinsell L W, Schlierf G, Kahlke W and Schettler G 1967 Essential hyperlipaemia. In Lipids and Lipidoses, ed. Schettler G, p 446–489. Springer-Verlag, Berlin

Kirkeby K 1966 Blood lipids, lipoproteins and proteins in vegetarians. Acta Medica Scandinavica 179, suppl. 443, 5–84

Kjeldsen K 1970 Carboxyhaemoglobin and serum cholesterol levels in smokers correlated to the incidence of occlusive arterial disease. In Atherosclerosis: Proceedings of the Second International Symposium, ed. Jones R J p 378–381. Springer-Verlag, Berlin

Klynstra F B and Böttcher C J F 1970 Permeability patterns in pig aorta. Atherosclerosis 11: 451–462

Lancet Editorial 1980 Why the American Decline in Coronary Heart Disease? Lancet i: 183–184

Langman M J S, Elwood P C, Foote J and Ryrie D R 1969 ABO and Lewis blood-groups and serum cholesterol. Lancet ii: 607–609

Lansing A I, Alex M and Rosenthal T B 1950 Calcium and elastin in human arteriosclerosis. Journal of Gerontology 5: 112/119

Lever W F, Smith P A J and Hurley N A 1954 Idiopathic hyperlipemic and primary hypercholesteremic xanthomatosis. I. Clinical data and analysis of the plasma lipids. Journal of Investigative Dermatology 22: 33–51

Levy R I, Rifkind B M 1980 The structure, function and metabolism of high-density lipoproteins: A status report. Circulation 62: Supplement IV 4–8

Lobstein J G C F M 1833 In Traite d'Anatomie Pathologique, p 550. Paris: Levrault

Lorenzen I 1963 In Experimental Atherosclerosis. Munksgaard, Copenhagen

McAndrew G M and Ogston D 1965 Arcus senilis in middle-aged men. British Medical Journal i: 425–427

Macaraeg P V J, Lasagna L and Snyder B 1968 Arcus not so senilis. Annals of Internal Medicino 68: 345–354

McCullagh E P and Lewis L A 1960 A study of diet, blood lipids and vascular disease in Trappist monks. New England Journal of Medicine 263: 569–574

McGill H C 1968 Geographic pathology of atherosclerosis. Progress in Biochemical Pharmacology 4: 26–29

Mcgill H C, Frank M H and Geer J C 1961 Aortic lesions in hypertensive monkeys. Archives of Pathology 71: 96–102

McGinley J, Jones H and Gofman J W 1952 Lipoproteins and xanthomatous diseases. Journal of Investigative Dermatology 19: 71–82

Maclagan N F and Billimoria J D 1964 Blood lipids in relation to coagulation. In Biological Aspects of Occlusive Vascular Disease, ed. Chalmers G G and Gresham G A, p 213–219. Cambridge University Press, London

Mahley R W, Innerarity T L, Weisgraber K H, Oh S Y 1976 Altered metabolism (in vivo and in vitro) of plasma lipoproteins after selective chemical modification of lysine residues of the apoproteins. Journal of Clinical Investigation 64: 743–750

Malmros H 1950 The relation of nutrition to health: A statistical study of the effects of the war-time on arteriosclerosis, cardiosclerosis, tuberculosis and diabetes. Acta Medica Scandinavica suppl. 246, p 137–153

Mancini R E, Vilar O, Dellacha J M, Davidson O W, Gomez C J and Alvarez B 1962 Extravascular distribution of fluorescent albumin, globulin and fibrinogen in connective tissue structures. Journal of Histochemistry and Cytochemistry 10: 194–203

Mathur K S, Patney N L and Kumar V 1961 Atherosclerosis in India: An autopsy study of the aorta and the coronary, cerebral, renal and pulmonary arteries. Circulation 24: 68–75

Medalie J H 1970 Current developments in the epidemiology of atherosclerosis in Israel. In Atherosclerosis: Proceedings of the Second International Symposium, ed. Jones R J, p 321–328. Springer-Verlag, Berlin

Meyer A C, Meyer B J, Verster F and Pepler W J 1964 Calcium and magnesium concentration in the aorta of whites and Bantu. South African Journal of Laboratory and Clinical Medicine 10: 99–101

Meittinen M, Turpeinen O, Karvonen M J, Eluoso R, Paavilainen E 1972 Effect of cholesterol-lowering diet on mortality from coronary heart disease and other causes. Lancet 2: 835–838

Miller G J, Miller N E 1975 Plasma high-density lipoprotein concentration and development of ischaemic heart disease. Lancet i: 16–19

Minick C R, Murphy G E and Campbell W G 1966 Experimental induction of athero-arteriosclerosis by the synergy of allegic injury to arteries and lipid-rich diet. I. Effect of repeated injections of horse serum in rabbits fed a dietary cholesterol supplement. Journal of Experimental Medicine 124: 635–652

Minick C R, Stemerman M B, Insull W W 1977 Effect of regenerated endothelium on lipid accumulation in the arterial wall. Proceedings of the National Academy of Sciences, USA 74: 1724–1728

Minick C R, Stemerman M B, Insull W W 1979 Role of endothelium and hypercholesterolaemia in intimal thickening and lipid accumulation. American Journal of Pathology 95: 131–158

Mitchell J R A 1964 Experimental Thrombosis. In Biological Aspects of Occlusive Vascular Disease, ed. Chalmers D G and Gresham G A, p 185–189. Cambridge University Press, London

Mitchell J R A and Schwartz C J 1965 Arterial Disease. Blackwell, Oxford

Moon H D and Rinehart J F 1952 Histogenesis of coronary arteriosclerosis. Circulation 6: 481–488

Moore R, Friedman R J, Singal D P, Gauldie J, Blajchman N H 1976 Inhibition of injury-induced thromboatherosclerotic lesions by anti-platelet serum in rabbits. Thrombosis and Haemostasis 35: 70–81

Moore S and Mersereau W A 1968 Microembolic renal ischaemia, hypertension, and nephrosclerosis. Archives of Pathology 85: 623–630

Morris C J, Bradby G V H, Walton K W 1978 Fibrous long spacing collagen in human atherosclerosis. Atherosclerosis 31: 345–354

Morris C J, Magnani H N, Walton K W 1983 Low-density lipoprotein sizes in hyperlipidaemias. In: DeGennes J L and Dairou F (eds) Latent Dyslipoproteinaemias, Raven Press, New York

Morris J N, Kagan A, Pattison D C, Gardner M M J and Raffle P A B 1966 Incidence and prediction of ischaemic heart disease in London busmen. Lancet ii: 553–559

Mustard J F, Rowsell H C, Murphy E A and Downie H G 1963 Intimal thrombosis in atherosclerosis. In Evolution of the Atherosclerotic Plaque, ed. Jones R J, p 183–203. Chicago University Press, Chicago

Myaskinov A L 1958 Influence of some factors on development of experimental cholesterol atherosclerosis. Circulation 17: 99–113

Nakamura M, Gorel I, Yabuta N, Torii S, Isihara Y, Tamari K and Imai T 1955 Acid mucopolysaccharides, cholesterol, calcium and magnesium content of Japanese aortas. Japanese Heart Journal 6: 20–39

Newcastle-upon-Tyne Physicians Group 1971 Trial of clofibrate in the treatment of ischaemic heart disease. British Medical Journal iv: 767–775

Nichols E F 1940 A study of syphilis of the aorta and aortic valve area. Annals of Internal Medicine 14: 960–977

Oliver M F 1981 Diet and coronary heart disease. British Medical Bulletin 37: 49–58

Oliver M F, Geizerova H, Cumming L A and Heady J A 1969 Serum cholesterol and ABO and Rhesus blood-groups, Lancet ii: 605–606

Oncley J L 1963 Lipid protein interactions. In Brain Lipids and Lipoproteins and the Leucodystrophies, ed. Folch-Pi J L and Bauer H, p 1–17. Elsevier, Amsterdam

Osborne J C, Brewer H B 1977 The plasma lipoproteins. Advances in Protein Chemistry 31: 253–337

Ott H, Lohss F and Gergely J 1958 Der Nachweis von Serumlipoprotein in der Aortenintima. Klinische Wochenschrift 36: 383–384

Page I H 1945 quoted by Hall E M 1948 In Pathology, ed. Anderson W A D p 565. Henry Kimpton, London

Pinto I J, Thomas P, Colaco F and Daley K K 1970 Current developments in India. In Atherosclerosis: Proceedings of the Second Internation Symposium, ed. Jones R J, p 328–35. Springer-Verlag, Berlin

Polano M K 1969 Cutaneous xanthomatosis in relation to the blood lipoprotein pattern. British Journal of Dermatology 81, suppl. 2. 39–48

Polano M K, Baes H, Lemmens H E F, Hulsmans H A M, Querido A, Pries C and van Gent C M 1970 Heredity in primary hyper β lipoproteinaemia with concomitant xanthomata. Acta Medica Scandinavica 188: 397–401

Pollak O J 1963 Discussion. In Evolution of the Atherosclerotic Plaque, ed. Jones R J, p 167. Chicago University Press, Chicago

Pomerantz H Z 1962 The relationship between coronary heart disease and the presence of certain physical characteristics. Canadian Medical Association Journal 86: 57–60

Poole J C F 1955 The significance of chylomicra in blood coagulation. British Journal of Haematology 1: 229–233

Poole J C F and French J E 1961 Thrombosis. Journal of Atherosclerosis Research 1: 251–282

Report from the Committee of Principal Investigators 1978 A co-operative trial in the primary prevention of ischaemic heart disease using clofibrate. British Heart Journal 40: 1069–1118

Retan J W and Miller R E 1966 Micro-embolic complications of atherosclerosis. Archives of Internal Medicine 118: 534–545

Rifkind B M 1965 The incidence of arcus senilis in ischaemic heart-disease: its relation to serum lipid levels. Lancet i: 312–314

Roberts J C and Straus R 1965 In Comparative Atherosclerosis. Hoeber, New York

Roberts W C, Levy R I and Fredrickson D S 1970 Hyperlipoproteinaemia. Archives of Pathology 90: 46–56

Robertson A L 1980 Arterial endothelium in the initial stages of atherosclerosis. In: Gotto A M, Smith L C, Allen B (eds) Atherosclerosis V, Springer-Verlag, New York, p 103–111

Robertson J S 1969 The water story (corr.). Lancet i: 1160

Rodstein M and Zeman F D 1963 Arcus senilis and arteriosclerosis in the aged. American Journal of the Medical Sciences 245: 70–77

Rokitansky C von 1852 In A Manual of Pathological Anatomy, vol. 4, p 261. Translated by G E Day. Sydenham Society, London

Rose G 1970 Current developments in Europe. In Atherosclerosis: Proceedings of the Second International Symposium, ed. Jones R J, p 310–314. Springer-Verlag, Berlin

Rosenberg H M, Klebba A J 1979 Trends in cardiovascular mortality with a focus on ischaemic heart disease, United States 1950–1976 In: Havlik R J, Feinleb M (eds) Proceedings of the Conference on the Decline in Coronary Heart Disease Mortality. National Institutes of Health Publication No 176–1610, p 11–57

Ross R, Glomset J 1976 The pathogenesis of atherosclerosis. New England Journal of Medicine 295: 369–377; 420–425

Ross R, Harker L 1976 Hyperlipidaemia and atherosclerosis Science 193: 1094–1110

Ross R, Vogel A, Raines E, Kariya B 1980 The platelet-derived growth factor. In: Gotto A M, Smith L C, Allen B (eds) Atherosclerosis V, Springer-Verlag, New York, p 442–449

Ross R S and McKusick V A 1953 Aortic arch syndromes. Archives of Internal Medicine 92: 701–740

Schaffner T, Taylor K, Bartucci E J, Fischer-Dzoga K, Beeson J H, Glagov S, Wissler R W 1980 Arterial foam-cells with distinctive immunomorphologic and histochemical features of macrophages. American Journal of Pathology 100: 57–80

Schettler G 1954 1st der sogenannte Greisenbogen der Hornhaut ein Heinweis auf Atheroskerlose? Deutsche medizinische Wochenschrift 79: 915–917

Schwartz C J, Gerrity R G, Sprague E A, Hagens M R, Reed C T, Guerrero D L 1980 Ultrastructure of the normal arterial endothelium and intima. In: Gotto A M, Smith L C, Allen B (eds) Atherosclerosis V, Springer-Verlag, New York, p 112–120

Scott P J, Dykes P W, Davies J W L and Walton K W 1963 Turnover studies of ^{131}I-labelled β-lipoprotein in health and in thyroid disease. In Biochemical Problems of Lipids, ed. Frazer A C, p 318–324. Elsevier, Amsterdam

Scott P J and Hurley P J 1969 Low-density lipoprotein accumulation in aortic and coronary artery walls. Israel Journal of Medical Sciences 5: 631–634

Scott P J and Hurley P J 1970 The distribution of radioiodinated serum albumin and low-density lipoprotein in tissues and the arterial wall. Atherosclerosis 11: 77–103

Scott P J and Winterbourn C C 1967 Low-density lipoprotein accumulation in actively growing xanthomas. Journal of Atherosclerosis Research 7: 207–223

Scottish Society of Physicians 1971 Ischaemic heart disease: a secondary prevention trial using clofibrate. British Medical Journal iv: 775–784

Shanoff H M and Little J A 1964 Studies of male survivors of myocardial infarction due to 'essential' atherosclerosis. III. Corneal arcus: Incidence and relation to serum lipids and lipoproteins. Canadian Medical Association Journal 91: 835–839

Shaper A G, Jones K W, Jones M and Kyobe J 1963 Serum lipids in three nomadic tribes of Northern Kenya. American Journal of Clinical Nutrition 13: 135–146

Shimamoto T 1963 The relationship of edematous reaction in arteries

to atherosclerosis and thrombosis. Journal of Atherosclerosis Research 3: 87–102

Shrire V and Asherson R A 1964 Arteries of the aorta and its major branches. Quarterly Journal of Medicine 33: 439–463

Silwer J, Cornberg S and Nilsson I M 1966 Occurrence of arteriosclerosis in von Willebrand's disease. Acta Medica Scandinavica 180: 475–484

Slack J 1969 Risks of ischaemic heart disease in familial hyperlipoproteinaemic states. Lancet ii: 1380–1382

Smith E B 1965 The influence of age and atherosclerosis on the chemistry of aortic intima II. Collagen and mucopolysaccharides. Journal of Atherosclerosis Research 5: 241–248

Smith E B 1970 Dicussion. In Atherosclerosis: Proceedings of the Second International Symposium, ed. Jones R J, p 106. Springer-Verlag, Berlin

Smith E B, Evans P H and Downham M D 1967 Lipid in the aortic intima: the correlation of morphological and chemical characteristics. Journal of Atherosclerosis Research 7: 171–186

Smith E B and Slater R S 1970 The lipoproteins of the lesions. In Atherosclerosis: Proceedings of the Second International Symposium, ed. Jones R J, p 42–49. Springer-Verlag, Berlin

Stamler J, Berkson D M, Young Q D, Hall Y and Miller W 1963 Approaches to the primary prevention of clinical heart disease in high-risk, middle-aged men. Annals of the New York Academy of sciences 97: 932–951

Starzl T E, Chase H P, Putnam C W, Porter K A 1973 Portacaval shunt in hyperlipoproteinaemia. Lancet i: 940–944

Starzl T E, Chase H P, Putnam C W, Nora J J 1974 Follow-up of patient with portacaval shunt for the treatment of hyperlipidaemia. Lancet 2: 714–715

Starzl T E, Kolp L, Weil R 1980 Portacaval shunt for Type II hyperlipidaemia. In: Gotto A M, Smith L C, Allen B (eds) Atherosclerosis V Springer-Verlag, New York, p 450–453

Stein E A, Glueck C J 1980 Homozygous hypercholesterolaemia: treatment by portacaval shunt. In: Gotto A M, Smith L C, Allen B (eds) Atherosclerosis V, Springer-Verlag, New York, p 474–477

Stewart J W and Acheson E D 1957 Atherosclerosis in a haemophiliac. Lancet i: 1121–1122

Strøm A and Jensen R A 1951 Mortality from circulatory diseases in Norway, 1940–1945. Lancet i: 126–9

Strong J P and Eggen D A 1970 Risk factors and atherosclerotic lesions. In Atherosclerosis: Proceedings of the Second International Symposium, ed. Jones R J, p 355–364. Springer-Verlag, Berlin

Subramaniam R and Kulangara A C 1967 Incidence of atherosclerotic lesions at Madras, South India. British Heart Journal 29: 333–336

Texon M 1957 A haemodynamic concept of atherosclerosis with particular reference to coronary occlusion. Archives of Internal Medicine 99: 418–427

Texon M 1963 The role of vascular dynamics in the development of atherosclerosis. In Atherosclerosis and its Origin, ed. Sandler M and Bourne G H, p 167–195. Academic Press, New York

Thannhauser S 1950 Lipidoses, 2nd Edn. Oxford University Press, New York

Thoma R 1883 Uber die Abhängigkeit der Hindegewebsneubildung in der Arterienintima von den mechanischen Bendingungen des Blutumlaufes. Virchows Archiv für pathologische Anatomie 93: 443–505

Thomas W A, Florentin R A, Nam S C, Daoud A S, Lee K T and Tiamson E 1970 Plasma lipids and experimental atherosclerosis. In Atherosclerosis: Proceedings of the Second International Symposium, ed. Jones R J, p 414–426. Springer-Verlag, Berlin

Thomas W A, O'Neal R M and Lee K T 1956 Thromboembolism, pulmonary arteriosclerosis and fatty meals. Archives of Pathology 61: 380–389

Thompson G R, Myant N, Oakley C, Steiner R, Sapsford R 1980 Combined medico-surgical strategy for severe familial hypercholesterolaemia. In: Gotto A M, Smith L C, Allen B (eds) Atherosclerosis V, Springer-Verlag, New York p 454–457

Thompson G R, Lowenthal R, Myant N B 1975 Plasma exchange in the management of homozygous familial hypercholesterolaemia. Lancet i: 1208–1211

Titus J L, Weilbaecher D G 1980 Smooth muscle cells in atherosclerosis. In: Gotto A M, Smith L C, Allen B (eds) Atherosclerosis V, Springer-Verlag, New York, p 126–129

Tracy R E, Merchant E B and Kao V C 1961 On the antigenic identity of human serum beta and alpha-2 lipoproteins and their identification in the aortic intima. Circulation Research 9: 472–478

Turnbull H M 1915 Alterations in arterial structure and their relation to syphilis. Quarterly Journal of Medicine 8: 201–254

Vakil R J 1963 Ischaemic heart disease in India. British Heart Journal 25: 283–290

Veress B, Balint A, Kóczé A, Nagy Z and Jellinek H 1970 Increasing aortic permeability by atherogenic diet. Atherosclerosis 11: 369–371

Virchow R von 1862 Phlogose und Thrombose in Gefassystem. Gesammelte Abhandlungen zur Wissenschaftlichen Medizin. Max Hirsch, Berlin

Walker H R P 1971 Sugar intake and coronary heart disease. Atherosclerosis 14: 137–152

Walker A R P and Arvidsson U P 1954 Fat intake, serum cholesterol concentration, and atherosclerosis in the South African Bantu. I. Low fat intake, and the age trend of serum cholesterol concentration in the South African Bantu. Journal of Clinical Investigation 33: 1358–1371

Walton K W 1952 The biological properties of a new anticoagulant possessing heparin-like properties. British Journal of Pharmacology 7: 370–391

Walton K W 1966 Lipoproteins in the vessel wall. Archives des Maladies du Coeur 59; Revue de Athérosclérose, 8, suppl. 2, p 41–47

Walton K W 1967 Fat transport by lipoproteins in health and disease. Journal of Atherosclerosis Research 7: 533–536

Walton K W 1969a The biology of atherosclerosis. In The Biological Basis of Medicine, Vol. 6, ed. Bittar E E and Bittar N, p 193–223. Academic Press, New York

Walton K W 1969b The metabolism of low-density (β) lipoproteins in health and disease. In Physiology and Pathophysiology of Protein Metabolism, ed. Birke G, Norburg R and Plantin L O Oxford: Pergamon Press

Walton K W 1969c Studies on the pathogenesis of atherosclerosis. Proceedings of the Royal Society of Medicine 62: 368–370

Walton K W 1970 Current concepts of the aetiology of atherosclerosis. Midland Medical Review 6: 183–205

Walton K W 1971 The role of low-density lipoproteins in corneal arcus formation. Annales de Biologie Clinique 29: 16–17

Walton K W 1972a Distribution of lipoproteins in arteries and tissues as determined by immunohistological and radioactive tracer methods. Protides of the Biological Fluids. Proceedings of the 19th Colloquium, 225–226

Walton K W 1972b Ischaemia, thrombosis and embolism. In Pathological Basis of Medicine, p 266. Edited by R C Curran and D G Harnden. Heinemann, London

Walton K W 1973 Studies on the pathogenesis of corneal arcus formation. I. Corneal arcus formation in the human and its relation to atherosclerosis as studied by immunofluorescence. Journal of Pathology 111: 263–274

Walton K W and Dunkerley D J 1974 Studies on the pathogenesis of corneal arcus formation. II. Immunofluorescent studies on lipid deposition in the eye of the lipid-fed rabbit. Journal of Pathology 114: 217–229

Walton K W, Dunkerly D J, Johnson A G, Khan M K, Morris C J, Watts R B 1976 Investigation by immunofluorescence of arterial lesions in rabbits on two different lipid supplements and treated with pyridinol carbamate. Atherosclerosis 23: 117–139

Walton K W and Scott P J 1964 Estimation of the low-density (β)

lipoproteins of serum in health and disease using large molecular weight dextran sulphate. Journal of Clinical Pathology 17: 627–643

Walton K W, Hitchens J, Magnani H N and Khan M 1974 A study of methods of identification and estimation of Lp(a) lipoprotein and of its significance in health, hyperlipidaemia and atherosclerosis. Atherosclerosis 20: 323–346

Walton K W, Morris C J 1977 Studies on the passage of plasma proteins across arterial endothelium in relation to atherogenesis. Progress in Biochemical Pharmacology 13: 138–152

Walton K W, Scott P J, Dykes P W and Davies J W L 1965 The significance of alterations in serum lipids in thyroid dysfunction. II. Alterations of the metabolism and turnover of ^{131}I-low-density lipoproteins in hypothyroidism and thyrotoxicosis. Clinical Science 29: 217–238

Walton K W, Scott P J, Verrier-Jones J, Fletcher R F and Whitehead T P 1963 Studies on low-density lipoprotein turnover in relation to Atromid therapy. Journal of Atherosclerosis Research 3: 396–414

Walton K W, Thomas C and Dunkerley D J 1972 The pathogenesis of cutaneous xanthomata. Journal of Pathology 109: 271–289

Walton K W and Williamson N 1968 Histological and immunofluorescent studies on the evolution of the human atheromatous plaque. Journal of Atherosclerosis Research 8: 599–624

Walton K W, Williamson N and Johnson A G 1970 The pathogenesis of atherosclerosis of the mitral and aortic valves. Journal of Pathology 101: 205–220

Wartman W B, Jennings R B and Hudson B 1951 Experimental arterial disease: The reaction of the pulmonary artery to minute emboli of blood clot. Circulation 4: 747–755

Wells N 1982 Coronary heart disease: The scope for prevention. Office of Health Economics, London

Wolf P 1967 The nature and significance of platelet products in human plasma. British Journal of Haematology 13: 269–288

Wood G C 1960 Formation of fibrils from collagen solutions. Biochemical Journal 75: 598–605; 605–612

World Health Chronicle 1967 The world health situation: A statistical review. 21: 350–356

World Health Organization 1958 Classification of atherosclerotic lesions. World Health Organisation Technical Report Series No. 143

Yates P O 1964 A change in the pattern of cerebrovascular disease. Lancet i: 65–69

Yates P O and Hutchinson E C 1961 Cerebral infarction: the role of stenosis of the extracranial cerebral arteries. Special Report Senes of the Medical Research Council (Lond.) No. 300.

Yudkin J 1957 Diet and coronary thrombosis. Hypothesis and fact. Lancet ii: 155–162

Yudkin J 1964 Dietary fat and dietary sugar in relation to ischaemic heart disease and diabetes. Lancet ii: 4–5

Yudkin J and Roddy J 1964 Levels of dietary sucrose in patients with occlusive atherosclerotic disease. Lancet ii: 6–8

Zelis R, Mason D T, Braunwald E and Levy R I 1970 Effects of hyperlipoproteinaemias and their treatment on the peripheral circulation. Journal of Clinical Investigation 49: 1007–1015

Zemplenyi T 1962 Enzymes of the arterial wall. Journal of Atherosclerosis Research 2: 2–24

Zinserling W D 1925 Untersuchungen über Atherosklerose. I. Uber die Aortaverfettung bei Kinder. Virchows Archiv für pathologische Anatomie und Physiologie 255: 677–705

The milieu interieur and aging

INTRODUCTION

The milieu interieur of Claude Bernard is more a hypothetical concept than a palpable entity (Bernard, 1865). Knowledge and understanding of its composition and function has been constantly refined and elaborated since the mid 17th century, as newer investigative tools and more experiments have led to a better understanding of what Bernard later called integrated physiology (Bernard, 1878). Cells require a precisely determined microenvironment — the milieu interieur — to operate optimally. The milieu interieur envelopes, supports and protects cells both from each other and from a potentially harmful milieu exterieur and maintenance of such an environment requires integrated function by all the body systems (Adolph, 1968) including the so-called higher order behavioural systems (Pavlov, 1927). Consideration of this vast area of normal and pathological homeostasis requires discussion of virtually the whole of human physiology and medicine. In the context of aging many of these topics are dealt with throughout this book under the various systematic chapter headings. In this section the milieu interieur and homeostasis will be discussed only in the context of whole body or inter-system regulation and will thus span that area of integrative physiology that lies across and between classical body systems. It is difficult to isolate aging changes in clinical physiology from age related diseases. The two areas are inter-related, and to some extent are inter-dependent one upon the other.

Since the time of Bernard a vast literature covering the interieur milieu and homeostasis has evolved. Most of the research reported in this area has been derived from studies of young adults, often for the sole reason that they are readily available in research environments. Less frequently are middle aged individuals studied, and it is even rarer for homeostatic mechanisms to be studied in the aged. Many research reports which include 'old' or 'elderly' in their titles limit their studies to individuals below the sixth decade. The recent past however has demonstrated a heartening increase in studies of old age as witnessed by the number of specialist journals devoted to aging in both man and other species. Much of gerontological research is still at the stage of descriptive study. Thus, in an aging study the average value or normal range of some variable is compared in young and old healthy individuals. Whilst age differences in such studies may be important, how the young and old respond if the variable is perturbed is much more important especially for the clinical practitioner.

Degradation or instability of homeostatic control mechanisms underlie many of the observed age differences (Fig. 11.1). Thus, how quickly and in what

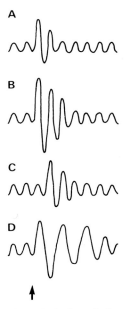

Fig. 11.1 Response to perturbation of a hypothetical system under feedback control. A — Young individual B–D — Effects of aging: B — Amplitude exaggerated. C — Initiation of response delayed. D — Phase of response delayed. The simplified function is of the form:

$$f(x) = A + A_0 \sin(\omega t + \phi) + A_1 e^{\theta_t} \sin(\omega_2 t + \phi_2)$$

Examination of age-changes in the parameters of such a function may provide insight as to where the 'age lesion' acts.

manner does an old person's system respond to perturbation may answer many questions and pose others leading to greater understanding of 'specific age lesions'. The acquisition of more quantifiable data from experiments as opposed to observation would allow much better formulation and testing of hypotheses. Indeed the elaboration of mathematical models (Fig. 11.1) of complicated aging homeostatic mechanisms would advance clinical medicine and biology (Donbal, 1982). The most important stress for the human body is produced by disease. It should be remembered that in the elderly, psychological and social trauma may disturb homeostasis more than pathology. Equally, degradation of homeostatic mechanisms will have important secondary effects on the pharmacokinetics and pharmacodynamics of drug metabolism in old age.

BODY COMPOSITION

From the moment of conception right into extreme old age the human body undergoes a considerable change in shape, size and composition (Cannon, 1932). The most dramatic changes in body composition take place during the first fraction of life, in utero, but change (maturation, development, senescence) is a continuous process and changes occurring in the latter half of the life span may have considerable import on the physiology, pharmacology and pathology of the older individual (Finch, 1972). Many of the age changes in body composition are brought about by developments and adaptations in the neuroendocrine system, but unfortunately only very few studies relating to aging have been reported.

Body weight

There are many reports of cross-sectional studies of the effects of aging on body weight in humans. Many of these reports reach variable or even conflicting conclusions. This is probably due to differences in culture or genetic make up of populations studied. Overall however beyond middle age changes in body weight well into old age are not gross.

In healthy individuals body weight generally reaches a plateau in middle life and is maintained to approximately the sixth decade, to be followed by a progressive decrease. Peak body weight is said to occur anywhere between the early 40's (Hejda, 1963; Damon et al, 1972) and the late 60's (Hollifield and Parson, 1959). However, most authors agree that following a gradual gain in body weight in early adult life there follows a somewhat elastic middle age plateau and thereafter a progressive decrease takes place into old age (Master et al, 1960). Over the whole adult life span the average changes in body weight are slight. Thus, because of the

more rapid loss of weight in old age comparison of 30 and 80 year old men will show similar weights, the elderly having shed their 'middle-aged spread' over the five decades. Women on the other hand do not seem to be so efficient and over the same age range old women may seem to have gained weight. However, on average they were heavier in their middle age. In old age the body weights of men and women are similar (Fig. 11.2). In general, men achieve a higher peak weight than women and tend to start to lose weight earlier, but at approximately the same rate as women. This rate is around 0.45 kg/year (1 lb/year) beyond the age of 45/50 years. Caution however needs to be applied to these cross-sectional studies because of secular changes and selective survivorship.

Dramatic improvements have taken place in the nutritional status of human beings in the last century in the Western World. The main impact has been infant and child nutrition, though the effects of better nutrition in early life are already being reflected in subsequent body composition in middle and old age. For example, over the last 100 years or so there has been a secular increase in height with each generation. The other factors affecting such cross-sectional studies of body weight are the problem of selective survivorship (only the fit survive into old age) and latent disease in elderly individuals. Thus, the average results for some physiological parameter in old people may be lower than in young individuals because in the former a common age related disease which is not yet manifest may be affecting a small number of older individuals bringing the average result to a lower level. Thus, for example, body weight and nutritional parameters may be less in old people because a number of the individuals are already affected by some undetected age-related cancer. In summary, changes in body weight with increasing age tend to be confounded by many other non-age-related factors which account for differences between surveys. Overall, however, body weight changes are not in themselves of great relevance or importance.

Fat and fat free mass

Within the somewhat minor age changes which are occurring in body weight, major redistributions of tissue proportions are taking place (Fig. 11.2). The weight of the body can be considered to be composed of only two simple components — fat, and the rest — fat free mass. Lean body mass is that component of the fat-free mass less the weight of bone and non-adipose fat. Whilst precise definitions of lean body mass vary slightly depending on measurement methods, for the purposes of this review of whole body composition the two will be treated as equivalent. Age changes in lean body mass and bones are essentially parallel so no significant systematic errors will be introduced (Munro, 1981). Fat

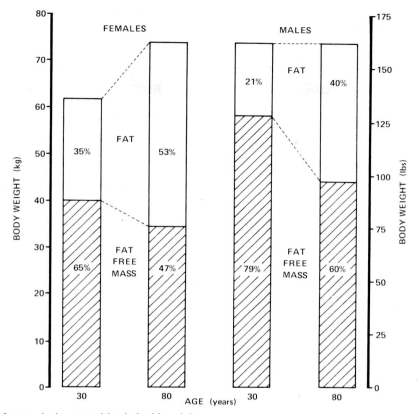

Fig. 11.2 Effects of age on body composition in healthy adults

is a relatively inert consumer of body energetics whilst the fat free mass is a measure of active organ and especially muscle mass (Moore et al, 1963). Thus, as was shown in a study of Scottish footballers, the proportion of fat free mass is a better predictor of physical fitness than body weight (Boddy et al, 1974). Similarly, lean body mass is closely related to the metabolic rate because muscle is the major consumer of oxygen (Miller and Blyth, 1952). This applies even into extreme old age. It may be suggested that the lean body mass or fat free mass should be used as a normalising factor for many physiological variables such as cardiac output, body potassium, or physical fitness (Cotes et al, 1973).

Measurement of fat free mass
There are many ways of measuring fat or its reciprocal fat free mass. Many studies have used elaborate methods but in clinical practice skinfold thickness measurements are to be preferred. The fat free mass can only be measured directly in cadaver studies and few have been reported (Shohl, 1939; Widdowson et al, 1951; Forbes and Lewis, 1956). Subjects reported in these studies have all been young, the oldest being 60 years. Because

73.2 per cent of the total body water is contained within the fat free mass, measurement of the total body water allows calculation of the fat free mass (Pace and Rathbun, 1945). Fat free mass can also be determined from measurements of body density using the fact that fat is anhydrous with a density of 0.90×10^3 kg/m^3 (Behnke et al, 1942; Durnin and Womersley, 1974). Whole body density can be determined by the technique of under-water weighing; then, using the equation of Siri (1956), the percentage of fat can be calculated. Unfortunately, underwater weighing is not a technique widely applicable in clinical practice, especially with elderly subjects. Direct chemical analyses in animals and man have demonstrated that fat tissue contains very little potassium (<8 mmol/kg), whereas muscle tissue and active organs contain high concentrations of potassium (>100 mmol/kg) (Shohl, 1939; Corsa et al, 1950; Widdowson et al, 1951; Woodbury, 1956). Knowledge of whole body potassium should allow calculation of fat free mass (Forbes, 1974). Unfortunately, recent studies have shown that the concentration of potassium in the fat free mass decreases with increasing age and cannot be used in the elderly as a measure of fat free mass

(Womersley et al, 1976; Lye, 1981). Body fat can also be determined from the absorption of cyclopropane and krypton (Davidsson et al, 1956; Lesser and Zak, 1963). Unfortunately, this method has not found much favour because of difficulties with the technique and has never been applied to studies of the elderly.

A relatively simple, non-invasive method of determining body fat and fat free mass involves the use of skinfold thickness measurements. This method does not require expensive equipment, is easy to use and can be repeated (Brozek, 1961). It is important to use good quality, calibrated skin calipers (Burgert and Anderson, 1979), to take the average of three readings at each site and to use at least three or preferably four sites for measurement (Durnin and Rahaman, 1967). This latter qualification is important because of the differential redistribution of body fat from the periphery to the centre which occurs with increasing age (Garn and Young, 1956; Parot, 1961; Wessel et al, 1963). The technique developed over a number of years by Durnin and colleagues seems to have much to recommend it (Durnin and Taylor, 1966; Durnin and Rahaman, 1967; Durnin and Womersley, 1974). These authors recommend that the average of three skinfold measurements should be taken at the biceps, triceps, subscapular and suprailiac, and the logarithm of the sum used to calculate the body density which can be then used in the equation of Siri (1956) to derive body fat. Comparative studies have confirmed the reliability of the technique (Womersley et al, 1972; Cotes et al, 1973; Womersley et al, 1976; Yang et al, 1977).

Aging and fat/fat free mass

Body fat. Cross-sectional studies in small mammals have given rise to conflicting reports of the effect of aging on body fat stores because of differences between species depending upon the anatomical site sampled. In the Osborne-Mendel rat perirenal adipose tissue increases throughout life-span by hypertrophy (Schemmel et al, 1970) and similarly in the Fischer 344 rat where the increase in perirenal fat was shown to be due to hyperplasia of adipocytes and not hypertrophy (Bertrand et al, 1978). In the same rat, however, epididymal fat increases by hyperplasia but the increase plateaus after mid-life span (Stiles et al, 1975). In the C57B mouse epididymal fat increases into mid-life span by hypertrophy and not hyperplasia (Greenwood et al, 1970). Total fat mass in the Fischer 344 rat strain increases for the first two-thirds of the life-span, then decreases significantly (Yu and Masoro, 1978). Thus, fat changes with age in small mammals vary considerably both between species and strains and also the manner of the fat increase (hyperplasia versus hypertrophy) varies.

Numerous cross-sectional studies using different techniques have consistently demonstrated significant increase in the body fat of humans with increasing age (Brozek, 1952; Anderson and Langham, 1959; Young et al, 1963a; Burmeister and Bingert, 1967; Parizkova et al, 1971; Boddy et al, 1972a; Novak, 1972; Durnin and Womersley, 1974; Edmonds et al, 1975; Lye, 1981). These results have been confirmed in a small number of longitudinal studies, though the rates of increase of body fat are somewhat less than in longitudinal studies, indicating a secular trend in body fat change (Forbes and Reina, 1970; Parizkova and Eiselt, 1971; Chien et al, 1975).

In spite of differences in technique and subject selection, the increase in body fat that occurs in Caucasians is remarkably similar in the different studies. Thus, using the data in the studies quoted above, weighted regression coefficients can be calculated to show that, on average, healthy males and females accumulate body fat at the approximate rate of 2.8 and 3.6 kg/decade (6.2 and 8.0 lb/decade) respectively (Fig. 11.3). These results, however, cannot be applied to non-Caucasians. In studies of primitive populations no increase in body fat with age has been observed (Bourlière and Parot, 1962; Glanville and Geerdink, 1970).

Fat free mass. Few studies of the effects of aging on lean body or fat free mass have been reported for small mammals. Lesser et al (1973) report that longitudinal studies in the rat show no change in lean body mass and this was the conclusion also of Yu and Masoro (1978). However, inspection of the latter's data does suggest quite a marked decrease in lean body mass of their very old rats, though this may be a pre-terminal event. It is well recognised that small mammals kept in animal houses invariably show a sudden decline in body weight preterminally (Rowlatt et al, 1976). In this case it would indeed be surprising if such mammals did not show some loss of lean body mass.

In the human, the situation is more clear. The majority of studies (for references see above) show a consistent decline in lean body or fat free mass with increasing age (Fig. 11.4). Even in primitive populations who demonstrate no increase in body fat because body weight tends to fall, especially in very old age, fat free mass must decrease *pari passu* (Bourlière and Parot, 1962). Moore has summed up the phenomenon pithily — 'The engine shrinks within the chassis' (Moore et al, 1963). From the literature the rate of decline in fat free mass can be calculated approximately as 2.8 kg/decade (6.2 lb/decade) in males and 1.0 kg/decade (2.2 lb/decade) in females (Fig. 11.4). Clearly men lose lean body mass at twice the rate of women and therefore sex differences in fat free mass become much less in old age because middle aged men have a higher fat free mass than similar aged women.

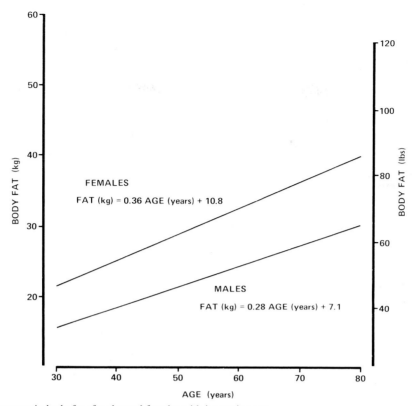

Fig. 11.3 Linear increase in body fat of males and females with increasing age

Significance of fat/fat free mass changes

The basal metabolic rate of man declines with increasing age (Boothby et al, 1936). However, if the basal metabolic rate is related to fat free mass the age effect is almost removed (Shock et al, 1963). Similarly it has been shown in cross-sectional (Robinson, 1938) and longitudinal studies (Robinson et al, 1975) that maximal oxygen consumption during exercise decreases as a function of increasing age. Miller and Blyth (1952) showed that most of this decrease in metabolic rate could be accounted for by the aging decrease in fat free mass. Later Tzankoff and Norris (1977) demonstrated that the decrease in metabolic rate could be more closely related to the decrease in muscle mass as determined from 24 hour creatinine excretion. These authors also showed that the proportion of oxygen consumption derived from non-muscle tissues (heart, liver, kidneys, brain, etc.) did not change with increasing age.

Thus, because the 'engine' of the body is shrinking, it is no surprise that physical fitness and working capacity also decline (Grimby and Saltin, 1966; Drinkwater et al, 1975; Robinson et al, 1975). The decline in physical fitness with age is less in physically active individuals (Wilmore et al, 1974; Robinson et al, 1976; Spirduso and Clifford, 1978) and can be halted or even reversed in some part by physical training (Robinson et al, 1975; Shephard, 1978; Dill et al, 1982). It is not known however whether the maintenance of physical condition preserves the engine (fat free mass) or is secondary to a decreased body fat.

Cardiac output decreases with increasing age, both at rest (Brandfonbrenner et al, 1955) and during exercise (Granath et al, 1964; Hossack and Bruce, 1982). If however the cardiac output is related to fat free mass, then the output is appropriate to the mass. This is because body fat which is increasing with age requires very little of the cardiac output for perfusion. In gerontological studies and also in geriatric practice the use of the fat free or lean body mass is likely to be a more appropriate normalising factor than body weight or body surface area. The age related accumulation of body fat has significant effects on pharmacokinetics. This phenomenon is well known to anaesthetists, especially in relation to halothane pharmacokinetics. Thus, Saraiva and colleagues (1977) demonstrated that people with higher body fat stores, measured from skinfold thick-

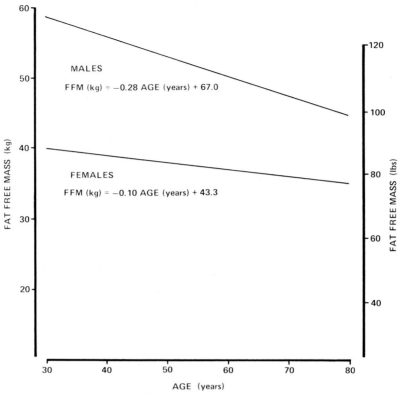

Fig. 11.4 Linear decrease in fat free mass of males and females with increasing age

nesses, had an increased intake of halothane and prolonged recovery times following halothane anaesthesia. They also found that age protected to a limited extent the effects of obesity, presumably secondary to a reduced cardiac output and hence fat perfusion with halothane. Thus the older patient is going to require more halothane to maintain a similar level of anaesthesia and is also going to take much longer to recover (Saraiva et al, 1977).

Aetiology of changes
The reason for the decrease in fat free mass and corresponding accumulation of body fat with increasing age is not obvious. Research in this area is hampered by the lack of any suitable animal model in which hypotheses can be tested. The situation is further confounded by the problem of *post hoc ergo propter hoc*, i.e. which is cause and which is effect.

Inactivity in whatever form leads to disuse atrophy (Chapter 40), and this is likely to affect muscle bulk, the main component of fat free mass. Is inactivity a consequence of increasing age? Certainly with increasing age there is a decrease in physical activity in both

mammals and healthy humans (Jones et al, 1953; Sidney and Shephard, 1977). Even in individuals continuing physical training into extreme old age, there is an inevitable reduction in physical fitness and fat free mass with increasing age (Grimby and Saltin, 1966). Alternatively, does the loss of lean body mass cause the decrease in physical fitness (Hossack and Bruce, 1982)? Does the decrease in cardiac output lead to muscle anoxia and hence reduction in fat free mass or is the decrease in cardiac output secondary to the reduced demands of a fat free mass? What are the roles of subnutrition or pathological processes? Before answers to these questions can be formulated more longitudinal studies of body composition need to be carried out. With the advent of non-toxic, non-invasive methods for measuring body composition such studies should be pursued in the near future.

Body compartments
Classical teaching divides the body fluid (total body water TBW) into two primary compartments, extracellular fluid (ECF) and intracellular fluid (ICF), neatly separated by a cell wall. This somewhat simplistic divi-

sion was modified by Robinson and McCance (1952) who suggested that the two fluid compartments are, in physiochemical terms similar to two phases of an emulsion, where ECF represents the continuous phase and ICF the disperse phase, thus emphasising that ECF is a transport medium serving the metabolic needs of the ICF. The ECF can be subdivided into intravascular and extravascular components, though apart from slight protein differences the two are identical in composition.

In Figure 11.5 the classical cation/anion balance between ECF (plasma) and ICF is depicted. There are differences between the chemical composition of ECF and ICF but also some similarities. The main cation in the ECF is sodium whereas in the ICF it is mainly potassium plus magnesium. It was suggested by MacCallum (1926) that this ionic difference was related to the fact that mammals had evolved from a 'primaeval soup', though this simple evolutionary idea has been questioned by Conway (1943).

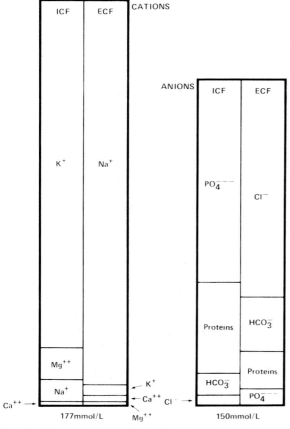

Fig. 11.5 The ionic composition of intracellular and extracellular fluids

Total body water

In view of the age changes in fat and fat free mass proportions discussed above it would be surprising if TBW did not fall with increasing age. However, studies have reported variable results. Thus, Edelman and colleagues (1952) and Shock et al, (1963) using antipyrine to measure TBW, report significant age decrements. Similarly Olbrich and Woodford-Williams (1956) reported a decrease in TBW but this was quite small. Young and colleagues (1963b) reported an overall average decrease with increasing age but there was considerable intersubject variation. Steele and colleagues (1950) found no significant decrease. Two recent studies from Scandinavia are pertinent. In a longitudinal study Steen et al, (1979) found that 70-year-old healthy, elderly subjects showed a decrease in TBW measured with tritiated water over 5 year intervals. Thus, males and females decrease by 3.0 and 2.0 litres respectively, whilst body weight decreased by 2.9 and 1.7 kg (6.4 and 3.7 lb) respectively over the same period. In a larger cross-sectional study of healthy elderly subjects (N = 134 males and 342 females), the same group reported that TBW decreased but in relation to body weight changed but little (Bruce et al, 1980). These studies suggest that TBW does decrease significantly with increasing age, but this is inkeeping with loss of body tissue (fat free mass) and does not represent a form of aging 'dehydration'. The decrease in TBW is more rapid before 50 years of age than after.

Intra and extracellular fluids. In the early days of body composition study it was thought that ECF increased with age (Lowry and Hastings, 1952) and then Shock and colleagues (1963) demonstrated from their own and other workers' data that there was no significant change in ECF after the age of 40 years though TBW continued to decrease (Fig. 11.6). Inspection of Table 11.1 reveals that the decrease in TBW occurs over the whole adult age range but is much steeper before the fifth decade than after due to a marked reduction in rate of loss of ECF after this age. After the fifth decade no

Table 11.1 Total body water (TBW), extracellular fluid (ECF) and intracellular fluid (ICF) by age group. (Calculated from the data of Shock et al, 1963. Weighted averages.)

Age (years)	TBW(L)	ECF(L)	ICF(L)	ECF/ICF
20–29	39.8	16.0	23.8	.67
30–39	38.3	13.9	24.4	.57
40–49	34.7	12.0	22.7	.53
50–59	35.0	12.4	22.6	.55
60–69	32.9	11.4	21.5	.53
70–79	31.6	11.8	19.8	.60
80–89	30.8	11.8	19.0	.62
90–99	30.1	11.4	18.7	.61

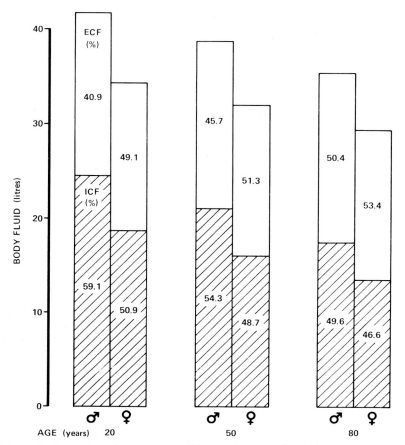

Fig. 11.6 Effects of age on absolute and relative proportions of intra and extracellular fluid values in men and women

further change occurs in ECF so that the decrease in TBW is accounted for by loss of ICF (Fig. 11.6).

Bruce and colleagues (1980) used tritiated water to measure TBW and derived ICF from whole body or exchangeable potassium measurements. They confirmed the trends in ECF and ICF found in the earlier non-isotopic studies. Their results differ slightly from the earlier reports, probably because the thiocyanate method of measuring ECF tends to overestimate the true value. Thus, the ratio ECF:ICF is slightly higher in the Scandinavian (Steen et al, 1979; Bruce et al, 1980) studies but the trends with age are of the same order as depicted in Table 11.1.

Blood/plasma volume
Both the total blood volume and plasma volume in healthy man are remarkably constant in spite of varying salt intake and cardiovascular activity (Strauss et al, 1958). There is no evidence of any systematic change in blood volumes with increasing age (Gibson and Evans, 1937; Cohn and Shock, 1949). Chien et al, (1966)

confirmed the earlier cross-sectional studies in a 16–17 year longitudinal follow up study. Because the ECF is not greatly affected by age beyond the 50's it can be assumed that the extravascular component of the ECF is not affected by age. A constant blood volume gives stability and is important for optimum performance of the circulatory system.

Regulation of body fluids
There are a number of mechano-volume (pressoreceptors and volume) receptors located throughout the vascular tree. The main receptors are located within the thorax (Epstein et al, 1972; Paintal, 1973; Epstein, 1976), arterial tree (baroreceptors) (Keeler, 1974) and in the kidneys (Burnett and Knox, 1980). Any decrease in volume sensed by these receptors is followed by a prompt increase in renal reabsorption of sodium. Similarly an increase in blood volume causes sodium excretion. The renal response is brought about by changes in glomerular filtration rate (de Wardener et al, 1961), aldosterone and angiotensin II (Johnson and

Malvin, 1977; Young and Guyton, 1977). Changes in volume or pressure also control the secretion of renin and arginine vasopressin (AVP), the latter is also under the control of plasma osmolarity, see below. For an excellent discussion of body fluid homeostasis the reader is referred to the review by Skorecki and Brenner (1981). As yet there are no reported studies of the effects of aging on these neurohumoral control systems, but it seems that those mechanisms which do show age-related effects, e.g. the arterial tree and kidney (see appropriate chapters in this volume) must be compensated by other mechanisms not affected by aging.

Blood constituents

The ionic composition of the ICF and ECF differ considerably (Fig. 11.5), but in clinical practice the composition of the ECF is assumed to be in equilibrium with the intravascular compartment and this is used in the assessment of overall electrolyte homeostasis, both in health and disease. The ionic differences between the ECF and ICF are maintained by energy dependent processes operating in the cell wall. The integrity of the cell wall is not impaired by aging unaccompanied by disease. Any difference found in old people in the ionic concentrations of ICF and ECF are likely to be due to latent or overt pathological processes or secondary to the action of drugs (Hodkinson, 1977).

Electrolytes

Sodium. The normal range of serum sodium does not change with increasing age in healthy individuals (Roberts, 1967; Leask et al, 1973; Bold and Wilding, 1975). There is however a small but significant increase in serum sodium round the time of the menopause (Wilding et al, 1972). Values in elderly hospitalised patients tend to be lower than age-matched healthy controls, though a few patients may exhibit hypernatraemia (Hodkinson, 1977).

Potassium. A number of cross sectional reports have stated that the mean value of serum or plasma potassium in healthy adults does not change with increasing age (Leask et al, 1973; Bold and Wilding, 1975; Hodkinson, 1977). However, Wilding et al (1972) in their survey of 4800 healthy individuals did demonstrate a systematic trend with age (Fig. 11.7 and 11.8). Their figures are in very good agreement with the results published by Leask and colleagues (1973) who confined their measurements to healthy individuals over the age of 65 years living in the community. Support for the idea that the serum potassium, especially in men, tends to rise with increasing age is provided by Hodkinson (1977). He showed that serum potassium levels are lower in ill old people compared with healthy age-matched controls. Thus, if unrecognized disease in the healthy populations studied was operating then the age-trend would be

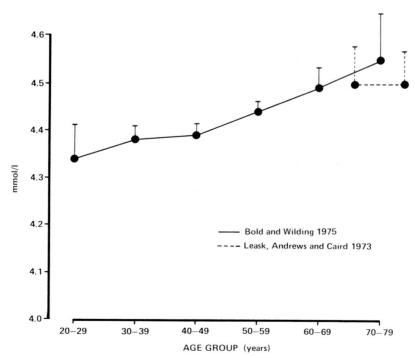

Fig. 11.7 Age changes in serum potassium of healthy males

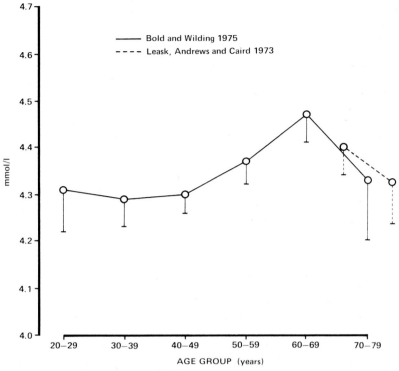

Fig. 11.8 Age changes in serum potassium of healthy females

towards a decrease and not an increase in serum potassium. The acute rise and fall in serum potassium around the menopause is unexplained though may be related to the simultaneous increase in blood urea and creatinine occurring at the same time.

Collection of blood specimens for the measurement of potassium requires care because the flux of the cation between red cells and plasma or serum is extremely labile. Thus haemolysis, prolonged storage and even minimal muscle exercise may lead to spurious results (Brown et al, 1970). Because elderly individuals may have poor superficial vein filling with difficulty in obtaining samples there is a tendency to perform forearm exercise before venepuncture which would lead to abnormally high values of serum potassium, perhaps even masking true hypokalaemia. Serum levels of potassium are slightly higher than plasma levels (Bold and Wilding, 1975) but, because the latter are less reliable, they are to be preferred in the research situation (Brown et al, 1970).

Chloride and bicarbonate. Measurements of the serum chloride and bicarbonate levels have shown no consistent trends with increasing age in healthy populations (Leask et al, 1973; Bold and Wilding, 1975; Hodkinson, 1977). Thus, the normal ranges applicable to young adults (98–108 and 22–26 mmol/l (mEq/l)

respectively) should be used for assessment of elderly subjects and patients.

Urea and creatinine. In general the blood urea is reported consistently to increase with increasing age in both sexes, though average values in women are lower than in men (Roberts, 1967; Keating et al, 1969; Wilding et al, 1972; Leask et al, 1973). There is an accelerated increase in blood urea of women around the menopause but in contradistinction to potassium it does not decline thereafter (Roberts, 1967; Wilding et al, 1972). Thus, the sex difference is negligible in the elderly. The approximate upper level for blood urea in elderly individuals (>65 years of age) in both sexes is 10.0 mmol/l (60 mg/100 ml). It is necessary to realise that blood urea is log normally distributed and mean values and normal ranges have been determined on the transformed values. This is particularly relevant in the consideration of ranges for hospital patients (Leask et al, 1973; Denham et al, 1975).

The serum creatinine follows the same pattern as urea with age. However, the sex difference is greater and the rise with age much less than that which occurs with the blood urea (Wilding et al, 1972; Leask et al, 1973). The upper limits for serum creatinine are given in Table 11.2. Whilst blood urea and serum creatinine are both related to renal function and in particular the glomerular

Table 11.2 Normal ranges for serum creatinine

	Age (Years)	
	65–74	75+
mmol/L		
Males	0.06–0.14	0.06–0.15
Females	0.04–0.12	0.04–0.14
mg/100 ml		
Males	0.65–1.60	0.70–1.70
Females	0.50–1.40	0.50–1.60

filtration rate, the relationship in *healthy individuals* is not very precise. Thus, urea and particularly creatinine measurements are influenced by the dietary intake of protein, the general state of catabolism and previous exercise. The attenuated increase in creatinine with age compared with that of urea can be attributed to these factors plus the reduction in lean body mass discussed previously (Rowe et al, 1976). The net result of these changes to some extent invalidates the use of serum creatinine as a measure of renal function in old people. Similarly it has been shown to be a poor predictor of dehydration in ill old people (Bahemuka et al, 1974).

Plasma proteins. Proteins in the plasma consist of three main groups determined electrophoretically. These are albumin, a heterogeneous group of globulins, and fibrinogen. The effects of aging on the absolute and relative amounts in the plasma vary between these groups. All are affected to some extent by virtually any pathological process and may be used as indicators of general health or otherwise.

Albumin. This low molecular weight protein is synthesized in the liver and provides colloid oncotic pressure within the intravascular space. Approximately 10 per cent per diem is destroyed and replaced. A number of surveys have shown that the absolute and relative concentrations of albumin fall with increasing age in healthy individuals (Rafsky et al, 1952; Karel et al, 1956; Keating et al, 1969; Hodkinson, 1977). Wilding et al (1972) showed significant sex differences up to the fifth decade with little difference thereafter. Levels in both sexes decreased throughout adult life. The average rate of decline from these studies is approximately 0.085 g/100 ml/year. Therefore the normal range for healthy elderly of both sexes is 38–46 g/l (3.8–4.6 g/100 ml) between 65 and 74 years and 35–42 g/l (3.5–4.2 g/100 ml) over the age of 75 years. Leask and colleagues (1973) comment that no decline in albumin occurred in subjects over the age of 65 years. Their values are however in general agreement with those quoted by other workers and within the suggested normal range quoted here.

As well as providing the intravascular colloid pressure albumin has a minor role in buffering pH changes. It may be speculated that the aging decrease in albumin

may make the elderly individual less efficient at keeping fluid in the vascular tree. This may partly explain the propensity of old people to develop immobility oedema so readily. The reduction in blood buffering ability has not been studied in detail. Albumin also acts as an important transport medium for compounds such as calcium, exogenous drugs and less importantly for cortisol and thyroid hormones. Thus, salicylates and phenylbutazone are strongly bound to albumin so that alterations in albumin concentration will greatly affect the amount of unbound metabolically active drugs (Wallace et al, 1976). Lewis and colleagues (1971) found that the high incidence of side-effects of prednisolone in the elderly could be largely explained by the lower albumin levels and thus binding of the drug. Recently this simple relationship has been questioned by Steele et al (1982) who studied in detail the pharmacokinetics of prednisolone binding in serum. Their conclusion that transcortin was more important than albumin in binding the steroid requires confirmation.

Globulins. The plasma globulins represent a heterogeneous group of proteins which include a group (γ globulins) of immunoglobulins IgA, IgG and IgM (see Chapter 5). No aging studies of the individual subsets of globulins have been reported in detail. The remaining globulins act as transport for various hormones, cholesterol, triglycerides, iron, etc. Aging has less effect overall on the globulins than it has on albumin. Thus Rafsky and colleagues (1952), Karel et al, (1956) and Roberts (1967) reported significant age increases, especially in the α_2 components. However, later workers have been able to demonstrate little if any change with increasing age (Wilding et al, 1972; Leask et al, 1973; Bold and Wilding, 1975). Hodkinson (1977) demonstrated a quite marked increase in total globulins with ill health and this probably explains the earlier results in that the authors did not screen their subjects to exclude minor degrees of pathology.

Fibrinogen. This high molecular weight protein is a precursor of fibrin in clots and the main determinant of the erythrocyte sedimentation rate in man (Lorand, 1965). Fibrinogen levels increase steadily with increasing age in healthy individuals (Cotton et al, 1968), though levels tend to plateau in extreme old age (Hamilton et al, 1974). These changes have no significant effect on blood coagulation. The relationship between age and erythrocyte sedimentation rate is discussed in a subsequent chapter of this book (Chapter 41).

Calcium. With age there is a tendency for the serum calcium to fall along with levels of 1,25-dihydrocholecalciferol and calcitonin whilst alkaline phosphatase levels tend to increase. There are a number of reasons for these changes and not all are due to direct effects of aging. Thus the rise in alkaline phosphatase is almost undoubtedly due to poor screening of populations for diseases. The regulation of calcium is complex and involves the gastrointestinal system, the liver, the kidneys, bone tissue and the parathyroid glands (Fig. 11.9). Behavioural patterns have important effects on calcium homeostasis. For example, the dietary intake of calcium and vitamin D and exposure to sunlight can alter over the long-term the levels of calcium within the blood and bones (Exton-Smith, 1971). The ability to measure various components within this complex chain (Fig. 11.9) has only been available within the last decade or so and few studies have looked at the effects of aging on various components of the system in healthy individuals.

The serum calcium tends to fall in healthy adults with increasing age, the fall in women being greater than that in men. The sex difference is presumably secondary to the effects of the menopause and loss of the oestrogenic stimulus to calcium absorption (Roberts, 1967; Keating et al, 1969; Reed et al, 1972; Leask et al, 1973). There is however some variation between these and other surveys, probably due in some cases to inadequate screening to ensure health status. As Roof and colleagues (1976) have shown there are marked differ-ences in serum calcium related to ethnic origin that cannot be explained by differences in sunlight exposure. It should be recalled that in the serum 50 per cent of calcium is bound to the plasma proteins including albumin, 5 per cent is bound to citrate, etc and only 45 per cent is ionized and therefore metabolically active. In the light of the changes in serum proteins, described above, age changes in total calcium may in part be explained by changes in these variables. Hodkinson (1977) has suggested a correction factor for these par-ameters which should be adopted more widely:

Corrected calcium (mmol/l) = serum calcium (mmol/l) − (Albumin (g/1) = 0.01833) − (globulin (g/1) = 0.00639)

All workers are agreed however that the first metabolite of cholecalciferol, 25-hydroxycholecalciferol is reduced in healthy elderly either as a result of malabsorption of the vitamin (Ackermann and Toro, 1953; Epstein et al, 1973; Ireland and Fordtran, 1973) or secondary to impaired hepatic metabolism (Bullamore et al, 1970; Stamp and Round, 1974; Brown et al, 1976; Morris and Peacock, 1976; Rushton, 1978; Gallagher et al, 1979; Baker et al, 1980). It has been demonstrated that the

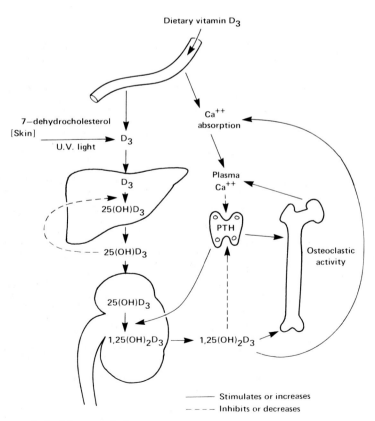

Fig. 11.9 Homeostatic control of calcium metabolism

serum level of 25-hydroxycholecalciferol exhibits a marked variation throughout the year with the nadir being reached in later winter and early spring (Stamp et al, 1976). This seasonal pattern is related to sunlight exposure both in young (Haddad and Hahn, 1973; Preece et al, 1975) and old individuals (Hodkinson et al, 1973; Lawson et al, 1979; Baker et al, 1980; Johnson et al, 1980). The plasma levels of the final active metabolite of cholecalciferol, 1,25-dihydroxycholecalciferol (Norman, 1974) also fall with age. The reduction is due to both reductions in its precursor, 25-hydroxycholecalciferol and subsequent impairment in renal conversion directly due to renal ageing (see below) (Deluca, 1975; Lund et al, 1975; Gallagher et al, 1979).

There are two final hormones concerned in calcium homeostasis which need to be considered in relationship to aging. Parathormone has a central role in regulation of calcium homeostasis (Fig. 11.9). The hormone is acutely sensitive to even minor changes in the serum ionised calcium. Thus, a 1 per cent drop in serum calcium will lead to a doubling of the parathormone output. The increase in serum parathormone will stimulate conversion of stored cholecalciferol within the liver into 25-hydroxycholecalciferol and then this metabolite is converted within the kidney into 1,25-dihydroxycholecalciferol which directly enhances intestinal absorption of cholecalciferol and calcium. Parathormone also stimulates osteoclastosis and the mobilisation of calcium from bone. Similarly parathormone increases renal tubular reabsorption of calcium and increasing renal excretion of phosphate. Thus, parathormone is uniquely placed to act as the conductor of the calcium orchestra (Guyton, 1976).

It is only in the last decade that the immunological assay of parathormone has become generally available (Arnaud et al, 1971) and surprisingly few studies of the elderly are reported. In 1972 Fujita and colleagues showed that age was associated with a decrease in parathormone in both males and females whereas Berlyne and colleagues (1975) showed the opposite effect in a population of young army cadets and nursing students compared with elderly residents of an old person's home. As the authors point out the latter group showed some significant degrees of osteoporosis and could not be considered healthy. Wiske and colleagues (1979) comparing similar groups again demonstrated significant age increases in parathormone levels. However, residents in old person's homes have limited access to sunlight and this factor would undoubtedly stimulate parathormone secretion. A final study (Roof et al, 1976) was unable to define consistent age effects on parathormone levels. This study is important because it used a specific immunoassay which only measured the active moiety of parathormone whereas the other studies used less specific methods which measure the inactive C-terminal

fragment which is more a reflection of the aging kidney's ability to excrete breakdown products than levels of the active hormone (Freitag et al, 1978). In an elegant study of parathyroidectomized male Wistar rats Kalu and colleagues (1982) have recently demonstrated a marked age-related attenuation of the calcium mobilizing action from bone of exogenous parathormone. This effect was not a consequence of renal dysfunction in the aged rats and they are unable to offer any explanation for their observation. A similar age effect in rats was reported for calcitonin by Hirsch and Munson (1969). They demonstrated that the diminished effectiveness of calcitonin to lower serum calcium was not compensated by the higher circulating levels found by them and others (Roos et al, 1978). In humans, calcitonin levels are higher in men and fall progressively with increasing age in both sexes (Deftos et al, 1980). These authors who studied well screened healthy individuals were also able to demonstrate a marked age related modulation of the calcitonin response to an infusion of 3 mg/kg calcium over 10 minutes. This finding confirmed a previous report of a lack of effectiveness of exogenous calcitonin in osteopaenia in the elderly (Care and Duncan, 1967). Deftos and colleagues (1980) speculated that the progressive calcitonin 'deficiency' with aging may be an aetiological factor in the development of osteopaenia in the elderly. However, this is unlikely as calcitonin only has very weak action in the healthy human (Guyton, 1976) compared with its potent action in other species (Watts et al, 1975; Roos et al, 1978; Deftos et al, 1979).

The serum alkaline phosphatase is used as a measure of bone turnover activity. Many earlier surveys showed significant increases in serum alkaline phosphatase with increasing age (Hobson and Jordan, 1959; Roberts, 1967; Keating et al, 1969; Reed et al, 1972; Sharland, 1972; Wilding et al, 1972; Leask et al, 1973). However, as shown by Hazell and Ortiz in 1966 and subsequently confirmed by Hodkinson and McPherson (1973) if the study population is very carefully screened to exclude the myriad other causes of a raised serum alkaline phosphatase (liver disease, Paget's disease, malignant bone deposits, etc.) no age effects can be demonstrated. Thus, it can be concluded that serum alkaline phosphatase does not rise in healthy people with increasing age and the normal range applicable to young individuals can continue to be used in the elderly.

The control of calcium homeostasis is very complex involving several hormonal control systems operating through a chain of enzymatic reactions involving several organ systems. The effects of aging on this system are not precisely delineated because of the problems of subject selection and difficulties in the assay of active hormones and intermediate metabolic products. At present the main significant effects of aging seem to be in the hydroxylation of cholecalciferol to 25-hydroxycholecalciferol in the liver (Rushton, 1978) and subsequent metabolism within the kidney to the active hormone 1,25-dihydroxycholecalciferol (Bullamore et al, 1970; Lund et al, 1975; Gallagher et al, 1978; Gallagher et al, 1979). The relationship of these biochemical age changes to the development of osteopaenia and osteoporosis in the elderly remains as obscure as it was in 1968 when Newton-John and Morgan concluded that these conditions represent a spectrum of aging. Subsequent work has not altered this concept though future studies may lead to a better understanding of age effects on calcium homeostasis which in turn may suggest better treatment for the severe forms of accelerated aging-osteopaenia and osteoporosis (Lund et al, 1975).

Acid base balance

In health the hydrogen ion content of the arterial blood, usually measured as pH, is kept constant in spite of changes in acid load produced by many metabolic processes and exercise — the normal range being between 36 and 43 mmol/l (pH 3.45 to 3.35) (Bold and Wilding, 1975). This resting basal level is the same in healthy elderly individuals as in youth (Shock and Yiengst, 1950). Acid base balance is regulated by rapidly acting changes in respiration and longer term adjustment is by renal excretory mechanisms (Guyton, 1976). Disturbances in acid base balance may be produced by primary changes in respiration, i.e. increased ventilation leading to respiratory alkalosis and vice versa producing respiratory acidosis. Acid loads from excess catabolism or exercise lead to primary metabolic acidosis: loss of acid, often in the elderly from gastrointestinal fluid losses, leads to primary metabolic alkalosis. In the clinical situation however it is unusual to have a single primary disturbance of acid base balance since the response of the body to such a primary disturbance is towards compensation by the unaffected system. Thus, a primary metabolic acidosis due to renal failure is in part compensated by a secondary respiratory alkalosis brought about by increased ventilation in response to the lowered pH. Thus, the interpretation of changes in acid base balance and pH require a consideration of the clinical circumstances and reliance upon laboratory results in isolation is fraught with danger.

Moderate exercise imposes an acid load on the body from working muscles, which, if the exercise becomes severe enough, may be supplemented by a lactic acid load due to utilisation of the pyruvate lactate anaerobic shunt. There is some evidence that the healthy elderly take longer to clear this metabolic load after exercise than young individuals (Dill et al, 1966; Bouhuys et al, 1966). Whether the elderly produce more acid for the same exercise stress as young people is not known. It is likely because the aging decrease in cardiac output and blood distribution to muscle should lead to anoxia at an earlier stage during exercise and thus more lactic acid should be generated. Unfortunately it is difficult to control for the effects of training and physical fitness when comparing age effects on aerobic or anaerobic metabolism. Considerable changes in the anatomy and physiology of mammalian and human lungs occur with healthy aging, such that the mechanical efficiency (oxygen cost of breathing) of the aged person's pulmonary system is significantly decreased when compared with the young individual (Norris et al, 1956; Briscoe and Dubois, 1958; Briscoe et al, 1959; Cohn and Donoso, 1963; Turner et al, 1968; Milne and Williamson, 1972; Ashley et al, 1974; Lye, 1975; Knudson et al, 1977; Colebatch et al, 1979; Mauderly, 1979). It is therefore not surprising that the ventilatory response to an acid load usually produced experimentally by increasing P_{CO_2} via rebreathing, is altered by increasing age. Kronenberg and Drage (1973) and Altose and colleagues (1977) found a 41 per cent and 33 per cent decrease in ventilatory response to CO_2 comparing young and elderly subjects, both decreases being significant. However, Patrick and Howard (1972) found only a non-significant decrease of 6 per cent and in a similar study Rubin et al, (1982) reported a 19 per cent non-significant decrease. Both authors point out that the differences between these studies can be largely accounted for by variability within the young controls due to differing degrees of athletic training. Thus, the ventilatory response to CO_2, ($\delta \dot{V}/\delta CO_2$, l/min/mmHg) of elderly subjects is remarkably constant between studies. The overall average being 2.39 ± 0.45 l/min/mmHg. The finding that the mouth pressure generated during airway occlusion (a measure of neuronal ventilatory drive) does not change with increasing age implies that any alteration with age in response to CO_2 is a function of lung mechanical changes and is not due to changes in sensitivity of chemodetectors or output of 'respiratory centres' (Rubin et al, 1982).

There have been studies of the ability of the aging kidneys to respond to changes in acid-base equilibrium. The only valid study is that of Adler and colleagues (1968) who challenged healthy individuals between the ages of 10 and 90 years with ammonium chloride and measured the rate of excretion of acid. They found that young people eliminated 35 ± 6 per cent of the acid load within 8 hours, whilst the elderly only excreted 18 ± 5 per cent over the same period. The correction of the arterial pH change was accomplished in 6–8 hours by the young and required 18–24 hours in the elderly. In large part the differences between young and old can be accounted for by reduced glomerular filtration due to aging nephron loss.

In the clinical sphere it is important that acid base function be closely monitored in ill old people because general principles and clinical experience suggest that the elderly tolerate such disturbances less than younger patients. It is also important not to be too enthusiastic in correcting pH disturbances, especially metabolic acidosis by the injudicious use of fluids. Correction of the underlying cause of the disturbance usually resolves the problem. Only with life threatening acidosis is direct correction with bicarbonate warranted. The usual formula used to calculate bicarbonate requirements in metabolic acidosis [$(25 - HCO_3) \times 0.5$ body weight (kg)] provides excess replacement. The formula proposed by Hazard and Griffin (1982) [$(0.5 \, P_{CO_2} - HCO_3^-) \times 0.5$ body weight] is much preferable in geriatric practice.

DISTURBANCES OF HOMEOSTASIS IN THE ELDERLY

The aging changes discussed so far in this chapter assume greater importance when the individual is stressed. The most important stress in an elderly subject from a clinical point of view is that produced by disease, the incidence of which itself increases with increasing age. As a consequence of this interaction between a fertile soil (the aged body) and a common seed (age-related disease), some health services have developed the specialty of geriatric medicine where both aspects of disordered function can be given due consideration. The interaction of disease and aging forms the bulk of the presentations in this book and the reader should consult the appropriate chapter. There are however two important areas of age-impaired homeostasis not covered in systematic reviews — salt and water homeostasis and potassium balance.

Fluid balance

Whilst fluid imbalance in middle-aged adults is not uncommon in surgical and medical practice there is a marked increase in both frequency and severity with increasing age of the patient. Thus, surgeons and physicians dealing with the aged see dehydration as a most important aspect of homeostatic impairment. Fluid balance requires the complex integration of several control systems ranging from psychological aspects of intake to renal excretion. The effect of aging upon renal function is discussed in Chapter 29 and will not be covered in great detail here. Elderly subjects with arthritis, stroke, etc. may have an inadequate fluid intake because of immobility leading to dehydration. Difficulty of communication may potentiate the problem. It has long been thought that the sensation of thirst may be decreased in the elderly and recently this clinical suspicion has been confirmed. Miller and colleagues (1982) recently demonstrated marked hypodipsia in six elderly patients with cerebrovascular

disease. None of the patients was aphasic or immobilised and likewise there was no evidence of hypothalamic or pituitary dysfunction and all were mentally alert. Despite access to fluids *ad libitum* all patients manifested significant hypernatraemia, plasma and urine hyperosmolality and volume depletion. No patient complained of thirst and the electrolytes of all responded to the prescription of fluid on a regular basis. Recently Phillips and colleagues (1983) have reported similar results in healthy elderly volunteers subjected to water deprivation. Thus, it can be concluded that the 'thirst mechanism' is significantly impaired with increasing age.

The neurohumoral control of sodium and water balance is complex and is still incompletely understood (for review see Bie, 1980 and Skorecki and Brenner, 1981). Renin is secreted by the juxtaglomerular apparatus of the kidney in response to decreased sodium delivery to the macula densa, decrease in renal blood pressure/flow, reduction in plasma potassium or a neurogenic or neurohumoral mechanism. There is good evidence that renin output by the kidney following sodium restriction is impaired in healthy subjects over the age of 60 years (Weidmann et al, 1975; Crane and Harris, 1976; Noth et al, 1977). The secretion of aldosterone by the adrenal zona glomerulosa is largely modulated by renin via angiotensin II. It is not surprising therefore that the stress-related output of aldosterone is also decreased with increasing age (Sambhi et al, 1973; Crane and Harris, 1976).

Arginine vasopressin (AVP) secreted by the hypothalamus in response to increases in osmolality acts on the distal renal tubules via cyclic AMP to increase water resorption (Vandersande et al, 1974; Handler and Orloff, 1981). AVP is probably the most sensitive regulator of water balance in man (Morgan and Thomas, 1979). Vernay (1946, 1948) was the first to introduce the concept of an osmoreceptor which sets a threshold for AVP release, which thereafter is linearly related to extracellular osmolality or tonicity (Hammer et al, 1980). The sensitivity of the system is such that urine flow can be halved or doubled by a one per cent change in plasma osmolality (Robertson et al, 1976; Morgan and Thomas, 1979). The osmoreceptor itself is not altered by osmolality but by changes in effective plasma volume (DeFronzo et al, 1976; Riegger et al, 1982). A decrease in plasma volume lowers the osmostat so that AVP is secreted at a much lower osmolality. The volume response overrides the osmolality control. Unfortunately there are few studies in man of the effects of aging on the AVP system.

Miller and Shock (1953) using an impure preparation of AVP, synthetic pitressin, demonstrated a significantly attenuated renal response to the hormone in old people. Later the same laboratory (Lindeman et al, 1966) showed that much of the reduced renal response to exogenous pitressin could be accounted for by the diminished renal maximal concentrating ability, this observation has subsequently been confirmed (Manson and Richards, 1968; Cowley et al, 1981) (see below). Posterior pituitary stores of AVP in rodents have been shown to decrease with age (Dunihue, 1965; Watkins and Choy, 1980; Sladek et al, 1981) but the opposite effect has been claimed to occur in humans (Robertson et al, 1979). As Wilkinson and Davies (1981) point out marked species differences make interpretation of quantitative histochemical data difficult. Measurements of AVP in the plasma of human subjects have given rise to conflicting reports. Thus, Helderman and colleagues (1978) using a sensitive AVP assay demonstrated that in their elderly subjects the suppression of AVP by alcohol was blunted whilst the response to saline was steeper than in young subjects. Robertson and Rowe (1980) showed that the increase in AVP response to head-up tilt was lower in old subjects. Seybold and Gessler (1981) claimed lower levels of basal AVP and a reduced response to stress in older subjects.

The different responses can be accounted for by the different stresses used in these experiments and the use of non-specific assay methods for AVP. The findings in the author's own laboratory using sensitive and specific radioimmunoassay methods have demonstrated that healthy old people have higher basal levels of AVP than younger subjects under identical conditions (Kirkland et al, 1983, unpublished observations). Similarly dehydration of elderly patients leads to a similar response of AVP as would be expected in younger dehydrated patients. Finally, Vargas and Lye (1983, unpublished observations) have demonstrated no difference between young and elderly healthy subjects in the AVP response to head-up tilt. The tentative conclusion therefore is that basal AVP levels in plasma probably rise with age and the response to stress is at least unaltered. Lack of effectiveness of AVP first demonstrated in 1953 by Miller and Shock is probably due to renal impairment in sensitivity to AVP or to a diminished capacity of the kidney to respond.

Hypernatraemia

Hypernatraemia, usually defined as a serum sodium concentration of more than 145 mmol(mEq)/l or a serum osmolality greater than 290 mosmol/kg, may be due to an increased body sodium or an absolute or relative decrease in body water (Bay and Ferris, 1976). Clinically the commonest cause of hypernatraemia is absolute water lack. In many cases this is associated with obvious excessive fluid loss. Thus, fluids lost from the gastrointestinal tract, acute or chronic diarrhoea, may be insufficiently replaced. A high solute load on the kidney as produced by uncontrolled diabetes mellitus and glycosuria soon leads to dehydration and hyperna-

traemia. Other causes of dehydration may be more subtle. Thus, the increased ventilation produced by respiratory infections in the elderly leads to excess fluid loss from the lungs which may further be exacerbated by pyrexia and sweating. Similarly, steroid therapy by increasing protein catabolism leads to increased urea production which provides another high renal solute load.

As detailed above the elderly are particularly at risk of becoming dehydrated and not replacing fluid loss because of age-related diminution in the thirst threshold (Miller et al, 1982; Phillips et al, 1983). Equally the kidney's ability to conserve water becomes impaired with age. Cross-sectional studies have shown considerable age-related reductions in renal blood flow and glomerular filtration rate (Lewis and Alving, 1938; Hollenberg et al, 1974; McLachlan, 1978; Epstein, 1979). Rowe and colleagues (1976) have confirmed in a longitudinal study that the creatinine clearance adjusted for body surface area in healthy individuals aged between 40 and 100 years falls by approximately 5 per cent per decade. They also noticed an increasing variability in creatinine clearances with increasing age. Of particular importance in the maintenance of body fluid is the ability to increase urinary concentration. Lewis and Alving (1938) found that the mean urinary specific gravity in healthy subjects in their ninth decade was 1.024 after 24 hours fluid restriction while in subjects in their fifth decade it was 1.029. They reported a 5 per cent per decade cross-sectional decline in maximum urinary concentration after age 40. Similar results were found in a longitudinal study (Rowe et al, 1976). This decreasing ability to conserve water can in part be corrected by exogenous AVP (Miller and Shock, 1953; Lindeman et al, 1966; Manson and Richards, 1968; Cowley et al, 1981).

The elderly are also more likely than the young to develop nephrogenic diabetes insipidus because of the age-related change in kidney function (Bay and Ferris, 1976). In the elderly diabetes insipidus is usually nephrogenic in origin though classical pituitary diabetes insipidus is also seen. The differentiation and the causes of hypernatraemia in an elderly patient is usually quite straightforward. Measurements of urinary osmolality or specific gravity and volume are all that are usually required (Table 11.3). Sometimes an elderly dehydrated patient may show little or no increase in urine osmolality because of inability to concentrate the urine. However, the urine output will always be low. Pituitary and nephrogenic diabetes insipidus can be separated by the response to exogenous AVP. Thus the patient with pituitary diabetes insipidus will show a response by increasing urine osmolality and decreasing urine volume. Those with the nephrogenic type will show no such change. If plasma AVP levels can be measured,

Table 11.3 Diagnosis of hypernatraemia

| | | Urinary | |
		Osmolality	Volume
Dehydration		↑	↓
Solute load	Diabetes insipidus	↑	↑
Pituitary		↓	↑
Nephrogenic		↓	↑

then low or absent levels would suggest a pituitary origin whereas in the nephrogenic form AVP levels tend to be high. In the elderly the fluid deprivation test (Dashe et al, 1963) or saline load (Jadresic and Maira, 1962) are too dangerous to be recommended.

The symptoms of hypernatraemia with or without ECF volume depletion are often non-specific in the early stages and are mimicked by many conditions prevalent in the elderly. Thus, the two prime symptoms, weakness and lethargy, are so common in geriatric practice as not to alert one to the presence of hypernatraemia. Severe (> 115 mmol(mEq)/1) hypernatraemia may cause drowsiness leading to coma, muscular rigidity and fits. If the hypernatraemia is due to dehydration, then symptoms may be ascribed to disease causing the dehydration. This is particularly likely to occur in elderly patients with respiratory infections. The depression of conscious level or fits demands that treatment be instituted promptly. Treatment of dehydration hypernatraemia is relatively straighforward — give water either orally or, if this is not feasible, by the intravenous route using 5 per cent dextrose. Careful monitoring of serum electrolytes, especially sodium and potassium, urine flow and central venous pressure should be carried out at frequent intervals. Prophylaxis requires the *prescription* of fluids as elderly patient will not respond to simple provision and encouragement (Miller et al, 1982). Like any other drug the nurse must ensure compliance. It is a personal view that where elderly patients are un-

Table 11.4 Aetiology of diabetes insipidus in the elderly

Pituitary	Nephrogenic
Iddiopathic	Obstructive uropathy
Tumour — metastases	Myeloma
— primary	Amyloidosis
Vascular accident	Potassium deficiency
Trauma — surgical	Hypercalcaemia
— fracture	Renal failure
Aneurysm	Hyperthyroidism
Encephalitis	Drugs — Lithium
Meningitis	
Tuberculosis	— Demeclocycline
Sarcoidosis	— Amphotericin
Guillain-Barre	— Vinblastine
	— Colchicine

able to maintain an adequate fluid intake they should be admitted to hospital. Patients with diabetes insipidus require detailed investigation bearing in mind the potential aetiologies outlined in Table 11.4

The treatment of diabetes insipidus is of the underlying cause wherever possible. Unfortunately, in geriatric practice this is unusual. Pituitary diabetes insipidus responds to AVP administered parenterally or by nasal insufflation. The new analogue 1-desaminodearginine vasopressin is less sensitizing and is now the drug of choice (Schrier and Leaf, 1981). If hypersensitivity does develop chlorpropamide and carbamazine can be tried. Nephrogenic diabetes insipidus can best be treated by reducing the ECF with salt restriction or thiazide diuretic. Contraction of the ECF enhances proximal absorption of sodium, thus reducing urinary flow and relieving to a greater or lesser extent the symptoms of polyuria. Indomethacin which acts directly on the distal tubule tends to cause excessive fluid retention and precipitate cardiac failure in the elderly.

Hyponatraemia

A diminution of serum sodium to below 135 mmol (mEq)/l represents an increase in the ratio of body water to sodium. Thus, hyponatraemia may represent a reduction in body sodium and an increase in body water (ECF), increased body sodium with a larger increase in body water or decreased body sodium with a lesser decrease in body water. Between these extremes a spectrum of conditions exists. Thus there is no one syndrome of hyponatraemia (Schwartz et al, 1957; Flear and Singh, 1973; Bay and Ferris, 1976; Berl et al, 1976). Detailed biochemical investigations of the hyponatraemic patient are usually unhelpful and much more information can be obtained by considering the biochemical abnormalities in the context of the clinical picture.

The symptoms of hyponatraemia depend on the cause, level of serum sodium and speed of development (Arieff and Guisado, 1976). Where the prime lesion is sodium depletion neurological symptoms (muscle twitching, fits, weakness) dominate and with water overload gastrointestinal symptoms (anorexia, nausea and vomiting) occur (Kennedy and Early, 1970; Demanet et al, 1971; Arieff et al, 1976). However, with severe hyponatraemia (less than 125 mmol(mEq)/1) all patients manifest neurological symptoms and signs. In the elderly confusion is the sign par excellence of hyponatraemia. Whilst there is no doubt that severe hyponatraemia is associated with increasing morbidity and mortality (Swanson and Iseri, 1958; Lipsmeyer and Ackerman, 1966; Logothetis, 1966; Arieff et al, 1976), recent work suggests that this pessimistic view may have been exaggerated (Thomas et al, 1978; Flear et al, 1981; Daggett et al, 1982).

Table 11.5 Classification of hyponatraemia

| Type | Sodium | | | Extracellular fluid volume |
	Body	Urine	Serum	
1	↓	↓*	↓↓	↓
2	↑	↓	↓	↑
3	±	↑	↓↓	± or sl ↑

* May be raised if renal lesion

The management of the hyponatraemic patient depends upon the underlying cause and whether the body sodium and ECF are increased or decreased (Table 11.5). Simple investigations and an appreciation of the clinical circumstances allow accurate differentiation into three main types. The level of serum sodium is a poor guide to the aetiology. Before embarking on the investigation of a low serum sodium factitious or pseudo-hyponatraemia needs to be excluded. Whilst laboratory errors do occur modern analytical techniques are unlikely to be in error on two separate occasions. Many patients with hyponatraemia are acutely ill and receiving intravenous fluids. It is not unknown for blood specimens to be collected downstream from a hypotonic saline or dextrose infusion giving rise to seemingly horrendous biochemical results (Berl et al, 1976; Flear et al, 1981). The concentration of sodium may be very low where there is an excess of large molecules in the plasma. This occurs because large molecules reduce the fractional water content of plasma (Waugh, 1969). In the elderly the commonest cause of pseudohyponatraemia is excess of paraproteins usually due to multiple myelomatosis (Frick et al, 1966). Occasionally hypertryglyceridaemia may be a cause (Flear et al, 1981). Severe paraproteinaemia and hyperlipidaemia may even mask hypernatraemia (Burn and Gill, 1979). In these situations a 'true' sodium level can be obtained by removing the large molecules by ultracentrifugation and measuring sodium in the clear supernatant fluid (Flear et al, 1981). Alternatively, the 'true' sodium can be measured directly with an ion-specific electrode (Swaminathan and Morgan, 1981). Severe hypoproteinaemia may lead to a reduction in the anion gap and in order to maintain electrochemical neutrality there is a compensatory fall in plasma sodium (Flear et al, 1981). This situation can be termed appropriate hyponatraemia and does not require treatment of the low sodium per se.

Classification of hyponatraemia (Table 11.5)

Type 1. Excessive loss of salt from the kidney or via extrarenal routes often leads to hyponatraemia and body depletion of sodium. In the elderly decreased renal concentrating ability (Rowe et al, 1978) tends to keep the loss of salt and water in balance making hypona-

traemia less likely. Renal diseases likely to be involved include polycystic kidneys, medullary cystic disease and nephrocalcinosis. Characteristically with renal disease the urinary sodium concentration is more than 20 mmol (mEq)/l. The more common cause of this type of hyponatraemia in the elderly is salt and fluid loss from diarrhoea, vomiting, burns and pancreatitis. Here the urinary sodium concentration is low (less than 10 mmol (mEq)/l). The depletion in ECF stimulates AVP secretion leading to water conservation and a dilutional hyponatraemia. Often the fluid losses are replaced by the patient with hypotonic or low salt fluids exacerbating the hyponatraemia. The treatment is adequate water and *salt* replacement. This can usually be achieved orally and on safety grounds is to be preferred in the elderly.

The over use of diuretics, especially of the thiazide type, or use where they are not indicated (immobility or postural oedema) may lead to hyponatraemia in the elderly. Similar results occur in young women using diuretics for slimming purposes (MacGregor et al, 1975). If there is elevation in blood urea and potassium accompanying a relatively high urine sodium output, adrenal insufficiency could be suspected as being the cause of hyponatraemia (Ahmed et al, 1967; McDonald et al, 1976). The management of these two conditions is obvious.

Type 2. Hyponatraemia may be associated with an *increase* in total body sodium accompanied by expansion of ECF. It has been known for many years that conditions most likely to lead to this situation are chronic cardiac failure, hepatic cirrhosis and nephrotic syndrome (White et al, 1953; Stein et al, 1954). In geriatric practice cardiac failure accounts for the vast majority of cases. The common factor leading to hyponatraemia in these syndromes is a reduction in effective blood volume. Thus cardiac failure is associated with reduced cardiac output, hepatic cirrhosis with decreased peripheral resistance and splanchnic pooling, whilst both cirrhosis and the nephrotic syndrome lead to hypoalbuminaemia. Reduction in effective blood volume stimulates volume receptors which override the osmoreceptors, reset the osmostat and increase the output of AVP leading to water retention inspite of a reduced plasma osmolality (DeFronzo et al, 1976; Riegger et al, 1982).

Unfortunately early measurements of AVP in congestive heart failure were inconsistent (Stein et al, 1954; Yamane, 1968; Schrier and Humphreys, 1971). The more specific radioimmunoassay methods measuring AVP in hyponatraemic patients with cardiac failure have shown that most patients have high or normal levels in the face of low plasma osmolality (Riegger et al, 1982). However, as these authors and others (Berliner and Davidson, 1957) point out the reduction in glomerular filtration rate produced by the cardiac failure itself will decrease delivery of tubular fluid to the distal diluting segment of the nephron favouring decreased urine output. As far as is known hormones apart from AVP play no role in this mechanism of fluid retention. Suppression of AVP with alcohol transiently increases urine output in many though not all patients with hyponatraemic heart failure or cirrhosis (Stein et al, 1954; Yamane, 1968; Berl et al, 1976).

The management of hyponatraemia with increased body sodium and ECF (oedema) may be difficult. Treatment of the underlying condition in order to maximize cardiac, hepatic or renal function is of paramount importance. Control of arrhythmias and perhaps long-term ionotropic agents (digoxin) may be of some benefit, but usually by this stage of cardiac failure left ventricular function is so compromised as to be unimprovable. Because total body salt and water is increased in these conditions giving salt orally or intravenously to treat the hyponatraemia can only make the situation worse (Berl et al, 1976). Restriction of water intake and perhaps also salt may help the metabolic state though this regimen finds little favour with elderly patients and cannot be continued for long. Judicious change of diuretic agent may be of benefit. The potassium sparing agents, especially amiloride, can usefully be substituted by other agents. The potassium sparing drugs are commonly associated with hyponatraemia especially in the elderly and have no benefits over and above the more potent loop diuretics (Tarssanen et al, 1981; Wan and Lye, 1980). The advantages of loop as compared with thiazide diuretics in increasing the urine osmolality and output in hyponatraemic states have recently been confirmed (Decaux et al, 1982; Szatalowicz et al, 1982). Finally, the introduction of orally active angiotensin converting enzyme (ACD) inhibitors for the treatment of cardiac failure (Turini, 1979) has proved a most useful approach in the management of metabolic problems in fluid retention diseases. By increasing renal plasma flow and reducing vascular resistance captopril enhances both glomerular filtration rate and creatinine clearance (Atkinson and Robertson, 1979). Thus captropil and other ACE inhibitors break the vicious circle in cardiac failure of decreasing urea, increasing sodium and improving heart failure (Montgomery et al, 1982).

Type 3. The association of decreased plasma sodium with an unchanged total body sodium and ECF has been termed the 'syndrome of inappropriate secretion of antidiuretic hormone (SIADH) (Bartter and Schwartz, 1967). Debate has continued since the introduction of this term as to whether the secretion of AVP is or is not appropriate to the clinical circumstances (Schrier, 1974; Berl et al, 1976; Morgan and Thomas, 1979; Flear et al, 1981). Suffice to say that AVP secretion is not only under the control of plasma osmolality, but also responds to changes in effective plasma volume (see

above). In addition, as Morgan and Thomas (1979) suggest in their hypothesis, brain cell volume may override the first two stimuli. With adequate investigation most cases of hyponatraemia will not fulfil the criteria of SIADH. SIADH is an overused term and is probably best discarded for at best it implies precision where there is none, and at worst precipitates inappropriate treatment response (Thomas et al, 1978).

Hyponatraemia without change in body salt or body fluid can be caused by a multiplicity of diseases (Table 11.6). The commonest in geriatric practice is a respiratory infection which may be viral or bacterial (Charles and Rees, 1975; Thomas et al, 1978). In most cases the hyponatraemia does not require active treatment; even in individuals with severe hyponatraemia [plasma sodium <125 mmol (mEq)/1] and symptoms fluid restriction is of doubtful value. As Thomas and colleagues (1978) point out most patients with hyponatraemia and respiratory infection correct their sodium before (i.e. <48 h) water deprivation could possibly work. In view of the dangers of dehydration in the elderly it is better to concentrate on treating the pneumonia as the best way of managing the hyponatraemia. It is not apparent why respiratory infections interfere with sodium homeostasis, though it has been suggested that the volume receptors in the left atrium are in some way induced to discharge by the respiratory infection thus stimulating AVP to produce a dilutional hyponatraemia (Morgan and Thomas, 1979).

Table 11.6 Hyponatraemia without gross disturbance of body fluid or body salt in the elderly

Respiratory infections
Malignant tumours
CNS lesions — stroke
              tumours
              meningitis
              encephalitis
              haemorrhage
              trauma
              Guillain-Barre
Stress
Drugs

Winkler and Crankshaw (1958) first described the association of bronchial carcinoma with chronic hyponatraemia. Since then other tumours including those arising from the pancreas, prostate and duodenum have been shown to cause hyponatraemia (Schwartz et al, 1957; Bartter and Schwartz, 1967; George et al, 1972; deTroyer and Demanet, 1976; Thomas et al, 1978). Bronchogenic carcinoma however is by far and away the commonest tumour causing hyponatraemia at any age. It is presumed in these cases that the malignant tissue is elaborating AVP or an AVP-like hormone and this has been confirmed in some but not all cases where AVP levels have been measured (Beardwell et al, 1975; Thomas et al, 1978). The production of AVP is usually uncontrolled but occasionally there is some feedback suppression (Padfield et al, 1976). Hyponatraemia in malignant disease is often persistent and usually associated with symptoms related to relative water overload (Arieff et al, 1976). Occasionally if the patient has consumed excess hypotonic fluids, including beer, a further drop in plasma sodium may occur precipitating a medical emergency (Daggett, 1979). In this situation urgent treatment with hypertonic saline intravenously is warranted. In the elderly this should be combined with frusemide to promote excretion of a hypotonic urine and prevent the development of cardiac failure (Hartman et al, 1973). In less urgent cases water deprivation or urea has been recommended (Decaux and Genette, 1981), though the elderly are not usually able to restrict fluids to less than the 500 ml/day required. Whilst chronic lithium has been recommended (White and Fetner, 1975) side effects limit its usefulness. Demeclocycline 600–1200 mg/day which produces a form of nephrogenic diabetes insipidus is the drug of choice, though it may lower the glomerular filtration rate and induce renal failure in the elderly (Singer and Rotenberg, 1973; Dousa and Wilson, 1974; deTroyer and Demanet, 1975).

Hyponatraemia has been discovered in numerous neurological and neurosurgical circumstances (Goldberg and Handler, 1960; Kaplan and Feigin, 1978, Lester and Nelson, 1981; Mather et al, 1981; Bouzarth and Shenkin, 1982). It is now apparent that trauma of any kind inducing stress provokes a transitory increase in AVP secretion (Moore, 1959; Cochrane et al, 1981). In neurological diseases the transient increase in AVP can be augmented by absolute recumbency as in coma (Auger et al, 1970) or intermittent pressure ventilation (Hemmer et al, 1980). In the elderly cerebrovascular accidents often cause transient hyponatraemia (Joynt et al, 1981). Rydin and Vernay recognised in 1938 that an emotional stress could inhibit diuresis. Since then pain (Moran et al, 1964) or relapse of psychotic illness (Dubovsky et al, 1973) has been shown to cause impairment of water excretion and hyponatraemia. Clinch (1982) describes an 86-year-old female patient who developed quite marked hyponatraemia — on one occasion following a bereavement and on another after a minor fall and hospital admission. Elderly patients with myxoedema may present with hyponatraemia (Discala and Kinney, 1971). It is not known whether this is due to increased stress and AVP release or low blood volume or due to hypometabolism affecting the kidney (Amidi et al, 1968; Emmanouel et al, 1974; McDonald et al, 1976). Treatment of the hypothyroid corrects the low sodium.

The management of 'stress induced' hyponatraemia is rarely a problem, especially when considered in the light of the condition causing the stress. Awareness of the problem can forestall much meddlesome investigation and potentially dangerous therapy. In clinical practice the emphasis on 'fluid balance' for the postoperative patient has allowed the pendulum to swing too far in favour of fluids. A rightful fear of excess salt in infusion therapy with the danger of precipitating heart failure (Moore, 1959) led to over reliance upon hypotonic dextrose solution. Bouzarth and Shenkin (1982) showed that by using only one litre per day of 2.5 per cent glucose in 0.45 per cent saline that the incidence of post-operative hyponatraemia on a neurosurgical unit could be reduced to zero. As Thomas and colleagues (1978) pointed out most medical cases of hyponatraemia are transient and resolve spontaneously. For persistent cases of hyponatraemia the judicious addition of sodium chloride tablets to the patient's regime is adequate. Use of hypertonic saline infusions is fraught with danger especially in the elderly (Flear et al, 1981).

Numerous drugs widely used in the elderly can cause hyponatraemia (Table 11.7) by stimulating release of AVP from the neurohypophyseal system, by potentiating the renal effects of endogenous AVP or by a combination of mechanisms (Bay and Ferris, 1976; Miller and Moses, 1976). Indomethacin and other nonsteroidal anti-inflammatory agents inhibit renal prostaglandin synthesis resulting in augmentation of AVP tubular activity and an antidiuresis (Silverstein et al, 1975). The antidiuretic activity of morphine and other narcotic agents can be reversed by narcotic antagonists which promote a diuresis (Nott and Jasinski, 1974). It is well recognized that phenothiazines may stimulate appetite, but often forgotten that they, and in particular thioridazine may also increase thirst, leading to water intoxication and a dilutional hyponatraemia (Cohen, 1956; Rao et al, 1975). Usually hyponatraemia secondary to drugs is asymptomatic, though occasionally the symptoms may be attributed to the primary disease

Table 11.7 Drugs causing hyponatraemia by stimulating release of AVP or augmenting AVP action on the kidney

	Augment AVP	Stimulate AVP
Chlorpropamide	+	+
Carbamazepine		+
Clofibrate		+
Indomethacin	+	
Narcotics		+
Amitriptyline		+
Acetaminophen	+	+
Nicotine		+
Vincristine		+

for which the drug was given. If the association is recognized, and this requires a high index of suspicion, the drug can be stopped and if necessary another drug with no effects on water homeostasis can be substituted.

Potassium homeostasis

Potassium plays a key role in many metabolic and enzymatic processes especially those involved in neuroexcitatory mechanisms and energy dependent cell membrane functions. The cation is uniquely placed within cells to perform these roles with very little potassium being extracellular. Overall body content of potassium decreases with increasing age though much of this loss can be accounted for by loss of potassium-containing cell mass, (see above). The relationship between intra and extra-cellular content is not fixed though it is controlled (Moore et al, 1954; Flear et al, 1957). Because 98 per cent of body potassium is intracellular and most metabolic functions of potassium depend upon the ratio between intra and extra-cellular content, knowledge of body content is not as important as was once thought. Thus in clinical practice knowledge of the concentration in the ECF which is the same as the plasma, is sufficient for most purposes. In very general terms a repeated plasma level of 3.0 mmol(mEq)/l in the absence of acid-base disturbance represents approximately 100–200 mmol(mEq) body loss (Kliger and Hayslett, 1978). Potassium homeostatic mechanisms operate to maintain a constant ECF concentration of potassium using the intracellular mass as a reserve or buffer.

The control of potassium homeostasis involves a number of systems which regulate distribution between extra and intra-cellular compartments and modulate urinary and faecal excretion of potassium. Thus a rise in ECF or plasma potassium increases potassium secretion by the colon (Schon et al, 1974). With a decrease in pH (acidosis) potassium migrates out of cells raising the plasma concentration and vice versa with an increase in pH (Mudge and Vislocky, 1949). The control parameter for this mechanism is probably not hydrogen ion concentration itself but the plasma bicarbonate level (Fraley and Adler, 1976). Insulin and noradrenaline both favour the transfer of potassium from the extra-cellular compartment into cells, and insulin has been used therapeutically to lower elevated plasma potassium (Andres et al, 1962; Todd and Vick, 1971). Approximately 90 per cent of potassium filtered by the glomerulus is passively reabsorbed by the proximal tubule and loop of Henle. In the distal nephron potassium is actively absorbed or secreted by an energy dependent mechanism which acts as a fine regulator of plasma potassium (Davidson et al, 1958; Malnic et al, 1966). In potassium depletion there remains an obligatory potassium excretion of 5–10 mmol(mEq)/day which cannot be reduced (Kliger and Hayslett, 1978). There is no evidence that this level changes with age (Lye, 1983 personal observation). The final mechanism by which the body can regulate potassium is via the colon, the mucosa of which acts very like the distal renal tubule actively varying potassium secretion (Berger, 1960).

Hyperkalaemia

The upper limit for the plasma potassium is set at 5.5 mmol(mEq)/l. Levels above this value result in abnormalities of the cardiovascular, neuromuscular and gastrointestinal systems (Kliger and Hayslett, 1978). Marked hyperkalaemia (> 8.0 mmol(mEq)/l) produces severe neuromuscular and cardiac dysfunction. Initially these include generalized and non-specific weakness and later ascending paralysis. Flaccid quadriplegia has been reported with severe hyperkalaemia (Bull et al, 1953). In the elderly, cardiac conduction defects are the most feared and every elderly patient with hyperkalaemia requires continuous ECG monitoring (Ettinger et al, 1974). The elderly patient with less severe hyperkalaemia may present with non-specific acute or acute on chronic confusion.

Hyperkalaemia may be caused by a shift of potassium from the intracellular to the extracellular compartment or alternatively due to overall body retention of the cation. In practice redistribution of potassium is the commonest cause of hyperkalaemia as no case of excess body potassium has ever been recorded (Wan and Lye, 1980). This may however be due to difficulty in defining the 'normal' body content of an individual (Lye and Faragher, 1982). Occasionally factitious hyperkalaemia may be due to in vitro haemolysis following prolonged storage of blood or increased red cell fragility. Blood specimens are sometimes taken down-stream of intravenous infusions containing potassium.

In the elderly the commonest cause of hyperkalaemia is related to the use of potassium-sparing diuretics or spironolactone. Not uncommonly patients may continue to take potassium supplements when their diuretic is changed to a potassium-sparing one. It is estimated that 12 per cent of patients taking a triamterene/hydrochlorothiazide diuretic will develop hyperkalaemia (Bender et al, 1967). A similar proportion become hyperkalaemic with spironolactone even without the addition of potassium supplements (Greenblatt and Koch-Weser, 1973). Because of the dangers of hyperkalaemia coupled with the observation that potassium-sparing agents lower glomerular filtration rate (Bailey, 1978; Wan and Lye, 1980) these agents should not be used if the creatinine clearance rate is less than 30 ml/min (Bennett et al, 1980). Many elderly have creatinine clearances of this order and a superadded infection perhaps with dehydration (see above) causes further deterioration leading to rapid and possibly fatal hyperkalaemia (Herman and Rado, 1966; Knight and Parkinson, 1967; Jaffey and Martin, 1981). Their widespread use cannot therefore be recommended in the elderly.

The plasma potassium rises with both respiratory and metabolic acidosis due to a shift of the cation from the intracellular compartment (Scribner et al, 1955). Tissue necrosis may release a large quantity of potassium which may not be eliminated fast enough if renal function is reduced by age or disease. In the elderly this may be seen following arterial surgery and restoration of blood flow to near necrotic limbs. The hyperkalaemia is partly caused by potassium release from severely damaged cells but the accompanying acid load also contributes to potassium shift. Many forms of renal failure lead to hyperkalaemia, especially if there is oliguria. In milder forms of renal failure excretion of potassium by the gut can often compensate (Hayes et al, 1967). Other causes of hyperkalaemia in the elderly such as haemolysis, hyperkalaemic periodic paralysis, hypoaldosteronism are rare.

Hypokalaemia
A plasma potassium of less than 3.0 mmol(mEq)/l is usually considered to be abnormal (Kliger and Hayslett, 1978). Hypokalaemia however is not synonymous with body potassium depletion though the likelihood of depletion being present rises if several consecutive plasma values are low (Moore et al, 1954; Flear et al, 1957). A shift of potassium from the ECF into cells is probably the commonest cause of hypokalaemia in all age groups. In the elderly persistent minor hypokalaemia may present with apathy, non-specific weakness or confusion (Judge, 1968). At values less than 2.5 mmol(mEq)/l more widespread and severe manifestations are apparent with paresis and ileus or constipation leading to faecal impaction (Welt et al, 1960; Pick, 1966). Cardiac conduction defects especially in the presence of digoxin or acute myocardial infarction may be prominent and require urgent treatment (Allison et al, 1972; Steiness and Olsen, 1976). Chronic hypokalaemia can lead to significant impairment of renal tubular function which is initially reversible but if prolonged may become permanent (Relman and Schwartz, 1956; Schwartz and Relman, 1967).

Hypokalaemia may be a prominent feature of conditions giving rise to extensive fluid loss from the gastrointestinal tract. Such conditions in the elderly include vomiting, diarrhoea from any cause, gastric aspiration and laxative abuse (Schwartz and Relman, 1953; Crane, 1965; Fleischer et al, 1969). Villous adenomas of the colon or rectum often present with profuse diarrhoea and hypokalaemia (Shields, 1966). It has been assumed that the hypokalaemia which develops in these conditions is secondary to the loss of the cation along with the gastrointestinal fluid. However other factors are important. Thus loss of gastric fluid causes metabolic alkalosis which in turn causes increased uptake of ECF potassium by cells (Mudge and Vislocky, 1949). Equally fluid loss leads to volume depletion which stimulates AVP and aldosterone secretion (see above). AVP by favouring water retention is likely to produce a dilutional component to hypokalaemia and increased aldosterone secretion produces increased urinary potassium excretion. These hormonal factors may be more important than the direct loss of electrolyte from the gut (Shields and Miles, 1965; Turnberg, 1970).

The kaliuretic action of thiazide and loop diuretics may lead to potassium depletion and hypokalaemia particularly in elderly individuals with chronic cardiac failure (British Medical Journal, 1978; Ibrahim et al, 1978). Early studies demonstrated that the total exchangeable potassium of patients with cardiac failure was between 13 and 37 per cent below the normal range (Moore et al, 1954; Aikawa and Fitz, 1956; Flear et al, 1966; White et al, 1969; Cox et al, 1971; Olsen and Valentin, 1973). Others who measured body potassium directly by whole body counting showed a much smaller decrease of around 5–10 per cent (Delwaide and Rorive, 1973; Davidson et al, 1976; Lawson et al, 1976; Thomas et al, 1978). The difference between the studies can be accounted for by the observation that exchangeable measurements of body potassium underestimate the body content in patients with a history of fluid retention (Boddy et al, 1972b; Boddy et al, 1978) including elderly patients with oedema-free cardiac failure (Lye and Winston, 1979). Most of the remaining 'depletion' of body potassium in both young and old patients can be explained by loss of potassium-rich body tissue (Thomas et al, 1979; Lye, 1982). Thus there is little evidence of significant loss of body potassium due to cardiac failure or it's treatment in old people and attention should be focused on plasma measurements. Estimates of the prevalence of hypokalaemia with thiazide diuretics average around 20 per cent (Manner et al, 1972; Leemhuis and Struyvenburg, 1973). The prevalence with loop diuretics is lower because of the smaller kaliuretic action of these drugs (Morgan and Davidson, 1980). There is evidence that the elderly are less likely to develop hypokalaemia with diuretic therapy than the young (Skovbo et al, 1972; Krakauer and Lauritzen, 1978). This is perhaps not surprising in view of the fact that plasma potassium tends to rise with increasing age (see Figs. 11.7 & 11.8). In elderly patients taking diuretics who develop hypokalaemia other causes for the low potassium should be sought. In particular minor degrees of diarrhoea should be considered. In the minority of patients with diuretic-induced hypokalaemia in whom no other cause for potassium wasting can be found potassium supplements should be prescribed. The dose required should be titrated against the response as often large doses of potassium are needed (Schwartz and Swartz, 1974). Occasionally diuretic induced hypomagnesaemia may produce refractory hypokalaemia which only responds to magnesium supplements (Sheehan and White, 1982).

Other causes of hypokalaemia such as primary hyperaldosteronism, Cushing's disease, Bartter's syndrome and renal tubular acidosis are thought to be uncommon in the elderly. Tumours of non-endocrine organs may produce ectopic ACTH and present with severe hypokalaemic alkalosis (Rees, 1975). In the elderly the commonest tumour is an oat cell carcinoma of the bronchus which may be small and difficult to detect (Azzopardi and Williams, 1968). Multiple pathology is common in old people and more than one cause of hypokalaemia is often found with detailed assessment and investigation. Thus hypokalaemia in a patient taking diuretics may be exacerbated by latent purgative abuse. Volume depletion of the ECF by excess diuretic dosage may lie behind hypokalaemia rather than simple potassium wasting. Hypokalaemia is not a diagnosis by itself. Efficient management requires full assessment and alleviation of underlying and contributory mechanisms. In this respect the elderly are the same as the young — there is no evidence that elderly patients have deficient potassium homeostatic control systems by virtue of age alone. Any higher prevalence of hypokalaemia is secondary to the higher disease load borne by the elderly.

REFERENCE

Ackermann P G, Toro G 1953 Calcium and phosphorus balance in elderly men. Journal of Gerontology 8: 289–300

Adler S, Lindeman R D, Yiengst M J, Beard E, Shock N W 1968 Effect of acute loading on urinary acid excretion by the aging human kidney. Journal of Laboratory and Clinical Medicine 72: 278–289

Adolph E F 1968 Origins of physiological regulations. Academic Press, New York

Ahmed A B J, George B C, Gonzalez-Auvert C, Dingman J F 1967 Increased plasma arginine vasopressin in clinical adrenocortical insufficiency and its inhibition by glucosteroids. Journal of Clinical Investigation 46: 111–123

Aikawa J K, Fitz R A 1956 Exchangeable potassium content of the body in congestive failure. Circulation 34: 1093–1098

Allen T H, Anderson E C, Langham W H 1960 Total body potassium and gross body composition in relation to age. Journal of Gerontology 15: 348–357

Allison S P, Morley C J, Burns-Cox C J 1972 Insulin, glucose, and potassium in the treatment of congestive heart failure. British Medical Journal 3: 675–678

Altose M D, McCauley W C, Kelsen S G, Cherniack N S 1977 Effects of hypercapnia and inspiratory flow resistive loading on respiratory activity in chronic airways obstruction. Journal of Clinical Investigation 59: 500–507

Amidi M, Leon D F, deGroot W J, Kroetz F W, Leonard J J 1968 Effect of the thyroid state on myocardial contractility and ventricular ejection rate in man. Circulation 38: 229–239

Anderson E C, Langham W H 1959 Average potassium concentration of the human body as a function of age. Science 130: 713–714

Andres R, Baltzan M A, Cader G, Zierler K L 1962 Effect of insulin on carbohydrate metabolism and on potassium in the forearm of man. Journal of Clinical Investigation 41: 108–115

Arieff A I, Guisado R 1976 Effects on the central nervous system of hypernatraemic and hyponatraemic states. Kidney International 10: 104–116

Arieff A I, Llach F, Massry S G 1976 Neurological manifestations and morbidity of hyponatraemia. Correlation with brain water and electrolytes. Medicine (Baltimore) 55: 121–129

Arnaud C D, Tsao H S, Littledike T 1971 Radioimmunoassay of human parathyroid hormone in serum. Journal of Clinical Investigation 50: 21–34

Ashley F, Kannel W B, Sorlie P D, Manson R 1974 Pulmonary function: relation to aging, cigarette habit and mortality. The Framingham Study. Annals of Internal Medicine 81: 739–749

Atkinson A B, Robertson J I S 1979 Captopril in the treatment of clinical hypertension and cardiac failure. Lancet 2: 836–839

Auger R G, Zehr J E, Siekert R G, Segar W E 1970 Position effect on antidiuretic hormone. Archives of Neurology 23: 513–517

Azzopardi J G, Williams E D 1968 Pathology of non-endocrine tumours associated with Cushing's syndrome. Cancer 22: 274–286

Bahemuka M, Hodkinson, H M, Denham M J, Padmore G R A 1974 Serum creatinine in a geriatric inpatient population. Age & Ageing 3: 43–48

Bailey R R 1978 Diuretics and the elderly. British Medical Journal 1: 1618

Baker M R, Peacock M, Nordin B E C 1980 The decline in vitamin D status with age. Age & Ageing 9: 249–252

Barter F C, Schwartz W B 1967 The syndrome of inappropriate secretion of antidiuretic hormone. American Journal of Medicine 42: 790–806

Bay W H, Ferris T F 1976 Hypernatraemia and hyponatraemia: disorders of tonicity. Geriatrics 31: 53–64

Beardwell C G, Geelen G, Palmer H M, Roberts D, Salamonson L 1975 Radioimmunoassay of plasma vasopressin in physiological and pathological states in man. Journal of Endocrinology 67: 189–202

Behnke A R, Feen B G, Welham W C 1942 The specific gravity of healthy men. Journal of the American Medical Association 118: 495–501

Bender A D, Carter C L, Hansen K B 1967 Use of a diuretic combination of triamterene and hydrochlorothiazide in elderly patients. Journal of American Geriatrics Society 15: 166–173

Bennett W M, Muther R S, Parker R A, Feig P, Morrison G, Golper T A, Singer I 1980 Drug therapy in renal failure: dosing guidelines for adults. Part II. Annals of Internal Medicine 93: 286–325

Berger E Y 1960 Intestinal absorption and excretion In: Comar C L, Bronner F (eds) Mineral metabolism — an advanced treatise. Academic Press, New York, Vol 1, p 249–286

Berl T, Anderson R J, McDonald K M, Schrier R W 1976 Clinical disorders of water metabolism. Kidney International 10: 117–132

Berlyne G M, Ben-Ari J, Kushelevsky A, Idelman I, Galinsky D, Hirsch M, Shainkin R, Yagil R, Zlotnik M 1975 The aetiology of senile osteoporosis: secondary hyperparathyroidism due to renal failure. Quarterly Journal of Medicine 44: 505–521

Bernard C 1865 Introduction a l'étude de la Medicine Experimentale. Bailliere, Paris

Bernard C 1878 Leçons sur les phenômenes de la vie. Cours de physiologie generale de Museum d'Histoire Naturelle, Paris

Bertrand H A, Masoro E J, Yu B P 1978 Increasing adipocyte number as the basis for perirenal depot growth in adult rats. Science 201: 1234–1235

Bie P 1980 Osmoreceptors, vasopressin, and control of renal water excretion, Physiological Review 60: 961–1048

Boddy K, King P C, Hume R, Weyers E 1972a The relation of total body potassium to height, weight and age in normal adults. Journal of Clinical Pathology 25: 512–517

Boddy K, Hume R, King P C, Weyers E, Rowan T 1974 Total body, plasma and erythrocyte potassium and leucocyte ascorbic acid in 'ultra-fit' subjects. Clinical Science and Molecular Medicine 46: 449–456

Boddy K, King P C, Lindsay R M, Winchester J, Kennedy A C

1972b Exchangeable and total body potassium in patients with chronic renal failure. British Medical Journal 1: 140–142

Boddy K, Davies D L, Howie A D, Madkour M, Mahaffy M E, Pack A I 1978 Total body and exchangeable potassium in chronic airways obstruction: a controversial area? Thorax 33: 62–66

Bold A M, Wilding P 1975 Clinical chemistry. Blackwell Scientific Publications, Oxford

Boling E A, Taylor W L, Entenman C, Behnke A R 1962 Total exchangeable potassium and chloride and total body water in healthy men of varying fat content. Journal of Clinical Investigation 41: 1840–1849

Boothby W M, Berkson J, Dunn H L 1936 Studies of the energy metabolism of normal individuals: a standard for basal metabolism with a nomogram for chemical application. American Journal of Physiology 116: 468–484

Bouhuys A, Pool J, Binkhorst R A, van Leeuwen P 1966 Metabolic acidosis of exercise in healthy males. Journal of Applied Physiology 21: 1040–1046

Bourlière F, Parot S 1962 Le vieillissement de deux populations blanches vivant dans des conditions ecologiques tres differentes, etude comparative. Revue Francaise d'Etudes Cliniques et Biologiques 7: 629–635

Bouzarth W F, Shenkin H A 1982 Is "cerebral hyponatraemia" iatrogenic? Lancet 1: 1061–1062

Brandfonbrenner M, Landowne M, Shock N W 1955 Changes in cardiac output with age. Circulation 12: 557–566

Briscoe A M, Loring W E, McClement J H 1959 Changes in human lung collagen and lipids with age. Proceedings of the Society for Experimental Biology 102: 71–74

Briscoe W A, Dubois A B 1958 The relationship between airway resistance, airway conductance and lung volume in subjects of different age and body size. Journal of Clinical Investigation 37: 1279–1285

British Medical Journal 1978 Diuretics in the elderly. British Medical Journal 1: 1092–1093

Brown I R F, Bakowska A, Millard P H 1976 Vitamin D status of patients with femoral neck fractures. Age & Ageing 5: 127–131

Brown J J, Chinn R H, Davies D L, Fraser R, Lever A F, Rae R J 1970 Falsely high plasma potassium values in patients with hyperaldosteronism. British Medical Journal 2: 18–20

Brozek J 1952 Changes of body composition in man during maturity and their nutritional implications. Federation Proceedings 11: 784–793

Brozek J 1961 Body measurements, including skinfold thickness, as indicators of body composition. In: Brozek J, Henschel (eds) Techniques for Measuring Body Composition. National Academy of Sciences N R C, Washington DC, p 3

Bruce A, Andersson M, Arvidsson B, Isaksson B 1980 Body composition. Prediction of normal body potassium, body water and body fat in adults on the basis of body height, body weight and age. Scandinavian Journal of Clinical Laboratory Investigation 40: 461–473

Bull A M, Carter A B, Lowe K G 1953 Hyperpotassaemic paralysis. Lancet ii: 60–63

Bullamore J R, Wilkinson R, Gallagher J C, Nordin B E C 1970 Effect of age on calcium absorption. Lancet 2: 535–537

Burgert S L, Anderson C F 1979 A comparison of triceps skinfold values as measured by the plastic McGaw caliper and the Lange caliper. American Journal of Clinical Nutrition 32: 1531–1533

Burmeister W, Bingert A 1967 Quantitative changes of the human cell mass between the 8th and 90th year of life, Klinische Wochenschrift 45: 409–416

Burn J, Gill G V 1979 Pseudohyponatraemia. British Medical Journal 2: 1110–1111

Burnett J C Jnr, Knox F G 1980 Renal interstitial pressure and sodium excretion during renal vein constriction. American Journal of Physiology 238: F279–F282

Cannon W B 1932 The wisdom of the body. Norton, New York

Care A D, Duncan T 1967 Age as a factor in the response to thyrocalcitonin secretion. Journal of Endocrinology 37: 107–108

Chamberlain M J 1964 Emergency treatment of hyperkalaemia. Lancet i: 464–467

Charles R, Rees J R 1975 Inappropriate secretion of antidiuretic hormone in pneumonia. Postgraduate Medical Journal 51: 663–664

Chien S, Usami S, Simmons R L 1966 Blood volume and age:

repeated measurements on normal men. Journal of Applied Physiology 21: 583–588

Chien S, Peng M T, Chen K P, Huang T F, Chang C, Fang H S 1975 Longitudinal measurements of blood volume and essential body mass in human subjects. Journal of Applied Physiology 39: 818–824

Clinch D 1982 Syndrome of inappropriate antidiuretic hormone secretion associated with stress. Lancet 1: 1131–1132

Cochrane J P S, Forsling M L, Gow N M, LeQuesne L P 1981 Arginine vasopressin release following operations. British Journal of Surgery 68: 209–213

Cohen I M 1956 Complications of chlorpromazine therapy. American Journal of Psychiatry 113: 115–121

Cohn J E, Donoso H D 1963 Mechanical properties of lung in normal men over 60 years old. Journal of Clinical Investigation 42: 1406–1410

Cohn J E, Shock N W 1949 Blood volume studies in middle-aged and elderly males. American Journal of Medical Sciences 217: 388–391

Colebatch H J H, Greaves I A, Ng C K Y 1979 Exponential analysis of elastic recoil and aging in healthy males and females. Journal of Applied Physiology: Respiratory, Environmental Exercise Physiology 47: 683–691

Conway E J 1943 The chemical evolution of the ocean. Proceedings of the Royal Irish Medical Academy B 48: 161–212

Corsa L, Olney J M, Steenburg R W, Ball M R, Moore F D 1950 The measurement of exchangeable potassium in man by isotope dilution. Journal of Clinical Investigation 29: 1280–1295

Cotes J E, Berry G, Burkinshaw L, Davies C T M, Hall A M, Jones P R M, Knibbs A V 1973 Cardiac frequency during submaximal exercise in young adults; relation to lean body mass, total body potassium and amount of leg muscle. Quarterly Journal of Experimental Physiology 58: 239–250

Cotton R C, Shaikh M S, Dent R V 1968 Heparin maintenance and plasma fibrinogen in elderly subjects with and without occlusive vascular disease. Journal of Atherosclerosis Research 8: 959–966

Cowley A W, Cushman W C, Quillen E W, Skelton M M, Langford H G 1981 Vasopressin elevation in experimental hypertension and increased responsiveness to sodium intake. Hypertension 3: Suppl I, 193–I100

Cox J R, Horrocks P, Speight C J, Pearson R E, Hobson W 1971 Potassium and sodium distribution in cardiac failure. Clinical Science 41: 55–61

Crane C W 1965 Observations on the sodium and potassium content of mucus from the large intestine. Gut 6: 439–443

Crane M G, Harris J J 1976 Effect of aging on renin activity and aldosterone excretion. Journal of Laboratory and Clinical Medicine 87: 947–959

Daggett P 1979 Endocrine emergencies. British Journal of Hospital Medicine 21: 38–44

Daggett P, Deanfield J, Moss F 1982 Neurological aspects of hyponatraemia. Postgraduate Medical Journal 58: 737–740

Damon A, Seltzer C C, Stoudt H W, Bell B 1972 Age and physique in healthy white veterans at Boston. Journal of Gerontology 27: 202–208

Dashe A M, Cramm R E, Crist C A, Habener J F, Solomon D H 1963 A water deprivation test for the differential diagnosis of polyuria. Journal of the American Medical Association 185: 699–703

Davidson C, Burkinshaw L, McLachlan M S F, Morgan D B 1976 Effect of long-term diuretic treatment on body potassium in heart disease. Lancet 2: 1044–1047

Davidson D G, Levinsky N G, Berliner R W 1958 Maintenance of potassium excretion despite reduction of glomerular filtration during sodium diuresis. Journal of Clinical Pathology 37: 548

Davidsson D, MacIntyre I, Rappaport A, Bradley J E·S 1956 Determination of total fat in vivo using ^{85}Kr. Biochemical Journal (London) 62: 34p

Deane N, Smith H W 1952 The distribution of sodium and potassium in man. Journal of Clinical Investigation 31: 197–199

Decaux G, Genette F 1981 Urea for long-term treatment of the syndrome of inappropriate secretion of antidiuretic hormone. British Medical Journal 283: 1081–1083

Decaux G, Waterlot Y, Genette F, Hallemans R, Demanet J C 1982 Inappropriate secretion of antidiuretic hormone treated with frusemide. British Medical Journal 285: 89–90

DeFronzo R A, Goldberg M, Zalman S A 1976 Normal diluting

capacity of hyponatraemia patients: reset osmostat of a variant of the syndrome of inappropriate antidiuretic hormone secretion. Annals of Internal Medicine 84: 538–542

Deftos L J, Krook L, Mayer G P 1979 Plasma calcitonin in the bovine species. Proceedings of the Society for Experimental Biology and Medicine 162: 150–151

Deftos L J, Weisman M H, Williams G W, Karpf D G, Frumar A M, Davidson B J et al 1980 Influence of age and sex on plasma calcitonin in human beings. New England Journal of Medicine 302: 1351–1353

Deluca H F 1975 The kidney as an endocrine organ involved in the function of vitamin D. American Journal of Medicine 58: 39–47

Delwaide P A, Rorive G L 1973 Interet de la determination du potassium total en cardiologie. Acta Cardiologica (Bruxelles) 17 Suppl. 282–290

Demanet J C, Bonnyns M, Stevens-Rocmans C 1971 Coma due to water intoxication in beer drinkers. Lancet ii: 1115–1117

Denham M J, Hodkinson H M, Fisher M 1975 Glomerular filtration rate in sick elderly inpatients. Age & Ageing 4: 32–36

deTroyer A, Demanet J C 1975 Correction of antidiuresis by demeclocycline. New England Journal of Medicine 293: 915–918

deTroyer A, Demanet J C 1976 Clinical, biological and pathogenic features of the syndrome of inappropriate secretion of antidiuretic hormone. Quarterly Journal of Medicine 45: 521–531

de Wardener H E, Mills I H, Clapham W F, Hayter C J 1961 Studies on the efferent mechanism of the sodium diuresis which follows the administration of intravenous saline in the dog. Clinical Science 21: 249–258

Dill D B, Phillips E E, MacGregor D 1966 Training: youth and age. Annals of the New York Academy of Science 134: 760–775

Dill D B, Yousef M K, Vitez T S, Goldman A, Patzer R 1982 Metabolic observations on Caucasian men and women aged 17 to 88 years. Journal of Gerontology 37: 565–571

Discala V A, Kinney M J 1971 Effects of myxoedema on the renal diluting and concentrating mechanism. American Journal of Medicine 50: 325–335

Donbal S 1982 Theory of reliability, biological systems and aging. Mechanisms of Aging and Development 18: 339–353

Dousa T P, Wilson D M 1974 Effects of demethylchlortetracycline on cellular action of antidiuretic hormone in vitro. Kidney International 5: 279–284

Drinkwater B L, Horvath S M, Wells C L 1975 Aerobic power of females ages 10 to 68. Journal of Gerontology 30: 385–394

Dubovsky S L, Groban S, Berl T, Schrier R W 1973 Syndrome of inappropriate secretion of antidiuretic hormone with exacerbated psychosis. Annals of Internal Medicine 79: 551–554

Dunihue F W 1965 Reduced juxtaglomerular cell granularity, pituitary neurosecretory material, and width of the zona glomerulosa in aging rats. Endocrinology 77: 948–951

Durnin J V G A, Rahaman M M 1967 The assessment of the amount of fat in the human body from measurements of skinfold thickness. British Journal of Nutrition 21: 681–689

Durnin J V G A, Taylor A 1966 Replicability of measurements of density of the human body as determined by underwater weighing. Journal of Applied Physiology 15: 142–144

Durnin J V G A, Womersley J 1974 Body fat assessed from total body density and its estimation from skinfold thickness: measurements on 481 men and women aged from 16 to 72 years. British Journal of Nutrition 32: 77–79

Edelman I S, Haley H B, Schloerb P R, Sheldon D B, Friis-Hansen B J, Stoll G, Moore F D 1952 Further observations on total body water. I — Normal values throughout life span. Surgery Gynaecology and Obstetrics 95: 1–12

Edmonds C J, Jasani B M, Smith T 1975 Total body potassium and body fat estimation in relationship to height, sex, age, malnutrition and obesity. Clinical Science and Molecular Medicine 48: 431–440

Emmanouel D G, Lindheimer M D, Katz A I 1974 Mechanism of impaired water excretion in the hypothyroid rat. Journal of Clinical Investigation 54: 926–934

Epstein M 1976 Cardiovascular and renal effects of head-out water immersion in man: application of the model in the assessment of volume homeostasis. Circulatory Research 39: 619–628

Epstein M 1979 Effects of aging on the kidney. Federation Proceedings 38: 168–172

Epstein M, Duncan D C, Fishman L M 1972 Characterization of the natriuresis caused in normal man by immersion in water. Clinical Science 43: 275–287

Epstein S, van Mieghem W, Sagel J, Jackson W P U 1973 Effect of single large doses of oral calcium on serum calcium levels in the young and the elderly. Metabolism 22: 1163–1173

Ettinger P O, Regan T J, Oldewurtel H A 1974 Hyperkalaemia, cardiac conduction and th EKG: a review. American Heart Journal 88: 360–371

Exton-Smith A N 1971 Nutrition of the elderly. British Journal of Hospital Medicine 5: 639–646

Finch C E 1972 Enzyme activities, gene function and aging in mammals. Experimental Gerontology 7: 53–57

Flear C T G, Singh C M 1973 Hyponatraemia and sick cells. British Journal of Anaesthesia 45: 976–994

Flear C T G, Cooke W T, Quinton A 1957 Serum potassium levels as an index of body content. Lancet 1: 458–459

Flear C T G, Gill G V, Burn J 1981 Hyponatraemia: mechanisms and management. Lancet II: 26–31

Flear C T G, Quinton A, Carpenter R G, Domenet J G, Sivyer A 1966 Exchangeable body potassium and sodium in patients in congestive heart failure. Clinica Chimica Acta 13: 1–12

Fleischer N, Brown H, Graham D Y, Delenna S 1969 Chronic laxative-induced hyperaldosteronism and hypokalaemia simulating Bartter's syndrome. Annals of Internal Medicine 70: 791–798

Forbes G B 1974 Stature and lean body mass. American Journal of Clinical Nutrition 27: 595–602

Forbes G B, Lewis A W 1956 Total sodium, potassium and chloride in adult man. Journal of Clinical Investigation 35: 596–600

Forbes G B, Reina J C 1970 Adult lean body mass declines with age: some longitudinal observations. Metabolism 19: 653–663

Fraley D S, Adler S 1976 Isohydric regulation of the plasma potassium by bicarbonate in the rat. Kidney International 9: 333–343

Freitag J, Martin K J, Hruska K A, Anderson C, Conrades M, Ladenson J et al 1978 Impaired parathyroid hormone metabolism in patients with chronic renal failure. New England Journal of Medicine 298: 29–32

Frick P G, Schmid J R, Kestler J H, Hitzig W M 1966 Hyponatraemia associated with hyperproteinaemia in multiple myeloma. Helvetica Medica Acta 33: 317–329

Fujita T, Orimo H, Okano K, Yoshikawa M, Shimo R, Inoue T, Itami Y 1972 Radioimmunoassay of serum parathyroid hormone in postmenopausal osteoporosis. Endocrinology Japan 19: 571–577

Gallagher J C, Riggs B L, DeLuca H F 1978 Effects of age on calcium absorption and serum 1,25(OH_2) D. Clinical Research 26: 680A

Gallagher J C, Riggs B L, Eisman J, Hamstra A, Arnaud S B, DeLuca H F 1979 Intestinal calcium absorption and serum vitamin D metabolites in normal subjects and osteoporotic patients. Effects of age and dietary calcium. Journal of Clinical Investigation 64: 729–736

Garn S M, Young R W 1956 Concurrent fat loss and fat gain. American Journal Physical Anthropology 14: 497–504

Gauer O H 1968 Osmocontrol versus volume control. Federation Proceedings 27: 1132–1136

George J M, Capen C C, Phillips A S 1972 Biosynthesis of vasopressin in vitro and ultrastructure of a bronchogenic carcinoma. Journal of Clinical Investigation 51: 141–148

Gibson J G, Evans W A Jr 1937 Clinical studies of the blood Volume: II The relation of plasma and total blood volume to venous pressure, blood velocity, physical measurements, age and sex in 90 normal humans. Journal of Clinical Investigation 16: 317–318

Glanville E V, Geerdink R A 1970 Skinfold thickness, body measurements and age changes in Trio and Wajana Indians of Surinam. American Journal of Physical Anthropology 32: 455–461

Goldberg M, Handler J S 1960 Hyponatraemia and renal wasting of sodium in patients with malfunction of the central nervous system. New England Journal of Medicine 263: 1037–1043

Granath A, Jonsson B, Strandell T 1964 Circulation in healthy old men studied by right heart catheterisation at rest and during exercise in supine and sitting position. Acta Medica Scandinavica 176: 425–446

Greenblatt D J, Koch-Weser J 1973 Adverse reactions to spironolactone. A report from the Boston Collaborative Drug

Surveillance Program. Journal of the American Medical Association 225: 40–43

Greenwood M R C, Johnson P R, Hirsch J 1970 Relationship of age and cellularity to metabolic activity in C57B mice. Proceedings of the Society for Experimental Biology and Medicine 133: 944–947

Grimby G, Saltin B 1966 Physiological analysis of physically well-trained middle aged and old athletes. Acta Medica Scandinavica 179: 513–526

Guyton A C 1976 Parathyroid hormone, calcitonin, calcium and phosphate metabolism vitamin D, bone and teeth. In: Textbook of Medical Physiology, 5th edn. W. B. Saunders, London, p 1052–1071

Haddad J G, Hahn T J 1973 Natural and synthetic sources of circulating 25- hydroxyvitamin D in man. Nature (London) 244: 515–517

Hamilton P J, Dawson A A, Ogston D, Douglas A S 1974 The effect of age on the fibrinolytic enzyme system. Journal of Clinical Pathology 27: 326–329

Hammer M, Ladefogerd J, Olgoord K 1980 Relationship between plasma osmolarity and plasma vasopressin in human subjects. American Journal of Physiology 238: E313–E317

Handler J S, Orloff J 1981 Antidiuretic hormone. Annual Review of Physiology 43: 611–624

Hartman D, Rossier B, Zohlman R 1973 Rapid correction of hyponatraemia in the syndrome of inappropriate secretion of antidiuretic hormone. Annals of Internal Medicine 78: 870–875

Hayes C P Jr, McLeod M E, Robinson R R 1967 An extrarenal mechanism for the maintenance of potassium balance in severe chronic renal failure. Transactions of the Association of American Physician 80: 207–216

Hazard P B, Griffin J P 1982 Calculation of sodium bicarbonate requirement in metabolic acidosis. American Journal of Medical Science 283: 18–22

Hazell K, Ortiz S 1966 The blood alkaline phosphatase level as an aid to diagnosis, treatment and prognosis. Gerontologia Clinica (Basel) 8: 111–117

Hejda S 1963 Skinfold in old and long-lived individuals. Gerontologia 8: 201–208

Helderman J H, Vestal R E, Rowe J W, Tobin J D, Andres R, Robertson G L 1978 The response of arginine vasopressin to intravenous ethanol and hypertonic saline in man: the impact of aging. Journal of Gerontology 33: 39–47

Hemmer M, Viquerat C E, Suter P M, Vallotton M B 1980 Urinary antidiuretic hormone excretion during mechanical ventilation and weaning in man. Anaesthesiology 52: 395–400

Herman E, Rado J 1966 Total hyperkalaemic paralysis associated with spironolactone. Observation on a patient with severe renal disease and refractory oedema. Archives of Neurology 15: 74–77

Hirsch P F, Munson P L 1969 Thyrocalcitonin. Physiological Review 49: 548–622

Hobson W, Jordan A 1959 A study of serum alkaline phosphatase levels in old people living at home. Journal of Gerontology 14: 292–293

Hodkinson H M 1977 Biochemical diagnosis of the elderly. Chapman and Hall, London

Hodkinson H M, McPherson C K 1973 Alkaline phosphatase in a geriatric inpatient population. Age & Ageing 2: 28–33

Hodkinson H M, Round P, Stanton B R, Morgan C 1973 Sunlight, vitamin D and osteomalacia in the elderly. Lancet 1: 910–912

Hollenberg N K, Adams D F, Solomon H S, Rashid A, Abrams H, Merrill J P 1974 Senescence and the renal vasculature in normal man. Circulation Research 34: 309–316

Hollifield G, Parson W 1959 Overweight in the aged. American Journal of Clinical Nutrition 7: 127–131

Hossack K F, Bruce R A 1982 Maximal cardiac function in sedentary normal men and women: comparison of age-related changes. Journal of Applied Physiology: Respiratory, Environmental and Exercise Physiology 53: 799–804

Hughes D, Williams R E, Smith A H 1967 Clinical studies on whole body potassium content measured by gamma-ray spectrometry in health and disease. Clinical Science 32: 495–502

Ibrahim I K, Ritch A E S, MacLennan W J, May T 1978 Are potassium supplements for the elderly necessary? Age and Ageing 7: 165–170

Ireland P, Fordtran J S 1973 Effect of dietary calcium and age on jejunal calcium absorption in humans studied by intestinal perfusion. Journal of Clinical Investigation 52: 2672–2681

Jadresic A, Maira J 1962 A simple test for the diagnosis of diabetes insipidus. Lancet I: 402–403

Jaffey L, Martin A 1981 Malignant hyperkalaemia after amiloride/hydrochlorthiazide treatment. Lancet 1: 1272

Johnson K R, Jobber J, Stonawski B J 1980 Prophylactic vitamin D in the elderly. Age & Ageing 9: 121–127

Johnson M D, Malvin R L 1977 Stimulation of renal sodium reabsorption by angiotensin II. American Journal of Physiology 232: F298–306

Jones D C, Kimeldorf D J, Rubadeau D O, Castanera T J 1953 Relationship between volitional activity and age in the male rat. American Journal of Physiology 172: 109–114

Joynt R J, Feibel J H, Sladek C M 1981 Antidiuretic hormone levels in stroke patients. Annals of Neurology 9: 182–184

Judge T G 1968 Hypokalaemia in the elderly. Gerontologia Clinica (Basel) 10: 102–107

Kalu D N, Hardin R R, Murata I, Huber M B, Roos B A 1982 Age-dependent modulation of parathyroid hormone action. Age 5: 25–29

Kaplan S L, Feigin R D 1978 The syndrome of inappropriate secretion of antidiuretic hormone in children with bacterial meningitis. Journal of Paediatrics 92: 758–761

Karel J L, Wilder V M, Beber M 1956 Electrophoretic serum protein patterns in the aged. Journal of the American Geriatric Society 4: 667–682

Keating F R, Jones J D, Elveback L R, Randall R V 1969 The relation of age and sex to distribution of values in healthy adults of serum calcium, inorganic phosphorus, magnesium, alkaline phosphatase, total proteins albumin and blood urea. Journal of Laboratory and Clinical Medicine 73: 825–834

Keeler R 1974 Natriuresis after unilateral stimulation of carotid receptors in unanaesthetised rats. American Journal of Physiology 226: 507–511

Kennedy R M, Early L E 1970 Profound hyponatraemia resulting from a thiazide-induced decrease in urinary diluting capacity in a patient with primary polydipsia. New England Journal of Medicine 202: 1185–1186

Kirkland J L, Vargas E, Goddard C, Davies I, Lye M 1983 Plasma arginine vasopressin in dehydrated elderly patients. (In preparation)

Kliger A S, Hayslett J P 1978 Disorders of potassium balance. In: Brenner B M, Stein J H (eds) Acid-base and potassium homeostasis, Churchill Livingstone, London.

Knight A H, Parkinson T 1967 Diuretic induced hypokalaemia. Lancet 1: 446–447

Knudson R J, Clark D F, Kennedy T C, Knudson D E 1977 Effect of aging alone on mechanical properties of the normal adult human lung. Journal of Applied Physiology: Respiratory Environmental and Exercise Physiology 43: 1054–1062

Krakauer R, Lauritzen M 1978 Diuretic therapy and hypokalaemia in geriatric outpatients. Danish Medical Bulletin 25: 126–129

Kronenberg R S, Drage C W 1973 Attenuation of ventilatory and heart rate responses to hypoxia and hypercapnia with aging in normal man. Journal of Clinical Investigation 52: 1812–1891

Lawson D E M, Paul A A, Black A E, Cole T J, Mandal A R, Davie M 1979 Relative contributions of diet and sunlight to vitamin D state in the elderly. British Medical Journal 2: 303–305

Lawson D H, Boddy K, Gray J M B, Mahaffy M, Mills E 1976 Potassium supplements in patients receiving long-term diuretics for oedema. Quarterly Journal of Medicine 45: 469–478

Leask R G S, Andrews G R, Caird F I 1973 Normal values for sixteen blood constituents in the elderly. Age & Ageing 2: 14–23

Leemhuis M P, Struyvenburg A 1973 Significance of hypokalaemia due to diuretics. Netherlands Journal of Medicine 16: 18–28

Lesser G T, Zak G 1963 Measurement of total body fat in man by the simultaneous absorption of two inert gases. Annals of New York Academy of Science 110: 40–54

Lesser G T, Deutsch S, Markofsky J 1973 Aging in the rat: longitudinal and cross-sectional studies of body composition. American Journal of Physiology 225: 1472–1478

Lester M C, Nelson P B 1981 Neurological aspects of vasopressin release and the syndrome of inappropriate secretion of antidiuretic hormone. Neurosurgery 8: 735–740

Lewis G P, Jusko W J, Burke C W, Graves L 1971 Prednisone side-effects and serum protein levels. Lancet 2: 778–781

Lewis W H, Alving A S 1938 Changes with age in the renal function in adult men. American Journal of Physiology 123: 500–515

Lindeman R D, Lee T D, Yiengst M J, Shock N W 1966 Influence of age, renal disease, hypertension, diuretics, and calcium on the anti-diuretic responses to suboptimal infusions of vasopressin. Journal of Clinical and Laboratory Medicine 68: 206–223

Lipsmeyer E, Ackerman G L 1966 Irreversible brain damage after water intoxication. Journal of the American Medical Association 196: 286–288

Logothetis J 1966 Neurologic effects of water and sodium disturbances. Postgraduate Medical Journal 42: 621–629

Lorand L 1965 Physiological roles of fibrinogen and fibrin. Federation Proceedings 24: 784–793

Lowry O H, Hastings A B 1952 Quantitative histochemical changes in ageing. In: Lansing A I (ed) Cowdry's problems of aging, 3rd edn. Williams and Wilkins, Baltimore, p 105–138

Lund B, Kjner I, Friis T, Hjorth L, Reimann I, Anderson R B, Sorenson O H 1975 Treatment of osteoporosis of aging with 1 (OH)D₃. Lancet 2: 1168–1171

Lye M 1975 Pulmonary function in relation to age. Modern Geriatrics 5: 30–36

Lye M 1981 Distribution of body potassium in healthy elderly subjects. Gerontology 27: 286–292

Lye M 1982 Body potassium content and capacity of elderly individuals with and without cardiac failure. Cardiovascular Research 16: 22–25

Lye M, Faragher E B 1982 Can body potassium of old people be predicted from anthropometric data? Clinical Physiology 2: 345–350

Lye M, Winston B 1979 Whole body potassium and total exchangeable potassium in elderly patients with cardiac failure. British Heart Journal 42: 568–572

MacCallum A B 1926 The paleochemistry of the body fluids and tissues. Physiological Review 6: 316–357

McDonald K M, Miller P D, Anderson R J, Berl T, Schrier R W 1976 Hormonal control of renal water excretion. Kidney International 10: 38–45

MacGregor G A, Tasker P R W, de Wardener H E 1975 Diuretic-induced oedema. Lancet I: 489–492

McLachlan M S F 1978 The aging kidney. Lancet 2: 143–146

Malnic G, Klose R M, Giebisch G 1966 Micropuncture study of distal tubular potassium and sodium transport in rat nephron. American Journal of Physiology 211: 529–559

Manner R J, Brechbill D O, De Witt K 1972 Prevalence of hypokalaemia in diuretic therapy. Clinical Medicine 79: 15–18

Manson J P, Richards P 1978 Age and urine concentration after desmopressin. British Medical Journal 1: 1054–1055

Master A M, Lasser R P, Beckman S 1960 Tables of average weight and height of Americans, aged 65–94 years: relationship of weight and height to survival. Journal of the American Medical Association 172: 658–662

Mather H M, Ang V, Jenkins J S 1981 Vasopressin in plasma and CSF of patients with subarachnoid haemorrhage. Journal of Neurology, Neurosurgery and Psychiatry 44: 216–219

Mauderly J L 1979 Ventilation, lung volumes and lung mechanics of young adult and old Syrian hamsters. Experimental Aging Research: 5: 497–508

Miller A T, Blyth C S 1952 Estimation of lean body mass and body fat from basal oxygen consumption and creatinine excretion. Journal of Applied Physiology 5: 73–78

Miller J H, Shock N W 1953 Age differences in the renal tubular response to antidiuretic hormone. Journal of Gerontology 8: 446–450

Miller M, Moses A M 1976 Drug-induced states of impaired water excretion. Kidney International 10: 96–103

Miller P D, Krebs R A, Neal B J, McIntyre D O 1982 Hypodipsia in geriatric patients. American Journal of Medicine 73: 354–356

Milne J S, Williamson J 1972 Respiratory function in older people. Clinical Science 42: 371–381

Montgomery A J, Shepherd A N, Emslie-Smith D 1982 Severe hyponatraemia and cardiac failure successfully treated with captopril. British Medical Journal 284: 1085–1086

Moore F D 1959 Metabolic care of the surgical patient. W B Saunders, Philadelphia

Moore F D, Edelman I S, Olney J M, James A H, Brook L, Wilson G M 1954 Body sodium and potassium. Metabolism 3: 334–350

Moore F D, Olsen K H, MacMurrey J D, Parker H V, Ball M R, Boyden C M 1963 The body cell mass and its supporting environment. Saunders, London

Moran W H, Miltenberger F W, Shuayb W A, Zimmerman B 1964 The relationship of antidiuretic hormone secretion to surgical stress. Surgery 56: 99–108

Morgan D B, Davidson C 1980 Hypokalaemia and diuretics: an analysis of publications. British Medical Journal 1: 905–908

Morgan D B, Thomas T H 1979 Water balance and hyponatraemia. Clinical Science 56: 517–522

Morris J F, Peacock M 1976 Assay of plasma 25-hydroxy vitamin D. Clinica Chimica Acta 72: 383–391

Mudge G H, Vislocky K 1949 Electrolyte changes in human striated muscle in acidosis and alkalosis. Journal of Clinical Investigation 28: 482–486

Munro H N 1981 Nutrition and ageing. British Medical Bulletin 37: 83–88

Newton-John H F, Morgan D B 1968 Osteoporosis: a disease or senescence? Lancet 1: 232–233

Norman A W 1974 1,25-dihydroxyvitamin D₃: a kidney produced hormone essential to calcium homeostasis. American Journal of Medicine 57: 21–27

Norris A H, Shock N W, Landowne M, Falzone J A Jr 1956 Pulmonary Function studies: age differences in lung volumes and bellows function. Journal of Gerontology 11: 379–387

Noth R H, Lassman N, Tan S Y 1977 Age and the renin-aldosterone system. Archives of Internal Medicine 137: 1414–1417

Nott J G, Jasinski D R 1974 Diuretic secretion of the narcotic antagonist oxilorphan. Clinical Pharmacology and Therapeutics 15: 361–367

Novak L P 1972 Aging, total body potassium fat free mass and cell mass in males and females between ages 18 and 85 years. Journal of Gerontology, 27: 438–443

Olbrich O, Woodford-Williams E 1956 Water distribution in the aged in correlation to cardiac and renal function. In: Verzar F (ed) Experimentelle Alternsforschung, Birkhauser Verlag, Basel, p 236–245

Olsen K H, Valentin N 1973 Total exchangeable potassium, sodium and chloride in patients with severe valvular heart disease during preparation for cardiac surgery. Scandinavian Journal of Thoracic Cardiovascular Surgery 7: 37–44

Pace N, Rathbun E N 1945 Studies on body composition. III — The body water and chemically combined nitrogen content in relation to fat content. Journal of Biological Chemistry 158: 685–691

Padfield P L, Morton J J, Brown J, Lever A F, Robertson I S, Wood M, Fox R 1976 Plasma arginine vasopressin in the syndrome of antidiuretic hormone excess associated with bronchogenic carcinoma. American Journal of Medicine 61: 825–831

Paintal A S 1973 Vagal sensory receptors and their reflex effects. Physiological Review 53: 159–227

Parizkova J, Eiselt E 1971 A further study on changes in somatic characteristics and body composition of old men followed longitudinally for 8–10 years. Human Biology 43: 318–326

Parizkova J, Eiselt E, Sprynarova S, Wachtlova M 1971 Body composition, aerobic capacity, and density of muscle capillaries in young and old men. Journal of Applied Physiology 31: 323–325

Parot S 1961 Recherches sur la biometrie du vieillissement humain. Bulletin et Memoires Societe d'Anthropologie de Paris 11: 299–308

Patrick J M, Howard A 1972 The influence of age, sex, body during CO_2 inhalation in Caucasians. Respiration Physiology 16: 337–350

Pavlov I P 1927 Conditional reflexes. Oxford University Press, London

Phillips P A, Rolls B J, Ledingham J G G, Crome M J, Wollner L 1983 Reduced thirst in the elderly after 24-hour water deprivation. Clinical Science 64: 61–62P

Pick A 1966 Arrhythmias and potassium in man. American Heart Journal 72: 295–306

Preece M A, Tomlinson S, Ribot C A, Pietrek J, Korn H T, Davis D M et al 1975 Studies of vitamin D deficiency in man. Quarterly Journal of Medicine 176: 575–589

Rafsky H A, Brill A A, Stern K G, Carey H 1952 Electrophoretic studies in the serum of normal aged individuals. American Journal of Medical Sciences 224: 522–528

Rao K J, Miller M, Moses A 1975 Water intoxication and thioridazine (Mellaril). Annals of Internal Medicine 82: 61

Reed A H, Cannon D C, Winkelman J W, Bhasin Y P, Henry R J, Pileggi V J 1972 Estimation of normal ranges from a controlled sample survey: 1. sex and age-related influence on SMA 12/60 screening group of tests. Clinical Chemistry 18: 57–66

Rees L H 1975 The biosynthesis of hormones by non-endocrine tumours — a review. Journal of Endocrinology 67: 143–175

Relman A S, Schwartz W B 1956 The nephrology of potassium depletion: a clinical and pathophysiological entity. New England Journal of Medicine 255: 195–203

Riegger G A J, Lieban G, Kochsiek K 1982 Antidiuretic hormone in congestive heart failure. American Journal of Medicine 72: 49–52

Roberts L B 1967 The normal ranges, with statistical analysis for seventeen blood constituents. Clinica Chimica Acta 16: 69–78

Robertson G L, Rowe J W 1980 The effect of aging on neurohypophyseal function. Peptides 1: Suppl 1, 158–162

Robertson G L, Sahid A 1976 The interaction of blood osmolality and blood volume in regulating plasma vasopressin in man. Journal of Clinical Endocrinology and Metabolism 42: 613–620

Robertson G L, Shelton R L, Athar S 1976 The osmoregulation of vasopressin. Kidney International 10: 25–37

Robertson G L, Mahr E A, Athar S, Sinha T 1973 Development and clinical application of a new method for the radioimmunoassay of arginine vasopressin in human plasma. Journal of Clinical Investigation 52: 2340–2342

Robertson G L, Rowe J, Helderman H, Andres R 1979 The effect of aging on the regulation of vasopressin secretion. Conference on Endocrine Aspects of Aging, Washington, NIH

Robinson J R, McCance R A 1952 Water metabolism. Annual Review of Physiology 14: 115–122

Robinson S 1938 Experimental studies of physical fitness in relation to age. Arbeitsphysiologie 10: 251–323

Robinson S, Dill D B, Robinson R D, Tzankoff S P, Wagner J A 1976 Physiological aging of champion runners. Journal of Applied Physiology 41: 46–51

Robinson S, Dill D B, Tzankoff S P, Wagner J A, Robinson R D 1975 Longitudinal studies of aging in 37 men. Journal of Applied Physiology 38: 263–267

Roof B S, Piel C F, Hansen J, Fudenberg H H 1976 Serum parathyroid hormone levels and serum calcium levels from birth to senescence. Mechanisms of Ageing and Development 5: 289–304

Roos B A, Cooper C W, Felinger A L, Deftos L J 1978 Acute and chronic fluctuations of immunoreactive and biologically active plasma calcitonin in the rat. Endocrinology 103: 2180–2186

Rowe J W, Shock N W, DeFronzo R A 1976 The influence of age on the renal response to water deprivation in man. Nephron 17: 270–278

Rowe J W, Andres R, Tobin J D, Norris A H, Shock N W 1976 Age-adjusted standards for creatinine clearance. Annals of Internal Medicine 84: 567–569

Rowe J W, Andres R, Tobin J D, Norris A H, Shock N W 1976 The effect of age on creatinine clearance in men: a cross-sectional and longitudinal study. Journal of Gerontology 31: 155–163

Rowlatt C, Chesterman F C, Sheriff M U 1976 Lifespan, age changes and tumour incidence in an aging C57BL mouse colony. Laboratory Animal 10: 419–442

Rubin S, Tack M, Cherniack N S 1982 Effect of aging on respiratory responses to CO_2 and inspiratory resistive loads. Journal of Gerontology 37: 306–312

Rushton C 1978 Vitamin D hydroxylation in youth and old age. Age and Ageing 7: 91–95

Rydin H, Vernay E B 1938 The inhibition of water diuresis by emotional stress and muscular exercise. Journal of Experimental Physiology 27: 343–374

Sambhi M P, Crane M G, Genest J 1973 Essential hypertension: new concepts about mechanisms. Annals of Internal Medicine 79: 411–424

Saraiva R A, Lunn J N, Mapleson W W, Willis B A, France J M 1977 Adiposity and the pharmacokinetics of halothane. Anaesthesia 32: 240–246

Schemmel R, Mickelsen O, Mostosky U 1970 Influence of body weight, age, diet and sex on fat depots in rats. Anatomical Record 166: 437–445

Schon D A, Silva P, Hayslett J P 1974 Mechanism of potassium excretion in renal insufficiency. American Journal of Physiology 227: 1323–1330

Schrier R W 1974 Appropriate versus inappropriate secretion of antidiuretic hormone. Western Journal of Medicine 121: 62–64

Schrier R W, Humphreys M H 1971 Factors involved in the anti-natriuretic effect of acute constriction of the thoracic and abdominal inferior vena cava. Circulation Research 29: 479–489

Schrier R W, Leaf A 1981 Effect of hormones on water, sodium chloride and potassium metabolism. In: Williams R H (ed) Textbook of Endocrinology, 6th edn. W.B. Saunders Co., Philadelphia, p 1032–1046

Schwartz W B, Relman A S 1953 Metabolite and renal studies in chronic potassium depletion resulting from over use of laxatives. Journal of Clinical Investigation 32: 258–271

Schwartz W B, Relman A S 1967 Effects of electrolyte disorders on renal structure and function. New England Journal of Medicine 276: 383–389

Schwartz A B, Swartz C D 1974 Dosage of potassium chloride elixir to correct thiazide-induced hypokalaemia. Journal of the American Medical Association 230: 702–704

Schwartz W B, Bennett W, Curelops S, Bartter F C 1957 Syndrome of renal sodium loss and hyponatraemia probably resulting from inappropriate secretion of antidiuretic hormone. American Journal of Medicine 23: 529–542

Scribner B H, Fremont-Smith K, Burnell J M 1955 The effect of acute respiratory acidosis on the internal equilibrium of potassium. Journal of Clinical Investigation 34: 1276–1285

Seybold D, Gessler N 1981 Wasser-, elektrolyt- und saure-basen-haushalt im alter. Zeitschrift Gerontologie 14: 370–381

Sharland D E 1972 Serum alkaline phosphatase: the levels and patterns of iso-enzymes in the non-hospitalised elderly. Age and Ageing 1: 168–176

Sheehan J, White A 1982 Diuretic associated hypomagnesaemia. British Medical Journal 285: 1157–1159

Shephard R J 1978 Physical activity and aging. Croom Helm, London

Shields R 1966 Absorption and secretion of electrolytes and water by the human colon with particular reference to benign adenoma and papilloma. British Journal of Surgery 53: 893–897

Shields R, Miles J B 1965 Absorption and secretion in the large intestine. Postgraduate Medical Journal 41: 435–439

Shock N W, Watkin D M, Yiengst M J, Norris A H, Gaffney G W, Gregerman R I, Falzone J A 1963 Age differences in the water content of the body as related to basal oxygen consumption in males. Journal of Gerontology 18: 1–8

Shock N W, Yiengst M 1950 Age changes in the acid base equilibrium of the blood of males. Journal of Gerontology 5: 1–4

Shohl A T 1939 Mineral metabolism. Rheinhold Publishing Co., New York

Sidney K H, Shephard R J 1977 Activity patterns of elderly men and women. Journal of Gerontology 32: 25–32

Silverstein M E, Feldman R O, Henderson L W, Engelman K 1975 Acute effects of indomethacin (Indo) and aspirin (ASA) on human renal function. Clinical Research 23: 374A

Singer I, Rotenberg D 1973 Demeclocycline-induced nephrogenic diabetes insipidus. In vivo and in vitro studies. Annals of Internal Medicine 79: 679–683

Siri W E 1956 Body composition from fluid spaces and density: analysis of methods. University of California Radiation Laboratory Report 3349, 1–29

Skorecki K L, Brenner B M 1981 Body fluid homeostasis in man: a contemporary overview. American Journal of Medicine 70: 77–88

Skovbo P, Bjerregaard P, Hvidt R 1972 Diuretika og hypokaliaemi. Ugeskrift for Laeger (Copenhagen) 134: 1043–1047

Sladek C D, McNeill T H, Gregg C M, Blair M L, Baggs R B 1981 Vasopressin and renin response to dehydration in aged rats. Neurobiology of Aging 2: 293–302

Spirduso W W, Clifford P 1978 Replication of age and physical activity effects on reaction and movement time. Journal of Gerontology 33: 26–30

Stamp T C B, Round J M 1974 Seasonal changes in human plasma levels of 25(OH)D. Nature (London) 247: 563–565

Stamp T C B, Haddad J G, Exton-Smith A N, Reuben A, Twigg C A 1976 Assay of vitamin D and its metabolites. Annals of Clinical Biochemistry 13: 571–577

Steele J M, Berger E Y, Dunning M F, Brodie B B 1950 Total body water in man. American Journal of Physiology 162: 313–317

Steele W H, Hawksworth G M, Barker H E 1982 The binding of

prednisolone in human serum and to recrystallised human albumin in vitro. British Journal of Clinical Pharmacology 14: 667–672

Steen B, Isaksson B, Svanborg A 1979 Body composition at 70 and 75 years of age: a longitudinal population study. Journal of Clinical and Experimental Gerontology 1: 185–200

Stein M, Schwartz R, Mersky I A 1954 The antidiuretic activity of plasma of patients with hepatic cirrhosis, congestive heart failure, hypertension and other clinical disorders. Journal of Clinical Investigation 33: 77–81

Steiness E, Olsen K H 1976 Cardiac arrhythmias induced by hypokalaemia and potassium loss during maintenance digoxin therapy. British Heart Journal 38: 167–172

Stiles J W, Francendese A A, Masoro E J 1975 Influence of age on size and number of fat cells in the epididymal depot. American Journal of Physiology 229: 1561–1568

Strauss M B, Lamdin E, Smith W P, Bleifer D J 1958 Surfeit and deficit of sodium: a kinetic concept of sodium excretion. Archives of Internal Medicine 102: 527

Swaminathan R, Morgan D B 1981 Pseudohyponatraemia. Lancet i: 96

Swanson A G, Iseri O A 1958 Acute encephalopathy due to water intoxication. New England Journal of Medicine 258: 831–834

Szatalowicz V L, Miller P D, Lacher J W, Gordon J A, Schrier R W 1982 Comparative effective of diuretics on renal water excretion in hyponatraemic oedematous disorders. Clinical Science 62: 235–238

Tarssanen L, Huikko M, Rossi M 1980 Amiloride induced hyponatraemia. Acta Medica Scandinavica 208: 492–494

Thomas R D, Silverton N P, Burkinshaw L, Morgan D B 1979 Potassium depletion and tissue loss in chronic heart failure. Lancet ii: 9–11

Thomas T H, Morgan D B, Swaminathan R, Ball S G, Lee M R 1978 Severe hyponatraemia. A study of 17 patients. Lancet 1: 621–624

Todd E P Vick R L 1971 Kalemotropic effect of epinephrine: analysis with adrenergic agonists and antagonists. American Journal of Physiology 220: 1964–1969

Turini G A, Brunner H R, Gribic 1979 Improvement of chronic congestive heart failure by oral captopril. Lancet 2: 1213–1215

Turnberg L A 1970 Electrolyte absorption from the colon. Gut 11: 1049–1054

Turner J M, Mead J, Wohl M E 1968 Elasticity of the human lungs in relation to age. Journal of Applied Physiology 25: 664–671

Tzankoff S P, Norris A H 1977 Effect of muscle mass decrease on age-related BMR changes. Journal of Applied Physiology: Respiratory, Environmental and Exercise Physiology 43: 1001–1006

Vandersande F, Demay J, Dierickx K 1974 Identification of neurophysin producing cells. 1. The origin of the neurophysin-like substance-containing nerve fibres of the external region of the median eminence of the rat. Cell Tissue Research 151: 187–200

Vernay E B 1946 Absorption and excretion of water. Lancet 2: 739–744

Vernay E B 1948 The antidiuretic hormone and the factors which determine its release. Proceedings of the Royal Society of London, Series B, 135: 25–106

Wallace S, Whiting B, Runcie J 1976 Factors affecting drug binding in plasma of elderly patients. British Journal of Pharmacology 3: 327–330

Wan H H, Lye M 1980 Moduretic induced metabolic acidosis and hyperkalaemia. Postgraduate Medical Journal 56: 348–350

Watkins W B, Choy V J 1980 The impact of aging on neuronal morphology in the rat hypothalamo-neurohypophyseal system: an immunohistochemical study. Peptides 1: Suppl 1, 239–246

Watts E G, Copp D H, Deftos L J 1975 Changes in plasma calcitonin and calcium during the migration of salmon. Endocrinology 96: 214–218

Waugh W H 1969 Utility of expressing serum sodium per unit of water in assessing hyponatraemia. Metabolism 18: 706–712

Weidmann P, de Myttenaere-Bursztein S, Maxwell M H, de Lima J 1975 Effect of aging on plasma renin and aldosterone in normal man. Kidney International 8: 325–333

Welt L G, Hollander W Jr, Blythe W B 1960 The consequences of potassium depletion. Journal of Chronic Diseases 11: 213–254

Wessel J A, Ufer A, Van Huss W D, Cederquist D 1963 Age trends of various components of body composition and functional characteristics in women aged 20–69 years. Annals of New York Academy of Sciences 110: 608–622

White A G, Rubin G, Leiter L 1953 Studies in edema: IV Water retention and the antidiuretic hormone in hepatic and cardiac disease. Journal of Clinical Investigation 32: 931–939

White M G, Fetner C B 1975 Treatment of the syndrome of inappropriate secretion of antidiuretic hormone with lithium carbonate. New England Journal of Medicine 292: 390–392

White R J, Chamberlain D A, Hamer J, McAlister J, Hawkins L A 1969 Potassium depletion in severe heart disease. British Medical Journal 2: 606–610

Widdowson E, McCance R A, Spray C M 1951 The chemical composition of the human body. Clinical Science 10: 113–125

Wilding P, Rollason J G, Robinson D 1972 Patterns of change for various biochemical constituents detected in well population screening. Clinica Chimica Acta 41: 375–387

Wilkinson A, Davies I 1981 The influence of age on the hypothalamo-neurohypophyseal system of the mouse: a quantitative ultrastructural analysis of the posterior pituitary. Mechanisms of Ageing and Development 15: 129–139

Wilmore J H, Miller H L, Pollock M L 1974 Body composition and physiological characteristics of active endurance athletes in their eighth decade of life. Medical Science and Sports 6: 44–48

Winkler A W, Crankshaw O F 1938 Chloride depletion in conditions other than Addison's disease. Journal of Clinical Investigation 17: 1–6

Wiske P S, Epstein S, Bell N H, Queener S F, Edmondson J, Johnston Jnr C C 1979 Increases in immunoreactive parathyroid hormone with age. New England Journal of Medicine 300: 1419–1421

Womersley J, Boddy K, King P C, Durnin J V G A 1972 A comparison of the fat free mass of young adults estimated by anthropometry, body density and total body potassium content. Clinical Science 43: 469–475

Womersley J, Durnin J V G A, Boddy K, Mahaffy M 1976 Influence of muscular development, obesity and age on the fat free mass of adults. Journal of Applied Physiology 41: 223–229

Woodbury D M 1956 Effects of acute hyponatraemia on the distribution of water and electrolytes in various tissues of the rat. American Journal of Physiology 185: 281–286

Yamane Y 1968 Plasma ADH levels in patients with chronic congestive heart failure. Japanese Circulation Journal 32: 745–759

Yang M U, Wang J, Pierson R M, van Itallie T B 1977 Estimation of composition of weight loss in man: a comparison of methods. Journal of Applied Physiology: Respiratory Environment Exercise Physiology 43: 331–338

Young C M, Blondin J, Tensuan R, Fryer J H 1963a Body composition studies of 'older' women, thirty to seventy years of age. Annals of New York Academy of Sciences 110: 589–607

Young C M, Blondin J, Tensuan R, Fryer J H 1963b Body composition of 'older' women. Journal of American Dietetic Association 43: 344–348

Young D B, Guyton A C 1977 Steady State aldosterone dose-response relationships. Circulation Research 40: 138–142

Yu B P, Masoro E J 1978 Age-related changes in the total body mass, lean body mass and adipose tissue mass, II. Gerontologist 18(Part II): 140

The cardiovascular system

PHYSIOLOGY AND PATHOLOGY OF THE CARDIOVASCULAR SYSTEM IN OLD AGE

Description of the changes in the senescent cardiovascular system is made difficult by the very frequent presence in old people of single or multiple pathological or disease processes which are clearly definable and identifiable. This is most obvious in the revolutionary change in thought about atherosclerotic coronary artery disease in the last three decades. Whereas the disease used to be considered as an inevitable 'degenerative' concomitant of aging, the elucidation of the various environmental and metabolic risk factors which contribute to its aetiology has made this simple view untenable, and strongly suggests that the fundamental aging processes by themselves are unlikely to be of basic importance in the pathogenesis of ischaemic heart disease. Yet the very great frequency of coronary artery disease and its consequences makes it extraordinarily difficult to determine what changes may be correctly attributed to aging, and what physiological consequences these may carry with them. It is, however, possible to give a reasonably coherent account of age-changes in the aorta, heart valves, myocardium, and conduction system, and of their physiological effects.

The aorta
It has long been known that the elasticity of the human aorta declines with increasing age (Roy, 1880; Bader, 1967; Gozna et al, 1974). This is accompanied by an increase in the calibre of the aorta demonstrable in vivo by angiocardiography (Dotter and Steinberg, 1949) and at autopsy (Suter, 1897; Fig. 12.1). The velocity of propagation of the pulse wave increases (Bramwell, 1924; Gozna et al, 1974).

These alterations result from changes in the aortic media, and do not reflect the very common intimal changes of atherosclerosis. Hass (1942, 1943) showed that, in addition to histologically demonstrable changes in the media (local atrophy and discontinuities in the elastic lamellae, and diffuse and focal increase in collagen), there are progressive changes in the functional

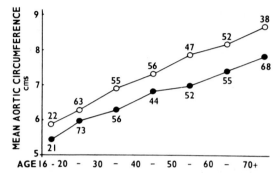

Fig.12.1 Increase with age in mean circumference of aorta at autopsy (Suter, 1897) (numbers refer to subjects in each group)
○—○ men of body length 161 to 165 cm
●—● women of body length 151 to 155 cm

characteristics of elastic tissue in the aorta (Bader, 1967; Baskett, 1982).

The principal physiological consequence of these changes is an increase in both pulse and systolic pressures, with little alteration in diastolic pressure. The increase in mean aortic pressure, and thus in cardiac work, is relatively small (Bader, 1967). The concomitant dilatation of the aorta acts to minimize the effects of these changes by increasing the size of the compression chamber into which the stroke volume is ejected. The aortic dilatation is responsible for the phenomenon of unilateral elevation of the jugular venous pulse (see below) and probably for 'isolated' aortic incompetence (see below).

The heart valves
A number of careful studies have elucidated the changes that occur with age in the valve cusps and rings, and in the associated 'fibrous skeleton' of the heart (McMillan and Lev, 1964; Sell and Scully, 1965; Pomerance 1967, 1976). These alterations differ somewhat from valve to valve.

In the aortic valve and its ring, the main changes consist of a decrease in the number of nuclei in the fibrous stroma of the valve, accumulation of lipid, degeneration of collagen and calcification of the valve fibrosa. These changes occur with the greatest intensity at the sites of maximum movement of the valve cusps, and show definite and steady increases in frequency with age. The resulting increased stiffness of the bases of the cusps seems likely to be the cause of the common ejection systolic murmur of the elderly (Bruns and van der Hauwert, 1958), and can also be shown by echocardiography (Manyari et al, 1982). There is a natural quantitative sequence between these changes and the variety of aortic stenosis without commissural fusion (Ashworth, 1946; Hultgren, 1948; Pomerance, 1976), so that the latter could reasonably be considered to be an exaggerated age-change. Other changes such as the formation of nodules and development of fenestrations on the cusp margins, and the appearance of small commissural adhesions, would seem unlikely to be true age-changes (Fig. 12.2).

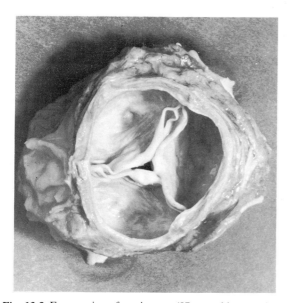

Fig. 12.2 Fenestration of aortic cusp (87-year-old woman)

Changes in the mitral valve may be similarly grouped. Decrease in the number and size of nuclei in the fibrous stroma, lipid accumulation, collagen degeneration, and calcification in the annulus increase in frequency with age (the last more commonly in women), but their severity is less than that in the aortic valve, for any given age. Other age-related changes are nodular thickening of the atrial surfaces of the cusps, together with lesser degrees of mucoid degeneration of the posterior cusp (Pomerance, 1976). Nodular thickening of the mitral valve occurs at the points of apposition of the cusps in systole, which are presumably the sites of maximum

mechanical stress. It is unrelated to blood pressure, but seems to be more common in those with chronic lung disease (Pomerance, 1966). Changes in the mitral valve, especially probably mucoid degeneration, are the cause of apical regurgitant murmurs without other clear cause heard in old people (see below), though such murmurs are commonly of ejection type (Davison and Friedman, 1968). Calcification of the mitral annulus may result in mitral incompetence when the posterior cusp can prolapse into the left atrium in systole, or, when a bar of calcium projects into and under the cusp, to mitral obstruction (Pomerance, 1976). In addition, the close relation of the mitral annulus to the main bundle of His means that calcification there may result in heart-block (Davies, 1971).

Essentially similar changes occur in the tricuspid and pulmonary valves, but their magnitude and frequency is very much less than in the mitral and aortic valves.

The myocardium

The classical age-change in the myocardium is 'brown atrophy', a decrease in heart weight accompanied by accumulation of lipofuscin in the myocardial fibres. Decrease in heart weight is probably related to the high frequency of death from diseases causing generalized wasting, while lipofuscin accumulation is probably a true age-change, though there is no good evidence that it is of any functional importance (Strehler et al, 1959). Rose and Wilson (1959) found it nearly twice as common in those without heart failure as in those with.

More important is the occurrence of fibrotic lesions between the myocardial fibres, or replacing them. Schwartz and Mitchell (1962) showed that these were of two different kinds. Large lesions, more than 2 cm long, having all the characteristics of myocardial infarcts, were more frequent in men than women, and their presence was well correlated with the severity of coronary artery disease. By contrast, lesions less than 2 cm long did not have the characteristics of infarcts, were equally common in men and women, increased in frequency with age, and were poorly correlated with coronary stenosis or the presence of cardiac failure. They probably represent myocardial scars following focal myocarditis. The significance of the large lesions is obvious, but it remains uncertain what effects, if any, the smaller lesions might have.

A third age-related pathological process has recently been shown to occur in the myocardium senile amyloidosis. The frequency of this condition rises steadily with age, and reaches 12 per cent in men aged over 80 (Pomerance, 1965a; Lenkiewicz et al, 1972). Women seem more prone to develop cardiac amyloid, but progression to a degree likely to be of clinical significance is more common in men (Pomerance, 1976). The amyloid material is more commonly found under the left atrial endocardium, but extensive deposits may occur between the myocardial fibres of the left ventricle. It remains uncertain whether senile cardiac amyloidosis can be considered a true age-change, perhaps of immuno-logical origin (Wright et al, 1969; Pomerance, 1976).

Conducting system

Age changes are described (Davies, 1976; Demoulin and Kulbertus, 1978) as consisting of a reduction in the number of pacemaker cells in the sinoatrial node (Davies and Pomerance, 1972; Thery et al, 1977), some increase in the amount of fibrous tissue and fat in the atrial myocardium with a decrease in the number of muscle fibres, and loss of fibres in the bifurcating main bundle of His (Hecht, 1980) and at the junction of the main bundle and its left fascicles, with lesser degrees of loss in the distal bundle branches. There is little if any alter-ation in the atrioventricular node.

PHYSIOLOGICAL CHANGES IN THE CARDIOVASCULAR SYSTEM IN OLD AGE

Heart rate

Although mean heart rate falls little with age, the inherent rhythmicity of the sinoatrial node declines as shown by the so-called 'intrinsic heart rate', i.e. the rate after 'pharmacological denervation' of the heart by simultaneous cholinergic and adrenergic blockade (Jose, 1966; Frick et al, 1967).

The maximum heart rate during exercise also declines with age (see Strandell, 1976). The relation between these interesting observations and the age-related changes in the sinoatrial node described above remains uncertain, but they at least suggest a lesser degree of reactivity to both sympathetic and vagal stimuli. Certainly both the former (Feely and Stevenson, 1979; Bertel et al, 1980) and the latter (Nalefski and Brown, 1950; Dauchot and Gravenstein, 1970) are documented.

Cardiac output and intracardiac pressures

Branfonbrener et al (1955) first demonstrated a decline in cardiac output with age, and this has been confirmed by studies reviewed by Strandell (1976), but not by Manyari et al (1982). At rest the fall is due to a reduction in stroke volume. An increase in arteriovenous oxygen difference indicates that the fall in cardiac output exceeds the fall with age in oxygen consumption. Since the stroke volume is reduced, but the duration of mechanical systole is unaltered, the systolic ejection rate must be reduced. Since the cardiac output is reduced and the mean blood pressure slightly increased, the systemic peripheral resistance is increased. Slowed mitral and aortic valve movement are compatible with

these changes (Gerstenblith et al, 1979; Manyari et al, 1982). Right heart catheterization shows that the pulmonary arterial diastolic and pulmonary 'capillary-venous' pressures are reduced [despite a decrease in pulmonary arterial distensibility (Gozna et al, 1974)], but the pulmonary vascular resistance increased. The changes found on exercise are parallel, with a lower output and higher arteriovenous oxygen difference than in younger subjects.

Exclusion of occult coronary artery disease is not easy, but Strandell (1976) points out that in myocardial failure the higher the filling pressure the lower the cardiac output, while in 'normal' old people the higher the filling pressure the higher the cardiac output. Increased stiffness of the myocardium could explain the latter finding (Manyari et al, 1982), and is supported by the demonstration of pressure patterns on cardiac catheter-ization which resemble those of cardiac constriction. At all events, age-related changes in myocardial function seem relatively small compared with the decline in oxygen consumption. There is no doubt that the elderly heart can increase both its output and its systolic press-ures, and can hypertrophy.

CARDIOVASCULAR DRUGS

There are many differences in cardiovascular drug therapy between the elderly and the young.

Digoxin

Digoxin is probably the drug whose clinical pharma-cology has been studied in most detail in the elderly. Its absorption and bioavailability are unaltered by age (Cusack et al, 1979), but its apparent volume of distri-bution is considerably reduced, from about 500 litres in middle age to about 300 litres. This is partly due to the smaller body size of the elderly, and partly to a reduc-tion in distribution volume per kg body weight, from 8–9 l/kg to 5–6 l/kg (Aronson and Grahame-Smith, 1977; Reid et al, 1982). In hyperthyroidism the apparent volume of distribution is increased (Lawrence et al, 1977; Shenfield et al, 1977). The cause of these changes is not known but may be related to alterations in the concentration of the postulated digoxin receptor Na-K ATPase (Repke, 1964), especially in the main site of digoxin uptake, skeletal muscle (Doherty et al, 1967). Much the most important age-related change in the kinetics of digoxin is in its elimination. Its renal clear-ance is reduced in proportion to the age- and disease-related reduction in creatinine clearance (Roberts and Caird, 1976), and its elimination half-life is increased. Hepatobiliary excretion, which accounts for about one-third of the elimination of digoxin, is also reduced, non-renal clearance values averaging 18–20 ml/min in the elderly, as against 50–60 ml/min in young adults (Roberts and Caird, 1976; Whiting et al, 1979).

Less is known of age-related changes in the dynamics of digoxin. In animals its inotropic effects are reduced but its cardiotoxic effects unchanged (Guarnieri et al, 1979; Gerstenblith et al, 1979), but there is as yet no good evidence that the same is true in man.

Indications for digoxin therapy

There are unaltered by age, and may be stated as: (1) supraventricular arrhythmias with a rapid ventricular response; (2) cardiac failure regardless of cardiac rhythm. There is doubt of its value in atrial fibrillation when spontaneous atrioventricular block leads to a slow ventricular rate, and also in cardiac failure in sinus rhythm after a few weeks of treatment (McHaffie et al, 1978; Johnston and McDevitt, 1979; Fleg et al, 1982). It is therefore reasonable to consider stopping digoxin in elderly patients in sinus rhythm whose cardiac failure has responded to treatment and who are in a steady state after 3 months. This is particularly the case when cardiac failure has been due to an extracardiac factor such as infection or anaemia, which has resolved, or to a cardiac disorder with a natural tendency to improvement, such as cardiac infarction (Dall, 1970).

Digoxin dosage

The altered kinetics of digoxin in old age necessitate changes in dosage. A number of nomograms and computer programmes have been devised to assist in this, but simple rules are also valuable (Caird and Kennedy, 1977). The reduced apparent volume of distribution reduces the loading dose needed, and a single dose of 0.5 mg or 0.75 mg is adequate, depending on body size. The maintenance dose is determined by renal function. If this is reasonable [serum urea less than 10 mmol/l (60 mg/100 ml) and creatinine less than 170 μmol/l (1.98 mg/100 ml)], the appropriate maintenance dose is 0.25 mg/day. If urea or creatinine levels are higher, then the maintenance dose should be 0.125 mg/day. Doses of 0.0625 mg/day rarely produce serum digoxin concentrations in the therapeutic range of 1–2 ng/ml, and there would seem to be no need for thrice daily doses of 0.0625 mg (Roberts and Caird, 1976).

Side effects

The toxic effects of digoxin encountered in the elderly differ from those common in the young, confusion being much more frequent (Dall, 1965a). 'Central' toxic effects such as nausea, vomiting, dizziness, confusion, hallucinations, and xanthospsia, occur at serum levels of 3 ng/ml or more (Reid et al, 1982), and atrioventricular block (partial or complete heart block, bradycardia in atrial fibrillation) at somewhat lower levels.

Many factors are involved in the genesis of digitalis intoxication in the elderly. Impaired renal function is the most important of these (Roberts and Caird, 1976), but increased sensitivity of the myocardium to digoxin may be due to myocardial depletion of potassium and perhaps magnesium. Potassium depletion with hypokalaemia is responsible for the most serious toxic effects of digitalis. Potassium loss due to diuretic therapy is the major factor, but the potassium intake of apparently healthy old people is often below the recommended level of 65 mmol (mEq) per day regarded as necessary for adults (Judge et al, 1974), due to the selection of foods with a low potassium content (Dall et al, 1971b). Magnesium is also lost during diuretic therapy, and animal experiments show that abnormal rhythms produced by digoxin can be corrected by giving magnesium (Neff et al, 1972). The possibility that the relative balance between calcium and potassium in the myocardial cells is important has been postulated from indirect observations on their serum levels (Sonnenblick and Dall, 1981). A relative depletion of calcium was associated with an impaired therapeutic response to digoxin and the absence of digoxin-induced automaticity despite adequate serum levels of digoxin. Conversely a relative deficiency of potassium increased sensitivity to digoxin and was associated with higher levels of digoxin-induced automaticity. This offers a possible explanation of why some old people are extremely sensitive and others apparently unresponsive to digoxin (Sonnenblick and Dall, 1981).

A dysrhythmia is the most frequent manifestation of digitalis intoxication in the elderly (Von Cappeler et al, 1959; Schott, 1964; Dall, 1965a; Chung, 1970). The abnormalities consists of a combination of increased cardiac irritability (atrial and ventricular ectopic beats, often regular (i.e. coupled), atrial tachycardia, atrial flutter, nodal or ventricular tachycardia) and impaired conduction (prolongation of the P-R interval, higher grades of heart block). One frequent combination is *atrial tachycardia* with atriventricular block; the pulse is regular, the ventricular rate not above 100, and unless an electrocardiogram is taken, the diagnosis of a potentially fatal condition may be missed (Dall, 1965b; Chung, 1970).

Other manifestations of digitalis toxicity may be difficult to evaluate in the elderly. Nausea and vomiting are late signs. Confusion may be the presenting feature; it occurs in about 25 per cent of cases (King, 1950; Church and Marriott, 1959; Dall, 1965a). Gynaecomastia and xanthopsia are rare. Refractory cardiac failure may result from the combination of digitalis overdosage and potassium depletion.

If digitalis intoxication is suspected, the drug should be stopped, potassium supplements begun, and the diagnosis confirmed by measurement of the serum concentration of digoxin. Propranolol may be used to control tachycardia provided there is no evidence of cardiac failure and care is used (Watt, 1968). Toxic manifestations usually disappear when the serum concentration falls to 2 ng/ml, but digoxin should not be restarted for 10–14 days, since especially in patients with severe renal impairment (those most likely to develop toxicity) excretion may be very slow. It is wise to confirm complete excretion by finding a negligible serum concentration.

Diuretics

Diuretics are one of the most widely prescribed groups of drugs in the elderly at home and in hospital (Law and Chalmers, 1976; Williamson and Chopin, 1980; Scott et al, 1982). The main indications for diuretic therapy are oedema and hypertension. Many old people receive long-term diuretic therapy unnecessarily. If no current indication is apparent, then these drugs should be withdrawn under careful supervision (Burr et al, 1977).

High efficacy diuretics

These potent or loop diuretics include frusemide (furosemide), bumetanide and ethacrynic acid; all work largely by blocking sodium reabsorption in the ascending limb of the loop of Henle. Oral administration promotes a diuresis within one hour, and the action is usually complete within 6 hours. Intravenous administration produces a peak effect within 30 minutes. Loop diuretics have a relatively steep dose response curve and raising the dose results in increased diuresis. Unlike other diuretics they are effective even in the presence of reduced renal perfusion.

Medium efficacy diuretics

This group includes the thiazides and related compounds, e.g. bendrofluazide, chlorthalidone and mefruside. They act mostly on the cortical diluting segment of the loop of Henle and at the beginning of the distal convoluted tubule, where they interfere with the active reabsorption of sodium ions. The onset of action of this group of drugs is slower than that of the high efficacy diuretics, and diuresis lasts longer. After oral administration the onset of action is within one or 2 hours and the effect lasts for 12–24 hours. The thiazides and their related compounds have a flat dose response curve; increasing the dose produces little extra diuresis. These agents tend to be ineffective when the glomerular filtration rate falls below 20 ml/min.

Low efficacy diuretics

This group includes the potassium-sparing diuretics,

amiloride and triamterene, and the aldosterone antagonist spironolactone. They act in the distal tubule where sodium-potassium exchange is inhibited.

Combination diuretic preparations

High and medium efficacy diuretics combined with potassium supplements are commercially available, and low efficacy diuretics are often combined with thiazides.

Indications for diuretic therapy

Heart failure. Diuretics diminish the venous return and thus the workload of the heart by decreasing blood volume. Oedema fluid is mobilised from the interstitial spaces back into the circulation and the excess fluid is then excreted in the urine. High-efficacy diuretics have a direct action on the blood vessels causing them to dilate and further reduce the cardiac workload.

Parenteral high efficacy diuretics are indicated in acute pulmonary oedema and often as the initial therapy in severe congestive cardiac failure in the elderly. When the oedema is controlled medium-efficacy diuretics are indicated for maintenance. If the heart failure is resistant to therapy then an aldosterone antagonist should be added to the diuretic regimen as secondary hyperaldosteronism is sometimes responsible for diuretic resistance.

Hepatic oedema. A slow and gradual diuresis should be promoted in patients with oedema due to hepatic disease. The high-efficacy loop diuretics should be avoided to prevent electrolyte imbalance, and a combination of a thiazide diuretic and an aldosterone antagonist is particularly useful.

Renal oedema. Thiazide diuretics may be adequate in the nephrotic syndrome but loop diuretics are frequently required. These must often be supplemented by potassium-sparing diuretics because of secondary hyperaldosteronism. If renal function deteriorates the potassium-sparing diuretic should be stopped because of the danger of hyperkalaemia.

Postural oedema. Although diuretics are often prescribed for postural or gravitational oedema of the legs in elderly patients, they are often unsatisfactory. Other factors must be considered and managed, for example prolonged immobility, varicose veins, and venous thrombosis. Tight bandaging of the legs and increasing the patient's mobility may well greatly improve the situation.

Hypertension. Diuretics have an anti-hypertensive effect which appears to be related to a reduction in the plasma volume and peripheral resistance. Thiazides are more effective in lowering the blood pressure than high-efficacy diuretics. There is some evidence that diuretics are particularly useful when hypertension is associated with low serum renin levels. In the elderly, hypertension can be managed with a thiazide combined with potassium-sparing agent, for example triamterene (Amery et al, 1978).

Side effects

A wide variety of side effects may be caused by diuretics (Table 12.1) and the elderly are particularly at risk. Hypovolaemia and postural hypotension may result from injudicious or excessive prescription of loop diuretics. All diuretics apart from potassium-sparing agents and the aldosterone antagonists can produce hypokalaemia, which can impair cardiac function, cause postural hypotension, and may increase cardiac sensitivity to digitalis compounds (MacLennan, 1981). Elderly cardiac patients may appear to be more susceptible to the hypokalaemic effects of diuretics as their total body potassium is already reduced (Ibrahim et al, 1978), and many elderly patients have poor dietary potassium intakes (Judge et al, 1974). The risk of potassium depletion from diuretic therapy in the elderly can be reduced by providing oral potassium supplements or combining high or medium efficacy diuretics with potassium-sparing agents or spironolactone. In these circumstances adequate monitoring of the serum potassium is necessary to avoid hyperkalaemia, particularly if there is any evidence of renal insufficiency. Sodium depletion may occur in elderly patients on loop diuretics associated with hypovolaemia and dehydration. Lethargy and confusion are prominent (and in more severe cases stupor and coma); the serum sodium concentration is usually below 120 mmol(mEq)/l. Diuretics can induce diabetes and occasionally control of known diabetes can be compromised, particularly by the use of long-acting diuretics. This effect is probably due to suppression of pancreatic insulin release. Long-term diuretic therapy may be associated with hyperuricaemia, but secondary gout is rarely a clinical problem. Urinary incontinence is a common problem for elderly patients on diuretic therapy, particularly if their mobility is compromised by arthritis or neuromuscular disorders. Acute retention of urine may be precipitated in elderly males with prostatic disease, this usually resolves when the patient is mobilized.

Beta-blocking agents

The actions of catecholamines on the beta-receptors are antagonised by the beta-blocking agents due to competitive inhibition. The elderly are known to show resistance to the beta-adrenergic-mediated responses to exercise and isoprenaline (Bertel et al, 1980). Aging is associated with an increase in plasma noradrenaline levels (Lake et al, 1977); this may compensate for reduced receptor sensitivity and might compete with isoprenaline or propranolol for beta-receptor binding sites in the heart (Vestal et al, 1979). The demonstration of reduced beta-adrenoceptors on human lymphocyte membranes (Schocken and Roth, 1977) with aging has been disputed (Abrass and Scarpace, 1981), but it is possible that these receptors might be reduced in other sites, such as the heart and peripheral blood vessels. Such a decrease in beta-receptors might produce an apparent age-associated loss of adrenergic responsiveness.

Clinically the beta-blockers are divided into the cardio-selective (e.g. metoprolol, atenolol) and the non-cardio-selective agents (e.g. propranolol, timolol, oxprenolol, pindolol). Cardio-selective agents should be preferred in patients with chronic lung disease or bronchospasm, peripheral vascular disease, and insulin-dependent diabetes. Beta-blockers with intrinsic sympathomimetic activity (e.g. oxprenolol, pindolol) are said to reduce the likelihood of cardio-depression, but exaggeration of left ventricular failure remains a hazard with all beta-blockers (Opie, 1980). The beta-blockers tend to reduce renal blood flow by reducing cardiac output. Because the ultimate excretion of beta-blockers is usually renal, doses must be reduced in renal failure. All beta-blockers have anti-renin properties and the non-cardio-selective agents may have a greater effect. The beta-blocking drugs are well absorbed following oral administration and peak plasma concentrations occur at from 1–3 hours. Several of this group of drugs undergo extensive first-pass hepatic metabolism and thus have a low bioavailability despite good absorption. The amount of drug metabolized varies from almost 100 per cent in the case of propranolol, through 40–60 per cent (pindolol), to virtually none (e.g. practolol, atenolol). Half-lives vary from 2 to 24 hours. Most beta-blockers are little protein-bound although propranolol is highly bound.

For angina, these drugs are usually given three to four

Table 12.1 Side effects of diuretics

	Common side effects	Less common side effects
General	Hypovolaemia	Gastrointestinal intolerance
	Postural hypotension	Skin rashes
	Potassium imbalance	Hypersensitivity reactions
	Sodium depletion	Marrow depression
	Alkalosis	Pancreatitis
	Impaired glucose tolerance	Cholestatic jaundice
	Urinary incontinence	Hypocalaemia
Specific	Frusemide Ethacrynic Acid } in high dose	Otoxicity
		Gastrointestinal haemorrhage
	Spironolactone	Gynaecomastia Impotence

times daily, because of their relatively short half-life, but their pharmacological effects are more prolonged in hypertension. Pharmacokinetic studies of the beta-blocking agents in the elderly have shown that practolol absorption is unimpaired (Castleden et al, 1977). The half-lives of practolol and of metoprolol are unchanged (Castleden et al, 1975; Lundborg and Steen, 1976). There are no apparent age-related changes in the clearance, volume of distribution or bioavailability of atenolol (Rubin et al, 1981).

An age-related increase in circulating plasma propranolol levels has been observed in the elderly, related to an increase in bioavailability due to diminished hepatic first-pass metabolism (Castleden and George, 1979). The elderly may, however, have reduced sensitivity to propranolol (Feely and Stevenson, 1979).

Indications for beta-blocking agents

Angina pectoris. The beta-blocking drugs reduce the oxygen demand of the heart and depress myocardial contractility. All are effective in the treatment of angina pectoris in the majority of patients, but the dose should be adjusted to maintain a resting heart rate of no less than 55–60 beats per minute.

Acute myocardial infarction. The role of beta-blocking agents as long-term prophylactics in elderly patients after acute myocardial infarction is not yet clarified. Aggregated results from published trials of beta-blockade after myocardial infarction have shown a reduction of death rate by about 25 per cent (Leading Article, 1982). In a controlled double blind study of alprenolol, the mortality of the elderly infarct patients was increased, although not significantly so (Anderson et al, 1979). In a study of timolol, mortality and re-infarction were reduced in men up to the age of 75 years (Norwegian Multicentre Study Group, 1981).

Hypertension. The anti-hypertensive action of the beta-blocking agents has not been fully elucidated, but these drugs are useful in addition to diuretic therapy in the management of elderly hypertensives. The plasma potassium concentration is slightly raised by beta-blockers and total body potassium gradually increases with chronic administration; this effect may offset the hypokalaemic effects of diuretics (Rogers et al, 1981). Once-daily combination preparations of a diuretic and a beta-blocker may improve compliance (Williams, 1982).

Cardiac dysrhythmias. Beta-blockers may be effective in the management of supraventricular and ventricular dysrhythmias, but their cardio-depressant action may preclude their use after acute myocardial infarction; alternatives are available. Beta-blockers are mainly used in chronic stable ventricular ectopic activity or in the therapy and prevention of supraventricular tachycardias. They are particularly effective in dysrhythmias associ-

ated with increased circulating catecholamines (e.g. anxiety, phaeochromocytoma) or in patients with an increased cardiac sensitivity to catecholamines as in thyrotoxicosis

Hypertrophic obstructive cardiomyopathy. Marked symptomatic improvement may result from propranolol therapy in elderly patients with hypertrophic obstructive cardiomyopathy (Berger et al, 1979).

Anxiety states. Beta-blockers may relieve the somatic manifestations of anxiety (e.g. palpitations or sinus tachycardia).

Parkinsonian tremor. Some elderly patients with Parkinsonism show a reduction in tremor when beta-blocking drugs are prescribed.

Side effects

Adverse reactions to propranolol have been reported as occurring more frequently in the elderly, but not significantly so (Greenblatt & Koch-Weser, 1972).

Serious cardiac depression is uncommon in patients receiving beta-blocking drugs, but heart failure may develop suddenly or slowly in elderly patients with poor left ventricular function. Beta-blockers should be given with caution to any patient with recent acute myocardial infarction. Beta-adrenergic blockade may lead to an increase in airway resistance and may aggravate bronchospasm. Propranolol will potentiate the hypoglycaemic action of insulin by reducing the compensatory effect of sympatho-adrenal activation. Insulin-dependent diabetics must be monitored carefully for the development of hypoglycaemia. Mild gastrointenstinal upsets may occur, and hallucinations, vivid dreams and depression have been reported. Cold extremities may be a problem, particularly in elderly patients with peripheral vascular disease.

Anti-hypertensive drugs

Adverse reactions to anti-hypertensive drugs are reported to be more common in elderly subjects (Williamson and Chopin, 1980). Arterial baroreceptor sensitivity decreases with age (Gross, 1970) and the renal capacity to conserve sodium and water is impaired (Swales, 1979). These factors may result in a reduced capacity to modify circulatory control when hypotensive stresses are introduced. Older hypertensive patients appear to preserve the ability to autoregulate the cerebral circulation if the blood pressure is gradually reduced to normal levels (Koch-Weser, 1979), but excessive or injudicious anti-hypertensive therapy may have unfortunate results (Jackson et al, 1976). Significant blood pressure reduction without major side effects may be achieved if therapy is introduced gently and gradually (Amery et al, 1978).

The blood pressure of elderly hypertensive patients can usually be controlled by diuretic drugs and/or beta-adrenergic blocking agents. These drugs are discussed on pages 234–235.

The adrenergic-neurone blocking agents guanethidine, bethanidine and debrisoquine should be avoided because they produce symptomatic postural hypotension. Reserpine is contraindicated in elderly patients because of its marked tendency to produce depression in adequate hypotensive doses.

Methyldopa acts by reducing the sympathetic output from the brain-stem vasomotor centre and has a lesser effect on the peripheral sympathetic nerves resulting in reduction of the peripheral resistance. Cardiac output is reduced in the elderly (Messerli et al, 1981). Methyldopa causes progressive reduction in blood pressure and heart rate, with an effect maximal at 4–6 hours, but persisting as long as 24 hours after a single oral dose. Plasma renin activity is reduced, and sodium and water retention may occur. Approximately 50 per cent of orally administered methyldopa is absorbed. It appears rapidly in the urine predominantly unaltered. Most of its side effects are dose-related. Drowsiness, postural hypotension, dry mouth, nasal congestion and fluid retention are not problems when total daily doses of 0.25 to 2 g are added to diuretic therapy in elderly hypertensive patients (Amery et al, 1978). Less common side effects include hepatitis and haemolytic anaemia. Methyldopa may be indicated in elderly hypertensives when beta-blockers or diuretics are contraindicated (e.g. in obstructive airways disease, diabetes, or gout).

The majority of elderly hypertensives will achieve satisfactory blood pressure control with thiazides and beta-blockers, but a small proportion may require 'third-line' additional drugs. Hydrallazine acts by producing arteriolar dilatation, but little is known about its effects in the elderly. It may increase arterial compliance and distensibility, and by itself shows some promise in small doses for the treatment of isolated or predominant systolic hypertension (O'Malley and O'Brien, 1980). Side effects may include a lupus-erythematosus-like syndrome or an acute rheumatoid state. Tachycardia, palpitation, headache, fluid retention, and facial flushing associated with nasal congestion may occur, but these side effects are minimised by restricting the total daily dose to 200 mg.

Prazosin has an anti-hypertensive effect due to peripheral vasodilatation. Absorption is reduced in the elderly; bioavailability and clearance appear unaffected by age (Rubin et al, 1981).

Calcium antagonists

The calcium antagonists or calcium-channel blockers inhibit the trans-membrane calcium influx necessary for cardiac and smooth muscle function. They decrease the peripheral resistance and reduce cardiac work. Coronary blood flow may be increased to ischaemic areas of the myocardium. This group of drugs includes verapamil, nifedipine, perhexiline, and prenylamine; their clinical effects differ.

Verapamil has vasodilator properties, and was first used as a treatment for angina pectoris. More recently its effects on supraventricular dysrhythmias have proved more important. Verapamil blocks slow channel conduction in the atrio-ventricular node and inhibits one limb of the re-entry circuit believed to underlie most paroxysmal supraventricular tachycardias. The ventricular rate in atrial flutter and fibrillation is reduced by an increase in atrio-ventricular block.

Verapamil is almost completely absorbed orally, but the bioavailability is only 10–20 per cent due to extensive first-pass hepatic metabolism. 90 per cent of the drug is protein-bound, and 70 per cent is excreted in the urine mainly as metabolites. The haemodynamic effects of intravenous verapamil are short-lived, with a peak at 5 minutes and a loss of activity by 10–20 minutes. However the peak effect on the atrioventricular node occurs after 10–15 minutes, and lasts for up to 6 hours; this suggests preferential binding by nodal tissues. Oral medication takes 2 hours to act and a peak serum level is reached at 5 hours. Therapeutic serum levels lie in the range of 100–200 ng/ml.

Verapamil is indicated in the treatment of paroxysmal supraventricular tachycardia, atrial fibrillation and atrial flutter.

Side effects include nausea, dizziness, and facial flushing. In patients with impaired sinus node function or A-V conduction, intravenous verapamil may cause sinus bradycardia, sinus arrest, hypotension, heart block and asystole. Contraindications to therapy include the sick-sinus syndrome, second or third degree A-V block, digitalis toxicity, and hypotension. In view of its negative inotropic effect, verapamil should be given with care in addition to beta-blocking agents.

Nifedipine has a powerful coronary vasodilator effect but does not share verapamil's effects on the conduction system. Nifedipine is almost fully absorbed after an oral dose and reaches peak serum levels in 20–45 minutes. It remains detectable in the serum for up to 6 hours and its duration of action is from 8–12 hours.

Nifedipine is indicated in the management of both stable and unstable angina, especially when associated with coronary spasm. It shows promise in the treatment of intractable angina in the elderly (Rothbaum, 1981), especially if beta-blocking drugs are contraindicated. Side effects include headache, dizziness, tremor, gastrointestinal upset and skin flushing.

Perhexiline has anti-anginal and anti-dysrhythmic activities. It has calcium-antagonist properties and additional quinidine-like and mild diuretic actions. It is metabolized by the liver and it may be effective in angina when other medical treatment fails. Side effects are usually transient, and may include dizziness and unsteadiness, headache, gastrointestinal upset, and peripheral neuropathy or myopathy, which is reversible. Hepatitis may occur and hypoglycaemia has been reported.

Anti-dysrhythmic drugs

The anti-dysrhythmic drugs have been divided into four main classes (Table 12.2) on the basis of their main mechanisms of action (Singh and Vaughan-Williams, 1972).

Quinidine is rapidly and most completely absorbed after oral administration. Peak plasma levels occur at 2–3 hours and nearly 80 per cent of the drug is protein-bound. Most of the drug is metabolized in the liver and 10–15 per cent is excreted unchanged in the urine. Quinidine clearance is reduced in the elderly, but there is no change in its volume of distribution (Ochs et al, 1978).

Table 12.2 Classification of anti-dysrhythmic agents

	Class	Drugs
I	Membrane-stabilising agents	A. Quinidine Procainamide Disopyramide B. Lignocaine Phenytoin Mexiletine C. Propranolol
II	Beta-blocking agents	
III	Widen action potential duration	Bretylium Amiodarone
IV	Calcium Antagonists	Verapamil

Indications for quinidine therapy include the treatment of premature beats, the restoration of sinus rhythm in atrial fibrillation or atrial flutter after initial digitalization, maintenance of sinus rhythm after electrical cardioversion, ventricular tachycardia, and the Wolff-Parkinson-White syndrome. Quinidine is contraindicated in patients with heart block, hyperkalaemia, digoxin intoxication, congestive cardiac failure and hypotension.

Side effects may develop soon after the first dose if the patient has idiosyncrasy, but most toxic effects are due to cumulative over-dosage. Side effects include mild gastrointestinal upsets, depression of conduction, cinchonism, thrombocytopenic purpura, and agranulocytosis. Quinidine may raise serum digoxin levels (Mungall et al, 1980).

Procainamide has similar effects to quinidine. It must be given frequently in high doses because of rapid renal elimination. Oral or intramuscular therapy is preferable, while the intravenous route should be reserved for life-threatening dysrhythmias that do not respond to oral or intramuscular therapy. Indications for the use of procainamide are similar to those for quinidine. Side effects include hypotension, heart block, rashes, fever and agranulocytosis. A lupus-erythematosus-like syndrome may develop in patients on long-term therapy.

Disopyramide has some properties similar to those of quinidine and lignocaine. About half of the drug is metabolized and the other half is excreted unchanged in the urine. It may be useful in the management of dysrhythmias after acute myocardial infarction. Most of its side-effects are associated with its anti-cholinergic effects (e.g. constipation and urinary difficulties). Contraindications for therapy with disopyramide include urinary retention, glaucoma and hypotension. Caution is thus required in elderly patients with benign prostatic hypertrophy and heart failure.

Lignocaine has become the standard parenteral agent for the suppression of dysrhythmias associated with acute myocardial infarction. Its bioavailability after oral administration is only 30 per cent due to pronounced first-pass hepatic metabolism. It is thus usually given intramuscularly or intravenously. 70–80 per cent of the drug is metabolized in the liver and its half-life increases when hepatic blood flow is reduced (e.g. in myocardial infarction or congestive cardiac failure). Lignocaine is substantially bound to proteins. Although its clearance is unchanged with age its plasma half-life is prolonged and there is an apparent increased volume of distribution (Triggs, 1978).

Lignocaine is usually administered as a bolus and then as a constant intravenous infusion. With higher infusion rates side effects are more likely; these include drowsiness, numbness, speech disturbances and dizziness. Focal and grand mal seizures may occur. Cardiovascular side effects include bradycardia, cardiac depression and asystole.

Phenytoin is particularly effective in ventricular dysrhythmias, especially if digitalis-induced. It is contraindicated in patients with a high degree of heart block or marked bradycardia, and should be given cautiously in patients with hypotension or cardiac failure. Dose-related side effects include nystagmus, ataxia, tinnitus, confusion and coma; others are hypotension, asystole, anaemia, pancytopenia and lymphadenopathy.

Phenytoin absorption is variable but slow, and peak serum levels may not occur until 12 hours after an oral dose. 90 per cent of the drug is metabolized in the liver; after conjugation it is excreted in the bile, re-absorbed, and re-excreted in the urine. The response of individual patients to standard doses is unpredictable and careful monitoring of plasma levels is thus necessary. There appears to be an increase in plasma clearance of the drug with age, but its kinetics are complicated in that they are both dose-dependent and influenced by protein binding (Stevenson et al, 1979).

Amiodarone is an effective agent for treating troublesome supraventricular and serious ventricular dysrhythmias. This drug has a variable bioavailability and a large volume of distribution. It is highly lipid-soluble and mainly eliminated through the biliary and gastrointestinal tracts. The terminal elimination half-life is usually 35–40 days, but it may be even longer in the elderly. A loading dose of 0.6–2 g daily for 1 to 8 weeks is usually followed by a maintenance dose of 200–400 mg daily. The elderly are particularly susceptible to side effects (McKenna et al, 1983), including skin reactions, sleep disturbances, resting tremor and less often gastrointestinal upset or peripheral neuropathy. Both hypothyroidism or thyrotoxicosis may occur as unwanted effects of this drug.

Vasodilators

Vasodilator drugs can improve cardiac performance in patients with acute and chronic heart failure (Chatterjee and Parmley, 1977). Most have no direct myocardial inotropic effect, and their main actions are on the precapillary resistance bed (preload) and the post-capillary capacitance bed (afterload). The vasodilators increase venous capacitance, reduce the intra-cardiac blood volume, and decrease the systemic and pulmonary and venous pressures. Arteriolar resistance is reduced with pressure unloading effects on the heart (Table 12.3).

Table 12.3 Vasodilators in cardiac failure

Agent	Afterload reduction	Preload reduction
Glyceryl trinitrate	±	−++
Isosorbide dinitrate	±	−++
Prazosin	+	−++
Nitroprusside	++	++
Phentolamine	++	−+
Hydrallazine	++	±

Phentolamine and *sodium nitroprusside* by intravenous infusion can produce marked improvement in acute and chronic heart failure, but this method of treatment is only practicable in intensive care units. Most of the nitrites will produce a significant reduction in the pulmonary and systemic venous pressures. They are useful in relieving venous congestion but have little effect on the cardiac output and are therefore not so effective in low cardiac output states. Sublingual *nitroglycerin* is useful in acute left heart failure but is short-acting; nitroglycerin ointment lasts for 3–5 hours. Sublingual *isosorbide dinitrate* requires frequent administration to maintain a reduction in preload.

Hydrallazine reduces afterload and produces an increase in the cardiac output. Longer term therapy may be combined with nitrites (Massie et al, 1981). *Prazosin* is an alpha-adrenergic blocking agent, which has the effect of reducing preload and afterload in refractory cardiac failure, although tachyphylaxis may be a problem.

The vasodilator drugs have marked beneficial effects in improving cardiac function in severe heart failure which is resistant to standard therapy, but there are no clear indications that long-term benefits accrue (Walsh and Greenberg, 1981).

The side effects of the vasodilators are not usually encountered in short-term therapy in acutely ill patients. The venodilators may reduce pulmonary venous congestion and relieve breathlessness at the expense of aggravating fatigue, and may produce wide and unpredictable swings in the blood pressure during changes in posture.

Anticoagulants

Heparin

The elderly, especially women, are more prone to bleeding episodes while on treatment with heparin (Jick et al, 1968). Since heparin is extensively bound to serum albumin, greater free drug concentrations may result from reduced binding in the presence of lowered serum albumin concentrations. Since heparin dosage is not fixed, but is individualized and controlled by the whole blood clotting time, rather than being given in fixed doses, these age-related changes in sensitivity should be relatively unimportant.

Warfarin

For long-term anticoagulant therapy warfarin is usually employed. The elderly are more sensitive to this drug than the young, and the mean dose required to produce an anticoagulant effect in the therapeutic range falls steadily with age (O'Malley et al, 1977). Since warfarin is bound to serum albumin, reduced albumin concentrations in sick old people may be partly responsible, but it has also been shown that the effect of warfarin on the hepatic vitamin-K dependent synthesis of clotting factors is increased in the elderly (Shepherd et al, 1977). There are thus both kinetic and dynamic reasons for the increased sensitivity of the elderly in warfarin. Other anticoagulants of the coumarin type have not been studied in detail, but it is likely that their activity will be similarly affected.

Warfarin therapy should be considered for elderly patients with leg-vein thrombosis, especially if the iliofemoral segment is affected, and if there is evidence of pulmonary embolism, in patients with systemic embolism complicating recent myocardial infarction or rheumatic heart disease, and in patients with prosthetic heart valves.

Control of anticoagulant therapy in elderly patients living at home is often very difficult, and it is rarely practical to contemplate its use beyond the restricted list of indications given. The potential advantage must always be weighed against the very real risks of serious haemorrhage due to excessive anticoagulant action or to an unsuspected source of bleeding, such as hiatus hernia or peptic ulcer.

SYMPTOMS, SIGNS AND INVESTIGATION OF HEART DISEASE IN THE ELDERLY

Two factors modify the cardinal symptoms of heart disease in old age. These are the mental manifestations of physical disease, which often obstruct history-taking and may make physical examination difficult, and the almost invariable coexistence of several pathological processes in the same patient. Thus one symptom may have more than one possible cause: breathlessness may be due to chronic lung disease, to obesity, or to anaemia, and ankle oedema to chronic venous insufficiency, or hypoproteinaemia, rather than to heart disease. Multiple pathology may also result in the paradoxical absence of symptoms, as when activity is so limited by arthritis, blindness, Parkinsonism, or hemiplegia, that an expected symptom, such as angina in clinically severe ischaemic heart disease, is absent.

Of the cardinal symptoms of heart disease, both cardiac pain and breathlessness are frequently modified in the elderly. Cardiac pain is often substantially reduced in severity, whether it arises on exertion or at rest. This is frequently due to the simultaneous presence of other symptoms, in particular breathlessness, in patients with cardiac infarction, and the fact that other symptoms are so obtrusive that chest pain is not noticed. However, even in patients who are mentally clear, and do not complain unduly of breathlessness, the apparent severity of cardiac pain may be much less than that experienced by younger people. Two speculative explanations, not mutually exclusive, may be advanced for this phenomenon. The first is that in the elderly, cardiac ischaemia may be due, more often than in younger patients, to disease of the smaller branch coronary arteries than to changes in the main vessels. The ischaemic or necrotic areas may thus be smaller, and so perhaps produce less pain. A second possibility is that afferent denervation of the heart may be responsible. It is known for instance that this occurs in tabes dorsalis (Sharpey-Schafer, 1956), and that there is substantial loss of sensory nerve endings elsewhere in the body in old age.

The second cardinal symptom of heart disease,

breathlessness, may also be modified. Many old people with heart failure complain not so much of breathlessness on exertion as of extreme fatigue, and inability to walk more than a few steps. This may be due to reduced cardiac output, with normal pulmonary vascular volumes and pressures (Caird, 1980). A complaint of fatigue of this severity should thus lead to a careful examination of the cardiovascular system and exclusion of cardiac failure. Attacks of breathlessness at night are as characteristic of left heart failure in the elderly as in the young, and should be ascribed to this cause in the first instance in old people.

Many other symptoms, such as confusion resulting from reduction in arterial blood pressure or cardiac output, vomiting and abdominal pain due to hepatic congestion, and insomnia due to paroxysmal nocturnal dyspnoea, may be due to heart disease in the elderly (Pathy, 1967). Only careful clinical examination will reveal their significance. On occasion syncopal episodes may be evidence of heart disease, in particular of Stokes-Adams attacks, or of transient hypotension, due for instance to cardiac infarction or pulmonary embolism. Other causes of transient loss of consciousness, in particular postural hypotension and epilepsy, should be excluded, the latter especially in the presence of focal neurological signs.

Physical signs
By contrast with the frequent variation in symptoms of cardiac disease in old age, the majority of cardiovascular signs are little modified. The pulse rate is essentially unaltered, sinus arrhythmia is not uncommon, and any irregularity of rhythm, apart from that due to occasional ectopic beats, requires explanation and investigation by electrocardiography. The arterial pulse wave is affected by the decreased elasticity of the large vessels, so that the upstroke becomes more rapid, and the peak systolic pressure higher. This change may sometimes cancel out the slowly rising pulse of aortic stenosis, and make it less clinically apparent (Bedford and Caird, 1960). Both sclerosis of the radial artery and the 'loco-motor brachial' should be ignored, however common they may be. The latter is evidence only of increased length and easier palpability of the brachial artery, which probably but not certainly accompanies increased length and tortuosity of the aorta, associated with the changes in its elasticity previously described.

The problems of assessment of the arterial blood pressure are discussed below. Interpretation of the venous pressure and pulse remains the same as in youth. The venous pulse is often more easily observed through the thin skin and subcutaneous tissues of the older person. One important modification is the frequent obstruction to venous return in the left innominate vein by an elongated and unfolded aorta. There is in consequence an elevation of the venous pressure in the left side of the neck (and also in the left arm and hand), the venous pulse being preserved. This has been clearly demonstrated as due to compression of the left innominate vein, particularly in systole, between the aortic arch and the back of the sternum (Sleight, 1962). On deep inspiration the obstruction disappears, and the venous pressure in the left external or internal jugular vein then falls to equal that on the right. Determination of the true central venous pressure, which is essential to the diagnosis of congestive heart failure, should therefore always be made from the right rather than the left neck veins, and if there is doubt, the effect of deep inspiration observed. In very rare instances both innominate veins may be compressed, and bilateral elevation in venous pressure may therefore occur. However, under these circumstances, deep inspiration still produces a dramatic fall in venous pressure, and the true central venous pressure must clearly be low. When elevation of the venous pressure is due to superior mediastinal obstruction, it does not fall on inspiration.

The position of the apex beat is frequently displaced by kyphoscoliotic chest deformity, so that its site is not necessarily evidence of the cardiac size. The character of the apical impulse can usually be correctly identified and both the forceful impulse of left ventricular hypertrophy, and the diffuse impulse of left ventricular dilatation correctly assessed. Gross right ventricular hypertrophy is rare in the elderly, and it is unusual for it to be severe enough to produce clinical evidence of its presence by a left parasternal heave. However, this important sign may on occasion be demonstrable in patients without lung disease and with severe chronic pulmonary hypertension due to rheumatic heart disease or atrial septal defect.

Auscultatory signs carry the same connotation at all ages, and should therefore receive special attention. The first and second hearts sounds can be clearly heard where they are normally heard, and additional atrial or ventricular gallop sounds can be recognized without undue difficulty, though a fourth heart sound is not necessarily evidence of heart disease in old age (Spodick and Quarry, 1974). Many elderly people have difficulty in conducting the respiratory manoeuvres necessary for proper identification of respiratory variation in splitting of the second heart sound, but it is frequently possible to identify normal splitting, increased width of splitting, and paradoxical splitting. Right-sided gallop sounds and murmurs show striking accentuation during inspiration, and occasionally left-sided sounds and murmurs may show accentuation on expiration.

Systolic murmurs

Systolic murmurs are very common in old people. Some studies have put their frequency at 60 per cent or more

(Bruns and van der Hauwert, 1958; Bethel and Crow, 1963). The basic principles which underlie the diagnosis of these murmurs are identical to those applicable in younger patients, but kyphosoliotic chest deformity and inadequate co-operation in respiratory manoeuvres may create difficulties.

There are three main types of systolic murmur encountered in elderly patients, ejection murmurs arising from the aortic valve, and regurgitant murmurs arising from either the mitral or the tricuspid valve. Ejection murmurs arising from the pulmonary valve are very rare (being almost confined to atrial septal defect), or are at least very rarely diagnosed. Ejection and regurgitant murmurs should be distinguished in the same way as in younger people. In practice the most useful point is to pay careful attention to late systole, when ejection murmurs are diminishing in intensity, and regurgitant murmurs are of undiminished or increasing intensity. Aortic ejection murmurs may be loudest not in the right second interspace but at the apex (Bedford and Caird, 1960), while on occasion mitral regurgitant murmurs may be well heard at the base of the heart. Triscuspid regurgitant murmurs are almost always associated with a systolic rise in venous pressure, and are substantially louder in inspiration than expiration. The site where a murmur is best heard is much less important than its other characteristics, but classical teaching is in general correct (Denham et al, 1977).

Investigation of heart disease in old age

Electrocardiography

The electrocardiogram is as important in the diagnosis of heart disease in the elderly as in the young. There are no 'normal' abnormalities of the electrocardiogram in old age. The only changes which seem to be genuinely related to ageing are a tendency for the P-R interval to increase, and for a minor degree of left axis deviation to develop (Harlan et al, 1967). Electrocardiographic abnormalities are very common in old age (Table 12.4), but almost all of them are accompanied by a worse prognosis for life (Caird et al, 1974). Exceptions include purely positional changes, voltage changes of left ventricular hypertrophy without S-T changes, incomplete right bundle branch block, and the pattern of left anterior hemiblock alone (Tammaro and Forin, 1977).

The electrocardiogram is diagnostic of dysrhythmias, and usually provides crucial evidence of digitalis intoxication (Dall, 1965b). Classical Q-wave changes are as definite signs of cardiac infarction in the elderly as in the young (Kurihara et al, 1967), while conduction disorders also carry the same significance. The electrocardiographic diagnosis of left ventricular hypertrophy presents similar problems at any age, but clinical experi-

Table 12.4 Percentage prevalence of electrocardiographic abnormalities in unselected old people. Studies by Ostrander et al (1965), Kitchin et al (1973), Campbell et al (1974), Cullen et al (1974) and Hedenrud et al (1980).

	Men	Women
Q/QS abnormalities★	8–10	2–7
T-wave abnormalities★	23–36	16–32
Left ventricular hypertrophy	4–13	10–15
Right ventricular hypertrophy	1	< 0.5
1st degree heart block	2–10	2–11
Left bundle branch block	0–2	2–4
Right bundle branch block	2–5	1–2
Frequent (> 10 per cent) ectopic beats	4–12	2–3
Atrial fibrillation	2–5	2–3

★ As defined by the Minnesota code

ence suggests that the combination of voltage changes with S-T and T-wave abnormalities are virtually always, and voltage changes alone usually, correlated with other evidence of left ventricular hypertrophy (Kennedy and Caird, 1972). The criteria of Goodwin and Abdin (1959) are adequate for the diagnosis of right ventricular hypertrophy in the elderly (Kennedy and Caird, 1972). The electrocardiogram may also provide very useful evidence of metabolic disorders, in particular hypothyroidism and potassium depletion.

Radiology

Radiological examination, in contrast to electrocardiography, has somewhat less value in cardiac diagnosis in old age. Kyphoscoliotic chest deformity and sternal depression may greatly affect apparent heart size, while the cardiothoracic ratio increases steadily with age, so that figures of over 50 per cent need not be taken to indicate cardiac enlargement in the elderly, especially in women, due mainly to increased kyphosis (Cowan, 1964, 1965).

If left ventricular enlargement may be difficult to assess in old age, left and right atrial enlargement can often be correctly diagnosed radiologically and carry the same significance as in the young, though echocardiographic evidence of left atrial enlargement increases with age (Manyari et al, 1982).

Cardiac calcification may be demonstrable in the coronary arteries, mitral annulus, aortic valve, myocardium (after a major infarct) and pericardium, but is always abnormal (Fig. 12.3). Lateral radiographs are often more helpful than postero-anterior in this connection, but image-intensification may be called for, particularly to demonstrate aortic valvular calcification. Allowance must be made for common extracardiac changes such as calcification of the costal cartilages and tracheobronchial tree.

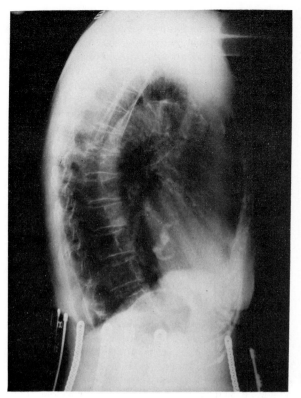

Fig. 12.3 Lateral chest radiograph of 87-year-old woman, showing calcification of costal cartilages, bronchi, aortic arch and its descending part, and mitral valve annulus

The aortic silhouette is frequently abnormal in old age, the increase in length giving rise to prominence of the ascending part to the right of the shadow of the superior vena cava, and often to greatly increased tortuosity of the descending part, which may curve back across the midline in its middle part. Increased calibre of the aorta is more difficult to demonstrate with certainty except by echocardiography, but increased prominence of the aortic knuckle is frequent.

Calcification is commonly seen in the left lower quadrant of the knuckle, where it represents calcified atheroma, the plaque being related to the insertion of the ductus arteriosus. The frequency of such calcification increases with age, and it is commoner and on average more severe in women than in men, perhaps because it is related to blood pressure (Caird, 1976). Linear calcification can also be seen in lateral radiographs in the descending aorta; here again it represents atheromatous lesions, usually around the orifices of the intercostal arteries (Fig. 12.3).

The radiological appearances of the pulmonary vasculature are the same in the elderly as in the middle aged

Undue prominence of the main pulmonary arteries indicates pulmonary hypertension, while Kerley's lines and the butterfly pattern of pulmonary oedema have the same significance at any age.

Other investigations

Other specialized investigations such as cardiac catheterization and angiocardiography are called for only in the rare instance when cardiac surgery is in question, but phonocardiography can be useful in determining the nature of doubtful sounds and murmurs (Fig. 12.4). The normal phonocardiogram has the same characteristics in the old as in the young (Aravanis and Harris, 1958; Bethel and Crow, 1963; Davison and Friedman, 1968). The apexcardiogram and the measurement of systolic time intervals can be combined with phonocardiography to elucidate abnormalities of the cardiac impulse and some disorders of left ventricular function (Caird et al 1973a; see Caird 1976). The apexcardiogram in general confirms signs clearly shown on clinical palpation. Impedance cardiography is a non-invasive technique which can be used to measure the cardiac output in the elderly (Williams and Caird 1980), and the impedance waveform is abnormal in major conduction disorders. Echocardiography can assist in the diagnosis especially of valve disorders (Feigenbaum, 1980), and can also be used to measure left ventricular function. The main changes in old age are a reduced rate of valve movement, especially of the mitral valve (Gerstenblith et al, 1979; Manyari et al 1982). Radionuclide measurements in old age show a reduced ejection fraction especially on exercise (Port et al, 1980), and a normal pulmonary blood volume (Caird, 1980), but have been little exploited.

Of more practical value are measurement of the peak

expiratory flow rate, or forced expiratory volume, to demonstrate the presence or absence of airways obstruction as a cause of dyspnoea, and determination of the blood gases in the diagnosis of cor pulmonale. Lung scanning should be used in the diagnosis of pulmonary embolism in the elderly as in the young.

CARDIAC DYSRHYTHMIAS AND CONDUCTION ABNORMALITIES

Any of the cardiac dysrhythmias may be encountered in the elderly. The identification of the significance of these dysrhythmias is a major clinical problem. Occasional ectopic beats, whether atrial or ventricular, have been recorded in routine electrocardiograms in 40 per cent of healthy older people (Kennedy and Caird, 1972). Ambulatory electrocardiography in a group of healthy elderly people showed a similar proportion (Clee et al, 1979). More serious dysrhythmias, including conduction defects and atrial fibrillation (Clarke et al, 1976; Patel, 1977) have been reported as occurring commonly in elderly people and not always in association with symptoms, although the possible importance in relation to the pathogenesis of falls, fractures, stroke and brain failure has been commented on (Livesley, 1977). A recent study comparing 20 asymptomatic elderly people, and 20 subjects with history of falls, collapse and dizziness as the major symptomatology revealed that cardiac dysrhythmias are equally common in both groups, particularly so in patients with cardiac disease (Rodrigues dos Santos and Lye, 1980).

The increased vulnerability of the aging heart to abnormal rhythms has been attributed to many factors. Age-related changes have been postulated in the sinoatrial node (Harris, 1976) with resultant reduction in the inherent rhythmicity of the node, and the likelihood that other abnormal rhythms will succeed in breaking through (Jose, 1966). Changes in the sinoatrial node and in the conducting tissue have also been described (Davies and Pomerance, 1972; Davies, 1976; see above p. 232). These structural alterations disturb the normal physiological properties of the heart and alter the excitability, irritability, rhythmicity, contractility and even conductivity. These alterations which are a feature of the aging heart are aggravated readily by common morbid processes to which the elderly are vulnerable: fever and infection, CO_2 retention, hypokalaemia and alterations in calcium and magnesium levels, as well as coronary disease, pulmonary thromboembolism, structural valvular disease and the toxic effects of many drugs in common use.

Many of the dysrhythmias in the elderly require no treatment at the time of record, but should be docu-

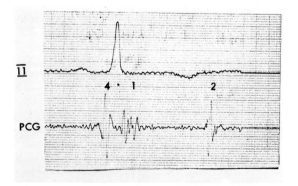

Fig. 12.4 Electrocardiogram (Lead II) and phonocardiogram (PCG) of a 90-year-old woman. Distinction between fourth and split first sound clinically difficult; phonocardiogram shows loud fourth sound (4) preceding first sound (I).

mented as it is likely that the pattern is one of change and deterioration. Although further experience of ambulatory monitoring is necessary, at present no treatment is indicated for occasional atrial or ventricular ectopic beats. There is little evidence that treatment for this complaint, even in the presence of symptoms, is of any value. A pattern of frequent ectopic beats is less common and may well be related to metabolic disorders, hypoxia or administered drugs, and these should be sought as the immediate cause of the problem.

Sinus arrhythmia is common in old age, (Harris, 1976) and may be phasic, with an increased rate associated with inspiration. Sinus bradycardia with rates of 60 per minute or less may be physiological, but should be kept on record as it may be a stage on the way to further change in the conducting tissue, if the obvious clinical problems of raised intracranial pressure, hypothyroidism, recent myocardial infarction and drug therapy with digoxin or beta blockade can be excluded. Treatment for sinus bradycardia is indicated if there is evidence of impaired cardiac output, limited exercise tolerance or signs of cardiac failure. If none of the mentioned precipitating causes are present, treatment with atropine or isoprenaline may be used as a temporary measure to increase the rate of the heart. Long-term drug therapy is rarely effective, and if the problem persists cardiac pacemaker implantation is usually required.

Conduction defects

Cardiac conduction defects are common in the elderly population (Table 12.4).

Sinoatrial block is purely an electrocardiographic diagnosis, with the complete absence of one cardiac cycle occurring at infrequent intervals. Its significance in the elderly is not clear, nor is any treatment indicated.

Bundle branch block

Bundle branch block arises for a variety of reasons, including age-related mechanical wear-and-tear, hypertension, ischaemic heart disease and ventricular hypertrophy (Davies, 1976).

Right bundle branch block is more common than left bundle branch block in old age, and may be present without other features of heart disease (Campbell et al, 1974). The diagnosis is confirmed by the electrocardiogram but may be suspected by fixed splitting of the second heart sound at the base on auscultation. Coexisting left bundle abnormalities are present in about half.

Left bundle branch block is usually associated with known pre-existing organic heart disease, such as hypertension, aortic stenosis or coronary artery disease. The clinical features include, again, splitting of the second

heart sound, but in this circumstance the splitting is reversed and is accentuated on expiration.

'Left anterior hemiblock' (Rosenbaum et al, 1970) describes a block in the anterior division of the left bundle and is characterized by the presence of left axis deviation. The significance of this abnormality in the older patient is not clear; it is not associated with reduction in life expectancy (Caird et al, 1974).

The bundle branch blocks are not in themselves necessarily associated with clinical symptoms, but they may well be indicators of existing heart disease and may in some cases proceed to complete heart block with Stokes-Adams attacks.

Atrio-ventricular block

Heart block is a conduction defect which is usually defined in three degrees. The first degree, or latent heart block, is an ECG abnormality with PR intervals prolonged beyond the upper limit of normal (0.22 seconds). Lengthening of the PR interval in the electrocardiogram with age has been reported (Harlan et al, 1967), prolonged intervals being more common over the age of 70 years. On the other hand, a recent study (Clark and Craven, 1981) of 691 patients with an age range from 65 to over 95, showed no evidence of age-related lengthening of the PR interval, but a marked increased in the length of the PR interval between the age 75 and 80 years. Although delay in the PR interval may be noted in association with myocardial infarction or digitalis therapy, latent heart block is seen in 2 per cent of the ECGs of otherwise healthy old people living in the community (Kennedy and Caird, 1972; Campbell et al, 1974).

Second degree heart block occurs either as Mobitz Type I (Wenckebach) where the PR interval lengthens progressively until a ventricular beat fails to occur, or as Mobitz Type II in which the PR interval remains constant, but dropped beats occur periodically. If this is occasional, the pulse will be irregular, but if it occurs in a regular sequence as in 2:1 or 3:1 heart block, then a bradycardia will be clinically apparent although the atrial rate may be fast.

While the aetiological significance of latent heart block is in some doubt, coronary artery disease is without doubt the commonest single underlying pathology in second degree and third degree block. Third degree or complete heart block occurs when there is no conduction between the atria and ventricles and each is controlled by a separate pacemaker. Coronary artery disease is the commonest cause, but chronic fibrosis in both bundle branches and cardiomyopathies may be found. Occasionally, heavy calcification round the aortic or mitral valves may involve the septum and lead to complete heart block (Davies, 1976). Symptoms arise

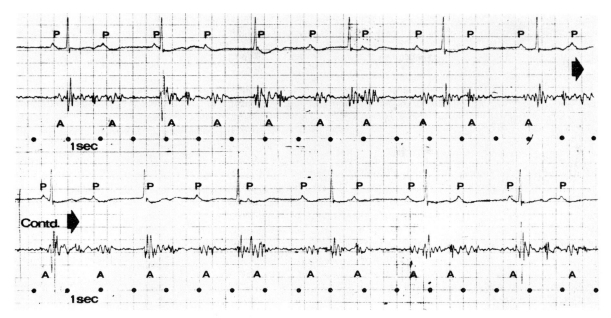

Fig. 12.5 Continuous electrocardiogram and phonocardiogram of 77-year-old patient with complete heart block. First heart sound varies in intensity, being loudest when atrial contraction immediately precedes or coincides with ventricular. Added atrial sounds shown were not clinically audible. (Reproduced by permission from Caird F I 1978 Investigation of the elderly patient. Medicine 1: 15–19)

mainly from bradycardia and include transient syncopal episodes associated with ventricular asystole (Stokes-Adams attacks), and cardiac failure. Other symptoms, such as confusion, have been related to impaired cerebral perfusion due to reduced cardiac output associated with the bradycardia or other dysrhythmias, such as ventricular tachycardia or fibrillation, which occasionally co-exist. The clinical signs are bradycardia, which is regular, and is associated with cannon waves in the jugular venous pulse; the first heart sound is of varying intensity and occasionally atrial sounds can be heard (Fig. 12.5). An ejection systolic murmur is usually present and will also vary in intensity.

Treatment

In acute myocardial infarction, atrio-ventricular block may occur in association with inferior infarcts, when it is usually temporary. Provided the patient survives the first 2 or 3 days, the outlook is good and sinus rhythm is usually spontaneously restored. In contrast, complete heart block in association with anterior myocardial infarction is associated with major damage to both bundle branches and wide-spread anteroseptal ischaemia (Davies, 1976). This is a much more grave condition and mortality is high; the block will usually persist, with the need for cardiac pacing in survivors.

In the management of acute complete heart block, an infusion of steroids in the first 24 hours may be valuable, and may enhance the recovery of sinus rhythm in those with an inferior myocardial infarction (Dall, 1964). If the rate has to be increased more immediately, an intravenous infusion of isoprenaline in a dosage of 0.02 to 0.1 mg/kg body weight/min. increases the ventricular rate. Continuous ECG monitoring is necessary as the danger of precipitating ventricular fibrillation is very real. The appearance of increased ventricular ectopic activity, or runs of ventricular ectopic beats, is an indication for terminating or reducing therapy. Oral isoprenaline is relatively unhelpful even in the chronic state. Under these circumstances, where the patient is symptomatic, a permanent pacemaker should be regarded as a necessary treatment. Expert cardiological advice should be sought and when in doubt, a useful test is to see whether the ventricular rate accelerates with atropine or exercise (Leading Article, 1979). On the whole, elderly patients tolerate a pacemaker well and once permanent pacing is established, the prognosis is that of the underlying heart disease.

Sick sinus syndrome

This syndrome is not uncommon in elderly patients with fairly extensive age changes in the atria, the sino-atrial node and the AV junctional pacemaker (Harris, 1970). Such patients may have episodes of extreme sinus bradycardia with or without symptoms, periods of sinus arrest, or occasionally runs of escape beats with atrial or junctional rhythms and thus a tachybradycardia syndrome, which can be very disabling. The condition has become much more widely recognized since the advent of 24-hour ECG monitoring, and where symptoms are disturbing and dangerous the insertion of a cardiac pacemaker is fully justified and greatly relieves symptoms.

Tachycardias

Atrial fibrillation is the commonest dysrhythmia other than occasional extrasystoles. It occurs in about 2 per cent of a population sample (see Table 12.4) and in about 15 per cent of elderly hospitalized geriatric patients (Bedford and Caird, 1960). Although common, this dysrhythmia may be temporary, paroxysmal, or chronic. In a temporary form it is associated with acute illness, including infection and pulmonary embolism, as well as with acute myocardial infarction.

Established chronic atrial fibrillation is associated with a variety of underlying pathologies, most of which are associated with chronic atrial dilatation and include ischaemic, valvular and amyloid heart disease, (Davies, 1976). Atrial fibrillation which responds poorly to digoxin is often the presenting feature of thyrotoxicosis (Staffurth et al, 1965).

Slow atrial fibrillation without other evidence of heart disease is seen in elderly men and appears to have no effect on survival. Symptoms are uncommon and treatment is unnecessary (Evans and Swan, 1954). Where symptoms occur, they are usually associated with congestive cardiac failure and include breathlessness, palpitation, confusion, syncope, and systemic emboli. The radial pulse is irregular and there is a pulse deficit between the auscultated rate at the apex of the heart, and the palpated rate at the radial pulse. The ECG is diagnostic, with the absence of P waves and irregular R-R intervals.

Rapid atrial fibrillation, with or without cardiac failure, requires urgent treatment with cardiac glycosides. Digoxin reduces the ventricular rate, allows increased ventricular filling, improves the coronary circulation and myocardial oxygenation. The resultant increase in the force and velocity of myocardial contraction improves the cardiac output. The purpose of treatment is to reduce the heart rate to between 60 and 80 beats per minute. Failure to achieve this readily should always indicate a review of the diagnosis to make sure that underlying conditions, such as thyrotoxicosis, pulmonary embolism or amyloid disease, have been excluded. In the absence of cardiac failure, a beta-adrenergic blocking agent will slow the heart and improve ventricular rate control (Wang et al, 1980), but should not be used where there is a history of recent cardiac

failure. Since digitalization is usually effective and easily achieved it is preferred to cardioversion by DC shock in the elderly because there is usually underlying pathology. The recurrence rate of atrial fibrillation is thus high (Rodstein, 1979).

Atrial flutter occurs in the presence of organic heart disease. In the absence of a recent myocardial infarction, pulmonary thromboembolism should be excluded. Treatment is aimed at control of the ventricular rate and this may be achieved with digitalization which converts flutter to fibrillation, and indeed sinus rhythm may recur. If digitalization is not successful, calcium antagonists such as verapamil or disopyramide may be tried. In the absence of symptoms of cardiac failure, beta blocking drugs given parenterally may be useful. If the situation is chronic or recurring, oral quinidine or digitalization is usually necessary.

Other supraventricular tachycardias are usually paroxysmal and may arise from the atria or from the junctional tissues. These cannot be differentiated clinically and are sometimes extremely difficult to differentiate on the ECG. As with atrial flutter, they are usually associated with ischaemic heart disease, but they are also important examples of the dysrhythmias which can arise as a toxic effect of digoxin. This may occur even when the serum levels of digoxin are known to be in the therapeutic range, if there is a sensitizing factor such as hypokalaemia. In the absence of digoxin as a precipitating cause, useful information can be obtained by carotid sinus massage which may stop the paroxysm. Where the patient is unresponsive to carotid massage, some other underlying pathology should be suspected including malignant pericardial infiltration. Prolonged attacks are associated with a considerable reduction in cardiac output and a consequent reduction in cerebral perfusion; cardioversion is fully justified. Maintenance therapy with digoxin, beta blocking agents or quinidine is needed.

Paroxysmal atrial tachycardia with atrio-ventricular block is usually due to digitalis over-dosage, and is an indication for stopping digoxin and correcting postassium depletion. If this is unsuccessful, a calcium antagonist such as nifedipine may be the drug of choice. Multifocal atrial tachycardia has been reported in association with severe heart disease or chronic lung disease (Clark, 1977). It is important to exclude electrolyte imbalance before attempting to control the rate with digoxin.

Ventricular dysrhythmias

Frequent, or multifocal ventricular ectopic beats are often attributed to smoking or excess tea or coffee drinking. No such association was found (Clee et al, 1979) in 24-hour ambulatory ECG monitoring in apparently healthy individuals, but the level of exposure was not excessive and may have been insufficient. Coronary artery disease is the most common cause, and if digoxin toxicity can be excluded, ischaemic heart disease should be presumed. The danger of ventricular ectopics has been illustrated in relation to recent acute myocardial injury. The same significance may not attach to observations on the ambulatory ECG record in apparently healthy old patients (Clee et al, 1979). Nonetheless, given the alteration in the physiological and biochemical milieu that occurs frequently in the older patient, these should still be regarded as dangerous. Treatment should be aimed at suppression in the absence of a correctable cause. Maintenance regimens should be reduced to the minimum level compatible with the therapeutic goal to avoid side effects. Where quinidine can not be tolerated, beta-blockade may be used provided there is no evidence of cardiac failure or bronchospasm.

Sustained ventricular tachycardia is regular, at a rate of 180–240/minute, and is a life-threatening dysrhythmia. It can result from digoxin overdosage, especially in the presence of serious hypokalaemia. More commonly, it occurs as a complication of acute myocardial infarction. The abrupt fall in cardiac output induced may produce loss of consciousness, confusion or stroke signs as well as cardiac failure. Intravenous lignocaine, in single doses of 50–100 mg, may halt the dysrhythmia and can be followed by an infusion of 2 mg/minute in the immediate recovery period. Hypokalaemia and acidosis should be corrected to decrease the risk of recurrence. For maintenance therapy, phenytoin 100 mg to 300 mg daily may be helpful. Where lignocaine is not effective, DC shock will be required.

Ventricular fibrillation is the most serious of all dysrhythmias and requires immediate resuscitative procedures. Like all the other dysrhythmias, it may occur for toxic reasons in association with digoxin therapy and is more liable to occur in the presence of acidosis or severe hypokalaemia. The most common event, however, is likely to be an acute myocardial infarction and it has been recorded in as many as 4 per cent of the elderly treated in coronary care units (Chaturvedi et al, 1972). Nevertheless, if treated energetically and appropriately with unsynchronized electrical shock in full doses, the prognosis is unaffected by age and is that of the underlying cause (Williams et al, 1976). Since the underlying cause is usually a serious myocardial infarction, or a major pulmonary embolism often with a saddle block of the pulmonary arteries, the prognosis must be regarded as poor unless the incident occurs within the coronary care unit or in some other situation with access to direct electrical current shock.

HYPERTENSION

The occurrence of hypertension in the elderly is widely accepted but what constitutes high blood pressure in old age is not so readily agreed. Nevertheless heart failure and stroke episodes occur in association with age and rising levels of blood pressure (Kannel et al, 1970), and there is evidence that successful treatment of hypertension probably reduces the frequency of these events (Hypertension Detection and Follow-up Programme, 1979; Kuramoto et al, 1981).

The prevalence of hypertension varies widely in the literature depending on the values accepted as normal and whether the readings are made in the recumbent or upright position, whether a single reading is used, or whether a series of readings is taken on several occasions. Master et al, (1958) reviewed the subject and reported a blood pressure in excess of 160/95 mmHg in between 30 per cent and 65 per cent of elderly men. In the 1962 National Health Documentation in the USA, systolic hypertension was reported in 15 per cent of white men aged 65–74 and 27 per cent of those aged 75–79. Among white women the prevalence was 31 per cent and 33 per cent. Blacks showed higher prevalences in both age groups, 26 per cent and 29 per cent for men, and 39 per cent and 43 per cent for women. The Community Hypertension Evaluation Clinic Programme (1977) recorded a single blood pressure in the sitting position and found the prevalence of high blood pressure to be 14 per cent for whites and 28 per cent for blacks over the age of 65 years.

The World Health Organization values of 160/90 mmHg as the upper limit of normal have been reinforced by the findings of the Framingham study (Kannel et al, 1971) and there is an increased incidence of stroke and heart failure at levels of blood pressure above these figures. Many trials use a diastolic figure of 95 mmHg, but in a review of published series, Moore-Smith (1980) showed that there was little convincing evidence of improvement where treatment was applied at levels of 180/95 mmHg or less. In practice, diastolic hypertension in excess of 100 mmHg is relatively uncommon in the elderly, and higher levels should suggest the possibility of renal vascular disease or dissecting aneurysm of the abdominal aorta. In contrast to younger age groups systolic hypertension is both more common in the elderly and more directly related to morbid events (Colandrea et al, 1970; Kannel et al, 1971).

Systolic pressure is more liable to be labile than diastolic, and the position of the subject during the recording is important. Caird et al (1973b) reported that a fall of 20 mmHg or more occurred on 24 per cent of 494 subjects of more than 65 years of age when standing erect for one minute. Of these, 9 per cent had a fall of 30 mmHg and 5 per cent had a fall of 40 mmHg. The frequency of a fall increased with age. It is important therefore not to establish a diagnosis of hypertension in old people which may give rise to consideration for treatment unless the blood pressure remains above the normal in the standing position. Failure to make this observation may result in unnecessary treatment and an unacceptable and precipitate fall in the blood pressure may result (Jackson et al, 1976).

The presence of significant postural hypotension even without symptoms in an elderly hypertensive patient should be a warning not to initiate hypotensive therapy as the patient is likely to be unable to prevent further falls in blood pressure which may be induced by anti-hypertensive therapy. Drug therapy with diuretics, phenothiazines, sedatives, tranquillisers, and anti-Parkinson regimens, as well as hypotensive agents are capable of inducing hypotensive attacks and are the most common cause of postural hypotension in the elderly. Other causes include Parkinsonism, which is associated with a failure of adequate reflex control due to a central effect, and diabetic neuropathy where the likely failure is in peripheral mechanisms of blood pressure regulation. Patients with any of these disorders should be assessed very carefully before any decision to start anti-hypertensive treatment is taken.

The decision to treat hypertension has long been influenced by consideration of a diastolic blood pressure which is the principal factor in hypertension of the young and middle-aged patient. Diastolic hypertension is mediated through disease of the small arterial vessels and is associated with a raised peripheral resistance. Hypertensive changes in the retina, the kidney and the heart have been considered for many years as evidence of target-organ damage due to established significant hypertension. In the absence of these features hypertension has usually been labelled as 'labile', 'essential', or 'benign'. In the last decade, however, largely due to evidence accumulated in the Framingham study, the importance of systolic hypertension has been increasingly recognised. The brain is the principal target organ for systolic hypertensive damage, and stroke disease may be the first event in as many as 30 per cent of cases (Colandrea et al, 1970; Kannel et al, 1971). A direct relationship between systolic hypertension and atherosclerosis is readily appreciated by examination of sections of the aorta removed from patients with coarctation of the aorta. The proximal segment is easily identified by the presence of excess atheroma in the wall.

The concept of systolic hypertension as the most important risk factor associated with stroke disease has been demonstrated as the Framingham cohort has advanced into the seventh decade (Kannel, 1982). Other risk factors such as obesity, cigarette smoking, and glucose intolerance have been shown to be of lesser importance in the elderly (Shekelle et al, 1974).

Assessment of the elderly hypertensive

At least three readings of the blood pressure should be taken by the same physician on three separate occasions. The elderly subject should be rested in the supine position for 5 minutes and the sphygmomanometer cuff should be applied evenly in the same arm on each occasion with no constricting garments. The systolic phase should be detected by taking the radial pulse to avoid missing an auscultatory gap and the fifth phase of the Korotkov sounds (disappearance of all sounds) should be noted. When this is difficult to detect, particularly in the presence of atrial fibrillation, then the fourth phase (muffling) should be documented and labelled as such in the case record. Supine and erect blood pressure measurements must be recorded to exclude the presence of significant postural hypotension. Less than 5 per cent of patients are likely to have secondary hypertension and most of these will have chronic renal disease or drug related hypertension. The likelihood of detecting such a correctable cause of hypertension in the elderly is small, as is the case in younger patients. Malignant or accelerated hypertension is rare in the elderly (Kincaid-Smith et al, 1958). This condition is associated with severe vascular damage and is usually associated with very high levels of blood pressure. A variety of drugs may induce or aggravate hypertension, e.g. steroids, non-steroidal anti-inflammatory drugs, liquorice, carbenoxolone, or sodium salts in patients with renal insufficiency. Reversible hypertension may be due to the ingestion of sympathomemetic amines, e.g. ephedrine or some of the constituents of nasal decongestant compounds.

Investigation

The investigation of the individual elderly hypertensive should include a careful clinical history, physical examination and relevant special investigations to elucidate the presence and degree of end-organ damage and where possible to detect any underlying cause.

Most elderly hypertensives have no symptoms, and the diagnosis of hypertension is usually made incidentally when the patient presents with another medical problem. Presenting symptoms may however include undue fatigue, dyspnoea, orthopnoea, ankle swelling, angina and headache. Failing memory and concentration may be due to hypertensive brain damage but are more likely to be due to side effects of drugs, particularly those anti-hypertensive agents with sedative actions.

The physical examination should include assessment of any evidence of brain damage, for example vascular dementia or focal neurological deficits. Fundal examination is often difficult to perform in the elderly. Grades 1 and 2 (Keith-Wagener classification) fundal changes of a marked light reflex and arteriovenous nipping are of little significance in old age (Garner and Ashton, 1979), but haemorrhages and exudates and papilloedema are highly significant findings and indicate the presence of malignant hypertension. Examination of the cardio-vascular system may show evidence of hypertensive cardiac damage including left ventricular enlargement or signs of left ventricular failure. Mitral systolic or aortic diastolic murmurs may be present and a soft ejection systolic murmur may occur.

Special investigations
Useful investigations in the elderly hypertensive include serum urea, electrolytes and creatinine, thyroid function tests, blood sugar and serum uric acid levels. Simple urine analysis will exclude proteinuria and infection. Many ECG abnormalities are common in the elderly (see Table 12.4) and the significance of voltage changes of left ventricular hypertrophy without ST-T abnormality is not clear (Caird et al, 1974). However left ventricular hypertrophy in association with ST-T change and left bundle branch block are likely to be indicative of hypertensive cardiac effects and are associated with an increased risk of mortality (Caird et al, 1974). There are often difficulties in the interpretation of chest radiographs in the elderly as the cardiothoracic ratio increases with age in the absence of heart disease and ratios of up to 54 per cent have been considered as normal in women over the age of 80 years (Cowan, 1964). Left ventricular enlargement may occur as a result of hypertension, but this appearance is not specific to hypertensive left heart disease. It is often technically very difficult to make accurate radiological measurements of ventricular size in elderly obese subjects. Characteristic features of pulmonary oedema may be observed in patients with left ventricular failure as a result of hypertensive disease.

Further extensive or invasive investigations are only justified in elderly patients if there is any convincing evidence of primary cause. Intravenous urography and separate renal function tests with renal arteriography and renin studies are only indicated if renal artery stenosis is suspected, and only in patients who are otherwise fit for surgical intevention. Further endocrine studies are rarely necessary but will help to exclude suspected rare adrenal lesions.

Treatment

In the management of hypertension in the elderly, the objective is to reduce the frequency of stroke disease and cardiac failure by gently lowering the blood pressure. Abrupt falls or swings in blood pressure are to be avoided. Gradual reduction in blood pressure levels is particularly important in relation to cerebral autoregulation. Too rapid reduction may reduce cerebral perfusion and result in confusion or focal neurological deficits. In the same way, altered renal perfusion may result in an abrupt deterioration in renal function, reflected by a rise in the blood urea and serum creatinine levels. Levels of 160/90 mmHg are regarded as upper

limits of 'normal' and should be the target figures for treatment. Patients with pressures above these levels should usually be treated, though where the blood pressure has been raised for many years and organ damage has already occurred, the objectives of treatment may have to be modified to reducing the risk of further damage without further compromising the function of organs already affected.

Drug therapy (see p. 235)
Much of the interest in the management of hypertension in the elderly arises because of the availability of new anti-hypertensive agents and combination preparations which can lower the blood pressure with relatively few side effects.

The severe depression often induced by reserpine and other central acting drugs is well documented in the literature of the 1950's and its use cannot be justified. Similarly the disabling postural hypotension, and abrupt swings of pressure from erect to standing position, induced by the early ganglion-blocking drugs with a peripheral action are too dangerous to be acceptable. Methyldopa is not without side effects but has remained an important drug because it is capable of reducing diastolic hypertension in a dose that may not cause significant side effects (see p. 236).

Satisfactory blood pressure control will normally be achieved in elderly patients with thiazides and or beta-blocking drugs and only a small minority will require a third line additional antihypertensive agent.

Supervision of treatment. During long-term hypotensive therapy the elderly patient should be supervised particularly carefully in the first three months of therapy to ensure a gradual reduction in the blood pressure with the minimum of unwanted effects. Erect and supine blood pressure should be checked at each visit to exclude the development of postural hypotension. After the first 3 months, 3-monthly blood pressure checks should be performed by the family physician if the blood pressure level remains satisfactory. Annual laboratory estimation of the serum urea, electrolytes, creatinine, blood sugar, and serum uric acid should be carried out, particularly in patients who are receiving a diuretic.

ISCHAEMIC HEART DISEASE

Ischaemic heart disease is quantitatively the most important form of heart disease in old age. It is the commonest single cardiac disease diagnosed in population studies, being found in 20 per cent of men and 12 per cent of women over the age of 65 (Kennedy et al, 1977). It is the commonest sole or contributory cause of cardiac failure in the elderly (Pomerance, 1965b), and the commonest variety of heart disease to be recorded on death certificates in old age. Though its pathological appearances show no striking differences from those found in the young and middle-aged, except that fibrous aneurysm and external cardiac rupture are more common (Pomerance, 1976), there are important modifications in its clinical presentation and management.

The most striking fact about ischaemic heart disease is the steady increase with age in its incidence and prevalence, accompanied by a steady decrease in the preponderance of men; women develop myocardial infarction about 10 years on average after men (Konu, 1977). This is shown in all clinical and autopsy studies, and is probably attributable to the withdrawal of the protective influence of female sex hormones at the menopause, a view supported by the high frequency of the disease in oophorectomized women (Oliver and Boyd, 1969). Pathologically a similar trend is seen in the prevalence and sex ratio of large myocardial lesions, both necrotic and fibrotic, which may be legitimately termed infarcts (Schwartz and Mitchell, 1962).

Angina pectoris

In the elderly angina pectoris is often associated with much less severe pain that in middle-aged patients though accompanying dyspnoea and the overriding need to stop the causal exertion remain. These features, when occurring on exercise and rapidly subsiding with rest, make clear the nature of even minor chest pain in the elderly. The radiation of pain follows that common in younger patients.

Physical examination is not usually contributory in the elderly patient with angina, but cardiac enlargement, an abnormal cardiac impulse, gallop rhythm or reversed splitting of the second sound may be present. The important investigations are the electrocardiogram, which often shows ischaemic changes or evidence of old infarction, and a blood count, to exclude a treatable anaemia as a cause of angina.

The management of angina follows the same lines as in younger patients. Retirement from active work and rearrangement of the social activities of the household may reduce exercise sufficiently to effect a great diminution in the frequency of angina. The patient should be encouraged to live up to but within the limits set by the symptom. Trinitrin is of value especially for use when activity resulting in angina can be predicted, and, provided serious hypotension can be avoided, beta-adrenergic blockade is useful in the elderly. Nifedipine (p. 237) is useful in the treatment of intractable angina in the elderly, particularly if beta-blocking agents are contraindicated (Rothbaum, 1981).

Coronary artery surgery

The main indication for coronary artery bypass surgery is for the relief of intractable angina not responding to adequate medical management. Advanced age is in itself not an absolute contraindication to myocardial revascularization procedures (Hamby et al, 1973; Ashor et al, 1972; Gann et al, 1977). Significant symptomatic improvement can now be expected in up to 95 per cent of elderly patients after aortocoronary bypass surgery (Du Cailar et al, 1980: Knapp et al, 1981). Operative mortality is higher in elderly patients (Tucker et al, 1977; Jolly et al, 1981) but with advances in myocardial protection techniques the mortality has recently been reduced considerably to less than 5 per cent in patients over 70 (Du Cailar et al, 1980; Knapp et al, 1981). Postoperative complications are more common than in younger patients but in one study of patients over the age of 65 the 5-year post-operative survival was 80 per cent; after a mean period of 30 months 94 per cent of patients were improved and 68 per cent asymptomatic (Du Cailar et al, 1980). In a study of patients over the age of 70 years, 95 per cent survived 3 years and 95 per cent of these were improved or angina-free (Knapp et al, 1981). The main prognostic factors for surgical success are related to the general medical condition of the patient, the adequacy of left ventricular function and the suitability of the distal coronary arterial tree for venous bypass grafting (Jolly et al, 1981).

Acute cardiac infarction

In the elderly acute cardiac infarction may show many clinical differences from the well-known picture in middle age but the classical presentation with chest pain and breathlessness is common (Williams et al, 1976; Macdonald et al, 1982). Pathy (1967) has described the varied ways in which this common illness can present in old age. Its frequent manifestations include an acute confusional state, syncopal episodes, hemiplegia (due to cerebral infarction following hypotension or to cerebral embolism), embolic occlusion of non-cerebral arteries, renal failure, vomiting, and intense weakness. There is no doubt however that absence of cardiac pain is a relatively frequent phenomenon in the elderly patient with cardiac infarction. Good evidence of this is provided by Rodstein's (1956) study, in which only 15 of 52 episodes (29 per cent) of myocardial infarction in residents in an old people's home were clinically typical, 21 (40 per cent) were atypical and 16 (31 per cent) entirely silent, in that the electrocardiogram provided the only clue to the diagnosis. Cardiac infarction should therefore be considered as a possible diagnosis in an old person whose general condition suddenly worsens, especially if dyspnoea, syncope or a confusional state are striking features, and whether or not there is a complaint of chest pain.

The physical signs of acute cardiac infarction in the

elderly do not differ from those in middle age. Dysrhythmias, hypotension, slight elevation of the venous pressure, gallop rhythm and reversed splitting of the second heart sound may be found. The electrocardiogram shows patterns identical to those in younger patients. Fever, leucocytosis, increased ESR and elevation of serum enzymes all follow the customary pattern.

Management of cardiac infarction

The management of acute infarction is often dictated by the presenting complex of symptoms. If the condition is clearly recognizable there is no reason other than purely economic considerations for initial management outside a coronary care unit (Chaturvedi et al, 1972; Semple and Williams, 1976), but management at home is indicated if the clinical severity of the infarct is mild and social circumstances favourable. There is little merit in complete bed rest in the very old. A deep comfortable armchair may be preferable to bed if dyspnoea is troublesome. Short periods out of bed each day may help to prevent venous thrombosis, hypostatic pneumonia and cardiovascular deconditioning (Fareeduddin and Abelmann, 1969). If there is no evidence of cardiac failure, gradual mobilization should begin after, at most, 7 to 10 days, but if there is, greater caution is necessary. The recurrence of dysponoea or tachycardia after the first few days should raise the suspicion of cardiac failure or pulmonary embolism.

There is often little indication in the acute stage for powerful analgesics, but morphine or diamorphine may be needed if pain is present, while chlordiazepoxide provides an adequate general sedative. Dyspnoea from left heart failure remains an indication for opiates, such as morphine 10 mg. Where anxiety and restlessness predominate, intramuscular diazepam 5 to 10 mg is valuable.

Dysrhythmias should be treated actively (see p. 238)

Anticoagulant therapy should be reserved for those patients who suffer a systemic embolus, or develop, or are at risk for, venous thrombosis and/or pulmonary embolism; these include the obese, the hemiplegic and those with pre-existing venous disease in the legs. There is no evidence that the elderly in general benefit from routine anticoagulant therapy for acute cardiac infarction but as a result of the indications cited a fair proportion of them in fact deserve this treatment.

Adequate psychological support is essential both in the acute stage (including when in the coronary care unit), and even more during and after rehabilitation. Elderly infarct patients have an increased tendency to continuing disability, especially anxiety, depression, dyspnoea and fatigue (Peach and Pathy, 1979). An optimistic outlook, with encouragement that return to previous activities is expected and prolonged invalidism and viability not in question, should be maintained by all concerned. The patient's spouse may have the same or even greater anxieties, and these should receive the necessary courtesy of explanation and reassurance. Cardiac infarction is a serious enough illness in old age without the unnecessary additional imposition of iatrogenic cardiac neurosis.

Hospital series show a steady increase in the mortality of cardiac infarction with age (Norris et al, 1969; Semple and Williams, 1976). Some of the complications appear to be related to age, including conduction defects, dysrhythmias, and 'shock' (Semple and Williams, 1976), while cardiac rupture (Sievers et al, 1961; Rasmussen et al, 1979) may be more common in the small heart of the older person. These increases with age may in part be due to selective admission of more severe cases in old age. Routine electrocardiographic and autopsy studies (Fisch et al, 1957; Gould and Cawley, 1958; Campbell et al, 1974) show a prevalence of totally unsuspected myocardial infarction of at least 5 per cent in the elderly. This indicates that the prognosis of all acute episodes must be much better than hospital statistics suggest.

There is no doubt than the long-term survival of elderly patients with myocardial infarction is better, relative to their natural expected mortality, than that of younger patients. Thus Bjorck et al (1958) found that the ratio of actual to expected mortality in the 5 years after discharge from hospital following acute cardiac infarction to be 4.6 in men in the sixth decade and 1.3 in the ninth. Other figures (Librach et al, 1976) are of the same order. In elderly patients who survive the first 3 months after the acute infarct, the expected survival is 71 per cent at three years (Pathy and Peach, 1981). This is the factual basis for optimism in considering the long-term prognosis of cardiac infarction in old age.

General anaesthesia after myocardial infarction

If general anaesthesia is required, age in itself does not appear to influence the incidence of re-infarction (Tarhan and Guiliani, 1974) or mortality (Skinner and Pearce, 1964) in patients who have suffered acute myocardial infarction. Patients over the age of 70 are however more at risk of perioperative cardiac complications (Goldman et al, 1977). The shorter the interval between an acute myocardial infarction and general anaesthesia, the greater is the risk of re-infarction. This is particularly so within the first 3 months (Howat, 1971; Sapala et al, 1975; Tarhan and Guiliani, 1974). Relative risks are reduced after 6 months have elapsed and the infarct is well compensated (Goldman et al, 1977; Fowler, 1981).

Myocardial re-infarction is especially likely to occur after surgery of the great vessels, lungs and upper abdomen (Tarhan and Guiliani, 1974). Infarction during anaesthesia may be precipitated by tachycardia, hypoxia, hypotension, haemorrhage and reduced cardiac output. The risk of perioperative cardiac complications can be minimized by the appropriate pre-operative management of dysrythmias, cardiac failure or other medical problems.

Elderly patients with well-compensated myocardial infarction of more than six months duration will tolerate elective surgical diagnostic and therapeutic procedures under any form of anaesthesia. Life-threatening surgical conditions, e.g. bowel strangulation, will require immediate surgical intervention regardless of the interval after acute myocardial infarction but the mortality in these circumstances may be as high as 90 per cent if the infarct has been very recent (Tarhan et al, 1972).

Secondary prevention

A number of pharmacological agents including aspirin, oral anticoagulants and beta-blockers have been proposed as useful forms of secondary prevention after acute myocardial infarction.

There is no convincing evidence that aspirin in conventional or lower dosage can reduce mortality after myocardial infarction (Mitchell, 1980) and, as yet, there are no clear recommendations for the use of aspirin or similar platelet anti-aggregants in survivors of infarction (International Society and Federation of Cardiology, 1981).

Despite earlier, less promising studies of the value of long-term oral anticoagulant therapy as a secondary prevention measure (International Anticoagulant Review Group, 1970) more recent work has observed a reduced re-infarction rate and mortality rate in selected elderly patients with good laboratory anticoagulant control (Sixty Plus Re-infarction Study Research Group, 1980, 1982).

It is not accepted that beta-blockers have a cardio-protective effect after acute myocardial infarction (Baber and Lewis, 1982). The mechanism is unclear but may be due to a combination of antidys-rhythmic, antihypertensive and antiplatelet effects. Oral timolol therapy (Norwegian Multicenter Study Group, 1981) and combined initial intravenous and oral long-term metoprolol therapy (Hjalmarson et al, 1981) lead to a reduction in mortality in elderly post-infarct subjects up to the age of 75. Timolol may also reduce the incidence of re-infarction (Norwegian Multicenter Study Group, 1981). The value of initial early intra-venous beta-blocker treatment has however not yet been established nor has the recommended duration of therapy been determined (Baber and Lewis, 1982). Beta blockade is contraindicated after acute myocardial infarction in patients with hypotension (systolic blood pressure <100 mmHg), bradycardia (<45 beats/minute),

overt heart failure, atrioventricular block or bronchial asthma (Hjalmarson et al, 1981).

VALVULAR DISEASE

Valvular disease is common in the elderly. It is easier to consider disorders of each valve separately.

Mitral valve disease

Rheumatic mitral valve disease

The prevalence of rheumatic mitral valve disease in elderly hospital patients is about 4 per cent (Bedford and Caird, 1960; Pomerance, 1976), and in the general elderly population perhaps 2 to 3 per cent. These figures are determined by the natural history of rheumatic heart disease and by the incidence of rheumatic fever during the childhood and adolescence of the patients in question. The incidence of rheumatic fever has been declining for many years (see, for example, Sievers and Hall, 1971), and so the frequency of rheumatic heart disease may also be expected to decline in the elderly as time passes. The relative importance of non-rheumatic mitral disease will thus increase.

About 40 per cent of elderly patients with mitral disease give a history of rheumatic fever or chorea in early life. The first rheumatic manifestation does not occur later in life in those patients who survive into old age, but recurrence of rheumatic fever is less common. Valvular deformity may perhaps have developed after a longer interval from the initial rheumatic episode in such patients (Bedford and Caird, 1960). Valve deform-ities in old people who do not give histories of rheumatic fever may also be due to valvulitis of other aetiologies (Pomerance, 1976), and it is now clear that many cases, particularly of mitral incompetence, are of non-rheumatic origin (see below).

In about one-third of patients the dominant lesion of the mitral valve is stenosis, while in the remainder incompetence predominates. About half also have evidence of disease of the aortic valve; this consists of incompetence alone in two-thirds, stenosis and incom-petence in a quarter, and pure stenosis in the remaining 15 per cent (Bedford and Caird, 1960). Of patients admitted to hospital, about half have no cardiac symp-toms; this proportion is doubtless considerably higher in elderly patients at home. About 40 per cent of patients seen in hospital have evidence of cardiac failure, and some 10 per cent have angina; almost all of the latter also have evidence of coronary artery disease. Systemic embolism is found in 6 per cent, particularly among those with dominant mitral stenosis. It rarely compli-cates predominant mitral incompetence except after coincidental myocardial infarction. Pulmonary embolism is largely a complication of cardiac failure, and infective endocarditis occurs in only the occasional case.

The physical signs are much as in younger patients. About one-third of hospital patients have atrial fibrillation. A malar flush is sometimes seen. Cardiac enlargement is common, and a left ventricular type of impulse will be felt in mitral incompetence, and rarely a right ventricular impulse in predominant stenosis. The first heart sound is loud in predominant stenosis, and if this is heard during tachycardia, a careful search should always be made for other signs of mitral disease when the heart rate is slower. An opening snap is not infrequent (Caird et al, 1973a), and may on occasion, particularly when the cardiac output is low, be the only sign. The classical mid-diastolic murmur is heard at the apex. In predominant incompetence a soft first heart sound, apical pansystolic murmur, third heart sound and short mid-diastolic murmur are the rule.

The electrocardiogram in mitral stenosis may show P mitrale or atrial fibrillation, but evidence of right ventricular hypertrophy is unusual. In predominant incompetence there may be signs of left ventricular hypertrophy. The chest X-ray often shows considerable left atrial enlargement, but Kerley's lines and any evidence of pulmonary hypertension are unusual.

These clinical, electrocardiographic and radiological signs may be modified by the simultaneous presence of aortic valve disease, especially when there is an important degree of aortic stenosis.

The cardiac output in valvular disease is only reduced if there is atrial fibrillation, cardiac failure, or both (Caird, 1982a).

Other causes of mitral valve disorder

Four other causes of mitral valve disorder require to be considered in the differential diagnosis. Taken together they may outnumber cases of rheumatic heart disease. 'Functional mitral imcompetence' is supposed to be due to variable dilatation of the mitral valve ring. It may well be a myth, and only the causes of true, fixed, or anatomical mitral incompetence require to be considered.

Papillary muscle dysfunction. Described by Goodwin (1968), this is usually secondary to ischaemic damage (De Pasquale and Burch, 1966) and may give rise to mitral incompetence. The resulting murmur is heard at the apex, and may be of ejection type; there are no signs of mitral obstruction.

Calcification of the mitral annulus. Described by Pomerance (1976), this is usually asymptomatic, and manifests as an abnormal radiological or echocardiographic appearance; the obliquely-set horseshoe of calcium is best seen on lateral radiographs, or may be diagnosed by echocardiography (Hirschfeld and Emilson, 1975). Occasionally a fibrotic and calcareous shelf may project below the cusps or into their bases and give rise to signs of mitral incompetence or stenosis (Simon and Liu, 1954; Korn et al, 1962; Kirk and Russell, 1969; Ostenberger et al, 1971; Bulkley and Roberts, 1975).

Mucoid degeneration of the mitral cusps. Not infrequently this is an incidental autopsy finding in the elderly (Pomerance, 1970; Devereux et al, 1976). Part of the posterior cusp and its attached elongated chordae may prolapse into the left atrium during systole, and so produce mitral incompetence. The characteristic pattern of physical signs (a midsystolic click followed by a late systolic murmur) may be difficult to recognize (Tresch et al, 1979). In some cases atrial fibrillation and cardiac failure develop, as may infective endocarditis, while rupture of the abnormal chordae (Tresch et al, 1979) may require mitral valve replacement or be fatal (Pomerance, 1976).

Left atrial myxoma. This may rarely be encountered in old age (Goodwin, 1963). The diagnosis should be suggested by rapidly advancing symptoms of mitral obstruction, with syncope (due to intermittent prolapse of the tumour into the mitral orifice and resultant cessation of forward flow), systemic embolic episodes, variable mitral systolic and diastolic murmurs, a raised ESR and abnormal plasma proteins. Detailed investigation by angiocardiography and/or echocardiography, and surgical treatment, are urgent, whatever the age of the patient.

Treatment of mitral valve disease

The treatment of rheumatic heart disease in old age is usually essentially medical, though the results of mitral valvotomy and valve replacement in the older age groups (Canepa-Anson & Emanuel, 1979; Jolly et al, 1981) are good enough, with 5-year survival rates of over 60 per cent, to encourage surgical treatment when there is evidence of severe mitral disease. Anti-coagulant therapy is essential in patients who have had systemic emboli, though this may need to be continued for only 6 months (Adams et al, 1974). It should also be considered for patients with mitral stenosis (but probably not mitral incompetence) and atrial fibrillation, as is now advised in younger patients. The difficulties of anticoagulant therapy in the elderly are discussed on page 239.

Aortic valve disease

Aortic stenosis

This valvular lesion is common in old age, the prevalence in geriatric hospital patients being about 4 per cent (Bedford and Caird, 1960), and in the elderly population probably little less. It seems to be more frequent in men under the age of 80, and in women over that age. Aortic valvular sclerosis, producing an ejection movement but no obstruction to ejection, is very common, but no more than the auscultatory evidence of an age change. About 20 per cent of cases of aortic stenosis are definitely due to rheumatic heart disease, and there is co-existent disease of the mitral valve. In the remainder there are three main processes (Pomerance, 1976). In the first or post-inflammatory variety, there is commissural adhesion and fibrous thickening of the valve cusps, giving rise to a triangular or eccentric buttonhole orifice (Fig. 12.6), in the second heavy calcific deposition mainly on the aortic aspects of the cusps, giving rise to rigid cusps with a triradiate orifice but normal commissures (Fig. 12.7), while in the third type there is calcification of a congenitally bicuspid valve, when the orifice is transverse or

Fig. 12.8 Heavy calcification of bicuspid aortic valve, with stenosis

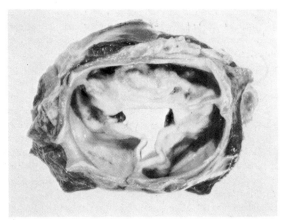

Fig. 12.6 Aortic valve showing commissural fusion, causing aortic stenosis and incompetence (72-year-old man)

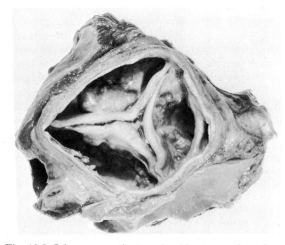

Fig. 12.7 Calcareous aortic stenosis without commissural fusion

slightly crescentic (Fig. 12.8). The second is the commonest variety, especially over the age of 75, and may represent an exaggerated age change. It is neither easy nor at present very important to attempt to distinguish clinically between these varieties of aortic stenosis in old age.

The majority of cases of aortic stenosis in the elderly have no cardiac symptoms, but about one-third of patients seen in hospital are dyspnoeic, and about 10 per cent have angina pectoris. A few have syncopal attacks, which usually occur on exertion. Patients in terminal cardiac failure may experience syncope at rest, accompanied by sweating, restlessness, confusion, cyanosis, irregular bradycardia and hypotension (see Bedford and Caird, 1960).

The physical signs in severe cases consist of a slowly rising pulse, low pulse pressure, left ventricular hypertrophy with a powerful slowly rising cardiac impulse, loud harsh ejection murmur maximal in the right second space, but also audible at the apex, sometimes showing expiratory accentuation radiating into the neck, and sometimes accompanied by a basal thrill, together with depression and reversed splitting of the second heart sound and, in over half, an aortic diastolic murmur, usually short and soft. In less severe cases the abnormality of the pulse is absent.

The electrocardiogram is rarely normal and shows evidence of left ventricular hypertrophy, usually with STT and T-wave changes. Left bundle branch block occurs in a few. Dysrhythmias are unusual unless there is mitral disease as well. The chest X-ray shows left ventricular enlargement, especially if there is aortic incompetence or cardiac failure. Calcification of the valve may be demonstrable on lateral radiographs or by image intensification; if present, it usually indicates severe stenosis. The cardiac output is unaltered except if there is cardiac failure (Caird, 1982a).

The principal problems in diagnosis of aortic stenosis in old age lie in distinguishing the murmur of aortic valvular sclerosis, without stenosis, and, if aortic incompetence is present, in distinguishing aortic stenosis with incompetence from the various forms of aortic incompetence. The former distinction is made from the loudness of the systolic murmur, which is greater in true aortic stenosis, from the presence of reduction in intensity and reversed splitting of the second sound and from evidence of left ventricular hypertrophy, which do not occur in valvular sclerosis. Phonocardiography and carotid systolic time interval tracings help to exclude severe aortic stenosis (Flohr et al, 1981). Most errors are of omission (Andersen et al, 1975), but it is at times impossible to make the distinction with certainty (cf. Rodstein and Zeman, 1967). The distinction from other causes of aortic incompetence is discussed below.

Surgical treatment of aortic valve disease in old age carries a reasonable prospect, with 5-year survival rates of over 50 per cent (Canepa-Anson & Emanuel, 1979; Jolly et al, 1981). It should be reserved for severe cases since the prognosis for life of cases seen in a geriatric unit is not very different from that of patients without valvular disease. The presence of cardiac failure worsens prognosis greatly, though not beyond that expected for congestive failure in non-valvular heart disease at the same age (Bedford and Caird, 1960).

Aortic incompetence

This is probably the commonest valvular lesion in old age. It has many causes, most of them very rare in the elderly: these include rupture of an aortic cusp, infective endocarditis, dissecting aneurysm of the aorta, incomplete aortic rupture (in which a tear in the aortic intima just above the aortic valve, similar to that in dissecting aneurysm, allows the adjacent cusp to prolapse into the left ventricle in diastole), and aortitis in ankylosing spondylitis. There are four common causes: rheumatic heart disease, calcareous disease of the aortic valve, syphilitic heart disease, and 'isolated non-syphilitic aortic incompetence' (Bedford and Caird, 1960; Pomerance, 1976).

About 40 per cent of cases of rheumatic heart disease in old age have aortic incompetence in addition to signs of mitral disease, and the combination is somewhat commoner in men than women. The murmur is heard at the usual site, at the base of the heart, down the left sternal edge, and at the apex, and is soft and usually short. The murmur of pulmonary incompetence should not give rise to difficulty, since it is excessively rare in old age, and should never be diagnosed unless there is

clear evidence of gross right ventricular hypertrophy. Aortic incompetence in calcareous aortic stenosis has been discussed.

Syphilitic heart disease is uncommon at any age, but in recent years one-third of cases have been over 70, especially in men. A past history of syphilis is rarely obtainable, but there is usually tabes dorsalis or taboparesis (Bedford and Caird, 1960). Cardiac symptoms are frequent and aortic incompetence clinically severe. There is usually an aortic ejection murmur, the aortic component of the second heart sound is loud and ringing, and there is a long aortic diastolic murmur widely heard over the praecordium. The electrocardiogram shows signs of left ventricular hypertrophy or myocardial ischaemia, and the chest radiograph shows irregular dilatation of the aorta, occasionally frank aneurysm formation, and especially calcification of the ascending aorta. The latter is characteristically thinner and more regular than that of atheroma, and retains its diagnostic significance in old age (Thorner et al, 1949). The serological tests for syphilis are positive (or have been in the past) in the blood or cerebrospinal fluid in the great majority of cases.

The diagnosis of syphilitic aortic incompetence is not usually difficult, and its prognosis is not unduly poor unless heart failure is present (Webster et al, 1953). Penicillin should be given if there is evidence of active infection; iodine therapy would seem unnecessary and undue fear of the Jarisch-Herxheimer reaction unreasonable.

Isolated aortic incompetence. It has long been recognized that aortic incompetence in old age may not be due to any of the commoner causes and may lack a clearly defined pathological basis. The underlying cause in these cases appears to be dilatation of the aorta due to the changes already described and concomitant increase in the circumference of the aortic ring, without any major abnormality of the aortic valve, though age-related changes in the valve (see above) are of course often present.

Clinical and autopsy data suggest that the frequency of 'isolated' aortic incompetence is about 1 per cent (Pomerance, 1976; Kennedy et al, 1977). It is almost always asymptomatic, and cardiac failure is no commoner than in elderly patients without aortic valve disease. Signs of 'free' or severe aortic incompetence are unusual, the pulse and pulse pressure are commonly normal, and there is only rarely clinical evidence of left ventricular hypertrophy. An aortic ejection murmur is common, the aortic component of the second sound is normal or loud, and the murmur of aortic incompetence usually short and heard only at the base or apex of the heart (Bedford and Caird, 1960).

The electrocardiogram may show signs of left ventricular hypertrophy, but the chest X-ray is unhelpful, because the degree of aortic dilatation is rarely great enough to be definitely recognizable.

It seems reasonable to regard the condition as a consequence of a normal age change, accelerated in some cases by hypertension. It carries a good prognosis.

Differential diagnosis. The differential diagnosis of aortic incompetence in old age may be summarized as follows: rheumatic aortic incompetence may be distinguished by the presence of signs of mitral disease; calcareous aortic valve disease by the louder, harsher systolic murmur and the reduced intensity of the aortic component of the second heart sound; and syphilitic aortic incompetence by signs of neurosyphilis, the usually more severe haemodynamic abnormality, the radiological changes, and the positive serology. The rarer causes may give rise to difficulty and there will inevitably be errors, but attention to the points mentioned will allow a correct diagnosis in the great majority of cases.

Tricuspid valve disease

Tricuspid stenosis usually occurs in severe multivalvular rheumatic heart disease, which is not in general compatible with long survival. It is therefore rare in the elderly, though the occasional case is encountered. It may complicate the carcinoid syndrome. In either case the diagnosis is suggested by gross elevation of the venous pressure with hepatomegaly but without frank cardiac failure, superior mediastinal obstruction having been excluded.

Tricuspid incompetence is by comparison common. Functional incompetence complicates right heart failure of whatever aetiology, as it is almost the rule when the right atrial pressure is grossly elevated. The diagnosis is made from the presence of a large positive systolic wave in the venous pulse, together with a regurgitant pansystolic murmur, maximal at the lower left sternal border and usually showing clear accentuation on inspiration. This murmur may be mistaken for that of mitral incompetence, and mitral disease thus diagnosed, if attention is not paid to the details mentioned. 'Organic' tricuspid incompetence, due to destructive changes in the valve, is, like tricuspid stenosis, decidedly rare in old people.

Pulmonary valve disease

This is extremely uncommon in the elderly. Pulmonary ejection murmurs are virtually always due to atrial septal defect (see below), while pulmonary incompetence is confined to very rare cases of severe chronic pulmonary hypertension, whether due to mitral valve disease or to chronic lung disease. This state is not compatible with long life.

PULMONARY HEART DISEASE

Chronic cor pulmonale

By far the commonest cause of pulmonary heart disease is severe chronic bronchitis, with respiratory failure, but often without emphysema (see Hanley, 1976, for review). This is rarely compatible with survival past the age of 80, so that this diagnosis should only occasionally be made over that age, but it is not infrequent under that age.

Chronic cor pulmonale may be diagnosed in the absence of cardiac failure by evidence of right ventricular hypertrophy in a patient with chronic lung disease. There is usually a long history, of many years or decades, of productive cough worse in winter. The great majority of patients are men, and have been cigarette smokers since early manhood, but there is a small group of cases in women who have never smoked. Breathlessness is usually severe, but chest pain unusual. Central cyanosis and right-sided gallop rhythm are the important physical signs, together with evidence of severe airways obstruction.

Cardiac failure is almost always precipitated by a respiratory infection and is signalled by worsening dyspnoea, and the appearance of orthopnoea and oedema. Regular tachycardia, elevation of the venous pressure in all phases of respiration, enlargement of the liver, as shown by percussion of the upper border and palpation of the lower, and basal crepitations (but only rarely pleural effusion) constitute the additional signs.

The electrocardiogram shows characteristic changes, with a P-wave axis of $+ 60°$ or more, right axis deviation, clockwise rotation with rS in V_5, a dominant R in V_4R and sometimes V_3R, and sometimes T inversion in V_3 and V_4. In patients without cardiac failure the cardiothoracic ratio may be normal, and the only useful radiological change is enlargement of the main pulmonary arteries; in those with cardiac failure the cardiothoracic ratio may exceed 50 per cent. Other investigations of value include measurement of the peak expiratory flow rate or forced expiratory volume. The former is usually less than 100 litres/minute and the latter less than 1 litre. The blood gases show hypoxaemia and hypercapnia.

The special features of the management of pulmonary heart failure are described below.

Occasional cases of cor pulmonale due to chronic diffuse interstitial fibrosis of the lungs (fibrosing alveolitis), and to pulmonary thromboembolism (see p. 745) are seen in old age. Again the diagnosis rests on the demonstration, almost always by electrocardiography, of right ventricular hypertrophy in the presence of pulmonary parenchymal or vascular disease. Kyphoscoliotic cor pulmonale is very rarely encountered in the elderly (Hanley, 1976).

MISCELLANEOUS FORMS OF HEART DISEASE

Congenital heart disease

Although occasional cases of patent ductus arteriosus, coarctation of the aorta and pulmonary stenosis have been reported as surviving into old age (Cooley et al, 1966; Perloff and Lindgren, 1974), only in atrial septal defect is this survival at all common.

The clinical, radiological and electrocardiographic features of atrial septal defect in the elderly are the same as in younger patients, except that disability from recurrent bronchitis and chronic congestive heart failure is almost always severe, and atrial fibrillation or flutter the rule (Coulshed and Littler, 1957; Markham et al, 1965). A murmur has often been heard in early or middle life. The heart is clinically enlarged, often with a pronounced parasternal heave indicating gross right ventricular hypertrophy. There is a loud ejection murmur maximum in the left second interspace, with wide splitting of the second heart sound and often a tricuspid regurgitant murmur.

The chest X-ray shows cardiac enlargement, and gross enlargement of the main pulmonary arteries (Colmers, 1958). The characteristic feature of the electrocardiogram is right bundle branch block, usually complete but sometimes incomplete.

The likelihood of irreversible changes in the pulmonary vasculature and parenchyma, and in the myocardium, makes surgical treatment only rarely practicable in the elderly but successful repair can be achieved (Cooley et al, 1966; Jolly et al, 1981). Medical management consists of protection against recurrent bronchitis with long-term antibiotic therapy, digoxin if there is an atrial dysrhythmia, and diuretics if cardiac failure develops.

Acute rheumatic fever

Rheumatic fever is characteristically a disease of childhood and young adult life, but about 10 per cent of cases of what is now a declining disease occur in patients over 60 (Kjorstad, 1957; Sievers and Hall, 1971). Fatal cases with the classical pathological appearances of acute rheumatic carditis are well described in old age (Rothschild et al, 1934; Grifone and Kitchell, 1954). Most clinically recognized cases present with malaise, fever, acute arthritis, and, on occasion, evidence of carditis such as changing murmurs and transient prolongation of the P-R interval. Many patients have had undoubted rheumatic fever in the past, or have signs of rheumatic heart disease. A rapid clinical improvement with salicylate therapy may be important diagnostic information.

The diagnosis is clearly difficult to make in the elderly, in view of the other much more common causes of acute arthritis, and the many possible causes of fever (Kjorstad, 1957), but the possibility should not be overlooked in the presence of suggestive features such as are mentioned above.

Infective endocarditis

In the past two decades there has been a substantial change in the clinical picture of infective endocarditis (Wilson, 1963; Hughes and Gauld, 1966; Shinebourne et al, 1969; Wedgwood, 1976; Schnurr et al, 1977). This is an uncommon illness but there has been an increase in the proportion of elderly patients affected (Schnurr et al, 1977; Moulsdale et al, 1980). Infective endocarditis often occurs in patients with no known valvular disorder (Anderson and Staffurth, 1955; Hughes and Gauld, 1966; Lerner and Weinstein, 1966; Schnurr et al 1977). The changing pattern of infective endocarditis over the last 30 years reflects the use of antibiotics, the decline of rheumatic fever and the increased survival of the elderly in the population, but there has also been a likely real increase in the incidence of the disease in old age (Leading Article, 1967).

The commonest infective organism is still the *Streptococcus viridans* (Moulsdale et al, 1980; Lowes et al, 1980) but other causes now include infection with other streptococci, staphylococci, pneumococci, coxiella, chlamydia and fungi. Clear-cut sources of infection are only detected in the minority of patients (Smith et al, 1976b). In the elderly, urological procedures or surgical treatment of the gall bladder or colon and even pressure sores are more likely to be the source of infection than dental procedures (Toh and Ball, 1960; Applefield and Hornick, 1974).

The largest single group of patients with infective endocarditis appear to have previously normal heart valves (Applefield and Hornick, 1974; Thell et al, 1975; Schnurr et al, 1977; Pomerance, 1981). Other possible predisposing cardiac lesions include calcific disease of the mitral and aortic valves, congenital bicuspid aortic valve, rheumatic valve disease, mucoid degeneration of the mitral valve and pacemaker wires or prosthetic valves.

The presenting features in the elderly are often bizarre and confusing (Wedgwood, 1976), but continuing fever, weight loss, embolism, either of a major artery (all too often cerebral) or as Osler's nodes, splenomegaly and microscopic heamaturia are all manifestations which should lead to urgent consideration of the diagnosis of infective endocarditis if they occur in a patient with a cardiac murmur, especially that of mitral incompetence (Anderson and Staffurth, 1955). The frequency of mental symptoms (Gleckler, 1958) and neurological signs (Applefield and Hornick, 1974) and of progressive renal failure (Zeman, 1945) has been stressed in the elderly. The presence of atrial fibrillation, once thought rare in infective endocarditis, should not deter the diagnosis (Eisinger, 1971).

Echocardiography may confirm the site of valve lesions and assist in visualising the vegetations (Hess et al, 1981). The crucial investigation, which is mandatory if the diagnosis is suspected, is blood culture, which may need to be repeated several times.

Treatment of infective endocarditis

Treatment should begin as soon as cultures have been taken because valve destruction may occur very early in the natural course of the illness. Antibiotic therapy should be bactericidal, should achieve high peak plasma concentrations and should be given parenterally. Intravenous infusion using a central subclavian line is to be preferred in the elderly when muscle wasting makes intramuscular injections distressing for the patient (Wedgwood, 1976). The majority of patients will respond to Penicillin G in doses of 10 megaunits in 24 hours combined with gentamicin 80 mg three times a day. Antimicrobial therapy should be carefully supervised by joint consultation between the clinician and the bacteriologist. Serum levels of the drugs prescribed should be carefully monitored. Antimicrobial therapy should be continued for at least 3 weeks, and for 6 weeks if the patient has an artificial heart valve (Oakley, 1978). Treatment should be continued until clinical signs of improvement occur: reduction in heart rate, fall in ESR, and disappearance of red cells from the urine. If emergency surgical intervention to eradicate the infective focus by a valve replacement is contemplated then a very high mortality must be expected (Smith et al, 1976a).

The prognosis of infective endocarditis in the elderly is poor, due mainly to delays in diagnosis and initiation of treatment, and partly to the frequent occurrence of damage to the aortic valve, with serious haemodynamic consequences and cardiac failure. The mortality rate rises to 25–50 per cent over the age of 60 years (Schnurr et al, 1977; Lowes et al, 1980). Death is usually due to cardiac failure and emboli and not as a result of failure to control the infective process (Smith et al, 1976b; Schnurr et al, 1977). Prevention is therefore more important, and antibiotic cover should be given for 24–48 hours to all old people with valvular disease who have a dental extraction or undergo any genitourinary procedure.

Senile cardiac amyloidosis

The prevalence of amyloidosis of the heart increases greatly with age. It is found at autopsy in 12 per cent of men dying over the age of 80 (Pomerance, 1965b). The amyloid material is most often found in the left atrial endocardium, but may be widespread throughout the ventricular myocardium. It is difficult to believe that the minor lesions demonstrable at autopsy can have great functional significance, except perhaps in the genesis of atrial arrhythmias, but it is clear that the widespread lesions can be a cause of cardiac failure (Pomerance, 1965b). The pathogenesis of senile cardiac amyloidosis is unknown. Amyloid deposition outside the heart is occasionally demonstrable, and it may perhaps be a variant of primary amyloidosis.

The clinical features of senile cardiac amyloidosis are mostly non-specific, and confident antemortem diagnosis is therefore very difficult. The most important pointers are probably the occurence of cardiac failure in a patient over the age of 80 without cardiac pain or evidence of valvular disease, with left ventricular enlargement, gallop rhythm and widespread T-wave changes on the electrocardiogram. The alkaline phosphatase may be raised (Hodkinson and Pomerance, 1974). A high frequency of digitalis toxicity has been reported, but this by itself is of little diagnostic value, as it is so common in all forms of cardiac disease in old age.

Cardiomyopathy

Primary disease of heart muscle (cardiomyopathy) is rare in the elderly, apart from cardiac amyloidosis. The occasional case of alcoholic cardiomyopathy and perhaps more often of hypertrophic obstructive cardiomyopathy will be encountered.

The former should be considered when congestive heart failure, usually with atrial fibrillation, substantial cardiac enlargement and marked gallop rhythm but without chest pain or electrocardiographic evidence of cardiac infarction, occurs in an alcoholic (Brigden and Robinson, 1964). There may be other evidence of alcoholism, such as hepatic cirrhosis or peripheral neuropathy. Routine treatment of the cardiac failure produces improvement, but the prognosis is poor.

Hypertrophic obstructive cardiomyopathy (Goodwin, 1970) usually masquerades as aortic stenosis and mitral incompetence. The oldest patient in Goodwin's series was 55 years old, but cases are certainly seen in later life (Berger et al, 1979; Petrin and Tavel, 1979). There is usually no relevant family history. Females predominate, and there is an association with hypertension (Petrin and Tavel, 1979). Patients may be asymptomatic, but the clinical presentation can include angina and dyspnoea on exertion; syncope is uncommon. Diagnosis is very difficult in the elderly, but should perhaps be suggested when aortic stenosis is considered but the aortic component of the second sound is normal in intensity. Phonocardiography (Tavel, 1968) and echocardiography (Berger et al, 1979) may help in the diagnosis.

Marked symptomatic improvement can be gained in this condition with propranolol (Berger et al, 1979), but digoxin, nitroglycerine and the excessive use of diuretics may be harmful. If medical treatment fails to produce a satisfactory response surgery may be indicated (Koch et al, 1980; Kafetz, 1981).

Thyrotoxic heart disease

Much has been written about the difference between the clinical picture of hyperthyroidism in young and middle-aged patients and in old age. It has been suggested that the presentation in the elderly is often atypical and diagnosis is in consequence difficult (Bartels, 1965; Locke, 1967). There is no doubt that the incidence of cardiac manifestations, and in particular atrial fibrillation, is greater in elderly patients with hyperthyroidism (Staffurth et al, 1965), and that hyperkinesia, palpitations and sweating are less common (Lazarus and Harden, 1969). But weight loss, tachycardia, heat intolerance, exophthalamos, lid lag and lid retraction are equally common. A goitre is demonstrable in 85 per cent, though it is often not large, is usually nodular, and may lack a bruit.

These manifestations of hyperthyroidism may be associated with signs of cardiac failure and, since other evidence of heart disease, for instance ischaemic or valvular (Bedford and Caird, 1956), may also be present, the diagnosis may hinge on the detection of a goitre, the demonstration of rapidly relaxing reflexes, or the observation that the ventricular rate does not respond to digitalis. Thyroid function tests should always be carried out if the diagnosis is suspected, but a therapeutic trial of antithyroid drugs can also be very valuable.

Radioiodine therapy is usually advocated for hyperthyroidism in the elderly (Sandler and Wilson, 1959; Staffurth et al, 1965) but more than one dose is often needed and the duration of hyperthyroidism and so of cardiac failure may be prolonged for several months before treatment becomes effective (Staffurth and Young, 1967). Initial control by antithyroid drugs combined perhaps with propranolol is more rapid, and thus often preferable, unless the goitre is large or retrosternal, when surgery after preliminary iodine therapy is the treatment of choice. Routine treatment with digitalis and diuretics will be needed to control cardiac failure until hyperthyroidism is suppressed. Atrial fibrillation usually but not always reverts spontaneously to sinus rhythm when the hyperthyroidism is controlled.

Anaemia and the heart

The response of the elderly heart appears to be quantitatively similar, if at a lower level, to that of the young. Cardiac output increases in proportion to the fall in haematocrit at least up to the age of 80. The response of the heart rate is unaltered (Caird, 1980).

Cardiac failure may complicate anaemia at any age, but even in the elderly is unusual until the haemoglobin falls below 7 g per 100 ml. Any type of anaemia may be responsible, but in the elderly anaemia of this severity is often megaloblastic.

The clinical features are those of severe anaemia and congestive heart failure of high output type, with warm hands, regular tachycardia, usually little cardiac enlargement (unless intrinsic heart disease is present), and almost always an ejection murmur.

A haematological diagnosis must be reached urgently. Patients with megaloblastic anaemia should receive the appropriate haematinic, but the hazard of potentially lethal potassium depletion must be remembered, and potassium supplements given as a routine (Lawson et al, 1972). Oedema may increase in the first few days and diuretics should not be withheld. Patients with anaemia of other origins usually require initial blood transfusion. Fear of precipitation of acute pulmonary oedema by transfusion is largely based on studies in which blood was given rapidly (Sharpey-Schafer, 1945). Packed cells from 1 litre of blood given over 6 to 8 hours are very well tolerated, and such small slow transfusions may need to be repeated every 2 or 3 days until a haemoglobin level of 10 g per 100 ml is reached (Bedford and Caird, 1960). Acute symptoms occurring during transfusion respond quickly to slowing of the infusion and administration of a rapidly acting loop diuretic.

Cardiac failure due to anaemia will not recur unless the anaemia recurs, and thus does not constitute an indication for long-continued therapy (Dall, 1970). The prognosis is that of the anaemia rather than that of cardiac failure (Bedford and Caird, 1956).

Vitamin B$_1$ deficiency (beri-beri)

Vitamin B$_1$ deficiency severe enough to give rise to beri-beri heart failure is not common in the elderly, but should be suspected when cardiac failure occurs with evidence of a high-output state, regular tachycardia, tender calf muscles and depressed reflexes in a patient with malnutrition and almost always chronic alcoholism (see Brigden and Robinson, 1964).

Digitalis and diuretics are said to be ineffective in controlling the cardiac failure, while a relatively rapid response, over a period of some days, to parenteral thiamine is diagnostic. Oedema may persist if there is hypoalbuminaemia, until this is corrected by a high-protein diet.

Paget's disease of bone

Paget's disease of bone is common in old age but usually only one or a few bones are affected. If lesions are extensive and active the increased vascularity of the bone is associated with a marked increase in the cardiac output, which may result in cardiac failure (Alpert, 1958; Acar et al, 1968). Cardiomegaly may occur and is in proportion to the extent of the bone lesions. An abnormal ECG may be found in more than three-quarters of those patients with generalised involvement of the skeleton (Acar et al, 1968). Such patients have clinically obvious Paget's disease with enlargement of the skull, bowing of the femora and tibiae, which are hot to touch, radiological evidence of abnormality of these and other bones, and a very high serum alkaline phosphatase, usually above 300 international units (Nagent de Deuxchaisnes and Rombouts-Lindermans, 1974). Metastatic calcification of the valve rings may occur with extension of the calcification to the intra-ventricular septum, and there may be associated con-duction defects (Harrison and Lennox, 1948).

High output cardiac failure associated with Paget's disease is an indication for prolonged calcitonin therapy (Woodhouse et al, 1975; Hosking, 1981), as the cardiac output is reduced to normal levels and symptomatic improvement can be expected (Woodhouse et al, 1975). Diphosphonates may be an alternative form of therapy in the high output cardiac failure state. Treatment for more than 6 months may be beneficial (Henley et al, 1976).

Pericardial disease
Acute pericarditis is not common in old age. A transient pericardial friction rub is heard in 10 per cent of elderly patients with acute myocardial infarction (Semple and Williams, 1976) and may rarely accompany left lower lobe pneumonia. Pyogenic pericarditis with cardiac tamponade is a very rare complication of pneumonia, but its recognition is of great importance, as aspiration of the pericardium and relief of cardiac compression is urgent.

The commonest cause of pericardial effusion in the elderly is undoubtedly malignant disease. Direct inva-sion of the pericardium with an effusion which is often blood-stained, may occur in bronchogenic carcinoma, especially of the left lower lobe, and in carcinoma of the left breast by spread through the chest wall. The important clinical signs are pulsus paradoxus and gross elevation of the venous pressure with the main com-ponent of the venous pulse a downward deflection. Diagnosis is best confirmed by echo-cardiography. Symptomatic relief is necessary by aspiration, and perhaps radio-therapy.

Chronic constrictive pericarditis
This is also rare in old age, but again its recognition is important, as it constitutes one of the curable forms of heart disease. Its clinical features are identical to those in younger patients. Important pointers are a grossly elevated venous pressure, hepatomegaly with ascites, and the combination of congestive failure and little or no radiological evidence of cardiac enlargement. Peri-cardial calcification will almost always be present, but

can also occur as an incidental finding in old people without symptoms or signs of heart disease, when it is probably a sequel to previous viral pericarditis. Oper-ative treatment of constrictive pericarditis should be carried out before prolonged elevation of the venous pressure produces irreversible hepatic damage.

CARDIAC FAILURE

Cardiac failure is a complex physiological state in which many organs other than the heart are involved. It occurs when the cardiac output falls, or fails to rise on exertion. The ventricular end-diastolic pressure and the pulmonary and/or systemic venous pressures rise; atrioventricular valves (commonly the tricuspid, probably rarely the mitral) may become incompetent because of dilatation of the valve ring. Reduced renal blood flow and glomerular filtration are associated with retention of sodium and water; in some cases a secondary increase in aldosterone secretion may further increase sodium retention and promote potassium loss.

The clinical picture is determined by whichever ventricle fails, and correct diagnosis, essential if grave errors of treatment are to be avoided, depends on the demonstration of the associated signs.

Left heart failure
This occurs in coronary artery disease, hypertension and aortic and mitral disease, and the main manifestations are due to pulmonary venous hypertension and increased stiffness of the lungs. Dyspnoea on effort, paroxysmal nocturnal dyspnoea and orthopnoea are accompanied by bilateral pulmonary signs (usually basal crepitations but occasionally patchy bronchial breathing), tachycardia and gallop rhythm. The appropriate murmurs will remain in valvular disease. In the elderly diagnosis may be made difficult by coexistent airways obstruction resulting from chronic bronchitis; but orthopnoea, left-sided gallop rhythm and especially the absence of purulent sputum, are usually enough to make it clear that dyspnoea has a major cardiac component. A chest radiograph will show cardiomegaly, pulmonary congestion and sometimes Kerley's lines. Other inves-tigations are unhelpful in diagnosing left heart failure, but are of importance in establishing its cause.

Right heart failure
The commonest cause of right heart failure is left heart failure, but chronic lung disease or multiple pulmonary emboli may precipitate it when the left heart is normal. Dyspnoea is often less urgent, and may be replaced by fatigue. Oedema of the legs is often the first symptom, but abdominal pain may be due to hepatic congestion, nausea and vomiting to congestion of the stomach or

small bowel, and confusion to hypoxaemia and reduced cerebral blood flow. The cardinal signs are the presence of visible dyspnoea, often with periodic breathing, symmetrical elevation of the venous pressure in all phases of respiration, positive hepato-jugular reflux, smooth hepatomegaly and oedema of both legs or sacrum. If oedema is asymmetrical, it cannot be solely due to cardiac failure, and venous disease is much the most likely cause. There are bilateral basal pulmonary signs, usually crepitations, but sometimes those of effusion. If all of these signs are present, the diagnosis of right heart failure is correct; if any one is absent, it is most unlikely.

In addition to making a correct diagnosis of the functional disorder of cardiac failure, it is important in any elderly patient to establish two further points both of which are vital in assessing the correct treatment and the prognosis: the type of heart disease responsible (the underlying cause) and the reason why the patient has cardiac failure at the time in question (i.e. the precipitating cause). It is important to establish the nature of the underlying heart disease because cardiac failure may result either from heart disease (primary cardiac failure) or from inability of the heart to achieve the output demanded by circumstances outside the heart (secondary cardiac failure). In the first instance treatment may need to be continued for life, in the second treatment of the extracardiac disease, especially severe anaemia or thyrotoxicosis, often results in the return of compensation and removes the need for continuing maintenance therapy (Dall, 1970). It is important to establish the precipitating cause of the episode of cardiac failure because many of these are either treatable (e.g. respiratory infection), tend to natural improvement (e.g. following myocardial infarction or pulmonary embolism), or can be guarded against (e.g. physical overexertion, or discontinuance of necessary therapy). Further, cardiac failure precipitated by a definite diagnosable event carries a better prognosis, if the event is not likely to recur, than failure occurring without a precipitating event, in the course of relentlessly progressive heart disease. The implication is that the heart disease is more serious in the second situation than the first. These principles apply to heart disease in the elderly as well as in the middle-aged.

Management of cardiac failure

The basic principles of management of cardiac failure are essentially the same at all ages, but allowance must be made for some special circumstances in old age.

Adequate rest must be ensured. This may not necessarily mean rest in bed, since orthopnoea often makes rest in a chair more comfortable. But walking must be prohibited in the early stages. Sedation with diazepam 5 mg or thioridazine 25 to 50 mg may be needed, and,

unless there is evidence of pulmonary disease, opiates in small doses (e.g. morphine 10 mg) may be used at night. But the best sedative for the elderly patient with cardiac failure is control of the failure. Severe and uncontrollable restlessness almost always implies a fatal outcome.

Oxygen therapy should be tried, again unless there is chronic lung disease. Its management in restless old people is often very difficult. A venti-mask delivering up to 40 per cent oxygen is safe and efficient, if it is tolerated. Fluid restriction is unncessary, and salt restriction need not be severe: no salt added to food is sufficient.

Digitalis remains the mainstay of therapy (see p. 232). The dangers of giving digitalis to the elderly have received much attention in the past 10 years; but provided there is a clear indication for the drug and the prescriber is aware of how the drug should be used in the elderly, age is no contraindication. The hazards result from the improper use of the drug, given in the wrong dose or for the wrong reasons (such as tachycardia alone, or breathlessness due to chronic bronchitis, or oedema due to immobility or chronic venous insufficiency).

The second mainstay of the treatment of cardiac failure is diuretic therapy (see p. 234). None of the commonly used drugs is contraindicated, but care is required with all of them. They should be given orally, except in the rare case of pulmonary oedema, when the rapid action of intravenous frusemide (40–80 mg) or ethacrynic acid (100 mg) may be life-saving. Those with a more rapid and intense action (frusemide, ethacrynic acid) should be given in the morning to avoid disturbance of sleep, but may overload the bladder and cause retention or overflow incontinence. The more slowly acting thiazides and chlorthalidone are thus preferable in some patients.

All thiazide and 'loop' diuretics should be assumed to produce potassium depletion (despite claims to the contrary). Potassium supplements should therefore be given as a routine. Twenty-four millimoles (mEq) per day is the amount required to protect against the development of hypokalaemia in elderly patients taking 40 mg of frusemide (furosemide) daily. Whatever preparation of potassium is best tolerated should be given.

Complex diuretic regimes involving the simultaneous use of several drugs are only very rarely needed. Spironolactone should be used only as part of one of these regimes. Amiloride may prove a useful alternative (Macfarlane and Kennedy, 1973). It augments sodium loss and reduces potassium loss when given with a thiazide; it may thus obviate the need for potassium supplements.

Patients with pulmonary heart failure due to chronic bronchitis should receive an antibiotic appropriate to any organism cultured from the sputum. Antibiotic therapy should be continued on a long-term basis, with ampicillin or tetracycline, as it is vital to attempt to prevent any recurrent infection. The regular use of a bronchodilator such as salbutamol or terbutaline is advisable for those whose airways obstruction is shown on testing to improve with treatment.

Control of treatment of heart failure
Clinical improvement, with reduction in breathlessness and oedema, fall in venous pressure and often improvement in mental state, constitutes the most important criterion of successful treatment. Much assistance may be gained from a weight chart; unless virtually moribund, no elderly patient is too ill to weigh. The information is much more valuable than a record of fluid output, particularly in an incontinent patient. Diuresis and loss of oedema results in a fall in weight, often of 10 kg or more, over a period of a week or so and the curve then levels off. It is useful, but not essential, to measure blood urea and electrolyte concentrations weekly. A rise in blood urea need not indicate a reduction in glomerular filtration rate, since urea production is often increased (Domenet and Evans, 1969). A minor fall in serum sodium and chloride should not be regarded as important, but a fall in the serum potassium level should be taken as an indication for increasing potassium supplements.

Once the patient is free of signs of cardiac failure, and weight loss has ceased, gradual mobilization should begin, first with walking to the toilet, then further about the ward or home, then on stairs. It is best to make changes no more often than weekly, and not to alter drug therapy during this phase, so that the effects of only one change at a time can be observed. Watch should ke kept for weight gain and the recurrence of oedema or nocturnal breathlessness. When a moderate degree of physical activity has been achieved, the drug regimen should be simplified as far as possible. It is usually possible to stop all cardiac therapy in patients with secondary cardiac failure as defined above, but apart from those patients whose failure was the result of a recent myocardial infarction, most other elderly patients who have been in 'primary' congestive heart failure require continuous therapy (Dall, 1970).

Resistant cardiac failure
A small proportion of elderly patients with congestive

failure do not respond rapidly to conventional therapy as outline above. Hope should not be abandoned, but a review made of the answers to the following questions. Is the diagnosis of cardiac failure correct? Is the diagnosis complete? Is therapy correct?

The accuracy of the diagnosis of congestive failure requires checking against the criteria mentioned. The completeness of the diagnosis needs to be assessed in the light of possible additional diagnoses, such as anaemia, thyrotoxicosis and infective endocarditis, possible complications such as pulmonary embolism, respiratory infection, pericardial effusion, chronic venous disease or hypoproteinaemia (as a cause of persistent oedema), digitalis intoxication, or severe electrolyte abnormality (Bedford and Caird, 1960). Any condition encountered will need to be treated in its own right before the cardiac failure is likely to respond completely. Treatment should be reviewed, with particular reference to exercise, digitalis and the efficacy of diuretic therapy. If none of these factors can be incriminated as the cause of resistance to treatment, severe myocardial disease must be assumed. In severe chronic heart failure, vasodilator therapy has been shown to improve performance and the response to exercise (Franciosa and Cohn, 1980). Despite encouraging initial reports and observations on haemodynamic parameters (Franciosa and Cohn, 1980), there has been difficulty in demonstrating sustained improvement in the management of chronic cardiac failure (Walsh and Greenberg, 1981).

Prognosis of cardiac failure
Twenty-five years ago, some 28 per cent of elderly patients admitted to a geriatric unit with congestive failure survived 2 years and 16 per cent 4 years (Bedford and Caird, 1956). Prognosis was worst in patients with cor pulmonale, syphilitic aortic incompetence and hypertensive heart failure with atrial fibrillation, and better in patients with coronary artery disease and rheumatic heart disease. Respiratory infection was the principal cause of death, but one death in seven was due to pulmonary embolism. Since that time it is likely that prognosis has improved because of earlier therapy with oral diuretics, while earlier mobilization may have reduced the frequency of venous thrombosis and pulmonary embolism, but clearly congestive heart failure is not 'terminal' in many old people. It should be correctly diagnosed and actively treated.

REFERENCES

Abrass I B, Scarpace P J 1981 Human lymphocyte beta-adrenergic receptors are unaltered with age. Journal of Gerontology 36: 298–301

Acar J, Delbarre F, Waynberger M 1968 Les complications cardio-vasculaires de la maladie osseuse de Paget. Archives des Maladies du Coeur et des Vaisseaux 6: 849–868

Adams G F, Merritt J D, Hutchinson W M, Pollock A M 1974 Cerebral embolism and mitral stenosis: survival with and without anticoagulants. Journal of Neurology, Neorosurgery and Psychiatry 37: 378–383

Alpert S 1958 Cardiovascular complications of Paget's disease. Annals of Internal Medicine 48: 871–876

Amery A, Berthaux P, Birkenhager W, et al 1978 Antihypertensive therapy in patients above 60 years (Fourth interim report of the European Working Party on high blood pressure in the elderly: EWPHE). Clinical Science and Molecular Medicine 55: 263–270

Andersen J A, Hansen B F, Lyngborg K 1975 Isolated valvular aortic stenosis. Acta Medica Scandinavica 197: 61–64

Anderson H J, Staffurth J S 1955 Subacute bacterial endocarditis in the elderly. Lancet ii:1055–1058

Anderson M P, Bechsgaard P, Frederiksen J, Hansen D, Jurgensen H J, Nielsen B, Pedersen F, Pederson Bjergaard O, Rasmussen S L 1979 Effect of alprenolol on mortality among patients with definite or suspected acute myocardial infarction. Lancet 2: 865–868

Applefield M M, Hornick R B 1974 Infective endocarditis in patients over age 60. American Heart Journal 88: 90–94

Aravanis C, Harris R 1958 The normal phonocardiogram of the aged. Diseases of the Chest 33: 214–219

Aronson J K, Grahame-Smith D G 1977 Monitoring digoxin therapy. II Determinants of the apparent volume of distribution. British Journal of Clinical Pharmacology 4: 233–237

Ashor G W, Meyer B W, Lindesmith G G, Stiles Q R, Walker G H, Tucker B L 1973 Coronary artery disease surgery in 100 patients 65 years of age and older. Archives of Surgery 107: 30–33

Ashworth C T 1946 Atherosclerotic valvular disease of the heart Archives of Pathology 42: 285–298

Baber N S, Lewis J A 1982 Confidence in results of beta-blocker postinfarction trials. British Medical Journal 284: 1749–1750

Bader H 1967 Dependence of wall stress in the human thoracic aorta on age and pressure. Circulation Research 20: 354–361

Bartels E C 1965 Hyperthyroidism in patients over 65. Geriatrics 20: 459–462

Baskett J J 1982 Biophysical ageing in systemic arteries. In: Isaacs B (ed) Recent Advances in Geriatric Medicine, Churchill Livingstone, Edinburgh, ch 3, p19

Bedford P D, Caird F I 1956 Congestive heart failure in the elderly. Quarterly Journal of Medicine NS 25: 407–426

Bedford PD, Caird F I 1960 Valvular disease of the heart in old age. Churchill, London

Berger M, Rethy C, Goldberg E 1979 Unsuspected hypertrophic subaortic stenosis in the elderly diagnosed by echocardiography. Journal of the American Geriatrics Society 27: 178–187

Bertel O, Buhler F R, Kiowski, W, Lutold B E 1980 Decreased beta-adrenoreceptor responsiveness as related to age blood pressure and plasma catecholamines in patients with essential hypertension. Hypertension 2: 130–138

Bethel C S, Crow E W 1963 Heart sounds in the aged. American Journal of Cardiology 11: 763–767

Bjorck G, Sievers J, Blomqvist J 1958 Studies in myocardial infarction in Malmo (III). Acta Medica Scandinavica 162: 81–97

Bramwell J C 1924 Arterial elasticity in man. Quarterly Journal of Medicine 17: 225–243

Branfonbrener M, Landowne M, Shock N W 1955 Changes in cardiac output with age. Circulation 12: 557–566

Brigden W, Robinson J 1964 Alcoholic heart disease. British Medical Journal ii: 1283–1289

Bruns D L, van der Hauwert L G 1958 The aortic systolic murmur developing with increasing age. British Heart Journal 20: 370–378

Bulkley B H, Roberts W C 1975 Dilatation of the mitral anulus. American Journal of Medicine 59: 457–463

Burr M L, King S, Davies H E F, Pathy M S 1977 The effects of discontinuing long-term diuretic therapy in the elderly. Age and Ageing 6: 38–44

Caird F I 1976 Clinical examination and investigation of the heart. In: Caird F I, Dall J L C, Kennedy R D (eds) Cardiology in old age, Plenum Press, New York and London, p 127–142

Caird F I 1980 Radionuclide studies of the circulation in the elderly. Journal of Clinical and Experimental Gerontology 2: 23–40

Caird F I 1982a Valvular disease of the heart. In: Platt D (ed) Geriatrics I, Springer-Verlag, Berlin, Heidelberg, New York, p 93–108

Caird F I 1982b The effect of age upon the cardiovascular response to anaemia: I Literature review, II Radionuclide studies in the elderly. Journal of Clinical and Experimental Gerontology 4: 179–192, 193–203

Caird F I, Andrews G R, Kennedy R D 1973b Effect of posture on blood pressure in the elderly. British Heart Journal 35: 527–530

Caird F I, Campbell A E, Jackson T F M 1974 Significance of abnormalities of electrocardiogram in old people. British Heart Journal 36: 1012–1918

Caird F I, Kennedy R D 1977 Digitalisation and digitalis detoxication in the elderly. Age and Ageing 6: 21–28

Caird F I, Kennedy R D, Kelly J C C 1973a Combined apexcardiography and phonocardiography in investigation of heart disease in the elderly Gerontologia clinica 15: 366–377

Campbell A E, Caird F I, Jackson T F M 1974 Prevalence of abnormalities of electrocardiogram in old people. British Heart Journal 36: 1005–1011

Canepa-Anson R, Emanuel R W 1979 Elective aortic and mitral valve surgery in patients over 70 years of age. British Heart Journal 41: 493–497

Castleden C M, George C F 1979 The effect of ageing on the hepatic clearance of propranolol. British Journal of Clinical Pharmacology 7: 49–54

Castleden C M, Kay C M, Parsons R L 1975 The effect of age on plasma levels of propranolol and practolol in man. British Journal of clinical Pharmacology 2: 303–306

Castleden C M, Volvans C N, Raymond K 1977 The effect of ageing on drug absorption from the gut. Age and Ageing 6: 138–143

Chatterjee K, Parmley W W 1977 Vasodilator therapy treatment for acute and chronic heart failure. British Heart Journal 39: 706–720

Chaturvedi N C, Shivalingappa G, Shanks P, McKay A, Cumming E, Walsh M J, Scaria K, Lynas P, Courtney D, Barber J M, Boyle D 1972 Myocardial infarction in the elderly. Lancet i: 280–282

Chung E K 1970 Digitalis induced cardiac arrhythmias. American Heart Journal 79: 845–848

Church G, Marriott J L 1959 Digitalis delirium. Circulation 20: 249–255

Clark A N G 1977 Multifocal atrial tachycardia (MAT). Gerontology 23: 445–461

Clark A N G, Craven A S H 1981 P R interval in the aged. Age and Ageing 10: 157–164

Clarke J M, Hamer J, Shelton J R, Taylor S, Venning G R 1976 The rhythm of the normal heart Lancet ii: 508–512

Clee M D, Smith N, McNeill F P, Wright D S 1979 Dysrhythmias in apparently healthy elderly subjects. Age and Ageing 8: 173–176

Colandrea M A, Friedman G D, Nichaman N Z, Lynd C S 1970 Systolic hypertension in the elderly: an epidemiologic assessment. Circulation 41: 239–245

Colmers R A 1958 Atrial septal defects in elderly patients. American Journal of Cardiology 1: 768–733

Community Hypertension Evaluation Clinic Hypertension Detection and Follow-up Program Cooperative Group 1977 Blood pressure studies in 14 communities. Journal of American Medical Association 237: 2385–2391

Cooley D A, Hallman G L, Hamman A S 1966 Congenital cardiovascular anomalies in adults. American Journal of Cariology 17: 303–309

Coulshed N, Littler T R 1957 Atrial septal defect in the aged. British Medical Journal i: 76–80

Cowan N R 1964 The heart-lung coefficient and the transverse diameter of the heart. British Heart Journal 26: 116–120

Cowan N R 1965 The frontal cardiac silhouette in older people. British Heart Journal 27: 231–235

Cullen K J, Murphy B P, Cumpston G N 1974 Electrocardiograms in the Busselton population. Australian and New Zealand Medical Journal 4: 325–330

Cusack B, Kelly J, O'Malley K, Noel J, Lavan J, Morgan J 1979 Digoxin in the elderly: pharmacokinetic consequences of old age. Clinical Pharmacology and Therapeutics 25: 772–776

Dall J L C 1964 The effects of steriod therapy on normal and abnormal A-V conduction. British Heart Journal 26: 537

Dall J L C 1965a Digitalis intoxication in elderly patients. Lancet i: 194–195

Dall J L C 1965b Digitalis intoxication. American Heart Journal 70: 572–574

Dall J L C, 1970 Maintenance digoxin in elderly patients. British Medical Journal i: 705–706

Dall J L C, Paulose S, Fergusson J A 1971 Potassium intake of elderly patients in hospital. Gerontologia Clinica 13: 114–118

Dauchot P, Gravenstein J S 1970 Effects of atropine on the

electrocardiogram in different age groups. Clinical Pharmacology and Therapeutics 12: 274–280

Davies M J 1971 Pathology of Conducting Tissue of the Heart. Butterworth, London

Davies M J 1976 Pathology of the conducting system In: Caird F I, Dall J L C, Kennedy R D (eds) Cardiology in Old Age, Plenum Press, New York and London, p 57–80

Davies M J, Pomerance A 1972 Quantitative study of aging changes in human sinoatrial nodes and interatrial tracts. British Heart Journal 34: 150–152

Davison E T, Freidman S A 1968 Significance of systolic murmurs in the aged. New England Journal of Medicine 279: 225–230

Demoulin J C, Kulbertus H E 1978 Histopathological correlates of sinoatrial disease. British Heart Journal 40: 1384–1389

Denham K J, Pomerance A, Hodkinson H M 1977 Pathological validation of auscultation of the elderly heart. Postgraduate Medical Journal 53: 66–68

DePasquale N P, Burch G E 1966 The necropsy incidence of gross scars or acute infarction of the papillary muscles of the left ventricle. American Journal of Cardiology 17: 169–170

Devereux R B, Perloff J K, Reichek N, Josephson M E 1976 Mitral valve prolapse. Circulation 54: 3–14

Doherty J E, Perkins W H, Flanigan W J 1967 The distribution and concentration of tritiated digoxin in human tissues. Annals of Internal Medicine 66: 116–124

Domenet J G, Evans D W 1969 Uraemia in congestive heart failure. Quarterly Journal of Medicine N S 38: 117–133

Dotter C T, Steinberg I 1949 The angiocardiographic measurement of the great vessels Radiology 52: 353–357

Du Cailar C, Chaitman B R, Castonguay Y 1980 Risks and benefits of aortocoronary by-pass surgery in patients aged 65 years or more. Canadian Medical Association Journal 122: 771–774

Eisinger A J 1971 Atrial fibrillation in bacterial endocarditis. British Heart Journal 33: 739–741

Evans W, Swann P 1954 Lone auricular fibrillation. British Heart Journal 16: 189–194

Fisch C, Genovese P D, Dyke R W, Laramore W, Marvel R J 1957 The electrocardiogram in persons over 70. Geriatrics 12: 616–620

Fareeduddin K, Abelmann W H 1969 Impaired orthostatic tolerance after bed rest in patients with myocardial infarction. New England Journal of Medicine 280: 345–350

Feely J, Stevenson I H 1979 The influence of ageing on propranolol concentration, binding and efficacy in hyperthyroid patients. Journal of Clinical and Experimental Gerontology 1: 173–184

Feigenbaum H 1980 Echocardiography. 2nd edn. Lea and Febiger, Philadelphia

Fleg J L, Gottlieb S H, Lakatta E G 1982 Is digoxin really important in treatment of compensated heart failure? American Journal of Medicine 73: 244–240

Flohr K H, Weir E K, Chesler E 1981 Diagnosis of aortic stenosis in older age groups using external carotid pulse recording and phonocardiography. British Heart Journal 45: 577–582

Fowler N O 1981 Noncardiac surgery in the elderly patient with heart disease, In: Noble R J, Rothbaum D (eds) Geriatric Cardiology, F A Davis Co, Philadelphia, p 211–220

Franciosa J A Cohn J N 1980 Sustained hemodynamic effects without tolerance during long-term isosorbide dinitrate treatment of chronic left ventricular failure. American Journal of Cardiology 45: 648–654

Frick M H, Kala R 1980 Once daily versus twice daily betablockers: effects on arrhythmias and hypertension. Lancet ii: 588

Frick M H, Heikkila J, Kahanpaa A 1967 Combined parasympathetic and beta-receptor blockade as a clinical test. Acta Medica Scandinavica 182: 621–627

Gann D, Colin C, Hildner F J, Samet P, Yahr W Z, Greenberg J J 1977 Coronary artery bypass surgery in patients seventy years of age and older. Journal of Thoracic and Cardiovascular Surgery 73: 237–241

Garner A, Ashton N 1979 Pathogenesis of hypertensive retionopathy; a review. Journal of Royal Society of Medicine 72: 362–365

Gerstenblith G, Spurgeon H A, Frohlich J P, Weisfeldt M, Lakatta E G 1979 Diminished inotropic responsiveness to ouabain in aged rat myocardium. Circulation Research 44: 517–523

Gleckler W J 1958 Diagnostic aspects of subacute bacterial endocarditis in the elderly. Archives of Internal Medicine 102: 761–765

Goldman L, Caldera D L, Nussbaum S R et al 1977 Multifocal index of cardiac risk in non-cardiac surgical procedures. New England Journal of Medicine 297: 845–850

Goodwin J F 1963 Diagnosis of left atrial myxoma. Lancet i: 464–468

Goodwin J F 1968 Mitral regurgitation in congestive cardiomyopathy. Postgraduate Medical Journal 44: 61–65

Goodwin J F 1970 Congestive and hypertrophic cardiomyopathies. Lancet i: 731–739

Goodwin J F Abdin Z H 1959 The cardiogram of congenital and acquired right ventricular hypertrophy. British Heart Journal 21: 523–544

Gould S E, Cawley L P 1958 Unsuspected healed myocardial infarction in patients dying in a general hospital. Archives of Internal Medicine 101: 524–527

Gozna E R, Marble A E, Shaw A, Holland J G 1974 Age-related changes in the mechanics of the aorta and pulmonary artery of man. Journal of Applied Physiology 36: 407–411

Greenblatt D J, Koch-Weser J 1973 Adverse reactions to propranolol in hospitalised medical patients: a report from the Boston Collaborative Drug Surveillance Programme. American Heart Journal 86: 478–484

Grifonse J W, Kitchell J R 1954 Active rheumatic heart disease in patients over 60. Journal of the American Medical Association 154: 1341–1343

Gross M 1970 Circulatory reflexes in cerebral ischaemia involving different vascular territories. Clinical Science 38: 491–502

Guarnieri T, Spurgeon H, Froehlich J P, Weisfeldt M L, Lakatta E G 1979 Diminished inotropic response but unaltered toxicity to acetylstrophanthidin in the senescent beagle. Circulation 60: 1548–1554

Hamby R I, Wisoff B G, Kolker P, Harstein M 1973 Intractable angina pectoris in the 65 to 79 years age group: a surgical approach. Chest 64: 46–50

Hanley T 1976 Pulmonary heart disease. In: Caird F I, Dall J L C, Kennedy R D (eds) Cardiology in old age. Plenum Press, New York and London, p 209–229

Harlan W R, Graybeil A, Mitchell R E, Oberman, A, Osborne R K 1967 Serial electrocardiograms: their reliability and prognostic validity during a 24-year period. Journal of Chronic Diseases 20: 853–867

Harris M 1968 Dissecting aneurysm of aorta due to giant cell arteritis. British Heart Journal 30: 840–844

Harris R 1970 The management of geriatric cardiovascular disease. Harris, R (ed) J B Lippincott Co, Philadelphia and Toronto

Harris R 1976 Cardiac arrhythmias in the aged. In: Caird F I, Dall J L C, Kennedy R D (eds) Cardiology in Old Age, Plenum, New York, p 315–346

Harrison C V, Lennox B 1948 Heart block in osteitis deformans. British Heart Journal 10: 167–176

Hass G E 1942 Elastic tissue II: a study of the elasticity and tensile strength of elastic tissue isolated from human aorta. Archives of Pathology 34: 971–981

Hass G E 1943 Elastic tissue. III: relation between the structure of the aging aorta and the properties of the isolated aortic elastic tissue. Archives of Pathology 35: 29–45

Hecht F M 1980 Studie uber quantitative Altersveranderungen am Hisschen Bundel des Menschen. Virchows Archiv: A: Pathological Anatomy and Histology 386: 343–356

Hedenrud B, Landahl S, Mellstrom, D, Rundgren A, Reupe S, Steen B 1980 Electrocardiogram at age 70 and 75: a longitudinal population study. Journal of Clinical and Experimental Gerontology 2: 231–244

Henley J W, Croxson R S, Ibbertson H K 1976 The cardiovascular system in Paget's disease of bone; the response to therapy with calcitonin and diphosphonate. New Zealand Medical Journal 84 (Abstr); 161

Hess T R, Hallam C C, Wann L S 1981 Echocardiography in the elderly. In: Noble R J, Rothbaum D A (eds) Geriatric Cardiology, F A Davis Co, Philadelphia, p 95–104

Hirschfeld D S, Emilson B B 1975 Echocardiogram in calcified mitral annulus. American Journal of Cardiology 36: 354–356

Hjalmarson A, Elmfeldt D, Herlitz A, Holmberg S, Malek I, Nyberg G, et al 1981 Effect on mortality of metoprolol in acute myocardial infarction. Lancet ii: 823–827

Hodkinson H M, Pomerance A 1974 Cardiac amyloidosis in the

elderly: associated elevation of serum alkaline phosphatase. Age and Ageing 3: 76–78

Hosking D J 1981 Paget's disease of bone. British Medical Journal 283: 686–688

Howat D D C 1971 Cardiac disease, anaesthesia and operation for non-cardiac conditions. British Journal of Anaesthesia 43: 288–298

Hughes P, Gauld W R 1966 Bacterial endocarditis: a changing disease. Quarterly Journal of Medicine NS 35: 511–519

Hultgren H N 1948 Calcific disease of the aortic valve. Archives of Pathology 45: 694–706

Hypertension Detection and Follow-up Program Cooperative Group 1979 Five year findings of the hypertension detection and follow-up program II: mortality by race, sex and age. Journal of the American Medical Association 242: 2572–2577

Ibrahim I K, Ritch A E S, MacLennan W J, May T 1978 Are potassium supplements for the elderly necessary. Age and Ageing 7: 165–170.

International Anticoagulant Review Group 1970 Collaborative analysis of long-term anticoagulant administration after acute myocardial infarction Lancet i: 203–209

International Society and Federation of Cardiology Scientific Councils on Arteriosclerosis, Epidemiology and Prevention, and Rehabilitation 1981 Secondary prevention in survivors of myocardial infarction. British Medical Journal 282: 894–896

Jackson G, Pierscianowski T A, Mahon W, Condon, J 1976 Inappropriate antihypertensive therapy in the elderly. Lancet ii: 1317–1318

Jick H, Slone D, Borda I T, Shapiro S 1968 Efficacy and toxicity of heparin in relation to age and sex. New England Journal of Medicine 279: 284–286

Johnston G D, McDevitt D G 1979 Is maintenance digoxin necessary in patients with sinus rhythm. Lancet i: 567–570

Jolly W W, Isch J H, Shumacker H B 1981 Cardiac surgery in the elderly. In: Noble R J, Rothbaum D A (eds) Geriatric Cardiology F A Davis Co, Philadelphia, p 195–210

Jose A D 1966 Effects of combined sympathetic and parasympathetic blockade on heart rate. American Journal of Cardiology 18: 476–478

Judge T G, Caird F I, Leask R G S, Macleod C C 1974 Dietary intake and urinary excretion of potassium in the elderly. Age and Ageing 3: 167–173

Kafetz K 1981 Surgical treatment of hypertrophic obstructive cardiomyopathy in the elderly Postgraduate Medical Journal 57: 604–606

Kannell W B 1982 Personal communication

Kannell W B, Gordon T, Schwartz M J 1971 Systolic versus diastolic blood pressure and risk of coronary heart disease — the Framingham Study. American Journal of Cardiology 1971: 335–346

Kannel W B, Wolf P A, Verter J, MacNamara P 1970 Epidemiological assessment of the role of blood pressure in stroke. Journal of the American Medical Association 214: 301–310

Kennedy R D, Andrews G R, Caird F I 1977 Ischaemic heart disease in the elderly. British Heart Journal 39: 1121–1127

Kennedy R D, Caird F I 1972 Application of the Minnesota code to population studies of the electrocardiogram in the elderly. Gerontologia Clinica 14: 5–16

Kincaid-Smith P. McMichael J, Murphy E A 1958 The clinical course and pathology of hypertension with papilloedema (malignant hypertension). Quarterly Journal of Medicine NS 27: 117–153

King J T 1950 Digitalis delirium. Annals of Internal Medicine 33: 1360–1372

Kirk R S, Russell J G B 1969 Subvalvular calcification of the mitral valve. British Heart Journal 31: 684–692

Kitchin A H, Lowther C P, Milne J S 1973 Prevalence of clinical and electrocardiographic evidence of ischaemic heart disease in the older population. British Heart Journal 35: 946–955

Kjorstad H 1957 Rheumatic fever in the aged. Acta Medica Scandinavica 158: 337–349

Knapp W S, Douglas J S, Crave J M, Jones E L, King III, Spencer B, Bone D K, et al 1981 Efficacy of coronary artery grafting in elderly patients with coronary artery disease. American Journal of Cardiology 47: 923–930

Koch J P, Maron B J, Epstein S E, Morrow A G 1980 Results of operation for obstructive hypertrophic cardiomyopathy in the elderly. American Journal of Cardiology 46: 963–966

Koch-Weser J 1979 Treatment of hypertension in the elderly. In: Crooks J, Stevenson I H (eds) Drugs and the Elderly, MacMillan, London, p 247–262

Konu V 1977 Myocardial infarction in the elderly Acta Medica Scandinavica Supplement 604: 9–68

Korn D, DeSanctis R W, Sell S 1962 Massive calcification of the mitral annulus. New England Journal of Medicine 267: 900–909

Kuramoto K, Matsushita S, Kuwajima I, Murakami M 1981 Prospective study of the treatment of mild hypertension in the aged Japanese Heart Journal 22: 75–85

Kurihara H, Kuramoto K, Terasawa F, Matsushita S, Seki M, Ideda M 1967 Reliability of abnormal Q and QS patterns classified by the Minnesota code for the diagnosis of myocardial infarction in aged people. American Heart Journal 8: 514–521

Lake C R, Ziegler M G, Coleman M G, Kopin I J 1977 Age-adjusted plasma norepinephrine levels are similar in normotensive and hypertensive subjects. New England Journal of Medicine 296: 208–209

Law R, Chalmers C 1976 Medicines and elderly people: a general practice survery. British Medical Journal 1: 565–568

Lawrence J R, Sumner D J, Kalk W J, Ratcliffe W A, Whiting B, Gray K, Lindsay M 1977 Digoxin kinetics in patients with thyroid dysfunction. Clinical Pharmacology and Therapeutics 22: 7–13

Lawson D H, Murray A M, Parker J L M 1972 Early mortality in the megaloblastic anaemias. Quarterly Journal of Medicine NS 41: 1–14

Lazarus J H, Harden R McG 1969 Thyrotoxicosis in the elderly. Gerontologia Clinica 11: 371–378

Leading Article 1967 Bacterial endocarditis: a changing pattern. Lancet 1: 605–606

Leading Article 1979 Asymptomatic complete heart block. British Medical Journal 2: 1245–1246

Leading Article 1982 Long term and short term beta blockade after myocardial infarction. Lancet i: 1159–1161

Lenkiewicz J E, Davies M J, Rosen D 1972 Collagen in human myocardium as a function of age. Cardiovascular Research 6: 549–555

Lerner P I, Weinstein L 1966 Infective endocarditis in the antibiotic era. New England Journal of Medicine 274:199–206, 259–266, 323–331, and 388–393

Librach G, Sschadel M, Seltzer M, Hart A, Yellin N 1976 Immediate and long-term prognosis of acute myocardial infarction in the aged. Journal of Chronic Diseases 29: 483–495

Livesley B 1977 Pathogenesis of brain failure in the aged. Age and Ageing Suppl 9–19

Locke W 1967 Hyperthyroidism in the aged. Geriatrics 22: 173–174

Lowes J A, William G, Tabaqchali S, Hill I M, Hamer J, Houang E, Shaw E J, Rees G M 1980 10 years of infective endocarditis at St Bartholomew's hospital: analysis of clinical features and treatment in relation to prognosis and mortality. Lancet i: 113–136

Lundborg P, Steen B 1976 Plasma levels and effect on heart rate and blood pressure of metoprolol after acute oral administration in 12 geriatic patients. Acta Medica Scandinavica 200: 397–402

Macdonald J B, Baillie J, Williams B O, Ballantyne D B 1983 Coronary care in the elderly. Age and Ageing 12: 17–20

MacFarlane J P R, Kennedy R D 1973 Clinical experience with amiloride in the elderly. Acta Cardiologica 28: 365–374

McHaffie D, Purcell H, Mitchell-Heggs P, Guz A 1978. The clinical value of digoxin in patients with heart failure and sinus rhythm. Quarterly Journal of Medicine (NS) 47: 401–419

McKenna W J, Rowland E, Krikler D M 1983 Amiodarone: the experience of the past decade. British Medical Journal 287: 1654–1656

Maclennan, W J 1981 The problem of potassium. In: Caird F I, Grimley Evans J (eds) Advanced Geriatric Medicine 1, Pitman, London, p 67–72

McMillan, J B and Lev, M 1964 The aging heart II: the valves. Journal of Gerontology 19: 1–14

Manyari D, Patterson C, Johnson L, Melendez L, Boughner D, Kostuk W, Cape R 1982 An echocardiographic study of resting left ventricular function in healthy elderly subjects. Journal of Clinical and Experimental Gerontology 4: 403–420

Markham P, Howitt G, Wade E G 1965 Atrial septal defect in the middle-age and elderly. Quarterly Journal of Medicine NS 34: 409–425

Massie B, Ports T, Chatterjee K, Parmley W, Ostland J, O'Young J, Haughom F 1981 Long term vasodilator therapy for heart failure : clinical response and its relationship to hemodynamic measurements. Circulation 63: 269–278

Master A M, Lasser R P, Jaffe H L 1958 Blood pressure in white people over 65 years of age. Annals of Internal Medicine 48: 284–299

Messerli F H, Dreslinski G R, Husserl F E, Suarez D H, MacPhee A A, Frohlich E D 1981 Antiadrenergic therapy of hypertension in the elderly. Hypertension 3 Suppl II: 226–229

Mitchell J R A 1980 Secondary prevention of myocardial infarction — the present state of the A.R.T. British Medical Journal 280: 1128–1130

Moore-Smith B 1980 The management of hypertension in the elderly In: Treatment of medical problems in the elderly, Denham M J (ed), MTP Press, Lancaster, p 117–158

Moulsdale M T, Eykn S J, Phillips I 1980 Infective endocarditis, 1970–1979 – a survey of culture-positive cases in St Thomas' Hospital. Quarterly Journal of Medicine (NS) 49: 315–328

Mungall D R, Robichaux R P, Perry W, Scott J W, Robinson A, Burelle T, Hurst D 1980 Effects of quinidine on serum digoxin concentration; a prospective study. Annals of Internal Medicine 93: 689–693

Nagent de Deuxchaisnes C N, Rombouts-Lindermans C 1974 Exploration biologique de la maladie de Paget. Journal Belge de Rheumatologie et de Medecine Physique — Acta Medica Belgica 29: 243–293

Nalefski L A, Brown C F G 1950 Action of atropine on the cardiovascular system of normal persons. Archives of Internal Medicine 86: 898–907

Neff M S, Mendlessohn S, Kun K E, Barch A, Swartz C Seller R E 1972 Magnesium sulphate in digitalis toxicity. Americal Journal of Cardiology 29: 377–382

Norris R M, Brandt P W T, Caughey D E, Lee A J, Scott P J 1969 A new coronary prognotic index. Lancet i: 274–278

Norwegian Multicenter Study Group 1981 Timolol-induced reduction in mortality and reinfarction in patients surviving acute myocardial infarction. New England Journal of Medicine 304: 801–807

Oakley C 1978 Use of antibiotics: endocarditis. British Medical Journal 2: 489–490

Ochs H R, Greenblatt D J, Woo E. Smith T W 1978 Reduced quinidine clearance in elderly persons. American Journal of Cardiology 42: 481–485

Oliver M F, Boyd G S 1959 Effects of bilateral ovariectomy on coronary artery disease and serum lipid levels. Lancet ii: 690–694

O'Malley K, O'Brien E 1980 Management of hypertension in the elderly. New England Journal of Medicine 302: 1297–1401

O'Malley K, Stevenson I H, Ward C A, Wood A J J, Crooks J 1977 Determinants of anticoagulant control in patients receiving warfarin. British Journal of Clinical Pharmacology 4: 309–314

Opie L H 1980 Beta-blocking agents. In: Opie L H Drugs and the Heart. Lancet, London

Ostenberger L E, Goldstein S, Khaja F, Lakier J B 1981 Functional mitral stenosis in patients with massive mitral annular calcification. Circulation 64: 472–476

Ostrander L D, Brandt R L, Kjelsberg M O, Epstein F H 1965 Electrocardiographic findings among the adult population of a total natural community, Tecumseh, Michigan. Circulation 31: 888–897

Patel K P 1977 Electrocardiographic abnormalities in the sick elderly. Age and Ageing 6: 163–167

Pathy M S 1967 Clinical presentation of myocardial infarction in the elderly. British Heart Journal 29: 190–199

Pathy M S, Peach H 1981 Change in disability status as a predictor of long term survival after myocardial infarction in the elderly. Age and Ageing 10: 174–178

Peach H, Pathy M S 1979 Disability in the elderly after myocardial infarction. Journal of the Royal College of Physicians of London 13: 154–157

Perloff J K, Lindgren K M 1974 Adult survival in congenital heart disease. Geriatrics 29: 94–104

Petrin T J, Tavel M E 1979 Idiopathic hypertrophic subaortic stenosis as observed in a large community hospital: relation to age and history of hypertension. Journal of the American Geriatrics Society 27: 43–46

Pomerance A 1965a Senile Cardiac amyloidosis. British Heart Journal 27: 711–718

Pomerance A 1965b Pathology of the heart with and without heart failure in the aged. British Heart Journal 27: 697–710

Pomerance A 1966 Pathogenesis of senile nodular sclerosis of atrioventricular valves. British Heart Journal 28: 815–823

Pomerance A 1967 Ageing changes in human heart valves. British Heart Journal 29: 222–231

Pomerance A 1970 Pathological and clinical study of calcification of the mitral valve ring. Journal of Clinical Pathology 23: 354–361

Pomerance A 1976 Pathology of the myocardium and valves. In: Caird F I, Dall J L C, Kennedy R D (eds) Cardiology in Old Age, Plenum Press, New York, p 11–55

Pomerance A 1981 Cardiac pathology in the elderly. In: Noble R J, Rothbaum D A (eds) Geriatric Cardiology, F A Davis Co, Philadelphia, p 9–45

Port S, Cobb F R, Coleman E, Jones R H 1980 Effect of age on the response of the left ventricular ejection fraction to exercise. New England Journal of Medicine 303: 1134–1137

Rasmussen S, Leth A, Kjoller E, Pederson A 1979 Cardiac rupture in acute myocardial infarction. Acta Medica Scandinavica 205: 11–16

Reid J, Kennedy R D, Caird F I 1982 Digoxin kinetics in the elderly. Age and Ageing 12: 29–37

Repke K 1964 Ueber den Biochemischen Wirkungsmodus von Digitalis. Klinische Wochenschrift 42: 157–165

Roberts M A, Caird F I 1976 Steady-state kinetics of digoxin in the elderly. Age and Ageing 5: 58–67

Rodrigues dos Santos A G, Lye M 1980 Transient cardiac arrhythmias in healthy elderly individuals: how relevant are they? Journal of Clinical and Experimental Gerontology 2: 245–258

Rodstein M 1956 The characteristics of non-fatal myocardial infarction in the aged. Archives of Internal Medicine 98: 84–90

Rodstein M 1979 Heart disease in the aged. In: Rossmann I (ed) Clinical Geriatrics, 2nd edn, J B Lippincott Co, Philadephia and Toronto, p 181–203

Rodstein M, Zeman F D 1967 Aortic stenosis in the aged: clinical pathological correlations. American Journal of the Medical Sciences 254: 577–583

Rogers H J, Spector R G, Trounce J R 1981 Cardiovascular drugs In: Rogers H J, et al (eds) A Textbook of Clinical Pharmacology. Hodder and Stoughton, London, Sydney, Auckland, Toronto, p 412

Rose G A, Wilson R R 1959 Unexplained heart failure in the aged. British Heart Journal 21: 511–517

Rosenbaum M B, Elizzari M V, Lazzari J O 1970 The hemiblocks. Tampa Tracings

Rothbaum D A 1981 Coronary artery disease. In: Noble R J, Rothbaum D (eds) Geriatric Cardiology. F A Davis Co, Philadelphia, p 105–118

Rothschild M A, Kugel M A, Gross L 1934 Incidence and significance of active infection in cases of rheumatic cardiovascular disease dying in various age periods. American Heart Journal 9: 586–595

Roy C S 1880 The elastic properties of the arterial wall. Journal of Physiology 3: 125–159

Rubin P C, Scott P J W, Reid J L 1981 Prazosin disposition in young and elderly subjects. British Journal of Clinical Pharmacology 12: 401–404

Rubin P C, Scott P J W, McLean K, Pearson A, Ross D, Reid J L 1982 Atenolol disposition in young and elderly subjects. British Journal of Clinical Pharmacology 13: 224–237

Sandler G, Wilson G M 1959 The nature and prognosis of heart disease in thyrotoxicosis. Quarterly Journal of Medicine NS 28: 347–369

Sapala J A, Ponka J L, Duvernoy W F C 1975 Operative and non-operative risks in the cardiac patient. Journal of the American Geriatrics Society 23: 529–534

Schnurr L P, Ball A P, Geddes A M, Gray J, McGhie D 1977 Bacterial endocarditis in England in the 1970's: a review of 70 patients. Quaterly Journal of Medicine (NS) 46: 499–512

Schocken D D, Roth G S 1977 Reduced beta-adrenergic receptor concentrations in ageing man. Nature 267: 856–858

Schott A 1964 Observations of digitalis intoxication — a plea. Postgraduate Medical Journal 40: 628–643

Schwartz C J, Mitchell J R A 1962 The relation between myocardial lesions and coronary artery disease. I: an unselected necropsy study. British Heart Journal 24: 761–786

Scott P J W, Stansfield J, Williams B O 1982 Prescribing habits and potential adverse drug interactions in a geriatric medical service. Health Bulletin 40: 5–9

Sell S, Scully R E 1965 Aging changes in the aortic and mitral valves. American Journal of Pathology 46: 345–365

Semple T, Williams B O 1976 Coronary care for the elderly. In: Caird F I, Dall J L C, Kennedy R D (eds) Cardiology in old age, Plenum Press, New York and London, p 297–313

Sharpey-Schafer E P 1945 Transfusion and the anaemic heart. Lancet 2: 296–299

Sharpey-Schafer E P 1956 Circulatory reflexes in chronic disease of the afferent nervous system. Journal of Physiology 134: 1–10

Shekelle R, Ostfield A, Klawans H 1974 Hypertension and risk of stroke in an elderly population. Stroke 5: 71–75

Shenfield G M, Thompson J, Horn D B 1977 Plasma and urinary digoxin in thyroid dysfunction. European Journal of Clinical Pharmacology 12: 437–443

Shepherd A M M, Hewick D S, Moreland T A, Stevenson I H 1977 Age as a determinant of sensitivity to warfarin. British Journal of Clinical Pharmacology 4: 312–320

Shinebourne E A, Cripps C M, Hayward G W, Shooter R A 1969 Bacterial endocarditis 1956–1965: analysis of clinical features and treatment in relation to prognosis and mortality. British Heart Journal 31: 536–542

Sievers J, Blomqvist G, Bjorck G 1969 Studies in myocardial infarction in Malmo, 1935–54 (VI). Acta Medica Scandinavica 169: 95–103

Sievers J, Hall P 1971 Incidence of rheumatic fever. British Heart Journal 3: 833–836

Simon M A, Liu S F 1954 Calcification of the mitral valve annulus and its relation to functional valvular disturbance. American Heart Journal 48: 497–505

Singh B N, Vaughan Williams E M 1972 A fourth class of antidysrhythmic action? Effect of verapamil on oubain toxicity on atrial and ventricular intracellular potentials and other other features of cardiac function. Cardiovascular Research 6: 109–119

Sixty Plus Reinfarction Study Research Group 1982 Risks of long-term oral anticoagulant therapy in elderly patients after myocardial infarction. Lancet 1: 64–68

Skinner J F, Pearce M L 1964 Surgical risk in the cardiac patient. Journal of Chronic Diseases 17: 57–72

Sleight P 1962 Unilateral elevation of the internal jugular pulse. British Heart Journal 24: 726–730

Smith J M, Lindsay W G, Lillehei R C, Nicoloff D M 1976a Cardiac surgery in geriatric patients. Surgery 80: 443–448

Smith R H, Radford D J, Clark R A, Julian D G 1976b Infective endocarditis : a survey of cases in the South East Region of Scotland, 1969–1972. Thorax 31: 373–379

Sonnenblick M, Dall J L C 1981 The importance of calcium in the action of digoxin. Journal of Clinical and Experimental Gerontology 2: 81–92

Spodick D H, Quarry V M 1974 Prevalence of the fourth heart sound by phonocardiography in the absence of cardiac disease. American Heart Journal 87: 11–14

Staffurth J S, Gibberd M B, Hitton P J 1965 Atrial fibrillation in thyrotoxicosis treated with radioiodine. Postgraduate Medical Journal 41: 663–671

Staffurth J S, Young J A 1967 ^{131}I in thyrotoxicosis. British Medical Journal 1: 629

Stevenson I H, Salem S A M, Shepherd A M M 1979. Studies on drug absorption and metabolism in the elderly In: Crooks J, Stevenson I H (eds) Drugs and the Elderly, MacMillan Press Ltd, London and Basingstoke, p 51–64

Strandell T 1976 Cardiac output in old age, In: Cardiology in Old Age, Caird F I, Dall J L C and Kennedy R D (eds) Plenum Press, New York and London, p 8–100

Strehler B L, Mark D D, Mildvan A S, Gee M V 1959 Rate and magnitude of age pigment accumulation in human myocardium. Journal of Gerontology 14: 430–439

Suter F 1897 Ueber das Verhalten des Aortenumfanges unter physiologischen und pathologischen Bedingungen. Archiv fur experimentelle Pathologie und Pharmakologie 39: 289–332

Swales J D 1979 Pathophysiology of blood pressure in the elderly. Age and Ageing 8: 104–109

Tammaro A E, Forin G 1977 Left fascicular hemiblocks in the elderly. Journal of the American Geriatrics Society 25: 439–442

Tarhan S, Guiliani E R 1974 General anesthesia and myocardial infarction. American Heart Journal 87: 137–138

Tarhan S, Moffitt E A, Taylor W F, Guiliani E R 1972 Myocardial infarction after general anaesthesia Journal of the American Medical Association 220: 1451–1454

Tavel M E 1968 Clinical phonocardiography. Its use in diagnosis of idiopathic hypertrophic subaortic stenosis. Journal of the American Medical Association 203: 285–286

Thell R, Martin F H, Edwards J E 1975 Bacterial endocarditis in subjects 60 years of age and older. Circulation 51: 174–182

Thery C, Gosselin B, Lekieffre J, Warembourg H 1977 Pathology of sinoatrial node: correlations with electrocardiographic findings in 111 patients. American Heart Journal 93: 735–740

Thorner M C, Carter R A, Griffith G C 1949 Calcification as a diagnostic sign of syphilitic aortitis. American Heart Journal 38: 641–653

Toh C C S, Ball K P 1960 Natural history of streptococcus faecalis endocarditis. British Medical Journal 2: 640–644

Tresch D D, Siegel R, Keeland M H Jr, Gross C M, Brooks H L 1979 Mitral valve prolapse in the elderly. Journal of the American Geriartrics Society 27: 421–414

Triggs E J 1979 Pharmacokinetics of lignocaine and chlormethiazole in the elderly; with some preliminary observations on other drugs. In: Crooks J, Stevenson I E (eds) Drugs and the Elderly, MacMillan, London, p 117–132

Tucker B L Lindesmith GG, Stiles Q R et al 1977 Myocardial revascularization in patients 70 years of age and older. Western Journal of Medicine 126: 179–183

Vestal R E, Wood A J J, Shand D G 1979 Reduced β-adrenoceptor sensitivity in the elderly. Clinical Pharmacology and Therapeutics 26: 181–186

Von Capeller D, Copeland G D, Stern T N 1959 Digitalis intoxication; a clinical report of 148 cases. Annals of Internal Medicine 50: 869–878

Walsh W F, Greenberg B H 1981 Results of long term vasodilator therapy in patients with refractory congestive heart failure. Circulation 64: 499–505

Wang R, Camm J, Ward D, Washington H, Martin A 1980 Treatment of chronic atrial fibrillation in the elderly, assessed by ambulatory electrocardiographic monitoring. Journal of American Geratrics Society 28: 529–534

Watt D A L 1968 Sensitivity to propanolol after digitalis intoxication. British Medical Journal 3: 414–415

Webster B, Rich, C, Jensen P M, Moore J E, Nicol C S, Padget P 1953 Studies in cardiovascular syphilis (III). American Heart Journal 46: 117–145

Wedgewood J 1976 Remediable heart disease. In: Caird F I, Dall J L C, Kennedy R D (eds) Cardiology in old age, Plenum Press, New York and London, p 249–265

Whiting B, Lawrence J R, Sumner D J 1979 Digoxin pharmacokinetics in the elderly. In: Crooks J, Stevenson I H (eds) Drugs and the Elderly, MacMillan, London, p 89–10

Williams B O 1982 Mechanism of combined treatment with beta-blockers and diuretics in elderly hypertensive patients. In: Lang E, Sorgel F, Blaha L (eds) Beta-blockers in the elderly. Springer-Verlag, Berlin, Heidelberg, New York p 41–45

Williams B O, Begg T B, Semple T, McGuinness J B 1976 The elderly in the coronary unit. British Medical Journal ii:451–452

Williams B O, Caird F I 1980 Impedance cardiography and cardiac output in the elderly. Age and Ageing 9: 47–52

Williamson J, Chopin J M 1980 Adverse reactions to prescribed drugs in the elderly: a multicentre investigation. Age and Ageing 9: 73–80

Wilson L M 1963 Pathology of fatal bacterial endocarditis before and since the introduction of antibiotics. Annals of Internal Medicine 58: 84–92

Woodhouse N J Y, Crosby W H, Mohamedally S M 1975 Cardiac output in Paget's disease: response to long-term salmon calcitonin therapy. British Medical Journal iv: 486

Wright J R, Calkins E, Breen W J, Stolte G, Shultz R T 1969. Relationship of amyloid to aging. Medicine (Baltimore) 48: 39–59

Zeman F D 1945 Subacute bacterial endocarditis in the aged. American Heart Journal 29: 661–684

The central nervous system — neuropathology of aging

INTRODUCTION

Just as the general problem of aging itself has been studied for many centuries, so more detailed examination of changes in one organ in later life — the brain — also goes back at least to the Middle Ages. Newer techniques and better understanding of basic pathological mechanisms have enabled us to define more accurately some of the alterations in the brain which are age-associated, and others which are secondary to disorders in other tissues and organs; however, we still have little understanding of the basic pathogenetic mechanisms involved, and in many instances even of the full range of their effects. There is still dispute about which, if any, of the changes in the brains of old people are 'physiological' consequences of aging and which might be 'pathological'.

For diagnostic purposes, as well as providing a framework of observations with which hypotheses can be matched, all the lesions can be regarded for the present as 'age-associated'; it is then possible in practice to analyse those which occur in apparently healthy old people and to compare them with the changes found in patients suffering from a variety of clinical disorders.

As man and animals age they gather the scars of many past illnesses and there are increasing opportunities for disorders in all their tissues to interact with each other. The neuropathology of old age, therefore, is inevitably a complex topic, made more difficult by the variety of cell types and the heterogeneity of the tissues affected, as well as by the diverse nature of the disease processes which must be considered. For practical reasons the contents of this chapter have been restricted to discussion of:

The aging brain
Changes associated with senescence in apparently healthy people, including lesions in the spinal cord and peripheral nerves.

Diseases without known external causative factors
1. Dementia in later life: senile dementia; Alzheimer's

and Pick's diseases; other conditions which cause similar pathological changes. Comparison of the lesions with those of normal aging.
2. Other degenerative disorders: idiopathic and other forms of Parkinsonism (postencephalitic Parkinsonism is dealt with here for convenience); Shy-Drager syndrome; olivopontocerebellar atrophy; Huntington's chorea; Steele-Richardson-Olszewski syndrome; other degenerations.

Diseases of the central nervous system with known or suspected external causative factors
1. Infective disorders: herpes zoster; subacute encephalitis; Jakob-Creutzfeldt disease.
2. Skeletal disorders: Paget's disease; cervical spondylosis.
3. Cerebrovascular disease: vascular pathology; arteriosclerotic dementia; vascular disorders of the spinal cord.

Many other disorders have been deliberately excluded because they also occur at other ages, and, although their clinical and pathological appearances may differ in the elderly, there are full accounts in standard monographs on neuropathology.

Major types of disease which are not discussed are: tumours, both primary and secondary; nutritional deficiencies, including subacute combined degeneration associated with Addisonian pernicious anaemia and sometimes with other syndromes; toxic disorders such as uraemia and liver failure; the effects of anoxia and profound systemic hypotension; such idiopathic degenerative disorders as motor neurone disease (amyotrophic lateral sclerosis) and certain rare degenerations and other inherited syndromes; trauma; and age-related changes in voluntary muscle (Tomlinson et al, 1969).

THE AGING BRAIN

The lesions found in the brains of apparently 'normal' healthy old people who have died from some non-neurological cause are multifarious, and, like so many of the basic data of gerontology, there is still dispute about their causes, severity and distribution.

External changes

These include gradual thickening and fibrosis of the dura and leptomeninges; increasing prominence of the Pacchionian granulations which lie along the sides of the longitudinal fissure and project into the sagittal sinus; occasional focal calcification in the leptomeninges; and formation of plaques of bone in the spinal leptomeninges (Schaltenbrand, 1955). The brain itself usually atrophies to some extent, a process most marked in the frontal halves of the cerebral hemispheres, where mild to moderate shrinkage of gyri and enlargement of sulci is commonly seen in patients more than 60 to 70 years old, and with relatively less effect on the posterior halves of the hemispheres, brain stem and cerebellum. In fixed specimens, the grey matter of the cerebral cortex and basal ganglia may sometimes have a yellow-brown tinge and the white matter may darken to a creamy shade, but both changes, which are due to the intracellular accumulation of lipofuscin pigments and scarring associated with loss of cells, are variable.

Internal changes

Of the internal structures of the brain, those which commonly show changes in the elderly are the basal ganglia and the ventricular system. In the former, especially the lentiform nuclei, it is common to find thickening of the walls of small perforating arteries and dilated perivascular spaces, both of which make the blood vessels stand out very clearly in slices of fixed specimens. The hilum of the dentate nucleus may show similar changes. It is difficult to know to what extent these changes really represent pathological lesions rather than just physiological aging changes, like the abnormalities which appear in the main cranial arteries, as described below.

The ventricular system is larger in many older subjects and although this change is most easily seen in the lateral (as rounding of the angles) and third ventricles, it also affects the aqueduct and fourth ventricle. Again, the amount of enlargement is variable, although it can be correlated loosely with increasing age and it may often be due, in part at least, to pathological changes. The lining of the ventricles often becomes slightly roughened by the formation of small, irregular knots of cells — ependymal granulations, formed by astrocytic proliferation in response to defects appearing in the ependymal membrane.

Attempts at quantitation of these changes have led to conflicting results, some of which have been reviewed by Morel and Wildi (1955), Wildi et al (1964) and Blinkov and Glezer (1968). In general, all these authors have agreed that the brain shrinks and the ventricles become larger in older subjects, but the exact form of the relationship is unclear.

Histologically, several important age-related changes may be seen in the different types of cells in the brain (Dayan, 1971a); one affects all cells (lipofuscin deposition) and is of uncertain significance; others occur in only one type of cell and, particularly in neurones, are probably of considerable pathological importance as evidence of senescence and because they appear to form a link with certain types of dementia.

Lipofuscin

A general phenomenon of aging in many tissues is the intracellular deposition of granules of lipofuscin, a yellow-brown, autofluorescent pigment, closely related to and probably identical with ceroid. Depending on the method employed to demonstrate this material, it can be detected in small amounts in glial cells and neurones by the age of 2 to 3 years and thereafter it increases in amount with age. Lipofuscin occurs as discrete granules occupying a well-defined crescentic zone extending around part of the nucleus, and eventually it may occupy most of the cell body (Fig. 13.1). It is composed of a complex and only partly analysed mass of phospholipids and proteins (Björkerud, 1964) and probably results from aberrant peroxidation of lipids. Lipofuscin also accumulates in large amounts during a variety of

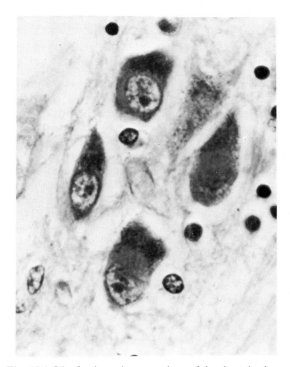

Fig. 13.1 Lipofuscin — large numbers of deeply stained granules in cytoplasm of pontine neurones (PAS × 400)

degenerative processes. This 'wear and tear' pigment is probably not itself harmful to cells, but it may be a pointer to the occurrence of potentially damaging aberrations of cellular metabolism (Mann and Yates, 1974). The detailed distribution of lipofuscin in the nervous system has been studied by many authors (see, for example, von Braunmühl, 1958; Brizzee et al, 1969), and striking regional differences have been claimed, although their importance has not been shown.

Changes in specific types of cell

Choroid plexus

There slowly accumulates during life twisted and coiled aygyrophilic fibrils within the epithelial cells (and sometimes in the related ependymal cells, too) — Biondi bodies (Schaltenbrand, 1955) which stain like amyloid (Schwartz, 1968). These can be regarded as an aging phenomenon, since — in contrast to other glial cells — ependyma and choroid plexus lose their regenerative capacity early (Chauhan and Lewis, 1979).

Interstitial fibrosis and the accumulation of fat-laden macrophages are common and so is the appearance in the stroma of rounded, laminated, haematoxyphilic, calcified psammoma bodies, apparently another type of degeneration of adventitial cells. Rarely, even in normal subjects, there are so many psammoma bodies that, together with more diffuse calcification of the stroma and blood vessels, the choroid plexus becomes visible radiologically.

Astrocytes

In the brains of the middle-aged and elderly, it is common to find prominent fibrillary astrocytes in both grey and white matter. This change, which may represent hyperplasia or hypertrophy, is usually focal and is concentrated around small blood vessels to which the cells are attached by thickened foot-processes. It is clearly seen in the cerebral and cerebellar cortex, and the subependymal layer around the lateral ventricles and basal ganglia, but is most obvious in the quadrigeminal plate, periaqueductal region, inferior olives, dentate nuclei and anterior grey matter of the spinal cord. There is no good evidence that it is pathological in the sense of being a response to a specific noxious stimulus, but it may represent the cumulative effects of minor physical or metabolic injuries. 'Gliosis' of this type is present to an increasing extent in parts of the brain stem and cerebellum from early childhood.

Corpora amylacea. A normal concomitant of aging is the appearance in astrocytic processes of these rounded structures, 5 to 15 nm in diameter. They may be found anywhere in the brain and spinal cord, but they appear to accumulate particularly in the subpial zones of the

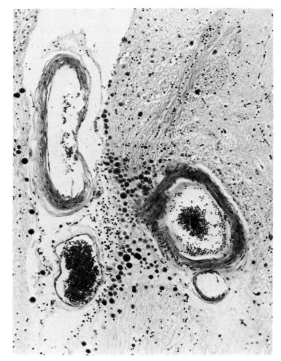

Fig. 13.2 Large numbers of rounded corpora amylacea near the edge of a perivascular space (HE × 100)

cerebral cortex, near the ependymal lining of the ventricular system, and around blood vessels especially in the white matter. In histological sections (Fig. 13.2) they have discrete margins, a central more densely staining core, are highly refractile and birefringent, and have the staining and histochemical properties of an insoluble, high-molecular-weight polysaccharide (Jasper and Prick, 1969). The name 'corpora amylacea' was coined by Virchow because of their superficial resemblance to starch granules. Electron microscopy has confirmed that they occur only within astrocytic processes and has shown that they have a complex structure consisting of a central, dense core surrounded by a mesh-work of fine fibrils (approximately 10 nm in diameter) in a finely granular matrix (Ramsey, 1965). Partial purification and analysis of corpora amylacea by Sakai et al (1969) has revealed that their major component is an unidentified glucose polymer related to the amylopectins.

There is no doubt that corpora amylacea are associated with aging; yet, as they are also found in increased numbers in many degenerative conditions, they cannot be regarded as specific for any particular disease process; nor do they necessarily imply a deleterious metabolic lesion of the affected glial cells as they appear to lie inertly in the tissues of the brain.

Neurones

For more than 70 years there has been controversy about the effects of senescence on neurones; particularly about whether there is a continual loss of nerve cells from the brain during life, about the pathogenesis of various intracellular inclusions and the significance of degenerative changes, e.g. neurofibrillary tangles and argyrophilic plaques.

Numbers of neurones. There are many conflicting reports about whether neurones are lost from the brain during life, and neither in man nor in animals have there been sufficiently well-controlled studies for any generalization to be safe (Blinkov and Glezer, 1968; Dayan, 1971a; Tomasch, 1971). Hanley (1974) reviewed evidence of nerve cell loss in a wide range of species, but was unable to discern any general trend. More recent quantitative studies in man have achieved precision by considerable effort. These have most recently been reviewed by Brody (1982). It has been shown that Purkinje neurones do disappear from the cerebellar cortex (Hall et al, 1975), but that cells in the ventral cochlear nucleus are not affected (Konigsmark and Murphy, 1972), nor are those in the inferior olive (Monagle and Brody, 1974). Some loss of neurones from the cortex in two elderly subjects was found by Colon (1973a), and Cragg (1975) has published similar results, which he has extended to the density of synapses. Using less accurate methods, Brody (1955, 1970) has demonstrated 'fall-out' of cortical nerve cells in later life. The occurrence of neuronal fall out is extremely important, because in the adult these cells are unable to undergo mitosis and any loss cannot be made good. The phenomenon of neuronal fall-out is one which is obscure but which merits the closest attention. What is the nature of the insults which cause nerve cell death?

Neuronal inclusions. Hyaline, eosinophilic and polygonal inclusion bodies have been described in the perikaryons of up to 30 per cent of certain groups of neurones in elderly men and animals (Fraser, 1969; Roesmann and McFarland, 1971). They appear to represent a distinctive degenerative process which results in an unusual type of membrane-bounded accumulation of protein-rich fibrils, apparently distinct from neurofibrillary tangles. These lesions are commonest in neurones in certain thalamic and lower brain stem nuclei.

Lewy bodies. They are rounded or spherical intraneuronal inclusions largely restricted to melanin-containing neurones in the midbrain and brain-stem, but widely distributed throughout nervous tissues (Lewis, 1971). They were noted by Lewy (1913) in cases of idiopathic paralysis agitans and all subsequent observers have stressed this association, although they are allegedly found less frequently and in much smaller

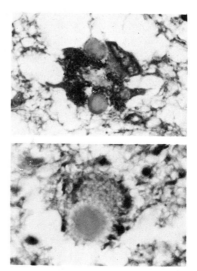

Fig. 13.3 Two views of intraneuronal Lewy bodies in pigmented neurones of the substantia nigra. They show a central core and a pale halo. (Klüver-Barrera × 500)

numbers in other diseases and as a concomitant of aging. One or sometimes two or more are found in affected cells. They measure up to 15 or 20 nm in diameter and consist of a homogeneous, hyaline, eosinophilic material, with a pale halo peripherally, and a central, more densely staining core (Fig. 13.3). Their histological appearances and staining reactions have been discussed and illustrated in detail by Greenfield and Bosanquet (1953), Woodard (1966), den Hartog Jager (1969) and Roy and Wolman (1969). Unlike the similar appearing corpora amylacea, Lewy bodies are not stained magenta by the periodic acid-Schiff technique and show none of the histochemical reactions of amyloid. Ultrastructurally, they consist of fine filaments, about 7 to 8 nm in diameter, often loosely packed and radially orientated peripherally, and densely compressed in the central core, which also contains granular debris. The Lewy bodies sometimes found in autonomic ganglia in Parkinsonism have a similar structure. Although bearing a superficial morphological resemblance to corpora amylacea and the Lafora bodies of myoclonus epilepsy Lewy bodies differ appreciably in their situation, ultrastructure and histochemical properties. They represent an independent type of age and disease-associated neuronal degeneration.

Neuroaxonal dystrophy. The development of homogenous eosinophilic and argyrophilic swellings on axis cylinders is a concomitant of slow degeneration of neuronal processes, possibly of the 'dying back' type (Cavanagh, 1964). This lesion, sometimes referred to as 'neuroaxonal dystrophy', is commonly seen in the gracile nuclei of as many as 30 to 40 per cent of all aged men and animals (Brannon et al 1967; Dayan, 1971a). The significance of this change is uncertain, but it is noteworthy that a degree of loss of posterior column function is a normal occurrence in aging (Garfield, 1982). The fascinating relationship of neuroaxonal dystrophy to vitamin E deficiency (which may also be related to lipofuscin accumulation) is discussed by Pallis and Lewis (1974).

It should be noted that the lesions presented so far (with the exception of Lewy bodies, which are believed by some authorities to denote idiopathic Parkinsonism) probably have little practical effect on the functioning of the nervous system and are of limited clinical significance. The changes described below — neurofibrillary tangles and argyrophilic plaques — are very important. They will be described first and then their occurrence in normal aging will be discussed.

Neurofibrillary tangles. These striking structures, first described by Alzheimer (1907) in the brain of a patient with dementia, have since been studied intensively by light and electron microscopy and by histochemistry. Light microscope findings have been well summarized by, amongst others, Divry (1952), von Braunmühl (1958) and Margolis (1959); those of electron microscopy by Kidd (1964), Terry and Wiśniewski (1970), Gonatas and Gambetti (1970), Terry (1971) and Wiśniewski et al (1976b).

Neurofibrillary tangles occur only within the cell bodies of neurones. They are best demonstrated by silver stains when they appear as elongated and often eccentric thickenings of normal neurofibrils; larger and possibly later lesions are formed by grossly enlarged bundles of densely argyrophilic material which fill a large part of the cytoplasm, and form curious shapes resembling a variety of skeletal structures (Fig. 13.4). The argyrophilic material is sometimes found near cell

processes but does not penetrate far into them. Using conventional non-metallic stains, small tangles are invisible by light microscopy and can be detected only as 'clear' cytoplasmic zones from which normal organelles have been displaced. The larger masses may be weakly amphophilic or eosinophilic; they stain like amyloid with dyes such as congo red and show its typical dichroism in polarized light. Other features of affected cells usually do not appear abnormal. The ultimate fate of the tangle-bearing cell is unknown but it presumably dies as there is some correlation between neurofibrillary tangle formation and loss of neurones in certain diseases (see below).

Knowledge about the biochemical nature and pathological significance of tangles has been greatly advanced by electron microscope and biochemical studies of the brains of aged humans and of animals with experimentally produced analogues of neurofibrillary tangles (Wiśniewski and Terry, 1970; Wiśniewski et al, 1970; Terry, 1971; Wiśniewski et al, 1976a; Tomlinson, 1979). They and others have shown in many disease states (and probably in normal aging) and there is depletion of the normal complement of 24 nm diameter microtubules in the neuronal perikaryon and their replacement by bundles of abnormal twisted tubule-like structures, 22 nm in diameter, which may be composed of two helically arranged filaments. The true 'neurofilament', which is about 10 nm wide, is not affected in most conditions in which tangles are formed, and in any case, may not be its precursor on the available biochemical and ultrastructural evidence. Analysis of preparations of the brain in cases of Alzheimer's presenile and senile dementia has revealed a unique protein in neurofibrillary tangles, unlike either of the monomers of tubulin, or the major neurofilament protein, although it could be derived from modified subunits from either source (Iqbal et al, 1975).

The normal functions of microtubules are partly skeletal, supporting cytoplasmic structures, and, possibly of greater import, providing one mechanism of intracellular transport (Shelanski and Taylor, 1970; Feit et al, 1971). It has been suggested that formation of a neurofibrillary tangle would impair neuronal ability to transport the metabolites and organelles required for continued existence and functioning of its distal processes (see, for example, Seitelberger and Friede, 1971). This might result in centripetal ('dying back') degeneration of the processes and thus to an anatomical lesion, as well, perhaps, to dysfunction at an earlier stage. There is no proof that either of these mechanisms is actually responsible for any of the clinical or pathological features which accompany the formation of neurofibrillary tangles, and there is some indirect evidence that at least a simple 'dying back' process may not be of importance (Dayan, 1971b), although Cragg

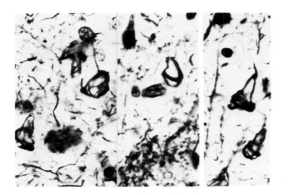

Fig. 13.4 Composite picture of neurofibrillary tangles, the almost triangular dense intraneuronal structures. Argyrophilic plaques are also present as larger and more fragmented areas of staining. (Da Fano × 880)

(1975) has published findings suggestive of loss of dendrites and synapses. The smaller size of nucleoli in tangle-bearing neurones than in normal cells suggests generalized impairment of metabolism (Dayan and Ball, 1973). The psychological and electrophysiological effects of tangles induced experimentally in the brains of animals by aluminium salts have been compared with the naturally-occurring lesions in man, and the latter attributed to aluminium poisoning (Crapper et al, 1976; but see Bowen and Davison, 1982).

Senile plaques. The extremely close connection between plaques and neurones was for long not appreciated and these structures were not formerly considered as a manifestation of neuronal degeneration.

Senile plaques, first described by Blocq and Marinesco (1892), have been repeatedly discussed from various aspects of light and electron microscopy and histochemistry (see Simchowicz, 1911; Divry, 1952; Margolis, 1959; Kidd, 1964; Gonatas and Gambetti, 1970; Terry and Wiśniewski, 1970; Tomlinson, 1979).

They are rounded foci of interstitial tissue degeneration in the cerebral cortex which result in the accumulation of granular and fibrillary argyrophilic material. Plaques are often solitary but may coalesce; they are approximately 10 to 100 nm in diameter. The smallest

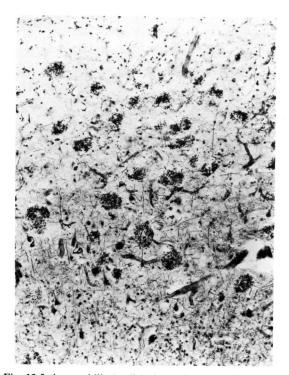

Fig. 13.5 Argyrophilic (senile) plaques in the cerebral cortex shown as rounded masses of irregularly thickened fibrils. Some contain more deeply staining cores. (Da Fano × 85)

lesion detectable by light microscopy ('primitive plaques' of Divry) consists of a minute, rounded focus of dust-like argyrophilic matter (Fig. 13.5); lesions just a little larger ('fibrillary plaques') contain coarser fibrils and often have densely staining cores; all types of plaques may be surrounded by a few hypertrophic microglia and occasional fibrillary astrocytes. The dense core has the staining reactions of amyloid and, in some instances, there may be fine radiating strands extending outwards from the centre into the peripheral zones of plaques.

By electron microscopy (reviewed by Terry and Wiśniewski, 1970; Tomlinson, 1979) the smallest plaques have been shown to consist of groups of a few degenerating neurites, probably terminal postsynaptic dendrites. Larger lesions all have central cores of the fine, distinctive amyloid fibrils which appear to be derived from adjacent mesodermal cells such as microglia. The largest plaques have extensive, dense, acellular cores of amyloid surrounded by smaller numbers of degenerating dendrites. Occasionally the 22 nm tubules characteristic of neurofibrillary tangles are found in nearby dendrites, but the majority of them show only less specific features of cellular damage. Electron microscope studies have shown that the initial lesion in the formation of senile plaques is degeneration of a small group of dendrites. As the lesion expands it is accompanied by dendritic changes in an increasingly large area and the local deposition of amyloid. A preliminary account of the biochemical composition of plaques has been published (Nikaido et al, 1971).

Distribution and frequency of neurofibrillary tangles and senile plaques in the brain in normal senescence. Ever since the detailed report by Simchowicz (1911) it has been claimed that both these lesions occur in the brains of apparently normal old people, although a major difficulty has been how to ensure that the subjects in the various published series were normal. Simchowicz (1911) did not discuss this point beyond stating that his patients were 'normal'; Grünthal (1927) gave detailed clinical accounts of his few cases; Gellerstedt's (1933) classical series consisted of patients who had only acutely fatal non-neurological diseases; Corsellis (1962) made a retrospective division of his 300 cases into those with 'functional' and those with 'organic' psychiatric disorders; Hirano and Zimmerman's (1962) patients all came from general medical wards; Matsuyama et al (1966) stated that their cases were 'normal'; Tomlinson et al (1968) undertook a careful psychiatric and psychometric assessment of their 28 cases; and Dayan's (1970a) series consisted of people who had died from sudden trauma, or unexpectedly from acute heart attacks. It is possible that all these series are biased to some extent, but, taken together, they probably provide a reasonable estimate of the changes found in aged men and women who did not suffer from significant psychiatric disorders.

Senile plaques and neurofibrillary tangles are uncommon in patients less than 50 to 60 years old, and thereafter there is a definite, although not identical, relationship between the frequency of occurrence of both these lesions and increasing age (Dayan, 1970a). More than 90 per cent of people aged 90 years or more probably have plaques and a similar proportion carry at least some neurofibrillary tangles.

Neither of these lesions is distributed uniformly in the brain and it has proved impossible to correlate exactly the occurrence of plaques with that of tangles, or to associate either of these changes with other abnormalities in the brain. It is generally accepted that plaques are slightly more common in the depths of sulci than in the exposed crests of gyri, perhaps because the packing density of neurones is greater at the former site. Simchowicz (1924) claimed that plaques were more common in the occipital than the frontal cortex, but this has not been confirmed, and they are now considered to be distributed uniformly throughout the neocortex. Plaques are more common in the hippocampus and other parts of the limbic system than elsewhere in the cerebral cortex (Morel and Wildi, 1955; von Braunmühl, 1958), and occasionally they have been reported in the hypothalamus and corpus striatum. Plaques have very rarely been described elsewhere and it has been doubted whether they occur at all outside these regions and have not been mistaken for artefacts, including Tinel's (1924) pseudo-plaques.

Neurofibrillary tangles have a different incidence and are not distributed in the same way as senile plaques. Simchowicz (1911), Newton (1948), Dayan (1970a) and Tomlinson et al (1968) have all described cases in whom tangles but not plaques were found; tangles are found at least twice as often and in larger numbers in the hippocampus than any other site in the brain, particularly in the end plate, Sommer sector and glomerular formations of the subiculum (von Braunmühl, 1958; Tomlinson et al, 1968), and their incidence and intensity are generally greater in the medial temporal region than elsewhere in the neocortex; third, unlike plaques, tangles may be widely distributed in the central nervous system for, as shown by Hirano and Zimmerman (1962) and Ishii (1966), they may occur in the hypothalamus, basal ganglia and even in nuclei in the brain stem.

In summary, senile plaques and neurofibrillary tangles represent different degenerative changes in neurones. They occur with increasing frequency in people over the age of 60 years but are not related directly to each other in terms of frequency, intensity or distribution. Plaques are most common in the hippocampus and limbic cortex. Tangles, too, occur very commonly at these sites but may be found over much wider areas of the archi- and neocortex as well as in central grey nuclei and the brain stem.

Granulovacuolar degeneration. Another histological lesion affecting certain neurones in the elderly is the 'granulovacuolar degeneration' also described by Simchowicz in 1911. It is restricted to neurones and almost exclusively those of the hippocampus, where it is particularly common in pyramidal cells in the centro-lateral quadrant (Woodard, 1962). Its exact incidence in normal aged man is unknown, but it has been said to be present to some extent in about 50 per cent of subjects more than 60 years old (Woodard, 1962; Tomlinson et al, 1968; Tomlinson and Kitchener, 1972), although usually only a few cells are affected (Woodard, 1962). These neurones show clusters of intracytoplasmic vacuoles, up to 5 nm in diameter, each of which contains a densely-staining, rounded central granule 0.5 to 1.5 nm across (Fig. 13.6). Affected cells usually contain several of these lesions. In areas where they are plentiful it is common to find some evidence of neuronal degeneration and gliosis.

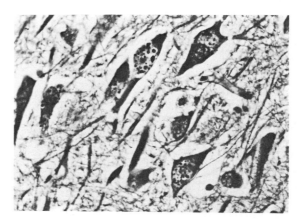

Fig. 13.6 Granulovacuolar degeneration of pyramidal neurones in Ammon's horn (Glees-Marsland × 500)

The electron microscopical appearances of this lesion show that it consists of a membrane-bounded vacuole containing a dense central core (Hirano et al, 1968). These appearances have been compared with those of residual lysosomes or dense bodies, but the normal structure from which granulovacuolar degeneration arises and its mechanism of formation are still uncertain.

Hirano bodies. These structures, described by Hirano et al (1968) are inconspicuous, erythrocyte-like bodies most easily found between hippocampal pyramidal cells, and in old brains. Their significance is unknown.

VASCULAR LESIONS AND NORMAL AGING

Apart from the specific pathological lesions of arterio-sclerosis and microaneurysm formation, which are discussed elsewhere, there are other changes in cerebral vessels which are found in almost everyone more than about 60 years of age.

A very high proportion of elderly people (Gellerstedt, 1933; Arab, 1959) show some reduplication and splitting of the elastic lamina and fibrosis and hyalinization of the media of intracerebral arteries and the larger arterioles (Baker, 1937). These changes affect vessels in the meninges, as well as in the grey and white matter of the brain and spinal cord, and are usually most severe in the perforating vessels in the basal ganglia.

The network of small arterioles and venules and their interconnecting capillaries also change with age, slowly becoming more complex as irregularities and abnormal or distorted channels accumulate (Hassler, 1967).

Encrustation of vessels with complex mineral deposits is common, particularly those of the pallidum and putamen and, to a lesser extent, of the thalamus, hippocampus and hilum of the dentate nucleus. The material, which may contain calcium, is basophilic, haematoxyphilic, has a polysaccharide-containing matrix and forms irregularly distributed granules, or concentric and often laminated cuffs around small blood vessels (Slager and Wagner, 1956).

A more striking lesion is the congophilic angiopathy of Scholz (1938), which has been extensively studied by Divry (1952), Morel and Wildi (1955) and Wildi et al (1964). The amyloid nature of the deposited material has been shown by conventional histochemistry and by electron microscopy (Pauli et al, 1971). This condition is relatively uncommon as not more than 15 per cent of people are affected (Surbek, 1961; Wildi et al, 1964). It takes the form of discontinuous and even nodular accumulations of amyloid in the walls of small arterioles, particularly in the meninges and cerebral cortex, and may extend into the intra-cerebral perivascular spaces. Usually only moderate amounts of amyloid are seen and only rarely does it appear to cause extreme narrowing of affected vessels. Glenner (1978) has briefly reviewed this subject. The pathogenesis of senile cerebral amyloid is obscure, and the rare familial form of cerebral vascular amyloidosis which predisposes to brain haemorrhage (Gudmundsson et al, 1972; Wattendorff et al, 1982) offers no clues.

SPINAL CORD AND PERIPHERAL NERVES

Within the spinal cord age-related changes appear to be of the same general type but less common than in the brain (Bailey, 1953). In addition to the neuroaxonal dystrophy mentioned above, from about the fifth decade onwards there is some associated loss of fibres and gliosis from the gracile fasciculus, manifested as pallor on myelin staining, and prominent accumulation of lipofuscin in larger neurones. Senile plaques and neuro-fibrillary tangles do not occur, nor does congophilic angiopathy, but arteriosclerotic degeneration of the small spinal arteries may be seen; calcification of the spinal dura is common, usually in the form of thin, white chalky plaques. Rarely do they become large enough to be visible on X-ray.

Peripheral nerves commonly show some degenerative features, apparently not due to specific causes, and generally correlated with increasing age. There is an increasing incidence in the elderly of random damage to individual Schwann cells, which can be detected histologically as scattered segmental loss, thinning or abnormal shortness of the myelin sheath around axis cylinders, and even some loss of nerve fibres with their replacement by finer axons (Lascelles and Thomas, 1966; Arnold and Harriman, 1970). Autonomic nerves show equivalent changes (Ochoa and Mair, 1969). The physiological results include slowing of conduction velocity and probably diminution or loss of reflexes (Norris et al, 1953).

DEMENTIA IN THE ELDERLY

As discussed above a great many changes are present in the brain of aged man, both at a macroscopical and a microscopical level. Some are so common, appear so early in life and are so widespread in their distribution that it is most unlikely that they can be considered as 'pathological' in the sense of indicating a significant disease process. Further, although of interest in terms of theories about the causes and mechanisms of aging, it is unlikely that these lesions are of much practical significance in the causation of neurological and psychiatric disease in the elderly (Dayan, 1972). Amongst these lesions, which must be recognized if only to be discarded in the present context of pathological changes which are concomitants or measures of brain damage, are the accumulation of lipofuscin, corpora amylacea, certain intracellular inclusions, though not Lewy bodies, perivascular calcification and amyloid deposition. There remains a small group of lesions, possibly related to each other pathogenetically and by having a common aetiological factor, which show a striking association with those psychiatric and physical symptoms and signs called *senile dementia*. Unfortunately, the pathological and no less the clinical study of patients suffering from this condition has been complicated and confused by the lack of qualitative specificity of many of the observed clinical disorders and pathological lesions, as superficially similar changes are found in apparently normal old people and in cases of the presenile dementia called Alzheimer's disease. The most important members of this group of lesions are argyrophilic plaques, neurofibrillary tangles and granulovacuolar degeneration. Needless controversy has continued for decades over the largely unrewarding problem of how to distinguish between this presenile condition and the pathologically comparable type of senile dementia and what significance, if any, can be attached to the distinction.

It can now be accepted, however, that cases of senile dementia and Alzheimer's disease have identical pathological lesions, and that the most striking differences so far detected between them and normal aging are quantitative rather than qualitative. This simplifying hypothesis, which is clearly discussed by Corsellis (1962, 1976) and Tomlinson et al (1970), contrasts with the claims by Grünthal (1927) and Rothschild (1937) that there were essential, albeit undetected, differences between the changes associated with normal aging and those of senile dementia (see Arab, 1960; Sourander and Sjögren, 1970). The present hypothesis may eventually prove to be an oversimplification, but currently there is no pathological evidence to contradict it.

In considering the pathological aspects of dementia in the elderly it is necessary to distinguish between disorders due to exogenous processes such as trauma, vascular disease, infections of the brain, metabolic diseases etc., and those associated with the idiopathic degenerative processes apparently restricted to the brain. The latter disorders, which are associated pathologically with the appearance of large numbers of argyrophilic plaques and neurofibrillary tangles may not often occur in pure form in clinical practice, as they are commonly combined with cerebrovascular disease. However, the pathology of the major types of disorders can be analysed satisfactorily if it is realized that patients show variable combinations of normal aging changes as well as some of the range of these pathological effects. This results in a complex summation of clinical and pathological disorders in which the most important process may well change as the patient's illness evolves. Furthermore, other diseases from which the patient suffers may affect the nature and extent of the pathological processes in the brain, or, by killing the patient, may cut short the expected natural history of an evolving neuropathological lesion.

Data about combinations of lesions have not yet been obtained from a sufficiently large series of patients studied both clinically and pathologically. It is impossible, therefore, to give more than a very approximate guide to the relative importance of different disease processes in a population of elderly subjects, especially as the relative incidence of cerebrovascular disease varies so greatly in different parts of the world and in the two sexes. The available information suggests that in a group of elderly demented patients sufficiently ill to require treatment in hospital, the proportion showing the change of 'senile dementia' alone would be about 40 per cent (Newton 1948), 20 per cent (Robertson and Mason Brown 1953), or 50 per cent (Tomlinson et al, 1970); the percentage with cerebral softenings and other changes due to vascular disease would be about 20 per cent (Tomlinson et al, 1970); and 20 per cent would show a combination of senile dementia and cerebrovascular disease. Other series collected and assessed in different ways are in general agreement with the trend of these figures (e.g. Corsellis, 1962). It should be noted that in any such group of patients there will be a few in whom standard neuropathological techniques will not reveal any anatomical lesion sufficient to account for the psychiatric disorder (Tomlinson et al, 1970). In such cases, there may have been a focal lesion at a crucial site which was so small that it was not detected, or some other general disorder, perhaps metabolic, which remained undiscovered.

The pathological features can now be considered of the different types of diseases associated with dementia in the elderly.

Senile dementia

The neuropathology of this disorder has been discussed in some detail by von Braunmühl (1958); Tomlinson et al (1970); and Jervis (1971a), and it has been compared with Alzheimer's disease by these authors, as well as by Smith (1969) and Sourander and Sjögren (1970).

In this disorder the brain shows a moderate but variable degree of atrophy, usually weighing between 1000 g and 1100 g (Fig. 13.7). It has been claimed that in younger patients with Alzheimer's disease, the brain more often weighs less than 1000 g (Tomlinson et al, 1970). The atrophy, shown by gaping sulci and shrunken gyri, is most marked in the frontal, occipital and temporal regions; and on coronal section, the amygdala and hippocampus are often seen to be affected as well. The lateral and third ventricles are dilated. To the naked eye the sizes of the basal ganglia appear in proportion to that of the brain, so they, too, must have atrophied. The cerebral cortical atrophy is normally uniform in affected areas, although selective damage, particularly to the temporal cortex (Tariska, 1970) and medial temporal structures (Corsellis, 1970; Sourander and Sjögren, 1970), is occasionally seen, which may account for certain clinical disorders (Brierley, 1966).

On microscopy three principal lesions are present, besides the normal concomitants of aging and other concurrent disorders. The important pathological changes are the appearance of argyrophilic plaques and

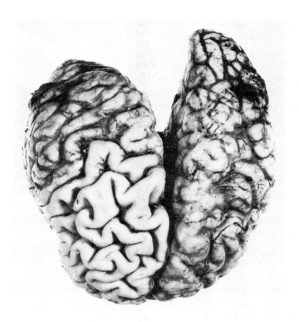

Fig. 13.7 Senile dementia. View from above of atrophic cerebral hemisphere on left (anteriorly the leptomeninges have been removed) and control from subject of same age on right. Note the shrunken gyri and gaping sulci in the patient's brain and the opalescence of the leptomeninges in the control.

neurofibrillary tangles and loss of neurones with reactive gliosis.

On light microscopy the plaques and tangles look exactly the same as in normal aging, and their ultra-structural appearances and probably their chemical composition are identical too (Terry, 1970; Iqbal et al, 1975). The most important difference between senile dementia and senescence is a quantitative one, i.e. the far greater number of these lesions present in demented patients. The problems of exact quantitation are formidable, not least those due to our uncertainty whether it is important to assess the entire cerebral cortex or whether to concentrate just on those areas which clinical disorders have suggested would be severely affected reviewed by Dayan, 1970b and 1971b). The attempts that have been made (Simchowicz, 1924; Grünthal, 1927; Gellerstedt, 1933; Jamada and Mehraein, 1968; Sourander and Sjögren, 1970; Tomlinson et al, 1970) have shown that all areas of the cerebral cortex in brains of patients with senile dementia contain many more plaques and tangles than normal controls of the same ages. Considerable disagreement still remains about the significance of the numbers of these lesions at different sites and even about the relative clinical importance of plaques and tangles. These arguments are largely academic and may even be unnecessary since electron

microscopy (Terry and Wiśniewski, 1970) has shown that many more plaques are present than are visible by light microscopy; and also because of uncertainty whether the same pathological mechanism causes both plaques and tangles. It probably does because they are rarely dissociated qualitatively in senile dementia. It may well be that the factor which ultimately causes the cerebral dysfunction is neither of these lesions but instead is the associated disruption of neuronal connec-tions brought about by the destruction of synapses, as shown by Gonatas and Gambetti (1970) and Cragg (1975), and perhaps the presumptive disorder of intra-neuronal transport (Terry, 1971).

In senile dementia there is a further problem about plaques and tangles, namely their distribution within the brain. They are found throughout the cerebral cortex; many authors have illustrated them in the amygdala and nearby structures (Corsellis, 1970); a smaller number have described both lesions in the hypothalamus (Hirano and Zimmerman, 1962; Ishii, 1966); and plaques and tangles have been reported separately and together in other basal ganglia, and even in the brain-stem (von Braunmühl, 1958; Hirano and Zimmerman, 1962; Ishii, 1966). The importance of this regrettably small number of reports is that extensive involvement of the various di- and mesencephalic structures could help to explain some of the visceral syndromes, such as wasting, from which these patients may suffer, as well as some of the abnormalities reported in CSF concen-trations of various catecholamine metabolites (reviewed by Dayan, 1971b).

A further lesion, which has proved difficult to study and so has had less attention, is loss of neurones. Many references have been made to loss of neurones from various parts of these atrophic brains. However, only limited quantitative information is available (Colon, 1973b), so, despite the frequent occurrence of diffuse gliosis in the cerebral cortex of cases of senile dementia, the amount and relative significance of neuronal loss remains to be determined. In almost all cases of senile dementia granulovacuolar degeneration is present in a very large number of pyramidal neurones in the hippo-campus (Woodard, 1962; Tomlinson et al, 1970; Tomlinson and Kitchener, 1972). More than 60 per cent of these cells may be affected (Woodard, 1962). This lesion is almost diagnostic of senile dementia because it is far less common in normal aging and otherwise occurs only in very uncommon diseases.

Another lesion sometimes associated with senile dementia is that of congophilic angiopathy. However, as shown by Wildi et al (1964), it is not unique to this disorder, and may be no more severe in such patients than in normal people of similar ages, except in rare cases, like those described by Corsellis and Brierley (1954). There is no direct link between the various forms of vascular disease, including arteriosclerosis and the occurrence of plaques and tangles (Arab, 1954; Corsellis, 1962; Wildi et al, 1964; Tomlinson et al, 1970).

The aetiology of senile dementia and Alzheimer's disease is not known. The finding of tangles in a number of other human diseases (Terry, 1971) is probably irrelevant because ultrastructurally and therefore biochemically the lesions are quite different. A form of dementia associated with Alzheimer's disease-like changes is rarely precipitated by trauma (Corsellis et al, 1973; Wiśniewski et al, 1976a). The suggestion that Alzheimer's disease might be a 'slow-virus' infection of the brain remains an unsupported speculation (Gajdusek and Gibbs, 1973). The experimentally produced tangles in animals may also not be strictly relevant because they, too, differ from the human lesion (Wiśniewski and Terry, 1970; *Lancet*, 1976).

Some research has been done into naturally-occurring lesion in the brains of aged animals (Dayan, 1971a). Plaque formation has been described only in the dog and the monkey (see Brizzee et al, 1978). Other lesions, including neuroaxonal dystrophy, intraneuronal inclusion formation and congophilic angiopathy occur frequently in aged animals (Dayan, 1971a). It is possible that sufficient numbers of really old animals have not been examined, that the intrinsic factors responsible for aging affect man and animals differently, or that extrinsic factors are involved which may exert different effects on different species.

Genetic studies in families and a large series of cases (Sjögren et al, 1952; Larsson et al, 1963; Pratt, 1970) have been made in attempts to distinguish between endogenous and exogenous factors in the aetiology and pathogenesis of Alzheimer's disease and senile dementia. Sjögren et al (1952) and Larsson et al (1963) concluded that these diseases were due to a single autosomal dominant gene. Others (Pratt, 1970) have considered that the findings were more in keeping with polygenic inheritance. There are no completely satisfactory reports of identical twins with typical Alzheimer's disease or senile dementia and there are reports of two sets discordant for these diseases (Hunter et al, 1972). All these results suggest that exogenous as well as endogenous factors may be involved in the aetiology of these forms of dementia in the elderly.

Pick's disease

Pick's disease is an unusual form of presenile dementia. It is characterized clinically by severe progressive dementia and signs of local cortical lesions, and pathologically by severe, localized cerebral atrophy.

The morbidity risk of Pick's disease has been calculated to be 0.05 per cent of the general population in Sweden (Sjögren et al, 1952) and its incidence as 0.2 per cent of all autopsies in a large American hospital (Neumann, 1949). Sjögren and colleagues and Pratt (1967) have discussed the genetic and family evidence which suggests that it may be due to an autosomal dominant gene affected by several modifier genes.

The apparent rarity of the condition has made it difficult to analyse either the clinical or pathological features adequately. The pattern of clinical illness has been reported to vary considerably although there are several fairly well-defined syndromes (Mansvelt, 1954). All patients have general intellectual deterioration, blunting of affect and loss of insight. Particularly severe lesions in the temporal lobes may result in memory disturbances and aphasia, and damage to the parietal lobes in dyslexia and agnosia, as well as in less common disorders such as the Klüver-Bucy syndrome.

Pathologically, the external appearances of the brain are striking, with severe, bilaterally symmetrical atrophy of particular areas of the cerebral cortex, most commonly in the frontal, temporal and parietal lobes (Fig. 13.8). The shrinkage is not uniform as, characteristically, anterior parts are most severely affected and the posterior parts of some gyri may look almost normal, thus giving the typical 'knife edge atrophy' appearance. Light microscopy shows disorganization of the cell pattern in affected parts of the cortex, severe loss of neurones and gliosis. There is also extensive loss of nerve fibres and gliosis in underlying parts of the white matter and basal ganglia, the caudate nuclei being most often affected (Jervis, 1971b). In addition, there are two lesions of neurones which are only infrequently seen in other types of dementia.

The first is swelling and pallor of affected neurones associated with loss of the intracytoplasmic Nissl bodies. It is well illustrated by von Braunmühl (1958), and affects neurones in the cortex, basal ganglia and midbrain. The other lesion is the formation of intraneuronal argyrophilic inclusions which may be up to 5 to 7 nm in diameter, are rounded and have a homogeneous or finely granular structure (Alzheimer, 1907). These bodies, which have been found in about half of all cases of Pick's disease, are most common in areas where swollen cells are also present. Typical senile plaques, neurofibrillary tangles and granulovacuolar degeneration do occur, too, but are much less common than in senile dementia (Hirano et al, 1968; Jervis, 1971b; Wiśniewski et al, 1972). The first authors also described an intracytoplasmic, eosinophilic, laminated rod-like structure ('Hirano body') in neurones in Sommer's sector of Ammon's horn in Pick's disease and occasionally in other disorders.

Although the clinical differentiation of Alzheimer's and Pick's diseases may sometimes be difficult, pathologically the two conditions are dissimilar. Cases of the former show diffuse cortical atrophy, and large numbers

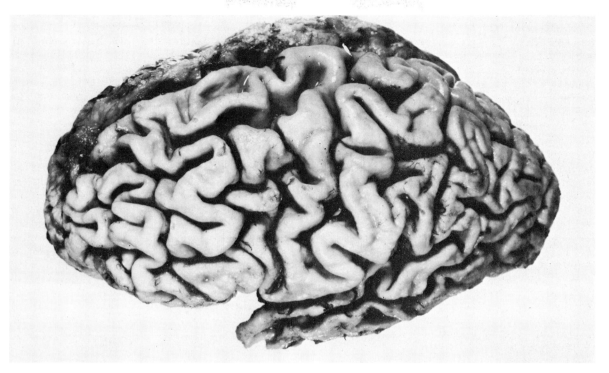

Fig. 13.8 Pick's disease. Side view of fixed brain showing extreme shrinkage of temporal lobe as well as generalized cerebral atrophy more marked anteriorly.

of argyrophilic plaques and neurofibrillary tangles, whereas in the latter there is localized atrophy of the brain and swollen cells and argyrophilic inclusions are common, but plaques and tangles are scarce.

DEGENERATIVE DISORDERS OF THE BASAL GANGLIA IN LATER LIFE

A considerable amount of ill-health and demand for medical attention in the elderly is due to various disorders of the basal ganglia, particularly those causing the different types of 'Parkinsonism'. Other, less common diseases are of concern because they raise problems of differential diagnosis and treatment, as well as of genetic counselling in cases of familial affection by inherited disorders.

The conditions of particular importance in patients suffering from the clinical syndrome of Parkinsonism are: idiopathic and postencephalitic Parkinsonism; striatonigral degeneration; progressive supranuclear palsy (Steele-Richardson-Olszewski syndrome); Shy-Drager syndrome; olivopontocerebellar atrophy; Huntington's chorea; and Jakob-Creutzfeldt disease. The last of these is discussed later (p. 285).

Parkinsonism (Paralysis agitans)

The clinical syndrome of Parkinsonism consists of variable manifestations of tremor, rigidity, brady- and hypokinesia combined in some cases with such disorders as oculogyric crises, psychiatric disturbances and dementia.

As discussed in detail by Eicke (1968), Selby (1968b) and Pallis (1971), the earliest descriptions of Parkinson's disease were purely clinical and relatively little information was available about the underlying pathology. The pandemic of encephalitis lethargica in the second and third decades of the twentieth century resulted in many more cases of postencephalitic Parkinsonism (a term coined especially to describe these patients), who were first recognized and studied in considerable detail by von Economo (1931). From about 1920 onwards it has been recognized that Parkinsonism is really a syndrome which may be due to several different causes, the two most important clinical forms being the postencephalitic and idiopathic (the latter is probably the type originally described by James Parkinson in 1817).

When considered together all types of Parkinsonism are one of the commoner forms of neurological disease in the adult. Their incidence has been calculated to be between 1.0 and 1.5/1000 of the adult population (Kurland, 1958), and, as the prevalence rises steeply with age, as many as 1 per cent of all people aged 50 or over have been reported to be affected to some degree.

It is probable that the incidence of Parkinsonism is changing slowly as surviving postencephalitic patients die. New cases of von Economo's disease still occur (see Rail et al, 1981), but are now extremely rare, so almost all new patients belong to the other major group of 'idiopathic' Parkinsonism (Duvoisin and Yahr, 1965; Pallis, 1971). The changing aetiology is reflected in a different pattern of age incidence in which the mean age of appearance of new cases is about 50 years, as in the period before 1917 (Schwab et al, 1956; Duvoisin et al, 1963). The postencephalitic cases were much younger, their mean age of onset being about 40 years, as this disease was most common in people aged 25 to 35 years, and their Parkinsonian syndrome appeared in 30 per cent within 3 years of the attack, and in 80 per cent of those affected within 10 years (Dimsdale, 1946; Duvoisin et al, 1963).

The idiopathic and postencephalitic forms of Parkinsonism can often be differentiated clinically and there are several consistent features which enable them to be distinguished pathologically. The neuropathological findings have been reviewed by Eicke (1968), Alvord (1971) and Lewis (1971). The features common to both major forms of Parkinsonism will be described first and then those characteristic of the idiopathic and postencephalitic forms.

General findings

The brain of a case of Parkinsonism appears normal externally, or will show only the usual changes of senescence. Cerebral atrophy may occur (Selby, 1968a) but is not usually severe unless some other disease is present, too. The lateral ventricles may be moderately enlarged. The only consistent abnormality is severe depigmentation of the substantia nigra which appears as a broad, pale brownish halo (Fig. 13.9a and b). In some cases depigmentation of the locus coeruleus in the pontine tegmentum is also visible to the naked eye.

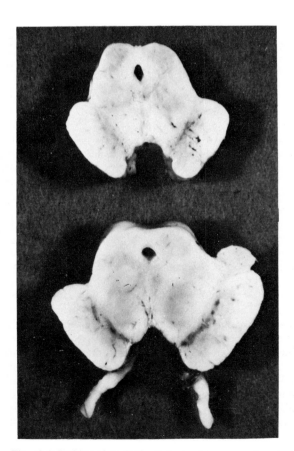 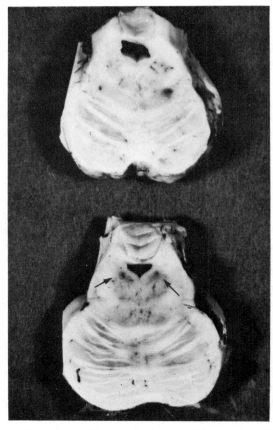

Fig. 13.9 Parkinsonism. Patient's brain above, normal control below. A. Severe pallor of substantia nigra. B. Disappearance of pigmented neurones of locus caeruleus (arrow).

Histologically, in both forms of Parkinsonism, the major lesion is destruction and loss of pigmented melanin-bearing neurones, particularly those in the substantia nigra, locus coeruleus, and dorsal motor nucleus of the vagus. Certain unpigmented nuclei in the brain-stem are also affected, particularly the reticular formation and hypoglossal nucleus (Greenfield and Bosanquet, 1953; Eadie, 1963; Earle, 1968). The affected areas show loss of neurones, less often occasional dying nerve cells surrounded by macrophages, gliosis which is most often marked in the central part of the substantia nigra, and melanin-containing macrophages concentrated around small blood vessels. Other lesions common to both types of Parkinsonism are more variable in their occurrence and probably represent the effects of concurrent senescence or cerebrovascular disease. These changes are slight cerebral atrophy with loss of neurones and the appearance of neurofibrillary tangles and argyrophilic plaques; inconstant loss of myelinated fibres and neurones from the outer segment of the globus pallidus and the putamen, perhaps representing loss of strionigral fibres and trans-synaptic degeneration of nerve cells; and enlarged perivascular spaces in the caudate nuclei and putamen.

The other lesions that have been described are far more closely associated with either idiopathic or post-encephalitic Parkinsonism and can be used pathologically to differentiate the two types.

Idiopathic Parkinsonism (true paralysis agitans)
Characteristically, surviving pigmented neurones contain Lewy bodies (see above). When sought for they have been found in more than 90 per cent of cases of paralysis agitans and in almost none of postencephalitic Parkinsonism in which there was a definite history of encephalitis (Greenfield and Bosanquet, 1953; Earle, 1968). Lewy bodies have been found elsewhere in the brain in idiopathic Parkinsonism (den Hartog Jager and Bethlem, 1960), in many diencephalic and brain-stem nuclei, lateral and posterior horns in the spinal cord and autonomic ganglia (Forno and Norville, 1976).

Postencephalitic Parkinsonism
Patients dying during or shortly after an attack of encephalitis lethargica showed the typical lesions of viral encephalitis, i.e. neuronal degeneration, glial stars, perivascular cuffing and gliosis. These changes were most marked in the brain-stem, mesencephalon and diencephalic and hypothalamic nuclei (von Economo, 1931; Greenfield and Blackwood, 1963). The brains of patients dying now, long after the initial attack, rarely show perivascular inflammatory infiltration but there is still evidence of damage and scarring in the affected areas. Many surviving pigmented and other neurones contain neurofibrillary tangles, very similar on light

microscopy to those found in senile dementia. The tangles are found in the substantia nigra and locus coeruleus, as well as in the hypothalamus, reticular formation, lower brain-stem and elsewhere (Greenfield and Bosanquet, 1953; Hirano and Zimmerman, 1962). Electron microscopy has shown that they consist of twisted, 22 nm diameter tubules like those found in senile dementia and some cases of subacute sclerosing panencephalitis. Although occasional tangles may be found in a case of paralysis agitans they follow the pattern of distribution found in senescence and do not occur in basal and brain-stem nuclei.

Another late feature of postencephalitic cases may be moderately severe, diffuse or patchy loss of neurones and scarring in the cerebral cortex, basal ganglia and especially in nuclei in the floor of the fourth ventricle, following the distribution of the acute inflammatory lesions of long ago.

The aetiology is unknown of both these forms of disease. There is a suggestion that some cases of apparently idiopathic Parkinsonism may really be an inherited degeneration (Pratt, 1967). The other 'postencephalitic' type of this disease has been so termed because of the descriptions of many cases which appeared during or after the world pandemic of encephalitis lethargica in the 1920s and which had certain clinical and pathological characteristics. No virus has ever been identified in these patients.

Biochemical research has improved our understanding of symptomatology and has helped to rationalise treatment of Parkinsonism (reviewed by Calne, 1970; Curzon, 1976). There is a marked reduction in the striatal content of the neurotransmitter dopamine and a corresponding fall in the CSF concentrations of it and its metabolites, due to degeneration of dopaminergic nigrostriatal nerve fibres caused by destruction of neurones in the substantia nigra.

Other causes of Parkinsonian-like disorders
Arteriosclerotic Parkinsonism. Clinically, a common cause of mild Parkinsonism in the elderly has often been considered to be arteriosclerosis, although it has not been possible to identify corresponding vascular lesions at any particular site in the brain. Denny Brown (1962) associated foci of damage to the lentiform nucleus (état criblé — see below) with clinical tremor and rigidity, but this pattern of damage is also found in many old people who do not have extra-pyramidal disorders. Arteriosclerotic Parkinsonism could in theory be due to micro-infarcts or minute zones of ischaemia affecting the nigrostriatal pathway, because its clinical features are similar to those of idiopathic Parkinsonism, but this remains to be proved. There is no morbid anatomical evidence of an excess of cerebrovascular disease in cases of true Parkinsonism (Eadie and Sutherland, 1964),

nor does clinical and biochemical evidence support the association (Parkes et al, 1974).

Benign essential tremor. This is a non-progressive disorder, usually familial, which is also known as 'senile tremor' if it first presents in later life. No significant pathological lesions were found in the case reported by Herskovits and Blackwood (1969).

Drug-induced Parkinsonism. Large does of certain drugs, especially phenothiazines, can produce Parkinsonian-like states, particularly affecting movements of the face and tongue (reviewed by Crane and Paulson, 1967). Patients with pre-existing brain damage are more liable to develop this complication and it may persist in them after the drug treatment has stopped. Accounts of the neuropathology are indefinite as it has not been possible to exclude changes due to other diseases of the brain which were also present (Hunter et al, 1968; Christensen et al, 1970).

Other intoxications. Parkinsonism may be caused by other poisons which affect the basal ganglia, in particular carbon monoxide, manganese and anoxia (Jellinger, 1968). Other very rare degenerations, often inherited, which may cause Parkinsonism, are discussed by Jellinger (1968).

Striatonigral degeneration

This very rare disease was first recognized as an entity by Adams, van Bogaert and van der Eecken (1961; 1964). Adams et al described four patients with rigidity and slowness of movement of one or more limbs which progressed to affect all four limbs as well as cranial and bulbar muscles. Clinically they appeared to be suffering from Parkinsonism, but pathologically they differed considerably from typical cases of postencephalitic or idiopathic Parkinsonism. The corpus striatum and pallidum were very shrunken macroscopically and there was some depigmentation of the substantia nigra. There was considerable loss of neurones from the putamen, and lesser degrees of loss from the caudate nuclei and substantia nigra. These areas all showed dense gliotic scarring (Fig. 13.10). The shrinkage of the globus pallidus was due to loss of myelinated striatopallidal fibres and the pallidal neurones were almost unaffected. Neurofibrillary tangles and Lewy bodies were not found.

The findings which distinguish these cases from more common varieties of Parkinsonism are the severity of the lesions in the putamen and caudate nuclei; and from Huntington's chorea — the lack of a family history and the amount of damage to the substantia nigra. One case resembled olivopontocerebellar atrophy and, in turn, cases of this disorder have been described in which there was severe damage to pigmented neurones. It is possible that this idiopathic disease is an intermediate form between Huntington's chorea, olivopontocerebellar atrophy and idiopathic Parkinsonism.

Shy-Drager syndrome

Another uncommon clinical syndrome consists of variable manifestations of mild extrapyramidal movement disorders, orthostatic hypotension, atonic bladder, incontinence and other features of damage to the autonomic nervous system (Shy and Drager, 1960; Chokroverty et al, 1969). The pathological lesions described have resembled olivopontocerebellar atrophy in some cases, whilst others have shown more diffuse system degenerations, including damage to the substantia nigra. Some cases have had intraneuronal inclusions resem-

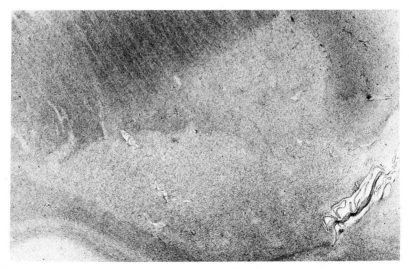

Fig. 13.10 Loss of large neurones and gliosis of striatum and shrinkage of pallidum in strionigral degeneration (PTAH × 8)

bling Lewy bodies in the central nervous system and peripheral autonomic ganglia (Johnson et al, 1966; Vanderhaeghen et al, 1969). Loss of intermediolateral spinal neurones occurs in the majority of cases, but not invariably (Evans et al, 1972). Familial incidence has been documented rarely (Lewis, 1964).

Huntington's chorea
This dominantly inherited degenerative disease usually presents in middle-aged patients and it is rare for it to appear first in older people. It has been extensively reviewed by Bruyn (1968).

The clinical characteristics include a family history of the disease, progressive intellectual and psychiatric impairment, choreic movements of the limbs and face and eventually of the trunk, and ultimately dystonic postures.

The neuropathological features were described by Jelgersma in 1909, and more fully in the 1920s by the German school of neuropathologists (e.g. Bielschowsky, 1922) as well as by Dunlap (1927). They have been reviewed by McCaughey (1961).

In Huntington's chorea the cerebral hemispheres are generally atrophic, and the entire brain weighs less than normal. The lateral ventricles are enlarged, due particularly to severe atrophy of the caudate nucleus and putamen (Fig. 13.11), which become brownish in colour, and to shrinkage of the centrum ovale. There is an ill-defined loss of neurones from the cerebral cortex accompanied by gliosis, which may be most severe in the occipital lobes. The caudate and putamen show a devastating loss of small neurones in particular and very severe fibrillary gliosis. These changes are most severe in the superoposterior parts of both nuclei. The large neurones may also be affected, although to a lesser extent. In the globus pallidus myelin stains show loss of the striopallidal fibres, and in some cases there may also be moderate loss of neurones. Other areas of the basal ganglia and brain-stem are sometimes affected, including the subthalamic and dentate nuclei. In an autopsy report on a rare rigid form of the disease, the putamen alone was said to be affected (Campbell et al, 1961).

Neurochemical changes observed in the striatum are an indication of functional neuronal damage. The cause of such damage remains unknown, and suggestions that Huntington's chorea is a DNA repair-deficient disorder (see e.g. Kidson et al, 1982) remain unconfirmed.

Progressive supranuclear palsy
Although recognized only relatively recently as a nosological entity (Steele et al, 1964), this disorder is not infrequent amongst patients with what appears to be 'atypical' Parkinsonism.

The clinical presentation and some features of the pathology have been discussed in detail by Behrman et al (1969) and Dix et al (1971). The majority of sufferers are men. The disease first appears in them about the age

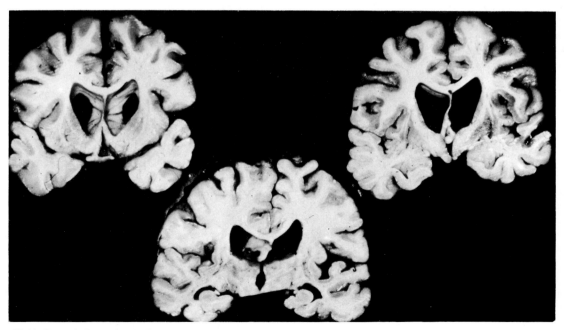

Fig. 13.11 Coronal slices of brain from a case of Huntington's chorea. They show severe atrophy of the head of the caudate nuclei and putamina, dilatation of the frontal horns of the lateral ventricles and moderate generalized cortical atrophy.

of 50 to 60 years, and death usually occurs after about 5 to 6 years. The more common early clinical features are ataxia, gaze palsies, and a characteristic progressive dementia attributed to subcortical lesions (Albert et al, 1974).

The pathological lesions described have been a somewhat heterogeneous multifocal degeneration of neurones associated with prominent neurofibrillary tangles in various brain stem nuclei (Steele et al, 1964; Behrman et al, 1969). There has usually been gliosis and loss of neurones from the globus pallidus, pretectal region in the forebrain, tegmentum of the midbrain and pons, substantia nigra, various oculomotor nuclei in the brainstem and the dentate nuclei. Neurofibrillary tangles, which resemble those of senile dementia and Alzheimer's disease under the light microscope, are found in neurones in the periaqueductal grey matter, oculomotor nuclei, substantia nigra, vestibular nuclei and elsewhere. Electron microscopy has shown that they consist of 10 nm filaments and not of the 22 nm twisted tubules found in senile dementia.

OTHER DEGENERATIVE DISORDERS OF THE CENTRAL NERVOUS SYSTEM

There are few other idiopathic degenerations of the nervous system which are particularly common in the elderly. Almost all the classical system degenerations are expressed earlier in life, although sufferers from the less severe or more indolent forms may have a nearly normal life span. The syndromes which do occur in elderly patients are too rare to justify full description here; they have been discussed generally by Greenfield (1954) and the one which appears to be most common — olivopontocerebellar atrophy — has been reviewed in detail by Konigsmark and Weiner (1970). The late onset spinocerebellar syndrome which is associated with this pathological picture may be related to deficits in cerebellar transmitter amine content.

Olivopontocerebellar atrophy is one of the neurological disturbances evident in patients with the most severe form of xeroderma pigmentosum, a rare inherited disorder in which there is defective repair of DNA damage induced by ultraviolet light and other agents. The significance of faulty DNA repair in aging is not yet known, but in a range of disorders affecting the nervous system DNA repair deficiency exists or is believed to occur (Arlett and Lehmann, 1978; Lewis and Corr, 1981). In theory, the failure of accurate macromolecule synthesis, consequent to breakdown of genetic information transfer stemming from abnormalities in DNA, could jeopardise the function and indeed survival of nerve cells (Andrews et al, 1978).

A further group of diseases of unknown aetiology which have sometimes been considered as 'degenerations', are the non-metastatic neurological complications of malignancy. They are not restricted to older people, but as the general incidence of neoplasia increases with age, so does the frequency of occurrence of these syndromes. Henson and Urich (1982) have described in detail the apparent association of neurological disease with cancer, and aspects of this problem have also been critically reviewed by Pallis and Lewis (1974). Apart from specific syndromes (limbic encephalitis, sensory ganglioradicomyeloneuropathy, and cerebellar cortical degeneration) almost always associated with bronchial cancer, current information suggests that paraneoplastic involvement of the central nervous system occurs rarely, if at all. The lymphoma-linked condition of progressive multifocal leukoencephalopathy is disseminated demyelination associated with infection of glial cells by a papova-like virus (Zu Rhein, 1969).

INFECTIONS OF THE NERVOUS SYSTEM

Pyogenic, viral and rarer fungal, protozoal and other infections of the nervous system are not restricted to the elderly. Their prevalence may differ at various stages during life because of a variety of bodily and environmental factors, and so may the severity of their clinical and pathological effects; in practice, however, only two conventional viral infections are of particular importance in older patients, namely herpes zoster and the much rarer 'subacute encephalitis of later life'. Another disorder, believed to be caused by a transmissible agent — Jakob-Creutzfeldt disease — will also be discussed here.

Herpes zoster

This disease is not specifically one of older people but it is much more common in them (Juel Jensen and McCallum, 1972). The basic neuropathological lesion is destruction of primary sensory neurones in posterior root ganglia or their cranial nerve equivalents due to infection with the varicella-zoster virus. Details of the pathology and clinical features of the various forms of zoster, including its symptomatic provocation, have been reviewed by Juel Jensen and McCallum (1972). They describe the vesicular lesion in the skin and the destruction of neural tissue, with its histological processes of widespread ganglion cell death, inflammatory infiltration and local vascular damage and subsequent scarring, as illustrated by Head and Campbell (1900) and Denny-Brown and Adams (1944). Electron microscopy and immunofluorescence have been employed by Esiri and Tomlinson (1972) to demonstrate the virus in affected ganglion cells, the sheath cells of their nerve fibres and the epidermis they innervate.

Localized bacterial infection of zosteriform lesions may occur and may be very troublesome, particularly if the eye is affected in ophthalmic zoster. The more direct complications of herpes zoster are: segmental or generalized encephalomyelitis due to uncommon, more diffuse invasion of the central nervous system by the virus (McCormick et al, 1969), of which segmental paresis is most frequent (Thomas and Howard, 1972); the rare generalized polyneuritis caused by demyelination of peripheral nerves (Dayan et al, 1972), perhaps an uncommon form of hypersensitivity triggered by an initial attack of 'shingles'; and the distressing and far more common 'postherpetic neuralgia', which is thought to be due to some disorder of central connections or information processing caused by the localized infection of sensory neurones.

The reason for the predilection of zoster for older patients is probably waning of immunity acquired in childhood, which permits lighting-up of an infection latent in the dorsal root ganglia since the initial attack of chickenpox (Hope-Simpson, 1965). The importance of local factors, too, is shown by the occurrence of 'symptomatic zoster' due to local damage to the sensory nerve supply to one segment.

Subacute encephalitis of later life

Under this heading, Brierley et al (1960) described 3 patients more than 50 years of age who had histories of organic mental disease for several months before death. At autopsy all had subacute encephalitis, shown by neuronal destruction, microglial and inflammatory cell infiltration, perivascular cuffing and gliosis maximal in the distribution of the limbic lobe. The aetiological agent was not identified. Other sporadic cases have since been described.

In the United Kingdom one of the commonest causes of encephalitis more or less restricted to the limbic lobe is herpes simplex infection, but other viruses also produce this pattern of attack, including members of the Coxsackie group (Heathfield et al, 1967), and it sometimes forms one of the non-metastatic complications of carcinoma (see above). Thus, limbic encephalitis may be due to several different aetiological agents.

Jakob-Creutzfeldt disease

This uncommon disorder of the nervous system has become very important as one of the only two diseases in man known to be transmissible by 'slow' viruses, i.e. infective agents which differ in many properties from typical viruses and which cause slowly evolving diseases characterized by degenerative rather than inflammatory lesions and by the absence of antibody responses.

The clinical and pathological features were reviewed by Kirschbaum in 1968, who summarized details of almost 200 cases which had been reported by then.

There are four variants of this disease, the distinctions depending on the presence or absence of a variety of clinical and histological features, viz. classical Jakob-Creutzfeldt disease; presenile dementia with cortical blindness (Heidenhain's syndrome); subacute spongiform encephalopathy with mental disorder, focal signs and myoclonus (Nevin-Jones disease); and subacute presenile polioencephalopathy (Brownell and Oppenheimer). Current practice is to designate all of these forms as Jakob-Creutzfeldt disease. All the patients have organic dementia associated with various motor and sensory disorders. Pathologically, the central nervous system shows loss of neurones, gliosis and spongy microvacuolation of cells and neuropil in various parts of the cerebral hemispheres, cerebellum and brain-stem. There are no features of inflammation.

Until 1968, this disorder was considered to be a 'degeneration'. It has since been transmitted to chimpanzees (Beck et al, 1969; Lampert et al, 1971) and it is now accepted as another example of a 'slow virus' infection (Daniel, 1971; Kimberlin, 1976), the unique group of diseases which also includes kuru in man, scrapie of sheep and the transmissible encephalopathy of mink. A full bibliography of recent clinical and experimental data, with notes on the problem of accidental transmission, is provided by Matthews (1982).

SKELETAL DISORDERS

Paget's disease

Paget's disease (osteitis deformans) occasionally causes damage to the nervous system. It does so because thickening and softening of skull bones may lead to platybasia and compression of cranial nerve foramina; and lesions in the spine may cause paraplegia by distorting the spinal canal and vertebrae (Barry, 1969).

Cervical spondylosis

Degenerative disease of the cervical spine accompanied by disc protrusion, osteophyte formation and thickening of the ligamenta flava may cause a variety of compressive and ischaemic lesions in the spinal cord and nerve roots (Hughes, 1966; Wilkinson, 1971). Corresponding to diverse clinical syndromes of radiculopathy and myelopathy, they range from loss of nerve fibres and fibrosis of spinal roots to cavitation in the cord with loss of anterior horn cells and extensive damage to the lateral and posterior columns.

CEREBROVASCULAR DISEASE

Vascular disease of the brain is probably the commonest cause of serious neurological disorders in the elderly in the United Kingdom. The actual incidence of clinically diagnosed strokes, by far the most important form, varies considerably with the age and sex composition of the population studies, but for all men and women more than 65 years of age, in Britain, there are at least 7 strokes per 1000 people per year (Acheson and Fairbairn, 1970); and about 130 000 people are alive at any one time who suffer appreciable ill health because they have suffered one or more strokes (Harris et al, 1971).

The following section summarizes very briefly points of major neuropathological concern about cerebrovascular disease.

Causes of strokes

In the great majority of patients cerebrovascular disease results either in cerebral infarction or haemorrhage and the relative incidence of these two pathological processes is about 8 : 1 (reviewed by Zülch, 1971; Yates, 1976). Either of these pathological end stages may result from combinations of several disease processes, but infarction, which may itself be haemorrhagic, is commonly due to arterial occlusion by atheroma, thrombosis and embolism; and haemorrhage to the effects of hypertension. The latter, however, is a very important cause of atheroma and so the pathological lesions which eventually occur in the brain may be complex and result from several different processes acting simultaneously at more than one site (McCall and Fletcher, 1975; Toole and Patel, 1975).

Cerebral infarction results from severe ischaemia, i.e. an inadequate supply of arterial blood. Failure of the arterial circulation may be due to general factors, e.g. systemic hypotension caused by cardiac infarction, gastrointestinal haemorrhage, etc., or, more commonly, to local obstruction to the arteries which supply the brain. The latter is usually due to the effects of atherosclerosis and other local disease processes affecting arteries at particular sites.

It has been known for many years that the artery which actually supplies an infarcted area of the brain is often still patent, e.g. in 60 per cent of the 100 cases examined by Hicks and Warren (1951). This has led to reconsideration and subsequently to rediscovery of the importance of atherosclerotic lesions in the proximal parts of the carotid and vertebral arteries in the neck as compared to distal lesions in named cerebral vessels (Fisher, 1954; Hutchinson and Yates, 1957; Yates and Hutchinson, 1961). These authors have shown a very strong association between severe atheromatous disease of the arteries in the neck and infarcts in the brain, albeit in areas apparently remote from the territory supplied by the most severely affected vessel. Stenosis of arteries caused by at atheroma associated with age (Schwartz and Mitchell, 1961) may not itself produce

infarction (Battacharji et al, 1967) as it has to be extremely severe to produce a marked drop in blood flow distally (Brice et al, 1964). It seems more likely that emboli, probably detached from mural ulcers and thrombi, are the underlying cause behind many episodes of cerebral infarction (McCall and Fletcher, 1975), and that the emboli consist of friable mixtures of platelets and atheromatous debris which break up too soon to be detected readily in life or after death (McBrien et al, 1963).

Other factors considered at some time to be generally important in producing strokes have included transient lowering of systemic arterial blood pressure, due to physiological variation or pathological effects, and embolization from mural thrombi in the left ventricle. Episodic hypotension has been largely discounted as a common cause of neurological disorders unless it is very severe (Kendell and Marshall, 1963). There is, however, increasing evidence of the importance of embolization from the heart as a cause of cerebral infarction (Blackwood et al, 1969), amounting perhaps to 60 per cent of all cases (McCall and Fletcher, 1975).

Etat Criblé & Lacunaire

Pierre Marie and O. and C. Vogt described small smooth walled cavities containing tortuous, patent blood vessels, in, respectively, the basal ganglia — *état lacunaire* (especially the putamen), and the white matter of the centrum ovale — *état criblé* (Fig. 13.12). Both lesions are common in the elderly and in hypertensive patients (Cole and Yates, 1968) and they should be regarded only as general evidence of moderate damage to blood vessels. There may be no correlation between their occurrence and clinical 'strokes', although lacunes due either to microhaemorrhage or localized arterial degeneration (Hughes, 1965), or to infarction (Fisher, 1969), are not always clinically silent.

Cerebral haemorrhages

Classical studies over many decades of the pathology of cerebral haemorrhages (summarized by Zülch, 1971) have shown that massive intracerebral lesions of this type usually occur in hypertensive patients in the basal ganglia in the region of the putamen, claustrum and the thalamus, and less commonly in the midbrain, brainstem and cerebellum.

The causes of such haemorrhages cannot always be proven with certainty, even at necropsy, but the available evidence favours direct damage to blood vessel walls causing fibrinoid degeneration and necrosis (Russell, 1954). Hypertensive patients also develop smaller haemorrhages and infarcts which are more evenly distributed in the brain near the cortical-white matter junction (Fig. 13.13) and which probably give rise by scarring to the smooth-walled cysts found in the

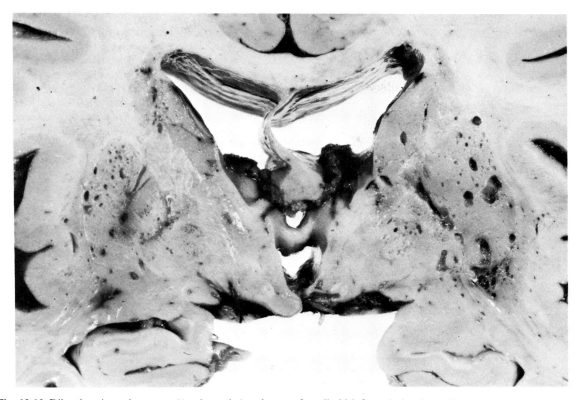

Fig. 13.12 Dilated perivascular spaces (état lacunaire) and scars of small old infarcts in basal ganglia

brains of the elderly (Cole and Yates, 1967, 1968). The cause of this type of lesion is uncertain, but it may be

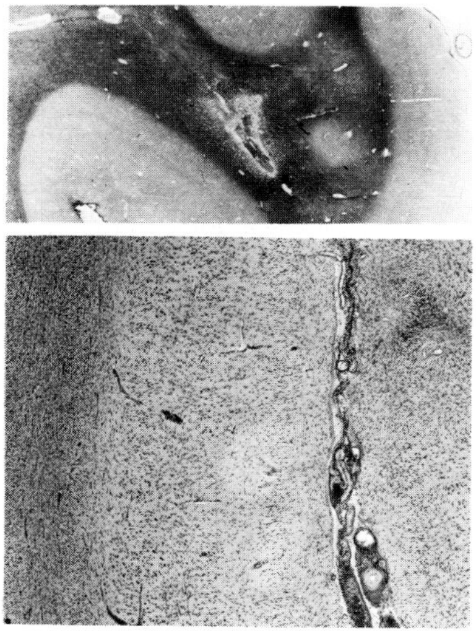

Fig. 13.13 Focal infarcts and scars in cerebral cortex and superficial white matter typical of severe hypertension (HVG × 15)

due to focal occlusion or haemorrhage from small arteries unrelated to microaneurysm formation.

Like any other large, rapidly expanding intracranial lesion, massive cerebral haemorrhages are liable to cause trans-tentorial herniation and 'coning' of the cerebellar tonsils and medulla. These processes in turn are liable to be associated with further haemorrhages in the midbrain, pons and medulla owing to damage to local arteries and veins.

Cerebral microaneurysms

Miliary aneurysms on cerebral arteries were first described by Charcot and Bouchard in 1868. They were almost entirely ignored subsequently until the 1960s, when autopsy injection and radiographic techniques were employed to show that they were common lesions at certain sites in the brain and that they were associated with aging and hypertension in 40 per cent of cases (Russell, 1963; Cole and Yates, 1967). These lesions may be the source of minor bleeds and microinfarcts, but they are unlikely to be the source of many large intracerebral haemorrhages.

They consist of focal, usually eccentric aneurysmal dilatations of the walls of arteries, 0.5 to 2.0 mm in

Fig. 13.14 Two microaneurysms in injected and cleared slice of brain. The crescentic rim on the upper lesion is due to a layer of thrombus ($\times$ 12). Reproduced by kind permission of the authors and Editor of the *Journal of Pathology*, from Cole and Yates (1967, Fig. 12).

diameter (Fig. 13.14), and may contain organizing thrombus. They are found on small branches of the striate arteries (70 per cent of Cole's and Yates' series) and in the superficial subcortical white matter (30 per cent). In the hindbrain they are most common in the midpart of the pes pontis and deep in the cerebellar white matter.

Cerebrovascular lesions in the elderly
In summary, the changes found in older patients who have no history of 'stroke' or other clinical disorders of the brain are, macroscopically, increasing atheroma and arteriosclerosis of major extra- and intracranial arteries and small 'lacunes' in the basal ganglia and cerebral white matter. Microscopically, there is also congophilic angiopathy, siderosis and calcification of small arteries and arterioles, medial fibrosis and hyalinization and microaneurysm formation.

The clinical disorder of 'stroke' may be due to cerebral haemorrhage and infarction. The former, which is strongly correlated with systemic hypertension, is commonly caused by rupture of arteries with damaged walls; the latter is more complex but most often is probably due to temporary occlusion of arteriosclerotic and atheromatous arteries by thrombi or emboli. Hypertension is a very important factor in damaging large and small cerebral arteries and also in causing the syndrome of subarachnoid haemorrhage due to rupture of aneurysms on large, named cerebral arteries (see comprehensive review by Sahs, 1969).

Arteriosclerotic dementia
A considerable number of clinical cases of dementia in the elderly are related to cerebrovascular disease. Both solitary or a few massive infarcts and multiple small ischaemic lesions can result in dementia, the former probably being more common (Corsellis, 1962; Tomlinson et al, 1970). Like arteriosclerotic Parkinsonism, which may also occur in these patients, the responsible vascular lesions have been found in many parts of the brain (Wildi et al, 1964). The most important ones are probably in the cerebral cortex rather than in the basal ganglia as described in Rothschild's (1942) account of this form of dementia, because other lesions in the latter structures do not usually cause similar intellectual disturbances and, in any case *état lucunaire* is a common necropsy finding in well-preserved elderly hypertensives. In the series of demented old people reported by Tomlinson et al (1970), like the general incidence of vascular disease, a much higher proportion of arteriosclerotic dementia occurred in males than in females, and it tended to occur in younger subjects.

Focal vascular lesions at particular sites will have profound clinical effects if they damage vital structures. Severe defects of memory, which are sometimes a prominent feature of dementia, can be caused by quite small bilateral lesions of the medial hippocampus, the forniceal system or mammillary bodies. Brierley (1966) has reviewed the pathology of these and other causes of amnesia.

Temporal arteritis
This is the only type of arteritis with a predilection for the aged. It is also known as granulomatous or giant-cell arteritis (Russell, 1959; Bruetsch, 1971). It is a true panarteritis which affects vessels of all sizes — from

Fig. 13.15 Temporal arteritis. Biopsy of temporal artery showing severe scarring, intimal proliferation, destruction of elastic laminae and inflammatory infiltration (Elastic van Gieson $\times$ 40)

large named arteries to small arterioles. The wall is thickened by granulomatous tissue containing epithelioid and multinucleate giant cells (related often to degeneration of internal elastic lamina),chronic inflammatory cell infiltration and, in the acute stage, polymorphs (Fig. 13.15; Bruetsch, 1971). Necrotic foci and areas of fibrinoid change may also be found in the media. Aneurysms sometimes develop if larger arteries are affected, and veins may be involved, too. An important feature is segmental occlusion of affected vessels by thrombosis and intimal proliferation. The pathological effect and clinical syndromes consequent upon them are of infarction of the tissues supplied, as in any other form of vasculitis.

The vessels most commonly affected are the temporal arteries and their branches, those of the visual system and sometimes leptomeningeal and cortical arteries (Hollenhorst et al, 1960). This disease is often a generalized one despite the greater prominence of cranial lesions (producing such well known symptoms as headache, scalp tenderness and jaw claudication) and changes may occur in arteries throughout the viscera (Hollen-

horst et al, 1960) and muscles, producing a wide variety of syndromes including some forms of 'polymyalgia rheumatica'.

Vascular disease of the spinal cord

Disorders of this type are uncommon at any age, but the elderly, because they exhibit many forms of vascular disease, are more liable to be affected. The commonest type is due to occlusion of the anterior spinal artery, which results in a sharply defined area of infarction in grey and white matter in the anterior two-third of the cord, with a consequent mixture of sensory and upper and lower motor neurone defects (Henson and Parsons, 1967; Lazorthes, 1972; Silver and Buxton, 1974; Toole and Patel, 1975). Posterior spinal artery occlusion is much rarer. Atheroma is probably the commonest cause of vascular damage, but the blood supply to the cord may also be jeopardized by dissecting aneurysm or coarctation of the aorta, as well as by postoperative hypotension and emboli. The effects of spondylosis on the cord may also be mediated by arterial insufficiency (Wilkinson, 1971; Hughes, 1976).

REFERENCES

Acheson R M, Fairbairn A S 1970 Burden of cerebrovascular disease in the Oxford area in 1963 and 1964. British Medical Journal 2: 621–626

Adams R D, van Bogaert L, van der Eecken H 1961 Degenerescences nigro-striées et cerebello-nigrostriées Psychiatria et Neurologia (Basel) 142: 219–259

Adams R D, van Bogaert L, van der Eeken, H 1964 Striatonigral degeneration. Journal of Neuropathology and Experimental Neurology 23: 584–608

Albert M L, Feldman R G, Willis Anne L 1974 The subcortical dementia of progressive supranuclear palsy. Journal of Neurology, Neurosurgery and Psychiatry 37: 121–130

Alvord E C, 1971 The pathology of Parkinsonism. In: Minckler J (ed) Pathology of the Nervous System, vol. 2, McGraw-Hill, New York, p 1152–1161

Alzheimer A 1907 Uber eine eigenartige Erkrankungen der Hirnrinde. Zbl Nervenheilk Psychiat 30: 177–179

Andrews A D, Barrett S F, Robbins J H 1978 Xeroderma pigmentosum neurological abnormalities correlate with colony-forming ability after ultraviolet radiation. Proceedings of the National Academy of Sciences of the United States of America 75: 1984–1988

Arab A 1954 Plaques séniles et artériosclerose cérébrale. Absence de rapporte de dépendance entre les deux processus. Etude statistique. Revue Neurologique 91: 22–36

Arab A 1959 Hyalinose arteriolaire cérébrale. Essai de synthése anatomo-clinique. Archives Suisses de neurologie, neurochirurgie et de psychiatrie

Arab A 1960 Unité nosologique entre démence sénile et maladie d'Alzheimer d'après une étude statistique et anatomo-clique. Sistema nervoso 12: 189–201

Arlett C F, Lehmann A R 1978 Human disorders showing increased sensitivity to the induction of genetic damage. Annual Review of Genetics 12: 95–115

Arnold N, Harriman D G F 1970 The incidence of abnormality in control human peripheral nerves studied by single axon dissection. Journal of Neurology, Neurosurgery and Psychiatry 33: 55–61

Baker A B 1937 Structure of the small cerebral arteries and their changes with age. American Journal of Pathology 13: 453–461

Bailey A A 1953 Changes with age in the spinal cord. Archives of Neurology and Psychiatry 70: 299–309

Barry H C 1969 In: Paget's Disease of Bone. Edinburgh: Livingstone

Battacharji S K, Hutchinson E C, McCall A J, 1967 Stenosis and occlusion of vessels in cerebral infarction. British Medical Journal iii: 270–274

Beck E, Daniel P M, Matthews W B et al 1969 Creutzfeldt-Jakob disease — the neuropathology of a transmission experiment. Brain, 92: 699–717

Behrman G, Carroll J D, Janota I, Matthews W B et al 1969 Progressive supranuclear palsy. Clinico-pathological study of four cases. Brain, 92: 663–678

Bielschowsky M 1922 Weitere Bemerkungen zur normalen und pathologischen Histologie des striären Systems. Journal für Psychologie ünd Neurologie 27: 233–288

Björkerud S 1964 Studies of lipofuscin granules of human cardiac muscle: II Chemical analysis of the isolated granules. Experimental and Molecular Pathology 3: 369–376

Blackwood W, Hallpike J F, Kocen R S et al 1969 Artheromatous disease of the carotid arterial system and embolism from the heart: a morbid anatomical study. Brain, 89: 897–910

Blinkov S M, Glezer I I 1968 In: The Human Brain in Tables and Figures. New York: Plenum Press

Blocq P, Marinesco G, 1892 Sur les lésions et la pathogénie de i'épilepsie dite essentielle. Semaine médicalo 12: 445–446

Bowen D M, Davison A N 1982 The neurochemistry of ageing and senile dementia. In: Recent Advances in Clinical Neurology 3 (ed) Matthews W B and Glaser G H, Edinburgh: Churchill Livingstone p 215–228

Brannon W, McCormick W, Lampert P 1967 Axonal dystrophy in the gracile nucleus of man. Acta Neuropathologica (Berlin) 9: 1–6

von Braunmühl A 1958 Alterserkrankungen des Zentralnervensystems: In: Hdbch spez path Anat (ed) Lubarsch O, Henke F, Rössle R, p XIII/1A, Berlin: Springer-Verlag 337–539

Brice J G, Dowsett D J, Lowe R D 1964 Haemodynamic effects of carotid artery stenosis. British Medical Journal ii: 1363–1366

Brierley J B 1966 The neuropathology of amnesic states. In: Amnesia, (ed) Whitty C W M, Zangwill O L London: Butterworths p 150

Brierley J B, Corsellis J A N, Hierons R, Nevin S 1960 Subacute encephalitis of later adult life, mainly affecting the limbic area. Brain, 83: 357–368

Brizzee K R, Cancilla P A, Sherwood N, et al 1969 The amount and distribution of pigments in neurons and glia of the cerebral cortex: autofluorescent and ultrastructural studies. Journal of Gerontology 24: 127–135

Brizzee K R, Ordy J M, Hofer H, Kaack B 1978 Animal models for the study of senile brain disease and aging changes in the brain. In: Alzheimer's disease: senile dementia and related disorders (Aging, vol. 7), Katsman R, Terry R D, Brick K L, (ed) New York: Rowen Press p 515–553

Brody H 1955 Organization of the cerebral cortex. III. A study of aging in the human cerebral cortex. Journal of Comparative Neurology 102: 511–556

Brody H 1970 Structural changes in the aging nervous system. Interdisciplinary Topics in Gerontology 7: 9–21

Brody H 1982 Age changes in the nervous system. In: Neurological Disorders in the Elderly, Caird F I (ed) Bristol: Wright p 17–24

Bruetsch W R 1971 Giant-cell arteritis. In: Pathology of the Nervous System, Minckler J (ed) vol. 2, New York: McGraw-Hill p 1456–1458

Bruyn G W 1968 Huntington's Chorea. In: Handbook of Clinical Neurology, Vinken P J, Bruyn G W (ed) Amsterdam: North Holland. Vol. 6, p 298–397

Calne D B 1970 In: Parkinsonism: Physiology, Pharmacology and Treatment. London: Arnold

Campbell A M G, Corner B, Norman R M, Urich H 1961 The rigid form of Huntington's chorea. Journal of Neurology, Neurosurgery and Psychiatry 24: 71–79

Cavanagh J B 1964 The significance of the 'dying back' process in experimental and human neurological disease. International Review of Experimental Pathology 3: 219–267

Chauhan A N, Lewis P D 1979 A quantitative study of cell proliferation in ependyma and choroid plexus in the postnatal rat brain Neuropathology and Applied Neurobiology 5: 303–309

Chokroverty A, Barron K D, et al 1969 The syndrome of orthostatic hypotension. Brain, 92: 743–768

Christensen E, Moller J E, Faurbye A, et al 1970 Neuropathological investigation of 28 brains from patients with dyskinesia Acta Psychiatrica at Neurologica Scandinavica 46: 14–23

Cole F M, Yates P O 1967 Intracerebral microaneurysms and small cerebrovascular lesions. Brain, 90: 759–768

Cole F M, Yates P O 1968 Comparative incidence of cerebrovascular lesions in normotensive and hypertensive patients. Neurology Minneapolis 18: 255–259

Colon E J 1973a The elderly brain: A quantitative analysis in the cerebral cortex of two cases. Psychiatria, neurologia, neurochirurgia 75: 261–270

Colon E J 1973b The cerebral cortex in presenile dementia. A quantitative analysis. Acta Neuropathologica (Berlin) 23: 281–290

Corsellis J A N 1962 In: Mental Illness and the Ageing Brain, London: O.U.P.

Corsellis, J A N 1970 The limbic areas in Alzheimer's disease and in other conditions associated with dementia. In: Alzheimer's Disease and Related Conditions. Wolstenholme G E W, O'Connor M (ed) London: Churchill p 37–50

Corsellis J A N 1976 Ageing and the dementias. In: Greenfield's Neuropathology. Blackwood W, Corsellis J A N (ed) 3rd edn. London: Arnold p 796–848

Corsellis J A N, Brierley, J B 1954 An unusual type of pre-senile dementia. (Atypical Alzheimer's disease with amyloid vascular change.) Brain, 77: 571–587

Corsellis J A N, Bruton, C J, Freeman-Browne, D, 1973. The aftermath of boxing. Psychological Medicine 3: 279–303

Cragg B G 1975 The density of synapses and neurones in normal, mentally defective and ageing human brains. Brain, 98: 81–90

Crane G E, Paulson, G E 1967 Involuntary movements in a sample of chronic mental patients and their relation to the treatment with neuroleptics. International Journal of Neuropsychiatry 3: 286–291

Crapper D R, Krishnan S S, Quittkat S 1976 Aluminium, neurofibrillary degeneration and Alzheimer's disease. Brain, 99: 67–80

Curzon G 1976 Transmitter amines in brain disease. In: Biochemistry and Neurological Disease Davison, A N (ed) Oxford: Blackwell p 168–227

Daniel P M 1971 Transmissible degenerative diseases of the nervous system. Proceedings of the Royal Society of Medicine 64: 787–796

Dayan A D 1970a Quantitative histological studies on the aged human brain I. Senile plaques and neurofibrillary tangles in 'normal' patients. Acta Neuropathologica (Berlin) 16: 85–94

Dayan A D 1970b Quantitative histological studies on the aged human brain II. Senile plaques and neurofibrillary tangles in senile dementia. Acta Neuropathologica (Berlin) 16: 95–102

Dayan A D 1971a Comparative neuropathology of aging. Studies on the brains of 47 species of vertebrates. Brain, 94: 31–42

Dayan A D 1971b Presenile dementia: some pathological problems and possibilities. Proceedings of the Royal Society of Medicine 64: 829–831

Dayan A D 1972 The brain and theories of aging. In: Ageing of the Central Nervous System. van Praag H, Kalverboer A F (ed) Haarlem: E F Bohn

Dayan A D, Ball M J 1973 Histometric observations on the metabolism of tangle-bearing neurons Journal of the Neurological Sciences 19: 433–436

Dayan A D, Ogul E, Graveson G S 1972 Herpes zoster polyneuritis. Journal of Neurology, Neurosurgery and Psychiatry 35: 170–175

Denny-Brown D 1962 The midbrain and motor integration. Proceedings of the Royal Society of Medicine 55: 527–538

Denny-Brown D, Adams R D 1944 Pathologic features of herpes zoster. Archs Neurol Psychiat, Chicago 51: 216–231

Dimsdale H 1946 Changes in the Parkinsonian syndrome in the twentieth century. Quarterly Journal of Medicine 15: 155–170

Divry, P 1952 La pathochimic generale et cellulaire des processus séniles et préséniles. Proceedings of the 1st Interantional Congress on Neuropathology. Turin: Rosenberg and Sellier. (Rome): 2:312–345

Dix M R, Harrison M J G, Lewis P D 1971 Progressive supranuclear palsy. A report of 9 cases with particular reference to the mechanism of the oculomotor disorder. Journal of the Neurological Sciences 13: 237–256

Dunlap C B 1927 Pathologic changes in Huntington's chorea with special reference to the corpus striatum. Archs Neurol Psychiat, Chicago 18: 867/943

Duvoisin R C, Yahr M D, Schweitzer M D, et al 1963 Parkinsonism before and since the epidemic of encephalitis lethargica. Archives of Neurology 9: 232–236

Duvoisin R C, Yahr M D 1965 Encephalitis and Parkinsonism. Archives of Neurology 12: 227/240

Eadie M J 1963 Pathology of certain medullary nuclei in Parkinsonism. Brain, 86: 781–792

Eadie M J, Sutherland J M 1964 Arteriosclerosis in Parkinsonism. Journal of Neurology, Neurosurgery and Psychiatry 27: 237–240

Earle K M 1968 Studies on Parkinson's disease including X-ray fluorescent spectroscopy of formalin-fixed brain tissue. Journal of Neuropathology and Experimental Neurology 27: 1–14

von Economo C 1931 Encephalitis Lethargica. Its Sequelae and Treatment. London: Oxford University Press

Eicke W J 1968 Pathology of the basal ganglia: a historical review. In: Handbook of Clinical Neurology, Vinken P J, Bruyn G W (ed) Amsterdam: North Holland. vol 6, p 56–89

Esiri M M, Tomlinson A H 1972 Herpes zoster Demonstration of virus in trigeminal nerve and ganglion by immunofluorescence and electron microscopy. Journal of the Neurological Sciences 15: 35–48

Evans D J, Lewis P D, Malhotra O, Pallis C 1964 Idiopathic orthostatic hypotension. Report of an autopsied case with histochemical and ultrastructural studies of the neuronal inclusions Journal of the Neurological Sciences 17: 209–218

Feit H, Dutton G R, Barondes L H, Shelanski M L, et al 1971 Microtubule protein. Incorporation in and transport to nerve endings. Journal of Cell Biology 51: 138–147

Fisher C M 1954 Occlusion of the carotid arteries. Archs Neurol Psychiat, Chicago 72: 187–204

Fisher C M 1969 The arterial lesions underlying lacunes. Acta Neuropathologica (Berlin) 12: 1–15

Forno L S, Norville R L 1976 Ultrastructure of Lewy bodies in the stellate ganglion. Acta neuropathologica (Berlin) 34: 183–197

Fraser H 1969 Eosinophilic bodies in some neurones in the thalamus of ageing mice. Journal of Pathology 98: 201–204

Gajdusek D C, Gibbs C J 1973 Subacute and chronic diseases caused by atypical infections with unconventional viruses in aberrant hosts. Perspectives in Virology 8: 279–307

Garfield J S 1982 Spinal lesions. In: Neurological Disorders in the Elderly, Caird F I (ed), Bristol: Wright. p 212–230

Gellerstedt N 1933 Zur Kenntis der Hirnveränderungen bei der normalen Altersinvolution. Upsala Läkareförenings Förhandlengar. 38: 194–408

Glenner G G 1978 Current knowledge of amyloid deposits as applied to senile plaques and congophilic angiopathy. In: Alzheimer's disease: senile dementia and related disorders (Aging, vol. 7), Katzman, R, Terry R D and Bick K L (ed), New York Rowen Press. p 493–501

Gonatas N K, Gambetti P 1970 The pathology of the synapse in Alzheimer's disease. In: Alzheimer's Disease and Related Conditions, Wolstenholme, G E W, O'Connor, M, (ed) London: Churchill p 169–179

Greenfield J G 1954 In: The Spino-Cerebellar Degenerations. Oxford: Blackwell

Greenfield J G, Blackwood W 1963 Encephalitis lethargica. In: Greenfield's Neuropathology, Blackwood, W, Meyer, A et al (ed) London: Arnold p 108–201

Greenfield J G, Bosanquet F D 1953 The brain-stem lesions of Parkinsonism. Journal of Neurology, Neurosurgery and Psychiatry 16: 213–226

Grünthal E 1927 Klinisch-anatomisch vergleichende Untersuchungen über den Greisenblödsinn. Zeitschrift für die gesamte Neurologie und Psychiatrie 111: 768–817

Gudmundsson G, Hallgrimson J, Jónasson T A, Bjarnasono 1972 Hereditary cerebral haemorrhage with amyoidosis. Brain 95: 387–404

Hall T C, Miller A K H, Corsellis J A N 1975 Variations in the human Purkinje cell population according to age and sex. Neuropathology and Applied Neurobiology 1: 267–292

Hanley T 1974 'Neuronal fall-out' in the aging brain: a critical review of the quantitative data. Age and Ageing, 3: 133–151

Harris A I, Cox E, Smith C R W 1971 In: Handicapped and impaired in Great Britain. Part I. London: HMSO

den Hartog Jager W A 1969 Sphingomyelin in Lewy body inclusion bodies in Parkinson's disease. Archives of Neurology (Chicago) 21: 615–619

den Hartog Jager W A, Bethlem, J 1960 The distribution of Lewy bodies in the central and autonomic nervous system in idiopathic paralysis agitans. Journal of Neurology, Neurosurgery and Psychiatry 23: 283–290

Hassler O 1967 Arterial deformities in senile brains. Acta Neuropathologica (Berlin) 8: 219–229

Head H, Campbell A W 1900 The pathology of herpes zoster and its bearing on sensory localization. Brain 23: 353–523

Heathfield K W G Pilsworth R, Wall B J, et al 1967 Coxsackie B5 infections in Essex, 1965, with particular reference to the nervous system. Quarterly Journal of Medicine 36: 579–595

Henson R A, Parsons M 1967 Ischaemic lesions of the spinal cord. Quarterly Journal of Medicine 36: 205–222

Henson R A, Urich H 1982 Cancer and the Nervous System. Blackwell Scientific, Oxford

Herskovits E, Blackwood W 1969 Essential (familial hereditary) tremor: a case report. Journal of Neurology, Neurosurgery and Psychiatry 32: 509–511

Hicks S P, Warren S 1951 Infarction of the brain without thrombosis Archives of Pathology 52: 403–412

Hirano A, Dembitzer H M, Kurland L T, Zimmerman H M 1968 The fine structure of some intraganglionic alterations. Journal of Neuropathology and Experimental Neurology 27: 166–182

Hirano A, Zimmerman H M 1962 Alzheimer's neurofibrillary changes. Archives of Neurology and Psychiatry 1: 227–242

Hogan E L, Krigman M R 1973 Herpes zoster myelitis, evidence for viral invasion of spinal cord. Archives of Neurology 29: 309–313

Hollenhorst R W, Brown J R, Wagener H P, Schic, R M 1960 Neurologic aspects of temporal arteritis. Neurology (Minneapolis) 10: 490–498

Hope-Simpson R E 1965 The nature of herpes zoster: a long term study and a new hypothesis. Proceedings of the Royal Society of Medicine 58: 9–20

Hughes J T 1966 In: Pathology of the Spinal Cord. London: Lloyd Luke

Hughes J T 1976 Diseases of the spinal cord. In: Greenfield's Neuropathology, Blackwood W, Corsellis J A N (ed) 3rd edn, Edinburgh: Arnold p 675–683

Hughes W 1965 Origin of lacunes. Lancet ii: 19

Hunter R, Blackwood W, Smith M C, Cumings J N 1968 Neuropathological findings in three cases of persistent dyskinesia following phenothiazine medication. Journal of the Neurological Sciences 7: 262–273

Hunter R A, Dayan A D, Wilson J 1972 Alzheimer's disease in one monozygotic twin. Journal of Neurology, Neurosurgery and Psychiatry 35: 707–710

Hutchinson E C, Yates P O 1957 Caroticovertebral stenosis. Lancet i: 2–8

Iqbal K, Wisniewski H M, Grundke-Iqbal I, Korthals J K, Terry R D 1975 Chemical pathology of neurofibrils. Neurofibrillary tangles of Alzheimer's presenile-senile dementia. Journal of Histochemistry and Cytochemistry 23: 563–569

Ishii T 1966 Distribution of Alzheimer's neurofibrillary changes in the brain stem and hypothalamus of senile dementia. Acta Neuropathologica (Berlin) 6: 181–187

Jamada M, Mehraein P 1968 Verteilungsmuster der senilen Veranderungen im Gehirn. Die Beteiligungen des limbschens Systems bei hirnatrophischen Prozessen des Seniums und bei Morbus Alzheimer. Archiv fur Psychiatrie und Nervenkrankheiten 211: 303–324

Jasper H H J, Prick J J G 1969 Morphology and histochemistry of the corpora amylacea in the brain. Proceedings. Koninklijké Nederlandse Akademie van Wetenschappen te Amsterdam, Series C. 72: 385–400

Jelgersma 1909 Neue anatomische Befunde bei Paralysis Agitans und bei chronischer Chorea. Zentralblatt für Neurologie 27: 995–996

Jellinger K 1968 Pallido-striatal degenerations and exogenous lesions. In: Handbook of Clinical Neurology. Vinken P J, Brugn G W (ed) Amsterdam: North Holland vol 6, p 632–693

Jervis G A 1971a Alzheimer's disease. In: Pathology of the Nervous System, Minckler J (ed) New York: McGraw-Hill vol 2, p 1385–1395

Jervis G A 1971b Pick's disease. In: Pathology of the Nervous System, Minckler J (ed) New York: McGraw-Hill vol 2, p 1395–1404

Johnson R H, Lee G de J, Oppenhelmer D R et al 1966 Autonomic failure with orthostatic hypotension due to intermediolateral column degeneration. Quarterly Journal of Medicine 35: 276–292

Juel Jensen B E, McCallum F O 1972 In: Herpes Simplex, Varicella and Zoster. London: Heinemann

Kendell R E, Marshall J 1963 Role of hypotension in the genesis of transient focal cerebral ischaemic attacks. British Medical Journal 2: 344–348

Kidd M 1964 Alzheimer's disease — an electron microscopical study. Brain, 87: 307–320

Kidson C, Chen P, Imray P 1982 Ataxia-telangiectasia heterozygotes: dominant expression of ionizing radiation sensitive mutants. In: Ataxia-telangiectasia — a cellular and molecular link between cancer, neuropathology and immune deficiency, Bridges B A, Harnden D G (ed) Chichester: Wiley p 363–372

Kimberlin R H 1976 In: Slow Virus Diseases of Animals and Man. Amsterdam: North Holland

Kirschbaum W R 1968 In: Jakob-Creutzfeldt Disease. New York: Elsevier.

Konigsmark, B W, Murphy, E A 1972 Volume of the ventral cochlear nucleus in man: its relationship to neuronal population and age. Journal of Neuropathology and Experimental Neurology 31: 304–316

Konigsmark B W, Weiner L P 1970 The olivopontocerebellar atrophies: a review. Medicine (Baltimore) 49: 227–242

Kurland L T 1958 Epidemiology, incidence, geographic distribution, genetic considerations. In: Pathogenesis and Treatment of Parkinsonism Fields W C (ed) Springfield: Thomas p 5–49

Lampert P W, Gajdusek D C et al 1971 Experimental spongiform encephalopathy (Creutzfeldt-Jakob disease) in chimpanzees. Electron microscope studies. Journal of Neuropathology and Experimental Neurology 30: 20–32

Lancet 1976 Aluminium and Alzheimer. (Editorial) ii: 1281–1282

Larsson T, Sjögren T, Jacobson G 1963 Senile dementia. Acta Psychiatrica Scandinavica 39: Suppl 167

Lascelles R G, Thomas P K 1966 Changes due to age in internodal length in the sural nerve in man. ibid. 29: 40–44

Lazorthes G 1972 Pathology, classification and clinical aspects of vascular diseases of the spinal cord. In: Handbook of Clinical Neurology, Vinken P J, Bruyn G W (ed) Amsterdam: North Holland vol 12, pt II: p 492–506

Lewis P 1964 Familial orthostatic hypotension. Brain 87: 119–128

Lewis P D 1971 Parkinsonism — neuropathology British Medical Journal 3: 690–692

Lewis P D and Corr, J B 1981 Increased radiosensitivity of skin fibroblasts in Friedreich's ataxia. Acta Neuropathologica (Berlin) Suppl VII: 230–232

Lewy F H 1913 Zur pathologischen Anatomie der Paralysis Agitans. Deutsche Zeitschrift für Nervenheilkunde 50: 50–55

McBrien D J, Bradley R D, Ashton N 1963 The nature of retinal emboli in stenosis of the internal carotid artery. Lancet, i: 697–697

McCall A J, Fletcher P J H 1975 Pathology. In: Strokes, Hutchinson E C, Acheson E J (ed) London: Saunders p 36–105

McCaughey W T E 1961 The pathologic spectrum of Huntington's chorea. Journal of Nervous and Mental Disease 133: 91–103

McCormick W F, Rodnitzky R L, Shochet S S et al 1969 Varicella-zoster encephalomyelitis. A morphologic and virologic study. Archives of Neurology Chicago 21: 559–570

Mann D M A, Yates P O 1974 Lipoprotein pigments in their relationship to agency in the human nervous system. Brain, 97: 481–488

Mansvelt J 1954 Pick's disease. A syndrome of lobar cerebral atrophy: its clinico-anatomical and histopathological types. Holland: Enschede

Margolis G 1959 Senile cerebral disease. Laboratory Investigation 8: 335–370

Matsuyama H, Namiki H, Watanabe I 1966 Senile changes in the brain in the Japanese. Incidence of Alzheimer's neurofibrillary change and senile plaques. Proceedings of the Vth International Congress on Neuropathology, Zurich: Excerpta Medica Congress Series 100: 979–980

Matthews W B 1982 Spongiform virus encephalopathy. In: Recent Advances in Clinical Neurology 3, Matthews W B, Glaser G H (ed) Edinburgh: Churchill Livingstone p 229–238

Monagle R D, Brody H 1974 The effects of age upon the main nucleus of the inferior olive in the human. Journal of Comparative Neurology 155: 61–66

Morel F, Wildi E 1955 Contributions á la connaissance des differentes altérations cérébrales du grand âge. Schweiz Archiv für Neurologie und Psychiatrie 76: 174–223

Neumann M A 1949 Pick's disease. Journal of Neuropathology and Experimental Neurology 8: 255–282

Newton R D 1948 Identity of Alzheimer's disease and senile dementia, and their relation to senility. Journal of Mental Science 94: 225–249

Nikaido T, Austin J, Rinehart R et al 1971 Studies in aging of the brain. The isolation and preliminary characterisation of Alzheimer plaques and cores. Archives of Neurology 25: 198–211

Norris A H, Shock N W, Wagman I H 1953 Age changes in the maximum conduction velocity of motor fibres of human ulnar nerves. Journal of Applied Physiology 5: 589

Ochoa J, Mair W C P 1969 The normal sural nerve in man. Part 2: Changes in the axons and Schwann cells due to ageing. Acta Neuropathologica (Berlin) 13: 217–239

Pallis C A 1971 Parkinsonism: natural history and clinical features British Medical Journal 3: 683–690

Pallis C A and Lewis, P D 1974 The neurology of gastrointestinal disease. London: Saunders

Parkes J D, Marsden C D, Rees J E et al 1974 Parkinson's disease, cerebral arteries and senile dementia. Quarterly Journal of Medicine 43: 49n62

Pauli B, Luginbül H R, Rössi G L 1971 Elektronenmikroskopische Untersuchungen der cerebralen Amyloidose bei alten Hunden und einen senilem Menschen. Acta Neuropathologica (Berlin) 19: 129–136

Pratt R T C 1967 Pick's disease. In: Genetics of Neurological Disorders. London: Oxford University Press p 76

Pratt R T C 1970 The genetics of Alzheimer's disease. In: Alzheimer's Disease and Related Conditions, Wolstenholme, O'Connor M, London: Churchill p 137–9

Rail D, Scholtz C, Swash M 1981 Post-encephalitic Parkinsonism: current experience. Journal of Neurology, Neurosurgery and Psychiatry 44: 670–676

Ramsey H J 1965 Ultrastructure of corpora amylacea. Journal of Neuropathology and Experimental Neurology 24: 25–29

Robertson E E, Mason Brown N L 1953 Review of mental illness in the older age group. British Medical Journal 2: 1076–1079

Roesmann U, McFarland D E 1971 Hyaline cytoplasmic inclusion in motor neurones. Journal of Neuropathology and Experimental Neurology 30: 551–556

Rothschild D 1937 Pathologic changes in senile psychoses and their psychobiologic significance. American Journal of Psychiatry 98: 324–333

Rothschild D 1942 Neuropathologic changes in arteriosclerotic psychoses and their psychiatric significance. American Medical Association Archives of Neurology and Psychiatry 48: 417–436

Roy S L, Wolman L 1969 Ultrastructural observations in Parkinsonism. Journal of Pathology 99: 39–44

Russell D S 1954 The pathology of spontaneous intracranial haemorrhage. Proceedings of the Royal Society of Medicine 47: 689–693

Russell R W R 1959 Giant-cell arteritis. Quarterly Journal of Medicine 28: 471–490

Russell R W R 1963 Observations on intracerebral aneurysms. Brain, 86: 425–441

Sahs A L 1969 In: Intracranial Aneurysms and Subarachnoid Haemorrhage. Philadelphia: Lippincott

Sakai M, Austin J, Witmer F et al 1969 Studies of corpora amylacea 1. Isolation and preliminary characterization by chemical and histochemical techniques. Archives of Neurology (Chicago) 21: 526–544

Schaltenbrand G 1955 Nervensystem. In: Hdbch Mikr Anat des Menschen, von Mollendorf W (ed) IV/2. Berlin: Springer-Verlag

Scholz W 1938 Die drusige Entartung der Hirnrinden-arterien und-capillaren eine Form seniler Gefa Berkrankung. Zentralblatt für die gesamte Neurologie und Psychiatrie 162: 694–715

Schwab R S, Doshay L G et al 1956 Shift to older age distribution in Parkinsonism. Neurology Minneapolis 6: 783–790

Schwartz P 1968 New patho-anatomic observations on amyloidosis in the aged. Fluorescence microscopic observations. In: Amyloidosis, Mandema E, Ruinen L, et al (ed) Amsterdam: Excerpta Medica p 400–417

Schwartz C J, Mitchell J R A 1961 Athroma of the carotid and vertebral arterial systems. British Medical Journal 2: 1057–1063

Seitelberger F, Friede R L 1971 Symposium on pathology of axons and aconal flow. Acta Neurophatologica Berlin, Suppl V

Selby G C 1968a Cerebral atrophy in Parkinsonism. Journal of the Neurological Sciences 6: 517–559

Selby G C 1968b Parkinson's disease. In: Handbook of Clinical Neurology, Vinken P J, Bruyn G W (ed) Amsterdam: North Holland vol 6, p 173–211

Shelanski M L, Taylor E W 1970 Biochemistry of neurofilaments and neurotubules. In: Alzheimer's Disease and Related Conditions. Wolstenholme G E W, O'Connor M (ed) London: Churchill p 244–262

Shy G M, Drager G A, 1960 A neurological syndrome associated with orthostatic hypotension. Archives of Neurology (Chicago) 2: 511–527

Silver J R, Buxton P H 1974 Spinal stroke. Brain, 97: 539–550

Simchowicz T 1911 Histologische Stüdien über die senile Demenz. Nissl-Alzheimer Pathol Arb 4: 267–443

Simchowicz T 1924 Sur le signification des plaques séniles et sur la formule de l'écorce cerebrale. Revue Neurologique 31: 221–227

Sjögren T, Sjögren H, Lindgren A G H 1952 Morbus Alzheimer and Morbus Pick. Acta Psychiatrica et Neurologica Scandinavica Suppl 82

Slager U T, Wagner J A 1956 The incidence, composition, and pathological significance of intracerebral vascular deposits in the basal ganglia. Journal of Neuropathology and experimental Neurology 15: 417–425

Smith W T 1969 Pathology of the organic dementias. In: Modern Trends in Neurology. Williams D, (ed) London: Butterworths vol 5 p 96–126

Sourander P, Sjögren H 1970 The concept of Alzheimer's disease and its clinical implications. In: Alzheimer's disease Disease and Related

Conditions. Wolstenholme G E W, O'Connor M, (ed) London: Churchill p 11–36

Steele J C, Richardson J C, Olszewski J 1964 Progressive supranuclear palsy. Archives of Neurology (Chicago)10: 333–359

Surbek E B 1961 L'angiopathie dyshorique (Morel) de l'écorce cérébrale. Etude anatomo-clinique et statistique; aspect génétique. Acta Neuropathologica (Berlin) 1: 168–197

Tariska I 1970 Circumscribed cerebral atrophy in Alzheimer's disease: a pathological study. In: Alzheimer's Disease and Related Conditions. Wolstenholme G E W, O'Connor M (ed) London: Churchill p 51–74

Terry R D 1971 Neuronal fibrous protein in human neuropathology. Journal of Neuropathology and Experimental Neurology 30: 8–19

Terry R D, Wisniewski H 1970 The ultrastructure of the neurofibrillary tangle and the senile plaque. In: Alzheimer's Disease and Related Conditions. Wolstenholme G E W, O'Connor M (ed) London: Churchill p 145–168

Thomas J E, Howard F M 1972 Segmental zoster paresis — a disease profile. Neurology Minneapolis 22: 459–466

Tinel J 1924 Les processus anatomo-pathologiques de la démence sénile. Revue Neurologique 11: 23–49

Tomasch J 1971 Comments on 'Neuromythology'. Nature, London 233: 60

Tomlinson B E 1979 The ageing brain. In: recent Advances in Neuropathology 1. Smith W T, Cavanagh J B (ed) Edinburgh: Churchill Livingstone p 129–159

Tomlinson B E, Blessed G, Roth M 1968 Observations on the brains of non-demented old people. Journal of the Neurological Sciences 7: 331–356

Tomlinson B E, Blessed G, Roth M 1970 Observations on the brains of demented old people. Journal of Neurological Sciences 11: 205–242

Tomlinson B E, Kitchener D 1972 Granulovacuolar degeneration of hippocampal pyramidal cells. Journal of Pathology 106: 165–185

Tomlinson B E, Walton J N, Rebeiz J J 1969 The effects of aging and of cachexia upon skeletal muscle. A histopathological study. Journal of the Neurological Sciences 9: 321–346

Toole J F, Patel A N 1975 In: Cerebrovascular Disorders. 2nd ed McGraw Hill: New York

Vanderhaeghen J-J, Périer O, Sternon J E 1969 Pathological findings in orthostatic hypotension. Its relationship with Parkinson's disease. Archives of Neurology (Chicago) 22: 207–216

Wattendorff A R, Bots G T A M, Went L N, Endtz L J 1982 Familial cerebral amyloid angiopathy presenting as recurrent cerebral haemorrhage. Journal of the Neurological Sciences 55: 121–135

Wildi E, Linder A, Costoulas G 1964 Étude statistique des altérations dégénératives cérébrales apparaissant au cours du vieillissement. Psychiatria et Neurologia (Basel) 148: 41–68

Wilkinson M 1971 In: Cervical Spondylosis. London: Heinemann

Wiśniewski H M, Goblentz J M, Terry R D 1972 Pick's disease, a clinical and ultrastructural study. Archives of Neurology (Chicago) 26: 97–108

Wiśniewski H M, Narang H K, Corsellis J A N, Terry R D 1976a Ultrastructural studies of the neuropil and neurofibrillary tangles in Alzheimer's disease and post-traumatic dementia. Journal of Neuropathology and Experimental Neurology 35: 367

Wiśniewski H M, Narang H K, Terry R D 1976b Neurofibrillary tangles of packed helical filaments. Journal of the Neurological Sciences 27: 173–181

Wiśniewski H, Terry R D 1970 An experimental approach to the problem of neurofibrillary degeneration and the argyrophilic plaque. In: Alzheimer's Diseasese and Related Conditions. Wolstenholme G E W, O'Connor M (ed) London: Churchill p 223–241

Wiśniewski H, Terry R D, Hirano A 1970 Neurofibrillary pathology. Journal of Neuropathology and Experimental Neurology 29: 163–178

Woodard J S 1962 Clinico-pathologic significance of degeneration in Alzheimer's disease. Journal of Neuropathology and Experimental Neurology 21: 85–91

Woodard J S 1966 Concentric hyaline inclusion body formation in mental disease. Analysis of twenty-seven cases. American Journal of Pathology 49: 1157–1169

Yates P O 1976 Vascular disease of the central nervous system. In: Greenfield's Neuropathology. Blackwood W, Corsellis J A N (ed) Arnold: London 3rd edn, p 86–147

Yates P O, Hutchinson E C 1961 Cerebral infarction: the role of stenosis of the extra-cranial vessels. Spec Rep Ser med Res Coun, no 300

Zülch K J 1971 Haemorrhage, thrombosis and embolism. In: Pathology of the Nervous System. Minckler J (ed) New York: McGraw-Hill vol. 2, pp 1499–1536

Zu Rhein G M 1969 Association of papova-virions with a human demyelinating disease (progressive multifocal leukoencephalopathy). Progress in Medical Virology 11: 185–247

The central nervous system — neurochemistry of the aging brain and dementia

INTRODUCTION

The concept that certain diseases of the central nervous system can be related to the degeneration of neuro-transmitter-specific groups of cells has been particularly fruitful. It has long been known from histological studies that neurone-specific degeneration may occur, but the demonstration that these neurones may also be biochemically distinct has considerably advanced our knowledge of the degenerative diseases of the central nervous system. This approach may not only provide insight into the pathophysiology of the disease, but it may offer an opportunity for therapeutic intervention by appropriate modulation of synaptic transmission.

Probably the best example of the value of the concept of neurotransmitter-specific cell degeneration is Parkinson's disease in which Ehringer and Horny-kiewicz (1964) demonstrated a reduced concentration of striatal dopamine. The subsequent introduction of levodopa therapy is well known (for review see Horny-kiewicz, 1976; Marsden, 1982). Although Parkinson's disease is the most eloquent example of this approach to degenerative disease, there is now a substantial amount of evidence to indicate that other diseases such as Alzheimer's Disease and Huntington's Disease may also involve selective neurotransmitter deficits. Similarly so called normal aging may involve selective changes in neurotransmitter systems.

The methodological approach used most commonly in the neurochemical analysis of aging and degenerative disease, is that of post-mortem tissue studies. Post-mortem tissue from a patient dying with the specific disease in question is compared with tissue from an age-matched normal control; factors such as drug history, sex and post-mortem delay, being closely matched.

Fortunately, a large number of neurotransmitters, neurotransmitter-related enzymes and receptors are stable post-mortem permitting analysis of routine autopsy material. However the interpretation of post-mortem neurochemical indices is difficult and the relation to synaptic transmission in vivo is not obvious. Subtle changes without cell loss may be difficult to

establish and, in general, neurotransmitter losses in degenerative diseases probably reflect neuronal losses, although the relationship is unlikely to be simple. Immunohistochemistry has recently provided further insight into the human central nervous system; it can be employed in post-mortem studies and may help to relate more precisely the measured neurotransmitter changes to cell loss. Analysis of cerebrospinal fluid (CSF) has the advantage that studies can be carried out in vivo, but lacks the anatomical specificty of post-mortem studies. (For reviews see Bird and Iversen 1982; Rossor and Emson, 1982).

A review of the aging brain should encompass both the changes associated with normal aging and those found in the age-related diseases. This chapter will adopt a neurotransmitter orientated approach and will not cover the many neurochemical changes which may occur for example, in pigment formation, structural proteins, lipids and energy metabolism. In addition to normal aging the neurotransmitter-related changes in Alzheimer's disease, Parkinson's disease and Huntington's disease will be reviewed.

'NORMAL' AGING

There is now a large body of animal and human data which reveal changes in neurotransmitter systems throughout the life-span of the organism. It is, however, important to distinguish those changes that are related to maturation from those that are related to senescence. For the purpose of this discussion the changes related to senescence will be those that occur with the passage of time, either because of the accumulation of environmental stresses or because of intrinsic molecular events, and which are associated with a decline in function after maturity.

A general feature of aging appears to be cell loss, and since neurones comprise a population of post-mitotic cells, there is limited capacity for cell regeneration, although there may be some opportunities for remodelling. Age-related cell death would be expected to result in a reduction in neurone numbers and indeed brain weight and volume decrease with age in several species, including man (Tomlinson, 1980; Lewis, see Ch. 13). Interestingly, however, neuronal loss in man does show some selectivity. Neurones of the cerebral cortex show substantial loss with age as do pigmented cells in the locus coeruleus, Purkinje cells of the cerebellum, and spinal cord motor neurones. In contrast, neuronal counts in the facial and trochlear nuclei, the ventral cochlear nucleus, the abducens nuclei and the inferior olive remain stable throughout life (Brody, 1955; Henderson and Tomlinson 1980; Tomlinson, 1980).

It might be expected that changes in neurotransmitter systems would reflect this differential propensity to cell death. Not surprisingly, the most detailed data are derived from animal studies in which the many variables can, to some extent, be controlled. At the present time data derived from a limited number of human post-mortem studies present many inconsistencies. Some discrepancies may be explained by the use of different dissection and assay techniques and to the fact that the age range studied may vary. Furthermore, a large number of anatomical areas may be analyzed with some observed changes occurring by chance.

From the point of view of clinical medicine, the most important questions are which neurotransmitter systems change with age and to what extent these changes reflect the functional impairments which may be observed in the elderly. It is not intended to review in detail the many studies in the literature, and the reader is referred to the reviews of Lal and Carroll (1979); Pradhan (1980) and Enna et al (1981), which provide extensive bibliographies in this area. In general the discussion will be confined to human data.

Monoamines

The dopaminergic and noradrenergic systems have been studied in some detail in the aging brain, and in particular, the dopaminergic nigrostriatal system. Reduced activities of the biosynthetic enzymes, tyrosine hydroxylase and dopa decarboxylase occur in the aging human striatum, although the main reduction in activity occurs in the age range 5–25 years, rather than senescence. This is in contrast to the reduction in cell counts of the substantia nigra, which mainly occur in old age and indicate that some of the alterations in enzyme activity relate to reduced activity within an extant neuronal population. (McGeer et al, 1977).

In contrast to biosynthetic enzymes, the degradative enzyme monoamine oxidase B (MAO-B) has been found to increase with age (Robinson, 1972). The increase in MAO-B may be due to a relative increase in the ratio of supporting tissue to neurones and the implications for the integrity of the dopamine neurones themselves are

unclear (Oreland et al, 1980). It has been argued that impaired dopaminergic transmission as reflected by reduced enzyme activities may underlie the motor deficits seen with advancing age (McGeer et al, 1977).

A number of studies report decreases in concentration of dopamine with age (Carlsson and Winblad, 1976). However, in the most comprehensive studies to date of normal control material, Spokes (1979) and Mackay et al (1982) found no statistically significant change in the dopamine concentration in either the striatum or substantia nigra with increasing age.

Similarly, some animal studies report relatively stable dopamine concentrations throughout life (Osterburg et al, 1981; Makman et al, 1979). The interpretation of the data is further complicated by the fact that tissue shrinkage with age may mark loss of neurotransmitters when these are expressed as concentrations. The current data probably indicate that although changes do occur they may be modest and that in terms of transmitter levels, there may be a capacity for the brain to compensate for neuronal loss.

With availability of a wide range of radioactively-labelled ligands, specific receptor binding can now be explored in brain tissue. A number of animal studies report reduced dopamine receptor binding with age in striatum (Makman et al, 1979; Stevenson and Finch, 1980). Using spiperone binding to define dopamine receptors, Mackay et al (1982) found a decrease with age in Bmax (i.e. the total number of binding sites) in human nucleus accumbens. Loss of pre-synaptic inputs generally results in an increase in post-synaptic receptors which can be observed in the mature or senescent organism as shown by the up-regulation in Parkinson's disease where there is an increase in striatal dopamine receptors early in the disease (Lee et al, 1978). If therefore, there is a selective loss of the pre-synaptic nigrostriatal pathway with age one might expect an increase in striatal dopamine receptors. It is not clear whether the absence of change indicates impaired receptor regulation or additional losses of post-synaptic striatal neurones (Bugiani et al, 1978).

In addition to the nigrostriatal system there are dopamine neurones in the retina, olfactory bulb, hypothalamic–pituitary axis and mesolimbic and mesocortical projections. These areas have been examined in less detail, although Spokes (1979) found no change in dopamine concentration in limbic areas and hypothalamus.

The other monoamine neurotransmitters, adrenaline, noradrenaline and 5-hydroxytryptamine (5HT) have been studied less intensively. Adrenaline is only found in low concentration in a few restricted areas of the brain, such as the hypothalamus and certain brain stem nuclei, and information on changes with age is not yet available. Robinson et al (1972) reported a reduction in noradrenaline concentration in whole hind brain with age, although Spokes (1979) found no statistically significant reductions in his large control series with the exception of the substantia nigra. In a smaller number of cases, dopamine-β-hydroxylase activity in cerebral cortex did not change with age (Cross et al, 1980). In contrast to the biochemical studies, cell counts within the locus coeruleus, a major origin of the noradrenergic projection to the forebrain, do decline with age (Tomlinson, 1980). Since the noradrenergic projection has been implicated both in motor and cognitive function, loss of neurones may underly some of the functional deficits in locomotion and cognition seen in the elderly. The minor changes in forebrain noradrenaline concentration and dopamine-β-hydroxylase activity may however, as with the nigrostriatal system, reflect biochemical compensation. Noradrenergic β-receptors are reduced in aged rat striatum and rat and human cerebellum although in humans the change occurs during maturation (Maggi et al, 1979; Greenberg and Weiss, 1978).

5-hydroxytryptamine and its metabolite 5-hydroxy-indoleacetic acid were found not to change with age in the study of Robinson et al (1972).

Acetylcholine

In a series of clinical studies, Drachman (1977) demonstrated that 'scopolamine dementia' — the cognitive impairment subsequent upon the administration of the anticholinergic agent scopolamine, bears a striking resemblance to that seen in the elderly. The effect of scopolamine was shown to be due to a selective action at the cholinergic synapse by the reversal of the 'dementia' by the anticholinesterase inhibitor physostigmine, but not by psychostimulants such as amphetamine. This has led to the proposal that certain aspects of the cognitive and memory decline in normal aging are due to inadequate function of the cholinergic system (for review see Bartus et al, 1982).

Cholinergic neurones are widely distributed throughout the brain and spinal cord. However, of particular interest in relation to dementia and geriatric memory dysfunction are the neurones projecting from the basal forebrain to the hippocampus and neocortex which appear to be involved in memory and learning (for review see Lewis and Shute, 1978, and section on Alzheimer's disease). Post-mortem biochemical evidence for changes in pre-synaptic cholinergic markers in human aging is inconsistent. Davies (1979) and Perry et al (1977a, 1980) reported substantial reductions in the activity of the cholinergic marker enzyme, choline acetyltransferase (ChAT) in the cerebral cortex in the aged, although other post-mortem series have failed to show any change with age (Spokes, 1979;

Bowen et al, 1979), and similarly no change in enzyme activity was found in temporal cortical biopsies (Bowen et al, 1979). In a more detailed post-mortem study, some areas of the cerebral cortex revealed a decline in activity with age, but the change was modest in degree and confined to only a few areas of the frontal lobe (Rossor et al, 1982b). Similarly the evidence for age related changes in striatal ChAT is conflicting (McGeer et al 1977; Perry et al 1977a; Bird and Iversen, 1974; Spokes, 1979; Bartus et al, 1982). Information on cell counts within the nuclei of origin of the cholinergic cortical projections is not yet available, although there is evidence of a loss of striatal neurons with age (Bugiani et al, 1978).

Perry and Perry (1980) have emphasized the greater age susceptibility of the pre-synaptic cholinergic marker ChAT compared with the density of muscarinic cholinergic receptors, which have been reported to be unchanged (Davies and Verth, 1978). However a number of studies have reported decreased muscarinic receptor binding in the cerebral cortex with increasing age (Perry and Perry, 1980; White et al, 1977) which is in accord with a number of animal studies (for review see Bartus et al, 1982). A reduction in receptors might be expected to lead to impaired cholinergic transmission especially if there is an additional pre-synaptic dysfunction. This has provided the basis for cholinergic therapy in geriatric memory dysfunction, and although precursor therapy has been disappointing, there have been some encouraging studies of the effect of the anti-cholinesterase physostigmine on cognitive performance in the elderly (Drachman and Sahakian, 1980; Bartus et al, 1982).

γ-Aminobutyric acid (GABA)

Neurones which utilise the inhibitory neurotransmitter γ-aminobutyric acid (GABA) are distributed widely throughout the central nervous system and GABA may be used by as many as a third of all synapses (Iversen, 1982). GABA is found particularly in local interneurones such as those within the cerebral cortex and since cortical neurones are lost with increasing age (Henderson et al, 1980; Tomlinson, 1980) concomitant changes in the GABA system might be expected. The activity of glutamic acid decarboxylase (GAD), the biosynthetic enzyme, and GABA concentrations are reduced with age in a number of cerebral cortical areas (Spokes, 1979; Spokes et al, 1980; Rossor et al, 1982b) whereas GABA receptor binding sites, appear to be increased or unchanged (Bowen et al, 1979; Maggi et al, 1979). GABA markers within the basal ganglia show less obvious age-related changes (Spokes, 1979; Spokes et al, 1980; Rossor et al, 1982b).

The functional implications of deficits within the

GABA systems in old age are not clear. The ubiquity of GABA neurones implies that impairment may relate to many of the declining functions in old age.

Other neurotransmitter systems

The recent discovery of a number of neuronally-localized peptides within the central nervous system has dramatically increased the number of neurotransmitter candidates. Knowledge of the role of many of these peptides in central nervous system function is rudimentary, and there is very little data as yet on changes with age. Crystal and Davies (1982) found a reduction in substance P in the hippocampus with increasing age although this observation has yet to be confirmed. Somatostatin and cholecystokinin have been found not to change with age (Davies et al, 1981; Perry et al, 1981a) although vasoactive intestinal polypeptide (VIP) has been reported to increase in the temporal lobe (Perry et al, 1981a). The functional implications of these peptide studies are not clear, although Dorsa and Bottemiller (1982) have proposed a relationship between decreased concentrations of extrahypothalamic vasopressin in rats and declining memory and cognitive function. No obvious age-related loss of vasopressin, however, has been found in human studies (Rossor et al, 1980).

SUMMARY OF AGE-RELATED CHANGES

The important questions which a neuropharmacology of aging should address are, firstly, whether the neurotransmitter parameters are lost selectively indicating impairment of synaptic transmission in specific systems, and secondly, whether the observed changes can be related to the functional decline of the aged. At the present time we fall far short of providing the answers to these questions. There are as yet few areas of agreement on the basic changes in neurotransmitter systems with senescence and even less agreement on the functional correlates. The two areas which at present provide the greatest scope for exploration are the roles of the cholinergic system in senescent forgetfulness and of catecholamines in hypokinesia. However the contribution of these two systems to the pathophysiology of senile dementia and Parkinson's disease are probably better understood and will now be considered.

SENILE DEMENTIA

Population studies of dementia indicate that as many as 15 per cent of those aged over 65 years of age may suffer from cognitive impairment and the prevalence rises to 20 per cent in those aged over 80 years of age (Kay et al, 1964). There are many different causes of the dementia syndrome, but the majority are due to Alzheimer's disease alone or in combination with vascular disease. Post-mortem analysis demonstrated Alzheimer type pathology (see chapter 13) in about 50 per cent of cases of dementia and in a further 15 per cent in association with vascular disease. A further 20 per cent can be attributed to multi-infarction (Tomlinson, 1980). Neurones may vary in their vulnerability to ischaemia, but it might be expected that in established cases of multi-infarct dementia non-specific neurochemical changes would reflect global tissue damage in the area of the infarct. In general patterns of neurotransmitter changes in multi-infarct dementia have been non-specific (Perry et al, 1977a; Rossor et al, 1982b) and will not be discussed further. The subsequent discussion of neurotransmitter abnormalities in senile dementia will be confined to Alzheimer's disease.

The term Alzheimer's disease has previously been used for cases of presenile dementia, and the term 'senile dementia of Alzheimer type', used for those patients aged over 65 years of age. In each instance, however, the diseases are characterized by widespread neocortical senile plaques and neurofibrillary tangles (see chapter 13), whereas in normal old age these changes are largely confined to the hippocampus. Although the histological and biochemical features may differ quantitatively there are no major qualitative differences and the distinction is somewhat arbitrary. For the purpose of the ensuing discussion the term Alzheimer's disease will be used irrespective of age.

The cortical cholinergic system

When one considers the global deterioration which may be encountered clinically and the atrophic brain which may be seen at autopsy in Alzheimer's disease, the question of neurotransmitter specificity seems unlikely to invite a positive answer. However, evidence that there may indeed be neurotransmitter-specific abnormalities in Alzheimer's disease came in 1976 and 1977 when three laboratories independently reported the now well established loss of choline acetyltransferase (ChAT) activity from the cerebral cortex. (Bowen et al, 1976; Davies and Maloney 1976; Perry et al, 1977b) Choline acetyltransferase is confined to acetylcholine neurones and the reduction in enzyme activity, therefore, indicates involvement of the cholinergic system: there are additional changes in acetylcholinesterase activity in Alzheimer's disease (Davies and Maloney, 1976; Perry et al, 1978), an observation originally made by Pope et al (1964). The observation of reduced cortical ChAT activity in Alzheimer's disease has now been amply confirmed but before considering the data it would be useful to review some aspects of the anatomy of the cerebral cortical cholinergic system.

Cholinergic neurones are distributed widely throughout the central nervous system from the anterior horn cells innervating skeletal muscle to the projections to the cerebral cortex (for review see Lewis and Shute, 1978). However, as will be discussed below, the main abnormalities in Alzheimer's disease appear to involve the cortical systems and evidence from animal studies now indicates that within the cortex there are few, if any, intrinsic cholinergic neurones (Emson and Lindvall, 1979; Wenk et al, 1980; Lehmann et al, 1980). Instead

the ChAT activity resides predominantly within nerve terminals projecting from perikarya which lie in the basal forebrain, and which can be stained using ChAT antisera (Kimura et al, 1981). Those neurones within the medial septal nuclei project largely to the hippocampus whereas those lying within the diagonal band of Broca and within the region of the substantia innominata project primarily to the neocortex (Wenk et al, 1980; Lehmann et al, 1980). Kainic acid injections into the basal forebrain, which selectively destroy cell bodies, result in substantial depletion of ChAT activity in the cortex, although a residual activity of about 30 per cent

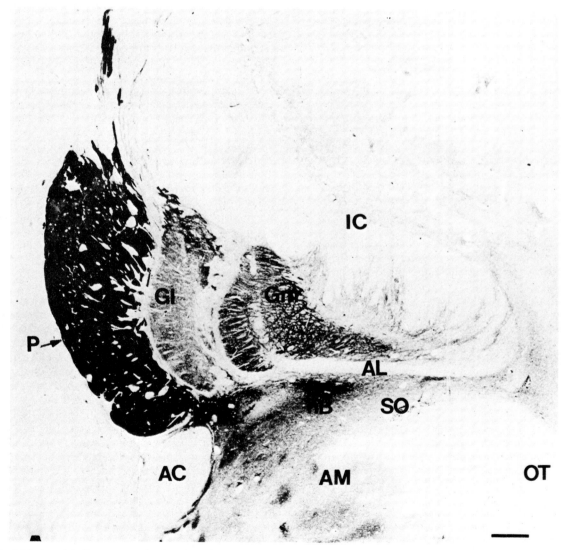

Fig. 14.1 Acetylcholinesterase-stained section of the human forebrain. AC, anterior commissure; AL, ansa lenticularis; AM, amygdala; GL, lateral division of globus pallidus; IC, internal capsule; nB, nucleus basalis; OT, optic tract; P, putamen; SO, supraoptic nucleus. Scale bar = 250 μm.

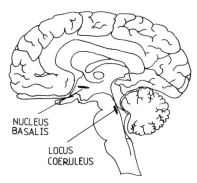

Fig. 14.2 The nucleus basalis (origin of the cholinergic projection) and the locus coeruleus (origin of the noradrenergic projection) projected onto a mid-sagittal section of human brain. (Adapted from Rossor, 1982).

may relate to a small population of intrinsic cortical cholinergic cells (Johnston et al, 1981). The homologous areas in the primate are the medial septal nucleus the diagonal band of Broca and the nucleus basalis of Meynert which lies within the substantia innominata. Combined acetylcholinesterase staining and horseradish peroxidase tracing has demonstrated a probable cholinergic projection from the region of the nucleus basalis to the neocortex in monkeys (Mesulam and Van Hoesen, 1976). Large intensely-cholinesterase stained cell bodies can also be demonstrated within the nucleus basalis in the human brain (Rossor et al, 1982b) (Figs 14.1 and 14.2)

The loss of cerebral cortical ChAT activity is consistent with damage to the ascending cholinergic projection from the basal forebrain (Rossor, 1982). The relationship between loss of enzyme activity, dying back of axons, and neuronal loss is not clear, although recently Whitehouse and colleagues (1982) have shown a reduced cell count within the nucleus basalis indicating that at least in the end-stage there is actual neuronal loss. Loss of ChAT activity has also been reported from the area of the nucleus basalis in Alzheimer's disease (Rossor et al, 1982b). An important question arising from the observation of reduced cortical ChAT activity is whether this is part of a widespread cholinergic dysfunction or whether it is confined to specific cholinergic systems. Davies (1979) found widespread reductions in ChAT activity in a group of severely demented patients who had died at a relatively young age. Other studies however, have reported variations in ChAT activity in different areas, (Perry and Perry 1980; Rossor et al, 1982b) with normal activity in some structures but reduced activity in those areas related to the cortical projections (Rossor et al, 1982b).

In addition to the analysis of pre-synaptic cholinergic markers, acetylcholine receptors have also been studied in Alzheimer's disease. Muscarinic receptors, measured using ^{3}H-quinuclidinyl benzylate binding in homogenates, have been found to be normal (Davies and Verth, 1979; Bowen et al, 1979; Perry and Perry, 1980). In some animal studies there is an increase in cortical muscarinic receptors following cholinergic lesioning or administration of anticholinergics (Westlind et al, 1981). The absence of up-regulation of receptors in Alzheimer's disease may indicate a concomitant loss of post-synaptic sites.

Two important lines of evidence suggest that the observed cholinergic deficit is important in the expression of the functional abnormalities and the histopathological features of Alzheimer's disease. Firstly, there is the animal evidence implicating the cholinergic synapse in memory (Deutsch, 1971) and the human studies of 'scopolamine dementia', (Drachman et al, 1977). In addition the extent of the ChAT deficit has been shown to correlate with the degree of dementia at the time of death (Perry et al, 1978). Secondly, a relationship to the histological abnormalities has been revealed by the close correlation between the enzyme activity and the density of senile plaques in the neocortex (Perry et al, 1978). This observation may only reflect a shared correlation between enzyme activity and histological abnormality with severity of disease. However, there is some evidence that the damage to the cholinergic projections may play a more integral role in senile plaque formation. Perry and Perry (1980), have demonstrated acetylcholinesterase staining of plaques, and Struble and colleagues (1982) have shown that in aged monkeys, early plaques stain intensely for acetylcholinesterase; the staining disappears with maturation to a burnt out plaque with an amyloid core. Although acetylcholinesterase staining is not specific to cholinergic neurones, and it remains to be shown that senile plaques stain for ChAT, it does suggest that damaged cholinergic axons may contribute to the dystrophic neuropil within plaques.

Non-cholinergic ascending projections
In addition to the cortical ChAT deficit early reports indicated abnormalities within the catecholamine systems. Reduced noradrenaline concentrations in the cortex have been reported in a number of series (Adolfsson et al, 1979; Windblad et al, 1982 and histochemical studies of cortical biopsy samples have revealed a reduction in staining of noradrenergic fibres (Berger et al, 1980). Further biochemical evidence of a noradrenergic deficit is provided by reduced activity of the noradrenergic marker enzyme, dopamine-β-hydroxylase (DBH) in post-mortem cerebral cortex (Cross et al, 1981) and of reduced noradrenaline uptake in cortical biopsy samples (Benton et al, 1982).

The noradrenergic input to the cerebral cortex is

comparable to the cholinergic in that it is an extrinsic system which arises from the subcortex. The cortical projection is derived primarily from perikarya lying within the locus coeruleus in the dorsal pons (see Fig. 14.2). As discussed in the previous section, there is an aged-related decline in locus coeruleus cell counts, but in Alzheimer's disease there is an additional cell loss (Bondareff et al, 1981; Tomlinson et al, 1981), which is most marked in the younger age group (Bondareff et al, 1981) (see Fig. 14.3). Although in some cases the histological and biochemical abnormalities in the noradrenergic system may be substantial, the noradrenergic deficit does not seem to be as widespread as the cholinergic deficit, and in one series all cases had a reduced cortical ChAT activity irrespective of whether there was substantial loss of locus coeruleus neurones (Perry et al, 1981b).

Post-mortem studies of dopamine have indicated some

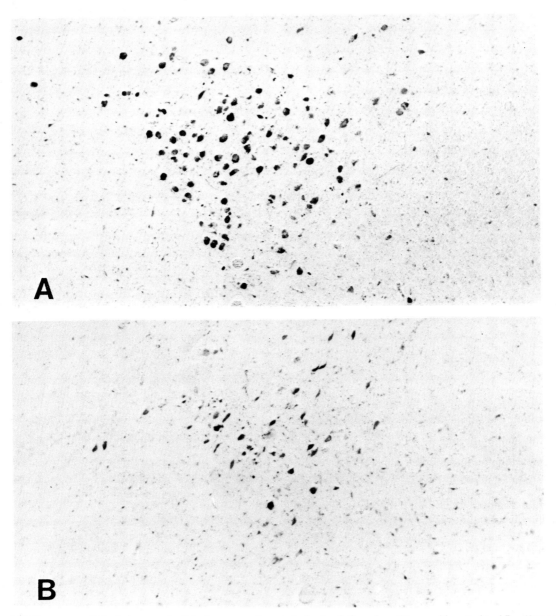

Fig. 14.3 Low power (2.5×) photograph of the locus coeruleus at similar levels from A an 88-year-old control and B a 69-year-old patient dying with Alzheimer's disease. (By courtesy of C. Mountjoy).

reduction in subcortical areas (Adolfsson et al, 1979; Winblad et al, 1982) although this has not been confirmed in other studies. Dopamine concentrations in the cerebral cortex are normal (Winblad et al, 1982). Early indications of dysfunction in the serotonergic system were provided by both histological and biochemical studies. As with the noradrenegic projections, the serotonin projection arises from the brainstem with perikarya predominantly in the dorsal râphé nucleus. Ishii (1966) reported a predilection of neurofibrillary tangle formation for the râphé nucleus and some post-mortem studies have shown reduced cortical concentrations of 5-hydroxytryptamine (Adolfsson et al, 1979; Winblad et al, 1982). Recently 5-hydroxytryptamine uptake has been found to be low in cortical biopsies (Benton et al, 1982).

Neurotransmitters intrinsic to the cerebral cortex

A striking feature of the abnormalities in the cholinergic, noradrenergic and serotonergic systems of the cortex in Alzheimer's disease is the fact that they are all ascending projections arising from perikarya in subcortical structures. Although there is some evidence that cholinergic terminals may be involved in senile plaque formation (Struble et al, 1982), neurofibrillary tangles are intraneuronal and reflect involvement in the disease process of intrinsic cortical neurones. Cortical neurone counts decrease with age (Henderson and Tomlinson, 1979) but it has been difficult to determine the extent of additional cortical cell loss in Alzheimer's disease. Colon (1973) reported substantial cell loss, although early studies using image analysis techniques found no difference in cell counts (Tomlinson, 1980). More recently, Terry et al (1982) have reported reduced cell counts to 60 per cent of age-matched controls, with the loss occurring primarily from the population of large neurones. Mountjoy et al (1983) have found that the cell loss is most marked in the younger cases and that in those dying above the age of 80 years there may be no significant reduction in cell counts in several cortical areas.

One can address the question of the integrity of cortical neurones neuropharmacologically by examining certain neurotransmitters which are found within intrinsic neurones. Immunohistochemical and lesioning studies in animals indicate that GABA, and the recently described neuropeptides, cholecystokinin, vasoactive intestinal polypeptide (VIP) and somatostatin are, within the cerebral cortex, confined to intrinsic neurones and therefore, can be used as intrinsic cortical markers (Fig. 14.4).

The biosynthetic enzyme glutamic acid decarboxylase (GAD) which is a specific GABAergic marker, has been found to be reduced in a number of cortical and subcortical areas (Davies, 1979; Perry et al, 1977a). However,

the post-mortem activity of GAD is profoundly affected by the agonal state, and the reduced activity may therefore relate more to the prolonged terminal illness of the patient than to the disease process. In support of this conclusion is the normal GAD activity found in cortical biopsy studies (Spillane et al, 1977). An alternative approach is to measure GABA itself; normal concentrations have been found in all subcortical areas examined, but reductions to about 70 per cent of control values were found in cerebral cortex, which were confined to the temporal lobe (Rossor et al, 1982b).

Of the cortical neuropeptides, cholecystokinin and VIP are found in normal concentrations (Rossor et al, 1982a), although in one study the concentration of cholecystokinin immunoreactivity was reduced in the temporal lobe of severe cases (Perry et al, 1981a). Somatostatin has been found to be reduced in all cortical areas to about 30 per cent of control value (Davies et al, 1980), although in a study of older cases the somatostatin reduction was confined to the temporal lobe, (Rossor et al, 1982a).

The reduced concentrations of somatostatin and GABA are consistent with reduced activity of β-galactosidase, a neuronal perikaryal marker, in temporal lobe (Bowen et al, 1977) and of the reported reduced cell counts (Terry et al, 1982; Mountjoy et al, 1983). The absence of substantial changes in cholecystokinin and VIP indicate that cortical neuronal loss may be relatively selective. It is of interest that the predominant loss occurs from the temporal lobe since cerebral atrophy in older cases is confined to the temporal lobe (Hubbard and Anderson, 1981) and this area appears to bear the brunt of the disease histologically.

The effect of age on the biochemical changes in Alzheimer's disease

Older cases of Alzheimer's disease show no qualitative histological differences from those dying at a younger age, although the changes may be less severe. The appreciation of the histological continuity between young and older cases has led to the avoidance of the terms presenile and senile dementia based upon an arbitrary age limit. However, comparison of young and old cases does reveal some clinical and pathological differences, and the age at death can also influence the neurochemical profile.

A number of studies have indicated that the ChAT deficit is more severe in the younger age group (Bowen et al, 1979; Rossor et al, 1982b). Moreover, in those patients dying over the age of 79 years, the cholinergic abnormality spares the frontal cortex (Rossor et al, 1982b). Changes in the noradrenergic and GABA systems are also age dependent with involvement of these systems occurring primarily in the younger age group. It is not known whether these differences rep-

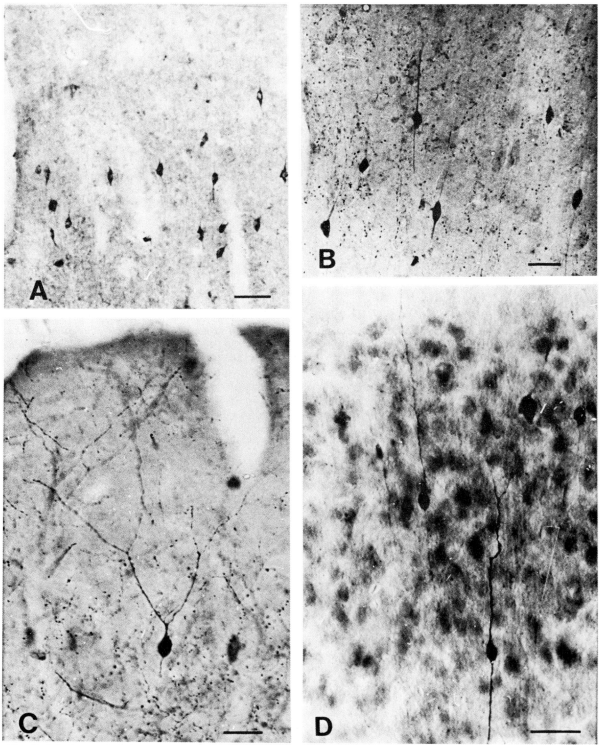

Fig. 14.4 A. Somatostatin immunoreactive neurons within the superficial layers (II–III) of the rat frontal cortex. Scale bar = 40 μm. B. Vasoactive intestinal polypeptide (VIP) immunoreactive neurons within the rat visual cortex. Scale bar = 25 μm. C. VIP immunoreactive neurons in the rat somatosensory cortex. Scale bar = 25 μm. D. Cholecystokinin immunoreactive neurons within the rat somatosensory cortex. Scale bar = 40 μm. (By courtesy of S. Hunt).

resent different disease processes, or whether the older patient succumbs at an earlier stage of the disease.

The cholinergic hypothesis and therapeutic implications

The involvement of the cholinergic synapse in cognition and memory, and the correlation of the biochemical deficit with clinical severity all suggest a central role for the cholinergic abnormality in the pathophysiology of the disease. This has led to the formulation of the 'cholinergic hypothesis', of Alzheimer's disease (Drachman 1977; Perry and Perry, 1980; Rossor, 1982; Bartus et al, 1982). This can simply be stated as, 'damage to the ascending cholinergic system is an important determinant of the functional deficits observed in Alzheimer's disease'. In this form the cholinergic hypothesis does not assume any direct relationship between the cholinergic abnormality and the pathological features, although as discussed above there is some evidence to suggest that dystrophic cholinergic terminals may contribute to senile plaque formation (Struble et al, 1982).

One of the attractions of the cholinergic hypothesis is that it offers a theoretical basis for therapy and a number of approaches have been employed in an attempt to enhance cholinergic transmission. One obvious strategy is to use precursor therapy in an analogous manner to the use of levodopa in Parkinson's disease. Both oral choline and lecithin have been reported to increase brain acetylcholine concentrations in animal studies although their clinical use has been disappointing in the short-term trials reported (Corkin et al, 1982; Bartus et al, 1982). Since ChAT is confined to cholinergic neurones one possible explanation for treatment failure is the fact that acetylcholine synthesis will depend upon the existence of a residual population of cholinergic neurones. A similar argument might militate against the use of acetylcholinesterase inhibitors although there have been reports of response to physostigmine. The use of direct agonists does not require presynaptic neurones, but such drugs as oxotremorine and arecholine have limiting side-effects.

The role of the other ascending systems (Rossor, 1982) is less well established and attempts at modulating catecholamine transmission using levodopa have been unsuccessful (Corkin et al, 1982). Further advances in the treatment of Alzheimer's disease may be dependent upon the development of non-toxic and specific direct agonists at cholinergic, noradrenergic and serotonergic synapses.

PARKINSON'S DISEASE

Although early onset cases of idiopathic Parkinson's

disease are well described, the peak age of onset is between 50 and 65 years of age, and as such represents one of the commonest neurological diseases of old age. Moreover it was probably the first disease which could be related to selective damage to a neurotransmitter-specific population of neurones and is therefore of particular importance in a discussion of the neurochemistry of old age. The ensuing discussion will be confined to idiopathic Parkinson's disease.

The original description of reduced dopamine concentration in the corpus striatum by Ehringer and Hornykiewcz (1963) is now well established and remains the most prominent abnormality in the disease (Marsden, 1982). The reduction is most profound in the putamen where values of about 10 per cent of control are found; but marked reductions are also found in the caudate and to a lesser extent the substantia nigra (Fig. 14.5). The reduced dopamine concentration provides the biochemical correlate to the observed loss of neurones from the substantia nigra, with concomitant Lewy body formation. Since the pigmented perikarya in the substantia nigra pars compacta send axons to the striatum which utilise dopamine, then the loss of this transmitter is presumed to be due to the neuronal loss. Loss of axons and reduction in neurotransmitter synthesis and release with surviving perikarya may occur early in the disease

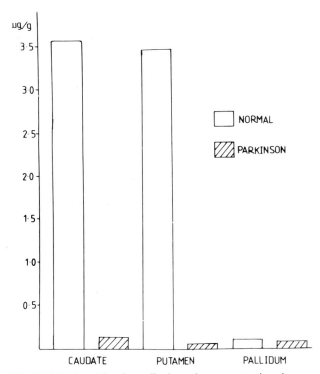

Fig. 14.5 Reduced basal ganglia dopamine concentrations in Parkinson's disease. (Adapted from Bernheimer et al, 1973).

but no information relating to the exact natural history is currently available.

There is good evidence that the dopamine deficiency is central to the functional deficit seen in Parkinson's disease. Depletion of central dopamine in animals results in a hypokinetic state which mimics that seen in Parkinson's disease and which can be reversed by giving dopaminergic drugs. Patients who have suffered hemi-parkinsonism and who have come to post-mortem have been found to have an asymmetric dopamine loss from the striatum and in post-mortem studies there is a correlation between the severity of akinesia and the degree of dopamine deficiency (Hornykiewicz, 1974). However, in the latter regard it is of interest to note that the nigrostriatal system appears to have considerable ability to compensate for neuronal loss, at least in early stages of the disease. Thus losses of 80–85 per cent appear to be necessary before the disease becomes overt (Bernheimer et al, 1973) and in the early stages there is an increase in the ratio of the metabolite homovanillic acid to dopamine in the striatum indicating increased turnover in the remaining neurons. In addition to the nigrostriatal pathway there are other central dopamine systems which may be involved, albeit to a lesser extent. Thus dopamine concentrations have also been found to be reduced in the cerebral cortical and striatal limbic areas which are supplied by projections from cell bodies in the ventral tegmental area (Javoy-Agid and Agid, 1980). Damage to these systems may contribute to the motor deficit but in addition it is tempting to speculate that they may underlie some of the affective and cognitive disturbances which may be seen in patients with Parkinson's disease.

Dopamine receptor binding in the striatum is increased in early untreated cases of Parkinson's disease, although later in the disease, and particularly in those patients on long-term dopaminergic drugs, there is a decrease in ligand binding to below control value (Lee et al, 1978). The changes in ligand binding are due to differences in Bmax, that is receptor numbers, rather than to changes in Kd or affinity. The rise in receptor numbers seen early in the disease is interpreted as an up-regulation in response to denervation and acts to compensate for nigrostriatal dopamine loss. The decrease in receptors later in the disease may be due to down-regulation in response to treatment or it may be due to loss of intrinsic striatal neurons (Reisine et al, 1977; Rinne, 1982).

The radioligands commonly employed in post-mortem studies, such as ^{3}H-spiperone, do not label all dopamine receptors. A number of different receptor classifications have been proposed and one of the simplest is that of Kebabian and Calne (1978) which distinguishes two classes of receptor based upon their linkage to the enzyme adenylate cyclase. D_1 receptors are linked to the enzyme, whereas D_2 receptors, which are labelled by ^{3}H-spiperone, are not enzyme linked. The dopamine receptors have a characteristic distribution (Kebabian and Calne, 1978) and there is now evidence that both D_1 and D_2 receptors may be reduced late in the disease (Shibuya, 1979).

Although the dopamine deficiency is the most prominent abnormality other neurotransmitter systems may also be involved in Parkinson's disease. Reduced concentrations of noradrenaline relate to the loss of pigmented cells from the locus coeruleus.

GABA neurones form a major output from the striatum to the pallidum and substantia nigra. GAD activity is reduced particularly in the substantia nigra (Lloyd and Hornykiewicz, 1973) and GABA receptors are normal in the striatum but reduced in the substantia nigra as a consequence of the loss of dopaminergic neurones on which they are located (Lloyd et al, 1977).

ChAT within the striatum is relatively unchanged, although there are some reductions in activity (Reisine et al, 1977) which may, like the reduction in ^{3}H-spiperone binding, relate to striatal neuronal loss. Of particular interest is the recent report of reduced cortical ChAT activity in Parkinsonian patients with dementia (Ruberg et al, 1982). Dementia may occur in as many as 30 per cent of late stage Parkinsonians (Marsden, 1982) and in a number of these the histological features of Alzheimer's disease may be present. The loss of cerebral cortical ChAT activity is presumably related to damage to the ascending cortical projection and indicates a degree of overlap with Alzheimer's disease.

Recently some studies of neuropeptides in Parkinson's disease have been undertaken. Met-enkephalin has been reported to be depleted in the substantia nigra (Tacquet et al, 1981) indicating that neuronal degeneration may be more widespread. The reported loss of cholecystokinin immunoreactivity (Studler et al, 1982) can be more easily related to the loss of dopamine neurones since cholecystokinin coexists with dopamine in some of the neurones of the mesolimbic and nigrostriatal systems. The functional significance of the peptide changes is unclear.

Therapeutic implications

Substrate precursor therapy using levodopa to enhance dopaminergic transmission is now well established. Since the majority of an oral levodopa load is metabolized peripherally, and dopamine cannot readily cross the blood-brain barrier, extracerebral dopa decarboxylase inhibitors have been introduced and now levodopa combined with carbidopa (Sinemet) or with benserazide (Madopar) forms the mainstay of treatment. The exact mode of action of levodopa is still not entirely clear. The loss of nigrostriatal neurones would be expected to lead to a loss of intraneuronal sites for dopamine synthesis, and this has been suggested as a cause for treatment failure. Levodopa may, however, be metabolized in other neurones, such as noradrenergic and serotonergic, at extraneuronal sites or even non-enzymatically (Hornykiewicz, 1974). Another intriguing question, which relates to neurotransmitter replacement in general, is how exogenous transmitter can mimic the information provided by neuronal transmitters which are released in response to impulse flow. It may be that some of the brain systems have a modulatory role and as such carry limited information (Iversen, 1982). These might be expected to be anatomically disperse systems, which are tonically active. The nigrostriatal dopamine systems and noradrenergic projection to the cortex share some of these characteristics.

In addition to levodopa, there are available a number of direct dopamine agonists. Bromocryptine has been most widely used and it is of interest that like many other direct agonists, it has a D_2 agonist action, and indeed is only a partial agonists at D_1 receptors. It has been proposed that the clinical features of Parkinson's disease relate to impaired transmission at D_2 receptors (Schachter et al, 1980) although further understanding of the role of the individual receptors awaits the development of specific D_1 agonists and antagonists. Other drugs used in Parkinson's disease also have actions at the dopamine receptor. Thus amantidine (Symmetrel) blocks dopamine reuptake, and selegiline (Eldepryl) prolongs dopamine action at the synapse by inhibiting the specific degradative enzyme, monoamine oxidase B. The anticholinergic drugs which have been in use since the previous century also inhibit dopamine re-uptake although their prime action is presumed to be via their blockage of cholinergic receptors, to restore dopamine/acetylcholine inbalance in the striatum.

The introduction of dopamine replacement has been one of the most exciting developments in the therapeutics of neurological disease. However, it is now becoming apparent that with passage of time, new problems arise in the management of these patients. After 5 years of treatment at least half will have lost some of the benefit derived from levodopa (Marsden and Parkes, 1977). The main problems are recurrence of akinesia and development of fluctuation in response to treatment. For discussion of the possible causes and management of these problems the reader is referred to the reviews by Marsden and Parkes (1977) and Marsden et al (1982).

HUNTINGTON'S DISEASE AND SENILE CHOREA

This autosomal dominant disorder, characterized by progressive chorea and dementia, may become manifest at any age from childhood to senescence, although in the majority the disease starts clinically between 30 and 50 years of age. The reason for including Huntington's disease in a chapter on the neurochemistry of aging is that since the disease is not apparent until later in life there is the intriguing possibility that the clinical expression is dependent upon an interaction of the aging process with the underlying disease-specific abnormality (Finch, 1980).

Histologically the disease is characterized by cortical thinning and gross atrophy of the corpus striatum with extensive loss of neurones in the caudate, putamen and pallidum with accompanying gliosis. One of the earliest reported biochemical abnormalities, the reduced GAD activity and GABA concentration in the striatum, indicated that the striatal GABAergic neurones might be predominantly affected (Perry et al, 1973; Bird and Iversen, 1974), and an increase in GABA receptors in the pallidum and substantia nigra is consistent with denervation supersensitivity (Enna et al, 1976). However the concept that the striatal pathology of Huntington's disease can be related to selective loss of GABA neurones is untenable since ChAT activity, and muscarinic receptors are also reduced, indicating additional damage to the cholinergic interneurones (Bird and Iversen, 1974; Spokes, 1980). Moreover the neuropeptides met enkephalin and substance P are reduced in the substantia nigra and globus pallidus indicating probable damage to additional striatonigral efferents (Emson et al, 1980).

In contrast to the widespread loss of striatal neurones is the relative preservation of the dopaminergic innervation from the substantia nigra. Increased dopamine concentrations are found in the striatum and nucleus accumbens (Spokes, 1980), and although there is a reduction in striatal dopamine receptors (Enna et al, 1976) the overall effect is to increase dopaminergic transmission in the striatum. By analogy with levodopa-induced dyskinesias in Parkinson's disease, the excessive dopaminergic stimulation of the striatum is believed to underlie, in part, the involuntary movement. This has provided the rational basis for the treatment of the chorea by dopamine antagonists. Attempts have been made to replace the GABA deficit using drugs such as sodium valproate, isoniazid and muscimol but without benefit.

So called senile chorea, in the setting of normal intellectual function, is occasionally seen in the elderly. It is not clear whether these patients constitute a distinct disease entity or whether some are cases of Huntington's disease, where by virtue of the late onset of clinical features the family history may not be apparent. Biochemical studies are not available and it is not known whether dopaminergic excess may also contribute to the involuntary movements in senile chorea.

CONCLUSION

In conclusion it can be said that both normal aging and the senile degenerative diseases demonstrate selective histological changes and that these can be related, to some extent, to alterations in specific neurotransmitter systems. There are many conflicting data from human post-mortem studies, but in general there are reductions in pre-synaptic markers which, against a background of degenerative diseases, are assumed to relate to cell damage or loss. There are in addition changes in neurotransmitter receptors which may reflect post-synaptic cell damage, but alternatively may reflect an impairment of the normal regulation of receptor density.

The overall effect of the observed neurotransmitter and receptor changes can be interpreted as reduced synaptic transmission, and an immediate question is whether this can be related to specific functional impairments. Knowledge of the functional roles of neurotransmitter systems is rudimentary but there is good evidence that the catecholamine and cholinergic disorders seen in Parkinson's and Alzheimer's disease contribute directly to the motor impairment and dementia respectively. Although we may be ignorant of the underlying mechanism of neuronal degeneration and death, the analysis of the neurotransmitter changes involved has provided a useful basis for the development of potential therapy.

REFERENCES

Adolfsson R, Gottfries C-G, Roos B E, Winblad B 1979 Changes in brain catecholamines in patients with dementia of Alzheimer type. British Journal of Psychiatry 135: 216–223

Bartus R T, Dean R L, Beer B, Lippa A S 1982 The cholinergic hypothesis of geriatric memory dysfunction. Science 217: 408–417

Benton J S, Bowen D M, Allen S J, Haan E A, Davison A N, Neary D et al 1982 Alzheimer's disease as a disorder of isodendritic core. Lancet i: 456

Berger B, Tassin J P, Rancurel G, Blanc G 1980 Catecholaminergic innervation of the human cerebral cortex in presenile and senile dementia: histochemical and biochemical studies. In: Usdin E, Sourkes T L, Youdin M B H (Eds) Enzymes and neurotransmitters in mental disease, John Wiley, New York, p 317–328

Bernheimer H, Birkmayer W, Hornykiewicz O, Jellinger K, Seitelberger F 1973 Brain dopamine and the syndromes of Parkinson's and Huntington. Clinical, morphological and neurochemical correlations. Journal of the Neurological Sciences 20: 415–455

Bird E D, Iversen L L 1974 Huntington's chorea — post-mortem measurement of glutamic acid decarboxylase, choline acetyltransferase and dopamine in basal ganglia. Brain 97: 457–472

Bird E, Iversen L L 1982 Human brain post-mortem studies of neurotransmitters and related markers. Handbook of Neurochemistry Vol 2, Lajtha A (Ed) 2nd Edn, Plenum Press, New York p 225–251

Bondareff W, Mountjoy C Q, Roth M 1981 Selective loss of neurones of origin of adrenergic projection to cerebral cortex (nucleus locus coeruleus) in senile dementia. Lancet i: 783–784

Bowen D M, Smith C B, White P, Davison A N 1976 Neurotransmitter-related enzymes and indices of hypoxia in senile dementia and other abiotrophies. Brain 99: 459–496

Bowen D M, Spillane J A, Curzon G, Meier-Ruge W, White P, Goodhardt M J et al 1979 Accelerated ageing or selective neuronal loss as an important cause of dementia. Lancet i: 11–14

Brody H 1955 Organisation of the cerebral cortex. 3. A study of ageing in the human cerebral cortex. Journal of Comparative Neurology 102: 511–556

Bugiani O, Salvarani S, Perdelli F, Mancardi G L, Leonardi A 1978 Nerve cell loss with ageing in the putamen. European Neurology 17: 286–291

Carlsson A, Winblad B 1976 Influence of age and time interval between death and autopsy on dopamine and 3-methoxytyramine levels in human basal ganglia. Journal of Neural Transmission 38: 271–276

Colon E J 1973 The cerebral cortex in presenile dementia: a quantitative analysis. Acta neuropathologica (Berlin) 23: 281–290

Corkin S, Davis K L, Growdon J H, Usdin E, Wurtman R J (eds) 1982 Alzheimer's disease: a report of progress in research. Ageing Vol XIX, Raven Press, New York

Cross A J, Crow T J, Perry E K, Perry R H, Blessed G, Tomlinson B E 1981 Reduced dopamine-beta-hydroxylase activity in Alzheimer's disease. British Medical Journal 282: 93–94

Crystal H A, Davies P 1982 Cortical substance P-like immunoreactivity in cases of Alzheimer's disease and senile dementia of the Alzheimer type. Journal of Neurochemistry 38: 1781–1784

Davies P 1979 Neurotransmitter-related enzymes in senile dementia of the Alzheimer type. Brain Research 171: 319–327

Davies P, Maloney A J 1976 Selective loss of central cholinergic neurones in Alzheimer's disease. Lancet ii: 1403

Davies P, Verth A H 1978 Regional distribution of muscarinic acetylcholine receptor in normal and Alzheimer-type dementia brains. Brain Research 138: 385–392

Davies P, Katzman R, Terry R D 1980 Reduced somatostatin-like immunoreactivity in cerebral cortex from cases of Alzheimer's disease and Alzheimer senile dementia. Nature 288: 279–280

Deutsch J A 1971 The cholinergic synapse and the site of memory. Science 174: 788–794

Dorsa D M, Bottemiller L 1982 Age-related changes of vasopressin content of microdissected areas of the rat brain. Brain Research 242: 151–156

Drachman D A 1977 Memory and cognitive function in man: does the cholinergic system have a specific role? Neurology 27: 783–790

Drachman D A, Sahakian B J 1980 Memory and cognitive function in the elderly. A preliminary trial of physostigmine. Archives of Neurology 37: 674–675

Ehringer H, Hornykiewicz O 1963 Verteilung von Noradrenalin und Dopamin (3-hydroxytyramin) im Gehirn des Menschen und Ihr Verhalten bei Erkrankungen des Extrapyramidalen Systems. Klinische Wochenschrift 41: 1236–1239

Emson P C, Lindvall O 1979 Distribution of putative neurotransmitters in the neocortex. Neuroscience 4: 1–30

Emson P C, Arregui A, Clement-Jones V, Sandberg B E B, Rossor M 1980 Regional distribution of methionine-enkephalin and substance P-like immunoreactivity in normal human brain and in Huntington's disease. Brain Research 199: 147–160

Enna S J, Bennett J P, Bylund D B, Snyder S H, Bird E D, Iversen L L 1976 Alteration of brain neurotransmitter receptor binding in Huntington's chorea. Brain Research 116: 531–537

Enna S J, Samorajski T, Beer B (eds) 1981 Brain neurotransmitters and receptors in ageing and age-related disorders. Ageing Vol. 17. Raven Press, New York

Finch C E 1980 The relationships of aging changes in the basal ganglia to manifestations of Huntington's chorea. Annals of Neurology 7: 406–411

Greenberg L H, Weiss B 1978 β-adrenergic receptors in aged rat brain: reduced number and capacity of pineal gland to develop supersensitivity. Science 201: 61–63

Henderson G, Tomlinson B E, Gibson P H 1980 Cell counts in human cerebral cortex in normal adults throughout life using an image analysing computer. Journal of the Neurological Sciences 46: 113–136

Hornykiewicz O 1974 The mechanisms of action of L-Dopa in Parkinson's disease. Life Sciences 15: 1249–1259

Hubbard B M, Anderson J M 1981 A quantitative study of cerebral atrophy in old age and senile dementia. Journal of the Neurological Sciences 50: 135–145

Ishii T 1966 Distribution of Alzheimer's neurofibrillary changes in the brain stem and hypothalamus of senile dementia. Acta Neuropathologica 6: 181–187

Iversen L L 1982 Neurotransmitters and CNS disease. Introduction. Lancet ii: 914–918

Javoy-Agid F, Agid Y 1980 Is the mesocortical dopaminergic system involved in Parkinson's disease? Neurology 30: 1326–1330

Johnston M V, McKinney M, Coyle J T 1981 Neocortical cholinergic innervation: a description of extrinsic and intrinsic components in the rat. Experimental Brain Research 43: 159–172

Kay D W K, Beamish P, Roth M 1964 Old age mental disorders in Newcastle-upon-Tyne. British Journal of Psychiatry 110: 146–158

Kebabian J W, Calne D B 1979 Multiple receptors for dopamine. Nature 277: 93–96

Kimura H, McGeer P L, Peng J H, McGeer E G 1981 The central cholinergic system studied by choline acetyltransferase immunohistochemistry in the cat. Journal of Comparative Neurology 200: 151–201

Lal H, Carroll P T 1979 Alterations in brain neurotransmitter systems related to senescence. In: Nandy K (ed) Geriatric Psychopharmacology, Elsevier, North Holland, p 3

Lee T, Seeman P, Rajput A, Farley I J, Hornykiewicz O 1978 Receptor basis for dopaminergic supersensitivity in Parkinson's disease. Nature (London) 273: 59–61

Lehman J, Nagy J I, Atmadja S, Fibiger H C 1980 The nucleus basalis magnocellularis: the origin of a cholinergic projection to the neocortex of the rat. Neuroscience 5: 1161–1174

Lewis P R, Shute C D 1978 Cholinergic pathways in the CNS. In: Iversen L L, Iversen S D, Snyder S H (eds) Handbook of Psychopharmacology. Vol IX. Plenum Press, New York, p 315–356

Llyod K G, Hornykiewicz O 1973 L-glutamic acid decarboxylase in Parkinson's disease. Nature 243: 521–523

Lloyd K G, Shemen L, Hornykiewicz O 1977 Distribution of high affinity sodium-independent (^{3}H-)gamma-aminobutyric acid (^{3}H-GABA) binding in the human brain: alterations in Parkinson's disease. Brain Research 127: 269–278

Mackay A V P, Iversen L L, Rossor M, Spokes E G S, Bird E, Arregui A et al 1982 Increased brain dopamine and dopamine receptors in schizophrenia. Archives of General Psychiatry 39: 991–997

Maggi, A, Schmidt M J, Ghetti B, Enna S J 1979 Effect of aging on neurotransmitter receptor binding in rat and human brain. Life Sciences 24: 367–374

Makman M H, Ahn H S, Thal L J, Sharpless N S, Dvorkin B, Horowitz S G, Rosenfield M 1979 Aging and monoamine receptors in brain. Federation Proceedings 38: 1922–1926

Marsden C D 1982 Neurotransmitters and CNS disease: basal ganglia. Lancet ii: 1141–1146

Marsden C D, Parkes J D 1977 Success and problems of long-term levodopa therapy in Parkinson's disease. Lancet ii: 345–349

Marsden C D, Parkes J D, Quinn N 1982 Fluctuations of disability in Parkinson's disease: clinical aspects. In: Marsden C D, Fahn S (eds) Movement disorders, Butterworths, London, p 96–122

McGeer P L, McGeer E G, Suzuki J S 1977 Aging and Extrapyramidal function. Archives of Neurology 34: 33–35

Mesulam M-M, Van Hoesen G W 1976 Acetylcholinesterase-rich projections from the basal forebrain of the rhesus monkey to neocortex. Brain Research 109: 152–157

Mountjoy C Q, Roth M, Evans N J R, Evans H M 1983 Cortical neuronal counts in normal elderly controls and demented patients. Neurobiology of Aging 4: 1–11

Oreland L, Fowler C J, Carlsson A, Magnusson T 1980 Monoamine oxidase-A and -B activity in the rat brain after hemitransection. Life Sciences 26: 139–146

Osterburg H H, Donahue H G, Severson J A, Finch C E 1981 Catecholamine levels and turnover during ageing in brain regions of male C 57BL/6J mice. Brain Research 224: 337–352

Perry E K, Gibson P H, Blessed G, Perry R H, Tomlinson B E 1977a Neurotransmitter enzyme abnormalities in senile dementia. Journal of the Neurological Sciences 34: 247–265

Perry E K, Perry R H, Blessed G, Tomlinson B E 1977b Necropsy evidence of central cholinergic deficits in senile dementia. Lancet i: 189

Perry E K, Tomlinson B E, Blessed G, Bergmann K, Gibson P H, Perry R H 1978 Correlation of cholinergic abnormalities with senile plaques and mental scores in senile dementia. British Medical Journal ii: 1457–1459

Perry E K, Perry R H 1980 The cholinergic system in Alzheimer's disease. In: Roberts P J (ed) Biochemistry of Dementia, John Wiley and Sons, Chichester, p 135–183

Perry E K, Blessed G, Tomlinson B E, Perry R H, Crow T J, Cross A J et al A 1981a Neurochemical activities in human temporal lobe related to aging and Alzheimer-type changes. Neurobiology of Ageing 2: 251–256

Perry E K, Tomlinson B E, Blessed G, Perry R H, Cross A J, Crow T J 1981b Noradrenergic and cholinergic systems in senile dementia of Alzheimer type. Lancet ii: 149

Perry T L, Hansen S, Kloster M 1973 Huntington's chorea: deficiency of gamma-aminobutyric acid in brain. New England Journal of Medicine 288: 337–342

Pope A, Hess, Lewin E 1964 Studies on the microchemical pathology of human cerebral cortex. In: Cohen M M, Snider R S (Eds) Morphological and Biochemical Correlates of Neural Activity, Harper and Row, New York, p 98–111

Pradhan S N 1980 Central neurotransmitters and aging. Life Sciences 26: 1643–1656

Reisine T D, Fields J Z, Yamamura H I, Spokes E G S, Bird E D, Schreiners P S, Enna S J 1977 Neurotransmitter receptor alterations in Parkinson's disease. Life Sciences 21: 335–344

Rinne U K 1982 Brain neurotransmitter receptors in Parkinson's disease. In: Marsden C D, Fahn S, (eds) Movement disorders, Butterworths, London, p 59–74

Robinson D S, Nies A, Davis J N, Bunney W E, Davis J M, Colburn RW et al 1972 Ageing, monoamines, and monoamine-oxidase levels. Lancet i: 290–291

Rossor M N 1982 Neurotransmitters and CNS disease: dementia. Lancet ii: 1200–1204

Rossor M N, Iversen L L, Hawthorn J, Ang V T Y, Jenkins J S 1981 Extrahypothalamic vasopressin in human brain. Brain Research 214: 349–355

Rossor M N, Emson P C 1982 Neuropeptides in degenerative disease of the central nervous system. Trends in Neurosciences 5: 399–401

Rossor M N, Emson P C, Iversen L L, Mountjoy C Q, Roth M, Fahrenkrug J, Rehfeld J F 1982a Neuropeptides and neurotransmitters in cerebral cortex in Alzheimer's disease. In: Corkin S, Davies K L, Growdon J H, Usdin E, Wurtman R J, (eds) Alzheimer's disease: a report of progress in research, Ageing Vol XIX, Raven Press, New York, p 25–33

Rossor M N, Garrett N J, Johnson A L, Mountjoy C Q, Roth M, Iversen L L 1982b A post-mortem study of the cholinergic and GABA systems in senile dementia. Brain 105: 313–330

Ruberg M, Ploska A, Javoy-Agid F, Agid Y 1982 Muscarinic binding and choline acetyltransferase activity in Parkinsonian subjects with reference to dementia. Brain Research 232: 129–139

Schachter M, Bedard P, Debono A G, Jenner P, Marsden C D, Price R et al 1980 The role of D-1 and D-2 receptors. Nature 286: 157–159

Severson J A, Finch C E 1980 Reduced dopaminergic binding during aging in the rodent striatum. Brain Research 192: 147–162

Shibuya M 1979 Dopamine-sensitive adenylate cyclase activity in the striatum in Parkinson's disease. Journal of Neural Transmission 44: 287–295

Spillane J A, White P, Goodhardt M J, Flack R H A, Bowen D M, Davison A N 1977 Selective vulnerability of neurones in organic dementia. Nature 266: 558–559

Spokes E G S 1979 An analysis of factors influencing measurements of dopamine, noradrenaline, glutamate decarboxylase and choline acetylase in human post-mortem brain tissue. Brain 102: 333–346

Spokes E G S 1980 Neurochemical alterations in Huntington's chorea. Brain 103: 179–210

Spokes E G S, Garrett N J, Rossor M N, Iversen L L 1980 Distribution of GABA in post-mortem brain tissue from control, psychotic and Huntington's chorea subjects. Journal of the Neurological Sciences 48: 303–313

Struble R G, Cork L C, Whitehouse P J, Price D L 1982 Cholinergic innervation in neuritic plaques. Science 216: 413–415

Studler J M, Javoy-Agid F, Cesselin F, Legrand J C, Agid Y 1982 CCK-8-immunoreactivity distribution in human brain: selective decrease in the substantia nigra from Parkinsonian patients. Brain Research 243: 176–179

Tacquet H, Javoy-Agid F, Cesselin F, Agid Y 1981 Methionine-enkephalin deficiency in brains of patients with Parkinson's disease. Lancet i: 1367–1368

Terry R D, Peck A, De Teresa R, Schechter R, Horoupian D S 1981 Some morphometric aspects of the brain in senile dementia of the Alzheimer type. Annals Neurology 10: 184–192

Tomlinson B E 1980 The structural and quantitative aspects of the dementias. In: Roberts P J (ed) Biochemistry of Dementia, John Wiley and Sons Ltd, Chichester, p 15

Tomlinson B E, Irving D, Blessed G 1981 Cell loss in the locus coeruleus in senile dementia of Alzheimer type. Journal of the Neurological Sciences 49: 419–428

Wenk H, Bigl V, Meyer U 1980 Cholinergic projections from magnocellular nuclei of the basal forebrain to cortical areas in rats. Brain Research Reviews 2: 295–316

Westlind A, Grynfarb M, Hedlund B, Bartfai T, Fuxe K 1981 Muscarinic supersensitivity induced by septal lesion or chronic atropine treatment. Brain Research 225: 131–141

White P, Hiley C R, Goodhardt M J, Carrasco L H, Keet J P, Williams I E I, Bowen D M 1977 Neocortical cholinergic neurones in elderly people. Lancet ii: 668–670

Whitehouse P J, Price D L, Struble R G, Clark A W, Coyle J T, De Long M R 1982 Alzheimer's disease and senile dementia: loss of neurones in the basal forebrain. Science 215: 1237–1239

Winblad B, Adolfsson R, Carlsson A, Gottfries C G 1982 Biogenic amines in brains of patients with Alzheimer's disease. In: Corkin S, Davies K L, Growdon J H, Usdin E, Wurtman R J, (eds) Alzheimer's disease: a report of progress in research, Ageing Vol XIX, Raven Press, New York, p 25–33

The central nervous system — dementia and delirium in old age

INTRODUCTION

It has not been long since dementia and delirium were topics generally ignored by health professionals. Cognitive deficits were the expected result of old age. Patients who developed dementia received no special assessment, treatment, or care, and generally did not survive more than a few years. Thus, society was under no real pressure to develop the resources to help this special population. Today, the situation has changed drastically. We now know that dementia is not an inevitable feature of aging, but rather a sign of a diseased brain. Concomitantly, medical science has progressed to the point where patients who develop dementia are physically maintained with much greater skill and care than before so that they often survive for 15 to 20 years. The current frequency of dementia is often stated as 5 per cent of the population age 65 and over, rising to 20 per cent or more beyond age 80. With the expansion of the number of patients suffering from dementia, the community resources needed to deal with them are being rapidly drained. Families are being overwhelmed by the emotional and financial cost. As the magnitude of the problem continues to increase, society has been appropriately increasing the pressure on the scientific community to develop the technology needed to correctly diagnose, treat, and prevent the dementias of old age.

Delirium, is generally recognized as a signal of widespread physical dysfunction requiring immediate assessment and intervention.

This chapter will review the common causes of dementia and delirium in old age. Before we continue, a few words on the mental status examination are in order. The mental status exam generally does not need to be extensive or require a large amount of time, in order to screen elderly patients for dementia or delirium. Many brief rating scales have been developed. Our own suggestion, as can be seen in Table 15.1, has the advantage of testing memory, language, calculations, and visuospatial skills, in usually under 4 minutes. If two or more errors are made, however, a more complete

Table 15.1 Brief mental status rating scale

Have the patient give:
1. Name
2. Date of birth
3. Age
4. Date and time of day
5. Season of the year
6. Address
7. Phone number
8. Name of the prime minister (or president)
9. Name of the previous prime minister (or president)
10. Name of several objects in the room, such as a watch, desk, shoelace, etc. (tests language)
11. Current news event (tests memory)
12. Reproduction of a simple drawing of a house (tests visuospatial skills)
13. Answers to several simple arithmetic problems (tests mental calculations)

evaluation is required. For an in-depth discussion of a complete mental status examination — often requiring up to two hours of time — the reader is referred to the work of Strub and Black (1977).

DELIRIUM

Delirium has had multiple synonyms over the years (Table 15.2). Despite the multiple terminology, there is

Table 15.2 Synonymous terminology in the literature on delirium (Reprinted with permission from Liston, 1982)

Acute brain failure	Metabolic encephalopathy
Acute brain syndrome	Pseudosenility
Acute cerebral insufficiency	Reversible cognitive dysfunction
Acute confusional state	Reversible dementia
Acute organic reaction	Reversible toxic psychosis
Acute organic psychosis	Subacute befuddlement
Acute psycho-organic syndrome	Toxic confusional state
Acute organic syndrome	Toxic delirious reaction
Cerebral insufficiency syndrome	Toxic encephalopathy
Exogenous psychosis	Toxic psychosis

less disagreement about its definition than that of dementia, and it is relatively easier to diagnose. ICD-9 states that delirium, although it is similar to dementia, has a short course. Moreover, in delirium, the features of dementia are 'overshadowed by clouded consciousness, confusion, disorientation, delusions, illusions and often vivid hallucinations.' The key to the diagnosis of delirium is finding multiple cognitive impairments in a patient who additionally has a clouding of consciousness, explained by Liston (1982) as a reduced clarity of awareness of the environment, and decreased attention (Table 15.3).

Table 15.3 Diagnostic criteria for delirium (From American Psychiatric Association: Diagnostic and Statistical Manual of Mental Disorders, Third edition, Washington D.C., 1980, p. 107, with permission)

A. Clouding of consciousness (reduced clarity of awareness of the environment), with reduced capacity to shift, focus, and sustain attention to environmental stimuli.
B. At least two of the following:
   1. perceptual disturbance: misinterpretations, illusions, or hallucinations.
   2. speech that is at times incoherent.
   3. disturbance of sleep–wakefulness cycle, with insomnia or daytime drowsiness.
   4. increased or decreased psychomotor activity.
C. Disorientation and memory impairment (if testable).
D. Clinical features that develop over a short period of time (usually hours to days) and tend to fluctuate over the course of a day.
E. Evidence, from the history, physical examination, or laboratory tests, of a specific organic factor judged to be aetiologically related to the disturbance.

A more complete description of the clinical features of delirium is given by Lipowski (1980) as follows:

'The patient manifests impairment in the areas of directed thinking, registration, recent memory, and orientation, at least in the time sphere. There is evidence of disturbance in the mobilization, focusing, maintaining, and shifting of attention. Arousal is either reduced with less than normal wakefulness and alertness or arousal is heightened with increased but indiscriminate response to external stimuli. The patient's sleep–wakefulness cycle is altered with either insomnia and daytime drowsiness or diurnal rhythm reversal. Defects in cognition and attention tend to fluctuate unpredictably and without regularity during the day and to become accentuated with insomnia. Behavioural manifestations include either decreased or increased psychomotor activity or wide swings from one to the other. Visual illusions and hallucinations are common, except in the aged as noted, and abnormalities of other perceptual modalities may be present as well, accompanied by restlessness and fear. Persecutory delusions which are poorly systematized and fleeting may be present and intermixed with hallucinations. At any time, the patient may enter a lucid interval or a period of improvement in attention span, reality testing, and other symptoms and signs.'

While many clinicians may be familiar with the more common agitated form of delirium, Morse and Litin (1971) have emphasized the importance of not overlooking the calm, hypoactive, or stuporous subtypes. Other features of delirium may include urinary incontinence, anorexia, or signs of the underlying medical illness (e.g. asterixis in liver failure, neurologic signs in stroke, dehydration in hyperglycemia, shortness of breath in hypoxemia, etc.). Delirium, however, may additionally occur in a patient with dementia. An example might be a patient with early Alzheimer's disease who develops delirium during a febrile episode of pneumonia.

The incidence of delirium in elderly patients has primarily been studied in hospitalized populations, where the frequency is surprisingly high. Reports from psychiatric wards have ranged from 10 to almost 40 per cent (Eisdorfer and Cohen, 1978; Kay, 1972; Simon and Cahan, 1963), a neurologic ward 40 per cent (Robinson, 1956), general medical and surgical floors 14–30 per cent (Merwin and Abram, 1977; Doty, 1946; Shevitz et al, 1976; Freemon, 1976). There is evidence indicating that delirium occurs twice as often in patients over 75 years of age compared to those between the ages of 65 and 74 years (Kay, 1972), but exact data on variations with age are not available. Additionally, reports on sex differences give conflicting data, the ratio of men to women varying between 1 : 1 (Morse and Litin, 1969) and 2 : 1 (Kay, 1972; Simon and Cahan, 1963).

The aetiology of delirium in the elderly has been said to cover virtually the entire spectrum of medical illness (Arie, 1978; Lipowski, 1983; Liston, 1982). Several of the most common medical causes are listed in Table 15.4. However, medications may be the most frequent cause of delirium in older patients (see Table 15.5), possibly because of age related sensitivity of the brain to the effects of drugs, as well as altered pharmacokinetics in geriatric patients (Greenblatt et al, 1982). Several of the most frequent offenders include long-acting minor tranquilizers (Abramowicz, 1981), analgesics (Gotz, 1978; Fraser and Isbell, 1960; Miller, 1975; Wood et al, 1974) antihypertensives (Levenson, 1979), digitalis (Greenblatt and Shader, 1972), cimetidine (Schentag et al, 1979; Jenike, 1982), and drugs with significant anticholinergic activity (Greenblatt and Shader, 1973) such as antidepressants, antiparkinsonian agents, and antihistamines. Table 15.5 includes other well documented agents, but no drug should be excluded from suspicion without a careful history and, if possible, diagnostic trial eliminating the drug temporarily.

In diagnosing delirium, the part of the mental status examination on which to focus includes tests of orientation, attention, and state of arousal, (such as the ability

Table 15.4 Disorders causing delirium in the aged (Reprinted with permission from Liston, 1982)

Central Nervous System disease	
Neoplasm	Primary intracranial neoplasm, metastatic neoplasm — bronchogenic carcinoma, breast carcinoma
Cerebrovascular disease	Arteriosclerosis, cerebral infarction, subarachnoid haemorrhage, transient ischaemic attacks, hypertensive encephalopathy, vasculitis (lupus), cranial arteritis, disseminated intravascular coagulation
Infection	Neurosyphilis, brain abscess, tuberculosis, meningoencephalitis (bacterial, viral, fungal), septic emboli (subacute bacterial endocarditis)
Head trauma	Chronic subdural haematoma, extradural haematoma, cerebral contusion, concussion
Ictal and post-ictal states	Idiopathic seizures, space-occupying lesion, post-traumatic lesions, electroconvulsive therapy
Cardiovascular disease	
Decreased cardiac output	Congestive heart failure, cardiac arrhythmias, aortic stenosis, myocardial infarction
Hypotension	Orthostatic hypotension, vasovagal syncope, hypovolaemia
Metabolic disorders	
Hypoxaemia	Respiratory insufficiency, anaemia, carbon monoxide poisoning
Electrolyte disturbance	Kidney disease, adrenal disease, diabetes mellitus, diuretics, oedematous states, inappropriate secretion of antidiuretic hormone, dehydration, starvation,
Acidosis	Diabetes mellitus, kidney disease, pulmonary disease, chronic diarrhoea
Alkalosis	Hyperadrenalcorticism, pulmonary disease, psychogenic hyperventilation
Hepatic disease	Acute hepatic failure, cirrhosis, chronic portahepatic encephalopathy
Uraemia	Chronic glomerulonephritis, chronic pyelonephritis, acute renal failure, obstructive uropathy
Endocrinopathies	Hypothyroidism, thyrotoxicosis, 'apathetic' hyperthyroidism, hypoglycaemia, hyperglycaemia, hypoparathyroidism, hyperparathyroidism, hypoadrenalcorticism, hyperadrenalcorticism
Deficiency states	Hypovitaminosis-thiamine, nicotinic acid, vitamin B_{12}, folate deficiency, iron deficiency
Other disorders	
Trauma	Burns, surgery, multiple injuries, fractures (fat embolism)
Sensory deprivation	Cataracts, glaucoma, otosclerosis, darkness ('sundown syndrome')
Exogenous toxins	Medications, alcohol, withdrawal syndromes, heavy metals, solvents, insecticides, pesticides, carbon monoxide
Temperature regulation	Exposure and accidental hypothermia, heat stroke, febrile illnesses

to repeat digits in reverse order) all of which are usually abnormal. More than one interview may be necessary to find the clinical features of delirium since the patient's symptoms typically fluctuate throughout the day, leaving the patient mentally clear on occasion. Reports from the nursing staff or a patient's family may prove to be invaluable and should never be ignored. Although not diagnostic, it is of interest that the EEG may reveal generalized slowing in delirium (Engel and Romano, 1959).

Once delirium has been diagnosed, it is of paramount importance to determine the cause as soon as possible. Hospitalization is required unless the aetiology is known or treatment not desired by the patient and family. The basic diagnostic procedures are similar to those described for dementia, and incude the tests listed in Table 15.6 as well as a complete physical examination.

DEMENTIA

ICD-9 defines dementia as: 'Syndromes in which there is impairment of orientation, memory, comprehension,

calculation, learning capacity and judgement. These are the essential features but there may also be shallowness or lability of affect, or a more persistent disturbance of mood, lowering of ethical standards and exaggeration or emergence of personality traits, and diminished capacity for independent decision. (Conditions are) . . . of a chronic or progressive nature, which if untreated are usually irreversible and terminal.'

In the USA, dementia has a similar definition with the important exception that there is no mention of duration or reversibility of disease. In brief, DSM-III (Diagnostic and Statistical Manual of the American Psychiatric Association, 1980) specifies five criteria: (1) loss of intellectual ability resulting in social or occupational impairment, (2) memory impairment, (3) impairment in abstract thinking, judgment, other higher cortical functions or a personality change, (4) clear state of consciousness and (5) documented or presumed evidence of an organic cause. As stated above, dementia is not a single disease but rather a clinical syndrome with a wide variety of possible aetiologies (Small and Jarvik, 1982) as listed in Table 15.7. The most common types

Table 15.5 Common medications causing delirium in the aged (Adapted with permission from Liston, 1982)

Disorder	Medication	Common examples
Cardiovascular conditions	Antiarrhythmics	Procainamide, propranolol, quinidine
	Antihypertensives	Clonidine, methyldopa, reserpine
	Cardiac glycosides	Digitalis
	Coronary vasodilators	Nitrates
Gastrointestinal conditions	Antidiarrhoeals	Atropine, belladonna, homatropine, hyoscyamine, scopolamine
	Antinauseants	Cimetidine, Cyclizine, homatropine-barbiturate preparations, phenothiazines
	Antispasmodics	Methanthelene, propantheline
Musculoskeletal conditions	Anti-inflammatory agents	Corticosteroids, indomethacin, phenylbutazone, salicylates
	Muscle relaxants	Carisoprodol, diazepam
Neurologic-psychiatric conditions	Anticonvulsants	Barbiturates, carbamazepine, diazepam, phenytoin
	Antiparkinsonism agents	Amantadine, benztropine, levopoda, trihexyphenidyl
	Hypnotics and sedatives	Barbiturates, belladonna alkaloids, bromides, chloral hydrate, ethchlorvynol, glutethimide, methaqualone
	Psychotropics	Benzodiazepines, hydroxyzines, lithium salts, meprobamate, monoamine oxidase inhibitors, neuroleptics, tricyclic antidepressants
Respiratory-allergic conditions	Antihistamines	Brompheniramine, chlorpheniramine, cyproheptadine, diphenhydramine, tripelennamine
	Antitussives	opiates, synthetic narcotics
	Decongestants and expectorants	Phenylephrine, phenylpropanolamine, potassium preparations
Miscellaneous conditions	Analgesics	Dextropropoxyphene, opiates, phenacetin, salicylates, synthetic narcotics
	Anaesthetics	Lidocaine, methohexital, methoxyflurane
	Antidiabetic agents	Insulin, oral hypoglycemics
	Antineoplastics	Corticosteroids, mitomycin, procarbazine
	Antituberculosis agents	Isoniazid, rifampin

belong to the primary dementias, i.e. the dementias due to degenerative brain diseases of unknown aetiology. The secondary dementias, i.e. those which result from a recognized aetiology, make up between 5 and 20 per cent of the dementias seen in old age.

Primary dementias

Dementia of the Alzheimer type (DAT)

Dementia of the Alzheimer type (DAT) refers to the clinical syndrome of a slowly progressive dementia of

Table 15.6 The laboratory investigation of dementia

Usually necessary	Often necessary
Complete blood count	Lumbar puncture
Sedimentation rate	Blood cultures
Kidney and liver function	Blood gases
Electrolytes, glucose	Toxic screen
Calcium, phosphorus	
Thyroid function	
B_{12}, folate	
Test for syphilis	
Chest X-ray	
Electrocardiogram	
Electroencephalogram	
Computerized tomography scan of brain	

unknown origin that is accompanied by characteristic pathologic alterations in the brain. Although traditional terminology separates the disease into senile and presenile forms, it is today's widespread belief that both types are part of the same process, which has a variable age of onset. As can be seen in Table 15.7, most studies have shown this process to be responsible for the cognitive decline in about 50 per cent of demented older adults, overall; several authors report that it may occur in association with multi-infarct disease in an additional 18–24 per cent. While the sex distribution remains unclear, it has been suggested that women may be affected up to twice as often as men (Roth, 1978).

Clinically, the typical course begins with anomia, short-term memory loss, and episodes of confusion. As the illness progresses, a general decline in cognition becomes evident and personality changes may occur. In these early stages, there may be diagnostic confusion. Depressive symptoms often predominate, raising the question of the dementia being secondary to depression alone. Patients treated with antidepressants may show improvement in symptoms of dementia, further confusing the diagnosis. Finally, affected individuals become completely disoriented, unable to recognize friends or relatives, with marked confusion, apraxia, agnosia, and aphasia, and totally unable to care for their own personal needs. Aimless wandering, lint picking (carphologia), and incontinence of both urine and faeces are common. Death eventually occurs from some other illness, often sepsis from pneumonia, urinary tract infection, or decubitus ulcers. Focal neurologic signs are absent throughout the disease although rigidity and seizure activity may occur in the final months. Frontal release signs such as snout, suck, palmomental, or grasp reflexes are often present and help confirm an alteration in brain functioning. A complete medical evaluation is important to rule out other causes of dementia, but adds no specific diagnostic confirmation. Whenever the diagnosis is in question, a computerized tomography (CT) scan of the brain is indicated. The purpose of CT scan is to search for a space occupying lesion, such as a brain tumour or subdural haematoma, rather than to look for atrophy, which is suggestive of a dementing process only

Table 15.7 Aetiologies of dementia expressed in percentages (Adapted from Strub R, Black F W 1981 Organic Brain Syndromes: An Introduction to Neurobehavioral Disorders. Davis F A, Philadelphia)

	Year	Number of Patients	Autopsy Study	MID*	NPH*	Mixed PDD/MID	Mass lesion	PDD*	Alcoholic dementia	Hutington disease	Creutzfeldt-Jacob	Other*
Sourander and Sjøgren	1970	258		51	28							21
Tomlinson et al	1970	50	X	50	18	18			2			12
Malamud	1972	1225	X	45†	29	23					3	
Marsden and Harrison	1972	84		56	10		10	6	7	4	4	3
Pearce and Miller	1973	63		92			3					3
Todorov et al	1975	675	X	40	29	24						7
Freemon	1976	60		43	8		3	12	7	7		20
Harrison and Marsden	1977	49		44	12		5	7	9			23
Smith and Kiloh	1981	164		50	14		2	5	19	3		7

* PDD = Primary degenerative dementia; MID = Multi-infarct dementia; NPH = Normal pressure hydrocephalus; Other includes chronic drug toxicity, post-trauma, post-subarachnoid haemorrhage, encephalitis, syphilis, subdural haematoma, hypothyroidism, depression, etc.
† Comprised of Alzheimer disease (42 per cent) and Pick disease (3 per cent).

when the distribution of the atrophy is unusual or asymmetric, or when the degree of atrophy far exceeds the age correction. EEG's tend to show generalized slowing and delta waves in patients with DAT, while focal abnormalities are more often seen in multi-infarct dementia or due to space occupying lesions.

Since the neuropathology and neurochemistry of the aging brain are well covered in chapter 14 of this textbook, we will not attempt to duplicate the material. We would like, however, to review several important points about DAT, a disease which may be aetiologically heterogeneous.

While the macroscopic pathologic finding of atrophy and ventricular enlargement that was considered highly suggestive of DAT in the past has also been found in age matched normals (Tomlinson et al, 1970; Bondareff et al, 1981), it has recently been suggested that weight and external size may not be adequate measures of atrophy since a sophisticated point-counting morphometric measurement was employed by Hubbard and Anderson (1981) to demonstrate a significant difference in several localized areas in brains from patients with DAT. The traditional method of definitive diagnosis of DAT has been to find the characteristic senile plaques, neurofibrillary tangles, and granulovacuolar degeneration of neurons on microscopic examination of selected brain areas — especially the hippocampus and cortex. The debate on these changes being specific to DAT or occurring also in normal elderly has not been resolved. These changes may represent a secondary reaction to a disease state, rather than a primary manifestation of DAT, as may also be true with the elevated concentration of aluminium in cells from the brain of a patient with DAT. It is important to remember, however, that in addition to the pathologic changes described above, the diagnosis of DAT must also include examination of enough of the brain to insure the absence of the minimum of 50 ml of stroke softened brain tissue, described by Roth (1978), which would suggest a mixed aetiology consisting of multi-infarct dementia in addition to DAT. Furthermore, infarcts that do occur must not be situated in areas critical to brain functioning such as the hippocampus or corpus callosum. Evidence of old trauma (Consellis, 1978) tumours, or suggestions of infection, would also prohibit a clear diagnosis of DAT despite consistent pathologic findings.

The widely accepted neurochemical finding of decreased cholinergic activity in DAT (Davies and Maloney, 1976; Davis et al, 1981; McGeer, 1978; Perry et al, 1977; Terry and Davies, 1980) was supported in one small autopsy series (Whitehouse et al, 1981) by the finding of a highly significant loss of neurons in the nucleus basalis (the major source of brain cholinergic innervation). The specificity of cholinergic neurotransmitter deficiencies was brought into question, however,

when a different group (Bondareff et al, 1982) reported an equally striking loss of 80 per cent of the neurons in the locus coeruleus (the major source of noradrenergic brain innervation) in another small autopsy series of patients with apparent DAT. In any case, the attempt to correct the cognitive dysfunction seen in DAT by increasing brain neurotransmitters (especially acetylcholine) has not been clinically successful and is discussed further in chapter 14.

The genetic deficit in DAT has not as yet been established. Postulated modes of inheritance include autosomal dominant with reduced penetrance and polygenic. It may be that there are aetiologically distinct subgroups of DAT with different modes of transmission. Clearly, families exist with sporadic forms as well as others with familial patterns. Heston et al (1981), has suggested that the risk of inheritance increases as a function of the severity of illness in the affected family member. A recent review (Matsuyama and Jarvik, 1982) combined data from several studies (one twin and eleven family studies in the literature) to recompute the morbidity risk for siblings based on 1146 siblings of 265 probands. They report a risk for siblings of 7.5 per cent up to 80 years and 11 per cent at age 85 with a probable further increase at older ages. Overall the risk appears to be three times that of the general population. A more positive way of looking at the same data was suggested by the calculation that at least 80 per cent of the siblings of an affected individual will be free of the disease even if they live to age 85.

Dementia due to Pick's disease

Pick's disease is a rare form of primary degenerative dementia (Table 15.7), well-known in the literature (Sjogren et al, 1952; Kahn and Thompson, 1934; Robertson et al, 1958; Stengel, 1943; Malamud and Waggoner, 1943; Schenk, 1959), but uncommonly recognized in clinical practice. This syndrome is often mistakenly diagnosed as DAT because of several similarities including age of onset, slowly progressive course, and lack of focal neurologic signs. Separation may, however, occasionally be possible early on, because of the characteristic pattern in Pick's disease of personality change and inappropriate social behaviour, in the relative absence of the anomia and memory loss usually seen in DAT. Patients with Pick's disease are usually unaware of these alterations, in contrast to patients with DAT in whom some degree of insight is generally preserved.

The clinical symptoms of Pick's disease may be explained by the predilection of the disease for the temporal and frontal lobes with relative sparing of the parietal areas. Thus, parietal signs often seen in DAT, such as agnosia, aphasia, and apraxia, are initially rare, while behavioural disturbances are prominent. At the current time, the CT scan may give a clue to the occurrence of Pick's dementia if atrophy is localized to the frontal and temporal lobes, but it is not diagnostic since an exact diagnosis can only be made postmortem. Several authors, however, have suggested that cerebral blood flow studies provide an acceptable in vivo measure of the dementia (Ingvar et al, 1978; Wisniewski et al, 1972). Further work in this area using positron emission tomography (PET scan) is in progress and may provide an adequate means of diagnosis in the near future.

Pathologically, the disease is characterized by symmetrical atrophy of the frontal and temporal lobes, the presence of Pick and Hirano bodies, and the relative absence of neurofibrillary tangles and plaques. The aetiology of the dementia remains unknown although a major study of the disorder described an autosomal dominant mode of inheritance with high penetrance (Sjogren et al, 1952). At the current time, only symptomatic treatment is available and the course of the dementia is similar to that of Alzheimer's disease, with a slowly progressive deterioration over one or two decades.

Dementia due to Creutzfeldt-Jakob disease

Creutzfeldt-Jakob disease is a very rare cause of dementia — one case per million in England and Wales (Matthews, 1975). Its importance lies in the scientific implications of its aetiology. Evidence suggesting an infectious aetiology includes the ability of brain suspensions from affected individuals to produce a spongiform encephalopathy in squirrel monkeys and a scrapie-like syndrome in goats, as well as intracerebral inoculation transferring the disease to chimpanzees and other laboratory animals (Gajdusek, 1977; Gibbs and Gajdusek, 1978; Merz et al, 1983). There are also reports of apparently accidental inter-human transmission, once by corneal transplantation (Duffy et al, 1974) and twice through the use of stereotaxic brain implants (Bernoulli et al, 1977). The infectious agent, presumably a virus, has not as yet been cultured. There has been concern about exposure among medical and laboratory personnel (Berncolli et al, 1977; Duffy et al, 1974; and Gajdusek et al, 1974). Although epidemiologic data have not demonstrated such a relationship, the concern would appear to be justified because of the reported resistance of this virus to boiling, ultraviolet irradiation, formaldehyde, proteases, and nucleases (Gajdusek, 1977). Brain pathology includes neuronal degeneration, extensive gliosis, and a spongy appearance of the grey matter with relative sparing of the parietal and occipital lobes.

A genetic aetiology (cf review by Matsuyama and Jarvik, 1980) is supported by reports of several families with an autosomal dominant pattern of inheritance (Brown et al, 1979a; May et al, 1968). Additionally, in 10 per cent of 449 cases summarized by Brown and

colleagues (1979b), at least one other family member was affected. Familial cases may be the result of a viral infection superimposed on a pre-existing genetically determined dysfunction or vulnerability.

Typically, the onset of the disease is between 50 and 60 years of age, although cases have been described in adults as young as 21 or as old as 79 years (May et al, 1968). Although symptomatology of the disease may be quite variable, initial symptoms such as fatigue, anxiety, apathy, irritability, and confusion are often followed by severe dementia and prominent neurological manifestations including myoclonic jerking, severe rigidity, motor tract damage, and asymmetric reflexes. Brown and colleagues (1979b) described a series of 124 cases where 39 per cent had a single presenting symptom; of these, the initial symptom was moderate to severe asthenia in 23 per cent, weight loss in 15 per cent, and sleep disturbance in 14 per cent. Once the dementia begins, death usually occurs within 6 to 9 months according to Roos and Johnson (1977) based on a series of autopsy confirmed cases.

While the rapid progression and various neurologic signs often make the diagnosis quite clear, occasional cases may be atypical. The EEG is frequently helpful since it is said to be abnormal in 90 per cent of cases (Haase, 1977). Initially, it has the characteristic appearance of diffuse slowing with occasional asymmetry, soon followed by the typical pattern of high voltage bursts of biphasic and triphasic slow waves (Haase, 1977). Spinal fluid examinations, however, are of little use in confirming the diagnosis, since unlike most conventional viruses, no inflammatory response occurs, and the spinal fluid is essentially free of cells and without elevation of protein (Gajdusek, 1977). Similarly, CT scans have not been helpful.

To date, there is no specific treatment for any aspect of Creutzfeldt-Jakob disease.

Dementia due to Huntington's disease

Huntington's disease is a familial disorder of unknown aetiology with an autosomal dominant pattern of inheritance manifesting apparently complete penetrance. The recent suggestion (Myers et al, 1983) of a maternally transmitted factor in late onset cases remains to be confirmed. The reported incidence is between two and seven per 100 000 (Heathfield, 1973). Usually the age at onset is in the mid-40s, but has been known to be as high as the 70s (Myrianthopoulos, 1966).

Classically, Huntington's disease begins with choreiform movements that resemble tardive dyskinesia, followed by personality changes and eventually dementia. The dementia may predate the movement disorder (Brackenridge, 1971). Early cognitive changes include a predominant loss of frontal lobe executive functions (e.g. the ability to plan and organize), while the cortical disturbances typically seen in Alzheimer's disease (e.g. amnesia, apraxia, aphasia, agnosia, and loss of insight) are usually absent (Aminoff et al, 1975; Caine et al, 1978). Muscle stretch reflexes increased in more than two-thirds of patients, with actual pathologic reflexes or clonus occurring in one-third (Otman and Friedman, 1961). Psychomotor retardation is also characteristic. It appears likely that the aetiology of Huntington's disease relates to neurotransmitter deficiencies in the caudate nucleus of the basal ganglia, including gamma aminobutyric acid (GABA) and possibly acetylcholine. A careful family history is essential. While there is still no specific treatment for this disorder, localization of the gene on chromosome 4, makes it likely that within the next few years it will be possible to identify carriers, of the gene long before they develop the disease.

Trials of L-Dopa have reportedly elicited movement disorders in apparently normal carriers of the gene, prior to the onset of any symptoms (Klawans et al, 1972). This diagnostic test has been challenged, however, since at least three cases of false negatives are now known (Myers et al, 1982). Currently, treatment consists primarily of the use of major tranquillizers to reduce the choreiform movements and temporarily improve the characteristic emotional instability and occasional psychosis. The progressive dementia cannot be stopped and death usually occurs within 15 years of the onset of the disease (Haase, 1977).

Dementia associated with Parkinson's disease

According to several authors, dementia occurs so frequently in patients with Parkinson's disease (incidence up to 80 per cent) (Martin et al, 1973; Marttila and Rinne, 1976; Sweet et al, 1976; Celesia and Wanamaker, 1972; Sroka et al, 1981) that it should be considered part of the basic Parkinsonian pathology. Others have disputed this claim and believe that the coexistence of the relatively common disorders (Parkinson's disease and Alzheimer type or multi-infarct dementia) explains the observed frequency of dementia. Others still, have reported histologic features of Alzheimer's disease to occur in 42 per cent (Boller et al, 1980) and 97 per cent (Hakim and Mathieson, 1979) of pathologic specimens from cases of clinically documented Parkinson's disease. According to classical thinking, the dementia associated with Parkinson's disease seems to follow rather than precede the prominent symptoms of the movement disorder allowing Parkinson's disease to be removed from the differential diagnosis of the dementia in any patient without clear neurologic signs. More recently, however, research findings have pointed to the simultaneous onset of both the mental and the motor symptoms (Mortimer et al, 1982).

The clinical features of the dementia associated with Parkinson's disease have also been described in conflicting terms, some authors (Asso, 1969; Loranger et al, 1972) stressing the relative preservation of memory and language thus differentiating it from Alzheimer type dementia, and others (Albert, 1977; Haaland and Matthews, 1977) emphasizing the decline in these same functions. In addition to changes in cognition, patients with Parkinson's disease tend to have a significantly higher incidence of depression than other physically disabled patients of similar age (Haaland and Matthews, 1977; Horn, 1974). When the depression precedes the other symptoms, it is usually treated with tricyclic antidepressants. The anticholinergic effects of these drugs may mask some of the Parkinsonian symptoms thus delaying the diagnosis. Other medications also confuse the association between dementia and Parkinson's disease. Extrapyramidal symptoms (EPS) of the Parkinsonian type may occur in patients with dementia under treatment with major tranquilizers (e.g. haloperidol). Treatment of EPS or true Parkinson's disease with anticholinergic medication may further impair cognition and should be avoided whenever possible in patients with dementia. Dopamine precursors, (e.g. L-dopa), while being the best treatment for true Parkinson's disease and the least likely to reduce cognition through an anticholinergic action, may cause episodes of confusion, or generally impair mental functioning (Barbeau, 1971; Goodwin, 1971). The early concept suggesting that the degree of dementia correlated with the amount of movement disorder (Riklan et al, 1959) prompted studies of the possible reversal of dementia by L-dopa. To date, several studies (Loranger et al, 1972; Marsh et al, 1971; Yahr et al, 1969) have failed to demonstrate any improvement in mood or cognition following reduction in Parkinsonian motor symptoms by the use of L-dopa.

Secondary dementias

Multi-infarct dementia

Less than two decades ago most clinicians believed the majority of dementias to be due to cerebral atherosclerosis. Currently, few believe that cerebral atherosclerosis is a significant cause of dementia in old age. Several authors are responsible for this shift in opinion, most notably Hachinski and colleagues (1974) who state: 'Progressive involvement of cerebral arteries by atherosclerosis does not critically stenose them and does not produce mental impairment; hence the term 'cerebral atherosclerosis' as applied to mental deterioration in the elderly is misleading and inaccurate . . . When vascular disease is responsible for dementia it is through the occurrence of multiple small or large cerebral infarcts.' According to Roth (1978) dementia occurs when 50–100 ml of cortical or subcortical areas have been softened by infarction. Multi-infarct dementia has now become the term for vascular dementias. This form of dementia can be differentiated from dementia of the Alzheimer type by its more sudden onset, focal neurologic signs, frequent association with hypertension, and step-wise decline in intellectual functioning (Fisher, 1968; Hachinski et al, 1974).

The statistics concerning the incidence of multi-infarct dementia are confusing, and vary from 8 to 29 per cent of all dementias. A review of nine well-known studies (see Table 15.7) suggests that lower incidences of multi-infarct dementia are reported when studies are based on clinical rather than on pathologic diagnosis. Possible reasons for this discrepancy include a lower incidence of autopsies for patients with primary degenerative than with multi-infarct dementia, a shorter lifespan for patients with vascular than with Alzheimer-type dementia, and the inclusion in pathologic studies of patients with major motor or clinically significant strokes who are generally excluded from clinical studies of progressive dementia. In our own clinical experience at our tertiary care geropsychiatry centre, the number of patients with pure multi-infarct dementia is far below the commonly quoted 18 per cent (Tomlinson et al, 1970) and much more like the 8 per cent reported by Freemon (1976). Regardless of the exact frequency of multi-infarct dementia, risk factors for stroke exist, and are essentially similar to those for cardiovascular disease. They include smoking, obesity, hyperlipidaemia, carotid bruits, atrial fibrillation, diabetes, history of cardiovascular disease, family history of cardiovascular disease, and especially hypertension. Men have a higher incidence than women (in the USA) for reasons that remain unclear, although a genetic contribution has been suggested (Matsuyama and Jarvik, 1980; Jarvik and Matsuyama, 1983).

In an attempt to reduce the diagnostic confusion between multi-infarct and Alzheimer-type dementia, Hachinski and colleagues (1975) developed an ischaemia rating scale, the score of which was intended to separate the two disorders. This scale was later modified by Rosen and associates (Table 15.8) according to data in their autopsy study of 14 patients (Rosen et al, 1980). The ischaemia scale is currently in everyday use and may prove to be more reliable than the CT scan, which often misses small infarctions. However, both clinical and autopsy validations are notable for their scarcity (Liston and La Rue, in press).

There have been no specific treatments, to date, with demonstrated efficacy in reversing the cognitive deficits of multi-infarct dementia (see chapter 17). There are, however, several measures which can be taken to reduce the likelihood of further progression. These include the reduction of risk factors, especially hypertension, and, whenever possible, the removal of embolic sources, such

Table 15.8 Clinical features of the modified Hachinski ischaemia score (Adapted from Rosen et al, 1980)

Feature	Point values
Abrupt onset	2
Stepwise deterioration	1
Somatic complaints	1
Emotional incontinence	1
History or presence of hypertension	1
History of strokes	2
Focal neurological symptoms	2
Focal neurological signs	2

A score of 4 or more is consistent with multi-infarct dementia

as carotid plaques and irregular cardiac rhythm. Large studies attempted to look at the potential of reducing the rate of stroke by the use of aspirin or sulfinpyrazone effects on platelets (Canadian Cooperative Study, 1978), but the studies did not deal with the problem of cognitive impairment. At least one small scale pilot study conducted under double-blind conditions, has demonstrated the lack of progression of an unseparated group of patients with dementia who were given warfarin (Ratner et al, 1972). Because of the likelihood that long-term anticoagulation will reduce the risk of further infarctions, many clinicians, including our own group, are prescribing aspirin in small doses (e.g. 30 mg every other day) to patients at risk. Geriatric psychiatry centres, including our own, tend to engage in clinical trials of new drugs in the hope of finding one which will unambiguously reduce or eliminate further infarctions.

Dementia due to normal pressure hydrocephalus
Two decades ago, interest in normal pressure hydrocephalus as a cause of dementia was stimulated by Adams and collaborators when they described a group of demented patients with normal spinal fluid pressure whose cognitive state improved following the shunting of fluid away from the ventricles (Hakim and Adams, 1965; Adams et al, 1965; McHugh, 1964). Since that time, the classic clinical triad of dementia, gait apraxia, and urinary incontinence has become widely popularized as one which is surgically reversible. The aetiology is often idiopathic, but the disorder has also been associated with many neurologic conditions (including tumour, stroke, subarachnoid haemorrhage, trauma, and infection).

The syndrome typically develops over weeks to months, beginning with a small-stepped apraxic gait and marked imbalance, in association with behavioural changes characteristic of frontal lobe disease (e.g., apathy, euphoria, irritability, or social disinhibition — Ojemann et al, 1969). Patients tend to be slow, cognitively dull, and mildly forgetful. Hyperactive reflexes, especially in the legs, are common along with Babinski signs. Urinary frequency or urgency may occur early in the disease. When neurologic signs occur in the absence of severe memory problems or emotional changes, patients are readily distinguished from those with dementia of the Alzheimer type, where minimal neurologic signs with prominent memory and behavioural disturbances are the rule. Later on, when dementia, urinary incontinence, and primitive reflexes (e.g. palmomental, suck, and grasp) occur in normal pressure hydrocephalus the differential diagnosis becomes increasingly difficult.

In general, the clinical features of normal pressure hydrocephalus result from enlargement of the anterior horns of the lateral ventricles and compression of the surrounding areas. Behavioural changes are typical of frontal lobe damage, while the gait, reflex, and bladder changes can theoretically be explained by the stretching and subsequent malfunction of the motor fibers to the legs and the autonomic tract, both of which run in close proximity to the anterior horns (Yakovlev, 1947). This significant anatomical correlation appears to explain why the best predictor of response in a large review series (62 patients) was the presence of the complete triad of dementia, gait disturbance, and urinary incontinence (Black, 1980). In this same study, 61 per cent of patients with the three classical signs showed significant improvement after shunting, while in 11 of the 13 patients who fully recovered, preoperative CT scans demonstrated the traditional findings of ventricular dilation without significant cortical atrophy. Surprisingly, response could not be correlated with age, degree of impairment, or duration of illness.

Another study (Fisher, 1976) of 30 patients who went to surgery, revealed that 75 per cent of the patients who responded had gait disturbances with minimal dementia preoperatively, while 81 per cent of treatment failures had prominent dementia. Several authors suggest that the best candidates for ventricular shunting are those with substantial gait disturbance, yet minimal cognitive change (Jacobs et al, 1976; Fisher, 1976; Shenkin et al, 1973). Early detection and intervention is said to be important since according to some (Jacobs et al, 1976) the degree of improvement is inversely proportional to the length of time the patient's symptoms have been present. Overall, 50 per cent of patients appropriately selected should demonstrate some improvement. Patients should be chosen carefully, however, since complications such as subdural haematoma and infection are common. The reason that shunting works remains elusive since the CSF pressure is initially normal, but most authorities suspect that cerebral decompression is somehow accomplished.

Once the diagnosis has been suggested by the clinical picture, the CT scan should be performed. Although not definitive, the classic appearance is prominent ventricular dilation in the absence of cortical atrophy. The lack of atrophy is explained by the space occupying effect of the enlarged ventricular horns pushing outwards. In the typical case, there are no sulcal markings and the width across the frontal horns of the lateral ventricles is said to be greater than 53 mm (Fisher, 1978). The next step in the evaluation should be the assessment of CSF pressure and flow dynamics, using a spinal tap and cisternogram, where a radioactive albumin tracer is injected into the subarachnoid space and the flow followed by several subsequent brain scans. Since the deficit is characterized by a decrease in absorption of the cerebrospinal fluid, an abnormal cisternogram is one where the tracer enters the ventricles within the usual 6 hours, but fails to circulate out of the ventricle within 24 hours (Benson et al, 1970; Lowry et al, 1977; Mathew et al, 1975). The procedure is not diagnostically definitive since many patients with dementia of the Alzheimer type will also demonstrate alterations in CSF flow dynamics (Sohn et al, 1973; Coblentz et al, 1973). At least one author (Fisher, 1978) has advocated the therapeutic removal of 20–25 ml of CSF and subsequent observation of the patient's clinical status for a week or two, with surgical shunting generally reserved for those patients who demonstrate unequivocal improvement. Although it is difficult to understand why this procedure should work since the amount of CSF removed is expected to be replaced within a few hours, it may be that the brief decrease in pressure allows the absorption of CSF to be normalized for a more prolonged period. In any case, the best patients for shunting are those who have a rapid clinical deterioration with the typical features of urinary incontinence, gait apraxia, dementia, markedly enlarged ventricles on CT scans, and abnormal cisternograms.

Dementia induced by drugs

The frequency of dementia due to prescription or over-the-counter medications is unknown, but generally considered so high that drugs are considered among the leading causes of secondary dementias. Contributing to the high frequency of drug induced dementia are the older patient's altered pharmacokinetics (Greenblatt et al, 1982), the high frequency of drug use in the upper age groups (Blaschke et al, 1981), and the age associated increased incidence of drug–drug and drug–disease interactions (Hurwitz, 1969; MacLennan, 1974). Moreover, geriatric patients appear to show increased vulnerability of higher cortical functions to the effects of medication unrelated to pharmacokinetics or patterns of usage.

Although every drug may potentially cause cognitive impairment, several classes of medications are more frequent offenders. Long-acting minor tranquillizers, such as diazepam and flurazepam (Abramowicz, 1981), have a much greater degree of accumulation in older patients than in younger adults with a subsequent build-up in blood levels over several weeks. Dementia, as well as delirium, sedation, ataxia and falling episodes may result. Analgesics (Fraser and Isbell, 1960; Gotz, 1978; Miller, 1975; Wood et al, 1974) of both the narcotic and non-narcotic type, may produce idiosyncratic cognitive impairment in elderly patients whose overall functioning has already been compromised by pre-existing physical disease or marginal mental reserve. Digitalis (Greenblatt and Shader, 1972) may cause cognitive change in a patient recently begun on it, as well as in patients who have been clinically maintained on a stable dose, the latter being due to the age-related reduction in renal clearance. Cimetidine (Jenike, 1982; Schentag et al, 1979), anti-hypertensive (Levenson, 1979), and anti-arrhythmic agents are all frequently prescribed for older patients. Each is capable of producing dementia. Drugs with a significant amount of anticholinergic activity (Greenblatt and Shader, 1973), including anti-depressants, antiparkinsonian agents, antihistamines, and non-prescription sedative/hypnotics, may produce dementia or delirium in an older patient without the other signs so typical of anticholinergic psychosis in younger patients (i.e., tachycardia, pupillary dilation, and facial flushing).

Usually, when questions arise concerning the role of a certain drug in the psychiatric symptoms exhibited by a geriatric patient, the preferred course of action is to eliminate the suspected agent and observe the patient closely for up to several weeks (depending on the half-life of the drug). Occasions do arise, however, when such action may not be in the best interest of the patient. Other approaches include the use of short-acting narcotic antagonists to assess the contribution of narcotic analgesics in producing cognitive impairment manifested by geriatric patients receiving such medication. These antagonists reverse not only the pain relieving action of narcotics, but also their effects on blood pressure and cognition. Similarly, physostigmine, a short-acting cholinergic agonist, may be administered under controlled conditions, to establish the role of anticholinergic medications in the production of a patient's altered mental functioning. Checking blood levels of medications (such as digitalis or anti-arrhythmics) and substituting agents with similar effects but alternative mechanisms of action are basic strategies in the evaluation of potentially drug-induced dementias.

Alcohol-induced dementia

Alcohol is a powerful neurotoxin, the chronic heavy use of which results in alterations in brain function in any age group. While these may be demonstrable clinically, they are more often detectable by neuropsychologic testing and possibly computerized cranial tomography (Wells, 1982). Moreover, these abnormalities appear independent of malnutrition, head trauma, or liver failure.

Basically, there are two types of chronic psychiatric disturbances. The first and best known is Korsakoff's syndrome. In this condition, often confused with dementia in older patients, there is an amnestic syndrome (DSM-III) with alterations in memory and new learning. It is not a dementia because of the restriction of the mental status changes. While it has generally been considered that this amnestic disorder is related to thiamine deficiency (Seltzer and Sherwin, 1978), it has become clear that not all chronic alcoholics develop this syndrome. It has been suggested that some drinkers are especially vulnerable due to a genetically transmitted transketolase deficiency (Blass and Gibson, 1977). In any case, the evaluation of amnesia in an older chronic alcoholic should include a search for other possible causes of amnesia (e.g. stroke and tumour).

Cutting (1978) has described an alcoholic dementia, with a gradually progressive dementing course and diffuse cerebral dysfunction, which may occur more frequently in older patients than Korsakoff's syndrome and has a higher incidence in women than in men. While it is not clear how much of alcoholic dementia or Korsakoff's syndrome will improve with cessation of drinking, clinical lore suggests that abstinence will halt the progression of both.

Dementia due to major depressive disorder

Depression in an older patient may be severe enough to actually interfere with normal cognition and produce the syndrome of dementia. While the original labelling of this form of dementia as 'pseudodementia' (Kiloh, 1961) drew much needed attention to its existence and the importance of prompt treatment, experience since then has made clear that it is as true a dementia as any other secondary dementia, with typical symptoms and a reversible cause (Post, 1975; Small and Jarvik, 1982). The frequency of this form of dementia ranges from under one per cent in tertiary referral centers to up to 20 per cent in the community (Small et al, 1981).

With a careful history and clinical examination, depression can often be separated from dementia. Several common features of dementia secondary to depression are listed in Table 15.9. Depressed patients tend to have a history of depression, poor motivation, decreased concentration, and make minimal efforts to compensate for any cognitive disturbance.

Because of the difficulty in distinguishing dementia secondary to depression from other types of dementia, a search has been under way to identify a biologic marker that would be capable of this task. The dexamethasone suppression test, recently widely studied in psychiatry, has been proposed as such a marker. Unfor-

Table 15.9 Clinical features of dementia secondary to depression (pseudodementia) and primary dementia (Adapted from Wells C E: The differential diagnosis of psychiatric disorders in the elderly, in Cole J O, Barrett J E (Eds): Psychopathology in the Aged, Raven Press, New York, 1980*)

	Dementia secondary to depression	Primary dementia
Duration of symptoms before physician consulted	Short	Long
Onset can be dated with some precision	Usual	Unusual
Family aware of dysfunction and severity	Usual	Variable (rare in early stages, usual in late stages)
Rapid progression of symptoms	Usual	Unusual
History of prior psychopathology	Usual	Unusual
Patient's complaints of cognitive loss	Emphasized	Variable (minimized in later stages)
Patient's description of cognitive loss	Detailed	Vague
Patient's disability	Emphasized	Variable minimized in later stages)
Patient's valuation of accomplishments	Minimized	Variable
Patient's efforts in attempting to perform tasks	Small	Great
Patient's efforts to cope with dysfunction	Minimal	Maximal
Patient's emotional reaction	Great distress	Variable (unconcerned in later stages)
Patient's affect	Depressed	Labile, blunted or depressed
Loss of social skills	Early	Late
Behaviour congruent with severity of cognitive loss	Unusual	Usual
Attention and concentration	Often good	Often poor
'Don't know' answers	Usual	Unusual
'Near miss' answers	Unusual	Variable (usual in later stages)
Memory loss for recent versus remote events	About equal	Greater
Specific memory gaps ('patchy memory loss')	Usual	Unusual
Performance on tasks of similar difficulty	Variable	Consistent

* Wells lists the characteristics of the later stages. In our clinical experience these manifestations are variable early in the course of dementia and are helpful in the differential diagnosis only if they are in the direction seen in later stages of dementia.

tunately, at least two groups (Spar and Gerner, 1982; Raskind et al, 1982) reported that serum cortisol failed to be suppressed by dexamethasone administration in up to one-half of all patients with Alzheimer type dementia even in the absence of any recognizable symptoms of depression. Until a reliable and accurate method of identifying dementia secondary to depression is found, patients should receive antidepressant treatment whenever the possibility of depression exists.

Dementia due to metabolic disturbances
A wide variety of metabolic disorders may be responsible for the production of dementia in elderly patients. These include liver failure (Victor et al, 1965), renal failure (Ryan et al, 1980), hyperglycaemia (Gautier-Smith, 1965; Heilman and Fisher, 1974), and hyperlipidaemic conditions. Disorders of fluid and electrolytes, especially hypercalcaemia, extreme alterations in sodium, and general dehydration (Jana and Romano-Jana, 1973; Seymour et al, 1980), are common causes of dementia in older patients. Interestingly, the degree of calcium elevation need not correlate with the severity

of the dementia (Weizman et al, 1979) and may depend on the patient's underlying vulnerability. Nursing home patients, especially when on tube feedings, tend to develop dementia as well as aspiration pneumonia secondary to dehydration.

In addition to the dementias related to tube feedings, nutritional deficiencies may produce dementias in geriatric patients through several other mechanisms including B-12 and folate depletion (Shulman, 1967; Strachan and Henderson, 1967). The B-12 deficiency has actually been reported to produce cognitive impairment in the absence of the typical changes expected in the bone marrow and peripheral blood (Strachan and Henderson, 1965). While the reversibility of the dementia these two vitamin deficiencies can produce has not been firmly established, clinical lore suggests that the longer the cognitive impairment has been present, the worse the prognosis.

Hormonal alterations can produce the dementia syndrome in geriatric patients through both primary and secondary effects (Lavis, 1981). These include parathyroid excesses (Weizman et al, 1979) and deficiencies

(Hyldstrup et al, 1981), thyroid excesses (Bulens, 1981) and deficiencies (Jellinek, 1962), cortisol excess (Whelan et al, 1980), and hypopituitarism (Hanna, 1970). Other hormones may also play a role but have not been as clearly documented to date.

Dementia due to space occupying lesions

Since different areas of the brain are responsible for specific functions such as motor activity, sensation, hearing, vision, memory, and personality, it is easily understood why physically compromising the space occupied by a section of the brain can produce an alteration in the function controlled by that area of the brain. The major causes of space occupying lesions in older patients are tumours (especially metastases), and haematomas produced either by stroke or trauma.

These three types of space-occupying lesions causing dementia can often be distinguished by clinical history. For malignancies, the history usually reveals other symptoms and physical signs; for stroke, hypertension and abrupt onset; while trauma often has the history of a fall. There is little reason to miss these diagnoses since they are generally apparent with the use of computerized tomography. Most of the causes of dementia on the basis of a space occupying lesion are potentially treatable, although few of us would be so bold as to encourage neurosurgery in a patient who has been profoundly demented for many years.

Cardiovascular-anoxic dementia

A variety of myocardial diseases has been reported to produce the clinical picture of dementia (Small and Jarvik, 1982; Rosenberg, 1981). It is tempting to believe that the dementia reported with acute myocardial infarction (Pathy, 1967), heart block (Dalessio et al, 1965), dysrhythmia (McCarthy and Wollner, 1977), and atrial myxoma (Hutton, 1981), is a result of cerebral anoxia. However, marked reduction in cerebral perfusion does not always appear to accompany the cognitive deficit, and the relationship between primary cardiac pathology and dementia remains in dispute (Emerson et al, 1981; McCarthy and Wollner, 1981). With advanced pulmonary disease, however, decreased cerebral oxygenation does appear to be an aetiologic factor in cognitive impairment (Austen et al, 1957). Improvement in dementia may be expected in patients with advanced obstructive pulmonary disease following oxygen supplementation.

Dementia due to infections

Although generalized infections with sepsis usually produce delirium rather than dementia, infections of the central nervous system, including meningitis (Dodge and Swartz, 1965), encephalitis (Glaser et al, 1968), and brain abscesses (Tarkkanen, 1963) may produce the picture of dementia through their localized effects on the brain. Tuberculosis and neurosyphilis (Nordenbo and Sorensen, 1981) can produce a wide variety of psychiatric symptoms including personality change, depression, hallucinations, and dementia. If an infectious aetiology is suspected as a cause of dementia, examination of spinal fluid becomes a virtual necessity.

It is important to remember that symptoms of delirium or dementia appearing in a patient undergoing antimicrobial treatment may indicate a reaction to the medication (e.g. penicillin or anti-fungal agents) rather than a spread of the infection to the central nervous system, sepsis, or a response to fever alone.

Subcortical dementias

Subcortical dementias denote a current concept promulgated primarily by Albert (1978) and by Cummings and Benson (1983) with the aim of separating the dementias into two main types: cortical and subcortical. The concept has found increasing prominence in the United States. The subcortical dementias include: Parkinson's disease, Huntington's disease, normal pressure hydrocephalus, and metabolic states. These dementias are characterized by symptoms which could be approximated by lesions in subcortical areas of the brain. By contrast, cortical dementias (e.g. DAT and Pick's disease) produce a clinical picture consonant with the disruption of cortical cells. Some dementias must be considered mixed, because symptoms mimic lesions in either cortical or subcortical areas. This last group would include dementias due to multiple infarcts or infections. A comparison of the clinical features seen in the cortical and subcortical dementias is contained in Table 15.10. The reader is referred to the work of Cummings and Benson (1983) for further details.

Table 15.10 Clinical features in cortical and sub-cortical dementias

Cortical dementias	Subcortical dementias
Aphasia	Slowing of cognition
Amnesia	Forgetfulness
Apraxia	'Dilapidation of intellect'*
Agnosia	Affective disturbance
Normal motor function and reflexes until late in the disease	Movement disorder
Normal speech	Dysarthria

* (Cummings and Benson, 1983)

Treatment of dementia

Definitive

To date, unfortunately, there are no known definitive treatments for any of the primary dementias or for the deficits in mentation that occur as a result of multiple infarcts, although reduction of the risk factors for stroke may prevent the progression. The drug therapy of cerebral dysfunction is discussed in chapter 17.

In most secondary forms of dementia as well as delirium, definitive treatment consists of attempts to correct the underlying dysfunction. For example, hypothyroid-induced dementia is treated by thyroid replacement. Specific treatment of delirium that accompanies pneumonia is directed towards elimination of the infection. Dementia or delirium resulting from digitalis intoxication will abate with the reduction of the toxic serum level. Normal pressure hydrocephalus producing dementia will often reverse with successful shunting of CSF. Dementia due to depression will often respond to antidepressant treatment, and so on.

Symptomatic
Despite the lack of definitive treatment for the most frequently encountered forms of dementia, many of the symptoms respond to treatment. Some, like the anxiety and agitation often accompanying dementia or delirium, require calm understanding, compassion, explanation, and attempts at reorientation. Even patients whose comprehension appears totally lacking often grasp the nurse's or physician's benevolent intent and feel reassured. A familiar person, reduction of external stimuli, and a relaxing atmosphere will often be enough to get a patient through a troubled period. The cause of the patient's irritation should be uncovered, listened to, and if possible, removed. If these measures are ineffective, more aggressive measures must be taken (including restraint and tranquillization), particularly for patients who are out of control and a danger to themselves or others. The medications of choice are potent major tranquillizers — such as haloperidol. Other major tranquillizers are equally effective, but patients who are demented or physically ill seldom can tolerate the added sedation that accompanies the less potent agents. When necessary, small doses of major tranquillizers as discussed above, or occasionally short-acting minor tranquillizers — such as oxazepam 10 to 15 mg every 8 hours, or lorazepam 0.5 to 1 mg every 12 hours — can be continued for a few days and the symptoms reassessed. Occasional patients may, however, experience a worsening of symptoms with minor tranquillizers. Usually, demented patients need only very low doses of major tranquillizers; they may, in fact, become obtunded by a dose of major tranquillizer minimally effective in a young schizophrenic. In the case of haloperidol, it is rarely neccesary to exceed one or 2 mg per day, and doses in excess of 4 mg per day are hardly ever justified.

Paranoid symptoms are often very difficult to treat in a demented patient. Supportive psychotherapy may be useful in communicating to patients that someone can understand how frightening it must be to believe that people are threatening them, stealing from them, or in some way endangering their safety. An open mind must always be kept, however, to the potential reality of their statements. Stealing from and physical abuse of impaired elderly patients is all-too-common. If it becomes apparent that the paranoid ideation is delusional, distressing, and/or interfering with their function, major tranquillizers are indicated in the lowest dose possible which will control their symptomatology. The use of major tranquillizers in an elderly person should, of course, never be taken lightly since the risk of tardive dyskinesia increases with age.

Insomnia, another symptom of dementia, often responds to treatment. First, an estimate should be obtained of the usual amount of sleep the patient required prior to the onset of the dementing illness. It is unrealistic to expect a demented person to sleep from 7 p.m. until 7 a.m., generally to allow caregivers a period of relief, when the person's premorbid need for sleep was only 7 or 8 hours per night. Once it becomes clear that the current sleeping pattern differs from the premorbid one, the next step is to establish the probable cause of the insomnia. If the insomnia is due to depression, the patient should be treated with antidepressant medication. Antidepressants with the fewest side effects — especially anticholinergic side effects — are preferred since anticholinergic activity may further impair cognition. Our current choice is trazodone, which has very little anticholinergic activity, with an initial dose of 25 mg per night or less.

If the insomnia is a result of anxiety, short-acting minor tranquillizers, such as oxazepam, lorazepam, or the newer agents, such as temazepam (15 mg), triazolam (0.125 to 0.25 mg), or nitrazepam (not yet available in the USA) may be tried. Alternatives are the old standbys of chloral hydrate 500–1000 mg per night or an antihistamine.

In contrast to insomnia, which responds relatively well to drug treatments, wandering is probably the least treatable and often most troublesome symptom of dementia. The reason for the aimless and often dangerous walking of some demented patients is not understood but may relate to the lack of memory of what to do next or to an alteration in neurotransmitters. Medications such as tranquillizers are of little use. They generally do not change the behaviour but cause the patient to become sleepy and contribute to the dangerousness of the situation. Sufficient quantities of drug effectively to control the wandering will require the patient to be asleep almost all day.

The best we have to offer these patients is protection from harming themselves during the wandering episodes. A locked setting may become necessary as may physical restraint. The best types of soft restraints are those which can be placed around a person's waist or chest and then tied to a bed or chair, thus immobilizing the patient, yet leaving the arms free to move and reducing the feeling of restriction.

The psychotherapy of depression in a demented individual differs from that in the depressed patient with normal cognition and is worth reviewing briefly (for greater detail, see Steuer, 1982). Overall, the type of psychotherapy felt to be most helpful to affected patients is best classified as supportive–directive. Patients often promote a dependent relationship and this should not be discouraged, as the goal of treatment is to support the patient rather than attempt a cure. The first rule, as always, is to listen to the patient's worries. The first tendency of clinicians is usually to project their own concerns about dementia onto a patient, often missing the real issue for the patient. For example, when we work with a dying patient we expect the patient to be afraid of death. Without carefully listening, we may not understand that the patient has accepted death and is concerned primarily about experiencing pain towards the end — an issue easily addressed with the explanation that most pain can be effectively removed with appropriate medication. With the demented patient, it might be our tendency to expect the main concern to be the loss of memory and higher mental facilities. Giving patients sufficient time and attention, and allowing them to express themselves, may reveal that they have come to terms with the reality of their memory loss and that their major concerns are long-term financial management, the care of spouse and children, the prospect of having life artifically prolonged, or a multitude of other considerations often far more readily remedied than the progressive memory loss.

The next principle is to be empathic with their worries and let them know that you are trying to understand how they feel. To tell an 80-year-old demented man that he is suffering less of a loss than he believes is inappropriate as well as counter-therapeutic. Ask for further clarification when the issue appears important and you do not understand.

With demented individuals, it is generally best to depart from the traditional non-directive model and give the patient suggestions as to what might be helpful. Usually, good advice will include mechanisms to compensate for memory impairment. Making lists, keeping an appointment book, and using visual imagery to aid memory tasks (such as remembering a person's name), are all useful suggestions. As the dementia advances, more basic strategies become necessary, such as clocks and calendars in sight (to aid orientation), dangerous doors (e.g. basement stairs, garage) kept closed at night, and the like.

Although no drug exists yet that improves a patient's ability to remember the location of the bathroom, or the need to remove underwear before urinating, it is important to check current medications for agents likely to impair memory (e.g. sedatives, hypnotics, tranquillizers and antidepressants). Specific aids to keep patients dry include underwear with specially designed pouches for absorbent pads and launderable sheets which absorb urine in a second layer, thereby keeping the patient's skin dry. Acute urinary incontinence requires careful examination of the patient (see chapter 30).

Urinary incontinence usually has an insidious onset, generally nocturnal at the beginning. The most common measures, such as regulating the time and amount of fluid intake, and the schedule and dosage of diuretics, as well as awakening patients during the night, may help to control, if not eliminate nocturnal enuresis. Anticholinergic agents are helpful in selected patients, but their desired action (blockade of the micturition reflex) must be weighed against their undesired side effects (e.g. impairment of cognition or production of anticholinergic psychosis).

Faecal incontinence, too, whether of the overflow or the neurogenic type, characteristically follows a chronic course. Again, timing is important, and caregivers rather than patients may need to be toilet trained. Immobility and low bulk diet tend to promote chronic constipation with overflow incontinence, so that high fibre diets are generally recommended (see chapter 26 for further details regarding management of faecal incontinence).

Experimental

Research aimed at reversing the cognitive decline associated with dementia of the Alzheimer type is discussed in chapter 17. Research into the aetiology and treatment of this type of dementia has been hampered by methodologic problems. Early studies were often uncontrolled and carried out in nursing homes without rigorous diagnostic distinction between the various forms of dementia. Assessments of drug response often included a large subjective component. Patients frequently received other medications concurrently with the medication under study, and at times were suffering from medical and psychiatric disorders in addition to the dementia. Improvements in cognition, anxiety and depression were not always separated. Furthermore, few studies dealt with the clinical issues most pertinent to the patient's need to be in a nursing home, such as the ability to bathe, eat, dress, ambulate independently, or maintain urinary and faecal continence.

Does this mean that medications previously tried may still prove to be useful? Possibly Alzheimer-type dementia may represent heterogeneous aetiologies which produce similar clinical pictures. Evidence in support of this includes the variable speed of progression, the variety of clinical symptoms seen, the finding in certain patients of deficits in the noradrenergic system while most have deficiencies in cholinergic neurotransmitters, and the occurrence of similar pathologic changes (specifically plaques and tangles) in both elderly normals as well as individuals with Alzheimer's disease. Additionally, occasional patients whose clinical state appears to be Alzheimer's disease, are found without plaques and tangles on post-mortem examination. It may be, that agents already in existence may benefit certain subtypes of DAT but not others (for review see Neshkes and Jarvik, 1983).

The family

If a demented patient has an involved relative, a family problem will exist and should always be treated. Generally, patients with dementia come to the attention of a physician when the family comes under stress. This may be in the form of financial concerns, sleepless nights, or intolerable incontinence. The family is usually aware of the 'senility' of the affected member and brings the person in, not expecting a cure, but rather hoping for some relief from the situation.

It is important to find out how the family is coping and what the problems really are. If possible, this should be done in the absence of the patient. It is usually a mistake to assume that demented individuals will not understand what is being said about them.

If the family is asking for some relief, one should attempt to provide it. Visiting nurses or day centres may be of great help (see chapter 49) in allowing family members some time for themselves. In addition, demented individuals will often enjoy a day centre, being around others with similar cognitive impairment, with activities suitable for them, and achieving some sense of independence from the family. Some patients can tolerate being away from their families more than others. Tranquillization may be helpful for those who have difficulty.

If the family is in need of supportive psychotherapy, this, too, should be arranged for them. If they have difficulty accepting this, it may be useful to have them return to the clinician more frequently for the purpose of checking the demented patient. At that time, the physician can provide family support.

If family members ask for information about their own risk of developing the disease, accurate information should be provided to them. Spouses should be informed that there is no evidence suggesting transmission among partners. Children should be told that there seems to be an increased risk of Alzheimer's disease for offspring of affected individuals, but data to predict the risk for a given family are generally inadequate. However, neither family members nor patients should ever be told there is no hope of improvement or finding a cure for Alzheimer's disease. The progress made in the last decade offers encouragement that within the next decade we will have the means to prevent, if not cure, most of the dementias afflicting the aged.

Conclusion

Dementia and delirium are not a normal consequence of aging. Even though good data are missing for much of the world, we can say that in the UK, Western Europe, and the USA, over 90 per cent of individuals over age 65, and 75 per cent of those over age 80, are not demented. When the dementia syndrome appears in the older adult, physicians should pursue an in-depth search for the underlying aetiology. They can expect to find some reversible cause in up to 20 per cent of patients. Even when no specific treatments are available to reverse the cognitive decline, substantial symptomatic treatment is available to effectively reduce the suffering of both patients and their caregivers, usually their families.

ACKNOWLEDGEMENT

This work was supported in part by National Institute of Mental Health Research Grants MH 36 205 and MH 31 357. Fellowship support for Dr Neshkes was provided by the Kaiser Foundation. The opinions expressed are those of the authors and not necessarily those of the Veterans Administration.

REFERENCES

Abramowicz M (ed) 1981 Medical letter on drugs and therapeutics. Choice of Benzodiazepines 23: 41–42

Adams R D, Fisher C M, Hakim S, Ojemann R C, Sweet W H 1965 Symptomatic occult hydrocephalus with 'normal' cerebrospinal fluid pressure. New England Journal of Medicine 273: 117–126

Albert M L 1978 Subcortical dementia. In: Katzman R, Terry R D, Bick K L (eds) Alzheimer's Disease: Senile Dementia and Related Disorders. Raven Press, New York

American Psychiatric Association 1980 Diagnostic and Statistical Manual of Mental Disorders, Third edition. Washington, D.C., APA

Aminoff M J, Marshall J, Smith E M et al 1975 Pattern of intellectual impairment in Huntington's chorea. Psychological Medicine 5: 169–72

Arie T 1978 Confusion in old age. Age and Ageing, 7 (suppl): 72–76

Asso D 1969 WAIS scores in a group of Parkinson patients. British Journal of Psychiatry 115: 555–556

Austen F K, Carmichael M W, Adams R D 1957 Neurologic manifestations of chronic pulmonary insufficiency. New England Journal of Medicine 257: 579–90

Barbeau A 1971 Long-term side-effects of levodopa. Lancet 1: 395

Benson D F, LeMay M, Patten D H, Rubens A B 1970 Diagnosis of normal-pressure hydrocephalus. New England Journal of Medicine 283: 609–615

Bernoulli C, Siegfried J, Baumgartner G et al 1977 Danger of accidental person-to-person transmission of Creutzfeldt-Jakob disease by surgery. Lancet 1: 478–479

Black P M 1980 Idiopathic normal-pressure hydrocephalus. Results of shunting in 62 patients. Journal of Neurosurgery 52: 371–377

Blaschke T F, Cohen S N, Tatro D S, Rubin P C 1981 Drug–drug interactions and aging. In Jarvik L F, Greenblatt D J, Harman D (Eds) Clinical Pharmacology and the Aged Patinet. New York, Raven Press

Blass J P, Gibson G E 1977 Abnormality of thiamine-requiring enzyme in patients with Wernicke-Korsakoff syndrome. New England Journal of Medicine 297: 1367–1370

Boller F, Mizutani T, Roessmann V et al 1980 Parkinson disease, dementia, and Alzheimer disease: Clinicopathological correlations. Annals of Neurology 7: 329–335

Bondareff W, Baldy R, Levy R 1981 Quantitative computed tomography in senile dementia. Archives of General Psychiatry 38: 1365–1368

Bondareff W, Mountjoy C Q, Roth M 1982 Loss of neurons of origin of the adrenergic projection to cerebral cortex (nucleus locus ceruleus) in senile dementia. Neurology 32: 164–168

Brackenridge C J 1971 The relation of type of initial symptoms and line of transmission to ages at onset and death in Huntington's disease. Clinical Genetics 2: 287–297

Brown P, Cathala F, Gajdusek D C 1979 Creutzfeldt-Jakob disease in France. III. Epidemiologic study of 170 patients dying during the decade 1968–1977. Annals of Neurology 6: 438–446 (a)

Brown P, Cathala F, Sadowsky D et al 1979 Creutzfeldt-Jakob disease in France. II. Clinical characteristics of 124 consecutive verified cases during the decade 1968–1977. Annals of Neurology 6: 430–437(b)

Bulens C 1981 Neurologic complications of hyperthyroidism. Archives of Neurology 38: 669–70

Caine E D, Hunt R D, Weingartner H et al 1978 Huntington's dementia. Archives of General Psychiatry 35: 377–384

Canadian Cooperative Study Group 1978 A randomized trial of aspirin and sulfinpyrazone in threatened stroke. New England Journal of Medicine 299: 53–59

Celesia G G, Wanamaker W M 1972 Psychiatric disturbances in Parkinson's disease. Diseases of the Nervous System 33: 577–583

Coblentz J M, Mattis S, Zingesser L H, Kasoff S S, Wisniewski H M, Katzman R 1973 Presenile dementia. Archives of Neurology 29: 299–308

Corsellis J A N 1978 Posttraumatic dementia. In: Katzman R, Terry R D, Bick K L (eds) Alzheimer's Disease: Senile Dementia and Related Disorders. Raven Press, New York, pp 125–133

Cummings J L, Benson D F 1983 Dementia: A Clinical Approach. Boston: Butterworths

Cutting J 1978 The relationship between Korsakov's syndrome and 'Alcoholic Dementia'. British Journal of Psychiatry 132: 240–251

Dalessio D J, Benchimol A, Dimond E G 1965 Chronic encephalopathy related to heart block. Neurology 15: 499–503

Davies P, Maloney A J R 1976 Selective loss of central cholinergic neurons in Alzheimer's disease. Lancet 2: 1403

Davis K L, Mohs R C, Davis B M et al 1983 Cholinominetic agents and human memory: clinical studies in Alzheimer's disease and scopolamine dementia. In: Crook T, Gershon S (eds) Strategies for the Development of an Effective Treatment for Senile Dementia. Powley M Associates, New Canaan, CT, pp 53–69

Dodge P R, Swartz M N 1965 Bacterial meningitis — a review of selected aspects. II. Special neurologic problems, postmeningitic complications and clinicopathological correlations. New England Journal of Medicine 272: 1003–10

Doty E J 1946 The incidence and treatment of delirious reactions in later life. Geriatrics 1: 21–26

Duffy P, Wolf J, Collins G et al 1974 Possible person-to-person transmission of Creutzfeldt-Jakob disease. New England Journal of Medicine 29: 692–693

Eisdorfer C, Cohen D 1978 The cognitively impaired elderly: Differential diagnosis. In Storandt M, Siegler I C, Elias M F (eds) The Clinical Psychology of Aging. New York, Plenum Press pp 7–42

Emerson T R, Milne J R, Gardner A J 1981 Cardiogenic dementia — a myth? Lancet 2: 743–4

Engel G L, Romano J 1959 Delirium: A syndrome of cerebral insufficiency. Journal of Chronic Diseases 9: 260–277

Fisher, C M 1968 Dementia and cerebral vascular disease. In: Cerebral Vascular Disease, Toole J F, Siekert R G, Whisnant J A (Eds) New York: Grune and Stratton

Fisher C M 1976 The clinical picture in occult hydrocephalus. Clinical Neurosurgery 24: 270–284

Fisher C M 1978 Communicating hydrocephalus Lancet 1: 37

Fraser H F, Isbell H 1960 Pharmacology and addiction liability of dl- and d-propoxyphene. Bulletin of Narcotics 12: 9–12

Freemon F R 1976 Evaluation of patients with progressive intellectual deterioration. Archives of Neurology 33: 658–659

Gajdusek D C 1977 Unconventional viruses and the origin and disappearance of Kuru. Science 197: 943–960

Gajdusek D C, Gibbs C J Jr, Earle K, Dammin G J, Schoene W C, Tyler H R 1974 Transmission of subacute spongiform encephalopathy to the chimpanzee and squirrel monkey from a patient with papulosis atrophicans maligna of Köhlmeier-Degos. In: Proceedings of the 10th International Congress of Neurology, Barcelona, Amsterdam: Excerpta Medica International Congress Series No. 319, Subirana A, Espadaler M, Burrows E H (Eds) 390–392

Gautier-Smith P C 1965 Clinical aspects of hypoglycaemia. In Cumings J N, Kremer M (Eds) Biochemical Aspects of Neurological Disorders (2nd series). Blackwell Scientific Publications, Oxford

Gibbs C J Jr, Gajdusek D C 1978 Subacute spongiform virus encephalopathies: The transmissible virus dementias. In: Katzman R, Terry R D, Bick K L (eds) Alzheimer's Disease: Senile Dementia and Related Disorders. Raven Press, New York, pp. 559–575

Glaser G H, Solitaire G B, Manuelidis E E 1968 Acute and subacute inclusion encephalitis. Association for Research in Nervous and Mental Disease Proceedings 44: 178–215

Goodwin F K 1971 Behavioral effects of l-dopa in man. Seminars in Psychiatry 3: 477–492

Gotz V 1978 Paranoid psychosis with indomethacin. British Medical Journal 1: 49

Greenblatt D J, Shader R I 1972 Digitalis toxicity. In Shader R I (Ed) Psychiatric Complications of Medical Drugs. New York, Raven Press

Greenblatt D J, Shader R I 1973 Drug therapy: Anticholinergics. New England Journal of Medicine 288: 1215–1219

Greenblatt D J, Sellers E M, Shader R I 1982 Drug therapy: Drug disposition in old age. New England Journal of Medicine 306: 1081–1088

Gusella J F, Wexler N S, Conneally P M et al 1983 A polymorphic DNA marker genetically linked to Huntington's disease. Nature 306: 234–238

Haaland K Y, Matthews G 1977 Cognitive and Motor Performance in Parkinsonism of Increasing Duration. Presented at the International Neuropsychology Society meeting, Sante Fe, New Mexico, February, 1977

Haase G R 1977 Diseases presenting as dementia. In Wells C E (Ed) Dementia, 2nd edn. Davis F A Philadelphia 27–67

Hachinski V C, Iliff L D, Zilhka E et al 1975 Cerebral blood flow in dementia. Archives of Neurology 32: 632–637

Hachinski V C, Lassen N A, Marshall J 1974 Multi-infarct dementia — a cause of mental deterioration in the elderly. Lancet ii: 207–209

Hakim A M, Mathieson G 1979 Dementia in Parkinson disease: A neuropathologic study. Neurology 29: 1209–1214

Hakim S, Adams R D 1965 The special clinical problem of symptomatic hydrocephalus with normal cerebrospinal fluid pressure: Observations on cerebrospinal fluid hydrodynamics. Journal of the Neurological Sciences 2: 307–327

Hanna S M 1970 Hypopituitarism (Sheehan's syndrome) presenting with organic psychosis. Journal of Neurology, Neurosurgery and Psychiatry 33: 192–193

Harrison M J G, Marsden C D 1977 Progressive intellectual deterioration. Archives of Neurology 34: 199

Heathfield K W 1973 Huntington's chorea: A centenary review. Postgraduate Medical Journal 49: 32–45

Heilman K M, Fisher W R 1974 Hyperlipidemic dementia. Archives of Neurology 31: 67–68

Heston L L, Mastri A R, Anderson V E, White J 1981 Dementia of the Alzheimer type: Clinical genetics, natural history, and associated conditions. Archives of General Psychiatry 38: 1085–1090

Horn S 1974 Some psychological factors in Parkinsonism. Journal of Neurology, Neurosurgery and Psychiatry 37: 27–31

Hubbard B M, Anderson J M 1981 A quantitative study of cerebral atrophy in old age and senile dementia. Journal of the Neurological Sciences 50: 135–145

Hurwitz N 1969 Predisposing factors in adverse reactions to drugs. British Medical Journal 1: 536–539

Hutton J T 1981 Atrial myxoma as a cause of progressive dementia. Archives of Neurology 38: 533

Hyldstrup L, Ladefoged S D, Astrup H 1981 Reversible dementia in idiopathic hypoparathyroidism. Danish Medical Bulletin 28: 74–5

Ingvar D H, Brun A, Hagberg B, Gustafson L 1978 Regional cerebral blood flow in the dominant hemisphere in confirmed cases of Alzheimer's disease, Pick's disease, and multi-infarct dementia: Relationship to chemical symptomatology and neuropathological findings. In: Katzman R, Terry R D, Bick K L (eds) Alzheimer's Disease: Senile Dementia and Related Disorders. Raven Press, New York, pp 203–211

Jacobs L, Conti D, Kinkel W R, Manning E J 1976 Normal pressure hydrocephalus. Journal of the American Medical Association 235: 510–512

Jana D K, Romano-Jana L 1973 Hypernatremic psychosis in the elderly: Case reports. Journal of the American Geriatrics Society 21: 473–7

Jarvik L F, Matsuyama S S 1983 Parental stroke: Risk factor for multi-infarct dementia? Lancet ii: 1025

Jellinek E H 1962 Fits, faints, coma and dementia in myxedema. Lancet ii: 1010–1012

Jenike M A 1982 Cimetadine in elderly patients. Journal of the American Geriatrics Society 30: 170–173

Kahn E, Thompson L J 1934 Concerning Pick's disease. American Journal of Psychiatry 90: 937–946

Kay D W K 1972 Epidemiological aspects of organic brain disease in the aged. In Gaitz C M (ed) Aging and the Brain. New York, Plenum Press pp 15–27

Kiloh L G 1961 Pseudo-dementia. Acta Psychiatrica Scandinavica 37: 336–51

Klawans H L Jr, Paulson G W, Ringel S P, Barbeau A 1972 Use of L-dopa in the detection of presymptomatic Huntington's chorea. New England Journal of Medicine 286: 1332–4

Lavis V R 1981 Psychiatric manifestations of endocrine disease in the elderly. In Levenson A J, Hall R C W (Eds) Neuropsychiatric Manifestations of Physical Disease in the Elderly. New York, Raven Press

Levenson A J (Ed) 1979 Neuropsychiatric Side Effects of Drugs in the Elderly. New York, Raven Press

Lipowski Z J 1980 Delirium: Acute Brain Failure in Man. Springfield, Illinois, Charles C Thomas

Lipowski Z J 1983 Transient cognitive disorders (delirium, acute confusional states) in the elderly. American Journal of Psychiatry 140: 1426–1436

Liston E H 1982 Delirium in the aged. In Jarvik L F, Small G W (eds) The Psychiatric Clinics of North America. W B Saunders Co. Philadelphia, p 49–66

Liston E H, LaRue A 1984 Clinical differentiation of primary degenerative and multi-infarct dementia: A critical review of the evidence. Part II: Pathological studies. Biological Psychiatry (in press)

Loranger A W, Goodell H, McDowell F H et al 1972 Intellectual impairment in Parkinson's syndrome. Brain 95: 405–12

Lowry J, Bahr A L, Allen J H Jr et al 1977 Radiological techniques in the diagnostic evaluation of dementia. In: Wells C E (ed) Dementia, 2nd ed. Davis F A, Philadelphia, pp 23–245

MacLennan W J 1974 Drug interactions. Gerontologia Clinica 16: 18–24

Malamud N 1972 Neuropathology of organic brain syndromes associated with aging In: Gaitz C M (ed): Aging and the Brain. Plenum, New York, pp 63–87

Malamud N, Waggoner R W 1943 Genealogic and clinicopathologic study of Pick's disease. Archives of Neurology and Psychiatry 50: 288–303

Marsden C D, Harrison M J G 1972 Outcome of investigation of patients with presenile dementia. British Medical Journal 2: 249–252

Marsh G G, Markham C M, Ansel R 1971 Levodopa's awakening effect on patients with parkinsonism. Journal of Neurology, Neurosurgery and Psychiatry 34: 209–218

Martin W E, Loewenson R B, Resch J A, Baker A B 1973 Parkinson's disease. Clinical analysis of 100 patients. Neurology 23: 783–790

Marttila R J, Rinne V K 1976 Dementia in Parkinson's disease. Acta Neurologica Scandinavica 54: 431–441

Mathew N T, Meyer J S, Hartmanm A, Ott E O 1975 Abnormal cerebrospinal fluid-blood flow dynamics. Archives of Neurology 32: 657–664

Matsuyama S S, Jarvik L F 1980 Genetics and mental functioning in senescence. In Birren J E, Sloane R B (eds): Handbook of Mental Health and Aging. p 134–148. Prentice-Hall, Inc, Englewood Cliffs, New Jersey

Matsuyama S S, Jarvik L F 1982 Genetics: What the practioner needs to know. Generations 7: 19–21

Matthews W B 1975 Epidemiology of Creutzfeldt-Jakob disease in England and Wales. Journal of Neurology, Neurosurgery and Psychiatry 38: 210–213

May W W, Itabashi H H, DeJong R N 1968 Creutzfeldt-Jakob disease II. Clinical, pathologic and genetic study of a family. Archives of Neurology 19: 137–149

McCarthy S T, Wollner L 1977 Cardiac dysrhythmias: Treatable cause of transient cerebral dysfunction in the elderly. Lancet ii: 2–203

McCarthy S T, Wollner L 1981 Cardiogenic dementia. Lancet 2: 1171

McGeer E G 1978 Aging and neurotransmitter metabolism in the human brain. In: Katzman R, Terry R D, Bick K L (eds) Alzheimer's Disease: Senile Dementia and Related Disorders. Raven Press, New York, pp 427–440

McHugh P R 1964 Occult hydrocephalus. Quarterly Journal of Medicine 33: 297–308

Merwin S L, Abram H S 1977 Psychological response to coronary artery bypass. Southern Medical Journal 70: 153–155

Merz P A, Somerville R A, Wisniewski H M 1983 Scrapie-associated fibrils in Creutzfeldt-Jakob disease. Nature 306: 474–476

Miller R R 1975 Clinical effects of pentazocine in hospitalized medical patients. Journal of Clinical Pharmacology 15: 198–205

Morse R M, Litin E M 1971 The anatomy of a delirium. American Journal of Psychiatry 128: 111–116

Morse R M, Litin E M 1969 Postoperative delirium: A study of etiologic factors. American Journal of Psychiatry 126: 388–395

Mortimer J A, Pirozzolo F J, Hansch E C, Webster D D 1982 Relationship of motor symptoms to intellectual deficits in Parkinson disease. Neurology 32: 133–137

Myers R H, Goldman D, Bird E D et al 1983 Maternal transmission in Huntington's disease. Lancet i: 208–210

Myers R H, Growden J H, Bird E D et al 1982 False-negative results with levodopa for early detection of Huntington's disease. New England Journal of Medicine 307: 561–562

Myrianthopoulos N C 1966 Huntington's chorea: Review article. Journal of Medical Genetics 3: 298–314

Neshkes R E, Jarvik L F 1983 Pharmacologic approach to the treatment of senile dementia. Psychiatric Annals 13: 14–30

Nordenbo A M, Sorensen P S 1981 The incidence and clinical presentation of neurosyphilis in Greater Copenhagen 1974 through 1978. Acta Neurologica Scandinavica 63: 237–246

Ojemann R G, Fisher C M, Adams R D, Sweet W H, New P F J 1969 Further experience with the syndrome of 'normal' pressure hydrocephalus. Journal of Neurosurgery 31: 279–294

Otman J E, Friedman S 1961 Comments on Huntington's chorea. Diseases of the Nervous System 22: 313–319

Pathy M S 1967 Clinical presentation of myocardial infarction in the elderly. British Heart Journal 29: 190–199

Pearce J, Miller E 1973 Clinical Aspects of Dementia. Bailliere-Tindall, London

Perry E K, Perry R H, Blessed G et al 1977 Necropsy evidence of central cholinergic deficits in senile dementia. Lancet i: 189

Post F 1975 Dementia, depression, and pseudodementia. In: Benson

D F, Blumer D (eds). Psychiatric Aspects of Neurological Disease. New York: Grune and Stratton 99–120

Raskind M, Peskind E, Rivard M et al 1982 Dexamethasone suppression test and cortisol circadian rhythm in primary degenerative dementia. American Journal of Psychiatry 139: 1468–1471

Ratner J, Rosenberg G, Kral V et al 1972 Anticoagulant therapy for senile dementia. Journal of the American Geriatrics Society 20: 556–559

Riklan M, Weiner H, Diller L 1959 Somato-psychologic studies in Parkinson's disease. I. An investigation into the relationship of certain disease factors to psychological functions. Journal of Nervous and Mental Disease 129: 263–272

Robertson E E, le Roux A, Brown J H 1958 The clinical differentiation of Pick's disease. Journal of Mental Science 104: 1000–1024

Robinson G W Jr 1956 The toxic delirious reactions of old age. In Kaplan O J (ed): Mental Disorders in Later Life, edition 2, Stanford University Press, California pp 332–351

Roos R P, Johnson R T 1977 Viruses and dementia. In Wells C E (ed). Dementia, 2nd ed. Davis F A, Philadelphia pp 93–112

Rosen W G, Terry R D, Fuld P A et al 1980 Pathological verification of ischemic score in differentiation of dementias. Annals of Neurology 7: 486–488

Rosenberg G M 1981 Neuropsychiatric manifestations of cardiovascular disease in the elderly. In Levenson A J, Hall R C W (ed) Neuropsychiatric Manifestations of Physical Disease in the Elderly. Raven Press, New York

Roth M 1978 Epidemiological studies. In Katzman R, Terry R D, Bick K L (eds) Alzheimer's Disease: Senile Dementia and Related Disorders. Aging, Vol 7. New York, Raven Press

Ryan J J, Souheaver G T, DeWolfe A S 1980 Intellectual deficit in chronic renal failure. Journal of Nervous and Mental Disease 168: 763–767

Schenk V W D 1959 Re-examination of a family with Pick's disease. Annals of Human Genetics 23: 325–333

Schentag J J, Calleri G, Rose J Q et al 1979 Pharmacokinetic and clinical studies in patients with cimetidine-associated mental confusion. Lancet i: 177–181

Seltzer B, Sherwin I 1978 Organic brain syndromes: an empirical study and critical review. American Journal of Psychiatry 135: 13–21

Seymour D G, Henschke P J, Cape R D T, Campbell A J 1980 Acute confusional states and dementia in the elderly: The role of dehydration/volume depletion, physical illness and age. Age and Ageing 9: 137–146

Shenkin H A, Greenberg J, Bourizarth W F, Gutterman P, Morales J O 1973 Ventricular shunting for relief of senile symptoms. Journal of the American Medical Association 225: 1486–1489

Shevitz S A, Silberfarb P M, Lipowski Z J 1976 Psychiatric consultations in a general hospital. A report on 1000 referrals. Diseases of the Nervous System 37: 295–300

Shulman R 1967 Psychiatric aspects of pernicious anaemia: A prospective controlled investigation. British Medical Journal 3: 266–270

Simon A, Cahan R B 1963 The acute brain syndrome in geriatric patients. Psychiatric Research Reports of the American Psychiatric Association 16: 8–21

Sjøgren T, Sjøgren H, Lindgren A G H 1952 Morbus Alzheimer and morbus Pick. Acta Psychiatrica Neurologica Scandinavica Supplement 82: 1–152

Small G W, Jarvik L F 1982 The dementia syndrome. Lancet ii: 1443–1446

Small G W, Liston E H, Jarvik L F 1981 Diagnosis and treatment of dementia in the aged. Western Journal of Medicine 135: 469–481

Smith J S, Kiloh L G 1981 The Investigation of dementia: Results in 200 consecutive admissions. Lancet i: 824–827

Sohn R S, Siegel B A, Gado M, Torack R M 1973 Alzheimer's disease with abnormal cerebrospinal fluid flow. Neurology 23: 1058–1065

Sourander P, Sjøgren H 1970 The concept of Alzheimer's disease and its clinical implications, in Wolstenholme G E W, O'Connor M (eds) Alzheimer's Disease and Related Conditions. Churchill, London pp 11–36

Spar J, Gerner R 1982 Does the dexamethasone suppression test distinguish dementia from depression? American Journal of Psychiatry 139: 238–240

Sroka H, Elizan T S, Yahr M D et al 1981 Organic mental syndrome and confusional states in Parkinson's disease: Relationship to computerized tomographic signs of cerebral atrophy. Archives of Neurology 38: 339–342

Stengel E 1943 A study of the symptomatology and differential diagnosis of Alzheimer's disease and Pick's disease. Journal of Mental Science 89: 1–20

Steuer J 1982 Psychotherapy with the elderly. In: Jarvik L F, Small G W (eds) Psychiatric Clinics of North American Saunders. Philadelphia pp 199–213

Strub R L, Black F W 1977 The Mental Status Examination in Neurology. Davis F A, Philadelphia

Strub R, Black F W 1981 Organic Brain Syndromes: An Introduction to Neurobehavioral Disorders. Davis, Philadelphia

Strachan R W, Henderson J G 1967 Dementia and folate deficiency. Quarterly Journal of Medicine 36: 189–204

Strachan R W, Henderson J G 1965 Psychiatric syndromes due to avitaminosis B_{12} with normal blood and marrow. Quarterly Journal of Medicine 34: 303–317

Sweet R D, McDowell F H, Feigenson J S, Loranger A W, Goodell H 1976 Mental symptoms in Parkinson's disease during chronic treatment with levodopa. Neurology 26: 305–310

Tarkkanen J V 1963 Otogenic brain abscess. Acta Otolaryngologica (Suppl) 185: 1–80

Terry R D, Davies P 1980 Dementia of the Alzheimer type. Annual Review of Neuroscience 3: 77–95

Todorov A B, Go R C P, Constantinidis J, Elston R C 1975 Specificity of the clinical diagnosis of dementia. 26: 81–98

Tomilinson B E, Blessed G, Roth M 1970 Observations on the brains of demented old people. Journal of the Neurological Sciences 11: 205–242

Victor M, Adams R D, Cole M 1965 The acquired (non-Wilsonian) type of chronic hepatocerebral degeneration. Medicine 44: 345–396

Weizman A, Eldar M, Shoenfeld Y, Hirschorn M, Wijsenbeek H, Pinkhas J 1979 Hypercalcaemia-induced psychopathology in malignant diseases. British Journal of Psychiatry 135: 363–366

Wells C 1982 Chronic Brain Disease: An update on Alcoholism, Parkinson's Disease and Dementia. Hospital and Community Psychiatry. 33: 111–126

Wells C E 1980 The differential diagnosis of psychiatric disorders in the elderly. In: Cole J O, Barrett J E (eds) Psychopathology in the Aged. Raven Press, New York

Whelan T B, Schteingart D E, Starkman M N, Smith A 1980 Neuropsychological deficits in Cushing's syndrome. Journal of Nervous and Mental Disease 168: 753–757

Whitehouse P J, Price D L, Clark A W et al 1981 Alzheimer disease: Evidence for selective loss of cholinergic neurons in the nucleus basalis. Annals of Neurology 10: 122–126

Wisniewski H M, Coblentz J M, Terry R D 1972 Pick's disease: A clinical and ultrastructural study. Archives of Neurology 26: 97–108

Wood A J J, Moir D C, Campbell C et al 1974 Medicines Evaluation and Monitoring Group: Central nervous system effects of pentazocine. British Medical Journal 1: 305–307

Yahr M D, Duvoisin R C, Schear M J et al 1969 Treatment of parkinsonism with levodopa. Archives of Neurology 21: 343–354

Yakovlev P I 1947 Paraplegias of hydrocephalics. A clinical note and interpretation. Journal of Mental Deficiency Research 51: 561–576

The central nervous system — the emotional disorders

GENERAL ORIENTATION

The minor and major emotional disorders encountered in old people are very similar in causation, symptomatology and response to treatment, to those of earlier life. Numerically, minor conditions are far more important than major emotional illnesses with their alterations of biological functions, disruptive psychopathology, and lack of illness insight. Both kinds of disorder may recur during old age from earlier life, or they may only arise towards its end. In that case, there have usually been present earlier flaws in personality structure and associated problems with personal relationships as well as disadvantaged economic and social positions. Physical ill health is frequently associated with the emotional disturbances in old age.

All emotionally disordered or ill old people require similar general management, approach, and psychotherapeutic guidance. With a few exceptions, specific therapies are available only for major depressions, manias, and paranoid psychoses, and these treatments are only symptomatic. As in all of geriatric medicine, continued supervision and treatment are almost always required. The various disorders will be described first and, to avoid repetition, treatment and its results will be dealt with, almost always, separately in the second part of this chapter. References have been chosen to enable more detailed enquiries and not to document every single statement.

MINOR CONDITIONS

Personality disorders

Very little is known about the consequences in old age of these usually life-long disorders and deviations. Aging of the personality, which is often thought of as implying increasing turning inward (Chap 6), is probably related to the impression that the aggressive kinds of personality dysfunction, especially most forms of delinquency, cause fewer problems with advancing age. By contrast, inadequate personalities seem to go down hill as life progresses, often to end in social isolation and destitution.

Senile character change has been regarded as exaggerations and caricaturing of lifelong personality traits: It has been long and often described in terms of surliness, suspiciousness, avarice or of garrulosity, empty emotionality and disinhibition. It does not seem to be known whether these changes do occur in old people who remain free of pathological cognitive decline, whether in other words they may not always be a prodrome or accompaniment of old age dementia. Only one disorder, senile seclusion, and one set of deviations (sexual) have been specifically studied.

Sexual problems

Old people very rarely complain of sexual dysfunctioning. Provided general health and the requisite setting are preserved, it is now generally accepted that full and normal sexual activity can continue to the highest age. Responses are slower, and can no longer be psychologically triggered; physical contact is required (Elias and Elias, 1977; Comfort, 1980). Many medications used in the elderly may produce impotence.

Exhibitionism and sexual offences against children by elderly men are over-represented in public imagination. Only 5 of 256 reported sexual offences were committed by persons over 60 (Epstein et al, 1970). They may, however, present as a family problem, and rarely as an early sign of one of the dementias. Where explanations and guidance fail, suppression with an anti-androgen, e.g. cyproterone acetate, 100–200 mg daily, has been found very useful.

Male homosexuals, especially when they have not enjoyed long lasting relationships, may be at special risks for emotional disorders in late life. They may be much helped by counselling (Kimmel, 1977).

Senile reclusion

This is a rare form of personality disorder with an annual incidence of only 0.5 in 1000 over 60. Probably men and women are equally affected. Most live alone, but a few share their seclusion with a sister or a spouse. They tend to be of at least average intelligence, to belong to the middle rather than the working class; also, poverty is conspicious by its absence. Senile recluses have always been independent and secretive persons, who have gradually withdrawn from society, and have finally come literally to lock themselves up in their homes. They bear witness to an almost unimaginable degree of self-neglect and hoarding (money under floor boards!). These persons tend to come to notice after many years only through complaints of neighbours or during a usually terminal illness. Where fit for mental examination, about half of them appear to be suffering from no circumscribed psychiatric condition. The remainder are reported to have developed by the time of discovery senile dementia or a more clear cut paraphrenic illness. The condition is not really a syndrome, but presents the end stage of a personality disorder; the term of Diogenes syndrome (Clark et al, 1975) seems also inappropriate in that this founder of the cynic school while living in a vat or dog kennel, did so to demonstrate his philosophy. Rehabilitation has been found to be possible (Macmillan and Shaw, 1966).

Alcoholism

This is the only habit disorder which is likely to come to attention in the elderly, but it should also be remembered that addictions to aperients or to night sedatives may be a causal factor of many geriatric disorders. There should be no need to stress the role of alcohol abuse in the accident surgery and medicine of the elderly.

Fortunately, older people as a group drink less than younger ones, and there are fewer elderly heavy drinkers. Among alcoholics, the elderly ones obviously form a group of survivors who have often reduced their drinking after the age of 50 on account of increasing health consciousness as well as of lowered income. All the same, alcoholism in the elderly is arousing increasing concern especially in the United States, where it has been well documented. Peak ages of incidence have been found to be at 45–54, but also at 65–75. The male over female predominance had decreased to 3 : 2 in the aged. In a psychiatric screening unit, 23 per cent of patients over 60 were classified as suffering from alcoholism, and an additional 5 per cent were regarded as heavy social drinkers. It has been estimated, however, that only 11 per cent of aged alcoholics had started to drink heavily recently (Simon, 1980).

As in the case of younger subjects, alcoholism as against social drinking should be suspected from the occurrence of shakiness, debilitating hang-overs, black-outs, memory loss, delirious episodes, and the need to arrange the day's schedule according to a drinking routine; finally, the presence of problem drinking should obviously be strongly suspected in persons with any alcohol-related disease. Lifelong alcohol abuse is associated with certain personality defects or with specific occupational risks, while excessive alcohol intake first becoming a problem only late in life has been linked to the minor forms of depression (Rosin and Glatt, 1971; Mishara and Kastenbaum, 1980), and often occurs in old people with previously stable personalities. Sometimes it is induced by relatives in an attempt at dealing with the old person's anxieties, their turns of feeling faint, their hypochondriacal complaints and general unhappiness.

Alcohol dependence in the old may well result from self medication for depression, and the treatment of depression may be all that is required; but it must be remembered that depression can also be the result of excessive and habitual alcohol consumption. Alcoholics who live alone should be admitted to hospital in the first instance, as withdrawal is otherwise unlikely to be successful. In the presence of confusion, gradual withdrawal is probably safer; otherwise sudden withdrawal under cover of chlormethiazole is indicated. Almost always the patient's social circumstances will make subsequent transfer to residential care imperative. However, most alcoholics can be treated in their own homes in co-operation with members of their family. Motivation may have to be stimulated and emotional cross currents may have to be dealt with; where this is not possible, initial hospital treatment may again be unavoidable. In view of the elderly alcoholic's satisfactory earlier psychological make-up, it is usually not too difficult to enforce total abstinence by encouragement and advice. Aversive techniques (e.g. with disulphiram) are thought to be too risky in older subjects. In them, the treatment of alcoholism is very often highly successful, even where there is a long history. Occasional, controlled drinking should probably be discouraged, but with an open mind.

Neurotic disorders

These cause variable degrees of disability in many people throughout life, usually at times of stress and on a background of personal vulnerabilities. Most more seriously and persistently ill neurotics improve as they get older. In addition, there are certain changes in the type of their symptomatology. The more demonstrative signs of anxiety and distress such as conversion hysteria and anxiety states with marked trembling, tachycardia and sweating give way to more inwardly disturbing disorders like situational phobias, fears of physical disease, and milder depressions in the widest sense of the word. The neuroses of old age have been rarely studied, even in relation to psychotherapy.

In a random community sample of 300 subjects 64–80 years old, from which those with major organic and functional psychiatric illnesses had been excluded, Bergmann (1971, 1978) found that only 49 per cent had always been entirely free of any psychopathology. Lifelong personality deviations had affected 6 per cent. In the majority of the remaining 45 per cent neurotic symptoms had occurred only occasionally and in a very mild form. They had been distressing in only 18 per cent of the sample, and in 11 per cent they had become so for the first time only in late life. Old women were about five times more frequently affected than men during later life.

Lifelong neurotics differed considerably from late-onset neurotics. Where neuroses had recurred throughout the life span they remained characterized by a variety of symptoms such as those of anxiety states, conversion hysteria, obsessional states, phobic disorders and mild depressive episodes. In late onset neurotics, attention seeking complaining (but never true hysterical conversions), phobias and obsessions might have been present also, but these features always occurred in the setting of depression, more rarely of anxiety, but often of anxiety-depression. Regardless of age of onset, the most prominent symptom of elderly neurotics was hypochondriasis, i.e. preoccupations with unpleasant physical sensations or non-delusional fears of somatic disease. These complaints and preoccupations were also frequent in elderly lifelong neurotics even though on the whole they were physically healthy. By contrast, late onset neurotics were very frequently afflicted with persistent and disturbing physical disorders. Cardiovascular and cardiopulmonary conditions were most frequently discovered, and on follow-up the death rate in this group was significantly higher than that of early onset neurotics. In contrast to them, late onset neurotics had had fewer childhood problems, but were not otherwise differentiated in terms of hereditary factors, marital or other earlier life stresses. However, in addition to more physical ill-health, late life neurotics were more disadvantaged financially, lonely, and restricted to their homes; there they tended to engage in ineffectual activities, sometimes resulting in objectively diminished self-care.

In recognizing elderly neurotics and their needs of treatment, attention should be paid to recent loss of social support and to untreated physical disabilities. Physical disease affecting oculo-vestibular mechanisms may result in a pseudo-agoraphobic syndrome (Marks, 1981). Recent worsening should suggest the development of depression, usually more characterized by increased physical complaints, diminishing interest, and social withdrawal than by an obvious mood of sadness. These late life neuroses probably shade over gradually into the therapeutically more responsive depressive illnesses. Their psychotherapeutic management will be discussed in the second half of this chapter.

MAJOR CONDITIONS

Of these the most common are the depressive illnesses, many of which, however, are not marked by severe mental disturbance or loss of insight. This is almost always absent in mania and in paranoid psychoses.

Depressions

Recent surveys of elderly community subjects (e.g. Stenbeck et al, 1979; Gurland et al, 1980; Blazer and Williams, 1980) have confirmed that only between 1.8 and 2.5 per cent of persons over 65 are discovered with severe depressive psychoses. By contrast, depressive preoccupations were entertained from time to time by some 70 per cent of aging people, who had been followed over a number of years (Gianturco and Busse, 1978) Depressive complaints which might suggest a clinical disorder as measured by a depression inventory had a point prevalence rate of 22 per cent (Gurland et al, 1980), but in only 13 per cent was the depression judged so marked as to evoke the concern of health care workers. Similarly, in Blazer and Williams' (1980) survey 11 per cent of depressed subjects exhibited fewer than four of the signs and symptoms of clinical depression on a list suggested by a statistical and diagnostic manual emanating from the American Psychiatric Association. To these mild disorders Blazer and Williams gave the label of dysphoric syndrome, a less pejorative one than that of senile demoralization.

Senile dysphoria is characterized by persistently reduced life satisfaction punctuated by periods of grief. Possibly, most aging persons pass through such a phase before making a satisfactory adjustment to the status of the aged. Where the condition persists it tends to be associated with physical ill-health in about half, and by social and economic disadvantages in most. Probably senile dysphoria overlaps with the late onset neuroses of the elderly, but is even less likely to come to the notice of psychiatrists rather than of general and geriatric physicians. It is also more likely to respond to simple environmental and psychotherapeutic measures rather than to antidepressant drugs, whose side effects may only add to the patients' problems.

Clinical depressions vary greatly in severity. In a consecutive series of patients requiring inpatient treatment (Post, 1972) 39 per cent had been mainly anxious with no or little overt sadness. They were chiefly preoccupied with unpleasant somatic sensations (e.g. 'butterflies in the stomach'), but there were usually also loss of interest — especially in food — irregularity of sleep, and on exploration some feelings of personal inadequacy or even of guilt. Most had come to be admitted on account of their restlessness, and the strain imposed on their families by their unceasing and importuning demands for reassurance, which had failed to be held in check by family doctor or psychiatric clinic treatment. The remaining 61 per cent were psychotic in the sense of having delusional ideas of guilt, poverty, dirtiness, or most frequently of physical disease, especially of alimentary or excretory obstruction. In 24 per cent overt depressive affect was not very severe and heavily overlaid by delusional beliefs of a depressive, but sometimes also paranoid nature. The remaining 37 per cent were severely agitated or retarded and communicated an affect of profound sadness and despair. They spoke little or uttered only repetitive depressive statements. Some were quite inaccessible, but only a few voiced nihilistic ideas, referring to emptiness of abdomen, of head or of bones, or even to their own non-existence. These impressive and classical symptoms of 'involutional' and 'senile melancholia' are now rarely seen, but less blatant nihilistic hypochondriacal beliefs may be discovered in some apparently, but moderately, ill aged (as also in younger) depressives.

Differential diagnosis of depression

Recognition and differential diagnosis gives rise to difficulties only occasionally. In mild cases, it may be a problem to decide whether depression is in fact due to an illness and therefore likely to respond to some specific antidepressant therapy. The presence of clinical depression rather than that of dysphoria is suggested by biological changes, in weight, appetite and sleep. An important indicator of clinical depression is an account of recent and fairly rapidly developing changes in personality functioning; loss of interest in activities and people, and in the case of neurotic old people, a clear increase of their neuroticisms.

In more severely depressed persons the differential diagnosis of dementia is frequently entertained. Much has been written about depressive pseudodementia (Post, 1975; Lishman, 1978; Wells, 1980), but its differentiation from true dementia is, as a rule easy: Depression is of recent onset, while dementia develops gradually, though acute confusional states may complicate depression through intercurrent physical illness or, more frequently, on account of injudicious antidepressive medication. Dements and sometimes their friends may be unaware of cognitive defects, while in the case of pseudo-dements both tend to complain vociferously of memory difficulties and disabilities in the performance of simple tasks, although latter is usually well maintained in the early stages of dementia. On examination, pseudo-dements in contrast to dements do not seem to try, and memory defects are mainly restricted to responses to specific questions. Cerebrally localized defect causing dysphasia, agnosia, or right-left disorientation, which are found in many, and especially in young-old dements, are hardly ever convincingly demonstrated. Patchy cognitive performance, however, can occur in both conditions, and so can approximate or near-miss answering. In very intelligent and educated persons it may be difficult to assess, in the presence of depression, the significance of surprising lapses of memory and of general information. It is probably a good rule to ignore pseudo-dementia, and to treat depression energetically, even with electro-convulsive therapies. Little harm will be done, if on some occasions the patient has begun to dement but is also depressed, a not uncommon concurrence.

Aetiology of depression

Turning to aetiology, in some 70 per cent of cases there is reliable evidence of disturbing and to the patient unusual life events having preceded the onset of depression by a few days, weeks or months. The most important ones are an acute illness, bereavement or threatened bereavement (e.g. serious illness of spouse), loss of home, moving away of children, and more rarely, retirement. Losses of this kind are sooner or later suffered by all aging persons. Why so few are so much more vulnerable to depression than others has gradually become clear. Certainly, the persistently physically disabled with impaired mobility are more often found among elderly depressives than among normal control subjects. Depressives in our age group are more often members of the lower socio-economic classes and have to contend with more poverty and poorer housing conditions. However, more important is the absence of any close and caring relationships, where the 'significant other' need not necessarily live close by or be at all frequently seen. Two-thirds of aged depressives with this lack had in fact never had such supportive relationships, and it has been suggested that the strongest predisposing factor to depression, just as in earlier life, is to be sought in the previous emotionally ambivalent personality (Murphy, 1982).

Furthermore, personality traits have been found to be strongly related to types of depression. Unstable and neurotic personalities have been found much more often in depressives remaining free of delusions, who in a setting of a relatively mild mood change, are a problem mainly because of their importuning behaviour, hypochondriacal complaints, and phobic, obsessional or hysteria-like symptoms. Otherwise these, descriptively speaking, neurotic depressives (at any rate when requiring hospital admission) have not been found to differ significantly from psychotic ones in terms of more frequent precipitation by life events or less frequent presence of a family history of affective illnesses (Post, 1972).

Some attempts have been made to discover factors responsible for old age depressions by comparing elderly patients with early as against late onsets of affective illness. First of all, hereditary factors have been found to be much weaker in late onset depressives by most investigators (Mendlewicz, 1976). Surprisingly, their illnesses are on the other hand, no more frequently precipitated by disruptive life events, and on the whole their personalities tend to have been more stable than those of depressives disabled by illnesses recurring since earlier life. At the same time, depression in old age is only very rarely an early sign of developing dementia; it is unnecessary to summarize the evidence for this once again (Post, 1968, 1972). However, there is mounting evidence supporting the hypothesis that simple aging of the brain short of Alzheimer or multi-infarct changes, may facilitate the occurrence (and the increasingly frequent recurrence) of depressions in later life. In comparison with early onset depressives, late onset cases tend to show mild cognitive impairment after full recovery, as well as some lasting abnormality of cortical evoked responses (Cawley et al, 1973; Hendrickson et al, 1979). Computed tomography has demonstrated in them the frequency of enlarged cerebral ventricles as well as a higher death rate, usually not however from direct cerebral causes (Jacoby et al, 1981). Even more impressive has been evidence for an age-wise increase of monoamine oxidase activity in many brain areas, especially in women, who are well known to suffer from depressions more frequently than men (Robinson et al, 1977). Other biological aging factors have been suggested by Lipton (1976).

Suicide
The incidence of suicide increases steeply with rising age, and this tendency is especially clearly maintained in the case of older men. In countries where 10–15 per cent of the population is over the age of 65 between 25 and 30 per cent of all suicides occur in the elderly. By contrast, only 5 per cent of all attempted suicides (parasuicide) have been registered in people over 65. This confirms clinical experience that, in contrast with the young, far fewer older people make suicidal gestures or attempts to seek attention, as a cry for help, or in a setting of drug abuse. Suicidal ideas, gestures, attempts, and completed suicide in the elderly almost always occur only during persistent depressions, and attempts are far more often repeated with fatal results than in younger persons. The lesson to be learnt is clear: in the case of the elderly, suicidal preoccupations should always lead to determined attempts at treatment of depression, and, unless the social setting is exceptionally favourable, in the first instance in hospital. The literature on suicidal behaviour of the aged, which is frequently associated with serious physical illness, has been summarized by Miller (1978) and by Shulman (1978), who also suggested some aetiological mechanisms for further study.

Mania
This severe mental illness is not as uncommon as used to be thought; estimates vary between 6.5 and 19 per cent of all affectively ill hospital patients over 60. Women are almost three times more often affected than men, rather more so than is the case for depression. When seen in old age, the first manic attack had usually occurred around the age of 60 and had been preceded by purely depressive illnesses in over two-thirds of cases. Many years may have passed before mania had supervened, up to 47 years, but on an average only 10 (Shulman and Post, 1980).

The clinical picture resembles closely that seen in younger people: elation, over-activity, aggressiveness when thwarted, sleeplessness, inattention to bodily needs, grandiose delusions of ability, wealth, and personal importance. Speech is excessive and characterized by flights of ideas. Possibly, in the elderly a mood of angry hostility or impatience is more common, and this may be related to a perhaps greater admixture in older patients of depressive mood and thought content.

Recognition may be difficult when the patient is highly disordered, in that an acute confusional state (brain syndrome) may at first be suspected. Observation will demonstrate that the patient may be playful in responding to test questions, but that there is no evidence of changed or fluctuating awareness. Patients with a mixture of manic and depressive symptoms may exhibit marked perplexity, and be wrongly thought to be confused. In hypomanics the elated mood may be mistaken for euphoria, and the speech disorder for circumstantiality and incoherence in an over active and seemingly cheerful type of senile dement. Apart from cognitive assessment, recording of speech may demonstrate the superficial associations characteristic of flight of ideas, which may be repetitive but do not exhibit incoherence or true perseveration. Where a history is obtainable, there will have been a rapid onset in a physically healthy person, possibly preceded by some depression and sleeplessness.

Paranoid psychoses
In later life, paranoid phenomena are far more restricted in form and content than those encountered in younger psychiatric patients. Grandiose paranoid delusions of being royal or religiously important personalities or of being persecuted on account of one's importance, are not encountered. Also, the paranoid delusions of older patients do not arise in a psychologically incomprehensible way: they are never true, autochthonous delusions,

but only delusional ideas elaborated from some recent life experiences or domestic situations. The content of the delusional ideas concerns persecutions by persons who envy the patient for his possessions, and less often for his good name. This kind of paranoid ideation is most uncommon in youth, but becomes more common with rising age, when there is increasing narrowing of the social circle, withdrawal to one's self, and awareness of belonging to an underprivileged minority, all factors promoting paranoid experiencing.

Possibly for these reasons paranoid symptoms are so common in older people, and may occur in numerous psychiatric settings. Especially when associated with illusions or hallucinations, paranoid beliefs and behaviour may heavily overlay acute and subacute brain syndromes. Recognition of the basic disorder may be difficult, as sometimes fluctuations in the level of awareness may be inconspicuous (much as in the amphetamine psychoses of younger subjects). The paranoid experiences tend to be fleeting and varied, and they will as a rule subside together with the organic confusional state in response to removal of the causative toxic factors. Brief paranoid episodes may be observed occasionally in old people where sudden removal from their home had been necessary. More persistent paranoid symptoms not infrequently accompany both types of late life dementia. To form paranoid beliefs, much cognitive ability must obviously remain preserved, and as dementia progresses paranoid contents will fade. However, differential diagnosis may remain unresolved for some time, especially as modern forms of therapy tend to be successful in the removal of paranoid symptoms even in the case of patients with cerebral pathology.

Depressive illnesses in later life not infrequently have persecutory content, and patients may show paranoid behaviour activated by paranoid delusions or even by persecutory voices. The content is not always clearly derivable from depressive unworthiness or guilt, and the differentiation of a depressive from a paranoid psychosis may have to await the response to specific therapies and the further course. There may be a small group patients, termed schizo-affective because they exhibit simultaneously or successively both reaction types. Finally, paranoid illnesses may become persistent in the absence of cerebral-organic changes or of depression. These 'functional' paranoid psychoses differ from the schizophrenias of earlier life by the finding that delusions and hallucinations are not accompanied by schizophrenic dilapidation of the personality, by catatonic features, or by the development of appreciable degrees of affective incongruity and flattening. The descriptive label of late or senile paraphrenia has, therefore, been applied to them (Roth, 1955; Kay and Roth 1961). Some 10 per cent of elderly hospital patients were found to be suffering from this condition, and to be generally physically healthy, and with a long survival rate.

Presenting features of paranoid psychosis
Regardless of its clinical setting, in later life paranoid symptomatology assumes one of three forms. These do not present stages in the disorder, but seem to remain stable for the individual patient. First of all, there is what might be termed a simple paranoid psychosis. This tends to be limited in its content and impact; families or the police may be able to cope with the patient's complaints, and doctors are perhaps only rarely involved. This may be the commonest form of the disorder. Typically, the patient believes himself persecuted by neighbours in his home, imagining them as envying his situation or his possessions. Noises and other nuisances are created, objects are moved about. Possibly, delusions of theft are particularly common in hoarding dements, so are often ridiculous but dangerous jealous delusions concerning the spouse. Occasionally there may also be auditory and other hallucinations.

Patients suffering from the other two types of paranoid psychosis usually come to medical attention on account of their much more disturbed condition. They suffer from widely spread delusions and hallucinations of much more general content. They believe themselves observed through peep holes or with special apparatus: smells or rays are directed against them, cars circle their home, shouts are directed at them at home and in the street, children cry under the floor boards, etc. etc. These patients may be said to be suffering from a schizophrenia-like psychosis. Finally, there are some patients who are in many ways very similar to younger paranoid schizophrenics, in that they believe themselves to be talked about by several persons discussing them or furnishing a running commentary on their activities. The patient usually also believes himself influenced in his thoughts and actions by telepathic communications, which may in the form of sensations enter his body (e.g. sexual hallucinations). He may hear his thoughts spoken out loud. (For details on this and other matters dealt with in this section see Post, 1980).

Differential diagnosis from organic and depressive conditions has already been dealt with. Recognition will be only difficult where delusions are narrowly confined, concealed from the doctor, or where they touch upon ordinary matters of domestic squabbling. Persistence of the same complaint as well as its improbable nature may indicate a pathological state which goes beyond querulous complaining, but quite likely the borders between this and a paranoid illness are indistinct and shifting.

Aetiology of paranoid psychosis
Regarding aetiology, once again the previous personality furnishes the most potent factors. Life events, which are

independent of the illness, play no role, and in contrast to depressives there is only rarely a history of early neurotic symptoms or breakdown. A family history of schizophrenia has been found significantly more frequently than in normals, but far less often than in younger schizophrenics. In most cases, longstanding personality defects are reported by informants. The patients are described as secretive, quarrelsome, and suspicious from a much earlier age. Their marriage rate and fertility are low. Their social associations have always been few and shallow, and have often been limited to membership of esoteric cult groups. Equally well documented has been the heavy incidence among elderly paranoids of social deafness (Cooper, 1976) which is not an age-linked nerve deafness, but long-standing deafness due to inflammatory or degenerative middle ear disease. This deafness may be partly respon-sible for the personality development (Cooper et al, 1976; Kay et al, 1976), from which the paranoid psychosis is precipitated by social age factors, or possibly by cerebral age changes similar to those suspected in old age depressions.

MANAGEMENT AND TREATMENT OF THE EMOTIONAL DISORDERS

The functional psychiatric disorders have been presented along a continuum as they disrupt increas-ingly severely the aging personality. Though their classi-fication is possible, the various conditions do not only overlap, but are practically always encountered in varying combinations. Discussion of treatment relating to each single condition would lead to a great deal of repetition, and for this reason this section on therapy has been left to the end of the chapter. Moreover, psychi-atric syndromes which are not secondary to any well understood physical malfunctioning (but which are the outcome of longstanding psychological dysfunctioning) cannot be expected to yield to simple causal therapies. Fortunately, there are numerous specific therapeutic procedures which are frequently successful in removing certain symptoms or symptom complexes. Anxiety may be alleviated by expertly conducted discussion and manipulation of the environment, or short-term treat-ment with minor tranquillisers; phobias may yield to behaviour therapy; depressive mood and its related thought content can usually be ameliorated or even removed by specific drug or by electroconvulsive therapy; more severe disruptions by schizophrenic types of delusions and of hallucinations can usually be suppressed by major tranquillizing drugs. All these specific therapies will be applied successfully only where an adequate relationship between patient and doctor has been established.

For all these reasons, management and treatment will be considered under three main headings relating to the general approach to the aging patient, to psychotherapy, and to somatic therapy.

General management

Doctor–patient relationship
Severe mental illness markedly impairs a person's ability to communicate, but even milder disturbances usually have this effect to some extent. Compared with others, many psychiatrically disabled patients tend for this reason to be called 'difficult'. A geriatrician (Williamson, 1978) has pointed out that the 'unlikable' patient should always be suspected of harbouring depression. It has been demonstrated that even demented old persons continue to sense whether an approach to them is merely mechanical or emotionally genuine (Bircher et al, 1978). So, the doctor will have to remind himself that mental suffering is as 'real' as physical pain and discomfort, even if the patient is often impatient, importuning, surly, hostile, or seemingly irrelevantly talkative. Only when he senses his doctor's sympathy will the patient open up and in due course comply with treatment. Thus a psychotherapeutically sophisticated approach may be required even for successful drug therapy.

In addition, allowance must be made for psychological age changes. Not only hearing, but also comprehension may be impaired. Slow repetition of questions and explanations is indicated. Too much abstraction in formulating to the elderly their problems and their poss-ible solutions should be avoided. Anxiety hinders comprehension, and challenges or helpfully-intended provocations should be employed only sparingly. For obvious reasons, denial is a mechanism much used by aging persons. It should be respected, and a review of previous life and of current relationships should be undertaken only where it seems therapeutically relevant. However, even sexual matters can be discussed, when indicated, with old people provided allowance is made for the attitudes of an older generation.

Family
Some patients may come for consultation on their own. They should be persuaded to allow contact with members of their family or with other close associates, especially when relationships appear to be disturbed, or where there are depressive or paranoid features to their disorder. Persistent refusal on the patient's part is unusual in our age group. Members of his entourage should preferably be interviewed initially on their own in order to minimize covering up. Immediate group discussions are only occasionally indicated: for instance, a few paranoid patients will divulge their beliefs and pathological experiences only when prompted by their

associates. The main role of group discussions will concern us in the section on psychotherapy.

The patient's associates should be encouraged to give vent to their ideas and opinions for as long as it seems profitable. In this way they will bring out their overt and covert feelings and attitudes towards the patient. While it is now generally recognized that the great majority of families are caring and concerned to the point of excessive protectiveness in the case of physically and mentally frail old members, neurotically complaining, importuning, miserable and accusatory old people tend to evoke mostly negative feelings and even physical maltreatment. Added to this, we saw earlier that many emotional disorders occur in later life in people burdened with earlier flaws in their personalities. Many of their relationships may have been problematical for many years, and it is not surprising that the appearance of the even more troublesome psychiatric symptoms may bring about a further deterioration in family atmosphere. In addition, depression, anxiety and paranoid beliefs may spread to close associates, especially spouses and single daughters living with their mothers. Under these circumstances, it may even be difficult to obtain a clear account of the patient's disorder, of the onset of a depressive condition, and of the circumstances and emotional undercurrents leading to decompensation. Negative family attitudes are likely to diminish compliance with treatment especially when, as is usual in neurotic disorders, results can be only gradually achieved.

In a few cases, hostility towards the patient may be so longstanding and rigid that family help and co-operation cannot be mobilized, at any rate initially, and the patient may then have to be treated in a hospital setting, even though the severity of his symptoms would hardly justify admission. Fortunately, in most cases the feelings of the patient's associates are ambivalent and mixed with a good deal of guilt. The doctor's concern, showing that he looks upon the patient as somebody who is suffering, will often come to be shared by his family, and the stage is then set for family meetings during which in the patient's presence feelings can be ventilated and modified. On the other hand, it may be discovered that close members of the patient's circle are themselves as disturbed as the patient, and they might respond to individual treatment. Finally, there are cases where it becomes clear that the patients are responding with neurotic symptoms to stresses arising from unreasonable demands made on them by others. Here firm instruction and energetic intervention (i.e. an authoritarian approach) may for once not be out of place (Kovacs, 1977), but we are now in an area where social workers skilled in family and group therapy may have to play a more active role than doctors.

So far, we have discussed in some detail matters with which every general physician, geriatrician, or psychiatrist in contact with elderly people must be familiar. By contrast, most of them cannot be expected to be experts in environmental manipulation, the various forms of psychotherapy, and the more specialized forms of somatic treatments. In the remainder of this chapter only guide lines will be given concerning the treatments available, their indications, and the results to be expected.

Social measures

In the case of emotionally disturbed or ill patients, the role of social work is more circumscribed than in situations surrounding old people severely handicapped by persistent physical or cognitive disabilities. Most problems of emotionally ill persons are intrapsychic or relate to intimate relationships, but as was pointed out earlier, neurotic, neurotically depressed, and unhappy old people have as a group been found more disadvantaged than their happier peers. They are more often unaware of the existence of economic and other social assistance, or are psychologically hindered in applying for it. They should be persuaded to allow a social worker to look into their affairs. Conversely, social workers in contact with old people are often more aware than the family doctor or the family of developing mental disturbance, and should often be instrumental in securing medical assessment. In the opposite direction, doctors should be more selective and thoughtful in their referrals to social workers than seems often the case.

Bergmann (1978) has tellingly made this point taking as an example the frequent complaint of loneliness, and many doctors' tendency to think of their patients' problems as due to too few social contacts. First of all, of course, many old people have outlived their associates and are alone. If they feel lonely, they may be guided by social workers into social activities with benefit. On the other hand, they may for many years have positively enjoyed the life style of the loner. In their case, social work should be limited to a watching brief, as isolated old people are obviously at risk of untreated physical and mental disorders. Secondly, whether or not they actually live alone, old persons may complain of loneliness, or may objectively lack in socialization. It is important to realize that loneliness may be the result of immobility, which requires the help, not of a social worker, but of a geriatrician. The complaint of loneliness and social withdrawal may also be due to developing depression and needs the attention of a doctor with psychiatric skills. Finally, and perhaps most frequently, loneliness is an aspect of what used to be called demoralization, and now more fittingly senile dysphoria. As we saw, this often shades over into a neurotic condition characterized by anxiety, depression and hypochondriacal concerns and complaints. Physical diseases and disabilities are unduly often present where these kinds of emotional disorders occur for the first time in old age, and it may be hoped (though this has not so far demonstrated) that morale may rise after successful physical rehabilitation. In addition, dysphoric old people should be helped by the provision of meaningful activities and company. Bergmann (1978) pointed out that neurotic old people often received the wrong sort of social treatment: they were more often than dements provided with domiciliary services, when what they needed were aids towards resocialization and towards domestic activities of their own.

Specific treatments

Psychotherapy

The psychological treatment of emotional disorders has been approached on the basis of two, perhaps only apparently, opposing causal theories. According to one, the patient is suffering from the results of faulty learning, and according to the other he is plagued by early memories of unfortunate experiences leading to lifelong anxiety about himself and his relation to others. Regardless of theories derived from different schools of psychiatry (which I have grossly over simplified), neurotic symptoms or states of varying psychological disability occur at times of stress. They may erupt repeatedly throughout the lifespan, but as we saw earlier they become a clinical problem for the first time only late in life under the impact of physical ill health, the loss of supporting persons, and possibly of retirement and financial stringency.

Behavioural psychotherapy. At the present, this still has limited application. It is most successful where there is a single symptom or a group of related ones, and behaviour therapy has been applied as in younger persons most frequently in phobic disorders. The commonest in the elderly is an overwhelming fear of staying alone at home or of going out alone or even in company. Very little has been published on behaviour therapy with older people (Brink, 1978; Garfinkel, 1979). On personal experience, the more complex methods involving imaginary desensitization are less successful than simple in vivo desensitization, where the patient is taught to tolerate situations, at first in the therapist's company, by stepwise progression. This method has proved highly successful, and has the advantage that at an early stage the practical therapeutic work can be taken over by nurses, members of the family or by voluntary workers, under the direction of the clinician or clinical psychologist. Far less certain, though always worth trying, is the effect of behavioural psychotherapy on obsessional rituals and ideas, and in illness phobias, i.e. a certain type of hypochondriasis. Nothing seems to have been published on old people treated for depres-

sion with cognitive therapy, which attempts to combat 'learned helplessness' and hopelessness. For more severely ill depressives requiring hospital treatment Goldstein (1979) has advocated ward measures designed to counter moaning, importuning and withdrawal from activities. The doctor should be seen as sympathetic and caring, but also as expecting the patient to function at his optimum level. His capacities should be carefully assessed and he should certainly not be pushed beyond them. However within the patient's limits, Goldstein directs that nurses and relatives should not respond to demands arising from helplessness and misery, and that even harsh measures should be adopted by often rather reluctant staff, such as removal of mattresses or threats of starvation in patients who withdraw to their beds or refuse to go to the dining room, to quote a few examples. Clearly, this type of approach requires scientific assessment, but it must be said that on the occasions when I encouraged enthusiastic junior doctors and nursing staff to use these methods orthodox treatment of the depressive state had to be employed in the end.

Dynamic psychotherapy. This has been shown to be indicated and applicable to old persons, and not only to younger patients with their allegedly greater plasticity. Regarding method, valuable advice has been given by Ingebretsen (1977), Wilensky and Weiner (1977), and by Brink (1977). The following are a few relevant points. Life review should be undertaken cautiously, as too much insight obtained by the patient may lead to too much guilt, while it is always important to increase an elderly patient's self-esteem. The therapist must guard against his own negative feelings (counter transference) aroused by the patient's apparently trifling and repetitive complaints. Dreams should not be interpreted along Freudian or Jungian lines, but their content might be made more hopeful by suggestion and autosuggestion. Current or recent problems should be discussed in a positive transference setting.

Group psychotherapy for older patients has been described by Krasner (1977), who points out that older groups do not tolerate much disturbance, and that in most instances individual sessions are required initially or during the course of group treatment.

Kahana (1979) has found it useful to divide neurotic old people into three groups. The first consists of essentially healthy persons with neurotic symptoms in a setting of good or fair general adjustment. In their case, therapy aimed at changing attitudes and limited aspects of psychic structure is often successful. At the opposite pole are persons who, though free of significant intellectual impairment, are debilitated by physical conditions, and who are also chronically unhappy and socially deprived. In their case, the main approach is to increase self-esteem, This may be achieved in brief but repeated sessions, in which the illusion is created in the patient of having vanquished the father-therapist. I have found it more satisfactory to admit to the patient, honestly, that his problems are too difficult for me, but that I shall be willing to discuss them with him sympathetically, as often and over as long a period as he finds it helpful. This has been accepted by many patients, who in this way have become an easier burden to their families, to whom a similar explanation had been given. Finally, Kahana (1979) described an intermediate and much smaller group, where more recent situational problems had led to consultation, and where the psychotherapist may have to step out of his role and pursue environmental changes. On the other hand, most of these patients suffer from anxious-depressive symptoms which invite also a more orthodox psychotherapeutic approach.

As we shall see, only relatively few older depressives are lastingly cured by somatic therapies, and most remain vulnerable to further breakdowns or are even lastingly afflicted. A psychotherapeutic approach, which might change basic attitudes and strengthen ego defences against losses of various kinds, would seem a more rational form of treatment. The resistance of psychotherapists against treating elderly depressives have been critically evaluated by Mintz et al (1981), and they also discussed the methods by which psychotherapy of elderly depressed patients might be experimentally studied. On their impression, the more economic group psychotherapy can be successful; controlled evaluative studies are on the way.

Somatic therapy

For the time being, treatment of emotional disorder is undertaken by physiological means far more frequently than by even the simplest forms of psychotherapy. In part this is due to the time consuming nature of psychotherapy, and the fact that in most areas of even the developed and industrial countries this form of treatment, where it goes beyond common sense on the one hand, and magic on the other, is simply not available even for younger people. Fortunately somatic therapies have been found in a considerable proportion of old patients to be effective, especially perhaps when they are used by doctors with psychological understanding. These forms of treatment shall be outlined under three headings: general physical measures, treatments aiming at normalizing mood, and drugs potent in suppressing symptoms of a schizophrenic type.

Treatment of concomitant physical disease. As was shown earlier, many mild and severe depressive conditions appear to be precipitated by physical illness, and many late life neurotics and depressives have been found to be suffering from persistent and disabling physical disorders. In addition, many of the remedies used in their treatment may produce not only acute or chronic deliria, but also depressive symptoms (see Chap.

8) It is, therefore, mandatory to review all medications recently taken by the emotionally ill patient, and to countermand all that are not urgently indicated. This usually includes also psychopharmacological preparations prescribed for longstanding anxiety or sleep disturbance. They may require gradual withdrawal.

Thorough physical examination and relevant investigations will confirm in most elderly depressives the presence of a number of disorders, and occasionally one may be discovered which is known to be associated with mood changes (e.g. parkinsonism, hypothyroidism, or incipient neoplasm). It is obviously good medicine to attend to all discovered treatable illnesses, but I have been disappointed by the very few instances in which their successful management has removed the depression. Even where it appears to have been precipitated by a physical illness, it seems as if clinical depression, once it has become established, runs its own, autonomous course. There is however the possibility that dysphoric and neurotic symptomatology may be ameliorated through effectively treated physical diseases and disabilities, and this needs to be investigated, urgently.

Somatic treatments of affective disorders. Three approaches are available. The first, and most acceptable one, is treatment with thymoleptic preparations (mood normalizers). The second method is with electroconvulsive therapies (ECT). Even more unpopular is the third, psychosurgery. In planning treatment of the depressed patient, some clinicians have advocated the immediate use of ECT for patients with depressive delusions or delusional ideas, under the impression that patients with such severely disruptive illnesses do not respond adequately to antidepressant drugs. From personal experience, this does not seem true, in that treatment with ECT as against that with drugs was followed by discharge from hospital only insignificantly more often in deluded than in non-deluded patients. Also, a number of depressives with delusions initially treated with ECT, became free of symptoms only after drug treatment had been substituted for unsuccessful electric shock therapy (Post, 1972).

Electroconvulsive therapy is sometimes the treatment of first choise because it usually produces improvement after three or four applications in patients who refuse food and fluids, or whose suicidal activities are difficult to control. It should now only be given under anaesthesia and with muscle relaxants, and obviously the doctor who administers the anaesthetic will have to be satisfied about the patient's fitness. Possibly a recent myocardial infarction is the only frequent contraindication to ECT. In a series of patients (most of whom admittedly were in the younger age groups) no lasting objective memory impairment was discovered regardless of whether the electrodes had been applied bilaterally or unilaterally (Weeks et al, 1980). However, especially for older patients, application to the non-dominant side is to be preferred, as postictal confusion is likely to be less, and thus the risk of accidents after each treatment diminished (Fraser and Glass, 1978). It is, however, sometimes difficult to decide whether a convulsion had actually been produced, and where unilateral treatment seems to be failing, treatment should be continued with bilaterally induced convulsions.

Thymoleptic drugs should be one's first choice in the great majority of patients with affective illnesses of clinical severity. The extent to which these remedies may also be effective in patients with milder depressions, e.g. those seen in geriatric departments, does not seem to have been scientifically evaluated. On personal impression, drug treatment of the concomitant and inconspicuous depression of elderly neurotics quite often diminishes hypochondriacal, phobic and obsessional concerns to an extent which makes further treatment unnecessary.

Once treatment with antidepressants has been decided, the clinician should use adequate doses of those drugs with which he has become familiar; also, there is no point, in case of failure, in substituting a drug with one belonging to the same group, i.e. one tricyclic for another. A minimum level of plasma concentration must be achieved, and this only partly depends in individual patients on dosage; for some drugs there may be a 'therapeutic window' (Montgomery et al, 1979), i.e. both too low and too high plasma levels fail to have therapeutic effects. Where estimations of plasma levels can be easily obtained it may be possible to determine correct dosages through a test dose (Dawling et al, 1981). However, in average practice drug level estimations will be considered only after the preparation concerned has failed to produce any improvement after about 3 weeks.

There has been increasing evidence that many tricyclic drugs used in elderly depressives, e.g. imipramine and amitriptyline, should be superseded by preparations which are more sedative, less anticholinergic, and more suitable for patients with cardiac problems, especially conduction defects (Burrows et al, 1976). Secunda (1980) is among those who have recently recommended doxepine: a daily dosage of around 200 mg is said to be required to produce therapeutic plasma levels, and there is supposed to be no 'therapeutic window'.

When a tricyclic preparation has failed in spite of adequate plasma levels, and especially when ECT is not acceptable, a tetracyclic drug like mianserin may be considered, but the risk of producing serious blood changes (Adams, 1982) should be considered. Monoamine oxidase inhibitors like phenelzine or tranylcypromine have been found useful in some older subjects (Ashford and Ford, 1979), but there have not been any properly controlled studies. A number of antidepressants, which are neither tricyclic, tetracyclic or MAOI substances, are at present under trial.

Lithium salts are highly effective in abolishing or greatly reducing manic symptoms at all ages. Where rapid control is essential, major tranquillisers, like haloperidol, are well tolerated by older subjects, at any rate up to a daily dose of around 9 mg. When lithium is used during the acute phase the plasma level should not rise much above 1.0 mmol (mEq)/1 (daily dosage usually 750–1000 mg of the carbonate) and for maintenance therapy should only be 0.4–0.7 mmol (mEq)/1. Manic illnesses always recur at short intervals in the elderly, and maintenance therapy is the rule. Frequently recurring depressions can also often be controlled by lithium maintenance therapy, checked by regular plasma level estimations. The dosages here recommended for both acute and for maintenance treatment are much lower than those used in younger adults because in the elderly renal clearance of lithium salts is much reduced, and toxic effects like tremor, anorexia, vomiting and diarrhoea are much more readily produced. Even on low dosages impairment of memory, and ultimately severe confusion may occur, and polydypsia and polyuria may become troublesome. Myxoedema may be precipitated in patients with marginal thyroid functioning. Electrolyte imbalance during physical illness or after commencing treatment with diuretics will cause lithium toxicity. In all these circumstances, frequent monitoring of lithium plasma levels and adjusting doses should make any, except temporary, discontinuation of therapy unnecessary and mental relapse avoidable.

Where all these forms of treatment have failed, and the patient has suffered without any significant relief for at least 18 months, natural remission is unlikely to occur for some years, if ever. One of the modern forms of psychosurgery, which produce only rarely lasting undesirable effect, should then be considered. The patient will have to be free of cerebral or significant physical deterioration or disease. Furthermore, he and his friends will have to give informed consent, and statutory regulations will have to be fulfilled. For all these reasons, few elderly depressives reap the benefit of psychosurgery, which continues to produce good results in a few apparently hopeless cases.

Somatic treatment of paranoid conditions. Some paranoid patients, especially those not suffering from the classical form of paranoid schizophrenia, may cease to be a problem on account of delusional complaints and hallucinations after being moved to sheltered and socially responsive surroundings. The great majority can be relieved only by major tranquillising drugs. Mainly in use are thioridazine, trifluoperazine and haloperidol. Chlorpromazine is alleged to cause jaundice especially frequently in older women. These drugs may be used briefly to deal with acute mental disturbances due to many causes, but their long-term use should be restricted to the treatment of persistent persecutory states. It is doubtful whether they are effective where paranoid delusions occur in a depressive psychosis, but they are highly successful in the management of late paraphrenics and also of dementing patients with troublesome and persistent paranoid symptoms.

It is inadvisable to exceed a daily dose of 500 mg of thioridazine, of 25 mg of trifluoperazine, or of 9 mg of haloperidol. Initial dosages should be about a tenth of the maximum doses, and treatment should be stepped up gradually over a number of weeks. Outpatient treatment should be attempted only in patients whose compliance can be assured. Compulsory admission is much more frequently necessary than in the case of severe depressives. Dosage increases should stop as soon as the patient ceases to be hallucinated or to elaborate fresh delusions. The maintenance dose will be much lower, just sufficient to suppress hallucinations and fresh delusions. Initial stepwise increase of medication should prevent acute dystonic reactions, but tardive dyskinesia can frequently not be avoided. However, the patients themselves are usually not aware of this condition, and many old people suffer from it without any exposure to causative drugs. However, every 6 months or so drug holidays should be attempted (Mehta et al, 1977). In my experience two thirds of previously successfully maintained patients are likely to relapse sooner or later after stopping their treatment (Post, 1980).

OUTCOME

Personality and neurotic disorders
There have been no critical studies of the outcome of any of these conditions in response to treatment, and neurotic disorders are likely to fluctuate in severity with the impact of external stresses and their relief through changes in life situations. If correctly approached, most patients tend to continue attending their doctors and often to be more grateful than some more 'successful' cases. It may therefore be assumed that skilful discussion and encouragement, as well as the promotion of increased self understanding, whose effects are difficult to measure, are all the same worthwhile and rewarding to both patients and doctors. The effects of psychological management on patients with persistent physical illnesses and disability should also be studied more closely.

Affective illnesses
By contrast, the results of treatment can be clearly summarized for the more severe forms of psychiatric illness. Quite likely, many patients with milder anxiety or depressive symptoms are successfully treated by their family doctors or geriatricians, but where they have not succeeded, or where the illness is more severe and persistent, results obtained in the psychiatric clinic are variable, though most certainly much better than before the introduction of modern treatment.

In the course of a 3-year follow-through of hospitalized depressives over the age of 60, only 26 per cent remained completely well over this period; 37 per cent had further depression, but made again full recoveries; 25 per cent remained vaguely unhappy, hypochondriacally complaining, and most of them also suffered from further more clear-cut depressive episodes; finally, 12 per cent remained significantly depressed throughout, though not usually requiring continuous hospital care. Of the 92 patients followed, seven became suicidal, and of these three killed themselves.

These at first sight disappointing results were achieved in spite of thorough and varied initial and maintenance treatment. All except the lastingly recovered patients received one or several of the recognised therapies during the follow-up period; more than one-third remained continuously on antidepressant drugs (Post, 1972). However, it should be added that recent studies have stressed that the long-term outcome of affective illnesses in younger people is also much worse than text books used to claim (Angst, 1978; Raskin et al, 1978).

Attempts to discover prognostic indicators for individual patients have proved unsuccessful. Only in general terms is the outlook worse for the patient over 70 or 75. Far more important is the malign influence of serious physical ill health, and a long previous history of continuous depression is usually unfavourable, especially perhaps when depressive breakdown had occurred for the first time only late in life.

Manic attacks always recur in the elderly within the next few months or year, usually interspersed with depressions. The effect of maintenance therapy with lithium remains to be investigated, but its benefit was manifest from a case note study in all but three of 27 consecutive elderly manics (Shulman and Post, 1980).

Paranoid illnesses
In the past, hardly any late paraphrenics recovered naturally; paranoid symptoms of dements obviously decrease and disappear with increasing cognitive decline. Major tranquillizers almost always remove or ameliorate paranoid delusions and hallucinations, but the patients remain handicapped by their previous personalities often compounded by deafness. In the long run, it turned out that only a quarter of patients remained ill; rather more than one-third pursued a fluctuating course, and rather less than one-third remained

well, half of them even having gained retrospective insight (Post, 1980). Prognosis depended on compliance with maintenance medication. This was favoured by complete initial remission, relatively good socialization, and no doubt related to this good rapport with the doctor.

CONCLUDING THOUGHTS

The purposes of this chapter have been to demonstrate that the emotional disorders of later life have with few exceptions close relationships to physical diseases and disabilities. Old people with persistent emotional disturbances also tend, in comparison with their more fortunate peers, to be more often economically disadvantaged and lacking loving and supporting family relationships. Their socially deprived circumstances are frequently the result of their own longstanding personality problems, of which many psychiatric illnesses arising in late life seem to be a later development.

On the other hand, in contrast with life-long psychiatric sufferers, those falling ill only at an older age tend to have rather more personality assests, and perhaps for this reason therapeutic results tend to be better than is so often the case with younger patients. Their psychotherapeutic management and the application of specific therapies are relatively easy and well within the province of all doctors and of their colleagues without medical qualifications.

REFERENCES

Adams P C 1982 Mianserin-induced agranulocytosis. Letter to British Medical Journal 285: 208–209

Angst J 1978 Verlauf endogener Psychosen. In: Finke J, Tölle R (eds) Aktuelle Neurologie und Psychiatrie, Springer-Verlag, Berlin, p 203–210

Ashford J W, Ford C V 1979 Use of MAO inhibitors in elderly patients. American Journal of Psychiatry 136: 1466–1467

Bergmann K 1971 The neuroses in old age. In: Kay D W K, Walk A (eds) Recent Developments in Psychogeriatrics, British Journal of Psychiatry Spec. Pub. No. 6, p 39–50

Bergmann K 1978 Neurosis and personality disorder in old age. In: Isaacs A D, Post F (eds) Studies in Geriatric Psychiatry, John Wiley & Sons, Chichester, p 41–75

Bircher M, Six W, Keller W 1978 Experiences in clinical psychotherapy with geriatric patients. Praxis 67: 990–995

Blazer D, Williams C D 1980 Epidemiology of dysphoria and depression in an elderly population. American Journal of Psychiatry 137: 439–444

Brink T L 1977 Dream therapy with the aged. Psychiatry: 354–360

Brink T L 1978 Geriatric rigidity and its psychotherapeutic implications. Journal of the American Geriatric Society 26: 274–277

Burrows G D, Vohra J, Davies B, Scoggins B A 1976 Cardiac effects of different tricyclic antidepressant drugs. British Journal of Psychiatry 129: 335–341

Cawley R H, Post F, Whitehead A 1973 Barbiturate tolerance and psychological functioning in elderly depressed patients. Psychological Medicine 1: 39–52

Clark A N G, Mankikar G D, Gray I 1975 Diogenes syndrome. A clinical study of gross neglect in old age. Lancet i: 366–373

Comfort A 1980 Sexuality in late life. In: Birren E J, Sloane R B (eds) Handbook of Mental Health and aging, Prentice-Hall Inc, Englewood Cliffs, N J, p 886–888

Cooper A F 1976 Deafness and psychiatric illness. British Journal of Psychiatry 129: 216–226

Cooper A F, Garside R F, Kay D W K 1976 A comparison of deaf and non-deaf patients with paranoid and affective psychoses. British Journal of Psychiatry 129: 532–538

Dawling S, Crome.P, Heyer E J, Lewis R R 1981 Nortriptyline therapy in elderly patients: Dosage prediction from plasma concentration at 24 hours after a single 50 mg dose. British Journal of Psychiatry 139: 413–416

Elias M F, Elias P K 1977 Motivation and Activity. In: Birren J E, Schaie K W (eds) Handbook of the Psychology of Aging, p 371–372, 376–378

Epstein I J, Mills C, Simon A 1970 Antisocial behaviour of the elderly. Comprehensive Psychiatry 11: 36–42

Fraser R M, Glass I B 1978 Recovery from ECT in elderly patients. British Journal of Psychiatry 133: 524–528

Garfinkel R 1979 Brief behaviour therapy with an elderly patient. Journal of Geriatric Psychiatry 12: 101–109

Gianturco D T, Busse E W 1978 Psychiatric problems encountered during a long-term study of normal ageing volunteers. In: Isaac A D, Post F (eds) Studies in Geriatric Psychiatry, John Wiley & Sons, Chichester, p 1–16

Goldstein S F 1979 Depression in the elderly. Journal of the American Geriatrics Society 27: 38–42

Gurland B J, Dean L, Cross P, Golden R 1980 The epidemiology of depression and dementia in the elderly: The use of multiple indicators of these conditions. In: Cole J O, Barrett J E (eds) Psychopathology in the Aged, Raven Press, New York, p 37–59

Hendrickson E, Levy R, Post F 1979 Averaged evoked responses in relation to cognitive and effective state of elderly psychiatric patients. British Journal of Psychiatry 134: 494–501

Ingebretsen R 1977 Psychotherapy in the elderly. Psychotherapy 14: 319–332

Jacoby R J, Levy R, Bird J M 1981 Computed tomography and the outcome of affective disorder: A follow-up study of elderly patients. British Journal of Psychiatry 139: 288–292

Kahana R J 1979 Strategies of dynamic psychotherapy with the wider range of older individuals. Journal of Geriatric Psychiatry 12: 71–100

Kay D W K, Roth M 1961 Environmental and herediatary factors in the schizophrenias of old age ('late paraphrenia') and their bearing on the general problem of causation in schizophrenia. Journal of Mental Science, 107: 649–686

Kay D W K, Cooper A F, Garside R F, Roth M 1976 The differentiation of paranoid from affective psychoses by patients' premorbid characteristics. British Journal of Psychiatry 129: 207–215

Kimmel D C 1977 Psychotherapy and the older gay man. Psychotherapy 14: 386–393

Kovacs H L 1977 Rapid intervention strategies in work with the aged. Psychotherapy 14: 368–372

Krasner J D 1977 Loss of dignity: Courtesy of modern science. Psychotherapy 14: 309–318

Lipton M A 1976 Age differentiation in depression: Biochemical aspects. Journal of Gerontology 31: 293–299

Lishman W A 1978 Organic Psychiatry. Blackwell Scientific Publications, Oxford, London, Edinburgh, Melbourne, p 571–574

MacMillan D, Shaw P 1966 Senile breakdown in standards of personal and environmental cleanliness. British Medical Journal 2: 1032–1037

Marks I 1981 Space 'phobia'; a pseudo-agoraphobic syndrome. Journal of Neurology, Neurosurgery and Psychiatry 44: 387–391

Mehta D, Mehta S, Matthew D 1977 Tardive dyskinesia in psychogeriatric patients: A five year follow-up. Journal of the American Geriatrics Society 25: 545–547

Mendlewicz J 1976 The age factor in depressive illness: Some genetic considerations. Journal of Gerontology 31: 300–303

Miller M 1978 Geriatric suicide: The Arizona Study. Gerontologist 18: 488–495

Mintz J, Steuer J, Jarvik L 1981 Psychotherapy with depressed elderly patients: Research consideration. Journal of Consultant Clinical Psychology 49: 542–548

Mishara B L, Kastenbaum R 1980 Alcohol and Old Age. Grune and Stratton, New York

Montgomery S A, McAuley R, Rani S J, Montgomery D B, Braithwaite R, Dawling S 1979 Amitriptyline plasma concentrations and clinical response. British Medical Journal 1: 230–231

Murphy E 1982 Social origins of depression in old age. British Journal of Psychiatry 141: 135–142

Post F 1968 The factor of ageing in affective illness. In: Coppen A, Walk A (eds) Recent Developments in Affective Disorders. British Journal of Psychiatry Spec. Pub. No. 2, p 105–116

Post F 1972 The management and nature of depressive illnesses in late life: A follow-through study. British Journal of Psychiatry 121: 393–404

Post F 1975 Dementia, depression and pseudo-dementia In: Benson D F, Blumer P (eds) Psychiatric Aspects of Neurologic Diseases, Grune and Stratton, New York, p 99–120

Post F 1980 Paranoid, schizophrenic-like and schizophrenic states in the aged. In: Birren J E, Sloane R B (eds) Handbook of Mental Health and Aging, Prentice-Hall Inc., Englewood Cliffs, N J, p 591–615

Robinson D S, Sourkes T L, Nies A, Harris L S, Spector S, Bartlett, D L 1977 Monoamine metabolism in human brain. Archives of General Psychiatry, 34: 89–92

Raskin A, Boothe H, Reatig N, Schulterbrandt J G 1978 Initial response to drugs in depressive illness and psychiatric and community adjustment a year later. Psychological Medicine 8: 71–79

Rosin A, Glatt M M 1971 Alcohol excess in the elderly. Quarterly Journal of Studies in Alcoholism 32: 53–59

Roth M 1955 The natural history of mental disorders in old age. Journal of Mental Science 101: 281–301

Secunda S K 1980 Doxepin: Recent plasmacologic and clinical studies. In: Mendels J, Amsterdam J D (eds) The Psychobiology of of Affective Disorders, S Karger, Basel, p 130–146

Shulman K 1978 Suicide and parasuicide in old age: A review. Age and Ageing 7: 201–209

Shulman K, Post F 1980 Bipolar affective disorders, in old age. British Journal of Psychiatry 136: 26–32

Simon A 1980 The neuroses, personality disorders, alcoholism drug use and misuse, and crime in the aged. In: Birren J E, Sloane R B (eds) Handbook of Mental Health and Aging, Prentice-Hall Inc, Englewood Cliffs, N J p 661–662

Stenback A, Kumperlainen M, Vauhkonen M L, 1979 A field study of old age depression. In: Orima H, Shimoda K, Inki M, Maeda D (eds) Recent Advances in Gerontology, International Congress Series, No. 469, Excerpta Medica, Amsterdam, p 193–194

Weeks K, Freeman C P L, Kendell R E 1980 ECT III. Enduring Cognitive Defecits? British Journal of Psychiatry 137: 26–37

Wells C E 1980 The differential diagnosis of psychiatric disorders in the elderly. In: Cole J O, Bennett J E (eds) Psychopathology in the Aged. Raven Bros., New York, p 19–36

Wilensky H, Weiner M B 1977 Facing reality in psychotherapy with the aging. Psychotherapy 14: 373–378

Williamson J 1978 Depression in the elderly. Age and Ageing 7 (Supp): 35–40

The central nervous system — cerebral function and drug therapy

In attempting to exert a favourable influence on cerebral function by the use of drugs, earlier approaches concentrated on vasodilators: by theoretical extrapolation, if a drug could dilate peripheral blood vessels it was considered probable that it could act similarly on cerebral vessels. It was assumed that cerebral arterial dilatation would improve cerebral function, and that successful cerebral vasodilatation would have no harmful effect.

It has become increasingly apparent, however, that these assumptions are not necessarily correct: rigid atherosclerotic vessels may not respond to the drugs, but more normal arteries might, so 'stealing' blood from the already ischaemic areas and actually aggravating the condition; and even where increased cerebal blood flow has been demonstrated there may not be concomitant or subsequent improvement in cerebral function. After all, deteriorating mental function may be due to primary neuronal degeneration quite apart from any changes in the cerebral circulation.

As a result, there has been a move away from the promulgation of 'cerebral vasodilators': the same drugs — and some newer ones — are now often promoted as agents for modifying the physical characteristics of the blood itself, so as to allow it to flow more readily through narrowed vessels; and there has been a wave of enthusiasm for drugs which are alleged to improve cerebral metabolism in various ways and — in some cases — to stimulate the failing cerebral neurons. It is now becoming commonplace to hear of 'vasoactive drugs', 'haemokinators', 'cerebral metabolic improvers' and 'cerebral activators'.

This chapter presents a review of these types of drugs and their effects on cerebral function. To do this is a formidable task, for the literature is vast and abounds with conflicting reports and research projects as variable in quality as in design. Furthermore, the topic is a highly controversial one; in the United Kingdom it is frequently regarded with scepticism but in Europe and North America such drugs find more ready acceptance and are used extensively.

THE CEREBRAL CIRCULATION

Anatomical considerations

The structure of the arterial walls show changes in senescence which resemble those seen in arteries elsewhere in the body — but these changes may develop more slowly in cerebral arteries (Bouissou et al, 1975). The smaller intraparenchymatous vessels show increased tortuosity, spirals, coils and sinusoidal formations as part of the normal aging process. Larger arterioles and cerebral and extracerebral arteries show medial fibrosis and loss of elasticity. These changes increase with each dacade from 55 years onward (Fung, 1976), and superimposed atherosclerotic changes are likely to occur. It is on this basis that lessened responsiveness to pharmacological agents is presumed.

Perhaps of more importance are changes in the microcirculation. In intracerebral capillaries the endothelial layer is continuous, and shares its basement membrane with the astrocyte sheath. This membrane increases in thickness and the endothelial cells become attenuated in the aging rat (Donahue and Pappas, 1961). Thinning of capillary walls due to loss and attenuation of endothelial cells has been reported in rats (Schwink and Wetzstein, 1966) and macaque monkeys (Burns et al, 1979). The latter authors found that the mean diameter of the capillary lumen was decreased in the aging primate, as reported in the rat (Bar, 1978). The capillaries and smaller arterioles have 85 per cent of their surface area covered by astroglial pseudopodia (Maynard et al, 1957) and oligodendrocytes are also in close perivascular relationships with these small vessels (Cammermeyer, 1960). These glial cells are not inert supporting cells: they are important in metabolism of neurons and transport of ions (Kuffler and Nicholls, 1966) and they *move*: e.g., oligodendrocytes in tissue culture show spontaneous rhythmic pulsatile activity (Lumsden and Pomerat, 1951; Pomerat, 1952) and respond to serotonin (Benitez et al, 1955). The perivascular arrangement of glial cells with these properties suggests that, by changes in their size, shape and motion, they may play a part in the local regulation of size of the lumen of the capillaries and small arterioles, thus influencing blood flow in the cerebral microcirculation (Cammermeyer, 1960; Wolff, 1968). Such a mechanism was considered by Chiang et al (1968) to play a part in the pathogenesis of the 'no-reflow' phenomenon seen after acute experimental ischaemia. More recent work has shown that capillary endothelial cells in the brain are also capable of contraction and relaxation (Owman et al., 1977).

If drugs can influence the size of the lumen of cerebral vessels, they may act by having agonist or antagonist effects on the autonomic nervous receptors in the vessel wall, or by direct effects on the vessel wall itself.

Deshmukh et al (1971–1972) described a dual adrenergic innervation of cerebral vessels in baboons: (a) *intraparenchymal arterioles* with little or no sympathetic innervation, their calibre being regulated locally by products of cerebral cellular metabolism or by changes in blood gases (see below); and (b) *extraparenchymal arteries* of and around the circle of Willis, with a rich adrenergic nerve supply and predominantly under autonomic control. These authors also showed a third category: (c) *pial arteries* with both neurogenic and metabolic control.

More recently it has been demonstrated that there is an extensive network of autonomic nerve fibres supplying cerebral arteries and arterioles (Zervas et al, 1975). Edvinsson and Owman (1975) have shown that parenchymal as well as pial arteries share in this abundant nerve supply, although fewer fibres reach the small intraparenchymal vessels, and associated with the smooth muscle of small cerebral arteries there are α- and β-adrenergic and cholinergic receptors and also H_1 and H_2 histaminergic and serotoninergic receptors. The receptors may not all be associated with the neurons, however.

The precise physiological role of the vasomotor nerves to cerebral blood vessels is the subject of considerable controversy. Some authorities (Sokoloff, 1960; Lassen, 1968; Skinhøj, 1972) dismiss this autonomic innervation as negligible in the regulation of cerebral blood flow in man (and thus consider that drugs influencing the autonomic nervous system are unlikely to be of use in therapy for impaired cerebral circulation). Others accept that there is evidence of some resting tonic activity (particularly with regard to vasoconstriction but also involving vasodilatation mediated by cholinergic influences) and see the neural contribution to the control of cerebral arterial tone and calibre as part of a balanced system which also involves those local metabolic and myogenic factors capable of influencing the vessels (see below). Thus, James et al (1969) suggested that the neural role becomes progressively more important as blood gas tensions or arterial pressure deviate from the physiological range; Zervas and colleagues (1975) consider that sympathetic innervation helps determine the 'set-point', at which blood vessels react to changes in local hydrogen-ion concentration.

Purves (1972) suggested that the most important function of vasomotor activity in cerebral vessels might be to integrate the responses of the cerebral vascular and other peripheral vascular beds. Mchedlishvili et al (1973) considered that the neural mechanism of autoregulation was more important than the humoral. The importance of neurogenic mechanisms has been stressed (Lundgren and Jodal, 1975; Obrist, 1975).

Cerebral blood flow (CBF)

The control of cerebral circulation is complex. Cerebral blood flow depends, as does flow in other vascular beds, upon perfusion pressure and resistance (see Olesen, 1974; Fieschi and des Rosiers, 1976).

Perfusion pressure depends on the arterial and venous pressures, but in health the mean arterial pressure may vary within a range of 80–140 mmHg without affecting cerebral blood flow because of the phenomenon of 'autoregulation'.

Resistance is made up of several factors, including the structure and tone of vessel walls and the physical properties of the blood.

Tone of vessel walls

Neurogenic influences have been described and evaluated above.

Myogenic influences are affected by perfusion pressure in certain conditions (see above).

Metabolic influences. The tone of intracerebral arteries is controlled mainly by the CO_2 tension of the arterial blood (Pa_{CO_2}). Increase in Pa_{CO_2} causes vasodilatation and lowered Pa_{CO_2} causes vasoconstriction. Although formerly considered a direct action of CO_2 on the cerebral vessels, the bulk of direct evidence now suggests that this effect of CO_2 is influenced by the autonomic innervation of the cerebral vessels (James et al, 1969; Purves, 1972) and by changes in pH in the cerebrospinal fluid around the vessels (Wahl et al, 1970), though Hernandez-Perez and Anderson (1976) found that CSF pH played no significant role in the autoregulation of CBF in Macaque monkeys.

Other metabolic changes influence cerebral blood flow. Increased hydrogen-ion concentration may increase CBF (the situation is complex, however) and decreased Pa_{O_2} has a similar effect; metabolic changes in the opposite direction have the converse effects. Pa_{O_2} may exert a direct effect on the vascular smooth muscle, but a reflex effect via carotid body and aortic chemoreceptors is also likely (James et al, 1969) and an influence on periarteriolar pH is also a possibility (Lassen and Skinhøj, 1975).

Metabolic influences decrease as the mean arterial pressure rises above 140 mmHg, and in old age (see below).

Physical properties of the blood
The flow of blood in small vessels and capillaries is greatly influenced by the viscosity of the blood. With a simple fluid such as water, viscosity is independent of flow-rate (or, more accurately, shear-rate) and the flow is termed newtonian. Blood, however, is a thixotropic fluid (Dintenfass, 1971) — i.e., its viscosity is inversely related to shear-rate, and this is reversible; the flow is non-newtonian. This is due to the flexibility of the red cells and their tendency to aggregate. (An emulsion of entirely non-aggregated particles has newtonian flow.) Aggregation is diminished when red cells become more rigid; rouleaux are not formed, and flow becomes newtonian, whilst at the same time blood viscosity increases because of the reduced flexibility of the red cells.

The main factors affecting blood viscosity are shear-rate, haematocrit, red-cell flexibility and aggregability, platelet aggregability, plasma viscosity (especially influenced by fibrinogen and other plasma protein concentrations), and vessel bore smaller than about 1 mm. Fåhraeus and Lindqvist (1931) observed an apparent decrease in the viscosity of blood flowing through capillary tubes of decreasing size below 300 mμ diameter. However, Dintenfass (1967) found that below a certain critical capillary radius (5–7 μ in his experimental conditions without platelet aggregates, but possibly much larger when red-cell flexibility falls and platelet aggregation occurs) a sudden and dramatic *increase* in resistance to flow occurs, with increase in apparent blood viscosity as the capillary radius is decreased further. He termed this the *inversion phenomenon*. Just prior to this critical diameter, the viscosity of blood is only 30 per cent greater than that of plasma, if the red cells have normal flexibility.

Red-cell flexibility decreases as the cells age and lose adenosine triphosphate (ATP) (Nakao et al, 1962) and the ability of red cells to assume rheologically favourable shapes depends on their ATP concentrations (Nakao et al, 1960). This is related to the ATP-modulated concentration of calcium ions in the red cells (Weed et al, 1969). The subject is discussed further by La Celle et al (1973), who point out that the passage of the more rigid ATP-depleted erythrocytes through the microcirculation may be markedly impaired.

Since the average erythrocyte diameter is 7.5 μ and since the smallest capillaries may be only 2 μ diameter the importance of red-cell flexibility is obvious: the behaviour of red cells in capillary flow is discussed by Charm and Kurland (1974).

Red cell shape and flexibility can also be affected by pH, Po_2 and Pco_2 (Weed et al, 1969; Lancet, 1978a), hypoxia can affect the haematocrit and the aggregability of red cells. Infection significantly increases the latter.

Some idea of the possible result of increased blood viscosity in the microcirculation, due to several of the influencing factors mentioned above, has been given by Dintenfass and Read (1968) in their hypothesis on the pathogenesis of heart-failure in acute-on-chronic respiratory failure: if the haematocrit exceeds 60 per cent, Pao_2 is less than 40 mmHg, and arterial blood pH approaches 7.0, in the presence of increased red-cell aggregation produced by infection, the viscous properties of the blood flowing slowly through small lung-vessels would approximate to that of a thick concrete sludge.

A small change in the rheology of blood might result in a multifold decrease in the rate of flow in the microcirculation; Pco_2 rises and this not only increases red-cell rigidity but also decreases the affinity of haemoglobin for oxygen. Decreased oxygen transport is the result.

Increase in haematocrit may be associated with low mean CBF (Thomas et al, 1977; Humphrey et al, 1979) and decreased cortical CBF (York and Sproule, 1978). In each of these studies reduction of haematocrit (by venesection) increased CBF. There was a correlation between blood viscosity and haematocrit, and an inverse relationship between blood viscosity and CBF (Humphrey et al, 1979).

One of the most fascinating therapeutic concepts at the present time is the possibility of improving the rheology of the blood by the use of 'vasoactive drugs' and other compounds alleged to improve cerebral metabolism; however, there is as yet incomplete evidence to confirm the potential value of these drugs in improving cerebral function.

Cerebral blood flow in old age
In normal old people CBF is usually considered to be the same as, or only slightly less than, that in young healthy controls (Sokoloff, 1966, 1975; Lassen and Ingvar, 1980). However, some authorities report a decline in CBF, as judged by the ^{133}Xe inhalation technique, with aging in normal subjects unselected except for their ability to function normally in their home environment (Obrist, 1980). In this work, CBF was correlated with cerebral metabolic rate and EEG changes, as well as intellectual function. For a fuller discussion, see Hoyer (1982). Autoregulation is normal with regard to the influences of both $Paco_2$ and blood-pressure changes (Meyer, 1978).

Vasomotor reactivity to $Paco_2$ has been reported as being slightly reduced in old age (Fazekas et al, 1952; Schieve and Wilson, 1953) and old rats showed a reduced ability to maintain a CBF response to prolonged hypercapnia (or hypoxia), when compared to young rats (Aukland, 1965; Haining et al, 1970). However, in the light of more recent evidence that cerebral vessels react normally to $Paco_2$ and arterial blood-pressure changes in dementia, whether multi-infarct or primary neuronal (see below), it seems most likely that normal old age does not bring about any significant change in immediate response to $Paco_2$ or blood-pressure.

Cerebral blood flow in disease states

Diseases associated with raised haematocrit. Older patients are less able to maintain CBF when increased haematocrit raises blood viscosity (Thomas et al, 1978).

Dementia. Cerebral arteriosclerosis, as a clinical diagnosis to explain mental deterioration in the elderly, has been severely criticized by Hachinski et al (1974). They point out that atherosclerosis causes dementia by producing multiple cerebral infarcts, some of which may be very small ('lacunes') (Fisher, 1965, 1969; Gautier, 1976). Dementia becomes apparent when the total volume of cerebral softenings exceeds 50 ml. Hachinski et al (1974) claimed that cerebral vasodilator drugs could hardly be expected to help such patients — although in a subsequent paper (Hachinski et al, 1975) they conceded that attempts to increase the blood supply to under-perfused but non-infarcted areas of brain tissue are certainly worthy of further exploration. Experiments reported by Heiss et al, (1976) demonstrate that ischaemic neurons do appear to have the potential for restoration of function, and an optimistic view appears justified (Millikan, 1978).

It has long been recognized that total CBF and mean cerebral oxygen uptake are decreased in some dementias, even though autoregulation remains normal (Freyhan, Woodford and Kety, 1951; Fazekas et al, 1953; Lassen et al, 1957). Munck et al (1968) confirmed these observations in studies of hemisphere flow, and bilateral studies showed that the reductions were more marked in the dominant hemisphere.

Much work has been done to study regional cerebral blood flow (rCBF) in various physiological and clinical states (Ingvar et al, 1965; Wilkinson et al, 1969; Lassen and Skinhøj, 1975) including dementia and pre-senile dementia (Ingvar et al, 1968; Obrist et al, 1970; Simard et al, 1971; Hachinski et al, 1975; Lavy et al, 1978). Some workers have tried to correlate the rCBF with the type of mental disturbance predominating in demented patients (Gustafson and Hagberg, 1975; Hagberg and Ingvar, 1976) but the validity of these correlations has been questioned (Leading article, British Medical Journal, 1976). Nevertheless, Obrist (1980) suggests that, haemodynamically, aging and dementia lie along a continuum, showing quantitative but not qualitative differences; when intellectual deterioration is present

CBF is reduced earlier and to a greater extent than in 'normal' aging.

It has been shown that focal increase in rCBF accompanies particular neurological and psychological activities — e.g., mental effort (Ingvar and Risberg, 1967; Risberg and Ingvar, 1968, 1973), speaking and reading (Ingvar and Schwartz, 1964), exercise of an arm (Olesen, 1971), stereognostic testing (Roland and Larsen, 1976) — and this has led to speculation as to whether reduced CBF in dementia is due to decreased metabolic demands in the grey matter (which is also reduced in amount (Hoedt-Rasmussen and Skinhøj, 1966; Ingvar et al, 1965, 1968) or is the underlying cause of the loss of grey matter.

The problem is simplified if senile dementia of Alzheimer type (SDAT) is considered separately from the dementia associated with cerebrovascular disease (multi-infarct dementia, MID). This differentiation can be made with a high degree of accuracy on clinical grounds (Hachinski et al, 1975; Todorov et al, 1975; Harrison et al, 1979). It is then found that hemisphere CBF is lower in cerebrovascular dementia than in SDAT, comparing patients of similar ages and degree of dementia (O'Brien and Mallett, 1970; Hachinski et al, 1975). This suggests that whereas vascular disease may lead to impairment of blood flow to the brain, it is more likely that in SDAT the reduced overall metabolic need determines a compensatory reduction in CBF, and a similar sequence may operate in multi-infarct dementia as well. Some support to this concept is given by oxygen-15 studies indicating reduced regional metabolic and circulatory distributions in two patients with dementia (Lenzi and Jones, 1980).

Metabolic mapping by the 18F-deoxyglucose technique may add information on anaerobic metabolism (Fieschi, 1980), but such new data are not yet available for dementia. The introduction of positron emission tomography will also be of potential value in this type of regional brain study (Benson, 1982).

Cerebral vasomotor reactivity to $Paco_2$ changes is preserved in both types of dementia (O'Brien and Mallett, 1970; Simard and colleagues, 1971) but the responses to hypercapnia were found to be less in MID than in SDAT (Yamaguchi et al, 1979). The same authors showed that the increase in CBF on mental activity is much reduced in patients with dementia.

Transient ischaemic attacks (TIA). Transient ischaemic attacks are common in the elderly, the incidence in the decade 65 to 74 years being given as 2 per 1000 (Whisnant, 1974). The risk of developing cerebral infarction within 5 years of TIA is about 30 per cent (Toole et al, 1975); the risk increases with age.

Disturbances of rCBF were observed by Skinhøj et al (1970) in 12 patients for up to one day after a transient ischaemic attack. Autoregulation was also altered temporarily, but re-established after a short interval. It is currently believed that TIA are due to platelet emboli or platelet-fibrin thrombi from ulcerated endothelial surfaces at the carotid bifurcation or in the heart.

Medical management. There are reports of reduced incidence of TIA in patients treated with cyclandelate and isoxsuprine (van der Drift, 1961). Van der Drift, 1961). Van der Drift and Kok (1971) consider that 'there is some evidence that vasoactive therapy is of more importance than was supposed one decade ago'. Some potential for benefit may be seen in view of the post-ischaemic disturbance of the cerebral microcirculation associated with swelling of capillary endothelium and perivascular glia, and increased blood viscosity (Scheinberg, 1979). However, this view is not shared by Easton and Byer (1980).

Focal neurological disease. Heiss (1973) investigated the effects of various drugs on rCBF in 175 patients with focal cerebrovascular disease and 36 with other neurological deficits; the results were compared with those in 36 untreated control subjects. Administration of β-receptor stimulants, such as isoxsuprine and nylidrin, produced a diffuse but significant fall in rCBF. The converse effect resulted from the use of hexobendine or low-molecular-weight dextran; however, intracerebral steal was noted in one patient given hexobendine. Interestingly, an 'inverse steal' phenomenon was seen after administration of a xanthine compound, papaverine-like drugs, and low-molecular-weight dextran.

Acute strokes. Autoregulation is lost focally and generally; changes in systemic arterial pressure will be reflected in changes in CBF, and this may be dangerous if there is marked hypertension or possibly drug-induced hypotension.

The consensus of opinion is therefore to avoid the use of vasodilator drugs in acute strokes; cerebral vasodilatation will already have occurred to a maximal extent due to occumulation of metabolites in and around the ischaemic area, and increasing capacitance of arteries elsewhere may only lead to the 'intracerebral steal' phenomenon, where blood is further diverted away from the ischaemic region of the brain (Lassen and Pálvölgyi, 1968). McHenry (1972, 1978) advocates a more aggressive approach to the use of vasoactive drugs in acute stroke, but only where rCBF measurements are available for monitoring purposes.

Recent experimental work in cats showed that some protection was afforded against acute focal cerebral ischaemia by intravenous administration of perfluorochemicals, inert oxygen-carrying blood substitutes (Peerless et al, 1981). The protection was attributed to support of the cerebral microcirculation by decreasing blood viscosity and by increasing availability of oxygen to the tissues; the protective effect was superior to that of mannitol.

Cerebral metabolism

The present discussion must touch on cerebral metabolism but cannot do more than make a few pertinent points. For more detailed information the reader is referred to Purves (1972); Harper et al, (1975); Himwich (1976a); Giacobini et al, (1982); Hoyer (1982); Meier-Ruge (1982).

Clearly, cerebral blood flow and metabolism are closely related, and, as has been emphasized above, the regulation of CBF depends very largely on local chemical control in brain tissue. Some specific metabolic features require particular mention.

Oxygen. The brain has a high demand for oxygen, requiring about 20 per cent of the total oxygen of the lungs under resting conditions. The cerebral metabolic rate for oxygen ($CMRO_2$) tends to parallel the CBF. There is little, if any, fall in normal old age (Sokoloff, 1975) but in genenral there is an inverse relationship between the degree of dementia and brain $CMRO_2$ (Obrist, 1980; Hoyer, 1982). Synaptic nerve-endings consume 40 per cent of the total oxygen used by the brain (Davison, 1976); therefore nerve-endings are particularly susceptible to hypoxia. However, enzyme 'markers' of synapses show no decreasing activities with advancing age (Davison, 1978)

Several vasoactive drugs are claimed to increase $CMRO_2$ as well as CBF.

Hyperbaric oxygen therapy has been advocated as helpful in the management of dementia (Jacobs et al, 1969) but this could not be confirmed by Goldfarb et al (1972) or by Thompson and his colleagues (1976). Critical reviews of hyperbaric oxygen therapy in dementia are provided by Eisner (1975) and Thompson (1975). According to Meyer et al (1976b) this therapy is not recommended, as it is 'impractical, expensive and not without danger'.

Glucose. This is of prime importance as the source of energy for neuronal metabolism; oxygen is required for the Embden-Meyerhof pathway citric acid cycle and, secondarily, for the pentose phosphate pathway. ATP is produced during these reactions, and is the power source; several control mechanisms exist to couple energy consumption tightly and rapidly to neuronal activity (Lowry, 1975). In animal studies local CBF correlates highly with local cerebral glucose utilization (Des Rosiers et al, 1974) and overall CBF correlates with both (Reivich et al, 1975). Sokoloff (1975) described significanlty reduced cerebral glucose consumption in both normal and asymptomatic arteriosclerotic groups of elderly subjects. The brain normally uses glucose and oxygen in stoichometric amounts, yet in these groups of elderly subjects the cerebral oxygen consumption was not altered (although the CBF fell in the atherosclerotic group). In dementia, a significant fall in cerebral glucose consumption is common, again without being necessarily accompanied by a fall in oxygen consumption or CBF (Hoyer, 1982).

The dissociation of cerebral glucose and oxygen consumption has been explained by the utilization of ketone bodies (Gottstein et al, 1972; Himwich, 1976b), although this presupposes elevated blood ketone levels in the elderly and there is insufficient evidence in this regard at the present time. Several studies have shown that aging brain has a decreased glycolytic capacity (see Meier-Ruge, 1982).

In normal aging rats, decreased glucose utilization was found to occur in specific brain regions, e.g., parietal cortex, and parts of the extrapyramidal and limbic systems (Smith, 1980). However, most of these age changes were present by mid-life and did not progress during senescence. In hypoxic rats it has been shown that significantly more glucose is metabolized via the pentose phosphate pathway than is the case in control animals (Hakim et al, 1976).

Several vasoactive drugs have been reported to increase cerebral glucose uptake, presumably by an effect on the blood-brain barrier (Brenner and Brenner, 1972; Meynaud et al, 1973). That intracellular brain glucose concentration can be increased by pharmacological intervention had been shown previously by Gottstein et al (1965).

Nucleotides, nucleosides and nucleic acids. Pyridine nucleotides (NAD, NADH) act as co-enzymes of the dehydrogenases in glycolytic and oxidative glucose degradation reactions. Increased glucose turnover is accompanied by increase in these nucleotides (Brenner and Brenner, 1972).

Adenine nucleotides are involved in the production and utilization of energy in the brain, as already indicated. Energy-rich phosphorylated compounds, notably ATP, are essential for (a) the maintenance of the normal sodium/potassium cationic pump, upon which the polarized condition of brain cells depends, and thus neuronal conduction and brain function; and (b) the synthesis, storage, release and re-uptake of the neurotransmitters in the synaptosomes — also essential for normal brain function. ATP may also play a role in the local regulation of CBF (Forrester et al, 1975a, b; Kozniewska et al, 1976).

A decreased supply of oxygen or glucose to cerebral tissues leads to depletion of ATP; thus in experimentally induced acute cerebral ischaemic lesions in animals, ATP levels fall progressively (Clendenon et al, 1971; Sundt and Michenfelder, 1971–1972). In chronic anoxic states, however, ATP levels may not be significantly reduced (Siesjö and Ljunggren, 1973; Siesjö et al, 1975). Decreased oxidative phosphorylation and ATP-ase activity in aging animals have been reported by Gold et al (1968) and Velkov (1973).

Experimental studies on the neurochemistry of the aging brain have been reviewed and extended by Meier-Ruge et al (1975). These authors consider the role of the cationic Na^+/K^+ pump and various enzyme changes, especially those which determine the levels of cyclic nucleotides (cAMP and cGMP). These cyclic nucleotides are the messengers of many hormone-induced activities throughout the body (Sutherland, 1970, 1972), and their role in the central nervous system has attracted much interest (Hertz and Schousboe, 1975; Daly, 1976). They may be involved in memory processes (McIlwain, 1977). There is evidence that cAMP levels may decrease with age in old rats (Zimmerman and Berg, 1974) and man (Robison et al, 1973). This may be secondary to decreased catecholamine concentrations in aging brain (see below). In anoxic rats, brain cAMP concentration increases (Stefanovich and John, 1974), possibly as a mediator of glycogenolysis, which is a metabolic reserve pathway for the brain. This effect is accompanied by an increase in tissue lactic acid; the fall in local pH may lead to vasodilatation of intracerebral arteries.

Meier-Ruge et al (1975) also consider the effect of certain drugs on brain metabolism, with particular reference to cyclic nucleotide enzyme activities and the Na^+/K^+ATP-ase dependent pump mechanism for sodium and potassium transport into and out of the brain cells. They showed that dehydrogenated ergot alkaloids had several effects on both systems which tended to normalize disturbed metabolism; (considered below under specific drugs).

Adenosine may be involved in the process of cerebral vasodilatation (Pull and McIlwain, 1972). There is also increasing interest in the possible role of adenosine as an inhibitory modulator of neurotransmission (Fredholm and Hedqvist, 1980; Burnstock, 1981; Daly et al, 1981). Adenosine receptors have been identified in brain membranes (Daly et al, 1981).

DNA shows little or no reduction in aged brains (Naber and Dahnke, 1979). RNA may decrease (Davis and Himwich, 1975; Ordy and Kaack, 1975), but neuronal RNA content and concentration show regional variations (Uemura and Hartmann, 1978, 1979a). In animals there is evidence of decreased synthesis of both messenger RNA (von Hahn, 1971) and ribosomal RNA (Strehler, 1976) in neurons. A relationship has been postulated between impaired RNA synthesis and the occurrence of neurofibrillary tangles (Uemura and Hartmann, 1979b; O'Brien et al, 1980).

Cerebral RNA increases during learning (Glassman, 1969), and RNA synthesis is involved in memory processes (Babich et al, 1965; Cameron, 1966).

Enzyme activities. Age changes in the activities of several cerebral enzymes have been studied histochemically (Emmenegger and Meier-Ruge 1968) and kinetically (Benzi et al, 1979, 1980; Meier-Ruge, 1982). Many (especially oxidative enzymes) show reduced activities with aging. These may be variably influenced by vasoactive drugs (Benzi et al, 1980).

Carbonic anhydrase inhibitors have been shown to increase cerebral blood flow since they lead to release of CO_2 locally (Ehenreich et al, 1961; Goto et al, 1966; Skinhøj, 1975). Kong et al (1969) recommended a combination of carbonic anhydrase inhibitors with hyperbaric oxygen but the comments on hyperbaric oxygen noted above should be borne in mind. Enzymes involved in the synthesis and breakdown of neurotransmitters are considered below.

Neurotransmitters. The role of neurotransmitters and their changes in aging and dementia are considered in Chapter 14. Only those aspects relevant to drug therapy are further considered here.

Acetylcholine. There is evidence that cholinergic nerve fibres accompany pial vessels (Lavrentieva et al, 1968) and that cholinergic receptors are situated in intracranial vessels (Edvinsson and Owman, 1975). Cholinergic stimulation causes vasodilatation and increases CBF and $CMRO_2$ (Purves, 1972; Matsuda et al, 1974). Other vasoactive neurotransmitters, especially the catecholamines (adrenaline, noradrenaline and dopamine) and serotonin, may be important in the pathogenesis of cerebral hypoxia (Zervas et al, 1975). Ischaemic areas of brain may release these monoamines into surrounding cerebral parenchyma, although transient anoxia suppresses brain catecholamine synthesis (Brown et al, 1974). It is now also considered that endogenous catecholamine can have a role in controlling the normal cerebral circulation (Edvinsson and Owman, 1975).

Serotonin and noradrenaline are probably potent spasmogens; dopamine may modulate the response of the cerebral arteries, the direction of the response varying with the concentration (Ekström-Jodal et al, 1973).

Catecholamines stimulate adenylcyclase and thus lead to increased levels of cAMP in brain cells. cAMP may have a basic role in the control of vascular reactivity and may facilitate vasodilatation (Flamm et al, 1975). They have also been implicated in memory processes (McGaugh, 1973; Squire, 1976). Catecholaminergic cells appear to decrease in number in the aging human brain (McGeer and McGeer, 1982). Age related declines have been reported for catecholamines (Robinson et al, 1977; Hervonen et al, 1978) including dopamine (Carlson and Windblad, 1976; Adolfsson et al, 1979). Enzymes concerned with catecholamine metabolism show marked regional differences in the age-related changes which have been reported (see McGeer and McGeer, 1982).

Variations in neuropeptides in normal aging are being studied (see Chapter 14); there is already evidence that certain neuropeptides are decreased in the brains of patients with Alzheimer's disease. Thus, significant reductions in somatostatin and substance P have been noted in some areas of cerebral cortex of these patients (Davies et al, 1982; Rossor et al, 1982), whereas vasointestinal peptide and cholecystokinin levels are unchanged (Rossor et al, 1982). Animal experiments have shown neuropeptides of hypothalamo-hypophysial origin to be involved in learning and memory processes (de Wied, 1977; de Wied and van Ree, 1982). Results in man have been conflicting (van Praag and Verhoeven, 1980; Keeb and Bloom, 1982).

Reviews of the effects of ACTH and its fragments on animal and human behaviour are given by Bohus (1979); van Praag and Verhoeven (1980); and de Wied and van Ree (1982).

Vasopressin is physiologically involved in memory processes. Administration of vasopressin enhances cognitive function in animals (de Wied, 1977; Keeb and Bloom, 1982; de Wied and van Ree, 1982). In man the results have been mixed (see section on individual drugs, below; also van Praag and Verhoeven (1980), Keeb and Bloom, 1982; and de Wied and van Ree, 1982. The possible mechanisms of these effects have been reviewed by Le Gros et al (1978) and Oliveros et al (1978). They include influences on rapid eye movement (REM) sleep (important in memory consolidation) and hippocampal theta rhythm (associated with learning and formation of memory) (Urban and de Wied, 1978). Such influences have been noted in the case of other drugs which enhance learning and memory in animals (Longo and Loizzo, 1973). There is also evidence that vasopressin facilitates memory consolidation by modulating noradrenergic neurotransmission in the limbic system (Kovács et al, 1979).

Endorphins have been the focus of intense research in the last decade. They have been connected with memory functions by van Ree and de Wied (1976) and Stein and Belluzzi (1978). However, their role is unclear (Keeb and Bloom, 1982); on the one hand the opiate antagonist naloxone has been shown to have memory-enhancing effects (Messing et al, 1979; Reisberg et al, 1983), but on the other hand, naloxone reduced vasopressin levels (Lightman and Forsling, 1980). Opiate receptor-binding sites may be concentrated in the limbic system (Kuhar et al, 1973), which is now recognized to be an important site of memory processes (Corsellis, 1976).

Other neuropeptides of current interest are discussed by Cooper et al (1978), Emson (1979) and Snyder and Innis (1979). Several neuropeptides show inter-relationships with ACh levels or turnover (Ebeid et al, 1979; Malthe-Sorensen and Wood, 1979; Davies et al, 1982).

The major age-related changes appear to be an increase in monoamine oxidase (MAO) (Robinson et al, 1977) and a sharp decrease in tyrosine hydroxylase and L-aromatic amino acid decarboxylase (dopa decarboxylase) in some brain regions (McGeer and McGeer, 1976; Davison, 1978).

Homovanillic acid (HVA), a stable dopamine metabolite, increases in the cerebrospinal fluid (CSF) with advancing years (Barbeau, 1976), and also in multi-infarct dementia (Meyer et al, 1976c). However, in SDAT the CSF levels of HVA have been reported to be normal or slightly reduced (Gottfries et al, 1969a) but decreased to a greater extent in the brain. It should be pointed out, however, that Yates et al (1979) found no decrease in dopamine in brain tissue from patients with SDAT, assessed histologically.

There is a significant reduction in beta-receptor sites in aged human cerebellum (Maggi et al, 1979); lymphocytes from elderly subjects also contain fewer beta-adrenergic receptors (Vestal et al, 1979).

There is lack of agreement about brain serotonin levels in aged humans; Nies et al (1973) reported no decrease, but Mackay et al (1978) found significant falls with aging in several areas of the brains of 10 neurologically normal individuals aged 46 to 74 years. The decreases may be due to increased MAO activity and/or to an age-related decline in serotonin turnover in the brain. There is also decreased affinity for serotonin in aging brains (Shih and Young, 1978). A possible role for serotonin in learning and memory has been shown in mice, with age changes in cerebral neurotransmitter levels which are quite different from those in man. There is, however, clear evidence for a dopaminergic-serotoninergic interaction (Roccatagliata et al, 1979), and a serotonin-acetylcholine interaction (Samanin et al, 1978) in the central nervous system — as indeed there is for interactions between other neurotransmitters (Karczmar, 1978). Carlsson et al (1980) reported significantly lowered serotonin levels in the hippocampus of patients with SDAT. GABA (gamma-aminobutyric acid) is the major inhibitory neurotransmitter throughout the brain. Its synthesis involves an enzyme, glutamic acid decarboxylase (GAD). Both GABA and GAD levels decrease with age in the thalamus (McGeer and McGeer 1976; Perry et al, 1979), and GAD losses also occur in cortical areas (McGeer and McGeer, 1976; Bowen et al, 1977).

ATP is involved in neurotransmitter physiology, as indicated earlier. Catecholamines and possibly serotonin and acetylcholine may be released complexed with other substances including ATP (McIlwain, 1972). There is also evidence for the existence of purinergic nerve fibres — i.e., ATP may itself act as a neurotransmitter or neuromodulator (Burnstock, 1975, 1981; Lancet, 1977b; Phillis et al, 1979).

Prostaglandins. These natural lipid local hormones have a wide range of biological effects. They are present in most organ systems, including the brain (Samuelsson, 1964; Wolfe and Coceani; 1979). The physiological and pathophysiological roles of prostaglandins (PGs) in the brain are not yet fully known, but it is now believed that PGs and related substances are important modulators of normal cerebrovascular tone and they may play a part in the tight coupling of cerebral metabolism to cerebral blood flow (Siesjö and Nilsson, 1982). PGE is a vasodilator in most vascular beds, but different effects of PGE_1 and PGE_2 have been reported on cerebral vessels (Pelofsky et al, 1972; Toda and Miyazaki, 1978). Prostacyclin (PGI_2) is the main product of arachidonic acid in blood vessels; it is a potent vasodilator and is probably more important in this respect than is PGE_2 (Armstrong et al, 1978; Lancet, 1978b; Moncada and Vane, 1979; Pickard et al, 1980).

PGI_2 has anti-aggregating properties, opposing the aggregating influence of platelet thromboxane. A shift in this equilibrium may occur in atherosclerosis and may play a part in the pathogenesis of TIAs or cerebral thrombosis (Moncada and Vane, 1979).

PGs also modulate adrenergic and possibly cholinergic neurotransmission (Hedqvist, 1977), but it is not certain if this modulating influence occurs in the central (as distinct from the peripheral) nervous system (Wolfe and Coceani, 1979).

The involvement of PGs with cyclic nucleotide systems is now controversial (Anggård, 1982).

The EEG in aging and dementia

The EEG changes progressively throughout life. In senescence, slow activity increases: the dominant alpha rhythm decreases in frequency, and there is an increase in the incidence of slower theta and delta waves (Obrist, 1980).

There is wide individual variation, and the tracing is influenced by the health of the subject.

An association between intellectual impairment and slow alpha rhythm has been described in psychogeriatric patients, and other elderly subjects in institutions, but this does not hold in relatively healthy old people (Obrist, 1980). However, diffuse slow (theta and delta) activity is related to moderate or more severe degrees of intellectual impairment. These and other EEG changes in SDAT and MID have been described by Soininen et al (1982). Such changes have prognostic value (Müller et al, 1975).

The EEG is more likely to show early abnormality in the course of a treatable than an irreversible dementia (Harner, 1975).

The EEG may sometimes be of help in overall asessment of the efficacy of psychoactive and vasoactive drugs (Matejcek et al, 1976, 1979; Fink and Irwin, 1978; Saletu and Grünberger, 1980).

Sleep in aging and dementia

Sleep patterns become fragmented in old age, with more and longer periods of awakening than in young adults. There is a marked reduction in Stage 4 (deep) sleep and a moderate decrease in rapid eye movement (REM) sleep. Characteristic EEG changes occur (Feinberg, 1976; Obrist, 1980). The decrease in REM sleep is highly correlated with impairment of memory and intelligence (Prinz, 1977). This change is particularly marked in SDAT (Prinz et al, 1982) and may reflect decreased cholinergic function (Serby, 1982).

THE DRUGS

Table 17.1 sets out a classification which attempts to include several vasoactive agents normally omitted from earlier classifications of 'vasodilator drugs'. The lists do not attempt to be fully comprehensive. Tables 17.2, 17.3 and 17.4 list drugs which are claimed to

Table 17.1 Vasoactive drugs

	UK trade name	USA trade name
I. *Drugs influencing autonomic nervous system receptors*		
(i) α-*adrenergic blockers*		
Dihydro-ergot alkaloids	Hydergine	Hydergine
Other ergot derivatives		
Ergot combinations		
Nicergoline		
Thymoxamine	Opilon	
Phenoxybenzamine	Dibenyline	Dibenzyline
Phentolamine	Rogitine	Regitine
Tolazoline	Priscol	Priscoline
(ii) β-*adrenergic stimulants*		
Isoxsuprine	Duvadilan	Vasodilan
	Defencin	
	Vasotran	
Nylidrin		Arlidin
II. *Drugs with relaxing effect on vascular smooth muscle*		
Papaverine		Pavabid and many others
Cyclandelate	Cyclospasmol	Cyclospasmol
Bencyclane	NCA	
Hexobendine		
Betahistine	Serc	
Nicotinic acid	Cosaldon	
(plus pentifylline)		
Nicotinic acid derivatives		
Inositol hexanicotinate	Hexopal	Hexanicotol
Nicotinoyl alcohol	Ronicol	Roniacol
tartrate		
Tetranicotinoyl fructose	Bradilan	
Xanthinol nicotinate	Complamex	
Methyl-xanthines		
Aminophylline	Phyllocontin	Lixaminol
		Phyllocontin
Pentifylline (with nicotinic acid)	Cosaldon	
III. *Antagonists of vasoconstriction (calcium entry blockers)*		
Cinnarizine	Stugeron	
Flunarizine		
Nifedipine	Adalat	Procardia
Nimodipine		
IV. *Drugs with combined effects*		
III. Oxpentifylline	Trental	
Suloctidil		
Naftidrofuryl	Praxilene	
V. *Drugs claimed to improve microcirculation*		
Dihydro-ergot alkaloids	Hydergine	Hydergine
Nicotinic acid derivatives		
Inositol hexanicotinate	Hexopal	Hexanicotol
Xanthinol nicotinate	Complamex	
Oxpentifylline	Trental	
Other drugs elevating ATP		
Naftidrofuryl	Praxilene	
Dextran (low molecular weight)	Rheomacrodex	Rheomacrodex
Newer drugs		
Buflomedil		

Table 17.2 Agents influencing cerebral cell metabolism

	UK trade name	USA trade name
Dihydro-ergot alkaloids	Hydergine	Hydergine
Nicotinic acid derivatives		
Inositol hexanicotinate	Hexopal	Hexanicotol
Xanthinol nicotinate	Complamex	
Naftidrofuryl	Praxilene	
Meclofenoxate	Lucidril	

Table 17.3 Agents enhancing cerebral acetycholine levels

Anticholinesterase (physostigmine)
Choline, lecithin, precursors (deanol, CDP-choline)
Dopaminergic drugs (levodopa)
Piracetam ('Noötropic' drugs)
Cholinomimetic agents (experimental)
Neuroactive peptides (under investigation)
— Vasopressin
— ACTH fragments
— Endorphins, naloxone

Table 17.4 Agents enhancing cerebral RNA levels

Pemoline
Vincamine and ethyl apovincaminate
1-Eburnamonine
Pyritinol

Table 17.5 Drugs described as cerebral 'activators'

	UK trade name	USA trade name
Piracetam	—	—
Deanol	—	Deaner
Pemoline	Kethamed	
	Ronyl	
	Cyclert	Cyclert
Meclofenoxate	Lucidril	—
Fencamfamin	Reactivan	
Methylphenidate	Ritalin	Ritalin hydrochloride

improve cerebral neuronal metabolism; they mainly appear again in Table 17.1, since cellular metabolism is closely related to microcirculation. Table 17.5 lists drugs promoted as cerebral 'activators', which need some discussion in a chapter on cerebral function. These various drugs will now be considered in more detail.

VASOACTIVE DRUGS

Drugs influencing autonomic nervous system receptors

α-Adrenergic blockers
α-blockers are usually better for dilating skin vessels than other vascular beds; they may dilate cerebral arteries,

though the evidence is conflicting except when used for spasm of cerebral arteries during or after neurosurgical operations.

Ergot alkaloids (Hydergine), co-dergocrine mesylate (UK), ergoloid mesylates (USA). Pharmacology: Hydergine was the first α-blocker, and has been extensively used for over a quarter of a century. It consists of the mesylates of dihydrogenated derivatives of the alkaloids of ergotoxine — i.e., dihydroergocornine, dihydroergocristine and dihydroergokryptine. Dihydrogenation eliminates the vasoconstrictor effects of ergotoxine and enhances its anti-serotonin and α-blocking properties. The resulting alkaloids share part of the same molecular structure as LSD, differing in the peptide moiety.

Reports on the effects of Hydergine on CBF have been conflicting. Evidence that parenteral Hydergine increases CBF in man has been presented by Heyck (1961) and Géraud et al (1963); and Herzfeld and Wittgen (1971) confirmed this in patients with 'cerebrovascular disease' treated with the drug for 3 to 8 weeks.

Mongeau (1974) corroborated these findings for patients with initially borderline or low cerebral perfusion rates as measured by cerebral circulation transit times, and Marc-Vergnes et al (1974), in a study of 10 drugs, found that only those containing Hydergine induced a significant increase in CBF and $CMRO_2$. Increased CBF has also been reported in baboons given intravenous Hydergine (Szewczykowski et al, 1970) and in cat brains perfused with Hydergine-containing fluid (Emmenegger and Meier-Ruge, 1968).

On the other hand, Hafkenschiel et al (1950) could find no increase in CBF after intramuscular Hydergine in man. Gottstein (1965, 1969) reported that there was no increase in CBF in older subjects given intravenous vasodilators, including Hydergine, although he had shown that intra-arterial injection could increase CBF markedly. Skinhøj (1972) states that α-blocking drugs — including Hydergine — do not alter CBF in man in doses allowed in human experiments and therapeutics. Gottstein (1969) pointed out that because of autoregulation the threshold for pharmacological effects on the cerebral circulation is at least 10 times higher than it is in peripheral blood vessels.

McHenry et al (1971) could not show acute effects of Hydergine on rCBF in patients with cerebrovascular disease, nor could Regli et al (1971a) find such changes in cats given ergotamine.

Those authors reporting increased CBF also reported decreased cerebrovascular resistance and increase in $CMRO_2$.

More recent studies with Hydergine have indicated that beneficial effects may relate less to improvement in total CBF or rCBF than to an effect on the metabolism of neurons and glial cells, and thus on the microcirculation (see above). These studies have included techniques to quantify brain electrical energy as recorded on electro-encephalographs and subjected to Fourier analysis; morphometric techniques; measurements of enzyme activities by histochemical and biochemical methods; metabolic studies of glucose and lactate, and hydrogen-clearance techniques for blood-flow measurements (for reviews see Meier-Ruge et al, 1975, 1978; Meier-Ruge, 1978; Berde and Schild, 1978; Loew, 1980; Loew and Weil, 1982).

The major effects of Hydergine are now thought to be:

Improved neuronal metabolism, as evidenced by changes in succinic dehydrogenase, monoamine oxidase and alkaline phosphatase activities and decrease in polysaccharide content.

Improved astrocyte metabolism, as evidenced by reductions in anaerobic glycolytic activity and lactate and polysaccharide content.

Favourable influence on cellular ATP balance: inhibition of rate of breakdown of ATP, leading to inhibition of anaerobic glycolysis via a feedback mechanism; increased aerobic metabolism of glucose reflected by decrease in blood lactate.

Stimulation of protein synthesis in the brain, due to activation of protein kinase by increased cAMP levels.

Increase in electrical activity of the brain, due to
— inhibition of catecholamine re-uptake;
— inhibition of catecholamine- or sympathetically-stimulated ATPases and adenyl cyclase;
— inhibition of brain-specific low-K_m cAMP-phosphodiesterase.

Improvement in brain microcirculation: when their metabolism is decreased, the brain cells accumulate water and glycogen, and swell, narrowing the capillaries (see above). Improvement in metabolism of the brain cells causes reduction in the swelling and improvement in the microcirculation (Emmenegger and Meier-Ruge, 1968; Hunziker et al, 1974). However, more recent evidence shows that, even without a net change in microcirculatory flow, beneficial effects of Hydergine on cell metabolism and EEG energy may be seen (Gygax et al, 1975); indeed, these authors revert to the argument that the disturbances of cell-metabolism are secondary to impaired microcirculation!

Other pharmacological effects. Hydergine has effects on the turnover of dopamine and serotonin and may interact with these neurotransmitters (Loew et al, 1976).Hydergine has been shown to accumulate in the synapses (Iwangogg et al, 1976), and binds to rat brain receptor sites specific for noradrenaline, dopamine and serotonin (Loew et al, 1979). Dopamine- and serotonin-agonist effects have been described (Corrodi et al, 1973; Bürki et al, 1978; Vigouret et al, 1978), and this would account for the marked inhibition of prolactin release

(Clemens and Fuller, 1978), although no correlation was noted between lowered serum prolactin and behavioural changes in elderly patients with organic brain syndrome treated with Hydergine (Gross et al, 1979).

Clinical value. Clinical experience with Hydergine for over a quarter of a century has probably exceeded that of any other drug mentioned in this chapter. Nearly 40 studies of this drug have been published; over half are well-designed and most of these show significant improvement in one or more psychological or behavioural parameters, considered to be of practical clinical benefit (Fanchamps, 1979; Hindmarch et al, 1979; McDonald, 1979; Yesavage et al, 1979a; Venn, 1980; Loew and Weil, 1982). Improvements were seen mainly in mild to moderate cases of brain failure and usually took 3 weeks to appear. Most studies were of short duration — usually 12 weeks, by which time maximum improvement had usually occurred; some studies showed more significant improvement after 16 weeks (Novo et al, 1978; Gaitz et al, 1977). Others showed a falling off of improvement after 12 weeks (Soni and Soni, 1975; Hollingsworth, 1980).

In a critical review of 12 studies, Hughes et al (1976) concluded that Hydergine was of little value in the treatment of dementia; but McDonald (1979), in a detailed review of 26 double-blind studies, with particular regard to methods of assessment of the patients, found that 13 symptoms improved significantly with Hydergine (in the areas of cognition, mood and global ratings — but not memory). Yesavage et al (1979a), reviewing 33 studies, stated that overall this drug has the best confirmed efficacy. It should be emphasized that even a little improvement may be of disproportionately great practical benefit in individual cases and may transform the quality of life for the patient and/or relatives.

Recent double-blind studies have mainly continued the trend of 12-week studies in patients with mild to moderate dementia. Cox et al (1978) reported highly significant global improvements in patients treated with co-dergocrine, 4.5 mg/day, and Matejcek et al (1979) reported a correlation between clinical improvement and EEG improvement, confirming the findings of Roubicek et al (1972), Arrigo et al (1973), Venn (1976), and Kugler et al (1978) — this last being a 15-month study at a dose of 4.5 mg/day. Oswald and Lang (1980) found that 3 mg/day of Hydergine improved the speed of cognitive performance in psychometric tests in residents of an old people's home. (This is consistent with the results of Hindmarch et al (1979) using high doses (12 mg/day) in normal volunteers.)

Enhanced cognitive performance may be due to an alerting effect of the drug; this could also explain the finding that Hydergine improved learning and recall in a word-list test (Yesavage et al, 1981).

A comparison of 6 mg with 3 mg daily doses of Hydergine over a 24-week period in senile dementia showed little evidence for superiority of the larger dose (Yesavage et al, 1977). However, the subjects were fairly severely demented institutionalized patients.

A Japanese multicentre double-blind study of Hydergine in 550 patients with various cerebrovascular disorders compared daily doses of 3 mg with 6 mg over a period of 12 weeks (Yoshikawa et al, 1983). Parameters evaluated included subjective and psychiatric symptoms and neurological disturbances. For each of these symptom-categories, global improvement ratings were significantly better in the patients receiving 6 mg of Hydergine daily. No serious side effects were noted at either dose. No placebo group was included; the authors considered that the effects of 3 mg/day vs placebo have been well-documented.

The patients studied mainly (86.5 per cent) suffered from sequelae of a cerebral infarction which had occurred not less than one month prior to entry to the study. Clearly, these patients are different from those with senile dementia studied by Yesavage et al (1979b). The implications would warrant further study.

Studies of Hydergine against papaverine have consistently favoured the former drug (Yesavage et al, 1979a; Loew and Weil, 1982).

Dosage: Over the years there has been a trend to increase the dosage from 1.5 mg to 4.5 mg daily. An 0.5 mg tablet has given way to a 1 mg tablet (USA) or a 1.5 mg tablet (UK). The question of dosage is important because the drug is irregularly absorbed (Hollister, 1975).

Side effects are few and uncommon: the sinus bradycardia reported by Cayley et al (1975) appears to be very rare. In 1593 elderly patients in 25 studies, the incidence of dizziness or hypotension was recorded as 1.82 per cent (Maclay, 1979).

Other ergot derivatives

Semisynthetic ergot alkaloids. Dihyroergonine and dihydro-beta-ergosin may have cerebral effects like those of co-dergocrine (Hauth and Richardson, 1977). Quantitative EEG evaluation suggested that dihydroergonine is 10 times as effective as co-dergocrine (Meier-Ruge et al, 1979) but this has not been translated into clinical application.

Bromocriptine is synthesized from ergokryptine; like the ergolines (see below) it has potent dopaminergic effects, and is used in the treatment of parkinsonism, as well as for neuroendocrinological disorders (Goldstein et al, 1980). It is considered further under 'Dopaminergic drugs,' below.

Ergolines. These synthetic ergot-derived compounds include two potent dopaminergic agents, lergotrile and pergolide, which have been studied in animals and in man as potential therapy for parkinsonism and various endocrine disorders (Lemberger and Crabtree, 1980). However, many toxic effects have been reported (Teychenne et al, 1979; Lemberger and Crabtree, 1980). These drugs appear to have no place in the treatment of dementia.

Ergot combinations

Nicergoline (Metergoline, formerly Nimergoline; Sermion — Europe). Nicergoline is a molecule in which a modified ergoline nucleus has been combined with a nicotinic acid moiety. It was developed as a stronger alpha-receptor blocking agent, but, like co-dergocrine, it has been shown in animal experiments to improve various cerebral metabolic processes, with consequent EEG improvements, after hypoxia or cerebral ischaemia (Moretti, 1979).

Pharmacological studies with nicergoline are reviewed by Moretti et al (1979). The drug showed marked alpha-blocking activity in vivo and in vitro in several animal species; blood flow increased in the brain and hind limbs, but splanchnic and aortic flow did not change. Acute and chronic toxicity were low.

Nicergoline and nicergoline tartrate increased learning ability in rats; brain extracts from these animals treated for long periods showed increased protein and RNA synthesis (Paul and Chandra, 1979). In normal elderly subjects, a double-blind crossover placebo-controlled study showed improved EEG patterns after administration of nicergoline 15 mg; 5 mg of co-dergocrine produced a similar effect (Saletu et al, 1979). These authors claimed that psychometric testing revealed a statistically significant improvement in learning ability after 30 mg nicergoline, as compared to 5 mg co-dergocrine or placebo.

Anti-aggregating and disaggregating effects on platelets have been described (Praga et al, 1979; Lagarde et al, 1980). Intravenous nicergoline (2 mg) increased CBF (measured by the ^{133}Xe method) in seven of 13 patients with cerebrovascular disease (10 with MID, three with TIA) (Iliff et al, 1979); yet Prencipe et al (1974) could find no increase in CBF after nicergoline treatment in patients with chronic or diffuse cerebrovascular pathology.

No adequate studies with oral nicergoline in senile dementia, of whatever type, have yet been reported. The drug is beginning to attract wider attention, partly because of the increasing interest in the neuropharmacology of ergot alkaloids generally (Meier-Ruge et at, 1979; Scott, 1979; Goldstein et al, 1980). Scientifically acceptable evaluation is still lacking in the clinical situation.

Other α-blockers

Of the other α-blockers, little need be said here.

Thymoxamine (Opilon) did not produce a significant change in CBF on intracarotid injection in the experimental studies by Deshmukh et al (1971–1972), nor when infused into normal resting man (Corbett et al, 1972). However, the latter authors showed that when normal volunteers hyperventilated, so producing cerebral vasoconstriction and 30 per cent decrease in CBF, the decrement in CBF could be reduced to 9 per cent after thymoxamine infusion. This was taken to support the concept that the sympathetic nervous system could control the reactivity of cerebral vessels, and that this control was susceptible to pharmacological modification.

Thymoxamine is not promoted as a cerebral vasoactive agent but only as a peripheral vasodilator.

Phenoxybenzamine (Dibenyline) is also marketed as a peripheral vasodilator; injections have been used to counter cerebral arterial spasm (Cummins and Griffith, 1971; Flamm et al, 1972) and have been shown to increase CBF in baboons (Kawamura et al, 1974). The drug produced slowing of cerebral metabolism in patients with subacute cerebral infarction (Meyer et al, 1974) but McGraw et al (1976), on the basis of their experimentally-produced strokes in gerbils, advise against the use of phenoxybenzamine in patients with acute cerebral infarction.

Phentolamine (Rogitine) is used in the diagnosis and medical management of phaeochromocytoma. Experimentally, small doses ($<50 \mu g$) have been shown to increase CBF in adult rhesus monkeys, but larger doses had the opposite effect (Raichle et al, 1975). In man, however, no such effects have been reported (Skinhøj, 1972).

Tolazoline (Priscol) is not recommended for cerebral problems. There is conflicting evidence with regard to cerebral vasodilatation by this drug (Whittier, 1964). Gottstein (1969) found no increase in CBF or CMRO$_2$ after tolazoline.

β-adrenergic stimulants

β-adrenergic stimulants are usually better for dilating vessels in skeletal muscle.

Isoxsuprine (Duvadilan, Defencin, Vasotran)

Pharmacology. Isoxsuprine is a phenylethylamine derivative of adrenaline and, though classified here as a β-stimulant, has in addition some α-blocking properties. The latter are seen with large doses, and may be used in treating ischaemic skin conditions. The β-mimetic effect is obtained with smaller doses, and causes relaxation of vascular smooth muscle.

It has been reported that CBF increases after administration of isoxsuprine (Gloning and Klausberger, 1958; Horton and Johnson, 1964) although the converse may also occur (Fazekas and Alman, 1964; Reiss et al, 1967;

Heiss and Podreka, 1978); and Marc-Vergnes et al (1974) found no effect.

Whittier and Dhrymiotis (1962) found that EEG changes due to hyperventilation-induced cerebral vasoconstriction could be returned to normal following intramuscular administration of a single dose of 10 mg isoxsuprine. This effect was seen in 100 per cent of 20 women aged 60 or over with a diagnosis of cerebral arteriosclerosis, and in 66 per cent of 20 younger women (35 years or below).

Miyazaki (1971–1972), using a Döppler ultrasound technique, found that in normal men 10 mg isoxsuprine intramuscularly increased brachial artery flow but did not alter internal carotid flow over the 13-minute period studied.

Isoxsuprine may decrease blood viscosity (Schlichting and Heidrich, 1976; Di Perri et al, 1978; Weber et al, 1980) and inhibit platelet aggregation (Di Perri et al, 1974; Weber et al, 1980) and red-cell clumping (Di Perri et al, 1977). This last effect, like part of the change in blood viscosity, may be due to lowered plasma fibrinogen levels (Di Perri et al, 1978).

Clinical evaluation

Cerebral arteriosclerosis. Uncontrolled trials by Job (1960) and Elliott et al (1973) claimed that elderly patients treated with isoxsuprine benefited mentally and physically.

Affleck et al (1961) reported a double-blind controlled trial in 20 elderly patients. The treatment group received 80 mg isoxsuprine daily by mouth for 14 weeks. There was a significant improvement in some intellectual performance as compared to the placebo group, but the latter adjusted more effectively to being hospitalized.

A double-blind controlled study of a graded-release preparation of isoxsuprine (Duvadilan Retard), 40 mg bd for 16 weeks, was reported in elderly patients with cerebrovascular disease by Hussain et al (1976). This study of 16 geriatric day-hospital patients used an automatically-controlled Questel picture-matching test to give objective assessments of mental performance, based on the principles described by Gedye and Wedgwood (1966) and used for assessment of cyclandelate (Gedye, 1970; Wedgwood, 1970), meclofenoxate (Gedye et al, 1972) and xanthinol nicotinate (Braverman and Naylor, 1975). The active-drug group showed a significantly greater improvement in mental performance than the placebo group ($p<0.05$); three patients in the placebo group showed deterioration.

Transient ischaemic attacks. Dhrymiotis and Whittier (1962) reported a reduction in transient ischaemic attacks in a double-blind controlled crossover trial lasting one year in 32 elderly patients. During treatment with isoxsuprine the frequency of transient ischaemic attacks was halved; but these patients showed no change in mental status or behaviour. The authors attributed these beneficial results to prevention of vasospasm; however, the idea that most transient ischaemic attacks are due to vasospasm was abandoned long ago, except in certain specific instances — e.g. migraine; after subarachnoid haemorrhage or intra-arterial injection of contrast media (Russell, 1976).

Elliott et al (1973) also found a lessened incidence of transient ischaemic attacks in their uncontrolled study.

Dosage. Isoxsuprine 80 mg daily, either as the resinate, one 40 mg capsule morning and evening, or as the tablets of the hydrochloride, 20 mg four times a day. Preparations of intravenous infusions are also available.

Side-effects are rare and transient (flushing and palpitation). High doses may cause hypotension.

Nylidrin (Arlidin, USA). This drug is structurally very similar to isoxsuprine, and has similar effects, but there is is some conflict over its effect on CBF. Klassen (1972) found increased CBF after intravenous injection of nylidrin, and Eisenberg et al (1960) showed a considerable increase in CBF in patients with cerebrovascular disease after 2 to 6 weeks on oral isoxsuprine; but Meyer et al (1967) found no change in CBF after intravenous nylidrin and Reiss et al (1967) and Heiss et al (1970) found decreased CBF following administration of nylidrin.

Though it has been used in USA with reports of benefit in cerebrovascular insufficiency (Winsor et al, 1960), mild to moderate chronic brain syndrome (Garetz et al, 1979) and labyrinthine ischaemia (Rubin and Anderson, 1958), nylidrin is not available in the UK.

DRUGS WITH RELAXING EFFECT ON VASCULAR SMOOTH MUSCLE

(Nitrites are omitted since they cause generalized vasodilatation and are not of practical value for improving cerebral function).

Papaverine (Pavabid, etc., USA)

Pharmacology and clinical evaluation. Papaverine acts directly on smooth muscle throughout the body; inhibition of cAMP-phosphodiesterase may contribute to this effect (Pöch and Kukovetz, 1971). In the brain, increased output of adenosine (Pull and McIlwain, 1972) may also be involved in the vasodilating effect.

Papaverine has been shown to decrease cerebral vascular resistance and increase CBF when given intravenously (Gottstein, 1965; McHenry et al, 1970; and Hadjiev, 1974*). All these studies were performed in

---

* Hadjiev (1974) reported even greater and more prolonged effects when papaverine was given in combination with ATP.

patients with strokes or cerebral vascular spasm. On the other hand, Shenkin (1951) — using smaller (60 mg) doses — found that decreased cerebral vascular resistance after papaverine was accompanied by a 10 per cent fall in systemic blood pressure and no net increase in CBF occurred; and Gottstein (1969) considered that the influence of intravenous vasodilators on the cerebral circulation was not really significant. Marc-Vergnes et al (1974) found no increase in CBF after intravenous papaverine.

Nevertheless, Meyer et al (1965) demonstrated that intravenous administration of 64 mg papaverine caused a significant increase of oxygen availability in stroke patients, and a controlled study in 70 patients with cerebral infarction showed that the clinical course could be improved, as judged by scored neurological assessments, by the use of papaverine (Gilroy and Meyer, 1966). A beneficial effect on cerebral glucose metabolism was shown by Meier-Ruge et al (1975) in their perfused cat brains; but the effect was less than with Hydergine and there was no effect on capillary morphometry.

McHenry et al (1970) showed that intravenous papaverine could increase regional CBF in some focal ischaemic areas in stroke patients, although they found no neurological improvements. Olesen and Paulson (1971) used 10 mg papaverine by intracarotid artery injection in 12 patients with presumed cerebral infarction or occlusive cerebrovascular disease and concluded that the drug decreased flow in pathological tissue and so had no place in the treatment of cerebrovascular disease; and Regli et al (1971) agreed with their interpretation of the data. However, McHenry (1972) re-examined that data and found that the evidence pointed to a definite increase in CBF and rCBF even in focal ischaemic areas, and the effect was greater than that due to intravenous administration of papaverine. McHenry (1972) emphasized that only carefully controlled clinical and laboratory evaluations of the effects of such drugs on rCBF and the clinical course would determine the policy to be recommended with regard to the use of vasodilators in stroke illness. He also stressed that the intracerebral steal phenomenon was written about frequently but seen only rarely in clinical practice; however, this statement should not allow relaxation of clinical vigilance if such treatment is being considered in stroke patients.

Oral dosage of papaverine has given less clear-cut results. Meyer et al (1971) found increased CBF and decreased arteriovenous oxygen difference within 20 to 60 minutes of oral administration of papaverine to baboons, and considered that such observations should be relevant to the treatment of patients with occlusive cerebrovascular disease. A double-blind cross-over study in healthy young adults showed that oral papaverine (300 mg b.d. for 7 days) produced small increases in

CBF during normal breathing and on hyperventilation (Wang and Obrist, 1976).

Results of double-blind controlled trials in elderly subjects have been conflicting. Long-term treatment improved dysautoregulation in patients with chronic cerebrovascular ischaemia (Shaw and Meyer, 1978) and with TIAs in the vertebrobasilar arterial system (Naritomi et al, 1979). Improvements have been reported in several clinical parameters, but these vary from one study to another, and it is difficult to arrive at general conclusions. Of 13 studies reviewed by Yesavage et al (1979a), nine were regared as well-designed. Of these, six reported some positive effects but only one claimed practical benefit (Ritter et al, 1971). More consistent improvements are seen in the EEG. The prevention by papaverine of the slowing of the EEG on hyperventilation was reported by Korenyi and Whittier (1969), although Meier-Ruge et al (1975) found that in perfused cat brains subjected to hypovolaemic oligaemia, papaverine decreased EEG activity further.

In five studies in which papaverine was compared with Hydergine (reviewed by Yesavage et al, 1979a), the latter was found to be superior in each study. Some authorities doubt the value of papaverine for 'cerebral vascular insufficiency' (Prien and Cole, 1978; Yesavage et al, 1979a); but Scott (1979) is less negative and aligns with Shader and Goldsmith (1976) and Branconnier Cole (1977) in speculating on the role of the dopaminergic-blocking effect.

Dosage. The drug is not used in the UK, but is widely used in the USA in a sustained-release form (Pavabid and other brand names). Ordinary papaverine hydrochloride is rapidly and completely absorbed from the gastrointestinal tract and peak plasma levels occur at 1 to 2 hours; it is almost completely metabolized, mainly by microsomal enzymes in the liver, where it is converted to phenolic metabolites which are excreted by the kidneys as glucuronide conjugates or without further transformation (Axelrod et al, 1958). Administration to human subjects in a dose of 200 mg 6-hourly gives a gradual rise in plasma levels; the sustained-release form allows a more practical therapeutic regimen, but the bioavailability of the US 150 mg sustained-release preparation may be less than that of the ordinary form (Kostenbauder, 1977). Clinical comparisons have favoured the ordinary form (Arnold et al, 1977; Lee et al, 1978) over the US sustained-release form. On the other hand, the sustained-release preparations in Europe appear to have excellent bioavailability (Maggi et al, 1977; Miller et al, 1978). There is evidence that a 300 mg sustained-release tablet is superior to a 300 mg capsule (Miller et al, 1978). The capsules may be given daily or twice daily; the usual dose is 600 mg daily but up to about 1 g has been used with reported benefit.

Side-effects. As expected with vasodilators, these may consist of flushing, tingling, headaches, dizziness, sweating and postural hypotension. Drowsiness and constipation have also been reported. Cardiac arrhythmias have been reported after intravenous papaverine (Elek and Katz, 1942). Hepatotoxicity is probably commoner than previously thought (Rønnov-Jessen and Tjernlund, 1969; Zimmerman, 1969; Kiaer et al, 1974); it is probably allergic and may manifest itself only as elevated serum levels of aminotransferases and alkaline phosphatase. Papaverine antagonizes the effect of L-dopa in patients with parkinsonism; the mechanism is unclear (Duvoisin, 1975).

Ethaverine is the tetraethoxy analogue of papaverine, with similar properties. It is used in the USA and Europe.

Cyclandelate (Cyclospasmol)

Pharmacology. Cyclandelate is the mandelic ester of 3,3,5-trimethylcyclohexanol; it is structurally somewhat similar to papaverine but unlike the latter it contains no nitrogen.

It has several actions:

Direct action on smooth muscle throughout the body. Bijlsma et al (1956) showed in animals that cyclandelate has three times the potency of papaverine, but is less toxic and does not affect the blood pressure or heart rate. In man its vasodilatory effect is weak. Increased CBF has been reported following cyclandelate administration, using a variety of techniques (Table 17.6).

Acceleration of the development of collateral vessels. Evidence for this effect is presented by van den Akker et al (1957) in hearts and skeletal muscle of cats, and by van Hell (1974) in the hind legs of rabbits.

Metabolic effect. This was suggested by Taylor (1971) and demonstrated in rats and mice by Funcke et al (1974). In these animals large doses of cyclandelate were compared with meclofenoxate (q.v.). Both drugs enhanced the resistance of the animals to hypoxia and increased glucose uptake in the brain.

Clinical evaluation. Open studies in patients with 'cerebral arteriosclerosis' suggested that cyclandelate treatment could improve mental performance. Double-blind studies are outlined in Table 17.7. In these studies, the best results appear to be in the 'younger old', aged below 75 years — as might be expected, for their disease states have had less chance to become advanced.

In all these studies there is the inconsistency of the pattern of improvements so commonly seen in assessment of such drugs. Aderman et al (1972) and Westreich et al (1975) each used a similar group of four mental tests (out of a battery of six) and found no benefit from the drug in these tests, although there was improvement in the other two in each study. The two tests which

Table 17.6 Clinical trials of cyclandelate on cerebral blood flow (CBF)

Authors	Year	Subjects	Technique	Controlled?	Results	Comments
Luisada et al	1966	26 CAS	Rheography	No	↑ CBF	Technique does not necessarily reflect arterial CBF. No correlation presented with clinical effects.
Kuhn	1966	25 CVD (focal cerebral ischaemia)	Angiography	No	↑ CBF and clinical correlations	Sparse data. Criteria of clinical improvement not given
Eichhorn	1965	40 CVD	Cerebral radiocirculography	Yes, D-B (random pairs)	↑ CBF	Sparse data on CBF and clinical effects
O'Brien and Veall	1966	9 CVD	^{133}Xe	Yes, each patient own control	↑ CBF in 7 of 9 after single dose	No comments on clinical value
Ball and Taylor	1967	32 long-stay geriatric patients	Cerebral radiocirculography	Yes, D-B	↑ CBF and mental function tests improved	No correlations between clinical improvements and ↑ CBF

CAS=cerebral arteriosclerosis; CVD = cerebrovascular disease; D-B = double-blind.

Table 17.7 Double-blind controlled trials of cyclandelate in 'cerebral arteriosclerosis'

Authors	Year	Subjects	Mean age (yr)	Dose	Duration	Trial design	Results
Eichhorn	1965	40 CVD	NG	800 mg/day	3/52	D-B random pairs	Sparse data, ?clinical improvement
Ball and Taylor	1967	32 long-stay geriatric patients	76.5	800 mg/day	4/12	D-B	Significant improvement in mental tests in treatment group; also in CBF but no individual correlations.
Rogers et al	1970	(a) 31 chronic CVD	Range mainly 60–90	800 mg/day	5/12	D-B cross-over with central 1/12 free of treatment	No improvements.
		(b) 16 CVD		800 mg/day	2/12	D-B	
Fine et al	1970	40 CAS	Range 62–75	800 mg/day	4½ months	D-B cross-over with central 2/52 free of treatment	Improved orientation, communication and socialization; lesser improvement in mood and self-care.
Aderman et al	1972	43 OPH	82.7	400 mg/day	6/52	D-B cross-over with central 2/12 free of treatment	Results not clear-cut; some psychological tests improved.
Young et al Hall	1974; 1976	21 CBS with CVD	69	1600 mg/day	1 year	D-B cross-over (6/12 & 6/12)	Less decline during active drug therapy. Best results in perception, conceptualization and memory.
Westreich et al	1975	24 CBS with CAS	70.8	800 mg/day	12/52	D-B cross-over	No benefit.

NG = not given; CVD = cerebrovascular disease; CAS = cerebral arteriosclerosis; CBS = chronic brain syndrome (dementia) of at least 6/12 duration; OPH = residents of old people's home; D-B = double-blind.

Judge et al (1973) found to improve significantly were not the two which were reported as improved in the papers just mentioned.

Capote and Parikh (1978) reported a double-blind placebo-controlled trial in patients with moderate senile dementia treated with cyclandelate, 1600 mg daily, or placebo for 16 weeks. Results suggested that cyclandelate was a 'moderately effective treatment for certain symptoms of senescence in carefully selected patients'.

Young et al (1974) make two comments worthy of

note: (1) *prevention of continuous decline may be the major role of such therapeutic endeavours*; (2) many previous marginally successful treatments for cerebral arteriosclerosis appear to have acted as antidepressants (see Hall and Harcup, 1969). However, in a double-blind placebo-controlled study in depressed and demented patients in a psychogeriatric unit (Davies et al, (1977)) there were no improvements noted in those patients receiving cyclandelate, 1200 mg daily, for 6 months.

On the other hand, Brasseur (1978) reported that concomitant treatment with tofenacine (an antidepressant) and cyclandelate in patients believed to have depression secondary to cerebrovascular insufficiency showed synergism between the two drugs.

One further study warrants mention. Judge et al (1973) carried out a double-blind cross-over trial of cyclandelate, 1200 mg/day for 2 months, in 54 'normal' elderly subjects, living at home. The results were interesting: the 23 men showed progressive intellectual and behavioural deterioration regardless of treatment; but the women showed significant improvement in some aspects of mental function, particular intelligence tests and Raven's Coloured Progressive Matrices; the paired-associate learning task just failed to show a significant difference.

The prophylactic effect of cyclandelate in patients suffering transient ischaemic attacks (van der Drift, 1961) could not be confirmed by Rogers et al (1970).

Large doses (1600–2400 mg daily) significantly improved sensorimotor recovery in patients started on cyclandelate at least 2 months after a stroke (Sourander and Blakemore, 1978).

Dosage. The manufacturer's recommended dose is 400 mg four times daily.

Side-effects. These are few and insignificant. Flushing, tingling, dizziness, headache, palpitation, sweating, nausea and heartburn have been reported.

Bencylane (Fludilat — FRG; Fluxeda — Italy)

Bencyclane acts directly on vascular smooth muscle, but does not inhibit phosphodiesterase (Kukovetz et al, 1975). It has in addition some alpha-lytic action (Aurousseau and Albert, 1978). Evidence that the drug increases CBF and has antiplatelet aggregating activity is reviewed by Hauth and Richardson (1977). There is also evidence suggesting a cerebral metabolic effect (Hapke, 1973). Clinical studies have been few and results mixed (Hauth and Richardson, 1977; Yesavage et al, 1979a); assessment of this drug's value is impossible at present.

Viquidil (Desclidium — France)

Viquidil increases CBF, acting like papaverine (DeValois, 1973).

Hexobendine (Ustimon — France, South Africa; Reoxyl — FRG)

This is a synthetic compound which has shown a prolonged vasodilator effect in animal preparations. An increase in CBF has been demonstrated in animal experiments (Meyer et al, 1970) and in man after parenteral injection (Hess et al, 1970; Meyer et al, 1971; McHenry et al, 1972). The increase in CBF in man was seen in ischaemic as well as non-ischaemic areas in patients with stroke or acute cerebrovascular spasm. Cerebral oxygen and glucose consumptions were unchanged. In 'cerebrovascular insufficiency', Heiss and Podreka (1978) found that hexobendine increased CBF but Herrschaft (1975) found no change in rCBF.

Minimal hypotension occurs with hexobendine, with correspondingly less chance of disturbance of cerebral autoregulation.

There is evidence that hexobendine potentiates the vasodilating effect of adenosine on the coronary arteries (Hansing et al, 1972), a mechanism which might also be relevant in the brain (see under Cerebral Metabolism).

Despite these promising data, this drug is not available in the UK, nor has it been approved for general use in the USA by the Food and Drugs Administration, but it has been widely used in Austria and Germany. There have apparently been no reports of the use of hexobendine in dementia due to cerebral arteriosclerosis.

Betahistine (Serc)

This drug, a β-2-pyridylalkylamine, is an histamine analogue with most of the H_2-receptor effects of histamine, but only a minimal effect on gastric secretion. Betahistine is widely used in the treatment of Ménière's disease, and has been shown to have a dilating effect on the microcirculation of the labyrinth (Suga and Snow, 1969; Martinez, 1972).

Evidence of increased CBF has come from Anderson and Kubicek (1971); Seipel (1971); Meyer et al (1974); Seipel and Floam (1975); Seipel et al (1975, 1977); Tomita et al (1978) and Hughes et al (1981). The drug appears to be particularly effective in increasing rCBF in the vertebro-basilar arterial system.

Clinical evaluation. Table 17.8 sets out the results of several double-blind controlled clinical trials in 'cerebral arteriosclerosis'. (Some of the patients are relatively young.) A variety of psychological tests were improved, as was vertigo in one study, but the incidence of TIAs was not affected. CBF and rCBF were increased.

In open studies, each lasting 6 months, improvements were reported: Botez (1975) found lessened incidence and severity of vertigo, and Seipel et al (1977) reported global improvement in dementia, together with a marked and highly-significant vasodilatation of cerebral and scalp arteries as assessed by rheoencephalography.

Meyer and colleagues (1974; 1976b) consider that oral

Table 17.8 Results of double-blind controlled clinical trials with betahistine in patients with 'cerebral arteriosclerosis' (including vertebrobasilar insufficiency and transient ischaemic attacks)

| Authors | Year | Patients | | Source | Dose | Design of trial | Duration | Results |
		No.	Mean age (yr)					
Esser and Reis	1968	20	NG (Range 55–70)	CAS	Increasing from 8 to 32 mg/day	D-B	5/52	Memory + (digit span test)
Rivera et al	1974	50	66.5	VBI +dementia	32 mg/day	D-B CO	12/52	Cognition, memory, perception, language+ Mean CBF & rCBF ↑
Spruill et al	1975	26	54.5	VBI with TIAs	32 mg/day	D-B CO	4/12	No change in frequency of TIAs. Subjective improvements
Pathy et al	1977	45	NG	CAS	24 mg/day	D-B	8/52	5/9 mental function tests+(orientation, digit retention, association learning, arithmetic, gen. knowledge)

CAS = cerebral atherosclerosis; VBI = vertebrobasilar insufficiency; TIAs = transient ischaemic attacks; NG = not given; + = significantly improved; D-B = double-blind; CO = cross-over.

betahistine is more effective than oral papaverine or hexobendine in patients with cerebral ischaemia.

Dosage. The dosage is 8–16 mg three times daily. Side effects include gastric disturbances, headache, flushing and faintness, although doses of 8 mg four times daily produced little change in blood pressure (Hughes et al, 1981).

This drug has not yet been granted approval in the USA.

Nicotinic acid and its derivatives

Nicotinic acid has a direct vasodilating effect, causing flushing but no significant increase in CBF (Loman et al, 1941; Scheinberg, 1950; Boudouresques et al, 1970). A decrease in CBF was reported by Gottstein (1965) and by Herrschaft (1975).

Nicotinic acid also has well-established effects on carbohydrate and lipid metabolism (Gey and Carlson, 1970; Levy, 1980).

Nicotinic acid needs to be given in large doses, at which side-effects are often a nuisance; however, even doses as large as 3 g/day did not produce significant benefit in elderly subjects (Smith et al, 1963). Lu et al (1971) reported that only small clinical changes could be observed during 3 months of treatment with nicotinic acid in a double-blind study in long-term psychogeriatric patients. Nicotinic acid is widely used, however, in smaller doses together with another agent, as in Cosaldon (see below), or a derivative is used which has fewer side-effects, either because of slow release of the

nicotinic acid (Bradilan, Hexopal) or differences in the molecular structure (Complamex).

In the past there was a vogue for giving nicotinic acid with a cerebral stimulant such as leptazol (pentylenetetrazol) for 'cerebral arteriosclerosis' (Levy, 1953; Thompson and Proctor, 1954; Bisley, 1960). A similar approach used a stimulant and a nicotinic acid derivative (see below).

Inositol hexanicotinate (Hexopal)

Pharmacology. This is a long-acting derivative of nicotinic acid, incorporating six nicotinic acid moieties in its molecule. Administration of Hexopal is followed by increased blood levels of nicotinic acid (Harthon et al, 1964; Sommer, 1965).

It has two major properties:

Vasodilatation. Although atherosclerotic vessels may show little response, the drug is claimed to dilate collateral vessels around ischaemic areas in the legs (Lindqvist, 1958; Kappert, 1961).

Metabolic effects. Stimulation of fibrinolysis (Kappert, 1961; Sommer, 1965); decrease in blood viscosity, surface tension and density (Goldstein et al, 1966); improvement in disturbed lipid metabolism (Goldstein et al, 1966; Hammerl et al, 1969; Rosier, 1975).

These metabolic effects may facilitate blood circulation in ischaemic areas even if the vasodilator effect is unobtainable.

Clinical evaluation in cerebral disorders. This has been limited, and the published data are unimpressive. Open studies have claimed that the drug improves mental function; focal symptoms and signs did not change. Reduction in serum triglycerides, reported by Rosier (1975), correlated with improved mental state.

Miller (1963) carried out a double-blind study of Hexopal and Leptazol in 30 long-stay geriatric patients with cerebrovascular insufficiency. Of the 24 patients completing the 6-month trial, 12 were in the 'active' group and 12 in the 'placebo' group. Only two patients — in the active group — showed possible improvement in behaviour. The Hexopal dose was low, however — only 200 mg tds. Sourander et al (1970) reported improved psychological test results in elderly patients treated with inositol hexanicotinate together with dixyrazine.

Dosage.   The dosage currently recommended is 3 to 4 g daily.

Side-effects.   Very few have been reported: feelings of warmth, slight perspiration, dyspepsia. These are rarely encountered and are then usually mild.

Tetranicotinoylfructose (Bradilan)

This compound is a fructose ester of nicotinic acid which releases nicotinic acid in the small intestine at alkaline pH; this, aided by an enteric coating of the tablet, ensures a gradual sustained release of the active agent, so avoiding gastric irritation and reducing flushing — both well-known side-effects of nicotinic acid ingestion.

Uncontrolled and controlled studies have established the value of this drug for dilatation of skin and muscle vessels (Andrews et al, 1973; Antcliff et al, 1974; Boroda, 1975), and Jaffé (1975), in a double-blind study, showed that tetranictinoylfructose had the statistical edge over inositol hexanicotinate in improving walking distance in 50 patients with intermittent claudication. Hypolipidaemic effects, stimulation of fibrinolysis and decrease in platelet stickiness have been described (Benaim and Dewar, 1975). These effects may contribute to improvement in blood flow.

Clinical evaluation in cerebral disorders.   There is little or no evidence of any value of this drug in cerebral disorders. Two papers attest to the usefulness of tetranicotinoylfructose combined with meclofenoxate in the treatment of psychiatric disorders, but the data are not impressive (Rabassini and Buoso, 1965; Viviano and Ceccarelli, 1966). These authors considered that tetranicotinoylfructose potentiated the meclofenoxate, allowing a lower dosage of the latter drug.

Dosage.   The starting dose is two 250 mg tablets three times a day, increasing if required to three or four tablets thrice daily — i.e. a maximum of 3 g daily.

Side-effects.   Rarely, a feeling of warmth may be experienced at the start of treatment, especially if alcohol is taken.

Nicotinyl alcohol tartrate (β-pyridylcarbinol, Ronicol — UK; Roniacol — USA & Canada)

This is the alcohol corresponding to nicotinic acid, with similar properties. During its metabolism, nicotinic acid is released: thus its action is more sustained than that of nicotinic acid itself. Its manufacturers recommend the use of Ronicol in peripheral vascular disease and make no claims for any value in cerebral disorders.

Heyck (1962) reported that nicotinyl alcohol produced dilatation of intracranial vessels in patients with cerebrovascular insufficiency (nitrous oxide technique). Becker et al (1970) found evidence to suggest increased CBF after oral doses of Ronicol (increasing from 500 mg to 5 g daily) over 18 days in patients with diffuse cerebrovascular insufficiency (circulation time technique). Boudouresques et al (1970) found increased rCBF (^{133}Xe method) in 12 of 20 patients treated with oral Ronicol for 6 weeks.

However, Gottstein (1969) found no increase in CBF (or $CMRO_2$) after intravenous Ronicol or other vasoactive drugs in normal subjects; and Herrschaft (1975) found that intravenous β-pyridylcarbinol (300 mg in 250 ml saline infused by drip over 20 minutes) caused a significant decrease in rCBF (^{133}Xe method) in patients with cerebrovascular insufficiency. Ammon et al (1970) found virtually no change in carbohydrate metabolism in the brains of mice treated with β-pyridylcarbinol, although Quadbeck et al (1964) had reported increased glucose uptake in animal experiments.

cAMP levels fall transiently in brain, liver and adipose tissue of rats treated with β-pyridylcarbinol orally, but the fall gives way to an even greater rise after one hour (Burkard et al, 1970).

Clinical evaluation in cerebral disorders.   Several European papers have reported beneficial effects from β-pyridylcarbinol in states of 'cerebral impairment'. Oesterreich and Tellenbach (1967) used repeated intravenous infusions of Ronicol as an adjuvant to other psychopharmacological treatment, or to ECT, and claimed excellent results in 180 patients — without control data. Cornu (1969) found that patients with brain failure showed improved drive, attentiveness and social contact which facilitated their nursing care, even in those with severe brain damage. Boudouresques et al (1970) studied 20 patients with diffuse chronic cerebrovascular insufficiency, treated for 3 weeks with a delayed-release form of Ronicol by mouth. Clinical effects were correlated with EEG and rCBF changes (^{133}Xe method). Overall improvement was recorded in 10 patients; increased rCBF was noted in 12 of the 20 patients.

An American double-blind study (Stuart, 1967) of nicotinyl alcohol in peripheral vascular disorders included nine patients with chronic brain syndrome; none of these showed significant improvement in mental state after 150 mg of the drug twice daily for 6 weeks.

Dosage. Each tablet of Ronicol contains 59.4 mg nicotinyl alcohol tartrate, equivalent to 25 mg nicotinyl alcohol. The recommended dosage is 1 to 2 tablets four times daily, for peripheral vascular disease.

Ronicol Timespan is a slow release tablet containing 357 mg of the tartrate, equivalent to 150 mg nicotinyl alcohol. Dosage is 1 to 2 tablets night and morning.

There is no 'recommended' dosage quoted for cerebrovascular indications in the UK. Stuart (1967) used 150 mg Ronicol Timespan bd; Boudouresques et al (1970) used two or three times that dose and recorded good tolerance except in one patient who had flushing of face and arms after a dose of 300 mg. On these larger doses a fall in blood pressure may occur and this is clearly undesirable.

Side-effects. Moderate doses are well tolerated. At optimum doses mild transient facial flushing and a sensation of warmth in the head may be noted.

Xanthinol nicotinate (Complamex — UK; Complamin — Europe)

This is a drug which consists of a xanthine base chemically combined with nicotinic acid. The effects of such a chemical combination appear to be superior to those of a mixture of theophylline and nicotinic acid.

Xanthines are discussed further below.

Xanthinol nicotinate has been reported to:

1. increase blood flow to skin and muscle (Bachmann, 1965; Klüken and Schmidt, 1972) and in the common carotid artery in rabbits (Winter et al, 1973). Schreiber (1960) had previously reported rheographical evidence of increased CBF due to Complamin;

2. increase stroke volume and blood flow velocity (Bachmann, 1965);

3. enhance development of collaterals — in the microcirculation (Davis and Rozov, 1973) and arterial collaterals (Schmitt and Drake, 1971);

4. activate fibrinolysis and lower plasma fibrinogen levels (but does not alter coagulation) (Cultrera et al, 1971; Davis and Rozov, 1973);

5. lower blood viscosity (Davis and Rozov, 1973);

6. exert a hypolipidaemic effect (Berkowitz, 1964; Davis and Rozov, 1973) — especially on cholesterol;

7. inhibit platelet aggregation when given intravenously (but not orally at a dosage of 900 mg daily) (Steger, 1973);

8. increase pyridine nucleotide levels in liver (Brenner, 1968) and brain (Brenner and Brenner, 1972);

9. increase adenine nucleotide levels in brain (Brenner and Brenner, 1972) and erythrocytes (Brenner, 1973);

10. increase oxygen uptake in brain and liver (Brenner, 1974), and increase glucose uptake in the brain (Brenner and Brenner, 1972).

In healthy adults rendered hypoxic, xanthinol nicotinate improved mental concentration (Held et al, 1973) and prevented a fall in erythrocyte ATP concentrations (Held, 1973).

It is of interest that the manufacturers of Complamex stress that the drug is *not* a vasodilator; it is said to increase circulation in the tissues by opening up the microcirculation and thus diminishing peripheral resistance, while simultaneously increasing stroke volume and minute volume of the heart. For these reasons it has been termed a 'haemokinator'. Various of the metabolic effects would also contribute to increased ease of blood flow (cf. oxipentifylline ('Trental') — see below).

Clinical evaluation in cerebral disease. Beneficial effects in patients with a diagnosis of cerebral circulatory insufficiency have been claimed from various uncontrolled trials.

Braverman and Naylor (1975) carried out a double-blind cross-over study with randomized selection of suitable patients, using a teaching machine to apply paired association tests. Results from 28 elderly demented patients were analysed after 22 weeks and compared with those from younger stroke patients in a rehabilitation centre. Of the 28 patients, 18 improved their score, seven showed no change and three reduced their score. Improvement persisted after the drug was stopped. This paper is also useful in discussing the rationale of the use of vasoactive drugs in the management of the elderly demented patient; the authors concluded that xanthinol nicotinate could produce beneficial effects in such patients, but that more and larger studies were required.

Dosage. Tablets of 150 mg and 300 mg are available: the dose is 300 mg tds with or immediately after meals. A retard preparation containing 500 mg xanthinol nicotinate is available in some countries. Parenteral administration is also possible.

Side-effects. Flushing (especially of the face and upper trunk), itching, fall in blood pressure and abdominal pain have been recorded. These — apart from flushing — are uncommon and slight. There is much individual variation in the incidence and degree of flushing: it is rarely a problem but patients should be warned of the possibility.

Nicergoline

Nicergoline has been considered earlier in this chapter.

Methylxanthines

Xanthine is a purine derivative; the methylxanthines include caffeine (1,3,7-trimethylxanthine) and theophylline (1,3-dimethylxanthine). These are cerebral stimulants, but also have peripheral vasodilator and diuretic properties.

Aminophylline is theophylline ethylene diamine and is well known as a respiratory stimulant, useful in the control of Cheyne-Stokes respiration. Formerly, it was held that aminophylline increased cerebral blood flow (Mainzer, 1949) and several authors recommended its use in acute strokes. However, it subsequently became apparent that this drug actually caused *constriction* of cerebral vessels in man (Wechsler et al, 1950; Moyer et al, 1952) and in animals (Koch and Schnellbächer, 1955). The subject is reviewed by Gottstein (1969), who studied the effects of intravenous aminophylline (240 to 480 mg) in man: normal volunteers showed a decreased CBF (nitrous oxide method), and patients with cerebrovascular disease had an even greater fall in CBF.

Herrschaft (1975) showed a fall of 20 per cent in rCBF in patients with cerebrovascular disease after intravenous aminophylline (450 mg). Skinhøj and Poulson (1970) confirmed the cerebral vasoconstricting effect, but considered that this could benefit some cases of acute vascular disorders by creating an 'inverse steal' phenomenon.

However, there is evidence that methylxanthines antagonize central adenosine receptors, (Daly et al, 1981), and since adenosine may be involved in cerebral vasodilatation (Pull and McIlwain, 1972), this may account for the cerebral vasoconstriction attributed to methylxanthines. It could also explain the central stimulant effect of these drugs, (Daly et al, 1981), probably better than the very weak inhibitory effects which methylxanthines exert on cyclic nucleotide phosphodiesterase (Iverson, 1983).

Pentifylline with nicotinic acid (Cosaldon)
Pentifylline is 1-hexyl, 3,7-dimethylxanthine; it dilates cerebral arteries (Cugurra and Echinard-Garin, 1960) and has metabolic and EEG effects (Quadbeck and Tarragó-Humet, 1972). All these effects are said to be potentiated by the addition of nicotinic acid. Evidence of benefit from Cosaldon in the elderly is scanty and unimpressive. Of the two published double-blind crossover studies with Cosaldon, one study reported improvements in patients wtth 'cerebral sclerosis' (Kirchberger et al, 1969) and the other reported improved psychological test results in 302 healthy volunteers over an age range from the third to the ninth decade (Amthauer, 1971). The design of both of these studies has been criticized (Drug Ther. Bull, 1972). Neubauer (1965) and Zielinski (1968) reported improved vision in various vascular disorders of the choroid and retina in some patients treated with Cosaldon for long periods (about a year or more).

Dosage. The tablet contains 200 mg of the xanthine derivative and 500 mg nicotinic acid. The makers recommend a dose of one tablet four times daily. This frequency of administration must itself impair its potential value as a therapy for dementia, at least in those patients living alone.

Side-effects. Flushing and gastrointestinal disturbances have been reported; they are likely to be transient.

Calcium entry blockers
This class of drugs has been the focus of a great burst of research and clinical interest in recent years. Muscle contraction requires free calcium ions (Ca^{++}) for activation. The excitation process at the membrane of the muscle cell produces a sudden influx of free Ca^{++} from the extracellular space to the interior of the cell, and Ca^{++} is also released from intracellular stores. Drugs which block the inward flux of Ca^{++} across the cell membrane are called calcium entry blockers, and were first studied in 1964 by Fleckenstein (see Fleckenstein 1977, 1981). Since then a great variety of such agents has been developed; these drugs do not form a homogeneous group, but vary in their properties with regard to such matters as effects on conducting tissues of the heart, myocardial cells (Henry, 1982) and vascular smooth muscle (Flaim, 1982). Structure-activity relationships are considered by Triggle (1982). Different vessels show varying degrees of response to these several drugs and some of the newer agents seem to be particularly effective in dilating cerebral arteries in animal models (see below, and Flaim, 1982).

One of the first calcium entry blockers studied was Cinnarizine.

Cinnarizone (Stugeron — UK; Stutgeron — Germany)
This is benzhydryl-4-cinnamyl piperazine and, being related to the cyclizines, has antihistamine properties and is well-known for its efficacy in motion sickness and vertigo. Cinnarizine antagonizes vasoconstrictor stimuli (Godfraind and Kaba, 1972); the manufacturers of this drug consider it to be not a vasodilator but rather a 'vasorelaxant' — i.e., a drug which acts to inhibit vasoconstriction produced by other stimuli. Such a concept has been compared to the protective effect of cromoglycate against bronchoconstriction, as distinct from the effect of bronchodilators in asthma (Emanuel and Will, 1977).

The drug may also reduce blood viscosity (Di Perri et al, 1977), attributed to increased erythrocyte flexibility.

Cinnarizine can increase CBF in man and animals (Behrens, 1966; Weigelin and Sayegh, 1968). Some double-blind studies in patients with 'cerebrovascular insufficiency' have been encouraging (Behrens, 1966; van der Meer-van Manen, 1967; Bernard and Goffart, 1968; Toledo et al, 1972; Staessen, 1977) but three such studies in the UK gave negative results: two of these were in severely affected patients, not always well-matched (Irvine et al, 1970; Droller et al, 1971) but the third examined less severely affected patients (General Practitioner Research Group, 1969).

Dosage. The drug is supplied in 15 mg tablets and (as cinnarizine forte) 75 mg capsules. Up to 75 mg tds may be used.

Flunarizine (Sibelium — Germany)

This difluoro-derivative of cinnarizine is more potent than cinnarizine (Verhaegen et al, 1974). It is even more selective than cinnarizine on calcium channels in vascular smooth muscle activated by vasoconstrictor agents (Van Nueten and Wellens, 1979), and effectively dilated vertebral arteries in anaesthetized dogs (Kato et al, 1981).

A multicentre double-blind study reported significant improvements in various 'symptoms of cerebral vascular insufficiency' (Nelson et al, 1978).

Newer calcium entry blockers

Recent interest in the effects of these drugs has been considerable. They include diltiazem, fendiline, nifedipine, perhexiline, prenylamine and verapamil. They show considerably greater activity than papaverine in suppressing potassium-induced spasm of strips of coronary arteries from pigs. For example nifedepine is several thousand times more potent than papaverine in this respect.

Nifedipine has been shown to inhibit the contractions induced by serotonin, phenylephrine or potassium in the canine basilar artery in vitro (Allen and Banghart, 1979); and sublingual administration of nifedipine reversed both acute and subacute vertebrobasilar arterial spasm produced in dogs by subarachnoid injection of blood (Allen and Bahr, 1979).

Nimodipine is an even newer calcium entry blocker. This drug is selective for cardiac and cerebral arteries and had undoubted cerebral vasorelaxant effects in experiments on cats (Kazda et al, 1979; Tanaka et al, 1980) and these effects persisted longer than those of cinnarizine or papaverine (Kazda and Hoffmeister, 1979). Nimodipine also protected rats against retrograde amnesia induced by hypoxia (Hoffmeister et al, 1979).

No reports have yet been found on the effects of nifedipine or nimodipine on cerebral blood flow and mental function in the elderly, but it is anticipated that such studies will be done. However, the effects of these drugs on systemic blood pressure must be taken into account. Nifedipine has been shown to reduce blood pressure and is used clinically in the treatment of some patients with hypertension (Olivari et al, 1979). It will be preferable to await the possible further development of a more selective calcium entry blocker.

DRUGS WITH COMBINED EFFECTS

Oxpentifylline (Trental)

This is 3,7-dimethyl-1-(5-oxohexyl) xanthine, intro-

duced as a peripheral vasodilator. It has two main properties:

Vasodilatation. By direct action on smooth muscle (Popendiker et al 1971), by potentiating β-sympathomimetic drugs (Stefanovich, 1978) and antagonizing the vasoconstrictor effects of adrenaline and noradrenaline (Boksay et al, 1971; Boksay and Bollman, 1971), and by inhibition of phosphodiesterase with consequent increase to cyclic AMP, which causes vascular smooth muscle to relax (Stefanovich, 1974; Hayashi and Ozawa, 1974).

Reduction in blood viscosity. Several mechanisms may operate including reduction in haematocrit (Hess et al, 1973; Heidrich and Ott, 1974) and increase of red cell flexibility by increase in erythrocyte ATP levels (Müller 1978). Incubation of blood with oxpentifylline also leads to improved flow properties (Ehrly, 1975). Inhibition of platelet adhesiveness and aggregation may also be involved (Gastpar, 1974a, b).

Intravenous use increases CBF (Koppenhagen et al, 1977), improves EEG patterns (Jovanović, 1976) and increases ATP concentrations in the brain (Jovanović, 1976).

Clinical evaluation has been beset with the usual problems of imprecision, but some double-blind studies have shown improvement in symptoms, mood and performance. Favourable results have followed its use after strokes (Janaki, 1980). Clinical experience is reviewed by Theis et al (1978); and 2 further double-blind placebo-controlled studies have been published (Dominguez et al, 1977; Harwart, 1979) showing significant benefits, but not the same benefits in the two studies.

Dosage. Initially, two 100 mg tablets tds; maintenance dose 100 mg tds.

Side-effects. Nausea, malaise, gastric upset, vertigo and flushing have been met with, usually mild and transient. The drug is probably best taken with food.

Suloctidil (Sulocton, — Europe)

A synthetic agent (1-[4-isopropylthiophenyl]-2 N octylaminopropanol) originally developed as a direct vascular relaxant, more potent than papaverine, suloctidil was later found to have various other properties which were considered of potential value in the treatment of arterial insufficiency and atherosclerosis, viz, reduction in plasma fibrinogen, blood viscosity and blood cholesterol; anti-platelet-aggregation and antithrombotic properties; and beneficial effects on cerebral metabolism reflected by increased cerebral ATP levels and improved EEG patterns (Roba et al, 1977). In 3-month double-blind studies on psychogeriatric patients, significant improvements have been reported in psychometric tests (Jacquy and Noel, 1977) and, especially in the third month of treatment, in behaviour and performance (Bargheon, 1977).

Dosage. 100 mg tds.

Naftidrofuryl (*Nafronyl oxalate, Praxilene — UK, Europe*)

This synthetic drug (a complex acid ester of diethylaminoethanol) is the acid oxalate of beta-naphthyl-l-beta'-tetrahydrofuryl diethanolamine isobutyrate. It has been used in Europe since 1968 for 'cerebral arteriosclerosis' and has multiple actions: direct vasorelaxant effect, sympatheticolytic effect, local anaesthetic properties, antagonism to serotonin, nicotine and bradykinin, and analeptic and antidepressant effects (Fontaine et al, 1968). In addition, it improves intracellular glucose and oxygen metabolism (Meynaud et al, 1975; Plotkine et al, 1975) by activation of succinate dehydrogenase (Shaw and Johnson, 1975). Increased cerebral ATP levels in mice were reported by Meynaud et al (1975), but Nickolson and Wolthuis (1976) could not confirm this in rats. Increased pyruvate; lactate ratio in cerebrospinal fluid was reported in patients with mild dementia given 400 mg nafronyl daily; this change was correlated with improvements in EEG, psychometric tests, and behavioural scales (Yesavage et al, 1982). There is conflicting evidence regarding changes in CBF attributable to nafronyl. Earlier studies showed some increase in subcortical rCBF (Pourrias and Raynaud, 1972) and in carotid artery flow (Plotkine et al, 1975), but Herrschaft (1975) and Heiss and Podreka (1978) found slight reductions in CBF after intravenous nafronyl. Other workers have found no change in CBF in elderly patients with cerebrovascular disease or dementia or both, after 120 mg nafronyl intravenously, although the vasodilator response to inhalation of 5 per cent carbon dioxide was attenuated (James et al, 1978). Oral nafronyl (200 mg tds for 6 weeks) also had no efect on CBF.

Clinical evaluation in cerebral disease. Several double-blind studies have attested to the value of nafronyl in dementia and 'cerebral arteriosclerosis' in the elderly (see Table 17.9). These must be criticized for variability in diagnostic precision, heterogeneous case-selection and inconsistency of assessment procedures. Of particular interest is the study by Judge and Urquhart (1972) in which significant and marked improvement in behaviour and intellect occurred in severely demented patients; although such dramatic results have not been found by others, many worthwhile gains have been reported. Yesavage et al (1979a) considered that nafronyl is one of the more promising new agents, but still in need of further study to define its specific effects. One such study was reported by Branconnier and Cole (1978b), using an 'Impairment Index' for assessment; another, from Yesavage et al (1982), correlated clinical improvement with biochemical changes in the CSF and EEG changes (quoted above). Admani (1978) reported benefit from nafronyl in recent acute stroke, but the trial design and the statistical procedures used were criticized by Steiner et al, (1979).

Dosage. 100 mg (1 capsule) tds. An injectable form is also available.

Side effects. These are rare and transient: headache, epigastric discomfort, heartburn, nausea, abdominal distension, diarrhoea, paraesthesiae and agitation have been reported.

DRUGS CLAIMED TO IMPROVE MICROCIRCULATION

Most have already been considered.

Dextran of low molecular weight (*Rheomacrodex*)

This is included because of its known effects on blood viscosity which may facilitate blood flow. Dextran is an synthetic dextrose polymer and a structural analogue of heparin. Dextrans of various molecular weights (MW) can be made: that with MW 70 000 (dextran 70) is used as a plasma expander and for its antithrombotic effect whereas that with MW 40 000 (dextran 40) may be infused for its antithrombotic effect or to improve microcirculatory flow (Atik, 1967). This last effect is the result of lowered blood viscosity (Lancet, 1977c) which is due in turn to haemodilution and possibly effects on erythrocyte and platelet aggregation (Atik, 1967).

Gottstein (1969) showed increased CBF after low MW dextran, and Gilroy et al (1969) noted benefit in patients with acute cerebral ischaemia and infarction due to atherosclerotic thromboembolism.

Increased rCBF was found after low MW dextran infusion in patients with focal cerebrovascular disease (Heiss, 1973; Heiss and Podreka, 1978) and in patients wiht cerebrovascular insufficiency (Herrschaft, 1975).

In the management of brain failure, this type of therapy is clearly of little practical value in view of the need for repeated infusions and the risks of increasing plasma volume in the elderly.

Buflomedil (*Fonzylane — France*)

This is a butyrophenone derivative claimed to improve microcirculation in ischaemic areas. Its mechanism of action is unclear: it has antiaggregating effects on platelets, but did not influence blood viscosity (Dubourg and Scamuffa, 1981). In a small double-blind crossover study, Dormandy and Ernst (1981) reported that infusion of buflomedil increased red cell flexibility to a significant extent.

An open randomized trial of buflomedil, 150 mg tds orally, against Hydergine, 1.5 mg tds orally, included 20 elderly patients with 'cerebrovascular insufficiency' in each treatment group (Demichelis Genesio and Cid Sanz, 1981). Buflomedil was judged superior to Hydergine in regard to neurological and psychological improvements.

Table 17.9 Results of double-blind controlled clinical trials with naftidrofuryl

Authors	Patients				Dose	Cross-over	Duration	Results
	Year	No.	Mean age (yr)	Source				
Robinson	1972	57	NG	CVI (hospitalized)	300 mg/day	No	2/12	Improved intellect and memory (subjective medical and nursing assessments)
Judge & Urquhart	1972	24	NG	Severely demented in-patients	300 mg/day	Yes	20/52 (4/52 central 'rest period' without treatment)	Improved intellectual function; 4 sent home. Beneficial effects persisted for 12/52 after drug stopped
Gerin	1974	20	78.8	Home for blind old people	150 mg/day	No	2/12	Recent memory and social behaviour +
Bouvier et al	1974	43	71.9	Chronic sick wards; advancing brain failure	150 mg/day for 7/52, then 300 mg/day for 7/52	No	14/52	Improved intellectual performance, especially in milder cases
Bargheon	1975	108	72	Old people's home	300 mg/day	No	12/52	Improved alertness, memory, orientation, motivation and self-care
Cox	1975	32	75.5	Confused, in geriatric or psychogeriatric wards	300 mg/day	No	2/12	Improved mood, memory, intellect and personality in significant proportion. Much individual variability
Adriaensen	1977	33	75.0	Long-stay geriatric in-patients	300 mg/day	No	2/12	Improved concentration, memory and social integration
Brodie	1977	60	76.0	60 confused patients from general practice	300 mg/day	No	2/12	Intellectual improvement, greater than in placebo group; significant improvement in DLA
Trouillas	1977	40	63.7	Neurological out-patients with CVI±dementia	300 mg/day	No	2/12	Improved recent memory, memory for numbers, and giddiness
Dartenuc et al	1978	36	75.6	Geriatric in-patients with CVI	300 mg/day	No	3/12	Very significant improvement in psycho-intellectual and functional aspects

CVI = cerebrovascular insufficiency; DLA = daily living activities; NG = not given.

In a double-blind study in 46 patients with advanced mental deterioration or psychosensory aphasia, buflomedil was compared to cinnarizine (Pacheco e Silva and Landi de Almeida, 1981). Both drugs had beneficial effects, with a slight advantage to buflomedil.

Dosage. 150 mg tds.

Side effects. digestive discomfort, headache, somnolence.

DRUGS INFLUENCING CEREBRAL CELL METABOLISM

Several of the drugs already considered are claimed to improve cerebral metabolism and the evidence has been presented in some detail. Several others require consideration.

Agents enhancing cerebral acetylcholine levels

Anticholinesterases

Physostigmine crosses the blood-brain barrier effectively; it improves memory which has been impaired by drugs with anticholinergic actions (e.g. tricyclic antidepressants or anti-parkinsonism drugs) (Granacher and Baldessarini, 1975; Ghoneim and Mewaldt, 1977) or by disease (Peters and Levin, 1977; Christie et al, 1981). It has improved long-term memory in normal subjects (Davis et al, 1978, 1979).

Evidence of improvement in selective mental functions has come from Muramoto et al (1979), Davis et al (1979) and Smith and Swash (1980). However, Peters and Levin (1979) found that physostigmine produced no facilitation of memory in three patients with Alzheimer's disease until lecithin was added to the treatment regimen, when long-term memory improved. Drachman et al (1982) reported that in 16 normal elderly subjects (mean age 70 years) neither intravenous physostigmine nor oral lecithin (nor the two drugs given together) had any effect on memory or learning.

In the management of SDAT the need for daily injections and the troublesome side effects make physostigmine an impracticable therapy, although concomitant injection of glycopyrrolate (Peters and Levin, 1979) or oral administration of methscopolamine bromide (Drachman et al, 1982) may be used to prevent peripheral cholinergic effects.

Oral physostigmine has been studied in patients with Alzheimer's disease, as sole therapy (Davis et al, 1983) or with concomitant choline (Bajada, 1982) or lecithin (Peters and Levin, 1982; Thal and Field, 1983). Modest improvements in memory were reported by all these authors except Bajada (1982). Further details of the concomitant-use studies are given below.

Comfort (1978) has advocated a search for a more selective cholinesterase inhibitor without peripheral effects — the cholinergic equivalent of carbidopa.

Choline

Choline is the precursor of ACh: in animal experiments, choline uptake by the brain correlates closely with cerebral ACh levels (Kuhar et al, 1973). Dietary choline consumption has increased brain concentrations of ACh in animals, along with brain and serum levels of free choline (Cohen and Wurtman, 1976; Hirsch et al, 1977); even where brain ACh has not increased, choline feeding led to behaviour changes in rats (Wecker and Schmidt, 1979) and may therefore affect cholinergic transmission without producing a net increase in brain ACh, possibly by increasing ACh turnover in the brain. Hanin (1979) has emphasized that the influence of choline on central cholinergic function is far from clear as yet, but evidence from in vitro models suggests that choline availability increases ACh release when neurons are depolarized or are made to fire rapidly (this could be the case in SDAT, where loss of some cholinergic neurons might lead to a compensatory increase in firing rates in those remaining (Lancet, 1980; Bartus et al, 1982)).

In man, fasting serum choline concentrations were similar in healthy young and old subjects, and did not relate to dietary choline content (Zeisel et al, 1982). Patients with Alzheimer's disease have normal CSF choline levels, but serum (and/or red cell) and CSF levels increased on choline administration in patients with Alzheimer's disease (Etienne et al, 1978a; Christie et al, 1979; Glen et al, 1981; Ferris et al, 1982) and with Huntington's chorea (Growdon et al, 1977).

Clinical evaluation. Bartus et al (1982) outlined 12 studies in which choline was administered — mainly to patients with various degrees of Alzheimer's disease (nine studies), also elderly outpatients and healthy elderly subjects, some of whom had demonstrated memory impairment. A further study was reported by Ferris et al, (1982). Results were not encouraging (although the studies were almost all of short duration, usually only 1 to 4 weeks). Levy (1978) emphasized the need for a long study with careful assessment. It is possible that subgroups of responders exist (Davis et al, 1982), but little or no improvements were found in well-controlled double-blind studies despite the use of a wide range of doses up to 15 g/day for 2 months, but no change was found in cognition, memory or behaviour in 18 patients (aged 57–84 years) with Alzheimer's disease.

It is possible that decreased choline acetyltransferase activity may prevent much additional ACh synthesis in the elderly brain despite choline therapy.

Lecithin

This natural source of choline is more effective in increasing blood choline levels in man (Wurtman et al,

1977) and has been found to increase ACh concentrations in rat brain (Hirsch and Wurtman, 1978). It may be preferable to choline for therapeutic use, as it produces fewer side effects than other cholinergic agents (Wurtman and Zeisel, 1982). A useful review of the effects of dietary influences on neurotransmitter synthesis in the brain of man and animals is given by Growdon and Wurtman (1979).

Clinical evaluation. The review of Bartus et al (1982) includes six studies in which lecithin was administered to patients with Alzheimer's disease (pre-senile and senile patients were studied). No significant or consistent improvements were noted in these studies. Three further negative studies were reported recently, involving patients with Alzheimer's disease (Heyman et al, 1982; Sullivan et al, 1982; Dysken et al, 1982).

Although the early results with choline and lecithin had shown some promise, the rapidly widening experience with those agents has not substantiated their value in the management of Alzheimer's disease.

Cytidine diphosphate choline (CDP-choline, Citicoline — Europe, Japan)

This compound is involved in the biosynthesis of lecithin and is used in the treatment of dementia in some countries. A precursor, CMP (cytidine monophosphate), and a combination of pyrimidine nucleosides have also been used. These compounds are claimed to improve cerebral glucose metabolism; but adequate clinical evaluation is lacking.

Combined therapy

Goldberg and his colleagues (Goldberg, 1982) have repeatedly shown that in vitro supplementation of media with choline does not enhance the spontaneous release of ACh until nerves are stimulated. This led to the concept that the effect of exogenous choline or lecithin on neuronal release of ACh is influenced by the rate of firing of neurons (Wurtman and Zeisel, 1982). Several studies have therefore been performed using concomitant therapy with choline (or lecithin) and a second agent which might enhance ACh levels and/or cerebral metabolism — e.g. an anticholinesterase (physostigmine or THA); a noötropic agent (piracetam — which is also said to enhance neuronal energy levels); or a dopaminergic drug (L-dopa). Such an approach, using piracetam and choline, produced highly significant improvements in memory in rats (P<0.001) (Bartus et al, 1981).

Ferris et al (1982) gave piracetam and choline concurrently for seven days to patients with mild to moderate Alzheimer's disease. Marked improvement in memory storage and retrieval was noted in four patients; this was not seen when each drug was taken individually. Erythrocyte choline levels were much higher in this subgroup

of 'responders' than in nonresponders, and may have predictive value.

Peters and Levin (1979) showed that physostigmine and lecithin can together improve verbal storage and retrieval in some patients with mild to moderate dementia. The same workers (Peters and Levin, 1982) examined the effect of oral physostigmine (0.5 to 3 mg tds) given concurrently with lecithin for up to 18 months to four patients with Alzheimer's disease, and again showed improved verbal memory.

A study of oral physostigmine (0.4 mg q4h) and choline in six patients with moderate to severe Alzheimer's disease was reported by Bajada (1982). No benefit was observed. Thal and Fuld (1983) reported memory improvement in eight out of 12 patients with early Alzheimer's disease who were given oral physostigmine, 2–2.4 mg six times daily, plus lecithin, 3.6 g tds (35 per cent phosphatidylcholine). Rechallenge (in a double-blind crossover study) confirmed these results. Another orally active anticholinesterase, tetrahydroamineacridine (THA) has been given (30 mg/day) together with lecithin (60 g/day) to 10 patients with primary degenerative dementia (Kaye et al, 1982). Mildly affected patients showed significantly improved performance on serial learning tests 2 hours after the last of three doses (at 10 p.m., 8 a.m. and 12 noon).

Concomitant therapy with L-dopa and lecithin was given for 9 weeks to a small number of patients with parkinsonism accompanied by definite intellectual deterioration; a control group received powdered skim milk as placebo along with their L-dopa (Gracia et al, 1982). Patients on lecithin improved in six of eight tests of cognition but deteriorated on vocabulary. The memory improvement reached statistical significance (P<0.05).

Deanol (Dimethylaminoethanol, DMAE)

Pharmacology. Du Vigneaud et al (1946) reported that 2-dimethylaminoethanol (DMAE) was a precursor of choline in rat tissue. Pfeiffer et al (1957) reported that DMAE had cerebral stimulant effects, possibly acting as a precursor of brain acetylcholine. Increased concentrations of acetylcholine in brains treated with DMAE or choline have been shown by Danysz et al (1967) and Haubrich et al (1975) in rats, and by Goldberg and Silvergeld (1974) in mice. Groth et al (1958) demonstrated that DMAE crossed the blood brain barrier far more effectively than choline and Honegger and Honegger (1959) showed that DMAE occurred naturally in animal tissues, including human brain. However, this observation and that of Goldberg and Silvergeld (1974) could not be confirmed by Zahmser and Hanin (1976).

Kostopoulos and Phillis (1975) confirmed the cholinomimetic action of deanol on single cerebral cortical neurones and supported the concept that the drug stimulated acetylcholine synthesis and release from presynaptic cholinergic nerve terminals.

Such data have been used as a basis for the treatment of various neurological disorders in which there is an underlying disorder of acetylcholine metabolism. The preparation used for this purpose has been the *p*-acetamidobenzoic acid salt (Deaner — USA). This drug, not marketed at presented in the UK, has been shown to extend the life span of senile male mice (Hochschild, 1973), as has also been shown for another DMAE derivative, meclofenoxate (see below).

Clinical evaluation. The earliest clinical usage was in schizophrenia (Pfeiffer et al, 1957, 1959; Pennington, 1959; Portnow et al, 1960), psychoneuroses and depression (Settel, 1959; Dominian, 1960) and subsequently in learning and behavioural disorders of children, including hyperkinetic states (see Jacobs, 1965; Ré, 1974).

In non-demented elderly subjects treated with 900 mg deanol daily for 21 days, no improvements were found in cognitive performance (Marsh and Linnoila, 1979), although enhanced average evoked potentials were seen on the EEG, suggesting that the drug was having some effect on brain function which was not revealed by the mental tests used. Ferris et al (1977) studied demented outpatients given doses of up to 1800 mg/day for 4 weeks and reported global and behavioural improvements in 10 patients, but no change in memory or in cognitive function.

Dosage. Deanol is available as the *p*-acetamidobenzoic salt of DMAE, (as Deaner in USA), in 25 mg, 100 mg, and 250 mg tablets. For adults, doses of up to 1 g daily have been suggested (Ré, 1974) and larger doses (up to 1800 mg/day) have been used (Ferris et al, 1977).

Side effects. Few have been reported, but severe cholinergic side-effects have been seen in a 37-year-old woman with tardive dyskinesia given doses reaching to 1.5 g daily (Nesse and Carroll, 1976). These observations are important in supporting the concept that deanol acts by conversion to choline and acetylcholine.

A related substance, diethylamineoethanol, is one of the metabolic products of procaine in the human body (the other is p-aminobenzoic acid). This is of interest because of the use of procaine (see below) in attempts to influence the effects of aging (Droller, 1960; Jarvik and Milne, 1975).

Dopaminergic drugs

Dopaminergic drugs increase ACh levels in the striatum of animal brains (Ladinsky and Consolo, 1979). Striatal dopamine loss may be associated with intellectual impairment, and derangement of mesocortical dopaminergic neurons may occur in SDAT (Phupradit et al,

1978). Histological evidence of Alzheimer's disease occurs more frequently in brains of patients with Parkinson's disease than in age-matched controls (Hakim and Mathieson, 1978).

Mean rCBF in parkinsonism was significantly lower than in age-matched controls (9.8 per cent fall, $P<0.001$) (Lavy et al, 1979), and this was most marked in older patients, aged 70 and above (18.8 per cent fall, $P<0.001$). The fall in rCBF was fairly uniform over the cortex in both hemispheres, even in patients with unilateral parkinsonism.

Dopamine promoted CBF in dogs (Von Essen, 1974) and L-dopa therapy restored the reduced mean rCBF to control levels (Lavy et al, 1979). There is thus a weight of evidence for the involvement of the cerebral cortex in parkinsonism.

There are conflicting reports on the effect of L-dopa on dementia associated with parkinsonism (Riklan, 1972; Murphy, 1973). Reports of mental deterioration (Sacks et al, 1970; Sweet and McDowell, 1975) came from experiences with doses of L-dopa which, by today's standards, would be considered high for elderly patients. Further, Lieberman, et al (1979) could find only one reported case in which a direct link between L-dopa therapy and the development of dementia seemed to be established — that of Wolf and Davis (1973). Some authors reported no effect on dementia (Van Woert et al, 1970; Kristensen et al, 1977) but there are also reports of beneficial mental changes (Beardsley and Puletti, 1971; Marsh et al, 1971; Loranger et al, 1972; Broe and Caird, 1973; Brachman and Stahl, 1975; Adolfsson et al, 1978). The most consistent of the improvements has been in intellectual function.

Results of L-dopa treatment in senile dementia without extrapyramidal features (i.e. in SDAT) appeared promising (Adolfsson et al, 1978; Lewis et al, 1978; Renvoize et al, 1978), but the improvement may not be maintained (Johnson et al, 1978). In the first controlled study (Kristensen et al, 1977) there had been no improvement in cognitive function. More positive results came from Jellinger et al (1981) and Adolfsson et al (1982), involving visually-related functions, long-term memory and dementia scores. However, Ferris et al, (1982) could find no benefit in these respects in their double-blind cross-over trial using choline and L-dopa separately in 112 patients with Alzheimer's disease.

Bromocriptine, which has enhanced cognitive function in rats (Loew et al, 1980), failed to improve intellectual function in seventeen elderly women with SDAT, despite reduction in serum prolactin (an indicator of its dopaminergic activity) (Smith et al, 1979).

Cholinomimetic Agents

In normal volunteers before and after scopolamine, arecoline (a natural alkaloid from the betal nut)

enhanced learning (Sitaram et al, 1978a), and in patients with presenile Alzheimer's disease intravenous injections of arecoline, 4 mg, significantly increased performance in a picture-recognition test (Christie et al, 1981).

Piracetam (2-oxo-pyrrolidine acetamide) (Nootropil — France; Normabrain — Germany)
This is a cyclic derivative of GABA. It has been termed a 'noötropic agent' (Giurgea, 1972), from the Greek *noos* = mind and *tropein* = toward. Its pharmacological effects are said to include protection of the brain against hypoxia and drug intoxications, facilitation of transfer of information between cerebral hemispheres, reinforcement of cortical control over subcortical neural structures, and facilitation of learning and memory (Giurgea, 1976). Its mechanism of action is unclear, but is it thought to increase the ATP/ADP ratio in brain cells and to enhance cerebral glucose metabolism (Pede et al, 1971; Gobert, 1972). It has also been suggested that piracetam might augment the release of acetylcholine (Wurtman et al, 1981).

Nickolson and Wolthuis (1976b) could not confirm that piracetam increased cerebral ATP in rats under normal conditions, but found that the drug stimulated adenyl kinase, which could prevent or lessen the fall in ATP which would be expected in hypoxia. Effects on cerebral protein metabolism have also been described (Nickolson and Wolthius, 1976a). Recently an antiplatelet aggregation effect has been demonstrated (Bick, 1979).

Absorption is rapid, peak plasma levels being attained 30–40 minutes after 2 g orally. Plasma half-life is 4.5 hours in man; the drug is only 30 per cent protein-bound.

Piracetam protected against mental effects of hypoxia in human volunteers (Lagergren and Levander, 1974; Demay and Bande, 1980), and improved verbal learning in healthy students (Dimond and Brouwers, 1976; Wilsher et al, 1979) and in dyslexic children (Wilsher et al, 1979). Piracetam aided in recovery of a normal level of consciousness in postoperative neurosurgical patients (Richardson and Bereen, 1977) and in recovery from postconcussional syndrome (Hakkarainen and Hakamies, 1978). Intravenous piracetam improved concentration and performance during recovery of alcoholic patients from a predelirial state (Meyer et al, 1979).

In aging individuals aged 47–73, with mild memory impairment, a double-blind placebo-controlled crossover study showed improved psychometric test performance after four weeks on piracetam, 4.8 g/day, but there was no difference in memory scores between piracetam and placebo treatment periods (Mindus et al, 1976). Improved EEG patterns have been reported on piracetam (Mindus, 1978).

In studies on psychogeriatric patients evidence of improvement was dose-dependent; significant results have been obtained using a dose of 4.8 g/day (Kretschmar and Kretschmar, 1976; Trabant et al, 1977; Bente et al, 1978; Born, 1978) but not usually with a dose of 2.4 g/day (Kretschmar and Kretschmar, 1976; Abuzzahab et al, 1977; Gedye et al, 1978). Since the main route of excretion is renal, the use of this drug in the elderly needs appropriate care. The promising results of using piracetam together with choline, both in animals and in patients with Alzheimer's disease, have been mentioned above. Further work is warranted in this direction.

Dosage. 2.4–4.8 g/day in divided doses (with 400 mg capsules this could mean taking 12 capsules daily!).

Side effects. Although Giurgea (1976) reported that virtually no side effects occur, Hakkarainen and Hakamies (1978) found side effects in 64 per cent of their postconcussion patients — however, 32 per cent of patients given placebo also experienced side effects, and Hakkarainen (1980) has pointed out the difficulty in interpreting such symptoms in postconcussion patients. Connell (1979) advises caution in the use of this drug until its relationship to other central nervous stimulants has been explored further.

Other noötropic agents are under investigation.

NEUROACTIVE PEPTIDES AND DRUGS AFFECTING THEM

Vasopressin and lysine-8-vasopressin (LVP) have been assessed without significant result (Tinklenberg et al, 1982; Durso et al, 1982).

1-desamino-8-d-arginine-vasopressin (DDAVP, desmopressin) and desglycinamide-9-arginine-8-vasopressin (DGAVP)
These are vasopressin analogues which retain behavioural activity but have fewer unwanted physiological effects.

DDAVP has little or no vasoactive properties but retains anti-diuretic activity; its half-life is considerably longer than that of LVP.

DGAVP is a newer analogue with positive behavioural effects in animals but without vasoactive, anti-diuretic or other endocrine effects.

DDAVP has improved aspects of learning, memory and mood in small numbers of patients with primary degenerative dementia and in younger subjects with or without cognitive deficits (Anderson et al, 1979; Gold et al, 1979; Weingartner et al, 1981; Tinklenberg et al, 1982). A study of DGAVP (Tinklenberg et al, 1982) showed no improvement.

Studies on the effects of injecting other neuropeptides into animals and man are under way (Kastin et al, 1979). For example, the endorphins are potent psychotropic agents (Way and Glasgow, 1978; Usdin, 1979) and injections of beta-endorphin improved patients with depression and schizophrenia (Kline et al, 1977).

Vincamine and Ethyl Apovincaminate

Vincamine (Devincan, Pervincamine — Europe) is a plant alkaloid obtained from *Vinca minor* (periwinkle). It has been used for many years as a cerebral vasodilator in Europe. Studies indicated that vincamine increased CBF and lowered cerebral vascular resistance and the drug was marketed thereafter as a cerebral vasodilator (Fekete, 1976). Ethyl apovincaminate was the result of a search for a more potent synthetic derivative.

Papers on the pharmacokinetics of vincamine and its effect on CBF appear in an issue of Arzneimittel-Forschung (1977). There is evidence that vincamine improves neuronal metabolism, increasing glucose utilization and CO_2 production. Witzmann and Blechacz (1977) review 33 international studies on vincamine, seven of them double-blind, and claim significant improvements, especially in memory and attention. Foltyn et al (1978) also report statistically significant improvement in a double-blind study of 40 psychogeriatric patients, and they emphasize the value of such treatment in facilitating the management of this type of patient. Scott (1979) is generally critical of the published claims for vincamine in the light of deficiencies of study design.

Another issue of Arzneimittel-Forschung (1976) contains a series of papers on ethyl apovincaminate (Cavinton, Vinpocetin — Europe) which appears to be not only more potent but also less toxic than vincamine.

Lim et al (1980) were unable to find a significant increase in CBF in six healthy volunteers (age 25–47) given infusions of vincamine and ethyl apovincaminate in a double-blind cross-over study. There was a high incidence of side effects in these subjects.

Dosage. Vincamine: 40–80 mg daily, in divided doses. *Ethyl Apovincaminate*: 5–10 mg tid; a more recent pharmacokinetic study suggested an initial dose of 10 mg followed by 5 mg tid (Vereczkey et al, 1979)

1-Eburnamonine (16-oxoeburnane, vincamone) (Eburnal, Cervoxan — Europe)

Structurally similar to vincamine, 1-eburnamonine is another alkaloid from *Vinca minor*; it had more pronounced beneficial cerebral metabolic effects than vincamine (Linée et al, 1978).

Manna et al (1982) reported significant improvements in EEG, clinical and neuropsychological parameters in eight patients with chronic cerebrovascular disorders treated with 1-eburnamonine for 30 days in an open study.

Dosage. 60–80 mg, in three divided doses, daily.

Newer derivatives of 1-eburnamonine are under study.

Pyritinol (Pyrithioxin) (Encephabol — Europe, South Africa, Australia; Enbel — Japan)

This drug is composed of two molecules of pyridoxine connected by a disulphide bridge. It increases CBF in animals (Dolce, 1970; Stoica et al, 1973) and in man (Herrschaft, 1978) and has a variety of effects on cerebral metabolism, including increased protein synthesis (Kanig, 1973).

In patients with organic dementia treated with pyritinol, favourable cerebral metabolic changes were unaccompanied by changes in CBF (Heyer et al, 1977).

Double-blind studies on healthy subjects indicated that pyritinol had significant effects on short-term memory and immediate recall (Deusinger and Haase, 1972).

The first double-blind controlled study with positive results was reported by Hamouz (1977); 60 elderly patients with moderate to severe 'organic psychosyndrome' were grouped in matched pairs and treated for 9 weeks with either 600 mg pyritinol daily or matching placebo. Global improvements in mental function were noted.

A series of multicentre controlled double-blind studies in 458 patients with a variety of cerebrovascular disorders — including 'cerebral arteriosclerosis' but excluding patients with marked dementia — was reported from Japan by Tazaki et al (1980). Pyritinol produced significant global improvement, and improvement in subjective symptoms, but not in behaviour, mobility, neurological or psychological features. EEG patterns showed improvements in more patients, and deterioration in less patients, in the pyritinol-treated group than in the placebo group.

Cooper and Magnus (1980) reported a randomized double-blind placebo-controlled trial of pyritinol (800 mg daily) in 40 patients with moderate dementia. Serial assessments were made using a modified Crichton Behavioural Scale: patients on pyritinol showed significantly greater degrees of improvement than patients on placebo.

Dosage. 600–1200 mg daily.

Pemoline (Cylert — USA, UK; Ronyl, Kethamed — UK)

(5-phenyl-2-imine-4-oxo-oxoazolidine) has been used as a cerebral stimulant since 1956 (Plotnikoff, 1971). Its effects resemble those of amphetamine. It increases the rate of cerebral dopamine synthesis (Valle-Jones,

1978). Magnesium pemoline may be more active than pemoline (Cameron and Brand, 1966); both produced improved performance in psychological tests in healthy adults (Dureman, 1962; East and Mann, 1966). However, most clinical studies in the elderly (Smart, 1967; Talland et al, 1967; Eisdorfer et al, 1968; Droller et al, 1971; Gilbert et al, 1973) have found no benefit to memory, although fatigue and apathy may lessen (Goldstein and Braunstein, 1968; Rickels et al, 1970).

Dosage. In the elderly, 5–20 mg daily.

The addition of pemoline (20 mg daily) to amantadine (200 mg daily) proved useful in the management of elderly patients with psychomotor retardation (Montanari et al, 1976); amantadine alone did not help these patients except in higher dosage (400 mg daily) which was then associated with a high incidence of side effects. The concomitant therapy had few side effects.

Meclofenoxate (Lucidril)

Pharmacology. In following up the work of Pfeiffer et al (1957) on DMAE, Thuillier et al (1959) found that this compound had only feeble and transient activity as a neurostimulant. They synthesized esters of DMAE and found one which they considered suitable for clinical trial: the DMAE ester of *p*-chlorophenoxyacetic acid, as the hydrochloride. This was known as ANP 235, and is now known as meclofenoxate. In countries other than the UK it is known as centrophenoxine.

In animals, increased cerebral glucose uptake and protection againt anoxia (Funcke et al, 1974) and cyanide poisoning (Rump and Edelwejn, 1968) have been reported.

A striking decrease in lipofuscin pigment was noted in neurons of old guinea pigs treated with meclofenoxate (Nandy and Bourne, 1966); Nissl substance (containing RNA) increases reciprocally. In old mice treated with meclofenoxate, improved learning and memory were associated with reduction in lipofuscin in cortical and hippocampal neurons, whereas impaired learning and memory in rats on a vitamin E-deficient diet was associated with increased neuronal lipofuscin (Nandy, 1978).

Nandy (1968) found many enzyme changes and suggested that the drug diverted glucose metabolism via the pentose phosphate shunt and decreased lysosomal degradation. It also increased cerebral glucose uptake and increased CBF (Herrschaft, 1975). It prolonged the life span of fruit flies and mice (Hochschild, 1971, 1973a,b). Its membrane-stabilizing effects are discussed by Scott (1979) and may be involved in its potentiation of alkylating cytotoxic drugs (Sladek, 1977). It increases choline levels markedly in rat brain (Wood and Peloquin, 1982), and in the hippocampus a new increased steady-state level of ACh was observed.

Clinical evaluation. Interest in the possibility of improving intellectual function in old age by the use of meclofenoxate was focused by leading articles in the *Lancet* (Leading articles, *Lancet*, 1969, 1970b). Gedye et al (1972) reported a small double-blind study of the effect of this drug in six matched pairs of elderly women in two short-stay geriatric units, using a teaching machine for the assessments. The treated group all improved with respect to their controls (P=0.025, one tail).

Marcer and Hopkins (1977) carried out a double-blind study of meclofenoxate in 62 normal elderly subjects in the community over a 9-month period: 6 months' treatment and 3 months' follow-up. Psychological and mental testing were performed every 3 months. In one psychological test — delayed free recall — there was a very significant difference in favour of the meclofenoxate-treated group (P<0.0001). This suggested that these subjects were able to process new information more efficiently, an area where the elderly are most vulnerable. Physically, feelings of well-being were more apparent in the meclofenoxate group. The authors suggest that some old people, who are finding everyday life harder to cope with, and may appear somewhat depressed, could be improved by the use of meclofenoxate rather than antidepressants or tranquillizers.

Dosage: One 300 mg tablet 3 to 5 times daily. An injectable form is available in Europe.

Side-effects. Stimulant effects may be excessive; euphoria, insomnia and confusion may result.

CEREBRAL 'ACTIVATORS'

This is a group of stimulants and their use has been reviewed by Lehmann and Ban (1975), Petrie and Ban (1978), and Reisberg et al (1981).

Amphetamine and its derivatives

Amphetamine

Known as a stimulant since 1930, d-amphetamine is more potent than l-amphetamine. It inhibits neuronal uptake and promotes release of catecholamines, and in animals it enhances learning and memory (McGaugh, 1973). It has many other effects and has been used for obesity, fatigue states, hyperkinesis, mild depression, and parkinsonism. However, its use has largely ended because of the possibility of addiction and of psychoses. It may have a limited use in the rehabilitable elderly with poor motivation (Clark, 1978), but should be used with care and for only a short time.

Dosage. 5–20 mg daily, given in 2 divided doses

(morning and midday). It is best to start with the lower dose and to increase gradually.

Pemoline has been considered above.

Methylphenidate (Ritalin, UK, USA; Methidate — Canada)

This is a cyclized amphetamine derivative containing a piperidine ring. It acts on several central nervous pathways. It may improve psychomotor performance in the elderly, particularly when apathy or depression retard rehabilitation effort (Miller and Nieburg, 1973; Kaplitz, 1975; Pritchard and Mykyta, 1975). The last-named authors also gave oxprenolol to counter sympathomimetic side effects and estimated that 50 per cent of the patients thus treated were prevented from becoming long-stay. Whether the beta-blocker contributed to improved learning is conjectural, but propranolol was found to do so in healthy old men (Eisdorfer et al, 1970), an effect attributed to attenuation of autonomic arousal which accompanies learning tasks.

Double-blind studies on methylphenidate in dementia have given conflicting results (Darvill, 1959; Holliday and Joffe, 1965; Lehmann and Ban, 1967; Gilbert et al, 1973; Kaplitz, 1975; Crook et al, 1977).

Dosage. 5 mg (half a tablet) morning and midday. This may be gradually increased to a maximum of 30 mg daily.

Side effects. Over-stimulation and sympathomimetic side effects may occur. Hepatotoxicity has been reported (Goodman, 1972) and long-term use has caused cardiomyopathy (Fischer and Barner, 1977).

Fencamfamin (Reactivan)

Fencamfamin is a camphor derivative which has a stimulant action on the reticular formation and cerebral cortex, said to be equivalent to amphetamine, but with no peripheral effects (Holliday and Devery, 1962). It is available as Reactivan in which it is combined with vitamins B_1, B_6, B_{12} and C. Reactivan has been widely used in Europe since 1960 for debility and fatigue states, and general practice studies in Britain have reported its value in this indication (G.P. Medical Research Unit, 1972; G.P. Group, 1974).

Evaluation in dementia. In double-blind trials Magnus and Cooper (1974) reported significant benefit from the drug in mild to moderate dementia, but Carney et al (1976) found no improvement in severely demented psychogeriatric patients.

Dosage. Tablets contain:

fencamfamin hydrochloride	10 mg
thiamine	10 mg
pyridoxine	20 mg
cyanocobalamin	10 µg
ascorbic acid	100 mg

The recommended dose is two tablets at breakfast and one at midday.

Side-effects. Restlessness and agitation may occur, but rarely sufficient to curtail the treatment. Increased motor activity may be channelled to good purpose in physiotherapy and occupational therapy departments.

MISCELLANEOUS OTHER DRUGS

Oxygen

Oxygen-enrichment of inspired air has improved psychomotor performance in stroke patients (Ben-Yishay et al, 1967) but hopes that it would improve mental function in demented old people (Ben-Yishay and Diller, 1973) were not realized, even when hyperbaric oxygen was part of the treatment program (Ben-Yishay et al, 1978; Raskin et al, 1978). Other studies have used hyperbaric oxygen alone: some were successful (Jacobs et al, 1969; Edwards and Hart, 1974) and some not (Goldfarb et al, 1972; Thompson et al, 1976). This treatment has been critically reviewed (Eisner, 1975; Thompson, 1975). However, in a double-blind controlled study, continuous normobaric portable oxygen therapy was given to healthy old men who had noted some memory impairment; statistically significant improvements in I.Q. and memory tests were found (Krop et al, 1977).

Carbonic anhydrase inhibitors

These may increase CBF, but the effect is not wholly due to local release of CO_2. $CMRO_2$ falls after the injection: carbonic anhydrase may play an important role in oxygen delivery to brain tissue via the Bohr effect (Laux and Raichle, 1978).

Of the available drugs, acetazoleamide ('Diamox') has been most used; its short-lived effects and its diuretic action make it unsuitable for attempts at long-term cerebral vasodilatation.

Procaine (H₃, GH₃, KH₃, Gerovital — UK, Europe, USA)

This local anaesthetic earned a new reputation in the controversy which has continued since Aslan (1956) first claimed its value in the prevention and treatment of various aspects of aging. It has been reported to be a cerebral stimulant and a week reversible competitive inhibitor of monoamine oxidase (MacFarlane and Besbris, 1974; Fuller and Roush, 1977), but has done little to live up to the early claims made for it. Several reviews of this agent have appeared in recent years; the most comprehensive is that of Ostfeld et al (1977), covering data from 285 sources and over 100 000 patients. The only benefit reported was a possible antidepressant effect; but many of the studies reported were of poor quality. In 1977, the US Food and Drugs Administration withdrew its permission for further studies with Gerovital because of lack of evidence of its safety and efficacy.

PERSPECTIVES IN DRUG THERAPY FOR DEMENTIA AND 'CEREBRAL ARTERIOSCLEROSIS'

The orthodox scientific attitude to this question is still that adequate and convincing double-blind trials are too few in number to support the routine or frequent use of such therapy. To those faced with these clinical problems such a nihilistic approach may seem too rigid in the light of the existing evidence as set out in this chapter; for a majority of the drugs considered there are published double-blind trials, some of which suggest that beneficial results may be obtained. Some of these trials are well planned and meticulously conducted; they suffer, however, from the frequent inhomogeneity of their case-selection and their protocols. For the future, more carefully-organized multi-centre trials may well be the best approach; for the present, we should base our attitude on what we are trying to achieve.

O'Brien (1971) points out that in patients whose reserve is already severely compromised a very small change in cellular metabolism may result in a worthwhile improvement in performance without any detectable changes in total CBF or metabolism demonstrable by present methods; and there is evidence that many drugs can influence cellular metabolism by a variety of means (some still more conjectural than proven) and in a variety of ways. No lesser authorities than Hachinski et al (1975) concede that attempts to increase blood supply to underperfused but non-infarcted brain tissue 'are certainly worthy of further exploration'; and this may well call for pharmacological manipulation of the micro-circulation rather than of larger vessels, or small changes in blood rheology leading to large changes in tissue blood flow and metabolism. Heiss et al (1976) give support to the feasibility of restoring function to ischaemic neurons by 'effective therapeutic measures'.

Thus, one's reaction to this controversy should presumably be influenced by the therapeutic optimism which is the *sine qua non* of those doctors dedicated to the care of the elderly: one should hope to influence neurons which are dormant rather than dead, underperfused yet still viable, and perhaps capable of being restored to activity by small increases in CBF or changes in cerebral metabolism.

These arguments should not be taken to imply that a 'blunderbuss' approach to such treatment is recommended. An intelligent appraisal of each patient on an individual basis is essential, as always, and careful selection of suitable patients at as early a stage as possible will give both patient and drug a reasonable chance. Indeed, interest is growing in testing such drugs in 'normal' old people in the community.

Assessments should be made over no less than 2 months, and possibly much more, and any 'carry-over' effect after treatment has stopped should be borne in mind. In the case of drugs with stimulant properties, this trial period may need to be shortened, but much depends on the patient's response; it is probably true to say that stimulant drugs have a smaller place in this realm of therapy than those having less dramatic effects on cerebral metabolism and function.

In conclusion, it would seem reasonable to follow Young et al (1974) in considering that the main aim of using drugs purporting to influence cerebral blood flow and metabolism may be to prevent a continuous decline rather than to obtain a dramatic reversal of that decline. Improvements relating to alleviation of depression might also be a worthwhile result (Young et al, 1974; Marcer and Hopkins, 1977).

The new antidepressants which act by blocking neuronal re-uptake of serotonin (zimelidine, alaproclate) may offer a new approach to improvement of SDAT (Carlsson, 1982) and clinical trials have been initiated to study this question. Noötropic agents and choline (or lecithin) may find greater application when used together.

REFERENCES

Abuzzahab F S, Merwin G E, Zimmermann R L, Sherman M C 1978 A double blind investigation of piracetam (Nootropil) versus placebo in the memory of geriatric inpatients. Psychopharmacology Bulletin 14: 23–25

Aderman M, Giardina W J, Koreniowski S 1972 Effect of cyclandelate on perception, memory and cognition in a group of geriatric subjects. Journal of the American Geriatrics Society 20: 268–271

Admani A K 1978 New approach to treatment of recent stroke. British Medical Journal 2: 1678–1679

Adolfsson R, Gottfries C G, Roos B E, Winblad B 1979 Post-mortem distribution of dopamine and homovanillic acid in human brain, variations related to age, and a review of the literature. Journal of Neural Transmission 45: 81–106

Adolfsson R, Gottfries C G, Oreland L, Roos B E, Winblad B 1978 Reduced level of catecholamines in the brain and increased activity of monoamine oxidase in platelets in Alzheimer's disease: therapeutic implications. In: Katzman R, Terry R D, Bick K L (eds) Alzheimer's disease: Senile dementia and related disorders (Aging 7). Raven Press, New York, p 441–451

Adolfsson R, Brane G, Bucht G, Karlsson I, Gottfries C G, Persson S, Winblad B 1982 A double-blind study with levodopa in dementia of Alzheimer type. In: Corkin S et al (eds) Alzheimer's disease: A report of progress in research (Aging 19). Raven Press, New York, p 469–473

Affleck D C, Treptow K R, Herrick H D 1961 The effects of isoxsuprine hydrochloride (Vasodilan) on chronic cerebral arterioscleriosis. Journal of Nervous and Mental Disease 132: 335–338

Allen G S, Bahr A L 1979 Cerebral arterial spasm: Part 10. Reversal of acute and chronic spasm in dogs with orally administered nifedipine. Neurosurgery 4: 43–46

Allen G S, Banghart S B 1979 Cerebral arterial spasm: Part 9. In vitro effects of nifedipine on serotonin-, phenylephrine- and potassium-induced contractions of canine basilar and femoral arteries. Neurosurgery 4: 37–42

Amaducci L, Davison A N, Antuono P (eds) 1980 Aging of the brain and dementia (Aging 13). Raven Press, New York

Ammon H P T, Estler C-J, Heim F 1970 Alteration of carbohydrate metabolism in liver, skeletal muscle and brain by nicotinic acid in mice. In : Gey K F, Carlson L A (eds) Metabolic effects of nicotinic acid and its derivatives. Proceedings of a workshop, Flims Huber, Bern, p 799–809

Amthauer R 1971 Veränderung psychischer Leistungen durch ein Pharmakon, das den Stoffwechsel im Gerhirn beeinflußt. (Changes in mental ability caused by a drug influencing cerebral metabolism.) Wiener Klinische Wochenschrift 83: 659–663

Anderson L T, David R, Bonnet K, Dancis J 1979 Passive avoidance-learning in Lesch-Nyhan disease. Effect of 1-desamino-8-arginine vasopressin. Life Sciences 24: 905–910

Anderson W D, Kubicek W G 1971 Effects of betahistine-HC1, nicotinic acid and histamine on basilar blood flow in anesthetized dogs. Stroke 2: 409–415

Andrews G, Judge T G, Walkey F 1973 The action of tetranicotinoylfructose in peripheral vascular disease. Practitioner 211: 83–85

Änggård E 1982 Essential fatty acids, prostaglandins and the brain. In: Corkin S, Davis K L, Growdon J H, Usdin E, Wurtman R J (eds) Alzheimer's disease: A report of progress in research (Aging 19). Raven Press, New York, p 295–302

Antcliff A C, Bouhoutsos J, Martin P, Morris T 1974 A plethysmographic study of the effect of tetranicotinoylfructose (Bradilan) on digital blood flow in primary and secondary Raynaud's phenomenon. Angiology 25: 312–316

Armstrong J M, Dusting G J, Moncada S, Vane J R 1978 Cardiovascular actions of prostacyclin (PGI_2), a metabolite of arachidonic acid which is synthesized by blood vessels. Circulation Research 43 (Suppl I): I-112–119

Arnold J D, Baldridge J, Riley B, Brody G 1977 Papaverine hydrochloride: the evaluation of two new dosage forms. International Journal of Clinical Pharmacology 15: 230–233

Arrigo A, Braun P, Kauchtschischwili G M, Moglia A, Tartara A 1973 Influence of treatment on symptomatology and correlated electroencephalographic (EEG) changes in the aged. Current Therapeutic Research, Clinical and Experimental 15: 417–426

Artom C, Crowder M 1949 Determination of dimethylethanolamine in biological materials. Federation Proceedings 8: 180–181

Arzneimittel-Forschung (1967) 26: No 10A, complete issue on ethyl apovincaminate, p 1905–1989

Arzneimittel-Forschung (1977) 27: No 6A, complete issue on vincamine, p 1238–1298

Aslan A 1956 A new method for the prophylaxis and treatment of aging with Novocain: Eutropic and rejuvenating effects. Therapiewoche 7: 14–22

Atik M 1967 Dextran 40 and Dextran 70. Archives of Surgery 94: 664–671

Auckland K 1965 Hydrogen polarography in measurement of local blood flow; theoretical and empirical basis. Acta Neurologica Scandinavica 14 (Suppl): 42–45

Aurousseau M, Albert O 1978 Cerebral circulatory and metabolic drugs. European Neurology 17 (Suppl 1): 73–86

Axelrod J, Shofer R, Inscoe J K, Wing W M, Sjoersma A 1958 The fate of papaverine in man and other mammals. Journal of Pharmacology and Experimental Therapeutics 124: 9–15

Babich F R, Jacobson A L, Bubash S, Jacobson A 1965 Transfer of a response to naive rats by injection of ribonucleic acid extracted from trained rats. Science 149: 656–657

Bachelard H S 1976 Biochemistry of coma. In: Davison A N (ed) Biochemistry and neurological disease. Blackwell, Oxford, p 228–277

Bachmann K 1965 Die photometrische Untersuchung der peripheren Durchblutung und ihrer pharmakoligischen Beeinflussung durch Complamin. Medizinische Klinik 60: 1413–1417

Bailey L E, Brown B B 1960 Central electrical effects of two CNS stimulants. Pharmacologist 2: 1

Bajada S 1982 A trial of choline chloride and physostigmine in Alzheimer's dementia. In: Corkin S et al (eds) Alzheimer's Disease: A Report of Progress in Research (Aging 19). Raven Press, New York, p 427–432

Ball J A C, Taylor A R 1967 Effect of cyclandelate on mental function and cerebral blood flow in elderly patients. British Medical Journal 3: 525–528

Bär T 1978 Morphometric evaluation of capillaries in different laminae of rat cerebral cortex by automatic image analysis: changes during development and aging. In: Cervos-Navarro J, Betz E, Ebhardt G, Ferszt R, Wüllenweber B (eds) Pathology of cerebral microcirculation (Advances in Neurology, 20). Raven Press, New York, p 1–9

Barbeau A 1976 L-Dopa and Parkinson's disease. In: Himwich H E (ed) Brain metabolism and cerebral disorders, 2nd edn. Spectrum Publications Inc, New York, p 283–210

Bargheon J 1975 Essai en double aveugle du Praxilène en gériatrie. (Double-blind trial of Praxilene in geriatrics.) Gazette Médicale de France 82: 4755–4758

Bargheon J 1977 Evaluation de l'activité thérapeutique du Suloctidil chez le vieillard atteint d'insuffisance cérébrovasculaire. Etude en double insu par comparaison à un placebo. Acta Clinica Belgica 32: 15–21

Bartus R T, Dean R L, Beer B 1980 Memory deficits in aged cebus monkeys and facilitation with central cholinomimetics. Neurobiology of Aging 1: 145–152

Bartus R T, Dean R L, Beer B, Lippa A S 1982 The cholinergic hypothesis of geriatric memory dysfunction. Science 217: 408–417

Bartus R T, Dean R L, Sherman K, Friedman E, Beer B 1981 Profound effects of combining choline and piracetam on memory enhancement and cholinergic function in aged rats. Neurobiology of Aging 2: 105–111

Beardsley J V, Puletti F 1971 Personality (MMPI) and cognitive (WAIS) changes after levodopa treatment: occurrence in patients with Parkinson's disease. Archives of Neurology 25: 145–150

Becker G, Tan A H, Stöcker G 1970 Diffuse Hirndurchblutungsverminderung weit gunstiger zu beeinflussen als lokale. (Diffuse reduced cerebral circulation much more easily influenced than local.) Medizinische Tribune, Ausg. Deutschland 5:1

Behrens E 1966 Medikamentöse Beeinflussung der Hirndurchblutung durch Stugeron. (Drug treatment of cerebral irrigation with Stugeron.) Medizinische Welt 38: 2029–2031

Benaim M E, Dewar H A 1975 The effect of tetranicotinoylfructose (Bradilan) on fibrinolytic activity, platelet stickiness and some other parameters. Journal of International Medical Research 3: 423–427

Benitez H H, Murray M R, Woolley D W 1955 Effects of serotonin and certain of its antagonists upon oligodendroglial cells. Proceedings o-f the 2nd International Congress on Neuropathology, London 2: 423–428

Benson D F 1982 The use of positron emission scanning techniques in the diagnosis of Alzheimer's disease. In: Corkin S et al (eds) Alzheimer's disease: A report of progress in research (Aging 19). Raven Press, New York, p 79–82

Bente D, Glatthaar G, Ulrich G, Lewinsky M 1978 Piracetam und Vigilanz: Elektroenzephalographische und Klinische Ergebnisse einer Langzeitmedikation bei gerontopsychiatrischen Patienten. Arzneimittel-Forschung 28 (II): 1529–1530

Ben-Yishay Y, Diller L 1973 Changing of atmospheric environment to improve mental and behavioral function. Applications in treatment of senescence. New York State Journal of Medicine 73: 2877–2880

Ben-Yishay Y, Haas A, Diller L 1967 The effects of oxygen inhalation on motor impersistence in brain-damaged individuals: a double-blind study. Neurology (Minneapolis) 17: 1003–1010

Ben-Yishay Y, Diller L, Reich T, Rosenblum J A, Rusk H A 1978 Can oxygen reverse symptoms of senility? New-York State Journal of Medicine 78: 914–919

Benzi G, Arrigoni E, Dagani F, Marzatico F, Curti D, Manzini A, Villa R F 1979 Effect of chronic treatment with some drugs on the enzyme activities of the rat brain. Biochemical Pharmacology 28: 2703–2708

Benzi G, Arrigoni E, Dagani F, Marzatico F, Curti D, Polgatti M, Villa R F 1980 Drug interference on the age-dependent modification of the cerebral enzymatic activities related to energy transduction. In: Amaducci L, Davison A N, Antuono P (eds) Aging of the Brain and Dementia (Aging 13). Raven Press, New York, p 113–117

Berde B, Schild H O (eds) 1978 Ergot alkaloids and related compounds. Springer-Verlag, New York

Berkowitz D 1964 Newer drugs in the treatment of hyperlipidemia. In: Brest A N, Moyer J H (eds) Cardiovascular Drug Therapy. 11th Hahnemann Symposium, Philadelphia. Grune and Stratton, New York, p 371–372

Bernard A, Goffart J M 1968 A double-blind cross-over clinical evaluation of cinnarizine. Clinical Trials Journal 5: 945–948

Bick R L 1979 In-vivo platelet inhibition by piracetam. Lancet ii: 752–753

Bijlsma U G, Funcke A B H, Tersteege H M, Rekker R F, Ernsting M J E, Nauta W T 1956 The pharmacology of Cyclospasmol. Archives Internationales de Pharmacodynamie et de Thérapie 105: 145–174

Bisley B 1960 Management of the geriatric patient in general practice. Evaluation of a new preparation. British Journal of Clinical Practice 14: 527–529

Bohus B 1979 Effects of ACTH-like neuropeptides on animal behavior and man. Pharmacology 18: 113–122

Boksay I, Bollmann V 1971 The effect of 3,7-dimethyl-l-(5-oxo-hexyl)-xanthine on the β-adrenergic receptors and on the activity of isoprenaline. Archives Internationales de Pharmacodynamie et de Thérapie 194: 174–180

Boksay I, Bollmanin V, Popendiker K 1971 Der Einfluss von 3,7-Dimethyl-l-(5-oxo-hexyl)-xanthin auf α-adrenerge Effekte. (The influence of 3,7-dimethyl-l-(5-oxo-hexyl)-xanthine on α-adrenergic effects.) Arzneimittel-Forschung 21: 1174–1177

Boroda C 1975 A clinical study of Bradilan (tetranicotinoylfructose) in diabetic patients with peripheral vascular disease. Journal of International Medical Research 3: 10–11

Botez M I 1975 La bétahistidine hydrochloride dans le traitement de l'insuffisance vertébro-basilaire. (Betahistidine hydrochloride in the treatment of vertebrobasilar insufficiency.) L'Encéphale 1: 279–286

Boudouresques J, Papy J J, Daniel F 1970 Une thérapeutique retard dans les insuffisances circulatoires cérébrales chroniques. (A long-acting treatment for chronic cerebral circulatory insufficiency.) Semaine Thérapeutique 46: 789–792

Bouissou H, Emery M C, Sorbara R 1975 Age-related changes of the middle cerebral artery and a comparison with the radial and coronary artery. Angiology 26: 257–268

Bouvier J B, Passeron O, Chupin M P 1974 Psychometric study of Praxilene. Journal of International Medical Research 2: 59–65

Bowen D M, Smith C B, White P, Davison A N 1976 Senile dementia and related abiotrophies: biochemical studies on histologically evaluated human postmortem specimens. In: Terry R D, Gershon S (eds) Neurobiology of Aging (Aging 3). Raven Press, New York, p 361–378

Bowen D M, Smith C B, White P, Goodhardt M J, Spillane J A, Flack R H A, Davison A N 1977 Chemical pathology of the organic dementias. Part I. Validity of biochemical measurements in human post-mortem brain specimens. Brain 100: 397–426

Branconnier R J, Cole J O 1977 Effects of chronic papaverine administration on mild senile organic brain syndrome. Journal of the American Geriatrics Society 25: 458–462

Branconnier R J, Cole J O 1978 The impairment index as a symptom-independent parameter of drug efficacy in geriatric psychopharmacology. Journal of Gerontology 33: 217–223

Brasseur R 1978 Clinical value of a combined anti-ischemic and anticholinergic substance with antidepressant properties. Angiology 29: 121–132

Braverman A M, Naylor R 1975 Vasoactive substances in the management of elderly patients suffering from dementia. Modern Geriatrics 5: 20–29

Brenner G 1968 Über den Einfluss von Xantinol-nicotinat auf die Biosynthese der oxydierten Pyridinnucleotide in der Rattenleber.

Eine Untersuchung am Normaltier und am lebergeschädigten Tier. (On the influence of xanthinol nicotinate on the biosynthesis of the oxidised pyridine nucleotides in the rat liver. A study on normal animals and such with experimental liver damage.) Arzneimittel-Forschung 18: 1153–1155

Brenner G 1973 Beeinflussbarkeit des ATP-Gehaltes menschlicher und tierischer Erythrozyten in vivo und in vitro durch Xantinol-nicotinat. (The influence of xanthinol nicotinate on the ATP content of human and animal erythrocytes in vivo and in vitro.) Arzneimittel-Forschung 23: 562–566

Brenner G 1974 Vergleichende Untersuchungen über die Beeinflussung von O_2-Aufnahme von Leber- und Hirnhomogenaten der Ratte durch xantinol-nicotinat und Nikotinsäure. (Comparative study on the influence of Xanthinol nicotinate and nicotinic acid on the oxygen uptake of liver and brain homogenates of rats.) Arzneimittel-Forschung 24: 321–325

Brenner G, Brenner H 1972 The effect of xantinol nicotinate on the metabolism of the brain. Arzneimittel-Forschung 22: 754–759

British Medical Journal 1976 Cerebral blood flow in dementia. British Medical Journal 1: 1487–1488

Brodie N H 1977 A double-blind trial of naftidrofuryl in treating confused elderly patients in general practice. Practitioner 218: 274–278

Broe G A, Caird F I 1973 Levodopa for parkinsonism in elderly and demented patients. Medical Journal of Australia 1: 630–635

Brown R M, Carlsson A, Ljunggren B, Siesjö B K, Snider S R 1974 Effect of ischemia on monoamine metabolism in the brain. Acta Physiologica Scandinavica 90: 789–791

Burkard W P, Lengsfeld H, Gey K F 1970 Cyclic adenosine 3′, 5′ — monophosphate and adenylcyclase in liver, adipose tissue and brain of rats treated with β-pyridylcarbinol or nicotinic acid. In: Gey K F, Carlson L A (eds) Metabolic Effects of Nicotinic Acid and its Derivatives. Proceedings of a workshop, Flims. Huber, Bern, p 379–386

Bürki H R, Asper H, Ruch W, Züger P E 1978 Bromocriptine, dihydroergotoxine, methysergide, d-LSD, CF 25–397 and 29–712: Effects on the metabolism of the biogenic amines in the brain of the rat. Psychopharmacology 57: 227–237

Burns E M, Kruckeberg T W, Comerford L E, Buschmann T 1979 Thinning of capillary walls and declining numbers of endothelial mitochondria in the cerebral cortex of the aging primate, Macaca nemestrina. Journal of Gerontology 34: 642–650

Burnstock G 1975 Purinergic transmission. In: Iversen L L, Iversen S D, Snyder S H (eds) Handbook of Psychopharmacology, vol 5, Plenum Press, New York, p 131–194

Burnstock G 1981 Neurotransmitters and trophic factors in the autonomic nervous system. Journal of Physiology 313: 1–35

Cameron D E 1966 Evolving concepts of memory. In: Wortis J (ed) Recent Advances in Biological Psychiatry, IX. Plenum Press, New York, p 1–12

Cameron D E, Brand M I 1966 Magnesium pemoline and memory. Proceedings of the IV world congress on Psychiatry 4. Excerpta Medica Foundation, Amsterdam, p 2558–2567

Cameron D E, Sved S, Solyom L, Wainrib B, Barik H 1963 Effects of ribonucleic acid on memory defect in the aged. American Journal of Psychiatry 120: 320–325

Cammermeyer J 1960 Reappraisal of the perivascular distribution of dendrocytes. American Journal of Anatomy 106: 197–219

Capote B, Parikh N 1978 Cyclandelate in the treatment of senility: a controlled study. Journal of the American Geriatrics Society 26: 360–362

Carlsson A 1982 Recent observations on new potential and established antidepressant drugs. Pharmacopsychiatria 15: 116–120

Carlsson A, Winblad B 1976 Influence of age and time interval between death and autopsy on dopamine and 3-methoxytyramine levels in human basal ganglia. Journal of Neural Transmission 38: 271–276

Carlsson A, Adolfsson R, Aquilonius S-M, Gottfries C-G, Oreland L, Svennerholm L, Winblad B 1980 Biogenic amines in human brain in normal aging, senile dementia, and chronic alcoholism. In: Goldstein M et al (eds) Ergot Compounds and Brain Function. Raven Press, New York, p 295–304

Carney M W P, Cashman M D, King A, Rogan P A, Sheffield B F 1976 Severely demented patients beyond help of drugs. Modern Geriatrics 7: 36–39

Cayley A C D, Macpherson A, Wedgwood J 1975 Sinus bradycardia following treatment with hydergine for cerebrovascular insufficiency. British Medical Journal 4: 384–385

Charm S E, Kurland G S 1974 Blood Flow and Microcirculation. John Wiley and Sons, New York

Chiang J, Kowada M, Ames A III, Wright R L, Majno G 1968 Cerebral ischemia. III. Vascular changes. American Journal of Pathology 52: 455–476

Christie J E, Shering A, Ferguson J, Glen A I M 1981 Physostigmine and arecoline: effects of intravenous infusions in Alzheimer presenile dementia. British Journal of Psychiatry 138: 46–50

Christie J E, Blackburn I M, Glen A I M, Zeisel S, Shering A, Yates C M 1979 Effects of choline and lecithin on CSF choline levels and on cognitive function in patients with presenile dementia of the Alzheimer type. In: Barbeau A, Growdon J H, Wurtman R J (eds) Nutrition and the Brain, vol 5. Raven Press, New York, p 377–388

Clemens J A, Fuller R W 1978 Chemical manipulation of some aspects of aging. In: Roberts J, Adelman R C, Cristafolo V J (eds) Pharmacological Intervention in the Aging Process (Advances in Experimental Medicine and Biology, 97). Plenum Press, New York, p 187–206

Clendenon N R, Allen N, Komatsu T, Liss L, Gordon W A, Heimberger K 1971 Biochemical alterations in the anoxic-ischemic lesions of rat brain. Archives of Neurology 25: 432–438

Cohen E L, Wurtman R J 1976 Brain acetylcholine: control by dietary choline. Science 191: 561–562

Comfort A 1978 Cholinesterase inhibition in the treatment of Alzheimer's dementia. Lancet i: 659–660

Connell P H 1979 Central nervous system stimulants and anorectic agents. In: Dukes M N G (ed) Side effects of Drugs Annual, 3. Excerpta Medica, Amsterdam, p 1–7

Cooper A J, Magnus R V 1980 A placebo-controlled study of pyritinol (Encephabol) in dementia. Pharmatherapeutica 2: 317–322

Cooper J R, Bloom F E, Roth R H 1978 The Biochemical Basis of Neuropharmacology, 3rd edn. Oxford University Press, New York, p 259–281

Corbett J L, Eidelman B H, Debarge O 1972 Modification of cerebral vasoconstriction with hyperventilation in normal man by thymoxamine. Lancet ii: 461–463

Cornu F 1969 Zur Kreislaufphysiologie und Biochemie zerebraler Abbauprozesse und der Verhaltensbeeinflussung von Kranken durch Pharmakotherapie. (The physiology of circulation and the biochemistry of cerebral breakdown processes and the influence exerted on the behaviour of patients by means of pharmacotherapy.) Wiener Klinische Wochenschrift 81: 426–431

Corrodi H, Fuxe K, Hökfelt T, Lidbrink P, Ungerstedt U 1973 Effect of ergot drugs on central catecholamine neurons: Evidence for a stimulation of central dopamine neurons. Journal of Pharmacy and Pharmacology 25: 409–412

Corsellis J A N 1976 Ageing and the dementias. In: Blackwood W, Corsellis J A N (eds) Greenfield's Neuropathology, 3rd edn. Edward Arnold, London, p 796–849

Cox J R 1975 Double-blind evaluation of naftidrofuryl in treating elderly confused hospitalised patients. Gerontologia Clinica 17: 160–167

Cox J R, Pandurangi V R, Wallace M G 1978 Drugs will help if dementing patients are caught early. Modern Geriatrics 8: 12–15

Coyle J T, Price D L, DeLong M R 1983 Alzheimer's disease: a disorder of cortical cholinergic innervation. Science 219: 1184–1190

Crook T, Ferris S, Sathananthan G, Raskin A, Gershon S 1977 The effect of methylphenidate on test performance in the cognitively impaired aged. Psychopharmacology 52: 251–255

Cugurra F, Echinard-Garin P 1960 Alcuni aspetti dell' attività farmacologica di un nuovo teofillinico: l'I-exil-3,7-dimetilxantine (SK-7). Archives Internationales de Pharmacodynamie et de Thérapie 123: 481–489

Cultrera G, Giarola P, Gibelli A, Baldoni E, Cuttin S, Galetti G, Serentha P 1971 Fibrinogen turnover during the treatment with xantinol nicotinate. Arzneimittel-Forschung 21: 954–957

Cummins B H, Griffith H B 1971 Intracarotid phenoxybenzamine for cerebral arterial spasm. British Medical Journal 1: 382–383

Daly J W 1976 The nature of receptors regulating the formation of cAMP in brain tissue. Life Sciences 18: 1349–1358

Daly J W, Bruns R F, Snyder S H 1981 Adenosine receptors in the central nervous system: relationship to the central actions of methylxanthines. Life Sciences 28: 2083–2097

Danysz A, Kocmierska-Grodzka D, Kostro B, Polocki B, Kruszewska J 1967 Własności farmakologiczne 2-dwumetyloamino-etanolu (DMAE) Cz. II. Analiza ośrodkowego działania farmakologicznego. (Pharmacological properties of 2-dimethylaminoethanol.) Dissertationes Pharmaceuticae i Pharmacologicae (Krakow) 19: 469–477

Dartenuc J-Y, Bellooussof T, Meriaud M, Cavel M, Choussat H 1978 Etude en double-aveugle du Praxilène dans l'insuffisance circulatoire cérébrale du vieillard. (Double-blind trial of Praxilene in cerebrovascular insufficiency in the aged.) Revue de Gériatrie 6: 325–327

Darvill F T 1959 Double-blind evaluation of methylphenidate (Ritalin) hydrochloride. Its use in the management of institutionalised geriatric patients. Journal of the American Medical Association 169: 1739–1741

Davies G, Hamilton S, Hendrickson E, Levy R, Post F 1977 The effect of cyclandelate in depressed and demented patients: a controlled study in psychogeriatric patients. Age and Ageing 6: 156–162

Davies P, Maloney A J F 1976 Selective loss of central cholinergic neurons in Alzheimer's disease. Lancet ii: 1403

Davies P, Katz D A, Crystal H A 1982 Choline acetyltransferase, somatostatin, and substance P in selected cases of Alzheimer's disease. In: Corkin S et al (eds) Alzheimer's disease: A report of progress in research (Aging 19). Raven Press, New York, p 9–14

Davis E, Rozov H 1973 The effects of xanthinol nicotinate on the small blood vessels. In: Ditzel J, Lewis D H (eds) 7th European Conference on Microcirculation, Aberdeen, 1972, part I (Bibliotheca Anatomica 11). Karger, Basel, p 334–339

Davis J, Himwich W A 1975 Neurochemistry of the developing and aging mammalian brain. In: Ordy J M, Brizzee K R (eds) Neurobiology of Aging. Plenum Press, New York, p 329–358

Davis K L, Mohs R C, Tinklenberg J R 1979 Enhancement of memory by physostigmine. New England Journal of Medicine 301: 946

Davis K L, Mohs R C, Rosen W G, Greenwald B S, Levy M I, Horvath T B 1983 Memory enhancement with oral physostigmine in Alzheimer's disease. New England Journal of Medicine 308: 721 (letter)

Davis K L, Mohs R C, Tinklenberg J R, Hollister L E, Pfefferbaum A, Kopell B S 1980 Cholinomimetics and memory: the effect of choline chloride. Archives of Neurology 37: 49–52

Davis K L, Mohs R C, Tinklenberg J R, Pfefferbaum A, Hollister L E, Kopell B S 1978 Physostigmine: improvement of long-term memory processes in normal humans. Science 201: 272–274

Davis K L, Mohs R C, Davis B M, Levy M I, Horvath T B, Rosenberg G S, Ross A, Rothpearl A, Rosen W 1982 Cholinergic treatment in Alzheimer's disease: Implications for future research. In: Corkin S, Davis K L, Growdon J H, Usdin E, Wurtman R J (eds) Alzheimer's Disease: A Report of Progress in Research (Aging 19). Raven Press, New York, p 483–494

Davison A N 1976 The pathology and biochemistry of the ageing brain. In: Davison A N, Hood N A (eds) Action on Ageing. MCS Consultants, Tunbridge Wells, p 9–10

Davison A N 1978 Biochemical aspects of the ageing brain. Age and Ageing 7 (Suppl): 4–11

De Feudis F V 1974 Central Cholinergic Systems and Behaviour. Academic Press, London

Demay F, Bande J 1980 The effect of piracetam on volunteers in a low-pressure tank. Journal of International Medical Research 8: 90–94

Demichelis Genesio M A, Cid Sanz M 1981 Evaluation of buflomedil in geriatric patients suffering from vascular cerebral insufficiency. Angiology 32: 717–728

Dereymaeker A, Theeuwissen-Lesuisse F, Buu-Hoï N P, Lapiere C 1962 L'anoxie cérébrale expérimentale; effect protecteur des dérivés de l'acide p-chlorophénoxyacétique. (Experimental cerebral anoxia: protective effect of derivatives of p-chlorophenoxyacetic acid derivatives.) Medicina Experimentalis (Basel) 7: 239–244

Deshmukh V D, Harper A M, Rowan J O, Jennett W B 1971–1972 Studies on neurogenic control of the cerebral circulation. European Neurology 6: 166–174

Des Rosiers M H, Kennedy C, Patlak C S, Pettigrew K D, Sokoloff

L, Reivich M 1974 Relationship between local cerebral blood flow and glucose utilization in the rat. Neurology (Minneapolis) 4: 389

Deusinger I M, Haase H 1972 Experimentelle Untersuchungen zur Wirkung von Pyrithioxin auf das Kurzzeitgedächtnis und das unmittelbare Behalten. Pharmakopsychiatrie Neuro-Psychopharmakologie 5: 283–294

Devalois J C 1973 Increase in cerebral blood flow in the rabbit by viquidil. Stroke 4: 218–220

De Wied D 1977 Peptides and behavior. Life Sciences 20: 195–204

De Wied D, Van Ree J M 1982 Neuropeptides, mental performance and aging. Life Sciences 31: 709–719

Dhrymiotis A D, Whittier J R 1962 Effect of a vasodilator (isoxsuprine) on cerebral ischemic episodes. Current Therapeutic Research, Clinical and Experimental 4: 124–129

Dimond S, Brouwers E Y M 1976 Improvement of human memory through the use of drugs. Psychopharmacology 49: 307–309

Dintenfass L 1967 Inversion of the Fåhraeus-Lindqvist phenomenon in blood flow through capillaries of diminishing radius. Nature 215: 1099–1100

Dintenfass L 1971 Blood Microrheology — viscosity factors in blood flow, ischaemia and thrombosis. Butterworths, London

Dintenfass L, Read J 1968 Pathogenesis of heart-failure in acute-on-chronic respiratory failure. Lancet i: 570–572

Di Perri T, Forconi S, Guerrini M, Agnusdei D 1977 In vitro activity of isoxsuprine on blood, plasma and serum viscosity. Pharmatherapeutica 1: 447–452

Di Perri T, Forconi S, Agnusdei D, Guerrini M, Laghi Pasini F 1978 The effects of intravenous isoxsuprine on blood viscosity in patients with occlusive peripheral arterial disease. British Journal of Clinical Pharmacology 5: 255–260

Di Perri T, Forconi S, Vittoria A, Laghi Pasini F, De-Gori V 1974 Action of isoxsuprine in vitro upon platelet aggregation by ADP, adrenaline and collagen. Bollettino della Società Italiana di Biologia Sperimentale 50: 1385–1390

Di Perri T, Forconi S, Guerrini M, Pasini F L, Del Cipolla R, Rossi C, Agnusdei D 1977 Action of cinnarizine on the hyperviscosity of blood in patients with peripheral obliterative arterial disease. Proceedings of the Royal Society of Medicine 70 (Suppl 8): 25–28

Dolce G 1970 Neurophysiologische Untersuchungen zur Wirkung von Pyrithioxin auf das Zentrale Nervensystem der Katze. Pharmakopsychiatrie Neuro-Psychopharmakologie 3: 355–370

Dominguez D, De Cayaffa C L, Gomensoro J, Aparicio N J 1977 Modification of psychometric, practical and intellectual parameters in patients with diffuse cerebrovascular insufficiency during prolonged treatment with pentoxifylline: a double-blind, placebo-controlled trial. Pharmatherapeutica 1: 498–506

Dominian J 1960 Deanol in depression: a controlled trial. Journal of Mental Science 106: 711–712

Donahue J, Pappas G D 1961 The fine structure of capillaries in the cerebral cortex of the rat at various stages of development. American Journal of Anatomy 108: 331–348

Dormandy J A, Ernst E 1981 Effects of buflomedil on erythrocyte deformability. Angiology 32: 714–716

Dorn M 1978 Piracetam bei vorzeitiger biologischer Alterung: Doppelblind-Prüfung nach medikamentöser Vorselektion. Fortschritte der Medizin 96: 1–6

Dott N M 1960 Brain, movement and time. British Medical Journal 2: 12–16

Drachman D A, Sahakian B J 1980 Memory and cognitive function in the elderly: a preliminary trial of physostigmine. Archives of Neurology 37: 674–675

Drachman D A, Stahl S 1975 Extrapyramidal dementia and levodopa. Lancet i: 809

Drachman D A, Glosser G, Fleming P, Longenecker G 1982 Memory decline in the aged: treatment with lecithin and physostigmine. Neurology 32: 944–950

Droller H 1960 The use of procaine injections in the treatment of degenerative deseases — a discussion with Professor Aslan. Gerontologia Clinica 2: 186–188

Droller H, Bevans H G, Jayaram V K 1971 Problems of a drug trial (pemoline) on geriatric patients. Gerontologia Clinica 13: 269–276

Droller H, Jayaram V K, Bevans H G, Bentinck S J 1971 A re-evaluation of cinnarizine with geriatric in-patients. Gerontologia Clinica 13: 89–95

Drug Therapy Bulletin 1972 Cosaldon for vascular disorders? 10: 66–68

Dubourg A, Scamuffa R F 1981 An experimental overview of a new vasoactive drug: buflomedil HCl. Angiology 32: 663–675

Dureman I 1962 Behavioral pattern of antibarbituric action after 5-phenyl-2-imino-4-oxo-oxazolidine, amphetamine and caffeine. Clinical Pharmacology and Therapeutics 3: 163–171

Durso R, Fedio P, Brouwers P, Cox C, Martin A J, Ruggieri S A, Tamminga C A, Chase T N 1982 Lysine vasopressin in Alzheimer disease. Neurology (New York) 32: 674–677

Du Vigneaud V, Chandler J P, Simmonds S, Moyer A W, Cohn M 1946 The rôle of dimethyl- and monomethyl-aminoethanol in transmethylation reactions in vivo. Journal of Biological Chemistry 164: 604–613

Duvoisin R C 1975 Antagonism of levodopa by papaverine. Journal of the American Medical Association 231: 845

East M O'N, Mann R D 1966 A clinical trial of magnesium and pemoline; a central nervous system stimulant. Journal of Therapeutics 1: 22–23

Easton J D, Byer J A 1980 Transient cerebral ischemia: medical management. Progress in Cardiovascular Disease 22: 371–377

Ebeid A M, Attia R R, Sundaram P, Fischer J E 1979 Release of vasoactive intestinal peptide in the central nervous system in man. American Journal of Surgery 137: 123–127

Edvinsson L, Owman C H 1975 Pharmacological identification of adrenergic (alpha and beta), cholinergic (muscarinic and nicotinic), histaminergic (H1 and H2), and serotonergic receptors in isolated intra- and extracranial vessels. In: Harper A M, Jennett W B, Miller J D, Rowan J O (eds) Blood Flow and Metabolism in the Brain. Churchill Livingstone, Edinburgh p 1.18–1.25

Edwards A E, Hart G M 1974 Hyperbaric oxygenation and the cognitive functioning of the aged. Journal of the American Geriatrics Society 22: 376–379

Ehrenreich D L, Burns R A, Alman R W, Fazekas J F 1961 Influence of acetazolamide on cerebral blood flow. Archives of Neurology 5: 227–232

Ehrly A M 1976 The effect of pentoxifylline on the flow properties of hyperosmolar blood. IRCS Journal of Medical Science 3: 465

Eichhorn O 1965 The effect of cyclandelate on cerebral circulation. A double-blind trial with clinical and radiocirculographic investigations. Vascular Disease 2: 305–314

Eisdorfer C, Conner J F, Wilkie F L 1968 Effect of magnesium pemoline on cognition and behavior. Journal of Gerontology 23: 283–288

Eisenberg S, Camp M F, Horn M R 1960 The effect of nylidrin hydrochloride (Arlidin) on the cerebral circulation. American Journal of the Medical Sciences 240: 85–92

Eisner D A 1975 Can hyperbaric oxygenation improve cognitive functioning in the organically impaired elderly?: a critical review. Journal of Geriatric Psychiatry 8: 173–188

Ekström-Jodal, von Essen C, Häggendal E, Roos B E 1973 Effects of noradrenaline, 5-hydroxytryptamine and dopamine on the cerebral blood flow in the dog. Stroke 4: 367–368

Elek S R, Katz L N 1942 Some clinical uses of papaverine in heart disease. Journal of the American Medical Association 120: 434–441

Elliott G G, Brown A L, Smith T C G 1973 Multicentre general practitioner trial of isoxsuprine in cerebrovascular disease: a pilot study. Current Medical Research and Opinion 1: 554–561

Emanuel M B, Will J A 1977 Cinnarizine in the treatment of peripheral vascular disease: mechanisms related to its clinical action. Proceedings of the Royal Society of Medicine 70 (Suppl 8): 7–12

Emmenegger H, Meier-Ruge W 1968 The actions of Hydergine® on the brain: A histochemical, circulatory and neurophysiological study. Pharmacology 1: 65–78

Emson P 1979 Peptides as neurotransmitter candidates in the mammalian CNS. Progress in Neurobiology 13: 61–116

Esser A H, Reis J 1968 Preliminary study of betahistine in chronic psychiatric patients with symptoms of arteriosclerosis cerebri. Current Therapeutic Research, Clinical and Experimental 10: 122–127

Essman W B 1978 Serotonin in learning and memory. In: Essman W B (ed) Serotonin in Health and Disease, vol III: the central nervous system. Spectrum Publications Inc, New York, p 69–143

Etienne P, Gauthier S, Johnson G, Collier B, Mendis T, Dastoor D,

Cole M, Muller H F 1978a Clinical effects of choline in Alzheimer's disease. Lancet i: 508–509

Etienne P, Gauthier S, Dastoor D, Collier B, Ratner J 1978b Lecithin in Alzheimer's disease. Lancet ii: 1206

Fåhraeus R, Lindqvist T 1931 The viscosity of the blood in narrow capillary tubes. American Journal of Physiology 96: 562–568

Fanchamps A 1979 Controlled studies with dihydroergotoxine in senile cerebral insufficiency. In: Nandy K (ed) Geriatric Psychopharmacology. Elsevier (North Holland), New York, p 195–212

Fang H C H 1976 Observations on aging characteristics of cerebral blood vessels, macroscopic and microscopic features. In: Terry R D, Gershon S (eds) Neurobiology of Aging (Aging 3). Raven Press, New York, p 155–166

Fazekas J F, Alman R W 1964 Comparative effects of isoxsuprine and carbon dioxide on cerebral hemodynamics. American Journal of the Medical Sciences 248: 16–19

Fazekas J F, Alman R W, Bessman A N 1952 Cerebral physiology of the aged. American Journal of the Medical Sciences 223: 245–257

Fazekas J F, Bessman A N, Cotsonas N J, Alman R W 1953 Cerebral hemodynamics in cerebral arteriosclerosis. Journal of Gerontology 8: 137–143

Fekete G 1976 Preface (to issue on ethyl on apovincaminate). Arzneimittel-Forschung 26: 1905

Ferrante G, Grassi M, Negro G 1960 A new vasodilator in the functional therapy of peripheral arteriopathies: 1-(p-hydroxphenyl)-2-(1-methyl-2-phenoxyethylamino)-propanol HC1. Minerva Cardioangiologica 8: 288–295

Ferris S H, Sathananthan G, Gershon S, Clark C 1977 Senile dementia: treatment with deanol. Journal of the American Geriatrics Society 25: 241–244

Ferris S H, Reisberg B, Crook T, Friedman E, Schneck R K, Mir P, Sherman K A, Corwin J, Gershon S, Bartus R T 1982 Pharmacological treatment of senile dementia: choline, L-DOPA, piracetam, and choline plus piracetam. In: Corkin S, Davis K L, Growdon J H, Usdin E, Wurtman R J (eds) Alzheimer's disease: A report of progress in research (Aging 19). Raven Press, New York, p 475–481

Fieschi C 1980 In vivo measurements of local cerebral energy metabolism: possible clinical relevance and perspectives. In: Amaducci L, Davison A N, Antuono P (eds) Aging of the Brain and Dementia (Aging 13). Raven Press, New York, p 123–125

Fine E W, Lewis D, Villa-Landa I, Blakemore C B 1970 The effect of cyclandelate on mental function in patients with arteriosclerotic brain disease. British Journal of Psychiatry 117: 157–161

Fisher C M 1965 Lacunes: small deep cerebral infarcts. Neurology (Minneapolis) 15: 774–784

Fisher C M 1969 The arterial lesions underlying lacunes. Acta Neuropathologica (Berlin) 12: 1–15

Flaim S F 1982 Comparative pharmacology of calcium blockers based on studies of vascular smooth muscle. In: Flaim S F, Zelis R (eds) Calcium Blockers: mechanisms of action and clinical applications. Urban and Schwarzenberg, Baltimore, p 155–178

Flamm E S, Kim J, Lin J, Ransohoff J 1975 Phosphodiesterase inhibitors and cerebral vasospasm. Archives of Neurology 32: 569–571

Flamm E S, Yasargil M G, Ransohoff J 1972 Control of cerebral vasospasm by parenteral phenoxybenzamine. Stroke 3: 421–426

Fleckenstein A 1977 Specific pharmacology of calcium in myocardium, cardiac pacemakers, and vascular smooth muscle. Annual Review of Pharmacology and Toxicology 17: 149–166

Fleckenstein A 1981 Pharmacology and electrophysiology of calcium antagonists. In: Zanchetti A, Krikler D (eds) Calcium antagonism in cardiovascular therapy: experience with Verapamil. Excerpta Medica, Amsterdam, p 10–29

Foltyn P, Groh R, Lücker P W, Steinhaus W 1978 Zur Problematik des Wirkamkeitsnachweises 'hirnaktiver' Pharmaka beim Alterspatienten. Ergebnisse einer randomisierten Doppelblindstudie mit einer vincaminhaltigen Spezialität. Arzneimittel-Forschung 28: 90–94

Fontaine L., Grand M, Chabert J, Szarvasi E, Bayssat M 1968 Pharmacologie générale d'une substance nouvelle vasodilatatrice, le naftidrofuryl. (General pharmacology of a new vasodilator drug, naftidrofuryl.) Bulletin de Chimie Thérapeutique 6: 463–469

Forrester T, Harper A M, Mackenzie E T 1975a Effects of intracarotid adenosine triphosphate infusions on cerebral blood flow and metabolism in the anaesthetized baboon. Journal of Physiology 250: 38P–39P

Forrester T, Harper A M, Mackenzie E T, Thomson E M 1975b Vascular and metabolic effects of systemic ATP on the cerebral circulation. In: Harper A M, Jennett W B, Miller J D, Rowan J O (eds) Blood Flow and Metabolism in the Brain. Churchill Livingstone, Edinburgh

Fredholm B B, Hedqvist P 1980 Modulation of neurotransmission by purine nucleotides and nucleosides. Biochemical Pharmacology 29: 1635–1643

Freyhan F A, Woodford R B, Kety S S 1951 Cerebral blood flow and metabolism in psychosis of senility. Journal of Nervous and Mental Disease 113: 445–456

Fuller R W, Roush B W 1977 Procaine hydrochloride as a monoamine oxidase inhibitor: implications for geriatric therapy. Journal of the American Geriatrics Society 25: 90–93

Funcke A B H, Van Beek M C Nijland K 1974 Protective action of cyclandelate in hypoxia. Current Medical Research and Opinion 2: 37–42

Gaitz C M, Varner R V, Overall J E 1977 Pharmacotherapy for organic brain syndrome in late life. Archives of General Psychiatry 34: 839–845

Garcia C A, Tweedy J R, Blass J P, McDowell F H 1982 Lecithin and parkinsonian dementia. In: Corkin S et al (eds) Alzheimer's Disease: a Report of Progress in Research (Aging 19). Raven Press, New York, p 443–449

Garetz F K, Baron J J, Barron P B, Bjork A E 1979 Efficacy of nylidrin hydrochloride in the treatment of cognitive impairment in the elderly. Journal of the American Geriatrics Society 27: 235–236

Gastpar H 1974a Inhibition of cancer cell stickiness by the blocking of platelet aggregation. South Arican Medical Journal 48: 621–627

Gastpar H 1974b The inhibition of cancer cell stickiness by the methylxanthine derivative pentoxifylline (BL191). Thrombosis Research 5: 277–289

Gautier J C 1976 Cerebral ischaemia in hypertension. In: Ross Russell R W (ed) Cerebral Arterial Disease. Churchill Livingstone, Edinburgh, p 181–209

Gedye J L 1970 The use of an interactive computer terminal to assess the effect of cyclandelate on the mental ability of geriatric patients. In: Stöcker G, Kuhn R A, Hall P, Becker G, van der Veen E (eds) Assessment in Cerebrovascular Insufficiency. Georg Thieme Verlag, Stuttgart, p 9–42

Gedye J L, Wedgwood J 1966 Experience in the use of a teaching machine for the assessment of senile mental changes. Proceedings of the 7th International Congress on Gerontology, Vienna 8: 205

Gedye J L, Exton-Smith A N, Wedgwood J 1972 A method of measuring mental performance in the elderly and its use in a pilot clinical trial of meclofenoxate in organic dementia (preliminary communication). Age and Ageing 1: 74–80

Gedye J L, Ibrahimi G S, McDonald C 1978 Double blind controlled trial of piracetam (2-pyrrolidone acetamide) on two groups of psychogeriatric patients. IRCS Journal of Medical Science 6: 202

General Practitioner Research Group 1969 Manifestations of cerebral arteriosclerosis unaffected by a vasodilator. Practitioner 203: 695–698

Géraud J, Bès A, Rascol A, Delpla M, Marc-Vergnes J P 1963 Mesure du débit sanguin cérébral au krypton 85. Quelques applications physiopathologiques et cliniques. Revue Neurologique (Paris) 108: 542–557

Gerin J 1974 Double-blind trial of naftidrofuryl in the treatment of cerebral arteriosclerosis. British Journal of Clinical Practice 28: 177–178

Gey K F, Carlson L A (eds) 1970 Metabolic Effects of Nicotinic Acid and its Derivatives. Proceedings of a workshop, Flims. Huber, Bern

Ghoneim M M, Mewaldt S P 1977 Studies on human memory. The interactions of diazepam, scopolamine and physostigmine. Psychopharmacology 52: 1–6

Giacobini E, Filogano G, Vernadakis A (eds) The Aging Brain: cellular and molecular mechanisms of aging in the nervous system (Aging 20). Raven Press, New York

Gibson G E, Jope R, Blass J P 1975 Decreased synthesis of acetylcholine accompanying impaired oxidation of pyruvic acid in rat brain minces. Biochemical Journal 148: 17–23

Gilbert J G, Donnelly K J, Zimmer L E, Kubis J F 1973 Effect of magnesium pemoline and methylphenidate on memory improvement and mood in normal aging subjects. International Journal of Aging and Human Development 4: 35–51

Gilroy J, Barnhart M I, Meyer J S 1969 Treatment of acute stroke with dextran 40. Journal of the American Medical Association 210: 293–298

Gilroy J, Meyer J S 1966 Controlled evaluation of cerebral vasodilator drugs in the progressive stroke. In: Siekert R G, Whisnant J P (eds) Cerebral Vascular Diseases. Transactions of the 5th Princeton conference. Grune and Stratton, New York, p 197–202

Giurgea C 1972 Vers une pharmacologie de l'activité intégrative du cerveau. Tentative du concept nootrope en psychopharmacologie. Actualités Pharmacologiques 25ème serie. Masson, Paris, p 115–156

Giurgea C 1976 Piracetam: nootropic pharmacology of neuro-integrative activity. In: Essman W B, Valzelli L (eds) Current Developments in Psychopharmacology, vol. 3. Spectrum Publications Inc, New York, p 221–273

Glassman E 1969 The biochemistry of learning: an evaluation of the role of RNA and protein. Annual Review of Biochemistry 38: 605–646

Glen A I, Yates C M, Simpson J, Christie J E, Shering A, Whalley L J, Jellinek E H 1981 Choline uptake in patients with Alzheimer pre-senile dementia. Psychological Medicine 11: 469–476

Gloning K, Klausberger E M 1958 Untersuchungen über die Hirngefäßfunktion im Bewegungsfilm. (Investigations on the cerebral-vessel function with the aid of motion pictures.) Wiener Klinische Wochenschrift 70: 145–149

Gobert J 1972 Genèse d'un médicament: le Piracétam, métabolisation et recherche biochimique. Journal de Pharmacie de Belgique 27: 281–304

Godfraind T, Kaba A 1972 The role of calcium in the action of drugs on vascular smooth muscle. Archives Internationales de Pharmacodynamie et de Thérapie 196 (Suppl): 35–49

Gold P H, Gee M V, Strehler B L 1968 Effect of age on oxidative phosphorylation of the rat. Journal of Gerontology 23: 509–512

Gold P W, Weingartner H, Ballenger J C, Goodwin F K, Post R M 1979 Effects of l-desamino-8-d-arginine vasopressin on behavior and cognition in primary affective disorder. Lancet ii: 992–994

Goldberg A M 1982 The interaction of neuronal activity and choline transport on the regulation of acetylcholine synthesis. In: Corkin S et al (eds) Alzheimer's Disease: a Report of Progress in Research (Aging 19). Raven Press, New York, p 327–330

Goldberg A M, Silbergeld E K 1974 Neurological aspects of lead induced hyperactivity. Transactions of the American Society of Neurochemistry 5: 185

Goldfarb A I, Hochstadt N, Jacobson J H, Weinstein E A 1972 Hyperbaric oxygen treatment of organic mental syndrome in aged persons. Journal of Gerontology 27: 212–217

Goldstein B, Burnet-Merlin J G, Herskiowiez A I, Fernandez E B, Galeano J C 1966 Probable mecanismo de accion del hexanicatinato de inositol en el tratamiento da las vasculopatias perifericas. (Probable mechanism of action of inositol hexanicotinate in the treatment of peripheral vascular disorders.) Semana Médica (Buenos Aires) 128: 502–505

Goldstein B J, Braunstein J 1968 Clinical evaluation of pemoline and magnesium hydroxide as a mild stimulant in geriatric patients. Current Therapeutic Research, Clinical and Experimental 10: 457–460

Goldstein M, Calne D B, Lieberman A, Thorner M O 1980 Ergot Compounds and Brain Function (Advances in Biochemistry and Psychopharmacology 23). Raven Press, New York

Gotoh F, Meyer J, Tomita M 1966 Carbonic anhydrase inhibition and cerebral venous blood gases and ions in man. Archives of Internal Medicine 117: 39–46

Gottfries C-G, Gottfries I, Roos B E 1969a The investigation of homovanillic acid in human brain and its correlation to senile dementia. British Journal of Psychiatry 115: 563–574

Gottfries C-G, Gottfries I, Roos B E 1969b Homovanillic acid and 5-hydroxyindoleacetic acid in the cerebrospinal fluid of patients with senile dementia, presenile dementia, and Parkinsonism. Journal of Neurochemistry 16: 1341–1345

Gottstein U 1965 Pharmacological studies of total cerebral blood flow in man with comments on the possibility of improving regional cerebral blood flow by drugs. Acta Neurologica Scandinavica 14 (Suppl): 136–141

Gottstein U 1969 The effect of drugs on cerebral blood flow especially in patients of older age. Pharmakopsychiatrie Neuro-Psychopharmakologie 2: 100–109

Gottstein U, Held K, Müller W, Berghoff W 1972 Utilization of ketone bodies by the human brain. In: Meyer J S, Reivich M, Lechner H (eds) Research on the Cerebral Circulation. 5th International Salzburg Conference 1970. C C Thomas, Springfield, Illinois, p 137–145

Gottstein U, Held K, Sebening H, Walpurger G 1965 Der Glukoseverbrauch des menschlichen Gehirns unter dem Einfluss intravenöser Infusionen von Glucose, Glucagon und Glucose-Insulin. Klinische Wochenschrift 43: 965–975

GP Group 1974 Studies with Reactivan in general practice. Medical Digest 19(4): 68–72

GP Medical Research Unit 1972 Double-blind comparison trial of Reactivan and placebo in the treatment of debility. Medical Digest 17(11): 64–73

Granacher R P, Baldessarini R J 1975 Physostigmine: its use in acute anticholinergic syndrome with antidepressant and antiparkinson drugs. Archives of General Psychiatry 32: 375–380

Green I 1965 Experiences in the management of geriatric patients with chronic brain syndrome. American Journal of Psychiatry 122: 586–589

Groth D P, Bain J A, Pfeiffer C C 1968 The comparative distribution of C14-labelled 2-dimethylaminoethanol and choline in the mouse. Journal of Pharmacology and Experimental Therapeutics 124: 290–295

Growdon J H, Wurtman R J 1979 Dietary influences on the synthesis of neurotransmitters in the brain. Nutrition Reviews 37: 129–136

Growdon J H, Cohen E L, Wurtman R J 1977 Effects of oral choline administration on serum and CSF choline levels in patients with Huntington's disease. Journal of Neurochemistry 28: 229–231

Gustafson L, Hagberg B 1975 Dementia with onset in the presenile period. A cross-sectional study. Acta Psychiatrica Scandinavica (Suppl) 257

Gygax P, Hunziker O, Schulz U, Schweizer A 1975 Experimental studies on the action of metabolic and vasoactive substances in the brain. Triangle 14: 80–89

Hachinski V C, Lassen N A, Marshall J 1974 Multi-infarct dementia. A cause of mental deterioration in the elderly. Lancet ii: 207–210

Hachinski V C, Iliff L D, Zilkha E, du Boulay G H, McAllister V L, Marshall J, Ross Russell R W, Symon L 1975 Cerebral blood flow in dementia. Archives of Neurology 32: 632–637

Hadjiev D 1974 Impedance methods for investigation of cerebral circulation. Progress in Brain Research 35: 25–85

Hafkenschiel J H, Crumpton C W, Moyer J H 1950 The effect of intramuscular dihydroergocornine on the cerebral circulation in normotensive patients. Journal of Pharmacology and Experimental Therapeutics 98: 144–146

Hagberg B, Ingvar D H 1976 Cognitive reduction in presenile dementia related to regional abnormalities of the cerebral blood flow. British Journal of Psychiatry 128: 209–222

Haining J L, Turner M D, Pantall R M 1970 Local cerebral blood flow in young and old rats during hypoxia and hypercapnia. American Journal of Physiology 218: 1020–1024

Hakim A M, Mathieson G 1978 Basis of dementia in Parkinson's disease. Lancet ii: 729

Hakim A M, Moss G, Gollomp S M 1976 The effect of hypoxia on the pentose phosphate pathway in brain. Journal of Neurochemistry 26: 683–688

Hakkarainen H 1980 Personal communication

Hakkarainen H, Hakamies L 1978 Piracetam in the treatment of post-concussional syndrome: a double blind study. European Neurology 17: 50–55

Hall P 1976 Cyclandelate in the treatment of cerebral arteriosclerosis. Journal of the American Geriatrics Society 24: 41–45

Hall P, Harcup M 1969 A trial of lipotropic enzymes in atheromatous ('arteriosclerotic') dementia. Angiology 20: 287–300

Hammerl H, Kränzl C, Pichler O, Studlar M 1969 Einfluss eines Inosit-Nikotinsäureesters (Hexanicit forte) auf Serumlipidveränderungen bei Gefässkranken. Münchener Medizinische Wochenschrift III: 1912–1916

Hamouz W 1977 The use of pyritinol in patients with moderate to severe organic psychosyndrome. Pharmatherapeutica 1: 398–404

Hanin I 1979 Choline and lecithin in the treatment of neurologic disorders. New England Journal of Medicine 300: 1113

Hansing C E, Folts J D, Alfonso S, Rowe G G 1972 Systemic and coronary hemodynamic effects of hexobendine and its interaction with adenosine and aminophylline. Journal of Pharmacology and Experimental Therapeutics 181: 498–511

Hapke H-J 1973 Tierexperimentelle Untersuchungen Zur Charakterisierung zentralnervöser Wirkungen von Bencyclan. Archives Internationales de Pharmacodynamie et de Thérapie 202: 231–243

Harner R W 1975 EEG evaluation of the patient with dementia. In: Benson D F, Billmer D (eds) Psychiatric Aspects of Neurological Diseases. Grune & Stratton, New York, p 63–81

Harper A M, Jennett W B, Miller J D, Rowan J O (eds) 1975 Blood Flow and Metabolism in the Brain. Churchill Livingstone, Edinburgh

Harrison M J G, Thomas D J, du Boulay G H, Marshall J 1979 Multi-infarct dementia. Journal of the Neurological Sciences 40: 97–103

Harthon J G L, Sigroth K J E, Sjöbom R A 1964 Ein Beitrag zur Klärung der Resorption des Hexanicotinsäureesters des Meso-Inosits im Organismus. (Contribution concerning the absorption of meso-inositol hexanicotinate in the organism.) Arzneimittel-Forschung 14: 126–128

Harwart D 1979 The treatment of chronic cerebrovascular insufficiency. A double-blind study with pentoxifylline ('Trental' 400). Current Medical Research and Opinion 6: 73–84

Haubrich D R, Wang P F L, Clody D E, Wedeking P W 1975 Increase in rat brain acetylcholine induced by choline or deanol. Life Sciences 17: 975–980

Hayashi S, Ozawa H 1974 Studies on 3,7-dimethyl-1-(5-oxo-hexyl)xanthine (BL 191). I. Cyclic 3'5'-nucleotide phosphodiesterase (PDE) in the inhibitory effect of BL 191 on PDE in rat brain and heart. Chemical and Pharmaceutical Bulletin 22: 587–593

Hedqvist P 1977 Basic mechanisms of prostaglandin action on autonomic neurotransmission. Annual Review of Pharmacology and Toxicology 17: 259–279

Heidrich H, Ott M 1974 Vasodilatantien und Blutviskosität. (Vasodilators and blood viscosity.) Herz/Kreislauf 6: 542–546

Heiss W-D 1973 Drug effects on regional cerebral flow in focal cerebrovascular disease. Journal of the Neurological Sciences 19: 461–482

Heiss W-D, Podreka I 1978 Assessment of pharmacological effects on cerebral blood flow. European Neurology 17 (Suppl 1): 135–143

Heiss W-D, Hayakawa T, Waltz A G 1976 Cortical neuronal function during ischemia. Effects of occlusion of one middle cerebral artery on single-unit activity in cats. Archives of Neurology 33: 813–820

Heiss W-D, Prosenz P, Gloning K, Tschabitscher H 1970 Regional and total cerebral blood flow under vasodilating drugs. In: Ross Russell R W (ed) Brain and Blood Flow. Pitman, London, p 270–276

Held K 1973 Experiments on effect and mechanism of xantinol nicotinate in man during oxygen deficiency. Therapiewoche 37: 3270–3275

Held K, Wünsche O, Reuter N 1973 The effect of xantinol nicotinate on man in altitude oxygen deficiency. Ärzneimittel Praxis 26: 91–93

Henry P D 1982 Comparative cardiac pharmacology of calcium blockers. In: Flaim S F, Zelis R (eds) Calcium Blockers: mechanisms of action and clinical applications. Urban and Schwarzenberg, Baltimore, p 135–153

Hernandez-Perez M J, Anderson D K 1976 Autoregulation of cerebral blood flow and its relation to cerebrospinal fluid pH. American Journal of Physiology 231: 929–935

Herrschaft H 1975 The efficacy and course of action of vaso- and metabolic-active substances on regional cerebral blood flow in patients with cerebrovascular insufficiency. In: Harper A M, Jennett W B, Miller J D, Rowan J O (eds) Blood Flow and Metabolism in the Brain. Churchill Livingstone, Edinburgh, p 11.24–11.28

Herrschaft H 1978 Die Wirkung von Pyritinol auf die Gehirndurchblutung des Menschen. Münchener Medizinische Wochenschrift 120: 1263–1268

Hertz L, Schousboe A 1975 Ion and energy metabolism of the brain at cellular level. International Review of Neurobiology 18: 141–211

Hervonen A, Vaalasti A, Partanen M, Kanerva L, Hervonen H 1978 Effects of aging on the histochemically demonstrable catecholamines and acetylcholinesterase of human sympathetic ganglia. Journal of Neurocytology 7: 11–23

Herzfeld U, Wittgen W 1971 Veränderung der zerebralen Zirkulationszeit unter dem Einfluß von Hydergin. (Changes of the cerebral circulation time influenced by Hydergine.) Arzneimittel-Forschung 25: 224–230 (English abstract)

Hess H, Franke L, Jauch M 1973 Medikamentöse Verbesserung der Fließeigenschaften des Blutes. Ein wirksames Prinzip zur Behandlung von arteriellen Durchblutungsstörungen. (Drug therapy to reduce the viscosity of the blood. An effective principle for the treatment of peripheral arterial disorders.) Fortschritte der Medizin 91: 743–748

Heyck H 1961 Der Einfluß der Ausgangslage auf sympathikolytische Effekte am Hirnkreislauf bei cerebrovasculären Erkrankungen. Arzneimittel-Forschung 15: 243–251 (English abstract)

Heyck H 1962 Der Einfluß der Nikotinsäure auf die Hirndurchblutung und den Hirnstoffwechsel bei Cerebralsklerosen und anderen diffusen Durchblutungsstörungen des Gehirns. Schweizerische Medizinische Wochenschrift 92: 226–231 (English abstract)

Heyman A, Logue P, Wilkinson W, Holloway D, Hurwitz B 1982 Lecithin therapy of Alzheimer' disease: a preliminary report. In: Corkin S et al (eds) Alzheimer's Disease: a Report of Progress in Research (Aging 19). Raven Press, New York, p 373–378

Himwich H E (ed) 1976a Brain Metabolism and Cerebral Disorders, 2nd edn. Spectrum Publications Inc, New York

Himwich H E 1976b Foodstuffs of the brain: ketone bodies. In: Himwich H E (ed) Brain Metabolism and Cerebral Disorders. Spectrum Publications Inc, New York, p 33–63

Hindmarch I, Parrott A C, Lanza M 1979 The effects of an ergot alkaloid derivative (Hydergine) on aspects of psychomotor performance, arousal and cognitive processing ability. Journal of Clinical Pharmacology 19: 726–732

Hirsch M J, Wurtman R J 1978 Lecithin consumption increases acetylcholine concentrations in rat brain and adrenal gland. Science 202: 223–225

Hirsch M J, Growdon J H, Wurtman R J 1977 Increase in hippocampal acetylcholine after choline administration. Brain Research 125: 383–385

Hochschild R 1971 Effect of membrane stabilizing drugs on mortality in Drosophila melanogaster. Experimental Gerontology 6: 133–151

Hochschild R 1973a Effect of dimethylaminoethanol on the life span of senile male A/J mice. Experimental Gerontology 8: 185–191

Hochschild R 1973b Effect of dimethylaminoethyl p-chlorophenoxyacetate on the life span of male Swiss Webster Albino mice. Experimental Gerontology 8: 177–183

Høedt-Rasmussen K, Skinhøj E 1966 In vivo measurements of the relative weights of the gray and the white matter in the human brain. Neurology (Minneapolis) 16: 515–520

Hoffmeister F, Kazda S, Krause H P 1979 Influence of nimodipine (BAY e 9736) on the postischaemic changes of brain function. Acta Neurologica Scandinavica 60 (Suppl 72): 358–359

Holliday A R, Devery W J 1962 Effects of drugs on the performance of a task by fatigued subjects. Clinical Pharmacology and Therapeutics 3: 5–15

Holliday A R, Joffe J P 1965 A controlled evaluation of protriptyline compared to a placebo and to methylphenidate hydrochloride (abstract). Journal of New Drugs 5: 257–258

Hollingsworth S W 1980 Response of geriatric patients from the satellite nursing homes of Maricopa County to Hydergine therapy: a double-blind study. Current Therapeutic Research, Clinical and Experimental 27: 401–410

Hollister L E 1974 Drugs for mental disorders of old age. Journal of the American Medical Association 234: 195–198

Honegger C G, Honegger R 1959 Occurrence and quantitative determination of 2-dimethylaminoethanol in animal tissue extracts. Nature 184: 550–552

Horton G E, Johnson P C 1964 The application of radio-isotopes to the study of cerebral blood flow, comparison of three methods. Angiology 15: 70–74

Hoyer S 1982 Cerebral blood flow, electroencephalography and behavior. In: Platt D (ed) Geriatrics I: Cardiology and vascular system; central nervous system. Springer-Verlag, New York, p 201–226

Hoyer S, Oesterreich K, Stoll K-D 1977 Effects of pyritinol-HCl on blood flow and oxidative metabolism of the brain in patients with dementia. Arzneimittel-Forschung 27: 671–674

Hughes J R, Williams J G, Currier R D 1976 An ergot alkaloid preparation (Hydergine) in the treatment of dementia: critical review of the clinical literature. Journal of the American Geriatrics Society 24: 490–497

Hughes R J D, James I M, Dijane A 1981 The effect of betahistine methanesulphonate upon cerebral blood flow. British Journal of Clinical Pharmacology 11: 308–310

Humphrey P R D, du Boulay G H, Marshall J, Pearson T C, Ross Russell R W, Symon L, Weatherly-Mein G, Zilkha E 1979 Cerebral blood-flow and viscosity in relative polycythaemia. Lancet ii: 873–877

Hunziker O, Frey H, Schulz U 1974 Morphometric investigations of capillaries in the brain cortex of the cat. Brain Research 65: 1–11

Hussain S M A, Gedye J L, Naylor R, Brown A L 1976 The objective measurement of mental performance in cerebrovascular disease. A double-blind controlled study, using a graded-release preparation of isoxsuprine. Practitioner. 216: 222–228

Iliff L D, du Boulay G H, Marshall J, Ross Russell R W, Symon L 1979 Wirkung von Nicergolin auf die Gehirndurchblutung. Arzneimittel-Forschung 29: 1277–1278

Ingvar D H, Risberg J 1967 Increase of regional cerebral blood flow during mental effort in normals and in patients with focal brain disorders. Experimental Brain Research 3: 195–211

Ingvar D H, Schwartz M S 1974 Blood flow patterns induced in the dominant hemisphere by speech and reading. Brain 97: 273–288

Ingvar D H, Risberg J, Schwartz M S 1975 Evidence of subnormal function of association cortex in presenile dementia. Neurology (Minneapolis) 25: 964–974

Ingvar D H, Cronqvist S, Ekberg R, Risberg J, Høedt-Rasmussen K 1965 Normal values of regional cerebral blood flow in man, including flow and weight estimates of gray and white matter. Acta Neurologica Scandinavica 14 (Suppl): 72–78

Ingvar D H, Obrist W, Chivian E, Cronqvist S, Risberg J, Gustafson L, Hägerdal M, Wittbom-Cigén G 1968 General and regional abnormalities of cerebral blood flow in senile and 'presenile' dementia. Scandinavian Journal of Clinical and Laboratory Investigation 22 (Suppl 102) XII: B

Irvine R E, Greenfield P R, Griffith D G C, Paget S C, Strouthidis T M, Vaughan V St G 1970 Cinnarizine in cerebrovascular disease. Gerontologia Clinica 12: 297–301

Iverson L L 1981 Another cup of coffee? Nature 301: 195

Iwangoff P, Meier-Ruge W, Schwieweck C H, Enz A 1976 The uptake of DH-ergotoxine by different parts of the cat brain. Pharmacology 14: 27–38

Jacobs E A, Winter P M, Alvis H J, Small S M 1969 Hyperoxygenation effects on cognitive functioning in the aged. New England Journal of Medicine 281: 753–757

Jacobs J 1965 A controlled trial of Deaner and a placebo in mentally defective children. British Journal of Clinical Practice 19: 77–86

Jacquy J, Noel G 1977 Double blind trial with Suloctidil, a new vasoactive agent, in elderly patients with psycho-organic brain syndrome. Acta Clinica Belgica 32: 22–26

Jaffe G 1975 Double-blind comparison of Bradilan (tetranicotinoylfructose) tablets and Hexopal (inositol hexanicotinate) tablets in the treatment of intermittent claudication. Journal of International Medical Research 3: 428–430

James I M, Millar R A, Purves M J 1969 Observations on the extrinsic neural control of cerebral blood flow in the baboon. Circulation Research 25: 77–93

James I M, Newbury P, Woollard M L 1978 The effect of naftidrofuryl oxalate on cerebral blood flow in elderly patients. British Journal of Clinical Pharmacology 6: 545–546

Janaki S 1980 Pentoxifylline in strokes: a clinical study. Journal of International Medical Research 8: 56–62

Jayne H W, Scheinberg P, Rich M, Belle M S 1952 The effect of intravenous papaverine hydrochloride on the cerebral circulation. Journal of Clinical Investigation 31: 111–114

Jellinger K, Flament H, Riederer P, Schmid H, Ambrozi I 1980 Levodopa in the treatment of (pre-) senile dementia. Mechanisms of Ageing and Development 14: 258–264

Job J 1960 Zur Frage der medikamentösen Beeinflussung der Zerebralsklerose. (The medicinal therapy of cerebral arteriosclerosis.) Münchener Medizinische Wochenschrift 102: 483–484 (English abstract)

Jovanović U J 1976 Statistical evaluation of polygraphic investigations of pentoxifylline. Journal of International Medical Research 4: 211–222

Judge T G, Urquhart A 1972 Natfidrofuryl — a double-blind crossover study in the elderly. Current Medical Research and Opinion 1: 166–172

Judge T G, Urquhart A, Blakemore C B 1973 Cyclandelate and mental functions: a double-blind crossover trial in normal elderly subjects. Age and Ageing 2: 121–124

Kanig K 1973 Encephalotropic drugs and cerebral RNA metabolism. In: Zippel H P (ed) Memory and Transfer of Information. Plenum Press, New York, p 571–582

Kaplitz S E 1975 Withdrawn, apathetic geriatric patients responsive to methylphenidate. Journal of the American Geriatrics Society 23: 271–276

Kappert A 1961 Experimental and clinical investigations with Hexanicit. Therapeutische Umschau und Medizinische Bibliographie 18: 303–309

Karczmar A G 1978 Multitransmitter mechanisms underlying selected functions, particularly aggression learning and sexual behavior. In: Deniker P, Radouco-Thomas C, Villeneuve A (eds) Neuro-psychopharmacology, vol 1 (Proceedings of the 10th Congress of the International College of Neuro-psychopharmacology, Quebec, 1976). Pergamon Press, Oxford p 581–608

Karlsberg P, Elliott H W, Adams J E 1963 Effect of various pharmacologic agents on cerebral arteries. Neurology (Minneapolis) 13: 772–778

Kastin A J, Olson R D, Schally A V, Coy D H 1979 CNS effects of peripherally administered brain peptides. Life Sciences 25: 401–414

Kato H, Kurihara M, Ishii K, Kasuy Y 1981 Vasodilating effect of flunarizine in anesthetized dogs. Archives Internationales de Pharmacodynamie et de Thérapie 249: 257–263

Kawamura Y, Meyer J S, Hiromoto H, Aoyagi M, Hashi K 1974 Neurogenic control of cerebral blood flow in the baboon. Effects of alpha adrenergic blockade with phenoxybenzamine on cerebral autoregulation and vasomotor reactivity to changes in $PaCO_2$. Stroke 5: 747–758

Kaye W H, Weingartner H, Gold P, Ebert M H, Gillin J C, Sitaram N, Smallberg S 1982 Cognitive effects of cholinergic and vasopressin-like agents in patients with primary degenerative dementia. In: Corkin S et al (eds) Alzheimer's Disease: a Report of Progress in Research (Aging 19). Raven Press, New York, p 433–442

Kazda S, Hoffmeister F 1979 Effect of some cerebral vasodilators on the postischaemic impaired cerebral reperfusion in cats. Archives of Pharmacology 307 (Suppl): R 43

Kazda S, Hoffmeister F, Garthoff B, Towart R 1979 Prevention of the postischaemic impaired reperfusion of the brain by nimodipine (BAY e 9736). Acta Neurologica Scandinavica 60 (Suppl 72): 302–303

Kent S 1982 The procaine 'youth' drugs. Geriatrics 37 (4) (April): 32–36

Kiaer H W, Olsen S, Rønnov-Jessen V 1974 Hepatotoxicity of papaverine: histologic lesions. Archives of Pathology 98: 292–296

Kimura H, McGeer P L, Peng F, McGeer E G 1981 The central cholinergic system studied by immunohistochemistry in the cat. Journal of Comparative Neurology 200: 151–201

Kirchberger F, Kehl R, Gutmann W 1969 Zur Behandlung zerebraler Ernährungsstörungen. Eine Doppelblind-Studie. (The treatment of disorders of cerebral nutrition — a double-blind study.) Medizinische Welt 22: 1542–1546

Klassen A C 1972 Treatment of cerebral ischemia with vasoactive drugs. Clinical Pharmacology and Therapeutics 15: 199–203

Kline N S, Li C H, Lehmann H E, Lajtha A, Laski E, Cooper T 1977 β-endorphin-induced changes in schizophrenic and depressed patients. Archives of General Psychiatry 34: 111–113

Klüken N, Schmidt H 1972 Investigación acerca del efecto del nicotinato de xanitinol sobre la irrigación de la musculatura de las extremidades y de la piel. (Studies on the effect of xantinol nicotinate on the blood flow in muscle and skin of the extremities.) Angiologia 24: 271–280 (English abstract)

Koch D, Schnellbächer F 1955 Über den Einfluss einiger Theophyllinderivate auf die Gehirndurchblutung. (The influence of a theophylline derivative on cerebral blood flow.) Klinische Wochenschrift 33: 668–674

Kong Y, Lunzer S, Heyman A, Thompson H K Jr, Saltzman H A 1969 Effects of acetazolamide on cerebral blood flow of dogs during hyperbaric oxygenation. American Heart Journal 78: 229–237

Koob G F, Bloom F E 1982 Behavioral effects of neuropeptides: endorphins and vasopressin. Annual Review of Physiology 44: 571–582

Koppenhagen K, Wenig H G, Müller K 1977 Measurement of cerebral blood flow following intravenous administration of pentoxifylline (Trental). Current Medical Research and Opinion 4: 521–528

Korenyi C, Whittier J R 1969 Prevention of brain vasospasm: effect of sustained release form of papaverine (Pavabid) on blocking of hyperventilation electroencephalogram in the human. Physicians' Drug Manual 1: 81–84

Kostenbauder H B 1977 Sustained-release papaverine hydrochloride. Journal of the American Pharmaceutical Association (NS) 17: 303–306

Kostopoulos G K, Phillis J W 1975 The effects of dimethylaminoethanol (deanol) on cerebral cortical neurons. Psychopharmacology Communications 1: 339–347

Kovács G L, Bohus B, Versteeg D H G 1979 The effects of vasopressin on memory processes: the role of noradrenergic neurotransmission. Neuroscience 4: 1529–1537

Kozniewska E, Trzebski A, Zielinski A 1976 Comparison of the effects of inorganic phosphate, adenosine and ATP on the cerebral blood flow in dogs. Journal of Physiology 256: 96P–97P

Kretschmar J H, Kretschmar C 1976 Zur Dosis-Wirkungs-Relation bei der Behandlung mit Piracetam. Arzneimittel-Forschung 26: 1158–1159

Kristensen V, Olsen M, Theilgaard A 1977 Levodopa treatment of presenile dementia. Acta Psychiatrica Scandinavica 55: 41–51

Krop H D, Block A G, Cohen E, Croucher R, Shuster J 1977 Neuropsychologic effects of continuous oxygen therapy in the aged. Chest 72: 737–743

Kuffler S W, Nicholls J G 1966 The physiology of neuroglial cells. Ergebnisse der Physiologie, Biologischen Chemie und Experimentellen Pharmakologie 57: 1–90

Kugler J, Oswald W D, Herzfeld U, Seus R, Pingel J, Welzel D 1978 Langzeittherapie altersbedingter Insuffizienzerscheinungen des Gehirns. Deutsche Medizinische Wochenschrift 103: 456–462

Kuhar M J, Pert C, Snyder S H 1973 Regional distribution of opiate receptor binding in monkey and human brain. Nature (London) 245: 447–450

Kuhar M J, Kethy V H, Roth R H, Aghajanian G K 1973 Choline: selective accumulation by central cholinergic neurons. Journal of Neurochemistry 20: 581–593

Kuhn R A 1966 Effect of cyclandelate upon cerebral blood flow in patients with 'stroke'. Angiology 17: 422–430

Kukovetz W R, Pöch G, Holzmann S, Paietta E 1975 Zum Wirkungsmechanismus von Bencyclan an der glatten Muskulatur. Arzneimittel-Forschung 25: 722–726

La Celle P L, Kirkpatrick F H, Udkow M P, Arkin B 1973 Membrane fragmentation and Ca^{++}-membrane interaction: potential mechanisms of shape change in the senescent red cell. In: Bessis M, Weed R I, Leblond P F (eds) Red cell shape. Springer-Verlag, Berlin, p 69–78

Ladinsky H, Consolo S 1979 The effect of altered function of dopaminergic neurons on the cholinergic system in the striatum. In: Tucek S (ed) The Cholinergic Synapse (Progress in brain research, 49). Elsevier, Amsterdam, p 411–419

Lagarde M, Guichardant M, Ghazi I, Dechavanne M 1980 Nicergoline, an anti-aggregating agent which inhibits release of arachidonic acid from human platelet phospholipids. Prostaglandins 19: 551–557

Lagergren K, Levander S 1974 Doppelblindstudie über die Wirkung von Piracetam auf perzeptorische und psychomotorische Leistung von Herz schrittmacher-Patienten bei verschiedenen Herzfrequenzen. Psychopharmacologia (Suppl 1): 97–104

Lancet 1969 Hyperbaric oxygen and senile psychosis. (Leading article). Lancet ii: 1348

Lancet 1970 A new line on age pigment. (Leading article). Lancet ii: 451–452

Lancet 1977a Cholinergic involvement in senile dementia. (Leading article). Lancet i: 408

Lancet 1977b Purinergic nerves. (Leading article). Lancet ii: 1331–1332

Lancet 1977c Hyperviscosity in disease. (Leading article). Lancet 2: 961

Lancet 1978a Red-cell deformability. (Leading article). Lancet ii: 1348

Lancet 1978b Circulating prostacyclin. (Leading article). Lancet ii: 21–22

Lancet 1980 Lecithin and memory. (Leading article). Lancet i: 293

Lassen N A 1968 Neurogenic control of CBF. Scandinavian Journal of Clinical and Laboratory Investigation 22 (Suppl 102) VI: F

Lassen N A, Ingvar D H 1980 Blood flow studies in the aging normal brain and in senile dementia. In: Amaducci L, Davison A N, Antuono P (eds) Aging of the Brain and Dementia (Aging 13). Raven Press, New York, p 91–98

Lassen N A, Pálvölgyi R 1968 Cerebral steal during hypercapnia and the inverse reaction during hypocapnia observed by the 133-Xenon technique in man. Scandinavian Journal of Clinical and Laboratory Investigation 22 (Suppl 102) XIII: D

Lassen N A, Munck O, Tottey E R 1957 Mental function and cerebral oxygen consumption in organic dementia. Archives of Neurology and Psychiatry (Chicago) 77: 126–133

Laux B E, Raichle M E 1978 The effect of acetazolamide on cerebral blood flow and oxygen utilization in the Rhesus monkey. Journal of Clinical Investigation 62: 585–592

Lavrentieva N B, Mchedlishvili G I, Plechkova E K 1968 Distribution and activity of cholinesterase in the nervous structures of the pial arteries (a histochemical study). Bulletin of Biological Medical Experiments in the USSR 64: 110–113

Lavy S, Melamed M, Bentin S, Cooper G, Rinot Y 1978 Bihemispheric decreases of regional cerebral blood flow in dementia: correlation with age-matched normal controls. Annals of Neurology 4: 445–450

Lavy S, Melamed M, Cooper G, Bentin S, Rinot Y 1979 Regional cerebral blood flow in patients with Parkinson's disease. Archives of Neurology 36: 344–348

Lawrence R M, Leichman N S 1965 Comparison of the effects of heparin sodium, xanthinol nicotinate (Complamin) and 2-dimethylaminoethanol (Deaner) in institutionalized geriatric groups. Journal of the American Geriatrics Society 13: 325–342

Lee B Y, Sakamoto H, Trainor F, Brody G, Cho Y W 1978 Comparison of soft gelatin capsule vs. sustained release formulation of papaverine HCl: vasodilation and plasma levels. International Journal of Clinical Pharmacology 16: 32–39

Legros J J, Gilot P, Seron X, Classens J, Adam A, Moeglen J M, Audibert A, Berchier P 1978 Influence of vasopressin on learning and memory. Lancet i: 41–42

Lehmann H E, Ban T A 1975 Central nervous system stimulants and anabolic substances in geropsychiatric therapy. In: Gershon S, Raskin A (eds) Aging 2. Raven Press, New York, p 179–202

Lemberger L, Crabtree R E 1980 Neuropharmacology of synthetic ergot derivatives in man. In: Goldstein M, Calne D B, Lieberman A, Thorner M O (eds) Ergot Compounds and Brain Function. Raven Press, New York, p 117–124

Lenzi G L, Jones T 1980 Cerebral metabolism-to-blood flow relationships with respect to aging and dementia. In: Amaducci L, Davison A N, Antuono P (eds) Aging of the Brain and Dementia (Aging 13). Raven Press, New York, p 99–102

Levy R 1978 Choline in Alzheimer's disease. Lancet ii: 944–945

Levy R I 1980 Drugs used in the treatment of hyperlipoproteinemias. In: Goodman A G, Goodman L S, Gilman A (eds) The Pharmacological Basis of Therapeutics, 6th edn. Macmillan, New York, p 839–840

Levy S 1953 Pharmacologic treatment of aged patients in a State mental hospital. Journal of the American Medical Association 153: 1260–1265

Lewis C, Ballinger B R, Presly A S 1978 Trial of levodopa in senile dementia. British Medical Journal 1: 550

Lieberman A, Dziatolowski M, Kupersmith M, Serby M, Goodgold A, Korein J, Goldstein M 1979 Dementia in Parkinson disease. Annals of Neurology 6: 355–359

Lightman S L, Forsling M L 1980 Evidence for endogenous opioid control of vasopressin release in man. Journal of Clinical Endocrinology and Metabolism 50: 569–571

Lim C C, Cook P J, James I M 1980 The effect of an acute infusion of vincamine and ethyl apovincaminate on cerebral blood flow in healthy volunteers. British Journal of Clinical Pharmacology 9: 100–101

Lindqvist T 1958 Klinisk prövning av Hexanicit, ett nikotinsyrapreparat med långvarig effekt. (Clinical testing of Hexanicit, a long-acting nicotinic acid preparation.) Svenska Läkartidningen 55: 1–15

Linée P, Lacroix P, Le Polles J B, Aurousseau M, Boulu R, Van den Driessche J, Albert O 1978 Cerebral metabolic, hemodynamic and antihypoxic properties of l-eburnamonine. European Neurology 17 (Suppl 1): 113–120

Lloyd K G, Davidson L, Hornykiewicz O 1973 Metabolism of levodopa in the human brain. Advances in Neurology 3: 173–188

Loew D M 1980 Pharmacologic approaches to the treatment of senile dementia. In: Amaducci L, Davison A N, Antuono P (eds) Aging of the Brain and Dementia (Aging 13). Raven Press, New York p 287–294

Loew D M, Weil C 1982 Hydergine in senile mental impairment. Gerontology 28: 54–74

Loew D M, Vigouret J M, Jaton A L 1976 Neuropharmacological investigations with two ergot alkaloids, Hydergine and bromocriptine. Postgraduate Medical Journal 52 (Suppl 1): 40–46

Loew D M, Vigouret J M, Jaton A L 1979 Effects of dihydroergotoxine mesylate (Hydergine®) on cerebral synaptic transmission. In: Meier-Ruge W (ed) CNS Aging and its Neuropharmacology (Interdisciplinary Topics in Gerontology, 15). S Karger, Basel, p 85–103

Loew D M, Vigouret J M, Jaton A L 1980 Neuropharmacology of bromocriptine and dihydroergotoxine (Hydergine). In: Goldstein M, Calne D B, Lieberman A, Thorner M O (eds) Ergot Compounds and Brain Function. Raven Press, New York, p 63–74

Loman J, Rinkel M, Myerson A 1941 The intracranial and peripheral vascular effects of nicotinic acid. American Journal of the Medical Sciences 202: 211–216

Longo V G, Loizzo A 1973 Effects of drugs on the hippocampal θ-rhythm: possible relationships to learning and memory processes. In: Pharmacology and the Future of Man. Proceedings of the 5th International Congress on Pharmacology, San Francisco, 1972, vol 4. S Karger, Basel, p 46–54

Loranger A W, Goodell H, Lee J E, McDowell F 1972 Levodopa treatment of Parkinson's syndrome: improved intellectual functioning. Archives of General Psychiatry 26: 163–168

Lowry O H 1975 Energy metabolism in brain and its control. In: Ingvar D H, Lassen N A (eds) Brain Work: The coupling of function, metabolism and blood flow in the brain. Munksgaard, Copenhagen, p 48–63

Lu L, Stotsky B A, Cole J O 1971 A controlled study of drugs in long-term geriatric psychiatric patients. Archives of General Psychiatry 25: 284–288

Luisada A A, Jacobs R, Bruce D, Bernstein J, MacCanon D M 1966 Action of a vasodilator on the circulation of the skull and brain. Vascular Diseases 3: 201–207

Lumsden C E, Pomerat C M 1951 Normal oligodendrocytes in tissue culture. Experimental Cell Research 2: 103–114

Lundgren O, Jodal M 1975 Regional blood flow. Annual Review of Physiology 37: 395–414

McDonald R J 1979 Hydergine: a review of 26 clinical studies. Pharmakopsychiatrie 12: 407–422

MacFarlane M D, Besbris H 1974 Procaine (Gerovital H3) therapy: mechanism of inhibition of monoamine oxidase. Journal of the American Geriatrics Society 22: 365–371

McGaugh J L 1973 Drug facilitation of learning and memory. Annual Review of Pharmacology 13: 229–241

McGeer E G, McGeer P L 1976 Neurotransmitter metabolism in the aging brain. In: Terry R D, Gershon S (eds) Neurobiology of Aging (Aging 3). Raven Press, New York p 389–403

McGeer E G, McGeer P L 1982 Neurotransmitters in normal aging.

In: Platt D (ed) Geriatrics I. Cardiology and vascular system; central nervous system. Springer-Verlag, New York, p 263–282

McGeer P L, McGeer E G 1979 Central cholinergic pathways. In: Barbeau A, Growdon J H, Wurtman R J (eds) Nutrition and the Brain, vol 5. Raven Press, New York, p 177–199

McGraw C P, Pashayan A G, Wendel O T 1976 Cerebral infarction in the Mongolian gerbil exacerbated by phenoxybenzamine treatment. Stroke 7: 485–488

McHenry L C 1972 Cerebral vasodilator therapy in stroke. Stroke 3: 686–691

McHenry L C 1978 Cerebral Circulation and Stroke. W H Geeen Inc, St Louis, Missouri, p 245–260

McHenry L C, Jaffe M E, Kawamura J, Goldberg H I 1970 Effect of papaverine on regional blood flow in focal vascular disease of the brain. New England Journal of Medicine 282: 1167–1170

McHenry L C, Jaffe M E, Kawamura J, Goldberg H I 1971 Hydergine effect on cerebral circulation in cerebrovascular disease. Journal of the Neurological Sciences 13: 475–481

McHenry L C, Jaffe M E, West J W, Cooper E S, Kenton E J, Kawamura J, Oshino T, Goldberg H I 1972 Regional cerebral blood flow and cardiovascular effects of hexobendine in stroke patients. Neurology (Minneapolis) 22: 217–223

McIlwain H 1972 Regulatory significances of the release and action of adenine derivatives in cerebral systems. Biochemistry Society Symposium 36: 69–85

McIlwain H 1977 Extended roles in the brain for second messenger systems. Neuroscience 2: 357–372

MacKay A V P, Yates C M, Wright A, Hamilton P 1978 Regional distribution of monoamines and their metabolites in the human brain. Journal of Neurochemistry 30: 841–848

Maclay W P 1979 Vasodilators in senile dementia. British Medical Journal 2: 866

Maggi A, Schmidt M J, Ghetti B, Enna S J 1979 Effect of aging in neurotransmitter receptor binding in rat and human brain. Life Sciences 24: 367–374

Maggi G C, Cerchiari D, Coppi G 1977 Papaverine blood levels after administration of a sustained-release preparation. Arzneimittel-Forschung 27: 1214–1215

Magnus R V, Cooper A J 1974 A controlled study of Reactivan in geriatrics. Modern Geriatrics 4: 270–277

Mainzer F 1949 Frühbehandlung des Schlaganfalls mit Aminophyllin. Schweizerische Medizinische Wochenschrift 79: 108–110

Malthe-Sørensen D, Wood P 1979 Modulation of acetylcholine turnover rate by neuropeptides. In: Tuček S (ed) The Cholinergic Synapse (Progress in brain research 49). Elsevier, Amsterdam p 486–487

Manna V, Conti L, Martucci N, Agnoli A 1982 EEG-pharmacological and neuropsychological study of (−) eburnamonine in patients with chronic cerebrovascular disorders. Current Therapeutic Research, Clinical and Experimental 32: 740–751

Marcer D, Hopkins S M 1977 The differential effects of meclofenoxate on memory loss in the elderly. Age and Ageing 6: 123–131

Marchi M, Hoffman D W, Giacobini E 1980 Aging alters acetylcholine metabolism in autonomic terminals. American Society of Neurochemistry (Abstract) 11: 84

Marc-Vergnes J-P, Bes A, Charlet J-P, Delpla M, Richardot J-P, Géraud J 1974 Pharmacodynamie de la circulation cérébrale. Bilan d'une étude de l'action de dix drogues sur débit sanguin et le métabolisme énergétique du cerveau chez les vasculaires cérébraux. (Pharmacodynamics of the cerebral circulation. Results of a study of the action of ten drugs on cerebral blood flow and metabolism in cerebrovascular insufficiency.) Pathologie et Biologie (Paris) 22: 815–825

Marsh G G, Markham C M, Ansel R 1971 Levodopa's awakening effect on patients with Parkinsonism. Journal of Neurology, Neurosurgery and Psychiatry 34: 209–218

Marsh G R, Linnoila M 1979 The effects of deanol on cognitive performance and electrophysiology in elderly humans. Psychopharmacology 66: 99–104

Martinez D M 1972 The effect of Serc (betahistine hydrochloride) on the circulation of the inner ear in experimental animals. Acta Otolaryngologica 305 (Suppl): 29–47

Matejcek M, Knor K, Piguet P-V, Weil C 1979 Electroencephalographic and clinical changes as correlated in geriatric patients treated three months with an ergot alkaloid preparation. Journal of the American Geriatrics Society 27: 198–202

Matsuda M, Meyer J S, Ott E O, Aoyagi M, Tagashira Y 1974 Cholinergic influence on autoregulation and CO_2 responsiveness of the brain. Circulation 50: III–90 (abstract)

Maynard E A, Schultz R L, Pease D C 1957 Electron microscopy of the vascular bed of the rat cerebral cortex. American Journal of Anatomy 100: 409–433

Meier-Ruge W (ed) 1978 Workship on advances in experimental pharmacology of Hydergine. Gerontology 24 (Suppl 1): 1–153

Meier-Ruge W 1982 Neurochemistry of the aging brain. In: Platt D (ed) Geriatrics I. Cardiology and vascular system; central nervous system. Springer-Verlag, New York, p 242–256

Meier-Ruge W, Gygax P, Emmenegger H, Iwangoff P 1979 Pharmacological aspects of ergot alkaloids in gerontological brain research. In: Cherkin A, Finch C E, Kharasch N, Makinodan T, Scott F L, Strehler B (eds) Physiology and Cell Biology of Aging (Aging 8). Raven Press, New York, p 203–221

Meier-Ruge W, Emmenegger H, Enz A, Gygax P, Iwangoff P, Wiernsperger N 1978 Pharmacological aspects of dihydrogenated-ergot alkaloids in experimental brain research. Pharmacology 16 (Suppl 1): 45–62

Meier-Ruge W, Enz A, Gygax P, Hunziker O, Iwangoff P, Reichlmeier K 1975 Experimental pathology in basic research of the aging brain. In: Gershon S, Raskin A (eds) Aging, vol 2. Raven Press, New York, p 55–126

Messing R B, Jensen R A, Martinez J L Jr, Spiehler V R, Vasquez B J, Soumireu-Mourat B, Liang D C, McGaugh J L 1979 Naloxone enhancement of memory. Behavioral and Neural Biology 27: 266–275

Meyer J S 1978 Improved method for noninvasive measurement of regional cerebral blood flow by ^{133}Xenon inhalation. Measurements in health and disease, part II. Stroke 9: 205–210

Meyer J S, Deshmukh V D, Welch K M A 1976a Experimental studies concerned with the pathogenesis of cerebral ischaemia and infarction. In: Ross Russell R W (ed) Cerebral Arterial Disease. Churchill Livingstone, Edinburgh, p 57–84

Meyer J S, Forst M, Meyer-Wahl L 1979 Verlauf des alkoholischen Prädelirs unter der Behandlung mit Piracetam. Deutsche Medizinische Wochenschrift 104: 911–914

Meyer J S, Mathew N T, Hartmann A 1976b Cerebral blood flow and metabolism changes in the epilepsies and during cerebral anoxia, ischemia and edema. In: Himwich H E (ed) Brain Metabolism and Cerebral Disorders, 2nd edn. Spectrum Publications Inc, New York, p 207–229

Meyer J S, Gotoh F, Akiyama M, Yoshitake S 1967 Monitoring cerebral blood flow, oxygen, and glucose metabolism. Analysis of cerebral metabolic disorder in stroke and some therapeutic trials in human volunteers. Circulation 36: 197–211

Meyer J S, Gotoh F, Gilroy J, Nara N 1965 Improvement in brain oxygenation and clinical improvement in patients with strokes treated with papaverine hydrochloride. Journal of the American Medical Association 194: 957–961

Meyer J S, Mathew N T, Hartmann A, Rivera V M 1974b Orally administered betahistine and regional blood flow in cerebrovascular disease. Journal of Clinical Pharmacology 14: 280–289

Meyer J S, Teraura T, Sakamoto K, Hashi K 1971 The effect of Pavabid (oral papaverine) on cerebral blood flow and metabolism in the monkey. Cardiovascular Research Centre Bulletin 9: 105–108

Meyer J S, Kondo A, Szewczykowski J, Nomura F, Teraura T 1970 The effects of a new drug (hexobendine) on cerebral hemodynamics and oxygen consumption. Journal of the Neurological Sciences 11: 137–145

Meyer J S, Kanda T, Shinohara Y, Fukuuchi Y, Shimazu K, Ericsson A D, Gordon W H Jr 1971 Effect of hexobendine on cerebral hemispheric blood flow and metabolism. Preliminary clinical observations concerning its use in ischemic cerebrovascular disease. Neurology (Minneapolis) 21: 691–702

Meyer J S, Shigemichi O, Shimazu K, Koto A, Ohuchi T, Sari A, Ericsson A D 1974a Cerebral metabolic changes during treatment of subacute cerebral infarction by alpha and beta adrenergic blockade with phenoxybenzamine and propranolol. Stroke 5: 180–195

Meyer J S, Welch K M A, Titus J L, Suzuki M, Kim H-S, Perez F I, Mathew N T, Gedye J L, Hrastnik F, Miyakawa Y, Achar V S, Dodson R F 1976c Neurotransmitter failure in cerebral

infarction and dementia. In: Terry R D, Gershon S (eds) Neurobiology of Aging (Aging 3). Raven Press, New York, p 121–138

Meynaud A, Grand M, Belleville M, Fontaine L 1975 Effet du naphtidrofuryl sur le métabolisme énergétique cérébral chez la souris. (Effect of naftidrofuryl on the energy metabolism of mouse brain.) Thérapie 30: 777–788

Miller E 1974 Deanol in the treatment of levodopa-induced dyskinesias. Neurology 24: 116–119

Miller E, Nieburg H A 1973 Amphetamines. New York State Journal of Medicine 73: 2657–2661

Miller R G 1963 Leptazol and mesoinositol hexanicotinate in the treatment of chronic cerebrovascular degenerative disorders. A double-blind study. Gerontologia Clinica 5: 95–102

Millikan C H, McDowell F H 1978 Treatment of transient ischemic attacks. Stroke 9: 299–308

Millington W R, McCall A L, Wurtman R J 1978 Deanol acetamidobenzoate inhibits the blood-brain barrier transport of choline. Annals of Neurology 4: 302–306

Mindus P 1978 Some clinical studies with piracetam — a 'nootropic' substance. In: Deniker P, Radouco-Thomas C, Villeneuve A (eds) Neuro-psychopharmacology, vol 1 (Proceedings of the 10th Congress Collagiate International on Neuro-psychopharmacology, Québec, 1976). Pergamon Press, Oxford, p 73–81

Mindus P, Cronholm B, Levander S E, Schalling D 1976 Piracetam-induced improvement of mental performance. A controlled study on normally aging individuals. Acta Psychiatrica Scandinavica 54: 150–160

Miyazaki H, Kagemoto A, Ishii M, Minaki Y, Nakamura K 1971 Uptake by brain and distribution of radioactivity after intravenous administration of ^{14}C-labelled meclofenoxate in mice. Chemical and Pharmaceutical Bulletin 19: 1681–1690

Miyazaki M 1971–1972 Effect of cerebral circulatory drugs on cerebral and peripheral circulation, with special reference to aminophylline, papaverine, cyclandelate and isoxsuprine. European Neurology 6: 162–165

Moncada S, Vane J R 1979 Pharmacology and endogenous roles of prostaglandin endoperoxides, thromboxane A_2 and prostacyclin. Pharmacological Reviews 30: 293–331

Mongeau B 1974 The effect of Hydergine on the transit time of cerebral circulation in diffuse cerebral insufficiency. European Journal of Clinical Pharmacology 7: 169–175

Montanari C, Vallecorsi G F, Bavazzano A, D'Ayalavalva G, Sanesi P 1976 Clinical trial with amantadine and pemoline in elderly patients. Age and Ageing 5: 6–11

Moretti A 1979 Metabolische und neurochemische Wirkung von Nicergolin auf das Zentralnervensystem. Übersicht über die experimentellen Untersuchungen. Arzneimittel-Forschung 29: 1213–1223

Moretti A, Arcari G, Pegrassi L 1979 Übersicht über pharmakologische Studien mit Nicergolin. Arzneimittel-Forschung 29: 1223–1227

Moyer J H, Tashnek A B, Miller S I, Snyder H, Bowman R O 1952 The effect of theophylline with ethylenediamine (Aminophylline) and caffeine on cerebral hemodynamics and cerebrospinal fluid pressure in patients with hypertensive headaches. American Journal of the Medical Sciences 224: 377–385

Muller H F, Grad B, Engelsmann F 1975 Biological and psychologic predictors of survival in a psychogeriatric population. Journal of Gerontology 30: 47–52

Munck O, Bärenholdt O, Busch H 1968 Cerebral blood flow in organic dementia measured with the Xenon-133 desaturation method. Scandinavian Journal of Clinical and Laboratory Investigation 22 (Suppl 102) XII: A

Muramoto O, Sugishita M, Sugita H, Toyokura Y 1979 Effect of physostigmine on constructional and memory tasks in Alzheimer's disease. Archives of Neurology 36: 501–503

Murphy D L 1973 Mental effects of L-dopa. Annual Review of Medicine 24: 209–216

Naber D, Dahnke H G 1979 Protein and nucleic acid content in the aging human brain. Neuropathology and Applied Neurobiology 5: 17–24

Nakajima H, Thuillier J 1964 Etude électroencéphalographique et électrocardiographique, chez le lapin éveillé, de l'anoxie histotoxique provoquée par le cyanure de potassium. Effects thérapeutiques de la centrophénoxine. (Electro-encephalographic and electrocardiographic study in the awake rabbit of the histotoxic anoxia provoked by potassium cyanide and the therapeutic effects of centrophenoxine.) Comptes Rendus des Séances de la Société de Biologie et de ses Filiales (Paris) 158: 982–985

Nakao M, Nakao T, Yamazoe S 1960 Adenosine triphosphate and maintenance of shape of the human red cells. Nature 187: 945–946

Nakao M, Wada T, Kamiyama T 1962 A direct relationship between adenosine triphosphate level and in vivo viability of erythrocytes. Nature 194: 877–878

Nandy K 1968 Further studies on the effects of centrophenoxine on the lipofuscin pigment in the neurons of senile guinea pigs. Journal of Gerontology 23: 82–92

Nandy K 1978 Centrophenoxine: effects on aging mammalian brain. Journal of the American Geriatrics Society 26: 74–81

Nandy K, Bourne G H 1966 Effect of centrophenoxine on the lipofuscin pigments in the neurons of senile guinea pigs. Nature 210: 313–314

Naritomi H, Sakai F, Meyer J S 1979 Pathogenesis of transient ischemic attacks within the vertebrobasilar arterial system. Archives of Neurology 36: 121–128

Nelson M, Dewitz G, Dom J, Horig C 1978 Prüfung der Wirksamkeit von Sibelium (flunarizin) bei Durchblutungsstörungen: eine multizentrische Doppelblindstudie. Medizinische Welt 29: 1175–1181

Nesse R, Carroll B J 1976 Cholinergic side-effects associated with deanol. Lancet ii: 50–51

Nickel J, Breyer U, Claver B, Quadbeck G 1963 Zur Wirkung von Aminoaethanol-Derivaten auf das Zentralnervensystem. (The effect of aminoethanol derivatives on the CNS.) Arzneimittel-Forschung 13: 881–883

Nickolson V J, Wolthuis O L 1976a Protein metabolism in the rat cerebral cortex in vivo and in vitro as affected by the acquisition-enhancing drug piracetam. Biochemical Pharmacology 25: 2237–2240

Nickolson V J, Wolthuis O L 1976b Effect of the acquisition-enhancing drug piracetam on rat cerebral energy metabolism. Comparison with naftidrofuryl and methamphetamine. Biochemical Pharmacology 25: 2241–2244

Nies A, Robinson D S, Davis J M, Ravaris L 1973 Changes in monoamine oxidase with aging. In: Eisdorfer C, Fann W E (eds) Psychopharmacology and aging: Advances in behavioral biology. Plenum Press, New York, p 41–54

Novack P, Shenkin H A, Bortin L, Goluboff B, Soffe A M 1953 The effects of carbon dioxide inhalations upon the cerebral blood flow and cerebral oxygen consumption in vascular disease. Journal of Clinical Investigation 32: 696–702

Novo F P, Ryan R P, Frazier E L 1978 Dihydroergotoxine mesylate in treatment of symptoms of idopathic cerebral dysfunction in geriatric patients. Clinical Therapeutics 1: 359–369

O'Brien I, Shelly K, Towfighi J et al 1980 Crystalline ribosomes are present in brains from senile humans. Proceedings of the National Academy of Sciences of the United States of America 77: 2260–2264

O'Brien M D 1971 Circulatory abnormalities in cerebrovascular disease. In: Stöcker G, Kuhn R A, Hall P, Becker G, Van der Veen E (eds) Assessment in Cerebrovascular Insufficiency. Georg Thieme Verlag, Stuttgart

O'Brien M D, Mallett B L 1970 Cerebral cortex perfusion rates in dementia. Journal of Neurology, Neurosurgery and Psychiatry 33: 497–500

O'Brien M D, Veall N 1966 Effects of cyclandelate on cerebral cortex perfusion rates in cerebrovascular disease. Lancet ii: 729–730

Obrist W D 1975 Cerebral blood flow and its regulation. Clinical Neurosurgery 22: 106–116

Obrist W D 1980 Cerebral blood flow and EEG changes associated with aging and dementia. In: Busse E W, Blazer D G (eds) Handbook of Geriatric Psychiatry. Van Nostrand Reinhold Co, New York, p 83–101

Obrist W D, Chivian E, Cronqvist S, Ingvar D H 1970 Regional cerebral blood flow in senile and presenile dementia. Neurology (Minneapolis) 20: 315–322

Oesterreich K, Tellenbach H 1967 Die Behandlung hirnatrophisch begründeter Versagenszustände mit Infusionen von Beta-Pyridyl-Carbinol (Ronicol). (The treatment of deficiency states due to cerebral atrophy with Ronicol infusions.) Nervenarzt 38: 34–36

Olesen J 1971 Contralateral focal increase of cerebral blood flow in man during arm work. Brain 94: 635–646

Olesen J 1974 Cerebral blood flow: methods for measurement, regulation, effects of drugs and changes in disease. Fadls Forlag, Copenhagen

Olesen J 1976 Effect of intracarotid prostaglandin E_1 on regional cerebral blood flow in man. Stroke 7: 566–569

Olesen J, Paulson O B 1971 The effect of intra-arterial papaverine on regional cerebral blood flow in patients with stroke or intracranial tumour. Stroke 2: 148–159

Olivari M T, Bartoreli C, Polese A, Fiorentini C, Moruzzi P, Guazzi M D 1979 Treatment of hypertension with nifedipine, a calcium antagonist agent. Circulation 59: 1056–1062

Oliveros J C, Jandali M K, Timsit-Berthier M, Remy R, Benghezal A, Audibert A, Moeglen J M, 1978 Vasopressin in amnesia. Lancet 1: 42

Ordy J M, Knack B 1975 Neurochemical changes in composition, metabolism and neurotransmitters in human brain with age. In: Ordy J M, Brizzee K R (eds) Neurobiology of Aging (Advances in behavioral biology 16). Plenum Press, New York, p 253–285

Ostfeld A, Smith C M, Stotsky B A 1977 The systemic use of procaine in the treatment of the elderly: a review. Journal of the American Geriatrics Society 25: 1–19

Oswald W D, Lang E 1980 Therapeutische Beeinflussung von Leistung und Selbstbild bei geriatrischen Patienten. Münchener Medizinische Wochenschrift 122: 59–62

Owman C, Edvinsson L, Hardebo J E, Gröschel-Stewart U, Unsicker K, Walles B 1977 Immunohistochemical demonstration of actin and myosin in brain capillaries. Acta Neurologica Scandinavica 56 (Suppl 64): 384–385

Pacheco e Silva A, Landi de Almeida S M 1981 Double-blind comparative study of cinnarizine and buflomedil in patients suffering from vascular cerebral insufficiency. Angiology 32: 728–732

Parkes J D, Marsden C D, Rees J E, Curzon G, Kantamaneni B D, Knill-Jones R, Akbar A, Das S, Kataria M 1974 Parkinson's disease, cerebral arteriosclerosis and senile dementia. Quarterly Journal of Medicine 63: 49–61

Pathy J, Menon G, Reynolds A, Van Strik R 1977 Bethahistine hydrochloride (Serc) in cerebrovascular disease: a placebo-controlled study. Age and Ageing 6: 179–184

Paul A, Chandra P 1979 Einfluß von Nicergolin auf molekularbiologische Prozesse im Gehirn und seine Auswirkung auf die Lernfähigkeit der Ratte. Arzneimittel-Forschung 29: 1238–1251

Pearse A G E 1977 The diffuse neuroendocrine system and the APUD concept: related 'endocrine' peptides in brain, intestine, pituitary, placenta and anuran cutaneous glands. Medical Biology 55: 115–125

Pede J P, Schimpfessel L, Crokaert R 1971 The action of piracetam on the oxidative phosphorylation. Archives Internationales de Physiologie et de Biochimie 79: 1036–1037

Peerless S J, Ishikawa K, Hunter I G, Peerless M U 1981 Protective effect of Fluosol-DA in active cerebral ischemia. Stroke 12: 558–568

Pelofsky S, Jacobson E D, Fisher R G 1972 Effects of prostaglandin E_1 on experimental cerebral vasospasm. Journal of Neurosurgery 36: 634–639

Pennington V M 1959 Clinical results with the use of deanol (Deaner) in schizophrenia. American Journal of Psychiatry 116: 165–166

Pepeu G, Freedman D X, Giarman N J 1960 Biochemical and pharmacological studies of dimethylaminoethanol (Deanol). Journal of Pharmacology and Experimental Therapeutics 129: 291–296

Perry E K, Perry R H, Blessed G, Tomlinson B E 1977 Necropsy evidence of central cholinergic deficits in senile dementia. Lancet i: 189

Perry T L, Kish S J, Buchanan J, Hansen S 1979 γ-Aminobutyric acid deficiency in brain of schizophrenic patients. Lancet i: 237–239

Peters B H, Levin H S 1977 Memory enhancement after physostigmine treatment in the amnesic syndrome. Archives of Neurology 34: 215–219

Peters B H, Levin H S 1979 Effects of physostigmine and lecithin on memory in Alzheimer disease. Annals of Neurology 6: 219–221

Peters B H, Levin H S 1982 Chronic oral physostigmine and lecithin administration in memory disorders of aging. In: Corkin S et al (eds) Alzheimer's Disease: a Report of Progress in Research (Aging 19). Raven Press, New York, p 421–426

Petrie W M 1978 Drugs in geropsychiatry. Psychopharmacology Bulletin 14: 7–19

Pfeiffer C C, Murphree H B Jr 1958 Stimulant effect of 2-dimethylaminoethanol in human subjects. Journal of Pharmacology and Experimental Therapeutics 122: 60A–61A

Pfeiffer C C, Groth D P, Bain J A 1959 Choline versus dimethylaminoethanol (deanol) as possible precursors of cerebral acetylcholine. In: Biological Psychiatry. Grune and Stratton, New York, p 259–272

Pfeiffer C C, Jenney E H, Gallagher W, Smith R P, Bevan W Jr, Killam K F, Killam E K, Blackmore W 1957 Stimulant effect of 2-dimethylaminoethanol — possible precursor of brain acetylcholine. Science 126: 610–611

Phillis J W, Edstrom J D, Kostopoulos G K, Kirkpatrick J R 1979 Effects of adenosine and adenine nucleotides on synaptic transmission in the cerebral cortex. Canadian Journal of Physiology and Pharmacology 57: 1289–1312

Phuapradit P, Phillips M, Lees A M, Stern G M 1978 Bromocriptine in presenile dementia. British Medical Journal 1: 1052–1053

Pickard J, Tamura A, Stewart M, McGeorge A, Fitch W 1980 Prostacyclin, indomethacin and the cerebral circulation. Brain Research 197: 425–431

Platt D (ed) Geriatrics I. Cardiology and vascular system; central nervous system. Springer-Verlag, New York

Plotkine M, Paultre C Z, Boulu R, Rossignol P 1975 Intérêt pharmacologique d'une technique d'enregistrement de la pO2 tissulaire du cortex cérébral chez le lapin. Réponse à la papavérine et au naftidrofuryl. (The pharmacological application of a method for the measurement of tissue pO2 in the cerebral cortex of the rabbit. Response to papaverine and to naftidrofuryl.) Thérapie 30: 713–723 (English abstract)

Plotnikoff N 1971 Pemoline: review of performance. Texas Reports on Biology and Medicine 29: 467–469

Pöch G, Kukovetz W R 1971 Papaverine-induced inhibition of phosphodiesterase activity in various mammalian tissues. Life Sciences 10(I): 133–144

Pomerat C M 1952 Dynamic neurogliology. Texas Reports on Biology and Medicine 10: 885–913

Popendiker K, Boksay I, Bollmann V 1971 Zur Pharmakologie des neuen peripheren Gefässdilatators 3,7-Dimethyl-l-(5-oxo-hexyl)-xanthin. (On the pharmacology of the new peripheral vasodilator 3,7-dimethyl-l-(5-oxo-hexyl)-xanthine.) Arzneimittel-Forschung 21: 1160–1171

Portnow S L, Ardis M B, Lubach J E 1960 The effect of Deanol on the activity of chronic schizophrenic patients. American Journal of Psychiatry 116: 748–749

Pourrias B, Raynaud G 1972 Action de quelques agents vaso-actifs sur l'irrigation sous corticale du lapin et du chien. (Effect of certain vasoactive agents upon subcortical blood flow in rabbit and dog.) Thérapie 27: 849–860 (English abstract)

Praga C, Tantalo V, Marangoni R 1979 Nicergolin und Thrombozytenaggregation: ein Überblick über experimentelle und klinische Studien. Arzneimittel-Forschung 29: 1270–1276

Prencipe M, Cecconi V, Pisarri F 1974 Osservazioni preliminari sull'azione del composto Nicergolina (F.I. 6714) sul flusso cerebrale. Il Farmaco (Ed Pr) 29: 278–284

Prien R F 1973 Chemotherapy in chronic organic brain syndrome. A review of the literature. Psychopharmacology Bulletin 9(4): 5–20

Prien R F, Cole J O 1978 The use of psychopharmacological drugs in the aged. In: Clark W G, del Giudice J (eds) Principles of Psychopharmacology. Academic Press, New York, p 593–605

Prinz P N 1977 Sleep patterns in the healthy aged: relationship with intellectual function. Journal of Gerontology 32: 179–186

Prinz P N, Peskind E R, Vitaliano P P, Raskind M A, Eisdorfer C, Zemcuznikov N, Gerber C J 1982 Changes in the sleep and waking EEGs of nondemented and demented elderly subjects. Journal of the American Geriatrics Society 30: 86–93

Pritchard J G, Mykyta L J 1975 Use of a combination of methylphenidate and oxyprenolol in the management of physically disabled, apathetic, elderly patients: a pilot study. Current Medical Research and Opinion 3: 26–29

Pull I, McIlwain H 1972 Output of (14C) adenine derivatives on electrical excitation of tissues from the brain: calcium ion-sensitivity

and an accompanying re-uptake process. Biochemical Journal 127: 91P

Purves M J 1972 The Physiology of the Cerebral Circulation. Cambridge University Press, Cambridge

Quadbeck G, Tarragó-Humet P 1972 Ricerche sperimentali sull'influenza dei derivati xantinici sul metabolismo cerebrale. (Experimental investigation of the effect of xanthine derivatives on cerebral metabolism.) Clinica Terapeutica 60: 125–133

Quadbeck G, Claver B, Minet G 1964 Einfluss von Stimulatien und Antidepressiva auf das Höhen-EEG der Ratte. Arzneimittel-Forschung 14: 563–565 (English abstract)

Rabassini A, Buoso M 1965 Sull'impiego di un'associazione di centrofenoxina e di tetranicotinoilfruttosio in psichiatria. (Psychiatric experience with an association of centrophenoxine and tetranicotinoylfructose.) Minerva Medica 56: 2467–2472

Raichle M E, Hartman B K, Eichling J O, Sharpe L G 1975 Central noradrenergic regulation of brain microcirculation. In: Harper A M, Jennett W B, Miller J D, Rowan J O (eds) Blood Flow and Metabolism in the Brain. Churchill Livingstone, Edinburgh, p 1.3–1.6

Raskin A, Gershon S, Crook T H, Sathananthan G, Ferris S 1978 The effects of hyperbaric and normobaric oxygen on cognitive impairment in the elderly. Archives of General Psychiatry 35: 50–56

Ré O 1974 2-dimethylaminoethanol (deanol): a brief review of its clinical efficacy and postulated mechanism of action. Current Therapeutic Research, Clinical and Experimental 16: 1238–1242

Regli F, Yamaguchi T, Waltz A G 1971a Responses of surface arteries and blood flow of ischemic and nonischemic cerebral cortex to aminophylline, ergotamine tartrate and acetazolamide. Stroke 2: 461–470

Regli F, Yamaguchi T, Waltz A G 1971b Cerebral circulation, effects of vasodilating drugs on blood flow and the microvasculature of ischemic and nonischemic cortex. Archives of Neurology 24: 467–474

Reisberg B, Ferris S H, Gershon S 1981 An overview of pharmacologic treatment of cognitive decline in the aged. American Journal of Psychiatry 138: 593–600

Reisberg B, Ferris S H, Anand R, Mir P, Geibel V, de Leon M J 1983 Effects of naloxone in senile dementia: a double-blind trial. New England Journal of Medicine 308: 721–722 (letter)

Reiss J, Standish M S, Rosomoff H J 1967 Effects of parenteral Vasodilan and Arlidin on cerebral and peripheral blood flow. Transactions of the American Neurological Association 92: 281–282

Reivich M, Sokoloff L, Kennedy C, Des Rosiers M 1975 An autoradiographic method for the measurement of local glucose metabolism in the brain. In: Ingvar D H, Lassen N A (eds) Brain Work: the coupling of function, metabolism, and blood flow in the brain. Munksgaard, Copenhagen, p 377–384

Renvoize E B, Jerram T 1979 Choline in Alzheimer's disease. New England Journal of Medicine 301: 330

Renvoize E B, Jerram T, Clough G 1978 Levodopa in senile dementia. British Medical Journal 2: 504

Richardson A E, Bereen F J 1977 Effect of piracetam on level of consciousness after neurosurgery. Lancet ii: 1110–1111

Rickels K, Gordon P E, Gansman D H, Weise C E, Pereira-Ogan J A, Hesbacher P T 1970 Pemoline and methylphenidate in mildly depressed outpatients. Clinical Pharmacology and Therapeutics 11: 698–710

Riklan M 1972 Levodopa and behavior. Neurology (Minneapolis) 22 (Suppl): 43–54

Risberg J, Ingvar D H 1968 Regional changes in cerebral blood volume during mental activity. Experimental Brain Research 5: 72–78

Risberg J, Ingvar D H 1973 Patterns of activation in the grey matter of the dominant hemisphere during memorizing and reasoning: a study of regional cerebral blood flow changes during psychological testing in a group of neurologically normal patients. Brain 96: 737–756

Rivera V M, Meyer J S, Baer P E, Faibish G M, Mathew N T, Hartmann A 1974 Vertebrobasilar arterial insufficiency with dementia. Controlled trials of treatment with betahistine. Journal of the American Geriatrics Society 22: 397–406

Roba, J, Roncucci R, Lambelin G 1977 Pharmacological properties of Suloctidil. Acta Clinica Belgica 32: 3–7

Robinson D S, Sourkes T L, Nies A, Harris L S, Spector S, Bartlett D L, Kaye I S 1977 Monoamine metabolism in human brain. Archives of General Psychiatry 34: 89–92

Robinson K 1972 A double-blind clinical trial of naftidrofuryl in cerebral vascular disorders. Medical Digest 17(12): 50–55

Roccatagliata G, Albano C, Cocito L, Maffini M 1979 Interactions between central monoaminergic systems: dopamine-serotonin. Journal of Neurology, Neurosurgery and Psychiatry 42: 1150–1162

Rogers W F, Shaikh V A R, Clark A N G 1970 Cyclandelate in long standing cerebral arteriosclerosis. Gerontologia Clinica 12: 88–93

Roland P E, Larsen B 1976 Focal increase of cerebral blood flow during stereognostic testing in man. Archives of Neurology 33: 551–558

Rønnov-Jessen V, Tjernlund A 1969 Hepatotoxicity due to treatment with papaverine: report of four cases. New England Journal of Medicine 281: 1333–1335

Rosier Y A 1975 Déficits circulatoires cérébraux et traitement des hyperlipidémies athérogènes. (Cerebral circulatory disorders and treatment of atherogenous hyperlipidaemias.) Cahiers de Médecine Lyonnais 51: 959–964

Rossor M N, Emson P C, Iversen L L, Neuropeptides and neurotransmitters in cerebral cortex in Alzheimer's disease. In: Corkin S et al (eds) Alzheimer's Disease: a Report of Progress in Research (Aging 19). Raven Press, New York, p 15–24

Rubin W, Anderson J R 1958 The management of circulatory disturbances of the inner ear. Angiology 9: 256–261

Rump S, Edelwejn Z 1968 Effects of centrophenoxine on electrical activity of the rabbit brain in sodium cyanide intoxication. International Journal of Neuropharmacology 7: 103–113

Russek H I, Zohman B L 1948 Papaverine in cerebral angiospasm (vascular encephalopathy). Journal of the American Medical Association 136: 930–932

Sacks O W, Messeloff C, Schartz W, Goldfarb A, Kohl M 1970 Effects of L-dopa in patients with dementia. Lancet i: 1231

Saletu B, Grünberger J 1980 Antihypoxidotic and nootropic drugs: proof of their encephalotropic and pharmacodynamic properties by quantitative EEG investigations. Progress in Neuro-psychopharmacology 4: 469–489

Saletu B, Grünberger J, Linzmayer L 1979 Bestimmung der enzephalotropen, psychotropen und pharmakoelektroenzephalographie und psychometrischer Analysen. Arzneimittel-Forschung 29: 1251–1261

Samanin R, Quattrone A, Consolo S, Ladinsky H, Algeri S 1978 Biochemical and pharmacological evidence of the interaction of serotonin with other aminergic systems in the brain. In: Garattini S, Pujol J F, Samanin R (eds) Interactions between Putative Neurotransmitters in the Brain. Raven Press, New York, p 383–399

Samuelsson B 1964 Identification of a smooth muscle stimulating factor in bovine brain. Biochimica et Biophysica Acta 84: 218

Sathananthan G L, Gershon S 1975 Cerebral vasodilators: a review. In: Gershon S, Raskin A (eds) Aging, vol 2. Raven Press, New York, p 155–168

Scheinberg P 1950 The effect of nicotinic acid on the cerebral circulation with observations on extracerebral contamination of cerebral venous blood in the nitrous oxide procedure for cerebral blood flow. Circulation 1: 1148–1154

Scheinberg P 1979 Survival of the ischaemic brain: a progress report. Circulation 60: 1600–1605

Schiebel M E, Lindsay R D, Tomisayu U, Schiebel A B 1975 Progressive dendritic changes in aging human cortex. Experimental Neurology 47: 392–403

Schiebel M E, Lindsay R D, Tomisayu U, Schiebel A B 1976 Progressive dendritic changes in aging human limbic system. Experimental Neurology 53: 420–430

Schieve J F, Wilson W P 1953 The influence of age, anesthesia and cerebral arteriosclerosis on cerebral vascular activity to carbon dioxide. American Journal of Medicine 15: 171–174

Schlichting K, Heidrich H 1976 Einfluss von Isoxsuprine auf die Blutviskosität. Vasa 5: 51–53

Schmidt L 1956 5-phenyl-2-imino-4-oxo-oxazolidin — ein zentral erregender Stoff. (5-phenyl-2-imino-4-oxo-oxazolidin — a central stimulating substance.) Arzneimittel-Forschung 6: 423–426

Schmitt G, Daake H 1971 Der Einfluss von Xantinolnicotinat auf die Vascularisation und auf die Ausbildung von Gefasskollateralen an Extremitätenarterien im Tierexperiment. (The influence of xantinol nicotinate on vascularisation and formation of vascular collaterals in extremity arteries in the animal experiment.) Arzneimittel-Forschung 21: 446–449

Schocken D D, Roth G S 1977 Reduced β-adrenergic receptor concentrations in aging man. Nature 267: 856–858

Schreiber H, 1960 Untersuchungen über die Änderung der Durchblutungsgröße des Gehirns unter 3-(Methyl-oxyäthylamino)-2-oxopropyl-theophyllin nikotinat mit Hilfe der Schädelrheographie. (Studies, with the aid of cranial rheography, of the alterations of cerebral blood supply under the influence of Complamin.) Medizinische Klinik 55: 509–511

Schwink A, Wetzstein R 1966 Die Kapillaren im subcommissuralorgan der ratte. Zeitschrift für Zellforschung und Mikroskopische Anatomie 73: 56–88

Seipel J H 1971 A rheoencephalographic study of the effect of betahistine hydrochloride on the normal human cerebral and scalp circulations. Federation Proceedings 30: 274

Seipel J H, Floam J E 1975 Rheoencephalographic and other studies of betahistine in humans. I. The cerebral and peripheral circulatory effects of single doses in normal subjects. Journal of Clinical Pharmacology 15: 144–154

Seipel J H, Fisher R, Floam J E, Bohm M 1975 Rheoencephalographic and other studies of betahistine in humans. II. The cerebral and peripheral microcirculatory effects of single doses in geriatric patients with 'pure' arteriosclerotic dementia. Journal of Clinical Pharmacology 15: 155–162

Seipel J H, Fisher R, Blatchley R J, Floam J E, Bohm M 1977 Rheoencephalographic and other studies of betahistine in humans. IV. Prolonged administration with improvement in arteriosclerotic dementia. Journal of Clinical Pharmacology 17: 140–161

Serby M 1982 REM sleep and senile dementia. Journal of the American Geriatrics Society 30: 422 (letter)

Settel E 1959 Stimulant therapy with deanol in depression, migraine and tension headaches. Journal of the American Geriatrics Society 7: 877–879

Shader R I, Goldsmith G N 1976 Dihydrogenated ergot alkaloids and papaverine: a status report on their effects in senile mental deterioration. In: Klein D F, Gittelman-Klein R (eds) Progress in Psychiatric Drug Treatment, vol 2. Brunner-Mazel, New York, p 540–554

Shaw S W J, Johnson R H 1975 The effect of naftidrofuryl on the metabolic response to exercise in man. Acta Neurologica Scandinavica 52: 231–237

Shaw T G, Meyer J S 1978 Double-blind trial of oral papaverine in chronic cerebrovascular ischemia. Angiology 29: 839–851

Shenkin H A 1951 Effects of various drugs upon cerebral circulation and metabolism of man. Journal of Applied Physiology 3: 465–471

Shih J C, Young H 1978 Alteration of serotonin binding sites in aged human brain. Life Sciences 23: 1441–1448

Siesjö B K, Ljunggren B 1973 Cerebral energy reserves after prolonged hypoxia and ischemia. Archives of Neurology 29: 400–403

Siesjö B K, Nilsson B 1982 Prostaglandins and the cerebral circulation. In: Oates J A (ed) Prostaglandins and the Cardiovascular System. Raven Press, New York, p 367–380

Siesjö B K, Johansson H, Norberg K, Salford L 1975 Brain function, metabolism and blood flow in moderate and severe arterial hypoxia. In: Ingvar D H, Lassen N A (eds) Brain Work: the coupling of function, metabolism and blood flow in the brain. Munksgaard, Copenhagen, p 101–119

Signoret J L, Whiteley A, Lhermitte F 1978 Influence of choline on amnesia in early Alzheimer's disease. Lancet ii: 837

Simard D, Olesen J, Paulson O B, Lassen N A, Skinhøj E 1971 Regional cerebral blood flow and its regulation in dementia. Brain 94: 273–288

Sitaram N, Weingartner H, Gillin J C 1978a Human serial learning: enhancement with arecholine and choline and impairment with scopolamine. Science 201: 274–276

Sitaram N, Weingartner H, Caine E D, Gillin J C 1978b Choline: selective enhancement of serial learning and encoding of low imagery words in man. Life Sciences 22: 1555–1560

Skinhøj E 1972 The sympathetic nervous system and the regulation of cerebral blood flow in man. Stroke 3: 711–716

Skinhøj E 1975 The effect of a new carbonic anhydrase inhibitor upon CBF and CMRO$_2$. In: Harper A M, Jennett W B, Miller J D,

Rowan J O (eds) Blood Flow and Metabolism in the Brain. Churchill Livingstone, Edinburgh, p 11.7–11.8

Skinhøj E, Paulson O B 1970 The mechanism of action of aminophylline upon cerebral vascular disorders. Acta Neurologica Scandinavica 46: 129–140

Skinhoj E, Hoedt-Rasmussen K, Paulson O B, Lassen N A 1970 Regional cerebral blood flow and its autoregulation in patients with transient focal cerebral ischemic attacks. Neurology (Minneapolis) 20: 485–493

Smart R G 1967 Magnesium pemoline. Science 155: 603–604

Smith C B 1980 Effects of aging on local rates of glucose utilization in the rat brain. In: Amaducci L, Davison A N, Antuono P (eds) Aging of the Brain and Dementia (Aging 13). Raven Press, New York, p 103–112

Smith C B, Swash M 1980 Effects of cholinergic drugs on memory in Alzheimer's disease. In: Amaducci L, Davison A N, Antuono P (eds) Aging of the Brain and Dementia (Aging 13). Raven Press, New York, p 295–304

Smith C M, Hoffer A, Dantow M, McIntyre S 1963 Nicotinic acid therapy in old age. The placebo effect and other factors in the collection of valid data. Journal of the American Geriatrics Society 11: 580–585

Snyder S H, Innis R B 1979 Peptide neurotransmitters. Annual Review of Biochemistry 48: 755–782

Soininen H, Partanen V J, Helkala E-L, Riekkinen P J 1982 EEG findings in senile dementia and normal aging. Acta Neurologica Scandinavica 65: 59–70

Sokoloff L 1960 The effect of carbon dioxide on the cerebral circulation. Anesthesiology 21: 664–673

Sokoloff L 1966 Cerebral circulatory and metabolic changes associated with aging. Research Publications, Association for Research in Nervous and Mental Disease 41: 237–254

Sokoloff L 1975 Cerebral circulation and metabolism in the aged. In: Gershon S, Raskin A (eds) Aging 2. Raven Press, New York, p 45–54

Sommer H 1965 Nicotinsäure — Spiegel im Blut und Fibrinolyse unter Einwirkung des Hexanicotinsäureesters des m-Inosits. Arzneimittel-Forschung 15: 1337–1339

Soni S D, Soni S S 1975 Dihydrogenated alkaloids of ergotoxine in nonhospitalized elderly patients. Current Medical Research and Opinion 3: 464–468

Sourander L, Blakemore C B 1978 Effects of cyclospasmol upon sensory parameters in patients recovering from cerebrovascular accidents. Angiology 29: 133–138

Sourander L, Ruikka I, Rautakorpi J 1970 Psychological methods applied to evaluation of symptomatic geriatric treatment. Geriatrics 25: 124–137

Spillane J A, Goodhardt M J, White P, Bowen D M, Davison A N 1977 Choline in Alzheimer's disease. Lancet ii: 826–827

Spruill J H Jr, Toole J F, Kitto W, Miller H E 1975 A comparison of betahistine hydrochloride with placebo for vertebral-basilar insufficiency: a double-blind study. Stroke 6: 116–120

Squire L R 1976 Amnesia and the biology of memory. In: Essman W B, Valzelli L (eds) Current Development in Psychopharmacology, vol 3. Spectrum Publications Inc, New York, p 1–23

Staessen A J 1977 Treatment of circulatory disturbances with flunarizine and cinnarizine. Vasa 6: 59–71

Stefanovich V 1974 Concerning specificity of the influence of pentoxifylline on various cyclic AMP phosphodiesterases. Research Communications on Chemical Pathology and Pharmacology 8: 673–680

Stefanovich V 1978 The biochemical mechanism of action of pentoxifylline. Pharmatherapeutica 2 (Suppl 1): 5–16

Stefanovich V, John J P 1974 The increase of cyclic AMP in rats' brain during anoxia. Research Communications on Chemical Pathology and Pharmacology 9: 591–593

Steger W 1973 Die Beeinflussung des Plättchenagglutinationstestes durch Xantinolnicotinat. (The effect of xantinol nicotinate on the platelet aggregation test.) Medizinische Welt 24: 301–302

Stein L, Belluzzi J D 1978 Brain endorphins and the sense of well-being: a psychological hypothesis. In: Costa E, Trebucchi M (eds) The Endorphins (Advances in Biochemical Psychopharmacology, 18). Raven Press, New York, p 299–311

Steiner T, Capildeo R, Rose F C 1979 New approach to treatment of recent stroke. British Medical Journal 1: 412

Stoica E, Meyer J S, Kawamura Y, Hiromoto H, Hashi K, Aoyagi M, Pascu I 1973 Central neurogenic control of cerebral circulation. Effects of intravertebral injection of pyrithioxin on cerebral blood flow and metabolism. Neurology (Minneapolis) 23: 687–698

Stuart S E 1967 Long-acting form of the peripheral vasodilator, nicotinyl alcohol: double-blind evaluation. Journal of the American Geriatrics Society 15: 780–785

Suga F, Snow J B Jr 1969 Cochlear blood flow in response to vasodilating drugs and some related agents. Laryngoscope 79: 1956–1979

Sullivan E V, Shedlack K J, Corkin S, Growdon J H 1982 Physostigmine and lecithin in Alzheimer's disease. In: Corkin S et al (eds) Alzheimer's Disease: a Report of Progress in Research (Aging 19). Raven Press, New York, p 361–367

Sundt T M, Michenfelder J D 1971–1972 Cerebral ATP and lactate levels with electrocorticogram correlation before, during, and after middle cerebral artery occlusion in the squirrel monkey. European Neurology 6: 73–77

Sutherland E W 1970 On the biological role of cyclic AMP. Journal of the American Medical Association 214: 1281–1288

Sutherland E W 1972 Studies on the mechanism of hormone action. Science 177: 401–408

Sweet R D, McCowell F H 1975 Five years' treatment of Parkinson's disease with levodopa: therapeutic results and survival of 100 patients. Annals of Internal Medicine 83: 456–463

Szewczykowski J, Meyer J S, Kondo A, Nomura F, Teraura T 1970 Effects of ergot alkaloids (Hydergine) on cerebral hemodynamics and oxygen consumption in monkeys. Journal of the Neurological Sciences 10: 25–31

Talland G A, Hogen D Q, James M 1967 Performance tests of amnesic patients with Cylert. Journal of Nervous and Mental Disease 144: 421–429

Tanaka K, Gotoh F, Muramatsu F, Fukuuchi Y, Amano T, Okayasu H, Suzuki N 1980 Effects of nimodipine (Bay e 9736) on cerebral circulation in cats. Arzneimittel-Forschung 30: 1494–1497

Taylor A R 1971 Speculation about the site of action of Cyclospasmol on cerebral metabolism. In: Stöcker G, Kuhn R A, Hall P, Becker G, van der Veen E (eds) Assessment in Cerebrovascular Insufficiency. Georg Thieme Verlag, Stuttgart, p 141–145

Tazaki Y, Omae T, Kuromaru S, Ohtomo E, Hasegawa K, Mori A, Kurihara M, Kutsusawa N, Okada T 1980 Clinical effect of encephabol (Pyritinol) in the treatment of cerebrovascular disorders. Journal of International Medical Research 8: 118–126

Terry R D, Gershon S (eds) 1976 Neurobiology of Aging (Aging 3). Raven Press, New York

Teychenne P F, Jones E A, Ishak K G, Calne D B 1979 Hepatocellular injury with distinctive mitochondrial changes induced by lergotrile mesylate: a dopaminergic ergot derivative. Gastroenterology 76: 575–583

Thal L-J, Fuld P A 1983 Memory enhancement with oral physostigmine in Alzheimer's disease. New England Journal of Medicine 308: 720 (letter)

Theis H, Lehrach F, Müller R 1978 A 5-year review of clinico-experimental and therapeutic experience with pentoxifylline. Pharmatherapeutica 2 (Suppl 1): 150–160

Thomas D J, DuBoulay G H, Marshall J, Pearson T C, Ross Russell R W, Symon L, Wetherley-Mein G, Zilkha E 1977 Effect of haematocrit on cerebral blood flow in man. Lancet ii: 941–943

Thompson L J, Proctor R C 1954 The effect of nicotinic acid and pentylenetetrazol in the therapy of psychiatric symptoms of cerebral arteriosclerosis. North Carolina Medical Journal 15: 596–598

Thompson L W 1975 Effects of hyperbaric oxygen on behavioral functioning in elderly persons with intellectual impairment. In: Gershon S, Raskin A (eds) Aging, vol 2. Raven Press, New York, p 169–177

Thompson L W, Davis G C, Obrist W D, Heyman A 1976 Effects of hyperbaric oxygen on behavioral and physiological measures in elderly demented patients. Journal of Gerontology 31: 23–28

Thuillier J 1960 Étude pharmacologique de l'ester diméthylaminoethylique de l'acide p-chlorophénoxyacétique (235 ANP.) (Pharmacological study on the dimethylaminoethyl ester of p-chlorophenoxyacetic acid (ANP 235).) Agressologie 1: 78–86 (English abstract)

Thuillier G, Rumpf, P. Thuillier J 1959 Préparation et étude pharmacologique préliminaire des esters diméthylaminoethyliques des divers acides agissant comme régulateurs de croissance des végétaux. Comptes Rendus Hebdomadaires des Séances de l'Académie des Sciences (Paris) 249: 2081–2083

Tinklenberg J R, Pigache R, Pfefferbaum A, Berger P A 1982 Vasopressin peptides and dementia. In: Corkin S et al (eds) Alzheimer's Disease: a Report of Progress in Research (Aging 19). Raven Press, New York, p 463–468

Toda N, Miyazaki M 1978 Responses of isolated dog cerebral and peripheral arteries to prostaglandins after application of aspirin and polyphloretin phosphate. Stroke 9: 490–498

Todorov A B, Go R C P, Constantinidis J, Elston R C 1975 Specificity of the clinical diagnosis of dementia. Journal of the Neurological Sciences 26: 81–98

Toledo J B, Pisa H, Marchese M 1972 Clinical evaluation of cinnarizine in patients with cerebral circulatory deficiency. Arzneimittel-Forschung 22: 448–451

Tomita M, Gotoh F, Sato T, Amano T, Tanahashi N, Tanaka K, Yamamoto M 1978 Comparative responses of the carotid and vertebral arterial systems of rhesus monkeys to betahistine. Stroke 9: 382–387

Tomlinson B E, Henderson G 1976 Some quantitative cerebral findings in normal and demented old people. In: Terry R D, Gershon S (eds) Neurobiology of Aging (Aging 3). Raven Press, New York, p 183–204

Toole J F, Janeway R, Choi K, Cordell R, Davis C, Johnston F, Miller H S 1975 Transient ischemic attacks due to atherosclerosis. Archives of Neurology 32: 5–12

Toyoda M, Takagi S, Seki T, Takeoka T, Gotoh F 1975 Effect of a new vasodilator (flunarizine) on the cerebral circulation. Journal of the Neurological Sciences 25: 371–375

Trabant R, Poljakovič Z, Trabant D 1977 Zur Wirkung von Piracetam auf das hirnorganische Psychosyndrom bei zerebrovasculärer Insuffizienz. Ergebnis einer Doppelblindstudie bei 40 Fällen. Therapie der Gegenwart 116: 1504–1521

Triggle D J 1982 Biochemical pharmacology of calcium blockers. In: Flaim S F, Zelis R (eds) Calcium blockers: mechanisms of action and clinical application. Urban and Schwarzenberg, Baltimore p 121–134

Uemura E, Hartmann H A 1978 RNA content and volume of nerve cell bodies in human brain. I. Prefrontal cortex in aging normal and demented patients. Journal of Neuropathology and Experimental Neurology 37: 487–496

Uemura E, Hartmann H A 1979a RNA content and volume of nerve cell bodies in human brain. II. Subiculum in aging normal patients. Experimental Neurology 65: 107–117

Uemura E, Hartmann H A 1979b Quantitative studies of neuronal RNA on the subiculum of demented old individuals. Brain Research Bulletin 4: 301–305

Urban I, De Wied D 1978 Neuropeptides: effects on paradoxical sleep and theta rhythm in rats. Pharmacologoy and Biochemical Behaviour: 8: 51–59

Urquhart N, Perry T L, Hensen S, Kennedy J 1975 GABA content and glutamic acid decarboxylase activity in brain of Huntington's chorea patients and control subjects. Journal of Neurochemistry 24: 1071–1075

Usdin E, Bunney W E Jr, Kline N S (eds) Endorphins in Mental Health Research. Macmillan and Co, New York

Valle-Jones J C 1978 Pemoline in the treatment of psychogenic fatigue in general practice. Practitioner 221: 425–427

Van den Akker S, Bijlsma U G, van Dongen K, ten Thije J H 1957 The effect of the 3,3,5-trimethylcyclohexanol ester of mandelic acid on artificially produced cardiac infarction and on experimentally produced necrosis of skeletal muscle. Arzneimittel-Forschung 7: 15–19

van der Drift J H A 1961 Ischemic cerebral lesions. Angiology 12: 401–418

van der Drift J H A, Kok N K D 1971 Transient ischaemic attacks. In: Stöcker G, Kuhn R A, Hall P, Becker G, van der Veen E (eds) Assessment in cerebrovascular insufficiency. George Thieme Verlag, Stuttgart, p 132–135

van der Meer-van Manen A H E 1967 Klinische evaluatie can cinnarizine bij geriatrische patienten. (Cinnarizine in the treatment of geriatric patients.) Nederlandsch Tijdschrift voor Geneeskunde 111: 256–261

van Essen C 1974 Effects of dopamine on the cerebral blood flow in the dog. Acta Neurologica Scandinavica 50: 39–52

van Hell G 1974 Action of cyclandelate on the development of collateral vessels in the rabbit. Current Medical Research and Opinion 2: 211–217

van Nueten J M, Janssen P A J 1973 Comparative study of the effects of flunarizine and cinnarizine on smooth muscles and cardiac tissues. Archives Internationales de Pharmacodynamie et de Thérapie 204: 37–55

van Nueten J M, Wellens D 1979 Mechanisms of vasodilatation and antivasoconstriction. Angiology 30: 440–446

van Ree J M, De Wied D 1976 Neurohypophyseal hormones and morphine dependence. In: Kosterlitz H W (ed) Opiates and Endogenous Opioid Peptides. North-Holland, New York, p 443–445

van Woert M H, Heninger G, Rathey U, Bowers M B Jr 1970 L-dopa in senile dementia. Lancet i: 573–574

Velkov V A 1973 Gerontological changes of ATP content and K-Na-ATPase activity in rat brain. Folia Morphologica (Praha) 21: 345–347

Venn D 1976 Electroencephalogram and ergot alkaloids. Postgraduate Medical Journal 52 (Suppl 1): 55–56

Venn R D 1980 Review of clinical studies with ergots in gerontology. In: Goldstein M, Calne D B, Lieberman A, Thorner M O (eds) Ergot Compounds and Brain Function. Raven Press, New York, p 363–377

Vereczkey L, Czira G, Tamás J, Szentirmay Z, Botár Z, Szporny L 1979 Pharmacokinetics of vinpocetine in humans. Arzneimittel-Forschung 29: 957–960

Verhaegen H, Roels V, Adriaensen H, Brugmans J, De Cock W, Dony J, Jageneau A, Schuermans V 1974 The arteriolar effects of cinnarizine and flunarizine. Multi-technical investigations in normal volunteers and in patients with occlusive disease of the extremities secondary to arteriosclerosis. Angiology 25: 261–278

Vestal R E, Wood A J J, Shand D G 1979 Reduced beta-adrenoreceptor sensitivity in the elderly. Clinical Pharmacology and Therapeutics 26: 181–186

Vigouret J M, Bürki H R, Jaton A L, Züger P E, Loew D M 1978 Neurochemical and neuropharmacological investigations with four ergot derivatives: bromocriptine, dihydroergotoxine, CF 25–397 and CM 29–712. Pharmacology 16 (Suppl 1): 156–173

Viviano M, Ceccarelli G 1966 L'impiego terapeutico dell'associazione necofuranosio-centrofenoxina nelle psicosi involutive. (Therapeutic use of an association of nicofuranose and Centrophenoxine® in involutional psychoses.) Minerva Medica 57: 3965–3969

Wahl M, Deetjen P, Thurau K, Ingvar D H, Lassen N A 1970 Micropuncture evaluation of the importance of the perivascular pH for the arteriolar diameter on the brain surface. Pflügers Archiv für die Gesamte Physiologie des Menschen und der Tiere 316: 152–163

Walker J E, Hoehn M, Sears E, Lewis J 1973 Dimethylaminoethanol in Huntington's chorea. Lancet 1: 1512–1513

Wang H S, Obrist W D 1976 Effect of oral papaverine on cerebral blood flow in normals: evaluation by the Xenon-133 inhalation method. Biological Psychiatry 11: 217–225

Way E L, Glasgow C E 1978 The endorphins: possible physiologic roles and therapeutic applications. Clinical Therapeutics 1: 371–386

Weber G, Kreisel T, Peter S, Künzel J 1980 A double-blind placebo-controlled cross-over study in patients with peripheral vascular diseases, using a new capillary viscometer. Angiology 31: 1–5

Wechsler R L, Kleiss L M, Kety S S 1950 The effects of intravenously administered aminophyllin on cerebral circulation and metabolism in man. Journal of Clinical Investigation 29: 28–30

Wecker L, Schmidt D E 1979 Central cholinergic function: relationship to choline administration. Life Sciences 27: 375–384

Wedgwood J 1970 Results of a pilot double-blind trial with cyclandelate (Cyclospasmol) in elderly patients with intellectual deterioration. In: Stöcker G, Kuhn R A, Hall P, Becker G, van der Veen E (eds) Assessment in Cerebrovascular Insufficiency. George Thieme Verlag, Stuttgart, p 43–50

Weed R I, La Celle P L, Merrill E W 1969 Metabolic dependence of red cell deformability. Journal of Clinical Investigation 48: 795–809

Weigelin E, Sayegh F 1968 Zur Objectivierung des zerebralen durchblutungsfördernden Effektes vasoaktiver Substanzen unter besonderer Berücksichtigung von Cinnarizin. (Objective evaluation of vasoactive drugs improving cerebral blood flow, and of cinnarizine in particular.) In: Heinrich K (ed) Aktuelle Probleme der psychiatrischen Pharmakotherapie in Klinik und Praxis. Schattauer, Stuttgart, p 3–12

Weingartner H, Gold P, Ballenger J C, Smallberg S A, Summers R, Rubinow D R, Post R M, Goodwin F K 1981 Effects of vasopressin on human memory functions. Science 211: 601–603

Wells R E 1964 Rheology of blood in microvasculature. New England Journal of Medicine 270: 832–839

Westreich G, Alter M, Lundgren S 1975 Effect of cyclandelate on dementia. Stroke 6: 535–538

Whisnant J P 1974 Epidemiology of stroke: emphasis on transient cerebral ischemic attacks and hypertension. Stroke 5: 68–70

Whittier J R 1964 Vasorelaxant drugs and cerebrovascular disease. Angiology 15: 82–87

Whittier J R, Dhrymiotis A D 1962 Prevention of slow wave response to hyperventilation in the human electroencephalogram by a vasodilator. Angiology 13: 324–327

Wilkinson I M S, Bull J W D, DuBoulay G H, Marshall J, Ross Russell R W, Symon L 1969 Regional blood flow in the normal cerebral hemisphere. Journal of Neurology, Neurosurgery and Psychiatry 32: 367–378

Wilsher C, Atkins G, Manfield P 1979 Piracetam as an aid to learning in dyslexia: preliminary report. Psychopharmacology 65: 107–109

Winsor T, Hyman C, Knapp F M 1960 The cerebral peripheral circulatory action of nylidrin hydrochloride. American Journal of the Medical Sciences 239: 594–600

Winter R, Schmitt G, Knoche H 1973 Durchblutungssteigerung verschiedener Organe nach Xantinol-nicotinat im akuten Tierexperiment. (Acute animal experiments on the increase in blood perfusion of various organs following xantinol nicotinate.) Arzneimittel-Forschung 23: 652–653

Witzmann H K, Blechacz W 1977 Zur Stellung von Vincamin in der Therapie zerebrovasculärer Krankheiten und zerebraler Leistungsminderungen. Arzneimittel-Forschung 27: 1238–1247

Wolf S M, Davis R C 1973 Permanent dementia in idiopathic parkinsonism treated with levodopa. Archives of Neurology 29: 276–278

Wolfe L S, Coceani F 1979 The role of prostaglandins in the central nervous system. Annual Review of Physiology 41: 669–684

Wolff J R 1968 Die Astroglia im Gewebsverband des Gehirns. (The role of the astroglia in the brain tissue) Acta Neuropathologica (Berlin) (Suppl 4): 33–39

Wurtman R J, Zeisel S H 1982 Brain choline: its sources and effects on the synthesis and release of acetylcholine. In: Corkin S, Davis K L, Growdon J H, Usdin E, Wurtman R J (eds) Alzheimer's disease: a report of progress in research (Aging 19). Raven Press, New York, p 303–313

Wurtman R J, Hirsch M J, Growdon J H 1977 Lecithin consumption raises serum-free-choline levels. Lancet ii: 68–69

Wurtman R J, Magil S G, Reinstein D K 1981 Piracetam diminishes hippocampal acetylcholine levels in rats. Life Sciences 28: 1091–1093

Wyper D J, McAlpine C J, Jawad K, Jennett B 1976 Effects of a carbonic anhydrase inhibitor on cerebral blood flow in geriatric patients. Journal of Neurology, Neurosurgery and Psychiatry 39: 885–889

Yamaguchi F, Meyer J S, Sakai F, Yamamoto M, Shaw T 1979 Behavioral activation testing in the dementias. In: Meyer J S, Lechner H, Reivich M (eds) Cerebral vascular disease 2 (Proceedings of the 9th International Salzburg Conference, September 27–30, 1978). Excerpta Medica, Amsterdam, p 121–132

Yates C M, Allison Y, Simpson J, Maloney A F J, Gordon A 1979 Dopamine in Alzheimer's disease and senile dementia. Lancet ii: 851–852

Yesavage J A, Hollister L E, Burian E 1979b Dihydroergotoxine: 6 mg versus 3 mg dosage in the treatment of senile dementia. Preliminary resport. Journal of the American Geriatrics Society 27: 80–82

Yesavage J A, Leirer V O, Becker L, Holman C 1981 Effect of an ergot preparation on cognitive ability and depression. Journal of Psychiatric Treatment and Evaluation 3: 153–156

Yesavage J A, Tinklenberg J R, Hollister L E, Berger P A 1979a Vasodilators in senile dementias. Archives of General Psychiatry 36: 220–223

Yesavage J A, Tinklenberg J R, Hollister L E, Berger P A 1982 Effect of nafronyl on lactate and pyruvate in the cerebrospinal fluid of patients with senile dementia. Journal of the American Geriatrics Society 30: 103–108

York E L, Sproule B J 1978 Cerebral blood flow and polycythaemia. Lancet i: 152–153

Yoshikawa M, Hirai S, Aizawa T, Kuroiwa Y, Gotoh F, Sofue I, Toyokura Y, Yamamura H, Iwasaki Y 1983 A dose-response study with dihydroergotoxine mesylate in cerebrovascular disturbances. Journal of the American Geriatrics Society 31: 1–7

Young J, Hall P, Blakemore C 1974 Treatment of the cerebral manifestations of arteriosclerosis with cyclandelate. British Journal of Psychiatry 124: 177–180

Zahniser N R, Hanin I 1976 Deanol and the cholinergic system: a gas chromatographic evaluation. Federation Proceedings 35: 801

Zeisel S H, Garry P J, Brigida M, Magil S G, Goodwin J S, Alvarez N 1982 Serum choline concentration in aged humans. In: Corkin S, Davis K L, Growdon J H, Usdin E, Wurtman R J (eds) Alzheimer's disease: a report of progress in research (Aging 19). Raven Press, New York, p 45–47

Zervas N T, Lavyne M H, Negoro M 1975 Neurotransmitters and the normal and ischemic cerebral circulation. New England Journal of Medicine 293: 812–816

Zielinski H W 1968 Zur Behandlung der arteriosklerotischen Chorioretinopathie. (On the treatment of arteriosclerotic chorioretinopathy.) Klinische Monatsblätter fur Augenheilkunde 172: 233–241 (English abstract)

Zimmerman H J 1969 Papaverine revisited as a hepatotoxin. New England Journal of Medicine 281: 1364–1365

Zimmerman I, Berg A 1974 Levels of adenosine 3',5' cyclic monophosphate in the cerebral cortex of aging rats. Mechanisms of Ageing and Development 3: 33–36

The central nervous system — clinical presentation and management of neurological disorders in old age

AGING AND NEUROLOGICAL SIGNS

The clinical presentation of neurological disorders in the elderly is frequently coloured by age-related changes in the central nervous system. Physical signs indicative of disease in the young may in the aged be unrelated to clinical nervous disorders. Normal neurological findings may be lost or exaggerated or signs primarily confined to infancy may reappear in old age. In the Goulstonian Lectures, Critchley (1931) highlighted the influence of aging on neurological signs.

Tendon reflexes
The ankle jerk is the first and most frequent tendon reflex to be lost in the elderly (Critchley, 1931; Howell, 1949; Smith, 1956; Bryndum and Marquarsden, 1964; Milne and Williamson, 1972; Bhattia and Irvine, 1973). The only recorded exception to these findings was in a community survey by Hobson and Pemberton (1955) who noted the knee and ankle tendon reflexes to be absent with equal frequency. Superficial reflexes become initially sluggish and commonly absent with advancing age (Critchley, 1931, 1956).

Primitive reflexes
These reflexes are normally found in early infancy, but disappear as the child matures. Their reappearance in old age is commonly due to diffuse irreversible brain disease (Paulson and Gottlieb, 1968). A number of primitive reflexes have been described, but only the more significant of these warrant discussion.

Sucking reflex
Light stroking of the lips produces sucking movement; if the stimulus is applied to the lateral margins of the lips, the head turns towards the source of the stimulus.

Pouting or snout reflex
Pouting the lips on lightly tapping the area above the upper lip or stroking the oral region may reappear in patients with bilateral corticospinal tract lesions above

the upper brain stem and is commonly found in chronic dementing states (Ajuriaguerra et al, 1963). The closely relating sucking and pouting reflexes have been noted following intensive phenothiazine therapy (Schmidt and Jarcho, 1966).

Nuchocephalic reflex
Rapid turning of the shoulders to the right or left is followed by turning of the head in the same direction. In infants and children up to age four the head remains central on rapidly moving the shoulders. This nucho-cephalic reflex reappears in early dementia, (Jenkyn et al, 1974).

Grasp reflex
This reflex is a flexion of the fingers with adduction of the thumb in response to stroking the palm of the hand. A closely related phenomenon of forced groping may be demonstrated when the eyes are closed and the palmar surface of the fingers lightly touched. The fingers close on the object and the hand and arm move towards the stimulus. A unilateral grasp reflex may be present in frontal lobe tumours and vascular accidents; in diffuse cortical atrophy the reflex may be bilateral (Rushworth and Denny-Brown, 1959). Analogous to the grasp reflex in the hand is flexion and adduction of the toes often associated with inversion and incurving of the foot when the sole is stimulated. This reflex response is almost invariably found in the newborn, but may re-emerge in senescence. As direct pressure on the sole of the foot may evoke the reflex, gait may be disturbed.

Palmomental reflex
Momentary contraction of the mentalis muscle elicited by stroking the thenar eminence of the ipsilated hand was first demonstrated by Marinesco and Radovici (1920). Otomo (1965) found a positive reflex in 2.3 per cent of students aged 15 to 24 years, 27.1 per cent of persons in the fifth decade and 53.5 per cent of subjects aged 60 and over, but the frequency of this reflex in healthy adults has varied in different reports,

(McDonald et al, 1963). A positive palmo-mental reflex is common in dementia, and in Parkinsonism. It may be an early sign of frontal lobe lesions (Bracha, 1958).

Gegenhalten (paratonia)

Increased muscle tone is commonly found in old age (Critchley, 1931; Prakash and Stern, 1973). Gegenhalten is a condition characterized by excessive motor tone during passive manipulation of the limbs, often suggestive of deliberate resistance, and may be accentuated by the rapid passive flexing and extending of the limbs — the resistance may be avoided if the movements are performed slowly. The rigidity of gegenhalten is inconstant in contrast to the plastic type of rigidity in Parkinsonism. Critchley noted that the tendency to a flexed posture with age may progress to marked general curvature. In advanced dementia this postural state may develop through a phase of paratonic rigidity to episodic flexion of arms and legs and finally sustained curving of the trunk and permanent flexion of upper and lower limbs (Yakolev, 1954).

Glabellar tap reflex

First described by Myerson (1944), this sign is a blink response to lightly tapping the glabella prominence. Blinking in response to the first few taps is common in normal subjects, but in Parkinson's syndrome (Myerson, 1944; Wartenberg, 1952; Garland, 1952, 1955; Schwab and England, 1958) the blink reaction continues with repeated taps and has been regarded as diagnostic of this disorder. Wright and Boyd (1964) found a positive glabellar tap sign in 60 per cent of patients over the age of 60 in the absence of clinical Parkinsonism. Parkes and Marsden (1973) regard the sign as of little diagnostic value in Parkinson's syndrome and noted it to be present in patients without this disease.

Corneo-mandibular reflex

This reflex is rarely found in healthy adults, but is present in 50 per cent of newborn infants (Paulson and Bird, 1971). The reappearance of this reflex is prominent in diffuse brain disease and may be a finding in Alzheimer's disease, multi-infarct dementia and motor neurone disease with mid-brain involvement. A unilateral corneomandibular reflex may be elicited in patients with a hemiplegia.

Sensory changes

Taste and smell significantly decline with age (Cooper et al, 1959; Grzegorczyk et al, 1979). Pain threshold is increased in the elderly (Procacci et al, 1970), but subjective sensory complaints are common, particularly formication and paraesthesiae (Pearson, 1928), and 'intractable symptoms of tic douloureux and postherpetic neuralgia are characteristic of old age' (Critchley,

1931). Vibration sensibility diminishes after the age of 50 (Pearson, 1928; Prakash and Stern, 1973), though postural sense is less often affected. Vibration sense is lost most frequently over bony prominences at the medial malleolus. Bender (1975) found that vibration sense might be present over bony prominences but absent in the soft tissues of the abdomen, thighs and legs and plantar surfaces of the toes in older subjects. In a series of 150 subjects aged 60 and over he found that 48 per cent had some defect of vibratory perception. The vibratory threshold is increased in the elderly (Whanger and Wang, 1974). Age-related neuronal degeneration occurs in the dorsal column of the spinal cord (Andrew, 1971) and this has been postulated as a possible explanation for diminished sensory awareness in later life. The decline in proprioceptive feedback performance with age is consistent with the hypothesis of impaired dorsal column function (Levin and Benton, 1973).

Other aspects of perceptual deficiency in later life have been documented. Bender et al (1951) and Fink et al (1952) noted an increased prevalence in later life of the inability to recognise as two separate stimuli the simultaneous touching of the subject's hand and face. Simple modification of the above test allowed assessment of an order of dominance in perceptual responses through the body and the detection of interaction between visual and tactile stimuli (Bender, 1970; Bender and Feldman, 1972; Green and Fink, 1974).

In subjects over 60 who were not colour-blind, Bender (1975) found that 48 per cent had had defects in colour perception. Using a test of large figures made up of a series of small figures, Bender and Feldman (1972) showed that patients with diffuse brain disease could usually see the small figures, but failed to perceive the large figure.

Tremor

Physiological tremor is present in the limbs at all ages and has a frequency of 6–15 Hz. Marshall and Walsh (1957) noted a lower frequency in children and old people, but Zwishenberger et al (1976) showed that amplitude and frequency of finger micro-tremor did not alter with age. Coakley and Thomas (1976) found no significant age-related change in the frequency of normal ocular microtremor. Considerable confusion exists over the distinction between types of tremor (Brumlik and Yapp, 1971). However, three types of physiological tremor have been characterized: rest tremor of the relaxed muscles which has a frequency range of 8–12 Hz; postural tremor illustrated when the subject holds out the arms with the muscles in a state of isometric contraction against gravity and having a tremor frequency of 8–12 Hz; action or volition tremor occurring during isotonic contraction of muscles with a frequency range of 7–12 Hz (Brimblecombe and Pinder,

1972). The incidence of clinical tremor in later life is controversial, but our experience is in accord with Critchley (1956a) who regarded tremor as uncommon in healthy old age. Seven per cent of subjects in the Duke Longitudinal Survey (Newman et al, 1970) had involuntary movements or tremor.

The label 'senile tremor' portrays a fine or coarse tremor of the hands of variable amplitude and not infrequently associated with rhythmical oscillation of the head anterio-posteriorly or from side to side. Careful enquiry will often establish the involuntary shaking as an exaggeration of a mild tremor extant for many years and a feature of familial or benign essential tremor. This form of tremor may be considered as enhanced physiological tremor (Marsden, 1978). Tremor associated with erratic choreiform movements may develop in progressive dementia (Allison, 1962).

Posture

Normal erect posture is relatively rare in late old age (Horenstein, 1974). A tendency to stand with slightly flexed hips and knees is common in the very elderly and is probably largely due to altered neuromuscular control, impaired muscle power and degenerative joint disease. Vestibular function plays little role in static posture or in righting reactions (Martin, 1967), but when sitting or standing on an unstable base, balance is seriously compromised if vestibular function is impaired (Martin, 1965).

Posture is dependent on proprioception where vision cannot be used as in blindness or darkness. Ability to cope in the dark progressively deteriorates with age and closely parallels the incidence of falls. In both situations women are considerably more affected than men.

Postural sway

Sway is a normal phenomenon and is determined by oscillations of two distinct frequencies. Fast oscillations are consequent on information from the ankle joints (Begbie, 1967) and feet (Orma, 1957). Slow oscillations appear to depend, at least in part, on vestibular influences. Looking at the feet aggravates normal postural sway probably due to reduction in peripheral visual information (Begbie, 1967). Hasselkus and Shambes (1975) showed that postural sway in female volunteers is significantly greater in the 70–80 year old than in subjects 20–30 years of age. Sheldon (1963) showed that control of stance as judged by static sway was poor in early childhood, but reaches an optimum in early adulthood and progressively deteriorates from the fifties onwards. Among the subjects of all age studied by Sheldon, one-third of those over the age of 60 were unable to minimize the amplitude of static sway by visual endeavour. This subgroup consisted predominantly of women and all had sustained one or more falls. Increased sway is most evident in old people with a history of falls due to drop attacks, loss of balance and giddiness (Overstall et al, 1977).

Gait

In the Duke Longitudinal Survey (1970) 15 per cent of subjects had some alteration in gait, most commonly a shortened stride or shuffling. Ten per cent showed loss of associated arm movement with walking.

Muscle change

Muscle atrophy is an age-related phenomenon and it is manifest before body weight declines (Fujisawa, 1974). The total number of muscle fibres diminishes with age and the size of the motor unit is reduced. Muscle wasting is most noticeable in the small muscles of the hand, particularly the first dorsal interosseus. Muscle strength in the arms and shoulders does not change significantly until after the middle 60s (Shock and Norris, 1970) but hand grip strength declines considerably after 50 years of age (Bourlière, 1963). McComas and his colleagues (1971; 1973) showed progressive loss of muscle units in small muscles of the hands and

Table 18.1 Main groups of atrophy (Gutmann, 1970)

Disuse	Denervation	'Functional' denervation	Hormone substrate deficiency
Reduction or loss of nerve-impulse activity	Absence of transmitter and/or neurotrophic agents released	Progressive reduction of spontaneous and impulse-directed transmitter release and other neurotrophic agents	Mixed metabolic and structural changes, more resembling simple atrophy
No or little decrease of spontaneous transmitter release			
'Simple' atrophy: reduction in size but not in number of muscle-fibres	Nerve degeneration Specific membrane and intracellular metabolic changes	Structural and metabolic changes intermediate between disuse and denervation	
Proportional decrease of enzyme activity	Fibrillation Increase of ACh sensitivity		

striking loss of motor neurones after aged 60. However, the experimental method used considered that all motor units have the same size. Gutmann and Hanzliková (1976) indicate that this assumption cannot be maintained. Table 18.1 shows the main groups of atrophy.

The pupils

The elderly pupil is characteristically small and minor differences in size of the two pupils are not uncommon. Relaxation and accommodation time increases progressively, reaching a maximum at about the age of 50. Critical flicker frequency decreases with age at all levels of brightness. The threshold of illumination rises through the second half of life (Birren and Shock, 1950).

CLINICAL FEATURES AND MANAGEMENT OF NEUROLOGICAL DISORDERS IN OLD AGE

Parkinson's syndrome

Epidemiological studies in the United States (Postkanzer and Schwab, 1963) and in the United Kingdom (Brown and Knox, 1972) have indicated an annual increase in the age of onset of Parkinson's syndrome, but this may represent improved recognition of the disease in an age group in whom widespread interest was hitherto conspicuous by its absence (Kurland et al, 1973). The proposition that Parkinson's disease is due to a single aetiology has been espoused by those who believe that the epidemic of encephalitis lethargica which swept the world from 1918–1926 provided the causal viral agent (Poskanzer and Schwab, 1963). Many of the clinical features of post-encephalitic parkinsonism (e.g. oculogyric crises) are not to be found in Parkinson's disease. In both presentations the substantia nigra is affected, but Lewy bodies are absent in post-encephalitic parkinsonism. Antigenic binding sites to influenza A virus are present in the brains of patients with the latter condition, but not in Parkinson's disease (Gamba et al, 1974).

A genetic basis has been documented in a small number of patients (Martin et al, 1973).

The possibility that aging may impair mechanisms which protect the monoaminergic cells from damage by the oxidative products of cellular metabolism has been postulated (Yahr, 1981). Cerebral atherosclerosis has been proposed as a major factor accounting for the increased incidence of the syndrome in advanced age. The general feature of the 'arteriopath' with historical and clinical evidence of minor strokes without limb paresis, with language disorder, deteriorating intellect and chaotic gait with abducted feet frequently 'freezing' to the ground, irregular length of stride, a trunk not uncommonly extended, difficulty in climbing stairs and a doubtful response to Levodopa, is in considerable contrast to Parkinsonism, though an immobile face, plastic rigidity and involuntary movements are points of resemblance. Evidence would suggest that multi-infarct disease rather than cerebral arteriosclerosis *per se* produces this picture (Hatchinski et al, 1974).

The phenothiazine group of drugs which block dopamine receptors in the brain is a significant cause of Parkinson's syndrome.

The general features of Parkinson's disease produce a distinctive picture, though individual elements may be clinically extreme or barely detectable. Early in the disease, symptoms may be firmly expressed, but parallel definitive findings absent. A common example is subjective weakness of a limb without objective confirmation. An animated account of symptoms in the absence of the normal numerous small movements of the head, hands and feet that characterize patients at a medical interview is of diagnostic import.

Facial immobility is usually pronounced, and the stare so familiar to this syndrome results from the infrequent blinking, diminished occular movement, widened palpebral fissure and static position of the head and neck. During speech there is poverty of facial expression, and the response to emotional events such as smiling has an artificial appearance as change slowly spreads and recedes across the face. When the articulatory muscles are involved, speech becomes slow, slurred and monotonous. The voice is soft and quiet and difficulty in initiating speech is not uncommon (Mawdsley, 1973). Occasionally bouts of rapid disjointed word fragments are interjected (Mawdsley and Gamsu, 1971). In advanced stages anarthria may occur. Dysphagia due to hypopharyngeal neuromuscular incoordination has been recorded (Palmer, 1974). Dopamine is of major importance in the act of spontaneous and reflex swallowing, particularly in initiating the act of swallowing (Bieger et al, 1977). It has been suggested that the dysphagia of Parkinson's disease may be due to dopamine acetylcholine imbalance (Bramble et al, 1978). Where akinesia is prominent difficulty in initiating sitting up, or turning in bed, or rising from a chair presents at a time when tremor or rigidity are barely evident. Fine finger movements are poor and micrographia is an early feature. Associated movements are often absent and arm swing is lost in walking. Rigidity does not appear to influence arm swing: indeed reciprocal arm swing may continue on walking even in the presence of marked muscle rigidity (Hallett et al, 1977).

Difficulty is often experienced in initiating the act of walking or in changing direction. Steps are short and the gait slow and shuffling with a marked tendency to propulsion or retropulsion. Stair-climbing and stepping over obstacles is often accomplished with surprising agility.

Two components can be identified in voluntary movements. 'Open-loop' movements which are pre-programmed and carried out independently of sensory input and 'closed-loop' movements where these factors are operative. Flowers (1976) produced experimental evidence to show that the ballistic or 'open-loop' type of movement is disrupted in Parkinsonism.

The general flexed attitudes graphically described by James Parkinson (1817) affects the neck and trunk, and the limbs exhibit both modest flexion and adduction (Fig. 18.1). In the fingers, flexion is initially in the metacarpophalangeal joints, but later involves the interphalangeal joints, though the thumb is adducted and extended.

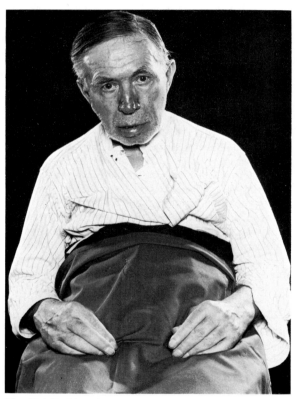

Fig. 18.1 Parkinsonism

Tremor may be the first symptom to herald Parkinsonism and may become severe and distressing or remain slight and only obvious during emotional stress. Resting tremor has a rate between 4 and 5 Hz and postural tremor a rate of 6–7 Hz. Postural tremor has been considered to be exaggerated physiological tremor (Lance et al, 1963), but this view has been refuted (Gesty and Findley, 1981). Resting or postural tremor is not a feature of drug-induced Parkinsonism. Tremor is depressed by muscle rigidity and tends to be predominant in the smaller and more peripheral muscles of the limbs. It is normally overtly present at rest and typically abolished by movement. Tremor usually commences in one upper limb, commonly followed by involvement of the lower limb of the same side, before the second upper limb is involved. Rhythmic flexion and extension of the metacarpo-phalangeal joints with adduction of the thumb is responsible for the classical pill-rolling movements. Tremor may move from one muscle group to another. In the lower jaw the movement is in a vertical plane. Head tremor is rare.

Rigidity is almost invariably present in the elderly with Parkinson's disease but may require careful attention to detail to elicit. Varying the rate at which passive movements at the joint is made or simultaneous movements in the opposite corresponding limb by a second observer may be helpful where doubt exists. The normal increased rigidity that may occur with age is readily distinguished by its uniformity at all joints. The ability to voluntarily relax muscles diminishes with the progress of Parkinson's disease and later continuous muscle contraction produces the characteristic flexed posture. When rigidity is severe, contractures may develop and restrict movement. Action tremor may add a 'cog-wheel' quality to the rigidity. Rigidity and akinesia in the absence of tremor is a feature of phenothiazine-induced Parkinsonism as is the intense desire to move the limbs without the ability to do so — akathisia.

Falls are common in Parkinsonism, and several factors may be inculpated. Trips may result from the shuffling gait. Following a sudden change in the centre of gravity, difficulty is experienced in restoring equilibrium due to the slowness of muscle movements and impairment of normal righting mechanisms. In a study of autonomic function in Parkinson's disease, Appenzeller and Goss (1971) found that compensatory vasoconstriction was defective in all patients tested by the Valsalva manoeuvre. Keenan (1970) noted orthostatic hypotension in 23 per cent of subjects with Parkinsonism treated with Levodopa, but there is no clear consensus of opinion on postural hypotension in untreated Parkinson's disease. Apenzeller and Goss suggested that postural blood change was insignificant in patients untreated with L-dopa, but Reid et al (1971); Bannister (1971) and Gross et al (1972) reported convincing postural falls of blood pressure in the absence of L-dopa administration. In our experience orthostatic hypotension is common in untreated elderly patients with Parkinsonism and accounts for a proportion of their falls.

Other features of Parkinsonism may at times dominate the clinical scene. Excessive salivation is the commonest autonomic disturbance and is persistent and intensely embarrassing. Akinesia of the muscles involved in swallowing is a major factor in the pooling of saliva in the mouth. Cutaneous vasodilation with undue feeling of warmth, even in a cold environment, may lead to hypothermia. Depression is the psychiatric disorder most frequently observed in Parkinsonism.

Treatment

In a disease with long-term disability, a general concept of management must take cognizance of the multifaceted social interactions that result from impaired functional capacity. In Parkinson's disease diminishing social contact with increasing isolation is common and the savour of life rapidly diminishes. This aspect is given preliminary emphasis lest we should overlook the broader realms of this disorder, whilst we are engrossed in specific therapy which does not invariably ameliorate symptoms. A return will be made to general measures after discussing the role of drug therapy.

The major neurochemical abnormality in Parkinson's disease is a reduction in neurotransmitter dopamine and its synthesising hormones, tyrosine hydrolase and dopa decarboxylase in the striatum and substantia nigra due to selective loss of melanin containing neurones (Ehringer and Hornykiewicz, 1960; Lloyd et al, 1975; McGeer and McGeer, 1976). There are other neurotransmitter disturbances particularly of noradrenaline but the most significant appears to be the alteration in the normal sensitive reciprocal relationship between dopamine and acetylcholine activity which leads to increased acetyl-choline activity as striatal dopamine production diminishes. Early in the disorder increased dopamine production by the remaining nigral neurones may possibly produce a compensated state and therapeutic strategy might be directed towards maintaining this balance.

Anticholinergic drug. The anticholinergic drugs have formed the basis of drug treatment of Parkinson's disease for over a hundred years. Since 1945 synthetic anticholinergic agents have progressively replaced the solanaceous alkaloids, but belladonna preparations remain useful in controlling excessive salivation. This group of drugs produces a modest reduction in rigidity and slight improvement in tremor. Benzhexol, perhaps one of the most effective of the synthetic anticholinergic drugs, produces confusion in a high proportion of the very old. Confusion is a much less common complication with the recently introduced, but related drug, benapyrazine.

De Smet and his colleagues (1982) have shown that anticholinergic drugs almost invariably produce confusion in Parkinsonian patients with pre-existing dementia.

Where phenothiazine preparations have induced Parkinsonism, treatment is withdrawal of the offending drug.

Levodopa. The enthusiasm of the 70's for early exhibition of levodopa has given way to a degree of pharmacological conservatism in the initial stages of the disorder (Lesser et al, 1979). Where there is no functional impairment, encouragement to continue a fully active lifestyle with low-profile surveillance is probably the most suitable approach.

The use of agents aimed at inhibiting the degradation of dopamine (e.g. deprenyl) as effective first line management in early Parkinson's disease has yet to be established.

Dopamine will not cross the blood-brain barrier, but its precursor, L-dopa does so readily. L-dopa remains the single most effective agent in symptomatic Parkinson's disease. The drug is now generally used in combination with a peripheral decarboxylase inhibitor either as carbidopa in a ratio of 1 : 10 (carbidopa: L-dopa) or more recently in the more effective ratio of 1:4 or as benzerazide/levodopa also in ratios of 1:4. The latter preparation commenced at the combined dose of 62.5 mg twice daily is well tolerated. It is rare to require in excess of 1.0 g of levodopa/benzerazide combination daily in divided doses and symptoms are controlled in the majority of patients by a half or less of this daily dose.

The predominant early side-effects of L-dopa therapy are nausea or vomiting, but depression, delusions and hyperactive confusional states are occasional adverse complications. Nausea may be controlled by the antiemetic metoclopramide, 10 mg to 30 mg daily, but multiple medication is frequently difficult to maintain in old age. Involuntary movements are a common late manifestation of well-controlled Parkinson's disease. They tend to be largely athetoid in nature and affect the tongue, mouth, neck and usually limbs. Myoclonic jerks may also occur. L-Dopa induced involuntary movements are closely dose-related and will usually subside with relatively small decrements of the drug. Unfortunately, optimum control of the Parkinsonian features also declines.

Rapid intermittent dyskinesia (on-off effect) occurs in about 10 per cent of patients treated with L-dopa for 2 years or more (Damasio et al, 1973).

End-of-dose akinesia. This is particularly evident in patients maintained on high-dose L-dopa regimen for several years and commonly occurs about 3 hours after each dose of drug.

Psychiatric symptoms which include reversible confusional states, hallucinations and nightmares may complicate long term L-dopa administration. Within 5–10 years of L-dopa treatment, there is significant diminuition of the therapeutic response which may be due to natural progress of the disease or to changes in dopamine receptor site sensitivity (Markham et al, 1974; Weiner and Bergman, 1977), or accumulation of dopa metabolites (other than dopamine) at striatal receptor sites (Lesser et al, 1979).

The treatment of the long-term side effects of levodopa and lack of responsiveness has been tackled by either adding or substituting other anti-Parkinsonian drugs or by manipulating the L-dopa regimen.

Drug holidays consisting of short term withdrawal of L-dopa therapy in hospital for 7–14 days have been suggested as a method of management of complications and failing therapeutic response (Wiener et al, 1979; Koller et al, 1980; Direnfeld et al, 1980). L-dopa withdrawal is followed by an intense exacerbation of symptoms requiring considerable medical and nursing supervision to prevent catastrophic complications, but up to a third of patients derive significant benefit (Feldman et al, 1979). Response to recommencing treatment is rapid and L-dopa dose requirement can be substantially reduced. Goetz and his colleagues (1981) reported significant benefit from a drug holiday for 2 days each week undertaken with the patient at home. Over 50 per cent of patients continued on the regimen for over 12 months. We have obtained similar results from using small doses of L-dopa/benzerazide e.g. 31.2 mg made up as a suspension, given hourly during the waking hours for 7–10 days.

Deprenyl. The monoamine oxidase inhibitor, deprenyl, inhibits the degradation of dopamine and is particularly useful in potentiating the anti-akinetic effect of L-dopa. In doses of 10 mg daily it significantly prolongs the beneficial effects of levodopa and is of particular value in over 50 per cent of patients with end of dose phenomena. Drug induced involuntary movements may be accentuated by deprenyl.

Bromocriptine. This drug is a dopaminergic ergot derivative. It potentiates the effect of L-dopa and usually allows dose reduction. It ameliorates some of the long term side effects of L-dopa, particularly akinesia and on-off reactions, but the benefit often only lasts for a few months. However, these side effects seem to rarely, if ever, occur where bromocriptine is used without L-dopa (Parks et al, 1976; Lieberman et al, 1979).

Initial dosing with 1.25 mg reduces the likelihood of side effects. Increments should be made over at least 2 months and maximum doses of 150 mg have been suggested, but we have found a maximum dose of 25 mg is appropriate.

The side effects include confusion and/or hallucinations, dyspnoea or overt signs of heart failure, postural hypotension and erythromelalgia. Though widely reported nausea has been uncommon in our experience. Liver enzymes may be raised and indicates a need for dose reduction.

Lergotrile and lisurmide have broadly similar effects to bromocriptine and are both postsynaptic dopamine receptor agonists. Hepatoxicity makes lergotrile unsuitable for prolonged use and the efficacy of both lergotrile and lisurmide decline after some months (Lieberman et al, 1981).

Amantadine produces some reduction in the disability of Parkinson's syndrome in about 25 per cent of patients. Improvement is rarely of the magnitude of that obtained with L-dopa therapy and is often not maintained for more than 6 to 12 months. In doses of 100 mg, 2 or 3 times daily, tolerance is good, but confusion, oedema and livido reticularis are side-effects. Postma and van Tilburg (1975) reported hallucinations and delusions in old age. Amantadine has an additive effect in some patients who are unable to tolerate optimum doses of L-dopa.

General management

As with any person with chronic disability, the patient with Parkinson's disorder is prone to social isolation, loneliness, lack of motivation and subsequent restriction of mobility, greater than that engendered by the physical ailment. Any programme of management will require to redress these factors in so far as it is possible. Succour and mutual support both for the patient and his relatives is often provided by associations catering specifically for this disability (in the United Kingdom, the Parkinson's Disease Society).

An interlude in physical activity of even a few days may be catastrophic. If intercurrent disease supervenes, significant bed-rest should be eschewed if at all possible. The time/pressure threshold to the ischaemic effect of compression of tissue between bone and mattress falls markedly with pyrexia (Pathy, 1959) and pressure necrosis is a major hazard in Parkinsonism.

Every effort is required to improve the level of mobility by gait retraining. It is regrettable that physical treatment is all too often omitted from the therapeutic equation in the early stages of disability. A patient barely able to stand can often walk upstairs and the barely ambulant can step over obstacles with unexpected agility. Passive swinging of the arms will significantly improve the lengths of stride. It is our experience that by using these observable features, the physiotherapist can often achieve gratifying improvement even with advanced disability.

Where functional retraining does not produce sufficient improvement for full personal independence, the redesign of clothing may be critical.

Subdural haematoma

Three forms may be recognized — acute, subacute and chronic. Though all three types may occur in the elderly, chronic subdural haematoma is the form so characteristic of old age that discussion will be limited to this presentation.

Gardener (1932) believed that lyses of the red cells of the haematoma increased the osmotic gradient and drew CSF into the encapsulated area. This view has been refuted by Weir (1980) who found no colloid osmotic pressure differences in subdural fluid and venous blood in affected patients. Evidence now suggests that the late increase in size of chronic subdural haematomas is due to repeated micro-haemorrhages from the highly vascular haematoma capsule (Ito et al, 1976).

Few neurological conditions are more frequently missed in life than chronic subdural haematoma. Constant clinical vigilance, a high index of suspicion and a positive attitude towards defining any progressive neurological abnormality of unknown cause are the critical ingredients if this eminently treatable disease is to be seriously considered as a diagnostic possibility.

A history of head injury may be absent due to confusion, alcoholism or lack of reliable witnesses. Head injury, frequently regarded as slight, may have other evidence to suggest that the degree of trauma was of some magnitude. Nevertheless there is a sufficient body of clinical experience to confirm that the head injury is indeed often relatively minor. Sometimes the injury is transmitted to the brain by a fall on the buttocks. Disorders of haemostasis or anticoagulant therapy (Wiener and Nathanson, 1962) enhance the liability to bleed following trivial blows to the head. Tearing of one or more of the veins crossing the subdural space to reach the dural sinuses leads to slow accumulation of blood in the subdural space. Chronic subdural haematomata may be large and bilateral. Within two to three weeks the haematoma becomes encased in a highly vascular membrane. The membranous walls may become grossly thickened or even calcified, but occasionally spontaneous reabsorption of the haematoma occurs. Because the subarachnoid space tends to be large in old age, the haematoma may increase in size considerably before producing obvious symptoms.

A history of head injury is obtainable in only a proportion of older patients. If a head injury can be established, symptoms develop in days or weeks, but rarely in months later. Confusion or impaired memory may result from the haematoma or may have preceded it due to other causes. A dull generalized headache which is usually persistent, but fluctuating in intensity, is commonly present. Mental function tends to fluctuate from cheerful alertness to apathetic confusion. Recent memory is impaired, focal epileptic fits may occur, and if the dominant hemisphere is involved dysphasia may develop. Later characteristic fluctuation in the level of consciousness occurs, the patient being quite wakeful at one time of the day and almost unrousable a few hours or a day later. Eventually stupor or coma persists.

Examination may reveal a mild hemiparesis in a proportion of patients with increased tendon reflexes and an extensor plantar response on the affected side. However, signs of corticospinal tract involvement may be bilateral. Dilation of the homolateral pupil, papilloedema and rarely a homonymous hemianopia, resulting from posterior cerebral artery compression, occur. If the haematoma continues to enlarge, brain-stem signs may supervene. Some elderly persons remain in an undiagnosed state of chronic dementia.

Diagnosis

The CSF is commonly xanthochromic with an increased protein content. A skull X-ray may show a shift of the calcified pineal, and echoencephalography may demonstrate a shift of midline structures and of the lateral ventricle. The EEG usually shows unilateral suppression or decreased voltage on the affected side or increased slow activity in the alpha and theta range. The decreased voltage is probably the result of the haematoma having a 'cushioning' effect on the electrical activity from the underlying brain.

Computerized tomography is the single most effective method of identifying a subdural haematoma. The haematoma is hypodense in relation to the surrounding brain in 70 per cent of cases during the chronic phase (Scotti et al, 1977). Various morphological changes in the scan outlines have been suggested to assist in diagnosis when the haematoma is isodense, (Marcu and Becker, 1977; Moeller and Erickson, 1979; Barmeir and Dubowitz, 1981). Where CT facilities are not available, scintiscanning will demonstrate the majority of chronic subdural haematomas.

Treatment

Mannitol and/or steroid administration may bring about a tardy resolution of symptoms, but the outcome with medical measures is uncertain at best. Evacuation of the haematoma through burr holes is well tolerated even in advanced old age (Markwallader, 1981; Markwallader et al, 1981).

Peripheral neuropathy

Defective structure or function of part or whole of peripheral motor, sensory or autonomic neurones are included under the broad term of peripheral neuropathy of which the causative factors are legion. Many attempts have been made not only to classify the whole spectrum of peripheral neuropathy (Bradley, 1974) but also to categorize some of its more complex components, such as diabetic neuropathy. With the latter, considerable debate exists on the feasibility of a realistic classification (Pirart, 1965; Greenbaum, 1964); others maintain that predominant features are identified by classifying diabetic neuropathy (Gilliatt, 1965; Bruyn and Garland, 1970; Thomas, 1973).

The WHO Study Group (1980) put forward an aetiopathological classification (Table 18.2) which they accept is open to the criticism that co-existing pathological involvement of both axon and myelin sheaths may occur, the category 'other type' is arbitrary, the role of some listed factors in peripheral neuropathy is equivocal and that the overall list is probably incomplete. Despite these drawbacks, the WHO classification brings some rational order to previous inadequate attempts to codify the peripheral neuropathies on a clinical basis. It is now

Table 18.2 Classification of peripheral neuropathies based on aetiopathology

Axonopathies*	Myelinopathies*	Other types
A. *Genetically determined*	A. *Genetically determined*	A. *Infections*
Peroneal muscular atrophy	Charcot-Marie-Tooth syndrome	Leprosy
Giant axonal neuropathy	Déjérine-Sottas disease	Herpes zoster
Hereditary sensory types	Roussy-Lévy syndrome	Viral
Ataxia telangiectasia	Refsum's disease	
Polyglucosan body axonopathy	Adrenoleucodystrophy	B. *Ischaemic*
Farby's disease	Metachromatic leucodystrophy	Collagen vascular
Tangier's disease	Krabbe's disease	disease
Bassen-Kornzweig disease	Pelizaeus-Merzbacher disease	Other vasculitides
Familial dysautonomia		Diabetes mellitus
Friedreich's ataxia		Atherosclerosis
Neuraxonal dystrophy		
Leigh's disease		
Agenesis of corpus callosum		
B. *Acquired*	B. *Acquired*	C. *Mechanical*
1. *Exogenous toxins and drugs*	1. *Idiopathic infectious or postinfectious*	Compression
(a) Metals: arsenic, mercury, gold alkyl tins,	(a) Acute (Guillain-Barré syndrome)	(entrapment)
aluminium, zinc, thallium	(b) Chronic	Stretch
(b) Solvents: hexane, carbon tetrachloride, carbon	(c) Relapsing	Severance
disulfide, methyl-*n*-butyl ketone, 2,5-hexanedione	(d) Brachial	D. *Miscellaneous*
(c) Miscellaneous: acrylamide, leptophos,	(e) Postvaccinal	Amyloid
organophosphates, carbon monoxide, nitrogen	(f) Infantile	Tumours (primary,
dioxide, 2,4-dichlorophenoxyacetic acid,	2. *Toxic*	secondary)
chlordecone	(a) Diphtheria	Mucopolysaccharidosis
(d) Medications: vincristine, nitrofurantoin, isoniazid,	(b) Lead	Thermal and electrical
adriamycin, clioquinol, thalidomide, disulfiram,	(c) Hexachlorophene	injury
dapsone, phenytoin, amitriptyline	(d) Tellurium	Perineuritis
(e) Dietary: neurolathyrism, ethanol	(e) Acetyl ethyl tetramethyltetraline	Idiopathic Bell's palsy
(f) Invertebrate poisons: botulin, black-widow-spider	(AETT)	Trigeminal neuralgia
venom, tick venom	(f) Cyanides (cassava)	
2. *Metabolic disorders*	3. *Metabolic*	
Diabetes mellitus	(a) Diabetes mellitus	
Renal failure	(b) Dysproteinaemias	
Hepatic failure		
Porphyria		
Hypoglycaemia		
Chronic hypothyroidism		
3. *Deficiency states*		
Thiamine (alcohol abuse)		
Vitamin B$_{12}$		
Folate		
Pyridoxine		
Protein malnutrition		
Niacin		
Pantothenic acid		
Riboflavin		
4. *Miscellaneous*		
Carcinoma		
Myeloma		
'Geriatric'		

* In some of the axonopathies and myelinopathies, coexisting involvement of the myelin sheath and axons may be found.
(W.H.O. Technical Report Series 654. 1980. Peripheral Neuropathies).

possible to characterize 75 per cent of patients with peripheral neuropathies (Dyck et al, 1981; Dyck, 1982).

This section is solely concerned with those forms of peripheral neuropathy which have particular reference to later life. This being so, it is germane to indicate peripheral changes that appear to be age-related. Nerve degeneration is readily detectable after 70 years of age, but there is evidence that the threshold for pressure sensation diminishes from the middle thirties (Dyck et al, 1972). Advancing age is accompanied by decreasing diameter of the larger nerve fibres and increasing irregularity of the inter-nodal (nodes of Ranvier) lengths associated with degenerative changes in the vaso vasorum, increased perineural fibrosis, segmental demyelination and axonal degeneration and regenerations (Vizoso, 1950; Lascelles and Thomas, 1966; Arnold and Harriman, 1970). These changes possibly account for the reduced nerve conduction velocity which is a feature of age. A decrease in maximum conduction velocity occurs in sensory and motor nerves (Kaeser, 1970).

The general clinical manifestations of peripheral neuropathy include numbness in the hands and feet, loss of joint position sense with unsteadiness of gait, impaired sensation of pain, heat or cold, or altered reactions to these stimuli, particularly hyperalgesia or hyperpathia. Patients with neuropathic pain use expressions such as dull, boring, aching, nagging, searing, in contradistinction to the sharp, lancinating character of neuralgic pain. A sensation of burning feet or more general dysaesthesia is common. Objective sensory loss may be partial or total and tendon reflexes may be diminished or lost. As the condition progresses, trophic changes in the limbs or digits occur and neuropathic ulcers or joints are more florid sequelae. Muscle weakness and wasting depending on the distribution of nerve involvement may develop quite insidiously or rapidly and progressively. The extraocular muscles may be involved.

Clinical features of autonomic nervous system involvement may be prominent and may present with tachycardia, excessive salivation, disorders of micturition, abnormal gastric and gut mobility with bouts of diarrhoea, orthostatic hypotension, lacrimation, pupillary abnormalities and trophic changes of the skin and nails.

Many aetiological causes of peripheral neuropathy are rare or are not seen in old age. Commonly the historical background of those who survive into old age with genetically determined neuropathies will help in diagnosis (see Fig. 18.4). Recent exposure to industrial chemicals is unlikely in old age, but drugs such as phenytoin, nitrofurantoin, isoniazide, amitriptyline or hydrallazine may be causal. Alcohol induced neuropathy has a prevalence from rare to common in different societies and is mainly seen in association with poor general nutrition.

Diabetic neuropathy
Oedema of the Schwann cells and segmental demyelination are the characteristic pathological findings. Schwann cell oedema is not solely due to increased cellular sorbitol concentration resulting from metabolic attempts to deal with excessive intracellular glucose by the enzyme, aldose reductase (Winegrad and Greene, 1976). The high intraneuronal-extracellular myoinositol concentration gradient is maintained in favour of intraneural excess by an active sodium dependent transport system that is competitively inhibited by hyperglycaemia (Greene and Lattimer, quoted by Clements and Bell, 1982). Reduction in intraneural myoinositol may lead to impaired Schwann cell function.

In diabetic mononeuropathy the affected peripheral nerves show evidence of multiple infarctions (Raff and Asbury, 1968) with demonstrable thickening and hyalinisation of the walls of the nutrient vessels.

The significance of the endoneural capillary changes in the pathogenesis of diabetic polyneuropathy is uncertain (Clements and Bell, 1982).

In the elderly, positive findings may be detected despite an unrevealing history. Symmetrical loss of sensibility for vibration, light touch and joint position in the lower limbs and sometimes blisters on the legs from close proximity to the fire indicate reduction in pain sensibility. Complaints of burning or aching pain in the feet and legs, particularly at night, are common. Numbness or marked hyperasthesiae and weakness in the lower limbs may be dominant features. Radiculopathy involving one or several nerve roots is not uncommon.

Weight loss may be severe and progressive and in diabetic amyotrophy it is associated with severe and disabling quadriceps wasting. Neuropathy may be accompanied by wasting of the interossei of the hands and feet giving rise to claw-shaped deformities.

Ataxia develops later, but is often of only moderate severity. Unilateral or bilateral foot drop and less commonly wrist drop may develop relatively acutely. Isolated cranial nerve involvement is not uncommon and the third nerve is most frequently affected, but fourth, sixth and seventh nerves may also be involved. Autonomic nervous system involvement is common, but often overlooked. Anhidrosis, disturbance of gastro-intestinal motility, particularly intractable diarrhoea, bladder atony, dysrhythmias and orthostatic hypotension are features which, in our experience, are frequently seen in conditions mild enough to be regarded as adequately controlled by diet or by oral hypoglycaemic agents.

Perforating ulceration of the foot and Charcot's

arthropathy are complications which are fortunately less commonly seen today.

Treatment. Obesity requires energetic management; strict blood sugar control appears to confer benefit. However, it is facile to believe that the majority of the elderly diabetic population will adhere to a precise diet. Therefore stabilization of the average elderly diabetic in hospital must take cognizance of this. It is generally accepted that careful insulin control is preferable to oral hypoglycaemic agents in patients with diabetic neuropathy.

Neuropathic pain may respond to simple analgesics, but for more severe symptoms a combination of a night dose of amitriptyline and, twice or thrice daily carbamazepine is often effective. Davis et al (1977) report the use of amitriptyline and fluphenazine in treating diabetic neuropathy, but the benefit of phenytoin in this condition remains debatable. Radiculopathic pain is usually self-limiting, but a nerve block may be appropriate in severe mononeuropathic pain. Transcutaneous nerve stimulation has a useful place in regional pain management.

Counselling on foot care is critical and regular skilled chiropody will minimize the risk of painless ulceration.

The metabolite myo-inositol is excreted in increased amounts in uncontrolled diabetes. Dietary supplementation with myoinositol has been put forward as a means of treating diabetic neuropathy, but its value is yet to be established.

A drop-foot caliper may be required if dorsiflexion is seriously impaired and a 'lively' finger and wrist support is useful if considerable wrist and finger weakness is present. However, more often a simple wrist support is required as the fingers may retain sufficient power.

Carcinomatous neuropathy

Since Denny-Brown (1948) described two cases of bronchogenic carcinoma associated with peripheral neuropathy, the peripheral neurological manifestations of primary malignant tumours have become widely recognized. The literature has been extensively reviewed by Hanson and Urich (1970) and Bruyn (1979). The primary lesion may occur almost anywhere, but lung, breast and stomach are the commonest sites. The neuropathic manifestations are commonly progressive sensory deficit or motor weakness. The onset of symptoms is typically swift and they tend to progress in distribution. The motor features are often those of heaviness and weakness of the lower limbs with ataxia, but very soon the paresis becomes florid and all movements rapidly decline. Cramp-like pains may occur early. Paraesthesiae rapidly followed by anaesthesia are evident. Particularly in old age the neurological symptoms may precede overt evidence of a primary malignancy by many months.

The onset is typically sudden and the progress measured in weeks, less often in months. Stabilization of symptoms may occur at any stage and for variable periods — sometimes many months — or the condition may advance relentlessly to end with profound disability. Paraesthesiae or mild or severe pain in the limbs may be the dominant symptoms. Sensory loss is often polymodal and may be associated with areflexia and ataxic features.

Treatment. If the primary lesion is operable, an attempt at removal should be made. The neurological features can be distressing in the extreme, persist for many months and kill the patient from recurrent urinary tract infection or extensive bed sores.

Entrapment or compression neuropathy

Compression may result from external causes such as overtight plaster of Paris splint or internal causes including fractures, tumours or haematomata, neural and perineural inflammations.

Gilliatt (1975) tabulated the degrees of injury that follow acute compressive nerve damage as — a) rapid reversible physiological block (Lewis et al, 1931); b) local demyelinating block (Denny-Brown and Brenner, 1944, and c) Wallerian degeneration, but changes of more chronic compression might be more readily located within the broader classification of Sunderland (1978):

1. Axonal conduction interrupted with maintenance of structural continuity.
2. Axonal continuity lost. Intact endoneurial sheath.
3. Loss of continuity of axon and endoneurium. Perineurium intact
4. Loss of continuity of nerve bundles. Epineurium intact.
5. Loss of continuity of nerve trunk.

The neuropathic changes derive from direct mechanical stress damaging the large myelinating fibres, although intrinsic ischaemia may contribute to the overall nerve injury (Gilliatt, 1975). The additive effects of noxious factors is demonstrated by the susceptibility of patients with one type of peripheral nerve disorder to develop more distal entrapment neuropathies, a finding recorded by Upton and McComas (1973) in their description of the association of carpal tunnel syndromes and of ulnar nerve compression at the elbow with cervico-thoracic root lesions under the title, 'The Double Crush in Nerve Entrapment Syndromes'.

Progressive constriction of peripheral nerves by anatomical structures at a number of sites form the entrapment neuropathies. The commonest example of this syndrome is compression of the median nerve in the carpal tunnel, a condition largely seen in older women, and variously due to increased fibrosis and oedema in the carpal tunnel, arthritis involving the wrist joints, elbow is flexed. Symptomatic ulnar nerve compression in the cubital tunnel may follow prolonged flexion of the elbow. Wadsworth and Williams (1973) and Wadsworth (1974, 1977) showed that this is particularly likely to occur when the flexed elbow is resting on a hard surface with the forearm pronated. The picture of the over sedated old person with her head resting on crossed and wasted forearms on a bare table is all too common. Deformities at the elbow consequent to injury or to bony overgrowth associated with osteoarthrosis may lead to secondary cubital tunnel syndrome.

Symptoms. Early symptoms are paraesthesiae over the inner one-and-a-half fingers and later objective sensory loss over the anterior and posterior surfaces of these digits and ulnar part of the hand. Weakness and wasting of muscles in the ulnar distribution may follow. The flexor carpi ulnaris is normally spared. In unrelieved pressure ulnar palsy may develop.

Treatment. Avoidance of prolonged flexion and prevention of pressure on the elbow will normally ensure restoration of early symptoms. Surgical relief of compression or occasionally transposition of the nerve to a protected position may be required.

Many other nerves may be involved in entrapment neuropathy including the radial, suprascapular, sciatic, amyloid infiltrations and hypothyroidism. Although the latter condition may cause entrapment neuropathy (Purnell et al, 1961), a more widespread neuropathy may also occur in this condition (Dyck and Lambert, 1970).

Symptoms are of burning pains, tingling and numbness in the thumb, index and middle fingers particularly at night, on hanging the arm down or after carrying heavy objects such as a full shopping basket. Cutaneous sensory loss over the affected digits impairs fine movement and associated wasting of the abductor pollicis brevis and opponens brevis cause conspicuous flattening of the thenar eminences. Pain may extend to involve the forearm, or even above, but the direction of radiation is invariably centripetal and, unlike the centrifugal pain of cervical nerve root compression (Downie, 1982).

Treatment. Any treatable underlying disease will clearly require specific attention. Resting the affected part with additional night splinting and corticosteroid injection into the carpal tunnel often relieve the symptoms. If these measures are unsuccessful, surgical division of the transverse carpal ligament is indicated.

Ulnar nerve entrapment

The ulnar nerve is particularly vulnerable to compressive injury at the elbow and it is susceptible to compression as it traverses the cubital tunnel (Feindel and Stratford, 1958). The size of the cubital space is maximal with the elbow extended and smallest when the

obturator, ilioinguinal, saphenous and peroneal (Koppel and Thomson, 1963) but many of these are occupational and less likely to be seen in the elderly.

Neuropathy due to rheumatoid arthritis

Active rheumatoid arthritis is largely a condition of younger adults, but we have been impressed by the development of an acute and rapidly progressive form of rheumatoid arthritis with widespread nodules and markedly raised rheumatoid factors occurring in old age. A proportion of these patients develop a peripheral neuropathy, usually involving motor nerves and initially asymmetrical in distribution. Corticosteroids do not appear to be of aetiological significance, though steroid therapy is said to enhance the likelihood of neuropathy (Ferguson and Slocumb, 1961).

The neuropathy of rheumatoid arthritis may fall into reasonably well-defined groups (Pallis and Scott, 1965). The presentations may be in the form of entrapment neuropathy; peripheral bilateral symmetrical sensory symptoms; digital sensory loss due to digital artery occlusion; and mixed progressive sensory and motor deficits in the upper and lower limbs.

Paraproteinaemias

The incidence of paraproteinaemias, both malignant and benign, increase with advancing age and their association with peripheral neuropathy is well established. Multiple myeloma (Victor et al, 1958; Silverstein and Doniger, 1963), macroglobulinaemia (Dayan and Lewis, 1966; Propp et al, 1975; Iwashita et al, 1974; Rowland et al, 1982), raised polyclonal immunoglobulin levels (Whitaker et al, 1973; Hobbs et al, 1976) and benign IgG paraproteinaemia (Chazot et al, 1976; Read et al, 1976) may at times be associated with peripheral neuropathy. Neuropathy may also be a significant feature of cryoglobulinaemia (Cream et al, 1974; Lapes and Davies, 1970). There is as yet no clear understanding of the interrelationship between the paraproteinaemias and neuropathic changes, though Chazot et al (1974) demonstrated autologous specific binding to peripheral nerves in IgG and IgA myelomas and in macroglobulinaemia.

Clinical evidence of neuropathy is recorded in 3 per cent of patients with multiple myeloma (Currie et al, 1970) but a third of myeloma patients have electrophysiological abnormalities (Walsh, 1971) and two-thirds have histological changes of demyelination (Hesselvick, 1969) characteristic of a neuropathic disorder.

Chronic polyneuropathy of old age

Under the title 'Late-life chronic peripheral neuropathy of obscure nature', Fisher (1982) described four elderly women with a chronic neuropathy involving only the lower limbs. The predominant features were sensory disturbances in patients and a symmetrical sensorimotor neuropathy progressing to bilateral foot-drop in two women. The condition appears to be relatively benign and progress to severe general disablement did not occur in Fisher's patients.

Vitamin B$_{12}$ neuropathy and subacute combined degeneration of the cord

In vitamin B$_{12}$ deficiency the major initial impact of nervous system change may be in the cord or in the peripheral nerves. Patchy demyelination in the dorsal columns of the mid-thoracic segments of the cord occur early, but later changes in the region of the corticospinal and ascending cerebellar tracts develop. Demyelination occurs in the peripheral nerves and moderate muscle atrophy may develop.

The clinical picture corresponds to the areas of nervous system involvement. The onset of symptoms is usually gradual, but occasionally so rapid that standing becomes impossible within three weeks. Typically paraesthesiae are the early dominant expression of neurological change and are variously described as a sensation of pins and needles, numbness, coldness or tightness in the toes, feet and later in the fingers. The patient may complain of difficulty in feeling the ground with the soles of his feet. Less common are complaints of stabbing or searing pain in the lower limbs and back. The muscles may become tender and sometimes excruciatingly so. Loss of sensation over the peripheral parts of the upper and lower limbs may be prominent. As the condition progresses, gait becomes disordered. The gait disturbance is dependent on the sites of nervous system involvement. With dorsal column disease ataxia of the limbs predominates, but weakness and spasticity suggest corticospinal tract damage. More often the gait shows features of weakness, ataxia and spasticity, and if peripheral nerve changes are marked, walking may be further aggravated by the presence of foot drop. Incoordination and spasticity may also become noticeable in the upper limbs, though somewhat later than in the lower limbs. Occasionally the picture is almost entirely of peripheral nerve involvement and only loss of vibration and appreciation of passive joint movement indicate posterior column cord damage.

The objective findings are those of early loss of vibration and joint position sensibility and later impaired perception of touch pain, heat and cold characteristically over the sock and glove areas. Reflexes may be absent if peripheral nerve involvement is dominant or exaggerated when lateral column changes are significant. Initially the plantars are flexor, but generally become extensor as the condition progresses. Sphincter disturbances are relatively common and initially hesitation of micturition and urinary retention occur followed later by incontinence. Autonomic nervous system involvement may account for the atonic bladder and for the occasional reduced intestinal motility.

Optic atrophy is present in less than 2 per cent of patients and external ophthalmoplegia has been reported (Gamstorp and Kupfer, 1961). Retrobulbar neuritis occurs in about 6 per cent of patients (Benedict, 1933). It is typically bilateral (Chisholm, 1979) and produces loss of central visual acuity.

The mental changes in pernicious anaemia are sometimes ill-defined and the alleged relationship to B$_{12}$ deficiency is not always proven. The dramatic presentation of acute psychotic reaction with hallucinations and paranoid delusions is seen occasionally (Chisholm, 1972) but response to adequate B$_{12}$ therapy is prompt and satisfying. The reported incidence of psychiatric disorders with pernicious anaemia is very variable and to a large extent appears to represent patient selectivity. Our own experience is in accord with that of Cox (1962) who noted mental symptoms in 2.5 per cent of patients with pernicious anaemia. Apathy or irritability and agitation, fluctuations of mood and impaired memory are not uncommon. We have noted the occasional development of confusion lasting for several weeks in patients with pernicious anaemia treated with large doses of vitamin B$_{12}$ in whom serum potassium levels were maintained within the normal range.

Prognosis

This largely depends on the degree of cord damage and the duration of symptoms before specific therapy is commenced. In general it may be said that where peripheral nerve involvement is the major cause of disability, recovery will eventually be complete. When cord damage is severe and protracted, residual damage is usual. Progress of the neurological disorder is arrested in all adequately treated cases. Where symptoms have been present for less than three months, the outlook for recovery is excellent.

Treatment

Initially an injection of 500 μg of hydroxocobalamine twice weekly for 6 weeks followed by a maintenance dose of 250 μg of hydroxocobalamine every 4 weeks is very generous replacement therapy. There is no evidence that larger doses achieve a more rapid or more certain effect. It is clear that coexisting folate or iron deficiency requires correction.

In the early stages of recovery, physical treatment is of crucial importance and it is basic that a multidisciplinary approach to the management of the sick and disabled person is not overlooked whilst wrangling over the precise number of micrograms of vitamin B$_{12}$ therapy.

Trigeminal neuralgia (Tic Douloureux)

This distressing condition is a disorder of older age and is rare before the age of 50. Females are affected more often than males in the proportion of three to two. The cause is unknown in the majority of patients. In younger patients a plaque of multiple sclerosis in the pons must be excluded and in the elderly rarely a tumour may compress the trigeminal nerve or ganglion and give rise to trigeminal pain. This disorder remains ill-understood, but it is probable that it is due to an abnormality of the trigeminal sensory root or ganglion (Kerr, 1979). Abnormal neurological signs are entirely absent and diagnosis rests on a meticulous history. The outstanding features are recurrent brief paroxysms of sharp, lancinating pain confined to an area of the face supplied by one or more divisions of the fifth nerve. The ophthalmic division is involved in less than 5 per cent of cases. The zones supplied by the second and third divisions of the nerve are affected with equal frequency. Though one or other of these divisions is initially involved, both divisions are usually affected in the course of time. Rarely are both sides of the face involved. Chewing or swallowing, touching or washing the affected side of the face or exposure to draughts may precipitate a severe paroxysm of pain. The patient will sometimes wear a scarf over the side of the face and barely move the face in talking. Reflex spasm of the muscles of the affected side may be induced by pain. Painful facial trigger points may be noted. During the early phase of trigeminal neuralgia, periods of complete freedom from pain ranging from weeks to months is common. However, as time passes, the attacks become more frequent and severe. The pain may disappear spontaneously for weeks or even years and recur for no apparent reason.

Treatment

Until the introduction of carbamazepine (Tegretol) in 1962 (Blom, 1962) no reliable medical treatment was available (Spillane, 1964). The drug is best introduced in doses of 200 mg daily, followed by a gradual increase until symptoms are controlled. Normally 400–600 mg is adequate, but doses up to 1 g or more may be required, though these larger doses are usually poorly tolerated by the old. Due to its relatively short half-life, the drug should preferably be divided into three to four doses per day. The main side effects of carbamazepine are nausea, vomiting, drowsiness, giddiness, or objective ataxia, occasionally associated with nystagmus. Skin rashes usually subside on temporarily discontinuing the preparation and reintroducing it in smaller doses. However, Donaldson and Graham (1965) considered a rash an absolute contraindication to further carbamazepine therapy. Phenytoin is much less effective.

If response to medical management is inadequate, injection or surgical treatment may be indicated. A number of complex factors largely determine the best procedure for a particular patient. Some physicians have acquired considerable expertise with injection techniques and some surgeons have outstanding results with surgical treatment. As Henderson (1965) so clearly put it: 'There is no single treatment for all cases of trigeminal neuralgia. Some patients will not tolerate injections and others are afraid of operations. There are individual considerations in every case, and the best treatment may be operation or Gasserian injection or peripheral nerve injection or tablets'.

Alcohol injection into the Gasserian ganglion requires introduction of the needle point to a depth of 8 cm or 9 cm into the foramen ovale with the patient sufficiently alert to respond accurately to sensory testing. Relief of symptoms averages 2 years, but may be as short as 2 months.

A number of surgical procedures have been used, but the extradural division of the sensory nerve behind the ganglion is a time-honoured procedure though rarely undertaken in frail old people by surgeons in the UK. Occasional sequelae to this operation are permanent analgesia of the lower part of the face, anaesthesia of the cornea and a transient facial palsy. The peripheral electrocoagulation technique developed at the Surgical Clinic of the University of Münster has proved safe and effective in many patients not responding to drug therapy. The procedure is carried out under local anaesthetic and the approach is via the infraorbital foramen, supraorbital notch, or mental foramen depending on the particular branch of the trigeminal nerve involved (Krasemann and Honkomp, 1968). Trew et al (1975) used the stereotaxic percutaneous approach to effect electrocoagulation of the trigeminal ganglion in over 300 patients with trigeminal neuralgia over a period of 5 years. More than 100 were over 65 years of age, and four were in excess of 90 years of age. By using successive radiofrequency lesions, the induced sensory deficit was sufficient to control pain, while preserving touch and motor function. Ninety-three per cent of patients over the age of 65 reported good-to-excellent results. Of the 7 per cent who had recurrent pain on follow-up, 5 per cent required recoagulation which was readily and successfully performed. However the recurrence rate is proportional to the duration of follow-up.

Herpes zoster

Since Garland (1943) suggested that Herpes zoster follows reactivation of the latent varicella virus, subsequent virological studies have amply confirmed this monistic concept of the varicella-zoster (VZ) virus, (Weller, 1953; Weller and Coons, 1954; Weller and Whitton, 1958; Weller, Whitton and Bell, 1958). There is no definitive evidence as yet to indicate whether the latency period of the varicella-zoster virus is due to a few virions being continuously elaborated or due to the persistence of the viral genome, but without viral replication.

The incidence of Herpes zoster increases markedly with age and the attack rate rises from 3.5 per 1000 under the age of 50 years to 10.1 per 1000 in the eighth decade (Hope-Simpson, 1965). In his study of a family practice in England, Hope-Simpson postulated that a decline in immunity to varicella-zoster virus with increasing age predisposed to reactivation of the latent virus in the posterior root ganglia and cranial nerves. However the varicella-zoster virus has never been recovered from these sites in asymptomatic individuals although in the few reported autopsies in patients who died during the course of zoster or chickenpox evidence of dorsal root ganglia involvement by the VZ virus has been forthcoming (Esiri and Tomlinson, 1972; Ghatak and Zimmerman, 1973; Bastian et al, 1972; Shibuta et al, 1974; Nagashima et al, 1975).

The relationship between immunity response to varicella antigen and age is controversial, largely due to semantic and technical differences in many studies. Tomlinson and MacCallum (1970) found that the lowest complement fixation (CF) titres to VZ antibody occurs at age 41–60 years, but that the CF titres rose after aged 60 (Wong et al, 1978).

The CF and immune adherence haemagglutination antibodies are at their lowest in the 31–40 age band and progressively rise with advancing age (Wong et al, 1978). In a study of subjects from 1 year to 85 years, Gershon and Steinberg (1981) noted that the proportion of seropositive persons identified by the sensitive fluorescent antibody to membrane antigen technique continued to rise with advanced old age. However Miller (1980) has demonstrated a striking decline in the cellular immune responses to VZ antigen which may seriously limit the ability of the cell mediated immune response to contain potential viral reactivation.

Trauma and radiotherapy to the spinal cord may precipitate Herpes zoster. Malignancy, chronic leukaemia, Hodgkin's disease and myelomatosis increase the likelihood of zoster, and in these instances there is often a widespread general eruption (see below).

The virus has a predilection for the posterior root ganglion. There is often a prodromal period of up to four days characterized by intense burning pain in the distribution of the dermatome of the affected nerve root or roots followed by cutaneous hyperaesthesia. A mild pyrexia is common. On the third to fourth day the skin of the affected area becomes erythematous and within hours superficial vesicles develop. The vesicles are thin-walled and initially contain clear fluid which becomes purulent if secondary infection supervenes. The lesions slowly dry to form scabs in one to two weeks and these

separate over a widely variable period to leave pink and subsequently white scars. The rash occurs on only one side of the body and trunk. At times the localized eruption of zoster is accompanied by a generalized eruption which may be sparse or profuse and has been referred to as herpes zoster with aberrant vesicles. This undesirable term masks the fact that the rash is that of chickenpox. Where the eruption is profuse, careful search is required to exclude malignancy or a reticulosis. Severe burning pain often persists at the site of scarring and in older age may last for months or years. Zoster of the ophthalmic divisions of the fifth nerve may involve the cornea causing permanent scarring. Herpes of the geniculate ganglion results in a vesicular eruption involving the external auditory meatus, tympanic membrane, and occasionally the homolateral fauces. Subsequently a lower motor neurone facial paralysis and loss of taste of the anterior two thirds of the tongue ensues (Ramsay Hunt syndrome).

Oculomotor paralysis (Parkinson, 1948) (see Fig. 18.2) and paralysis of skeletal muscles probably due to anterior horn cell involvement occur occasionally (Taterka and O'Sullivan, 1943) (see Fig. 18.3). Shivalingappa (1970) described a woman of 80 years with hemidia-

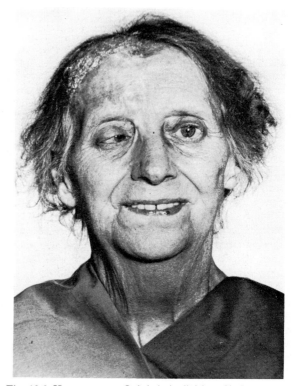

Fig. 18.2 Herpes zoster. Ophthalmic division. Sixth nerve palsy

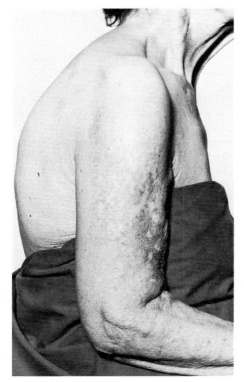

Fig. 18.3 Herpes zoster. Deltoid paralysis

phragmatic paralysis following herpes zoster. Recovery of motor paresis may be slow or incomplete (Taterka and O'Sullivan, 1943; Thomas and Howard, 1972; Pathy, 1979). Encephalomyelitis is uncommon and is generally seen in the immuno-compromised patient.

Concomitant encephalopathy and Guillain-Barre type neuropathy has been described (Twomey and Jefferson, 1981).

Treatment
In the acute stage of the eruption, the topical application of lint well moistened with 40 per cent idoxuridine dissolved in dimethylsulphoxide relieves pain and appears to reduce the incidence of postherpetic neuralgia if commenced early and continued for at least 4 days (Drawber, 1974). The use of amantadine hydrochloride may reduce the duration and incidence of postherpetic neuralgia in the elderly if it is administered during the acute phase of zoster (Galbraith, 1973). Intravenous acyclovir decreases enythema and prevents the formation of new lesions (Bean et al, 1982). The drug does not appear to prevent postherpetic neuralgia (Bean et al, 1982; Van Der Meer and Versteeg, 1982). Oral cyclovir appears effective (Timbury, 1982). It is given in doses of 1 g daily taken in five divided doses.

Postherpetic neuralgia
Melzack and Wall (1965) put forward a 'gate' theory postulating that stimuli via larger diameter afferent fibres close, but that small diameter fibres open a gate which allows the incoming stimuli to give rise to pain. Nathan (1976) points out that non-myelinated nerves are predominantly polymodal nocioceptors and are specific in as much as they are nocioceptors. In this respect these fibres are akin to the small fibres of the gate control theory.

Russell et al (1957) have advocated a programme of vigorous exercise to increase the input of afferent impulses from muscles and thereby raise the pain threshold. They further noted the value of electric vibrators as a procedure in diminishing the sensitivity of hyperaesthetic postherpetic areas. Transcutaneous nerve stimulation has given encouraging results in our hands over the last 6 years.

Spinal artery ischaemia
Déjèrine (1911) described the condition of intermittent claudication of the spinal cord in which affected patients experience a feeling of heaviness or weakness in the lower limbs on walking, occasionally associated with sphincter disturbance. Symptoms rapidly subside with rest. The presence of upper motor neurone signs indicates involvement of the spinal cord. The condition has to be distinguished from the Leriche syndrome of intermittent claudication, often in the buttocks and thighs, and wasting and ischaemic changes in the lower limbs due to occlusion of the descending aorta and from 'claudication' of the cauda equina due to intervertebral disc protrusion (Blau and Logue, 1961).

In a review of ischaemic lesions of the spinal cord, Henson and Parsons (1967) point out that anatomical variations of the blood supply to the cord are largely responsible for the variable clinical features of ischaemia of the spinal cord and they emphasize that atherosclerosis is the commonest cause of the ischaemic changes. Marked atheromatous change in the aorta is a significant factor in a proportion of cases with atherosclerotic vascular disease of the spinal cord (Gruner and Lapresle, 1962). Wells (1966) noted the importance of aortic atheroma in chronic myelopathy. The areas of the spinal cord particularly susceptible to ischaemic events are those at the periphery of the territory supplied by a main contributory vessel, and as Silver and Buxton (1974) indicate, these areas are not only at risk from damage to one of these vessels, but also from severe general hypoxia or a fall in perfusion pressure as may occur in severe shock or cardiac arrest. Acute obstruction of the origins of the thoracic and lumbar segmental arteries from dissection of the aorta may precipitate a spinal stroke (Kalischer, 1914; Hughes & Takaro, 1974). The widespread introduction of aortic surgery was frustrated at times by disasterous spinal cord ischaemic events. A greater awareness of the anatomical and haemodynamic vulnerability of the cord has lead to a considerable reduction in the incidence of this complication (El-Torraei and Juler, 1979). Extensive cord softening may result from spinal thrombophlebitis (Garland et al, 1966).

In recent years increasing attention has been focussed on the findings of partial or patchy cord infarction due to occlusion of one of the main radicular tributaries to the anterior spinal artery. It seems certain that transient episodes of weakness and paraesthesiae of the lower limbs may be due to transient ischaemia of the spinal cord or corda equina (Wells, 1966; Garland et al, 1966; Henson and Parson, 1967).

Anterior spinal artery occlusion due to thrombosis or embolism is an uncommon disorder. It has been described in association with cervical spondylosis (Hughes and Brownwell, 1964). Diabetes and syphilis may be predisposing factors, though the latter is now rarely a cause in the UK. Dissecting aneurysm of the aorta is one of the commoner causes of anterior spinal artery cord infarction (Marcus, 1972).

The clinical onset is usually abrupt with flaccid paraplegia, loss of pain and temperature sensation to a level of about the tenth thoracic segment and sphincter paralysis. Vibration and joint position senses are preserved. With anterior lumbar and sacral segment destruction, flaccid paralysis remains with subsequent muscle wasting and absent tendon reflexes. Where the lateral columns are most extensively involved, a spastic paraplegia may develop after the initial phase of spinal shock has passed. Occlusion of the anterior spinal artery near its origin may result in a quadriplegia due to ischaemia of the pyramidal fibres and their decussation (Marshall, 1976).

Treatment

With extensive infarction of the anterior two-thirds of the cord, management is that of the paraplegia and incontinence with emphasis on prevention of pressure sores and improvement of power in the upper limbs and trunk, directed towards wheelchair independence. However, often the ischaemic damage is transient or patchy and the resulting disability is short-lived or capable of progressive improvement with physical retraining. With recurrent transient episodes, drugs which reduce platelet aggregation such as aspirin or sulphinpyrazone are worthy of consideration although there is as yet no confirmation of their effectiveness in this condition.

Cauda equina claudication

Blau and Logue (1961) described six elderly patients who complained of severe discomfort in the lower limbs on exercise. All were due to chronic lumbar disc protrusion and were relieved by laminectomy. The condition is now widely recognized and is characterized by burning pain or severe numbness or paraesthesiae usually involving the whole lower limb and brought on by exercise and relieved by rest. Exercise may induce a sense of heaviness or weakness in the legs. Objective sensory signs are normally absent, though slight sensory impairment may be present over the sacral area. Peripheral arterial pulsation is normal unless coincidental peripheral arterial disease is present.

Other conditions narrowing the spinal canal in the region of the cauda equina may give rise to this disorder. The diagnosis is confirmed by myelography and laminectomy gives excellent results.

Vertebrobasilar syndrome

Pathology

The effect of narrowing or occlusion of an artery supplying the circle of Willis will depend on anatomical variations and on the integrity of the remaining vessels contributing to or forming the circle itself. Stenosis or even occlusion of one artery may produce no symptoms if the remaining vessels are adequately patent. Martin et al (1960) found occlusive cervical arterial disease in 20 per cent of consecutive routine autopsies in the absence of recorded symptoms. Cerebral infarction occurs more readily where intracranial and extracranial occlusions are associated (Hutchinson and Yates, 1957; Stein et al, 1962; Wiener et al, 1964). Congenital anomalies of one or more vessels of the circle of Willis are common (Alpers et al, 1959) and may affect the outcome of arterisclerotic narrowing of the remaining vessels. Disease of the internal carotid or vertebral arteries is most often due to atheroma, but occasionally the arterial lesion is due to giant cell arteritis (Whitfield et al, 1963; Hamrin et al, 1965).

Clinical features

The clinical picture is characterized by episodic symptoms indicating involvement of more than one part of the brain at a time. The disturbance of function may involve brain-stem, occipital cortex or possibly temporal lobe. Symptoms are variable and may indicate involvement of first one side and then the other. Vertigo and ataxia are often cardinal features of vertebrobasilar disease. Visual hallucinations in the form of bright refractile spots or more highly organized coloured spectra point to occipital lobe involvement. Ivanov and Matev (1973) found transient visual phenomena in 83 per cent of patients with vertebrobasilar insufficiency associated with cervical spondylosis. Less frequent is the occurrence of diplopia or visual field defects. Deafness, often with associated tinnitus, may uncommonly be a presenting symptom. Transient recurrent dysarthria, dysphagia or hemiplegia are encountered but eventual progress to established hemiplegia may occur. Patrick et al (1980) characterize the temporal profile of verte-brobasilar infarction (Tables 18.3, 18.4). Involvement of one side of the face and contralateral side of the body is indicative of brain-stem lesion. Paraesthesia over the face or upper limb or transient facial weakness is seen. Occipital headache, often intense and sometimes accom-

Table 18.3 Presenting symptoms and mode of onset in 39 patients with vertebrobasilar infarction (from Patrick et al, 1980, by permission of the American Heart Association Inc.)

Symptoms	Total patients	Sudden onset (27 patients)	Gradual onset (9 patients)
Weakness	14	10	4
Ataxia	13	8	5
Vertigo	11	10	1
Nausea and vomiting	11	9	2
Numbness	11	8	3
Dysarthria	10	7	3
Dizziness	8	6	2
Obtundation	6	4	2
Diplopia	6	6	0
Dysphagia	6	3	3
Loss of consciousness	6*	4*	2†
Blurred or loss of vision	5	5	0

* In 3 of these patients, the mode of onset could not be determined
† One of these patients regained consciousness

Table 18.4 Neurological findings on initial examination in 39 patients with vertebrobasilar infarction (from Patrick et al, 1980, by permission of the American Heart Association Inc.)

Deficits	Patients
Facial (VII cranial nerve) weakness	25
EOM disorders	18
Altered LOC	17
Weakness	15
Nystagmus	11
Ataxia	11
Dysmetria	11
Hypaesthesia	7
Pupillary abnormalities	7
Central unilateral	20
Peripheral unilateral	4
Peripheral bilateral	1
Comatose since onset	5
Hemiparesis	8
Monoparesis	6
Quadriparesis	1
Horizontal only	4
Vertical only	3
Both and rotatory	4

panied by marked tenderness over the back of the scalp and upper neck, may prove misleading.

The *drop attack* so well described by Sheldon (1960) in his review of falls in 500 older people is an important manifestation of vertebrobasilar disease, though its frequency in this condition has been over emphasized in the past. It is rare for drop attacks to be due to vertebro-basilar disease in the absence of other features indicating brain stem involvement (Kubala and Millikan, 1964). It is believed that momentary failure of blood supply to the reticular formation is responsible for drop attacks (Marshall, 1976). Turning or extension of the neck is a frequent precipitating factor. Drop attacks particularly affect elderly females and occur without warning, the patient suddenly falling on to her flexed knees and hands. Consciousness is either retained or only momentarily lost and the patient is normally able to rise to her feet immediately. Sheldon emphasized the transient flaccid state that may be exhibited in some patients. Angiography may be justified in selected cases to establish the presence of vertebral artery stenosis. Direct puncture of the diseased vessel is far too hazardous in the elderly. Aortic arch angiography via a high branchial artery approach is safe and informative.

Vertebrobasilar disease and cervical spondylosis
The vertebral arteries arise from the first part of the subclavian arteries and run cranially in the transverse foramina of the upper six cervical vertebrae.

Yates (1967) observed that the vertebral arteries may be displaced laterally or forward by osteophytes in the region of the neurocentral or apophyseal joints respectively.

Hutchinson and Yates (1957) showed that turning the head may arrest blood flow in the vertebral arteries. Toole and Tucker (1960) perfused the carotid and vertebral arteries of cadavers and were able to demonstrate that certain positions of the neck obstructed the flow of fluid in the cervical vessels. In the presence of cervical spondylosis and vertebral artery atheroma, quite minor neck movements could arrest flow in the vertebral arteries. Bauer et al (1961) and Bauer et al (1962) confirmed the effect of cervical spondylosis on vertebral artery blood flow by angiographic studies.

Drop attacks are one of the more dramatic clinical manifestations of transient abolition of blood flow in the vertebral vessels. A common situation is when the old person turns his head prior to crossing the road or extends the cervical spine when reaching to a high shelf.

The effect of vertebral artery compression may be influenced by the state of the circulation in the internal carotid arteries. The contralateral internal carotid artery may be compressed against the lateral process of the atlas on head rotation (Hardesty et al, 1960). Forty-one per cent of patients studied by Bauer et al (1961) only showed abnormal EEG changes on head-turning if the carotid artery was digitally compressed.

Basilar impression. Transient symptoms of vertebro-basilar insufficiency can be induced by rotation of the head in a patient with basilar impression (Janeway et al, 1966).

Hypotension. As the systemic blood pressure falls, cerebrovascular resistance diminishes in response to hypotension (Finnerty et al, 1954). The mean arterial pressure has to fall to an average of 29 mmHg before signs of cerebral ischaemia occur. In subjects with essential hypertension, the response to hypotension is similar, but signs of cerebral ischaemia occur with an average mean arterial pressure of 47 mmHg. Finnerty and his co-workers emphasize that an overall decrease in cerebrovascular resistance in subjects with cerebral arteriosclerosis does not necessarily indicate that all cerebral vessels are capable of undergoing the same degree of relaxation. The elderly with orthostatic hypotension (see below) and vertebrobasilar insufficiency are particularly vulnerable to frequent and unexpected falls.

Other causes of falls

Other causes of falls with or without syncope must be distinguished from the drop attacks of vertebrobasilar disease. True drop attacks are either not associated with loss of consciousness or at most a momentary syncopal episode. Impaired circulation in the vertebrobasilar territory may complicate falls due to other factors.

Cough syncope, micturition syncope, carotid sinus syncope and orthostatic hypotension are considered on pages 464–465. Defaecation syncope was recently described by Pathy (1975).

Subclavian steal syndrome. If the proximal part of a subclavian artery is significantly stenotic or occluded, the reduced pressure beyond the stenosis causes blood to flow down the ipsilateral vertebral artery into the subclavian artery beyond the obstructions and the vertebro-basilar system thereby contributes to the blood supply of the upper limb. Exercise of the arm on the affected side may shunt sufficient blood from the brain-stem and occipital lobes to induce transient ischaemic manifestations. The importance of arm movements in producing symptoms has been over-stressed in the past. The integrity of the vertebrobasilar and internal carotid circulation is the critical factor determining the occurrence of ischaemic symptoms. The signs and symptoms are essentially those noted under the vertebrobasilar syndrome. Falls occur occasionally. Pulses may be absent or differ appreciably from one side to the other in the upper limbs, and significant differences of brachial blood pressure of at least 20 mmHg systolic and 10 mmHg diastolic are common. Retrograde brachial

angiograms will demonstrate retrograde flow in the cerebral artery of the affected side.

Anaemia. There may be an association between moderately severe anaemia and intermittent focal cerebral ischaemia (Siekert et al, 1960). Giddiness and falls occur, but the symptoms respond to correction of the anaemia.

Cardiac disorders. Heart disease and vertebrobasilar insufficiency are not infrequently found together in the elderly. Difficulties in interpreting the primary cause of falls in these subjects may be considerable. An accurate history from the patient and from an observer, if available, is often crucial. Heart block, paroxysmal tachycardia and arrhythmias, aortic stenosis and myocardial infarction (Pathy, 1967) may cause falls with or without transient syncope. Using a Medilog cassette recorder Goldberg et al (1975) showed transient dysrrhythmias in 74 per cent of elderly subjects with a history of syncope or giddiness. More recent experience in ambulatory monitoring has shown that transient dysrhythmias are common in healthy old people. These rhythm changes are brief and usually ectopic beats. More serious dysrhythmias such as brady-tachycardias may certainly produce falls and syncopal attacks.

Epileptic fits. Epilepsy occurring the first time in later life is nearly always due to clearly defined pathology. Cerebral arterial disease is undoubtedly the major cause of fits at this age. Where fits are witnessed the nature of the attacks is rarely in dispute. In old people living alone it is surprising how frequently epileptic episodes are undiagnosed and the patient seeks medical attention for his recurrent falls or 'blackouts'.

Treatment. It is mandatory to identify factors precipitating episodes of vertebrobasilar insufficiency if management is to be successful. Where cervical spondylosis plays a contributory role, restriction of movement of the cervical spine is the most successful single procedure in reducing the frequency of falls.

Drop attacks from vertebrobasilar disease carry a relatively good prognosis, apart from the risk of injury. If they are accompanied by other signs of transient ischaemic attacks, the prognosis should be more guarded. Where repeated transient hemiparesis dominates the clinical scene in normotensive subjects, anticoagulant therapy should be seriously considered. The risk of anticoagulation in the elderly has been considerably overemphasized. If anticoagulant therapy is initiated, it should be continued for at least one year and tapered off gradually (Marshall and Reynolds, 1965).

The surgical treatment of vertebrobasilar insufficiency is only exceptionally indicated in the elderly. The relative inaccessibility and small size of the vertebral artery and the frequency of congenital anomalies makes surgery on the vessel less successful than with the internal carotid artery. However, stenosis or occlusion of the vertebral artery at or near its origin may be amenable to surgery in early old age. Depending on the degree and extent of the occlusion, a patch graft, or endarterectomy and patch graft to enlarge the circumference of the affected vessel restores vertebral artery blood flow.

Subclavian steal syndrome. In the face of minimal symptoms, the patient only requires reassurance. If symptoms are mainly associated with upper limb activity, moderate restriction of limb use may be sufficient to control symptoms. Where symptoms are frequent or disabling, a bypass operation or endarterectomy may be considered. In frailer candidates the vertebral artery on the affected side may have to be ligatured to prevent blood being shunted to the basilar region.

Cervical spondylosis

Cervical spondylosis refers to the degenerative changes in the cervical intervertebral discs leading to secondary changes in adjacent vertebrae. The progressive desiccation (Püschel, 1930) and diminution of the protein mucopolysaccharide complex (Taylor, 1953) of the nucleus pulposus as age advances encourages disc degeneration. Secondary osteophytic outgrowths may form bony bars or spondylotic ridges and enlarge backwards. Loss of height in the cervical spine from multiple disc degeneration may lead to tortuosity and kinking of the vertebral arteries. Frykholm (1951) classified disc protrusions into four main types based on the predominant site of disc change.

The apophyseal joints of the cervical spine are in posterior relationship to the vertebral arteries, and the neurocentral joints — present only in the third to seventh cervical vertebrae — lie just medial to the vertebral vessels. Both are diarthrodial joints and subject to the changes of osteoarthrosis. Cervical spondylosis and osteoarthrosis are so frequently associated in old age that for practical convenience the two conditions are always considered under the broad heading of cervical spondylosis.

Bony spurs from arthrotic changes in these joints may project into the inter-vertebral foramina and compress the spinal nerve roots.

The presenting features of cervical spondylosis are largely those of root compression, cord compression or vertebrobasilar insufficiency, though there may be a variable admixture of these components in the individual subject.

Cervical radiculopathy

The radicular nerves may be compressed by dorsolateral or intraforaminal disc protrusion (Frykholm, 1951), apophyseal osteoarthrosis or by dural root sleeve fibrosis (Frykholm, 1951; Wilkinson, 1960). In a study of 201

patients with cervical spondylosis, Phillips (1975) found that two groups could be distinguished both on the clinical manifestations and on the level of disc involvement. He noted that in patients with brachial neuritis in the absence of evidence of myelopathy there was a striking incidence of involvement of disc at C5 to C6 and C6 to C7, whereas cases with cord compression had disc changes at a higher level.

Correlation between the degree of foraminal encroachment and radiculopathy is frequently poor, but the dynamic reduction in size of the intervertebral foramina during extension of the neck may play a significant role in producing intermittent root compression (Hadley, 1956; Waltz, 1967).

The date of onset of symptoms is historically often difficult to ascertain with precision as early symptoms are mild and evanescent. Initially, aching in the back or side of the neck spreading later to involve the arm, occurs, but symptoms tend to fluctuate both in duration and severity. Less frequently pain is moderate or severe and persistent. Exacerbations in the severity of pain can at times be related to episodes of physical activity involving the upper limbs. An acute onset of pain in the neck and arms in the absence of earlier symptoms is less common. Many older persons present with a history of recurrent falls and only after direct questioning can a complaint of root pain be elicited. A sensation of numbness or 'pins and needles' of unpleasant quality is common. Significant weakness in the upper limbs is uncommon and when present is rarely severe and usually in only one arm. In the absence of evidence of myelopathy, muscle wasting is minimal and may involve the deltoid, triceps and the intrinsic hand muscles. Objective physical signs are normally few or absent. The triceps tendon jerk may be lost. A plethora of signs with marked muscle wasting and corticospinal involvement is clearly indicative of cord compression.

Cervical myelopathy

Cervical spondylosis is the commonest cause of cervical cord compression in old age. An appreciation of the variation in size of the normal spinal canal and the anatomical relationships within the cervical spine is essential to an understanding of symptoms of cervical spondylosis. The cervical spinal cord has a diameter of 9.5 mm (Crandall and Hanafee, 1964; Wolf et al, 1956).

Burrows (1963) found the average sagittal diameter of the spinal canal (C.3 to C.7) in normal subjects to be 17 mm. In patients with evidence of myelopathy due to cervical spondylosis, Payne and Spillane (1957) noted that the sagittal diameter of the canal averaged 14 mm, but that this diameter might be further reduced by infoldings of the ligmenta flava. Posterior osteophytes might reduce the sagittal diameter by as much as 3 mm (Wilkinson, 1960). Spinal cord compression is likely to occur if, as judged on a lateral radiograph, the distance from the cortical line of the spinous process to the posterior aspect of the cervical spinal body or an osteophytic spur on the body is less than 11 mm. Adams and Logue (1971) emphasize the importance of traction of the spinal cord over osteophytes projecting into the spinal canal. Brownwell and Hughes (1975) presented autopsy evidence that 10 per cent of hospital subjects over the age of 70 have observable degeneration of the cervical cord due to compression by spondylotic bars.

Considerable evidence has been advanced to support a vascular basis for myelopathy (Brain, 1948; Chakravorty, 1969; Mayfield, 1979).

The spectrum of symptoms is wide and any part may dominate the clinical scene. The picture of incomplete and patchy cord involvement is a characteristic feature. Frequently the onset is insidious, and commonly medical advice is sought only after symptoms have been present for several months or even years. Symptoms may be both motor and sensory. Motor involvement may be found in the upper limb, but the resulting symptoms are initially often unimpressive and are commonly accepted as an inconvenience of advancing age. Positive findings are often detected only during examination for an unrelated clinical event. Clinically a complaint of weakness and signs of muscle wasting of variable degree at sites determined by the level of cord compression may be evident. Involvement of the anterior horn cells of the upper part of the cervical enlargement produces wasting in the deltoids, biceps, triceps, spinati, pectoralis major and the extensors of the wrists and fingers. Compression of the lower part of the cervical enlargement is manifested by wasting of the flexors of the fingers and wrists. Muscle wasting is rarely severe. Hypertrophic arthrotic changes in the apophyseal joints (Epstein et al, 1978), infolding (Adornato and Glasberg, 1980) or calcification of the ligamenta flava or calcification of the posterior longitudinal ligament (Tsukimoto, 1960; Murakami et al, 1978) may further compromise available spinal canal space and lead to spinal cord compression in the presence of a constitutionally narrowed spinal canal.

The motor features of cervical myelopathy are often asymmetrical in distribution and severity and symptoms parallel this patchy cord involvement.

Heaviness or weakness of one or both upper limbs or clumsiness of hand movement with impairment of grip are common symptoms. Where anterior horn cell damage is extensive muscle fasciculation of slight to modest degree is detectable and the intrinsic muscles of the hands are wasted (Fig. 18.4). Changes in the tendon reflexes are determined both by the level and major site of cord involvement, and characteristically some reflexes are exaggerated and others absent or lost due to a combination of anterior horn and pyramidal tract involvement. The triceps jerk is commonly lost as the

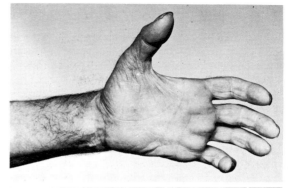
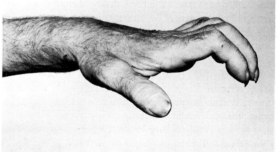

Fig. 18.4 Wasting of the small muscles of the hands

sixth cervical segment is frequently damaged. With involvement of the fifth cervical segment, the triceps jerk is preserved or exaggerated and tapping the lower end of the radius evokes reflex flexion of the fingers (inverted radial reflex). Spasticity may be evident in the upper limbs, but it is uncommon for it to be as marked as in the lower limbs.

Progressive impairment of gait with dragging of the feet when walking and a sensation of heaviness and weakness in the lower limbs is the characteristic presentation of spondylotic myelopathy.

A mild to moderate degree of ataxia may be evident. Examination reveals an incomplete spastic paraplegia. Rarely is the paraplegia severe enough to produce total immobility. Nurick (1970) showed that the presence of generalized vascular disease did not influence the severity of paraparesis. Vibration and position sense may be impaired. Muscle wasting of more than marginal degree is rare in the lower limbs.

Sensory symptoms of myelopathy are common, but rarely severe enough to be the cardinal feature of cord damage.

Paraesthesia and numbness in one or both upper and lower limbs or in the digits with variable impairment of appreciation of light touch, pin prick and tactile discrimination, and diminished vibration sense over the legs are the predominant findings.

Sphincter disturbance develops only in the late stage of myelopathy.

Anterolateral cord compression may occasionally produce a Brown-Sequard syndrome of ipsilateral pyramidal signs with contralateral anaesthesia below the level of the lesion.

Vertebrobasilar involvement has been considered earlier (p. 408).

Diagnostic procedures

Radiology. Pallis et al (1954) recorded radiological evidence of cervical spondylosis in 50 per cent of persons over the age of 50 and 75 per cent for those over the age of 65. McRae (1960) observed disc thinning and osteophytosis in 50 per cent of subjects over 40 years of age. He concluded that radiological changes of cervical spondylosis were likely to be of diagnostic significance only if they closely corresponded to the level of neurological disturbance. The minimum radiographic examination, based on the suggestions of Bull (1948) and Brain (1963), would be anteroposterior and laterals in flexion and extension and two oblique views. Narrowing of the intervertebral space due to disc degeneration is the radiological hallmark of spondylosis. C5–C6 and C6–C7 are the discs most frequently involved. Sclerosis of cortical bone in juxtaposition to the disc with secondary osteophytosis is usual, though not invariable. Osteophytes may develop anteriorly, but it is the posterior osteophytes that are of neurological significance as they encroach on the spinal canal or on the intervertebral foramina if they grow in a posterolateral direction. (Fig. 18.5) Posterolateral disc osteophytes are best demonstrated in the oblique radiograph. Osteophytic change in the neurocentral joints may also be visualized in this view or from an anteroposterior film. Osteoarthrosis of the apophyseal joints is apparent in the lateral radiograph but if the joint change is gross it will be seen also on an anteroposterior view.

The sagittal diameter from the posterior aspect of the vertebral body to the cortical line of the spinous process (Wolf et al, 1956) is often 10 mm or less in cervical myelopathy.

Myelography. Positive contrast myelography may be essential to exclude a second pathology in the presence of known cervical spondylosis, and in cases of spondylotic cord or root compression where surgery is contemplated. Cervical spondylosis produces one or several central or lateral filling defects in the myelogram.

Management of cervical spondylosis

Radiculopathy. If the onset is acute with severe pain in the neck and upper limb we have found the following regime effective:

1. Immediate provision of a Platazote collar which can be cut and shaped to fit each individual
2. Prohibition of undue physical activity involving the upper limbs, including avoidance of lifting or carrying heavy objects, e.g. buckets of coal.
3. The administration of one of the non-steroidal anti-inflammatory drugs for 2 weeks. In less severe cases simple analgesics may suffice.

Rarely bed rest for 2–3 days with constant cervical traction may be indicated.

Though intermittent traction may produce temporary relief, we have found that the overall results are no better than simple immobilization with a cervical collar. Locally applied heat is often of value in the acute phase.

With chronic long-standing pain in the neck, back of the head and/or arm with dysaesthesia, the use of a cervical collar for a few hours each day and mild analgesics are often all that is required. Unless symptoms are sufficiently distressing, patient compliance to wearing a cervical collar is unreliable.

Long-term forms of heat therapy are time-consuming and rarely achieve more than can be obtained from locally applied counter-irritant creams or the injection of local anaesthetic into tender trigger areas.

When pain has subsided, the muscles of the shoulder girdles and neck should be strengthened by active resisted exercises followed by relaxation exercises.

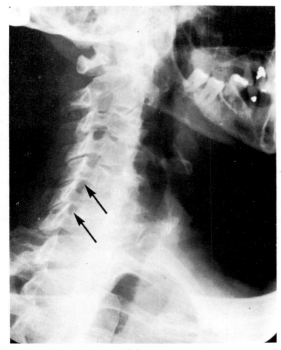

Fig. 18.5 Cervical spine 10/1/77. Degenerative changes are present with particular narrowing of the distances between C6/7. There is associated osteophyte formation with encroachment on the intervertebral foramina

Myelopathy. Care has to be exercised when considering the incidence of the major complications of cervical spondylosis reported in studies from major neurological or neurosurgical centres. These centres of excellence cater for a highly selected clientele whose constellation of clinical findings are unrepresentative of the usual clinical pattern of cervical spondylosis as seen in the general population. No surgical interference is required by the vast majority of elderly people with symptoms clearly attributable to cervical spondylosis. Fifty-three per cent of patients may improve symptomatically without treatment (Lees and Turner, 1963).

A number of surgical procedures have been advocated for the relief of the sequelae of cervical spondylosis. The main procedures that are in vogue are decompression surgery involving removal of (1) laminae (laminectomy), (2) bone around the intervertebral foramina (foraminotomy), and (3) the anterior intraspinal fusion technique described by Cloward (1958). Gregorius et al (1976) carried out a long-term follow-up study on 96 patients surgically treated for cervical spondylosis. The mean period of follow up after surgery was 7 years. They point out that the natural history of persistent symptomatic cervical spondylosis is one of progressive disability. Patients with myelopathy, particularly if very elderly or with severe gait disorder, did not always improve from surgery, but in general those subjected to anterior interbody fusion progressively improved whereas disability gradually worsened after any form of laminectomy, despite a phase of initial improvement in some patients. Recent studies have questioned the benefits of surgery over conservative management (Lunsford et al, 1980).

Giant cell arteritis

Giant cell arteritis (GCA) has been well reviewed by Hamilton (1971), Hamrin (1972), Hunder and Allen (1978–9). The disorder is characterized by a proliferative granulomatous arteritis of the aorta and its major arteries. Histological evidence of giant cell change is not invariable. Cohen and Smith (1974) maintain that skip areas of normal histology do not occur, but these areas have been clearly demonstrated in a few patients (Klein et al, 1976). The cervical segments of the internal and external carotid arteries and the temporal, ophthalmic and occipital arteries are particularly affected. Those portions of the carotid and vertebral arteries with a high elastic tissue content are particularly prone to be involved, (Wilkinson and Russell, 1972).

Aetiology

Giant cell arteritis is a condition of old age and is rare before age 50. Women are affected more often than men. The disease appears to occur most commonly in Northern areas and has a predilection for persons of Scandinavian descent. Familial aggregation is recorded

rarely (Liang et al, 1974). The possibility of abnormal immunological response to infection has been suggested (Bacon et al, 1975; Tan and Pearson, 1972; Liang et al, 1974).

Association with polymyalgia rheumatica. Nosologically, giant cell arteritis and polymyalgia rheumatica (PMR) are probably different manifestations of the one disorder (Huston et al, 1978). Polymyalgic symptoms frequently herald the localized symptoms of GCA and about a third of patients with PMR develop GCA at some stage in the course of the disease. About half of the patients with PMR have evidence of giant cell arteritis on routine biopsy (Dixon et al, 1966; Fourchard et al, 1972).

Clinical features

The mode of onset depends on the vessels involved, but typically the presentation is with pain in one or both fronto-temporal areas with tenderness, redness and diminished or absent pulsation over the temporal arteries. Hamilton has emphasized that there is no single reliable diagnostic sign and global evaluation of each individual case is critical. Headache may be localized or radiate to face, jaw or neck. It may be severe and boring in quality or diffuse and non-specific. Tenderness of the scalp may cause sleeplessness due to pain on touching the pillow. Combing or brushing the hair may be intolerable.

Intermittent claudication in the tongue is highly suggestive of the diagnosis and infarction of the lingular artery may ensue (Fig. 18.6).

Sudden partial or complete blindness in one or both eyes is the most frightening complication of this disorder. Visual complications may be the consequence of ischaemic optic or retrobulbar neuritis or of occlusion of the central retinal artery. Visual field defects occur occasionally. When diplopia occurs, it frequently presages visual loss.

Symmetrical peripheral neuropathy is an uncommon presentation (Warrell et al, 1968).

The vertebral arteries are more extensively involved than the internal carotids (Wilkinson and Russell, 1972) and brain stem or occipital lobe infarction may be a manifestation of giant cell arteritis. A lateral medullary syndrome is particularly likely to announce vertebral artery and its posterior inferior cerebellar artery branch involvement.

Pyrexia, anorexia, weight loss and depression are common features of GCA and may precede local symptoms by several weeks.

Joint pains may precede local symptoms by considerable periods, but evidence of objective synovitis is normally absent (O'Duffy et al, 1976).

Laboratory findings. A markedly elevated ESR often exceeding 100 mm in 1 hour (Westergren) is the characteristic finding.

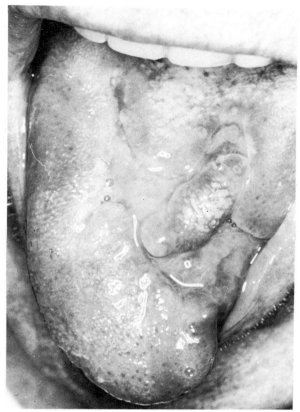

Fig. 18.6 Lingular artery infarction involving lateral aspect of tongue

Temporal artery biopsy is of value in confirming the diagnosis, (Fig. 18.7) but specific changes are not always found.

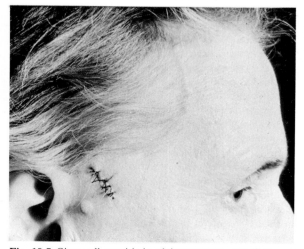

Fig. 18.7 Giant cell arteritis involving temporo mandibular artery. Biopsy of artery performed

Treatment

With adequate initial steroid therapy symptoms subside within 48 hours, though blindness remains permanent. Treatment with maintenance doses of steroid is required for at least 18 months, but often for considerably longer.

Transient global amnesia

Transient global amnesia (TGA) is a well defined clinical syndrome with a characteristic clinical picture of sudden transient memory loss. This clinical entity was first described under the name of transient global amnesia by Fisher and Adams (1958, 1964), though an earlier description of the syndrome was given by Bender (1956). It is predominantly a condition of elderly men and is rarely seen before the age of 50. The pathogenesis of TGA remains obscure and it is generally regarded as a benign condition (Godwin-Austen, 1982). Fisher and Adams (1964) considered a possible epileptic basis, but supportive features of epilepsy are rarely evident and epileptogenic focal abnormalities in the EEG are almost invariably absent. Godlewski (1968) noted symptoms suggestive of transient ischaemic attacks in the vertebro-basilar territory in some cases, but without neurological sequelae. Neuropsychological testing during an episode of TGA suggests that ischaemia in the medial temporal area around the hippocampus is responsible for the memory impairment (Ponsford and Donnan, 1980). Jensen and Olivarius (1980) discussed 10 cases with transient global amnesia all of whom had TIA's and six of the cases eventually developed a completed stroke. Migraine has been recorded in association with TGA (Olivarius and Jensen, 1979; Caplan et al, 1981) and Corston and Godwin-Austen (1982) have described the condition in four brothers.

The clinical picture is surprisingly well-defined. The onset is abrupt with the patient continuing a series of relevant and apparently normal activities for which he is subsequently amnesic. During an attack the patient may be agitated and may repeatedly ask where he is. On recovery there is complete amnesia for the period of the attack, but subsequent memory is normally unimpaired. However, Mathew and Meyer (1974) and Jensen and Olivarius (1980) record permanent short term memory loss in those cases complicated by strokes in the verte-brobasilar territory.

Frequently only one amnesic episode occurs, but a history of multiple attacks over several years is not uncommon.

Treatment

Most cases are regarded as benign and it would seem reasonable to provide simple reassurance. However, Jensen and Olivarius (1980) believe that transient global amnesia should be regarded as a symptom of vertebrobasilar insufficiency and that drugs that reduce platelet aggregation should be considered.

Progressive supranuclear palsy

Progressive supranuclear palsy (PSP) was first described as a clinico-pathological entity by Richardson et al in 1963. Symptoms develop in the 6th and 7th decade and run a progressive course to death in 4 to 7 years, but survival to 12 years may occur. The causation of PSP is unknown, but a viral role has been suspected in the aetiology (Steele, 1975).

The characteristic histopathological findings are the presence of neuronal loss, neurofibrillary tangles and astrocytic gliosis, particularly in the brain stem, diencephalon and cerebellum.

Progressive supranuclear palsy may present with insidious personality change progressing to overt dementia in about one-third of patients. Albert and his colleagues (1974) suggest that the dementia is typically subcortical in character. Non-specific gait impairment, visual disorders, slurred speech and dysphagia may be early features but the overall picture unfolds slowly over months or years.

A supranuclear ophthalmoplegia for vertical gaze is a consistent and characteristic finding and indeed it is a feature which may dominate the course of the disease from an early stage. A disturbance in lateral gaze is less common and usually occurs later in the disease. The eyes usually move fully if the gaze is fixed and the head moved passively, but difficulty in ocular fixation may be experienced. Ocular convergence is commonly impaired and this is associated with miosis and loss of pupillary response to accommodation.

The facial muscles are often rigid giving an immobile but furrowed facies. Increased tone may be evident on flexing and extending the neck, but not on rotation.

The position of the neck is commonly extended and in the presence of ophthalmoplegia it may make walking hazardous in the extreme. Richardson and his associates recorded axial dystonia and rigidity in the limbs as other significantly disabling manifestations of PSP.

Features of pseudobulbar palsy are commonly present and may progress relentlessly until the patient succumbs to an aspiration pneumonia. Emotional lability is not a pronounced feature, but spastic dysarthria may progress to anarthria. The jaw jerk is brisk, but increased tendon reflexes and the presence of an extensor plantar response is variable and usually a late feature.

Treatment

Treatment is largely supportive and symptomatic as with so many chronic progressive disabling disorders. Ophthalmoplegia (Mendell et al, 1970) and rigidity and bradykinesia (Dehaene and Bogaerts, 1970) have been reported to show some response to L-dopa therapy.

Motor neurone disease

The term motor neurone disease (MND) is commonly used to include progressive muscular atrophy (PMA), amyotrophic lateral sclerosis (ALS) and progressive bulbar palsy (PBP), but MND and ALS have been used interchangeably with little benefit to clarity.

MND is a disorder of world wide distribution affecting males more often than females. The disease is rarely evident before the age of 50 and it has a peak incidence at age 70. The point prevalence of MND is 5 per 100 000 in most populations (Kurtzke, 1982).

The disease in its classical distribution occurs spontaneously and its origin is unknown. 5–10 per cent of sporadic cases are familial (Horton et al, 1976). The Western Pacific form of ALS seen predominantly in the Chamorro tribe of Guam and among the population of the Kii peninsula of Japan is identical with the sporadic form, but occurs 50–100 times more frequently. About 10 per cent of these patients develop a Parkinsonian-dementia complex (Gajdusek, 1979). Trauma in the previous 5 years (Kondo and Tsubaki, 1981) particularly fractures of the limbs (Kurtzke and Beebe, 1980), appear to occur significantly more frequently than in the general population.

Pathologically there is demyelination of the antero-lateral tracts, particularly the pyramidal tracts, and loss of anterior horn cells and motor nuclei of the brain stem.

Clinical features

Anyone of the three components of MND may predominate, but it is uncommon for any one of the three to continue in its 'pure' form throughout its course. The disorder almost invariably progresses relentlessly with the worst prognosis in patients who present with bulbar palsy and the longest survival among those cases where progressive muscular atrophy continues in the absence of bulbar and pyramidal features.

Weakness and wasting most commonly first occur in the upper extremities and about equally in the lower limbs and bulbar region. Upper and lower motor neurone features frequently coexist and bulbar palsy is an early presentation in 30 per cent of cases.

Progressive muscular atrophy occasionally continues in the absence of upper motor neurone signs. Wasting of the small muscles of the hands with early involvement of the thenar eminence is followed by changes in the forearm flexors and biceps and later by more generalized spread to all muscle groups in the upper limbs including the shoulder girdle and the neck. Foot-drop may be the presenting feature of involvement of the lower limb muscles (Fig. 18.8).

Fasciculation is a prominent finding and may be localized to overtly wasted muscles or it may be more widespread. Tapping the affected muscles sharply may

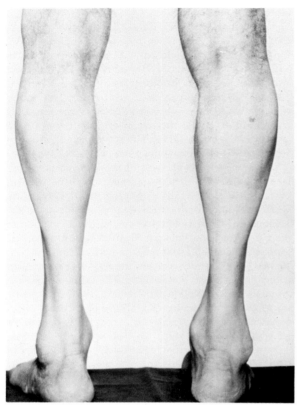

Fig. 18.8 Perineal muscular atrophy with bilateral foot drop

enhance the fasciculation. Involvement of the tongue is common and of particular diagnostic import.

Upper motor neurone signs are common and include hyperreflexia and hypertonus, particularly in the lower limbs, and ankle clonus. The jaw jerk is exaggerated. An extensor plantar response is present in only 20 per cent of cases (Bonduelle, 1975).

Bulbar palsy may present with dysarthria or dysphagia. The bulbar symptoms are most commonly due to lower motor neurone involvement (chronic bulbar palsy) and wasting and fasciculation of the tongue may be prominent. Involvement of the palate and usually the extrinsic muscles of the pharynx and larynx occur shortly after the tongue changes. The muscles of the lips are usually affected at much about the same time.

Fluids are particularly difficult to swallow and often regurgitate through the nose. Speech is nasal and involvement of the orbicularis oris impairs the ability to pronounce labials and dentals.

Upper motor neurone bulbar lesions are less common in motor neurone disease and produce the picture of pseudobulbar palsy with spastic dysarthria, dysphagia

and emotional lability. The spastic tongue is difficult to protrude. The jaw and glabella jerks are particularly brisk.

Signs of posterior column involvement are uncommon though most frequently found in familial cases of MND.

Hudson (1981) reviewed the evidence on the occurrence of dementia and/or Parkinsonism in sporadic ALS and believes that all three conditions are part of the same process.

Treatment
Treatment is symptomatic. In the presence of chronic bulbar palsy food is best taken in a semisolid form with careful checks on temperature. Salivation should be appropriately reduced with anticholinergic drugs and prostigmine may help swallowing.

Where aphonia occurs a small digital communicator (e.g. Cannon Communicator) may facilitate communication considerably. However, many patients manage adequately with pencil and paper.

Normal pressure hydrocephalus
The term normal pressure hydrocephalus was introduced by Adams et al (1965) when they reported three patients with progressive dementia associated with disordered gait who dramatically improved subsequent to the insertion of a ventriculoatrial shunt.

The absorption of cerebrospinal fluid is almost wholly via the arachnoid villi and arachnoid granulations (Oldenorf, 1972; Pollay, 1972). These structures are believed to function as collapsible unidirectional valves transmitting the flow of CSF from the subarachnoid space into the lumen of the superior sagital sinus and neighbouring venous lakes (Cutler et al, 1968; Potts et al, 1972). The pressure gradient between the subarachnoid space and the venous sinus may induce separation of the endothelial cells and facilitate unidirectional pinocytosis (Bradbury, 1979). Diffuse fibrosis may be found in the arachnoid granulations in old age. Wolf (1959) has indicated that these changes may impair CSF absorption and account for part of the dilatation of the ventricular system seen in old age, though hitherto age-related ventricular dilatation has been considered to be entirely secondary to cortical atrophy. The fibrosis with reduction of the intracranial subarachnoid space and involvement of the arachnoid granulations may be aggravated by previous subarachnoid haemorrhage, meningitis and brain trauma. Associated hypertensive cerebrovascular disease has been reported in some patients (Earnest et al, 1974; Buerger et al, 1976; Coblentz et al, 1973; Shukla et al, 1980).

Normal pressure hydrocephalus, which is essentially a condition of later life, may be defined as a communicating hydrocephalus in which 'the flow of CSF is obstructed in the intracranial subarachnoid spaces or the arachnoid granulations so that it cannot be absorbed into the venous circulation' (Kieffer, 1974). By definition the CSF pressure is less than 180 mm of water.

The mechanism of normal pressure hydrocephalus is not fully understood. Hakim and Adams (1965) considered that an initially raised pressure is required, but that once ventricular dilatation develops, the increased ventricular surface area exerts greater force with normal pressure — Pascal's principle of expansile force being equal to the product of pressure and area. More complex mathematical concepts have been advanced to explain the progressive ventricular dilatation in the presence of a normal CSF pressure (Epstein, 1974; Block and Tallala, 1976; Hakim et al, 1976; White et al, 1979).

The production of acute hydrocephalus in the experimental animal is followed by rapid ventricular dilatation in a matter of hours with flattening of the ventricular ependymal cells and the development of progressively enlarging gaps between the cells (Clarke and Milhorat, 1972; Milhorat et al, 1970). The seepage of CSF through the gaps between the ventricular ependymal cells into the adjacent brain substance has been put forward as a compensatory mechanism when normal CSF absorption is impaired (Milhorat et al, 1970).

The clinical onset of normal pressure hydrocephalus is commonly rapid with a generally recognized triad of progressive dementia, spastic ataxic gait and incontinence of urine and faeces. Mild short-term memory loss, apathy and personality change may be the initial manifestations of dementia, but symptoms often accelerate rapidly with marked deterioration of intellect and sometimes indifference of striking degree which may progress to akinetic mutism. The disorder of gait is variable, but it is essentially a spastic ataxia. Difficulty in initiating movement is common and a *marche de petits pas* may be evident. Postural maintenance is often poor and repeated falls are not uncommon. Motor tone is increased, tendon reflexes exaggerated and plantar responses are extensor. Occasionally pouting and sucking reflexes can be elicited. Tremor and muscle rigidity of Parkinsonian type is less common. Sphincter disturbance, particularly urinary incontinence, is a common but not invariable feature of this disorder.

Diagnosis

Evaluation of current diagnostic techniques is controversial. Daily lumbar puncture over two days often produces observable short-lived improvement in mental state and gait and has limited diagnostic value. Wikkels et al (1982) noted that the temporary improvement following the removal of 40–50 ml. CSF at lumbar puncture correlated well with the improvement following shunt operation.

Air-contrast studies produce a temporary exacerbation of symptoms. The diagnostic value of air encephalography is hotly disputed. Using pneumoencephalographic criteria, Kieffer (1974) was unable to distinguish patients with normal pressure hydrocephalus who should benefit from a shunt operation from those with hydrocephalus secondary to cerebral atrophy who do not benefit by surgery. Benson (1974) found air-contrast studies to be of considerable value. Pneumoencephalography is not necessary where CT is available.

Scinticisternography. Scinticisternography is a useful diagnostic procedure in assessing whether patients with suspected normal pressure hydrocephalus will be helped by a shunting operation. A number of isotopes have been used for scinticisternography, but [99 m]Tc-labelled albumin is probably the most suitable due to its short half-life. The labelled technetium is introduced into the subarachnoid space via a lumbar puncture and the brain is scanned at 24-hour intervals for 2 days. In normal pressure hydrocephalus, the cerebral ventricles are visualized as being densely filled with isotope, with no radiosensitivity detected over the cerebral surfaces due to subarachnoid block.

Long-term pressure recording. This technique of long-term intracranial pressure measurements may provide appropriate information to identify those patients who will respond well to shunt procedures, (Symon and Hinzpeter, 1976; Chawla et al, 1974). However it is clear that a chronic history and the presence of all features of the classical triad of symptoms, particularly gait disturbance are among the most effective predictors of a good outcome from a shunt operation.

C.T. Scan. The presence of enlarged ventricles with little or no cortical atrophy is not only the single most useful evidence of normal pressure hydrocephalus, but these two findings closely correlate with a good outcome from shunting (Black, 1980).

Treatment

General treatment is the symptomatic management of dementia, gait disorders and urinary incontinence. A few patients with normal pressure hydrocephalus subsequent to subarachnoid haemorrhage will recover spontaneously in a matter of months. With these exceptions the condition progresses to profound dementia and immobility unless cerebrospinal fluid can be constantly removed to an extracranial site by some form of shunting procedure. The original techniques involved shunting CSF, from a lateral cerebral ventricle to the left atrium of the heart or to the peritoneal cavity (ventriculoatrial and ventriculoperitoneal shunts respectively). A more recently introduced shunt from the lumbar subarachnoid sac to the peritoneum is technically less complicated and does not involve intracranial surgery. Each procedure is subject to technical complications, particularly involving the maintenance of optimum CSF flow, and to medical complications.

The latter include subdural haematoma due to rupture of cortical emissary veins consequent to relief of intra-cerebral tension, embolus formation, meningitis and brain abscess. Ojemann et al (1969) summarized their experience of ventriculoatrial shunting. Of 13 patients where the causes of hydrocephalus with normal pressure was unknown, 8 improved. All 4 patients whose hydrocephalus was subsequent to a subarachnoid haemorrhage improved dramatically and 4 cases in whom cerebral trauma was considered causal showed moderate improvement. In a study of 125 patients with progressive dementia, Kieffer (1974) found that of the 26 patients submitted to ventriculoatrial shunt procedures, improvement was recorded in those patients who showed persistent ventricular reflux associated with a delay in subarachnoid flow on scinticisternography. No patient with normal subarachnoid flow benefited from a shunt operation.

In the study by Black (1980) computerized tomography showing large ventricles and little atrophy predicted improvement to shunting in 11 out of 13 patients. Before contemplating a shunt procedure it should be recalled that complications occur in about a third of these elderly patients (Laws and Mokri, 1977; Greenberg et al, 1977; Black, 1980).

Intracranial tumours

McKeown (1965) found primary brain tumours in 14 per cent of a series of 1500 autopsies on persons aged 70 years and over. In both general neurosurgical and autopsy series, gliomas account for rather over 40 per cent of tumours, whereas metaplastic lesions comprise about 5 per cent of tumours in neurosurgical series, but form 25 per cent of intracranial malignancy in post-mortem studies. The incidence of metastatic tumours increases with age (Palma, 1972). Primary benign and malignant intracranial tumours occur throughout the age spectrum, but certain tumours have a proclivity for particular age groups. McKeown recorded a high post-mortem diagnosis of meningiomas in the elderly, and Hurwitz and Swallow (1971), in a study of 60 patients presenting with dementia, found 7 proven tumours, 5 of which were meningiomas. The investigators themselves remarked on the striking reversal of the usual incidence of cerebral tumour pathology. Moersch et al (1941) reviewed 100 patients aged 60 and over with brain tumours and found only 1 case with astrocytoma, but Knox and Adams (1969) reported 5 patients with a hemiplegic presentation of a brain tumour and 4 had astrocytomas. Bonnaud et al (1974) noted that the early presentation of intracerebral metastases often simulated a cerebrovascular accident, and Padt et al (1973) noted that 2.5 per cent of patients with brain tumours presented as acute intracerebral haemorrhage.

Hurwitz and Swallow (1971) found that 11.7 per cent

of elderly persons with dementia had a proven intracranial tumour. Dementia has been reported in association with carcinomatous infiltration of the leptomeninges (Fischer-Williams et al, 1955). The clinical presentation of intracranial tumours in the elderly is essentially similar to that in younger adults and only those points of reasonable differences have received comment. Diagnosis will largely rest on historical and objective clinical findings, but supplementary diagnostic procedures may be essential.

Investigations

Radiology of the chest to exclude a primary brochogenic carcinoma is essential and of the skull is sometimes useful. In the latter an abnormal area of calcification, pineal shift or bony erosion may be of diagnostic importance. Pituitary adenoma 'balloons' the sella and an acoustic neuroma may expand and erode the internal auditory meatus. Most often the skull X-ray reveals little or nothing of diagnostic value. A focal abnormality of the EEG is valuable in the absence of clinical evidence of a cerebrovascular accident. Angiography often provides localizing and diagnostic information, but is potentially hazardous in the elderly.

Computed tomography (CT) scanning offers a safe, non-invasive method of diagnosing brain tumours. An early review of 366 patients, Ambrose et al (1975) quantified the diagnostic accuracy of computerized transverse axial scanning in intracranial tumours. As a screening technique it was found to have an accuracy of 96 per cent in their hands. The CT scan defined a structural abnormality and enabled a diagnosis to be made or a lesion to be excluded in 92.3 per cent of patients, results comparable to that which Ambrose and his colleagues obtained with angiography and pneumoencephalography.

Gliomas commonly show a variable diminished density or a mixture of increased and diminished density. Meningiomas appear as areas of increased density. Metastases are characterized by being multiple separate lesions often surrounded by a zone of low density due to oedema.

Treatment

Benign lesions such as meningiomas may be amenable to surgery if not too large or inaccessible. Few malignant lesions are surgically treatable in the elderly. Fager (1975), however, firmly believes that solitary intracranial secondaries from breast or kidney should be removed, as probably should also a secondary from an asymptomatic bronchogenic primary.

General management. Pain should always be controlled by adequate analgesia, but mental alertness maintained as far as possible. Agitation or restlessness may require major tranquillizers. The air of pessimism that so often surrounds patients with incurable disease is to be avoided. Gait difficulties may be helped by a simple walking frame. The patient and his family require supervised encouragement and tangible help. If family support is fragile, residential care may be required in the terminal phase. The specialized homes or institutions for cancer patients play an important supportive role in all stages of incurable malignancy, but hospital care may ultimately be required in many areas.

Isotope brain scanning

Technetium (99 Tc) is the radioisotope commonly used for brain scanning. The dose of radiation is minimal and the half-life is only 6 hours. The scan is performed shortly after the intravenous injection. The isotope concentrates in several tumours and in abscesses, infarcts and subdural haematomas and the gamma emissions are detected by a rectilinear scanner. Photoscans can be obtained using a gamma camera system.

Computed tomography

This method of tomography, introduced by Nobel Prizewinner, Godfrey Hounsfield, uses multidirectional X-ray scanning of transverse 'slices' of brain and the X-ray photons are received by multiple detectors and are converted into scintillations. The vast amount of information generated requires computerization for image processing.

The information is usually presented on the cathode ray tube in grey scale with the most dense tissues appearing white and the least dense, shades of grey. Dense tissues absorb more X-ray photons than less dense tissue.

Contrast enhancement of the images following intravenous injection of contrast material improves definition in those structures in which the iodine concentration is selectively increased (tumours, abscesses, infarcts,

aneurysms). Subdural haematoma may be hyperdense, isodense or hypodense depending on the stage of the lesion.

The introduction of more complex computer analysis now makes it possible to image the brain in sagittal and coronal planes as well as conventional CT views. CT directed biopsy and preoperative CT scanning during craniotomy is now possible (Brown et al, 1981; Kelly et al, 1981).

Digital vascular imaging (digital subtraction angiography)

This system of vascular imaging is still in the development stages but holds great promise for the safe investigation of the vascular system by intravenous injection of contrast material using image intensification with television recording. The computer processed information subtracts the imaging change before and after contrast injection using real-time and provides immediate display which can be recorded for storage.

Nuclear magnetic resonance (NMR)

Nuclear magnetic resonance is based on the physical properties exhibited by nuclear protons of responding to exposure to specific radiofrequency waves when placed in a strong magnetic field by resonating at the same frequency. Varying the magnetic field strength allows detection of differences in body composition. The grey and white matter of the brain can be readily distinguished (Bydder et al, 1982; Pollett et al, 1981).

The bony skull is not visualized and the technique has been suggested to be of value in defining subdural haematomas. The use of ^{31}p with NMR is likely to allow precise characterization of cerebrovascular occlusions. The technique is apparently safe and the only currently identified potential biological hazard is heating.

REFERENCES

Adams C B T, Logue V 1971 Studies in cervical myelopathy. Brain 94: 557–568

Adams R D, Fisher C M, Hakim S 1965 Symptomatic occult hydrocephalus with 'normal' cerebrospinal fluid. A treatable syndrome. New England Journal of Medicine 273: 117–126

Adornato B T, Glasberg M R 1980 Diseases of the Spinal Cord in Neurology Science and Practice of Clinical Medicine Rosenberg R N (ed), Vol 5, p 392–433. N Y Grune and Stratton

Ajuriaguerra J, Reggo A, Rissot R 1963 The oral reflex and various oral activities in dementia syndromes of old age: their significance in psychomotor disintegration. Encéphale 52: 189–219

Albert M L, Feldman R G, Willis A L 1974 The 'subcortical dementia' of progressive supranuclear palsy. Journal of Neurology, Neurosurgery and Psychiatry 37: 121–130

Allison R S 1962 The Senile Brain. A Clinical Study. Arnold E, London

Alpers B J, Berry R G, Paddison R M 1959 Anatomical studies in the circle of Willis in normal brain. Archives of Neurology and Psychiatry (Chicago) 81: 409–418

Ambani L M, Van Woert M H 1973 Start hesitation: a side effect of long-term Levodopa therapy. New England Journal of Medicine 288: 1113–1115

Ambrose J, Gooding M R, Richardson A E 1975 An Assessment of the accuracy of computerized transverse axial scanning (EMI scanner) in the diagnosis of intra-cranial tumour. Brain 98: 561–581

Andrew W 1971 The Anatomy of Aging in Man and Animals. New York: Grune and Stratton

Appenzeller O, Goss J E 1971 Autonomic deficits in Parkinson's syndrome. Archives of Neurology 24: 50–57

Arnold N, Harriman D G F 1970 The incidence of abnormalities in control of human peripheral nerves studied by single axon dissection. Journal of Neurology, Neurosurgery and Psychiatry 33: 55–61

Bacon P A, Doherty S M, Zuckerman A J 1975 Hepatitis-B antibody in polymyalgia Rheumatica. Lancet ii: 476–478

Bannister R 1971 Degeneration of the autonomic nervous system. Lancet ii: 175–179

Bannister R, Ardhill L, Fentem P 1967 Defective autonomic control of blood vessels in idiopathic orthostatic hypotension. Brain 90: 725–746

Barmeir E, Dubowitz B 1981 Grey-white matter interface (G-WMI) displacement: a new sign in the computed tomographic diagnosis of subtle subdural hematomas. Clinical Radiology 32: 393–396

Bastian F O, Rabson A S, Yee C L et al 1972 Herpes virus hominis: Isolation from human trigeminal ganglion. Science 178: 306–307

Barbeau A, Gillo-Joffroy L, Boucher R, Nowaczynski W, Genest J 1969 Renin aldosterone system in Parkinson's disease. Science, N.Y. 165: 291–292

Barbeau A 1971 Long term side effects of Levodopa. Lancet i: 395

Bauer R B, Sheehan S, Wechsler N, Meyer J S 1962 Arteriographic study of sites, incidence and treatment of arteriosclerotic cerebrovascular lesions. Neurology (Minneapolis) 12: 698–711

Bauer R B, Wechsler N, Meyer J S 1961 Carotid compression and rotation of the head in occlusive vertebral artery disease: relation to carotid sinus sensitivity. Annals of Internal Medicine 55: 283–291

Bean B, Braun C, Balfour H H 1982 Acydovirus therapy for acute herpes zoster. Lancet 2: 118–121

Begbie G H 1967 Myotatic, Kinesthetic and Vestibular Mechanisms. Ciba Foundation Symposium, de Reuck A V S, Knight J (ed), p 80–92. J & A Churchill, London

Bender M B 1956 Syndrome of isolated episode of confusion with amnesia. Journal of the Hillside Hospital 5: 212–215

Bender M B 1970 Perceptual Interactions. In: Williams D (ed) Modern trends in neurology, Butterworth, London

Bender M B 1975 The Incidence and Type of Perceptual Deficiencies in the Aged. In: Fields W S (ed) Neurological and sensory disorders in the elderly, p 15–31. Medical Book Corporation, Stratton Intercontinental, New York

Bender M B, Feldman M 1972 The so-called 'visual agnosias'. Brain 95: 173–186

Bender M B, Fink M, Green M 1951 Patterns in perception on simultaneous tests of face and hand. Archives of Neurology and Psychiatry (Chicago) 66: 355

Benedict W L 1933 Retrobular neuritis and disease of the nasal accessory sinuses. Proceedings of Staff Meetings of the Mayo Clinic 8: 147–149

Benson F 1974 Normal pressure hydrocephalus. A controversial entity. Geriatrics 83: 125–132

Bhattia S P, Irvine R E 1973 Electrical recording of the ankle jerk in old age. Gerontologia Clinica 15: 357–360

Bieger D, Giles S A, Hockman C H 1977 Dopaminergic influences on swallowing. Neuropharmacology 16: 243–252

Birren J E, Shock N W 1950 Age changes in rate and level of visual dark adaptation. Journal of Applied Physiology 2: 407–411

Black P McL 1980 Idiopathic normal pressure hydrocephalus. Results of shunting in 62 patients. Journal of Neurosurgery 52: 371–377

Blau J N, Logue V 1961 Intermittent claudication of the cauda equina. Lancet i: 1081–1086

Bloch R, Talalla A 1976 A mathematical model of cerebrospinal fluid dynamics. Journal of the Neurological Sciences 27: 485–498

Blom S 1962 Trigeminal neuralgia: its treatment with a new anticonvulsant drug. Lancet i: 839–840

Bonduelle M 1975 Amyotrophic Lateral Sclerosis. In Vinken P J, Bruyn G W (ed) Handbook of clinical neurology, vol 22, North Holland Publishing Co. Amsterdam, p 281–338

Bonnaud E, Latinville D, Henry P, Lowseau P 1974 Un aspect tromper des metastases cérébrales les formes pseudovasculaires. Bordeaux Medecin 7: 1137–1142

Bourlière F 1963 Principles et méthodes de mesure del'âge biologique chez l'homme. Bulletin et Memoires de la Societe d'Anthropologie, Paris 4: 561–583

Bradbury M 1979 The Concept of a Blood Brain Barrier. John Wiley, Chichester

Bradley W G 1974 In: Disorders of Peripheral Nerves. Blackwell Scientific Publications, Oxford

Brain W R 1956 Some aspects of neurology of cervical spine. Journal of the Faculty of Radiologists 8: 74–91

Brain W R 1963 Some unsolved problems of cervical spondylosis. British Medical Journal 1: 771–777

Bramble M G, Cunliffe J, Dellipiani A W 1978 Evidence for a change in neurotransmitter affecting oesophageal motility in Parkinson's disease. Journal of Neurology, Neurosurgery and Psychiatry 41: 709–712

Brimblecombe R W, Pinder R M 1972 In: Tremors and Tremogenic Agents. Scientechnica Publishers Ltd, Bristol

Brown E L, Knox E G 1972 Epidemiological approach to Parkinson's disease. Lancet i: 974–979

Brown R A, Roberts T, Osborne A G 1981 Simplified CT-guided stereotaxic biopsy. American Journal of Neuroradiology 2: 181–184

Brownwell B, Hughes J T 1975 Necropsy observations on the damage to the nervous system in degenerative disease of the cervical spine. Proceedings of the 5th International Congress on Neuropathology 551–554

Bull J W D 1948 Discussion on the rupture of the intervertebral disc in the cervical region. Proceedings of the Royal Society of Medicine 41: 513–516

Bull J W D, Nixon W L B, Pratt R T C 1955 The radiological criteria and familiar occurrence of primary basilar impression. Brain 78: 229–247

Brumlik J, Yapp G B 1971 In Normal Tremor, A Comparative Study. Springfield, Illinois: C C Thomas

Bruyn G W 1979 'Carcinomatous polyneuropathy' In: Vinken F J, Bruyn G W (eds) Handbook of clinical neurology 38, p 679–693. North-Holland, Amsterdam

Bruyn G W, Garland H 1970 Neuropathies of endocrine origin. In: Vinken P J, Bruyn G W (eds) Handbook of Clinical Neurology, vol 8, p 29–71. North-Holland, Amsterdam

Bryndum B, Marquardsen J 1964 The tendon reflexes in old age. Gerontologia Clinica 6: 257–265

Buerger, P C, Burch J G, Kunze U 1976 Subcortical arteriosclerotic encephalopathy (Binswanger's disease). A vascular etiology of dementia. Stroke 7: 626–631

Burrows E H 1963 The sagittal diameter of the spinal cord in cervical spondylosis. Clinical Radiology 14: 77–86

Bydder G M, Steiner R E, Young I R et al 1982 Clinical NMR imaging of the brain: 140 cases. American Journal of Roentgenology 139: 215–236

Caplan L, Chedru F, Hermitte F, Mayman C 1981 Transient global amnesia and migraine. Neurology (N.Y.) 31: 1167–1170

Chakravorty B G 1969 Arterial supply of the cervical spinal spondylosis. Annals of the Royal College of Surgeons of England 45: 232–251

Chawla J C, Hulme A, Cooper R 1974 Intracranial pressure in patients with dementia and communicating hydrocephalus. Journal of Neurosurgery 40: 376–380

Chazot G, Berger G, Bady B, Dumas R, Crevsel R, Tommasi M et al 1974 Neuropathie périphérique an coms des dysglobulinemies malignes. Nouvelle Presse Medicale 3: 1355–1358

Chazot G, Berger B, Carrier H, Barbaret C, Bady B, Dumas R, Creyssel R, Schott R 1976 Manifestations neurologiques des ganorapathies monoclonales. Revue Neurologique 132: 195–212

Chisholm I A 1972 The dyschromatopsia of pernicious anaemia. Modern Problems of Ophthalmology 11: 130–135

Chisholm I A 1979 Anaemia: general and neuro-ophthalmic features in Handbook of Clinical Neurology 38, eds. P J Vinken, G W Bruyn, p 15–32, North-Holland, Amsterdam

Clements R S and Bell D S H 1982 Diabetic neuropathy: peripheral and autonomic syndromes. Postgraduate Medicine 71: 50–67

Cloward R B 1958 Anterior approach for removal of ruptured cervical discs. Journal of Neurosurgery 15: 601–617

Coakley D, Thomas J G 1976 The effect of age and eye-position on the normal ocular microtremor record. Proceedings of the Physiological Society Sept. C 25: 31–32

Coblentz J M, Mathis S, Zingesser L H et al 1973 Presenile dementia. Clinical aspects and evaluation of cerebrospinal fluid dynamics. Archives of Neurology 29: 299–308

Cohen D N, Smith R T 1974 Skip lesions in temporal arteritis: myth versus fact. Transactions of the American Academy of Ophthalmology and Otolaryngology 78: 772–778

Cooper R, Balish I, Zubek J 1959 The effect of age on taste sensitivity. Journal of Gerontology 14: 56–58

Corston R N, Godwin-Austen R B 1982 Transient global amnesia in four brothers. Journal of Neurology, Neurosurgery and Psychiatry 45: 375–377

Cotzias G C, Papavasiliou P S, Tolosa E S, Mendez J S, Bell-Midura M 1976 Treatment of Parkinson's disease with aporphines. New England Journal of Medicine 11: 567–572

Cox E V 1962 The clinical manifestations of vitamin B_{12} deficiency in Addisonian pernicious anaemia. Vitamin B_{12} and intrinsic factor. 2.

Europaisches symposium. Hamburg, 1961, ed. Henrich H C, p 590. Stuttgart: Enke

Crandall P H, Hanafee W M 1964 Cervical spondylotic myelopathy studies by air myelography. American Journal of Roentgenology 92: 1260–1269

Cream J J, Hern J E C, Hughes R A C, Mackenzie I C K 1974 Mixed or immune complex cryoglobulinaemia and neuropathy. Journal of Neurology, Neurosurgery and Psychiatry 37: 82–87

Critchley M 1931 Neurology of old age. Lancet i: 1119–1127; 1221–1230; 1331–1336

Critchley M 1956a Neurological changes in the aged. Journal of Chronic Diseases 3: 459–477

Critchley M 1956b Neurological changes in the aged. Proceedings of the Society for Research into Nervous and Mental Disease 35: 459–477

Currie S, Henson R A, Morgan H G, Poole A J 1970 The incidence of non-metastatic neurological syndromes of absence origin in the reticulosis. Brain 93: 629–640

Cutler R W P, Page L, Galicich J 1968 Formation and absorption of cerebro-spinal fluid in man. Brain 91: 707–720

Damasio A R, Castro-Caidas A, Levy A 1973 The on-off effect. Advances in Neurology, ed. Calne D B, vol 13, 11–22. New York: Raven Press

Daniels L E 1940 Paraplegia in flexion. Archives of Neurology and Psychiatry (Chicago) 43: 736–764

Davis J L, Lewis S B, Gerich J E, Kaplan R A, Schultz T A, Wallin J D 1977 Peripheral diabetic neuropathy treated with amitriptyline and fluphenazine. Journal of the American Medical Association 238: 2291–2292

Dayan A D, Lewis P D 1966 Demyelinating neuropathy in macroglobulinaemia. Neurology (Minneapolis) 16: 1141–1144

Dehaene L, Bogaerts M 1970 L-dopa in progressive supranuclear palsy. Lancet 2: 470

Déjérine J 1911 La claudication intermittente de la moelle épiniére. Presse méd. 19: 981–984

De Kleyn A, Nieuwenheyse P 1927 Schwindelpnfalle und nystagmus ber einder besbimmetmen. Stellung des Kopfes. Acta Otolaryngologica Stockholm 11: 155–157

Denny-Brown D 1948 Primary sensory neuropathy with muscular changes associated with carcinoma. Journal of Neurology, Neurosurgery and Psychiatry 11: 73–87

Denny-Brown D, Brenner C 1944 Paralysis of nerve induced by direct pressure and by tourniquet. Archives of Neurology and Psychiatry 51: 1–26

Desmet Y, Ruberg M, Serdaru M, Dubois B, Lhermitte F, Agid Y 1982 Confusion, dementia and anticholinergics in Parkinson's disease. Journal of Neurology, Neurosurgery and Psychiatry 45: 1161–1164

Direnfeld K L, Feldman R G, Alexander M P, Kelly-Hayes M 1980 Is levodopa drug holiday useful? Neurology (N.Y.) 30: 785–788

Dixon A S, Beardwell C, Kay A et al 1966 Polymyalgia rheumatica and temporal arteritis. Annals of the Rheumatic Diseases 25: 203–208

Donaldson G W K, Grahan J G 1965 Aplastic anaemia following the administration of Tegretol. British Journal of Clinical Practice 79: 699–702

Downie A 1982 Peripheral nerve compression syndromes. In: Matthews W B, Glaser G H (eds) Recent advances in clinical neurology, Churchill Livingstone, Edinburgh, p 48–66

Drawber R 1974 Idoxuridine in herpes zoster; further evaluation of intermittent topical therapy. British Medical Journal 2: 526–527

Dyck P J 1982 Current concepts in neurology. The causes, classification and treatment of peripheral neuropathy. New England Journal of Medicine 307: 283–286

Dyck P J, Lambert E H 1970 Polyneuropathy associated with hypothyroidism. Journal of Neuropathology and Experimental Neurology 29: 631–658

Dyck P J, Oviatt K F, Lambert E H 1981 Intensive evaluation of unclassified neuropathies yields improved diagnosis. Annals of Neurology 10: 222–226

Dyck P J, Schultz P W, O'Brien P C 1972 Quantitation of touch-pressure sensation. Archives of Neurology and Psychiatry (Chicago) 26: 465–473

Earnest M P, Fahn S, Karp J H et al 1974 Normal pressure

hydrocephalus and hypertensive cerebrovascular disease. Archives of Neurology 31: 262–266

Ehringer H, Hornykiewicz O 1960 Verteilung von noradrenalin und dopamin (3-hydroxytramin) im Gehirn des menschen und ihr verhalten bei erkankungen des extrapyramisdalen system. Klinische Wochenschrift 38: 1236–1239

Ellis F G 1962 Acute polyneuritis after nitrofurantoin. Lancet ii: 1136–1138

El-Toraei I, Juler G 1979 Ischemic myelopathy. Angiology 30: 81–94

Epstein C M 1974 The distribution of intracranial forces in acute and chronic hydrocephalus. Journal of the Neurological Sciences 21: 171–180

Epstein J A, Epstein B S, Lavine L S, Carras R, Rosenthal A D 1978 Cervical myeloradiculopathy caused by arthrotic hypertrophy of the posterior facets and luminae. Journal of Neurosurgery 49: 387–392

Esiri M M, Tomlinson A H 1972 Herpes zoster. Demonstrations of virus in trigeminal nerve and ganglion by immunofluorescence and electron microscopy. Journal of the Neurological Sciences 15: 35–48

Fager C A 1975 Indications for neurosurgical intervention in metastatic lesions of the central nervous system. In: Oberfield R A (ed) The Medical Clinics of North America, W B Saunders Co, Philadelphia, 59: 481–493

Fauchald P, Rygold O, Oystese B 1972 Temporal arteritis and polymyalgia rheumatica. Clinical and biopsy findings. Annals of Internal Medicine 77: 845–852

Feindel W, Stratford J 1958 The role of the cubital tunnel in tardy ulnar palsy. Canadian Journal of Surgery 1: 287–300

Feldman R G, Direnfeld L, Alexander M, Kelly-Hayes M. Is L-Dopa 'Drug Holiday' useful? Neurology 29: 553

Ferguson R H, Slocumb C H 1961 Peripheral neuropathy in rheumatoid arthritis. Bulletin of the Rheumatic Diseases 11: 251–254

Fink M, Green M, Bender M B 1952 The face-hand test as a diagnostic sign of organic mental syndrome. Neurology 2: 46

Finnerty F A JR, Witkin L, Fazekas J F 1954 Cerebral haemodynamics during cerebral ischaema induced by acute hypotension. Journal of Clinical Investigation 33: 1227–1232

Fischer-Williams M, Bosanquet F D, Daniel P M 1955 Carcinomatosis of the meninges; a report on three cases. Brain 78: 42–58

Fisher C M, Adams R D 1958 Transient global amnesia. Transactions of the American Neurological Association 83: 143–145

Fisher C M, Adams R D 1964 Transient global amnesia. Acta Neurologica Scandinavica 40 Suppl. 9: 1–83

Fisher C M 1982 Late-life chronic peripheral neuropathy of obscure nature. Archives of Neurology 39: 234–235

Flowers K A 1976 Visual closed loop and open loop characteristics of voluntary movement in patients with Parkinsonism. Brain 99: 269–310

Frykholm R 1951 Cervical nerve root compression resulting from disc degeneration and root sleeve fibrosis. Acta Chirurgica Scandinavica suppl. 160

Fujisawa K 1974 Some observations on the skeletal musculature of aged rats. 1. Histological aspects. Journal of the Neurological Sciences 22: 353–366

Gajdusek D C 1979 A focus of high incidence amyotrophic lateral sclerosis and Parkinsonism and dementia syndromes in a small population of Auyn and Jakai people of Southern West New Guinea. In: Tsubaki T, Toyokura Y, (eds) Amyotrophic lateral sclerosis, p 287–305. University Park Press, Baltimore (Japan Medical Research Foundation Publ. No. 8)

Galbraith A W 1973 Treatment of acute zoster with ammantadine hydrochloride (Symmetrel). British Medical Journal 4: 693–695

Gamba E T, Wolfe A, Yahr M D, Harter D H, Duffy F E, Barden H, Hsu S C 1974 Influenza virus antigen in postencephalitic Parkinsonism brain. Archives of Neurology 31: 228

Gamstorp I, Kupfer C 1961 Denervation of extra ocular and skeletal muscles in a case of pernicious anaemia. Neurology (Minneapolis) 11: 182–184

Gardner W J 1932 Traumatic subdural hematoma with particular reference to the latent period. Archives of Neurology and Psychiatry 27: 847–858

Garland J 1943 Varicella following exposure to herpes zoster. New England Journal of Medicine 228: 336–337

Garland H G 1952 Parkinsonism. British Medical Journal 2: 153–155

Garland H G 1955 Some clinical aspects of Parkinsonism. Proceedings of the Royal Society of Medicine 48: 867–868

Garland H J, Greenberg J, Harriman D E F 1966 Infarction of the spinal cord. Brain 89: 645–662

Gelhorn E 1958 Surgical treatment of cervical spondylosis. Confinia Neurologica 24: 1–24

Gelhorn E 1964 Neurophysiology of associated movements in hemiplegia. Confinia Neurologica 24: 1–24

Gershon A A, Steinberg S P 1981 Antibody response to varicella zoster virus and the role of antibody in hos defense. American Journal of the Medical Sciences 282: 12–17

Ghatak N R, Zimmerman H M 1973 Spinal ganglion in herpes zoster. A light and electron microscopic study. Archives of Pathology 95: 411–415

Gilliatt R W 1965 Clinical aspects of diabetic neuropathy, p 117–142. In Biochemical Aspects of Neurological Disorders, ed. Cummings J N, Kremer M 2nd series. Oxford: Blackwell Scientific Publications

Gilliatt R W 1975 Peripheral nerve compression and entrapment. In: Lant A F (ed) Eleventh Symposium on Advanced Medicine, p 144–163. Pitman Medical, Tunbridge Wells

Godlewski S 1968 Les episodes amnesiques (Transient global amnesia). Etude clinique basée sur 33 observations inétites. Semaine des hôpitaux de Paris 44: 553–577

Godwin-Austen R B 1982 Where am I? British Medical Journal 285: 85–86

Goetz C G, Tanner C M, Nausieda P A 1981 Weekly drug holiday in Parkinson disease. Neurology (N.Y.) 31: 1460–1462

Goldberg A D, Rafferty E B, Cashmann P M M 1975 Ambulatory electrocardiographic records in patients with transient cerebral attacks or palpitation. British Medical Journal 4: 569–571

Goldstein K 1938 Tonic foot response to stimulation of sole: its physiological significance and diagnostic value. Brain 61: 269–283

Graham J G, Oppenheimer D R 1969 Orthostatic hypotension and nicotine sensitivity in a case of multiple system atrophy. Journal of Neurology, Neurosurgery and Psychiatry 32: 28–34

Green M, Fink M 1974 Simultaneous tactile perception in patients with conversion sensory deficits. Mount Sinai Journal of Medicine 41: 141–143

Greenbaum D 1964 Observations on the homogenous nature of diabetic neuropathy. Brain 87: 215–232

Greenberg J O, Shenkin H A, Adam R 1977 Idiopathic normal pressure hydrocephalus — a report of 73 patients. Journal of Neurology, Neurosurgery and Psychiatry 40: 336–341

Gregorius F K, Estrin T, Crandall P H 1976 Cervical spondylotic radiculopathy and myelopathy. Archives of Neurology 53: 618–625

Gresty M A, Findley L J 1981 Tremors in Parkinson's disease. In Research in Parkinson's Disease, ed. F C Rose, R Capildeo. Pitman Medical, p 75–87

Gross M, Bannister R, Godwin-Austen R 1972 Orthostatic hypotension in Parkinson's disease. Lancet 1: 174–176

Gruner J, Lapresle J 1962 Etude anatome pathologique des medullopathies d'origine vasculaire. Revue Neurologique 106: 592–631

Grzegorczyk P B, Jones S W, Mistretta C M 1979 Age-related differences in salt taste acuity. Journal of Gerontology 34: 834–840

Gutmann E 1970 Nervous and hormonal mechanisms in the aging process. Experimental Gerontology 5: 357–366

Gutmann E, Hanzlíková V 1972 In: Age changes in the neuromuscular system 1–195. Scientechca Publishers Ltd, Bristol

Gutmann E, Hanzlíková V V 1976 Fast and slow motor units in aging. Gerontology 22: 280–300

Hatchinski V C, Lassen N A, Marshall J 1974 Multi-infarct dementia — a cause of mental deterioration in the elderly. Lancet 2: 207–209

Hadley L A 1956 Secondary ossification centres and the intra-articular ossicle. American Journal of Roentgenology 76: 1095–1101

Hakim S, Adams R D 1965 The special clinical problems of symptomatic hydrocephalus with normal cerebro-spinal fluid pressure: observations on cerebro-spinal fluid hydrodynamics. Journal of the Neurological Sciences 2: 307–327

Hakim S, Venegas J G, Burton J D 1976 The physics of the cranial cavity, hydrocephalus and normal pressure hydrocephalus: mechanical interpretation and mathematical model. Surgical Neurology 5: 187–210

Hallett M, Shahani B T, Young R R 1977 Analysis of stereotyped voluntary movements at the elbow in patients with Parkinson's disease. Journal of Neurology, Neurosurgery and Psychiatry 40: 1129–1135

Hamilton C R Jr 1971 Giant cell arteritis: including temporal arteritis and polymyalgia rheumatica. Medicine (Baltimore) 50: 1–27

Hamrin B 1972 Polymyalgia arteritica. Acta Medica Scandinavica Suppl. 533: 1–131

Hamrin B, Jonsson N, Landberg T 1965 Involvement of large vessels in polymyalgia arteritica. Lancet i: 1193–1196

Hardesty R H, Roberts B, Tole J F, Roystea H P 1960 Studies in carotid artery blood flow in man. New England Journal of Medicine 263: 944–946

Hasselkus B R, Shambes G M 1975 Aging and postural sway in women. Journal of Gerontology 30: 661–667

Henderson W R 1965 The anatomy of the Gasserian ganglion and the distribution of pain in relation to injections and operations for trigeminal neuralgia. Annals of the Royal College of 37: 346 –358

Henson R A, Parsons M 1967 Ischaemic lesions of the spinal cord. An illustrative review. Quarterly Journal of Medicine 36: 205–222

Henson R A, Urich H 1970 Peripheral neuropathy associated with malignant disease. In: Vinken P J, Bruyn G W (eds) Handbook of clinical neurology 8, p 131–148. North-Holland, Amsterdam

Hesselvik M 1969 Nemopathological studies on myelomatosis. Acta Neurologica Scandinavica 45: 95–108

Hobbs J R, Carter P M, Cooke K B, Foster M, Oon C J 1976 IgM paraproteins. Journal of Clinical Pathology 28 Suppl. t6: 54–64

Hobson W, Pemberton J 1958 The health of the elderly at home. British Medical Journal i: 587–593

Hohl R, Frame B, Schatz I J 1965 The Shy-Drager variant of idiopathic orthostatic hypotension. American Journal of Medicine 39: 134–141

Hope-Simpson R E 1965 The nature of herpes zoster: a long-term study and a new hypothesis. Proceedings of the Royal Society of Medicine 58: 9–20

Horenstein S 1974 Managing gait disorders. Geriatrics 29: 86–94

Horton W A, Eldridge R, Brody J A 1976 Familial motor neurone disease. Evidence for at least three different types. Neurology (N.Y.) 26: 460–465

Howell T H 1949 Senile deterioration in the central nervous system. British Medical Journal 1: 56–68

Howell T H 1966 Neurological problems in the elderly. Gerontologia Clinica 8: 77–94

Hudson A J 1981 Amyotrophic lateral sclerosis and its association with dementia, Parkinsonism and other neurological disorders: a review. Brain 104: 217–247

Hughes J T, Brownwell B 1964 Cervical spondylosis complicated by anterior spinal artery thrombosis. Neurology (Minneapolis) 14: 1073–1077

Hunder G C, Allen G L 1978–79 Giant cell arteritis: a review. Bulletin of the Rheumatic Diseases 29: 980–986

Huston K A, Hunder G G, Lie J T, Kennedy R H, Elverback L R 1978 Temporal arteritis: A 25 year epidemiologic, clinical and pathologic study. Annals of Internal Medicine 88: 162–167

Hutchinson E G, Yates P O 1957 Cortico-vertebral stenosis. Lancet i: 2–8

Hurwitz L J 1969 Proceedings of the 8th International Congress on Gerontology 1: 235–238

Hurwitz L J, Swallow M 1971 An introduction to the neurology of aging. Gerontologia Clinica 13: 97–113

Ito H, Yamamoto S, Komai T et al 1976 Role of local hyperfibrinolysis in the etiology of chronic subdural hematoma. Journal of Neurosurgery 45: 26–31

Ivanov I, Matev I 1973 Visual phenomena in cervical spondylosis with transitory vertebro-basilar obstruction. Ophthalmologia 21: 26–28

Iwashita H, Argyrakis A, Lowitzsch K, Sparr F W 1974 Polyneuropathy in Waldenstrom's macro globulinaemia. Journal of the Neurological Sciences 21: 341–354

Janeway R, Toole J F, Leinback L B, Miller H S 1966 Vertebral artery obstruction with basilar impression. An intermittent phenomenon related to head turning. Archives of Neurology 15: 211–214

Jenkyn L R, Walsh D, Culver C, Reeves A G 1974 The nuchocephalic reflex in diffuse cerebral disease. Neurology (Minneapolis) 24: 358–363

Jensen T S, Olivarius B, de Fine B 1980 Transient global amnesia as a manifestation of transient cerebral ischemia. Acta Neurologica Scandinavica 61: 115–124

Kaeser H E 1970 Nerve conduction velocity measurements. In: Vinken P J, Bruyn G W (eds) Handbook of clinical neurology, vol 7, p 116–196. North-Holland Publishing Company, Amsterdam

Kalisher O 1914 Demonstration eines praparates (aneurysma dissecans der aorta mit paraplegie). Klinische Wochenschrift 51: 1286–1287

Keenan R E 1970 The Eaton collaborative study of levodopa therapy in Parkinsonism; a summary. Neurology 20: 46–59

Kelly P J, Alker G J Jr, Goerss S 1982 Computer assisted stereotactic microsurgery for the treatment of intracranial neoplasms. Neurosurgery 10: 324–331

Kerr F W L 1979 Craniofacial neuralgias. In: Bonia J J, Liebeskind J C, Albe-Fessard D G (eds) Advances in pain research and therapy, vol 3, p 283–295. Raven Press, New York

Kieffer S A 1974 Normal pressure hydrocephalus. Geriatrics 29: 77–88

Klein R G, Campbell R J, Hunder G G 1976 Skip lesions in temporal arteritis. Mayo Clinic Proceedings 51: 504–508

Knox E W, Adams G F 1969 The hemiplegic onset of brain tumours. Gerontologia Clinica 11: 1–12

Koller W C, Weiner W J, Perlik S, Naksieda P A, Klawans H L 1980 Long term efficacy of drug holiday in the management of the complications of chronic levodopa therapy in parkinsonism. Neurology (N.Y.) 30: 1257–1261

Kondo K, Tsubaki T 1981 Case-control studies of motor neurone disease. Association with mechanical injuries. Archives of Neurology 38: 220–226

Koppel H P, Thompson W S A 1963 In Peripheral Entrapment Neuropathies. Williams and Wilkins, Baltimore

Krasemann P H, Honkomp J 1968 Eine einfache Behandlungsmethode der Trigeminusneuralie erfahrungsbericht uber eiwa 1000 periphere elektroagulationen langenbecks. Archiv für klinische Chirurgie 322: 581

Kurland L T, Kurtzke J E, Oldberg I D 1973 Epidemiology of Neurologic and Sense Organ Disorders. Oxford University Press, London

Kurtzke J F, Beebe G W 1980 Epidemiology of amyotrophic lateral sclerosis. I. A case-control comparison based on ALS deaths. Neurology (N.Y.) 30: 453–462

Kurtze J F 1982 Motor neurone disease. British Medical Journal 1: 141–142

Lance J W, Schwab R S, Peterson E A 1963 Action tremor and the cogwheel phenomenon in Parkinson's disease. Brain 86: 95–110

Lapes M J, Davis J S 1970 Arthalgia-Purpura weakness — cryoglobulinaemia. Archives of Internal Medicine 126: 287–289

Lascelles R G, Thomas P K 1966 Changes due to age in internodal length in the sural nerve in man. Journal of Neurology, Neurosurgery and Psychiatry 29: 40–44

Laws E R Jr, Mokri B 1977 Occult hydrocephalus. Results of shunting correlated with diagnostic tests. Clinical Neurosurgery 24: 316–333

Lees F, Turner J W 1963 Natural history and prognosis of cervical spondylosis. British Medical Journal 5373: 1607–1610

Lesser R P, Fahn S, Snider S R et al 1979 Analysis of the clinical problems in Parkinsonism and the complications of long-term levodopa therapy. Neurology (N.Y.) 29: 1253–1260

Levin H S, Benton A L 1973 Age effects in proprioceptive feedback performance. Gerontologia Clinica 15: 161–169

Lewis T, Pickering G W, Rothschild P 1931 Centripetal paralysis arising out of arrested bloodflow to the limb, including notes on a form of tingling. Heart 16: 1–32

Liang G C, Simkin P A, Hunder G G, Wilske K R, Healey L A 1974 Family aggregation of polymyalgia rheumatica and giant cell arteritis. Arthritis and Rheumatism 17: 19–24

Lieberman A, Neophytides A, Kupersmith M et al 1979 Treatment of Parkinson's disease with dopamine agonists: a review. American Journal of the Medical Sciences 278: 65–76

Lieberman A, Goldstein M, Neophytides A et al 1981 Lisuride in Parkinson disease: Efficacy of lisuride compared to levodopa. Neurology (N.Y.) 31: 961–965

Lloyd K G, Davidson L, Hornykiewicz O 1975 The neurochemistry of Parkinson's disease: effect of L-dopa therapy. Journal of Pharmacology and Experimental Therapeutics 195: 453–464

Lunsford L D, Bissonette D J, Zorub D S 1980 Anterior surgery for cervical disc disease. Part 2. Treatment of cervical spondylotic myelopathy in 32 cases. Journal of Neurosurgery 53: 12–19

McComas A J, Fawcett P R W, Campbell A J, Sica R E P 1971 Electrophysiological estimation of the number of motor units within a human muscle. Journal of Neurology, Neurosurgery and Psychiatry 34: 121–131

McComas A J, Upton A R M, Sica R E P 1973 Motorneurone diseases and aging. Lancet ii: 1476–1480

McGeer P L, McGeer E G 1976 Enzymes associated with the metabolism of catecholamines, acetylcholine and gaba in human controls and patients with Parkinson's disease and Huntington's chorea. Journal of Neurochemistry 26: 65–76

McKeown E F 1965 In: Pathology of the aged. Butterworth, London

McRae D L 1960 The significance of abnormalities of the cervical spine. American Journal of Roentgenology 84: 3–25

Marcu H, Becker H 1977 Computed-tomography of bilateral isodense chronic subdural hematomas. Neuroradiology 14: 81–83

Marcus E M 1972 Anterior spinal artery thrombosis. In: Curtis B A, Jaobson S, Marcus E M (eds) An Introduction to the Neurosciences, p 184. W B Saunders Co, Philadelphia

Marinesco G, Radovici A 1920 Sur un réflexe cutané nouveau: réflexe palmomentonnier. Revue Neurologique 27: 237–240

Markham C, Treciokas L J, Diamond S G 1974 Carbidopa in Parkinson disease and in nausea and vomiting of levodopa. Archives of Neurology 31: 128–133

Markwalladder T M 1981 Chronic subdural haematomas: a review. Journal of Neurosurgery 54: 637–645

Markwalladder T M, Steinsiepe K, Rohner M, Reichenback W, Markwalladder T M 1981 The course of chronic subdural haematomas after burr-hole craniostomy and closed system drainage. Journal of Neurosurgery 55: 390–396

Marsden C D 1978 The mechanism of physiological tremor and their significance for pathological tremors. In: Desmedt J E (ed) Physiological Tremor, Pathological Tremor and Clonus, vol 3, p 1–77. Basel, Karger

Marshall J 1976 In: The Management of Cerebro-Vascular Disease. 3rd edn Blackwell Scientific Publications, Oxford

Marshall J, Reynolds E H 1965 Withdrawal of anticoagulants from patients with transient ischaemic cerebrovascular attacks. Lancet i: 5–6

Marshall J, Walsh E 1957 Physiological tremor. Journal of Neurology, Neurosurgery and Psychiatry 19: 260–274

Martin J P 1965 Tilting reactions and disorders of the basal ganglia. Brain 88: 885–874

Martin J P 1967 Myotatic Kinesthetic and Vestibular Mechanisms. Ciba Foundation Symposium, de Reuck A V A, Kim J (ed), p 92. J & A Churchill Ltd, London

Martin J, Travis R, Van De Noort S 1965 Centrally mediated orthostatic hypotension. Archives of Neurology 19: 163–173

Martin J M, Whishnant J P, Sayre G P 1960 Occlusive vascular disease in the extracranial cerebral circulation. Archives of Neurology 3: 530–538

Martin W E, Young W I, Anderson V E 1973 Parkinson's disease: A genetic study. Brain 96: 495–506

Mathew N, Meyer J S 1974 Pathogenesis and natural history of transient global amnesia. Stroke 5: 303–311

Mawdsley C 1973 In: Calne D E (ed) Advances in neurology, vol 3, p 33–47. Raven Press, New York

Mawdsley C, Gamsu C V 1971 Periodicity of speech in Parkinsonism. Nature 231: (5301), 315–316

Mayfield F H 1979 Cervical spondylotic radiculopathy and myelopathy. Advances in Neurology 22: 307–321

Melzack R, Wall P D 1965 Pain mechanisms: a new theory. Science 150: 971–979

Mendell J R, Chase T N, Engel W K 1970 Modification by L-dopa of a case of progressive supranuclear palsy. Lancet 1: 593–594

Milhorat T H, Clarke R G, Hammock M K 1970 Structural, ultra structural and permeability changes in the ependyma and surrounding brain favouring equibration in progressive hydrocephalus. Archives of Neurology 22: 397–407

Miller A E 1980 Selective decline in cellular immune response to varicella-zoster in the elderly. Neurology 30: 582–587

Milne J S, Williamson J 1972 The ankle jerk in older people. Gerontologia Clinica 14: 86–88

Moeller A, Erickson K 1979 Computed tomography of iso attenuating subdural hematomas. Radiology 130: 149–152

Moersch F P, Craig W McK, Kernohan J W 1941 Tumours of brain in aged patients. Archives of Neurology and Psychiatry (Chicago) 45: 235–245

Murakami N, Muroga T, Sobue I 1978 Cervical myelopathy due to ossification of the posterior longitudinal ligament: a clinicopathologic study. Archives of Neurology 35: 33–36

Murnaghan G F 1961 Neurogenic disorders of the bladder in Parkinsonism. British Journal of Urology 33: 403–409

Myerson A 1944 Tap and blink responses in Parkinson's Disease. Archives of Neurology and Psychiatry (Chicago) 51: 480

Nagashima K, Nakazawa M, Endo H et al 1975 Pathology of the human spinal ganglia in varicella zoster virus infection. Acta Neuropathologica (Berlin) 33: 105–117

Nathan P N 1976 The gate control theory of pain. Brain 99: 123–158

Newman G, Dovenmuehle R H, Busse E W 1970 Alterations in neurological status with age. Duke Longitudinal Study 1955–1968, Palmore E (ed), p 47–50. University Press, Durham NC

Nurick S 1970 The Natural History of the Neurological Complications of Cervical Spondylosis. M D Thesis, Oxford University

O'Duffy J D, Wahner H W, Hunder G G 1976 Joint imaging in polymyalgia rheumatics. Mayo Clinic Proceedings 51: 519–524

Ojemann R F, Fisher C M, Adams R D, Sweet W H 1969 Further experience with the syndrome of 'normal' pressure hydrocephalus. Journal of Neurosurgery 31: 279–294

Oldenorf W H 1972 Cerebrospinal fluid formation and circulation. Progress in Nuclear Medicine 1: 336–358

Olivarius B D, Jensen T S 1979 Transient global manesia in migraine. Headache 19: 335–338

Otomo E 1965 The palmomental reflex in the aged. Geriatrics 20: 901–905

Overstall P, Immis F, Exton-Smith A N, Thornton C 1975 Causes of Falls and their Relationship to Postural Imbalance. Paper read at British Geriatrics Society, London, 1975

Overstall P W, Exton-Smith A N, Imms F J, Johnson A L 1977 Falls in the elderly related to postural imbalance. British Medical Journal 1: 261–264

Padt J P, De Reuck J, Vad Der Ecken H 1973 Intracerebral haemorrhage as initial symptom of brain tumours. Acta Neurologica et Psychiatrica Belgica 73: 241–251

Pallis C, Jones A M, Spillane J D 1954 Cervical spondylosis. Brain 77: 274–289

Pallis C A, Scott J T 1965 Peripheral neuropathy in rheumatoid arthritis. British Medical Journal 1: 1141–1147

Palma A 1972 Tumores metastasicos del encephalo. Neurocirugia 30: 211–218

Palmer E D 1974 Dysphagia in Parkinsonism. Journal of the American Medical Association 229: 1349

Parkes J D, Marsden C D 1973 The treatment of Parkinson's disease. British Journal of Hospital Medicine 10: 284–294

Parkes J D, De Bono A G, Marsden C D 1976 Bromocriptine in Parkinsonism: long-term treatment, dose response, and comparison with levodopa. Journal of Neurology, Neurosurgery and Psychiatry 39: 1101–1108

Parkinson T 1948 Rare manifestations of herpes zoster. British Medical Journal 1: 8–10

Pathy M S 1959 Some Factors Responsible for the Formation of Pressure Sores. Paper given to British Geriatrics Society, Aylesbury

Pathy M S 1967 Clinical presentation of myocardial infarction in the elderly. British Heart Journal 29: 290–299

Pathy M S 1975 Defaecation Syncope. Paper given to British Geriatrics Society, London

Pathy M S 1979 Motor complications of herpes zoster. Age and Ageing 8: 75–80

Patrick B K, Ramirez-Lassepas M, Snyder B D 1980 Temporal profile of vertebrobasilia territory infarction. Stroke 11: 643–648

Paulson G, Gottlieb G 1968 The re-appearance of foetal and neonatal reflexes in aged patients. Brain 91: 37–52

Payne E E, Spillane J D 1957 The cervical spine: an anatomico-pathological study of 70 specimens with particular reference to the problem of cervical spondylosis. Brain 1957, 80: 571–596

Pearson H G J 1928 Effects of age on vibratory sensitivity. Archives of Neurology and Psychiatry (Chicago) 20: 482–496

Phillips D G 1973 Surgical treatment of myelopathy with cervical

spondylosis. Journal of Neurology, Neurosurgery and Psychiatry 36: 879–884

Phillips D G 1975 Upper limb involvement in cervical spondyloses. Journal of Neurology, Neurosurgery and Psychiatry 38: 386–390

Pirart J 1965 Diabetic neuropathy: a metabolic or a vascular disease. Diabetes 14: 1–19

Pollay M 1972 C S F formation and mechanism of drainage. Progress in Nuclear Medicine 1: 336–358

Pollett J E, Sharp P F, Smith F W, Davidson A I, Miller S S 1981 Intravenous radionuclide cystography for the detection of vesicorenal reflux. Journal of Urology 125: 75–78

Ponsford J L, Donnan G A 1980 Transient global amnesia. Journal of Neurology, Neurosurgery and Psychiatry 43: 285–287

Poskanzer D C, Schwab R S 1963 Cohort analysis of Parkinson's syndrome: Evidence for a single etiology related to subclinical infarction about 1920. Journal of Chronic Diseases 16: 961–973

Postma T J, Van Tilburg W J 1975 Visual hallucinations and delirium during treatment with Amantadine (Symmetrel). Journal of the American Geriatrics Society 23: 212–215

Potts D G, Reilly K F, Deonarine V 1972 Morphology of the arachnoid villi and granulations. Radiology 105: 333–341

Prakash C, Stern G 1973 Neurological signs in the elderly. Age and Aging 2: 24–27

Procacci P, Bozza G, Buzzelli G, Della Corte M 1970 The cutaneous pricking pain threshold in old age. Gerontologia Clinica 12: 213–218

Propp R P, Means E, Deibel R, Sherer G, Barron K 1975 Waldenström's macroglobulinaemia and neuropathy. Neurology (Minneapolis) 25: 980–988

Purnell D C, Daly D D, Lipscombe P R 1961 Carpal tunnel syndrome associated with myxoedema. Archives of Internal Medicine 108: 751–756

Püschel J 1930 Beiträge zur pathologischen Anatomie und zur allgemeinen Pathologie. Beitrage zur pathologischen Anatomie 84: 123

Raff M C, Asbury A K 1968 Ischemic mononeuropathy and mononeuropathy multiplex in diabetes mellitus. New England Journal of Medicine 279: 17–22

Read D J, Vanhegan R I, Matthews W B 1978 Peripheral neuropathy and benign IgG paraproteinaemia. Journal of Neurology, Neurosurgery and Psychiatry 41: 215–219

Reid J L, Calne D B, George C F, Pallis C, Vakil S D 1971 Cardiovascular reflexes in Parkinsonism. Clinical Science 41: 63–67

Richardson J C, Steele J, Olsjewski J 1963 Supranuclear ophthalmoplegia, pseudobulbar palsy, nuchal dystonia and dementia. Transactions of the American Neurological Association 88: 25–27

Roberts M A, Caird F I 1976 Computerized tomography and intellectual impairment in the elderly. Journal of Neurology, Neurosurgery and Psychiatry 39: 986–989

Rowland L P, Defendini R, Sherman W, Hirano A, Olarte M R, Latov N, Lovelace R, Inoue K, Osserman E 1982 Macroglobulinaemia with peripheral neuropathy simulating motor neurone disease. Annals of Neurology 11: 532–536

Rushworth G, Denny-Brown D 1959 The two components of the grasp reflex after ablation of frontal cortex in monkeys. Journal of Neurology, Neurosurgery and Psychiatry 2: 91–98

Russel R W, Espir M L E, Morgenstern F S 1957 Treatment of post-herpetic neuralgia. Lancet i: 242–245

Schmidt W R, Jarcho L W 1966 Persistent dyskinesias following phenothiazine therapy. Archives of Neurology and Psychiatry (Chicago) 14: 369–377

Schwab R S, England A C 1958 Parkinson's disease. Journal of Chronic Diseases 8: 488–509

Schwab R S, England A C 1958 Diseases of the Basal Ganglia. In Handbook of Clinical Neurology, ed. Vinken P J, Bruyn G W, vol 6, p 228. North-Holland, Amsterdam

Scotti G, Terbrugge K, Melancon D et al 1977 Evaluation of the age of subdural hematomas by computerized tomography. Journal of Neurosurgery 47: 311–315

Sethi G K, Hughes R K, Takaro T 1974 'Dissecting aortic aneurisms'. Collective Review. Annals of Thoracic Surgery 18: 201–215

Sheldon J H 1960 Natural history of falls in old age. British Medical Journal 2: 1685–1690

Sheldon J H 1963 The effect of age on the control of sway. Gerontologia Clinica 5: 129–138

Shibuta H, Ishikawa T, Hondo R et al 1974 Varicella virus isolation from spinal ganglion. Archiv für die gesamte Virusforschung 45: 382–385

Shivalingappa G 1970 Diaphragmatic paralysis following herpes zoster. Gerontologia Clinica 12: 283–287

Shock N W, Norris A H 1970 Neuromuscular co-ordination as a factor in age changes in muscular exercise. In: Jokl E, Brunner D, (ed) Physical activity and exercise, vol 4, p 92–99. S Karger, Basel

Shukla D, Singh B M, Strobos R J 1980 Hypertensive cerebrovascular disease and normal pressure hydrocephalus. Neurology 30: 998–1000

Siekert R G, Whisnant J P, Millikan C H 1960 Anaemia and intermittent focal cerebral arterial insufficiency. Archives of Neurology 3: 386–390

Silver J R, Buxton P H 1974 Spinal stroke. Brain 97: 539–550

Silverstein A, Doniger D 1963 Neurological complications of myelometosis. Archives of Neurology (Chicago) 9: 534–544

Smith R C F 1956 The elicitation and incidence of neurological signs in the aged. Practitioner 177: 59–66

Spillane J D 1964 The treatment of trigeminal neuralgia. Practitioner 192: 71–77

Steele J C 1975 Progressive supranuclear palsy. In: Vinken P H, Bruyn G W (ed) Handbook of clinical Neurology, vol 22, p 217–227. Elsevier, Amsterdam

Stein B M, McCormick W F, Rodriguez J N, Taveras J H 1962 Postmortem angiography of cerebral vascular system. Archives of Neurology 7: 545–559

Sunderland S 1978 Nerves and Nerve Injuries. 2nd Edn. Churchill Livingstone, Edinburgh

Symon L, Hinzpeter T 1977 The enigma of normal pressure hydrocephalus: tests to select patients for surgery and to predict shunt function. Clinical Neurosurgery 24: 285–315

Tan E M, Pearson C M 1972 Rheumatic disease sera reactive with capillaries in the mouse kidney. Arthritis and Rheumatism 15: 23–28

Taterka J H, O'Sullivan M E 1943 The motor complications of herpes zoster. Journal of the American Medical Association 122: 737–739

Tatlow W F T, Bammer H G 1957 Syndrome of vertebro-artery compression. Neurology (Minneapolis) 7: 331–340

Taylor A R 1953 Mechanism and treatment of spinal cord disorders associated with cervical spondylosis. Lancet i: 717–720

Thomas J E, Howard F M J 1972 Segmental zoster paresis — a disease profile. Neurology (Minneapolis) 22: 459–466

Thomas P K 1973 Metabolic neuropathy. Journal of the Royal College of Physicians of London 7: 154–160

Timbury M C 1982 Acyclovir. British Medical Journal 2: 1223–1224

Tomlinson A H, MacCallum F O 1970 The incidence of complement fixing antibody to varicella-zoster virus in hospital patients and blood donors. Hygiene 68: 411–415

Toole J F, Tucker S H 1960 Influence of head position upon cerebral circulation. Archives of Neurology 2: 616–623

Trew J M, Lockwood P, Mayfield F H 1975 Treatment of trigeminal neuralgia in the aged by a simplified surgical approach (percutaneous electrocoagulation). Journal of the American Geriatrics Society 23: 426–430

Tsukimoto H 1960 A case report: Autopsy of syndrome of compression of spinal cord owing to ossification within spinal canal of cervical spine. Archiv für jupanische Chirurgie 29: 1003–1007

Twomey J A, Jefferson D 1981 Encephalitis and polyneuritis complicating varicella zoster infection. Postgraduate Medical Journal 57: 507–508

Upton A R M, McComas A J 1973 The double crush in nerve entrapment syndromes. Lancet 2: 359–361

Van Der Meer J W M, Versteeg J 1982 Acyclovir in severe herpes virus infections. American Journal of Medicine 73: 271–274

Victor M, Banker B, Adams R D 1958 The neuropathy of multiple myeloma. Journal of Neurology, Neurosurgery and Psychiatry 21: 73–88

Virtama P, Kivalo E 1957 Impressions on the vertebral artery by deformation of the unco-vertebral joints. Post mortem angiographic studies. Acta Radiologica 48: 410–412

Vizoso A D 1950 The relationship between internodal length and growth in human nerves. Journal of Anatomy 84: 342–353

Wadsworth T G, Williams J R 1973 Cubital tunnel external compression syndrome. British Medical Journal 1: 662–666

Wadsworth T G 1974 The cubital tunnel and the external compression syndrome. Anesthesia and Analgesia 53: 303–307

Wadsworth T G 1977 The external compression syndrome of the ulnar nerve at the cubital tunnel. A clinical study of external compression ulnar neuropathy at elbow level and a classification of the cubital tunnel syndrome. Clinical Orthopaedics 124: 189–204

Walsh J C 1971 Neuropathy of multiple myeloma. Archives of Neurology (Chicago) 25: 404–414

Waltz T A 1967 Physical factors in the production of the myelopathy of cervical spondylosis. Brain 90: 395–404

Warrell D A, Godfrey S, Olsen E G J 1968 Giant cell arteritis with peripheral neuropathy. Lancet 1: 1010–1013

Wartenberg G 1948 Winking jaw phenomenon. Archives of Neurology and Psychiatry (Chicago) 59: 734–753

Wartenberg R 1952 Early diagnosis of Parkinsonism. Archivos de neuro-psiquiatria (S. Paulo) 10: 139–146

Weiner W J, Bergman D 1977 In: Klavans H L (ed) Clinical Neuropharmacology, Vol. 2. Raven Press, New York

Weiner W J, Perlik S, Koller W C, Navsieda P A, Klawans H L 1979 The role of drug holiday in the management of Parkinson's disease. Neurology (N.Y.) 29: 553–556

Weir B 1980 Oncotic pressure of subdural fluids. Journal of Neurosurgery 53: 512–515

Weller T H 1953 Serial propagation in vitro of agents producing inclusion bodies derived from varicella and herpes zoster. Proceedings of the Society for Experimental Biology and Medicine 83: 340–346

Weller T H, Coons A H 1954 Fluorescent antibody studies with agents of varicella and herpes zoster propagated in vitro. Proceedings of the Society for Experimental Biology and Medicine 86: 789–794

Weller T H, Whitton H M, Bell E J 1958 The etiologic agents of varicella and herpes zoster; isolation, propagation, and cultural characteristics in vitro. Journal of Experimental Medicine 108: 843–868

Weller T H, Whitton H M 1958. The etiologic agents of varicella and herpes zoster; serologic studies with the viruses as propagated in vitro. Journal of Experimental Medicine 108: 869–890

Wells C E C 1966 Clinical aspects of spinovascular disease. Proceedings of the Royal Society of Medicine 59: 790–796

Whanger A D, Wang H S 1974 Clinical correlates of the vibratory sense in elderly psychiatric patients. Journal of Gerontology 29: 39–45

Whitaker J M, Sciabbarrasi B S, Engel W K, Warmolts J R, Strober W 1973 Serum immunoglobulin and complement C_3 levels. A study in adults with idiopathic chronic polyneuropathies and motor neurone diseases. Neurology (Minneapolis) 23: 1164–1173

White D N, Wilson K C, Curry G R, Stevenson R J 1979 The limitation of pulsatile flow through the aqueduct of Sylvius as a cause of hydrocephalus. Journal of the Neurological Sciences 42: 11–51

Whitfield A G W, Bateman M, Cooke W T 1963 Temporal arteritis. British Journal of Ophthalmology 47: 555–566

Wiener L M, Berry R G, Kundin J 1964 Intracranial circulation in carotid occlusion. Archives of Neurology 11: 554–561

Wiener L M, Nathanson M 1962 The relationship of subdural haematoma to anticoagulant therapy. Archives of Neurology and Psychiatry (Chicago) 6: 282–286

Wikkels C, Andersson H, Blomstrand C, Lindqvist G 1982 The clinical effect of lumbar puncture in normal pressure hydrocephalus. Journal of Neurology, Neurosurgery and Psychiatry 45: 64–69

Wilkinson M 1960 The morbid anatomy of cervical spondylosis and myelopathy. Brain 83: 589–617

Wilkinson M S, Russell R W R 1972 Arteries of the head and neck in giant cell arteritis. Archives of Neurology 27: 378–391

Willett R W 1963 Peripheral neuropathy due to nitrofurantoin. Neurology (Minneapolis) 13: 344–345

Winegrad A J, Greene D A 1976 Diabetic polyneuropathy: the importance of insulin deficiency. Hyperglycaemia and alterations in myoinositol metabolism in its pathogenesis. New England Journal of Medicine 295: 1416

Wolf A 1959 Clinical Neuropathology in relation to the process of aging. In: Birren J E, Innis H A, Windle W F, (eds) The process of Aging in the Nervous System, C C Thomas Springfield, Illinois

Wolf B S, Khilnani M, Malis L I 1956 The sagittal diameter of the bony cervical spinal canal and its significance in cervical spondylosis. Journal of the Mount Sinai Hospital 23: 283–292

Wong C L, Castriciano S, Chernesky M A, Rawls W E 1978 Quantitation of antibodies to varicell-zoster virus by immune adherence hemagglutination. Journal of Clinical Microbiology 7: 6–11

World Health Organization 1980 Peripheral Neuropathies. Technical Report Series 654

Wright W B, Boyd R V 1964 The glabellar tap sign in the elderly patient. Gerontologia Clinica 6: 124–128

Yahr M D 1981 Introduction to Research Progress in Parkinson's Disease, F C Rose, R Capildeo (ed), p 3–8. Pitman Medical

Yakolev P I 1954 Paraplegia in flexion of cerebral origin. Journal of Neuropathology and Experimental Neurology 13: 267–296

Yates P O 1967 In: Williams D (ed) Modern Trends in Neurology, vol 4, p 180–192. Butterworth, London

Zwischenberger H, Mamolu B, Mifka K 1976 Finger microtremor, an experimental study. Electroencephalography and Clinical Neurophysiology 41: 190

The central nervous system — stroke

INTRODUCTION

Stroke has for years been an embarrassment to physicians. It is a disease with a swift beginning and a slow end, a vascular lesion in neurological territory. It is too acute to be chronic and too chronic to be acute. It is too common in young people to be 'geriatric' and too common in old people to be 'medical'. Its management needs non-medical skills more than it needs medical skills. Stroke strikes at the seat of the intellect, the emotions, the means of communication, the very personality, and is thus a uniquely poignant illness. Yet stroke has suffered comparative neglect, and most physicians would admit to knowing more about damage to the heart — a mere pump, than damage to the brain — the supreme achievement of the evolutionary process of Nature.

The appearance in the recent past of new technical methods for the demonstration of abnormal structure and disturbed function of the brain — such as cerebral angiography, radionuclide scanning, and computerized tomography, and of new surgical methods of approach — such as endarterectomy, clot removal and extracranial–intracranial bypass, have greatly increased interest in the disease in specially equipped centres. But there remains a pressing need for the average stroke patient at home, in a general medical ward or in a geriatric unit, to be comprehensively diagnosed, assessed, treated and rehabilitated, making full use of simple inexpensive effective methods which should be available in the humblest medical setting.

This chapter will concetrate on some of the major changes in knowledge and outlook which have influenced the management of stroke illness in older patients in recent years.

Definition of stroke

Stroke is now defined in clinical terms as 'a persisting focal neurological deficit due to a cerebrovascular lesion' (Marshall, 1979); or for survey purposes, as a 'clinical syndrome consisting of a constellation of neurological findings, sudden or rapid in onset, which persists for more than 24 hours, and whose vascular origins are limited to:

1. thrombotic or embolic occlusion of a cerebral artery resulting in infarction, or
2. spontaneous rupture of a vessel resulting in an intracerebral or subarachnoid haemorrhage.' (Walker et al, 1981).

The latter definition includes subarachnoid haemorrhage and excludes occlusion or rupture of a blood vessel due to traumatic, neoplastic or infectious processes which produce vascular pathology.

Previous definitions which spoke of a 'presumed' vascular cause (Royal College of Physicians, 1974) are considered no longer appropriate, since the diagnosis can now be firmly established. But not all units have access to CT scanners; and even these can make their errors (Norris and Hachinski, 1982). Indeed while the scan approaches 100 per cent accuracy in the diagnosis of cerebral haemorrhage it identifies a lesion in cerebral infarction at the onset of the stroke in little more than one half of cases. Unsuspected tumours and other non-vascular lesions are picked up in special centres sufficiently often in patients presenting clinically as a 'stroke' (Weisberg and Nice, 1977) to justify retention of the word 'presumed' in the clinical definition.

The CT scan has also increased the accuracy of the clinical classification of stroke into the pathological categories of intracerebral haemorrhage and infarction; and the location of the lesion in carotid or vertebrobasilar territory, and in cortical or deep areas of the brain (Nelson et al, 1980). Better identification of possible embolic sources of infarction is also possible as the result of greater awareness of the significance of carotid bruits (Sandok et al, 1982); cardiac dysrhythmia and recent myocardial infarction (Chin et al, 1977; Dimant and Grob, 1977; McAllen and Marshall, 1977; Fisher, 1978); hypotension (Mitchinson, 1980); and prolapsing mitral valve (Kostuk et al, 1977; Barnett, 1982). Jones and Millikan (1976) showed that one-quarter of a group of patients with non-haemmorrhagic infarction in the carotid territory had a progressive or remitting and relapsing course; and similar findings were reported by Jones et al (1980) in respect of infarction in the vertebral-basilar system. Thus the older classification of 'stroke-in-evolution' and 'completed stroke' (Carter, 1964) is now known to bear little relationship to the pathogenesis and should be discarded.

The definitions of transient ischaemic attack (TIA) and recurrent ischaemic neurological deficit (RIND) are discussed below.

Classfication

The classification of stroke used by the WHO in its International Classification of Diseases dissatisfies epidemiologists, especially by its retention of the catagories of 'cerebral thrombosis' (a diagnosis which is now rarely made) and 'acute but ill-defined cerebral vascular disease'. An elaborate but logical alternative has been proposed by Capildeo et al (1977, 1978) which could help to answer some puzzling questions in epidemiology and treatment. This provides a 'unique number' for every stroke patient, in which is embedded information about the anatomical and pathological diagnosis, the investigations, associated conditions, disability on admission and on discharge, and outcome.

Epidemiology

Incidence
The conclusion of the Royal College of Physicians Report (1974) that the incidence of stroke is of the order of 1.5 new cases per 1000 of population per year has been confirmed in most recent studies (Baum and Robins, 1981; Waters and Perkin, 192); although Weddell and Beresford (1979) in a community survey in southern England found a distinctly lower incidence; while Hansen and Marquardsen, (1977) reported a higher incidence in Scandinavia. As the population of all Western countries ages the significance of relating incidence to age and sex increases. In each decade from age 45 to 85 the incidence of new stroke doubles (Robins and Baum, 1981). The growing number of people surviving into late life means that most first strokes now occur in old people in whom complicating illnesses are prevalent. In the United States 50 per cent of male patients entering hospital with a first stroke had already celebrated their 71st birthday; and 50 per cent of female patients had attained the age of 74. (Walker et al, 1981).

The incidence of stroke in the two sexes is almost equal in the younger patients, but the male to female ratio increases slightly with increasing age. Amongst all admissions to American hospitals with stroke there was a 44 per cent excess of males over females, but this figure may partly reflect a greater likelihood for male patients to be hospitalized.

It seems likely that the major centres attract rather younger patients, and doctors working in district general hospitals should be cautious about extrapolating research findings unless the ages are clearly stated.

Type of stroke
The proportion of strokes due to intracranial haemorrhage declines with increasing age, and the proportion due to atherothrombotic infarct rises. In the U.S. national survey of hospitalized strokes, mainly from non-specialist centres, 80 per cent of cases were of thrombotic origin and only 6 per cent each were due to intracerebral haemorrhage, embolism and subarachnoid (Walker et al, 1981).

Is the incidence of stroke falling?
Is the incidence of stroke falling? It has long been known that the number of deaths registered as being due to cerebral haemorrhage has been on the decrease, but as this was accompanied by an increase in the certification of cerebral thrombosis (Bronte-Stewart, 1964) it was possible that the cause was merely a change in certifying practice. However, much evidence is now available from the United States of a substantial and continuing reduction in age-adjusted mortality rate from stroke (Soltero et al, 1978) and in age-adjusted rates for both cerebral thrombois (Garraway et al, 1979a) and haemorrhagic stroke (Furlan et al, 1979; Garraway et al, 1979b). This evidence from the Mayo Clinic is based on accurate records of the stable community of Rochester, Minnesota.

In Rochester, the incidence of cerebral thrombosis appears to be declining more rapidly in women than in men, and in older rather than younger subjects. Although these trends are not general, death certification data from the United Kingdom (Haberman et al, 1978) and from Japan (Ueda et al, 1981) confirms a falling mortality from both cerebral haemorrhage and cerebral thrombosis. The degree of reduction is striking. In Rochester, for every 100 deaths attributed to stroke in the years 1945–49, there were only 55 in 1970–74 (Garraway et al, 1979b).

It has not escaped notice that the decline began just as antihypertensive treatment was beginning, and accelerated in the 1960's when, at least in the United States, effective antihypertensive agents were being widely prescribed. At about the same time the American way of life was beginning to change, with a reduction in the amount of cholesterol in the diet and a greatly increased use of exercise. It would be a triumph of preventive medicine if indeed this improved attention to positive health and pre-emptive treatment could be causally related to the falling stroke mortality. However, Stallones, (1979) after taking a hard look at the epidemiological evidence, is not satisfied that the facts can be thus explained. The declining mortality preceded significant changes in diet, exercise and antihypertensive therapy; it affected equally males and females, young and old, and different racial groups who did not equally pursue the good life. Stallones thinks it probable that the combination of environmental factors responsible for the falling mortality of stroke illness is more complex than we can unravel.

One factor that is not sufficiently stressed in the literature is that the survival of stroke patients, especially older ones, is not necessarily accompanied by functional recovery. This will lead to an increased prevalence of disabled stroke survivors, with an increasing need for rehabilitation and social support.

Stroke and hypertension

The predominant role of hypertension as a factor in the causation of stroke was brought out in many earlier studies (Friedman et al, 1968; Dayton et al, 1970; Wylie, 1970; Kannel, 1971). More recent information from the Framingham Study has yielded the crucial information that for men and women aged 45–74, the probability of developing a stroke was related to the level of blood pressure on entry. The relationship extended over the whole range of blood pressure. It applied to the casual as well as to the resting blood pressure; and, equally to the systolic and to the diastolic blood pressure. The risk ranged from less than 1 per 1000 for patients with systolic blood pressure of less than 110 mmHg to about 10 per 1000 with patients for blood pressure in excess of 190 mmHg (Kannel et al, 1976).

Other population studies demonstrating the link between blood pressure level and subsequent development of stroke have come from Shekelle et al (1974) and from the Veterans' Administration Hospital Trial (1973).

A higher proportion of patients with recent onset of stroke have an elevated blood pressure than is the case for the population in general. This relationship applies to both haemorrhagic and thromboembolic strokes. In patients with completed stroke, the probability of the subsequent development of a recurrent stroke is related to the level of blood pressure. Patients with diastolic pressure of more than 105 mmHg are at increased risk of stroke and most of this increased risk is in the first few months after the onset of transient ischaemic attacks (Whisnant, 1976).

The mortality of stroke victims during their initial hospital stay is related to the level of blood pressure found on admission to hospital as is the mortality over subsequent months and years.

Antihypertensive therapy in stroke victims reduces the risks of both fatal and non-fatal recurrences (Carter, 1970; Beevers et al, 1973; Australian Trial 1980).

In patients with transient ischaemic attacks, the probability of subsequent development of a stroke is related to the level of blood pressure (Whisnant, 1976), while the mortality rate is higher in patients with raised blood pressure that it is in those with normal blood pressure (Whisnant, 1976).

Death in hypertensive stroke patients is more often due to heart disease than to any other cause.

Ross Russell (1975) has explained stroke in hypertensive patients as being due to dilatation of small blood vessels and the formation of microaneurysms, with the occurrence of lipohyaline and subsequent tendency to haemorrhage.

In subjects over the age of 65 participating in the Framingham Study (Kannel et al, 1981) systolic hypertension, defined as a systolic blood pressure of 160 millimetres or over with a diastolic blood pressure of less than 90 millimetres of mercury, was strongly associated with stroke as was hypertension with an elevated diastolic blood pressure. Evans and Caird (1982) questioned this interpretation, quoting British work in which no association was found between the level of systolic or diastolic blood pressure in elderly people and the subsequent development of a stroke, and advancing the view that the risk of stroke in old age is defined by the height of the blood pressure in middle life rather than the level which it may have attained in later years. This debate has implications for the use of antihypertensive drugs in the hope of preventing stroke in old age. This is recommended by Kannel et al (1981), although they admit that no direct evidence exists of the efficacy of such a measure.

Other aetiological factors

Heart disease. The relationship between stroke and rheumatic heart disease, particularly atrial fibrillation with mitral stenosis, is well attested. A very high proportion of patients with mitral stenosis are likely to suffer cerebral embolism by the age of 40 unless operated on, and valve replacement is now standard practice. Recent advances in heart valve surgery have made this operation common for aortic incompetence, but earlier types of ball-and-cage valve were associated with a high incidence of cerebral embolism. The newer homograft techniques are much safer in this respect. Stroke may also result from cerebral embolization after recent myocardial infarction. Easton and Sherman (1980) showed that the use of anticoagulant drugs in patients with rheumatic heart disease and those with recent myocardial infarction reduced the occurrence of stroke to one-quarter or less of the expected incidence. Artery-to-artery embolism e.g. from atheromatous ulcers in the internal carotid or middle cerebral artery are a common mechanism of stroke (Ueda et al, 1980); while increase in the cholesterol/triglyceride ratio raises the risk of transient ischaemic attack but not of carotid stroke.

Contraceptive pill. Evidence incriminating the contraceptive pill, first produced in 1968 (Inman and Vessey, 1968; Vessey and Doll, 1968) has been strengthened by recent studies. Vessey (1973) has now demonstrated that the risk of a non-pregnant woman aged 15 to 45 suffering a stroke is increased ninefold by the use of oestrogen-containing contraceptive tablets, but even so this remains a very small risk.

Environmental temperature. Bull and Morton (1975), extending previous interest in the relationship between environmental temperature and stroke, showed that a definite increase occurred in mortality attributed to stroke some seven days after periods of particularly low or high temperature.

Water softness. The relationship between stroke and the softness of the water supply reported by Crawford et al in 1968 remains unexplained.

Biochemical factors. In the Framingham Study, which convincingly incriminated hypertension as a major factor in stroke, no other important cause was identified. However, three abnormalities, when present in association with hypertension, further increased the risk. These were (1) serum cholesterol greater than 9.33 mmol/l (335 mg/100 ml), (2) glucose intolerance, (3) left ventricular hypertrophy (Kannel et al, 1975).

Heredity. Family clustering of strokes, probably related to hypertension, was reported by Heyden et al (1969) and by Marshall (1971b). A Japanese multivariate analysis of risk factors for cerebrovascular disease found that family history was a weak predictive factor, and only age and blood pressure were important discriminators.

Mitral valve prolapse. In the 1970's excitement was generated by the discovery of an association between prolapse of the mitral valve, diagnosed by echocardiography, and the occurrence of transient ischaemic attacks and cerebral emoblism. It is now recognized that mitral valve prolapse is a common condition, and its association with stroke is probably quite incidental, except in younger patients (Barnett, 1982).

Haematocrit. The Framingham Study revealed by chance an association between the incidence of stroke in the community and a high level of haemoglobin. Subsequent studies showed that an elevated haematocrit reading was associated with a distinct reduction in cerebral blood flow (Thomas et al, 1977; Tohgi et al, 1978; Humphrey et al, 1979). Not only does a high haematocrit level predispose to strokes and to transient ischaemic attacks, but, in the presence of carotid stenosis, patients with viscous blood associated with high haematocrit are liable to suffer a larger infarct than are those with normal haematocrit, presumably because of a reduced collateral circulation, (Harrison et al,

1981). The elevated haematocrit found in these patients is not due to polycythaemia or to dehydration and may be associated with cigarette smoking. Reduction in haematocrit level by repeated venesection is recommended as a possible means of preventing stroke, the aim being to reduce the haematocrit to around 40–43 per cent (Thomas, 1982).

Diabetes. The association between diabetes and stroke is well known and has been thought to be indirect. However, Riddle and Hart (1982) found an elevation of glycosylated haemoglobin in stroke patients, and considered that hyperglycaemia might be a direct risk factor for stroke and also for transient ischaemic attacks. Gerlis (1981), on the other hand, stressed the relationship between unrecognized nocturnal hypoglycaemia and transient hemiparetic attacks.

TRANSIENT ISCHAEMIC ATTACKS

Transient ischaemic attacks (TIA) are defined in the WHO Report (1971) as 'the sudden occurrence of usually repeated episodes of sensory or motor impairment, caused by temporary inadequacy of blood flow to a localized area of the brain and disappearing completely within 24 hours'. Yates (1976) stressed that it is the symptoms rather than the underlying pathological manifestations which should be properly considered 'transient'. The term 'transient ischaemic attacks' should be confined to cases where there is definite evidence of neurological deficit, and should not be used to describe patients with transient symptoms of dizziness, unsteadiness, syncope or falls. In most cases the symptoms last for only a few minutes and disappear as rapidly as they appear. Characteristic symptoms of TIA in the carotid distribution include clumsiness and weakness of the arm and leg on the same side, paraesthesiae of the same distribution, homonymous hemianopia and transient dysphasia (Genton et al, 1977). TIA in the vertebral basilar distribution is characterized by motor weakness in any combination of the four limbs, perioral paraesthesiae, facial weakness, ataxia, dysarthria and diplopia.

Transient monocular blindness (amaurosis fugax) is a transient ischaemic attack affecting the ophthalmic branch of the internal carotid artery. This may be due to embolization of the retinal vessels by clot or cholesterol or to reversal of flow in the ophthalmic artery at its anastomosis with the external maxillary artery. In its natural history this condition is similar to TIA (Parkin et al, 1982).

Reversible ischaemic neurological deficits (RIND) are attacks of focal neurological deficit with manifestations similar to those of TIA but with persistence of symptoms and signs for a few days or even weeks before complete recovery occurs. Their significance and prognosis is similar to that of TIA (Wiebers et al, 1982).

Transient cerebral ischaemia without focal signs is characterized by brief attacks of impaired consciousness or confusion which are completely reversible. TIA has to be distinguished from other transient disturbances of cerebral function, including migraine attacks, epilepsy, hypertensive encephalopathy and meningism. Labyrinthine attacks are characterized by vertigo without focal neurological signs. Hypoglycaemia can closely mimic TIA (Shaw, 1981).

Shaw has characterized the mechanisms of TIA as embolic, haemodynamic and haematological. Embolic causes include the well known plaques and ulcers in the great vessels, especially the internal carotid artery at its bifurcation; and cardiac causes which include mitral stenosis and other valve lesions arising from rheumatic heart disease accompanied by atrial fibrillation; recent myocardial infarction, prosthetic valves, atrial myxoma valve prolapse and subacute bacterial endocarditis. The haemodynamic causes, which are associated with non-focal signs, are disturbances of cardiac rhythm and hypotension. The haematological causes include polycythaemia, anaemia, hypoglycaemia and hyperglycaemia.

The diagnosis of TIA depends largely on a carefully taken history confirmed by corresponding clinical signs. The discovery of a bruit on auscultation over the carotid artery in the neck is of great value, especially when this corresponds to the clinical picture. In patients with non-focal signs, 24-hour tape recording of the ECG is a necessary diagnostic test, (Jonas et al, 1977).

The great importance attached to the diagnosis of TIA lies in the fact that a proportion of patients go on to have a stroke quite soon; and if the cause can be found and dealt with there is a possibility of rescuing some patients from this tragic consequence. Most of the research on this topic comes from neurology departments to which these patients tend to present, and much of it relates to relatively young patients; so that the possibilities afforded to practising geriatricians of preventing strokes in patients with TIA are relatively limited.

Risk of stroke

There are now many long-term studies of the outcome of TIA, although few of these are in untreated groups. McDowell (1979) stated that in one-third of patients the ischaemic attacks stop spontaneously, in one-third they persist, and one-third of patients go on to suffer strokes. The greater risk of stroke is in the first few weeks or months after the appearance of the first transient ischaemic attack when 15 per cent of patients are likely to suffer a stroke (Millikan, 1979). Cartlidge et al (1977) put the risk to TIA victims of a stroke during the first year after the first attack at nearly 20 times that of the

general population, and after the first year at nearly 10 times. The risk is highest in hypertensive subjects. (Whisnant, 1976). Mortality in patients who have suffered TIAs is about three times that of the general population (Heyden et al, 1978); but in older patients it is only about twice as high (Whisnant, 1976). The commonest cause of death is heart disease from myocardial infarction or from congestive heart failure, with stroke and other causes of death being less common but still excessive (Cartlidge et al, 1977). Hypertension and diabetes are commoner accompaniments but are not thought to play any part in the excess mortality of TIAs (Heyden et al, 1978).

Management

The diagnosis of TIA carries a responsibility for further investigation and treatment, If a single atheromatous plaque can be found in one carotid artery while the other vessels are clear then direct surgical attack by removal of the plaque carries an excellent prognosis (Ford et al, 1975; Easton and Sherman, 1977; Kusunoki 1978; Byer and Easton, 1980). When disease of one carotid is more extensive there is scope for the new operation of extra-cranial –intracranial bypass (Greenalgh et al, 1979). This restores circulation to ischaemic areas of the brain by bringing a branch of the superficial temporal artery, nourished by the intact external carotid artery, through the skull to anastomose with the middle cerebral artery beyond the point of stenosis (Reichman, 1975). Much experience has now been gained with this operation which is being carefully evaluated (Amaducci et al, 1982).

If the possibility of direct surgical attack is being considered then it is essential to display the state of the great vessels. The definitive method is by four vessel cerebral angiography which, despite refinement of technique, remains risky especially to the older patient (Galligioni, 1979). In well-selected cases angiography reveals a definite treatable lesion in 50 per cent of cases, a doubtful one in 25 per cent, and no abnormality in 25 per cent.

Recently many new investigations have been introduced which are 'non-invasive' and which may eventually replace angiography. These rarely yield false positive results, but the occasional occurrence of false negative results means that angiography remains the definitive test.

Döppler ultrasonography is the most promising of the non-invasive methods (Barnes et al, 1976; Lewis et al, 1979) The Döppler probe is moved over the carotid arteries in the neck and yeilds quantitative information on the direction and velocity of flow and the degree of flow disturbance within the sample volume (Blackshear, et al 1978). In cases of occlusion of the internal carotid artery the Döppler can detect reversed flow in the collateral channels of the facial, ophthalmic and temporal arteries. This technique can detect complete occlusion of the internal carotid artery in 100 per cent of cases and severe stenosis in 90 per cent (Bes et al, 1979). False negatives are sufficiently uncommon to make this an acceptable screening technique; but it does not yet replace angiography (Hames et al, 1981; Lakeman et al 1981).

Radionuclide angiography

The method of Mettinger et al (1978) involves the intra-venous injection of radioactive fibrinogen which is taken up by artherosclerotic plaques. Screening over the neck with a Gamma camera immediately and after 4 and 24 hours may detect the plaque. This method, which is still being developed, may prove helpful in demonstrating intra-cerebral haematomas, tumours and malformations (Amaducci et al, 1979).

Some laboratories continue to find that ocular pneu-moplethysmography and carotid audiofrequency analy-sis are suitable additional tests (Raines et al 1978; Goran and Moore 1980). Cerebral blood flow measure-ments may contribute to localization of the deficit (Thomas et al, 1979). Other methods undergoing exper-imental evaluation include positron imaging of cerebral blood flow during continuous inhalation of carbon dioxide labelled with a short-life isotope. $^{15}O_2$ only obtainable from a cyclotron (Ackerman et al, 1980); and the study of brain stem auditory evoked potentials (Raggazoni et al, 1982). The advent of the new technique of nuclear magnetic resonance is awaited.

These technical advances are likely to remain confined to the larger neurological centres, and will make little difference to diagnosis in the ordinary elderly patients attending a district general hospital, in whom clinical diagnosis remains paramount.

Medical treatment

When the clinical picture makes it unlikely that a surgi-cally correctable lesion will be found, medical treatment is required and this is well summarized by millikan and McDowell (1978). In cases of presumed embolic origin the choice lies between anticoagulant and antithrombo-tic drugs.

Anticoagulants. Anticoagulant therapy for TIA has been in vogue for more than 20 years (Siekert et al, 1961). Twelve published studies were critically reviewed by Brust (1977) who concluded that the case for their effectiveness remained unproved. Subsequently, in a well controlled study from Rochester, Minnesota, Whis-nant et al (1978) demonstrated no effect of anticoagu-lant therapy on survival — not surprisingly since death after TIA is related largely to myocardial infarction which is not prevented by anticoagulants. There was a reduction in the expected occurrence of stroke in

patients with vertebral-basilar TIAs but not in those with carotid TIAs. There was also an increase in the occurrence of intra-cerebral haemorrhage, especially in older patients. Muuronen and Kaste (1982) found a higher incidence of ischaemic stroke in TIA patients treated with anticoagulants than in an untreated group. This and other evidence no longer justifies the use of anticoagulant drugs in the prevention of stroke in older patients with TIA.

Antithrombotic agents. More recently hopes have turned towards the use of aspirin, dipyridamole and sulfinpyrazone. These drugs have the property, by different mechanisms, of reducing platelet adhesiveness. It was hoped that administration of these drugs to patients with TIA might prevent subsequent strokes. Three large trials have been completed which sought to evaluate the efficacy of this approach. None of these has produced conclusive results.

In the US multi-centre trial (Fields et al, 1977, 1978) patients were randomly allocated to either aspirin 1300 mg daily or placebo. Five per cent of the patients in this study were aged 75 and over and 30 per cent were aged 65–74. Aspirin appeared to reduce the likelihood of all unfavourable end points, especially in patients with multiple TIAs in the carotid territory, or in whom lesions were demonstrated which were appropriate to the symptoms. The evidence that aspirin actually prevented strokes in these patients was however inconclusive.

In the Canadian trial (Canadian Cooperative Study Group, 1978) patients whose ages are not stated, received either aspirin 1300 mg daily, sulfinpyrazone 800 mg daily, both drugs or neither. Aspirin, given alone or in combination with sulfinpyrazone, reduced the risk of continuing ischaemic attacks, stroke or death from all causes in men but not in women. Sulfinpyra-zone alone was not significantly effective. In the Italian study (Candelise et al, 1982), all of whose patients were under the age of 70, patients received either aspirin 500 mg daily or sulfinpyrazone 400 mg daily. Male patients treated with aspirin benefited and so, but to a non-significant extent, did female patients treated with sulfinpyrazone.

The methodology and conclusion of these trials have been attacked, e.g. by Kurtzke (1979) and particulary in swashbuckling fashion by Mitchell (1981); and have been defended (Barnett et al, 1978). No matter how carefully such large scale trials are planned, executed and analysed doubt creeps in about the methods used and the applicability to other patient groups. (Armitage, 1979) The only fact unequivocally to emerge is that these drugs can be given in substantial doses for long periods without serious side-effects. Guidelines for management which make the best use of published information are printed by Sandok et al (1978) and by McDowell et al (1980).

Conclusion

Geriatricians see few TIAs in the high age group. When they do they should treat associated diseases, especially hypertension, cardiac dysrhythmia, cardiac failure, and possibly polycythaemia. Anticoagulants should not be used. In the few cases where a carotid bruit is associated with symptoms in the appropriate distribution and the patient is otherwise fit, investigation of the blood vessels should be undertaken initially by non-invasive methods, with a view to possible endarterectomy or EC-IC bypass. In other cases aspirin may be given in a dose of from 800–1300 mg daily, for one year, provided that the patient is not sensitive to this drug. However, the physician who decides to do nothing will find support for his caution in the uncertain results of today's drugs and in the melancholy history of previous therapies.

THE COMPLETED STROKE

Diagnosis

Diagnosis in the stroke patient resolves itself into seeking answers to the following questions:

1. Is there any reasonable doubt, from the history and physical findings, that this is other than a vascular stroke; and if so, what further safe, practical and informative measures can be taken to establish the true diagnosis?

2. Given that the stroke has a vascular origin, is it one of the treatable types; and what further measures must be taken to establish this with a higher degree of probability?

3. What can be inferred from the clinical findings regarding the nature, locus and extent of the causal lesion?

4. What functional disturbances have resulted from the stroke, and what is their neurological mechanism?

5. What is the patient's general state of health; in particular what general disease underlies the stroke?

6. Who suffered the stroke?

These will now be separately discussed.

The following are among the diseases which may present in older people with symptoms and signs similar to a stroke:

1. Intracranial tumour, primary or secondary
2. Subdural haematoma
3. Cerebral abscess
4. Post-traumatic encephalopathy
5. Meningitis and meningoencephalitis
6. Epilepsy (Todd's palsy)
7. Meningovascular syphilis
8. Giant-cell arteritis

The clinical differentiation of these conditions is discussed by Jennett (1968). Knox and Adams (1969)

detected cerebral tumours in 2 per cent of patients admitted with a diagnosis of stroke, while Heasman and Lipworth (1966) found that in 10 per cent of cerebral tumours demonstrated at postmortem a clinical diagnosis of stroke had been made.

In the initial examination attention is paid to the level of consciousness, the integrity of swallowing reflexes and of bladder and bowel function, the status of the skin, the state of hydration and electrolyte balance, the tone of the muscles and the posture of trunk and limbs.

Once the patient's co-operation is assured a comprehensive examination is undertaken of physical function, neurological status and personality factors. The assessment covers the following main areas:

1. Movement
2. Balance
3. Communication
4. Sensation
5. Vision
6. Cognition
7. Autonomic function
8. Emotional expression

For practical bedside use a scheme of examination is required which will quickly and clearly delineate the major functional disturbances. This will allow rational planning of a rehabilitation programme. The principal tests required are as follows:

Motor function. Observe voluntary movement of individual limbs and classify into no movement, some movement and full movement. Observe the movement of face, lips and tongue.

Observe the ability to turn in bed, to sit up from the lying position, to transfer to a chair, to sit unsupported in a chair, to stand up from the chair, to remain standing. No attempt should be made to observe the patient's gait until a physiotherapist is in attendance. Balance should be tested in the sitting position and, when appropriate, with the patient standing. The standard neurological tests of cerebellar function should be performed. The range of passive movement, particularly of the shoulder joint, should be observed, and observation should be made of the muscle tone. The testing of tendon reflexes seldom contributes any useful information.

Communication. The patient's hearing should always be carefully assessed with and without a portable hearing aid if necessary. Note the articulation and the quality of 'speech melody', i.e. the pitch and rhythm variation. Note the speed of talking and the clarity of articulation. The examination of specific language deficit is considered below under the section on 'aphasia'.

Cognition. The stroke patient is, by definition, brain-damaged and does not necessarily think in a normal way even although he may be able to express himself clearly. The more striking abnormalities to look for in all stroke patients are:

1. Slowness of mentation
2. Difficulty in word finding
3. Difficulty in the formation of abstract concepts
4. Difficulty in grasping reality

Sensation. Test for the perception of light touch by touching the back of each hand lightly with the finger successively and then touching both hands simultaneously. The patient may either fail to perceive the touch on the affected side (hemianaesthesia) or he may perceive the affected side when it is touched singly but fail to perceive it when both are touched simultaneously (suppression).

Pin-prick. The backs of both arms are pricked successively until the patient winces.

Proprioception. This is tested by the thumb-finding test (Allison, 1966) in which the patient's affected arm is supported by the examiner and he is asked to grasp the affected thumb under visual observation. He is then told to let the thumb go. His eyes are covered, the arm is moved into a different position by the examiner, and the patient is asked to feel the thumb again. Proprioceptive loss is indicated by the patient grasping the air at the point formerly occupied by the affected thumb.

Somatoception. The patient is asked directly if he has experienced the sensation that his arm does not belong to him (Ullman, 1962).

Vision. The two main defects to be looked for are hemianopia and unilateral visual neglect. The simplest way to differentiate them is to give the patient something to read. The hemianopic patient turns his head towards the side of the hemianopia in order to bring the material into the unaffected visual field. The patient with unilateral neglect looks straight ahead but fails to see the material on the affected side. Lesser degrees of unilateral neglect are demonstrated by the posting-box test (Isaacs and Marks, 1973).

In the aphasic patient, hemianopia may be demonstrated by Cohn's test (1973) in which two large, brightly coloured objects are suddenly held up, one in each visual field. If the patient is hemianopic his eyes suddenly move in the direction of the normal side.

Autonomic function. Bladder function is usually examined only on the basis of nursing reports, and attention should be paid to the possibility of retention with overflow in the early stages of stroke. Enquiries should be made about the integrity of bladder sensation, the presence of 'urge', the time and frequency of micturition and the patient's awareness of his inability to use the toilet independently.

Emotion. Stroke patients experience a wider range of emotional changes than is usually appreciated. In addition to the expected anxiety, bewilderment and depression, they may show elation, indifference, inappropriate humour, aggression, disinhibition or callousness (Gainotti, 1972). Inappropriate weeping may occur and may be distressing to patients and relatives but is not induced by sadness.

This set of tests and observations can be quickly and easily performed without special apparatus or ancillary help and should go far towards localizing the lesion, determining the patient's potential for rehabilitation, and indicating the kind of obstacles that may be experienced. In complex cases further tests may be required to identify specific disabilities.

The results of this evaluation should be made known to all those in the rehabilitation team. Further information on behavioural responses will emerge from the observations of the nurses, physiotherapists, occupational therapists and speech therapists while they work with the patient in such stressful and complex neurophysiological tasks as the attempts to walk and to dress. Information of this type contributes important data to the clinical understanding of the patient.

Aphasia

Aphasia is the most dramatic, the most tragic and the most controversial of the clinical manifestations of stroke. It is perhaps best for the geriatrician to admit that, unless he is prepared to devote a great deal of time to the study of the vast literature on the subject, he will never really grasp its complexity. This section will be confined to the presentation of the important practical issues.

The questions to be discussed here are:

1. How common is aphasia in stroke?
2. How should the dysphasic patient be examined by the doctor?
3. What indications are there for prognosis?
4. What system of management should be employed in hospital?
5. What can be done for the patient by the speech therapist, the nursing staff, relatives, friends and others?

Those wishing to read further into the subject might like to start with Schuell's book (1975) or with short articles by Geschwind (1971) and Luria (1972).

1. Aphasia is found in from one-half (Brust et al, 1976) to two-thirds (Marquardsen, 1969) of cases of right hemiplegia admitted to hospital.

2. The doctor can glean useful information by engaging the patient in informal conversation. He has to learn to interpret the patient's comprehension and must insert questions and give instructions the understanding of which depend on the syntactical structure of the sentence, as well as offering material which can be comprehended from the substantives alone. He must

also learn to avoid giving visual and expressive clues while he is assessing verbal comprehension.

A quick simple scheme, which is helpful but has no theoretical basis, is to consider the following 'levels' of verbal language expression:

1. *Propositional* — the formulation of new sentences specific to the situation.
2. *Clichés* — sustaining conversation by the use of familiar 'ready made' phrases which do not contain new ideas.
3. *Indiscriminate* — the indiscriminate use of words or phrases which may or may not be appropriate to the situation.
4. *Rote* — the inability to use words in conversation but the ability to repeat rote-learned series such as numbers or days of the week.
5. *Melodic* — the inability to form words except when singing a familiar song.
6. *Total loss* — no word formulation possible.

The patient is first addressed by a simple open-ended question which requires a phrase or sentence in response, such as: 'Tell me what family you have'. From the reply the questioner detects whether the patient is functioning at, above or below level three. The questioning is then, as it were, moved up and down the scale to find a level at which the patient functions.

The doctor should also look for grammatical and syntactical errors and for paraphasias and neologisms. He should test repetition of verbal statements, reading, writing and copying.

It is desirable to have a tentative classification in mind while interrogating the patient. The classification of Geschwind (1971) was designed for this purpose. It has not proved universally acceptable, and it can be criticized on the grounds of failing to delineate distinct types of language deficit; but it has the advantage of being related to a very simple test schedule, and this puts it within the reach of the average doctor. The classification distinguishes first between 'fluent' and 'non-fluent' aphasia. The patient with fluent aphasia speaks without effort, articulates well, uses long phrases or sentences with normal rhythm and speech melody, but these are largely devoid of meaning. He makes frequent use of non-specific words and phrases, verbal and phonemic paraphasias and neologisms. By contrast the patient with non-fluent aphasia makes a great effort to try and express himself, articulates poorly, speaks slowly and produces only a small quantity of speech. His sentences lack grammatical structure, and the non-substantives are often omitted. Geschwind acknowledges that mixed types are commoner than the 'pure' varieties, which diminishes the value of the classification. Fluent aphasia is subdivided into four groups according to the results of tests of comprehension and repetition. All fluent patients have difficulty in naming objects. Those in whom both comprehension and repetition of a simple sentence are impaired are described as suffering from Wernicke's type, with a lesion in the posterior superior temporal lobe. Those in whom both comprehension and repetition are unimpaired suffer from the anomic type with a lesion in the angular gyrus. When comprehension is unimpaired but repetition is impaired, the patient has the conduction type with a lesion deep in the parietal lobe; while when the reverse is the case, i.e. comprehension is impaired but repetition is unimpaired, the condition is described as being of the 'isolation' type with a lesion that surrounds the speech areas but does not involve them. Brust (1976) succeeded in classifying most of his patients on this scheme and found that one-third of his cases were of fluent type — half of these being of Wernicke type — while two-thirds were non-fluent, most of these being mixed.

CT scanning has confirmed this association between the site of the lesion and the clinical features.

Gechwind's classification is a useful shorthand but does not replace the more complete traditional testing systems. In Schuell's textbook (1975) there is a comparative classification of classifications; while Luria (1973) has made his remarkable original insights into aphasia available in semipopular form.

Eslinger and Damasio (1981), in a small retrospective study, noted that patients with the Broca and conduction types of dysphasia were on average 10 to 15 years younger than those with the Wernicke and global types, a surprising finding which has not been explained adequately.

Prognosis in aphasic patients
The prognosis for early and late survival in aphasic patients is poorer than that for non-aphasics with comparable physical disability but no language disturbance (Marquardsen, 1969). Even if this is due to some extent to the greater size of aphasia-producing lesions, it is possible that the poor prognosis is in part a consequence of the loss of communication between patient and treatment team. The early mortality in non-fluent aphasics is higher that that in fluent aphasics (Brust et al, 1976).

Left hemiplegia with perceptual disturbances
A common stroke syndrome is the occurrence of left hemiplegia in association with hemianaesthesia, hemianopia, neglect of half of external space, loss of proprioception on the affected side, disturbed awareness of the affected half of the body particularly the upper limb, inattention to stimuli emanating from the left side, unawareness or denial of disability, inappropriate behaviour and emotions, loss of sitting and standing balance and of righting reflexes and apathy or indifference. This

syndrome is usually associated with a major infarct in the right hemisphere, usually attributed to occlusion of the internal carotid or middle cerebral artery, and involving infarction in the frontal, temporal and parietal lobes. A corresponding syndrome is occasionally observed in the presence of right hemiplegia (Welman, 1969).

Patients with this disability sit slumped in a chair falling over to the affected side. They seem inattentive to their surroundings and their head and eyes are deviated away from the paralysed side. When approached from this side they may reply quite promptly but without turning head or eyes towards the speaker, although they are capable of effecting this movement. They fail to perceive passive movement or displacement of the affected limb. When given a newspaper to read they may omit the first words in each line without evidently appreciating that what they read is nonsensical; although in other respects they may be surprisingly shrewd. They are incapable of making rational abstractions from perceived data and may thus be disoriented in space. They often experience bizarre delusions about the nature of their environment, for example that they are in a subterranean building such as a cellar, a prison or the Spanish inquisition. They may have even stranger delusions about their own body, and sometimes startle staff by talking of their two left arms. Their failure to appreciate reality may be simply tested by asking them if they are car owners and , if so, do they believe themselves capable of driving their car in their present state. Very often the patients believe that they are able to do so.

This common clinical picture is a vivid reminder of the immense range of cerebral functions which can be disrupted by a brain lesion. The unsophisticated may attribute inappropriate motives to the patient, such that he does not want to get better or he is not trying hard enough. Such attitudes are inimical in themselves to successful rehabilitation. The prognosis for such patients is not, however, invariably bad and in the series of Isaacs and Marks (1973) of 28 patients with severe perceptual loss accompanying left hemiplegia 12 were able to leave hospital substantially improved.

The neurological mechanisms underlying these curious manifestations are well described by Luria (1973).

Hind-brain strokes

Vertebrobasilar insufficiency may be due to lesions in the arteries of the system itself, to kinking or compression of the vertebral artery in the neck, or to stenotic or occlusive lesions of large thoracic vessels causing reversed flow in the vertebral system, the so-called 'cervical steal syndrome' (Reivich et al 1961). Depending on the exact site of the lesion and the nature of the blood supply, hind-brain strokes are characterized by paralysis or paresis of one or more limbs on one or both sides of the body accompanied by numbness or hypoaesthesia which may be on the same or on the opposite side of the body. Blurring of vision, abnormalities of the pupils, oculomotor paralysis and ptosis may also occur. Severe hind-brain strokes are characterized by dysarthria, dysphonia and dysphagia and can then be life-threatening. In many cases the cerebellum is involved with nystagmus, dysarthria and ataxia. The uncommon syndrome of infarction of the cerebellum alone has been described by Sypert and Alford (1975), whose patients presented with dizziness or falling and inability to stand, accompanied by vomiting, dysarthria and in some cases transient disturbances of consciousness. Duncan et al (1975) described a similar syndrome due to involvement of the anterior inferior cerebellar artery. Brain stem infarction following anaesthetic and surgical procedures such as oesophagoscopy was described by Fogelholm and Karli (1975). Patients with brain-stem signs are severely disabled from persistent dizziness and ataxia and full recovery may be delayed.

Gerstmann's syndrome. This syndrome of finger agnosia, agraphia, acalculia and constructional apraxia has long been attributed to lesions of the left parietal lobe. This syndrome in its pure form is not often seen, and its significance has been doubted. Geschwind (1970) critically reviewed the evidence for its existence and believes that a single conceptual defect related to the ordering of information may account for the clinically observed features. Luria (1973) adopted a somewhat similar view of the function of the left parietal lobe.

'Confusion'

Many stroke patients are 'confused' because of their inability to perceive or to conceptualize their environment adequately or to give proper language expression to what they do perceive. This is not surprising when thought is given to the extraordinarily unique exteroceptive and proprioceptive stimuli which flood the damaged brain of the recent stroke victim. His troubles are added to by difficulty in registering and retaining recent information and by the emotional turmoil which he experiences.

Mesulam et al (1976) drew attention to the common occurrence of acute confusional states as a manifestation of infarction in the territory of the right middle cerebral artery. The confusional state can occur in the absence of paralysis. Occlusion of the posterior cerebral artery leads to a characteristic amnesic syndrome (Benson et al 1974) while the syndrome of 'akinetic mutism' in which the patient is drowsy and apathetic, refuses food, does not speak and pays no attention to what is said to him is caused by occlusion of a branch of the bifurcation of the basilar artery (Segarra, 1970).

The emotional responses of patients with brain lesions were studied systematically by Gainotti (1972). Uncontrolled weeping, swearing and aggressive behaviour were common features in those with left-sided brain lesions, while in those whose lesion was on the right side of the brain emotional apathy and indifference, denial or minimization of disability and a bland indifference to their own state and to the effect on others were commonly noted.

The thought processes of the brain-damaged patient are characterized by loss of the capacity to form abstract ideas and dependence on 'concrete' thought (Goldstein and Schearer, 1941). Brain responses are slowed because of the asynchronous activity of the two hemispheres (Belmont, 1971) while the impersistence of cerebral traces is a major interfering factor in the acquisition of new information (Ben-Yishay et al, 1968).

Fascinating insights into the thought processes of the stroke patient are given in two accounts of their own strokes by doctors. One, a distinguished neuroanatomist with a pure motor stroke, was astonished at the slowness of the responses of his muscles to his will, and he reflected deeply on the origin of this slowing and its consequences on his behaviour (Brodal, 1973). Another, a general practitioner, admitted that it had never occurred to him that he might suffer a stroke, although he was mentally well prepared for a possible occurrence of a myocardial infarction (Kyle, 1976).

The behaviour of the stroke victim must be understood as a consequence of the limitations imposed on him by the disease and the environment, combined with the disturbance of bodily responses, perceptions and conceptual processes created by the brain damage.

Complications

Incontinence. Although urinary incontinence frequently accompanies the onset of stroke and may persist throughout the course of the illness, there do not appear to have been any systematic studies of the frequency with which this complication occurs, of its mechanism or prognosis. In the early stages of stroke catheterization is frequently resorted to, but not always is a distinction made between retention of urine with overflow and incontinence due to loss of cortical control of inhibition as an indication for catheterization.

Loss of inhibition, reduced bladder sensation and loss of locomotor ability seem to be the major factors in causing disturbances of continence in the stroke patient. Early removal of the catheter or avoidance of catheterization, and early active encouragement towards toilet independence are the basis of management. In an unpublished study Fletcher (1971) observed the spontaneous regaining of control of micturition in stroke patients. This occurred on average some 4 to 6 weeks after onset in those with recovery of ambulation.

Spasticity. Spasticity, formely looked upon as part of the normal genesis of stroke (Twitchell, 1951), is now recognized as a preventable complication. It affects distal muscles more than proximal ones, and is characterized by an increasing resistance as the velocity of stretch is increased and by radiation of reflex activity (Herman et al, 1974). The discharge of the primary endings of the muscle spindles of extensors, but not of flexors, is enhanced by the release of the dynamic fusimotor neurones. The process of the development of spasticity is described by Bobath (1970) and by Kottke (1974).

Spasticity, once established, greatly complicates treatment, and its avoidance requires the co-ordinated activities of the therapeutic team.

Contractures. Contractures of muscles, tendons, ligaments and joint capsules were in the past the all too common consequences of inadequate rehabilitation in the early stages of stroke. Corrective surgery, for example tendon transplantation, has been widely used in some centres for their relief (Nickel, 1976). Orthotic appliances are frequently prescribed, not always appropriately. Proper posturing and an appropriate exercise programme should prevent these painful and restricting complications.

Shoulder pain. The painful shoulder is a most unhappy consequence of stroke. It can gravely disturb the patient's morale and it interferes with attempts at upper-limb rehabilitation. Shoulder pain was in the past often ascribed to the so-called 'thalamic' syndrome. but mechanical causes are probably even more common. Spencer (1974) lists, amongst others, the following causes of painful hemiplegic shoulder:

1. Traction and pressure neuropathy of cervical roots or brachial plexus
2. Impacted fracture of the surgical neck of the humerus
3. Rotator cuff or biceps tendon injuries
4. Subluxation of the glenohumeral joint
5. Capsulitis around the shoulder joint
6. The shoulder-hand syndrome of reflex sympathetic dystrophy
7. Contracture from disuse

Najenson et al (1972) studied 32 stroke patients with complete paralysis of the upper limb by arthrography, and found rupture of the rotator-cuff ligament in one-third of these, almost all of whom had severe shoulder pain. Glenohumeral displacement was also a feature of these patients. The injuries were believed to be caused by inappropriate handling of the paralysed limb in the early stages of the stroke. Malalignment of the shoulder was a common finding in the study of Smith et al (1982).

Heart disease. Stroke victims often suffer from widespread vascular disease. In an electrocardiographic study of 252 patients aged 50 years and over with stroke, Steinmann (1975) found evidence of old myocardial infarction in 15 per cent and of recent myocardial infarction in 1 per cent. Two-thirds of his patients had electrocardiographic evidence of myocardial damage and 20 per cent suffered from atrial fibrillation. Similar findings were reported by Dimant and Grob (1977) Marshall and Kaeser (1961), Adams (1965, 1971) and Bourestom (1967). These have been supplemented by long-term studies from Denmark by Marquardsen (1969), from the United States ny Katz et al (1966), and Baker et al (1968a, b) and by Acheson (1971) and Acheson and Hutchinson (1971) from Britain.

Deep vein thrombosis

Deep vein thrombosis has been identified in the hemiplegic leg in half of all hospitalized cases (Warlow et al, 1976) and is a contributory cause of unilateral leg oedema (Gibberd et al, 1976). However, the proportion of cases in which this finding has real clinical significance is much lower, and pulmonary embolism is an infrequent complication.

Prognosis

Harmsen and Tibling (1972) in a small series of patients under the age of 65 found that nearly three-quarters of their patients with intra-cerebral haemorrhage were dead within 6 months, compared with rather less than half of those with thromboembolic lesions. Five per cent of Harmsen and Tibling's community sample were dead before admission and one-third died while in hospital. Only two of those discharged from hospital died within 6 months of onset, and 60 per cent of these patients were alive 6 months after onset. Oxbury et al (1975) confirmed the relationship between conscious level on admission and outcome in non-haemorrhagic cerebral infarction. There was no mortality among 52 patients who were fully conscious on admission, but one-third of those who were drowsy or confused and one-half of those who were unresponsive or unconscious died within 3 weeks.

The functional level both at the time of admission and at the time of discharge influence the prognosis. Haerer (1975) showed that two-thirds of patients who were able to walk at the time of discharge from hospital following a stroke survived for 5 years, compared with less than a quarter of those who were unable to walk at the time of discharge.

The experience at Framingham, Massachusetts, has been published by Sacco et al (1982); and also from the United States comes a national survey of all hospital admissions (Weinfeld 1981). There is a large Canadian study by Abu-zeid et al (1978) and a Japanese one by Fujishima et al (1976). All these studies confirm an early mortality of around 40 per cent in the first 6 months,

most of this being in the first 30 days after the onset of the stroke; with a continuing mortality of 6–7 per cent of the survivors annually over the next 5 years.

Clinical factors which influence outcome and which have been studied in detail include:

Pathogenesis. Whisnant (1976), in the Rochester study, found that of patients with embolic stroke one-third died within a month of onset, one-half within 6 months and two-thirds within 2 years; while of those with non-embolic stroke one-quarter died within 3 months, and one-third within one year; but half the patients survived for 4 years after their stroke. In the Framingham Study (Sacco et al, 1982) there was no difference in the 30-day case-fatality rate between patients with cerebral infarction and those with cerebral embolus, of whom one-sixth died within that period; but 82 per cent of patients with intracerebral haemorrhage died within the first month.

Hypertension. The presence of hypertension exerts an adverse effect on outcome. (Fujishima et al, 1976). In the Framingham Study hypertension greatly increased early mortality from stroke in men but not in women.

Heart disease. Coronary heart disease and congestive cardiac failure preceding and accompanying the stroke exert a profound effect on early mortality in men and a lesser but still significant effect in women (Sacco et al, 1982).

Age and sex. Age exerts an adverse effect on mortality (Weinfeld, 1981); but in patients under the age of 65 intracerebral haemorrhage is a relatively common cause of stroke and carries a high mortality (Harmsen and Tibbling, 1972). The greater mortality of males than females is noted in all studies.

Clinical features

In non-haemorrhagic cerebral infarction mortality is related to the conscious level on admission (Oxbury et al, 1975). Patients who were fully conscious on admission suffered no mortality. One-third of those who were drowsy and confused died within 3 weeks of admission as did one-half of those who were unresponsive or unconscious.

Patients with accompanying renal failure have an adverse prognosis (Frithz and Werner, 1976). Feigenson et al (1977) and Feigenson and McCarthy (1977) analysed the clinical findings which were associated with rapid recovery.

Andrews et al (1981) stressed that most recovery took place in the first 3 months after onset with some continuation for up to 6 months; but thereafter improvement was mainly in walking and mobility and related to better use of residual function rather than to neurological recovery. Andrews et al (1980) found that amongst the many predictors of outcome none was more valuable nor more simple than the analysis of the patient's ability to draw pictures of simple objects, like a house, 2 weeks after the onset. Haerer (1975) showed that two-thirds of patients who were able to walk at the time of discharge from hospital following a stroke survived for 5 years, compared with less than a quarter of those who were unable to walk at the time of discharge.

Other factors. As new forms of investigation have made their appearance, so their findings have been related to long term prognosis. Thus Miller and Myamoto (1979) were able to show that the size and nature of the lesion as located by CT scanning was closely related to the outcome. Cerebral blood flow shows a similar relationship, patients with a normal flow at onset having a better survival and functional recovery rate than those with reduced flow (Fujishima et al, 1977; Heiss et al, 1977).

La Joie et al (1982) noted that patients with a normal or diminished somatosensory evoked potential recorded over the contralateral parietal cortex after stimulation of the sensorimotor nerves of the involved extremity showed better functional gain in the arm than did those in whom this response was absent.

Studies on prognosis are reviewed by Bloch and Bayer (1978).

TREATMENT OF STROKE

The search for a specific treatment of stroke continues. The search has concentrated on drugs which, when administered as soon as possible after the onset of the stroke, will arrest the brain damage, improve the circulation or nutrition of jeopardized areas at the edges of the infarct, or prevent or arrest the processes of thrombosis and blood coagulation. Attempts have also been made to reduce cerebral oedema and to improve the nutrition of sick neurones. These efforts have been summarized by Millikan and McDowell (1978) in the bleak statement: 'There is no known method of treatment which will limit infarction once it starts or reverse it once it occurs.' This statement embraces unconfirmed claims or cirtical reports made on behalf of agents which reduce cerebral oedema (Fieschi et al, 1977), including dextran. (Matthews et al, 1976), glycerol (Antonini et al, 1977; Fawer et al, 1918); vasodilators (Capon et al, 1977; Pathy et al, 1977) hyperbaric oxygen (Sukoff, 1978), steroids (Norris, 1976) and even barbiturates (Agnoci et al, 1979). Admani (1978) published a controlled trial of naftidrofuril which showed a significant difference in outcome in recent stroke patients in favour of those treated with this drug; but his findings have not yet been confirmed.

Parsons-Smith (1979, 1981) urged the instant intravenous administration of dexamethasone to every stroke victim as soon as he was seen by a doctor, and ideally within 4 hours of onset. He argued by analogy from animal experiments and from clinical experience in conditions other than stroke, that early administration would reduce brain damage and limit infarct size, and he criticised published studies which failed to confirm this expectation on the grounds that the injection was given too late. It would be difficult to organize a trial to support this claim. In the ordinary conditions of admission, Mulley et al (1978) attempted a clinical trial in which alternate stroke patients were given dexamethasone as soon as possible after admission, and failed to reveal any significant difference between the treated and untreated group. Despite many trials over many years, some of them admittedly defective, insufficient evidence has been amassed to justify the use of this drug in the emergency treatment of stroke disease.

Surgery

The advent of computerized tomography has been of immense help in the identification of surgically treatable lesions. Surgical evacuation is recommended for large superficial haematomas, and occasionally for deeper ones, occurring in non-comatose patients with modest neurological deficits, especially when the lesion is in the non-dominant hemisphere. Large cerebellar haematomas with compression of the brain stem may also be suitable for surgical evacuation (Feindel, 1979).

Although anticoagulants in general are inappropriate in acute stroke low dose heparin can be given safely as a prophylaxis against deep vein thrombosis (McCarthy et al, 1977).

Rehabilitation

Until recently little interest in the rehabilitation of stroke patients was evident from perusal of the British medical literature. McLeod and Williamson (1967) viewed the situation thus: 'The onus appeared to rest with the patient to demonstrate that he could do better, rather than upon the doctor to discover how much functional recovery was possible'. Interest in the United States was more active. In the last few years a number of guides to stroke rehabilitation have appeared (e.g. Bobath, 1970; Brunnstrom, 1971; Zankel, 1971; Manning, 1974; Licht, 1975).

While there is general agreement on the imperative need for early active prolonged multidisciplinary rehabilitation in at least the more severely disabled stroke patient, there is as yet no properly structured body of information to give the doctor active guidance on exactly what should be done. The present discussion will deal with the following topics:

1. Neurophysiological principles
2. Disability rating

3. Physiotherapy methods
4. Mechanical, electronic and orthotic devices
5. Principles of management
6. Resources
7. Evaluation of effectiveness of treatment.

Neurophysiology

How do patients get better from stroke? Do sleeping brain cells wake up? Are ischaemic areas revascularized? Do broken neuronal networks regrow? Do other parts of the brain assume the functions of the damaged areas? These questions are much debated with little evidence. However there is much evidence of repair procedures in the damaged brain, particularly of neuronal dendritic growth and of the appearance of new synapses after damage to neural structures (Bach-y-rita, 1981). It has recently been recognized that well-attested repair processes may indeed play some part in stroke rehabilitation, but as yet there is no knowledge of how these processes can be influenced to accelerate recovery.

The neurophysiological principles which should underlie the management of the stroke patient were described by Bobath (1970), Brunnstrom (1971), Atkinson (1974) and extensively by Kottke (1975). Kottke emphasized the key roles in all motor function of facilitation or sensory activation of internuncial neurones and motor neurones and the inhibition of excitation in the internuncial pool to prevent involuntary activation of motor neurones. Damage to the corticospinal tract upsets the delicate balance. Injury to sensory pathways and to the reticular formation interferes with the sensory component vital for normal movement and with the control of postural reflexes. Damage to the inhibitory system in the mid-brain and cerebellum may result in spasticity and rigidity. Non-responsive muscles must be activated by appropriate sensory stimulation, while muscles whose activity is unwanted must be inhibited by appropriate movements or postures. Facilitation of the weakened muscle can be obtained by use of the primary stretch reflex and by proprioceptive facilitation. Specifically this can be achieved by moving the muscle through its range of motion, by manual vibration and by stimulating the skin with ice, brushing, stroking or by iontophoresis. The unresponsive muscle may be further facilitated by inhibition of the spastic antagonist by such techniques as the use of ice. The desired movement can also be facilitated by activation of reflex synergies, i.e. the basic reflex patterns of musclar contraction on which the higher centres act to produce voluntary motion.

General reflex tone is influenced by the position of the body in relation to gravity. In the supine position there is increased extensor tone in the lower extremities and increased flexor tone in the upper extremities. Reflex extension in the lower limb is facilitated by the static labyrinthine reflex.

Bobath (1970) advocated the use of postures which inhibit reflexes and abnormal movements. Extension of the neck and spine, external rotation and extension of the arm, abduction, external rotation and extension of the hips and knees achieve this purpose, while the opposite postures, which are often adopted bypatients, have the undesired effect of increasing muscle tone and promoting spasticity.

The revolution in physiotherapy practice has been almost complete and it is now rare to see hemiplegic patients with flexed and adducted arms and dropped wrists leaning on a tripod stick, stepping forward with the good leg and sweeping an abducted extended spastic leg behind them. Physiotherapists select their style of rehabilitation however from the experience of many teachers, giving as much weight to personal experience as to theory; as is well described in the text of Johnstone (1978). The physician should acquaint himself with the methods used in his physiotherapy department so that he can provide leadership and guidance to relatives, general practitioners and other members of the rehabilitation team.

The enthusiasm with which neurophysiological methods have been adopted has caused some scepticism, and although many apparent benefits have been documented they have not been evaluated. However, no one has devised an ethical and accurate method of evaluating rehabilitation programmes. Anderson et al (1979) found that 27 per cent of stroke patients who had no rehabilitation became independent. Most treatment programmes can beat this. Lind (1982), in analysing methodologically imperfect trials, concluded that there was no clear evidence that the functional gains claimed were due to anything other than natural recovery; but conceded that rehabilitation probably increased the patient's sense of independence. Certainly trials cannot measure the transmission to the patient by the physiotherapist of hope enthusiasm, concern, confidence or affection. It remains unclear whether physiotherapy, as it is practised in the average hospital with the average stroke patient, accelerates functional recovery through neurophysiological or psychological means, or whether it merely enables the patient to make more effective use of residual function.

Feigenson et al (1977a) reviewed the clinical, social and administrative factors which influenced outcome and length of stay.

Attempts have also been made to evaluate specific methods of treatment with clearly defined and limited objectives. For example De Souza et al (1980a, b) described tests for the recovery of upper limb function which measured the way in which muscle groups were brought into play in the performance of a rotating task.

Merletti et al (1978), used the measurement of muscle force in the lower limb to evaluate functional electrical stimulation. Takebe and Basmajian (1976) used gait analysis to assess the treatment of drop foot; while Wall and Ashburn (1979) demonstrated the value of simple time and distance factors in the analysis of gait as an overall measure of progress.

New methods of treatment

The proponents of biofeedback believe that functional improvement in gait and balance can result from the use of the EMG signal from the paretic limb as the afferent loop. In controlled trials improvement has been demonstrated in drop foot (Burnside et al, 1982); in the lower as compared with the upper limb (Wolf et al, 1979); and, in combination with electrical stimulation, as a form of 'automated treatment' (Bowman et al, 1979). The training of sensory awareness, especially in left hemiplegics with proprioceptive loss, is treated by placing a pneumatic cuff on the upper limb (Johnstone, 1978). This also prevents contracture. Biofeedback is used in this type of case as well (Weinberg et al, 1979).

Defeated by the attempt to evaluate individual treatment methods, some researchers have faced the task of evaluating total regimes, but have encountered many practical difficulties (Sheikh et al, 1978). Smith et al (1981) compared three regimes of out-patient management for patients who had been discharged from hospital after stroke illness with continuing disability. They found that this form of management was applicable to only a small minority of stroke patients among whom the best results were obtained with the most intensive treatment; but as this required the attendance of the patient at the hospital on four full days a week for up to 6 months the question has to be faced whether the results are justified by the costs.

Treatment of dysphasia

Controversy has long surrounded the question of whether the treatment of dysphasia by speech therapists is beneficial. Basso et al (1979) reported a large series which appeared to show that improvement could be objectively demonstrated and was independent of the type of aphasia. Improvement was greatest in the less severely affected patients and in those in whom treatment was started early.

The use of volunteers in the treatment of aphasic patients is discussed in the following section.

Management

Three questions have been extensively debated:

1. Should stroke patients be treated at home or in hospital?

2. Should hospitalized stroke patients be treated in special stroke units and if so of what type?

3. What role can volunteers play in stroke rehabilitation, especially in the management of the dysphasic patient?

Home or hospital

In the United States and other countries where the cost of hospital treatment is high (Adelman, 1981) patients are usually admitted to a department of acute internal medicine or neurology for an average period of under 3 weeks (Walker et al 1981) along with subsequent but by no means invariable referral to a rehabilitation unit. In the United Kingdom whether a stroke patient is admitted to hospital or not seems to depend more on social factors — whether relatives able and willing to nurse him at home are available — rather than on identified medical factors, such as the need for investigation and rehabilitation. (Brocklehurst et al, 1978a). A patient treated in a general hospital may or may not receive an adequate course of rehabilitation; and paradoxically those who receive most treatment are the ones with the least likelihood of recovery: an indication perhaps of the continuing concern of the physiotherapist for her patient rather than of a critical audit of cost effectiveness. The attainment of functional independence in hospital is not necessarily sustained when patients return home (Garraway et al, 1980b); and stroke patients do not always undertake the activities in their homes which they are capable of doing in rehabilitation departments. (Andrews and Stewart, 1979). These findings are used as rather flimsy evidence in support of a greater use of home rehabilitation (Vetter, 1980), which is also advocated for terminally ill cases by Wright and Robson (1980). Stroke illness is highly complex, necessitating a wide range of medical and therapeutic activities, in addition to skilled nursing; and home management seems justified only when a keen general practitioner can introduce into a supportive home all the necessary domiciliary services; has high expectation of outcome; and remains determined to achieve this and to turn to other aids if required (Waters and Perkin, 1982). In any one practice so few cases of stroke will be seen that these circumstances must rarely be realized. If however the alternative is hospital admission without any guarantee of an adequate length of stay or of the provision of intensive and well ordered rehabilitation, the home option may be preferred.

Stroke units

The advocates of stroke units believe that hospital management flourishes when a multi-disciplinary team concentrates their efforts on the complex problems of the stroke patient, both those encountered by the patient himself in hospital and those which will be faced when he returns to an anxious and possibly over-protective family. Stroke units with a major emphasis on rehabilitation have been advocated by Hewer (1976), Norris and Hachinski (1976), Isaacs (1977), Feigenson et al (1977b), Feigenson (1981) Brocklehurst et al (1978b) and Blower and Ali (1979). All of these units presented excellent results, gave much of the credit to the team spirit, and stressed the educational and exemplary value of their units. Objective evidence of the superiority of the results of a stroke unit over the performance of the general medical wards of a district general hospital was sought by Garraway et al (1981a). They excluded from their study patients thought likely to get better without rehabiliation and those considered too ill to benefit from the rehabiliation; and concentrated on this 'middle band' which comprised only 25 per cent of all stroke patients. The initial results (Garraway et al, 1981b) showed that patients admitted directly to the stroke unit had a significantly higher level of functional independence at the time of discharge from hospital than those admitted to the general medical wards.

The major difference in management between the two groups was a greater use of occupational therapy in the specialized unit; while the stroke unit patients also made more effective use of community health and social services (Garraway et al, 1981b). The stroke unit patients curiously received less physiotherapy over a shorter period of time than did the medical unit patients; and, as in the study of Brocklehurst et al (1978b) it was the patients who remained dependent who had most physiotherapy (Smith et al, 1981). Unfortunately the benefit of treatment in a stroke unit was not sustained when the patients were re-examined at home one year later (Garraway et al, 1980b) suggesting that family influences on stroke outcome exert a powerful late effect, a subject dealt with in more detail in the next section.

Conclusion

The objective evidence collected by Garraway and his team suggests that the rehabilitation services are most effectively deployed in the management of the stroke patient when these are concentrated in a specialized stroke unit. The opinion of those who have worked in these units is that the extent of working together generates enthusiasm and awareness which are reflected in a better quality of life for patients, relatives and indeed staff. The resources required are no greater than those employed in the management of the same patients when these are dispersed in a number of wards (Isaacs, 1977).

In a population of 250 000, that is the population served by the average British district general hospital,

about one fresh stroke occurs each day. If all of these were admitted to hospital, and if they remained there on average for 30 days, then a stroke unit receiving all stroke patients would require 30 beds. In practice stroke units usually manage with about half that number, which should be sufficient, provided the 'triage' system of pre-admission selection is practised, with a stroke unit concentrating on 'middle band' cases; and with some outlet to longer stay units for patients who fail to recover and are unable to return home.

The stroke patient goes home

The discharge home of the stroke patient is preceded by final evaluation of his capacity to function in his home environment, by means of a predischarge visit to his home in the company of the physiotherapist and occupational therapist of the unit; and sometimes perhaps by a trial weekend. Other activities at this stage include provision of domiciliary services, and adaptations to the house to provide freedom of egress and ingress, safety in the bathroom and functional efficiency in the kitchen. Attention is also paid to the height of the patient's bed and chair, the suitability of floor coverings, staircases and door handles. Special provision is required for wheelchair users. Domiciliary physiotherapy (Adams et al 1957) or day hospital attendance may be arranged (Brocklehurst, 1970). The services available to the patient in the United Kingdom include home help, district nurse, health visitor, meals on wheels, luncheon club, physiotherapy, occupational therapy, chiropody, general practitioner service, residential home, convalescent home, short-term hospital admission, help from voluntary organizations with club attendance, gardening, decorating, holidays, crafts. Home care has also been successful in the United States (Rogoff et al 1964).

With all these services available to him, what is the quality of the patient's life in the 3 to 5 years or longer which he survives in comparatively good health after the stroke? The studies of Collins et al (1960); Isaacs et al (1976); and Mackay and Nias (1979) revealed that a substantial proportion of recovered stroke victims, especially the younger ones and those who had been in full-time employment before their stroke, suffered prolonged misery and frustration as a result of their inability to resume their former role in life and, by their behaviour and attitude, inflicted strain and distress on their relatives. Similar evidence of mutual incomprehension between patients and relatives and of maladaptation to the changes in potential and personality were presented by Christie and Lawrence (1978); Lawrence and Christie (1979); Labi et al (1980) and Brocklehurst et al (1981). Folstein et al (1977) looked upon mood disorder as a specific complication of stroke; and Feibel and Springer (1982) using a rating scale, described 26 per cent of a group of stroke victims as 'depressed' when they examined them 6 weeks after the onset of the stroke. In this study no relation was found between depression and any neurological feature, but there was a close relationship with failure of the patient to resume his pre-stroke activities. Sexual function in stroke survivors has been studied by Sjögren and Fugl-Meyer (1981) and by Bray et al (1981). These studies were of patients under the age of 60 interviewed 3 to 6 months after stroke and they had resumed fairly normal sexual activity, but with some reduction in quality.

Stroke is a family illness, as the title of Valerie Eaton-Griffith's book (1975a) reminds us. The patient may have lost the use of his arm and leg, but the wife has lost the use of her husband. She too suffers great disruption and may not get back to anything approaching her previous pattern of normal living. Kinsella and Duffy (1980) interviewed 79 spouses of stroke patients and found amongst them an over-riding sense of anxiety, guilt, over-protection and a lack of realism. These relatives did not know what to do for the best, and claimed to have received little guidance. Many attributed the patient's stroke and his failure to recover to their own inadequacies, and created a situation in which the resumption of normal living became difficult. In a parallel study of relatives of patients with aphasia (Kinsella and Duffy, 1979) the most prominent consequences were found to be impairment of social and leisure activitives of the spouse. Marital relationships were more reduced in aphasics than in non-aphasic patients, and there was a significantly raised incidence

amongst these spouses of minor psychiatric disorder.

Attempts have been made to anticipate these difficulties and to help relatives by counselling them before the patient returns home and after his return (Mulhall, 1980); but far more effective has been the very rapid growth of the Stroke Club movement. Stroke Clubs are to be found in all parts of the United Kingdom, most of them providing a weekly club meeting, some for patients only, some for relatives only, and some for both groups. These gatherings enable stroke patients and relatives to compare their lot with that of others, and to share experiences, ideas and happy social activities. They have made life more bearable for many hundreds of people.

The United Kingdom has also pioneered the use of volunteers to supplement the treatment given to the dysphasic patients (Eaton-Griffith, 1975b; Eaton-Griffith and Miller, 1980) In this scheme dysphasic patients have allotted to them a small number of volunteers who visit them at their home and engage them in conversation about everyday activities, encouraging them to widen their range of interests. Accompanying this is a weekly club where the emphasis is on having an enjoyable time and playing games which call for skill and for language use, but which are adapted to the special difficulties of the stroke patient. Patients benefit greatly from the improved level of socialisation and quality of life (Lesser and Watt, 1978); and their use of language seems to improve also (Meikle et al, 1979). Extension of these schemes will do much to improve the hard lot of stroke patients and their families.

REFERENCES

Abrams H L, Mcneil B J 1976 Medical implications of computed tomography (CAT scanning). New England Journal of Medicine 298: 255–261

Abu-zeid H A H, Nung Won Choi, Ping-Hwa Hsu, Maini K K 1978 Prognostic factors in the survival of 1484 stroke cases observed for 30 to 48 months. 1: Diagnostic types: clinical variables. Acta Neurologica 35: 121–125

Acheson J 1971 Factors affecting the natural history of 'focal cerebrovascular disease' Quarterly Journal of Medicine 40: 25–46

Acheson J, Hutchinson E C 1971 The natural history of 'focal cerebral vascular disease' Quarterly Journal of Medicine 40: 15–23

Ackerman R H, Subramanyam R, Correia J A, Alpert N M, Taveras J M 1980 Positron imaging of cerebral blood flow during continuous inhalation of $C^{15}O_2$ Stroke 11: 45–49

Adams G F 1965 Prospects for patients with strokes, with special reference to the hypertensive hemiplegic. British Medical Journal ii: 253–259

Adams G F 1971 Clinical outlook for stroke patients. Gerontologia Clinica 13: 181–188

Adams G F, McQuitty F M, Flint M Y 1957 Rehabilitation of the elderly invalid at home. The Nuffield Provincial Hospital Trust, London

Adelman S M 1981 Economic impact. In: Weinfeld FD (ed) The National Survey of Stroke, Stroke Supplement I: I 69–I 78

Admani A K 1978 New approach to treatment of recent stroke. British Medical Journal 2: 1678–1679

Agnoci A, Palesse N, Ruggieri S, Leonardis G, Benzi G 1979 Barbiturate treatment of acute stroke. Advances in Neurology 25: 269–274

Allison R S 1966 Perseveration as a sign of diffuse and focal brain damage British Medical Journal ii: 1027–1032, 1059–1101.

Amaducci L, Framm E S, Haynes R B, Mohr J P, Peerless S J, Robertson J T, Tulleman C A F, Yonekawa Y 1982 The international EC/IC bypass study. Stroke 13: 247–255

Amaducci L, Voegelin M R, Cappelli G, Masi R 1979 Radionuclide angiography. Advances in Neurology 25: 227–235

Anderson T P, Baldridge M, Ettinger M G 1979 Quality of care for completed stroke without rehabilitation: evaluation by assessing patient outcomes. Archives of Physical Medicine Rehabilitation 60: 103–107

Andrews K, Stewart J 1979 Stroke recovery: he can but does he? Rheumatology and Rehabilitation 18: 43–48

Andrews K, Brocklehurst J C, Richards B, Laycock P J 1980 The prognostic value of picture drawings by stroke patients. Rheumatology and Rehabilitation 19: 180–188

Andrews K, Brocklehurst J C, Richards B, Laycock P J 1981 The rate of recovery from stroke and its measurement. International Rehabilitation Medicine 3: 155–161

Antonini F M, Bertini G, Fumagalli C, Fieschi C, Battistini N, Violante F, Nori A 1977 Effects of intravenous infusion of glycerol on regional cerebral blood flow in cerebral infarction. Gerontology 23: 376–380

Armitage P 1979 Controversy in the interpretation of clinical trials. Annals of Neurology 5: 601–602

Atkinson H W 1974 Principles of treatment. In: Cash J (ed) Neurology for Physiotherapists, Faber, London

The Australian therapeutic trial in mild hypertension 1980. Lancet i: 1261–1267

Bach-y-Rita P 1981 Brain plasticity as a basis for the development of rehabilitation procedures for rehabilitation. Scandinavian Journal of Rehabilitation Medicine 13: 78–83

Baker R N, Ramseyer J C, Schwartz W S 1968 Prognosis in patients with transient cerebral ischaemic attacks. Neurology 18: 1157–1165

Barnes R W, Bone G E, Reinertson J, Slaymaker E E, Hoklanson D E, Stradness D E 1976 Noninvasive ultrasonic carotid angiography in prospective validation by contrast arteriography. Surgery 80: 328–335

Barnett H J M 1982 Embolism in mitral valve prolapse. Annual Review of Medicine 33: 489–507

Barnett H J M, McDonald J W D, Sackett D L 1978 Aspirin — effective in males threatened with stroke. Stroke 9: 295–298

Basso A, Capitani E, Vignolo L A 1979 Influence of rehabilitation on language skills in aphasic patients: a controlled study. Archives of Neurology 36: 190–196

Baum H M, Robins M 1981 Survival and prevalence. In: Weinfeld F D (ed), The National Survey of Stroke, Stroke 12: Supplement 1: I 59–I 68

Beevers D G, Farman M J, Hamilton M, Harper J E 1973 Hypertensive treatment and the course of established cerebrovascular disease. Lancet i: 1407–1409

Belmont I, Karp E, Birch H G 1971 Hemispheric inco-ordination in hemiplegia. Brain 94: 337–348

Benson D F, Marsden C D, Meadows J C 1974 The amnesic syndrome of posterior cerebral artery occlusion. Acta Neurologica Scandinavica 50: 133–145

Ben-Yishay Y, Diller L, Gerstman L, Haas A 1968 The relationship between impersistence, intellectual function and outcome of rehabilitation in patients with left hemiplegia. Neurology 18: 852–861

Bes A, Guell A, Braak A, Geraud G, Jauzac P 1979 Doppler sonography in the diagnosis of occlusion or stenosis of the internal carotid artery. Advances in Neurology 25: 211–221

Blackshear W M, Phillips D J, Bodily K C, Strandness D E 1978 Ultrasonic demonstration of external and internal carotid patency with common carotid occlusion: a preliminary report. Stroke 11: 249–252

Bloch R, Bayer N 1978 Prognosis in stroke. Clinical Orthopaedics and Related Research 131: 10–14

Blower P, Ali S 1979 A stroke unit in a District General Hospital: The Greenwich experience. British Medical Journal 2: 644–646

Bobath B 1970 Adult Hemiplegia; Evaluation and Treatment. Heinemann, London

Bourestom N C 1967 Predictions of long-term recovery in cerebrovascular disease. Archives Physical Medicine Rehabilitation 48: 415–419

Bowman B R, Baker L L, Waters R L 1979 Positional feedback and electrical stimulation: an automated treatment for the hemiplegic unit. Archives of Physical Medicine and Rehabilitation 60: 497–502

Bray G P, Defrank R S, Wolfe T L 1981. Sexual functioning in stroke survivors. Archives of Physical Medicine and Rehabilitation 62: 286–288

Brocklehurst J C 1970 The Geriatric Day Hospital London: King Edward's Hospital Fund for London.

Brocklehurst J L, Andrews K, Morris P, Richards B R, Laycock P L 1978 Why admit stroke patients to hospital? Age and Ageing 7: 100–108

Brocklehurst J C, Andrews K, Richards B, Laycock P J 1978b How much physical therapy for patients with stroke? British medical Journal 1: 1307–1310

Brocklehurst J C, Morris P, Andrews K, Richards B, Laycock P 1981 Social effects of stroke. Social Sciences and Medicine 150: 35–39

Brodal A 1973 Self-observations and neuroanatomical considerations after stroke Brain 96: 675–694

Bronte-Stewart R 1964 The epidemiology of stroke. In: Anderson W F, Issacs B (eds) Current Achievements in Geriatrics, Cass London, p 49–55

Brunnstrom S 1971 Movement Theory in Hemiplegia In: a Neurophysiological Approach. Harper and Rowe, New York

Brust J C M 1977 Transient ischaemic attacks: natural history and anticoagulation. Neurology 27: 701–707

Brust J C M, Shafer S Q, Richter R W, Bruun B 1976 Aphasia in acute stroke. Stroke 7: 167–174

Bull G M, Morton J 1975 Seasonal and short-term relationships of temperature with deaths from myocardial and cerebral infarction. Age and Ageing 4: 19–31

Burnside I G, Tobias S, Burshill D 1982 Electromyographic feedback in remobilisation of stroke patients: controlled trial. Archives of Physical Medicine and Rehabilitation 63: 217–222

Byer J A, Easton J D 1980 Transient cerebral ischaemia: review of surgical results. Progress in Cardiovascular Diseases 32: 389–396

Canadian Co-operative study Group 1978 A randomised trial of aspirin and sulfinpyrazone in threatened stroke. New England Journal of Medicine 299: 53–59

Candelise L, Landi G, Perrone P, Bracchi M, Brambilla G 1982 A randomised trial of aspirin and sulfinpyrazone in patients with TIA. Stroke 13: 175–179.

Capildeo R, Haberman S, Rose F C 1977 New classification of stroke: preliminary communication. British Medical Journal 2: 1578–1580

Capildeo R, Haberman S, Rose F C 1978 The definition and classification of stroke: a new approach. Quarterly Journal of Medicine 47: 177–196

Capon A, deRood M, Vervist A, Fruhling J, 1977 Action of vasodilators on regional cerebral blood flow in subacute or chronic cerebral ischaemia. Stroke 8: 25–29

Carter A B 1964 Cerebral Infarction. Pergamon Press, Oxford

Carter A B 1970 Hypotensive therapy in stroke survivors. Lancet i: 485–489

Cartlidge N E F, Whisnant J P, Elveback L R 1977 Carotid and vertebral-basilar transient cerebral ischaemic attacks: a community study, Rochester, Minnesota. Mayo Clinical Proceedings 52: 117–120

Chin P L, Kaminski J, Rout M 1977 Myocardial infarction coincident with cerebrovascular accidents in the elderly. Age and Ageing 6: 29–37

Christie D, Lawrence L 1978. Patients in hospitals: a study of the attitudes of stroke patients. Social Science and Medicine 12: 49–51

Cohn R, 1972 Eyeball movements in homonymous hemianopia following simultaneous bitemporal object presentation. Neurology 22: 12–14

Collins P, Marshall J, Shaw D A, 1960 Social rehabilitation following cerebrovascular accidents. Gerontologia Clinica 2: 246–256

Crawford M D, Gardner M J, Morris J N 1968. Mortality and hardness of local water supplies. Lancet i: 827–831

Dayton S, Chapman J M, Pearce M L, Popjak G J 1970 Cholesterol, artherosclerosis, ischaemic heart disease and stroke. Annals of Internal Medicine 72: 97–109

De Souza L H, Langton Hewer P, Miller S 1980a Assessment of recovery of arm control in hemiplegic stroke patients. 1: Arm funtion tests. International Rehabilitation Medicine 2: 3–9

De Souza L H, Langton Hewer R, Lynn P A, Millers S, Reed G A L 1980b Assessment of recovery of arm control in hemiplegic stroke patients. 2: Comparison of arm function tests and pursuit tracking in relation to clinical recovery. International Rehabilitation Medicine 2: 10–16

Dimant J, Grob D 1977 Electrocardiographic changes and myocardial damage in patients with acute cerebrovascular accidents. Stroke 8: 448–455

Duncan G W, Parker S W and Fisher C M 1975 Acute cerebellar infarction in the PICA territory. Archieves of Neurology 32: 364–368

Easton J D, Sherman D G 1977 Stroke and mortality rate in carotid endarterectomy: 228 consecutive operations. Stroke 8: 565–568

Easton J D, Sherman P G 1980 Management of cerebral symbolism of cardiac origin. Stroke 11: 433–422

Eaton-Griffith V 1975b A Stroke in the Family. Wilwood, London

Eaton-Griffith V 1975b Volunteer scheme for dysphasic patients with stroke. British Medical Journal 3: 633–635

Eaton-Griffith V, Miller C L 1980 Volunteer stroke scheme for dysphasic patients with stroke. British Medical Journal 281: 1605–1607

Eslinger P J, Damasio A R 1981 Age and type of aphasia in patients with stroke. Journal of Neurology, Neurosurgery and Psychiatry 44: 377–381

Evans J G, Caird F I 1982 Epidemiology of neurological disorders in old age. In: Caird F I (ed) Neurological Disorders in the Elderly, Wright, Bristol

Fawer R, Justafré J C, Berger J P, Schelling J L 1978 Intravenous glycerol and cerebral infarction: a controlled four-month trial. Stroke 9: 484–486

Feibel J H, Springer J C 1982 Depression and failure to resume social activities after stroke. Archives of Physical Medicine and Rehabilitation 63: 276–278

Feigenson J S, McCarthy M L, Meese P D, Fekenson W D, Greenberg S D, Rubin E, McDowell F H 1977 Stroke rehabilitation: I — Factors predicting outcome and length of stay. New York State Journal of Medicine 77: 1426–1430

Feigenson J S, McCarthy M L 1977 Stroke rehabilitation: II — Guidelines for establishing a stroke rehabilitation unit. New York State Journal of Medicine 77: 1430–1434

Feigenson J S 1981 Stroke rehabilitation: outcome studies and guidelines for alternative levels of care. Stroke 12: 372–375

Feindel W 1979 Management of intracerebral haemorrhage. Archives of Neurology 25: 293–300

Fields W S, Lemak N A, Frankowski R F, Hardy R J 1967 Controlled trial of aspirin in cerebral ischaemia. Stroke 8: 303–314

Fields W S, Lemak N A, Frankowski R F, Hardy R J 1978a Controlled trial of aspirin in cerebral ischaemia. Stroke 9: 303–309

Fields W S, Lemak N A, Frankowski R F, Hardy R J 1978b Controlled trial of aspirin in cerebral ischaemia: Part II — surgical group. Stroke 9: 309–317

Fieschi C, Battistini N, Nardini M, D'Ettore M, Volante F, Zangtte E 1977 Clinical management of cerebrovascular disease. Arteriosclerosis Reviews 2: 155–174

Fisher M 1978 Holter monitoring in patients with transient focal cerebral ischaemia. Stroke 9: 514–516

Fletcher M 1971 Disturbances of bladder and bowel in stroke patients. Unpublished observations

Fogelholm R, Karli P 1975 Iatrogenic brain stem infarction. European Neurology 13: 6–12

Folstein M F, Maiberger R, McHugh P R 1977 Mood disorder as a specific complication of stroke. Journal of Neurology, Neurosurgery and Psychiatry 40: 1018–1020

Ford J J, Baker W H, Ehrentraft J L 1975 Carotid endarterectomy for non-hemisphereic transient ischaemic attacks. Archives of Surgery 110: 1314–1317

Friedman G D, Loveland D B, Ehrlich S P 1968 Relationship of stroke to other cardiovascular disease. Stroke 38: 533–541

Frithz G, Werner I 1976 Studies on cerebrovascular strokes: II — Clinical findings and short-term prognosis in a stroke material. Acta Medica Scandinavia 199: 133–140

Fujishima M, Omae T, Takeya Y, Takeshita M, Ogata J, Ueda K 1976 Prognosis of occlusive cerebrovascular diseases in normotensive and hypertensive subjects. Stroke 7: 472–476

Fujishima M, Nishimaru K, Omae T 1977 Long-term prognosis for cerebral infarction in relation to brain circulation — a seven-year follow up study. Stroke 8: 680–683

Furlan A J, Whisnant J P, Elveback L R 1979 The decreasing incidence of primary intracerebral haemorrhage: A population study. Annals of Neurology 5: 367–373

Gainotti, G 1972 Emotional behaviour and hemispheric side of the lesion Cortex 8: 41–55

Galligioni F 1979 Angiography. Advances in Neurology 25: 223–226

Garraway W M, Whisnant J P, Kurland L T, O'Fallon W M 1979a Changing pattern of cerebral infarction: 1945–1974. Stroke 10: 657–663

Garraway W M, Whisnant J P, Furllan A J, Phillips L H, Kurland L T, O'Fallon W M, 1979b The declining incidence of stroke. New England Journal of Medicine 300: 449–452

Garraway W M, Akhtar A J, Prescott R J, Hockey L 1980a Management of acute stroke in the elderly: preliminary results of a controlled trial. British Medical Journal 280: 1040–1043

Garraway W M, Akhtar A J, Prescott R J, Hockey L 1980b Management of acute stroke in the elderly: follow-up of a controlled trial. British Medical Journal 281: 827–829

Garraway W M, Akhtar A J, Smith D L, Smith M E 1981a The triage of stroke rehabilitation. Journal of Epidemiology and Community Health 35: 39–44

Garraway W M, Walton M S, Akhtar A J, Prescott R J 1981b The use of health and social services in the management of stroke in the community: results from a controlled trial. Age and Ageing 10: 95–104

Genton E, Barnett H J M, Fields W S, Gent M, Hoak J C 1977 Report of the Joint Committee for Stroke Resources XIV. Cerebral ischaemia: the role of thrombosis and of anti-thrombotic therapy. Stroke 8: 150–175

Gerlis L S 1981 Transient hemisparetic attacks due to unrecognised nocturnal hypoglycaemia. British Medical Journal 282: 401

Geschwind N 1970 The clinical syndromes of the cortical connections. In: Williams D (ed) Modern Trends in Neurology, Butterworth, London, vol 5, p 29–40

Geschwind N 1971 Aphasia. New England Journal of Medicine 284: 654–656

Gibberd F B, Gould S R, Marks P 1976 Incidence of deep vein thrombosis and leg oedema in patients with strokes. Journal of Neurology, Neurosurgery and Psychiatry 30: 1222–1225

Goldstein R, Schearer M 1941 Abstract and concrete behaviour: an experimental study with special tests. Psychological Monographs No. 239

Goran A, Moore G 1980 Value of the non-invasive cerebrovascular laboratory in diagnosis of extracranial carotid artery disease: an analysis of 159 studies in 157 patients. Stroke 11: 325–328

Greenhalgh R M, Illingworth R D, McFie J, Mills S P, Perkin G O, Rose F C 1979 Extracranial to intracranial micro-revascularisation for the treatment of completed ischaemic stroke. British Medical Journal 2: 18–19

Haberman S, Capildeo R, Rose F C Q 1978 The changing mortality of cerebrovascular disease. Quarterly Journal of Medicine 47: 71–88

Haerer A F, Woolsey P C 1975 Prognosis and quality of survival in a hospitalised stroke population from the south. Stroke 6: 543–548

Hames T K, Humphries K V, Powell T V, McLellan D L 1981 Comparison of angrography with continuous wave Doppler ultrasound in the assessment of extracranial arterial disease. Journal of Neurology, Neurosurgery and Psychiatry 44: 661–669

Hansen B S, Marquardsen J 1977 Incidence of stroke in Frederiksberg, Denmark. Stroke 8: 663–65

Harmsen P, Tibling G 1972 A stroke register in Goteborg, Sweden. Acta Medica Scandinavia 191: 463–470

Harrison M JG, Pollock S, Kendall B E, Marshall J 1981 Effect of haematocrit on carotid stenosis and cerebral infarction. Lancet ii: 114–115

Heasman M A, Lipworth L 1966 Accuracy of certification of cause of death. General Register Office Studies on Medical and Population Subjects, No. 20 H.M.S.O., London

Heiss W D, Zeiler K, Havelec L, Reisner T, Bruck J 1977 Long-term prognosis in stroke related to cerebral blood flow. Archieves of Neurology 34: 671–676

Heler R L 1976 Stroke Rehabilitation In: Gillingham F J, Mawdsley C, Williams A E (eds) Stroke, Churchill Livingstone, Edinburgh

Herman R, Freedman W, Mayer N 1974 Neurophysiological mechanisms of hemiplegic and paraplegic spasticity: implications for therapy. Annals of Physical Medicine Rehabilitation 55: 338–343

Heyden S, Heyman A, Complong L 1969 Mortality pattern among patients with atherosclerotic cerebrovascular disease. Journal of Chronic Diseases 22: 105–110

Heyden S, Heiss G, Heyman A, Tyroler A H, Hames C G, Patzschke V, Manegold C 1978 Cardiovascular mortality in transient ischaemic attacks. Stroke 11: 252–255

Humphrey P R D, Du Boulay G H, Marshall J, Pearson T C, Ross Russell R W, Symon L, Wetherlet-Mein G, Zilkha E 1979. Cerebral blood flow and viscosity in relative polycythaemia. Lancet ii: 873–876

Inman W H W, Vessey M P 1968. Investigation of deaths from pulmonary, coronary and cerebral thrombosis and embolism in women of child-bearing age. British Medical Journal ii: 193–199

Isaacs B 1977 Five years' experience of a stroke unit. Scottish Health Bulletin 35: 93–98

Isaacs B, Marks M 1973 Determinants of outcome of stroke rehabilitation. Age and Ageing 2: 139–149

Isaacs B, Neville Y, Rushford I 1976 The stricken: the social consequences of stroke Age and Ageing 5: 188

Jenkins J J, Jiménez-Pabón E, Shaw R E, and Sefer J W 1975. Schuell's aphasia in adults: diagnosis, prognosis and treatment. 2nd edn, Harper & Row, Hagerston, Maryland

Jennett W B 1968 Strokes in the elderly — a problem in diagnosis. Gerontologia Clinica 10: 17–83

Johnstone M 1978 Restoration of motor function in the stroke patient. Churchill Livingstone, Edinburgh

Jonas S, Klein I, Dimant J 1977 Importance of Holter monitoring in patients with periodic cerebral symptoms. Annals of Neurology 1: 470–474

Jones H R, Millikan C H 1976 Temporal profile (clinical course) of acute carotid system cerebral infarction. Stroke 7: 64–71

Jones J R, Millikan C H, Sandok B A 1980 Temporal profile (clinical course) of acute vertebrobasilar system cerebral infarction. Stroke 11: 173–177

Kannel W B 1971 Current status of the epidemiology of brain infarction associated with occlusive arterial disease. Stroke 2: 295–318

Kannel W B, Dawbert T R, Sorlie P, Wolf P A 1976 Components of blood pressure and risk of artherothrombotic brain infarction. The Framingham Study. Stroke 7: 327

Kannel W B, Wolf P A, McGee O L, Dawber T R, McNamara P, Castelli W P 1981 Systolic blood pressure, arterial rigidity and risk of stroke. Journal of the American Medical Association 245: 1225–1229

Katz S O, Ford A B, Chinn A B, Newhill W A 1966 Prognosis after strokes. Part II. Long-term course of 159 patients. Medicine (Baltimore) 45: 236–246

Kiloh L G, Osselton J W 1961 Clinical Electroencephalography. Butterworth, London

Kinsella G J, Duffy F D 1979 Psychosocial readjustment in the spouses of aphasic patients. Scandinavian Journal of Rehabilitation Medicine 11: 129–132

Kinsella G J, Duffy F D 1980 Attitudes towards disability expressed by spouses of stroke patients. Scandinavian Journal of Rehabilitation Medicine 13: 73–76

Knox E W, Adams G F 1969 The hemiplegic onset of brain tumour. Gerontologica Clinica 11: 1–12

Kostuk W J, Boughner D R, Barnett H J R, Silver M D 1977 Strokes: a complication of mitral-leaflet prolapse. Lancet 2: 313–316

Kottke F J 1975 Neurophysiologic therapy for stroke. In: Licht S (ed) Stroke and its Rehabilitation, Waverley Press, Baltimore

Kurtzke J F 1979 Controversy in neurology: the Canadian study on TIA and aspirin: a critique of the Canadian TIA study. Annals of Neurology 5: 597–599

Kusunoke T, Rowed D W, Tator C G, Lougheed W M 1978 Thromboendarterectomy for total occlusion of the internal carotid artery: a reappraisal of risks, success rate and potential benefit. Stroke 9:34–38

Kyle D 1976 Personal View. British Medical Journal i: 895

Labi M L C, Phillips T F, Gresham G E 1980 Psychosocial disability of physically restored long term stroke survivors. Archives of Physical Medicine and Rehabilitation 61: 561–565

La Joie W J, Reddy N M, Melvin J L 1982 Somatosensory evoked potentials: their predictive value in right hemiplegia. Archives of Physical Medicine and Rehabilitation 63: 223–226

Lakeman M J, Sherriff S B, Martin T R P 1981 A prospective study of the accuracy of Doppler ultrasound in detecting carotid artery disease. Journal of Neurology, Neurosurgery and Psychiatry 44: 657–660

Lawrence L, Christie D 1979 Quality of life after a stroke: a three-year follow-up. Age and Ageing 8: 167–172

Lesser R, Watt M 1978 Untrained community help in the rehabilitation of stroke sufferers with language disorder. British Medical Journal 2: 1045–1048

Lewis R R Beasley M G, Gosling R G 1979 Disease at the carotid bifurcation: diagnosis by Doppler ultrasound imaging. Gerontology 25: 291–298

Licht S, (ed) 1975 In Stroke and its Rehabilitation. Waverley Press, Baltimore

Lind K 1982 A synthesis of studies of stroke rehabilitation. Journal of Chronic Diseases 35: 133–149

Luria A R 1972 Aphasia reconsidered. Cortex 8: 34–40

Luria A R 1973 The Working Brain: An Introduction to Neuropsychology. Penguin, London

McAllen P M, Marshall J 1977 Cerebrovascular incidents after myocardial infarction. Journal of Neurology, Neurosurgery and Psychiatry 40: 951–955

McCarthy S T, Turner J J, Robertson O, Hawkey C J, Macey D J 1977 Low-dose heparin as a prophylaxis against deep-vein thrombosis after acute stroke. Lancet 2: 800–801

McDowell F H 1979 Prevention of subsequent infarctions and transient ischaemic attacks. Advances in Neurology 25: 277–286

McDowell F H, Millikan C H, Goldstein M 1980 Treatment of impending stroke. Stroke 11: 1–3

McLeod R D M, Williamson J 1967 Problems of stroke assessment and rehabilitation. Scottish Medical Journal 12: 384–389

Mackay A, Nias B C 1979 Strokes in the young and middle-aged: consequences to the family and to society. Journal of the Royal College of Physicians 13: 106–112

Manning J 1974 Hemiplegia. In: Cash J (ed) Neurology for Physiotherapists, Faber, London

Marquardsen J 1969 The natural history of acute cerebrovascular disease: a retrospective study of 769 patients. Acta Neurologica Scandinavica 45: Suppl. 38

Marshall J 1979 Differential diagnosis of stroke. Advances in Neurology 25: 177–179

Marshall J, Kaeser A C 1961 Survival after non-haemorrhagic cerebrovascular accidents: a prospective study. British Medical Journal ii: 73–77

Marshall J 1971b Familial incidence of cerebrovascular disease. Journal of Medical Genetics 8: 84–89

Matthews W B, Oxbury J M, Grainger K M R, Greenhall R C D 1976 A blind controlled trial of Dextran 40 in the treatment of ischaemic stroke. Brain 99: 193–206

Meikle M, Wechsler E, Tupper A, Benson M, Butler J, Mulhall D, Stern G 1979 Comparative trial of volunteer and professional treatment of dysphasia after stroke. British Medical Journal 2: 87–89

Merletti R, Zelaschi F, Latella D, Galli M, Angeli S, Sessa M B 1978 A Control study of muscle force recovery in hemiparetic patients during treatment with functional electrical stimulation. Scandinavian Journal of Rehabilitation Medicine 10: 147–154

Mesulam M-M, Waxman S G, Geschwind N, Sabrin T D 1976 Acute confusional states with right middle cerebral artery infarctions. Journal Neurology, Neurosurgery and Psychiatry 39: 84–89

Mettinger K L, Larsson S, Fricson K, Casseborn S 1978 Detection of atherosclerotic plaques in carotid arteries by the use of ^{123}I-Fibrinogen. Lancet 1: 242–244

Miller L S, Miyamoto A T 1979 Computed tomography: its potential as a prediction of function of recovery following stroke. Archives of Physical Medicine and Rehabilitation 60: 108–114

Millikan C H, McDowell F H 1978 Treatment of transient ischaemic attacks. Stroke 9: 299–308

Millikan C 1979 The transient ischaemic attack. Advances in Neurology 25: 135–140

Mirchell J R A 1981 Anticogulants, aspirin and anturan in transient cerebral ischaemic attacks. In: Turnbridge W M G (ed) Advanced Medicine Newcastle upon Tyne, Pitman Medical, London, p 276–286

Mitchinson M J 1980 The hypotensive stroke. Lancet i: 244–246

Mulhall D J 1980 Stroke rehabilitation: counselling relatives towards a helping relationship. Geriatric Medicine 10: 39–42

Mulley G, Wilcox R G, Mitchell J R A 1978 Dexamethasone in acute stroke. British Medical Journal 2: 994–996

Muuronen A, Kaste M 1982 Outcome of 314 patients with transient ischaemic attacks. Stroke 13: 24–31

Najenson T, Yacobovich E, Pikielni S S 1971 Rotator cuff injury in shoulder joints of hemiplegic patients. Scandinavian Journal of Rehabilitation Medicine 3: 131–137

Nelson R F, Pullicino P, Kendall B E, Marshall J 1980 Computed tomography in patients presenting with lacunar syndromes. Stroke 11: 256–261

Nickel V L 1976 Physical rehabiliation of the stroke patient with emphasis on the needs for integration into the community. Stroke: Proceedings of the Ninth Pfizer Symposium. Churchill Livingstone, Edinburgh

Norris J W 1976 Steroid therapy in acute cerebral infarction. Archives of Neurology 33: 69–71

Norris J W, Hachinski V C 1976 Intensive care management of stroke patients. Stroke 7: 573–577

Norris J W, Hachinski V C 1982 Misdiagnosis of stroke. Lancet i: 328–331

Oxbury J M, Greenhall R C D, Grainger K M R 1975 Predicting the outcome of stroke: acute stage after cerebral infarction. British Medical Journal iii: 125–127

Parkin P J, Kendall B E, Marshall J, McDonald W I 1982. Amaurosis Fugax: some aspects of management. Journal of Neurology, Neurosurgery and Psychiatry 45: 1–6

Parsons-Smith B G 1979 First aid for acute cerebral stroke. Practitioner 223: 553–557

Parsons-Smith B G 1981 Neurological emergencies. Practitioner 225: 1135–1140

Pathy J, Menon G, Reynolds A, Van Strik R 1977 Betahistine hydrochloride (Serc) in cerebrovascular disease: a placebo controlled study. Age and Ageing 6: 179–184

Raggazoni A, Amantini A, Rossi L, Pagnini P, Arnetoli G, Marini P, Nencioni C, Versari A, Zappoli R 1982 Brain-Stem auditory evoked potentials and vertebral-basilar reversible ischaemic attacks. Advances in Neurology 32: 187–194

Raines J K, Schlaen H H, Brewster D C, Abbott W M, Darling R C 1978 Experience with a non-invasive evaluation for cerebral vascular disease. Angiology 30: 600–609

Reichman O H 1975 Extracranial and intracranial arterial lesions. In: Whisnant N, Sandok B (eds) Conference of Cerebrovascular Diseases, Crane Sutton, New York

Reivich M, Holling H E, Roberts B, Toole J F 1961 Reversal of blood flow through the vertebral artery and its effect on cerebral blood flow. New England Journal of Medicine 265: 878–885

Riddle M C, Hart J 1982 Hyperglycaemia recognised and unrecognised as a risk factor for stroke and transient ischaemic attacks. Stroke 13: 356–359

Robins M, Baum H M 1981 Incidence. In: Weinfeld F R (ed) The National Survey of Stroke, Stroke 12: Supplement I: I 45–I 57

Rogoff J B, Cooney D V, Kutner B 1964 Hemiplegia: a study of home rehabilitation. Journal of Chronic Diseases 17: 539–550

Ross Russell R W 1975 How does blood pressure cause stroke? Lancet ii: 1283–1286

Royal College of Physicians 1974 Report of geriatric working group on stroke. RCP, London

Sacco R L, Wold P A, Kannel W B, McNamara P M 1982 Survival and recurrence following stroke: the Framingham Study. Stroke 13: 290–295

Sandok B A, Furlan A J, Whisnant J P, Sunot T M 1978 Guidelines for the management of transient ischaemic attacks. Mayo Clinic Proceedings 53: 665–674

Sandok B A, Whisnant J P, Furlan A J, Mickell J 1982 Carotid artery bruits: prevalence survey and differential diagnosis. Mayo Clinic Proceedings 57: 227–230

Segarra J M 1970 Cerebral vascular disease and behaviour. I. The syndrome of the mesencaphalic artery. (Basilar artery bifurcation). Archives of Neurology 22: 408–418

Shaw D A 1981 Transient ischaemic attacks: clinical management. In: Tunbridge W M G (ed) Advanced Medicine, Newcastle upon Tyne, Pitman Medical, London, p 287–294

Sheikh K, Smith D S, Meade T W, Brennan D J 1978 Methods and problems of a stroke rehabilitation trial. British Journal of Occupational Therapy 41: 262–265

Shekelle R S, Ostfield A S, Khaurans H L 1974 Hypertension and risk of stroke in an elderly population. Stroke 5: 71–75

Siekert R G, Millikan C H, Whisnant J P 1961 Anticoagulant therapy in intermittent cerebrovascular insufficiency. Journal of the American Medical Association 176: 19–22

Sjogren K, Fugl-Meyer A R 1981 Sexual problems in hemiplegia. International Rehabilitation Medicine 3: 26–31

Smith D S S, Goldenberg E, Ashburn A, Kinsella G, Sheikh K, Brennan P J et al J S 1981 Remedial therapy after stroke: a randomised controlled trial. British Medical Journal 282: 517–520

Smith R G, Cruickshank J G, Dunbar S, Akhtar A J 1982 Malalignment of the shoulder after stroke. British Medical Journal 284: 1224–1226

Spencer R 1974 Painful neuroplegic shoulder. Australian Journal of Physiotherapy 20: 186–190

Smith M E, Garraway W M, Smith D L, Akhtar A J 1982 Therapy impact on functional outcome in a controlled trial of stroke rehabilitation. Archives of Physical Medicine and Rehabilitation 63: 21–24

Soltero I, Lin K, Cooper R, Stamler J, Garside D 1978 Trends in mortality from cerebrovascular disease in the United States 1960–1975. Stroke 9: 549–558

Stallones R A 1979 Epidemiology of stroke in relation to the cardiovascular disease complex. Advances in Neurology 25: 117–126

Steinmann B 1975 Care, rehabilitation and follow-up of the stroke patient. Age and Ageing suppl. 31–40

Sukoff M H 1978 Experience in the treatment of cerebrovascular problems with hyperbaric oxygenation. Stroke 9: 110

Sypert G W, Alford E C 1975 Cerebellar infarction: a clinicopathological study. Archives of Neurology suppt. 31–40

Takebe K, Basmajian J V 1976 Gait analysis in stroke patients to assess treatment of foot-drop. Archives of Physical Medicine and Rehabilitation 57: 305–310

Thomas D J 1982 Whole blood viscosity and cerebral blood flow. Stroke 13: 285–287

Thomas D J, DuBoulay G H, Marshall J, Pearson T C, Ross Russell R W, Symon L et al 1977 Effect of haematocrit on cerebral blood flow in man. Lancet 2: 941–943

Thomas D J, Zilkha E, Redmond S, Duboulay G H, Marshall J, Ross Russell R W, Symon L 1979. An intravenous $_{133}$Xenon clearance technique for measuring cerebral blood flow. Journal of Neurological Sciences 40: 53–63

Tohgi H, Yamanouchi H, Murakami M, Kameyama A 1978 Importance of the haematocrit as a risk factor in cerebral infarction. Stroke 9: 369–374

Twitchell T 1951 The restoration of motor function following hemiplegia in man. Brain 74: 443–480

Ueda K, Howard G, Toole J F 1980 Transient ischaemic attack and cerebral infarction: a comparison of predisposing factors. Journal of Chronic Diseases 33: 13–19

Ueda K 1981 Decreasing trend in incidence and mortality from stroke in Hisayama residents. Stroke 12: Supplement I: I 3–1 5

Ullman M 1962 Behavioural Changes in Patients Following Strokes. Charles C. Thomas, Springfield, Illionois

Vessey M P 1973 Oral contraceptives and stroke. New England Journal of Medicine 288: 906–907

Vessey M P, Doll R 1968 Investigation of relation between use of oral contraceptives and thromboembolic disease. British Medical Journal ii: 199–205

Veterans' Administration Hospital Trial 1973 Anticoagulants in acute myocardial infarction. Journal American Medical Association 225: 726–729

Vetter N J 1980 Home or hospital for the stroke patient. Lancet ii: 1254

Walker A E, Robins M, Weinfeld F D 1981 Clinical findings. Stroke 12: Supplement Number 1: I 13–I 44

Wall J C, Ashburn A 1979 Assessment of gait disability in hemiplegics: hemiplegic gait. Scandinavian Journal of Rehabilitation Medicine 11: 95–103

Warlow C, Ogston D, Douglas A S 1976 Deep venous thrombosis of the legs after strokes. Part I — Incidence and predisposing factors; Part II — Natural history. British Medical Journal 2: 1178–1183

Waters H J, Perkin J M 1982 Study of stroke patients in a single geriatric practice. British Medical Journal 284: 791–794

Weddell J M, Beresford A A 1979 Planning for stroke patients: a four year descriptive study of home and hospital care. Her Majesty's Stationery Office, London

Weinberg J, Diller L, Gordon W A, Gerstman L J, Lieberman A, Lakin P, Hodges G, Ezrachi O 1979 Training sensory awareness and spatial organisation in people with right brain damage. Archives of Physical Medicine and Rehabilitation 60: 491–496

Weinfeld F D 1981 The National Survey of Stroke. AHA monograph Number 75. Stroke 12: Supplement 1.

Weisberg L A, Nice C N 1977 Intracranial tumours simulating the presentation of cerebrovascular syndromes: early detection with cerebral computed tomography. American Journal of Medicine 63: 517–524

Welman A J 1969 Right-sided unilateral visual spatial agnosia, asomatognosia and anosognosia with left hemisphere lesions. Brain 571–580

Whisnant J P 1976 A population study of stroke and transient ischaemic attacks: Rochester, Minnesota, In: Stroke: Proceedings of Ninth Pfizer Symposium, Churchill Livingstone, Edinburgh

Whisnant J, Cartlidge N E F, Elveback L R 1978 Carotid and vertebral basilar transient ischaemic attacks: effect of anticoagulants, hypertension and cardiac disorders on survival and stroke occurrence — a population study. Annals of Neurology 3: 107–115

Wiebers D O, Whisnant J P, O'Fallon W M 1982 Reversible ischaemic neurologic deficit (RIND) in a community. Rochester, Minnesota. Neurology 32: 459–465

Wolf S L, Baker M P, Kelley J L 1979 EMG feedback in stroke: effect of patient characteristics. Archives of Physical Medicine and Rehabilitation 60: 96–102

World Health Organisation 1971 Cerebrovascular diseases: prevention, treatment and rehabilitation. World Health Organization Technical Report Series Number 469

Wright W B, Robson P 1980 Crisis procedure for stroke at home. Lancet ii: 249–250

Wylie C M 1970 Death statistics for cerebrovascular disease: a review of recent findings. Stroke 1: 184–193

Yates P O 1976 The pathogenesis of transient ischaemic attack. In: Stroke: Proceedings of the Ninth Pfizer Symposium, Churchill Livingstone, Edinburgh.

Zankel H T 1971. Stroke Rehabilitation. A Guide to the Rehabilitation of an Adult Patient Following a Stroke. Charles C. Thomas, Springfield, Illinois

The autonomic nervous system

'I propose the term "Autonomic Nervous System" for the sympathetic system and the allied nervous system of the cranial and sacral nerves and for the local nervous system of the gut' (Langley, 1898). These are efferent (effector) systems but for the most part they are not as autonomous as Langley may have thought, for like the rest of the nervous system they largely depend for their functioning on reflexes. The afferent side of the reflex arc sometimes comprises fibres travelling with autonomic nerves, but commonly does not. For instance, a cardinal reflex in the control of the circulation is from the baroreceptors mainly in the carotid sinus, and the afferents travel in the ninth cranial nerve. Cutaneous blood flow is constantly changing and an important factor in its control is skin temperature. Body temperature is partly controlled by nervous activity originated by temperature receptors within the brain, and partly by receptors in the skin. It is the abnormal functioning of these reflexes and other mechanisms especially in the elderly which is the subject of this chapter.

There is experimental evidence in animals and man that with increasing age the influence of the autonomic nerves decreases and the sensitivity of the cells to humoral factors increases (Frolkis, 1967; Frolkis et al, 1975). In aging in animals synthesis and hydrolysis of acetylcholine decreases and the sensitivity of various organs and systems to cholinergic substances increases (Frolkis et al, 1973). Haemodynamic reflexes from the mechanoreceptors of the carotid sinus are decreased (Frolkis et al, 1977). Baroreceptor sensitivity in man decreases with age (Cokkinos et al, 1979) as does the skin potential reflex (Nomura et al, 1981). The importance of disturbance of body temperature and blood pressure regulation in the elderly due to disruption of autonomic activities has become increasingly recognized in recent years (Wollner, 1966, 1967; Brocklehurst, 1975; Exton-Smith, 1977; Collins et al, 1980). Disorders of the human autonomic nervous system are reviewed by Johnson and Spalding (1974, 1976).

Bladder and bowel function are largely under autonomic control and are discussed in Chapters 26 and 30. Elderly patients with atonic bladders may have impaired circulatory reflexes (Collins et al, 1980). In multiple system atrophy with autonomic failure the sacral para-sympathetic neurons may atrophy giving rise to bladder dysfunction and impotence (Sung et al, 1979). Neuronal changes in aging people have been reported in the jejunum (Israilov et al, 1978). Peripheral vascular disease can be due to vasospasm, but is largely due to obliterative vascular disease which is dealt with in Chapter 10. Hypertension is dealt with in Chapter 12. It has been suggested that hypertension in renal failure may be more readily induced when uraemic neuropathy impairs baroreflex sensitivity (Tomiyama et al, 1980).

TEMPERATURE REGULATION

The normal regulation of body temperature

The ability to maintain a constant central temperature whilst peripheral tissues undergo wide fluctuations is an important factor in determining survival (Hardy, 1961; Cranston, 1966; Cooper, 1965, 1968). There is diurnal variation, the temperature being highest in the evening and lowest in the morning, provided the normal rhythm of waking and sleeping is maintained (Lewis and Lobban, 1957a, b; Mills, 1966; Corbett and Johnson, 1968). Diurnal variation persists in old age (Fox et al, 1973). The central temperature is accurately reflected by the temperature of the oesophagus or the covered external auditory meatus (Cooper et al, 1964). For clinical purposes, changes in rectal temperature reflect variations in central temperature, and this is useful in the management of accidental hypothermia (Cooper and Kenyon, 1957). The temperature of urine as it is passed may be measured with the Uritemp apparatus (Brooke et al, 1973). It has been regarded as a measure of the central temperature, a urine temperature of 34.8°C being equivalent to a rectal temperature of 35°C. This and the gradient between urine and hand temperatures have been used in surveys of elderly people in the community (Fox et al, 1971, 1973). Urinary bladder temperatures measured by an intravesical thermocouple correlate well with oesophageal, rectal and pulmonary arterial blood temperatures (Lilly et al, 1980).

The temperature of the mouth is not reliable as a measure of central temperature, particularly in elderly people, unless special methods are used, partly because of the difficulty of assuring adequate mouth closure (Barley and Evans, 1970).

Control of body temperature is dependent on the integrated activity of the nervous system. The afferent pathway leads from skin receptors to central structures in the brain in which the hypothalamus plays an important part. There are also receptors in the brain which themselves respond to temperature changes. The efferent pathways descend in the lateral columns of the spinal cord. Sympathetic fibres synapse with cells in the intermediolateral column from which preganglionic fibres pass to the sympathetic ganglia. Postganglionic fibres innervate cutaneous blood vessels and sweat glands. Somatic motor fibres innervate striated muscle where shivering may occur. Non-thermal stimuli such as consumption of alcohol and drugs produce vasomotor changes which can affect temperature regulation. Acclimatization can occur as a result of exposure to a particularly cold or hot environment (Burton and Edholm, 1955; Hong and Rahn, 1967; Fox et al, 1963a, b; Johnson and Spalding, 1974).

When a normal subject is exposed to cold, heat is conserved by cutaneous vasoconstriction, and there is an increase of heat production from shivering. Appreciation of cold at a conscious level influences the decision to exercise, to increase clothing and to move out of the cold environment. Conversely, exposure to heat induces heat loss by vasodilatation and sweating. Appreciation of heat will influence the decision to remove clothing and to move into a cooler environment (Johnson, 1965). In the elderly, however, responses to heat stress have a high threshold and are less efficient (Crowe and Moore, 1974), and appreciation of skin temperature is poorer than in the young (MacMillan et al, 1967; Wagner et al, 1972; Wagner et al, 1974; Fennell and Moore, 1973; Cowburn and Fox, 1974; Crowe and Moore, 1974). There is an association of deaths with environmental temperatures above +20°C and below −10°C and this association is more marked in the elderly (Bull and Morton, 1978).

ACCIDENTAL HYPOTHERMIA IN THE ELDERLY

The term 'accidental hypothermia' was introduced to distinguish it from hypothermia induced for therapeutic reasons. It includes all conditions associated with a rectal temperature of 35°C (95°F) or less. It can occur in normal subjects of any age in response to sufficient cold stress. It is a cause of death in hill climbers and hill walkers caught in bad weather with inadequate protection (Pugh, 1966; Stewart, 1972), in cavers (Lloyd, 1964), and in those who are in water for a long time as in long distance swimmers (Keatinge, 1976), in boating accidents (Golden and Rivers, 1975) or after shipwreck or aircraft disaster (Keatinge, 1969).

There have, however, been many reports of elderly people found in a state of hypothermia in no more hostile an environment than their own homes (Emslie-Smith, 1958; Rees, 1958; Fruehan, 1960; Duguid et al, 1961; Prescott et al, 1962; Trafford and Hopkins, 1963; McNichol and Smith, 1964; Paulley et al, 1964; Rosin and Exton-Smith 1964; Mills, 1974; MacLean and Emslie-Smith, 1977). A survey was undertaken by the Royal College of Physicians in 1965 to establish the incidence of hypothermia in patients admitted to 10 British hospitals during 3 winter months; this was 0.68 per cent of admissions. Forty-two per cent of the patients with hypothermia were elderly (over age 65) and most of the remainder were infants (Royal College of Physicians, 1966). If these were representative of all hospital admissions in England and Scotland, nearly 4000 patients over age 65 would have been admitted to hospital with hypothermia during that period. Moreover in a later survey in 2 London hospitals during 3 winter months an even larger number of elderly patients (3.6 per cent) than in the 1965 survey (1 per cent) were hypothermic (Goldman et al, 1977).

In a national survey in Britain 0.52 per cent of 1020 elderly people living at home and 0.38 per cent of another 1000 elderly people in London were hypothermic (urine temperature of less than 34.8°C (94.6°F) equivalent to a rectal temperature of less than 35°C (95°F)). Ten per cent of these 2020 elderly subjects had a urine temperature of 35.5°C (95.5°F) and have, therefore, been considered at risk of developing hypothermia (Fox et al, 1973). These figures do not, however, include those who were treated at home, those in whom the condition was not recognized, and those who were found dead in their own homes (Howitt, 1971). In the United States of America the mortality from accidental hypothermia is increased about five times over the age of 75 (Rango, 1980). Accidental hypothermia can occur in the aged poor even in warm climates such as Florida (Altus et al, 1980).

Aetiology

Accidental hypothermia has four main causes: exposure, impaired thermoregulatory reflexes, decreased metabolism, and the effect of drugs. As in so many disorders of the elderly, multiple factors are usually involved.

Exposure

Exposure to cold usually plays an important part when

an elderly person is found hypothermic in his own home. There is a clear relationship between the prevalence of hypothermia and the environmental temperature. Inadequate insulation from insufficient clothing and loss of subcutaneous tissue increases the risk from exposure (Keatinge, 1965; 1969; Pugh, 1966). Elderly people living at home who have a low body temperature have some common characteristics: they are single, or widowed, live alone, have no heating in bedrooms, lack basic amenities, are on supplementary pensions and have a high incidence of impaired mobility, nocturia, insomnia and liability to falls (Fox et al, 1973; Collins et al, 1977). Some cannot afford adequate heating, whereas others neglect themselves because of physical illness, forgetfulness, or depression. A common story is that of an old person who falls whilst attempting to get out of bed at night and remains on the floor for several hours or even days before being found. Elderly people demonstrate a less precise control of environmental temperature and allow larger swings in temperature to occur than the young. This may be due to impaired cutaneous temperature discrimination in those over age 60; they may also tend to find cold environments more comfortable (Collins, 1981).

Exposure, however, in many cases is minimal; indeed some elderly people develop hypothermia in mild weather. They may be found well covered in bed and even in a heated room. In these patients exposure alone is not enough to account for hypothermia, and other factors are of greater importance.

Impairment of thermoregulatory reflexes
This has been demonstrated in survivors of accidental hypothermia in the elderly. On moderate cooling shivering was absent, the metabolic rate did not rise, and there was defective vasoconstriction. As a result the central temperature fell abnormally and progressively (Fig. 20.1). The resting temperature was also low, yet the patient did not feel cold. The defect of temperature regulation was found up to 3 years after hypothermia (Macmillan et al, 1967). These patients are at special risk of developing further attacks of hypothermia. Recurrent attacks may occur and are often precipitated by small doses of drugs with a hypothermic action.

In a study of 150 elderly people living at home abnormal peripheral blood flow in response to moderate cooling and warming was found in 56 per cent of men and 42 per cent of women. Shivering on cooling occurred in only 12 per cent (Collins et al, 1977). Perception of cold by the finger was impaired in the elderly as shown by failure to discriminate temperature differences of 5°C (9°F) as compared with 0.5°C (0.9°F) in younger subjects (Cowburn and Fox, 1974). When the 43 survivors of these elderly subjects were reinvestigated 4 years later 14 of them (33 per cent) had

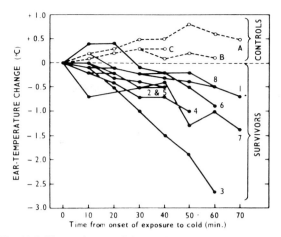

Fig. 20.1 Change in central (external auditory meatus) temperature on exposure to cold.
A, B, C: Elderly controls (aged 70 to 94)
1 to 8: Survivors of accidental hypothermia (aged 66 to 89) (from MacMillan et al, 1967)

abnormal peripheral blood flow to cooling; only six of these had this abnormality 4 years earlier. A significantly greater increase in deep body temperature was required to initiate sweating in the later as compared with the earlier study (Collins et al, 1977).

It is likely that the defect of temperature regulation precedes the hypothermic state rather than being due to damage by the low body temperature. Some patients with a moderately low resting temperature later develop hypothermia (Wollner, 1967), some even in a warm environment (Johnson and Park, 1973a). Defective vasoconstriction also produces an impaired thermal insulation index (Fig. 20.2) (MacMillan et al, 1967) due to an increased core-periphery temperature gradient (Fox et al, 1973). This defect of temperature regulation is not an inevitable accompaniment of old age as three normal subjects aged 84 to 93 years had normal thermoregulatory responses on cooling (Fig. 20.1) (Macmillan et al, 1967). Oral temperature readings taken in the customary way are open to wide errors (Barley and Evans, 1970). Indeed oral temperature readings are unreliable as a measure of deep body temperature when compared with rectal or urine temperatures (MacPherson and Ofner, 1965; Fox et al, 1971; Salvaso et al, 1971).

The evidence therefore indicates a group of elderly people with impairment of temperature regulation who are at risk of developing hypothermia. This disturbance of thermoregulation becomes more common with increasing age, and could be regarded as a normal aging process; advanced old age, however, is compatible with normal temperature regulation. Those at risk of hypothermia also have a higher incidence of postural hypotension (Collins et al, 1977).

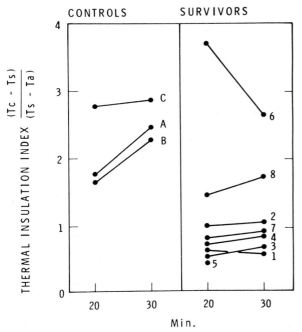

Fig. 20.2 Thermal insulation index for anterior chest after 20 and 30 minutes exposure to cold.
Tc — central temperatures; Ts — skin temperature; Ta — air temperature. (from MacMillan et al 1967)

Impaired thermoregulatory reflexes have been demonstrated in patients with head injuries and other lesions, especially in the neighbourhood of the hypothalamus (Duff et al, 1961; Hockaday et al, 1962; Gubbay and Barwick, 1966; Shapiro et al, 1969; Fox et al, 1970; Sadowsky and Reeves, 1975); in Wernicke's encephalopathy (Koeppen et al, 1969; Phillips and Smith, 1973; Ackerman, 1974; Hunter, 1976; British Medical Journal, 1979; Macaron et al, 1979); in spinal cord lesions (Comarr, 1958; Guttman et al, 1958; Pledger, 1962; Johnson, 1971); extensive skin lesions (Fox et al, 1965; Warshaw, 1973), and steatorrhoea (Dent et al, 1961). In central lesions two types of chronic hypothermia have been described: in one there is loss of the normal temperature regulating mechanisms, whereas in the other body temperature is regulated at unusually low levels (Hockaday et al, 1962). Periodic hypothermia with episodes of shivering and sweating has also been described. This may be associated with a lesion of the corpus callosum or with epilepsy (Thomas and Green, 1973). In the common form of accidental hypothermia in the elderly, however, no pathological lesion has so far been demonstrated. There is, however, an association between impaired thermoregulation and postural hypotension in some elderly people (Wollner, 1967; Collins et al, 1977).

Metabolic change

Decreased metabolism may be due to primary hypothyroidism or hypopituitarism (Sheehan and Summers, 1952). Hypothermic myxoedema is reviewed by Hyams (1963); it probably accounts for only a small number of cases, perhaps 5 per cent of patients admitted to hospital with accidental hypothermia.

Diminished exercise may play a part; a large proportion of the heat generated in the body is derived from muscular activity, and immobility from various causes such as hemiplegia, paraplegia, Parkinsonism, severe arthritis fractures, or indeed just a prolonged illness in bed could be expected to play an important part. Such patients, however, only rarely develop hypothermia and diminished exercise is probably not significant unless exposure or impaired thermoregulation coexist. Coma from various causes, but in particular diabetic or insulin coma, can be associated with hypothermia. Diabetic ketoacidosis with hypothermia has a high mortality (Gale and Tattersall, 1978). Malnutrition can also be a predisposing factor even in warm climates (Sadikali and Owor, 1974).

Brown adipose tissue is important in thermoregulation in the newborn (Dawkins and Hull, 1964) and it has been suggested that in the elderly also, depletion of brown adipose tissue can be a cause of hypothermia (Aherne and Hull, 1965; Heaton, 1973).

Drug effects

Drugs may have a direct effect on the temperature regulating centre, inhibit shivering, or cause peripheral vasodilatation. Advantage is taken of these actions in their use in intentionally induced hypothermia.

Phenothiazines are particularly liable to precipitate hypothermia (Mitchell et al, 1959; Jones and Meade, 1964); in patients with already impaired thermoregulatory reflexes very small doses, such as 25 mg of chlorpromazine, may cause hypothermia. Nevertheless, large doses are not uncommonly given for confusion which is itself a common manifestation of developing hypothermia. Other drugs with hypothermic action include barbiturates (Lee and Ames, 1965); diazepam (Fell and Dendy, 1968a), glutethimide (Irvine, 1966); imipramime (McGrath and Paley, 1960); reserpine (Matthews, 1967); nitrazepam (Impallomeni and Ezzat, 1976); and morphia. Carbon monoxide poisoning may also do so. Alcohol (Fruehan, 1960; Day and Morgan, 1974; Weyman et al, 1974; Davidson and Grant, 1981) may precipitate the condition and in some countries is the commonest recorded cause of hypothermia. When these drugs give rise to an impaired level of consciousness this in itself can lead to exposure to cold.

Clinical features

The striking feature is that the skin, particularly that of

the abdomen, feels very cold and so does the rectum. A low reading thermometer (down to 24°C (75°F)) is necessary to establish the diagnosis. The skin is usually pale and of waxy appearance although pallor sometimes is not marked. Shivering is usually absent.

Consciousness

As the central temperature falls consciousness becomes impaired and this eventually leads to coma. At first the patient may be aware of being cold but too apathetic to do anything about it, even if mobility is retained. Disorientation, listlessness, hallucinations, or paranoid features are early manifestations and restlessness may result in falls with further exposure to cold. Paradoxical undressing as hypothermia develops has been decribed (Wedin et al, 1979).

Neurological features

These include slurred speech, ataxia and extensor plantar responses; a tremor is usual; occasionally there is a flap; muscular rigidity is common and may be so marked that neck stiffness can be mistaken for meningism. Reflexes show both a slow contraction and relaxation time. A photometrogram of the Achilles tendon reflex has been found helpful in differentiating primary hypothermia from hypothermic myxoedema where the relaxation time is selectively prolonged (Maclean et al, 1973b). As the temperature falls to low levels reflex responses are abolished. Deep posterior tibial compression has been described after hypothyroid hypothermia (Coni, 1981).

Circulatory features

Sinus bradycardia is probably due to the effect of cold on the pacemaker. Cardiac dysrhythmias are very common as seen by continuous monitoring, and these include supraventricular extrasystoles and tachycardia, atrial fibrillation, ventricular extrasystoles, ventricular tachycardia and ventricular fibrillation. Some degree of heart block occurs in most cases, with an increased P-R interval, reversible A-V block has been demonstrated by His-bundle electrocardiographic studies (Jacob et al, 1978), and intraventricular conduction delay is also seen. Complete heart block may occur at any time and this and ventricular fibrillation or asystole may give rise to cardiac arrest, particularly at rectal temperatures below 32.2°C (90°F).

The Q-T interval may be prolonged and there is inversion of the T-wave (Emslie-Smith, 1958; Prescott et al, 1962; Ree, 1964; Schwab et al, 1964). The ECG often shows a 'J'-wave (Osborne, 1953) (Fig. 20.3), and this and the 'J'-loop on vectorcardiography (Pr'eda and Kenedi, 1973; Maclean and Emslie-Smith, 1974) are almost pathognomonic of hypothermia but have little prognostic value. The 'J'-wave has occasionally been

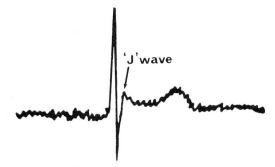

Fig. 20.3 Electrocardiogram showing 'J'-wave in patient aged 74 with accidental hypothermia (from Wollner, 1967)

seen with a rise in arterial P_{CO_2} (Altschule and Sulzbach, 1947) or a fall in pH or a rise in serum calcium (Hegnauer and Govino, 1956) in the absence of hypothermia. The blood pressure falls, and this is due to the net effect of decreased cardiac output and a varying degree of fall in peripheral resistance. A detailed haemodynamic study using right heart and aortic catheterization during prolonged deep hypothermia and after fast rewarming demonstrated the importance of hypovolaemia as a cause of low cardiac output and low arterial pressure in these patients (Harari et al, 1975). However, non-cardiac pulmonary oedema has been reported (O'Keefe, 1980). There is a tendency to sequestration of blood in venous pools in areas of low blood flow. This could give rise to unrepresentative samples being taken; estimations should therefore be made on arterial blood (Cooper and Sellick, 1960; Cooper, 1968).

Respiratory effects

In severe hypothermia respirations are slow and shallow and hypopnoea can lead to apnoea. Periodic respiration is common. The P_{O_2} in the arterial blood is low. The oxygen dissociation curve is altered so that less oxygen is given up to the tissues at a given partial pressure of oxygen; cyanosis is therefore less likely to appear than at normal temperature. The effect is to produce tissue anoxia and this may be an important adverse factor in prognosis (McNichol and Smith, 1964; McNichol, 1967). In severe hypothermia the P_{CO_2} is often low because of low production of CO_2. However, when hypopnoea is marked the P_{CO_2} may be so greatly elevated as to give rise to respiratory failure (Buchanan et al, 1967). Bronchopneumonia is very difficult to diagnoze because of minimal signs. As the temperature rises the patient with bronchopneumonia may hyperventilate and the P_{CO_2} may fall below normal; this can also occur as a result of pulmonary oedema which may be difficult to differentiate.

Alimentary tract

Gastric dilatation is common; there is a risk that aspiration of gastric contents may occur. Extensive necrosis of the oesophageal mucosa has been described (Brennan, 1967). Acute pancreatitis seems to be related to the duration of hypothermia, but may give rise to few signs. A rise in serum amylase is common, but this rise can occur in the absence of pancreatic disease (Maclean et al, 1968; Maclean .et al, 1973a).

Hepatic function is impaired partly due to the effect of cold and partly due to a rise in central venous pressure. Serum transaminases are frequently raised, but this can occur in the absence of hepatic dysfunction (Maclean et al, 1968). The ability of the liver to detoxify and excrete drugs may be greatly reduced.

The kidney

Renal plasma flow and glomerular filtration rate decrease and tubular function is impaired (Moyer et al, 1957), Oliguria is very common and may be due to the direct effect of cold on the kidneys or to ischaemia and acute tubular necrosis (Precott et al, 1962; Fell and Dendy, 1968b; McKean et al, 1970).

The blood

The haemoglobin and haematocrit may be raised because of a fall in plasma volume. Transient leucocytosis is common, but marked leukopenia may occur (Tolman and Cohen, 1970; Weyman et al, 1974). This could be an important factor in some cases with bronchopneumonia. Thrombocytopenia is not uncommon and there is experimental evidence that this is due to sequestration of platelets in the liver, spleen, and possibly elsewhere (Villabos· et al, 1958; Wensel and Bigelow, 1959). Thrombocytopenia can give rise to bleeding. Disseminated intravascular coagulation has been described in accidental hypothermia (Mahood and Evans, 1978). Of 11 patients with hypothermia, who also had alcoholism or diabetes mellitus, four died: all four had thrombocytopenia or low levels of fibrinogen, and at necropsy intravascular thromboses and multiple infarcts were found (Tolman and Cohen, 1970). Excess cryofibrinogen, determined by the plasma cryotest, was found in 30 per cent of 33 elderly patients with hypothermia and this was significantly related to mortality (Goodall et al, 1975). Multiple infarcts may occur in the myocardium, viscera, or limbs (Duguid et al, 1961) or the pancreas (Savides and Hoffbrand, 1974). 'Sludging' is thought to be another possible cause of multiple infarcts (Duguid et al, 1961).

Hormonal effects

It has not been clearly established whether in man adrenal cortical hormone output is decreased as occurs in experimental cooling of the adrenals in animals (Bern-hard, 1956). In patients with hypothermia plasma cortisol levels are raised (Sprunt et al, 1970; Stoner et al, 1980) which suggests a stress response of normally functioning adrenals. As there is increased binding of cortisol to corticosteroid-binding globulin (Transcortin) at low temperatures it is possible that available free cortisol may be diminished (Slaunwhite and Sandberg, 1959). Increase in plasma cortisol in response to adrenocorticotrophic hormone (ACTH) is also impaired during hypothermia, recovering after rewarming (Felicetta et al, 1980). There is clinical evidence that corticosteroids raise the blood pressure and improve the prognosis of elderly patients with accidental hypothermia (Mitchell et al, 1959; Duguid et al, 1961), but whether this is due to its endocrine function has not been established.

The diagnosis of primary hypothyroidism is difficult to confirm as some tests of thyroid function are unreliable in hypothermia (Rosin and Exton-Smith, 1964). TSH may be raised in hypothyroid hypothermia but not in primary. hypothermia (Woollf et al, 1972). Growth hormone levels may be independent of changes in plasma glucose concentration (Woollf et al, 1972).

Metabolic effects

Tissue metabolism and oxygen consumption are decreased in severe hypothermia. As the temperature rises and the metabolic rate increases, tissue anoxia and a metabolic acidosis may ensue if the circulation is inadequate (McNichol and Smith, 1964). In severe hypothermia respiratory alkalosis may be present from reduced CO_2 production, and at a later stage from hyperventilation due to pulmonary infection or pulmonary oedema. Insulin is inactive in hypothermia so that the blood sugar may rise although the patient does not have impaired glucose tolerance. As the temperature rises on rewarming, glucose goes back into the cells and hypoglycaemia may result; this is particularly important in the diabetic patient on hypoglycaemic therapy (Wynn, 1954). Spontaneous hypoglycaemia, however, may be found at the onset of hypothermia (Maclean et al, 1974). This may occur in the presence of renal glycosuria (Fitzgerald, 1980). Hypokalaemia is particularly likely to develop on rewarming although it may be present during hypothermia; it increases the risk of serious cardiac dysrhythmias. Although haemoconcentration may be associated with raised plasma sodium levels, hyponatraemia is more common, particularly in myxoedema where it may be due to inappropriate ADH secretion (Cornu et al, 1973; Newmark et al, 1974). The uric acid may be raised during hypothermia but falls rapidly after rewarming (Meriwether and Goodman, 1972). Severe hypophosphataemia has been reported as a complication of the treatment of hypothermia and may need correction (Levy, 1980). Serum creatine kinase may be raised due to damaged cardiac or skeletal muscles (MacLean et al, 1968; Carlson et al, 1978).

Studies of hypothermia induced in man suggest that the hypothermic state is associated with movements of water within the body, and there is probably leakage of capillaries which allows the accumulation of tissue oedema, and also increases the risk of pulmonary oedema (Cooper, 1968). Generalised oedema is indeed common in accidental hypothermia and can be so marked that the patient gives the appearance of 'myxoedema', although thyroid function later proves to be normal (Duguid et al, 1961). This movement of water into the tissues may be associated with a fall in plasma volume and a fall in arterial pressure (Cooper, 1968). On rewarming, water moves back into the circulation and this too can give rise to pulmonary oedema.

Management

Rewarming

Hypothermia is a serious condition and should be considered a medical emergency. The management of patients with accidental hypothermia is reviewed by Maclean and Elmslie-Smith (1977) and the British Medical Journal (1978).

Rapid surface rewarming. Rapid surface re-warming in a hot bath at 41°C–45°C (106°F–113°F) or with a heat cradle is the treatment of choice for most hypothermic young subjects; it has also been successfully used in younger alcoholics (Fernander et al, 1970; Weyman et al, 1974) and in some elderly patients (Meriwether and Goodman, 1972; Ledingham and Mone, 1974, 1980).

In the elderly, however, rapid surface rewarming can be dangerous in the majority of patients. This is probably due to the effect of extensive cutaneous vasodilatation which results in a fall of arterial blood pressure and inadequate coronary perfusion. In some cases also the vasodilatation allows cool blood to reach the core of the body and this causes a further fall in central temperature. This 'after drop' may then induce cardiac dysrhythmias and cardiac arrest.

Slow surface rewarming. Slow surface rewarming using space blankets in a warm room [25°C (77°F)] can often be effective in the elderly. The patient is rewarmed at 0.5°C (1°F) per hour. The rectal temperature is monitored continuously and the blood pressure taken at half-hourly intervals. If the blood pressure falls as the temperature rises the patient is immediately cooled by fans and when the blood pressure is stabilized the patient is gradually rewarmed (Wollner, 1967).

Rapid core rewarming. This has been achieved in a number of ways: inhalation of gases warmed either by the interaction of carbon dioxide and soda lime in a carbon dioxide absorber (Lloyd, 1972, 1973) or by a heated humidifier with mechanical ventilation (Shanks and Marsh, 1973). Hot fluids, however, are more efficient than air in transferring heat. Peritoneal dialysis with fluids at 38°C–43°C (100.5°F–109.5°F) (Grossheim 1973; Desmeules and Blais, 1979; Davis and Judson, 1981) or haemodialysis (Lee and Ames, 1965) can be used. Warm mediastinal irrigation after thoracotomy has been successful (Linton and Ledingham, 1966; Ledingham and Mone 1980). Gastric rewarming through a tube has been used (Khalil and MacKeith, 1954; Pickering et al, 1977), but this carries the danger of inhalation. Extra-corporeal blood rewarming with cardiopulmonary by-pass may be necessary in patients with very low temperatures or circulatory failure (Fell and Dendy, 1968b; Towne, 1972; Schissler et al, 1981). Ventricular fibrillation may not respond to electrical cardioversion until the core temperature is above 30°C (86°F).

In the elderly *mild hypothermia* (deep body temperature 32°C–35°C (89.5°F–95°F)) usually responds to simple methods of slow rewarming. *Moderate hypothermia* (deep body temperature 28°C–32°C (82.5°F–89.5°F)) may respond to slow rewarming, but needs careful observation, preferably with intensive care. If the temperature or circulation fails to respond rapid core rewarming is indicated. *Severe hypothermia* (deep body temperature below 28°C (82.5°F)) generally requires rapid core rewarming in an intensive care unit.

General measures

Cardiac monitoring. This is helpful during hypothermia. Reference has already been made to the frequent occurrence of cardiac dysrhythmias, and antidysrhythmic drugs should be used but may not be effective until the patient is rewarmed. The correction of acidosis by intravenous bicarbonate may also correct cardiac dysrhythmias. Ventricular fibrillation may be difficult to reverse at low temperatures but should be treated electrically. A longer period is available for the correction of ventricular fibrillation because of the protective effect of hypothermia (Ross, 1957). If there is severe bradycardia atropine may increase the heart rate even at low temperatures with an increase in cardiac output and perfusion; if this fails cardiac pacing can be effective.

Protection and maintenance of the airway. These are of importance in patients with hypothermia as in other patients with an impaired level of consciousness. Aspiration of vomitus may well be the cause of many cases of bronchopneumonia. If the airway cannot be kept clear a cuffed endotracheal tube should be inserted. Gastric contents should only be aspirated with an endotracheal tube in place. Oxygen should be given routinely by a Venturi or similar mask; a very high inspired oxygen should be avoided as otherwise carbon dioxide retention may occur. Adequate fluid repletion and correction of hypoxaemia, if necessary by endotracheal intubation and mechanical ventilation in an intensive care environment has been recommended (Ledingham and Mone, 1980)

Fluids and electrolytes

Fluids warmed to room temperature should be given intravenously in the early stages and fluid balance be carefully controlled. There is considerable risk of inducing pulmonary oedema from overhydration (Cooper and Sellick, 1960); a central venous catheter may give a guide to fluid requirements. Oliguria is common and mannitol or frusemide may be required to induce a diuresis (McKean et al, 1970). Blood urea and electrolytes and blood gases should be estimated from arterial blood when the patient is first seen, and must be corrected for temperature. Rapid changes in serum potassium may occur; electrolyte estimations should therefore be repeated after 12 and 24 hours and frequently during the first week. Acidosis should be corrected by intravenous bicarbonate. During the diuretic phase considerable elevation of blood urea may take place and be associated with low serum potassium levels.

Drugs

Hydrocortisone. Intravenous hydrocortisone should be given to patients whose temperature is below 32.2°C (90°F) or when the systolic blood pressure is below 100 mm Hg. It can usually be discontinued when the body temperature has returned to normal (Duguid et al, 1961). ACTH may be ineffective (Felicetta et al, 1980).

Antibiotics. Ampicillin is used routinely since the normal clinical criteria for the diagnosis of bronchopneumonia may be absent. It is best given parenterally as absorption may not be satisfactory in the presence of hypothermia (Tadzer, 1961).

Thyroid hormone. This need not be given since patients with hypothermic myxoedema will warm up without it, at least to about 32°C (90°F). Myxoedematous patients, however, often remain mildly hypothermic and occasionally in coma when the temperature has returned to normal; tri-iodothyronine 10µg 8-hourly should then be given. Larger doses may increase the metabolism too greatly and give rise to cardiac complications (Hyams, 1963; Verbow, 1964). If hypopituitarism is suspected, cortisone has to be continued since acute adrenal insufficiency can otherwise be precipitated. Intramuscular Vitamin B$_1$ should be given when Wernicke's encephalopathy is suspected (Macaron et al, 1979).

Prognosis

The lowest temperature from which recovery from accidental hypothermia has been reported was 18°C (64.4°F) (Laufman, 1951), but this was in a young person. Mortality in several published series in elderly patients is high, varying from 30 to 75 per cent (Duguid et al, 1961; Prescott et al, 1962; McNichol and Smith, 1964; Paulley et al, 1964; Rosin and Exton-Smith, 1964; Ledingham and Mone, 1972, 1980). When the temperature is above 32.2°C (90°F) recovery from hypothermia is the rule unless death occurs from a condition which is not directly related. The inclusion of patients within this temperature range in some reports but not others affects the interpretation of the mortality rates. The prognosis often depends on the associated conditions which vary widely in reported series. This makes it difficult to compare different methods of treatment such as rapid rewarming in an intensive care unit (Ledingham and Mone, 1980). In a study of primary hypothermia in the elderly with a rectal temperature of less than 35°C (95°F) the mortality was 38.5 per cent (Goldman et al, 1977). Another variable is the time between diagnosis and death which varies between 24 hours and several months in different series. Mills (1973) using slow rewarming reported an immediate mortality of 12.5 per cent within 24 hours, and a mortality after one month of 50 per cent in elderly patients admitted with a rectal temperature below 32.2°C (90°F). Recovery of elderly patients is possible, both from very low temperatures and in advanced old age.

If death occurs necropsy is reported to show raised acetone levels in the urine. Haemorrhage in deep muscles such as the ileopsoas and punctiform haemorrhages in the gastric mucosa were also characteristic findings (Schneider and Klug, 1980).

Prevention

There is much that can be done in the prevention of accidental hypothermia in the elderly (British Medical Association, 1964; MacLean and Emslie-Smith, 1977). Elderly people should be advised that bedrooms should always be heated and the windows kept closed at night. This not only applies to private homes but also to old people's homes and hospital wards where the temperature may fall to very low levels especially at night (Taylor, 1964; Salvaso et al, 1971). A survey of accommodation in London during the winter showed that 13 per cent of dwellings had obvious signs of damp; 50 per cent of the bedrooms on the top floor had a calculated temperature of only 10°C (50°F) (Fox et al, 1973). In a national survey in Britain 75 per cent of elderly people were living at home in the winter with room temperatures below 18°C (65°F), 50 per cent below 16°C (60.8°F) and 10 per cent below 12°C (53.6°F).

Much could be achieved by establishing a standard warmth for old people's dwelling and by the wider use of storage and central heating (Ministry of Housing, 1961; 1962). Assistance can be obtained for extra fuel allowance, clothing and bedding but many old people are either too disabled or too proud to take advantage of these facilities. Lists of elderly people are maintained by some Local Authorities and Age Concern Committees and regular visiting can be arranged (Anderson, 1971). Some elderly people often also suffer from undernutrition which may be a contributory factor to the development of hypothermia (Taylor, 1964). Those who visit should be aware that when an elderly person becomes confused or takes to bed during the winter months hypothermia may be the cause. Drugs with a hypothermic action such as phenothiazines should be used cautiously in elderly people. Other measures should include the development of warning systems to detect low temperature, the use of electrically safe 'extra-low-voltage' underblankets, and measures to improve space heating and insulation in the houses of those at risk (Fox et al, 1973).

The oral temperature should be taken routinely in elderly patients to see whether it is below normal. An oral temperature below 35°C (95°F) is not necessarily significant, but if confirmed by rectal temperature the patient is hypothermic: slow rewarming is indicated and in most cases hospital admission is advisable. It should be noted that the standard clinical thermometer does not read below 35°C (95°F) and that hypothermia cannot be diagnosed without the use of a low-temperature recording thermometer. This should be carried by every general practitioner, district nurse and health visitor, and be standard equipment in every hospital department (Exton-Smith, 1968).

FEVER IN THE ELDERLY

An abnormally raised body temperature (fever, pyrexia, hyperthermia) may occur from exposure to excessive heat, impaired thermoregulatory reflexes, or the effect of pyrogens (Cooper, 1968). In investigating a puzzling case of apparent fever the possibility that the 'fever' is factitious should be borne in mind (Petersdorf and Bennett, 1957; Cranston, 1969).

Heat illness

A normal subject exposed to sufficient external heat may be unable to increase his heat loss adequately by vasodilatation and sweating, and the temperature then rises. There may be a period of intense sweating followed by anhidrosis, and if this occurs the body temperature rises rapidly and dangerously (heat stroke). In the normal subject this only occurs in very severe heat stress and particularly in unacclimatized subjects (Leithead and Lind, 1964; Eichler et al, 1969). A haemodynamic study in young men with heat stroke showed that there are two types (O'Donnell and Clowes, 1972):

1. The hyperdynamic response with a high cardiac index, raised mean arterial pressure, raised pulmonary vascular resistance, and increase in central venous pressure.
2. The hypodynamic response with low cardiac index, fall in mean arterial pressure, but raised central venous pressure.

Hyperventilation due to heat stress may produce a fall in P_{CO_2} which itself can raise the central temperature by causing a shift of blood from the skin or by inhibiting sweating. Hyperventilation could therefore exacberbate heat stroke (Robinson and King, 1971). Dangerous increase in body temperature is more likely to occur in elderly than in younger patients, particularly when high external temperatures are liable to continue for some days. In one series in North America the average age of death from this cause was 78 years; only 12 per cent were under age 70. The average rectal temperature was 41.3°C (106.4°F). There was a high incidence of other pathology: 72 per cent had evidence of ischemic heart disease, 32 per cent of cerebrovascular disease, 52 per cent of diabetes mellitus (Levine, 1969).

Mortality from all causes increases dramatically during heat waves in people over the age of 50, and progressively with increasing age (Ellis, 1972; Ellis et al, 1975; Ellis et al, 1980). In New York City excess deaths were recorded as mainly due to ischaemic heart disease or to a lesser extent cerebrovascular disease. None of the deaths was certified as being due to heat illness and only in a small proportion was heat illness mentioned as a contributory factor (Ellis et al, 1975). It is likely that heat illness as a cause of both morbidity and mortality is much more common than is recognized. It is also a particular hazard when unclimatized elderly people go on holiday (Exton-Smith, 1969). It can occur during a heat wave even in Britain. It is advisable during a heat wave to monitor the temperature of ill patients particularly in the afternoons to allow prompt treatment (Lye and Kamal, 1977).

Heat illness may occur in hot climates without direct exposure to the sun. In one series 4 per cent of elderly patients residing in nursing homes developed a fever above a temperature of 37.8°C (100°F) in facilities which were not air-conditioned (Rossman, 1971). Deaths have occurred when air-conditioning has failed (Sullivan-Bolyai et al, 1978).

Patients with impaired thermoregulatory reflexes, however, may be unable to control their body temperature on exposure to only moderate heat. This has been reported in lesions of the hypothalamus (Hockaday et al, 1962), of the spinal cord (Comarr, 1958; Pledger, 1962) or in extensive skin lesions (Fox et al, 1965). Some patients have lost all their mechanisms of temperature regulation and are poikilothermic (Hockaday et al, 1962).

Compared with younger subjects elderly people show a higher threshold of central temperature to sweating and sweat loss for a given heat load; in consequence there is a greater rise in central temperature (Lind et al, 1970; Fennell and Moore, 1973; Crowe and Moore, 1974). Fortytwo per cent of elderly men and 62 per cent of elderly women at home, when exposed to an ambient temperature of 45°C (113°F) for 46 minutes, failed to sweat on the forehead as younger subjects do (Foster et al, 1976). Peripheral blood-flow patterns to warming were also abnormal (Collins et al, 1977) and there was impaired warm and cold perception (Cowburn and Fox, 1974). Impaired temperature regulation from diminished or absent sweating is probably the main factor responsible for the increased mortality in the elderly population in heat waves (Foster et al, 1976).

Certain steroids, including etiocholanolone, raise the body temperature, but their clinical significance in the production of febrile illness is not clear (Bondy et al, 1958; George et al, 1969). The administration of a general anaesthetic on rare occasions causes hyperpyrexia in susceptible subjects. This condition which has a high mortality is inherited and associated with a myopathy (Denborough and Lovell, 1960; Denborough et al, 1970). Creatine phosphokinase estimations have been recommended to identify those at risk (King et al, 1972; Isaacs and Barlow, 1973; Zsigmond et al, 1978) but have not always proved satisfactory (Morikawa et al, 1979). Hyperpyrexia which may be fatal may occur after a combination of tricyclic antidepressants and monoamine oxidase inhibitors (Pollock and Watson, 1971).

Fever due to pyrogens

Infections usually cause fever by the action of endogenous leucocyte pyrogens on the brain, probably by raising the set point of the temperature regulating mechanisms; regulation of body temperature occurs normally around the raised set point (Cooper, 1965). The normal febrile response to infection usually occurs in advanced old age (Macpherson and Ofner, 1971). In the elderly, however, a substantial infection can occur with much less change in temperature than would be expected in younger subjects. The absence of fever in an elderly person should therefore not preclude careful investigation for possible sites of infection. In some elderly patients the rectal temperature may indicate a febrile response when the oral temperature is normal, and therefore in cases of doubt the rectal temperature should be taken. Fever is not infrequently caused by cardiac infarction, cerebral infarction or haemorrhage, tumour, or other causes of inflammation or necrosis. In these conditions pyrogens from damaged tissues probably induce fever in a similar way to pyrogens arising in infection (Cranston et al, 1971).

Clinical features of fever

In the elderly, *fever* gives rise to headache, dizziness, restlessness and confusion which may be the main clinical manifestation. Delusions, hallucinations and paranoia may occur. Both pulse and respiratory rates are increased. Since in the elderly thirst is a poor indicator of water depletion, dehydration can occur rapidly and give rise to circulatory insufficiency or postural hypotension. In *heat stroke*, cessation of sweating occurs in most cases, but may not be noticed by the patient. Impairment of consciousness may lead to coma. Cardiac dysrhythmias, pneumonia, purpura and gastrointestinal bleeding are common. Peripheral circulatory failure from sodium and water depletion may occur (Leithead and Lind, 1964; Shibolet et al, 1967; Levine, 1969).

Management

In *moderate fever*, antipyretics such as soluble aspirin and the correction of the underlying cause may be all that is required. Salicylates probably act by antagonizing the action of endogenous pyrogens within the central nervous system (Rawlins et al, 1971). Ice-cold sponging may prove helpful. Early correction of dehydration is important. In *high fever* as in heat stroke, speed is essential to avoid permanent brain damage. Immersion in ice-water, ice-cold sponging, a cold-water spray, and wet blankets with evaporated cooling by fans are effective. Protection of the airway and the adequate replacement of fluids and electrolytes is most important; over 12 litres in 4 hours may be required in severe cases. Antibiotics may be necessary (Leithead and Lind, 1964: Shibolet et al, 1967; Eichler et al, 1969; Levine, 1969; Lye and Kamal, 1977). Intravenous isoprenaline can be effective in patients with the hypodynamic type of heat stroke (O'Donnell and Clowes, 1972).

Prognosis

In fever due to pyrogens the prognosis usually depends on the underlying condition. In heat stroke the mortality rises with rate of rise of body temperature. It varies between 30 per cent and 70 per cent and is higher in the elderly. In one series 36 per cent of patient died within 24 hours and a further 40 per cent within one week (Levine, 1969).

THE CIRCULATION

Normal regulation of the circulation

The circulation is under both reflex and humoral control. Both the peripheral circulation and the heart rate depend on a number of circulatory reflexes, and in particular on those which originate in baroreceptors.

The nervous pathways lead from baroreceptors in the carotid sinus and perhaps in the aorta and elsewhere to the brain; from there they influence the sympathetic nervous system via the intermediolateral columns and the peripheral sympathetic nerves. The efferent pathway leads from the spinal cord via the preganglionic fibres to the sympathetic chain and from there via postganglionic fibres to the blood vessels and sweat glands. These reflexes also influence the parasympathetic activity and in particular the vagus.

When a normal subject stands up or is tipped into the erect posture from the horizontal position the systolic pressure may fall 10 to 15 mmHg and the diastolic pressure may fall or rise 5 mmHg; the mean arterial pressure remains almost unchanged (Currens, 1948). Although cardiac output falls due to decreased venous return baroreceptors react by vasoconstriction of arteries and veins together with an increase in heart rate to maintain the mean arterial pressure constant (Brigden et al, 1950; Burch, 1960). The increase in heart rate on standing (Hellström, 1961; Strandell, 1964) and on exercise (Bertel et al, 1980) diminishes with age due to a reduction in sympathetic activity on the heart. Variations in heart rate with respiration (sinus arrhythmia) also diminish with advancing age due to a reduction in parasympathetic activity (Davies, 1975; Hellman and Stacy, 1976; Vargas and Lye, 1980). Some normal elderly subjects on tilting head up show a fall in peripheral resistance with a rise in cardiac output. This indicates a failure of vasoconstrictor response (Thangarjah et al, 1980).

Control of the blood supply to the brain differs from that elsewhere. Within wide limits the cerebral blood flow is unaltered in spite of changes in arterial pressure. Cerebral blood vessels, therefore, show autoregulation. The principal agent affecting cerebral blood flow is carbon dioxide; low carbon dioxide causes a reduction in cerebral blood flow, and high carbon dioxide an increase. It has been claimed that carbon dioxide acts directly on the cerebral blood vessels but there is evidence that autonomic innervation may also play a part (Gotoh et al, 1971). When systemic arterial pressure falls cerebral vessels dilate so that cerebral blood flow is maintained until mean arterial pressure falls below 60 mmHg and this is not affected by ageing (Dekoninck et al, 1977; Arnold, 1981). In patients with autonomic degeneration, autoregulation of cerebral blood flow was found by some to be impaired (Meyer et al, 1972, 1973; Caronna and Plum, 1973; Depresseux et al and Franck, 1979) but not by others. (Skinhøj et al, 1971; Nanda et al, 1975; Thomas and Bannister, 1980). In elderly patients with symptoms of postural hypotension cerebral autoregulation may fail bilaterally or unilaterally; this impairment was not seen in asymptomatic patients with postural hypotension. Patients with impaired cerebral autoregulation may be at risk of brain damage from minor falls in blood pressure (Wollner et al, 1979).

Impaired autonomic control of the circulation

Impairment of circulatory reflexes can be demonstrated in a number of ways: heart rate changes can be observed in response to change in posture, to respiration (sinus arrhythmia) and to exercise. Beat-to-beat variations in heart rate are conveniently measured by the R-R interval of the electrocardiogram (Ewing, 1978). The immediate rate response to standing is a tachycardia, maximal at about the 15th beat, followed by a relative bradycardia most pronounced at the 30th beat. In normal subjects aged 48 to 67 with a resting R-R interval of 890 msec the R-R interval at the 15th beat is about 700 msec and at the 30th beat about 820 msecs. Heart rate change in patients with vagal neuropathy is diminished or absent and this has been particularly demonstrated in diabetic patients (Ewing et al, 1978) even without symptoms of autonomic neuropathy (Sundkvist et al, 1980). There is, however, evidence that in the elderly without autonomic neuropathy the normal changes in the R-R interval after standing may be impaired (MacLennan and Ritch, 1978; Oliver, 1978); this could be due to an aging process affecting the vagus. Variation in heart rate with respiration, (sinus arrhythmia) provides another simple test of vagal function. The subject breathes as hard as possible while an electrocardiogram is recorded. In normal subjects the R-R interval is shortened during inspiration and prolonged during expiration. A difference of 10 per cent or less indicates vagal dysfunction as has been shown particularly in diabetics (Sundkvist et al, 1979).

The blood pressure response to sustained handgrip at 30 per cent of the maximum voluntary contraction has been suggested as a non-invasive test of autonomic function. A rise of less than 15 mmHg of diastolic blood pressure during handgrip is abnormal (Ewing, 1978).

In the Valsalva manoeuvre a rise in intrathoracic pressure is produced by forced expiration against a closed glottis. In normal subjects the release of intrathoracic pressure is followed by an 'overshoot' of blood pressure above the resting level with reflex bradycardia (Fig. 20.4(1)). In subjects with a baroreceptor block these changes do not occur (Fig. 20.4(2)) (Sharpey-Schafer, 1955). Baroreceptor function can also be tested by observing circulatory effects of change in posture or by simulating change by lower body suction (Brown et al, 1966; Vargas and Lye, 1980). For a given fall in systolic pressure caused by lower body suction the rise in heart rate is less in the elderly than in the young (Collins et al, 1980). Baroreflex action has been tested by suction over the carotid sinus (Ludbrook et al, 1977).

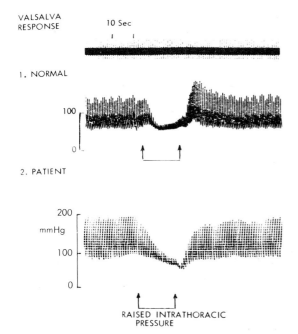

Fig. 20.4 The effect of Valsalva's manoeuvre on the blood pressure.
1. In normal subject.
2. In patient aged 80 with postural hypotension. (from Johnson et al, 1965)

Baroreceptor sensitivity can be tested by measuring the increase in R-R interval which occurs reflexly in response to a rise in systolic pressure induced by intravenous phenylephrine. Baroreceptor sensitivity falls with increasing age (Gribbin et al, 1971). It has also been found abnormal in diabetics (Bennett et al, 1976).

Methods are also available which help to localize the block (Prout, 1968). They include the effect on arterial blood pressure and hand blood flow of mental arithmetic, hyperventilation, cold, sudden noise (central and efferent pathways), sudden voluntary inspiration (spinal reflex), the effect of intradermal histamine on the axon flare, or of intradermal acetylcholine on sweating and piloerection (postganglionic pathways), the effect of intravenous noradrenaline on peripheral blood vessels, and of atrophine on the heart rate (for details see Johnson and Spalding, 1974).

POSTURAL (ORTHOSTATIC) HYPOTENSION IN THE ELDERLY

In a patient with postural hypotension the systolic, diastolic and pulse pressures fall beyond the normal on assuming the erect posture. This is because baroreceptor reflexes are either blocked or are ineffective, for instance, when they are fully in operation and have no reserves. If baroreceptor reflexes are absent blood is allowed to pool in the dependent veins and other capacity vessels in the standing position. This leads to decreased venous return and a fall in cardiac output. Reflex vasoconstriction of arteries and veins does not occur, the heart rate does not rise, and the systemic arterial pressure falls (Sharpey-Schafer, 1961; Glezer and Moskalenilo, 1972; White, 1980). On exercise the blood pressure may fall even in the recumbent position because of vasodilation in muscles (Marshall et al, 1961; Bevegård et al, 1962).

Postural hypotension is common in elderly patients (Wollner, 1978); it occurs spontaneously or following the use of small doses of drugs with a hypotensive action. In an acute geriatric ward at Oxford a fall of 20 mmHg systolic blood pressure was found in 17 per cent and of 40 mmHg in 5 per cent of patients over the age of 65 who had not received any drugs with a hypotensive action (Johnson et al, 1965). In an extended care ward in New York, however, 46 patients, with a mean age of 78 years, and with no obvious abnormality which could cause postural hypotension, had their blood pressure taken lying down and every 30 seconds for 5 minutes after standing; none showed a fall of more than 20 mmHg systolic blood pressure (Gorgy et al, 1973). Nevertheless in people over the age of 65 living in the community in Scotland a fall of 20 mmHg systolic blood pressure was seen in 24 per cent and of 40 mmHg in 5 per cent of apparently healthy elderly people. The only significant associations were with varicose veins and multiple minor abnormalities (Caird et al, 1973). In idiopathic postural hypotension spontaneous fluctuations in supine blood pressure may occur due to variations in total peripheral resistance (Niarchos et al, 1978). Symptomatic postural hypotension can be precipitated in some elderly patients by a moderate fall in cardiac output or peripheral resistance. This suggests that these patients may have a defect of vasomotor control. There is direct evidence that baroreceptor function becomes less efficient with increasing age and this could be due to an aging process (Appenzeller and Descarries, 1964; Bristow et al, 1969).

Aetiology
Impaired baroreceptor reflexes have been shown to give rise to postural hypotension in the following disorders:

Afferent block
Tabes dorsalis (Sharpey-Schafer 1956); diabetic neuropathy (Sharpey-Schafer, and Taylor, 1960); acute polyneuropathy (Johnson, 1966; Patte et al, 1980); car-

cinoma (Park et al, 1972; Boasberg et al, 1977; Carr-Locke, 1979; Green et al, 1979).

Central block in the brain
Cerebrovascular disease (Appenzeller and Descarries, 1964; Gross, 1970); Landry-Guillain-Barré syndrome (Appenzeller and Marshall, 1963); trigeminal zoster (Bhowmick and Arnold, 1976); Parkinsonism (Appenzeller and Goss, 1971; Gross et al, 1972); Wernicke's encephalopathy (Birchfield, 1964); tumours (Wagner, 1959; Thomas et al, 1961).

Central block in spinal cord
Traumatic spinal cord lesions above T6 (Guttmann et al, 1963); syringomyelia (Aminoff and Wilcox, 1972); transverse myelitis (Spingarn and Hitzig, 1942); intermediolateral column autonomic degeneration (Johnson et al, 1966) as seen in autonomic degeneration of the Shy-Drager syndrome, multiple system disease (Bradbury and Eggleston, 1925; Shy and Drager, 1960; Bannister et al, 1967; Spokes et al, 1979; Oppenheimer, 1980).

Efferent block
Alcoholism (Duncan et al, 1980); amyloidosis (Burns et al, 1971; Gaan et al, 1972; Low et al, 1981), chronic renal failure (Zuccalà et al, 1978; O'Hare and Murnaghan, 1981); diabetes mellitus (Bárány and Cooper, 1956; Ewing et al, 1980); mitral valve prolapse (Santos et al, 1981); rheumatoid arthritis (Edmonds et al, 1979); acute pandysautonomia (Hopkins et al, 1974; Young et al, 1975); Parkinsonism (Rajput and Rozdilsky, 1976); pernicious anaemia (White et al, 1981) and acute and chronic peripheral neuropathies from other causes (Watson, 1962; Barraclough and Sharpey-Schafer, 1963; Spalding and Smith, 1963; Brooks 1980). Chronic renal failure with dialysis has been accompanied by postural hypotension and baroreflex failure, but the lesion has not been explained (Bach et al, 1979).

In most *elderly patients* with postural hypotension none of these causes can be identified although cerebrovascular disease is very common. Investigation of some elderly patients with postural hypotension suggested that the lesion was in the brain. Although cerebrovascular disease was present at post-mortem examination in four patients who died, infarcts were not demonstrated in the brainstem and the pathology remained uncertain (Johnson et al, 1965).

Acute postural hypotension can occur in elderly patients at the onset of a stroke. There may be chronic impairment of baroreceptor function and any fall in cardiac output or peripheral resistance may precipitate postural hypotension.

Drugs may produce a block at one or more sites or

Table 20.1 Drugs commonly given to elderly patients and capable of producing postural hypotension

Hypotensive agents
Thiazides and other diuretics
Phenothiazines
Tricyclic antidepressants
Butyrophenones: haloperidol
Benzodiazepines: diazepam
Levodopa
Bromocryptine
Barbiturates
Antihistamines
Alcohol
Glyceryl trinitrate
Isosorbide dinitrate

act directly on the blood vessels. Many drugs have a hypotensive action (Table 20.1). They may, even in small doses, precipitate postural hypotension in patients with autonomic impairment, especially if taken in combination.

Other disturbances of vasomotor control
Patients with loss of baroreceptor reflexes may nevertheless be able to maintain a normal blood pressure with change in posture (SharpeySchafer, 1961; Johnson et al, 1969; Gross, 1970). On the other hand, patients with cerebrovascular disease or with Parkinsonism may have postural hypotension despite a normal Valsalva manoeuvre (Bannister, 1971; Gross et al, 1972). This may indicate poor sensitivity of the Valsalva manoeuvre in demonstrating baroreceptor function. There are, however, other mechanisms which influence the blood pressure and which may compensate for loss of baroreceptor function.

Blood vessels. The blood vessels themselves show local regulation to changes in intramural pressure (Bannister et al, 1967). It has been suggested that increased arterial and arteriolar rigidity may be a factor in postural hypotension (MacLennan et al, 1980).

In some patients the autonomic failure is *hypoadrenergic* with low basal levels of plasma noadrenaline and failure of the normal rise in response to standing (Cryer and Weiss, 1976; Mathias et al, 1976) associated with diminished noradrenergic innervation of blood vessels (Klein et al, 1980). In others it is *hyperadrenergic* with high noradrenaline stores, and an exaggerated rise of plasma noradrenaline on standing and normal noradrenergic innervation of blood vessels. Intermediate cases also occur (Ziegler et al, 1977; Cryer et al, 1978; Lake, 1979; Klein et al, 1980; Ninet et al, 1980; De Rohan-Chabot et al, 1980; Bannister et al, 1981; Polinski et al 1981a). There may also be an inadequate catecholamine response to injected insulin (Polinski et al, 1980), but glucagon, growth hormone and cortisol responses are normal (Polinski et al, 1981b).

Plasma renin activity and aldosterone. These may rise normally with standing or may remain unchanged (Chokroverty et al, 1969; Wilson et al, 1969; Johnson and Park, 1973b, Love et al, 1971; Wilcox et al, 1974a). When healthy elderly people stand up they have lower plasma renin, higher plasma dopamine, and lower urinary catecholamines and aldosterone than younger subjects. Similar changes occur in younger subjects when exposed to beta-blockade (Hork'y et al, 1975). Hyperbradykinism due to impaired destruction of bradykinin has been described as a familial orthostatic syndrome (Streeten et al, 1972)

Blood volume. A fall in blood volume may be an important factor in inducing postural hypotension (Bannister et al, 1969). This may be associated with hyponatraemia (Fine, 1969). Patients with blocked baroreceptor reflexes lose more sodium and free water in the urine in the recumbent position than normal subjects (Wilcox et al, 1974b) and do not show the normal rise in aldosterone when salt-depleted (Mills, 1970). Postural hypotension may be the early and only clinical manifestation of Addison's disease; possible causes include loss of blood volume, sodium depletion, and reduction in cortisol, necessary for noradrenaline vasoactivity. In diabetes mellitus insulin injections may precipitate postural hypotension (Page and Watkins, 1976; Palmer et al, 1977). Endogenous hyperinsulinaemia has also been reported as a factor in postprandial hypotension in autonomic failure (Turnbull et al, 1981).

Potassium deficiency. Potassium deficiency as shown by exchangeable potassium even when the serum potassium is normal, may be associated with postural hypotension (Cox et al, 1973). This can sometimes be controlled with potassium alone (Wagner, 1959; Cox et al, 1973). A blocked Valsalva response in patients with primary hyperaldosteronism may be corrected with potassium repletion (Biglieri and McIlroy, 1966). Potassium deficiency is common in elderly patients partly due to the effect of diuretic therapy and partly because of inadequate intake in the diet.

Prolonged bed rest alone impairs the efficiency of baroreceptor reflexes (Taylor et al, 1949). After cardiac infarction the blood pressure may be maintained by near maximum vasoconstriction (Fareeduddin and Abelmann, 1969). On assuming the erect posture there may be too few reserves to call on and then the blood pressure falls; this is even more conspicuous when the patient is hypotensive when recumbent. A similar situation arises with severe loss of blood volume as seen in haemorrhage or other causes of vasomotor shock. Myocardial insufficiency may also be a factor in postural hypotension in the elderly (Ibrahim et al, 1974).

Postural hypotension has also been reported in cardiomyopathy (Michardiere et al, 1978).

Clinical features

The clinical effects vary from nothing more than a little dizziness on standing up quickly to loss of consciousness on sitting up (Wollner, 1966, 1978). The common clinical picture is that of a patient whose legs give way when an attempt is made to stand him. This is often associated with clouding of consciousness, confusion, pallor, cyanosis, tremor, and finally loss of consciousness. These symptoms recover rapidly on return to the recumbent position. Because these patients are unable to cooperate when they stand up they are sometimes misdiagnosed as being unco-operative or lazy. Syncopal attacks lead to falls, and fractures, particularly of the neck of femur, may result. The differential diagnosis is from other causes of syncope (p. 464). Postural hypotension can be associated with increased sway but this may not be due to the fall in blood pressure (Overstall et al, 1978). In a patient who had had a previous cerebral infarct orthostatic hypotension induced new focal transient neurological signs with corresponding electrocardiographic changes referable to the compromised hemisphere (Riley and Friedman, 1981).

The diagnosis is established by demonstrating a fall in systolic blood pressure of 20 mmHg or more, often associated with a diastolic fall of 10 mmHg or more on change from the supine to the standing position. The fall in the systolic blood pressure is usually sufficient to be detected by palpation of the radial pulse; care has, however, to be taken not to compress the upper arm while holding the patient up and palpating the radial pulse. The examination is made easier by the use of a tilting bed.

Elderly patients with postural hypotension may have an abnormally low blood pressre of less than 100 mmHg systolic in the supine position, or on exercise, particularly when drugs with a hypotensive action are used, even in small doses (Barraclough and Sharpey-Schafer, 1963). When postural hypotension has been confirmed by manometry, investigations should establish any underlying neurological disorders and any precipitating factors, notably drugs. A silent cardiac infarction, or pulmonary emboli are also common findings.

Management

Drugs with a hypotensive effect should be discontinued or the dose reduced.

Parenteral vitamin B_1 should be given routinely (Barraclough and Sharpey-Schafer, 1963; Birchfield, 1964; Paulley, 1965) particularly as vitamin B_1 deficiency is common in elderly patients in hospital (Griffiths et al, 1967; Brocklehurst et al, 1968).

The benefit of frequent changes of posture has been

demonstrated in patients with spinal cord lesions (Guttman, 1946) and also in elderly patients with postural hypotension (Johnson et al, 1965). This may be due to training of baroreceptor reflexes which become less effective if they are not used (e.g. in prolonged recumbency or weightlessness). It has been said that blood vessels recover their own tone (Sharpey-Schafer, 1961).

Orthostatic tolerance can also be developed by keeping the patient in the semi-upright position — by progressive elevation of the head of the bed; the blood pressure, however, needs to be carefully observed until the patient can be sat out of bed. In the semi-upright position the raised intramural pressure induces local reactive vasoconstriction of blood vessels and sodium is also retained (Wilson et al, 1969); this tends to restore the blood volume which falls during recumbency (Stead and Ebert, 1941; Bannister et al, 1969). It does not affect the blocked Valsalva manoeuvre nor increase circulating catecholamines (Guttman et al, 1963; Johnson et al, 1969).

An atrial pacemaker at a rate of 100 per minute has been effective (Moss et al, 1980).

Antigravity measures

Antigravity support of the lower extremities reduces the pooling of blood on standing. Nursing horizontal may be required at first but as soon as possible the patient should be sat out of bed. Elastic stockings or tight bandages, preferably including the thigh (Palmer, 1980) are effective. They should be kept on day and night. If the patient should get up in the middle of the night without support, falls may result. For this reason a G-suit, although effective (Levin et al, 1964; Rosenhamer and Thornstrand, 1973), should if possible be avoided in the elderly.

Increasing blood volume

An increase in blood volume by the early and effective replacement of loss of blood or plasma is important. Dextran and intravenous albumin can also be used; 9-alpha-fluorohydrocortisone can be very effective, although in some cases the effect may not persist (Hickler et al, 1959; Soloman and Kuhn, 1960). It increases the blood volume but also has vasoconstrictor effects (Bannister et al, 1969). This may be due to supersensitivity of blood vessels to vasoconstrictor substances (Davies et al, 1979). It is usual to start with 0.1 mg daily and this can be increased gradually to 2 mg provided signs of significant fluid retention and a raised blood pressure do not occur.

Vasoconstrictor drugs

These can produce an increase in peripheral vascular resistance and in venous tone (Sharpey-Schafer and Ginsburg, 1962). Where sympathetic denervation has taken place an exaggerated response to catecholamines and angiotensin can be expected (Bannister et al, 1969). It is therefore reasonable to try sympathomimetic drugs in combination with plasma expanders. Ephedrine is often ineffective and the effect of vasopressin is short-lived; both have unpleasant side effects. Phenylephrine is effective but only for short periods and in small doses even in eyedrops (Robertson, 1979) can give rise to hypertension (Parks et al, 1961; Bannister et al, 1969). Etilefrin has also been recommended (Birke, 1977). Midodrine, an alpha-agonist can be effective but may cause supine hypertension (Schirger et al, 1981). Mono-amine oxidase inhibitors with tyramine (Diamond et al, 1970; Frewin et al, 1973; Guillevin et al, 1980), with amphetamine (Lewis et al, 1972), or with levodopa (Sharpe et al, 1972; Boisson et al, 1977; Corder et al, 1977) can improve postural hypotension. The rise in blood pressure when tyramine is given with a mono-amine oxidase inhibitor is associated with a rise in plasma noradrenaline and adrenaline (Nanda et al, 1976). It can work when all other methods have failed, but if not carefully controlled can produce dangerous hypertension (Davies et al, 1978) and should therefore be used with care in the elderly. Dihydroergotamine has been shown in haemodynamic and clinical studies to correct postural hypotension when given intravenously or intramuscularly (Fouad et al, 1981).

Oral medication in doses of 4–10 mg has been used (Bevegård et al, 1974). Others recommend 20 mg as the effective oral dose (Jennings et al, 1979). Variations in effective dose may be related to varying blood levels achieved (Bobik et al, 1981; Fouad et al, 1981; Oliver et al, 1980). Although it has a selective vesoconstrictor effect in both animals and man (Mellander and Norden-felt, 1970; Nordenfelt and Mellander, 1972) it probably also has a significant effect on arterial vasoconstriction in denervated vessels (Bevegård et al, 1974). A combination of dihydroergotamine and etilefrin has also been used (Muth and Jansen, 1980; Bracharz and Polzien, 1981; Hengstmann et al, 1982). It has been used successfully with 9-alphafluorohydrocortisone (Jennings et al, 1979). Indomethacin inhibits the vasodilator activity of prostaglandins and has been helpful in improving postural hypotension and raising systemic vascular resistance (Abate et al, 1979), but it is not always effective (Crook et al, 1981; Davies et al, 1980). Flubiprofen, another prostaglandin synthetase inhibitor, has also been used alone and in combination with fludrocortisone (Watt et al, 1981). The betablockers propanolol and pindolol have been found effective in some cases possibly by reducing vasodilatation or by acting as an alpha-agonist, but they are not always satisfactory and can cause cardiac failure (Davies et al, 1981; Goldstraw and Waller, 1981).

Once hypotension has been controlled the blood pressure may stabilize without further treatment; these patients, however, remain at risk of postural hypotension and drugs with a hypotensive action should not be used (Wollner, 1966).

SYNCOPE IN THE ELDERLY

The term syncope is applied to transient loss of consciousness due to failure of an adequate cerebral blood supply. This is a common and important cause of falls in the elderly and may lead to fractures particularly of the femoral neck of the femur (Abdon and Nilsson, 1980). The blood flow to the brain is dependent on the relationship of the blood pressure and the cerebrovascular resistance. In old age adaptation of the cerebral circulation to a fall in arterial blood pressure may be less easily accomplished than in younger subjects (Wollner et al, 1979).

Aetiology
Syncope can be caused by a fall in cardiac output, a fall in peripheral resistance of the systemic circulation, or due to local abnormality of the blood vessels supplying the brain (Shillingford, 1970) (see also Ch. 18).

Cardiac syncope
Syncope is not uncommonly due to cardiac dysrhythmias as shown by continuous electrocardiographic monitoring (McCarthy and Wollner, 1977; Camm et al, 1978; Gordon, 1978; Brown and Anderson, 1980; Abdon, 1981). It may occur in slow or fast dysrhythmias, including the sick sinus syndrome (Cabeen et al, 1978). It also occurs in cardiac infarction or angina which may produce syncope from dysrhythmias, myocardial insufficiency, or vasovagal phenomena. Prolongation of the Q-T interval especially due to quinidine, prenylamine or disopyramide may be associated with paroxysmal ventricular tachycardia and syncope (Di Segni et al, 1980; Grenadier et al, 1980; Riccioni et al, 1980; Steinbrecher and Fitchett, 1980; Schottelndreier, 1981). Lithium may cause syncope due to depressed sinus node function (Hagman et al, 1979). Syncope can be caused by severe aortic stenosis (Gann et al, 1979; Vilhemsen et al, 1979), mitral stenosis, aortic incompetence, left atrial myxoma or ball-valve thrombus of the mitral valve. It is seen in pulmonary hypertension, and pulmonary emboli are also an important cause of syncope in the elderly (Thames et al, 1977).

Vasovagal syncope
In vasovagal attacks bradycardia from excessive vagal tone is associated with peripheral vasodilatation in muscles. Anxiety, pain, emotional stress or standing for long periods in crowded places may precipitate a vasovagal attack. Syncope may also occur in cardiac infarction, in glossopharyngeal neuralgia (Khero and Mullins, 1971; Taylor et al, 1977; Jacobson and Russell, 1979) after a cold drink (Rainsford, 1972) swallowing food (Grützmacher et al, 1978) or due to oesophageal dilatation or spasm (Levin and Posner, 1972; Alstrup and Pedersen, 1973) or endoscopy (Goncalves, 1979), with venepuncture and minor surgical or dental procedures, and even during rectal and prostatic examinations (Bilbro, 1970). Vasovagal attacks are the commonest cause of syncope in younger people; in the elderly, however, they are a less common cause than other conditions.

Peripheral vasodilatation may occur in vasovagal attacks, and can cause syncope in the absence of bradycardia (Greenfield, 1951; Weissler et al, 1957; Blair et al, 1959; Glick and Yu, 1963; Roddie and Shepherd, 1963). There is usually a combination of factors which tend to lower the blood pressure; for instance, a hot room or hot bath, micturition, or most importantly in old age the effect of drugs. Many drugs act on the sympathetic nervous system to produce a fall in peripheral resistance with or without an associated fall in venous tone and a fall in cardiac output. Impairment of baroreceptor reflexes is common in older patients and even small doses of drugs may precipitate syncopal attacks, especially the phenothiazines, tricyclic antidepressants and drugs used in the treatment of hypertension. Syncope from peripheral vasodilatation due to histamine has been reported in mastocytosis (Lapresle et al, 1978).

Carotid sinus syncope
Carotid sinus hypersensitivity can give rise to extreme sinus bradycardia or asystole or to acute peripheral vasodilatation (Weiss and Baker, 1933; Draper, 1950). It can be confirmed by carotid sinus compression with continuous electrocardiographic recording, although this must be undertaken with great care particularly in elderly people and only on one side at a time (Nelson and Mahru, 1963; Smiddy et al, 1972). It particularly occurs in old men, notably with cardiovascular disease (Heron et al, 1965). It can be precipitated by drugs, including digitalis (Lown and Levine, 1961), propanolol (Reyes, 1973) and alphamethyldopa (Bauernfeind et al, 1978)

Cough syncope
Cough syncope can result from diminished venous return, from raised intrathoracic pressure or from a reflex from baroreceptors stimulated by pressure transients from repeated coughing (Sharpey-Schafer, 1953a, b).

Micturition syncope
This has been ascribed to failure of venous return

especially when straining. Circulatory changes similar to those accompanying a Valsalva manoeuvre have been demonstrated in both males and females by direct arterial blood pressure measurements (Littler et al, 1974); this may be exacerbated by prostatic hypertrophy (Lyle et al, 1961; Coggins et al, 1964; Lukash et al, 1964; Donker et al, 1972). Bladder contraction sets off a sympathetic reflex through the spinal cord and withdrawal of this vasoconstrictive activity at the end of micturition may be an important factor in micturition syncope (Guttman and Whitteridge, 1947; Corbett et al, 1971; Debarge et al, 1974; Johnson and Spalding, 1974).

Defaecation syncope
Defaecation syncope may occur in the elderly of either sex especially at night (Pathy, 1978). Circulatory changes as seen in the Valsalva manoeuvre have been recorded during defaecation (Littler et al, 1974).

Postural hypotension is discussed on page 460. It is a common cause of syncope in the elderly.

Cerebrovascular disease. Transient ischaemic attacks can cause attacks of loss of consciousness without focal signs (These are discussed further on p. 430).

Clinical features and diagnosis
The characteristic symptoms are a feeling of dizziness, visual disturbance, nausea, hyperventilation and pallor followed by loss of consciousness; recovery occurs usually within 2 or 3 minutes in the recumbent position. There may, however, still be a feeling of faintness which may last up to half-an-hour or more and syncope may recur if the patient is stood up too quickly. The limbs are flaccid so that the patient tends to collapse like a house of cards.

An exception can be the Stokes-Adams attacks when there is sudden loss of consciousness without warning but rapid recovery within about 30 seconds and flushing as the peripheral vessels are dilated when the cardiac output is re-established.

In transient cerebral ischaemic attacks, loss of consciousness is usually associated with transient neurological signs, but when this is not the case the diagnosis can be difficult. Loss of consciousness for longer than 3 minutes in the recumbent position is, however, rarely due to vasomotor syncope and increases the probability that the patient had a cerebrovascular incident.

The differential diagnosis of syncope is from vertigo, 'drop' attacks, hyperventilation, narcolepsy, catalepsy, and hypoglycaemia but the main condition from which it has to be differentiated is epilepsy. In epilepsy, there are either no prodromal symptoms or a characteristic aura; it is not related to posture; limbs are usually hypertonic at the time of the loss of consciousness and the patient tends to fall to the ground in a rigid position. In epilepsy there may be a characteristic picture of a full blown grand mal attack, but in minor attacks the loss of consciousness may be so brief that the patient does not fall. Although brief convulsions can develop as a result of syncope, when the clonic movements precede the loss of consciousness this is always due to epilepsy.

The diagnosis of the cause of syncopal attacks from epilepsy and the cause of syncopal attacks themselves is not always easy in elderly patients because of the difficulty of obtaining an accurate history. Yet this is the most important way of establishing the diagnosis and no effort should be spared in obtaining an accurate history both from the patient and also from relatives, neighbours or attendants. In this way, the diagnosis can usually be established but an electrocardiogram (ECG) should be done as a routine. Twenty-four-hour continuous ECG monitoring may, however, be necessary to demonstrate cardiac dysrhythmias as the cause of syncopal attacks. The electroencephalogram is less useful in elderly patients because it is so often abnormal in the absence of any symptoms. An ambulatory electroencephalogram may, however, record an attack.

Management
Syncopal attacks are particularly dangerous in old people since falls may result in head injury or fracture. Also, because of other disabilities an elderly patient may not be able to get up following a fall and may lie on the floor sometimes for days with resultant hypothermia. The management of patients with postural hypotension is discussed elsewhere in this chapter. Great care must be taken with drugs with a hypotensive action which should always be started in small doses in elderly patients and stopped altogether if postural hypotension occurs.

Patients with micturition syncope should attempt micturition in the sitting position and a wall bar which they can use in getting on and off the commode is helpful.

Carotid sinus hypersensitivity may respond to atropine and can be treated with surgical stripping of the carotid vessels (Cheng and Norris, 1973; Knobel et al, 1978; Trout et al, 1979). The most effective treatment, however, is the introduction of a demand pacemaker (Christian and Schwartz, 1973; Ramirez, 1973; Davies et al, 1979a; Poggi et al, 1981; Kaliman et al, 1982) which has also been used for syncope caused by glossopharyngeal neuralgia (Khero and Mullins, 1971). In syncope with oesophageal spasm oesophagomyotomy may be helpful (Alstrup and Pederson, 1973). Hypokalaemia should be corrected (McCarthy and Wollner, 1981).

Correction of cardiac dysrhythmias, if necessary, by a pacemaker is often effective (Dimarco et al, 1981).

Transient loss of consciousness is frequently considered in the elderly to be due to 'little strokes'. It may indeed be so, but there are many other causes which should be considered and appropriate treatment given.

REFERENCES

Abate G, Polimeni R M, Cuccurullo F, Puddu P, Lenzi S 1979 Effects of indomethacin on postural hypotension in Parkinsonism. British Medical Journal 2: 1466–8

Abdon N J 1981 Frequency and distribution of long-term ECG-recorded cardiac arrhythmias in an elderly population. With special reference to neurological symptoms. Acta Medica Scandinavica 209: 175–83

Abdon N J, Nilsson B E 1980 Episodic cardiac arrhythmia and femoral neck fracture. Acta Medica Scandinavica 208: 73–76

Ackerman W J 1974 Stupor, bradycardia, hypotension and hypothermia. A presentation of Wernicke's encephalopathy with rapid response to thiamine. Western Journal of Medicine 121: 428–429

Aherne W, Hull D 1965 Brown adipose tissue. Lancet i: 765

Alstrup P, Pedersen S A 1973 A case of syncope on swallowing secondary to diffuse oesophageal spasm. Acta Medica Scandinavica 193: 365–368

Altschule M D, Sulzbach W M 1947 Tolerance of the human heart to acidosis. American Heart Journal 33: 458–463

Altus P, Hickman J W, Pina I, Barry P P 1980 Hypothermia in the sunny south. Southern Medical Journal 73: 1491–2

Aminoff M J, Wilcox L S 1972 Autonomic dysfunction in syringomyelia. Postgraduate Medical Journal 48: 113–115

Anderson W F 1971 Practical Management of the Elderly, 2nd edn, p 319. Blackwell Scientific Publications, Oxford, London, Edinburgh, Melbourne

Appenzeller O, Descarries L 1964 Circulatory reflexes in patients with cerebrovascular disease. New England Journal of Medicine 27: 820–823

Appenzeller O, Goss J E 1971 Autonomic deficits in Parkinson's syndrome. Archives of Neurology and Psychiatry (Chicago) 24: 50–57

Appenzeller O, Marshall J 1963 Vasomotor disturbance in Landry-Guillain-Barré syndrome. Archives of Neurology and Psychiatry (Chicago) 9: 368–372

Arnold K G 1981 Cerebral blood flow in Geriatrics — a review. Age and Ageing 10: 5–9

Bach C, Iaina A, Eliahou H E 1979 Autonomic Nervous System disturbance in patients on chronic haemodialysis. Israel Journal of Medical Science 15: 761–4

Bannister R 1971 Degeneration of the autonomic nervous system. Lancet ii: 175–179

Bannister R, Ardill L, Fentem P 1967 Defective autonomic control of blood vessels in idiopathic orthostatic hypotension. Brain 90: 725–746

Bannister R, Ardill L, Fentem, P 1969 An assessment of various methods of treatment of idiopathic orthostatic hypotension. Quarterly Journal of Medicine 38: 377–395

Bannister R, Crowe R, Eames R, Burnstock G 1981 Adrenergic innervation in autonomic failure. Neurology 31: 1501–6

Bárány F R, Cooper E H 1956 Pilomotor and sudomotor innervation in diabetics. Clinical Science 15: 533–540

Barley S L, Evans E J 1970 Hypothermia in the elderly. Lancet i: 1003–1004

Barraclough M A, Sharpey-Schafer E P 1963 Hypotension from absent circulatory reflexes. Lancet i: 1121–1126

Bavernfeind R, Hall C, Denes P, Rosen K M 1978 Carotid sinus hypersensitivity with alpha methyldopa. Annals of Internal Medicine 88: 214–5

Bennett R, Hosking D J, Hampton J R 1976 Baroreflex sensitivity and responses to the Valsalva manoeuvre in subjects with diabetes mellitus. Journal of Neurology, Neurosurgery and Psychiatry 39: 178–83

Bernhard W F 1956 In: Dripps R D (ed) The physiology of induced hypothermia, Publ. 451, p 175. National Academy of Sciences, Washington D.C.

Bertel O, Bühler F R, Kiowski W, Lütold B E 1980 Decreased Beta-adrenoreceptor responsiveness as related to age, blood pressure, and plasma catecholamines in patients with essential hypertension. Hypertension 2: 130–8

Bevegård S, Castenfors J, Lindblad L E 1974 Haemodynamic effects of dihydroergotamine in patients with postural hypotension. Acta Medica Scandinavica 196: 473–477

Bevegård S, Jonsson B, Karlöf, I 1962 Circulatory response to recumbent exercise and head up-tilting in patients with disturbed sympathetic cardiovascular control (postural hypotension). Acta Medica Scandinavica 172: 623–636

Bhowmick B K, Arnold J P 1976 Trigeminal zoster producing facial paralysis and postural hypotension. British Medical Journal 1: 131–132

Biglieri E G, McIlroy M B 1966 Abnormalities of renal function and circulatory reflexes in primary aldosteronism. Circulation 33: 78–86

Bilbro R H 1970 Syncope after prostatic examination. New England Journal of Medicine 282: 167–168

Birchfield R I 1964 Postural hypotension in Wernicke's disease. American Journal of Medicine 36: 404–414

Birke E R 1977 On the action of anti-hypotensive agents in sympathicotonic orthostatic hypotension in geriatric patients: comparison with placebo and etilefrin. Medizinische Klinik 72: 1696–702

Blair D A, Glover W E, Greenfield A D M, Roddie I C 1959 Excitation of cholinergic vasodilator nerves to human skeletal muscles during emotional stress. Journal of Physiology (London) 148: 633–658

Boasberg P D, Henry J F, Rosenbloom A A, Hall T C, Rose M, Fisher D A 1977 Case reports and studies of paraneoplastic hypotension: abnormal low pressure baroreceptor responses. Medical and Paediatric Oncology 3: 59–66

Bobik A, Jennings G, Skews H, Esler M, McLean A 1981 Low oral bioavailibility of dihydroergotamine and first-pass extraction in patients with orthostatic hypotension. Clinical Pharmacology and Therapeutics 30: 673–9

Boisson D, Annat G, Aimard G, Pequignot J N, Grivet B, Devici M 1977 Treatment of a case of grave orthostatic hypotension (Shy-Drager's syndrome) by an association of L-dopa and mono-amine-oxidase inhibitor. Nouvelle Press Medicale 6: 3839–41

Bondy P K, Cohn G L, Herrman W, Crispell K R 1958 The possible relationship of etiocholanolone to periodic fever. Yale Journal of Biology and Medicine 30: 395–405

Bracharz E, Polzien P 1981 Treatment of hypotensive circulatory dysregulation with a combination of dihydroergotamine and etilefrine. Münchener Medizinische Wochenschrift 123: 177–80

Bradbury S, Eggleston C 1925 Postural hypotension. American Heart Journal 1: 73–86

Brennan J L 1967 Case of extensive necrosis of the oesophageal mucosa following hypothermia. Journal of Clinical Pathology 20: 581–584

Brigden W, Howarth S, Sharpey-Schafer E P 1950 Postural changes in the peripheral blood flow of normal subjects with observations on vasovagal fainting reactions as a result of tilting; the lordotic posture and spinal anaesthesia. Clinical Science 9: 79–91

Bristow J D, Gribbin B, Honour A J, Pickering T G, Sleight P 1969 Diminished baroreflex sensitivity in high blood pressure and aging man. Journal of Physiology (London) 202: 45P–46P

British Medical Association Special Committee 1964 Accidental hypothermia in the elderly. British Medical Journal 2: 1255–1258

British Medical Journal: Leading Article 1978 Treating accidental hypothermia. British Medical Journal 2: 1383–4

British Medical Journal: Clinicopathological Conference 1979 Royal College of Physicians of London. British Medical Journal 1: 1768–73

Brocklehurst J C 1975 Aging of the autonomic nervous system. Age and Ageing Suppl. 7–17

Brocklehurst J C, Griffiths L L, Taylor G F, Marks J, Scott D L, Blackley J 1968 The clinical features of chronic vitamin deficiency. Gerontologia Clinica 10: 309–320

Brooke D G, Collins J E, Fox R H, James S, Thornton O 1973 Evaluation of a method for measuring urine temperature. Journal of Physiology (London) 231: 91P–93P

Brooks A P 1980 Abnormal vascular reflexes in Charcot-Marie-Tooth disease. Journal of Neurology, Neurosurgery and Psychiatry 43: 348–50

Brown A K, Anderson V 1980 The contribution of 24-hour ambulatory ECG monintoring in a general medical unit. Journal of the Royal College of Physicians of London 14: 7–12

Brown E, Goei J S, Greenfield A D M, Plassaras G 1966 Circulatory responses to stimulated gravitational shifts of blood in man induced by exposure of the body below the iliac crests to subatmospheric pressure. Journal of Physiology (London) 183: 607–627

Buchanan K D, McKiddie M T, Reid J M 1967 Respiratory acidosis in hypothermic myxoedema coma. Postgraduate Medical Journal 43: 114–116

Bull G M, Morton J 1978 Environment, Temperature and Death Rates. Age and Ageing 7: 210–224

Burch G E 1960 Influence of the central nervous system on veins in man. Physiological Reviews 40, Suppl. 4: 50–56

Burns R J, Downey J A, Frewin D B, Whelan R F 1971 Autonomic dysfunction with orthostatic hypotension. Australian and New Zealand Journal of Medicine i: 15–21

Burton A C, Edholm O G 1955 In: Man in a Cold Environment. Edward Arnold, London

Cabeen W R, Roberts N K, Child J S 1978 Syncope and Sick Sinus Syndrome. Western Journal of Medicine 129: 452–55

Caird F I, Andrews G B, Kennedy R D 1973 Effect of posture on blood pressure in the elderly. British Heart Journal 35: 527–530

Camm A J, Ward D E, Spurell R A J 1978 Arrhythmias in Ambulatory Persons. Biotelemetry and Patient Monitoring 5: 167–81

Carlson C J, Emilson B, Rapaport E 1978 Creatine phosphokinase MB isoenzyme in hypothermia: case reports and experimental studies. American Heart Journal 95: 352–8

Caronna J J, Plum F 1973 Cerebrovascular regulation in preganglionic and postganglionic autonomic insufficiency. Stroke 4: 12–19

Carr-Locke D L 1979 Autonomic neuropathy and inappropriate secretion of antidiuretic hormone. Occurence in a patient with bronchogenic carcinoma. Journal of the American Medical Association 241: 2298

Cheng L H, Norris L W 1973 Surgical management of the carotid sinus syndrome. Archives of Otolaryngology 97: 395–398

Chokroverty S, Barron K D, Katz F H, Del Greco F, Sharp J T 1969 The syndrome of primary orthostatic hypotension. Brain 92: 743–768

Christian N, Schwartz H 1973 Treatment of carotid sinus syncope with demand pacemaker. Geriatrics 28: 131–133

Coggins C H, Lillington G A, Gray C P 1964 Micturition syncope. Archives of Internal Medicine 113, 14–18

Cokkinos D V, Haralambakis A G, Thalassinos N C, Heimonas E T, Demopoulos I N, Voridis E M, Gardikas C D 1979 Effect of digitalis on diminished baroreceptor sensitivity in diabetics. Angiology 30: 549–57

Collins K J 1981 Thermal comfort and hypothermia. Royal Society of Health Journal 101: 16–18

Collins K J, Dore C, Exton-Smith A N, Fox R H, McDonald I C, Woodward P M 1977 Accidental hypothermia and impaired temperature homeostasis in the elderly. British Medical Journal 1: 353–356

Collins K J, Exton-Smith A N, James M H, Oliver D J 1980 Functional changes in autonomic nervous responses with ageing. Age and Ageing 9: 17–24

Comarr A E 1958 Differential diagnosis of high fever peculiar to spinal cord injury patients. Journal of the Indian Medical Profession 5: 2223–2236

Coni N K 1981 Deep posterior tibial compartmental syndrome after accidental hypothermia in an elderly hypothyroid patient. Journal of the American Geriatrics Society 29: 77–79

Cooper K E 1965 In: Scientific Basis of Medicine. Annual Reviews, p 239. Athlone Press, London

Cooper K E 1968 In: Baron D N, Compston N D, Dawson A M (eds) Recent Advances in Medicine, 15th edn. p 333. Churchill, London

Cooper K E, Cranston W I, Snell E S 1964 Temperature in the external meatus as an index of central temperature changes. Journal of Applied Physiology 19: 1032–1035

Cooper K E, Kenyon J R 1957 A comparison of temperature measurement in the rectum, oesophagus, and on the surface of the aorta during hypothermia in man. British Journal of Surgery 44: 616–619

Cooper K E, Sellick B A 1960 In: Cooper K E, Ross D N (ed) Hypothermia in Surgical Practice. p I. Cassell, London

Corbett J L, Johnson R H 1968 Circadian changes in body temperature and renal excretion of Bedouin Arabs, non-Bedouin Arabs and Europeans. Journal of Physiology 198: 105P–106P

Corbett J L, Frankel H L, Harris P J 1971 Cardiovascular reflex responses to cutaneous and visceral stimuli in spinal man. Journal of Physiology (London) 215: 395–409

Corder C N, Kanefsky T M, McDonald R H Jr, Gray J L, Redmond D P 1977 Postural hypotension: adrenergic responsivity and levodopa therapy. Neurology 27: 921–7

Cornu P, Bickert P, Segrestaa J M, Marsan C, Ertel M, Manicalli M, Laffay J, Lanotte M 1973 Myxoedema coma. Study of 3 cases. Semaine des Hopiteaux de Paris 49: 1449–1458

Cowburn E J, Fox R H 1974 A technique for studying thermal perception. Journal of Physiology 239: 77–78P

Cox J R, Admani A K, Agarwal M F, Abel P 1973 Postural hypotension: body fluid compartments and electrolytes. Age and Ageing 2: 112–120

Cranston W I 1966 Temperature regulation. British Medical Journal 2: 69–75

Cranston W I 1969 Factitious fever. British Journal of Hospital Medicine 2: 1075–1078

Cranston W I, Rawlins M D, Luff R H, Duff G W 1971 In: Wolstenholm G E W, Birch J (ed) Pyrogens and Fever, p 155. Churhill Livingstone, Edinburgh and London

Crook J E, Robertson D, Whorton A R 1981 Prostaglandin suppression: inability to correct severe idiopathic orthostatic hypotension. Southern Medical Journal 73: 318–24

Crowe J P, Moore R E 1974 Proceedings: Physiological and behavioural responses of aged men to passive heating. Journal of Physiology (London) 236: 43P–45P

Cryer P E, Silverberg A B, Santiago J V, Shah E D 1978 Plasma catecholamines in diabetes. The syndromes of hypoadrenergic and hyperadrenergic postural hypotension. American Journal of Medicine 64: 407–16

Cryer P E, Weiss S 1976 Reduced plasma norepinephrine response to standing in autonomic dysfunction. Archives of Neurology and Psychiatry (Chicago) 33: 275–277

Currens J H 1948 Comparison of blood pressure in lying and standing positions: study of 500 men and 500 women. American Heart Journal 35: 646–654

Davidson M, Grant E 1981 Accidental hypothermia: a community hospital perspective. Postgraduate Medicine 70: 42–9

Davies A B, Stephens M R, Davies A G 1979a Carotid sinus hypersensitivity in patients presenting with syncope. British Heart Journal 42: 583–6

Davies B, Bannister R, Mathias C, Sever P 1981 Pindolol in postural hypotension: the case for caution. Lancet 2: 982–3

Davies B, Bannister R, Sever P 1978 Pressor amines and monoamine-oxidase inhibitors for treatment of postural hypotension in autonomic failure. Limitations and hazards. Lancet i: 172–5

Davies B, Bannister R, Sever P, Wilcox C S 1979b The pressor actions of noradrenaline, angiotensin II and saralasin in chronic autonomic failure treated with fludrocortisone. British Journal of Clinical Pharmacology 8: 253–260

Davies H E F 1975 Respiratory change in heart rate, sinus arrhythmia in the elderly. Gerontologia Clinica 17: 96–100

Davies I B, Bannister R, Hensby C, Sever P S 1980 The Pressor Actions of Noradrenaline and Angiotensin II in chronic autonomic failure treated with Idomethacin. British Journal of Clinical Pharmacology 10: 223–239

Davis F M, Judson J A 1981 Warm peritoneal dialysis in the management of accidental hypothermia: report of five cases. New Zealand Medical Journal 94: 207–9

Dawkins M J R, Hull D 1964 Brown adipose tissue and the response of the new-born rabbit to cold. Journal of Physiology (London) 172: 216–238

Day E A, Morgan E B 1974 Accidental hypothermia: report of a case following alcohol and barbiturate overdose. Anaesthesia and Intensive Care 2: 73–76

Debarge O, Christensen N J, Corbett J L, Eidelman B H, Frankel H L, Mathias C J 1974 Plasma catecholamines in tetraplegics. Paraplegia 12: 44–49

Dekoninck W J, Collard M, Noel G 1977 Cerebral vasoreactivity in senile dementia. Gerontology 23: 148–160

Denborough M A, Ebeling P, King J O, Zapf P 1970 Myopathy and malignant hyperpyrexia. Lancet i: 1138–1140

Denborough M A, Lovell R R H 1960 Anaesthetic deaths in a family. Lancet ii: 45

Dent L E, Stokes J F, Carpenter M E 1961 Death from hypothermia in steatorrhoea. Lancet i: 748–749

Depresseux J C, Rousseau J J, Franck G 1979 The autoregulation of cerebral blood flow, the cerebrovascular reactivity and their interaction in the Shy Drager syndrome. European Neurology 18: 295–301

Desmeules H, Blais C 1979 Accidental hypothermia: treatment of a case using peritoneal irrigation. Canadian Anaesthetists Society Journal 26: 506–9

Diamond M, Murray R, Schmid P 1970 Idiopathic postural hypotension: physiologic observations and report of a new mode of therapy. Journal of Clinical Investigation 49: 1341–1348

Dimarco J P, Garan H, Harthorne J W, Ruskin J N 1981 Intracardiac Electrophysiological techniques in recurrent syncope of unknown cause. Annals of Internal Medicine 95: 542–548

Disegni E, Klein H O, David D, Libhaber C, Kaplinsky E 1980 Overdrive pacing in quinidine syncope and other long QT-interval syndromes. Archives of Internal Medicine 140: 1036–40

Donker D N, Robies De Medina E O, Kieft J 1972 Micturition Syncope. Electroencephalography and Clinical Neurophysiology 33: 328–331

Draper A J 1950 The cardioinhibitory carotid sinus syndrome. Annals of Internal Medicine 32: 700–716

Duff R S, Farrant P C, Leveaux V M, Wray S M 1961 Spontaneous periodic hypothermia. Quarterly Journal of Medicine 30: 329–338

Duguid H, Simpson R G, Stowers J M 1961 Accidental hypothermia. Lancet ii: 1213–1219

Duncan G, Johnson R H, Lambie D G, Whiteside E A 1980 Evidence of vagal neuropathy in chronic alcoholism. Lancet ii: 1053–7

Edmonds M E, Jones T C, Saunders W A, Sturrock R D 1979 Autonomic neuropathy in rheumatoid arthritis. British Medical Journal 2: 173–5

Eichler A C, McFee A S, Rott H D 1969 Heat Stroke. American Journal of Surgery 118: 855–863

Ellis F P 1972 Mortality from heat illness and heat-aggravated illness in the United States. Environmental Research 5: 1–58

Ellis F P, Nelson F, Pincus L 1975 Mortality during heat waves in New York City, July 1972 and August and September 1973. Environmental Research 10: 1–13

Ellis F P, Princé H P, Lovatti G, Whittington R M 1980 Mortality and Morbidity in Birmingham during the 1978 Heatwave. Quarterly Journal of Medicine 49: 1–8

Emslie-Smith D 1958 Accidental hypothermia. Lancet ii: 492–495

Ewing D J 1978 Cardiovascular reflexes and autonomic neuropathy. Clinical Science 55: 321–7

Ewing D J, Campbell I W, Murray A, Neilson J M, Clarke B F 1978 Immediate heart-rate response to standing: simple test for autonomic neuropathy in diabetes. British Medical Journal 1: 145–7

Ewing D J, Hume L, Campbell I W, Murray A, Neilson J M 1980 Autonomic mechanisms in the initial heart rate response to standing. Journal of Applied Physiology 49: 809–14

Exton-Smith A N 1968 Accidental hypothermia in the elderly. Practitioner 200: 804–812

Exton-Smith A N 1969 Hazards of the elderly on holiday. Community Health (Bristol) i: 52–56

Exton-Smith A N 1977 Functional consequences of aging: clinical manifestations. In: Exton-Smith A N, Grimley-Evans J (eds) Care of the Elderly, Meeting the Challenge of Dependency, Academic Press, London

Fareeduddin K, Abelmann W H 1969 Impaired orthostatic tolerance after bed rest in patients with myocardial infarction. New England Journal of Medicine 280: 345–350

Felicetta J V, Green W L, Goodner C J 1980 Decreased adrenal responsiveness in hypothermic patients. Journal of Clinical Endocrinology and Metabolism 50: 93–97

Fell R H, Denny P R 1968a Severe hypothermia and respiratory arrest in diazepam and glutethimide intoxication. Anaesthesia 23: 636–640

Fell R H, Dendy P R 1968b Severe hypothermia as a result of barbiturate overdose complicated by cardiac arrest. Lancet i: 392–394

Fennell W H, Moore R E 1973 Responses of aged men to passive heating. Journal of Physiology (London) 231: 118P–119P

Fernander J P, O'Rourke R A, Ewy G A 1970 Rapid active external rewarming in accidental hypothermia. Journal of the American Medical Association 212: 153–156

Fine W 1969 Some common factors in the causation of postural hypothension. Gerontologia Clinica ii: 206–215.

Fitzgerald F T 1980 Hypoglycaemia and Accidental hypothermia in an alcoholic population. Western Journal of Medicine 133: 105–107

Foster K G, Ellis F P, Doré L, Exton-Smith A N, Weiner J S 1976 Sweat responses in the aged. Age and Ageing 5: 91–101

Fouad F M, Tarazi R C, Bravo E L 1981 Dihydroergotamine in idiopathic orthostatic hypotension: short-term intramuscular and long-term oral therapy. Clinical Pharmacology and Therapeutics 30: 782–9

Fox R H, Davies T W, Marsh F P, Vrich H 1970 Hypothermia in a young man with an anterior hypothalamic lesion. Lancet ii: 185–188

Fox R H, Goldsmith R, Kidd D J, Lewis H E 1963a Acclimatization to heat in man by controlled elevation of body temperature. Journal of Physiology (London) 166: 530–547

Fox R H, Goldsmith R, Kidd D J, Lewis H E 1963b Blood flow and other thermoregulatory changes with acclimatization to heat. Journal of Physiology (London) 166: 548–562

Fox R H, Schuster S, Williams R, Marks J, Goldsmith R, Condon R E 1965 Cardiovascular metabolic and thermoregulatory disturbances in patients with erythrodermic skin diseases. British Medical Journal 1: 619–622

Fox R H, Woodward P M, Exton-Smith A N, Green M F, Donnison D V, Wicks M H 1973 Body temperature in the elderly: a national study of physiological, social and environmental conditions. British Medical Journal 1: 200–206

Fox R H, Woodward P M, Fry A J, Collins J C, Macdonald I C 1971 Diagnosis of accidental hypothermia in the elderly. Lancet i: 424–427

Frewin D B, Robinson S M, Willing R L 1973 The use of a new mode of therapy in the management of orthostatic hypotension. Australian and New Zealand Journal of Medicine 3: 180–183

Frolkis V V 1967 The autonomic nervous system in the aging organisms. Triangle 8: 322–328

Frolkis V V, Bezruvov V V, Duplenko Y K, Shchegoleva I V, Shevtchuk V G, Verkhratsky N S 1973 Acetycholine Metabolism and Cholinergic regulation of functions in Aging. Gerontologia 19: 45–47

Frolkis V V, Bezrukov V V, Shevchuk V G 1975 Hemodynamics and its regulation in old Age. Experimental Gerontology 10: 251–271

Frolkis V V, Bogatskaya L N, Stupina A S, Shevchuk V G 1977 Experimental analysis of development of cardiac insufficiency in old age. American Heart Journal 93: 334–48

Fruehan A E 1960 Accidental hypothermia. Archives of Internal Medicine 106: 218–229

Gaan D, Mahoney M P, Rowlands D J, Jones A W 1972 Postural hypotension in amyloid disease. American Heart Journal 84: 395–400

Gale E A, Tattersall R B 1978 Hypothermia: a complication of diabetic ketoacidosis. British Medical Journal 2: 1387–9

Gann D, Fernandes H, Samet P L 1979 Syncope and aortic stenosis: significance of conduction abnormalities. European Journal of Cardiology 9: 405–13

George J M, Wolff S M, Diller E, Bartter F C 1969 Recurrent fever of unknown aetiology: failure to demonstrate association between fever and unconjugated etiocholanolone. Journal of Clinical Investigation 48: 558–563

Glezer G A, Moskalenilo N P 1972 The physiological and pathological haemodynamic changes in subjects with normal arterial pressure. Cor et Vasa 14 265–277

Glick G, Yu P N 1963 Haemodynamic changes during spontaneous vasovagal reactions. American Journal of Medicine 34: 42–51

Golden F S, Rivers J F 1975 The immersion incident. Anaesthesia, 30: 364–373

Goldman A, Exton-Smith A N, Francis G, O'Brien A 1977 Report on a pilot study of low temperatures in old people admitted to hospital. Journal of the Royal College of Physicians ii: 291–306

Goldstraw P, Waller D G 1981 Pindolol in orthostatic hypotension. British Medical Journal 283: 310

Goncalves D 1979 Endoscopic procedure hazard — vasovagal syncope with heart standstill due to ERCP. Arquivos de Gastroenterologia 16: 200–202

Goodall H B, Todd A S, Maclean D, Henderson R, King J F 1975 Proceedings: Cryofibrinogenaemia and activation of the coagulation lysis systems in accidental hypothermia of the elderly. Journal of Clinical Pathology 28: 758

Gordon M 1978 Occult cardiac arrhythmias associated with falls and dizziness in the elderly. Detection by Holter monitoring. Journal of the American Geriatrics Society 26: 418–423

Gorgy A N, David S B, Friedman S A 1973 Vasomotor tone in the aged. Archives of Neurology 29: 439–440

Gotoh F, Ebihara S, Toyoda M, Shinohara X 1971 Role of autonomic nervous system in autoregulation of human cerebral circulation. Panminerva Medica 13: 175

Green C J, Breckenbridge A M, Wright F K 1979 Severe orthostatic hypotension associated with carcinoma of bronchus. Postgraduate Medicine 55: 426–9

Greenfield A D M 1951 An emotional faint. Lancet i: 1302–1303

Grenadier E, Keidar S, Alpan G, Marmor A, Palant A 1980 Prenylamine-induced ventricular tachycardia and syncope controlled by ventricular pacing. British Heart Journal 44: 330–4

Gribbin B, Pickering T G, Sleight P, Peto R 1971 Effect of Age and High Blood Pressure on Baroreflex sensitivity in Man. Circulation 29: 424–31

Griffiths L L, Brocklehurst J C, Scott D L, Marks J, Blackley J 1967 Thiamine and ascorbic acid levels in the elderly. Gerontologia Clinica 9: 1–10

Gross M, 1970 The effect of posture on subjects with cerebrovascular disease. Quarterly Journal of Medicine 39: 485–491

Gross M, Bannister R, Godwin-Austen R 1972 Orthostatic hypotension in Parkinson's disease. Lancet i: 174–176

Grossheim R L 1973 Hypothermia and frostbite treated with peritoneal dialysis. Alaska Medicine 15: 53–55

Grützmacher J, Horstkotte W, Kitzing J 1978 Syncope on swallowing Medizinische Klinik 73: 1218–20

Gubbay S S, Barwick D D 1966 Two cases of accidental hypothermia in Parkinson's disease with unusual E.E.G. findings. Journal of Neurology, Neurosurgery and Psychiatry 29: 459–466

Guillevin L, Dumas P, Bletry O, Serdaru M, Brunet P, Godeau P 1980 Treatment of neurogenic orthostatic hypotension by an association of tyramine and a monoamine oxidase inhibitor. Annales de Medecine Interne 131: 504–7

Guttman L 1946 Rehabilitation after injuries to the spinal cord and cauda equina. British Journal of Physical Medicine 9: 162–171

Guttman L, Munro A F, Robinson R, Walsh J J 1963 Effect of tilting on the cardiovascular responses and plasma catecholamine levels in spinal man. Paraplegia i: 4–18

Guttman L, Silver J, Wyndham C H 1958 Thermoregulation in spinal man. Journal of Physiology (London) 142: 406–419

Guttman L, Whitteridge D 1947 Effects of bladder distension on autonomic mechanisms after spinal cord injuries. Brain 70: 361–404

Hagman A, Arnman K, Rydén L 1979 Syncope caused by lithium treatment. Report on two cases and a prospective investigation of the prevalence of lithium-induced sinus node dysfunction. Acta Medica Scandinavica 205: 467–71

Harari A, Regnier B, Rapin M, Lenaire F, Le Gall J R 1975 Haemodynamic study of prolonged deep accidental hypothermia. European Journal of Intensive Care Medicine i: 65–70

Hardy J D 1961 Physiology of temperature regulation. Physiological Reviews 41: 521–606

Heaton J M 1973 A study of brown adipose tissue in hypothermia. Journal of Pathology 110: 105–108

Hegnauer A H, Govino B G 1956 In: Dripps A D (ed) Physiology of Induced Hypothermia, Publ. 451, p 327. National Academy of Sciences, Washington D.C

Hellman J B, Stacy R W 1976 Variations of respiratory sinus arrhythmia with age. Journal of Applied Physiology 41: 734–8

Hellström R 1961 Body build, muscular strength and certain circulatory factors in military personnel. Acta Medica Scandinavica 170 suppl. 371: 1–84

Hengstmann J H, Hengstmann R, Schwonzen S, Dengler H J 1982 Dihydroergotamine increases the bioavailability of orally administered etilefrine. European Journal of Clinical Pharmacology 22: 436–67

Heron J R, Anderson E G, Noble I M 1965 Cardiac abnormalities associated with carotid sinus syndrome. Lancet ii: 214–216

Hickler R B, Thompson G R, Fox L M, Hamlin J T 1959 Successful treatment of orthostatic hypotension with 9-alpha-fluorohydrocortisone. New England Journal of Medicine 261: 788–791

Hockaday T D R, Cranston W I, Cooper K E, Mottram R F 1962 Temperature regulation in chronic hypothermia. Lancet ii: 428–432

Hong S K, Rahn H 1967 The diving women of Korea and Japan. Scientific American 216: 34–43

Hopkins A, Neville B, Bannister R 1974 Autonomic neuropathy of acute onset. Lancet i: 769–771

Hork'y K, Marek J, Kopeck A J, Gregorov'a I 1975 Influences of age on orthostatic changes in plasma renin activity and urinary catecholamines in man. Physiologia Bohemoslovaca 24: 481–488

Howitt L F 1971 Death in Scotland from malnutrition and/or hypothermia, 1968 Health Bulletin (Edinburgh) 29: 43–49

Hunter J M 1976 Hypothermia and Wernicke's encephalopathy. British Medical Journal 2: 563–564

Hyams D E 1963 Hypothermic myxoedema coma. British Journal of Clinical Practice 17: 1–14

Ibrahim M M, Tarazi R L, Dunstan H P, Bravo E L 1974 Idiopathic orthostatic hypotension: circulatory dynamics in chronic autonomic insufficiency. American Journal of Cardiology 34: 288–294

Impallomeni M, Ezzat R 1976 Hypothermia associated with nitrazepam administration. British Medical Journal 1: 223–304

Irvine R E 1966 Hypothermia due to diazepam. British Medical Journal 2: 1007

Isaacs H, Barlow M B 1973 Malignant hyperpyrexia: further muscle studies on asymptomatic carriers identified by creatine phosphokinase screening. Journal of Neurology, Neurosurgery and Psychiatry 36: 228–243

Israilov B, Maiorov V N, Soloviov N A 1978 Morphometic features of changes in the neurones of the jejunum in the ageing body. Arkhiv Anatomi Gistologii Embryologii 75: 53–6

Jacob A I, Lichstein E, Ulano S D, Chadda K D, Gupta P K, Werner B M 1978 A-V block in accidental hypothermia. Journal of Electrocardiology 11: 399–402

Jacobson R R, Russell R W R 1979 Glossopharyngeal neuralgia with cardiac arrhythmia: a rare but treatable cause of syncope. British Medical Journal 1: 379–80

Jennings G, Esler M, Holmes R 1979 Treatment of orthostatic hypotension with dihydroergotamine. British Medical Journal 2: 307

Johnson R H 1965 Neurological studies in temperature regulation. Annals of the Royal College of Surgeons of England 36: 339–352

Johnson R H 1966 The autonomic nervous system and body temperature. Proceedings of the Royal Society of Medicine 59: 463–546

Johnson R H 1971 Temperature regulation in paraplegia. Paraplegia 34: 562–570

Johnson R H, Lee de G, Oppenheimer D R, Spalding J M K 1966 Autonomic failure with orthostatic hypotension due to intemediolateral column degeneration. Quarterly Journal of Medicine 35: 276–292

Johnson R H, Park D M 1973a Intermittent hypothermia. Independence of central and reflex thermoregulatory mechanisms. Journal of Neurology, Neurosurgery and Psychiatry 36: 411–416

Johnson R H, Park D M 1973b Effect of change of posture on blood pressure and plasma renin concentration in men with spinal transections. Clinical Science 444: 539–546

Johnson R H, Smith A C, Spalding J M K 1969 Blood pressure response to standing and to Valsalva's manoeuvre. Clinical Science 36: 77–86

Johnson R H, Smith A C, Spalding J M K, Wollner L 1965 Effect of posture on blood pressure in elderly patients. Lancet i: 731–733

Johnson R H, Spalding J M K 1974 In: Disorders of the Autonomic Nervous System, p 129–147. Blackwell Scientific Publications, Oxford, London, Edinburgh, Melbourne

Johnson R H, Spalding J M K 1976 Widespread autonomic failure. British Journal of Hospital Medicine 15: 266–274

Jones I H, Meade T W 1964 Hypothermia following chlorpromazine therapy in myxoedematous patients. Gerontologia Clinica 6: 252–256

Kaliman J, Weber H, Scheibelhofer W, Fuchs J, Lederbauer M, Probst P 1982 Diagnosis and therapy of carotid sinus syndrome. Acta Medica Austriaca 9: 45–9

Keatinge W R 1965 Death after shipwreck. British Medical Journal 2: 1537–1541

Keatinge W R 1969 In: Survival in Cold Water. Blackwell Scientific Publications, Oxford

Keatinge W R 1976 Collapse during Channel swim. Lancet ii: 692

Khalil H H, MacKeith R C 1954 A simple method of raising and lowering body temperature. British Medical Journal 2: 734–736

Khero B A, Mullins C B 1971 Cardiac syncope due to glossopharyngeal neuralgia. Treatment with a transvenous pacemaker. Archives of Internal Medicine 128: 806–808

King J O, Denborough M A, Zapf P W 1972 Inheritance of malignant hyperpyrexia. Lancet i: 365–370

Klein R L, Baggett J M, Thureson-Klein A, Langford H G 1980 Idiopathic orthostatic hypotension: circulating noradrenaline and ultrastructure of saphenous vein. Journal of the Autonomic Nervous System 2: 205–22

Knobel E, Lopes A C, Korn D, De Andrade L A, Gebara M B, Sustovich D R 1978 Carotid sinus syncope: report of a case subjected to surgical treatment. Arquivos Barasileiros de Cardiologia 31: 325–8

Koeppen A H, Daniels J C, Barron K D 1969 Subnormal body temperatures in Wernicke's encephalopathy. Archives of Neurology 21: 493–498

Lake C R 1979 Relationship of sympathetic nervous system tone and blood pressure. Nephron 23: 84–90

Langley J N 1898 On the union of cranial autonomic (visceral) fibres with the nerve cells of the superior cervical ganglion. Journal of Physiology (London). 23: 240–270

Lapresle J, Verret J M, Doubrère J F, Enjoiras O 1978 Syncope and transitory amaurosis during mastocytosis. Annales de Medicine Interne 129: 601–4

Laufman H 1951 Profound accidental hypothermia. Journal of the American Medical Association 147: 1201–1212

Ledingham I McA, Mone J G 1972 Treatment after exposure to cold. Lancet i: 534–535

Ledingham I McA, Mone J G 1974 Management of severe Accidental Hypothermia. In: Ledingham I McA (ed) First World Congress on Intensive Care, p 292

Ledingham I M, Mone J G 1980 Treatment of accidental hypothermia: a prospective clinical study. British Medical Journal 280: 1102–5

Lee H A, Ames A C 1965 Haemodialysis in severe barbiturate poisoning. British Medical Journal 1: 1217–1219

Leithead C S, Lind A R 1964 In: Heat Stress and Heat Disorders, p 195. Cassell, London

Levin B, Posner J B 1972 Swallow syncope. Report of a case and review of the literature. Neurology (Minneapolis) 22: 1086–1093

Levin J M, Ravenna P, Weiss M 1964 Idiopathic orthostatic hypotension. Treatment with a commercially available counterpressure suit. Archives of Internal Medicine 114: 145–148

Levine J A 1969 Heat stroke in the aged. American Journal of Medicine 47: 251–258

Levy L A 1980 Severe hypophosphataemia as a complication of the treatment of hypothermia. Archives of Internal Medicine 140: 128–9

Lewis R K, Hazelrigg C G, Fricke F J, Russel R O 1972 Therapy of idiopathic postural hypotension. Archives of Internal Medicine 129: 943–949

Lewis P R, Lobban M C 1957a The effects of prolonged periods of life on abnormal time routines upon excretory rhythms in human subjects. Quarterly Journal of Experimental Physiology and Cognate Medical Sciences 42: 356–371

Lewis P R, Lobban M C 1957b Dissociation of diurnal rhythms in human subjects on abnormal time routines. Quarterly Journal of Experimental Physiology and Cognate Medical Sciences 42: 371–386

Lilly J K, Boland J P, Zakan S 1980 Urinary bladder temperature monitoring: a new index of body core temperature. Critical Care Medicine 8: 742–4

Lind A R, Humphreys P W, Collins K J, Forster K, Sweetland K F 1970 Influence of age and daily duration of exposure on responses of men to work in heat. Journal of Applied Physiology. 28: 50–56

Linton A L, Ledingham I McA 1966 Severe hypothermia with barbiturate intoxication. Lancet i: 24–26

Littler W A, Honour A J, Sleight P 1974 Direct arterial pressure, pulse rate and electrocardiogram during micturition and defaecation in unrestricted man. American Heart Journal 88: 205–210

Lloyd E Ll 1972 Diagnosic problems and hypothermia. British Medical Journal 3: 417

Lloyd E Ll 1973 Accidental hypothermia treated by central rewarming through the airway. British Journal of Anaesthesia 45: 41–48

Lloyd O C 1964 Cavers dying of cold. Bristol Medico-Chirurgical Journal 79: 1–5

Love D R, Brown J J Chinn R H, Johnson R H, Lever A F, Park D M, Robertson J I 1971 Plasma renin in idiopathic orthostatic hypotension: differential response in subjects with probably afferent and efferent autonomic failure. Clinical Science 41: 289–299

Low P A, Dyck P J, Okazaki H, Kyle R, Fealey R D 1981 The splanchnic autonomic outflow in amyloid neuropathy and Tangiers disease. Neurology 31: 461–3

Lown B, Levine S A 1961 The carotid sinus: clinical value of its stimulation. Circulation 23: 766–789

Ludbrook J, Mancia G, Ferrari A, Zanchetti A 1977 The variable-pressure neck-chamber method for studying the carotid baroreflex in man. Clinical Science 53: 165–71

Lukash W M, Sawyer G T, Davies J E 1964 Micturition syncope produced by orthostasis and bladder distension. New England Journal of Medicine 270: 341–344

Lye M, Kamal A 1977 Effects of a heatwave on mortality rates in elderly inpatients. Lancet ii: 529–531

Lyle C B, Monroe J T, Flinn D E, Lamb L E 1961 Micturition syncope. New England Journal of Medicine 265: 982–986

Macaron C, Feero S, Goldflies M 1979 Hypothermia in Wernicke's encephalopathy. Postgraduate Medicine 65: 241–2

McCarthy S T, Wollner L 1977 Cardiac dysrhythmias: Treatable cause of transient cerebral dysfunction in the elderly. Lancet 2: 202

McCarthy S T, Wollner L 1981 Falls and funny turns: a possible complication of hypokylaemia. Royal Society of Medicine International Congress and Symposium Series 44: 25–28

McGrath M D, Paley R G 1960 Hypothermia induced in a myxoedematous patient by imipramine hydrochloride. British Medical Journal 2: 1364

McKean W I, Dixon S R, Gwynne J F, Irvine R O H 1970 Renal failure after accidental hypothermia. British Medical Journal 2: 463–464

Maclean D, Emslie-Smith D 1974 The J-loop of the spatial vectorcardiogram in accidental hypothermia in man. British Heart Journal 36: 621–629

Maclean D, Emslie-Smith D 1977 Accidental Hypothermia. Blackwell Scientific Publications, Oxford, London

Maclean D, Griffiths P D, Browning M C, Murison J 1974 Metabolic aspects of spontaneous rewarming in accidental hypothermia and hypothermic myxoedema. Quarterly Journal of Medicine 43: 371–387

Maclean D, Griffiths P D, Emslie-Smith D 1968 Serum enzymes in relation to electrocardiographic changes in accidental hypothermia. Lancet ii: 266–271

MacLennan W J, Hall M R P, Timothy J I 1980 Postural hypotension diabetic ketoacidosis in accidental hypothermia and hypothermic myxoedema. British Medical Journal 4: 757–761

Maclean D, Taig D R, Emslie-Smith D 1973b Achilles tendon reflex in accidental hypothermia and hypothermic myxoedema. British Medical Journal ii: 87–90

MacLennan W J, Ritch A E S 1978 Heart rate response to standing as a test for autonomic neuropathy. British Medical Journal 1: 505

MacLennan W J, Hall M R P, Timothy J I 1980 Postural hypotension in old age: is it a disorder of the nervous system or blood vessels? Age and Ageing 9: 25–32

Macmillan A L, Corbett J L, Johnson R H, Smith A C, Spalding J M K, Wollner L 1967 Temperature regulation in the survivors of accidental hypothermia in the elderly. Lancet ii: 165–169

McNichol M W 1967 Respiratory failure and acid-base status in hypothermia. Postgraduate Medical Journal 43: 674–676

McNichol M W, Smith R 1964 Accidental hypothermia. British Medical Journal 1: 19–21

Macpherson R K, Ofner F 1965 Heat and the survival of the aged and chronically ill. Medical Journal of Australia i: 292–295

Macpherson R K, Ofner F 1971 The febrile response in the aged. Medical Journal of Australia 58: 1386–1387

Mahood J M, Evans A 1978 Accidental hypotermia, disseminated intravascular coagulation and pancreatitis. New Zealand Medical Journal 87: 283–284

Marshall R J, Schirger A, Shepherd J I 1961 Blood pressure during supine exercise in idiopathic orthostatic hypotension. Circulation 24: 76

Matthews J A 1967 Accidental hypothermia. Postgraduate Medical Journal 43: 622–667

Mathias C J, Christensen N J, Corbett J L, Frankel H L, Spalding J M K 1976 Plasma catecholamines during paroxysmal neurogenic hypertension in quadriplegic man. Circulation Research 39: 204–208

Mellander S, Nordenfelt I 1970 Comparative effects of dihydroergotamine and noradrenaline on resistance exchange and capacitance function in the peripheral circulation. Clinical Science 39: 183–201

Meriwether W D, Goodman R M 1972 Severe accidental hypothermia with survival after rapid rewarming. Case report, pathophysiology and review of the literature. American Journal of Medicine 53: 505–510

Meyer J S, Shimazu K, Fukuuchi Y, Ohuchi T, Erilsson A D 1972 Dysautoregulation in patients with central neurogenic orthostatic hypotension. Neurology 22: 407–408

Meyer J S, Shimazu K, Fukuuchi Y, Ohuchi T, Okamoto S, Koto A, Erilsson A D 1973 Cerebral dysautoregulation in central neurogenic orthostatic hypotension (Shy-Drager Syndrome). Neurology (Minneapolis) 23: 262–273

Michardiere A, Almange C, Revillon L, Laborgne P 1978 Orthostatic hypotension and obstructive hypertrophic cardiomyopathy. Semaine des Hopitaux de Paris 54: 1425–9

Mills G L 1973 Accidental hypothermia in the elderly. British Journal of Hospital Medicine 10, 691–699

Mills G L 1974 Management of Accidental Hypothermia in the Elderly. In: Ledingham I McA (ed), First World Congress on Intensive Care, p. 112

Mills I H 1970 Regulation of sodium excretion: intra- and extrarenal mechanisms. Journal of the Royal College of Physicians of Lond 4: 335–350

Mills J N 1966 Human circadian rhythms. Physiological Reviews 46: 128–171

Ministry of Housing and Local Government 1961 Homes for Today and Tomorrow, p. 15. HMSO, London

Ministry of Housing and Local Government 1962 Some Aspects of Designing for Old People. Design Bull. I, p 4. HMSO, London

Mitchell J R A, Surridge D H C, Willison R G 1959 Hypothermia after chlorpromazine in myxoedematous psychosis. British Medical Journal 1: 932–933

Morikawa S, Murata M, Murata H, Iwai S 1979 Evaluation of preoperative creatin phosphokinase (CPK) level — usefulness as a screening test for malignant hyperpyrexia. Masui. Japanese Journal of Anaesthesiology 28: 187–96

Moss A J, Glaser W, Topol E 1980 Atrial tachypacing in the treatment of a patient with primary orthostatic hypotension. New England Journal of Medicine 302: 1456–7

Moyer J H, Morris G, De Bakey M E 1957 Hypothermia. I. Effect on renal hemodynamics and on excretion of water and electrolytes in dog and man. Annals of Surgery 145: 26–40

Muth H H, Jansen W 1980 Dihydroergot plus in the long-term therapy of orthostatic hypotension in older patients. Fortschritte der Medizin 98: 1571–4

Nanda R N, Johnson R H, Keogh H J 1976 Treatment of neurogenic orthostatic hypotension with a mono-oxidase inhibitor and Tyramine. Lancet ii: 1164

Nanda R N, Wyper D J, Harper M A, Johnson R H 1975 In: Harper A M, Jennett W B, Miller J D, Rowen J O (ed), Blood Flow and Metabolism in the Brain, p 2.22 Churchill Livingstone, Edinburgh

Nelson D A, Mahru M M 1963 Death following digital carotid artery occlusion. Archives of Neurology 8: 640–643

Newmark S R, Himathomkam T, Shane J M 1974 Myxoedema coma. Journal of the American Medical Association 230: 884–885

Niarchos A P, Magrini F, Tarazi R C, Bravo E L 1978 Mechanism of spontaneous supine blood pressure variations in chronic autonomic insufficiency. American Journal of Medicine 68: 547–52

Ninet J, Annat G, Boisson D, Michel D, Schott B, Devil M et al 1980 Hypotension orthostatique primitive. Nouvelle Presse Medicale 9: 1875–79

Nomura S, Yamazak K, Sawa Y, Yamauch T, Nakazawa T 1981 Palmar skin potential reflex and serum dopamine-beta-hydroxylase activity of the aged. Folia Psychiatrica et Neurologica Japonica 35: 3–9

Nordenfelt I, Mellander S 1972 Central haemodynamic effects of dihydroergotamine in patients with orthostatic hypotension. Acta Medica Scandinavica 191: 115–120

O'Donnell T F Jr, Clowes G H Jr 1972 The circulatory abnormalities of heat stroke. New England Journal of Medicine 287: 734–737

O'Hare J A, Murnaghan D J 1981 Postural hypotension in chronic renal failure due to autonomic neuropathy. Irish Journal of Medical Science 150: 270–275

O'Keeffe K M 1980 Noncardiogenic pulmonary oedema from accidental hypothermia. A case report. Colorado Medicine 77: 106–7

Oliver D J 1978 Heart rate response to standing as a test of autonomic neuropathy. British Medical Journal 1: 1349–50

Oliver N O, Jennings G L, Bobik A, Esler M 1980 Low bioavailability as a cause of apparent failure of dihydroergotamine in orthostatic hypotension. British Medical Journal 28: 275–6

Oppenheimer D R 1980 Lateral horn cells in progressive autonomic failure. Journal of Neurological Science 46: 393–404

Osborne J J 1953 Experimental hypothermia, respiratory and blood-gas changes in relation to cardiac function. American Journal of Physiology 175: 389–398

Overstall P W, Johnson A L, Exton-Smith A N 1978 Instability and falls in the elderly. Age and Ageing Suppl 92–6

Page M McB, Watkins P J 1976 Provocation of postural hypotension by insulin in autonomic neuropathy. Diabetes 25: 90–95

Palmer K 1980 Graduated compression stockings. British Medical Journal 28: 389–90

Palmer K T, Perkins C J, Smith R B 1977 Insulin aggravated postural hypotension Australian and New Zealand Journal of Medicine 7: 161–2

Park D M, Johnson R H, Crean G P, Robinson J F 1972 Orthostatic hypotension in bronchial carcinoma. British Medical Journal iii: 510–511

Parks V J, Sandison A G, Skinner S L, Whealan R F 1961 Sympathomimetic drugs in orthostatic hypotension. Lancet i: 1133–1136

Pathy M S 1978 Defaecation syncope. Age and Ageing 7: 233–6

Patte L, Raphael J L, Salmeron M, Goester C 1980 Postural blood pressure variations in primary acute polyradiculitis. Annales de Medicine Interne 131: 494–8

Paulley J W 1965 Posture and blood pressure in the elderly. Lancet, i: 1076–1077

Paulley J W, Jones R A, Hughes J P, Porter D I 1964 Old people in the cold. British Medical Journal 1: 428

Petersdorf R G, Bennett I L 1957 Factitious fever. Ann. Intern. Med. 46: 1039–1062

Phillips G, Smith J F 1973 Hypothermia and Wernicke's encephalopathy. Lancet ii: 122–124

Pickering B G, Bristow G K, Craig D B 1977 Case history number 97: core rewarming by peritoneal irrigation in accidental hypothermia with cardiac arrest 56: 574–7

Pledger H G 1962 Disorders of temperature regulation. Journal of Bone and Joint Surgery 44B: 110–113

Poggi L, Aubry J, Eisinger F, Kohler J L, Casanova P 1981 Syncope and lipothymia of carotid sinus origin. Apropos of 13 cases of carotid sinus syndrome of the cardio-inhibitor form. Revue de Medicine Interne 2: 95–107

Polinski R J, Kopin I J, Ebert M H, Weise V 1980 The adrenal medullary response to hypoglycaemia in patients with orthostatic hypotension. Journal of Clinical Endocrinology and Metabolism 51: 1401–6

Polinsky R J, Kopin I J, Ebert M H, Weise V 1981a Pharmacologic distinction of different orthostatic hypotension syndromes. Neurology 31: 1–7

Polinski R J, Kopin I J, Ebert M H, Weise V, Recant L 1981b Hormonal responses to hypoglycaemia in orthostatic hypotensive patients with adrenergic insufficiency. Life Sciences 29: 417–25

Pollock R A, Watson R L 1971 Malignant hypothermia associated with hypocalcaemia. Anaesthesiology 34: 188–194

Pr'eda I, Kenedi P 1973 ECG and VCG in accidental and experimental hypothermia. Acta Medica Academiae Scientiarum Hungaricae 30: 67–77

Prescott L F, Peard M C, Wallace I R 1962 Accidental hypothermia. British Medical Journal 2: 1367–1370

Prout B J 1968 Postural hypotension. British Journal of Hospital Medicine 2: 1269–1276

Pugh L G C E 1966 Accidental hypothermia in walkers, climbers and campers: report to the Medical Commission on Accident Prevention. British Medical Journal i: 123–129

Rainsford D J 1972 Cold drink and syncope. British Medical Journal iii: 475

Rajput A H, Rozdilsky B 1976 Dysautonomia in Parkinsonism: A clinicopathological study. Journal of Neurology, Neurosurgery and Psychiatry 39: 1092–1100

Ramirez A 1973 Demand pacemaker for the treatment of carotid sinus syncope. Journal of Thoracic and Cardiovascular Surgery 66: 287–289

Rango N 1980 Old and cold: hypothermia in the elderly. Geriatrics 35: 93–96

Rawlins M D, Rosendorff C, Cranston W I 1971 In: Wolstenholme G E W, Birch J (ed), Pyrogens and Fever, p 175, Churchill Livingstone, Edinburgh and London

Ree M J 1964 Electrocardiographic changes in accidental hypothermia. British Heart Journal 26: 566–571

Rees J R 1958 Accidental hypothermia. Lancet i: 556–559

Reyes A J 1973 Propranolol and the hyperactive carotid sinus reflex syndrome. British Medical Journal 2: 662

Riccioni N, Bartolmei C, Soldani S 1980 Prenylamine-induced ventricular arrythmias and syncopal attacks with Q-T prolongation. Cardiology 66: 199–203

Riley T L, Friedman J M 1981 Stroke, orthostatic hypotension and focal epilepsy. Journal of the American Medical Association 245: 1243–4

Robertson D 1979 Contraindications to the use of ocular phenylephrine in idiopathic orthostatic hypotension. American Journal of Ophthalmology 87: 819–22

Robinson S M, King A B 1971 Hypocapnia-induced increases in rectal temperature in man during heat exposure. Journal of Applied Physiology 31: 656–658.

Roddie I C, Sherherd J T 1963 Nervous control of the circulation in skeletal muscle. British Medical Bulletin 19: 115–119

De Rohan-Chabot P, Said G, Ziza J M 1980 Idiopathic orthostatic hypotension and the Shy-Drager syndrome: haemodynamic and pharmocological studies in seven patients. Annales de Medicine Interne 131: 483–8

Rosenhamer G, Thornstrand C 1973 Effect of G-suit in treatment of postural hypotension. Acta Medica Scandinavica 193: 277–280

Rosin A J, Exton-Smith A N 1964 Clinical features of accidental hypothermia with some observations on thyroid function. British Medical Journal 1: 16–19

Ross D N 1957 Problems associated with the use of hypothermia in cardiac surgery. Proceedings of the Royal Society of Medicine 50: 76–78

Rossman L 1971. In: Rossman I (ed), Clinical Geriatrics, p 471, J B Lippincott, Philadelphia

Royal College of Physicians of London 1966 Report of the Committee on Accidental Hypothermia. Royal College of Physicians, London

Sadikali F, Owor R 1974 Hypothermia in the tropics: a review of 24 cases. Tropical and Geographical Medicine 26: 265–270

Sadowsky D, Reeves A C 1975 Agenesis of the corpus callosum with hypothermia. Archives of Neurology 32: 774–776

Salvaso C B, Payne P R, Wheeler E F 1971 Environmental conditions and body temperatures of elderly women living alone or in Local Authority homes. British Medical Journal 4: 656–659

Santos A D, Mathew P K, Hilal A, Wallace W A 1981 Orthostatic hypotension: a commonly unrecognised cause of symptoms in mitral valve proplapse. American Journal of Medicine 71: 746–50

Savides E S, Hoffbrand B I 1974 Hypothermia, thrombosis and acute pancreatitis. British Medical Journal 1: 614

Schirger A, Sheps S G, Thomas J E, Fealey R D 1981 Midodrine. A new agent in the management of idiopathic orthostatic hypotension and Shy-Drager syndrome. Mayo Clinic Proceedings 56: 429–33

Schissler P, Parker M A, Scott S J Jr 1981 Profound hypothermia: value of prolonged cardiopulmonary resuscitation. Southern Medical Journal 74: 474–7

Schneider V, Klug E 1980 Death by hypothermia. Are there any new diagnostic aspects? Zeitschrift fur Rechtsmedizin. Journal of Legal Medicine 86: 59–69

Schottelndreier M A 1981 Syncope associated with prolonged QT-interval on the electrocardiogram. Nederlands Tijdschrift voor Geneeskunde 125: 726–30

Schwab R H, Lewis D W, Killough J H, Templeton J Y 1964 Electrocardiographic changes in rapidly-induced deep hypothermia. American Journal of the Medical Sciences 248: 290–303

Shanks C A, Marsh H M 1973 Simple core rewarming in accidental hypothermia. British Journal of Anaesthesia 45: 522–525

Shapiro W R, Williams G H, Plum F 1969 Spontaneous recurrent hypothermia accompanying agenesis of the corpus callosum. Brain 92: 423–436

Spalding J M K, Smith A C 1963 In: Clinical Practice and Physiology of Artificial Respiration. Blackwell Scientific Publications, Oxford

Sharpe J, Marquez-Julio A, Ashby O 1972 Idiopathic orthostatic hypotension treated with levodopa and MAO inhibitor: a preliminary report. Canadian Medical Association Journal 107: 296–300

Sharpey-Schafer E P 1953a The mechanism of syncope after coughing. British Medical Journal 2: 860–863

Sharpey-Schafer E P 1953b Effect of coughing on intrathoracic pressure and peripheral blood flow. Journal of Physiology (London) 122: 351–357

Sharpey-Schafer E P 1955 Effects of Valsalva's manoeuvre on the normal and failing circulation. British Medical Journal i: 693–695

Sharpey-Schafer E P 1956 Circulatory reflexes in chronic disease of the afferent nervous system. Journal of Physiology (London) 134: 1–10

Sharpey-Schafer E P 1961 Venous tone. British Medical Journal 2: 1589–1595

Sharpey-Schafer E P, Ginsburg J 1962 Humeral agents and venous tone. Lancet ii: 1337–1340

Sharpey-Schafer E P, Taylor P J 1960 Absent circulatory reflexes in diabetic neuritis. Lancet i: 559–562

Sheehan H L, Summers V K 1952 Treatment of hypopituitary coma. British Medical Journal i: 1214–1215

Shibolet S, Coll R, Gilat T, Sohar E 1967 Heatstroke: its clinical picture and mechanism in 36 cases. Quarterly Journal of Medicine 36: 525–548

Shillingford J P 1970 Syncope. American Journal of Cardiology 26: 609–612

Shy G M, Drager G A 1960 A neurological syndrome associated with orthostatic hypotension. Archives of Neurology 2: 511–527

Skinhøj E, Olesen J, Strandgaard S 1971 Autoregulation and the sympathetic nervous system: a study in a patient with idiopathic orthostatic hypotension. In: Ross Russel R W (ed) Brain and Blood Flow, pp 351–353. Pitman, London

Slaunwhite W R, Sandberg A A 1959 Transcortin: a corticosteroid-binding protein of plasma. Journal of Clinical Investigation 38: 384–391

Smiddy J, Lewis H D Jr, Dunn M 1972 The effect of carotid massage in older men. Journal of Gerontology 271: 209–211

Soloman A, Kuhn L A 1960 Posteral hypotension, American Journal of Medicine 28: 328–332

Spingarn C L, Hitzig W M 1942 Orthostatic circulatory insufficiency. Archives of Internal Medicine 69: 23–40

Spokes E G S, Bannister R, Oppenheimer D R 1979 Multiple system atrophy with autonomic failure. Journal of the Neurological Sciences 43: 59–82

Sprunt J G, Maclean D, Browning M C K 1970 Plasma-corticosteroid levels in accidental hypothermia. Lancet i: 324–326

Stead E A, Ebert R V 1941 Postural hypotension. Archives of Internal Medicine 67: 546–562

Steinbrecher U P, Fitchett D E 1980 Torsade de pointes. A cause of syncope with atrioventricular block. Archives of Internal Medicine 140: 1223–6

Stewart T 1972 Treatment after exposure to cold. Lancet i: 140

Stoner H B, Frayne K N, Little R A, Threlfall C J, Yates D W 1980 Metabolic aspects of hypothermia in the elderly. Clinical Science 59: 19–27

Strandell T 1964 Circulatory studies in healthy old men. Acta Medica Scandinavica 175, suppl 414: 1–44

Streeten D H, Kerr C B Prior J C, Dalakos T G 1972

Hyperbradykinism: a new orthostatic syndrome. Lancet
ii: 1048–1053
Sullivan-Bolyai J Z, Lumish R M, Smith E W P, Howell J T,
Bregman D J, Lund M, Page R C 1978 Hyperpyrexia due to air-
conditioning failure in a Nursing Home. Public Health Reports
94: 466–470
Sundkvist G, Almér L-O, Lilja B 1979 Respiratory influence on heart
rate in diabetes mellitus. British Medical Journal 1: 924–5
Sundkvist G, Lilja B, Almér L O 1980 Abnormal diastolic blood
pressure and heart rate reactions to tilting in diabetes mellitus.
Diabetologia 19: 433–8
Sung J H, Mastri A R, Segal E 1979 Pathology of Shy-Drager
syndrome. Journal of Neuropathology and Experimental Neurology
38: 353–68
Tadzer I S 1961 Influence of hypothermia on intestinal absorption.
Acta Medica Iuagoslavica 15: 302–306
Taylor G 1964 The problem of hypothermia in the elderly.
Practitioner 193: 761–767
Taylor H L, Henschel A, Brožek J, Keys A 1949 Effects of bed rest
on cardiovascular function and work performance. Journal of
Applied Physiology 2: 223–239
Taylor P H, Gray K, Bicknell P G, Rees J R 1977 Glossopharyngeal
neuralgia with syncope. Journal of Laryngology and Otology
91: 859–68
Thames M D, Alpert J S, Dalen J E 1977 Syncope in patients with
pulmonary embolism. Journal of the American Medical Association
238: 2509–10
Thangarjah N, Hames T, Mubako H, Patel J, MacLennan W J 1980
The use of impedence cardiography in the young and elderly during
postural stress. Age and Ageing 9: 235–245
Thomas D J, Bannister R 1980 Preservation of autoregulation of
cerebral blood flow in autonomic failure. Journal of the
Neurological Sciences 44: 205–12
Thomas D J, Green I D 1973 Periodic hypothermia. British Medical
Journal 2: 696–697
Thomas J E, Schirger A, Love J G, Hoffman D L 1961 Postural
hypotension as the presenting sign in craniopharyngioma.
Neurology (Minneapolis) II: 418–423
Tolman K G, Cohen A 1970 Accidental hypothermia. Canadian
Medical Association Journal 103: 1357–1367
Tomiyama O, Shiigai T, Ideura T, Tomita K, Mito Y, Shinohara S,
Takeuchi J 1980 Baroreflex sensitivity in renal failure. Clinical
Science 58: 21–7
Towne W D 1972 Intractable ventricular fibrillation associated with
profound accidental hypothermia successfully treated with partial
cardiopulmonary by pass. New England Journal of Medicine
287: 1135
Trafford J A P, Hopkins A 1963 Deadly cold. British Medical Journal
1: 400
Trout H H 3rd, Brown L L, Thompson J E 1979 Carotid sinus
syndrome: treatment by carotid sinus denervation. Annals of
Surgery 189: 575–80
Turnbull C J, Palmer K T, Taylor B B 1981 Autonomic failure with
postprandial hypotension: case report. New Zealand Medical
Journal 93: 6–8
Vargas E, Lye M 1980 The assessment of autonomic function in the
elderly. Age and Ageing 9: 210–4
Verbow J L 1964 Modern treatment of myxoedema associated with
hypothermia. Lancet i: 194–196
Vilhelmsen R, Wennevold A, Olesen K H 1979 Syncope in aortic
stenosis. Ugeskrift for Laeger 141: 2754–2757
Villabos T J, Adelson E, Riley P A Jr, Crosby W H 1958 A cause of
the thrombocytopenia and leukopenia that occur in dogs during
deep hypothermia. Journal of Clinical Investigation 37: 1–7
Wagner H N 1959 Orthostatic hypotension. Bulletin of the Johns
Hopkins Hospital 105: 322–359
Wagner J A, Robinson S, Marino R P 1974 Age and temperature
regulation of humans in neutral and cold environments. Journal of
Applied Physiology 37: 562–565

Wagner J A, Robinson S, Tzankoff S P, Marino R P 1972 Heat
tolerance and acclimatization to work in the heat in relation to age.
Journal of Applied Physiology 33: 616–622
Warshaw T G 1973 Thermal studies in psoriasis. Journal of
Investigative Dermatology 60: 91–93
Watson W E 1962 Some circulatory responses to Valsalva's manoeuvre
in patients with polyneuritis and spinal cord disease. Journal of
Neurology, Neurosurgery and Psychiatry 25: 19–23
Watt S J, Troke J E, Perkins C M, Lee M R 1981 The treatment of
idiopathic orthostatic hypotension: a combined fludrocortisone and
flubiprofen regime. Quarterly Journal of Medicine 50: 205–12
Wedin B, Vanggaard L, Hirvonen J 1979 Parodoxical undressing in
fatal hypothermia. Journal of Forensic Sciences 24: 543–53
Weiss S, Baker J P 1933 The carotid sinus reflex in health and
disease: its role in the causation of fainting and convulsions.
Medicine 12: 297–354
Weissler A M, Warren J V, Estes E H 1957 Vasodepressor syncope:
factors influencing cardiac output. Circulation 15: 875–882
Wensel R H, Bigelow W G 1959 The use of heparin to minimise
thrombocytopenia and bleeding tendencies during hypothermia.
Surgery 45: 223–228
Weyman A E, Greenbaum D M, Grace W J 1974 Accidental
hypothermia in an alcoholic population. American Journal of
Medicine 56: 13–21
White N J 1980 Heart-rate changes on standing in elderly patients
with orthostatic hypotension. Clinical Science 58: 411–3
White W B, Reik L Jr, Cutlip D E 1981 Pernicious anaemia seen
initially as orthostatic hypotension. Archives of Internal Medicine
141: 1543–4
Wilcox C S, Aminoff M J, Kurtz A B, Slater J D H 1974a
Comparison of the renin response to dopamine and noradrenaline in
normal subjects and patients with autonomic insufficiency. Clinical
Science and Molecular Medicine 46: 481–488
Wilcox C S, Aminoff M J, Penn W 1974b Basis of nocturnal polyuria
in patients with autonomic failure. Journal of Neurology,
Neurosurgery and Psychiatry 37: 677–684
Wilson R J, Mills I H, De Bono E 1969 Cardiovascular reflexes and
the control of aldosterone production and sodium excretion.
Proceedings of the Royal Society of Medicine 62: 1257–1258
Wollner L 1966 In: Agate J N (ed), Medicine in Old Age, p 208.
Pitman Medical Publishing Co. Ltd., London
Wollner L 1967 Accidental hypothermia and temperature regulation in
the elderly. Gerontologia Clinica 9: 347–359
Wollner L 1978 Postural hypotension in the elderly. Age and Ageing
Suppl 112–8
Wollner L, McCarthy S T, Soper N D, Macey D J 1979 Failure of
cerebral autoregulation as a cause of brain dysfunction in the
elderly. British Medical Journal 1: 1117–8
Woollf P D, Hollander C S, Mitsuma T, Lee L A, Schach D S 1972
Accidental hypothermia: endocrine function during recovery.
Journal of Clinical Endocrinology Metab. 34: 460–466
Wynn V 1954 Electrolyte disturbances associated with failure to
metabolise glucose during hypothermia. Lancet ii: 575–578
Young R R, Asbury A K, Corbett J L, Adams R D 1975 Pure pan-
dysautonomia with recovery. Brain 98: 613–636
Ziegler M G, Lake C R, Kopin I J 1977 The sympathetic-nervous-
system defect in primary orthostatic hypotension. New England
Journal of Medicine 296: 293–297
Zsigmond E K, Starkweather W H, Anido V, Kothary S P, Flynn
K B 1978 Increased serum CPK activity and abnormal serum CPK
isoenzyme patterns in MH probands and MH families. In: Aldrete
J A, Britt B A (eds) Malignant hypothermia, Grune and Stratton,
p 239–41
Zuccalà A, Esposti E D, Sturani A, Chiarini C, Santoro A 1978
Autonomic function in haemodialyzed patients. International
Journal of Artificial Organs 1: 76–82

Special senses — aging of the eye

INTRODUCTION

An important external characteristic of old age is the sunken appearance of the eyes. This is due to a loss of orbital fat. It accounts for laxity of the eyelids resulting in senile ptosis and redundancy of skin on the eyelids. The pupil is small and an arcus senilis can be seen on the cornea. Visual acuity is diminished and the visual field shrunken (Weale, 1963a, b). Weale (1975) suggests that an important component of this is a 2.5 per cent loss of cerebral cells per annum. (See also p. 271.) The crystalline lens has long been unable to adapt its shape to permit the focusing of near objects, a state of presbyopia. Frequently in old age, physiological changes in ocular tissues overlap pathological conditions, the dividing line being poorly defined. This is particularly true of the crystalline lens in cataract.

Age changes in the eye can be fairly easily studied by the use of the slit-lamp microscope, ideally in cohort or longitudinal studies.

Some eyeball measurements are distributed normally in populations. As in diseases like essential hypertension and diabetes, so in eye diseases of senescence, important parameters in affected patients fit into an upper or lower 'tail' or 'cut-off' of distribution. An example is open angle glaucoma in which raised intraocular pressure is important. Population surveys show that both the mean and standard deviation or scatter of intraocular pressure increase in successively older age-groups. Thus an increasing proportion of the population fits into the upper 'tail' of the distribution of intraocular pressure with increasing age. This rise in intraocular pressure with increasing age is paralleled by an increase in the prevalence of open angle glaucoma. It is interesting that people with a family history of glaucoma fit into the group of subjects in the population whose intraocular pressure increases with age (Armaly, 1965).

The size of the crystalline lens and its increase in size with increasing age are probably modified by genetic and environmental factors. A large lens is clearly of importance in angle-closure glaucoma. Also important in this condition are a small cornea and small size of

eyeball which also seem to be genetically determined. It is therefore not difficult to see why glaucoma often seems to have an hereditary basis. It is probably either a dominant or polygenic multifactorial condition.

Ophthalmologists have long been aware that some eye diseases in aging patients have an hereditary basis. Waardenburg et al (1961a, b) mention that familial senile cataract was reported in 1834 and familial glaucoma in 1853. Nordmann (1965) has referred to senile cataract as 'an hereditary exaggeration of physiological aging'.

EYELIDS

In senile *entropion* of the lower eyelid (Plate 21.1) the eyelashes cause irritation by rubbing against the cornea and conjunctiva. This probably results from loss of orbital fat causing backward displacement of the eye and consequent laxity of the eyelids (Fox, 1959; Foulds, 1961). The only effective treatment is a simple operation, e.g. a resection of the lower eyelid and excision of redundant skin (Foulds, 1961, 1962).

Laxity of the eyelids is probably also an important mechanism in *ectropion* of the lower eyelid which results in epiphora. Wedge resection of the lower eyelid, sometimes associated with insertion of a skin graft into the lower lid, is the method of treatment.

Trichiasis, or ingrowing eyelashes is a troublesome condition requiring repeated epilation.

Senile ptosis (Plate 21.2) also results from a backwards displacement of the eyeball with increasing age but very seldom requires treatment.

Basal cell carcinoma of the eyelids (Plate 21.2) is treated by excision and a skin graft rather than by radiotherapy. Enlarging malignant melanomas of the eyelids are treated similarly, sometimes after biopsy.

LACRIMAL APPARATUS

Epiphora is common in old patients and is most often due to obstruction of the nasolacrimal duct. Conditions which cause an excessive production of tears, for example, corneal and subtarsal foreign bodies, and corneal ulcers should be looked for in patients with watery eyes. The only effective treatment of nasolacrimal duct obstruction in old patients is an operation to bypass the obstruction. In dacryocystorhinostomy, the lacrimal sac is anastomosed to the mucosa of the middle meatus of the nose through a bony ostium made in the lacrimal bone. This operation is not often justified in aged patients who merely have epiphora. Acute dacryocystitis causes an inflammatory swelling at and just below the medial canthus of the eye. Incision and evacuation of a lacrimal abscess as well as treatment with antibiotics is then often needed. After resolution of inflammation, dacryocystorhinostomy or dacryocystectomy (excision of the lacrimal sac, a surprisingly effective operation) should be undertaken since recurrence of the acute dacryocystitis is common.

CORNEA AND CONJUNCTIVA; SCLERA

In arcus senilis or gerontoxon (Plate 21.3) lipid substances are deposited at the periphery of the cornea. A narrow interval separates this from the whiteness of the sclera. Marin-Amat (1956) showed that with increasing age a transition from 'with-the-rule' to 'against-the-rule' corneal astigmatism occurs. Hence in aged eyes, a greater vertical than horizontal corneal radius is much commoner than in young patients (Fig. 21.1). This is again believed to be due to a progressive loss of orbital fat with increasing age and a backwards displacement of the eyeball. The eyelids then press less heavily against the eyeball (Weale, 1963c).

Priestley Smith (1890) found that the horizontal diameter of the cornea was smaller in the old than in the young and he suggested this might indicate a reduction

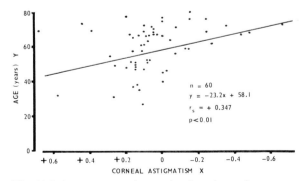

Fig. 21.1 A scattergram of corneal astigmation and age. 'Against the rule' astigmatism is found in old patients due to loss of orbital fat and backwards displacement of the eyeball. Another result of this is senile entropion. (Data from Leighton and Tomlinson, 1972, unpublished observations).

in volume of the whole eyeball with increasing age. Ultrasonic measurements of eyeball axial length in 72 normal subjects by Leighton and Tomlinson (1972) supported this view.

Keratoconjunctivitis sicca is particularly common among patients with rheumatoid arthritis. Because of reduced formation of tears, the normal lubrication of the conjunctiva and cornea is lacking. Affected patients complain of irritation and dryness of the eyes. 'Artificial tears' are prescribed in the form of guttae methylcellulose 1 per cent. Necrotizing sclero-keratitis is an occasional and severe condition also found in patients with rheumatoid arthritis.

Tumours at the limbus, the junction between cornea and sclera are liable to occur in old patients, the commoner ones being epithelioma and malignant melanoma. These are usually excised and a corneal graft inserted if necessary. In advanced cases the eye is enucleated.

THE UVEAL TRACT

The pupil is small in old age, possibly due to atrophy and increased rigidity of the iris (Weale, 1963d). A shallow anterior chamber is also common in old patients (see below) and predisposes to angle-closure glaucoma. Caution is therefore required in dilating the pupil, especially in patients with a shallow anterior chamber.

Choroidal sclerosis in old patients, an appearance familiar to ophthalmoscopists, probably indicates vascular sclerosis of the choroid. A familial incidence of central, circumpapillary and generalized types is described by Sorsby (1970a).

Malignant melanomas sometimes occur in the iris and ciliary body, when they may be associated with cataract, but are much more common in the choroid. Malignant melanoma of the choroid is the most common of all intraocular tumours. It presents as a gradually increasing visual field defect, but is frequently not noticed by the patient until an occasion when he closes his opposite eye. By then the tumour may be quite large. A retinal detachment is seen which is partly solid, partly fluid in appearance.

Treatment is usually enucleation of the eye, but local excision of the tumour if possible or radiotherapy are preferred if there is little sight in the opposite eye.

Metastases arising from tumours of the breast, bronchus and other sites are occasionally seen, and are often bilateral. They are treated with radiotherapy.

ANTERIOR CHAMBER

Intraocular pressure and glaucoma

Aqueous humour is formed in the ciliary body by ultra-

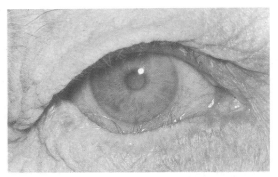

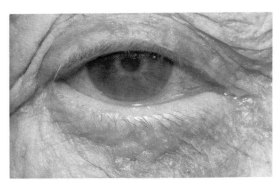

Plate 21.1. Senile entropion. The margin of the lower eyelid has rolled backwards and the eyelashes are brushing against the conjunctiva and cornea.

Plate 21.2. Senile ptosis is present and an early basal cell carcinoma of the lower eyelid can be seen.

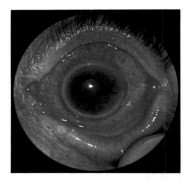

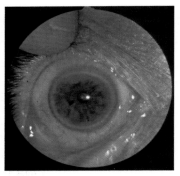

Plate 21.3. Acute closed angle glaucoma.
(**a**) Affected eye. Conjunctival hyperaemia and a relatively dilated pupil are seen. A dull appearance of the cornea due to oedema is also evident.

(**b**) Unaffected eye of same patient. No conjunctival hyperaemia is present and the pupil is relatively small. A bright lustre of the cornea is evident in contrast to the affected eye. A prominent arcus senilis is present.

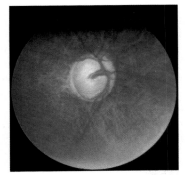

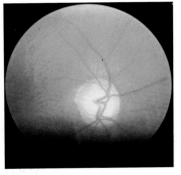

Plate 21.4. (**a**) Glaucomatous cupping of the optic disc. Following elevation of intra ocular pressure, a normal physiological excavation has changed to an appearance of pathological excavation with pallor.

(**b**) Optic disc in the contralateral eye of the same patient showing an optic cup which is still within normal limits of size and colour.

filtration and active transport mechanisms (Duke-Elder, 1968). It passes through the pupil to enter the anterior chamber, escaping from the eye through the filtration angle of the anterior chamber at the junction of cornea with iris and ciliary body. Here aqueous passes through the trabecular meshwork and into Schlemm's canal. Electron microscopic studies (1965) show that aqueous probably passes by micropinocytosis as vacuoles through the endothelial cells lining the inner trabecular wall of Schlemm's canal. Aqueous leaves Schlemm's canal by collector channels in which it passes to the episcleral veins. These were named 'aqueous veins' by Ascher (1942). He was the first to describe laminar flow in them, i.e. in the same vessel a column of aqueous is seen alongside a column of blood.

The intraocular pressure is largely determined by the rate of formation of aqueous and the resistance to its escape from the eye. The normal intraocular pressure has been investigated in population surveys, e.g. Armaly (1965), Hollows and Graham (1966), Bankes et al (1968). The incidence of glaucoma in these surveys has been found to be about 0.5 per cent of the population over the age of 40 years. The distribution of intraocular pressure as measured by tonometry in these population surveys was only roughly Gaussian. Thus when successively older age-groups were analysed, the distribution became increasingly skewed due to the inclusion of an increasing proportion of persons with intraocular pressures in the high to normal range. The mean intraocular pressure rose, also suggesting that a rise in a portion of the population occurs with increase in age. This trend is more marked in females than males in the age-group 60 to 69 years and also in those with a family history of glaucoma (Armaly, 1965).

Aqueous outflow resistance can be measured in patients by a tonometer, adapted for the purpose, although the results are not accurate enough to be of any real practical value in the management of patients. Weekers et al (1956), Becker (1958) and Boles-Carenini and Cambiaggi (1959) showed that outflow resistance increased with age, although Grant (1951), de Roetth and Knighton (1952) and Spencer et al (1955) reported that it was not age-dependent.

Glaucoma in adult and aged patients (other than secondary glaucoma due, for example, to iridocyclitis, cataract and some ocular tumours) is classified as either angle-closure glaucoma or open-angle glaucoma according to the classification suggested by Barkan (1938). In angle-closure glaucoma the mechanism for the rise in intraocular pressure is now fairly clearly understood (see below).

Angle-closure glaucoma

Clinical picture. A rise in intraocular pressure results from blockage of the filtration angle of the anterior chamber by the iris, in an eye predisposed to angle closure by a shallow anterior chamber and a narrow angle. In acute cases a large portion of the circumference of the filtration angle suddenly becomes blocked by the iris and a sudden and marked rise in intraocular pressure occurs. This causes severe pain in and over the eyes often associated with vomiting. Oedema of the cornea also occurs leading to blurring of vision and a misty appearance of the cornea. The pupil becomes dilated, oval and unresponsive to light (see Plate 21.3). Such a severe attack is often preceded by mild self-limiting angle closure attacks. These occur chiefly in the evening with slight ocular pain, blurring of vision, and with haloes round lights, in which all the spectral colours are seen. A survey of patients presenting with angle-closure glaucoma (Leighton et al, 1971) showed that an acute or subacute attack had occurred in half the total number of cases. A further third presented with a chronic insidious onset, by which time prolonged elevation of intraocular pressure had usually resulted in damage to the optic disc.

Mechanism. It has long been known that hypermetropia is common in patients with angle-closure glaucoma (Fuchs, 1923; Sugar, 1941; Davenport, 1959). Hypermetropic eyes tend to be small and to have shallow anterior chambers (Rosengren, 1931, 1950; Sorsby et al, 1957; Grieten and Weekers, 1962a). The latter was noted to be a prominent feature of many cases of glaucoma by Priestley Smith (1911), Rosengren (1950), and of angle-closure glaucoma by Törnquist (1956), Grieten and Weekers (1962a) and Lowe (1968). The depth of the anterior chamber becomes reduced with increasing age (Raeder, 1922; Rosengren, 1950). The size and position of the structures bordering the anterior chamber, i.e. the cornea, iris and lens, determine its depth. Hence in angle-closure glaucoma, lens thickness measured antero-posteriorly is greater than in normal eyes (Aizawa, 1960; Gernet and Jürgens, 1965; Lowe, 1969; Storey and Phillips, 1971). Corneal diameter (Grieten and Weekers, 1962b; Storey and Phillips, 1971), corneal height, measured from the plane of the junction between sclera and cornea, to the apex of the cornea (Storey and Phillips, 1971) and axial length of eyeball (Lowe, 1970; Storey and Phillips, 1971) are all smaller in angle-closure glaucoma eyes than in normal eyes. Priestley Smith (1911) suggested that the lens may be abnormally large in proportion to the corneoscleral envelope in glaucoma. The following characteristics, a thick lens, small corneal diameter and height, and a small axial length of eyeball all contribute to shallowness of the anterior chamber. When a critical amount of shallowing of the anterior chamber has occurred, the iris tends to billow forward in the stream of aqueous which flows through the pupil and blocks the angle of the anterior chamber. This appearance is known as Iris

Bombé. Instillation of mydriatic eyedrops can in such predisposed eyes result in angle-closure glaucoma.

The lens not only increases in size with increasing age (Priestley Smith, 1883, see Fig. 21.2) but also comes to lie with its anterior surface further forward (Lowe, 1970a). These are two important factors in the reduction of anterior chamber depth with increasing age. Priestley Smith (1890) found that the horizontal diameter of the cornea is less in the old than in the young (as did Storey and Phillips, 1971), and suggested this may indicate that the volume of the whole eyeball becomes reduced with increasing age. Age changes in the collagen of the corneoscleral envelop might account for a reduction in the size of the cornea and the whole eyeball (Leighton and Tomlinson, 1972), either of which could be a factor in reduction in depth of the anterior chamber with increasing age.

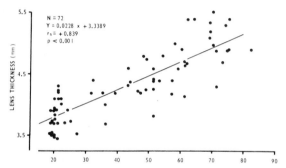

Fig. 21.2 A scattergram of lens thickness and age. Anteroposterior thickness of the crystalline lens was measured by ultrasonics in 72 normal subjects (Leighton and Tomlinson, 1972, unpublished observations).

Treatment. The emergency treatment of angle-closure glaucoma is best undertaken in an eye ward. Initially the affected eye is treated intensively with guttae pilocarpine 2 per cent, i.e. one drop every second five times, one drop every minute five times, one drop every five minutes five times and thereafter one drop every half hour until an ophthalmologist arrives. To the unaffected eye which is predisposed to angle closure, guttae pilocarpine 0.5 per cent is given every three hours. Prompt constriction of the pupil in the affected eye usually indicates that the filtration angle has opened and treatment has been effective. Even if treatment with guttae pilocarpine is continued, angle closure is very likely to return, an event which will probably be prevented by a prompt iridectomy operation. If the pupil is still dilated and the intraocular pressure raised about three hours after the start of treatment, an intramuscular injection of 500 mg acetazolamide (Diamox) is given. This suppresses aqueous formation. Operation

to relieve the raised intraocular pressure is performed soon afterwards. If treatment has not opened the filtration angle, a drainage operation (usually an iris inclusion operation) is done. General anaesthesia is preferred although local anaesthesia can be used. In chronic closed-angle glaucoma, either an iridectomy or a drainage operation is carried out depending on the state of the angle.

Winter (1955) and others have shown that 40 to 60 per cent of unaffected though predisposed eyes of patients presenting with acute closed-angle glaucoma, develop angle closure within five years even if treated with guttae pilocarpine. A prophylactic peripheral iridectomy is therefore performed almost routinely in these unaffected eyes. A high degree of protection against angle closure results, probably because the tendency for the iris to billow forwards is reduced.

Open angle glaucoma

Patients with open angle glaucoma, as well as those with chronic closed-angle glaucoma, usually present to ophthalmologists when an asymptomatic and prolonged elevation in intraocular pressure has resulted in pathological cupping or abnormal excavation of the optic disc and in visual field defects called arcuate scotomata. In open angle glaucoma the filtration angle is seen to be unobstructed by the iris. The patient often only seeks medical attention when a visual field defect begins to threaten the central part of his vision. Otherwise his glaucoma may be detected by an optician, or during a medical examination when a definitely pathological or suspicious appearance of the optic disc is seen with an ophthalmoscope (see Plate 21.4). Ophthalmoscopy by an experienced observer even without measurement of the intraocular pressure is probably at present as good a method as any of screening for glaucoma (Graham and Hollows, 1966). Especially in pedigrees with a high prevalence of glaucoma, the screening of first-degree relatives of glaucoma patients is worthwhile (Becker, Kolker and Roth, 1960; Miller and Paterson, 1962; Graham, 1966; Leighton, 1976).

Mechanism. In open angle glaucoma, raised intraocular pressure is probably due to an abnormally high resistance to outflow of aqueous from the eye in the trabecular meshwork and possibly other outflow channels. The precise reason for this is not known. The trabecular meshwork has been of interest to many research workers. Only minimal differences between the appearances of the collagen in the trabecular meshwork in glaucomatous eyes and in normal eyes of corresponding age have so far been found (Rohen, 1970).

A search for characteristic ocular dimensions in open angle glaucoma has been unproductive (in contrast to angle-closure glaucoma) except for anterior chamber depth which has been reported by some to be slightly, though significantly, shallower than in controls (Törnquist and Brodén, 1958; Tomlinson and Leighton, 1972) and by others as of normal depth.

A high incidence of myopia in open angle glaucoma has been reported by Weekers et al (1958) and others. The large eyeball in myopia may be unduly susceptible to raised intraocular pressure, especially as eyeballs with a high axial length have been shown by Tomlinson and Phillips (1969) to have more extensive physiological cupping than small eyeballs. Armaly (1969) has suggested that the size of the physiological cup, i.e. the cup/disc ratio, may be a factor determining the susceptibility of eyes with raised intraocular pressure to visual field defects. Abdalla and Hamdi (1970) showed that myopic eyes have higher intraocular pressures than emmetropic eyes. Tomlinson and Phillips (1970) showed that large eyeball size as well as myopia was associated with higher intraocular pressure than small eyeball size and emmetropia or hypermetropia. This also perhaps helps to explain the high prevalence of myopia in cases of open angle glaucoma.

Some workers believe that inadequate blood supply to the optic disc is important in the pathogenesis of visual field defects in glaucoma. Drance (1968) for example suggests that atherosclerotic disease in the small vessels to the optic disc is important in open angle glaucoma. There is probably a tendency to high blood pressure in glaucoma (Kümmell, 1911; Vele, 1933; Leighton and Phillips, 1972). This might predispose to atherosclerotic disease in the optic disc. Leighton and Phillips (1972) also found a significant correlation between intraocular pressure and blood pressure in cases of open angle glaucoma.

Treatment. The aim of treatment in open angle glaucoma is to prevent any further deterioration of the visual fields by medical control of the intraocular pressure, e.g. guttae pilocarpine 1 to 4 per cent, guttae phospholine iodide (β blockers) and guttae tosmilen bromide, or guttae adrenaline. Diamox is only occasionally used as a long-term medication because of its liability to cause renal calculi. If, in spite of medical treatment, the visual field defects enlarge, and the intraocular pressure remains high, a drainage operation, e.g. a trabeculectomy, will allow escape of aqueous from the anterior chamber and its absorption in the sub-conjunctival space, thereby controlling the intraocular pressure.

Heredity and glaucoma
There have been many reports of inheritance in glaucoma. For example, Waardenburg et al (1961) mention reports of many dominant, some recessive and a few examples of X-linked recessive transmission. Francois and Heintz de Bree (1966) showed that there is a very variable prevalence of open angle glaucoma in families with affected members. Hence in the families of 26

index patients, 47 other cases of open angle glaucoma were found out of 186 relatives who were examined. A penetrance of 98 per cent for a dominant gene was calculated in these families. However, from the families of another 43 index patients only one additional case of glaucoma was found out of 322 relatives examined. Surprisingly these authors supported the view of a dominant heredity in open angle glaucoma with variable penetrance of the gene.

Families of patients with angle-closure glaucoma would probably show a similar variation in prevalence to the condition although Törnquist (1953) and Miller (1970) suggest a dominant heredity in angle-closure glaucoma. Sorsby (1970b) stated that 'whether glaucoma is monofactorial or polygenic, is still open to question'. He suggested that environment plays an important part in the aetiology of glaucoma.

Lowe (1970b) suggests a polygenic aetiology in angle-closure glaucoma. Size and growth of the crystalline lens, corneal dimensions and eyeball size which contribute to a shallowness of the anterior chamber found in the condition, are likely to be controlled by genetic and environmental factors. Genetic control of size of lens, cornea and whole eyeball may be determined for each dimension separately (i.e. polygenetically) or for all dimensions together (by a single dominant gene).

A polygenic aetiology has been suggested in open angle glaucoma by Armaly (1967a, b) who showed that size of physiological cup and cup/disc ratio and intraocular pressure are genetically determined. It is interesting that Pickering (1968) suggested a multifactorial aetiology in essential hypertension.

CRYSTALLINE LENS

Presbyopia
The focusing power of the average eye will, by the age of 45 to 50 years, have become so reduced that clarity of vision for near objects will only be possible at an uncomfortably long distance from the eye to the object of attention, e.g. newsprint can be focused clearly only if the newspaper is held at arm's length. Relaxation of the suspensory ligament of the lens by the action of the ciliary muscle will result in only a limited amount of forward bulging of the anterior pole of the lens, and thickening of the antero-posterior diameter of the lens. Thus the lens is no longer able to alter its shape and become sufficiently convex to permit focusing of close objects, since it has set in its flat unaccommodated form (Weale, 1963e). There is also a reduction in elasticity of the lens capsule (Fisher, 1969).

Glasses will have now become necessary for reading and close work, and as the power of accommodation dwindles still further a progressive increase in the strength of the near correction will be needed.

In non-Caucasians, the onset of presbyopia is usually appreciably earlier than 45 years and often as early as 40 years.

Cataract

Nordmann (1965) regards senile cataract as 'an hereditary exaggeration of physiological aging', and suggests that investigation of the problem of senile cataract involves geneticists, morphologists and biochemists. The lens in old age will accordingly be considered under these three headings.

Heredity. Waardenburg et al (1961b) report many examples of heredity in senile cataract. Nordmann (1965) in speculating about future trends in research on cataract, believed the one-gene-one-enzyme hypothesis may help in the understanding of the problem of cataract.

Morphology. The crystalline lens is probably a unique structure in that new lens fibres are constantly being formed throughout life and old lens fibres are not lost, but come to lie progressively deeper and more distant from the capsule of the lens. Hence the lens increases in size throughout life. Priestley Smith (1883) was the first to demonstrate this. Figure 21.2 shows a scattergram of lens thickness and age. Increase in lens size results in an increased rigidity of the lens which probably leads to presbyopia and is also an important factor in the aetiology of angle-closure glaucoma (see above).

As the lens ages, its nucleus becomes increasingly hard (Weale, 1963f), a feature well known to ophthalmic surgeons and affecting the management of cataract. Nuclear sclerosis aptly describes a type of cataract in old patients, so common as to be regarded as a normal age change, in which the lens nucleus is hard, dense, usually has a high refractive index, and is relatively opaque.

Sippel (1965) suggests that the reduction in metabolic activity in the lens with increasing age, which accompanies nuclear sclerosis, occurs because as the lens grows its increase in volume is relatively great compared to its increase in surface area.

Fisher (1970, 1973) demonstrated that the shear stresses between human lens fibres during accommodation were likely to be at a maximum between the ages of 55 and 60 years, resulting in the familiar wedge-shaped lens opacities.

Maclean and Taylor (1981) outline an objective clinical method of quantitation of cortical cataract in patients using a pattern analysing computer.

Black et al (1960) first described posterior subcapsular cataracts of a characteristic appearance in patients taking cortisone by mouth. No biochemical explanation for the appearance of these cataracts has yet been found.

Biochemistry. The metabolism of the lens and its abnormalities leading to cataract is a highly complex subject and very imperfectly understood (See Nordmann (1965), Kinoshita (1973) and Bloemendal (1981) for reviews of the subject).

Duncan and Bushell (1975) contrasted the ionic constituents of cataracts, and found that Na^+, K^+, Ca^{++}, Mg^{++} and Cl^-, tended to be present in relatively normal concentrations in nuclear cataract, but were abnormal in other types of cataract.

Of particular interest is the metabolism of glutathione, a tripeptide, which is present in high concentrations in the normal lens and is reduced in concentration in almost all types of cataract (see Reddy, 1971).

Low-molecular-weight soluble proteins have been of interest to research workers. Hence Francois et al (1965) noted a reduction in levels in the lens with increasing age and also found reduced amounts in cataract. This decrease in concentration may result from a conversion to insoluble protein (Pirie, 1968; Sheridan and Zigman, 1971) or leakage from the lens through its capsule (Charlton and van Heyningen, 1968). Spector (1973) found a shift to higher molecular weight alpha crystalline with increasing age.

Pirie (1965) combined epidemiological and biochemical studies in a fairly well-defined population and showed that operations for senile cataract were necessary in four to six times as many diabetics as non-diabetics, and that poorly controlled diabetics are more likely to require cataract extraction than well-controlled diabetics. The same author found greater quantities of sorbitol, glucose and fructose in diabetic than in non-diabetic lenses.

Ohrloff et al (1980) demonstrated by an immunological technique, a reduction of activity in nearly all those lenticular enzymes involved in carbohydrate metabolism.

Hockwin and Ohrloff (1981) in a review article indicate a greater heterogeneity of the structure of enzymes in the crystalline lens with increasing age, including the formation of metenzymes, which they regard as the consequence of post-translational modifications rather than to transcription or translational errors. A lack of enzymal effectiveness results. Such age-dependent changes in enzymes are relatively easily demonstrated even within the highly complex labyrinths of lens metabolism and probably give insight into the fundamental nature of aging.

Management of cataract

Increasing myopia is frequently found in patients with nuclear sclerosis, hence a change of glasses is often all that is needed in early cataract. Central lens opacities can also be treated by a dilatation of the pupil using guttae homatropine if there is no danger that closure of the aqueous filtration angle might result.

In unilateral cataract it is important to exclude trauma, intraocular foreign bodies and tumours. Otherwise such unilateral cataracts are not removed unless complications arise in the affected eye, e.g. secondary closed-angle glaucoma or phako-anaphylactic uveitis, or unless the vision is poor in the other eye for some other reason. The decision to remove a cataract is made when poor sight interferes with normal activities sufficiently to justify operation. Cataracts do not necessarily need to reach 'maturity' before removal. There is an increasing preference for general anaesthesia by ophthalmic surgeons rather than local anaesthesia which can be very troublesome especially in restless, apprehensive or deaf patients. Improvements in the technique of cataract extraction, i.e. better suturing materials and the insertion of several sutures into the corneoscleral incision, have coincided with a realization of the need for early mobilization. Thus the time spent in hospital following a cataract operation need only be two to seven days.

The aging patient, compared to a younger patient, faces a testing time after he obtains the glasses which correct his aphakic condition. An average correction is +11 dioptres with 1 to 2 dioptres of astigation for distance. This results in a $1.3 \times$ magnification of the image. Also, spherical aberration results in much distortion of peripheral vision; straight objects appear curved. Contact lenses can offset these undesirable optical side-effects of cataract removal but are often far too troublesome for old patients. Increasing use is being made by ophthalmic surgeons of the insertion of an artificial intraocular lens at the time of cataract extraction, held in position by a constricted pupil or by means of a deliberately retained lens capsular 'bag' when an 'extra-capsular' method of cataract extraction is used. Alternatively fixation is achieved by an intraocular lens which crosses a diameter of the anterior chamber and engages by means of suitably elongated processes into the irido-corneal angle. Such techniques require the highest microsurgical standards, as well as optimal anaesthesia. Potential consequences are compromised function of the decreasing (age-dependent) corneal endothelial cell population resulting in loss of corneal transparancy.

The known increased risk of retinal detachment and glaucoma in patients who have had cataracts removed can discourage ophthalmologists from extracting either the patient's second cataract or a uniocular cataract.

VITREOUS AND RETINA

Optic nerve
Progressive degeneration of the vitreous body occurs with increasing age, accelerated by myopia and pathological conditions such as uveitis. Often vitreous opacities result and patients describe these as black objects or 'floaters' in their vision. The chief importance of these symptoms is that they should be carefully differentiated from the early symptoms of retinal detachment. This is often heralded by the sudden appearance of such 'floaters' which coincide with the appearance of a vitreous haemorrhage due to the formation of a retinal hole. As the retina detaches, a corresponding visual field defect results. Prompt referral to an ophthalmologist is necessary.

Senile changes are seen in the retinal blood vessels with increasing age. Involutionary arteriosclerosis (Duke-Elder, 1967) indicated by a diffuse narrowness and straightness of the arterioles, which tend to obscure venules at crossing points, is described in senile eyes. These changes are believed to occur quite independently of hypertension and it is upon these changes that the appearances of true hypertensive retinopathy are superimposed. Fundus appearances must always be evaluated against this background of normal change with aging, an important point to be borne in mind in the management of hypertension in the old.

A common feature of aged eyes is colloid bodies or drusen. These are seen in the fundus as small pale patches especially round the posterior pole. They consist of hyaline degeneration and are situated in Bruch's membrane of the choroid. Senile macular degeneration is quite common in old patients, the typical appearance being a coarse dark mottling around the macula. The 'Moorfields Macular Study Group' (1982) in a controlled trial of argon laser photocoagulation in macular degeneration could not demonstrate any significant visual benefits in this treatment though some types may be improved. Otherwise the only treatment for the resultant poor vision is strong reading glasses and a low-vision aid, e.g. a magnifying glass. The condition may be genetically determined (Duke-Elder, 1966; Sorsby, 1970c).

Diabetic retinopathy is a fairly common cause of blindness in the older age groups although it is already an important cause in middle life (Sorsby, 1973). The most important principle of treatment is, of course, the careful control of blood sugar levels; light coagulation (Xenon arc or laser) is occasionally used.

It is generally assumed that the optic disc becomes paler with increasing age.

Occlusive disease of the retinal blood vessels requires careful evaluation to detect underlying pathological conditions. These include hypertension, atheromatous disease either local or in the carotid or vertebral systems, conditions of abnormal blood viscosity, temporal arteritis and glaucoma. The last two conditions demand especially great care in the management of both eyes, because the unaffected eye may be in imminent danger. Hence immediate measurement of the blood sedimentation rate and the intraocular pressure are obligatory in all cases of occlusive retinal vascular disease.

Sudden loss of vision occurs and this is more profound in arterial than venous occlusions. In temporal arteritis there is often general malaise, headache, anorexia and sometimes polymyalgia rheumatica.

Ophthalmoscopy in central or branch retinal arterial occlusion reveals a pallor of the retina due to coagulative necrosis especially at the posterior pole. This obscures choroidal structures except at the fovea centralis where the pinkness of the choroidal circulation will still be seen as a 'cherry-red spot'. Stasis in the retinal circulation is seen. Often in temporal arteritis, retinal structures appear normal, but the optic disc is pale and swollen with a few small haemorrhages surrounding it, i.e. 'ischaemic papillopathy'. However, the loss in vision will be just as serious as in central retinal artery occlusion. In a central or branch vein occlusion, haemorrhages along retinal veins, posterior polar oedema and some optic disc oedema are seen.

Emergency treatment is aimed at overcoming the obstruction in central retinal artery occlusion by vasodilator drugs, but the chance of relieving obstruction more than two hours after its onset is slight. Immediate referral to an ophthalmologist for retrobulbar injection of isoxsuprine HC1 is necessary. Treatment will otherwise be to the underlying cause, e.g. in the case of temporal arteritis, the immediate commencement of a course of systemic cortisone. Anticoagulants are not of any proven value.

Patients with tobacco amblyopia are mostly pipe-tobacco smokers who complain of poor vision in both eyes. A scotoma between the blind spot and fixation is found. Detection is most important because treatment with neocytamen injections (hydroxocobalamin, and not cyanocobalamin) brings about a very marked improvement in vision, even if (against advice) the patient continues to smoke.

REFERENCES

Abdalla M I, Hamdi M 1970 Applanation ocular tension in myopia and emmetropia. British Journal of Ophthalmology 54: 122–125

Aizawa K 1960 Studies on the depth of the A C The axial depth of the A C in glaucomatous eyes. Acta Societa Ophthalmologica Japonica 64: 869–888

Armaly M F 1965 On the distribution of applanation tension. Archives of Ophthalmology (New York) 73: 11–18

Armaly M F 1967a Genetic determination of cup/disc ratio of the optic nerve. Archives of Ophthalmology (New York) 78: 35–43

Armaly M F 1967b The genetic determination of ocular pressure in the normal eye. Archives of Ophthalmology (New York) 78: 187–192

Armaly M F 1969 Cup/disc ratio in early open angle glaucoma. Documenta Ophthalmologica 26: 526–533

Ascher K W 1942 The aqueous veins. American Journal of Ophthalmology 25: 1174–1209

Bankes J L K, Perkins E S, Tsolakis S & Wright J E 1968 Bedford Glaucoma Survey. British Medical Journal i: 791–796

Barkan O 1938 Glaucoma: classification, causes and surgical control. American Journal of Ophthalmology 21: 1099–1113

Becker B 1958 The decline in aqueous secretion and outflow facility with age. American Journal of Ophthalmology 46: 731–736

Becker B, Kolker A E, Dale Roth F 1960 Glaucoma family study. American Journal of Ophthalmology 50: 557–567

Black R L, Oglesby R B, von Sallmann L, Bunim J J 1960 Subcapsular cataracts induced by cortico-steroids in patients with rheumatoid arthritis. Journal of the American Medical Association 174 (No. 2): 166–171

Bloemendal H (ed) 1981 Molecular and Cellular Biology of the Eye Lens. Wiley-Interscience, New York, Chichester, Brisbane, Toronto

Boles-Carenini B, Cambiaggi A 1959 Are aqueous humour dynamics influenced by aging? American Journal of Ophthalmology 44: 395–401

Charlton J M, van Heyningen R 1968 An investigation into the loss of proteins of low molecular size from the lens in senile cataract. Experimental Eye Research (London) 7: 47–55

Corsellis J A N, Alston R L, Miller A K H 1975 Cell counting in the human brain: traditional and electronic methods. Postgraduate Medical Journal 51: 722–726

Davenport R C 1959 Facets of glaucoma. Transactions of the Ophthalmological Societies of the United Kingdom 79: 3–14

Drance S M 1968 Some studies of the relationships of haemodynamics and ocular pressure in open angle glaucoma. Transactions of the Ophthalmological Societies of the United Kingdom 88: 633–640

Duke-Elder S 1966 System of Ophthalmology, Vol. IX, Diseases of the Uveal Tract. p 613. London: Kimpton

Duke-Elder S 1967 System of Ophthalmology, Vol. X, Diseases of the Retina. p 305. London: Kimpton

Duke-Elder S 1968 System of Ophthalmology, Vol. IV, The Physiology of the Eye and of Vision, p 186. London: Kimpton

Duncan G, Bushell A R 1975 Ion analyses of human cataractous lenses. Experimental Eye Research (London) 223–230

Fisher R F 1969 The significance of the shape of the lens and the capsular energy changes in accommodation. Journal of Physiology 201: 1, 21–47

Fisher R F 1970 Senile cataract: a comparative study between lens-fibre stress and cuneiform opacity formation. Transactions of the Ophthalmological Societies of the United Kingdom 90: 93–109

Fisher R F 1973 Human lens fibre transparency and mechanical stress. Experimental Eye Research (London) 16: 41–49

Foulds W S 1961 Surgical cure of senile entropion. British Journal of Ophthalmology 45: 678–682

Foulds W S 1962 Correspondence. British Journal of Ophthalmology 46: 634

Fox S A 1959 The aetiology of senile entropion. American Journal of Ophthalmology 48: 607–611

Francois J, Rabaey M, Stockmans L 1965 Gel filtration of the soluble proteins from normal and cataractous human lenses. Experimental Eye Research (London) 4: 312–318

Francois J, Heintz De Bree C 1966 Personal research on the heredity of chronic simple (open-angle) glaucoma. American Journal of Ophthalmology 62: 1067–1071

Fuchs E 1923 Textbook of Ophthalmology, 7th edn (trans. Duane), p 795–796. London and Philadelphia: Lippincott

Gernet H, Jürgens V 1965 Echographische befunde beim primär-chronischen Glaukom. Albrecht Von Graefe's Archiv fur Klinische und Experimentelle Ophthalmologie 168: 419–422

Graham P A 1966 Screening for chronic glaucoma. Proceedings of the Royal Society of Medicine 59: 1215–1220

Graham P A, Hollows F C 1966 Glaucoma, Epidemiology, Early Diagnosis and Some Aspects of Treatment. ed. Hunt L B, p. 114. Edinburgh and London: E & S Livingstone

Grant W M 1951 Clinical measurements of aqueous outflow. Archives of Ophthalmology (New York) 46: 113–131

Grieten J, Weekers R 1962a Étude des dimensions de la chambre antérieure de l'oeil humaine. Ophthalmologica (Basel) 143: 56–66

Grieten J, Weekers R 1962b Étude des dimensions de la chambre antérieure de l'oeil humaine. III. Dans le glaucome à angle fermé et dans le glaucome à angle ouvert. Ophthalmologica (Basel) 143: 409–422

Hall T C, Miller A K H, Corsellis J A N 1975 Variations in the human Purkinje cell population according to age and sex. Neuropathology and Applied Neurobiology 1: 267–292

Hockwin O, Ohrloff C 1981 In: Bloemendal H (ed) 'Molecular and Cellular Biology of the Eye Lens' Enzymes in Normal, Aging and Cataractous Lenses; p 367–413

Hollows F C, Graham P A 1966 Intra-ocular pressure, glaucoma and glaucoma suspects in a defined population. British Journal of Ophthalmology 50: 570–586

Holmberg A S 1965 Schlemm's canal and the trabecular meshwork. An electron microscopic study of the normal structure in man and monkey (Cercopithecus Ethiops). Documenta Ophthalmologica 19: 339–373

Kinoshita J H 1973 Lens and development. Experimental Eye Research (London) 15: 143–264

Kronfeld P C 1953 Eye changes due to advanced age. Illinois med. J. 103: 104–107

Kümmell R 1911 Untersuchungen über Glaukom und Blutdruck. Albrecht Von Graefe's Archiv fur Klinische und Experimentelle Ophthalmologie 79: 183–209

Leighton D A 1976 A survey of the first-degree relatives of glaucoma patients. Transactions of the Ophthalmological Societies of the United Kingdom 96: 28–32

Leighton D A, Phillips C I, Tsukahara S 1971 Profile of presenting states of eyes in angle-closure glaucoma. British Journal of Ophthalmology 55: 577–584

Leighton D A, Phillips C I 1972 Systemic blood pressure in open angle glaucoma, low tension glaucoma and the normal. British Journal of Ophthalmology 56: 447–453

Leighton D A, Tomlinson A 1972 Changes in axial length and other dimensions of the eyeball with increasing age. Acta Ophthalmologica 50: 815–826

Leighton D A, Tomlinson A 1972 Unpublished observations

Lowe R F 1968 Time-amplitude ultrasonography for ocular biometry. American Journal of Ophthalmology 66: 913–918

Lowe R F 1969 Causes of shallow anterior chamber in primary angle-closure glaucoma. American Journal of Ophthalmology 67: 87–93

Lowe R F 1970a Anterior lens displacement with age. British Journal of Ophthalmology 54: 117–121

Lowe R F 1970b Aetiology of the anatomical basis for primary angle-closure glaucoma. Biometric comparisons between normal eyes and eyes with primary angle-closure glaucoma. British Journal of Ophthalmology 54: 161–169

Maclean H, Taylor C J 1981 Experimental Eye Research 33: 597–602. An objective staging for cortical cataract in vivo aided by pattern analysing computer

Marin-Amat M 1956 Les variations physiologiques de la courbure de la cornée pendent la vie. Leur importance et transcendance dans la réfraction oculaire. Bulletin de la Societe Belge d'Ophthalmologie 113: 251–293

Miller S J H, Paterson G D 1962 Studies on glaucoma relatives. British Journal of Ophthalmology 46: 513–522

Miller S J H 1970 Genetics of closed angle glaucoma. Journal of Medical Genetics 7: 250–252

'The Moorfields Macular Study Group' 1982 British Journal of Ophthalmology 66: 576–579. Retinal pigment epithelial detachments in the elderly; a controlled trial of argon laser photocoagulation

Nordmann J 1965 Present state and perspectives in research of the lens. Investigative Ophthalmology 4: 384–397

Ohrloff C, Bensch J, Jaeger M, Hockwin O 1980 Experimental Eye Research (London) 31: 573–579. 'Immunologic detection of inactive enzyme molecules in the aging lens'

Pickering G W 1968 High Blood Pressure 2nd edn, p 275. London: Churchill

Pirie A 1965 Epidemiological and biochemical studies of cataract and diabetes. Investigative Ophthalmology 4: 629–637

Pirie A 1968 Colour and solubility of the proteins of human cataracts. Investigative Ophthalmology 7: 634–650

Raeder J C 1922 Die Lage und Dicke der Linse bei Emmetropen,

Hypermetropen und myopen Albrecht Von Graefe's Archiv fur Klinische und Experimentelle Ophthalmologie 110: 73–108

Reddy V N 1971 Metabolism of glutathione in the lens. Experimental Eye Research (London) 11: 310–328

Rohen J W 1970 The morphologic organization of the chamber angle in normal and glaucomatous eyes. Advances in Ophthalmology 20: 80–92

De Roeth A, Knighton W S 1952 Clinical evaluation of the aqueous flow test. Archives of Ophthalmology (New York) 48: 148–153

Rosengren B 1931 Studien über die Tiefe der vorderen Augenkammer mit besonderer Hinsicht auf ihr Verhalten beim primären Glaukom. Acta Ophthalmologica 9: 103–179

Rosengren B 1950 Studies in the depth of the anterior chamber of the eye in primary glaucoma. Archives of Ophthalmology (New York) 44: 523–528

Sheridan E J, Zigman S 1971 Fate of human lens soluble proten during cataractogenesis. Experimental Eye Research (London) 12: 33–38

Sippel T O 1965 Energy metabolism in the lens during aging. Investigative Ophthalmology 4: 502–513

Smith, Priestley 1883 On the growth of the crystalline lens. Transactions of the Ophthalmological Societies of the United Kingdom 3: 79–99

Smith, Priestley 1890 On the size of the cornea in relation to age, sex, refraction and primary glaucoma. Transactions of the Ophthalmological Societies of the United Kingdom 10: 68–78

Smith, Priestley 1911 Glaucoma problems. Ophthalmic Review 30: 97–107

Sorsby A 1970 In Ophthalmic Genetics, 2nd edn (a) p 144; (b) p 36; (c) p 151. London: Butterworth

Sorsby A 1973 Prevention of blindness: present prospects. Health Trends 5: 7–9

Sorsby A, Benjamin B, Davey J B, Sheridan M, Tanner J M 1957 Emmetropia and its Aberrations. Special Report Series of the Medical Research Council No. 293. London: HMSO

Spector A 1973 The aging of alpha-crystallin: a review. Experimental Eye Research (London) 16: 115–121

Spencer R W, Helminck E D, Scheie H G 1955 Tonography: technical difficulties and control studies. Archives of Ophthalmology (New York) 54: 515–527

Storey J K, Phillips C I 1971 Ocular dimensions in angle-closure glaucoma. British Journal of Physiological Optics 26: 228–242

Sugar H S 1941 The mechanical factors in the aetiology of acute glaucoma. American Journal of Ophthalmology 24: 851–873

Tomlinson A, Phillips C I 1969 Ratio of optic cup to optic disc in relation to axial length of eyeball and refraction. British Journal of Ophthalmology 53: 765–768

Tomlinson A & Phillips C I 1970 Applanation tension and axial length of eyeball. British Journal of Ophthalmology 54: 548–553

Tomlinson A, Leighton D A 1972 Ocular dimensions in low tension glaucoma compared with open angle glaucoma and the normal. British Journal of Ophthalmology 56: 97–105

Törnquist R 1953 Shallow anterior chamber in acute glaucoma. A clinical and genetic study. Acta Ophthalmologica suppl. 39

Törnquist R 1956 Chamber depth in primary acute glaucoma. British Journal of Ophthalmology 40: 421–429

Törnquist R, Broden G 1958 Chamber depth in simple glaucoma. Acta Ophthalmologica KBH 36: 309–323

Vele M 1933 Sui rapporti tra arteriosclerosi e glaucoma. Annali di ottalmologia e clinca occelista 61: 511–520

Waardenburg P J, Franceschetti A, Klein D 1961 Genet Ophthal, vol. I (a) p 604; (b) p 910. Assen, Netherlands: Royal Van Gorcum

Weale R A 1963 The Aging Eye. (a) p 144; (b) p 142; (c) p 33; (d) p 56; (e) p 112; (f) p 85. London: H K Lewis & Co. Ltd

Weale R A 1975 Senile changes in visual acuity. Transactions of the Ophthalmological Societies of the United Kingdom 95: 36–38

Weekers R, Watillon M, De Rudder M 1956 Experimental and clinical investigations into the resistance to outflow of aqueous humour in normal subjects. British Journal of Ophthalmology 40: 225–233

Weekers R, Lavergne G, Prijot E 1958 La correction des mesures tonométriques chez les sujets à rigidité basse en haute. Annales d'oculistique 191: 26–31

Winter F C 1955 The second eye in acute primary shallow-chamber angle glaucoma. American Journal of Ophthalmology 40: 557–558

Special senses — the aging auditory system

SYMPTOMS

Hearing is impaired with advancing age, both as the result of physiological effects of aging itself and also by the superimposition of pathological changes. Several functional abnormalities associated with the aging auditory system can be identified: impaired sensitivity; derangement of loudness perception; disturbance of localization and direction detection; decline in discrimination, especially of speech; decrease in time-related processing abilities; tinnitus. An increased, age-related prevalence of vertigo is the result of aging processes which affect the whole labyrinth including the vestibular portion.

Impaired sensitivity

It has been confirmed that from the third decade of life onwards the threshold of people who have normal hearing in early adulthood tends to deteriorate as a result of age. Population studies clearly demonstrate this hearing loss (Hinchcliffe, 1959a; Glorig et al, 1957) in which, first of all, sensitivity at the upper end of the auditory scale (high frequencies) declines gradually.

Threshold of hearing for pure tones as a function of age was measured on random samples of representative rural populations (that is, not exposed to excessive noise) in Great Britain (Hinchcliffe, 1959b). This made it possible to calculate the average amount of loss at a given age (Fig. 22.1) and it was possible to calculate then a probable maximum limit of impairment at each decade (Fig. 22.2). This was confirmed by a more recent investigation by Siegalaub et al (1974) who examined the auditory sensitivity of 33 146 subjects aged 30 to 59. The greatest differences in hearing loss of 40 dB or more at 4000 Hz were those between men and women: 2.5 to 5 times more men had hearing loss. The next largest differences were related to age; losses ranged from 1.5 to 4 times more frequent in each older decade compared with the preceding one. The knowledge of the average amount of hearing loss that might be expected to have occured at a given age has acquired important legal significance. When a person claims damages as a result

Correction of Pure Tone Audiograms

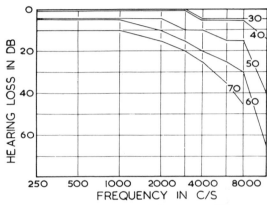

Fig. 22.1 Hearing loss due to the aging process. The curves indicate an average amount of hearing loss that might be expected to have occurred at given ages. (From Hinchcliffe, 1959c).

of noise damage, one can estimate to what degree age-related hearing loss contributed to the total defect.

This gradual age-related impairment is sensorineural, in which generally there is a tendency for the high

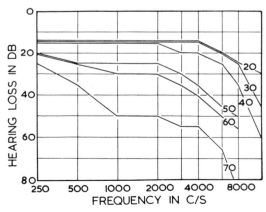

Fig. 22.2 The curves indicate a *probable maximum* limit of hearing loss at each decade (From Hinchcliffe, 1959c)

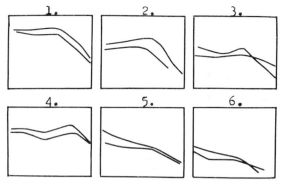

Fig. 22.3 Audiograms of elderly subjects. There is a considerable variation in the degree of hearing loss.

frequencies to be affected first. High frequency hearing is phylogenetically a younger development. Younger structures are also more complex, with a greater metabolic rate and therefore more vulnerable to certain unfavourable influences. The high frequency component can thus be damaged selectively (Fisch, 1970), as often happens in sensorineural hearing loss.

When elderly subjects with hearing difficulty are examined by pure tone audiometry, we do not always obtain the regular curves as shown in the average audiograms from population studies. A variety of patterns will be noted with an emphasis on the decline for the higher notes, usually the same in both ears.

Recent surveys (Chamberlain, 1971; Fisch, 1971) revealed audiograms as illustrated in Figure 22.3. They can be classified according to their patterns and summarized as follows:

1. Within normal limits (loss in essential frequencies not greater than 20 dB)
2. Slight impairment (loss up to 30 dB, but not above)
3. Moderate impairment (loss between 30 and 40 dB)
4. Moderately severe impairment (loss between 30 and 50 dB)
5. Severe impairment (loss between 50 and 70 dB)
6. Very severe impairment (loss 70 dB or more).

An audiometric survey by Milne and Louder (1975) confirmed the result obtained by previous investigators.

The threshold audiometric test is easily applied and is still the most useful hearing test in existence. For this reason a preoccupation with changes of sensitivity to pure tones prevailed for a long time. Although a test of absolute sensitivity to pure tones reveals useful information about the physiological condition of the hearing apparatus, it does not disclose some important aspects of deterioration.

Difficulty in hearing speech

There is a close relationship between loss of hearing for

pure tones and for hearing speech but no complete overlap between the two. The audiogram does not enable us to forecast *precisely* how hearing for speech will be affected. We can do so within certain limits. For example, the impairments illustrated in the audiograms in Figure 22.3 can be translated approximately into the following categories as regards hearing speech in ordinary, reasonably favourable, circumstances.

Within normal limits
   Slight impairment. Some difficulties but a somewhat louder voice should be heard well.
   Moderate impairment. Difficulties in hearing a quiet voice or even a normal conversational voice in somewhat less favourable conditions.
   Moderately severe impairment. Considerable difficulties in hearing normal conversational voice, but speech heard properly when voice moderately loud and combined with lip-reading; understanding of speech still good.
   Severe impairment. Impossible to hear normal voices even in best conditions. Difficulties in understanding even a very loud voice without lip-reading.
   Very severe impairment. Normal voice not heard at all. Very loud voice heard but impossible to understand. Communication difficulties severe even with lip-reading.

Many attempts to standardize the evaluation of hearing of speech from pure tone audiometric results have been made. The usual method is to average the hearing loss in the essential frequencies important for hearing speech sounds.

Compared to normal hearing, an average hearing level of 15 dB at the frequencies of 1000, 2000 and 3000 Hz will indicate: (1) negligible impairment in understanding sentences heard under conditions of complete quiet; (2) an 8 per cent impairment in understanding sentences heard in a mild background of noise, and (3) pronounced impairment in conditions of increased noise stress, frequently distortions of the speech signal and use of individual words out of sentence context. (The American Academy of Ophthalmology and Otolaryngology.)

Tests of sensitivity for hearing speech can be carried out by listening to undistorted test words above threshold intensities, in favourable conditions without the presence of background noise. The number of correctly repeated words is scored and a graph compiled (speech audiometry). This test has been thought to reflect *all* the difficulty which a person with hearing impairment may have in understanding speech.

Within certain limits, correlation between the two types of sensitivity tests, pure tone and hearing speech, is quite a good one. It is closer in younger than in older age groups, because of difficulties in the latter in speech discrimination even when audiograms are similar (Pestalozza and Shore, 1955).

Many elderly people with hearing impairment have considerable difficulty in understanding speech when circumstances are less favourable (background noise, bad acoustic conditions, speech a little faster than normal). This difficulty is greater than one would expect from both the pure tone and the speech articulation tests. Obviously such tests do not reveal additional inherent difficulties in the elderly. Fournier (1954) considered the reduced speech perception in aged persons to be due in part to a lengthening of time required by the higher listening centres to identify the message. Calearo and Lazzaroni (1957) found that with an increase in the speed of speech, younger listeners could still achieve good understanding, although they required a slight increase in the intensity of the signal. Older listeners, however, could no longer understand much of the speech at any intensity.

It seems that the time factor plays a complex role in processing information transmitted by auditory communication. The duration of various components of speech varies greatly. When the time-component of reaction is distorted, understanding of speech may be distorted. Consonants have durations not much longer than 10 seconds (Littler, 1965). Signals of this duration are dealt with by an auditory mechanism which is separate from that dealing with longer duration tones (Baru, 1966, 1967; Gabor, 1946, 1947, 1953).

The time factor is probably also influenced by a certain degree of demyelination which consequently slows down the speed of signal transmission in the nervous pathway. Generally, speech sounds last on the average 4 milliseconds or so and there are rapid changes between them, for instance from vowels to plosives. In a communication system when such a quick succession of signals is essential for its efficiency, a very fast transmission is necessary. The aging system is less able to cope with the necessary speed of transmission.

Bergman (1971) pointed out that although tests for undistorted and uncompeted speech samples may not show much decline in hearing speech with advancing age, tests of understanding speech under difficult conditions still reveal progressive decline. For these reasons, tests based on articulation scores for undistorted and uncompeted test words and sentences must be augmented by tests in which selection of a desired signal and rejection of an undesired competing signal is involved. This will reflect the real difficulties in communicating by speech in social circumstances, which is one of the outstanding symptoms of hearing difficulty in the elderly. Study of the relationship of aging and auditory performance by such methods reveals difficulties inherent in older age.

There are other influences which affect intelligibility of speech. Various forms of distorted speech are less intelligible to the elderly than to the young (Bocca, 1958). Speech occurring in rooms with long reverberation is also much less intelligible to the elderly (Schubert, 1958). Auditory temporal discrimination (Weiss, 1959) and auditory reaction time (Feldman and Roger, 1967) and frequency discrimination (König, 1957) also decline.

Various degrees of hearing loss for the different frequencies play an important role in understanding speech well. High frequency loss itself contributes significantly and in more severe cases decisively to the difficulty in understanding speech. Vowel sounds (which are of longer duration) are mainly in the lower range of notes; consonant sounds (which are of shorter duration) are mainly in the higher range. Much of the information in speech is encoded in the consonant sounds. When these cannot be heard well, speech may become quite unintelligible. Fortunately, many consonants can be lip-read and lip-reading can compensate to a large extent in the understanding of speech in high frequence hearing loss. With elderly deaf people this helps, but even then the time factor in processing the information remains.

From a practical point of view all the separate reasons which cause difficulty in understanding speech fuse and come to the surface during group conversation. In the great majority of elderly hard of hearing people the greatest single social disability is created by the difficulty in understanding speech in group conversation. They may be able to understand (possibly with moderate amplification) in face to face conversation with one person, but are totally unable to do so in group conversation and this becomes a disability which causes the greatest concern and distress.

Tinnitus

Tinnitus is an internal noise, generated within the hearing system. It can be a most distressing symptom. Although many types of hearing disorder at all ages are associated with tinnitus, it seems that a much higher proportion of old people suffer from it.

Data for prevalence of tinnitus vary in different surveys. Hinchcliffe (1961) gave 37 per cent as the prevalence in the age group 65 to 75 years. In a USA survey (US Department of Health Education and Welfare Report, 1968), the prevalence rate for tinnitus was assessed. In the 18 to 24 year group 3 per cent complained of severe tinnitus; in the 55 to 64 year group it had increased to 9 per cent and in the 65 to 74 year group to 11 per cent. These figures apply to both sexes. When men and women were assessed separately it transpired that more women complained of tinnitus than men. For example, in the 65 to 74 year group 10 per cent of men and 12.5 per cent of women complained of severe tinnitus.

Tinnitus is experienced by many people with normal hearing (Hempstock and Atherley, 1971). A study of elderly people by Milne (1976) also disclosed that tinnitus in the elderly is not necessarily related to hearing loss.

Some elderly people with considerable hearing loss associated with tinnitus consider the internal noise as the principal symptom ('I don't mind being deaf, if only I could get rid of this noise').

The degree of tolerance or distress from tinnitus varies. It is not necessarily related to the intensity of the noise but is modified by various aspects of mental and physical health.

Some people who suffered extreme distress (not infrequently with suicidal tendencies) benefited from psychiatric treatment which made it possible for them to tolerate their tinnitus (Goldie, 1977).

Drugs, so far, have been disappointing in the treatment of tinnitus.

Some progress has been made by the use of the 'tinnitus masker' in alleviating the distressing effect of the internal noise. These are hearing aid type instruments which generate a noise which masks the tinnitus. To many sufferers this particular noise is more bearable. The type of noise generated by the instrument is adjusted according to the type of tinnitus.

Abnormal loudness perception

This occurs in two forms: hypersensitivity to sounds of high intensity and the 'loudness recruitment' phenomenon. In the latter the rate of loudness-increase in sounds of gradually increasing intensity is greater than in a normally hearing subject. Amplified sound to a person with loudness recruitment feels unpleasantly harsh and difficult to tolerate.

Hypersensitivity is noted by many elderly subjects with hearing loss. This becomes apparent when a speaker is asked to speak louder, or the output of a hearing aid is increased, in the hope of achieving better intelligibility. An intensity level which would be still tolerable to a normal person, becomes then intolerable or even painful to the elderly person with hearing loss.

The loudness recruitment phenomenon occurs in sensorineural hearing loss when the disorder lies in the sensory hair cells in the inner ear (Yantis, 1955). It is not identical with hypersensitivity but in some cases they are related. It makes discrimination of amplified sound much more difficult. The prevalence of the loudness recruitment phenomenon among the aged deaf is not known with any degree of accuracy, but approximate figures suggest that it occurs in about 50 per cent of cases (Pestalozza and Shore, 1955).

Sound localization

Sound localization contributes to effectiveness of signal detection and helps with discrimination (for example hearing the wanted signal against a background of ambient noise). Loss of directional hearing results in greater hearing difficulty in a noisy environment. Localization and direction detection can be disrupted for several reasons. First of all, this happens when the hearing loss is strongly asymmetric but it can be also of central origin.

Localization is based on (1) a timing delay in the arrival of the signal in the two ears, but also on (2) comparison of intensities detected at each ear. The timing delay is manifested in two aspects of the auditory signal. First, the sound begins and ends sooner in the ear closer to the source ('transient disparity') and secondly, throughout the duration of the sound the sound waves reaching the far ear will be slightly delayed ('ongoing disparity'). Humans rely on both transient and ongoing disparity to determine the source of a sound (Knudsen, 1981).

The signals are also subjected to neural processing in parts of the auditory pathway and the various cues delivered by the peripheral receptors are converted into spatial information in certain parts of the auditory system. In the elderly, apart from reasons located in the peripheral receptors, disturbed localization of the sound source can be also the result of deterioration in the central auditory pathway.

Vertigo

The age function for vestibular behaviour does not exhibit a simple parallel to hearing. The vestibular portion of the labyrinth has an inherent capacity to resist change as compared with greater vulnerability of the cochlear portion. However, the prevalence of vertigo increases with age but with a fall in the prevalence in the oldest men. Sheldon (1948) gave prevalences in persons of 65 years and over of 39 per cent in men and 57 per cent in women. Approximately the same figures are given in the US National Health Survey (1968) with the same observation of a fall in prevalence in older age groups.

Vestibular responsivity is measured by the caloric test (warm and cold irrigation) and observation of resulting nystagmus. Bruner and Norris (1971) found that all parameters of nystagmus showed increased responsivity with age into the sixties, followed by a decline. Age-related increments in nystagmus were more marked for warm stimuli than cold. Spontaneous or positional nystagmus did not vary in incidence with age.

Age-related histological changes were described in detail in the cochlear portion of the labyrinth but corresponding changes in the vestibular portion have not been documented as well. Johnsson and Hawkins (1972) observed degeneration of the macula of the saccule with severe loss of its otoconia. There was less severe degeneration of the utricular macula. Loss of otoconia and sacular degeneration may be important causes of vestibular disturbances in elderly people.

The complexity of the disorder

It is evident that auditory dysfunction in the elderly is a complex disorder with various contributing and interacting factors. Apart from the deterioration which can certainly be attributed to impairment in the auditory system, a considerable amount of evidence suggests that some of the difficulties originate from deterioration in other systems as well.

The rate of information processing over the sensory channels of the aged is reduced (Talland, 1968). For a given rapid rate of information, the old people would be expected to perform more poorly than the young. This suggests a narrowing of the communication channel capacity (Miller, 1956) which results in a reduced rate in processing information.

PATHOLOGY

To what extent can the various manifestations of disordered hearing in the elderly be supported by evidence of pathological or morphological change? Some claim that specialized speech tests are useful in differentiating brain-stem and cortical lesions (Calearo, 1957; Matzker, 1959; Sanchez Longo, 1957; Jerger, 1960). Bocca (1958) found that the performance of the elderly on various types of distorted speech material is similar to that of subjects with temporal lobe tumours. By inference he concluded that auditory discrimination problems of the aged are primarily cortical in nature. Cawthorne (1951), König (1957), Klotz and Kilbane (1962) and Calvi and Finzi (1957) are of the same opinion.

There is no evidence available according to which one could determine reliably, by hearing tests alone, the site of lesion.

Histological findings in the inner ear

Schuknecht (1955), from histological studies of animal and human cochlea, has described two types of presbyacusis. The first, referred to as epithelial atrophy, commences in middle life. It is characterized by progressive degeneration of the structures of the cochlea from base to apex. Both afferent and efferent nerve fibres are affected. The second, neural atrophy, begins late in life. It is superimposed on epithelial atrophy and is associated with degeneration of the spiral ganglion cells in the base of the cochlea. In the cochleas of 30 aged people, Nomura and Kirikae (1968) found loss of sensory cells (most severe near the basal end of the cochlea). Both afferent and efferent nerve fibres showed marked changes (near the basal

end and less towards the apex). Johnsson and Hawkins (1972) observed in cochleas of 150 subjects (including foetuses to a person 97 years of age) that hair cell degeneration in the organ of Corti can be observed at a very young age. With aging, hair cell and nerve degeneration progressed to involve mainly the first half of the basal turn. In the elderly, degeneration of outer hair cells in the apical turn was a regular finding. In most cases hair cell degeneration preceded nerve degeneration, which occurs secondarily. Only a few cases of neural presbyacusis were seen with primary nerve degeneration and preservation of the organ of Corti. Fleischer (1952) reported atrophy of the stria vascularis, restricting thus the blood supply of the neurosensory receptor. The stria vascularis must play a vital rôle in inner ear function. Morphological changes in this structure of the cochlea should provide important clues for the study of various types of deafness. In histological studies of cochleas of subjects of various ages (free from infection) no atrophic changes were found in specimens from children, but atrophy appeared as age increased, especially above 60 years (Takahashi, 1971). Degeneration of the stria vascularis was noted most often in the apical and lower basal turn of the cochlea after the age of 60 years. Gacek (1968) identified four histopathological types of presbyacusis according to the morphological changes in the cochlea.

Sensory. The effect of aging on the organ of Corti consisting of a loss of hair cells and supportive cells.

Neural. Loss of neurons in the cochlea (and in the auditory pathways).

Metabolic. The pathological correlate is atrophy of the stria vascularis.

Mechanical. Loss of elasticity in the vibrating partition (the basilar membrane).

A progressive narrowing of the inner auditory canal (*porus acousticus int.*), thus pressing on the eighth nerve, was also observed (Sercer and Krmpotic, 1958).

Michael and Wells (1981) reviewed the pathological changes in conjunction with the resulting audiometric patterns in the different types of presbyacusis:

1. *Sensory.* Deafness commences in middle age and is very slowly progressive. The audiogram shows an abrupt high-tone hearing loss. The cochlea shows atrophy of the organ of Corti in the basal turn. The supporting and basal cells are atrophied. These changes may be associated with secondary degeneration.

2. *Neural.* This form of presbycusis can commence at any age. Speech discrimination is poor as compared to thresholds on pure tone audiogram. There is degeneration of cochlear neurones in the entire cochlea, worse in the basal turn.

3. *Vascular.* Hearing loss is insidious in onset between the third and sixth decades of life and is progressive. Audiometric pattern is flat with good speech discrimination. The stria vascularis may show

partial or diffuse atrophy. Cystic structures may sometimes be seen in the stria vascularis.

Histological findings in the central nervous system

Undoubtedly many of the features of auditory disorders associated with age are not peripheral in origin. In some cases the inner ear may not even be involved (Hallpike, 1962).

Kirikaé et al (1964) reported changes in the major nuclei of the auditory pathway, including atrophy and pyknotic nuclei of the ganglion cells. Hansen and Reske-Nielsen (1965, 1968) reported changes in the cortical areas concerned with hearing.

The middle ear

There is some evidence that age changes occur also in the conductive system. Nixon et al (1962) noted how the tympanic membrane thickens and loses its elasticity. They suggest that there is a diminution of the mechanical efficiency of the articulation of the ossicular chain. All this would result in a conductive hearing loss.

The differential diagnosis between conductive and sensorineural hearing loss is usually not difficult. A test in which hearing by air conduction is compared to that by bone conduction usually provides the answer. A gap between the two types of hearing (bone conduction better than air conduction) indicates a conductive loss. Glorig and Davis (1961) compared the air and bone conduction thresholds of 164 men aged 25 to 80 years. Their findings suggested that the air–bone gap is a function of age. This has not been confirmed by other workers (van der Waal, 1962; Sataloff et al, 1965; Miller and Ort, 1965).

Since a new technique for assessing accurately middle ear function has become available (impedance measurement), the question to what degree 'stiffening' of middle ear structures contributes to presbyacusis should be resolved.

Bone conduction tests may present some difficulty in some of the elderly people but the use of impedance testing for assessing middle ear function can easily resolve this problem.

This technique should enable us for the first time to assess precisely the mobility of the tympanic membrane, the dynamics of the ossicular chain and the middle ear pressures in the elderly. The test is easy to apply, the results are recorded automatically and no active co-operation is required from the subject (all he has to do is to sit quietly for about a minute). The new technique for assessment of middle ear function has made a significant contribution to more accurate diagnosis. Impedance measurements should be now part of the routine investigation of hearing loss in the elderly. Treatment of the conductive element, superimposed on a sensorineural loss, may improve hearing considerably in many cases.

Conductive loss may be present as a result of obstruction by wax. Green (1970) found that in one-third of those elderly patients who complained of deafness, wax (cerumen) in the external meatal canal contributed to or even caused it. In another enquiry (Williams, 1970), in 49 out of 283 elderly people with hearing impairment there was wax in both ears and in 61 in one ear. Thus 110 subjects had ears that were blocked by wax.

Milne (1976) found in a sample of 487 elderly people wax in 45 per cent of men and 38 per cent of women. Strangely enough he stated that 'the presence of wax was not associated with any increase in hearing loss'. But he tested (by audiometry) only at two frequencies (1000 Hz and 4000 Hz). Wax notoriously impairs hearing mainly for low frequencies. This illustrates the inadequacy of audiometry when only a limited range of frequencies is used.

Pathological and environmental influences

Three major influences seem to enhance the progression of hearing loss with advancing age — previous middle-ear disease, vascular disease and exposure to noise (Schmidt, 1967). The picture is complicated by the fact that it is not easy to distinguish between the physiological processes of normal aging and pathological changes which would cause hearing impairment of their own.

Exposure to noise is particularly blamed as a contributory factor. The difference in the degree of hearing loss between elderly men and women found in some population studies (Hinchcliffe, 1959a, b) is attributed to the greater noise exposure of men. Noise-induced hearing loss shows specific characteristics and by careful study, taking into account the corrections appropriate for an age group, one could differentiate between the two pathologies (Hinchcliffe, 1971). Data are available to make presbyacusis corrections to data for noise-exposed populations (Robinson, 1968, 1971).

This problem has gained importance in relation to assessment of the degree of disablement from noise damage for purposes of compensation. Dixon Ward (1971) stated that one of the most persistent medico-legal problems in the area of occupational deafness involves the so-called correction for presbyacusis. Opinions vary as regards age-related hearing loss correction in occupational (noise-induced) deafness. According to Dixon Ward there is no experimental evidence that sensorineural hearing losses are additive.

When the effect of aging in cases of deafness from acoustic trauma or other wartime noise exposure was tested audiometrically (Macrae, 1971), it was found that threshold levels at both 1000 and 4000 Hz had increased by approximately the amounts predicted by presbyacusis curves. The results support the hypothesis that presbyacusis and noise-induced hearing loss are independent.

Vascular disease is blamed by several workers. There

are some indications that the severity of hearing loss is related to the degree of degenerative arterial disease (Fabinyi, 1931). This was reasserted by Rosen (1969) and Bochanek and Jachowska (1968). Rosen and Olin (1966) stated that a longitudinal study had shown that the institution of a nonatherogenic diet is associated with better hearing levels. These trends are reversed when the diets of the control and the experimental groups are interchanged (Rosen, 1969).

Hansen (1968) studied the relation of arterial hypertension to neurosensory hearing loss but found no correlation between the two.

There is no direct evidence to show that vascular lesions alone can be responsible for extensive damage to the organ of Corti. Comparison between a group of old people in good health and a group of individuals with cardiovascular disorders, hypertension, familial history of deafness and metabolic disease, does not show a significant difference in so far as the relation between hearing loss and discrimination loss is concerned. Health conditions do not seem to influence the amount of hearing loss in people of the same age group (Pestalozza and Shore, 1955).

The relative contributions of various pathological influences towards hearing difficulties are not known on a population basis. Clark (1971), on the basis of a clinical study of 204 elderly patients in an otological outpatients' department, estimated that 46 per cent had middle-ear disease, 54 per cent inner-ear disease, 14 per cent neural disease and 23 per cent central disease (many patients having multiple pathology).

It has been suggested that ototoxic drugs may affect the aging auditory system to a greater extent, as compared with the younger one. This concerns specially the ototoxicity of aminoglycosides (such as gentamycin). McDowell (1982) carried out animal experiments to find out if age is a predisposing factor. He examined the hair cell loss in guinea pig ears and he found no difference in the younger and older age groups as far as ototoxic effects of gentamycin are concerned; in both groups he found the same degree of cochlear hair cell loss.

The syndrome of presbyacusis

Deterioration of sensory preception with advancing age is not limited to the hearing system. Sensory systems which are not subjected to environmental assaults to the same degree as the hearing system also deteriorate with advancing age in a similar proportion (Hinchcliffe, 1962).

The available evidence indicates that what is known as 'presbyacusis' or 'old age deafness' is a complex clinical and pathological entity. Pestalozza and Shore (1955) stated that the specific hearing loss associated

with advancing age can be considered as a syndrome when the following criteria are fulfilled:

1. Negative otoscopic and rhinoscopic findings and no previous ear diseases
2. No previous severe general diseases
3. Sixty years of age or older
4. Audiometric indication of sensory neural hearing loss
5. Pure tone audiogram shows a gradually increasing loss for the higher frequencies
6. Onset of deafness gradual and progressive for less than 10 years before the test
7. Bone conduction almost equal to air conduction
8. Right and left ear air conduction almost equal (not differing by more than 15 dB at any frequency)
9. Average hearing loss for pure tones (500 to 200 Hz) between 10 and 60 dB.

There is enough evidence to show that, in spite of the complexity of the clinical and pathological picture, there is a distinct progressive sensorineural hearing loss showing certain characteristics, which is the function of advancing age, and that the deterioration is not limited to the peripheral sensory receptor. In spite of all the above-mentioned investigations, it still remains a puzzle why in some elderly people, the hearing can remain only slightly impaired or very nearly normal, while in others without any obvious reason a very severe progressive hearing loss can develop. It is quite possible that this relates simply to the effectiveness of blood supply to the brain and may be related to the size of the carotid artery which is subject to natural variation. A good blood supply will certainly help to maintain good function for a much longer time. Further detailed investigation based on well controlled population survey is required.

PREVALENCE

Reported prevalence of impaired hearing in the elderly differs accroding to criteria which have been used to estimate it.

Good data are available on the distribution of hearing impairment based on pure tone audiometry. Hinchcliffe (1959a, b) in a population survey in British rural areas found that in the age group 65 to 74 years, 21 per cent had a hearing loss greater than 25 dB. He also found a significant sex difference in the age group of 55 years and over for certain frequencies (3000 to 8000 Hz). A US survey (US Department of Health Education and Welfare, 1965) revealed 28 per cent of those aged 65 to 74 years and 48 per cent of those aged 75 to 79 years had a hearing loss greater than 15 dB.

In a sample of 6672 persons representing non-institutionalized adults in the USA, aged 18 to 79 years (US

Dept. Health Education and Welfare, 1968), it was found that hearing levels for men and women steadily deteriorated from the youngest to the oldest age group and beginning with age 65 years the threshold of hearing rose with each successive age group, increasing more rapidly at 2000 Hz. Above 2000 Hz, women had substantially better hearing. For men the increase per decade of age from the youngest to the eldest age group ranged from two decibels at 500 Hz to 10 decibels at both 4000 and 6000 Hz.

A stratified random sample of the population was examined by Wilkins (1948). His findings are shown in Table 22.1. They show 12.2 per cent hearing difficulty for the population aged 64 to 74 years. It is considered that this survey underestimated the prevalence of hearing difficulties in the elderly population. Another survey undertaken in the same year (Sheldon, 1948) produced a figure of 31 per cent, for all of pensionable age, while Hobson and Pemberton (1955) have come up with a figure as high as 39.5 per cent. A survey by Harris (1962) revealed that 30 per cent of people over 65 admitted hearing 'difficulties' and that a further 1.5 per cent had such difficulties without admitting them. Over 50 per cent (1116 out of 2081) of a sample of people over 80 questioned, had impaired hearing (Lempert, 1958). A survey of persons aged 65 and over, carried out throughout Britain in 1962 (Government Social Survey, 1962), found that 27.9 per cent admitted difficulty in hearing and a further 3.8 per cent were considered by the interviewers to have such difficulty, making a total of 31.7 per cent. In a national survey of people over 65 years (367 000 persons) conducted by Townsend and Wedderburn (1965), over 30 per cent had difficulty in hearing.

Table 22.1 Hearing difficulty in a random population sample of persons (Wilkins, 1948)

Age group	Difficulties in hearing (%)
25 to 34	1.6
44 to 54	4.7
64 to 74	12.2
74+	27

Investigations have been carried out in various special groups. Williams (1970) studied 283 applicants to the Local Authorities for social welfare services, aged 70 years and over. Eighty-eight had difficulty in communicating by speech because of hearing difficulty. Millard (1969) found that, in patients of 70 years of age and over in general practice, 27 per cent could not hear a normal voice in a test. Fawcus (1971) found that of 244 patients

in geriatric wards of a hospital, 69 (28 per cent) had a hearing loss and of these 12 per cent were severely handicapped by their difficulty. Fisch (1971) tested 100 patients in a home for the elderly. In 84 a threshold audiometric test was possible. Results are shown in Table 22.2; about 27 per cent had a hearing loss which would produce a significant difficulty in hearing speech. Maclean (1971) reports the investigations by Townsend concerning hearing problems of elderly people living in institutions. A significantly higher proportion of these people had hearing difficulties, both with and without treatment, than of those living in the community.

Table 22.2 Hearing loss among old people in a residential home

Hearing loss in both ears (dB)	NO. of patients (total 84)
30 to 40	14
40 to 60	16
60	2
Total	32 (27%)

When the number of deaf in Great Britain, as found in some of the population surveys, was related to the 1961 census, the total deaf in the country was 2 235 000 and of these 1 178 000 were under the age of 65 years and 1 057 000 over the age of 65 years. Therefore, somewhat over 40 per cent of the total number of people with hearing impairment were over the age of 65 years.

All the available evidence shows that about one-third of the population of 65 years and over suffers from a hearing impairment which can have unfavourable social consequences.

In surveys the commonest tests for detecting a hearing difficulty are pure tone audiometry, the individual's own assessment of his hearing or the observer's impression of the subject's ability to communicate by hearing.

Population studies using a pthological classification of hearing loss face many problems at present and their use is limited to patients seeking advice.

Many studies were conducted by interviewing or by questionnaires. The questionnaire responses may be affected by refinement in wording of the question and different attitudes towards problems of deafness. This transpired from USA Survey (US Dept. Health Education and Welfare, 1968). The hearing status was determined by audiometric tests, self-evaluation of 'hearing trouble' (trouble or none), household interview of the examinee or a knowledgeable adult in his famijy. Levels were quoted as 'Hearing impairment', 'Hearing loss' or 'Hearing poor, fair or good'. These findings are shown in Table 22.3.

Table 22.3 Effect of wording of questions on results of survey of hearing disability (figures %)

Age group	Hearing trouble	Hearing poor	Hearing impairment	Hearing loss
18 to 24	5.6	0.9	1.5	0.8
40 to 50	17.2	2.6		4.3
65 to 74	27.0	9.9	17.0	28.2
75 to 79	35.0	16.0	22.5	48.0

Milne (1976), in a survey of a sample of elderly people (215 men and 272 women), tested the accuracy of assessment of their own hearing. The questions asked were: Do you suffer from deafness? Are you hard of hearing? The results suggested that questions about deafness would wrongly classify as deaf a large number of people probably without disability and a smaller number of those with a hearing disability would be missed. The discrepancies in various surveys based on questioning the subjects about their hearing loss are so great that the use of such methods should not be encouraged. Minor changes in the wording of the question may affect the results. The same applies not only in population surveys but also when trying to assess individual patients.

There is no single test available which could assess in an all embracing manner the communication difficulties produced by hearing impairment in the elderly population.

Atherley and Noble (1971) have devised a comprehensive 'multilateral' assessment of hearing difficulty ('the Hearing Measurement Scale'). The purpose was the assessment of disability in those with sensorineural hearing loss. It comprises 42 scoring items in seven sections: (1) speech hearing, (2) non-speech sounds, (3) localization, (4) emotional response to hearing loss, (5) distortion of speech, (6) tinnitus, (7) personal opinion of hearing. This type of assessment may turn out to be the best definitive measure of hearing problems in the elderly, not only in population studies but also for a comprehensive assessment of an individual.

Thomas and Ring (1981) carried out a validation study of the hearing measurement scale and they concluded that the overall validity was confirmed but there were two areas of doubt. One concerns the poor differentiation of the first two sections of the scale and they thought that section five may not be a valid measure of speech distortion.

IDENTIFICATION AND CARE

Several studies have indicated a large pool of both undiagnosed and ineffectively managed deafness among the elderly.

The number of elderly people who have sought and obtained medical care for hearing problems is not known exactly, but it falls far short of the number shown to be deaf in the various prevalence surveys. In a national survey of people over 65, Townsend and Wedderburn (1965) found that only 6.3 per cent had a hearing aid, although over 30 per cent had difficulty in hearing. Among those who complained of severe difficulty in hearing only 34 per cent possessed an aid. Forty-one per cent of those with hearing difficulties had never had an aural examination and a further 23 per cent had not had one during the last five years.

In Wilkins' (1948) survey all subjects who reported any degree of deafness were questioned as to whether they had sought medical advice. Only half those suffering from mild and moderate degrees of hearing loss did so. Men under 65 years of age sought advice almost twice as often as those over the age of 65 years for similar degrees of deafness.

In another survey, 88 of 283 subjects with hearing difficulties never had a hearing test or treatment (Williams, 1970). Harris (1962) found that 55 per cent of those interviewed had informed their doctors of hearing difficulty, but that only 36 per cent of these had hearing aids. Millard (1968) found that a quarter of those who said that their hearing was inadequate for their needs had never had their ears examined.

In a survey of morbidity in general practice (Logan and Cushion, 1958), it was found that for every 1000 people aged 65 years and over, 5 or 6 would consult their doctor about deafness in any one year. In addition, however, 13 out of every 1000 would have their ears syringed for wax and there may well have been some cases of presbyacusis in this group. In one study of elderly people (Government Social Survey, 1962), only one-third of deaf people, who said their doctor knew of their disability, had hearing aids.

In a USA National Health Survey (1968), it was found that 34 per cent of persons with bilateral hearing loss had never been tested by a doctor and that only 18 per cent had had their hearing tested within the two years prior to the interview.

If Townsend's (1965) figures, collected in 1962, still apply nationally in Great Britain, it is estimated from the home population in 1968, that there are about 1 300 000 people over the age of 65 who have hearing problems, but only 400 000 of them have aids. It is possible that many elderly people regard increasing deafness as an inevitable part of aging and hence do not seek help, or they are not aware of the possibilties of treatment and remedial measures. This attitude may also be present in many of their medical advisers.

The difficulties and inadequacies of the present system of providing care for the elderly deaf have been described by Gregory (1964). Difficulties were met at each stage, i.e. general practitioner level, ENT consultation, provision of a hearing aid, further rehabilitation measures; all reflecting the low priority accorded to hearing loss in the elderly as a disability.

There is an almost universal lack of specialized audiological facilities for the elderly. While the care of children with hearing impairment developed into a system of paediatric audiology of high standard, including early detection by screening, detailed diagnostic and assessment facilities, parent guidance and early training, the care of elderly people with socially handicapping hearing impairment remains largely neglected. It is impossible to provide the necessary detailed diagnostic and assessment facilities and organize rehabilitation via an ENT outpatient department. Otolaryngological surgeons usually have no facilities, nor the time and training which is required for an effective geriatric audiological service. Experience shows that such care requires an audiology team, headed by an audiological physician and including an audiological scientist, hearing therapists and social workers.

Data on prevalence as reviewed here lean heavily on surveys carried out in Great Britain and the United States. A review of conditions in various countries by direct enquiry (Chamberlain et al, 1970), including most European countries, showed no significant differences. As far as an organized system of care for the elderly deaf is concerned, none exists anywhere in the world with the notable exceptions of Denmark and Sweden.

Reliable statistical information concerning hearing loss is lacking not only in relation to elderly deaf, but in all age groups. The problem very often is terminology — what to include in the population called 'deaf' or 'hearing impaired'? For example, should one include unilateral hearing loss, conductive hearing losses, minor high frequency losses which initially do not cause social disability etc., etc? In many population surveys these factors are not defined precisely enough and in spite of many surveys, even now we are not certain about the statistics. This is also the reason for the great variation given by numbers of authors who carried out surveys without stating precisely the terms of reference. For example, the number of hearing impaired people whose impairment causes a social disability: even when we would select those who have a hearing aid as a basis for statistical analysis, we would arrive at false figures. The elderly deaf notoriously request a hearing aid only after many years of suffering a hearing loss, and even then come to clinics as a result of pressure from relations, and many do not come at all, assuming that nothing can be done about their hearing loss. However, one thing is certain that the size of the problem is seriously underestimated.

Studies by Humphrey et al (1981) confirmed the difficulties concerning identification and care. They examined the characteristics of the hearing impaired elderly without aids and tried to gain some understanding of the factors which lead people to seek rehabilitation.

The two major single determinants of seeking help were found to be: severity of impairment and onset of deafness before reaching retirement age. Almost half of all the deaf who admitted impairment were those who became hard of hearing before retirement. They were also very much more likely to feel handicapped and to have seen a doctor about their hearing loss (Herbst, 1980).

Attitudes to a disorder first suffered at a stage in life when it was felt to be untimely are different from the response to the same disorder encountered at a stage where it is conventionally expected as part of a 'normal running down' and indeed has become literally a norm (Herbst, 1980).

Screening

The large numbers of elderly people with socially handicapping hearing impairment who do not receive help raises the question of desirability and feasibility of screening.

Theoretically, screening should be desirable but in practice it cannot be considered in isolation, separate from the system of general care for the elderly in society. Screening for hearing loss must be considered as part of a system of care for the elderly deaf, which should incorporate not only facilities for detection but also those for diagnosis, assessment and rehabilitation. Unless organized care for those with hearing impairment exists, there is no point in screening the whole elderly population. At present, even those who are presenting themselves on a symptomatic basis cannot be guaranteed the care they require.

The next difficulty is created by the fact that we have no entirely satisfactory single screen test for the detection of the elderly with socially handicapping hearing impairment.

Pure-tone audiometry is potentially the best test but conditions must be satisfactory. Besides, in a small number of subjects, it may not be possible to apply it because of lack of the required co-operation.

Speech perception ability tests can be applied for screening (repetition of test words and sentences and scoring the result), but again acoustic conditions must be reasonably good.

Methods based on self-estimates of hearing ability contain inherent difficulties already mentioned, although some authors claimed that self-estimates of the *degree* of hearing handicap made by elderly subjects correlate fairly well with measured speech discrimination difficulties (Blumenfeld et al, 1969). A study by Chamberlain (1971) showed, in a small number of subjects (85), that a combination of the subject's opinion of his hearing and the observer's impression of it is a more sensitive measure of hearing impairment than repetition of word lists in a formal test.

Much more research is necessary to elaborate a method which would fulfil all the criteria of a satisfactory screen test.

REHABILITATION

Social consequences of hearing difficulty

Impaired ability to communicate leads to loss of independence and to social isolation — conditions for which the old person may already be greatly at risk.

Persistent irritation and unhappiness is undoubtedly caused by hearing difficulty. Psychological consequences can be more serious. Deaf people generally feel left out in group conversation, become suspicious and feel people talk about them, mainly when they are turned away and lip-reading is impossible. Paranoid tendencies can increase to almost intolerable degrees and relations and friends can be affected.

The prevalence of old people with hearing impairment in institutions is higher than outside. Hearing difficulty might be considered as a precipitating factor in relation to need for residential care (Maclean, 1971).

The implications of the communication difficulty in the elderly are not fully appreciated. Deafness stands low in the hierarchy of disabilities. While other disabled groups of all ages may have attributed to them compensatory characteristics, such as the blind having more acute hearing, the deaf tend to elicit only negative attributes such as slowness. Many elderly people in their relations may accept hearing difficulty as a natural part of aging not amenable to treatment or they may see deafness as a stigmatized condition and be unwilling to identify themselves with a negatively valued group (Maclean, 1971).

Difficulties in group conversation are especially grave. Many who have no particular difficulty in face-to-face conversation cannot participate in group conversation and this is their principal social handicap. The difficulties of the elderly deaf in this respect should be stressed.

Amplification

Reduced sensitivity is physically equivalent to sound attenuation which can be corrected by amplification. Because of preoccupation with impaired sensitivity, many otologists consider amplification to be the only necessary and possible rehabilitative measure. Amplification does help but almost invariably only in combination with other measures. In some it helps only to a limited degree or not at all.

A limitation is imposed by oversensitivity to sounds of high intensity and by the recruitment phenomenon. The elderly person hopes to increase intelligibility of speech by increasing the volume which, however, soon becomes harsh and intolerable. The next limitation is imposed by the high frequency hearing loss. Consonant sounds cannot be heard well even when amplified and therefore intelligibility of speech remains low.

One of the serious problems of the elderly deaf is created by the difficulty of communication between husband and wife, mainly at the initial stages when neither of them realises or accepts that one of them is hard of hearing. This causes needless friction and when both are hard of hearing, may create serious difficulties. This can be sorted out only by expert advice. Often when one spouse attends the clinic it is revealed that the other one is also hard of hearing, although no request has been made for a hearing aid or hearing test. In these cases it is pointless to fit hearing aids only to one.

Hearing aids

The most accepted method of amplification is by a wearable electronic amplifier, a hearing aid. The aid is most useful in face-to-face conversation, when lip-reading helps considerably with the understanding of speech. As soon as one gets away from this situation, difficulties develop. When the distance from the source of the desired sound increases, ambient noise and reverberant sound interfere more and more with what one wants to hear. The old person with hearing difficulty whose vision is also impaired is doubly handicapped because of decreased ability to lip-read.

The limitations of the instrument must be understood and expectation must not exceed its potential usefulness. If it is not made clear at the very beginning that the instrument is primarily for face-to-face conversation and that difficulties will arise as soon as one departs from this situation, the user may discard the aid when found useless in various other situations. It is a matter for careful instruction to achieve the correct degree of expectancy. The disappointment and consequent depression from unsuccessful use of an aid hopefully acquired, can be considerable.

Good maintenance and advisory facilities must be provided, including adequate follow-up. Six to eight weeks after receiving the aid is the most important time when advice concerning the various problems, which are bound to emerge, should be available. Without such follow-up the majority will either not use the aid properly or discard it altogether.

A small behind-the-ear hearing aid which, acoustically, may be suitable for an elderly person could be quite useless when such a person is unable to manipulate the minature controls. For example people with arthritis in their hands, may be unable to manipulate the controls and to place the aid themselves properly in the ear. They rely on others to do it for them thereby losing independence. Without proper attention the elderly person may find that he is not able to use the aid given to him. Commercial and political pressure stimulated the provision of behind-the-ear hearing aids to the elderly deaf, many of whom are unable to use them and would benefit much more from body-worn aids which are easier to control. There is no reason why they should not have both types at the same time: a behind the ear aid used for social occasions and a body worn aid used at home and other occasions, when it gives better results in any case and it can be amplified independently by the person concerned.

Considerable progress has been made in producing a greater variety of aids. Better methods of selection, with the necessary adjustments, make it possible to provide a more suitable and effective aid. But this needs a properly established audiology centre with equipment for selection of hearing aids for each individual patient.

There are no hearing aids designed specifically for the elderly. This is surprising, since they comprise such a large section of all hearing aid users. In the United Kingdom, 60 per cent of all hearing aids are issued under the National Health Service to people over the age of 65 (Knight, 1971). It would seem justifiable to pay special attention to designing aids for the elderly.

Technically there are no reasons why certain modifications should not be incorporated into the instruments to help to overcome the specific difficulties of aged users. Special output-limiting devices (to prevent sudden surge of sound) and controls specially designed for easy manipulation are desirable. The ergonomic aspects of hearing aid design are specially important for the elderly.

Binaural use of the hearing aid improves intelligibility and the use of two instruments (especially of the head-worn, postaural type) improves stereophonic hearing and intelligibility of speech in group conversation. The headworn (behind the ear) hearing aid can be used successfully by many elderly people. From the acoustical point of view it could give better results. Unfortunately, with these smaller instruments the controls are more difficult to manipulate and many old people may not be able to cope effectively with them although they are socially much more acceptable.

The importance of social acceptance of a hearing aid for elderly people is underestimated. It is a visible sign of a handicap low in social estimation and many elderly people reject it on this account.

When the elderly deaf do eventually get round to reporting their impairment to their doctor, the findings suggest that a very substantial proportion (55 per cent) are not referred on for aids or other rehabilitation. This number is too large to be dismissed simply as representing those deaf for whom hearing aids would be regarded as clinically inappropriate or unhelpful, nor can the non-referral be attributed merely to unwillingness to accept recommendation for an aid among the elderly themselves, since many (59 per cent) of these same respondents were only too glad to be referred to a hearing-aid centre when this was suggested by a research team (Herbst and Humphrey, 1981).

Non-wearable amplifiers

Desk amplifiers can be, in many circumstances, more useful than a hearing aid worn on the body or behind the ear. The quality of sound is much better (the speaker or speakers use a microphone and the listener uses earphones). Various modifications make it possible to use such amplifiers in conjunction with television, radio, recorded music. Good quality amplifiers of this type should be available in institutions, homes for the elderly, meeting places, etc.

The already-mentioned difficulty in group conversation cannot be overcome by the conventional wearable hearing aid and special types of amplifiers will have to be elaborated for this specific purpose.

In most institutions or homes for the elderly there are no aids for communication and staff are unaware of the nature of the difficulties and how to overcome them. But relatively simple and inexpensive aids can help greatly both the elderly deaf and those who care for them.

A good compromise between the wearable aid and the speaking tube is provided by the 'lorgnette' type of instrument when the speaker uses a microphone and the listener holds to his ear an earphone incorporated into a handle which holds the amplifier and the controls of the aid.

Mechanical amplification

In many cases when a hearing aid is of little use, mechanical amplification, for example by a speaking tube, can still help. There is less distortion and less intrusion of ambient noise, but mechanical amplifiers are often socially unacceptable. Since small wearable electronic aids came into use the mechanical ones have been pushed aside as inferior and their considerable usefulness unjustly underestimated.

Various types of communication

Apart from direct face-to-face conversation, in some circumstances other forms of communication may become even more important. This concerns the telephone, radio, television and essential warning signals such as door bells and fire alarms. Difficulties in this respect may increase the isolation of the elderly or even create dangerous situations.

In the course of a study to investigate the effect of severe hearing loss on family life it became apparent that many of the difficulties encountered could have been alleviated by the acquisition or better use of appropriate environmental aids. In some cases the problems were practical and in others social or psychological in nature (Harris et al, 1981)

A special hearing-aid telephone can be provided in place of a conventional type by fitting a miniature amplifier into the instrument. In conjunction with the telephone bell a lamp signal can be made to operate the house lights, flashing on by day and off by night, when the telephone rings. Extension bells can also be fitted. Extra earpieces can be connected by means of an extending flex and used with benefit by a deaf person to listen with both ears or by a second person to help the deaf answer a call. Loud-speaking telephones can be installed. An induction loop incorporated in the hearing aid makes it possible to listen to the telephone through the aid. Simple prearranged coded signals can be transmitted by the telephone to those who have difficulty in understanding more complex messages. Equipment which converts handwriting from a special pen into signals which are sent by telephone and reconverted at the other end into writing, should fulfil many essential needs for the elderly with hearing impairment. Such 'electrowriters' are already available but still very expensive.

Television and radio

The importance of television and radio for the elderly population has greatly increased. A survey (Meyrick and Cox, 1969) revealed that in 1969, 90 per cent of elderly people listened to the radio, 88 per cent watched television (as opposed to 59 per cent in 1961) and 46 per cent had a telephone. In the same survey it transpired that the proportion of elderly living alone increased from 15 per cent to 22 per cent from 1961 to 1968. Obviously, as isolation increases, the importance of various communication media is also growing.

Various adaptors can be installed to bring sound from the television set directly to the listener through an earpiece which can sometimes be his own hearing aid receiver. A control box contains a volume control to adjust loudness to suit the deaf subject. There is a great variety of similar devices which make listening to television and radio much easier.

Extreme loudness of television, demanded by the hard of hearing, can be frustrating or even intolerable to other members of the family or neighbours and may lead to acute distress. Installing suitable adaptors can solve this problem at once.

Warning signals

Light-flashing door bells can be installed to overcome considerable difficulties of the elderly deaf in this respect. There are several systems available which activate lights in the house when the door bell is pushed. A warning door mat has the same function. When anyone steps on it, a light comes on inside the house. Light-flashing alarm clocks exist or a vibrating pillow can be connected to the alarm clock (Royal National Institute for the Deaf, 1968).

The quality of voice

Subjects with severe hearing impairment are unable to control the volume of their voices because of absence of auditory feedback. It is characteristic that elderly people with a severe hearing loss shout. This is irritating and embarrassing, especially in public. The affected person is unaware that he speaks too loud. Generally the quality of voice deteriorates with age by losing power and the effort an elderly person has to make when hoping to hear his own voice, by raising it, is considerable.

It is possible to train a person with hearing impairment to modify the voice and reduce the volume to a tolerable level. When a hearing aid is used it is possible by talking into it to re-establish auditory feedback The pitch of the voice tends to increase with age, articulation deteriorates and speech is slurred, consequently the voice is less pleasing. A speech therapist can give useful instructions to the elderly, teaching them how to reduce the level of voice, improve its quality and articulation. When successful, there is considerable improvement in social life.

Treatment by drugs

Four main groups of drugs have been widely used for the treatment of presbyacusis: vitamins, hypophyseal hormones, sex hormones and androgen-oestrogen preparations. The claims for improvement are very unconvincing (Schmidt, 1967).

The annoyance feature of tinnitus may be eased by psychotrophic drugs. However, the advantages to be gained may be offset by their prolongation of auditory reaction time.

How to talk to the elderly deaf

The most important aspect of helping elderly people with a socially handicapping hearing impairment is the degree of understanding and co-operation by all those who are in social and professional contact with them. Without this, even the most sophisticated amplifiers may prove to be useless. Much of the advice or instruction, following diagnosis and assessment of communication needs, must be directed towards relations, friends and those who look after the elderly professionally, including doctors, social workers, etc.

First of all, they must know how to talk to the elderly deaf. This should be done:

1. Clearly, in a moderately loud voice, but not shouting
2. Face-to-face, with the light falling on the speaker's mouth
3. At a somewhat slower speed
4. Leaving somewhat longer intervals between sentences
5. Eliminating distractions as much as possible.

When a hearing aid is used, one should check that it functions; the microphone must be turned to the speaker: it may be better to hold the aid in the hand and to speak clearly but without shouting.

In some cases when the hearing aid does not help or is difficult to use, a simple speaking tube can be most effective. All those who are professionally involved with the care of the elderly will find it useful to carry a speaking tube with them as part of their equipment.

In group conversation the elderly person should face as many people in the group as possible. This may require special arrangements for seating. People should realize that the elderly person will be unable to follow fast interchanges of speech between the members of the group. If they want the elderly person with hearing impairment to join in, certain conditions must be fulfilled even at the cost of the free-and-easy exchanges usually enjoyed in lively conversations. However, considering that this may effectively reduce the elderly persons isolation, the sacrifice is relatively small.

PROGNOSIS

Care of the elderly deaf is improving in various countries. For example, in the United Kingdom, with the emergence of audiology as an independent specialty, departments of audiology are being created where the elderly deaf can be better assessed and rehabilitation organised effectively. A significant development is the establishment of a new profession, Hearing Therapists, attached either to an ENT Department or to a special Audiology Centre. They are specially trained in the rehabilitation of the adult and elderly with impaired hearing. Without such a service it is difficult to carry out the increasingly complex measures required for rehabilitation. Now there is greater awareness that simply to provide a hearing aid is not enough, further guidance and training are needed, relations and friends must be involved and proper instruction in the use of various amplification aids (including 'environmental aids') is essential. Understanding of the nature of the communication difficulty of the elderly deaf by all those who are in social or professional contact with them, is essential. Improvements in communication aids and the techniques have created a very promising future as far as alleviation of hearing loss in the elderly is concerned. Provided all the potentialities are fully exploited, the unfavourable consequences of hearing loss in the elderly can be considerably reduced. Geriatric physicians should be fully aware of these possibilities.

REFERENCES

Atherley G R C, Noble W G 1971 Clinical picture of occupational Hearing loss obtained with hearing measurement scale. In: Robinson D W (ed) Occupational Hearing Loss, Academic Press, London p 193

Baru A V 1966 On the role of temporal parts of the cerebral cortex in the discrimination of acoustic signals of different duration. Zhurnal Vysshei Nervnoi Deiatelnosti Imeni I P Parlova 16: 655–665

Baru A V 1967 Peculiarities of the detection of acoustic signals of different duration under the action of some drugs. Zhurnal Vysshei Nervnoi Deiatelnosti Imeni I P Parlova 17: 107

Bergman M 1971 Hearing and aging. Implications of recent research findings. Audiology, 10: 164–170.

Blumenfeld V G, Bergman M, Millner E 1969 Speech discrimination in an aging population. Journal of Speech and Hearing Research 12: 210–217

Bochenek Z, Jachowska A 1968 Atherosclerosis, accelerated presbyacusis and acoustic trauma. Internal Audiology 7: 509–510

Bocca S 1958 Clinical aspects of cortical deafness. Laryngology, 68: 301–309

Bruner A, Norris T W 1971 Age-related changes in caloric nystagmus. Acta Otolaryngologica, suppl 282

Calearo C 1957 Binaural summation in lesions of the temporal lobe. Acta Otolaryngologica 47: 392–395

Calearo C, Lazzaroni A 1957 Speech intelligibility in relation to the speed of the message. Laryngology, 67: 410–419

Calvi L A, Finzi A 1957 Rhythme, langeur et signification des messages verbeaux dans le presbyaecie. Revue d' Oto-Neuro-Ophthalmologie 29: 226–239

Cawthorne T 1951 Hearing and deafness. Acta otolaryngologica 40: 257–263

Chamberlain J 1971 Evaluation of screening tests for unreported disability in the elderly. Dept. Publ. Health, London School of Hygiene and Tropical Medicine. Personal communication from unpublished research

Chamberlain J, Fisch L, Hinchcliffee R 1970 Personal communication from members of Working Party (Dept. Health and Soc. Sec. U.K.), on screening for hearing impairment in the elderly

Clark D 1971 A system of care for the elderly with hearing impairment. Symposium on Hearing Loss and Communication Difficulties in the Elderly. (Unpublished. Papers available from British Society of Audiology)

Dixon Ward W 1971 Presbyacusis, sociocusis and occupational noise-induced hearing loss. Proceedings of the Royal Society of Medicine Medicine 64: 200–203

Fabinyi G 1931 Regarding morphological and functional changes of the internal ear in arteriosclerosis. Laryngology, 41: 663–670

Fawcus M 1971 A survey of communication problems in a geriatric hospital. Symposium on Hearing Loss and Communication Difficulties in the Elderly. (Unpublished. Papers available from British Society of Audiology)

Feldman R M, Roger S N 1967 Relations among hearing, reaction time and age. Journal of Speech and Hearing Research 479–495

Fieandt H von, Saxen A 1937 Pathologie und Klinik der Alterschwerhörigkeit. Acta Acta Otolaryngologica (suppl. 23)

Fisch L 1970 The selective and differential vulnerability of the auditory system. In: Ciba Foundation Symposium on Sensorineural Hearing Loss: 101–126. J A Churchill, London

Fisch L 1971 The nature of communication difficulties in the elderly. Symposium on Hearing Loss and communication Difficulties in the

Elderly. (Unpublished. Papers available from British Society of Audiology)

Fleischer K 1952 Uber Vorgänge des Alterns am Gehörorgan. Zeitschrift für Alternforshung

Fournier J E 1954 L'analyse et J'identification du message sonore. Journal of Oto-Rhino-Laryngology

Gabor D 1946 The theory of communication. JIEE 93:429–457

Gabor D 1947 Acoustical quanta and theory of hearing. Nature, 159: 591–594

Gabor D 1953 Communication Theory. Butterworth, London

Gacek R A 1968 The pathology of presbyacusis. Internat Audiology 7: 445–446

Glorig A, Wheeler D, Quiggle R, Grings W, Summerfield A 1957 1954 Wisconsin State Fair Hearing Survey. Report to Amer. Acad. Ophthalm. Otolaryng. Research Centre, Los Angeles

Glorig A, Davis H 1961 Age, noise and hearing loss. Annals of Otology, Rhinology and Laryngology 70: 556–571

Goetzinger C P, Proud G O, Dirks D, Embrey A J 1961 A study of hearing in advanced age. Archives of Otology

Goldie L 1977 Psychiatric treatment of tinnitus. (Unpublished. Paper obtainable from British Society of Audiology)

Government Social Survey 1962 Old People in Lewisham. King Edward VII Hosp. Fund, Lond., p. 43

Green M F 1970 Incidence of deafness from wax. Paper read at British Geriatrics Society

Gregory R 1964 Deafness and Public Responsibility. Occas. Paper on Social Administration. No 7 Codicode Press, England

Hallpike C S 1962 Vertigo of central origin. Proceedings of the Royal Society of Medicine 55: 364–370

Hansen C C 1968 Perceptive hearing loss and arterial hypertension. Archives of Otolaryngology 87: 119–122

Hansen C C, Reske-Nielsen E 1968 Cochlear and cerebral pathology in aged patients. Internal Audiology 7: 450–452

Hansen C C, Reske-Nielsen E 1965 Pathological studies in presbyacusis. Archives of Otolaryngology. 82: 115–132

Harris A 1962 Government social survey. Old People in Lewisham. King Edward VII Hosp. Fund, Lond

Harris M, Thomas A, Lamont M 1981 Use of environmental aids by adults with severe sensorineural hearing loss. British Journal of Audiology 15: 101–106

Hemstock T I, Atherley G R C 1971 Tinnitus and noise-induced tinnitus. In: Occupational Hearing Loss. Robinson D W (ed) Academic Press, London and New York

Herbst G K R, Humphrey C M 1981 The prevalance of hearing impairment in the elderly living at home. Journal of the Royal College of General Practitioners (in press)

Herbst G K R, Humphrey C M 1980 Hearing impairment and mental state in the elderly living at home. British Medical Journal 281: 903–905

Herbst G K R 1983 Psycho-social consequences of disorders of hearing in the elderly. In: Hinchcliffe R (ed) Hearing and balance in the elderly. Churchill Livingstone, Edinburgh. Chapter 8

Hinchcliffe R 1959a The threshold of hearing as a function of age Acoustica, 9: 303–308

Hinchcliffe H 1959b The threshold of hearing of a random sample rural population. Acta Otolaryngologica 50: 411–422

Hinchcliffe R 1959c Correction of pure-tone audiograms for advancing age. Journal of Laryngology and Otology 73: 12, 830–832

Hinchcliffe R 1961 Prevalence of the commoner ear, nose and throat condition in the adult rural population of Great Britain. British Journal of Preventive and Social Medicine 15: 128–139

Hinchcliffe R 1962 Aging and sensory thresholds. Journal of Gerontology 17: 45–50

Hinchcliffe R 1970 Noise and hearing loss. Sound, Feb. issue. Royal National Institute for the Deaf. London

Hinchcliffe R 1971 Auditory dysfunction in the elderly. Symposium on Hearing Loss and Communication Difficulties in the Elderly. (Unpublished. Papers available from British Society of Audiology)

Hobson W, Pemberton J 1955 The Health of the Elderly at Home. Butterworth, London

Humphrey C, Herbst G K R, Faurqi S 1981 Some characteristics of the hearing-impaired elderly who do not present themselves for rehabilitation. British Journal of Audiology 15: 25–30

Jerger J F 1960a Observations on auditory behaviour in lesions of the central auditory pathways. American Medical Association Archives of Otolaryngology 71: 797–806

Jerger J F 1960b Audiological manifestations of lesions in the auditory nervous system. Laryngology, 70: 417–425

Johnsson L G, Hawkins J E 1972 Sensory and neural degeneration with aging as seen in microdissection of the human inner ear. Annals of Otology, Rhinology and Laryngology 81: 179–193

Kirikaé I, Sato T, Skitara T, Skitara T 1964 Auditory function in advanced age with reference to histological changes in the central auditory system. Laryngology, 74: 205–220

Klotz, R S, Kilbane M 1962 Hearing in an aging population. New England Journal of Medicine 266: 277–280

Knight J 1971 Hearing aid service and follow-up for the elderly. Symposium on Hearing Loss and Communication Difficulties in the Elderly. (Unpublished. Papers available from British Society of Audiology)

Knudsen E L 1981 The hearing of the barn owl. Scientific American 245: 82

Konig J 1957 Pitch discrimination and age. Acta Otolaryngologica 48:–489

Lempert S M 1958 Report on the survey of the aged in Stockport, County Borough of Stockport

Littler T S 1965 The Physics of the Ear. Pergamon, London

Logan W P D, Cushion A 1958 Studies on Medical and Population Subjects, No 14, Vol iii. HMSO, London

Maclean M 1971 Social factors affecting the diagnosis and management of deafness in the elderly. Symposium on Hearing Loss and Communication Difficulties in the Elderly. (Unpublished. Papers available from British Society of Audiology)

Macrae T H 1971 Noise-induced hearing loss and presbyacusis. Audiology, 10: 5–6, 323–333

McDowell B 1982 Patterns of cochlear degeneration following gentamicin administration in both old and young guinea pigs. British Journal of Audiology 16: 123–129

Matzker J 1959 Two new methods for the assessment of central auditory function in case of brain disease. Annals of Otolaryngology 68: 118–1197

Meyrick R L C, Cox A 1969 A geriatric survey repeated. Lancet, i: 1146–1149

Millard P H 1969 Paper given at the British Geriatrics Society

Millard P H 1971 Communication problems in the elderly. Symposium on Hearing Lost and Communication Difficulties in the elderly. (Unpublished. Papers available from British Society of Audiology)

Miller G A 1956 The magical number seven, plus or minus two: some limits on our capacity for processing information. Psychological Review, 63: 81–97

Miller M M, Ort R G 1965 Hearing problems in a home for the aged. Acta Otolaryngologica 59: 333–44

Milne J S 1976 Hearing loss related to some signs and symptoms in older people. British Journal of Audiology 10: 65–73

Milne J S, Lauder I J 1975 Pure-tone audiometry in old people. British Journal of Audiology 9: 50–58

Milne J S, Maule M, Williamson J 1971 Method of sampling in a study of older people with comparison of respondents and non-respondents. British Journal of Preventive and Social Medicine 25: 37–41

Nixon J C, Glorig A, High W S 1962 Changes in air and bone conduction threshold as a function of age. Journal of La Laryngology and Otology 76: 288–298

Nomura Y, Kirikae I 1968 Presbyacusis: a histological histochemical study of the human cochlea. Acta Otolaryngologica 66: 17–24

Pestalozza G, Shore I 1955 Clinical evaluation of presbyacusis on the basis of different test of auditory function. Laryngology, 65: 1136–1163

Robinson D W 1968 NPL Aero Report. Ac. 32. Nat. Phys. Lab. (also append. 10, Burns, Robinson. Hearing and Noise in Industry. HMSO, London)

Robinson D W 1971 in Occupational hearing loss, loc. confer. Brit. Acoust. Soc., Academic Press, London, New York

Rosen S 1969 Dietary prevention of hearing loss — long-term experiment. IX Exerpta Medica VIII, 189: 134–135

Rosen S, Olin P 1966 Hearing loss and coronary heart disease. Internal Audiology 5: (2) 156–158

Sanchez Longo L P, Forster F M, Auth T L 1957 A clinical test for sound localization and its applications. Neurology, 7: 655–663

Sataloff J, Vassalo L, Menduke M 1965 Presbyacusis air and bone conduction thresholds. Laryngology, 75: 889–901

Schmidt P H 1967 Presbyacusis: the present status. Internat Audiology suppl i: 1–36

Schubert K 1958 Sprachh; und methoden, Grundlagen, Würdigung und Anwendung bei Begutachtung und Hörgerateanpassung. Thieme, Stuttgart

Schuknecht H 1955 Presbyacusis. Laryngology, 65: 402–419

Sercer A, Krmpotic J 1958 Uber die ursacher der progressiven altersschwerhörigkeit (Presbyacusis). Acta Otolaryngologica suppl 143: 1–36

Sheldon J H 1948 The Social Medicine of Old Age. Oxford University Press, London

Siegelaub B, Friedman G D, Adnour K, Seltzer C C 1974 Hearing loss in adults: relation to age, sex, etc. Archives of Environmental Health 29: 107–109

Sticht T G, Gray B B 1969 The intelligibility of time compressed words as a function of age and hearing loss. Journal of Speech and Hearing Research 12: 443–448

Takahashi T 1971 Ultrastructure of the pathologic stria vascularis and spiral prominence in man. Annals of Otology, Rhinology and Laryngology 80: 721–735

Talland G A 1968 Human Aging and Behaviour. Academic Press, New York

Thomas A, Ring J 1981 A validation study of the hearing measurement scale. British Journal of Audiology 15: 55–60

Townsend P 1962 The Last Refuge: A survey of residential institutions and homes for the aged in England and Wales. Routledge and Kegan Paul, London

Townsend P, Wedderburn D 1965 The aged in the Welfare State: p 55–58. Occas. paper in social administration.G. Bell and Sons, London

US Dept. Health Education and Welfare Education and Welfare Reports 1965 Hearing Levels of Adults by age and sex. USA 1960–1962.

US Dept. Health Education and Welfare Reports 1965 Hearing Levels of Adults by age and sex. USA 1960–1962. National Centre for Health Statistics Ser ii, No 11

US Dept. Health Education and Welfare Reports 1968 Hearing status and ear examinations 1960–1962. National Centre for Health Statistics Ser ii, No 32

US National Health Survey 1968 Hearing before sub-committees on consumer interests of the elderly. Spec. Committee on Aging. US Senate, 90th 2nd Congress 2nd session

Wall J van D 1962 Het. Loren van hepaarden. Thesis: Leiden

Weiss A D 1959 Sensory Functions. In: handbook of aging and the individual: Birren J E (ed), p 503–542. Univ. of Chicago Press, London

Williams L 1970 In: Medical Assessment in Helping the Aged, Goldberg E M (ed) Allen and Unwin, London

Williamson J, Skokoe I H, Gray S, Fisket M, McGhee A, Stephenson E 1964 Old people at home. Lancet, i: 1117–1120

Wilkins L T 1948 The Prevalence of Deafness in the Population of England, Scotland and Wales. Central Office of Information, London. Revised Dec. 1949

Yantis Ph A 1955 Locus of the lesion in recruitment ear. Archives of Otoleryngology 62: 625–631

The gastrointestinal system — the oral tissues

All the tissues that make up the stomatognathic system (appertaining to the teeth and jaws) are affected by increasing age. The age changes found in the mouth are a reflection of the general aging process but may well be complicated by:

1. Normal wear of remaining teeth (attrition and abrasion)
2. Loss of teeth as a result of caries and/or periodontal disease
3. Migration of teeth following loss of teeth in the same or opposing jaw
4. Decreased masticatory efficiency following loss of teeth
5. Deterioration in oral hygiene
6. The effects of dentures on the oral tissues.

Changes in the teeth, their supporting structures including the oral mucosa and the alveolar bone, influence markedly the dental treatment of the aging patient.

AGE CHANGES IN THE TEETH AND THEIR SUPPORTING TISSUES

Before considering how the teeth are affected by age, it is pertinent to consider briefly the structures involved. A natural tooth consists of three calcified tissues, enamel, dentine and cement, and a specialized mass of connective tissue within the calcified structures known as the pulp.

Enamel, which is of epithelial origin, is the hardest of the dental tissues. Once formed and exposed in the mouth, the enamel is cut off from any cellular elements and therefore does not have any powers of reaction to injury or repair. Dentine and cement are mesodermal in origin and their organic matrices of collagen are similar to that of bone. Dentine is permeated by a system of minute tubules which contain protoplasmic processes of the odontoblasts which line the surface of the pulp. Formation of dentine and cement may continue throughout life. In the case of dentine, additions occur on the surface adjacent to the pulp

(secondary dentine) and with cement, on its outer surface.

Age changes in enamel

Teeth become darker with age and, although this may be due to a deepening of the colour of the dentine showing through the enamel, it may be that the enamel itself darkens either because of an increase in pigmentation of its organic content or by absorption of coloured substances from the oral cavity. The permeability of enamel decreases with age, but because of ionic interchange between enamel and saliva, there may be changes, after eruption, in the composition of the outer layer of enamel. For example, there may be an increased concentration of fluorine, although this tends to reach a peak by about 30 years of age.

The most obvious change in the teeth with advancing age is attrition (wear), which results in a gradual loss of enamel over the cusps of posterior teeth and the incisal edges of anterior teeth. The amount of attrition varies tremendously and is influenced by such factors as diet, habits, type of occlusion, muscular power and the loss of other teeth. When the dentine has been exposed on the occlusal or incisal surfaces, it wears at a faster rate than enamel, leading to the formation of concave dentine surfaces surrounded by sharp cutting edges of

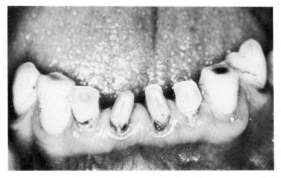

Fig. 23.1 Severe attrition of lower incisors in a man aged 70 years

enamel (Fig. 23.1). Where a number of natural teeth have been lost, the pattern of attrition may be complex and lead to abnormalities of the relation of jaws in vertical and horizontal planes. However, where the process of attrition is slow yet progressive compensatory eruption, possibly associated also with an increase in alveolar bone growth (Murphy, 1959; Berry and Poole, 1976) may maintain the height of the face. Wear of the enamel at the contact points of teeth causes a gradual reduction of their mesiodistal dimensions. The enamel of other surfaces of the teeth may be subject to wear by excessive toothbrushing or be chemically eroded in those who consume large quantities of acid drinks.

Age changes in dentine
During the life of a tooth, a mineralized tissue known as peritubular dentine is laid down on the inner aspects of the walls of the dentinal tubules. There is a relation between the formation of this tissue and the rate of attrition. In heavily worn teeth the peritubular dentine layer is thicker and the tubules frequently become completely occluded. In the dentine of the root there is a similar mineral occlusion of the tubules by a process akin to peritubular dentine formation. Secondary dentine is also laid down on the surface adjacent to the pulp throughout the functional life of a tooth. Regular (or physiological) dentine forms continuously but slowly and cannot be distinguished from the primary dentine of the tooth. Irregular (or pathological) dentine is formed as a response to traumas such as caries, attrition or abrasion and is laid down quickly (Osborn, 1981). Both lead to a gradual reduction in the size of the pulp cavity.

Age changes in cement
There is continued slow deposition of cement which increases the thickness of the cement covering of the root dentine, particularly at the apex. Resorption of cement frequently occurs but is usually repaired by further deposition of cement. A marked thickening may occur as a result of chronic inflammation; if the thickening is localized in the apical area of the root, extraction of the tooth may be difficult. With recession of the gingival tissues, the cement will become gradually exposed to the oral environment. It becomes non-vital as its nutritional supply from the gingival tissues and the periodontal ligament is cut off. The exposed cement is particularly prone to wear by toothbrushing and to attack by caries.

Age changes in the pulp
As the odontoblasts continue to lay down secondary dentine throughout life, the dentine becomes thicker whilst the pulp decreases in size. With increasing age, there is a reduction in the number of cellular elements and an increase in fibrous tissue with appreciable amount of mature collagen, so that eventually the pulp resembles scar tissue. Calcification is common in the form of large masses throughout the pulp or more localized as pulp stones. Individual odontoblasts undergo atrophy, so that the dentine-forming tissue becomes discontinuous, and there is also a reduction in blood vessels and nervous tissue. Thus there is a decreased vitality of pulp tissue and a reduced response to stimulation.

Age changes in the gingival tissues
With age, there tends to be continuous apical migration of the gingival tissues leading to a gradual exposure of the cement-covered root. As this proceeds proceeds, there may be a compensatory elongation of the root by deposition of layers of cement at the apical end, thus preserving the functional root area for support purposes. If the recession of the gingival tissue is accentuated by a descending infection from the mouth (periodontal disease), there will be a progressive destruction of the fibres of the periodontal ligament and resorption of the surrounding alveolar bone. The affected tooth therefore becomes increasingly more mobile.

Age changes in alveolar bone
It is reasonable to expect alveolar bone to follow the pattern of age changes in bone in general where there is a trend towards osteoporosis, and this has been confirmed by microradiography in the mandible (Manson and Lucas, 1962). The complete loss of an alveolar ridge in the edentulous person is, however, not inevitable and there are many examples of aged edentulous patients who present with well-formed alveolar ridges, particularly if they have been rendered edentulous at an early age because of gross caries. In contrast, when teeth are lost later in life because of severe periodontal disease, the residual alveolar ridges often undergo a rapid reduction in height and width. There is no evidence that porotic alveolar bone is more likely to undergo rapid resorption, but the reduced mass of bone per unit area, together with the reduced bone turnover that occurs with age, may render it more susceptible to functional forces directed from a denture — frequency, intensity, duration and direction. Such forces are translated into cellular activity resulting in either bone formation or bone resorption. Therefore, in the aging person where the emphasis is on resorption, more rapid reduction of the ridge may occur than would be the case with similar loading in a young person.

Age changes in the temporomandibular joint
Although many studies have suggested that a dyfunction of the stomatognathic system, including the temporomandibular joint, is more commonly found in the 20-

to 40-year age group and with a feminine dominance, a more recent epidemiological survey (Agerberg and Osterberg, 1974) has shown that symptoms are very common in the elderly. There may be crepitus or clicking on joint movement, pain in the masticatory muscles, limitation of opening and tenderness of the joint area. Radiographs often show marginal erosions and flattening of the joint surfaces and macroscopic and histological studies of postmortem material have shown that a high proportion of joints of the elderly have changes of a degenerative nature comparable with those of osteoarthrosis. Other laboratory studies have demonstrated that remodelling of the joint surfaces is common (Blackwood, 1966; Toller, 1973). The remodelling appears to be more related to functional factors than to age.

Disagreement exists in the literature as to whether the temporomandibular joint is stress bearing or non-stress bearing. A recent study using the adult *Macaca arctoides* (stump-tailed monkey) in which a 9-micron-thick pressure sensitive foil was inserted inferior to the meniscus showed that the condylar head was loaded during molar chewing with a maximum load of 1 to 3 lb (0.45 to 1.35 kg). The condylar head showed a larger loading of 3 to 4 lb (1.35 to 1.8 kg) during incision (Brehnan et al, 1981). This study is the first to actually measure loads directly at the articulating surfaces of the condyle.

Following loss of some teeth and their non-replacement, changes in the occlusion occur which may cause a disturbance of the mechanism of the joint. With good tooth contacts allowing bilateral mastication and equal use of both joints, the loads of mastication are mainly transmitted via the teeth to the alveolar bone. In a crippled dentition, however, excessive stresses may be transmitted through the joints with the emphasis perhaps on degenerative changes rather than on remodelling.

Age changes in saliva
Although salivary secretion decreases with senility and those in poor health produce less saliva, xerostomia is not likely to arise as a result of the aging process (Mason and Chisholm, 1975; Bertram 1976). Ostlund (1953) showed that the secretion of the mucous glands of the posterior part of the hard palate is reduced in old people. Mucous secretion is an important aid to the retention of a complete denture particularly in the early stages before muscular control has been learnt. The reduction in secretion may therefore provide difficulties of retention of dentures in the elderly.

THE LOSS OF TEETH

The most apparent change in the mouth with increasing age is loss of the natural teeth caused by the two main diseases that the dentist has to combat, namely dental caries and periodontal (gum) disease. Both, if untreated, are likely to cause pain and result in tooth loss and may affect general health. Successive tooth loss leads to the edentulous state which is so commonly seen in the middle-aged and in the elderly in the civilized world. Tooth loss, however, is not an inevitable sequel to aging as is shown by studying elderly Australian aborigines living in their natural environment. Their oral health is generally excellent with little evidence of caries or periodontal disease. However, their coarser diet results in marked attrition (Murphy, 1959).

Caries and periodontal disease account for more than 90 per cent of extractions in modern society. A major Government Social Survey in England and Wales (Gray et al, 1970) revealed the poor state of dental health of the population. Of people in England and Wales aged 16 years and over at the time that the survey was carried out in May and June 1968, 36.8 per cent had no natural teeth. Of significance to those dentists practising in working-class areas, was the relation between total tooth loss and household social class. For the social classes IV non-manual, IV manual and V, the proportion of edentulous persons was very similar and considerably higher than that found in other social classes. A regional variation was found particularly with social classes IV and V where 57.3 per cent in the North were edentulous compared with 37.1 per cent in London and the South East. The survey showed clearly that there was an obvious difference in oral health between those who attended the dentist regularly and those who did not. The regional variation was also associated with variations in the availability of dental manpower.

In 1968, the majority of elderly persons in England and Wales were already edentulous (for example 63.6 per cent in the age group 55 to 64 and 78.9 per cent in the age group 65 to 74) and there is no reason to believe that there has been a significant change during the last 10 years. Figure 23.2 shows the percentage of persons edentulous at different decades of life in various countries. The wide variations are thought to be due to differences in social class and attitude, and to the dentist: patient ratio which varies from country to country (Anderson and Storer, 1981).

Ten years later there was a further survey that covered the whole of the United Kingdom (Todd et al, 1982). The 1978 Survey showed that 29 per cent of adults of all ages were edentulous. This compared favourably with the 36.8 per cent found to be endulous in 1968 and the situation was improved in each age group. The change was only marginal for people aged 65 and over; in those age groups the levels of edentulousness were obviously affected by previous dental history. Because some people lose all of their teeth early in life and have

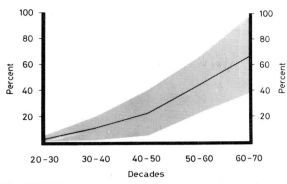

Fig. 23.2 Mean and range of percentage of persons edentulous at various decades of life (reproduced by permission of Blackwell Scientific Publications)

many years of life ahead of them, they will number amongst the edentulous for 50 years. Therefore the overall proportion edentulous cannot be drastically reduced rapidly. For example, in the 1968 Survey there were some in the age group 16 to 24 who had already lost all their teeth, so even if from 1968 onwards not one more person was rendered edentulous it would still take until 2028 before the total population was dentate. Therefore large improvements for the whole population in the 10 year period 1968 to 1978 cannot be expected although it is obvious that in particular age groups considerable changes have occurred. The 1978 survey has demonstrated a significant improvement in adult dental health and this, together with a decreasing caries experience for young children in many parts of the country, beholds well for the future.

The percentage of teeth lost to caries and periodontal disease varies with age. Dental caries, which is a bacterial disease (Hartles et al, 1969), is recognized as a disease of the young, but following a period in middle life when caries is less active, there is generally an increase in activity in the aging patient. This may be related to various factors including decreased oral hygiene, a preference for softer foods with a high carbohydrate content and a reduced salivary secretion. The incidence and severity of periodontal disease increases with age and is the major cause of the loss of otherwise sound teeth in the aging patient. The recession of the gingival tissues that occurs with age predisposes to the accumulation of food débris, plaque and calculus on and between the teeth, leading to a chronic inflammatory condition. This in turn results in breakdown of the supporting tissues of the teeth which become increasingly more mobile. The condition is particularly prevalent in the United Kingdom as is shown by the studies of Sheiham (1971), who reported that by 55 to 59 years, over 90 per cent were affected by the 'terminal' stages of the disease and were about to lose teeth because of it.

Gradually the importance of the retention of as many natural teeth as possible is being recognized by the population. But if the ultimate sequelae of untreated periodontal disease is avoided by the elderly, it is likely that the remaining natural teeth will have been so heavily restored and be so mobile that their retention for the remainder of the patient's life will often present the dentist with unsurmountable problems (Hobdell, 1973).

TREATMENT PLANNING IN THE ELDERLY PATIENT

The aim of dental treatment in elderly patients is the maintenance of a good standard of oral health with a functional efficiency that is *adequate* although not necessarily optimal. The degree of functional efficiency to be achieved will be regulated by an interpretation of the patient's total state — physical and mental status, expectation of life, the immediate environment, the social status and the personal needs of the patient.

Many aging patients drift into the edentulous state because of a series of badly planned and unsuccessful partial dentures. Others are rushed into the wearing of complete dentures prematurely because the value of retaining several mobile teeth for the retention of a transitional, but well-planned partial denture, has not been appreciated (Anderson and Storer, 1981).

The extent of dental treatment provided will vary in relation to the physician's assessment of the person's life expectancy. For example, an 80-year-old person with advanced degenerative disease whose life expectancy is short may not be a good case for new complete dentures. But a person of similar age in good physical health will be perfectly suited to all aspects of rehabilitive dentistry. A person of 60 years or over, having survived some of the ravages of dental disease might have 16 natural teeth remaining (Jackson and Murray, 1972). Extrapolating from these data, Manson (1973) has suggested that 'the average' could be 10 teeth in the lower jaw and 6 in the upper. In such a case all the possible clinical problems — periodontal, endodontic, prosthodontic and restorative — are presented to the dentist for solution.

The most significant and perhaps the most difficult dental problem in the aging person is the evaluation of the remaining natural teeth, particularly when they are mobile. In considering their retention or extraction, it is important to recognize two classes of persons: those in middle age who are entering the period when age changes become manifest and those in old age where the changes are already well advanced. Likewise the clinician should appreciate the difference between the biological age of the tissues and the chronological age of the individual — a difference that is likely to be mirrored in the mouth and in the response to dental care. An assessment of the biological age in relation to the chronological age is an important aid to correct treatment planning.

All persons over the age of 55 should be carefully assessed for prognosis of tooth retention and for signs of aging of the oral tissues (Storer, 1965). Where the dentist considers the loss of all the remaining natural teeth is inevitable, a decision to extract should be made when the environmental musculature can still adapt to and control complete dentures; for it must be remembered that age changes in the central nervous system affect the functional elements of the cerebral cortex and subcortical structures involved in the learning process. Therefore, the older the person the longer is the period required for adaptation to and control of dentures.

The decision whether to extract in cases of periodontal disease is particularly difficult. Further research is required before precise knowledge can be claimed on the effect of tooth retention or tooth loss on the eventual shape and degree of permanence of the edentulous ridge. There are situations where extractions can be delayed for several years by correct periodontal treatment often including partial dentures designed to splint mobile teeth.

When an old person presents for dental treatment with some mobile and carious teeth, when there has already been considerable alveolar bone loss elsewhere in the mouth and where there is evidence of age changes in the oral tissues, the severe problems of accommodation to complete dentures if the natural teeth are extracted must be considered. Here there is much to be said for the use of mobile, restored teeth as abutments for partial dentures. It seems that moderately mobile teeth in the elderly respond well to periodontal management and occlusal adjustment. In fact the greater the age, possibly the better the prognosis for mobile teeth. Since periodontal disease is generally a chronic process, it is possible that delayed breakdown of tissues indicates a higher resistance. If the loss of remaining natural teeth is inevitable in the old person, replacement by immediate dentures is particularly important in order to avoid interruption of function which itself is likely to have an adverse effect on the aging oral tissues.

The actual timing of extraction depends on how much comfort and efficiency the person is enjoying with the remnants of the natural dentition. Some prefer to continue with their natural teeth for a longer period and are ready to accept the lesser denture efficiency that may result. Others prefer to play safe on the future denture comfort and efficiency and will accept the edentulous state at an earlier date.

Probably the most important factor in keeping the natural teeth is the person's co-operation. With good oral hygiene and a slow loss of supporting alveolar bone, he and the dentist working together can often avoid the edentulous state. In addition, satisfactory function can be achieved from a few molar teeth in contact and, therefore, a mutilated and reduced dentition unacceptable in a younger person may be adequate in the elderly.

THE EFFECTS OF DENTURE WEARING ON THE ORAL TISSUES

Although well-designed and well-maintained dentures are likely to keep the supporting tissues in good condition particularly if the patient recognizes the importance of denture hygiene, denture trauma is commonly seen in elderly mouths. The oral mucosa shows signs of atrophy with increasing age. The surface epithelial layers are reduced in number and the mucosa shows an overall decrease in thickness. As the submucosa also becomes thinner, any edentulous areas are likely to have a soft tissue covering that is less resilient than found in younger persons. The general dehydration of the body tissues that accompanies aging has an added effect in reducing the resilience of the tissues covering edentulous alveolar ridges (Storer, 1965).

There is a predisposition to earlier signs and symptoms of denture trauma when there are, in addition, manifestations of tissue change due to the aging process. Although the changes in the mucosa are not considered to be of a dangerous nature, it is obvious that the dentist should recognize that it is his responsibility to prevent chronic oral irritation in the aging patient and to take steps to ensure that the dentures are as atraumatic to the tissues as possible. The commonest forms of denture trauma are (1) denture hyperplasia and (2) denture stomatitis.

Denture hyperplasia

This is seen as a flap or roll of tissue usually found at the mucosal reflection and is related to the border of the denture. The flaps may be single or multiple and where multiple are separated by clefts. The usual cause is

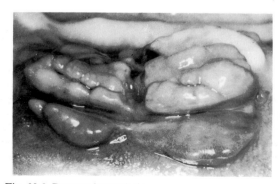

Fig. 23.3 Denture hyperplasia

sinkage of the denture due to continued alveolar bone resorption and the condition is most frequently seen in the lower anterior area of the mouth (Fig. 23.3).

Denture stomatitis

In this condition the mucosa beneath the denture appears deep red in colour, bruised and oedematous. It is usually seen under the upper denture, and although localized in the early stages often spreads to present as a general inflammation of the entire denture-bearing area. The area of redness is limited to the area covered by the denture (Fig. 23.4). The condition is usually painless.

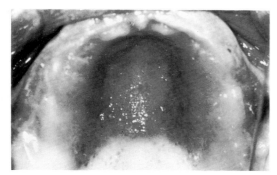

Fig. 23.4 Denture stomatitis

An assessment of cases of denture stomatitis suggests that apart from trauma, infection by *Candida albicans* is an important aetiological factor. Trauma may result from a rough denture fitting surface, inadequate adaptation to the tissues or faults in tooth contacts. There is still controversy over whether the inflammatory condition is due to primary infection by *C. albicans* or whether yeasts are secondary invaders of traumatized tissues. Studies have shown a 90 per cent positive yield of yeast-like fungi in patients with denture stomatitis, compared with 40 per cent in a control group of patients with dentures, but not showing signs of denture stomatitis.

It seems probable that trauma of the oral mucosa predisposes to growth of *C. albicans*, although fungi may be isolated from inflamed mucosa beneath apparently non-traumatic dentures and also, of course, from non-inflamed mucosa. By removing trauma, inflamed areas often resolve and there is usually a concomitant reduction in candida growth. But there appears also to be a significant correlation between poor denture hygiene and candida growth. Organisms may be isolated from the fitting surface of a denture as well as from the soft tissues. Persons with denture stomatitis in which candida growth is confirmed are more likely to exhibit

also signs and symptoms of angular cheilitis and glossitis.

Many cases of denture stomatitis are referred to hospital with a 'query allergy' diagnosis. The patients themselves often firmly believe they are allergic to the plastic denture material. But allergy to acrylic is rare. In contrast to denture stomatitis, where the tissue reaction is confined to the denture-bearing area, in cases of true allergy all tissues in contact with polished or fitting surfaces of the denture would be affected.

The treatment of denture stomatitis includes the correction of denture faults, the prescribing of antifungal agents and instruction in denture hygiene (Anderson and Storer, 1981; Budtz-Jørgensen and Bertram, 1970).

The climacteric and the oral tissues

If it is accepted that aging is a life-long phenomenon, a period of particular significance is that phase of life known as the climacteric. The oral symptoms that may occur in a small percentage of women include a burning sensation related particularly to the sides, tip and base of the tongue and any edentulous areas covered by a denture, an atrophic glossitis, abnormal taste sensations and a generalized oral discomfort. Where dentures are present, the patient usually blames them for the oral symptoms even though they may be technically and functionally perfect. Clinically, the mucosa usually appears pale and parchment-like, but occasionally, in contrast, it may be reddened, swollen and glossy with bleeding a predominant feature. Apart from the effects of a low oestrogen level, the adverse mucosal changes at the climacteric may be related to malnutrition, for dietary neglect and peculiar dietary habits are often encountered. The unpleasant taste sensations prevent the enjoyment of food and the result is that the person forgoes regular meals and takes a poorly balanced diet (Storer, 1965).

It is not uncommon to observe a rapid loss of alveolar bone, particularly in the mandible, at the climacteric. This may be associated with bone changes that occur elsewhere at this time of life.

Denture hygiene

Deposits such as microbial plaque, calculus and food debris can cause various problems including denture stomatitis, angular stomatitis, unpleasant tastes, odours and an unsightly appearance. Effective cleaning of dentures is therefore of considerable importance to the patient's oral health (Basker et al, 1976). The simplest way to keep dentures clean is by the regular use of soap, water and a soft nylon brush. The importance of removing all deposits, not just the more obvious stains and food particles, should be emphasised. In addition to brushing the dentures the occasional use of a proprietary cleanser is also necessary. Of these the alkaline peroxide cleansers are the most widely used and are effective due to the formation of small bubbles of oxygen which dislodge loosely attached material from the denture surface.

In cases of denture stomatitis, meticulous cleaning of the dentures is particularly important. Two solutions have been shown to be effective in removing microbial plaque, a proprietary hypochlorite denture cleanser and 0.1 per cent aqueous chlorhexidine gluconate. Overnight immersion is necessary if either solution used.

The replacement of dentures

At some stage during the life of any denture, consideration must be given to whether its deficiencies should be corrected by modification of the existing denture or whether it should be replaced by a new denture.

Patients are frequently seen who have continued to wear the same dentures for far too long — sometimes the period has extended into several decades. In many instances this has occurred simply because the patient had not been told of the importance of regular inspection of the dentures and their supporting tissues. With others, the cost of replacement dentures may have acted as a deterrent. In either event, the philosophy of the patient is likely to have been 'why interfere with something that is comfortable?' The dentist must therefore educate the edentulous patient to the need for regular inspection of the dentures and supporting tissues. The patient should be warned that the continued wearing of dentures which have become ill-fitting is likely to result in considerable damage to the supporting tissues with consequent difficulties in wearing dentures later in life. The dentist must forewarn his patient of the necessity for eventual replacement of the dentures due to long-term changes in the jaws and in the dentures themselves.

However, it is not possible to state a definite time after which a denture must be replaced, because the two most important indications for replacement — those of tissue change and denture deterioration — vary with each case.

If the dentures are not maintained by regular correction of the fitting surface and occlusal adjustment, then replacement is usually necessary after a 5-year period. With regular maintenance, however, dentures may last for upwards of 10 years and only require replacement because of deterioration of the tooth material.

The special needs

Fortunately the majority of elderly persons are in good general health and are able to obtain treatment in the dentist's surgery. There are those, however, who need special help, the homebound, the chronic sick, the mentally retarded and the physically handicapped. It is these who, in many parts of the country, are forgotten as far as dentistry is concerned. Apart from those confined to their homes, there are many elderly persons living in council homes and homes organized by voluntary organizations, and in hospital geriatric and psychogeriatric units.

The amount of dental care provided for those who require special consideration varies from none to complete, but surveys indicate that dental neglect is widespread, particularly in the smaller institutions. Unfortunately a comprehensive dental examination of the mouth in those confined to one institution or another is uncommon, and generally the dentist is only called when a patient is complaining of pain.

Apart from his responsibility to eradicate the usual dental diseases in such patients, the dentist should examine the mouth as a whole to ensure that all tissues are healthy. Oral carcinoma is comparatively rare, but it is significant that it commonly occurs in the elderly and that it is too frequently diagnosed at an advanced stage (Storer, 1972). The reasons for late diagnosis may be many, but certainly if regular oral examinations are carried out for those in homes and hospitals, the tragic consequences of oral carcinoma could be avoided.

In providing treatment for the elderly person, the dentist has an opportunity to enhance the quality of his or her life. Great benefit can result from the provision of a satisfactory dentition, be it natural or artificial. A more balanced diet may then be taken in contrast to the high carbohydrate, low protein diet of the dental cripple. The psychological benefits of a healthy mouth can be quite dramatic — the elderly person looks and feels so much better.

REFERENCES

Agerberg G, Österberg T 1974 Maximal mandibular movements and symptoms of manidbular dysfunction in 70-year-old men and women. Svensk Tandlakare-Tidskrift 67: 147–163

Anderson J N, Storer R 1981 Immediate and Replacement Dentures, 3rd edn, Blackwell Scientific, Oxford, p 8, 14–23, 228

Basker R M, Davenport J C, Tomlin H R 1976 Prosthetic treatment of the Edentulous Patient, 1st edn, pp 70 and 164. London: MacMillan

Berry D C, Poole D F G 1976 Attrition: possible mechanisms of compensation. Journal of Oral Rehabilitation 3: 201–206

Bertram U 1976 Xerostomia Acta. Odontologica Scandinavica 25, Supplement 49

Blackwood H J 1966 Adaptive changes in the mandibular joints with function. Dental Clinics of North America November, 559–566

Brehnan K, Boyd R L, Laskin J, Gibbs C H, Mahan P 1981 Direct Measurement of Loads at the Temporomandibular Joint in *Macaca Arctoides*. Journal of Dental Research 60: 1820–1824

Budtz-Jørdensen E, Bertram U 1970 Denture stomatitis. Acta Odontologica Scandinavica 28: 71–92; 283–304; 551–579

Gray P G, Todd J E, Slack G L, Bulman J S 1970 Adult Dental Health in England and Wales in 1968. London: HMSO

Hartles R L, Darling A I, König K G, Mühlemann H R, Bowen W H 1969 The aetiology of dental caries. British Dental Journal 126: 136–138

Hobdell M H 1973 Epidemiology of the impaired dentition. Proceedings of the Royal Society of Medicine 66: 589–594

Jackson D, Murray J J 1972 The loss of teeth in dentate populations. Dental Practitioner and Dental Record 22: 186–189

Manson J D 1973 The elderly dental cripple. Proceedings of the Royal Society of Medicine 66: 597–598

Manson J D, Lucas R B 1962 Microradiographic study of age changes in the human mandible. Archives of Oral Biology 7: 761–769

Mason D K, Chisholm D M 1976 Salivary Glands in Health and Disease, 1st edn, pp 228–230. London: Saunders

Murphy T R 1959 Compensatory mechanisms in facial height adjustment to functional tooth attrition. Australian Dental Journal 4: 312–323

Osborn J W 1981 Editor Dental Anatomy and Embryology. Vol 1 Book 2. A companion to Dental Studies, 1st edn, pp 166–174. Blackwell Scientific, Oxford

Ostlund Stig G: Son 1953 Palatine glands and mucin factors influencing retention of dentures. Odontologisk tidskrift 62: 1–12

Sheiliam A 1971 The prevention and control of chronic periodontal disease. Dental Health 10: 1–6

Storer R 1965 The effect of the climacteric and of aging on prosthetic diagnosis and treatment planning. British Dental Journal 119: 349–354

Storer R 1972 Oral cancer. Lancet i: 430

Todd J E, Walker A M, Dodd P 1982 Adult Dental Health, Volume 2, United Kingdom in 1978. London: HMSO

Toller P A 1973 Osteoarthrosis of the mandibular condyle. British Dental Journal 134: 223–231

The gastrointestinal system — the upper gastrointestinal tract

INVESTIGATION OF THE ELDERLY PATIENT WITH SUSPECTED UPPER GASTROINTESTINAL DISEASE

In the management of the elderly patient with symptomatology suggesting disease in the oesophagus, stomach or small bowel the importance of a good history cannot be emphasized strongly enough. Since symptoms may be relatively non-specific, close questioning for a history of vomiting, heartburn, dysphagia or abdominal pain is essential. In addition to full haematological, biochemical and serological examination, a stool examination for occult blood, a barium swallow and meal may be required including screening in the Trendelenburg position to exclude a hiatus hernia and upper-intestinal endoscopy.

Gastric secretion tests should include measurement of the acid secretion under basal conditions (the basal acid output) and either the insulin or pentagastrin-stimulated secretion. Insulin has its effect on the vagus-stimulated component of acid secretion. In patients who have previously had gastric surgery for peptic ulceration, this test will indicate if a vagotomy is complete or not. In the patient with an intact vagus there is a rise in acid secretion of at least 15 mmol per litre compared with the basal period (Baron, 1970).

Pentagastrin (Peptavlon, ICI) is the physiologically active synthetic C-terminal pentapeptide of gastrin and stimulates acid secretion from the parietal cells by a direct action. The use of pentagastrin in a dose of 6 μg per kg body weight by a subcutaneous injection has largely replaced the augmented histamine test (Makhlouf et al, 1966) and has the advantage of not producing systemic effects. An antihistamine is not required. Pentagastrin-stimulated acid secretion is a good indication of the size and activity of the parietal cell mass in the stomach and is increased in patients with duodenal ulceration and reduced in gastric carcinoma and following gastric surgery.

Upper gastrointestinal tract endoscopy has become freely applicable to elderly patients since the introduction in the late 1950s of fibre-optic instruments. Until that time endoscopy with rigid or semirigid instruments had been a difficult and sometimes hazardous procedure. The new flexible instruments are relatively safe. Indeed Ariga (1966) records a complication rate of only 0.003 per cent in a series of 829 000 examinations. Fibre-optic instruments are presently available with either side- or end-viewing optics. The tip of these instruments is fully controllable and can be rotated through a full range of movements including inversion to a J-shape for examination of the blind area of the fundus. Internal channels allow biopsies to be performed, and photographic facilities are available. Oesophagus, stomach or duodenum, or all three may be examined in the same patient at one instrumentation. Routine preparation for this includes the use of local anaesthetic lozenges to anaesthetize the throat, atropine to reduce gastric and oral secretions and diazepam 5 to 10 mg or midazolam 2.5 to 10 mg intravenously as a sedative. We frequently examine older patients and a recent examination in a 93-year-old man showed that a suspicious lesion on barium meal appeared benign endoscopically. This was confirmed by the histology of the biopsy, thus saving an unnecessary laparotomy.

The main use of flexible endoscopes is in the management of patients with suspected gastric ulceration, oesophageal or gastric carcinoma, atrophic gastritis or with post-gastric-surgery symptoms. In most instances it should be possible to differentiate between benign and malignant lesions although a barium meal examination may be used as well. Kato (1966) reported accurate differentiation in 93 per cent of cancers and 87 per cent of gastric ulcers. With the further development of endoscopic equipment and supporting apparatus these now constitute an important investigative and therapeutic technique in elderly patients. It is now possible to use cytology brushes directly applied to the suspected lesion, diathermize polyps, electrocoagulate bleeding lesions, or even to inject sclerosants into bleeding oesophageal varices. Laser therapy holds out great possibilities. A major development in the past few years has been the production of the Eder-Puestow oesophageal dilator which allows the management of benign oesophageal structures during a routine endoscopy examination. This simple apparatus has now been adapted to allow the insertion of a Celestin type tube at the same time.

THE MOUTH

Common findings in healthy old people

Apart from dental studies there has been little published work on this subject. Bhaskar (1968) examined 785 healthy residents (774 men and 11 women) of an Old Soldiers' Home in Washington, DC, for changes in the oral mucosa. Sixty-four per cent of his subjects were over the age of 60 and there were 233 aged 71 and over. The commonest feature that he found was varicosity of mucosal vessels, usually on the underside of the tongue. These changes were present in almost 49 per cent of his subjects; an incidence so high that it could well be considered a normal aging phenomenon. White hyperkeratotic lesions of the oral mucosa were found in almost 21 per cent. Bhaskar pointed out that he had found about 12 per cent of such lesions to be premalignant, and he stressed the need for careful observation and mucosal biopsy.

Xerostomia

Dry mouth is most commonly associated with mouth breathing or insufficient fluid intake. There have been few studies on changes in parotid secretion with age. In one such study by Kamocka (1970) parotid secretion was significantly reduced in individuals aged 70 to 88 years compared with a younger control group. Cheraskin and Ringsdorf (1969) interviewed 67 edentulous patients, and 20 per cent of them reported xerostomia, which was, however, usually mild and intermittent. Sjögren's syndrome, in which xerostomia and keratoconjunctivitis sicca are frequently associated with enlargement of the parotid and/or lacrimal glands, has been reported most frequently in middle-aged patients. Thus, in the review of 62 patients by Bloch et al (1965) only 15 were aged over 55 at the time of onset. Their oldest patient was aged 75 years. Dysphagia is quite a common associated symptom in Sjögren's syndrome, and may be associated with postcricoid narrowing or web formation (Doig et al, 1971). Whaley et al (1972) compared the incidence of xerostomia and keratoconjunctivitis sicca in hospital patients of various age groups. Their series included 130 patients aged 31 to 80 and 122 patients aged 81 to 93. They found no evidence of xerostomia in the younger patients, but in the elderly group 18.2 per cent of the females and 2.8 per cent of the males had xerostomia. Although Sjögren's syndrome is usually associated with evidence of autoimmune disorder, such as the presence of rheumatoid factor in the serum, Whaley and colleagues found no such correlation and they suggest that in the very elderly the disorder may result from acinar atrophy rather than chronic inflammation association with an autoimmune process.

Disorders of taste

It is generally believed that the sensations of taste and smell decline with age, but there is a lack of precise information. Harris and Kalmus (1949) found in a group of 441 males aged 10 to 91 years that there was a steady decline with age in ability to taste phenylthiourea.

Snapper (1967) has well reviewed the causes of normal and abnormal patterns of taste sensation from the anatomical, clinical, experimental and cultural points of view. Taste may be affected, for instance, by lesions of the facial nerve during its passage through the temporal bone, and by lesions in the medulla, thalamus or temporal lobe.

It seems unlikely that simple loss of taste sensation is an important cause of malnutrition whereas abnormal taste patterns can certainly lead to reduced food intake. Epstein (1967) has shown experimentally that rats can vary their food intake normally even when they can neither taste nor smell the food they are eating. Shafar (1965) described 4 elderly patients with abnormal taste patterns (dysgeusia) in whom food tended to taste foul and disagreeable. His patients were aged between 68 and 78 (mean 74). Cerebral neoplasm, psychoneurosis, and psychosis were excluded, but congestive heart failure was an associated disorder in 3 of the 4 patients. This unpleasant abnormality of taste affected all food and drink and led to weight loss. Spontaneous recovery occurred after 1 to 16 weeks in 3 of his patients. Henkin et al (1971) reviewed 35 patients with a more widespread syndrome of hypogeusia, dysgeusia, hyposmia and dysosmia, for which no cause was apparent. The mean age was 53 years. The syndrome did not tend to recover spontaneously, but they found that oral zinc sulphate produced good symptomatic improvement.

THE PHARYNX AND OESOPHAGUS

Pharyngeal and oesophageal motility in old age

Motility in the pharynx has been reviewed by Kilman and Goyal (1976) and by Palmer (1976). These authors emphasize the complex shape, innervation and musculature of the buccopharyngeal area and point out the crucial role of the cricopharyngeus muscle which functions as the upper oesophageal sphincter. Piaget and Fouillet (1959) studied 100 individuals over the age of 65, and in 22 cases found evidence of pharyngeal muscle weakness and abnormal relaxation of the cricopharyngeus muscle. Passage of food from the pharynx to the oesophagus depends on relaxation of the cricopharyngeus, and following the early work of Kaplan (1957), other workers, including Mills (1973), have found that surgical section of this muscle may relieve intractable upper dysphagia in a number of neurological disorders, including cerebrovascular disease and motor neurone disease.

Two early papers concerning oesophageal motility came from the same group of workers (Soergel et al, 1964; Zboralske et al, 1964). They studied patients aged between 90 and 98 who were free of gastric and oesophageal disease. The first report detailed cineradiographic and motility studies with pressure readings and balloon kymograph on 15 individuals and the second dealt with cineradiographic observations on 41 individuals. They found that relaxation of the lower oesophageal sphincter occurred in only 44 per cent of swallows, compared with between 90 and 100 per cent in young adults. The proportion of abortive swallows increases in the elderly and there is a reduction in the amplitude of manometrically measured oesophageal contractions (Khan et al, 1977). Other abnormalities found were reduced or absent peristalsis, frequent tertiary contractions, delay of oesophageal emptying and dilation of the oesophagus. The authors emphasize that these changes, for which they use the term 'presbyoesophagus', must be differentiated from the better-known disorders of oesophageal spasm, achalasia, scleroderma and oesophagitis. Castell (1976), however, points out that many of the extremely old individuals investigated by Soergel and colleagues had diabetes mellitus, senile dementia, peripheral neuropathy or all three disorders, which may have affected motility. Hollis and Castell (1974) investigated patients over 70 without diabetes mellitus or neurological disease and found only a decrease in the amplitude of oesophageal peristalsis. Castell considered that previously reported disordered motility in elderly patients was most likely to be due to associated disease rather than to aging *per se*. This does not deny the practical significance of Soergel's observations in view of the high frequency of neurological disorder and diabetes in the higher age groups.

Differentiation between oesophageal and cardiac pain

This is important because conditions which cause oesophageal pain are common in the elderly and also because cardiac pain is often much less dramatic and clear cut in its presentation in this age group. Bennet and Atkinson (1966a), in a detailed study, reviewed the case records of 124 emergency admissions with praecordial pain. They noted that 23 per cent of these patients were found to have only alimentary disease, as follows:

Oesophagitis only	20 cases
Oesophagitis and peptic ulcer	4 cases
Peptic ulcer only	3 cases
Diffuse oesophageal spasm	1 case

They noted that the pain usually described was 'burning' in oesophageal disease. Dyspnoea was commoner with cardiac pain and acid regurgitation with oesophageal pain. Three factors found four to six times as commonly in oesophageal as in cardiac pain, were: relation to posture, relation to meals, and relief by antacids.

In a second paper Bennet and Atkinson (1966b) describe the results of oesophageal perfusion with dilute hydrochloric acid in the diagnosis of praecordial pain. They found that in 29 patients with reflux oesophagitis an identical pain was produced by hydrochloric acid perfusion in 28 cases. Moreover, in 22 patients who presented diagnostic difficulties the results of oesophageal acid perfusion correlated well with the final diagnosis. They recommend an oesophageal acid perfusion (Bernstein) test as a diagnostic aid in this situation.

Dysphagia in the elderly

In old age dysphagia is frequently caused by extra-oesophageal disease. The commonest example is pseudobulbar palsy due to cerebrovascular disease. Intrathoracic lesions such as a bronchial carcinoma or lymph nodes enlarged by metastatic spread may press on or invade the oesophagus. Not uncommonly, more than one possible cause of dysphagia may coexist in the same patient. Thus a mild or severe stroke may bring on dysphagia and investigation may reveal, for instance, a stricture of the lower oesophagus requiring instrumental dilation.

Dysphagia due to age changes in the great vessels

Aneurysms of the arch and descending aorta are a recognized cause of dysphagia and regurgitation (Avery-Jones et al, 1968). Coppola (1964) described an unusual case of severe dysphagia due to elongation and tortuosity of the left common carotid artery, in a 75-year-old woman. Her symptoms were cured by surgical relocation of the vessel towards the left side.

Impaction of a food bolus in the lower end of the oesophagus

This occurs especially after certain foods such as bread and meat. As mentioned by Avery-Jones et al (1968) it can occur when a constricting ring develops at the oesophagogastric junction in patients with a sliding hiatus hernia. In these patients the bolus usually passes into the stomach within a few hours and recurrences can be minimized by a suitable choice of diet.

Pelner and Levy (1960) report the case of a female patient of 76 years with mild achalasia who presented with persistent vomiting due to an impacted bolus of fish roe. She was treated with frequent oral doses of an enzyme mixture. Recovery began after three doses and was complete six hours later.

Diffuse oesophageal spasm
This clinical syndrome has been well described by Creamer et al, (1958), whose studies included clinical, radiological and manometric observations. In 15 of their patients with both radiological and pressure changes the average age was 60 years (range 35 to 76). Symptoms were intermittent and comprised dysphagia and retrosternal pain which might resemble cardiac pain. This pain could occur on swallowing or at other times. Manometric studies showed that in the lower half of the oesophagus the normal peristaltic wave was replaced by a simultaneous and prolonged rise in pressure. This abnormal pressure pattern was also found in 16 out of 58 patients with symptoms suggestive of the syndrome but without the characteristic radiological changes. Clinical points regarding this syndrome and related conditions affecting the lower oesophagus are discussed by Avery-Jones et al (1968).

Dysphagia due to moniliasis
The frequent use of antibiotics in frail patients not uncommonly leads to monilial infection. Although this usually affects the mouth, where it is easily detected, it can involve the oesophagus without significant oral changes. This is being increasingly recognized as a cause for dysphagia or a loss of desire to eat in the elderly. The painful swallowing which these patients experience is characteristic and can occur with even bland liquids such as milk or water.

Buckle and Nichol (1964) described two patients who developed painful retrosternal dysphagia without typical signs in the mouth. The characteristic appearances on barium swallow were of great assistance in both cases, and the symptoms cleared in four days on nystatin therapy. The use of endoscopy in these patients produces a higher diagnostic yield than barium studies and is the investigation of choice. Sarner and Rooke (1971) point out the need for adequate clinical and radiological follow-up after treatment for oesophageal candidiasis because similar X-ray appearances may be seen in association with oesophageal carcinoma. The condition responds readily to antifungal therapy such as nystatin. The use of the tablet form of the medication if preferable and the patient should be instructed to suck these over as long a period of time as possible so as to bathe the infected area with anti-fungal.

Achalasia of the cardia
There is less bias towards the older age groups in this condition than with carcinoma. In Barrett's (1964) series

of 122 cases there were nine over the age of 70. It is important not to overlook it, however, because it can be improved by relatively minor surgical procedures. The older patient is more at risk from chest infection due to spill-over into the lungs in the recumbent posture.

Gastro-oesophageal reflux
Gastro-oesophageal reflux is one of the commonest causes of dyspepsia in this country. The chief symptom is chest pain which the patient usually describes as heartburn (usually made worse by stooping, straining or lying in bed at night). In most patients the underlying pathology is a hiatus hernia but it may also occur in obese patients and in the presence of pyloric stenosis. In almost every patient with gastro-oesophageal reflux the pain can be simulated by the infusion of weak hydrochloric acid into the lower oesophagus. In some few patients with achlorhydria a similar pain may occur and has been attributed to the reflux of bile or pancreatic juice.

The differential diagnosis of this pain from that of cardiac origin may be difficult even with the aid of electrocardiography (Master, 1964) although endoscopy is of considerable help in demonstrating an oesophagitis not shown on barium meal.

Reflux oesophagitis
The reflux of acid gastric contents into the lower oesophagus usually produces in due course a reflux oesophagitis. Lyall (1937) distinguished two types of reflux oesophagitis which he named superficial ulcerative oesophagitis and localized penetrating ulceration. The latter type is least frequent but when present has the histological characteristics of a peptic ulcer and also has a tendency to perforate or penetrate through the wall. In the superficial ulcerative type the ulceration does not usually extend beyond the muscularis mucosae although fibrosis does involve deeper layers. Usually the lowermost portion of the oesophagus is spared as this part is usually kept closed by the sphincter. The absence of pain should not cause a reflux oesophagitis to be overlooked since it is a frequent cause of alimentary bleeding in the elderly (Atkinson, 1965).

Hiatus hernia
Hiatus hernia is usually an acquired condition, the causes of which are still poorly understood. Akërlund's (1926) original concept of a congenitally short oesophagus is now regarded as being unlikely in most instances. Allison (1951) has since shown that the shortening of the oesophagus results from muscular contraction and fibrosis due to associated oesophagitis. Whilst many other theories have been advanced over the years a discussion on these is beyond the scope of this chapter.

Hiatus hernia occurs with increasing frequency in later years, and in one large series (Brick and Amory, 1950) only 18 per cent of patients were less than 50 years of age whilst 28 per cent were over the age of 70 years. The same authors found an incidence of asymptomatic herniae of 1.3 per cent in older men. There is a greater frequency of the condition in females compared with males.

On anatomical grounds hiatus hernia is usually divided into three types.

In the *sliding* type, the most common, the oesophago-gastric junction moves up through the diaphragmatic hiatus into the chest and produces a bell-shaped deformity. These are small herniae with frequent symptoms from gastro-oesophageal reflux. At a late stage when there is an active oesophagitis progressing to fibrosis the oesophagus becomes shortened.

In the *paraoesophageal* or 'rolling' type of hiatus hernia the fundus of the stomach herniates through the hiatus alongside the cardia, which retains its normal position. This type is more common in younger patients although symptoms are less frequent and reflux and oesophagitis are uncommon.

In the *mixed* type features of both the rolling and sliding type of herniae are present and this is more common than a pure paraoesophageal hernia. Symptoms of dysphagia occur not infrequently.

The symptoms of hiatus hernia are varied. In many instances the patient never seeks medical advice and this group may represent up to 25 per cent of all those with a hernia. The principal symptoms are those of gastro-oesophageal reflex with heartburn and acid regurgitation. Belching, chest pain and dysphagia also occur. The initial presentation may be that of anaemia from occult alimentary bleeding.

The diagnosis is usually suspected clinically and can be substantiated by a barium meal examination including a head-down view or endoscopy. Only in complicated cases are manometric studies really indicated.

In most instances the management is medical and only rarely is surgery contemplated in the elderly. Medical management includes weight reduction if the patient is obese, and attention to posture with the avoidance of stooping or bending and lifting of heavy loads. In addition, the head of the bed should be elevated about 3 inches on blocks. This is more satisfactory than using an extra pillow.

If the patient has pyloric stenosis then the symptoms will continue until the stenosis is relieved. An anticholinergic drug sometimes provokes gastric retention with symptoms of gastro-oesophageal reflux which clear when the drug is withdrawn.

Antacids form the mainstay of treatment given as regular doses every two or three hours and on retiring at night. Alternatively the combination of metoclopramide (Maxolon; Primperan) in a dosage of 5 to 10 mg before meals combined with a surface-acting agent such as Gaviscon or Gastrocote will usually prove most effective although one must be careful of the dystonia which may occasionally occur with metoclopramide in full dosage. In some patients with severe oesophagitis and in whom surgery cannot be contemplated, it has recently been advocated that low-dosage irradiation to the gastric parietal cell area may sufficiently reduce the acid production to allow the inflammation to respond to simple medical measures. In the more severe forms of oesophagitis and ulceration, the use of an H_2 receptor antagonist such as ranitidine or cimetidine (see below) is recommended in combination with metoclopromide.

Benign oesophageal stricture

Benign oesophageal stricture is about one-third as common as carcinoma of the oesophagus and should only be diagnosed after carcinoma has been adequately excluded. It usually occurs as a complication of reflux oesophagitis, a penetrating peptic ulcer of the oesophagus or following the swallowing of corrosives. Oesophagoscopy with biopsy is essential to exclude malignancy.

The treatment of this condition is either the progressive dilatation with bougies or the use of the Eder-Puestow dilators described above, and correction of the underlying condition if possible. The more recent development of transluminal balloon dilatation catheters, used in conjunction with endoscopy, will allow the stretching of benign strictures under direct vision and in a controlled manner without recourse to surgery. The prognosis is good although further dilatation at a later date may be required.

Oesophagitis and oesophageal ulceration induced by potassium preparations

In the early 1960's clinicians became aware of increasing numbers of patients who were presenting with small-intestinal ulceration or stricture formation. Eventually these were causally related to the use of enteric-coated potassium preparations which were usually administered in association with diuretics. It was believed that these were produced by the release of large concentrations of the potassium salts in a localized area of the gut causing local irritation, inflammation and ultimately ulceration followed by stricture formation. These enteric-coated preparations then fell into disfavour and were gradually replaced by either syrups and other forms of liquid therapy or by slow-release tablets such as Slow K.

More recently the clinicians have come to recognise upper alimentary lesions associated with these slow-release compounds. The lesions have usually been oesophageal in the form of an oesophagitis, but oesophageal ulceration and stricture formation can also occur. In this situation, there may be an abnormality of oesophageal motility, but the presence of cardiomegaly may produce compression of the oesophagus with temporary arrest of the ingested tablets at that area and consequent release of the irritant potassium salts.

Similar irritation and inflammation may occur in the stomach and duodenum. The lesions respond to appropriate medication and the use of an alternative form of potassium supplement.

Oesophageal carcinoma

In a series of 405 patients with carcinoma of the oesophagus and cardia described by Miller (1962), the average age was 60.7 years, and 98 of his patients were over 70 years old. There is a steady rise in the incidence of carcinoma of the oesophagus with increasing age (Langman, 1971) and it is about twice as common in men as in women. There is an increased incidence of carcinoma of the upper oesophagus in patients with sideropenia, and of carcinoma of the middle oesophagus in patients with achalasia of the cardia.

The decision whether to treat oesophageal cancer by surgery or radiotherapy depends both on the level of the lesion and on whether it is a squamous or adenocarcinoma as determined on a biopsy specimen. Lesions of the lower oesophagus are the most amenable to surgery and squamous carcinoma responds quite well to radiotherapy. Miller found that in his older patients the surgical prognosis was better than might be expected. A much higher proportion were operable than was the case in younger patients. Not unexpectedly, intercurrent disease became a more frequent cause of late deaths with increasing age. Pearson (1971) has made a special study of the value of radiotherapy in the management of squamous oesophageal cancer. He considers that with improved techniques the results of radiotherapy may compared well with surgery for squamous lesions even in the lower oesophagus, though he stresses that more experience is required before definite comparisons can be made.

In the very frail old patient there are practical advantages in using radiotherapy rather than surgery. Useful palliation may be obtained in some patients who cannot be cured. The decision whether to aim at palliation by radiotherapy or by the insertion of a Mousseau-Barbin or Souttar's tube can be a difficult one and will need careful consideration in each case. Important factors are, for instance, suitability of the lesion for insertion of a tube, and the patient's cardiopulmonary condition in relation to his tolerance of radiotherapy. Successful introduction of a Clestin tube using fibre-optic endoscopy for inoperable neoplasms at or near the cardia has been reported by Atkinson and Ferguson (1977).

THE STOMACH AND DUODENUM

Age changes in acid secretion and in the gastric mucosa

It has been suspected for many years that there are changes in the gastric mucosa, related to age, which lead to altered secretory function. Earlier studies concentrated on the incidence of achlorhydria at different ages in groups of normal people. They revealed that the incidence of achlorhydria increases with advancing years and that this tendency is notably greater in females. Keefer and Bloomfield (1926), using fractional gastric analysis, found achlorhydria in 20 per cent of subjects aged 50 to 60 years and in 35 per cent of those over 60. Vanzant et al (1932) in a large series of 3381 subjects found the incidence of achlorhydria in various age groups as shown in Table 24.1.

Table 24.1 Percentage incidence of achlorhydria in different age groups

Age group	Percentage incidence of achlorhydria	
	Males	Females
40 to 49	9.9	13.0
50 to 59	18.2	18.0
60 to 69	23.1	27.6
70 to 79	20.0	19.4

Bockus et al (1932), using somewhat stricter criteria for the diagnosis of achlorhydria but still the fractional gastric analysis method, confirmed in general the findings of Vanzant as did Polland (1933) in whose series of 654 normal people, incidence of achlorhydria in comparable groups of people was if anything slightly higher. This was despite the fact that Polland used histamine as a stimulant whereas Vanzat did not do so.

All these earlier studies are subject to the criticism that the procedures used would nowadays be considered inadequate to establish the diagnosis of achlorhydria. However, the earlier methods would only exaggerate the actual incidence of achlorhydria. The demonstration with these methods of an increasing tendency to achlorhydria with advancing years would appear to be beyond this criticism. In fact Baron et al (1963) using a modification of Kay's augmented histamine test on 40 normal people noted that both basal and maximal gastric secretion declined with age, more so in females. Thus there does appear to be an increasing incidence of gastric secretory failure with advancing age.

A review of the literature suggests that this may be due to gastric mucosal changes although for obvious reasons there are not many reports of gastric mucosal biopsy studies in normal old people. Palmer (1954) studied gastric biopsies of 30 normal people aged over 60 years. In 27 the mucosa was normal. In three there were minor atrophic changes but the chief and parietal cells were still normal. On the other hand others, e.g. Andrews et al (1967) and Siurala et al (1968), have related chronic idiopathic gastritis to age and Edwards and Coghill (1966) in a non-ulcer dyspepsia series should find only one-fifth of patients over 60 years of age with an entirely normal gastric mucosal biopsy. Andrews et al (1967) studied histologically and histochemically the gastric mucosal biopsy of 24 asymptomatic subjects aged 64 to 87 who also had acid-secretion tests. All but one showed some degree of chronic atrophic gastritis. Acid secretion decreased progressively with increasing severity of the gastritis.

In summary, evidence hitherto available shows an increasing tendency to achlorhydria with advancing age. It appears that this tendency is associated with atrophic changes in the gastric mucosa. Whether a diminished maximal secretory function of the remaining cells contributes to this tendency as suggested by Fikry (1965) requires further study.

Peptic ulceration

While the pathology of peptic ulcer in old age is similar to that in younger patients, the clinical features may vary considerably. Whilst many patients have classical post-prandial epigastric discomfort relieved by food or antacids, others present with vague abdominal discomfort, weight loss, anorexia or vomiting. Sometimes the initial presentation is when the ulcer perforates or bleeds.

Peptic ulcer is a general term, being first employed by Quincke (1882) to indicate ulceration in any area bathed in peptic juice. The five classical sites for peptic ulcers are: the lower end of the oesophagus, the stomach, the first and second parts of the duodenum, in heterotopic gastric mucosa in a Meckel's diverticulum and in the jejunum at the site of a gastroenterostomy. Peptic ulcers may occur in any of these sites in older patients though those in a Meckel's diverticulum are much less common than in younger age groups.

The aetiology of peptic ulcer remains a matter of dispute. It seems certain, however, that the development of a chronic peptic ulcer is the balance between aggressive factors acting on the gastrointestinal mucosa and defensive mechanisms (Rivers, 1939; Hollander, 1954). The main aggressive factors include gastric acid and pepsin secretion and other factors such as antral drive, cephalic stimulation, the parietal cell mass and local trauma, whilst the defensive factors include mucosal resistance, gastric mucus, mucosal blood flow and the inhibitory effect of duodenal acidification on parietal cell activity. In addition, other elements may be indluential including hormonal factors and blood groups. Individuals of blood-group O are more liable to develop ulcers than those with other blood groups, whilst those who are blood-group O and do not secrete blood-group substances in their gastric juice, group O non-secretors, are twice as liable to develop an ulcer as secretors of other blood groups (Clarke et al, 1959). Hormonal factors are also important, there being a marked increase in the incidence in female individuals after the menopause whilst those premenopausal women who do develop a peptic ulcer almost invariably experience a remission in pregnancy which lasts until the third or fourth month of the puerperium (Clarke, 1953). Also important may be the 'permissive' role of adrenal secretions in peptic ulceration (Engel, 1955) and parathromine, there being a high incidence in hyperparathyroidism (Wilder et al, 1961). One additional factor deserves special mention, namely the Zollinger-Ellison syndrome or gastrinoma. These patients have an area of adenoma formation in the pancreatic islet cells or a hyperplasia of the same cells or of the G-cells of the gastric antrum. In this situation there is often a fulminant diathesis with recurrent peptic ulceration in various sites. This situation is uncommon in the elderly and the reader is referred to one of the specialist gastroenterology texts.

Gastric ulceration

Gastric ulcers occur frequently in the elderly, Mulsow (1941) finding that 10 per cent of all ulcers occurred in patients over the age of 60 years, whilst one-third of all ulcer deaths occur in this age group. Other authors report incidence figures ranging from 5.2 per cent (Smith, 1950) for patients over 65 years of age to 8.5 per cent in the over-70 age group (McKeown, 1965) but both these latter reports are from autopsy data. In McKeown's (1965) series of 128 patients with a chronic peptic ulcer at autopsy, 65 were in the stomach of which 48 were chronic, 9 acute and 8 had healed. The sex distribution was almost equal there being a slight preponderance of males. However, in 34 of the 65 patients the ulcer was the principal cause of death. In 18 patients the ulcer had bled, producing uncontrollable haemorrhage and in 14 patients the ulcer had perforated. Two patients died following gastric surgery. Others authors have reported similar statistics with an equal sex incidence in the elderly and a high incidence of fatal complications (Howell, 1970; Boles and Dunbar, 1946; Strange, 1963). This is not a condition to be treated lightly.

Presentation of gastric ulceration in old age is characterized by the paucity of specific symptoms and the high incidence and severity of the complications. Weight loss with vomiting and vague upper abdominal pain are frequent symptoms and a high index of suspicion is important to make the diagnosis. Barium meal examination is mandatory and may reveal a large chronic ulcer. McKeown (1965) noted a correlation between the size of ulcer and the duration of symptoms, the larger ulcers occurring in patients with the longest duration of symptoms. At one time it was believed that these large ulcers were more likely to be malignant but this view is no longer held (Strange, 1959). The current view is that site is more important than size, malignant ulcers being most common along the greater curvature. If any doubt exists gastroscopy should help to differentiate, including if need be biopsies from the ulcer margin.

It is rare nowadays for gastric ulcers to require surgical treatment. Supportive measures such as a nutritious high-protein diet, antacid therapy and a mild sedative undoubtedly assist ulcer healing. Bed-rest alone is beneficial though the risks of bed-rest may outweigh these advantages and specific drugs are preferred which allow the patient to remain ambulant.

Carbenoxolone sodium (Biogastrone) is a triterpenoid derivative from glycyrrhetinic acid, a constituent of liquorice. Several clinical trials have confirmed the ability of this agent to heal gastric ulcers (Doll et al, 1962; Turpie and Thomson, 1965) although it may be accompanied by side-effects which can hinder its use in the elderly. These are fluid retention, a rise in blood pressure and hypokalaemia. Several reports (Mohammed et al, 1966) have documented dangerous hypokalaemia and in view of the known tendency for elderly subjects to develop hypokalaemia (Judge, 1968) this drug must be used with caution. Fluid retention and hypertension can be prevented by the use of a thiazide diuretic but must be accompanied by adequate potassium supplementation. In using carbenoxolone sodium the patient should be seen at weekly intervals for electrolyte checks together with recording of the blood pressure and body weight.

An alternative preparation, deglycyrrhizinized liquorice, i.e. liquorice without the glycyrrhetinic acid, is available as Ulcedal (Boehringer) or as Caved S (Tillotts) in which it is compounded with antacids and frangula. Caved S has a tendency to produce diarrhoea and the pure preparation seems preferable. It appears to heal ulcers as effectively as carbenoxolone (Russell and Dickie, 1968; Turpie et al, 1969) and does not appear to produce fluid retention or hypokalaemia.

A colloidal bismuth preparation, tripotassium dicitrate bismuthate (DeNol), has been shown to be effective in healing gastric ulceration without the production of any significant side-effects (Boyes et al, 1975). Although the mode of action is not certain it is thought to be a local one by coating the base of the ulcer. The rate of healing and the percentage reduction in ulcer size with this preparation is in the order of 90 per cent whilst that with carbenoxolone is usually quoted as being approximately 70 per cent. At the present time DeNol, in either liquid or tablet form, is the drug of choice in the management of gastric ulceration.

The mode of action of these preparations is as yet unknown.

The H_2 receptor antagonists are also useful and have often replaced the above preparations although the healing rate may be lower than with DeNol and recurrence more frequent (see below).

Surgery for gastric ulceration

If medical treatment fails, surgery must be considered because of the high risk of fatal complications. The standard Billroth I type of partial gastrectomy with a gastroduodenal anastomosis is a major operation in the elderly and postoperative nutritional problems are common. Reports (Clarke et al, 1972; Kennedy et al, 1972) of the use of vagotomy and drainage procedure (pyloroplasty or gastroenterostomy) in gastric ulceration are of interest in view of the lower operative risk and the lower incidence of postoperative complications.

Duodenal ulceration

In all age groups duodenal ulcers are more common than gastric ulcers. There is a steady chance of a man developing a chronic duodenal ulcer from the age of 20 to over the age of 60 (Doll et al, 1951). The male: female sex ratio is usually about 7 : 1 or 8 : 1 (Doll and Pygott, 1952).

In McKeown's (1965) autopsy series a duodenal ulcer was found in 63 patients in 30 of whom it had been the principal cause of death. In 51 of the 63 patients the ulcer was chronic, in 6 acute and in 6 it had healed. The principal complications were haemorrhage in 15 patients and perforation in 13. There was 1 postoperative death.

The symptomatology of duodenal ulceration in the elderly is similar to that in younger age groups although epigastric tenderness tends to be less common. Barium meal examination is of importance though the demonstration of acute ulcers may be more difficult. In this situation gastric acid secretion tests or endoscopy may be of value.

Medical treatment

The medical management of duodenal ulcer has limitations and the best the physician can hope for is to produce a remission to facilitate the strong natural tendency to heal. The mainstay of medical management is a good antacid regime. The adsorbent antacids magnesium trisilicate and aluminium hydroxide are best, but in view of the tendency of the former to produce loose bowel motions and of the latter to cause constipation it is wise to use a balanced mixture of these two. They should be taken regularly every 2 hours with a final dose at bedtime, in this way hoping to neutralize acid secretion throughout the day. There is no place for their use after meals as at this time the food contents of the stomach are acting as a neutralizing agent. For many years it was usual to prescribe a bland diet with the avoidance of fat and fried foods but this has been shown to be of little value and only causes inconvenience at home. Free food intake with small but more frequent meals should be allowed avoiding any food known to irritate or caused dyspepsia. Anticholinergic drugs, such as poldine and propantheline may produce urinary retention or constipation in the elderly and are best avoided. As yet there is little proof that either carben-oxolone or deglycyrrhizinized liquorice have any effect in duodenal ulceration. Tripotassium dicitrato bismu-thate (DeNol) is also effective in duodenal ulcertaion usually producing a remission in symptoms within 4 or 5 days of commencing treatment. It is an effective ulcer-healing preparation, the results in several published series being of the order of 90 per cent healing at one month (Salmon, 1975; Shreave, 1975; Moshal, 1975). No significant side-effects have been recorded. The usual dose is 5 ml four times per day.

The development of H_2 receptor antagonists has revolutionized the medical treatment of peptic ulceration and other disorders associated with gastric acid hyper-secretion or reflux. They are effective in reducing acid secretion and thereby allow the natural healing of the ulcer or inflammation. Two preparations are in wide-spread use. Cimetidine (Tagamet) has been in use for the past seven or eight years. Given in a dosage of 200 mg t.d.s. and 400 mg nocte it achieves healing in almost 70 to 80 per cent of patients with duodenal ulcer with only slightly lower healing rates in gastric ulcer-ation (Wormsley, 1981). After healing of a duodenal ulcer maintenance therapy as 400 mg nocte may be given to prevent ulcer recurrence. In one large series the recur-rence rate at one year in the placebo treated patients was 54 per cent compared with 17 per cent in the cimetidine treated group.

Ranitidine (Zantac) has been introduced more recently and has similar healing properties and at least an equivalent success rate. It has the advantage over cimetidine in that it does not interfere with the cyto-chrome P450 enzyme system or androgen receptors which cimetidine can do. The effects of cimetidine can result in interactions with beta blocking drugs, antico-agulants and the benzodiazepines. For these reasons many clinicians regard ranitidine as the preparation of choice. The usual therapeutic dose is 150 mg twice daily and the maintenance dose is 150 mg nocte.

Both preparations are ideally given for 6 weeks to achieve ulcer healing. They may also be employed to reduce the risk of alimentary haemorrage in at-risk situ-ations such as in acute liver failure. They do not have an accepted role in the management of either actively bleeding peptic ulcers but are of value in recurrent ulceration and oesophageal ulceration and oesophagitis (Tytgat, 1981).

With any form of peptic ulceration it is important that analgesics used for other conditions should be carefully screened. Aspirin, phenylbutazone and indomethacin may all irritate peptic ulcers and indeed the latter prep-aration may even produce them *de novo*. The only really safe analgesic is paracetamol although in special circum-stances the use of an enteric coated preparation of aspirin may be justified.

Surgery for duodenal ulceration

If emergency surgery is necessary for perforation or haemorrhage the simplest and least major procedure should be performed.

Elective surgery for duodenal ulceration in the elderly requires careful consideration and preparation. An important indication is a history of gastrointestinal haemorrhage in a patient with known vascular disease. The danger of massive haemorrhage may outweigh the risk of surgery provided that the patient's general condition is reasonable. As with gastric ulceration the present standard treatment is vagotomy combined with a drainage procedure (Gillespie, 1969). For many patients a gastroenterostomy without a vagal nerve section may well be adequate; results of this simple operation in patients with low gastric acid secretion are encouraging (Small et al, 1971).

Pyloroduodenal obstruction

Gastric outlet obstruction occurs not infrequently in old age and appears to be most common in elderly men. The commonest lesion in the older age groups is an infil-trating carcinoma of the antrum or pylorus. Ulceration, which is most common in younger patients, is less frequent in the old. Indeed McKeown (1965) was able to record only one death due to ulceration and stenosis in her autopsy series.

The clinical presentation with copious vomiting of gastric contents is often similar to that in younger patients but the effects of dehydration, hypotension and electrolyte imbalance are more severe. In some patients weight loss may be the presenting complaint. Early and adequate replacement of both fluids and electrolytes, especially potassium, is essential and surgery is usually required at an early stage. Preparation for surgery includes free fluids with a homogenized diet by day and aspiration of residual gastric contents in the evening. Half the aspirated fluid volume is replaced as half normal (N/2) saline with 2 g of potassium chloride and it is usually possible to allow the secondary oedema at the pylorus to settle permitting a more leisurely surgical approach.

Symptoms of pyloroduodenal obstruction occasionally occur with an amotile stomach, produced by anticholin-ergic or antidepressant drugs. Simple withdrawal of the drug usually allows the symptoms to settle.

The effects of gastric operations

It has been estimated that in 1961 some 26 000 patients in the UK were subjected to a partial gastrectomy and that at the present time some 80 000 patients have some form of gastric surgery in any given year. Between 5 and 15 per cent of these patients develop some form of post-gastrectomy syndrome though this may take many years to manifest itself clinically. Four main groups of symptoms or syndromes may occur. These are: dumping, regurgitation or vomiting, diarrhoea or malabsorptive states, deficiency syndromes.

Dumping

This term includes postprandial sweating, unpleasant warmth, flushing, nausea, abdominal fullness, borborygmi and occasionally diarrhoea. The more extensive the operation the more likely this is to appear. Three main predisposing factors are the rapid passage of food into the proximal small bowel, the high osmotic power of food causing fluid to accumulate in the gut lumen and predisposing factors such as a psychological instability or a past history of allergic states. These symptoms tend to improve with time. Revisional surgery is only undertaken as a last resort and in most instances the symptoms can be controlled by avoiding the particular foodstuffs which provoke the symptoms together with an alteration in fluid intake at meal times (Williams, 1970).

Vomiting and regurgitation

These symptoms occur after partial gastrectomy or gastroenterostomy but are less frequent after pyloroplasty. They are usually due to stenosis or obstruction at the site of the stoma or in the proximal small bowel, or to the regurgitation of bile and pancreatic juice into the gastric remnant. In its most severe form there is vomiting of copious quantities of bile (the afferent-loop syndrome) mainly after meals. This is produced by free regurgitation of duodenal juices into the stomach. Revisional surgery usually with restoration of normal alimentary continuity is often necessary (Williams, 1970).

Diarrhoea and malabsorptive states

These occur fairly commonly after either partial gastrectomy or vagotomy. They present either with frequent passage of loose or steatorrhoeic stools or intermittenly with watery diarrhoea at irregular intervals, usually with minimal warning. Symptomatic measures with codeine, kaolin or anticholinergic drugs and the avoidance of provocative dietary constituents such as milk may be all that can be offered to help.

Deficiency states

These represent the main cause of postgastrectomy symptoms in the elderly and in most instances the deficiency does not develop until many years after surgery (Adams, 1968). Iron-deficiency anaemia is frequent and may develop in up to 50 per cent of patients (Weir et al, 1963). Reduced dietary intake, failure to absorb iron because of the duodenal bypass and blood loss from the mucosa adjacent to the anastomosis (Adams, 1968) may all contribute. Pre- or perioperative intestinal bleeding markedly predisposes the individual to subsequent iron deficiency (Dymock et al, 1972a). Vitamin B_{12} deficiency may occur in up to 16 per cent of patients after a gastrectomy (Hines et al, 1967) and is probably due to lack of gastric intrinsic factor. This does not usually occur after vagotomy. When vitamin B_{12} deficiency develops it rarely does so in less than 4 years (Adams, 1968). Subnormal folate levels also occur frequently (Gough et al, 1965), but rarely do these contribute to the anaemia (Hines et al, 1967). This folate deficiency is probably due to a combination of dietary deficiency and failure of absorption. Other vitamin deficiency states may also develop in these patients including scurvy and beri-beri (Dymock et al, 1972b).

Vitamin D deficiency with osteomalacia is important (Thompson et al, 1966) though it now appears that bone loss is more common than a true osteomalacic state. In patients over the age of 60 years particularly, bone loss is accelated by partial gastrectomy (Morgan et al, 1966). Patients who have had vagotomy and drainage are not at risk to the same extent.

Almost all patients also lose weight after a partial gastrectomy.

With all these problems in mind Williams (1966) has suggested daily oral supplements for all patients after partial gastrectomy with an iron salt 300 mg, vitamin B_{12} 500 μg, folic acid 500 μg, vitamin D 500 iu and a calcium salt 500 mg. This is still a matter of discussion but its usefullness in the elderly with their known tendency to vitamin deficiency seems beyond doubt.

Gastritis

The literature on gastritis is varied and confusing largely due to an inadequate nomenclature and the inappropriate interchange of clinical and pathological syndromes. Four main types of gastritis now recognized are: acute gastritis, chronic atrophic gastritis, chronic hypertrophic gastritis, giant hypertrophic gastritis.

Acute gastritis usually follows a specific injury to the mucosa from the local application of some damaging agent such as the staphylococcal toxins in food poisoning, coliform organisms in gastroenteritis, alcohol and drugs. It is usually self-limiting after a few days.

Chronic atrophic gastritis oocurs in several different forms. The mildest is superficial gastritis with infiltration of lymphocytes and plasma cells and flattening of the superficial epithelium but preservation of the underlying glandular structure. The ability to secrete acid is reduced but not absent. Chronic atrophic gastritis itself has more severe changes with involvement of the tubules of the glands and a reduction in their numbers. Mucosal atrophy is a third form with thin mucosa and almost complete absence of gastric glands. There is a minimal inflammatory cell infiltration and frequently intestinal metaplasia.

These three pictures may represent varying degrees or stages of the same pathological process and there is certainly a progressive reduction in the ability of the stomach to secrete acid. In one study Siurala et al (1968) found these changes in almost half of all subjects whom he examined and there is a correlation with the presence of parietal cell antibodies in the serum. This pattern of mucosal damage may be found with pernicious anaemia (Bardhan et al, 1969), iron-deficiency anaemia (Davidson and Markson, 1955), chronic alcoholism and pancreatitis (Joske et al, 1955), virus hepatitis and after irradiation to the abdomen (Palmer, 1954a and b) or in the postoperative period (Wall et al, 1967) following gastric surgery. These patients may lose iron from the gastric mucosal cells which are shed and a secondary iron deficiency anaemia may occur (Croft, 1970).

In many of these patients there are no specific symptoms but in some there is a vague epigastric discomfort. There is no specific treatment for chronic atrophic gastritis although small doses of dilute hydrochloric acid may sometimes be beneficial.

Chronic hypertrophic gastritis is largely a gastroscopic diagnosis when the mucosal folds are seen to be prominent, rigid and stiff with a superficial erythema. The ability to secrete acid is little affected and there is no typical histological picture.

Both the above varieties of gastritis have an increased incidence in the elderly and may be the cause of dyspeptic symptoms in patients with a normal barium X-ray examination. In some instances these symptoms respond to metoclopramide 10 mg three times daily.

Giant hypertrophic gastritis, also known as Ménétrier's disease or giant rugal hypertrophy, is a rare condition with the production of large hypertrophic gastric mucosal folds easily seen on gastroscopy or on barium meal examinations. The cause is unknown.

Carcinoma of the stomach

Carcinoma of the stomach is one of the commonest malignancies in the elderly and is at least as common as carcinoma of the colon and rectum in this country. It is most commonly seen in the sixth and seventh decades but the peak incidence is between the ages of 75 and 85 years (McKeown, 1965). Males are affected twice as frequently as females.

The aetiology of gastric carcinoma remains unknown although certain predisposing factors are now recognized. Environmental factors are important, there being a high incidence in Japan where it is twice as common as in the United Kingdom and four times as common as in the United States. Hereditary factors are also involved, the children of a parent with a gastric carcinoma having five times the expected chance of developing this malignancy (Macklin, 1956). Patients with blood-group A have a higher incidence than those with blood-group O (Aird et al, 1953) and conditions associated with an atrophic gastritis, such as penicious anaemia, have a threefold increase in the incidence compared with a control group (Mosbech and Videback, 1950). Other gastric disorders may predispose to the development of a gastric carcinoma such as polyps and gastric ulceration though the role of gastric ulcers has recently been questioned and it is suggested that in these patients the gastric ulcer has been malignant from the outset (Gear et al, 1969).

The flatulent dyspepsia syndrome

A frequent cause of dyspepsia and abdominal pain without any underlying organic pathology has become increasingly recognized in recent years. Usually termed the flatulent dyspepsia syndrome it is characterized by upper abdominal pain usually located in or radiating to the left hypochondrium and often accompanied by a feeling of fullness, with nausea and frequent eructation of air. The symptoms are often worse after meals and towards evening and the patient may be unable to eat large meals and is easily replete. There may also be sensations of churning or 'butterflies' in the abdomen. The condition is produced by aerophagy, almost always subconsciously, and is usually precipitated by underlying stress or anxiety. This is a diagnosis of exclusion and gall bladder and gastro-oesophageal pathology should be eliminated by appropriate investigations.

The treatment of this condition is best tackled by symptomatic measures such as metoclopramide (Maxolon) 5 or 10 mg thrice daily before meals or domperidone (Motilium) in a similar dosage, together with treatment of the underlying psychological upset.

Duodenal diverticular disease

Diverticula in the duodenum occur with increasing frequency in the elderly, being rare before the age of 40. Bockus (1963) has suggested that the incidence may be as high as 10 per cent after the age of 55. Colonic diverticula occur more frequently and jejunal diverticula less frequently.

The symptomatology is varied and may include diarrhoea, dyspepsia, anaemia, weight loss or mental confusion. Clark (1972) has described 15 patients over the of 70 with a variety of symptoms attributable to duodenal diverticula. In his series there were 12 women and 3 men with an average age of 80. Nine patients had single diverticula but in 6 they were multiple and in one of these there were 5 separate pouches. The commonest site was in the second part of the duodenum in the periampullary area but they could occur at any point along its course. In Clark's series 5 patients presented with diarrhoea (episodic in 3), 5 with iron deficiency anaemia, and 3 each with dyspepsia, weight loss or anorexia. At the time of hospital admission 3 of the 15 had a mental confusional state and 2 had clinical, radio-logical and biochemical evidence of osteomalacia.

Low levels of iron, folate and B_{12} were frequently noted and 2 patients had biochemical steatorrhoea. The diagnosis was usually only made with a barium meal examination.

The cause of symptoms in these patients is not clear but it seems likely that intestinal bacterial colonization is important. Some may even have associated peptic ulceration and bleed. Duodenal diverticula are probably not the innocuous and incidental finding they were once thought to be (Avery-Jones et al, 1968).

REFERENCES

Adams J F 1968 The clinical and metabolic consequences of total gastrectomy. Scandinavian Journal of Gastroenterology 3: 137

Aird I, Bentall H H, Fraser Roberts J A 1953 A relationship between cancer of the stomach and ABO blood groups. British Medical Journal 1: 799–801

Akërlund, A 1926 Hernia diaphragmatic hiatis oesophagi vom anatomischen und roentgenologischen geschtpunkt. Acta Radiologica 6: 3

Allison P R 1951 Reflux oesophagitis, sliding hiatal hernia and the anatomy or repair. Surgery, Gynecology and Obstetrics 92: 419–431

Anderson B, Belcher E H, Chanarin I, Mollin D L 1960 The urinary and faecal excretion of radioactivity after oral doses of 3h folic acid. British Journal of Haematology 6: 439–455

Andrews G R, Haneman B, Arnold B J 1967 Atrophic gastritis in the aged. Australasian Annals of Medicine 16: 230–235

Ariga K 1966 Gastrointestinal endoscopy. Gastroenterology 8: 7

Atkinson M 1965 Recent Advances in Gastroenterology. Badenoch J, Brooke B N (ed), p 49. Churchill, London

Atkinson M, Feruguson, R 1977 Fibreoptic endoscopic palliative intubation of inoperable oesophagogastric neoplasms. British Medical Journal 1: 266–267

Avery-Jones F, Gummer J W P, Lennard-Jones J E 1968 In: Clinical Gastroenterology. Blackwell Scientific Publications, Oxford

Barker K W, Remine W H, Priestly J T, Gage P R 1963 A critical evaluation of total gastrectomy. Archives of Surgery (Chicago) 87: 23

Bardhan K D, Wangel A G, Spray G H, Callender S T 1969 Latent pernicious anaemia. Quarterly Journal of Medicine 38: 525

Baron J H 1963 Studies basal and peak acid output with an augmented histamine test. Gut 4: 136–144

Baron J H 1970 The clinical use of gastric function tests. Scandinavian Journal of Gastroenterology 5 suppl 6: 9

Barrett N R 1964 Achalasia of the cardia. British Medical Journal 1: 1135–1140

Bennet J R, Atkinson M 1966a The differentiation between oesophageal and cardiac pain. Lancet ii: 1123–1127

Bennet J R, Atkinson M 1966b Oesophageal acid perfusion in the diagnosis of precordial pain. Lancet ii: 1150–1152

Bhaskar S N 1968 Oral lesions in the aged population. Geriatrics 23: 137–149

Bloch J J, Buchanan W W, Wohl M J, Bunim J 1965 Sjögren's syndrome. Medicine (Baltimore) 44: 187–231

Bockus H L, Bank J, Willard J H 1932 Achlorhydria with a review of 210 cases in patients with gastrointestinal complaints. American Journal of the Medical Sciences 184: 185–20

Boles R S, Dunbar W 1946 Peptic ulcer in the elderly. Geriatrics 1: 217

Boyles B E, Woolf I L, Wilson R Y, Cowley A J, Dymock I W 1975 Treatment of gastric ulceration with bismuth preparation. Postgraduate Medical Journal 51: 29–33

Brick I B, Amory H I 1950 Incidence of hiatus hernia in patients without symptoms. Archives of Surgery (Chicago) 60: 1045–1050

Buckle R M, Nichol W D 1964 Painful dysphagia due to monilial oesophagitis. British Medical Journal 1: 821–822

Butterfield W J H 1964 Summary or results of Bedford Diabetes Survey. Proceedings of the Royal Society of Medicine 57: 196–200

Castell D O 1976 Achalasia and diffuse esophageal spasm. Archives of Internal Medicine 136: 571–579

Cheraskin E, Ringsdorf W M 1969 The edentulous patient. Part 1. Xerostomia and the serum cholesterol level. Journal of the American Geriatrics Society 17: 962–965

Clark A N G 1972 Deficiency states in duodenal diverticular disease. Age and Ageing 1: 14–23

Clarke C A, Prive Evans D A, McConnell R B, Sheppard D M 1959 Secretion of blood group antigens and peptic ulcer. British Medical Journal 1: 603–607

Clarke D H 1953 Peptic ulcer in women. British Medical Journal 1: 1254–1257

Clark R J, Lewis D L, Williams J A 1972 Vagotomy and pyloroplasty for gastric ulcer. British Medical Journal 2: 369

Comfort M W, Gray H K, Dockerty M B, Gage R P, Dornberger G R, Solis J, Epperson D P, MacNaughton R A 1954 Small gastric cancer. Archives of Internal Medicine 94: 513–524

Coppola E D 1964 Dysphagia caused by elongation and tortuosity of the common carotid artery. New England Journal of Medicine 270: 572–574

Creamer B, Donoghue F E, Code C F 1958 Pattern of oesophageal motility in diffuse spasm. Gastroenterology 34: 782–796

Croft D N 1970 Body iron loss and cell loss from epithelia. Proceedings of the Royal Society of Medicine 63: 1221

Davidson W M B, Markson J L 1955 The gastric mucosa in iron deficiency anaemia. Lancet ii: 639–643

Dawson J L 1969 Carcinoma of the stomach. In: Diseases of the Digestive System. British Medical Association, London

Doig J A, Whaley K, Dick W C, Nuki G, Williamson J, Buchanan W W 1971 Otolaryngological aspects of Sjögren's syndrome. British Medical Journal 2: 460–463

Doll R, Avery-Jones F, Buckatsch M 1951 Occupational factors in the aetiology of gastric and duodenal ulcers. M.R.C. Special Report No 276. HMSO, London

Doll R, Hill R D, Hutton C, Underwood D J 1962 Clinical trial of a triterpenoid liquorice compound in gastric and duodenal ulcer. Lancet ii: 793–796

Dyer N H, Dawson A M 1969 Diseases of the Digestive System. British Medical Association, London

Dymock I W, Allan N C, Small W P 1972a Unpublished observations

Dymock I W, Hilton A M, Boyles B E 1972b Unpublished observations

Edwards F C, Coghill N F 1966 Aetiological factors in chronic atrophic gastritis. British Medical Journal 2: 1409–1415

Engel F L 1955 Addison's disease and peptic ulcer. Journal of Clinical Endocrinology and Metabolism 15: 1300–1307

Epstein A N 1967 Feeding without oesopharyngeal sensations. In: The Chemical Senses and Nutrition, Kare M R, Maller O, (ed) p 263–280. Johns Hopkins Press, Baltimore

Fikry M E 1965 Gastric secretory functions in the aged. Gerontologia Clinica 7: 216–226

Foroozan P, Trier J S 1967 Mucosa of the small intestine in

pernicious anaemia. New England Journal of Medicine
277: 553–559

Frank B W, Kern F 1967 Ménétrier's disease. Gastroenterology
53: 953–960

Friedman J W 1968 Dentistry in the geriatric patient. Geriatrics
23: 98–107

Gear M W L, Truelove S C, Williams D G, Massarella G R,
Boddington M M 1969 Gastric cancer simulating benign gastric
ulcer British Journal of Surgery 56: 739–742

Gillespie I E 1969 Duodenal ulcer. In Diseases of the Digestive
System. British Medical Association, London

Girdwood R H, Delamore I W 1961 Observations on tests of folic
acid absorption and clearance. Scottish Medical Journal 6: 44–59

Glass G B J, Goldbloom A, Boyd L H, Laughton R, Rosen S, Rich
M 1956 Intestinal absorption and hepatic uptake of radioactive vit.
B_{12} in various age groups and the effects of intrinsic factor
preparations. American Journal of Clinical Nutrition 4: 124–133

Gorbach S L, Nahas L, Lerner P I, Weinstein L 1967 Studies of
intestinal microflora. i. Effects of diet, age and periodic sampling
on numbers of faecal microorganisms in man. Gastroenterology
53: 845–855

Gough K R, Thirkettle J L, Read A E 1965 Folic acid deficiency in
patients after gastric resection. Quarterly Journal of Medicine
34: 1–14

Harris H, Kalmus H 1949 The measurement of taste sensitivity to
phenylthiourea (PTC). Annals of Eugenics 15: 24–31

Henkin R I, Schiechter P J, Hoye R, Mattern C F T 1971 Idiopathic
hypogeusia with dysgeusia, hyposmia and dysosmia. Journal of the
American Medical Association 217: 434–440

Hines J D, Hoffbrand A V, Mollin D L 1967 The haematological
complications following partial gastrectomy. American Journal of
Medicine 43: 555

Hollander F 1954 The two component mucous barrier. Archives of
Internal Medicine 93: 107–120

Hollis J B, Castell D O 1974 Esophageal function in elderly men.
Annals of Internal Medicine 80: 371–374

Howat, H T 1969 Aprotinin (Trasylol) in acute pancreatitis.
Prescribers J 9: 82–84

Howell, T H 1970 A Student's Guide to Geriatrics. London: Staples

Huete-Armijo A, Exton-Smith A N 1962 Causes and diagnosis of
jaundice in the elderly. British Medical Journal 1: 1113–1114

Hyams D E 1964 The absorption of vit. B_{12} in the elderly.
Gerontologia Clinica 6: 193–206

Joske R A, Finckh E S, Wood I J 1955 Gastric biopsy. Quarterly
Journal of Medicine 24: 269–294

Judge T G 1968 Hypokalaemia in the elderly. Gerontologia Clinica
10: 102–107

Kamocka D 1970 Quoted in Excerpta Medica, 13: 412

Kaplan S 1957 Paralysis of the swallowing mechanism following
bulbar poliomyelitis: surgical restoration of function. Archives of
Otolaryngology 65: 495–498

Kato Y 1966 Analysis on the diagnosis of the surgical gastric disease
by gastrocamera — particularly on diagnostic accuracy by combined
method with x-ray examination, gastrocamera and exfoliative
cytology. Gastroenterological Endoscopy (Tokyo 8: 293

Katz J H, Dimase J, Donaldson R M 1963 Simultaneous
administration of gastric juice bound and free radio-active
cyanocobalamin: rapid procedure for differentiating between
intrinsic factor deficiency and other causes of vit. B_{12}
malabsorption. Journal of Laboratory and Clinical Medicine
61: 266–271

Keefer C S, Bloomfield A L 1926 The significance of gastric
anacidity. Bulletin of the Johns Hopkins Hospital 34: 304

Kennedy T, Kelly J M, George J D 1972 Vagotomy for gastric ulcer.
British Medical Journal 2: 371–373

Kennedy Watt J, Watson W C, Haase S 1967 Chronic intestinal
ischaemia British Medical Journal 2: 199

Khan T A, Shragge B W, Crispin J S, Lind J F 1977 Oesophageal
motility in the elderly. American Journal of Digestive Diseases
22: 1049–1054

Kilman W J, Goyal R K 1976 Disorders of pharyngeal and upper
esophageal sphincter motor function. Archives of Internal Medicine
136; 592–601

Langman M J 1968 In: Symposium on Carcinoma of the Oesophagus.
British Society for Gastroenterology, London

Langman M J S 1971 Epidemiology of cancer of the oesophagus and
stomach. British Journal of Surgery 58: 792–793

Longmire W P, Kuzma J W, Dixon W J 1968 The use of
triethylenethiophosphoramide as an adjuvant to the surgical
treatment of gastric carcinoma. Annals of Surgery 167: 293

Lyall A 1937 Chronic peptic ulcer of the oesophagus. British Journal
of Surgery 24: 534–547

Macklin M T 1956 Role of heredity in gastric and intestinal cancer.
Gastroenterology 29: 507–514

Makhlouf G M, McManus J P A, Card W I 1966 Action of ICI
5 0123 on gastric secretion in man. Gastroenterology 51: 455

Master A M 1964 Spectrum of anginal and non-cardiac pain. Journal
of the American Medical Association 187: 894–899

Manor G E, Lyall A D, Chrystal K M R, Tsagopas M 1963
Observations on experimental occlusion of the superior mesenteric
artery. British Journal of Surgery 50: 219

McKeown F 1965 Pathology of the Aged, p 219–220 Butterworths,
London

Miller C 1962 Carcinoma of thoracic oesophagus and cardia. A review
of 405 cases. British Journal of Surgery 49: 507–522

Mills C P 1973 Dysphagia in pharyngeal paralysis treated by
cricopharyngeal sphincterotomy. Lancet i: 455–457

Mohammed S D, Chapman R S, Crooks J 1966 Hypokalaemia, flaccid
quadriparesis and myoglobinuria with carbenoxolone. British
Medical Journal 1: 1581–1582

Morgan D B, Pulvertaft C N, Fourman P 1966 The effects of age on
the loss of bone after gastric surgery. Lancet ii: 772–773

Mosbech J, Videbaek A 1950 Mortality from and risk of gastric
carcinoma among patients with pernicious anaemia. British Medical
Journal 2: 390

Moshal M G 1975 Treatment of duodenal ulceration with TDB —
duodenal double-blind cross-over investigation. Postgraduate
Medical Journal 51: 36–50

Mulsow F W 1941 Peptic ulcer of the aged. American Journal of
Digestive Diseases 8: 112

Palmer E D 1954a The state of the gastric mucosa of elderly persons
without upper gastrointestinal symptoms. Journal of the American
Geriatrics Society 2: 171–173

Palmer E D 1954b Gastritis: a revaluation. Medicine 33: 199

Palmer E D 1976 Disorders of the cricopharyngeus muscle: a review.
Gastroenterology 71: 510–519

Pearson J G 1968 In: Symposium on Carcinoma of the Oesophagus.
British Society for Gastroenterology, London

Pearson J G 1971 The value of radiotherapy in the management of
squamous oesophageal cancer. British Journal of Surgery
58: 794–798

Pelner L, Levy A 1960 Impaction of food bolus in the oesophagus.
Journal of the American Medical Association 172: 1922–1923

Piaget F, Fouillet J 1959 Le pharynx et l'esophage seniles: Etude
clinique, radiologique et radiocinématographique. Journal de
Médecin de Lyon 40: 951–966

Plaut A G, Gorbach S L, Nahas L, Weinstein L, Spanknebel G,
Levitan R 1967 Studies of intestinal microflora. (III) The microbial
flora of human small intestinal mucosa and fluids. Gastroenterology
53: 768–821

Polland W S 1933 Histamine test meals. An analysis of 988
consecutive tests. Archives of Internal Medicine 51: 903–919

Quinke H 1882 Deutsche Medizinische Wochenschrift 8: 79

Rivers A B 1939 Peptic Ulcer. In: Cyclopaedia of Medicine Surgery
and Specialities, 14, p 340. Davis, Philadelphia

Russell R I, Dickie J E N 1968 Clinical trial of a deglycyrrhizinized
liquorice preparation in peptic ulcer. Journal of Therapeutic Clinical
Research 2: 2

Salmon P R 1975 Evaluation of TDB in the treatment of duodenal
ulceration employing endoscopic selection and follow-up.
Postgraduate Medical Journal 51: 26–28

Sarner M, Rooke H W P 1971 Oesophageal candidiasis and carcinoma
of the oesophagus. Lancet ii: 1259

Schreeve D R 1975 A double-blind study of tripotassium di-citrato
bismuthate in duodenal ulceration. Postgraduate Medical Journal
51: 33–36

Shafar J 1965 Dysageusia in the elderly. Lancet i: 83–84

Sherwood L, Gorbach A L, Tabaqchali S 1969 Bacteria, bile and the
small bowel. Gut 10: 963–972

Siurala M, Isokoski M, Varis K, Kekki M 1968 Prevalence of gastritis in a rural population. Scandinavian Journal of Gastroenterology 3: 211

Small W P, Falconer C W A, Smith A N, McManus J P A, Sircus W 1971 Gastroenterostomy — an obsolete operation. Paper at British Society for Gastroenterology. Newcastle

Smith G S 1950 Causes of death in the aged. Lancet i: 24

Snapper I 1967 The aetiology of different forms of taste behaviour. In: The Chemical Senses and Nutrition, Kare M R, Maller O (ed), p 337–346. Johns Hopkins Press, Baltimore

Soergel K H, Zboralske F F, Amberg J R 1964 Presbyesophagus: oesophageal motility in nonagenarians. Journal of Clinical Investigation 43: 1472–1479

Strange S L 1959 Giant innocent gastric ulcer. British Medical Journal 1: 476

Strange S L 1963 Giant innocent gastric ulcer in the elderly. Gerontologia Clinica 5: 171

Tabaqchali S, Booth C C 1967 Relationship of the intestinal bacterial flora to absorption. British Medical Bulletin 23: 385–390

Thompson G R, Lewis B, Booth C C 1966 Vitamin-D absorption after partial gastrectomy. Lancet i: 457–458

Turpie A G G, Runcie J, Thomson T J 1969 Clinical trial of deglycyrrhizinized liquorice in gastric ulcer. Gut 10: 299–302

Turpie A G G, Thomson T J 1965 Carbenoxolone sodium in the treatment of gastric ulcer. Gut 6: 591–594

Tytgat G N S 1981 Assessment of the efficacy of cimetidine and other drugs in oesophageal reflux disease. In: Cimetidine in the 80s. J H Baron (ed) Churchill Livingstone, Edinburgh p 153–166

Vanzant Frances R et al 1932 The normal range of gastric acidity from youth to old age: an analysis of 3,746 records. Archives of Internal Medicine 49: 345–359

Wall A J, Ungar B, Baird C W, Langford I M, Mackay I R 1967 Malnutrition after partial gastrectomy. American Journal of Digestive Diseases 12: 1077

Weir D G, Temperley I J, Gatenby P B B 1963 Anaemia following gastric operations for peptic ulceration in Dublin. Irish Journal of Medical Science 488: 151

Whaley K, Williamson J, Wilson T, McGavin D D M, Hughes G R V, Hughes H, Schmulian L R, MacSween R N M, Buchanan W W 1972 Sjögren's syndrome and autoimmunity in a geriatric population. Age and Ageing 1: 197–206

Wilder W T, Frame B, Hanbrich W S 1961 Peptic ulcer in primary hyperparathyroidism. Annals of Internal Medicine 55: 885–893

Williams J A 1966 Postgastrectomy bone disease. In: Post-Graduate Gastroenterology, Thomson T J, Gillespie I E (ed) Ballière, Tindall and Cassell, London

Williams J A 1970 The effects of gastric operations. Annals of the Royal College of Surgeons of England 48: 54

Wormsley K G 1981 Short Term Treatment of Duodenal Ulceration. In: Cimetidine in the 80s. Baron J H (ed) Churchill Livingstone, Edinburgh, p 3–13

Zboralske F F, Amberg J R, Soergel K H 1964 Presbyesophagus, Cineradiographic manifestations. Radiology 82: 463–467

The gastrointestinal system — the pancreas and the small bowel

THE PANCREAS

Age changes in the pancreas

Structural changes

Even after death, study of the pancreas is difficult because of rapid autolysis. Changes in pancreatic size in old age have not been noted. Kreel and Sandin (1973) found the pancreatic position to be altered in elderly subjects, the pancreas sometimes being sufficiently ptosed for the papilla of Vater to be below the level of the L_3 vertebra. Andrew (1944) studied the pancreas of Wistar rats of various ages and made comparisons with human tissue. His main conclusion in both species was that duct hyperplasia occurs with increasing age. The proliferating duct cells extend both into the lumen of the ducts and between the pancreatic lobules. This results in both alveolar degeneration and duct obstruction. The latter may progress to locule formation, which was in fact the most obvious change seen in the aged human pancreas. Finally, adipose tissue invasion was seen to occur as a replacement phenomenon.

McKeown (1965) confirmed these changes in routine postmortems in the elderly. More recent support has been provided by the postmortem retrograde pancreatography carried out by Kreel and Sandin (1973). Ducts with a diameter as great as 1 cm were seen but without any evidence of obstruction. Ductular ectasia was also seen with cysts of 1 to 2 cm in diameter.

Infiltration of various organs by amyloid tissue and lipofuscins occurs in old age. Amyloidosis is most marked in the islets of Langerhans, involving both intra and peripancretic vessels, but secretory epithelial changes are thought to be rare. Pancreatic fat and connective tissue may also show amyloid degeneration (Schwartz, 1970). Lipofuscin granules have been demonstrated in the acinar cells of the pancreas (Wolman, 1969).

Functional changes

Necheles et al (1942) compared the duodenal juice of young subjects (mean age 23.4 years) with that of elderly subjects (mean age 66.5 years) following the adminis-

tration of oleic acid. They found no reduction in amylase or bicarbonate content with age, but lipase was reduced by 21 per cent in the elderly. Trypsin and total volume were not affected by age. Thaysen et al (1964) was able to confirm that total volume and amylase content were constant on aging. Bartos and Groh (1969) found that stimulation of the pancreas by injections of pancreozymin and secretin induced similar volumes of pancreatic juice production, irrespective of age, but repeated stimulation became less effective in the elderly subjects.

Garcia et al (1955) and Becker et al Meyer and Necheles (1950) both found impaired fat absorption in healthy elderly subjects consistent with reduced pancreatic lipase excretion. These changes are not considered sufficiently great to cause any significant handicap during normal daily life, and therefore pass unnoticed. Webster et al (1976) also reached the same conclusion after comparing fat absorption in young and old.

Disorders of the exocrine pancreas

Malignant disease and pancreatitis are the principal disorders. Carcinoma of the pancreas unfortunately remains difficult to diagnose in its early stages. Its treatment is therefore frequently delayed and the results disappointing.

Pancreatitis is now subdivided into the following four groups: acute pancreatitis, recurrent acute pancreatitis, chronic relapsing pancreatitis and chronic pancreatitis. Descriptions are clear cut and well defined only in the first and last subgroups, the intermediate divisions having a mixture of symptoms and signs. Acute pancreatitis is often dramatic in presentation and has a high acute fatality rate. The chronic form usually causes prolonged discomfort and ill-health, but is rarely fatal.

Acute pancreatitis

Aetiology. In all age groups, a large proportion of cases of acute pancreatitis have no clear cause; the bulk of the remaining cases are secondary to biliary tract disease, leaving a small minority due to metabolic disorders (Trapnell, 1966). Many cases in the idiopathic group may be due to ischaemia and it is tempting to think that this proportion will be increased in the aged population. However, Norris and Good (1961) found that there was no increase in vascular disease in elderly patients with pancreatitis compared with age-matched controls. Postoperative pancreatitis is also increased in the elderly; again this may be due to damage to the blood supply of the pancreas caused at operation, especially during biliary tract surgery, but this is an unsatisfactory explanation after such procedures as prostatectomy.

The incidence of biliary tract disease in Norris and Good's older patients was greater than in age-matched controls. Rittenbury (1961) also found that gall stones were more frequent in his series of patients over 60 years of age than would be expected.

Alcholism in Britian was said to be a rare cause of pancreatitis. However, James et al (1974) report that the previously accepted incidence of 10 per cent has now increased to almost 50 per cent. In America, alcohol has been long accepted as a more frequent cause of pancreatitis than in the United Kingdom, but Rittenburg found it to be less important in his older subjects.

Of the other metabolic causes, hypercalcaemia would not appear to be more common in the elderly and hyperlipaemia is less common. However, hypothermia and carbon monoxide poisoning, although rare, are both hazards to which the elderly are more prone than the general population, and both are known to be complicated by pancreatitis on some occasions.

Presentation. Nausea and vomiting are early symptoms, but affect only about one-third of elderly patients with acute pancreatitis. Such dyspeptic symptoms are most likely in patients with associated gall stones.

When pain occurs, it is usually dramatic and the patient will be able to give precise details of its sudden onset. The pain is usually epigastric (70 per cent of cases) but in half it also radiates into the back. In the elderly, pain is less likely to be in the right hypochondrium and more common in the lower abdomen (Hoffman et al, 1959; Rittenbury, 1961).

Unconciousness on presentation becomes more common in patients over 50 years of age (present in 24 per cent). It is a poor prognostic sign as 48 per cent succumb (Hoffman et al, 1959). In patients with mild chronic brain syndrome confusion may be precipitated by an attack of acute pancreatitis. The hypokalaemia which accompanies the acute episode may also contribute to their impaired cerebration.

The most interesting difference between age groups is the increased freqency of 'silent' attacks in old age. Although pain free, these attacks are often fatal and the diagnosis is only made at postmortem. Norris and Good (1961) described three cases of acute pancreatitis diagnosed after death, and of these two were aged 78 and 83 years.

In the most severe cases, the patient is shocked and abdominal examination will reveal the changes of peritonitis and ileus. When hypotension occurs, there is always the risk of distant catastrophies being precipitated in a frail, elderly patient. Evidence may therefore be found of complications such as a myocardial or cerebral infarction. Abdominal masses will only be found if a pseudocyst or abscess has occurred and these appear to be more rare in the elderly.

Grey Turner's and Cullen's signs are classical features of pancreatitis and reflect changes which occur in blood coagulation. However, they would seem to be rare in the elderly as reported series contain no examples.

Investigation. The most useful test in the diagnosis of acute pancreatitis is the serum amylase level. Gross elevation is usually good confirmation of the diagnosis, but some other abdominal emergencies, such as perforation of a peptic ulcer or dissection of an aortic aneurysm, may also produce high levels. Another reason for caution is that impaired renal function may artificially raise the serum amylase level and reduce urinary estimations.

Management. Laparotomy can usually be avoided, but if it is the only possible way of confirming the diagnosis, it appears safe provided the patient is well prepared preoperatively, especially regarding fluid and electrolyte replacement. Surgical action may prove lifesaving if symptoms are due to a perforated duodenal ulcer, and nothing is lost if pancretitis is confirmed.

In the majority of patients with acute pancreatitis, surgery has a place only in the treatment of complications (e.g. pancreatic abscess or pseudocysts). The main goal in the acute management is fluid replacement, initially with saline and potassium supplements, but with plasma or blood if hypotension occurs. The mortality of acute pancreatitis is highest in the elderly probably because of their inability to withstand the fluid loss. Replacement must therefore be as rapid and complete as possible. The use of a central venous pressure recorder will help to make these objectives possible without causing further difficulties.

Powerful analgesics may be required and none available is ideal. Morphia in particular is best avoided because of its effect on the sphincter of Oddi. Pentazocine is perhaps the analgesic of choice, although some elderly patients react unfavourably. Antispasmodics are of little value in the elderly as the large doses required produce dangerous side-effects.

Continuous duodenal aspiration is the most effective way of 'resting the pancreas' and also relieves the patient's nausea and vomiting. Aprotinin (Trasylol) has still not proved its value in the treatment of acute pancreatitis, and until evidence of benefit is better documented should not generally be used.

Chronic pancreatitis

Aetiology. Chronic pancreatitis is usually the end result of repeated episodes of damage due either to pancreatitis secondary to gall stones or alcoholic overindulgence.

Presentation. Pain is likely to be the most troublesome symptom. It is usually less severe than in acute pancreatitis and less frequently radiates away from the epigastrium. When radiation does occur it is most likely to move through to the back or shoulder. Attacks are sometimes precipitated by alcohol consumption. Half of the patients with chronic pancreatitis complain of nausea and vomiting, compared with only one-third of patients with acute pancreatitis.

The combination of the above symptoms is probably responsible for the anorexia and weight loss which may occur. Malabsorption of fat and fat-soluble nutrients may also lead to a fall in body weight. Although steatorrhoea might be expected in chronic pancretitis, constipation seems to be twice as common as diarrhoea in the elderly. Cases of diarrhoea are generally half as frequent in old victims as in young.

Jaundice can occur in pancreatitis, and elderly patients with the chronic disease tend to have the highest serum bilirubin levels (Rittenbury, 1961; Hoffman et al, 1959).

Hyperglycaemia and/or glycosuria occur twice as frequently in old as in young patients.

Investigation. In chronic pancreatitis, serum enzyme levels are of little value and are usually within normal limits. However, changes brought about by the use of intravenous secretin may be helpful, especially if there is an element of duct obstruction when it may produce an increase in serum amylase.

There is a natural reluctance to use tests requiring intubation to assess pancreatic function. The Lundh test (1962) is the most commonly used and gives valuable results in chronic pancreatitis — where tryptic activity is markedly reduced. A tubeless test would be a great convenience and the fluorescein dilaurate test described by Barry (1982) may prove itself reliable when more experience has been gained in its use.

Stool examination also has considerable drawbacks. Enzyme estimations are not very reliable, and faecal fat determinations may be misleading. For other tests concerning fat absorption, see the section on investigation of the small bowel (p. 527).

A straight X-ray of the abdomen may show evidence of pancreatic calcification, but similar lesions in the splenic vessels can lead to confusion.

With all these tests in suspected chronic pancreatitis it should be remembered that abnormal results will be helpful in confirming the diagnosis, but normal results have no value in excluding pathology.

Management. If steatorrhoea is present, then replacement of the exocrine secretions by pancreatic extract is necessary. This may improve both bowel habit and the absorption of fat-soluble vitamins and other nutrients. Treatment of the sometimes persistent pain is difficult and often only partly successful, even with potent analgesics. Anticholinergic drugs such as propantheline are more likely to be of value than in acute pancreatitis, but must be pushed to the point of tolerance.

Biliary bypass operation, sphincterotomy and removal of gall stones may all be indicated when the latter are thought to be responsible for the disease.

Carcinoma of the pancreas

Carcinoma of the pancreas has a peak incidence in the over 80s. It is also more common among diabetics, although it is not always clear as to whether the abnormal carbohydrate metabolism preceeds or follows the development of the carcinoma.

Presentation. Painless obstructive jaundice is the classical presentation of carcinoma of the pancreas (Bard and Pic, 1888), but drug-induced jaundice also needs to be considered in such patients. In obstructive jaundice due to malignant disease, about half have the responsible lesion in the head of the pancreas (Heute-Armijo and Exton-Smith, 1962). Biliary tract lesions and metastases account for the remainder. Pain frequently does occur in patients with a pancreatic carcinoma. Fifty-six per cent of patients are affected in the early stages (Bell, 1957) and the incidence rises as the disease progresses. Pain is usually epigastric, of a boring nature, with radiation into the back but relief is sometimes obtained by leaning forward.

Anorexia, weight loss and weakness may occur as early symptoms in about one-eight of patients. Although the stools will be pale, actual steatorrhoea appears to be rare. Melaena may occur if erosion into the stomach or duodenum takes place.

Patients are often initially thought to be hysterical or hypochondriacal, perhaps because the early symptoms of carcinoma of the pancreas are vague and often unsupported by abnormal laboratory results. Fras et al (1967) reported that 76 per cent of patients they investigated for carcinoma of the pancreas had psychiatric symptoms (depression, anxiety and premonitions of serious illness were characteristic). In over half their patients these symptoms preceded all others.

Episodes of vascular occlusion are also common in patients with pancreatic malignancy. Thompson and Rodgers (1952) found 95 episodes in 157 autopsy records. Sproul (1938) demonstrated the association between venous thrombosis and carcinoma of the pancreas, particularly lesions situated in the body and tail. Although less common, the non-bacterial thrombotic endocarditis described in malignant disease by Oelbaum and Strich (1953) must be considered as a possible cause of arterial occlusions.

Liver enlargement is found in 66 per cent of patients and is twice as common as an epigastric tumour or ascites. Thompson and Rodgers (1952) found a clinically palpable gall bladder in only 18.5 per cent, but postmortem examination increased the incidence to 44 per cent, indicating the difficulty in palpation of this viscus.

Auscultation of the abdomen should not be omitted. Partial obstruction of the splenic vessels is common (65 per cent of cases) according to Serebro (1965). In his case a bruit was recorded in 14 per cent. This sign is most likely to be present in cases of carcinoma of the body and tail, lesions which are usually more difficult to detect, but more rewarding to treat.

Investigation. Serum enzyme levels are usually normal. However, amylase levels may rise after an injection of secretin or pancreozymin if there is significant duct obstruction by the carcinoma. Conversely, a reduction in enzyme levels and total volume will be observed if duodenal aspirates are studied. In the elderly, there are considerable practical difficulties in tests requiring intubation for either biochemical or cytological investigations on secretions.

A simple and worthwhile investigation in patients with suspected carcinoma of the pancreas is the barium meal.

In 100 cases, Broadbent and Kerman (1951) recorded changes which made a definite clinical diagnosis in 54 per cent, and in a further 25 per cent there were suspicious signs on the films. X-ray finding of value were: alterations of duodenal mucosa suggesting invasion, pressure on the duodenal mucosa, distortion, irregularity, rigidity, constant filling defects and abnormal displacements of neighbouring structures.

The radiologist should be fully informed of the suspected diagnosis in order that special views may be taken. The technique of hypertonic duodenography may increase the diagnostic yield in suspected cases of pancreatic malignancy.

In cases of obstructive jaundice, where drug toxicity and carcinomatosis have been excluded, tests will be needed to determine the nature and site of the obstruction. Investigations of value in differentiating bile-duct growths, gall stones and carcinoma of the head of the pancreas are percutaneous cholangiography (followed by laparotomy, if necessary) and endoscopic retrograde pancreatography. The latter has been made possible by the development of flexible fibre-optic endoscopes and the increasing skill of their operators.

The results from isotope scanning using selenium-tagged methionine have been dispointing in attempts to demonstrate masses in the pancreas (Cotton et al, 1975).

Management. Because carcinoma of the pancreas tends to have a late presentation, the results of surgical removal are poor. An extensive mutilating procedure is often needed and postoperative complications will often lead to failure even if the entire tumour is removed. Lesions of the tail have the best prognosis but are notorious for being even more 'silent' and difficult to diagnose early than are lesions of the head.

Imaging of the pancreas

The investigation of structural and functional changes in the pancreas remains difficult. The latter because of a natural reluctance to resort to tests which require intubation, the former because of the deep position of the gland. Straight radiography and contrast barium studies tend only to show abnormalities in the late stages of disease — e.g. calcification in chronic pancreatitis and distortion of the duodenal loop in malignant disease. Arteriographic studies and cholangiograms are considered too invasive and complicated for routine use. The results of isotope scintilograms have been disappointing.

However, ultrasonography is proving itself to be of great value and is becoming increasingly available. Coles et al (1982) have shown that use of ultrasound is acceptable and valuable in geriatric practice. Lees et al (1979) reported great accuracy in identifying (94 per cent) and differentiating between chronic pancreatitis and carcinoma of the pancreas. They recorded no false negatives in their study. Ducan et al (1976) used ultrasound to observe progress in patients after an episode of acute pancreatitis. They found it a good technique for the identification of pseudocysts and were able to differentiate between cystic lesions and inflammatory masses. The spontaneous resolution of the latter was conveniently monitored.

Fawcitt et al (1978) published their experience with computed tomography in pancreatic disease. They found a 90 per cent accuracy in recognizing chronic pancreatitis and carcinoma and were easily able to differentiate between the two diagnoses.

Computer assisted tomography is not freely available so it is reassuring that its accuracy does not surpass that of ultrasonography. Mackie et al (1979) compared multiple techniques (including CT scanning) for the investigation of pancreatic disease and recommended ultrasound examination as the most fruitful. If further information was required they favoured endoscopic retrograde cholangiopancreatography with pancreatic juice assay and cytological examination of the fluid.

The patients being investigated for painless jaundice should initially undergo ultrasound examination of their liver. If dilated ducts are demonstrated the precise sit and nature of the obstruction is best revealed either by percutaneous cholangiography or endoscopic retrograde cholangiopancreatography — depending on the facilities and skills available locally.

THE SMALL BOWEL

Age changes in the small bowel

Structural changes
The little information available concerning age changes in the small bowel has been gained mainly from animal studies. That similar changes occur in aging man awaits confirmation.

Baker, Mathan and Cherian (1963) showed that the finger-like villi in neonatal rats gradually alter to become leaf-shaped and then parallel ridges in adult animals. Mathis (1928) and Van Lennep (1962) demonstrated a similar progression in bats and bandicoots.

Shortening of villi in very old rats has also been confirmed by Clarke (1977). Hohn et al (1978) also reported proximal villus atrophy in aged rats which was associated with irregularity of the normal villus architecture and reduction in enzyme activity. These changes were however restricted to the proximal small bowel. The enzymetic reduction was considered to be a reflection of the observed reduced number of cells in the aged villi. Penzes and Skala (1977) measured small bowel length in rats of different ages and recorded a shortening as the animals matured. Varga (1976) however found the converse. These changes may not be universal as Moog (1977) found the total weight of the small intestine of mice increased with age. She describes this change as being due to increased cellularity of the epithelium with elongation of the villi. A concurrent increase in enzyme activity was also reported. The changes were noticed to be most marked in the distal small bowel where the intestine was also thickened due to amyloid deposition.

The earliest age-change reported in man was the reduction in intestinal weight recorded by Vierordt in 1906. Jungman and Cosin (1948) and Portis and King (1952) demonstrated an increased coarseness of the small bowel mucosa radiographically. Using post mortem material, Chacko et al (1969) found that in an Indian population the shape of villi changed on aging. The youngest subjects had finger-shaped villi, but the frequency of broad villi and convolutions increased in specimens from older people. Webster and Leeming (1975a) described similar changes when fresh jejunal specimens from geriatric patients were compared with normal young controls. They found that in the elderly broader villi were more common, and in addition the villi were significantly shorter.

At a cellular level, age changes have only been studied in animals. Andrew and Andrew (1957) noticed an increase in the amount of fibrous tissue between the crypts of Lieberkuhn and a general reduction of cellularity in older mice. Suntzeff and Angeletti (1951) had described similar changes but also noted an increase in goblet cells in older animals, and found that villi were also shorter. Wulff et al (1961), using tritiated cytidine, found that 450-day-old mice incorporated the cytidine into villous cells more slowly than 15-day-old animals. Lesher et al (1961), Lesher and Sacher (1968) and Fry et al (1961), using autoradiography and tritiated thymidine, showed a prolonged generation time for duodenal crypt cells in old animals and an increased cell transit time (for cells to progress from the crypts to villous tips).

In conclusion, the possible expected age changes in the small bowel of man are an increase in broad villi, with a reduction in villous height. Consequently there would be a reduction in the surface area available for absorption. Warren et al (1978) have been able to estimate the surface area of small bowel biopsies taken from subjects of varying ages. They have demonstrated a significant reduction on aging. These structural changes could result from reduced cell production in the mucosa.

Functional changes
Meyer et al (1943) was probably the first to demonstrate an age difference in small bowel absorption. Using the galactose tolerance test, he showed a slow rise in blood levels of the monosaccharide in old subjects which failed to reach a peak as high as that in young controls. Webster and Leeming (1975b), using a modified xylose tolerance test, also showed poor absorption of monosaccharide in old subjects (26 per cent of a group of geriatric patients absorbed less efficiently than a young group of volunteers).

Most fat absorption studies in the elderly do not exclude the effect of maldigestion, due to pancreatic changes. However, Citi and Salvine (1964) studied oleic acid .which does not require digestion and found evidence of impaired absorption in old people.

Impairment of calcium absorption in elderly man has been demonstrated by Bullamore et al (1970) and Alevizaki et al (1973). Animal studies by Hansard and Crowder (1957), Hansand et al (1954), Henry and Kon (1953) and Schachter et al (1960) have all shown that with increasing age the ability to absorb calcium declines, but factors not related to mucosal function may be of significance. Thomson (1979, 1980) has reported a reduction in jejunal permeability for glucose and fatty acids as rabbits age.

Yeh et al (1965) concluded from their rat experiments that iron absorption falls with age and that this change does not reflect a reduced iron requirement. Marx (1979) could find no age-related reduction in the ability to absorb ferrous sulphate in both normal and iron depleted subjects. Jacobs and Owen (1969) showed a reduction in ability to absorb ferric citrate in the elderly but no differences when absorption of haem iron was studied. Such changes may reflect the increased incidence of gastric atrophy in old subjects.

Of the vitamins, there is evidence, although sometimes indirect, to suggest that some are not as efficiently absorbed by the old as by the young. Wright and Milner (1965) reported that serum carotene levels were lower in the elderly. Yiengst and Shock (1949) found that peak levels of vitamin A were reached later in old subjects following an oral dose, suggesting delayed absorption. Rafshy and Newman (1948) discovered that it was necessary to give old subjects a larger oral dose of vitamin A than younger controls in order to increase the serum levels, although this could indicate a pre-existing deficiency. Andrews et al (1969) found that geriatric patients who had been saturated with vitamin C were only able to maintain normal levels of ascorbic acid if given doses in excess of the recommended daily requirements calculated for young subjects (an increased need in old age is an unlikely alternative explanation). Thiamine absorption was found to be reduced in old rats compared with young in the investigations of Draper (1958), but no information is available for man. Baker et al (1978) demonstrated the poor absorption by the elderly of complicated forms of dietary folate. It has been suggested that this change may be due to changes in the mucosal enzyme content.

Other enzyme changes in mucosal cells may occur with increasing age and affect the function of the small bowel. The lactase content of cells may be reduced in aging man as in the baboon (Welsh et al, 1974). The alkaline phosphatase content may also fall. The staining technique used by Suntzeff and Angeletti (1951) showed no change in distribution with age, but there is a reduction in intensity of staining in older mice. Welsh et al (1974) found the same fall with age in baboons. Maldigestion due to atrophic changes in the stomach, pancreas and small bowel villi may play a significant role in some cases of nutrient deficiency found in old age. Poor intake and malabsorption will also be contributing in some instances.

Investigation of small-bowel function in the elderly

The investigation of small-bowel function in old people is complicated by changes occurring in other systems and organs. These may significantly alter the value of measurements used in standard tests, e.g. changes in renal (Davies and Shock, 1950) and hepatic function (Thompson and Williams, 1965).

Both physical and mental disabilities will make many tests unsuitable and prevent full patient co-operation in prolonged and complicated procedures. Therefore, the ideal test needs to be quick and simple, requiring minimum patient co-operation, and should be uninfluenced by changes in other systems. Obviously these criteria can only rarely be satisfied. Compromises have to be made and the subsequent limitations must not be overlooked. The investigation of a particular geriatric patient will only be justified if valuable and reasonably accurate results can be obtained without undue inconvenience to the patient and with the prospect of therapeutic benefit.

Fat absorption

The demonstration of excess faecal fat excretion is perhaps the most frequently used test to demonstrate impaired small-bowel function. However, the accuracy of such tests depends on a complete faecal collection for 3 to 5 days and the daily intake of a reasonable fat load (i.e. 60 to 100 g daily). Both may be difficult to achieve in the aged, however this remains the most readily available and trusted test.

An alternative method of estimating fat malabsorption, based on the microscopic examination of faeces for neutral and split fats, has been described by Drummey et al (1961).

Isotopic methods are not as accurate as would be desired (Pimparker et al, 1960) mainly because of the unstable nature of the combination between ^{131}I and fat: once separated the radioactive iodine follows its own metabolic course. Examination of residual radioactivity in the faeces has the same disadvantages as a standard faecal fat test.

Another approach to the quantification of fat absorption is the examination of blood following a fat meal and estimation of the various products of fat absorption. Serum chylomicron counts after a fatty meal have been demonstrated to alter with age (Garcia et al, 1955) but there has been no attempt to correlate chylomicron counts with efficiency of absorption. Serum turbidity following a fat meal was compared with the estimates of fat absorption using a radioiodinated protein test by Gabriel et al (1963). They report that low optical density occurs in all patients with steatorrhoea whilst normal radioactive fat absorption is associated with high optical density. Unfortunately a number of patients with normal fat absorption had an intermediate optical density value. However, this turbidity test may easily be used in geriatric practice. A high result would exclude steatorrhoea although a low result could be associated with either normal or impaired fat absorption.

Penfold (1967) measured the rise in serum lipids following a standardized fat meal and compared the results with faecal fat balance tests. In 98 per cent of normal subjects with normal faecal fat estimations, the serum lipid rose within four hours and was greater than 90 mg per 100 ml. In comparison, those with excessive faecal fat showed a serum lipid rise of less than

90 mg/100 ml. Like the serum turbidity test this offers the possibility of estimating fat absorption in patients not suitable for the more familiar tests.

The vitamin-A test was once used as an indicator of fat absorption since the vitamin is fat soluble. This was, however, a tolerance test depending on blood levels, and the effect of removal could not be differentiated from accumulation in the blood.

The triolein breath test Newcome et al (1979) based on the measurement of ^{14}C in expired carbon dioxide after the ingestion of labelled triolein offers an alternative method of assessing fat absorption. However, false positive results have occured in the obese and difficulties may be encountered in the elderly with resporatory disease.

Carbohydrate absorption
Xylose, a pentose absorbed from the proximal small bowel, has proved of great value in assessing small-bowel function. The standard xylose test of 25 g (or sometimes 5 g) given orally followed by the estimation of urinary excretion of xylose over the next five hours has fallen into disrepute in the elderly because of the high frequency of low urinary values without evidence of malabsorption. Such results have usually been considered a reflection of impaired renal function. Attempts have been made to circumvent this complication. Guth (1968) estimated blood levels in addition to urinary excretion of xylose, but here too renal function can interfere as the blood levels are dependent not only on rate of xylose absorption but also on its rate of removal — including renal excretion. Kendall (1970) compared the urinary excretion of xylose after oral and intravenous administration, both results being equally affected by any impairment of renal function. Using this method he reports normal absorption of xylose in healthy old people, and therefore this new approach to the problem may again make xylose a useful tool in investigating small-bowel absorption in the elderly (see Webster and Leeming, 1975).

In young persons the glucose tolerance test is often used as a test of small-bowel function, a poor rise in blood glucose suggesting malabsorption. However, in the elderly the frequency of impaired glucose tolerance may give rise to erroneous conclusions. Similarly, the starch tolerance test is unsuitable in old people because impaired digestion secondary to poor pancreatic function will effect blood glucose levels in addition to the difficulties noted above.

Tolerance tests are suitable in the elderly in the search for disaccharidase deficiencies, where the patient is used as his own control. Blood-sugar levels are estimated and compared with results obtained when the constituent monosaccharides are given independently (McGill and Newcomer, 1967; McMichael et al 1965). Although

lactose tolerance has been shown to be reduced with increasing age, the significance of this change is uncertain and its incidence in the elderly population is not known. However, these tests are simple, can be carried out without undue inconvenience to the patient and may reveal a definite diagnosis. Disaccharide intolerance can also be confirmed in the elderly by barium studies with and without the disaccharide under suspicion.

Examination of a small-bowel biopsy for evidence of disaccharidase activity will depend on local facilities and also on the patient's ability to co-operate during the biopsy procedure.

As the measurement of faecal pH is simple there may be a temptation to use this test in screening for disaccharide intolerance, but the test is of no value except during infancy since the adult colon probably corrects any pH change (McMichael et al, 1965).

Protein absorption
Protein absorption and loss is difficult to measure in all patients because isotopic labels applied to proteins are often unstable and may be independently recirculated and taken up by tissues. The use of synthetic substances instead of proteins solves some problems but is still not ideal (Dawson et al, 1961). In the aged there is the additional problem of specimen collection.

Vitamin B_{12} absorption
Impaired renal function and urine collection difficulties impair the usefulness of the Schilling test in old age. The double isotope method of Campbell and Craswell (1970), using ^{51}Cr as an unabsorbed marker, appears attractive for geriatric use as only an isolated sample and not a continuous collection of faeces is required. However, in practice the prolonged transit time makes it difficult to know when the ideal sample should be collected, and the amount of radioactivity measured during our own experience with the technique was so low as to make the calculations of absorption unreliable.

Surface-counting methods (Finlayson and Simpson, 1970), after the administration of radioactively lavelled vitamin B_{12}, also suffer from the slower intestinal emptying of the elderly. Whole-body counting (Finlayson and Simpson, 1970), after complete intestinal emptying, of a labelled dose would be the easiest way of measuring the absorption of vitamin B_{12} but such facilities are not widely available. McEvoy et al (1982) confirm the problems of prolonged transit times when whole body radiation measurement is used to assess the absorption of radioactive vitamin B_{12}. They recommend that the body count should made at 14 days rather than the more usual 7 day interval used in younger patients.

The use of plasma radioactivity measurements after oral administration of labelled vitamin B_{12} has generally been thought unreliable because of the overlap between normality and patients with vitamin B_{12} malabsorption. However, a large parenteral injection of unlabelled vitamin B_{12} given early in the test appears to separate normal subjects and others when plasma radioactivity is measured 8 to 12 hours after the beginning of the test (Amstrong and Woodliff, 1966). The commercially prepared Dicopac test incorporating two isotopes, one of which is combined with intrinsic factor, is an easy method for excluding pernicious anaemia (i.e. the major cause) as the reason for vitamin B_{12} deficiency.

The subject of vitamin B_{12} absorption is more fully discussed in chapter 41.

Folate absorption

The majority of tests used to estimate folate absorption require the patient to be saturated with parenteral folic acid prior to the test to ensure that the administered test dose does not disappear into the folate stores and become unavailable for easy measurement. This has the serious disadvantage that the saturating process will correct any folate deficiency which itself may be the cause of the small-bowel functional impairment. Moreover, these tests do not always clearly differentiate between normal and abnormal. It must also be remembered that the Figlu test is a test for folate deficiency irrespective of its cause, and not a direct test of small-bowel absorption of folate.

Folate absorption is more fully discussed in chapter 41.

Iron absorption

Iron absorption can be measured using radioactive isotopes (Lunn et al, 1967) but the procedures will have more disadvantages in older patients with limited co-operation. Absorption of iron from food is the most physiological process to measure and may be carried out more easily using a whole-body counter (Callender, 1971). The results, however, are so dependent on other dietary factors and gastric acid secretion that these tests are not justified as a routine clinical investigation for small-bowel function.

Calcium absorption

Because of the incidence of metabolic bone disease in elderly patients the intestinal absorption of calcium may merit investigation in some geriatric patients. Nordin et al (1968) and Bullamore et al (1970) describe methods based on the blood levels of radioactivity following the oral administration of labelled calcium, allowing for the rate of isotope removal from plasma. Using this technique, they have found better absorption in normal elderly subjects than in osteomalacic patients.

Small-bowel biopsy

The primary indication for a small-bowel biopsy in old age is to exclude or confirm the diagnosis of the adult coeliac disease arising late in life. Rare infiltrative conditions of the mucosal lining may also be demonstrated — e.g. lymphosarcoma (Linaker and Calam, 1978).

Changes have also been reported in pernicious anaemia, postgastrectomy patients (Scott et al, 1964), ulcerative colitis (Salem and Trulove, 1965) and neoplastic disease (Dymock et al, 1967), but these changes are minimal and do not contribute to making a diagnosis or planning treatment. Should a small-bowel biopsy be required the technique of Evans et al (1970), using a rigid outer cuff in addition to the usual flexible radio-opaque tubing of the Crosby capsule, greatly speeds up the procedure. With this modification it will be possible in most patients to obtain a suitable biopsy within 15 minutes although delay may occur in patients with hiatus hernia. Premedication with metoclopramide will also shorten the time taken (Mitchell and Parkins, 1969). Such time saving is particularly valuable in old people, as many are unable to tolerate prolonged procedures, rapidly tire and may become uncooperative.

Small bowel biopsy is not without risk. Linaker and Calam (1978b) reported 2 cases of perforation in patients over the age of 65 years — giving a high complication rate of 3.8 per cent in their elderly group. In one of their cases the perforation only became clinically apparent 4 days after the procedure — prolonged observation is therefore recommended when this technique is used in older patients.

Bacterial flora of the small bowel

Studies of the bacterial flora in the small bowel may be useful in conditions where stasis occurs. Culture of organisms from a blind loop or diverticulum require the full co-operation of both patient and bacteriology laboratory. Intubation will be unacceptable to many geriatric patients and difficulty may be experienced in accurately guiding the tube to the correct site. There are also many problems in cultivating the fluids obtained.

The indirect test of measuring urinary indicans may be helpful, high levels suggesting heavy bowel contamination.

Increased numbers of metabolically active bacteria in the upper gut will lead to the increased deconjugation of bile salts. The giving of radioactively labelled glycocholic acid (^{14}C) and the subsequent measurement of the radioactivity of expired air has been found to be a useful test (Parkin et al, 1972). High recovery rates in the breach indicate abnormal bacterial colonization.

X-ray studies

The use of the barium meal and follow-through is limited in the investigation of malabsorption particularly in the elderly, where poor quality films reduce its value even further.

The malabsorption pattern of flocculated barium and dilated loops of bowel is very non-specific. However, the demonstration of small-bowel diverticular disease is very helpful and probably the only justification for a follow-through in old age.

Malabsorption syndrome in the elderly

Malabsorption syndromes are conditions in which the mucosal lining of the small bowel or deeper structures are unable to perform their normal functions efficiently. It is the consequential development of deficiency disorders which frequently bring the patient to seek medical advice. In the elderly, deficiencies may arise rapidly and when the functional ability of the small bowel is only marginally impaired because they are less able to compensate by increasing the quantity and quality of their nutritional intake. However, recognition and reporting of symptoms is often delayed.

Anaemia is the most frequent presenting disorder. It occured in all 9 of Ryder's (1963) patients over 60 years of age with steatorrhoea and in one-third of Clarke's (1972) 15 patients with duodenal diverticular disease. A hypochromic microcytic picture is the most common appearance. However, evidence of folate and vitamin B_{12} deficiency may be revealed in many cases when the serum levels of these vitamins are assayed. In other cases a truly macrocytic picture due to either severe folic acid or vitamin B_{12} deficiency will be observed.

Disturbances of bone metabolism due to deficiencies of calcium and vitamin D are also not uncommon. Two of Clark's (1972) patients (13 per cent) presented in this fashion. Eight per cent of Chalmers's (1968) 93 patients with osteomalacia, of which over 80 per cent were aged 60, had an intestinal cause (excluding postgastrectomy patients). One-quarter of the 12 patients with osteomalacia described by Webster et al (1976) had evidence of impaired small-bowel function.

An increased frequency of bowel habit appears to be less conspicuous in the elderly (occurring in none of Ryder's patients, and in only five (33 per cent) of Clarke's — persistent in only two.

Montgomery et al (1978) investigated 33 patients with symptoms or abnormal biochemical and haematological results consistent with a degree of malabsorption. They confirmed impaired gastrointestinal function in 45 per cent of their patients, but also in 12 per cent of their elderly control group! Significant impairment of gut function may therefore not only be more frequent than previously realised, but also surprisingly silent.

Radiographic series have repeatedly shown how common and silent abnormalities in the gastrointestinal tract can be amongst old people.

Coeliac disease

Coeliac disease may be diagnosed for the first time in subjects over 60 years of age. Badenoch (1960) reported four such cases in his series. However, the true incidence of the condition in the elderly is not known but would appear to be low. As in younger patients, the diagnosis should depend on the histological and morphological appearances of the jejunal mucosa as seen on biopsy obtained with a Crosby capsule or similar instrument. Ideally, improvement after gluten restriction should also be demonstrated.

Management in the elderly will generally consist solely of replacement of nutritional deficiencies. The instigation of a strict gluten-free diet will not be justified unless severe abdominal discomfort and diarrhoea are symptoms affecting the patient. The very commendable reasons for strict dietary control in younger victims are not relevant to most geriatric patients.

Bacterial colonization

Of more relevance to geriatric practice, but with the magnitude of the problem again unknown, is the effect of abnormal bacterial colonization on the small-bowel lumen.

Important, and confirmed, causes of this condition are postgastrectomy states with blind loops (discussed above), duodenal and jejunal diverticular disease, and changes proximal to strictures whatever their aetiology. These opportunist bacteria may upset the patient's metabolic equilibrium in several ways. They may alter the mucosal cells of the jejunum and reduce their absorptive function. They may directly compete with the host for available vitamin B_{12} and lead to a B_{12} deficiency megaloblastic anaemia (in contrast, the patient may be protected against folic acid deficiency by the production of this substance by the bacteria). These bacteria may also interfere with bile-salt metabolism with a resultant effect on the absorption of fat and fat-soluble vitamins.

Another cause of abnormal bacterial colonization is abnormality of the gut flora of elderly subjects without obvious anatomical changes because circumstances for bacterial growth are more favourable in this age group. The higher incidence of hypo- and achlohydria removes a normally effective barrier to bacterial entry and the reduced gut motility may also encourage bacterial growth (as occurs in patients with scleroderma affecting the small bowel).

Roberts et al (1977) reported five elderly patients with evidence of bacterial overgrowth and malnutrition but without any structural abnormality on radiological examination. All these patients improved dramatically after treatment with a broad spectrum antibiotic.

Treatment of the condition is correction of the reason

for stasis (removal of the blind loop, diverticula or stenosis). If this is not possible, either due to the patient's condition or because of the extensive nature of the lesion (i.e. multiple diverticula), sterilization of the gut by the use of tetracycline will be effective, but recolonization is an ever-present risk.

Small-bowel ischaemia

As all vascular disease increases with age, it is not surprising that small-bowel ischaemia should be a cause of dysfunction in the elderly. For convenience, the disorders will be subdivided into their acute and chronic forms.

Acute mesenteric obstruction. This is usually a dramatic incident ushered in by abdominal pain and distension, from a gangrenous, non-functioning, length of small bowel. The cause of the vascular obstruction may be obvious, such as an embolus from a mural thrombus following a myocardial infarction or from an infected valve in subacute bacterial endocarditis. In other patients the events may only be a final incident in a long episode of chronic mesenteric ischaemia due to atherosclerotic changes. A previous clinical history of abdominal symptoms may then be the only guide to the diagnosis.

In most cases, treatment will be surgical with complete removal of the affected segment of gut, although cases have recovered spontaneously. These latter have usually been less extensive infarction, especially those resulting from embolism. Treatment of the underlying source of emboli or prevention of extension of the block may then be sufficient.

Chronic mesenteric ischaemia. This is sometimes known as abdominal angina and has long been recognized but, because of the nature of its symptoms and difficulty in confirmation, it is a diagnosis which is often missed.

The most common symptom is pain after food, usually of a cramp-like nature and situated in the epigastrium or umbilical region. Because of its site and precipitation, confusion with peptic ulceration is common. Cholelithiasis is another diagnosis often made erroneously. A useful distinguishing feature is the lack of alleviation of symptoms by antacids or further food. Evidence of ischaemia elsewhere is helpful supporting evidence but not absolute confirmation of the diagnosis.

Malabsorption of nutrients may occur and can be demonstrated as described above.

Arteriography is the only conclusive method of confirming the diagnosis (Dick et al, 1967). However, this technique will often be unsuitable. The presence of calcification of the aorta is sometimes a useful clue as it is usually present when the mesenteric vessels are narrowed, but the converse is not true.

Treatment will usually be conservative. Small and frequent meals will be beneficial in reducing symptoms and in helping to regain weight. It is interesting that such a dietary pattern has been suggested for the elderly for many centuries (e.g. by Thomas Elyot in *The Castel of Health* in 1534).

Malabsorption as a manifestation of a systemic disease. Certain systemic disorders may be associated with a malabsorption syndrome but need only a brief mention here. They include amyloidosis, scleroderma, diabetes mellitus (Berge et al, 1956), malignant disease (Dymock, 1967), skin disease (Marks and Shuster, 1970), rheumatoid arthritis (Pettersson et al, 1970), and chronic congestive heart failure (Hyde and Loehry, 1968). In addition drugs such as neomycin and phenindione have been incriminated.

REFERENCES

Alevizaki C C, Ikkos D G, Singhelakis P 1973 Progressive decrease of true intestinal calcium absorption with age in normal man. Journal of Nuclear Medicine 14: 760–762

Andrew W 1944 Senile changes in the pancreas of Wistar Institute rats and of man, with special regard to the similarity of locule and cavity formation. American Journal of Anatomy 74: 97–128

Andrew W, Andrew N W 1957 An age involution in the small intestine of the mouse. Journal of Gerontology 12: 136–149

Andrews J, Letcher M Brook M 1969 Vitamin C supplementation in the elderly. A 17-month trial in an old people's home. British Medical Journal ii: 416–418

Armstrong B K, Woodlife H J 1966 Absorption studies, comparison of 58_{co} B_{12} Schilling test and 57_{co} B_{12} plasma level. Medical Journal Australia 1: 709–712

Badenoch J 1960 Steatorrhoea in the adult. British Medical Journal ii: 880

Baker S J, Mathan V I, Cherian V 1963 The nature of the villi in the small intestine of the rat. Lancet, i: 860

Baker H, Jaslow, S P, Frank O 1978 Severe impairment of dietary folate utilization in the elderly. Journal of the American Geriatrics. Society 26: 218–221

Bard L, Pig A 1888 Revenue Medicale (Paris) 8: 257

Barry R E, Barry R, Ene M D, Parker G 1982 Flourescein dilaurate — tubeless test for pancreatic exocrine Lancet ii: 742–744

Bartos V, Groh J 1969 The effect of repeated stimulation of the pancreas on the pancreatic secretion in young and aged men. Gerontologia Clinica 11: 56–62

Becker G H, Meyer J, Necheles H 1950 Fat absorption in young and old age. Gastroenterology 14 80–92

Bell E T 1957 Carcinoma of the pancreas. 1. A clinicial and pathological study of 609 necropsied cases. 2. The relation of carcinoma of the pancreas to diabetes mellitus. American Journal of Pathology 33 499–523

Berge K G, Sprague R G, Bennett, W A 1956 Intestinal tract in diabetic diarrhoea: pathologic study Diabetes 5: 289–294

Broadbent T R, Kerman H D 1951 100 cases of carcinoma of the pancreas, a clinical and roentgenological analysis. Gastroenterology 17: 163–177

Bullamore J R, Gallagher J C, Wilkinson R, Nordin B E C Marshall D H 1970 Effect of age in calcium absorption. Lancet ii: 535–537

Callender, S T 1971 Iron absorption from food. Gerontologia Clinica 13: 44–51

Campbell C B, Craswell P W 1970 A double isotope method to measure vit. B_{12} absorption. Australian Annals of Medicine 1: 42–46

Chacko C J G, Paulson K A, Mathan V I, Baker S J 1969 The villus architecture of the small intestine in the tropics — a necropsy study. Journal of Pathology and Bacteriology 98: 146–151

Chalmers J 1968 Osteomalacia: a review of 93 cases. Journal of the Royal College of Surgeons of Edinburgh 13: 255–275

Citi S, Salvini L 1964 The intestinal absorption of ^{131}I-labelled olein and triolen of ^{58}Co, vit. B_{12} and ^{59}Fe, in aged subjects. Giornale de gerontologia 12: 123–126

Clarke A N G 1972 Deficiency states in duodenal diverticular disease. Age and Ageing 1: 14–23

Clarke R M 1977 The effects of age on mucosal morphology and epithelial cell production in rat small intestine. Journal of Anatomy 123: 805–811

Coles J A, Beynon G P J, Lees W R 1982 The use of ultrasound in Geriatric Medicine. Age and Ageing 11: 145–152

Cotton P B, Ponder B A J, Beales J S M, Croft D N 1975 Pancreatic diagnosis: comparison of endoscopic pancreatography (ERCP), isotope scanning, and secretin tests in 62 patients Gut 16: 405

Davies D F, Shock N W 1950 Age changes in glomerular filtration rate, effective plasma flow and tubular excretary capacity in adult males. Journal of clinical Investigation 29: 496–507

Dawson A M, Williams R, Williams H S 1961 Faecal PVP excretion in hypoalbuminaemia and gastro-intestinal disease. British Medical Journal ii: 667–670

Dick A P, Graff R, Greig D McG, Peters N, Sarner M 1967 An arteriographic study of mesenteric arterial disease. Gut 8: 206

Draper H H 1958 Physiological aspects of aging. 1. Efficiency of absorption and phosphorylation of radiothamine. Proceedings of the Society for Experimental Biology and Medicine 97: 121–124

Drummey, G D, Benson J A, Jones, C M 1961 Microscopical examinations of the stool for steatorrhoea. New England Journal of Medicine 264: 85–97

Dymock I W, Mackay N, Miller V, Thomson T J, Gray B, Kennedy E H, Adam J F 1967 Small intestinal function in neoplastic disease. British Journal of Cancer 21: 505–511

Evans N, Farrow L J, Harding A, Stewart J S 1970 New techniques for speeding small intestinal biopsy. Gut 11: 88–89

Fawcitt R A, Forbes W A C, Isherwood I, Braganza J M, Howat H T 1978 Computed tomography in pancreatic disease. British Journal of Radiology 51: 1–4

Finlayson N D, Simpson J D 1970 Whole body counting of vit B_{12} Co^{58} absorption supplemented by profile scanning. Scandinavian Journal of Gastroenterology 5: 261–264

Fras J, Liten E M, Pearson J S 1967 Comparison of psychiatric symptoms in carcinoma of the pancreas with those in some other intra-abdominal neoplasma. American Journal of Psychiatry 123: 1553–1562

Fry R J M, Lester S, Kohn H I 1961 Age effect on cell-transit time in mouse jejunal epithelium. American Journal of Physiology 201: 213–216

Gabriel J B, Vorsanger E, Beer D T, Sass M 1963 Evaluation of a serum optical density method for excluding malabsorption. American Journal of Clinical Pathology 39: 456–461

Garcia P, Roderick C, Swanson P 1955 The relation of age to fat absorption in adult women with observations on concentration of serum cholesterol. Journal of Nutrition 55: 601–609

Guth P H 1968 Physiological alterations in small bowel function with age. American Journal of Digestive Diseases 13: 565–571

Hansard S L, Comar L, Davis G K 1954 Effects of age upon the physiological behaviour of calcium in cattle. American Journal of Physiology 177: 383–389

Hansard S L, Crowder H M 1957 The physiological behaviour of calcium in the rat. Journal of Nutrition 62: 325–339

Henry K M, Kon S K 1953 The relationship between calcium retention and body stores of calcium in the rat. Effect of age and vitamin D British Journal of Nutrition 7: 147–159

Heute-Armijo A, Exton-Smith A N 1962 Causes and diagnosis of jaundice in the elderly. British Medical Journal 1: 1113–1114

Hoffman E, Perez E, Somera V 1959 Acute pancreatitis in the upper age groups. Gastroenterology 36: 675–685

Hohn P, Gabbert H, Wagner R 1978 Differentiation and ageing of the rat intestinal mucosa II Morphological, enzyme histochemical

and disc electrophoretic aspects of the ageing of the small intestinal mucosa. Mechanisms of Ageing and Development 7: 217–226

Hyde G H, Loehry C A 1968 Folic acid malabsorption in cardiac failure Gut 9: 717–721

Jocobs A M, Owen G M 1969 The effect of age on iron absorption. Journal of Gerontology 24: 95–96

James O, Agnew J E, Bouchier I A 1974 Chronic pancreatitis in England: a changing picture? British Medical Journal 11: 34–38

Jungman H J, Cosin L 1948 Radiology of the small intestine in old age. Journal of Gerontology 3: 297

Kendall M J 1970 The influence of age on the xylose absorption test. Gut 11: 498–501

Kreel L, Sandin B 1973 Changes in pancreatic morphology associated with aging. Gut 14: 962–970

Lees W R, Vallon A G, Denyer M E, Vahl S P, Cotton P B 1979 Prospective study of ultrasonography in chronic pancreatic disease. British Medical Journal 1: 162–164

Lesher S, Fry R J M, Kohn H I 1961 Influence of age on transit time of cells of mouse intestinal epithelium. Laboratory Investigation 10: 291–300

Lesher S, Sacher G A 1968 Effects of age on cell proliferation in mouse duodenal crypts. Experimental Gerontology 3: 211–217

Linaker B D, Calam J 1978 Is jejunal biopsy valuable in the elderly. Age and Ageing 7: 244–245

Linaker B D, Calam J 1978b Jejunal biopsy with the Watson capsule and perforation in the elderly. Gastroenterology 75: 723–725

Lundh G 1962 Pancreatic exocrine function in neoplastic and inflammatory disease — a simple and reliable new test. Gastroenterology 42: 275–280

Lunn J A, Richmond J, Simpson J D, Leask J D, Tothill P 1967 Comparison between three radioisotope methods for measuring iron absorption. British Medical Journal iii: 331–33

McEvoy A W, Fenwick J D, Boddy K, James O T W 1982 Vitamin B_{12} absorption from the gut does not decline with age in normal elderly humans. Age and Ageing 11: 180–183

McGill D B, Newcomer A D 1967 Comparison of venous capillary blood samples in lactose tolerance testing. Gastroenterology 55: 371–374

McKeown F 1965 In: Pathology of the Age, p 210–220. Butterworth, London

Mackie C B, Cooper M J, Lewis M H, Moossa A R 1979 Non-operative differentiation between pancreatic cancer and chronic pancreatitis. Annals of Surgery 189: 400–487

McMichael H B, Webb J, Dawson A M 1965 Lactase deficiency in adults: a cause of functional diarrhoea. Lancet i: 717–720

Marks J, Shuster S 1970 Dermatogenic enteropathy. Gut 11: 292–298

Marx J J M 1979 Normal iron absorption and decreased red cell iron uptake in the aged blood 53: 204–211

Mathis J 1928 Beiträge zur kenntris das Fledermaus darmes. Zeitschrift fur Mikroskopisch-Anatomische Forschung 12: 595–647

Meyer J, Sorter H, Oliver J, Necheles H 1943 Studies in Old Age. VII. Intestinal absorption in old age. Gastroenterology 1: 876–881

Mitchell A B S, Parkins R A 1969 metaclopramide as an adjunct to small bowel intubation. Gut 10: 690

Montgomery R D, Haeney M R, Ross I N, Sammons H G, Barford A V, Balakrishnan S, Mayer P P, Culank L S Field J, Gosling P 1978. The ageing gut: a study of intestinal absorption in relation to nutrition in the elderly. Quarterly Journal of Medicine 186: 197–211

Moog F 1977 The small intestines in old mice; growth, alkaline phosphatase and disaccharidase activities and deposition of amyloid. Experimental Gerontology 12: 223–235

Necheles H, Plotke F, Meyer J 1942 Studies in old Age V. Active pancreatic secretion in the aged. American Journal of Digestive Diseases 9: 157–159

Newcomer A D, Hofmann A F, Dimagno E P, Thomas P J, Carlson G L 1979 Triolein breath test. A sensitive and specific test for fat malabsorption. Gastroenterology, 76: 6–13

Nordin B E C, Young M M, Oxby C, Bulusu L 1968 Calculation of calcium absorption rate from plasma radioactivity. Clinical Science 35: 177–182

Norris T St M, Good C J 1961 Pancreatitis: a retrospective review of 92 cases. Postgraduate Medical Journal 37: 792–797

Oelbaum M H, Strich S J 1953 Thrombo-phlebitis migrans and

carcinoma of the body and tail of pancreas. British medical Journal ii: 907–909

Parkin D M, O'Moore R R, Cussons D J, Warwick R R C, Rooney P, Percy-Robb I W, Shearman D J C 1972 Evaluation of the 'Breath Test' in the detection of bacterial colonisation of the upper gastrointestinal tract. Lancet ii: 777–780

Penfold W A F 1967 Serum lipid levels following a fatty meal as a test of steatorrhoea. Proceedings of the Association of Clinical Biochemists 4: 205–209

Penzes L, Skala I 1977 Changes in the mucosal surface area of the small gut of rats of different ages. Journal of Anatomy 124: 217–222

Pettersson T, Wegelius O, Skrifuars 1970 Gastro-intestinal disturbances in patients with severe rheumatoid arthritis. Acta Medica Scandinavica 188: 139–144

Pimparker B D, Tulsky E G, Kalser M H 1960 Correlation of radioactive and chemical faecal fat in different malabsorption syndromes. British Medical Journal ii: 894–900

Portis S A, King J C 1952 The gastrointestinal tract in the aged. Journal of the American Medical Association 148: 1073–1079

Rafshy H A, Newman B 1948 A study of the vitamin A and carotene tolerance tests in the aged. Gastroenterology 10: 1001–1006

Rittenbury M 1961 Pancreatitis in the elderly patient. American Surgeon 27: 475–494

Roberts S H James O, Jarvis E H, 1977 Bacterial overgrowth syndrome without 'blind loop'. A cause for malnutrition in the elderly. Lancet ii: 1193–1195

Ryder J B 1963 Steatorrhoea in the elderly. Gerontologia Clinica 5: 30–37

Salem S N, Truelove S E 1965 Small intestinal and gastric abnormalities in ulcerative colitis. British Medical Journal i: 827–831

Schachter D, Dowdle E B, Schenker H 1960 Active transport of calcium by the small intestine of the rat. American Journal of Physiology 198: 263–274

Schwartz P 1970 In: Amyloidosis: Cause and Manifestation of Senile Degeneration: p 111–114. Charles C Thomas, Springfield, Illinois

Scott G B, Williams M J, Clark C G 1964 Comparison of jejunal mucosa in post-gastrectomy states, idiopathic steatorrhoea and controls using the dissecting microscope and conventional histological methods. Gut 5: 553–562

Serebro H 1965 A diagnostic sign of carcinoma of the body of the pancreas Lancet i: 85–86

Sproul E E 1938 Carcinoma and venous thrombosis; the frequency of association of carcinoma in the body or tail of the pancreas with mulitple venous thrombosis. American Journal of Cancer 34: 566–585

Suntzeff V, Angeletti 1951 Histological and histochemical changes in intestine of mice with aging. Journal of Gerontology 16: 225–229

Thaysen E H, Mullertz S, Worning H, Bang H O 1964 Amylase concentration of duodenal aspirates after stimulation of the pancreas by a standard meal. Gastroenterology 46: 23–31

Thomson A B R 1979 Unstirred water layer and age-dependent changes in rabbit jejunal D-glucose transport. American Journal of Physiology 236: E685–91

Thomson A B R 1980 Effect of age on uptake of homologous series of saturated fatty acids into rabbit jejunum. American Journal of Physiology 239: G363–371

Thompson C M, Rodgers L R 1952 Analysis of the autopsy records of 157 cases of carcinoma of the pancreas with particular reference to the incidence of thromboembolism. American Journal of the Medical Sciences 223: 469–478

Thompson E N, Williams R 1965 Effect of age on liver function with particular reference to bromsulphthalein excretion Gut 6: 266–269

Trapnell J E 1966 The natural history and prognosis of acute pancreatitis: Annals of the Royal College of Surgeons of England 38: 265–287

Varga F 1976 Transit time changes with age in the gastro-intestinal tract of the rat. Digestion 14: 319–324

Van Lennep E W 1962 The histology of the mucosa of the small intestine of the long-nosed bandicoot with special reference to intestinal secretion. Acta Anatomica 50: 73–89

Vierordt H 1906 In: Datan und tabellen für medizine (3rd edn). G Fischer, Jena

Warren P M, Pepperman M A, Montgomery R D 1978 Age changes in small intestinal mucosa. Lancet ii: 849–850

Webster S G P, Leeming J T 1975a The appearance of the small bowel mucosa in old age Age and Ageing 4: 168–174

Webster S G P, Leeming J T 1975b Assessment of small bowel function in the elderly using a modified xylose tolerance test. Gut 16: 109–113

Webster S G P, Leeming J T, Wilkinson E M 1976 The causes of osteomalacia in the elderly. Age and Ageing 5: 119–122

Webster S G P, Wilkinson E M, Gowland E 1977 A comparison of fat absorption in young and old subjects Age and Ageing 6: 113–117

Welsh J D, Russell L C, Walker J A W 1974 Changes in intestinal lactase and alkaline phosphatase activity level with age in the baboon. Gastroenterology 66: 993–997

Wolman M 1969 In: Pigments in Pathology: p 199. Academic Press, New York and London

Wright W B, Milner A R 1965 The serum carotene level in elderly patients Gerontologia Clinica 7: 120–127

Wulff V J, Quastler N, Sherman F G 1961 The incorporation of H^3 Cytidine in mice of different ages. Archives of Biochemistry 95: 548–549

Yeh D J, Soltz W, Chow B F 1965 The effect of age on iron absorption in rats Journal of Gerontology 20: 177–180

Yiengst M J, Shock N W 1949 Effect of oral administration of vitamin A on plasma levels of vitamin A and carotene in aged males. Journal of Gerontology 4: 205–211

The gastrointestinal system — the large bowel

ANATOMICAL CHANGES

The normal anatomy of the large bowel has been well reviewed by Christensen (1971). However, little consideration has been given to age associated anatomical changes. Yamagata (1965) compared biopsy specimens obtained from the colon from 222 healthy subjects with those obtained at autopsy from 160 hospital cases. He paid special regard to changes of senescence. Aging changes include atrophy of the mucosa, morphological abnormality of the intestinal glands, cell infiltration of the lamina propria and mucosae, hypertrophy of the lamina muscularis mucosae, increase in connective tissue, atrophy of the muscle layer and arteriolar sclerosis. Electron microscopic examination of the epithelial cells showed an increase in small vacuoles, abnormalities in the nucleus and an increase in electron density of the cell and its nucleus, with advancing age. Mars and Buogo (1967) reported on colonic anatomy in 104 random autopsies from a geriatric institution. They noted a very high incidence of colonic diverticula — 55 per cent in females and 34 per cent in males with an overall incidence of 47 per cent. They found an increase in connective tissue spaces around blood vessels but no histological difference between subjects with and without diverticula.

Arteriosclerosis affecting the coeliac axis and mesenteric vessels leads to very important age associated change which will be discussed under ischaemic colitis.

PHYSIOLOGY

The nature of motility within the large bowel has been the subject of a great deal of investigation. This is likely to be particularly important in relation to bowel function in old people because of diseases and age-associated changes in the nervous system which may have an effect on bowel motility.

So far little research has been undertaken in the relationship of senescence and altered motility. Motility within the colon has been investigated by the use of balloons and open-ended tubes inserted through the anus or through colostomy openings: also by pressure telemetering capsules which may be swallowed; by cineradiography, and by noting the progress of variously shaped radio-opaque markers in their passage through the colon. Early investigations (White et al, 1940) were based on the application of the principle of the cystometrogram to the lower bowel. A 'colonmetrogram' was made by distending the colon with fluid from a reservoir and noting the pressure reactions to distension. White and his colleagues investigated a series of neurologically affected patients by this means and their findings were exactly the same in the colon as in the bladder, i.e. that lesions above the sacral cord led to an increase in motility resulting from distension. These findings were in keeping with those of Denny Brown and Robertson (1935) but are at variance with more recent investigations made with miniature balloons (e.g. Connell et al, 1963).

Since the colon is in fact an open-ended cylinder the recording of pressure changes within it presents a more difficult problem than in a closed organ such as the urinary bladder. Ritchie et al (1962) have discussed this question very completely and have indicated that while balloons record isotonic contractions, open-ended tubes record isometric contractions and neither one alone will adequately record both types. They demonstrate also the dual nature of pressure changes in a given segment of the colon resulting from both inflation and contraction. In the former the gut size is increased and thus direct pressure on a balloon may be diminished while the pressure as measured by an open-ended tube increases. With contraction, the lumen of the bowel is diminished leading perhaps to direct contraction of the balloon so that greater pressure may be recorded in the balloon than that measured by an open-ended tube. They suggest the use of a differential unit employing both the balloon and an open-ended tube in order to try to overcome these difficulties.

Despite these problems, the recording of pressure changes through miniature balloons continues to be used as a research tool and by this means different patterns of motility have been demonstrated in different conditions (for instance in comparing diarrhoeal states with non-diarrhoeal states). For interpretation of the data obtained in this way Painter and Truelove (1964) describe a colonic motility index and Misiewicz et al (1968) have devised a method of finding the motility index using a digital computer.

Another shortcoming of this type of recording is the unpredictable nature of colonic motility and the fact that motility patterns are not necessarily reproducible in one individual throughout subsequent periods. One method of overcoming this is by maximally stimulating colonic motility using neostigmine (Prostigmin) (Misiewicz et al, 1966) or by a meal (Meunier et al, 1979). By these various means a number of findings have become well established.

Motility increases during and after food but this is rarely associated with propulsive activity in the resting patient although propulsion does occur in physically active patients (Holdstock, 1970). This may be a factor of importance in the causation of constipation in immobile elderly patients (see below). Hypomotility is associated with the use of the drugs pethidine and propanthelene and with diarrhoeal states (Misiewiez et al, 1966). Hypermotility on the other hand is caused by morphine and by Prostigmin. It is associated also with diverticular disease (Painter and Truelove, 1964). Its well documented association with constipation has recently been questioned (Meunier et al, 1979).

As well as the intrinsic contractions which are measured in the motility index, peristaltic 'stripping' waves are found down the whole length of the descending colon ending at the rectosigmoid junction, but not extending into the rectum. These have been demonstrated by Mann and Hardcastle (1970) who show that they occurred very occasionally (4 were seen in over 48 patient hours of observation). Their incidence is greatly increased by administration of a contact laxative (e.g. bisacodyl) which produced the same waves with a frequency of up to one minute for a period of up to 45 minutes.

Rectal distension causes discomfort. Frenckner and Ihre (1976) reported a slight continuous feeling of distension in normal subjects after the injection of 36 ml of air into the rectum, and maximal tolerable discomfort with 363 ml. An increase with age in the volume of rectal distension required to produce discomfort was reported by Newman and Freeman (1974), who also showed the rectums of constipated subjects to be even less sensitive than others.

So far no investigation of the effect of aging on any aspect of colon motility has been reported other than the effects resulting from rectal distension. Brocklehurst (1951, 1972) compared the effects of balloon distension of the rectum in young and old men and the relationship between balloon distension of the rectum and fluid distension of the bladder (recorded at different times) in aged women.

Gastrocolic reflex

The so-called 'gastrocolic reflex' has always been thought important in initiating mass peristalsis in the colon and leading to the call to defaecation. This is discussed by Christensen (1971) in a very good review of the physiology of the large bowel. The increased colonic activity which has been noted following food ingestion occurs even in the denervated colon and persists following thoraco-lumber spinal cord transection (Roman and Gonella, 1981). Transmission, therefore, appears to be hormonal. It has been shown above that this response is increased in association with physical activity. Holdstock and Misiewicz (1970) associate the so-called 'gastrocolic reflex' rather with the entry of food into the small intestine by showing that not only is the reflex independent of vagal innervation but also that it occurs in the absence of the stomach, of gastric acidity, and of antral gastrin.

Defaecation

The physiology of defaecation has been reviewed by Davenport (1966). Three or four times a day part of the caecal contents passes into the transverse colon and on to the descending colon and rectum by strong and massive contraction of the caecum and colon; the resulting mass distends the rectum and arouses the distension reflex which is centred in the sacral cord. If this reflex is not inhibited then defaecation involving co-ordinated movements of both voluntary and involuntary muscles follows. If the reflex is inhibited the rectum relaxes; stimulation in its wall disappears and defaecation is postponed. Co-ordination of defaecation with other body effects results from a defaecation 'centre' in the medulla situated close to the vomiting centre. As with micturition there are centres higher than this (in the diencephalon and in the cerebral cortex) with affect defaecation.

The phenomena associated with defaecation were investigated by Halls (1965) on 18 normal volunteers who swallowed radio-opaque markers of different shapes. By this means he was able to show that each meal taken was spread over a wide area of the colon and that there was some premixing in the right side. He found no gross change in movement of the markers to account for the call to stool but found that resistance to the call to stool may lead to faecal reflux from the rectum back into the colon. In one case the markers returned from the rectosigmoid junction to the distal transverse colon. No obvious correlation between the amount of faeces in the colon and the length of the segment involved in defaecation was found. The amount of faeces passed varied from time to time, sometimes the whole left side of the colon from the splenic flexure emptying at a defaecation and at other times only partial emptying of the rectum occurring. He also found, in contradiction to the commonly held view that the rectum is normally empty, that 17 of the 18 volunteers had faeces in the rectum unassociated with any urge to defaecate.

Denny Brown and Robertson (1933) showed that distension of a balloon within the rectum caused a sensation of distension which lasted for about 5 to 10 minutes and then the balloon tended to ascend within the rectum. Parks et al (1962) indicated that sensation within the rectum came from stretch receptors in the rectal wall but Lane and Parks (1977) showed that the inflation reflex — rise of intra-rectal pressure together with relaxation of the internal sphincter — occurred in patients following excision of the rectum. They proposed that the sensors lie among the fibres of the levator ani muscle. Rectal distension leads at first to an increase in the contractility of the anal sphincter, followed almost at once by inhibition of discharge (Parks et al, 1962; Schulster et al, 1965; Frenckner, 1975). Freckner and Ihre (1976) by combined pressure recording from the anus and electromyographic recording from the external sphincter, showed that the drop in pressure was entirely due to the internal sphincter — and that some subjects maintained external sphincter discharge during rectal distension. Tucker (unpublished) has shown no impairment of this reflex with aging, even in faecally incontinent old people.

The distending balloon may be discharged involuntarily (equivalent to faecal incontinence) in a number of situations, e.g. paraplegia (Parks et al, 1962), normal subjects with low spinal anaesthesia (Freckner and Ihre, 1976) and faecally incontinent elderly men (Brocklehurst, 1951).

Tonic discharge in the normal external anal sphincter is present at rest and during sleep and is also present in patients with spinal cord transection above L.3 (Parks et al, 1962). In tabes dorsalis there is no resting activity but voluntary contraction is possible. Coughing causes increased activity within the external sphincter which starts before the cough. This also remains in transection of the cord above L.3. Bearing down and attempted micturition both diminish the tone in the external sphincter.

Duthie and Bennett (1963) investigated sensation in the anal canal and suggested that some relaxation of the anus on distension of the rectum allowed the sensory anal canal to 'sample' the bolus contained within the rectum since he found that the sensation resulting from contact with the sphincter was different from the sensation due to distension. This may help to explain the ability to distinguish between faeces, fluid and flatus within the rectum, a distinction which is important in the maintenance of continence and which may possibly be impaired in very old people.

Continence mechanisms

There are three mechanisms involved in maintaining continence. First is the ano-rectal angle, (Fig. 26.1) maintained principally by the pubo-rectalis sling. Continence depends on this angle being less than 115° (Kerremans, 1969). Second is the 'flutter valve' mechanism of the slit shaped anal canal (Philips and Edwards, 1965). Third is the muscular sphincter mechanism at the anus. In part this is due to opposing loops of the

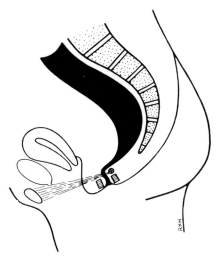

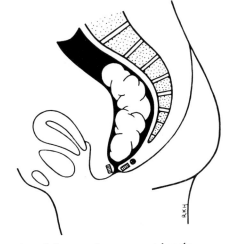

A   B

Fig. 26.1 (a) Pubo-rectalis sling maintaining ano-rectal angle. (b) Faecally-distended rectum loses ano-rectal angle.

external sphincter (Shafick 1975); in part due to the continuous contraction of the internal and external sphincter (Frenckner and Ihre, 1976)

Bowel habit

The variations in bowel habit of people living in the United Kingdom were described by Connell et al (1965). They interviewed 1455 subjects, of whom 125 were over 60; they found that 99 per cent had a bowel habit which lay between 3 defaecations a day and 3 defaecations a week and that there was no difference in bowel habit between those under 60 and those over 60. Milne and Williamson (1972) in a random sample from 27 000 people aged 62 and over in Edinburgh (the total sample being 215 men and 272 women) recorded the frequency of defaecation. 71 per cent of the men and 67 per cent of the women claimed to have a bowel movement once daily. The range of frequency was from less than twice a week to more than twice a day.

CONSTIPATION

It is a generally held impression that people tend to become more constipated as they get older. However, as indicated above, there is no evidence in support of this fact. The impression probably results from two main factors; the first is that old people often complain of constipation almost as non-specific evidence of malaise, possibly because it is a symptom that seems clear to them and seems important. The second and related factor is that people who are old today, certainly in the United Kingdom, have lived through the medical profession's great myth about autointoxication from the colon and the supposed resulting evils of infrequent bowel actions. There can be little doubt that a fad which led eminent surgeons to the performance of colectomies in order to overcome the ill-effects of autointoxication must have had a profound affect on the lay public who were at an impressionable stage of their lives during that era. This emphasis of the virtue of regular and frequent bowel actions led to a whole generation of children being brought up on at least once-weekly purgation; the use of vegetable laxatives in the armed services has become a music hall joke. No less an intellect than Bertrand Russell was persuaded, albeit lightheartedly, to attribute his longevity to having a regular bowel motion twice a day (Russell, 1970).

There have been few serious attempts to determine the limits of 'normality' in frequency of bowel motions. The most important are those of Connell et al (1965) and Milne and Williamson (1972) already referred to. Both papers report a distinct age associated difference in frequency of laxative taking. Although, as indicated above, this is likely to be cultural and reflect a lifelong

habit rather than evidence of recently developing symptoms, nevertheless, it may be that if this older group were not taking laxatives to the extent that it reported, some age related association between lesser frequency of bowel motions and increasing age may have emerged. Connell and his colleagues defined regular laxative taking as more often than once a week. They found none of the subjects aged 10 years and below fell into this category, 16 per cent of those between 10 and 59 did and 30 per cent of those over the age of 60.

The first importance of constipation in old age is the possibility that it is a symptom of underlying disease, among which must be considered carcinoma of the colon. Hinton and Lennard-Jones (1968) have reviewed the definition and classification of constipation admirably and their differential diagnostic list is shown in Table 26.1. In the elderly, hypothyroidism and depression are two particularly important and insidious illnesses which may include constipation among their symptoms.

Table 26.1 Aetiology of constipation

LESIONS OF THE GUT
  Aganglionosis
  Obstruction
  Idiopathic megacolon
NEUROLOGICAL
METABOLIC
  Hypercalcaemia
  Porphyria
  Drugs
ENDOCRINE
  Hypothyroidism
PSYCHIATRIC
  Depression
GENERAL
  Immobility

Definition

As to definition, 'constipation' is a term used in two principal and different ways. One is that frequency of bowel action seems to the patient to be insufficient, the other is that the stools may be hard and difficult to pass. In a number of old people neither of these causes may be present and the really constipated person with a gradually impacting mass of faeces in the rectum and descending colon may have a bowel motion every day which, far from being hard, may present as a spurious diarrhoea.

One way of measuring constipation is by estimating *transit time* through the alimentary tract. Various methods of measuring transit time have been used including the ingestion of dyes, millet seed and glass beads. These early methods have been well reviewed by Truelove (1966). More recently radio-opaque markers have been used which can either be monitored by regular X-ray examination of the abdomen or by X-raying each day's stool, collected in plastic containers. Hinton et al (1969) used this latter method and investigated transit times in 25 normal male subjects. They showed that all subjects had passed the first marker by the end of the third day and all but one had passed 80 per cent by the end of the fifth day. This they regarded as the upper limit of normal transit time. As to lower limits they found that no normal subject had passed 80 per cent of the markers at the end of the first day. These findings are very much in keeping with those of workers using other methods although mean transit times, as opposed to 80 per cent limit times, are much shorter (e.g. 54 hours) (Cummings et al 1976). These findings apply to a Euro-American culture and since transit time appears to be affected by the amount of roughage in the diet, findings from people with a different dietary habit are different. Burkitt et al (1972) compared mean 80 per cent transit times in different ethnic groups and linked these with the bulk of their diet — unrefined (high in natural fibre) 36 hours, mixed diet — 45 hours, refined 48–83 hours. Cummings et al (1976) claimed mean transit time in healthy subjects to drop from 2.4 to 1.6 days when additional dietary fibre was used. Other workers have reported variable effects of added dietary bran on transit time — generally showing that transit time is speeded up where it was previously slow, but unchanged or even slowed, where it was previously rapid (Harvey et al Payler et al, 1975).

Eastwood et al (1973) found no increase in transit time, but only an increase in stool weight, with added dietary bran.

Transit-time studies among elderly people have been carried out by Brocklehurst and Khan (1969) but these were almost entirely confined to long-stay hospitalized geriatric patients. Brocklehurst and Khan compared 8 long-stay geriatric patients with 4 non-hospitalized active elderly people. The latter had all passed all the markers by the 7th day and their transit time may, therefore, be regarded as normal. Only 1 of the long-stay patients, however, had passed 80 per cent of the markers by the 7th day although they had all passed 80 per cent by the 14th day. The long-stay geriatric patients were mainly bedfast or chairfast and the majority of them suffered from disabling neurological disease.

In a further study (Brocklehurst et al, 1983) 37 long stay geriatric patients were all found to have 80 per cent transit times in excess of 6 days and 30 per cent of them still had markers in situ after 14 days.

In the majority of cases the markers had reached the descending colon fairly rapidly and were held up at that level; they may thus be described as the Terminal Reservoir Syndrome, a title used by Bodian et al in 1949.

Idiopathic megacolon

Two important complications of constipation in old people are faecal incontinence (see below) and idiopathic megacolon. The causes of megarectum and megacolon in the adult have been reviewed by Todd (1971) who suggested a primary muscular disorder or degeneration as accounting for a small group of them in whom no neurological cause could be found, while it seems likely that the majority of cases presenting among institutionalized older people are secondary to constipation. Nevertheless the possibility of an acquired lesion of the myenteric plexuses similar to Hirchsprung's disease has been raised by Smith (1968) who showed that degeneration of the plexuses occurred in mice given anthraquinone purgatives in large doses and also in patients suffering from the cathartic colon syndrome, who had been taking purgatives for 30 to 40 years.

Idiopathic megacolon in old people presents as gross tympanitic abdominal distension, usually associated with diarrhoea and faecal incontinence. The diagnosis is easily made on the X-ray findings (see Fig. 26.2). Treatment is unsatisfactory. It should include the maintenance of an empty colon by frequent and regular enemas and possibly the use of neostigmine (Connell, 1961). More of these cases may be shown in due course to be due to degeneration of the myenteric plexuses and this may be why the result of treatment is so often unsatisfactory. Diarrhoea due to anaerobic bacterial colonization may require treatment with metronidazole. The main danger of idiopathic megacolon is that of developing volvulus of the sigmoid.

Volvulus of the colon

Volvulus of the colon is a disorder particularly of institutionalized and immobile patients and descriptions of it have come mainly from mental hospitals. It has also been described in patients with Parkinsonism (Caplan et al, 1965) where it may be associated with the use of anticholinergic drugs. The disorder is more common in Africa than in the United Kingdom where it is associated not with mental hospital patients but with a high-residue diet (Annotation, 1968).

Table 26.2 shows some findings from a number of reviews of sigmoid volvulus. The early diagnosis of this condition requires a high index of suspicion since it tends to occur in long-stay, institutionalized patients and the presenting symptoms may not be marked. They include abdominal distension which may be minor or may be considerable, cramping abdominal pain and constipation; hypercalcaemia, high-residue diet and explosive treatment of constipation have been suggested as possible associated factors. The mortality is high and no doubt this is, in part, due to the tardiness in making the diagnosis. String and DeCosse (1971) say 'long delays before recognition and management especially in

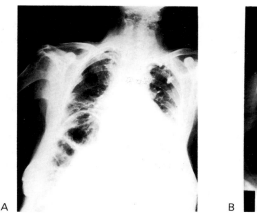
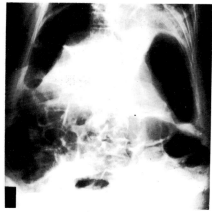

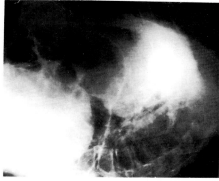

Fig. 26.2 X-rays of patient with megacolon

patients already in the hospital for another disease correlated prominently with the increased mortality'.

Sigmoidoscopy itself is sometimes all that is required
to reduce the volvulus but over 50 per cent of the cases
require operative intervention.

Treatment of constipation

The use of laxatives, suppositories and enemas among
elderly people, particularly those in hospital, often has
no more rational basis than the experience and the preju-
dices of the nurse or relative in charge of the case. The
traditional classification of laxatives and purgatives into
the three categories of bulk, lubricant and irritant is still

applicable although one or two of the more recently
introduced substances require a rather liberal interpretation of these terms. Indeed the whole basis of this classification has been questioned by Binder (1977) who
suggests that most laxatives have their effect by fluid
accumulation caused by active ion secretion.

Bulk purgatives on the whole are not popular among old
people and would seem to be particularly contraindicated in those who are immobile and likely to be
suffering from the terminal reservoir syndrome. Their
use might, therefore, be thought of as preventative, but
with the exception of bran-containing foods it seems
doubtful whether pharmacological agents should be used

Table 26.2 Some findings from reported series of cases of sigmoid volvulus

	No. of patients	Mean age at onset	Percentage over 70 years	Percentage with psychiatric disorder	Mortality
Ingalls et al (1964)	18	—	—	100	—
Wuepper et al (1966)	39	67	50	60	—
String & DeCosse (1971)	25	61	—	50	28%
Arnold & Nance (1973)	99	66	53	30	28%

for this purpose on the present evidence. Cleave et al (1969) strongly advocate the use of unrefined flour (or added bran) in the prevention of constipation and their case for this would seem to be a good one. Clark and Scott (1976) found 15 g added wheat bran to be effective in the treatment of constipation among long-stay geriatric patients in males but not in females. The bran had to be completely mixed with the food to prevent it being inhaled. Side-effects occurred only in men who reported depressed appetite (42 per cent) and abdomen fullness (25 per cent). Enthusiastic support for the use of bran comes from Hull et al (1980) who investigated its use in a 300-bedded geriatric centre (average age 80 years and many patients immobile). After one year the use of laxatives was virtually eliminated — with considerable financial saving. They do not however discuss different effects between patients with varying mobility. They describe the three recipes that were used successfully.

Saline purgatives are probably very popular as forms of self-medication in the elderly but are best avoided as a drug prescribed by the physician, except in very special circumstances as in preoperative preparation of the bowel.

Other bulk purgatives include the celluloses and hydrophilic colloids. Among these ispaghulia has been favourably compared with bran in diverticular disease (see below).

The lubricant purgatives used to consist principally of liquid paraffin popularized by Arbuthnot Lane, but now another group of drugs might be admitted to this category — those which lower the surface tension of the faeces and allow water to penetrate them. They are sometimes called faecal softeners. Dioctyl sodium sulphasuccinate (DSS) has been used most commonly for this purpose. A comparison with dioctyl calcium sulphasuccinate (DCC — Surfak) by Fain and colleagues (1980) among institutionalized elderly people showed DCS to be superior. DSS and poloxalkol (a further stool softener) are available in combination with irritant purgatives (e.g. Dorbanex, Normax). These are widely used among the elderly and few side-effects have been reported. They may be most rationally used in the prevention of faecal impaction among those who are at risk because of their immobility.

The case against mineral oil was made by Becker (1952). Its disadvantages include diminished absorption, by the direct coating of the mucosa with oil and the preferential solution of fat-soluble vitamins, pleuritis, lipid pneumonia and a possible carcinogenic factor.

The irritant purgatives include many that are now superseded. Those in common use include cascara sagrada, senna in the form either of infusion or of the standardized product Senokot, bisacodyl and picosulphate. The first two are anthracine purgatives which are absorbed from the small bowel and excreted into the

colon where they are broken down to various products including the active principle emodine which has a direct stimulant affect on the myenteric plexuses. Hardcastle and Wilkins (1970) have shown that a senna concentrate, if incubated with either faeces or *Escherichia coli* for a period of 6 to 12 hours and then inserted into the rectum, shows a response within 10 minutes, followed by continuous contractions, whereas the untreated concentrate inserted into the rectum shows no response.

The fact that anthracine purgatives given over a long period of time damage the myenteric plexuses has been referred to above (p. 538). Recent work by Tucker (unpublished) demonstrated a relationship between loss of the rectal-anal sphincter reflex in elderly people who have been on long-term authrocines.

Havard and Hughes-Roberts (1962) reported the use of Senokot in the treatment of constipation in large numbers of patients in a mental hospital, including a number with chronic organic brain disease. They noted a temporary period of faecal incontinence but this was overcome in most cases by giving Senokot at night and sitting the patient on a commode first thing in the morning. High doses were used and no 'griping' was reported. It was also shown that in most cases after a period of regular purgation by this means for about three months the drug could be withdrawn altogether. Picosulphate was found to be as effective as standardized senna in 50 long-stay geriatric patients (MacLennan and Pooler, 1975).

Bisacodyl is not absorbed from the gut and has its stimulant effect directly on the myenteric plexus. It may thus be given orally or rectally, but is probably most popularly given by the latter route. Deiling et al and (1959) report a review of this drug and show that evacuation occurs in 85 per cent of cases between 35 and 75 minutes after insertion of the suppository. Warman (1961) also writes enthusiastically about the use of this drug in geriatric patients. Brocklehurst (1964) compared bisacodyl suppositories with miniature enermas (containing dioctyl potassium sulphasuccinate, glycerin and soft soap to a total volume of 5 ml) and also a control enema of 5 ml of soap solution given in the same way as the miniature enermas. Evacuation occurred within three hours in 85 per cent of both groups on the active drugs and 50 per cent of those on the placebo. The stool was similar in all groups but more complete evacuation was obtained more often with bisacodyl than with the miniature enema containing dioctyl potassium sulphasuccinate.

In general the use of bisacodyl suppositories is popular and effective among elderly people and has the advantage of producing an action within a reasonable period of time.

Another drug which hardly fits into any of the three

normal categories is lactulose. This was the subject of a double-blind trial carried out by Wesselius-DeCasparis et al (1968) in 103 elderly people. It was found that 50 per cent of these did not need laxatives although they generally considered themselves chronically constipated. Among the remainder lactulose was used with a success rate of 80 per cent compared to a plain syrup placebo which produced a success rate of 33 per cent. The only side-effects were transient gas formation and intestinal bloating.

The use of lactulose was also reported in geriatric patients by Ryan et al (1974) with particular reference to its effect on faecal incontinence (see below).

Lactulose and a combination of poloxalcol and di-hydroxianthroquinalone (Dorbanex) were compared as to their effectiveness in preventing constipation in a group of long-stay geriatric patients (Brocklehurst et al, 1983). While both were better than no treatment neither of them normalized the transit time.

Enemas

Large bulk soap and water enemas are not generally in geriatric patients. Small bulk enemas have been found to be just as effective and are particularly convenient since they are prepared in a prepacked for which is easy to administer [Phosphates enema B.P.C. (Fleet enema) — each of these contains 128 ml including 10 per cent sodium acid phosphate and 8 per cent sodium phosphate]. One and quite often two of these are required. Injury from phosphate enemas has been reported (Pietsch et al, 1977). Mucosal damage from the hard plastic nozzle together with the effect of the hypertonic solution caused tissue necrosis.

Whole gut irrigation — a method of clearing a very constipated or even impacted colon in one procedure, was described by Smith et al (1978). Intravenous injections of frusemide 40 mg and (separately) metoclopramide 10 mg are given, a nasogastric tube passed and isotonic saline at roughly body temperature infused at a rate of 2.5–3 litres an hour. Smith reported the precedure in 70 patients (mean age 80 years) using a mean quantity of 8 litres of irrigant. Irrigation was continued until effluent began to clear. The precedure failed in only one patient. It should not be used in subjects in heart failure.

Mannitol 200 g, cooled and flavoured with fruit juice has also been used as a single treatment. A high rate of colic has been reported (Lee, 1982).

The treatment of constipation may be summed up as follows. No preventive methods are necessary in old people unless experience has shown that they have been the subject of recurring bouts of constipation. The use of a high-residue diet and even added bran or stone-milled flour is to be encouraged, and exercise or mobility is clearly an important factor in preventing the onset of constipation. Patients who have become faecally impacted on one or more occasions might be retained on a regular dose of dioctyl sodium sulphasuccinate or a combination of poloxalkol and anthroquinone (e.g. Dorbanex). In such case this should probably be combined with a regular enema perhaps once a week. Patients must, of course, be treated individually both as to dose and as to frequency and where possible the active ingredients taken by mouth should be diminished as much as they can be. The alternative drug to use in this situation is Senokot which is again found to be very satisfactory. In the treatment of acute episodes of constipation bisacodyl suppositories or small bulk phosphate enemas may be recommended. It is worth noting in a number of the trials reported above how prominent placebo effects are in relation to laxatives and purgatives.

An excellent critical review of therapeutic agents in the management of constipation is that of Godding (1972).

FAECAL INCONTINENCE

Faecal incontinence ranks second only to urinary incontinence as one of the major problems in the care of geriatric patients. It is secondary to urinary incontinence because it is less frequent and because it is more readily managed but it exceeds urinary incontinence in the unpleasantness it produces both for the patient and for his nurses. Brocklehurst (1951), in his survey of incontinence of patients in 5 Glasgow hospitals, found an incidence of 23 per cent of incontinence in a geriatric hospital and 11 per cent among the medical wards of the other general hospitals. This was among a total of 2223 patients surveyed and included a total of 312 who were incontinent. Of these 25 per cent were incontinent of urine only, 72 per cent were incontinent of urine and faeces, and only 3 per cent were incontinent of faeces alone. A study of patients in long-stay geriatric wards (Brocklehurst et al 1977) showed a faecal incontinence rate of 45 per cent. They also showed faecal incontinence to be a positive correlate of bacteriuria.

Classification

There are three main causes of faecal incontinence in old age. The first is symptomatic of underlying disease either of the colon or rectum or of the anal sphincter. The second is faecal impaction, and the third a neurogenic change which is analogous to that found in the bladder of the majority of incontinent elderly people (see Chapter 30).

Faecal incontinence may be a symptom and indeed may be the presenting symptom of carcinoma of the colon or rectum. It may be the result of diverticular disease, ischaemic colitis, proctocolitis, diabetic neuro-pathy (see Pallis and Lewis, 1974; British Medical Journal, 1979) or any other disorder causing diarrhoea in an elderly person. It may be the side-effect of purga-tive drugs or drugs such as iron. Finally it may be associated with disruption of the anal sphincter as a result of surgery for haemorrhoids or with prolapse of the rectum. In each of these cases the treatment is that of the underlying cause.

Old people may be predisposed to incontinence in diarrhoeal states because of denervation of the striated fibres of the pubo-rectalis, external sphincter and levator ani muscles. (Parks et al, 1977; Henry and Swash, 1978; Beersiek et al, 1979; Percy et al, 1982). This may cause diminution or loss of anorectal sensation, loss of the anal reflex, impairment of the rectal angle or a patulous anus.

Constipation of long standing in an older person leads imperceptibly to faecal impaction in which the consti-pating mass becomes gradually dehydrated and hard and the resulting scyballa, by irritating the mucosa of the colon and rectum, cause an outpouring of mucus. This in turn carries liquid faeces beyond the scyballous masses and leads to the spurious diarrhoea characteristic of this type of faecal incontinence. Although on many occasions the hard impacting mass can be felt on rectal examination this is by no means always the case. Brock-lethurst and Khan (1969) showed that even in patients with transit times in excess of 7 days, faeces in the rectum may be soft. On a series of rectal examinations at weekly intervals in a group of faecally incontinent elderly people (3 examinations each in 20 patients) the rectum was found to be empty on 13 occasions, contained soft faeces on 16 occasions and hard faeces on 31 occasions.

Watkins' (unpublished) findings (on examining 177 long-stay geriatric patients) are as follows:

Incontinent patients. Rectum empty 11 per cent; large quantity of faeces 60 per cent.
Non-incontinent patients. Rectum empty 27 per cent; large quantity of faeces 40 per cent.

Neurogenic incontinence is in some ways a theoretical concept. A number of experimental findings in support of it may be quoted. White et al, in 1940, in their colon-metrogram experiments (p. 534) found a reaction to distension of the rectum in patients with neurological lesions to be similar to the reaction of the urinary bladder to distension in similar patients, confirming the findings of Denny Brown and Robertson (1935). Parks et al (1962) also showed that a balloon distended in the rectum of paraplegic patients might be extruded.

Brocklehurst (1951) recorded the intrinsic contrac-tions arising from within the rectum as a result of its distension by a large balloon with increments of 50 ml of air. Measurements were taken directly from the

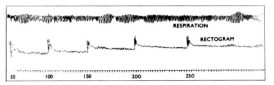

Fig. 26.3 Rectal tracing taken from a distended balloon within the rectum in a normal elderly male. The balloon is distended by air in 50 ml increments to a total of 250 ml. No intrinsic rectal contractions are seen.

distending balloon. Consistent results emerged when 19 elderly men suffering from faecal incontinence and 11 men of various ages who were not particularly inconti-nent were compared. The balloon was distended, where possible, to a total of 250 ml of air; none of the control patients evacuated the balloon and in 7 of them no intrinsic contractions arising within the rectum were seen as a result of balloon distension (Fig. 26.3). More than one-third (7 of the 19) incontinent men passed the balloon during the period of distension, in each case preceded by intrinsic rectal contractions (Fig. 26.4). Such contractions were present in 16 of the 19 incon-tinent males; thus the reaction of these 2 groups of patients to balloon distension within the rectum was different. In the majority of cases this distension gave rise to a series of intrinsic rectal contractions which the incontinent patients were unable to inhibit and which often led to the passing of the balloon. A sensation of distension was noted in only 4 of the control patients and 2 of the 19 incontinent patients. These findings are in keeping with the hypothesis that distension of the rectum in a group of incontinent elderly people (resulting perhaps from the mass movement of faeces as a result of the gastrocolic reflex) is followed by intrinsic rectal contractions and by the inhibition of contraction in the anal sphincter (see p. 536) to the point that the distending bolus is passed in many cases. Such a process is clearly analogous to that described in relation to the uninhibited neurogenic bladder in the chapter on urinary incontinence. Many of these incontinent elderly men had overt neurological disorders, others were suffering from arteriosclerotic dementia.

Fig. 26.4 Tracing from intrarectal balloon in an elderly male with faecal incontinence. Intrinsic contractions are seen from 200 ml and the balloon is passed after a series of contractions at 250 ml.

In order to compare the response of the bladder and of the rectum to distension in a group of incontinent elderly people, Brocklehurst and Freeman (Brocklehurst, 1972) performed cystometrograms, and tracings of balloon distension of the rectum, in the same patients at different times. In this case the rectum was distended by a large balloon with 50 ml increments of air to a maximum of 250 ml and rectal motility was recorded by a small balloon high in the rectum, proximal to the larger balloon. Of 10 patients, 6 passed the large balloon before it was fully distended, and 4 retained it after full distension. Figure 26.5 represents the findings in these 10 patients and it is seen that 5 of those who passed the balloon before full distension also had an abnormally low bladder capacity. They all showed both intrinsic rectal activity and unihibited bladder contractions. It may be argued, therefore, that these 5 patients, 1 of whom had a right hemiplegia and the other 4 were suffering from dementia, showed loss of inhibition of both bladder and rectal contractions (and undue inhibition of the external anal sphincter) as a result of disease of their cerebral cortex. Three of the other patients, who retained the balloon even when it was fully distended, had the highest bladder capacities. In 2 of these the bladder capacity was within the normal range and in the third just below it. Two of these patients were

mentally clear and 1 was demented. In only 2 of the 10 patients were the findings in the bladder and the rectum inconsistent (patients 9 and 10, both suffering from dementia).

In the case of demented patients it is difficult to argue that this loss of control is anything other than unaware-ness of the environment and of the need to show socially acceptable behaviour in their excretory habits. Never-theless, the majority of these patients are not antisocial in other ways and many patients with serious dementia are not incontinent. Certainly those with neurological lesions and faecal incontinence who are mentally aware have no reason to abandon the normal code of social behaviour. The probability is, therefore, that the third or neurogenic group of faecal incontinence is a real one in old age and is, in many ways, comparable to the urinary incontinence associated with the uninhibited neurogenic bladder.

Clinical presentation
There may be a difference in clinical presentation between incontinence associated with constipation and that which has a neurogenic basis. In the former case the patient tends to be continually lying in a mass of semi- or unformed faeces. In the latter the incontinence may only occur perhaps once or twice a day in associ-ation with the gastrocolic reflex and a formed stool is passed.

The treatment of faecal incontinence
The successful treatment of faecal incontinence has two prerequisites — the first an adequate investigation to discover its cause and the second a determination on the part of the physician and transmitted by him to the ward staff that treatment is worthwhile and can be successful. Once symptomatic causes have been excluded it is prob-ably best, in the first instance, to regard all faecally incontinent patients as being constipated; particularly since the findings on rectal examination do not always reflect this. The first thing to do then is to empty the rectum and the larger part of the colon, a procedure which can most effectively be undertaken by giving one or two phosphate enemas daily for a period of 7 to 10 days until there is no return or using whole gut irri-gation or mannitol (see p. 541). If constipation has been the cause of faecal incontinence then the latter will have cleared up and the next important matter is to prevent its recurrence. This may be done either by the use of a mild laxative containing a wetting agent (see above) or by regular use of enemas — perhaps once weekly. Of course, if the immobility which has been associated with the incontinence has disappeared as a result of rehabili-tation, then no further treatment may be required.

If this course of treatment is not successful in stop-ping faecal incontinence then it may be assumed that

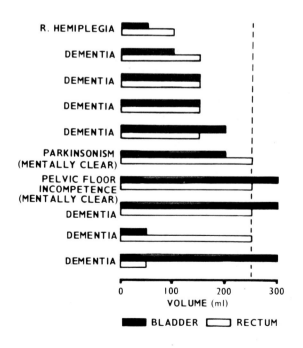

Fig. 26.5 Comparison of the reaction of the rectum and the bladder to distension in a group of long-stay elderly patients

this is of a neurogenic type and a therapeutic trial of the appropriate treatment for this condition undertaken.

Neurogenic incontinence should be treated on the principle of induced constipation with periodic planned evacuation. This may be achieved by giving alternating courses of treatment with a constipating agent such as chalk and opium, and one which has the opposite affect such as a mild laxative or an enema. Jarratt and Exton-Smith (1960) describe a 12-hourly alternation of kaolin and morphine (given in the morning) and Senokot (given in the evening). Brocklehurst (1972) prefers longer periods of the constipating drug, given two or three times a day, as may be necessary, and the planned evacuation to be obtained on the 5th, 6th or 7th day by the use of enermas or suppositories. For practical purposes, particularly in patients at home, an enema may be given first and after this has had its effect a bisacodyl suppository left in the rectum to produce a further action in an hour to an hour-and-a-half.

A third method of control has been reported by Kaplan (1970) from his experience in a spinabifida unit; here a conditioned reflex was produced by reinforcing the gastrocolic reflex with neostigmine (15 to 30 mg) given before a meal on two or three days a week; one-and-a-half hours later or soon after the meal, two glycerin suppositories are given rectally or if these cannot be retained the larger glycerin ovule which is normally available for vaginal use; 20 minutes later the patient is seated on the toilet for 10 minutes and if at the end of this time there has been a small result or no result then an enema is given. Kaplan claims that by frequent trial over a number of weeks or months the neostigmine dosage can be reduced and finally discontinued. A similar approach, using biofeedback has been described by Macleod (1979) and Cerulli et al (1979).

The use of electronic stimulators also requires consideration. Caldwell (1963) first introduced the concept of implanting electrodes into the area of the external sphincter and maintaining a constant tetanic current from a battery by means of apparatus worn over the implanted system. This method has been considerably developed and the need for surgery obviated by the production of an intra-anal plug containing the electrode around which the anal muscles contract and thus hold it in position when the current is running. This has been reviewed by Glenn (1971) by Hopkinson and Lightwood (1966) and by Collins et al (1969). In general, the method is of use where the defect lies within the anal sphincter or the supporting pelvic musculature. The rate of patient acceptability is not high. Collins found, for instance, that of 12 patients with faecal incontinence only 4 were suitable for long-term electrical treatment. Matheson and Keighley (1981) reported good results combining it with pelvic floor exercises.

DIVERTICULAR DISEASE

Diverticular disease of the colon is essentially a disease of middle and old age. It is also a disease apparently becoming more common with the passage of time. Thus, in 1937 Kocour, in 700 consecutive autopsies, found the prevalence of diverticular disease in patients aged 70 and over as follows:

White males 17 per cent; females 15 per cent
Coloured males 2 per cent; females 3 per cent

More recent figures show a much higher prevalence amongst elderly people. Thus Mars and Buogo (1967), among 104 randomly selected individuals from an old peoples' home, found that 47 per cent had bowel diverticula (55 per cent of the females and 34 per cent of the males) and that in 85 per cent of cases these were localized in the sigmoid colon. Manousos et al (1967) in a series of 109 subjects without gastrointestinal symptoms, the majority being healthy volunteers, found the age incidence of colonic diverticula as follows:

40 to 59 years	18.5 per cent
60 to 79 years	29 per cent
80 years and over	42 per cent

As might be expected with an age-associated pathological abnormality the age of onset of symptoms associated with this shows a similar spread. Parks (1969), reviewing 521 patients with diverticular disease found the age at onset of symptoms as follows:

20 to 49 years	12 per cent
50 to 59 years	24 per cent
60 to 69 years	32 per cent
70 years and over	32 per cent

He also found that the number of diverticula was greater in the older patients. It would seem that the diverticula are of late onset since the length of the history was under one month in 50 per cent of his cases and under a year in 75 per cent.

The aetiology of diverticular disease has been extensively studied by Painter, who reviewed his hypothesis in 1969 and again with Burkitt in 1971. Painter and Burkitt point out that diverticulitis was almost an unknown disease prior to 1900 but has since become the commonest affliction of the colon in Western Europe and that this has happened in 70 years, the traditional lifespan of man. They show the striking geographical prevalence, in that this is a disease of Western cultures and that it is extremely rare in Africa, Malaya, China, India, Singapore, Fiji, New Guinea and Korea. Painter and Burkitt link both these historical and geographical features by attributing them to differences in diet. Thus in 1880, roller milling of flour was introduced in Britain which removed two-thirds of the remaining fibre from the flour. At about the same time the average intake of refined sugar had doubled; thus dietary residue became greatly diminished at the end of the last century. These historical facts have been disputed by Eastwood et al (1974) who quote evidence that low fibre flour was popular in England from the 18th century. However it is in those parts of the world where this type of diet is the custom that the disease has emerged, whereas in those areas in which it is uncommon, a high-residue diet is the rule. Brodribb and Humphries (1976) showed that the crude fibre intake of patients with diverticular disease was significantly lower than controls.

The disease is also less common in vegetarians (Gear et al, 1979).

Painter's previous work (reviewed in 1964) showed that colonic segments bearing diverticula had certain motility responses which differentiated them from the colon of patients without diverticular disease. In particular there was very much greater increase of motility and of areas of high pressure in diverticula-bearing segments when morphine or prostigmine were injected. Painter showed that these areas of high pressure were associated with the formation of small 'bladders' in the colon by contraction of the bands of circular muscle and thus the pressure within these affected segments of the colon could be raised (just as in the urinary bladder with an obstructed outlet). This high pressure is associated with muscular hypertrophy (Hughes, 1969; Jalan et al, 1970) and could thus cause the formation of diverticula.

Painter linked all these findings by suggesting that a high-residue diet prevented the formation of these colonic 'bladders' either by preventing the complete closure of the circular muscle fibres or else because the sigmoid colon acted as a functional sphincter above the rectum by the action of its circular muscle bands. In the presence of a low-residue diet the muscle would have to work much harder to maintain this effect and thus become hypertrophied. This theory would also seem to gain some support from Manousos et al (1967), who showed that transit time was shorter in those with diverticular disease than in normal people.

There is also experimental evidence to support Painter's findings in that Carlson and Haelzel (1949), in a study of rats, maintained during their lifetime on different kinds of diet, a low-residue diet was associated with the formation of diverticula whereas a high-residue diet was not. The greatest number of diverticula occurred in rats who began on a high-residue diet and in which this was subsequently changed to a low-residue diet. Similar findings in rabbits were reported by Hodgson (1972).

Clinical findings

These have been well reviewed by Parks (1969) in his survey of the natural history of 521 patients presenting with diverticular disease at hospital. Change in bowel habit was an important symptom; 19 per cent of his patients showing diarrhoea, 35 per cent showing constipation and 9 per cent alternating constipation and diarrhoea — a total of 63 per cent of the patients. Rectal bleeding occurred in 30 per cent, abdominal pain in 78 per cent (which had various qualities and while being most commonly present in the lower abdomen also occurred in other areas). Urinary symptoms occurred in 13 per cent and flatulence and heartburn also occurred in the majority of the patients. Nausea and vomiting were present in 20 per cent.

A mass was palpable in the left lower quadrant either abdominally or rectally in one-fifth of the cases, there was an associated hiatus hernia in 7 per cent and cholecystitis or gall stones in 14 per cent but the patients were not fully investigated to exclude these diseases. A review of 296 cases of diverticular disease in Finland (Havia, 1971) shows a broadly similar clinical pattern with abdominal pain in 58 per cent, disturbance of bowel habit in 46 per cent (constipation being more common than diarrhoea), but a palpable mass in only 8 per cent. An association between diverticular disease of the colon and hiatus hernia is well known. Bertrand and Trestard (1970) showed that patients with diverticulosis had a 29 per cent incidence of muscular defects (hiatus hernia, abdominal hernia or eventration and vaginal prolapse), compared to an incidence of only 11.5 per cent of these defects in a series of patients without colonic diverticula. This would then suggest some aetiological factors in common in these condition, all of which are associated either with local changes in muscular and connective tissue sheets or else with areas of high pressure. Brodribb and Humphries (1976) showed an association between diverticular disease and haemorrhoids, varicose veins, abdominal hernias and gallstones and proposed that the common aetiological factor was a low fibre diet. An association with ischaemic heart disease has also been reported (Foster et al, 1978). They are all, of course, age-associated phenomena.

Presence of the disease is confirmed by barium enema (Fig. 26.6).

Complications of diverticular disease include perforation with peritonitis, with abscess formation or with the formation of fistula into the bladder or vagina. Colo-vesical fistula shows faecal matter in the urine in only one third of patients. The commonest symptom is pneumaturia — gas passed after the urine. The fistula is found at cystoscopy in less than 40 per cent of cases (Small and Smith, 1975). Intestinal obstruction is another not uncommon complication. Diverticular

Fig. 26.6 Diverticular disease. X-ray shows a number of large sigmoid diverticula. The outline of a calcified fibroid is also seen in the pelvis.

disease does not appear to predispose to carcinoma of the colon (Parks and Connell, 1970). Bleeding occurred in 20 per cent of Havia's series, a figure supported by the many other series that he reviews. Parsa et al (1975) reported 83 patients with bleeding colonic diverticulosis. Eighty-six per cent were aged 60 and over, and there was a high incidence of associated disease. Bleeding is due to the intimate association of the diverticulum, as it develops, with a perforating branch of the marginal artery (Meyers et al, 1976). Heald and Ray (1975) related bleeding from colonic diverticula both to advanced age and to hypertension. They found bleeding did not relate to pain (other than mild colic), pyrexia or leucocytosis and concluded that diverticulitis (infection) did not cause bleeding.

The majority of cases of diverticular disease require medical treatment and symptoms appear to persist or recur, no matter what type of treatment is used. Thus Parks and Connell (1970), investigating 445 patients admitted for the treatment of diverticular disease, found that two-thirds of these were treated medically and that in 43 per cent of them symptoms persisted or recurred, although in only 5 per cent were these symptoms severe. Of the one-third of the patients who had surgical treatment, 33 per cent had continuing or recurring symptoms. A more optimistic claim is made by Painter (1972) for the treatment of symptoms by use of added bran to increase the residue of the diet, treatment which is clearly rational if his theories of aetiology are correct. He treated 70 patients for an average period of 21 months with bran added to their diet. All had diverticular disease with symptoms and in 85 per cent those symptoms were markedly relieved. Eastwood et al (1974) showed that 20 g unprocessed bran daily reduced

transit time and reduced intra-luminal pressure in the distal colon in response to stimuli. Brodribb (1977) demonstrated the value of bran in a double-blind controlled trial in 18 patients. Not only was there significant relief of symptoms (despite a high initial placebo effect) but the extent of relief increased over a prolonged period of time. Srivastava et al (1976) used the bulk laxative sterculia, together with a smooth-muscle relaxant (alvarine citrate), and found this as effective as bran and, therefore, useful to patients who could not tolerate the latter. Eastwood et al (1978) compared bran, ispaghula (Fybogel) and the laxative lactulose: all produced symptomatic improvement, bran decreased transit time, ispaghula increased stool weight, and the effect on motility (in which a decrease would be expected with increasing bulk) was a decrease with bran, but a significant increase with ispaghula. Most recently, Ornstein and his colleagues (1981) in a controlled trial comparing bran, ispaghula and placebo in 58 patients over 4 months, showed no benefit from either fibre preparation in any symptom except constipation. In this ispaghula had a greater effect than bran. This paper — contrary to current orthodoxy — created a flurry of correspondence. Further studies may now be expected.

The medical treatment of diverticular disease involves essentially the use of a chemotherapeutic agent or antibiotic, phthalyl sulphathiozole or tetracycline or septrin (the last being the first choice in view of the dangers of tetracycline in association with reduced renal function in the elderly). Probanthine is also used for symptomatic relief. Bleeding is successfully treated by blood transfusion in most cases, but recurrence occurs in about 25 per cent (Parsa et al, 1975). Current therapy is well reviewed by Hughes (1975).

ISCHAEMIC COLITIS

Since atherosclerosis is such a common pathological process in old age and since in most parts of the body (e.g. brain, myocardium, extremities) it is the major cause of morbidity in the elderly, it might be expected that its effects would be equally prominent and equally important in relation to the blood supply of the alimentary tract. That this is not the case is due to the remarkably effective anastomotic channels in the mesenteric circulation, and in particular to the marginal artery of the colon. This is in effect a long artery extending from the superior to the inferior mesenteric arteries and receiving a blood supply successively from the various branches of these two major vessels (Fig. 26.7). The anastomosis is continued upwards through the superior pancreaticoduodenal branch of the coeliac axis and

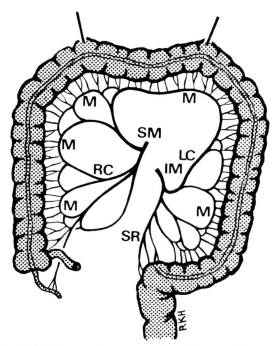

Fig. 26.7 Diagrammatic representation of the arterial blood supply to the colon showing important anastamotic function of the marginal artery. M = marginal artery; SM = superior mesenteric; IM = inferior mesenteric; RC = right colic; LC = left colic; SR = superior rectal.

indeed in the absence of arterial disease the entire colon and rectum may be vascularized from the superior mesenteric artery. Marcuson et al (1969) showed that ligation of the inferior mesenteric artery in a series of dogs produced little effect and that a more extensive ligation was needed to produce even the transient diarrhoea and mucosal sloughing of mild ischaemic colitis. The most critical point in the blood supply to the colon is in the region of the splenic flexure which represents the junction between the superior and inferior mesenteric arteries, and where there may be some narrowing of the marginal artery (Griffiths, 1956). Griffiths performed aortograms on 71 cadavers with peripheral vascular disease and found that the inferior mesenteric artery was outlined in only 20 of these. By arteriography studies in 58 cadavers, Meyers (1976) confirmed that the anastomosis at 'Griffith's point' was present in 48 per cent; poor or tenuous in 9 per cent and absent in 43 per cent.

It is certainly in the region of the splenic flexure that the majority of cases of ischaemic colitis present. For example, in 15 cases confirmed by X-ray and reported by Marston and colleagues (1966) the lesion was in the splenic flexure in 12, in the ascending colon, sigmoid colon and transverse colon in 1 each. In 7 of the 12 cases

where the splenic flexure was involved the lesion extended into the sigmoid.

The incidence and site of atheroma has been studied in a series of 119 autopsies by Koikkalainen et al (1968) and their findings are shown in Table 26.3. They found complete occlusion of the inferior mesenteric artery in 16 of their cases and lesions in 2 or more vessels at one time in only 7.6 per cent of the cases. They noted that angina does not seem to occur until 2 or even 3 arteries are affected. Morson (1968) discusses the effect of blood pressure on flow within the mesenteric arteries and points out that within the physiological range the flow does not vary much with changes of pressure at the origin of the main vessel but that with very low pressures there is a rapid lowering of blood flow. Age-related changes in the long colic arteries (between the marginal arteries and the gut) have been demonstrated by post-mortem angiography (Binns and Isaacson 1978). Increased tortuosity is strikingly demonstrated in their specimens. This may reflect further loss of blood supply.

Table 26.3 Incidence of moderate and severe arteriosclerosis of different age groups in the various arteries to the alimentary tract. (All figures per cent) (Koikkalainen et al, 1968)

Age	Coeliac axis	Superior mesenteric artery	Inferior mesenteric artery	Total autopsies
20 to 39	0	0	14	7
40 to 59	14	6	22	36
60 to 79	50	26	32	66
80+	70	60	40	10

Digitalis has been incriminated as a cause of colonic ischaemia (Gazes et al, 1961; Ko, 1974) and indeed Withering himself in 1785 described frequent motions resulting from intoxication with the foxglove. Pawlik and Jacobson (1974) demonstrated in dogs that digoxin infusion into an intestinal artery caused a decrease of blood flow and oxygen consumption in the relevant segment of gut. Other aetiological factors are polycythaemia, arteritis and diabetes (Marcuson and Farman, 1971).

Having in mind the lavish vascular provision indicated above, it becomes less surprising that ischaemic disease of the alimentary tract should be so much less common than that of other organs. Ischaemic colitis is certainly a rare disease or at least a disease in which the diagnosis is rarely made even among the very old. Almost the entire literature dates only from the last 20 years although the clinical entity of visceral angina was discussed in 1921 by Davies and in 1933 by Connor.

Clinical features

These are reviewed by Morson (1968), Ottinger (1974) and O'Connell et al (1976). Berger and Byrne (1961) found heart disease in 21 of 23 cases of bowel infarction without mesenteric block and Jordan, Boulafendis and Quinn (1970) in 4 of 5 similar cases. In ischaemic colitis itself heart disease has not been reported with this high frequency. Pheils (1969), for instance, reports it in 6 out of 42 cases. In addition to vascular occlusion a frequent precipitating factor is impaired perfusion due to low blood pressure in association with congestive heart failure, dehydration or haemorrhage. Other precipitating factors include polycythaemia and diabetes (Marcuson and Farman, 1971).

Symptoms and signs

An intense fear of food, occurring in an elderly patient, should raise suspicion. The two presenting symptoms are, however, abdominal pain and a loose stool containing red blood or clots. The onset is usually sudden and may be associated in addition with vomiting, pyrexia and leucocytosis; bowel motions will probably have been irregular. A bruit may be heard over the superior mesenteric artery. In less acute cases the abdominal pain may be up to 2 months duration.

The two conditions which must be considered in differential diagnosis are Crohn's disease and proctocolitis. The rectum is affected in 50 per cent of the former and 95 per cent of the latter but not in ischaemic colitis. Ischaemic colitis is transitory and may be associated with the diseases noted above. Final differentiation should be possible on a barium enema, which should be carried out as soon as the disease is suspected.

X-ray findings

In ischaemic colitis X-ray appearances are typical and fall into three main groups in the barium enema. They are first:

Thumb printing in which there is the appearance of indentatien of the colon as though a thumb were compressing it, secondly:

Saw tooth which is a more extensive series of indentations and, thirdly:

Sacculation due to the formation of a pseudo-diverticulum. The first two findings are due to the extensive oedema and submucous haemorrhage in the affected segment. These findings are transitory, and serial X-rays may be needed to demonstrate them. In lesions of sufficient severity they may be replaced by the appearance of stricture.

The X-ray findings are well reviewed by Schwartz et al (1968).

Management

Massive mesenteric artery occlusion associated with ganerene is a surgical problem requiring emergency treatment. Lesser degrees of ischaemic colitis should be treated expectantly since they are transitory. Antibiotics and low-molecular-weight dextran may be used. If a stricture results then elective surgical excision of this may be required. It is important to look for underlying associated causes and in particular to check electrolytes and review the drugs that are being taken.

ULCERATIVE COLITIS

Ulcerative colitis may have its onset in late life. Its incidence is bimodal, with a watershed between the modes at age 55. In each of the two groups, the age incidence by decades from age of onset is similar, and while the possibility of this representing two separate diseases has been considered, there is little convincing evidence that this is the case (Evans and Acheson, 1965). The only difference which Evans and Acheson could show between the two groups was that diarrhoea was a more common presenting symptom and rectal bleeding a less common presenting symptom in the elderly. Gebbers and Otto (1975) found a difference in the inflammatory exudate in the age groups above and below 50 with fewer plasma cells and more lymphocytes in the older age group. Ritchie and her colleagues (1978) reviewed 269 patients presenting at St Mark's Hospital between 1966 and 1975 with a history of less than six months duration at presentation who were then followed up for 11 years. Twenty per cent of their patients were over 60 and 7 per cent over 70.

The disease varies considerably in its extent and severity. Ritchie et al (1978) found it confined to the rectum in 28 per cent of their cases within the first 3 months, and of these 76 patients it had extended above the rectum by 5 years in only five. They estimated the likelihood of spread of proctitis to the sigmoid colon in 10 years to be about 30 per cent and to the whole colon to be between 5 and 10 per cent.

The risk of developing malignancy is low in the first 10 years (even among those with onset in old age). The risk thereafter is higher in patients who have suffered a severe first attack or who have extensive involvement of the colon and chronic continuous symptoms. There seems a special likelihood of it developing in those with onset in childhood or adolescence (Edwards and Truelove, 1964). Potentially dangerous complications in old people are perforation and acute toxic dilatation of the colon (Toghill and Benton, 1973).

The diagnosis is based on history of diarrhoea and the passage of blood. There may be urgency, tenesmus, lower abdominal colicky pain, weight loss, fever and anaemia. Generalized associated findings include mouth ulcers, erythema nodosa, acute arthropathy and uveitis.

The diagnosis requires a barium enema and sigmoid-oscopy. On the latter the findings may vary from a granular and hyperaemic appearance to an appearance of frank ulceration and bleeding. The rectal biopsy will confirm the diagnosis, although there may be difficulty in the differential diagnosis with Crohn's disease (see below).

Treatment

Sulphasalazine and steroids (orally or rectally) are the principle forms of treatment for acute exacerbations and sulphasalazine on a long-term basis to prevent relapse. The subject was reviewed in 1981 in the British Medical Journal and more recently by Lennard Jones (1983). In mild cases sulphasalazine half a gram twice a day increasing to 1 gram three times daily or else prednisolone 20 mg a day are required. If the disease is confined to the rectum, steroids are satisfactorily given as suppositories or enema. More severe attacks require high doses and in severe attacks with six or more bowel motions a day and systemic signs, immediate admission to hospital is required with day to day monitoring. Disodiumcromoglycate has been used more recently in preventing recurrence but the results are disappointing (Willoughby et al, 1979).

Surgical treatment consists of panproctocolectomy with the formation of an ileostomy. The most common indications for this are the failure of medical treatment to control the acute condition or in patients at risk of developing malignant change (i.e. severe disease present for more than 10 years and continuous rather than remitting). Surgery is also required should systemic complications such as iritis or arthritis develop. An acute surgical emergency is dilatation of the colon presenting in patients with acute fulminating ulcerative colitis.

CROHN'S DISEASE

Like ulcerative colitis Crohn's disease also has a bimodal distribution with a second peak of incidence at age 70 (British Medical Journal, 1973, leading article). Two epidemiological studies — in Basle and Aberdeen — showed the proportion aged 60 and over at onset of the disease to be 15 to 16 per cent (Fahrlander and Baerlocher, 1971; Kyle, 1971). Later onset of Crohn's disease is more likely to occur in females and more likely to be confined to the left side of the colon and the rectum. It therefore may present considerable problems in diagnosis from diverticulitis, particularly since a quarter or more of late onset cases of Crohn's disease will co-exist with diverticulosis.

The natural history of Crohn's disease was reported by Cooke et al (1980) from a series of 174 patients who had been followed up for at least 20 years and some for 45 years. Only six of their patients were over 60 at the time of diagnosis. The increased mortality rate compared to that which would otherwise have been expected was 1.5. The great majority of patients had initial onset in the distant ileum (47 per cent) or the distant ileum and right colon (29 per cent). Ninety-six per cent of the series had undergone one or more abdominal operations and approximately one third had developed a fistula. Ten per cent had serum negative arthropathy. It was concluded that an optimistic attitude to the eventual outcome of Crohn's disease is justified.

When it was first described Crohn's disease was regarded as a granulomatous disease, but it is now known that the non-caseating giant cell granulomata once thought to be the hallmark occurs in only about half of the cases (Morson and Dawson, 1972) and had also been described in some cases of ulcerative colitis (Gonzales-Licea and Yardley, 1966).

The criteria for diagnosis in Crohn's disease defined by Lennard Jones and colleagues (1976) were set as follows:

Discontinuous disease
Terminal ileum affected
Deep fissures on radiographs or surgical specimen
Enterocutaneous fistula
Chronic anal lesion
Normal mucin content of epithelial cells in the presence of mucosal inflammation on biopsy
Lymphoid aggregates in the mucosa and sub-mucosa

If epitheliod cell granulomata are present at least one of these features should also be present, or in the absence of granulomata at least three should be present to make the diagnosis.

Radiology may be useful in showing skip lesions and other characteristics are 'rose thorn spike ulceration' and fistulae. Colonoscopy at an early stage shows discrete ulcers (rather like aphthous ulcers) surrounded by normal looking mucosa. If doubt exists about the diagnosis, multiple biopsies can be taken.

Occasional difficulty exists in the diagnosis of tuberculosis of the ileocaecal region of the colon or lymphoma of the ileocaecal region (Chadwick, 1982).

Treatment

There have been several recent reviews of the treatment of Crohn's disease (Chadwick, 1982; Lennard Jones, 1980; Goodman, 1980). Specific medical therapy is similar to that for ulcerative colitis. Sulphasalazine or corticosteroids (20–60 mg daily) are both useful in treating the acute disease, particularly when of recent onset, the combination is not superior to either alone. Neither has been shown to prevent relapse. Azothioprin and 6-mercaptopurine are being assessed and final judgement is premature, but both have considerable side-effects. Cromoglycate is not effective.

Surgery is required either in the treatment of complications (such as abscess, fistula, perforation, stenosis) or in failed medical therapy. Ileal or colonic resection will relieve symptoms but not protect against recurrence.

Attention to nutrition may be very important and the place of parenteral nutrition has recently been reviewed by Powell-Tuck (1980). Symptomatic treatment with antidiarrhoeal agents may be helpful but should be avoided in severe active cases of the disease in whom they may precipitate toxic dilatation of the colon. Long-term treatment with fibre-rich unrefined carbohydrate diet was reported by Heaton et al (1979) who showed significantly fewer and shorter hospital admissions in a group so treated compared with a matched control group studied retrospectively. The same authors also reported the pre-illness diet of patients with Crohn's disease as being substantially higher in refined carbohydrate and lower in dietary fibre than a group of controls (Thornton et al, 1979).

Malignancy
While malignancy is not as important a complication as in ulcerative colitis, Crohn's disease does involve some risk. Gyde (1980) showed an increased risk of 1.7 times in cancer at all sites and 3.3 times for tumours within the digestive system.

ANTIBIOTIC ASSOCIATED COLITIS

Roddis (1978) reviewed 15 cases of colitis associated with antibiotics. In nine the histology was of pseudo-membranous colitis and in the remainder of 'non-specific' colitis. Many antibiotics were involved — usually in combinations — but the common were the penicillins (especially penicillin and ampicillin). Half were aged 65 and over. Sigmoidoscopy showed patchy membrane easily scraped from a reddened, non-friable mucosa. Mortality rate was 70 per cent of the pseudo-membrane and 14 per cent of the non-specific type. Pseudomembranous colitis presents with intense watery diarrhoea which is usually blood-stained and the patient suffers a rapid downhill course leading to dehydration and shock. Toxic dilatation of the colon has been reported.

CARCINOMA OF THE COLON AND RECTUM

Colo-rectal carcinoma shows a linear increase in incidence with advancing age (as indeed do all epithelial cancers). The sex incidence of carcinoma of the colon

Table 26.4 Annual age-specific incidence of colo-rectal cancer 1973–1976. Figures per 100 000 population, West Midlands Cancer Registry.

Age group	Colon		Rectum	
	Males	Females	Males	Females
0	0.0	0.0	0.0	0.0
1–4	0.0	0.0	0.0	0.0
5–9	0.0	0.4	0.0	0.0
10–14	0.6	0.2	0.0	0.0
15–19	0.3	1.6	0.0	0.0
20–24	1.0	0.6	0.0	0.0
25–29	1.6	1.5	0.0	0.2
30–34	2.5	2.5	1.1	0.9
35–39	3.9	3.8	3.2	3.6
40–44	6.2	8.0	4.4	5.4
45–49	14.3	14.2	8.0	12.4
50–54	20.8	29.3	19.3	23.5
55–59	37.1	44.9	25.2	45.7
60–64	60.6	55.2	38.8	66.9
65–69	80.9	78.2	41.8	102.7
70–74	132.5	119.4	62.6	139.0
75–79	204.1	142.1	89.9	182.2
80–84	223.0	216.0	96.4	171.6
85+	239.2	209.8	141.6	225.8

is similar but carcinoma of the rectum is twice as common in women over 65 and in men over 65. Table 26.4 shows recent age and sex specific annual incidence rates recorded by the Regional Cancer Registry in Birmingham, England. The annual incidence of colonic carcinoma has an enormous geographical variation (in the range of 3 per 100 000 in Africa and Asia to 30 per 100 000 in Western Europe, Australasia and North America). It is thought that dietary variation accounts for these differences and it is known for instance that natives of low risk countries who move to high risk countries and conform to their diet increase their risk of lower bowel cancer. One striking piece of evidence is that Seventh Day Adventists in the United States (who are vegetarians) have an incidence which is half that of Americans in general.

The place of diet in the aetiology of lower bowel cancer has been recently reviewed by Heaton (1977). It must be emphasized that all the evidence in this regard is epidemiological and therefore indirect. The closest correlations are between lower bowel cancer and the consumption of meat and animal fat. Meat eaters have bile salts in higher concentration and in more degraded forms than vegetarians and have also been shown to have more anaerobic bacteria which may degrade bile. The major dietary theory is that unsaturated bile acids produced by bacteria in the colon are the important aetiological factor.

Some supportive evidence for the increased bile acids theory comes from two recent studies. Linos et al (1981) in a study of patients who had undergone cholecystectomy found carcinoma of the colon developed in more patients (of 1681 whom they followed up) than would have been expected. This was a significant finding in females, particularly for carcinoma of the colon. Rundgren and Mellstrom (1983) in a prospective longitudinal study of subjects between the ages of 70 and 75 found a correlation between previous cholecystectomy and the development of colonic carcinoma. Their subjects who developed cancer also had significantly higher body weights at aged 70.

Correlations have also been shown between high fibre-containing diets and the incidence of lower bowel cancer (Lancet, 1977). The effect of high fibre diet may be twofold — first, by increasing the bulk of the stool and diminishing the transit time it dilutes the bile acid and speeds its passage through the colon; and secondly those who take high fibre diets are more likely to be vegetarians and also are less likely to consume refined sugar as well as fat. It is the high intake of fat and refined sugar which characterizes much of Western diet and causes overnutrition leading to obesity. Obesity is more common in patients with carcinoma of the lower bowel than in controls or in the general population (Wynder and Shigematsu, 1967).

Patients with ulcerative colitis also have a cancer risk which is 5–10 times greater than that of the comparable population. This is particularly so of those with chronic continuous disease. Morson (1977) proposes either that they should have a colonoscopy with biopsies from all regions repeated every 3 to 5 years or a 6-monthly rectal biopsy. Patients with Crohn's disease also have a higher malignancy rate than expected — both in the upper and in the lower bowel (Gyde et al, 1980).

The great majority of carcinomas of the colon and rectum develop from adenomas. This development takes at least 5 years and usually 10–15 years (Morson, 1977; British Medical Journal, 1980). The three main types of adenoma and their malignancy rates are shown in Table 26.5.

Adenomas of less than one centimetre diameter rarely show malignant change. Adenomas are found especially in the rectum and have been noted in 95 per cent of rectums removed for carcinoma.

Because of the origin of carcinomas from adenomas, it is not surprising that 20 per cent of all patients with carcinoma have other tumours (malignant or benign) in the lower bowel.

A new method for diagnosis of colo-rectal carcinoma by the use of an anti-tumour monoclonal antibody has recently been described (Farrands et al, 1982). This uses a special monoclonal antibody which reacts with human malignant colo-rectal cells and is detected by a radioimmunodetection method. Farrands describes a successful diagnosis in 10 out of 11 patients — and the eleventh had received radiotherapy to his tumour 2 weeks previously.

Treatment

Surgery is the only effective method of treatment at the present time. Chemotherapy and immunotherapy have nothing to offer. Radiotherapy preoperatively (supravoltage irradiation) has been shown to diminish lymph node metastases — in one series of cases from 40 per cent to 27 per cent (Sischy and Remington, 1975).

The outcome of surgery depends in part on whether it is carried out in a specialist centre receiving principally selected cases for elective procedures or district hospitals where surgery may include emergencies as well as elective procedures. Results from a series of general hospitals in England were reported by Till (1977). Collected statistics for different hospitals at periods between 1950 and 1972 showed that 65 per cent of their cases were admitted as emergencies and that the diagnosis was found to be mistaken at operation in 7–8 per cent. However, a false negative diagnosis leading to delay in ultimate diagnosis was made in 19.6 per cent. The operative mortality in those undergoing elective surgery varied from 4–23 per cent. The crude 5-year survival figures for all patients admitted were 24 per cent and for those undergoing radical surgery only, 30–32 per cent (Table 26.6).

Table 26.5 Relative frequency and malignancy of different colo-rectal adenomas (from Morson 1977)

	Frequency (%)	Malignancy (%)
Tubular adenoma (Adenomatous polyp)	75	5
Tubulo-villous adenoma (villo-glandular)	15	22
Villous adenoma	10	40

Table 26.6 5-year survival figures (percentages) for colo-rectal cancer. Four District Hospitals 1950–1960 compared with a specialist hospital (1947–67). Figures derived from Hawley (1977) and Till (1977).

	4 District Hospitals	Specialist Hospital	
	Crude survival	Crude	Corrected
All ca colon		52.5	62.9
All ca rectum	20–24	47.1	56.7
Radical surgery:			
Ca colon	38–42.3	66	73.8
Ca rectum	0–39.8	52.7–66.7*	63.8–79.4*

* First figure represents simultaneous combined resection. Second figure represents anterior resection

A more recent study of all cases of colorectal carcinoma treated in hospitals in the Grampian region of Scotland in 1968–69 (Clarke et al, 1980) showed 5-year survival for radical surgery between 62 and 70 per cent in the rectum and 77–79 per cent for the colon with a perioperative mortality of 9 per cent. Of the 433 patients in this study, 89 per cent came to laparotomy, 50 per cent had a radical operation and 22 per cent a palliative resection. Only 3 per cent of those undergoing palliative surgery survived 2 years. The authors' comment was that the overall picture for the treatment of colorectal carcinoma did not seem to have changed in the previous 20 years.

The outcome of treatment from a specialist centre (St Mark's Hospital, London) was reported by Hawley (1977) and is shown in Table 26.6 and it is seen that overall the 5-year survival rates are in these selected cases somewhat greater.

Screening

In view of the importance of surgery in colorectal cancer, the question of screening for unidentified cases has been considered. In one study (Larkin, 1980) 5840 individuals entered a screening programme and the yield was four cases of colorectal carcinoma (0.07 per cent). In addition there were seven cases of adenoma (0.03 per cent). A series of 8925 patients in a general practice were offered haemoccult test (Farrands et al, 1981). Of these 2489 accepted and from this population 12 bowel tumours were identified of which four were malignant. The cost of the exercise was £12 500 per tumour. From both of these studies it was concluded that screening by faecal examination for occult blood is not a cost-effective exercise.

Winawer (1981) however outlines a scheme for annual occult blood screening of high risk groups which he describes as being cost-effective. Even serial faecal occult blood testing will produce false negative results in non-ulcerating cancers (Griffith et al, 1981).

ANGIODYSPLASIA OF THE COLON

Since the introduction of flexible colonoscopy and aortography it has become apparent that a great deal of bleeding from the lower bowel in elderly patients derives from vascular ectasias of the colon. They are not associated with angioma of the skin or other viscera though Wolf et al (1977) reported three cases, one of whom had a telangiectatic lesion on the linner side of the lower lip. They occur either in the caecum or proximal ascending colon, are usually less than 5 mm in diameter, may be multiple and are rarely diagnosed at surgery or indeed at autopsy. They require direct visualization through the flexible colonoscope (revealing a raised cherry red lesion with spreading 'foot processes') or demonstration of the bleeding vessel by selective mesenteric arteriography with rapid segmental filming (Allison, 1980).

Boley et al (1977) suggest that these are age-associated lesions caused by chronic, intermittent, low grade obstruction to the blood flow through the submucosal veins due to muscle contraction over a long period of time. This leads to dilatation and tortuosity, initially of the submucosal veins, but ultimately the precapillary sphincters lose their competence and small arteriovenous communications are produced,

Treatment

Clinical presentation is often by chronic anaemia although they may also present as major lower gastrointestinal bleeding — and indeed some suggest that these lesions are the commonest cause of rectal bleeding in the elderly. Treatment is by endoscopie coagulation or surgical resection (for review see Leading Article, Lancet, 1981).

THE INVESTIGATION OF LOWER BOWEL DISORDERS

Tests for occult blood in the faeces have had an unhappy history. Ross and Gray (1964) compared the orthotolidine test, the hematest, the Occultest tablet and the hemastix strip test by an isotopic method and found a large proportion of false positives and false negatives with all of these. Indeed their conclusion was that no value could be attached to the results of any of the chemical tests alone and they questioned whether such tests ought to be retained in modern medicine. They suggested that the best method was to deploy two tests, one relatively insensitive producing a large number of false negatives — the hematest, and one extremely sensitive producing a large number of false positives — the orthotolidine test. The conclusion would then be that a positive result with the hematest would suggest bleeding and a negative result with the orthotolidine test would suggest the absence of bleeding. Holt and Simpson (1970) compared the benzedine test, orthotolidine test, hematest and a modified guaiacum test. The benzedine test had the largest number of positives and the guaiacum the largest number of negatives. They indicated that both benzedine and orthotolidine (which they regarded as best) are carcinogenic and conclude that the only useful test available at the present time remains the guaiacum test.

Flexible fibreoptic sigmoidoscopy is advocated as an outpatient examination in preference to rigid sigmoidoscopy and two recent papers (Vellacott and Hardcastle, 1981; Leicester et al, 1982) reported on a comparison between the two methods. One to two phosphate enemas were given as preparation and the examination carried out, without sedation, 10–15 minutes later. In each case the duration (7.6–8 mins) and the length of insertion (50.8–60 cms) were similar. Inadequate preparation was described in 4.6 and 17.8 per cent (paradoxically the larger figure in the study where two enemas were given) and the yield of pathological findings compared to rigid sigmoidoscopy was 30 per cent compared to 6.5 per cent in one series and 36.2 per cent compared to 14.7 per cent in the other. Further evidence for the use of this method in geriatric patients was presented by Holt and Wherry (1979).

REFERENCES

Allison D J, Hemingway A P 1981 Angiodysplasia — does old age begin at 19? Lancet 2: 979–980

Arnold G J, Nance F C 1973 Volvulus of the sigmoid colon. Annals of Surgery 177: 527–537

Becker G L 1952 The case against mineral oil. American Journal of Digestive Diseases 19: 344–348

Beersiek F, Parks A G, Swash M 1979 Pathogenesis of ano-rectal incontinence. Journal of the Neurological Sciences 42: 111–127

Berger R L, Byrne J J 1961 Intestinal gangrene associated with heart disease. Surgery, Gynecology and Obstetrics 112: 529–533

Bertrand J, Trestard A 1970 Les deficiences de la musculature abdominale dans la diverticulose colique. Cahiers de Médecine 11/6: 457–462

Binns J C, Isaacson P 1978 Age-related changes in the colonic blood supply: their relevance to ischaemic colitis. Gut 19: 384–390

Bodian M, Stephens F D, Ward B C H 1949 Hirschsprung's disease and idiopathic megacolon. Lancet i: 6–11

Boley S J, Sammartano R, Adams A, Diabiasea, Kleinhaus S, Sprayregan S 1977 On the nature and aetiology of vascular ectasias of the colon. Gastroenterology 72: 650–660

British Medical Journal 1968 Volvulus of the sigmoid colon. Annotation i: 264–265

British Medical Journal 1973 Crohn's disease in the elderly: a diagnostic problem Editorial British Medical Journal 1: 188–189

British Medical Journal 1980 Evolution of Colonic Polyps. Editorial British Medical Journal 3: 257–258

British Medical Journal 1981 Treatment of ulcerative colitis. Editorial British Medical Journal 282: 1255–1256

Brocklehurst J C, 1951 In: Incontinence in Old People. Edinburgh: Livingstone

Brocklehurst J C 1964 Treatment of constipation and faecal incontinence in old people. Practitioner 193: 779–782

Brocklehurst J C 1972 Bowel management in the neurologically disabled. The problems in old age. Proceedings of the Royal Society of Medicine 65: 66–69

Brocklehurst J C, Bee P, Jones D, Palmer M C 1977 Bacteriuria in geriatric hospital patients: its correlates and management. Age and Ageing 6: 240–245

Brocklehurst J C, Khan Y 1960 A study of faecal stasis in old age and use of Dorbanex in its prevention Gerontologia Clinica 11: 293–300

Brocklehurst J C, Kirkland J L, Martin J, Ashford J 1983 Constipation in longstay elderly patients: its treatment and prevention by Lactulose, Poloxalkol, Dihydroxyanthroquinolone and phosphate enema. Gerontology 29: 181–184

Brodribb A J M, Humphreys D M 1976 Diverticular disease: three studies. Part I — Relation to other disorders and fibre intake. British Medical Journal 1: 424–430

Brodribb A J M 1977 Treatment of symptomatic diverticular disease with a high-fibre diet. Lancet ii: 664–666

Burkitt D P, Walker A R P, Painter N S 1972 Effect of dietary fibre on stools and the transit time and its role in the causation of disease. Lancet ii: 1408

Caldwell K P S 1963 Electrical control of sphincter incompetence Lancet ii: 174–175

Caplan L H, Jacobson H G, Rubenstein B N, Rottman M S 1965 Megacolon and volvulus in Parkinson's disease. Radiology 85: 73–79

Carlson A J, Hoelzel F 1949 Relation of diet to diverticulosis of the colon in rats. Gastroenterology 12.1: 108–115

Cerulli M A, Nikoomanesh P, Schuster M M 1979 Progress in biofeedback conditioning for fecal incontinence. Gastroenterology 76: 742–746

Christensen J 1971 The controls of gastrointestinal movements: Some old and new views. New England Journal of Medicine 285: 85–98

Chadwick V S 1982 Diagnosis and medical management of Crohn's disease British Journal of Hospital Medicine 27: 472–480

Clark A N G, Scott J S 1976 Wheat bran in dyschezia in the aged. Age and Ageing 5: 149–154

Clarke D N, Jones P F, Needham C D 1980 Outcome in colorectal carcinoma: seven year study of a population. British Medical Journal 280: 431–435

Cleave T L, Campbell G D, Painter N S 1969 In: Diabetes, Coronary Thrombosis and the Saccharine Disease, (2nd edn) Bristol: Wright

Collins C D, Brown B H, Duthie H O 1969 An assessment of intraluminal electrical stimulation for anal incontinence. British Journal of Surgery 54: 542–546

Connell A M 1961 The motility of the pelvic colon. Gut II: 175–186

Connell A M, Frankel H Guttman L 1963 The motility of the pelvic colon following complete lesions of the spinal cord. Paraplegia I: 98–115

Connell A M, Hilton C, Irvin G, Lennard-Jones J E, Misiewicz J J 1965 Variations in bowel habit in two population samples. British Medical Journal ii: 1095–1099

Connor L A 1933 A discussion of the role of arterial thrombosis in visceral diseases of middle life based upon analogies drawn from coronary thrombosis. American Journal of the Medical Sciences 185: 13–21

Cooke W T, Mallass E, Prior P, Allen R N 1980 Crohn's disease — treatment and long term prognosis. Quarterly Journal of Medicine 49: 363–384

Cummings J H, Jenkins D J A, Wiggins H S 1976 Measurement of the mean transit time of dietary residue through the human gut. Gut 17: 210–218

Davenport H W 1966 Physiology of the digestive tract. In: Year Book Medical Publishing Incorporation: Chicago

Davies D B 1921 In: Nebraska Medical Journal 6: 101

Deiling D A, Fischer R A, Fernandez O 1959 The therapeutic usefulness of Dulcalax. American Journal of Digestive Diseases 4: 311

Denny Brown D, Robertson E G 1933 On the physiology of micturition. Brain 56: 149–190

Denny Brown D, Robertson E G 1935 Involuntary nervous control defaecation. Bran 58: 256

Duthie H L, Bennet R C 1963 The relation of sensation in the anal canal to the functional anal sphincter. A possible factor in anal incontinence. Gut 5: 179–182

Eastwood M A, Kirkpatrick J R, Midgell W D, Bone A, Hamilton T 1973 Effects of dietary supplements of wheat bran and cellulose on faeces and bowel function. British Medical Journal ii: 392–394

Eastwood M A, Smith A N, Bridon W G, Pritchard J 1978 Comparison of bran, ispaghula and lactulose on colon function in diverticular disease. Gut 19: 1144–1147

Eastwood M A, Fisher N, Greenwood C T, Hutchinson J B 1974 Perspectives on the bran hypothesis. Lancet 1: 1029–1032

Edwards F C, Truelove S C 1964 The course and prognosis of ulcerative colitis Gut 4: 2–315

Evans J G, Acheson E D 1965 An epidemiological study of ulcerative colitis and regional enteritis in the Oxford area. Gut 6: 3121–324

Fahrlander H, Baerlocher C H 1971 Clinical features and epidemiological data on Crohn's disease in the basal area. Scandinavian Journal of Gastroenterology 6: 657–662

Fain A M, Susat R, Herring M, Dorton K 1978 Treatment of constipation in geriatric and chronically ill patients: a comparison. Southern Medical Journal 71: 677–680

Farrands P A, Griffiths R, Britton R 1981 The Frome experiment — value of screening for colorectal cancer. Lancet 2: 1231–1232

Farrands P A, Perkins A C, Pimm M V, Hardy J D, Embleton M J, Baldwin R W, Hardcastle J D 1982 Radioimmunodetection of human colorectal cancers by an anti-tumour monoclonal antibody. Lancet 2: 397–400

Foster K J, Holstock G, Whorwell P J, Guyer P, Wright R 1978 Prevalence of diverticular disease of the colon in patients with ischaemic heart disease. Gut 19: 1054–1056

Frenckner B 1975 Function of the anal sphincters in spinal man. Gut 16: 638–644

Frenckner B, Ihre T 1976 Influence of the autonomic nerves on the internal anal sphincter in man. Gut 17: 306–312

Gazes P C, Holmes C R, Moseley V, Pratt-Thomas H R 1961 Acute haemorrhage and necrosis of the intestines associated with digitalisation. Circulation 23: 358–363

Gear J S S, Brodribb A J M, Ware A, Mann J I 1981 Fibre and bowel transit times. British Journal of Nutrition 45: 77–82

Gebbers J O, Otto H F 1975 Ulcerative colitis in the elderly. Lancet 2: 714–715

Glenn E S, 1971 Effective and safe control of incontinence by the intra-anal plug electrode. British Journal of Surgery 58: 249–252

Godding E W 1972 In: Management of Constipation, (ed.) Avery-Jones, Godding, p 25–76. Oxford: Blackwell Scientific Publications

Gonzales Licea A, Yardley J H 1966 Nature of the tissue reaction in ulcerative colitis. Light and electron microscopic findings. Gastroenterology 51: 825–840

Goodman M J 1980 The case for conservative treatment. In: Truelove S C, Kennedy A J (eds) Topics in Gastroenterology 8. Blackwell, Oxford, p 123–140

Griffith C D M, Turner D J, Saunders J H 1981 False negative results of Hemoccult test in colorectal cancer. British Medical Journal 283: 472

Griffith J D E 1956 Surgical anatomy of blood supply of the distal colon. Annals of the Royal College of Surgeons of England 19: 241–256

Gyde S N, Prior P, Macartney J C, Thompson H, Waterhouse J A H, Allan R N 1980 Malignancy in Crohn's disease. Gut 21: 1024–1029

Halls S J 1965 Bowel contents shift during normal defaecation Proceedings of the Royal Society of Medicine 58: 859–860

Hardcastle J B, Wilkins J L 1970 The action of sennosides and related compounds on the human colon and rectum. Gut 11: 1038–1042

Hawley P R 1977 The results of Surgery in a specialised hospital, In: Truelove F C, Lee E (eds) Topics in Gastroenterology 5. Blackwell Scientific, Oxford, p 65 and 76

Harvey R F, Pomare E W, Heaton K W 1973 Effects of increased dietary fibre on intestinal transit. Lancet i: 1278–1280

Harvard L R C, Hughes-Roberts H E 1962 The treatment of constipation in mental hospitals. Gut 3: 85–90

Havia T 1971 Diverticulosis of the colon — a clinical and histological study. Acta Chirurgica Scandinavica: 137/415S

Heald R J, Ray J E 1971 Bleeding from diverticular of the colon. Diseases of the Colon and Rectum 14: 420–427

Heaton K W 1977 Cancer of the large bowel: dietary factors. In: Truelove F C, Lee E (eds) Topics in Gastroenterology 5, Blackwell Scientific, Oxford, p 29–44

Heaton K W, Thornton J R, Emmett P M 1979 Treatment of Crohn's disease with an unrefined carbohydrate fibre rich diet. British Medical Journal 2: 764–766

Henry M M, Swash M 1978 Assessment of pelvic floor disordersand incontinence by electrophysiological recording. Lancet 1: 1290–1291

Hinton J M, Lennard-Jones J E 1968 Constipation: definition and classification. Postgraduate Medical Journal 44: 720–723

Hinton J M, Lennard-Jones J E, Young A G 1969 A new method of studying gut transit times using radio-opaque markers. Gut 10: 842–847

Hodgson W J B 1972 An interim report on the production of colonic diverticula in the rabbit. Gut 13: 802–804

Holdstock D J 1970 Propulsion (mass movements) in the human colon and its relationship to meals and somatic: activity. Gut 11: 91

Holdstock D J, Misiewicz J J 1970 Factors controlling colonic motility: colonic pressures and transit after meals in patients with total gastrectomy, pernicious anaemia or duodenal ulcer. Gut 11: 100–110

Holt D C, Simpson R G 1970 Occult blood in faeces. Lancet 1: 39

Holt R W, Wherry D C 1979 Why flexible fiberoptic sigmoidoscopy is important in the geriatric patient. Geriatrics 34: 85–88

Hopkinson B R, Lightwood R 1966 Electrical treatment of anal incontinence. Lancet i: 344–351

Hughes L E 1969 Postmortem survey of diverticular disease. Gut 10: 336–351

Hughes L E 1975 Complications of diverticular of disease, inflammation, obstruction and bleeding. Clinics in Gastroenterology 4: 147–170

Hull C, Greco R S, Brooks D L 1980 Alleviation of constipation in the elderly by dietary fibre supplementation. Journal of the American Geriatrics Society 28: 410–414

Ingalls J F, Lynch M F, Schilling J A 1964 Volvulus of the sigmoid in mental institution. American Journal of Surgery 108: 339–343

Jalan K M, Walker R J, Prescott R J, Butterworth S T G, Smith A N, Sircus W 1970 Faecal stasis and diverticular disease in ulcerative colitis. Gut 11: 688–696

Jarratt A S, Exton-Smith A N 1960 Treatment of faecal incontinence. Lancet i: 925

Jordan P H, Boulafendis D, Quinn G A 1970 Factors other than major vascular occlusion that contribute to intestinal infarction. Annals of Surgery 171: 189–194

Kaplan B J 1970 Pharmacological aid for faecal incontinence. British Medical Journal i: 113

Kerremans R 1969 Morphological and physiological aspects of anal continence and defecation. Presses Academiques Europeennes SC.

Ko H S 1974 Intestinal ischaemia and digitalis. Journal of the American Medical Association 227: 1263

Kocour E J 1937 Diverticulosis of the colon. American Journal of Surgery 37: 433–439

Koikkalainen K, Laustela E, Tala P 1968 Pathological study of arteriosclerosis in the coeliac and mesenteric circulation. Annales Chirurgiae et Gynaecologiae Fenniae 57: 234–238

Kyle J 1971 An epidemiological study of Crohn's disease in North East Scotland. Gastroenterology 61: 826–833

Lancet 1977 Dietary fibre. Lancet Editorial ii: 337–338

Lancet 1981 Angiodysplasia Lancet Editorial 2: 1086–1087

Lane R H S, Parkes H E 1977 Function of the anal sphincters following colo-anal anastomosis. British Journal of Surgery 64: 596–599

Larkin K K 1980 Mass screening in colorectal cancer. Australia and New Zealand Journal of Surgery 50: 467–469

Lee J R 1982 Faecal peritonitis after laxative preparation for barium enema. British Medical Journal 284: 740

Leicester R J, Hawley P R, Pollett R J, Nicholls R J 1982 Flexible fibreoptic sigmoidoscopy as an outpatient precedure. Lancet i: 34–35

Lennard Jones J E 1980 An overall view. In: Truelove S C, Kennedy A J (eds) Topics in Gastroenterology 8, Blackwell Scientific, Oxford, p 85–104

Lennard Jones J E 1983 Towards optimal use of corticosteroids in ulcerative colitis and Crohn's disease. Gut 24: 177–181

Lennard Jones J E, Ritchie J K, Zohrab W J 1976 Proctocolitis and Crohn's disease of the colon: a comparison of the clinical course. Gut 17: 477–482

Linos D A, Beard C M, O'Fallon W M, Dockerty M B, Beart R W, Kurland L T 1981 Cholecystectomy and carcinoma of the colon Lancet ii: 379–381

McKeown F 1965 In: Pathology of the Aged. London: Butterworths

MacLennan W J, Pooler A F W M 1975 A comparison of sodium picosulphate (Laxoberal) with standardised senna (Senokot) in geriatric patients. Current Medical Research and Opinion 2: 641–647

MacLeod J H 1979 Biofeedback in the management of partial anal incontinence. Diseases of the Colon and Rectum 22: 169–171

Mann C V, Hardcastle J D 1970 Recent studies of colonic and rectal motor action. Diseases of the Colon and Rectum 13: 225–230

Manousos O N, Truelove S C, Lumsden K 1967 Transit times of food in patients with diverticulosis or irritable colon syndrome and normal subjects British Medical Journal iii: 760–762

Marcuson R W, Arthur J F, Chapman M, Manton A 1969 Experimental aspects of ischaemic colitis. Proceedings of the Royal Society of Medicine 62: 711–713

Marcuson R W, Farman J 1971 Intestinal arterial disease. Proceedings of the Royal Society of Medicine 64: 1079–1083

Mars G, Buogo A 1967 Considerazioni sui diverticoli del colon nell eta avanzata. Giornale di gerontologia 15: 1243–1266

Marston A, Pheils M T, Thomas M L, Morson B C 1966 Ischaemic colitis. Gut 7: 1–15

Matheson D M, Keighley M R B 1981 Manometric evaluation of rectal prolapse and faecal incontinence. Gut 22: 126–129

Meunier P, Rochas A, Lambert R 1979 Motoactivity of the sigmoid colon in chronic constipation. A comparative study with normal subjects. Gut 20: 1095–1101

Meyers M A 1976 Griffiths' point critical anastomosis at the splenic flexure. American Journal of Roentgenology 126: 77–94

Meyers M A, Alonso D R, Gray G F, Baer J W 1976 Pathogenesis of bleeding colonic diverticulosis. Gastroenterology 71: 577–583

Milne J S, Williamson J 1972 Bowel habit in older people. Gerontologia Clinica 14: 56–60

Misiewicz J J, Connell A M, Pontes F A 1966 Comparison of the effect of meals and prostigmine on the proximal and distal colon in patients with or without diarrhoea. Gut 7: 468–473

Misiewicz J J, Waller J S, Healy S L, Piper E A 1968 Computer analysis of intraluminal pressure record. Gut 9: 232–236

Morson B C 1968 Ischaemic colitis. Postgraduate Medical Journal 44: 665–666

Morson B C 1977 Cancer of the large bowel: predisposing factors. In: Truelove S C, Lee E (eds) Topics in Gastroenterology 5. Blackwell Scientific, Oxford, p 15–28

Morson B C, Dawson I M P 1972 Disorders of muscular function In: Gastrointestinal pathology, Blackwell Scientific, Oxford, p 502

Newman H F, Freeman J 1974 Physiologic factors affecting defecatory sensation. Journal of the American Geriatrics Society 22: 553–554

Ornstein M H, Littlewood E R, Baird I M, Fowler J, North W R S, Cox A G 1981 Are fibre supplements really necessary in diverticular disease of the colon: a controlled clinical trial. British Medical Journal 282: 1353–1356

Ottinger L W 1974 Non-occlusive mesenteric infarction. Surgical Clinics of North America 74: 689–698

O'Connell T C, Cadell B, Tompkins R K 1976 Ischaemia of the colon. Surgery, Gynecology and Obstetrics 142: 337–342

Painter N S 1969 Diverticular disease of the colon: the disease of the century. Lancet ii: 586–588

Painter N S, Burkitt D P 1971 Diverticular disease of the colon: a deficiency disease of western civilisation. British Medical Journal ii: 440–445

Painter N S, Almeida A S, Colebourne K W 1972 Unprocessed bran in treatment of diverticular disease of the colon. British Medical Journal ii: 137–140

Painter N S, Truelove S C 1964 The intraluminal pressure patterns in diverticulosis of the colon. Gut 5: 201–213, 365–373

Painter N S, Truelove S C, Ardran G M, Tuckey M 1965 Effect of morphine, prostigmine, pethidine and probanthine on the human colon in diverticulosis studied by intraluminal pressure recording and cineradiography. Gut 6: 57

Pallis C A, Lewis P D 1974 In: The Neurology of Gastro-Intestinal Disease, p 252–254. London: W B Saunders & Co. Ltd

Parks A G, Porter N H, Melyatt J 1962 Experimental study of the reflex mechanism controlling the muscles of the pelvic floor. Diseases of the Colon and Rectum 5: 407–414

Parks T G 1969 Natural history of diverticular disease of the colon. British Medical Journal iv: 639–645

Parks T G, Connell A M 1970 The outcome in 455 patients admitted for treatment of diverticular disease of the colon. British Journal of Surgery 57: 775–778

Parks A G, Swash M 1979 Denervation of the anal sphincter causing idiopathic anorectal incontinence. Journal of the Royal College of Surgeons of Edinburgh 24: 94–96

Parks A G, Swash M, Urich H 1977 Sphincter denervation in anorectal incontinence and rectal prolapse. Gut 18: 656–665

Parsa F, Gordon H E, Wilson S E 1975 Bleeding diverticulosis of the colon — a review of 83 cases. Diseases of the Colon and Rectum 18: 37–41

Pawlik W, Jacobson E D 1974 Effects of digoxin on the mesenteric circulation Cardiovascular Research Centre Bulletin 12: 80–84

Payler D K, Pomare E W, Heaton K W, Harvey R F 1975 The effect of wheat bran on intestinal transit. Gut 16: 209–213

Percy J P, Neill M E, Kandiah T K, Swash M 1982 A neurogenic

factor in faecal incontinence in the elderly. Age and Ageing 11: 175–179

Pheils M T 1969 Ischaemic colitis. Medical Journal of Australia 2: 715–716

Phillips S F, Edwards A W 1965 Some aspects of anal incontinence and defaecation. Gut 6: 396–405

Pietsch J B, Shizgal H M, Meakins J L 1977 Injury by hypertonic phosphate enema. Canadian Medical Journal 116: 1169–1170

Powell-Tuck J 1980 Nutritional methods. In: Truelove S C, Lee E (eds) Topics in Gastroenterology 8. Blackwell, Oxford pp 105–121

Ritchie G M, Ardran M D, Truelove S 1962 Motor activity of the sigmoid colon of humans. Gastroenterology 43(6): 642–668

Ritchie J K, Powell-Tuck J, Lennard-Jones J E 1978 Clinical outcome of the first ten years of ulcerative colitis and proctitis. Lancet i: 1140–1143

Roddis M J 1978 Antibiotic associated colitis. Age and Ageing 7: 182–188

Roman C, Gonella J 1981 Extrinsic control of digestive tract motility. In: Johnson L R (ed) Physiology of the Gastrointestinal Tract, Raven Press, New York, p 289–333

Ross G, Gray C H 1964 Assessment of routine tests for occult blood in faeces. British Medical Journal 1: 1351–1354

Rudgren A, Mellstrom D 1983 Cholecystectomy and colon cancer in the elderly. Age and Ageing 12: 44–49

Russell B 1970 In: Autobiography. London: Allen & Unwin

Ryan D, Wilson A, Muir T S, Judge T G 1974 The reduction of faecal incontinence by the use of Duphalac in geriatric patients. Current Medical Research and Opinion 2 (6): 329–334

Schulster M M, Hookman P, Henrix T R and Mendeloff A I 1965 Bulletin Johns Hopkins Hospital 116: 79–88

Shafiek A 1975 A new concept of the anatomy of the anal sphincter mechanism and the physiology of defaecation. Investigative Urology 12: 412–419

Schwartz S, Boley S J, Robinson K, Kreiger H, Schultz L, Allen A C 1968 Roentologic features of vascular diseases of the intestines. Radiological Clinics of North America 2: 71–87

Sischy B, Remington J H 1975 Malignant tumours of the rectum radiotherapy in Clinics in Gastroenterology 4, p 571–581

Small W P, Smith A N 1975 Fistula and conditions associated with diverticular disease of the colon. Clinics in Gastroenterology 4: 171–199

Smith B 1968 The effect of irritant purgatives on the myenteric plexus in man and mouse. Gut 9: 139–143

Smith R G, Curry A E J, Walls A D F 1978 Whole gut irrigation, new treatment for constipation. British Medical Journal 3: 396–397

Srivastava G S, smith A N, Painter N S 1976 Sterculia bulk-forming agent with smooth-muscle relaxant versus bran in diverticular disease. British Medical Journal i: 315–318

String S T, Decosse J J 1971 Sigmoid volvulus. American Journal of Surgery 121: 293–297

Thornton J R, Emmett P M, Heaton K W 1979 Diet and Crohn's disease — characteristics of the pre-illness diet. British Medical Journal 2: 762–764

Till A S 1977 The results of treatment in district general hospitals. In: Truelove S C, Lee E (eds) Topics in Gastroenterology 5. Blackwell Scientific, Oxford. p 77–85

Todd L P 1971 Some aspects of adult megacolon. Proceedings of the Royal Society of Medicine 64: 561–565

Toghill P J, Benton P 1973 Ulcerative colitis in elderly patients. Gerontologia Clinice 15: 65–73

Truelove S C 1966 Movement of the large intestine. Gut 46: 457–512

Vellacott K D, Hardcastle J D 1981 An evaluation of flexible fibreoptic sigmoidoscopy. British Medical Journal 283: 1583–1586

Walker A R P, Walker B F, Richardson B D 1970 British Medical Journal iii: 48

Warman S 1961 Standardized treatment of chronically constipated dependent geriatric patients. Journal of the American Geriatrics Society 9: 285

Wesselius-DeCasparis A, Braad Baart S, Vdbergh-Bohlken G E, Micica M 1968 Treatment of chronic constipation with 'lactulose' syrup. Results of a double-blind study. Gut 9: 84–86

White J C, Verlot M G, Ehrengheill O 1940 Neurogenic disturbances of the colon and their investigation by the colonmetrogram. Annals of Surgery 112: 1042–1057

Willoughby C P, Heyworth M F, Pris J, Truelove S C 1979

Comparison of disodium cromoglycate and sulphasalazine as maintenance therapy for ulcerative colitis. Lancet i: 119–122

Winawer S J 1981 Preventative screening and early diagnosis. Large Bowel Cancer — Clinical Surgery International 1. In: DeCosse J J (ed), Churchill Livingstone, Edinburgh

Woolff W I, Grossman M B, Sinya H 1977 Angioplasia of the colon. Diagnosis and treatment. Gastroenterology 72: 329–333

Wuepper K B, Otterman M G, Staklgram L H 1966 An appraisal of the operative and non-operative treatment of sigmoid volvulus. Surgery, Gynecology and Obstetrics 122: 84–88

Wynder E L, Shigematsu R 1967 Environmental factors of cancer of the colon and rectum. Cancer 20: 1520–1561

Yamagata A 1965 Histopathological studies of the colon in relation to age. Japanese Journal of Gastroenterology 62: 229–235

The gastrointestinal system — the liver and biliary system

THE LIVER

Changes with aging

Structural changes

Macroscopic. The liver loses weight from 50 years onwards (Boyd, 1933). Thompson and Williams (1965) found that liver weight correlated with total body weight; both fell after 50 years of age. Liver weight, greater in males than females, varies with the metabolic demands made on it, and may be reduced in under-nutrition (Everitt, 1957) or after thyroidectomy (Walter and Addis, 1939).

There appear to be racial and/or environmental differences in the change in liver weight in old age (Tauchi and Sato, 1975).

Microscopic. There is a moderate increase in fibrous tissue (Andrew, 1971; Wilson and Franks, 1975).

Andrew et al (1959) and Van Bezooijen et al (1974) found little evidence of cell loss with age in the rat, and no marked differences in fine structure between hepatocytes isolated from old and young rats. Nevertheless, there are now several studies describing morphological changes in the livers of old animals and of man. Tauchi and Sato (1962, 1975) observed a decreased number of hepatocytes in the aging human liver at autopsy and little change in size of hepatocytes. Several papers have since reported an increase in their size in rat liver (Andrew, 1968; Van Bezooijen et al, 1972, 1974; Schmucker, 1976). There is increasing binuclearity of the cells (Wheatley, 1972; Engelmann et al, 1981) later replaced by an increase in volume of individual nuclei (Tauchi and Sato, 1962, 1975; Schmucker, 1976; Meinhuizen and Blausjaar, 1980). Giant nuclei are common in the livers of man and of rodents in old age and invaginations of the nuclear membrane lead to the formation of intranuclear inclusions, which are entrapped masses of cytoplasm, sometimes containing mitochondria or fragments of endoplasmic reticulum (Andrew, 1971).

It is not known why the hepatocytes change with age. Tauchi and Hasegawa (1972) have also shown increase in hepatocyte size, with a decrease in number, and an increase in size of nuclei with increased frequency of binucleate cells. When old rats were made parabiotic with young rats, there was a slight increase in number of cells with fewer being binucleate, which indicates some degree of regeneration. Of far greater significance was the finding that the cells in the young rats became much more like those in old rats in every way. It was concluded that proliferation is inhibited in the young rats by a factor or factors from the old rats. A more recent publication (Pieri et al, 1980) has shown that the nuclear changes in rat liver cells from old rats can be modified by the grafting of young thymus. There is a reduction in nuclear volume, but this has no effect on hepatocyte volume.

Chromosome aberrations were described in livers of aging animals by Curtis and Miller (1971). Organelles such as microbodies (Tauchi et al, 1974) and lysosomes (Comolli et al, 1972; Schmucker, 1976; Meinhuizen and Blausjaar, 1980) increase in number and the latter increase in volume, while the surface area of the Golgi membrane decreases linearly with aging (Schmucker, 1976).

The hepatic Golgi membrane system is thought to be involved in various synthetic activities, such as bile acids (Story and Kritchevsky, 1974), lipoprotein (Kritchevsky, 1972; Bizzi and Marsh, 1973), albumin (Jones and Mills, 1973) and bile secretion (Cooper et al, 1974). Lipofuscin accumulates (Bachman, 1953) and is associated with the lysosomes. Fragmentation, dispersion and loss of the rough areas of the endoplasmic reticulum (ER) have been described (Ohnishi et al, 1974; Pieri et al, 1975a), but Schmucker (1976) reported a linear increase in the amounts of both rough and smooth ER in the livers of aging rats. Meinhuizen and Blausjaar (1980) have demonstrated increases in the volume density of smooth endoplasmic reticulum and lysosomes in all areas of the liver of old rats. This does not necessarily imply that increases in the amounts of enzymes concerned in drug metabolism occurred; proliferation of hepatocyte smooth ER which was not associated with increased drug metabolizing enzyme activity has been described frequently (Fouts, 1971; Koff et al, 1973; Anthony and Jones, 1976). Indeed, the evidence available suggests that hepatic drug-metabolizing enzyme activity is reduced in older animals (Conney, 1967; Kato and Takanaka, 1968a,b,c,; Baird et al, 1975). Furthermore, tthe number of active ribosomes in mouse liver decrease in number with aging, as observed in senescent mice of 28 months (Kurtz, 1978).

Mitochondria are of great importance in various aspects of cellular metabolism and are accessible for structural and functional study. Because of this a sizable literature exists concerning mitochondrial changes in the livers of aging and old animals and man. It is possible that these studies will afford insights into biological aging itself. There is controversy about the number of mitochondria per liver cell. In the liver of man after 60, Tauchi and Sato (1968) report a decrease and this is confirmed in aging and senile mice (Herbener, 1976). However, Kwent et al (1966) report an increase and Boulière (1946) states there is no change. There are also conflicting reports about the size of the hepatic mitochondria in old age: in mice, Herbener (1976) found no change, but Wilson and Franks (1975) found 60 per cent increase in mean size and an increased proportion of larger mitochondria in livers of old animals. In man, hepatic mitochondria showed increase in size in biopsies from subjects aged above 65 (Sato and Tauchi, 1975). This increased size was achieved either by fusion (Kimberg and Loeb, 1972) or — more likely — by the synthesis of new material (Albring et al, 1973). There are also differences in the density of cristae (increased in man (Sato and Tauchi, 1975) and decreased in mice (Tate and Herbener, 1976)). The inner membrane becomes more permeable with aging which is shown by increased loss of protein matrix in hypo-osmolar medium (Spencer and Horton, 1978). In passing, it may be noted that Tate and Herbener (1976) showed that liver and heart mitochondria behaved differently in aging mice; they deduced that mitochondrial outer and inner membranes had a semi-independent existence. The effect of race and environment on age changes in the structure of the liver is considered by Sato et al (1970) and Tauchi and Sato (1975). The amount of lipofuscin pigment accumulation in hepatocytes varies between races (Tauchi and Hanenoucki, 1980) but this appears not to to be a true aging phenomenon.

Functional changes

Biochemical changes. Liver glycogen and ascorbic acid may decrease and lipid may increase in livers of old animals (Weinbren, 1961; Meinhuizen and Blausjaar, 1980) and some elderly humans (Findor et al, 1973). There is evidence of reduced protein synthesis (Hrachovec, 1969, 1971; Mainwaring, 1969; Buetow and Gandhi, 1973; Cooke and Buetow, 1981). A study in rats has shown an increase in protein synthesis (leucine incorporation) in rats aging from 24 to 36 months (Van Bezooijen et al, 1981). This appears to be compensation for protein loss by the kidneys. Individual proteins may show differences and some authors report increased albumin synthesis in old rats (Obenrader et al, 1974a). These workers also showed (1974b) that after partial hepatectomy in old rats the regenerated liver showed 'rejuvenated' functional properties, viz. decrease in albumin synthesis and reduced half-life of ferritin, for several weeks; by 12 weeks, however, the 'old' functional properties were restored. These findings suggested that the age changes in liver protein metabolism were not due to somatic mutations. It is interesting to compare these functional changes in regenerating liver with the structural changes reported by Pieri and colleagues (1975b) in old rats subjected to two-thirds hepatectomy: here the regenerated liver cells showed a similar degree of aging change in the rough ER to that in old control animals, but the mitochondria showed 'rejuvenation' changes. These authors suggested that their findings could lend support to the concept of somatic mutations being involved in the aging process, though they admit that they have not offered proof.

Devi et al (1963) reported decreased RNA content in livers from old rats, and Pyhtila and Sherman (1969) found gradual reduction in RNA and protein in chromatin obtained from livers of aging rats. Zs-Nagy et al (1977) noted age dependent loss of perichromatin granules (RNA) in various tissues, including liver cells. Wust and Rosen (1972) reported qualitative and quantitative changes in transfer RNA (tRNA) of rat liver and spleen, but Comolli (1973) found that tRNA from old and young rat livers accepted ^{14}C-leucine to the same extent. Decreased template activity occurs in old animals (Zhelabovskaya and Berdyshev, 1972; Ryan and Cristofalo, 1975). Samis et al (1964) reported that despite decreased extractable RNA from nuclei of old rat livers, incorporation of ^3H-cytidine into that RNA was increased; this suggested increased activity of fewer genetic loci, lending support to von Hahn's (1966) theory that aging results from progressive irreversible repression of genetic information. Amici et al (1974), however, reported no difference in the amount of RNA extractable from young and old rat livers. Protein synthesis decreased in senescent Wistar rats, which was due to changes in transfer RNA synthetase, transfer RNA and the polysomes (Cooke and Buetow, 1981).

Thermal stability of hepatic DNA increases in old age due to differences in DNA-protein binding and the composition of the associated protein (von Hahn and Fritz, 1966; Zhelabovskaya and Berdyshev, 1972; Berdyshev and Zhelabovskaya, 1972; Stein et al, 1973; Pieri et al, 1976). Tas (1976) showed that liver chromatin from older rats had an increased number of disulphide bonds; this accorded with the known increase in the glutathione/reduced glutathione ratio in aging rat liver (Harisch and Schole, 1974).

Increased incorporation of ^{3}H-thymidine into rat liver DNA with aging was reported by Samis et al (1966). Although DNA polymerase activity appears to be unchanged in the livers of old rats, there is a diminished capacity to repair bleomycin-induced damage in the old animals (Ove and Coetzee, 1978).

Age changes have been described in the polyamine content of the liver (Janne et al, 1964; Ferioli and Comolli, 1975). The polyamines (spermine, spermidine) are ubiquitous substances which are implicated in the control of protein synthesis; their levels increase when RNA and protein are being synthesized actively. Comolli (1973) studied the effects of polyamines on protein synthesis in liver microsomes from rats of different ages, and found that the inhibition of protein synthesis associated with old age could be reversed by polyamines, in a selective way: spermine was most effective with microsomes from old livers, and spermidine with 'young' microsomes in 'old' cell sap.

Enzyme changes. Aging has no consistent effect on enzyme activity within the liver. Enzyme levels may be increased or decreased in the livers of old animals, according to the enzyme and the state of nutrition (Ross, 1968). Finch (1972) reviewed the age changes recorded in the literature on 21 liver enzymes, and summarized his findings thus:

Little change with age	(< 25 per cent)	80 per cent
Big increase	(> 25 per cent)	13 per cent
Big decrease	(> 25 per cent)	7 per cent

He discusses the biological factors which could account for the many conflicting reports.

An even more comprehensive review of enzyme changes in aging mammals is given by Wilson (1973). She, too, emphasized the complex pattern of age changes and the wide variations and frequent discrepancies in the literature. Undoubtedly part of the difficulty arises from lax interpretation of the terms 'aging' and 'aged'. Some experiments on 'aging' animals fail to include any which could be regarded as 'old' at all: this is perfectly legitimate since aging might be said to begin at conception; but the relevance of the ages included in any given study must be kept clearly in mind when evaluating its significance.

The overall picture is of a decrease in the activities of respiratory enzymes and an increase in hydrolytic enzymes. However, liver mitochondria do not always show the enzyme changes often described in mitochondria from other organs (Wilson et al, 1975), and Menzies and Gold (1971) and Comolli et al (1972) were unable to show any age change in mitochondrial protein turnover. Nevertheless, in the abnormally large liver mitochondria induced by cortisone administration (Kimberg and Loeb, 1972) there were multiple defects in the respiratory chain, and the same could be true for senes-cent livers (Wilson and Franks, 1975). Liver mitochondrial cytochrome oxidase activity does not change with age in rat liver (Paterniti et al, 1980). There is a decline in the respiratory control ratio of rat liver mitochondria in old age (Horton and Spencer, 1981)

The increase in lysosomal enzymes may be found despite an overall decrease in lysosomal protein synthesis and turnover (Comolli et al, 1972).

Some liver enzymes change very markedly in old age, e.g. cathepsins increase considerably (Barrows and Roeder, 1961) and glucose-6-phosphatase decreases greatly (Grinna and Barber, 1972; Gold and Widnell, 1974). Grinna and Barber (1975b) made a kinetic analysis of the age-related differences in the activity of the latter enzyme and showed that the velocity of its reaction in old livers is only half that in young livers; and it remains slowed even after activation of the enzyme by biochemical manipulations. Hepatic microsomal NADPH cytochrome c reductase and cytochrome P450 appear to decline in old age (Schmucker and Wang, 1981).

Wilson (1973) is careful to point out that the total amount of an enzyme may not be the most important aspect; adaptability or inducibility (the latter being associated with increase in ER and *de novo* protein synthesis) are probably of greater significance. There is some evidence of diminution of both these responses in old age, but the effects may be quite complex. Rahman and Peraino (1973) and Adelman (1975) found a general impairment of adaptation in several enzymes studied, but Britton et al (1976) could find no age-effect on the adaptive increase in tyrosine aminotransferase activity in vitro in isolated hepatocytes incubated with hydro-cortisone: the time-course and the magnitude of the increase were independent of the age of the donor rats. These authors considered that previously reported age changes in liver enzyme behaviour probably reflected alterations in extrahepatic regulatory mechanisms.

On the other hand, Platt and Pauli (1972) showed that the induction of lysosomal enzymes in the rat liver was decreased by aging, despite increase in the amount of smooth ER. Adelman (1971) studied 19 separate examples of enzymes in tissues of mouse, rat and rabbit whose inductions were subject to an age-dependent modification. Although decreased enzyme activity was apparent with single measurements, kinetic analysis showed a lag period, proportional to age; maximal production of the enzyme was not age-related. Adelman considered that the lag period might be used as a molecular parameter of biological aging, but Baird et al (1975) could not confirm any lag in enzyme-induction with advancing age, although like Adelman (1975) and other workers they had demonstrated decreased efficiency in the hepatic microsomal mixed-function oxidase system which metabolizes many drugs. Yet Eisenbach et al

(1976) found that certain liver enzymes were practically non-inducible in old mice.

A more recent study confirms that inducibility decreases with age. This was shown by measuring the rate of enzyme and haemoprotein induction during chronic phenobarbital stimulation (Schmucker and Wang, 1981). It is concluded that there is a reduction in the capacity of the microsomal mixed function oxidase system to respond in old age.

The rate of degradation of enzymes in old age may be reduced (Haining and Correll, 1969; Comolli et al, 1972; Haining and Legan, 1973) or increased (Wulf and Cutler, 1975). Clearly such changes may influence studies of enzyme kinetics.

There is evidence that enzymes in senescent animals may have greatly reduced activity (Gershon and Gershon, 1973) or increased thermolability (Grinna and Barber, 1975a; Wulf and Cutler, 1975). These observations are consistent with those of Holliday and Tarrant (1972) and Holliday et al (1974) in tissue-culture experiments, and support the hypothesis that altered protein synthesis occurs as part of the aging process (Orgel, 1963, 1973). On the other hand, Yagil (1976) and Schofield et al (1978) could find no appreciable amounts of altered glucose-6-phosphate dehydrogenase in livers of aged mice, and Kahn et al (1977) found no altered enzymes in senescent cultured cells from human livers.

Isoenzyme patterns may change during aging (Wilson, 1973).

Rothstein (1975) also reviews the alteration of enzymes with aging. There may be a release of lysosomal enzymes into cell cytoplasm with aging (Björkerud et al, 1967; Goto et al, 1969) and this might cause structural changes in the cell (Weissmann, 1967).

Hepatic drug metabolism in old age
Reduced hepatic blood-flow in old age was suggested by the work of Sherlock et al (1950) and Bender (1965). Tesauro et al (1969) showed reduced flow in subjects over 50 years of age. Altered hepatic blood flow can affect the rate of metabolism of some drugs (Leevy and Kiernan, 1975; Nies et al, 1976), and probably accounts for the decreased metabolism in old age (Crooks et al, 1976). The intrinsic hepatic clearance of a drug (Wilkinson and Shand, 1975) may also change with age (Nation et al, 1976).

Observations of decreased hepatic microsomal drug metabolism in rats have been made by Kato et al (1964) and Kato and Takanaka (1968a,b,c) and by Baird et al (1975). but no direct data are available on age-related microsomal drug metabolism in human liver. These changes are thought to acccount for the observation that aging affects the response to certain drugs. In aged experimental animals there is increased sensitivity to

certain drugs such as alcohol (Chen and Robbins, 1944a), morphine (Henderson and Chen, 1948) and secobarbital (Chen and Robbins, 1944b) which are known to be metabolized within the liver. Indirect evidence from plasma clearance studies (Hayes et al, 1975) and measurement of half-life values (O'Malley et al, 1971) or both (Flanagan et al, 1977) in man, for various drugs, confirm that elderly patients are more sensitive to these drugs. It is suggested that changes within the aging liver might account for these differences. We have already seen that the microsomal mixed function oxidase system is less able to respond to induction in the old rat (Schmucker and Wang, 1981). This would contribute to the increased sensitivity to ethanol, morphine and barbiturates already mentioned. But for many drugs it is not so simple, and it is difficult to extrapolate from experimental animal to man. Klotz et al (1975) reported a positive correlation between plasma half-life of diazepam and age of the subject between youth and the ninth decade, but this was compensated for by an increased apparent volume of distribution of the drug so that the plasma clearance showed no age-related change. This could be due to the increased fat-content of tissues in the elderly (Rossman, 1971) since diazepam is a highly lipid-soluble compound. The elderly are more sensitive to benzodiazepines, yet there is no evidence to support the hypothesis that the healthy elderly show a different pharmacokinetic profile (Castleden and George, 1979). In the case of nitrazepam, the problem appears to rest with sensitivity of the brain.

Increasing age also appears to contribute to increased sensitivity to the anticoagulant warfarin (O'Malley et al, 1974). This has been looked at in some detail (Shepherd et al, 1979). Warfarin clearance and receptor sensitivity are not altered in old age. However, the plasma clearance of vitamin K_1 does appear to be increased in old age, which might result in a relative deficiency. It is postulated that reduced efficiency of carboxylation of precursor proteins and of NADH-dependent reduction of vitamin K_1 account for the increased warfarin sensitivity. These processes take place within the liver.

Diazepam (Berkowitz et al, 1975), lignocaine (Oldendorf et al, 1972) and prazosin (Jick et al, 1968) all show prolonged half life in the elderly. However, this is not due to any change in clearance but rather to altered distribution. These three drugs are metaboliized by demethylation within the liver.

Antipyrine (Bellville et al, 1971) and chlormethiazole (Chan et al, 1975) have prolonged half lives in the elderly which appears to result from reduced clearance. These drugs are hydroxylated within the liver. Propranolol is degraded within the liver by a complex pathway which includes hydroxylation. In a study of elderly patients from long-term care wards, half life was prolonged and clearance reduced (O'Malley et al, 1977).

However, healthy elderly volunteers did not show the same changes (Shepherd et al, 1977).

The possible effects of aging on the liver are complex and it is likely that different metabolic pathways are influenced to different extents. There is much more work that needs to be done before any firm conclusions can be reached.

Further discussion of the role of the liver in the metabolism of drugs in the aged is to be found in reviews of pharmacokinetics in the elderly (Triggs and Nation, 1975; Crooks et al, 1976; Hollister, 1981).

Changes in liver function tests

A large number of tests have been introduced to help in the diagnosis of liver disease. Most are redundant and are of marginal value (Knill-Jones, 1975). The tests that are commonly included in biochemical profiles are serum bilirubin, transaminases (aspartate aminotransferase and alanine aminotransferase), alkaline phosphatase, gamma glutamyl transpeptidase and lactate dehydrogenase. Serum albumin and total protein levels are also measured. These tests are sufficient for the diagnosis of most forms of liver disease. There are many other tests of liver function which have been in use in the past. Most are now redundant and because of that will not be considered in great depth.

Bromsulphthalein (BSP) retention test is of extremely limited value; its use is now relegated to diagnosis of rare forms of hereditary genetic liver disease. BSP retention, storage capacity and maximum biliary excretion have been extensively studied in normal people of different ages. A review of this information leads us to the conclusion that there is no consistent change in any aspect of BSP metabolism with age.

Turbidity and flocculation tests are no longer used diagnostically and will not be considered further.

Serum bilirubin does not change in old age (Reed et al, 1972; Sharland, 1972; Leask et al, 1973; Kampmann et al, 1975).

Serum transaminase elevation is a sensitive indicator of hepatocellular damage and the normal range does not change in old age (Reed et al, 1972).

Much interest has been shown in the levels of serum alkaline phosphatase (SAP) in old age. Age-related increases above the 'normal' have been reported by Clark et al, (1951); Hobson and Jordan (1959); Klaassen (1966); Roberts (1967); Keating et al (1969); Chen and Millard (1972): the first 3 series contained few subjects over 60 years. Heino and Jokipii (1962) reported a slight age-related increase but all levels remained within the usually-accepted range of normal.

Several authors have found no evidence of increased SAP in 'normal' old age — Mulay and Hurwitz (1938); Thompson and Williams (1965); Canapa-Anson and Rowe (1970); Hodkinson and McPherson (1973), and Kampmann et al (1975). Sewell (1960) reported an age-related increase up to 60 years, followed by a fall at higher ages. Recent work has shown that elderly patients treated over a period of time with such compounds as phenytoin, which are capable of enhancing hepatic drug-metabolizing enzyme activity, have increased SAP levels, together with lowered serum-free bilirubin concentrations and increased urinary D-glucarate excretions. This drug-mediated increase in SAP activity may explain some of the previous observations of raised levels in the elderly.

The interpretation of elevated SAP levels in 'normal' old people is not easy; occult liver or bone disease may be difficult or virtually impossible to exclude. The best evidence would appear to be from the sort of study performed by Kampmann et al (1975) where old people were selected because their liver biopsies were normal; their SAP levels were found to be normal. In hospital series, about 10 per cent of elderly patients have raised SAP (Hazell and Ortiz, 1966; Hodkinson and McPherson, 1973; Sharland, 1975) and the cause can be established in most cases, if necessary, with the help of isoenzymes (Burke, 1974); the majority prove to be due to bone disease, such as Paget's disease and osteomalacia, but the possible effect of drug therapy on SAP must be remembered.

We conclude that there is no change in serum alkaline phosphatase levels with aging. Finding an elevated SAP in an elderly patient warrants further investigation. Perhaps the initial test that needs to be carried out is one that will help in determining the site of origin of the elevated SAP: isoenzyme measurement, 5'-nucleotidase or gamma glutamyl transpeptidase (GGT). Serum 5'-nucleotidase, which is of liver origin, was found to be elevated in 15 of 70 subjects who were considered to be normal (Sharland, 1972). GGT is the test most frequently included in biochemical profiles; it is of liver origin. If GGT is elevated at the same time as SAP, then it indicates the latter is most likely of liver origin. There are no data available on the normal range for GGT in old age. It is likely to be unaltered. It should be remembered that GGT elevation has been reported in many other conditions which are common in old age, such as myocardial infarction, left ventricular failure, pulmonary embolism, epilepsy or cerebrovascular disease (Roselski, 1975).

Lactate dehydrogenase does not change with age (Reed et al, 1972).

Serum albumin is synthesized within the liver and is low in the presence of significant liver disease. Interpretation of this test in the elderly is difficult as serum albumin may be lower in old age (Keating et al, 1969). However, surveys of fit elderly people in the community reveal values significantly higher than those in hospitalized elderly patients (Leask et al, 1973; Hodkinson,

1977). The normal range in the fit elderly is somewhat lower than younger adults, being 33–49 g/1 (Leask et al, 1973). A fall in serum albumin or the finding of a low value may result from a number of disease states, including liver disease. For this reason it has a limited place as a test of liver function in old age.

Conclusions. It is always difficult to define normal old age, and the study of Kampmann et al (1975) must therefore carry much weight since the normality of the structure of the subjects' livers was shown by histology of biopsy material. Their inability to find any functional defect over the range of tests studied suggests that much of the discord in the previous literature on the subject may well be explained by the true degree of health in the 'normal' individuals studied.

There appears to be no significant age-related alteration in hepatic organic anion transport (bilirubin, BSP, rose bengal) or serum transaminases or alkaline phosphatase. However, synthetic functions (protein synthesis) and microsomal mixed-function oxidase activity (drug- and steriod-metabolism) are reduced in old age.

The main implications for geriatric medicine relate to those plasma proteins which bind ions, hormones and drugs, and the hepatic metabolism of drugs.

Resistance to hepatotoxins. This is generally considered to be higher in old than in young liver cells (MacNider, 1936; Reuber and Lee, 1968; Reuber et al, 1969), but Wiberg et al (1970) noted increased ethanol toxicity in old rats despite increased hepatic alcohol dehydrogenase.

Regeneration. Bucher (1963) found only a slight slowing of regenerative processes in the livers of old rats. Structural and functional changes in regenerated liver in old animals have been considered above.

Investigation of liver disease in the elderly

The value of a good history (including a drug history) and clinical examination cannot be overemphasized. For further investigation the usual tests are used, and age is no contraindication of the use of the most appropriate diagnostic technique. Techniques of investigation have been introduced in recent years which are less invasive but yield much more information. These are entirely appropriate to the diagnosis of liver disease in old age.

Biochemical tests

Urine and stools. Bile pigments behave similarly in old and young subjects. Normal urine contains no bilirubin and only a little urobilinogen. Bilirubinuria indicates obstructive jaundice. Complete biliary obstruction leads to an absence of urobilinogen in the urine, whereas haemolysis or hepatocellular damage increases urinary urobilinogen. Stool colour and faecal occult blood tests should be performed repeatedly; they are more impor-

tant (and practicable) than quantitative estimations of faecal stercobilin.

Liver function tests. Liver function tests should be kept to a minimum to avoid confusion and only the most useful and discriminatory tests should be used. Liver function tests obtained from the routine biochemical screen may reveal two things — first that normal liver function is disturbed and second, the nature of that disturbance.

Elevation of serum bilirubin indicates the presence of jaundice and remains a valid test in old age. Measurement of conjugated and unconjugated fractions is of little value except in mild jaundice where haemolysis is a strong possibility.

Serum alkaline phosphatase (SAP) has been discussed and a value above the normal range (20–85 IU/1) is pathological in old age. Gamma glutamyl transpeptidase (GGT) elevation in association with this indicates that the SAP is of liver origin. A normal GGT would suggest that the source of the increased SAP was bone. GGT is raised in all types of liver disease but the highest levels are recorded in cholestasis and malignancy. Transaminases are elevated in liver disease and finding this in association with raised bilirubin, GGT and SAP indicates liver pathology. The nature of the liver disturbance is determined by the amount of elevation of the different tests. Very high SAP and GGT with only moderate elevation of transaminases indicates cholestatic or obstructive liver disease. Very high transaminases with modest elevation of SAP and GGT indicate hepatocellular damage, the highest levels being seen in acute hepatitis. In malignant liver disease all tests may be high but the pattern with very high SAP and LDH is very suggestive of this diagnosis.

The changes in liver function may be secondary to problems elsewhere, most of which are common in geriatric medical practice. Perhaps the most frequently seen result from liver congestion in congestive cardiac failure, and very high levels of transaminases have been recorded (Bloth et al, 1976). Liver function tests may also rise, particularly SAP, with pneumonia and also with malignancy elsewhere in the body, particularly hypernephroma.

None of these tests change only with liver disease. For example, SAP changes with bone disease; transaminases with cardiac infarction; and GGT with administration of enzyme-inducing drugs.

Serum albumin will be low in advanced liver disease such as cirrhosis, but it is of poor discriminating value because it is reduced in so many other common problems in old age.

Other blood tests. The results of liver function tests will have indicated the presence of liver disease and its type. These will also indicate the need for further investigations. There are various blood tests available which might be valuable in establishing a diagnosis. These include tests for hepatitis antigens (A, B-surface, B-core and e) and antibodies. Alpha$_1$ fetoprotein is positive in a number of patients with primary liver cell cancer, and is indicated if this diagnosis is suspected (Kew, 1975).

If the possibility is raised of a chronic liver disease such as primary biliary cirrhosis or chronic active hepatitis, the autoantibody tests are useful. Antibodies to smooth muscle, nuclear antigens and mitochondria may be positive.

Mitochondrial antibodies are found in 98 per cent of cases of primary biliary cirrhosis and in less than 10 per cent of cases of biliary obstruction from other causes. They are also found in 30 per cent of cases of chronic active hepatitis and cryptogenic cirrhosis. About 0.5 to 1 per cent of normal persons show these antibodies and this incidence increases with age (Doniach, 1972).

Haematology

Anaemia is common in liver disease, especially cirrhosis. Several factors play a part: liver dysfunction, blood loss (the major factors); malnutrition, hypersplenism and haemolysis.

Liver disease itself may be associated with depressed erythropoiesis and shortened red-cell life-span; alcohol ingestion may contribute its own toxic effects on the marrow. Obstructive jaundice is associated with changes in shape and size of red cells, which become less fragile, e.g. target cells and bizarre shapes may occur, presumably due to the presence of bile-salts in the blood. These changes are not related to the degree of anaemia which may be present.

Anaemia is usually moderate; if severe, blood loss or malnutrition should also be suspected. It may be normocytic and normochromic or macrocytic. Macrocytes may be thin, thick or 'target' cells. A moderate reticulocytosis (about 5 per cent) is common. The severity of the anaemia does not correlate with the severity of the liver lesion nor with the duration of the disease.

The marrow is not diagnostic.

The liver plays an important part in folic acid metabolism, and folate deficiency makes its effects felt more readily if there is liver dysfunction. In such cases a megaloblastic picture may ensue.

Raised serum vitamin B$_{12}$ levels have been reported in acute hepatitis and cirrhosis; but autopsy evidence has revealed a greatly reduced liver content of vitamin B$_{12}$ (Swendseid et al, 1957) although these values did not show any correlation with the degree of anaemia in life. Megaloblastic anaemia is not seen in uncomplicated liver disease. Intestinal absorption of iron may be increased even in the absence of sideropenia, and plasma iron may be elevated for this reason as well as by cell-necrosis and haemolysis. An opposing tendency is due to bleeding and malnutrition. Total iron-binding capacity (TIBC) may fall because of the liver disease, and increased saturation of IBC results. Serum ferritin levels are raised.

Blood loss may occur from oesophageal varices or haemorrhoids. In severe liver disease it is aggravated by a coagulation defect, which may lead to epistaxis or haemoptysis. Gastritis and peptic ulcer may also occur in association with cirrhosis.

Malnutrition. Protein, iron, folic acid and even (rarely) vitamin B$_{12}$ deficiencies may contribute. Chronic alcoholism is an important aetiological factor here.

Hypersplenism. Splenomegaly due to portal hypertension and chronic splenic congestion may lead to the picture of 'hypersplenism', with anaemia and possibly leucopenia and/or thrombocytopenia.

Haemolysis. Rarely, a frank acquired haemolytic anaemia is seen; the Coombs test may be positive. Note that the body's immunological system may be disturbed in liver disease.

Patients with alcoholic fatty liver and cirrhosis may develop episodes of haemolytic anaemia, hyperlipaemia and jaundice (Zieve's syndrome) (Zieve, 1958).

Defects in haemostasis. These may occur due to faulty synthesis of some clotting factors, impaired vitamin K absorption, and possibly increased fibrinolysis (Ollendorff et al, 1966); the importance of vitamin K in the elderly was emphasized by Hazell and Baloch (1970). Haemostatic abnormalities in liver disease are reviewed by Parbhoo (1975) and Aledort (1976).

X-Rays

A plain X-ray of the abdomen may show gall stones, which are very common in the elderly, but they may be incidental and many are radiolucent. The liver and spleen may be seen as soft tissue shadows (see also under Biliary system).

Oral cholecystography. This is often disappointing in old people with liver and/or gall-bladder disease; it should never be attempted if jaundice is present.

Intravenous cholangiography. This has its main use after cholecystectomy if symptoms recur, or when cholecystography has failed. It is unlikely to succeed if the serum bilirubin is much over 34 μmol/l (2 mg/100 ml), even if high dose infusion techniques and tomography are used.

Endoscopic retrograde cholangio-pancreatography (ERCP). This is a technique of great value in the diagnosis of jaundice (Salmon, 1975; Ayoola et al, 1976; Cotton, 1976; Maffioli et al, 1976; Elias, 1976; Zimmon et al, 1979). With a side-viewing fibreoptic panendoscope the papilla of Vater is cannulated under direct vision and contrast material is injected into the common bile duct and pancreatic duct. X-ray screening is then carried out.

The advantages of this technique are that minimal patient sedation is required: in the hands of a skilled operator the test can be completed in 15 minutes (these advantages are especially useful in elderly and frail patients); the pancreatic duct system is included in the examination; and endoscopic examination of the stomach and duodenum may be achieved at the same time. Periampullary carcinoma can be seen, and biopsies and brush cytology taken before the contrast medium is injected. Pure bile can be aspirated and manometry performed. With this technique an unnecessary laparotomy may be avoided.

Good tolerance and safety of ERCP in elderly patients has been reported by Wong and Schuman (1976), who stressed that it could prove the existence of biliary or pancreatic disease which might not be diagnosed by any other technique. Their indications included not only jaundice but also upper abdominal pain or a mass suspected of being related to the biliary tract or pancreas.

The complication rate is 2 to 3 per cent and includes sepsis and pancreatitis. The mortality rate is low (usually due to sepsis) at 0.1 per cent.

Percutaneous transhepatic cholangiography. This has been made safer by the introduction of a fine needle, which has reduced the risks of haemorrhage and bile peritonitis. It is less costly than ERCP, requires less expertise, and has a very high success rate in visualizing dilated bile ducts; but it is usually done preoperatively or with a surgeon standing by. When the ducts are not dilated it may be less successful than ERCP (Elias et al, 1975). In the elderly it can only rarely have an application, and in any case ERCP should be carried out first. Only those patients who can co-operate fully should be considered for this investigation.

Open transhepatic cholangiography. Carried out via a small incision under local anaesthetic, this has been advocated where other procedures fail (Stein, 1975). It is rarely indicated in the elderly.

Percutaneous trans-splenic portal venography. This can surely have no place in the elderly. For the investigation of portal hypertension, selective coeliac and superior mesenteric angiography are preferred.

Barium studies. These may be relevant to show oesophageal varices, to exclude peptic ulcer, to show a distorted duodenal loop due to carcinoma of the head of the pancreas, or to show a primary growth in some cases with hepatic metastases. However, the use of barium studies has been diminished by the introduction of fibreoptic endoscopy (see below).

The use of the double-contrast barium meal promises far greater resolution of mucosal details down to 2 to 3 mm diameter but this is not in wide use (Scott Harden, 1974; Laufer, 1975; Lavelle et al, 1976; Stevenson et al, 1976).

Laparoscopy

Laparoscopy is popular in Europe, where it may be performed in 'difficult' cases of cholestatic jaundice before ERCP (Etienne et al, 1976). Its value in the investigation of hepatobiliary disorders has been put forward in the USA by Scott et al (1968) and Anselm and Gluckmann (1974), and in the UK by Cuschieri (1975), Balfour (1976) and Woolf and Williams (1976a). It is useful in patients in whom accurate diagnosis is problematic, and especially so for directing the site for biopsy in primary or secondary malignant tumours in the liver. While it may not have much application in the elderly, it may occasionally save an unnecessary laparotomy, and may be performed under local anaesthesia (Hall et al, 1980).

Liver biopsy

Liver biopsy is a procedure which carries a low mortality (Zamcheck and Klausensotck, 1953) and a low risk of complications. It is a very valuable technique in establishing diagnoses in patients with liver disease. Age is no contraindication and the indications for liver biopsy are the same in the elderly as at any age. The Menghini needle is most widely used (Menghini, 1970), but disposable needles (Trucut) are also available. The use of needle liver biopsy in old age has been advocated by several authors (Munzer, 1966; Eastwood, 1971), but not by others (Agate, 1970). The risks appear to be no greater in the elderly if the usual precautions are taken, and the rewards are as good as in any age group.

Liver imaging

Radioisotope methods. A gamma-emitting radioisotope is injected intravenously. The agents used fall into three groups: (1) those taken up and metabolized by hepatocytes and excreted into bile (^{131}I-rose bengal). These agents have fallen into disuse but in recent years have gained acceptance for the demonstration of the biliary tract; (2) labelled colloids taken up by Kupffer cells (^{198}Au, ^{113m}In ferrous hydroxide, ^{99m}Tc sulphur colloid); these may also be used as an indirect method of estimating hepatic blood flow; (3) a miscellaneous group (^{75}Se-selenomethionine, ^{67}Ga citrate) taken up by abnormal tissue and useful in evaluating lesions seen with colloids. Technetium (^{99m}Tc) is a synthetic isotope prepared from ^{99}molybdenum; it has a short half-life and a high energy and is the most popular agent. It gives good results with the gamma camera, which is easier to use with ill or immobile patients than is the scintiscanner.

Lesions which do not take up the isotope (e.g. secondary carcinoma, cysts, abscesses) show up as filling defects, but 'false positive' filling defects occur in about 21 per cent and false negatives in about 23 per cent of scans (Rosenthal, 1976). Rothschild (1976) showed that the 'false' results were related to the type of liver disease present; best results are seen in neoplastic involvement of the liver.

[75]Se-selenomethionine and [67]gallium are taken up by growing lesions e.g. neoplasms or abscesses, which show up as 'hot areas'. ^{131}I-labelled rose bengal or technetium labelled HIDA (an imino-diacetic acid derivative) are used to visualize the biliary tract. These agents are extracted from the blood and rapidly excreted through the hepatocyte to be concentrated in the bile. HIDA scanning is possible in jaundiced patients provided the serum bilirubin is no more than twice the upper limit of normal. It can be used to diagnose acute cholecystitis and a patient's common bile duct and occluded cystic duct will be seen. It is also used post-operatively in those patients who have had biliary tract surgery to assess the status of the biliary tract.

Ultrasound. The liver is acoustically homogeneous and ultrasound is of use in detecting cysts or abscesses in the liver. The portal vein, inferior vena cava and aorta are routinely visualised, but a normal biliary tree is not seen. It is essential in the diagnosis of jaundice and is more important than radioisotope scans or radiological procedures, since the gall bladder, cystic duct, common bile duct and branching intrahepatic ducts will all be enlarged in extraheptic obstructive jaundice, and gall stones may be visualized down to 3 mm diameter in the gall bladder; the cause of the obstruction may also be visualized, though stones in the common bile duct may be missed. Various liver lesions may be seen and adjac-

ent structures evaluated. The false positive rate is 3 per cent, but the false negative rate is 32 per cent — mainly in diffuse liver disease (Lomonaco et al, 1975). This technique may allow guidance of a needle for biopsy or aspiration. It is also useful in diagnosing ascites (see Fig. 27.1).

EMI scanning. Computerized transverse axial tomography is likely to become a most valuable technique for the study of abdominal structures and in particular offers a non-invasive method for diagnosis of carcinoma of the pancreas and periampullary region, common causes of obstructive jaundice in the elderly (Alfidi et al, 1976; Abrams and McNeil, 1978). The technique is of value in haemochromatosis, where the radiological density is increased (Chapman et al, 1980). Its place in geriatric practice, in the diagnosis of other problems, has not yet been established (see Fig. 27.2).

Relative value of imaging techniques. Recent reviews are those of Carlsen (1975), Lomonaco et al (1975), Rosenthal (1976), Rothschild (1976), Andersen et at (1976), Biello et al (1978) and Snow et al, (1979). In practice some of the methods are best regarded as complementary to each other and to other investigative procedures. These non-invasive techniques are clearly of considerable value in geriatric practice (Poe and Bennett, 1971).

Jaundice in the elderly

Formal accounts of bilirubin metabolism and detailed

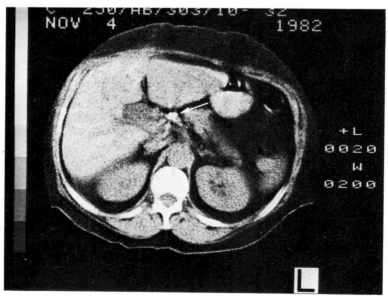

Fig. 27.1 An example of a gall stone impacted in the common hepatic duct at the junction of the cystic duct (arrow). There is dilatation of the common hepatic and main intra-hepatic ducts proximally. The dilated ducts are shown as areas of reduced attenuation within the porta hepatis and within the liver parenchyma. (Courtesy of Dr St Clair Forbes)

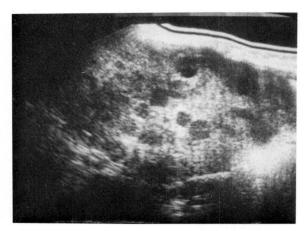

Fig. 27.2 Primary prostatic carcinoma. There is extensive involvement of the liver by hypo-echoic and hyper-echoic metastases. (Courtesy of Dr Rowland Wood)

consideration of the classification and causes of jaundice may be found in standard texts (Sherlock, 1981) and a review of diagnosis and management is given by Murray-Lyon and Reynolds (1976).

The assessment and management of jaundice are no different in elderly and younger adults.

A simple classification depends on whether the predominant pigment is unconjugated or conjugated bilirubin and whether the cause is prehepatic, hepatic, or posthepatic.

Unconjugated hyperbilirubinaemia (Prehepatic)
The commonest cause in the elderly is breakdown of haemoglobin from a pulmonary infarct in a patient with cardiac failure. If cardiac failure is absent, pulmonary infarcts do not produce jaundice (Sherlock, 1981) so some impairment of function of the congested liver presumably contributes (see Chronic cardiac failure below).

Conjugated hyperbilirubinaemia
Hepatic. Hepatocellular damage may be associated with cardiac failure, hepatitis or cirrhosis.

Intrahepatic cholestasis is due to drugs, hepatitis, macronodular or primary biliary cirrhosis, or associated with other diseases (hepatic infiltrations, ulcerative colitis).

Posthepatic. Extrahepatic cholestasis due to gall stones or carcinoma in the ampullary region. The term 'obstructive jaundice' includes both intra- and extra-hepatic cholestasis. Huete-Armijo and Exton-Smith (1962) found that obstructive jaundice was far commoner (73 per cent) than hepatocellular jaundice (16 per cent) in a study of 80 elderly jaundiced patients. Malignant causes of obstruction (44 per cent) outnumbered gall-

stone jaundice (29 per cent); in each case the sex incidence was equal. Jaundice was drug-induced in only 6 cases (7.5 per cent).

Elmslie (1966) found that 20 of 27 aged jaundiced patients had obstructive causes; 8 of these were malignant. A false diagnosis of hepatitis had often been made; in fact no hepatocellular jaundice occurred in this series, but two patients had chlorpromazine jaundice. Elmslie writes as a surgeon and his advice is to presume an obstructive cause until proved otherwise in aged jaundiced patients.

Naso and Thompson (1976) reported their findings in 100 patients aged over 50 years with hyperbilirubinaemia >34 µmol/l (2mg/100 ml). Extrahepatic biliary obstruction was present in only 33 cases; 20 of these were due to malignancy (10 primary colonic carcinomas with hepatic metastases, 5 carcinomas of pancreas, 3 primary carcinomas of common bile duct and 2 of gall bladder). Twenty-nine patients had gall bladder disease, 13 with common bile duct stones. There were 22 cases of cirrhosis, 8 of hepatitis, 4 of fatty liver, and 14 'medical causes' — but none due to drugs. Three were of unknown aetiology. This series presumably reflects the high incidence of alcoholism in American practice.

O'Brien and Tan (1970) reported that, of 50 jaundiced geriatric patients, in whom all diagnoses were confirmed by liver biopsy or autopsy, parenchymal types of jaundice (62 per cent) were commoner than obstructive (36 per cent). Only 3 cases (6 per cent) were drug-induced. The only case of haemolytic jaundice was due to septicaemia.

Eastwood (1971) surveyed 102 patients over 65 years old presenting with jaundice in a London hospital. Neoplasm was the cause in 35 cases (primary in 23, secondary in 12) and gall stones caused 16 cases. Drug-induced jaundice occurred in 21 cases (20 due to intra-hepatic cholestasis). Ten cases of cirrhosis presented with jaundice. Infectious hepatitis occurred in 15 and haemolytic anaemia in five. The high incidence of drug-induced jaundice should be contrasted with earlier series: Eastwood found 17 instances of chlorpromazine jaundice in his 102 patients (16.7 per cent) as against the 5 per cent of Huete-Armijo and Exton-Smith (1962), the 8.4 per cent of Elmslie (1966), the absence of this condition in the series of Naso and Thompson (1967), and the 6 per cent of O'Brien and Tan (1970).

Obstructive jaundice
Certain aspects may conveniently be emphasized here. Differential diagnosis of obstructive jaundice, often difficult, has been made easier by the development of methods of investigation as outlined above.

Malignant obstruction. This is the commoner cause, and usually due to carcinoma of the head of the pancreas or to secondary deposits in the liver or at the porta hepatis. Primary carcinoma may also affect the ampulla of Vater, the bile ducts or the gall bladder, and primary hepatic carcinoma occurs rarely.

Calculous obstruction.   This is due to a gall stone in the common bile duct; it may be a painless illness in the elderly, so that differential diagnosis from malignancy may be difficult; further, pain is often present in malignant cases. Fluctuation in the depth of the jaundice is more likely to be due to a gall stone than a neoplasm, but can occur in the latter also.

Laparotomy has no place in the diagnosis of jaundice, the advent of modern non-invasive techniques of investigation having eliminated it.

Huete-Armijo and Exton-Smith (1962) and Fenster (1965) point out how hepatitis can lead to errors in diagnosis and unwarranted laparotomy. The former authors found that such diagnostic errors were made in five of their 13 patients with hepatocellular jaundice; all five had viral hepatitis, three with intrahepatic cholestasis, but liver function tests showed little or no abnormality and the serum alkaline phosphatase was only slightly elevated at 98 to 182 u/l (14 to 26 KA units). Four of the five had a laparotomy, but there was no ill-effect from the operation. Of particular interest was the high accuracy of diagnosis in the other types of jaundice. Of the 80 cases, 72 (90 per cent) had a correct diagnosis.

Once jaundice is established and the clinical features and biochemical tests point to the diagnosis of obstructive jaundice, further investigation is indicated. The first test is ultrasonography. This will usually reveal the presence of a mechanical obstruction and its nature. If there is no evidence of obstruction and bile ducts appear normal in size, a liver biopsy needs to be considered next.

An equivocal ultrasound is an indication for further investigation of the biliary tract and ERCP is usually the next step. In all but the most difficult cases a diagnosis will be reached using these three diagnostic techniques along with the usual biochemical tests.

Circulatory disturbances of the liver

Acute cardiac failure and shock
Centrilobular congestion, haemorrhage and necrosis may occur, but the reticulin framework remains intact. Occasionally the left lobe is more affected than the right. Liver function is impaired, and serum transaminases increase, sometimes to very high levels (Bloth et al, 1976).

Chronic cardiac failure
Chronic congestion produces a large firm liver, but if cardiac cirrhosis develops the liver shrinks and becomes fibrous.

At post-mortem the cut surface of the large chronically congested liver has a 'nutmeg' appearance, with centrilobular congestion and haemorrhages surrounded by fatty yellow zones; there is also gross distension of hepatic veins. Microscopically, centrilobular liver cells show degenerative changes and accumulation of brown pigment; the cells atrophy, the reticulin stroma condenses, and proliferation of reticulin and collagen may follow. In very chronic or recurrent cases, rings of fibrous tissue come to surround the portal areas ('reversed lobulation' of cardiac cirrhosis).

The centrilobular changes are due to hepatic anoxia and increased venous pressure causing haemorrhage from distended sinusoids: the most severe changes occur in long-standing cases and centrilobular cell loss is greatest in tricuspid incompetence or constrictive pericarditis.

Clinical features.   Pain or discomfort in the right hypochondrium and epigastrium are due to stretching of Glisson's capsule as the liver enlarges. Jaundice may occur, especially in very chronic cases. Usually mild, it may occasionally be marked and green, suggesting an obstructive cause. In fact there are probably several contributory factors, hepatocellular, cholestatic and haemolytic. The commonest cause of jaundice in chronic congestive cardiac failure is the development of pulmonary infarction, where the increased pigment derived from the liberated haemoglobin in the infarct overloads the anoxic liver cells (see above).

On examination, the liver is enlarged, firm, smooth and tender. Bimanual palpation may reveal pulsation of the liver if tricuspid incompetence is present, unless there is cardiac cirrhosis. Ascites may occur, especially when there is high hepatic venous pressure, low serum protein and sodium retention.

Hepatic failure is rare.

Cardiac cirrhosis cannot be diagnosed clinically with confidence.

Biochemical changes.   The serum bilirubin is raised and the alkaline phosphatase normal. Transaminases and GGT are increased.

Urinary urobilinogen is increased if there is jaundice, and in severe cases bilirubin may be found.

Stercobilinogen is increased, producing dark stools; pale stools occur only if there is a marked obstructive element to the jaundice.

The comparative value of laboratory investigations in the difficult diagnosis of chronic hepatic congestion due to cardiac failure is discussed by Cassan et al (1976).

Treatment.   Treatment is that of the underlying cause of cardiac failure.

Hepatic vein occlusion
Hepatic vein occlusion is rare. It produces a severe 'nutmeg' liver.

The condition should be suspected if a patient with

malignant disease in or near the liver, or with polycy-thaemia vera, develops a large tender liver and gross ascites. Congestive heart failure and cirrhosis must be excluded.

Characteristic liver-scan findings have been reported (Meindok and Langer, 1976).

Treatment is symptomatic, together with that of any discoverable cause.

Toxic liver injury

Hepatotoxic agents include drugs, chemicals, irradia-tion, plants and fungi and they produce their effects on the liver in different ways, e.g. by a direct, predictable, dose-dependent toxic effect causing necrosis and/or fatty change; by producing a hepatitis-like reaction; by producing intrahepatic cholestasis, which is sometimes due to a hypersensitivity reaction; or by combinations of these effects.

Hepatic necrosis

Direct hepatotoxicity is an attribute of halogenated hydrocarbons (such as carbon tetrachloride), heavy metals, and cytotoxic drugs, and it has been recorded after ferrous suphate and paracetamol overdosage, and intravenous tetracycline. Other agents include yellow phosphorus, DDT, paraquat, tannic acid, benzene derivatives, *Amanita* species, irradiation burns and hyperpyrexia.

In 1965, 84 people in Epping became jaundiced after eating bread made from flour contaminated by an aromatic amine. Some elderly patients had few symp-toms but presented with deep jaundice and a large liver. Liver biopsies showed hepatic cell necrosis and some-times cholangitis (Kopelman et al, 1966b).

Fatty liver

Lipids reach the liver as free fatty acids from adipose tissue stores and as triglycerides (neutral fats) in chylo-microns from the intestines. The liver converts the tri-glyceride into fatty acids and then resynthesizes triglycer-ide — some of which combines with a protein to form lipoprotein, which can then leave the liver and be trans-ported in the blood to adipose tissue. Any disturbance of these various mechanisms involving the liver can result in the accumulation of excessive lipid in the liver. A huge literature exists on the subject of fatty liver, in experimental animals and in man. From a practical viewpoint, fatty liver in man is seen mainly in the kwashiorkor syndrome — not of immediate concern to the geriatrician — and in some alcoholic patients. The subject of alcohol and the liver is reviewed by Brunt (1971), Leevy et al (1975) and Lieber (1973, 1978). Various organic and inorganic chemicals, drugs and physical agents may produce fatty changes in the liver. Some fatty change may also occur in livers of obese

patients, especially diabetics, in ulcerative colitis, and in severe anaemia.

Hepatitis-like reaction

A number of drugs may produce liver changes indistin-guishable from those of infective hepatitis. The mech-anism is obscure; hypersensitivity may be involved.

Mortality may exceed greatly that of infective hepa-titis. Jaundice may appear several weeks after the drug is stopped.

The main drugs which have been implicated are monoamine oxidase inhibitors, antidepressants, anticon-vulsants, antituberculous drugs, antirheumatic drugs, appetite suppressants; ethacrynic acid, dichloralphena-zone and certain anaesthetic agents (notably halothane).

Halothane hepatitis has aroused much interest in recent years. It is rare, and probably due to hypersen-sitivity. The subject is reviewed by Klatskin and Smith (1975), Simpson et al (1975) and Drug and Therapeutics Bulletin (1975).

Other drugs worthy of note in this respect are meth-yldopa (Lancet 1976c) and dantrolene (Ogburn et al, 1976; Schneider and Mitchell, 1976).

A granulomatous hepatitis is sometimes seen after methyldopa (Miller and Reid, 1976) or chlorpropamide (Rigberg et al, 1976) and has been reported as a reaction to malignant neoplasms (Saunders, 1976) (see review by Fauci and Wolff, 1976).

Perhexiline is used as an anti-anginal agent and has been implicated in several cases of toxic liver damage. The hepatitis and subsequent cirrhosis is similar to that found in alcohol-induced disease, but Mallory's hyaline is prominent (Pessayre et al, 1979), and steatosis less prominent (Forbes et al, 1979).

Intrahepatic cholestasis

There are two main types, one due to hypersensitivity and one not. Women are usually affected more than men by both types.

Hypersensitivity

This type is characteristically seen with phenothiazine drugs, notably chlorpromazine (Isselbacher and Lesser, 1975). It occurs in less than 0.5 per cent of those taking the drug, and is unrelated to dose (it has occurred after a single tablet) or duration of therapy. It may come on in the first month of treatment, or 1–3 weeks after the drug is stopped. If the drug is restarted, the reaction recurs in nearly half the cases. Other phenothiazines may or may not cause recurrence.

Other drugs implicated include antidepressants, benzodiazepines, oral hypoglycaemic agents, thiazide diuretics, antithyroid drugs and phenylbutazone. Some reactions to PAS and sulphonamides fall into this cat-egory, others are part of a generalized hypersensitivity reaction. Some of these drugs may cause a hepatitis-like reaction.

Histological features. Cholestasis, with a marked portal infiltration of mononuclear and eosinophilic leucocytes is found. Degenerative changes occur in liver cells.

Clinical picture. A prodromal period with anorexia and malaise may occur for a few days. Jaundice follows, often with pruritus (this may appear first). A skin rash and an eosinophilia may occur; occasionally there is leucopenia in the early stages. The serum alkaline phosphatase is usually elevated above 210 μu/l (30 KA units/100 ml); transaminases may be moderately raised and usually do not exceed 100 μu/100 ml. Recovery is usual, in a matter of weeks, but the jaundice may persist for months or even years; in prolonged cases, steatorrhoea, weight-loss, xanthomata and osteomalacia may occur. Such cases resemble biliary cirrhosis, with high serum alkaline phosphatase and cholesterol levels but mitochondrial antibody is usually negative. Bilirubinuria occurs, urinary urobilinogen is decreased. Hepatic histology may not be conclusive in these chronic cases and it is necessary to exclude extrahepatic biliary obstruction. Symptomatic treatment may be required, e.g. cholestyramine resin for pruritus. Corticosteroids may reduce the serum bilirubin but do not affect the course of the illness, and are contraindicated.

Non-sensitivity cholestasis

This type of cholestasis is related to dose and duration of therapy. The cholestasis is unaccompanied by hepatic necrosis or portal tract inflammation. It was first reported after methyltestosterone but has occurred after various C-17 alkyl-substituted testosterone compounds, e.g. methandienone (Dianabol), norethandrolone (Nilevar), and certain related steroids; it does not occur with testosterone propionate or nandrolone (Durabolin). Therefore, when anabolic steroid therapy is required in the elderly this type of jaundice may be avoided by using Deca-Durabolin injections rather than the oral agents.

Mixed pictures may occur with some drugs, e.g. antituberculous drugs, sulphonamides, oral antidiabetic agents, methyldopa and erythromycin estolate.

Drug interactions

In the last few years much information has become available about the mechanisms of drug interactions, which may have detrimental effects on the patient. Elderly patients, so often the recipients of polypharmacy, are particularly vulnerable to such problems (MacLennan, 1974) and in view of the likelihood of impaired drug metabolism in old age, all clinicians treating the elderly must be aware of the dangers which may be present.

Many drugs may induce hepatic enzymes which diminish their own effectiveness or that of another drug. Phenobarbitone is well known in this respect; if given with warfarin the dose of the latter may need to be increased. If the phenobarbitone is then stopped the existing dose of warfarin may prove to be too great, with potentially hazardous consequences.

Phenobarbitone (little used, one hopes, in geriatric practice) will also accelerate the metabolism of nortriptyline and digoxin.

Chlorpromazine may decrease the effect of meprobamate by a similar mechanism, but may increase the effect of tricyclic antidepressants by competition for the same degradation enzyme (Gram and Overt, 1972).

Monoamine-oxidase inhibitors depress hepatic microsomal enzymes and may thus enhance the effect of certain other drugs.

In view of the multiple pathology characteristic of illness in old age, drug interactions may be difficult to recognize: it is possible that with the increasing awareness of the possibility of such interactions many more will come to light as time goes by.

Hepatitis in the elderly

Viral hepatitis

The two major forms of viral hepatitis, formerly described as infective and serum, are now termed hepatitis A and B respectively. Non-A, non-B hepatitis is now also recognized.

Hepatitis A occurs mainly in children and young adults. Elderly patients, especially females, have a more severe form of the disease, often with a prolonged course: jaundice may last for 6 weeks or more, and a fatal outcome may ensue, especially during epidemics (Binder et al, 1965). Sporadic viral hepatitis has been little discussed in geriatric literature.

Fenster (1965) discussed this subject and described 23 elderly patients with viral hepatitis. Twenty presented with jaundice; one patient presented with oesophagitis, and jaundice was found on examination; and in another jaundice and stupor rapidly supervened on the initial confused state. One patient presented with ascites. The prodromal features usually described ('gastric flu' — anorexia, nausea, abdominal discomfort and perhaps fever) were present in 50 per cent of cases. Pruritus occurred in 26 per cent. Weight loss was a common and prominent feature. Mental changes were common.

Clinical examination and laboratory tests showed no particular differences from younger patients but the diagnostic accuracy was only 52 per cent. This was partly due to a low index of suspicion: the patient's age, loss of weight and jaundice with obstructive features often led to the mistaken diagnosis of neoplasm. Three patients had a laparotomy (and two of these died). It was felt in retrospect that too much importance had been placed on a previously abnormal cholecystogram in some of the patients.

Ten patients had proven subacute hepatic necrosis or fulminating hepatitis and four others had a prolonged and/or progressive course. There were six deaths, i.e. a mortality of 26 per cent. Possible contributory factors in the high morbidity and mortality of viral hepatitis in these elderly patients included malnutrition, associated diseases (especialy neoplasia), and a long delay before admission to hospital.

Hepatitis B has a more insidious onset and a higher mortality than hepatitis A, since it tends to affect older and more debilitated patients.

The identification of hepatitis B antigen (HBAg) has led to the finding of a relationship between hepatitis B and chronic hepatitis, cirrhosis and hepatoma (Dudley et al, 1972; British Medical Journal, 1975a; Woolf and Williams, 1976b).

Another antigen called the e-antigen, is said to have prognostic significance for hepatitis B (Norkans et al, 1976); this e-antigen is less often found in asymptomatic HBAg carriers as age increases, whereas antibody to e (anti-e) increases with age (Ohbayashi et al, 1976). This finding may relate to lesser infectivity of the older subjects.

Acute viral hepatitis is reviewed by Woolf and Williams (1977).

Non-A, non-B hepatitis is being increasingly recognized, especially after blood transfusion (British Medical Journal, 1978).

Recent developments in the therapy of viral hepatitis have been discussed by Hollander (1973) and Murray-Lyon and Reynolds (1976). The use of corticosteroids may tend to chronicity, especially in antigen-positive type B hepatitis.

'Non-specific reactive hepatitis' is a term applied by Schaffner and Popper (1959) to the histological changes which they found in liver biopsies from 94 elderly subjects. It seems likely that these were pathological changes of varied aetiology in a group of infirm persons. Sklar et al (1956) could find no changes in liver histology in 300 subjects over the age of 65. Non-specific reactive hepatitis is seen in the liver of those patients who have significant pathology elsewhere, such as pneumonia or tumour.

Chronic hepatitis
Chronic persistent hepatitis. This is a benign self-limiting condition which usually follows on from an episode of acute viral hepatitis. It is characterized by persisting symptoms of general malaise and right upper quadrant discomfort. Serum transaminases remain high, usually with the other biochemical tests being close to normal. No treatment is indicated.

Chronic active hepatitis
This is known by several other names: active chronic hepatitis, chronic aggressive hepatitis or lupoid hepatitis. It merges imperceptibly into cryptogenic cirrhosis which is discussed later. This condition almost always progresses to cirrhosis.

There may be an association with hepatitis B or A, or occasionally drugs such as methyldopa, oxyphenisatin (as in Bydolax), or alcohol.

It occurs characteristically in young women but a wide age range may be affected and Woolf et al (1974) described three elderly patients with the syndrome. All three presented differently, and two atypically, one with xerostomia and one with a confusional state. Biochemical findings were atypical in one patient. Histology was characteristic in all three and they all responded to corticosteroids. Williams et al (1976) described a case in a lady of 70 whose sister, aged 72, had primary biliary cirrhosis and myxoedema. Four out of 23 relatives in this family had autoantibodies to various tissues.

Immunological aspects are important — polyclonal hypergammaglobulinaemia (mainly IgG) and commonly a significant titre of autoantibodies. Smooth muscle antibody is the most frequently positive, in about two-thirds, but antinuclear and antimitochondrial antibodies are also found.

For further details of chronic hepatitis see Boyer (1976) and Popper and Schaffner (1976). Active chronic hepatitis is reviewed by Joske (1975) and the modern approach to its treatment is discussed by Summerskill et al (1975) and Murray-Lyon and Reynolds (1976). If the diagnosis of chronic active hepatitis is made and any aetiological factors such as drugs or hepatitis B excluded, then the patient should be treated with corticosteroids. This has been shown to be beneficial therapy (Cook et al, 1971).

Cirrhosis

Classification
There has been further progress in the classification of cirrhosis of the liver. Old terminology, such as 'portal' (Laennec's) and 'postnecrotic', is no longer acceptable. The terms 'micronodular' and 'macronodular' replaced these, but mixed pictures are seen morphologically and the terms are of little clinical value on their own.

A new classification was adopted at the 1974 meeting of the International Association for the Study of the Liver to take into account modern concepts of pathology, pathogenesis and clinical aspects (Galambos, 1975). Two criteria are now used — the morphological and the aetiological; to those may be added functional staging based on regeneration histology and clinical activity (Brunt, 1976).

Aetiology

The incidence of cirrhosis was said to increase markedly with advancing years (Dublin and Lotka, 1937) but Feldman did not find this in his autopsy studies (Morgan and Feldman, 1957). International mortality trends reported for the period 1950–1971 (Massé et al, 1976), show a general increase in many countries, especially after the age of 45 years.

In Denmark and Japan the most notable increases were in females over 75 years of age. In France and USA there is a decrease after 75 years; in France, where there has been a very sharp increase, especially in men, the peak mortality is between 65 and 74 years in both sexes, and in USA it has moved from the over-75's to the 55 to 64 age group in both sexes. In the UK the mortality figures for cirrhosis are generally low relative to the other countries reported, but are increasing due to alcohol (Saunders et al, 1981).

Cirrhosis may follow viral hepatitis (usually type B), alcoholism, disturbed immunity, prolonged cholestasis, circulatory disturbances, iron overload, and may occur in various other diseases not seen in geriatric practice.

Any condition causing fatty change may lead to cirrhosis; therefore malnutrition and some chemical toxins may play a part, and cirrhosis may also result from jejunoileal bypass operations for obesity (Lancet, 1976c).

Cryptogenic cirrhosis

The aetiology of this condition is unclear and in the UK about one-third of all patients with cirrhosis fall into this category. The condition is closely related to chronic active hepatitis, the two merging imperceptibly. Once the diagnosis of cirrhosis is established, aetiological categories should be looked for; these include hepatitis B, alcohol, drugs and iron overload. The remaining mixture is designated cryptogenic, and it is undoubtedly composed of differing disease states. Cryptogenic cirrhosis has not changed in frequency of occurrence in the UK in the last 20 years, but the incidence of alcoholic cirrhosis in the UK has increased and now accounts for two-thirds of cases of cirrhosis (Saunders et al, 1981). The 5-year survival for cryptogenic cirrhosis is 14 per cent, which has not been altered by modern forms of treatment in the last 20 years (Saunders et al, 1981).

'Cirrhosis of the aged' and 'senile cirrhosis' are terms which have been used for cirrhosis seen in the eighth and ninth decades, especially by European writers. At this time of life the classical overt picture of cirrhosis, with an atrophic liver, ascites, portal hypertension and hepatic failure, is relatively uncommon. The commonest variety of cirrhosis in the elderly is a latent cryptogenic cirrhosis with a liver which is granular, not atrophic, and usually micronodular, and which is usually asymptomatic and without ascites or signs of portal hypertension or liver failure. The subject is reviewed by Ludwig et al (1970) and Ludwig and Baggenstoss (1970). Note that splenomegaly is a common feature and may be the initial clue to the diagnosis. Kraft and Finby (1970), in a radiographic survey of the abdomens of geriatric patients, found that the liver was often small and sometimes associated with an enlarged spleen, suggesting the diagnosis of latent cirrhosis. Some impairment of liver function may be found in these patients, especially with the BSP test; this is important if surgery is contemplated, since such patients tolerate surgery badly. It is also necessary to take special care when prescribing for cirrhotic patients (Brunt, 1976), especially in old age.

Cirrhosis may present in old age with the typical features of hepatocellular failure or portal hypertension. The principles of treatment are the same in all age groups. However, the elderly fare badly with regard to bleeding as a result of portal hypertension and liver failure. Surgery is unlikely to be beneficial.

Biliary cirrhosis

Primary biliary cirrhosis.   This is classically a disease of middle-aged females but was found more commonly in the 70 to 90 year age group in the series of Ludwig and Baggenstoss (1970). It is a chronic non-suppurative destructive cholangitis (Rubin et al, 1965) and is associated with considerable immunological disturbances, particularly positive antimitochondrial antibodies and raised serum IgM levels. These tests help to differentiate this condition from extrahepatic biliary obstruction (and may prevent unnecessary laparotomy) and from other intrahepatic causes of chronic cholestasis.

Pruritus is an early feature; jaundice may not appear for months or years. Steatorrhoea develops and may lead to osteomalacia and aggravate osteoporosis in the elderly. Skin pigmentation is usual, and xanthomata common. Clubbing occurs late. Bleeding may occur. The liver is very large, firm and smooth, and splenomegaly is common. Portal hypertension and liver failure may ensue.

The condition is frequently detected in its asymptomatic form, which was first recognised by Fox et al (1973). A recent study from Newcastle-upon-Tyne revealed that the disease is more common than was previously thought (James et al, 1981) and half of the 93 patients reported were symptom free. They were detected by the finding of positive antimitochondrial antibodies or abnormal liver function tests. It is interesting that the mean age of the asymptomatic group was 61 years. These elderly patients may remain symptom free and treatment is not indicated.

Little work has been done on the aetiology of this condition. Most authors have pointed to an immunological disturbance. A recent paper suggests that environmental factors might be of great importance (Triger, 1980).

Treatment with fat-soluble vitamins, A, D, and K, and calcium supplements should be started as soon as a diagnosis is made and before some of the advanced complications develop. Pruritus can be relieved by oral cholestyramine (Questran) — a resin which binds bile acids in the gut and increases their excretion — but this may aggravate steatorrhoea. If biliary obstruction is complete, no bile salts enter the gut, and norethandrolone (Nilevar) may be used to relieve intractable pruritus, but this will increase the jaundice. New forms of treatment to try to eradicate the disease have been tried, such as penicillamine or the immunosuppressive agent, azathioprine. These have little to offer and symptomatic treatment remains the best available.

Secondary biliary cirrhosis. This occurs after longstanding extrahepatic biliary obstruction (see below). Ascending cholangitis may produce intermittent fever with rigors (Charcot's intermittent biliary fever). Mitochondrial antibody is usually negative.

Haemochromatosis

Cirrhosis with iron overloading of tissues is a disease of middle and old age. Iron absorption is increased, due to a presumed failure of the 'mucosal block' control mechanism in the small intestine, but the cause for this is unknown. Genetic factors are important; 70 per cent of asymptomatic relatives have excess liver iron, and 55 per cent have increased iron absorption. There is an association with HLA 3, HLA B14 and HLA B7. The condition appears to be inherited as on autosomal dominant. Alcoholism is a common association. Sex incidence is equal in the elderly; at younger ages females are much less often affected due to menstruation and pregnancy.

Clinical features. Slaty pigmentation of the skin and sometimes buccal mucosa, hepato-(spleno-)megaly, diabetes mellitus, cardiomyopathy with heart failure, and testicular atrophy are the major features, but in older patients a progressive polyarthritis with chondrocalcinosis is a common association (Hamilton et al, 1968; Whelton, 1970; Dymock, 1975; Hirsch et al, 1976). Abdominal pain is also more common in the elderly, as is the development of primary hepatocellular carcinoma (Sherlock, 1975). Other complications include cardiac arrhythmias, peripheral neuropathy, and mental disturbances.

Diagnosis. Liver function tests are often normal. Serum iron is raised due to increased (90 per cent) saturation of serum transferrin. Serum ferritin is increased and correlates with mobilizable iron stores, but there is an imbalance between transferrin iron and chelatable iron, on the one hand, and ferritin on the other. Iron absorption in this disease is correlated with the ratio of chelatable iron to serum ferritin (Walters et al, 1975). Iron absorption may be little raised when the patient first presents but increases strikingly when venesection is started as treatment.

Iron stores may be assessed by measurement of serum ferritin; the concentration is proportional to the body iron stores. It is measured by radioimmunoassay.

The most accurate method of measuring iron overload is to quantitate the amount of iron in the liver from a needle biopsy specimen. Chelation tests are no longer used. The CT scan will show a uniformly increased absorption coefficient of liver with excess iron deposition.

Anaemia is unlikely unless there is concomitant folate or vitamin B_{12} deficiency. Sideroblastic anaemia may occur and may respond to pyridoxine.

Other findings include an abnormal glucose tolerance test, ECG changes, and chondrocalcinosis.

Treatment. *Removal of iron* — venesections of 500 ml blood remove only 250 mg iron and must be performed regularly until 7 to 45 grams of iron have been removed: this may take 2 years. The frequency of venesections may be two or three times a week in younger patients, but weekly intervals are probably adequate in the elderly. Maintenance venesections of 4 litres of blood annually may be required; the aim should be to reduce transferrin saturation to 30 to 40 per cent (the normal figure). There is evidence that such treatment improves survival (Bomford and Williams, 1976) and reduces symptoms such as abdominal pain.

Chelation therapy removes iron less effectively. Desferrioxamine can remove 10 to 20 mg iron daily, decreasing with repeated treatment.

Reduction of iron absorption may be achieved by phosphate administration.

Both of these methods are ineffective compared with venesection.

Diabetes and other features are treated in the usual way. An overall review of haemochromatosis is given by Dymock (1975), and Sherlock (1981) reviews the course and modern treatment of this disease.

Cardiac cirrhosis has been considered in an earlier section (Chronic cardiac failure).

Portal hypertension

The elderly tolerate gastrointestinal bleeding less well than younger patients (Avery-Jones, 1956; Schiller et al, 1970; Walls et al, 1971; Logan and Finlayson, 1976).

After the age of 50 the morbidity and mortality of bleeding oesophageal varices becomes particularly high (Wells, 1973) but that author emphasized that an aggressive approach to detecting and correcting treatable lesions was essential.

Fibreoptic endoscopy is safe and well-tolerated in elderly patients (Anselm et al, 1971; Gibbins et al, 1974; Stevenson et al, 1976). It may allow visualization of the site of bleeding and is widely regarded as superior to barium studies in rapidly making an accurate diagnosis (Forrest and Finlayson, 1974; Cotton, 1976). Morris et al (1975) state that this is especially true in the case of oesophageal varices; only 50 per cent of their patients with varices and bleeding were actually bleeding from the varices. McGinn et al (1975) found endoscopy more accurate than barium X-ray, but the use of both tests gave even better results. Stevenson, Cox and Roberts (1976) obtained a high degree of accuracy with double-contrast barium studies, but the results with endoscopy were even better.

Another advantage of endoscopy in bleeding varices is the possibility of injecting sclerosant solution directly into them (British Medical Journal, 1976b).

Despite all this enthusiasm for early endoscopy, Logan and Finlayson (1976) considered that early diagnosis might make little difference to the overall mortality in view of the increasing proportion of high-risk patients (often elderly) in most series today.

The prognosis of bleeding oesophageal varices in cirrhosis is related to liver function and to age. Liver function is likely to be worse in alcoholic than in non-alcoholic patients. Gastrointestinal bleeding aggravates impaired liver function in cirrhosis and may precipitate liver failure.

Portasystemic shunt operations are more likely to lead to encephalopathy as age increases (Read et al, 1961) and Hourigan et al (1971) do not recommended this operation in patients over 40 years of age.

Liver failure

Note that this term has been broadened to include the neuropsychiatric syndrome of portal systemic encephalopathy, even if there is little hepatocellular damage (e.g. 'shunt encephalopathy').

Chronic forms may lead to cerebellar and basal ganglia signs, possibly with parkinsonism, and dementia may ensue (Read et al, 1967).

Full descriptions of portal hypertension, hepatocellular failure, and hepatic coma and precoma are given by Sherlock (1981). The principles of treatment include the removal or treatment of any precipitating factor such as gastrointestinal haemorrhage, hypotension, electrolyte disturbance or constipation. Protein is severely restricted and the bowel is cleared. The latter is achieved with magnesium sulphate purgation, and absorption of nitrogenous waste products is kept to a minimum by administration of neomycin and lactulose. Sedatives are avoided.

The management of liver failure is considered in more detail by Miller et al (1975) and Williams (1975, 1976)

and the classification, pathogenesis, and therapy of hepatic encephalopathy and coma by Lunzer (1975), Fischer and Baldessarini (1976) and Sherlock (1977).

INFILTRATIONS OF THE LIVER

Malignant disease

This has been reviewed by Terblanche (1977).

Secondary carcinoma

The liver is the commonest site for metastases from many primary sites; they should be suspected when marked hepatomegaly is found. Involvement of peritoneum may produce ascites; involvement of bile ducts in the porta hepatis produces obstructive jaundice. Direct spread to hepatic veins or inferior vena cava may occur; the portal vein is rarely involved. Cirrhotic livers are rarely affected by metastases.

Clinically, right-sided abdominal discomfort and tenderness are associated with hepatomegaly; a distended abdomen may contrast with generalized wasting. Hepatomegaly varies from minimal to gross; the surface may feel undulant and hard; individual deposits may be palpable and umbilicated. Jaundice is inconstant.

Associated features depend on the primary lesion and the sites of other metastases.

Liver function tests are often little altered; but if serum alkaline phosphatase and aminotransferases (transaminases) are normal there is only a 10 per cent chance that hepatic metastases are present. The characteristic pattern of change in metastasis is elevation of SAP, GGT and LDH. Liver biopsy may carry an increased risk due to bleeding, but should be performed to establish a diagnosis if this will significantly alter management. Plain abdominal X-ray and barium studies are of limited diagnostic value. Diagnosis can usually be established by one of the non-invasive visualizing techniques — ultrasonography, radioisotope scanning or CAT scan.

Once metastatic carcinoma is established, further investigation is not warranted. There is no point in establishing the primary location unless new forms of chemotherapy or immunotherapy are worthwhile in specific types of tumour.

Treatment. This will be symptomatic. Cytotoxic drugs are likely to make the patient more ill, and partial hepatectomy of a localized deposit is very rarely feasible. These measures would usually be regarded as more meddlesome than therapeutic in elderly patients.

Primary carcinoma of the liver

Hepatoma is an hepatocellular tumour and cholangioma is a rarer tumour from bile ducts.

Macronodular cirrhosis is a very frequent antecedent to primary liver cell carcinoma, but not to cholangioma. The association has marked geographical differences; it is very striking in South and East Africa and Indonesia; in Britain about 15 per cent of cirrhotics have liver cell carcinoma present when they die. Haemochromatosis is a rare condition but frequently leads to liver cell carcinoma. Other possible aetiological factors include thorotrast (formerly used as a contrast medium in radiology) and clonorchiasis infection.

The association between hepatitis B infection, persistent HBsAg in the blood, and chronic liver disease, including cirrhosis and primary hepatic carcinoma, has been mentioned above.

The tumour may occur as a single mass or multicentric nodules. Morphological aspects are reviewed by Brocheriou et al (1975).

Clinical features. Primary carcinoma of the liver should be suspected in cirrhotic patients who deteriorate, develop abdominal pain and possibly a hard irregular abdominal mass, or appear to have resistant ascites or precoma.

An arterial murmur over the enlarged liver is highly suggestive of this diagnosis, but false positives occur in alcoholic hepatitis.

Porphyria may develop in patients with primary hepatic carcinoma. Brocklehurst et al (1965) and Eddleston et al (1971) described two such cases, and Keczkes and Barker (1976) reported another and reviewed the literature, analysing data on nine other patients with hepatic cutaneous porphyria and liver tumours. All were over 60, one had a benign adenoma, three had hepatic metastases and five had primary carcinoma of the liver. These authors point out that porphyria cutanea tarda is well known to occur with cirrhosis even if there is no evidence of neoplasm.

Other features are caused by the cirrhosis, and possibly local or general spread.

Biochemical tests. Liver function tests may simply reflect 'cirrhosis'. Various other biochemical abnormalities have been noted: hypercalcaemia, hypoglycaemia, dysproteinaemia.

Serological tests. Alpha-fetoprotein may appear in the serum and strongly suggests the diagnosis.

Haematology. Anaemia is not marked and erythrocytosis may occur. Polymorphonuclear leucocytosis is common, eosinophilia occurs occasionally. There may be thrombocytosis. Fibrinolysis tends to decrease.

Hepatic imaging, X-ray investigation, liver biopsy and laparoscopy may be helpful as outlined earlier.

The value of selective hepatic venography in primary carcinoma of the liver has been decribed by Williams et al (1976).

Treatment. Treatment is usually symptomatic with pain relief. Solitary tumours may be surgically resectable in younger age groups. Surgery is almost never possible in the presence of cirrhosis, although transplantation has been done with very limited success.

Adriamycin (doxorubicin) induces remissions in approximately one-third of patients with primary liver cancer (Johnson et al, 1978). Infusion of chemotherapeutic agents such as fluorouracil into the hepatic artery has been tried but with limited success. This may be useful in controlling local symptoms of pain.

Haemangiosarcoma of the liver
This is a rare tumour arising from Kupffer cells. It has developed many years after thorotrast injection, or in chronic arsenic poisoning, and in recent years it has been related to working with vinyl chloride.

Malignant lymphoma
(see Kim et al, 1976).

Amyloidosis
Primary amyloid rarely affects the liver; secondary amyloid frequently does, in conditions of chronic sepsis or chronic inflammations, rheumatoid arthritis, myelomatosis, Hodgkin's disease, Crohn's disease and ulcerative colitis.

The liver is smooth, firm and rubbery, and nontender; it may be enlarged. Hepatic impairment is mild and it is renal involvement which produces most symptoms and signs and perhaps a fatal outcome; splenomegaly is common. Serum IgM levels may be increased. Rarely, obstructive jaundice occurs (Levy et al, 1971). Diagnosis by the Congo red or Evans blue tests is not without risk, and is now superseded by rectal, liver and perhaps renal biopsy.

In primary amyloidosis, hepatic ^{99m}Tc scanning shows hepatomegaly with homogeneous or heterogeneous uptake (Sostre et al, 1975), and decreased ^{67}Ga uptake has been reported (Goergen et al, 1976).

A false positive liver scan has been reported in secondary hepatic amyloidosis (Suzuki et al, 1976).

Treatment is that of the underlying cause and this may lead to regression of the amyloid.

For further details refer to Cohen (1967) and Hodkinson (1971).

THE LIVER IN SYSTEMIC DISEASES

Chronic bowel inflammation
Impaired liver function occurs in ulcerative colitis and Crohn's disease, and is associated with rather nonspecific histological changes (fatty change, periportal inflammatory cells), although long-standing colitis may lead to cirrhosis, occasionally of the chronic aggressive hepatitis type. Jaundice may occur in severe relapses.

Occasionally it is prolonged, due to intrahepatic cholestasis, possibly due to pericholangitis or sclerosing cholangitis; biliary cirrhosis may supervene.

These changes may be due to nutritional, toxic and immunological factors.

The subject is reviewed by Kern (1976).

Diabetes mellitus

Diabetes occurs more commonly in chronic liver disease than in the general population. Impaired glucose tolerance is common in cirrhosis, though overt diabetes may be coincidental; the incidence of cirrhosis in diabetics is not higher than in the general population, although hepatomegaly and fatty change are common in untreated diabetics.

Infections of the liver

Any severe infection can produce jaundice which is mainly cholestatic, though haemolysis and hepatocellular impairment may play a part.

Ascending cholangitis follows bile stasis usually due to extrahepatic biliary obstruction from a gall stone or carcinoma. The former may produce the picture of Charcot's intermittent biliary fever, with bouts of Gram-negative septicaemia.

Age over 70 years appears to predispose to bacterial infection in bile (Keighley et al, 1976a).

Pyogenic liver abscess is increasing in incidence whereas portal pyaemia secondary to purulent infection in the gut is now less common. There are two types: multiple abscesses associated with an obvious acute infection, e.g. cholangitis or bowel sepsis, and often with jaundice; and solitary abscess with no obvious source of infection, an insidious onset and a long history (even up to 3 years — Butler and McCarthy, 1969), in patients who are often elderly but less often jaundiced (25 per cent). In solitary abscess, the right lobe is usually involved.

Presentation may be as pyrexia of unknown origin and possibly tender hepatomegaly, night sweats, anorexia, vomiting, malaise and weight-loss. Guarding and rigidity are not common (Young, 1976). X-rays may show a high, immobile right diaphragm, and fluid levels may be present in the liver. Repeated blood cultures must be taken. Localization is assisted by scanning, etc. Treatment is drainage and antibiotics; treat any underlying cause. Anaerobic organisms are of great importance in the pathogenesis of liver abscess (Sabbaj et al, 1972).

Despite modern antibiotics, mortality is high. The subject is reviewed in Lancet (1976a).

Chronic inflammations include tuberculosis and brucellosis. Miliary tuberculosis may be clinically undramatic in the elderly; it may present as an anaemia.

Infectious mononucleosis is very rare in old age. Liver dysfunction is more marked in elderly patients with this condition, two of whom were reported by Horwitz et al (1976) as part of their series of seven patients over the age of 40 years.

THE BILIARY SYSTEM

Changes with aging

Bile

There is little available information on changes in composition and volume of bile in old age. Bertolini (1969) states that the bile of the elderly is reduced in amount, thicker, and richer in cholesterol than that of younger subjects; there is a relative decrease in inorganic constituents. There is experimental evidence to suggest decreased hepatobiliary transport (uptake and secretion of bile acids) in old rats (Kroker et al, 1977).

Gall bladder — structural changes

The musculature may hypertrophy but there is a tendency to ptosis of the gall bladder due to decreased elasticity of its walls (Ivy and Grossman, 1952). In old dogs the mucosa of the gall bladder is thickened (Goodpasture, 1918).

Gall bladder — functional changes

The main functions of the gall bladder are to concentrate hepatic bile and to evacuate it. Delayed filling of the gall bladder was described by Seyss (1967). Concentrating power and emptying-time seem unaltered (Ivy and Grossman, 1952).

Investigation of diseases of the biliary system in the elderly

Biochemical tests

These are relevant mainly in the differential diagnosis of jaundice (see above). Prolonged obstructive jaundice may lead to intestinal malabsorption with its attendant deficiencies. Pancreatic function tests also may be required for full elucidation of some patients with biliary-tract disease and associated pancreatic abnormalities.

Radiology

X-rays have been discussed in the corresponding section on the liver, but a little more may be added about plain films of the abdomen. Apart from showing radio-opaque gall stones, a calcified gall bladder wall may be seen; it is rare to see a distended gall bladder as a soft tissue shadow, but a carcinoma of the gall bladder may show up in this way.

Radio-opaque bile may occur in chronic cholecystitis where calcium carbonate is excreted and concentrated in the bile.

Gas shadows may occur in the biliary system, due to a biliary fistula, or regurgitation through an incompetent sphincter of Oddi associated with biliary-tract disease, or after choledochoduodenostomy.

DISEASES OF THE BILIARY SYSTEM

These are common and important in geriatric practice: gall stones and cholecystitis are by far the commonest of them. Biliary-tract disease has been said to be the commonest pathological finding requiring abdominal surgery in the aged (Strohl et al, 1964).

Gall stones

The incidence of gall stones increases with advancing age (e.g. Crump, 1931; Bateson and Bouchier, 1975). Mitmaker et al (1964) noted that the incidence of gall stones (and cholecystitis) at necropsy had increased over the years from 1939 (3 per cent) to 1960 (23 per cent) in their hospital in Montreal, but Bateson and Bouchier (1975) found no increase in the age-sex standardized prevalence rate between 1902–1909 and 1953–1973 in over 10 000 necropsy records from two large general hospitals in Dundee. They point out that apparent increases were due to increased age of the patients in the later period, and stress that overall prevalence rates must not be applied direct to the community at large because hospital series contain far more elderly subjects than does the community. McKeown (1965) stated that estimates varied from 8 to 25 per cent in routine autopsy material; in her analysis of 1500 post-mortems in patients aged 70 years and over, the incidence of gall stones was 20 per cent (26 per cent female, 14 per cent male). In 100 post-mortems over the age of 90 years the overall incidence of gall stones was 21 per cent (McKeown, 1976). Glenn (1969) states that 15 to 20 per cent of the population of the USA have gall stones but that the figure is much higher after the age of 65. Other authors have given figures in excess of 50 per cent after 70 years (Strohl and Diffenbaugh, 1953). As is well known, gall stones are commoner in women than in men; in women there is a correlation with parity (Friedman et al, 1966; Bernstein et al, 1973). Lieber (1952) states that stone-formation is most active in females between 50 and 60 years and in males between 60 and 70 years, and the sex difference lessens from the seventh decade onwards; but Bernstein et al (1973), in their survey of obese women, showed that the incidence per 100 women per decade of life was relatively constant, the lowest figures being obtained in the sixth decade. Nevertheless, the overall occurrence rate rose steadily from the age of 20 upwards, since the data are cumulative decade by decade. Thus in the 4002 women aged 60 and over, the occurrence rate was 27 per cent.

Various types of stones occur; by far the most common is the mixed stone, but pure cholesterol, calcium bilirubinate and pure calcium palmitate stones may occur, and pigment stones occur in haemolytic states. More than one mechanism of formation of gall stones must therefore operate, and these are discussed by Bouchier (1971, 1975), Coyne and Schoenfield (1976), and Coyne et al (1977). It appears that the bile produced by the liver in patients with gall stones is abnormal in having decreased ability to keep cholesterol in solution, due to an increased ratio of cholesterol to bile salts-plus-phospholipid. There is, however, no correlation between the presence of gall stones and the serum cholesterol (Friedman et al, 1966; Hove and Geill, 1968), although there is a relationship, in Caucasians, with body weight (Friedman et al, 1966) and diet. In recent years there has been much interest in the role of diets low in natural fibre and high in refined carbohydrate as possible contributory factors in the development of various common diseases, notably diverticular disease of the colon, diabetes mellitus, and coronary thrombosis (Cleave and Campbell, 1969). Gall stones have been included in this list of diseases. Bateson and Bouchier (1975) could not support this concept from their data, and Bouchier (1976) concluded that there is no acceptable evidence that gall stone disease is influenced by any particular diet.

Hepatic factors include diminished bile salts and/or phospholipids, and possibly altered enterohepatic circulation of bile salts. There is a strong association with cirrhosis, the incidence rising dramatically in patients with cirrhosis (Bouchier, 1969). Disease of the terminal ileum or ileal resection also leads to increased risk of gall stones. Gall bladder factors such as rate of emptying, mucus-formation or transformation, degree of concentration, and infection, are also involved. Iatrogenic gall stones may occur, e.g. after clofibrate treatment (British Medical Journal, 1976a).

Clinical features. Gall stones are often symptomless, especially in the elderly. If they migrate into or through the common bile duct they may remain silent or produce biliary colic; partial obstruction to the common bile duct may ensue, with obstructive jaundice which may be intermittent as the calculus may act as a ball-valve in the duct. Ascending cholangitis may develop behind the obstruction, and may become suppurative, with liver abscesses. Long-standing obstruction may lead to sclerosing cholangitis and biliary cirrhosis.

Migration of stones to the neck of the gall bladder causes obstruction of the cystic duct which leads to stasis and infection (acute or chronic cholecystitis). In these conditions an internal biliary fistula may occur into an adjacent viscus (especially the duodenum) and the stone may (rarely) impact in the ileum and cause gall stone ileus or even perforate the small bowel.

Carcinoma of the gall bladder may develop after some years.

Clinical relationships of gall stones, including the association with other gastrointestinal disorders, coronary artery disease, and diabetes, have been discussed by Kaye and Kern (1971).

A general discussion on gall stones is given by Bouchier (1975).

Silent gall stones

Much argument has raged about the advisability of cholecystectomy for silent gall stones. The incidence of silent stones increases with age (Sato and Matsushiro, 1974), and so does the incidence of complications due to gall stones (Strohl et al, 1964; Glenn, 1965); 40 to 45 per cent of patients with silent gall stones will have significant trouble within 5 to 20 years (Comfort et al, 1948; Lund, 1960; Colcock et al, 1967); often with an abrupt onset (Sato and Matsushiro, 1974). Thus the decision regarding elective cholecystectomy will depend largely on the risks of the operation relative to those of 'waiting to see'. The mortality rate of cholecystectomy below the age of 60 years is usually below 1 per cent (Colcock and Perey, 1963; Wright et al, 1963); although some authors state that there is no increased mortality in older patients (Hoerr, 1963; Wright et al, 1963), or only very little (Wenckert and Robertson, 1966), the majority consider that such an increased mortality rate does occur (Braasch, 1965; Shelby and Lorhan, 1968; Hermann and Martin, 1969; Elbhar et al, 1972; Myline and Karnauchow, 1974). Amberg and Zboralske (1965) state that the mortality of cholecystectomy, in their series of 1057 patients over 70 years of age, was 7.4 per cent, which was higher than that in unoperated cases. They advocated a conservative approach for silent gall stones in the elderly. This view was also taken by Newman and Northup (1964), who calculated that whereas a patient aged 45 with gall stones had a 1.4 per cent chance of developing carcinoma of the gall bladder, at 65 the chance was only 0.44 per cent, which was better than the operative mortality. Bouchier (1976) also favours a conservative approach if the gall stones are totally silent clinically; dissolution therapy (see below) might be tried, but most truly silent gall stones are discovered on plain X-rays because they are radio-opaque, and these stones are not suitable for dissolution treatment.

Postoperative complications are undoubtedly commoner in the elderly (Griffiths, 1972; Szauer and Zukaukas, 1975). There seems widespread agreement that elective cholecystectomy for silent gall stones should be considered only before the age of 60 years (Braasch, 1965) or, if possible, before 50 years (Mitmaker et al, 1964), to prevent the development of complications and to reduce the need for emergency surgery in later life, which carries a much higher mortality and morbidity (Griffiths, 1972; Grodsinsky et all, 1972; Ziffren and Hartford, 1972; Sullivan et al, 1982).

Medical treatment. By increasing the total bile salt pool radiolucent gall stones may be dissolved. The first successful agent used was chenodeoxycholic acid (Bell et al, 1972; Danzinger et al, 1972; Bell, 1974; Bouchier, 1976, Dowling, 1977). Treatment is successful in about two-thirds of patients provided the radiolucent stones are less than 15 mm diameter. Recurrence rate is about 30 per cent at one year. The most common side effect is diarrhoea which is dose dependent. Ursodeoxycholic acid, derived from bear bile, is much less toxic, rarely produces diarrhoea and is better at dissolution (Maton et al, 1977). Other agents such as Rowachol, a mixture of essential oils, have been used successfully for dissolution.

There are limitations to this form of therapy in that it is useful only for small radiolucent stones in a functioning gall bladder. Nevertheless it has a potential role in the sick or frail elderly patient.

Gall stones in the common bile duct

These occur twice as often in the elderly as in younger subjects. The clinical picture of biliary colic and obstructive jaundice will not be elaborated further here. Some aspects have been discussed under 'Jaundice'; it should be stressed that the jaundice may occur without any history of biliary colic.

Apart from symptomatic treatment of biliary colic, treatment is surgical: exploration of the common bile duct and removal of all stones, and cholecystectomy. Acute obstructive cholangitis requires urgent decompression of the bile duct. These operations carry a considerably higher mortality than elective cholecystectomy, especially in the elderly. Great importance is attached to full preoperative medical assessment, correction of fluid and electrolyte imbalance and anaemia, and intramuscular vitamin K if jaundice is present (Glenn, 1969). Further advances in preoperative management include the prevention of the hepatorenal syndrome by forced diuresis with mannitol, continued during the operation (Szauer and Zukaukas, 1975; Murray-Lyon and Reynolds, 1976). Intravenous antibiotics may also be needed. The importance of operative cholangiography in all cases is emphasized by Hermann and Martin (1969) and Murray-Lyon and Reynolds (1976), and Sherlock (1981) advocates repeating this postoperatively before removing the tube draining the common bile duct. Some surgeons advocate protective choledecho-duodenostomy in elderly patients with multiple common bile duct stones following earlier cholecystectomy or other biliary tract operation (Moesgaard et al, 1982).

Recently retained stones at the lower end of the common bile duct have been removed by papillotomy or sphincterotomy via a fibreoptic endoscope (Cotton et al, 1976; Safrany, 1977). This is an important advance for patients unfit for further surgery; two-thirds of Safrany's 243 patients were aged 60 or above, and 40 per cent were over 70. Mee et al (1981) report their experience of this procedure in 71 patients over the age of 70. The overall success rate was 92 per cent; complications occurred in 13 per cent. Another possibility is to dissolve the stone(s) in situ. This can be achieved with sodium cholate but this usually produces diarrhoea (Way et al, 1972). More recently heparin (Chary, 1977) or, better still, mono-octanoin (Thistle et al, 1980) have been used successfully.

Gall stone ileus

This is rare but occurs mainly in elderly women. Gall stones causing intestinal obstruction are over 2.5 cm in diameter; impaction takes place most often in the ileum, but occasionally in higher or lower parts of the intestine. There is a gradual onset of diffuse abdominal colic and distension, nausea and vomiting; the obstruction is intractable and nearly always requires surgical intervention. There may be features of cholangitis. There are usually symptoms of chronic cholecystitis leading up to these new developments. X-rays of abdomen may show, apart from distended loops of bowel with fluid levels, air in the biliary tract and presence of a gall stone; but these features may be absent. Preoperative diagnosis is made in only a third of cases (Kirkland and Croce, 1961) but is more likely if a high index of suspicion is sustained in the case of the aged with small-bowel obstruction of obscure aetiology (Safaie-Shirazi and Printen, 1972).

Treatment. It is rare for irrigations or barium enema to remove the stone and enterotomy is usually required after careful preoperative preparation of the patient. More than one stone may be found.

The prognosis is poor: the mortality rate is higher than that for other causes of intestinal obstruction. Maingot (1964) reported a 26.1 per cent mortality in 700 cases; Manax (1969) had 4 deaths in 11 patients. In successful cases a subsequent elective cholecystectomy is advisable (Thomas et al, 1962). Rarely an ischaemic bowel may be perforated by the gall stone (Brown et al, 1966).

Cholecystitis

Acute or chronic cholecystitis is usually associated with gall stones, and, like the latter, has an increased incidence in the elderly. Full descriptions are given by Clark (1968) and Sherlock (1981).

Acute cholecystitis

Acute cholecystitis must be differentiated from retrocaecal appendicitis, perforated peptic ulcer, acute pancreatitis, myocardial infarction, pleurisy and renal stone or pyelonephritis. The diagnosis may well be difficult (Halasz, 1975); ultrasound (Crow and Bartrum, 1976) or HIDA scan (Elias, 1976) may help.

The acute attack may be mild or fulminating, and is often an exacerbation of chronic cholecystitis. The organism is usually a coliform, especially *Escherichia coli*, or a streptococcus, staphylococcus or clostridium.

Treatment. Supportive and symptomatic treatment (avoiding morphine) should be supplemented by broad-spectrum antibiotics in patients over 60 years (Kune and Burdon, 1975).

The penicillins, cephalosporins and cephamycins provide the drugs most suitable for treating acute cholecystitis since therapeutic levels in the bile are obtained. However, serum concentrations of the drugs appear to be equally important (Keighley et al, 1976a). Ampicillin, metronidazole or trimethoprim are satisfactory antibacterial agents for most patients with acute cholecystitis.

The timing of surgical intervention has been, and still is, the subject of much controversy. American surgeons favour early surgery — not as an emergency, which carries a high mortality, but within a few days of the onset, which allows time for full evaluation and preoperative preparation. Even so, the mortality may be as high as 10.6 per cent in expert hands (Glenn, 1965). Despite antibiotic cover, postoperative infection still causes much morbidity and mortality (Raine and Gunn, 1975; Gagic et al, 1975). Chetlin and Elliott (1971) reported that two-thirds of their patients had a positive bile-culture. Bacteraemic shock, biliary peritonitis, subphrenic abscess and wound infections are commoner than after elective operations on the biliary system

Nielsen and Justesen (1976) found that age above 60 years predisposed to bacteria in the bile in biliary-tract diseases; in their series the overall incidence of biliary infection was 87 per cent if the common bile duct was obstructed by stones or a stricture, and 22 per cent if there was gall bladder disease with a normal common bile duct. They reported that anaerobic organisms were frequently present, with or without aerobic organisms.

It would seem that antibiotic therapy before, during and after surgery on the biliary tract is likely to be of value mainly in reducing the incidence of wound infections and septicaemias, but is less likely to prevent local septic complications such as empyema of the gall bladder or pericholecystic abscess formation (Kune and Burdon, 1975; Morrow et al, 1978).

Keighley and colleagues (1976b) advise prophylactic antibotics for biliary-tract surgery if one or more 'high risk' factors are present; these are: age over 70, common bile-duct obstruction, stones in the bile duct, previous biliary tract operation, jaundice at the time of operation, recent rigors, emergency operation, or an operation within 4 weeks of an emergency admission. By using mutivariate analysis they found that the presence of one 'high risk' factor was associated with infected bile in 53 per cent of patients; four 'high risk' factors together were associated with infected bile in 87 per cent of cases. The elderly are particularly vulnerable because exploration of the common bile duct, and stones therein, are common in this age group, and the elderly have a higher incidence of emergency operations.

The decision on early operation must be made in the light of the knowledge that the elderly have a greater tendency to develop complications of acute cholecystitis, such as gangrene and perforation of the gall bladder (Becker, 1957), empyema of the gall bladder, internal biliary fistula, perhaps with gall stone ileus — since all require emergency operation — and hepatic abscesses (Morrow et al, 1978). The operation of choice is cholecystectomy unless the patient's general condition is poor, in which case cholecystostomy is performed as an interim measure (Chaitin, 1974). Anatomical difficulties at the operation site may also indicate the latter operation (Glenn, 1969; Chaitin, 1971, 1974). Murray-Lyon and Reynolds (1976) also advocate this approach in frail, ill patients in whom a large mucocele or empyema of the gall bladder is usually found at operation. Raine and Gunn (1975) point out, however, that cholecystostomy may fail to decompress the common bile duct effectively and may thus allow hazardous cholangitis to continue. Crosby and Ziffren (1965) recommend cholecystostomy as a definitive procedure in the elderly with acute cholecystitis where cholangiography shows no obstruction to the free flow of bile; but Hays and Glenn (1955) state that if life expectancy after the operation exceeds 2 years, over half the patients will need further surgery, and it is usual to plan an elective cholecystectomy at a later date.

Du Plessis and Jersky (1973) recommend a conservative approach since emergency diagnosis may be uncertain and since the risks of emergency operations on elderly patients with multiple pathology are considerable; they also point out the low mortality rate of conservative treatment. Grodsinsky et al (1972) agree that conservative treatment is usually satisfactory, but point out that all too often aged patients refuse a subsequent elective cholecystectomy and may later need emergency surgery with its much increased risk. This point deserves due emphasis in arriving at a decision on an individual elderly patient. In fact, in the UK most surgeons tend towards conservative management of acute cholecystitis (British Medical Journal, 1975b; Murray-Lyon and Reynolds, 1976).

In a controlled double-blind trial (McArthur et al, 1975), conservative and surgical methods of management of acute cholecystitis were compared. Several categories of patients, including those over 80 years of age (whose numbers are, however, increasing) were eliminated and the hospital facilities for investigation and surgery were sophisticated. The surgical patients did well, but in less satisfactory circumstances conservative management is said to be undoubtedly the safer approach to take (British Medical Journal, 1975b).

Chronic cholecystitis

This condition almost always occurs with cholelithiasis, and is thus the commonest disease of the biliary system. The gall bladder becomes shrunken and fibrotic, with ulcerated and scarred mucosa. The bile in it is turbid and 'muddy'.

Clinically the onset is insidious; the condition rarely follows an initial acute attack, although the course may be punctuated by acute exacerbations. Symptoms are often vague (nausea, vomiting, 'flatulent dyspepsia', especially after fatty food, pain or discomfort in the right hypochondrium, right scapular region or right shoulder). There may be tenderness over the gall bladder, and a positive Murphy's sign. The clinical picture is often atypical, however.

Differential diagnosis is from hiatus hernia, peptic ulcer, colonic disorders, and urinary infections.

Oral cholecystography helps clinch the diagnosis, but is not infallible, since some cases have a normally functioning gall bladder, and in any case various technical difficulties may arise in the elderly.

Acalculous cholecystitis is imperfectly documented, and must be diagnosed only by exclusion (Adams and Foxley, 1976).

Treatment. Medical treatment (weight-reduction, alkalis and restriction of fat, especially cooked fat) is mainly for patients in whom cholecystectomy is considered inadvisable, i.e. uncertain diagnosis or patient-factors which prevent surgery; it is also best in acalculous cases, which rarely improve after cholecystectomy.

Cholecystectomy is the definitive treatment. Its risks have been mentioned earlier, and are increased if the common bile duct is explored. This is the major issue requiring fine clinical judgement in the elderly case; it is clearly bad practice to overlook a stone in the common bile duct, and further surgery is hazardous and undesirable in the elderly. Operative cholangiography may be a useful investigation in this situation.

If common bile duct calculi are found it may be wise to perform biliary fenestration (in effect a wide choledochoduodenostomy) in selected elderly patients (Magarey, 1966); or sphincterotomy (Niederle, 1967).

The possibility of endoscopic sphincterotomy and extraction of common bile duct stones has already been mentioned.

Malignant disease

Carcinoma of the gall bladder

This is rare but important. Of 396 943 collected autopsies in the USA, gall bladder carcinoma was the cause of death in 0.4 per cent (Newman and Northup, 1964). It causes under 1 per cent of all cancer deaths in Great Britain (Cooke et al, 1953).

Gall stones were found in 75 per cent of 1120 patients with gall bladder carcinoma by Newman and Northup (1964), but the reported incidence varies from 54 per cent (Solan and Jackson, 1971) to 99 per cent (Mitmaker et al, 1964). Of patients aged over 70 years with biliary-tract disease, 11 per cent may have carcinoma (McLaughlin, 1964).

The tumour may be an adenocarcinoma, squamous-celled, scirrhous or, rarely, anaplastic. Early lymphatic spread involves the glands at the porta hepatis, producing obstructive jaundice.

The condition is commonest in elderly women. Pre-operative diagnosis is correct in only 10 per cent of cases, and is rarely enough to permit extirpation of the growth.

A non-functioning gall bladder in a patient over 60 years should be regarded with suspicion, especially if symptoms have recently changed, with persistent pain or weight-loss or deterioration of health. In such cases intravenous cholangiography is indicated, and coeliac axis angiography may be advisable, especially if there is doubt about performing cholecystectomy for the 'chole-cystitis'. The value of ultrasonics in the diagnosis of biliary tract neoplasms has been mentioned earlier, and is further discussed by Goldberg (1976) and Reid (1976).

The prognosis is very poor; the 5-year cure rate is less than 3 per cent (Newman and Northup, 1964; Vaittinen, 1970; Solan and Jackson, 1971). Results are best with a small carcinoma found unexpectedly during routine cholecystectomy (Nevin et al, 1976) and early operation is essential in established cases.

Prophylactic surgery involves routine cholecystectomy for gall stones when the expectation of life is long enough to permit a significant risk of carcinoma developing. It is probably too late to recommend this after 65 years of age, and effort must be concentrated on patients in middle age (Newman and Northup, 1964).

Richard and Cantin (1976) report a series of 108 patients with primary carcinoma of the gall bladder, mainly elderly women over 60 years old.

Carcinoma of the bile ducts

This is an even rarer condition, and may affect extra- and intrahepatic ducts (Strohl et al, 1963). In the region of the ampulla of Vater it simulates carcinoma of the head of the pancreas; higher parts of the common bile duct are less often involved, the cystic duct never. The right or left main hepatic duct is not infrequently the site of origin.

These tumours occur in late middle-age or in the elderly; males are affected more often than females. Deep obstructive jaundice presents which is occasionally intermittent (Phatak, 1974). Pain is mild, weight-loss and hepatomegaly marked. The clinical and pathological features of periampullary carcinoma are described by Wise (1976) and Balasegaram (1976).

Hypertonic duodenography and ERCP have helped in earlier diagnosis, and endoscopic retrograde brush cytology of the biliary ducts may be valuable (Osnes et al, 1975). Newer angiographic findings in cholangiocarcinoma are described by Walter, Bookstein and Bouffard (1976).

The tumour grows slowly but by virtue of its site it is usually inoperable. Palliative surgery is valuable, however, and radiotherapy may be given.

The prognosis of carcinoma of the ampulla of Vater is better than that of carcinoma of the head of the pancreas, although the 5 year survival rate is still only 36 per cent (Longmire, 1973) and may be as low as 11 per cent (Blumgart and Kennedy, 1973). Preoperative duodenoscopy and biopsy may help prognosis by avoiding dissemination of the tumour at operation (Longmire, 1973; Phatak, 1974).

Perspectives in hepatobiliary disorders in the elderly

The major conditions affecting these systems in the elderly are: jaundice, often due to malignant biliary obstruction; gall stones and cholecystitis; congestive heart failure; drug effects on the liver; and metastatic carcinoma in the liver. Cirrhosis is commoner than previously thought, and clinically-apparent viral hepatitis is relatively rare. Carcinoma of the gall bladder is important out of proportion to its incidence because of the risk of its development in patients who have had gall stones for many years and its poor prognosis.

Modern advances in diagnostic and therapeutic procedures have much application to the improved management of the elderly with jaundice and/or gall stones.

REFERENCES

Abrams H L, McNeil B J 1978 Medical implications of computed tomography ('CAT scanning'). New England Journal of Medicine 298: 255–310

Adams T W, Foxley E G Jr. 1976 A diagnostic technique for acalculous cholecystitis. Surgery, Gynecology and Obstetrics 142: 168–170

Adelman R C 1971 Age-dependent effects in enzyme induction — a biochemical expression of aging. Experimental Gerontology 6: 75–87

Adelman R C 1975 Impaired hormonal regulation of enzyme activity during aging. Federation Proceedings 34: 179–182

Agate J 1970 The Practice of Geriatrics (2nd edn): p 152. Heinemann, London

Albring M, Radsak K, Thoens W 1973 Enhanced DNA synthesis in isolated megamitochondria. FEBS Letters 35: 4–5

Aledort L M 1976 Blood clotting abnormalities in liver disease. Progress in Liver Diseases 5: 350–362

Alfidi R J, Haaga J R, Havrilla T R et al 1976 Computed tomography of the liver. American Journal of Roentgenology 127: 69–74

Amberg J R, Zboralske F F 1965 Gall stones after 70. Requiescat in pace. Geriatrics 20: 539–542

Amici D, Gianfranceschi G L, Marsill G, Michetti L 1974 Young and old rats. ATP, alkaline phosphatase, cholesterol and protein levels in the blood. DNA and RNA contents of the liver. Regulation by an aqueous thymus extract. Experientia 30: 633–635

Andersen H, Pedersen L, Svendsen K N, Peters N D, Kilstrup M, Thaysen E H 1976 The diagnostic value of liver scanning. A retrospective study. Scandinavian Journal of Gastroenterology 11: 241–248

Andrew W, 1968 The fine structural and histochemical changes in aging. In: Bittar E E, Bittar N (ed) The Biological Basis of Medicine, vol 1: p 461–492 Academic Press, London

Andrew W 1971 In: The Anatomy of Aging in Man and Animals: p 161–171. Heinemann, London

Andrew W, Shock N W, Barrows C H Jr, Yiengst M J 1959 Correlation of age changes in histological and chemical characteristics in some tissues of the rat. Journal of Gerontology 14: 405–414

Anselm K, Gluckmann R M 1974 Peritoneoscopy in geriatric patients. Journal of the American Geriatrics Society 22: 193–197

Anselm K, Schuman B M, Priest R J 1971 Fiberoptic esophagoscopy in geriatric patients. Journal of the American Geriatrics Society 19: 167–171

Anthony L E, Jones A L 1976 Lack of enhanced microsomal enzyme activity by oxandrolone, an inducer of hepatic smooth endoplasmic reticulum. Biochemical Pharmacology 25: 1549–1551

Ayoola E A, Vennes J A, Silvis S E, Rohrman C A, Ansel H J 1976 Endoscopic retrograde intrahepatic cholangiography in liver disease. Gastrointestinal Endoscopy 22: 156–159

Bachman K D 1953 Uber das Lipofuscin der Leber. Virchows Archiv A Pathological Anatomy and Histology 323: 133–142

Baird M B, Nicolosi R J, Massie H R, Samis H V 1975 Microsomal mixed-function oxidase activity and senescence. I. Hexobarbital sleep time and induction of components of the hepatic microsomal enzyme system in rats of different ages. Experimental Gerontology 10: 89–99

Balasegaram M 1976 Carcinoma of the periampullary region: a review of a personal series of 87 patients. British Journal of Surgery 63: 532–537

Balfour T W 1976 Laparoscopy in liver disease. Lancet i: 612–613

Barrows C H, Roeder L M 1961 Effect of age on protein synthesis in rats. Journal of Gerontology 16: 321–325

Bateson M C, Bouchier I A D 1975 Prevalence of gallstones in Dundee: a necropsy study. British Medical Journal iv: 427–430

Becker W F 1957 Perforated gall bladder. Surgery, Gynecology and Obstetrics 105: 636–641

Bell G D 1974 The present position concerning gallstone dissolution. Gut 15: 919–929

Bell G D, Whitney B, Dowling R H 1972 Gallstone dissolution in man using chenodeoxycholic acid. Lancet ii: 1213–1216

Bellville J W, Forrest H, Miller E, Brown B W 1971 Influence of age on pain relief from analgesics: A study of post-operative patients. Journal of the American Medical Association 217: 1835–1841

Bender A D 1965 Efect of increasing age on the distribution of peripheral blood flow in man. Journal of the American Geriatrics Society 13: 192–198

Berdyshev G D, Zhelabovskaya S M 1972 Composition, template properties and thermostability of liver chromatin from rats of various age at deproteinization by NaCl solution. Experimental Gerontology 7: 321–330

Berkowitz B A, Ngai S H, Yang J C, Hempstead J, Spector S 1975 The disposition of morphine in surgical patients. Clinical Pharmacology and Therapeutics 17: 629–635

Bernstein R A, Werner L H, Rimm A A 1973 Relationship of gallbladder disease to parity, obesity and age. Health Service Reports 88: 925–936

Bertolini A M 1969 Gerontologic Metabolism. Thomas, C C Springfield, Illinois

Biello D R, Levitt R G, Siegel B A et al 1978 Computed tomography and radionuclide imaging of the liver: comparative evaluation. Radiology 127: 159–163

Binder L, Ferencz A, Vidor E 1965 A hepatitis epidemica jelentősége idos korban. (The importance of epidemic jaundice in the elderly). Orvosi Hetilap 106: 108–110. [English abstract: Excerpta Medica, Section XX (1965) 8, no 2189]

Bizzi A, Marsh J 1973 Further observations on the attachment of carbohydrate to lipoproteins by rat liver Golgi membranes. Proceedings of the Society for Experimental Biology and Medicine 144: 762–765

Björkerud S, Björntorp P, Schersten T 1967 Lysosomal enzyme activity in human liver in relation to the age of the patient and in cases with obstructive jaundice. Scandinavian Journal of Clinical and Laboratory Investigation 20: 224–230

Bloth B, DeFair A, Edhag O 1976 Extreme elevation of transaminase levels in acute heart disease — a problem in differential diagnosis. Acta Medica Scandinavica 200: 281–288

Blumgart L H, Kennedy A 1973 Carcinoma of the ampulla of Vater and duodenum. British Journal of Surgery 60: 33–40

Bomford A, Williams R 1976 Long term results of venesection therapy in idiopathic haemochromatosis. Quarterly Journal of Medicine 45: 611–623

Bouchier I A D 1969 Postmortem study of the frequency of gall stones in patients with cirrhosis of the liver. Gut 10: 705–710

Bouchier I A D 1971 Gall stone formation. Lancet i: 711–715

Bouchier I A D 1975 Gallstones. In: Read, A E (ed) Modern Trends in Gastroenterology 5: 203–230 Butterworth, London

Bouchier I A D 1976 Gallstones. British Medical Journal ii: 870–872

Boulière F 1946 Recherches physiologiques sur la senescence des mammiferes III. L'involution anatomique au cours de la senescence chez le rat. Bulletin de la Société de Zoologie 71: 204–207

Boyd E 1933 Normal variability in weight of the adult human liver and spleen. Archives of Pathology 16: 350–372

Boyer J L 1976 Chronic hepatitis: a perspective on classification and determinants of prognosis. Gastroenterology 70: 1161–1171

British Medical Journal 1975a After type B hepatitis. Leading article iv: 311–312

British Medical Journal 1975b Management of acute cholecystitis. Leading article iv: 607–608

British Medical Journal 1976a Iatrogenic gallstones. Leading article i: 859–860

British Medical Journal 1976b Bleeding oesophageal varices. Leading article ii: 603

British Medical Journal 1978 Non-A, non-B hepatitis. Leading article i: 942–943

Britton G W, Britton V J, Gold G, Adelman R C 1976 The capability for hormone-stimulated enzyme adaptation in liver cells isolated from aging rats. Experimental Gerontology 11: 1–4

Brocheriou C, Auriol M, Ajebo M, Chomette G 1975 Les hepatomes. Dénombrement nécropsique et aspect morphologique à partir de 3700 nécropsies. Hepatomas. Autopsy evaluation and morphologic aspect of 3700 autopsies. Annales de Médecine Interne, Paris 126: 265–268

Brocklehurst J C, Humphreys G S, Gardner-Medwin D 1965 Porphyria in old age. Gerontologia Clinica 7: 83–91

Brown D B, Kerr I F, Livingstone D J 1966 Gall stone obstruction. British Journal of Surgery 53: 672–675

Brunt P W 1971 Alcohol and the liver. Gut 12: 222–229

Brunt P W 1976 Cirrhosis. Medicine, London, 2nd series No 21: p 991–997

Bucher N L R 1963 Regeneration of mammalian liver. International Review of Cytology 15: 245–300

Buetow D E, Gandhi P S 1973 Decreased protein synthesis by microsomes isolated from senescent rat liver. Experimental Gerontology 8: 243–249

Burke M D 1974 Hepatic function tests. Geriatrics 29: 75–80

Butler T J, McCarthy C F 1969 Pyrogenic liver abscess. Gut 10: 389–399

Canapa-Anson R, Rowe D J F 1970 Electrophoretic separation of tissue-specific serum alkaline phosphatases. Journal of Clinical Pathology 23: 499–508

Cardell R R Jr 1971 Action of metabolic hormones on the fine structure of rat liver cells: I. Effects of fasting on the ultrastructure of hepatocytes. American Journal of Anatomy 131: 21–53

Carlsen E N 1975 Liver, gallbladder and spleen. In: Sanders R C (ed) Symposium on B-scan ultrasound. Radiological Clinic of North America 13: 543–556

Cassan P H, Coulbois J, Dupuy P, Dorra M 1976 Chronic cardiac liver of difficult diagnosis. Comparative value of laboratory investigations. Nouvelle Presse Médicale (Paris) 5: 1899–1900 English Abstract

Castleden C M, George C F 1979 Increased sensitivity to benzodiazepines in the elderly. In: Crooks J, Stevenson I H (ed) Drugs and the elderly: Perspectives in Geriatric Clinical Pharmacology: pp 169–178. Macmillan Press, London

Chaitin H 1971 Cholecystostomy in geriatric surgery. Geriatrics 26: 57–60

Chaitin H 1974 Cholecystostomy in geriatric surgery. Modern Geriatrics 4: 140–142

Chan K, Kendall M J, Mitchard M, Wells W D E 1975 The effect of ageing on plasma pethidine concentration. British Journal of Clinical Pharmacology 2: 297–302

Chapman R W G, Williams G, Bidder G et al 1980 Computed tomography for determining liver iron content in primary haemochromatosis. British Medical Journal i: 440–442

Chary S 1977 Dissolution of retained bile duct stones using heparin. British Journal of Surgery 64: 347–351

Chen F W K, Millard P H 1972 The effect of aging on certain biochemical values. Modern Geriatrics 2: 92–106

Chen K K, Robbins E B 1944a Influence of age of mice on the toxicity of alcohol. Journal of the American Pharmaceutical Association 33: 62–80

Chen K K, Robbins E B 1944b Age of animals and drug action. Journal of the American Pharmaceutical Association 33: 80

Chetlin S H, Elliott D W 1971 Biliary bacteremia. Archives of Surgery 102: 303–307. Chicago

Clark C G 1968 Cholecystitis. British Journal of Hospital Medicine 1: 40–45

Clark L C Jr, Beck E I, Shock N W 1951 Serum alkaline phosphatase in middle and old age. Journal of Gerontology 6: 7–12

Cleave T L, Campbell G D 1969 In: Diabetes, Coronary Thrombosis and the Saccharine Diseases. Wright, Bristol

Cohen A S 1967 Amyloidosis. New England Journal of Medicine 277: 522–530, 574–583, 628–638

Colcock B P, Perey B 1963 The treatment of cholelithiasis. Surgery, Gynecology and Obstetrics 117: 529–534

Colcock B P, Killen R B, Leach N G 1967 The asymptomatic patient with gallstones. American Journal of Surgery 113: 44–48

Comfort M W, Gray H K, Wilson J M 1948 The silent gall stone: a ten to twenty year follow up study of 112 cases. Annals of Surgery 128: 931–937

Comolli R 1973 Polyamine effects on ^{14}C-leucine transfer to microsomal protein in a rat liver cell free system during aging. Experimental Gerontology 8: 307–313

Comolli R, Ferioli M E, Azzola S 1972 Protein turnover of the lysosomal and mitochondrial fractions of rat liver during aging. Experimental Gerontology 7: 369–376

Conney A H 1967 Pharmacological implications of microsomal enzyme induction. Pharmacological Reviews 19: 317–366

Cook G C, Mulligan R, Sherlock S 1971 Controlled prospective trial of corticosteroid therapy in active chronic hepatitis. Quarterly Journal of Medicine 40: 159–185

Cooke J R, Buetow D E 1981 Decreased protein synthesis by polysomes, tRNA and aminoacyl-t-RNA synthetase isolated from senescent rat liver. Mechanisms of Ageing and Development 17: 41–52

Cooke L, Avery Jones F, Keech M K 1953 Carcinoma of the gallbladder, a statistical study. Lancet ii: 585–587

Cooper A D, Jones A L, Koldinger R E, Ockner R K 1974 Selective biliary obstruction: a model for the study of lipid metabolism in cholestasis. Gastroenterology 66: 574–585

Cotton P B, Chapman M, Whiteside C G, Le Quesne L P 1976 Duodenoscopic papillotomy and gallstone removal. British Journal of Surgery 63: 709–714

Coyne M J, Schoenfield L J 1976 Gallstone formation and dissolution. Progress in Liver Diseases 5: 622–635

Coyne M J, Marks J, Schoenfield L J 1977 Mechanism of cholesterol gallstone formation. Clinics in Gastroenterology 6: 129–139

Crooks J, O'Malley K, Stevenson I H 1976 Pharmacokinetics in the elderly. Clinical Pharmacokinetics 1: 280–296

Crosby V A, Ziffren S E 1965 Cholecystostomy as definitive therapy in the aged with acute cholecystitis. Journal of the American Geriatrics Society 13: 496–500

Crow H C, Bartrum R J 1976 Ultrasound in diagnosis of acute cholecystitis. Journal of the American Medical Association 235: 2389

Crump C 1931 The incidence of gall stones and gall bladder disease. Surgery, Gynecology and Obstetrics 53: 447–455

Curtis H J, Miller K 1971 Chromosome aberrations in liver cells of guinea pigs. Journal of Gerontology 26: 292–293

Cuschieri A 1975 Value of laparoscopy in hepatobiliary disease. Annals of the Royal College of Surgeons of England 57: 33–38

Danzinger R G, Hofmann A F, Schoenfield L J, Thistle J L 1972 Dissolution of cholesterol gall stones by chenodeoxycholic acid. New England Journal of Medicine 286: 1–8

Devi A, Mukundan M A, Srivastava U, Sarkar N K 1963 The effect of age on the variations of DNA, RNA, and total nucleotides in liver, brain and muscle of the rat. Experimental Cell Research 32: 242–250

Doniach D 1972 Autoimmune aspects of liver disease. British Medical Bulletin 28: 145–148

Dowling R H 1977 Chenodeoxycholic acid therapy of gallstones. Clinics in Gastroenterology 6: 141–163

Drug and Therapeutics Bulletin 1975 Halothane and the liver 13: 49–51

Dublin L I, Lotka A J 1937 In: Twenty-five years of health progress: pp 397–398. Metropolitan Life Insurance Co, New York

Dudley F J, Scheuer P S, Sherlock S P V 1972 Natural history of hepatitis-associated antigen-positive chronic liver disease. Lancet ii: 1388–1393

Du Plessis D J, Jersky J 1973 The management of acute cholecystitis. Surgical Clinics of North America 53: 1071–1077

Dymock T W 1975 Haemochromatosis. In: Read A E (ed) Modern Trends in Gastroenterology-5: p 345–372. Butterworth, London

Eastwood H D H 1971 Causes of jaundice in the elderly. Gerontologia Clinica 13: 69–81

Eddleston A L W F, Rake M O, Pagaltsos A P, Osborn S B, Williams R 1971 ^{75}S-selenomethionine in the scintiscan diagnosis of primary hepatocellular carcinoma. Gut 12: 245–249

Eisenbach L, Shimron F, Yagil G 1976 The effect of age on the regulation of glucose-6-phosphate dehydrogenase in mouse liver. Experimental Gerontology 11: 63–72

Elbhar G, Vuagnat P, Rudler J C 1972 A study of 1103 case records of surgical treatment of gallstones. Annales de Chirurgie 26: 951–965

Elias E 1976 Cholangiography in the jaundiced patient. Gut 17: 801–811

Elias E, Hamlyn A N, Jain S, Long R, Summerfield J A, Dick R, Sherlock S 1975 A randomized trial of percutaneous transhepatic cholangiography versus endoscopic retrograde cholangiography for bile duct visualization in cholestasis. Gut 16: 831

Elmslie R G 1966 Jaundice in the aged. Postgraduate Medicine 40: 103–106

Engelman G L, Richardson A, Katz A, Fierer J A 1981 Age related changes in isolated rat hepatocytes: comparison of size, morphology, binucleation and protein content. Mechanisms of Ageing and Development 16: 385–395

Etienne J P, Chaput J C, Chousterman M 1976 Laparoscopy in liver disease. Lancet i: 1191

Everitt A V 1957 The senescent loss of body weight in male rats. Journal of Gerontology 12: 382–387

Fauci A S, Wolff S M 1976 Granulomatous hepatitis. Progress in Liver Diseases 5: 609–621

Fenster L F 1965 Viral hepatitis in the elderly. Gastroenterology 49: 262–271

Ferioli M E, Comolli R 1975 Changes of liver and kidney polyamine levels during aging. Experimental Gerontology 10: 13–15

Finch C E 1972 Enzyme activities, gene function and aging in mammals Review. Experimental Gerontology 7: 53–67

Findor J, Perez V, Igartua E B, Giovanetti M, Fioravantti N 1973 Structure and ultrastructure of the liver in aged persons. Acta Hepato-gastroentologica 20: 200–204

Fischer J E, Baldessarini R J 1976 Pathogenesis and therapy of hepatic coma. Progress in Liver Diseases 5: 363–397

Forbes G B, Rake M O, Taylor D J E 1979 Liver damage due to perhexiline maleate. Journal of Clinical Pathology 32: 1282–1285

Forrest J A H, Finlayson N D C 1974 The investigation of upper gastrointestinal haemorrhage. British Journal of Hospital Medicine 12: 160–165

Fouts J R 1971 Some morphological characteristics of hepatocyte endoplasmic reticulum and some relationships between endoplasmic reticulum, microsomes and drug metabolism. In: Brodie B B, Gillette J R (ed) Concepts in Biochemical Pharmacology Vol II: pp 243–250. Springer Verlag, Berlin

Fox R A, Scheuer P J, Sherlock S 1973 Asymptomatic primary biliary cirrhosis. Gut 14: 444–447

Friedman G D, Kannel W B, Dawber T R 1966 The epidemiology of gall bladder disease: observations in the Framingham study. Journal of Chronic Diseases 19: 273–292

Gagic N, Frey C F, Gaines R 1975 Acute cholecystitis. Surgery, Gynecology and Obstetrics 140: 868–874

Galambos J T 1975 Classification of cirrhosis. American Journal of Gastroenterology 64: 437–451

Gershon H, Gershon D 1973 Inactive enzyme molecules in aging mice: liver aldolase. Proceedings of the National Academy of Sciences of the United States of America 70: 909–913

Gibbins F J, Collins H J, Hall R G P, Dellipiani A W 1974 Endoscopy in the elderly. Age and Ageing 3: 240–244

Glenn F 1965 Surgical treatment of acute cholecystitis. Geriatrics 20: 728–738

Glenn F 1969 Indications for operation in biliary tract disease among the elderly. Geriatrics 24: 98–103.

Goergen T G, Taylor A, Alazraki N 1976 Lack of gallium uptake in primary hepatic amyloidosis. American Journal of Roentgenology 126: 1246–1248

Gold G, Widnell C C 1974 Reversal of age-related changes in microsomal enzyme activities following the administration of triamcinolone, triiodothyronine and phenobarbital. Biochimica et Biophysica Acta 334: 75–85

Goldberg B B 1976 Ultrasonic cholangiography. Radiology 118: 401–404

Goodpasture E W 1918 An anatomical study of senescence in dogs with especial reference to the relation of cellular change of age to tumours. Journal of Medical Research 38: 127–190

Goto S, Takano T, Mizumo D, Nakano T, Imaizumi K 1969 Aging and location of acid ribonuclease in liver of various animals. Journal of Gerontology 24: 305–308

Gram L F, Overt K F 1972 Drug interaction: inhibitory effect of neuroleptics on metabolism of tricyclic antidepressants in man. British Medical Journal i: 463–465

Griffiths J M T 1972 Surgical policy in the over seventies. Gerontologia Clinica 14: 282–296

Grinna L S, Barber A A 1972 Age-related changes in membrane lipid content and enzyme activities. Biochimica et Biophysica Acta 288: 347–353

Grinna L S, Barber A A 1975a Age-related thermolability of liver and kidney glucose-6-phosphatase. Experimental Gerontology 10: 239–240

Grinna L S, Barber A A 1975b Kinetic analysis of the age-related differences in glucose-6-phosphatase activity. Experimental Gerontology 10: 319–323

Grodsinsky C, Brush B E, Ponka J L 1972 Management of complicated biliary-tract disease in geriatric patients. Journal of American Geriatrics Society 20: 531–536

Hahn H P von 1966 A model of regulatory aging of the cell at the gene level. Journal of Gerontology 21: 291–294

Hahn H P von, Fritz E 1966 Age-related alterations in the structure of DNA. Gerontologia 12: 237–250

Haining J L, Correll W W 1969 Turnover of tryptophan-induced tryptophan pyrrolase in rat liver as a function of age. Journal of Gerontology 24: 143–148

Haining J L, Legan J S 1973 Catalase turnover in rat liver and kidney as a function of age. Experimental Gerontology 8: 85–91

Halasz N A 1975 Counterfeit cholecystitis. A common diagnostic dilemma. American Journal of Surgery 130: 189–193

Hall T J, Donaldson D R, Brennan T G 1980 The value of laparoscopy under local anaesthesia in 250 medical and surgical patients. British Journal of Surgery 67: 751–753

Hamilton E, Williams R, Barlow K A, Smith P M 1968 The arthropathy of idiopathic haemochromatosis. Quarterly Journal of Medicine 37: 171–182

Harisch G, Schole J 1974 Der Glutathionstatus der Rattenleber in Abhangigkeit vom Lebensalter und akuter Belastung. The status of glutathione of the rat liver and its dependence on the age and acute stress (English Abstract). Zeitschrift für Naturforschung, Section C, Biosciences 27c: 261–266

Hayes M J, Langman M J S, Short A H 1975 Changes in drug metabolism with increasing age. 2 Phenytoin clearance and protein binding. British Journal of Clinical Pharmacology 2: 73–79

Hays D M, Glenn F 1955 The fate of the cholecystomy patient. Journal of the American Geriatrics Society 3: 21–30

Hazell K, Ortiz S 1966 The blood alkaline phosphatase level as an aid to diagnosis, treatment and prognosis. Gerontologia Clinica 8: 111–117

Hazell K, Balock K H 1970 Vitamin K deficiency in the elderly. Gerontologia Clinica 12: 10–17

Heino A E, Jokipii S G 1962 Serum alkaline phosphatase levels in the aged. Annales Medicinae Internae Fenniae 15: 105–109

Henderson F G, Chen K K 1948 Effect of age upon the toxicity of methadone. Proceedings of the Society for Experimental Biology and Medicine 68: 350–354

Herbener G H 1976 A morphometric study of age-dependent changes in mitochondrial populations of mouse liver and heart. Journal of Gerontology 31: 8–12

Hermann R E, Martin J C 1969 Biliary disease and advancing age. Geriatrics 24: 139–145

Hirsch J H, Killen F C, Troupin R H 1976 The arthropathy of hemochromatosis. Radiology 118: 591–596

Hobson W, Jordon A 1959 A study of serum alkaline phosphatase levels in old people living at home. Journal of Gerontology 14: 292–293

Hodkinson H M 1971 Amyloidosis in the elderly Modern Geriatrics 1: 312–315

Hodkinson H M 1977 Biochemical Diagnosis of the Elderly. Chapman and Hall Ltd, London

Hodkinson H M, McPherson C K 1973 Alkaline phosphatase in a geriatric inpatient population. Age and Ageing 2: 28–33

Hollander D 1973 Recent developments in viral hepatitis therapy. Geriatrics 28: 100–103

Holliday R, Tarrant G M 1972 Altered enzymes in aging human fibroblasts. Nature 238: 26–30

Holliday R, Porterfield J S, Gibbs D D 1974 Premature aging and occurrence of altered enzyme in Werner's syndrome fibroblasts. Nature 248: 762–763

Hollister L E 1981 General principles of treating the elderly with drugs. In: Jarvik L F, Greenblatt D J, Harman D (ed) Clinical Pharmacology and the Aged Patient (Aging, vol. 16), pp 1–9 Raven Press, New York

Horton A A, Spencer J A 1981 Decline in respiratory control ratio of rat liver mitochondria in old age. Mechanisms of Ageing and Development 17: 253–259

Horwitz C A, Henle W, Henle G, Segal M, Arnold T, Lewis F B, Zanick D, Ward P C J 1976 Clinical and laboratory evaluation of elderly patients with heterophil-antibody positive infectious mononucleosis. Report of seven patients, ages 40–78. American Journal of Medicine 61: 333–339

Hourigan K, Sherlock S, George P, Mindel S 1971 Elective end-to-side portacaval shunt: results in 64 cases. British Medical Journal iv: 473–477

Hove E, Geill T 1968 Serum cholesterol and incidence of gallstones. Analysis of one year autopsy material. Geriatrics 23: 114–118

Hrachovec J P 1969 Age changes in amino-acid incorporation by rat liver microsomes. Gerontologia 15: 52–63

Hrachovec J P 1971 The effect of age on tissue protein synthesis. I. Age changes in amino-acid incorporation by rat liver purified microsomes. Gerontologia 17: 75–86

Huete-Armijo A, Exton-Smith A N 1962 Causes and diagnosis of jaundice in the elderly. British Medical Journal i: 1113–1114

Isselbacher K J, Lesser P B 1975 Phenothiazine jaundice. In: Gerok W, Sickinger K (ed) Drugs & the Liver, p 359–365. Schattauer, Stuttgart

Ivy A C, Grossman M I 1952 Digestive system. In: Lansing A (ed) Cowdry's Problems of Aging (3rd edn): p 481–526. Williams & Wilkins, Baltimore

James O, Macklon A F, Watson A J 1981 Primary biliary cirrhosis — a revised clinical spectrum. Lancet i: 1278–1281

Jänne J, Raina A, Siimes M 1964 Spermidine and spermine in rat tissues at different ages. Acta Physiologica Scandinavica 62: 352–358

Jick H, Stone D, Borda I T, Shapiro S 1968 Efficacy and toxicity of heparin in relation to age and sex. New England Journal of Medicine 279: 284–286

Johnson P J, Williams R, Thomas H et al 1978 Induction of remission in hepatocellular carcinoma with doxorubicin. Lancet i: 1006–1009

Jones A L, Mills E S 1973 Ultrastructural contributions to molecular pharmacology. In: Featherstone R (ed) Modern Pharmacology — a guide to molecular pharmacology — toxicology, Vol 1 Part I: p 83–140. Marcel Dekker, N Y

Joske P A 1975 Active chronic hepatitis. In: Read A E (ed) Modern Trends in Gastroenterology — 5: p 418–443. Butterworth, London

Kahn A, Guillouzo A, Cottreau D, Marie J, Bourel M, Boivin P, Dreyfus J-C 1977 Accuracy of protein synthesis and in vitro aging: search for altered enzymes in senescent cultured cells from human liver. Gerontology 23: 174–184

Kampmann J P, Sinding J Møller-Jørgensen I 1975 Effect of age on liver function. Geriatrics 30: 91–95

Kato R, Takanaka A 1968a Metabolism of drugs in old rats (I) Activities of NADPH-linked electron transport and drug-metabolizing enzyme systems in liver microsomes of old rats. Japanese Journal of Pharmacology 18: 381–388

Kato R, Takanaka A 1968b Metabolism of drugs in old rats (II) Metabolism in vivo and effect of drugs in old rats. Japanese Journal of Pharmacology 18: 389–396

Kato R, Takanaka A 1968c Effect of phenobarbital on the electron-transport system and reduction of drugs in liver microsomes of rats of different ages. Journal of Biochemistry (Tokyo) 63: 406–408

Kato R, Vassanelli P, Frontino G, Chiesara E 1964 Variation in the activity of liver microsomal drug-metabolising enzymes in rats in relation to age. Biochemical Pharmacology 13: 1037–1051

Kaye M D, Kern F 1971 Clinical relationships of gall stones. Lancet i: 1228–1230

Keating F R Jr, Jones J D, Elveback L R, Randall R V 1969 The relation of age and sex to distribution of values in healthy adults of serum calcium, inorganic phosphorus, magnesium, alkaline phosphatase, total proteins, albumin and blood urea. Journal of Laboratory and Clinical Medicine 73: 825–834

Keczkes K, Barker D J 1976 Malignant hepatoma associated with acquired hepatic cutaneous porphyria. Archives of Dermatology and Syphilology 12: 78–82

Keighley M R B, Drysdale R B, Quoraishi A H, Burdon D W, Alexander Williams J 1976a Antibiotics in biliary disease: the relative importance of antibiotic concentrations in the bile and serum. Gut 17: 495–500

Keighley M R B, Flinn R, Alexander-Williams J 1976b Multivariate analysis of clinical and operative findings associated with biliary sepsis. British Journal of Surgery 63: 528–531

Kern F Jr 1976 Hepatobiliary disorders in inflammatory bowel disease. Progress in Liver Diseases 5: 575–589

Kew M C 1975 Alpha-fetoprotein, In: Read A E, (ed) Modern Trends in Gastroenterology 5: pp. 91–114. Butterworth, London

Kim H, Dorfman R F, Rosenberg S A 1976 Pathology of malignant lymphomas in the liver: application in staging. Progress in Liver Diseases 5: 683–698

Kimberg D V, Loeb J N 1972 Effect of cortisone administration on rat liver mitochondria. Support for the concept of mitochondrial fusion. Journal of Cell Biology 55: 635–643

Kirkland K C, Croce E J 1961 Gallstone intestinal obstruction. Journal of the American Medical Association 176: 494–497

Klaassen C H L 1966 Age and serum-alkaline-phosphatase. Lancet ii: 136†

Klatskin G, Smith D P 1975 Halothane-induced hepatitis. In: Gerok W, Sickinger K (ed) Drugs and the Liver: pp 289–296. Schattauer, Stuttgart

Klotz U, Avant G R, Hoyumpa A, Schenker S, Wilkinson G R 1975 The effects of age and liver disease on the disposition and elimination of diazepam in adult man. Journal of Clinical Investigation 55: 347–359

Knill-Jones R P 1975 The diagnosis of jaundice by the computation of probabilities. Journal of the Royal College of Physicians of London 9: 205–210

Koff R S, Davidson L J, Gordon G, Sabesin S M 1973 D-galactosamine hepatotoxicity. III. Normoactive smooth endoplasmic reticulum and modification by phenobarbital. Experimental and Molecular Pathology 19: 168–177

Kopelman H, Robertson M H, Sanders P G, Ash I 1966 The Epping jaundice. British Medical Journal i: 514–516

Kopelman H, Scheuer P J, Williams R 1966b The liver lesion of the Epping jaundice. Western Journal of Medicine 35: 553–564

Kraft E, Finby N 1970 Abdominal survey radiography of geriatric patients in a neuropsychiatric hospital. Journal of the American Geriatrics Society 18: 391–395

Kritchevsky D 1972 Lipid metabolism in aging. Mechanisms of Ageing and Development 1: 275–284

Kroker R, Hegner D, Answer M S 1977 The age dependence of bile acid metabolism in rats. Aktuelle Gerontologie 7: 539–545

Kune G A, Burdon J G W 1975 Are antibiotics necessary in acute cholecystitis? Medical Journal of Australia 2: 627–630

Kurtz D I 1978 A decrease in the number of active mouse liver ribosomes during ageing. Experimental Gerontology 13: 397–402

Kwent V A, Liebetseder J, Burger H 1966 Gerontologische Untersuchungen an Rattenherz mitochondren. Gerontologia 12: 193–199

Lancet 1976a Pyogenic liver abscess: a continuing problem of management. Leading article i: 1170–1171

Lancet 1976b Methyldopa hepatitis. Leading article ii 299

Lancet 1976c The liver after jejunoileal bypass. Leading article ii: 666–667

Laufer I 1975 A simple method for routine double-contrast study of the upper gastrointestinal tract. Radiology 117: 513–518

Levelle M I, Venables C W, Douglas A P, Thompson M H, Owen J P, Hacking P M 1976 A prospective endoscopically controlled trial of double contrast against single contrast barium meals. Gut 17: 396–397

Leask R G S, Andrews G R, Caird F I 1973 Normal values for sixteen blood constituents in the elderly. Age and Ageing 2: 14–23

Leevy C M, Kiernan T H 1975 Drugs and hepatic blood flow. In: Drugs and the Liver: Gerok W, Sickinger K (ed) p 241–251. Schattauer, Stuttgart

Leevy C M, Tamburro C H, Zetterman R 1975 Liver disease of the alcoholic. Medical Clinics of North America 59: 909–918

Levy M, Fryd C H, Eliakim M 1971 Intrahepatic obstructive jaundice due to amyloidosis of the liver. A case report and review of the literature. Gastroenterology 61: 234–238

Lieber C S 1973 Hepatic and metabolic effects of alcohol (1966–1973). Gastroenterology 65: 821–846

Lieber C S 1978 Pathogenesis and early diagnosis of alcoholic liver injury. New England Journal of Medicine 298: 888–893

Lieber M M 1952 The incidence of gall stones and their correlation with other diseases. Annals of Surgery 135: 394–405

Logan R F A, Finlayson N D C 1976 Death in acute upper gastrointestinal bleeding. Can endoscopy reduce mortality? Lancet i: 1173

Lomonaco A, Kline P, Halpern S, Leopold G 1975 Nuclear medicine and ultrasound: correlation in diagnosis of disease of liver and biliary tract. Seminars in Nuclear Medicine 5: 307–324

Longmire W P 1973 Periampullary tumours. Journal of the Royal College of Surgeons of Edinburgh 18: 131–136

Ludwig J, Baggenstos A H 1970 Cirrhosis of the aged and senile cirrhosis — are there two conditions? Journal of Gerontology 25: 244–248

Ludwig J, Garrison C O, Baggenstoss A H 1970 Latent hepatic cirrhosis: A study of 95 cases. American Journal of Digestive Diseases 15: 7–14

Lund J 1960 Surgical indications in cholelithiasis: prophylactic cholecystectomy elucidated on the basis of long-term follow-up on 526 non-operated cases. Annals of Surgery 151: 153–162

Lunzer M 1975 Encephalopathy in liver disease. British Journal of Hospital Medicine 13: 33–44

McArthur P, Cuschieri A, Sells R A, Shields R 1975 Controlled clinical trial comparing early with interval cholecystectomy for acute cholecystitis. British Journal of Surgery 62: 850–852

McGinn F P, Guyer P B, Wilken B J, Steer H W 1975 A prospective comparative trial between early endoscopy and radiology in acute upper gastrointestinal haemorrhage. Gut 16: 707–713

McKeown F 1965 In: Pathology of the Aged: p 165. Butterworth, London

McLaughlin C W Jr 1964 Carcinoma of the gall bladder, an added hazard in untreated calculous cholecystitis in older patients. Surgery 56: 757–759

MacLennan W J 1974 Drug interactions. Gerontologia Clinica 16: 18–24

MacNider W de B 1936 The resistance to chloroform of a naturally acquired atypical type of liver epithelium occurring in senile animals. Journal of Pharmacology and Experimental Therapeutics 56: 382–387

Maffioli C, Brunetaud J M, Butel J, Coudoux P, Geoffroy H 1976 The value of endoscopic retrograde opacification of biliary-pancreatic ducts in icterus. International Surgery 61: 173–175

Magarey J R 1966 Biliary fenestration. British Journal of Surgery 53: 41–46

Maingot R 1964 Biliary fistulae and gall stone ileus. In: Smith R, Sherlock S, (ed), Surgery of the Gall Bladder and Bile Ducts: p 309–317. Butterworth, London

Mainwaring W I 1969 The effect of age on protein synthesis in mouse liver. Biochemical Journal 113: 869–878

Manax S J 1969 Gall stone ileus. Abdominal Surgery 11: 182–187

Massé L, Juillan J M, Chisloup A 1976 Trends in mortality from cirrhosis of the liver, 1950–1971. World Health Statistics Report 29: 40–67

Maton P N, Murphy G M, Dowling R H 1977 Ursodeoxycholic acid. Treatment of gall stones. Lancet ii: 1297–1301

Mee A S, Vallon A G, Croker J R, Cotton P B 1981 Non operative removal of bile duct stones by duodenoscopic sphincterotomy in the elderly. British Medical Journal 283: 521–523

Meindok H, Langer B 1976 Liver-scan in Budd-Chiari syndrome, Journal of Nuclear Medicine 17: 365–368

Meinhuizen S P, Blausjaar N 1980 Stereological analysis of liver parenchymal cells from young and old rats. Mechanisms of Ageing and Development 13: 111–118

Menghini G 1970 One-second biopsy of the liver — problems of its clinical application. New England Journal of Medicine 283: 582–585

Menzies R R, Gold P H 1971 The turnover of mitochondria in a variety of tissues of young adult and aged rats. Journal of Biological Chemistry 246: 2425–2429

Miller A C Jr, Reid W M 1976 Methyldopa-induced granulomatous hepatitis. Journal of the American Medical Association 235: 2001–2002

Miller D J, Saunders S J, Hickman R, Terblanche J 1975 Acute hepatic necrosis: a review of causes and management of fulminant hepatic failure. In: Read A E (ed) Modern trends in gastroenterology — 5: p 64–90. Butterworth, London

Mitmaker B, Margolese R, Guttman F, Ballon H C 1964 Gallbladder carcinoma associated with cholelithiasis: surgical implications. Journal of the American Geriatrics Society 12: 180–187

Moesgaard F, Nielsen M L, Pedersen T, Hansen J B 1982 Protective choledochoduodenostomy in multiple common duct stones in the aged. Surgery, Gynecology and Obstetrics 154: 232–234

Morris D W, Levine G M, Soloway R D, Miller W T, Marin G A 1975 Prospective, randomized study of diagnosis and outcome in acute upper gastrointestinal bleeding: endoscopy v. conventional radiography. American Journal of Digestive Diseases 20: 1103–1109

Morrow D J, Thompson J, Wilson S E 1978 Acute cholecystitis in the elderly. Archives of Surgery 113: 1149–1152

Mulay A S, Hurwitz S 1938 Normal plasma phosphatase values. Journal of Laboratory and Clinical Medicine 23: 1117–1119

Munzer D 1966 The importance of liver biopsy in middle and old age, Geriatrics 21: 144–148.

Murray-Lyon I M, Reynolds K 1976 Jaundice. British Medical Journal ii: 923–925

Myline G E, Karnauchow P N 1974 Cholecystectomy and related procedures in two community hospitals. Canadian Journal of Surgery 17: –24

Naso F, Thompson C M 1967 Hyperbilirubinaemia in the patient past 50. Geriatrics 22: 206–212

Nation R L, Learoyd B, Barber J, Triggs E J 1976 The pharmacokinetics of chlormethiazole following intravenous administration in the aged. European Journal of Clinical Pharmacology 10: 407–415

Nevin J E, Moran T J, Kay S, King R 1976 Carcinoma of gallbladder. Staging, treatment, and prognosis. Cancer 37: 141–148

Newman H F, Northup J D 1964 Gall bladder carcinoma in cholelithiasis. A study of probability. Geriatrics 19: 453–455

Niederle B 1967 Sphincterotomy in biliary surgery. Journal of the Royal College of Surgeons of Edinburgh 12: 330–336

Nielsen M L, Justesen T 1976 Anaerobic and aerobic bacterial studies in biliary tract disease. Scandinavian Journal of Gastroenterology 11: 437–446

Nies A S, Shand D G, Wilkinson G R 1976 Altered hepatic blood flow and drug disposition. Clinical Pharmacokinetics 1: 135–155

Norkrans D, Magnius L, Iwarson S 1976 e antigen in acute hepatitis. British Medical Journal i: 740–742

Obenrader M, Chen J, Ove P, Lansing A I 1974a Etiology of increased albumin synthesis in old rats. Experimental Gerontology 9: 173–180

Obenrader M, Chen J, Ove P, Lansing A I 1974b Functional regeneration in liver of old rats after partial hepatectomy. Experimental Gerontology 9: 181–190

O'Brien G F, Tan C V 1970 Jaundice in the geriatric patient. Geriatrics 25: 114–127

Ogburn R M, Myers R L, Burdick G E 1976 Hepatitis associated with dantrolene sodium. Annals of Internal Medicine 84: 53–54

Ohbayashi A, Matsuo Y, Mozai T, Imai M, Mayumi M 1976 Decreasing frequency of e antigen in serum of symptom-free carriers of hepatitis B antigen. Lancet ii: 577–578

Ohnishi N, Tsukuda S, Ogawa N 1974 Effects of cytochrome c on the liver function of aged rats. Japanese Journal of Pharmacology 24: 15–21

Oldendorf W H, Hyman S, Braun L, Oldendorf S Z 1972 Blood-brain barrier: penetration of morphine, codeine, heroin and methadone after carotid injection. Science 178: 984–986

Ollendorff P, Rasmussen J, Astrup T 1966 Blood coagulation and plasma fibrinolysis in geriatric patients with decreased liver function. Acta Medica Scandinavica 179: 101–111

O'Malley K, Crooks J, Duke E, Stevenson I H 1971 Effect of age and sex on human drug metabolism. British Medical Journal iii: 607–609

O'Malley K, Stevenson I H, Ward C A 1974 In: Morselli L, Garattini S, Cohen S N (ed) Drug Interactions: p 309–316. Raven Press, New York

O'Malley K, Stevenson I H, Ward C A, Wood A S, Crooks J 1977 Determinants of anticoagulant control in patients receiving warfarin. British Journal of Clinical Pharmacology 4: 309–314

Orgel L E 1963 The maintenance of the accuracy of protein synthesis and its relevance to aging. Proceedings of the National Academy of Sciences of the United States of America 49: 517–521

Orgel L E 1973 Aging of clones of mammalian cells. Nature 243: 441–445

Osnes M, Serck-Hanssen A, Myren J 1975 Endoscopic retrograde brush cytology (ERBC) of the biliary and pancreatic ducts. Scandinavian Journal of Gastroenterology 10: 829–831

Ove P, Coetzee M L 1978 A difference in bleomycin-induced DNA synthesis between liver nuclei from mature and old rats. Mechanisms of Ageing and Development 8: 363–375

Parbhoo S 1975 The measurement of bleeding in liver disease. British Journal of Hospital Medicine 12: 17–28

Paterniti J R, Lin C P, Beattie D S 1980 Regulation of heme metabolism during senescence. Activity of several heme-containing enzymes and heme oxygenase in the liver and kidney of ageing rats: Mechanisms of Ageing and Development 12: 81–91

Pessayre D, Bichara M, Feldmann G, Deggott C, Potet F, Benhamou J P 1979 Perhexiline maleate induced cirrhosis. Gastroenterology 76: 170–177

Phatak P S 1974 Intermittent jaundice due to a carcinoma of the ampulla of Vater. Proceedings of the Royal Society of Medicine 67: 1025–1026

Pieri C, Zs-Nagy I, Mazzufferi G, Giuli C 1975a The aging of rat liver as revealed by electron microscope morphometry. I. Basic parameters. Experimental Gerontology 10: 291–304

Pieri C, Zs-Nagy I, Giuli C, Mazzufferi G 1975b The aging of rat liver as revealed by electron microscope morphometry. II. Parameters of regenerated old liver. Experimental Gerontology 10: 341–349

Pieri C, Giuli C, Del Mono M, Piantanelli E M 1980 Morphometric analysis of mouse liver. II Effect of ageing and thymus transplantation in old animals. Mechanisms of Ageing and Development 13: 275–283

Platt D, Pauli H 1972 Age-dependent determinations of lysosomal enzymes in the liver of spironolactone and aldosterone pre-treated rats. Experimental Gerontology 7: 1–7

Poe N D, Bennett L R 1971 The proven value of liver scanning. Geriatrics 26: 123–133

Popper H, Schaffner F 1976 Chronic hepatitis: taxonomic, etiologic, and therapeutic problems. Progress in Liver Diseases 5: 531–558

Pyhtilä M J, Sherman F G 1969 Influence of age on rat liver and kidney chromatin. Gerontologia 15: 321–327

Rahman Y E, Peraino C 1973 Effects of age on problems of enzyme adaptation in male and female rats. Experimental Gerontology 8: 93–100

Raine P A M, Gunn A A 1975 Acute cholecystitis. British Journal of Surgery 62: 697–700

Read A E, Laidlaw J, Sherlock S 1961 Neuropsychiatric complications of portal caval anastomosis. Lancet i: 961–963

Read A E, Sherlock S, Laidlaw J, Walker J G 1967 The neuropsychiatric syndromes associated with chronic liver disease and an extensive portal-systemic collateral circulation. Quarterly Journal of Medicine 36: 135–150

Reed A H, Cannon D C, Winkelman J W, Bhasin Y P, Henry R H, Pileggi V J 1972 Estimation of normal ranges from a combined sample survey. I. Sex- and age-related influence on the SMA 12/60 screening group of tests. Clinical Chemistry 18: 57–66

Reid M H 1976 Focused ultrasound for bile ducts. Radiology 118: 155–158

Reuber M D, Lee C W 1968 Effect of age and sex on hepatic lesions in Buffalo strain rats ingesting diethylnitrosamine. Journal of the National Cancer Institute 41: 1133–1140

Reuber M D, Glover E L, Dove L F 1969 Hepatic lesions in aged rats given carbon tetrachloride. Gerontologia 15: 7–13

Richard P F, Cantin J 1976 Primary carcinoma of the gallbladder: study of 218 cases. Canadian Journal of Surgery 19: 27–32

Rigberg L A, Robinson M J, Espiritu C R 1976 Chlorpropamide-induced granulomas. A probable hypersensitivity reaction in liver and bone marrow. Journal of the American Medical Association 235: 409–410

Roberts L B 1967 The normal ranges with statistical analysis for 17 blood constituents. Clinica Chimica Acta 16: 69–78

Rosalski S B 1975 Gamma glutamyl transpeptidase In: Bodansky O, Latner A L (ed) Advances in clinical chemistry vol 17: p 53–107

Rosenthal S N 1976 Are hepatic scans overused? American Journal of Digestive Diseases 21: 659–663

Ross M H 1969 Aging, nutrition, and hepatic enzyme activity patterns in the rat. Journal of Nutrition 97: Suppl I: 563–601

Rossman I 1971 The Anatomy of Aging. In: Rossman I (ed) Clinical geriatrics: p. 12. Lippincott, Philadelphia

Rothschild M A 1976 Hepatic radionuclide imaging: an effective diagnostic procedure! American Journal of Digestive Diseases 21: 655–659

Rothstein M 1975 Aging and the alteration of enzymes: a review. Mechanisms of Ageing and Development 4: 325–338

Rubin E, Schaffner F, Popper H 1965 Primary biliary cirrhosis. Chronic non-suppurative destructive cholangitis. American Journal of Pathology 46: 387–407

Ryan J M, Cristofalo V J 1975 Chromatin template activity during aging in WI38 cells. Experimental Cell Research 90: 456–458

Sabbaj J, Sutter V L, Finegold S M 1972 Anaerobic pyogenic liver abscess. Annals of Internal Medicine 77: 629–638

Safaie-Shirazi S, Printen K J 1972 Gallstone ileus: review of 40 cases. Journal of the American Geriatrics Society 20: 335–339

Safrany L 1977 Duodenoscopic sphincterotomy and gallstone removal. Gastroenterology 72: 338–343

Salmon P R 1975 Endoscopic retrograde choledochopancreatography (ERCP). In: Read A E (ed) Modern Trends in Gastroenterology — 5: p 231–249. Butterworth, London

Samis H V, Wulfe V J, Falzone J A Jr 1964 The incorporation of H3-cytidine into RNA of liver nuclei of young and old rats. Biochimica et Biophysica Acta 91: 223–232

Samis H V, Falzone J A Jr, Wulff V J 1966 H3-thymidine incorporation and mitotic activity in liver of rats of various ages. Gerontologia 12: 79–88

Sato T, Matsushiro T 1974 Surgical indications in patients with silent gallstones. American Journal of Surgery 128: 368–375

Sato T, Tauchi H 1975 The formation of enlarged and giant mitochondria in the aging process of human hepatic cells. Acta Pathologica Japonica 25: 403–412

Sato T, Miwa T, Tauchi H 1970 Age changes in the human liver of the different races. Gerontologia 16: 368–380

Saunders J 1976 Lymph node and hepatic granulomata associated with carcinoma. British Medical Journal i: 437–438

Saunders J B, Walters J R F, Davies P, Paton A 1981 A 20 year prospective study of cirrhosis. British Medical Journal 282: 263–266

Schaffner F, Popper H 1959 Non-specific reactive hepatitis in aged and infirm people. American Journal of Digestive Diseases 4: 389–399

Schiller K F R, Truelove S C, Williams D G 1970 Haematemesis and melaena, with specific reference to factors influencing the outcome. British Medical Journal ii: 7–14

Schmucker D L 1976 Age-related changes in hepatic fine structure: a quantitative analysis. Journal of Gerontology 31: 135–143

Schmucker D L, Wang R K 1981 Effects of ageing and phenobarbitol on the rat liver microsomal drug metabolising system. Mechanisms of Ageing and Development 15: 189–202

Schneider R, Mitchell D 1976 Dantrolene hepatitis. Journal of the American Medical Association 235: 1590–1591

Schofield J D 1978 Age related alterations in the heat lability of mouse liver glucose-6-phosphate dehydrogenase. Experimental Gerontology 13: 147–157

Scott N M Jr, Hitzelberger A L, Parker G W, Durden W D, Langdon D E 1968 Role of peritoneoscopy in diagnosis of intra-abdominal disease. Archives of Internal Medicine 120: 207–213

Scott-Harden W G 1974 Radiology of acute upper digestive tract bleeding. Journal of the Royal College of Physicians of London 8: 365–374

Sewell S 1960 Serum acid and alkaline phosphatase values in the adult male. American Journal of the Medical Sciences 240: 593–598

Seyss R 1967 Zur Spätfultung der Gallenblase. (Delayed filling of the gall bladder). (English abstract)-Excerpta medica Sect. XX 1968 11: no 126

Sharland D E 1972 Serum alkaline phosphatase: the levels and patterns of isoenzymes in the non-hospitalised elderly. Age and Ageing 1: 168–176

Sharland D E 1975 Clinical value of serum alkaline phosphatase isoenzyme estimations in the elderly. Age and Ageing 4: 1–7

Shepherd A M M, Wilson N, Stevenson I H 1979 Warfarin sensitivity in the elderly. In: Crooks J, Stevenson I H Drugs and the Elderly: p 199–209. Macmillan Press Ltd, London

Shepherd A M M, Havick D S, Morland T W, Stevenson I H 1977 Age as a determinant of sensitivity. British Journal of Clinical Pharmacology 4: 309–320

Sherlock S 1975 Diseases of the Liver and Biliary System (5th edn). Blackwell, Oxford

Sherlock S 1976 Hemochromatosis — course and treatment. Annual Review of Medicine 27: 143–149

Sherlock S 1977 Hepatic encephalopathy. British Journal of Hospital Medicine 17: 144–159

Sherlock S 1981 Diseases of the Liver and Biliary System (6th edn). Blackwell Scientific Publications, London

Sherlock S, Bearn A G, Billing B, Paterson J G S 1950 Splanchnic blood flow in man by the bromsulfalein method: the relation of peripheral plasma bromsulfalein level to the calculated flow. Journal of Laboratory and Clinical Medicine 35: 923–932

Simpson B R, Strunin L, Walton D 1975 Halothane and jaundice. British Journal of Hospital Medicine 13: 433–439

Sklar M, Kirsner J B, Palmer W L 1956 Symposium on medical problems of the aged: gastrointestinal disease in the aged. Medical Clinics of North America 40: 223–237

Snow J H Jr, Goldstein H M, Wallace S 1979 Comparison of scintigraphy, sonography and computed tomography in the evaluation of hepatic neoplasms. American Journal of Roentgenology 132: 915–917

Solan M J, Jackson B T 1971 Carcinoma of the gall bladder. A clinical appraisal and review of 57 cases. British Journal of Surgery 58: 593–597

Sostre S, Martin N D, Lucas R N, Strauss H W 1975 Scintigraphic findings in primary amyloidosis. Radiology 115: 675–677

Spencer J A, Horton A A 1978 An age dependent release of matrix proteins from rat liver mitochondria. Experimental Gerontology 13: 227–232

Stein G S, Wang P L, Adelman R C 1973 Age-dependent change in the structure and function of mammalian chromatin. I. Variations in chromatin template activity. Experimental Gerontology 8: 123–133

Stein H D 1975 The diagnosis of jaundice by the minilaparotomy open transhepatic cholangiogram. Annals of Surgery 181: 386–389

Stevenson G W, Cox R R, Roberts C J C 1976 Prospective comparison of double-contrast barium meal examination and fibreoptic endoscopy in acute upper gastrointestinal haemorrhage. British Medical Journal ii: 723–724

Story J A, Kritchevsky D 1974 Cholesterol oxidation by rat liver preparations: effect of age. Experientia 30: 242–243

Strohl E L, Reed W H, Diffenbaugh W G, Anderson R E 1963 Carcinoma of the bile ducts. Archives of Surgery (Chicago) 87: 567–577

Sullivan D M, Hood T R, Griffin W O Jr 1982 Biliary tract surgery in the elderly. American Journal of Surgery 143: 218–220

Summerskill W H J, Korman M G, Ammon H V, Baggenstoss A H 1975 Prednisone for chronic active liver disease: dose titration, standard dose and combination with azathiaprine compared. Gut 16: 876–883

Suzuki K, Okuda K, Yoshida T, Kanda Y 1976 False positive liver scan in a patient with hepatic amyloidosis: case report. Journal of Nuclear Medicine 17: 31–32

Swendseid M E, Hvollboll E, Schick G, Halsted J A 1957 Vitamin B_{12} content of human liver tissue and its nutritional significance. Blood 12: 24–28

Szauer J S, Zukaukas C 1975 The problems of abdominal operations in elderly patients. Geriatrics 30: 52–64

Tas S 1976 Disulfide bonding in chromatin proteins with age and a suggested mechanism for aging and neoplasia. Experimental Gerontology 11: 17–24

Tate E L, Herberne G H 1976 A morphometric study of the density of mitochondrial cristae in heart and liver of aging mice. Journal of Gerontology 31: 129–134

Tauchi H, Hanenoucki M 1980 Accumulation of lipofuscin pigment in human hepatic cells from different races and in different environmental conditions. Mechanisms of Ageing and Development 12: 183–195

Tauchi H, Hasegawa K 1972 Changes in the hepatic cells in parabiosis between old and young rats. Mechanisms of Ageing and Development 6: 333–339

Tauchi H, Sato T 1962 Some micromeasuring studies of hepatic cells in senility. Journal of Gerontology 17: 254–259

Tauchi H, Sato T 1968 Age changes in size and number of mitochondria of human hepatic cells. Journal of Gerontology 23: 454–461

Tauchi H, Sato T 1975 Effect of environmental conditions upon age changes in the human liver. Mechanisms of Ageing and Development 4: 71–80

Tauchi H Sato T, Kobayashi H 1974 Effect of age on ultrastructural changes of cortisone-treated mouse hepatic cells. Mechanisms of Ageing and Development 3: 279–290

Terblanche J 1977 Liver tumours. British Journal of Hospital Medicine 17: 103–114

Tesauro P, Manduco A, Corsini G G, De Gaetano M N, Cicala V 1969 Il comportamento del flusso sanguino epatico, determinato mediante la clearance dei radiocolloidi, in soggetti in età senile, con epatiticroniche e cirrosi epatiche. Giornale di Gerontologia 17: 721–728

Thistle J L, Carlson G L, Hofman A F et al 1980 Mono-octanoin, a dissolution agent for retained cholesterol bile duct stores: physical properties and clinical application. Gastroenterology 78: 1016–1022

Thomas H S, Cherry J K, Averbrook B D 1962 Gall stone ileus. Journal of the American Medical Association 179: 625–629

Thompson E N, Williams R 1965 Effect of age on liver function with particular reference to BSP excretion. Gut 6: 266–269

Triger D R 1980 Primary biliary cirrhosis: an epidemiological study. British Medical Journal 281: 772–775

Triggs E J, Nation R L 1975 Pharmacokinetics in the aged: a review. Journal of Pharmacokinetics and Biopharmaceutics 3: 387–418

Vaittinen E 1970 Carcinoma of the gall-bladder. A study of 390 cases diagnosed in Finland, 1953–1967. Annales Chirurgiae et Gynaecologiae Fenniae 59, Suppl 168.

Van Bezooijen C F, De Leeuw-Israel F R, Hollander C F 1972 On the role of hepatic cell ploidy changes in liver function with age and following partial hepatectomy. Mechanisms of Ageing and Development 1: 351–358

van Bezooijen C F, van Noord M J, Knook D L 1974 The viability of parenchymal liver cells isolated from young and old rats. Mechanisms of Ageing and Development 3: 107–119

van Bezooijen C F, Sakker A N, Knook D L 1981 Sex & strain dependency of age-related changes in protein synthesis of isolated rat hepatocytes. Mechanisms of Ageing and Development 17: 11–18

Walls W D, Glanville J N, Chandler G N 1971 Early investigation of haematemesis and melaena. Lancet ii: 387–390

Walter F, Addis T 1939 Organ work and organ weight. Journal of Experimental Medicine 69: 467–483

Walter J F, Bookstein J J, Bouffard E V 1976 Newer angiographic observations in cholangiocarcinoma. Radiology 118: 19–23

Walters G O, Jacobs A, Worwood M, Trevett D, Thomson W 1975 Iron absorption in normal subjects and patients with idiopathic haemochromatosis: relationship with serum ferritin concentration. Gut 16: 188–192

Way L W, Admirand W H, Danphy J E 1972 Management of choledocholithiasis. Annals of Surgery 176: 347–359

Weinbren K 1961 Aging changes in the liver. In: Bourne G H (ed) Structural Aspects of Ageing: p 217–226. Pitman, London

Weissman G 1967 The role of lysosomes in inflammation and disease. Annual Review of Medicine 18: 97–112

Wells R F 1973 Management of bleeding esophageal varices in the elderly. Geriatrics 28: 90–93

Wenckert A, Robertson B 1966 The natural course of gallstone disease. 11 year review of 781 non-operated cases. Gastroenterology 50: 376–381

Wheatley D N 1972 Binucleation in mammalian liver. Experimental Cell Research 74: 455–465

Whelton M J 1970 Arthropathy and liver disease. British Journal of Hospital Medicine 3: 243–247

Wiberg G S, Trenholm H L, Coldwell B B 1970 Increased ethanol toxicity in old rats: changes in LD_{50} in vivo and in vitro metabolism, and liver alcohol dehydrogenase activity. Toxicology and Applied Pharmacology 16: 718–727

Wilkinson G R, Shand D G 1975 A physiological approach to hepatic drug clearance. Clinical Pharmacology and Therapeutics 18: 377–390

Williams M, Smith P M, Doniach D 1976 Primary biliary cirrhosis and chronic active hepatitis in two sisters. British Medical Journal ii: 566

Williams R 1975 Management of liver failure. In: Walker W F, Taylor D E (ed) Intensive Care: p 160–170. Churchill Livingstone, Edinburgh

Williams R 1976 Hepatic failure and development of artificial liver support system. Progress in Liver Diseases 5: 418–435

Wilson P D 1973 Enzyme changes in aging mammals. Gerontologia 19: 79–125

Wilson P D, Franks L M 1975 The effect of age on mitochondrial ultrastructure. Gerontologia 21: 81–94

Wilson P D, Hill B T, Franks L M 1975 The effect of age on mitochondrial enzymes and respiration. Gerontologia 21: 95–101

Wise L 1976 Periampullary cancer: a clinicopathologic study of 62 patients. American Journal of Surgery 131: 141–148

Wong K H, Schuman B M 1976 The value of endoscopic study of the bile ducts and the pancreas in the elderly. Geriatrics 31: 61–67

Woolf I L, Boyes B E, Leeming J T, Dymock I W 1974 Active chronic hepatitis in the elderly. Age and Ageing 3: 226–228

Woolf I L, Williams R 1976a Laparoscopy in liver disease. Lancet i: 807

Woolf I L, Williams R 1976b Significance of perisitent HBs antigenaemia. British Medical Journal ii: 807–808

Woolf I L, Williams R 1977 Acute viral hepatitis. British Journal of Hospital Medicine 17: 117–124

Wulf J H, Cutler R G 1975 Altered protein hypothesis of mammalian aging processes — I. Thermal stability of glucose-6-phosphate dehydrogenase in C57BL/6J mouse tissue. Experimental Gerontology 10: 101–117

Wust C J, Rosen L 1972 Aminoacylation and methylation of tRNA as a function of age in the rat. Experimental Gerontology 7: 331–343

Yagil G 1976 Are altered glucose-6-phosphare dehydrogenase molecules present in aged liver cells? Experimental Gerontology 11: 73–78

Young A E 1976 The clinical presentation of pyogenic liver abscess. British Journal of Surgery 63: 216–219

Zamchek N, Klausenstock O 1953 Liver biopsy III. The risk of needle biopsy. New England Journal of Medicine 249: 1062–1069

Zhelabovskaya S M, Berdyshev G D 1972 Composition, template activity and thermostability of the liver chromatin in rats of various age. Experimental Gerontology 7: 313–320

Zieve L 1958 Jaundice, hyperlipemia and hemolytic anemia: a heretofore unrecognized syndrome associated with alcoholic fatty liver and cirrhosis. Annals of Internal Medicine 48: 471–496

Ziffren S E, Hartford C E 1972 Comparative mortality for various surgical operations in older versus young age groups. Journal of the American Geriatrics Society 20: 485–489

Zimmon D S, Chang J, Clemett A R 1979 Advances in the management of bile duct obstruction. Medical Clinics of North America 63: 593–609

Zs-Nagy V, Bertoni-Freddari C, Zs-Nagy I, Pieri C, Giuli C 1977 Alterations in the numerical density of perichromatin granules in different tissues during aging and cell differentiation. Gerontology 23: 267–276

The gastrointestinal system — nutrition

The differences between physiological aging — 'a process of unfavourable progressive change . . . becoming apparent after maturity' (Lansing, 1951) or a 'deterioration process . . . a decrease in viability and an increase in vulnerability' (Comfort, 1956) — and the pathological conditions commonly encountered in elderly people, have been discussed elsewhere in this book. These differences have implications in relation to nutrition. As one example, gross arthritic changes will obviously affect the ability to move the limbs, will reduce physical activity and may considerably influence the development or treatment of obesity, whereas 'normal' physiological degeneration is a relatively slow process which will still allow a way of life which includes active work or recreation into advanced age.

With certain limitations, the amount of physical activity in the elderly is probably the most critical factor in affecting nutritional status. This whole problem is discussed in greater depth later in this chapter, but it is salutary to mention briefly the difficulties presented by circumstances which markedly diminish physical activity in the elderly. When physical activity falls, energy expenditure also lessens, the energy required to replace that energy is similarly reduced, appetite deteriorates, and the amount of food eaten is proportionately less. Since the fact of being elderly had already reduced the food requirements, this further diminution may well result in an intake of several nutrients which will be marginally adequate or perhaps patently inadequate. The nutritional status of the elderly person will become less favourable, although this may frequently be difficult to detect. Further pathological deterioration following the malnutrition may induce a steadily worsening situation.

Thus, it is worth while putting considerable effort into maintaining or increasing physical movement and activity in elderly men and women. The improvement is not only local, because of better muscle tone and mobility, but general as well, if the increased food eaten corrects or improves nutrient deficiencies.

Nutrition in the elderly involves several different areas — food intake, nutritional status (including anthropometric, biochemical and clinical assessment), changes in some aspects of body composition, and physical activity and energy expenditure.

Several of these topics may pose considerable problems to the conscientious physician. Undoubtedly, a certain amount of nutritional disability is preventable. But most physicians have not been adequately taught, in a modern context, about the significance of the nutritional value of individuals foods nor of eating habits; nutritional status is often extremely difficult to define and measure; and the role of physical activity in relation to its degree of severity and its duration and frequency is poorly understood in a medical context.

The education of the elderly in eating and exercise habits is one of the duties of the physician which is demonstrably beneficial, but it is a task which should not be deferred until the patient is already elderly.

The physical deterioration which accompanies aging and which involves a nutritional component, begins (especially in women) in middle age and the importance of nutrition and exercise for health needs to be emphasized by the doctor at that stage in a patient's life.

Thus, the doctor has an important task in firstly being carefully on the look-out for indications of malnutrition and secondly in encouraging the patient to adopt habits which will tend to minimize the likelihood of malnutrition developing.

NUTRITIONAL REQUIREMENTS

General

The requirement for energy and the various nutrients for the elderly are incorporated in the reports of various national and international committees. Many of the actual values quoted in these tables are the result of a mixture of experimental data — often inadequate and of highly variable quality — and intelligent guesswork. Because of this and of the very large variability of these requirements when applied to individual men and women, they are of very little practical use to assess the nutritional status of a single patient. Indeed, unless the intake of energy or of a nutrient by an individual is grossly at variance with the supposed requirement, no attention should be paid to it as an indicator of the nutritional state of the patient. It may, however, be useful when applied to groups of individuals — e.g. old people living in an institution — both in the assessment of the likely adequacy of a diet or in the construction of a satisfactory diet.

The requirement of specific nutrients for elderly individuals falls into one or other of two categories, according to whether or not the amount of the nutrient is a function of energy intake; that is, some nutrients are required in amounts which vary directly with the total energy intake, others are independent of energy intake.

The requisite energy content of the diet obviously depends upon the energy expenditure and will therefore be usually, but not always, dependent upon body size, body composition and sex, and will vary to a large extent with the amount of physical activity.

Protein needs reflect body size and composition and are almost unrelated to total energy output. The minerals, calcium and iron, are required also in quantities which are related to body size and not to energy expenditure and while their minimal requirements are relatively low for elderly people it is certainly possible, and sometimes quite common for some individuals to obtain less than the desirable amounts. Sodium, chloride, magnesium, phosphorus, fluoride, copper, manganese, cobalt, selenium, molybdenum and chromium are all present in sufficient measure, even in apparently frugal diets, in elderly men and women and, although they may on occasion be deficient, this has not, up to now, been thought to be other than a rare occurrence. However, information on the trace elements is still very inadequate (WHO, 1973). Again, usually their need does not apparently vary with factors other than body size. Zinc may sometimes be deficient in the diet (Sandstead et al, 1982). This will be discussed later.

The importance of potassium in nutrition is a subject of some dispute. Potassium deficiency is found in some old people admitted to hospital and living in institutions (Judge, 1979; Vir and Love, 1979) and even living a normal social life at home (Borgstrom et al, 1979), and very low intakes of the mineral in the diet may be a causative factor. Quite plausible arguments implicating dietary deficiency in these people have been suggested by Judge et al (1974), in spite of the fact that intakes of potassium in the diet of old people living at home would be expected to be considerably in excess of requirement (Dall et al, 1971).

Some of the vitamins show different characteristics. Thiamine for example, is related properly to carbohydrate intake, since it is concerned in carbohydrate metabolism, but, in practice, it can be reasonably associated with total energy intake. Riboflavine, and nic-

otonic acid, although sometimes expressed as functions of energy intake, are probably dependent only on body size and composition. Similarly, cobalamin, pantothenic acid, biotin, ascorbic acid and retinol all have requirements which depend on the size of the individual elderly person; and calciferol, tocopherol and vitamin K, although perhaps having special implications for the elderly, are in the same category.

The role of energy expenditure

Whether the standards for most nutrients are met for any individual man or woman will often depend more on the total quantity of food eaten than on the composition of the diet. This statement is clearly not always true but, in general, unless a diet is quite an unusual one, most nutrients will be supplied in more or less adequate quantities if the total amount of food eaten is reasonable. Of course, some isolated elderly people, with little motivation to cooking adequate meals, have a diet consisting of little more than bread, margarine and jam. If the individual is house-bound and eating only small amounts, malnutrition may result.

Nevertheless, a mixture of foods — which can often be very simple, such as porridge, bread, potatoes, some vegetables, a little meat or fish, and some milk — can usually provide a sufficiency of nutrient intake if the total energy of the diet reaches somewhere around the recommended energy requirements.

Thus energy expenditure in many ways is the critical component for good nutrition. Energy intake is primarily dependent on the energy expenditure. Any imbalance will result either in the individual gaining or losing weight and the amount of the imbalance need be only of small degree — say 100–200 kcal (approximately 400–800 kJ) per day — for very considerable differences in body weight and in body composition to occur. Thus a satisfactory energy intake ought to result from an energy expenditure of the recommended levels, and an examination of the variables which influence energy expenditure in the elderly would be useful. Some of these variables might be related to body build and body composition, and they will also include disease and disability.

One of the considerable difficulties in discussing nutrition in the elderly is the variability of the population. The range is in reality too extreme to examine in any satisfactory manner so that, initially, this discussion is mainly about 'elderly' people, as opposed to 'old' people, and covers the ages of approximately 60–75 years.

Body mass and body composition

Body mass frequently diminishes with aging. The lower body weight, by itself, will reduce the total energy expenditure and thus the intake of food. While there is often a remarkably low correlation between body weight and energy expenditure in groups of individuals, with values of the correlation coefficient around +0.4 (Durnin, 1973), it is probable that this relationship is much closer within an individual when he or she changes the body weight by moderate amounts. Thus, a man who weighs 70 kg when he is 40 years old and who weighs 65 kg when he is 65 years old may well have reduced his energy expenditure approximately proportionately in resting situations or when he is engaged in any more or less standardized activity — such as walking to catch a bus or a train, or digging the garden, or working. However, there is the added complication with aging that, outwith the resting state, physical activity may not be carried out in the same way at the age of 65 as it was at 40; walking may be slower, digging may involve longer rest pauses and be done less energetically, and so on. Therefore, theoretically, changes in body mass with aging may be accompanied by more than simply a proportionate change in energy expenditure.

Alterations in body mass with aging are not well documented. Most cross-sectional data show decreases in *height*, which may be as much as 5–7 cm for some groups, between 30 years and 70 years but which may be significantly affected by occupation and socio-economic class (Miall et al, 1967).

Alterations in *weight* seem more complex and differ between the sexes so that men may appear to have a slightly lower body weight at 65–70 years compared to that at 40 years whereas women frequently show an increasing body weight over this period. Much of the data is cross-sectional. In a study in Czechoslovakia on 170 normal men between 55–79 years of age (Table 28.1), Parizkova and Eiselt (1966) found a small decrease in the body weight of just over 2 kg in 'active' men at age 73 compared to age 60 but no change in weight between inactive men. In a more recent longitudinal study (Parizkova and Eiselt, 1980) on the same indiviuals followed after 16 years, they found some interesting results (Table 28.2), on weight — a loss of 1.7 kg, height — a loss of 1.5 cm, but of sitting height a loss of 2.6 cm — suggesting some unusual alterations in posture.

The Health and Nutrition Examination Survey (the HANES project: Abraham et al, 1979) in the US provides us with the largest number of measurements

Table 28.1 Changes in height and weight in Czecho-Slovak men (cross-sectional study) (Parizkova and Eiselt, 1966)

	Active		Inactive	
Age (y)	60	73	63	69
Weight (kg)	73.4	71.3	70.7	71.3
Height (cm)	170.8	169.7	168.9	168.9

Table 28.2 Changes in height and weight in Czecho-Slovak men (longitudinal study) (Parizkova and Eiselt, 1980)

			Difference
Age (y)	65	81	16
Weight (kg)	70.9	69.2	−1.7
Height (cm)	169.7	168.2	−1.5
Sitting height (cm)	88.8	86.2	−2.6

Table 28.3 Height and weight measurements by age — the Health and Nutritional Examination Survey USA 1971–1974 (Abraham et al, 1979) and UK (1981) data

	Age (y)	Height (cm)		Weight (kg)	
			UK		UK
Men	25–34	176.8	(175.1)	80.0	(74.0)
	45–54	175.0	(173.1)	79.5	(76.3)
	55–64	173.5	(170.8)	77.7	(74.1)
	65–74	170.9		74.5	
Women	25–34	162.8	(161.9)	63.6	(60.6)
	45–54	161.5	(160.2)	67.7	(64.3)
	55–64	159.5	(159.0)	67.7	(64.6)
	65–74	158.2		66.4	

on height and weight so far published (Table 28.3). The sample included between 600 and 1900 individuals in each decade between 25–34 years and 65–74 years, and is hopefully large enough to be reasonably representative.

In 1981, a random sample of 10 021 adults aged 16–64 years was measured for height and weight in the UK (OPCS — private communication). The number in each sub-group in the table is approximately 1000 individuals.

The results show changes in height which are more or less consistent between the two countries and between the sexes, but the changes in body weight differ between men in the USA and men in the UK, and also between men and women.

Although it is not certain what happens to skeletal mass, the density of the skeleton seems to decrease with aging. A cosniderable volume of published literature on the analyses of various parts of the skeleton suggests that there may be a fall in the mineral content of the skeleton of 8–15 per cent in men between the age of 50 and 75; for women, it seems to be much higher, about 18 to 30 per cent of a decrease between the same ages. Such alterations will affect the density of the fat-free mass of the body and will have an influence on the calculation of the fat component of the body if this is measured by the technique of densitometry (Durnin and Womersley, 1974).

The fat mass of the body has frequently been compared in groups of individuals of different ages, although virtually no truly representative data are available. Data obtained on heights and weights e.g. the HANES data in the USA or the OPCS data in the UK, cannot properly be extrapolated, by the use of a formula such as W/H^2, to give an estimate of fatness. In some recent investigations on more than 5000 men and 1000 women it is obvious that no height and weight index can eliminate the possibility of very considerable errors if it is used to estimate fatness (McKay et al, 1981).

Using measurements of fatness by densitometry on 103 men between 20 and 55 years old, Brozek (1952) found that although there had been an increase in total weight of about 6 kg, the fat mass had increased by 9 kg so that the fat free mass (FFM) had actually decreased during this time by about 3 kg, apparently the result of a reduction in muscle mass. In fact, the reduction in the FFM might have been even greater than the 3 kg since the increase in body fat of 9 kg would be accompanied by an addition to the FFM of perhaps 1–3 kg: when the body gets fatter, it is not only fat which is deposited but also there is an increase in the cellular elements of the adipose tissue, connective tissue and fluid.

Brozek thought that the decreased mass of muscle and increased fatness might have been caused by reduced physical activity. Whether reduced activity leads to fatness or vice versa is however a disputed question.

Other published work on cross-sectional data supports the probability that fat mass increases with aging, at least to some extent. Noppa et al (1979) studied Swedish women, Tzankoff and Norris (1977) measured US men, and their findings seem to demonstrate a fall in FFM (probably muscle) and an increase in fat mass with aging. Brozek also described a redistribution of fat, subcutaneous fat being deposited more on the trunk in the elderly than on the limbs, compared to younger people. It has also been found (Durnin and Womersley, 1974) that there is a change in the ratio of fat between the subcutaneous and the deeper, truncal areas with aging, more of the fat being in the deeper regions in older people.

Other functional characteristics alter with aging and may contribute indirectly to changes in energy expenditure. Larson (1978) has shown that independent of reduction in muscle mass, there are changes in the structure of skeleton muscle with aging. Type II fibres decrease in size and this is associated with a diminished strength of contraction even though the size of the total muscle may not have appreciably lessened.

The classical experiments of Dill (1961) on his own capacity for exercise throughout much of his adult life up to an age in the late 60's and the Swedish studies of Åstrand (1968) demonstrate clearly that there is a considerable fall in maximal exercise capacity, in cardiac output, in stroke volume, and in maximal heart rate with aging. Blood volume and total haemoglobin do not appear to change. Bengtsson et al (1978) have published comparable data on women.

The importance of these reductions as far as energy expenditure is concerned is that the stress of physical exercise is often very largely a function of its proportion of the maximal exercise capacity (Vo$_2$ max). That is, if the Vo$_2$ max is the equivalent of 15 kcal/min (63 kJ/min) then activity at a level of 7 kcal/min (29 kJ/min) is quite tolerable. If the Vo$_2$ max is 10 kcal/min (42 kJ/min) then an exercise at 7 kcal/min (29 kJ) would be quite stressful.

Therefore elderly people with markedly reduced Vo$_2$ max would be unlikely voluntarily to undertake any physical activity of more than rather light degree.

However, improvement in the ability to exercise can certainly still be accomplished in the elderly. A monograph published by WHO (Denolin et al, 1982) gives illustrations of what can be accomplished by training: 10–15 per cent increases in Vo$_2$ max by men between 65 and 69 years, increases of 20 per cent in vital capacity, improvements in lung diffusion, a lower systolic BP, and greater strength. There may also be a considerable increase in the release of some of the adrenal and pituitary hormones.

Digestion and absorption

Another of the changes in function which is commonly believed to occur in the elderly, relative malabsorption of foods, is potentially of some importance in nutrition. Good scientific evidence in favour of this is hard to come by. Southgate and Durnin (1970) measured, by chemical means and by bomb calorimetry, the total food eaten and the urine and faeces excreted by groups of young and elderly men and women. Table 28.4 summarises the results and shows no evidence of decreased efficiency of digestion and absorption with aging. However, Webster et al (1977) found minor degrees of impairment of fat absorption in old age.

Table 28.4 Digestibility of 'energy', protein, fat and pentosan (Southgate and Durnin, 1970)

Group	Energy	Protein	Fat	Pentosan
Young men	96.6	89.6	96.4	95.3
Elderly men	96.8	91.4	95.1	96.8
Young women	96.5	92.1	96.7	93.9
Elderly women	96.0	92.9	94.6	97.8

In the elderly, energy expenditure may be affected in several ways, the most important of which are: (1) via the BMR, (2) changes in the amount of physical activity, and (3) alterations in the efficiency of muscular activity and of movement.

Basal metabolic rate (BMR)

A reduction in BMR with aging is, superficially, a biological fact. All tables of BMR show metabolic rates, quoted as kcal (or kJ) per m² per unit time which show a progressive decrease from birth up to old age. For example, one of the best of these tables, those of Fleisch (1954) gives a BMR for a woman aged 40 as 34.9 kcal/m²/h and at age 70 it is 31.7 kcal/m²/h; the equivalent values for a man are 36.3 at age 40 and 33.8 at age 70.

However, these conclusions are based on cross-sectional studies, and the few longitudinal investigations, together with a more biologically searching approach to the problem, provide an alternative view. If elderly people have avoided the marked changes in body composition, with reduced muscle mass and increased fat mass, which usually occur as most of us get older, then BMR will not necessarily become lower. The studies of Tzankoff and Norris (1977, 1978), and indeed the data (with one exception) in the classical study of Benedict et al (1914), support this contention.

It may be concluded that most populations, and for most individuals within these populations, a reduction in BMR of about 10 per cent probably occurs between the age of young adulthood and about 60 years, and another 10 per cent of decline by 75 years.

Physical activity

The second factor which may reduce total daily energy expenditure in the elderly is the decline in the amount of physical activity. This is undoubtedly a factor of considerable — but variable — importance. The energy expenditure of an office worker, perhaps 2500 kcal (10.5 MJ)/day, compared to a factory worker at about 3000 kcal (12.6 MJ)/day, and an agricultural or forestry worker at 3500 kcal (14.5 MJ)/day demonstrates the very obvious influence of physical activity. Even within one occupation group, e.g. office workers, the difference between a man whose leisure time is more-or-less quite inactive (the 'norm' in our society) — and someone who enjoys walking and some form of active sports, can easily reach several hundred calories (up to 2000 kJ) per day. Most elderly people who have retired will automatically reduce their energy expenditure.

Work and leisure. Occupation alone, has probably become less important in the face of increasing mechanization. If a man is still at work at age 60, or 65, or 70, he will often be expending as much energy during his job as he did at age 25 or 30. In occupations where much physical effort is needed, as in some forms of agriculture, in forestry work, or in mining, aging, sometimes up to the mid-70's, may still have relatively little influence.

Physical activity in leisure time may be more important. Physically active leisure is a pursuit which seems to be on the increase. Jogging is a good example. What is lacking in the statistics of this leisure activity is its prevalence and age distribution. It probably still affects small numbers of the general population to any significant extent and there are relatively few elderly among them.

Fatness and activity. Fatness increases with aging and increasing fatness could well have an influence in decreasing physical activity. Only limited information is available on this but Table 28.5 shows some data collected on about 284 men and 208 women, working in various occupations, and aged 45 to 70 years (Durnin, 1967). Less time is spent in physical activity as body fat increases but since most of the activity of the men is necessitated by the occupation, either the more obese men tended to gravitate to lighter jobs or else the physical activity of the work helped to prevent the addition of much extra fat.

Table 28.5 Duration (min/day) of moderate physical activity related to body build in men and women over 45 years of age (Durnin, 1967)

Body build	Men		Women
	Total	At work	
'Thin'	152	130	80
Average	112	83	67
'Mildly obese'	88	68	33

Similar data was obtained in the Michigan study of Montoye et al (1977).

Activity and disease. Another feature of aging which may restrict physical activity is the increased liability to suffer from one or more of the degenerative diseases of the circulatory and respiratory systems, and particularly of the bones and joints.

The proportion of elderly people who suffer from joint disabilities sufficient to incapacitate or inhibit movement is unknown and probably varies considerably for different countries, climates, occupations, etc. However, some very informative data has been published recently in the US (Maurer, 1979) in a report by the Department of Health, Education and Welfare on 'Basic Data on Arthritis'. Table 28.6 shows the

Table 28.6 Percentage of 'normal' men and women related to arthritis of knees, hips and sacro-iliac joints (from: Basic Data on Arthritis, Mauser, 1979)

Age (y)	Knees		Hips		S–I joints	
	M	F	M	F	M	F
35–44	98	98	100	—	99	—
55–64	92	89	97	96	96	99
65–74	86	75	94	96	98	98

'normal' population, the remainder being 'sufferers'. Even then never more than 1 per cent of the group had a 'severe' grade of the condition. The possibility arises, therefore, that degenerative arthritic changes may not be such an important factor for most people in inhibiting physical activity.

Physical activity in the elderly is thus exposed to the sort of variation found in a younger group of reasonably healthy people, but the variation may be skewed to the lower end of the range because of those elderly people who suffer disability, loss of muscle tone, and increasing fatness.

Mechanical efficiency. The third factor, after BMR and physical activity, which may influence energy expenditure is the reduction in the mechanical efficiency of the limbs, and in the control of balance, associated with aging (see e.g. Norris et al, 1955; Durnin and Mikulicic, 1956; Hellon et al, 1956). A fairly typical set of results is shown in Table 28.7. Two groups, each of 12 men, one group aged 20–30 years and the other 55–67, were compared. All were unskilled labourers working the building industry. They performed two grades of standardized exercise involving arm work, and walked at 2 levels of standard exercise on the treadmill. The experiment was designed in the form of a Latin square to minimize the effects of fatigue and of other uncontrollable variables. There were no significant differences in energy expenditure in either of the 2 arm exercises between the young and elderly men, although the exercises involved moderate and moderately-heavy exertion. In the walking exercises, the older men expended 17 per cent more in the lighter exercise and 21 per cent more at the heavier work load.

Table 28.7 Energy expenditure (kcal/min) of young and elderly men during standardized exercise

Exercise	Elderly men	Young men
Arm ergometer 1	4.36	4.12
Arm ergometer 2	5.89	5.82
Treadmill 1	6.68	5.72
Treadmill 2	8.50	7.04

Thus, the general conclusion of the effects of these 3 factors on energy expenditure — i.e. BMR, physical activity, and mechanical efficiency – is somewhat indefinite because of the complexity of the problem.

Two other relevant areas should be mentioned. *Firstly*, increasing unemployment involving both the developed and the developing countries. It may be that for the unemployed, the difference in the energy expenditure of elderly and young people will diminish. And *secondly*, this whole problem has been discussed without

reference to the housewife. Her energy expenditure starts to decrease at age 45–50, and falls proportionally more than that of a man up to 70 years or so.

Published reports on energy expenditure

The foregoing account is partly a hypothesis based on a certain amount of scientifically collected data. It would be interesting to compare the theory with actual measurements of energy expenditure in elderly people.

How difficult it is! There appear to have been no studies published since 1970 on the energy expenditure of either elderly men or elderly women.

Prior to 1970, various groups of elderly people were studied (c.f. Durnin, 1978). The energy expenditures of crofters (peasant farmers) living in a harsh environment in the highlands of Scotland, of farmers in moderately rich agricultural land in Central Scotland, of steel workers, factory workers, forestry workers (all living and working in the West of Scotland), of some elderly retired men, and of some Swiss peasants are shown in Table 28.8. These men were in their sixties and seventies.

Table 28.8 Levels of daily energy expenditure of elderly men (kcal/day)

	Mean	Minimum	Maximum
Retired	2330	1750	2810
Factory workers	2840	2180	3710
Crofters	2920	2360	3350
Steel workers	3280	2600	3960
Farmers	3500	2450	4670
Forestry workers	3670	2860	4600
Swiss peasants	3530	2210	5000

The mean values, and the ranges between the minimum and the maximum, are very interesting. One can only assume that they are not completely representative of elderly people – although there seemed no bias in the selection of subjects from the particular population — because they could all easily have been obtained on young populations. Even the energy expenditure of the elderly retired men is not very much lower than that found in many young office workers. Some of the individual results are quite remarkable; almost 4000 kcal (16.7 MJ)/day by a farmer and 5000 kcal (21 MJ)/day by a Swiss peasant. In all of these studies food intake was also measured and the mean values were very similar for both energy intake and energy expenditure.

Table 28.9 shows data on energy expenditure obtained by Wirths (1963) on 33 elderly men and 48 women working in a variety of jobs in Germany. Again, the energy values seem comparatively high. The second

Table 28.9 Daily energy expenditures (kcal/day) of elderly men and women in Germany and influence of body weight (Wirths, 1963)

	Men		Women	
Age				
under 70		3410		2960
71 to 75		2990		2860
		Energy		Energy
Body wt (kg)	Total	at work	Total	at work
below 50	2850	1750	2700	1610
51 to 60	2970	1700	2830	1640
61 to 70	3220	1860	2790	1520
71 to 80	2820	1300	2810	1450
81 to 90	2750	1110	2550	1070
over 90	2200	370	2450	880

Table 28.11 Recommended daily intakes of energy and nutrients for elderly people in the UK (DHSS, 1978)

	Men		Women	
	65 to 74	75+	55 to 74	75+
Energy				
(kcal)	2400	2150	1900	1680
(MJ)	10.0	9.0	8.0	7.0
Protein (g)	60	54	47	42
Thiamine (mg)	1.0	0.9	0.8	0.7
Riboflavine (mg)	1.6	1.6	1.3	1.3
Nicotinic Acid				
(mg equivalents)	18	18	15	15
Ascorbic Acid (mg)	30	30	30	30
Vitamin A				
(ug retinol equivalents)	750	750	750	750
Vitamin D				
(ug cholecalciferol)	*	*	*	*
Calcium (mg)	500	500	500	500
Iron (mg)	10	10	10	10

* If inadequate exposure to sunlight is suspected, a supplement of 10 mg is recommended.

part of the table gives an interesting illustration of the influence of body weight on these values; there is an increase with body weights up to 70 kg in the men and then a steady decline — presumably due to increasing obesity. The women have a much more extended 'plateau', from a weight of 51 up to 80 kg, suggesting yet another sign of the quite different meaning of moderate obesity in men (where it is abnormal) and in women (where it is biologically normal).

Table 28.10 gives the much smaller amount of data available on women. One would be compelled to repeat that again the Swiss peasants have extraordinary high levels. Again, food intake measurements were also measured and were similar to the energy expenditures.

Table 28.10 Levels of daily energy expenditure of elderly women (kcal/day)

	Mean	Minimum	Maximum
Women (60–69) Living alone	1990	1490	2410
Women (54–66) with varying sized families	2130	1510	2740
Swiss peasants	2890	2200	3860

RECOMMENDED INTAKES OF NUTRIENTS

There are many national and international standards of 'requirements' or 'recommended' intakes for populations. The standard 'international' report on energy and protein requirements is that from FAO/WHO (1973). The currently recommended values for the UK are contained in Report 120 on Public Health and Medical Subjects from the Department of Health and Social Security (1979). The recommended intakes for elderly people in the UK are extracted from this report and given in Table 28.11. The values for energy are similar to the published values of FAO/WHO for elderly men, but the UK values for elderly women are higher than the international standards and indeed higher than most other national standards.

Diet surveys, 'nutritional status' and malnutrition
The commonest way by which populations are assessed in relation to the adequacy of their nutritional status is by measuring the intake of energy and nutrients provided by their normal diet. In considering the nutrition of elderly people, it is especially necessary that dietary studies and biochemical and clinical assessments are carried out in a careful, critical, scientific fashion, with the use of control groups where necessary. Such care often makes experiments difficult but it is scientifically unjustifiable to do otherwise, since conclusions from inadequately controlled studies may be misleading and may sometimes inhibit progress. As well as to dietary studies, these criticisms apply particularly to the interpretation of clinical signs of malnutrition, biochemical analyses of serum, etc., and 'malabsorption syndromes'.

Survey methods
Exton-Smith (1982) has written an excellent account of the methods and importance of dietary surveys among the elderly. He describes the more note-worthy objectives as follows: (1) To assess the nutritional status of the elderly population and to ascertain to what extent this differs from that of younger adults. (2) To identify malnutrition and the factors involved in its causation. (3) To investigate the effects of aging in nutritional

status and on nutritional requirements in old age. (4) To formulate recommendations for dietary allowances in old age. (5) To ascertain the range of 'normal' biochemical and haematological values in old age with particular relevance to those related to nutrition. (6) To investigate the effects of nutrition on morbidity and mortality in the elderly and in particular to investigate the role of nutritional factors in the aetiology of specific diseases, for example, osteoporosis and ischemic heart disease. (7) To determine whether the health of the elderly can be improved by dietary modifications.

Both cross-sectional and longitudinal surveys can become very biased by uncontrollable variables, (e.g. large secular changes, sociocultural developments, morbidity and mortality influences), with the result that interpretation of the data requires great care and considerable qualification. Method also may produce extremely biased results. In general, the only data examined in this chapter have been obtained by weighing the food eaten or measuring it by 'household measures', and little emphasis has been placed on information obtained by questionnaire.

Macleod and her colleagues (Macleod, 1970) have carried out dietary studies on elderly people of an uncommon and valuable kind since the original sample was a random one from the whole population over 65 years in the district (although, with refusals and rejections, the final group can, naturally, no longer be completely random). However, the limitations of dietary studies on their own are well illustrated by Macleod's excellently gathered results. Mention is made of the apparently inadequate nutrient and energy intakes of some of these elderly individuals but no other evidence is provided of the presence of malnutrition. Similarly, Lonergan et al (1975) suggest that low intakes of energy and nutrients were associated with mental illness in women and deafness and severe dyspnoea in men, but not that the nutritional factors were causative.

Low intakes of energy (perhaps less that 1500 kcal per day) and of nutrients in individuals in our Western 'developed' societies are often difficult to explain but do not necessarily indicate undernutrition. For example in a survey on 74 dentists and their wives, mostly aged between 30 and 50 years, in the USA, Cheraskin et al (1967) found that 10 out of 41 of the men and 23 out of the 33 women were eating less than 2000 kcal per day (8.4 MJ) of energy and nine of the women consumed less than 1400 kcal per day (5.9 MJ).

The low intakes of some of the elderly individuals in the UK is considered in more detail below.

There is need for research in depth into such individuals so that the real significance of low nutrient intakes can be assessed.

At present with our limited knowledge of the extent of variability between healthy individuals in their energy and nutrient intakes, it is not justifiable to equate these intakes with 'nutritional status', and they should probably be utilised solely as indicators of possible malnutrition.

There is much evidence to suggest that dietary surveys should always, if at all possible, be done on individuals and not on families or households. Marr (1971) has written an excellent and exhaustive review of 'individual diet studies'. Where family studies are used to extract data which can be applied to individuals within the family, deductions may be difficult and can sometimes lead to quite large errors (Buzina, 1968).

Prevalence of malnutrition

The prevalence of malnutrition in the elderly community of developed countries is a subject where extremes of viewpoint are held. Thus Taylor (1968) in the UK and the report of the Citizens' Board of Inquiry into Hunger and Malnutrition in the United States (1968) imply that malnutrition is a widespread problem in the elderly. Taylor particularly states that 'classic standard clinical signs of vitamin deficiencies (are) found very commonly in elderly people in Britain and elsewhere . . .'. On the other hand, in a survey in the UK (Department of Health and Social Security, 1970, 1972) the nutritional disability which accounted for almost half of the small total number of 'malnourished' individuals was obesity — hardly a strong indication that an inadequate intake of nutrients was a common phenomenon.

In a follow-up to this survey (Department of Health and Social Security, 1979), only 6 per cent of the men and 5 per cent of the women under 80 years were described as 'undernourished'.

In the USA, preliminary analyses of the first HANES survey (1975) – i.e. the large-scale Health and Nutrition Examination Survey – showed that clinical signs of nutrient deficiency were uncommon in the elderly.

Therefore, there seems some uncertainty whether there is much relationship between the prevalence of clinical signs of nutritional deficiency and the actual intake of energy and nutrients, which is often low.

Several surveys have been carried out, using reasonably accurate methodology, on the dietary intake of elderly people in the UK, Holland, Sweden and the USA. The classical studies in California by Morgan and her colleagues (Gillum and Morgan, 1955; Gillum et al, 1955a, b, c; Morgan et al, 1955a, b) showed that although the intake of energy and nutrients fell with increasing age, when these results were expressed as units per kg body weight, there was an insignificant decrease with ageing (Table 28.12). The economic status of the population covered the entire spectrum and there was no sign that aging, *per se*, in this group, exerted a deleterious influence on nutritional intake.

Apart from a general reduction in all nutrients, there

Table 28.12 Body weight and mean daily nutrient intakes of elderly Californians (Morgan et al, 1955)

	Male			Female		
	55 to 64	65 to 74	75+	55 to 64	65 to 74	75+
'n'	73	71	31	105	68	36
Wt (kg)	74	71	69	66	65	61
Protein (g)	92	71	69	66	65	61
Protein (g/kg)	1.2	1.1	1.1	0.9	1.0	0.8
Fat (g)	107	93	89	73	74	58
% energy from fat	38	38	37	38	37	36
CHO (g)	284	267	257	210	208	187
kcal	2570	2260	2190	1760	1760	1485
kcal/kg	34	32	32	26	27	25
Iron (mg)	16	14	14	11	11	9
Iron (mg/kg)	0.21	0.19	0.20	0.17	0.17	0.15

were few changes of nutritional significance in this Californian population after a 14 year follow-up (Steincamp et al, 1965). In the UK, the results obtained by Lonergan (1971) on energy intake of elderly men were similar to those of the Californian men. She weighed the food eaten during two consecutive days by 14 men, mean age 70 years, and 26 women, mean age 69 years, living in Edinburgh. The mean energy intake of the men was 2250 kcal per day (9.4 MJ) and for the women 1510 kcal per day (6.2 MJ). The intake of energy and of the nutrients for some of the individuals, especially the women, was low, although no mention is made of signs of clinical malnutrition in their subjects.

Essentially similar results on a much larger population – 212 men and 263 women, aged 62–90 years – were found by the same group working in Edinburgh (Lonegan et al, 1975). Roughly comparable data were obtained by Macleod et al (1974) in the West of Scotland on elderly men and women living at home, although 31 out of 264 subjects had notably low intakes of either protein or energy. In this group, mostly women, the mean energy intake was between 1200 and 1300 kcal/day, and at these levels there would seem to be a real danger of eventual nutritional deficiency developing.

In a study on a random sample of 100 men and women receiving 'meals-on-wheels' in Portsmouth, England, Davies and Holdsworth (1978) found some rather unusual energy intakes. Ten men aged between 65–74 had 2160 kcal (9.0 MJ)/day and 16 men aged over 75 consumed the same quantity — 2150 kcal (9.0 MJ)/day. Comparable results on women showed an intake of 1600 kcal (6.7 MJ)/day by 24 women aged 65–74 and 1750 kcal (7.3 MJ)/day by 50 women over 75. These unexpected results were not commented upon by the authors. Intakes of protein, calcium, iron, riboflavin, ascorbic acid and cholecalciferol were all above, or about equal to, the recommended levels.

Vir and Love (1979) surveyed groups of men and women over 65 years of age and living in long-stay

geriatric wards, in residential institutions, or at home, all of them in Belfast, Northern Ireland. As well as the dietary investigation, clinical examinations, and biochemical analyses of albumin, calcium, iron, folate, vitamin B_{12}, ascorbic acid, thiamin, riboflavin, vitamins B_6, D and A, and alkaline phosphatase were done on blood samples. As might be expected, there was much variability in intakes of energy and nutrients and in the biochemical data. In general, most of the mean results for energy and protein were reasonable but the authors thought the intakes most deficient were of potassium, magnesium, vitamin D, and vitamin B_6. Signs of clinical deficiency were rare. However, biochemical levels of many of the minerals and vitamins were considered to indicate deficiency and there is a recommendation that desirable intakes of some minerals and many of the vitamins should be increased.

A very comprehensive investigation of 17 men and 20 women, aged 67 years and living in Dalby, Sweden, was undertaken by Borgstrom et al (1979). Intakes of energy, protein, calcium, iron, vitamin B_{12} and folate seemed adequate, but potassium, magnesium and zinc were present in the diet in lower quantities than are recommended.

In the United States, a summary of some of the dietary studies on older Americans has been given by O'Hanlon and Kohrs (1978). Most of these studies were done either prior to 1970 (and therefore perhaps not too relevant now) or by a 24 hour recall method which, as a scientific tool for research, is of far too uncertain accuracy to be acceptable. Most of the more reliable data appear to indicate a comparative absence of deficiences.

An extension to this type of review (Bowman and Rosenberg, 1982) has made some analyses of a study on 100 men and women in Oregon (Yearick et al, 1980) and also of some of the HANES data. Again, the conclusion seems to be that calcium, perhaps iron, and the vitamin B group are most likely to be deficient but that overt clinical signs of malnutrition are uncommon. The authors consider that 'sub-clinical' nutrient deficiency, with symptoms of fatigue, irritability, loss of appetite, anxiety etc. may be much more prevalent. However, thare is remarkably little evidence in the nutritional literature in support of a marked improvement in these symptoms with nutrient supplementation.

Dietary intakes of 270 free living residents of the Albuquerque area, New Mexico were assessed by Garry et al, (1982). Most of them were between the ages of 65–75 years. Intakes of energy were 2170 kcal/day for the men and 1650 kcal/day for the women. Dietary intakes of the nutrients were considered to be adequate, with the possible exception of vitamin D and calcium in the women (raw data are not given for most nutrients so it is difficult to form an independent opinion). Clinical examination revealed no signs of malnutrition.

Problems in assessing whether malnutrition is present
The principal problem in diagnosing malnutrition is that it becomes obvious only when clinical signs appear, and this may occur at a comparatively late stage of the process. It is noteworthy that in most surveys on the elderly, when malnutrition might be expected in at least a small proportion of the population, clinical signs of malnutrition are rarely present. The presumption is made therefore that, excluding frank signs of malnutrition, the possibility of its presence may be deduced from either (1) low intakes of energy and nutrients in the diet or (2) low levels of the relevant nutrients in the blood.

Both of these assumptions produce their own problems. Firstly, in relation to the dietary intake, the method of measuring this needs to produce reliable and reproducible results. Unforunately few published accounts of measurements of the food intake of elderly people satisfy these criteria. Very many of these studies employ a 24 hour recall technique — a notoriously unsatisfactory method, the accuracy of which is seldom tested and is almost infinitely variable depending on the skill and experience of the investigator, the type of individual being measured and the sort of diet eaten – but even more laborious and more stringent methods may not provide accurate data. However, undoubtedly the first requirement is to obtain as valid information as possible, in a quantative sense, of the intake of energy and of nutrients of the appropriate population.

Also, since the variability found in an elderly population is likely to be considerable, the technique must be suitable for obtaining reliable data on each individual and not simply reasonably satisfactory for the whole group. A mean intake for a group which appears acceptable has limited value if 20 per cent of the population is deficient but the individual data must be sufficiently accurate for there to be reasonable confidence in the validity of the finding.

Secondly, the low values in the biochemical findings in the blood are also, like the dietary data, not necessarily related to the development of malnutrition.

In this potentially important context there is a great need to acquire more definitive information. One approach might be to examine much more carefully any improvement in signs or symptoms in elderly people (related to 'sub-clinical' malnutrition) when the nutritional state of the patient is bettered, either by changing the diet or giving supplements. Well-controlled prospective studies are desperately needed in this field.

At the present juncture, it is unwise to place too much reliance on either dietary or biochemical findings, but the benefit of the doubt ought to be given to the elderly. A suspicion of malnutrition, reasonably based, should be adequate justification for intervention.

Protein
All of the studies quoted thus far in this chapter have shown intakes of protein in the diets of elderly people which would almost always be adequate for each individual. Even on relatively low energy intakes, the protein content of the diet will be adequate, as long as energy imbalance is not present. Marked deficiency of energy intake seems seldom to occur — presumably because low energy intakes are counterbalanced by a reduced BMR and concomitantly low activity levels. However, if, perhaps for short periods, the elderly person is receiving less food energy than he is expending, then the protein in the diet will be used as an energy source and protein deficiency may ensue, in spite of what may appear a superficially adequate intake of protein. This seems a rare situation.

Opinions on protein requirements in general, and specifically in relation to the elderly, differ considerably. Whether protein intake is related to tissue degeneration with aging is also uncertain.

Widdowson and Kennedy (1952) showed that rats, whether fed initially on high or on low nutritional planes and then allowed to eat, *ad lib*, identical food for the rest of their lives, lost weight as they became elderly and that the weight loss included the fat-free mass in both groups. Therefore apparently a negative nitrogen balance was occurring in these rats in spite of an unrestricted energy intake and it is at least possible that a similar situation exists in elderly people. Loss of the fat-free mass of the body may not be a preventable phenomenon, although the influence of physical activity is an undetermined factor.

Nitrogen balance studies, in general, do not show significant differences between young and elderly people, though there are some discrepancies. Thus, Swendseid and Tuttle (1961) considered that there was an indication that men over 50 years required more nitrogen and, in particular, more methionine and lysine than younger men. On the other hand, Horwitt (1953),

Schulze (1954) and Watkin (1964) on various diets, found nitrogen balances at levels ranging from as low as 0.35 g protein per kg, with no differences between young and old subjects.

Tuttle and colleagues (1957) considered that their male subjects aged 52 to 68 had higher requirements than younger men for some of the essential amino-acids. However, similar experiments by Watts and co-workers (1964) did not demonstrate this extra need. Other studies (Roberts et al, 1948; Albanese et al, 1957) all seemed to indicate that protein requirements are no different in the elderly than in young adults.

More recent studies by Cheng et al (1978) and by Zanni et al (1979) show protein requirements to be either similar to those of a control group of young adults or of a level comparable to the supposed young adult recommendation.

Munro (1972), on the basis of the very few nitrogen balance studies carried out on the elderly, has calculated that protein requirements are about 0.6 g/kg per day, which corresponds to an intake of 40 g of protein or less per day. This agrees with the findings of Zanni et al (1979).

In spite of the fact that there is argument about whether this quantity is adequate (Uauy et al, 1978; Gersovitz et al, 1982), the general statement made above still remains true — that protein deficiency is an unusual phenomenon in the elderly.

Mitchell and Lipschitz (1982) point out that a possible explanation for alterations in the dietary protein needs of the elderly may be related to changes in whole-body protein metabolism. The rate of whole-body protein turnover has been shown to decline with age. There is also redistribution of protein metabolism found in the elderly, with muscle making a smaller contribution to whole body protein synthesis and breakdown. The effect of these changes in muscle and whole-body protein metabolism on the ability of the elderly to adapt to periods of stress combined with low protein intake is not known.

Calcium

The exact role of calcium in the diet of elderly people, in relation to loss of bone mass and the increased risk of fracture, has been the subject of considerable controversy. Several excellent review papers have been published recently. The views, postulated for many years by Nordin and his colleagues and reviewed by them in 1979 (Nordin et al, 1979) that dietary intakes of calcium are often low especially in women, and that this may have a significant influence on the development of osteoporosis, have received increasing support. Heaney et al (1978) have calculated bone loss to be about 1.5 per cent per year in normal post-menopausal women on calcium intakes of 500 mg/day. Avioli (1977, 1981)

considers the US Recommended Allowance of 800 mg/day to be potentially inadequate and suggests that bone loss may begin in women as early as in the second and third decade of life. Some interesting brief reviews in this general area were published in a symposium in Federation Proceedings (Draper, 1981).

Two excellent and extremely comprehensive reviews on calcium, particularly related to the elderly, were published in 1982. Allen (1982) examined calcium availability and absorption in a basic exhaustive account, dealing with techniques of calcium balance, the forms in which calcium is absorbed and the proportion of dietary calcium likely to be absorbed in different circumstances (infancy, adulthood, pregnancy and lactation, the elderly), the effects of other dietary constituents (fibre, protein, fat, alcohol, vitamin D, phosphorus), and the influence of disease and surgery. It is concluded that several of the factors commonly thought to affect calcium absorption have, in fact, either no effect or a relatively unimportant one; these include phosphorus, protein, oxalate, and phytate. In contrast, there may be concern about possible deleterious effects of fibre on calcium balance.

The second review (Heaney et al, 1982) can also be confidently recommended. The authors consider that it is well established that calcium absorption decreases with aging (they examine the physiological reasons for this). Like Allen (1982) they also attempt to determine the importance of phosphorus, protein, fibre, drugs, and alcohol which might also form part of the intake of a patient. The general role of the menopause, illness, and exercise is also analysed.

They conclude that the requirement for calcium in the elderly remains controversial, although more recent evidence indicates the requirement may be higher than previously thought. This evidence comes from several sources and can be summarized briefly as follows. Studies performed in actual elderly subjects (as contrasted with young adults) have uniformly revealed mean intake requirements for calcium balance above the current RDA for the United States (and hence for the UK allowances higher still). Further, calcium supplementation in the elderly has produced some degree of slowing of age-related bone loss, calcium balance improvement, or decrease in fracture prevalence. Essentially all published reports agree in these respects.

Controversy continues to surround this issue principally because most of the World's population ingests less calcium than the RDA for the US and is nevertheless manifestly able to grow and form a skeleton satisfactory for ordinary adult function. This apparent contradiction appears to be explained by several recent observations. First, calcium absorption efficiency declines with age, and hence an intake adequate to grow a skeleton may not be adequate to maintain it. Second, there are now recognized to be important differences between lesser developed countries and industrialized nations which make comparison of calcium intake requirements hazardous. These differences include lower protein intakes and heavier mechanical loading in lesser developed countries, both of which favour calcium retention. Additionally, ethnic differences between populations in lesser developed countries and industrialized nations (e.g. larger skeletons in African Blacks and their descendents) imply a genetic basis for differences in efficiency of calcium utilization. Third, only recently have we began to realize that all persons lose bone with age and that peak bone mass achieved at 30–35 is an important determinant of fracture risk 40 or more years later. Thus, since bone mass normally continues to increase until age 30 to 35, an intake found to be sufficient to maintain zero balance in young adults can no longer be considered to provide adequate nutrition. Some degree of positive balance, as during the years of linear growth, is the criterion of adequacy until age 30 to 35. Current knowledge does not permit us to define either what that degree of positive balance ought to be, or the extent to which peak adult bone mass can be influenced by calcium intake in the early adult years.

This paper summarizes the situation as follows:

The average elderly person is in negative calcium balance and accordingly is losing bone mass. While factors such as decreased mechanical loading of the skeleton undoubtedly figure in this age-related loss, a growing body of evidence suggests that inadequate calcium intake may contribute to this loss. On any given day, men and women in the USA 65 years of age or older ingest about 600 and 480 mg calcium respectively. Calcium intake in the elderly is less than in the young, and reduced absorption efficiency further lowers effective intake. Additionally, other nutrients such as protein and fiber, taken in excess, effectively increase the calcium requirement. Estrogen withdrawal at menopause leads to a decrease in intestinal calcium absorption efficiency and in renal calcium conservation, both effects equivalent to an effective increase in calcium intake requirement.

Thus it is not surprising that all studies of mean requirements for zero balance performed in elderly subjects have yielded values above the current RDA for the USA. The available evidence thus suggests that the RDA for adults should surely not be lowered below its current level (800 mg), but that, instead, it ought to be raised. It is not possible to say with certainty to exactly what level, but available evidence is compatible with allowances of at least 1200 to 1500 mg/day.

Further, the evidence indicates that the mean requirement ought to be thought of as a complex function of age, sex, absorption efficiency, intake of protein, fiber and probably other nutrients, estrogen status and mechanical loading. Extensive experience with calcium supplements indicates that daily intakes up to at least 2.5 g of elemental calcium are quite safe in all persons except for certain subsets of the population uncommon among the elderly (e.g. those with sarcoidosis, active tuberculosis, or other absorptive hypercalciuric syndromes).

At the same time it must be said that osteoporosis is a complex, multifactorial disorder, and that factors unrelated to calcium nutrition undoubtedly play important, even dominant roles in many — perhaps most — osteoporotics. The available evidence, taken together, does not indicate that raising calcium intake will abolish the problem of osteoporosis. It does indicate, however, that calcium nutrition is considerably more important in the genesis of osteoporosis than has been commonly thought for the past 35 years. The full extent of that importance, in both pathogenesis and prophylaxis, remains to be elucidated. In the meanwhile we believe that the balance of risks and benefits involved in a general increase in calcium intake clearly favours some degree of upward adjustment of both the RDA and some change of calcium fortification policies for basic food stuffs.

Iron, copper and zinc

The recommended intakes of these minerals depend upon surveys of the levels in the diets of apparently healthy men and women, and also on balance studies. Balance studies of any nutrient are notoriously difficult to carry out, usually because of the necessity for long-term, well-controlled investigations, and also because of the difficulty in measuring precisely enough the losses in hair, sweat, nails etc. Turnland et al (1981), in a study of zinc, copper and iron balance in elderly men, have discussed some of these problems, and have concluded that recommended intakes of 15 mg/day of zinc and 2–3 mg/day of copper are adequate. On intakes of 10 mg/day of iron, most of their subjects were in negative balances but the authors do not consider this definitive enough, in the light of the methodological problems, to suggest that this level of intake is too low. It is also well known that the absorption of iron from the diet is a complex phenomenon depending on the source of the iron (Hallberg and Bjorn-Rasmussen, 1972) and on the iron stores and needs of the body (Heinrich, 1975). Iron storage in the liver does not seem to vary between young and elderly people (Charlton et al, 1970; Celada et al, 1980).

In any case, the problems about eating a diet containing large quantities of iron should be taken into account. It is unrealistic to expect elderly people — indeed even young people — to eat foods which will provide much more than 10–12 mg/day. It is often expensive to do so, because of the nature of foods rich in iron, and the selection of these foods makes it unlikely to occur in the normal dietary of many elderly people. Supplementation may need to be considered if such high intakes are thought desirable, but the problems then become more pharmacological than nutritional. On the whole, there seems little evidence that iron deficiency is other than an uncommon phenomenon on dietary intakes of even less than 10 mg/day.

Zinc in an average adult diet contains about 10–15 mg (Sanstead et al, 1967; Schröeder et al, 1967) and the effective absorption is believed to be about half of that (Underwood, 1971). It is quite probable that the diets of many elderly people contain less than the recommended allowance of 10–15 mg and it is equally possible that zinc, and other trace elements, may have importance in the nutritional state of elderly people. However, at the present time, there does not appear to be much convincing evidence that malnutrition, as a consequence of inadequate dietary intake of zinc, is a major problem in the elderly, and specific advice about diet in relation to zinc or the giving of zinc supplements is probably rarely required.

Copper can be assessed in a similar manner to zinc. It is an essential element for the body, it is present in certain foodstuffs, but its inadequacy seems to be rare and specific advice about its intake is probably unnecessary.

Two very extensive reports on very large numbers of the population in the USA are relevant. One of these (National Centre for Health Statistics, 1982a) deals with various relationships between diet and iron status. The other (National Centre for Health Statistics, 1982b) presents descriptive data on, among other things, diet and serum iron, total iron-binding capacity, transferrin saturation, serum zinc and serum copper. Similar data on the elderly populations of European countries would be most instructive.

Vitamins

The vitamins which are likely to be present in inadequate amounts in the diets of elderly people are some of the B group, vitamin C and vitamin D.

Many studies have attempted to assess both dietary intakes and blood levels of these vitamins with, on occasion, some health parameters which might be related to them (Weber et al, 1973; Harrill and Cervone, 1977; Vir and Love, 1977; Baker et al, 1979; Rutishauser et al, 1979; Fidanza and Losito, 1981; Wyse and Hansen, 1981; Goodwin and Hunt, 1982).

While some of the implications of these findings are considered in more detail later in this chapter, in the context of the DHSS study in the UK (1979), it can be said now that the picture seems very unclear. Incontrovertible evidence that deficiency of any of the vitamins in the diet causes ill health in the elderly is almost uniformly absent from the literature nor is there evidence of a marked response if supplements are given or the diet altered, e.g. Schorah et al (1981). On the basis of low levels in the plasma and in leucocyte vitamin C of 94 elderly 'long-term' institutionalized elderly people in Leeds, England, supplements were given to some of them in a randomized double-blind trial using placebos as well. Blood levels of the vitamin increased considerably after 2 months accompanied by significant increases in body weight for those receiving the supplement — but of only 0.4 kg, which, at least over that

period, can hardly be regarded as of much importance. There were also small improvements indicated by reductions in purpura and petechial haemorrhages, but there were no benefits in altered mood or mobility.

In the light of this the following conclusions may be justified. Firstly, that it is probably difficult, time-consuming, and expensive to demonstrate clearly, in individual patients, that low dietary intake and low blood levels are accompanied by specific signs of ill health. Secondly, there might therefore be a persuasive case for providing or advising routine vitamin supplements for most old people, i.e. for almost all people over the age of 75. Multi-vitamin capsules are relatively cheap and are almost entirely innocuous should they prove unnecessary.

Fibre

The role of fibre in the diet of elderly people is that of a mixed blessing. In preventing constipation it is likely to be beneficial. On the other hand, moderate amounts of fibre in the diet will interfere with the digestion and absorption of other nutrients — fats, proteins, calcium (Southgate and Durnin, 1970) — and in situations where the intake of these nutrients is marginally adequate, it is possible that long-term disadvantages may arise for the individual. Each case will have to be weighed-up; in general, the benefits are likely to outweigh the drawbacks and diets containing fruit, vegetables and wholemeal bread should be recommended.

Obesity

Obesity is supposedly relatively common in some elderly populations, especially in women (Borgstrom et al, 1979; DHSS, 1979; Kohrs et al, 1980; Clarke et al, 1981). However, its importance in the elderly is not always easy to distinguish. It may not be closely linked, as it is in younger adults, with hypertension and diabetes (DHSS, 1979) and its significance may be mainly related to its mechanical disadvantages — i.e. as a factor in osteoarthritis, in general mobility, in skin disorders, lung conditions, etc. If no obvious related disabilities are present, advice about its treatment may be unnecessary.

Treating the elderly obese may also be inadvisable since in order to produce an important weight loss, a low food intake may be required during several months with the concomitant danger of producing a dietary deficiency in one of the nutrients. If at all possible, treatment of the elderly obese should be oriented towards increasing energy expenditure by encouraging more physical activity together with only modest reductions in diet — cutting down on fats and fatty foods. Only in situations of very considerable inconvenience to the patient or to the persons caring for the elderly should much stress be laid on large reductions on food intake.

UK studies on nutrition of the elderly — Department of Health and Social Security

The most informative picture of the general state of nutrition of elderly people in the United Kingdom, in relation to energy and to the important nutrients, comes from three reports issued by the Department of Health and Social Security.

The first report by the Panel on Nutrition of the Elderly in the UK (1970) was concerned with elderly people living in their own homes. The report included studies of food intake, evidence from consultant physicians to geriatric departments of hospitals, and other specialized reports, as, for example, on osteomalacia and osteoporosis, iron-deficiency anaemia, deficiences of folate and B_{12}, of vitamins, and of protein. The panel concluded that there was no doubt that some elderly people were malnourished but the number was probably small. A much larger group might have been suffering from subclinical malnutrition but the evidence was still insufficient.

Probably the largest study on the nutrition of elderly people was published by the Department of Health and Social Security (1972). This was a comprehensive survey carried out in 1967 and 1968 of people aged 65 and over in the UK living alone, or with spouses, relatives or friends, but not in institutions.

Few such studies have been carried out. A large-scale study of elderly people was made in two areas of Holland (de Wijn et al, 1979) but it was restricted to healthy individuals, and obesity seemed to be a more widespread problem in Holland than in the UK.

In the UK survey the investigations were of several types:

1. Food intake was assessed by means of a written diary which recorded the foods eaten during seven days and a 'dietary investigator' called at the house to attempt to quantify the food eaten.

2. Most subjects underwent a clinical examination at a hospital or clinic — although some agreed only to a medical examination at home — and an X-ray of the left hand was also taken.

3. Biochemical analyses were made on a sample of blood from each subject.

4. Various socioeconomic pieces of information were elicited including 'physical and mental competence'.

Six areas throughout the UK were surveyed, two being predominantly rural and the other four various types of urban community.

Selection of the subjects was initially by apparently random selection but there was considerable variation between the areas in the numbers of subjects who eventually participated compared to the initial eligible populations — 51 per cent in Portsmouth, 79 per cent in Cambridgeshire, 69 per cent in Sunderland, 92 per cent in Rutherglen, 73 per cent in Angus and 74 per cent in Camden.

In all, 879 people, 425 men and 454 women, were studied, aged as follows:

	65–74 years	75+ years
Men	231	194
Women	236	218

Only a very small percentage — about 3 per cent — were judged to be mentally confused, although 22 per cent were 'of limited physical competence' and 1.5 per cent were helpless.

Of the 879 subjects who had either a medical, a dietary or a socioeconomic investigation, 789 had all three, 52 had a medical examination only and 38 a dietary cum socio-economic investigation only.

Thirteen per cent of the men and 40 per cent of the women lived alone (72 per cent of all the men compared to only 33 per cent of the women had a living spouse).

Table 28.13 shows the estimated intake of energy and

Table 28.13 Daily intake of energy and nutrients of 425 elderly men and 454 elderly women in the UK (DHSS, 1979)

	Men		Women	
	65 to 74	75+	65 to 74	75+
Energy				
(kcal)	2340	2100	1790	1630
(MJ)	9.8	8.8	7.5	6.8
Protein (g)	75	68	59	54
CHO (g)	266	244	200	187
Fat (g)	110	98	87	78
Calcium (mg)	910	880	795	725
Iron (mg)	12	11	9	9
Riboflavine (mg)	1.6	1.4	1.3	1.1
Ascorbic Acid (mg)	43	38	40	34
Vitamin D (i.u.)	133	107	92	84
Vitamin A (i.u.)	3790	3650	3420	2960
Thiamine (mg)	1.1	0.9	0.8	0.7
Nicotinic Acid (mg)	16.8	13.6	11.5	10.2
Pyridoxine (mg)	1.4	1.2	1.0	0.9

Table 28.14 Intake as a percentage of 'recommended intake' (DHSS, 1979)

	Men		Women	
	65 to 74	75+	65 to 74	75+
Energy	98	98	92	97
Protein	125	126	126	129
Calcium	182	177	159	145
Iron	120	110	90	90
Thiamine	110	100	100	100
Riboflavine	100	88	100	85
Ascorbic Acid	143	127	133	113
Vitamin A	151	146	137	118

nutrients and Table 28.14 gives these intakes as percentages of the levels recommended for the UK by the report of the Department of Health and Social Security (1979).

Of the different groupings of foodstuffs, cakes, puddings, biscuits, etc. provided the main contribution to the energy value of the diet, with meat and meat dishes taking second place — the average daily intake of meat was 2.8 oz (78 g). 12 oz (336 g) of milk were taken per day on average. Meat and milk were the main sources of protein, and milk also supplied most of the calcium. Vitamin C was mainly (66 per cent) derived from potatoes, green vegetables and tomatoes and citrus fruits.

When energy intake was related to the nutritional state, in three of the four groups of subjects (the exception being the women of 75 or over) those with the highest intakes were judged to be in better health but otherwise no relationship seemed to be present (i.e. those who were 'better', 'worse' or 'much worse' than average could not be distinguished by the energy intake of their diet). Also 'thinness' (assessed by skinfold thickness) was not related to energy intake; although the report makes some point out of a table which is stated to show 'that in general fat people eat fewer calories than thin people', this is not borne out by the table quoted, which shows no statistical validity for the statement.

Some interesting pointers towards a reduced food intake by the 'poor' masticators is provided in one of the tables.

The intake of protein is perhaps surprisingly high and no indication of inadequate protein intakes because of poor diet is demonstrated by the results.

Of the 789 subjects who had both medical and dietary examinations, 57 were diagnosed as having either angular stomatitis or cheilosis, although only four could be related to riboflavine deficiency. No relationship could be established either to sublingual haemorrhages or varicosities, nor with purpura of flat nails.

In two subjects, scurvy was definitely diagnosed, and it was suspected in another two subjects but the intakes of vitamin C of three of these four people was not at the low levels usually associated with scurvy.

The values of vitamin D intake were low enough to have been related to osteomalacia, and showed some association with constant low back pain, but the biochemical analyses did not correlate very well with these findings.

The overall picture of malnutrition presented by this survey is one which is reassuring for the elderly in the UK. Of the 841 subjects examined by the clinicians who participated in the six areas of the country, only 27 were diagnosed as malnourished (this figure, however, does not include those suffering from obesity). The 27 were subdivided as follows: eight subjects had angular stomatitis diagnosed as of nutritional origin; two definite and two tentative diagnoses of scurvy were made; 12 subjects, all in one area, were said to show protein–calorie malnutrition, although this must be a very difficult diagnosis to make in an elderly subject and the biochemical blood analyses and the intakes of protein and energy in their diets supported the diagnoses in only one or two of the 12.

The picture, then, of 'clinical' malnutrition makes it a very uncommon condition in these elderly subjects — possibly only about 2 per cent of the sample being affected.

However, a search was made for more information on all the people on low energy intakes — i.e. 41 men whose intake was less than 1500 kcal per day (6.3 MJ) and 47 women with less than 1200 kcal per day (5.0 MJ). Of these 88 people, 14 (all women) were reported as obese and were 'dieting'. Twenty-two of the remaining 74 were assessed by their clinicians as having a 'better than average' general condition of health; none had low serum pseudocholinesterase values (this enzyme is thought to be related to protein-energy malnutrition Hutchinson et al, 1951). A third group of 24 had nonnutritional diseases which affected their food intake — e.g. very reduced physical activity because of strokes, crippling arthritis, mental depression, or they suffered from gastrointestinal disease; two of these people had reduced levels of serum pseudocholinesterase. A further 17 subjects had defects which interfered with food preparation (very poor vision, osteoarthritis of the hand, etc.) and four of these had a low serum pseudocholinesterase and a low serum albumin.

The remaining seven subjects suffered from 'senile degenerative states'; two had reduced serum pseudocholinesterase.

Of these 88 people on low energy and nutrient intakes, six were diagnosed by the clinicians as being under-nourished. By the biochemical analyses, as has been documented above, eight were possibly suffering from protein–energy malnutrition. Again, therefore, it seems as if malnutrition (excluding obesity) was an uncommon condition.

'Meals-on-wheels' were being received by 21 subjects, five of whom had been diagnosed as malnourished by their clinicians. Among 35 others in the total group who said they would like to receive such meals, only seven seemed to have any real need ('they were thin') and one had been diagnosed as malnourished.

From the socioeconomic information collected, the only group who were stated to suffer because of their mode of living (and this is not reflected by their food intake) were the men aged 75 and over who lived alone and cared for themselves. Also, perhaps surprisingly, the comment is made the 'the dietary and physical differences consequent on income are unimpressive, and their causes are indirectly rather than directly economic'.

Of the factors with which are commonly supposed to render the elderly particularly vulnerable to malnutrition — apathy, disinterest, ignorance, alcoholism, food faddism, limited mobility, loneliness and social isolation, mental disturbance, poverty, ill-fitting dentures and poor dentition — the only one which was shown to have more than minor importance was 'limited mobility'. 'The outstanding impression', it is stated, 'was that the most important reason for mal- or undernutrition, when it occurred, was because the subject was biologically very old or was infirm, often with multiple pathology.'

The third report describes a follow-up survey of the surviving participants of the 1967–68 investigation (DHSS, 1972), and was carried out 5 years afterwards, i.e. in 1972–73 (DHSS, 1979). Of the 879 original men and women, 277 were known to have died and some others could not be traced. This left 563 eligible persons but 59 refused to participate again, 21 were now living in institutions, leaving 486 who co-operated and still lived at home.

The survey followed the same pattern as that in the 1967–68 study. In general, the results are also comparable.

Foods eaten and the dietary pattern were similar to those of younger adults. The energy and nutrient intakes of the men and women, divided into two age groups, is shown in Table 28.15. The results are very similar to those of the earlier survey, except that — as would be expected — they are all slightly lower in quantity.

In part the reduced food intake may have been due to impaired health because the incidence of disease was greater and the dietary intake smaller in the subjects who were aged 80 years or over compared with those aged under 80 years. Moreover, for subjects who were classified as much better than average in health there was no significant difference in dietary intakes between those above and below the age of 80, whereas subjects who were not healthy and were classified as much worse than average had significantly smaller intakes than those classified as healthy and better than average.

The incidence of malnutrition was 7 per cent and was twice as large among the subjects aged 80 years or more compared with those under 80 years of age. In all except perhaps one subject, malnutrition was associated with non-nutritional disease. Three of the malnourished subjects had scurvy, two had osteomalacia and 13 had nutritional anaemias associated with haematological evidence of iron, folate and vitamin B_{12} deficiency. The figure of 7 per cent is almost certainly an overestimate of malnutrition in elderly people because all of the factors which made the sample nationally unrepresentative operate in the same direction.

The diets of the malnourished were generally of poor quality; over the age of 80 the mean daily intakes of animal protein, vitamin C and vitamin D by the malnourished were significantly smaller than the expected mean intakes standardised for area.

Malnutrition was associated with both medical and social 'risks factors'. Among these, certain medical conditions — chronic bronchitis and emphysema,

Table 28.15 Mean daily intakes of energy and nutrients for all men and women in the survey in two age groups (DHSS, 1979)

Daily Intake		Sex and Age Group							
		Under 80 yrs (111 men)		80 yrs and over (58 men)		Under 80 yrs (125 women)		80 yrs and over (71 women)	
		Mean	s.d.	Mean	s.d.	Mean	s.d.	Mean	s.d.
Energy	kcal	2217	(522)	2024	(498)	1679	(416)	1559	(358)
	MJ	9.3	(2.2)	8.5	(2.1)	7.0	(1.7)	6.5	(1.5)
Animal Protein	g	47.5	(12.9)	47.8	(14.3)	39.3	(10.7)	36.4	(9.5)
Total protein	g	71.2	(15.6)	68.9	(17.5)	57.5	(13.7)	52.6	(12.1)
Fat	g	100	(27.4)	93	(27.9)	81	(23.8)	72	(19.1)
Carbohydrate	g	255	(67.5)	235	(63.1)	189	(56.8)	182	(52.8)
Calcium	mg	890	(285)	870	(311)	780	(251)	690	(184)
Iron	mg	11.6	(3.01)	11.0	(3.06)	9.3	(3.09)	8.6	(2.74)
Vitamin A	μg	1120	(728)	1050	(689)	1050	(1161)	980	(776)
Thiamine	mg	1.0	(0.27)	0.9	(0.26)	0.8	(0.27)	0.7	(0.20)
Riboflavine	mg	1.5	(0.62)	1.4	(0.47)	1.3	(0.53)	1.1	(0.40)
Nicontinic Acid	mg	14.4	(5.97)	12.3	(4.02)	10.3	(3.45)	9.7	(2.86)
Pyridoxine	mg	1.3	(0.41)	1.2	(0.37)	0.9	(0.26)	0.9	(0.29)
Vitamin C	mg	46	(28.2)	38	(31.1)	40	(29.3)	37	(25.1)
Vitamin D	μg	2.4	(1.64)	2.7	(2.01)	2.1	(1.79)	2.3	(2.61)

dementia, depression, long-term effects of gastrectomy, difficulty in swallowing, poor dentition — and certain social factors — conditions associated with being housebound, men living alone, having no regular cooked meals, bereavement, being in social classes IV and V and in receipt of supplementary benefit — were associated with a higher incidence of malnutrition. Subjects affected by several risk factors were particularly prone to malnutrition.

The housebound, who accounted for 12.6 per cent of the survey population over the age of 70, were the most important single group at risk of malnutrition. The higher incidence of malnutrition among the housebound was associated with significantly smaller dietary intakes and abnormalities of biochemical measurements for certain nutrients. In particular, the housebound women had a poorer vitamin D status than the non-housebound subjects which was probably attributable to not taking vitamins and (for vitamin D) to a lack of exposure to sunlight. Since housebound elderly people are a readily identifiable group, they present the best opportunities for proplylaxis of malnutrition.

Single clinical signs and isolated biochemical findings were considered to be unreliable evidence of malnutrition. The diagnosis required an assessment of all the information available from clinical, dietary, biochemical and haematological studies.

CONCLUSION

In this assessment of nutrition in the elderly, no attempt has been made to present a complete all-embracing picture. Many excellent reviews (such as that of Holtmeier and Heilmeyer, 1968, based on their studies at the Department of Nutritional Physiology at Freiburg in Breisgau, and of Esposito et al, 1969) and original articles have not been referred to, and apologies must be given to authors whose work might justifiably have been included had this been a comprehensive review of all the literature on nutrition as it concerns elderly people.

The emphasis here has been biased towards the elderly in the United Kingdom and perhaps in the USA, although data on similar populations in other countries have occasionally been used. This approach has not been entirely for parochial reasons: the nutrition of a population of any age group will show considerable variability for reasons of socioeconomic, climatic and other environmental factors. Where elderly people are concerned,

the differences in the way of life within the continent of Europe alone, to say nothing of, for example, the Indian subcontinent and Africa, are of such import that, even if data were available, it would be beyond the scope of this chapter to attempt a proper appraisal.

The general conclusion from the assessment presented here must be that malnutrition in the elderly appears not to be, at least for the moment, a problem of wide importance. The incidence seems low and the severity, when it occurs, seems moderate. Nevertheless, this conclusion is still based on limited information and may not be strictly accurate. Although the average clinician treating elderly people is not likely to encounter malnutrition as a significant predisposing factor to ill-health on more than infrequent occasions, he should still bear the possibility in mind — as he would any relatively uncommon condition.

The likely nutrients in short supply in the diet of the elderly are calcium, potassium, vitamin C, and some of the vitamin B group. Prevention of these deficiencies, and also of possible sub-clinical conditions, could be at least partly brought about by good nutrition education which, ideally, should start early, i.e. at age 60 or younger. A short interesting account of one method of approaching this is given by Holdsworth and Davies (1982). Education authorities might contribute by organizing evening classes specifically oriented to the elderly. Nutrition Foundations might consider producing a booklet which physicians could distribute (together with helpful encouragement) to their elderly patients.

As far as vitamins are concerned, although blunderbuss therapy is generally to be discouraged, there might be a strong case for multi-vitamin supplements to be taken almost routinely by people over 75 years old.

Physical activity should be strongly recommended. It has enormous benefits of a wide-ranging nature — in increasing mobility, energy expenditure, food intake – which includes the various nutrients – preventing or reducing obesity, and providing the opportunity for psychological and social stimulus.

Apart from the somewhat negative attitude to nutrition embodied in this chapter, where the concern has been largely with the prevention of undernutrition, the positive pleasures and benefits to be obtained from a good varied diet, well cooked and presented, also need emphasis — particularly in the elderly. Good nutrition involves more than just adequate intakes of energy and nutrients.

REFERENCES

Abraham S, Johnson C L, Najjar M F 1979 Weight and height of adults 18–74 years of age. National Center for Health Statistics: Health and Nutrition Examination Survey. US Government Printing Office, Washington

Albanese A A, Higgins R A, Orto L A, Zavattaro D N 1957 Protein and amino acid needs of the aged in health and convalescence. Geriatrics 12: 465–475

Allen L H 1982 Calcium bioavailability and absorption: a review. American Journal of Clinical Nutrition 35: 783–808

Avioli L V 1977 Osteoporosis: pathogenesis and therapy. In: Avioli L V, Krane S M (eds) Metabolic Bone Disease, Academic Press, New York, p 307–370

Avioli L V 1981 Postmenopausal osteoporosis: prevention versus cure. Federation Proceedings 40: 2418–2422

Baker H, Frank O, Thind I S, Jaslow S P, Louria D B 1979 Vitamin profiles in elderly persons living at home or in nursing homes, versus profile in healthy young subjects. Journal of the American Geriatric Society 27: 444–450

Benedict F G, Emmes L E, Roth P, Smith H M 1914 The basal gaseous metabolism of normal men and women. Journal of Biological Chemistry 18: 139–155

Borgstrom B, Norden Å, Åkesson B, Abdulla M, Jagerstad M (eds) 1979 Nutrition and old age. Scandinavian Journal of Gastroenterology 14: supp 52

Bowman B B, Rosenberg I H 1982 Assessment of the nutritional status of the elderly. American Journal of Clinical Nutrition 35: 1142–1151

Brozek, J 1952 Changes of body composition in man during maturity and their nutritional implications. Federation Proceedings 11: 784–793

Buzina, R 1968 Nutrition surveys carried out in Yugoslavia and their relationship to the general problem of assessment of the nutritional status of populations. In: Vitamins in the Elderly, Exton-Smith A N, Scott D L (eds), p 5–11. John Wright, Bristol

Celada A, Herreros V, de Castro S 1980 Liver iron storage in Spanish aging population. American Journal of Clinical Nutrition 33: 2662–2664

Charlton R W, Hawkins D M, Mavor W O, Bothwell T H 1970 Hepatic storage iron concentrations in different population groups. American Journal of Clinical Nutrition 23: 358–371

Cheng A H R, Gomez A, Bergen J G, Lee T-C, Monckeberg F, Chichester C O 1978 Comparative nitrogen balance study between young and aged adults using three levels of protein intake from a combination of wheat-soy-milk mixture. American Journal of Clinical Nutrition 31: 12–22

Cheraskin E, Ringsdorf W M, Setyaadmadja A T H, Barrett R A 1967 Thiamine consumption and cardiovascar complaints. Journal of the American Geriatrics Society 15: 1074–1079

Citizens Board of Inquiry into Hunger and Malnutrition in the United States 1968 Hunger U.S.A., Citizens Crusade against Poverty (Chairman, W P Reuther), Washington, D.C. p 1–100

Clarke R P, Schlenker E D, Merrow S B 1981 Nutrient intake, adiposity, plasma total cholesterol, and blood pressure of rural participants in the (Vermont) Nutrition Program for Older Americans (Title III). American Journal of Clinical Nutrition 34: 1743–1751

Comfort A 1956 The Biology of Senescence, p 257. New York: Rinehart

Dall J L, Paulose S, Fergusson J A 1971 Potassium intake of elderly patients in hospital. Gerontologia Clinica 13: 114–118

Davies L, Holdsworth M D 1978 The place of milk in the dietary of the elderly. Journal of Human Nutrition 32: 195–200

Department of Health and Social Security 1970 First Report by the Panel on Nutrition of the Elderly. Report on Public Health and Medical Subjects. no 123. London: HMSO

Department of Health and Social Security 1972 Nutrition Survey of the Elderly Report on Public Health and Medical Subjects no 3. London: HMSO

Department of Health and Social Security 1979a Recommended daily amounts of food energy and nutrients for groups of people in the United Kingdom. Report on Health and Social Subjects no 15, London: HMSO

Department of Health and Social Security 1979b Nutrition and Health in Old Age. Report on Health and Social Subjects no 16, London: HMSO

Dill D B 1961 The physiology of aging in man. George Cyril Graves Lecture. Department of Anatomy and Physiology, Bloomington

Draper H H 1981 Nutrition and aging bone loss. Federation Proceedings 40: 2417

Durnin J V G A 1967 Activity patterns in the community. Canadian Medical Association Journal 96: 882–886

Durnin J V G A 1973 Body weight, body fat and the activity factor in energy balance. In: Apfelbaum (ed) Energy Balance in Man, Paris: Masson, p 141–150

Durnin J V G A, Mikulicic, V 1956 The influence of graded exercises on the oxygen consumption, pulmonary ventilation and heart rate of young and elderly men. Quarterly Journal of Experimental Physiology 41: 442–452

Durnin J V G A, Womersley J 1974 Body fat assessed from total body density and its estimation from skinfold thickness: measurements on 481 men and women aged from 16 to 72 years. British Journal of Nutrition 32: 77–97

Esposito S J, Vinton P W, Rapuano J A 1969 Nutrition in the aged: review of the literature. Journal of the American Geriatrics Society 17: 790–806

Exton-Smith A N 1982 Epidemiological studies in the elderly: methodological considerations. American Journal of Clinical Nutrition 35: 1273–1279

FAO/WHO: Expert Committee on Energy and Protein Requirements 1973. Geneva: WHO

Fleisch A 1954 Nouvelles Méthodés d'Etude des Echanges Gaseux et de la Fonction Pulmonaire. Basel: Schwabe

Fidanza F, Losito G 1981 Nutritional status of the elderly. Bibliotheca Nutritio et Dieta 30: 70–80

Garry P J, Goodwin J S, Hunt W C 1982 Nutritional status in a healthy elderly population: riboflavine. American Journal of Clinical Nutrition 36: 902–909

Garry P J, Goodwin J S, Hunt W C, Hooper E M, Leonard A G 1982 Nutritional status in a healthy elderly population: dietary and supplemental intakes. American Journal of Clinical Nutrition 36: 319–331

Gersovitz M, Motil K, Munro H N, Scrimshaw N S, Young V R 1982 Human Protein requirements: assessment of the adequacy of the current Recommended Dietary Allowance for dietary protein in elderly men and women. American Journal of Clinical Nutrition 35: 6–14

Gillum H L, Morgan A F 1955 Nutritional status of the aging. Journal of Nutrition 55: 265–288

Gillum H L, Morgan A F, Jerome D W 1955a Nutritional status of the aging. Journal of Nutrition 55: 449–468

Gillum H L, Morgan A F, Sailer F 1955b Nutritional status of the aging. Journal of Nutrition 55: 655–670

Gillum H L, Morgan A F, Williams R I 1955c Nutritional status of the aging. Journal of Nutrition 55: 289–303

Hallberg L, Bjorn-Rasmussen E 1972 Determination of iron absorption from whole diet. Scandinavian Journal of Haematology 9: 193–197

Harrill I, Cervone N 1977 Vitamin status of older women. American Journal of Clinical Nutrition 30: 431–440

Heaney R P, Recker R R, Saville P D 1978 Menopausal changes in calcium balance performance. Journal of Laboratory and Clinical Medicine 92: 953–963

Heaney R P, Gallagher J C, Johnston C C, Neer R, Parfitt A M, Whedon G D 1982 Calcium nutrition and bone health in the elderly. American Journal of Clinical Nutrition 36: 986–1013

Heinzich H C 1975 Definition and pathogenesis of iron deficiency. In: Kief H (ed) Iron Metabolism and its Disorders. American Elsevier Publishing Co, New York p 113

Hellon, R F, Lind A R, Weiner J S 1956 The physiological reactions of men of two age groups to a hot environment. Journal of Physiology 133: 118–131

Holdsworth M D, Davies L 1982 Nutrition education for the elderly. Human Nutrition: Applied Nutrition 36A: 22–27

Holtmeier, H J, Heilmeyer L 1968 Ernahrung des alternden Menschen. Stuttgart: Georg Thiéme Verlag

Horwitt M K 1953 Dietary requirements of the aged. Journal of the American Dietetic Association 29: 443–448

Hutchinson A O, McCance R A, Widdowson E M 1951 Serum cholinesterase. In: Studies of Undernutrition, Wuppertal 1946–9. Spec Rep Ser Med Res Coun Lond No 285. London: HMSO

Judge T G 1972 Potassium metabolism in the elderly. In: Carlsson L A (ed) Nutrition in old age, Almqvist & Wiksell, Uppsala, p 86

Judge T G, Caird F I, Leask R G S, Macleod C C 1974 Dietary intake and urinary excretion of potassium in the elderly. Age and Ageing 3: 167–173

Kohrs M B, Nordstrom J, Plowman E L, O'Hanlon P, Moore C, Davis C, Abrahams O, Eklund D 1980 Association of participation in a nutritional program for the elderly with nutritional status. American Journal of Clinical Nutrition 33: 2643–2656

Lansing A I 1951 Some physiological aspects of ageing. Physiological Reviews 31: 274–284

Lonergan M E 1971 Nutritional survey of the elderly. Nutrition (London) 25: 30–36

Lonergan M E, Milne J S, Maule M M, Williamson J 1975 A dietary survey of older people in Edinburgh. British Journal of Nutrition 34: 517–527

Macleod, C C 1970 Dietary intake of older people. Nutrition (London) 24: 24–29

Macleod C C, Judge T G, Caird F I 1974 Nutrition of the elderly at home. I. Intakes of energy, protein, carbohydrates and fat. Age and Ageing 3: 158

Marr J W 1971 Individual dietary surveys: purposes and methods. World Review of Nutrition and Dietetics 13: 105–164

Miall W E, Ashcroft M T, Lovell H G, Moore F 1967 A longitudinal study of the decline of adult height with age in two Welsh communities. Human Biology 39: 445–454

Mitchell C O, Lipschitz D A 1982 Detection of protein–calorie malnutrition in the elderly. American Journal of Clinical Nutrition 35: 398–406

Montoye H J, Lock B W D, Metzner H, Keller J B 1977 Habitual physical activity and glucose tolerance Diabetes 26: 172–176

Morgan A F, Gillum H L, Williams R I 1955a Nutritional status of the aging. Journal of Nutrition 55: 431–448

Morgan A F, Mural M, Gillum H L 1955b Nutrional status of the aging. Journal of Nutrition 55: 671–685

Munro H N 1972 In: Nutrition in Old Age, Carlson L A, (ed) Almqvist and Wiksell, Stockholm

National Center for Health Statistics, Singer J D, Granahan P, Goodrich N N 1982a Diet and iron status, a study of relationships: United States, 1971–1974. Vital and Health Statistics, Series II, No 229, Public Health Service, Washington

National Center for Health Statistics, Fulwood R, Johnson C L, Bryner J D 1982b Hematological and nutritional biochemistry reference data for persons 6 months–74 years of age: United States, 1976–1980. Vital and Health Statistics, Series II, No 232, Public Health Service, Washington

Nordin B E C, Horsman A, Marshall B H, Simpson M, Waterhouse G M 1979 Calcium requirement and calcium therapy. Clinical Orthopaedics and Related Research 140: 216–239

Norris A H, Shock N W, Yiengst M J 1955 Age differences in ventilatory, and gas exchange responses to graded exercise in males. Journal of Gerontology 10: 145–155

O'Hanlon P, Kohrs M B 1978 Dietary Studies of older Americans. American Journal of Clinical Nutrition 31: 1257–1269

Parizkova J, Eiselt E 1980 Longitudinal changes in body build and skin folds in a group of old men over a sixteen year period. Human Biology 52: 803–809

Roberts P H, Kett C H, Ohlson M A 1948 Nutritional status of older women; nitrogen, calcium, phosphorus retention of nine women. Journal of the American Dietetic Association 24: 292–299

Rutishauser I H E, Bates C J, Paul A A, Black A E, Mandal A R, Patnaik B K 1979 Long-term vitamin status and dietary intake of healthy elderly subjects. I. Riboflavine. British Journal of Nutrition 42: 33–42

Sanstead H H, Prasad A S, Schulert A S, Farid Z, Miale A, Bassily S, Darby W J 1967 Human Zinc deficiency, endocrine manifestations and response to treatment. American Journal of Clinical Nutrition 20: 422–442

Sandstead H H, Henricksen L K, GregerJ L, Prasad A S, Good R A 1982 Zinc nutriture in the elderly in relation to taste activity, immune response, and wound healing. American Journal of Clinical Nutrition 36: 1046–1059

Schorah C J, Tormey W P, Brooks G H, Robertshaw A M, Young G A, Talukder R, Kelly J F 1981 The effect of vitamin C supplements on body weight, serum proteins, and general health of an elderly population. American Journal of Clinical Nutrition 34: 871–876

Schroeder H A, Nason A P, Tipton I H, Balassa J J 1967 Essential trace elements in man: zinc. Journal of Chronic Diseases 20: 179

Schulze W 1954 Int Cong Geront III, Lond. p 122

Simms H S, Stolman A 1937 Changes in human tissue electrolytes in senescence. Science, 86: 269–270

Southgate D A T, Durnin J V G A 1970 Calorie conversion factors. An experimental reassessment of the factors used in the calculation of the energy value of human diets. British Journal of Nutrition 24: 517–535

Srinivasan V, Christensen N, Wyse B W, Hansen R G 1981 Panthothenic acid nutritional status in the elderly — institutionalized and non-institutionalized. American Journal of Clinical Nutrition 34: 1736–1742

Steincamp R C, Cohen N L, Walsh H E 1965 Resurvey of an aging population: fourteen year follow-up. Journal of the American Dietetic Association 46: 103–110

Swendseid M E, Tuttle S G 1961 Publications of the National Research Council (Washington) no 843

Taylor G F 1968 A clinical survey of elderly people from a nutritional standpoint. In: Vitamins in the Elderly, Exton-Smith A N, Scott D L, (ed) p 51–56. John Wright, Bristol

Turnlund J, Costa F, Margen S 1981 Zinc, copper and iron balance in elderly men. American Journal of Clinical Nutrition 34: 2641–2647

Tuttle S G, Swendseid M E, Mulcare D B, Griffith W H, Basset S H 1957 Study of the essential amino acid requirements of men over 50. Metabolism, 6: 564–573

Tzamnoff S P, Norris A H 1977 Effect of muscle mass decrease on age related BMR changes. Journal of Appied Physiology 43: 1001–1006

Tzamnoff S P, Norris A H 1978 Longitudinal changes in basal metabolism in man. Journal of Applied Physiology 45: 536–539

Uauy R, Scrimshaw N S, Young V R 1978 Human protein requirements: nitrogen balance response to graded levels of egg protein in elderly men and women. American Journal of Clinical Nutrition 31: 779–785

Underwood E J 1971 Zinc. In: Trace Elements in Human Nutrition, Academic Press, New York

Vir S C, Love A H G 1977 Nutritional evaluation of B groups of vitamins in institutionalized aged. International Journal for Vitamin and Nutrition Research 47: 211–218

Vir S C, Love A H G 1979 Nutritional status of institutionalized and non-institutionalized aged in Belfast, Northern Ireland. American Journal of Clinical Nutrition 32: 1934–1947

Watkin D M 1964 In: Mammalian Protein Metabolism, 2, Ch 17, Munro H N, Allison J B (ed), p 247–263. Academic Press, New York

Watts J H, Mann A N, Bradley L, Thompson D 1964 Nitrogen balances of men over 65 fed the FAO and milk patterns of essential amino acids. Journal of Gerontology 19: 370–374

Weber F, Glatzle D, Wiss O 1973 Symposium on recent advances in the assessment of vitamin status in man. The assessment of riboflavin status. Proceedings of the Nutrition Society 32: 237–241

Webster S G P, Wilkinson E M, Gowland E 1977 A comparison of fat absorption in young and old subjects. Age and Aging, 6: 113–117

Widdowson E M, Kennedy G C 1962 Rate of growth, mature weight and life-span. Proceedings of the Royal Society. Series B. 156: 96–108

Wirths, von W 1963 Die Relation von Arbeits- und Grundumsatz zum Gesamtumsatz bei alteren Personen mit körperlicher Belastung. Gerontologia, 8: 209–232

WHO 1973 Trace Elements in Human Nutrition. Techn Rep Ser No 532. Geneva: WHO

WHO 1973 Energy and Protein Requirements. Techn Rep Ser No 522. Geneva: WHO

Yearick E S, Wang M L, Pisias S J 1980 Nutritional status of the elderly: dietary and biochemical findings. Journal of Gerontology 35: 663–671

Zanni E, Calloway D H, Zezulka A Y 1979 Protein requirements of elderly men. Journal of Nutrition 109: 513–524

The genitourinary system — the aging kidney

INTRODUCTION

The study of the aging process in the kidney is beset by difficulties. One major problem, as in all gerontological research, is to distinguish between changes influenced by 'normal' aging, and those influenced by disease.

With the possible exception of the lung, the changes in kidney function with normal aging are the most dramatic of any human organ or organ system. In a normal young adult renal capacity far exceeds the ordinary demands for solute and water conservation and excretion. In old age, renal function, while substantially diminished, still provides under ordinary circumstances for adequate regulation of the volume and composition of extracellular fluid. However, the reduced function of the aged kidney has important clinical implications for diagnosis and treatment of many disorders and clearly reduces the individual's capacity to respond to a variety of physiologic and pathologic stresses.

Epidemiology and symptomatology of renal disease in the elderly, diagnostic difficulties, and response to treatment are problems about which there is still a lack of basic information. In general, renal disease in the aged is often caused by several concomitant pathoanatomical changes. Arteriosclerosis, infection and age-induced changes might occur simultaneously. The diagnostic entities are not so clear cut as in younger individuals.

ANATOMIC CHANGES

Changes in the nephron

Age-induced renal changes are manifested macrosopically by a reduction in weight of the kidney and a loss of parenchymal mass. According to Oliver (1952), the average combined weight of the kidneys in different age groups is as follows: 60 years, 250 g; 70 years, 230 g; 80 years, 190 g. The decrease in weight of the kidneys corresponds to a general decrease in the size and weight of all organs (Roessle and Roulet, 1932). Microscopically the most impressive changes are a reduction in the number of nephrons and a reduction in the size of the

nephron. Loss of parenchymal mass leads to a widening of the interstitial spaces between the tubules. There is also an increase in the interstitial connective tissue with age.

The total number of identifiable glomeruli falls with age, roughly in accord with the changes in renal weight (McLachlan, 1974). The number of hyalinized or sclerotic glomeruli identified on light microscopy increases from 1–2 per cent during the third to fifth decade, to 12 per cent after age 70 (McLachlan, 1977; Sworn and Fox, 1972; Kaplan, 1975).

Aging is associated with a loss of lobulation of the glomerular tuft, thus decreasing effective filtering surface. Although the total number of nuclei per glomerulus is unchanged with age, the filtering surface is diminished by a progressive increase of the number of mesangial cells after age 40 years, and a reciprocal decrease in the number of epithelial cells. The mesangium, which accounts for roughly 8 per cent of total glomerular volume at age 45 years, increases to nearly 12 per cent by age 70 years (Sorenson, 1977). Although the glomerular basement membrane thickens with age, studies of glomerular filtration characteristics show no difference in permeability with aging (Artursen et al, 1971).

Darmady and his colleagues (1973) have shown an interesting change in the distal convoluted tubule. They observed that the number of diverticula in the distal convoluted tubules increased with age. They thought that these diverticula might play a part in the production of pyelonephritis, and in harbouring organisms and causing and maintaining recurrence of renal infection in the aged. Figure 29.1 shows the increase in the number of diverticula per 100 distal tubules consequent upon advancing age. It has been suggested that these diverticula represent the origin of the simple retention cysts commonly seen in the elderly (McLachlan, 1978; Baert and Steg, 1977).

Vascular changes

Changes in the intrarenal vasculature with age, independent of hypertension or other renal disease, are prob-

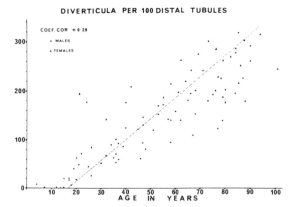

DIVERTICULA PER 100 DISTAL TUBULES

Fig. 29.1 Increase in the number of diverticula per 100 distal tubules (Darmady et al, 1973)

ably responsible for most clinically relevant changes in renal function with age. Normal aging is associated with variable sclerotic changes in the walls of the larger renal vessels. These sclerotic changes do not encroach on the lumen, and are augmented in the presence of hypertension (McLachlan, 1978). Smaller vessels appear to be spared, with fewer than 20 per cent of senescent kidneys from non-hypertensive individuals displaying arteriolar changes (Moritz and Oldt, 1973).

Combined microangiographic and histologic studies have identified very distinctive patterns of change in arteriolar-glomerular units with senescence (Taka-zakura, 1972; Ljungqvist and Lagerggen, 1962). In the cortex, hyalinization and collapse of the glomerular tuft is associated with obliteration of the lumen of the preglomerular arteriole and a resultant loss in blood flow. Changes in the juxtamedullary area are characterized by the development of anatomic continuity between the afferent and efferent arterioles during glomerular sclerosis. The end point is thus loss of the glomerulus and shunting of blood flow from afferent to efferent arterioles. Blood flow is maintained to the arteriolar rectae verae, the primary vascular supply of the medulla, which are not decreased in number with age (Fig. 29.2)

It is difficult to differentiate between age-induced changes and changes caused by past renal disease. Changes due to arteriosclerosis in connection with hypertension, diabetes and pyelonephritis are very common.

The appearance of a normal, histological kidney structure in the elderly is rare. According to Brocklehurst (1971) an analysis of 100 consecutive autopsies on geriatric patients at Farnborough Hospital, England, showed normal histology in only 3 per cent of the cases.

FUNCTIONAL CHANGES

Renal physiology

Renal blood flow
A progressive reduction in renal plasma flow of approximately 10 per cent per decade from 600 ml/min in

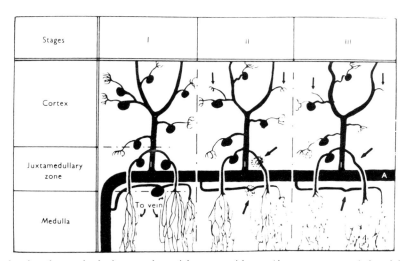

Fig. 29.2 Diagram showing changes in the intrarenal arterial pattern with age. (A, arcuate artery. 1, interlobular artery.) Stage I — Basic adult pattern showing glomerular arterioles. Stage II — Partial degeneration of some glomeruli. Two cortical afferent arterioles ramify into remnants of glomerular tufts (small arrows). Two juxtamedullary arterioles pass through partially degenerated glomeruli (large arrows). There is slight spiraling of interlobular arteries and afferent arterioles. Stage III — Two cortical afferent arterioles now end blindly (small arrows), and two juxtamedullary arterioles are aglomerular (large arrows). The corresponding glomerular tufts have degenerated completely. The spiraling of interlobular arteries and afferent arterioles is now more pronounced. (From Ljungqvist and Lagergren, 1962, Journal of Anatomy 96: 285, by permission of the publisher.)

young adulthood to 300 ml/min by 80 years of age is well established (Wesson, 1969). Detailed studies indicate selective loss of cortical vasculature with preservation of medullary flow. These cortical vascular changes probably account for the patchy cortical defects commonly seen on renal scans in healthy old adults. This histologic and functional demonstration of selective decrease in cortical flow may explain the observation that filtration fraction (the fraction of renal plasma flow that is filtered at the glomerulus) actually increases with advancing age, since outer cortical nephrons have a lower filtration fraction than juxta-medullary nephrons.

Glomerular filtration rate

The major clinically relevant renal functional defect arising from these histologic and physiologic changes is a progressive decline after maturity in the glomerular filtration rate (GFR), whether estimated by the clearance of inulin or creatinine. Age-adjusted normative standards for creatinine clearance have recently been established (Rowe et al, 1976). Creatinine clearance is stable until the middle of the fourth decade when a linear decrease of about 8.0 ml/min/1.73 m²/decade begins (Fig. 29.3).

A major clinical relevance of the decrease in GFR with age relates to the absence of a reciprocal elevation in serum creatinine (Rowe et al, 1976). Since muscle mass, from which creatinine is derived, falls with age at roughly the same rate as GFR, the rather drastic age-related loss of renal function is not reflected in an elevation of

serum creatinine. Thus serum creatinine overestimates GFR in the elderly. Depressions of GFR so severe as to result in elevation of serum creatinine above 132 μmol/l (1.5 mg/dl) are rarely due solely to normal aging and indicate the presence of an additional disease state.

Tubular function

Both excretory and reabsorptive capacities of the renal tubules decrease as age increases (Shock, 1968). The decrease in tubular secretion of diodrast and para-amino-hippuric acid in the aged reveals a decrease in tubular function. Ammonia excretion studies indicate a slight decrease of the ammonia production of the aged kidney. This impairment of the renal metabolic function is of importance in acidosis. The kidney of an old individual is, however, generally capable of maintaining a normal acid-base balance.

Mechanism of age-related reductions in renal function

Brenner and his colleagues (1982) have recently presented an innovative unitary hypothesis to explain the progressive nature of the reduction in renal function that characterizes nomal aging in man and a number of other mammals as well as a number of renal disease states. They suggest that the high protein content of most human diets and the resultant high solute load delivered to the kidneys is associated with chronic renal vasodilatation. The resultant persistent high renal capillary pressure and blood flow may lead to extravasation of macromolecules into the glomerular me-

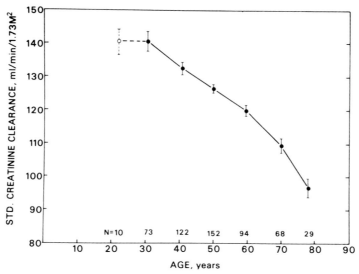

Fig. 29.3 Cross-sectional differences in standard creatinine clearance with age. The number of subjects in each age group is indicated above the abscissa. Values plotted indicate mean ± SEM The data represent creatinine clearance determinations based on measure of true creatinine. Creatinine autoanalyzer determinations in common clinical use will yield creatinine clearance values approximately 20–25 per cent lower than results shown here. Values in women are approximately 20 per cent lower than men. (From Rowe et al, 1976, Journal of Gerontology 31: 155 by permission of the publisher.)

sangium thus setting up a mesangial reaction which leads to progressive glomerular sclerosis. As glomeruli drop out the solute load per nephron is increased and the deteriorative process accelerates.

DIAGNOSTIC PROBLEMS OF RENAL DISEASE IN THE AGED

The diagnosis of renal disease in the elderly is characterized by the following difficulties:

1. The unspecifiable nature of the symptoms and often even the complete absence of the classical symptoms associated with younger patients,

2. The concomitant occurrence of diseases other than renal; diabetes, cardiac failure, arteriosclerotic vascular disease — confuse both the clinical picture and the symptomatology, and as a result the clinical diagnosis often overlooks renal disease,

3. The interpretation of clinical findings, such as the urinary findings and clearance estimations, is often difficult without special knowledge of alterations induced by the aging process.

These diagnostic difficulties indicate the need to check renal involvement in all geriatric patients. The basic examinations which must be performed as a matter of routine on all patients are as follows: haemoglobin value, blood-urea nitrogen and/or serum creatinine value, and examination of urine from a mid-stream-voided, clean-catch sample, including tests for albumin, sugar, pH, microscopic examination of the urinary sediment and screening for bacteria.

Collection of urine samples

Obtaining the urine for examination is of special importance because, in elderly women, there is frequent contamination of the sample. The bedridden, female patient of advanced years is the most difficult subject, and therefore the nursing staff needs special training in collecting urine samples. According to Roberts et al (1967) the best method is to clean with water without adding any disinfecting agents. The specimen is best obtained in the morning when the urine has been in the bladder all night. A large diuresis might reduce the concentration of bacteria, and therefore impede interpretation of the bacterial count. It is of the utmost importance that the laboratory data be obtained under controlled conditions.

The best method for collecting representative samples of bladder urine is bladder puncture. Suprapubic aspiration is both safe and accurate, but it is technically difficult in the elderly and has a consistent success rate of only 65 per cent, making it impractical as a routine procedure (Moore-Smith, 1974).

According to Moore-Smith (1974) the mid-stream urine (MSU) has an incidence of doubtful results between 17.5 per cent and 28 per cent, while frankly contaminated results may be as high as 31 per cent.

The incontinent elderly patient must be catheterized to obtain the urine sample, but it must be kept strictly in mind that catheterization can infect the urinary tract, and therefore this procedure must be performed only when necessary.

Interpretation of urinary sediment

Microscopic examination of sediment often reveals an increased number of leucocytes, and epithelial cells. If the bacteriological findings reveal a mixed infection then inefficient sampling, and contamination, must be suspected. In these cases the urinary examination should be repeated. An increase in the number of leucocytes — more than ten per millilitre — is regarded as being pathological in younger patients, but is not always a sign of an infection of the urinary tract in the elderly. The occurrence of a normal number of leucocytes does not exclude the possibility of infection. In an epidemiological study in Turku (Sourander, 1966) a random sample of 405 elderly inhabitants of the city was examined for significant bacteriuria, and in this study the correlation between significant bacteriuria and the increased number of leucocytes in the high-power field of urinary sediment was significant.

Screening for bacteria

Screening for bacteria in the urine with the quantitative colony count method described by Kass, or using the calibrated-loop streak culture method is the only accurate method for establishing the diagnosis of urinary tract infection. This method is, however, in practice a difficult one because the bacteria must be cultivated immediately after obtaining the sample, and a sufficiently equipped laboratory is required. Storing urine at usual refrigeration temperatures after sampling is absolutely necessary if the culture cannot be started immediately.

Guttmann and Naylor (1967) have devised a simple and useful method for bacteriological screening: a dipslide consisting of a microscopic slide coated with nutrient-Agar on one side and MacConkey's agar on the other, is equipped with a cylindrical container. Cohen and Kass (1967) have modified this method by substituting eosin methylene blue for MacConkey's agar. The dipslide is immersed in the urine specimen and incubated in the container at 37 °C for 18 to 24 hours. The incubated dip-slide is then compared with a photographic standard. The reliability of this method is very high — there is at least a 95 per cent correlation with pour-plate cultures.

A number of chemical tests have been developed for detecting significant bacteriuria. These methods are useful only as screening methods, and their value depends on the accuracy of the negative test results. Cases showing positive results must be followed with a more elaborate, bacteriological check up.

DISEASES OF THE KIDNEY IN THE AGED

Renovascular disease

Nephrosclerosis

Arteriosclerotic changes in the kidneys with advancing age are obviously responsible for a great number of cases of renal failure in the elderly. Destruction of the glomeruli is a result of vascular changes affecting the afferent glomerular arterioles. Arteriosclerotic changes and narrowing of the interlobular arteries induce renal ischaemia. The condition is often called nephrosclerosis and is characterized by the concomitant occurrence of malignant hypertension and a rapid progress of the disease terminating in uraemia and death. The clinical diagnosis is often overlooked because of the scarce urinary findings. The differential diagnosis between renovascular disease and chronic pyelonephritis is often very difficult and the two conditions might coexist quite often.

Isothenuria and a usually slight proteinuria, granular casts and hyaline cylinders in the high-power field of the urinary sediment, are typical laboratory findings.

Renovascular disease and concomitant hypertension in old age, however, are not generally of the malignant type. Progress is often very slow and subjective complaints few. It must be regarded as exceptional when malignant hypertension ocurs in a geriatric patient.

Renal arterial emboli and thrombosis

Occlusive arterial disease is an important cause of both acute and chronic renal failure in the elderly. Renal arterial emboli occur in any setting associated with peripheral embolization, such as acute myocardial infarction, chronic atrial fibrillation, subacute bacterial endocarditis and aortic surgery or aortography. The manifestations of renal emboli in the elderly may vary from an essentially clinically silent event to a full blown syndrome of severe flank pain and tenderness, hematuria, hypertension, spiking fevers, marked reduction in renal function and elevations of serum lactate dehydrogenase. Small emboli are very difficult to detect since renal scans may show focal perfusion defects in many apparently normal elderly patients. Major emboli may be suggested by findings of differential contrast excretion on pyelography and confirmed by renal scanning and aortography. Surgery is generally not indicated and anticoagulant therapy may be of major benefit. In cases where renal function is discernibly impaired,

improvement may occur over a period of several days to weeks.

Thrombotic occlusive renal arterial disease frequently complicates severe aortic and renal arterial atherosclerosis, especially in the setting of decreased renal blood flow caused by congestive heart failure or volume depletion. Renal artery stenosis secondary to dysplastic changes in the arterial walls is essentially limited to young age groups and is not an important disorder in a geriatric population. Symptoms of renal arterial occlusion may be remarkably absent. In cases in which renal function was previously good, the only manifestation of unilateral thrombosis may be a doubling of serum blood urea nitrogen (BUN), creatinine, and perhaps a modest increase in blood pressure. In cases with pre-existing renal impairment and azotemia, renal arterial occlusion may precipitate congestive heart failure, marked hypertension and the emergence of the uraemic syndrome. Intravenous pyelography is generally of less diagnostic benefit than renal scanning and definite diagnosis is made angiographically. There should be a careful evaluation for coexisting abdominal aortic aneurysm which may lead to renal arterial occlusion by extension of atheromata or dissection. Angiography should involve the least amount of contrast possible in order to minimize the likelihood of a nephrotoxic reaction which, while generally limited to several days of oliguria and mild azotemia, may take the form of severe acute oliguric renal failure. When technically feasible, surgical revascularization should be carefully considered. Substantial return of renal function can be obtained after prompt revascularization, and, in some cases, recovery occurs even if surgery is delayed until several months after the vascular occlusion.

Pyelonephritis

The commonest renal disease in the aged is pyelonephritis. The prevalence of this disease has been repeatedly studied in autopsy series, but a great discrepancy in the results is observable, depending obviously, on the different series and the various interpretations placed on the findings. Raschou (1948) studied an autopsy series of 3107 patients aged 10 years and over. He reported pyelonephritis in 28 per cent of the cases. Kimmelstiel (1964) studied the results of 3393 autopsies and detected chronic pyelonephritis in 2.8 per cent of cases. Baumanis and Russell (1959), who studied a series of 900 autopsies obtained from a hospital for chronic diseases, reported chronic pyelonephritis in 185 instances — 20 per cent of the cases. These authors considered the infection haematogenic in 20 of the cases and ascending in 165. The ages of the subjects varied from 50 to 101 years. Brückel and Wincker (1963) reported that pyelonephritis occurred in 28 per cent of an autopsy series obtained from a hospital for chronic diseases. Numerous other authors report a prevalence of pyelonephritis varying between these percentages (Lieberthal, 1939; Bell, 1942; Prewitt, 1943; Jackson et al, 1955; Sanjurjo, 1959; Kleeman and Freedman, 1960).

An important feature of chronic pyelonephritis in the old is the asymptomatic course of the disease. Kass (1955) claims that pyelonephritis is clincally diagnosed in one-fifth of those cases detected at autopsy. Many cases of chronic pyelonephritis in the aged are detected when the patients have been admitted into hospital for other reasons and the disease has often attained an advanced level with uraemia.

In many cases of chronic pyelonephritis it is not possible to detect bacteria in the urine despite progressive renal infection. In a few cases viruses may have caused the infections although such cases presumably are rare. It is also possible that a few cases are due to focal bacterial infections without the excretion of bacteria into the urine. It is possible that bacterial endotoxins can induce prolonged damage in the renal tissue after the disappearance of detectable bacteria in the tissue. As has been pointed out by Freedman (1967) the features of non-obstructive chronic pyelonephritis are not sufficeiently specific to establish the role of bacterial infection on the basis of morphological criteria alone. Freedman reported a review of autopsies during three 2-year intervals between 1957 and 1964 and showed a progressive decline in the frequency of pathoanatomical diagnosis of chronic pyelonephritis (excluding urinary obstruction, diabetes mellitus, or bloodstream infections arising in other organs). The decline was greater in men than in women and was considered most likely to be due to a growing appreciation of the non-specificity of the pathological features of chronic pyelonephritis.

Relationship with bacteriuria

The question of the correlation of asymptomatic bacteriuria and pyelonephritis is an important geriatric problem which until now has not been solved. The correlation between the bacteriuria and autopsy findings has been the subject of many investigations. MacDonald et al (1957) compared the bacterial count with the pathoanatomical changes in the kidneys and noted a correlation between pyelonephritis and a bacterial count of at least 100 000 bacteria per millilitre of urine. They studied the correlation by means of puncturing the bladder post mortem and performing the bacterial count according to the method described by Kass. In their material pathoanatomical changes due to urinary tract infection were found in 20 instances. Seventeen of these belonged to the group of 40 cases with more than 100 000 bacteria per millilitre of urine. In 14 of these 17 cases pyelonephritis was noted and in three instances cystitis without pyelonephritis. Active pyelonephritis

was noted in three instances without bacteria occurring in the urine — two of these had been intensively treated with antibiotics. Kleeman and Freedman (1960) reported that in their autopsy series chronic pyelonephritis without obstruction occurred as often in women as in men. They concluded that pathoanatomical changes characteristic of pyelonephritis may be caused by factors other than bacterial infection.

It is clear that significant bacteriuria occurs very often in the aged and increases with age.

In the epidemiological study in Turku, Sourander (1966) showed that significant bacteriuria occurred in 20 per cent of the population aged 65 or over. Compared with the findings of Brocklehurst et al. (1968) in a similar study in London the percentages are very similar. In an examination 5 years later Sourander, Ruikka and Kasanen (1970) found that the infection continued in 35 per cent of the cases — in 14 per cent of men and 41 per cent of women. New infections had developed in 7 per cent of the men and in 13 per cent of the women. The total frequency of urinary tract infection — 16.5 per cent (24 per cent of women and 8 per cent of men) — is about the same as found five years earlier. The infected cases had not increased in number though over the 5-year period some of the previously non-infected patients had become infected. Urinary tract infection seems, however, to be quite persistent and in a great number of the subjects the infection is continuous.

Dontas and Kasviki-Chervali (1976) have drawn attention to the significance of diuresis-provoked bacteriuria. In their series of clinically healthy ambulant elderly subjects 21 per cent of those who were found to have negative cultures excreted bacteria in the urine under forced hydration and frusemide treatment. These patients were thought to have infection of the upper urinary tract.

Dontas et al (1981) studied the effect of asymptomatic bacteriuria on survival in 342 healthy residents of a home for the aged in Athens. Out of these 76 subjects (22 per cent) had bacteriuria. The authors found a reduction in survival of 30 to 50 per cent among subjects with bacteriuria. There were no differences in age distribution, blood pressure, hematocrit, smoking habits, cholesterol, or myocardial changes between bacteriuric and non-bacteriuric subjects. Bacteriuric subjects had a median survival of 30 to 34 months regardless of sex or age at entry, in contrast to non-bacteriuric subjects, who survived for 20 to 41 months longer than bacteriuric subjects. The authors claimed that bacteriuria is an important factor associated with a statistically significant reduction of survival in both sexes, that the effect of bacteriuria overrides that of age and sex, and that in contrast to bacteriuria, extremes of blood pressure do not appear to influence survival.

The conclusions made by Dontas et al have been criticized by Kirkland and Robinson (1981), who draw attention to the fact that diseases of the central nervous system, cerebrovascular accidents and senile dementia could account for both reduced life expectancy and bacteriuria. They stressed that it may be premature to consider treating elderly patients with asymtomatic bacteriuria in the expectation that treatment will improve their survival. According to Dontas even if the relation between bacteriuria and shortened survival is shown to be non-causal, well-controlled trials of long-term treatment should be carried out to test the potential reversibility of this condition.

An interesting question is the role the L-forms of the bacteria play in causing recurrent pyelonephritis. The L-forms are bacterial cells without a solid wall structure. The bacteria can change into L-forms after being exposed to agents which damage the surface. These agents can be, for instance, antibiotics or enzymes. The L-forms do not grow in common broths used in bacterial cultivation. They need their own cultivation techniques and during the cultivation they return to their 'normal' forms. Virulence of the L-forms is low but after returning to their normal bacterial forms the virulence is restored. The L-forms survive in the tissues for a long time. The same is true of endotoxins (Turck et al, 1968; Wittler, 1968; Feingold, 1969).

L-forms have been isolated in most cases in old patients with chronic urinary infections, often with severe underlying diseases (Guttman et al, 1965; Conner et al, 1968).

The L-forms might play a part in the development of recurrent urinary tract infections in the aged and contribute to the renal damage inflicted by chronic pyelonephritis; their significance, however, is not clarified.

Bacteriuria and hypertension

The relationship between significant bacteriuria and hypertension in the aged is an interesting question. In younger age groups the occurrence of hypertension in connection with chronic pyelonephritis is a well-established fact and studies strongly indicate a relationship between significant bacteriuria and hypertension — for example, Kass et al (1961) showed this in their studies in Jamaica. Marketos et al (1970) studied this relationship quite extensively. They studied two groups — one consisting of 477 elderly, ambulant residents of a welfare home, and the other of 302 chronically ill, elderly patients of a medical department. The average occurrence of bacteriuria in the first-mentioned group was 18.7 per cent and in the second group 57.9 per cent, and of hypertension, respectively, 25.6 per cent and 48.7 per cent. Among the residents of the welfare home no significant difference was demonstrated in the occurrence of hypertension in bacteriuric and non-bacteriuric subjects, or in the occurrence of bacteriuria in hypertensive and non-hypertensive subjects. Among the hospitalized patients, of the bacteriurics 69.7 per cent had elevated diastolic pressure, and of the hypertensives, 83 per cent had significant bacteriuria. The differences in the occurrence of hypertension in bacteriuric and non-bacteriuric patients, and of bacteriuria in hypertensive and non-hypertensive patients, were statistically significant. The authors claim that a causal relationship between bacteriuria and arterial hypertension exists.

These findings of Marketos and colleagues are valuable in interpreting the importance of significant bacteriuria in the aged. The fact that the relationship between bacteriuria and hypertension was only established in chronically ill, hospitalized patients, leads us to assume that there are other factors which can induce this positive relationship, and that the relationship is not necessarily causative. A well-known fact among geriatricians is the occurrence of urinary tract infection, especially in the elderly who are chronically ill and bedridden due to severe diseases such as cerebrovascular disease and encephalopathy (see Brocklehurst et al, 1977). Arterial hypertension is common in these patients. Significant bacteriuria, in fact, occurs with great frequency in bedridden patients and in patients whose movements are limited. This relationship was clearly demonstrated in the epidemiological study of urinary tract infection in Turku (Sourander, 1966). Thus it appears reasonable to assume that the relationship between bacteriuria and hypertension is more coincidental than causative.

Renal function

According to Kasanen and Salmi (1959), the specific gravity of morning urine and the haemoglobin value are the most sensitive indicators renal insufficiency due to pyelonephritis. The next most sensitive indicator is the phenolsulphonphthalein excretion test. Glomerular filtration and effective renal flow decrease much later.

Hagenfeldt et al (1962) observed no correlation between significant bacteriuria and renal function as far as the serum creatinine level was concerned in their study of hospital patients with urinary tract infection. Nor did Marner and Faurschou-Jensen (1963) report a decrease in renal function in their series of hospital patients. These series consisted of patients from medical wards and only some of them were elderly. Bengtsson (1962) reported a series of patients with pyelonephritis and decreased renal function in which the decrease was of the same degree in patients with and without symptoms. Studying patients with hypertrophy of the prostate and concomitant urinary tract infection, Olbrich et al (1950) discovered that the maximal tubular excretory capacity was considerably decreased. Mitchell and Valk (1953) compared the renal function in aged patients with and without urinary obstruction using inulin clearance and para-amino hippurate clearance. They could not find any significant difference in renal function between the groups.

Sourander (1966) studied the epidemiology of urinary tract infection in the aged including estimations of endogenous creatinine clearance and phenolsulphonphthalein excretion tests. The mean serum creatinine value did not differ in the groups with or without bacteriuria. Nor did the phenolsulphonphthalein excretion test values differ significantly. The same was found in the case of the specific gravity of the morning urine. The endogenous creatinine clearance values were somewhat better in both men and women who were free of significant bacteriuria; the differences between the means were, however, not statistically significant. (Endogenous creatinine clearance for men with bacteriuria was 82.6 ± 7.70 ml per min and in women 82.2 ± 6.40 ml per min. The corresponding figures in the groups free of significant bacteriuria were 93.3 ± 4.12 ml per min for men and 98.2 ± 4.45 ml per min for women.)

Development of renal failure in the aged seems in the first instance to be induced by vascular changes, perhaps in association with hypertension. As has been shown by several authors, the intrarenal infection accelerates the evolution of pre-existing renovascular disorders (Bengtsson et al, 1968; Dontas et al., 1968; Marketos et al, 1969).

An epidemiological study of uraemia in the aged was performed in south-west Finland by Sourander et al (1979), and 668 cases of uraemia — a serum creatinine value exceeding 230 μmol/litre (2.6 mg/dl) — detected. Out of these 372 were 65 years or older. This means that more than half of the uraemic subjects in the region concerned were aged. Compared with younger age groups both prevalence and incidence rates of uraemia were about 10-fold in the aged. Fifty-one per cent of the women suffered from chronic pyelonephritis, which was more common in women than in men. The most common cause of uraemia in men was postrenal obstruction, in 35 per cent, most of whom also suffered pyelonephritis. Prerenal uraemia was present in 31 per cent of the women and in 29 per cent of the men. Among other diagnoses the following were most frequent: nephrosclerosis, diabetic nephropathy, amyloidosis and myeloma.

Sixty-four per cent of the subjects with pyelonephritis had received long-term treatment for infection — such treatment had not affected the death rate. Obviously long-term treatment in advanced cases of uraemia caused by chronic pyelonephritis has no or very little effect on the prognosis.

Predisposing factors
Hydrokinetic mechanisms are weakened by anatomical

changes in the bladder and by disturbed neuromuscular function of the bladder. The presence of obstruction is very clearly a leading cause in the development of renal infection in men. Prostatic hypertrophy and carcinoma account for the vast majority of infections in men. Obstruction can also be promoted by changes in the bladder neck, malformations, nephro- and ureterolithiasis and neoplasms. In women prolapse conditions and even slight descensus of the vagina increase the possibility of urinary tract infection (Sourander et al, 1965). In both sexes neurological disorders and diabetes are important factors in the development of urinary tract infection. An atonic bladder is at risk of infection. The protective effect of prostatic secretion against bacterial infection might partly explain the great difference in the occurrence of non-obstructive infection in males and females.

Other protective mechanisms are localized to the bladder mucosa. These are, however, not clear. Postmenopausal changes in women with estrogen deficiency are probably factors which decrease the mucosal resistance to infection in elderly women.

An important factor promoting urinary tract infection is the use of indwelling catheters in the aged. In 100 consecutive autopsies performed on geriatric patients Carty et al (1981) found chronic pyelonephritis in 22 patients and acute pyelonephritis in four patients. In 14 of these 22 patients with chronic pyelonephritis there had also been significant bacteriuria in life; in seven cases of the autopsied pyelonephritis patients no significant bacteriuria obtained. There was a clear correlation between infected renal pathology and indwelling catheter in life. The findings showed that in 30 per cent of the clinically manifest urinary tract infection cases there were patho-anatomical changes of renal infection.

Escherichia coli causing urinary tract infection mostly originate from the intestine. Because of special affinity for the urogenital mucosa or abundance in the stool flora (Turck et al, 1962; Gruneberg, 1969; Lidin Janson et al, 1977) bacteria proceed to colonize the outer genital (Stamey et al, 1971) and periurethral areas (Bollgren and Winberg, 1976) and ascend the urinary tract. Bacteria ascend and remain in the urinary tract despite the urine flow. Only bacteria with ability to attach to the mucosal lining have been thought capable of resisting elimination at voiding and of producing significant bacteriuria. Binding to slime may have a dual effect: it may be a defense for the host since bacteria trapped in slime may easily be excreted or, alternatively bacteria bound to slime overlying the mucosa may remain in the bladder and cause infection (Svanborg Eden et al, 1982).

A relationship has been shown between ability to attach to human uroepithelial cells in vitro and severity of infection produced in vivo (Svanborg Eden et al, 1978). Capacity to attach to the epithelium is a virulence factor for *E. coli* causing urinary tract infection. This attachment is specific for the epithelium of the urogenital tract (Korhonen and Svanborg Eden, 1981). *Proteus mirabilis* strains show an adhesion pattern different from *E. coli* (Svanborg Eden et al, 1980). They attach only to squamous and not to transitional epithelial cells.

The most obvious predisposing factor causing urinary tract infection and pyelonephritis in the aged is urinary obstruction. In men prostatic hypertrophy and carcinoma of the prostate account for the vast majority of infections (Sourander, 1966). Digital examination of the prostate is not satisfactory — even an apparently normal finding does not exclude enlargement of the prostate and bladder neck obstruction.

In both sexes the occurrence of malformation, nephro- and uretero-lithiasis and neoplasms are factors which cause obstruction and infection. In women, however, the vast majority of infected cases show no such obstruction. Some of these cases have coexistent prolapse conditions (Sourander et al, 1965). Figure 29.4 shows the occurrence of therapy-resistant urinary tract infection and recurrent urinary tract infection in a hospital series consisting of geriatric patients with a high incidence of infection.

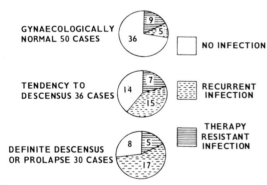

Fig. 29.4 Urinary infection in gynaecologically different groups (Sourander et al, 1965)

The occurrence of these two types of infection is correlated with the presence of laxity of the vaginal wall with a tendency to descensus and definite vaginal or uterine prolapse. Those patients in this study in whom urinary tract infection had been found once or several times during their stay in hospital, but whose urine was sterile and sediment normal at intervals, can be regarded as recurrent. Those cases in which pyuria or bacteriuria persisted in spite of a number of courses of treatment with different antimicrobial drugs can be regarded as therapy-resistant and incurable.

Cases established as having recurrent urinary tract infection are, apparently, influenced by anatomical

changes of the bladder, and frequently show cystocele caused by vaginal descensus or uterine prolapse. Bladder capacity is often decreased in such cases, as is shown by cystometry. Even slight gynaecological changes further urinary tract infection of the recurrent type.

Cases established as therapy-resistant are less influenced by these changes and are represented in equal proportions in all groups. The similarity in the amount of residual urine both in correlation to gynaecological findings and to infection suggests the minor significance of this factor in promoting urinary tract infection in elderly females.

The authors believed that anatomical prolapse conditions were important in promoting urinary tract infection in female hospital patients of advanced years, but not significant in cases with a continuous therapy-resistant infection — these apparently having a true pyelonephritis. The cases considered to have pyelonephritis formed one-third of the total of all patients with urinary tract infection.

The role of reflux in the pathogenesis of pyelonephritis is not clear but may play an important part. Parvinen et al (1965) studied the correlation between radiographic findings at micturition cystography and evidence of urinary infection in a group of elderly, hospitalized women. A unilateral, ureteral reflux was observed in 3 patients out of 37 with urinary tract infection. Among the 22 patients without urinary tract infection no cases of reflux were found. Diverticula, trabeculation and deformation were present in both groups, and normal cystographic findings were not significantly more frequent in the group without infection. These findings support the opinion that vesico-ureteral reflux and urinary tract infection are concomitant features in a small number of elderly women.

The increased incidence and severity of infection in geriatric patients may be induced by a lowered antibody response and a weakened resistance to infection. Kaarsal et al (1964) studied the problem and vaccinated 36 geriatric patients and 33 medical students with salmonella (TAB)-vaccine. Only persons without demonstrable antibodies prior to vaccination were selected. The mean age of the geriatric patients was 72 years and that of the students 21 years. The two groups responded similarly to the flagellar antigens, but with a significant difference in the case of the somatic antigens. Antibodies to somatic antigens were obtained in 94 per cent of the students and in 50 per cent of the geriatric patients. Of the geriatric patients who responded to immunization the titres were high or higher than was the case with the group of students.

Sourander et al (1967) compared the differences in antibody-forming capacity between an adult and a geriatric group of patients with urinary tract infection after vaccination with salmonella vaccine. In the geriatric patients with urinary tract infection the somatic agglutinin increased more often than was the case with the younger group of adult patients with urinary tract infection. The authors concluded that the antibody formation after a salmonella vaccination is decreased in adults with urinary tract infection but not in a corresponding group of the elderly, and that the reason for this may be because younger people suffer more often from a haematogenic urinary tract infection and the aged more often from urinary tract infections induced by local, predisposing factors.

Although the antibody formation is decreased in the aged this seems not to be of importance as an aetiological factor causing urinary tract infection.

Urological sepsis

Sepsis from Gram-negative pathogens is a grave disorder which must be considered possible in all aged patients with unexplained fever. Seneca and Grant (1976) have reviewed urologic sepsis/shock and claim that older patients are susceptible to the consequences of instrumentation and surgical operations involving the genitourinary tract. An early diagnosis and vigorous treatment decreases the mortality dramatically. Repeated blood cultures from samples drawn during the rise of fever are essential in establishing the diagnosis.

Renal papillary necrosis

Renal papillary necrosis is not uncommon in the aged. The disease can be defined as a severe form of chronic pyelonephritis with ischaemic necrosis of the papillae and the medullary pyramid. Necrotic papillae migrate through the urinary passages and are often detected macroscopically in the urine. The patients suffer from haematuria, urinary colic and very often from fever, which may be high. The disease often has a quite rapid course resulting in uraemia and death. Diabetes and vascular diseases are of importance as aetiological factors. The role played by the consumption of analgesics — especially phenacetin — may be of importance. Clinical experience favours the opinion that continuous prolonged use of analgesics is connected with the development of papillary necrosis in the aged. Nevertheless Ruikka and Sourander (1967) could not find any correlation between phenacetin consumption and urinary tract infection in the aged.

Kasanen and Vasama (1964) reported their findings in a series of autopsies consisting of 111 cases of papillary necrosis, and observed a substantial increase in the incidence of renal papillary necrosis during a 10-year period. The number of persons abusing phenacetin-containing drugs was 25 per cent, while other predisposing factors were observed in 9 cases (urological obstruction, radiotherapy to the pelvic region and perhaps a long-term course of cortisone).

Women totalled 60 per cent: their mean age was 61 years. Only 41 per cent had micturition difficulties, the others had general symptoms. Mild proteinuria was established in 30, haematuria in 50, leucocyturia in 62 and bacteriuria in 45 per cent.

The majority of the patients did not seek admission to hospital until they were uraemic. The serum creatinine was normal in only 12 patients. Two-thirds of the patients had renal anaemia on admission.

Acute glomerulonephritis

Acute glomerulonephritis is generally considered practically non-existent in the aged. In recent years there have, however, been several reports of acute glomerulonephritis in old people. Arieff et al reported some cases in 1971 and gave a review of the literature summarizing the principal facts in 86 cases of acute glomerulonephritis in the aged. These reports indicate that acute glomerulonephritis in the elderly is far more common than is generally realized, that the aetiology of the disease in the age group is diverse and is not limited to streptococcal infection and that the prognosis is not as unfavourable as is generally believed. According to these authors the initial diagnostic impression in elderly patients with acute glomerulonephritis is usually that of congestive heart failure or infection, and renal disease is not considered. The most common manifestations are those of oedema, dyspnoea, circulatory congestion, infection and nonspecific symptoms such as anorexia, nausea, vomiting, diarrhoea and muscular pain. Hypertension is less common.

Laboratory findings may be nonspecific. Azotaemia, anaemia, elevated erythrocyte sedimentation rate and hypoalbuminaemia are variable. Although protein, red blood cells, and red blood cell casts are usually present in the urine, their absence does not rule out this diagnosis.

Since many elderly patients have a variety of concomtant degenerative diseases, such as diabetes, congestive heart failure, hypertension and arteriosclerotic peripheral vascular disease, the presence of haematuria, proteinuria, circulatory congestion, and mild azotaemia will often be attributed to an exacerbation of one of these diseases. Because of this tendency, many cases of acute glomerulonephritis in the elderly are not diagnosed ante-mortem (Nesson and Robbins, 1960; Berlyne et al, 1964; Boswell and Eknovan 1968). It appears that renal biopsy is necessary for diagnosis (Lee et al, 1966; Berlyne et al, 1964).

These observations indicate that this entity should be considered in old patients in the presence of urinary abnormalities, even though the disease may be apparently of a completely different nature.

The prognosis of acute glomerulonephritis in the elderly is not as grave as has been thought. The most common cause of death is pulmonary oedema secondary to circulatory congestion.

Nephrotic syndrome

As is the case with acute glomerulonephritis, the nephrotic syndrome has generally been considered to be uncommon in the elderly. Fawcett et al (1971) reported a series of 100 consecutive adult cases of nephrotic syndrome, of which 25 were 60 years or over. Patients with known chronic glomerulonephritis who became nephrotic during the period were excluded from this series. Patients with diabetes were also excluded. Six (24 per cent) of the older patients had the minimal change lesion, compared with 16 per cent of the younger adults. The incidence of membranous glomerulonephritis was similar in the two age groups, but proliferative glomerulonephritis was more common in the younger (29 per cent) than in the older group (16 per cent). Amyloidosis did not have a higher incidence in the higher age group. Five of the elderly patients with minimal change lesion were treated with prednisone — in four a complete remission from the nephrotic syndrome followed, while the fifth patient's course was unknown. Finkelstein and Hayslett (1976) have reviewed the nephrotic syndrome in the elderly and indicate that nephrotic syndrome in these age groups is often associated with a systemic disease, especially diabetes mellitus but also renal amyloidosis, malignancies, systemic lupus erythematosus, polyarteritis, renal vein thrombosis and congestive heart failure.

The correct treatment of the nephrotic syndrome is only possible when a diagnosis of the underlying renal condition has been made. In some cases this requires a needle biopsy. The histological changes in the aged patients are, however, often difficult to interpret.

The restriction of sodium intake is of utmost importance in patients with the nephrotic syndrome. The nephrotic syndrome secondary to lipid nephrosis without focal glomerulosclerosis responds to steroid treatment with a complete resolution of proteinuria. An alternative treatment is cyclophosphemide which is perhaps the drug of choice for aged patients (Finkelstein and Hayslett, 1976).

The development of osteoporosis during prolonged corticosteroid treatment is well known, as is the occurrence of fracture of the vertebral bodies due to osteoporosis. Immunosuppressive therapy and steroids have not been beneficial in membranous nephropathy. In diabetic nephropathy corticosteroids are not indicated. The treatment with steroids of nephrosis due to amyloidosis is also contraindicated.

Diabetic nephropathy

Nephropathy is a complication of diabetes, occurring in the elderly as in the young. Since Kimmelstiel and Wilson in 1936 described intercapillary glomerulosclerosis there have been numerous histological studies of this phenomenon. Clinically there is nothing specific about the diabetic nephropathy. The kidney-function tests are gradually decreased and the disease terminates in uraemia. It is usual for the nephropathy to begin clinically with proteinuria, and it is connected with nephrogenic anaemia. The course can be either rapid or slow. The evolution of renal lesion does not depend on the degree of 'good control' of diabetes: it may be minimal in poorly controlled diabetics and advanced in spite of strict dietetic or other therapy.

Diabetics appear to be especially at risk for irreversible loss of renal function as a complication of the use of radiographic contrast agents such as those employed in intravenous pyelography and angiography. Such studies should be used sparingly and with great caution in diabetics and the patients should be well hydrated prior to study, to establish a brisk diuresis and minimize the risk of contrast induced nephrotoxicity (Diaz-Buxo et al, 1975; Hackonen and Kjellstrand, 1977; Kamdar et al, 1977).

Obstructive nephropathy

The commonest cause of urinary obstruction in old age is prostatic hypertrophy. Olbrich et al (1957) reported a 30 to 50 per cent decrease of glomerular filtration rate and renal plasma-flow in aged males with prostatic hypertrophy. After prostatectomy the renal plasma flow increased slightly but the means of the glomerular filtration rate values before and after the operation did not differ significantly.

The increased intrapelvic pressure caused by urinary obstruction has been considered to be transmitted back through the tubular lumina and induce pressure atrophy of the renal parenchyma. Renal failure caused by obstruction is, however, restored after removal of obstruction if the renal trauma is not irreversible.

Other renal diseases in the aged

Urogenital tuberculosis in the aged must be suspected in the same way as in younger age groups when the clinical findings give reason for this suspicion. In the light of autopsy findings renal tuberculosis seems to be uncommon in aged hospital patients. There are, perhaps, geographical differences in the incidence. Tumours of the kidneys are found under the same conditions as in younger age groups. The same applies to nephrolithiasis. Renal calculi and calcifications following hyperparathyroidism are occasionally found in the elderly.

Polycystic renal disease occasionally presents in old age with haematuria, recurrent urinary infections, or azotaemia. The progress is usually slow. Treatment of urinary tract infection and hypertension is indicated in patients with this disorder (Ralston, 1975). Clinical experience indicates that renal involvement in myelomatosis and in connective tissue diseases is not uncommon. Nephropathy of hypercalcaemia also occurs in the aged as well as nephropathy of potassium depletion.

SPECIAL PROBLEMS OF TREATMENT

Treatment of infection

The treatment of renal diseases in the aged corresponds very closely to that generally accepted for patients in younger age groups. Since pyelonephritis is the most common renal disease in old age, and asymptomatic bacteriuria is closely related to this disease, one of the major questions in geriatrics is how to treat the considerable number of elderly patients who show a significant bacteriuria. The need for treatment of patients with asymptomatic bacteriuria has been criticized by Petersdorf (1966), according to whom elderly patients with asymptomatic bacteriuria should not be treated. Petersdorf claims that these patients have relatively normal renal function, have few acute flare-ups, and are unlikely to have shortened life-spans as a result of urinary infection. Furthermore, Petersdorf points to the fact that the toxic side-effects of drugs, the risk of superinfection, and the expense involved, in addition to the high failure rate of therapy, all argue against therapy of asymptomatic urinary infections in this group.

Brocklehurst et al (1968b, 1977) have studied the problem of treating urinary tract infections in the elderly and are of the opinion that patients without subjective complaints of urinary infection should not be treated, though patients who have various distressing symptoms should, as is the case with younger age groups, be given adequate therapy with antimicrobial drugs. These opinions are in accord with the present interpretation of the relationship between significant bacteriuria and renal involvement in the aged. Therapy for significant bacteriuria is unnecessary in protecting against renal damage, but is helpful in mitigating distressing symptoms. There are, however, some patients with significant bacteriuria and nonspecific symptoms, like fatigue, dizziness, psychic deterioration, who perhaps can benefit from treatment of the urinary infection.

A short-term course of therapy for all hospitalized and institutionalized patients manifesting significant bacteriuria seems indicated regardless of the symptoms. Foul smells and social handicap can be a big problem for the aged, and successful treatment of a urinary tract infection is of great importance for these patients. The prevention of hospital infections is also a strong indication for the treatment of significant bacteriuria.

Several recent studies have shown that the administration of a single dose of any of a variety of antibiotics (amoxicillin 2 grams p.o, sulfisaxazole 1 gram p.o, trimethoprimsulfa-methoxazole 160/800 mg (one double strength tablet) is effective in the treatment of uncomplicated symptomatic lower urinary tract infection (Fang et al, 1978; Rubin et al, 1980).

While these studies have generally included only young patients it is likely that this approach, which minimizes non-compliance, cost and risk of adverse reactions, will prove beneficial in the elderly.

Treatment of elderly patients with acute pyelonephritis follows the same principles as with younger patients. The same can be said of cases where chronic pyelonephritis is clinically manifest. If the patients have flare-ups with fever, or if there are signs of papillary necrosis in combination with bacteriuria, intensive treatment followed by long-term treatment is strongly indicated.

Since the bacteria which are found in the urine often are in vitro resistant to antimicrobial drugs, due to the fact that the patients concerned have often been repeatedly treated, it is necessary to discuss the treatment of urinary tract infection in the aged with different drugs. The best method is to begin the treatment with a sulphonamide. If there is a clinical failure of the treatment it should be continued with some other drug according to the in vitro sensitivity tests. Nitrofurantoin is also important as a primary treatment. The combination of sulphamethoxazole and trimethoprim has proved to be very effective. In a series of 117 geriatric patients Sourander et al (1967) got a positive response in the treatment of 109 cases. Antibiotic treatment with cephalexin — a cephalosporin derivative — seems to be both effective for the elderly patients, and well tolerated by them (Saarimaa et al, 1971).

An important question is the indication for long-term treatment of urinary-tract infection in the aged. This applies only to a relatively small group of patients — those with distressing symptoms and a high recurrence rate. The benefits are, of course, quite limited. The urine remains sterile a little longer than it would without treatment.

With a long-acting sulphonamide Sourander et al (1965) found that the patients were in 65 per cent of cases free of bacteriuria after a 6-month course of treatment. In a corresponding group of patients without treatment 35 per cent of cases were free of bacteriuria. The bacterial strain which caused the reinfection was in all cases a strain that was resistant to the drug used in long-term treatment. The benefit derived from long-term treatment with a combination of sulphamethoxazole and trimethoprim is established. Sourander and Havas (1969) treated two similar groups of geriatric hospital patients with significant bacteriuria, giving to one group a short-term sulphamethoxazole-trimetho-

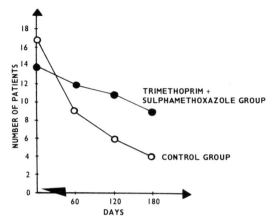

Fig. 29.5 Results of long-term treatment of urinary tract infection with sulphamethoxazole-trimethoprim (see text) (Sourander and Havas, 1969)

prim treatment and to the other a short-term treatment with ampicillin. After getting the patients' urine sterile they administrered to the first group long-term treatment with sulphamethoxazole-trimethoprim (sulphamethoxazole 800 mg and trimethoprim 160 mg daily, divided into two doses). The latter group received long-term treatment with a placebo. The urine of the patients in the first group was sterile for an average of 195 days, and in the placebo-treated group for an average 113 days (Fig. 29.5).

The attitude towards the use of long-acting sulphonamides has in recent years been more restrictive because of reported cases of the Stevens-Johnson syndrome developing in some treated patients. The development of superimposed infection during antibiotic treatment is quite frequently seen in geriatric practice. The development of vulvovaginitis in patients receiving antibiotics which afford high urinary concentration, needs special attention.

Long-term treatment with nitrofurantoin can lead to the development of chronic pulmonary fibrosis. The acute reactions to nitrofurantoin therapy — polyneuritis and pulmonary infiltrates — are well known. The complications of long-term administrations of nitrofurantoin were first described by Sollacio et al (1966) who during long-term therapy observed slowly progressing lung infiltrates and severe dyspnoea. Ruikka et al (1971) reported a case of progressive pulmonary fibrosis leading to death.

It has been shown that urinary bacteria commonly originate in the intestinal flora (Vahlne, 1945; Turck, Petersdorf and Fournier, 1962). Lincoln et al (1970) have claimed that treatment with sulphonamides may cause a change in the resistance pattern of the intestinal flora which then plays a part in subsequent urinary

infection. In their series of children the resistance patterns of urinary bacteria in recurrent infections closely reflected preceding changes in the intestinal flora. The authors point out that the current use of very potent new antibiotics also causes profound changes in the intestinal flora. The discrepancy between urinary and faecal flora is explained according to Lincoln et al by serial cultures from faeces and urethra which showed how an acquired, resistant strain disappeared from the faeces but persisted in the urethra.

Bacterial resistance to antimicrobials is a problem in geriatric hospital wards. Since urinary tract infections are derived from the faecal flora, the development of resistance of the bowel flora is of utmost importance. Long-term suppressive treatment with antibiotics and chemo-therapeutics can alter the sensitivity pattern. The transferable resistance is of special interest. In this case molecules of DNA, R-plasmids, carry genes that determine resistance to antibacterial agents. These R-plasmids are transferable between bacteria and can also be transferred between different Enterobacteriaceae. In long-term treatment of urinary tract infections nitrofurantoin is suitable because R-plasmid resistance is unknown for nitrofurantoin.

There is obviously a great need for a critical attitude and a restrictive treatment policy for the use of antibiotics in hospitals. Gruneberg and Bendall (1979) reported a hospital outbreak of plasmid-borne trimethoprim resistance in pathogenic coliform bacteria which was associated with heavy use of co-trimoxazole, sulphonamides and ampicillin, but was controlled by isolation of the patients and restriction of antibiotic use.

These observations have not been confirmed in old age but it seems highly probable that the frequent occurrence of multiple-resistant, coli strains causing urinary tract infections and pyelonephritis in the aged is not simply a result of treatment of urinary infections with antibiotics and chemotherapeutic agens, but that it is also a result of treatment of other infections, with a change in the faecal bacterial resistance-pattern and subsequent reinfection of the urinary tract. This might explain the high degree of recurrent urinary tract infection with multiple resistant bacterial strains in geriatric hospitals, and also explain the failure of the long-term administration of sulphonamides to prevent reinfection.

Observations of Lincoln et al suggests that nitrofurantoin may be a drug which combines a good antibacterial effect in the urinary tract with little or no effect on intestinal flora. The same can be said of cephalexin which is absorbed almost totally in the upper gastrointestinal tract, and rapidly excreted in the urine in high concentration.

The dosages of antimicrobial drugs must be lowered in cases of renal failure. The actual serum creatinine values must be taken into account and the dosage adapted to a level which corresponds with the decreased renal function. Estimation of the concentration of non-acetylated sulphonamide in serum is of great value and can successfully be used in securing long-term treatment with sulphonamide in patients with renal failure. Methenamine hippurate 1 g morning and evening gives a fairly good prophylaxis when abacteruria has been achieved after primary treatment of the infection with antibiotics. During a 16-month follow up the reinfections were reduced to two-thirds (Nilsson, 1975). Both mandelate and hippurate is well tolerated in aged patients.

A method of long-term treatment comprises the oral administration of an antimicrobial drug in the evening and maintaining a sufficient diuresis during the day.

Treatment of anaemia

Anaemia associated with renal disease is generally considered as a poor subject for treatment. Uraemic patients, especially aged, should be very cautiously treated with blood transfusions to avoid the development of acute pulmonary oedema. Instead of blood, erythrocyte suspensions are better tolerated. Some benefit has been obtained from the administration of cobalt chloride (Geill, 1969). Haemoglobin values can usually be raised by about 1 to 2 g per 100 ml after a three-week course with cobalt chloride. The drug is, however, potentially toxic, particularly in old people, and may cause a confusional state that is irreversible (Brocklehurst, 1971). (See also pp. 858–859).

Acute renal failure

Age influences renal disease by either altering the prevalence of specific diseases or by affecting the presentation, course, and response to treatment of conditions seen in both early and late adult life. Acute renal failure is seen more frequently in old patients simply because the common inciting events, including hypotension associated with marked volume depletion, major surgery, sepsis, major angiographic procedures or the injudicious use of antibiotics, are more common in multiply impaired elderly who are often at increased risk because of pre-existing moderate renal insufficiency.

The management of acute renal failure in the elderly is a complex and demanding task worthy of the effort. The aged kidney retains the capacity to recover from acute ischaemic or toxic insults over the course of several weeks. While the usual 'acute tubular necrosis' (ATN) with 2–10 days of oliguria followed by a diuretic phase preceding recovery of function is seen in the elderly, 'non-oliguric' acute renal failure is being recognized with increasing frequency. In these cases, renal function, as reflected in serum BUN and creatinine levels, is impaired for several days after a brief hypotensive episode associated with surgery, sepsis, over-medication or volume depletion or after the administration of neph-

rotoxic radiographic contrast agents. After this brief period of azotaemia renal function gradually returns to its previous level. Despite this transient and reversible loss of renal function, oliguria is not a prominent component of the clinical picture. Since the clinical hallmark of renal failure is generally thought to be a dramatic reduction in urine output, cases of non-oliguric acute renal failure may go unrecognized. This may result in the inadvertent overdose of patients during the period of impaired renal function with medications excreted predominantly via renal mechanisms, including digitalis preparations and aminoglycoside antibiotics such as gentamicin.

The management of elderly patients with full-blown acute renal failure complicated by oliguria is guided by the same principles employed in younger patients. The most important principle is the careful exclusion of urinary obstruction as a cause of the renal failure. This is particularly true in men with prostatic hypertrophy or prostatic carcinoma or in women with gynaecologic malignancy.

The major causes of death during acute renal failure are volume overload precipitating acute pulmonary oedema, hypertensive crisis, hyperkalaemia and infection. Dialysis, whether it be haemodialysis or peritoneal dialysis, is effective in the elderly and the complication rate seems more to be dictated by coincident cardiovascular disease rather than the patient's age. Dialysis often substantially simplifies management. Thus one should not wait until an emergency situation is present before initiating dialysis in a patient with acute renal failure. It is more prudent to initiate dialysis early in cases in which it is very likely that renal function will not return before the dialysis will be needed. The immediate indications for emergency dialysis include pulmonary oedema unresponsive to diuretics, hyperkalaemia, uraemic pericarditis, and seizures or uncontrolled bleeding on a uraemic basis. The use of intravenous catheters placed in the femoral vein for dialysis has been a recent major advance in the management of elderly patients with acute renal failure. These catheters are easily placed, may be left in for several days to a week with a very low incidence of infection or thrombosis and circumvent the need for implantation of arterio-venous shunts for access for dialysis in acute renal failure.

Aside from the initiation of dialysis, careful attention to the balance of several factors is necessary. Water and salt balance must be monitored carefully. Due to catabolism, the usual patient with acute renal failure will lose about about 0.5 kg of body mass per day. Attempts to keep body weight constant will result in the gradual expansion of the extracellular fluid and consequent increase in blood pressure and risk of precipitation of cardiac failure. Similarly, overzealous fluid restriction will impair the patient's general condition and central nervous system function and may delay the recovery of renal function. In general, the administration of approximately 600 ml of fluid a day, in addition to repletion of insensible losses, provides adequate fluid balance.

Potassium balance is crucial and hyperkalaemia must be avoided if possible and treated promptly if present. Acidosis progresses with the length and degree of renal failure and sodium bicarbonate should be administered in an effort to maintain circulating bicarbonate levels in the range of 15–19 mEq per litre. Administration of sodium bicarbonate may expand extracellular fluid volume and thus patients should be watched carefully for the development of congestive failure.

Infection is a common and lethal complication of acute renal failure. Urine infection secondary to unnecessary urinary catheterization is particularly common. Little is gained from placing a urinary catheter in an oliguric patient in whom volume status and serum levels of BUN, creatinine, and potassium are better guides to progress and treatment than his urinary output. Infection of intravenous lines is also common, and these should be scrupulously monitored and discontinued when possible.

Additional routine measures include the administration of oral phosphate binding agents in an effort to mimimize the elevation of serum phosphorus associated with acute renal failure and the administration of diet limited in protein content in order to blunt the rise in BUN. Of major importance is careful attention to the alteration in dose interval of medications excreted via the kidney and recognition of the enhanced sensitivity of elderly uraemic patients to psychotropic medication such as hypnotics and major tranquilizers.

Chronic renal failure

Many forms of chronic renal failure are more commonly seen late in life because the renal disease is secondary to other age-dependent diseases. Examples include prostatic hypertrophy or cancer leading to hydronephrosis, renovascular hypertension or renal failure secondary to atherosclerosis, multiple myeloma, drug-related causes of renal insufficiency and, perhaps most common, pre-renal azotaemia from congestive heart failure or volume depletion.

While the general principles of the management of renal failure are similar in young and old adults, the geriatric patient with chronic renal insufficiency presents several special considerations. With regard to diagnosis, serum creatinine generally fails to rise to as high levels in the elderly as in young despite equivalent levels of residual renal function. This is because muscle mass, the ultimate source of creatinine, falls with age, particularly in the presence of nutritional deficits such as seen in uraemia. Since serum creatinine underestimates the degree of renal failure many debilitated uraemic elderly

patients will not be recognized as uraemic since their creatinine levels may be less than 264 µmol/l (3.0 mg/dl) while substantially higher levels are common in younger uraemic patients.

Another factor often delaying recognition of chronic renal failure in the elderly is the presentation of renal failure as decompensation of a previously impaired organ system before the emergence of specific symptoms of uraemia. Examples include worsening of pre-existing heart failure or hypertension due to inability to excrete salt and water, gastrointestinal bleeding in the presence of GI malignancy or ulcer, or mental confusion in a border-line demented patient who becomes increasingly azotaemic.

Once the presence of chronic renal failure is established the definitive cause should be identified. Most renal failure in the elderly is due to chronic glomerulonephritis, hypertensive and atherosclerotic vascular disease, diabetes, or in some cases, late-presenting polycystic kidney disease. The most important diagnostic consideration is strict exclusion of potentially reversible causes such as urinary tract obstruction — particularly in men with symptoms of prostatism — renal arterial occlusion which may be repairable, hypercalcaemia or the administration of nephrotoxic agents.

If no reversible component is identified, the patient should be followed closely so that the rate of loss of renal function can be accurately judged. Appropriate adjustments to account for the renal failure should be made in the doses and dose schedules of all medications, especially digoxin. Hypertension should be carefully controlled. As serum phosphate rises, phosphate-binding antacids should be given, with meals, in order to suppress hyperphosphataemia, hypocalcaemia and the resultant adverse effects on bone. As serum phosphate falls in response to treatment, serum calcium will generally rise towards the normal range. If hypocalcaemia persists after normalization of phosphate this should be treated with preparations of Vitamin D or its congeners (Vitamin D — 50 000 unit tablets, b.i.d. to t.i.d.; Dihydrotachysterol, 0.2–0.4 mg b.i.d. or 1,25-dihydroxy Vitamin D_3, 0.25–0.5 mg b.i.d.) in order to increase intestinal calcium absorption.

Anaemia associated with chronic renal failure often requires more aggressive management in elderly patients because of co-existing cardiac disease. Red cell indices are not a reliable estimate of iron deficiency in uraemia. Iron deficiency should be excluded by evaluation of serum iron and ferritin and oral or parenteral iron supplements administered if indicated. In the absence of iron deficiency anaemia of chronic renal failure will respond to monthly injections of androgens (nandrolone decanlate, 200 mg i.m.). If symptomatic anaemia persists, which it often does, regular transfusions of red cells are indicated.

Dietary management of elderly with chronic renal failure is often overdone, thus compounding the nutritional impact of the disease. Protein and salt restriction is often needed in young individuals to suppress the volume expansion and BUN elevations. Many elderly patients ingest only 60–70 g of protein daily and 4–5 g of salt under normal conditions and strict limitations of these dietary constituents is often unnecessary. Similarly, hyperkalaemia should be avoided and dietary potassium controlled but the reductions required in the elderly are often moderate. Acidosis should be controlled with the addition of oral sodium bicarbonate tablets with the aim to keep serum bicarbonate levels near 18–20 mEq/L. The best approach to these modifications is careful alteration of the diet to the proven needs of the individual patient.

Pruritus is a major problem in elderly uraemic patients, especially the presence of co-existing xerosis. In addition to skin moisteners, ultra-violet treatments have been found effective and safe for elderly uraemics. Administration of so-called 'anti-pruritic' agents such as anti-histamines and ataractics are rarely helpful since they act primarily by causing sedation and may have adverse nervous system effects in the elderly.

Dialysis in the elderly

Chronic maintenance dialysis — generally haemodialysis but occasionally chronic ambulatory peritoneal dialysis — is an effective safe treatment for elderly uraemic patients. Elderly patients often do very well on dialysis with the frequency of complications seemingly more related to the coexisting extra-renal disease than age itself. Psychologically, elderly patients often are more able to adapt to chronic dialysis than their younger counterparts. Once it is clear that a patient will need dialysis at some time in the near future, and the decision is made that dialysis will be available to the patient, early creation of an arterio-venous fistula for access to haemodialysis is important. This is particularly so in the elderly since such fistulas often mature rather slowly. At present renal transplantation is generally not considered in individuals over age 60 years.

REFERENCES

Arieff A J, Anderson R J, Massry S G 1971 Acute glomerulonephritis in the elderly. Geriatrics 26: 74–84

Artursen G, Groth T, Grotte G 1971 Human glomerular membrane porocity and filtration pressure: dextran clearance data analyzed by theoretical models. Clinical Science 10: 137

Attman P-O, Bucht H 1971 Erfarenheter av höga doser furosemid vid avancerad njurinsufficiens. Läkartidningen 68, suppl iv: 49–57

Baehler R W, Galla J H 1976 Conservative management of chronic renal failure. Geriatrics 31: 46–50

Baert, Stegg 1977 Bartecchi C E 1975 When should peritoneal dialysis be considered in elderly patients? Geriatrics 30: 47–51

Baumanis J, Russell H K 1959 Pyelonephritis in a chronic disease hospital. Geriatrics 14: 25–37

Bell E T 1942 Exudative interstitial nephritis (pyelonephritis). Surgery II: 261–280

Bengtsson U 1962 A comparative study of chronic non-obstructive pyelonephritis and renal papillary necrosis. Acta Medica Scandinavica suppl 388

Bengtsson U, Hogdahl A, Hood B 1968 Chronic non-obstructive pyelonephritis and hypertension: a long term study. Quarterly Journal of Medicine 37: 361–377

Berlyne G M, Baker S B, De C 1964 Acute anuric glomerulonephritis. Quarterly Journal of Medicine 33: 105–115

Bollgren I, Winberg J 1976 The periurethral aerobic flora in girls highly susceptible to urinary infection. Acta Paediatria Scandinavica 65: 81–87

Boswell D C, Eknovan G 1968 Acute glomerulonephritis in the aged. Geriatrics 23: 73–80

Brenner B M, Meyer T W, Hostetter T H 1982 Dietary protein intake and the progressive nature of kidney disease. New England Journal of Medicine 307: 652 .

Brocklehurst J C 1971 In: Rossman I (ed) Clinical geriatrics p 227. J B Lippincott Philadelphia and Toronto

Brocklehurst J C, Dillane J B, Griffiths L, Fry J 1968a The prevalence and symptomatology of urinary infection in an aged population. Gerontologia Clinica 10: 242–253

Brocklehurst J C, Dillane J B, Griffiths L, Fry J 1968b A therapeutic trial in urinary infection of old age. Gerontologia Clinica 10: 345

Brocklehurst J C, Bee P, Jones D, Palmer M 1977 Bacteriuria in geriatric hospital patients: its correlates and management. Age and Ageing 6: 240–245

Brückel R W, Wincker H J 1963 Clinical aspects of urinary tract infections in geratrics. 6th International Congress of Gerontology Copenhagen (Excerpta medica Congr. ser. 57)

Carty M, Brocklehurst J C, Carty J 1981 Bacteriuria and its correlates in old age. Gerontology 27: 72–75

Cohen S N, Kass E H 1967 A simple method for quantitative urine culture. New England Journal of Medicine 277: 176–180

Conner J F, Coleman S E, Davis J L, McGaughey F S 1968 Bacterial L-forms from urinary-tract infections in a veterans' hospital population. Journal of the American Geriatrics Society 16: 893–900

Diaz-Buxo J A, Wagoner R D, Hattery R R, Palumbo P J 1975 Acute renal failure after excretory urography in diabetic patients. Annals of Internal Medicine 8–3: 155

Darmady E M, Offer J, Woodhouse M A 1973 The parameters of the aging kidney. Journal of Pathology 195–209

Dontas A S, Kasviki-Charvati P 1976 Significance of diuresis-provoked bacteriuria. Journal of Infectious Diseases 134: 174–180

Dontas A S, Rasviki-Charvati P, Chem L, Papanayioto P C, Marketos S G 1981 Bacteriuria and survival in old age. New England Journal of Medicine 304: 939–943

Dontas A S, Papanayiotou P, Marketos S, Papanicolaou N 1968 The effect of bacteriuria on renal functional patterns in old age Clinical Science 34: 73–81

Dontas A S, Papanayiotou P, Marketos S, Papanicolaou N, Economou P 1966 Bacteriuria in old age. Lancet ii: 305–306

Fang L S T, Tolkoff-Rubin N E, Rubin R H 1978 Efficacy of single-dose and conventional amoxicillin therapy in urinary-tract infection localized by the antibody-coated bacteria technic. New England Journal of Medicine 298: 413–416

Fawcett I W, Hilton P J, Jones N F, Wing A J 1971 Nephrotic syndrome in the elderly British Medical Journal 2: 387–388

Feingold D S 1969 Biology and pathogenicity of microbial spheroplasts and L-forms. New England Journal of Medicine 281: 1159–1170

Finkelstein F O, Hayslett J P 1976 Nephrotic syndrome: Etiology, diagnosis and treatment. Geriatrics 31: 39–48

Freedman L R 1967 Chronic pyelonephritis at autopsy. Annals of Internal Medicine 66: 697–710

Geill T 1969 On the treatment of the nephrogenic anaemias with a combined cobalt-iron preparation. Gerontologia Clinica II: 48–55

Gruneberg R N, Bendall M J 1979 Hospital outbreak of trimehoprim resistance in pathologenic coliform bacteria. British Medical Journal 2: 7–9

Guttmann D, Naylor G R E 1967 Dip-slide: an aid to quantitative urine culture in general practice. British Medical Journal 3: 343–345

Gutmann L T, Turck M, Petersdorf R G, Wedgwood R J 1965 Significance of bacterial variants in urine of patients with chronic bacteriuria. Journal of Clinical Investigation 44: 1945–1952

Hagenfeldt L, Wester P O, Lithander A, Eliash H 1962 The incidence of urinary tract infection in hospitalized patients. Scandinavian Journal of Clinical and Laboratory Investigation, suppl 64: 77–83

Harkonen S, Kjellstrand C M 1977 Exacerbation of diabetic renal failure following intravenous pyelography. American Journal of Medicine 673: 939

Jackson G G, Dallenbach F D, Kipnis G P 1955 Symposium on clinical advances in medicine; pyelonephritis; correlation of clinical and pathologic observations in antibiotic era. Medical Clinics of North America 39: 297

Kaarsalo E, Kasanen A, Laurent B, Sourander L 1964 Antibody response, haptoglobin and immunoglobins in geriatric patients after vaccination against salmonellosis Annals of Internal Medicine 53: 21–24

Kamdar A, Weidmann P, Markoff D L, Marssy S G 1977 Acute renal failure following intravenous use of radiographic contrast dyes in patients with diabetes Mellitus. Diabetes 26: 643

Kaplan C, Pasternack B, Shah B 1975 Age-related incidence of sclerotic glomeruli in human kidneys. American Journal of Pathology 80: 227

Kasanen A, Salmi H 1959 Significance of some renal function tests in the early diagnosis of chronic pyelonephritis. Acta Medica Scandinavica 165: 147–152

Kasanen A, Vasama R 1964 Renal papillary necrosis. Duodecim 80: 446–453 Helsinki

Kass E H 1955 Chemotherapeutic and antibiotic drugs in management of infection of urinary tract. American Journal of Medicine 18: 764–781

Kass E H 1956 Asymptomatic infections of the urinary tract. Transactions of the Association of American Physicians 69: 56–67

Kass E H 1962 Chemotherapy of infections of the urinary tract. Practitioner 188: 22–26

Kass E H, Miall W E, Stuart K L 1961 Relationship of bacteriuria to hypertension; an epidemiological study. Journal of Clinical Investigation 40: 1053

Kimmelstiel P 1964 The nature of chronic pyelonephritis. Geriatrics 19: 145–157

Kimmelstiel P, Wilson C 1936 Intercapillary lesions in the glomeruli of the kidney. American Journal of Pathology 12: 83–98

Kirkland J L, Robinson J M 1981 Bacteriuria and survival in old age. New England Journal of Medicine 305: 586–587

Kjellstrand C M, Shideman J R, Lynch R E, Buselmeier T J, Simmons R L, Najarian J S 1976 Kidney transplants in patients over 50. Geriatrics 31: 65–73

Kleeman S E, Freedman L R 1960 The finding of chronic pyelonephritis in males and females at autopsy. New England Journal of Medicine 263: 988–992

Lee H A, Stirling G, Scharpstone P, 1966 Acute glomerulonephritis in middle-aged and elderly patients. British Medical Journal 2: 1361–1363

Lidin Janson G, Hanson L A, Kaijser B et al 1977 Comparison of Escherichia coli from bacteriuric patients with those from gaeces of health school children. Journal of Infectious Diseases 136: 346–353

Lieberthal F 1939 Pyelonephritic contracture of the kidney. Surgery, Gynecology and obstetrics 69: 159–171

Lincoln K, Lidin-Janson G, Winberg J 1970 Resistant urinary infections resulting from changes in resistance pattern of faecal flora induced by sulphonamide and hospital environment. British Medical Journal 3: 305–309

Ljungqvist A, Lagerggen C 1962 Normal intrarenal arterial pattern in adult and aging human kidney. Journal of Anatomy (London) 96: 285

MacDonald R A, Levitin H, Mallory G K, Kass E H 1957 Relation between pyelonephritis and bacterial counts in the urine: an autopsy study. New England Journal of Medicine 256: 915–922

Machachlan 1978

McLachlan M S F, Guthrie J C, Anderson C K 1977 Vascular and glomerular changes in the aging kidney. Journal of Pathology 121: 65

McLachlan M S F 1978 The aging kidney. Lancet 2: 143

Marketos S G, Dontas A S, Papanayiotou P, Economous P 1970 Bacteriuria and arterial hypertension in old age. Geriatrics 25: 136–146

Marketos S G, Papanayiotou P, Dontas A S 1969 Bacteriuria and non-obstructive renovascular disease in old age. Journal of Gerontology 23: 33–36

Marner I L, Faurschou-Jensen S 1963 Infektiøse nyrelidelser i en almenmedicinsk afdeling Ugeskrift for Laeger 125: 556–563

Miller J H, MacDonald R K, Shock N W 1951 Renal extraction of PAH in the aged individual. Journal of Gerontology 6: 213–216

Mitchell A D, Valk W L 1953 Renal function in the aged. Geriatrics 8: 263–266

Moore-Smith B 1974 The treatment of urinary tract infections in elderly women. Modern Geriatrics 4: 408–414

Mortiz A R, Oldt M R 1973 Arteriolar sclerosis in hypertensive and non-hypertensive individuals. American Journal of Pathology 13: 679

Nesson H R, Robbins S L 1960 Glomerulonephritis in older age groups. Archives of Internal Medicine 105: 47–56

Nilsson S 1975 Long-term treatment with methenamine hippurate in recurrent urinary tract infection. Acta Medica Scandinavica 198: 1–2, 81–85

Olbrich O, Ferguson M H, Robson J S, Stewart C P 1950 Renal function in aged patients. Edinburgh Medical Journal 57: 112–121

Olbrich O, Woodford-Williams E, Irvine R E, Webster D 1957 Renal function in prostatism. Lancet i: 1322

Oliver J 1952 Urinary system. In: Cowdry E V (ed) Problems of Aging. Williams and Wilkins, Baltimore

Parvinen M, Sourander L B, Vuorinen P 1965 Cystographic studies of old women. Gerontologia Clinica 7: 343–347

Petersdorf R G 1966 In: Ingelfinger F J, Relman A S, Finland M (ed) Controversy in Internal Medicine, p 311. W B Saunders Co, Philadelphia and London

Prewitt G 1943 Pyelonephritis. Western Journal of Surgery 51: 393

Raaschou F 1948 Studies of Chronic Pyelonephritis with Special Reference to Kidney Function. Munksgaard, Copenhagen

Ralston A J 1975 Renal disease. Modern Geriatrics 5: 10–14

Reynes M, Caulet T, Diebold J 1968 Microvascularisation du rein normal et senescent. Pathologie et Biologie 16: 1081–1089

Roberts A P, Robinson R E, Beard R W 1967 Some factors affecting bacterial colony counts in urinary tract infection. British Medical Journal 1: 400–403

Roessle R, Roulet F 1932 Mass und Zahl in der Pathologie: p 63. Springer, Berlin

Rowe J W, Andres R, Tobin J D, Norris A H, Shock N W 1976 The effect of age on creatinine clearance in man: a cross-sectional and longitudinal study. Journal of Gerontology 31: 155

Rubin R H, Fang S T, Jones S R, Munford R S, Slepack J M, Verga P A 1980 Single-dose amoxicillin therapy for urinary tract infection. Journal of the American Medical Association 244: 561–564

Ruikka I, Sourander L B 1967 Phenacetin consumption, occurrence of urinary tract infection and renal function in a series of aged hospital patients. Gerontologia Clinica 9: 99–102

Ruikka I, Vaissalo T, Saarimaa H 1971 Progressive pulmonary fibrosis during nitrofurantoin therapy. Scandinavien Journal of Respiratory 52: 162–166

Saarimaa H, Sourander L B, Arvilommi H 1971 Treatment of urinary tract infections with Cephalexin. Advances in antimicrobial and antineoplastic chemotherapy. Proceedings of the VIIth International Congress of Chemotherapy, Prague: 1347–1349

Sanjurjo L A 1959 The problem of chronic pyelonephritis. Medical Clinics of North America 43: 1601–1610

Seneca H, Grant J P Jr 1976 Urologic sepsis/shock. Journal of the American Geriatrics Society 24: 292–300

Shock N W 1952 In: Cowdry's Problems of Ageing (3rd edn): p 614. Williams and Wilkins, Baltimore

Shock N W 1968 The physiology of aging. In: Powers J H (ed) Surgery of the Aged and Debilitated Patient: p 17. Saunders, London

Snyder A, Brest A N 1966 Chronic renal insufficiency treated with anabolic steriods: effects on acid-base balance, protein metabolism and hematopoiesis. Journal of the American Geriatrics Society 14: 21–32

Sollacio P A, Ribaudo C A, Grace W J 1966 Subacute pulmonary infiltration due to nitrofurantoin. Annals of Internal Medicine 65: 1284–1286

Sorenson F 1977 Quantitative studies of the renal corpuscles. Acta Pathologica et Microbiologica Scandinavica 85: 356

Sourander L B 1966 Urinary tract infection in the aged. An epidemiological study. Annales medicinae internae Fenniae suppl 45: 56

Sourander L B, Havas L 1969 Langzeitbehandlung chronischer Harnwegsinfekte bei geriatrischen Patienten mit einem neuen Chemotherapeuticum. Paper read at 13 Kongresskreuzfahrt, Wiener Medizinische Akademie für ärztliche Fortbildung

Sourander L B, Kaarsalo E, Kasanen A 1967 Antibody formation after vaccination against salmonellosis in adults and geriatric patients with urinary tract infection. Gerontologia Clinica 9: 103–106

Sourander L B, Kasanen A 1965 En dos 'långtids' sulfonamid i veckan (4-sulfanilamido-5-6-dimetoxypyrimidin) vid behandling av urinvägsinfektioner hos åldringar. Nordisk Medicin 74: 1229–1230

Sourander L, Kasanen A, Pasternack A, Kaarsalo E 1979 Uraemia in the aged in South-Western Finland. A longitudinal study. In: Orimo H, Shimada K, Iriki M, Maeda D (eds) Recent advances in gerontology. International congress series 469 Excerpta Medica, Amsterdam, Oxford, Princeton, p 540–546

Sourander L B, Ruikka I, Gronroos M 1965 Correlation between urinary tract infection, prolapse conditions and function of the bladder in aged female hospital patients. Gerontologia Clinica 7: 179–184

Sourander L B, Ruikka I, Kasanen A 1970 A health survey of the aged with a 5-year follow-up. Acta Sociomedica Scandinavica, suppl 3

Sourander L B, Saarimaa H, Arvilommi H 1972 Treatment of sulfonamide-resistant urinary tract infections with a combination of sulfonamide and trimethoprim. Acta Medica Scandinavica 191: 1–3

Sourander L B, Werner G E 1967 Efficacy and tolerance of sulphonamide-trimethoprim combinations in geriatric patients with bacteriuria. Proceatings of the 5th International Congress on Chemotherapy: 199–211. Vienna

Stamey T A, Timothy M, Miller M, Mihara G 1971 Recurrent urinary infections in adult women. The role of introital enterobacteria. California Medicine 115: 1–19

Stewart C P 1959 Renal function in the aged. Gerontologia Clinica I: 160

Svanborg Eden C 1978 Attachment of Escherichia coli to human uroepithelial cells. An in vitro test system applied in the study of urinary tract infection. Scandinavian Journal of Infectious Diseases Suppl 15: 1–74

Sworn M J, Fox M 1972 Donor Kidney selection for transplantation. British Journal of Urology 44: 377

Takazakura E, Sawabu N, Handa A, Takada A, Shinoda A, Takeuchi I 1972 Intrarenal vascular changes with age and disease. Kidney International 2: 224

Tauchi H, Tsuboi K, Okutomi J 1971 Age changes in the human kidney of the different races. Gerontologia 17: 87

Turck M, Gutman L T, Wedgwood R J, Petersdorf R G 1968 In: Guze L B (ed) Microbial Protoplasts, Spheroplasts and L-forms: p 415. Williams and Wilkins, Baltimore

Turck M, Petersdorf R G, Fournier M R 1962 The epidemiology of non-enteric Escherichia coli infections: prevalence of serological groups. Journal of Clinical Investigation 41: 1760–1765

Vahlne G 1945 Serological typing of the colon bacteria. Acta Pathologica et Microbiologica Scandinavica, suppl 62

Vallery-Radot P, Delafontaine P 1930 Le rein des vieillards. Presse Médicale 38: 265–269

Vertes V, Bloomfield D K, Patel R, Gary M 1967 Peritoneal dialysis in the geriatric patient. Journal of the American Geriatrics Society 15: 1019–1024

Walker P J, Ginn H E, Johnson H K, Stone W J, Teschan P E, Latos D, Stouder D, Lamberth E L, O'Brien K 1976 Long-term hemodialysis for patients over 50. Geriatrics 31: 55–61

Wesson L G 1969 Physiology of the Human Kidney. Grune and Stratton, New York, p 98

Wittler R G 1968 In: Guze L B (ed) Microbial Protoplasts, Spheroplasts and L-forms: p 200. Williams and Wilkins, Baltimore

Woodford Williams E 1960 Renal function in the aged. British Journal of Clinical Practice 14: 351–359

Zollinger H U 1966 Niere und ableitende Harnwege In: Doerr W, Uehlinger E (ed) Spezielle pathologische Anatomie vol 3: p 116. Springer-Verlag, Berlin

The genitourinary system — the bladder

INTRODUCTION

Impairment of functional efficiency is the most important practical problem relating to the bladder in old age, and is the main concern of this chapter. The causes are multifactorial and their consideration must be preceded by a brief survey of recent concepts of bladder anatomy and physiology. This is followed by a review of such age changes as are known to occur. The aetiology and management of age-related bladder dysfunction are then discussed in detail.

Important conditions such as papilloma, carcinoma and calculus which present in the aged as in those of middle age, are the concern of textbooks of surgery and are not dealt with here. The management of prostatic hypertrophy, a major urological problem of old age, is discussed in Chapter 31.

Embryology

The main part of the bladder, the detrusor muscle, is formed from the entodermal cloaca. This also forms most of the female urethra and the male posterior urethra, the prostate and the paraurethral glands. The mesonephric Wolffian ducts which are of mesenchymal origin, constitute an island of mesoderm on the base of the bladder which extends from the ureteric orifices to the urethra, and becomes the trigone. Other associated structures of entodermal origin are the vagina, uterus and Fallopian tubes. The skin of the external urethral meatus and of the vulva, and of the distal urethra in the male are ectodermal.

All of these facts are generally agreed, but there is much less certainty as to the final epithelial covering of the trigone and female urethra. Arey (1965) suggests that encroaching entodermal epithelium replaces that of the trigone. Zuckermann (1940), studying the oestrogen sensitivity of tissues in the bladder, suggested there was an invasion of the mesenchymal trigone tissues by entoderm, and of the entodermal tissues in the urethra by ectodermal epithelium.

Histology

The trigone would seem to be a mixtures of tissues, reacting in different ways to oestrogen stimulation. This may be of some importance in the aetiology of bladder changes in elderly women, and may also be relevant to the treatment of some forms of dysuria. Burns (1939) showed that animals given oestrogens replaced the normal tissues of the urethra and trigone by stratified squamous epithelium. Tyler (1962) in an autopsy study of 107 subjects found squamous epithelium covering the trigone in 86 per cent of premenopausal and 50 per cent of postmenopausal women, in only 1 of 23 males (and he was on estrogens for carcinoma of the prostate) and in no stillbirths, new-born or children. Henry and Fox (1971) described this oestrogen-sensitive area as 'greyish heaped-up mucosa with a serpiginous margin, surrounded by a cuff of hyperaemia'. It contains vacuoles and glycogen and shows a sudden change at its edge to transitional epithelium. They found similar changes in the trigonal area of males on oestrogen therapy.

That similar age change which affects the vagina also affects the urethra has been shown by several workers (Youngblood et al, 1958; von Rutte and Delnon, 1968; Smith et al, 1970; Smith, 1972).

All of these various findings were drawn together by Packham (1971) who related changes in oestrogen-sensitive squamous epithelium in the trigone of premenopausal women with the condition of 'abacterial recurrent cystitis' or the urethral syndrome. He limited this syndrome to oestrogen changes occurring throughout the menstrual cycle; thus, times of high oestrogen level led to marked keratinization of the squamous epithelium, and times of low oestrogen level showed this epithelium to be red and granular — the latter may be associated with symptoms characteristic of the urethral syndrome.

The epithelium lining the remainder of the bladder (apart from the trigone) is transitional — 3 to 4 cells deep. Jacob et al (1978) described the electron microscope appearance in biopsies from 8 subjects aged 61–82 years. These showed areas in which the the epithelium was only one cell deep — a change which they attributed to aging.

Other changes commonly found in the urothelium of elderly subjects are Von Brunn's Nests and cystitis cystica. Wiener et al (1979) found the former in 89 per cent and the latter in 60 per cent of 100 grossly normal bladders at autopsy in subjects of all ages. They regard these as normal findings.

The possibility of a female homologue of the prostate gland contributing of bladder outlet obstruction in the female has been a matter of discussion for a very long time. Embryologically the paraurethral glands of the female would seem to be direct homologues of the prostate, and in 1853 Virchow noted concretions in these glands in elderly women which were similar to the calcification occurring in the prostates of old men. Beneventi (1943) differentiated between the normal paraurethral glands of full-time female infants which he said never occurred posteriorly, and two out of 21 specimens he examined which showed posterior glands indistinguishable from those of the male prostate. The subject is further discussed by Moore (1960) but he found no evidence to suggest that tissue excised from the bladder neck of the female simulated the adenomatous appearance of prostatic enlargement in the male. The general consensus of opinion would seem to be that, while there is an embryological homology between the paraurethral glands and the prostate, the former do not become enlarged in older age groups as does the prostate, and they do not seem to be an important element in bladder neck obstruction in the female.

The aging of the individual epithelial cells lining the bladder has been described by Mooney and Hinman (1974).

Connective tissues

Tissue changes with age have been described in mice (Phillips and Davies, 1981) and in the human (Brocklehurst and Phillips, unpublished). In mice the only bladder change was an increased cellularity of the lamina propria but in the urethra there was a quantitative loss of smooth muscle which was replaced by fibrous tissue. In the human female urethra a similar change was seen with an increase in collagen/smooth muscle mixed area of tissue and diminution in pure smooth muscle. These changes may explain the lower urethral closing pressure noted by several workers (e.g. Raz and Haufman, 1977).

Mucosal prolapse of the urethral epithelium at the external meatus is commonly seen in old women. Dymock (unpublished) examined 100 female geriatric patients and found statistically significant correlations between urethrocele of this type and incontinence, but not with parity or urinary infection. Although all

patients with vaginal prolapse showed some degree of urethrocele, this only accounted for nine of the 69 patients with urethrocele. The cause and significance of these findings is not proven. The urethrocele could be prolapsing or oedematous mucosa.

Anatomy

The anatomy of the bladder musculature has been well described, particularly by Tanagho et al (1968) and Woodburne (1961). They indicate that detrusor muscle fibres are continued into the urethra as longitudinal fibres, and form the major part of the urethral wall. By their contraction, they tend to shorten the urethra (the whole female urethra and the prostatic urethra in the male). The trigone and the detrusor are intimately related to each other, but the trigone muscle fibres which rise as a continuation of the fibres of the ureter, and which extend medially to form the inter-ureteric bar, also extend down into the bladder outlet to be inserted in the *verumontanum urethrae* in the male, and in the terminal part of the urethra in the female. Contraction of this muscle will therefore produce an initial funnelling of the bladder outlet, which is subsequently maintained by further contractions of the detrusor.

The muscles of the urogenital diaphragm, including the external urethral sphincter and the pelvic muscles are under voluntary control. Gosling et al (1981) compared the external sphincter and the levator ani muscles in the human and showed a number of important differences. The fibres of the external urethral sphincter were one-third of the diameter of those of the levator ani and contained no spindles. They were classified as Type 1 fibres (slow twitch) whereas the levator ani was mixed Type 1 and Type 2. They concluded that the external urethra was capable of maintaining tone over a prolonged period without fatigue, a finding which is in keeping with that of Garry and colleagues (1959) that the external sphincter at rest shows a tonic discharge and this tends to increase with bladder filling. However, several workers have shown that the external sphincter is not necessary for the maintainance of continence in normal people (e.g. Sundin and Peterson, 1975). Neither does bilateral section of the pudendal nerves lead to leakage or incontinence (Langworthy et al, 1940; Emmet et al, 1948). Ardvan and colleagues (1967b) showed that the urethra of the dog can be cut leaving only the proximal 0.25 cm, (thus removing the external sphincter) and continence retained.

Rossier and colleagues (1982) from work using pudendal nerve block suggest that the striated urethral muscle contributes approximately 50 per cent of the maximum urethral closure pressure.

The question of 'tone' in bladder muscle has been the

subject of a number of experiments. It seems clear that the bladder muscle has no tone in the sense of a degree of maintained contraction which can be increased or diminished by interference in the peripheral nerves or central nervous system. Such tone as there is appears to be a physical property of the muscle itself, and is always the same for any single bladder, even when the central nervous system effect is removed, either by anaesthesia or by death. This tone will be altered only by exposure of the bladder to varying degrees of distension. For instances, Schmaelze et al (1969) showed that bladders of dogs, kept empty for a period of 6 weeks by diversion of the ureters, showed a capacity diminished to 12.5 per cent of the original, and that when bladder filling was resumed capacity was restored to 88 per cent of the former level.

Innervation

Bladder innervation has been the subject of a considerable amount of research and controversy. In simple terms it may be represented as a sacral micturition reflex through the pelvic (parasympathetic) nerves to a centre in the second, third and fourth sacral segments of the spinal cord, which is affected (either facilitated or inhibited) by an ascending series of centres. This is represented in Figure 30.1. The classical view of micturition is that the sacral segments of the cord contain a centre which is entirely adequate for bladder filling and emptying (e.g. Denny Brown and Robertson, 1933). However, recent investigations of subjects with detrusor sphincter dyssynergia (a condition in which the bladder contracts but its outlet does not relax) indicates that complete bladder emptying requires involvement of the pontine centre and so the effective bladder reflex is a supraspinal one (Bradley et al, 1974; Siroky and Krane, 1982; Blaivas, 1982). The highest centre, which has an inhibitory influence over those beneath it, has been shown by Andrew and Nathan (1964) to lie in the superior medial part of the middle of the frontal lobe, in the anterior end of the cingulate gyrus and in the

white matter between these areas and the genu of the corpus callosum. This centre must be receiving information about the state of the bladder, and mediates conscious or unconscious impulses to it.

There is some evidence also that the basal ganglia may affect bladder function (stimulation causing inhibition and ablation causing detrusor hyperreflexia (Lewin et al, 1967).

Sensory receptors in the bladder submocosa are principally free nerve endings (Fletcher and Bradley, 1978). They are sensitive to distension and to mucosal deformation — as well as to touch and pain. They relay through the sacral (parasympathetic) innervation, except those from the trigone which are in the lumbar (sympathetic) innervation. The tracks decusate in the lumbo-sacral cord and relay through the spino-thalamic tracts. Some afferent axones also cross to the opposite side in the bladder wall.

In the spinal cord the efferent pathways serving micturition lie in the lateral columns in line with the central canal (Nathan and Smith, 1958).

Peripherally there seems to be no doubt that bladder detrusor contractions are mediated by cholinergic neurotransmission (Diokno et al, 1973) although there is uncertainty on the place of adrenergic effects in micturition. Gosling and Dixon (1975) confirm that in animals there is a rich supply of catacholamine containing nerves in the muscle coat of the urethra (as reported by Rohner et al, 1971). Examining the bladder neck and proximal urethra in human material they found adrenergic innervation only in the proximal urethra of the male where it may well be involved in ejaculation (Gosling et al, 1977). Pharmacological and animal experiments however, indicate widespread α-adrenergic innervation of the smooth muscle of the urethra in both sexes (e.g. Caine, 1977; McGuire and Herlihy, 1979 — see also review by Creed and Tulloch, 1978).Current opinion is that α-adrenergic innervation is predominant in contraction of the smooth muscle of the urethra and while most of the experimental work is in animals evidence in man rests on changes in the urethral closing pressure as measured in the urethral pressure profile (e.g. Caine, 1977; Caine et al, 1978).

The maintenance of continence

As long as the closing pressure of the urethra is greater than the intravesical pressure continence will be maintained. The continence mechanisms in the urethra and bladder therefore will be considered separately.

The slit shape of the urethra itself provides a closure mechanism which has the nature of a flutter valve (Pullen et al, 1982; Hickey et al, 1982). To this must be added the effect of connective tissue and of the rich plexus of venous sinuses in the submucosa, (Tulloch, 1974; Fletcher and Bradley, 1978), the smooth muscle compo-

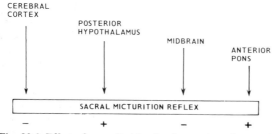

Fig. 30.1 Effect of ascending levels of control on the sacral micturition reflex. − = inhibition + = facilitation (Cerebral cortex — enters consciousness; anterior pons — co-ordinates detrusor and external sphincter) (After Tang and Ruch, 1956)

nent and possibly a striated muscle component. Rud et al (1980) suggested (from work in cats) that the closing pressure of the urethra was derived one-third from the vascular component, one-third from the smooth muscle and one-third from striated muscle. Another important feature, particularly in the female is the intra-abdominal part of the proximal urethra which is subject to the same rise in intra-abdominal pressure as is the bladder (e.g. in coughing which thus increases the closure pressure, McGuire, 1977).

The mechanics of opening and closure of the bladder itself are more uncertain. Hutch (1972) proposed a theory depending on the 'base plate' of the bladder. He described this as consisting of the trigone and circular detrusor fibres arranged as shown in Figure 30.2. As long as the base plate is flat its muscle components draw together around the bladder outlet, maintaining it closed. If the base plate is broken the same muscle bands then form a diminishing cone which contributes to bladder emptying. Dislocation of the base plate occurs from the action of the posterior longitudinal layer of the detrusor muscle acting as shown in Figure 30.2.

Other theories are that the trigone opens the bladder neck (Tanagho et al, 1968), and that the longitudinal smooth muscle fibres in the urethra are a continuation of those of the detrusor and by their contraction they open the urethra.

The last word has still to be said on how the bladder

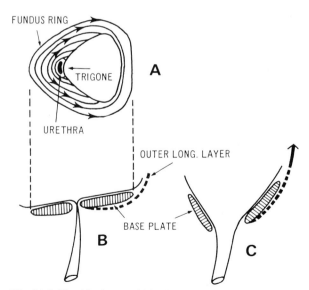

Fig. 30.2 Hutch's theory of bladder emptying showing the base plate (A and B) and dislocation of the base plate by contraction of the outer longitudinal muscle (C). (From Hutch, J. (1972) *Anatomy and Physiology of the Bladder, Trigone and Urethra*. Courtesy of Appleton-Century-Crofts, publishing division of Prentice-Hall)

functions. In general terms voluntary micturition begins with relaxation of the striated muscles of the pelvic floor and cessation of cortical inhibition. Lower cerebral reflexes then facilitate the development of detrusor contractions, the bladder neck is opened, the urethra shortened and urine is passed. Supplementary mechanisms include an increase in abdominal pressure but this is not necessary.

Abnormalities of micturition

This complicated process of micturition may be interrupted by disease and injury at various levels within the central nervous system. These produce the different types of neurogenic (or neuropathic) bladder and these have been the subject of a number of different classifications. Perhaps the simplest is to describe the neurogenic bladder as being either hyperreflexive or areflexive (directly analogous to upper and lower motor neurone lesions). The areflexive bladder is associated with lesions within the sacral segments of the cord and the hyperreflexive bladder with lesions above this level. A more comprehensive classification was propounded first by McLennan (1939) who described four types of neurogenic bladder as follows:

The autonomous bladder. Both afferent and efferent sides of parasympathetic innervation are destroyed by lesions involving destruction of the corda equina (e.g. by tumour). Vague sensation may remain through the sympathetic innervation, but in general the autonomous bladder is devoid of effective sensation and empties incontinently and inefficiently from time to time, as a result of local and axonal reflexes.

The atonic neurogenic bladder. This is the overdistended bladder which occurs typically in tabes dorsalis with destruction of the posterior nerve roots. Some power of voluntary micturition remains, but because the patient is so constantly unaware of bladder filling, the bladder tends to become overdistended leading eventually to retention and overflow. A similar type of bladder is sometimes found in patients with diabetic autonomic neuropathy.

The reflex neurogenic bladder. This is one in which the sacral bladder centre remains intact, but both the afferent and efferent connections with higher centres are destroyed. This is the typical paraplegic bladder, which is devoid of sensation, and empties incontinently from time to time. This bladder is associated with a degree of residual urine since emptying is impaired by diminished or absent coordination between the detrusor muscle and the smooth or the striated urethral muscles. Thus the detrusor may contract against a closed bladder outlet — leading to trabeculation and diverticula formation and proceeding to the 'fir tree' appearance of the advanced paraplegic bladder. The paraplegic may be above to initiate micturition reflexly by various forms of sensory stimulation in the area of the second, third and fourth sacral dermatomes.

The uninhibited neurogenic bladder. Here, sensation is retained, but the ability to inhibit spontaneous contractions is lost. This is usually the result of a lesion in the frontal cortex and may occur in patients with stroke or with frontal lobe tumour.

For general purposes this is a good working classification although, because many lesions in the cord are only partial, the distinction between the reflex and uninhibited neurogenic bladders is not always clear.

Psychological effects

Disorders of micturition may arise not only from organic changes within the central nervous system but also from functional changes. The acquisition of continence in the early years of life requires an awareness by the young child of the sensation of bladder distension, an awareness of the social necessities to postpone micturition until time and place are appropriate and the ability, by an act of will, to inhibit reflex contractions developing through the sacral segment of the cord and reflex emptying which involves the pontine centre. The 'toilet training' by which this ability is acquired tends to be based on systems of rewards and punishments. It is also a subject which carries social taboos and it is not surprising therefore that for many people the whole process of micturition has strong emotional overtones. Many have difficulty in initiating micturition in the company of others and it is almost a universal experience that episodes of mental stress can be associated with a degree of frequency and urgency of micturition (e.g. before sitting examinations). The whole subject has been well reviewed by Wells (1984). Some children acquire control of micturition late and spend numbers of years as enuretics and some acquire it precariously so that the control is more easily lost than in other people.

The unstable bladder (detrusor instability)

The unstable bladder is one which develops uninhibited intrinsic bladder contractions either as a response to filling or as a response to provocative stimuli such as coughing, laughing or changing position. The unstable bladder is generally regarded as any bladder which on cystometry develops contractions greater than 15 cm of water at a time when the subject is not attempting to micturate. A provocative stimulus may be required to demonstrate this. The term unstable bladder or detrusor instability is used in two different ways at the present time. One is to describe as unstable any bladder in which uninhibited contractions of 15 cm of water and above develop, either in the presence or absence of overt disease within the central nervous system. Thus all hyperreflexive bladders and all uninhibited and reflex neurogenic bladders would be regarded as unstable, by

this usage. The term is also used to designate bladders in patients who show no overt evidence of disease within the central nervous system but who show the features of detrusor instability. This second usage (which would seem the more appropriate) describes a condition which is common in subjects of all ages and which may be present in association with pathology within the pelvis e.g. cystitis, prostatic enlargement, prolapse and with previous pelvic surgery. The unstable bladder may be asymptomatic or it may be associated with the symptoms of frequency, nocturia, urgency and urge incontinence. It would seem that the process of cortical inhibition has been imperfectly acquired and is precariously maintained. This is sometimes called ideopathic detrusor instability. It would seem to be a functional disorder as evidenced by the very high response to placebos in drug trials and the very good response to behavioural therapy (see below).

The bladder in old age

Anatomically the main changes in the lower urinary tract associated with aging are histological and have already been described. Basically they consist of areas of diminished epithelial thickness and in the urethra of some replacement of smooth muscle by connective tissue. However, the gross changes of trabeculation, cellule and diverticula are common in the elderly (see Figs. 30.3, 30.8, 30.9). In some males these are associated with bladder outlet obstruction due to benign prostatic hypertrophy. However, in other men and in women they are almost certainly the accompaniment of some impairment of cerebral control of micturition — that is of the uninhibited neurogenic bladder. Brocklehurst and Dillane (1967) described a series of micturating cystograms 23 of which showed trabeculation, diverticula formation and cellular formation. 19 of these showed uninhibited bladder contractions and all 23 showed evidence of organic cerebral disease.

INVESTIGATION OF BLADDER FUNCTION

Four important approaches to the investigation of bladder function in elderly patients are as follows:

History and clinical examination

History of bladder function should always be obtained in the medical examination of elderly people. It should include the number of micturitions during the night, the frequency of micturition by day, the presence or absence of precipitancy, scalding, dribbling and incontinence including the differentiation of stress incontinence. Knowledge of the presence or absence of any of these symptoms, together with their duration, is an essential premliminary to the diagnosis of dysuria. If incontin-

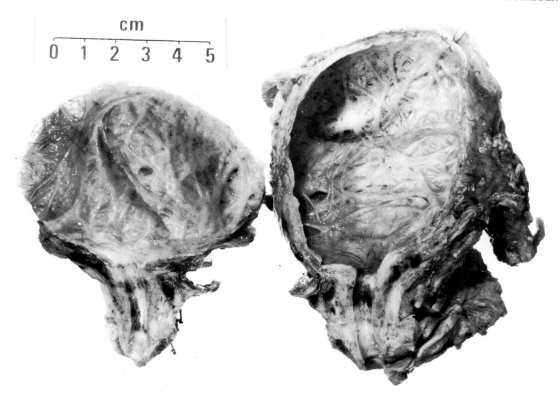

Fig. 30.3 Bisected female bladder showing trabeculation and cellule formation

ence is present, then its pattern must also be enquired into; also whether or not the patient is aware of impending micturition.

A bladder chart kept either by the nursing staff or by the patient if at home, is a most useful addition to the history. Bladder charts should indicate not only the time of the wetting but also the time of every visit to the lavatory and whether or not urine was passed on each occasion. In hospitals it is useful to have such a chart maintained 4, 3 or 2 hourly (Brocklehurst, 1972) but with patients at home a less structured chart is often more acceptable.

Clinical examination should include inspection of the vulva and urethra and digital examination of the rectum. The state of the reflexes in the legs and the presence or absence of a palpable bladder are also very relevant.

A number of methods have been devised to provide objective measurement of the extent of incontinence. Early among these was the Urilos nappy described by James et al (1971) which measures the time of first wetting but does not provide a reliable quantitative measurement over a period of time (Wilson et al, 1980).

A simple method of quantifying urine loss over a period of time is by the use of a series of pads which are changed at regular intervals and weighted. (Walsh and Mills, 1981).

Cystometry

Essentially a cystometer consists of a manometer attached to a catheter in the bladder; it thus shows pressure changes occurring within the bladder as it fills. For convenience this is generally linked to a recording device, and a further addition may be that of a reservoir so that the bladder may be filled either continously or by increments of 25, 50 or 100 ml of fluid at a time. Carbon dioxide gas is also used for filling (see review by Bradley et al, 1975). The cystometer then allows the observation of the bladder's reaction to increasing distension and to certain provocative stimuli (e.g. change of position, coughing). The complete investigation will give information on the following heads: residual urine; capacity: intravesical pressure at various stages; the presence or absence of uninhibited bladder contractions; the point at which desire to void is first felt.

It is suggested that, when the bladder is filled by the patient's own secretion of urine only, a more physiological situation is present, and Comarr (1957) showed

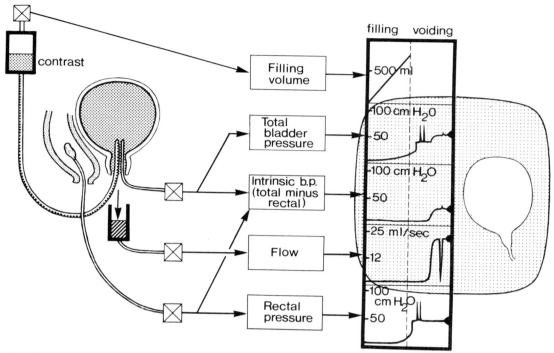

Fig. 30.4 Simultaneous cystometry and cystourethrography, with videotape recording. (Reproduced from the *British Journal of Urology*, with permission)

differences in the capacity attained by these different methods. Most observers found little difference between the incremental and the drip method and, indeed, very close correlations have been observed (Brocklehurst and Dillane, 1966a). In any event, if one method is used consistently in any department, it will provide a very useful comparative study of bladder function. The reproducibility of cystometrograms even after many months has been shown by Booth et al (1981), although they had to discount pressure measurements.

Additional equipment allows simultaneous subtraction of intra-abdominal pressure (as measured in the rectum) from total bladder pressure giving a true picture of pressure arising solely from the bladder wall. This eliminates pressure rises resulting from coughs, movements, etc. This system is also linked with video-cystourethrography, so that on a screen a picture of the bladder outline and the tracings of true bladder pressure are shown simultaneously. This is all recorded on video-tape and so can be recalled, or viewed, at any point as

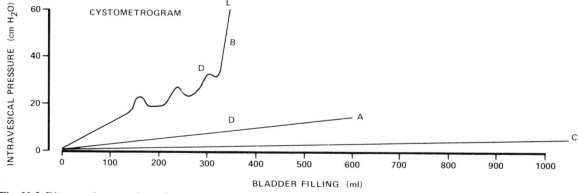

Fig. 30.5 Diagramatic comparison of cystometrograms. A: Normal; B: Uninhibited neurogenic or unstable bladder; C: Atonic bladder; D: First desire to void; L: Leakage.

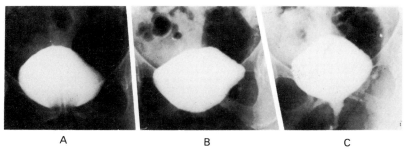

Fig. 30.6 Micturating cystogram showing descent of bladder due to pelvic floor incompetence in erect position and funnelling on micturition: A. Recumbent. B. Erect. C. Micturating.

a 'still' (see Fig. 30.4 Bates et al, 1970; Bates, 1971).

Simultaneous recording of intra-vesical and intra-urethral pressures with subtraction and digital display is also available.

All methods of cystometry will differentitate the various types of neurogenic bladder described above, and this is the most important function of the investigation in relation to the dysuria of old age. They also identify the unstable bladder in which contractions can be provoked by an extravesical stimulus. Cystometrograms are illustrated diagramatically in Figure 30.5.

Micturating cystourethrography

X-raying the bladder after filling it with a radio-opaque fluid is a method of recording bladder morphology and changes in the bladder and urethral flow during micturition. It has been described by many authors (e.g. Bates et al, 1970; Bhatia et al, 1982). The development of image-intensification and videotape recording has simplified this procedure. Its linkage with simultaneous cystometry, described above, and with a recording of the rate both of bladder filling and of bladder emptying have been further refinements. This interesting investigation may, in the elderly, assist in differentiating the various types of neurogenic and unstable bladder. Genuine stress incontinence with abnormal descent of the bladder base on assuming the erect posture, an open proximal urethra, funnelling of the bladder outlet during micturition and the movement of urine into the urethra on coughing is usually well demonstrated (Fig. 30.6, 30.7). Bladder outlet obstruction whether due on the one hand to anatomical causes such as stric-

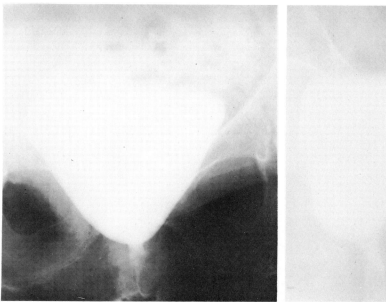
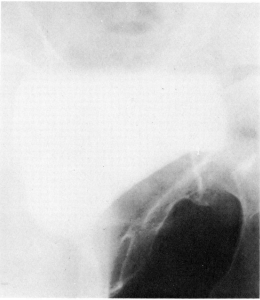

Fig. 30.7 Micturating cystogram showing funnelling: A. Antero-posterior. B. Lateral.

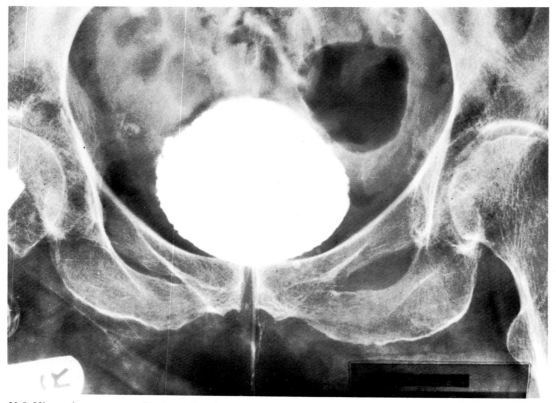

Fig. 30.8 Micturating cystogram showing trabeculation

ture of the urethra or enlargement of the prostate, or on the other, to functional causes as in the reflex and uninhibited neurogenic bladders, will be shown by the presence of trabeculation, cellule and possible diverticula formation (Fig. 30.8 and 30.9).

The urethral pressure profile

This technique, first reported by Brown and Wickham (1969) allows a record of the urethral length, and of its closing pressure at various points, to be made. Length, maximal closing pressure and shape of the

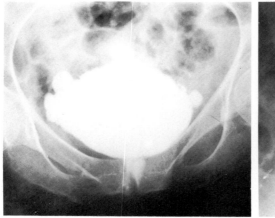
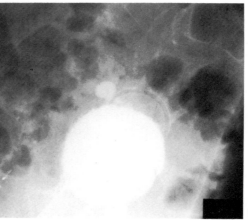

Fig. 30.9 Micturating cystogram showing diverticula formation: A. Antero-posterior. B. Lateral.

profile all have some significance in different types of bladder and urethral disorders. Its usefulness was reviewed by Edwards and Malvern in 1974.

In elderly females the maximum closure pressure is lower e.g. 50 cm water compared to 75 cm water in younger women (Raz and Kaufman, 1977) though the measurement is subject to a good deal of variation.

Measurement of urinary flow The Uroflow meter (Randell, 1975) by measuring the rate of flow provides information about the patency of the bladder outflow tract and the strength of detrusor contractions. The peak flow rate depends on the volume voided. In males it is diminished in old age (e.g. an average of 20 ml per second when 300–499 ml voided — Drach et al, 1979). In females the flow rate is higher and is not affected by age.

Other investigations which may be occasionally useful in elderly women include the fluid bridge test (Sutherst and Brown, 1981) which is a simple method of detection of early grades of genuine stress incontinence; very occasionally electromyography of the pelvic floor in elucidation of spinal cord lesions (Thomas, 1979).

A more recently introduced technique which may have future application in the elderly is the use of evoked responses (Haldeman et al, 1982). These may be developed to indicate the level in the brain and spinal cord of neurological lesions affecting micturition.

Cystoscopy

Cystoscopy will complete the investigation of the bladder. While this procedure is generally regarded as the prerogative of the surgeon, there is no reason why a physician in geriatric medicine should not become competent in the use of an examining cystoscope, especially in female patients who provide the majority of the problems in relation to bladder function. Cystoscopy will indicate the various types of inflammation, will show clearly trabeculation and diverticula formation, and will also show occasional unexpected causes of dysuria in the elderly such as papilloma, stone and carcinoma.

FUNCTIONAL CHANGES IN OLD AGE

As in the case in many conditions in old age, most of the surveys which have been carried out on urinary dysfunction have related to people who are inpatients in hospital. This is a very select group and cannot be extrapolated to represent old people in general. Nevertheless, the prevalence of dysuria, and particularly incontinence, in hospital patients is of the greatest importance, partly because it offers such a tremendous nursing problem, and secondly because it is often the most important single factor which prevents the discharge of an elderly patient from hospital.

Table 30.1 shows the prevalence of urinary incontinence in various surveys of hospitalized geriatric patients. This shows a considerable variability, as might be expected, from different institutions, and various sampling techniques. It is seen that the range lies somewhere between 25 per cent and 40 per cent (and approaches 100 per cent in some psychogeriatric institutions); the condition is rather more common in women. It might be expected that the developing specialty of geriatric medicine over the last 25 years would lead to an increasing concentration of irremediably incontinent patients in hospitals, as more and more of those who did not require long-stay hospital care were picked out and discharged. There is some evidence that this is the trend, but it is not entirely consistent. In residential homes the prevalence of incontinence has been estimated by McLauchlin and Wilkin (1982) as 17 per cent.

Table 30.1 Prevalence of urinary incontinence among institutionalized old people

Type (reference)	Definition	No/Sex	% Incontinence
Psychogeriatric patients UK McLaren et al, 1981	Incontinence at least once in three weeks	81 F	89.3
Nursing Home USA Ouslander et al, 1982	Any uncontrolled leakage of urine	842 M + F	50★
Geriatric patients UK Isaacs and Walkey, 1964	Incontinence in previous twenty four hours	274 M 248 F	40 46
Willington, 1969	Established incontinence	411 M 489 F	16 13
Residential Homes UK McLauchlan and Wilkin, 1982	Excluding occasional accident and those continent with regular toileting	864 M + F	17

★ includes 28% with indwelling and 10% with external catheters

Table 30.2 Prevalence of urinary incontinence in the community

Reference	Definition	Age	No/Sex	% Incontinence M	F	Amount which is severe	
Sheldon, 1968	Voiding — unconsciously or without control	60 (F) 65 (M)	456 M+F	7	12.7		
Brocklehurst et al, 1971	'Urine comes away and you get wet'*	65+	182 M 375 F	17	23		
Milne, 1972	4 questions*	62+	215 M 272 F	25	42	5% M	4.5% F
Yarnell et al, 1979	Any leakage of urine in past 12 months?	65+	388 M+F	11	17	3% daily	
Thomas et al, 1980	Involuntary leakage of urine at inappropriate places and times at least twice monthly	70+	1280 M+F	6.9	11.4	1.2%M†	4.0%F†
Vetta et al, 1981	Do you ever wet yourself if unable to get to the lavatory when you need to?	65+	1102 M 1562 F	7.3	18.1	5% daily	

* Do you lose control if unable to go to the lavatory as soon as you need to?
 Does urine come away when you cough or sneeze?
 Are you wet at night?
 Are you wet at any other time?
† Extra laundry, pads or expenses; some restriction in activities.

In the community the prevalence of incontinence is a good deal less than among hospital patients (see Table 30.2). Each of the samples, shown is a representative sample of the population but the variability in the prevalence reflects varying definitions of the word 'incontinence'. The sample interviewed by Brocklehurst and colleagues comprised 577 people. They were regarded as suffering from incontinence if they replied in the affirmative to the following question: 'Does urine every come away unexpectedly, and without your being able to stop it, and you get wet?' Of the 116 people who were incontinent, 51 suffered from stress incontinence only (including, no doubt, cases of the unstable bladder) and this comprised 3 per cent of the males in the series and 12 per cent of the females.

Other definitions are described in Tables 30.1 and 30.2. In general it may be concluded that about 12 per cent of men and 20 per cent of women over 65 have some degree of incontinence — and this compares with 1.6 per cent and 6.9 per cent respectively of those aged 15 to 64 (Thomas et al, 1980). Of the elderly about 4 per cent in both sexes is really severe.

Symptoms of dysuria other than incontinence have been investigated in detail by Brocklehurst et al (1968, 1971) and also by Milne et al (1972). They have also been referred to by Sheldon (1948) and Sourander (1966). The results are shown in Table 30.3. All authors discuss the incidence of diurnal and nocturnal frequency of micturition, and their findings are very similar.

Nocturnal frequency of micturition is the most common symptom. It also increases in severity with increasing age.

Table 30.3 Other abnormalities in micturition among old people living in the community (all figures %)

Symptoms		Sheldon (1948)	Sourander (1966)	Brocklehurst et al (1968)	Milne et al (1972)
Daytime frequency	M	29	25	28	33
	F	35	26	32	23
Nocturnal frequency	M	—	56	70	49
	F	—	67	61	67
Scalding	M	—	6	7	—
	F	—	13	13	—
Difficulty	M	—	22	13	—
	F	—	7	3	—

Scalding on micturition was present in similar numbers of both series in which it was recorded. *Difficulty* in micturition is also found among both sexes, in a significant number of people.

These, then, are the symptoms of bladder dysfunction in elderly people, and the important matter is to decide what aetiological factors underlie these various symptoms. They may be due to anatomical changes affecting the bladder itself, or affecting the supporting muscles of the pelvic diaphragm; they may result from infection of the bladder or be associated with vaginitis; they may have a mainly neurogenic basis associated with cerebrovascular disease, or with the neurological changes of aging itself; finally they may be due to mental confusion and clouding of consciousness leading to behavioural abnormality. These aetiological factors will be considered individually.

Causes of urinary symptoms

Urinary infection. The relationship between urinary infection and symptoms of dysuria is referred to in Chapter 29. In studying the prevalence of dysuria in a normal population, Brocklehurst et al (1968) also related these symptoms to the presence or absence of chronic bacteriuria. They found among females that there was a statistical correlation between precipitancy of micturition and difficulty in passing urine, and infection, but there was no correlation between infection and any other symptoms. In men they found no correlation at all.

Senile vaginitis. An association between incontinence and senile vaginitis has been reported by Wilson (1948), and this association may well reflect the common embryological origin of some of these tissues referred to above. Senile vaginitis is associated with urethritis and trigonitis. The effect of oestrogens in these conditions is discussed below.

Pelvic floor incompetence. There is no doubt that some of these symptoms are related to changes in the bladder outlet associated with prolapse of the uterus of greater or lesser degree. Such a finding is confirmed when funnelling is seen on the micturating cystogram. This was seen in 50 per cent of incontinent elderly women (Brocklehurst and Dillane, 1967a) and a relationship between stress incontinence and surgical interference at parturition was a statistically significant finding in the series reported above (Brocklehurst et al, 1971). On the other hand, no correlation has been reported between any aspect of dysuria and the parity of the female.

There is some relationship between the amplitude of the urethral pressure profile (UPP) and genuine stress incontinence (Edwards and Malvern, 1974; Kaufman, 1979; Godec et al, 1980). The UPP may, therefore, be of assistance in diagnosing genuine stress incontinence. However, the most useful investigation is simultaneous urethrocystography and cystometry (which will identify those patients whose leak following a cough or movement is due to the unstable bladder).

Neurogenic bladder. That evidence of the uninhibited neurogenic bladder is common among elderly people has been demonstrated by Brocklehurst and Dillane (1966a) in cystometrograms among a series of 40 non-incontinent elderly women. Sixteen of these had evidence of neurological lesions, including 9 who suffered from right hemiplegia. The remaining 24, however, had no evidence of neurological involvement.

Figure 30.10 represents these cases in relation to bladder capacity (a) and the presence of uninhibited intrinsic bladder contractions (b). Of the 24 cases with no overt neurological disease 18 (75 per cent) had unstable bladders. Unfortunately no further reports of the prevalence of detrusor instability in old people have been published. However, it is suggested that these

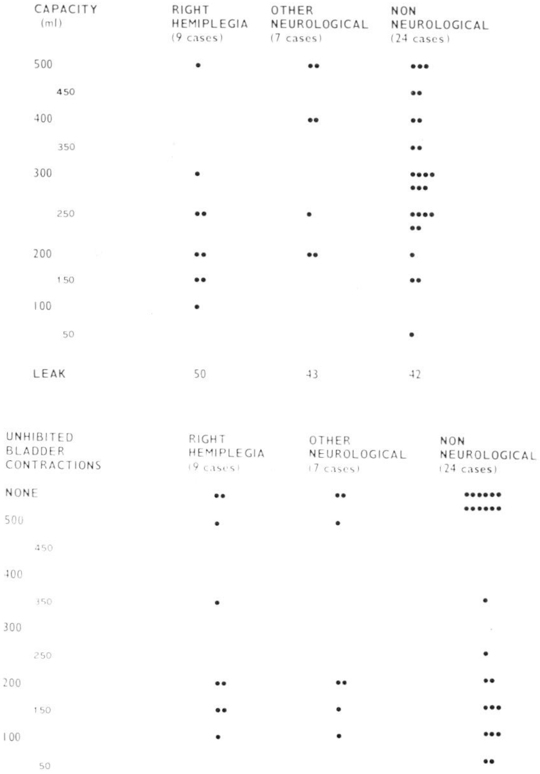

Fig. 30.10 Upper. Scatter of bladder capacity in non-incontinent elderly women according to neurological disease. Also shows percentage who leaked during cystometrogram. Lower. Scatter of degree of filling at first onset of uninhibited bladder contractions in relation to neurological disease.

findings together with the age-associated increase in nocturnal frequency comprise evidence that there is some impairment in the cortical control of micturition in large numbers of elderly people. It is no unreasonable to expect that this is secondary to age changes involving the number and function of cortical neurones.

The relationship of neurogenic changes in the bladder to the presence of incontinence is well documented. This was first demonstrated by Wilson (1948) who investigated bladder function in 36 patients selected at random in a chronic sick ward. Twenty-one of these were incontinent. The incontinent cases showed early onset of uninhibited contractions without accompanying desire to micturate. These findings have subsequently been confirmed by Brocklehurst (1951), Thompson (1964), and Brocklehurst and Dillane (1966b). The last showed that among 100 incontinent aged women, cystometrograms had the characteristics of either a reflex or an uninhibited neurogenic bladder in 85. They found that these neurogenic changes were also associated with significant loss of orientation, of intellectual capacity, and with the presence of bilateral hyper-reflexia. These correlations were also shown by Isaacs and Walkey (1964) who found 83 per cent of incontinent patients were non-ambulant, and that a significant proportion had evidence of brain damage and were also unable to feed and dress themselves.

Other studies have shown similar abnormalities. Eastwood (1979) though using cystometric criteria not directly comparable, showed only 8 per cent of 182 incontinent old people as having cystometrically normal bladder. He found 60 per cent hyperreflexic and 17 per cent areflexic. Castleden et al (1981) reviewed 100 patients attending an incontinence clinic, 38 of whom had clinically detectable neurological lesions, 16 per cent were normal, 3 per cent unstable or 'irritable' and 11 per cent atonic.

There is little need to refer to the place of hyperplasia of the prostate in the cause of incontinence in elderly men, since this is well known and, in fact, is all to often regarded as responsible for incontinence when it is not the cause. However, among the symptoms of prostatic hypertrophy must be counted incontinence of urine and other related dysuric symptoms. The most important point in this respect is that the clinician should always have in mind the possibility of a double aetiology for these symptoms, and removal of the prostate may not lead to automatic alleviation of the symptoms, should a neurogenic bladder be present at the same time.

URINARY INCONTINENCE

The importance of urinary incontinence as a manifestation of the aging bladder has been referred to above. Urinary incontinence occurs in a number of otherwise healthy old people who usually do not report it to their medical attendant. Its incidence among hospitalized old people is very great. It is now necessary to consider a classification of the causes of incontinence, and on this basis its management and treatment.

Classification
A useful clinical classification of incontinence begins by dividing it into transient and established incontinence (Table 30.4).

Transient incontinence Transient incontinence is that which accompanies other underlying acute disease, and in which the incontinence clears up as the disease is successfully treated. Thus, any condition causing an acute confusional disorder (such as respiratory infection, myocardial infarction, various toxaemias, and minimal cerebral infarcts) may be associated with incontinence which is of short duration. An acute stroke may be associated with incontinence which is transient because

Table 30.4 Cause of urinary incontinence in old age

Transient Incontinence
Acute confusional disorder
Acute cerebrovascular accident
Acute urinary tract infection
Environmental change
— becoming bedfast
Psychological
Retention with overflow
— faecal impaction
— drug effect (anticholinergic)

Established Incontinence
Unstable bladder
Uninhibited neurogenic bladder
— stroke
— focal frontal lobe lesion
— dementia
— Parkinsonism
— normal pressure hydrocephalus
Reflex neurogenic bladder
— spinal cord lesion (disc prolapse, infarct etc.)
Prostatisim
Carcinoma or calculus in bladder
Retention with overflow
— atonic neurogenic bladder (diabetes, tabes)
— urethral stricture
— prostatic enlargement

it is cerebral oedema which affects the bladder control pathways rather than the infarct itself. It will often clear up within a few days — a particularly important reason for not inserting an indwelling catheter if it can be avoided. An acute urinary tract infection (UTI) also is very often accompanied by incontinence in old people. A third, and perhaps all-important cause of transient incontinence, is the simple fact of becoming bedfast for whatever reason, and thus being no longer able to get independently to the lavatory, or to a commode, as quickly and as often as needed. This is especially likely to be the case when nurses or other attendants are unaware of the limited nature of the elderly patient's bladder function, and perhaps do not realize that before she became ill and bedfast, the old lady got up two or three times at night to empty her bladder, and had to do the same every three or four hours during the day. If the nurse is not able to assist her patient to a commode as regularly as this, then incontinence may be the inevitable result.

Retention of urine as a cause of incontinence is not at all uncommon. If it is secondary to constipation then the incontinence is likely to be of both urine and faeces. Among the many drugs which may cause retention are the tricyclic antidepressants, some of the anti-Parkinsonian drugs and the spasmolytics used in the treatment of gastrointestinal disease and those used in the treatment of the uninhibited neurogenic, or unstable, bladder (see below). In the latter case incontinence from one cause may be converted to incontinence due to chronic retention without the attending physician being aware of this fact.

Established incontinence. Established incontinence is that which continues after the above causes have been successfully treated and the patient's rehabilitation is progressing well. Established incontinence may also be the principle presenting symptom in someone in whom it is unaccompanied by other acute disease. The most common cause is the uninhibited neurogenic bladder associated with global or focal disease of the brain and particularly multi-infarct dementia. Spinal cord disease including the effect of disc prolapse, tumours, demyelinating disease and spinal artery thrombosis may enter the differential diagnosis. Spinal cord lesions because of their partial and variable distribution may present with variable cystometric patterns. Lumbar spondylosis, for instance (a common condition in old age) may present with urgency or with retention (Sharr et al, 1976).

Other important causes include prostatic enlargement leading to incontinence as a result of distortion of the bladder outlet or due to retention of urine with overflow. The latter may also be due to urethral stricture and occasionally occurs with an atonic neurogenic bladder associated with diabetic neuropathy or tabes dorsalis.

Weir and Jaques (1974) studied 109 patients with excessively large bladder capacities. The cause was obstructive in 32 per cent males and 15 per cent females, and an atonic bladder in 12 per cent males and 13 per cent females; however the bladder was normal in 33 per cent of males and 21 per cent of females, indicating that capacities in excess of 800 ml may be within the range of normality. However, a large residual urine is probably abnormal and requires investigation.

Psychological factors producing detrusor instability have been considered above (page 630). There is no estimate of how common they are in the elderly but it is probable that they are a less frequent cause of incontinence in old people than in the young and middle aged.

Parkinsonism is also reported to be associated with incontinence although the causes are uncertain — some patients having uninhibited and others atonic bladders (Murnaghan 1961; Porter et al, 1969; Aminoff and Wilcox, 1971).

Finally, another useful method of classification of aetiological factors in incontinence which brings together most of those referred to above is to divide these into *predisposing* and *precipitating* factors (Brocklehurst, 1951). The predisposing factors are those which lead to an inefficient and maimed bladder with which the elderly person copes as long as her normal environment is undistrubed. This is some degree of the uninhibited neurogenic bladder. The *precipitating* factors are those which are superadded and which tilt the balance

so that the bladder with impaired control can no longer be contained and incontinence results. As has been said above, perhaps most important among these precipitating factors are the bedfast state and dependency upon nurses, who either do not understand the condition, or who are so over-worked as, with the best intentions, to be unable to give the necessary attention. They also include acute infections and the various other precipitating factors referred to above.

Treatment of incontinence

Transient incontinence

First exclude (or treat) an acute UTI, constipation and the side effects of drugs. Treatment is then that of the underlying acute condition, and this together with adequate and sympathetic nursing is usually all that is required. At this stage the use of an indwelling catheter should be resisted since it will almost certainly introduce infection into a bladder which may be sterile. Catheters are usually introduced on the understanding that incontinence may lead to the formation of a pressure sore. Other methods should be taken to prevent this, including the use of alternating (Ripple) mattress. If the patient is incontinent or immobile at this stage, then a sheath urinal or even a length of Paul's tubing attached to the penis will provide a successful drainage system in the male. Appropriate protective pads may be used in females. If the patient is conscious then every effort should be made to get her up to a bedside commode every two hours. This is facilitated if the patient is nursed in a low bed.

If an indwelling catheter is regarded as essential at this stage, because of a severe urine rash or existing ulceration of the skin, then some attempt to maintain sterility of the bladder should be made with a closed system of drainage. This may be provided by a disposable tidal drainage system, by anchoring the catheter so that it does not slide up and down within the urethra and by applying antiseptic spray to the external urethral meatus several times during the day. A high fluid intake should be maintained. Urinary antiseptic or even an antibiotic may be given at this point, to maintain the sterility of the urine. This regime, however, can hardly be continued for more than a week, and should only be envisaged for a few days to overcome the most acute part of the illness, and that only in the most exceptional circumstances.

Incontinence associated with urinary retention and overflow will require slow decompression of the bladder by catheter over a period of 12 to 24 hours. Drugs must be used with care during this period because of the extrarenal uraemia which may be present. Recurrence of the retention should be prevented wherever possible, and in particular the presence of severe constipation requires immediate treatment by a series of enemas. Normal micturition should be assisted by allowing the patient to sit on a commode or go to the lavatory, or micturate standing. Micturating in a lying position is difficult for many, and impossible for some. If retention tends to recur the use of cholinergic drugs or prostaglandin instillation may help (see below).

Established incontinence

The treatment of established incontinence first requires a firm diagnosis to be made. This does not necessarily demand a urodynamic assessment. Hilton and Stanton (1981) devised an algorithm and reported on its use in 100 women aged 65 and over. They compared the outcome by this method with that of full urodynamic assessment and found that the same recommendations as to treatment would be made in 83 per cent of cases. The remaining 17 were wrongly diagnosed as detrusor instability. Since urodynamic investigation showed these to have stable bladders they concluded that 12 should have been cystoscoped, that one had stress incontinence and four had voiding difficulty.

A few general principles underlying treatment are as follows:

1. Exclude (or treat) atrophic vaginitis and prostatic enlargement. Rectal and/or vulval examination are essential.

2. If the main symptom is urge incontinence there is an 80 per cent probability of detrusor instability. A trial of bladder training together with anticholinergic drugs may reasonably be undertaken for four weeks.

3. If the main symptom is leak on coughing and leakage can be seen to coincide with the cough, pelvic floor exercises should be prescribed.

4. If incontinence persists then cystometry (including provocation tests) should be carried out. If this is normal cystoscopy is necessary.

5. By this stage only relatively rare conditions (e.g. detrusor sphincter dyssynergia, vesico-vaginal fistula) may remain undiagnosed and specialist opinion should be sought.

Some general points to be borne in mind in the management of incontinence are as follows:

1. Urinary tract infection may be a complication of an obstructed or neurogenic bladder. Incontinence in this case may be due to the underlying cause and the infection incidental. Treatment of infection will then not eliminate the incontinence. A general rule is to treat UTI when it is first diagnosed in an incontinent patient, but to look for other causes if the incontinence persists and not to treat recurrent infection in such cases.

2. Prostatic enlargement may coexist with detrusor instability and prostatectomy will not always cure associated incontinence. Most usually, however, prostatic obstruction causes incontinence due to chronic retention.

3. Apparent stress incontinence may be due to detrusor instability. That which is due to pelvic floor (or sphincter) weakness is now called 'genuine stress incontinence' and should be carefully diagnosed before gynaecological surgery is carried out.

4. Post-prostatectomy incontinence (and some cases of genuine stress incontinence) may be improved by treatment with alpha-adrenergic stimulant drugs (see below). Conversely, detrusor sphincter dyssynergia may be successfully treated with alpha-adrenergic inhibitors.

The treatment of established incontinence falls under three headings — general measures, drug treatment, and the use of catheters and appliances.

If the patient is in hospital then first among the general methods of treatment should be the use of an incontinence chart. The continence chart will not only show the incidence of incontinence through the 24 hours, and its pattern throughout a number of days, but will also indicate whether or not other measures of treatment are having effect, and will in itself, if properly used, ensure the regular nursing attention which is so essential. Incontinence charts should be made out 4-hourly in the first place throughout the 24 hours, and if this shows a considerable proportion of episodes of wetting, then charting should be done every 2 hours (see p. 631).

The question of fluid restriction should also be mentioned. A general restriction of fluid is contraindicated and, indeed, the incontinent patient may well have been restricting her own fluids for some time before coming into hospital, in an attempt to treat the incontinence herself. For this reason she may be dehydrated. An adequate fluid intake must be assured, both for its obvious general needs, and also to combat urinary infection. It is wise, however, in a patient who is wet during the night to regulate the fluid so that she does not have a large drink within two or three hours of going to sleep. Other general measures include the use of a low bed (for this reason variable height beds are of great importance in the geriatric ward). A commode should be available at the bedside.

Drug treatment

This, again, falls under three main headings — antidiuretic drugs, drugs to diminish or increase bladder excitability and oestrogens. The use of posterior pituitary in the form of pituitrin snuff to diminish diuresis during the night in patients suffering from nocturnal incontinence has been reported both in children and in elderly people (Jones and Tibbetts, 1959; Dequeker, 1965). Neither report was very enthusiastic. More recently another preparation of antidiuretic hormone (Desmopressin) given as nasal spray has been described with benefit in nocturnal frequency and also for short term occasional use on 'social' occasions (Hilton and Stanton, 1982). These drugs are contraindicated in patients with ischaemic heart disease and hypertension.

Pharmacological blockade. The use of antiparasympathomimetic drugs to produce a pharmacological blockade of the uninhibited sacral micturition reflex has a very large literature, both in children and in patients suffering from neurological disorders, as well as old people. Atropine, ephedrine and belladonna were among those used in the first place, but almost any drug which produces urinary retention as a side-effect may be considered for possible use. In addition to the solanaceous alkaloids these include the ganglion blocking agents such as tetraethylammonium bromide and more modern drugs used in the treatment of hypertension (but the coexisting hypotension rules them out for practical use). Anticholinergic drugs used for their effects on the bladder include propanthaline, emepronium bromide, imipramine, dicyclomine and orphenadrine hydrochloride. They have been reviewed by Brocklehurst (1984).

Emepronium bromide has been described as having a beneficial effect both on nocturnal frequency of micturition and on incontinence, in two double blind trials (Brocklehurst et al, 1969; Brocklehurst et al, 1972). It may be used in a dose of 150 to 200 mg two to four times a day. Others have failed to show any effect on the unstable or uninhibited neurogenic bladder when emepronium is given by mouth (Rich et al, 1977; Walker et al, 1982). In the latter trial in 20 old people of both sexes with unstable bladder, there was a cure rate of 79 per cent with both the active drug and the placebo. Briggs et al (1980) compared parental and oral treatment with emepronium bromide in six elderly patients and showed little effect on cystometrograms with intravenous therapy and no effect on incontinence by oral therapy. Robinson and Brocklehurst (1983) showed some limited improvement on a combination of emepronium and flavoxate compared to placebo.

Mouth ulcerations may occur with emepronium bromide in aged patients who do not swallow the tablets but keep them in their mouth. Ulceration of the lower end of the oesophagus has also been reported (Habeshaw and Bennet, 1972; Strouthidis et al, 1972; Kenwright and Norris, 1977).

Propanthaline bromide has also been the subject of a good deal of investigation — the parental preparation diminishing uninhibited contractions and the oral preparation abolishing incontinence, for instance in 31 per cent of one series (Blaivas, 1980). Dicyclomine has been similarly reported (Fisher et al, 1978; Awad et al, 1977) and was shown to be superior to propanthaline in a comparative trial by Beck et al (1976). Flavoxate (Urispas) is a more recently introduced quaternary ammonium compound which selectively reacts on the smooth-muscle autonomic receptor. Trials comparing its effect in urinary incontinence with propantheline (Kohler and Morales, 1968) and emepronium bromide (Stanton, 1973) suggest its superiority. The dose is 200 mg to 600 mg for 24 hours. Since flavoxate, propantheline and emepronium bromide act at different pharmacological sites, there may well be advantages in using combined therapy.

Imipramine (150 mg at night) was shown to diminish nocturnal incontinence in a group of 10 old people (Castleden et al, 1981) — although work on animals (Creed and Tulloch, 1982) indicates that the effect of imipramine on the bladder may not be an anticholinergic effect.

Two other groups of drugs have been assessed for their ability to diminish uninhibited bladder contractions and prevent incontinence. The prostaglandin inhibitor flurbiprofen (50 mg three times daily) showed some improvement in a double blind trial although the rate of side effects was high (Cardazo et al, 1980). The calcium antagonists introduced for use in cardia arrhythmias have an effect on the bladder also (by preventing the release of calcium into the myofibrils which is necessary to initiate muscle contraction). This action on the bladder was first described by Van Duzen (1954) and the use of calcium antagonists in women with unstable bladders has been described recently e.g. nifedipine (Rud et al, 1978) and flunarazine (Palmer et al, 1981).

It will be apparent from the variety of responses described in these various drugs intended to diminish bladder excitability that no ideal agent has yet been produced. The quaternary ammonium compounds are poorly absorbed by mouth and the prostaglandin inhibitors and calcium antagonists have as yet not undergone sufficient trial. At the present time, therefore, the best recommendations that can be made are for combinations of drugs acting at different sites to be used and this might be either propanthaline, emepronium bromide or dicyclomine in combination with flavoxate or imipramine, or alternatively with flurbiprofen or flunarazine. In the ideopathic unstable bladder there is likely to be a very high placebo reactor rate and in the uninhibited neurogenic bladder in patients with global cerebral disease the results with any of them will be disappointing. Their best use therefore is probably in patients with uninhibited neurogenic bladder due to focal cerebral lesions (particularly stroke) who have intractable incontinence.

Other drugs affecting the autonomic nervous system

Alpha-adrenergic stimulators. Ephedrine (which has both alpha-and beta-adrenergic stimulatory effects) has long been known as a drug which can produce retention of urine (Balyeat and Rinkel, 1932) and its principle effect is probably in alpha stimulation of the smooth muscle of the urethra increasing urethral closing pressure. Thus its beneficial effect in patients with non-neurogenic stress incontinence and post prostatectomy incontinence were described by Diokno and Paul (1975). Phenylpropanol amine has also been reported to improve these conditions in which there is impairment of urethral closure — e.g. Stewart et al (1976), Awad et al (1978). Some serious side effects have been reported (Mueller, 1983).

Alpha-adrenergic blockers. Alpha-adrenergic blocking agents have been used for conditions in which the bladder smooth muscle does not relax when the detrusor contracts (a form of detrusor-sphincter dyssynergia). Caine (1977) and Caine et al (1981) also reported the use of this drug in the treatment of males with prostatic obstruction who were unfit for surgery, with a very considerable improvement in symptoms although 10 per cent of their 200 patients had to stop the medication because of side effects.

Cholinergic drugs. Cholinergic drugs (particularly bethanechol chloride) have been used in the management of recurring retention of urine (Lapides, 1964). The effects of this drug have been criticised on two counts — first because of poor absorption when given by mouth (Diokno et al, 1976; Sonder et al, 1979). The second problem is that while bethanechol causes contraction of bladder muscle fibres and a rise of intravesical pressure it does not stimulate a bladder contraction (Wein et al, 1980). Most studies have been carried out on patients with degrees of residual urine which do not amount to chronic retention. Taplan et al (1978) suggested that the drug was more effective in lower motor neurone bladder lesions (which are those likely to cause retention), whereas much of the experimental work has not been done on patients with such lesions.

Another approach is to use a drug which has anti-cholinesterase effect and distigmine bromide had been advocated. However, trials indicate no benefit in patients with lower motor neurone lesions (Yeo et al, 1974; Smith et al, 1974). A third approach to the management of chronic retention is the use of prostaglandins instilled directly into the bladder (PGE_2 1.5 mg in alcohol solution) and left for one hour. Good effects were reported by Bultitude et al (1976) and by Desmond et al (1980) who showed immediate improvement in 72 per cent and prolonged improvement in 39 per cent — but no improvement in those with lower motor neurone lesions. However, no therapeutic result was found in a series of 13 women reported by Delaere et al (1981).

The present situation, therefore, would suggest that if chronic retention tends to recur after any causative agents have been removed and the bladder emptied,

then a course of subcutaneous bethanechol (7.5–10.0 mg, 4-to 6-hourly) followed by 100 mg by mouth once residual has been reduced to 100 ml, is worth a trial in patients with lower motor neurone lesions and the installation of prostaglandin E_2 in those without such lesions. Failing this the only alternative at present available is indwelling catherization — although some urologists accept chronic retention without treatment, provided the blood urea does not actually rise.

Oestrogens. The beneficial effect of estrogens in urinary incontinence in old people was first noted by Wilson (1948) who used stilboestrol cream in the treatment of senile vaginitis. Their use for this purpose in postmenopausal women was also described by Geist and Salmon in 1943.

A double blind trial with oestradiol 2 mg together with oestriol 1 mg daily was reported by Walter et al (1978) on a group of 29 post-menopausal women with a mean age of 56 years. There was a significant cure rate among those who suffered from frequency, urgency and urge incontinence but no change in the urethral closure pressure or functional length. On the other hand Rud (1980) showed some statistically significant improvement both in urethral closing pressure and functional length and in the symptoms of stress incontinence in a group of post menopausal women treated with oestrogens. Robinson (1984) showed a variable effect of oestrogens on incontinence in a series of aged women with atrophic vaginal smears.

The conclusion is that all women with established urinary incontinence should have a vaginal smear carried out. If the cells are atrophic or if there is clear clinical evidence of atrophic vaginitis then a month's course of treatment with an oral oestrogen preparation should be carried out. In a proportion of women this will be effective and in that group it may require to be repeated twice a year.

Behavioural therapy and bladder training

Since the ideopathic unstable bladder probably has a strong functional component (see above) it is not surprising that behavioural therapy has been reported to have very good effects (as indeed have placebos). A series of studies reported by Jarvis and colleagues (Jarvis and Miller, 1980; Jarvis, 1981; 1982 a, b) have analysed the effect of bladder drill. Patients were diagnosed by cystometry and cystoscopy. All had urgency and urge incontinence and a high proportion had stress incontinence. All had diurnal frequency and most had nocturnal frequency. In their first study (Jarvis and Miller, 1980) urethral dilatation was also carried out and no drugs were used. Patients were admitted to hospital and instructed to pass urine at specific intervals during the day (usually starting at $1\frac{1}{2}$ hours) being told that they must not do so earlier or later than this. Frequency at night was ignored. Once the target interval was reached it was increased by $\frac{1}{2}$ hour daily until the patients were voiding 4-hourly. They maintained a fluid balance chart themselves and part of the treatment involved being introduced to someone previously successfully treated. The length of stay in hospital varied from 5 to 16 days and the effect of treatment was good. Urgency, nocturnal and diurnal frequency all diminished by approximately 50 per cent and incontinence was cured in 90 per cent. Follow-up at 3 months showed 65 per cent totally symptom free with stable bladders. The age ranges of the patients in these trials was up to 69. A trial of outpatient bladder training was reported by Frewen (1982) in a consecutive series of 90 women aged up to 75 with a history of urge incontinence, frequency and enuresis present for several years. After 3 months treatment 86 per cent were free of all abnormal urinary symptoms.

No account of this form of bladder training has yet been reported in aged patients with uninhibited urogenic bladders. However, several reports of behavioural therapy and its effectiveness in both demented and non-demented old people have been reported. The whole subject has been well reviewed by Whitehead et al (1984).

Bladder distension

The use of prolonged bladder distension under anaesthesia has shown some success in treatment of the uninhibited neurogenic and unstable bladders (Dunn et al 1974; Whitfield and Mayo, 1975; Ramsden et al, 1976). This may be considered if other treatments fail.

Treatment of stress incontinence

Genuine stress incontinence due to pelvic floor (sphincter) weakness may be treated by physiotherapy, by the use of a pessary or by gynaecological surgery. The importance of a critical diagnosis and particularly the exclusion of an underlying unstable bladder as the cause has been considered above. For patients without any significant degree of uterine descent, pelvic floor exercises taught by a physiotherapist, and practiced several times every day, have been shown to be strikingly effective. The exercises include teaching the woman to stop micturating in mid-stream, to be aware of the pubococcygeal muscle and learn to appreciate its contraction by palpating it. The use of bio feedback may increase the effectiveness of the exercises and a special and simple perineometer was described many years ago by Kegel and Powell (1950) and is now available commercially. If the woman is able to understand and cooperate then physiotherapy is a very important method of treatment (see Mandelstam, 1980). If this

fails then a vaginal pessary may be necessary or a gynaecological operation. This subject has been recently reviewed by Stanton (1977) and McGuire (1981).

The use of appliances and catheters

These may be required in two main situations. In the first place to provide a drainage system for a short period of incontinence associated with an acute illness or state of unconsciousness, and secondly, as a long-term measure for the management of established incontinence when other methods have failed. The use of a catheter for this first purpose should be avoided if possible. In males, either the condom urinal or length of Paul's tubing may be helpful during this short period, particularly in patients who are unconscious.

The condom urinal (Texas catheter) is useful also in co-operative males for the management of intractable incontinence. They do, however, have drawbacks in sometimes producing irritation and infection of the penis. A simple protective device for males who have dribbling incontinence is the 'dribbler bag' which is a pouch containing some absorbent material worn over the penis or penis and scrotum. More massive portable urinals, including the pubic pressure urinal are also available and useful to an occasional co-operative and ambulant man. For the female there is no satisfactory appliance available as a body-worn urinal but incontinence in women may sometimes be prevented by providing them with appropriate portable urinals (see review by Mandelstam, 1977).

Indwelling catheters

Finally, there remains the question of *long-term indwelling catherization*. While it is possible to maintain a closed sterile system and sterility of the urine for short-term catherization, this is virtually impossible when the catheter has to remain *in situ* for longer than a week. In paraplegic patients with significant residual urine, self-catheterization every few hours is now practised (Lapides et al, 1974, 1976; Orikasa et al, 1976), but it seems unlikely that many aged people will adopt this method.

The decision whether or not to use an indwelling catheter must be made individually in each case. The main consideration is to weigh the risk of infection against the patient's prognosis as regards life, and the benefit which the indwelling catheter will produce. Although ascending infection will eventually produce renal infection and, possibly, abscess, this is a process which seems to take a matter of 7 or 8 years rather than a shorter period. Talbot et al (1959) investigated 50 consecutive unselected patients who had worn indwelling catheters for at least a year. They all suffered from spinal injury or disease, and of the 2 who died, 1 died of coronary artery thrombosis after a period of 8 years, with unaffected kidneys. The other who had numerous pressure sores died of amyloid. Carty et al (1981) in a post-mortem study of renal histology showed pyelonephritis to be associated with use of an indwelling cather in life.

Elderly women with intractable incontinence usually suffer from some degree of cerebrovascular disease, and their prognosis is usually limited to one or two years. In such a situation the indwelling catheter provides no risk of any importance. If it can allow the old lady to be dry and perhaps leave hospital for the last year or two of her life, rather than spend this time in a state of constant wetness, possibly in a long-stay hospital ward, then the use of the indwelling catheter is to be welcomed.

Three catheters in common use at the present time are 100 per cent silicone catheters, siliconized latex and teflon-coated catheters. The 100 per cent silicone catheters are 10 times more costly than the others — a difference which will only be justified if they remain *in situ* for a much longer period, or are significantly more comfortable. In old people (for various reasons) little difference has been shown between these catheters and the siliconized latex either in comfort or length of time *in situ* (Brocklehurst and Brocklehurst, 1978; Kennedy and Brocklehurst, 1984). Catheter by-passing is common — partly due to encrustation, partly to kinking and partly also to over distension of the urethra. Small diameter catheters are associated with less by-passing (Kennedy et al, 1983). Problems in the management of indwelling catheters were reviewed by Kennedy and Brocklehurst (1983) — who showed that many old people were needlessly catheterized.

The catheter should be worn attached to a bag suspended from a waistband (e.g. the Shepherd sporran) and not one which is fixed to the furniture or left lying on the floor. Such a bag with a flutter valve can be worn both day and night, and is unobtrusive and unobjectionable. It is important to avoid catheter blockage. This can be achieved by washing out the bladder every week with solutions such as chlorhexidine (1 : 5000), noxithiolin or neomycin 0.2 per cent solution.

It is not usually necessary to use continuous cover of antibiotics since this is only likely to produce a successive series of resistant organisms. Neither will continuous urinary antiseptics maintain a sterile urine (Brocklehurst and Brocklehurst, 1978).

REFERENCES

Abrams P H, Feneley R C L 1976 The actions of prostaglandins on the smooth muscle of the human urinary tract in vitro. British Journal of Urology 47: 909–915

Affleck J W 1947 The chronic sick in hospital; a psychiatric approach Lancet ii: 533–537

Aminoff M J, Wilcox C S 1971 Assessment of autonomic function in patients with a Parkinsonian syndrome. British Medical Journal 4: 80–84

Andrew J, Nathan P W, 1964 Lesions of the anterior frontal lobes and disturbances of micturition and defaecation Brain 87 233–262

Ardvan G M, Cope V, Essenheigh D M, Tuckey M 1967a The primary vesical sphincter. British Journal of Urology 39: 329–333

Ardvan G M Cop V, Essenheigh D M, Tuckey M 1967b Observations on the function of the bladder neck and urethra in the dog. British Journal of Urology 39: 334–340

Arey L B 1965 In: Development Anatomy, pp. 295–314 Philadelphia: Saunders

Awad S A, Bryniak S, Downie J W, Bruce A W 1977 Treatment of the uninhibited bladder with dicyclomide. Journal of Urology 117: 161–163

Awad S A, Downie J W, Kiruluta H G 1978 Alpha-adrenergic agents in urinary disorders of the proximal urethra. British Journal of Urology 50: 332–335

Balyeat R M, Rinkel H J 1932 Urinary retention due to the use of ephedrine. Journal of the American Medical Association 98: 1545

Bates C P 1971 Continence and incontinence — a clinical study of the dynamics of voiding and of the sphincter mechanism. Annals of the Royal College of Surgeons 49: 8–35

Bates C P, Whiteside C G, Turner-Warwick R 1970 Synchronous cine/pressure/flow/cysto-urethrography with special reference to stress in urge incontinence. British Journal of Urology 42: 714–723

Beck R P, Arnusch T, King C 1976 Results in treating 210 patients with detrusor over-activity incontinence of urine. American Journal of Obstetrics and Gynecology 125: 593–596

Beneventi F A 1943 Study of the posterior urethra in newborn female. Surgery, Gynecology and Obstetrics 76: 64–76

Bhatia N N, Bradley W E, Haldeman S 1982 Urodynamics: continuous monitoring. Journal of Urology 128: 963–968

Blaivas J G, Labib K B, Michalik S J, Zayed A A H 1980 Cystometric response to propantheline in detrusor hyperreflexia: therapeutic implications. Journal of Urology 124: 259–262

Bors, E, Mar K T, Parker R V 1956 Observations of some modalities of bladder sensation. Journal of Urology 76: 566–575

Booth C M, Whiteside C G, Turner-Warwick R T 1981 A long-term study of the persistence of the urodynamic characteristics of the unstable bladder. British Journal of Urology 53: 310–341

Bradley W E, Fletcher T E 1969 Innervation of the mammalian bladder. Journal of Urology 101: 846–853

Bradley W E, Timm G W, Scott F B 1975 Cystometry. Urology 5: 843–848

Bradley W E, Rockswold G L, Tim G W, Scott F B 1976 Neurology of Micturition. Journal of Urology 115: 481–486

Briggs R S, Castleden C M, Asher M J 1980 The effects of flavoxate on uninhibited detrusor contractions and urinary incontinence in the elderly. Journal of Urology 123: 665

Brocklehurst J C 1951 Incontinence in Old People. Edinburgh: Livingstone

Brocklehurst J C 1972 Bladder outlet obstruction in elderly women. Modern Geriatrics 2: 108–113

Brocklehurst J C, Brocklehurst S 1978 The management of indwelling catheters. British Journal of Urology 50: 102–105

Brocklehurst J C, Dillane J B 1966a Studies of the female bladder in old age. I. Cystometrograms in non-incontinent women. Gerontologia Clinica 8: 285–305

Brocklehurst J C, Dillane J B 1966b Studies of the female bladder in old age. II. Cystometrograms in 100 incontinent women. Gerontologia Clinica 8: 306–319

Brocklehurst J C, Dillane J B 1967a Studies of the female bladder in old age. III — Micturating cystograms in incontinent women. Gerontologia Clinica 9: 47–58

Brocklehurst J C, Dillane J B 1967b Studies of the female bladder in old age. IV. Drug effects in urinary incontinence. Gerontologia Clinica 9: 182–191

Brocklehurst J C, Dillane J B, Criffiths L, Fry J 1968 The prevalence and symptomatology of urinary infection in an aged population. Gerontology Clinica 10: 242–53

Brocklehurst J C, Dillane J B, Fry J, Armitage P 1969 Clinical trial of emepronium bromide in nocturnal frequency of old age. British Medical Journal ii: 216–218

Brocklehurst J C, Fry J, Griffiths L L, Kalton G 1971 Dysuria in old age. Journal of the American Geriatrics Society 197: 582–592

Brocklehurst J C, Fry J, Griffiths L L, Kalton G 1972 Urinary infection and symptoms of dysuria in women aged 45–64 years: Their relevance to similar findings in the elderly. Age and Ageing I: 41

Brown M, Wickham J E A 1969 The urethral pressure profile. British Journal of Urology 41: 210–217

Bultitude M I, Hills N H, Shuttleworth K E D 1976 Clinical and experimental studies of the action of prostaglandins and their synthesis inhibitors on detrusor muscle, in vitro and in vivo. British Journal of Urology 48: 631–637

Burns R K Jr 1939 Effects of female sex hormones in young opossums. Proceedings of the Society for Experimental Biology and Medicine 41: 270–272

Caine M 1977 The importance of adrenergic receptors in disorders of micturition. European Urology 3: 1–6

Caine M, Perlberg S, Meretyk S 1978 A placebo controlled double-blind study of the effect of phenoxybenzamine in benign prostatic obstruction. British Journal of Urology 50: 551–554

Caine M, Perlberg S, Shapiro A 1981 Phenoxybenzamine for benign prostatic obstruction. Urology 17: 542–546

Cardozo L D, Stanton S L 1980 Detrusor dynamics 2 — a comparison between bromocriptine and indomethacin in the treatment of detrusor instability. Journal of Urology 123: 399–400

Carty M, Brocklehurst J C, Carty J 1981 Bacteriuria and its correlates in old age. Gerontology 1981 27: 72–75

Castleden C M, Duffin H M 1981 Guide lines for controlling urinary incontinence without drugs or catheters. Age and Ageing 10: 186–190

Castleden C M, Duffin H M, Asher M J 1981 Clinical and urodynamic studies in 100 elderly incontinent patients. British Medical Journal 282: 1103–1105

Castleden C M, George C F, Renwick A G, Asscher M J 1981 Imipramine — a possible alternative to current therapy for urinary incontinence in the elderly. Journal of Urology 125: 318–320

Comarr A E 1957 Excretory cystometry. Journal of Urology 7: 622

Creed K E, Tulloch A G S 1978 The effect of pelvic nerve stimulation and some drugs on the urethra and bladder of the dog. British Journal of Urology 50: 398–405

Creed K E, Tulloch A G S 1982 The action of imipramine on the lower urinary tract of the dog. British Journal of Urology 54: 5–10

Delaere K P J, Thomas C M G, Moonen W A, Debruyne F M J 1981 The value of intravesical prostaglandin E_2 and F_2alpha in women with abnormalities of bladder emptying. British Journal of Urology 53: 306–309

Denny Brown D, Robertson G 1933 On the physiology of micturition. Brain 56: 149–190

Dequeker J 1965 Drug treatment of urinary incontinence in the elderly. Gerontologia Clinica 7: 311–317

Desmond A D, Bultitude M I, Hills N H, Shuttleworth K E D 1980 Clinical experience with intravesical prostaglandin E_2. British Journal of Urology 52: 357–366

Diokno A C S, Lapides J 1977 Action of oral and parenteral bethanecol on decompensated bladder. Urology 10: 23–24

Diokno A C, Davis R, Lapides J 1973 The effect of pelvic nerve stimulation on detrusor contraction. Investigative Urology 11: 178–181

Diokno A C, Taub M 1975 Ephedrine in the treatment of urinary incontinence. Urology 5: 624

Drach G W, Layton T N, Binard W J 1979 Male peak urinary flow rate — relationships to volume voided and age. Journal of Urology 122: 210–214

Dunn M, Smith J C, Ardrang 1974 Prolonged bladder distension as a treatment of urgency and urge incontinence of urine. British Journal of Urology 40: 645–652

Eastwood H D H 1979 Urodynamic studies in the management of urinary incontinence in the elderly. Age and Ageing 8: 41–48

Edwards L 1976 Electronic Control. In Incontinence in the Elderly, Willington F L (ed) p 162. Aademic Press, London

Edwards L, Malvern J 1974 The urethral pressure profile; theoretical considerations and clinical application. British Journal of Urology 46: 325–329

Emmett J L, Daut R V, Dunn J H 1948 Role of the external urethral sphincter in the normal bladder and cord bladder. Journal of Urology 59: 439–454

Farrer D J, Osborne J L 1976 The use of bromocriptine in the treatment of the unstable bladder. British Journal of Urology 48: 235–238

Fisher C P, Diokno A, Lapides J 1978 The anticholinergic effects of dicyclomine. Journal of Urology 120: 328–329

Fletcher T F, Bradley W E 1978 Neuroanatomy of the bladder/urethra. Journal of Urology 119: 153–159

Frewen W K 1982 A reassessment of bladder training in detrusor dysfunction in the female. British Journal of Urology 54: 372–373

Gardner H S, Campbell J A, Garnett R A, Schell H A 1961 Cine radiographic studies of female urinary continence. American Journal of Obstetrics and Gynecology 82: 1112

Garry R C, Roberts T D M, Todd J K 1959 Reflexes involving the external urethral sphincter in the cat. Journal of Physiology (London) 149: 653–665

Geist S K, Salmon U J 1943 The relationship of oestrogens to dysuria and incontinence in post-menopausal women. Journal of the Mount Sinai Hospital 10: 208–211

Gerstein A R, Okun R, Gonick H C, Wilner H I, Kleeman C R, Maxwell H H 1968 The prolonged use of methenamine hippurate in the treatment of chronic urinary tract infection. Journal of Urology 100: 767–771

Gibson G R 1970 A clinical appraisal of methenamine hippurate in urinary tract infections. Medical Journal of Australia i. 167–169

Godec C J, Esho J, Cass A S 1980 Correlation among cystometry, urethral pressure profilometry and pelvic floor electromyography in the evaluation of female patients with voiding dysfunction symptoms. Journal of Urology 124: 687–682

Gosling J A, Dixon J S 1975 The structure and innervation of smooth muscle in the wall of the bladder neck and proximal urethra. British Journal of Urology 47: 549–558

Gosling J A, Dixon J S, Lendon R G 1977 The autonomic innervation of the human male and female bladder neck and proximal urethra. Journal of Urology 118: 302–305

Gosling J A, Dixon J S, Critchley H O D, Thompson S 1981 A comparative study of the human external sphincter and periurethral levator ani muscle. British Journal of Urology 53: 35–41

Habeshaw T, Bennet J R 1972 Ulceration of mouth due to emepronium bromide. Lancet ii: 1422

Haldeman S, Bradley W E, Bhatia N 1982 Evoked responses from the pudendal nerve. Journal of Urology 128: 974–980

Henry L, Fox M 1971 Histological findings in pseudo-membraneous trigonitis. Journal of Clinical Pathology 24: 605–608

Heymann A 1906 Die cystitis trigoni der frau. Zentralblatt Krankh Sexualogr 16: 422–428

Hickey D S, Phillips J I, Hukins D W L 1982 Arrangements of collagen fibrils and muscle fibres in the female urethra and their implications for the control of micturition. British Journal of Urology 54: 556–561

Hilton T, Stanton S L 1981 Algorithmic method for assessing urinary incontinence in elderly women. British Medical Journal 282: 940–942

Hilton T, Stanton S L 1982 The use of desmopressin (DDAVP) in nocturnal urinary frequency in the female. British Journal of Urology 54: 252–255

Hukins D W L, Hickey D S, Kennedy A P 1982 Catheter encrustation by struvite. British Journal of Urology

Hutch J A 1972 Anatomy and Physiology of the Bladder, Trigone and Urethra. Butterworth, London

Isaacs B, Walkey F A 1964 A survey of incontinence in the elderly. Gerontologia Clinica 6: 367–376

Jacob J, Ludgate C A, Forde J, Tullock W S 1978 Recent observations on the ultra structure of the human urothelium — normal bladder of elderly subjects. Cell and Tissue Research 193: 543–560

Jarvis J 1981 A controlled trial of bladder drill and drug therapy in the management of detrusor instability. British Journal of Urology 53: 565–566

Jarvis J 1982a Bladder drill for the treatment of enuresis in adults. British Journal of Urology 54: 118–119

Jarvis J 1982b The management or urinary incontinence due to primary vesical sensory urgency by bladder drill. British Journal of Urology 54: 374–376

Jarvis G J, Miller D R 1980 Control trial of bladder drill for detrusor instability. British Medical Journal 281: 1322–1323

Jones K S, Tibbetts R W 1959 Pituitary snuff, propanthalene and placebos in treatment of enuresis. Journal of Mental Science 105: 371–381

Judge T G 1969 The use of quinoestradol in elderly incontinent women — a preliminary report. Gerontologia Clinica 11: 159–164

Kaplan P E, Nanninga J B, Lal S 1978 Urinary bladder smooth muscle electrical activity — response to atropine and bethanechol. Archives of Physical Medicine and Rehabilitation 59: 454–458

Kaufman J M 1979 Urodynamics in stress urinary incontinence. Journal of Urology 122: 778–782

Kegale A H 1956 The physiologic treatment of urinary stress incontinence. Journal of Internat. College of Surgeons 20: 487–499

Kegel A 1948 Progressive resistance exercise in the functional restoration of the perineal muscles. American Journal of Obstetrics and Gynecology 56: 238

Kennedy A P, Brocklehurst J C 1982 The nursing management of patients with long-term indwelling catheters. Journal of Advanced Nursing 7: 411–417

Kennedy A P, Brocklehurst J C, Lye M, 1983 Factors related to problems of long-term catheterisation. Journal of Advanced Nursing 8: 207–212

Kenwright S Norris A D C 1977 Oesophageal ulceration due to emepronium bromide. Lancet i: 548

Kohler F P, Morales P A 1968 Cystometric evaluations of flavoxate hydrochloride in normal and neurogenic bladder. Journal of Urology 100: 729–730

Langworthy O R, Kolb L C, Lewis L G 1940 In: Physiology of Micturition. Williams and Wilkins, Baltimore

Lapides J 1964 Urecholine regime for rehabilitating the atonic bladder. Journal of Urology 91: 658–659

Lapides J, Diokno A C, Goulde F R, Lowe B S 1976 Further observation on self-catheterisation. Journal of Urology 116: 169–171

Lapides J, Diokno A C, Lowe B S, Kalish M D 1974 Follow-up on the unsterile intermittent self-catheterisation. Journal of Urology 111: 184–187

Lewin R J, Dillard G U, Porter R W 1967 Extrapyramidal inhibition of the urinary bladder. Brain Research 4: 301–307

McGuire E J, Diddel G, Wagner J F 1977 Balanced bladder function in spinal cord injury patients. Journal of Urology 118: 626–628

McGuire J, Herlihy E 1979 Bladder urethral responses to sympathetic stimulation. Investigative Urology 17: 9–15

McLauglan S, Wilkin D 1982 Levels of provision and dependency in residential homes for the elderly — implications for planning. Health Trends 14: 63–65

McLennan F C 1939 The Neurogenic Bladder. C C Thomas, Springfield

Mandelstam D 1977 Incontinence. Disabled Living Foundation, London

Milne J S, Williamson J, Maule M M, Wallace E T 1972 Urinary symptoms in older people. Modern Geriatrics 2: 198–213

Montgomery E 1974 Regaining Bladder Control. Bristol: John Wright

Mooney J K, Hinman F 1974 Aging and replacement of the luminal cells in the mammalian bladder studied by scanning electron microscopy. Investigative Urology 11: 396–401

Moore T 1960 The female prostate: bladder neck obstruction in women. Lancet i: 1305–1309

Moore T, Schofield P N 1967 The treatment of stress incontinence by maximal perineal electrical stimulation. British Medical Journal iii: 150–151

Mueller S M Phenylpropanolamine, a non-prescription drug with potentially fatal side-effects. New England Journal of Medicine 308: 653

Muellner S R 1949 The physiological components of the urinary bladder: their clinical significance. New England Journal of Medicine 241: 769–772

Murnaghan G F 1961 Neurogenic disorders of the bladder in Parkinsonism. British Journal of Urology 33: 403–409

Nathan P W, Smith M C 1958 Pathway for micturition within spinal cord. Journal of Neurology, Neurosurgery and Psychiatry 21: 177

Orikasa S, Koyanagi T, Motomura M, Kudo T, Togashi M, Tsuji I 1976 Experience with non-sterile intermittent self-catheterization. Journal of Urology 115: 141–142

Packham D A 1971 The epithelial lining of the female trigone. British Journal of Neurology 43: 201–205

Palmer J H, Worth P H L, Exton-Smith A N 1981 Flunarazine — a once daily therapy for urinary incontinence. Lancet ii: 279–281

Parvinen M, Sourander L B, Vuorinen P 1965 Cystographic studies of old women. Gerontologia Clinica 7: 343–347

Phillips J I, Davies I 1981 A comparative morphometric analysis of the component tissues of the urethra in young and old female C57BL/Icrfat mice. Investigative Urology 18: 422–425

Plum F, Colfelt R H 1960 The genesis of vesical rhythmicity American Medical Association Archives of Neurology 2: 487–496

Porter R W, Bors E, Hyman W 1969 In: Gillingham F J, Donaldson I M C (eds) Third Symposium on Parkinson's diseases. Livingstone, Edinburgh, p 124–128

Pullen B R, Phillips J I, Hickey D S 1982 Urethral lumen cross-sectional shape and relationship to function. British Journal of Urology 54: 399–407

Ramsden P D, Smith J C, Dunn M, Ardron G M 1976 Distension therapy for the unstable bladder: later results including assessment of repeated distensions. British Journal of Urology 48: 623–629

Randell N J 1975 A new uroflow meter for routine clinical use. Biomedical Engineering 21: 24

Raz S, Kaufman J J 1977 Carbon dioxide urethral pressure profile in female incontinence. Journal of Urology 765–769

Ritch A E S, George C F, Castleden C M, Hall M R P 1977 A second look at emepronium bromide in urinary incontinence. Lancet i: 504–506

Roberts G R 1969 Dependent drainage ballon catheter. British Medical Journal i: 705

Robinson J M 1983 Atrophic vaginitis: its prevalence and treatment in elderly women with incontinence. Presented at British Geriatrics Society Meeting, Liverpool

Robinson J M, Brocklehurst J C 1983 Emepronium bromide and flavoxate hydrochloride in the treatment of urinary incontinence associated with detrusor instability in elderly women. British Journal of Urology 55: 371–376

Rohner T J, Raeger D M, Wein A J, Schernberg H W 1971 Contractile responses of dog bladder neck. Journal of Urology 105: 657–661

Rossier A B, Fam Bushra A, Lee Il Y, Mehdi S, Evans D A 1982 Role of striated and smooth muscle components in the urethral pressure profile in traumatic neurogenic bladder: a neuropharmacological and urodynamic study. Preliminary report. Journal of Urology 128: 529–535

Rud T 1980 The effect of oestrogens and gestagens on the urethral pressure profile in urinary continent and stress incontinent women. Acta Obstetrica et Gynecologica Scandinavica 59: 265–270

Rud T, Andersson K E, Ulmstem U 1978 The effects of calcium antagonists in women with unstable bladders. Proceedings of the 8th Internation Continence Society Meeting. Manchester: Pergamon Press p 53–57

Rud T, Andersson A E, Asmussen M, Hunting A, Ulmsten U 1980 Factors maintaining the intra-urethral pressure in women. Investigative Urology 17: 343–347

Rutte B Von, Delnon I 1968 Die Urethralzytologie und ihre bedeutung zur Diagnose hormonal bedingter miktionsstorungen. Praxis 16: 555–560

Schmaelze J F, Cass A S, Hinison F 1969 Effect of disuse and restoration of function on vesical capacity. Journal of Urology 101: 700–705

Seabury J C, Boyarsky S 1968 Evaluation of silastic coated ballon catheters. Journal of Urology 100: 90–91

Sharr M M, Garfield J S, Jenkins 1976 Lumbar spondylosis and neuropathic bladder: investigation of 73 patients with chronic urinary symptoms. British Medical Journal 1: 695–697

Sheldon J H 1948 In: Social Medicine of Old Age. London: Nuffield Foundation, O.U.P

Siroky M B, Krane R J 1982 Neurologic aspects of detrusor-sphincter dyssynergia with reference to the guarding reflex. Journal of Urology 127: 953–957

Smith P 1972 Age changes in the female urethra. British Journal of Urology 42: 667–676

Smith P H, Cook J B, Prasad E W M 1974 The effect of Ubretid on bladder function after recent complete spinal cord injury. British Journal of Urology 46: 192

Smith P, Roberts M, Slade N 1970 Urinary symptoms following hysterectomy. British Journal of Urology 42: 3–9

Sonda L P, Gershon C, Diokno A C, Lapides J 1979 Further observations on the cystometric and uroflowmetric effects of bethanechol chloride on the human bladder. Journal of Urology 122: 775–777

Sourander L B 1966 Urinary tract infection in the aged. Epidemiological Study. Annals Medicinae internae Fenniae, suppl. 45: p. 55

Stanton S L 1973 A comparison of emepronium bromide and flavoxate hydrochloride in the treatment of urinary incontinence. Journal of Urology 110: 529–532

Stewart B H, Banowsky L H W, Montague D K 1976 Stress incontinence: conservative therapy with sympathomimetic drugs. Journal of Urology 115: 558–559

Strouthidis T M, Mankika R G D, Irvine R E 1972 Ulceration of mouth due to emepronium bromide. Lancet i: 72

Sundin T, Peterson I 1975 Cystometry and simultaneous electro-myography from the striated urethral and anal sphincters and from the levator ani. Investigative Urology 13: 40–46

Sutherst J R, Brown M 1981 Detection of urethral incompetence. Erect studies using the fluid bridge test. British Journal of Urology 53: 360–363

Talbot H S, Mahonery E M, Joffee S J 1959 The effects of prolonged urethral catheterization of normal renal structure and function. Journal of Urology 81: 138

Tanagho E A, Smith D R, Meyers F H 1968 The trigone: anatomical and physiological considerations. 2. In relaton to the bladder neck. Journal of Urology 100: 633–639

Tang P R, Ruch T C 1956 Localization of brain-stem and drencephalic areas controlling the micturition reflex. Journal of Comparative Neurology 106: 213–231

Tanner E R 1969 Pelvic muscle dysfunction in urinary incontinence. Physiotherapy:372–375

Thomas D 1979 Clinical urodynamics in neurogenic bladder dysfunction. Urological Clinics of North America 6: 237–253

Thomas T M, Flymat K R, Blannin J, Meade T W 1980 Prevalence of urinary incontinence. British Medical Journal 281: 1243–1245

Thompson J 1964 Cystometry in investigation of urinary incontinence. Current Achievements in Geriatrics. London: Cassell

Tulloch A G S 1974 The Vascular contribution to intra-urethral pressure. British Journal of Urology 46: 659

Tyler D E 1962 Stratified squamous epithelium in the vesical trigone and urethra: findings correlated with the menstrual cycle and age. American Journal of Anatomy 111: 319–325

Underwood R 1970 Cellulose gel pads in the control of incontinence in elderly women. Practitioner 205: 224–225

Van Duzen R A 1954 Pharmacological effects of various drugs on micturition. Journal of the American Medical Association 156: 1393

Virchow R 1853 Prostataconcretionen Beim Weib. Archiv für pathologise hes Anatomie 5: 403–444

Von Brunn A 1839 Archiv für mikroskopische Anatomie 41: 294

Warrell D W, Watson B W, Shelley T 1963 Intravesical pressure measurement in women during movement using a radio pill and air probe. Journal of Obstetrics and Gynaecology of the British Commonwealth 70: 959–967

Walter S, Hansen J, Hansen L, Maegaard E, Meyhoff H H, Nordling J 1982 Urinary incontinence in old age — a controlled clinical trial of emepronium bromide. British Journal of Urology 54: 249–251

Walter S, Wolf H, Barlebo H, Jensen H K 1978 Urinary incontinence in post-menopausal women treated with oestrogens. Urology International 33: 135–143

Wein A J, Raezer D M, Malloy T R 1980 Failure of the bethanechol supersensitivity test to predict improved voiding after subcutaneous bethanechol administration. Journal of Urology 123: 202–204

Weiner D P, Koss L G, Sablay B Freed S Z 1979 The prevalence and significance of Brunn's nests, cystitis cystica and squamous metaplasia in normal bladders. Journal of Urology 122: 317–321

Weir J, Jaques P F 1974 Large capacity bladder. Urology IV: 544–548

Wells T 1984 Social and psychological implications of incontinence. In: Brocklehurst J C (ed) Urology in the Elderly. Churchill Livingstone, Edinburgh

Whitfield H M, Mayo M E 1975 Prolonged bladder distension in the treatment of the unstable bladder. British Journal of Urology 47: 635–639

Whitehead W E 1984 Behavioural methods in assessment and treatment of urinary incontinence. In: Brocklehurst J C (ed) Urology in the Elderly. Churchill Livingstone, Edinburgh

Willington F L 1969 Problems in urinary incontinence in the aged. Gerontologia Clinica 11: 330–356

Willington F L 1976 Hygienic Methods of Management of Incontinence. In: Incontinence in the Elderly (ed) Willington F L, p 227. London: Academic Press

Wilson T S 1948 Incontinence of urine in the aged. Lancet ii: 374–377

Woodburne R T 1961 The sphincter mechanism of the urinary bladder and urethra. Anatomical Medicine 141: 11

Yeo J, Southwell P, Rutowski S, Marchant-Williams H 1974 A further report on the effect of distigmine bromide (Ubretid) on the neurogenic bladder. Medical Journal of Australia 2: 201–203

Youngblood V H, Tomlin E M, Williams J O, Kimilstein P 1958 Exfoliative cytology of the senile female urethra. Journal of Urology 79: 110–113

Zuckerman S 1940 The histogenesis of tissues sensitive to oestrogens. Biological Reviews of the Cambridge Philosophical Society 15: 231–271

The genitourinary system — the prostate

INTRODUCTION

It is important in the consideration of aging of the prostate and the clinical effects this may have that there is an understanding of the pathology of the gland and its related structures. The prostate is a heterogeneous structure closely related to the detrusor and trigonal muscles of the bladder above and the external sphincter muscle of the pelvic floor below. There is muscular continuity between the trigone of the bladder and the voluntary pelvic floor sphincter (external sphincter) in the striated muscle of the urethra (Fig. 31.1). This anterior muscular investment of the gland and a downward extension of the deep trigonal muscle into it are two examples of the close interrelationship between gland parenchyma and fibromuscular structures which can be

simultaneously involved in involutionary changes and the symptoms which arise from these. Although the basic functional anatomy can usually be identified throughout life there is considerable morphological change at the time of maturation of the gland (puberty) and in later life as a result largely of focal atrophy and benign hyperplastic change. The typical location respectively of benign prostatic hyperplasia (BPH) and carcinoma differ and this accounts for the different clinical presentation.

The hormone sensitivity of the stroma and epithelium of the parenchyma and the innervation of the musculature of the fibro-muscular stroma are important both in involutional changes and in modifying the symptoms caused by these. This is the basis for the use of hormones and neural blocking agents in the management of some forms of prostatic disease.

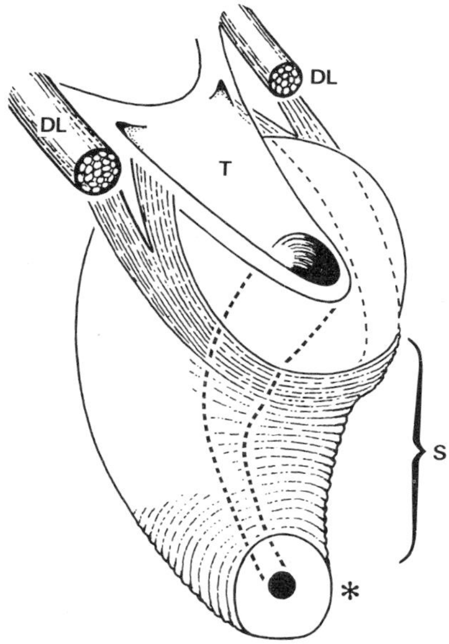

MORPHOLOGY

Previous descriptions of the morphology of the parenchyma of the prostate have largely been superceded by that of McNeal (1972) who interpreted the subdivisions of the parenchyma of the prostate in a different way and provided for these a new terminology. His intentions in appealing for this new nomenclature was to overcome the confusion of descriptive terms wherein it was impossible to know whether reference was being made to normal functional tissue or pathology. The previous descriptions had used the term 'lobe' to describe various parts of the prostate e.g. middle, lateral and posterior and the same nomenclature, i.e. 'middle' and 'lateral' lobe, is the standard description for pathological entities of BPH. In papers, both clinical and research, it was impossible to know whether the author was describing normal functional tissue or pathological entities. This nomenclature also probably gave rise to the erroneous belief that the operation of 'prostatectomy' removes the whole gland whereas in fact all that is removed surgically is the hyperplastic tissue leaving the functional tissue or its compressed remnant in situ. There is no doubt that

Fig. 31.1 The striated sphincter muscle of the urethra (S) is inserted into the deep trigonal muscle (T) above and is continuous below with the external sphincter (*). DL — detrusor loop.

McNeal's use of the term 'zone' to describe normal functional prostatic parenchyma provides the means for a clearer understanding of the anatomy and the differentiation between ostensibly normal and pathological tissue.

McNeal's interpretation of a dual morphology of the functional state has been confirmed by others (Blacklock, 1976) and there is additional confirmatory evidence from embryological studies and comparative anatomy.

The morphology is best appreciated from mid saggital and coronal sections (Fig. 31.2).

It is important to appreciate that the urethra lies in front of the normal prostatic parenchyma which is disposed posterior and postero-lateral to it. It is only

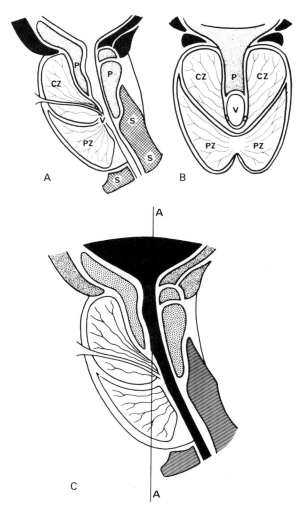

Fig. 31.2 (a) mid sagittal and (b) coronal sections through prostate. CZ: central zone; PZ: peripheral zone; V: verumontanum; P: preprostatic sphincter; S: striated sphincter of the urethra. (c) — AA shows plane of coronal section

when prostatic hyperplasia takes place that an abnormal parenchyma lies in front. The urethra is surrounded in its upper part — above the verumontanum — by the downward extension of the trigone forming a circular fibro-muscular tube which McNeal has termed the preprostatic sphincter. This terminates about the level of the verumontanum and is overlapped in front at this point by the upward prolongation of the striated muscle of the urethra which is continuous below with the external sphincter and pelvic floor musculature.

McNeal (1968, 1972) described two sub-divisions of the prostatic parenchyma which resembled other descriptions for instance by Lowsley (1912) if Lowsley's posterior and lateral lobes were considered as one. McNeal identified a central zone just beneath the trigone which extends down to the level of the verumontanum and this is partially enclosed by the peripheral zone laterally, the peripheral zone extending inferiorly to form the apex of the gland. The central zone completely surrounds the ejaculatory ducts so that at no point do these come into contact with the peripheral zone in their course through the gland to the urethra. The central zone composes approximately one-third of the functional gland mass.

The differentiation into these zones is made from the size and shape of the individual prostatic acini, the fibromuscular stroma and the lining epithelium. The fibromuscular stroma of the central zone is more prominent and the acini are large and rectangular in cross-section with prominent intraluminal partitions. The lining epithelium is compound with multiple layers of cells which have vacuolated opaque cytoplasm. In contrast the peripheral zone has a finer stroma and a simpler form of duct branching. The smaller acini are in general round with a simpler more regular epithelial lining of cells which have pale, granular cytoplasm and small dark nuclei.

The embryological support for this dual functional morphology is provided in a number of descriptions. Glenister (1962) described the rudiments of prostatic ducts at two levels one group above and the other below the seminal colliculus in a 125 mm foetus. The site of origin of these rudiments is of significance since the primordia of the cranial entity (central zone) lie in the region of confluence of the urogenital sinus, the mesonephric and paramesonephric ducts; since this part of the urethra is also represented in the female the central zone of the prostate is embryologically homologous with the female paraurethral glands or female prostate. The primordia of the lower group of prostatic ducts rises from that part of the urogenital sinus which later is only represented in the male. These origins suggest a differential steroid hormone sensitivity of the epithelium of each.

The comparative anatomy of the lower orders of

animals in respect of the prostate is confusing since in the rodent there is a multi-lobular prostate parts of which do not appear to have their representation in the human. The primate however provides a replica of the human anatomy as described by McNeal, there being a cranial and caudal lobe with virtual separation between these two moieties. The inference is that the cranial lobe of the primate is homologous with the central zone in the human and the caudal lobe with the human peripheral zone.

The clinical application of this anatomy arises from its functional considerations. Firstly the innervation of the pre-prostatic sphincter — which is intimately associated with the process of BPH — is largely alpha-adrenergic. The innervation of the striated sphincter of the urethra is probably both noradrenergic and cholinergic as well as voluntary. A specific function of the pre-prostatic sphincter is the closure of the bladder neck at the time of ejaculation to prevent reflux of seminal fluid into the bladder and there is a similar alpha-adrenergic innervation of the musculature of the seminal vesicles, ejaculatory ducts and prostatic acini. The role of the preprostatic sphincter in continence is less clear although it may be responsible for resting continence. The 'milk-back' phenomenon is most probably accomplished by the striated muscle of the urethra since this is a rapid movement usually complete up to the level of the bladder neck and the characteristics of its contraction are suggestive of striated muscle action. The presence of the two sphincter formations — pre-prostatic sphincter and the striated sphincter of the urethra — in combination with the external sphincter provides the reason for the maintenance of continence after prostatectomy in which the pre-prostatic sphincter is either ablated or compromised. The alpha-adrenergic nerve supply of this sphincter however provides the explanation for some cases of acute urinary retention precipitated by cold weather and other stresses which increase, however temporarily, the secretion of noradrenalin. For the same reason however, episodes of retention precipitated in this way are frequently reversible as this stimulation of the muscles recedes. Such a history however is also indicative of the presence of a degree of prostatic hyperplasia and usually means that the episode will be repeated if the condition remains untreated.

The embryological origin of the two zones of the prostate just described suggests the greater androgen sensitivity of the epithelium and stroma of the peripheral zone compared with the central zone and this is strengthened by the observation in the primate of a significantly greater number of androgen receptors in the caudal compared with the cranial lobe (Ghanadian et al, 1977).

AGE RELATED CHANGES AND PATHOLOGY

The prostatic parenchyma remains for some time after birth as a fibro-muscular stroma penetrated by the prostatic ducts without much in the way of acinar structure. Just before puberty an acinar structure develops in the central zone (less androgen dependent) whereas the acinar anatomy of the peripheral zone (more androgen dependent) occurs after puberty (Blacklock, 1976). Thereafter the morphology is relatively static until the fifth decade when there are the beginnings of nodular hyperplasia. Atrophic change may occur at this time but has also been observed in earlier years usually in conjunction with debilitating illness when it is surmised that androgen utilization may be less.

Prostatitis

Although this may occur at any age it is more common in its pure form during the second, third, fourth and fifth decades in association with sexual activity. The inflammatory change is within the ducts and acini and in the stroma in juxtaposition to these. It is an ascending infection and affects the peripheral zone significantly more frequently than the central. Resolution usually occurs with adequate antibiotic treatment but chronicity may become established with focal inflammatory infiltration and destruction of parenchyma. In some cases abscess formation takes place and the abscess may drain either through the urethra, via the perineum or burst into the rectum. This however is unusual except in the debilitated old man since antibiotic treatment will usually prevent suppuration.

One form of prostatitis which is a feature in the older man is granulomatous inflammation characterized by infiltration with chronic inflammatory cells including macrophages, lymphocytes and plasma cells. There is fibrosis and destruction of acinar anatomy and the condition is much more generalized throughout the gland than bacterial prostatitis which tends to be focal in its distribution.

The cause of granulomatous prostatitis is not known and may be an autoimmune phenomenon. Although it can give rise to irritative symptoms and even prostatism it is frequently silent and only found incidentally during digital examination of the prostate per rectum when it tends to be confused with carcinoma since the palpable characteristics are the same. The gland is uniformly hard but usually regular. Biopsy however provides the diagnosis.

Atrophy

One of the earlier changes within the gland is focal atrophy, and it can be found from the fifth decade onwards. As it is so often seen in association with chronic inflammatory infiltration and stromal fibrosis it may be a basically inflammatory process. One of the features is the degeneration present in both the acinar anatomy and the stroma itself. Although focal it may involve a large area of the gland (McNeal 1968).

The distribution of the atrophic change associated with aging is more diffuse and may be due to either deprivation of androgens — general or local — or to a diminished utilisation as may occur in chronic debilitating disease including malignancy. This atrophy is not usually accompanied by inflammatroy infiltration and the stromal destruction is not as great. Either of these processes may be the basis for the small fibrous gland of old age in which the fibrosis extends to involve the preprostatic sphincter and, at the level of the bladder neck, the fibrosis can lead to narrowing with the production of a poor flow and the secondary effect of detrusor hypertrophy, bladder diverticulum and, in the advanced case, dilatation of the upper tract. It is this type of prostate which specifically requires management by transurethral resection since enucleation is impossible and failure to recognise the pathology for what it is can lead to surgical mishap.

Benign prostatic hyperplasia

This nodular hyperplasia which involves both epithelial and stromal elements in varying degree arises in three characteristic locations which are in juxtaposition. The submucosal glands enclosed within the preprostatic sphincter are involved as is the fibro-muscular stroma of the preprostatic sphincter itself. An additional segment of the parenchyma lying just external to the pre-prostatic sphincter at its lower border also participates and McNeal has described this as a 'transitional' zone (Fig. 31.3). The hyperplastic process tends to involve the intergrity of the fibro-muscular stroma of the pre-prostatic sphincter leading to its progressive destruction. There is some continuity in the hyperplastic process although there may be the development of separate nodules and this typically occurs as three entities — two anterolaterally and one posteriorly in the subcervical position at the bladder neck. In this position the hyperplasia gives rise to typical intra-urethral protrusions which are located antero-laterally in this upper part of the prostatic urethra and in the midline posteriorly at the level of the neck of the bladder. The location of the beginnings of the process are shown in Figure 31.4 in a coronal section and the progression of this to the fullblown condition is depicted in Figure 31.5. In this illustration the reason is clear for the characteristic elongation of the urethra in BPH together with the manner in which the hyperplasia intrudes into the cavity of the bladder. In all of these diagrams and in a cross section (Fig. 31.6) the disposition of the areas

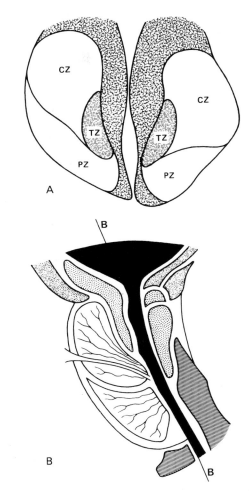

Fig. 31.3 (a) Diagrammatic coronal section through prostate showing location of transitional zone (TZ) in relation to central zone (CZ) and peripheral zone (PZ). (b) — BB shows plane of coronal section

of hyperplasia can be seen together with their relationship to the functional prostate which is pushed peripherally and posteriorly and becomes compressed. There is usually atrophic change of the functional parenchyma where it is contiguous with the hyperplastic nodule and this can give rise to cystic degeneration which can define a plane of surgical cleavage between the nodule and the underlying tissue. This is seen in a cross section of a gland in which antero-lateral hyperplastic nodules are well developed (Fig. 31.7).

The intimate relationship of the hyperplastic process to alpha-adrenergically innervated muscle both of the pre-prostatic sphincter and of the investing striated sphincter muscle of the urethra has already been referred to in respect of the influence this may have in

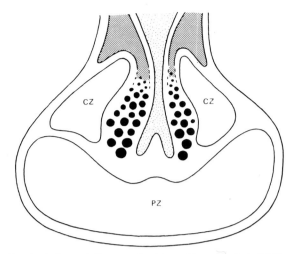

Fig. 31.4 Coronal diagram of origins of hyperplasia in BPH in relationship to central zone (CZ) and peripheral zone (PZ)

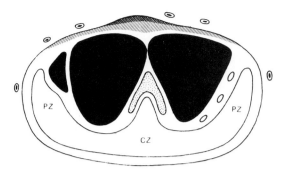

Fig. 31.6 Diagram of transverse section of prostate showing disposition of hyperplasia in relation to urethra and displacement of lower central zone (CZ) and peripheral zone (PZ)

aggravating the mechanical effects of the hyperplasia itself. What may be only minor obstructive effects can be precipitated into occlusion by alpha-adrenergically induced spasm of the muscles surrounding the hyperplasia.

Carcinoma

Carcinoma arises predominantly in the peripheral zone of the prostate but may spread from this to involve other areas and areas of hyperplasia. Carcinoma 'in situ' can also be found on occasions within areas of hyperplasia. It is frequently multi-focal within the peripheral zone

of the gland and a histological feature is the heterogeneity of the tumour between one focus and another. The origins are therefore separate and most probably involve different clones of cells so that it is easy to understand that one clone may be more dependent upon androgen than another hence a differential response to treatment by hormone ablation or treatment with oestrogenic and progestogenic hormones. Situated in the periphery of the gland the tumour does not usually give rise to prostatism until it is advanced such as to occupy the greater part of the gland and infiltrate the sphincter. For this reason a cancer is frequently quite far advanced at the time of presentation and it is not unusual for the presentation to be with metastatic lesions which are characteristically in the bones of the pelvis, the spine and in the upper parts of the femur. Local spread, in addition

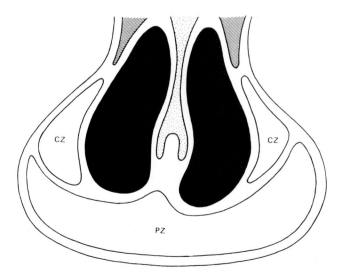

Fig. 31.5 Coronal diagram of location and disposition of advanced BPH. Note elongation of prostatic urethra and displacement of central (CZ) and peripheral zone (PZ)

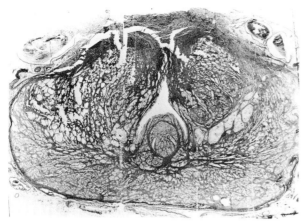

Fig. 31.7 Cross-section of prostate which is the seat of BPH. Cystic degeneration has taken place between the hyperplastic nodule on the right side and the peripheral zone posteriorly. This would facilitate enucleation of the 'adenoma'.

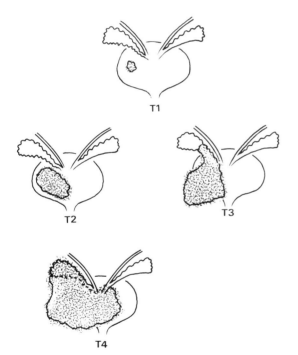

Fig. 31.8 TNM classification of prostatic cancer (UICC, 1978).
T0 — small focus of cancer usually undetectable clinically except by biopsy or resection of an apparently benign gland.
T1 — a palpable tumour confined to one part of the gland.
T2 — a palpable tumour involving a greater part of the gland but still confined within the capsule.
T3 — a palpable tumour involving the gland to greater or lesser extent and also extending beyond the confines of the capsule.
T4 — extensive tumour within the gland and extending widely into the surrounding tissues.

to involving the urethra, may infiltrate the base of the bladder and silently engulf the lower ureters with progressive obliteration of the lumen and obstructive nephropathy.

Although metastases are characteristically blood-borne in prostatic cancer there is also spread to involve both the regional and juxta-regional glands and, again, presentation may be a mass of glands in the inguinal region.

In the staging of prostatic cancer the tumour-lymph node-metastasis (TNM) classification (UICC, 1978) is increasingly used and provides considerable advantages in allowing objective comparison between one regime of management and another. This classification in respect of prostatic cancer is depicted in Figure 31.8.

The usual location of cancer in the peripheral zone of the prostate, behind hyperplasia when this is present, leaves the potential for malignancy or actual malignancy even after enucleation or resection procedures have been carried out for hyperplasia. In view of this it is customary for perineal prostatic biopsy to be carried out in all cases having resection or enucleation procedures for BPH. The biopsy needle introduced through the perineum and guided by the finger in the rectum can be made to sample the tissues which are most likely to be the seat of neoplasia.

CLINICAL

Urinary tract infection

Whereas in the younger male and adult lower urinary tract infection is usually synonymous with prostatitis, urinary tract infection as a disease in the older man is usually associated with some degree of outflow obstruction and residual urine. Foci of inflammation are found in areas of BPH and these may be due to localized infarcts or the result of infection introduced at the time of catheterization.

A urinary infection in a man over the age of 60 requires the evaluation of the prostate and investigation by excretion urography to define whether there is residual urine.

The infection is usually heralded by the characteristic symptoms of urinary irritation and frequency with terminal dysuria and these may be superimposed upon symptoms for a longer time of outflow obstruction/ (prostatism). A febrile episode is unusual unless there is an established prostatitis with focal inflammation and even abscess formation.

These infections may be complicated by an epididymitis in which case there is usually a systemic reaction with fever and where this occurs with one of the more resistant pyogenic organisms (*B.proteus*, *B.pyocyaneus*) toxaemia may be considerable.

The physical evaluation of the patient must always include digital examination of the prostate per rectum. If the gland is the seat of focal infection or an abscess there will characteristically be exquisite tenderness and the surface characteristics of the gland will be difficult to determine on account of this. Palpation of the lower abdomen should also be carried out to detect a palpable residue of urine.

Apart from the routine bacteriological scrutiny of the urine, excretion urography should be carried out after the infection has been fully treated with the appropriate antibiotic since bladder emptying may be impeded during the infective episode either from oedema of the prostate or irritative sphincter spasm giving rise to a false impression of the amount of residual urine. Where the residual urine is significant in amount and there have been symptoms of prostatism prior to the infective episode, consideration should be given to prostatic surgery.

Benign prostatic hyperplasia (BPH)

BPH occurs in a significant proportion of men as they age and it has been estimated that about 10 per cent of men over the age of 40 will subsequently require some form of prostatectomy. Whilst this applies in Europe, North America and the other technically advanced countries it also occurs in the African Negro but is not as common in Arabia and Japan and is even less common in mainland China. Apart from the interest of these epidemiological differences there is the suggestion from them of an aetiology which probably bears upon dietary habit.

BPH or fibrous stenosis of the bladder neck gives rise to the characteristic symptoms of deterioration of the urine flow, difficulty in the initiation of urination and the tendency for post micturitional dribbling of urine (prostatism). The difficulty in initiation of urination and the sometimes interrupted urine flow is an indication of the irritability of alpha-adrenergically supplied muscles at the bladder neck and surrounding the hyperplasia and these symptoms are aggravated under states of mental or physical stress. The frequency which characterises some cases is a manifestation of the secondary change of hypertrophy of the bladder which has occurred to overcome the outflow obstruction. It is noteworthy that frequency on its own is not an indication for surgery as long as bladder emptying is complete since this will usually respond to a drug with anticholinergic effect which reduces the irritability of the detrusor. Whilst nocturia may be another manifestation of the same change particular note must be made not only of the number of times that voiding occurs during the night but also of the amount voided on each occasion. Where frequent nocturnal voiding is associated with the passage of only small amounts of urine it is likely that bladder hypertrophy and an irritable detrusor is the cause. If the nocturnal voiding is characterized by the passage of large volumes of urine this is unlikely to be prostatic in origin and is more suggestive of a cardiovascular cause with a failing circulation and pooling of fluid in the peripheral tissues during day time activity. For this reason the evaluation of these urinary symptoms is best accomplished by providing the patient with a frequency/volume chart in which not only are the times of urination noted but the volume of urine passed each time.

Haematuria and dysuria are uncommon features of BPH. Haematuria however may occur with varices in the prostatic urethra and dysuria can occur where prostatitis supervenes or there is infection in residual urine. One of the modes of presentation with BPH is uraemia or pre-uraemia due to obstructive nephropathy. In these the bladder is usually painlessly distended and there is a history of prostatism of varying degree over a period of years.

A dribbling urinary incontinence is a further type of presentation and this is usually of the 'overflow' variety occurring with a distended bladder. The other type of incontinence is 'urge' incontinence which is characterized by the subjective desire urgently to urinate against which sphincteric control may be inadequate. This symptom complex occurs in association with significant hypertrophy of the detrusor of the bladder.

In addition to the examination of the abdomen and the prostate there is the necessity to investigate renal function biochemically and to evaluate the cardio-respiratory reserve since operative treatment will usually be necessary.

The digital examination of the prostate per rectum will allow a crude estimate of the gland size and the main use of the examination is to exclude the presence of obvious prostatic neoplasia. Small glands may be accompanied by gross micturitional disturbance for the reasons of pathology and physiology already described. The gland size is the main criterion of the type of operative approach since the biggest glands are still more satisfactorily treated by open operation than by transurethral resection.

It is customary for intravenous urography to be done in these cases but this is not mandatory unless there has been complaint of haematuria such as to suggest neoplasia in the bladder or upper tracts. In other words if time on a waiting list may be significantly increased by delaying for intravenous urography it is reasonable to omit this procedure if all of the other methods of evaluating the case are used.

In some centres where there are the facilities renography is used in the assessment since this can detect the earliest stages of differential diminution in function and delay in elimination of the isotope from the upper urinary tract. If combined with gamma camera techniques the tracts on each side can be visualized and also the presence of residual urine. This type of investigation is more cost effective than IVU and is a preferred alternative for all of these reasons.

More recently the advent of ultrasonic techniques can now provide an objective estimate of prostatic size and also the degree of hypertrophy of the bladder neck. The technique requires a rectal probe. In addition to providing an estimate of size however, perhaps its more important application is in defining the homogeneity or otherwise of the parenchyma and identifying areas of infiltration, either neoplastic or inflammatory. It also accurately defines the location of prostatic calculi. Whilst this sophisticated technique of investigation is probably only justified for the moment in larger centres there is the possibility that its modification will allow greater control over resection procedures and, specifically, the retrieval of tissue from demonstrably suspect areas of the prostate either with the resectoscope or with the biopsy needle.

Computerized tomography can provide some estimate of prostatic size but this is crude in comparison with the image produced by ultrasound. There is certainly no value in its routine use in cases of BPH.

Carcinoma

Prostatic cancer accounts for an increasing proportion of the cancer mortality of men. Observations of various clinical series suggest that latent cancer is present in between 10 and 20 per cent of men in their sixties and between 20 and 40 per cent in those over 70. These are morphological but not necesarily invasive cancers and observations of those found to have these TO or TI lesions (see Fig. 31.8) have shown survival rates which are comparable with cases of BPH within the same age range.

The disease appears to occur with fairly even frequency in Europe, North America and the developed world but like hyperplasia is uncommon in China and Japan. Again this interesting epidemiological difference suggests some environmental factors in aetiology which are likely to be associated with dietary structure.

As already described the clinical presentation of these cases is frequently incidental — the result of a digital examination of the gland carried out for other reasons than prostatism. The presence of carcinoma may also be detected during the routine histology of resected or enucleated hyperplastic tissue. Presentation of the case may also be as the result of symptoms due to a metastasis. A feature in local symptoms when they occur is the association of pain with prostatism in the absence of infection. This can occur as the result of sphincter involvement by extension of a tumour.

Diagnosis of the condition may be apparent from the physical features of the gland but on occasion these are not diagnostic and can be confused with granulomatous prostatitis.

A tumour marker in this instance is the prostatic acid phosphatase but its significance is still questionable in the early stages of the disease although the new techniques using radio-immunoassay, counter immuno-electrophoresis and immunofluorimetric assay provide hope that it may soon be possible to detect a focal lesion by these means. For the moment elevation of prostatic acid phosphatase in the serum is suggestive of metastatic disease either bone or lymphatic. Other markers are of little value but these include alkaline phosphatase — often raised in metastic disease — carcino-embryonic antigen (CEA) and hydroxyproline (HP) excretion in the urine. This latter estimation is of value in monitoring the patient with metastases (Mundy, 1979).

The full assessment of the case necessitates intravenous urography since infiltration of the ureters may occur and with more extensive involvement of these may bring the presentation of such a patient in uraemia. There is unlikely to be much if any distortion of the cystogram in these cases. More sensitive as an indicator of upper tract involvement, as in the case of BPH, is renography using a gamma camera. This also provides the most sensitive indication of progression or remission.

Ultrasonography using a rectal probe is now able to delineate suspicious areas within the prostate and allow their biopsy specifically for diagnosis. This also allows the definition of the capsule of the gland and provides evidence of infiltration of tumour through the capsule and more accurate staging than was possible before. Whilst the finger may detect such infiltration when it occurs postero — laterally, ultrasound can show breach of the capsule in the previously 'silent' areas antero-laterally.

Computerized tomography is also useful in the evaluation of the extent of the disease and has the advantage in the old of its relative non-invasiveness. It is able to detect glandular metastases in the pelvis and para-aortic regions.

Where carcinoma has been confirmed histologically either by transperineal prostatic biopsy or transurethral resection full assessment of the case requires radioisotope bone scan. The optimum scanning agent is Technetium-99 methylenediphosphate. Twenty per cent of patients presenting with prostatic cancer already have a positive bone scan (Chisholm, 1980). The bone scan may be positive for as long as 18 months before there is skeletal X-Ray evidence and this simple, relatively non-invasive test is of great value in the assessment, follow up and monitoring of response to treatment.

MANAGEMENT

The prostatism of the older man bears careful evaluation to guide the decision on the most effective and least traumatic management. It is here that the frequency volume chart provides invaluable information and may suggest the trial of bladder relaxant drugs, e.g. emepronium bromide, as a first resort. Ninety per cent of all prostates are dealt with by transurethral techniques, open surgery being reserved for the biggest glands.

Transurethral surgery minimizes tissue trauma and confines it to the lesion with over-all benefit to the patient and the result of this is manifest in the much shorter period of time spent in bed post-operatively and much shorter hospital stay which is important in the case of the old who depend so much on a minimal separation from their familiar home surroundings. This operation is almost specifically indicated for the old man and for this reason open operation using either the transvesical or retropubic techniques should be specifically reserved for glands which cannot be satisfactory dealt with otherwise. From this point of view it may be preferable even with the biggest glands to attempt a partial trans-urethral resection with the considerable chance that such partial removal of obstructive tissue will at least allow resumption of urination and better bladder emptying. Resort to this may be necessary if there is severe accompanying systemic disease or feebleness.

Another refinement in operative management which is of further advantage to the old is the availability of epidural anaesthesia which is quite the best anaesthetic in this procedure. The patient is conscious throughout the operation or only slightly drowsy with respiratory and cough reflexes intact. Furthermore the blocking effect of the anaesthetic on sympathetic impulses from the traumatised area minimizes or diminishes the metabolic response to trauma which is not to the patient's advantage. On return to the ward from a transurethral resection of prostate in which epidural anaesthesia has been used the old man is able immediately to have fluids and to eat and is minimally disturbed by the procedure. Post-operatively the urethral catheter is removed rather earlier after transurethral operations than open and ambulation is earlier. All of these are in the best interests of the old, allowing an earlier return to home surroundings.

In some cases of chronic atonic bladder distension, the atonicity of the bladder perpetuates a retention of urine even although the outlet obstruction at the bladder neck has been satisfactorily removed. These cases require a cholinergic bladder stimulant and an indwelling catheter on continuous drainage to allow the recovery of bladder tone. The patient is best to return to his home surroundings whilst recovery is taking place since this may be prolonged.

Where atonic bladder distension persists or where there is incontinence following prostatectomy due to sphincter deficiency resort must be had to continuing definitive management by indwelling catheter or incontinence device where this is acceptable to the patient and effective.

Carcinoma

The management of this disease is influenced by what is now known of the natural history particularly that a significant proportion of patients when they present (20 per cent) already have skeletal metasases. Chisholm (1980) found that 52 per cent of cases already have evidence of local spread outside the confines of the prostate when first seen. This is perhaps the main reason why radical prostatectomy is so rarely considered in treatment. Both for this reason and the severity of the operation it will never be considered a choice of treatment in the case of the older patient.

Patients with focal disease (TO/1/2) show comparable survival rates over a 5 year period with cases of benign hyperplasia within the same age range (Byar 1977) so that there is some justification for an expectant approach to management unless or until there is the evidence of progression of the neoplasm locally or by metastases. While hormone manipulation using oestrogen (stilboestrol) may appear simple and easy for the patient this is now recognized to be accompanied by considerable risk of cardiovascular complications whose effects are more lethal than the disease. There is furthermore now some evidence to suggest that a longer remission may be obtained if hormonal manipulation is delayed until there is the evidence of progression of the disease (Lepor et al, 1983). A modifying factor however is the degree of differentiation of the histology since those with poorer differentiation are most likely to be accompanied by early spread both local and metastatic, and there may be the indication then even with localized disease to commence treatment.

Where the disease is more extensive within the prostate but still confined within it, management policy is once again influenced by the degree of differentiation of the tumour. Where this is poor there is probably the indication for some form of management and the bias for the moment is towards radiotherapy rather than use of hormones. The results from a number of series treated in this way are awaited. A further possibility at this stage is the implantation of Iodine 125 seeds and favourable reports have been received of 90 per cent 5 year survival rates of patients who had T3 tumours without metastases at the time of presentation (Chisholm, 1981).

Where the disease has become locally advanced

although not yet clinically metastatic management may either be by hormonal means or radiotherapy. Again, because of the potential complications using oestrogens, orchidectomy has become the more common form of hormonal manipulation and one present trial is combining this with radiotherapy. This trial continues.

Although the management of the earlier local disease is controversial, particularly so in the older patient, the lines of management become clearer with later disease. With the morbidity and mortality ascribable to oestrogen therapy shown in an extensive earlier trial (Byar, 1977) a low dose of an oestrogen (stilboestrol 1 mg tds) is used and comparison with larger dosages has shown that this is as effective and carries with it fewer cardiovascular complications. Even this low dose oestrogen treatment however is contraindicated in those patients with a history of cardiovascular disease both on account of the haemocoagulation problems and fluid retention which accompanies this treatment. There is little advantage in other oestrogen preparations although in the patient admitted in acute pain from bone secondaries quicker relief may be obtained with the intravenous preparation of tetrasodium fosfestrol (Honvan) (diethylstilboestrol diphosphate — stilphostrol). After the initial relief of symptoms treatment can be continued with stilboestrol 1 mg tds.

The alternative hormone manipulation to estrogen treatment, and one which carries with it no risk of cardiovascular complications, is orchidectomy. Subscapsular orchidectomy is as effective as removal of the testis and epididymis and is a lesser operative procedure and therefore the desirable one in the old. In addition to avoiding the risk of cardiovascular complications orchidectomy overcomes the risk in an old patient of forgetfulness to take necessary regular treatment. Furthermore the complication of gynaecomastia is avoided. There is some evidence however that oestrogen may be more effective than orchidectomy in preventing cancer deaths (Byar, 1977).

Another form of oestrogen therapy which may be especially indicated in the forgetful old man is an injection — oestradiol phosphate (Estradurin) — which is given monthly and is said to be less accompanied by side effects.

There is little place for the use of the other drugs in the older man as their evaluation is still awaited.

Hormone manipulation by castration or oestrogen therapy will cause remission of the disease for a variable period of time and in some may permit the patient to die of some unrelated disease. The response to hormone manipulation is governed by the androgen dependence of the neoplastic cells. Approximately 20 per cent of tumours are hormone dependent, and therefore do not respond to treatment. Furthermore although there may be initial response to this form of management 'escape' may occur which is most likely due to the growth and predominance of a clone of neoplastic cells which are androgen independent.

When a patient who has previously responded to management with an oestrogen is subsequently found to have objective evidence of progression of the disease it is unlikely that any other form of hormonal manipulation will influence the course of the disease. Specifically in the older patient there can be no indication for adrenalectomy to remove other sources of androgen although hypophysectomy as a means of pain relief may be an indication if there is troublesome generalised bone pain.

There is little indication so far of the ideal chemotherapeutic drug or drug combination in prostatic cancer. Estracyt is a combination of oestradiol with an alkylating agent, normustine. This combination was formulated so that the hormone would carry the alkylating agent to the tumour where it would be released in high concentration. The anti-tumour effect can be dramatic and subjective responses of as much as 20–30 per cent are reported. This drug and another — Prednimustine (an ester of chlorambucil with prednisone) — await further longer term evaluation. These and other agents probably have a place in the management of old patients who have escaped hormone manipulation or radiotherapy but their use is modified by the need to avoid the further compromize of bone marrow already probably infiltrated and destroyed by tumour.

In the advanced case of prostatic malignancy with localized bone pain there is a specific indication for the use of radiotherapy for the control of symptoms.

REFERENCES

Byar D P 1977 VACURG studies on prostatic cancer and its treatment. In: Tannenbaum M (ed) Urologic Pathology; the prostate, Lea and Febiger, New York, Ch 13, p 241–267

Blacklock N J 1976 The Anatomy of the Prostate In: Chisholm G D, Williams D I (ed) Scientific Foundations of Urology, Heninemann, London, p 113–125

Chisholm G D 1981 Perspectives and prospectives in prostatic cancer. In: Duncan W (ed) Prostatic Cancer, Springer Verlay, Berlin, p 181

Chisholm G D Habib F R 1980 Prostatic cancer; experimental and clinical advances. In: Hendrie W S (ed) Recent Advances in Urology/Andrology, Churchill Livingstone, Edinburgh, p 211–232

Chisholm G D 1980 Urological malignancy; prostate. In: Chisholm G D (ed) Tutorials in Postgraduate Medicine; Urology, Heinemann, London, Ch 15, p 223–246

Ghanadian R, Smith C B, Chisholm G D, Blacklock N J 1977 Differential androgen uptake by the lobes of the rhesus monkey prostate. British Journal of Urology 49: 701–704

Glenister T W 1962 The development of the utricle and the so called 'middle' or 'median' lobe of the human prostate. Journal of Anatomy (London) 96: 443–445

Lepor H, Ross A, Walsh P C 1983 The influence of hormonal therapy on survival of men with advanced prostatic cancer. Journal of Urology (in press)

Lowsley O S 1912 The development of the human prostate gland with reference to the development of other structures in the neck of the urinary bladder. American Journal of Anatomy 13: 299–349

McNeal J 1968 Regional morphology and pathology of the prostate. American Journal of Clinical Pathology 49: 347–357

McNeal J 1972 The prostate and prostatic urethra: a morphologic synthesis. Journal of Urology 107: 1008––1016

Mundy A R 1979 Urinary hydroxproline excretion in carcinoma of the prostate; a comparison of four different modes of assessment and its role as a marker. British Journal of Urology 51: 570–574

UICC Union Internationale Contre le Cancer 1978 TNM Classification of malignant tumour. 3rd edn International Union against cancer, Geneva

The genitourinary system — gynaecological disorders in the elderly

AGE CHANGES IN THE GENITAL TRACT

Hormone production and effects

Ovary

The physiological aging process, particularly in the genital tract, accelerates after the menopause. The remaining ovarian primordial follicles, which are usually but not always present, do not respond even to greatly increased pituitary gonadotrophin stimulation. In the reproductive years the ovary has three compartments for steroid biosynthesis which are the maturing follice, the functional corpus luteum and the stroma; after the menopause only the stroma remains active in steroidogenesis. This has been demonstrated by in vitro studies (Mattingly and Huang, 1969), and the steroids are produced in the interstitial glands which arise from degenerating medium-sized and antral follicles (Mossman et al, 1964) which have the characteristics of steroid secreting cells (Deane et al, 1962). Thus the ovary remains active for many years after the menopause but there is a different pattern in steroidogenesis.

Oestrogen production continues after the menopause and total urinary oestrogens do not change in the first 10 years (Grattarola et al, 1975). McLennan and McLennan (1971) showed that approximately 40 per cent of postmenopausal women have oestrogenized vaginal smears until after the age of 75 years. Oestradiol is the dominant oestrogen in the reproductive years; its blood levels are reduced in perimenopausal women (Sherman et al, 1976) and by approximately 90 per cent after the menopause (Longcope, 1971). Ovarian oestradiol secretion is minimal after the menopause (Judd et al, 1976).

Oestrone is the major postmenopausal oestrogen and approximately 40 μg are produced in 24 hours. It is derived from conversion of androgens, mainly androstenedione, which takes place predominantly in adipose tissue (Hemsell et al, 1974). This process is increased with advancing age and obesity and is altered by liver disease and hyperthyroidism (Southren et al, 1973). Androgens are secreted by the adrenal glands in approximately the same quantities before and after the meno-

pause, while ovarian output increases postmenopausally (Judd et al, 1974; Greenblatt et al, 1976). Longcope (1974) suggested that the ovary is the major source of androgens in the climacteric.

Oestriol, a weak oestrogen, is produced before and after the menopause, but its metabolism is not well documented and its possible postmenopausal role has not been established. Pregnanediol levels decline after the menopause, and Vermeulen (1976) demonstrated that progesterone and 17-hydroxyprogesterone are derived almost entirely from the adrenal glands.

Pituitary gonadotrophins

The high concentrations of follicular stimulating hormone (FSH) and luteinizing hormone (LH) found after the menopause are due to the loss of feedback inhibition normally exerted by oestradiol. The levels of gonadotrophins remain elevated throughout the remainder of the patient's life although they decline somewhat after the age of about 70 years. Once the gonadotrophin levels have risen, much higher doses of oestrogen and progesterone are required to suppress them and this ability depends on the time of administration after the onset of the menopause (McPherson et al, 1975); this suggests a change in hypothalamic sensitivity after oestrogen deprivation which may be relevant to hormone replacement therapy. Hot flushes and night sweats are the most frequent symptoms of the climacteric. Their cause is not completely known but is probably related to low oestrogen levels, elevated gonadotrophins, adrenalin and the potent vasodilators, bradykinin and histamine (Studd et al, 1977).

Gonadotrophins do not increase suddenly at the menopause as there is a change in hypothalamo-pituitary-ovarian relations over the whole climacteric. Reyes et al (1976) studied gonadotrophins and gonadal steroid levels in groups of regular menstruating women of increasing ages; while FSH levels rose gradually from 34 to 39 years, no changes were noted in LH or oestradiol levels, and progesterone levels were on average slightly lower. These findings suggest the existence of a non-oestrogenic feedback factor whose lack results in

FSH increase. The human male possesses this factor, called inhibin, which is involved in a negative feedback on FSH secretion (Baker et al, 1976).

Anatomic changes

Age changes in the genital tract are influenced by the normal degenerative process, progressive diminution of hormone stimulation and reduced or absent function; the onset and rapidity of these effects varies. The major change is atrophy which results in smaller and smoother structures, flattened epithelial surfaces, fibrous stroma and much reduced vascularization and fat content.

Vulva

Vulval atrophy is characterized by shrinkage and wrinkling of the skin, loss of prominent landmarks and sparse greying hair. Histologically, the epidermis is thinner although there may be increased keratinization; in the dermis there are fewer blood vessels, but ischaemia does not usually occur as arteriolar sclerosis is not a prominent feature (Lang and Aponte, 1967). These vulval changes may become severe with increasing age, leading to disorders described later.

Vagina

Vaginal atrophy results in a pale, foreshortened and narrow structure and the external urethral meatus may recede along the anterior vaginal wall (Parsons and Sommers, 1962). The epithelium is thinner and less cellular so that there is reduced or absent interaction between cellular glycogen and Doederlein's bacilli which normally react to produce lactic acid; thus the vaginal secretions are reduced, the reaction becomes alkaline and a potent vaginal defence mechanism is lost. Progressive weakness of the vaginal walls is sometimes seen because connective tissue is affected by oestrogen lack (Suntzeff et al, 1940) and aging skeletal muscle becomes replaced by adipose tissue (Frantzell and Ingelmark, 1951). Uterovaginal prolapse may supervene if the supports have been weakened previously, for example during childbirth.

Uterus

The major change is a reduction in size so that the ratio of uterine body to cervix reverts from 4 : 1 in reproductive life to the childhood ratio of 2 : 1. The cervical squamous epithelium sometimes extends into the endocervical canal (Lang, 1962) which may lead to stenosis of the cervical os. The endometrium consists of a single layer of flat or cuboidal cells with few glands which are frequently cystic and the stroma becomes fibrous and hyalinized. In the myometrium there is interstitial fibrosis and the blood vessels are thickened due to obliterative subintimal sclerosis. Woessner (1963) studied tissue change in the aging human uterus and

noted that the wet weight, collagen and elastin increased to a maximum by 30 years of age, remained constant for 20 years and declined from 50 to 65 years by approximately 50 per cent.

Ovary

As function diminishes the ovary becomes smaller until finally it is sclerotic and convoluted. Germinal inclusion cysts may be seen, there is hyalinizing stromal fibrosis and obliterative arteriolar sclerosis (Lang and Aponte, 1967). The remnants of corpora albicantia coalesce into amorphous masses and atretic follicles disappear.

POSTMENOPAUSAL BLEEDING

This condition requires detailed investigation because of the association with, and the increased incidence of, genital tract malignancy in the elderly. Procopé (1971) investigated 667 cases of postmenopausal bleeding of which 154 (23.1 per cent) had carcinoma, 19.8 per cent showed endometrial hyperplasia, 19.6 per cent had endometrial polyps and 33.3 per cent showed atrophic endometrium. Keirse (1973) analysed 160 patients and noted a malignancy rate of 23.7 per cent of which endometrial adenocarcinoma was found in 13.1 per cent and cervical squamous cell carcinoma in 7.5 per cent. However, Gambrell (1974) studied 363 patients and found only 3 per cent with endometrial adenocarcinoma; 29 patients were aged 60 years or over and one had endometrial adenocarcinoma, 10 showed endometrial hyperplasia and 16 had atrophic endometrium. Thus carcinoma is a major cause of postmenopausal bleeding but the commonest finding is atrophic epithelium involving part or the whole of the genital tract.

Oestrogen therapy, given orally or applied locally, may cause postmenopausal bleeding, particularly with long courses or high doses. In view of the increasing use of this treatment in Great Britain it is necessary to record the patient's recent drug treatment. Oestrogen replacement therapy has been prescribed for many years in America, and in 218 patients with postmenopausal bleeding Gambrell (1977) noted that 100 (46 per cent) were taking oestrogen; 15 of his series were aged 60 years or over and oestrogen had been prescribed in seven.

Benign conditions which may cause bleeding include urethral caruncle, cervical or endometrial polyps, decubital ulceration of the cervix, and occasionally, vaginal infection and ulceration due to a long-forgotten ring pessary. Other milignant growths which should be considered are vulval carcinoma and hormone-secreting tumours of the ovary; the latter may present with vaginal bleeding due to endometrial hyperplasia. The lower urinary and intestinal tracts also may require investigation as the origin of the bleeding may be mistaken, particularly in the elderly.

Investigation includes bimanual examination, cervical cytology, biopsy of suspicious areas and endometrial curettage. Cystoscopy is recommended to exclude a bladder tumour — not uncommon in the elderly. In Great Britain dilatation and curettage under general anaesthesia are usually performed to obtain an endometrial biopsy as this allows more detailed examination of the abdomen and pelvis. In patients at risk from even a short anaesthetic or where no obvious pelvic abnormality is found, vacuum curettage using a small suction aspirator and local anaesthetic has been recommended. This technique is rapid, safe, provides a high degree of accuracy (Saunders and Roland, 1972), and it has the advantages of not requiring hospital admission or general anaesthetic and does not restrict the patient's mobility. The pain experienced with this technique is usually minimal.

The treatment of postmenopausal bleeding depends upon the cause and it is outlined in the appropriate section. The role of hormone replacement therapy is discussed in the section 'Conditions of the vagina'. Recurrent bleeding requires reinvestigation including sigmoidoscopy. If no cause is found, total hysterectomy and bilateral salpingo-oophorectomy are necessary as a small tumour in the ovary or uterus may have been overlooked.

VULVAL DISORDERS

Pruritis valvae

This common symptom is associated with many conditions, including vaginal infection, poor hygiene, glycosuria, allergy and drug sensitivity, such deficiency states as avitaminosis A and B_2 and lack of iron, folic acid and vitamin B_{12} (Jeffcoate, 1975) and epithelial disorders. Detailed examination and investigation and appropriate treatment are essential as empirical medication with pessaries, ointment or anaesthetic cream are unhelpful and may lead to a long-term problem often with serious consequences.

Vulval epithelial disorders

These conditions represent an advanced stage of the common atrophic change. They are called sometimes vulval dermatoses or vulval epithelial dystrophies, but implied in the term dystrophy is some degree of epithelial atypia which may or may not be present. The epithelial disorders are important because of the severity and chronicity of their symptoms, the commonest and dominant one being pruritis, and the possible association with carcinoma. There are conflicting views concerning their terminology, pathogenesis, aetiology and diagnosis as well as their relationship to carcinoma. The commonest subgroups are leukoplakia, kraurosis and *lichen sclerosus et atrophicus*, but as there are many common features these diagnostic terms are of little significance clinically or histologically. Generalized skin diseases, particularly psoriasis, must also be considered as there may be similar macroscopic vulval lesions and little involvement elsewhere.

The vulval disorders are difficult to distinguish from each other particularly in the presence of secondary inflammation with bacterial or mycotic organisms or when chronic scratching has occurred. The gross features include thickened grey-white plaques of keratin or pale or reddish areas where keratin is much reduced. Histologically, the epidermis is frequently thickened and there may be increased mitotic activity associated with chronic inflammation. The pattern may vary throughout the vulva. Therefore multiple biopsies are necessary to exclude atypical elements elsewhere.

The term leukoplakia, strictly used, describes the macroscopic appearance of thickened white plaques on the vulva (Berkeley and Bonney, 1909) which covers orderly or atrophic epithelium. More recently this term has been used to describe irregular cell morphology in the vulval epithelium which is called dysplasia in other squamous epithelia; this cellular atypism is generally accepted as unstable and at risk of eventual maligant change (Wallace and Whimster, 1951; McAdams and Kistner, 1958). Thus confusion has arisen from these different interpretations. Leukoplakia may affect a localized area, the whole vulva, or occasionally it spreads more widely.

Kraurosis has characteristic dry and shiny mucosa which usually involves the vestibule, urethral orifice, vagina and inner aspects of the labia major only. The introitus becomes progressively narrowed and the lesion may be painful. Histologically, the mucus membrane shows atrophy and sometimes inflammatory change. It is not known if this condition is separate from, or an end stage of, leukoplakia. Lichen sclerosus is a similar condition to kraurosis but it affects areas outside the vulva.

A retrospective histological survey of specimens was carried out by Leighton and Langley (1975); they classified the conditions into three categories – hypertrophic vulvitis, neurodermatitis (due to chronic scratching) and lichen sclerosus. The first two categories were similar and were therefore differentiated according to the site of occurrence: neurodermatitis arose in the hair-bearing areas while hypertrophic vulvitis was confined to the hairless areas medial to the inner aspects of the labia majora.

In view of the problems of classifying these vulval disorders it has been suggested that the subdivisions should be abandoned and an assessment of the skin changes made according to their basic nature. Thus, Woodcock (1973) defined three categories: degenerative, inflammatory, and dysplastic. The clinician may therefore decide more easily on methods of treatment and when dysplasia is present appropriate steps may be taken to prevent future development of carcinoma

Association of vulval epithelial disorders with carcinoma

The incidence of carcinoma arising in vulval disorders is approximately 5 per cent (Jeffcoate, 1966). While the development of carcinoma from leukoplakia is well documented the relationship between the other disorders and malignancy is not understood. Carcinoma may arise in lichen sclerosus (Wallace, 1962), but it is not known if this change occurs directly or involves leukoplakia.

Squamous cell carcinoma

Squamous cell carcinoma of the vulva is most frequently seen in the sixth and seventh decades and accounts for about 5 per cent of genital cancers; it is the commonest vulval tumour. The patient may complain of pruritis or discomfort or she may notice a lump. The aetiology is unknown, but suggested predisposing factors include long-standing irritative agents (chemical, infective or mechanical), poor hygiene or epithelial dysplasia (Jeffcoate, 1975).

The lesion arises in any part of the vulva but usually the labium majus and spread is by direct invasion or the lymphatics. The major vulval lymph channels run anteriorly along the labium majus (Parry-Jones, 1976) and drain to the superficial inguinal nodes; from there the deep inguinal and external iliac nodes become involved. Contralateral lymphatic spread also may occur. Diagnosis is made by biopsy as infection and ulceration often coexist causing a slough of fibrin, pus cells and necrotic tissue which makes cytological examination difficult.

MANAGEMENT OF VULVAL DISEASE

Epithelial disorders

Diagnosis is made by biopsy of suspicious areas with a minimum of three specimens from the anterior, middle and posterior areas of each labium because of the possiblility of abnormal foci elsewhere. Treatment of the benign conditions depends upon the cause. Where a factor is found, for example anaemia, glycosuria or candidiasis, appropriate treatment is prescribed. Empirical measures are often necessary but they tend to provide temporary relief only; these include local corticosteroid preparations which arrest the epithelial reaction, antihistamines which have a sedative effect and antibiotics for treating secondary infection. Oestrogen therapy is not likely to reverse these long-standing

changes but it may reduce the possibility of secondary infection. Two per cent testosterone in vaseline is proving to be an effective application in many patients (Freidrich, 1976). Improvement of local hygiene is essential, the vulva should be kept dry and hospital admission for diagnosis and initial treatment is helpful. Simple vulvectomy (local removal) has been advocated, but as epithelial changes and symptoms often recur it is not recommended.

With premalignant disease, simple vulvectomy including a margin of normal skin is usually effective. Long-term follow-up of all patients is necessary, and if exacerbation occurs detailed reinvestigation is required.

Squamous cell carcinoma

Radical vulvectomy is the most effective treatment of squamous cell cancer and the operation consists of vulval excision and bilateral superficial and deep lymphadenectomy. Few gynaecological surgeons have wide experience of this condition therefore, where possible, the patient should be referred to a gynaecological oncology centre where the best results are achieved. Vulval cancer is associated with elderly patients, therefore fitness for surgery is a major problem. In general, the operation is tolerated well, particularly when a one-stage procedure is performed. The extent of lymphadenectomy is important as the more extensive procedures are associated with higher operative and postoperative risks. Te Linde (1970) and Way (1954) recommended that if, at frozen section, the proximal node in the deep inguinal glands is involved further lymphadenectomy is necessary.

Radiotherapy is of limited value because the surrounding normal vulval tissue is even more sensitive than the tumour, and a persistent and violent skin reaction results (Woodcock, 1973). However, radiotherapy may be used to reduce tumour mass and make surgery possible. Coagulation diathermy and cryosurgery are palliative techniques used only to control bleeding or reduce a large fungating mass (Chamberlain, 1975). In early cases a 5-year survival of approximately 75 per cent may be expected.

CONDITIONS OF THE VAGINA

Atrophic vaginitis

Atrophic vaginitis is also described as senile vaginitis; the term senile is inappropriate in the author's view as it is somewhat pejorative. The condition is due to the thin inactive epithelium becoming less resistant to pathogenic organisms. This process may involve the vulva, uterine endometrium or lower urinary tract which are affected also by hormone deficiency. Blood-stained vaginal discharge with or without pruritis is a common presentation and frequency and urgency of urination or dysuria may be noted. The presence of small red spots are diagnostic of atrophic change and excoriation of the vagina may occur in advanced stages leading to adhesions between the anterior and posterior walls.

Atrophic change should be diagnosed as the cause of postmenopausal bleeding only after the detailed examination and investigation outlined previously. The disorder is due to oestrogen deficiency, therefore replacement therapy should be considered. It is accepted generally that oestrogen replacement just after the menopause may be beneficial but its long-term value continues to be debated vigorously. Its use in Great Britain is increasing but less than in the United States where a survey by Barrett-Connor et al (1979) found that 24 per cent of women over 70 years were taking oestrogens.

The main advantage of long-term therapy is the prevention of osteoporosis provided it is started shortly after the monopause (Lindsay et al, 1976; Hutchinson et al, 1979). It has been observed that 25 and 50 per cent of Caucasian women have osteoporotic vertebral fractures by the ages of 50 and 75 respectively (Greenblatt et al, 1979). However when the oestrogens are stopped there is accelerated bone loss so that the patient may be no better off (Lindsay et al, 1978), also the current data relate to treatment for the first 10 postmenopausal years, therefore, the long-term benefits and risks are not known. Other advantages claimed for this therapy are reduced rates of skin atrophy, coronary heart disease and aging as well as improved libido, however, the data are unsubstantiated (Utian, 1982).

The main disadvantage of oestrogen replacement is endometrial hyperplasia which in susceptible patients may lead to endometrial carcinoma; this risk is reduced by the addition of cyclical progestogens for 7–13 days (Studd and Thom, 1981). Unfortunately, progestogens are implicated in the development of stroke and ischaemic heart disease (Meade et al, 1980): to overcome these problems synthetic anabolic steroids have been used which prevent bone loss and do not affect the endometrium (Lindsay et al, 1980). Other potential risks of long-term oestrogen treatment in postmenopausal women have been studied. Postmenopausal bleeding (either 'breakthrough', while taking the pill, or 'withdrawal', after cessation,) may occur due to endometrial stimulation. Uterine curettage in all cases may be recommended by some clinicians but it is reasonable initially to observe the effect of stopping the hormone. If bleeding persists investigation is necessary. With long-term therapy 1-2-yearly curettage is advised (Cooke, 1983).

There is unconfirmed evidence of a slight increase in breast cancer associated with long-term oestrogens but this seems to be related to continuous and high dose treatment (Hoover et al, 1976). The data concerning the oral contraceptive pill and breast cancer are more encouraging as no relationship has been found between the two (Utian, 1982).

In spite of the established association between combined oral contraceptives and deep venous thrombosis and thromboembolism, this phenomenon has not been found in postmenopausal oestrogen-takers. The reason is unknown but may be related to differences in type and/or potencies of oestrogen (Notelovitz and Ware, 1982). Nevertheless oestrogen should not be used in such high risk women as those with a past history of thromboembolism, liver disease or homone-dependant tumour, or who are obese, have severe hypertension or are heavy smokers. The incidence of gallstones requiring surgery is increased by 2.5 times (Boston Collaborative Drug Surveillance Programme, 1974) but carbohydrate metabolism is little altered with correct oestrogen use. In diabetic patients and those at risk of developing it, investigation is necessary before starting treatment (Utian, 1982).

Oral oestrogens are most frequently prescribed and a variety of natural and synthetic preparations is available. At present either type is acceptable provided it is prescribed cyclically and combined with progesterone (Cooke, 1983). Such combined oestrogen and progesterone preparations as Menophase*, Prempak† or Cyclo-Progynova‡ (in US — Biosterone§) may be used. The length of treatment depends on clinical response but usually a 2–3 month course is sufficient initially. The patient must be warned of such possible side-effects as breast discomfort and vaginal bleeding.

Oestrogen cream is useful to treat atrophic vaginitis particularly when there are such symptoms as vulval soreness, vaginal dryness and dyspareunia. Oestrogen absorption through the vagina is rapid and leads to hormone levels which are equivalent to those observed in ovulating women (Widholm and Vartiainen, 1974; Rigg et al, 1978). Thus the absorptive capacity of the vaginal epithelium and gastrointestinal tract are similar so there are the same absolute and relative contraindications to oestrogen use whatever the route of administration (Whitehead et al, 1978). These authors showed following cream application to the vagina that a maximal response is not obtained for 2 weeks and the duration of the carry-over effect after stopping therapy is 2 weeks; they recommend that an initial course of 2 weeks should be followed by 2 nights' application each week thereafter. If this treatment is continued for more than 2–3 months then cyclical oral progesterone therapy

* Syntex
† Ayerst
‡ Schering
§ Myers Carter

should be given (e.g. Norethisterone, 5 mg) to prevent endometrial hyperplasia and possible carcinoma. A problem of this treatment in the elderly is reduced acceptability and manual dexterity required for self-administration, therefore, the district nurse may be required to teach and encourage the use of cream and its vaginal applicator.

UTEROVAGINAL PROLAPSE

The supports of the uterus and vagina are closely related and should be considered together. Prolapse of the anterior and posterior vaginal walls may occur independently or together resulting in any combination of urethrocele, cystocele, rectocele and enterocele which are displacements of the underlying urethra, bladder base, rectum and Pouch of Douglas (and any contents) respectively. Uterine prolapse may predominate, but usually this is associated with some degree of vaginal wall laxity. Uterovaginal prolapse may be caused by congenital or developmental weakness of the pelvic organ supports (Jeffcoate, 1975) or it may follow childbirth (although the exact mechanism is unknown), hormone deficiency and the natural aging process.

Supports of the genital organs
The main supports of the uterus and upper vaginal are the transverse cervical, or cardinal, ligaments which arise from the supravaginal cervix and upper vagina and are inserted into the pelvic side walls. These ligaments extend anteriorly to form the pubocervical fascia which supports the bladder base, urethra and anterior vaginal wall as it travels to the insertion in the symphysis pubis. The posterior extensions of the transverse cervical ligments — the uterosacral ligaments — also contribute to uterine support (Jeffcoate, 1975). The lower vagina is supported by fibres of the levatores ani muscles which are inserted into its side walls, by the urogenital diaphragm and perineal muscles. The anterior wall rests on the posterior vagina and perineal body when the patient is erect and the posterior wall is strengthened by the rectovaginal fascia and the perineal body.

Major degrees of prolapse are nowadays less common because of improved obstetric management. The patient usually presents with a dragging, or bearing down, sensation of gradual onset which is worse with activity and settles with rest. A lump may be felt. Urinary symptoms do occur, but these are just as likely to be related to atrophic change, inflammation, infection or uninhibited detrusor muscle activity as to the mechanical effect of the prolapsed bladder or urethra. Nevertheless distortion of the bladder outlet may lead to incomplete bladder emptying and urinary infection. Thus, digital replacement of the anterior, or indeed posterior, vaginal wall is sometimes necessary before micturition, or defaecation, may proceed.

With prolonged uterine descent oedema occurs due to interference with venous and lymphatic drainage leading to hyperkeratinization of the epithelium, elongation of the cervix and decubital ulceration; bleeding may result but carcinoma rarely develops.

The management of uterovaginal prolapse depends on severity of symptoms, degree of incapacity and the patient's fitness for surgery. When treatment is necessary surgery is most effective and may consist of anterior colporrhaphy, amputation of the elongated cervix or vaginal hysterectomy and posterior colpoperineorrhaphy. This often leads to improved mobility and a return to an independent life. Most patients tolerate this surgery well because of improved anaesthetic techniques and the limited postoperative morbidity.

When surgery is contraindicated or refused, conservative measures may be used. A soft polyvinyl or hard polyethylene pessary may be inserted into the vagina; the former is advised as it is more easily inserted and removed. Four-monthly vaginal inspection and cleaning of the pessary are necessary because mucosal ulceration commonly occurs. Regular use of oestrogen cream as described previously may reduce or prevent ulceration; when it does occur removal of the pessary and cream application will produce healing and thickening of the epithelium. Douching with plain water or a mild antiseptic solution is not often necessary.

URINARY INCONTINENCE

Urinary incontinence is particularly disabling in elderly patients, but with modern methods of investigation and treatment symptoms may be alleviated if not cured (Brown, 1977). Uninhibited detrusor muscle contractions (detrusor instability) are usually the cause in elderly patients due to age-related changes in the central nervous system (see Chapter 30). Incontinence may also be caused by intrinsic weakness, or dysfunction, of the urethral closure mechanism which is best described as genuine stress incontinence (International Continence Society, 1976); this is the most common cause of incontinence in the reproductive and early postmenopausal years. Successful management of incontinence depends on (1) adequate assessment which includes a detailed urinary history incorporating daily urination and incontinence charts (Wilson et al, 1980), (2) accurate cystometry which measures vesical and rectal (similar to abdominal) pressures and involves multiple provocative tests, for example coughing with a full bladder in the supine and erect positions. Endoscopy should be performed when appropriate, for instance when there is haematuria. The problem is discussed in detail in Chapter (30).

CARCINOMA OF THE UTERUS

In the last two decades there has been an improved prognosis for cervix and corpus cancer, due mainly to earlier diagnosis and also to more precise histopathological classification of tumours which has influenced treatment selection (Kolstad, 1982). Furthermore there is an increasing trend for patients with gynaecological cancer to be centralized in units staffed by experienced gynaecological oncologists so that their care and treatment can be improved (RCOG Working Party Report, 1982). In general, mortality occurs more commonly from cervical than endometrial carcinoma, but the latter is more frequent in elderly patients.

Carcinoma of the cervix uteri

Carcinoma of the cervix is the commonest genital cancer and occurs most frequently in the sixth decade. Squamous cell carcinoma accounts for approximately 95 per cent of the primary neoplasms. The aetiology is not completely understood, but coitus and an early age of onset of coitus have been established as major prerequisites for the disease (Gagnon, 1950; Towne, 1955; Rotkin, 1967). Other relevant factors are the number of sexual partners, sexually transmitted diseases and prostitution, all of which are related to each other and with the established factors. Racial traits have been implicated and the evidence suggests that different cultural habits related to sexual activity are more important than such physical characteristics as circumcision (Coppleson, 1969). Lower socio-economic groups have a higher incidence of cervical cancer and many explanations have been put forward but, again, early age at first intercourse and marriage may be relevant: also these groups tend to underuse screening facilities and seek help late when symptoms develop.

The debate continues concerning the value of cytological screening for cervical cancer but when screening is continued for 10–15 years the incidence and mortality of invasive carcinoma are reduced (Fidler et al, 1970; MacGregor, 1976).

Blood-stained vaginal discharge is a common presentation and secondary infection occurs frequently with advanced lesions producing a characteristic offensive odour. Pain is usually a late symptom. Tumour spread is by direct invasion of lymph or blood vessels. Approximately 30 per cent of early lesions have some degree of lymph channel spread within the pelvis; with advanced disease the inguinal and aortic nodes become involved. Diagnosis is achieved from biopsy of suspicious areas under general anaesthesia and concomitantly an assessment of the degree of spread, called staging, is made. Appropriate treatment may then be decided.

Early cervical cancers are treated by radical (Wertheim) hysterectomy, which involves lymph node dissection, or radiotherapy as both have similar 5-year survival rates of approximately 80 per cent. However, each gynaecologist encounters relatively few cases; therefore it is not justifiable for him/her to perform the radical operation necessary as results of this occasional surgery are worse than those achieved by a competent radiotherapy unit. Later stages of the disease are treated by intracavitary and external megavoltage radiation. Unfortunately this tumour is generally insensitive to chemotherapy.

Carcinoma of the corpus uteri

Aetiology and pathogenesis of adenocarcinoma of the endometrium

Endometrial cancer is the commonest gynaecological malignancy in elderly patients with a mean age of 62 (Studd and Thom, 1981). Many factors have been implicated in the aetiology and pathogenesis of endometrial carcinoma, but our present knowledge is incomplete. Fox and Sen (1970), Brown (1974) and MacMahon (1974) have demonstrated a significant association between endometrial carcinoma and the single state, nulliparity, reduced fertility and a late menopause. MacMahon (1974) and Fox and Sen (1970) showed also an association with obesity and hypertension respectively.

The effect of diabetes mellitus on endometrium is not clear as the association with endometrial carcinoma ranges from 1 to 50 per cent. This variation is due to different criteria being used for assessment as some groups have related the number of frankly diabetic patients with endometrial cancer while others have used abnormal glucose tolerance tests as the criterion. Carbohydrate tolerance is affected by such factors as genetic traits, obesity, malignant disease and circulating oestrogen levels; therefore an association of diabetes with endometrial carcinoma may be due to one or more of these factors.

Endometrial hyperplasia is a precursor of adenocarcinoma in some patients. Cystic glandular hyperplasia does not predispose to endometrial cancer as Schröder (1954) and McBride (1959) found an association only in approximately 0.3 per cent; however, endometrial cancer is related to atypical hyperplasia (Gusberg and Kaplan, 1963), and its incidence increases with greater degrees of atypia (Campbell and Barter, 1961).

The role of oestrogens in the aetiology of endometrial adenocarcinoma is receiving considerable attention due to the increasing use of oestrogen replacement therapy. This subject is dealt with elsewhere (p. 663), but it is relevant to consider the problem briefly in this discussion. There is evidence which links endogenous oestrogen production with endometrial carcinoma. A relationship between ovarian granulosa and theca cell tumours and adenocarcinoma has been demonstrated by Koller (1966) and Fox et al (1975), who found an incidence of 6.5 per cent. Also patients with Stein-Leventhal syndrome, which is characterized by hyperoestrogenism, have an increased incidence of endometrial carcinoma (Sommers et al, 1949; Reicher and Phillips, 1961).

The effect of exogenous oestrogens on endometrium is uncertain as many poorly controlled series of long-term oestrogen therapy have produced widely divergent results. Reports have shown increased incidences of endometrial carcinoma in young women taking sequential oral contraceptives (Silverberg and Makowski, 1975; Lyon, 1975) as well as in postmenopausal patients receiving conjugated oestrogens (Smith et al, 1975; Ziel and Finkle, 1975). Criticism of these reports has been made on the grounds of poor patient selection, equivocal histological evidence, high doses of hormones and doubtful statistical evaluation. As a result of the controversy aroused by the findings of Smith et al (1975) and Ziel and Finkle (1975) the Obstetric and Gynecology Advisory Committee of the American Food and Drug Administration considered the evidence in 1975 and decided that no conclusions could be drawn from the evidence and that more prospective studies were necessary. Studd and Thom (1981) have reviewed the subject and they suggest that possible causes of the increased incidence of endometrial carcinoma in American studies include (1) an increased detection rate of occult tumours due to oestrogen use, (2) lack of regular endometrial sampling, (3) use of continuous and excessive oestrogens, (4) incorrect histopathological diagnosis and (5) failure to use progestogen. They concluded that the proliferative effect of oestrogen may damage the uterine endometrium and in susceptible patients lead to malignancy; however this change may be prevented by adding towards the end of the low dose cyclical oestrogen 7–13 days of progestogen. The optimal levels of these hormones have still to be decided.

Staging of endometrial carcinoma

Treatment of endometrial adenocarcinoma depends on such factors as clinical staging and histological differentiation. The International Federation of Gynaecology and Obstetrics (FIGO) classifies uterine corporeal cancer into: Stage 0 — carcinoma in situ. Histological findings suspicious of malignancy; Stage I — limited to the corpus, with subdivisions depending on uterine cavity size; Stage II — extension to the cervix; Stage III — extension from the uterus but within the pelvis excluding vesical and rectal mucosa; and Stage IV —

involvement of vesical or rectal mucosa or spread outside the pelvis. The FIGO classification also includes the histological grading of these tumours and this is related to lymphatic involvement. Thus, Grade I describes well-differentiated adenocarcinoma and has the best prognosis, G2 indicates differentiated carcinoma with solid areas and G3 denotes a solid or undifferentiated tumour which has the worst prognosis.

Treatment of endometrial carcinoma

At present approximately 70 per cent of patients presenting for treatment are Stage I cancers (Joelson et al, 1973) and this has contributed to improved survival rates. The treatment of endometrial adenocarcinoma may be surgery, radiotherapy or a combination of both, and it depends on the factors already mentioned as well as fitness for operation and surgical pathology of the excised specimen. With the high age incidence of this malignancy patients frequently have associated conditions, for example cardiovascular disease, diabetes or obesity. Thus in many reported series a significant proportion of patients is unfit for surgery. Stage 0 carcinoma is usually seen around the menopause and treated by hysterectomy.

Stage I cancer. Total hysterectomy and bilateral salpingo-oophorectomy are the treatment of choice with some centres giving pre-operative intracavitary or external radiation. Vaginal irradiation may be given post-operatively, depending on the histopathology of the specimen, as this reduces vault recurrence from about 10 to 12 per cent (Kolstad, 1982). Lymph node involvement has been noted in approximately 10 per cent of these patients (Boronow, 1976), therefore external irradiation may be considered when the myometrium is deeply invaded or the tumour is poorly differentiated.

Stage II cancer. Combination therapy is used because of the higher incidence of node involvement. A common treatment plan is a preoperative intracavitary source then surgery followed later by external irradiation to the maximum dose, depending on the surgical pathology. Radiotherapy may be given before or after hysterectomy and good results have been achieved by both methods. Preoperative radiation has the advantage of sterilizing the cancer cells so that there is less spill of viable tumour at operation; also the uterus is a useful container for radium implants. However, post-operative radiotherapy is more accurately calculated when tumour differentiation and spread are known. Wertheim hysterectomy has been advocated (Stallworthy, 1971) but it is associated frequently with increased post-operative morbidity, for example pulmonary embolus and urinary fistulae; in general the reported results are no better than for less radical surgery and radiotherapy.

Progestational agents. These have been used to treat early endometrial cancer because regression of hyperplasia and carcinoma in situ of the endometrium after treatment with progesterone has been demonstrated (Kistner, 1959). However, the value of this treatment is uncertain; in a multicentre trial of patients with uterine corporeal cancer alone Lewis et al (1974) found no difference in the survival rates in 285 patients treated with medroxyprogesterone acetate (Provera) and 287 patients given a placebo.

Advanced endometrial carcinoma. Stage III and IV endometrial cancer are treated mainly by radiotherapy although surgery is considered later if response to treatment is good. Progestational agents are of value in recurrent or advanced disease and particularly when lung metastases are present. Reifenstein (1974) reported a series of 314 patients with advanced cancer and noted a 37 per cent objective response to progesterone with an average survival of 27 months which was four times the average of non-responders. Progesterone and oestrogen receptor studies are giving useful information on the response to hormone treatment of advanced disease (Kauppila et al, 1980).

OVARIAN TUMOURS

Ovarian enlargement in the elderly must be regarded with suspicion because of its high incidence of malignancy. Ovarian tumours may arise from epithelial or connective tissue elements. The sex cord stromal tumours (granulosa cell and thecoma) are also common. While primary neoplasms are most frequently encountered, secondary deposits in the ovary do occur from breast, stomach or large intestine cancer. Ovarian malignancy is the third most common gynaecological cancer, but it has the highest mortality because the onset and development of disease are silent and the condition is diagnosed usually at an advanced stage. A high index of suspicion is necessary if early diagnosis and successful treatment are to be given.

A variety of benign and malignant ovarian tumours is seen in elderly patients but certain neoplasms are more frequent in this age group.

Granulosa cell tumour

This is the commonest sex cord ovarian tumour, and approximately 40 to 60 per cent occur after the menopause. It arises from the adult cells of the medulla. Characteristically it is small, grey or yellow and unilateral. The clinical presentation is similar to other ovarian neoplasms although their hormone-producing ability may result in related symptoms, for example vaginal bleeding due to endometrial hyperplasia. Oestrogenic activity is not always present — Kecskés et al (1963) found no oestrogen in pure granulosa cell tumours. Thus, since many sex cord tumours are a mixed type of granulosa cell and thecoma, it may be that thecal, but

not granulosa, cells are able to produce oestrogen (Govan, 1976). Granulosa cell tumours are generally regarded as malignant, although rates vary from 10 per cent (Hodgson et al, 1945) to 50 per cent (Haines and Jackson, 1950). Evidence has been presented earlier of the association with endometrial carcinoma.

Thecoma

This neoplasm is even more characteristic of the aging female and it arises from the stroma of the ovarian cortex. It is almost as common as the granulosa cell tumour with which it shares many clinical and pathological features. Symptoms associated with hormone upset are more common — oestrogen production has been demonstrated frequently. It is generally regarded as benign although metastases have been noted and it is associated also with endometrial adenocarcinoma.

Brenner tumour

This epithelial tumour is seen predominantly in adult life and approximately 50 per cent occur after the fifth decade. The neoplasm is usually small, grey and unilateral; it grows slowly and is rarely malignant. There are no peculiar clinical features except endometrial hyperplasia which has been noted in less than 10 per cent of cases (Idelson, 1963). The origin of the tumour is not known, but it has been suggested that it is derived from coelomic or urinary tract epithelium or that it originates in the ovarian medulla (Jorgensen et al, 1970).

In contrast with endometrial cancer, approximately 70 per cent of patients with ovarian carcinoma present with advanced disease and this affects the clinical presentation. The initial symptoms noted in patients treated by Clark et al (1976) are listed in Table 32.1. Pain and swelling in the abdomen and vaginal bleeding are most frequently seen. Investigation includes a detailed history and physical examination, full haematological and biochemical profiles as well as radiological assessment including chest, intravenous urogram (to exclude

Table 32.1 Presenting symptoms with ovarian cancer (From Clark et al, 1976)

Abdominal pain	133
Abdominal swelling	117
Abnormal vaginal bleeding	108
Palpable mass	87
Gastrointestinal	31
Weakness fatigue	20
Urinary	17
Respiratory	9
Weight loss	3
None	
(Physical examination	43)
(Incidental	9)
(Unknown	25)

ureteric obstruction and retroperitoneal node involvement) and barium enema.

The diagnosis is established at laparotomy when staging and initial treatment are undertaken. Preliminary dilatation and curettage are indicated when bleeding has occurred. The FIGO classification of ovarian tumours is Stage I – tumour limited to the ovaries, with subdivisions for involvement of one or both ovaries or ovarian capsule, or the presence of ascites; Stage II — spread within the pelvis, with subdivision for the nature of the spread or the presence of ascites; Stage III — tumour spread outside the pelvis, for example to small bowel or omentum; and Stage IV — such distant metastases as liver nodules or pleural effusion with positive cytology.

Treatment of ovarian tumours

Surgery

All ovarian tumours in the elderly should be considered malignant until proved otherwise and the standard treatment of an encapsulated, possibly benign, tumour and Stage I and II cancers is hysterectomy, bilateral salpingo-oophorectomy and omentectomy. The omentum should be removed as it is involved frequently in microscopic disease, and if peritoneal instillations are to be given better distribution will be achieved. With advanced disease (Stage III and IV) the aim of surgery is to remove as much primary tumour as possible as adjuvant treatment will be more effective and ascites better controlled. If the patient's general condition is unsatisfactory the extent of surgery is, of course, modified.

Radiotherapy

Radiotherapy may be given alone or in combination with surgery and/or chemotherapy. In general, ovarian cancers are radiation insensitive, except granulosa cell tumours, but it may be necessary when surgery is contraindicated or there is advanced disease. Radiation is most effective in the presence of minimal tumour. The whole abdomen should be irradiated because usually there is spread outside the pelvis, even in Stage I disease; this may be associated with early and late complications, particularly of the gastrointestinal tract. In debilitated elderly patients prolonged radical treatment is poorly tolerated and therefore a simpler regime and chemotherapy are necessary.

In Stage I disease postoperative radiation using intraperitoneal instillation of radiocolloids is recommended by Clark et al (1976). In a series of 85 patients treated postoperatively with ^{32}P chromic phosphate they reported a 5-years survival of 90 per cent compared with a 65 per cent survival in 30 postoperative patients who did not receive radiation.

Chemotherapy

Chemotherapy is primarily used for advanced or recurrent disease or radioresistant tumours. Alkylating agents, for example Cyclophosphamide, Chlorambucil, Melphalan (phenylalanine mustard), or Thiotepa, are the most effective preparations, and their response rates are equivalent. Masterson and Nelson (1965) and Wallach et al (1970) reported initial responses of between 50 and 64 per cent and a 2-year remission in 14 and 25 per cent respectively. Administration is by loading and maintenance doses given orally or intermittent intravenous therapy; these methods are equally effective, but intraperitoneal instillation is less efficient than the intravenous route (Smith and Rutledge, 1970).

The value of these agents in prolonging survival has been demonstrated by Burns et al (1967) who showed a mean survival time of 33.5 months and 9.3 months in a double blind randomized study of patients treated with Chlorambucil and placebo respectively.

Non-alkylating agents have been used less frequently and only after other treatments have failed. Young et al (1974) evaluated the effect of 5-fluouracil and progestogens on ovarian cancer and found tumour regression in approximately 30 and 10 per cent respectively. Combined therapy has been tested such as cyclophosphamide, actinomycin-D, 5-fluouracil (Park et al, 1980) and high remission rates are accompanied by greater toxicity and little difference in long-term survival. Cis-diaminodichloroplatinum (Cis-platin), a metallic compound, is being used singly and in regimes as it has the unusual property of inducing second remissions (Wiltshaw and Kroner, 1976). The toxic Vinca alkaloids such as vinblastine and vincristine are also used in combination therapies (Hudson, 1982). These plant derivatives have a different mode of action which involves poisoning the spindles during mitosis. They have little single agent activity.

Ascites.   Ascites is a common sequal to ovarian cancer and it may arise from venous obstruction or exudation from the primary tumour or serosal implantation of tumour cells. Limited ascites is treated with systemic chemotherapy, while the advanced state requires removal of tumour bulk followed by radiation or chemotherapy. Paracentesis is necessary when severe discomfort or respiratory embarrassment is present, but the associated protein and electrolyte depletion may be aggravated and fluid accumulation tends to recur rapidly.

REFERENCES

Baker H W G, Burger H G, De Kretser D M, Bulmanis A, Eddit L W, Hudson B et al 1976 Testicular control of follicle stimulating hormone secretion. Recent Progress in Hormone Research 32: 429–476

Barrett-Connor E, Brown W V, Turner J, Austin M, Criqui M H 1979 Heart disease link factors and hormone use in postmenopausal women. Journal of the American Medical Association 241: 2167–2169

Berkeley C, Bonney V 1909 Leukoplakic vulvitis and its relation to kraurosis vulvae and carcinoma vulvae. British Medical Journal ii: 1739–1744

Boronow R C 1976 Endometrial Cancer. Not a benign disease. Obstetrics and Gynaecology 47: 630–634

Boston Collaborative Drug Surveillance Program 1974 Surgically confirmed gallbladder disease, venous thromboembolism and breast tumors in relation to postmenopausal estrogen therapy. New England Journal of Medicine 290: 15–19

Brown A D G 1977 Postmenopausal Urinary Problems. Clinics in Obstet. Gynaec. Greenblatt R B, Studd John (ed) vol 4 10: p 181–206. Saunders, London

Brown R 1974 Clinical Features associated with endometrial carcinoma. Journal of Obstetrics and Gynaecology of the British Commonwealth 81: 933–939

Burns B C Jr, Rutledge F N, Smith J P, Delclos L 1967 Management of Ovarian Carcinoma, Surgery, Radiation and Chemotherapy. American Journal of Obstetrics and Gynecology 98: 374–386

Campbell P E, Barter R A, 1961 The significance of atypical endometrial hyperplasia. Journal of Obstetrics and Gynaecology of the British Commonwealth 68: 668–672

Chamberlain G 1975 Cryosurgery in Gynaecology. British Journal of Hospital Medicine 14: 26–37

Clark D G C, Hilaris B S, Ochoa M 1976 Treatment of cancer of the ovary. Clinics in Obstet. Gynae. MacNaughton M C, Govan A D T (ed), vol 3 no 1, chap 6: p 159–179 Saunders, London

Cooke I D 1983 Personal communication

Coppleson M 1969 Carcinoma of the cervix: Epidemiology and aetiology. British Journal of Hospital Medicine 2: 961–980

Deane H W, Lobel B L, Romney S L 1962 Enzymic histochemistry of normal ovaries of the menstrual cycle, pregnancy and the early puerperium. American Journal of Obstetrics and Gynecology 83: 281–294

Fidler H K, Boyes D A, Nichols T M, Worth A J 1970 Cervical cytology in the control of the cervix. Modern Medicine of Canada 25: 9–15

Fox H, Agrawal K, Langley F A 1975 A clinico-pathological study of 92 cases of granulosa cell tumour of the ovary with special reference to factors influencing prognosis. Cancer 35: 231–241

Fox H, Sen D K 1970 A controlled study of the constitutional stigmata of endometrial adenocarcinoma. British Journal of Cancer 24: 30–36

Frantzell A, Ingelmark B E 1951 Occurrence and distribution of fat in human muscles at various age levels: a morphological and roentgenologic investigation. Acta Societalis Medicorum 56: 58–87

Freidrich E G Jr 1976 Vulvar Disease. W B Saunders. p 58

Hoover R, Gray L A Sr, Cole P, MacMahon B 1976 Menopausal estrogens and breast cancer. New England Journal of Medicine 295: 401–405

Hudson C N 1982 Chemotherapy in gynaecological malignant disease. In: Studd J (ed) Progress in Obstetrics and Gynaecology 2, Churchill Livingstone, Edinburgh, p 136–150

Hutchinson T A, Polansky S M, Feinstein A R 1979 Postmenopausal oestrogens protect against fractures of hip and distal radius. A case-control study. Lancet ii: 705–9

Idelson M G 1963 Malignancy in Brenner tumours of the ovary with comments on hertogenesis and possible estrogen production. Obstetrical and Gynecological Survey 18: 246–267

International Continence Society 1976 First report on the standardization of terminology of lower urinary tract function. British Journal of Urology 48: 39–42

Jeffcoate T N A 1966 Chronic vulval dystrophies. American Journal of Obstetrics and Gynecology 95: 61

Jeffcoate T N A 1975 Principles of Gynaecology. p 365–383. Butterworth & Co, London

Jensen J G 1970 Danish Medical Bulletin 7: 199–202

Joelsson I, Sandri A, Kotimeier H L 1973 Carcinoma of the uterine corpus. Acta Radiologica, Supplement 334

Jorgensen E O, Dockerty M B, Wilson R B, Welch J S 1970 Clinico-pathologic study of 53 cases of Brenner's tumours of the ovary. American Journal of Obstetrics and Gynecology 108: 122–127

Judd H L, Judd G E, Lucas W E, Yen S S C 1974 Endocrine function of the postmenopausal ovary: concentration of androgens and estrogens in ovarian and puerperal vein blood. Journal of Clinical Endocrinology 309: 1020

Judd H L, Lucas W E, Yen S S C 1976 Serum 17-estradiol and estrone levels in postmenopausal women with and without endometrial cancer. Journal of Clinical Endocrinology 43: 272–278

Kauppila A, Jarme O, Kujansuu E, Vihko R 1980 Treatment of advanced endometrial carcinoma with a combined cytologic therapy. Predictive value of cytosol estrogen and progestin receptor levels. Cancer 46: 2162–2167

Kecskés L, Mutschler F, Kóbor J 1963 Oestrogens in ovarian tumours. Zentralblatt fur Gynkologie 85: 325–328

Keirse M J N C 1973 Aetiology of postmenopausal bleeding. Postgraduate Medical Journal 49: 344–348

Kistner R W 1959 Histological effects of progestins on hyperplasia and carcinoma in situ of endometrium. Cancer 12: 1106–1110

Koller O 1966 Granulosa and theca cell tumour and genital cancer. Acta Obstetrica et Gynecologica Scandinavica 45: 114–120

Kolstad P 1982 Advances in the treatment of carcinoma of the cervix and corpus uteri. In: Bonnar J (ed) Recent advances in Obstetrics and Gynaecology, 14, Churchill Livingstone, Edinburgh, p 325–340

Lang W R 1962 Cervical portio from menarche on a colposcopic study. Annals of the New York Academy of Sciences 97: 653

Lang W R, Aponte G E 1967 Gross and microscopic anatomy of the aged female reproductive organs. In: Lang W R (ed) Clinical Obstet. Gynec vol 10 no 3, chap. 2: p. 454–465 Harper and Row, New York

Leighton P C, Langley F A 1975 A clinicopathological study of vulval dermatoses. Journal of Clinical Pathology: 394–402

Lewis G C, Slack N H, Mortel R, Bross I D J 1974 Adjuvant progestin therapy in the primary definitive treatment of endometrial cancer. Gynaecological Oncology: 368–376

Lindsay R, Hart D M, Aitken J M, MacDonald E B, Anderson J B, Clarke A C 1976 Long-term prevention of postmenopausal osteoporosis by oestrogen. Lancet i 41: 1038–40

Lindsay R, MacLean A, Kraszewski A, Hart D M, Clarke A C, Garwood J 1978 Bone response to termination of oestrogen treatment. Lancet i: 1325–7

Lindsay R, Hart D M, Kraszewski A 1980 Prospective double-blind trial of synthetic steroid (ORG OD 14) for preventing postmenopausal osteoporosis. British Medical Journal 280: 1207–9

Longcope C 1971 Metabolic clearance and blood production rates of oestrogen in postmenopausal women American Journal of Obstetrics and Gynecology II: 778

Longcope C 1974 Steroid production in pre-and postmenopausal women. In: Greenblatt R B, Makesk V B, McDonough P E, (ed) The Menopausal Syndrome. p 6–11. Medcom Press, New York

Lyon F A 1975 The development of adenocarcinoma of the endometrium in young women receiving long-term sequential oral contraception. American Journal of Obstetrics and Gynecology 123: 299

Masterson J G, Nelson H H Jr 1965 The role of chemotherapy in the treatment of gynaecological malignancy. American Journal of Obstetrics and Gynecology 93: 1102–1111

Mattingly R F, Huang W Y 1969 Steroidogenesis of the menopausal and postmenopausal ovary. American Journal of Obstetrics and Gynecology 111: 778

McAdams A J Jr, Kistner R W 1958 The relationship of chronic vulvar disease, leukoplakia and carcinoma in situ of the vulva. Cancer (Philadelphia) II: 740–757

McBride J M 1959 Premenopausal cystic hyperplasia and endometrial carcinoma. Journal of Obstetrics and Gynaecology of the British Empire 66: 288–296

MaCgregor J E 1976 Evaluation of mass screening programmes for cervical cancer. Tumori 62: 287–295

McLennan M T, McLennan C E 1971 Oestrogenic status of menstruating and postmenopausal women assessed by cervico-vaginal smears. Obstetrics and Gynecology 37: 325

McMahon B 1974 Risk factor for endometrial cancer. Gynaecological Oncology 2: 122–129

McPherson J C III, Costoff A, Mahesh V B 1975 Influence of estrogen-progesterone combinations on gonadotrophin secretion in castrate female rats. Endrocrinology 97: 771

Meade T W, Greenberg G, Thomson S G 1980 Progestogens and cardiovascular reactions associated with oral contraceptives and a comparison of the safety of 50- and 30-ug oestrogen preparations. British Medical Journal 280: 1157–61

Mossman H W, Koering J M, Ferry D 1964 Cyclic changes of interstitial gland tissue of the human ovary. American Journal of Anatomy 115: 235–256

Notelovitz M, Ware M 1982 Coagulation risks with postmenopausal oestrogen therapy In: Studd J (ed) Progess in Obstetrics and Gynaecology, 2, Churchill Livingstone, Edinburgh, p 228–240

Park R C, Blom J Di Saia P J, Lagasse L D, Blessing J A 1980 Cancer 5: 2529–2542

Parry-Jones E 1976 The management of premalignant and malignant conditions of the vulva. In: Langley F A (ed) Clinics in Obstetrics and Gynaecology, vol 3 no 2, chap. 2: p 229–241. Saunders, London

Parsons L, Sommers S C 1962 Gynaecology: p 1175. W B Saunders, Philadelphia

Procopé B J 1971 Aetiology of postmenopausal bleeding. Acta Obstetrica et Gynecologica Scandinavica 50: 311–313

Reicher N B, Phillips R S 1961 Carcinoma of the endometrium. American Journal of Obsterics and Gynecology 82: 417

Reifenstein E C 1974 The treatment of advanced endrometrial cancer with hydroxyprogesterone caproate. Gynaecological Oncology 2: 377–414

Reyes F I, Winter J S D, Faiman C 1976 Transition in pituitary-ovarian relationships preceding the menopause. Journal of Clinical Endocrinology In press

Rigg L A, Hermann H, Yen S C 1978 Absorption of estrogens from vaginal creams. New England Journal of Medicine 298: 195

Rotkin I D 1967 Adolescent coitus and cervical cancer: Associations of related events with increased risk. Cancer Research 27: 603–617

Royal College of Obstetricians and Gynaecologists 1982 Report of the R.C.O.G. working party on further specilization within OB/GYN. Whitfield C R (ed) p 65

Saunders P, Rowland R 1972 Vacuum curettage of the uterus without anaesthesia. Journal of Obstetrics and Gynaecology of the British Commonwealth 79: 168–174

Schröder R 1954 Endometrial hyperplasia in relation to genital function. American Journal of Obstetrics and Gynecology 68: 294–309

Sherman B M, West J H, Korenman S G 1976 The menopause transition: Analysis of LH, FSH, estradiol and progesterone concentration during menstrual cycles of older women. Journal of Clinical Endocrinology 42: 629

Silverberg S G, Makowski 1975 Endometrial carcinoma in young women taking oral contraceptive agents. American Journal of Obstetrics and Gynecology 46: 503

Smith D C, Prentice R, Thompson D J, Herrman W L 1975 Association of exogenous oestrogen and endometrial carcinoma. New England Journal of Medicine 293: 1164

Smith J P, Rutledge F 1970 Chemotherapy in the treatment of cancer of the ovary. American Journal of Obstetrics and Gynecology 107: 691–700

Sommer S C, Hertig A T, Bengloff H 1949 Genesis of endometrial carcinoma II: Cases 19–35 years old. Cancer 2: 957

Southren A L, Olivo J, Gordon G G, Brenner J, Raffi F 1973 Conversion of androgens to oestrogens in hyperthyroidism. Proceedings of the Endocrinological Society: p 181. Abstract

Stallworthy J A 1971 Surgery of endometrial cancer in the Bonney tradition. Annals of the Royal College of Surgeons of England 48: 293–305

Studd J, Chakravarti S, Oram D 1977 The Climacteric. In: Greenblatt R B, Studd J (ed) Clinics in Obstetrics and Gynecology 4: 3–29

Studd J, Thom M H 1981 Oestrogens and endometrial cancer. In: Studd J (ed) Progress in Obstetrics and Gynaecology, Churchill Livingstone, Edinburgh, p 182–198

Suntzeff V, Babcock R S, Loeb L 1940 Reversibility of hyalinization in mouse uterus produced by injections of oestrogen and changes in mammary gland and ovaries after cessation of injections. American Journal of Cancer 38: 217–233

Te Linde R W 1970 Operative gynaecology (4th ed) p 682–695. Lippincott, Philadelphia and Toronto

Towne J E 1955 Carcinoma of the cervix in nulliparous and alibate women. American Journal of Obstetrics and Gynecology 69: 606–613

Utian W H 1982 Cost-effectiveness of hormone therapy after the menopause. In: Bonnar J (ed) Recent advances in Obstetrics and Gynaecology, 14, Churchill Livingstone, Edinburgh, p 307–323

Vermeulen A 1976 The hormonal activity of the postmenopausal ovary. Journal of Clinical Endocrinology 42: 247

Wallace H J 1962 Vulval leukoplakia. Journal of Obstetrics and Gynaecology of the British Commonwealth 69: 865

Wallace H J, Whimster L W 1951 Vulval atrophy and leukoplakia. British Journal of Dermatology 63: 241–257

Wallach R C, Kabakow B, Blinick G, Antopol W 1970 Thio-tepa chemotherapy for ovarian carcinoma. Obstetrics and Gynecology 35: 278–286

Way S 1954 Results on a planned attack on carcinoma of the vulva. British Medical Journal ii: 780–782

Whitehead M I, Minardi J, Kitchin Y, Sharples M J 1978 Systemic absorption of estrogen from Premarin vaginal cream. In: Cooke I D (ed) The role of Estrogen/Progestrogen in the management of the menopause, p 63–75. MTP Press Ltd, Lancaster

Widhome O, Vartiainen E 1974 The absorption of conjugal and sodium oestrone sulphate from the vagina. Annales Chirurgicae et Gynaecologiae Fenniae 63: 186–190

Wilson P D, Al Samarai Ai M T, Brown A D G 1980 Quantifying female incontinence with particular reference to the urilos system. Urologia Internationalis 35: 298–302

Wiltshaw E, Kroner T 1976 Phase II study of cis-diaminodichroplatinum (III) (NSC 119875) in advanced adenocarcinoma of the ovary. Cancer Treatment Reports 60: 55–60

Woessner J F Jr 1963 Age-related changes of the human uterus and its connective tissue framework. Journal of Gerontology 18: 220–226

Woodcock A S 1973 Pathology of the vulva In: Fox H, Langley F A (ed) Obstetrical and Gynaecological Pathology: p 51–70

Young R C, Hubbard S P, De Vita V T 1974 The chemotherapy of ovarian carcinoma. Cancer Treatment Reviews I: 99

Ziel H K, Finkle W D 1975 Increased risk of endometrial carcinoma among users of conjugated oestrogens. New England Journal of Medicine 293: 1157

The endocrine system — the hypophysoadrenal axis

THE HYPOTHALAMUS, THE HYPOPHYSOADRENAL AXIS AND THE AGING PROCESS

That the hypothalamus and the endocrine system are intimately connected with the aging process seems an attractive hypothesis. Deficiencies in the hypophyso-tropic peptides (so-called hypothalamic regulating hormones) such as thyrotrophin releasing hormone (TRH) or gonadotrophin releasing hormone (LHRH), a hypophyseal hormone such as thyroid stimulating hormone (TSH) or adrenocorticotrophic hormone (ACTH) or a target hormone such as cortisol or thyroxine, often lead to changes which give the appearance of aging. These may be reversed by appropriate replacement therapy. Nevertheless, perhaps because their symptoms mimic the signs and symptoms of advancing age they have given rise to such hypotheses as the 'hypothyroid hypothesis', the 'hypopituitary hypothesis' the 'pituitary hypothesis' and most recently, the 'neurotransmitter hypothesis'. It has also been proposed that hormones secreted are inactive (Segall, 1979) though another explanation might be that target organ receptors are diminished so that cellular responses are reduced. These hypotheses and others such as 'the ageing clock' hypothesis have been excellently reviewed by Everitt (1976, 1980) — see also Chapter 4.

Recently Russian workers in Kiev and Leningrad have extended their studies on what Everitt (1980) terms, 'the hypothalamic disregulation hypothesis' and 'the hypothalamic elevation hypothesis'. Frolkis and his colleagues (1979) in Kiev have shown that the hypo-thalamic–hypophysoadrenal axis plays a part in the regulation of RNA synthesis and of induction of some enzymes of carbohydrate and amino acid metabolism and that these functions are diminished in age. This clearly suggests that homeostatic and repair mechanisms may be influenced and gives some support to an underlying role for the neuroendocrine system, in the aging process.

Dilman (1979), on the other hand, proposes that the main defect in the hypothalamus is elevation of the hypothalamic threshold to negative feed-back leading to over secretion of hormones. He suggests for instance, that the hypothalamic threshold of sensitivity to glucose suppression is elevated. As a result there is a relative excess of growth hormone (GH), an enhanced contra-insular effect (whatever this may be), hyperglycaemia and hyperinsulinaemia leading to obesity and increased levels of free fatty acids (FFA) which should then operate as a feed-back mechanism to the hypothalamus inhibiting production of GH. However, this does not happen and a lipid shunt develops — FFA's being utilized instead of glucose as the main source of energy. This then leads to the development of vascular disease, hypertension, diabetes mellitus and other conditions often associated with aging, morbidity and death.

These hypotheses are interesting but as yet are unproven. They can, however, be tested and will hopefully lead us to a better understanding of the role the hypothalmus and the endocrine system has to play in the ageing process. At the present time doubt exists, for Greenblatt et al (1979) suggest its function remains unaltered in aged women. Moreover, on the one hand there is circumstantial evidence that dimunition of hormonal secretion may hasten it, either directly or through the effect of hormones on tissue enzyme processes. The appearances of premature senility are seen in patients with Simmonds' disease, but pituitary deficiency has been sought unsuccessfully in patients with progeria and Werner's syndrome. On the other hand patients with Cushing's syndrome (hyperadreno-corticism, pituitary basophilism) show many features of premature aging. Animal studies have tended to confirm these observations but there are anomalies and different tissue responses. Bellamy (1968), for instance, suggests that predisolone prolongs the life-span of a short-lived strain of mouse while Asling et al (1954) suggest that hypophysectomy retards the growth and aging of bone.

These anomalous findings may be due to alteration of end organ response, perhaps, as has already been suggested, due to alteration in receptor function or density, since Avissan et al (1981) have suggested that the density of muscarinic receptors in the rat adeno-hypophysis diminishes with age.

Hypophysoadrenal hormones and stress

Since the ability to respond or adjust to stress declines with age and since variations in responses of the hypophysoadrenal axis are shown to be associated with adjustment of the body to stress and shock, it is not unreasonable to suppose that the function and structure of the component parts will be altered in aged humans. It has also been suggested, that stressfull stimuli accelerate aging (Selye and Tuchweber, 1976) and Arvay (1976) has shown that aging of collagen fibres in the rat tail tendon is increased by exposure of animals to various stresses. However, whether the damage, which can undoubtedly be provoked by stress, to various systems such as the cardiovascular system, gastrointestinal system or immune system is due to altered function of the hypothalamo–hypophysoadrenal axis is doubtful.

Studies have in the main been directed towards the measurement of hormone levels in the plasma or their metabolic breakdown products in the urine. Verzar (1966) has pointed out the inaccuracies which may exist in the methods used to assess function. It has, for instance, long been agreed that urinary excretion of 17-ketosteroids diminishes with age but it is also universally recognized that excretion of a hormone or its breakdown products is a poor estimate of glandular function. This may apply even more in the old since renal function is reduced and low urinary levels may only be a reflection of this reduction. Further, when plasma level of the various hormones has been measured it has usually followed the maximal stimulation of the glandular cell under consideration. This is necessary so that statistical analysis of results from groups of people of different ages may be comparable. Nevertheless, it means that the actual measurement is of total glandular function which may bear little relation to daily output of specific hormone and its level as a response to the stress which an old person experiences during the course of daily life, i.e. daily glandular function. Again, maximal stimulation of a gland may not always be achieved by the chosen method and this may account for some of the differences described by some workers. For instance, Hochstaedt et al in 1961 showed that while the response of the adrenal cortex (as measured by serial determinations of the plasma free and conjugated 17-hydroxy-corticosteroids (17-OHCS) in young and old), was similar following administration of corticotrophin (ACTH), it was significantly diminished in response to injection of insulin. These workers considered that insulin-induced hypoglycaemia was a general unspecific stress, and that, since the adrenal cortex produced similar amounts of hormone in young and old when stimulated directly by corticotrophin, the hypothalmic

hypophyseal centres were the source of the decreased adrenocortical response. However, in this study it was shown that the degree of hypoglycaemia was the main stimulus for the increase in plasma 17-OHCS levels. Greenwood et al (1966) suggests that the degree of hypoglycaemia produced should be at least 50 per cent of fasting values. In Hochstaedt's study, the fall in blood sugar was only equal to 40 per cent of the fasting value, and this may have been inadequate for sufficient stimulation of the hypothalamic–hypophyseal centres in the elderly to achieve 17-OHCS levels comparable to the young. Other factors too may play a part, such as reduced cellular response to hypoglycaemia. However, Cartlidge et al (1970) showed that a sample of elderly aged 82–95 years had a similar response to insulin induced hypoglycaemia to young subjects. GH, FFA and cortisol levels were measured in this study and the result confirms that the response of the hypothalamic–hypophysoadrenal axis to maximal stimulation is intact with age. A similar response to insulin was found by Kalk et al (1973) but Lanon et al (1970) found lower levels in response to the stress of exercise.

Nevertheless, the variability of the observations in the work quoted does suggest that differences exist between young and old in their response to a given stimulus or stress. These observations gain in importance when it is realized that insulin-induced hypoglycaemia is thought to be the test which is best related to surgical stress (Jensen and Blichert-Toft, 1970). Hence if the response of elderly subjects to hypoglycaemia is poor, so may be their response to surgery.

The problem with all the studies is that they have been cross-sectional or point-of-time studies and are consequently only able to measure age differences as opposed to age changes. Point-of-time studies can only indicate changes which may take place in individuals, and only by studying an individual's glandular function consecutively over a period of time will it be possible to say whether these are truly age differences or not, (Shock, 1967).

Until recently the functional assessment of endocrine glands, particularly the pituitary, has been by indirect measurement. The ability to measure hormone levels direct as a result of radioimmune assay techniques has meant that glandular function can be assessed directly and compared to that occurring in the young. It should, however, be pointed out that these techniques are not always easy to apply. The method of measurement may be difficult to establish and high levels of quality control and comparison between laboratories is essential if accurate interpretation of results is to be achieved. Unless methods of measurement can be easily and correctly reproduced, and are truly sensitive enough to measure change, controversy over results will be inevitable and difficult to resolve.

Many gaps still exist in our knowledge. These particularly relate to our knowledge of the protein binding of hormones in old age, their peripheral utilization and their receptor mechanisms. The ability to define and measure receptors and elucidate their function is a great advance and will increase our knowledge. Roth and Adelman (1975) suggest that specific binding to target cells by hormones may be altered in old age and this may account for some of the unresponsiveness seen.

Until recently researchers studying the effect of stress on the hypothalamo–hypophysoadrenal axis had almost entirely concentrated on the central role of the adenohypophysis (anterior pituitary) and little attention had been paid to the neurohypophysis (posterior pituitary). This was probably because it was thought the high blood concentrations necessary for vasopressin to produce its pressor, inotropic and other haemodynamic effects hardly ever occurred in man. However, in stress situations (Felsl et al, 1978) in man and following acute haemorrhage in rats (Laycock et al, 1979) levels (150–200 m/ml), high enough to produce cardiovascular effects, are reached. Frolkis and his colleagues (1982) have recently studied the effect of vasopressin in adult and old rats, rabbits and dogs as well as estimating blood vasopressin in healthy human subjects aged 20–80 years. Vasopressin was measured by both biological and radioimmunoassay methods with comparable results. They found that vasopressin concentrations rises in the blood of both humans and animals. There was however, only a four-fold rise in the elderly, levels being 13.2 + — 1.8 pmol/ml. They suggest that old vessels are more sensitive to vasopressin in that ECG changes occurred in old rats with very low doses. Similarly, the fall in cardiac cAMP was greater in young than old and though the blood pressure rose in both young and old it fell after the initial rise in the old, possibly due to bradycardia and diminished cardiac output. They also found that vasopressin levels were higher in elderly suffering from hypertension and ischaemic heart disease than in age matched controls.

The peptide hormones of the neurohyphosis, vasopressin and oxytocin are secreted in the hypothalamus, mainly in the supraoptic nucleus (SON) and then transported and stored in the neurohypophysis (Morris et al, 1978). Obviously, disturbance in the secretion of these peptide hormones will have an effect on homeostasis and inability to maintain homeostasis will obviously have a detrimental effect on the organism. Recently, Davies and Fotheringham, (1981) have shown a qualitative difference in the ultrastructure of the cells of SON in old mice (28 months) as well as a quantitative difference, in response to an osmotic load producing salt-stress. While it would not appear from this work that hormone production is affected by these changes it is possible that the changes seen will have an effect on cellular metabolic

functions such as recovery and repair. Continuing stress, might, therefore, eventually have a deleterious effect upon hormone production.

A similar stress (i.e. salt loading for 2 hours) in elderly humans produces an increased production of arginine vasopression (Helderman et al, 1978).

Morphology

The histological appearances of hypophysis and adrenal differ little in the young and old though in some glands changes which may be termed 'age changes' (since they occur in other organs in old people) have been described. Fazekas and Jobba (1970) describe age changes in the hypophysis which they term as being consistent with *hypophysis naviculare*. In this condition a diffuse fibrosis is the prominent feature and there is loss of basophilic cells. Adenoma may also occur in the hypophysis in old age but rarely produce symptoms. The commonest is the chromophobe, and the oldest individual described by Kernohan and Sayre (1956) was 85 years. Nevertheless the chance finding of a small hypophyseal adenoma at routine autopsy examination of the hypophysis would seem to increase with age — Costello (1936), in a study of 1000 glands, found adenomas present in 22.5 per cent while McKeown (1965), in a series of 1500 autopsies over 70 years old found a total of 39 cases.

Electronmicrography has shown that chromophobe cells do not exist, only cells with varying numbers of granules. It is possible to identify acidophilic cells containing prolactin and growth hormone (GH or somatotrophin, STH) and basophilic granules for ACTH, thyroid-stimulating hormone (TSH), luteinizing hormone (LH) and follicle-stimulating hormone (FSH), so that further study of the aged hypophysis may alter our views concerning its function, but as yet no studies of man have been reported.

On the other hand, McKeown (1965) found little abnormality in the adrenals of her subjects, finding only one example each of Addison's disease, Cushing's syndrome, adrenal cortical carcinoma and phaeochromocytoma. This is contrary to our experience that adrenal adenoma in the aged is quite often found at autopsy. Indeed, these were first described by Letulle in 1889 and have recently been studied or reviewed by Dobbie (1969). He describes two series, the first of 71 abnormal adrenals from 50 patients and the second a study of 113 consecutive autopsies. In this very detailed study he showed that 35 per cent of autopsies had a normal cortical appearance, 50 per cent had mild cortical nodularity and 14 per cent showed distinct nodularity comparable to those in the selected first series.

Cortical nodularity might be multifocal and bilateral; atrophic segments of cortex were also found. Sometimes nodules are large, more than 20 mm in diameter, their centres contining angiomatous formations. Haemorrhage from these vascular spaces into surrounding areas of myxomatous degeneration may occur. There was no evidence of pleomorphism or mitotic figures. However, areas of myelolipomatous metaplasia such as are seen in functioning adrenal adenomata were found. No intrinsic medullary lesions were seen in any gland though the medulla was often constricted and infiltrated by discrete tongues of cortical cells. The most striking concomitant feature was the frequency and severity of the degenerative changes in the capsular arteries and arterioles. Obliteration of the lumen in the capsular arteries was seen in 42 per cent (occurring in the 50- to 80-year age group in 80 per cent of the cases). Dobbie suggests that this nodular hyperplasia arises as a result of the arteriopathy which is secondary to hypertension in the majority of cases. A local arteriopathy occasionally occurs. These lesions may be capable of secreting steroids but owing to the vascular damage insufficient steroid is released into the circulation to produce symptoms of hypercorticoadrenalism.

PHYSIOLOGY

Control mechanisms

Much research into the hypophysoadrenal axis has recently been directed towards control mechanisms. It would seem that many dissimilar messengers act by way of the adenyl cyclase system, indicating that adenosine-3', 5'-monophosphate (3', 5'-cyclic-AMP) plays a part in the production and mediation of both hypophyseal and adrenal hormones. However, no work has as yet been done in old animals or cells.

Comparative studies of hypophysoadrenal function in animals

Animal work supports the hypothesis that hypophysoadrenal function is reduced with age. Hess and Riegle (1970) for instance have studied the functional reserve capacities of young and old, male and female Long-Evans rats by measuring the increase in plasma corticosterone concentration following ether vapour stress and ACTH stimulation. No age-related differences in resting corticosterone levels were found, but following exposure to either ether vapours or doses of exogenous ACTH sufficient to stimulate maximally the adrenal cortex, old rats, both male and female, showed significantly lower plasma corticosterone levels than young male and female rats receiving the same stimulus. Breznock and McQueen (1970) suggest that adrenocortical function, while remaining excellent in dogs, does tend to decrease slightly in response to ACTH with age. Further, decreased adrenal cortical response to ACTH infusion has been shown in older cattle, decreased adrenal cortical reserve with increasing age in goats (Riegle and Nellor, 1968) and lower levels of circulating corticosterone in aged mice (Grad and Khalid, 1968).

Dynamic tests of glandular function in humans

It is generally agreed that glandular function is best assessed by tests which directly provoke hormonal secretion, followed by the measurement of those secretions in the plasma. Hypophyseal function is usually assessed by the response to acute stress, while the adrenal is stimulated by direct challenge, following injection of ACTH.

In the case of the hypophysis the problem is two-fold — firstly, is the stress to which the individual is subjected great enough to produce an adequate response? Secondly, is it likely to be dangerous to the patient — especially an elderly patient? Consequently, in assessing hypophyseal function several types of test have been tried. Mostly these are mediated through the hypothalamic receptors or by blocking the feed back mechanism.

Figure 33.1 shows the schematic association between the hypothalamus, hypophysis and target gland such as the adrenal. Physiological or pharmacological stimuli may be used and the tests which vary in their value with regard to the trophic hormone to be measured are shown in Table 33.1.

Studies of hypophysoadrenal response

Experience in the use of most of the tests shown in Table 33.1 has come from the study of patients with known or suspected hypothalamic-pituitary adrenal disease.

Insulin-induced hypoglycaemia. Carroll et al (1969) have compared insulin-induced hypoglycaemia, administration of pyrogen and the administration of lysine vasopressin in 44 normal subjects and 140 patients, while Jacobs and Nabarro (1969) have similarly reviewed these tests in addition to metyrapone as stimuli to ACTH release. These authors suggest that insulin-induced hypoglycaemia is the most sensitive test of pituitary function, especially when growth hormone levels are measured along with plasma 11-hydroxy-corticosteroids (cortisol). Nevertheless, insulin-induced hypoglycaemia did not always produce an adequate response and a second test may often need to be employed in cases of doubt. This second test may be the lysine vasopressin test or the arginine infusion test as suggested by Raiti et al (1967). Penny et al (1969) have devised a combined sequential arginine infusion-insulin hypoglycaemia test which is probably the simplest and most effective way of measuring ACTH reserve in the elderly as well as GH response (Lazarus and Eastman, 1976). In this test fasting subjects are given a 30-minute infusion of arginine (0.5 g per kg or 40 g maximum) followed after 30 min by 0.075 units of insulin per kg

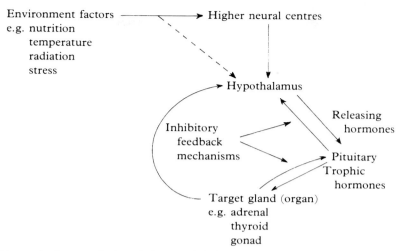

Fig. 33.1 Patterns of interaction between the hypothalamus and the hypophysoadrenal axis

intravenously. The usual dose of insulin is 0.1 units per kg (range 0.05 to 0.6 units per kg) but this dose should be given with great caution in the elderly, and screening for extreme hypoglycaemia sensitivity with a standard dose of 1.5 units may be a justifiable precaution. One of the eight subjects studied by Cartlidge et al (1970) was found to respond quite adequately to this small dose.

Glucagon stimulation test. The glucagon stimulation test may also be of value in the elderly. Mitchell et al

(1970) consider it an innocuous, reliable means of distinguishing normal adults from those with growth hormone deficiency. Fasting subjects are given 1 mg glucagon subcutaneously or intramuscularly. This test is probably safer in subjects with extreme insulin hypoglycaemic sensitivity but these subjects also suffer after glucagon.

Metyrapone test. The metyrapone test would appear unreliable for when given by mouth it may cause dizziness, nausea and vomiting as well as an Addisonian-type

Table 33.1 Stimulatory and inhibitory tests of hypophyseal trophic hormones

	Physiological	Test Pharmacological
Trophic hormone Growth hormone (GH)	1. Exercise 2. Sleep	1. Insulin-induced hypoglycaemia 2. Arginine infusion 3. Glucagon stimulation
Adrenocorticotrophic hormone (ACTH)	1. 9.0 a.m. Circulating basal ACTH levels	1. Insulin-induced hypoglycaemia 2. Pyrogen 3. Lysine vasopressin 4. Metyrapone (metopirone) 5. Dexamethasone suppression 6. Tetracosactrin response 7. Glucagon stimulation
Thyroid-stimulating hormone (TSH)	1. Circulating basal TSH levels	1. Thyrotropin-releasing hormone (TRH) stimulation
Follicle-stimulating hormone (FSH) Luteinizing hormone (LH)	1. Circulating basal gonadotrophin levels	1. Clomiphene stimulation 2. Luteinizing hormone releasing hormone (LHRH) stimulation
Prolactin	1. Basal levels	1. Insulin-induced hypoglycaemia 2. Chlorpromazine (CPZ) stimulation 3. TRH stimulation 4. L-Dopa suppression test

crisis in some elderly patients. Moreover, patients taking sedatives and antidepressants such as chlorpromazine, chlordiazepoxide and amitriptyline may have diminished or absent responses. Further it is a lengthy procedure and involves admission to hospital and urine collections which may be unreliable in the elderly. Intravenous metyrapone infused over 4 hours may be safer and more pleasant according to Jensen and Blichert-Toft (1970). They compared 12 subjects, average age 77 years, with 11 control subjects. Intravenous infusions of 5 g of metyrapone were given and plasma cortisol and plasma compound-S were checked over a period from 8 a.m. to 8 p.m. The results produced in young and old were very similar with no significant statistical difference. They found that metyrapone given intravenously was quite safe and produced little in the way of side-effects. Indeed, the usual side-effects seen when this substance is given by mouth were not seen when it was given intravenously. Jensen and Blichert-Toft conclude that the intravenous metyrapone test is a safe method for the indirect assessment of the pituitary gland's ability to produce ACTH, the feedback mechanism being the stress factor. They point out that all other tests of pituitary function (insulin-induced hypoglycaemia, the vasopressin test and the pyrogen test) are potentially dangerous, and the metyrapone test is a safe way of assessing the efficiency of the hypophysoadrenal axis. While previous studies had revealed a lack of association between the response to metyrapone stimulation and surgical stress, because a negative metyrapone test did not necessarily exclude adequate surgical response, use of the intravenous route now avoids this criticism. Further work by Blichert-Toft (1975) has confirmed that there is no age-related difference in ACTH secretion in response to metyrapone administered intravenously and that no GH (STH) response to this test was demonstrated.

Russian workers Svechnikova and Bekker (1970) have found that in apparently healthy human subjects, changes in the content, spontaneous excretion and the total amount of reserve capacity of adrenal hormones occur with age. Laron et al (1967), in a study of 19 elderly patients, found impaired human growth hormone response to insulin hypoglycaemia in four. However, in three of these the hypoglycaemic stimulus was not satisfactory, while the fourth patient had previously been treated for carcinoma of the breast and it is well recognized that deposits in the hypophyseal hypothalamic region are common.

Friedman et al (1969) investigated 20 unselected hospitalized subjects with a mean age of 81 years. At the time of investigation, the patients were in the recovered phase of their illness and were mentally normal. The hypophysoadrenal axis was assessed by measuring plasma cortisol response to insulin-induced hypogly-caemia and to a maximal stimulation with exogenous and synthetic ACTH. In addition, dexamethasone suppression tests were performed and plasma cortisol levels estimated. In a further group of 23 patients the diurnal rhythm of cortisol secretion was studied. They found that there was no evidence of a decrease in the functional integrity of the hypothalamic–hypophysoadrenal axis in any of these subjects. Dexamethasone suppression was within normal limits confirming that there was no alteration in the negative feedback control of ACTH release and response to synthetic ACTH (Tetracosactrin) was also normal. Response to exogenous ACTH gel, however, was excessive, and midnight plasma cortisol levels were much higher than in younger subjects, findings which are in keeping with the response to surgical stress studied by Blichert-Toft (1975).

Cartlidge and his colleagues (1970) investigated the function of the hypophysoadrenal axis in eight elderly subjects aged 80 to 95. Plasma cortisol, plasma-free fatty acids (FFA) and serum-growth hormone (GH) were measured following insulin-induced hypoglycaemia. The results were compared to those which had been obtained in younger subjects. The serum GH response to insulin was normal in all cases. As one would expect, the FFA recovery index was also normal. The maximum plasma cortisol level achieved after insulin was also normal although the maximum increment of plasma cortisol was in fact reduced in four subjects.

Growth hormone in exercise and sleep. Laron et al (1970) have studied GH output during exercise in men and women over the age of 70 years and found that GH output was not increased. Nevertheless GH was excreted even though 50 per cent of the subjects studied had reduced reserve. It must be remembered that the size of GH response to exercise is proportional to the severity of the exercise, and consequently unless exercise is maximal, response may not be adequate. Subjects to be exercised should therefore be carefully examined before testing and monitored with a continuous electrocardiographic record during the test.

Similarly, though GH (STH) levels rise with sleep in the young, it would seem that this is not so in the elderly. This is possibly due to the fact that testing is less easy in the old so that they are wakened by the sampling procedures.

Cortisol and ACTH stimulation test. West et al (1961) studied adrenocortical function in old age to observe the apparent decreased cortisol utilization which seems to occur in the old. They measured free and conjugated 17-OHCS in the plasma following standard infusions of cortisol and the ACTH stimulation test. Three groups of old men, divided by decades, were compared to a group of 15 normal subjects with an average age of 33 years. The results showed that following intravenous administration, cortisol is removed from the circulation at a progressively slower rate with advancing age. West (1961) suggests that since there is a normal rise in the concentration of plasma 17-OHCS during ACTH stimulation the adrenal cortex is less responsive with aging, for if the decreased rate of cortisol utilization is taken into account one would expect higher levels than one gets in the young. Their study, however, failed to establish an entirely satisfactory explanation for the inhibitory effect of aging on cortisol utilization. This may be associated with the reduction in the basal metabolic rate which occurs with aging (probably unrelated to thyroid function). Another possibility is that the prolongation of the half-life of cortisol is due to reduced liver metabolism. Thirdly, the decreased consumption of cortisol may correlate with the decreased muscle bulk that occurs with age. Work by Romanof et al (1961) tends to support this view. Until recently Romanof's study was the only published report on cortisone production rate (CPR) in elderly patients. This omission has been rectified by Murray et al (1981) who measured CPR in a small group of 20 hospitalized patients (13 men, 7 women) aged 70–95 years. The CPR levels in this group were no different to reference ranges published for younger groups. There was also correlation between CPR and urinary 'free' cortisol levels as determined by radioimmunoassay thereby confirming a similar observation in younger subjects between CPR and urinary cortisol measured fluorimetrically. This study confirmed the elevation of midnight cortisol levels in men found by Friedman et al (1969). It also showed that CPR was related to creatinine output but not to creatinine clearance. This later observation supports the view that muscle mass may have some influence on cortisol secretion.

This study tends to refute the suggestion that hypophysoadrenal cortical activity decreases with advancing age because of decreasing basal glucocorticoid turnover in the elderly and supports the work of Blichert-Toft (1971). He studied serum corticotrophin in 22 subjects with an average age of 82 years. In 5 the nycterohemeral variation in the concentrations of serum corticotrophin and plasma cortisol was observed simultaneously. The results were compared to younger subjects and were similar. This paper suggests that corticotrophin concentrations are similar in old age and though there is a slight tendency for these to decrease, the change is not significant.

While dynamic tests show that the axis is usually intact in old age, an equal rise in plasma cortisol in both long and short duration corticotrophin stimulation suggests a reduced adrenal response in the aged, since cortisol is elminated more slowly and also the cortisol distribution space is unchanged with age (West et al, 1961). This observation, however, is probably of no

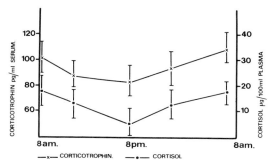

Fig. 33.2 Diagram to show the mean corticotrophin and cortisol levels found in the elderly over a period of 24 hours

clinical relevance unless exhaustion of elderly subjects stress response is expected.

Serio et al (1970) have also studied the circadian rhythm of plasma cortisol in subjects over the age of 70 years. They concluded that a circadian rhythm in plasma cortisol persists in aged subjects, and the timing of the rhythm, irrespective of the presence of sleep disturbances, appears to be later than that of younger control subjects. The type of pattern seen in the levels of corticotrophin and cortisol may be diagrammatically represented as shown in Figure 33.2.

Hypophysoadrenal function in relation to surgery

The proper functioning of the hypophysoadrenal axis in response to stresses of surgery is one of the major theoretical considerations when contemplating surgery in the aged patient. Blichert-Toft (1975) has reviewed the literature and studied the effect of surgical stress on both ACTH and GH (STH) release. The group of patients studied contained 25 young (7 female, 18 male) and 22 elderly (10 female, 12 male) whose age range was 65 to 86 years. ACTH release was estimated by the glucocorticoid response and found not to be reduced in age; neither was evidence of postoperative exhaustion found. On the other hand GH (STH) response to surgery was variable, lack of response among elderly subjects being more common than in the young group; GH (STH) response in surgery would, therefore, seem to be dissociated from the ACTH response. Routine preoperative use of tests of hypothalamic–hypophysoadrenal function would seem to be unnecessary, though Blichert-Toft et al (1970) felt that an evaluation of the hypophysoadrenal axis and its capacity might be of value in aged chronically ill patients, and in patients who had previously received or were receiving steroid, therapy, either locally or parentally. Further, it should be recognized that other groups of patients may have diminished hypophysoadrenal function, in particular those elderly patients with chronic subnutrition (Cooke et al, 1964). Carroll (1969) has also shown that patients with depressive illness may suffer from hypothalamic-hypophyseal insensitivity.

Studies of hypophysothyroid response in aged humans

Plasma TSH levels are slightly higher in the elderly than those in younger subjects (Mayberry et al, 1971; Kobayashi et al, 1973). The normal range in most laboratories is from 1.0 to 4.5 μu/ml. and in the elderly normal levels of between 5 and 6 μu/ml are often found. Levels higher than this usually indicate primary hypothyroidism (the simplest method of diagnosing the doubtful case and differentiating primary from secondary hypothyroidism).

The thyrotrophin releasing hormone (TRH)-stimulation test is the most effective method of assessing hypophyseal TSH reserve and a normal TSH response excludes hypophyseal TSH deficiency. Absent responses are found in patients with hyperthyroidism (Ormiston et al, 1971) and euthyroid Graves' disease (Lawton et al, 1971). TRH may be given intravenously as a single injection of 400 μg as the response is dose-dependent in younger subjects though this may not be so in the elderly (Kobayashi et al, 1973). The oral dose is 20 to 40 mg and following this there is a sustained rise in plasma TSH, T_3 and T_4 levels, which is probably sustained in the elderly (Lazarus and Eastman, 1976) though no definitive studies have yet been performed.

Contrary to the evidence quoted, a recent study by Blichert-Toft et al (1975) of 170 healthy volunteers aged 18 to 94, no difference was found in fasting morning TSH levels, nycterohemeral TSH rhythm and TSH response to TRH in young or old.

Studies of other hypophyso-target organ response in aged humans

Plasma gonadotrophin concentrations rise steadily with age and may be useful in assessing the hypothalamic–hypophyseal axis. Stimulation of gonadotrophins in response to clomiphene is retained in older subjects (Wise et al, 1973). Similarly, synthetic luteinizing hormone releasing hormone (LHRH) may be used for the same purpose but as yet has not been studied in old age, though Lazarus and Eastman (1976) found a similar response in elderly and young men: in elderly postmenopausal women the response is accentuated.

Prolactin levels in old age are similar to those in younger age groups and the serum prolactin concentration in the basal state is less than 30 g/ml. A low serum prolactin concentration is consistent with diminished hypophyseal prolactin reserve. However, this may not be helpful in establishing a diagnosis of hypofunction since prolactin levels are very variable in normal adults. The finding of a high level in the absence of renal and thyroid disease is indicative of a hypothalamic disorder or hypophyseal tumour and should be investigated further, (Lazarus and Eastman, 1976).

Adrenal medullary function

Adrenal medullary secretion has been comparatively little studied in old age. McKeown (1965) points out that phaeochromocytoma is rare in the aged.

Fisher (1971) studied the urinary excretion of 4-hydroxy-3-methoxymandelic acid (VMA) in 50 hospital patients — 31 women and 19 men aged 69 to 96. Levels were found to be slightly higher in men than women and there was little decrease in the mean amount with age. This is at variance with previous studies of Karki (1957), Masse (1960) and Herbeuval et al (1963) who showed a decrease with age in the urinary catechol amine secretion. It would seem, however, from this work of Fisher's that the sympatheticoadrenal function is well preserved in the elderly.

PATHOLOGY

The anterior pituitary

Hyperfunction of the gland in old age is extremely uncommon, though with modern techniques it is by no means unusual for patients with adenomas to survive into the older age groups. Consequently it is quite easy to find patients over the age of 60 years in many series. For instance, Landon et al (1966) had nine out of 34 subjects over the age of 60 amongst the patients that they studied with hypopituitary function. Eight of these patients had chromophobe adenomas and one had an acidophilic adenoma. Three had had hypophysectomies — the oldest a man of 73 years. Hypopituitarism results from the tumour and its treatment.

Hypopituitarism

This condition may present for the first time in old age. Patients who have suffered pituitary necrosis following postpartum haemorrhage may rarely present in old age. Autoimmune hypophysitis has, however, been described in younger patients, and it is certain that this condition will also occur in older patients. It is likely to be associated with autoimmune thyroiditis since this association has been described in a young woman (Goudie and Pinkerton, 1962) while Maisey and Lessor (1969) and Maisey and Stevens (1969) have drawn attention to the association of idiopathic Addison's disease and autoimmune disease of the thyroid gland.

Posterior pituitary

Disease of the neurohypophysis is usually mimicked in the elderly subject by neoplasms which secrete a substance with an antidiuretic-hormone-like effect.

Recently, however, Saito et al (1970) described a case of chronic hypernatraemia associated with inflammation of the neurophypophysis which occurred in a 66-year-old woman. Hypernatraemia in the elderly, however, unassociated with severe dehydration, must be extremely rare, and consequently, if found, this condition must be borne in mind as a possible cause.

Considerable evidence exists that antidiuretic hormone (ADH) secretion is diminished in old Wistar rats. The evidence has been reviewed in detail by Turkington and Everitt (1976). There is little evidence that secretion of neurohypophyseal hormones is altered in man despite minor histological changes in the structure of the gland occurring with age. It has recently been shown that quite significant changes occur in ultrastructure of the neurohypophysis of mice (Wilkinson and Davies, 1981). Nevertheless, the content of neuro-secretory granules in those animals seems similar to that in younger controls. Consequently hormonal responses are likely to be retained. However, for how long this may occur in face of the 'degenerative' change remains in doubt.

The responses of the neurohypophysis to stress in humans and animals has already been described earlier in this chapter. The very interesting hypothesis of Frolkis et al (1982) on the role of vasopressin in the pathogenesis of vascular disease undoubtedly needs further study.

The hypothalamic-hypophyseal hormones and memory
The high incidence of 'brain failure' (Isaacs and Caird, 1976) in old age has led to investigation of the role of neurotransmitters in the genesis of senile brain changes unassociated with cerebral infarction or other definable cause. The close involvement of neurotransmitters with the neuroendocrine system has inevitably focused attention on the hypophyseal hormones. In a recent study, Oram et al (1981) looked at cerebrospinal fluid (CSF) neuropeptides in dementia. They measured TRH, LHRH and somatostatin (ST) in the lumbar CSF in patients with dementia and compared these to a control group with other neurological conditions. Significantly lower levels of all these 'so called' hypothalmic hormones were found in the demented group. The CSF levels of vasopressin were in the low normal range. This suggests that there may be some differential involvement of production of hypothalamic hormones, only some peptidergic secretory neurones being affected. Hypophyseal hormones on the other hand appeared non-affected in these subjects. The subject has recently been reviewed in a Lancet leader (1982). It would seem that ACTH, alpha-melanocyte-stimulating hormone (α-MSH) and vasopressin can all influence learning and forgetting in animals. Whether they do so in man has yet to be determined. Nevertheless, this opens up a new field for further study.

Adrenal cortex
Hyperfunction of the adrenal cortex and consequent Cushing's syndrome is extremely rare. Soffer et al (1961) suggested that the oldest patient on record was 70 years. Adrenal hypofunction, however, may be much more common in old people, particularly since patients with Addison's disease may survive for long periods with modern therapy. Nevertheless in the very large series reported in the literature, it is most unusual to find patients over the age of 70. However, it is possible that more cases may occur as more people live longer. Maisey and his colleagues (1969) at Guy's Hospital have drawn attention to the association between idiopathic Addison's disease and thyroid disease. The pattern they describe is certainly consistent with the concept that idiopathic atrophy can be an autoimmune disease regularly affecting the thyroid gland as well. Physicians treating elderly patients should certainly be aware that autoimmune adrenalitis with a resultant Addisonian picture may occur in their patients.

The adrenal medulla
Phaeochromocytoma does occur in the aged, though again like other tumours of the hypophysoadrenal axis it is uncommon. Eisenberg and Wallerstein (1932) described four cases with this form of tumour. The oldest was 82 years.

THE HYPOPHYSOADRENAL AXIS AND MALE HORMONAL AGING

Sexual intercourse has an added function in humans as opposed to animals, since in addition to its purely reproductive aspect it has sociological and psychological attributes, serving deeply felt personal needs and reinforcing pair bonding, thereby adding to the stability of society. This latter aspect has tended to become the province of psychiatrists, psychologists and sociologists rather than doctors or physiologists. In the last edition of this textbook, Felix Post suggested that the great majority of men have become impotent by the age of 75, yet sexual activity could be 'continued far beyond this age in a happy marriage of healthy spouses'. Is therefore, the development of impotence in the male, like many things, a disuse/atrophy response or does it follow age or disease changes in the neuroendocrine system? It has long been a myth that the vigour of old men is maintained by their having a young mistress. If hypophyseal function is defective no amount of erotic stimulus will restore potency!

The hypothalamic-hypophysoadrenal-testicular axis

Physiology
Figure 33.3 shows the relationship that exists between

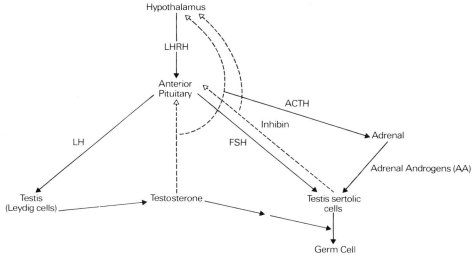

Fig. 33.3 Diagram to show the relationships involved in reproductive endocrine physiology. LHRH, luteinizing hormone releasing hormone; FSH, follicle-stimulating hormone; LH, luteinizing hormone

the various organs and structures. Release of the deca-peptide luteinizing hormone-releasing hormone (LHRH) promotes the secretion of two glycoproteins, luteinizing hormone (LH) which acts on the Leydig cells of the testis to release steroid hormones (mainly testosterone) and follicle-stimulating hormone (FSH) which stimulates the growth and function of the seminiferous tubules. Those tubules contain the germinal epithelium and Sertoli cells and FSH acts in conjunction with testosterone to promote germ cell maturation and thereby sperm production.

In addition to its role in the reproductive process, testostrone has many other actions which are summarized in Table 33.2. It circulates in the plasma loosely bound to albumin and firmly bound to globulin (TeBG) and is in equilibrium with a small amount of free hormone. The free hormone is available for target cells and when taken up is converted into 5-dihydrotestosterone (DHT) by the action of 5-reductase. The target

cell contains a specific protein which binds to DHT to form a receptor-DHT complex which enables the target cell to fulfil its appropriate function. Cells without the specific protein won't respond but there are exceptions such as bone and voluntary muscle and possibly nerve cells. Other tissues such as skin and liver will convert testosterone to oestradiol which then re-enters the circulation. This may account for some of the feminizing features seen in old men such as gynaecomastia.

Brandes and Garcia-Bunnel (1978) in an excellent review on aging and male sex accessary organs, suggest that the hormonal control of these organs may be altered in four ways:

1. A decline in Leydig cell function reducing testosterone levels.
2. Decrease in the binding of testosterone by target cells.

Table 33.2 The physiological effects of testosterone

Male sexual organs	Growth of penis, prostate, seminal vesicles Secretory activity of prostate, seminal vesicles Maturation of germ cells (with FSH) Development of rugal pattern and darkening of scrotal skin
Secondary sex characteristics	Growth of beard, axillary and pubic hair, increased muscle mass, apocrine sweat glands Enlargement of larynx (deep voice) Genetically determined baldness
Metabolic	Bone growth, epiphyseal closure, calcium and protein metabolism
Endocrine	Conversion to oestrogen (peripheral) Inhibits LHRH and LH secretion

3. Alteration of hormone metabolism within accessory organs.
4. Decreased target organ response to testosterone (androgens).

While it is not too difficult to study the first of these hypotheses, proof to substantiate the other three is less easy for at the present time little work seems to have been done in man. However it would appear from animal work that a decrease in specific binding of DHT may occur either due to a reduction of binding sites or reduction in binding capacity. That the response of target tissue to hormones alters with age can be deduced from tissue culture and transplantation studies which suggest that old tissue can be rejuvenated by a 'young environment'. In similar ways it can be shown that altered hormonal metabolism such as decreased conversion of DHT to androstanediol could result in cellular prolifiation and thereby prostatic glandular hyperplasia.

Hormonal age changes
As has been previously emphasised in this chapter, it is difficult to be certain what age changes occur. Methodology with regard to estimation of hormone levels may be difficult so that interpretation of results is not easy and studies are often incomparable and inadequately controlled. A good example of this difficulty is illustrated by a study of 5-dihydrotestosterone (DHT) levels. It would appear that these increase with age but the evidence is conflicting and there is a wide scatter of results. Moreover, DHT probably promotes more prostatic growth than testosterone. On the other hand, testosterone is converted by the prostate to DHT so that raised DHT levels in old age may simply reflect the amount of benign prostatic hypertrophy present in the old age population. Similarly, TeBG increases with age but the free testosterone fraction falls. Again there is considerable scatter and one is faced with a *post hoc ergo propter hoc* situation for the increased TeBG liver production may be the effect of androgen diminution and oestrogen increase.

The topic has been excellently reviewed by Harman (1978). From this it would seem that while anomalies exist, some things are certain. Firstly, the decrease in androgen level correlates with reduction in the Leydig cell mass. Human chorionic gonadotrophin (hCG) stimulation of Leydig cells show that base line and maximally stimulated testosterone levels are depressed though the per cent response as expressed by maximum levels/base line levels are about the same. This can be explained by a loss in cell mass. There may also be a reduction in response to hCG as well as reduced hypophyseal function. Since Leydig cell reserve for testosterone secretion is preserved it might be expected, if hypothalamic hypophyseal function were intact, that the

feed-back system would step up gonadotrophin secretion either to raise testosterone levels to normal or until the reserve was exhausted. This does not happen, even though LH and FSH levels are persistently raised in old age, in some cases to levels as high as those seen in castrates. FSH levels are higher than LH levels but this may also be a matter of interpretation for LH response is more easily measurable than FSH and increased oestrogen levels may suppress LH. Although hypophyseal response to LRHR is variable and equivocal, it would seem that relative and absolute LH response is diminished. Therefore, hypothalamic function is probably normal but hypophyseal function diminished.

Support for this is presented in a recent paper by Parker et al (1981) who have shown that adrenal androgens such as dehydroepiandrosterone (DHA) and dehydroepiandrosterone sulphate (DHAS) decrease with age due to decreased production. ACTH stimulation shows impaired reserve of DHA and androsteredione and a complete lack of ability to produce DHAS. While this might be due to an age-related loss of adrenal enzymes, or cell populations which produce adrenal androgens or loss or decreased function of ACTH receptors specific to adrenal androgens (as previously suggested by Roth and Adelman (1975) as a reason for reduced endocrine function), it could be explained by the loss of a hypophyseal factor needed for adrenal androgen production.

Hormonal changes in relation to prostatic disease
The role of 5-dihydrotestosterone (DHT) in promoting prostatic growth has already been mentioned but other changes have also been reported. However, most studies have been uncontrolled and many have studied hospital populations in which the subjects have been sick as well as old (Harman, 1978). The fact therefore, that testosterone levels have been found to be low in benign prostatic hypertrophy and even lower in carcinoma may reflect the debilitated state of the patient rather than an age change. (A similar situation occurs when vitamin D levels are measured in geriatric ward populations). It is possible that low FSH and LH levels may be associated with larger testes and benign prostatic hypertrophy, FSH and LH being suppressed by some steroid hormone possibly DHT. While such hypotheses can be proposed, proof will almost certainly have to await the results of a prospective study which undertakes to measure hormone levels in healthy young normals and follow these at regular intervals to observe the changes which take place with the development of benign prostatic hypertrophy and carcinoma of the prostate.

Sexual behaviour and hormones
The reduction in testosterone described is accompanied by a reduction in sexual activity and to a lesser extent interest as age progresses. Since these two

observations seem to be linked, the question has to be asked, as to whether hormone replacement therapy will improve male sexual function? This is particularly pertinent if testosterone plays a part in maintaining mental alertness and an aggressive attitude to life, since in androgen deficient men, weepiness and lethargy may be abolished by testosterone, (Harman, 1978). However, although replacement therapy, may restore function in the castrate, it would not appear to be so successful in the elderly. While there appears no doubt that androgen deficiency causes reduction in both libido and potency, no adequately controlled studies of the benefits of replacement therapy have, as yet, been published and those studies reporting benefit have been anecdotal. Moreover, androgens may actually be harmful, increasing the risk of vascular disease. Castrated men, for instance, may survive longer than those who are intact.

CLINICAL FEATURES OF ABNORMAL HYPOPHYSOADRENAL FUNCTION

General
The symptoms and signs of abnormal endocrine function are described in considerable detail in standard textbooks of endocrinology but some features are worthy of special consideration in the elderly.

Anterior pituitary

Hypofunction (hypopituitarism)
Some of the causes of hypopituitarism have already been described earlier in this chapter. Of most concern to the clinical gerontologist is destruction of the gland following infarction, tumours and granulomas or as part of an autoimmune process. Infarction may follow circulatory collapse after a post-partum haemorrhage (Simmonds Disease, Sheehan's syndrome), or more rarely blood loss from other causes. Other causes of infarction include temporal arteritis, carotid artery thrombosis, cavernous sinus thrombosis, head injury and diabetes mellitus. Destruction of the pituitary may result from extrinsic tumours such as the craniopharyngioma or intrinsic tumours such as a chromophobe adenoma. Necrosis of a large chromophobe adenoma or healing of a large granuloma may give rise to the 'empty sella syndrome'.

Diagnois of this condition in old age may be very difficult since many of the clinical features are often found in the sick old person. Lethargy and general malaise and a 'failure to thrive' may be easily attributed to depression, loneliness and even hypochondriasis. Palor of the skin, fine wrinkling of face and loss of body hair may suggest anaemia and aging. A low blood pressure associated with orthostatic symptoms such as faints and falls may be attributed to autonomic degeneration particularly if a history of diabetes is obtained. These patients are often mentally abnormal, tending to hide from the world and often have avoided medical attention. Past medical history may be difficult to obtain and general practitioners may have little information. A past history of post-partum haemorrhage or a history of diabetes mellitus which suddenly has improved so that less treatment is necessary, should alert one to the potential diagnosis.

While such patients are not common, sufficient do survive and present in old age for the physician in geriatric medicine to be aware of this possibility. The larger active geriatric unit may well see one patient with hypopituitarism admitted as a 'new case' each year.

Diagnosis is not difficult if it is suspected, and it should be remembered that they can sometimes present dramatically with collapse and coma (and even die) associated with an acute illness or surgical operation, even 30–40 years after a post-partum haemorrhage. Skull X-ray may show an empty sella but most of the changes are biochemical. Hyponatraemia and an inability to handle a water load may precipitate coma. Cortisol secretion is almost nil. ACTH levels will also be nil, if these can be measured, as are LH and FSH levels which do not respond to LHRH. TSH is also immeasurable and there is no respone to TRH. Prolactin levels are low and there is no response of GH to insulin and hypoglycaemia is marked.

All such biochemical findings however, will only be found in the presence of panhypopituitarism. Often only some are abnormal. For instance, a high prolactin may indicate a chromophobe adenoma which has destroyed the pituitary. In making the diagnosis the extreme sensitivity of these patients to insulin may be valuable and a very small dose, initially not more than a total of 1.5 units should be given. If this fails to produce a fall of blood sugar of over 50 per cent then a larger dose, (0.05 units/kg) can be tried. The standard dose of 0.1 units/kg can then be used on those suspected cases which haven't responded. Treatment is simple using appropriate replacement with hydrocortisone and thyroxine.

Hyperfunction
Acromegaly.   This condition may be seen in old age (Fig. 33.4). Diagnosis is not usually difficult since the facies suggest it. Confirmation is also easy since the fasting morning GH level is over 10 mU/l and often very much higher. The level does not fall after an oral 50 g glucose load.

Patients can be treated, if necessary with Bromocriptine, but prognosis is not good since many organs are affected and the condition is complicated by heart

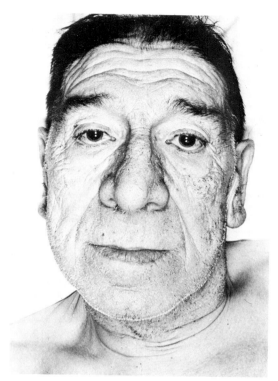

Fig. 33.4 Elderly male patient with acromegaly

failure, cardiorespiratory disease and cerebrovascular accidents.

Cushing's syndrome. This is rare in the elderly but this may be because many of the characteristic symptoms are common concomitants of old age. A recent referral for instance, with cardiac failure, diabetes mellitus and immobility for rehabilitation from an acute medical ward revealed also a depressed, irritable man with truncal obesity, a buffalo hump and marked pigmentation. His immobility was due to muscle weakness. But diagnosis was still difficult for a skull X-ray showed a normal dorsum sellae. Visual fields however, showed a bitemporal hemianopia. This patient was 76 years old and had been receiving treatment for hypertension for 5 years and for diabetes for 18 months. Plasma cortisol was high and suppression could not be obtained during a high dose dexamethasone test.

Cushing's syndrome also arises as a result of an adrenal adenoma or carcinoma or as a result of steroid therapy (iatrogenic). The latter is probably the commonest cause seen in old age. Other clinical features include osteoporosis, polycythaemia and biochemical abnormalities. Changes in the electrolytes may sometimes be seen, hypernatraemia, hypochloraemia and hypokalaemia being accompanied by an alkalosis. Cortisol levels are raised and a high post-prandial blood sugar is

common. Now ACTH levels can be measured the differentiation of the cause, i.e. primary pituitary or primary adrenal, is easier and fasting levels taken at 9 a.m. seem capable of differentiation (Horrocks and Landon, 1982). X-rays, particularly computerised tomography, may be particularly helpful in differentiating the site of the lesion.

Posterior pituitary

Hypofunction (diabetes insipidus)
Diabetes insipidus is due to deficiency of antidiuretic hormone (ADH). It is usually due to destruction of the posterior pituitary following surgery and consequently is unlikely to present *de novo* in old age.

Hyperfunction
Tumours of neuro-secretory cells don't occur so that the clinical syndrome of excess ADH secretion is due to inappropriate secretion or Schwartz-Bartter syndrome.

Carcinoma of bronchus is the commonest cause of ectopic secretion but some other cancers will also do this. Presenting symptoms are drowsiness, confusion, aggression, and headache. A low sodium of less than 120 mmol/l (120 mEq/l) usually confirms the diagnosis. The condition responds sometimes to radiotherapy. As mentioned earlier, a primary cause associated with inflammation of the neurohyphophysis has been described.

Adrenal

Hypofunction (Addison's disease)
The condition follows destruction of the adrenal, either from autoimmune disease or from a chronic infection such as tuberculosis. Patients present in a similar manner to those with hypopituitaism except they are pigmented rather than pale. Pigmentation of mucous membranes may also occur and is diagnostic. In the elderly, however, sublingual varices may sometimes cause confusion.

Diagnosis is usually not too difficult since electrolyte disturbance is common, hyponatraemia and hyperkalaemia occurring so that the Na: K ratio is low. Plasma cortisol levels are low and do not rise after injection of tetracosactrin (synacthen). Similarly urinary 17-OHCS levels don't respond to the long acting tetracosactrin zinc (synacthen retard).

Hydrocortisone is an efficient replacement therapy and most subjects respond to 40 mg daily, i.e. 20 mg b.d.

Adrenal cortex

Hyperfunction (Cushing's syndrome)
This has already been described.

Adrenal medulla

Hyperfunction (Phaeochromocytoma)

As mentioned earlier in this chapter this is rare in old age. It should be excluded in patients with unexplained high blood pressure. Diagnosis is now easier since non-invasive methods of radioisotope scanning with metaiodo-benzyle-guanidine labelled with ^{131}I is now available.

REFERENCES

Asling C W, Simpson M E, Li C H, Evans H M 1954 The effects of chronic administration of thyroxine to hypophysectomised rats on their skeletal growth, maturation and response to growth hormone. Anatomical Record 119: 110–120

Array A 1976 Aging in the hypothalamic-hypophyseal ovarian axis in the rat. In: Everitt A V, Burgess J A (eds) Hypothalamus, pituitary and aging, Thomas, Springfield, Illinois, p 376–418

Avissan S, Egozi Y, Sokolovsky M 1981 Aging process decreases the density of muscarinic receptors in rat adenohypophysis. FEBS Letters 133: 275–278

Bellamy D 1968 Long-term action of prednisolone sulphate on a strain of short-lived mice. Experimental Gerontology 3: 327–330

Blichert-Toft M 1971 Assessment of serum corticotrophin concentration and its nycterohemeral rhythm in ageing. Gerontologia Clinica 13: 215–220

Blichert-Toft M 1975 Secretion of corticotrophin and somatotrophin by the senescent adrenoanophysis in man. Acta Endocrinologica (Copenhagen) suppl. 195

Blichert-Toft M, Blichert-Toft B, Jensen H K 1970 Pituitary adrenocortical stimulation in the aged as reflected in levels of plasma cortisol and compounds. Acta Chirurgica Scandinavica 136: 665–670

Blichert-Toft M, Hummer L, Dige-Petersen H 1975 Human serum thyrotrophin level and response to thyrotrophin-releasing hormone in the aged. Gerontologia Clinica 17: 191–203

Brandes D, Garcia-Bunuel R 1978 Aging of the male sex accessory organs In: Schneider E L (ed) The ageing reproductive system (Aging, Vol 4) Raven Press, New York

Bresnock E M, McQueen R D 1970 Adrenocortical function during aging in the dog. American Journal of Veterinary Research 31: 1269–1272

Carroll B J 1969 Hypothalamic-pituitary function in depressive illness, insensitivity to hypoglycaemia. British Medical Journal iii: 27–28

Carroll B J, Pearson J M, Martin R I R 1969 Evaluation of three acute tests of hypothalamic-pituitary adrenal function. Metabolism 18: 476–483

Cartlidge N E F, Black M M, Hall M R P, Hall R 1970 Pituitary function in the elderly. Gerontologia Clinica 12: 65–70

Cooke J N C, James V H T, Landon J, Wynn V 1964 Adrenocortical function in chronic malnutrition. British Medical Journal i: 662–666

Costello T Y 1936 Subclinical adenoma of the pituitary gland. American Journal of Pathology 12: 205–215

Davies I, Fotheringham A P 1981 The influence of age on the response of the supraoptic nucleus of the hypothalamo-neurohypophyseal system to physiological stress. I ultrastructural aspects. Mechanisms of Ageing and Development 15: 355–366

Davies I, Fotheringham A P 1981 The influence of age on the response of the supraoptic nucleus of the hypothalamo-neurohypophyseal system to physiological stress II Quantitative morphology. Mechanisms of Ageing and Development 15: 367–378

Dilman V M 1979 Hypothalamic mechanisms of aging and of specific age pathology V A model for the mechanism of human specific age pathology and natural death. Experimental Gerontology 14: 287–300

Dobbie J W 1969 Adrenocortical nodular hyperplasia; the ageing adrenal. Journal of Pathology and Bacteriology 99: 1–18

Eisenberg A A, Wallerstein H 1932 Phaeochromocytoma of the suprarenal medulla. Archives of Pathology (Chicago) 14: 818–828

Everitt A V 1976 Aging and its hypothalamic-pituitary control. In: Everitt A V, Burgess J A (ed) Hypothalamus, pituitary and ageing, p 676–699. Thomas, Springfield, Illinois

Everitt A V 1980 The neuroendocrine system and aging. Gerontology 26: 108–119

Fazekas I G, Jobba G 1970 Beitraz zur morphologie der senilen hypophyse. Acta Morphologica Academiae Scientiaram Hungaricae 18: 74–89

Felsl I, Gottsmann M, Evesmann T, Jehle W, Uhlech E 1978 Influence of various stress situations on vasopressin excretion in man. Acta Endocrinologica (Copenhagen) 87 (suppl. 215): 122–23

Fisher R H 1971 The urinary excretion of 4-hydroxy-3-methoxy-mandelic acid in the elderly. Gerontologia Clinica 13: 257–260

Friedman M, Green M F, Sharland E 1969 Assessment of hypothalamic-pituitary-adrenal function in the geriatric age group. Journal of Gerontology 24: 292–297

Frolkis V V, Bezyukov V V, Muradian K K 1979 Hypothalamic-pituitary-adrenocortical regulation of induction of some enzymes of carbohydrate and amino acid metabolism in aging. Experimental Gerontology 14: 65–76

Frolkis V V, Bezyukov V V, Muradian K K 1979 Hypothalamic-pituitary adrenocortical regulation of RNA synthesis in ageing. Experimental Gerontology 14: 77–85

Frolkis V V, Golovchenko S F, Medred V I, Frolkis R A 1982 Vasopressin and cardiovascular system in aging. Gerontology 28: 290–302

Goudie R B, Pinkerton P H 1962 Anterior hypophysitis and Hashimoto's disease in a young woman. Journal of Pathology and Bacteriology 83: 584–585

Grad B, Khalid R 1968 Circulating corticosterone levels in young and old, male and female C57B1/6J mice. Journal of Gerontology 23: 522–528

Greenblatt R B, Natrajam P K, Tzingounis V 1979 Role of the hypothalamus in the aging woman. Journal of the American Geriatrics Society 27: 97–103

Greenwood F C, Landon J, Stamp T C B 1966 The plasma sugar, free fatty acid, cortisol and growth hormone in response to insulin in control subjects. Journal of Clinical Investigation 45: 429–437

Harman S M 1978 Clinical aspects of aging of the male reproductive system. In: Schneider E L (ed) The ageing reproductive system (Aging, vol 4). Raven Press, New York, p 29–58

Helderman J H, Vestal R E, Rowe J E, Tobin J D, Andres R, Robertson J L 1978 The response of arginine vasopressin in intravenous ethanol and hypertonic saline in man: The impact of aging Journal of Gerontology 33: 39–47

Herbeuval R, Masse G, Cuny G, Guerci O 1963 L'excretion des catecholamines dans l'hypertension des vieillards. Revue Francaise de Gérontologie 9: 75–76

Hess G D, Riegle, G D 1970 Adrenocortical responsiveness to stress and ACTH in ageing rats. Journal of Gerontology 25: 354–358

Hochstaedt B B, Schneebaum M, Shadel M 1961 Adrenocortical responsivity in old age. Gerontologia Clinica 15: 239–246

Horrocks P M, Landon D R 1982 Diagnostic value of 9 a.m. plasma adrenocorticotrophic hormone concentrations in Cushing's Disease. British Medical Journal 285: 1302–1303

Isaacs B, Caird F I 1976 'Brain failure': a contribution to the terminology of mental abnormality in old age. Age and Ageing 5: 241–244

Jacobs H S, Nabarro J D N 1969 Tests of hypothalamic-pituitary-adrenal function in man. Quarterly Journal of Medicine 38: 475–492

Jensen H K, Blichert-Toft M 1970 Pituitary-adrenal function in old age evaluated by the intravenous metyrapone test. Acta Endocrinologica (Copenhagen) 64: 431–438

Kalk W J, Vinik A I, Pimstone B L, Jackson W P U 1973 Growth hormone response to insulin hypoglycaemia in the elderly. Journal of Gerontology 28: 431–00

Karki N T 1957 The urinary excretion of noradrenaline and adrenaline in different age groups, its diurnal variation and the effect of muscular work on it. Acta Physiologica Scandinavica 39 suppl: 132

Kernohand J W, Sayre G P 1956 In: Tumours of the pituitary gland and infundibulum. Armed Forces Institute of Pathology

Kobayashi T, Shiraishi M, OHara H 1973 Studies on the thyroid function in the aged as viewed from TRH-TSH system, Japanese Society for Internal Medicine 62: 610–619

Lancet 1982 Drugs and memory ii: 474–476

Landon J, Greenwood F C, Stamp T C B, Wynn V 1966 The plasma sugar, free fatty acid, cortisol and growth hormone response to insulin and the comparison of this procedure with other tests of pituitary and adrenal function. II. In patients with hypothalmic or pituitary dysfunction or anorexia nervosa. Journal of Clinical Investigation 45: 437–449

Laron Z, Doron M, Amikan B 1970 Plasma growth hormone in men and women over 70 years of age. In: Medicine and sport IV, p 136–141. Petah Tigra-Karger Basel

Lawton N F, Ekins R P, Nabarro J D N 1971 Failure of pituitary response to thyrotropin-releasing hormone in euthyroid Grave's disease. Lancet ii: 14–16

Laycock J F, Penn W, Shirley D G, Walter S J 1979 The role of vasopressin in blood pressure regulation immediately following acute haemorrhage in the rat. Journal of Physiology 296: 267–275

Lazarus L, Eastman C J 1976 Assessment of hypothalamic pituitary function in old age. In: Everitt A V, Burgess J A (ed) Hypothalamus, Pituitary and Aging, p 97–122. Thomas, Springfield, Illinois

Letulle M 1889 Note sur la degenerescence graisseuse de la capsule surenale. Bulletins et mémoires de la Société d'Anatomie Paris, 64: 264–266

McKeown F 1965 In: Pathology of the Aged. Butterworth, London

Maisey M N, Lessor M H 1969 Addison's disease: a clinical study. Guy's Hosp. Rep. 118: 363–372

Maisey I, Stevens A 1969 Addison's disease at Guy's Hospital: a pathological study. Guy's Hospital Reports 118: 373–385

Masse G 1960 Etude des variations de l'eau, des catecholamines urinaires au cours de la senescence. Comptes rendus des séances de la Société de biologie et ses filiales 154: 2112–2114

Mayberry W E, Gharib H, Bilstad J M, Sizemore G W 1971 Radioimmunoassay for human thyrotropin: clinical value in patients with normal and abnormal thyroid function. Annals of Internal Medicine 74: 471

Mitchell M L, Byrne M J, Sanchez Y, Swain C T 1970 Detection of growth hormone deficiency: glucagon stimulation test. New England Journal of Medicine 282: 539–541

Morris J F, Nordmann J J, Dyball R E J 1978 Structure — function correlation in mammalian neurosecretion. International Review of Experimental Pathology 18: 1–95

Murray D, Wood P J, Moriarty J, Clayton B E 1981 Adrenocortical Function in old age. Journal of Clinical and Experimental Gerontology 3: 255–269

Oram J J, Edwardson J, Millard P H 1981 Investigation of cerebrospinal fluid neuropeptides in idiopathic senile dementia. Gerontology 27: 216–223

Ormston B J, Garry R, Cryer R J, Besser G M, Hall R 1971 Thyrotropin-releasing hormone as a thyroid-function test. Lancet ii: 10

Parker L, Gral T, Perrigo V, Skowksy R 1981 Decreased adrenal androgen sensitivity to ACTH during aging. Metabolism 30: 601–604

Penny R, Blizzard R M, Davis W T 1969 Sequential arginine and insulin tolerance tests on the same day. Journal of Clinical Endocrinology 29: 1499–1501

Raiti S, Davis W T, Blizzard R M 1967 Comparison of the effects of insulin hypoglycaemia and arginine infusion on release of human growth hormone. Lancet ii: 1182–1185

Riegle G D, Nellor J E 1968 Changes in adrenocortical responsiveness to ACTH infusion in aging goats. Journal of Gerontology 23: 187–190

Romanoff L P, Morris C W, Welch P, Rodriguex R M, Pincus G 1961 The metabolism of cortisol-4-C[14] in young and elderly men. I. Secretion rate of cortisol and daily excretion of tetrahydrocortisol, allotetrahydrocortisol, tetrahydrocortisone and cortolone (20 and 20). Journal of Clinical Endocrinology and Metabolism 21: 1413–1425

Roth G S, Adelman R C 1975 Age related changes in hormone binding by target cells and tissues, possible role in altered adaptive responsiveness. Experimental Gerontology 10: 1–13

Saito T, Yoshida S, Nakao K, Takanashi R 1970 Chronic hypernatraemia associated with inflammation of the neurohypophysis. Journal of Clinical Endocrinology 31: 391–396

Segall P E 1979 Interrelations of dietary and hormonal effects in aging. Mechanisms of Ageing and Development 9: 515–525

Selye H, Tuchweber B 1976 Stress in relation to aging and disease. In: Everitt A V, Burgess J A (ed) Hypothalamus, Pituitary and Aging, p 553–559. Thomas, Springfield, Illinois

Serio M, Piolanti P, Romano S, DeMagistris L, Guisti G 1970 The circadian rhythm of plasma cortisol in subjects over 70 years of age. Journal of Gerontology 25: 95–97

Shock N W 1967 Current trends in research on the physiological aspects of aging. Journal of the American Geriatrics Soceity 15: 995–1000

Soffer L J, Doreman R I, Gabrilove J L 1961 In: The Human Adrenal Gland. Kimpton, London

Svechnikova N V, Bekker V I 1970 Functional condition of the adrenal cortex in the process of ageing. Problemy Endocrinologii 16: 3–7

Turkington M R, Everitt A V 1976 The neurohypophysis and aging, with special reference to the antidiuretic hormone. In: Everitt A V, Burgess J A, (ed) Hypothalamus, Pituitary and Aging, p 123–137. Thomas, Springfield, Illinois

Verzar F 1966 Anterior pituitary function with age. In: Harris G W, Donovan B T (ed) The Pituitary Gland, p 444–459. Butterworth, London

West C D, Brown H, Simons E L, Carter D B, Kumagal L F, Englert E Jr 1961 Adrenocortical function and cortisol metabolism in old age. Journal of Clinical Endocrinology and Metabolism 21: 1197–1207

Wilkinson A, Davies I 1981 The influence of age on the hypothalamo-neuro-hypophyseal system of the mouse: a quantitative ultrastructural analysis of the posterior pituitary. Mechanisms of Ageing and Development 15: 129–139

Wise A J, Gross M A, Schalch D S 1973 Quantitative relationships of the pituitary gonadal axis in post-menopausal women. Journal of Laboratory and Clinical Medicine 81: 28–32

The endocrine system — thyroid disease in the elderly

AGE CHANGES

Thyroid size

Aging has long been known to be accompanied by atrophy and involution. Although there are many individual exceptions most organs become smaller in senescence and show a decrease in weight relative to the body as a whole. This was shown to be true of the rat thyroid by Koronchevsky (1961). The older literature, reviewed by McGavack (1951), suggested that the human thyroid also follows this rule. Hull's (1955) research supported this view.

McGavack and Seegers (1956, 1959) made clinical estimates of the size of the thyroid in more than 600 residents from an American chronic disease hospital and home for the aged. They found that the number of subjects with normal-sized glands decreased and the number with small glands increased with each decade up to 70. Above 70 two-thirds of the subjects had small glands but there was no further increase in the proportion over the next two decades. Even among the nonagenarians one-third had glands of normal size. Other studies also indicate that the thyroid gland becomes smaller with age, though there are considerable individual variations (Mochizuki et al, 1963; Verdy et al, 1971). In a large necropsy study from France the majority of glands weighing over 20 g came from subjects under 70, and the majority of glands less than 10 g came from those over 90. Glands weighing 10 to 20 g were found in similar proportions in each decade up till 90, after which small glands predominated (Chomette et al, 1966).

However, Mortensen et al (1955) suggest that the thyroid size increases with age. They base this view on an autopsy series of 821 patients with no evidence of clinical thyroid disease and in whom the thyroid was impalpable in life. Whilst thyroid weight tended to increase with age, 21 per cent of glands had palpable nodules and a further 20 per cent nodules revealed by serial sectioning. The apparent weight increase with age might thus be attributable to the rising prevalence of nodularity alone. Furthermore, as McGavack and

Seegers (1959) point out, these patients came from the American goitre belt.

Denham and Wills (1980), reporting from the non-goitrous London area, found that there was no relationship between thyroid gland weight and age after exclusion of nodular glands in an autopsy series of patients over 60. The upper limit for weight of the normal thyroid for their elderly patients, 33 g, is closely similar to that cited for series of younger patients, which ranged from 23 to 35 g. Thus, though the evidence is somewhat contradictory, there would appear to be no substantial change in thyroid size with age, at least up to the age of 90, except when nodules develop.

Microscopic changes

Evidence concerning microscopic changes in the thyroid with age is of necessity derived from necropsy material. It is known that the height of the follicular epithelial cells correlates with gland function, tall cells being associated with an active gland and flat cells with an inactive gland (Doniach, 1967). On the basis of the predominant cell type, Koronchevsky (1961) classified the glands from 202 women free of endocrine disease and cancer as normal, hyperplastic or atrophic. Only a fifth of the glands from subjects over 70 showed atrophic changes and more than a third were normal. Chomette and colleagues (1966) stress the variation found in old age, describing how the gland shows 'functional asynergy'. Most of the follicles are resting, but some are hyperactive. Mustacchi and Lowenhaupt (1950) compared 40 glands from old people with those from younger subjects. In two-thirds of the elderly glands they found an increase in connective tissue, in half a decrease in follicle size and in one-third a reduced amount of colloid. In many instances, however, the glands from old people were indistinguishable from those of younger subjects. Stoffer et al (1961) noted that the average diameter of the follicles and the average height of the follicular epithelium decreased between the ages of 20 and 50, but thereafter showed little change. In older glands they confirmed the presence of increased fibrosis and found that the colloid showed a tendency to basophilic staining. They found little evidence of arterio-sclerosis in contrast to Donini and Cella (1956) who claimed that in many elderly thyroids obliteration of the blood supply was sufficient in itself to account for the changes of aging. It seems likely that, while a certain amount of atrophy often occurs with advancing age, sufficient functional units normally remain, even in the oldest gland, to satisfy the demand for thyroid hormone during senescence.

Another feature of the aging thyroid is infiltration with small round cells. These changes resemble those noted in low-grade autoimmune thyroiditis. In younger patients the histological appearances of autoimmune thyroiditis correlate with the presence of thyroid anti-bodies (Goudie et al, 1959). A similar correlation has been observed in old age (Fedelli et al, 1963; Chomette et al, 1966).

Denham and Wills (1980) showed that histological examination of macroscopically normal glands showed tiny follicles, microscopic colloid nodules and fibrosis in many. Nodular glands had the features of long-standing colloid nodular goitre whilst focal lymphocytic thyroid-itis was found in a fifth. They were not able to relate histological changes with in vivo thyroid function results.

Nodules

Thyroid nodules are found at many routine necropsies (Ibbertson, 1964). Their incidence increases with age (Fig. 34.1). Nodules are commoner in females and may be of any size (McKeown, 1965). The presence of nodules can be reliably detected only by serial section. Clinical impression and even palpation at postmortem can be very misleading. Mortensen et al (1955) showed that only one-third of glands found to contain multiple

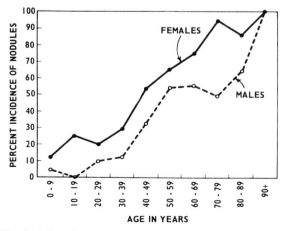

Fig. 34.1 Relationship of age and sex to incidence of nodularity in clinically normal thyroids (After Mortensen et al, 1955)

nodules on serial section were correctly identified by palpation at postmortem, while two-thirds of glands with apparently single nodules were found to be multi-nodular on section. These authors classified nodules as involutional (the great majority), inflammatory and neoplastic. A surprising finding was the large number of small adenomata and a 2 per cent incidence of symptomless carcinoma in situ. Their work relates to goitrous area, but in a non-goitrous area Denham and Wills (1980) still found 27 per cent of elderly subjects to have thyroid nodules at postmortem.

The evolution of the thyroid nodule has been studied experimentally by Taylor (1958) in iodine-deficient rats. Iodine deficiency leads to the formation of hyperplastic nodules. These eventually break down with haemor-rhage and necrosis and are replaced by cysts filled with non-iodine-containing colloid. There is, however, little evidence of iodine deficiency severe or widespread enough to account for nodules on the scale found post-mortem in man.

The high prevalence of nodularity of the thyroid gland in the elderly is of more than academic interest, for Denham and Wills (1980) found a significant corre-lation between such postmortem findings and borderline abnormalities of thyroid function in life. Nodularity and other structural changes probably underlie both the higher prevalence of thyroid disorders in old age (Jefferys, 1972) and the greater vulnerability of the elderly gland as exemplified by the relative frequency of transient disturbances of thyroid function following iodine medication (Denham and Himsworth, 1974).

Changes in thyroid function with age

There is considerable evidence that the functional activity of the thyroid decreases with age (Pittman, 1962; Gregerman, 1967; Ingbar, 1976). This is the result and not the cause of the aging process.

Gregerman et al (1962) estimated from thyroxine turnover studies that the production rate of thyroid hormone decreased by 50 per cent between the ages of 20 and 80 (Fig. 34.2). This was confirmed by Oddie et al (1966a) in Australia and by Nielsen and Friis (1973) in Denmark. Azizi et al (1975) studied the thyroid hormone responses to large doses of thyrotropin-releasing hormone (THR). T_4 levels rose equally in young and old subjects, but the rise in T_3 was less in the elderly, particularly among the men. Whether these changes represent intrinsic failure of the thyroid or a diminution of the drive which it receives from the pitu-itary is not known. Blichert-Toft et al (1975) found little evidence that age affected the pituitary response to TRH. Failure of the thyroid is associated with raised basal levels of TSH but levels in the elderly do not rise except where thyroid antibodies are positive (Tunbridge et al, 1977).

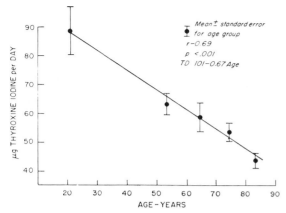

Fig. 34.2 Relationship of age to daily thyroxine degradation, by age groups. The regression line is calculated from the regression analysis based on individual values for 72 subjects. The vertical lines represent one standard error above and below the mean for each group. (From Gregerman et al, 1962, by permission of the Journal of Clinical Investigation)

Basal metabolic rate (BMR)

The BMR is no longer used in the diagnosis of thyroid disease but has been of gerontological interest in the past. Early workers found falls with age but Shock et al (1963) were able to show that, while the oxygen consumption of the body did indeed decline with age, when related to the total body water (which also declines with age) it remained constant (Fig. 34.3). They concluded that the fall in oxygen consumption was related to a reduction in the mass of functioning cells rather than to a decline in their metabolic activity. Keys et al (1973) suggest from their results based on longitudinal data that previous cross-sectional studies may have exaggerated the extent of falls in BMR with age.

Radioactive iodine uptake

There is an extensive older literature which generally supports the occurrence of falls in radioactive iodine uptake with age. Gaffney et al (1962) noted an age-dependent reduction at 2 and 6 hours after the administration of radioactive iodine, but there was no change with age at 24 hours. They attributed this to diminished renal function in the elderly which delays the excretion of iodine. Oddie et al (1966b) confirmed that the renal clearance of radioactive iodine decreases with age in parallel with the glomerular filtration rate.

Oddie et al (1960), working in Australia, noted a difference between the sexes. In males the uptake fell steadily from puberty to the age of 70. In women it remained steady until the menopause and then began to decline. Later Oddie et al (1968) correlated their results not only with age and sex, but also with diet. Males were found to have a dietary iodine intake one-third higher than women in middle life, but after the age of 70 the intake of iodine was reduced in both sexes. A smaller intake of dietary iodine leads to an increased uptake of radioactive iodine, and this might explain the levelling off phenomenon mentioned above. On the other hand in Glasgow, Thompson et al (1972) found normal levels of plasma inorganic iodine and no evidence of iodine deficiency in a group of old people living at home. Dietary iodine is a factor that has always to be taken into account when interpreting the results of uptake tests. In the United States, because of an increase in the iodine content of food, the standards for radioactive iodine uptake have had to be revised downwards (Pittman, Dailey and Beschi, 1969; Oddie et al, 1970; Robertson et al, 1975). A recent review (Ingbar, 1978) suggests that the falls in radioactive iodine uptake with age may simply reflect compensation for the decreasing rate of peripheral conversion of thyroxine.

Thyroid function tests in old age

With the advent of general availability of direct hormone measurements, older tests such as radioactive iodine uptake have been largely supplanted. This is also true of protein-bound iodine which, though formerly extensively used as a measure of thyroid hormones, is now only of historical interest, but the impressive review by Acland (1971) may be consulted for details of its variations in health and disease.

Thyroxine (T_4)

Thyroxine, T_4, is quantitatively the predominant thyroid hormone (Fig. 34.4). The extrathyroidal pool of T_4 contains some 800 μg of T_4, two-thirds of which is intracellular; one-third, bound to protein, is intravascular (Refetoff, 1975) and can be measured in the serum. About 10 per cent, 80 μg, is removed from the pool each day, 40 per cent of it through conversion to

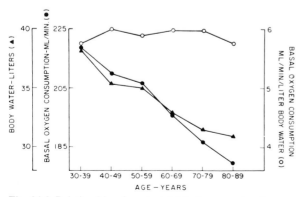

Fig. 34.3 Relationship of age to total body water, basal oxygen consumption, and basal oxygen consumption per unit of body water. (From Gregerman, 1967, drawn from data presented by Shock et al, 1963, in Journal of Gerontology)

Thyroxine, T4

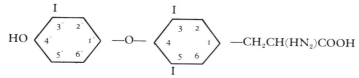

T4 is 3 : 5 : 3′ : 5′-tetra-iodothyronine

Tri-iodothyronine, T3

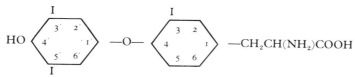

T3 is 3 : 5 : 3′-tri-iodothyronine

Reverse Tri-iodothyronine, RT3

HO ⟨3′ 2′ 4′ 1′ 5′ 6′⟩ —O— ⟨3 2 4 1 5 6⟩ —CH₂CH(NH₂)COOH

RT3 is 3 : 3′ : 5′-tri-iodothyronine

Fig. 34.4 Thyroid hormones and RT₃

T_3, an iodine atom being removed in the peripheral tissues (Braverman et al, 1970; Nicoloff et al, 1972; Surks et al, 1973). It now seems clear that T_4 exerts its major biological effect through its conversion to T_3, but it is still uncertain whether it is exclusively a pro-hormone without intrinsic metabolic activity (Chopra et al, 1973; Oppenheimer and Surks, 1975).

Thyroxine is readily estimated and is still the most generally useful guide to thyroid status. The original chemical tests for thyroxine iodine and the competitive protein-binding techniques are being replaced by radioimmunoassay (Ratcliffe et al, 1974; Seth et al, 1975). This is cheaper, more accurate and easily automated. Serum T_4 levels show little change throughout life in healthy people, though Evered et al (1978) found a slight rise with age in males and a trivial increase in females in a large community based survey in Northern England.

Some investigators have found mean T_4 levels in the elderly to be marginally lower than in younger patients, though still well within the normal range (Carter et al, 1974; Herrman et al, 1974; Kind and Ghosh, 1976; Lee et al, 1978). Others have found higher mean values in the elderly, extending into the thyrotoxic range in a proportion of undoubtedly euthyroid hospital patients (Britton et al, 1975b; Burrows et al, 1975; Baruch et al, 1976). Such high figures were not due to elevation of the levels of binding proteins, as the free thyroxine index was also abnormally high. In one series the possibility of occult thyrotoxicosis was excluded by the finding of normal levels of free T_4 and free T_3, measured directly (Britton et al, 1975b). One explanation for these anomalous high T_4 values is the effect of drugs. Hodkinson (1974) found transient high values after the administration of levodopa, while Baruch et al (1976) showed that elevated T_4 values were also associated with the administration of digitalis preparations, diuretics and cotrimoxazole. However, high levels may also relate to the lower peripheral conversion rate to T_3 in ill old people and represent a compensatory mechanism (Birkhäuser et al, 1977).

Tri-iodothyronine (T_3)

Tri-iodothyronine, T_3, is present in much smaller amounts than T_4, though its turnover is faster. The extrathyroidal pool contains only about 50 μg of T_3 in contrast to 800 μg of T_4. Ninety per cent of this is in the cells. Only about 10 per cent is intravascular and available for measurement. Most of the body's T_3 comes from the peripheral deiodination of T_4. Normally only about 20 per cent is contributed by direct secretion from the gland. Tri-iodothyronine is the hormone through which metabolism is directly controlled, and specific binding sites for it have been identified in cell nuclei (Oppenheimer and Surks, 1975; Refetoff, 1975).

Serum T_3 concentrations, which are very much lower than those of T_4, are measured by radioimmunoassay (Larsen, 1972; Lieblich and Utiger, 1972; Hesch and Evered, 1973). The normal range of total T_3 levels in the elderly is somewhat lower in men but is unchanged in women (Evered et al, 1977). However, other workers report falls in both sexes (Herrmann et al, 1981). Low T_3 levels are common in non-thyroidal illness (Bermudez et al, 1975), and many investigators have noted a reduction of T_3 in old age, sometimes to as little as half the levels found in younger people (Brunelle and Bohuon, 1972; Rubenstein et al, 1973; Herrmann et al, 1974; Britton et al, 1975b; Burrows et al, 1975). Recent work suggests that these falls in T_3 are related more to illness than to age itself (Olsen et al, 1978; Caplan et al, 1981).

Reverse Tri-iodothyronine (RT₃)

Thyroxine, T_4, consists of a tyrosyl ring joined to a phenolic ring, each carrying 2 atoms of iodine. The positions on the tyrosyl ring are marked 1, 2, 3, 4, 5, 6 and those on the phenolic ring 1', 2', 3', 4', 5', 6'. The four iodine atoms of T_4 are in the 3, 5, 3' and 5' positions, so that thyroxine is chemically 3:5:3':5'-tetra-iodothyronine. When T_4 is deiodinated in the tissues of the body it may lose an iodine atom from the 5' position on the phenolic ring to produce 3:5:5'-trio-iodothyronine, T_3, or it may lose it from the tyrosyl ring to produce 3:3':5'-tri-iodothyronine, which is known as reverse T_3 (RT₃: Fig. 34.4). Each substance can be measured separately by radioimmunoassay (Chopra, 1974). Reverse T_3 is metabolically inactive (Pittman et al, 1962).

More than four-fifths of the thyroid's daily output of T_4 is converted into T_3 or RT₃ (Chopra, 1976). In thyroid disease the blood levels of RT₃ follow those of T_4 and T_3. In thyrotoxicosis the levels of RT₃ are increased, and in hypothyroidism they are reduced (Chopra, 1974; Wenzel and Meinhold, 1975). In non-thyroidal illness, however, a reciprocal relationship obtains between the levels of T_3 and RT₃ (Chopra et al, 1975). When T_3 levels are reduced, levels of RT₃ rise. This has been shown to be true for acute medical illness (Burger et al, 1976), after surgical operations (Burr et al, 1975, 1979) and following a single dose of dexamethasone (Burr et al, 1976). It has also been noted in liver disease (Kodding et al, 1976), in starvation and in other chronic illness (Chopra et al, 1975). Burrows et

al (1977) have shown that low T_3 values in the elderly hospital patient are associated with high levels of RT₃. This is in contrast to the situation in healthy old people where lower T_3 values are not accompanied by elevation of RT₃ (Herrmann et al, 1981).

Serum binding of thyroid hormones

Thyroxine is about 99.96 per cent protein bound, principally to a specific alpha-globulin, thyroxine-binding globulin (TBG), which carries about 75 per cent of the hormone, but also to thyroxine-binding prealbumin (TBPA) and albumin which carry about 15 per cent and 10 per cent respectively (Oppenheimer, 1968). In old age TBG tends to increase and TBPA to decrease (Braverman et al, 1966). Binding of T_3 to carrier proteins is far less strong, but still amounts to about 99.5 per cent. Routine methods which measure total serum levels of PBI, T_4 and T_3 are thus profoundly influenced by changes in the concentration of the binding proteins, particularly TBG (Osorio, 1967).

It is now well known that oestrogens increase TBG (Engbring and Engstrom, 1959) whilst androgens and anabolic steroids lower it (Rosenberg et al, 1962). Corticosteroids decrease T_4 binding by TBG and increase that of TBPA (Oppenheimer and Werner, 1966). There is some evidence that TBG may be increased by perphenazine (Oltman and Friedman, 1964). Severe illness is another important cause of lowered TBG (Harvey, 1971; McLarty et al, 1975). In many old people the serum albumin is lower than in younger patients and the alpha-2-globulin a little higher (Haferkamp et al, 1966). These changes may be due to concomitant disease rather than to age (Meindok and Franks, 1969; Hyams, 1973). This is a particularly important factor in the elderly. Twenty per cent of tests from patients admitted to the geriatric unit at North-wick Park Hospital showed disturbances reflecting abnormally low TBG levels, often associated with a fall in albumin (Jefferys et al, 1972). Interpretation of PBI levels was found to be misleading unless the test was combined with a T_3 uptake test to correct for changes in the binding proteins. Burr et al (1977) suggest that measurement of TBG by radioimmunoassay gives a better correction for thyroid hormone levels than the T_3 uptake test but this assay is not yet generally available.

T₃-uptake tests

Although thyroid hormones are almost completely bound to their carrier proteins, the binding sites are never fully saturated and are always available to take up added radioactive T_3. The T_3-uptake tests depend on the partition of the labelled T_3 between the binding sites on the patients' proteins and an additional binding material such as charcoal, sephadex or resin. These methods are possible because T_3 has a lower affinity for the binding sites than T_4. Added T_3 does not disturb T_4 that is already bound.

The original versions of the test measure the uptake of radioactive T_3 by the binding material. In hyperthyroidism there are fewer free binding sites available on the carrier proteins, so the uptake by the binding material is increased. In hypothyroidism there are more free binding sites available and uptake by the binding material is decreased. A popular version is the Triosorb test (Abbott Laboratories Ltd). The results may be expressed as the percentage of radioactive T_3 taken up by the binding material or as a ratio relative to the results obtained with pooled normal serum.

Other techniques measure directly the uptake of radioactive T_3 by unoccupied binding sites on the carrier proteins. This is the principle of the Thyopac 3 test (Radiochemicals Ltd), currently the most widely used uptake test in Great Britain. In this test a low figure is found in hyperthyroidism and a high figure in hypothyroidism. The results are expressed as a percentage of the uptake by pooled normal serum. It is important for the physician to understand the test which his laboratory is using, since the word 'uptake' has two different meanings, uptake by the binding material and uptake by the unoccupied binding sites on the carrier proteins. High and low figures have a reciprocal relationship and opposite implications according to the method used. T_3 uptake tests reflect not only changes in thyroid hormone levels, but also alterations in the carrier proteins. An increase in the level of TBG increases the number of free binding sites and leads to a higher Thyopac 3 uptake. Age affects the test through changes in the serum proteins. In health, Thyopac 3 rises slightly with age (Evered et al, 1977; Hodkinson and Denham, 1977). Severe non-thyroidal illness affects the serum proteins, and low Thyopac 3 results were noted by Jefferys et al (1972) among ill old people, usually in association with lowered serum albumin. Using an older technique, Rosin and Exton-Smith (1964) found similar results in patients with hypothermia. Anomalous results have been found in renal failure (Joasoo et al, 1974). Hodkinson (1975) has found that the Thyopac 3 uptake is a powerful prognostic indicator in patients admitted to a geriatric department. A low uptake indicates a poor prognosis. T_3 uptake tests are also affected by drugs such as phenytoin and salicylates, which preferentially occupy the binding sites. Under these circumstances fewer binding sites are available and the Thyopac 3 uptake is reduced. Wood and Crooks (1973) gave a neat summary of the effects of drugs on thyroid function.

T_3 uptake tests are of little use as the sole measure of a patient's thyroid status (and they cost three to four times as much as an estimation of serum thyroxine) but they have proved invaluable through their contribution to the free thyroxine index.

Free thyroxine index (FTI)

The difficulty that measures of total hormone in the serum are affected by the binding proteins can fortunately be overcome by calculation of the free thyroxine index (Clark and Horn, 1965). This relates the total hormone concentration to the T_3 uptake and corrects for anomalies caused by changes in the thyroid binding proteins (TBP). A similar index, the free tri-iodothyronine index (FT_3I) can be calculated for total T_3 which is also affected, though to a lesser extent than T_4, by binding protein changes.

When, as in the Triosorb Test, T_3 uptake by the added binding material is being measured the FTI is given by the product of total T_4 or PBI concentration and the T_3 uptake. When the test is measuring directly the uptake of T_3 by unoccupied sites on the patient's serum, as in Thyopac 3, the FTI is given by dividing total T_4 (or PBI) by the T_3 uptake, thus:

$$FTI = \frac{Total\ T_4\ (or\ PBI)\ concentration}{Thyopac\ 3\ uptake} \times 100$$

Both methods give comparable results, though the range for the Thyopac 3 FTI is a little higher than for the Triosorb FTI (Clark and Brown, 1970a, b). The FTI correlates closely with direct estimates of free thyroxine (Wellby and O'Halloran, 1966). It has, in general, been found reliable for both well and ill old people (Rosin and Farran, 1968; Jefferys et al, 1972; Taylor, Thompson and Caird, 1974; Kind and Ghosh, 1976). Bayliss and Hall (1975) conclude that the FTI is the most reliable single indicator of thyroid secretory function for routine use. Bahemuka and Hodkinson (1975) have shown that it can be used effectively in screening the elderly for inapparent disease.

There is some overlap in FTI between the results from euthyroid patients and those with hypothroidism and thyrotoxicosis, but Britton and his colleagues (1975a) have shown how a simple strategy can facilitate interpretation. The appropriate normal range for the elderly remains to be determined. Among healthy old people living in the community the range of 0.58 to 1.24 (Hodkinson and Denham, 1977) is narrower, particularly at its upper end, than it is at 0.54 to 1.59 for hospital inpatients (Hodkinson, 1975).

An alternative to the FTI is to perform a combined test such as the effective thyroxine ratio (ETR) rather than the separate T_4 and T_3 uptake tests (Mincey et al, 1971). Although on theoretical grounds the ETR would be expected to correlate closely with the FTI, D'Haene et al (1974) found the correlation to be worse than expected and concluded that ETR gave a less trustworthy correction for protein abnormalities. Wellby et al (1974), however, found ETR to discriminate better than either FTI or free thyroxine between euthyroid subjects and those with thyroid disease. Lee et al (1978) found that in old age there was less change in the ETR than in the FTI.

Direct estimation of free hormone

The free thyroxine and free tri-iodothyronine indices correlate well with direct hormone measurements, but they remain an indirect method. The ideal is to measure directly the levels of free T_4 and free T_3. This is technically possible, and such methods are now beginning to be introduced as practical routine assays have become available for routine use (Midgley and Wilkins, 1981). Herrmann et al (1974) have reported lower values for free T_3 and T_4 in elderly subjects.

Table 34.1 gives a representative range of normal values for thyroid function tests. It is important to note that different laboratories have different ranges and different nomenclature. It would be valuable if the names of the tests could be standardized, as suggested by the American Thyroid Association (1976).

THYROTOXICOSIS

Thyrotoxicosis results from increased secretion of the hormones T_3 and T_4. There is preferential production of T_3, the synthesis of which may increase seven-fold from about 35 to over 200 μg per day (Nicoloff et al, 1972). Almost all of this comes from direct secretion by the thyroid and not by conversion from T_4 peripherally (Larsen, 1975). The production of T_4 increases only three-fold from approximately 100 to 300 μg per day.

Tri-iodothyronine toxicosis.   In most patients the levels of both hormones are increased and the patient can be said to be suffering from T_3/T_4 toxicosis (Sterling et al, 1970b; Hollander et al, 1972), but in up to 30 per cent

of patients with thyrotoxicosis the level of T_3 may be raised while that of T_4 remains within the normal range (Shalet et al, 1975). Other authors report a much lower incidence (Hollander and Shenkman, 1972; Patel and Burger, 1973). Sometimes T_3 toxicosis represents an early stage in the development of conventional thyrotoxicosis with raised levels of both hormones (Hollander et al, 1971). Tri-iodothyronine toxicosis occurs in the elderly and among patients with every kind of goitre, but there may be a special association with solitary toxic adenoma, which is commoner in late life (Marsden et al, 1975).

Thyroxine toxicosis.   Some authorities believe that the level of T_3 is raised in all patients with thyrotoxicosis, except those with low levels of TBG (Burke and Eastman, 1974). But cases have been reported where T_4 levels were raised while T_3 remained within the normal range (Stoffer and Hamburger, 1975; Hadden et al, 1975). Some such patients have been elderly (Kirkegaard et al, 1975; Turner et al, 1975a, b; Joasoo, 1975). Such patients are said to have T_4 toxicosis, certainly a much rarer entity than T_3 toxicosis.

Incidence

Thyrotoxicosis, though formerly regarded as relatively rare in old age, has now been established as a fairly common condition by the application of routine screening tests for thyroid disease to elderly populations. Jefferys (1972), in one of the earliest reports of such screening experiences, found a prevalence of 2.3 per cent in a series of patients admitted to a geriatric department. A subsequent larger series from the same department revised this prevalence figure to 1.1 per cent however (Bahemuka and Hodkinson, 1975). Similar prevalences in geriatric patients have been reported from overseas, for example Palmer (1977) from New Zealand.

Table 34.1 Normal values for thyroid hormones

Test	Old units	Normal range	SI units	Normal range
*Total T_4	μg/100 ml	4.5–9.9	nmol/1	58–128
Free T_4	pg/ml	8–21	pmol/1	10–27
Triosorb T_3 uptake	% of dose	25–35	% of dose	25–35
*Thyopac 3 T_3 uptake	% of standard	93–125	% of standard	93–125
*FT$_4$ index	T_4/Thyopac 3 × 100	4.5–9.6	T_4/Thyopac 3 × 100	0.58–1.24
ETR	ratio to normal	0.86–1.13	ratio to normal	0.86–1.13
NTR	ratio to normal	0.88–1.11	ratio to normal	8.88–1.11
Total T_3	ng/100 ml	70–200	nmol/1	1.23–3.07
Free T_3	pg/ml	3.5–6.5	pmol/1	5.4–10.00
FT$_3$ index	T_3/Thyopac 3 × 100	70–200	T_3/Thyopac 3 × 100	1.23–3.07
Reverse T_3	ng/100 ml	25–65	nmol/1	0.27–0.53
TSH	μu/ml	0.8–3.5	mu/1	0.8–3.5

NB. Normal range differs in different laboratories.
* Reference ranges for healthy elderly subjects (Hodkinson and Denham, 1977).

The experience of specialist thyroid clinics is also of relevance, thyrotoxicosis being increasingly thought of as a disease of the elderly. Thus, in Paris, Moreau (1966) reported that 18 per cent of his thyrotoxic patients were over 60. In Glasgow, Lazarus and Harden (1969) reported 15 per cent. In Denmark, Iversen (1953) reported 9 per cent, but 21 years later from the same country Ronnov-Jessen and Kirkegaard (1973) reported that 28 out of 49 patients recognized as thyrotoxic by a general medical service were over 60.

Although the incidence in the elderly appears to be increasing this is probably the result of increased interest in geriatric medicine and the much larger numbers of old people in all countries. In Olmsted County, Minnesota, where records have been kept for 33 years, the incidence of thyrotoxicosis remains constant at 30.5 per 100 000 women of all ages (Becker and Hurley, 1972). All investigators agree that the disease is commoner in women with a female preponderance of 4:1 or more. In a recent series from New York the female preponderance was 9.6:1 (Davis and Davis, 1974).

A recent large community survey (Tunbridge et al, 1977) found an overall prevalence of 1.1 per cent for thyrotoxicosis. There was a 12:1 female preponderance and average at diagnosis was 48 years.

Aetiology

Any of the recognized causes of thyrotoxicosis may be encountered in elderly subjects though their relative frequencies are altered. Multinodular goitres are common in the elderly at post mortem, even though they are often clinically inapparent, and these abnormal glands appear to predispose to hyperthyroidism (Denham and Wills, 1980). Diffuse goitres may also be difficult to palpate on clinical examination.

A special problem in the elderly is the large number of hyperthyroid patients in whom there is no detectable thyroid enlargement. Such patients accounted for 37 per cent of a recent American series (Davis and Davis, 1974). On scintiscan, however, such glands behaved in the same way as the diffusely enlarged glands of Graves' disease. A few showed a small 'hot' nodule that had been missed. None was multinodular. In the same series the patients with thyroid enlargement were almost equally divided into those with diffuse goitres, multinodular goitres and solitary nodules. Among the goitrous patients, those with nodular glands outnumbered those with diffuse enlargement by two to one, but in the series as a whole a diffuse pattern was the most common.

The controversial issues concerning non-toxic goitres, diffuse and nodular, which may precede the onset of thyrotoxicosis have been well expounded by Maloof et al (1975), but much uncertainty remains.

The main causes of thyrotoxicosis in old age appear to be classical Graves' disease, toxic multinodular goitre, Plummer's disease, thyroiditis and iodine induced hyperthyroidism (Jod Basedow phenomenon). Other rarer causes listed by Hoffenberg (1974) include TSH and T_4 secreting tumours and overdosage of thyroid hormones.

Graves' disease

Classical Graves' disease or toxic diffuse goitre seems to be relatively uncommon in old age in comparison to its predominance in younger age groups. This is believed to account for the relative rarity of such clinical features as eye signs, ophthalmopathy and pretibial myxoedema which appear to be specifically associated with Graves' disease and not with other varieties of thyrotoxicosis (Havard, 1981). The immunological aspects of Graves' disease, the role of long-acting thyroid stimulator LATS, LATS protector and the immunoglobulin human-specific thyroid stimulator HTS, are beyond the scope of this chapter. Readers are referred to the excellent reviews of Hoffenberg (1974), Kendall-Taylor (1975) and Mackenzie and Zakarija (1976).

Toxic multinodular goitre

Most cases of thyrotoxicosis in old age occur in the presence of multinodular glands. Such toxic nodular goitres appear to be a heterogenous group for excessive secretion of thyroid hormones may arise either in the glandular tissue between the nodules (Werner, 1971) or, very much more commonly, in one or more of the nodules. There is thus overlap in the first instance with classical Graves' disease whilst the secretory nodules are a form of Plummer's disease.

Plummer's disease

Toxic adenomas, 'hot' nodules, Plummer's disease, are classically solitary (Molnar et al, 1965; Ramsay et al, 1972) but may be multiple. Because they contain functional thyroid tissue they are avid for iodine and are normally recognized by scintiscan. Their essential feature is their autonomy. They are not dependent on TSH or on any other form of stimulation. Because of this they are not suppressed by T_3, unlike normal thyroid tissue under TSH control. They may be of any size from a nodule several centimetres in diameter to a lesion too small to be palpable. They may occur in a previously non-toxic nodular goitre. Some undergo necrosis and cyst formation, one reason perhaps why more of them do not cause hyperthyroidism (Miller, 1975) though increased peripheral conversion of T3 to RT3 may help maintain euthyroid status (Bianchi et al, 1979). Indeed, only a minority ever secrete sufficient hormone to cause hyperthyroidism. Those which do are likely to have been present for many years and are seen mainly in older women (Ferriman et al, 1972).

The secretory capacity of an adenoma depends on its mass and the amount of iodine which it can obtain. In some adenomas hypersecretion only begins when the patient increases his intake of iodine through a change of diet or medication (see below). When a patient is euthyroid the adenoma may secrete enough hormone to suppress the rest of the gland by the pituitary feedback mechanism, and this will certainly occur should the patient by thyrotoxic. The suppressed tissue can be made temporarily functional again by the administration of TSH. The hormone which the adenoma secretes may well be T_3 rather than T_4 so that the patient presents as a case of T_3 toxicosis (Marsden et al, 1975). Even when the patient is euthyroid there may be just enough hypersecretion of T_3 to suppress the pituitary response to TRH (Evered et al, 1974).

Iodine-induced thyrotoxicosis
In several parts of the world the addition of iodine to table salt or bread has been followed by an increased incidence of hyperthyroidism, particularly among older people of both sexes. The most recent epidemic occurred in Tasmania (Adams et al, 1975; Stewart and Vidor, 1976). Iodide given medicinally to patients with autonomous nodules (Ermans and Camus, 1972) and even to patients with apparently normal glands (Savoie et al, 1975) has also been reported to cause hyperthyroidism.

In a geriatric unit, Denham and Himsworth (1974) reported three patients who became thyrotoxic after receiving potassium iodide in the course of a ^{125}I fibrinogen test for venous thrombosis. Thyrotoxicosis has also been reported after the administration of iodine-containing contrast media in urography (Blum et al, 1974) and cholecystography (Fairhurst and Naqui, 1975) and with the use of the iodine containing drug, amiodarone (Jonckheer, 1980). Of course, only a small minority of patients exposed to iodine respond by becoming hyperthyroid, and they must in some way be primed to show this unusual response. The most plausible reason may be a pre-existing 'hot nodule'. The mechanism by which iodine induces hyperthyroidism in these and other patients is not understood, but the possibilities are discussed in the reviews of Hoffenberg (1974) and Vagenakis and Braverman (1975).

Thyroiditis
Classical autoimmune Hashimoto's thyroiditis is not common in old age. However, a less florid, painless thyroiditis is becoming increasingly recognized (British Medical Journal Editorial, 1977). A form of this gives rise to temporary hyperthyroidism without clinical goitre (Dorfman et al, 1977). It is not yet clear how frequent this might be in old age though its occurrence in a woman of 93 has been reported (Gordon, 1978).

Clinical features of thyrotoxicosis
Though thyrotoxicosis in younger patients may often be accompanied by a goitre with a bruit and exophthalmos, indicating an autoimmune aetiology (Davis and Davis, 1974), these signs are rarely found in elderly patients (Ronnov-Jessen and Kirkegaard, 1973) as they are not associated with Plummer's disease. Old people stand the stress of hypermetabolism badly and are made ill in many ways by minor degrees of hyperthyroidism (Havard, 1981), thyroid hormone levels being elevated to a lesser extent in elderly patients than in younger ones at the time of diagnosis of thyrotoxicosis (Nightingale et al, 1978). In one series the diagnoses made when the patient was first seen by a doctor included carcinoma of the stomach, pyloric stenosis, carcinoma of the colon, ischaemic heart disease, cerebrovascular disease, osteoporosis, hyperparathyroidism, depression and even myxoedema (Ronnov-Jessen and Kirkegaard, 1973). Mental disturbances are common and may obscure the clinical picture. Thyrotoxicosis may be an incidental finding in a patient admitted for other reasons such as a stroke, a fall, a confusional episode, a respiratory infection or dementia. The clinical picture was 'atypical' in all the thyrotoxic patients detected in the Northwick Park Survey (Jefferys, 1972) and it might well be said that typically the presentation of thyrotoxicosis in a geriatric setting is atypical.

The patient may be unwell for a long time before thyrotoxicosis is recognized. In a French series it was noted that in the absence of goitre or eye signs the duration of symptoms before diagnosis averaged two-and-a-half years (De Gennes et al, 1961). Moreover a goitre may be present for many years before the patient becomes toxic (Bartels, 1962; Locke, 1967). This is particularly true of Plummer's disease and of Graves' disease when it supervenes in a pre-existing nodular goitre. Old people with more obvious thyrotoxicosis and fewer concurrent diseases tend to go to the thyroid clinic where the diagnosis is made as quickly as it is in younger patients (Lazarus and Harden, 1969).

Ophthalmopathy
Ophthalmopathy accompanying thyrotoxicosis in the elderly is usually mild and affects only a minority of patients. In a Danish series, exophthalmos affected only 1 patient out of 28 (Ronnov-Jessen and Kirkegaard, 1973), and in an American study 7 out of 85 (Davis and Davis, 1974). Dalrymple's sign, retraction of the upper eyelid, is reported in about 25 per cent of patients in most series. Widening of the palpebral fissure and a staring expression is, however, common in old age from causes other than thyroid disease, particularly Parkinsonism. Ectropion should be easily distinguished.

Endocrine exophthalmos or ophthalmic Graves' disease occurs occasionally in late life (Hall et al, 1970a).

Malignant exophthalmos requiring steroid treatment or orbital decompression is exceedingly rare in the elderly (Cullen and Irvine, 1970).

Masked hyperthyroidism

The hyperactivity, restlessness, and irritability which characterize Graves' disease in younger patients, occur in only one in four of the elderly. Some old people with hyperthyroidism may appear normal but are more likely to feel weak, lethargic and depressed and to appear wasted, chronically ill or apathetic. Their condition is then called 'masked' or 'apathetic' hyperthyroidism (Thomas et al, 1970), and any one of the numerous other features of hyperthyroidism may come to dominate the clinical picture. The more unusual of these have been reviewed by Gorman (1972). Apathetic T_3 toxicosis has been described by Fairclough and Besser (1974).

Circulation

Tri-iodothyronine and thyroxine sensitize the heart to catecholamines (Spaulding and Noth, 1975), increasing the heart rate, stroke volume and cardiac output, shortening left ventricular ejection time and speeding up the circulation (De Groot, 1972). All this may be too much for the older person, and cardiac symptoms, palpitation, dyspnoea and angina are experienced by the majority of elderly patients with hyperthyroidism (Havard, 1981). Moreover, any discussion of the circulatory effects of hyperthyroidism in the elderly must be coloured by the high incidence of concurrent ischaemic heart disease. Tachycardia is the rule, but in one series the pulse rate was below 100 in half the patients and below 80 in a quarter (Davis and Davis, 1974). Ectopic beats are common, but paroxysmal dysrhythmias other than atrial fibrillation are surprisingly rare (Vazifdar and Levine, 1966). The commonest rhythm disturbance is established atrial fibrillation present in almost half of patients (Davis and Davis, 1974). ST and T wave changes are also very frequent on the ECG.

Another common finding — in perhaps 50 per cent of old people with thyrotoxicosis — is oedema of the legs. In only half of these is it due to congestive cardiac failure (Davis and Davis, 1974). Leg oedema is, of course, a common finding in old people generally and is often due to venous insufficiency and stasis. The incidence of congestive heart failure and atrial fibrillation in thyrotoxic patients increases with age. This has been attributed to concurrent ischaemic heart disease. Thyrotoxicosis may supervene in patients with other forms of heart disease (Symons et al, 1971); but some patients die in congestive failure with no evidence of any disease other than thyrotoxicosis. A feature of thyrotoxic heart disease is the rapid improvement once the hyperthyroidism is controlled. A specific form of thyrotoxic cardiomyopathy with permanent damage to the heart has been described (Hausmann, 1975).

Cardiomegaly may occur without atrial fibrillation and in two patients out of three systolic or diastolic murmurs may be heard, attributable to the hyperkinetic circulation (Davis and Davis, 1974). The increased circulation is also responsible for the common finding of warm, moist hands. When the patient is in heart failure, however, the hands may feel cold. The increased circulation is no doubt also the reason for the rather full right ventricular outflow tract noted by some observers (Thomas, 1972). The accelerated circulation can be measured by timing the interval between the Q wave of the electrocardiogram and the Korotkoff sounds at the elbow, using a phonocardiograph (Young et al, 1976).

In thyrotoxic heart disease an apparently poor response to digoxin has long been observed and occurs because the blood levels are lower. The increased circulation leads to enhanced glomerular filtration and more rapid excretion (Croxson and Ibbertson, 1975).

Despite the hyperdynamic circulation, arterial embolism is particularly common where thyrotoxicosis is accompanied by atrial fibrillation so that routine anticoagulant therapy has been recommended in such circumstances (Straffurth et al, 1979).

Alimentary tract

Weight loss is a classical feature of thyrotoxicosis. It was the only constant feature in Ronnov-Jessen and Kirkegaard's (1973) series, and was the commonest presenting symptom in an Australian study (Stiel et al, 1972). There was, however, no weight loss in a quarter of the patients reported by Davis and Davis (1974). Appetite is classically increased in thyrotoxicosis (Kimberg, 1971), despite the weight loss, but hyperphagia is present in less than a quarter of elderly patients. Anorexia on the other hand may be present in a third (Davis and Davis, 1974) to a half (Ronnov-Jessen and Kirkegaard, 1973) of elderly thyrotoxics. Loss of appetite is very likely when the patient is in heart failure.

Anorexia and weight loss may be associated with other gastrointestinal symptoms including abdominal pain, nausea and intractable vomiting, sufficient to suggest the possibility of carcinoma of the stomach (Ronnov-Jessen and Kirkegaard, 1973; Rosenthal et al, 1976). Weight loss in thyrotoxicosis may also be due to intestinal hurry which can be associated with steatorrhoea (Thomas et al, 1973).

Diarrhoea is classically associated with thyrotoxicosis (Kimberg, 1971), which increases the frequency of bowel actions (Baker and Harvey, 1971). In the elderly, however, the patient is just as likely to be constipated (Ronnov-Jessen and Kirkegaard, 1973; Davis and Davis, 1974).

Liver

The liver is an important reservoir of thyroid hormones and holds 25 per cent of the body's exchangeable T_4 (Oppenheimer, 1972). Liver function tests were abnormal in 15 per cent of a large American series not confined to the elderly (Ashkar et al, 1971) and in a larger proportion in a study restricted to elderly patients (Davis and Davis, 1974). Serum bilirubin, alkaline phosphatase and transaminase levels may all be raised, but seldom grossly. Liver flocculation tests may be positive. Liver biopsy in thyrotoxicosis reveals depletion of glycogen and increased fatty change (Montgomery and Welbourn, 1975). There is little correlation between histology and liver function tests (Dooner et al, 1967).

Clinical jaundice is very rare. Hepatomegaly in an elderly thyrotoxic patient may well be due to heart failure, cancer or previous cirrhosis. Occasionally no cause other than thyrotoxicosis is apparent. A few have associated splenomegaly though splenic atrophy has also been noted in Graves' disease (Brownlie et al, 1975).

Failure of the liver to conjugate oestrogen may explain the high blood levels of the oestrogen E2 which have been found in hyperthyroid men (Chopra et al, 1972). This could account for the occurrence of gynaecomastia which has been reported in old as well as younger men with thyrotoxicosis (Becker et al, 1968). There may, however, be other explanations (Chopra, 1975).

Neuromuscular changes

The weight loss of thyrotoxicosis is caused in part by generalized muscle wasting. About half the patients complain of weakness and in the elderly, such muscle weakness may lead to falls and cause difficulty in climbing stairs or rising from a chair (Satoyishi et al, 1963). Cramps may be a troublesome feature in some cases (Kennedy, 1965). Myopathic changes, detectable by electromyography, are present in the limb girdles of 90 per cent of thyrotoxic patients whether there is gross wasting or not (Havard et al, 1963; Ramsay, 1965, 1966). Thyrotoxic myopathy responds well to the correction of the hyperthyroidism, but myasthenia gravis, another neuromuscular disorder occasionally associated with hyperthyroidism, does not (Engel, 1972).

Tremor is a classical sign of hyperthyroidism, but is so common in the elderly for other reasons that it is of little significance in diagnosis.

Glucose tolerance

Evidence for the increased incidence of diabetes in patients with thyroid disease is conflicting, but diabetes is probably only slightly more common in patients with thyrotoxicosis than in the general population (Kozak, 1971). The incidence of thyroglobulin antibodies is 10 per cent higher in diabetic patients than in normal controls (Simkins, 1968). The association is stronger in those who need insulin (Whittingham et al, 1971) and in older age groups (Ikejiri et al, 1978).

Impairment of glucose tolerance and raised fasting blood sugar levels were present in a third of the patients in the New York series. Most of them were already known to be diabetic before thyrotoxicosis supervened (Davis and Davis, 1974). It is also known that latent diabetes may be unmasked by thyrotoxicosis and difficulty in stabilizing a diabetic patient may be the first clue to the presence of the thyroid disorder (Hall et al, Anderson and Smart, 1969). Any patient with thyrotoxicosis and diabetes should be carefully reassessed when he becomes euthyroid as he may be found to have regained normal glucose tolerance (Kreines et al, 1965).

Anaemia

Anaemia is uncommon in thyrotoxicosis as thyroid hormones tend to promote erythropoesis, increasing the blood volume and red cell mass. Nevertheless, anaemia does occur in some thyrotoxic patients and may be microcytic, normocytic or macrocytic (Fein and Rivlin, 1975). Pernicious anaemia and Graves' disease are both autoimmune disorders which is probably why they occur together more often than would be expected from a chance association (Schiller et al, 1968). The anaemia is more likely to follow than to precede the thyrotoxicosis, sometimes after a long interval (Furszyfer et al, 1971). This can be understood in the light of the lesser importance of autoimmune disease as a cause of thyrotoxicosis in the elderly.

Other autoimmune links with thyrotoxicosis. In a retrospective survey 5 out of 59 women, mainly elderly, suffering from giant cell arteritis, were found to have a history of thyrotoxicosis and both diseases occurred simultaneously in two (Thomas and Croft, 1974) — a much stronger association than was found in a control group. Vitiligo also has been found to be associated not only with thyrotoxicosis, but with Hashimoto's disease, myxoedema, and with pernicious anaemia (Cunliffe et al, 1968).

Calcium metabolism

Thyrotoxic patients have a high turnover of calcium (Eisenberg and Gordon, 1961). The serum calcium level is often slightly raised (Ronnov-Jessen and Kirkegaard, 1973). Curiously, in spite of the raised serum calcium levels, absorption of calcium from the gut may be defective, perhaps due to intestinal hurry (Shafer and Gregory, 1972). Hyperthyroid patients have depressed levels of parathormone, suggesting that the disease causes functional hypoparathyroidism (Bouillon and De Moor, 1974).

Occasionally osteoporosis or a disturbance of calcium metabolism may be the predominant clinical feature.

Hyperthyroid patients run an increased risk of fracture because of their osteoporosis (Fraser et al, 1971). Where there is gross hypercalcaemia there may be severe prostration and vomiting (Parfitt and Dent, 1970).

Death from thyrotoxicosis

Death from thyroid crisis in the elderly is very rare. Most patients who die while thyrotoxic succumb to congestive heart failure or to major embolism. A significant number die suddenly without obvious clinical cause, but presumably due to cardiac arrest. Only 16 deaths from cardiac infarction in thyrotoxic patients have been recorded in the literature to 1973 (Parker and Lawson, 1973).

Laboratory diagnosis

In the elderly the diagnosis of thyrotoxicosis is often difficult and every help is needed from the laboratory.

Total T4 and FTI

Estimation of the serum level of total T_4 is the screening test most generally available. However two groups of workers have found raised T_4 levels in a sufficient number of undoubtedly euthyroid old people to show that a raised T_4 level cannot invariably be taken as diagnostic of thyrotoxicosis. Even the FTI may be misleading, usually because of drug effects (see p. 691).

Total T3 and free tri-iodothyronine index (FT3I)

Serum T_3 and T_4, or preferably free levels or FTIs, are now the main routine tests for the diagnosis of thyrotoxicosis. We have seen how they may be affected by non-thyroidal illness and have noted the uncertainties surrounding the concepts of T_4-toxicosis and of sick euthyroid hyperthyroxinaemia (Britton et al, 1975; Mankikar and Clark, 1981). T_3-toxicosis, i.e. toxicosis with a raised T_3 but normal T_4, appears to be quite common, Caplan and his colleagues (1978) finding this in 14 per cent of a series of elderly cases. Serum T_3 determinations must therefore be regarded as the more important of the two determinations. Not only will it pick up patients with T_3 toxicosis who are missed when only T_4 is estimated, but it will detect more quickly treated patients who are in relapse (Jacobs et al, 1973; Marsden and McKerron, 1975). T_3 values are either normal or low in euthyroid old people, so a raised level is likely to be significant of hyperthyroidism. Because of these difficulties, diagnosis may remain uncertain. Havard (1981) points out the importance of demonstrating the autonomy of thyroid gland function in order to clarify the diagnosis in such circumstances.

TRH test

Thyroid-stimulating hormone levels are always very low or undetectable in thyrotoxicosis. They make no contribution to the routine diagnosis of hyperthyroidism, but they may be most helpful in the thyrotrophin-releasing hormone (TRH) test. Normally 200 μg of TRH given intravenously stimulates the pituitary to release TSH within a few minutes. In thyrotoxicosis the response of the pituitary is suppressed by the excess of circulating thyroid hormones. A normal response excludes hyperthyroidism.

Partial or complete suppression may also occur in conditions of so-called subclinical hyperthyroidism, euthyroid patients with ophthalmic Graves' disease or Plummer's disease and those on antithyroid drugs. There are certain other drugs also which interfere with the response, notably levodopa, corticosteroids and thyroxine in doses of more than 0.2 mg daily. Failure to respond is also seen in patients with pituitary disease, but this is unlikely to be confused with thyrotoxicosis (Fig. 34.5). The test is easy to perform and unlikely to upset the patient. Some people experience mild nausea or a desire to pass water. Care should be taken in patients with airways obstruction as TRH may precipitate asthma (Hall et al, 1973).

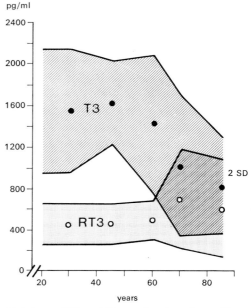

Fig. 34.5 Serum RT3 and T3 as a function of age. (From Nicod et al, 1976)

The test gives the same kind of information about the state of the pituitary as was obtained from the T_3 suppression test which it has replaced. It is safer, quicker and much more convenient.

Thyroid antibodies

Thyroid antibody tests are of little clinical value in hyperthyroidism. In patients being considered for surgery, however, they give warning of an increased risk of postoperative hypothyroidism. The detection of thyroid-stimulating immunoglobulin remains a research procedure, but if a routine test were to be developed it would be the ideal way to distinguish Graves' disease from Plummer's disease.

Radioactive isotope studies

The uptake of radioactive isotopes, nowadays technetium 99 rather than radioactive iodine (Goolden et al, 1971; Van't Hoff et al, 1972), has lost its importance as a means of establishing the diagnosis of thyrotoxicosis. But isotopes retain their value in the assessment of patients with nodular goitre. A scintiscan enables the function of a nodule to be determined, whether it is 'hot' or 'cold' and whether the rest of the gland is suppressed or functioning. A scintiscan is an essential step in the diagnosis of Plummer's disease. The 20-minute uptake is also the only test capable of revealing the underlying functional state of the thyroid during treatment with antithyroid drugs. Some authorities advocate a 20-minute uptake test every 1 to 3 months using it like an ESR during treatment of TB and rheumatic fever (Alexander et al, 1973).

Treatment

Thyrotoxicosis in the elderly can be treated, as in the young, by drugs, surgery or radioactive iodine. Antithyroid drugs may be used as the sole treatment in mild cases of Graves' disease, when their reversibility gives them an advantage over destructive methods. They are used to prepare patients for surgery, but their main use in the elderly is to bridge the gap until radioactive iodine treatment can become effective. Individual clinicians show considerable variation and inconsistency in their choice of treatment methods (Aitchison et al, 1973).

Thionamides

The thionamide drugs (thiouracils and imidazoles) block the organification of iodine. Propyl thiouracil is preferred in the United States, carbimazole in Great Britain. Propyl thiouracil has an additional action not shared by carbimazole. It inhibits the peripheral de-iodination of T_4 to T_3 (Oppenheimer et al, 1972; Saberi et al, 1974), but there is no evidence that this gives it any therapeutic advantage. To be fully effective thionamide drugs should be given every six hours, which is not easy for an old lady living at home. The initial dose of carbimazole is 40 to 60 mg daily. The maintenance dose, once euthyroidism is re-established, is titrated against the patient's clinical and biochemical state. It is usually 5 to 20 mg daily.

An alternative method of treatment is the 'block replace' regime. A full blocking dose of thionamide is given continuously together with a replacement dose of thyroid hormone, 0.15 mg of T_4 (Wise et al, 1973) or 60–80 μg of T_3 (Alexander et al, 1973). Such regimes have the advantage of simplicity. They are less confusing to an old person and reduce the need for frequent outpatient attendance. In a patient with nodular goitre, who for any reason refuses radioactive iodine, drug treatment may be continued indefinitely. In patients with Graves' disease, in whom spontaneous remissions may occur eventually, drug treatment is usually given for about 2 years. When the treatment is stopped, about half the patients will remain in remission. The other half will require continued therapy.

The thionamide drugs act rapidly. Hormone levels begin to fall within 5 days (Abuid and Larsen, 1974) and become normal in 1 to 5 weeks (Muhlen et al, 1975), but it takes 1 to 2 months before the patient is euthyroid (Mortimer et al, 1977). The 20-minute uptake of radioactive iodine or technetium is unaffected by drug treatment and remains high until the disease goes into remission (Alexander et al, 1973). The TRH test eventually shows a normal response, once remission has occurred, but is not suitable for the control of drug therapy (Muhlen et al, 1975). Side-effects are rare and seldom serious. Skin rashes clear when the drug is changed. Agranulocytosis occurs in the first month, if it is going to appear at all. It affects only about 1 patient in 200 and there is a 90-per-cent chance of recovery if the drug is withdrawn promptly. Patients are, therefore, urged to report any sore throat or malaise occurring in the first month of treatment, but routine white counts are not necessary (Harvard, 1974).

Potassium perchlorate

Potassium perchlorate interferes with the transport of iodine into the thyroid. It acts more slowly than the thionamides and is counteracted by iodine which must not be given concurrently. The risk of agranulocytosis is greater. It should only be used in patients who have developed hypersensitivity to all the thionamides, a very rare situation indeed. The initial dose is 200 mg 6-hourly.

Iodides

Iodides in full doses temporarily increase the storage and diminish the release of thyroid hormones. Blood levels of T_4 and T_3 fall to about half their initial levels in 4 to 10 days, but soon begin to rise again (Emerson et al, 1975), confirming the long-established clinical observation that the effect of iodine on patients with thyrotoxicosis is only transient. The only indication for iodine therapy is the very rare situation of thyroid crisis (Evered, 1976).

Lithium

Lithium carbonate in a dose of 800 to 1200 mg daily reduces the synthesis and blocks the release of thyroid hormones. T_3 and T_4 levels fall rapidly and the patient becomes euthyroid in about a fortnight (Lazarus et al, 1974). It acts as quickly as the thionamides (Kristensen et al, 1976). Given in small doses for a short time it has been claimed as a valuable adjunct to radioactive iodine, improving its uptake by the gland (Turner et al, 1976). There are, however, many potential side-effects, especially in patients with impaired renal function, and blood levels must be monitored weekly. Toxic effects include tremor, confusion, bowel upsets and electrolyte disturbances with weight gain and oedema. Many authorities consider that there is no place for this drug in the treatment of thyroid disease (Evered, 1976). Its proper place is in psychiatry.

Beta adrenergic blockade

Hyperthyroid patients show an increased response to adrenergic stimulation and this has been attributed to potentiation of catecholamines by thyroxine (Harrison, 1964). The truth of this is now in question (Spaulding and Noth, 1975), but there is no doubt that many of the clinical features of hyperthyroidism, the tachycardia, the anxiety, the sweating, and the tremor, resemble the effects of sympathetic overactivity and can be controlled by beta adrenoceptor blocking drugs. More recent work has shown that propanolol blocks the peripheral conversion of T_4 to T_3 and that this effect is independent of its beta-blocking properties (Heyma et al, 1980). Furthermore this effect is not common to other beta-blocking drugs (Jones et al, 1980). In doses of 40 mg four times a day propranolol abolishes palpitation, tremor and sweating. Maximal slowing of the pulse is achieved in four days (Toft et al, 1976a). Even thyrotoxic myopathy is improved (Pimstone et al, 1968). Propranolol does not affect bowel function or any of the eye signs, including lid retraction and lid lag (Shanks et al, 1969). Nor does it alter the underlying hypermetabolism. Patients do not put on weight. Their thyroid function tests are unaltered and their lack of response to TRH remains the same (Epstein et al, 1975). Cardiac failure may be made worse, Ikram (1977) having found a 30 per cent fall in cardiac output in patients with thyrotoxic heart failures who were given propranolol. Propranolol, although a most useful therapeutic agent, is no more than an adjuvant. Its value is to 'hold the patient pending definitive therapy' (Levey, 1975). It allows for rapid symptomatic treatment while the patient is undergoing investigation or awaiting a response to thionamides or radioactive iodine. Propranolol can shorten the preparation time before surgery (Hadden et al, 1968; Plimstone and Joffe, 1970), and, because it reduces the vascularity of the gland, has been claimed

as the best preparation for partial thyroidectomy (Michie et al, 1974). Although it does not affect the underlying thyrotoxic process, some patients go into spontaneous remission while taking propranolol alone (McLarty et al, 1973). Propranolol given intravenously contributes to the management of thyroid crisis (Das and Krieger, 1969; Havard, 1974).

Propranolol is contraindicated in patients prone to bronchospasm. It reduces cardiac output and is, therefore, normally avoided for patients in cardiac failure. If, however, the patient is first digitalized and treated with diuretics, the benefits of the slower heart rate are likely to outweigh the disadvantages of the reduced cardiac output (Levey, 1975).

Surgery

Surgery plays only a small part in the management of thyrotoxicosis in the elderly. The main indication for partial thyroidectomy is a large nodular goitre causing pressure symptoms. Goitres may also be removed because they are unsightly, but old people are seldom impressed by such cosmetic considerations. They have usually had their goitres too long and have got used to them. Clark and Demling (1976) have reviewed the criteria for selection of elderly patients with thyroid nodules for surgical treatment. Surgery is good treatment also for an isolated toxic adenoma, but radioactive iodine is equally effective and more often used (Ramsay et al, 1972; Miller 1975). A cold nodule of recent onset is an indication for surgery as it may be malignant (Thomas, 1975). Surgery is not undertaken until the patient has become euthyroid after medical treatment. Carbimazole supplemented by thyroxine 0.15 mg daily to prevent overstimulation of the blocked gland by TSH is now the method of choice (Evered, 1976). Most surgeons aim to leave a remnant of about 8 g of thyroid tissue in the hope that this will maintain normal thyroid function (McDougal and Greig, 1971; Hedley et al, 1972). The early complications of surgery include laryngeal palsy in 2 to 5 per cent of patients, about half of whom recover spontaneously, and hypoparathyroidism with tetany and paraesthesiae in 2 per cent (Cooke, 1973). Late complications include recurrent hyperthyroidism in 4 per cent (Hedley et al, 1971; Evered et al, 1975), and hypothyroidism in a much larger number — 30 per cent within 5 years according to one investigation (Hedley et al, 1970), 49 per cent in another (Michie et al, 1972), and on occasion 20 years or more after operation (Van Welsum et al, 1974). In some cases, however, hypothyroidism in the first few months may be only temporary (Toft et al, 1976a).

Radioactive iodine

Radioactive iodine progressively destroys the secretory epithelium of the thyroid by preventing cell replication.

Though slower to correct hyperthyroidism than partial thyroidectomy or antithyroid drugs, it is probably the most generally useful method of treatment for elderly patients (Goolden, 1969; Greig, 1973). It is also the treatment of choice for those who relapse after surgery (McLarty et al, 1969) and for many patients with Plummer's disease (Miller, 1975). Any lingering doubts about its safety should be dispelled by the massive American study which showed no increase in thyroid carcinoma or leukaemia after radioiodine treatment of 36 000 patients (Dobyns et al, 1974). Iodine-131 remains the isotope of choice. The theoretical advantages of ^{125}I, which it was hoped would spare the cell nucleus, have proved illusory (Chapman, 1971; Weidinger et al, 1974; Bremner et al, 1976).

The administration of radioiodine is followed by a transient thyroiditis, sometimes accompanied by discomfort and tenderness in the gland. More importantly there is an immediate outpouring of thyroid hormones with a rise in blood levels of T_3 and T_4. This lasts only a few days, but is the probable explanation for the occasional thyroid crisis or early death after radioiodine treatment (Parker and Lawson, 1973; Shafer and Nuttall, 1975).

Until the mid-1960s it was standard practice to give a fairly large dose, 7 to 10 mCi. Remission was usually achieved after a few months but 10 to 20 per cent of patients became hypothyroid in the first year. From the second year onwards the increase in hypothyroidism was cumulative reaching 80 per cent after 15 years (Greig, 1973). Postradiation hypothyroidism is not related to the age of the patient or to the nodularity of the gland (Lazarus and Harden, 1969). For the past 10 years low-dose treatment has been in vogue, giving about half the radiation previously employed (Smith and Wilson, 1967; Hagen, 1968; Glennon et al, 1972; Greig, 1973; Sterling, 1975). Smaller doses have always been used in Plummer's disease. Low-dose treatment reduces the incidence of hypothyroidism in the first year, but after the second year the cumulative increase occurs at the same rate, about 4.5 per cent a year whether the dose is low or high (Malone and Cullen, 1976). Isotope treatment has to be supplemented by antithyroid drugs for as long as two years (Goolden and Fraser, 1969a and b). It is open to question whether for the elderly patient this is the highest priority. Provided the patient is followed up carefully it is easy to institute replacement therapy with thyroxine when it is needed.

Where radioiodine therapy is readily available it may be best to start treatment with the isotope, especially in mild cases. Antithyroid drugs are begun, once the iodine has been absorbed by the thyroid, about a week later. Thyroxine 0.15 mg is added when the patient becomes euthyroid. Where the disease is more severe, or where radioiodine treatment takes time to arrange, it may be better to begin with antithyroid drugs and administer the isotope when the patient has become euthyroid. The drugs should be stopped for a week before the isotope is given to ensure a good uptake. Antithyroid drugs and thyroxine are continued for a year. They are then stopped for a period while the patient's thyroid status is re-assessed. If he is still hyperthyroid a second dose of radioiodine is given (Evered, 1976).

The pendulum may now be beginning to swing away from small dose treatments to the other extreme, intentional thyroid ablation with planned thyroxine replacement. By giving an ablative dose of 10 to 20 mCi three-quarters of the patients can be rendered hypothyroid in 3 months and virtually all in 6 months. Thyroxine is then started, and maintained indefinitely. At present this technique, which is cheap and extremely simple, is only suitable for patients with Graves' disease and diffuse glands (Adams, 1973; Wise et al, 1975). It is the best treatment for patients with heart failure. However, where an elderly patient is known to have Plummer's disease, which in contrast to Graves' disease has a low post-treatment incidence of hypothyroidism, it has been shown that a single standard dose of 15 mCi ^{131}I rendered 29 of 30 patients euthyroid and only one subsequently developed hypothyroidism (Ng Tang Fui and Maisey, 1979).

Follow up

Patients treated for hyperthyroidism need lifelong follow up, and the elderly are no exception. Clinical observation of the patient's general health, weight, and pulse rate should be supplemented by laboratory tests. The three fundamental tests are the levels of T_3, T_4 and TSH. All can be estimated from a single 10 ml specimen of clotted blood (Bellabarba et al, 1972). Raised levels of T_3 and T_4 with low or undetectable TSH imply that the patient is still thyrotoxic. Low levels of T_4 and T_3 and a raised TSH indicates hypothyroidism. Normal levels of T_3, T_4 and TSH indicate that the patient is euthyroid. Some patients remain clinically euthyroid with low T_4 levels but with normal T_3 and a raised TSH (Sterling et al, 1971). After drug treatment of thyrotoxicosis the likely problem is early relapse in half the patients, mostly within a year (Hershman et al, 1966; McDougall and Greig, 1971; Alexander et al, 1973). Patients who have achieved a remission on drugs alone require frequent follow up. They should be seen every 3 months for the first 2 years. Thereafter annual review is probably appropriate. A few relapse only after 10 or more years. A rising T_3 level is an early pointer to relapse (Marsden et al, 1975).

After partial thyroidectomy the risk of relapse into hyperthyroidism is small, but the risk of hypothyroidism is considerable and persists for many years. Hyperthyroidism may remain after radioactive iodine treatment if the dose has been inadequate, but once euthyroidism has been achieved the only risk is hypothyroidism, which will be permanent (Einhorn and Wicklund, 1966). In these patients T_4 and TSH estimations are the crucial tests.

Patients should be reassessed three monthly for the first year to pick up those with early hypothyroidism. They may show a fall in T_4 before a rise in TSH (Toft et al, 1974). After a year or so, however, the patients will sort themselves out into those with raised TSH levels, who should be seen every 3 months in the second year and annually thereafter, and those with normal TSH levels, who should be seen once or twice during the second year but thereafter need only attend every 2 or 3 years. Those with raised TSH levels and low T_4 levels are likely to develop clinical signs of hypothyroidism eventually, though many will remain unchanged for some years (Tunbridge et al, 1974; Toft et al, 1975).

HYPOTHYROIDISM

Hypothyroidism is the result of suboptimal secretion of thyroid hormones. An important advance has come from the demonstration that hypothyroidism is not an 'all or none' disease, but a graded phenomenon. Patients with overt myxoedema represent only the tip of an iceberg. As well as these there are patients with mild or indefinite symptoms and others without symptoms, but evidence from hormone studies of compensated thyroid failure (Evered et al, 1973a).

Thyroid hormones in hypothyroidism
In overt hypothyroidism the serum concentration of T_4 is subnormal. When the thyroid is failing, the gland compensates by the preferential secretion of T_3, which is both more active and more economical in iodine. Preferential secretion of T_3, first demonstrated in iodine-deficient rats (Greer et al, 1968), has been noted in patients with autoimmune thyroiditis (Gharib et al, 1972), with endemic goitre (Pharaoh et al, 1973) and after treatment of thyrotoxicosis (Braverman and Ingbar, 1969).

Preferential secretion of T_3, enough to maintain clinical euthyroidism in spite of subnormal levels of T_4, is most often seen after treatment for thyrotoxicosis. Some patients go on to become overtly hypothyroid. Others remain euthyroid and the T_4 eventually rises to normal levels. A few appear to continue the preferential secretion of T_3 indefinitely perhaps because of a 'resetting' of the pituitary feedback mechanism (Hoffenberg, 1973; Patel and Burger, 1973).

Aetiology
Hypothyroidism in old age may have a number of causes. These include autoimmune thyroiditis, radiotherapy, surgery and drugs. Pituitary failure is a rare cause.

Autoimmune thyroiditis. Autoimmune thyroiditis (AIT) causing hypothyroidism may present with a goitre as in Hashimoto's disease or, more commonly, with thyroid atrophy. The literature of the 1960s is authoritatively reviewed by Delespesse et al (1972). The two disease variants form a continuous spectrum (Buchanan and Harden, 1965). Four out of five patients with hypothyroidism have thyroid antibodies, often in high titre (Doniach, 1973). There is often a family history of thyroid disease (Hall et al, 1960) and an association with other autoimmune disorders such as vitiligo and pernicious anaemia (Cunliffe et al, 1968). Both cell-mediated immunity involving T lymphocytes and humoral immunity involving B lymphocytes are necessary for the full expression of autoimmune thyroiditis (Volpe, 1975). The natural history of the condition has been described on the basis of follow-up of 163 subjects with either positive thyroid antibodies, raised TSH or both together (Tunbridge et al, 1981). In women with both abnormalities, hypothyroidism developed at the rate of 5 per cent a year.

Radiotherapy. The cumulative incidence of hypothyroidism following radioactive iodine treatment of thyrotoxicosis is discussed in the section on thyrotoxicosis. Zellman (1968) comments that in America, where patients of all ages have been given radioactive iodine, this is likely to become the commonest cause of hypothyroidism.

Surgery. Total thyroidectomy for malignant disease will inevitably be followed by hypothyroidism. After partial thyroidectomy the removal of too much tissue with too small a remnant is the most important cause of hypothyroidism, which develops within a year in almost half the patients (Michie et al, 1972). An additional factor may be the degree of lymphocytic infiltration found in the gland at the time of operation (Green and Wilson, 1964; Olsen et al, 1970). Later hypothyroidism several years after surgery is associated with an autoimmune process (Van Welsum et al, 1974).

Drugs. Hypothyroidism may come on within a few weeks of overdosage with antithyroid drugs. Certain other drugs, such as the sulphonylureas (Hunton et al, 1965; Burdick and Brice, 1968), PAS (Munkner 1965) and resorcinol (Bull and Fraser, 1950) are mildly goitrogenic and have been reported as causing hypothyroidism. Recently lithium carbonate, now increasingly used in psychiatry, has been added to the list (Candy, 1972; Crowe et al, 1973; Brownlie, 1976).

Iodide goitre. An unusual form of drug-induced hypothyroidism is iodide goitre (Morgans and Trotter, 1959; Begg and Hall, 1963; Murray and Stewart, 1967; Wolff, 1969). Patients with asthma may take Felsol powder containing iodopyrine, a compound of iodine and phenazone. Both substances have a synergistic effect on thyroid metabolism (Pasternak et al, 1969). A similar synergism between iodide and lithium has been documented (Shopsin et al, 1973).

Excess iodine given for a few days inhibits thyroid hormone synthesis — the Wolff-Chaikoff effect (Wolff and Chaikoff, 1948a, b) — but the effect of iodine is normally short-lived, an escape mechanism coming into play. The gland ceases to absorb iodine and the intrathyroidal concentration of iodide falls below the level at which hormone synthesis is inhibited.

In patients predisposed by autoimmune thyroiditis (Braverman et al, 1971), radiotherapy (Braverman et al, 1969), or synergistic drugs, this escape mechanism fails. Trapping continues, hormone production falls, TSH levels rise and a goitre develops, accompanied in about half the cases by overt hypothyroidism. Thyroid hormone levels are normal or low in these patients, but protein-bound iodine levels are high owing to iodine contamination. Withdrawal of iodide leads to recovery and provides the most convincing evidence of the diagnosis. The review of Vagenakis and Braverman (1975) should be consulted for further details.

Omission of thyroxine. Failure to take thyroxine by a patient previously known to have hypothyroidism is always a possibility in old age, when he becomes forgetful or leaves the care of the doctor who originally started treatment. There may be a tendency among new doctors to question the original diagnosis because the patient looks so well and to stop the thyroxine and see what happens. This is one of the reasons why it is so important to document a diagnosis of hypothyroidism by appropriate tests rather than to start treatment on clinical impression alone.

When the patient develops another illness the thyroxine may be overlooked among a plethora of other treatment. Overt hypothyroidism may occur in a forgetful patient attending a geriatric day hospital because both the hospital and the general practitioner think that the other is supervising treatment and supplying the drugs.

The pituitary in hypothyroidism
The activity of the thyroid is normally controlled by the pituitary through its secretion of thyroid stimulating hormone (TSH). The thyroid-pituitary feedback mechanism is extremely sensitive and a reduction of less than 0.25 ng per 1 in the serum concentration of T_3 is followed by an immediate rise in the level of TSH (Vagenakis et al, 1975). A high TSH level (usually above 20 μu per ml) is the most consistent feature in primary hypothyroidism (Hershman and Pittman, 1971a; Mayberry et al, 1971). Only in the rare situation of hypothyroidism secondary to pituitary failure is this rise not seen. Although raised levels of TSH are an invariable accompaniment of primary thyroid failure, they do not necessarily indicate clinical hypothyroidism. They are found also in patients with subclinical hypothyroidism (Evered et al, 1973a) whether this be due to autoimmune thyroiditis, to previous treatment for thyrotoxicosis or to residence in an area of endemic goitre (Carlson and Hershman, 1975). The pituitary itself is under the control of the hypothalamus through its secretion of thyrotophin-releasing hormone (TRH) (Hall et al, 1970b; Ormston et al, 1971a and b; Shenkman et al, 1972). Very small reductions in circulating T_3 levels not only increase the level of TSH but heighten the sensitivity of the pituitary to TRH (Vagenakis et al, 1975). It is, however, not necessary to perform a TRH test to diagnose hypothyroidism. A single estimation of TSH is equally informative in all except borderline situations (Snitcher et al, 1976).

Hypopituitarism. Pituitary disorders, usually diagnosed before the age of 45 (McKeown, 1965), have occasionally been reported in old age (Coni, 1973). Hypopituitarism in late life may be due to Sheehan's syndrome of many years standing or more often to a cranopharyngioma. Hypothyroidism is then usually part of a much wider spectrum of endocrine failure, but it can occur in isolation, when the clinical picture is indistinguishable from primary hypothyroidism (Sawin and McHugh, 1966). However, there is a low, instead of a high, TSH and an absent or impaired response to TRH instead of an exaggerated one.

Incidence of hypothyroidism
In old age hypothyroidism occurs more often than thyrotoxicosis, two to three times more commonly in patients referred to geriatric units (Bahemuka and Hodkinson, 1975). Women with hypothyroidism outnumber men by five to one or more.

Hypothyroidism is readily treated at any age and a routine search for it in elderly patients has been advocated for many years, but only recently has it become possible to apply this policy to unselected patients admitted to a geriatric unit. At Northwick Park Hospital 3.8 per cent of 300 consecutive admissions had biochemical evidence of hypothyroidism and in some the diagnosis would not have been suspected on clinical grounds alone (Jefferys, 1972). This research was later extended to cover 2000 consecutive admissions, among whom were 46 (2.3 per cent) in whom a diagnosis of hypothyroidism was confirmed. Less than a third were typical cases of overt hypothyroidism. The majority had nonspecific symptoms (Bahemuka and Hodkinson, 1975). These patients represent acute admissions to a geriatric unit. Studies of hospital series in New Zealand (Porteous, 1979) and USA (Atkinson et al, 1978) have shown comparable prevalences of hypothyroidism — 3.8

and 2.2 per cent respectively. A similar percentage were found among 95 long-stay patients in a geriatric unit, but there were none among 100 old people's home residents examined concurrently (Kind and Ghosh, 1976). However, Gonzalez and Sullivan (1979) found 3 per cent of hypothyroidism among 125 nursing home residents in USA. Studies of the incidence of hypothyroidism in the community are few. A survey in northeast England suggested that 1 in 500 of the adult population is hypothyroid, and a similar estimate was made in Finland (Evered and Hall, 1972). Among 291 old people living at home in Scotland a study of protein-bound iodine levels revealed 1 subject only with hypothyroidism (Thompson et al, 1972). A later survey revealed a further 4 cases among 97 additional subjects (Taylor et al, 1974).

Pathology

The morbid anatomy of myxoedema has been well documented (Sclare, 1963; Bastenie et al, 1972). At postmortem the thyroid is often atrophic or a fibrous remnant. Sometimes the gland is not greatly reduced in size, however, but shows the changes of autoimmune thyroiditis. Histologically, epithelial atrophy, fibrosis and infiltration with lymphocytes, plasma cells and giant cells are present in varying degrees. In the skin, tongue, vocal cords, heart, gut and other organs there is infiltration with myxoedema proteins (Hamolsky et al, 1961; Vanhaelst et al, 1967), extracellular deposits of a mucopolysaccharide protein complex containing hyaluronic acid and chondrointin sulphuric acid. Serial skin biopsies have demonstrated the disappearance of this material over six to eight weeks of treatment with thyroxine (Gabrilove and Ludwig, 1957). The pituitary may be enlarged. The thyrotroph cells are increased in size and number, sometimes with adenoma formation (Herlant and Pasteels, 1972; Lawrence et al, 1973).

Clinical features

The main characteristic of hypothyroidism at any age, but especially in the elderly, is its insidious onset. Symptoms are likely to have been present for 3 to 5 years before the diagnosis is made (Lloyd and Goldberg, 1961). The mental and physical slowing, the deafness and cold intolerance in an elderly patient are likely to be attributed to aging alone. Indeed all these symptoms are common euthyroid subjects (Billewicz et al, 1969). In old age the problem of multiple pathology is ever present. It has been pointed out that apathy and depression may prevent the patient from seeking medical help. He may make a few spontaneous complaints, but many more may be elicited by careful enquiry (McKerron, 1971). Asher (1960) claimed that hypothyroidism is one of the few conditions in medicine where the physical examination may be more important than the history.

If the doctor does not suspect the diagnosis as the patient walks into the room, he may not make it at all.

Non-specific picture. This is still true of overt hypothyroidism, but every clinician knows that he meets many old people in whom hypothyroidism is suspected and not confirmed and, with routine screening for thyroid function, many more in whom the disease is present without any of the classical signs. It may well be true nowadays that a non-specific picture is commoner than a classical one. Two-thirds of the patients admitted to a geriatric unit and found to have hypothyroidism by Bahemuka and Hodkinson (1975) presented a non-specific picture of impaired mobility and general health, sometimes with apathy and depression.

Face and skin. In advanced hypothyroidism not only is there swelling of the face but there may be puffiness of the neck, wrists and ankles. Most of this is due to myxoedematous infiltration, but there may also be hypertrophy of brown adipose tissue under stimulation by TSH (Doniach, 1975). The skin is dry and coarse and the excretion of sebum measurably diminished (Goolamali et al, 1976). Infiltration of the face may be generalized or confined to the cheeks (Lloyd and Mawdsley, 1967). Any patient with baggy eyelids should be suspected of hypothyroidism. The yellowish colour of the skin is due to staining with carotene (Wayne, 1960). There may be some loss of hair, but thinning of the outer third of the eyebrows is of no diagnostic value in old age. *Erythema ab igne* may be suggestive.

Special senses. Patients with hypothyroidism, like many others in old age, are likely to be deaf. Much of this is due to old age and not reversible, but the occasional patient hears better after treatment with thyroxin. He is likely to have a reversible serous effusion into the middle ear. Serous effusions may also affect the eye, causing retinal detachment (Sachdev and Hall, 1975). Defects of taste and smell, reversible by thyroxine, have been documented (McConnell et al, 1975).

The voice. The gruff voice of myxoedema is very characteristic and is at least as valuable a diagnostic aid in the elderly as the facial appearance. Asher's (1949) description has never been bettered: 'The voice is like a bad gramophone record, running down, of a drowsy and slightly intoxicated person with a bad cold and a quinsy.'

The limbs. Limb pains are common in hypothyroidism. They may be caused by muscle stiffness, entrapment neuropathy or arthralgia (Bland and Frymoyer, 1970; Golding, 1970). Muscular weakness, too, is a feature and may be related to a low total exchangeable potassium (Misra et al, 1974). Myopathy has been recorded (Gaede, 1977) but limb pain or paraesthesiae are more often due to entrapment neuropathy. This usually takes the form of carpal tunnel syndrome, but similar paraesthesiae have been reported in the legs (Golding, 1971). Claims have been made for the existence of a specific peripheral neuropathy because of delayed conduction in the ulnar nerve which is not subject to compression in the carpal tunnel (Fincham and Cape, 1968). Arthralgia in a patient with hypothyroidism is most likely to be due to concomitant osteoarthrosis, but joint pain and swelling with synovial thickening may be the direct result of hormonal deficiency. In such patients the joint fluid is 'non-inflammatory', increased in volume and of high viscosity, but with normal protein and cells (Golding, 1971). Wordsworth et al (1980) showed thyroid autoantibodies to be present. However, Delamere et al (1982) found that in four of 26 patients with arthralgia associated with thyroid disease rheumatoid arthritis and myxoedema had had a simultaneous onset.

All these symptoms respond to thyroxine. Carpal tunnel decompression is not needed.

The ankle jerk. Delayed relaxation of the ankle jerk has been noted in hypothyroidism for almost a century and is a useful physical sign. However, diagnostic tests involving measurement of relaxation time have become obsolete given the general availability and reliability of thyroid hormone and TSH determinations.

Ataxia. Some degree of ataxia is present in many elderly patients, and it is not easy to be sure, except in retrospect, whether it is due to hypothyroidism or to concomitant degenerative changes in the central nervous system. Cerebellar signs such as intention tremor, nystagmus and general inco-ordination have been reported (Jellinek and Kelly, 1960) and specific myxoedema bodies have been described in post-mortem material from the cerebellum (Price and Netsky, 1966). Syncope, drop attacks and epilepsy have also been recorded and may bring the patient to hospital with a fracture (Jellinek, 1962). A comprehensive review of the neurological aspects of hypothyroidism is given by Cremer et al (1969).

Constipation. Constipation is common in old age, but patients with hypothyroidism have more infrequent motions than the average (Baker and Harvey, 1971). In overt hypothyroidism there may be myxoedematous infiltration of the gut. This can lead to ileus, (Wells et al, 1977).

Metabolic effects include the syndrome of inappropriate ADH secretion (De Troyer and Demanet, 1975) and serum enzyme elevations, particularly of creatine kinase (Gaede, 1977).

Appetite and weight. Some weight gain, usually with decreased appetite, is common, but gross obesity is rare (Wayne, 1960). The patient may be sufficiently apathetic to stop eating and so lose weight.

Circulation

A slow pulse is a traditional sign of hypothyroidism, but it is of limited diagnostic value. It is as likely to be above 70 beats per minute as below (Wayne, 1960). Dysrhythmias are rare because the hypothyroid heart loses its sensitivity to catecholamines. The heart is quiet and isovolumetric relaxation time is prolonged (Manns et al, 1976), and interesting parallel with the ankle jerk. The heart may be enlarged by myxoedematous infiltration of the myocardium, concomitant hypertension, ischaemic heart disease or pericardial effusion (Vanhaelst et al, 1967). In addition to pericardial effusion there may be ascites and pleural effusions, sometimes unilateral. Recently hydrocoele has been added to the list of serous effusions (Isaacs and Havard, 1976). The pathogenesis of these effusions is obscure. The fluid has a protein content similar to that of other exudative effusions. It has been suggested that extravasation of hygroscopic mucopolysaccharides is primarily responsible, but increased capillary permeability and inappropriate secretion of antidiuretic hormone may also play a part (Sachdev and Hall, 1975). It is uncertain whether heart failure occurs from hypothyroidism alone, and catheter studies show normal pressures in the right atrium (Graettinger et al, 1958). The electrocardiogram is abnormal in the majority of cases, the commonest abnormality being flattening or inversion of the T waves, which become normal after treatment. The total exchangeable body potassium is reduced in elderly patients with hypothyroidism and returns to normal after treatment with thyroxine. This may be the reason for the electrocardiographic changes (Misra et al, 1974). It has been suggested that there is a link between hypothyroidism and abdominal aneurysm (Niarchos and Finn, 1973).

Mental change

Irreversible dementia associated with hypothyroidism was reported by Jellinek (1962), but in old age dementia is seldom due to lack of thyroid hormones. Organic brain syndromes have been noted in 22 per cent of those over 80 (Kay et al, 1970), and such people have the same chance as the rest of the population to develop hypothyroidism. In the Northwick Park study, Bahemuka and Hodkinson (1975) found no excess of mental impairment among their hypothyroid patients and no patient with dementia improved on thyroxine. This was in contrast to those in whom hypothyroidism was associated with functional mental disorder, depression, delirium and paranoid states. In these patients functional mental disturbances were three times as common as in a group of matched controls, and they responded to thyroxine. These authors stress depression as a presenting symptom of hypothyroidism rather than the more florid psychoses described by Asher (1949) in his celebrated paper on myxoedematous madness.

Coma. Patients with myxoedema, often accompanied by mental impairment, may slip into coma, sometimes accompanied by fits, particularly during the winter months (Impallomeni, 1977). The precipitants are probably cold and infection, which increase the demand for thyroid hormone (Harvey, 1971). Elderly patients with hypothyroidism are also extremely sensitive to sedative drugs (Zellman, 1968) which may precipitate coma.

Myxoedema coma involves a heterogenous group of mechanisms which vary in individual cases. Hypothermia, hyponatraemia, hypoglycaemia, respiratory insufficiency and shock may variously occur. McConahey (1978) reviews the treatment of this highly lethal condition.

Anaemia

In hypothyroidism the red cell mass falls in response to reduced metabolic demand. The process is mediated through the hormone erythropoietin, the level of which falls in hypothyroidism, particularly when the patient is anaemic (Das et al, 1975).

Anaemia is present in about one-third of those with hypothyroidism (Tudhope and Wilson, 1960). Although men become hypothyroid less often than women they are more likely to become anaemic if they do. There is no close correlation between the severity and duration of the hypothyroidism and the degree of anaemia. The anaemia has been variously ascribed to iron deficiency, pernicious anaemia, folate deficiency and to the direct effects of thyroid hormone lack. Recent work from Northwick Park Hospital suggests that hormone deficiency is the principal mechanism (Horton et al, 1976). Macrocytosis is the commonest manifestation of hypothyroidism being present in a third of cases. The degree of macrocytosis was no greater in those with deficiencies of vitamin B_{12} and folate than in those with thyroid hormone deficiency alone. The MCV fell with thyroxine treatment even when there was no anaemia. Acanthocytes, small, irregularly contracted red cells first noted by Wardrop and Hutchinson (1969) in hypothyroidism, were present in one-fifth of the blood films but they seldom constituted more than 0.5 per cent of the red cells. The commonest biochemical abnormality was a low serum iron level, but half the patients with low serum iron levels were not anaemic and the classical microcytic anaemic of iron deficiency occurred in less than 5 per cent. Low levels of B_{12} were found in less than 10 per cent of the subjects, and low folate levels in a similar number, but less than half the patients with these deficiencies were anaemic. The authors concluded that the anaemia of hypothyroidism is most commonly attributable solely to the endocrine deficiency.

From the same hospital Bahemuka and Hodkinson (1975) observed that macrocytosis was a useful pointer to the possibility of hypothyroidism.

Laboratory diagnosis

Serum TSH and T_4 are the most useful tests in the diagnosis of hypothyroidism. Where T_4 is in the subnormal range and supports the clinical impression, nothing more is needed. But in hypothyroidism there is often a slight increase in thyroid-binding protein and this may be enough to raise a subnormal figure into the low normal range. So it is better to include a T_3 uptake test and to calculate the free thyroxine index. This will correct for the error introduced by the binding protein abnormality and gives a better separation between normal and subnormal.

The total T_3 level is a less good test for hypothyroidism because there is a greater overlap with normal. It is nevertheless helpful to have a total T_3 estimation if the clinical situation is in doubt. If the T_4 and T_3 levels are both subnormal, there can be no doubt that the patient is hypothyroid. If only the T_4 level is low and the T_3 is normal, the patient's condition is one of T_3 euthyroidism or compensated hypothyroidism.

Hypothyroidism, except in the minority of cases due to pituitary failure, is associated with elevation of TSH and a value of 10 mu/l or more occurring in association with a low FTI virtually confirms the diagnosis of primary hypothyroidism (Britton et al, 1975a). Serum TSH is the most sensitive indicator of primary hypothyroidism and modest elevation of TSH accompanied by a T_4 value within the normal range is likely to indicate compensated thyroid failure (Havard, 1981). TRH tests are not generally helpful in the further investigation of cases of suspected hypothyroidism with minor elevation of TSH as the response will almost always be exaggerated. A low TSH level, when other tests confirm hypothyroidism, will suggest failure of the pituitary or hypothalamus.

Treatment

The treatment of hypothyroidism consists of appropriate hormone replacement.

Thyroxine

The preparation of choice is synthetic thyroxine sodium, T_4. It is normally given by mouth and is well absorbed, though somewhat less well when taken with food (Wenzel and Kirshsieper, 1977).Parenteral preparations are rarely required but are available in America. A single dose by mouth begins to act in 4 days and reaches its maximum effect in 10. At least one-third of the T_4 given by mouth is deiodinated within the body and changed to T_3 (Braverman et al, 1970). It exerts most, if not all, of its metabolic effect after this conversion (Refetoff, 1975). Thyroxine can be given to all patients with primary hypothyroidism. Caution is needed in pituitary failure since thyroxine may provoke acute adrenal insufficiency unless corticosteroids are given first.

Old people with hypothyroidism are exquisitely sensitive to thyroid hormones and the initial dose should be small, 25 μg (0.025 mg) or half a 50 μg tablet daily. The dose can be increased to 50 μg after 2 weeks and to 100 μg after a month. The proper dose is that which will raise the T_4 level and lower the TSH level to within the normal range (Cotton et al, 1971). This is normally achieved with doses of 100 to 200 μg daily (Stock et al, 1974). In one trial more than half the subjects showed TSH suppression on 100 μg daily. Larger doses were required only for those with more advanced degrees of thyroid failure (Evered et al, 1973b). Old people are likely to need smaller rather than larger doses. Thyroxine is long acting. It need never be given more than once a day to produce a steady blood level of both T_4 and T_3 throughout 24 hours. In children who could not be relied upon to take tablets regularly once weekly medication was successful (Sekadde et al, 1974). This method has not been tried in the elderly but might be worth considering where a forgetful patient is, perhaps,

visited once a week by a district nurse. The dose required would be about 1 mg per week.

Tri-iodothyronine

Thyroxine is converted to T_3 in the body, so it might seem more rational to use T_3 for replacement therapy. T_3, tri-iodothyronine (Liothyronine), is three to five times more active than thyroxine (Lavietes and Epstein, 1964), is more completely absorbed (Hays, 1968) and its turnover in the body is faster (Nicoloff et al, 1972; Surks et al, 1973). After a single dose blood levels rise to a peak in 3 to 4 hours and return to baseline levels within 24 hours (Saberi and Utiger 1974). Such peaks and troughs are unphysiological and are not therapeutically desirable. The only indication for T_3 replacement is in the crisis of hypothyroid coma, though even here Holvey et al (1969) claimed good results with thyroxine. T_3 should be given intravenously in small doses, 10 μg every 6 to 12 hours (Smart, 1972) (Fig. 34.6).

THYROID CARCINOMA

Carcinoma of the thyroid is seen only very occasionally among patients in the geriatric age group. It is usually subdivided into four types, papillary accounting for 60

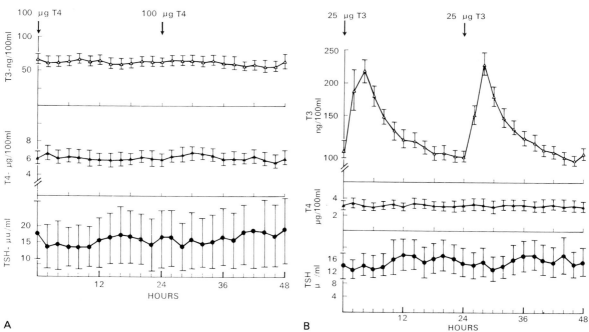

Fig. 34.6 Results of serum T_3, T_4 and TSH determinations at 2-hr intervals for 48 hr in 8 hypothyroid patients receiving (A) 100 μg T_4, (B) 25 μg T_3, once daily. The vertical bars indicate ± 1 s.e. mean. (After Saberi and Utiger, 1974, by courtesy of the Editor of Journal of Clinical Endocrinology and Metabolism)

per cent, follicular for 20 per cent, anaplastic for 15 per cent and medullary for 5 per cent of cases overall (Kark and Gueret Wardle, 1980). However, in old age, anaplastic carcinoma predominates and papillary cancer accounts for only some 20 per cent whilst follicular and medullary types are very infrequent (Havard, 1981; Kark and Gueret Wardle, 1980). Thyroid carcinoma may arise in either a normal sized gland or in one already affected by goitre.

Thyroid cancer in the elderly is typically a highly aggressive tumour with a propensity to metastasise to bone. Subtotal thyroidectomy, which may need to be accompanied by dissection of neck glands, is treatment of choice for papillary and follicular growths but total thyroidectomy is preferred for medullary carcinoma. However, surgery has very little to offer for the more frequent anaplastic tumours which have an extremely unfavourable prognosis (Kark and Gueret Wardle, 1980). These authors point out that, although anaplastic thyroid carcinoma is the commonest cause of recent rapid enlargement of a goitre in an elderly patient, a substantial minority prove to have a lymphoma which may respond reasonably well to a combination of surgery and radiotherapy.

REFERENCES

Abuid J, Larsen P R 1974 Triiodothyronine and thyroxine in hyperthyroidism: a comparison of acute changes during therapy with antithyroid agents. Journal of Clinical Investigation 54: 201–208

Acland J D 1971 The interpretation of the serum protein bound iodine — a review. Journal of Clinical Pathology 24: 187–218

Adams D D, Kennedy T H, Stewart J C, Utiger R D, Vidor G I 1975 Hyperthyroidism in Tasmania following iodide supplementation: measurement of thyroid stimulating auto-antibodies and thyrotropin. Journal of Clinical Endocrinology and Metabolism 41: 221–228

Adams P 1973 The treatment of hyperthyroidism. Prescribing Journal 13: 7–14

Aitchison J, Moore M F, West S A, Taylor T R 1973 Consistency of treatment allocation in thyrotoxicosis. Quarterly Journal of Medicine (NS) 42: 575–583

Alexander L 1975 Ophthalmic Graves' disease. Hospital Update 1: 325–329

Alexander W D, McLarty D G, Horton P, Pharmakiotis A D 1973 Sequential assessment during drug treatment of thyrotoxicosis. Clinical Endocrinology 2: 43–50

American Thyroid Association 1976 Revised nomenclature for tests of thyroid hormones in the serum. Journal of Clinical Endocrinology and Metabolism 42: 595–598

Asher R 1949 Myxoedematous madness. British Medical Journal ii: 555–562

Asher R A J 1960 The diagnosis and treatment of myxoedema. Postgraduate Medical Journal 36: 471–476

Ashkar F S, Miller R, Smoak W M, Gilson A 1971 Liver disease in hyperthyroidism. Southern Medical Journal 64: 462–465

Atkinson R L, Dahms W T, Fisher D A, Nichols A L 1978 Occult thyroid disease in an elderly hospitalized population. Journal of Gerontology 33: 372–376

Azizi F, Vagenakis A G, Portnay G I, Rapoport B, Ingbar S H, Braverman L E 1975 Pituitary thyroid responsiveness to intramuscular thyrotropin-releasing hormone based on analyses of serum thyroxine, triiodothyronine and thyrotropin concentrations. New England Journal of Medicine 292: 273–277

Bahemuka M, Hodkinson H M 1957 Screening for hypothyroidism in elderly patients. British Medical Journal 2: 601–603

Baker J T, Harvey R F 1971 Bowel habit in thyrotoxicosis and hypothyroidism. British Medical Journal i: 322–323

Bartels E C 1962 Obscure hyperthyroidism in the elderly patient with long-standing nodular goitre. Surgical Clinics of North America 42: 667–672

Baruch A L H, Davis C, Hodkinson H M 1976 Causes of high free thyroxine index values in sick euthyroid elderly patients. Age and Aging 5: 224–227

Bastenie P A, Bonnyns M, Vanhaelst L 1972 Thyroiditis and acquired hypothyroidism in adults. In: Bastenie P A, Ermans A M (ed), Thyroiditis and Thyroid Function, pp. 211–228. Pergamon, Oxford

Baylis R I S, Hall R 1975 The Thyroid gland. Medicine-Monthly Add On (2nd ser.) 7: 297–319

Becker D V, Hurley J R 1972 Impact of technology on clinical practice in Graves' disease. Mayo Clinic Proceedings 47: 835–847

Becker K L, Winnacker J L, Matthews M J, Higgins G A 1968 Gynaecomastia and hyperthyroidism: an endocrinal and histological investigation. Journal of Clinical Endocrinology and Metabolism 28: 277–285

Begg T B, Hall R 1963 Iodide goitre and hypothyroidism. Quarterly Journal of Medicine 32: 351–362

Bellabarba D, Bernard B, Langlois M 1972 Pattern of serum thyroxine, triiodothyroine and thyrotropin after treatment of thyrotoxicosis. Clinical Endocrinology 1: 345–353

Bermudez F, Surks M I, Oppenheimer J H 1975 High incidence of decreased serum triiodothyronine concentration in patients with non-thyroidal disease. Journal of Clinical Endocrinology and Metabolism 41: 27–40

Bianchi R, Zucchelli G C, Gianessi D, Pilo A, Cazzuola F, Del Corso L, Molea N, Carpi A, Toni M G, Mariani G 1979 Triiodothyronine turnover studies in euthyroid patients with autonomous thyroid nodules. Metabolism 28: 163–168

Billewicz W Z, Chapman R S, Crooks J, Day M E, Gossage J, Wayne E, Young J A 1969 Statistical methods applied to the diagnosis of hypothyroidism. Quarterly Journal of Medicine 38: 255–266

Birkhäuser M, Burr Th, Busset R, Burger A 1977 Diagnosis of hyperthyroidism when serum-thyroxine alone is raised. Lancet ii: 53–56

Bland J H, Frymoyer J W 1970 Rheumatic syndromes of myxoedema. New England Journal of Medicine 282: 1171–1174

Blichert-Toft M, Hummer L, Dige-Petersen H 1975 Human thyrotropin level and response to thyrotropine-releasing hormone in the aged. Gerontologia Clinica 17: 191–203

Blum M, Weinberg U, Shenkman L, Hollander C S 1974 Hyperthyroidism after iodinated contrast medium. New England Journal of Medicine 291: 24–25

Bouillon R, De Moor P 1974 Parathyroid function in patients with hyperthyroidism and hypothyroidism. Journal of Clinical Endocrinology and Metabolism 38: 999–1004

Braverman L E, Dawber N A, Ingbar S H 1966 Observations concerning the binding of thyroid hormone in sera of varying ages. Journal of Clinical Investigation 48: 1273–1279

Braverman L E, Woeber K A, Ingbar S H 1969 Induction of myxoedema by iodide in patients euthyroid following radioiodine or surgical treatment of diffuse toxic goitre. New England Journal of Medicine 281: 816–821

Braverman L E, Ingbar S H 1969 Preferential synthesis of triiodothyronine (T_3) after thyroid radiation. Clinical Research 17: 458

Braverman L E, Ingbar S H, Sterling K 1970 Conversion of thyroxine (T_4) to triiodothyronine (T_3) in athyreotic human subjects. Journal of Clinical Investigation 49: 855–864

Braverman L E, Ingbar S H, Vagenakis A G, Adams L, Maloof F 1971 Enhanced susceptibility to iodide myxoedema in patients with Hashimoto's disease. Journal of Clinical Endocrinology and Metabolism 32: 515–521

Bremner W F, Spencer C A, Ratcliffe W A, Greig W R, Ratcliffe J G 1976 The assessment of 125I treatment of thyrotoxicosis. Clinical Endocrinology 5: 225–234

British Medical Journal Editorial 1977 Painless thyroiditis. British Medical Journal 2: 248–349

British Medical Journal Editorial 1981 Management of angina and hypothyroidism. British Medical Journal 282: 1818–1819

Britton K E, Quinn V, Brown B L, Ekins R P 1975a A strategy for thyroid function tests. British Medical Journal 3: 350–352

Britton K E, Quinn V, Ellis S M, Cayley A C D, Miralles J M, Brown B L, Ekins R P 1975b Is T₄ toxicosis a normal biochemical finding in elderly women? Lancet ii: 141–142

Brownlie B E W, Chambers S T, Sadler W A, Donald R A 1976 Lithium associated thyroid disease — a report of 14 cases of hypothyroidism and 4 cases of thyrotoxicosis. Australian and New Zealand Journal of Medicine 6: 223–229

Brownlie B E W, Hamer J W, Cook H B, Hamwood S M 1975 Thyrotoxicosis associated with splenic atrophy. Lancet ii: 1046–1047

Brunelle P, Bohuon C 1972 Baisse de la thiiodothyronine serique avec l'âge. Clinica Chimica Acta 42: 201–203

Buchanan W W, Harden R M 1965 Primary hypothyroidism and Hashimoto's disease — a continuous spectrum. Archives of Internal Medicine 115: 411–417

Bull G M, Fraser R 1950 Myxoedema from resorcinol ointment applied to leg ulcers. Lancet i: 851–855

Burdick C O, Brice L T 1968 Hypothyroidism after sulphonylurea. Lancet i: 97

Burger A, Nicod P, Sutor P, Vallotton M B, Vagenakis A, Braverman L 1976 Reduced active thyroid hormones levels in acute illness. Lancet i: 653–655

Burke C W, Eastman C J 1974 Thyroid hormones. British Medical Bull. 30: 93–99

Burr W A, Griffiths R S, Black E G, Hoffenberg R, Meinhold H, Wenzel K W 1975 Serum triiodothyronine and reverse triiodothyronine concentrations after surgical operations. Lancet ii: 1277–1279

Burr W A, Ramsden D B, Griffith R S, Back E G, Hoffenberg R 1976 Effect of a single dose of dexamethasone on serum concentration of thyroid hormones. Lancet ii: 58–61

Burr W A, Ramsden D B, Evans S E, Hogan T, Hoffenberg R 1977 Concentration of thyroxine-binding globulin: value of direct assay. British Medical Journal 1: 485–488

Burrows A W, Cooper E, Shakespear R A, Aickin C M, Fraser S, Hesch R D, Burke C W 1977 Low serum L-T₃ levels in the elderly sick: protein binding, thyroid and pituitary responsiveness and reverse T₃ concentrations. Clinical Endocrinology 7: 289–300

Burrows A W, Shakespear R A, Hesch R D, Cooper E, Aickin C M, Burke C W 1975 Thyroid hormones in the elderly sick: T₄ euthyroidism. British Medical Journal 4: 437–439

Candy J 1972 Severe hypothyroidism — an early complication of Lithium therapy. British Medical Journal 3: 277

Caplan R H, Glasser J E, Davis K, Foster L, Wickus G 1978 Thyroid function tests in elderly hyperthyroid patients. Journal of the American Geriatrics Society 16: 116–120

Caplan R H, Wickus G, Glasser J E, Davis K, Wahner H W 1981 Serum concentrations of the iodothyronines in elderly subjects: decreased triiodothyronine (T₃) and free T₃ index. Journal of the American Geriatrics Society 29: 19–24

Carlson H E, Hershman J M 1975 The hypothalamic-pituitary-thyroid axis. Medical Clinics of North America 59: 1045–1051

Carter J N, Eastman C J, Corcoran J M, Lazarus J 1974 Effect of severe chronic illness on thyroid function. Lancet ii: 971–974

Chapman E M 1971 Which radioiodide? New England Journal of Medicine 285: 1142–1145

Chomette G, Pinaudeau Y, Brocheriou C, Auriol M, Pfister A 1966 La thyroide du viellard; caractères anatomiques et essai d'interpretation physiopathologique. Archives d'anatomie pathologique 14: 233–245

Chopra I J 1974 A radioimmunoassay for measurement of 3:3':5'-triiodothyronine (reverse T₃). Journal of Clinical Investigation 54: 583–592

Chopra I J 1975 Gonadal steroids and gonadotrophins in hyperthyroidism. Medical Clinics of North America 59: 1109–1121

Chopra I J 1976 An assessment of the daily production and significance of thyroidal secretion of 3:3':5'-triiodothyronine (reverse T₃) in man. Journal of Clinical Investigation 58: 32–40

Chopra I J, Abraham G E, Chopra U, Solomon D H, Odell W D 1972 Alteration in circulating estradiol 17B in male patients with Graves' disease. New England Journal of Medicine 286: 124–129

Chopra I J, Chopra U, Smith S R, Reza M, Solomon D H 1975 Reciprocal changes in serum concentration of 3:3':5'-triiodothyronine (reverse T₃) and 3:5:3'-triiodothyronine (T₃) in systemic illness. Journal of Clinical Endocrinology and Metabolism 41: 1043–1049

Chopra I J, Solomon D H, Chua Teco G N 1973 Thyroxine — just a prohormone too? Journal of Clinical Endocrinology and Metabolism 36: 1050–1057

Chopra I J, Solomon D H, Hepner G W, Morgenstein A A 1979 Misleadingly low free thyroxine index and usefulness of reverse triiodothyronine measurement in nonthyroidal illnesses. Annals of Internal Medicine 90: 905–912

Clark F, Horn D B 1965 Assessment of thyroid function by the combined use of serum protein bound iodine and resin uptake of ₁₃₁I triiodothyronine. Journal of Clinical Endocrinology and Metabolism 25: 39–45

Clark F, Brown H J 1970a Evaluation of thyopac-3 test in the in vitro assessment of thyroid function. British Medical Journal i: 713–715

Clark F, Brown H J 1970b Free thyroxine index. British Medical Journal ii: 543, 672

Clark O H, Demling R 1976 Management of thyroid nodules in the elderly. American Journal of Surgery 132: 615–619

Cohen R D, Lloyd-Thomas H G 1966 Exercise electrocardiogram in myxoedema. British Medical Journal ii: 327–329

Coni N K 1973 Disorders of thyroid function. Modern Geriatrics 3: 544–552

Cooke S A R 1973 Thyroid surgery-after care. Update 7: 173–176

Cotton G E, Gorman C A, Mayberry W E 1971 Suppression of thyrotropin in serums of patients with myxoedema of varying aetiology treated with thyroid hormones. New England Journal of Medicine 285: 529–533

Cremer G M, Goldstein N P, Paris J 1969 Myxoedema and ataxia. Neurology (Minneapolis) 19: 37–46

Crowe M J, Lloyd G G, Block S, Rosser R M, 1973 Hypothyroidism in patients treated with lithium. Psychological Medicine 3: 337–342

Croxson M S, Ibbertson H H K 1975 Serum digoxin in patients with thyroid disease. British Medical Journal 3: 566–567

Cullen D R, Irvine W J 1970 Exophthalmos. British Journal of Hospital Medicine 5: 41–48

Cunliffe W J, Hall R, Newell D J, Stevenson G J 1968 Vitiligo, thyroid disease and autoimmunity. British Journal of Dermatology 80: 135–139

Das G, Krieger M 1969 Treatment of thyrotoxic storm with intravenous propranolol. Annals of Internal Medicine 70: 985–988

Das K C, Mukherjee M, Sarkar T K, Dash R J, Bastogi G K 1975 Erythropoiesis and erythropoietin in hypothyroidism and hyperthyroidism. Journal of Clinical Endocrinology and Metabolism 40: 211–220

Davis P J, Davis F B 1974 Hyperthyroidism in patients over the age of 60 years. Medicine (Baltimore) 53: 161–182

De Gennes L, Batrinos M L, Moreau L, Deschamps H 1961 L'hyperthyroidie due sujet âge de plus de 60 ans (A propos de 86 cas). Presse médicale 69: 2425–2427

De Groot L J 1972 Thyroid and the heart. Mayo Clinic Proceedings 47: 864–871

Delamere J P, Scott D L, Felix-Davies D D 1982 Thyroid dysfunction and rheumatic diseases. Journal of the Royal Society of Medicine 75: 102–106

Denham M J, Himsworth R L 1974 Hyperthyroidism induced by potassium iodide given in the course of 125I fibrinogen test. Age and Aging 3: 221–225

Denham M J, Wills E J 1980 A clinico-pathological survey of thyroid glands in old age. Gerontology 26: 160–166

Deslespesse G, Bastenie P A, Vanhaelst L, Neve P 1972 In: Bastenie P A, Ermans A M (ed), Thyroiditis and Thyroid Function, p. 39. Pergamon, Oxford

De Troyer A, Demanet J C 1976 Clinical, biological and pathogénic features of the syndrome of inappropriate secretion of antidiuretic hormone. Quarterly Journal of Medicine 45: 521–531

D'Haene E G M, Crombag F J L, Tertoolen J F W 1974 Comparison between determination of free thyroxine index and effective thyroxine ratio in human serum. British Medical Journal 3: 708–711

Dobyns B M, Sheline G E, Workman J B, Tompkins E, McConahey W M, Becker D V 1974 Malignant and benign neoplasms of the thyroid in patients treated of hyperthyroidism: a report of the Thyrotoxicosis Co-operative (Thyrotoxicosis Therapy Follow-up Study). Journal of Clinical Endocrinology and Metabolism 38: 976–998

Doniach D 1967 The structure of the thyroid gland. Journal of Clinical Pathology 20: Suppl. 309–17

Doniach D 1973 Progress report on thyroid autoimmune disease. In: Walker G (ed), Ninth Symposium on Advanced Medicine; - Proceedings of a Conference held at the Royal College of Physicians of London, pp. 27–37. Pitman, London

Doniach D 1975 Possible stimulation of thermogenesis in brown adipose tissue by thyroid-stimulating hormone. Lancet ii: 160–161

Donini I, Cella C 1956 Radiographic and anatomical observations on the aging of the thyroid arteries. Giornale di gerontologia 4: 316–321

Dooner H P, Parada J, Ahago C, Hoyl C 1967 The liver in thyrotoxicosis. Archives of Internal Medicine 120: 25–32

Dorfman S G, Coopermann M T, Nelson R L, Depuy H, Peake R L, Young R L 1977 Painless thyroiditis and transient hyperthyroidism without goitre. Annals of Internal Medicine 86: 24–28

Einhorn J, Wicklund H 1966 Hypothyroidism following 131I treatment for hyperthyroidism. Journal of Clinical Endocrinology and Metabolism 26: 33–36

Emerson C H, Anderson A J, Howard W J, Utiger R D 1975 Serum thyroxine and triiodothyronine concentration during iodide treatment of hyperthyroidism. Journal of Clinical Endocrinology and Metabolism 40: 33–37

Engbring N H, Engstrom W W 1959 Effects of oestrogen and testosterone on circulating thyroid hormone. Journal of Clinical Endocrinology and Metabolism 19: 783–796

Engel A G 1972 Neuromuscular manifestations of Graves' disease. Mayo Clinic Proceedings 47: 919–925

Epstein S, Pimstone B L, Vinick A I, McLaren H 1975 Failure of adrenergic alpha and beta receptor blockade to elevate the TST in prolactin response to TRH in hyperthyroidism. Clinical Endocrinology 4: 501–504

Ermans A M, Camus M 1972 Modification of thyroid function induced by chronic administration of iodide in the presence of autonomous thyroid tissue. Acta endocrinologica (Copenhagen) 70: 463–475

Evered D C 1976 Treatment of thyroid disease. British Medical Journal 1: 264–266, 335–336

Evered D C, Hall R 1972 Hypothyroidism. British Medical Journal 1: 290–293

Evered D C, Clark F, Petersen V B 1974 Thyroid function in euthyroid subjects with autonomous thyroid nodules. Clinical Endocrinology 3: 149–154

Evered D C, Ormston B J, Smith P A, Hall R, Bird T 1973a Grades of hypothyroidism. British Medical Journal 1: 657–662

Evered D C, Tunbridge W M G, Hall R, Appleton D, Brewis M, Clark F, Manuel P, Young E 1978 Thyroid Hormone concentrations in a large scale community survey. Effect of age, sex, illness and medication. Clinica Chimica Acta: 223–229

Evered D C, Young E T, Ormston B J, Menzies R, Smith P A, Hall R 1973b Treatment of Hypothyroidism; a reappraisal of thyroxine therapy. British Medical Journal 3: 131–134

Evered D, Young E T, Tunbridge W M G, Ormston B J, Green E, Petersen V B, Dickinson P H 1975 Thyroid function after subtotal thyroidectomy for hyperthyroidism. British Medical Journal 1: 25–27

Fairclough P D, Besser G M 1974 Apathetic T_3 toxicosis. British Medical Journal 1: 364–365

Fairhurst B J, Naqui N 1975 Hyperthyroidism after cholecystography. British Medical Journal 3: 630

Fedelli S, Regazzini A, Mars G, Chiesa R 1963 Latex antithyroglobulin test in the elderly — il test antitireoglobulina nel vecchio. Giornale di clinica medica 44: 1125–1133

Fein H G, Rivlin R S 1975 Anaemia in thyroid diseases. Medical Clinics of North America 59: 1133–1145

Ferriman D, Hennebry T M, Tassopoulos C N 1972 True thyroid adenoma. Quarterly Journal of Medicine (NS) 41: 127–139

Fincham R W, Cape C A 1968 Neuropathy in myxoedema: a study of sensory nerve conduction in the upper extremities. Archives of Neurology and Psychiatry (Chicago) 19: 464–466

Francis R M, Barnett M J, Selby P L, Peacock M 1982 Thyrotoxicosis presenting as fracture of femoral neck. British Medical Journal 285: 97–98

Fraser S A, Anderson J B, Smith D A, Wilson G M 1971 Osteoporosis and fractures following thyrotoxicosis. Lancet i: 981–983

Furszyfer J, McConahey W M, Kurland L T, Maldonado J E 1971 On the increased association of Graves' disease with pernicious anaemia. Mayo Clinic Proceedings 46: 37–39

Gabrilove J L, Ludwig A W 1957 The histogenesis of myxoedema. Journal of Clinical Endocrinology and Metabolism 17: 925–932

Gaede J T 1977 Serum enzyme alterations in hypothyroidism before and after treatment. Journal of the American Geriatrics Society 15: 199–201

Gaffney G W, Gregerman R I, Shock N W 1962 The relationship of age to the thyroidal accumulation, renal excretion and distribution of radioiodide in euthyroid man. Journal of Clinical Endocrinology and Metabolism 22: 784–794

Gardner M J, Barker D J P 1975 Diagnosis of hypothyroidism: a comparison of statistical techniques. British Medical Journal 2: 260–262

Gharib H, Wahner H W, McConahey W M 1972 Serum levels of thyroid hormones in Hashimoto's thyroiditis. Mayo Clinic Proceedings 47: 175–179

Glennon J A, Gordon E S, Sawin C T 1972 Hypothyroidism after low dose ^{131}I treatment of hyperthyroidism. Annals of Internal Medicine 76: 721–723

Golding D N 1970 Hypothyroidism presenting with musculoskeletal symptoms. Annals of the Rheumatic Diseases 29: 10–14

Golding D N 1971 The musculoskeletal features of hypothyroidism. Postgraduate Medical Journal 47: 611–614

Gonzalez S M, Sullivan H 1979 Occult hypothyroidism in a nursing home population. Arizona Medical Journal 36: 24–25

Goolamali S K, Evered D, Shuster S 1976 Thyroid disease and sebaceous function. British Medical Journal 1: 432–433

Goolden A W G 1969 Radiotherapy in thyroid disease. British Journal of Clinical Practice 23: 251–258

Goolden A W G, Fraser T R 1969a Treatment of thyrotoxicosis with low doses of radioactive iodine. British Medical Journal iii: 442–443

Goolden A W G, Fraser T R 1969b Treatment of pretreatment with carbimazole in patients with thyrotoxicosis subsequently treated with radioactive iodine. British Medical Journal 3: 443–444

Goolden A W G, Glass H J, Williams E D 1971 Use of 99 Tc^m for routine assessment of thyroid function. British Medical Journal 4: 396–399

Gordon M 1978 'Silent' thyroiditis with symptomatic hyperthyroidism in an elderly patient. Journal of the American Geriatrics Society 16: 375–377

Gorman C A 1972 Unusual manifestations of Graves' disease. Mayo Clinic Proceedings 47: 926–933

Goudie R B, Anderson J R, Gray K G 1959 Complement fixing antithyroid antibodies in hospital patients with asymptomatic thyroid lesions. Journal of Pathology and Bacteriology 77: 389–400

Graettinger J S, Muenster J J, Checchia C S, Grisson R I, Campbell J A A 1958 A correlation of clinical and haemodynamic studies in patients with hypothyroidism. Journal of Clinical Investigation 37: 502–510

Green M, Wilson G M 1964 Thyrotoxicosis treated by surgery or iodine 131 with special reference to development of hypothyroidism. British Medical Journal 4: 1005–1010

Greer M A, Grimm Y, Studer H 1968 Qualitative changes in the secretion of thyroid hormones induced by iodine deficiency. Endocrinology 83: 1193–1198

Gregerman R I 1967 The age related alteration of thyroid function and thyroid hormone metabolism in man. In: Gitman L (ed), Endocrines and Aging, pp. 161–173. C C Thomas, Springfield, Illinois

Gregerman R I, Gaffney G W, Shock N 1962 Thyroxin turnover in euthyroid man with special references to changes with age. Journal of Clinical Investigation 41: 2065–2074

Greig W R 1973 Radioactive iodine treatment of thyrotoxicosis: the current problem. In: Walker G (ed), 9th Symposium on Advanced Medicine, pp. 38–64. Pitman, London

Hadden D R, Montgomery D A D, Shanks R G, Weaver J A 1968 Propranolol and iodine 131 in the management of thyrotoxicosis. Lancet ii: 852–854

Hadden D R, McMaster A, Bell J K, Weaver J A, Montgomery D A D 1975 Does T$_4$ toxicosis exist? Lancet i: 745–755

Haferkamp O, Schlettwein-Gsell D, Schwick G H, Storiko K 1966 Serum proteins in an aging population. Gerontologia 12: 30–35

Hagen G A 1968 Treatment of thyrotoxicosis with 131I and post therapy hypothyroidism. Medical Clinics of North America 52: 417–428

Hall R 1970 Hyperthyroidism — pathogenesis and diagnosis. British Medical Journal 1: 743–745

Hall R, Anderson J, Smart G S 1969 Fundamentals of Endocrinology, pp. 73, 86. Pitman, London

Hall R, Doniach D, Kirkham K, El Kabir D 1970a Ophthalmic Graves' disease — diagnosis and pathogenesis. Lancet i: 375–378

Hall R, Amos J, Garry R, Buxton R L 1970b Thyroid stimulating hormone response to synthetic thyrotrophin releasing hormone in man. British Medical Journal ii: 274–277

Hall R, Evered D, Tunbridge W M G 1973 Role of TSH and TRH in thyroid disease. In: Walker G (ed), 9th Symposium on Advanced Medicine, pp. 16–26. Pitman, London

Hall R, Owen S G, Smart G A 1960 Evidence for genetic predisposition to formation of thyroid autoantibodies. Lancet ii: 187–188

Hall R, Saxena K M, Owen S G 1962 A study of the parents of patients with Hashimoto's disease. Lancet ii: 1291–1292

Hamolsky M W, Kurland G S, Friedberg A S 1961 The heart in hypothyroidism. Journal of Chronic Diseases 14: 558–569

Harrison T S 1964 Adrenal medullary and thyroid relationships. Physiological Reviews 44: 161–185

Harvey R F 1971 Serum thyroxine and thyroxine binding globulin in seriously ill patients. Lancet i: 208–212

Hausmann W 1975 Thyrotoxic cardiomyopathy complicated by systemic and pulmonary embolism. Proceedings of the Royal Society of Medicine 68: 327

Havard C W H, Campbell E D R, Ross H B, Speare A W 1963 Electromyographic and histological findings in the muscles of patients with thyrotoxicosis. Quarterly Journal of Medicine 32: 145–163

Havard C W H 1974 Management of thyrotoxicosis. British Journal of Hospital Medicine 11: 893–904

Havard C W H 1981 The thyroid and aging. Clinics in Endocrinology and Metabolism 10: 163–178

Hays M T 1968 Absorption of oral thyroxine in man. Journal of Clinical Endocrinology and Metabolism 30: 675–677

Hedley A J, Flemming C J, Chesters M I, Michie W, Crooks J 1970 Surgical treatment of thyrotoxicosis. British Medical Journal 1: 519–523

Hedley A J, Michie W, Duncan T, Hems G, Crooks J 1972 The effect of remnant size on the outcome of subtotal thyroidectomy for thyrotoxicosis. British Journal of Surgery 59: 559–563

Hedley A J, Ross I P, Beck J S, Donald D, Albert-Recht L, Michie W, Crooks J 1971b Recurrent thyrotoxicosis after sub-total thyroidectomy. British Medical Journal 4: 258–261

Herlant M, Pastells J L 1972 Pituitary changes in myxoedema and chronic thyroiditis. In: Bastenie P, Ermans A M (ed), Thyroiditis and Thyroid Function, pp. 251–260. Pergamon, Oxford

Herrmann J, Rusche H J, Kroll H J, Hilger P, Krusemper H L 1974 Free triiodothyronine and thyroxine levels in old age. Hormone and Metabolic Research 6: 239–240

Hershman J M, Givens J R, Cassidy C E, Astwood E B 1966 Long term outcome of hyperthyroidism treated with anti-thyroid drugs. Journal of Clinical Endocrinology and Metabolism 26: 803–807

Hershman J M, Pittman J A 1971a Control of thyrotrophin secretion in man. New England Journal of Medicine 285: 997–1006

Hershman J M, Pittman J A 1971b Utility of radioimmunoassay of serum thyrotrophin in man. Annals of Internal Medicine 74: 481–490

Hesch R D, Evered D 1973 Radioimmunoassay of triiodothyronine in unextracted human serum. British Medical Journal 1: 645–648

Heyma P, Larkins R G, Higginbotham L, Ng K W 1980 D-propranolol and DL-propranolol both decrease conversion and L-thyroxine to L-triiodothyronine. British Medical Journal 281: 24–25

Hodkinson H M 1975 In: Diagnostic and Prognostic Aspects of Routine Laboratory Screening of the Geriatric Inpatient. D M Thesis, Oxford

Hodkinson H M, Denham M J 1977 Thyroid function in the elderly in the community. Age and Aging 6: 67–70

Hoffenberg R 1973 Triiodothyronine. Clinical Endocrinology 2: 75–87

Hoffenberg R 1974 Aetiology of hyperthyroidism. British Medical Journal 3: 452–455, 508–510

Hollander C S, Sheuhman L, Mitsuma T, Blune M, Kastin A J, Anderson D G 1971 Hypertriiodothyroninaemia as a premonitory manifestation of thyrotoxicosis. Lancet ii: 731–3

Hollander C S, Mitsuma T, Nihei N, Shenkman L, Bunday S Z, Blum M 1972 Clinical and laboratory observations in cases of triiodothyronine toxicosis confirmed by radioimmunoassay. Lancet i: 609–611

Hollander C S, Shenkman L 1972 T$_3$ Toxicosis. British Journal of Hospital Medicine 6: 393–395

Holvey D N, Goodmer C J, Nikoleff J T, Dawling J T 1969 Treatment of myxoedema coma with intravenous thyroxine. Archives of Internal Medicine 113: 89–96

Horton L, Coburn R J, England J M, Himsworth R L 1976 The Haematology of hypothyroidism. Quarterly Journal of Medicine (NS) 45: 101–124

Hull O H 1955 Critical analysis of 221 thyroid glands. Archives of Pathology 59: 291–311

Hunton R B, Wells M V, Skipper E W 1965 Hypothyroidism in diabetics treated with sulphonylurea. Lancet ii: 449–451

Hyams D E 1973 Plasma proteins. In: Brocklehurst J C (ed), Textbook of Geriatric Medicine and Gerontology, 1st edn. p. 529. Churchill Livingstones, Edinburgh

Ibbertson H K 1964 In: Bacon D N, Compston N, Dawson A M (ed), Recent Advances in Medicine, 14th edn, p. 353. Churchill, London

Ikejiri K, Yamada T, Ogura H 1978 Age-related glucose intolerance in hyperthyroid patients. Diabetes 27: 543–549

Ikram H 1977 Haemodynamic effects of beta-adrenergic blockage in hyperthyroid patients with and without heart failure. British Medical Journal i: 1505–1507

Impallomeni M G 1977 Unusual presentation of myxoedema coma in the elderly. Age and Aging 6: 71–76

Ingbar S H 1978 The influence of Aging on the human thyroid hormone economy. In: Greenblatt R B (ed), Geriatric Endocrinology, pp. 13–31. Raven Press, New York

Isaacs A J, Havard C W H 1976 Myxoedema and hydrocoele. British Medical Journal i: 322

Iversen K 1953 Thyrotoxicosis in aged individuals. Journal of Gerontology 8: 65–69

Izumi M, Larsen P R 1978 Correlation of sequential changes in serum thyroglobulin, triiodothyronine and thyroxine in patients with Graves' disease and subacute thyroiditis. Metabolism 27: 449–460

Jacobs H S, Mackie D B, Eastman C J, Ellis S M, Ekins R P, McHardy Young S 1973 Total and free triiodothyronine and thyroxine levels in thyroid storm and recurrent hyperthyroidism. Lancet ii: 236–238

Jefferys P M 1972 The prevalence of thyroid disease in patients admitted to a geriatric department. Age and Aging 1: 33–37

Jefferys P M, Farran H E A, Hoffenberg R, Fraser P M, Hodkinson H M 1972 Thyroid function tests in the elderly. Lancet i: 924–927

Jellinek E H 1962 Fits, faints, coma and dementia in myxoedema. Lancet ii: 1010–1015

Jellinek E H, Kelly R E 1960 Cerebellar syndrome in myxoedema. Lancet ii: 225–227

Joasoo A 1975 T$_4$ thyrotoxicosis with normal or low serum T$_3$ concentration. Australian and New Zealand Journal of Medicine 5: 432–434

Joasoo A, Murray I P C, Parkin J, Robertson M R, Jeremy D 1974 Abnormalities of in vitro thyroid function tests in renal disease. Quarterly Journal of Medicine (NS) 43: 245–261

Jonckheer M H 1980 Amiodarone and the thyroid gland. A review. Acta Cardiologica 46: 199–205

Jones M K, John R, Jones G R 1980 The effect of oxprenolol, acebutolol and propranolol on thyroid hormones in hyperthyroid subjects. Clinical Endocrinology 13: 343–347

Kark A E, Gueret Wardle D F 1980 Management of malignant disease in old. In: Denham M J (ed), The treatment of medical problems in the elderly, pp. 333–417. MTP Press, Lancaster

Kay D W, Bergmann K, Foster E M, McKechnie A A, Roth M 1970 Mental illness and hospital usage in the elderly. Comprehensive Psychiatry 11: 26–35

Kendall-Taylor P 1975 The aetiology of thyrotoxicosis. British Journal of Hospital Medicine 9: 638–643

Kennedy W R 1965 Muscle disease of older patients. Geriatrics 20: 964–968

Keys A, Taylor H L, Grande F 1973 Basal metabolism and age of adult man. Metabolism 22: 579–587

Kimberg D V 1971 Hyperthyroidism: gastro-intestinal tract. In: Werner S C, Ingbar S H (ed), The Thyroid: a Fundamental and Clinical Text, p. 565. Harper and Rowa, New York

Kind P R N, Ghosh S 1976 Observations on thyroid function tests in the elderly. Age and Aging 5: 141–148

Kirkegaard C, Nielsen K S, Friis T, Rogowski P 1975 Does T_4 toxicosis exsit? Lancet i: 868

Kodding R, Janzen J, Schmidt E, Hesch K D 1976 Reverse triiodothyronine in liver disease. Lancet ii: 314

Koronchevsky V 1961 In: Bourne G H (ed), Physiological and Pathological Aging, pp. 40–44, 311–315. Karger, Basel

Kozak G P 1971 The thyroid gland and diabetes. In: Marble A, White P, Bradley R E, Krall L P (ed), Joslin's Diabetes Mellitus, 11th edn, pp. 671–679. Lea and Febiger, Philadelphia

Kreines K, Jett M, Knowles H C JR 1965 Observations in hyperthyroidism of abnormal glucose tolerance and other traits related to diabetes mellitus. Diabetes 14: 740–74

Kristensen O, Harrestrup Andersen H, Pallisgaard G 1976 Lithium carbonate in the treatment of thyrotoxicosis: a controlled trial. Lancet i: 603–605

Krugman L G, Hershman J M, Chopra I J, Levine G A, Pekary A E, Geffner D L, Chua Teco G H 1975 Pattern of recovery of hypothalmic-pituitary-thyroid axis in patients taken off chronic thyroid therapy. Journal of Clinical Endocrinology and Metabolism 41: 70–80

Larsen P R 1972 Direct immunoassay of triiodothyronine in human serum. Journal of Clinical Investigation 51: 1939–1949

Larsen P R 1972 Triiodothyronine: review of recent studies of its physiology and pathophysiology. Metabolism 21: 1073–1092

Larsen P R 1975 Thyroidal triiodothyronine and thyroxine in Graves' disease: correlation with pre-surgical treatment, thyroid status and iodine content. Journal of Clinical Endocrinology and Metabolism 41: 1098–1105

Larsen P R 1975 Tests of thyroid function. Medical Clinics of North America 59: 1063–1074

Lavietes P H, Epstein F H 1964 Thyroid therapy and myxoedema: a comparison of various agents with a note on the composition of thyroid secretion in man. Annals of Internal Medicine 60: 79–89

Lawrence A M, Wilber J F, Hagen T C 1973 The pituitary and primary hypothyroidism. Archives of Internal Medicine 132: 327–333

Lazarus J H, Harden R, McG 1969 Thyrotoxicosis in the elderly. Gerontologia Clinica 11: 371–378

Lazarus J H, Richards A R, Addison G M, Owen G M 1974 Treatment of thyrotoxicosis with lithium carbonate. Lancet ii: 1160–1163

Lee N D, Henry R J, Golub O J 1964 Determination of free thyroxine content of serum. Journal of Clinical Endocrinology and Metabolism 24: 486–495

Leeper R D, Benna R S, Brener J L, Rawson W 1960 Hyperuricaemia in myxoedema. Journal of Clinical Endocrinology and Metabolism 20: 1457–1466

Levey G S 1975 The heart and hyperthyroidism: use of beta adrenergic blocking drugs. Medical Clinics of North America 59: 1193–1201

Lieblich J, Utiger R D 1972 Triiodothyronine radioimmune assay. Journal of Clinical Investigation 51: 157–163

Lloyd W H, Goldberg I J L 1961 Incidence of hypothyroidism in the elderly. British Medical Journal ii: 1256–1259

Lloyd W H, Mawdsley C 1967 The face in hypothyroidism. Medical and Biological Illustration 17: 12–19

Locke W 1967 Hyperthyroidism in the aged. Geriatrics 22: 173–174

McConahey W M 1978 Diagnosing and treating myxoedema and myxoedema coma. Geriatrics 33: 61–66

McConnell R J, Menendez C E, Smith F R, Henkin R I, Rivlin R S 1975 Defects of taste and smell in patients with hypothyroidism. American Journal of Medicine 59: 354–364

McDougall I R, Greig W R 1971 Pathogenesis and treatment of thyrotoxicosis. Scottish Medical Journal 16: 519–531

McGavack T H 1950 Hormonal therapy in the aging. Geriatrics 5: 151–158

McGavack T H 1951 In: The Thyroid, p. 111. Mosby, St. Louis

McGavack T H, Seegers W 1956 Thyroid function and disease in old age. Journal of the American Geriatrics Society 4: 535–541

McGavack T H, Seegers W 1959 Status of the thyroid gland after age 50. Metabolism 8: 136–150

McKenzie J M, Zakarija M 1976 A reconsideration of thyroid stimulating immunoglobulin as the cause of hyperthyroidism in Graves' disease. Journal of Clinical Endocrinology and Metabolism 42: 778–784

McKeown F 1965 Pathology of the Aged, pp. 210–214. London: Butterworth

McKerron C G 1971 Hypothyroidism. Update Plus 1: 727

McKerron C G, Howorth P J N 1971 Thyroid function tests. Update 3: 1409–1417

McLarty D G, Alexander W D, Harden R McG, Clark D H 1969 Results of treatment of thyrotoxicosis after post-operative relapse. British Medical Journal 3: 200–203

McLarty D G, Brownlie B E W, Alexander W D, Papetrou P D, Horton L 1973 Remission of thyrotoxicosis during treatment with propranolol. British Medical Journal 2: 332–334

McLarty D G, Ratcliffe W A, McColl K, Stone D, Ratcliffe J G 1975 Thyroid hormone levels and prognosis in patients with serious non-thyroidal illness. Lancet ii: 275–276

Malone J F, Cullen M J 1976 Two mechanisms for hypothyroidism after 131I therapy. Lancet ii: 73–75

Maloof F, Wang C A, Vickery A L 1975 Non-toxic goitre — diffuse or nodular. Medical Clinics of North America 59: 1221–1232

Mankikar G D, Clark A N G 1981 Euthyroid 'Thyroxine Toxicosis'. Journal of the American Geriatrics Society 19: 331–333

Manns J J, Shepherd A M M, Crooks J, Adamson D G 1976 Measurement of cardiac muscle relaxation in hypothyroidism. British Medical Journal 2: 1366–1368

Marsden P, Facer P, Acosta M, McKerron C G 1975 Serum triiodothyronine in solitary autonomous nodules of the thyroid. Clinical Endocrinology 4: 327–330

Marsden P, Howorth P J N, Chalkley S, Acosta M, Leatherdale B, McKerron C G 1975 Hormonal pattern of relapse in hyperthyroidism. Lancet i: 944–947

Marsden P, McKerron C G 1975 Serum triiodothyronine concentration in the diagnosis of hyperthyroidism. Clinical Endocrinology 4: 183–189

Mayberry W E, Gharib H, Bistead J M, Sizemore G W 1971 Radioimmunoassay for human thyrotrophin: clinical value in patients with normal and abnormal thyroid function. Annals of Internal Medicine 74: 471–480

Meindok H, Franks W M 1969 Serum proteins, protein bound iodine and triiodothyronine resin uptake in the elderly. Journal of the American Geriatrics Society 17: 451–458

Michie W, Pegg C A S, Bewsher P D 1972 Prediction of hypothyroidism after partial thyroidectomy. British Medical Journal 1: 13–17

Michie W, Hamer-Hodges D W, Pegg C A S, Orr F G G, Bewsher P D 1974 Beta blockade and partial thyroidectomy for thyrotoxicosis. Lancet i: 1009–1011

Midgley J E M, Wilkins T A 1981 The direct estimation of free hormones by a simple equilibrium radioimmunoassay. The Radiochemical Centre, Amersham

Miller H M 1975 Plummer's disease. Medical Clinics of North America 59: 1203–1216

Mincey E K, Thorson S C, Brown J L 1971 A new in vitro blood test for determining thyroid status — the Effective Thyroxin Ratio. Clinical Biochemistry 4: 216–221

Misra D P, Staddon G, Powell N, Jackson P 1974 Assessment of potassium metabolism, using 42K in cases of myxoedema before and after treatment with thyroxine. Age and Aging 3: 245–248

Mitsuma T, Nihei N, Geischengorn M C 1971 Serum triiodothyronine measurements in human serum by radioimmunoassay with corroboration by gas liquid chromatography. Journal of Clinical Investigation 50: 2679

Mochizuki Y, Mowafy R, Pasternak B 1963 Weights of human thyroids in New York City. Health Physics 9: 1299–1301

Molnar G D, Wilber R D, Lee R E, Woolner L B, Keating F R 1965 On the hyperfunctioning solitary thyroid nodule. Mayo Clinic Proceedings 40: 665–684

Montgomery D A D, Welbourn R B 1975 In: Medical and Surgical Endocrinology, p. 292. Arnold, London

Morgans M E, Trotter W R 1959 Iodopyrine as a cause of goitre. Lancet ii: 374–375

Mortensen J D, Woolner L B, Bennett W H 1955 Gross and microscopic findings in clinically normal thyroid glands. Journal of Clinical Endocrinology and Metabolism 15: 1270–1280

Mortimer C H, Anderson D C, Liendo-Ch P, Fisher R, Chan V, Self M, Besser G M 1977 Thyrotoxicosis: relations between clinical state and biochemical changes during carbimazole treatment. British Medical Journal 1: 138–141

Mühlen A Von Zur, Hesch R D, Köbberling J 1975 The TRH Test in the course of treatment of hyperthyroidism. Clinical Endocrinology 4: 165–167

Munkner T 1965 The influence of paraaminosalicylic acid on $_{131}$I metabolism. Acta radiologica (Diagnosis) suppl. 234, p. 44

Murray I P C, Stewart R H D 1967 Iodide goitre. Lancet i: 922–926

Mustacchi P O, Lowenhaupt E 1950 Senile changes in the histologic structure of the thyroid gland. Geriatrics 5: 268–273

Niarchos A P, Finn R 1973 Association between hypothyroidism and abdominal aneurysm. British Medical Journal 4: 110

Nicoloff J T, Low J C, Dussault J H, Fisher D H 1972 Simultaneous measurement of thyroxine and triiodothyronine peripheral turnover kinetics in man. Journal of Clinical Investigation 51: 473–483

Nielsen L K S, Friis T 1973 Age dependence of thyroxine metabolism in euthyroid patients. Ugeskrift for Laeger 135: 640–644

Nightingale S, Vitek P J, Himsworth R L 1978 The haematology of hypothyroidism. Quarterly Journal of Medicine 47: 35–47

Ng Tang Fui S C, Maisey M N 1979 Standard dose of ^{131}I therapy for hyperthyroidism caused by autonomously functioning thyroid nodules. Clinical Endocrinology 10: 69–77

Oddie T H, Fisher D A, McConahey W M, Thompson C S 1970 Iodine intake in the United States — a reassessment. Journal of Clinical Endocrinology and Metabolism 30: 659–665

Oddie T H, Meade J H JR, Fisher D 1966a An analysis of published data on thyroxine turnover in human subjects. Journal of Clinical Endocrinology and Metabolism 26: 425–435

Oddie T H, Meade J H JR, Myhill J, Fisher D A 1966b Dependence of renal clearance of radioiodide on sex, age and thyroidal status. Journal of Clinical Endocrinology and Metabolism 26: 1293–1296

Oddie T H, Myhill J, Pirnique F G, Fisher D A 1968 Effect of age and sex on radioiodine uptake in euthyroid subjects. Journal of Clinical Endocrinology and Metabolism 28: 776–782

Oddie T H, Thomas I D, Rundle F, Myhill T, Carr B 1960 Diagnostic limits for ^{131}I uptake rates. Journal of Clinical Endocrinology and Metabolism 20: 389–400

Olsen T, Laurberg P, Weeke J 1978 Low serum triiodothyronine and high serum reverse triiodothyronine in old age: an effect of disease not age. Journal of Clinical Endocrinology and Metabolism 47: 1111–1115

Olsen W R, Nishiyama R H, Graber L W 1970 Thyroidectomy for hyperthyroidism. Archives of Surgery 101: 175–180

Oltman J E, Friedman S 1964 Further report on protein bound iodine in patients receiving perphenazine. American Journal of Psychiatry 121: 176–182

Oppenheimer J H 1968 Role of plasma proteins in the binding distribution and metabolism of the thyroid hormones. New England Journal of Medicine 278: 1153–1162

Oppenheimer J H 1972 Thyroid hormones in the liver. Mayo Clinic Proceedings 47: 854–863

Oppenheimer J H, Schwartz H L, Surks M 1972 Propyl thiouracil inhibits conversion of T_4 to T_3. Journal of Clinical Investigation 51: 2493–2497

Oppenheimer J H, Surks M I 1975 Peripheral action of thyroid hormones. Medical Clinics of North America 59: 1055–1061

Oppenheimer J H, Werner S C 1966 Effect of prednisone on thyroxine binding protein. Journal of Clinical Endocrinology and Metabolism 26: 715–720

Ormston B J, Kilbon J R, Garry R, Amos J, Hill R 1971a Further observations on the effect of synthetic thyrotrophin-releasing hormone in man. British Medical Journal 2: 199–202

Ormston B J, Garry R, Cryer R J, Besser G M, Hall R 1971b Thyrotrophin-releasing hormone as a thyroid function test. Lancet ii: 10–14

Osorio C 1967 Carriage of circulating thyroid hormones and the estimation of total plasma hormone levels. Journal of Clinical Pathology 20, suppl. 335–343

Otten M H, Hennermann G, Docter R, Visser T J 1980 The role of dietary fat in peripheral thyroid hormone metabolism. Metabolism 29: 930–935

Palmer K T 1977 A prospective study into thyroid disease in a geriatric unit. New Zealand Medical Journal 86: 323–324

Parfitt A M, Dent C E 1970 Hyperthyroidism and hypercalcaemia. Quarterly Journal of Medicine 39: 171–187

Parker J L W, Lawson D H 1973 Death from thyrotoxicosis. Lancet ii: 894–895

Pasternak D P, Socolow E L, Ingbar S H 1969 Synergistic interaction of phenazone and iodide on thyroid hormone biosynthesis in the rat. Endocrinology 84: 769–777

Patel Y C, Burger H G 1973 Serum triiodothyronine in health and disease. Clinical Endocrinology 2: 330–340

Pharoah P O, Lawton N F, Ellis S M, Williams E S, Ekins R P 1973 The role of triiodothyronine (T_3) in the maintenance of euthyroidism in endemic goitre. Clinical Endocrinology 2: 193–199

Pimstone B, Joffe B 1970 The use and abuse of beta-adrenergic blockade in the surgery of hyperthyroidism. South African Medical Journal 44: 1059–1061

Pimstone N, Marine N, Pimstone B 1968 Beta-adrenergic blockade in thyrotoxic myopathy. Lancet ii: 1219–1220

Pittman J A 1962 The thyroid and aging. Journal of the American Geriatrics Society 10: 10–21

Pittman J A, Brown R W, Register H B 1962 Biological activity of 3:3′:5′-triiodothyronine. Endocrinology 70: 79–83

Pittman J A, Dailey G E, Beschi R J 1969 Changing radioiodine uptake. New England Journal of Medicine 280: 1431–1434

Porteous W M 1979 Hypothyroidism in elderly hospital patients. New Zealand Medical Journal 89: 81–83

Price T R, Netskey M C 1966 Cerebellar alterations and neural myxoedema bodies. Neurology (Minneapolis) 16: 957–967

Ramsay I D 1965 Electromyography in thyrotoxicosis. Quarterly Journal of Medicine 34: 255–267

Ramsay I D 1966 Muscle dysfunction in hyperthyroidism. Lancet ii: 931–935

Ramsay I, Marsden P, Richardson P J, McKerron C G 1972 Thyroid hot nodules. Postgraduate Medical Journal 48: 577–583

Ratcliffe W A, Ratcliffe J G, MacBride A D, Harland W A, Randall T W 1974 The radioimmunoassay of thyroxine in unextracted human serum. Clinical Endocrinology 3: 481–487

Ray T 1977 What to look for in diagnosing hypothyroidism. Geriatrics 32: 55–59

Refetoff S 1975 Thyroid hormone therapy. Medical Clinics of North America 59: 1147–1162

Robertson J S, Nolan N G, Wahner H W, McConahey 1975 Thyroid radioiodine uptakes and scans in euthyroid patients. Mayo Clinic Proceedings 50: 79–84

Ronnov-Jessen V, Kirkegaard C 1973 Hyperthyroidism: a disease of old age. British Medical Journal 1: 41–43

Rosenberg I N, Alan C S, Mitchell M L 1962 Effect of anabolic steroids on circulating thyroid hormones. Journal of Clinical Endocrinology and Metabolism 22: 612

Rosenthal F D, Jones C, Lewis S I 1976 Thyrotoxic vomiting. British Medical Journal 3: 209–211

Rosin A J, Exton-Smith A N 1964 Clinical features of accidental hypothermia with some observations on thyroid function. British Medical Journal 1: 16–19

Rosin A J, Farran H E A 1968 Factors influencing in vitro tests of thyroid function in the elderly. Journal of the American Geriatrics Society 16: 1030–1038

Rubenstein H A, Butler V P, Werner S C 1973 Progressive decrease in serum T_3 with human aging. Journal of Clinical Endocrinology and Metabolism 37: 247–253

Saberi M, Sterling F H, Utiger R D 1974 Reduction in extrathyroidal triiodothyronine production by propyl thiouracil in man. Journal of Clinical Investigation 55: 218–223

Saberi M, Utiger R D 1974 Serum thyroid hormone and thyrotrophin concentrations during thyroxine and triiodothyronine therapy. Journal of Clinical Endocrinology and Metabolism 39: 923–927

Sachdev Y, Hall R 1975 Effusions into body cavities in hypothyroidism. Lancet i: 564–566

Satoyishi E, Murahami K, Kowa H, Kimoshita M, Noguchi K, Hoshina S, Nishiyama Y, Ito K 1963 Myopathy in thyrotoxicosis. Neurology (Minneapolis) 13: 645–658

Savoie J C, Massin J P, Thomopoulos P, Leger F 1975 Iodine-induced thyrotoxicosis in apparently normal thyroid glands. Journal of Clinical Endocrinology and Metabolism 41: 685–691

Sawin C T, Chopra D, Albano J, Azizi F 1978 The free triiodothyronine (T_3) index. Annals of Internal Medicine 88: 474–477

Sawin C T, McHugh J E 1966 Isolated lack of thyrotropin in man. Journal of Clinical Endocrinology and Metabolism 26: 955–959

Schiller K R F, Spray G H, Wangel A G, Wright R 1968 Clinical and precursory forms of pernicious anaemia in hyperthyroidism. Quarterly Journal of Medicine 37: 451

Sclare G 1963 The thyroid in myxoedema. Journal of Pathology and Bacteriology 85: 263–278

Sekadde C S, Slaunwhite W R, Aceto T, Marnay K 1974 Administration of thyroxine once a week. Journal of Clinical Endocrinology and Metabolism 39: 759–764

Seth J, Rutherford F, McKenzie I 1975 Solid phase radioimmunoassay of thyroxine in untreated serum. Clinical Chemistry 21: 1406–1413

Shafer R B, Gregory D H 1972 Cause of negative calcium balance in hyperthyroidism. Gastroenterology 63: 235–239

Shafer R B, Nuttal F Q 1975 Acute changes in thyroid function in patients treated with radioactive iodine. Lancet ii: 635–637

Shalet S M, Beardwell C G, Lamb A M, Gowland E 1975 Value of routine serum triiodothyronine estimation in the diagnosis of thyrotoxicosis. Lancet ii: 1008–1010

Shanks R G, Hadden D R, Lowe D C, McDevitt D G, Montgomery D A D 1969 Controlled trial of propranolol in thyrotoxicosis. Lancet i: 993–994

Shenkman L, Mitsuma T, Suphavai A, Hollander C S 1972 Triodothyronine and thyroid stimulating hormone response to thyrotrophin releasing hormone: a new test of thyroidal and pituitary reserve. Lancet i: 111–113

Shock N W, Watkin D M, Yienst M J, Norris A H, Gaffney G W, Gregerman R I, Falzone J A 1963 Age differences in water content of the body as related to basal oxygen consumption in males. Journal of Gerontology 18: 1–10

Shopsin B, Shenkman L, Blum M, Hollander C S 1973 Iodine and lithium induced hypothyroidism. American Journal of Medicine 55: 695–699

Simkins S 1968 Antithyroglobulin antibodies in diabetes mellitus. Diabetes 17: 136–140

Smart G A 1972 The treatment of myxoedema. Prescribing Journal 12: 112–117

Smith R N, Wilson G M 1967 Clinical trial of different doses of ^{131}I in treatment of thyrotoxicosis. British Medical Journal 1: 129–132

Snitcher E, Nye L, Landon J 1976 The assessment of thyroid function. Update 12: 209–218

Spaulding S W, Noth R H 1975 Thyroid catecholamine interactions. Medical Clinics of North America 59: 1123–1132

Sterling K 1975 Radioactive iodine therapy. Medical Clinics of North America 59: 1217–1220

Sterling K, Brenner M A, Newman E S 1970a Conversion of thyroxine to triiodothyronine in normal human subjects. Science 169: 1099–1100

Sterling K, Brenner M A, Newman E S, Odell W D, Bellabarba D 1971 The significance of triiodothyronine in the maintenance of euthyroid status after treatment for hyperthyroidism. Journal of Clinical Endocrinology and Metabolism 33: 729–735

Sterling K, Refetoff S, Selenkow H A 1970b T_3 thyrotoxicosis: thyrotoxicosis due to elevated serum triiodothyrone levels. Journal of the American Medical Association 213: 571–575

Stewart A G 1975 Endocrine disturbances in the older patient. Practitioner 215: 623–631

Stewart J C, Vidor G J 1974 Endocrine disorders in the elderly. British Medical Journal 2: 672

Stewart J C, Vidor V I 1976 Thyrotoxicosis induced by iodine contamination of food: a common unrecognized condition. British Medical Journal 1: 372–375

Stiel J N, Hales I B, Reeve T S 1972 Thyrotoxicosis in an elderly population. Medical Journal of Australia 2: 986–988

Stock J M, Surks M J, Oppenheimer J H 1974 Replacement dosage of L-thyroxine in hypothyroidism. New England Journal of Medicine 290: 529–533

Stoffer R P, Hellwig C A, Welch J W, McCusker E N 1961 The thyroid gland after age 50. Geriatrics 16: 435–443

Stoffer S S, Hamberger J 1975 T_4 Toxicosis. Lancet ii: 660

Staffurth J S, Gibberd M C, Ng Tang Fui S 1977 Arterial embolism in thyrotoxicosis with atrial fibrillation. British Medical Journal ii: 688–690

Surks M I, Schadlow A R, Stock J M, Oppenheiner J H 1973 Determination of iodothyronine absorption and conversion of 1-thyroxine to 1-triiodothyronine (T_3) using turnover rate techniques. Journal of Clinical Investigation 52: 805–811

Symons C, Richardson P J, Wood J B 1971 Unusual presentation of thyrocardiac disease. Lancet ii: 1163–1167

Taylor B B, Thompson J A, Caird F I 1974 Further studies of thyroid function tests in the elderly at home. Age and Aging 3: 122–125

Taylor S 1958 The thyroid nodule. Lancet i: 751–754

Thomas A J 1972 Thyrotoxic heart disease. Modern Geriatrics 2: 147–149

Thomas C G 1975 The surgery of the thyroid. Medical Clinics of North America 59: 1247–1261

Thomas F B, Caldwell J H, Greenberger N J 1973 Steatorrhoea in thyrotoxicosis. Annals of Internal Medicine 78: 669–675

Thomas F B, Mazaferri E L, Skillman T G 1970 Apathetic thyrotoxicosis: a distinctive clinical and laboratory entity. Annals of Internal Medicine 72: 679–685

Thomas R D, Croft D N 1974 Thyrotoxicosis and giant cell arteritis. British Medical Journal 2: 408–409

Thompson J A, Andrews G R, Caird F I, Wilson R 1972 Serum protein bound and plasma inorganic iodine in the elderly at home. Age and Ageing: 158–161

Toft A D, Hunter W M, Seth J, Irvine W J 1974 Plasma thyrotrophin and serum thyroxin in patients becoming hypothyroid in early months after 131 Iodine. Lancet i: 704–705

Toft A D, Irvine W J, Campbell R W F 1976a Assessment by continuous cardiac monitoring of minimum duration of preoperative propranolol treatment in thyrotoxic patients. Clinical Endocrinology 5: 195–198

Toft A D, Irvine W J, McIntosh D, Seth J, Cameron E H D, Lidgard G P 1976b Temporary hypothyroidism after surgical treatment of thyrotoxicosis. Lancet ii: 817–818

Toft A D, Irvine W J, Seth J, Hunter W M, Cameron E D H 1975 Thyroid function in the long-term follow up of patients treated with 131 Iodine for thyrotoxicosis. Lancet ii: 576–578

Tudhope G R, Wilson G M 1960 Anaemia in hypothyroidism. Quarterly Journal of Medicine 29: 513–537

Tunbridge W M G, Evered R, Hall R, Appleton D, Brewis M, Clark F, Grimley Evans J, Young E, Bird T, Smith P A 1977 The spectrum of thyroid disease in a community. The Whickham Survey. Clinical Endocrinology 7: 481–493

Tunbridge W M G, Harsoulis P, Goolden A W G 1974 Thyroid function in patients treated with radioactive iodine for thyrotoxicosis. British Medical Journal 3: 89–92

Tunbridge W M G et al 1981 Natural history of autoimmune thyroiditis. British Medical Journal 282: 258–262

Turner J G, Brownlie B E W, Sadler W A 1975a Does T_4 toxicosis exist? Lancet i: 407–408

Turner J G, Brownlie B E W, Sadler W A 1975b Does T_4 toxicosis exist? Lancet i: 1292–1293

Turner J G, Brownlie B E W, Rogers T G H 1976 Lithium as an adjunct to radioiodine therapy for thyrotoxicosis. Lancet i: 614–615

Vagenakis A G, Braverman L E 1975 Adverse effects of iodides on thyroid function. Medical Clinics of North America 59: 1075–1088

Vagenakis A G, Rapoport B, Azizi F, Portnay G, Braverman L E, Ingbar S H 1975 Hyper-response to thyrotropin releasing hormone accompanying small decreases in serum thyroid hormone concentration. Journal of Clinical Investigation 54: 913–918

Vanhaelst L, Neve P, Chailly P, Bastenie P 1967 Coronary artery disease in hypothyroidism. Lancet ii: 800–802

Van't Hoff W, Pover G C, Eiser W M 1972 Technetium 99m in the diagnosis of thyrotoxicosis. British Medical Journal 3: 203–206

Van Welsum M, Feltkamp T E W, De Vries M J, Docter R, Van Zijl J, Henneman G 1974 Hypothyroidism after thyroidectomy for Graves' disease: a search for an explanation. British Medical Journal 4: 755–757

Vazifdar J P, Levine S A 1966 Rarity of atrial tachycardia and acute myocardial infarction in thyrotoxicosis. Archives of Internal Medicine 118: 41–42

Verdy M, Brosseau A, Brochu P 1971 La glande thyroide: revue de 400 autopsies et examen de 400 malades. Union médicale du Canada 100: 259–266

Volpe R 1975 Thyroiditis: current views of pathogenesis. Medical Clinics of North America 59: 1163–1175

Wahner H W 1974 Diagnosing thyroid disease by selected laboratory tests. Geriatrics 29: 83–94

Wardrop C, Hutchinson H E 1969 Red cell shape in hypothyroidism. Lancet i: 1243

Wayne E J 1960 Clinical and metabolic studies in thyroid disease. British Medical Journal 1: 1–11, 78–90

Weidinger P, Johnson P M, Werner S C 1974 Five years' experience with 125 iodine therapy of Graves' disease. Lancet ii: 74–76

Wellby M L, O'Halloran M W 1966 Measurement of plasma free thyroxin level as a test of thyroid function. British Medical Journal 2: 668–670

Wellby M L, O'Halloran M W, Marshall J 1974 A comparison of effective thyroxine ratio, free thyroxine index and free thyroxine concentration in correcting for thyroxine binding abnormalities in serum. Clinical Endocrinology 3: 63–68

Wells I, Smith B, Hinton M 1977 Acute ileus in myxoedema. British Medical Journal 1: 211–212

Wenzel K W, Kirschsieper H E 1977 Aspects of the absorption of oral L-thyroxine in normal man. Metabolism 16: 1–8

Wenzel K W, Meinhold H 1975 Triiodothyronine/reverse triiodothyronine balance and thyroxine metabolism. Lancet ii: 413

Werner S C 1971 Physical Examination in: The Thyroid, ed. Werner S C, Ingbar S H, pp. 340–341, 499–502. Harper and Rowa, New York

Whittingham S, Matthews J D, Mackay I R, Stocks A E, Ungar B, Martin F R 1971 Diabetes, autoimmunity and aging. Lancet i: 763–767

Wise P H, Ahmad A, Burnet R T S 1975 Intentional radioiodine ablation in Graves' disease. Lancet ii: 1231–1233

Wise P H, Marion M, Pain R W 1973 Single-dose 'block replace' drug therapy in hyperthyroidism. British Medical Journal 3: 143–145

Wolff J 1969 Iodine goitre and the pharmacologic effects of excess iodide. American Journal of Medicine 47: 101–123

Wolff J, Chaikoff I L 1948b Plasma inorganic iodide as homeostatic regulator of thyroid function. Journal of Biological Chemistry 174: 555–560

Wolff J, Chaikoff I L 1948a The inhibitory action of excessive iodide upon the synthesis of diiodotyrosine and thyroxine in the thyroid gland of the normal rat. Endocrinology 43: 174–179

Wood A J J, Crooks J 1973 Effect of drugs on thyroid function tests. Prescribing Journal 13: 94–99

Wordsworth P, Ebringer R, Jones D, Bedi S 1980 Thyroid antibodies in synovial effusions. Lancet i: 660

Young R T, Van Herle A J, Rodbard D 1976 Improved diagnosis and management of hyper and hypothyroidism by timing the arterial sounds. Journal of Clinical Endocrinology and Metabolism 42: 330–333

Zellman H E 1968 Unusual aspects of myxoedema. Geriatrics 23: 140–148

The endocrine system — diabetes

DEFINITION

Diabetes mellitus is a descriptive term for a group of disorders in which there is a breakdown of the normal mechanisms which keep the blood glucose at a constant level. The condition may range in its clinical manifestation from the totally asymptomatic to a severe metabolic disorder which may lead to rapidly fatal ketoacidosis. It is both clinically and genetically heterogeneous. If the disease is prolonged it may, even in its mildest form, be complicated by degenerative changes in the cardiovascular system, the retina, the renal glomerulus and the nervous system.

HISTORY

The first systematic description was written by Aretaeus in the first century AD. He interpreted the disease as 'a melting down of the flesh into urine' and named the condition diabetes, from the Greek word for syphon, because of the characteristic polyuria. Willis, in 1679, commented on the sweet taste of the urine, and in 1776 Dobson recognized that this was due to sugar. Minkowski, in 1889, produced the disease by pancreatectomy in dogs, and the discovery of insulin in 1921 by Banting and Best, led to the conclusion that the disease was due to insulin deficiency. More recently, the discovery that some adult onset diabetics have appreciable amounts of circulating insulin has led to the hypothesis that in some cases there is resistance to the action of insulin. The discovery of the sulphonylureas, and biguanides in the 1950's enabled some types of diabetes to be treated without the use of insulin injections.

Although the neurological complications of diabetes were described in the last century, the renal and retinal lesions were only recognized in the 1940's perhaps because before the discovery of effective treatment, diabetics did not in general survive long enough to develop these complications.

CLASSIFICATION

A recent classification of diabetes mellitus is shown in Table 35.1 (National Diabetes Data Group, 1979).

The old terms 'juvenile onset' diabetes and 'maturity onset' diabetes have been replaced by the more informative terms 'insulin-dependent' diabetes and 'non-insulin-dependent' diabetes. The term 'impaired glucose tolerance' recognizes a category of borderline subjects. They have an increased risk of developing unequivocal diabetes, but the group includes some who revert to normal glucose tolerance, who should not be categorized as being diabetic.

Type 1 insulin-dependent diabetes mellitus. This is characterized by abrupt onset of symptoms, insulinopoenia and dependence on insulin, with the tendency to develop ketosis. Although this condition occurs more

Table 35.1 Classification of diabetes mellitus and allied categories

CLINICAL CLASSES
Diabetes
Insulin-dependent type (Type 1, IDDM)
Non-insulin-dependent type (Type 2, NIDDM)
   a. Non-obese
   b. Obese
Secondary diabetes mellitus in association with:
   a. Pancreatic diseases
   b. Hormonal disorders
   c. Drug or chemical agents
   d. Insulin receptor abnormalities
   e. Genetic syndromes
   f. Miscellaneous
Impaired glucose tolerance
   a. Non-obese
   b. Obese
   c. With known drug or disease associations
STATISTICAL RISK CLASSES
(Normal glucose tolerance but increased statistical risk for diabetes)
   a. Previous abnormality of glucose tolerance (prev AGT)
      (Latent Diabetes)
   b. Potential abnormality of glucose tolerance (pot AGT)
      (Potential Diabetes)

commonly in the younger age groups, it may be recognized and become symptomatic at any age, and the elderly patient may present in ketoacidosis without any previous indication of the presence of diabetes.

Type 2 non-insulin-dependent diabetes. This type frequently presents with minimal or no symptoms of diabetes mellitus. Patients are not dependent on insulin and are not prone to ketosis. They may require insulin for correction of symptomatic or persistent hyperglycaemia if this cannot be controlled by diet or oral agents, and such patients may develop ketosis under special circumstances such as severe stress, precipitated by infection or trauma. Although most patients develop this type of diabetes over the age of 40, it may occur in the young.

Secondary diabetes. This class includes diabetes secondary to pancreatic disease, acromegaly, pheochromacytoma and various genetic syndromes. It also includes diabetes secondary to drugs, such as diuretics and antihypertensives, corticosteroids and oral contraceptives, and resulting from abnormalities of insulin receptors.

Impaired glucose tolerance. This class recognizes a group of borderline subjects in whom minor degrees of glucose tolerance are present without satisfying the criteria for diabetes. The group carries an increased risk of 2–4 per cent per annum of developing diabetes, although glucose tolerance may revert to normal. The risk of developing retinopathy in this group is very small, but the increased risk of cardiovascular disease is said to be equal to that of the diabetic. Many elderly patients fall into this category, and although no treatment is required, it is important that they are followed up. A glucose tolerance test is required for classification in this group.

Statistical risk classes

Previous abnormality of glucose tolerance (Prev AGT). This class is restricted to persons who have normal glucose tolerance, but who have previously demonstrated diabetic hyperglycaemia, for example gestational diabetics, and diabetes occuring at times of stress or trauma. The older term of 'latent diabetes' is better.

Potential abnormality of glucose tolerance (Pot AGT). This class includes persons who have never shown abnormal glucose tolerance, but who are at increased risk of developing diabetes, for example close relatives of diabetics, mothers of babies weighing more than 4 kg (9 lb), members of ethnic groups with high prevalence of diabetes. This used to be called potential diabetes.

Evolution of the disease

It is important to emphasize that patients may change from one category to another. Thus 'impaired glucose tolerance' can become 'non-insulin dependent' and 'non-insulin-dependent' can become 'insulin-dependent'. In general mild disease becomes more severe over many years, but rarely the reverse may occur. Classifications have their limitations!

AETIOLOGY

Diabetes is not a single disease entity, and there is no single factor responsible for its development. A variety of factors, including inheritance, autoimmunity, infections and obesity have been implicated as being of importance. There is good genetic and immunological evidence which suggests that the aetiology of insulin-dependent and non-insulin-dependent diabetes is different (Albin and Rifkin, 1982).

Inheritance

The importance of genetic factors in the development of diabetes has been recognized for a long time. Like all chronic diseases cases tend to cluster in families. There is a wide variability in prevalence between different ethnic groups, for example, diabetes is almost non-existant in the Eskimo, but is found in about 50 per cent of Pima Indians. However, the mode of inheritance is difficult to establish, and almost every type of genetic transmission has been proposed, including simple recessive, autosomal dominance with incomplete penetrance and multifactoral inheritance.

Evidence for separate inheritance of insulin-dependent and non-insulin-dependent diabetes comes from twin studies and from discoveries in the human histocompatibility complex. The concordance rate for insulin-dependent diabetes in monozygotic twins is less than 50 per cent, whereas that for non-insulin-dependent diabetes is greater than 90 per cent, suggesting a relatively greater role for environmental factors in the development of insulin-dependent diabetes. Further evidence for a different genetic basis comes from the observation that the prevalence of non-insulin-dependent diabetes in relatives of insulin-dependent diabetics is no greater than in the relatives of non-diabetics. However, that there is some inherited predisposition to insulin dependent diabetes has been demonstrated by histocompatibility studies. A positive association has been found with several HLA antigens, and a particularly strong association is demonstrable with antigens DW_3 and DW_4. The risk is additive in subjects with two high risk alleles. Other antigens, e.g. DW_2 are associated with a reduced risk of developing diabetes. The non-diabetic twin of a monozygotic pair discordant for diabetes will carry the same high risk alleles, indicating the operation of an environmental influence.

The high concordance rate for non-insulin-dependent twins suggests that this type is predominantly genetically determined. There is no association with HLA antigens. A particularly clear pattern of inheritance has been described for an uncommon subgroup of young, non-insulin-dependent diabetics (maturity onset diabetes in youth, MODY). These patients have mild symptoms, are controlled without insulin, and are not prone to ketoacidosis. There is often a strong family history with dominant inheritance, and these patients are less liable to microvascular complications.

Autoimmunity

There is an association between insulin-dependent diabetes and auto-immune organ specific diseases such as Hashimoto's thyroiditis, and pernicious anaemia. Serological studies have shown an increased incidence of organ specific antibodies directed at thyroid adrenal and gastric parietal cells in insulin-dependent diabetics. Circulating pancreatic islet cell antibodies are also present in diabetics with autoimmune disease. Indeed it is now known that islet cell antibodies are detectable in 50–85 per cent of newly diagnosed insulin-dependent diabetics, whereas they are demonstrable in only 5 per cent of non-insulin-dependent diabetics and 2 per cent of the general population (Lendrum et al, 1976). The incidence of these antibodies decreased with duration of the disease, but whether they are a factor in the development of pancreatic damage or arise secondary to it, is not certain. It has also been suggested that there is a subset of older, apparently non-insulin-dependent diabetics, in whom circulating islet cell antibodies are present, who go on to show metabolic deterioration and come to require insulin (Irvine et al, 1977). This group of patients resemble insulin-dependent diabetics in their HLA type.

Viruses

An association between diabetes and previous mumps infection was first reported in 1899. More recently the observation that the incidence of insulin-dependent diabetes in young patients is seasonal (Gamble and Taylor, 1969) and possibly associated with previous infection with Coxsackie B4 virus has led to speculation that in genetically susceptible individuals, B cell damage occurs as a result of virus infection. This could be virus damage either direct or mediated by autoimmune antibodies. It is difficult to assess the relevance of this to the development of insulin-dependent diabetes in the elderly. In any case it is very difficult to be sure at what stage islet cell damage occurs. It may antedate the appearance of clinical diabetes by many months.

Obesity

Obesity is the major non-genetic factor in the development of non-insulin-dependent diabetes mellitus. The incidence of obesity in this group is, depending on definition, in the range of 60–85 per cent. In the obese population an increased prevalence of diabetes is observed which depends on the duration rather than the degree of obesity. In some very highly inbred and very obese groups (e.g. Pima Indians, Nauruan Micronesions) over 50 per cent of the population become diabetic by the age of 60 years. Changes in body weight probably explain the increase in prevalence of diabetes seen in some ethnic groups when a change of life style allows for more to eat. The mechanism by which diabetes develops is probably related to the insulin resistance which accompanies excessive weight gain. In the genetically susceptible individual, the development of obesity may engender a demand for insulin which the secretory capacity of the B cell is unable to meet, resulting in hyperglycaemia. In many of these patients, reduction of weight results in improved glucose tolerance.

PATHOGENESIS

Insulin

Insulin is synthesized by the β cells of the islets of Langerhans as a single chain precursor, proinsulin, in which the two polypeptide chains (the A and B chains) are joined by a connecting peptide (C peptide). Proinsulin is converted to insulin within the β cell secretory granules and C peptide and insulin are secreted in equimolar concentrations. This equal relationship is not preserved in the peripheral circulation because of different metabolic clearance rates, but insulin and C peptide concentrations in the peripheral circulation show a high degree of correlation. The recent development of an assay for C peptide has enabled endogenous β cell secretion to be measured in the presence of exogenous insulin, and has provided a means of investigating β cell function in insulin-dependent diabetes.

Insulin is secreted by the β cell in response to the blood glucose concentration, possibly triggered by a membrane bound glucoreceptor. The insulin response is biphasic, with an initial rapid secretory burst, followed by a second, more gradual output. The former represents release of preformed insulin from β cell granules, and the latter release of newly synthesized insulin. The response to oral glucose is greater than that to an intravenous dose, and this augmentation of insulin response is attributed to release of gastrointestinal hormones, particularly GIP (gastric inhibitory polypeptide) upon contact of glucose with the gut mucosa.

There is strong evidence that the effects of insulin are triggered by binding of the hormone to a specific receptor on the cell membrane. Insulin receptors have been demonstrated not only in target cells (liver, muscle, fat) but also in a variety of other cell types. Binding is specific for insulin, rapid and reversible, and maximum biological action occurs when only about 10 per cent are occupied. The number of receptors is regulated by the ambient glucose concentration, so that hyperinsulinaemia leads to a reduction in the number of insulin binding sites. This process is known as down-regulation.

Insulin deficiency and insulin resistance

Following the discovery of insulin by Banting and Best in 1921 the assumption was made that diabetes was due to insulin deficiency. The introduction of a radioimmunoassay for circulating insulin by Berson and Yallow in 1960 led to confirmation that absolute deficiency of insulin is found in insulin-dependent diabetics. However, initial investigations in non-insulin-dependent diabetics failed to demonstrate a similar deficiency and there were insulin concentrations comparable to those in normal subjects. These studies failed to take into account the importance of obesity and the ambient glucose concentration, and when obese diabetics were compared with weight matched controls, a decrease in insulin secretion particularly in the early phase, was observed. In other words, the insulin response of normal subjects to hyperglycaemia was found to exceed that of the diabetic. Therefore it seems that the hyperinsulinaemia of obese diabetics is a consequence of obesity but compared with the obese non-diabetic there is still a relative deficiency in insulin secretion. The mechanism of the delayed insulin response is not clear. It does not appear to be related to gastrointestinal hormones and a defect in the glucoreceptor has been suggested.

There are, however, a group of non-obese, non-insulin-dependent diabetics in whom insulin deficiency is not present, and normal or even elevated plasma levels are found. In these patients we must suppose there is peripheral resistance to the action of insulin. Evidence for this comes from the demonstration of hyperglycaemia in the presence of hyperinsulinaemia and the reduced effectiveness of exogenous insulin. A variety of mechanisms have been suggested for this insulin resistance, including changes in receptor function and the presence of circulating insulin antagonists.

Whether the reduction in the number of receptors is a cause or a consequence of hyperinsulinaemia is not certain. There is no good evidence that circulating nonhormonal insulin antagonists are responsible for insulin resistance. However counter regulatory hormones such as glucagon, cortisol, growth hormone and adrenaline, exacerbate the effect of insulin lack, and account for increased need for exogenous insulin during infection and other stress.

In summary, insulin deficiency is found in insulin-dependent diabetes, but in non-insulin-dependent diabetics, there is both relative insulin deficiency and poor peripheral response to its action (Sherwin and Felig, 1978).

GLUCOSE TOLERANCE AND AGING

There is a decrease in glucose tolerance with age, beginning in the third or fourth decade and continuing throughout the adult life. This has only a small effect on fasting plasma glucose, which increases by only 1 mg/100 ml per decade. Whether the decrease in glucose tolerance represents the emergence of diabetes mellitus or is a change in the 'normal' distribution of values in the elderly is a matter for some debate (Davidson, 1979; De Fronzo, 1981).

Several factors may be important. Changes in body mass occur with age, with a decrease in lean body mass and an increase in adiposity without a significant change in the total body weight. As obesity is known to effect insulin secretion, and to be associated with insulin resistance, it is possible that an age-related increase in adiposity may alter the response to insulin. However on aggregate these increases in adiposity are relatively small, and are probably not enough to result in significant insulin resistance.

It is known that physical activity enhances insulin sensitivity and as older subjects are frequently less active, a decline in tissue responsiveness to insulin may occur, although this is likely to be important only in combination with other factors. The presence of other physical disorders in the elderly may well influence glucose tolerance, particularly if this necessitates treatment with diabetogenic drugs. Thus the thiazide diuretics are widely used in the treatment of oedema, congestive cardiac failure and hypertension, and the extent to which this contributes to impairment of glucose tolerance although not known could well be significant.

There have been several studies of the effect of age on insulin secretion. The results are conflicting, with some investigations finding a rise in insulin levels with age while others found no change (De Fronzo, 1981).

This may be explained by a difference in criteria for patient selection. In a group of patients selected on the basis of strictly normal glucose tolerance, an increase in the insulin response to a glucose lead was seen with age (Chlouverakis et al, 1967). However in patients who already had impaired tolerance there was little change in insulin levels. Taken together, these results suggest that normal glucose tolerance is maintained in the elderly only in the presence of higher circulating insulin levels.

Other work using the clamp technique to study

'glucose' insulin responses in the elderly, found no evidence of an age-related change in the total plasma insulin response to physiological elevation of blood glucose, although the insulin response to above normal elevation was impaired (De Fronzo, 1981). However, an age-related decline in total glucose metabolized was observed, suggesting that decreased tissue responsiveness to insulin may be the primary cause of a deterioration in glucose metabolism. As hepatic responsiveness to insulin did not change it was inferred that the site of resistance was the peripheral tissues. Whether this is due to a defect in the insulin receptor, or to some other factor, is not known. As these studies were performed using intravenous glucose, the gastrointestinal–pancreatic axis was bypassed, but there is no evidence to suggest impaired secretion of gastrointestinal hormones in the elderly.

Animal studies on the response of the β cell to glucose have found an age-related decrease in the amount of insulin secreted per β cell but an increase in the proportion of large islet cells, suggesting that an increased number of large islets compensates for an age-related decrease in sensitivity to hyperglycaemia (Reaven et al, 1979). If man behaves similarly there may be a decrease in sensitivity of the individual β cell to hyperglycaemia which is offset by an increase in large islet cell number and in insulin content.

The observations made on the decline in glucose tolerance with age have led to difficulties in interpretation of minor degrees of glucose tolerance, as it is not clear whether this represents a normal aging phenomenon or the emergence of true diabetes in the elderly. Using the old criteria based on the glucose tolerance test, approximately 20 per cent of the over-60 population could be considered diabetic. It has been suggested that adjustments should be made for age, and several methods have been proposed, the simplest being the addition of 0.6 mmol/l (10 mg/100 ml) after an oral glucose load.

The introduction of the term 'impaired glucose tolerance' and the raising of the diagnostic blood values for diabetes (see classification) has provided a more satisfactory basis for the interpretation of minor degrees of intolerance in the elderly (Table 35.2). The revised criteria are based on the results of several prospective population studies, including those in Birmingham and Bedford, in which individuals with minor abnormalities of glucose tolerance were observed over a 10 year period (Keen et al, 1979). The proportion of individuals in this group progressing to overt diabetes was 2–4 per cent per annum, with a similar proportion reverting to normal glucose tolerance and the rest remaining in the borderline category of impaired glucose tolerance. The development of overt diabetes was not influenced by treatment with a carbohydrate restricted diet or oral hypoglycaemic agents. New cases of clinical diabetes occurred from the normal 'surveyed population'. Those with impaired glucose tolerance do not carry an increased risk of developing retinopathy, cataract or proteinuria, but the risk of developing coronary, cerebrovascular and peripheral vascular disease may be similar to that of the diabetic.

On the basis of these findings it is recommended that the term diabetes be avoided in these borderline individuals, because of the psychological and social implications of such a diagnosis. However, it is important that they are followed , so that those who do progress to diabetes can be identified.

The introduction of this group has particular relevance to the elderly. However, it must not be forgotten that whatever the arguments about minor degrees of glucose intolerance, the incidence of overt diabetes increases with age, and many elderly patients present with symptoms and unequivocally raised blood glucose values.

Symptoms

The most characteristic symptom of severe diabetes is thirst. It is due to dehydration as the result of the osmotic diuresis provoked by hyperglycaemia. Thus, polyuria, especially at night, is also a classical symptom of diabetes and needs to be distinguished from the

Table 35.2 Diagnostic glucose concentrations

		Venous whole blood	Capillary whole blood	Venous plasma
Diabetes mellitus	Fasting	>7 mmol/litre (120 mg/100 ml)	>7.0 mmol/litre (120 mg/100 ml)	>8.0 mmol/litre (140 mg/100 ml)
	2 hr blood sugar	>10 mmol/litre (180 mg/100 ml)	>11.0 mmol/litre (200 mg/100 ml)	>11.0 mmol/litre (200 mg/100 ml)
Impaired glucose tolerance	Fasting	<7 mmol/litre (120 mg/100 ml)	>7.0 mmol/litre (120 mg/100 ml)	<8.0 mmol/litre (140 mg/100 ml)
	2 hr blood sugar	>7.0 <10.0 ml/l (120–180 mg/100 ml)	>8.0 <11.0 mmol/l (140–200 mg/100 ml)	>8.0 <11.0 mmol/l (140–200 mg/100 ml)

effects of insidious renal failure. In the elderly, diabetic polyuria also needs to be distinguished from the frequency of micturition found in prostatic hypertrophy or cystitis. Thirst does not correlate well with the degree of hyperglycaemia and may pass unnoticed. Wasting as a symptom of diabetes is due to calorie loss due to the glycosuria which often exceeds 100 g a day. It is often insidious and elderly patients frequently recall a gradual decline in weight, often from excessive levels 5 to 10 years before diagnosis. Fatigue and muscle weakness are also common but are too non-specific to be helpful in diagnosis. Pruritus vulvae is an extremely common symptom in diabetic women of all ages. It is accompanied by labial reddening and swelling which in severe cases spreads to the perineal skin and thighs. *Candida albicans* is nearly always found in the lesions, presumably related to the glycosuria since the lesion clears rapidly when the urine is made sugar-free. The male counterpart of balanitis is also a symptom of diabetes.

The protein nature of diabetic symptomatology can be realized when it is understood that in the elderly the first complaints may be those of long-term complications. Thus, visual deterioration, neuritic pain or weakness or lesions of the feet cause the patient who presumably has had asymptomatic diabetes for many years, to seek medical attention for the first time. The diagnosis is usually not difficult provided urine testing for glycosuria is made a routine part of the clinical examination. If this rule is neglected, however, the possibility of diabetes may be far from obvious, particularly in confused elderly patients with concomitant illness.

DIAGNOSIS

In the presence of the symptoms of thirst, polyuria and weight loss, with glycosuria, a single estimation of the blood sugar should be sufficient to confirm the diagnosis of diabetes, and even in the absence of symptoms or signs, a fasting blood glucose greater than 8 mmol/l (140 mg/100 ml) or a post-absorptive glucose in excess of 11 mmol/l (200 mg/100 ml) is enough to confirm an abnormality. A normal fasting blood glucose does not exclude diabetic glucose tolerance but, a post-absorptive value of less than 6 mmol/l (110 mg/100 ml) indicates that the subject is normal. When values are equivocal, or when it is necessary to exclude the possibility of diabetes, a glucose tolerance test is required.

It should be noted that the finding of glycosuria in an elderly patient is highly suggestive of diabetes, as the rise in renal threshold with age means that glycosuria is almost always associated with a significantly raised blood glucose. However, the diagnosis should always be confirmed by a blood test, and the figure recorded carefully for posterity.

Glucose tolerance tests

A glucose load of 75 g glucose in 250–350 ml of water is now the standard recommendation for the adult glucose tolerance test. Blood samples are taken fasting and at half, one, one-and-a-half and two hours after the dose. The patient should be seated during the test, and should not smoke.

Several factors may influence the test and result in incorrect interpretation. There is a diurnal insulin response to a glucose load, and a normal blood glucose response with maximal insulin release is found only if the test is done in the morning after an overnight fast. The fast should be of at least 10 hours duration, but no longer than 16 hours. Severe restriction of dietary carbohydrate before the test can produce a diabetic abnormality, carbohydrate intake should be not less than 250 g per day for the 3 days before the test. Those patients who have recently been subject to stress, for example, following trauma, myocardial infarction or infection may show transient abnormalities of glucose tolerance, and the test should not be performed during the immediate recovery period. Even when all the requirements are met, the test is not always reproducible. While some individuals may show a stable response to a glucose load, stress may produce very variable readings, and this is particularly common in the elderly.

Diagnostic values for diabetes mellitus have been raised above those generally in use over the last 25 years and the introduction of the category of impaired glucose tolerance for more minor abnormalities makes adjustment for age unnecessary. The diagnostic glucose concentrations for diabetes mellitus and impaired glucose tolerance are shown in the table.

Capillary samples give higher readings than venous samples by up to 1.67 mmol/l (30 mg/100 ml). The peak difference occurring one hour after the glucose load. Blood specimens which are not tested immediately should be stored in fluorinated tubes to inhibit glycolysis.

MANAGEMENT

In the elderly there can be no arguments about the benefits of the energetic treatment of symptomatic diabetes. It is easy if the patient complains of all the 'right things'. In practice it is not so easy to be sure about the need to treat moderate hyperglycaemia in the feeble patient with other disorders. On the one hand treatment may be very successful in restoring well being, on the other hand, it is wrong to impose dietary restrictions and the risk of hypoglycaemia without obvious clinical improvement. The theoretical benefit of good blood glucose control in preventing diabetic vascular complications are long term and for obvious reasons do not apply in old age. Successful treatment is always dependent on patient understanding and compliance and in those with mental impairment good control is unlikely to be possible. When in doubt there is a lot to be said for a trial of treatment and it takes time and further observation to make a judgement. Finally it must be reiterated that diabetes can and does deteriorate and the need for treatment can change.

Diet

Many patients can be satisfactorily controlled on diet alone, but it is equally important for those treated with oral hypoglycaemics and insulin to be given careful dietary instruction. The diet should be simple and flexible, as elderly people find it difficult to change their habits and are easily confused by too many instructions. Too rigid a diet may result in poor compliance or dietary deficiencies and the emphasis should be on the simple instructions to avoid sugar, sweet drinks, pop, confectionery, jam and cakes, etc.

Contrary to folklore there is no need to advise any restriction of bread or potatoes, provided the patient is not obese. Meal times do need to be regular, and it is very important that the food is palatable and well presented. Proper variety should ensure that the intake of other nutrients is adequate. There need be no prohibition of alcohol. Proprietary special diabetic foods are expensive, and since they use sorbitol as a sweetener, they are laxative if taken in any quantity.

Obese patients need be advised to reduce their total calorie intake by restriction of both carbohydrate and fat. Those patients requiring insulin will need more detailed advice about the spacing of carbohydrate especially the importance of the bed-time snack to avoid nocturnal hypoglycaemia.

Dietary advice is best given initially by a dietician, then reinforced if necessary by a health visitor. If possible, relatives should be instructed at the same time as the patient. Even when great care is taken, the effectiveness of advice is limited and perhaps only about 30 per cent of all diabetics adhere to their regimen. The increased cost of the diabetic diet should be borne in mind when dealing with the pensioner.

Oral hypoglycaemics

In general, oral hypoglycaemic agents are indicated when the post prandial blood glucose is consistently elevated above 10 mmol/l (180 mg/100 ml) on dietary treatment. However, in the elderly patient, higher blood glucose levels may be accepted as long as the patient is asymptomatic and is not losing weight. It is probably wise to treat all patients in whom the post prandial blood sugars are consistently above 14 mmol/l (250 mg/100 ml).

Many newly diagnosed patients can be treated by diet alone for 3–4 weeks and their response assessed, before a decision about the need for an oral agent is taken. However, there are patients with severe symptoms and substantial hyperglycaemia who need immediate oral treatment. The need for maintenance on an oral agent can be reassessed later. Oral hypoglycaemic agents are not indicated in patients with significant ketonuria, ketoacidosis or hyperosmolar states when insulin is always necessary.

Sulphonylureas

In 1970 doubts were cast on the long-term safety of both the sulphonylureas and the biguanides. It was reported there was an increased risk of cardiovascular deaths, compared with insulin or dietary therapy. These conclusions were never accepted in Europe or the UK where the sulphonylureas continue to be used on a very large scale. In the USA the use of oral agents remains restricted. The results of the original study have never been confirmed.

These drugs act primarily by stimulation of insulin release from the β cells but also have extra-pancreatic hypoglycaemic effects by their action on hepatic and peripheral tissues. The exact mechanism and which effect is most important in diabetic patients is not known. Tolbutamide is the shortest acting and least potent, having a half life of $3\frac{1}{2}$ hours. It is excreted in the urine after carboxylation in the liver. The short duration of action makes it the most suitable drug for use in the elderly, as it is least likely to produce hypoglycaemia. The converse is true of chlorpropamide which is more potent and has a half-life of about 30 hours. It is excreted unchanged in the urine. Its persistence enhances the risk of hypoglycaemia particularly in the confused elderly person who forgets to eat. Impaired renal function and excessive alcohol intake depressing gluconeogenesis further increases this risk. The drug should therefore be used with great caution and a dose of 500 mg/day should not be exceeded. Chlorpropamide has mild antidiuretic effects, which may be significant in the patient with congestive cardiac failure and which may rarely lead to impairment of consciousness from hyponatraemia. Some patients develop facial flushing with alcohol. Glibenclamide (Daonil in USA) is as potent as chlorpropamide in a much smaller dose of 2.5–5 mg daily, and has a shorter duration of action. It is of value if a more potent drug than tolbutamide is required, but there is a risk of hypoglycaemia. Several other sulphonylurea drugs are available, for example, glipizide, tolazamide, glymidine, but they have no clear advantages over the three mentioned. There is no value in combining more than one sulphonylurea.

The hypoglycaemic effects of the sulphonylureas is potentiated by salicylates, sulphonamides and phenylbutazone but this does not seem of much clinical importance. In obese patients the insulin-like action may result in undesirable weight gain.

A small proportion of patients unexpectedly fail to respond to oral therapy. The dose-effect relationship of sulphonylureas is limited, and a response will be seen within 4 weeks if the drug is to be effective. There is little point in increasing the dose above the maximum levels already stated. In other patients a failure to respond may develop later, sometimes after very many years of satisfactory control. For this reason, all patients receiving sulphonylureas need regular review to ensure that they are continuing to respond to therapy.

Biguanides

The mechanism of action of the biguanide compounds, phenformin and metformin, is not clear. The blood sugar is lowered only in the diabetic, and this action does not depend on the presence of islet tissue. They probably have several effects, including enhancement of peripheral uptake of glucose, inhibition of hepatic glycogen breakdown and depression of glucose absorption from the bowel.

Phenformin has been associated with an increased risk of lactic acidosis and has recently been withdrawn. Although clinical lactic acidosis is far less commonly associated with metformin, it has been reported. The risk is increased in those patients who are prone to tissue hypoxia (e.g. microvascular disease, ischaemic heart disease, cardiac failure) and those with renal or hepatic impairment. As these conditions are seen so commonly in the elderly, quite apart from the common side effects, metformin is frequently contraindicated in this age group.

The indication for the use of metformin is in the very obese, without other impairment, in whom dietary treatment has failed. The effectiveness of the drug in these circumstances is probably due to its anorexic effect. Gastrointestinal side effects are common, and include anorexia, metallic taste in the mouth, nausea, vomiting, abdominal pain and diarrhoea and many patients are unable to tolerate the drug. Metformin may sometimes be combined with a sulphonylurea if this has become ineffective on its own, as the hypoglycaemic effect of the two drugs is additive, but in many a change to insulin is preferable when this stage has been reached.

Insulin

Insulin is always required in the treatment of ketoacidosis and in hyperosmolar non-ketotic coma. It may also be required in elderly patients with acutely disordered diabetes, for example, associated with infection or myocardial infarction, or when symptoms on initial presentation are particularly severe. Many of these patients do not require long-term insulin therapy, and once the acute episode is over and the diabetes

controlled, a change to tablets should be considered. There is, however, a small group of patients in whom true insulin-dependent-diabetes presents in old age. These patients are often at, or below, ideal body weight, with acute onset of symptoms, severe hyperglycaemia and ketonuria. They may be difficult to identify, and in some cases a carefully monitored trial of tablets is necessary before a decision on treatment can be made.

A number of patients who have been satisfactorily controlled on tablets for many years may come to need insulin in old age, because of the development of symptomatic hyperglycaemia on maximum oral doses. These patients often respond well to insulin, but the possibility of an underlying cause for the loss of control should always be considered, and every patient should be screened for infection and myocardial infarction.

Insulin is sometimes indicated in patients with long-term complications of diabetes, for example, those with neuritic symptoms, and it may be necessary in order to obtain the best possible control in those patients with retinopathy or foot lesions.

When the decision to treat an elderly person with insulin is taken, it is necessary to assess the circumstances carefully. Many old people find it difficult to learn and are too anxious to cope with the injections. In these cases, and when there is mental impairment, confusion or when vision is poor, injections should be administered by the district nurse. However, many old people are alert and independent and easily master the new techniques. These patients often benefit from a few days in hospital at the start of insulin therapy, where they can receive frequent instruction and gain confidence in secure surroundings. This is particularly valuable for the patient who lives alone. In all elderly patients, careful instruction on recognition and prevention of hypoglycaemia is essential.

There is a wide variety of insulin preparations available, in different species, strengths and degrees of purity. The availability of two strengths, 40 units/ml and 80 units/ml has been a source of dosage errors in the past, and the introduction of single strength 100 units/ml insulin should simplify matters. New syringes are needed calibrated directly in units so that the old confusion between marks and units is now avoided. Two sizes of syringe are available, 0.5 ml for administration of up to 50 units and 1.0 ml for 50–100 units. Most preparations, both bovine and porcine, are now available in a highly purified form, which has a reduced incidence of local reaction and antibody formation. New diabetics should be started on the purer insulins, but there is little reason to change those satisfactorily controlled on older preparations, as long as they remain available. A change to highly purified insulin may be accompanied by a reduction in dose requirement and care should be taken to avoid hypoglycaemis. Human insulin, prepared either by substitution of amino acids in the porcine molecule, or by production from genetically altered *E. coli*, is now available, but has no clear advantage over the pure porcine and bovine insulins.

The many insulin preparations available can be grouped according to their duration of the action: short (with rapid onset), medium and long, and these may be used singly or in combination. In the elderly patient a single daily injection is usually best, and a long-acting preparation may be satisfactory. When a combination of insulins is required, premixed preparations (such as Neulente, Monotard, Mixtard) although less flexible are simpler for the older patient to use.

There is no 'formula' or working out the correct dose of insulin. When starting a new patient it is wise to begin with a small dose of 16–20 units in case of unexpected hypoglycaemia. The dose can then be increased by about 20 per cent every 3 days until there is glycaemic control. Care is required to simulate the patients normal meal times and usual activity.

Assessment of control

Regular urine testing is still a valuable method of monitoring diabetic control, as long as the limitations in the elderly are recognized. The rise in renal threshold with age means that negative tests should be interpreted with caution, as hyperglycaemia may still be present. On the other hand, glycosuria almost always indicates significant hyperglycaemia, and the blood sugar should then be estimated. The value of a random blood sugar is limited, especially if the patient has missed a meal to get to the hospital on time. In younger patients, frequent self-monitoring of blood glucose has been a valuable addition to urine tests, but it is rarely worthwhile burdening an elderly patient with this.

The discovery of glycosylated haemoglobin has brought a new method of assessing control (Gabbay, 1982). Haemoglobin A_1C is a minor component of haemoglobin A, and is structurally identical apart from a glucose group linked to the terminal amino acid of the β chains. In normal individuals, haemoglobin A_1C comprises 3–6 per cent of total haemoglobin, but in poorly controlled diabetics it may be up to 20 per cent. The proportion of haemoglobin A_1C is directly related to the glucose concentration in the blood. Once formed, glycosylated haemoglobin will stay in the circulation for the remaining life span of the red cell, and can therefore be used as an index of the general level of glycaemia over the preceding 6 weeks. Improved control is followed after a time lag of several weeks by a fall in haemoglobin A_1C concentration. A falsely low value is seen in haemolytic anaemia, blood loss and after blood transfusion. The test is valuable in the elderly when a change in treatment is contemplated and the adequacy of the current treatment needs further assessment.

Hypoglycaemia

Hypoglycaemia may occur both in patients on insulin and those taking oral hypoglycaemic agents. It is particularly dangerous in the elderly, as it is more likely to result in irreversible brain damage because of coexisting cerebrovascular disease. Animal studies have shown that the combination of a local arterial lesion and a lowering of the blood glucose can result in a permanent hemiplegia.

The most frequent causes of hyperglycaemia in the elderly patient are omission of meals and administration of an incorrect insulin dose, which may occur either because of poor eyesight or because of confusion, which may sometimes result in a dose being taken twice. In some patients dosage requirements may fall, often for no apparent reason, although a deterioration in renal function should then be looked for.

The initial symptoms are due to catecholamine release and include shaking, sweating, palpitations, weakness and hunger. Cerebral symptoms include headaches, blurred vision, perioral parasthesia and behavioural changes. In the absence of treatment there may be progression to drowsiness, confusion and focal cerebral dysfunction, resulting in hemiparesis, convulsions or brain stem disorders. It follows that any elderly person presenting as an emergency with a stroke should have a blood sugar estimation to exclude hypoglycaemia, because the fact that they are on insulin may be overlooked.

The early symptoms may be reversed by the administration of carbohydrate, but once consciousness has been lost, intravenous glucose is required. On occasions, spontaneous recovery may occur, but if it does not, the elderly person living alone is at risk of developing irreversible brain damage, hypothermia and bronchopneumonia from prolonged hypoglycaemia. Once the acute problem has been treated, the cause of the hypoglycaemia should be considered. If there is no apparent cause, insulin dose should be reduced, or if oral agents are used they should either be stopped or changed to a shorter-acting preparation. The importance of regular meals and a snack before bedtime should be stressed to the patient, and if vision is poor, or the patient confused, injections should be administered by the district nurse. The daily contact resulting from this arrangement is often of great value in the elderly.

In some cases, chronic mild hypoglycaemia may occur, resulting in intellectual impairment and confusion. It is particularly difficult to diagnose, but should be suspected if the blood sugar is persistently below 5 mmol/l (100 mg/100 ml) in a confused patient.

Ketoacidosis

About 20 per cent of all cases of ketoacidosis occur in patients over the age of 60 (Fig. 35.1) and although

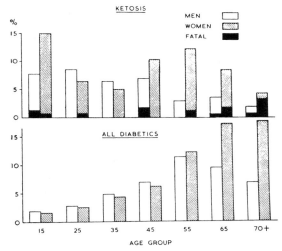

Fig. 35.1 Incidence of severe ketosis for men and women in 10-year age groups compared with the prevalence of clinical diabetes in the same age group (FitzGerald et al, 1961).

many of these are longstanding diabetics, a proportion present for the first time in ketosis. The most common precipitating factor is infection, which may be quite trivial. Other causes include stroke, trauma, myocardial infarction, inadequate insulin dosage and previously undiagnosed diabetes.

Symptoms include thirst, polyuria, vomiting and confusion. Most elderly patients have impaired consciousness. The prognosis is grave if the patient is comatose. Dehydration and hyperventilation (Kussmaul respiration) are important diagnostic signs and the hyperventilation may be mistaken for bronchopneumonia in the elderly. The breath smells of acetone and there is tachycardia and hypotension, with peripheral vasodilatation due to acidaemia. This may lead to hypothermia and very few patients have a fever, even in the presence of severe infection.

Initial investigations should include blood glucose and ketone bodies, urea and electrolytes, pH and packed cell volume. The use of Diastix to test the urine is unreliable in ketoacidosis, as falsely low values are obtained in the presence of ketones. If the diagnosis is certain, treatment should begin without waiting for laboratory confirmation. Fluid replacement is most important as tissue perfusion must be improved before insulin can have an effect. The fluid deficit is usually about 5–6 litres, and in the elderly replacement should be monitored with a central venous pressure line. Continuing urinary losses of water may be large in the first few hours and it is important to take this into account when calculating replacement volumes. Normal saline should be used unless the plasma sodium rises above 155 mmol/l (155 mg/100 ml) in which case half normal

saline should be substituted. Regular plasma electrolyte estimations are an important part of management.

The use of frequent small doses of insulin is now established, and soluble insulin should be given intramuscularly in an initial dose of 20 units, followed by 6 units hourly. If the blood glucose has not fallen after 6 hours, fluid replacement should be reassessed and insulin administration changed to carefully monitored continuous intravenous infusion at a rate of 6 units/hour. Intravenous bolus injections are of little value, as the half life of insulin in the circulation is only 4–5 minutes. When the blood glucose falls below 15 mmol/l (270 gm/100 ml) an infusion of 5 per cent dextrose should be started (continuing saline if the patient is still dehydrated) and the insulin changed to 6 units intramuscularly 2-hourly (Alberti, 1977).

Potassium replacement should begin when the first dose of insulin is given, monitored by frequent laboratory estimations and ECG. Sodium bicarbonate can be used with caution if the pH is less than 7.0 (100 mmol in one hour, initially) and discontinued when the pH rises above 7.0.

Other measures include the use of antibiotics after urine and blood have been sent for culture either because there is suspicion of infection following the use of central venous or bladder catheter. Semiconscious or unconscious patients need a nasogastric tube.

The mortality for even the uncomplicated cases of ketoacidosis is high over the age of 65. Arterial occlusion may develop in a variety of sites, and the combination of myocardial infarction and ketosis is particularly ominous.

Hyperosmolar non-ketotic coma

About 10 to 20 per cent of severe hyperglycaemic comas present without marked ketoacidosis and the majority occur in middle-aged and elderly patients, many of whom were not previously known to be diabetic. The pathogenesis is uncertain, but the condition has been associated with a high carbohydrate intake, particularly carbohydrate rich drinks, taken in larger quantities to quench the thirst of diabetes, and some drugs have been implicated, including propranolol, thiazide diuretics and corticosteroids.

There is often a history of thirst and polyuria for several days or weeks, followed by impairment of consciousness, which may come on gradually over 1–2 days. The conscious level is directly related to the degree of hyperosmolarity. Focal neurological signs may develop, and fits occur in 25 per cent of cases.

There is marked dehydration, often with hypotension as a result of the severe osmotic diuresis. Respiration is shallow, without acetone on the breath, but the presence of ketones in the urine does not exclude the diagnosis.

Laboratory findings usually include a very high blood

glucose value of greater than 50 mmol/l (900 mg/100 ml) but ketone bodies are absent from the blood and the pH is normal. Plasma urea is usually above 20 mmol/l (120 mg/100 ml) and plasma osmolarity is greater than 360 mmol/l. In about 50 per cent of cases the plasma sodium exceeds 150 mmol/l (150 mg/100 ml) which obviously contributes to the hyperosmolar state but both sodium and potassium levels may be normal or even low.

Treatment consists of replacement of lost fluid with saline, which should be isotonic if the plasma sodium is below 150 mmol/l, but half normal otherwise. Several litres will be necessary to replace the deficit, and their administration needs to be monitored by central venous pressure line. Insulin should be given in small frequent intramuscular doses as for ketoacidosis, and potassium replacement started immediately unless there is hyperkalaemia.

The incidence of disseminated intravascular coagulation and post-coma thrombosis is high, and the use of subcutaneous heparin should be considered.

Clinical improvement tends to be slower than in ketoacidosis, and impaired consciousness may persist for 24–48 hours, with eventual full recovery. Mortality is high, rates of 40–50 per cent being reported, and many deaths result from arterial occlusions (Podolsky, 1978).

Lactic acidosis

Its presence should be suspected when there is a low pH in the absence of ketonuria. Expert laboratory help is needed to confirm the presence of massive lactate excess, and the analysis made on immediately deproteinized chilled blood specimens.

This is a rare cause of metabolic acidosis in the elderly diabetic. The incidence has fallen since the decrease in the use of phenformin. It may complicate major illness, such as pulmonary embolus or myocardial infarction, and should be suspected in acidotic patients taking biguanides. Large amounts of bicarbonate are recommended for treatment, but in the elderly the mortality is very high.

COMPLICATIONS

Most of the complications of diabetes are attributable to vascular disease. The atheromatous changes occurring in the major arteries are indistinguishable from those occurring in non-diabetics, but usually occur earlier and more extensively. Changes which are specific for diabetes are found in the small blood vessels. In the capillaries, the basement membrane is thickened, and the degree of thickening is almost always present in long established diabetes, whether there is clinical evidence of microangiopathy or not.

Debate continues as to whether the changes observed are related to the metabolic defect (i.e. hyperglycaemia, or some other consequence of insulin deficiency) or whether they arise as an independently inherited abnormality. The bulk of evidence favours a relationship between metabolic defect and microangiopathy (Stowers, 1975). Thus those patients who develop diabetes secondary to pancreatic disease, haemochromatosis or endocrine disorders are also susceptible to microangiopathy. Changes typical of diabetic vascular disease may be observed in the kidney of a non-diabetic donor after transplant to a diabetic patient and in animal studies, typical retinal and renal lesions are produced in experimentally induced diabetes (Cameron et al, 1975). Against these arguments is the observation that microvascular disease can develop before clinically detectable diabetes, but the presence of fluctuations of glucose tolerance before diagnosis cannot be excluded.

In diabetes the prevalence of microvascular disease is very high, increasing in frequency with increasing duration of the disease. The commonest effect is retinopathy, which is readily seen on opthalmoscope in 50 per cent of patients who have had the disease for more than 20 years. Clinical evidence of nephropathy is present in 25 per cent of patients who have had the disease 15 years, but the frequency is much higher if the kidneys are examined histologically. However, there are some patients who are totally free of clinically detectable diabetic vascular disease after 20 years. Why this should be so is one of the most important questions in clinical diabetes. Perhaps there are important genetic differences between the two groups of patients.

Whether good diabetic control can prevent or delay the development of microvascular disease is the subject of much discussion. Animal experiments in the dog and cat suggest that the incidence and severity of retinopathy and nephropathy is decreased in the presence of good control (Fox et al, 1977; Bloodworth et al, 1973). In humans the evidence is less direct, but improvement is sometimes seen in retinopathy and nephropathy with change from poor control to good control (Miki et al, 1969; Stowers, 1975).

Much of the tissue pathology of diabetes has been likened to a premature aging process. Cataract occurs at an earlier age and the development of atherosclerosis is premature and accelerated in the diabetic. This could partly result from age-related changes in arterial smooth muscle and endothelial cells. Thickening of the capillary basement membrane also increases with age in healthy individuals and this universal change may just be accelerated in diabetes. Accelerated aging of collagen also occurs in the diabetic, and fibroblasts from diabetic patients show the decreased life span and replication rates in culture which again are universal features of cell aging (Bierman, 1980).

The impaired glucose tolerance of the elderly diabetic may itself be due to relatively early development of the aging process in the islet β cells, with loss of sensitivity to the glycaemic stimulus, or of the total insulin secretory capacity of the β cell mass. (See Glucose tolerance and aging, p. 718).

Arterial disease

Coronary, cerebral and ilio-femoral atherosclerosis is the major cause of chronic ill health and premature death in both insulin-dependent and non-insulin-dependent diabetics.

The excess mortality is greatest in the younger age groups, falling off in the elderly, but not to the level of the general population. Mortality is particularly high in middle-aged women, whose death rate is equal to that of the men. There seems to be little correlation with the duration or severity of diabetes, and those with merely impaired glucose tolerance may also carry an increased risk.

The risk of dying immediately following myocardial infarction is twice as high in the diabetic compared with an age-matched non-diabetic control. The reason for the increased susceptibility of the diabetic to atherosclerosis is not clear, although there is an increased frequency of such risk factors as hypertension and abnormalities of plasma lipids.

Atherosclerosis occurs earlier in diabetics and is more likely to affect the smaller vessels. Although the indicators for arteriography and arterial surgery are the same as for the non-diabetic, treatment is often less successful presumably because of the concomitant small vessel involvement. It hardly needs saying that no diabetic should smoke cigarettes.

Renal

The commonest and most important changes seen in the kidney in diabetes occur in the glomeruli. The diffuse form of glomerulosclerosis consists of thickening at the centre of the glomerular lobules, accompanied by a variable degree of thickening of the peripheral basement membrane. The characteristic nodular lesions seem to be a manifestation of the same underlying process (Fig. 35.2). The lesions are found in patients of all ages, and the original description by Kimmelstiel and Wilson in 1936 included several elderly patients.

The incidence of both diffuse and nodular glomerulosclerosis increases with the duration of diabetes, and at least 80 per cent of patients with nephropathy also have retinopathy. In the elderly patient nephropathy, like retinopathy, may be recognized at, or soon after, diagnosis.

The first clinical sign is proteinuria, but this is not specific for nephropathy. Although oedema may occur, a true nephrotic syndrome is rare. Hypertension is a late complication, and renal failure may develop, but progression is usually slow, and death is more likely to be from coexisting coronary artery disease.

Urinary tract infection is not more frequent in diabetics than in non-diabetics, but the effect may be more severe. It may be the cause of deterioration in diabetic control, especially in the elderly. The condition of renal papillary necrosis, which is a rare complication of renal infection, is more common in diabetics, but may

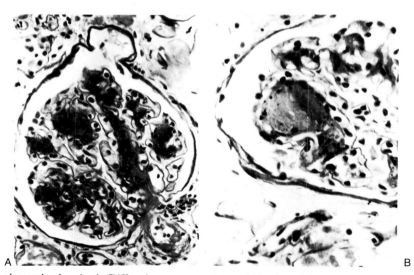

Fig. 35.2 Diabetic glomerulosclerosis. A: Diffuse basement membrane thickening with quite marked sclerosis in the centre of lobules. B: A typical Kimmesstiel-Wilson nodule.

range in severity from an asymptomatic post mortem finding to a severe pyelonephritis with deterioration in renal function.

Ocular

The ocular complications of diabetes are important in old age, not only because they are a common cause of visual impairment and blindness, but also because they may lead to the diagnosis of diabetes in a previously unrecognized case. One in every eight diabetics over the age of 70 presents with an ocular complaint, most often cataract, and 12 per cent of elderly patients have retinopathy at diagnosis, therefore the routine screening of elderly patients for glycosuria at eye clinics is worthwhile.

Retinopathy

About 40 per cent of all diabetics over the age of 60 show evidence of retinopathy, although this is usually of the background type. Even so, the incidence of blindness due to retinopathy over the age of 70 is about 20 times that of the 30–50 age group. Every newly diagnosed diabetic should have careful opthalmoscopic examination of the fundi with the pupil fully dilated, but in the elderly patient it may be difficult to distinguish changes due to retinopathy from those of hypertension, atherosclerosis and retinal vein thrombosis.

Mild background retinopathy produces no visual symptoms and advances slowly and good vision is maintained for many years. However, regular examination is necessary so that action can be taken early if deterioration occurs. The lesions, microaneurysms, dot haemorrhages and exudates are scattered, but often most marked just lateral to the macula (Figs 35.3, 35.4). The development of maculopathy occurs most commonly in non-insulin-dependent diabetes of the middle aged and elderly. The term implies haemorrhages and exudates encroaching on the macula causing ischaemia and oedema. Even slight visual deterioration is a serious sign in these circumstances, and the elderly often do not complain until there is marked visual loss. Visual deterioration is more rapid if the diabetes is diagnosed late in life, and the lesions tend to be more advanced and less likely to respond to treatment.

Proliferative retinopathy may occur in any age group, but is more common in the young and middle-aged. It is often the final cause of visual loss, but is asymptomatic until a complication such as vitreous haemorrhage occurs. New vessels may arise at any part of the retina, but those at the optic disc are of more serious prognostic significance than those at the periphery. In all cases referral to an opthalmologist is essential. 'Pre-proliferative' changes, indicating ischaemia and imminent formation of new vessels include multiple cotton wool

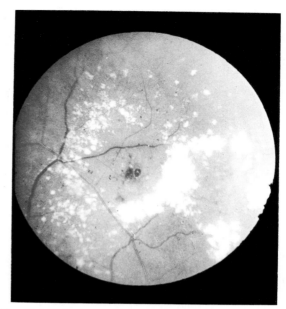

Fig. 35.3 Diabetic retinopathy showing circinate deposits of hard exudate. In the central area are microaneurisms and haemorrhages.

spots, multiple haemorrhages, venous loops and venous bleeding. The development of vitreous haemorrhage, fibrous tissue formation and thrombotic glaucoma indicates end stage retinopathy. Even at this stage, treatment may preserve partial vision.

Treatment has been revolutionized by the development of photocoagulation and vitrectomy techniques, and vision can now be maintained in about 70 per cent of patients who would otherwise have gone blind. Indications for photocoagulation are maculopathy and proliferative retinopathy. Treatment of new vessels arising at the disc is urgent and may produce dramatic improvement in what is a poor prognostic group. Maculopathy should be treated early, as the condition tends to be arrested rather than improved. Vitrectomy techniques have developed considerably in the last few years, but a successful outcome cannot be guaranteed. Although there is no firm evidence that good diabetic control will prevent or arrest the progress of retinopathy, there is sufficient indirect evidence to make the attempt worthwhile.

Cataract

Lens opacities are no commoner in older diabetics than in non-diabetics, but cataract extraction is needed 3–4 times more commonly, suggesting that the progression of the cataract is more rapid. The results of surgical removal should be good provided there is no underlying diabetic or senile macular disease.

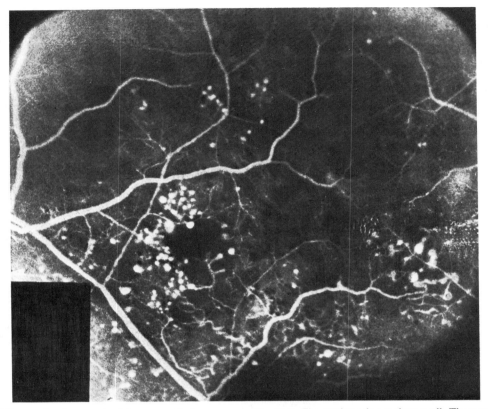

Fig. 35.4 Fluorescein photograph of the same retinal area seen in Fig. 35.3. The exudates do not show at all. The central area can now be seen to be avascular but surrounded by multiple microaneurisms.

Neuropathy

The disturbances of peripheral nerve function associated with diabetes are more complex than in most other types of neuropathy, suggesting that the underlying pathogenic mechanisms are likely to be varied. Estimates of the incidence of neuropathy are difficult because although a high proportion of diabetics show abnormalities of nerve conduction, only some of these will have clinical signs or symptoms (Mayne, 1965).

Diabetic neuropathy can be classified into two major groups, the symmetrical polyneuropathies, with a predominance of sensory and autonomic manifestations, and the asymmetrical syndromes, comprising mononeuropathies, multiple mono-neuropathies and radiculopathies. However, mixed syndromes occur frequently.

Symmetrical sensory polyneuropathy is the commonest form of diabetic neuropathy, and is usually a complication of long-standing diabetes, although elderly patients may have symptoms of neuropathy on presentation. It is frequently asymptomatic, the only detectable abnormality being the absence of ankle jerks and loss of vibration sense. As these abnormalities are frequently present in the non-diabetic elderly subject exact diagnosis may be uncertain. If pain and light touch sensation are also lost, this should be regarded as evidence of neuropathy.

When symptoms are present, these are usually of numbness and paraesthesiae in the feet. The fingers are less often affected, but blind diabetics may find that loss of fine sensation prevents them from reading Braille. Pain is often a significant feature, taking the form of stabbing or burning sensations in the lower limbs, and this tends to be most troublesome at night. If severe, it may cause insomnia and depression, and should be treated by good diabetic control, non-addictive analgesics and antidepressants. Severe sensory polyneuropathy is irreversible, and the major hazard to the diabetic is the risk of injury, ulceration and sepsis developing in the insensitive foot. Some patients develop neuropathic (Charcot) joints.

Autonomic neuropathy, if of sufficient severity to give rise to symptoms, is associated with the presence of sensory polyneuropathy. It is probably present in a mild form in many longstanding diabetics. Disturbances include postural hypotension, with syncopal episodes on standing, cardiac denervation, abnormalities of sweating, diarrhoea, which tends to be nocturnal and may respond to treatment with broad spectrum antibiotics, impaired gastric motility, constipation, bladder atony and impotence. Many of the symptoms are self-limiting but distressing.

Mononeuropathies and multiple mononeuropathies are not specific for diabetes. The onset is often acute, sometimes following a period of poor control, and recovery usually occurs, although the time course may be variable. Cranial nerves, particularly the third and sixth, may be involved, as may isolated peripheral nerves, particularly those susceptible to pressure palsies. Manifestations may be sensory, mixed motor and sensory or purely motor. A common form of mononeuropathy is femoral mononeuropathy (diabetic amyotrophy) in which the femoral nerve or nerve roots are involved. The condition usually occurs in the elderly patient, either recently diagnosed or not previously known to be diabetic. There is pain in the thighs, with asymmetrical weakness and wasting, loss of knee jerks and no objective sensory loss. Plantar responses may become extensor and CSF protein is usually elevated. Slow, spontaneous recovery usually occurs, particularly in well controlled cases and the condition is an indication for strict control. Radiculopathy may cause pain in any part of the trunk. The pain is frequently misdiagnosed.

There is evidence to suggest that the acute forms of neuropathy respond to improved control. Poorly controlled patients have a greater reduction in nerve conduction velocity and this improves following treatment in newly diagnosed cases. There is greater risk of isolated nerve lesions in poorly controlled cases, and this may be reduced by good control. The benefit of good control in longstanding neuropathy is less clear, but further deterioration may be prevented.

Diabetic foot

The most important effect of diabetic neuropathy is to impair sensation in the feet. The results of this may exist in a 'pure' form but more often they are combined with the effects of ischaemia and sepsis. The contribution of each element has to be considered carefully in each case and the blanket term diabetic gangrene is perhaps best avoided. Loss of pain sensation may cause burns on the feet, either from hot water bottles or from sitting close to a fire. Damage may also result from ill-fitting shoes or from nails projecting from the sole of the shoe. Blistering of the toes may occur without recognized trauma. Pressure ulceration of the heel occurs after prolonged bed rest. A common presentation is the perforating ulcer over the metatarsophalangeal joints following clawing of the feet. At first the lesion is painless and indolent. Eventually there is extension into the metatarsophalangeal joint with infection which often spreads to involve the fascial web spaces of the foot and at this stage the

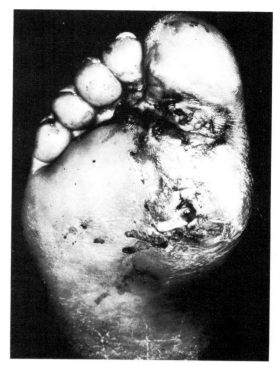

Fig. 35.5 Neuropathic perforating foot ulcer with sepsis in the foot. Foot pulses were present.

foot becomes painful (Fig. 35.5). Bone necrosis with a 'sucked candy' appearance of the metatarsal heads, unsuspected fractures and neuropathic destruction of the tarsal bone (Charcot's joints) are all radiological features of neuropathy.

Much can be done to avoid the disastrous consequences of sensory deprivation of the diabetic foot by regular attention to cleanliness and footwear. The services of a chiropodist are important (particularly for the elderly with failing vision), both for the care of the nails and to remove hard skin over pressure areas. Provided the arterial circulation is adequate, there is scope for local surgery to the foot such as local removal of toes, ray amputation and mid-tarsal amputation for the more serious septic neuropathic lesions. Ischaemia of the diabetic foot is due to athersclerosis affecting the aortoiliac system or the run off from the femoral vessels. There has been much debate as to whether ischaemia is also due to a more specific diabetic arteriolar or capillary lesion. Mönckeberg's sclerosis causing calcification of the digital arteries of the feet is often found as a radiological appearance but is not of functional importance. It has been calculated that 50 per cent of elderly men and 80 per cent of elderly women with arteriosclerotic gangrene are diabetics. The indications for arteriography and arterial surgery for ischaemia of the legs and feet are similar to the non-diabetic but in general the results both for salvaging the limb and ultimate survival are disappointing.

LONG-TERM CARE

Once diabetes has been diagnosed and the appropriate treatment instituted it is important to establish some kind of routine for follow up. Diabetic patients, if ambulant, are best seen collectively, but particularly in the elderly, there is no need for them to travel long distances to attend hospital clinics. A group practice of 10 000 patients will yield enough diabetic patients (about 60) to make it worthwhile for specialist help to be available if the patients are seen together, and it is hoped that this pattern of collaboration between hospital and general practice will increase in the future. Many of the problems concern general medicine and are the province of the family doctor. However, the weight, the result of a urine test and blood sugar need recording routinely in all the patients. An enquiry should be made about diabetic symptomatology and the side-effects of treatment. Especial attention should be directed to the state of the eyes and the feet. Individual patients often need to be considered over a very long time-span. In general, diabetes is a progressive disease and patients who at first may be well controlled on diet or oral therapy often come to need insulin after a number of years.

REFERENCES

Alberti K G M M 1977 Low dose insulin in the treatment of diabetic ketoacidosis. Archives of Internal Medicine 137: 1367–1376
Albin J, Rifkin H 1982 Etiologies of diabetes mellitus. In: Raskin P (ed) Medical Clinics of North America: Diabetes Mellitus Vol 66, Saunders, Philadelphia, p 1209–1226
Bierman E L 1980 In: Annual review of Gerontology and Geriatrics. Eisdorfer (ed) Springer, New York
Bloodworth J M B, Engerman R L 1973 Diabetic microangiopathy in the experimentally diabetic dog and its prevention by careful control with insulin (abstract). Diabetes 22 (suppl 1): 290
Cameron J S, Ireland J T and Watkins P J 1975 The kidney and renal tract. In: Keen H, Jarrett R J (eds) Complications of Diabetes, p 99–150
Chlouverakis C, Jarrett R J, Keen H 1967 Glucose tolerance, age and circulating insulin. Lancet i: 806–809
Davidson M B 1970 The effect of ageing on carbohydrate metabolism. A review of the English literature and a practical approach to the diagnosis of Diabetes Mellitus in the Elderly. Metabolism 28: 688–705
DeFronzo R A 1981 Glucose intolerance and ageing. Diabetes Care 4: 493–501
FitzGerald M G, O'Sullivan D J, Malins J M 1961 Fatal diabetic ketosis. British Medical Journal 1: 247–250
Fox C J, Darby S C, Ireland J T, Sonksen P H 1977 Blood glucose control and glomerular capillary basement thickening in experimental diabetes. British Medical Journal 2: 605–607
Gabbay K H 1982 Glycosylated haemoglobin and diabetes mellitus. In: Raskin P (ed) Medical Clinics of North America: Diabetes Mellitus Vol 66. Saunders, Philadelphia, p 1309–1315
Gamble D R, Taylor K W, Cumming H 1973 Coxsackie viruses and diabetes mellitus. British Medical Journal 4: 260–262
Irvine W J, McCallum C J, Gray R S, Campbell C J, Duncen L J P,

Farquhar J W et al 1977 Pancreatic islet cell antibodies in diabetes mellitus correlated with the duration and type of diabetes, coexistent autoimmune disease and HLA type. Diabetes 26: 138–147
Keen H, Jarrett R J, Alberti K G M M 1979 Diabetes Mellitus: A new look at diagnostic criteria. Diabetologia 16: 283–285
Lendrum R, Walker G, Cudworth A G, Theophenides C, Pyke D A, Bloom A, Gamble D R 1976 Islet cell antibodies in diabetes mellitus. Lancet 2: 1273–1276
Mayne N 1965 Neuropathy in the diabetic and non-diabetic populations. Lancet 2: 1313–1316
Miki E, Fukude M, Kuzuya T, Kosake K, Nakao K 1969 Relation of the course of retinopathy to control of diabetes, age and therapeutic agents in diabetic Japanese agents. Diabetes 18: 773–780
Miki E, Kuzuya T, Ide T, Nakao 1972 Frequency, degree and progression with time of proteinuria in diabetic patients. Lancet 1: 922
National Diabetes Data Group 1979 Classification and diagnosis of diabetes mellitus and other categories of glucose intolerance. Diabetes 28: 1039–1057
Podolsky S 1978 Hyperosmolar non ketotic coma in the elderly diabetic. Medical Clinics of North America: Diabetes Mellitus Vol 62. Saunders, Philadelphia, p 815–828
Reaven E P, Gold G, Reaven G M 1979 Effect of age on glucose-stimulated insulin release by the β cell of the rat. Journal of Clinical Investigation 64: 591–99
Sherwin R, Felig P 1978 Pathophysiology of diabetes mellitus. In: Podolsky S (ed) Medical Clinics of North America: Vol 62 No 4, Saunders, Philadelphia, p 695–711
Stowers J M 1975 Complications in relation to diabetic control — general review. In: Complications of Diabetes Ed Keen and Jarrett p 1–5

The respiratory system

ANATOMICAL CHANGES

Abnormalities of the chest wall are common in old people with about two-thirds of them exhibiting a degree of kyphosis. Decalcification of the ribs is usual and results, especially in women, in some reduction of the transverse thoracic diameter and a false radiological appearance of cardiomegaly. Increased calcification of the costal cartilages occurs and contributes to the overall increase in chest wall rigidity. Because the rib cage is less mobile the diaphragm and abdominal wall muscles become more important than those of the rib cage in effecting ventilation (Rizzato and Marazzini, 1970). During resting breathing the limitation of movement is more evident during expiration than inspiration, perhaps because there are no efficient accessory muscles of expiration.

The bronchi are little altered by normal aging. There is no change in the quantity of bronchial cartilage (Bedrossian et al, 1977), and a large scale autopsy study (Ryder et al, 1971) found no alteration in the bronchial mucous gland volume even in advanced old age. Other unaltered tissues include goblet cells (Anderson et al, 1970) and bronchial epithelium (Auerbach et al, 1962). Mucous gland volume and epithelial abnormalities increase in cigarette smokers in whom smoking and aging may act synergistically to enhance histopathological changes in the small airways (Cosio et al, 1980).

The alveolar surface area falls by approximately 4 per cent per decade from its average value of about 75 m² at age 30 (Thurlbeck, 1981). Although some old people have lungs which are morphologically indistinguishable from those of young adults, in most the alveoli become flatter and shallower while the alveolar ducts enlarge so that the proportion of the lung volume formed by alveolar air decreases. These changes are associated with reduced extensibility of the alveolar wall (Sugihara et al, 1971) with some increase in the resting length of alveolar tissue altering the internal geometry of the lung. The alveolar wall is thinner and contains fewer capillaries (Reid, 1967).

The alveolar wall consists of alveolar epithelium and capillary endothelium with their basement membranes and an interstitium of connective tissue fibres and mesenchymal cells. Small collagen fibres form a continuous mesh in a helical configuration in the alveolar wall. Larger fibres pass across the thickness of the wall and are closely applied to the capillaries; even larger fibres form the supportive struts of the alveolar wall as they cross it (Rosenquist, 1981). This configuration supports a mechanically stable duct system and permits varying linear and circumferential airway dimensions (Young et al, 1980). Elastic tissue follows the same arrangement. There is probably no change in the total lung content of collagen or elastic tissue with age. Some reduction in the number and thickness of elastic fibres around the alveolar ducts and the mouths of the alveoli has been observed (Wright, 1961), and may contribute to the dilating of these structures. An electron microscopy study (Adamson, 1968) did not find any age related quantitative differences in elastic tissue or collagen with aging and there was no calcification, disruption or increasing fragmentation of elastic fibres. Elastin, which is the major component of elastic tissue, shows some increase with age but this is confined to the pleura and septa (Pierce and Ebert, 1965).

The role of collateral ventilatory pathways in health and disease is unknown and the effects of aging unclear. Pores of Kohn, inter-bronchiolar channels of Martin and alveolar-bronchiolar channels of Lambert are possible pathways (Menkes and Traystman, 1977) but at Functional Residual Capacity (FRC) the resistance to flow along collaterals is high in healthy people suggesting they are of little importance during normal breathing. The resistance to collateral air flow is greater in old subjects than young though in emphysematous patients it may be less than the resistance to flow in airways (Terry et al, 1978) and hence play a part in maintaining alveolar ventilation.

The pulmonary artery and its main branches exhibit a steady increase with age in wall thickness, radius and cross-sectional area. There are no such concomitant changes in the main pulmonary veins (Speransky, 1978) so that in old people the ratio of outflow to inflow cross-sectional area is about 1 compared with a ratio of 2 in young adults. Smaller arteries and veins show a steady fall in medial collagen content with age though thickness of the media is little changed (MacKay et al 1978). The vessels become less extensible and there is loss of elastic tissue in the smaller arteries (Semmons, 1970). Thickening of the intima occurs (Wagenvoort and Wagenvoort, 1975). Deposition of amyloid material is a frequent finding in very old lungs, being present in more than 20 per cent of people aged 85 years and over (Kunze, 1979). The commonest pattern is a combination of vascular and alveolar septal deposition. Less frequently the amyloid is found only in the alveolar septa.

PHYSIOLOGICAL CHANGES

Lung volumes

A large scale cross-sectional spirometric study of healthy non-smokers living in an environment free of significant air pollution (Morris et al, 1971) showed that both the forced expired volume in one second (FEV1) and the forced vital capacity (FVC) decline from about the age of 20 years. Only 8 per cent of their population was over 64 years old and Figure 36.1, which is derived from their data, includes extrapolation. As in most similar studies FEV1 falls more steeply than FVC and the changes are more pronounced in men. The FEV1 declined on average by about 32 ml per year in men and about 25 ml per year in women, after standardization for height. In all such reports there is a wide range of variation from mean values which is not attributable to age,

sex or height; this limits the value of spirometry in the detection of early abnormalities. The many other reports of lung volume changes with age have one or other defect such as being cross-sectional, including too few very old subjects, not excluding smokers and those living in industrial areas and people with a history of chest illness. Milne and Williamson (1972) reported upon a random sample of 214 men and 272 women aged 62 to 90 years including some cigarette smokers. These cross-sectional data indicated no age-related change in FEV1 or FVC or their ratio FEV1/FVC percentage in men and though there was some fall in women the values stayed within the range of predicted normality. However when the same subjects were re-tested after 5 years (Milne, 1978) the rate of loss by the older subjects was appreciably higher than in Morris' study. Aged urban residents appear to lose FEV1 and FVC at rates of about 60–100 ml per year (Bosse et al, 1981; Schmidt et al, 1973), but many of these will be smokers, ex-smokers or have chronic bronchitis. A 10-year longitudinal study of younger (40–64 years) rural dwellers in Finland (Huhti and Ikkala, 1980) suggests figures of about half of those quoted above for old people with non-smokers at the lower end and persistent smokers the upper end of the range. The FEV1/FVC percentage falls somewhat in old people, the lower limit of normality becoming 65–70 per cent.

With advancing age Residual Volume (RV) increases and comes to occupy an increasing proportion of the TLC which remains largely unaltered (Boren et al, 1966). There is some increase in both anatomical and physiological dead space.

Ventilation, perfusion and compliance

In the region of spontaneous breathing the compliance of the lungs ie the change in volume per unit change in pressure, increases with age because of declining lung elasticity. This increased lung extensibility is counterbalanced in vivo by increased rigidity of the chest wall so that the compliance of the total respiratory system is somewhat lessened by the age of 60 years (Turner et al, 1968). The reduced elastic recoil is probably present in both airways and parenchyma and contributes to the increased alveolar size. It is qualitatively similar to changes present in other body elastic tissue, occurs independently of smoking and is unlikely to be due to minor degrees of emphysema (Gibson et al, 1976).

The loss of elastic recoil and consequent susceptibility to airway collapse is mainly responsible for altering the distribution of ventilation. In young people during resting tidal volume breathing inspired air passes preferentially to the lower zones. This is not so in the old because of airway closure in the lower zones (Holland et al, 1975). The Closing Volume (i.e. the lung volume at which small airways start to close) increases linearly

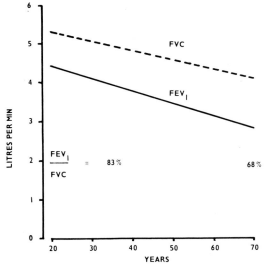

Fig. 36.1 Age-associated changes in lung function

with age (Begin et al, 1975). On expiration, therefore, this volume is reached sooner by older subjects and from about the age of 68 years airway closure occurs during expiration and distorts the balance of ventilation and perfusion. The effect is exacerbated by high expiratory flow rates such as may occur on exercising because at high flow rates airway resistance becomes more important than is the case during quiet breathing. Airway resistance is chiefly determined by lung volume and is not influenced by age (Briscoe and Dubois, 1958).

In comparison with young subjects there is increased blood flow to the upper lung zones, though the flow is still predominently to the lower zones (Holland et al, 1968). The increased apical blood flow may be partly due to the modest increase in pulmonary artery pressure which is known to occur with aging and perhaps also the increased lower zone vascular resistance arising as a consequence of loss of elastic recoil. Total pulmonary vascular resistance at rest is the same in old and young but does increase more in old people on exercise i.e. with increased blood flow (Emirgil et al, 1967) which is as expected; the pulmonary arteries are known to be less distensible with age. There is some fall in capillary blood volume from about the age of 50 years (Georges et al, 1978) in keeping with anatomical findings of reduced numbers of capillaries in the alveolar walls and presumably also with the known decline in cardiac output. There is an accompanying fall in pulmonary diffusing capacity both at rest and with exercise but this is due more to ventilation-perfusion imbalance than to capillary losses. It is not of clinical significance.

Blood gas changes
The alveolar-arterial oxygen difference increases progressively with age due to falling arterial oxygen tension (Raine and Bishop, 1963). Anatomical shunting accounts for only a small part of this and it is mainly due to there being closed unventilated alveoli which are only inflated by deep breaths, and to the cyclical airway closure during normal breathing described above. With added inspired oxygen the difference not due to anatomical shunting is largely abolished (Harris et al, 1974). The same effect can be achieved by deep breathing; a point of considerable importance in the post-operative period. The arterial carbon dioxide pressure does not alter with age.

Control of respiration
It is not known if age-related changes in the central nervous system have any effect upon the neurological control of respiration. A study of stroke patients (Klassen et al, 1980) demonstrated an increased ventilatory response to carbon dioxide in those with lesions of a hemisphere but not in patients with brain stem infarcts. The effect may be due to loss or decrease of

cerebral inhibition of brain stem mediated autonomic responses to hypercapnoea. Evidence for possible insensitivity of the chemoreceptor responses is provided by an investigation of the ventilatory and heart rate responses to hypoxia and hypercapnoea (Kronenberg and Drage, 1973). Eight men aged 64–73 years were compared with young controls and the ventilatory response to hypoxia was found to be strikingly diminished in the older subjects.

A failure to increase tidal volume and respiratory rate when hypoxic may have clinically significant consequences and help to explain why some old people with pneumonia do not have tachypnoea (Freeman et al, 1982). The response to hypercapnoea is also diminished in the elderly though less so than for hypoxia; some old people with respiratory failure are relatively lacking in symptoms. Hypercapnoea produces little change in the heart rate of old men in whom hypoxia also causes less of a tachycardia than in young subjects. These ventilatory and cardiac responses to blood gas changes are oddly similar to those of athletes (Byrne-Quinn et al, 1971). Peterson et al (1981) confirmed the altered ventilatory responses but noted that the changes in the aged are largely those of tidal volume. They could not find any differences between old and young in the control of respiratory timing; i.e. the duration of inspiration was the same proportion of the respiratory cycle in the two groups. There was no observed change in the rib cage contribution to breathing and it appears that diminished neural output to the respiratory muscles is the likely explanation for the ventilatory response change. Whether this is due to altered central processing or perception is unknown though there is some evidence (Tack et al, 1981) that old people perceive added resistive and elastic loads to breathing differently from young people. As one might expect, old people can not achieve the same maximal inspiratory and expiratory pressures of young adults; such manoeuvres reflect the strength of the respiratory muscles.

RESPIRATORY SYMPTOMATOLOGY

Although there are no respiratory diseases which are unique to old age many diagnostic problems result from the different ways in which ailments present and the modification of symptoms by physiological aging.

Cough
Some old people are hardly aware that they have a cough. They wrongly regard their early morning bronchitic throat clearing as a normal phenomenon which, in a statistical sense, it may be in industrial areas. Others have been frightened by the widely publicised association of smoking with lung cancer and are reluctant to

admit to the symptom. The commonest causes of persistent cough in old people are chronic bronchitis and bronchial asthma but these are not usually diagnostic problems. Coughs lasting for more than 3 weeks are regarded as chronic but the cause can usually be found. Irwin et al (1981) investigated 49 patients aged 17–88 years who had persistent coughs. Almost a third of them had chronic post-nasal drip associated with allergy, perennial rhinitis or sinusitis. A quarter of the series were found to have bronchial asthma but many did not wheeze and the diagnosis was established only by a bronchial activity test. Gastro-oesophageal reflux was also common, especially in the older subjects, and a few proved to have heart failure, lung cancer or other paren-chymal disease.

In old people any condition predisposing to aspiration of pharyngeal secretions, such as Parkinsons disease, should be considered. Less common causes include inhaled foreign bodies, subphrenic disease and reflexly reproduced cough, e.g. by irritation of the external auditory meatus.

History-taking therefore covers allergy, nasal catarrh, possible aspiration, dyspnoea, wheezing and gastro-intestinal symptoms. Physical examination will include the naso-pharynx and ears. A chest X-ray will be needed to exclude parenchymal or space occupying lesions and may show evidence of pulmonary congestion. Sinus X-rays may be indicated. A simple lung function test will help to diagnose airway obstruction in bronchitis or asthma. If all these are normal, gastro-oesophageal reflux should be excluded. It is well worth persisting as most causes of this symptom are amenable to treatment. Habit cough or neurosis are diagnoses of exclusion.

Chest pain

The rising pain threshold of advancing years makes old people better able to tolerate painful conditions. An important exception is shingles which poses no diag-nostic problems after the appearance of the rash. Unfor-tunately old people have a much increased susceptibility to post-herpetic neuralgia. This pain may be life-long. Complaints of aching and tenderness around the rib cage may be associated with osteomalacia or other causes of soft tissue tenderness such as polymyalgia rheumatica, Vitamin B group deficiencies and alcoholism. With or without bone disease in old people relatively slight trauma may fracture a rib and the pain of this may last several weeks, the original injury having long been forgotten by the time of presentation. An unsuspected crush fracture of a vertebra sometimes sends pain radiating around the chest wall. A rare cause of pain over the lower ribs occurs in severely kyphotic individ-uals whose bony deformity forces the lower ribs into frictional contact with the iliac crest. In patients with suspected cardiac neurosis, tenderness in the precordial

area is a useful clinical pointer away from ischaemic heart disease. Most chest pain of respiratory, cardiac or gastrointestinal origin has no age related distinguishing features but an important diagnostic difficulty arises with central chest pain on exertion occurring in elderly bronchitics; namely the distinction of angina pectoris from dyspnoea. Both may be described by the patient as central, caused by exertion and soon relieved by rest. An account of radiation down the arm or obvious wheezing is usually lacking. Sometimes the patient has no pain whatever and describes his symptoms in col-loquial terms such as 'my legs won't go' or 'I just can't walk'. A trial of anti-anginal treatment and perhaps an exercise ECG will be needed.

Dyspnoea

The causes of breathlessness of acute onset are much the same at any age with pulmonary oedema and pulmonary embolism common. Bronchial asthma occasionally presents for the first time in old age. Pneumothorax tends to occur mainly in association with emphysema in this age group. Partial or complete collapse of a lung is usually initially associated with chest pain but the breathlessness may persist; the physical signs however are usually obvious on examination. Dyspnoea on exer-tion in the elderly usually has some obvious cause in the respiratory or cardiovascular system but it is often not reported by the patients many of whom wrongly regard it as no more than an everyday manifestation of normal ageing. Landahl et al (1980) reported a large series of elderly people who complained of breathlessness. Respiratory disease and cardiac failure were common but about one-third of the men and half of the women had neither of these. In such patients there is a strong possibility that their symptom is angina pectoris. Inter-mittent interstitial pulmonary oedema may not be diag-nosable from a random chest X-ray. When the history raises this possibility a trial of diuretic therapy is indi-cated; it is usually associated with ischaemic heart disease. Fluid retaining drugs, especially anti-arthritics or liquorice derivatives are occasional contributory factors.

In the series of Landahl and colleagues (1980), a quarter to a third of all dyspnoeic elderly patients were found to have psychiatric evidence of irritability or emotional lability and in rather more there was no detectable organic disease. Before attributing the symptom to depression or neurosis such basic tests as haemoglobin, chest X-ray, ECG and simple pulmonary function tests will have been done. If these, the history, and physical examination are unhelpful, gross organic pathology is unlikely. Even so, some conditions such as diffuse interstitial fibrosis may escape detection in their early stages and more detailed lung function testing including blood gas studies may be required. Rarely, dyspnoea is the presenting symptom of generalized neuromuscular disorders including motor neurone disease (Nightingale et al, 1982).

After excluding the hypoxic, stagnant and anaemic types of hypoxia the remote possibility will remain of chronic carbon monoxide poisoning or methaemoglobinaemia.

Exercise

Few elderly people regularly undertake much exercise. The resulting loss of fitness contributes to subsequent exertional dyspnoea. This can be corrected; old age does not debar physical exertion. De Vries (1970) instituted a vigorous training programme for 112 men aged 58–87 years which produced much improvement in effort tolerance without untoward effects. He found trainability to be unrelated to the subjects' previous exercising habits. Training programmes do not, however, improve static lung volumes, closing volume or pulmonary diffusing capacity (Niinimaa and Shephard, 1978a).

In untrained people there is a fall with advancing age in the maximal oxygen consumption when measured at maximal exercise capacity (Reinhard et al, 1979) and although training increases maximal oxygen uptake it appears that the improvements are due to increased cardiovascular efficiency rather than to lung changes. Compared with young, older people on exercise meet a larger proportion of their oxygen requirements by increasing the peripheral utilization of oxygen; in them the benefits of training are associated with a reduction of both the resting heart rate and cardiac output at a given work level and with an increased cardiac reserve (Niinimaa and Shephard, 1978b).

PNEUMONIA

Acute infections of the lower respiratory tract are particularly frequent in old age in both community and hospital populations. Hospital based reports suggest a mortality of 25 per cent or more for people over 70 years with pneumonia. About half of all patients dying on long-stay wards are found to have some degree of pneumonia at autopsy and on average patients living in such wards have more than one chest infection every 2 years.

Pathogenesis

No single reason for this susceptibility to lower respiratory tract (LRT) infections has been established; old people seem no more vulnerable than young people to infections of the upper airways (Logan and Cushion, 1958). It must partly be associated with the increased prevalence of conditions known to predispose to respiratory infection such as chronic bronchitis, pulmonary oedema, diabetes mellitus, neoplasms and other debili-

tating disease. Stroke and neuromuscular diseases may lead to aspiration effects. Sedatives, codeine derivatives, alcohol and other drugs depress respiration and the protective reflexes of the airways which form a part of the lung's complex defensive system.

Protective reflexes

Depression of the cough reflex contributes to a failure to clear inhaled material. Pontoppidan and Beecher (1960) studied the effect of inhaled dilute ammonia gas on a large number of healthy males and found that with advancing age there is a progressive loss of the protective laryngeal response. The threshold for provocation increased six-fold from the second to eighth decades with the main change occurring after middle age. Alcohol has the same effect.

Mucociliary clearance

The bronchial tree is lined by ciliated epithelium as far down as the respiratory bronchioles. Inhaled particles lodging on it are removed either by coughing or by the normal upward movement of mucus and are swallowed when they pass the epiglottis. There is much variation in the rate of mucociliary clearance both between individuals and in the same person measured at different times. Clearance rates fall steeply during sleep (Bateman et al, 1978) thus contributing to retention of secretions. Tracheal mucous velocity is somewhat reduced in elderly people (Goodman et al, 1978) though this is not invariable; a centenarian described by Pavia and Thomson (1970) had unimpaired action despite having smoked regularly for 80 years. Clearance is worsened in a wide range of conditions including chronic bronchitis, severe asthma, infections by influenza A virus and *Mycoplasma pneumoniae*, cigarette smoking and bronchiectasis.

Phagocytosis

Inhaled bacteria which reach the alveoli are normally quickly rendered non-viable by the phagocytic action of the pulmonary alveolar macrophages. Animal studies (Green and Kass, 1964; Kass et al, 1966) show that the rate of removal varies with the bacterial species, and the action of the macrophages is influenced by a variety of clinically relevant factors. Virus infections inhibit the clearance of staphylococci but there is a 6–8 day delay before this becomes maximal, as there often also is when staphylococcal pneumonia complicates influenza. Alcohol has a similar depressant effect which is dose related and not due to respiratory depression; polymorphonuclear phagocytosis is unaffected. Acute hypoxia, renal failure, acidosis, cold stress and corticosteroids have all been shown to depress pulmonary alveolar macrophage function. In contrast the phagocytic activity of neutrophils in the blood appears to be normal in healthy aged people

(Phair et al, 1978). Even when macrophage activity is overwhelmed, however, as in diffuse interstitial fibrosis, pulmonary oedema or grossly disturbed local function, respiratory infections are quite uncommon (Turner-Warwick, 1975) owing to a variety of immunological defences.

Immunity

In human bronchial mucosa the majority of immuno-globulin-producing cells make Immunoglobulin A (IgA). This secretory IgA is the predominent antibody of the respiratory tract and is also present in saliva and nasal fluid. It differs from serum IgA in its sedimentation rate, amino-acid complement and antibody activity (Tomasi, 1968) and is known to possess several antibody functions including antibacterial and antiviral activity. Clinical recovery from some URT virus infections is more closely related to secretory than serum IgA levels. There may be some fall in nasal secretory IgA with age (Alford, 1968) but age-related changes in the lung's immune system have not been explored. Serum IgA level is not changed by age (Czlonkowska and Korlak, 1979) and no consistent changes in other serum immunoglobulins have been described. It is not known if the dynamic response to infection of the lung's immune system is altered by aging. The systemic response to vaccination by influenza virus (MacKenzie, 1977) and pneumococcal antigen (Ammann et al, 1980) seems much the same in old and young people.

Clinical

The clinical picture of primary pneumonia in young people with the abrupt onset of a productive cough, pyrexia, pleurisy and signs of consolidation is less often seen in the elderly. Any of these features may be present but are usually much less dramatic and the illness is usually insidious in its onset, presenting with a non-specific deterioration of health in much the same way as many other acute illnesses present in old age. Secondary pneumonia is frequently overlooked when such deterioration is wrongly attributed to the worsening to a known co-existing illness. Spontaneous cough may be slight and consist of little more than throat clearing; persuading a patient to cough and listening for evidence of retained mucus is often useful. Breathlessness when present is usually accompanied by cough but is rarely a cause of spontaneous complaint. On specific enquiry about half of pneumonic old people admit to this symptom. Chest pain and haemoptysis are uncommon. Ancillary signs and symptoms such as sore throat, shivering and muscle aches are often present but again must be specifically enquired after as pneumonia in old age is frequently accompanied by some depression of the conscious level. This drowsiness is often a part of a delirium (acute confusional state) but is frequently not recognized as such because it is not always realized that depression of wakefulness and psychomotor behaviour is as typical a feature of delirium as is overactivity.

Signs of consolidation may be lacking on routine examination but this may be due to shallow breathing; the physiological response to increased lung rigidity is to reduce tidal volume and maintain the minute volume by increasing the respiratory rate (Marshall and Christie, 1954); this saves energy. The signs can often be brought out by instructions to breathe deeply. Crepitations are sometimes heard at the lung bases in normal old people and can cause diagnostic confusion. They are probably due to the lower zone airway closure previously discussed and if so they will be gravity dependent and change their position with patient movement. Two physical signs, raised respiratory rate and increased pulse rate, are of particular help as diagnostic indicators but of course they are not specific. The normal resting respiratory rate in geriatric patients is 16–25 min. (McFadden et al, 1982) and although some with pneumonia will be within the normal range a figure in excess of it usually indicates respiratory dysfunction. Pyrexia and other features of acute infection such as leukocytosis and a raised ESR may each be entirely absent but one or more of these factors is invariably abnormal.

Aetiological agents

The investigation of pneumonia is little affected by age though it may be difficult to obtain satisfactory specimens for examination from weak old people. Sputum cultures are not entirely reliable because of nasopharyngeal contamination but an immediate Gram stain may offer a useful guide to therapy pending other reports. To avoid nasopharyngeal contaminants, especially in suspected aspiration pneumonia, transtracheal aspiration can be performed. It is commonly used in the USA but less so in the UK; there is a small but definite morbidity. It can be safely performed in old people after proper physician training (Berk et al, 1981). Blood cultures are valuable when positive but are less likely to be so in old age with about 10 per cent or less positive (Denham and Goodwin, 1977). Other culture and serological methods are unaffected by age.

The frequency with which different pathogenic organisms are found varies greatly with both the intensity of the search for them and the nature of the population studied. Macfarlane et al (1982) made a detailed study of 127 cases in patients less than 80 years old and found the cause in 124. These patients were all admitted to hospital with pneumonia from the community and did not have major co-existing illness. Pneumococcal infection was found in about three-quarters, Legionnaires disease in about 15 per cent. Virus infections were uncommon. The authors note that most of the pneumococcal infections would have been undiagnosed had not counter-current immunoelectrophoresis (CIE) been done; this point helps to explain why in many previous reports no aetiological agent is found in about one-third of all cases (Fiala, 1969; Mufson et al, 1967) as does the increasing awareness of Legionnaires disease. The pneumococcus is the commonest bacterial cause of pneumonia in all age groups though elderly patients may have a somewhat increased frequency of Gram-negative infections (Ebright and Rytel, 1980). Such organisms together with anaerobes and staphylococci are commoner in those acquiring infection in hospital or nursing homes, when there is co-existing debilitating illness and following antibiotic therapy.

The influenza group are the commonest respiratory viruses in old people; the incidence of virus infection seems increased in the aged (Mufson et al, 1967). It may well be that viruses which causes mainly URTI in young people cause pneumonia in old owing to faulty protective mechanisms.

Pneumococcal pneumonia
Many different pneumococcal serotypes cause pneumonia in old age (Valenti et al, 1978) and the mortality varies somewhat with the capsular type (Austrian and Gold, 1964), the distribution of which may be altered in old age. Patients with cardiac or renal failure, hepatic cirrhosis, malignant neoplasms and diabetes mellitus are particularly vulnerable to pneumococcal infections. The prognosis is influenced by the extent of the consolidation though in older people this is less likely to be the characteristic homogenous lobar consolidation. Most deaths occur soon after onset and even early appropriate antibiotic therapy does not much improve the prospects of survival in the first 5 days. Bacteraemic pneumonia is most likely in hospital acquired infection and tends to occur soon after discontinuation of previous antibiotic therapy (Mylotte and Beam, 1981). A small but increasing proportion of pneumococcal isolates exhibit resistance to penicillin.

Haemophilus influenzae
This rare pneumonia produces a high mortality rate in old age. The radiological appearance is occasionally of lobar consolidation but more usually is multisegmental or multilobar infiltrates without cavitation. Bacteraemia is common (Wallace et al, 1978).

Legionnaires disease
Legionella pneumophila is a small Gram-negative bacillus with fastidious culture requirements. Clinically, (Swartz, 1979) after an incubation period of about 2–10 days prodromal symptoms of malaise, headache and myalgia develop followed by fever, chills and prostration. Diarrhoea may be prominent. By the second or third day there is a dry cough with mucoid sputum; small

haemoptyses may occur and pleuritic pain is common as is acute confusion which may seem out of proportion to any pyrexia or hypoxia which is present. Signs of pulmonary involvement tend to be lacking until consolidation develops. The chest X-ray however shows some signs of bilateral involvement from the onset in about 70 per cent of patients and the lesions tend to progress and enlarge, are often multi-lobar and may opacify an entire lung. They do not cavitate and may take several weeks, sometimes months to clear. Pleural effusions are usually small and have no characteristic features. The total white cell count is usually only modestly raised and they are chiefly neutrophils. The lymphocyte count is frequently low. Biochemical changes include raised liver cell enzymes and hypophosphataemia. Hyponatraemia occurs but may be due to accompanying diarrhoea and vomiting. Microscopic haematuria is found in up to 10% of patients.

The clinical diagnosis (Miller, 1979) is strongly suggested by a combination of at least three of the following;
— virus-like prodromal illness with pyrexia
— dry cough or confusion or diarrhoea
— lymphopenia without marked neutrophilia
— hyponatraemia.

Other Gram-negative bacilli
Respiratory infections with species of Pseudomonas, Proteus, Klebsiella and other Gram-negative organisms occur mainly in an institutional setting. These organisms act as opportunistic pathogens when broad spectrum antibiotic therapy kills off their competitors or the immune system is compromised. Other predisposing factors are serious systemic disease, bronchiectasis and tracheal intubation. Their presence in the respiratory tract does not necessarily indicate significant infection as they may be harmless colonists. Oropharyngeal colonization is particularly likely to occur in the disabled elderly (Valenti et al, 1978b) irrespective of previous antibiotic usage but it may be temporary and does not increase the risk of pneumonia (Irwin et al, 1982) unless other factors are operative. These infections have a high fatality rate (Tillotson and Finland, 1969) but lack distinctive clinical features.

Aspiration pneumonia
Pneumonia or lung abscess may follow the aspiration of nasopharyngeal material. This mainly happens following unconsciousness, excess alcohol or postoperatively. Commonly, aerobic and anaerobic organisms co-exist and this is especially likely with infections acquired in hospital (Bartlett et al, 1974). The anaerobic component may well be overlooked on routine culture studies and only become apparent following failure to respond to standard therapy. The anaerobic infections particularly

tend to putrid sputum and the development of lung abscess. X-ray changes vary from small patchy infiltrates to abscesses with either smooth or irregular walls and tend to worsen during the first few days of treatment; the abscess cavity usually contains little fluid (Landay et al, 1980).

Old age may be less of a risk factor for postoperative pneumonia than was once thought. Garibaldi et al (1981) reported a large series and found that susceptibility was chiefly related to male sex, gross obesity, chronic pulmonary disease, the duration of prior hospitalization and the duration and site of surgery. After correcting for these there was no significant correlation with age.

An entirely different type of aspiration pneumonia occurs following the inhalation of gastric contents. An early chemical pneumonitis results which is bacteriologically sterile. Secondary infection may follow in a few days but prophylactic antibiotic therapy is usually unavailing.

Viral and mycoplasmal infections

Most respiratory virus infections typically involve the upper airways but any of this group may cause pneumonia in old people. It is not possible to distinguish them by clinical evidence owing to the considerable overlap in the range of symptoms produced and the lack of specific features.

Repeated serological examination of hospital long-stay residents (Freeman et al, 1982) demonstrated more virus activity than anticipated though these serological conversions were not always associated with overt respiratory infection. In such institutions these viruses are common causes of minor afflictions.

Influenza viruses

Influenza A infections are not more common in the elderly but the incidence of LRT complications is much increased. They occur in more than half of affected old people with a high mortality rate (Miller and Lee, 1969). Symptoms of headache, chills, malaise, myalgia and sore throat are followed by some combination of tracheitis, bronchitis and bronchiolitis. Debility may persist for several weeks perhaps because even without pneumonia restrictive ventilatory defects occur in a proportion of patients and cause persisting hypoxia by small airway or parenchymal involvement (Johanson et al, 1969). Primary influenzal pneumonia may rarely be present from the start or develop after a few days. Bacterial pneumonia may co-exist or follow after about a week. It is usually pneumococcal but there is an increased likelihood of staphylococcal infection.

Patients suspected of having influenza should be isolated as this contagious disease may quickly involve other residents in a ward or old peoples home. During an outbreak of Influenza A in a geriatric unit (Gowda,

1979) all of those affected became pyrexial and confused with headache, myalgia, asthenia, dry cough and tachycardia. Influenza B produces a similar but less severe illness which affects mainly children as adults retain immunity to it. This is not so for Influenza A because of changes in its antigenic structure between epidemics.

Parainfluenza viruses

These have a predilection for the larynx and may cause severe illness in old people with aggravating and persistent dry cough. About 10 per cent of isolations are from the aged.

Respiratory syncitial virus

Although usually thought of as a cause of acute bronchiolitis of children this virus affects old people also. In 17 of the 40 residents in a psycho-geriatric home (Harvie and Gray, 1980) it produced an illness like mild influenza. Mathur et al (1980) reported another outbreak, this time in a community hospital for ambulatory elderly and chronic sick patients. There were concurrent infections with infleunza A and the two viruses produced much the same symptoms and signs.

Mycoplasma pneumoniae

The incidence of mycoplasmal infections is probably little influenced by age (Balassanian and Robbins, 1967). About 15 per cent of cases are asymptomatic and otherwise the signs and symptoms resemble those of virus infection. Older patients are more likely to develop pneumonia in which case cold agglutinins are likely to be present. The organism may persist in the lower respiratory tract for many weeks. It is highly infectious and continues among family groups for several months. Acute confusional states develop in a small number of patients even in the absence of pneumonia.

Management

Many patients are successfully treated in their own homes and hospital admission is essential only when adequate supervision is not available or skilled nursing is needed. There have been few trials of different treatment regimens in old age.

Antibiotics

In old people it is usual to use bactericidal rather than bacteriostatic drugs because of presumed impaired resistance to infection. During the first few days parenteral administration is preferred as absorption from the gut is unreliable. The choice of antibiotic is guided by consideration of the likely infecting organism and the patients clinical state. Although pneumococcal infections almost always respond to benzyl penicillin, in practice it is often difficult to exclude acute bronchitis so a broad spectrum drug, active against *H. influenzae*, is preferred. If lobar pneumonia is confirmed benzyl penicillin is indicated. In mild or moderate infections in patients admitted from the community and without other serious illness ampicillin, amoxycillin and co-trimoxazole are of about equal efficacy. Most such patients have pneumococcal infection and clinical improvement is expected in 36 to 48 hours. Lack of recovery indicates that either the organism is insensitive to the antibiotic used or the diagnosis is wrong or incomplete. By this time culture and radiological studies will be available.

The chest X-ray will help to exclude bronchial obstruction, pulmonary embolism, pleural effusions and tuberculosis. It will not usually guide the choice of antibiotic though multiple cavities suggest staphylococcal or klebsiella infection; the latter sometimes causes a bulging inter-lobar fissure.

When seriously ill patients are admitted from the community all likely organisms must be treated from the start and if the patient was previously fit a combination of ampicillin and erythromycin is reasonable. If Legionnaires disease is confirmed treatment with erythromycin continues for at least 2 weeks. During influenza epidemics flucloxicillin is added because of the risk of staphylococcal infection.

Those acquiring their infections in geriatric nursing homes (Garb et al, 1978) or long-stay wards have an increased risk of Gram-negative infections. If not acutely ill, cefuroxime can be given pending culture studies. Otherwise gentamycin should be added. If associated illness might have caused aspiration then metronidazole may also be needed. It is sometimes impossible to exclude staphylococcal infection in which case a fourth drug, flucloxacillin, is added. This 'blunderbus' therapy is usually only needed for a day or two until reports become available. The identification of an unusual resistant organism prompts a clinical assessment of its role — i.e. is it causing the pneumonia or is it merely colonising the respiratory tract? The sensitivity patterns of such organisms vary from place to place and early consultation with a bacteriologist is indicated.

No effective treatment is available for virus pneumonia. Mycoplasmal infections are not usually diagnosed until the patient is recovering and their clinical course is little influenced by antibiotic therapy.

Oxygen

Continuous oxygen therapy during the acute stage is an essential part of the treatment and an important preventive measure against cardiac complications. There is no reason why it should not be given in the patient's home. In chronic bronchitis a careful watch for respiratory failure whether due to oxygen therapy or infection is needed. In severely ill patients' blood gas monitoring is advisable. 28 per cent or 35 per cent oxygen given by Ventimask is usually adequate.

Sputum production

The gradual development of illness with a poor fluid intake over several days results in many patients becoming dehydrated. This is often severe enough to cause a pre-renal uraemia. The dehydration makes the bronchial secretions viscid and difficult to expectorate leading to physical exhaustion and sputum retention. Early fluid replacement, by infusion if necessary, is the best treatment. Inhalations of steam are useful. Chest physiotherapy is particularly valuable in encouraging the clearance of secretions. Some improvement in oxygenation results (Holody and Goldberg, 1981) but it does not influence the course of the illness (Graham and Bradley, 1978) as judged by the speed of radiological clearing, duration of pyrexia, length of hospital stay or mortality.

Cardiac complications

Next to ischaemic heart disease insidious respiratory infections are the commonest cause of congestive heart failure developing without apparent reason. The cardiac complication may not be gross and sometimes consists only of sub-acute pulmonary oedema, so that the patient may be more breathless than expected and the physical signs may be misleading and suggest only congestion. The combination of infection and congestion, which is frequently found at autopsy, is probably commoner than is generally realized; the parenchymal involvement by infection alone is insufficient to explain the increased lung rigidity associated with pneumonia (Marshall and Christie, 1954). Cardiac arrhythmias, especially atrial fibrillation, occuring in the acute stages will often revert spontaneously as the infection subsides so that it is not necessary to continue treatment with digitalis and diuretics.

Acute confusional states

Delirium, in greater or lesser degree, complicates up to one-third of pneumonic episodes in old people. The onset may be acute and violent but more often consists of the gradual development of clouding of consciousness, disturbed sleep and disorientation with memory impairment. Perceptive disorders including hallucinations may be subtle and easily overlooked. Motor and psychological activities may be either increased or depressed. The severity of the confusional state is unrelated to the extent of the pneumonia and indeed may occur with upper respiratory tract infection. There is no definite evidence that it is due to arterial hypoxia though doubtless this sometimes contributes. Demented patients are probably no more likely than others to develop this complication and its onset does not imply the presence of pre-existing brain damage. In a small proportion of cases the mental disorder persists as a chronic confusional state. Confusion is particularly likely during pyrexial illnesses though there is no known relationship with particular infecting organisms. It is especially important not to overlook the possible associated presence of any of the many non-infective causes of delirium. In old people drug toxicity, heart failure, alcoholism, vitamin deficiency and hypothyroidism are likely. Encephalitis and brain abscess need to be excluded. When symptoms begin the day after hospital admission they may be due to inadvertent failure to prescribe previously taken sedatives, especially barbiturates and benzodiazepines. Withdrawal symptoms which have all the manifestations of a delirium may result. Prompt sedation of overactive patients is essential to prevent acute heart failure and self injury. Haloperidol by intramuscular injection is the treatment of choice. Phenothiazines are less satisfactory because of the risk of producing hypotension. Chlormethiazole by intravenous infusion is an alternative approach but needs careful monitoring during the induction phase to prevent over-sedation. Oxygen and B group vitamins by injection are also given, the latter to ensure that a possible contributory nutritional deficiency does not go untreated.

Pleurisy, effusions and empyema

Pleuritic pain is best treated with an analgesic unlikely to depress respiration or cough, such as paracetamol. Local heat may help. Sometimes cough is so troublesome that a small dose of codeine phosphate is needed. Small effusions are common in all forms of pneumonia but mostly clear spontaneously. There are no clinical differences between patients with and without effusion and the fluid's protein content or white cell count is not a good guide to pleural infection (Light et al, 1980). A glucose level below 40 mg% is suggestive of infection. If the fluid collection is large enough it should be tapped to prevent loculation and a diagnostic aspiration will be required if the fluid persists for more than a week or pyrexia continues. Drainage is likely to be necessary if pus is found or organisms are identified but repeated aspiration plus intra-pleural instillation of antibiotics may suffice if the effusion is recent and the pus thin.

Duration of treatment

Antibiotic therapy continues for 7–10 days. As long as clinical progress is satisfactory there is no need for repeated chest X-rays but it is always advisable for a repeat film after about 6 weeks to confirm complete radiological clearing and the absence of an underlying lesion. Prolonged antibiotic therapy predisposes to secondary infection.

Prevention of pneumonia

Amantidine hydrochloride 100 mg daily is partly effective in preventing influenza A 2 infection and the illness is probably milder in those infected during its use (Smorodintsev et al, 1970). It is of no value as an active treatment and is specific for that particular virus. It may be worth using in closed communities during an influenza epidemic. Vaccination against influenza confers a substantial degree of protection when the vaccine used corresponds with the antigenic structure of the virus (Barker and Mullooly, 1980). There is no age-related difference in either the height or duration of the antibody response to vaccination (Mackenzie, 1977). Clinical benefit from annual vaccination has not been definitely established in groups of old people but it is reasonable to vaccinate those with chronic lung or heart disease, especially before an expected epidemic.

Amman et al (1980) found that aged women responded as well as young control subjects to vaccination with pneumococcal capsular types 3 and 8. Though they started and finished with lower absolute levels, the antibodies produced should afford protection. Theoretically vaccination against the pneumococcus should be cost-effective in old people (Willems et al, 1980), but no definite immunization policy has yet been established (see also p 1012). Severe reaction to the vaccine sometimes occurs. Protection should last at least 3 years.

CHRONIC OBSTRUCTIVE AIRWAYS DISEASE

Definition

Simple chronic bronchitis is defined as a chronic or recurrent increase in the volume of mucoid bronchial secretions sufficient to cause expectoration on most days during three consecutive months, for more than two successive years (Medical Research Council, 1965). Mucopurulent and obstructive types are self explanatory.

Emphysema is a condition of the lungs characterized by an abnormal increase in the size of air spaces distal to the terminal bronchiole, with destruction of their walls (World Health Organization 1961).

It is clinically unsatisfactory to define conditions either solely by a symptom or by an inaccesible histological finding — furthermore in practice these two conditions frequently co-exist. The less specific term chronic obstructive airway disease (COAD) or some variant of it is used when precise definition is impossible.

Incidence

Chronic bronchitis usually begins in young or middle-aged adults and the incidence falls off in old age. The prevalence however continues to rise so that in industrial areas up to 40 per cent of old men and 20 per cent of old women have the symptoms (Caird and Akhtar, 1972).

The manner in which emphysema begins and develops is obscure. Even when groups of patients with COAD are followed-up the development of radiological signs of generalised emphysema is rarely observed (Jones et al, 1967). Autopsy studies (Sutinen et al, 1978) do not indicate an age-association with prevalence. Males and females are about equally affected.

Pathogenesis

Chronic bronchitis

The increased sputum production is associated with hypertrophy of the bronchial mucous gland layer which increases the thickness of the bronchial walls; goblet cells also increase (Reid, 1967). The viscid sputum tends to obstruct small airways while permanent structural damage and loss of support for their walls from infection and inflammation contribute to the obstruction (Lamb, 1970). Some hyperplasia of the bronchial muscles (Hossein and Heard, 1970) involves the large airways. The physiological consequences are a susceptibility to both airway obstruction and airway collapse leading to alveolar underventilation and ventilation: perfusion imbalance, i.e. with underventilated lung remaining well perfused. Hypoxia and hypercapnoea eventually result.

Emphysema

Recent attention has concentrated on the role of alpha 1 antitrypsin deficiency though only a small proportion of patients have demonstrable deficiency. Eriksson (1964) demonstrated its inheritance as an uncommon recessive trait, and in those with homozygous deficiency (PiZZ phenotype) severe panlobular emphysema develops in early adult life. Heterozygotes show intermediate deficiency. A few old people with homozygous deficiency without evidence of emphysema have been reported (Eriksson, 1970). Concentrates of cigarette smoke cause the release of elastase from pulmonary alveolar macrophages and polymorph neutrophil leucocytes and in patients with deficiency it is thought that a failure to neutralize elastase leads to local destructive lesions of both alveolar wall and lung parenchyma.

In early emphysema there is dilatation of some alveoli. These then fuse with neighbouring alveoli to form minute cysts while fenestrae develop between them. The destructive process eventually involves several alveoli with disappearance of adjacent capillaries (Pump, 1976). In all age groups the histological changes are more severe in cigarette smokers. The centrilobular type is the most common but more than one type is often present.

The physiological results are variable and sometimes at autopsy severe emphysema may be found without there having been notable disturbances of pulmonary function during life. The alveolar changes lead to loss of diffusing capacity and inefficient gas mixing while loss of parenchymal elasticity contributes to airway collapse.

Signs and symptoms

In the early stages of chronic bronchitis a little mucoid sputum is produced after awakening or during the winter months. A few never progress much beyond this stage but more commonly the cough worsens over the years and becomes a part of everyday life. Wheezing and breathlessness develop. Episodes of acute infection punctuate the illness and may precipitate heart failure of either right ventricular or congestive type. In the later stages acute respiratory failure may supervene on the chronic hypoxia which determines many of the secondary features. There are no distinctive radiological changes.

In emphysema without bronchitis the chief symptom is progressive breathlessness with or without obvious wheezing. Loss of cardiac and hepatic dullness to percussion is a distinctive finding. The chest X-ray (Fig. 36.2) shows, in advanced cases, low flat diaphragms with the retrosternal translucency much increased. The heart tends to be narrow while the hilar vessels are prominent with relatively small mid-lung vessels. Bullae may be obvious. The chest X-ray may appear quite normal at an earlier stage.

In COAD the chest may assume a barrel-like shape. Elevation of the sternum reduces the length of trachea palpable above the sternal notch. Tracheal descent on

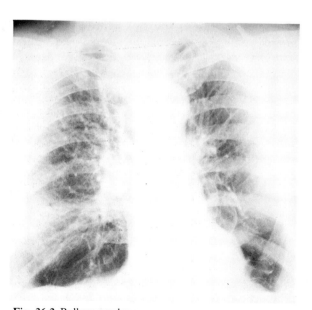

Fig. 36.2 Bullous emphysema

inspiration is seen and use of the accessory muscles of respiration at rest can be felt. Indrawing of the supra-clavicular and intercostal tissues may be seen (Campbell, 1969). Most of these signs may also be observed in some normal old people due to chest wall rigidity and other aging changes.

Course and prognosis

Burrows et al (1965) comparing old and young people with COAD found the two groups to have the same length of history though older people were less likely to have muco-purulent sputum. It is the young subjects who seem unable to compensate for the physiological changes as in them hypoxia and hypercapnoea are significantly more frequent. So too is electrocardio-graphic evidence of right ventricular hypertrophy. These differences are found even in groups with comparable lung volumes and the reason for them is unknown; it may be related to better collateral venti-lation in the elderly. X-ray evidence of emphysema is equally present in old and young.

The best available predictor of mortality from this condition in old people is the post-bronchodilator FEV_1, though this is still far from satisfactory (Traver et al, 1979). The FEV_1 correlates well with such clinical features as a raised resting heart rate, breathlessness and hypercapnoea so that clinical assessment of these factors provides a good guide to prognosis. The severity of cough, sputum and wheezing and X-ray evidence of bullae do not help in this assessment. Over the years the rate of fall of ventilatory function in patients with COAD is greater than would be expected from aging alone and the deterioration is most rapid in those with initially more severe obstruction. Once mild dyspnoea (FEV_1 1–2 litres) develops, only 6–10 years is needed for progression to severe disability (FEV_1 less than 1 litre). By this stage the death rate is about 10 per cent per year (Diener and Burrows, 1975).

Factors in the long-term management

There is no available therapy which can be relied upon to halt or reverse the progress of the established condition, though in some progress may be so slow that clinical complications are never a problem.

Tobacco and environmental effects

There is no doubt that cigarette smoking is the chief initiating and potentiating agent in the development of COAD. It stimulates mucous gland hypertrophy, predisposes to infection and inhibits the inactivation of elastase even when alpha 1 antitrypsin is present in normal concentrations. The ventilatory function of smokers deteriorates more quickly than age-matched controls and it is possible, but unproven, that aging and smoking act synergistically.

With advancing age there is a spontaneous reduction in tobacco consumption and a concomitant increase in the proportion of ex-smokers in the population (McKennell and Thomas, 1967). Many elderly people have little difficulty in giving up the habit; the benefits include less coughing, reduction in sputum production and a diminished risk of respiratory infection. The deterioration in FEV_1 and FVC slows quite quickly in ex-smokers and assumes a rate of fall between that of non-smokers and continuing smokers (Bosse et al, 1981). Stopping smoking, even in old age, reduces the death rate (Gentleman et al, 1978).

The role of long-term exposure to the many atmos-pheric pollutants (Boren, 1967) is unclear. It is well known that symptoms are worsened when the levels of atmospheric pollutants are high; old people are particu-larly vulnerable (Carnow et al, 1969).

Respiratory infection

Acute respiratory infections are more common in chronic bronchitics than the general population. There is no evidence that acute infection plays a significant part in initiating the disease process even though many patients date the onset of their illness to such an infec-tion. The acute episode prompts awareness of chronic symptoms. It is possible, but unproven, that repeated respiratory infections in childhood increases later susceptibility to the effects of smoking (Burrows et al, 1977). During acute infection, arterial oxygen tension and ventilatory function usually worsen but this lasts for only a limited period; up to a few weeks. Permanent worsening is not seen. Infective episodes become more common over the years as lung function worsens.

The commonest responsible bacteriae are *H. influ-enzae* and *S. pneumoniae*. These two organisms are common upper respiratory tract commensals so that routine sputum cultures in acute exacerbations are of little value. Serological methods are available for diag-nosis, if required. Other bacteriae are rarely found. Treatment with ampicillin, amoxycillin or cotrimoxazole should be effective against either pathogen. Tetracycline is just as good but is usually avoided in the elderly because of its anti-anabolic effects. Trimethoprim may well be as efficient as cotrimoxazole (sulphamethoxazole-trimethoprim) in lower respiratory tract infection but this is not yet proven. For the domiciliary management of patients with renal failure either erythromycin or doxycycline can be used. For severe infection, or when pneumonia is suspected, the choice of antibiotic is guided by the principles detailed in the section on pneumonia.

Attempts to prevent infective exacerbations have been unconvincing. In those with mild bronchitis winter long treatment with oxytetracycline produced no real benefits (Medical Research Council, 1966) but there may be some reduction in the number of episodes in those having frequent exacerbations i.e. those with more advanced disease (Johnston et al, 1969). In cooperative patients a supply of antibiotic may be provided with instructions to start taking it as soon as symptoms begin. One reason for the failure of prophylactic methods using antibiotics is that the cause is often viral or mycoplasmal (Smith et al, 1980; McHardy et al, 1980). In many cases even detailed study fails to identify a pathogen.

Medication

Certain drugs should be either prescribed with caution or avoided in COAD. Cough suppressants and analgesics may cause sputum retention and depress respiration. Sedatives and tranquillisers also depress respiration; none of them is without this effect. Beta-adrenergic receptor blockers, such as propranolol, increase airway resistance by inducing bronchoconstriction. Oxygen must be administered with care whenever respiratory failure is possible. In patients with chronic or recurrent hypercapnoea there may be some loss of the ventilatory response to carbon dioxide with dependance on the hypoxic stimulus to respiration. In such patients uncontrolled oxygen therapy may cause apnoea.

Antispasmodics

The use of bronchodilators to ease breathlessness by relieving airway obstruction is much less successful than in asthma. Simple pulmonary function tests to confirm that some degree of airway obstruction reversibility is present should be carried out before beginning treatment. The individual response varies and if one drug fails another is tried. Salbutamol and aminophylline derivatives are well tolerated by old people. They can be given in combination for additional effect. Ephedrine is effective but may precipitate urinary retention and sleeplessness. Metered-dose aerosols of beta 2 adrenergic receptor stimulators such as salbutamol, or drugs with atropine-like effects such as ipratropium bromide can be tried. A synergistic effect is sometimes obtained from the use of both together. The patient needs to be instructed in the technique of inhalation. After the first dose the patient waits for a minute or two. A second dose may then penetrate previously constricted airways.

Corticosteroids have little to offer in most cases but in a few a dramatic response is made owing to the presence of an unrecognized asthmatic element. The dangers of long-term systemic corticosteroid therapy make it important to secure objective evidence of improvement and exclude a placebo effect. They are worth trying in all patients with advanced and unresponsive symptoms but if no improvement is achieved in 1–2 weeks they should be discontinued. Metered-dose aerosols of corticosteroids are available and in many patients their use avoids the need for systemic therapy. Occasional patients benefit from suppositories of aminophylline taken at night. Nocturnal worsening of symptoms however is more likely in asthma than in COAD.

Expectorants

These have not been shown to be of any value other than as a placebo. The same is largely true of mucolytic agents. Inhalation of steam sometimes helps expectoration and inhalations of hypertonic saline are sometimes effective, probably by increasing mucociliary clearance (Clarke et al, 1980).

Heart failure

In bronchitic patients recurring episodes of cardiac failure occur usually in association with acute respiratory infection. Although this is often of the expected right ventricular type, in association with pulmonary hypertension, in practice congestive failure is also common owing to co-existing ischaemic heart disease. Left ventricular dysfunction occasionally occurs independently of coronary artery occlusion (Baum et al, 1971). A good response to diuretic therapy is usual in the earlier of these episodes and treatment need not necessarily be continued when the acute features have subsided. By the time chronic heart failure becomes established digitalis can be added, though its value in this condition is not established. The treatment of heart failure is not influenced by age. In emphysema (without bronchitis) cardiac failure occurs late in the course and is often the terminal event.

Respiratory failure

The management of acute respiratory failure is largely unaffected by age though the mortality rate is higher in the old (Warren et al, 1980). Careful monitoring of blood gases is essential. 24 per cent oxygen is usually sufficient to avoid the serious consequences of hypoxia without depressing respiration further. In a very few patients 24 per cent will be too high a concentration and this will be detected by checking arterial levels after starting the treatment. The aim is to achieve an arterial oxygen tension of about 50 mmHg. without provoking acidosis. Frequent chest physiotherapy, every 2 hours or so, may be needed to clear secretions and during the acute stages this must be continued through the night. Encouraging the patient to cough is an important part of the treatment and any drug, especially sedatives, which might inhibit this action must be avoided.

An unusual form of respiratory failure is the hypoxic episodes during sleep which are common in patients with COAD, even when not hypercapnoeic. They tend to occur during the REM phase of sleep and are most likely in those with a low ventilatory response to carbon dioxide (Fleetham et al, 1980; Wynne et al, 1980). In those with chronic carbon dioxide retention treatment with medroxyprogesterone acetate effects a modest improvement by increasing tidal volume (Skatrud et al, 1980).

Rehabilitation

When people become breathless on exertion they avoid exercise. The resulting loss in physical fitness may itself contribute to subsequent exertional dyspnoea. Obese patients should be encouraged to lose weight. Patients should be advised to exercise as far as they are able and gradually to increase their efforts. Walking is a suitable exercise though more active physical training programmes are also feasible and improve the subjective sense of well-being (Brundin, 1974) without however, improving ventilatory function or blood gases. Prior inhalation of a bronchodilator improves exercise tolerance. Recovery from exertional dyspnoea is speeded by oxygen, now widely used in domiciliary practice. The concentration should be controlled by a suitable mask; 28 per cent is usually satisfactory. It is of no value taken before exercise and is unfortunately often used by patients while they are inactive when its value is probably negligible.

Trials of long term oxygen therapy in severely disabled patients, (Medical Research Council Working Party, 1981) suggest a modest improvement in mortality but it is not clear that the quality of life is improved by this expensive manoeuvre which necessitates breathing oxygen for at least 15 hours per day.

Simpler methods of improving everyday life include the alteration of living arrangements, such as sleeping downstairs and using a commode to reduce the need to climb stairs. It can be helpful to have an oxygen cylinder at the top of stairs. Provision of an appropriate wheelchair or invalid car should be considered for those who would otherwise be housebound.

Depression is common, as in all chronic disease, and often manifests itself as irritability and querulousness. Such people are difficult to live with and spouses observing an apparent discrepancy between effort and symptoms may suspect malingering; explanations are required. The spouses are sometimes right, in a sense, as neurotic dyspnoea is not infrequent. It presents as complaints of severe exertional dyspnoea by individuals whose performance is far worse than one would expect from their lung function tests and clinical assessment. This also may be a feature of depressive illness. A trial of antidepressant therapy will be worthwhile.

BRONCHIAL ASTHMA

This condition is characterized by recurring episodes of breathlessness and wheezing with varying periods of remission. Asthmatics may be regarded as having persistently increased bronchial reactivity and in them asthma develops after exposure to various agents which do not cause symptoms in normals.

Epidemiology

The onset is usually in early life but can be at any age. No precise figures of incidence or prevalence are possible as there is no universally accepted definition. In old people the condition may co-exist with chronic bronchitis, or be indistinguishable from chronic bronchitis with reversible airway obstruction. Burr et al (1979) surveyed a random sample of people over 70 years old in South Wales. They found 5.1 per cent of men and 1.8 per cent of women to have bronchial asthma (2.9 per cent overall), defined by the patient having (1) wheezing and breathlessness during the previous year, (2) an FEV_1 which increased by at least 15 per cent after salbutamol inhalation and (3) a consistent response to corticosteroids or bronchodilators. An additional 3.6 per cent of the aged population were ex-asthmatics or mild asthmatics not entirely conforming to the definition used. In about one-fifth of the total, onset had been in youth. When the onset is in old age asthma is more likely to be of the intrinsic type — i.e. with no demonstrable causal allergen. The extrinsic type may rarely occur and sometimes co-exists with the intrinsic type. Even in old age there is a somewhat increased likelihood of positive skin tests for allergens, systemic eosinophilia and a positive family history of asthma.

Clinical

Acute

Symptoms of cough, sputum production and wheezing tend to be more common in older asthmatics, especially in smokers. These symptoms may present acutely or worsen somewhat before an acute attack. For some weeks poor control of symptoms may not occasion undue alarm. Rapid deterioration may then occur (Bellamy and Collins, 1979). No single clinical or laboratory factor provides a satisfactory guide to the severity of the attack. Anxiety, sometimes panic, exaggerates the clinical features so that the degree of breathlessness and wheezing may appear excessive. Use of the accessory muscles of respiration is probably the best single guide to severity (McFadden et al, 1973). Tachycardia, tachypnoea and sometimes pulsus paradoxus occur, together with pallor and sweating. Signs of carbon dioxide retention such as drowsiness and confusion, which may be due to sedation, indicate profound physiological disturbance and a near terminal state. Radiography is of little diagnostic value but helps to exclude pneumothorax which is a common cause of sudden worsening. The pathological changes of bronchial mucosal oedema, thick adherent sputum, bronchial plugging and smooth muscle contraction lead to a variety of physiological changes. Hypoxia is usual though the patient hyperventilates and the Pa_{CO_2} is usually low or normal. Ventilation: perfusion defects occur with underventilated areas remaining well perfused.

Older patients take longer to recover, perhaps because of associated bronchitis (Smith, 1981). Fatal attacks of asthma not infrequently occur within a few weeks of discharge from hospital and are more likely in old people. Sometimes steroid therapy has been tapered off too quickly (Poukkula et al, 1979).

Chronic

The distinction from chronic bronchitis is difficult. A productive cough may be present in both, and sometimes in asthma a chronic cough is the sole presenting symptom (Corrao et al, 1979). Nocturnal worsening is more suggestive of asthma than bronchitis. The presence of eosinophilia in the sputum is not diagnostic for asthma though bronchial casts (Curschmann's spirals) are more helpful. Skin testing for allergens is of no value and attempts at desensitization are ineffective. Bronchial provocation tests have no place in old age. Chronic asthma may mimic advanced chronic bronchitis and the main practical point is the importance of a trial of corticosteroids (as previously discussed). A life-enhancing improvement occasionally results.

Treatment

Antibiotics

Only a small proportion of acute exacerbations are due to respiratory infections (Clarke, 1979), and a trial of routine antibiotic therapy did not show any advantage (Graham et al, 1982). Where acute bronchitis is suspected however, this will have to be treated. Following respiratory infections the airways of asthmatic subjects exhibit increased reactivity and this often responds best to anticholinergic therapy.

Bronchodilators

The same drugs can be used as described for chronic obstructive airways disease. The response is better in asthma. There is some evidence that beta receptor stimulators by inhalation are more effective in younger patients and ipratropium bromide in older patients (Ullah et al, 1981) but the difference is not of practical significance. The two may be given together for additional benefit. A worsening response to continued usage is an important sign of clinical deterioration and possible acute attacks. Sodium cromoglycate (cromolyn sodium) is of use in some older chronic asthmatics (Gillard et al, 1979) despite the illness being non-atopic.

It can also be tried in the rare patient with exercise-induced asthma. Treatment should continue for some weeks to allow a proper assessment of its place. It is of no value during acute attacks.

The absorption and elimination of theophylline is unaffected by age (Cusack et al, 1980), though elimination is increased in smokers in whom higher doses may be needed. Most asthmatics quickly learn to stop smoking. Slow-release oral preparations are particularly useful; they can be taken at night by those with nocturnal worsening. An aminophylline suppository is an alternative line of treatment. In acute asthma, treatment by intravenous aminophylline has largely been replaced by intravenous salbutamol. When given in this way care must be taken to administer the dose slowly. In those who have previously been taking an aminophylline derivative dangerously toxic levels may be reached. Paradoxically, hypoxia sometimes worsens because the pulmonary blood flow to underventilated areas is increased.

Inhaled corticosteroids (beclomethasone or betamethasone) are valuable in chronic asthma. Systemic absorption does not occur in doses of up to about 12 puffs daily. Oral thrush is an occasional complication. The maximum response occurs after about 10 days treatment so it is best to delay reducing systemic steroid therapy by this time when substituting inhalations (Gaddie et al, 1973). Inhaled steroids are only an adjunct to systemic therapy in the treatment of acute asthma.

Oesophageal disease. It has recently been observed that a surprisingly high proportion of asthmatics have disorders of oesophageal function (Kjellen et al, 1981a), including hiatus hernia and abnormal motility. Improvement in the asthma is often effected by treating the alimentary problem with simple measures including bed-head elevation, abstaining from late night food and antacid therapy (Kjellen et al, 1981b). This has no effect on pulmonary funtion tests.

PULMONARY EMBOLISM

Incidence

Pulmonary embolism increases in frequency with advancing age being found in 14 per cent of all deaths of patients over 70 years in one large hospital autopsy series (McKeown, 1965). It was however judged responsible for only 3.5 per cent of the deaths. Higher figures have been reported but much depends on the selection of the series studied. In a group containing many postoperative patients deaths were attributable to pulmonary embolism in 14 per cent (Morrell and Dunnill, 1968) while in a general medical department (Nielsen et al, 1981), in nearly all fatal cases the condition was thought to have only slightly modified life-expectancy because of the frequent co-existance of other severe illness.

Causation

Most cases are consequent upon thrombosis in the leg or pelvic veins, and anything which encourages that may lead to pulmonary embolism. It is not certain that aging as such is one of these causes. In old people the common factors include myocardial infarction, congestive cardiac failure, fractures of the hip, surgical operations, malignancy, stroke or any other cause of either prolonged immobility or altered blood coagulation. Gross obesity, varicose veins and the post-phlebitic syndrome add to the risk. In the presence of more than one risk factor the chances of embolism are multiplied. Anyone who has previously had a pulmonary embolus remains at increased risk of another. In stroke patients the embolus almost always originates in the paralysed leg (Byrne and O'Neil, 1952), rarely the arm. Although venous thrombosis frequently develops during the first few days after a stroke (Warlow et al, 1976) fatal emboli tend to occur after the first week (Brown and Glassenberg, 1973). They usually happen unexpectedly and quite without clinical warning.

Postoperative changes in blood coagulation have been described in elderly patients but their significance is unclear. Evidence of hypercoagulability 7-days post-operatively is reported by Feruglio et al (1960).

Mechanical and stasis factors are more likely causes. Thrombosis begins in the calf and tends to extend upwards (Kakkar et al, 1969). The risk of embolism is somewhat higher when the thrombus originates in the pelvic or thigh veins rather than the calf.

Non-thrombotic emboli (e.g. septic, fat etc.) are not considered here.

Clinical

Acute massive emboli cause immediate right ventricular failure and shock. They are usually rapidly fatal in old people.

Acute minor emboli may or may not cause infarction. The presentation may be relatively non-specific and is not always sudden, with patients sometimes complaining of increasing dyspnoea on exertion or tightness in the chest; at other times hypotension or cardiac arrhythmias occur without obvious cause. More typically the onset is with acute breathlessness or chest pain, often pleuritic. Haemoptysis may be present from the start or appear during the first few days. Sometimes it is absent throughout. Pyrexia is common, especially with infarction (Murray et al, 1979). Even with quite large emboli physical signs in the chest may be strikingly lacking. At other times observation indicates tachycardia and tachypnoea with unilaterally diminished thoracic movements. Wheezing and bronchospasm may be obvious

and right ventricular strain evident. Signs of either consolidation or collapse may be present, perhaps with evidence of a pleural effusion. The chief differential diagnosis is from pneumonia, and clinical evidence may not allow the distinction. The two conditions may co-exist.

Investigations

Blood enzyme studies are of little value. With infarction the serum bilirubin may be somewhat elevated, but only when liver function is compromised. Finding blood in aspirated pleural fluid is a suggestive confirmatory sign. Blood gas studies will show arterial hypoxia and the carbon dioxide level will be low or normal. The electrocardiogram is likely to show evidence of right ventricular stain and tachycardia with clockwise rotation and a P pulmonale. These findings are not specific.

Plain X-rays of chest are of most value when infarction has occurred. The most useful signs are of an elevated hemidiaphragm, small atelectases and small unilateral effusion. The absence of vascular shadows is an unreliable guide (Talbot et al, 1973). Effusions tend to occur early and are usually associated with pleuritic pain. Late increase in their size suggests repeated embolism (Bynum and Wilson, 1978). Wedge-shaped parenchymal opacities extend to a pleural surface and eventually heal as linear scars.

Diagnostic accuracy is much improved by the use of ventilation and perfusion scans. Unfortunately perfusion scans are likely to be abnormal with any lung disease including COAD. Pulmonary embolism is unlikely when a perfusion defect is substantially smaller than the corresponding lesion on a plain chest X-ray. When the perfusion defect is substantially larger, pulmonary embolism is highly likely. A ventilation scan showing normal ventilation to an area of poor perfusion increases the likelihood of pulmonary embolism (Biello et al, 1979).

In the absence of scanning facilities peripheral venography may demonstrate clot formation and provide useful indirect evidence of embolism. Pulmonary artery angiography is used only as a prelude to operative intervention and will rarely be appropriate for old people.

Resolution

Infarcts eventually heal completely though this may take several weeks and even when the chest X-ray appears normal perfusion defects may be present. About half of all infarcts leave residual scars and the proportion seems to be the same at all ages (McGoldrick et al, 1979). Acute minor, and massive infarcts do not progress to chronic pulmonary hypertension. This is not the case with the fortunately rare condition of chronic pulmonary embolism. There is usually no apparent predisposing cause and the prognosis is poor because of the progressive development of right ventricular failure and pulmonary hypertension (Sutton et al, 1977).

Treatment

Prevention
The first step is to assess the various risk factors in any susceptible patient. In a surgical series (Hills et al, 1972) considerable success in preventing deep vein thrombosis (DVT) was achieved by applying intermittent pneumatic compression of the calves from shortly before operation to the time mobilization began. The method was particularly advantageous for old patients who tolerated this prolonged treatment well. A similar attempt to prevent DVT in stroke patients (Prasad et al, 1982) failed, possibly because the intermittent compression was applied three times daily rather than continually. A widely-used and successful technique of preventing postoperative DVT is with low dose heparin (Kakkar et al, 1982). Its effectiveness has been shown in stroke patients (McCarthy et al, 1977), and it can also be used in old patients with heart failure and other predisposing factors.

Anticoagulants
The active treatment of pulmonary embolism is largely uninfluenced by age. Thrombolytic therapy is rarely used. Anticoagulant treatment does not appear to be associated with a significantly increased risk of bleeding disorders in old people (Second Report, 1982) but there are many possible contraindications to its use. These include peptic ulcers, and other likely causes of bleeding, frequent falls, uncertain patient cooperation and likely interaction with other medication being taken. Except when there has been recent bleeding these are all relative contraindications, to be assessed in each individual.

There have been no completely satisfactory trials to determine the optimum duration of treatment and there seems no good reason to prolong it beyond 6 weeks after the resolution of any underlying cause (O'Sullivan, 1972).

DIFFUSE INTERSTITIAL FIBROSIS

Some disorders which differ slightly in their reported pathology appear to be variants of the same condition. Pseudonyms include Fibrosing Alveolitis and Desquamative Interstitial Pneumonia. The aetiology is unknown but the increased incidence of connective tissue disorders and various antibodies suggest it to be an autoimmune disease. In the desquamative type, which may represent early changes, there is a sparse interstitial infiltration with plasma cells and eosinophils while monocytes are found in small air spaces. There is little proteinaceous exudate in the alveoli. In other patients a dense cellular interstitial infiltration with lymphocytes and monocytes occurs. There is some proteinaceous exudate in the alveoli whose walls may show some fibrosis (Carrington, et al 1978). With advancing disease, cellular infiltration of the alveolar wall increases while fibrosis there and in the interstitium progresses. Cystic degeneration eventually occurs. Evidence of small airways involvement is sometimes found; it takes the form of an obstructive or obliterative bronchiolitis.

The physiological consequences are the development of a restrictive lung defect with reduced FEV_1, FVC and TLC. Lung rigidity increases. Ventilation: perfusion defects occur. Hypoxia is usual and the arterial carbon dioxide tension is normal or low because of hyperventilation.

Clinical
The onset of this rare condition is typically in late middle-age. A sub-acute form progresses to death over a period of a few months, but more usually the course is of several years duration with young patients and women surviving the longest. The main symptoms (Stack et al, 1965; Turner-Warwick et al, 1980a) are dyspnoea and poor effort tolerance. Dyspnoea may persist for years, having been troublesome from the earliest stages when other clinical and radiological signs may be minimal. Cough is frequent and may follow a deep inspiration. It is often dry. Finger clubbing may precede the onset of respiratory symptoms or eventually develop. Auscultation reveals crackles at the lung bases and these are usually widespread and often sound characteristically metallic and louder than congestive adventitae. Joint signs of rheumatoid arthritis or a polyarthropathy occur in 10–20 per cent of cases. In a few patients the disease process appears to halt spontaneously, but in most death eventually results from the disease itself, cardiac failure, respiratory infection or from some complication of immunosuppressive therapy. There is an increased incidence of carcinoma of the bronchus.

Investigations
In younger patients both open lung biopsy and bronchoalveolar lavage may be done, sometimes for diagnostic purposes but also to allow an assessment of the likely response to corticosteroids. In biopsies (Winterbauer et al, 1978) the more interstitial fibrosis present the less likely a response, while in lavage material (Rudd et al, 1981) lymphocyte counts are higher, and eosinophil and neutrophil counts lower in responders. Such methods are rarely used in old age.

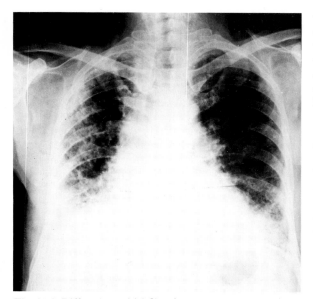

Fig. 36.3 Diffuse interstitial fibrosis

The chest X-ray may be quite normal at first but later small irregular or rounded opacities cause a mottled appearance in the lower zones (Fig. 36.3). This may extend upwards.

Translucencies appear later to give a honeycombed appearance which is rarely gross. Pleural effusions are uncommon.

Lung function tests show the expected restrictive defect and a low diffusing capacity. These tests are used to follow progress. A positive latex test and raised antinuclear antibody titres plus a high ESR are common.

Differential diagnosis
The diagnosis may be surprisingly easy when a suggestive history combines with basal crackles and finger clubbing. The chief distinction to be made is from rheumatoid arthritis and other collagen diseases affecting the lungs; extrapulmonary clues are often present. Sarcoidosis, xanthomatous disease, idiopathic haemosiderosis and alveolar proteinosis are uncommon in old people. Chronic lipid pneumonitis is excluded by a relevant history and sputum examination: the symptoms are usually less than would be expected from the X-rays. Lymphangitis carcinomatosis may be difficult to exclude. Asbestosis and other occupational lung disorders have to be considered. Miliary tuberculosis can usually be excluded on clinical grounds, but if not, both steroids and antituberculosis drugs are given.

Treatment
Corticosteroids, in substantial dosage, are the only drugs to which this condition is likely to respond. Responders tend to be younger patients with cellular histology (Turner-Warwick et al, 1980b). About half of those treated experience subjective improvement, but objective evidence of it is only found in a minority. It is not clear that the treatment much improves survival and it should be tailed off if no clinical or physiological improvement results.

CARCINOMA OF THE BRONCHUS

The mortality from this condition rises throughout adult life and in 1980 the death rates per million in England and Wales for those aged 75–84 years were 8117 (men) and 1237 (women). It is only slightly less in those even older. By comparison, in the same year the rates for ages 55–64 years were 2425 (men) and 762 (women). Cigarette smoking is the chief aetiological agent. Pipe and cigar smokers are at less risk. Altered smoking habits probably explain the increasing incidence in women. Other causes include exposure to radioactivity, asbestos and other occupationally linked factors.

The histological changes seen in bronchial epithelium as a result of smoking are reversible and normal histology may be restored within about 2 years of giving up the habit (Bertram and Rogers, 1981). This may not benefit old people in whom a higher proportion of tumours are slow growing. From the onset of malignant epithelial change it may take 30 years for a tumour with a slow doubling-time to present clinically so that after stopping smoking such a tumour may take many years to show itself (Geddes, 1979). Old people, at the time they stop smoking, are thus much more likely to be harbouring a malignancy than are younger ones with their more rapidly growing tumours. A slower rate of tumour growth helps to explain the likelihood of old people having less advanced disease at the time of presentation (Holmes and Hearne, 1981); this includes a reduced frequency of metastases (Suen et al, 1974). Presumably in old age the squamous cell type of carcinoma is relatively commoner than the more aggressive small cell (oat cell) type or adenocarcinoma, though there are no authoritative data on this point. Alveolar cell carcinoma is uncommon at any age.

Clinical features
The main respiratory symptoms are cough, chest pain and haemoptysis. The section on 'respiratory symptomatology' (p. 733) details the altered ways of presentation in old age. The cough has no distinctive characteristics and often presents as a worsening of pre-existing bronchitis. Chest pain may be due to pleurisy, pneumothorax, rib erosion or a Pancoast syndrome. Other pressure-related effects include superior vena caval obstruction, paralysis of the recurrent laryngeal or

phrenic nerves, Horner's syndrome and oesophageal compression. Bronchial occlusion may cause stridor or lung collapse.

In some there are no obvious thoracic signs or symptoms and the presentation is with some manifestation of metastatic disease. Bone pain tends to be constant; its importance may be overlooked in those with arthritis. Epilepsy or stroke occur, the latter following haemorrhage into an intracranial deposit. Multiple cerebral deposits cause a subacute confusional state.

A number of extrathoracic manifestations which are unrelated to metastases have been described. Finger clubbing and hypertrophic pulmonary osteoarthropathy are the best known but neurological, metabolic and endocrine disorders also occur. None of them is known to have a particular relationship with aging. They all increase in frequency with advancing disease. Of the neurological abnormalities, a symmetrical peripheral neuropathy is the commonest. Other forms are relatively rare; they include mononeuropathies, which are sometimes multiple, cerebellar degeneration, the myasthenic syndrome of Eaton-Lambert and motor neurone disease. Polymyositis and dermatomyositis may occur. In elderly men, neoplastic disease is a common cause of symmetrical proximal muscle weakness. Among the endocrine and metabolic group hypercalcaemia is the commonest. Cushing's syndrome and the syndrome of inappropriate ADH secretion are not infrequent. They are due to the manufacture by the tumour of hormones or substances with hormone-like activity (Gropp et al, 1980).

Diagnostic methods

Many cases are discovered when a chest X-ray is performed for some unrelated reason. A chest film should be part of the routine examination of all new geriatric patients. Cytological examination of sputum produces few false positives in experienced hands. Bronchoscopy is not contraindicated by old age. It allows both histological diagnosis and an assessment of the feasibility of operation. Sometimes osteoarthritis of the cervical spine will not permit the necessary neck extension and there may then be some danger of cord damage in those with spondylosis.

Computed tomography of the thorax (Kreel, 1978; Felson and Jacobson, 1979) is a highly sensitive diagnostic technique capable of detecting small lesions which are not apparent on conventional films. It allows accurate assessment of the hilar and mediastinal structures, and can be used to detect recurrences and monitor the response to treatment. It will be valuable in geriatric practice wherever it is available.

Radioisotope scanning is useful for detecting secondary deposits in brain, bone and liver (Kelly et al, 1979). Gallium seems to be a particularly sensitive diagnostic tool in this respect with the added advantage that it picks out lung primaries (DeMeester et al, 1979). It is not generally available. Such scans form part of the preoperative assessment.

Ultrasound of the pleura is of occasional use; it distinguishes fluid from solid lesions and may indicate the best site for a diagnostic aspiration (Lipscomb et al, 1981).

Management

Early diagnosis, preferably with histological proof, is important to allow authoritative advice, accurate treatment and the avoidance of the disaster of leaving a misdiagnosed benign condition untreated.

Prevention and screening

Apart from the causes related to industrial agents the only known effective means of prevention is reducing tobacco consumption. Patients diagnosed by random X-ray examination tend to have relatively early disease but it is not completely clear that their prognosis is better as a result. Brett (1968) could not demonstrate a reduction in mortality in those diagnosed by regular 6-monthly X-ray surveillance, but it remains possible that concentrating attention on heavy smokers will be more productive. Woolner et al (1981) are doing this using a combination of chest X-ray and sputum cytology at 4-monthly intervals. Perhaps unexpectedly the X-ray has proven best at detecting early tumours but the cytological method is better for picking up central lung lesions which may be missed radiologically. As yet there is insufficient evidence to justify community screening programmes.

Surgery

There is no doubt that surgery offers the best prospect of a cure to those with localised disease. Unfortunately the majority of patients are found to be unsuitable for resection because of location, intrathoracic spread, metastases or co-existing illness. In one large series (Evans, 1973) the resection rate was only 15 per cent and was the same in old and young.

The preoperative phase should include explanation of the procedure and of such potentially frightening postoperative necessities as intrathoracic drains and intravenous infusions, together with reassurance, sedation and chest physiotherapy (Okinaka and Holman, 1966). An ECG will be useful for comparison with postoperative tracings. Some test of ventilatory function is advisable. It may be worse than expected, especially in bronchitics, and a successful pneumonectomy may produce a respiratory cripple. Due regard must be given to the amount of lung lost to the tumour; when it is substantial, resection may cause little further worsening. The published normal lung volumes are not entirely reliable for very old people and some also use an exercise test (Butland et al, 1982) as a general guide to cardio-respiratory function. Some method of preventing deep vein thrombosis should be considered.

The commonest postoperative complications are cardiac arrhythmias, retained secretions which may necessitate therapeutic bronchoscopy and problems related directly to the surgical procedure. In old people respiratory infections, hypotension, electrolyte disturbances, urinary retention and gastric dilatation occur (Okinaka and Holman, 1966). The incidence of major problems does not seem to be related to age (Breyer et al, 1981). For those undergoing resection 5-year survival rates of about 20 per cent are typical.

Radiotherapy

For those unfit for surgery, or refusing it, radiotherapy offers some hope of cure. A radical course, though debilitating, is reasonably well tolerated by old people in whom complications are not more severe or frequent (Aristizabal et al, 1976). The survival rate at 3 years is about 20 per cent and is best for the squamous cell type (Coy and Kennelly, 1980).

Palliative radiotherapy is of especial value in venous and bronchial obstruction, painful bone secondaries and ulcerating skin deposits (Hope-Stone, 1967). Whole-brain irradiation is sometimes used to relieve the sub-acute confusional symptoms of multiple brain metastases (Nisce et al, 1971). There seems to be little difference between tumour cell types in their frequency of response (Slawson and Scott, 1979).

Cytotoxic therapy

Small cell cancers respond poorly to surgery or radiotherapy (they metastasize early) and chemotherapy using several cytotoxic agents, with or without radiotherapy, is being developed. Greco et al (1979) achieved a 1-year survival rate of 75 per cent in a small series using repeated courses of drugs and radiotherapy plus prophylactic whole-brain irradiation. Livingston et al (1978) managed remission rates up to 40 per cent with a similar regimen. Not surprisingly toxic effects were frequent and serious, but the untreated prognosis of these patients was a few months at most. Intrapleural instillation of cytotoxic drugs plays a valuable part in the management of malignant effusions.

TUBERCULOSIS

The numbers of new cases and the mortality from all forms of tuberculosis have been declining steadily throughout this century. Over the last 15 years the rate of fall of respiratory tuberculosis has levelled off and the numbers of new cases of extra-respiratory tuberculosis has changed little.

In 1980 in England and Wales for all ages and all types of tuberculosis, there were 9145 new cases notified and 608 reported deaths. Figure 36.4 shows the age-specific notification rates for men and women of different ages for respiratory tuberculosis. It is remarkable that the condition becomes very much more

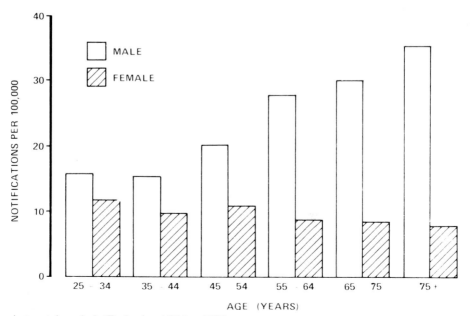

Fig. 36.4 Respiratory tuberculosis (England and Wales, 1980)

common in older men while not increasing at all in women. For extrapulmonary disease there is a considerable fall in the number of new cases in older men and a lesser fall in women who constitute the majority of cases at all ages.

The death rate from the respiratory form rises throughout adult life until in the very old it is about 156/million (men) and 39/million (women).

Morbidity

These epidemiological changes have magnified the importance of the condition in old age. The reasons for the high death rate in old people (British Thoracic and Tuberculosis Society, 1971) constitute mainly a mixture of under-diagnosis and management failure. There is some self-neglect and under-reporting of symptoms by old people, especially those with mental disorders and alcoholism, and residents in common lodging houses, so that the condition may be far advanced by the time of presentation. Attack rates are higher in single and widowed men. In clinical practice tuberculosis has become a rare condition and may not be considered either because of failure to recognized uncommon forms (Greenbaum et al, 1980), incorrect assumption of malignancy or because the clinical features are disguised by immunosuppressive treatment or severe co-existing illness. A substantial proportion of cases are discovered at autopsy, especially in miliary tuberculosis.

Clinical

Symptoms are initially innocuous; it is characteristic of this condition for the disease to be more advanced than one would expect from the signs and symptoms. Cough is usual, haemoptysis sometimes occurs, breathlessness is unlikely unless the disease is advanced. Tuberculous bronchitis may cause wheezing. Non-specific but common symptoms include lethargy, weight loss, night sweats and the usual features of chronic ill health. Abnormal physical signs may be lacking. Some crackles over an upper lobe may be detectable. Signs of lung contraction usually indicate old fibrous disease. Pyrexia is not invariably present. Any anaemia is likely to be mild and the white cell count may be either somewhat raised or lowered. Hypokalaemia, hyponatraemia or hypercalcaemia are occasional findings. The syndrome of inappropriate ADH secretion is a rare complication. Arthralgia may be present especially in immigrants. Although most cases in old age are of the post-primary type a small number of cases of primary tuberculosis are seen. In them, pleural effusions are more likely and, uncommonly, a tuberculous lobar pneumonia may be present, especially in immigrants.

Diagnostic methods

The usual techniques of microscopy and culture of sputum are used. When sputum samples cannot be produced inhalations of either steam or hyperosmolar saline (Elliott and Reichel, 1963) help. Cultures of gastric aspirates or laryngeal swabs may otherwise be used. Most cases are diagnosed by X-ray. In doubtful cases it is particularly helpful to secure any previous films for comparison. The radiological signs vary from minimal changes with a barely detectable soft infiltrate, to advanced bilateral cavitating disease. Primary tuberculosis may produce unilateral effusions, hilar adenopathy or basal infiltrates of a pneumonic type (Kahn et al, 1977). Small lesions without cavitation are not necessarily inactive. Large lesions may be mistaken for a lung abscess or aspiration pneumonia (Miller and MacGregor, 1978). A normal chest X-ray does not exclude miliary tuberculosis.

The tuberculin test is of little value in the diagnosis of individual cases.

Miliary tuberculosis

This extremely rare condition poses difficult diagnostic problems. There is usually some other severe pathology present which could account for all the patient's symptoms, or perhaps they are disguised by immunosuppressive treatment. The clinical course (Grieco and Chmel, 1974) is of non-specific deterioration with cough, weight loss, debility and fever. The condition must be considered in all pyrexias of unknown origin. Sputum cultures and the tuberculin test are frequently negative. The chest X-ray may be normal until a late stage.

Cultures of bone marrow are sometimes positive, and positive urine cultures may be obtained even in the absence of abnormal cells in the urine. A wide variety of haematological abnormalities (Glasser et al, 1970) may be present including leucocytosis, leucopenia and monocytosis. Leukaemic appearances and pancytopenia may indicate a pre-existing haematological disease.

The clinical examination is usually unhelpful, other than the exceptional circumstance of choroidal tubercles being present. The liver and spleen are often enlarged but rarely by much.

A substantial proportion of these patients are diagnosed only at autopsy (Fullerton and Dyer, 1965), so that if the condition is suspected, but proof is lacking, there may be no alternative to a therapeutic trial. Such a trial should be with drugs likely to act only on the tubercle bacillus, such as isoniazid and ethambutol.

Tuberculin testing

The Mantoux test consists of the intradermal injection of a measured amount of purified protein derivative (PPD) into the volar skin of the forearm. The test is read at 48–96 hours. Only induration is measured. A positive result is 5 mm or more of induration (using

PPD BP). Ten tuberculin units (TU), i.e. intermediate strength, are usually given. Cross-reactions with other mycobacteriae occur and are more likely with higher doses. There are other types of tuberculin test in use and several different antigens.

The proportion of old people with positive reactions has fallen over the years. Fifty years ago almost all would have been positive. Johnston et al (1963), using the Heaf test, in the UK found 60 per cent of geriatric ward residents were positive and the same was found in the United States (Chesrow and Norah, 1967). Nowadays only about one-third of geriatric long-stay residents are positive to 10 TU. These changes reflect a lack of recent exposure to tuberculosis in the community owing to the reduced prevalence of the condition, and perhaps also some waning of tuberculin sensitivity with advancing age.

When negative responders are re-tested a week or so later with the same dose of tuberculin a small proportion are found to have become positive, i.e. converted. This so-called 'boosting phenomenon' (Thompson et al, 1979) is more common in the aged being seen in about 7 per cent of a personal series. The clinical implication is that an unrepeated negative test may be misleading and a later positive response may be wrongly regarded as a conversion indicating recent infection.

About 30 per cent of elderly people with active tuberculosis have negative tuberculin tests compared with 20 per cent for all ages (Holden et al, 1971). This is probably due to the response being suppressed by malnutrition and the greater likelihood of the disease being severe in old age (Rooney et al, 1976).

Of the many factors which may cause negative tuberculin reactions (American Thoracic Society, 1981a) virus infections, severe nutritional or metabolic disease, neoplasms, immunosuppressive therapy and faulty testing techniques are the most likely.

Tuberculosis in institutions

Within a closed community such as an old people's home a single active case may cause an outbreak lasting months. Stead (1981) gives a detailed account of how such a case infected 10 residents, an employee and a visitor to a home. The closer the personal contact the more likely the infection. The outbreak was not halted until all at risk had been repeatedly tuberculin tested and isoniazid prophylaxis was used for converters.

The management of such an incident involves the chest X-ray and tuberculin testing of all at risk, including care staff. Repeat tuberculin testing after one week will detect boosters. Negative responders will require to be re-tested after about 2 months. If their chest X-ray is clear tuberculin converters can be treated with isoniazid alone. Active cases should be segregated

from previously unexposed individuals until treatment is underway but strict isolation is not essential.

Domestic arrangements to reduce the risk of infection include adequate ventilation to expel infective sputum droplets; they are detailed elsewhere (American Thoracic Society, 1981b).

Treatment

The aims of treatment are to kill all the bacilli and prevent resistant strains emerging. A small proportion of the progeny of a multiplying tubercle bacillus will be resistant to at least one drug so multiple therapy is mandatory. Prolonged treatment is needed as some organisms are dormant within macrophages (Dickinson and Mitchison, 1981).

Chemoprophylaxis

When very few bacilli are present it can be assumed that resistant organisms are unlikely. A single drug may then be used to treat minimal lesions of doubtful activity or recent tuberculin converters thought to have been infected. True prophylaxis is sometimes used in those at risk of reactivation of old infection by planned corticosteroid therapy. Isoniazid prophylaxis is little used in old people because of the increased risk of liver toxicity (Byrd et al 1979), which may, however, partly be due to the usual use of 300 mg daily irrespective of age or weight.

Chemotherapy

The disease responds to treatment just as well in old as young people provided the treatment is taken. Patient compliance with prolonged courses is a problem at all ages, but especially in the elderly who may well be taking other medication and are more likely to experience side effects or be forgetful. The issuing of drugs in regular monthly prescriptions facilitates supervision. Such social factors as nutrition and housing do not influence the rate of recovery as long as effective treatment is being taken. Admission to hospital is not essential but does impress the importance of the situation on the patient and allows observation of the likely future cooperation to be expected. In Britain the recommended regimen (British Thoracic Association, 1980) consists of an initial 2 months of treatment with isoniazid (200–300 mg daily), rifampicin (rifampin) (450–600 mg daily) and ethambutol (15 mg per kg body weight/day). This is followed by another 7 months of daily treatment with isoniazid and rifampicin in the same doses. A valid alternative which allows supervision of medication is for the continuation phase to be with isoniazid and rifampicin twice weekly in increased doses (Singapore Tuberculosis Survey, 1977). It should be noted that regimens using only two drugs from the start are widely used elsewhere, especially in the USA (American Thoracic Society, 1980), and have been shown to be effective in extrarespiratory tuberculosis (Dutt et al, 1981). In the UK (Monie et al, 1982) and the USA (Leff et al, 1981) there is considerable variation between treatment centres in the regimens used, but it should be emphasized that failure to adhere to a proven regimen is a likely cause of relapse.

A full discussion of the chemotherapy of tuberculosis is beyond the scope of this chapter. General aspects are reviewed by Crofton and Douglas (1981) and short-course chemotherapy by Fox (1981).

REFERENCES

Adamson J R Jr 1968 An electron microscopic comparison of the connective tissue of the lungs of young and elderly subjects. American Review of Respiratory Diseases 98: 399–406

Alford R H 1968 Effect of chronic bronchopulmonary disease and aging on human nasal secretion IgA concentrations Journal of Immunology 101: 984–988

American Thoracic Society 1980 Guidelines for short-course tuberculosis chemotherapy. American Review of Respiratory Diseases 121: 611–614

American Thoracic Society 1981a The tuberculin skin test. American Review of Respiratory Diseases 124: 356–363

American Thoracic Society 1981b Diagnostic standards and classification of tuberculosis and other mycobacterial diseases (14th edu.). American Review of Respiratory Diseases 123: 343–345

Amman A J, Schiffman G, Austrian R 1980 The antibody responses to pneumococcal capsular polysaccharides in aged individuals. Proceedings of the Society for Experimental Biology and Medicine 164: 312–6

Anderson A E Jr, Furlaneto J A, Foraker A G 1970 Bronchopulmonary derangements in nonsmokers. American Review of Respiratory Diseases 101: 518–527

Aristizabal S A, Meyerson M, Caldwell W L, Mayer E G 1976 Age as a prognostic indicator in carcinoma of lung. Radiology 121: 721–723

Auerbach O, Stout A P, Hammond E C, Garfinkel L 1962 Changes in bronchial epithelium in relation to sex age residence smoking and pneumonia. New England Journal of Medicine 267: 111–119

Austrian R, Gold J 1964 Pneumococcal bacteraemia with especial reference to bacteremic pneumococcal pneumonia. Annals of Internal Medicine 60: 759–776

Balassanian V, Robbins F C 1967 Mycoplasma pneumoniae infection in families. New England Journal of Medicine 277: 719–725

Barker W H, Mullooly J P 1980 Influenza vaccination of elderly persons. Journal of the American Medical Association 244: 2547–2549

Bartlett J G 1979 Anaerobic bacterial pneumonitis. American Review of Respiratory Diseases 119: 19–23

Bateman J R M, Pavia D, Clarke S W 1978 The retention of lung secretions during the night in normal subjects. Clinical Science and Molecular Medicine 55: 523–527

Baum G L, Schwartz A, Llamas R, Castillo C 1971 Left ventricular function in chronic obstructive lung disease. New England Journal of Medicine 285: 361–365

Bedrossian C W M, Anderson A E Jr, Foraker A G 1977 Bronchial morphometry in emphysema and senescence. Experimental and Molecular Pathology 27: 44–50

Begin R, Renzetti A D, Bigler A H, Watanabe S 1975 Flow and age dependence of airway closure and dynamic compliance. Journal of Applied Physiology 38: 199–207

Bellamy D, Collins J V 1979 'Acute' asthma in the elderly. Thorax 34: 36–39

Berk S L, Holtsclaw S A, Kahn A, Smith J K 1981 Transtracheal aspiration in the severely ill elderly patient with bacterial pneumonia. Journal of the American Geriatrics Society 29: 228–231

Bertram J F, Rogers A W 1981 Recovery of bronchial epithelium on stopping smoking. British Medical Journal 283: 1567–1569

Biello D R, Mattar A G, McNight R C, Siegel B A 1979 Ventilation-perfusion studies in suspected pulmonary embolism. American Journal of Roentgenology 133: 1033–1037

Boren H G 1967 Pathobiology of air pollutants. Environmental Research 1: 178–197

Boren H G, Kory R C, Syner J C 1966 The Veterans Administration-Army cooperative study of pulmonary function II. The lung volume and its subdivision in normal men. American Journal of Medicine 41: 96–114

Bosse R, Sparrow D, Rose C L, Weiss S T 1981 Longitudinal effect of age and smoking cessation on pulmonary function. American Review of Respiratory Diseases 123: 378–381

Brett G Z 1968 The value of lung cancer detection by six-monthly chest radiographs. Thorax 23: 414–420

Breyer R H, Zippe C, Pharr W F, Jensik R J, Kittle C F, Faber L P 1981 Thoracotomy in patients over age seventy years. Ten year experience. Journal of Thoracic and Cardiovascular Surgery 81: 187–193

Briscoe W A, Dubois A B 1958 The relationship between airway resistance, airway conductance and lung volume in subjects of different age and body size. Journal of Clinical Investigation 37: 1279–1285

British Thoracic and Tuberculosis Association 1971 A survey of tuberculosis mortality in England and Wales in 1968. Tubercle 52: 1–18

British Thoracic Association 1980 Short-course chemotherapy in pulmonary tuberculosis. Lancet i: 1182–1183

Brown M, Glassenberg M 1973 Mortality factors in patients with acute stroke. Journal of the American Medical Association 224: 1493–1495

Brundin A 1974 Physical training in severe chronic obstructive lung disease. Scandinavian Journal of Respiratory Diseases 55: 25–36

Burr M L, Charles T J, Roy K, Seaton A 1979 Asthma in the elderly: an epidemiological survey. British Medical Journal 1: 1041–4

Burrows B, Niden A H, Barclay W R, Kajik J E 1965 Chronic obstructive lung disease. American Review of Respiratory Diseases 91: 521–540

Burrows B, Knudson R J, Lebowitz M D 1977 The relationship of childhood respiratory illness to adult obstructive airway disease. American Review of Respiratory Diseases 115: 751–760

Butland R J A, Pang J, Gross E R, Woodcock A A, Geddes D M 1982 Two six and twelve minute walking tests in respiratory disease. British Medical Journal 284: 1607–8

Bynum L J, Wilson J E III 1978 Radiographic features of pleural effusions in pulmonary embolism. American Review of Respiratory Diseases 117: 829–834

Byrd R B, Horn B R, Solomon D A, Griggs G A 1979 Toxic effects of isoniazid in tuberculosis chemoprophylaxis. Role of biochemical monitoring in 1000 patients. Journal of the American Medical Association 241: 1239–1241

Byrne J J, O'Neij E E 1952 Fatal pulmonary emboli. American Journal of Surgery 83: 47–49

Byrne-Quinn E, Weil J V, Sodal I E, Filey G F, Grower R F 1971 Ventilatory control in the athlete. Journal of Applied Physiology 30: 91–98

Caird F I, Akhtar A J 1972 Chronic respiratory disease in the elderly. Thorax 27: 764–768

Campbell E J M 1969 Physical signs of diffuse airways obstruction and lung distension. Thorax 24: 1–3

Carnow B W, Lepper M H, Shekelle R B, Stamler J 1969 SO_2 levels and acute respiratory illness in patients with chronic bronchopulmonary disease. Archives of Environmental Health 18: 768–776

Carrington C B, Gaensler E A, Coutu R E, Fitzgerald M X, Gupta R G 1978 Natural history and treated course of usual and desquamative interstitial pneumonia. New England Journal of Medicine 298: 801–809

Chesrow E J, Norah J B 1967 Tuberculin testing of the aged. Diseases of the Chest 51: 635–636

Clarke C W 1979 Relationship of bacterial and viral infections to exacerbations of asthma. Thorax 34: 344–347

Clarke S W, Thomson M L, Pavia D 1980 Effect of mucolytic and expectorant drugs on tracheobronchial clearance in chronic bronchitis. European Journal of Respiratory Diseases 61 suppl 110: 179–191

Corrao W M, Braman S S, Irwin R S 1979 Chronic cough as the sole presenting manifestation of bronchial asthma. New England Journal of Medicine 300: 633–637

Cosio M G, Hale K A, Niewohner D E 1980 Morphologic and morphometric effects of prolonged cigarette smoking on the small airways. American Review of Respiratory Diseases 122: 265–271

Coy P, Kennelly G M 1980 The role of curative radiotherapy in the treatment of lung cancer. Cancer 45: 698–702

Crofton J, Douglas A 1981 Respiratory Diseases 3rd edn Blackwell Scientific, Oxford, p 281–301

Cusack B, Kelly J G, Lavan J, Noel J, O'Malley K 1980 Theophylline kinetics in relation to age; the importance of smoking. British Journal of Clinical Pharmacology 10: 109–114

Czlonkowska A, Korlak J 1979 The immune response to aging. Journal of Gerontology 34: 9–14

De Meester T R, Golomb H M, Kirchner P, Rezai-Zadeh K, Bitran J D, Streeter D L, Hoffman P C, Cooper N 1979 The role of Gallium-67 scanning in the clinical staging and preoperative evaluation of patients with carcinoma of the lung. Annals of Thoracic Surgery 28: 451–464

Denham M J, Goodwin G S 1977 The value of blood cultures in geriatric practice. Age and Ageing 6: 85–88

De Vries H A 1970 Physiological effects of an exercise training regimen upon men aged 52 to 88. Journal of Gerontology 25: 325–336

Dickinson J M, Mitchison D A 1981 Experimental models to explain the high sterilizing activity of rifampicin in the chemotherapy of tuberculosis. American Review of Respiratory Diseases 123: 367–371

Diener C F, Burrows B 1975 Further observations on the course and prognosis of chronic obstructive lung disease. American Review of Respiratory Diseases 111: 719–724

Dutt A K, Moers D, Stead W W 1981 Results of short course chemotherapy in extrapulmonary tuberculosis. American Review of Respiratory Diseases 123: 255

Ebright J R, Rytel M W 1980 Bacterial pneumonia in the elderly. Journal of the American Geriatrics Society 28: 220–223

Edelman N H, Mittman C, Norris A H, Shock N W 1968 Effects of respiratory pattern on age differences in ventilation uniformity. Journal of Applied Physiology 24: 49–53

Elliott R C, Reichel J 1963 The efficacy of sputum specimens obtained by nebulization versus gastric aspirates in the bacteriological diagnosis of pulmonary tuberculosis. American Review of Respiratory Diseases 88: 223–227

Emirgil C, Sobol B J, Campodonico S, Herbert W H, Mechicati R 1967 Pulmonary circulation in the aged. Jounal of Applied Physiology 23: 631–640

Eriksson S 1964 Pulmonary emphysema and alpha 1 — antitrypsin deficiency. Acta Medica Scandinavica 175: 197–205

Eriksson S 1970 Antitrypsin deficiency in chronic obstructive lung disease. Lancet i: 891–892

Evans E W T 1973 Resection for bronchial carcinoma in the elderly. Thorax 28: 86–87

Felson B, Jacobson H G 1979 The role of computerized tomography in the diagnosis of diseases of the thorax. Journal of the American Medical Association 241: 933–936

Feruglio G, Sandberg H, Bellet S 1960 Postoperative changes in blood coagulation in elderly patients. American Journal of Cardiology 5: 477–482

Fiala M 1969 A study of the combined role of viruses, mycoplasmas and bacteria in adult pneumonia. American Journal of the Medical Sciences 257: 44–51

Fleetham J A, Mezon B, West P, Bradley C A, Anthonisen N R, Kryger M H 1980 Chemical control of ventilation and sleep arterial oxygen desaturation in patients with COPD. American Review of Respiratory Diseases 122: 583–589

Fox W 1981 Whither short-course chemotherapy. British Journal of Diseases of the Chest 75: 331–357

Freeman E, Sutton R N P, Cevikbas A 1982 Respiratory infections on longstay wards. Journal of Infection 4: 237–242

Fullerton J M, Dyer L 1965 Unsuspected tuberculosis in the aged. Tubercle 46: 193–198

Gaddie J, Petrie G R, Reid I W, Sinclair D J M, Skinner C, Palmer K N V 1973 Aerosol beclomethasone diproprionate in chronic bronchial asthma. Lancet i: 691–693

Garb J L, Brown R B, Garb J R, Tuthill R W 1978 Differences in aetiology of pneumonias in nursing home and community patients. Journal of the American Medical Association 240: 2169–2172

Garibaldi R A, Britt M R, Coleman M L, Reading J C, Pace N L 1981 Risk factors for postoperative pneumonia. American Journal of Medicine 70: 677–680

Garvie D G, Gray J 1980 Outbreak of respiratory syncitial virus infection in the elderly. British Medical Journal 281: 1253–1254

Geddes D M 1979 The natural history of lung cancer: A review based on rates of tumour growth. British Journal of Diseases of the Chest 73: 1–17

Gentleman J F, Brown K S, Forbes W F 1978 Smoking and its effect on mortality of the aged. American Journal of the Medical Sciences 276: 173–183

Georges R, Saumon G, Loiseau A 1978 The relationship of age to pulmonary membrane conductance and capillary blood volume. American Review of Respiratory Disease 117: 1069–1078

Gibson G J, Pride N B, O'Cain C, Quagliato R 1976 Sex and age differences in pulmonary mechanics in normal nonsmoking subjects. Journal of Applied Physiology 41: 20–25

Gillard C, Dierckx JP, Jorde W, Werdermann M, Matthys H, Cegla V H et al 1978 Sodium cromoglycate with and without isoprenaline in older patients with bronchial obstruction. Journal of Pharmacotherapy 1: 78–83

Glasser R M, Walker R I, Herion J C 1970 The significance of haematologic abnormalities in patients with tuberculosis. Archives of Internal Medicine 125: 691–695

Goodman B M, Yergin B M, Landa J F, Golinvaux M H, Sackner M A 1978 Relationship of smoking history and pulmonary function tests to tracheal mucous velocity in nonsmokers, young smokers, ex-smokers and patients with chronic bronchitis. American Review of Respiratory Diseases 117: 205–214

Gowda H T 1979 Influenza in a geriatric unit. Postgraduate Medical Journal 55: 188–191

Graham V A L, Milton A F, Knowles G F, Davies R J 1982 Routine antibiotics in hospital management of acute asthma. Lancet i: 418–420

Graham W G B, Bradley B S 1978 Efficacy of chest physiotherapy and intermittent positive-pressure breathing in the resolution of pneumonia. New England Journal of Medicine 299: 624–627

Greco F A, Richardson R L, Snell J D, Stroup S L, Oldham R K 1979 Small cell lung cancer. Complete remission and improved survival. American Journal of Medicine 66: 625–630

Green G M, Kass E H 1964 Factors influencing the clearance of bacteria in the lung. Journal of Clinical Investigation 43: 769–776

Greenbaum M, Beyt B E Jr, Murray P R 1980 The accuracy of diagnosing pulmonary tuberculosis at a teaching hospital. American Review of Respiratory Diseases 121: 477–481

Grieco M H, Chmel H 1974 Acute disseminated tuberculosis as a diagnostic problem. American Review of Respiratory Diseases 109: 554–560

Gropp C, Havemann K, Scheuer A 1980 Ectopic hormones in lung cancer patients at diagnosis and during therapy. Cancer 46: 347–354

Harris E A, Kenyon A M, Nisbet H D, Seelye E R, Whitlock R M L 1974 The normal alveolar-arterial oxygen tension gradient in man. Clinical Science and Molecular Medicine 46: 89–104

Hills N H, Pflug J J, Jeyasingh K, Boardman L, Calnan J S 1972 Prevention of deep vein thrombosis by intermittent pneumatic compression of the calf. British Medical Journal 1: 131–135

Holden M, Dubin M R, Diamond P H 1971 Frequency of negative intermediate-strength tuberculin sensitivity in patients with active tuberculosis. New England Journal of Medicine 285: 1506–1509

Holland J, Milic-Emili J, Macklem P T, Bates D V 1968 Regional distribution of pulmonary ventilation and perfusion in elderly subjects. Journal of Clinical Investigation 47: 81–92

Holmes F F, Hearne E III 1981 Cancer stage-to-age relationship: implications for cancer screening in the elderly. Journal of the American Geriatrics Society 29: 55–57

Holody B, Goldberg H S 1981 The effect of mechanical vibration on arterial oxygenation in acutely ill patients with atelactasis or pneumonia. American Review of Respiratory Diseases 124: 372–375

Hope-Stone H F 1967 Radiotherapy in the management of carcinoma of the lung. British Journal of Diseases of the Chest 61: 57–70

Hossein S, Heard B E 1970 Hyperplasia of bronchial muscle in chronic bronchitis Journal of Pathology 101: 171–184

Howells C H L, Vesselinova-Jenkins L K, Evans A D, James J 1975 Influenza and mortality from bronchopneumonia in the elderly. Lancet i: 381–383

Huhti E, Ikkala J 1980 A 10 year follow-up study of respiratory symptoms and ventilatory function in a middle-aged population. European Journal of Respiratory Diseases 61: 33–45

Irwin R S, Corrao W M, Pratter M R 1981 Chronic persistent cough in the adult. American Review of Respiratory Diseases 123: 413–417

Irwin R S, Whitaker S, Pratter M R, Millard C E, Tarpey J T, Corwin R W 1982 The transiency of oropharyngeal colonization with gram-negative bacilli in residents of a skilled nursing facilty. Chest 81: 31–35

Johanson W G Jr, Pierce A K, Sanford J P 1969 Pulmonary function in uncomplicated influenza. American Review of Respiratory Diseases 100: 141–146

Johnston R N, Ritchie R T, Murray I H F 1963 Declining tuberculin sensitivity with advancing age. British Medical Journal 2: 720–724

Johnston R N, McNeill R S, Smith D H, Dempster M B, Nairn J R, Purvis M S, Watson J M, Ward F G 1969 Five-year chemoprophylaxis for chronic bronchitis. British Medical Journal 4: 265–269

Jones N L, Burrows B, Fletcher C M 1967 Serial studies of 100 patients with chronic airway obstruction in London and Chicago. Thorax 22: 327–335

Kakkar V V, Howe C T, Flanc C, Clarke M B 1969 Natural history of postoperative deep vein thrombosis. Lancet 2: 230–232

Kakkar V V, Djazaeri B, Fok J, Fletcher M, Scully M F, Westwick J 1982 Low-molecular-weight heparin and prevention of postoperative deep vein thrombosis. British Medical Journal 284: 375–379

Kass E H, Green G M, Goldstein E 1966 Mechanisms of antibacterial action in the respiratory system. Bacteriological Reviews 30: 488–496

Kelly R J, Cowan R J, Ferree C B, Raben M, Maynard D 1979 Efficacy of radionuclide scanning in patients with lung cancer. Journal of the American Medical Association 242: 2855–2857

Khan M A, Kovnat D M, Bachus B, Whitcomb M E, Brody J S, Snider G L 1977 Clinical and roentgenographic spectrum of pulmonary tuberculosis in the adult. American Journal of Medicine 62: 31–38

Kjellen G, Brundin A, Tibling L, Wranne B 1981a Oesophageal function in asthmatics. European Journal of Respiratory Diseases 62: 87–94

Kjellen G, Tibling L, Wranne B 1981b Effect of conservative treatment of oesophageal dysfunction on bronchial asthma. European Journal of Respiratory Diseases 62: 190–197

Klassen A C, Heaney L M, Lee M C, Kronenberg R S 1980 Altered cerebral inhibition of respiratory and cardiac responses to hypercapnoea in acute stroke. Neurology 30: 951–955

Kreel L 1978 Computed tomography of the thorax. Radiological Clinics of North America 16: 575–584

Kronenberg R S, Drage C W 1973 Attenuation of the ventilatory and heart rate responses to hypoxia and hypercapnia with aging in normal man. Journal of Clinical Investigation Pathology, Research and Practice 52: 1812–1819

Kunze W-P 1979 Senile pulmonary amyloidosis. Pathology, Research and Practice 164: 413–422

Lamb D 1970 In: Orie N G B, Van DerLende R (eds) Bronchitis III. Proceedings of the Third International Symposium on Bronchitis. Van Goram and Co. N.V. Assen, The Netherlands, p 149–159

Landahl S, Steen B, Svanborg A 1980 Dyspnoea in 70-year-old people. Acta Medica Scandinavica 207: 225–230

Landay M J, Christensen E E, Bynum L J, Goodman C 1980

Anaerobic pleural and pulmonary infections. American Journal of Roentgenology 134: 233–240

Leff A R, Leff D R, Brewin A 1981 Tuberculosis chemotherapy practices in the major metropolitan health departments in the United States. American Review of Respiratory Diseases 123: 176–180

Light R W, Girard W M, Jenkinson S G, George R B 1980 Parapneumonic effusions. American Journal of Medicine 69: 507–512

Lipscomb D J, Flower C D R, Hadfield J W 1981 Ultrasound of the pleura: an assessment of its clinical value. Clinical Radiology 32: 289–290

Livingston R B, Moore T N, Heilbrun L, Bottomley R, Lehane D, Rivkin S E, Thigpen T 1978 Small cell carcinoma of the lung. Combined chemotherapy and radiation. Annals of Internal Medicine 88: 194–199

Logan W P D, Cushion A A 1958 Morbidity statistics in General Practice. London, Vol 1, p 36

Macfarlane J T, Finch R G, Ward M J, Macrae A D 1982 Hospital study of adult community-acquired pneumonia. Lancet ii: 255–258

Mackay E H, Banks J, Sykes B, Lee G De J 1978 Structural basis for the changing physical properties of human pulmonary vessels with age. Thorax 33: 335–344

MacKenzie J S 1977 Influenza subunit vaccine: antibody responses to one and two doses of vaccine and length of response, with particular reference to the elderly. British Medical Journal 1: 200–202

Marshall R, Christie R V 1954 The visco-elastic properties of the lungs in acute pneumonia. Clinical Science 13: 403–408

Mathur U, Bentley D W, Hall C B 1980 Concurrent respiratory syncytial virus and influenza A infections in the institutionalized elderly and chronically ill. Annals of Internal Medicine 93: 49–52

McCarthy S T, Turner J J, Robertson J, Hawkey C J 1977 Low-dose heparin as a prophylaxis against deep-vein thrombosis after acute stroke. Lancet ii: 800–801

McFadden E R Jr, Kiser R, Degroot W J 1973 Acute bronchial asthma: relations between clinical and physiological manifestations. New England Journal of Medicine 288: 221–225

McFadden J P, Price R C, Eastwood H D, Briggs R S 1982 Raised respiratory rate in elderly patients: a valuable physical sign. British Medical Journal 284: 626–627

McGoldrick P J, Rudd T G, Figley M M, Wilhelm J P 1979 What becomes of pulmonary infarcts? American Journal of Roentgenology 133: 1039–1045

McHardy V U, Inglis J M, Calder M A, Crofton J W, Gregg I, Ryland D A et al 1980 A study of infective and other factors in exacerbations of chronic bronchitis. British Journal of Diseases of the Chest 74: 228–238

McKennell A C, Thomas R K 1967 Adults and adolescents smoking habits and attitudes. A report on a survey carried out for the Ministry of Health, 55353/B, HMSO, London

McKeown F 1965 Pathology of the aged. Butterworths. London

Medical Research Council 1965 Definition and classification of chronic bronchitis for clinical and epidemiological purposes. Lancet 1: 775–778

Medical Research Council 1966 Value of chemoprophylaxis and chemotherapy in early chronic bronchitis. British Medical Journal 1: 1317–1322

Medical Research Council Working Party 1981 Long term domiciliary oxygen therapy in chronic hypoxic cor pulmonale complicating chronic bronchitis and emphysema. Lancet i: 681–685

Menkes H A, Traystman R J 1977 Collateral ventilation. American Review of Respiratory Diseases 116: 287–309

Miller A C 1979 Early clinical differentiation between Legionnaires disease and other sporadic pneumonias. Annals of Internal Medicine 90: 526–532

Miller D L, Lee J A 1969 Influenza in Britain 1967–68. Journal of Hygiene 67: 559–572

Miller W T, MacGregor R R 1978 Tuberculosis: frequency of unusual radiographic findings. American Journal of Roentgenology 130: 867–875

Milne J S 1978 Longitudinal respiratory studies in older people. Thorax 33: 547–554

Milne J S, Williamson J 1972 Respiratory function tests in older people. Clinical Science 42: 371–381

Monie R D H, Hunter A M, Rocchiccioli K, White J, Campbell I A, Kilpatrick G S 1982 Survey of pulmonary tuberculosis in South and West Wales (1976–8). British Medical Journal 284: 571–573

Morrell M T, Dunnill M S 1968 The post-mortem incidence of pulmonary embolism in a hospital population. British Journal of Surgery 55: 347–352

Morris J F, Koski A, Johnson L C 1971 Spirometric standards for healthy nonsmoking adults. American Review of Respiratory Diseases 103: 57–67

Mufson M A, Chang V, Gill V, Wood S C, Romansky M J, Chanock R M 1967 The role of viruses, mycoplasmas and bacteria in adult pneumonia in civilian adults. American Journal of Epidemiology 86: 526–544

Murray H W, Ellis G C, Blumenthal D S, Sos T A 1979 Fever and pulmonary thromboembolism. American Journal of Medicine 67: 232–235

Mylotte J M, Beam T R Jr 1981 Comparison of community-acquiacquired and nosocomial pneumococcal bacteria. American Review of Respiratory Diseases 123: 265–268

Nielsen H K, Bechgaard P, Nielsen P F, Husted S E, Geday E 1981 178 fatal cases of pulmonary embolism in a medical department. Acta Medica Scandinavica 209: 351–355

Nightingale S, Bates D, Bateman D E, Hudgson P, Ellis D A, Gibson G J 1982 Enigmatic dyspnoea: an unusual presentation of motor neurone disease. Lancet 1: 933–935

Niinimaa V, Shephard R J 1978a Training and oxygen conductance in the elderly. I The respiratory system. Journal of Gerontology 33: 354–361

Niinimaa V, Shephard R J 1978b Training and oxygen conductance in the elderly. II The cardiovascular system. Journal of Gerontology 33: 362–367

Nisce L Z, Hilaris B S, Chu F C H 1971 A review of experience with irradiation of brain metastasis. American Journal of Roentgenology 111: 329–334

Okinaka A J, Holman C W 1966 Carcinoma of the lung in the elderly. American Review of Respiratory Diseases 93: 579–586

O'Sullivan E F 1972 Duration of anticoagulant therapy in venous thrombo-embolism. Medical Journal of Australia 2: 1104–1107

Pavia D, Thomson M G 1970 Unimpaired mucociliary clearance in the lungs of a centenarian smoker. Lancet ii: 101–102

Peterson D D, Pack A I, Silage D A, Fishman A P 1981 Effects of aging on ventilatory and occlusion pressure responses to hypoxia and hypercapnia. American Review of Respiratory Diseases 124: 387–391

Phair J P, Kauffman C A, Bjornson A, Gallagher J, Adams L, Hess E V 1978 Host defences in the aged. Journal of Infectious Diseases 138: 67–73

Pierce J A, Ebert R V 1965 Fibrous network of the lungs and its change with age. Thorax 20: 469–476

Pontoppidan H, Beecher H K 1960 Progressive loss of protective reflexes in the airway with the advance of age. Journal of the American Medical Association 174: 2209–2213

Poukkula A, Huhti E, Kaipainen W J 1979 Fatal asthma: circumstances at death. Annals of Clinical Research 11: 13–17

Prasad B K, Banerjee A K, Howard H 1982 Incidence of deep vein thrombosis and the effect of pneumatic compression on the calf in elderly hemiplegics. Age and Ageing 11: 42–44

Pump K K 1976 Emphysema and its relation to age. American Review of Respiratory Diseases 114: 5–13

Raine J M, Bishop J M 1963 A-a difference in O_2 tension and physiological dead space in normal man. Journal of Applied Physiology 18: 284–288

Reid L 1967 The Pathology of Emphysema Lloyd-Luke, London

Reinhard V, Muller P H, Schmulling R M 1979 Determination of anaerobic threshold by the ventilation equivalent in normal individuals. Respiration 38: 36–42

Rizzato G, Marazzini L 1970 Thoracoabdominal mechanics in elderly men. Journal of Applied Physiology 28: 457–460

Rooney D J, Crocco J A, Kramer S, Lyons J A 1976 Further observations on tuberculin reaction in active tuberculosis. American Journal of Medicine 60: 517–522

Rosenquist T H 1981 Organisation of collagen in the human pulmonary alveolar wall. Anatomical Record 200: 445–459

Rudd R M, Haslam P T, Turner-Warwick M 1981 Cryptogenic fibrosing alveolitis. Relationships of pulmonary physiology and

bronchoalveolar lavage to response to treatment and prognosis. American Review of Respiratory Diseases 124: 1–8

Ryder R C, Dunnill M S, Anderson J A 1971 A quantitative study of bronchial mucous gland volume, emphysema and smoking in a necropsy population. Journal of Pathology 104: 59–71

Schmidt C D, Dickman M L, Gardner R M, Brough F K 1973 Spirometric standards for healthy elderly men and women. American Review of Respiratory Diseases 108: 933–939

Second Report of the Sixty Plus Reinfarction Study Research Group 1982 Risks of long-term oral anticoagulant therapy in elderly patients after myocardial infarction. Lancet 1: 64–68

Semmons M 1970 The pulmonary artery in the normal aged lung. British Journal of Diseases of the Chest 64: 65–72

Simon G 1964 Radiology and emphysema. Clinical Radiology 15: 293–306

Singapore Tuberculosis Service/British Medical Research Council 1977 Controlled trial of intermittent regimens of rifampin plus isoniazid for pulmonary tuberculosis in Singapore. The results up to 30 months. American Review of Respiratory Diseases 116: 807–820

Skatrud J B, Dempsey J A, Bhansali P, Irwin C 1980 Determinants of chronic carbon dioxide retention and its correction in humans. Journal of Clinical Investigation 65: 813–821

Slawson R G, Scott R M 1979 Radiation therapy in bronchogenic carcinoma. Radiology 132: 175–176

Smith C B, Golden C A, Kanner R E, Renzetti A D 1980 Association of viral and mycoplasma pneumoniae infections with acute respiratory illness in patients with chronic obstructive pulmonary disease. American Review of Respiratory Diseases 121: 225–232

Smith A P 1981 Pattern of recovery from acute severe asthma. British Journal of Diseases of the Chest 75: 132–140

Smorodintsev A A, Zlydnikov D M, Kiseleva A M, Romanov J A, Kazantsev A P, Rumovsky V I 1970 Evaluation of amantadine in artificially induced A2 and B influenza. Journal of the American Medical Association 213: 1448–1454

Speransky U S 1978 Morphometrical study of gross lung vessels. Anatomischer Anzeiger 144: 469–475

Stack B H R, Grant I W B, Irvine W, Moffat M A J 1965 Idiopathic diffuse interstitial lung disease. American Review of Respiratory Diseases 92: 939–948

Stead W W 1981 Tuberculosis among elderly persons; an outbreak in a nursing home. Annals of Internal Medicine 94: 606–610

Suen K C, Lau L L, Yermakov V 1974 Cancer and old age. Cancer 33: 1164–1168

Sugihara T, Martin C J, Hildebrandt J 1971 Length-tension properties of alveolar wall in man. Journal of Applied Physiology 30: 874–878

Sutinen S, Vaajalahti P, Paako P 1978 Prevalence severity and types of pulmonary emphysema in a population of deaths in a Finnish city. Scandinavian Journal of Respiratory Diseases 59: 101–115

Sutton G C, Hall R J C, Kerr I H 1977 Clinical course and late prognosis of treated subacute massive, acute minor, and chronic pulmonary embolism. British Heart Journal 39: 1135–1142

Swartz M N 1979 Clinical aspects of Legionnaires disease. Annals of Internal Medicine 90: 492–495

Tack C M, Cherniak N S, Altose M D 1981 Effect of aging on the perception of resistive respiration loads. American Review of Respiratory Diseases 123: 182

Talbot S, Worthington B S, Roebuck E J 1973 Radiographic signs of pulmonary embolism and pulmonary infarction. Thorax 28: 198–203

Terry C B, Traystman R J, Newball H H, Batra J, Menkes H A 1978 Collateral ventilation in man. New England Journal of Medicine 298: 10–15

Thompson N J, Glassroth J L, Snider D E Jr, Farer L S 1979 The booster phenomenon in serial tuberculin testing. American Review of Respiratory Diseases 119: 587–597

Thurlbeck W M 1981 The ageing lung. In: Scadding J G, Cumming G (eds) Scientific Foundations of Respiratory Medicine, Heinemann, London, p 108–109

Tillotson J R, Finland M 1969 Bacterial colonization and super-infection of the respiratory tract complicating antibiotic treatment of pneumonia. Journal of Infectious Diseases 119: 597–624

Tomasi T B 1968 Human immunoglobulin A. New England Journal of Medicine 279: 1327–1330

Traver G A, Cline M G, Burrows B 1979 Predictors of mortality in chronic obstructive pulmonary disease. American Review of Respiratory Diseases 119: 895–902

Turner J M, Mead J, Wohl M E 1968 Elasticity of human lungs in relation to age. Journal of Applied Physiology 25: 664–671

Turner-Warwick M 1975 Clinical aspects of protective immunity of the respiratory tract. Thorax 30: 601–611

Turner-Warwick M, Burrows B, Johnson A 1980a Cryptogenic fibrosing alveolitis: clinical features and their influence on survival. Thorax 35: 171–180

Turner-Warwick M, Burrows B, Johnson A 1980b Cryptogenic fibrosing alveolitis: response to corticosteroid treatment and its effect on survival. Thorax 35: 593–599

Ullah M I, Newman G B, Saunders K B 1981 Influence of age on response to ipratropium and salbutamol in asthma. Thorax 36: 523–529

Valenti W M, Jentzer M, Bentley D W 1978 Type-specific pneumococcal respiratory disease in the elderly and chronically ill. American Review of Respiratory Diseases 117: 233–238

Valenti W M, Randall G T, Bentley D W 1978 Factors predisposing to oropharyngeal colonization with gram-negative bacilli in the aged. New England Journal of Medicine 298: 1108–1111

Wagenvoort C A, Wagenvoort N 1965 Age changes in the muscular pulmonary artery. Archives of Pathology 79: 524–528

Wallace R J, Musher D M, Martin R R 1978 Haemophilus infleunzae pneumonia in adults. American Journal of Medicine 64: 87–93

Warlow C, Ogston D, Douglas A S 1976 Deep venous thrombosis of the legs after stroke. British Medical Journal 1: 1178–1183

Warren P M, Flenley D C, Millar J S, Avery A 1980 Respiratory failure revisited: acute exacerbations of chronic bronchitis between 1961–68 and 1970–76. Lancet i: 467–471

Willems J S, Sanders C R, Raddiough M A, Bell J C 1980. Cost effectiveness of vaccination against pneumococcal pneumonia. New England Journal of Medicine 303: 553–559

Winterbauer R H, Hammar S P, Hallman K O, Hays J E, Pardee N E, Morgan E H et al 1978 Diffuse interstitial fibrosis. Clinicopathologic correlations in 20 patients treated with prednisone/azothiaprine. American Journal of Medicine 65: 661–672

Woolner L B, Fontana R S, Sanderson D R, Miller W E, Muhm J R, Taylor W F, Uhlenhopp M A 1981 Mayo lung project: Evaluation of lung screening through December 1979. Mayo Clinic Proceedings 56: 544–555

World Health Organization 1961 Chronic cor pulmonale. Report of an expert committee. Technical Report Series Number 213, Geneva

Wright R R 1961 Elastic tissue of normal and emphysematous lungs. A tridimensional histologic study. American Journal of Pathology 39: 355–363

Wynne J W, Block A J, Hemenway J, Hunt L A, Flick M R 1979 disordered breathing and oxygen desaturation during sleep in patients with chronic obstructive lung disease (COLD). American Journal of Medicine 66: 573–579

Young C D, Moore G W, Hutchins G M 1980 Connective tissue arrangement in respiratory airways. Anatomical Record 198: 245–254

The musculoskeletal system — bone aging and metabolic bone disease

Metabolic bone disease is always generalized, affecting the whole skeleton. The two common forms in old age are osteoporosis and osteomalacia. As is the case with many common diseases in the elderly they may occur together. Hyperparathyroidism and renal osteodystrophy are occasionally seen and must be considered in differential diagnosis. Paget's disease is also frequently found in old people, but though it may be diffuse it is never generalized. Changes in bone have an important influence on the epidemiology of fractures in old age.

AGING IN BONE

Aging is accompanied by loss of bone from the skeleton; atrophy of bone corresponds to atrophy of other tissues which occurs with increasing age. There are, however, other factors. There are considerable differences in the patterns of development and bone loss between males and females. Garn et al (1967) have suggested that while all people lose bone ultimately with age, there are some factors (e.g. gastrectomy) which increase bone loss while others such as tall stature (Garn and Hull, 1966) may be associated with a decrease in the rate of loss. The study of these factors requires an accurate method for measuring amount of bone in the skeleton.

Methods

Visual inspection of standard radiographs gives only an approximate indication of bone density. Accuracy can be improved by photoelectric densitometry in which the density of bone is compared with that of a standardized aluminium step-wedge; but this method, too, has its limitations due to variations in radiographic techniques (Garn, 1962). The more recently introduced photon absorption method (Cameron and Sorenson, 1963; Strandjord and Lanzl, 1966) is proving much more promising. The absorption in bone is measured by scanning, using a low-energy source (for example ^{125}I). So far data are limited (Davis et al, 1966; Nordin et al, 1970).

Measurements on hand radiographs have been exten-sively used as a simple method for estimating the amount of bone in the skeleton. The length (L) of the bone (usually the second metacarpal or the third proximal phalanx) is measured with a millimetre rule and at the midpoint the diameters of the medullary canal (d) and the periosteal envelope (D) are measured with a Vernier Caliper. The transverse cross-sectional cortical area of the third proximal phalanx as calculated from measurements of X-rays, correlates well with the ash content as determined by incineration (Exton-Smith et al, 1969a); a similar relationship exists for the second metacarpal (Gryfe et al, 1972).

Garn and his colleagues have mainly used measurements of cortical thickness (D − d) and they have contributed valuable information on normal developmental patterns, racial factors and nutritional status as they relate to the skeleton (Garn et al, 1964b, 1967); more recently derived parameters (Garn, 1970) have been presented.

When using morphometric methods of this kind it is necessary to make a correction for skeletal size in order to compare the amount of bone in different individuals. Nordin (1971) has employed the ratio of cortical area to total area, $(D^2 − d^2)$, while we have used the ratio of cortical area to surface area, $(D^2 − d^2)$ (Exton-Smith et al, 1969b; Gryfe et al, 1971), which we have shown compensates for differences in skeletal size between individuals and between the sexes.

Pattern of bone development and loss

By measurements made on a large number of individuals of different ages it is possible to obtain mean values for the amount of bone in each five-year age group. Nordin (1971) has plotted data for normal men and women using the metacarpal cortical area/total area ratio showing the mean and the standard error. Using the ratio cortical area/surface area it has been possible to construct percentile ranking curves for the normal population of men and women between the ages of 2 and 85 years (Exton-Smith et al, 1969b; Gryfe et al, 1971). These curves not only indicate the variance but also the distribution about the mean (Fig. 37.1).

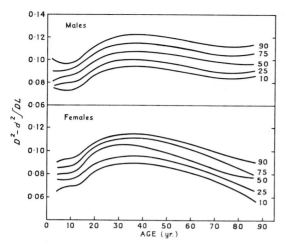

Fig. 37.1 Percentile ranking curves for amount of bone in males and females aged 3 to 85 years

Some of the characteristics of the curves are:

The curves for the percentile ranks (10, 25, 50, 75 and 90) remain roughly parallel with age; that is, the variance remains unchanged with age and the distribution at each age group is normal.

There is a rapid increase in the amount of bone during the period of growth (up to the age of 17), but the increase continues at a slower rate for another 12 years or so after increase in height has ceased.

Loss of bone is steady after about the age of 45, occurring more rapidly in women than in men.

There are some individuals aged 80 who have more bone than others at the age of 30.

These data are based on cross-sectional studies; that is, measurements made in one age-group are compared with those in other groups. In this type of study, secular influences are observed and it is rarely possible to assess their contribution to the observed age differences. There is an exception to this, however, when measurements of the length of long bones are made. Thus the length of the metacarpal when measured in old age is an indication of skeletal size at maturity since there is no change in the length of the bone after growth has ceased. It has been found that the mean length of the second metacarpal in men aged 75 is 1.5 mm less than that for men aged 25 to 30 years (Exton-Smith, 1970). This corresponds to a difference in height of about 1.5 inches; that is, the present generation of 75-year-olds were in earlier adult life 1.5 inches shorter than those aged 25 today. This estimate is close to that reported by Khosla and Lowe (1968) who found that there has been an increase in mean height of the adult male population in this country of 1 inch per generation since the beginning of the century.

A cohort effect is clearly seen in the different pattern

of bone loss in men during old age. Following a flattening off of the curves at about the age of 75 there is a slight rise in the 80s. Undoubtedly true age changes have been masked in these cross-sectional studies by secular differences between individuals in the various age groups. Compared with men in their 70s the higher proportion of those in their 80s with good skeletal development suggests the view that the older individuals form a highly selected group. They represent a biological elite; not only do they have better developed bones but their sustained health and physical vigor have enabled them to survive to extreme old age. This is in accord with clinical experience; Sheldon (1948) has shown that for men, but not for women, the proportion of individuals in exceptionally good health rises abruptly to a maximum after the age of 80.

A serious limitation of our knowledge about aging in bone (and aging processes generally) is imposed by reliance on cross-sectional studies. There is an urgent need for serial measurements on the amount of bone in different individuals. Only a limited number of such longitudinal studies have been conducted; some of these include repeated measurements on older people for periods up to 15 years (Garn et al, 1964c); on postmenopausal women (Davis et al, 1966); on elderly subjects over a period of 6½ years (Exton-Smith et al, 1969b) and on patients with idiopathic osteoporosis and hyperparathyroidism (Gryfe et al, 1971; Gryfe, 1972).

Factors influencing amount of bone

In old age considerable variation is observed in the amount of bone in the skeleton of different individuals. Some of the factors concerned are:

Amount of bone at maturity. Although some reservation must be placed on the interpretation of cross-sectional data, the fact that the percentile ranking curves remain parallel with age suggests that the amount of bone in adult life and old age is determined by the skeletal development at maturity. Skeletal status in childhood may be influenced by physical activity, disease, nutrition and by endocrine and racial factors. The importance of each of these factors has yet to be assessed.

Poorer skeletal development of girls. By the age of 17 the bone mass/body weight ratio is 20 per cent lower in girls than in boys (Gryfe et al, 1971). This relatively lower bone mass in girls may be one of the factors accounting for the higher incidence of osteoporosis in older women.

Postmenopausal bone loss. There is a rapid bone loss during the first 10 years after the menopause. The administration of oestrogens (Davis et al, 1966) prevents this initial rapid loss; but loss still continues at a slower rate with the curves parallel at a higher level.

Excessive bone loss. It is known that excessive bone

loss occurs in a number of conditions, and to demonstrate it serial measurements are required (see above). Increased rate of loss has been clearly demonstrated in juvenile osteoporosis, but the cause is ill understood. Excessive loss has also been observed following partial gastrectomy, immobilization and the administration of corticosteroids.

Whatever be the relative importance of these factors, it seems likely that people with densely calcified bones in early life will have some protection against developing the clinical syndrome of osteoporosis when, in later life, part of the bone mineral is lost.

OSTEOPOROSIS

Osteoporosis is not a single disease entity but it has characteristic clinical, radiological and pathological features which can usually distinguish it from other forms of metabolic bone disease. It is the end result of a number of processes which lead to a diminution in the amount of bone in the skeleton. The condition was recognized many years ago by German anatomists (Pommer, 1885; Gerth, 1930) who clearly distinguished it from osteomalacia. At the clinical level the distinction was only made more recently by Albright et al (1941).

Definition

The classical definition of osteoporosis by Albright is 'too little bone, but what bone there is, is normal', and he believed the disorder was a failure to make bone matrix. Now we no longer include aetiology within the definition, attributing osteoporosis solely to a hormonal imbalance affecting bone formation.

The original definition has its limitations on other counts. It does not define 'too little bone'; usually this has been taken to mean diminution in the amount of bone as assessed by standards for adults at maturity. But in the definition we ought to distinguish between the phenomenon of gradual bone loss as an accompaniment of aging and the fact that bone loss, whether normal or excessive, leads ultimately to structural failure of the skeleton (fracture) or its likely risk. The normal age-related loss is sometimes called 'physiological osteoporosis' to distinguish it from 'pathological osteoporosis' in which the clinical syndrome is characterized by collapse of the vertebral bodies and liability to fracture of certain long bones.

Thus the cut-off point between physiological and pathological osteoporosis is taken to be the stage when the process incapacitates the patient. But the practice of geriatric medicine is rightly concerned with the prevention of disability and it is just as important to recognize osteoporosis in the patient on the day before she has a fracture as on the day after. There is here a close analogy

with hypertension; but unlike blood pressure measurements there is no simple uniformly accepted method for measurement of the mineral content of bone.

In the original definition the bone in osteoporosis is taken to be normal; this is true when the method of study is by histology or organic analysis. It has, however, recently been shown (Posner, 1970) that the per cent crystallinity can change and that mineral form can affect bone strength as much as the mineral content. Thus, as methods improve, several diseases at present grouped as osteoporosis may be separately identified.

Aetiology

Some of the important factors influencing the amount of bone in old age have already been discussed (see page 759). These include the skeletal status at maturity, the loss of bone with age in later life in both sexes, and the more rapid bone loss following the menopause in women. Thus those individuals who have densely calcified bones at maturity may be at an advantage; the skeleton will remain adequate even when, in later life, part of the bone mineral is lost. Newton-John and Morgan (1968), from a model of bone loss in women, consider that these factors alone can be responsible for the clinical syndrome of osteoporosis and that it develops earlier in those whose initial skeletal development is poor.

There is evidence that in most cases osteoporosis is not a disorder which develops suddenly in middle or old age, but it is a condition to which all people progress gradually, beginning soon after the age of 25 years (Rose, 1970). Nevertheless this hypothesis does not account for all the features of the disease since in some patients there seems to be an additional process which accelerates the osteoporosis. Dent and Watson (1966) believe that this process, which is of uncertain origin, is self-limiting; it produces the clinical signs of an acute attack of osteoporosis. During these attacks they have demonstrated easily measurable negative calcium balances (200 to 400 mg per day).

Immobilization

It is well known that osteoporosis can be induced by immobilization. Immobility due to fracture, joint disease, splinting and hemiplegia (Hodkinson and Brain, 1967) leads to localized osteoporosis. Dietrick et al (1948) immobilized normal young men in bed and demonstrated marked negative calcium balances. On remobilization, balances became no more positive than they had been prior to immobilization. The extent to which the process can be reversed is debatable; Rose (1970) believes that bone remineralization does not usually occur, but Whedon (1970) has shown that the results of long-term studies indicate that restoration on remobilization can occur in considerable degree.

Dent and Watson (1966) consider that osteoporosis due to immobilization may complicate other forms and initiate a vicious circle. In particular, many old people, mainly women, become largely sedentary, a situation almost certainly to blame in part for their frequent osteoporosis. According to Jowsey (1966), osteoporotic patients are more sensitive than normal to increased bone resorption on immobilization. Immobility may be a factor in the increased rate of bone loss seen in some of the cases in the $6\frac{1}{2}$ years follow-up, reported by Exton-Smith et al (1969b).

Hyperadrenocorticism
Osteoporosis is a well-known clinical feature in patients with Cushing's syndrome. It also develops in patients treated for a number of years with corticosteroids for rheumatoid arthritis, asthma and skin diseases.

Rheumatoid arthritis
McConkey et al (1962) drew attention to the occurrence of transparent skin both in patients with osteoporosis and in those with rheumatoid arthritis and to the common association of rheumatoid arthritis with osteoporosis which they thought was unrelated to treatment of the rheumatoid arthritis with corticosteroids.

Nutritional factors
Calcium deficiency. Several studies have shown that osteoporosis can be induced in growing rats fed on a low-calcium diet (Gershon-Cohen et al, 1962; El Maraghi et al, 1965). Nordin (1960) on the basis of dietary studies suggested that dietary calcium deficiency was a major cause of osteoporosis, but a later dietary investigation (Nordin et al, 1964) did not confirm the earlier claim. Garn et al (1967) have shown that calcium intakes of 1500 mg daily are not protective against bone loss, nor are intakes of 300 mg daily associated with increased loss.

Dent and Watson (1966) refer to one of their cases of severe osteoporosis occurring in a 7-year-old boy who had a calcium intake of 120 mg per day over a prolonged period; he made a full, but slow, recovery when a normal diet was instituted without any other treatment. They agree with the FAO/WHO Report (FAO Nutritional Studies, 1961) that there is no convincing evidence for calcium deficiency disease in the human.

Nordin (1971) has since revised the calcium deficiency theory. He has shown that the fasting urinary calcium of postmenopausal women is raised and that the overnight or early morning excretion of calcium exceeds the amount that can be stored during the day. The increased bone resorption in the fasting state is attributed to the loss of the protective action of oestrogens against parathyroid hormone and supports Heaney's view (1965,

1970) that the negative calcium balance results from increased sensitivity of end organs to parathormone.

Vitamin D deficiency. A further factor in senile osteoporosis may be a fall in calcium absorption which, according to Bullamore and colleagues (1970), occurs in men and women after the age of 70. In part impaired calcium absorption may be due to vitamin D deficiency which is not uncommon in the elderly, especially women. In the majority of cases the vitamin D deficiency is not detected until severe enough to cause osteomalacia (see page 756). Correction of the deficiency promotes the absorption of calcium.

Vitamin C deficiency. It has long been known that severe osteoporosis and other bone lesions occur in scurvy. The characteristic radiological signs of osteoporosis are present (Joffe, 1961; Hyams and Ross, 1963). Ascorbic acid is necessary for collagen synthesis, and vitamin C deficiency probably exists when the leucocyte ascorbic acid level is less than 15 µg per 10^8 WBC (Windsor and Williams, 1971). Low ascorbic acid levels in the leucocytes are commonly present in old people but the extent to which deficiency of the vitamin is responsible for osteoporosis has not yet been established.

Protein deficiency. Experimentally, Platt and Stewart (1962, 1968) produced osteoporosis in growing pigs and dogs fed on a low-protein diet but there is little evidence that protein deficiency in the human causes osteoporosis. In the nutrition survey conducted by the Department of Health and Social Security (1972) it was found that the bone mass in the second metacarpal was unrelated to the dietary protein intake in old age.

Fluoride. Bernstein and his colleagues (1966) demonstrated in an epidemiological study in North Dakota that women living in a high fluoride area (4 to 5.8 ppm) had significantly less osteoporosis as measured radiologically than those living in a low fluoride area (0.15 to 0.3 ppm). This relationship between osteoporosis and the fluoride content of the water supply, however, pertained only to women and not to men. Although there is no adequate explanation for these sex differences it has been suggested that the particular group of men was engaged in relatively hard physical labour (farming) which may have cause an increased number of traumatic fractures. It was not possible to determine which crush fractures were traumatic and which were secondary to osteoporosis. Nordin (1970) examined the amount of bone per unit volume in the iliac crest of patients coming to postmortem in Leeds and in West Hartlepool. The fluoride content of the water supply in Leeds is less than 0.3 ppm and in West Hartlepool it has been 2 to 3 ppm for the last 30 to 40 years. Although more fluoride was found in the bone ash of people in West Hartlepool there was no difference in the amount of bone in the iliac crest corrected for age and sex in people from the two places. Thus the evidence from the studies of Bernstein and of Nordin is conflicting.

Experimentally it has been shown that an increased amount of fluoride in the diet causes greater crystallinity of the bone mineral. The reduction in dental decay by fluoride administration is known to be apparent only during the period of formation of the teeth and it is possible that the influence of fluoride is exerted only during the period of bone growth in childhood rather than in adult life; that is, the action of fluoride, like that of other nutrients, in the prevention of osteoporosis in old age may be exerted maximally in the first 20 years of life.

Gastrectomy. Morgan et al (1966) have pointed out that gastrectomy accelerates the effects of aging on loss of bone from the skeleton. This effect is more marked in women than in men. Histological section reveals that following gastrectomy there is an excessive amount of thin osteoid seams, whereas in simple osteoporosis osteoid seams are absent. The distinctive findings in postgastrectomy cases are considered to be due to calcium deficiency.

Clinical features
The symptoms range from no complaint at all to attacks of severe backache which may be completely disabling. The backache may be precipitated by muscular effort, e.g. turning the trunk in reaching to lift an object from a wall shelf, and this points to collapse of a vertebral body which is subsequently revealed on X-ray examination. The pain may last a few weeks followed by a period in which the pain is completely absent. According to Urist et al (1970), who have followed 100 patients with osteoporosis for 7 to 20 years, the latent intervals of relatively little discomfort may be as brief as 1 year and as long as 11 years. In other cases pain persists as more or less chronic backache with sudden severe exacerbations which may not be related to trauma or muscular strain. Indeed osteoporosis is probably the commonest cause of backache in the elderly (Dent and Watson, 1966). The pain is felt in the back occasionally radiating to the buttocks and down the legs. It is usually relieved by immobilization and made much worse by movement — patients often remark that it is worse when try to turn their position in bed at night.

Associated with the back pain there is some immobility of the spine which is marked during acute episodes. But in the intervening periods spinal movements are not especially limited even in the presence of crush fractures or spinal deformity. Nerve root compression is rare and spinal cord damage does not occur even in the presence of severe deformity.

An important early sign in osteoporosis is loss of height due to shortening of the trunk (Dent, 1955). This can only accurately be assessed by serial measurements. Elderly patients seldom remember their maximum height during the prime of life. It is a common finding in osteoporosis that the crown-pubis distance is less than pubis to heel and Dent and Watson (1966) have observed shrinking of as much as 21 cm in the trunk of patients with severe osteoporosis. Urist and his colleagues (1970) have drawn attention to the folding of the anterior cortex or wedging of the midthoracic vertebrae which occurs early in the course of the disease to produce the dowager's hump deformity; this is later followed by spontaneous crush fractures of the dorsilumbar region. The collapse fractures lead to progressive incremental loss of height. The lower ribs in severe cases often over-ride the iliac crests. Dent et al (1953) have pointed out that the transverse band of keratinized skin which appears over the upper abdomen is highly suggestive of osteoporosis and is rarely present in other conditions causing vertebral collapse.

Radiology
Increased translucency of bone is the main feature. This affects all bones, but trabecular bone in the spine appears relatively more affected. Lachman (1955) found that at least 50 per cent of the mineral content of the bone must be lost before the diminished radiographic density is detected by eye. Owing to the greater involvement of the horizontal trabeculae in the vertebral bodies the vertical trabeculae appear more prominent. Later the vertebral bodies appear hollow, outlined by the shell of cortical bone. Doyle et al (1967) have assessed some of these criteria for the radiological diagnosis of osteoporosis in the spine pointing out that a slight tilt in the sagittal axis of the spine gives rise to difficulties in interpretation through:

1. Alterations in the apparent density of the vertebral bodies.
2. Changes in the apparent thickness of the vertebral end-plates.
3. Variations in the degree of concavity of the lumbar vertebral bodies again due to differences in angles of incidence of the X-ray beam (Fig. 37.2).

Impaction fractures of the brittle bones occur, affecting the midthoracic vertebrae; but the vertebral bodies are not uniformly involved so that some retain their shape with collapsed vertebrae intervening. The bodies of the lumbar vertebrae become biconcave due to the expansion into them of the intervertebral discs. Sometimes localized protusions of the nucleus pulposus occur giving rise to Schmorl's nodes. Although biconcavity in the lumbar region is the typical appearance and is seen in very old people it can only occur at a stage when the disc is fluid and capable of expansion. But, as the disc becomes rigid with advancing age, the lumbar

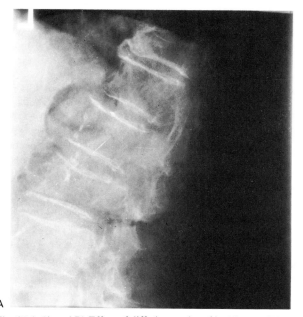
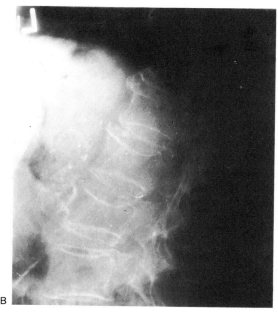

Fig. 37.2 (A and B) Effect of differing angles of incidence of X-ray beam; radiographs from the same patient

vertebral bodies may become wedged similar to the thoracic vertebrae.

In the long bones diminution in cortical thickness is the salient feature; this is mainly the result of endosteal absorption (Stewart et al, 1972). Signs of other forms of metabolic bone diseases are absent, such as bending of the sternum and long bones, triradiate deformity of the pelvis and subperiosteal erosions.

Biochemistry

The serum calcium, inorganic phosphorus and alkaline phosphatase are normal in osteoporosis. Sometimes a moderate rise in the serum alkaline phosphatase occurs following fractures; even a small fracture can induce a temporary elevation lasting several weeks. When active absorption is occurring there is usually a slight increase in urinary calcium excretion.

Treatment

One of the chief difficulties in assessing the results of treatment is the episodic nature of the disorder and the fact that the acute episodes characterized by crush fractures are self-limiting. Thus, when the patient seeks treatment for the sudden onset of backache, spontaneous remission occurs within a few weeks irrespective of what drug therapy is given.

It is important to avoid immobilization, which can only aggravate loss of bone, except in occasional cases during the acute phases. Thus, spinal supports and braces which few elderly patients tolerate have little

place in treatment. It is better to improve muscular support by exercises, if necessary relieving pain by analgesics or the injection of local anaesthetic. Some patients gain confidence from the temporary use of a lumbar sacral elastic support and at the same time are encouraged to remain active by walking with a stick.

The most effective treatment is that advocated by Albright, who showed that use of sex hormones will reduce negative nitrogen and calcium balance. Stilboestrol (1 to 3 mg) or dienoestrol (0.3 to 0.9 mg) are given daily in courses of 4 to 5 weeks with 1 week's gap in between. Patients should be warned that withdrawal bleeding may occur after each course. Using such a regime Henneman and Wallach (1957), reviewing the results in over 200 women with post-menopausal osteoporosis, found that they had fewer fractures and stopped losing height when treated for months or years.

In Leeds Nordin and his colleagues (Horsman et al, 1977; Nordin et al, 1979; Nordin, 1980) have randomly allocated patients with osteoporosis to one of six different therapeutic regimes or to a no treatment group. The long-term results were assessed by means of sequential measurements of mean metacarpal cortical area (MCA) and by vertebral fracture progression using measurements of height. There was a gain in the MCA in the group treated with oestrogens and oestrogens plus 1α-hydroxyvitamin D (1α-OHD), no significant change in MCA in the group on calcium supplementation, a significant loss of bone in the untreated cases, but an even greater loss in the groups on vitamin D and 1α-

OHD; the vitamin D plus calcium group occupied an intermediate position. Similar results were obtained when change in standing height was used as the method of assessment. Thus the most effective therapy appears to be a combination of hormones with 1α-OHD. Vitamin D and 1α-OHD by themselves and in the doses used appear to do more harm than good and this is attributed to the resorbing action of these agents, but Nordin considers that it may be possible to find a dose level sufficient to correct calcium malabsorption but not so large as to increase bone resorption.

The use of an anabolic steroid, methandrostenolone, in the treatment of osteoporosis has been assessed by Chestnut et al (1977, 1979). Determination of the total body calcium (TBC) by neutron activation analysis performed at 6-monthly intervals was used as the measure of total bone mass. Those treated with methandrostenolone showed an average gain of 2 per cent in TBC while those on placebo showed an average loss of 3.1 per cent during the 26 month period of the study; the differences between the two groups were significant (P<0.01). Moreover the differences in the percentage TBC between the two groups increased in a linear fashion with time indicating a continuation of the drug effect throughout the 26 months.

Although the role of deficient fluoride intake in the causation of osteoporosis is uncertain, Rich et al (1964) have suggested that fluoride might be a useful agent for the treatment of osteoporosis on the basis of the production of osteosclerosis by fluoride ingestion. Jowsey et al (1968) have shown that fluoride administration causes osteoblastic stimulation, when biopsy specimens are examined during the course of treatment, but the newly formed bone tissue is poorly mineralized resulting in the histological appearances of osteomalacia. Moreover, animal experiments have shown that fluoride also produces increased bone resorption due to the development of secondary hyperparathyroidism. Both these abnormalities can be prevented by increasing the intakes of vitamin D and calcium. Jowsey et al (1972) have recently evaluated in patients with osteoporosis the effects of fluoride administration combined with vitamin D and calcium. The optimum regime was found to be 50 mg sodium fluoride and 900 mg supplemental calcium per day and 50 000 iu vitamin D twice a week. Eleven patients with progressive osteoporosis which was of sufficient severity to cause deformity of the vertebral bodies were treated for a period of at least one year. Bone resorption and formation were assessed using a quantitative microradiographic technique on bone specimens taken from the iliac crest at the commencement and at the end of the treatment. In all but one patient bone formation was increased after treatment and the group mean was significantly higher than before treatment; the newly formed bone was histologically normal

in appearance. The degree of bone resorption was also significantly less after treatment than at the beginning of the study and this change in resorption was significantly correlated with the amount of supplemental calcium administered.

Although these studies have shown that fluoride administration increases bone mass the effects on bone strength have not yet been assessed; it is believed that fluoride causes an increase in crystallinity of bone structure and the bone may be more fragile than normal. Indeed in Jowsey's series four out of 11 patients developed additional crush fractures during treatment, but it is considered that they may have occurred before therapy was able to changed the bone mass significantly. Mitchell et al (1975) used a similar treatment regime in 14 osteoporotic patients over a period of 12–18 months and in this study no further fractures occurred during the period of observation. But the most convincing evidence of the effectiveness of fluoride has come from a report of investigators at the Mayo Clinic (Riggs et al, 1982). In this study 5 different treatment regimes were compared: placebo, calcium alone, fluoride and calcium, oestrogen and calcium and fluoride, oestrogen and calcium. Some of the patients in each treatment group also received vitamin D (50 000 IU once or twice per week). Oestrogen, calcium and calcium plus fluoride significantly reduced the vertebral fracture rate compared with no treatment. The most dramatic reduction in fracture rate was achieved when fluoride, oestrogen and calcium were given together and was more effective than any other combination (P<0.001). Although all patients received a multivitamin preparation containing 400 IU vitamin D daily the addition of very large doses of vitamin D provided no extra benefit, and indeed in some patients it caused hypercalcaemia and hypercalciuria. In spite of the overall remarkable results a minority of patients failed to respond to fluoride even after 4–6 years of therapy; Riggs and his colleagues considered that these patients may have an intrinsic abnormality of osteoblast function which prevents stimulation of bone formation.

Prognosis

Most patients with long-standing osteoporosis, even with severe changes in the spine X-ray, remain well in themselves and life expectancy is good. Thus it is important to maintain an optimistic outlook in dealing with these patients and avoid using such terms as 'crumbling spine' which to the lay mind has a sinister connotation. The only two conditions which directly threaten life are a fracture, especially of the femoral neck, and diminution in the vital capacity of the lungs which places the patient at a disadvantage should bronchopneumonia develop.

OSTEOMALACIA

Definition

Osteomalacia is a generalized disease of bone characterized by deficient calcification of a normal bone matrix. Histological examination reveals an increase in the amount of osteoid, that is, non-calcified matrix around the bone trabeculae (Fig. 37.3). It is a disease produced by lack of vitamin D.

Prevalence in old age

Although the incidence of osteomalacia is not confined to any particular age group, in old age there are many conditions which can give rise to it and consequently it is not uncommon. Anderson and his colleagues (1966) have drawn attention to osteomalacia occurring in old people in Glasgow. They investigated a group of 100 women aged 68 to 93 years who had been newly admitted to a geriatric department and who had a possible clinical indication of osteomalacia (see Table 37.1). In this group 16 cases of osteomalacia were discovered. Subsequently 100 consecutive patients admitted to the female wards were investigated and the incidence of osteomalacia was shown to be 4 per cent of elderly women admitted to this geriatric department. Chalmers (1967), an orthopaedic surgeon in Edinburgh, and his colleagues have described the clinical features of 37 recently recognized cases of osteomalacia. Thirty-four of the 37 cases were in women; their ages ranged from 39 to 89 years and the majority of patients were over the

Table 37.1 Possible indications for diagnosis of osteomalacia (Anderson et al, 1966)

Vague and generalized pain
Low backache
Muscle weakness and stiffness
Waddling gait
Skeletal deformity
Bone tenderness
Malabsorption states
Long confinement indoors
Malnutrition

age of 70. They consider that osteomalacia is not uncommon in elderly women among whom it is likely to be confused with senile osteoporosis, and that there is a need for a thorough screening of all elderly patients presenting with weakness, skeletal pain, pathological fractures or with diminished radiographic density of bone.

Following the dietary studies in the King Edward's Hospital Fund survey (Exton-Smith and Stanton, 1965) three-quarters of the subjects agreed to attend a hospital for clinical assessment, X-ray densitometry of the bones of the hand, and biochemical investigations. Rather more than one-quarter of the subjects were found to have marked skeletal rarefaction. This, in the main, was due to osteoporosis rather than to osteomalacia; but when subjects having skeletal rarefaction were compared with age-matched individuals in the survey whose bones

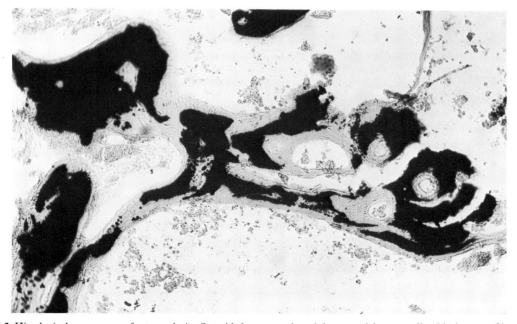

Fig. 37.3 Histological appearance of osteomalacia. Osteoid shown as pale staining material surrounding black areas of bone.

were of good density, it was found that there was a significant difference in their vitamin D intakes. Moreover, the vitamin D intakes were correlated with the changes in serum levels of calcium, inorganic phosphorus and alkaline phosphatase (Exton-Smith et al, 1966). Thus the evidence suggests that osteomalacia often contributes to the skeletal rarefaction which occurs in old age and this in turn is frequently due to dietary lack of vitamin D.

Smith and his colleagues (1964) in the United States compared a group of elderly women (average age 60.6 years) living in Michigan with a group of similar age living in Puerto Rico. In the Michigan group the level of vitamin D in the blood (serum anti-rachitic activity) was significantly lower in those subjects with lower bone density compared with those having normal bones; the level showed marked seasonal variation, being considerably lower in the winter than in the summer months, and it was related to the serum levels of calcium, phosphorus and alkaline phosphatase. On the other hand, in Puerto Rico, where there is much greater exposure to sunlight, the incidence of skeletal rarefaction was found to be much lower, the blood levels of vitamin D were much higher and there was no seasonal variation.

AETIOLOGY

There are many causes of osteomalacia in old age and often the condition is caused by several factors coexisting in the same individual.

The main causes include inadequate dietary intake of vitamin D, lack of exposure to sunlight, malabsorption, gastrectomy, impaired hydroxylation of cholecalciferol in the liver and reduced conversion of 25-hydroxycholecalciferol to the active 1,25-dihydroxycholecalciferol due to impairment of renal function.

Simple vitamin D lack. According to Gough et al (1964) only three cases of osteomalacia due to dietary lack of vitamin D had been reported in this country up to 1962 and consequently it was rarely thought to be purely dietary in origin. They described three further cases of osteomalacia in old people proved histologically after bone biopsy. One of their cases, a spinster aged 84 years with marked radiological changes of osteomalacia, had an average daily intake of vitamin D of 24 iu. Her diet had been extremely poor for many years and consisted of tea, bread and butter, and occasionally supplemented by egg and milk puddings provided by her niece. The 'rheumatic' pains associated with the osteomalacia were so crippling that she had been unable to leave her room for 10 years and consequently her ability to obtain and to prepare food was greatly impaired.

A number of investigations, to which reference has already been made (Smith et al, 1964; Anderson et al, 1966; Exton-Smith et al, 1966), all indicated that dietary vitamin D deficiency is not uncommon in the old, especially in women. In addition, deficient vitamin D synthesis in the skin due to lack of exposure to sunlight associated with the housebound state is believed to be important (Department of Health and Social Security, 1972). Since approximately 10 per cent of the elderly population are housebound (Sheldon 1948) this represents a sizable medical and social problem.* Moreover, the housebound often have very low nutrient intakes; Exton-Smith et al (1972) in a nutritional study of the housebound showed that the vitamin D intakes were significantly lower than those of active old people.

Stamp and Round (1974) have shown seasonal variations in both young and old subjects of plasma levels of 25-hydroxycholecalciferol when measured by radiostereo assay techniques. The old people had much lower levels than those found in the younger subjects. They conclude that summer sunlight is an important, and possibly the chief, determinant of vitamin D nutrition in Britain.

Malabsorption. Minor and even more severe degrees of malabsorption are not uncommon in old age. Enteropathy due to rye and wheat gluten sensitivity similar to that causing childhood coeliac disease is still seen in patients in their 70s. Although in most instances malabsorption presenting as steatorrhoea is recognized before there is bone disease, in some cases osteomalacia can overshadow all other manifestations (Moss et al, 1965). Biliary obstruction producing steatorrhoea can lead to osteomalacia if the patient lives long enough. The stagnant loop syndrome due to jejunal diverticulosis is a well-recognized cause of osteomalacia. Duodenal diverticula are usually regarded as innocuous; but in a series of 15 elderly patients with large primary duodenal diverticula reported by Clark (1972) 2 had osteomalacia. It has yet to be determined how often malabsorption is due to intestinal ischaemia resulting from atherosclerosis of the mesenteric arteries. The ingestion over many years of large amounts of liquid paraffin which interferes with the absorption of vitamin D can also cause osteomalacia.

Gastrectomy. Osteomalacia may develop 5 to 20 years after gastrectomy. It is a complication of Polya type gastrectomies more frequently than Billroth. It is believed to be due to a diminished intake and/or defective absorption of vitamin D. The development of osteomalacia, however, is not related to the severity of steatorrhoea which in some cases is minimal or absent.

* On the basis of 7.38 million persons of retirement age in England and Wales in 1966 the number of housebound old people is just over 700 000.

In some reported series the incidence has been high (Clark et al, 1964; Deller et al, 1964); but Morgan et al (1965), in a large survey, found osteomalacia in only 3 per cent of women and less than 1 per cent of men after a Polya type gastrectomy.

Hepatic disorders.   Liver and biliary tract disease can lead to osteomalacia due to impaired absorption of vitamin D and its reduced conversion to 25-hydroxy-cholecalciferol. Dent et al (1970) have drawn attention to the occurrence of osteomalacia in patients receiving anticonvulsant drugs which lead to hepatic enzyme induction. This form of therapy increases the catabolism of both dietary and endogenously produced vitamin D and diverts it towards biologically inactive metabolites. In consequence, body stores of vitamin D are depleted and plasma concentrations of 25-hydroxycholecalciferol are diminished (Hahn et al, 1975). When combinations of anticonvulsant drugs are used the effects on micro-somal enzymes are additive, leading to a greater inci-dence of hypocalcaemia, reduced bone mineral density and histological evidence of osteomalacia.

Renal impairment.   Fraser and Kodicek (1970) have shown the importance of adequate renal function for the conversion of 25-hydroxycholecalciferol to the active 1,25-dihydroxycholecalciferol. It is uncertain to what extent impaired metabolism of vitamin D can be attrib-uted to an age-related physiological decline in renal function which is believed to affect all individuals. Osteomalacia can occur in renal failure due to both glomerular and tubular disorders and following ureteros-sigmoidostomy. Eastwood et al (1976) have investi-gated the plasma 25-hydroxyvitamin D levels and the histological appearances of bone in 22 patients with stable chronic renal failure. Osteomalacia occurred only in those patients with relatively low levels of 25-hydroxyvitamin D. They conclude that the osteomalacia of chronic renal failure results from a lack of 25-hydroxyvitamin D superimposed on a deficiency of 1,25-dihydroxyvitamin D rather than from a lack of 1,25-dihydroxyvitamin D alone.

Clinical features

In the early stages the disease is often missed altogether because the bodily pains are thought to be due to 'rheu-matism'. When patients complain of inconstant pains in a variety of sites they tend to be dismissed as neurotic. Owing to the poor localization of the pain, attention may not be directly focused on the bones. Later, pain is nagging, persistent and unremitting and its results from strain on tender soft bone, rather than fracture of non-tender brittle bone as in osteoporosis. In some cases the pain is very severe, even breathing becomes difficult and the weight of bedclothes pressing upon the ribs becomes unbearable.

Muscular weakness is often striking. This has been regarded as a typical feature of rickets for many years but it is only recently that the frequent occurrence of muscle weakness in osteomalacia has been recognized. A proximal myopathy was first reported by Ekbom in Sweden in 1964. It affects chiefly the gluteal muscles but the shoulder girdle may also be involved. In 1965, Prineas et al described two cases: one patient had hyper-calcaemia (due to hyperparathyroidism) and the other hypocalcaemia. More recently, Stern and Smith (1968) demonstrated proximal myopathy in a high proportion of patients with osteomalacia. In spite of the hypotonia and muscle weakness the knee jerks are often exagger-ated. It now seems unlikely that this myopathy occurs in primary hyperparathyroidism. The patient may complain of difficulty in climbing stairs or getting up from a chair, difficulty in lifting the feet from the ground when walking and this leads to a typical 'waddling gait'. If the shoulder girdle is involved the patient may be unable to brush her hair.

The patient becomes shorter owing to deformities of the trunk — usually kyphosis but less often scoliosis. The softening of the bones lead to angulation of the sternum, deformities of the pelvis and bending of the femoral necks. Finally, on account of painful move-ments and skeletal deformities, the patient is forced to her bed.

Radiography

There is diminished radiographic density of bone and deformities may occur in the softened bone. Thus the pelvic brim may become bent as the result of the inward pressure of the femoral heads. The intervertebral discs are often ballooned and the soft vertebral bodies become biconcave in shape ('cod-fish vertebrae'). Although typically the vertebral bodies are evenly involved in osteomalacia coexistent osteoporosis is so often present that there is an irregular distribution of crush fractures. Thus this point of distinction from osteoporosis, although useful in younger patients, is less reliable in old age.

A characteristic finding is the appearance of Looser's zones or pseudofractures. These are bands of decalcifi-cation perpendicular or oblique to the surface of the bone, and on either side of the translucency there may be a denser band of callus which makes the Looser's zone appear more obvious (Fig. 37.4). They occur only in osteomalacia and when present make a certain differ-entiation from osteoporosis. The common sites are the axillary border of the scapula, the pubic rami, the ribs, the neck of the humerus and near the lesser trochanter of the femoral neck.

Sometimes the bone changes of secondary hyperpar-athyroidism are present with, for example, the appear-ance of subperiosteal erosions in the metacarpals or phalanges.

Fig. 37.4 Osteomalacia showing Looser's zone near lesser trochanter

Biochemistry

The typical biochemical findings are a low or normal serum calcium, low serum inorganic phosphorus, raised serum alkaline phosphatase and a diminished urinary calcium excretion. These findings, however, may vary considerably from time to time in the same patient, especially when the cause is simple vitamin D lack. In particular, the serum calcium and phosphorus levels vary according to the immediate state of vitamin D repletion and small doses can correct the abnormalities rapidly. But the serum alkaline phosphatase follows the bone changes and there is a delay in response to vitamin D. Thus a patient with long-standing osteomalacia may show normal serum calcium and phosphorus levels soon after treatment is started whilst the bone changes and the raised alkaline phosphatase remain unchanged for many months. Difficulties in diagnosis also arise in some cases of undoubted osteomalacia because the serum alkaline phosphatase is normal.

Diagnosis

According to the definition given, the diagnosis of osteomalacia can only be made on histological examination with the finding of increased amount of osteoid. In the majority of cases, however, diagnosis rests on the history of bone pains and muscular weakness, the radiological finding of Looser's zones, typical serum biochemical findings and a history of one of the disorders producing osteomalacia. When histological confirmation is necessary bone biopsy must be performed and undecalcified sections examined.

There will be some cases in which the diagnosis remains in doubt; in such instances a therapeutic trial with vitamin D is the most satisfactory means of confirming the presence of osteomalacia. All cases respond to vitamin D but clinical improvement may be slow. Thus monitoring of treatment should be undertaken by such procedures as demonstrating the rise in total hydroxyproline excretion in response to vitamin D (Smith and Dicks, 1968),the decreased proportion of osteoid with a calcification front and its increase with therapy (Bordier et al, 1968), and the rise in serum inorganic phosphorus in response to intravenous vitamin D_3 (Whittle et al, 1969).

Treatment

Calciferol should be given orally in doses of 0.025 to 0.125 mg (1000 to 5000 iu) daily for 1–3 months. Within 1–2 weeks the serum calcium and inorganic phosphorus reach normal values but the serum alkaline phosphatase does not fall to normal for several months. There is striking symptomatic improvement with disappearance of muscular weakness and bone pains. The Looser's zones gradually heal. In order to counteract the hypocalcaemia occurring immediately after the commencement of treatment (and possibly producing tetany) it is usual to give calcium supplements orally in the form of calcium hydrogen phosphate (1 g) daily.

When malabsorption is present and it is due to gluten sensitivity a gluten-free diet should be instituted but the response may be slow over a period of months. If the cause of malabsorption cannot be corrected the oral dose of vitamin D must be much greater but it is rarely necessary to give it by injection.

SKELETAL STATUS AND FRACTURES

Fracture epidemiology

Major advances in orthopaedic surgery have led to new techniques in the treatment of fractures which are generally considered to be surgical problems in the individual rather than a hazard to society as a whole. Fractures in the elderly differ markedly from those in the younger adult. In the adult (aged 20 to 60) considerable violence, usually direct trauma to the affected part, is required. In the young and in the elderly, fractures result from minimal or moderate violence; moreover, the site of fracture is usually cancellous bone next to a joint rather than the shaft of a bone.

In younger adults fracture incidence is lower in females than in males (the latter usually sustain fractures in motor accidents or industrial injuries). In the elderly, however, the sex and age corrected incidence of fractures is considerably higher in females than in males, especially for fracture of the vertebral bodies, the hip and lower end of the forearm.

Newton-John and Morgan (1968) pointed out that if there is a general loss of bone with age in the population and if this loss of bone causes structural weakening, then there might be expected to be a critical level below which the risk of fracture would be significantly increased and it would be expected that the fracture rate of the population would rise as more and more individuals fell below this critical level. They and other investigators have been able to test this hypothesis from data on the amount of bone and fracture rates at different ages.

Femoral neck fracture

Alffram (1964) made an epidemiological analysis of fracture of the hip involving 1664 cases observed over a 13-year period in the population of Malmo. In both males and females the incidence was negligible below the age of 50 and it apparently doubled for each 5-year increment after the age of 60. The incidence in females was 2.4 times that in males.

Bauer (1970) has calculated the annual number of fractures of the upper end of the femur in the female population of the USA from 1900 to 1960. The total female population trebled from 31 million in 1900 to 91 million in 1960, but during the same period the total annual number of fractures increased from 11 000 to 62 000; that is, the fracture rate rose twice as quickly as the population, because of the rapid rise in the age groups susceptible to fracture of the upper end of the femur.

Role of osteoporosis. Newton-John and Morgan (1968) were able to show a close parallelism between the fracture rate of the femoral neck and the frequency with which the amount of bone in the population falls below a critical level. In this and other studies, the cortical thickness of the metacarpal was used to estimate the amount of bone. Nordin (1971) used his data on the metacarpal cortical area/total area ratios in normal men and women by decades and found an inverse relationship with the femoral neck fracture rate derived from the data of Knowelden et al (1964). Nordin suggests that the metacarpal cortex reflects the bone loss which predisposes to fractures of the proximal femur and this is confirmed by the low metacarpal cortical area/total area ratios found in actual hip fracture cases.

Exton-Smith (1976) calculated the metacarpal cortical ratio based on measurements made on hand radiographs of patients with fracture of the femoral neck. The individual values were plotted on the percentile ranking curves for the general population (see Fig. 37.1). Although the mean value for both the male and female fracture cases were less than those for the general population in the corresponding age groups and some of the fracture cases had greatly dminished amounts of bone well below the 10th percentiles, there was found to be a wide scatter of values and many were in the higher percentile ranges. These results fail to support the hypothesis that there is a single critical level of bone mass below which fracture of the femoral neck is likely to occur, but there may be a critical level for each individual. The results also indicate that there may be factors other than osteoporosis which contribute to fracture of the femoral neck.

Role of vitamin D deficiency. Aaron et al (1974a) in Leeds have shown that 20 to 30 per cent of women and about 40 per cent of men with fracture of the femoral neck have histological evidence of osteomalacia. Later they showed (Aaron et al, 1974b) that the proportion with osteomalacia varied with the season of the year. The highest proportion of bone biopsy specimens with abnormal calcification fronts (43 per cent) was observed in February to April and the lowest (15 per cent) in October to December. The highest frequency of abnormal osteoid covered surfaces (47 per cent) was observed in April to June and the lowest (13 per cent) in October to December. They conclude that variation in hours of sunshine is responsible for a seasonal change in incidence of femoral neck fractures and possibly for osteomalacia in the elderly population as a whole. The significance of vitamin D deficiency as an important factor in fracture of the proximal femur has been confirmed by the study of Faccini et al (1976). The mean value of trabecular osteoid area in the fracture group was 4 per cent compared with 1 per cent in a control group matched for age and sex. The difference was also striking in the proportion of trabecular surface covered by osteoid; the mean value for the fracture group was 24.5 per cent compared with 7.9 per cent for the control group. Brown and his colleagues (1976) found significantly lower levels of plasma 25-hydroxy-cholecalciferol in patients with fracture of the femoral neck compared with those in controls of similar age from whom blood samples were taken at the same time of the year. This is believed to be a reflection of the decreased out-of-doors activity of the patients prior to their fracture.

Fracture of the forearm

The effects of age and sex on the incidence of wrist fractures are also clearly seen. There is a high incidence in the young, both in boys and girls, a low incidence in adults and a steep rise in aging women, unaccompanied by any corresponding change in men (Bauer, 1970). Nordin (1971) compared the radius and ulna 'density' value in normal men and women based on his own data (Nordin et al, 1970) with the annual age-specific wrist fracture rate in the normal population derived from the data of Knowelden et al (1964), it was found that the fracture rate in the normal population was inversely related to the mean density of the lower end of the radius.

Vertebral compression fractures

Measurements of peripheral bone status (for example, in the second metacarpal) in patients with vertebral compression fractures yield inconclusive results. Certainly younger patients with vertebral collapse have an amount of bone in the metacarpal which is below the normal range for their age (Fig. 37.5); in the elderly, however, values quite commonly fall within the normal range (Nordin, 1971). Nevertheless patients with the most severe degrees of osteoporosis of the spine also have low values of bone mass in the metacarpal. Nordin, using spinal densitometry, has shown that crush fracture cases generally suffer from a more severe degree of spinal osteoporosis than other individuals of the same age (Nordin et al, 1968, 1970). He considers that differences between the vertebral and peripheral bone status may depend on the rate at which osteoporosis develops. The vertebral bodies consist largely of trabecular bone, which with its large surface area/volume ratio is preferentially absorbed. Thus in the early stages severe spinal osteoporosis may exist with relatively normal peripheral bones. Peripheral bone loss lags behind the resorption of the vertebral bodies.

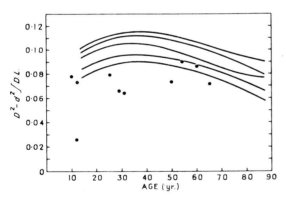

Fig. 37.5 Percentile ranking curves showing individual values for younger patients with idiopathic osteoporosis

Thus both osteoporosis and osteomalacia contribute to the rising incidence of fractures at the three common sites in the elderly — the hip, wrist and spine. In osteomalacia there is an obvious change in the quality of bone, but in osteoporosis there may also be a change in bone quality which is not revealed by histological examination. A complete explanation of the fracture patterns in old age must depend on satisfactory studies of bone-breaking strength and other parameters of bone quality in relation to age and disease states.

HYPERPARATHYROID BONE DISEASE

The distinction between osteitis fibrosa and other forms of bone disease was first made by Von Recklinghausen. The cause of primary hyperparathyroidism is an adenoma of the parathyroid glands. Secondary hyperparathyroidism most often results from osteomalacia which leads to compensatory hypertrophy of the parathyroids. In some of these cases autonomous development of adenoma occurs (tertiary hyperparathyroidism). The condition can occur at almost any age including extreme old age. It is more common in women than in men, especially in women after the menopause.

Clinical features

Many cases of hyperparathyroidism remain asymptomatic for years and the diagnosis is only suspected when routine estimations of serum calcium carried out in the investigation of other disorders reveals hypercalcaemia. When symptoms are present they are usually the result of hypercalcaemia, renal stones and bone disease. Hypercalcaemia leads to weakness and lassitude, to gastrointestinal disturbances, mental disorders, to thirst and polyuria.

Gastrointestinal symptoms

Anorexia and vomiting are prominent manifestations and lead to loss of weight. These symptoms may simulate those of peptic ulcer. Peptic ulceration is common in hyperparathyroidism but it is uncertain whether the frequency is greater than in the general population and it is possible that hyperparathyroidism accentuates symptoms of peptic ulcer rather than being a primary cause. Both acute and chronic pancreatitis may be a complication of hyperparathyroidism. Sometimes in acute pancreatitis there is a fall in the serum calcium concentration and in these cases diagnosis of hyperparathyroidism may be difficult.

Mental symptoms

Toxic confusional states are especially common in older patients and many are inappropriately admitted to mental hospitals with the diagnosis of senile dementia. These symptoms are directly related to hypercalcaemia and if the serum calcium concentration can be lowered the mental disturbances quickly remit.

Renal lesions

Polyuria is a prominent feature of hyperparathyroidism and it leads to dehydration and to thirst. In some cases the thirst is out of proportion to the degree of polyuria yet it disappears when a parathyroid adenoma is removed at operation. All patients presenting with renal calculi must be investigated for possible hyperparathyroidism which is responsible for 5 per cent of renal stones and for 15 per cent of cases of recurrent stones. The calculi consist of calcium salts of phosphate or oxylate and they may cause renal colic, infection, haematuria or renal failure. Hyperparathyroidism may be complicated by the deposition of calcium in the renal parenchyma (nephrocalcinosis). The condition is probably quite common but diagnosis is only rarely made since considerable deposition of calcium must occur before radiographic changes are apparent. Stones and renal calcification lead to renal failure consequent upon glomerular and tubular damage and the patient may die of uraemia.

Metastatic calcification

The only other common site for metastatic calcification in hyperparathyroidism apart from calcium deposition in the kidney is in the cornea. This leads to 'band keratopathy' and it is usually best revealed by tangential illumination from a slit lamp.

Bone lesions

Skeletal pain is often prominent in hyperparathyroidism. It may be localized to the limbs, the spine or the ribs and it is often severe by the time the radiographs reveal loss of bone tissue. Spontaneous fractures may occur. The ends of the fingers become stubbed due to disintegration of the terminal phalanges and loss of support to the soft tissues. The typical bone lesion in hyperparathyroidism is the giant cell-tumour or osteoclastoma. The tumour can occur in the jaw (epulis) or at the end of a long bone. Swelling and pain occur at the site of the tumour. Only about one-third of cases of hyperparathyroidism have the typical bone changes.

Radiography

Loss of bone tissue from the skeleton is a constant finding in hyperparathyroidism making the bones abnormally translucent with thinning of the cortex. When the metacarpal cortical indices for patients with hyperparathyroidism are plotted on percentile ranking curves it is found that they have significantly less bone than the normal population of corresponding age and sex (Gryfe, 1973). Spontaneous fractures and deformities of the bone can occur. In the spine crush fractures may be present and in these instances it may be difficult to distinguish the X-ray appearance of hyperparathyroidism from that of osteoporosis. The distinction can be more readily made, however, in those cases of hyperparathyroidism which show patchy increase in bone density (osteosclerosis). This tends to occur at sites in the vertebral bodies adjacent to the end plates and produces the so called 'rugger-jersey'sign with alternate bands of increased density and translucency. Loss of calcium from the skull produces a granular mottling which is characteristic. If this is combined with areas of

patchy density then the flat bones of the skull have a woolly appearance. In those old people who have retained their teeth the dense alveolar bone which surrounds the roots of the teeth (lamina dura) disappears. When present, pathognomonic findings in the hands are subperiosteal erosions which are due to irregular loss of bone from the outer cortex of the metacarpals or phalanges. The ends of the distal phalanges disappear completely. In some cases a diagnosis of hyperparathyroidism can be made from the appearance of bone cysts in the long bones. They are produced by giant-cell tumours or osteoclastomas. The cortex over the tumour is usually very thin and a pathological fracture may occur.

Biochemistry

In hyperparathyroidism the total calcium concentration may range from normal to twice normal values in severe cases. In the elderly in particular it is important to calculate the ionized fraction of serum calcium since protein-bound calcium may be reduced by the fall in serum albumin which is common in old age and in disease states. Thus a rise in the ionized fraction may be significant even though the total serum calcium is normal. The 'adjusted calcium value' can be calculated using a modification of the formula proposed by Berry et al (1973): Adjusted calcium = observed calcium (mmol/l) − 0.023 (albumin (g/l) − 46). Serum inorganic phosphorus is generally reduced although there are many cases of hyperparathyroidism where the values fall within the normal range. This is likely to be the case when renal impairment is present since this leads to an elevation of serum inorganic phosphorus. The serum alkaline phosphatase activity is always increased in patients with radiological abnormalities of the bones but the activity is normal in those patients without evidence of bone disease (Dent and Harper, 1962). The net excretion of calcium in the urine is usually increased due to the elevation of serum calcium levels.

Diagnosis

The problems to be considered in the differential diagnosis of hyperparathyroidism concern hypercalcaemia, renal lesions, bone lesions and the differentiation of primary and secondary hyperparathyroidism.

Hypercalcaemia

When the serum calcium level is elevated and the serum inorganic phosphorus is reduced the diagnosis of hyperparathryoidism is rarely in doubt. Apart from some cases of malignant disease this finding is characteristic. It is unusual for the serum inorganic phosphorus to be diminished in other diseases producing hypercalcaemia such as sarcoidosis, multiple myeloma, thyrotoxicosis, Paget's disease, vitamin D intoxication and milk-alkali syndrome. Most of these conditions producing hyper-calcaemia can usually be distinguished on clinical grounds. In sarcoidosis, malignancy and vitamin D intoxication the administration of cortisone (150 mg daily for 10 days) reduces the serum calcium but corti-sone usually does not influence the hypercalcaemia of hyperparathyroidism (Dent, 1956). Fraser and her colleagues (1971) have drawn attention to the value of discriminant function analysis in the differential diag-nosis of hypercalcaemia. They have shown that multi-variate analysis of readily available biochemical data (serum inorganic phosphorus, alkaline phosphatase, chloride, bicarbonate and urea) obtained from hyper-calcaemia patients on admission to hospital led to diag-noses which coincided in 90 per cent of cases with the diagnosis reached after a long period of detailed clinical investigation.

Renal lesions

Patients in whom renal stones or nephrocalcinosis are the only manifestations of hyperparathyroidism may show only minor or intermittent elevation in the serum calcium concentration. It is in these cases that problems in the diagnosis of hyperparathyroidism arise since the small increase in serum calcium may be the only feature to enable the distinction to be made from patients in whom stones are not due to hyperparathyroidism. The best way for making the diagnosis is to make repeated accurate determinations of the serum calcium paying particular attention to the corrections for abnormally low serum albumin levels.

Bone lesions

Patients with hyperparathyroidism showing radiological findings of osteosclerosis must be distinguished from other causes of patchy increase in bone density such as Paget's disease and osteosclerotic secondary deposits especially from malignant disease of the prostate. In the earlier reported cases of osteoclastoma confusion often arose between hyperparathyroidism and polyostotic fibrous dysplasia. This latter condition, however, is not a generalized bone disease and there is no disturbance of calcium metabolism. Moreover, the symptoms of polyostotic fibrous dysplasia usually begin in late childhood.

Secondary hyperparathyroidism

Patients with hyperparathyroidism secondary to renal failure (uraemic osteodystrophy) may have radiological changes in bone similar to those occurring in primary hyperparathyroidism. Uraemic osteodystrophy, however, usually occurs in children rather than in older adults and although periosteal erosions and patchy osteosclerosis may be found on radiographic examination, osteoclas-tomas are rare. It should be borne in mind, however, that primary hyperparathyroidism may be superimposed on secondary hyperparathyroidism when an autonomous adenoma develops in a hyperplastic parathyroid gland.

In the majority of cases of hyperparathyroidism diag-nosis can be made on the basis of biochemical and radio-logical findings in patients with renal stones or bone lesions. When the diagnosis remains in doubt the blood parathormone level should be determined by means of radioimmunoassay.

Treatment

The treatment of hyperparathyroidism is generally surgical but the main problem is to find the adenoma at operation. The surgeon must identify all four glands but even when these are normal there is still the possi-bility of an adenoma being present. When there is no adenoma and the parathyroid glands are hyperplastic the major part of the parathyroid tissue must be removed. Following a successful parathyroid operation serum calcium levels quickly return to normal but there is considerable risk of subsequent hypocalcaemia and the development of tetany. This can usually be treated by intravenous infusion of calcium gluconate. Patients with severe bone disease in whom hypocalcaemia is likely to persist following operation should be treated with vitamin D (2.5 mg calciferol daily).

Elderly patients with marginal hypercalcaemia and who are not submitted to surgical operation may main-tain normal health for many years without complica-tions. The risk of stone formation can be reduced by the use of a calcium restricted diet. In elderly women with mild hyperparathyroidism bone resorption leading to accelerated osteoporosis can be controlled by the admin-istration of oestrogens (Gallagher and Nordin, 1972). In elderly patients who are unfit for operation successful control of hypercalcaemia can sometimes be achieved by the use of an oral phosphate supplement, disodium hydrogen phosphate 10–15 g daily (Dent, 1962).

OSTEITIS DEFORMANS (PAGET'S DISEASE)

Osteitis deformans was first described by Sir James Paget in 1877. It is a common bone disorder in the elderly affecting 2–4 per cent of people over the age of 60 but there is no convincing proof that the condition is due to metabolic disorder. It is characterized by a combination of excessive bone resorption and deposi-tion. These processes can result in enlargement of bones and in severe deformity of the skeleton.

Clinical features

Paget's disease can occur at almost any site but the tibia, the bones of the pelvic girdle and the skull are most commonly involved. The polyostotic form of the disease affects multiple areas of the skeleton but bone involvement is never generalized. In 10 per cent of Paget's disease the condition is monostotic involving a single bone or a single area. Some patients are greatly disabled by severe unremitting bone pain. Transverse fractures, particularly of the shaft of the femur occur. Bone enlargement can lead to pressure on other structures producing such minifestations as deafness, back pain radiating in a radicular distribution due to pressure on nerve roots and paraplegia due to spinal cord compression (in this latter case often only one vertebral body is involved). In a large number of patients, however, the disease is completely asymptomatic and is found when radiographic examination is carried out for the investigation of other disorders. High output cardiac failure is a rare complication of Paget's disease resulting from multiple small arterio-venous fistulae in areas of affected bone. Cardiac failure, however, is not uncommon and is usually due to associated ischaemic heart disease. The development of osteogenic sarcoma is rare but it is the most serious complication of Paget's disease.

Diagnosis

When such characteristic features such as enlargment of the skull and bowing of the long bones are present the diagnosis is readily made. Radiographs show cortical thickening, destruction of the normal trabecular pattern and patches of rarefaction and sclerosis. The serum calcium and inorganic phosphorus levels are usually normal although hypercalcaemia can occur in the active phase of the disease especially when the patient is immobilized. Typically the serum alkaline phosphatase activity is elevated, often markedly so. Total hydroxyproline excretion in the urine is raised and this indicates increased collagen turnover. In men the condition with which Paget's disease is most likely to be confused is sclerotic bone metastases from carcinoma of the prostate but this is not associated with any enlargement or deformity of bone.

Treatment

Prior to the introduction of calcitonin there was no effective treatment of Paget's disease. Calcitonin can be administered in porcine, human or salmon form and all three hormones have produced a similar degree of clinical, biochemical and radiological improvement. The salmon and porcine preparations, however, are potentially antigenic. A dose of 50 MRC Units daily for a period of 3 to 6 months produces a response in the majority of patients; thereafter the dosage can often be reduced to 50 MRC Units three times a week. Most patients with Paget's disease do no require treatment and the main indications for the use of calcitonin are bone pain, neurological complications, high output cardiac failure, the reduction in hypercalcaemia and stone formation associated with immobilization and in the prophylaxis of orthopaedic complications such as fracture of the tibia and femur, protusio acetabulae in pelvic disease, and crippling deformity from advance of the disease. The effects of treatment can be monitored by the reduction in serum alkaline phosphatase activity and in total hydroxyproline excretion.

REFERENCES

Aaron J E, Gallagher J C, Anderson J, Stasiak L, Longton E B, Nordin B E C, Nicholson M 1974a Frequency of osteomalacia and osteoporosis in fractures of the proximal femur. Lancet i: 229–233

Aaron J E, Gallagher J C, Nordin B E C 1974b Seasonal Variation of histological osteomalacia in femoral neck fractures. Lancet ii: 84–85

Albright F, Smith P H Richardson A M 1941 Post-menopausal osteoporosis. Journal of the American Medical Association 116: 2465–2474

Alffram P A 1964 An epidemiological study of cervical and trochanteric fractures of the femur in an urban population. Acta Orthopaedica Scandinavica Supp 65

Anderson I, Campbell A E R, Dunn A, Runciman J B M 1966 Osteomalacia in elderly women. Scottish Medical Journal 2: 429–436

Bauer G C H 1970 In: Barzel U S (ed) Osteoporosis. Grune and Stratton, New York

Bernstein D S, Sadowsky N, Hegsted D M, Guri C D, Stare F J 1966 Prevalence of osteoporosis in high- and low-fluoride areas in North Dakota. Journal of the American Medical Association 198: 499–504

Bordier P, Matrajt, H, Hioco D, Hepner G W, Thompson G R, Booth C C 1968 Subclinical vitamin D deficiency following gastric surgery. Lancet i: 437–440

Brown I R F, Bakowska A, Millard P H 1976 Vitamin D status of patients with femoral neck fractures. Age and Ageing 5: 127–131

Bullamore J R, Gallagher J C, Wilkinson R, Nordin B E C, Peacock M 1970 Effect of age on calcium absorption. Lancet ii: 535–537

Cameron J R, Sorenson J 1963 Measurement of bone mineral in vivo: An improved method. Science 152: 230–232

Chalmer J, Conacher W D H, Gardner D L, Scott P F 1967 Osteomalacia a common disease in elderly women. Journal of Bone and Joint Surgery 49B: 403–423

Chesnut C H, Nelp W B, Baylink D J, Denney J D 1977 Effect of methandrostenolone on postmenopausal bone wasting as assessed by changes in total bone mineral mass. Metabolism 26: 267–277

Chestnut C H, Ivey J L, Nelp W B, Baylink D J 1979 Assessment of anabolic steroids and calcitonin in the treatment of osteoporosis. In: Barzel U S (ed) Osteoporosis II: p 135–150. Grune & Stratton, New York

Clark A N G 1972 Deficiency states in duodenal diverticular disease. Age and Ageing I: 14–23

Clark C G, Crooks J, Dawson A A, Mitchell P E G 1964 Disordered calcium metabolism after Polya partial gastrectomy. Lancet i: 734–738

Davis M E, Strandjord N M, Lanzi L H 1966 Estrogens and the aging process. Journal of the American Medical Association 196: 219–224

Deller D J, Begley M D, Edwards R G, Addison M 1964 Metabolic effects of partial gastrectomy with special reference to calcium and folic acid. I. Changes in calcium metabolism and the bones. Gut 5: 218–225

Dent C E 1955 Idiopathic osteoporosis. Proceedings of the Royal Society of Medicine 48: 574–578

Dent C E, Watson L 1966 Osteoporosis. Postgraduate Medical Journal Suppl 42: 583–608

Dent R V, Miline M D, Roussak N J, Steiner G 1953 Abdominal topography in relation to senile osteoporosis of the spine. British Medical Journal 2: 1082–1084

Dent C E Richens A, Rowe D J F, Stamp T C B 1970 Osteomalacia with long-term anticonvulsant therapy in epilepsy. British Medical Journal 4: 69–72

Department of Health and Social Security 1972 A Nutrition Survey of the Elderly. H.M.S.O., London

Dietrick J E, Whedon G D, Shorr E 1948 Effects of immobilization upon various metabolic and physiologic functions of normal men. American Journal of Medicine 4: 3–36

Doyle F H, Gutteridge D H, Joplin G F, Fraser R 1967 An assessment of radiological criteria used in the study of spinal osteoporosis. British Journal of Radiology 40: 241–250

Eastwood J B, Harris E, Stamp T C B, DeWardener H E 1976 Vitamin D deficiency in the osteomalacia of chronic renal failure. Lancet ii: 1209–1211

El-Maraghi N R H, Platt B S, Stewart R J C 1965 The effect of the interaction of dietary protein and calcium on the growth and maintenance of the bones of young, adult and aged rats. British Journal of Nutrition 19: 491–509

Exton-Smith A N 1970 Cross-sectional and longitudinal studies of aging. Experimental Gerontology 5: 273–280

Exton-Smith A N 1976 The management of osteoporosis. Proceedings of the Royal Society of Medicine 69: 931–934

Exton-Smith A N, Stanton B R 1965 Report of an Investigation into the Dietary Habits of Elderly Women Living Alone. King Edward's Hospital Fund, London

Exton-Smith A N, Hodkinson, H M, Stanton B R 1966 Nutrition and metabolic bone disease in old age. Lancet i: 999–1001

Exton-Smith A N, Millard P H, Payne P R, Wheeler E F 1969a Method for measuring quantity of bone. Lancet ii: 1153–1154

Exton-Smith A N, Millard P H, Payne P R, Wheeler E F 1969b Pattern of development and loss of bone with age. Lancet ii: 1154–1157

Exton-Smith A N, Stanton B R, Windsor A C M 1972 Nutrition of Housebound Old People. King Edward's Hospital Fund, London

FAO Nutritional Studies 1961 Calcium Requirements. Report of an FAO/WHO Expert group, Rome

Faccini J M, Exton-Smith A N, Boyde A 1976 Disorders of bone and fracture of the femoral neck. Lancet i: 1089–1092

Fraser D R, Kodicek E 1970 Unique biosynthesis by kidney of a biologically active vitamin D metabolite. Nature 288: 764–765

Garn S M 1962 An annotated bibliography on bone densitometry. American Journal of Clinical Nutrition 10: 59–67

Garn S M 1970 The Earlier Gain and Later Loss of Cortical Bone. Thomas C C, Springfield, Illinois

Garn S M, Hull E I 1966 Taller individuals lose less bone as they grow older. Investigative Radiology I: 255–256

Garn S M, Pao E M, Rihl M E 1964a Compact bone in Chinese and Japanese. Science 143: 1438–1439

Garn S M, Rohmann C G, Behar M, Viteri F, Guzman M A 1964b Compact bone deficiency in protein-calorie malnutrition. Science 145: 1444–1445

Garn S M, Rohmann C G, Nolan P 1964c The developmental nature of bone changes during aging. In: Birren J E, (ed) Relations of Development and Aging. Thomas C C, Springfield, Illinois

Garn S M, Rohmann C G, Wagner B 1967 Bone loss as a general phenomenon in man. Federation Proceedings (Federation of American Societies for Experimental Biology) 26: 1729–1736

Gershon-Cohen J, Jowsey J 1964 The relationship of dietary calcium to osteoporosis. Metabolism 13: 221–226

Gershon-Cohen J, McClendon J F, Jowsey J, Foster W C 1962 Osteoporosis produced and cured in rats by low and high calcium diets. Radiology 78: 251–252

Gerth E 1930 Dur frage der osteoporose. Virchows Archiv für pathologische Anatomie und Physiologie 277: 311–325

Gough K R, Lloyd O C, Wills M R 1964 Nutritional osteomalacia. Lancet ii: 1261–1264

Gryfe C I 1973 Bone loss in primary hyperparathyroidism. Canadian Medical Association Journal 109: 479–482

Gryfe C I, Exton-Smith A N, Payne P R, Wheeler E F 1971 Pattern of development of bone in childhood and adolescence. Lancet i: 523–526

Gryfe C I, Exton-Smith A N, Stewart R J C 1972 Determination of the amount of bone in the metacarpal. Age and Ageing 1: 213–221

Hahn T J, Hendin B A, Scharp C R, Boisseau V C, Haddad J G 1975 Serum 25-hydroxycalciferol levels and bone mass in children on chronic anticonvulsant therapy. New England Journal of Medicine 292: 550–552

Heaney R P 1965 A unified concept of osteoporosis. American Journal of Medicine 39: 877–880

Heaney R P 1970 In: Barzel U S (ed) Osteoporosis Grune and Stratton, New York

Henneman P H, Wallach S 1957 The use of androgens and estrogens and their metabolic effects: A review of the prolonged use of estrogens and androgens in post-menopausal and senile osteoporosis. Archives of Internal Medicine 100: 715–723

Hodkinson H M, Brain A T 1967 Unilateral osteoporosis in longstanding hemiplegia in the elderly. Journal of the American Geriatrics Society 15: 59–64

Horsman A, Gallagher J C, Simpson M, Nordin B E C 1977 Prospective trial of oestrogen and calcium in postmenopausal women. British Medical Journal 2: 789–792

Hyams D E, Ross E J 1963 Scurvy, megaloblastic anaemia and osteoporosis. British Journal of Clinical Practice 17: 332–340

Joffe N 1961 Some radiological aspects of scurvy in the adult. British Journal of Radiology 34: 429–437

Jowsey J 1965 The indirect measurement of bone resorption. Journal of Clinical Endocrinology 25: 429–25: 1408–1426

Jowsey J, Riggs B L, Kelly P J, Hoffman D L, 1972 Effect of combined therapy with sodium fluoride, vitamin D and calcium in osteoporosis. American Journal of Medicine 53: 43–49

Jowsey J, Schenk R K, Reutter F W 1968 Some results of the effect of fluoride on bone tissue in osteoporosis. Journal of Clinical Endocrinology and Metabolism 28: 869–874

Khosla T, Lowe C R 1968 Height and weight of British men. Lancet i: 742–745

Knowelden J, Buhr A J, Dunbar O 1964 Incidence of fractures in persons over 35 years of age. British Journal of Preventive and Social Medicine 18: 130–141

Lachman E 1955 Osteoporosis. The potentialities and limitations of its roentgenological diagnosis. American Journal of Roentgenology 74: 712–715

McConkey B, Fraser G M, Bligh A S 1962 Osteoporosis and purpura in rheumatoid disease: Prevalence and relation to treatment with corticosteroids. Quarterly Journal of Medicine 31: 419–427

Mitchell C J, Parsons V, Dische F 1975 The treatment of osteoporosis with sodium fluoride, vitamin D and calcium supplements. Quarterly Journal of Medicine 44: 636–637

Morgan D B, Paterson C R, Woods C G, Pulvertaff C N, Fourman P 1965 Search for osteomalacia in 1228 patients after gastrectomy and other operations on the stomach. Lancet ii: 1085–1089

Morgan D B, Pulvertaft C N, Fourman P 1966 Effects of age on the loss of bone after gastric surgery. Lancet ii: 772–773

Moss A J, Waterhouse C, Terry R 1965 Glutensensitive enteropathy with osteomalacia but without steatorrhoea. New England Journal of Medicine 272: 825–830

Newton-John H F, Morgan D B 1968 Osteoporosis: disease or senescence? Lancet i: 232–233

Nordin B E C 1960 Osteoporosis and calcium deficiency. Proceedings of the Nutrition Society 19: 129–137

Nordin B E C, 1971 Clinical significance and pathogenesis of osteoporosis. British Medical Journal 1: 571–576

Nordin B E C 1980 Calcium metabolism and bone. In: Exton-Smith A N and Caird F I (eds) Metabolic and nutritional disorders in the elderly p 123–145. Wright, Bristol

Nordin B E C, Dallas I, MacGergor J, Smith D A 1964 In: Hioco D J (ed) L'Osteoporose. Masson & Cie, Paris

Nordin B E C, Horsman A, Marshall D H, Hanes F, Jakeman W 1979 The treatment of post-menopausal osteoporosis. In: Barzel U S (ed) Osteoporosis II pp 183–204. Grune & Stratton, New York

Nordin B E C, Young M M, Bentley B, Ormondroyd P, Sykes J 1968 Lumbar spine densitometry. Clinical Radiology 19: 459–464

Nordin B E C, Young M M, Bulusu L, Horsman A 1970 In: Barzel U S (ed) Osteoporosis. Grune and Stratton, New York

Platt B S, Stewart R J C 1962 Transverse trabeculae and osteoporosis in bones in experimental protein-calorie deficiency. British Journal of Nutrition 16: 483–495

Platt B S, Stewart R J C 1968 Effects of protein-calorie deficiency on dogs. I. Reproduction, growth and behaviour. Developmental Medicine and Child Neurology 10: 3–24

Pommer G, 1885 Untersuchungen uber Osteomalacie und Rachitis. Leipzig

Posner A S 1970 In: Barzel U S (ed) Osteoporosis. Grune and Stratton, New York

Prineas J W, Mason A S, Henson R A 1965 Myopathy in metabolic bone disease. British Medical Journal 1: 1034–1036

Rich C, Ensinck J, Ivanovich P 1964 The effects of sodium fluoride on calcium metabolism of subjects with metabolic bone diseases. Journal of Clinical Investigation 43: 545–555

Riggs B L, Seeman E, Hodgson S, Taves D R, O'Fallon W M 1982 Effect of the fluoride/calcium regimen on vertebral fracture occurrences in postmenopausal osteoporosis. New England Journal of Medicine 306: 446–450

Rose G A 1970 In: Barzel U S (ed) Osteoporosis. Grune and Stratton, New York

Sheldon J H 1948 The Social Medicine of Old Age. Oxford University Press, London

Smith R, Dick M 1968 Total urinary hydroxyproline excretion after administration of vitamin D to healthy human volunteers and a patient with osteomalacia. Lancet i: 279–281

Smith R W, Rizek J, Frame B, Mansour J 1964 Determinants of serum anti-rachitic activity. Special reference to involutional osteoporosis. American Journal of Clinical Nutrition 14: 98–108

Stamp T C B, Round J M 1974 Seasonal changes in human plasma levels of 25-hydroxyvitamin D. Nature 247: 563–565

Stern G, Smith R 1968 Myopathy and Metabolic Bone Disease. Paper read to joint meeting of Royal College of Physicians, London, and American College of Physicians

Stewart R J C, Sheppard H G, Preece R F, Exton-Smith A N 1972 Bone resorption in the elderly. Age and Ageing 1: 1–13

Strandjord N M, Lanzl L H 1966 Estrogens and post-menopausal osteoporosis. In: Progress in Development of Methods in Bone Densitometry, p 115–126. NASA SP-64

Urist M R, Gurvey M S, Fareed D O 1970 In: Barzel U S (ed) Osteoporosis. Grune and Stratton, New York

Whedon G D 1970 In: Barzel U S (ed) Osteoporosis. Grune and Stratton, New York

Whittle H et al 1969 Intravenous vitamin D in the detection of vitamin D deficiency. Lancet i: 747–750

Windsor A C M, Williams C B 1970 Urinary hydroxyproline in the elderly with low leucocyte ascorbic acid levels. British Medical Journal 1: 732–733

The musculoskeletal system — aging of articular cartilage

INTRODUCTION

The disorders of cartilaginous joints become increasingly common as age advances. Both hyaline and fibrocartilages undergo material failure. Abnormalities of major synovial joints such as osteoarthrosis (OA) of the hips, knees and fingers, and of major fibrocartilaginous joints such as intervertebral (IV) disc disease of the spine, culminate in disability, pain and deformity, loss of stature, diminished strength and incapacity. These age-related changes, hallmarks of the molecular disorganization of the articular connective tissues, are accompanied and exacerbated by alteration in bone density, in ligament and tendon strength and in meniscal elasticity. In 'third world' countries such as Brazil, Argentina and India, where life expectation is much less than in Europe and North America, the degenerative disorders of cartilage may be secondary to infection and trauma. In the older populations of Western Society, the causes for the onset of the age-related degenerative diseases of cartilage are not clear and the reasons for their occurrence are therefore still sought in the process of aging itself.

Although aging of articular tissues can be said to begin at the time of their intrauterine formation, growth and maturation overshadow morphological age changes until skeletal development is complete; normal modifications of the structure and function of the articular tissues begin in infancy and evolve through childhood and adolescence. They are often overlooked when the broader issues of senescence are debated.

AGING OF HYALINE CARTILAGE

Important reviews are those of Schofield and Weightman (1978) and Stockwell (1979).

Changes in chemical composition

The main physical attributes of hyaline articular cartilage are determined by the presence of water (Muir, 1979). Water normally constitutes ~ 70 per cent of adult cartilage and is retained within the domains of the giant proteoglycan (PG) molecules that comprise ~ 30 per cent of the dry weight of cartilage. These PGs are expanded to an extent determined by the strength and integrity of the numerous type II collagen (COL) fibres (Fig. 38.1) that form a meshwork, holding PGs in place. COL constitutes ~ 70 per cent the dry weight of the tissue.

As age advances, the cells of cartilage become less numerous: their synthetic and metabolic activities change and decline. There is a gradual decrease in the content of water (Venn and Maroudas, 1977; Venn, 1978). This suggests that, in advancing age, the COL meshwork, in which increasingly numerous cross-links form with time, expands to a diminishing degree. The amount of PG changes little (Bayliss et al, 1983). The aggregation of PG with hyaluronate (HA) is preserved but smaller PG monomers come to form a larger proportion of the total, and the glycosaminoglycans (GAG) that are the side chains of the PGs, alter in amount and in composition (Elliott and Gardner, 1979). In older cartilage, the chondroitin sulphates (ChS) that form so much of the normal population of GAGs diminish and in the deep zone are replaced to an increasing extent by keratan sulphate (KS).

Collagen structure appears to alter little with age but a growing body of evidence confirms that COL cross-links increase in number and in strength. COL and PG molecules are closely associated. Electron microscopy (EM) demonstrates that labelled PG is associated with COL periodic structure (Fig. 38.2) (Orford and Gardner, 1984) and bound ionically. It is reasonable to assume that these COL-PG links are modified with age but evidence to establish this alteration is not yet available.

In this account we adopt the following definitions: Age= the length of life*; aging= the process of growing old†; old= advanced in age*; senescence= growing old*; maturity= full, natural development*.
(*Concise Oxford English Dictionary; †Chambers Twentieth Century Dictionary).

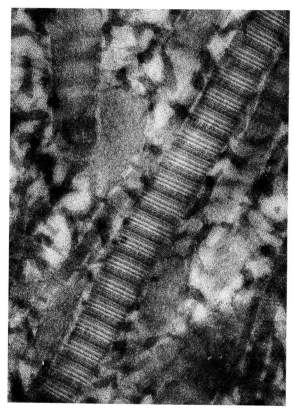

Fig. 38.1 Collagen (COL) fibril. Transmission electron microscopic (TEM) view of type II COL fibril from zone IVb of 10 month old dog. Femoral condylar articular cartilage. Glutaraldehyde/cupromeronic blue-phosphotungstic acid and uranyl acetate, × 103 800.

Fig. 38.2 Articular cartilage. TEM view of baboon cartilage from zone I of femoral condyle. Note proteoglycan (PG)-dye complexes, indicated as dark deposits, aligned at regular intervals along unstained COL fibrils. Arrangement suggests orderly interaction between PG and COL at specific sites on COL fibrils. Glutaraldehyde/cupromeronic blue, × 76 500.

A difficulty in interpreting the state of COL cross-links in hyaline cartilage is that much of the evidence has been derived from tissues other than human cartilage and from young, growing, rather than from mature tissues. With maturation, the *reducible* cross-links gradually disappear: total cross-linking, however, increases and must therefore be of a stable, non-reducible kind (Schofield and Weightman, 1978). How this is brought about is not certain but new forms of cross-links have been identified (Bailey et al, 1980). It has also been established that the large amianthoid COL fibres that form during aging, in costal cartilage at any rate, correspond to an increased orientation of COL fibres in affected parts as revealed by high-angle X-ray diffraction studies (Aspden and Hukins, 1979).

Cartilage metabolism declines with age but it is widely suspected that this may be a reflection of diminished cellularity. That there are qualitative changes in metabolism is strongly suggested by the altered nature of the PG secreted by the remaining cells. Sulphate uptake, an index of GAG synthesis, is not changed but the aggregation of PGs is impaired. The formation of amyloid (Fig. 38.3) is characteristic of many aging tissues (Glenner and Page, 1976) and it is of interest that amyloid is being discovered with increased frequency in older, osteoarthrotic (OA) cartilage (Goffin et al, 1981; Egan et al, 1982).

Young cartilage has a delicate blue-white colour and is almost translucent (Gardner, 1984b). As age advances, the cartilage assumes a yellow-brown colour and becomes increasingly opaque. The pigment is an acid glycoprotein. It is unrelated to the iron-containing pigments of haemophilia and haemochromatosis which aggregate in, but do not significantly colour, the matrix. Haemochromatotic iron deposition is commonly accompanied by chondrocalcinosis, the accumulation of calcium pyrophosphate. It is absolutely distinct from the melanin-like pigment, the particulate deposits of which impregnate articular cartilage in ochronosis resulting from the rare disorder, hereditary alkaptonuria.

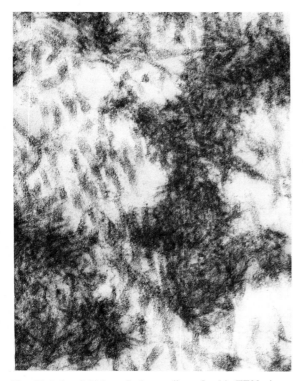

Fig. 38.3 Amyloid in articular cartilage. In this TEM view note dark fibrillar masses in clusters deposited among COL fibrils of the superficial, zone I articular cartilage from the femoral condyle of a 70-year-old woman. Glutaraldehyde/osmium tetroxide-uranyl acetate and lead citrate, × 66 400.

Whereas ochronotic pigment deposits have a drastic effect on cartilage strength, the pigment of aging appears to be without functional significance.

Changes in cells and in tissue structure (*see review by Silberberg, 1972*)

Fetal cartilage displays a very high cell density. The number of cells per unit volume is large. Cell density decreases quickly in the periods of growth and maturation. There is thereafter a diminution in the cellularity of intact cartilage which differs both anatomically and in the degree to which the perpendicular zones of cartilage are affected (Stockwell, 1979). Between the ages of 25 and 85 there is no overall decline in the cell density of humeral head and femoral condylar cartilage when the *whole thickness* of the tissue is assessed. When, however, the superficial zone of the femoral condyles is considered independently, it is found that there is a substantial reduction in cell density which accompanies a significant increase in cell density of the deeper zones: the overall cell density remains unchanged. This pattern is not reduplicated in the femoral *head* where the decline

in cell density of the superficial zone cartilage is sufficient to account for an age-related fall in the mean cellularity of the whole tissue.

There is no evidence that the cellularity of the much thinner cartilages of large congruent joints such as the ankle or of small condylar joints such as those of the fingers and toes, declines with age. Since a reciprocal relationship exists between cell density and cartilage thickness, a relationship evident when analogous joints of large and of small mammalian species are compared (the scale effect) (Simon, 1971), it is, however, probable that the same substantial changes in cell density will be found in the hyaline cartilage of smaller synovial joints as in the large.

Changes in cartilage thickness

The older view that cartilage becomes thinner with age (Barnett et al, 1963) was probably based on observations of specimens with advanced fibrillation in which a breaking away of hyaline cartilage may have led to the exposure of bone. More recent evidence does not support this belief: the mean thickness of intact but aging human humeral cartilage (Meachim, 1971) and of patellar cartilage (Simon, 1971) does not decrease. However, few systematic attempts have been made to measure the thickness of hyaline articular cartilage in even the most important joints; and fewer still have taken account of the asymmetry of the major articulations.

Recognizing the need for additional information on the thickness and volume of the hyaline cartilage of those human joints in which OA is a common clinical problem, Armstrong and Gardner (1977) tested 28 normal human hip joints, obtained post-mortem, and measured the thickness of the articular cartilage from radiographs made in the lateromedial plane (Fig. 38.4). The articular surface was defined without the use of the

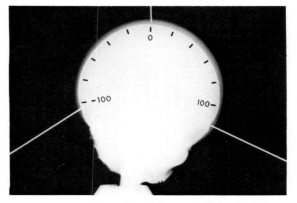

Fig. 38.4 Human femoral head. Lateromedial radiograph from normal adult hip showing zenith (0°) and orientation for measurement of cartilage thickness.

special contrast media developed for measuring cartilage thickness in whole joints in vitro (Armstrong et al, 1979). The zenith of the femoral head was identified in a preliminary test of each specimen; in this way, cartilage thickness measurements in the latero-medial plane could be exactly related to points on the femoral head circumference. Radiographs were amplified by television, and measurements of cartilage thickness were made around the femoral head circumference. In the age range 20–50 years, the thickest zone of normal femoral head cartilage lay ~ 20° anterior to the zenith. The mean thickness of the hyaline cartilage from males and females in this age range increased with age (Fig. 38.5) and the greatest increase was in the thickest, anterior part.

It is of interest that the cartilage zone of the human femoral head found to be thickest, and to increase in thickness to the greatest extent between age 20 and 50 years (Armstrong and Gardner, 1977) is not a zone found to display the limited non-progressive, age-related cartilage changes (p 783) (Byers et al, 1970); neither is it a zone obviously susceptible to the progressive changes of OA.

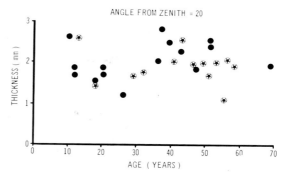

Fig. 38.5 Measurement of cartilage thickness of femoral heads from 28 normal persons aged 10 to 68 years. Note that, after age 20, there is a significant rise in cartilage thickness until aged 50, ✱ male; ● female.

Important aspects of the mechanical properties of hyaline cartilage are determined by the junction between the deepest, calcified zone of cartilage (zone V) and the underlying bony end plate. This is a site for horizontal microfractures in OA. Measurements of the thickness

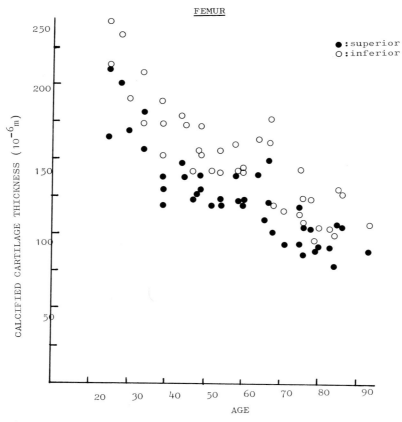

Fig. 38.6 Calcified cartilage and age. The relation of the thickness of the layer of calcified cartilage to age (from Lane and Bullough, 1980).

of the calcified cartilage show that there is a decrease with age (Lane and Bullough, 1980) (Fig. 38.6). Changes in the thickness of this zone depend upon endochondral ossification which leads to added subchondral bone and thinning of the calcified cartilage. In turn, there is an incorporation of non-calcified articular cartilage into the calcified zone by advancement of the calcification front, indexed by duplication of the tidemark (Fig. 38.7). This age-related change should lead to an increase in the thickness of the calcified cartilage. That there is a thinning with age indicates that increased endochondral ossification at the deeper aspect of the zone of calcification is relatively greater than advancing calcification at the superficial margin. This dynamic change may determine the altered geometry of the ar-

ticular surfaces described in older persons (Bullough et al, 1973; Freeman, 1975).

Changes in cartilage mechanics

The peak loads applied to major joints such as the hip are very large: the forces may be almost 5 times that of body weight during walking. These loads are applied on many millions of occasions in a life span of 70 years. The forces exerted in *compression* are resisted by the swelling pressure of the matrix PGs and the water retained within their domains. The COL fibrils that retain PG within a fibre skeleton, resisting swelling pressure under both normal and abnormal circumstances, are, however, continually subjected to critical *tensile* stresses: a tearing of the COL fibres may allow the escape of PG and the

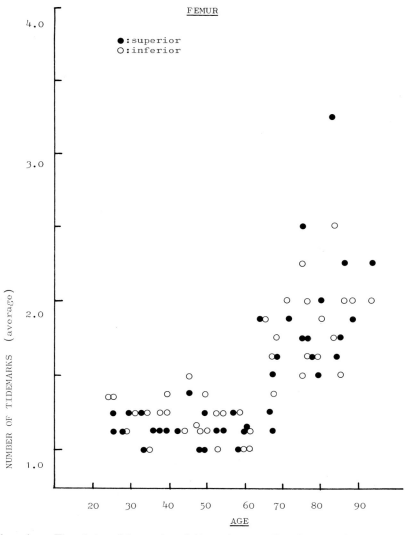

Fig. 38.7 Tide marks and age. The relation of the number of tide marks to age (from Lane and Bullough, 1980).

loss of cartilage elasticity. There would be a corresponding increase in deformability.

Mechanical tests of aging cartilage have been made both in tension and in compression.

The *tensile* stiffness, fracture strength and fatigue resistance all deteriorate with increasing age (Kempson, 1979). There is a linear relationship between these properties and the COL content. It is widely assumed that it is the cross-linking of COL, not its absolute amount, which mainly regulates tensile strength. Since cross-linking increases, a concept has emerged that some other change such as an age-related decrease in COL alignment, may be responsible for diminishing tensile strength. Among additional evidence for COL change is increased cartilage water content in OA, indicating increased COL extensibility, particularly in mid-zone cartilage.

Compressive tests showed that the deformations of femoral head articular cartilage under peak loads in the intact hip joint were non-uniform and increased greatly with age (Armstrong et al, 1979). For these tests, whole normal human hip joints were obtained post-mortem. A cartilage-binding, radiopaque medium was introduced into the joint which was placed inverted in a hydraulic test rig. Under peak loads corresponding to those sustained during the normal walking cycle, at the toe-off position, the femoral cartilage of young adult joints was almost incompressible whereas in old (> 80 years) persons, reductions in thickness of up to 15 per cent occurred under load (Fig. 38.8). When measurements were made of femoral head cartilage from 28 normal

persons in the age range 28–85 years the degree of compressibility, i.e. the compliance, was found to be directly related to age. There was no corresponding age-related change in creep compliance when this was measured in 12 specimens under similar conditions. In a single preliminary test, instantaneous deformability of the very thick residual cartilage of a femoral head with grade III OA was very large.

Much of the published evidence on compression has been derived from isolated specimens tested with an indentor. By contrast with tests conducted on *whole* hip joints, indentation tests reveal no significant alteration with age in Young's modulus of the cartilage on the superior surface of the femoral head (Armstrong et al, 1980). It appears that the testing of the intact joint enables the detection of fluid expressed during the first 30 seconds of loading, a change not recognizable by indentation procedures (Kempson et al, 1970).

These results suggest that the changes with age in the chemical composition and water content of articular cartilage can lead to a vicious circle in which normal peak loads cause increased disruption with disorganization and increased susceptibility to injury. The thickened cartilage of older persons, increasingly compliant, responds by excessive deformation to the forces imposed by normal cycles of movements such as walking. Eventually, distortion may bring about the mechanical failure of COL, with the fatigue fractures envisaged by Freeman (1975). Accelerated breakdown, with the development first of minimal, later of overt fibrillation, and the onset of cartilage loss, eburnation, osteophytosis and remodelling, may ensue (Gardner, 1983, 1984b).

Changes in cartilage surfaces

The surfaces of the load-bearing synovial joints were regarded as remarkably smooth (Hunter, 1742–43; Davies, 1969). More recently, it has become evident that the articulating surfaces of hyaline cartilage are not only not smooth in the sense of 'absence of roughness' (SOED), but are normally characterized by the presence of several orders of microscopic irregularity that are superimposed on the primary anatomical contours of the articulating surfaces (Gardner, 1984b). A hand lens reveals 0.4–0.5 mm (2ry) irregularities; a dissecting microscope reveals a large number of randomly arranged shallow (3ry) undulations that are approximately the same diameter as the most superficial chondrocytes whose location they probably represent (Middleton et al, 1984). Reaching beyond the limits of resolution of the light microscope, the scanning EM (SEM) reveals still finer (4ry) irregularities some of which may be artefactual and the transmission EM (TEM), used to examine very thin replicas made at low temperature, identifies a further (5ry) order of microstructure (Fig. 38.9) (Gardner et al, 1983).

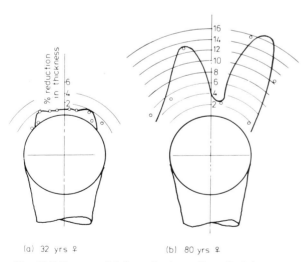

(a) 32 yrs ♀   (b) 80 yrs ♀

Fig. 38.8 Patterns of deformation in cartilage of *whole* normal human hip joints produced by applying loads in range of those sustained during daily movement, i.e. ca. 5 MN/m^{-2} Observe the large increase in compliance in aged (right) cartilage compared to young adult (left).

Fig. 38.9 Articular cartilage — normal. Surface of normal dog femoral condylar cartilage seen as TEM view of platinum/carbon replica made at low temperature. Note the regular cross-striations of the superficial COL fibrils and the intervening 5th order prominences, × 14 700.

Taking advantage of reflected light interference microscopy (RLIM), Longmore and Gardner (1975, 1978) analyzed the surfaces of the lateral femoral condyles of 20 normal human subjects aged 0–47 years. They found that the load-bearing surfaces, entirely smooth to the naked eye, bore a pattern of 3[ry] hollows. Prominences predominated in the very young. Hollows became less frequent in number as age advanced, an observation of considerable interest since it is known from studies of perpendicular sections that the cell density of cartilage diminishes with increasing age with a relative increase in the proportion of the extra-cellular fibrous and non-fibrous matrix. This increased proportion of matrix may contribute to the altered frequency of the surface features.

Systematic measurements of the diameter, depth and frequency of the tertiary surface undulations have shown that their dimensions are also age-related (Longmore and Gardner, 1975, 1978). These investigations have confirmed that progressive and extensive microscopic disruption of the load-bearing surfaces of the knees of normal individuals can be seen with the light microscope as early as 25 years; by the age of 35 years, disorganization of the cartilage surfaces has become so pronounced that studies by reflected light interference

microscopy and by SEM become very difficult.

Several techniques have helped understanding of the surface structure of hyaline cartilage. Replicas of surfaces can be made in latex by simple one-stage techniques; either the replicas or the original material can be examined by a diamond stylus (Talysurf) instrument that passes over the surface, recording an amplified contour pattern (Sayles et al, 1979). Reflected light interference microscopy allows the diameter, depth and frequency of the surface irregularities to be measured on fresh samples: there is no restriction to fixed tissue and no requirement for desiccation. Delicate 2-stage replicas can be made of the surfaces of fixed tissue and the carbon casts made in this way can be examined at high resolution in the TEM. Recent advances have also taken place in techniques for the examination of articular surfaces with low temperature methods. Rapid freezing in nitrogen slush at −210° (63K) permits surface blocks of cartilage to be prepared without artefact; and a new generation of low temperature stages made for the SEM (Oates, 1983) allows the surfaces of this unfixed, hydrated material to be scanned at −192° (81K) for long periods without significant electron beam damage (Gardner et al, 1981) (Fig. 38.10). An advance in replication techniques enables the surfaces of very rapidly frozen material to be reduplicated; and replicas made in this way from unfixed, hydrated tissue can be surveyed at high resolution by TEM (Fig. 38.9) (Gardner et al, 1983).

The microscopic disorganization of aging articular surfaces to which reference has already been made, determines that traces, 2-stage replicas and RLIM images made from femoral condylar cartilages from subjects aged more than 45 years are complex and difficult to interpret.

Age-related disorders of cartilage

As age advances, selected areas of normal hyaline cartilage surfaces come to display areas of *fibrillation*, a non-uniform disorganization of the surface which varies in extent and severity from one individual to another and from one area in a particular joint to another. Fibrillation (Figs. 38.11, 38.12) is a 'fraying and splitting of cartilage, seen in material which still presents an exposed surface to the synovial cavity without a covering of new fibrous or bony tissue' (Meachim and Stockwell, 1979). Fibrillation is said to be 'overt' when it can be detected by the naked eye; this is easiest after a fresh cartilage surface has been painted with dilute Indian ink in isotonic solution. When fibrillation is recognizable only by incident LM or by SEM (Figs. 38.13, 38.14) it is said to be 'minimal'.

Fibrillation is therefore an age change of many, if not all, normal human synovial joints. The patterns of fibrillation recognizable on glenoid, humeral head, acetabular, femoral head, patellar, tibial condylar, distal tibial and lateral malleolar, and talar surfaces have been

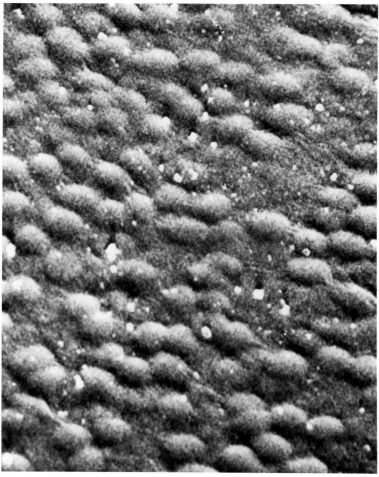

Fig. 38.10 Articular cartilage — normal. Scanning electron microscopy (SEM) view of surface of normal, fully hydrated dog femoral condylar articular cartilage viewed at low temperature (−192°), × 700.

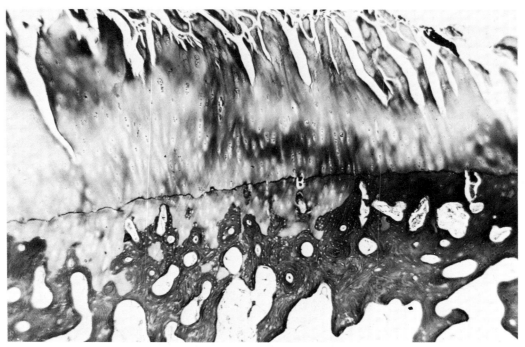

Fig. 38.11 Knee joint cartilage. Light microscope, perpendicular section of femoral condylar cartilage from knee of 62 year old male. The tangential perpendicular splits (fibrillation), would appear *en face* as over fibrillation. One split extends almost to the thin dark tideline (centre). Note slight osteosclerosis of underlying bone. Haematoxylin and eosin (HE), × 125.

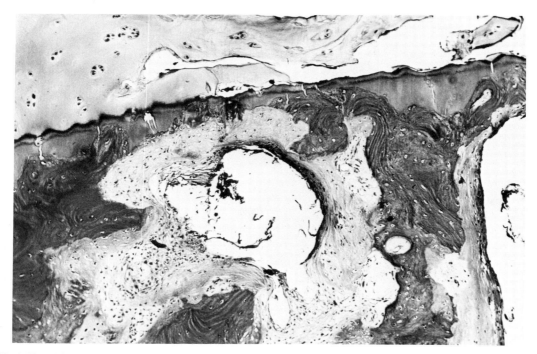

Fig. 38.12 Knee joint cartilage — osteoarthrosis. Overt fibrillation has progressed (at right) to whole thickness loss of cartilage from part of cartilage articular surface. Note (top left) chondrones of dividing chondrocytes forming small cell clusters and (at bottom) loose pale grey fibrous tissue among trabeculae of sclerotic bone. HE, × 125.

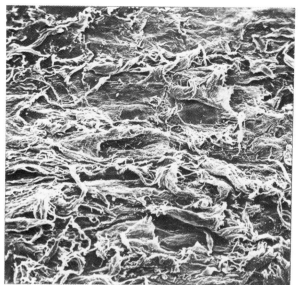

Fig. 38.13 Articular cartilage — fibrillation. SEM view of part of articular cartilage surface from femoral condyle of 70 year old human knee. The disorderly surface structure seen at low magnification represents minimal fibrillation.
Glutaraldehyde-propylene oxide and vacuum drying, × 210.

carefully plotted for a Liverpool necropsy series by Meachim and his colleagues (see Freeman and Meachim, 1979). It is evident that fibrillation is an age change; by itself, it cannot be termed a disease.

Nevertheless, when large numbers of articular surfaces from series of older persons are examined, it becomes clear that fibrillation is not always restricted to the limited but age-related changes so carefully demonstrated by Meachim. More advanced lesions with whole-thickness loss of cartilage, eburnation and osteophyte formation (Gardner, 1984c) are detected. A subpopulation of advanced cartilage degradation and loss emerges to which the term *osteoarthrosis* (OA) can be applied (Figs. 38.15, 38.16). Two distinct patterns of change were recorded by Byers et al (1970) for the femoral head. The first pattern of fibrillation was anatomically restricted and structurally non-progressive, related to age in its frequency. The second pattern, termed OA, much less common, found in a different

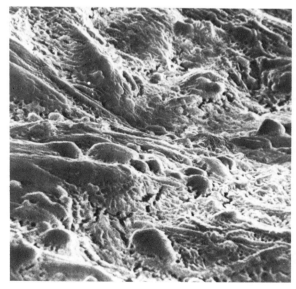

Fig. 38.14 Articular cartilage — fibrillation. Surface of femoral condylar cartilage of 76-year-old human, viewed at low temperature with cartilage water present. Tissue unfixed. Note rounded prominences that may be surface chondrocytes, nearby splits, lacunae from which PG may have been lost and disorderly state of surface. Unfixed — viewed at −192°, × 1500.

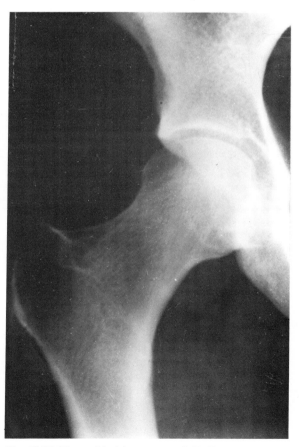

Fig. 38.15 Human hip joint — normal. Radiograph showing intact, normal acetabulum with femoral head and neck. Note orderly structure of joint space and bone density.

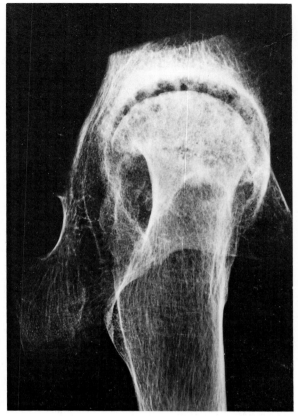

Fig. 38.16 Human hip joint — osteoarthrosis. Radiograph of human hip joint with severe osteoarthrosis. Note dense, sclerotic bone adjoining articular space which is poorly defined. Remaining bone of pelvis and of femoral shaft is osteoporotic.

Fig. 38.17 Articular cartilage — normal. TEM view of articular surface and zone I superficial cartilage of femoral condyle of 24 year old normal human female. Note closely packed COL fibrils forming bundles arranged parallel to the articular surface and seen in longitudinal and cross-section. Glutaraldehyde/osmium tetroxide-phosphotungstic acid, uranyl acetate and lead citrate, × 11 000.

distribution, was progressive in structural terms but not related to age in its frequency. These important, but largely unconfirmed, observations have lent support to the view (Sokoloff, 1969) that OA, as a disease, is not solely an aging phenomenon. The numerous factors that may contribute to OA have recently been reviewed (Gardner, 1983).

Late in the natural history of the disease there may occur inflammation secondary (1) to the presence of fragments of bone and cartilage within the synovia and (2) to the crystals of calcium pyrophosphate and of apatite that are responsible for the chondrocalcinosis and apatite deposition commonplace in longstanding OA. Pain may result both from this synovitis and from the exposure of nerve endings within exposed bone. At this stage disability and deformity evoke the need for arthroplasty and the other surgical measures that are proving so successful in eradicating the local disease.

Transmission electron microscopy (Figs. 38.17, 38.18, 38.19, 38.20) has been used to confirm the extent

and form of the earliest aspects of hyaline articular cartilage fibrillation. The selection of material for ultrastructural study is difficult since the usual techniques for the recognition of minimal and overt fibrillation, incident light microscopy and Indian ink painting respectively, select material that, by TEM standards, is grossly disturbed. However, by choosing, for TEM study, cartilage *adjoining* areas of minimal fibrillation, a compromise can be reached and blocks of tissue collected that are, presumably, neither normal nor overtly fibrillated.

On this basis, the work of Weiss (Weiss and Mirow, 1972; Weiss, 1979) and of Mitchell and Shepard (1981) has attracted particular interest. Analogous studies of dog cartilage fibrillation and of experimental OA have been made (Orford et al, 1983). In affected cartilage, the normal arrangement of the COL in the superficial cartilage zones is lost and the quantity of highly hydrated, interfibrillar matrix increased. Collagen fibres display a wider and more variable range of diam-

Fig. 38.18 Human articular cartilage — fibrillation. TEM view of articular surface and of superficial, zone I cartilage of femoral condyle from 64-year-old human male. Dark-grey, electron-dense deposits form a thick lamina at the cartilage surface, separating COL fibrils of matrix. Compare with Figure 38.17. Glutaraldehyde/osmium tetroxide-phosphotungstic acid, uranyl acetate and lead citrate, × 11 000.

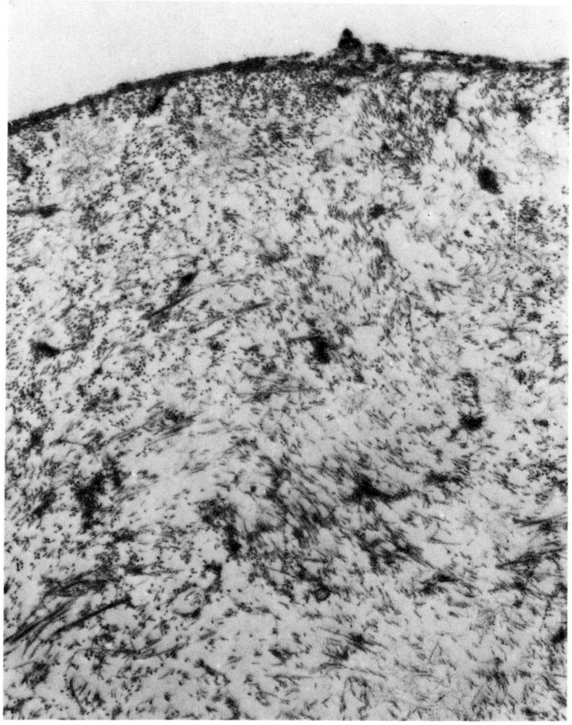

Fig. 38.19 Articular cartilage surface. TEM view of articular surface and superficial, zone I matrix of femoral condylar cartilage from 64-year-old human male. Note, by comparison with Figure 38.17, the disorderly arrangement of the COL fibrils which are separated by apparently electron-lucent spaces. Glutaraldehyde/osmium tetroxide-phosphotungstic acid, uranyl acetate and lead citrate, × 11 000.

eters than normal and occasional giant fibres are seen. 'Microscars' are identified where the loss of chondrocytes has resulted in a focus of condensed COL. The intercellular matrix includes more vesicles than normal. There is a suggestion that the ultramicroscopic aggregates of calcium hydroxyapatite crystals associated with these vesicles, constitute structural nonhomogeneities in the cartilage and foci for stress concentrations, facilitating material failure and cartilage disruption.

Weiss (1979) recognized two morphologically distinct clones of chondrocytes in the early fibrillation of OA. The first category had intensely staining pericellular halos, the second had not. With advancing age, chondrocyte degeneration became more frequent. Eventually, the fragments of the degraded cells remain as the only evidence of chondrocyte injury. The loss of chondrocytes corresponded with the progression of the matrix change seen as fibrillation. There was little evident repair and no sign that the remaining clones of reacting chondrocytes were capable of providing suffi-

cient new matrix PG or of constructing a new COL microskeleton.

AGING IN FIBROCARTILAGE

Although cartilage with a very high COL content, fibrocartilage, is recognized in articular discs, menisci and labra, it is in the intervertebral joints that the age changes of fibrocartilage assume their greatest significance. The aging of fibrocartilage will therefore be considered in the light of data on the intervertebral (IV) discs.

Changes in composition (*Beard and Stevens, 1980*)
When normal young IV discs are divided or excised and placed in physiological saline, the disc swells. Swelling is particularly conspicuous in the nucleus pulposus where the PG and water content are high. The swelling pressure is exerted by disc PG and opposed by COL fibres. The COL fibres of the nucleus pulposus are few,

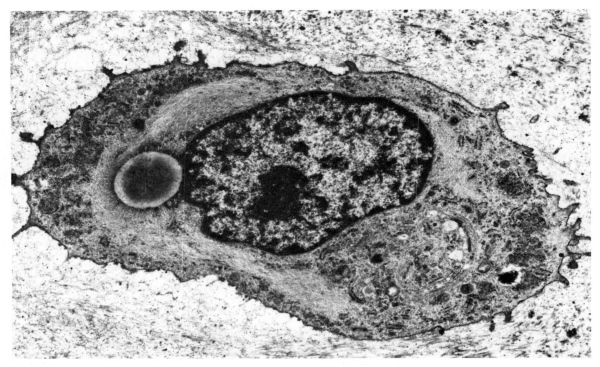

Fig. 38.20 Mature cartilage cell. TEM view of chondrocyte from zone II femoral condylar cartilage of mature dog. Note the central nucleus containing a grey-black nucleolus and the processes that extend from the edge of the cell into the adjoining matrix. Within the cell, much of the cytoplasm is occupied by fine, concentric filaments, characteristic of the aging cell. Glutaraldehyde/osmium tetroxide-uranyl acetate and lead citrate, × 10 800.

the PG content high: the tendency of the exposed or divided nucleus to swell is therefore very great and under circumstances of sudden increased mechanical load or of congenital or acquired defects of the cartilage end-plate the swelling pressure may be sufficient for the displaced nucleus to penetrate nearby osteoporotic bone (Figs. 38.21, 38.22).

The PG of IV discs contains ChS and KS attached to a protein core. Although the protein core, like that of hyaline cartilage, has three regions, one lacking GAG, one rich in KS and one rich in ChS, the IV disc PGs contain more KS and protein and less ChS and are substantially smaller than those of hyaline cartilage. There is a shorter region of core protein bearing the ChS chains. Differences exist between the PGs of the human disc nucleus and annulus: a greater proportion of PG in the latter can bind to HA. The molecular weight of IV disc PG decreases with age. The water content of the disc also declines, an age change that accompanies an increase in the KS/Ch-4-S ratio. The altered water content is not the result of changed PG osmotic properties.

There is a much higher concentration of PG in the young disc nucleus than in the annulus. There is an increasing gradient in the concentration of GAG from the outer annulus to the central part of the nucleus (Szirmai, 1970) an observation confirmed by measurements of fixed charge density.

Normally, GAG, and presumably PG, are associated with the COL fibrils of the annulus of the IV disc (Butler and Heap, 1982). A similar intimate relationship has been demonstrated for rat tail COL (Scott and Orford, 1981) and it is suspected for the COL of hyaline cartilage (Orford and Gardner, 1984). In the IV disc, as in hyaline cartilage in OA, a disturbance of the COL/PG relationship may be an important molecular explanation for subsequent mechanical failure.

Intervertebral disc COL is abundant, particularly in the annulus fibrosus where it is arranged in interlacing concentric bundles the disposition of which gives great strength. In the annulus there is much type I COL, particularly in the outer regions; there is little type I COL in the nucleus pulposus. The outer annulus resembles a perichondrium. Anti-type II COL antisera stain the nucleus and the whole of the annulus except the outer lamellae. There is therefore an inverse relationship between the amounts of type I and type II COL in the annulus relative to the nucleus. Small amounts of type

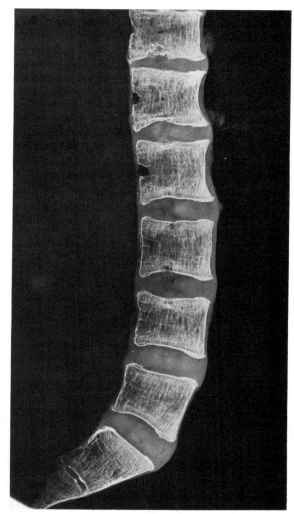

Fig. 38.21 Spine — osteoporosis. Radiograph of sagittal section of lumbar and sacral spine in osteoporosis. Note gentle protrusion of intervertebral disc material into osteoporotic bone. The vertebral bodies are beginning to assume a fishtail appearance.

III COL are now known to be present in the pericellular regions of chondrocytes in adult IV discs.

Much less is known of the COL of aging and of abnormal IV discs than of normal (Akeson et al, 1977); there is little understanding of how such changes contribute to mechanical defects. Tensile properties including stiffness increase up to age 26 years but not beyond (Galante, 1967). Biochemical measures of IV disc composition do not correlate with biomechanical properties; in particular, hydroxyproline content as an index of COL does not change with age.

The COL fibrils of human fetal annulus fibrosus do not increase in diameter from the time at which they are first deposited, at age 10 weeks, to an age of at least 24 weeks (Hickey and Hukins, 1981). Whether there is a similar constancy of COL fibril diameter at later ages is not established. Evidence derived from SEM of glutaraldehyde-fixed, critical point dried human lumbar IV discs, some treated with chymotrypsin, suggests that this may not be so and that fibril diameter increases markedly to an adult level during maturation, thereafter again remaining constant (Takeda, 1975).

Normal IV discs contain a small quantity of solvent-extractable lipid. The lipid content of the nucleus pulposus and of the hyaline cartilage plate of the IV disc is approximately the same and constitutes ~ 0.6 per cent of the tissue wet weight after dry extraction, ~ 1.8 per cent after wet extraction (Franklin and Hull, 1966).

The orientation of COL fibrils in the IV disc annulus has been measured by X-ray and neutron diffraction (Berthet et al, 1978). The fibrils are wound round the annulus at a specific orientation to the axis of the vertebral column; the two dimensional structure of the COL fibrils is different from that of COL in the rat tail tendon. Fixation before X-ray diffraction causes the COL molecules to become more closely packed although the distribution of COL in the tissue is not affected (Hickey and Hukins, 1979).

There is a change in chemical composition of human lumbar IV discs not only with age but with anatomical location. At age 44, but not at age 16, the COL content of the annulus increases distally. An analogous change in GAG composition is shown by the increasing glucosamine/galactosamine ratios down the spine both in annuli and in nuclei (Adams and Muir, 1976).

Changes in mechanics
The 23 IV discs of the normal vertebral column of man are very strong: they provide a flexible, firm union between adjacent vertebral bones and, with the intervertebral and interspinous ligaments, the apophyseal joints and the paravertebral muscles, form an axial skeletal framework that moves readily from extreme flexion to 10° of extension and laterally by approximately 30°. When a 75 kg 24-year-old normal man holds a 750 N weight, the forward bending moment acting at the L5-S1 intervertebral joint is 485 Nm^{-2}. The total compressive force acting on L5 is 9.0 KN, a force largely attributable to extensor muscle activity; this value is close to the average compressive breaking load for lumbar vertebral bodies of 7.1–8.8 KN in the 20–30 year male age group. However, experimental testing reveals that this compressive breaking load of lumbar vertebrae at physiological strain rates varies very greatly across the population, ranging from 0.8 KN to nearly 16 KN (Hutton et al, 1979). The difference in compressive strength between upper and lower lumbar vertebrae is not significant.

A

B

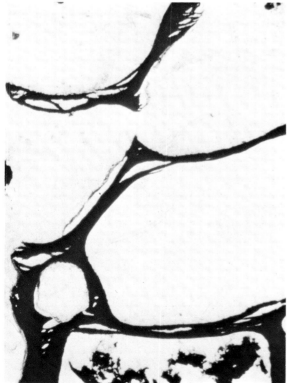

C

Fig. 38.22 Osteoporotic bone. Cut sections from slight (a), moderate (b) and severe (c) osteoporosis. von Kossa silver nitrate/neutral red, × 165.

Age-related disorder: intervertebral disc degeneration

Disc degeneration in its common form is age-related (Ball, 1978) but the relationship is complex. The inner part of the degenerate annulus is frayed and the nucleus pulposus appears more fibrous, contains more chondrones and a granular age-pigment that may be a PG-lipid complex derived from degenerate cells.

Tears in the IV disc predominate in the posterior annulus fibrosus (Fig. 38.23): they are relatively rare in the rounded contour of the upper lumbar discs, a region where torsion is resisted by the vertical orientation of the facet joints. Posterior tears in the annulus predominate in the L4 and L5 discs, particularly before age 50 years. However, tears of the anterior annulus fibrosus are conspicuous above the L2 level in the middle aged and elderly. Age appears to influence the integrity of the anterior annulus to a greater degree in the L2–D10 region than at lower levels (Hilton et al, 1977; Ball, 1978). The anterior part of the disc, it is suggested, may be a more important cause of low back pain than has previously been supposed. Anterior disc herniation has been successfully reproduced experimentally (Lipson and Muir, 1981).

In terms of the distribution and severity of anterior and posterior annular tears in the spine between D11 and S1, no significant sex difference has been detected (Hilton et al, 1980). The number of tears increases with age. There are differences between the frequency of anterior and posterior tears in the older and younger age groups and the evidence suggests that at least 2 factors cause annular tears: one factor affects L4 and L5 in young adults and may be mechanical; the second factor operates at a later age, promotes widespread disc involvement and may be of a degenerative character.

Fig. 38.23 Sagittal section of upper lumbar vertebrae from an elderly male. The intervertebral disc (at centre) displays 2 main horizontal fissures or tears. At the anterior margin (left) the rims of the adjoining vertebrae are fused in the process of ankylosing hyperostosis.

Fig. 38.24 Intervertebral disc — chondrocalcinosis. (a) Stipled appearance of island of calcium pyrophosphate crystals seen (at centre) in part of annulus fibrosus of IV disc. (b) Polarised light view of same material displaying the characteristic rhomboidal crystals. HE, × 500.

CPPD deposits. With advancing age, deposits in the articular connective tissues of calcium pyrophosphate dihydrate (CPPD) become common (Fig. 38.24). Such deposits are encountered as calcific foci in IV discs, and are a form of chondrocalcinosis. Disc degeneration results. CPPD deposition is often unexplained but the presence of CPPD crystals in a degenerate disc where they are found when discectomy is performed, may be an early sign of primary hyperparathyroidism and other occult conditions associated with CPPD deposition (Ball, 1978; Hamilton et al, 1981).

Degenerative spondylosis. Pathological changes in the IV discs, osteophytes formed at the vertebral body margins and OA of the apophyseal joints are common and probably inter-related disorders (Vernon-Roberts, 1980). They are embraced by the collective term degenerative spondylosis. The changes of spondylosis are found much more often pathologically than radiologically. In the 4253 specimens examined by Schmorl and Junghanns (1971) there was degenerative disease in 60 per cent of women and 80 per cent of men by age 49 years, in 95 per cent of both sexes by age 70 years. More recently, Vernon-Roberts and Price (1977) found changes from the normal morphology of young adults in the IV discs of all persons by middle age and in many by age 30 years. It is clear that the presence of these abnormalities does not necessarily contribute to back pain.

Degenerative changes in the IV discs are very frequent and become more common with age. With time, the nucleus pulposus becomes brown, desiccated and friable, losing its normal turgidity. Splits and clefts appear in the annulus, particularly between the disc centre and the cartilage end plates to which they run parallel. The clefts extend posteriorly and posterolaterally. At the same time, congenital deficiencies may persist in the cartilage end plates.

IV disc protrusion. Single episodes of major mechanical stress, or repeated smaller loads, may displace the nucleus in one of two main directions; *vertically* into the nearby cancellous bone of the vertebrae where the displaced material constitutes a Schmorl's node; or *postero-laterally*, where the nuclear tissue protrudes into the intervertebral foramina or into the spinal canal, or prolapses more completely.

IV disc prolapse. Fracture of the vertebral end-plate permits part of the nucleus to escape under load into the bone of the vertebral body, constituting a Schmorl's node. The affected disc is mechanically defective. These nodes are more frequent in the T10–L1 region than at lower levels and correlate positively with IV disc degeneration in each of the T10–L1 segments. The extent of degeneration is higher in those segments with Schmorl's nodes at all ages between 10 and 96. The finding of Schmorl's nodes as often *before* the age of 50 as *after*, suggests that Schmorl's nodes arise early in life, predisposing to disc degeneration (Ball, 1978). The nodes are not related to bone density, are more common in the lower than in the upper vertebral endplate and are distributed differently from micro-fractures (Vernon-Roberts and Pirie, 1973). A developmental rather than a traumatic origin is suggested.

Vertical prolapse, with the formation of one or more Schmorl's nodes, is very frequent (Fig. 38.25). Recent observations show that nodes are present in ~ 76 per cent of spines and with equal frequency above and below age 50 (Hilton et al, 1976). Protrusion of the nucleus, it is therefore now believed, is only likely when the material of the nucleus retains the semifluid consistence of youth or early adult life. Prolapse is clearly most probable when defects occur also in the cartilaginous end plates or when abnormally large mechanical forces are applied.

Posterior prolapse of the nucleus pulposus is much less frequent than posterolateral because of the site of the lateral extensions of the posterior intervertebral ligaments. In one study, posterior displacements were found post-mortem in 11.5 per cent of male spines, in 18.7 per cent of female. Others have confirmed that posterior prolapse may also be found before the age of 30 years when surgical treatment may be required.

The functional significance of vertical nuclear prolapse is a disturbance of the distribution of forces within the vertebrae. New bone formation is stimulated at disc margins anterolaterally, with osteophytosis. When prolapse is multiple, a consequential dorsal

Fig. 38.25 Intervertebral disc prolapse. Sagittal slices of parts of two vertebral columns displaying protrusion of nuclei pulposus of IV discs into adjoining vertebral body bone.

kyphosis develops, exacerbated in the elderly by the coexistence of osteoporosis and bony collapse.

The functional significance of posterolateral prolapse is irritation and compression of the spinal nerves as they pass through the intervertebral foramina. Since osteophyte formation at the edges of the apophyseal joints may also reduce the diameter of those foramina, protrusions may compress the nerves of the cauda equina.

When IV disc changes are severe, there are invariably alterations in the forces exerted upon the posterior intervertebral (apophyseal) joints. These synovial joints therefore commonly display the pathological changes of OA but bony ankylosis is rare except in the presence of ankylosing spondylitis or ankylosing hyperostosis (Forestier's disease).

ACKNOWLEDGEMENTS

In this section we have been privileged to be allowed to draw freely on the original investigations of Dr R. B. Longmore, Mr N. H. F. Wilson, Dr R. J. Elliott, Dr C. R. Orford, Mr K. Oates and Dr C. G. Armstrong to whom our thanks are due. We acknowledge the expert technical assistance of P. Sullivan, Carolyn Bartley, Janet Brereton and M. Hollinshead and we are grateful to Anne Mellor for the preparation of the manuscript. The continued work of this laboratory has been made possible by the support of the Medical Research Council, of the Arthritis and Rheumatism Council for Research and of Ciba-Geigy (Pharmaceuticals).

REFERENCES

Adams P, Muir H 1976 Qualitative changes with age of proteoglycans of human lumbar discs. Annals of the Rheumatic Diseases 35: 289–296

Akeson W H, Woo S L-Y, Taylor T K F, Ghosh P, Bushell G R 1977 Biomechanics and biochemistry of the intervertebral discs: the need for correlation studies. Clinical Orthopaedics and Related Research 129: 133–140

Armstrong C G, Bahrani A S, Gardner D L 1979 In vitro measurements of articular cartilage deformations in the intact human hip joint under load. Journal of Bone and Joint Surgery 61-A: 744–755

Armstrong C G, Bahrani A S, Gardner D L 1980 Changes in the deformational behaviour of human hip cartilage with age. Journal of Biomechanical Engineering 102: 214–220

Armstrong C G, Gardner D L 1977 Thickness and distribution of human femoral head articular cartilage. Annals of the Rheumatic Diseases 36: 407–412

Aspden R M, Hukins D W L 1979 Determination of the direction of preferred orientation and the orientation distribution function of collagen fibrils in connective tissues from high-angle X-ray diffraction patterns. Journal of Applied Crystallography 12: 306–311

Bailey A J, Light N D, Atkins E D T 1980 Chemical cross-linking restrictions on models for the molecular organization of the collagen fibre. Nature 228: 408–409

Ball J 1980 New knowledge of intervertebral disc disease. Journal of Clinical Pathology 31 supp. (Roy Coll. Path), 12: 200–204

Barnett C H, Cochrane W, Palfrey A J 1963 Age changes in articular cartilage of rabbits. Annals of the Rheumatic Diseases 22: 389–400

Bayliss M T, Venn M, Maroudas A, Ali S Y 1983 Structure of proteoglycans from different layers of human articular cartilage. Biochemical Journal 209: 387–400

Beard H K, Stevens R L 1980 Biochemical changes in the intervertebral disc. In: Jayson M I V (ed) The Lumbar Spine and Back Pain, 2nd edition. Tunbridge Wells, Pitman Medical, p 407–436

Berthet C, Hulmes D J S, Miller A, Timmins P A 1978 Structure of collagen in cartilage of intervertebral disk. Science 199: 547–549

Bullough P, Goodfellow J, O'Connor J 1973 The relationship between degenerative changes and load-bearing in the human hip. Journal of Bone and Joint Surgery 55-B: 746–758

Butler W F, Heap P 1982 An ultrastructural study of glycosaminoglycans associated with collagen and other constituents of the rat annulus fibrosus. Histochemical Journal 14: 113–124

Byers P D, Contepomi C A, Farkas T A 1970 A post-mortem study of the hip joint including the prevalence of the features of the right side. Annals of the Rheumatic Diseases 29: 15–31

Davies D V 1969 The biology of joints. In: Copeman W S C (ed) Textbook of the Rheumatic Diseases. (4th edn) E and S Livingstone, Edinburgh, London, p. 40–86

Egan M S, Goldenberg D L, Cohen A S, Segal D 1982 The association of amyloid deposits and osteoarthritis. Arthritis and Rheumatism 25: 204–208

Elliott R J, Gardner D L 1979 Changes with age in the glycosaminoglycans of human articular cartilage. Annals of the Rheumatic Diseases 38: 371–377

Franklin L, Hull E W 1966 Lipid content of the intervertebral disc. Clinical Chemistry 12: 253–257

Freeman M A R 1975 The fatigue of cartilage in the pathogenesis of osteoarthrosis. Acta Orthopaedica Scandinavica 46: 323–328

Freeman M A R, Meachim G 1979 Ageing and degeneration. In: Freeman M A R (ed) Adult Articular Cartilage, 2nd edition. Tunbridge Wells, Pitman Medical, p 487–543

Galante J O 1967 Tensile properties of human annulus fibrosus. Acta Orthopaedica Scandinavica (supp) 100: 8–91

Gardner D L 1983 The nature and causes of osteoarthrosis. British Medical Journal 286: 418–424

Gardner D L 1984a The Connective Tissue Diseases: their Pathological Basis. Edward Arnold, London (In press)

Gardner D L 1984b Structure and function of connective tissue and joints. In Scott J T (ed) Copeman's Textbook of the Rheumatic Diseases, 6th edition Churchill Livingstone, Edinburgh London New York (In Press)

Gardner D L 1984c Osteoarthrosis in man with particular reference to the hip and knee joints. In: Jasani K (ed) The Protection of Cartilage during the treatment of Osteoarthritis and Osteoarthrosis. Academic Press, New York London (In press)

Gardner D L, O'Connor P, Oates K, Orford C R 1983 An investigation by transmission electron microscopy of freeze replicas of dog articular cartilage surfaces: the fibre-rich surface structure. Journal of Anatomy 137: 573–582

Gardner D L, O'Connor P, Oates K 1981 Low temperature scanning electron microscopy of dog and guinea-pig hyaline articular cartilage. Journal of Anatomy 132: 267–282

Glenner G G, Page D L 1976 Amyloid, amyloidosis and amyloidogenesis. In: Richter G W, Epstein M A (ed) International Review of Experimental Pathology Volume 15. Academic Press, New York, San Francisco, London p 1–81

Goffin Y A, Thoua Y, Potuliege P R 1981 Microdeposition of amyloid in the joints. Annals of the Rheumatic Diseases 40: 27–33

Hamilton E B D, Bomford A B, Laws J W, Williams R 1981 The natural history of arthritis in idiopathic haemochromatosis — progression of the clinical and radiological features over 10 years. Quarterly Journal of Medicine 50: 321–330

Hickey D S, Hukins D W L 1979 Effects of methods of preservation on the arrangement of collagen fibrils in connective tissue matrices: an X-ray diffraction study of annulus fibrosus. Connective Tissue Research 6: 223–228

Hickey D S, Hukins D W L 1981 Collagen fibril diameters and elastic fibres in the annulus fibrosus of human fetal intervertebral disc. Journal of Anatomy 133: 351–359

Hilton R C, Ball J, Benn R T 1976 Vertebral end-plate lesions (Schmorl's nodes), in the dorso-lumbar spine. Annals of the Rheumatic Diseases 35: 127–132

Hilton R C, Ball J, Benn R T 1979 In-vitro mobility of the lumbar spine. Annals of the Rheumatic Diseases 38: 378–383

Hilton R C, Ball J, Benn R T 1980 Annular tears in the dorsolumbar spine. Annals of the Rheumatic Diseases 39: 533–538

Hunter W (1742–43) Of the structure and diseases of articulating cartilages. Philosophical Transactions 42: 514–521

Hutton W C, Cyron B M, Stott J R R 1979 The compressive strength of lumbar vertebrae. Journal of Anatomy 129: 753–758

Kempson G E 1979 Mechanical properties of articular cartilage. In: Freeman M A R (ed) Adult Articular Cartilage. Tunbridge Wells, Pitman Medical, p 333–414

Kempson G E, Muir H, Swanson S A V, Freeman M A R 1970 Correlations between stiffness and the chemical constitutents of cartilage on the human femoral head. Biochimica et Biophysica Acta 215: 70–77

Lane L B, Bullough P G 1980 Age-related changes in the thickness of the calcified zone and the number of tidemarks in adult articular cartilage. Journal of Bone and Joint Surgery 62-B: 372–375

Lipson S J, Muir H 1981 Experimental intervertebral disc degeneration — morphologic and proteoglycan changes over time. Arthritis and Rheumatism 24: 12–21

Longmore R B, Gardner D L 1975 Development with age of human articular cartilage surface structure. Annals of the Rheumatic Diseases 34: 26–37

Longmore R B, Gardner D L 1978 The surface structure of ageing human articular cartilage: a study by reflected light interference microscopy (RLIM). Journal of Anatomy 126: 353–365

Meachim G 1971 Effect of age on the thickness of adult articular cartilage at the shoulder joint. Annals of the Rheumatic Diseases 30: 43–46

Meachim G, Stockwell R A 1979 The matrix. In: Freeman M A R (ed) Adult Articular Cartilage, Tunbridge Wells, Pitman Medical, p 1–68

Middleton J F S, Oates K, O'Connor P, Orford C R, Gardner D L 1984 Surface structure of dog articular cartilage: scanning electron microscopy and X-ray microanalysis of bulk material at low temperature. Connective Tissue Research (In press)

Mitchell N, Shepard N 1981 Pericellular proteoglycan concentrations in early degenerative arthritis. Arthritis and Rheumatism 24: 958–964

Muir I H M 1979 Biochemistry. In: Freeman M A R (ed) Adult Articular Cartilage, Pitman Medical, London p 145–214

Oates K 1983 Personal communication

Orford C R, Gardner D L 1983 Proteoglycan association with collagen d band in hyaline articular cartilage. Connective Tissue Research (In press)

Orford C R, Gardner D L, O'Connor P 1983 Ultrastructural changes in dog femoral condylar cartilage following anterior cruciate ligament section. Journal of Anatomy 137: 653–663

Sayles R S, Thomas T R, Anderson J, Haslock I, Unsworth A 1979 Measurement of the surface microgeometry of articular cartilage. Journal of Biomechanics 12: 257–267

Schmorl G, Junghanns H 1971 The Human Spine in Health and Disease. Grune and Stratton, New York London

Schofield J D, Weightman B 1978 New knowledge of connective tissue ageing. Journal of Clinical Pathology 31 (Supp.) Roy. Coll. Path. 12: 174–180

Scott J E, Orford C R 1981 Dermatan-sulphate rich proteoglycan associates with rat tail tendon collagen at the d band in the gap region. Biochemical Journal 197: 213–216

Silberberg R 1972 Articular aging and osteoarthrosis in dwarf mice. Pathologia et Microbiologica 38: 417–430

Simon W H 1971 Scale effects in animal joints. II. Articular cartilage indentability and thickness. Arthritis and Rheumatism 14: 493–502

Sokoloff L 1969 The Biology of Degenerative Joint Disease. The University of Chicago Press, Chicago London

Stockwell R A 1979 Biology of Cartilage Cells. Cambridge University Press, New York Melbourne London Cambridge p 245–247

Szirmai J A 1970 Structure of the intervertebral disc. In: Balazs E A (ed) Chemistry and Molecular Biology of the Intercellular Matrix. Volume 3. Academic Press, London

Takeda T 1975 Three-dimensional observation of collagen framework of human lumbar discs. Journal of Japanese Orthopaedics 49: 45–57

Venn M F, Maroudas A 1977 Chemical composition and swelling of normal and osteoarthrotic femoral head cartilage. Annals of the Rheumatic Diseases 36: 121–129

Venn M F 1978 Variation of chemical composition with age in human femoral head cartilage. Annals of the Rheumatic Diseases 37: 168–174

Vernon-Roberts B 1980 The pathology and interrelation of intervertebral disc lesions, osteoarthrosis of the apophyseal joints, lumbar spondylosis and low back pain. In: Jayson M I V (ed) The Lumbar Spine and Back Pain. 2nd edition. Tunbridge Wells, Pitman Medical, p 83–114

Vernon-Roberts B, Pirie C J 1973 Healing trabecular microfractures in the bodies of lumbar vertebrae. Annals of the Rheumatic Diseases 32: 406–412

Vernon-Roberts B, Pirie C J 1977 Degenerative changes in the intervertebral discs and their sequelae. Rheumatology and Rehabilitation 16: 13–21

Weiss C 1979 Normal and osteoarthritic articular cartilage. Orthopaedic Clinics of North America 10: 175–189

Weiss C, Mirow S 1972 An ultrastructural study of osteoarthritic changes in the articular cartilage of human knees. Journal of Bone and Joint Surgery 54-A: 954–972

The musculoskeletal system — disease of the joints

OSTEOARTHROSIS

It is a moot point whether osteoarthrosis is in reality merely an exaggerated reflection of the aging process. Certainly the incidence of osteoarthrosis shows a very significant positive correlation with age (Lawrence et al, 1966; Silberberg et al, 1959). It has been estimated that 80 per cent of those over the age of 60 have some evidence of osteoarthrosis (Favour et al, 1956). In an English population survey (Kellgren and Lawrence, 1957) no less than 87 per cent of females and 83 per cent of males aged between 55 and 64 years showed X-ray evidence of osteoarthrosis. Only 22 per cent and 15 per cent, respectively, of these patients had symptoms. Cobb et al (1957), in a survey in Pittsburgh, found that 30 per cent of subjects with osteoarthrosis on X-ray experienced pain in the corresponding joints. Wood (1972) found that 8 per cent of patients with radiological osteoarthrosis of the hip and 12 per cent with changes in the knee were asymptomatic. Despite the fact that osteoarthrosis encountered radiologically may be asymptomatic, Gresham and Rathey (1957) have shown a significant correlation between the occurrence of clinical manifestations and the severity of the X-ray changes

More recently an American survey (Wilcock, 1979) undertaken in a population of 838 patients above the age of 66 years revealed that 5.6 per cent had symptoms that were suggestive of osteoarthrosis of the hip. Of these, 0.7 per cent had been operated on and a further 0.5 per cent would have benefited from hip replacement. An additional 1.3 per cent could have benefitted but were excluded on medical grounds as being unfit for surgery.

The incidence of osteoarthrosis is influenced by many factors other than age, including heredity, previous joint disease and trauma, metabolic factors (e.g. in ochronosis) and diet (e.g. Kashin Beck disease). Indeed, Dequeker et al (1969) showed, in a population of 140 women of various ages in a large psychiatric hospital, that whereas loss of stature, skin thickness and osteoporosis correlated strikingly with age, the correlation between osteoarthrosis and age was much weaker.

Clinical features

For a complete description of the clinical features of the various forms of osteoarthrosis the reader is referred to one of the standard textbooks on clinical rheumatology. It serves the present purpose to highlight some of the more common sources of error in diagnosis and treatment. In general terms, osteoarthrosis is not a difficult condition to diagnose. Classical features such as joint pain, stiffness and deformity unaccompanied by the signs of inflammation should lead one to suspect this condition. Difficulty arises when the condition is polyarticular, such as commonly occurs in the hands. The Heberden's node is rarely missed, but the less familiar Bouchard's node, which is the equivalent lesion in the proximal interphalangeal joint, is frequently misdiagnosed as rheumatoid arthritis, merely because of its unfamiliar situation (Fig. 39.1a). Fortunately, the X-ray appearances (Fig. 39.1b) are so characteristic as to make the distinction easy. Nor is this merely an academic exercise, for correct management will depend on an accurate diagnosis. Osteoarthrosis of the larger joints of the upper limb (e.g. wrist, elbow and shoulder) will manifest painful restriction of movement without much deformity. All these are relatively uncommon sites for the disease and in the case of the shoulder, osteoarthrosis is much rarer than capsulitis (see below).

Osteoarthrosis of the lower limbs may seriously impair the gait. With osteoarthrosis of the hip, the patient walks with a painful limp and finds difficulty in negotiating stairs and getting in and out of the bath. He may also have difficulty in rising from a low chair. A patient with bilateral osteoarthrosis of the hips is severely disabled and walks with a shuffling gait.

Involvement of the knees is probably the most potent source of morbidity from osteoarthrosis because of its high prevalence. In early cases the chief symptom is pain on certain activities such as climbing stairs, accompained by 'articular gelling', i.e. stiffness after a period of immobility. At this stage, the only significant physical sign may be crepitus felt on passive flexion of the joint, accompanied perhaps by some quadriceps wasting. Only

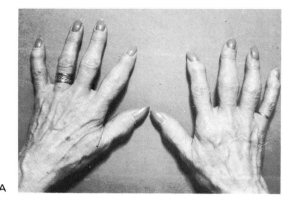

A

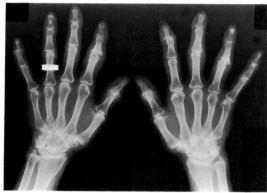

B

Fig. 39.1 (a) Polyarticular osteoarthrosis of the hands affecting the distal and proximal interphalangeal joints. (b) X-ray of the hands of the patient shown in (a) showing the characteristic radiological features of osteoarthrosis, *viz.* narrowing of joint space, sclerosis of juxta-articular bone and osteophyte formation.

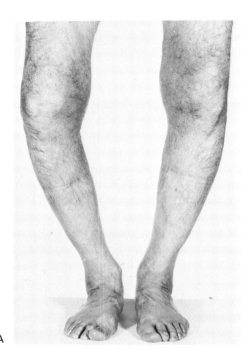

A

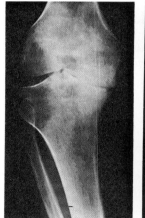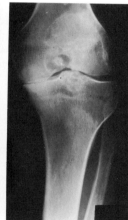

B

Fig. 39.2 (a) *Genu varum* produced by bilateral osteoarthrosis of the knees. (b) X-rays of patient shown in (a).

later does the joint lose its full range of flexion and extension. While the former is undesirable, the latter is much more serious in that it places the quadriceps at a serious disadvantage with a resulting loss of knee joint stability. This is responsible for the patient's complaint that the knee 'lets him down'. Furthermore, in the later stages, owing to the major brunt of the disease falling on the medial compartment, a *genu varum* deformity may occur (Fig. 39.2). Alteration of the centre of gravity in relation to the feet may cause a serious problem of balance. Though signs of inflammatory change in the joint are usually absent in this disease, one exception may be in the knee, which not infrequently shows an effusion.

The inflammatory exudate shows a low cell count (less than $0.5 \times 10^9/l$), low protein content (less than 3 g per dl) and high viscosity indicating that the inflammatory component is mild. Synovial biopsy shows a mild non-specific synovitis. This inflammatory reaction

almost certainly occurs in response to the presence within the joint of loose particles of degenerating cartilage. Evidence that this may be the result of inflammation caused by hydroxyapatite particles within the joint has been reported by Dieppe et al (1976).

The presence of an effusion within the knee joint in an ambulant patient may result (irrespective of the cause of the effusion) in the formation of a synovial cyst. Thus it is not unusual to palpate a cystic swelling within the popliteal fossa (Baker's cyst) which may on occasions

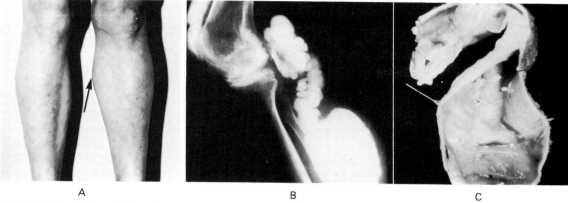

A   B   C

Fig. 39.3 (a) Synovial cyst of the calf. (b) Contrast arthrogram of patient shown in (a). (c) Cyst dissected out at operation (same patient as (a) and (b)).

spread down within the substance of the calf (Fig. 39.3). Though often symptomless, the synovial cyst may cause local pain, compress the popliteal vein and sometimes rupture and expel its contents into the tissues of the calf, producing the syndrome of 'acute synovial rupture'. This comprises pain, subcutaneous oedema and a positive Homan's sign which may be misinterpreted and diagnosed as a deep vein thrombosis.

Osteoarthrosis of the ankle is rare except after a Pott's fracture. In the feet the most common site of osteoarthrosis is the first metatarsophalangeal joint where it is commonly associated with long-standing hallux valgus.

The term generalized osteoarthrosis is defined as involvement of three or more joint groups. Three types have been described:

1. Primary generalized osteoarthrosis (Kellgren and Moore, 1952) in which Heberden's nodes are a prominent feature. This form is seen predominantly in females at around the time of the menopause. As age progresses, osteoarthritis of the hands becomes increasingly prevalent in both sexes with particular involvement of the distal inter-phalangeal joints (Heberden's nodes) of the index and middle fingers, whereas in the proximal interphalangeal joints no fingers are particularly favoured (Caird et al, 1973) (See Fig. 39.1).

2. Non-nodal generalized osteoarthrosis — more common in males — either following inflammatory polyarthritis of the metacarpophalangeal joints or occurring in hyperuricaemic subjects (Kellgren et al, 1963; Lawrence, 1969).

3. A recently described third variety affecting mainly males over the age of 60 and associated with hypertension. The hip and knees, carpometacarpal and metacarpophalangeal joints are mainly affected. Avascular necrosis of the femoral head is particularly common in this group (Lawrence, 1975).

Treatment of osteoarthrosis

General

While presently available treatment for this condition leaves much to be desired, nevertheless symptoms can be alleviated and joint function improved. Dietary restriction is advocated by most authorities for obese patients suffering from osteoarthrosis of the weight-bearing joints. This view has recently been challenged by Boyle and Buchanan (1971).

Drug therapy

Where pain is a troublesome symptom relief can be obtained with the use of simple analgesics, e.g. paracetamol, dihydrocodine, dextro-popoxyphene or pentazocine. Many patients, however, seem to derive more benefit from non-steroidal anti-inflammatory analgesic drugs (NSAID), particularly when inflammation (usually mild) is present. The whole question of the use of NSAID's in the elderly is considered on pp. 803 to 805.

Local treatment

Physical therapy. Various forms of physiotherapy, e.g. radiant heat, short-wave diathermy, wax baths, are soothing but on their own have no lasting benefit. When combined with active exercises, however, improvement, albeit temporary, may result. The purpose of these active exercises is two-fold. Firstly, to improve the range of joint movement, which has been reduced as a result of the disease; secondly, to improve the condition of the muscles that activate the diseased joint. Once the vicious circle (painful joint — muscle inhibition — muscle atrophy — impaired joint stability — worsening of joint disease) is broken, it is often possible to achieve considerable improvement in joint function by the use of physiotherapy in this way.

Intra-articular steroid injections. Local steroid injections into the joint are only likely to be of value in the presence of an inflammatory reaction. In clinical terms this usually means that an effusion is detectable and the joint may be warm. Such injections are likely to be most valuable in the presence of a transient synovitis precipitated by traumatising an osteoarthrotic joint. Persistent synovitis is less amenable (Friedman and Moore, 1980), and in the absence of synovitis the injections are not indicated. Details of the preparations used are given below.

Radiotherapy. Though radiotherapy has been advocated for the treatment of osteoarthrosis, a recent controlled clinical trial (Gibson et al, 1973) has shown that it is of no greater value than the standard course of physiotherapy in osteoarthrosis of the knee joint.

Surgery. Recent years have seen a movement away from arthrodesis and osteotomy towards arthroplasty, although osteotomy is still advocated for early osteoarthrosis of the hip and in cases of osteoarthrosis of the knee where realignment of the limb is required as in *genu varum.*

Earlier methods of hip arthroplasty such as the Smith-Petersen vitallium cup, the Austin-Moore and the Judet prostheses are now considered to be obsolete though there are many elderly patients about who still have them. Tillberg (1969) stressed the disappointing results of the vitallium cup prosthesis in 404 patients with osteoarthrosis of the hip whom he had followed for up to 11 years. Few surgeons now perform these operations, and the field had largely been taken over by the various forms of total hip replacement arthroplasty. Because they have been available for only a comparatively few years and their durability is therefore uncertain, surgeons are reluctant to perform these operations on young patients. The methods most commonly used in this country at the present time are:

1. The low friction arthroplasty (Charnley, 1965) composed of a stainless steel 'head' which articulates with the high density polyethylene socket.

2. The McKee-Farrar prosthesis (McKee and Watson-Farrar, 1966) incorporates a metal-on-metal vitallium device which is cemented into the femur and pelvis.

3. The Ring prosthesis (Ring, 1968), a two-piece prosthesis of chrome and cobalt alloy. The acetabular component is screwed into the pelvis in the direction of the sacroiliac joint but no cement is used.

Although encouraging results have been obtained in the short follow-up time available by the protagonists of these three total hip replacement prostheses, caution is advised until longer follow-up has been possible and the hazards of mechanical failure and infection assessed. Sepsis in relation to a cemented prosthesis is a disastrous complication, since it necessitates the removal of the prosthesis, a very formidable undertaking. Occasionally the prosthesis may fail through fracture or dislodgement. Notwithstanding these comments, it should be emphasized that many patients who have been subjected to one or other of these prosthetic operations have undoubtedly benefited to a very large degree.

The development of a satisfactory knee prosthesis presents serious technical problems. There are two main types. The first, such as the Waldius (1957) and the Shiers (1960), involves resection of the joint and replacement by a plastic or metal hinge. In the second, a mould is interposed between the bony surfaces after excision of the articular cartilage and synovial membrane. Platt (1969) has developed a stainless steel mould and has reported a favourable outcome in 49 patients after 10 years. When the disease is chiefly confined to either the lateral or medial compartments of the knee, a metallic plateau such as that designed by Mackintosh (1958) or McKever (1960) may be inserted on to the tibial table. A series of such operations in patients suffering from osteoarthrosis of the knee reported by Potter (1969) has given favourable results in 90 per cent of cases.

More recently a newer generation of knee replacement prostheses has been developed in which the tibial and femoral condyles have been replaced by separate components one of which is metal, the other high density polyethylene. They have the advantage of requiring less cement, sacrifice of less bone with fewer complications, e.g. infection and loosening. A number of such devices are available of which the polycentric (Gunston, 1971) and the Geomedic (Coventry et al, 1972) have been the most widely used.

In summary, it might be said that the current trend in surgical treatment of osteoarthrosis is towards the replacement of the badly affected joint with a prosthesis which is mechanically sound and which at the same time provokes no tissue reaction. The need for careful clinical evaluation backed by substantial follow-up explains the slow but encouraging progress in this field of research.

DEGENERATIVE DISEASE OF THE SPINE

Degenerative changes similar to those seen in osteoarthrosis of peripheral joints frequently occur with advancing age in the apophyseal joints, the neurocentral joints and the costovertebral joints. The situation is complicated by degenerative changes which occur in the intervertebral discs. Epidemiological studies have demonstrated the high prevalence of cervical disc degeneration in particular. In one study, 87 per cent of males and 74 per cent of females between the ages of 65 and 74 years showed radiological evidence of cervical disc degeneration (Lawrence et al, 1963). The same survey revealed radiological evidence of lumbar disc degeneration in 60 per cent of males and 44 per cent of females over the age of 35 years. Not only is it more common in men but there is a clear-cut correlation with heavy manual work (e.g. dock-workers). Other factors which predispose to premature disc degeneration include kyphoscoliosis, postural disorders and ochronosis.

In a survey of 4500 residents of the American town of Tecumseh the increasing prevalence of cervical spondylosis with age was clearly demonstrated in both sexes (Mikkelsen et al, 1970).

Clinical picture
The majority of patients who show radiological evidence of degenerative disease of the spine are symptom-free. In some cases, the onset of symptoms may be related to a traumatic episode, but in many others the precipitating factor or factors are not known. The clinical picture will depend on which region of the spine is involved.

Cervical spine
In the cervical region a number of syndromes can be delineated as follows:

1. Pain arising in the apophyseal joints — leading to reduced range of movement and accompanied by reflex muscle spasm.

2. Nerve root irritation resulting from cervical disc protrusion or foraminal encroachment by osteophytes.

3. Cervical myelopathy which results from cervical cord compression and manifests as long-tract signs, in particular pyramidal signs in the lower limbs.

4. Vertebrobasilar artery obstruction resulting in transient brain-stem ischaemia.

A patient with cervical spondylosis may thus complain of local pain arising from apophyseal joints, radicular pain, paraesthesiae, numbness or weakness in the arms, ataxia and weakness in the legs, or symptoms of brain-stem ischaemia or any combination of these. It should be reiterated that he may complain of no symptoms at all and this is probably the case in the majority. A careful neurological assessment is clearly of extreme importance and undue emphasis should not be given to X-ray findings in the absence of any neurological disturbance.

Treatment of cervical spondylosis. In the absence of symptoms or evidence of neurological disorder no treatment is required, other than reassurance. It is important to avoid any unwarranted invalidism resulting from the patient's anxiety about her X-ray appearances which may have been imparted to her.

If the symptoms are limited to local pain and there is no evidence of neurological disturbance, treatment usually consists of rotation exercises in flexion preceded by a period of radiant heat. Some schools advocate

manipulation but it should be avoided in elderly subjects, unless the physician or therapist is well experienced in this technique. Maitland's (1973) mobilizations are now widely used by physiotherapists to treat those patients who fail to respond to exercise therapy. Being a much gentler form of treatment than manipulation, it is much safer and is applicable to elderly subjects with neck stiffness due to spondylosis without neurological sequelae.

Radicular symptoms almost invariably respond to the application of a cervical collar. 'Plastizote', which was recently introduced, appears to be more effective and more comfortable than the more rigid polythene varieties and certainly more effective than a soft foam rubber which does little to immobilize the neck. The collar should be worn continuously and particularly at night as radicular symptoms are troublesome at this time. In most cases, there will be a favourable outcome in a few weeks, and once the symptoms have subsided the collar may be left off.

It is only rarely necessary to advocate traction, which should be used with great caution in elderly patients. A collar is also helpful in those who develop basilar ischaemia as a result of their cervical spondylosis.

In the presence of evidence of cord compression a neurosurgical opinion should be sought. A myelogram would then be indicated as a preoperative procedure. The occurrence of acute radicular pain, which may or may not be accompanied by sensory symptoms or signs of sensory or motor loss, may herald the onset of an acute prolapsed cervical intervertebral disc. This is not a common lesion but requires prompt management. The patient should be nursed flat in bed where feasible with the head immobilized between sandbags or by the use of a well-fitting collar. Analgesics should be given as required and the patient treated thus until the acute symptoms subside. At his stage, he may be allowed up in the collar and gradually resume normal activities.

(Cervical spondylosis — presentation and management — see also pp. 410, 411)

The dorsal spine
The dorsal spine is commonly a site of spondylosis but this only rarely produces symptoms. Occasionally, there will be localized pain in the dorsal region (with or without radiation to the appropriate intercostal space) which may be exacerbated by percussion and palpation of the individual affected area or by rotating the upper part of the truck in either direction. In old people it is important to exclude metastatic or myelomatous deposits in the spine if the pain is recent. This applies in particular to the dorsal region, which should therefore be X-rayed. Treatment includes short-wave diathermy, mobilizing exercises, Maitland's mobilizations or a dorsolumbar spinal support.

The lumbar spine

The lumbar spine is also predisposed to spondylotic changes: degenerative changes may arise as part of a generalized disorder associated with advancing age or may result from disc lesions acquired earlier in life. Backache is the usual presenting symptom. Physical examination reveals loss of the normal lumbar curve and reduction in the range of spinal movements in all directions. As in the cervical region, radicular pain such as sciatica or anterior thigh pain as in L.4 lesions may result from osteophytic involvement of nerve root foramina or, if of sudden onset, indicate an acute intervertebral disc protrusion. It is not widely appreciated that acute disc lesions are common in elderly people. The clinical presentation often differs from the classical picture of the acute lumbar prolapsed intervertebral disc seen in younger subjects. In young adults, the commonly affected discs are the L.4–5 and the L.5–S.1 discs which result in classical sciatica. In elderly subjects, it is common to encounter disc lesions involving the upper lumbar nerve roots. Compression of these roots by an acutely prolapsed disc results in pain which is often appreciated in the groin or anterior thigh and is commonly misdianosed as disease of the hip or knee joint. Neurological signs may be absent or inconspicuous, an absent knee jerk being the only abnormality detected. However, the femoral nerve-stretch test is a very helpful indication that this referred pain is arising in the upper lumbar nerve roots. In this test the patient lies prone on the bed, the knee is passively flexed, and if the test is positive a sudden pain is produced in the distribution of the femoral nerve, i.e. in the anterior region of the thigh. It is a useful test not only in diagnosis but in gauging the response to treatment. It is the upper lumbar equivalent of the straight leg raising test described by Lasègue for detecting tension in the sciatic nerve or its roots. As has recently been shown in our own studies of 377 patients admitted to hospital for back-pain problems, that cruralgia (pain in the anterior thigh) as a manifestation of root compression was significantly more common in those over the age of 60 years than in younger subjects (Grahame, 1977).

Another cause of backache in elderly subjects which may be difficult to diagnose clinically but is readily revealed on X-ray examination is spondylolisthesis. This lesion, which most commonly occurs at the L.4–5 or L.5–S.1 levels, probably develops as a result of advanced degenerative changes in the apophyseal joints at these levels.

As with the cervical spine, a conservavative approach to the problem of lumbar spondylosis and disc degeneration in elderly subjects is generally advocated. The acute lumbar disc prolapse almost invariably settles with a few days of lying flat in bed and it is only very rarely that other procedures such as traction, epidural corti-costeroid injections or surgical intervention are needed. Traction is rarely tolerated by elderly subjects and is an unsuitable form of treatment in this age group. Epidural injections of methyl prednisolone in normal saline by the translumbar route have been shown in a controlled trial to be effective in the management of lumbar disc lesions with nerve root compression (Dilke et al, 1973). Their prompt effect in an otherwise prostrating condition is of especial value in elderly subjects, although technical difficulties may occasionally be encountered in entering the epidural space in the presence of gross spondylotic changes. Many patients with backache associated with lumbar spondylosis will respond to a short course of physiotherapy in the form of heat and mobilizing exercises. In others, gentle manipulation may be advocated. Where these methods fail, a surgical corset will often relieve symptoms. It is not possible to predict which patient will respond to which form of treatment and in the large multi-centre trial involving 456 patients with low back pain, randomly allocated to one of the following: manipulation, physiotherapy (other than manipulative), surgical corset or analgesic tablets, no one form of therapy showed itself to be superior to any of the others (Doran and Newell, 1975) A corset is the treatment of choice in spondylolisthesis though, where this is not tolerated or where it fails, a spinal fusion operation will be necessary.

Vertebral ankylosing hyperostosis. An entity likely to be confused with either ankylosing spondylitis or spondylosis is called vertebral ankylosing hyperostosis or Forestier's disease (Forestier and Lagier, 1971). It is characterized by continuous or discontinuous bony outgrowths over the anterior convexities of vertebral bodies and their corresponding discs. Thus, in the cervical and the lumbar regions, bony spurs occur, while in the dorsal region adjacent spurs coalesce to form bony bridges. In cervical involvement both cord compression (Gibson and Schumacher, 1976) and dysphagia (Meeks and Renshaw, 1973) have been reported. The intervertebral discs themselves are intact as are the apophyseal and sacroiliac joints (Fig. 39.4). Similar 'fluffy' bony outgrowths may be seen in relation to the larger peripheral joints notably the hip (Harris et al, 1974). Unlike osteophytes, these are para-articular and are not part of arthrotic remodelling. Two-thirds of cases are in males and 88 per cent occur over the age of 50. A prevalence rate of 1.3 per cent has been reported by Julkunen et al (1974), the prevalence rising with age. There appears to be a definite association with diabetes mellitus and acromegaly. Pain, decreased mobility and deformity are minimal and the condition is usually discovered by radiography. The pathogenesis of the condition is unknown but heavy physical labour is not a predisposing factor. Patients are generally thickset and obese.

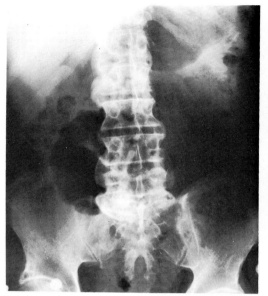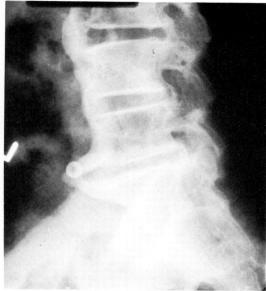

Fig. 39.4 Antero/posterior and lateral views of the lumbar spine of a patient suffering from vertebral ankylosing hyperostosis, showing development of florid bony osteophytic bridging with normal sacroiliac joints.

Other causes of back pain in the elderly

Although, without doubt, degenerative spinal disease is the most common cause of back pain in elderly subjects, the possibility that it might be due to bone pathology of an infective, metabolic or neoplastic origin should be bourne in mind. This is particularly so where fever, weight loss or anaemia are present. Pyogenic discitis, tuberculosis of the spine, multiple myeloma or spinal metastases from primary carcinoma of the lung, breast, thyroid, adrenal or prostate may all present with back pain and these are all diseases whose prevalence increases with advancing age (Sarkin, 1977). The reader is referred to the relevant chapters of this book.

RHEUMATOID ARTHRITIS AND RELATED DISEASES

The pattern in old age

With the possible exception of early infancy, rheumatoid arthritis may commence at any age. Because of the chronicity and low mortality of the disease many patients carry their rheumatoid disease with them into old age. In some the disease will have become inactive. In others persistent activity may continue over many years or decades so that fresh joint damage may occur in the latter years. In yet a third group, the disease may manifest itself for the first time in old age. It is with this group that this section is largely concerned. A number of recent studies have emphasized the way in which rheu-matoid disease presenting in old age differs from that seen in younger patients.

Ehrlich et al (1970) studied 79 patients over the age of 60 who were suffering from 'definite' or 'classical' rheumatoid arthritis according to the ARA criteria. They compared the 36 who developed the disease before their sixtieth birthday with the 43 whose disease commenced after that age. The average age of onset in the two groups was 46.4 and 66.9 years respectively. The sex ratio female: male was 5 : 1 in the younger onset group and 2.5 : 1 in the older onset group. The distribution of joint involvement was similar in the two groups, but synovitis of the ankles and wrists was significantly less frequent in both sexes and the hip less frequent in males in the older onset group. There appeared to be no difference in the incidence of Sjögren's syndrome, of rheumatoid nodules, or of positive Latex fixation tests for rheumatoid factor in the two groups. Radiological changes were more severe in the group with the later age of onset, but there was less deformity in those cases. The response to gold therapy was better in those patients whose disease started over the age of 60. In both groups systemic features such as weight loss, lymph node and splenic enlargement and prolonged morning stiffness were much less common than in a group of young patient who were also studied.

In a smaller series, Adler (1966) studied 20 patients whose disease started over the age of 55 years. Deformities were rare and nodules occurred in none of the patients.

Ebert (1967) described 67 patients whose disease commenced over the age of 60 (87 per cent Latex positive). The outcome was benign in 10, progressive in 36 and explosive or malignant in 21. Brown and Sones (1967) studied a series of 156 patients from the Mayo Clinic whose rheumatoid disease began after the age of 65 years. The sex incidence was equal; the onset insidious in 69 per cent, abrupt in 26 per cent and episodic in 4 per cent. Morning stiffness in excess of two hours was present in 35 per cent. Joints affected in descending order of frequency were metacarpophalangeal, knee, shoulder, proximal interphalangeal, metatarsophalangeal, ankle and elbow joints. Anaemia was present in one-third of cases and in 15 per cent the ESR was in excess of 60 mm in one hour. One interesting finding was that a malignant process developed in 9 patients from 1 to 10 years after the onset of joint symptoms (see 'Arthritis and Malignant Disease').

Moesmann (1968) reported 85 consecutive patients with rheumatoid arthritis whose disease commenced after the age of 50. The female to male sex ratio was 1.29: 1. An abrupt onset was very common and 85 per cent of patients sought medical advice within one month of symptoms. The prognosis was no better than in the earlier onset type.

In a further series of 24 patients whose rheumatoid disease commenced over the age of 60 years, Oka and Kytila (1957) noted a female: male ratio of 1.1 : 1, an acute onset in one-third of cases, a predilection for involvement of the foot, wrist and knee and a tendency towards a high sedimentation rate.

In our own small series (Gibson and Grahame, 1971) 12 patients suffering from sero-positive rheumatoid arthritis with acute onset after the age of 70 were studied. The average age of onset was 79 years (range 70 to 88). The mean length of follow-up was 1.5 years and the mean duration of symptoms prior to examination was 5 weeks. Morning stiffness was present in three patients and nodules in one-quarter of the patients. Joint involvement was similar to that in younger patients. Erosions were seen on X-ray in half the patients and osteoporosis in one. The average sedimentation rate at onset was 69 mm and in four patients it rose to above 100 mm. The average differential agglutination titre was 1 : 128, though in some cases it rose to 1 : 1024. The Latex test was positive in all cases.

On follow-up, seven showed inactive disease at the end of the survey, six were treated with prednisolone (up to 7 mg per day) with satisfactory results, and one died.

A group of seven sero-negative patients, average age 73.5 years, was also followed up with exactly similar findings (including an average sedimentation rate of 69 mm). After 15 months, five were symptom-free and one had died.

One variant of rheumatoid arthritis which is seen in elderly subjects whose disease has been present for decades and who have led a life of enforced immobility is known as 'ankylosing rheumatoid arthritis'. It is characterized by widespread bony ankylosis of peripheral and central joints particularly those of the cervical spine. These patients can be distinguished from patients with ankylosing spondylitis by the absence of sacro-iliac joint involvement and of the antigen HLA B27 (Grahame et al, 1975).

The essentially benign prognosis has been recently confirmed in an Australian study (Corrigan et al, 1974) of 110 patients who developed their rheumatoid arthritis over the age of 60 years. They distinguished two subgroups: a larger group (74 per cent), whose disease was not noticeably different from that seen in younger patients, and a smaller group (26 per cent), who exhibited an explosive onset with marked systemic upset but whose disease remitted within 18 months in all cases.

From these various surveys (with occasionally contradictory findings) the following conclusions may be reached.

Rheumatoid arthritis commences in the latter decades of life in a substantial proportion of patients. The female preponderance seen in younger rheumatoid subjects tends to disappear. The onset is often abrupt, even explosive. The joints involved are as in the young. The sedimentation rate is often markedly elevated and may remain so despite the later subsidence of clinical arthritis. Tests for rheumatoid factor often show a particularly high titre, not necessarily associated with a bad prognosis. Erosions and nodules are less common than in younger subjects, and rheumatoid arteritis distinctly rare in subjects developing rheumatoid disease in old age. With the exception of anaemia, extra-articular manifestations, e.g. pulmonary involvement, neuropathy and digital ischaemia, are not commonly seen.

Rheumatoid arthritis may be confused with polymyalgia rheumatica (PMR) (see chapter 18) and vice versa. The reason for this is two-fold. Firstly, some elderly rheumatoid patients experience diffuse muscle pains without synovitis in the earlier stages (Dimant, 1979: Weinberger, 1980), and secondly, occasionally polymyalgia rheumatica itself may be accompanied by synovitis in joints (Bruk, 1967; Henderson et al, 1975).

Management

The general principles of treatment in the elderly are the same as in other patients. The following points, however, deserve special mention:

Rest

Prolonged bed rest during the acute phase of the disease

should be applied with caution because of the risks of bed sores and deep vein thrombosis in this age group.

Splintage

Elderly subjects are particularly prone to develop contractures so that splinting of the inflamed joints especially wrists and knees is of particular importance (Fig. 39.5).

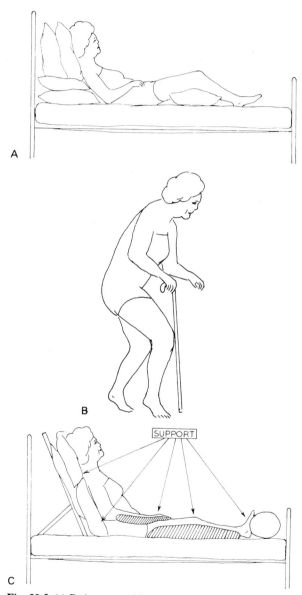

Fig. 39.5 (a) Patient nursed incorrectly without splinting of the knee or wrist. (b) Same patient when later attempting to walk. She is severely handicapped by the resulting fixed flexion deformities. (c) Correct method of supporting wrist, knee, spine and ankle in the course of active joint disease (reproduced by courtesy of the Editor, *Nursing Times*).

Intra-articular steroids

Intra-articular injections of corticosteroid preparations are often beneficial during phases of acute or recurrent joint inflammation in rheumatoid arthritis and related diseases: also in some cases of osteoarthrosis accompanied by inflammation (see above). Care to avoid introducing infection is particularly important in elderly and debilitated subjects whose resistance to infection may be impaired; also avoid such injections in joints already infected by bacteria or viruses. Thus, synovial fluid should always be aspirated before the steroid is injected and if the fluid is purulent or merely suspected of being purulent, the steroid should not be injected until the results of bacteriological culture are available.

The preparations currently available are (in alphabetical order):

Dexa-methasone sodium phosphate (Dose 0.8–4 mg)
Hydrocortisone acetate (5 and 50 mg)
Methylprednisolone acetate (4–80 mg)
Prednisolone acetate (5–25 mg)
Prednisolone pivalate (10–50 mg)
Prednisolone sodium phosphate (1.6–24 mg)
Triamcinolone acetonide (2.5–40 mg)
Triamcinolone hexacetonide (2–30 mg)

Of these hydrocortisone acetate and prednisolone acetate have the shortest action and are the cheapest, whereas the remaining preparations are believed to have a longer action and are considerably more expensive. Repeated intra-articular injections carry a greater risk of introducing iatrogenic infection, but the deleterious effect on articular cartilage previously ascribed to repeated steroid injections has probably been exaggerated (Gibson et al, 1977).

Non-steroidal anti-inflammatory drugs (NSAID's)

The last decade has seen a veritable explosion in the introduction of new NSAID's, widely used in the treatment of a variety of rheumatic diseases. The availability varies from country to country but at the time of writing, no less than 26 distinct drugs in this category are available in the United Kingdom (British National Formulary, 1982). In the United States only nine are available (Hunder and Bunch, 1982).

Because they combine analgesia with an anti-inflammatory effect, NSAID's have wide application in Rheumatology. Thus, they are effective in acute gout (see page 809), rheumatoid arthritis and other forms of chronic inflammatory joint diseases, where they form the mainstay of drug therapy in the early stages; in osteoarthrosis where they tend to be more effective than simple analgesics (such as paracetamol, dextropropoxyphene and pentazocine) and in a variety of soft tissue conditions where they give little more than symptomatic relief (Hart, 1976).

The rationale behind the NSAID explosion lies in the high incidence of side-effects experienced with the older druges in this category — aspirin, phenylbutazone, indomethacin. The quest has been for drugs with equivalent potency but with improved tolerability. Although the newer drugs have a lower incidence of serious adverse reactions, notably on bone marrow, their record in terms of gastric irritation and even haemorrhage in not as good as had been hoped. This latter effect reflects the potent blocking effect on prostaglandin synthesis which characterizes the mode of action of most members of this group of drugs. This problem has been aptly illustrated in a recently published gastroscopic study of over 200 patients with rheumatoid arthritis and osteoarthritis which showed that 31 per cent in both disease catagories had gastric erosions (23 per cent in patients receiving a single drug and 51 per cent in patients receiving combined treatment). The patients in question had all been receiving one or more of 12 anti-inflammatory drugs, none of which was exonerated although aspirin-treated patients had the greatest incidence and sulindac and diflunisal the least (Caruso and Porro, 1980).

Although comparative trials have been undertaken between newer NSAID's and either placebo or the older drugs in this category, it is very difficult to perceive an overall picture of relative efficacy between the members of this very large group of agents. One trial attempted to place four non-steroidal drugs, fenoprofen, ibuprofen, ketoprofen and naproxen in rank order of greatest efficacy and least toxicity in 90 patients with rheumatoid arthritis (RA). In that trial naproxen scored highest (Huskisson et al, 1976). More recently, the same investigators compared naproxen with two newer NSAID's, diclofenac sodium, an acetic acid derivative and diflunisal, a fluorinated derivative of aspirin in 90 patients with RA (Huskisson et al, 1982). The efficacy of the three drugs was similar though some trends favoured diclofenac. Side effects were generally mild and were equally distributed among the three drugs. By and large, the choice of a NSAID for an individual patient rests on a basis of trial and error. There is probably little to choose between the various drugs in terms of efficacy although individual patients do appear to derive better results with certain drugs. Variation in tolerability is wide and difficult to predict in individual patients. The risks of NSAID treatment should not be underestimated, particularly in the elderly and consequently they should be used with discretion and after carefully weighing up the benefits and possible hazards. This is particularly aposite in cases where it would be more appropriate to use local treatment, e.g. local corticosteroid injections and/or physiotherapy in soft tissue lesions, when non-steroidal drugs are hardly justified.

Table 39.1 sets out currently available drugs according to their chemical classification and gives details of indications, dose, side-effects and interactions with particular regard to elderly subjects.

Gold

Many authors have stressed that gold is frequently efficacious in the treatment of rheumatoid disease in old people. With due care in the early recognition of side-effects (notably repeated and frequent examination of the peripheral blood, urine and skin), there is no reason why this form of treatment should not be used.

Providing patients respond and are not troubled by side-effects chrysotherapy can be continued indefinitely to good effect. Recent practice has been towards more flexibility in dosage. The original Empire Rheumatism Council Trial (1961) advocated 50 mg of sodium aurothiomalate (myocrysin; myochrysine) weekly to a total of 1 g and this has become the established accepted dose. A weekly dosage of 10 mg appears to be as effective as 50 mg (McKenzie, 1981). In responders it is customary to continue with monthly injections of myocrysin 50 mg providing there are no side-effects. There appears to be no advantage in increasing the maintenance injections to fortnightly (Griffin et al, 1981).

However, there is some evidence to suggest that advancing age is associated with a less favourable therapeutic response to gold (Billings et al, 1975), and a greater liability to toxic reactions (DeBosset and Bitter, 1975).

D-penicillamine

Since the publication of the multicentre trial of d-penicillamine in the treatment of rheumatoid arthritis (1973) this drug has been widely used and it may be more effective than gold in delaying the progression of radiographic erosions (Gibson et al, 1976). Side-effects, though frequent, are usually not severe. However, a careful watch should be kept for skin reactions, proteinuria and thrombocytopaenia and the drug stopped in all cases (except for minor rashes). Frequent blood and platelet counts are mandatory as irreversible aplastic anaemia has been reported.

Corticosteroids

Most authorities condemn the widespread use of systemic corticosteroids in the treatment of rheumatoid arthritis because of the serious side-effects that may occur: in particular, osteoporosis, skin atrophy, cataract, suppression of the hypothalamic-pituitary-adrenal (HPA) axis, predisposition to infection and peptic ulceration. First impressions are that in frail elderly people side-effects would be particularly hazardous and therefore steroids contraindicated. However, it has recently been shown (Grahame, 1969) that in the case of skin atrophy a correlation exists between the thinning effect and the

Table 39.1 Non-steroidal anti-inflammatory drugs available in the United Kingdom in 1984

Class	Drug	Total daily dose	Dose interval (hours)	Tolerability in elderly	Special comments	References
Salicylates	Aspirin			Poor		Fowler, 1967; Inman, 1977
	Aspirin Dispersable	4 g	4	Moderate	Risk of gastric erosion	
	Aspirin Enteric Coated			Moderate		
	Aloxiprin			Moderate		
	Benorylate	8 g	12	Good	Ester of aspirin and paracetamol	
	Choline Magensium Trisalicylate	2–3 g	12			
	Salsalate	3–4 g	8			
	Sodium Salicylate					
	Diflunisal	0–5–1 g	12		Of use in rheumatic fever	
Pyrazoles	Phenylbutazone	200–600 mg	8	Poor	Risk of aplastic anaemia, GI bleeding — best avoided	Powell-Jackson, 1977; Ritch et al 1982
	Oxyphenbutazone	400–600 mg	8–12	Poor		
	Feprazone	200–600 mg	8–12			
	Azapropazone	1.2 g	6–12		Interaction with Warfarin; reduced renal clearance in elderly	
Indenes	Indomethacin	50–200 mg	8–12	Poor	High risk of gastric ulcer, giddiness, headache common	O'Brien, 1968
	Sulindac	200–400 mg	12	Good		Khan, 1980; Ghosh and Rastogi, 1981
Fenamates	Mefanamic Acid	1.5 G	8	Good		
	Flufenamic Acid	400–600 mg	8			
Propionic acid derivatives	Ibuprofen	0.6–1.6	6	Good		Choussat et al, 1978; Buckler, 1975
	Ketoprofen	100–200 mg	6–12	Good		Khan, 1980; McMahon, 1976; Innes, 1977; Brook and Jackson, 1982
	Naproxen	0.5–1 g	12	Moderate		
	Fenoprofen	0.9–2.4 g	6–8	Moderate		
	Flurbiprofen	150–300 mg	6–8			
	Fenbufen	600 mg–900 mg	12–24			
Aryl acetic acid derivatives	Fenclofenac	600–1200 mg	12	Poor		Swain et al, 1980
Pyrrole-acetic acid derivatives	Diclofenac	50–150 mg	8–12	Good	Pharmacokinetics = young adults (6)	Willis et al, 1978; Cannella et al, 1979
	Tolmetin	0.6–1.8 g	6–12			
Oxicams	Piroxicam	20 mg	24	Good	Beware occasional GI haemorrhage	Dessain et al, 1979; Emery et al, 1982
Thienylacetic acid derivative	Tiaprofenic Acid	600 mg	8	Good		Meurice 1982

total dose of corticosteroid administered over the years. Since life expectancy is short it follows that steroid therapy is likely to be required for a relatively short period in old age. The chance of developing this particular complication is correspondingly small. The same may apply to other long-term complications of steroid therapy. This premise may justify the limited use of steroids in active rheumatoid disease in elderly subjects. In practice, with a dose of up to 7.5 mg of prednisolone daily, side-effects do not pose any serious problem, and in most cases this dose is sufficient to control the activity of the disease. Often it enables the elderly patient who is virtually immobilized by joint stiffness to become once again fully mobile and active. High-dose steroids should be avoided as elderly subjects are particularly prone to develop vertebral collapse, diabetes, psychosis and hypertension (Davison, 1980).

Immunosuppressive drugs

In the small proportion of patients whose rheumatoid disease activity is unresponsive to the drugs mentioned above immunosuppressive drugs may be required. These are hazardous drug particularly in elderly subjects because of their liability to cause bone marrow depression. They should, therefore, be used with extreme caution and only when other measures have failed. Of the various drugs available in this category azathioprine is the one that has been most extensively tried. By and large the results indicate efficacy that is comparable with gold, chloroquine (Dwosh et al, 1977) and d-penicillamine (Berry et al, 1976), but with a higher incidence of side-effects.

Antimalarials

Chloroquine and hydroxychloroquine have both been shown in clinical trials to possess remission-inducing properties in rheumatoid arthritis but their effect is weaker than that of gold of penicillamine. It is thought that chloroquine is twice as affective through twice as toxic as hydroxychloroquine (McConkey, 1982). The overriding side-effect is retinal damage which once established may be permanent. This has, undoubtedly, reduced the popularity of this drug in rheumatoid arthritis. However, it is now clear that provided the patient is examined by an ophthalmologist at 6-monthly intervals and is given no more than 250 mg chloroquine or 400 mg hydroxychloroquine daily the chances of serious retinal damage are minimal.

Surgery

In the presence of active rheumatoid synovitis, persisting despite the use of the various general and local measures referred to above, the operation of synovectomy should be considered. In this operation, the inflamed synovial membrane is removed as completely as possible, often with very satisfactory relief in pain, swelling and disability. The success of the operation largely depends on the absence of gross destructive change within the joint. The knee joint has been most widely submitted to this procedure but others, including the wrist, metacarpophalangeal and proximal interphalangeal joints of the hands, and occasionally the elbow and shoulder joint, have also been treated in this way. Marmor (1967) has performed synovectomy of the knee in 58 subjects over the age of 50, 17 of whom were aged between 60 and 69 years and 10 between 70 and 79 years. One patient was 83 years old. The length of follow-up ranged from 6 months to 3 years and pain relief was reported as pronounced in all cases after the operation. There were no instances of recurrence of synovitis.

Where considerable joint destruction has occurred, alternative operations are required. In the wrist, arthrodesis results in a pain-free, stable joint with a beneficial effect on hand function. This operation is widely used to good effect. In cases of gross destruction of the knee or hip, arthrodesis is sometimes performed, though many surgeons now advocate a replacement arthroplasty. Prosthetic arthroplasty is also available for destructive arthritis affecting the small joints of the hands or in the presence of fixed swan-neck deformity of the proximal interphalangeal joints.

For the hands the Flatt (1963) stainless steel alloy hinge arthroplasty (available in five sizes) and the Swanson (1968) silicone rubber prosthesis are also available. The latter consists of a central block and two stems which are inserted into the medullary canals of the articulating bones. Flexion and extension result from the intrinsic elasticity of the prosthesis itself. Many surgeons have reservations about the use of either of these two prostheses and the outcome of long-term follow-up studies is awaited with interest.

Rehabilitation

The general principles of rehabilitation and their applicability to joint disease are described in chapter 51. A recent review is that of Gibson and Grahame (1981).

Ulnar deviation in the elderly

Ulnar deviation is a common and well-recognized manifestation of metacarpophalangeal involvement in rheumatoid and related diseases. However, caution must be used in ascribing ulnar deviation to an arthropathy in elderly subjects in the absence of pain, stiffness and swelling of the metacarpophalangeal joints, since ulnar deviation may occur as a normal phenomenon of aging. Wigsell (1976), in a study of 100 elderly female subjects aged 70 to 90 years, found the mean ulnar deviation of the middle finger to be 7.55° on the left and 6.31° on the right. Twenty-five per cent showed a deviation of between 11° and 25°. There was no correlation between handedness or previous manual labour.

Sero-negative polyarthritis

Of the sero-negative polyarthritides, sero-negative rheumatoid disease has been dealt with above and crystal synovitis is the subject of the next section. Ankylosing spondylitis, Reiter's disease, Behçet's syndrome and arthropathies associated with regional enteritis, ulcerative colitis and Whipple's disease rarely commence in old age and will not therefore be considered further.

Psoriatic arthritis

Of a group of 227 patients with psoriatic arthritis, only 6 per cent of males and 16 per cent of females developed their articular symptoms after the age of 65 years (Roberts et al, 1976). The males in this age group exhibited the distal interphalangeal joint variety while the females belonged exclusively to the group in which the arthropathy was indistinguishable from rheumatoid disease.

Systemic disorders of connective tissue

This group of diseases includes systemic lupus erythematosus, systemic sclerosis, polyarteritis nodosa (PAN) and dermatomyositis (described in chapter 40). They are characterized by multisystem involvement and heightened immunological reactivity. They are not commonly encountered in elderly subjects and by and large the clinical features do not differ from those seen in young patients. However, certain differences have been described.

Systemic lupus erythematosus (SLE)

An insidious onset with polymyalgia rheumatica-like or rheumatoid arthritis-like symptoms typified nine SLE patients diagnosed after the age of 60 years out of 86 patients described by Soad and colleagues (1972). Their patients showed a strikingly benign prognosis and symptoms were controlled. In another series (Baker et al, 1979) of 31 SLE patients whose disease commenced after the age of 60 years, pleurisy and pericarditis were the most common presenting features whilst pulmonary involvement was considered to be more common than in SLE occurring early in life. They too stressed the better prognosis with 92 per cent of patients surviving 5 years. In view of this they recommended a conservative approach to treatment. There is general agreement that arthritis, alopoecia, Raynaud's phenomenon and neuropsychiatric manifestations are less common in the elderly group (Urowitz, 1967; Gibson and Myers, 1976; Catoggio and Manson, 1982) whilst the incidence of renal involvement has been shown to decline linearly with age (Wilson et al, 1981).

Differences have also been noted in serological responses. Anti-dsDNA antibodies and immune complexes (as determined by C1q binding) occurred less frequently in the older patients (Wilson et al, 1981). Out of Cataggio and Maddison's series of 10 patients eight showed positive ANA and only four had antibodies to DNA. Nine (90 per cent) had antibodies to the cellular antigen Ro (compared to 37 per cent in a younger group). Seven also had antibodies to the antigen La. These authors suggest the possibility that testing for anti-Ro and anti-La might be useful in identifying this group of atypical SLE patients. Drug-induced SLE is seen in elderly subjects, most commonly in procainamide-treated patients illustrating the wide use of the drug in this age group (Hess, 1981). As with younger SLE subjects suffering from drug-induced lupus, the clinical features tend to be milder than in the spontaneous variety of the disease.

Systemic sclerosis (scleroderma)

Unlike SLE which has its highest incidence and mortality during the childbearing years, systemic sclerosis displays increasing incidence as age progresses. About 10 per cent of scleroderma commences after the age of 60. Medsger and Masi (1971) in their large epidemiological study found that over the study period the average incidence of new cases overall was 2.7 per million of the population. They found a progressive increase in this incidence as age advanced, reaching a peak for those of over 65 years of 7.6 per million, thereby confirming Rodnan's (1963) earlier observation.

Scleroderma appears to follow a mild form in old age with a favourable prognosis. Hodgkinson (1971) described 15 patients over the age of 70 years (in nine of whom the disease actually commenced over the age of 70 years). All were female and 10 of them manifested the calcinosis-Raynaud's phenomenon-sclerodactyly-telangiectasia tetrad, the so-called 'CRST syndrome' which is generally associated with a benign prognosis. The atypical presentation of scleroderma in the elderly has also been highlighted by Dalziel and Wilcock (1979). They described two patients who presented over the age of 80 with Raynaud's phenomenon and arthritis. They both appeared to have oesophageal involvement but lacked the classical skin changes of scleroderma. These authors make the point that systemic sclerosis is probably undiagnosed in the elderly age group where multi-system symptomtology are more likely to be attributed to multiple pathology in old age rather than a unifying multisystem connective tissue disorder.

CRYSTAL SYNOVITIS

An acute inflammatory synovial reaction resulting from the physical presence of microcrystals within the synovial cavity occurs in two naturally occurring conditions: (1) classical gout in which the offending crystal is monosodium urate monohydrate and (2) pyrophosphate arthropathy (pseudogout) caused by crystals of calcium pyrophosphate dihydrate.

Classical (urate) gout

A recent computer-assisted clinical survey of 354 patients with gout (Grahame and Scott, 1970) has shown that although the peak decade of onset is the 5th in males and 6th in females, no less than 11.6 per cent of the total series experienced their first attack of clinical gout after they had reached the age of 60 years. It has been known since the writings of Hippocrates that gout in women is rare before the menopause. It is not surprising, therefore, that gout first presenting after the age of 60 years shows a female incidence of 29 per cent compared to 7 per cent below that age. The predilection of gout for higher social strata seen in the younger onset age group does not apply to those in whom the disease developed later in life (Fig. 39.6). There is also significantly lower incidence of positive family history in the latter group.

Other differences between gout with onset at younger and older ages are shown in Table 39.2. The higher incidence of renal impairment in the older onset group

Table 39.2 Incidence of certain features among 354 patients with gout related to age of onset

	Onset 59 years or less %	Onset 60 years or more %	Probability
Positive family history	36	12	<0.01
Obesity	47	44	NS
Underlying blood dyscrasia	3.5	12	<0.05
Moderate hypertension	42	54	NS
Severe hypertension	9	5	NS
Regular alcohol consumption	38	27	NS
Clinical tophi	22	17	NS
X-ray changes	35	39	NS
Blood urea >7.1 mmol/l	22	46	<0.01
Proteinuria (45 mg per 100 ml)	22	24	NS
Joint involved at any time:			
Big toe	75	80	NS
Ankle/foot	54	28	<0.01
Finger	24	25	NS
Wrist	9	10	NS
Elbow	11	5	NS
Knee	33	22	NS

might be explained by their increasing age; no such increase in proteinuria was apparent nor of moderate or severe hypertension. Severe hypertension was less common in this group. It is associated with gout which commences in the first three decades of life.

Secondary gout resulting from a blood dyscrasia was over three times more common in the older onset group.

Other features which showed no difference between the two age onset groups in this survey are:

1. The incidence of obesity, of regular alcohol consumption, of clinical tophi and of radiological changes.

2. Involvement of great toe, of finger/hand and of wrist joints.

3. The pretreatment level of uric acid.

In the older onset group, on the other hand, the ankle/foot, elbow and knee joints were less frequently involved.

Thus, gout beginning in old age is characterized by an increased female incidence, an increased incidence of an underlying blood disorder and a reduced incidence of inherited and social factors.

Diagnosis of gout in elderly subjects

Little difficulty is usually encountered with the diagnosis of gout in its most classic form of acute podagra (arthritis of the first metatarsophalangeal joint), particularly when this is accompanied by a significantly raised

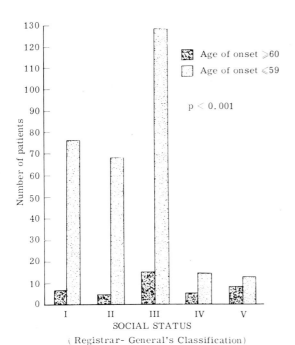

Fig. 39.6 Social status in male gouty patients related to age of onset. In those in whom the disease commenced over the age of 60 years the predilection for the upper social strata seen in the early onset group disappears.

plasma urate level (more than 0.42 mmol/l (7.0 mg per 100 ml)). Other joints, of course, may be involved and the immediate diagnosis may in consequence not be obvious. Further caution is needed in the interpretation of hyperuricaemia in old age. Many old people may be taking oral diuretics and their raised plasma uric acid level may be an incidental rather than an aetiological finding. It is, therefore, of immense value to be able to confirm the diagnosis of urate gout beyond question by finding intraleucocytic crystals in the synovial fluid aspirated from the inflamed joint. In practice this is usually only possible when the knee joint is involved. Using a system of compensated polarizing microscopy, crystals may be identified according to their optical properties. Monosodium urate monohydrate crystals are negatively birefringent whereas calcium pyrophosphate dihydrate crystals (see below) show weak positive birefringence. Examination of the synovial fluid by polarizing microscopy is essential in all cases of synovitis in whom the diagnosis is uncertain and in which a specimen may be obtained for examination. For further details the reader is referred to McCarty and Hollander (1961).

Treatment of gout in old age

Acute attack

The three drugs in common use for the treatment of acute gouty arthritis are colchicine, pheylbutazone and indomethacin. They may all be used in elderly patients, although side-effects are not infrequent. Gastrointestinal intolerance may occur with all three, and fluid retention commonly occurs with phenylbutazone. Many of the newer NSAID's have been tried in the treatment of acute gout apparently with success and without adverse effect. In comparative trials naproxen 750 mg as a single dose followed by 250 mg three times a day for 48 hours has appeared to be equally effective as phenylbutazone 200 mg four times daily given for a similar period (Sturge et al, 1977). Other propionic acid derivatives tried include fenoprofen (800 mg 6-hourly for between 3 and 8 days (Wallace, 1975), and ketoprofen given intramuscularly in a dose of 100 mg twice daily (Eberl et al, 1973). Of the more recently introduced NSAID's pyroxicam has been shown to be effective in an open study at a dosage of 40 mg once daily for an average of 5 days in eleven patients with acute gout. It was well-tolerated. The mean age was 65.2 years, range 31–77 (Widmark, 1978). Similarly, fenbufen given in daily divided doses of between 600 and 1000 mg has given good results in an open study in nine out of 10 patients within 4 days of beginning treatment (Vertzman et al, 1976).

Long-term treatment

In the presence of tophi and/or repeated attacks of acute gouty arthritis the plasma uric acid should be lowered by long-term therapy, either by means of uricosuric treatment, e.g. probenecid, or with the xanthine oxidase inhibitor allopurinol. In early uncomplicated gout there is little to choose between these two drugs (Scott et al, 1966). However, in the presence of large tophaceous deposits, renal failure, gout with urate stone production and with overproduction of uric acid, in gout secondary to a blood dyscrasia or where intolerance to uricosuric drugs occurs it is advisable to use allopurinol. Both probenecid and allopurinol are well tolerated in old age and the incidence of side-effects is very low. The patient should be aware of the possibility of acute attacks during the first few months of treatment with either drug. To offset this a small dose of colchicine (e.g. 0.5 mg twice daily) or indomethacin (25 mg twice daily) for the first few months of treatment is a useful prophylactic. Recent evidence suggests that the gradual decline in renal function seen in untreated gout patients or those treated with colchicine alone does apparently not occur in those patients treated with colchicine and allopurinol. Thus the hypouricaemic effect of allopurinol may actually counter the adverse effects of hyperuricaemia on renal function in gouty subjects (Gibson et al, 1982).

Pyrophosphate arthropathy (pseudogout)

This disease of advancing years, despite its similar pathogenetic mechanism, differs in many ways from classical or urate gout. In McCarty's series (1966) of 80 cases, men predominated in a ratio of 1.35: 1. The mean age was 71.9 years (range 38 to 92). The acute attacks showed a predilection for the larger synovial joints, notably the knee. As in urate gout systemic features including fever may be present leading to an erroneous diagnosis of septic arthritis (Angevine and Jacox, 1973; Bong and Bennett, 1981). There is a distinct familial tendency (Zitnan and Sitaj, 1963).

During the acute attack examination of the joint aspirate by polarizing microscopy will reveal the intraleucocytic positively birefringent crystals of calcium pyrophosphate dihydrate. The essential prerequisite for a diagnosis of pyrophosphate arthropathy is the finding on X-ray of articular calcification (chondrocalcinosis). This is most commonly seen in the fibrocartilage of the knee (the menisci), the symphis pubis or the inferior radial ulnar joint. It may also be seen in the articular cartilage of involved joints as a thin line of calcification or in the synovial membrane or capsule actually around the hip or shoulder joints (Fig. 39.7). Chondrocalcinosis is not always very obvious and may be missed unless the X-rays are submitted to close scrutiny. Pathological examination of articular tissues affected with chondrocalcinosis has shown a widespread deposition of crystals within the cartilage, ligaments, synovial membrane and capsule of affected joints. The crystals have also been

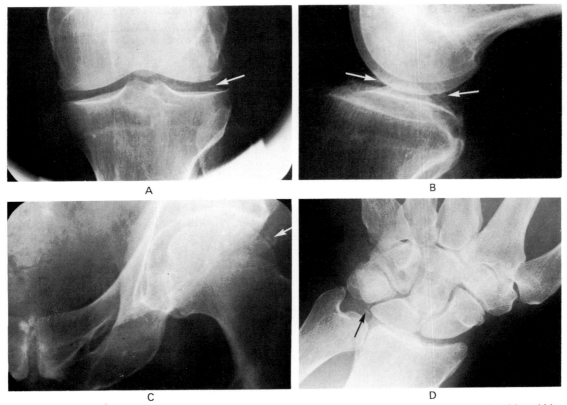

Fig. 39.7 Articular calcification seen in (a) meniscus of knee joint; (b) articular cartilage of knee; (c) symphysis pubis and hip joint; (d) inferior radioulnar joint fibrocartilage (reproduced by courtesy of the Editor, *Annals of Rheumatic Diseases*)

identified by X-ray diffraction as calcium pyrophosphate dihydrate.

There is a definite association between diffuse chondrocalcinosis and two metabolic disorders, namely, hyperparathyroidism (Dodds and Steinbach, 1968) and haemochromatosis (Hamilton et al, 1968; Dorfman et al, 1969). It is, therefore, of great importance to estimate plasma calcium, phosphate, alkaline phosphatase, iron and iron-binding capacity in all cases of chondrocalcinosis.

The actual prevalence of pyrophosphate arthropathy is unknown but a number of studies have been undertaken to assess the incidence of articular calcification. In a study of 800 menisci from 215 anatomy cadavers performed by McCarty et al (1966) deposits of calcium pyrophosphate dihydrate were identified in all 4 menisci from 7 cadavers (3.2 per cent). Bocher et al (1965) performed AP X-rays of the knees in 455 patients who were selected at random from old-age homes. The prevalence of chondrocalcinosis was 7 per cent. None of these patients with radiological abnormalities had suffered any episode suggestive of pyrophosphate arthropathy. A similar study by Dodds (1969) showed

that the prevalence of calcification of the triangular ligament of the wrist in a group of 200 elderly persons was 2.5 per cent. More recently Ellman and Levin (1975), using the more sensitive industrial X-ray film, detected a much higher incidence of chondrocalcinosis (27.6 per cent) amongst a series of 58 residents of an old people's home with a mean age of 82.6 years (range 70 to 94). Again there was no correlation between the presence of chondrocalcinosis and inflammatory arthritis. Chondrocalcinosis is thus a not infrequent finding in X-rays of elderly patients. Although it may be related to a co-existent acute arthropathy it may also be an incidental finding. It is, therefore, important to confirm the diagnosis of pyrophosphate arthropathy when it is suspected, by a polariscopic examination of synovial fluid along the lines mentioned earlier.

Treatment

The treatment of an acute attack of pyrophosphate arthropathy is similar to that of gout, and though information in the literature is confusing the drugs recommended for acute gouty arthritis are often used with benefit. Where an acute episode occurs in the knee, merely aspirating the joint will abort the attack in many cases. There is no known method of reversing articular calcification in the idiopathic group and there is no information as yet to suggest that treatment of the hyperparathyroidism or haemochromatosis will reverse the articular calcification in those cases in which it is an associated phenomenon. On the contrary, with regard to hyperparathyroidism there is evidence that chondro-calcinosis progresses after successful parathyroidectomy with correction of hypercalcaemia (Glass and Grahame, 1976).

Chronic crystal synovitis

Occasionally a patient presents with a chronic progressive polyarthritis similar to rheumatoid arthritis which may be due either to urate gout or to the deposition of calcium pyrophosphate within the joint. In the latter case the destructive changes seen particularly in the metacarpophalangeal wrist, shoulder, hip and knee joints may be particularly severe (Richards and Hamilton, 1974).

SOFT-TISSUE LESIONS

This section includes a variety of unrelated conditions affecting tendons and ligaments of the locomotor system. Although most of these conditions are benign and self-limiting, they do give rise to a considerable amount of pain and disability in old age.

Adhesive capsulitis of the shoulder

This condition is frequently seen in old age. Of a series of 186 patients, 27.3 per cent presented over the age of 65 years (Wright and Haq, 1976). It may occur either spontaneously or in relation to a variety of predisposing conditions such as trauma, or any painful condition of an upper quadrant of the body which results in a period of immobility of the upper limb. It is commonly seen in old people after a myocardial infarction, a hemiplegia or pneumonia.

To a considerable extent this condition may be prevented by the judicious use of prophylactic active and passive exercises in susceptible subjects. This is particularly important in patients suffering from hemiplegia (Jayson, 1981). The possibility that psychological factors might play a part in the pathogenesis of this condition has been raised. In one study of 56 patients with adhesive capsulitis personality profile showed more evidence of somatic anxiety in female subjects (but not in males) than in controls (Fleming et al, 1976). An earlier report (Bulgen et al, 1976) linking adhesive capsulitis with the tissue type HLA B27 has not been confirmed.

Fig. 39.8 Adhesive capsulitis of the shoulder

The symptoms consist of pain, often felt around the region of the insertion of the deltoid muscle, accompanied by inability to raise the arm (Fig. 39.8). This latter causes difficulty in combing the hair and dressing.

Physical examination reveals, in addition to inability to elevate the arm actively, a loss of passive movement of the shoulder joint when tested with the scapula fixed by the examining physician. Tenderness where present tends to be diffuse rather than localized. An X-ray is helpful to exclude other conditions whicy may mimic adhesive capsulitis. Usually the X-ray appearances of the shoulder are normal but in long-standing cases it is not infrequent to appreciate sclerosis of the tip of the greater tuberosity and osteoporosis of the humeral head. The vast majority of these conditions remit spontaneously within 6 to 24 months and it is doubtful to what extent treatment shortens this period. Active exercises of the shoulder region preceded by the application of either heat or cold (ice therapy) do appear to increase the range of shoulder movement if undertaken frequently over several months.

A study comparing the use of analgesic tablets with hydro-cortisone injections to the joint combined with exercises, hydro-cortisone injected into the region of the biceps tendon combined with exercises, and heat and exercises alone showed that all the active forms of treatment produced better results than analgesic tablets alone. There was no significant difference between the three active treatment groups (Lee et al, 1974).

In resistant cases manipulation under local or general anaesthesia have been widely used in the past. The use of manipulation had been controversial; some workers reporting benefits (Bloch and Fisher, 1961) and others were less impressed (Hazelman, 1972). However, a recent comparative trial comparing manipulation after intravenous diazepam combined with an intra-articular injection, hydro-cortisone into the shoulder, was compared with treatment with the local injection alone. Although at the end of 1 month there was little difference between two treatment groups, at 3 months the group treated by manipulation appeared to be better, although the numbers were too small for statistical analysis (Thomas et al, 1980).

Supraspinatus tendinitis

This is another condition seen frequently in elderly subjects who have injured their shoulder, usually from a fall directly on to the shoulder. The patient experiences pain on active abduction of the upper limb and often finds that sleeping on the affected side is unbearably painful.

On physical examination a full range of passive movement is usually retained but characteristically abduction of the arm against resistance is acutely painful. The other characteristic feature is localized tenderness on palpation of the supraspinatus tendon as it courses over the superior aspect of the shoulder joint.

This condition may frequently be associated with the presence of calcific deposits (hydroxyapatite) within the supraspinatus tendon. The mechanism by which this calcific material is deposited is not known but as is seen in the X-rays shown in Figure 39.9 it may disappear spontaneously with the passage of time. Occasionally a very acute painfully stiff shoulder may result probably due to the rupture of calcific material into the subdeltoid bursa. In some cases it is possible to obtain chalky fluid from the bursa by aspiration. Examining this material under the polarizing microscope reveals that it is optically inert — a feature of hydroxyapatite.

Treatment of supraspinatus tendinitis consists of injecting hydrocortisone into the affected region leading in a majority of cases to a rapid relief of symptoms; on occasions, repeated injections are required. Physiotherapy has a limited part to play in this condition — only when there is a secondary adhesive capsulitis.

Shoulder-hand syndrome

This term was originally coined by Steinbrocker (1947) to designate a condition characterized by diffuse, tender swelling of the fingers and hand in association with a painful stiff shoulder. In addition, vasomotor changes, later giving rise to atrophy of muscles and skin with formation of contractures of the fingers are seen. The characteristic X-ray abnormality is patchy osteoporosis of the head of the humerus and of the bones of the wrist and hand which in the course of time becomes diffuse. This condition occurs particularly in old age and as with adhesive capsulitis is seen in association with myocardial infarction, cervical disc lesions, trauma, hemiplegia and a variety of other conditions. In a quarter of cases there is no obvious cause and in a similar number the condition is bilateral.

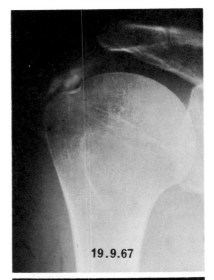

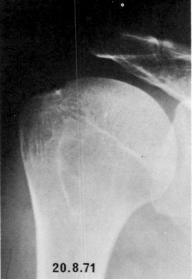

Fig. 39.9 Calcification in the supraspinatus tendon which disappeared spontaneously

Recent reports suggest that drugs, notably the anti-tuberculosis drugs isoniazid and ethionamide (Good et al, 1965; Lequesne and Moghtader, 1966) and phenobarbitone (van der Korst et al, 1966) may be implicated in the causation. The pathogenesis of this condition still remains uncertain. One favoured theory is that it is a reflex neurovascular dystrophy which occurs in response to a painful lesion. It is believed that a barrage of afferent impulses arriving at the spinal cord activate the lateral sympathetic horns which control the vasomotor efferents to the upper limb via internuncial reflexes.

The correct method of treatment is uncertain. Active and passive exercises are advised to prevent contractures and promote active movements of both the hand and shoulder thus counteracting the tendency to atrophy of skin, muscle and bone of the extremity and stiffness of the shoulder. Stellate ganglion block has been advocated but controlled studies have not been performed.

Miscellaneous

A variety of other soft-tissue lesions may occur in elderly subjects. These include tennis elbow (lateral epicondylitis), golfer's elbow (medial epicondylitis), carpal tunnel syndrome, plantar fasciitis, bursitis affecting the trochanteric, olecranon, achilles, calcaneal, ischial and prepatella bursae and tenosynovitis of the hand and wrist regions. There are no characteristic features concerning their clinical presentation or treatment in old age. They will not, therefore, be considered further. The reader should refer to a standard textbook on clinical rheumatology.

NEUROPATHIC ARTHROPATHY

Where the ability to perceive pain is impaired or lost while motor function is retained, the joint is subjected to abnormal stresses without the benefit of the protective function rendered by pain. The result is a highly destructive lesion of the joint which is termed neuropathic arthropathy. Though comparatively rare, it should be suspected in any elderly patient who presents with a relatively pain-free but severe destructive joint lesion.

The most common causes are: tabes dorsalis (Charcot's joints), syringomyelia, diabetic neuropathy, congenital indifference to pain.

In tabes the larger joints of the lower limbs, notably the hip and knee, are usually affected though occasionally it may affect the spine or upper limbs. In syringomyelia the upper limbs are favoured. In diabetic neuropathy it is usually the tarsal joints that become involved while in congenital indifference to pain the disease may occur in any joint. Where a peripheral joint is involved, the onset is usually insidious, with increasing enlargement of the joint due to an effusion associated with instability. Because of the disproportionately mild discomfort, the patient continues to use the joint freely without seeking medical attention.

Where an effusion is present there is often increased warmth, with occasional tenderness and pain on movement, though these are less marked than would have been expected from the appearance of the joint. Where the feet, hips or vertebrae are involved, the disturbance of joint function may be very much less apparent and diagnosis in these regions is usually based on radio-logical findings. With foot involvement, as in diabetes, there is typically a painless swelling of the foot without redness or increase in temperature. Secondary local infection may be present, occasionally with osteomyelitis. As progressive destruction occurs there are increasing shortening and deformity of the foot.

Other occasional causes of neuropathic arthropathy include spinal cord injury, subacute combined degeneration of the cord and peripheral nerve injury.

In recent years repeated intra-articular steroid injections, notably to weight-bearing joints (hip or knee) have been implicated as a further cause of neuropathic arthropathy. It has been suggested that the relief of pain gained from the use of these steroids has resulted in over-use of the joints causing accelerated progressive destruction of the articular structures (Steinberg et al, 1962; Sweetnam et al, 1960). Hollander et al (1961) have estimated that the incidence of instability in a weight-bearing joint as a result of repeated intra-articular steroid injections is less than 1 per cent; in only 4 joints out of approximately 4000 patients did they observe extensive absorption of bone. Nevertheless, it would seem advisable to avoid repeated injections of corticosteroids into synovial weight-bearing joints and in particular the hip joint.

ARTHRITIS AND MALIGNANT DISEASE

As age progresses there is an increasing prevalence of both joint disorders and malignant disease. It is not surprising, therefore, that many elderly patients manifest both conditions coincidentally. The association between neoplasia and diffuse disorders of connective tissue, notably dermatomyositis and polymyositis, has been referred to in Chapter 40 in describing polymyalgia and polymyositis.

The articular manifestations of malignant disease

Hypertrophic osteoarthropathy

Most important under this heading is the condition known as hypertrophic osteoarthropathy — clubbing of the fingers and toes and enlargement of the extremities resulting from periarticular and periosteal thickening. The joints themselves may be swollen, painful and warm. There is wide variation in the degree of pain and stiffness in the affected extremities. It is seen in a wide variety of intrathoracic tumours but particularly in bronchogenic carcinoma. In a series of 76 cases of this condition reported by Hatch and Knudson (1967) osteoarthropathy was present in 23 while clubbing alone was found in 52. In primary lung cancer, squamous cell tumours, peripheral tumours and those with central necrosis have been found to be most frequently associated with osteoarthropathy (Knowles and Smith, 1960). The incidence of osteoarthropathy is even greater in extrapulmonary tumours such as pleural mesothelioma (Clagett et al, 1952; Wierman et al, 1954), and diaphragmatic neurilemmoma (Trivedi, 1958).

The features that help to distinguish hypertrophic osteoarthropathy due to tumours from that due to nonmalignant conditions have been summarized by Calabro (1967). They include an acute form of clubbing preceding the onset of signs of the tumour by a short period; warmth and burning of the finger tips; a painful polyarthritis resembling rheumatoid disease; the appearance of periosteal proliferation on X-ray examination (Fig. 39.10) and occasionally sweating of the hands and feet and thickening of the skin or scalp. Examination of synovial fluid shows a low cell count (less than 2000 per mm³, mainly lymphocytes) and all the other features of a non-inflammatory synovial reaction. Histological examination shows only a moderate degree of synovial hyperplasia with minimal lymphocytic and plasma cell infiltration.

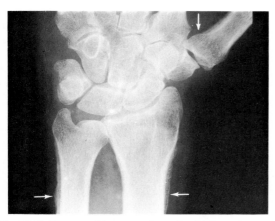

Fig. 39.10 Hypertrophic osteoarthropathy (N.B. periosteal new bone formation)

Treatment of hypertrophic osteoarthropathy is essentially that of the underlying condition. Where feasible, removal of the offending tumour may result in a complete resolution. Sometimes unilateral or bilateral vagotomy will have a similar beneficial effect. Where these measures are not feasible, the condition may be treated symptomatically with the usual antirheumatic drugs or corticosteroids.

Myeloproliferative disorders
Myeloproliferative disorders and malignant lymphomas may produce joint symptoms in a variety of ways. Secondary hyperuricaemia and gout may occur in acute

and chronic leukaemias, malignant lymphomas and occasionally in multiple myeloma. A particularly common cause is polycythaemia rubra vera (Grahame and Scott, 1970). Hyperuricaemia in these cases is due to an overproduction of uric acid from an increased turnover of tissue nucleoproteins. Even where this complication has not occurred spontaneously it is likely to result from the treatment of these conditions by cytotoxic agents. Under these circumstances an extremely high level of circulating plasma uric acid may occur resulting in an acute obstructive uric acid nephropathy which may lead to anuria. This potentially disastrous complication of cytotoxic treatment may be adequately prevented by pretreatment of the patient with allopurinol (Watts et al, 1966). The same drug is equally effective in correcting the hyperuricaemia and reducing the incidence of attacks of gouty arthritis in all patients suffering from secondary gout.

Joint symptoms may arise in patients suffering from acute leukaemia and more rarely in those with chronic leukaemia or malignant lymphomas, as a result of direct deposition of malignant tissue within the synovial membrane or the juxta-articular bone.

In multiple myeloma, in addition to the more familiar skeletal symptoms of pain in the bones resulting from myelomatous deposits within them, a polyarthritis affecting small joints may occur closely resembling rheumatoid arthritis. The similarity is enhanced by the presence in some of these patients of nodules over the extensor surfaces of both ulnars and by the presence of the carpal tunnel syndrome (Goldberg et al, 1964). Such manifestations are due to the extensive deposition of amyloid in the synovial membrane and para-articular tissues. These authors reviewing the literature were able to find six such cases and added a seventh of their own. Hamilton and Bywaters (1961) reviewed 46 cases of myelomatosis seen over a 10-year period, in whom the diagnosis had been unequivocally confirmed histologically. In this series involvement of the joints or tendon sheaths was present in only six of the patients and in only one was para-amyloid infiltration observed. In the remainder the joint symptoms were explicable either on the basis of secondary gout or of an unassociated osteoarthrosis or traumatic synovitis. Myeloid leukaemia may also develop in patients suffering from ankylosing spondylitis who have been treated previously with radiotherapy (Court Brown and Doll, 1965). Of over 14 500 patients who had received radiotherapy between 1935 and 1944, 14 had died from myeloid leukaemia up to 15 years after receiving the X-ray therapy. This is 10 times the expected incidence.

Rheumatoid disease and malignancy
Recent large series have suggested that visceral malignancy is no more common amongst patients suffering

from rheumatoid arthritis than in the population as a whole. Surveying 374 patients suffering from rheumatoid arthritis, Ragan and Snyder (1955) noted a development of malignant disease in only 2 per cent after 5 years. More recently, Owen et al (1970) compared 169 patients with rheumatoid arthritis satisfying the ARA criteria for classical or definite disease followed for 1 month to 24 years (mean 49.5 months). This group was compared with 125 patients suffering from a variety of non-rheumatoid arthritides observed for a similar period and matched with the original group. There was no significant difference between the incidence of malignancy in the 2 groups; 8 patients of the rheumatoid group and 5 of the control group were found to have systemic malignancies. Taking both groups together, they further observed that, whereas only 16.5 per cent of the 308 patients without malignancy had received corticosteroids, 46.1 per cent of the 13 patients with malignancy had been on steroids. The difference is statistically significant and the authors infer that in the age group concerned (50 to 74 years) malignancy may be more closely associated with steroid therapy than with rheumatoid disease itself. This inference would need to be confirmed by other studies.

Litwin et al (1966) reported a 43-year-old woman in whom a pulmonary neoplasm was accompanied by the development of a strongly sero-positive polyarthritis with histologically confirmed rheumatoid nodules. The rheumatoid disease in all its clinical and serological aspects appeared to disappear after the resection of the lung growth. When the tumour recurred there was a return of the rheumatoid factor in the serum terminally. Although the authors were convinced that the removal of the tumour was directly responsible for the disappearance of the rheumatoid disease, Calabro (1967) offers an alternative explanation, namely that the cancer surgery may have induced a temporary remission in this case.

Evidence for the existence of a specific 'cancer polyarthritis' has been put forward by Lansbury (1963), Sperling (1961), Standberg and Jarlov (1961) and Mackenzie and Sherbel (1963). In these various small series, joint manifestations preceded the development of the malignant neoplasm (which included a variety of epithelial and lymphatic tumours) by a period of several months. In the large majority of cases the polyarthritis was seronegative. Mackenzie and Sherbel inferred that carcinoma polyarthritis is distinguishable from 'true' rheumatoid disease by the acute late onset, and asymmetrical joint involvement with sparing of the wrist and small joints of the hand. In their series of 18 patients, rheumatoid nodules were absent whilst rheumatoid factor was present in only 1 patient. There were no characteristic histological abnormalities. Many of the features referred to by Mackenzie and Sherbel are those seen in rheumatoid disease of late onset (see p. 801).

It may be concluded that the existence of a specific 'cancer polyarthritis' is for the moment unproven, and that cases referred to by the various authors under this heading probably represent no more than the coincidental occurrence of two reasonably common diseases.

Finally, an association has been reported between Sjögren's syndrome (the triad of keratoconjunctivitis sicca (dry eyes), xerostomia (dry mouth) and rheumatoid disease or one of the other connective tissue disorders) and lymphoma. In 1964, Talal and Bunim reported extrasalivary lymphomata in 3 out of 56 patients with Sjögren's syndrome. Subsequently this has been confirmed by other authorities (Miller, 1967).

PSYCHOGENIC RHEUMATISM

Elderly patients presenting with musculoskeletal symptoms for which no objective evidence of organic disease exists may be suffering from depression or psychoneurosis. Assessment of the patient's affect and emotional state is therefore always important. The term psychogenic rheumatism is restricted to those patients whose symptoms of pain, stiffness and a subjective feeling of swelling or loss of movement of joints are intensified or precipitated by emotional influences. Such patients will usually also show other features of psychoneurosis.

Therapy should be directed towards treatment of the underlying psychological disturbance, and where necessary the patient referred for a psychiatric opinion.

INFECTIVE ARTHRITIS

Despite its infrequent occurrence, infective arthritis should be suspected in any arthritis (particularly a monarthritis) in which the cause is not obvious. In any such circumstances bacteriological examination of the synovial fluid is very important. In some cases, particularly if tuberculous arthritis is suspected, a diagnostic synovial biopsy should be undertaken. Although a variety of micro-organisms including viruses, bacteria and fungi may infect one or more synovial joints, for practical purposes pyogenic arthritis is the main type. This results from infection with staphylococcus, streptococcus, gonococcus, meningococcus, pneumococcus, coliform bacillus, salmonella, haemophilus and, uncommonly in the United Kingdom, brucellosis. An unrecognized and therefore untreated pyogenic arthritis may cause total loss of function, possibly with bony ankylosis.

Pre-existing joint disease, for example, rheumatoid arthritis, predisposes to the development of pyogenic arthritis, a risk which is increased in patients receiving oral corticosteroids. Local corticosteroid injections are occasional sources of septic arthritis. Pyogenic bacteria may also gain access to a healthy joint as a result of blood-stream spread from a focus elsewhere.

In a recent study of 75 cases of pyogenic arthritis 29.4 per cent of the patients had pre-exisiting rheumatoid disease, and in these the foot was the most common site of primary infection and *Staphylococcus aureus* was the most common organism involved (Morris and Eade, 1978).

Gibson and Grahame (1971) described 52 patients aged 70 years and over who developed an acute arthritis. Two (4 per cent) of these were pyogenic, diagnosis being discovered only on routine culture of aspirate during investigation of the arthritis. Willkens et al (1960) described 19 cases of acute septic arthritis occurring in two hospitals in Seattle over a period of 5 years. They also stress that this condition is not rare in elderly debilitated patients, that joint aspiration is the essential diagnostic examination and that adequate response to systemic antibiotics together with repeated aspirations and intra-articular injections of antibiotics results in a favourable outcome in the majority of cases; only where this regime fails is it necessary to resort to surgical drainage. Newman (1976), reviewing 134 cases of septic arthritis who presented to the Nuffield Orthopaedic Centre, Oxford, over the past 30 years, draws attention to the increasing incidence of this condition in the elderly in the past decade. The knee was the most common joint involved. In this series only eight of the 20 cases occurring over the age 60 years regained good joint function because of the difficulty in mobilizing an affected joint after a period of immobilization. They recommended a period of not longer than 2 weeks' immobilization provided that a satisfactory response to antibiotics is obtained and that no focus of bone infection exists.

Tuberculous arthritis should be suspected in a monarthritis, showing insidious development and which gives rise to destructive changes in the bones, but often with preservation of articular cartilage until late in the disease. Although becoming increasingly rare, it is seen particularly in elderly males suffering from pulmonary tuberculosis. Treatment consists of antituberculous therapy, combined where necessary with appropriate surgical correction.

'SENILE MONOARTICULAR ARTHRITIS'

The term 'senile monoarticular arthritis' was coined by Benians (1969) who described an acute arthropathy affecting a single joint in elderly patients. Over a 3-year period he collected 31 cases, of whom seven were male and 24 female; with the exception of two patients all were aged 70 years or over. The favoured joints to be involved were the knee, wrist, shoulder, ankle and small joints of the hand. The duration of symptoms could not be accurately determined but appeared to be short. In all cases the arthropathy was responsible for the patient's admission to hospital.

Laboratory and other investigations were restricted to the Hyland R. A. screening test which was performed in 30 cases and positive in two. The serum uric acid was measured in 11 cases and raised in one. Joint X-ray was performed in only four cases. The author noted that phenylbutazone produced a rapid relief of symptoms within 48 hours in most cases.

To substantiate (or refute) the existence of 'senile monoarticular arthritis' as a distinct clinical entity the present author undertook a detailed survey of all patients aged 70 years or more who presented with an acute arthropathy of one or more joints of less than three months' duration (Gibson and Grahame, 1971). All patients were submitted to a clinical evaluation, radiology and full laboratory investigation.

Table 39.3 Diagnosis in 52 cases of acute arthritis in the elderly (Gibson and Grahame, 1971)

Diagnosis	No.	%
Sero-positive R. A.	12	23
Sero-negative polyarthritis	5	9
Osteoarthrosis	8	16
Pseudogout	4	8
Gout	2	4
Pyogenic arthritis	2	4
Psoriatic arthritis	2	4
Traumatic synovitis	2	4
Capsulitis	1	2
Indeterminate	14	28

By the end of 2 years, 52 patients had been admitted and an accurate diagnosis made with reasonable confidence in 38 of these (Table 39.3). The 14 remaining patients formed an 'indeterminate' group. Eight of these had radiological evidence of osteoarthrosis, chondrocalcinosis, hyperuricaemia or any combination of the three. Precise diagnosis is difficult without examination of synovial fluid for crystals by polarizing microscopy. Of the remaining six patients, one subsequently came to synovectomy and the histological appearance was identical with that of rheumatoid disease.

There remain five cases out of 52 in whom the diagnosis was obscure. These bore little resemblance to one another or to the cases described by Benians. Further evidence will be required if 'senile monoarticular arthritis' is to be sustained as a viable clinical entity.

REFERENCES

Adler E 1966 Rheumatoid arthritis in old age. Israel Medical Journal 2 (5): 607

Angevine C D, Jacox R F 1973 Pseudogout in the elderly. Archives of Internal Medicine 131: 693–696

Baker G B, Rovira J R, Campion E W, Mills J A 1979 Late onset systemic lupus erythematosus. American Journal of Medicine 66: 727–723

Benians R G 1969 Senile monoarticular arthritis. Gerontologia Clinica 11: 109

Berry H, Lyanage S P, Durance R A, Barnes C, Berger L, Evans S 1976. Azathioprine and Penicillamine in the Treatment of Rheumatoid Arthritis: A Controlled Trial. British Medical Journal 1: 1052–1054

Billings R, Grahame R, Marks V, Wood P J, Taylor A 1975 Blood and urine gold levels during chrysotherapy for rheumatoid arthritis. Rheumatology and Rehabilitation 14: 13

Bloch J, Fisher F K 1961 Frozen Shoulder. Documenta, Rheumatologica, Geigy No. 15

Bocher J, Mankin H J, Berk R N, Rodnan G P 1965 Problems of calcified meniscal cartilage in elderly persons. New England Journal of Medicine. 272 (91), 1093

Bong D, Bennett R 1981 Pseudogout mimicking systemic disease. Journal of the American Medical Association 246: 1438–1440

Boyle J A, Buchanan W W 1971 In: Clinical Rheumatology, p 49. Blackwell Scientific Publications, Oxford and Edinburgh

British National Formualry, No. 3, 1982 British Medical Association and the Pharmaceutical Society of Great Britain, pp 260–267

Brook P G, Jackson D 1982 European Journal of Rheumatology and Inflammation 5: 326

Brown J W, Sones D A 1967 The onset of rheumatoid arthritis in the aged. Journal of the American Geriatrics Society 15, 873

Bruk M I 1967 Articular and vascular manifestations of polymyalgia rheumatica. Annals of the Rheumatic Diseases 26: 103

Buckler J W, Hall J E, Rees J A, Sheldrake F E Miller A B 1975 Tolerance and acceptability of Ibuprofen (brufen) in the elderly patient. Current Medical Research 3: 558

Bulgen D Y, Hazelman B L, Voak D 1976 HLA B27 and Frozen Shoulder, Lancet i: 104

Caird F I, Webb J, Lee P 1973 Osteoarthrosis of the hands in the elderly. Age and Ageing 2: 150–156

Calabro J J 1967 Cancer and arthritis. Arthritis and Rheumatism 10 (6), 553

Cannella J J, Brobyn R D, Albert M, Morton G 1979 A multi clinic comparative double blind evaluation of tolmetin. Current theraputic research 25: 447–56

Caruso I, Forro G B 1980 Gastroscopic evaluation of anti-inflammatory agents. British Medical Journal 1: 75–78

Cataggio L J, Maddison P J 1982 Systemic lupus erythematosus in the elderly. Annals of the Rheumatic Diseases 41: 201–202

Charnley J 1965 Low friction arthroplasty of the hip joint. In: Dixon A St J (ed) Progress in clinical rheumatology, 339–347 Churchill, London

Choussat H, Dartenuc J-Y, Belloussoff I, Parigent N, Poch H 1978 L'interêt clinique de brufen en rhumatologie gériatique. Revue Gériatrique (France) 3 (3), 161–164

Clagett O T, McDonald J R, Schmidt H W 1952 Localized fibrous mesothelioma of the pleura. Journal of Thoracic Surgery 24: 213

Cobb S, Merchant W R, Rubin T 1957 The relationship of symptoms to osteoarthritis. Journal of Chronic Diseases 5: 197–204

Corrigan A B, Robinson R G Terenty R, Dick-Smith J B, Walters D 1974 Benign rheumatoid arthritis of the aged. British Medical Journal 1: 444

Court Brown W M, Doll R 1965 Mortality from cancer and other causes after radiotherapy for ankylosing spondylitis. British Medical Journal 2: 1327

Coventry M B, Finerman G A M, Riley L H, Turner R H, Upshaw J E 1972 A new geometric knee for total knee arthroplasty. Clinical Orthopaedics 83–157

Dalziel J A, Wilcock G K 1979 Progressive systemic sclerosis in the elderly. Postgraduate Medical Journal 55: 192–193

Davison S 1980 Rheumatic Disease in the Elderly. Mount Sinai Journal of Medicine 47: 175–180

DeBosset P L, Bitter T 1975 Factors governing safety and success of gold salt therapy in rheumatoid arthritis. A prospective study. Annals of the Rheumatic Diseases 34: 196

DeQueker J V, Baeyens J P, Claessens J 1969 The significance of stature as a clinical measurement of aging. Journal of the American Geriatrics Society 17: 169

Dessain P, Estabrooks T F, Gordon A J 1979 Piroxicam in treatment of osteo-arthritis. Journal of Internal Medicine 7: 335

Dieppe P A, Huskisson E C, Crocker P, Willoughby M D 1976 Apatite deposition disease. Lancet i: 266

Dilke T F W, Burry H C, Grahame R 1973 Extradural corticosteroid injection in the management of lumbar nerve root compression. British Medical Journal 2: 635

Dimant J 1979 Rheumatoid Arthritis in the Elderly presenting as Polymyalgia Rheumatica. Journal of American Geriatrics Society, 37: 183–185

Dodds W J 1969 Triangular cartilage calcification in the wrist — its incidence in the elderly. American Journal of Roentgenology 105: 850

Dodds W J, Steinbach H L 1968 Primary hyperparathyroidism and articular cartilage calcification. American Journal of Medicine 104: 884

Doran D M I, Newell D T 1975 Manipulation in the treatment of low back pain: a multi-centre study. British Medical Journal 2: 161–164

Dorfman E, Solnica J, Menza Cl. Di, Seze S De 1969 Les arthropathies des hémochromatoses Hôpital (Paris) 45: 516

Dwosh I L, Stein H B, Urowitz M B, Smythe H A, Hunter T, Ogryzlo M A 1977 Azathioprine in Early Rheumatoid Arthritis. Comparison with Gold and Chloroquine. Arthritis and Rheumatism 20: 685–692

Eberl R, Tausch G, Siegmeth W, Broll H 1973 Essai comparatif ketoprofene contre phenylbutazone dans la goutte. 13th International Congress of Rheumatology, Kyoto, 1973. Pub. Rhumatologie, 199

Ebert H 1967 Der Verlauf der im alter auftrenden chronische Polyarthritis. Zeitschrift für Alternforschung 20: 259

Ehrlich G E, Katz W A, Cohen S H 1970 Rheumatoid arthritis in the elderly. Geriatrics 2: 103

Ellman M H, Levin B 1975 Chondrocalcinosis in elderly persons. Arthritis and Rheumatism 18: 43

Emery P, Grahame R 1982 Gastro-intestinal blood loss and piroxicam. Lancet i: 1362–3

Empire Rheumatism Council, Research Sub-Committee, Gold Therapy in Rheumatoid Arthritis. Final Report of a Multi-Centre Controlled Trial 1961. Annals of the Rheumatic Diseases 20: 315

Favour C B, Ritts R E J, Bayles T B 1956 Arthritis research. New England Journal of Medicine 254: 1078

Flatt A E 1963 In: The Care of the Rheumatoid Hand. Mosby, St Louis

Fleming A, Dodman S, Beer T C, Crown S 1976 Personality in Frozen Shoulder, Annals of the Rheumatic Diseases, 35: 456–457

Foad B H J, Sheon R P, Kirsner A S 1972 Systemic lupus erythematosus in the elderly. Archives of Internal Medicine 130: 743

Forestier J, Lagier R 1971 Vertebral ankylosing hyperostosis In: Hill A G S (ed) Modern trends in rheumatology — 2: 323–337

Fowler P D 1967 Marrow toxicity of the pyrazoles. Annals of the Rheumatic Diseases 26 (4), 344

Friedman D M, Moore M E 1980 The efficacy of intra-articular steroids in osteoarthritis. Journal of Rheumatology 7: 850–856

Ghosh A K, Rastogi A K 1981 A randomised comparison between sulindac and ibuprofen in osteoarthritis of the aged. Current Medical Research and Opinion 7: 482–487

Gibson T J, Grahame R 1971 Acute arthritis in the elderly. Proceedings of the 7th European Congress on Rheumatism Brighton

Gibson T, Grahame R 1981 Rehabilitation of the Elderly Arthritic Patient. Clinics in Rheumatic Diseases 7 (2), 485–495

Gibson T, Myers A K 1976 Nervous system involvement in systemic lupus erythematosus. Annals of the Rheumatic Diseases 35: 398–406

Gibson T, Schumacher H R 1976 Ankylosing hyperostosis with

cervical cord compression. Rheumatology and Rehabilitation 15: 67–70

Gibson T J, Winter J, Grahame R 1973 Treatment of osteoarthrosis by radiotherapy. Rheumatology and Rehabilitation 12: 42

Gibson T, Burry H D, Poswillo D, Glass J 1977 Effect of intra-articular cortico steroid injections on primate cartilage. Annals of the Rheumatic Diseases. 36: 74–49

Gibson T, Rodgers V, Potter C, Simmonds H A 1982 Allopurinol treatment and its effect on renal function in gout: a controlled study Annals of the Rheumatic Diseases 41: 59–65

Gibson T, Huskisson E C, Wojtulewski J A, Scott P J, Balme H W, Burry H C, Grahame R, Hart F D 1976 Evidence that d-penicillamine alters the course of rheumatoid arthritis. Rheumatology and Rehabilitation 15: 211

Glass J S, Grahame R 1976 Chondrocalcinosis after para-thyroidectomy. Annals of the Rheumatic Diseases 35: 521–525

Goldberg A, Brodsky I, McCarty D 1964 Multiple myeloma with para-amyloidosis presenting as rheumatoid disease. American Journal of Medicine 37: 653

Good A E, Green R A, Zarafonetis C J D 1965 Rheumatic symptoms during tuberculous therapy. A manifestation of izoniazid toxicity? Annals of Internal Medicine 63: 800

Grahame R 1969 Elasticity of human skin in vivo. A study of physical properties of the skin in rheumatoid arthritis and the effect of corticosteroids. Annals of Physical Medicine 10: 130

Grahame R Cruralgies d'origine discales aspects cliniques, therapeutiques et pronostiques, 1977. Actualités en Réducation Fonctionnelles et Readaptation. 2 ième Série Masson Paris pp 91–95

Grahame R, Scott J T 1970 Clinical survey of 354 patients with gout. Annals of the Rheumatic Diseases 99: 461

Grahame R, Calin A, Tudor M, Kennedy L, Perrin A 1975 Ankylosing Rheumatoid Arthritis. Rheumatology and Rehabilitation 14: 25–30

Gresham G E, Rathey U K 1975 Osteoarthritis of knees of aged persons. Relationship between roentgenographic and clinical manifestations. Journal of the American Medical Association 233, 2: 168–170

Griffin A J, Gibson T, Huston G, Taylor A 1981 Maintenance, chrysotherapy in rheumatoid arthritis: a comparison of 2 dose schedules. Annals of the Rheumatic Dieases 40: 250–253

Gunston F H 1971 Polycentric knee arthroplasty. Journal of Bone and Joint Surgery 53B–272

Hamilton E B D, Williams R, Barlow K A, Smith P M 1968 The arthropathy of idiopathic haemochromatosis. New England Journal of Medicine 37: 145

Hamilton E B D, Bywaters E G L 1961 Joint symptoms in myelomatosis and similar conditions. Annals of the Rheumatic Diseases 20: 353

Harris J, Carter A R, Glick E N, Storey G O 1974 Ankylosing hyperostosis. I. Clinical and radiological features. Annals of the Rheumatic Diseases 33: 210

Hart F D 1976 Which anti-rheumatic drug? Drugs, II: 451–460

Hatch H B, Knudson R J 1967 Extrathoracic manifestations of bronchogenic carcinoma. Medical Clinics of North America 51 (4): 1041

Hazelman B L 1972 The Painful Stiff Shoulder. Rheumatology Physical Medicine 11: 413–421

Henderson D R F, Tribe C R, Dixon A St J 1975 Synovitis in polymyalgia rheumatica Rheumatology and Rehabilitation 14: 244–250

Hess E V 1981 Introduction to drug-related lupus. Proceedings of the KROC Foundation Conference on drug-induced lupus. Arthritis and Rheumatism 24: vi–x

Hodkinson H M 1971 Scleroderma in the elderly with special reference to the C.R.S.T. syndrome. Journal of the American Geriatrics Society 19: 224

Hollander J L, Jessar R A, Brown E M Jr 1961 Intra-synovial corticosteroid therapy. A decade of uses. Annals of the Rheumatic Diseases 11: 239

Hunder G G, Bunch T W 1982 Treatment of RA. Bulletin on the Rheumatic Diseases 32: 1–7

Huskisson E C, Dieppe P A, Scott S, Jones H 1982 Diclofenac sodium, diflusinal and naproxen: patient preferences for anti-inflammatory drugs in rheumatoid arthritis. Rheumatology and Rehabilitation 21: 238

Huskisson E C, Woolf D L, Balme H W, Scott J, Franklin S 1976 Four anti-inflammatory drugs: responses and variations, British Medical Journal 1: 1048–1049

Inman W H W 1977 Study of fatal bone marrow depression with special reference to phenylbutazone. British Medical Journal 1: 1500

Jayson M I V 1981 Frozen Shoulder: Adhesive Capsulitis. British Medical Journal 283: 1005–1006

Julkunen H, Heinonen O P, Pyörälä K 1974 Hyperosostis of the spine in an adult population: its relation to hyperglycaemia and obesity. Annals of the Rheumatic Diseases 30: 605–612

Kellgren J H, Moore R 1952 Primary generalised osteoarthrosis. British Medical Journal 1: 181

Kellgren J H, Lawrence J S 1957 Radiological assessment of osteoarthrosis. Annals of the Rheumatic Diseases 16: 494

Kellgren J H, Lawrence J S, Bier F 1963 Genetic factors in generalised osteoarthrosis. Annals of the Rheumatic Diseases 22: 237

Khan A U 1980 Drugs for the elderly. European Journal of Rheumatology and Inflammation. 3: 205–209

Knowles J H, Smith L H Jr 1960 Medical progress. Extrapulmonary manifestations of bronchogenic carcinoma. New England Journal of Medicine 262: 505

Korst J K Van Den, Colenbrander I, Cats A 1966 Phenobarbital and the shoulder hand syndrome. Annals of the Rheumatic Diseases 25: 553

Lansbury F J 1953 Collagen disease complicating malignancy. Annals of the Rheumatic Diseases 12: 301

Lawrence J S 1969 Generalised osteoarthrosis in a population sample. American Journal of Epidemiology 90: 381

Lawrence J S 1975 Hypertension in relation to musculo skeletal disorders. Annals of the Rheumatic Diseases 34: 457

Lawrence J S, Bremner J M, Bier E 1966 Osteoarthrosis. Annals of the Rheumatic Diseases 25: 1

Lawrence J S, De Graff R, Laine V A I 1963 Degenerative joint disease in random samples and occupational groups. In: Kellgren J H, Jeffrey M R, Ball J (ed) The Epidemiology of Chronic Rheumatism, vol 1, p 98. Blackwell Scientific Publications, Oxford

Lee P N, Lee M, Haq A M M, Longton E B, Wright V 1974 Periarthritis of the shoulder. Trial of treatments investigated by multivariant analysis. Annals of the Rheumatic Diseases, 33: 116–119

Lequesne M, Moghtader R 1966 L'algodystrophie de l'isoniazide et de l'ethionamide. Revue du Rheumatisme et des maladies Ostéo-articulaires 33: 727

Litwin S D, Allen J C, Kunkel H G 1966 Disappearance of the clinical and serological manifestations of rheumatoid arthritis following a thoracotomy for a lung tumour. Arthritis and Rheumatism 9: 865

McCarty E J 1966 Pseudo-gout: articular chondrocalcinosis. In: Hollander J L, (ed) Arthritis and allied conditions, 8th edn, pp 947–964. Lea and Febiger, Philadelphia

McCarty E J, Hollander J L 1961 Identification of urate crystals in gouty synovial fluid. Annals of Internal Medicine 54: 452

McCarty G D J, Hogan J M, Gatter R A, Grossman M 1966 Studies in the pathological calcification in human cartilage. Journal of Bone and Joint Surgery 48A: 309

McConkey B 1982 Remission Inducing Drugs in Rheumatoid Arthritis. Reports on Rheumatic Diseases. No 82

McKee G K, Watson-Farrar J 1966 Replacement of arthritic hips by the McKee-Farrar prosthesis. Journal of Bone and Joint Surgery 48B: 245

McKenzie J J M 1981 Report of a double blind trial comparing small and large doses of gold in the treatment of rheumatoid disease. Rheumatology and Rehabilitation 21: 198–202

Mackenzie E H, Sherbel A L 1963 Connective tissue syndromes associated with carcinoma. Geriatrics 18: 745

McKever D C 1960 Tibial plateau prosthesis. In: Palmer A F de (ed) Clinical Orthopaedics, Lippincott, Philadelphia

McMahon F G, Jain A, Onel A 1976 A controlled evaluation of fenoprofen in geriatric patients with osteo-arthritis. Journal of Rheumatology Supplement 2: 76–83

Mackintosh D L 1958 Hemiarthroplasty of the knee using a space occupying prosthesis for painful valgus deformities. Journal of Bone and Joint Surgery 40A: 1431

Maitland G D 1973 In: Vertebral Manipulation, 3rd edn. Butterworth, London

Marmor L 1967 Surgery of the rheumatoid knee in a geriatric patient. Geriatrics 22: 97

Medsger T A, and Masi A T 1971 Epidemiology of systemic sclerosis (scleroderma). Annals of Internal Medicine 74: 714–721

Meeks L W, Renshaw T S 1973 Vertebral osteophytosis and dysphagia. Journal of Bone and Joint Surgery 55A: 197–201

Meurice J 1982 Evaluation of Surgam — Longterm tolerance. Rheumatology (Basel) 7: 182

Mikklesen E M, Duff I F, Dodge H J 1970 Age — Specific prevalence of radiographic abnormalities of the joints of the hands, wrist and cervical spine of adult residents of Tecumseh. Journal of Chronic Diseases 23: 151–159

Miller D G 1967 The association of immune disease and malignant lymphoma. Annals of Internal Medicine 66: 507

Moesmann G 1968 Sub-acute rheumatoid arthritis in old age. 1. Acta Rheumatica Scandinavica 14: 14

Morris I M, Eade A W T 1978 Pyogenic Arthritis and Rheumatoid Disease: The Importance of the Infected Foot. Rheumatology and Rehabilitation, 17: 222–226

Multicentre Trial Group 1973 Controlled trial of d-penicillamine in severe rheumatoid arthritis. Lancet i: 275

Newman J H 1976 Review of septic arthritis throughout the antibiotic era. Annals of the Rheumatic Diseases 35: 198

O'Brien W A 1968 Indomethacin a survey of clinical trials. Clinical Pharmacology and Therapeutics 9: 94

Oka M, Kytila J 1957 Rheumatoid arthritis with onset in old age. Acta Rheumatica Scandinavica 3: 249

Owen D S Jr, Waller M, Toone E C Jr 1970 Rheumatoid arthritis and malignancy. Bulletin of the Medical College of Virginia 6: 8–10

Platt G 1969 Mould arthroplasty of the knee — a 10 year follow-up. Journal of Bone and Joint Surgery 51B (1): 76

Potter T A 1969 Arthroplasty of the knee with tibial metallic implants of the McKever and MacIntosh design. Surgical Clinics of North America 49: 903

Powell-Jackson P R 1977 Interaction between azapropazone and warfarin. British Medical Journal 1: 1193–1194

Ragan C, Snyder A I 1955 Rheumatoid arthritis D. M. (Disease-A-Month) Nov. 1

Ring P A 1968 Complete replacement arthroplasty of the hip by the Ring prosthesis. Journal of Bone and Joint Surgery 50B: 720

Richards A J, Hamilton E B D 1974 Destructive arthropathy in chondrocalcinosis articularis. Annals of the Rheumatic Diseases 53: 196–203

Ritch A E S, Perera W N R, Jones C J 1982 British Journal of Pharmacology 14: 116–119

Roberts M E T, Wright V, Hill A G S, Mehra A C 1976 Psoriatic arthritis: follow-up study Annals of the Rheumatic Diseases 35: 206

Rodnan G P 1963 A review of recent observations and current theories on the aetiology and pathogenesis of progressive systemic sclerosis (diffuse scleroderma). Journal of Chronic Diseases 16: 929

Sarkin T L 1977 Back ache in the aged. South African Medical Journal 51: 418–420

Scott J T, Hall A D, Grahame R 1966 Allopurinol in treatment of gout. British Medical Journal 2: 321

Shiers L G P 1960 Arthroplasty of the knee. Journal of Bone and Joint Surgery 42B: 31

Silberberg M, Frank E L, Jarrett S R, Silberberg R 1959 Aging and osteoarthritis of the human sterno-clavicular joint. American Journal of Pathology 35: 851

Sperling I L 1961 The relationship of malignant disease and rheumatic syndromes. Proceedings of the 10th International Congress of Rheumatology Vol. II, p 590. Turin: Minerva

Standberg B, Jarlov N V 1961 Cancer arthritis and rheumatoid arthritis. Archives of Physical Medicine 42: 273

Steinberg C L, Duthie R B, Piva A E 1962 Charcot-like arthropathy

following intra-articular hydrocortisone Journal of the American Medical Association 181: 851

Steinbrocker O 1947 The shoulder-hand syndrome. American Journal of Medicine 3: 402

Sturge R A, Scott J T, Hamilton E B D, Lyanage S P, Dixon A St J, Davies J, Engler C 1977 Multicentre trial of naproxen and phenylbutazone in acute gout. Annals of the Rheumatic Diseases 36: 80–82

Swain M C, Smith D W, Goldberg A A J 1980 Fenclofenac — a five year study of patient tolerance. International Conference Symposium number 28, Academic Press London

Swanson A 1968 Silicone rubber implants for replacement of arthritic or destroyed joints in the hands. Surgical Clinics of North America 48: 1003

Sweetnam D R, Mason R M, Murray R A 1960 Steroid arthropathy of the hip. British Medical Journal 1: 92

Tallal N, Bunim J J 1964 The development of malignant lymphoma in the course of Sjögren's syndrome. American Journal of Medicine 36: 529

Thomas D, Williams R A, Smith D S 1980 The Frozen Shoulder: A Review of Manipulative Treatment. Rheumatology and Rehabilitation, 19: 173–179

Tillberg B 1969 Results of arthroplasty with vitallium cup because of coxarthrosis. Acta Orthopaedica Scandinavica 40 (3): 373

Urowitz M B, Stevens M B, Shulman L E 1967 The influence of age on the clinical pattern of systemic lupus erythematosus arthritis and rheumatism. Arthritis and Rheumatism 10: 319–320

Vertzman L, Lederman R, Rubenstein J, Lite N H, Guimaraes S J 1976 Fenbufen (a propionic acid derivative) in the treatment of acute gouty arthritis. A Folha Medica, 1973, 1

Waldius B 1957 Arthroplasty of the knee using an endoprosthesis. Acta Orthopaedica Scandinavica, supp. 24

Wallace S L 1975 Colchicine and new anti-inflammatory drugs for the treatment of gout. Arthritis and Rheumatism 18: 847–851

Watts R W E, Watkins P J, Matthias J Q, Gibbs G A 1966 Allopurinol and acute uric acid nephropathy. British Medical Journal 1: 22

Weinberger K A 1980 Rheumatoid arthritis masquerading as polymyalgia Rheumatica: A report of two cases. Journal of the American Geriatrics Society 38: 523–524

Widmark P 1978 Safety and efficacy of piroxicam in the treatment of acute gout. European Journal of Rheumatology and Inflammation 1: 346–349

Wierman W H, Clagett O T, McDonald J R 1954 Articular manifestations in pulmonary diseases. Analysis of the occurrence in 1024 cases in which pulmonary resection was performed. Journal of the American Medical Association 155: 1459

Wigsell F W 1976 Ulnar deviation of the fingers as a clinical sign in the elderly. Age and ageing 5: 132

Wilcock G K 1979 Prevalence of osteoarthritis of the hip requiring total hip replacement in the elderly. International Journal of Epidemiology 8: 247–250

Willis J V, Kendall M J 1978 Pharmacokinetic studies on Diclofenac. Scandinavian Journal of Rheumatology Supplement 2: 233–41

Willkens R F, Healer L A, Decker K L 1960 Acute infectious arthritis in the aged and chronically ill. Archives of Internal Medicine 106: 354

Wilson H A, Hamilton M E, Spyker D A, Brunner C M, O'Brien W M, Davis J S, Winfield J B 1981 Age influences the clinical and serological expression of systemic lupus erythematosus. Arthritis and Rheumatism 24: 1230–1235

Wood P H N 1972 Radiology in the diagnosis of arthritis and rheumatism. Transactions of the Society of Occupational Medicine 22: 69–73

Wright V, Haq A M M M 1976 Periarthritis of the shoulder. I. Aetiological considerations with particular reference to personality factors. Annals of the Rheumatic Diseases 35: 213

Zitnan D M, Sitaj S 1963 Articular chondrocalcinosis. Annals of the Rheumatic Diseases 22: 142

The musculoskeletal system — skeletal muscle

INTRODUCTION

Skeletal muscle is post mitotic at birth and consists of an aggregation of cylindrical cells or fibres which are polygonal in cross section and contain multiple peripherally situated nuclei. Fibre lengths may vary considerably according to the muscles in which they are situated, from a few millimetres in the extra ocular muscles to 10 cm in soleus. Fibre diameter varies in a similar fashion but in addition, is very sensitive to habitual activity, increasing with exercise and decreasing with disuse.

Several elongated sub-units termed myofibrils are arranged longitudinally within each muscle fibre. These sub-units contain the contractile proteins which are the source of the characteristic cross striations seen in longitudinal section (see Plate 40.1). The contractile proteins themselves are arranged in sub-units called sarcomeres which increase in number as muscle elongates during growth (Williams and Goldspink 1971).

The sarcoplasmic reticulum and transverse (T) tubules are two systems of channels which invest and invade the muscle fibre forming an intimate network around each myofibril. The sarcoplasmic reticulum which contains calcium, is an invagination of the sarcolemma and is arranged longitudinally; it does not connect with the extracellular space. The T tubules are an invagination of the plasma membrane, containing extracellular fluid and conduct it to each myofibril. The two systems are in intimate electrical contact at junctions called triads which consist of a central T tubule bounded on each side by an expansion of the sarcoplasmic reticulum called a 'terminal cistern'. These terminal cisterns contain a further reserve of calcium.

Contraction

In response to a nerve impulse, an action potential is produced at the motor end plate which is then propagated throughout the muscle fibre via the T tubules. At the triad, depolarization of the terminal cistern occurs and in response to this, calcium is released into the myofibril initiating contraction. This process is called excitation-contraction coupling. In order for this sequence to occur, the negative electropotential of the intracellular space must be maintained by a Na/K dependent membrane pump.

There are four contractile proteins, actin, myosin, tropomyosin and troponin. In a highly energy dependent process, actin and myosin combine to form cross bridges which then slide over each other producing contraction. In the relaxed state, troponin and tropomyosin inhibit cross bridge formation. Calcium combines with these two proteins inhibiting their action and allowing actin and myosin to combine.

Relaxation occurs by active sequestration of calcium into the terminal cistern by an energy-dependent membrane pump. In the total absence of ATP, cross bridges cannot be broken and muscular rigidity results. This is the biochemical basis of rigor mortis and also of rigidity in malignant hyperpyrexia.

Energy supply

Ultimately energy is supplied by ATP stored as phosphorylcreatine. Sufficient is present for only a few contractions and continuous work depends on rapid replacement by either aerobic or anaerobic tissue respiration (Holloszy, 1982) (Table 40.1). During gentle exercise or at rest, energy supply is by aerobic metabolism. Heavy exercise demands more energy than the aerobic system can supply and anaerobic respiration then provides an increasing proportion. For instance, during a fast sprint or in lifting a heavy weight, virtually all the energy required is generated anaerobically. In an unfit subject, climbing a few stairs may constitute heavy exercise and require a large anaerobic contribution. A

Table 40.1 Energy metabolism

ATP $\rightleftharpoons$ ADP + inorganic phosphate + ENERGY
Phosphorylcreatine + ADP $\rightleftharpoons$ Creatine + ATP
Glycogen + inorganic phosphate + ADP $\rightarrow$ H$^+$ + lactate + ATP
Glucose/free fatty acids + O$_2$ + inorganic phosphate + ADP $\rightarrow$ H$_2$ + CO$_2$ + ATP

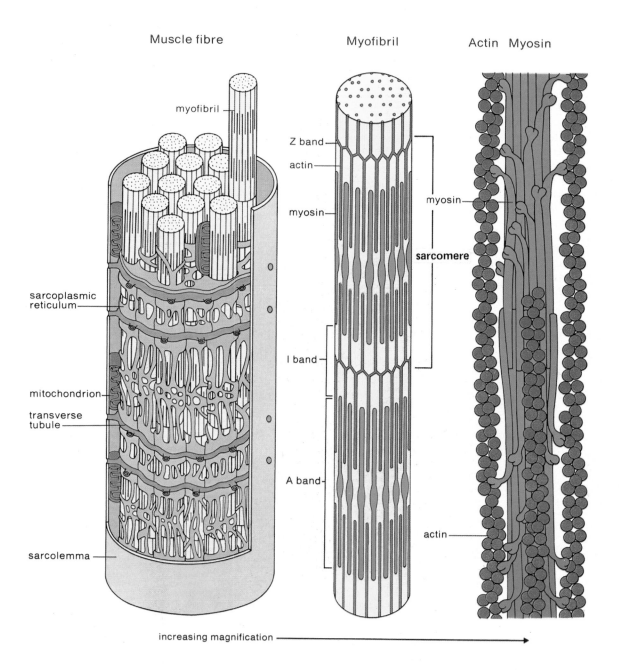

Muscle fibre

Myofibril

Actin   Myosin

myofibril

Z band
actin

myosin

sarcomere

myosin

sarcoplasmic
reticulum

mitochondrion

transverse
tubule

I band

A band

actin

sarcolemma

increasing magnification

Plate 40.1 Sub-divisions of skeletal muscle indicating the structural network involved in the conversion of relative molecular movement into muscular force. Reproduced by permission of Professor R H T Edwards and Imperial Chemical Industries from 'Muscle Weakness and Fatigue'.

similar circumstance arises in an ischaemic muscle where, although the level of activity is low, oxygen availablity becomes a limiting factor.

The problem with anaerobic respiration is that fatigue rapidly sets in due to intracellular lactate accumulation which inhibits metabolism. This is felt subjectively as heavy, painful, tired muscle. Aerobic respiration however, is relatively fatigue-resistant and exercise maintained by this means may continue for prolonged periods.

The major fuels are fatty acid and carbohydrate, both of which may be metabolized aerobically but only carbohydrate is metabolized anaerobically (Felig and Wahren, 1975). Only under prolonged intensive exercise does substrate supply become a limiting factor in young people. The situation in elderly subjects has not been studied.

Fibre types

There are two fibre types differentiated by their response to a single neuronal impulse, slow twitch — type I and fast twitch — type II. This probably reflects different types of myosin in each fibre (Holloszy, 1982).

The fibre types may also be distinguished histochemically (Gutmann and Melichna, 1979) (Table 40.2).

Table 40.2 Muscle fibre types

I	II$_a$	II$_b$
Slow twitch	Fast twitch	Fast twitch
Fatigue resistant	Fatigue resistant	Rapidly fatigue
Tonic activity	Phasic activity	Phasic activity
	Endurance	
		Power

It will be seen that type II fibres may be further subdivided into II$_a$ and II$_b$. Type II$_b$ fibres have predominantly anaerobic enzymes and rapidly fatigue. Type II$_a$ fibres have an admixture of aerobic and anaerobic systems. In the trained subject, the respiratory enzymes may be similar to type I fibres and in sedentary subject, almost completely anaerobic as in II$_b$ fibres.

Cross innervation experiments have shown that fibre types are determined by their innervation (Karpati and Engel, 1967)

In man most muscles have an admixture of type I and II fibres in proportions that are characteristic of that muscle. In addition, there are inter-individual differences which are determined genetically (Johnson et al,

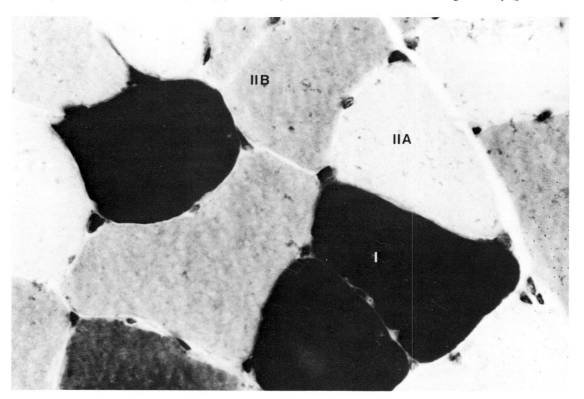

Fig. 40.1 Myosin ATP'ase. pH 4.6 Staining characteristics of type I, type II$_a$ and type II$_b$ fibres are shown. Original magnification × 216

1973; Komi et al, 1977). Muscles with a predominantly phasic action have mainly type II fibres e.g. extra ocular muscles, whereas tonic muscles, e.g. soleus have mainly type I fibres. Quadriceps which exhibit phasic and tonic activity comprises about 40 per cent type I and 60 per cent type II fibres. Histochemically, a characteristic feature is that the muscle fibres are arranged in a mosaic 'checkerboard' fashion (Fig. 40.1). Groups of one or other fibre type do not occur together in young healthy muscle.

The motor unit

The motor unit as defined by Sherrington, consists of an anterior horn cell, nerve axon and a number of muscle fibres. The numbers of muscle fibres varies considerably between small and large muscles, e.g. 10 fibres in extra ocular muscles and 2000 in soleus.

Each motor unit consists of only one fibre type and the territories of each motor unit overlap.

During muscle contraction, each motor unit functions as a single entity and all fibres are in the same state of contraction at the same time. With increasing demand for force, motor units are recruited in a fixed order, with the smallest units recruited first. In all movements, type I and II_a fibres are recruited from the outset, but type II_b seem to be recruited only during near maximal contractions (Holloszy, 1982).

The effects of exercise and disuse

Lifting heavy weights produces type II fibre hypertrophy, in particular of type II_b fibres. Endurance exercises, such as jogging and long distance walking produce minimal fibre hypertrophy but increase the concentrations of aerobic enzymes in type I and II_a fibres, increase the size and numbers of mitochondria and increase the capillary blood supply.

Disuse is generally accepted to cause type II fibre atrophy. Sargeant (1977) demonstrated type I and II fibre atrophy in the quadriceps of young soldiers immobilised in plaster due to leg fractures. It may be that in this case, some of the observations may have been due to lack of stretch, which is known to induce hypertrophy (McComas, 1976).

Pathological changes in muscle

Two major groups of changes can be seen. Neuropathic, secondary to neuronal damage or denervation, and myopathic, secondary to primary muscle disease. During severe denervation, secondary myopathic changes may also occur.

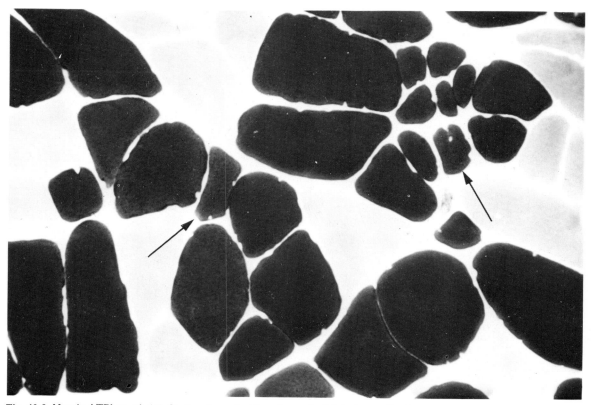

Fig. 40.2 Myosin ATP'ase. ph 4.6. Scattered angular fibres (arrows). Original magnification × 165

When a motor neurone is damaged, the fibres it innervates will atrophy. If the process is due to generalized denervation then atrophy of both fibre types is seen, distributed amongst relatively normal fibres. This is called disseminated neurogenic atrophy (Fig. 40.2). Following denervation, the atrophied fibres are adopted by neighbouring healthy motor neurones which develop sprouts and reinnervate the fibres. This results in fewer but larger motor units being formed. If the fibre is adopted into a motor unit of a different fibre type then it will gradually change to the type of the adopting unit. If this process is prolonged and repetitive then the checkerboard appearance of fibre types is lost and large groups of one or other fibre type are seen. This appearance is called fibre type grouping and is pathognomonic of chronic denervation and reinnervation (Fig. 40.3). If the axon supplying one of these large grouped motor units is then damaged, grouped atrophy will result (Fig. 40.4).

In long standing denervation, myopathic changes may occur including variation in fibre size, fibre splitting, central muclei and necrotic fibres.

These processes are readily seen histochemically in fresh, frozen muscle but are not reliably demonstrated by conventional electromyography. The investigations are therefore effectively limited to neurological centres with a special interest in muscle disease.

For further details, the reader is referred to the works of Walton (1981), McComas (1977), Swash and Schwartz (1981), De Girolami and Smith (1982).

AGING SKELETAL MUSCLE

Performance

Muscle strength and the ability to maintain co-ordinated muscle work decrease with increasing age from a maximum in young adults of 30 years of age (Norris and Shock, 1960)

Anderson and Cowan (1966) and MacLennan et al (1980) established values for hand grip pressure in healthy adults aged 60–80 years. Males had a stronger hand grip than females and there was a linear decline in strength with increasing age. The exact relationship between hand grip pressure and the strength of other muscles is unknown and in addition, forearm muscles are not easily studied electrophysiologically or by biopsy. The quadriceps, which does not suffer from these disadvantages, has been studied in more detail.

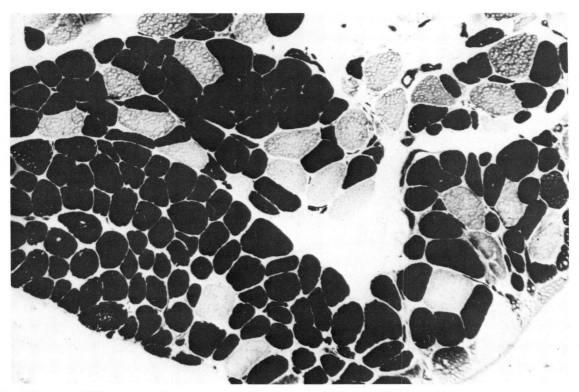

Fig. 40.3 Myosin ATP'ase. ph 4.6. Grouping of type I fibres is shown. Original magnification × 90

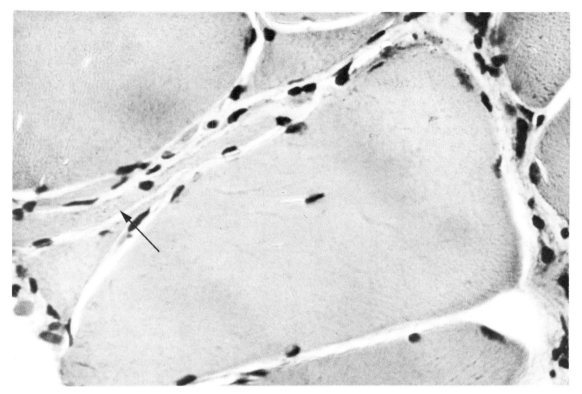

Fig. 40.4 Myosin ATP'ase. ph 4.6 'Grouped' angular fibres (arrows). Hand E, original magnification × 216

Larsson (1978) showed that isometric and isotonic quadriceps strength increased from 10–14 years old to 20–29 years, remained unchanged until 40–49 years and then gradually declined. This decrease was not associated with a reduction in thigh circumference but it correlated with a reduction in fat free mass, a relationship which has been confirmed by other workers (Clarkson, 1979; Aniansson, 1980; Aniansson et al, 1981). Independent of this correlation, there was a significant reduction in muscle strength directly related to increasing age.

Training programmes in 64–79 year old subjects have increased quadriceps strength by up to 22 per cent, an improvement comparable to that seen in young adults (Aniansson et al, 1980; Aniansson and Gustaffson, 1981).

Histology and histochemistry
Serratrice and Roux (1968) studied 12 elderly subjects with progressive weakness and muscle wasting and demonstrated a variety of non-specific 'myopathic changes'. They extensively reviewed the literature. Tomlinson et al (1969) studied patients who had died with muscle wasting associated with old age and/or prolonged coma due to head injury and dementia.

Marked evidence of denervation and type II fibre atrophy were seen.

Jennekens et al (1971a) studied post-mortem specimens of 8 cases aged 65–92 years whose pre-mortem levels of activity were unknown. Fibre type grouping was seen especially in extensor digitorum brevis where the usual checkerboard appearance was notably absent. However, the same authors (1971b) have observed similar changes in extensor digitorum brevis in patients aged 19–51 years dying suddenly. They postulate that chronic trauma to this nerve may produce these appearances and caution against drawing any general conclusions from this muscle (Jennekens et al, 1972)

Tomonaga (1977) studied intra-operative biopsies of patients aged 60–90 years with various pathologies including carcinoma, but with no overt neuromuscular disease. Denervation was noted at several sites, but especially in the distal limb musculature. In addition, type II fibre atrophy and myopathic features with central nuclei and necrosis were seen.

There have been several studies using needle biopsy. Changes of denervation have been seen by Grimby et al (1982) in the quadriceps of healthy subjects aged 78–81 years and by Cheshire and Cumming (1983) in healthy subjects in their seventh decade. However, Larsson

(1978), Aniansson (1980) and Aniansson and Grimby (1981) specifically note the absence of denervation in subjects up to the age of 70 years.

Type II fibre atrophy (especially of type II$_b$) is a consistent finding (Tomonaga, 1977; Larsson et al, 1978; Clarkson et al, 1979; Aniansson et al, 1981; Grimby et al, 1982; Cheshire and Cumming, (unpublished). This change may be reversed by a training programme (Larsson, 1978; Aniansson et al, 1981).

In young adults it is axiomatic that muscle strength varies directly with type II fibre area and this relationship has been demonstrated by Larsson (1978) and Grimby et al (1982). However, Aniansson et al (1981) were unable to demonstrate this in sedentary elderly subjects until after a 3 months training programme which had reversed the type II fibre atrophy seen in their original biopsies. The relevance of this observation is uncertain.

Electrophysiological studies
Campbell et al (1973) demonstrated electrophysiologically a decrease in the number of functioning motor units in extensor digitorum brevis. In a 92-year-old man only one functioning motor unit was identifiable and during a 5 week period, the function of this declined. Borg (1981) demonstrated slightly decreased axonal velocities in the nerve to extensor digitorum brevis in healthy elderly subjects. It has already been emphasized that this muscle may appear grossly abnormal in young people. The relevance of these findings is therefore unknown.

Newer methods of study
Crowe et al (1982) measured the cross sectional area of the thigh muscle in young and elderly women, using ultrasonography. There was a highly significant correlation between muscle strength and cross sectional area throughout the whole age range. They suggested that the decreased strength in elderly women could be explained by the smaller size of the muscle. It will be interesting to see whether this can be confirmed by other workers or using CAT scanning.

Summary
Muscle strength declines from the fifth decade and it is likely that this is a direct reflection of a reduction in muscle bulk. This is paralleled by a reduction in the area of type II muscle fibres and most workers have shown a significant correlation between this and declining muscle strength. At all ages, it seems that a programme of exercises can increase strength and increase type II fibre area, which in the elderly results in a reversal of the type II fibre atrophy.

Biopsy changes of chronic denervation have been seen more commonly in the very elderly.

The changes of myopathy with central nuclei, fibre splitting and necrotic fibres are seen but are not prominent. How far this reflects secondary myopathic changes is unknown.

Electrophysiological studies have been performed on extensor digitorum brevis but the changes in this muscle may not represent changes seen in other parts of the body.

Theories of muscle weakness in old age
Immobility causes muscle weakness. It has therefore been postulated that relative immobility and a gradual change to a sedentary existence may be responsible for the weakness of old age. Since this reduction in activity is universal, the hypothesis is effectively untestable. The fact that muscle strength in the elderly increases with training does not support the general argument that weakness in old age is due to immobility. Training at all ages increases strength.

The changes of denervation are commonly seen, but what causes denervation? In the extensor digitorum brevis, this may well be due to chronic trauma. In rats, Gutmann and Hanzlikova (1972) used the term functional denervation to explain the changes seen in muscle at a time when there was no evidence of anterior horn cell fall out. However, the ratio of nerve axon to muscle fibres cannot be counted in vivo and therefore this theory cannot be studied in man.

There is evidence that the numbers of both fibre tracts and anterior horn cells decrease with increasing age (Corbin and Gardner, 1937; Gardner, 1940; Tomlinson et al, 1973). This may account for some of the changes seen.

There is little, if any evidence, that the physiological decline in strength in the elderly is due to primary change within the muscle.

Androgen levels decline from middle age and androgen supplementation will increase muscle strength (Norris and Shock, 1960). There is however, no evidence that physiological decline in sex hormones is causally related to muscle weakness in old age.

The suggestion that there is a causal relationship between dietary potassium intake and muscle strength (Judge and Cowan, 1971) was refuted by Burr et al (1975).

There is no evidence that fibrous tissue replacement of muscle tissue (MacLennan et al, 1980) is the cause of muscle weakness in old age.

Summary
The cause of muscle weakness and wasting in old age is probably multifactorial. Changes within the central and peripheral nervous systems seem to be fundamental. The cumulative effects of intermittent systemic illness

and joint disease are unknown but the level of habitual exercise is probably important.

Limitations in methodology raise many questions of interpretation. The spatial distribution of fibre types within the quadriceps of old people is not well documented and Nygaard (1982) has questioned the validity of needle biopsy in the detection of fibre type grouping in the elderly. This problem is currently being investigated (Cumming, 1983). Although age-related changes have been demonstrated in autopsy studies of the spinal cord, the effects of these on the peripheral nervous system are unknown.

Single fibre electromyography can identify individual motor units and methods are available to study the monosynaptic reflex and long loop reflexes within the spinal cord and cerebral cortex. These sophisticated new techniques now allow muscle and its control mechanisms to be studied dynamically. Research into the aging neuromuscular system with these techniques has not yet been performed but provides exciting possibilities for the future.

INVESTIGATION OF NEUROMUSCULAR DISEASE

Old people will tolerate muscle weakness and to a lesser extent pain and stiffness for a long time, regarding them as inevitable concomitants of aging. It is only when the ability to perform some well established task is lost that these symptoms may be reported to the physician. Proximal muscle weakness will usually be tolerated for longer than distal weakness. For example difficulty in rising from a low chair or in climbing stairs may be seen as normal whereas catching the foot on the stairs or experiencing difficulty in depressing the pedals while driving are quickly recognized as abnormal. Similarly in the upper limbs difficulty in reaching up to a shelf or combing the hair may be tolerated whereas that in turning a key or opening a bottle is not. Pain or stiffness in addition to weakness may initially be attributed to 'arthritis'. In many cases the family will initiate the referral on the basis that their relative is 'slowing up'.

History
The commonest presenting symptoms of muscle disease are weakness and pain. Proximal weakness is common in diseases of the muscle fibres themselves (myopathic weakness) and in many of the inherited spinal muscular atrophies (neurogenic weakness). Distal weakness occurs main in myotonic dystrophy. Weakness of the cervical muscles may lead to the head falling forward and having to be supported by the hand. Weakness related to exercise is characteristic of the myasthenia gravis while another disease of neuromuscular trans-

mission — the myasthenic syndrome (Eaton Lambert) weakness which is present at the beginning of exercise improves as exercise continues. Myotonia (delayed relaxation) is uncommon in the elderly and usually signifies myotonic dystrophy.

Muscle pain is relatively non-specific and often poorly described. As a presenting feature it is only commonly seen in inflammatory myopathy of acute or sub-acute onset and in polymyalgia rheumatica.

Specific enquiry about other family members should be made. The spinal muscular atrophies (SMA) and the myotonic disorders are inherited. Myotonic dystrophy (autosomal dominant inheritance) can present in later life and patients with SMA may survive into old age.

Examination
The terms limb girdle dystrophy (LGD) and fascio-scapulo-humeral dystrophy (FSH) describe the pattern of weakness in an individual and do not in any sense indicate the underlying pathology (Walton, 1981). They should be referred to as 'syndromes'. In the limb girdle syndrome the proximal upper and lower limb girdles are affected with preservation of strength in the distal muscles of arms and legs. In FSH the orbicularis oculi and orbicularis oris muscles and the proximal upper limb muscles are first involved and lower limb muscles later. The LG and FSH syndromes account for the majority of patients with neuromuscular disease.

Two other patterns are occasionally encountered. Scapuloperoneal weakness involves the proximal upper limb muscles and the distal lower limb muscles. The second is Distal weakness which involves the forearm and hand muscles in the upper limb and the anterior and posterior tibial compartment in lower. This occurs in some forms of spinal muscular atrophy (SMA) and in myotonic dystrophy.

Weakness in myopathic diseases (those involving the muscle fibre) is symmetrical and all of the muscles around the joint will be involved to about the same degree. In neurogenic diseases (where the abnormality lies in the anterior horn cell or in the peripheral nerve) asymmetry and unequal involvement around a joint are seen. With the exception of motor neurone disease (MND) tone and reflexes in muscle diseases are either normal or more commonly, reduced. Fasiculations will be seen most frequently in MND but they are a feature of any denervating neuromuscular disease. Fasiculations of the tongue are best seen with the tongue lying at rest in the floor of the mouth. Apparent fasiculation may be seen in normal individuals with the tongue in any other position.

Investigations
Confirmation of the diagnosis usually involves the appli-

cation of electrophysiological, pathological and bio-chemical techniques. In most cases this involves the estimation of the serum enzymes, electromyography and nerve conduction studies; and muscle biopsy.

Serum enzymes

Serum creatine kinase (CK) is the most sensitive index of muscle necrosis both primary (as in polymyositis) and secondary (myopathic change in long standing dener-vation). CK consists of three separate izoenzymes; (MM) derived from skeletal muscle; (MB) derived largely from cardiac muscle; and (BB) derived mainly from brain. In normal serum the major izoenzyme is MM with about 6 per cent MB. The proportion of the latter rises in acute myocardial injury. Alterations in the serum CK will be discussed in the appropriate sections.

Neurophysiological studies

These provide detailed information on the integrity of the peripheral nerve, neuromuscular junction and the muscle. Measurement of nerve conduction velocities and terminal latency allow for the differentiation of axonal and demyelinating peripheral neuropathies. Repetitive stimulation gives information on the integrity of the neuromuscular junction. The electromyogram (EMG) gives evidence of either neurogenic atrophy or myopathy (Table 40.3). Recent developments in clinical neuro-physiology, including single fibre EMG and macro EMG, are reviewed by Stalberg and Young (1981).

Table 40.3 EMG findings in neuro-muscular disease

Neurogenic atrophy
— +ve sharp waves.
— spontaneous fibrillation potentials
— reduced number of motor units
— giant motor units (long-standing denervation)
Primary muscle disease
— absent spontaneous activity
— motor units polyphasic and of short duration

Muscle biopsy

The final diagnosis of muscle disease can only be made on muscle biopsy. Needle muscle biopsy (described by Edwards et al, 1973) can be performed on out-patients and repeatedly if necessary. The application of histo-chemical techniques to fresh frozen muscle permits the differentiation of muscle fibre types (see above) and can be used to study the distribution of cellular enzymes and metabolic reserves. Routine histological stains can also be used with fresh frozen material. The problems involved in processing and interpretation of muscle biopsies make the technique unsuitable for routine

laboratories and muscle samples should be sent to special neuromuscular laboratories or to experienced pathology centres. The pathological changes seen on biopsy will be described below. Developments in the field of radiology are beginning to have an impact on neuromuscular investigation. CT scanning of muscle, and ultrasound and isotope imaging, will probably become routine within the next few years.

NEUROMUSCULAR DISEASE IN THE ELDERLY

A description of the nosology of muscle diseases is not appropriate in the present context and detailed recent reviews are those of Munsat (1979) and Walton and Gardner-Medwin (1981) and of inherited neuromuscular disease — Walton (1981).

Inflammatory myopathy

The inflammatory myopathies can be broadly sub-divided into infective (bacterial, viral and parasitic) and autoimmune (idiopathic). The first group is the most common worldwide but in western societies idiopathic inflammatory myopathy accounts for the greatest proportion of acquired primary myopathies.

The idiopathic group comprises:

— polymyositis (PM)
— dermatomyositis (DM)
— PM-DM in association with connective tissue disorders
— PM-DM in association with malignancy

The current system of classification is as follows (Hudgson and Walton, (1979):

Group 1 — Pure 'PM'
Group 2 — PM-DM in association with other auto-immune diseases
Group 3 — PM-DM in association with malignancy

Polymyositis-dermatomyositis complex

This is considered an autoimmune disorder mainly because of its association with conditions such as SLE and because mononuclear cells are frequently seen on muscle biopsy. Circulating antibodies however, are rarely found and cell mediated immunity is probably the main cause.

Clinical features

PM-DM can occur at any age but it peaks in both child-hood and late middle age. The overall incidence is 4 to 5 per million population (Rose and Walton, 1966) affecting women more often than men (DeVere and Bradley 1975). It presents with weakness, skin rash and joint or muscle pain and progresses over weeks or months rather than years. A rare hyperacute presentation with subcutaneous oedema, intense muscle pain and myoglobinuria has been described (Bohan and Peter, 1975). Weakness always occurs, usually the limb girdle type, and wasting is seen in about 50 per cent of cases. Other muscle involvement is of distal muscles in about 30 per cent and pharyngeal muscles in 50 per cent (Currie, 1981). Predominantly distal weakness is rare (Hollinrake, 1969) as is scapulohumeral weakness (Bates et al, 1973) and localized nodular myositis (Cumming et al, 1977). In this variant painful nodules, which may be misdiagnosed as deep venous thrombosis, occur before the myopathy.

The rash occurs in about one-third of cases typically involving the face in a butterfly distribution which may spread to periorbital areas. Extensor surfaces of arms and legs involved with dusky red patches over elbows, knuckles and to a lesser extent knees and medial malleoli. Grottron's papules and periungal telangiectases are uncommon skin manifestations (Callen 1982a).

Joint involvement occurs in 25 per cent of patients and some with long standing rheumatoid arthritis may develop proximal myopathy with evidence of muscle necrosis on biopsy as a late complication (Haslock et al, 1970). Dysphagia, Raynauds phenomenon and articular symptoms are more common in PM-DM associated with systemic collagen-vascular disease (Mastaglia and Walton, 1982).

Involvement of other organ system is rare although heartblock has been described (Henderson et al, 1980) as has parenchymal lung involvement with fibrosing alveolitis (Plowman and Stablethorn, 1977).

PM-DM and malignancy

The reported incidence of malignancy in PM-DM varies from 5 to 35 per cent of all cases (Callen, 1982b). This disparity is not unexpected since many case reports are anecdotal and the diagnostic criteria vary (see DeVere and Bradley, 1978; Bohan et al, 1977). The onset of symptoms of the malignancy usually coincides with those of PM-DM although there are exceptions (Barnes, 1976). The most common sites of malignancy in women are breast, ovary, uterus and colon and in men lung, prostate and colon (Barnes, 1976). Response to treatment is still uncertain.

Investigation

The serum CK will usually be elevated, often into the range 1000–2000 IU/1 and sometimes higher. Serum myoglobin may also be estimated as a marker of muscle necrosis (Nashikai and Reichlin, 1977). The EMG shows a triad of features in classical PM-DM (Currie, 1981) — spontaneous activity with fibrillation, positive potentials and increased insertional activity: small amplitude, short duration polyphasic potentials on volitional activity: 'pseudomyotonic' discharges provoked by mechanical stimulation. Muscle biopsy is diagnostic in 70 per cent of cases, false negative results being due to the patchy nature of the disease. The biopsy shows necrosis, phagocytosis and regeneration with varying inflammatory infiltrates.

Treatment

In the majority of cases oral steriods (e.g. prednisone) in high dose and for an adequate period is required. Usual initial dose is 1–2 mg per kilogram body weight daily. This should be maintained until there is clear clinical evidence of improvement and then change to alternate day therapy which may need to be continued for several years. Clinical criteria of improvement rather than CK levels should be used, since although initial CK levels are significantly related to the degree of muscle necrosis, this is not the case when treatment has been started (Bunch et al, 1980). Serial testing of muscle strength has been shown to parallel metabolic function studies of muscle breakdown and repair (Edwards et al, 1979). Since steroids produce a non-specific fall in the serum CK this measurement is not reliable. Serum myoglobin measurement may be a more useful guide to disease activity during therapy. Diminution in muscle strength during the course of treatment may indicate recrudescence of myositis or the development of a steroid myopathy. It is important to distinguish these two possibilities on repeat muscle biopsy. Late secondary steroid myopathy appears to be a major contributor to the poor prognosis recorded in some series of PM-DM.

Azothioprine in doses of 1–2 mg/kg has improved functional ability over a period of 3 years with considerable steroid sparing effect (Bunch, 1981).

Prognosis

In uncomplicated PM-DM the prognosis has been improved by the use of steroid (with or without azathioprine), particularly in those patients in whom treatment was initiated early in the course of the disease. Bohan et al (1977) found a mortality rate of 14 per cent overall the poorest response being found in those patients with malignancy and in the older age groups.

Polymyalgia rheumatica

This disorder is characterized by pain and stiffness occurring in the proximal muscles, particularly in the upper limbs. There is usually evidence of an underlying systemic disorder with malaise, weight loss, anaemia and an elevated ESR. Despite its name and similarities to PM/DM, Polymyalgia rheumatica however is not a myopathy in that the muscles are not primarily involved. Muscle weakness occurs late, if at all.

Polymyalgia rheumatica only rarely occurs under the age of 50 and peak incidence rates occur between the ages of 70 and 79. There is a female to male ratio of 1.7 : 1 (Chuang et al, 1982). In addition to an elevated ESR, a mild anaemia is seen in some patients. A positive antinuclear factor and abnormal liver function tests are seen in about 20 per cent of patients. An association with giant cell arteritis is seen in 15 per cent of patients. Muscle biopsy shows changes consistent with disuse (type II$_b$ fibre atrophy: Brooke and Kaplan, 1972). The CK is normal.

Treatment in the majority of patients is with steroids, the most commonly used being prednisolone. Initial doses of 60 to 80 mg daily produce an improvement in clinical symptomatology and the ESR within 72 hours but complete resolution of symptoms may take up to 3 months.

The average duration of disease is 1 year. This is however, some evidence to suggest that two populations of patients exist. One group appears to have a self-limiting illness and requires treatment between 11 and 16 months, whereas those who have a more persistent illness have treatment durations of 36 to 40 months (Chuang et al, 1982; Von Knorring, 1979).

Motor neurone diseases

Motor neurone disease (MND) is the collective term which comprises the three disorders of progressive muscular atrophy, progressive bulbar palsy and amyotrophic lateral sclerosis. In the USA amyotrophic lateral sclerosis (ALS) is more commonly used as the collective term. MND can present at any age, but it has a predilection for older age groups. In the series of Jokelainen (1977), 36 per cent of patients had an onset between 50–60 years, 39 per cent between 60–70 years and 6 per cent over 70. Outside the Western Pacific Islands, where atypical forms of the disease occur, there is a male: female ratio of 1.6: 1, except in the 5–10 per cent of familial cases where the sex ratio is equal (Kurland and Mulder, 1955).

Sporadic MND

The disease most commonly presents in the upper limbs (40 per cent of cases) with wasting and weakness of the intrinsic hand muscles. Frequent muscle cramps may preceed the onset of weakness by months (Bonduelle, 1975) The weakness gradually spreads to involve the whole limb and then starts in the opposite limb. With time, the bulbar muscles and the lower limbs become involved.

Upper motor neurone symptoms of spastic weakness and reflex nocturnal spasms may dominate the early stages (ALS). The patient may be aware of 'flickerings' under the skin, even in normal muscles, indicating fasciculations. In progressive bulbar palsy the first manifestation may be indistinct speech followed by dysphagia. These symptoms preceed clinically obvious wasting or fasciculation in the early stages of the disease. Weakness may remain confined to the bulbar muscles for months before becoming generalized.

Irrespective of the initial mode of presentation, the disease runs a steadily progressive course over 3–4 years (Campbell and Liversedge, 1981). Eventually all limb, trunk, head and neck muscles, with the exception of extra-ocular muscles, become paralyzed. Death usually results from respiratory insufficiency.

Familial MND

The mean age of onset, the clinical presentation and the course of the disease is similar in familial and sporadic MND (Campbell, 1979). There may be considerable variation both in presentation and course between family members.

Sensory symptoms occur, including numbness, deadness and paraesthesia, but objective sensory signs are rare. Clinical examination reveals a combination of upper and lower motor neurone signs, depending on the stage of the disease at the time of examination. Increased tone in the lower limbs is common and correlates with the preserved or increased reflexes seen despite the degree of weakness. At some time during the course of the disease, extensor plantar responses will occur.

Investigation. There is no specific diagnostic test for MND. The most useful investigation is EMG which shows fasciculations and a reduced number of motor units on recruitment. These changes are seen in clinically uninvolved muscle, whereas in cervical spondylosis presenting with weakness of the hand, signs of denervation are found in a radicular pattern.

Treatment. There is no specific treatment for MND. A wide range of therapies have been tried all with no clear benefit (for review see Campbell and Liversedge, 1981). In patients with bulbar symptoms leading to marked pooling of saliva, pyridostigmine may be of temporary benefit. In patients with dysphagia, crico-pharyngeal myotomy, which lowers the intrapharyngeal pressure, may be of major benefit (Loizou et al, 1980). The timing of this proceedure is of importance and best results are obtained when tongue movement is less impaired than swallowing. In patients with marked dysphonia, the provision of electronic communicators (e.g. Canon) can be of benefit. However for the majority of patients general supportive care of the patient and family is the mainstay of treatment.

Myasthenia gravis

Although myasthenia gravis is generally considered to be a disease of younger patients, about 10 per cent of patients with both generalized and ocular onset have their first symptoms after the age of 60 years (Grob,

1983). In this group of patients the disease is more common in males in contradistinction to patients with earlier onset where females outnumber males.

In most cases, it presents with fatiguable weakness, initially of the extraocular muscles with ptosis (25 per cent) and diplopia (25 per cent) as the major symptoms. Less common presenting symptoms are lower limb weakness (13 per cent), fatigue (6 per cent), difficulty in chewing (6 per cent), slurred and nasal speech (5 per cent), difficulty chewing (4 per cent), weakness of arms, neck or face (3 per cent) and weakness of trunk or shortness of breath (1 per cent). In only very few patients is a precipititing cause found and this is usually an upper respiratory tract infection. In the first few months after the initial symptom 40 per cent will develop generalized symptoms, 40 per cent will have only ocular mainfestations, 10 per cent will have only limb symptoms and 10 per cent only bulbar or oculobulbar symptoms. The most common progression of symptoms is extraocular muscles, face, swallowing, speech, jaw, tongue, neck, shoulders, arms hands, hips, legs, trunk and respiration (Grob et al, 1981).

The 'Tensilon' test confirms the diagnosis by a rapid improvement following the intravenous infusion of Edrophonium. Decrement of repetitive stimuli and increased 'jitter' on single fibre EMG are the main features seen with electrophysiology (for review see Desmedt, 1983).

Understanding of the pathogenesis of myasthenia gravis has led to the development of the anti-acetylcholine receptor antibody (Anti AChR-Ab) assay. The weakness and fatiguability is thought to be due to interference with neuromuscular transmission that follows binding of antibody to post-junctional acetylcholine receptors. Anti AChR-Ab is present in 85–90 per cent of patients with generalized disease and false positive results are rare (Compston et al, 1980). On the basis of multiple analyses, this group have identified three groups of patients with myasthenia gravis of which two are important in the elderly. These are Group A which is characterized by the presence of thymoma, high titres to anti AChR-Ab and the presence of striated muscle antibody and Group C where no thymoma is demonstrated in patients presenting over the age of 40. This group have variable titres of anti-AChR-Ab; low frequency of striated muscle antibody; and a high frequency of other antibodies but a low frequency of other autoimmune disease. The presence of thymic abnormalities is best investigated with CT scanning of the thorax.

Treatment

Treatment of MyG involves the use of anticholinesterase agents, steroids, plasmapheresis, immunosupression and thymectomy. The role of each of these is not clearly defined and there is no single correct therapy for all patients. In patients with pure ocular disease, anticholinesterases and or steroids are to be preferred to more complex treatment regimes. In the patient with generalized disease anticholinesterases have long been the main form of therapy. However 'crises' either myasthenic or cholinergic (see below), may occur especially with intercurrent infection. The value of thymectomy in the elderly patient has been demonstrated (Olanow et al, 1982). Steroids may initially increase the degree of disability and should therefore only be commenced as inpatient therapy. Plasmapheresis is of great value in the short term.

In the patient with progressive generalized disease, a logical approach to therapy is plasmapheresis to improve the condition prior to thymectomy, using either plasmapheresis or steroids/immunosupression for late relapse. The respective value of these different treatment regimes will become more clearly defined in the next few years.

'Crises'. In some patients the neuromuscular block in myasthenia gravis is not or is only partially reversible by anticholinesterases. This may occur during exacerbations of the disease or they may be made unresponsive by excessive doses of drugs. This insensitivity of the motor end plate is responsible for the failure of drugs to restore muscle strength. A further increase in drugs fails to improve strength (myasthenic crisis) and excess dosages result in increasing weakness (cholinergic crisis). No reliable clinical features distinguish between the different mechanisms. In most patients, reduction or cessation of medication for a few days, with ventilator support if necessary, may be followed by a return of responsiveness (Grob, 1983).

Neuromuscular diseases in malignancy

In the aging population the frequency of carcinoma increases and therefore the incidence of neuromuscular disorders associated with malignancy also increases. This subject has been reviewed in detail by Kula (1979) and Henson and Urich (1982). The incidence of these disorders is 5 per cent in unselected patients with cancer (Croft and Wilkinson, 1965). Henson and Urich (1982) have defined three major groups of disorders: polymyopathy; disorders of neuromuscular transmission; and PM-DM complex (see above).

Polymyopathy

Cachectic myopathy. In this condition there is loss of body fat then protein with muscle wasting, weakness, and anaemia. The clinical features are well recognized with loss of subcutaneous fat, and diffuse muscle wasting, involving proximal and distal muscles equally. Despite the degree of wasting, muscle strength is well maintained until the final stages of the disease when weakness becomes profound. Muscle biopsy shows scattered fibre atrophy, changes which are similar to those found in any wasting process (Schmitt, 1978).

Proximal muscle weakness (*carcinomatous neuromyopathy*). In these patients, weakness in the proximal and axial muscles is found initially with little evidence of wasting. The weakness may preceed the symptoms of carcinoma by months or years. The common tumoursites are lung, breast and GI tract. Muscle biopsy shows evidence of denervation. It has been suggested that the tumour has a remote effect on the distal axons of motor nerves (Barron and Heffner, 1978).

Disorders of neuromuscular transmission — myasthenic syndrome (Eaton-Lambert)

The clinical picture is mainly of fatiguability with background weakness. Initially the weakness is confined to the pelvic gridle and proximal lower limb muscles and later spreads to the proximal upper limb muscles. The facial and ocular muscles are involved late in the disease which helps distinguish the condition from myasthenia gravis. Facilitation, increase in power with repeated contraction, is seen in some patients. Diffuse muscle aching is common. Examination often fails to reveal gross abnormalities. The reflexes are depressed or absent. The disease affects men more often than women (4:1). The commonest tumor site is lung but cases have been reported in association with carcinoma of breast, prostate, rectum and stomach.

The response to intravenous Tensilon is poor although some patients have a good response. Electrophysiological investigation shows an increase of the evoked potential with repetitive stimulation (Elmqvist and Lambert, 1968). The disease has been shown to be due to an underlying defect in acetylcholine release (Lindstrom and Lambert, 1978).

The prognosis is that of the underlying tumour. The value of tumour removal on the course of the disease is disputed. In patients who can tolerate the drug, guanidine HCL (35 mg/kg daily) provides the best symptomatic relief. Prednisolone and 4-aminopyridine may be of value in some patients (Lundh et al, 1977).

Drug-induced myopathy

Agents causing disorders of neuromuscular transmission have been reviewed by Argov and Mastaglia (1979) who cite 30 drugs in common use. Hudgson (1982) has reviewed the literature with respect to peripheral neuropathy, neuromuscular transmission and myopathy.

Impaired neuromuscular transmission. The clinical features of drug-induced disorders of neuromuscular transmission are postoperative respiratory depression, precipitation or aggravation of myasthenia gravis and myasthenic-like syndromes. Antibiotics, particularly of the aminoglycoside group (neomycin, streptomycin and kanomycin) can produce all three types of neuromuscular disorders. The most common antirheumatic drug which influences neuromuscular transmission is penicillamine. This produces a syndrome indistinguishable from myasthenia gravis is patients taking 0.5–1 g daily for periods of up to 8 years (Hudgson, 1982). The patients improve slowly on cessation of therapy although anti-cholinesterases may be required. Anti AChR-Ab titres may be raised (Fawcett et al, 1982). Cardioactive drugs have been described as worsening myasthenia gravis (procainamide, quinidine) or producing a myasthenic like syndrome (propanolol, oxprenolol, practolol). The anticonvulsant phenytoin has been reported to produce a myasthenic-like syndrome.

Myopathy. The clinical features of drug induced myopathy are those of the induced disorder. Hudgson (1982) has subdivided these on the basis of the pathological reaction in muscle. Thus muscle cramps without weakness are seen with clofibrate, lithium, cimetidine and salbutamol. Fibrosis and contracture is seen with repeated injections of irritant antibiotic injections at one site. Acute muscle necrosis with renal failure is seen with aminocaproic acid (used to reduce the risk of rebleeding after subarachnoid haemorrhage). Chronic painless myopathy is seen with steroids (see below) and chloroquine. Hypokalaemic myopathy is seen with thiazide diuretics, carbenoxolone and chronic purgation. Inflammatory myopathy is seen with penicillamine, procainamide and hydralazine.

Steroid induced myopathy is the commonest drug-induced myopathy encountered in clinical practice. The onset is usually slow as is the course. In all respects it resembles Cushing's disease. There is proximal muscle weakness of the lower limbs with slight involvement of the upper limbs. The CK is usually normal or only slightly raised and conventional EMG is normal although changes may be seen on quantitative EMG. Muscle biopsy shows selective atrophy of Type II_b fibres. The recovery of muscle function following withdrawal of the drug is protracted and may take years. In some cases the weakness is irreversable (Mastaglia et al, 1970). The pathogenesis of the condition is unknown.

Endocrine myopathy

Muscle involvement in endocrine disease is rare. It has recently been reviewed by Hudgson and Hall (1982). Muscle disease is most often seen in patients with thyroid disease and in Cushings syndrome (discussed under steroid myopathy).

Thyrotoxicosis. Clinical evidence of proximal weakness is present in the majority of patients with thyrotoxicosis and in rare cases can be the presenting feature. Localised paresis of the extraocular muscles, a myasthenic-like syndrome, and attacks of periodic paralysis have been described. Fasiculations are seen in some patients. The CK is normal and EMG and muscle biopsy show non-specific changes. The weakness rapidly resolves on treatment.

Hypothyroidism. The commonest symptoms in patients with hypothyroid myopathy are aches and pains, muscle stiffness and cramp which can simulate arthritic disease (Golding, 1970). Apparent muscle hypertophy and myotonia (Hoffmann's syndrome) is seen in some cases. The serum CK is almost always elevated and may reach values of 1000–2000. Muscle biopsy shows a change in the proportions of Type 1 and 2 fibres with much higher percentages of Type 1. This change in the Type 1 proportion changes only slowly with therapy (McKeran et al, 1975) whereas the clinical symptoms and the CK levels rapidly return to normal.

REFERENCES

Aniansson A 1980 Muscle function in old age with special reference to muscle morphology, effect of training and capacity in activities of daily living. Department of rehabilitation, medicine and geriatric and long term care medicine. University of Goteburg, Goteburg, Sweden.

Aniansson A, Grimby G, Rundgren A, Svanborg A, Orlander J 1980 Physical training in old men. Age and Ageing 9: 186–187

Aniansson A, Gustaffson E 1981 Physical training in elderly men with special reference to quadriceps muscle strength and morphology. Clinical Physiology 1: 87–98

Aniansson A, Grimby G, Hedberg M, Krotkiewski M 1981 Muscle morphology, enzyme activity and muscle strength in elderly men and women. Clinical Physiology 1: 73–86

Anderson W F, Cowan N R 1966 Hand grip in old people. British Journal of Preventative and Social Medicine 20: 141–147

Argov Z, Mastaglia F L 1979 Disorders of neuromuscular transmission caused by drugs. New England Journal of Medicine 301: 409–413

Barnes B E 1976 Dermatomyositis and malignancy. A review of the literature. Annals of Internal Medicine 84: 68–76

Barron S A, Heffner R R 1978 Weakness in malignancy; evidence for a remote effect of tumour on distal axons. Annals of Neurology 4: 268–274

Bates D, Stevens J C, Hudgson P 1973 'Polymyositis' with involvement of facial and distal musculature. Journal of the Neurological Sciences 19: 105–108

Bohan A, Peter J B 1975 Polymyositis and Dermatomyositis. New England Journal of Medicine 292: 344–347, 403–407

Bohan A, Peter J B, Bowman R L, Pearson C M 1977 A computer assisted analysis of 153 patients with polymyositis and dermatomyositis. Medicine (Baltimore) 56: 255–286

Bonduelle M 1975 Amyotrophic lateral sclerosis. In: Vinken P J, Bruyn G W (eds) Handbook of Clinical Neurology, North Holland, Amsterdam, p 281–338

Borg J 1981 Properties of single motor units of the extensor digitorum brevis in elderly humans. Muscle and Nerve 4: 429–434

Brooke M H, Kaplan H 1972 Muscle pathology in rheumatoid arthritis, polymalgia rheumatica and polymyositis. A Histochemical study. Archives of Pathology 94: 101–115

Bunch T W 1981 Prednisone and Azathioprine for polymyositis. Long-term follow up. Arthritis and Rheumatism 24: 45–48

Bunch T W, Worthington J W, Combs J J, Ilstrup D M, Engel A G 1980 Azathioprine with prednisone for polymyositis. Annals of Internal Medicine 92: 365–369

Burr M L, St Leger A S, Wetlake C A, Davis H E F 1975 Dietary potassium deficiency in the elderly: a controlled trial. Age and Aging 4: 148–151

Callen J P 1982a Dermatomyositis and Malignancy. Clinics in Rheumatic Diseases 8: 369–381

Callen J P 1982b The value of malignancy evaluation in patients with dermatomyositis. Journal of the American Academy of Dermatology 6: 253–259

Campbell M J 1979 Genetic aspects of motor neurone disease. In: Behan P O, Rose F C (eds) Progress in Neurological Research, Pitman, London, p 135–144

Campbell M J, Liversedge L A 1981 The motor neurone diseases. In: Walton J N W (ed) Disorders of Voluntary Muscle, 4th end, Churchill Livingstone, Edinburgh, p 725–752

Campbell M J, McComas A J, Petito F 1973 Physiological changes in aging muscle. Journal of the Neurological Sciences 36: 174–182

Chaung T, Hunder G G, Ilstrup D M, Kurland L T 1982 Polymyalgia Rheumatica. A 10-year epidemiologic and clinical study. Annals of Internal Medicine 97: 672–680

Clarkson P M, Kroll W, Melchionda A M 1981 Age, isometric strength, rate of tension development and fibre type composition. Journal of Gerontology 36: 648–653

Compston D A S, Vincent A, Newson-Davis J, Batchelor J R 1980 Clinical, pathological, HLA antigen and immunological evidence for disease heterogeneity in myasthenia gravis. Brain 103: 579–601

Corbin K B, Gardner E D 1937 Decrease in the number of myelinated fibres in human spinal roots with age. Anatomical Record 68: 63–74

Croft P B, Wilkinson M 1965 The incidence of carcinomatous neuromyopathy in patients with various types of carcinoma. Brain 88: 427–434

Crowe M, Stokes M, Young A 1982 Non-invasive measurements of quadriceps muscle strength and cross sectional area in the elderly. Paper presented at the Autumn meeting of the British Geriatric Society.

Cumming W J K 1983 Unpublished data.

Cumming W J K, Weiser R, Hudgson P, Walton J N 1977 Focal Nodular Myositis. Quarterly Journal of Medicine 46: 531–546

Currie S 1981 Inflammatory Myopathies. In: Walton J N (ed) Disorders of Voluntary Muscle, 4th edn, Churchill Livingstone, Edingburgh, p 525–568

De Girolami V, Smith T W 1982 Pathology of Skeletal Muscle Diseases. A teaching monograph. American Journal of Pathology 107 (2): 235–276

De Vere R, Bradley W G 1975 Polymyositis: Its presentation, morbidity and mortality. Brain 98: 637–666

Desmedt J E 1983 Electrophysiological validation of myasthenia gravis. In: Albuquerque E X, Eldefrawi A T (eds) Myasthenia Gravis, Chapman and Hall, London, p 249–274

Edwards R H T, Maunder C, Lewis P D, Pearse A G E 1973 Percutaneous Needle biopsy in diagnosis of muscle disease. Lancet ii: 1070–1071

Edwards R H T, Wiles C M, Round J M, Jackson M J, Young A 1979 Muscle breakdown and repair in Polymyositis: A case study. Muscle and Nerve 2: 223–228

Elmqvist D, Lambert E H 1968 Detailed analysis of neuromuscular transmission in a patient with the myasthenic syndrome sometimes associated with bronchogenic carcinoma. Mayo Clinic Proceedings 43: 689–713

Fawcett P R W, McLachlan S M, Nicholson L V B, Mastaglia F L 1982 d-Penicillamine associated myasthenia gravis: Immunological and electrophysiological studies. Muscle and Nerve 5: 328–334

Felig P, Wahren J 1975 Fuel Homeostasis in exercise. New England Journal of Medicine 293: 1078–1084

Gardner E 1940 Decrease in human neurones with age. Anatomical record 77: 529–536

Golding D N 1970 Hypothyroidism as a cause of rheumatic pain. Annals of the Rheumatic Diseases 29: 10–16

Grimby G, Danneskiold-Samsoe B, Hvid K, Saltin B 1982 Morphology and enzymatic capacity in arm and leg muscles in 78–81 year old men and women. Acta Physiologica Scandinavica 115: 125–134

Grob D 1983 Clinical manifestations of Myasthenia Gravis. In:

Albuquerque E X, Eldefrawi A T (eds) Myasthenia Gravis, Chapman and Hall, London, p 319–346

Grob D, Brunner N G, Namba T 1981 The natural history of myasthenia gravis and effect of therapeutic measures. Annals of the New York Academy of Sciences 377: 652–669

Guttmann E, Hanzlikova V 1972 Age Changes in the Neuromuscular System. Scientecnica Limited, Bristol

Guttmann E, Melichna J A 1979 Contractile and histochemical properties of denervated and reinnvervated fast and slow skeletal muscles of new-born and adult guinea-pigs. Physiologia Bohemoslovaca 28: 35–42

Haslock D I, Wright V, Harriman D G F 1970 Neuromuscular disorders in Rheumatoid Arthritis. A motor point muscle biopsy study. Quarterly Journal of Medicine 39: 335–349

Henderson D, Cumming W J K, Hudgson P, Williams D W 1980 Cardiac abnormalities in polymyositis. Journal of the Neurological Sciences 47: 425–428

Henson R A, Urich H 1982 Muscular and Neuromuscular disorders associated with malignant disease. In: Henson R A, Urich H Cancer and the Nervous System, Blackwell Scientific Publications, Oxford, p 406–431

Hollinrake K 1969 Polymyositis presenting as distal muscle weakness. Journal of the Neurological Sciences 8: 479–481

Holloszy J O 1982 Muscle metabolism during exercise. Archives of Physical Medicine and Rehabilitation 63: 231–234

Hudgson P 1982 Adverse Drug reactions in the neuromuscular apparatus. Adverse Drug Reaction and Acute Poisoning Reviews 1: 35–64

Hudgson P, Hall R 1982 Endocrine Myopathies. In: Mastaglia F L, Walton J N (eds) Skeletal Muscle Pathology, Churchill Livingstone, Edinburgh, p 393–408

Hudgson P, Walton J N 1979 Polymyositis and other Inflammatory Myopathies. In: Vinken P J, Bruyn G W (eds) Handbook of Clinical Neurology Vol 41, North Holland, Amsterdam, p 51–93

Irving D, Rebeiz J J, Tomlinson B E 1974 The numbers of limb motoneurones in the individual segments of the human lumbosacral spinal cord. Journal of the Neurological Sciences 21: 203–212

Jennekens F G I, Tomlinson B E, Walton J N 1971a Histochemical aspects of five limbs muscles in old age. An autopsy study. Journal of the Neurological Sciences 14: 259–276

Jennekens F G I, Tomlinson B E, Walton J N 1971b The sizes of the two main histochemical fibre types in five limb muscles in man. An autopsy study. Journal of the Neurological Sciences 13: 281–292

Jennekens F G I, Tomlinson B E, Walton J N 1972 The extensor digitorum brevis. Histological and Histochemical aspects. Journal of Neurology, Neurosurgery and Psychiatry 35: 124–132

Johnson M A, Polgar J, Weightman D, Appleton D 1973 Data on the distribution of fibre types in thirty six human muscles. An autopsy study. Journal of the Neurological Sciences 18: 111–129

Jokelainen M 1977 Amyotrophic Lateral Sclerosis in Finland. Acta Neurologica Scandinavia 56: 185–193,194–204

Karpati G, Engel W K 1967 Transformation of the histochemical profile of skeletal muscle by foreign innervation. Nature 215: 1509–1510

Komi P U, Viilasolo J H Y, Havu M, Thorstensson A, Sjodin B, Karlsson J 1977 Skeletal muscle fibres and muscle enzyme activities in monozygous and dizygous twins of both sexes. Acta Physiologica Scandinavica 100: 385–392

Kula R W 1979 Neuromuscular disorders associated with systemic neoplastic disease. In: Vinken P J, Bruyn G W (eds) Handbook of Clinical Neurology, vol 41, North Holland, Amsterdam, p 317–404

Kurland L T, Mulder D W 1955 Epidemiologic investigations of Amyotrophic Lateral Sclerosis. Neurology 5: 249–269

Larsson L 1978 Morphological and functional characteristics of aging skeletal muscle in man. Acta Physiologica Scandinavica Supplement 457

Larsson L, Sjodin B, Karlsson J 1978 Histochemical and biochemical changes in human skeletal muscle with age in sedentary males aged 22–65 years. Acta Physiologica Scandinavica 103: 31–39

Lindstrom J M, Lambert E H 1978 Content of acetyl receptor and antibodies to receptor in myasthenia gravis, experimental

autoimmune myasthenia gravis and Eaton Lambert syndrome. Neurology 28: 130–138

Loizou L A, Small M, Dalton G A 1980 Cricopharyngeal myotomy in Motor Neurone Disease. Journal of Neurology, Neurosurgery and and Psychiatry 43: 42–45

Lundh H, Nilsson O, Rosen I 1977 4-Aminopyridine. A new drug tested in the treatment of Eaton-Lambert syndrome. Journal of Neurology, Neurosurgery and Psychiatry 40: 1109–1112

McComas A J 1977 Neuromuscular function and disorders. Butterworths, London

McKeran R O, Slavin G, Andrew T M, Ward P, Mair W P G 1975 Muscle fibre type changes in hypothyroid myopathy. Journal of Clinical Pathology 28: 659–664

MacLennan W J, Hall M R P, Timothy J I, Robinson M 1980 Is weakness in old age due to muscle wasting? Age and Ageing 9: 188–192

Mastaglia F L, Walton J N 1982 Inflammatory Myopathies. In: Mastaglia F L, Walton J N (eds) Skeletal Muscle Pathology, Churchill Livingstone, Edinburgh, p 360–392

Mastaglia F L, McCollum J P K, Larson P F, Hudgson P 1970 Steroid myopathy complicating McArdle's disease. Journal of Neurology, Neurosurgery and Psychiatry 33: 111–120

Munsat T L 1979 The Classification of human Myopathies. In: Vinken P J, Bruyn G W (eds) Handbook of Clinical Neurology, vol 40: North Holland Publishing Company. Amsterdam, p 275–293

Norris A H, Shock N W 1960 Exercise in the adult years with special reference to the advanced years. In: Johnson W R (ed) Science and Medicine of Exercise and Sport, Harper, New York, ch 24, p 466–499

Nygaard E, Sanchez J 1982 Intramuscular variation of fibre types in brachial biopsies and lateral vastus of elderly men. How representative is a small biopsy sample? Anatomical Record 203: 451–40

Olanow C W, Lane R J M, Roses A D 1982 Thymectomy in late onset myasthenia gravis. Archives of Neurology 39: 82–83

Plowman P N, Stableforth D E 1977 Dermatomyositis with fibrosing alveolitis. Response to treatment with cyclophosphamide. Proceedings of the Royal Society of Medicine 70: 738–739

Rose A L, Walton J N 1966 Polymyositis: A survey of 89 cases with particular reference to treatment and prognosis. Brain 89: 747–771

Sargeant A J, Davies C T M, Edwards R H T, Maunder C, Young A 1977 Functional and Structural change after disuse of human muscle. Clinical Science and Molecular Medicine 52: 337–342

Schmitt H P 1978 Quantitative analysis of voluntary muscles from routine autopsy material with special reference to the problem of remote carcinomatous changes ('Neuromyopathy'). Acta Neuropathologica 43: 815–817

Serratrice G, Roux H, Aquaron R 1968 Proximal muscle weakness in elderly subjects. Report of twelve cases. Journal of the Neurological Sciences 7: 275–299

Stalberg E, Young R R 1981 Clinical Neurophysiology. Butterworths, London.

Swash M, Schwartz M S 1981 Neuromuscular Diseases. A practical approach to diagnosis and management. Springer-Verlag, Berlin

Tomlinson B E, Walton J N, Rebeiz J J 1969 The effects of ageing and cachexia upon skeletal muscle. A histopathological study. Journal of the Neurological Sciences 9: 321–346

Tomonaga M 1977 Histochemical and Ultrastructural changes in senile human skeletal muscle. Journal of the American Geriatric Society 25: 125–131

Von Knorring J 1979 Treatment and prognosis in polymyalgia rheumatica and temporal arteritis: a ten-year survey of 53 patients. Acta Medica Scandinavica 205: 429–435

Walton J N (ed) 1981 Disorders of Voluntary Muscle. 4th edn, Churchill Livingstone, Edinburgh

Walton J N, Gardner-Medwin D 1981 Progressive muscular dystrophy and the Myotonic disorders. In: Walton J N (ed) Disorders of Voluntary Muscle, 4th edn, Churchill Livingstone, Edinburgh, p 481–524

Williams P E, Goldspink G 1971 Longitudinal growth of striated muscle fibres. Journal of Cell Science 9: 751–767

The blood

CHANGES ASSOCIATED WITH AGING

Peripheral blood

Formed elements
In describing aging changes in blood cells there are two aspects to consider, aging of individual cells and cell changes in aging organisms.

Red blood cells
Aging of red cells. Each red cell undergoes biophysical and biochemical changes as it ages and these are widely assumed to represent a metabolic 'lesion' causing red cell senescence and ultimately its destruction and removal from the circulation.

The biophysical changes have been reviewed by Danon (1975): they include increased density, decreased flexibility, decreased osmotic and mechanical resistance, and reduction in surface charge density.

Biochemical changes have been reviewed by Bunn (1972), Brewer (1974a), Eaton and Brewer (1974) Berlin and Berk (1975), Ganzoni et al (1976), Dreyfus et al (1979) and Nakao et al (1979) and may be summarized: aging red cells lose water, potassium, phospholipid, adenosine triphosphate (ATP), 2, 3-diphosphoglycerate (DPG), glycolytic enzymes (notably hexokinase and aldolase), enzymes of the pentose phosphate shunt (notably glucose-6-phosphate dehydrogenase (G6PD)), sulphydryl groups (especially those of reduced glutathione), transaminases, acid phosphatase, various other enzymes, and protoporphyrin. Increases have been reported in ionic calcium, sodium, long-chain fatty acids, cholesterol, methaemoglobin, haemoglobin A_3, and oxygen affinity for haemoglobin.

The increased Hb-O_2 affinity results from the decreased DPG and ATP levels (Brewer 1974b; Huehns, 1974a) and results in diminution of oxygen-release in the tissues. Decreased ATP levels are partly due to the reduced activity of the pentose phosphate shunt, but there is also decreased utilization of ATP for glycolysis (Sass, 1973) which falls off markedly. The diminished ability to maintain glutathione in reduced form reduces the integrity of the red cell.

The shape and flexibility of red cells depend on their levels of ATP; decrease in ATP leads to loss of biconcavity and more spherical and less flexible red cells (Nakao et al, 1960; Bessis et al, 1973; Lessin et al, 1976). This effect is thought to be mediated by increased calcium ion levels in the erythrocytes, reacting with a protein at the inner membrane surface (Weed et al, 1969). The passage of these more rigid erythrocytes through restricted regions of the microcirculation may be markedly impaired (LaCelle et al, 1973).

The addition of adenosine to the incubation medium of senescent erythrocytes in vitro reverses these changes in shape and rigidity (Weinstein, 1974).

Peroxidation of membrane lipids may lead to polymerization of membrane components, and this change may contribute to the altered biochemical and mechanical properties of aging red cells (Jain and Hochstein, 1980).

Red cells in aging organisms. For practical purposes, the red cells of old people cannot be distinguished from those of young people, but subtle differences have been described.

Mean cell diameter increases slightly after the age of 50 (Spriggs and Sladden, 1958) and mean corpuscular volume behaves similarly (Okuno, 1972; Htoo et al, 1979; Bowdler et al, 1981). These changes are insufficient to have clinical significance in old people (Powell, 1978).

Osmotic fragility increases (Detraglia et al, 1974; Araki and Rifkind, 1980; Bowdler et al, 1981). The last named authors found that the age-related effect increased both the mean values for red cell fragility and the variability of the fragilities of the cells within individual blood samples. These changes were correlates of increased isometric sphering at isotonicity, which was considered to be insufficient to affect capillary perfusion significantly in normal subjects. However, the authors suggested that the changes in cell shape would increase the vulnerability of the elderly to abnormalities of the microvasculature.

Despite the increased osmotic fragility, it has been reported that the rate of haemolysis actually decreases with aging (Araki and Rifkind, 1980). — attributed to an increase in cholesterol content of the red cell membrane in older subjects. Red cell longevity was reported to be normal by Hurdle and Rosin (1962) and Woodford Williams et al (1962). These last authors noted a significant reduction in red cell mass, haematocrit and blood volume in ambulant subjects aged over 80 years as compared with young students: and Milne and Williamson (1972b) reported a significant regression of packed cell volume on age in elderly men (but not women) in a random population sample in Edinburgh. (See also Table 41.2.)

Red cell count and haemoglobin values will be considered later, in the section on anaemia.

There is relatively little information on changes in red cell enzymes and metabolism in aging organisms. Enzyme changes are reviewed by Wilson (1973) and Rothstein (1975), and metabolic changes by Brewer (1974b). It is noteworthy that although decreased erythrocyte ATP levels have been reported with increasing age in man (Gross et al, 1963; Brewer, 1967; Brain and Card, 1972; Sakuta, 1981) and rats (Brewer and Coan, 1969), these data mostly compare children with adults. Similarly, red cell DPG decreases with age in man (Brain and Card, 1972) and rats. The mechanisms for such decreases have not yet been clarified, and the effects of senescence of the organism have not been investigated. Nevertheless, it has been reported that deformability of erythrocytes was lower in a group of old people (aged 69 to 91 years) than in a young control group (aged 12 to 29 years) (Cerny et al, 1972) and a decrease in deformability index of red cells with advancing age was reported in healthy subjects and, even more markedly, in patients with cerebrovascular disorders (Sakuta, 1981).

It would thus appear worth while to measure the ATP levels in erythrocytes from elderly subjects (particularly in view of the current trend towards explaining the mechanism of action of vaso active drugs in terms of elevation of subnormal red cell ATP levels). On the other hand, Tweeddale et al (1976) could find no significant age-variation in red cell DPG levels (which usually parallel ATP levels in erythrocytes) in a study of 47 healthy volunteers aged from 18 to 90 years.

Red cell sodium increases with age in women (Beilin et al, 1966; Naylor, 1970). Naylor et al (1977) showed that this is due to increased passive transport, whereas active transport decreased along with decreased erythrocyte Na^+-K^+-ATPase. (No elderly subjects were included in these studies.)

Red cell potassium is a useful indicator of potassium status in the elderly, whereas serum potassium levels are unreliable (Bahemuka and Hodkinson, 1976.)

Erythrocyte transaminases may show a fall with age (Jacobs et al, 1968) with evidence of pyridoxine deficiency (q.v.). Erythrocyte glutathione increases in older subjects (Bertolini, 1969).

White blood cells

Aging of white cells. Most granulocytes become senescent after less than one day in the circulation (Cronkite and Fliedner, 1964). Clein (1972) states that neutrophils persist in the blood stream for only about 10 hours, and the blood granulocyte pool is replaced from the marrow two and a half times each day.

In contrast, lymphocytes are longer-lived. Everett et al (1964) suggested that lymphocytes might live for days or years according to their origin. Norman et al (1965) estimated a lymphocyte life-span of 530 ± 64 days in women.

In the last few years an enormous literature has built up concerning the lymphocytes. There is now clear evidence that lymphocytes are heterogeneous in origin, life-cycle and function. Two main types are usually described — T-cells, processed by the thymus and concerned with cell-mediated immunity (40 to 70 per cent of total lymphocytes), and B-('bursa-equivalent') cells, possibly produced in the bone marrow in man, independent of thymic control, and concerned with humoral immunity, i.e. they produce circulating antibodies and co-operate with T-cells in immune processes (Greaves et al, 1973; Burnet, 1974b; Rowlands and Daniele, 1975). T-cells have been further subdivided into T_1 and T_2 cells (Raff and Cantor, 1971) and these can be distinguished by their differential responses to the mitogens phytohaemagglutinin and concanavalin A (Stobo and Paul, 1973).

About 10 per cent of lymphocytes are neither T- nor B-cells; these include K-('killer') cells (Forman and Möller, 1973; Perlmann et al, 1973; Calder and Irvine, 1975).

In mice, thoracic duct T-lymphocytes have an average life-span of 4 to 6 months (Sprent and Basten, 1973). Gillette (1975) estimated that T_2 lymphocytes had a life of 6 to 7 months. Buckton et al (1967) found that lymphocytes had a life-span of 4.4 years in men irradiated as treatment for ankylosing spondylitis.

Plasma cells have a half-life of 4.7 days in mice (Mattioli and Tomasi, 1973).

Monocytes have an intravascular half-life of 3 days in the rat (Whitelaw, 1966), and 22 hours in the mouse (Cline, 1975). In normal man, the half-life is 8.4 hours; this decreases in acute infection and increases in monocytosis and rises to 3 days in patients with monocytic leukaemia (Meurat and Hoffman, 1973). Monocytes, like granulocytes, leave the circulation in random fashion, independently of their age (Cline, 1975) — although a small aging factor is possibly involved in the case of granulocytes (Fliedner et al, 1964).

White cells in aging organisms. The consensus of opinion is that the white cells from old people show no significant morphological change from those of young people (Shapleigh et al, 1952; Otani, 1958; Corberand et al, 1981) but Olbrich (1947) described more marked lobulation and less marked granulation* in granulocytes of old persons as compared with those of young adults. Brueschke et al (1960) noted more four-lobed than two-lobed nuclei in granulocytes ('shift to the right') from elderly subjects as compared with young subjects; they also described an increased osmotic resistance in the granulocytes.

Normal subjects have less than 3 per cent polymorphs with five or more lobes (Herbert, 1959), but Adam et al (1973) found hypersegmentation (defined as 10 per cent or more five-lobed nuclei in an Arneth-Cooke count of 100 neutrophil polymorphs in a well-made film) in a few elderly hospital patients — although this finding was often a valuable indicator of a megaloblastic marrow. Sheridan et al (1974) also found a significant correlation between polymorph lobe-counts and serum vitamin B_{12} and folate values.

Sahi et al (1972) reported that the azurophil granules of lymphocytes (usually large lymphocytes) were slightly fewer in old than in young subjects, and related this finding to the impairment of immune function characteristic of the aged.

Beregi et al (1980) reported age-related mitochondrial changes in peripheral blood lymphocytes from healthy subjects, and similar changes in spleen and lymph-node lymphocytes of rats and mice.

Lymphocyte RNA increases and incorporation of C^{14}-leucine into lymphocyte protein (in vitro) decreases steadily with age (Sakai et al, 1968).

However, no change in thymidine incorporation was found by Agarwal et al (1978).

Membrane microviscosity of peripheral blood lymphocytes increases progressively with age and is correlated with the ratio of cholesterol to phospholipids in the serum (Rivnay et al, 1980).

Leucocyte peptidase increases with age (Stern et al, 1951) and granulocyte pyruvate kinase (Rubinson et al, 1976) increases in old age. Leucocyte alkaline phosphatase decreases with age, sometimes markedly in old people (Ray and Pinkerton, 1969). The pentose phosphate metabolizing activity of leucocytes, as assessed by their transketolase activity, decreases with advancing age of the subject (Markkanen, Peltola and Heikinheimo, 1972). This age decrement is less than that seen in red cells from aging individuals (Markkanen, Heikinheimo and Dahl, 1969).

Leucocyte ascorbic acid is more conveniently discussed in the section on plasma vitamins (p. 841).

White cell counts in the elderly. Several studies in the literature show no change of total and differential leucocyte count with age (Sanders, Orr and Evans, 1968; Corberand et al, 1981). However, sex differences in total leucocyte and neutrophil counts after the menopause have been described (Cruickshank and Alexander, 1970; Friedman et al, 1973; Richards and Wilding, 1973; Helman and Rubinstein, 1975).

There is now increasing evidence that changes in leucocyte counts may indeed occur with aging. Caird, Andrews and Gallie (1972) investigated the 'normal' range for the total and differential white counts in nearly 500 old people living at home who were without acute illness. They reported that the leucocyte counts of these 'relatively fit' old people showed a tendency to leucopenia and a more definite tendency to lymphopenia. They suggest that the normal range for the total leucocyte count in old age might well be considered to be 3000 to 8500/mm³ (3.0 to 8.5 × 10^9 1).

There have been conflicting reports on the peripheral lymphocyte count in old age. Some studies have indicated a decrease (Díaz-Jouanen et al, 1975; MacKinney, 1978) and some have shown no change (Zacharski et al, 1971; Sparrow et al, 1980; Pepys et al, 1982).

There does seem to be clear evidence of a reduced proportion of T-cells in the elderly, even though the absolute numbers of T-cells remain within the normal range (Pepys et al, 1982).

The B-cell population is maintained normally in old age (Díaz-Jouanen et al, 1975; Davey and Huntington, 1977; Pepys et al, 1982). The relative proportion of 'null' cells increases (Pepys et al, 1982). Changes in lymphocyte function in old age, relating to changes in the immune system, are considered in Chapter 5.

Cytogenetic studies have shown chromosome changes in cultures of leucocytes from elderly persons: the commonest finding is aneuploidy, especially in women after the age of 60 years (Jacobs, Court Brown and Doll, 1961; Jacobs and Court Brown, 1966; Fitzgerald, 1975; Mattevi and Salzano, 1975). Jarvik et al (1976) confirmed this phenomenon in a six-year longitudinal study. Similar chromosome losses have been reported in marrow cultures (Pierre and Hoagland, 1972; Martin et al, 1980). Phair et al (1978) found defective chemotaxis in 5 of 70 healthy volunteers aged 65 to 88 years. Silverman and Silverman (1977) showed that granulocyte adherence was greater in subjects aged over 60 years. These changes were confirmed by Corberand et al (1981), in a study of 285 healthy subjects aged 20 to 97 years. These workers also found reduced microbicidal activity in older subjects.

Impaired phagocytosis by neutrophils in the aged was reported by Moroni et al (1976) and Ivanova (1978). Bacterial killing by neutrophils from elderly subjects has

---

* The granules are now thought to be lysosomes (Cohn and Hirsch, 1960; Hirschhorn and Weissmann, 1965; Clein, 1972).

been reported variously as normal (Moroni et al, 1976; Palmblad and Haak, 1978) or diminished (Phair et al, 1978). Candida killing activity was found by Corberand et al (1981) to be significantly decreased in subjects aged over 80 years. These workers found no change in neutrophil alkaline phosphatase or myeloperoxidase in aging subjects.

Impaired macrophage function with aging was reported by Weeks (1979).

Platelets

Aging of platelets. Platelets survive for 10 to 12 days in the circulation. Earlier studies gave somewhat conflicting results which cast doubt on the part played by aging of platelets in their survival. More sophisticated techniques have made it possible to follow a platelet from its birth to its death, and careful studies comparing young and old platelets biochemically, biophysically and functionally strongly support the existence of human platelet senescence. Kinetic studies suggest that the larger, heavier platelets are young platelets and the smaller, lighter platelets are old ones, although there is some disagreement about this (Paulus, 1975). Young platelets are more efficient biochemically and functionally (haemostasis). Large platelets are an index of the number of megakaryocytes in the marrow.

The subject is reviewed by Karpatkin (1972), Caen et al (1977) and Karpatkin et al (1978).

Platelets in aging organisms. No morphological change with aging has been reported, and platelet count and function were considered to be normal in the elderly (Shapleigh et al, 1952). However, Brueschke et al (1961) reported diminished clot retraction, and Nilsson (1964) noted some increased platelet adhesiveness in the elderly. Adams (1966) reported that there was a wide scatter of platelet adhesiveness in old people, with some high values in normals and in stroke patients but no consistent trend.

Bankowski et al, (1967) found that the ability of collagen to aggregate platelets diminishes with aging, but platelet agglutination in response to adenosine diphosphate (ADP) was reported as increased in elderly subjects (Crolle et al, 1968; Reading and Rosie, 1980). Lombardi et al (1968) noted increased adhesiveness of platelets from old subjects to glass beads.

Bentzen et al (1972) performed 172 such measurements on 63 elderly patients under long-term psychiatric care and found a wide scatter of of results with no age-related variation detectable: these workers studied the effects of dietary unsaturated fatty acids on platelet adhesiveness in these patients.

Szanto (1972) studied the electrophoretic mobility of blood platelets from elderly patients with primary neuronal dementia and with vascular dementia, and showed that the latter group showed an increased

sensitivity of their platelets to ADP added to the suspending plasma in vitro. The difference in behaviour appeared to be due to a transferable plasma factor, possibly a plasma lipid abnormality as suggested by Bolton et al (1967) in arteriosclerosis.

Banerjee and Etherington (1974a) reported detailed studies of platelet function in 14 'normal' old people aged 67 to 94 years (mean age 80 years) and 27 healthy younger control subjects aged 20 to 63, mean age 36 years. Platelet counts were significantly higher, and platelet functions generally impaired, in the older group. The tests showing impairment were: speed of aggregation in response to ADP, adhesiveness to glass beads, and to some extent release of platelet factor 3. The response to collagen was not impaired in these studies.

More recent studies of platelet function in the elderly have suggested an enhanced platelet 'release reaction' in old age (Zahavi et al, 1980; Sie et al, 1981) — evidenced by increased plasma β-thromboglobulin and platelet factor 4 levels, and diminished platelet density and granular content.

Plasma

The osmotic pressure of the plasma does not change with age (Shock, 1958). Alkali reserve and blood pH decrease very slightly (Shock and Yiengst, 1950). A slow adaptation to induced acid-base disequilibrium was described in elderly subjects by Shock and Yiengst (1948) and Hilton et al (1955).

Plasma volume. Although total body water decreases with aging (Edelman et al, 1952; Olbrich et al, 1957), extracellular fluid volume shows no consistent age change (Shock et al, 1953) and plasma volume was reported as unchanged (Gibson and Evans, 1937; Cohn and Shock, 1949; Gersovitz et al, 1980). Hall (1968), however, related plasma water to the fat-free solid mass of plasma and noted a minimum value at 45 years followed by progressive rehydration.

Plasma proteins. There are many conflicting reports in the literature regarding total plasma protein levels and the various plasma protein fractions in old age. The main problem, as so often seems to be in distinguishing between physiological old age and the effects of concomitant disease processes. Thus, Bock (1948) reported a decrease in total protein in the elderly, mainly due to decreased albumin levels and Pryce et al (1969) and Reed et al (1972) reported significant falls in plasma proteins with age.

Reductions in serum albumin have also been described by Weeke and Krasilnikoff (1972), and 13 per cent of the 879 elderly subjects living at home and studied in the DHSS national Nutrition Survey of the Elderly (Department of Health and Social Security, 1972) had low serum albumin (< 3.5 g/100 ml). In this survey, there was a greater incidence of lower levels of serum albumin in women aged 65 to 74 who were living alone. Lyngbye and Krøll (1971) and Earney et al (1975) also found reductions in serum albumin in elderly subjects in the community.

In contrast to these reports, Leask et al (1973) found no significant changes in total protein or albumin or globulin levels in a random sample of the elderly living at home in Glasgow and Kilsyth; however, amongst the (nearly) 500 persons (aged over 65 years) studied there was a slightly reduced mean total protein after the age of 75, and a slight sex difference in the albumin and globulin levels, the means of which were slightly increased in women and men respectively.

It should be noted that ill elderly people in hospital have even lower mean serum albumin levels than do 'normal' old people living at home (Hodkinson, 1973; Flanagan et al, 1977; MacLennan et al, 1977).

Yan and Franks (1968) found low serum albumin levels in 5 of 6 healthy elderly subjects in whom they studied albumin metabolism. Although intravascular and interstitial albumin compartments were diminished, the studies on albumin flux and catabolism were normal. Misra et al (1975) studied albumin metabolism in 14 elderly hospital patients who were not acutely ill: 5 had low plasma albumin levels (below 3 g/100 ml), reduced albumin pools, but increased fractional catabolic rates for albumin. These authors considered that there was impairment of the mechanism controlling degradation of albumin in these 5 elderly patients, so that the decrease in degradation which would normally occur to compensate for the albumin deficiency failed to occur.

Both these studies were criticized methodologically by Gersovitz et al (1980), who evaluated albumin synthesis in five young and six elderly males on low and normal protein intake. Serum albumin was lower in the elderly regardless of protein intake and did not change. The rate of albumin synthesis was sensitive to protein intake only in the young. These findings are compatible with the lack of change in serum albumin after food supplementation in 50 long-stay elderly patients studied by Banerjee et al (1981). MacLennan et al (1977) found a correlation between dietary protein intake and serum albumin in long-stay elderly female patients but not in males.

Many authors have described reductions in albumin/globulin ratio due to increased globulins with or without decreased albumin (Woodford Williams et al, 1964/5; Meindok and Franks, 1969; Thomas and Powell, 1971). Such changes are usually ascribed to morbid processes such as infection, neoplasm or malnutrition, but even simple immobility has been implicated (Woodford Williams et al, 1964/5). The increased globulins are usually gamma-globulins, but increases in beta-globulins (Rafsky et al, 1952; Nöcker and Bemm, 1955/6) and alpha-globulins (Nöcker and Bemm, 1955/6; Meindok and Franks, 1969; Salatka et al, 1971) have been noted.

As noted earlier, plasma β-thromboglobulin levels increase in old age (Zahavi et al, 1980; Sie et al, 1981). Several studies have shown an increase in level of all globulin fractions with age (Walford, 1969). Acheson and Jessop (1962) reported that peak levels of gamma-globulins were reached (in men) in the 7th and 8th decades; thereafter the levels fell in extreme old age. Kipshidze (1968) found a rise in gamma-globulin from youth to the 7th decade, a fall in the 8th decade, then an even greater level in the 9th decade and beyond.

Very high gamma-globulin levels may be *formes frustes* of myelomatosis (Martin, 1961).

Alterations in immunoglobulins (Ig) may occur with aging, but the reported studies show much variation. Grundbacher and Schreffler (1970), Kalff (1970), and Finger et al (1973) reported elevated IgG and IgA levels but little change in IgM. Schwick and Becker (1969) could find no rise of IgG with increasing age, but IgM levels were reduced. Buckley and Dorsey (1970) found decreased IgG and IgM after the age of 60; but in a more recent longitudinal study Buckley et al (1974) also reported increased IgG and IgA in two-thirds of the aging subjects studied. Hallgren et al (1973) found increased IgG and IgA after the seventh decade. The Ig levels did not correlate with changes in cellular and humoral immunity as demonstrated by these authors. Radl et al (1975) described Ig patterns in 73 very old volunteers aged over 95 years. Total Ig levels were slightly increased; there were more marked increases in IgG and IgA. Such changes in very old people have been equated with survival (Buckley and Roseman, 1976). These authors claim that Ig assay can predict survival better than conventional estimates of risk of disease and death. They also suggest that similar measurements may help identify older persons who have the greatest need for health care resources — presumably related to the decreased 'immune surveillance' in old age (Burnet, 1974a, b).

A circadian rhythm for IgA, IgG and IgM was found in 36 elderly ambulant subjects by Casale et al (1983), with peak values in the early afternoon.

In a normal population 1 per cent of persons may show minor serum protein abnormality; the tendency increases in old age, and abnormal immunoglobulins have been reported in the sera of 3 per cent of healthy persons over 70 years of age (Hallén, 1963, 1966; Derycke et al, 1965) with a sharp increase in the 9th decade, rising to 19 per cent after the age of 90 (Englisova et al, 1968; Kohn and Srivastava, 1973; Radl et al, 1975). This subject is discussed further in the section on paraproteinaemias.

There is an age-related increase in incidence of auto-antibodies, and their female preponderance in younger adult life alters to a more equal sex incidence in old age (Burnet, 1974a, b; Cheney and Walford, 1974: Díaz-Jouanen et al, 1975; Fixa et al, 1975). One noteworthy point is the dip in the curve of incidence of autoantibodies at about 75 years of age, followed by a sharp rise after 85, reported by Mackay (1972). Similar dips have been found at about this time for mortality findings in the population studied by Mackay and his colleagues (Mackay, 1972), and for serum Ig levels (Acheson and Jessop, 1962) and gamma-globulins (Kipshidze, 1967). Burnet (1974b) suggests that this may be explained by two populations being concerned, one with a 'standard' life-span of 65 to 70 years, the other longer lived, but in both a rise in the incidence of autoantibodies may indicate a major process leading to death. This would lend much support to the importance of autoimmunity in the final operative stage of aging. Autoimmune disease may be the consequence of deficient T-cell function (Kay, 1976; Davey and Huntington, 1977).

The presence of an abnormal Ig or an autoantibody should lead to full investigation for underlying diseases, and prolonged follow-up is mandatory.

Other antibodies decline with age — those which result from foreign antigens (Schwick and Becker, 1969; Mackay, 1972). There is a decrease in delayed hypersensitivity reactions in old age (Waldorf et al, 1968; Mackay, 1972; Toh et al, 1973) and other forms of allergy may be less marked (Leach, 1976). Blood group antibodies decrease with increasing age (Somers and Kuhns, 1972).

There is an increased incidence of lymphocytotoxic reactions in the sera of aging subjects (Ooi et al, 1974). Lymphocytotoxins may arise from exogenous stimuli, e.g. after viral infections, or by cell mutations. Such reactions may reflect minor histoincompatibility and may be involved in the process of aging itself (Walford, 1969).

For general accounts of the immunobiology of aging see chapter 5.

Age-related changes in proteins involved in haemostasis will be considered under that heading.

Plasma iron, total iron-binding capacity (TIBC) and ferritin. Plasma iron levels are lower in old than in younger subjects. There is a progressive fall after the age of 30 (Pirrie, 1952; Bothwell and Finch, 1962), although the level may rise again in women after 60 years of age (Powell et al, 1968; Thomas, 1971). Values in men are generally higher than in women, though this sex difference may disappear in late life.

Total iron-binding capacity also falls with aging (Bothwell and Finch, 1962; Thomas, 1971), but there is no sex difference. Powell and Thomas (1969) showed that in hospital patients the highest levels were at 50 to 60 years, and thereafter there was a progressive fall with aging.

The iron-binding protein (transferrin) is decreased in elderly subjects (Weeke and Krasilnikoff, 1972). It is normally one-third saturated with iron (Card et al, 1964) though the range may be wide in the elderly (MacLennan et al, 1973).

It is difficult to be dogmatic about normal values for plasma iron and TIBC in the elderly. Average 'normal adult' values are:

plasma iron — men 23 μmol/l (125 μg per 100 ml)
— women 20 μmol/l (110 μg per 100 ml)
TIBC   — 53 to 71 μmol/l (300 to 400 μg per 100 ml).

In the elderly apparently normal plasma iron values may reach as low as 9 μmol/l (50 μg per 100 ml); the mean values are often 11–14 μmol/l (60 to 80 μg per 100 ml), but MacLennan and colleagues (1973) in a study of elderly people living at home found in 188 subjects a mean serum iron of 19.5 ± 5.4 (109 ± 30 μg per 100 ml) with a range of 8.8 to 30.3 μmol/l (49 to 169 μg per 100 ml). Their corresponding findings for TIBC were: mean 63 ± 12 (352 ± 67 μg per 100 ml); range 38.3 to 87.0 μmol/l (214 to 486 μg per 100 ml).

It is necessary to consider these values together when interpreting their significance (see section on iron deficiency). It may be noted here, however, that the plasma iron level and the degree of transferrin saturation are closely related but do not correlate well with the haemoglobin level (Powell et al, 1968; Britton, 1969a); they do show a significant correlation with mean corpuscular haemoglobin concentration (MCHC) (Powell et al, 1968).

Temporal variation in serum iron and TIBC levels has been demonstrated by Pathy and Newcombe (1980): these values fell significantly from 8 a.m. to 8 p.m. in their study; at follow-up after 1 year serum iron had fallen but TIBC had not. Food intake did not influence these levels in the short term.

Ferritin, formerly considered an intracellular protein which entered the plasma only after cellular necrosis (e.g. acute liver damage), has now been identified as a normal constituent of both serum (Jacobs et al, 1972; Siimes et al, 1974) and circulating blood cells (Summers et al, 1974). The prime value of serum ferritin estimation is that it reflects iron stores in the reticuloendothelial system at all storage levels from deficiency to gross overload (Worwood, 1982). One microlitre of ferritin per litre of serum is normally equivalent to 8 mg storage iron (Walters et al, 1975) and there is a rough correlation with the amount of stainable marrow iron (Hussein et al, 1975).

Normal values for adults are 15 to 300 μg ferritin per litre serum; males have higher values than females *except* in old age. There is a progressive increase with age after 20 in men; in women the increase starts after the menopause. This increase in serum ferritin in old age reduces the value of this test for the evaluation of iron status in the elderly (Cook et al, 1976).

Plasma vitamins. Low levels of vitamin A were reported in elderly women who were apparently on adequate dietary intake of the vitamin (Harrill and Cervone, 1977). Impaired vitamin A absorption is a possible cause although Hollander and Morgan (1979) found that in rats intestinal absorption of vitamin A actually increases linearly with age, possibly due to a decreased thickness of the unstirred water layer at the luminal surface of the absorbing cells.

Vitamin B complex plays various roles in haematopoeisis, some very important. Evidence for a low plasma levels of thiamine (B_1) comes from several sources (e.g. Griffiths et al, 1967; Dibble et al, 1967; Markkanen et al, 1969; Hoorn et al, 1975). Since absorption of thiamine is normal in old age (Thomson, 1966) the apparent deficiency is presumably dietary. Riboflavine (B_2) is unchanged in the blood (Suvarnakich et al, 1952). Nicotinic acid (niacin) may be diminished in the elderly since nicotinamide-containing coenzymes are diminished in the blood of old people and plasma nicotinates are often reduced (Baker et al, 1979). Pantothenic acid and pyridoxine (B_6) levels fall in old age according to Fulford-Jones (1970) and Baker et al (1979), but no fall in serum B_6 was discovered (between ages 65 and 90) in the Department of Health and Social Security (1972) Nutritional Survey. Pyridoxine deficiency is occasionally associated with a form of sideroblastic anaemia (*q.v.*).

Low blood plasma and leucocyte levels of Vitamin C have been reported by many authors (e.g. Batata et al, 1977; Griffiths et al, 1967; Mitra, 1970; Loh and Wilson, 1971; Burr et al, 1974, 1982). There is a seasonal variation, levels being higher in the second than in the first half of the year (Milne et al, 1971). Vitamin C supplementation restores the levels to those seen in younger subjects (Griffiths et al, 1967; Andrews et al, 1969; Burr et al, 1975). The true significance of these low levels has yet to be determined. An association has been demonstrated between mortality and low levels of vitamin C in the elderly in hospital (Hodkinson and Exton-Smith, 1976) and in the community (Burr et al, 1975). It should be noted that leucocyte ascorbic acid levels show an inverse relationship with the leucocyte count in young and old healthy subjects (Loh and Wilson, 1971; Vallance, 1979) and with the polymorph count in old age (MacLennan and Hamilton, 1976).

Very low plasma levels of 25-hydroxyvitamin D_3 in elderly long-stay geriatric patients compared to younger controls were reported by Corless et al (1975). Others have also reported low vitamin D concentrations in old age (Lester, Skinner and Wills, 1977; MacLennan et al, 1979; Hodkinson and Hodkinson, 1980).

Seasonal variation in circulating levels of 25 hydroxy vitamin D_3 in the elderly have been demonstrated (Brown et al, 1976).

Erythrocyte sedimentation rate (ESR)
The ESR is deceptively simple to perform, yet requires careful standardization (Lane and Gill, 1974): the result varies with room temperature, dilution factors, the anticoagulant used and the delay between taking the blood and performing the test. This is not surprising since the ESR depends upon the dynamic interaction between the surfaces of living red cells and their plasma environment. A detailed discussion of the factors influencing the ESR is given by Zacharski (1976) but little mention is made of age as a physiological variant.

There is not general agreement on the effect of age on the ESR. Westergren (1957) gave up to 5 mm in the first hour as normal for men and 10 to 15 mm for women. There is a growing literature suggesting that higher values than these may be associated with 'normal' health in old age (Olbrich, 1948; Wilhelm and Tillisch, 1951; Renbourn and Ellison, 1952; Ansell and Bywaters, 1958; Dawson, 1960; Hilder and Gunz, 1964; Gilbertsen, 1965; Weinsaft and Haltaufderhyde, 1965; Boyd and Hoffbrand, 1966; Böttiger and Svedberg, 1967; Cotton et al, 1968; Harris, 1972; Milne and Williamson, 1972a; Hamilton et al, 1974a; Hayes and Stinson, 1976; Sharland, 1980; Sparrow et al, 1981).

Gilbertsen (1965) reported a steady rise of ESR with age in over 4000 healthy adults aged 45 to 79. Over half the women and a third of the men in his series had values over the 'accepted normal' range (5 to 20 mm for women, 5 to 15 mm for men); and of the 532 women aged 65 to 79 years, as many as 75 per cent had an ESR of 20 mm or more. If 'normal' means 'ranges including 90 per cent of asymptomatic persons studied', Gilbertsen found the following normal ranges: aged 65 to 69 years, 0 to 35 mm for men, 1 to 50 mm for women; aged 70 to 79 years, 0 to 38 mm for men, 1 to 53 mm for women. The median value for women in this large series was twice that for men.

Böttiger and Svedberg (1967) suggested that the upper limit of normal after the age of 50 was 20 mm for men and 30 mm for women. Ansell and Bywaters (1958), Harris (1972) and Milne and Williamson (1972a) took 20 mm as the upper limit of normal, but accepted that values above this could not always be explained and might be compatible with 'normal' health. Harris (1972) considered that the tendency for the ESR to rise above 20 mm started at about 60 years. Boyd and Hoffbrand (1966) found that even 40 mm might occur in apparently normal subjects and Caird (1973) and Rai (1979) agreed. Careful clinical follow-up is advisable in such cases however.

Hayes and Stinson (1976) studied 169 patients awaiting elective eye or ear, nose and throat operations, but without apparent disease or medication which was likely to affect the ESR. They found that the mean ESR (Wintrobe) rose with each decade of life; the percentage of patients with ESR over 20 mm increased in each decade until the age of 60, after which it increased more sharply and remained at the higher level until 89 (the oldest person studied). Sparrow et al (1981) also found a significant correlation between age and ESR in a community survey.

Not all authors find a raised ESR in healthy old persons. Pincherle and Shanks (1976b) found a rise in ESR with age but a flattening out after age 60. Gibson (1972) studied 442 hospital inpatients aged over 60 years and 118 controls in a similar age group (treated for pernicious anaemia and observed over a prolonged period). Sixty-seven of the 442 inpatients came to post-mortem, and 51 were thought to have a known cause for a high ESR, but 34 of these had a *further* possible cause found only at post-mortem, frequently a malignant tumour. Only 7 per cent of all ESR abnormal values were unexplained; there was no link with age, but the diagnostic process was much more difficult in the females. From her data she concluded that a normal old person should have an ESR of 10 mm or less.

This was not the view of Sharland (1980), who found that elevated ESRs up to 69 mm in 1 hour were compatible with continuing good health in normal, non-hospitalized people aged 70–89 years, followed-up for up to 11 years. Similar conclusions were reached in a larger community sample (of men) followed-up for 10 years by Sparrow et al (1981).

Hospital studies, e.g. Boyd and Hoffbrand (1966); Harris (1972); Kulvin (1972), naturally tend to reveal a higher incidence of raised ESR levels than do community studies such as those of Milne and Williamson (1972a), Sharland (1980) and Sparrow et al (1981), but investigation and follow-up usually explain a high proportion of these. Much interest has centred on the very high ESR level and this is reviewed by Zacharski (1976) who concludes that such a finding is not invariably evidence of serious disease. For instance, Liljestrand and Olhagen (1955) and Olhagen and Liljestrand (1955) followed up 21 patients with an ESR of 100 mm or over for up to 20 years and found them to be free of serious disease. Nevertheless, in a majority of such cases a definitive diagnosis is often found quite readily and multiple diagnoses are common (Ford et al, 1979); and even in more elusive clinical situations detailed investigation may eventually reveal such diseases as myelomatosis, blood dyscrasias, neoplastic or renal disease, or cranial arteritis. Care must be taken in evaluating different published analyses of very high ESRs since some series derive from general hospitals (Abengowe, 1975) and some from specialized clinics (Zacharski and Kyle, 1967).

It is possible that increases in ESR in healthy old age are related to changes in plasma constituents. It is widely accepted that the ESR depends more on plasma fibrinogen levels than on the other plasma proteins (Wintrobe, 1967), but the albumin: fibrinogen and globulin: fibrinogen ratios may be more relevant (Dintenfass and Stewart, 1974). There is considerable evidence of increased plasma fibrinogen levels in old age (see below) and there may be reductions in plasma albumin (see above).

Even more important than fibrinogen, however, is the amount of fibrin monomer (Lipinski et al, 1969): this is the first fibrinogen breakdown product during in vivo thrombin formation.

Hyperlipidaemia is known to increase ESR (Böttiger, 1973; Scherer et al, 1976) and Böttiger et al (1973) found a high incidence of ischaemic changes in the ECGs of their 101 patients who had a raised ESR and marked (but asymptomatic) hyperlipidaemia. They postulated that the raised ESR was due to silent vascular disease brought on by the high lipids. Wardle (1973) agreed that a high ESR might mean hidden vascular disease but considered that the effect of hyperlipidaemia was due to its enhancement of platelet aggregation with release of platelet factor 4, leading to in vivo thrombin formation and thus elevated plasma fibrin monomer levels.

Zacharski (1976) also considers causes of a very low ESR. Some of these are to be found in the elderly (e.g. polycythaemia, hypochromic microcytic anaemia, hyperproteinaemia associated with hyperviscosity, congestive heart failure, cachexia, anti-inflammatory drugs, and Coombs-positive haemolytic anaemia) but a low ESR is of little help in most instances, being within the normal range.

Milne and Williamson (1972a) conclude that the ESR is of doubtful value as a test or in multiphasic screening in older people and much of the foregoing discussion would seem to support that opinion. In many situations where the ESR is likely to be abnormal the diagnosis can be made without it. Nevertheless, it may indicate the presence of organic disease in cases where there is doubt as to the diagnosis, and may help in distinguishing between organic and psychological diseases. It is also of value in following the progress of a disease, before or after treatment (e.g. cranial arteritis, polymyalgia rheumatica).

New variations of the 'standard' ESR have been devised: the zeta sedimentation ratio (ZSR) (Lancet, 1976a) has several technical advantages over the ESR and it is independent of sex and haematocrit; the sigma SR uses the sum of ESR values at 20, 30, 40 and 50 minutes, routinely corrected to a standard haematocrit of 35 per cent and is claimed to correlate more closely with clinical changes than does the 'standard' ESR

(Pawlotsky et al, 1978). However, the ZSR requires special equipment and the SSR is cumbersome to perform.

Plasma viscosity. Harkness (1971) and Harris (1972) found plasma viscosity more useful than the ESR as a diagnostic test in the elderly. Eastham (1973) confirmed this; normal viscosity excludes inflammation from any cause and increased viscosity is a useful though non-specific index of disease, calling for further investigation. A low viscosity suggests low protein levels. Many elderly people have a normal plasma viscosity even if the ESR is raised (Harris, 1972). Roe and Harkness (1975) carried out 500 plasma viscosity tests on 420 unselected in- and outpatients aged 65 or over. They found that values in 64 of their subjects with no apparent active disease were slightly higher than values in younger subjects; but in diseases of various degrees of severity the values were lower in the elderly than in younger patients similarly afflicted. Nevertheless, there was significant differentiation between groups of different severity, viscosity rising as severity of disease increased. These authors, as well as Eastham (1973), point out the practical advantages of viscosity measurements — the test is cheap, rapid, accurate and safe. Reproducibility varies from one laboratory to another, however.

The slight increase in plasma viscosity with increasing age was confirmed by Lowe et al (1980), who showed that the age-related differences were more apparent in non-smokers.

Whole blood viscosity. Dintenfass et al (1966) found no change in viscosity of whole blood in normal donors aged 18 to 80 years, but there was an increase of viscosity in elderly patients with vascular disease. Ditzel and Kampman (1971) reported that healthy women (but not men) aged 56 to 80 years had slightly higher blood viscosity than did those aged 15 to 35; they related this to an increase in plasma fibrinogen with age (see below), which is more pronounced in females than in males. Lowe et al (1980) reported increased blood viscosity with increasing age.

Cerny et al (1972) reported that plasma viscosity did not change in old age, but whole blood viscosity did show an increase, and they attributed this to decreased deformability of the red cell; they did not measure fibrinogen levels. These workers also showed that the degree of haemoglobinization and the size of the red cells influenced whole blood viscosity — thus viscosity fell in normochromic normocytic anaemia, and intermediate values were seen in macrocytic anaemias. These findings were again interpreted as being due to changes in red-cell flexibility. The subject is reviewed by Chien (1975).

Phillips and Harkness (1976) relate whole blood viscosity to specific clinical situations; it may also be affected by drugs such as beta-blockers (Dintenfass and Lake, 1976) and oral anticoagulants (Mayer, 1976).

Haemopoietic system

Bone marrow
Active haemopoietic marrow gradually diminishes as age advances, being replaced by fatty marrow (Custer and Ahlfeldt, 1932; Schroder and Tougaard, 1977). This involution occurs earliest in long bones; it is slower in flat bones, so that marrow may be obtained by sternal puncture in the elderly. Vertebral marrow is the last bony site to show fatty change, which begins after the age of 60 (Tanaka and Inoue, 1976).

Hartsock et al (1965) described variations with age in the amount of haemopoietic tissue in the anterior iliac crest in 177 cases of sudden death examined at necropsy. The cellularity of red marrow here was maximal in the first decade (79 per cent), falling until the age of 30 and then stationary until 60. After 60 years a further fall occurred so that in the eighth decade cellularity was only 29 per cent.

Cellular composition of red marrow in the elderly shows no significant difference from younger subjects (Reich et al, 1944; Shapleigh et al, 1952), reflecting the essential similarity in peripheral blood counts between old and young.

Lymph nodes and spleen
Changes in these tissues are considered by Carlson (1954), Oliver (1954) and Andrew (1971).

Dynamic aspects of haemopoiesis
There has been increasing interest in the effect of aging on haemopoiesis.

Erythropoiesis. There are many stimuli to red-cell production, including erythropoietin, hormones, anoxia, bleeding and haemolysis, and in the elderly there are likely to be several factors operating simultaneously. Bone marrow can increase its red-cell production up to 13 times normal without any marked expansion, but prolonged and pronounced marrow stimulation will lead to replacement of yellow (fatty) marrow by red haemopoietic marrow (Van Dyke et al, 1964; Van Dyke and Anger, 1965). This functional reserve capacity may be diminished in the elderly, but in practice response to haemorrhage may be just as satisfactory in the old as in the young.

Leucopoiesis. Timaffy (1962) and Cream (1968) reported decreased leucopoietic reserve capacity in the elderly.

Haemopoiesis in aging animals. There is growing evidence from animal experiments, mainly in mice, that the number of haemopoietic stem-cells in the bone marrow remains virtually constant throughout life

(Chen, 1971; Coggle et al, 1975), although the number in the spleen decreased markedly in old age.

Haemopoietic function does not seem to decline in the marrow stem-cells of old animals. The proliferative capacity of erythropoietic stem-cell lines in aging mice has been reviewed by Harrison (1979). The erythropoietic capacity of old and young marrow grafts in mice are similar. However, recovery after irradiation is impaired in stem-cells in old mice (Chen, 1974), and slow recovery after bleeding has been reported in old rats (Grant and Le Grande, 1964; Roylance et al, 1969) and mice (Harrison, 1975). Harrison's (1975) study is especially interesting; the initial response to bleeding in old mice was normal but fell off markedly from the 4th day onwards; young mice recovered rapidly over a 9- to 10-day period. Marrow from young mice failed to improve the recovery rate in old mice. Taken with the previous evidence of normal stem-cell functions, these results are interpreted as follows: old mice have normal production of erythropoietin and normal responses to it at first, but the response cannot be sustained at the normal rate for younger mice; the defect appears to be in the haemopoietic microenvironment, possibly influenced by long-term nutritional or other factors.

Leucopoietic capacity seems substantially normal in marrow stem cells in old animals (Silini and Andreozzi, 1974; Silini et al, 1974), but some doubt has been cast on their ability to generate B lymphocytes (Stoltzner and Makinodan, 1975; Kishimoto et al, 1976).

Plasma factors in haemopoiesis

Various factors stimulating the production of the different types of blood cells are now known, or at least there is good evidence for their existence. The best-known is erythropoietin, but there are also probably granulocytopoietin, lymphocytopoietin, and so on. The subject is well reviewed by Kelemen (1969), Hardisty and Weatherall (1974), Nakao et al (1975) and Cline (1975). Prostaglandins may also be involved in erythropoietin production (Fisher, 1980a) and in haem synthesis (Dukes et al, 1975). Inhibitors of granulopoiesis have been reviewed by Vogler and Winton (1975).

There is little information about the effects of age on these plasma factors (Harrison, 1975; Earney et al, 1975).

Haemostasis and the coagulation mechanism

It has been stated that no decrease in clotting factors occur in old age (Nilsson, 1964; Todd et al, 1973). However, Hamilton et al (1974b) found a fall in factors XI and XII in men (but a rise in women) aged over 65; factors X, VII and V were elevated in both sexes, but in extreme old age all these clotting factors decreased. Factor VIII levels were not changed, confirming the results of Preston and Barr (1964). Antithrombin III levels are increased in postmenopausal and elderly women (Fagerhol and Abildgaard, 1970; Hamilton et al, 1974b) but reduced in elderly men along with heparin co-factor activity (Ødegård, 1976).

Plasma fibrinogen increases with aging (Ogston and Ogston, 1966; Cotton et al, 1968; Lowe et al, 1980), although some authors could not confirm this (Harris, 1972; Böttiger, 1973). Hamilton et al (1974a) found an age-related rise in fibrinogen levels up to 85 years; after this age the levels fell — as previously indicated by Ogston and Ogston (1966). The reason for this late fall is unknown. The ESR paralleled the plasma fibrinogen levels in this study.

There is much conflict in the literature over the fibrinolytic activity of the blood in the elderly. Brunetti et al (1967) and Bychikhin and Volchkova (1970) reported a decrease, whereas Swan (1963), Guest and Bond (1964) and Tepper and Bratchik (1966) found it increased. Others have found no relation with age (Nilsson, 1964; Moser and Hajjar, 1966), but Fearnley et al (1963) described low activity in the blood of atherosclerotic postmenopausal women.

Hamilton et al (1974a) studied the effect of age on the fibrinolytic enzyme system in young and old healthy volunteers. Apart from the fibrinogen changes described above, they also found that fibrinogen-related antigen (FR-A) was increased in the elderly group, and so were the principal antiplasmins in the blood, α_1-antitrypsin and α_2-macroglobulin. Plasminogen activator levels rose and plasminogen itself fell after the age of 75. In males the blood fibrinolytic activity was inversely related to obesity.

Overall, there is probably no increase in agglutinability of the blood (Landsteiner, 1939; Nilsson, 1964) although Bychikhin and Volchkova (1970) did report such an increase. Cotton and colleagues (1968) noted increased heparin-resistance in the blood of the elderly.

DISEASE OF THE BLOOD AND BLOOD-FORMING ORGANS

Anaemia

Definition

Anaemia exists when the quantity or quality of circulating erythrocytes falls below normal (Britton, 1969b).

The normal erythrocyte count for men varies from 4.7 to 6.5 million per mm³ of blood, and the normal haemoglobin (Hb) level is 14 to 18 g per dl. Women have lower levels than men.

A WHO study group (World Health Organization, 1959) gave values below which anaemia can be diagnosed in adults (Table 41.1).

Table 41.1 World Health Organization (1959) criteria for diagnosis of anaemia in adults

Sex	Hb g per dl	RBC 10^6 per c mm	PCV %	MCHC %
Male	14	4.7	42	34
Female	12	4.0	35	34

A subsequent report (World Health Organization, 1968) recommended that for males the critical Hb level could be reduced to 13 g per dl.

Normal old people are not anaemic, and there is no justification for neglecting an anaemia in an old person 'because it is due to old age'.

Recently a new trend has been developing, in the USA particularly, to accept the existence of an 'anaemia of senescence' (Vogel, 1980; Lipschitz et al, 1981). Part of the reason for this trend seems to be the use of a lower limit of haemoglobin of 14 g per dl according to WHO criteria. Lipschitz et al (1981) were impressed with the incidence of leucopenia and neutropenia in their anaemic subjects and they suggested that this indicated an overall reduction in haemopoiesis in the elderly — hence an 'anaemia of senescence'. Despite their observations most other authorities do not agree with this (see Table 41.3; and Walsh, 1981). Htoo et al (1979) and Freedman and Marcus (1980) advise against creating new norms for the elderly.

Table 41.2 sets out some representative studies which show no significant decreases in Hb and red cell (RBC) counts in elderly subjects considered to be 'healthy' or in random samples of the population. In addition, Pincherle and Shanks (1976a) found no fall in haemoglobin with aging in 2000 business executives, of whom 306 were over 60 years of age.

However, Hawkins et al (1954) found a gradual decrease in Hb, RBC and packed cell volume (PCV) in men and women after 60 years, and Elwood (1971) also showed small decreases in mean haemoglobin and PCV after 65 years. These changes were not considered to have clinical significance. Milne and Williamson (1972b) found significant age regressions for haemoglobin and PCV in men only, but the levels were all well within the normal range. Brunning (1974) stated that haemoglobin falls by 1.5 g per dl per decade in men after the age of 60 years, whereas it remains stable in women after that age. Williams (1980) states that haemoglobin in males falls slowly after age 70. Zaino (1981) found modest reductions in haemoglobin and PCV in nonagenarian males in a residential home for the elderly and suggested that a realistic criterion for anaemia in nonagenarians should be haemoglobin 11 g per dl. Thus he joins the battle for 'anaemia of senescence', at least in the 10th decade.

Incidence of anaemia among the elderly
Surveys have been performed on communities and in hospital geriatric departments. These will be considered separately.

Community surveys
Table 41.3 shows the results obtained in several surveys, although differences in techniques, sampling and criteria of anaemia make comparisons difficult. Note the high incidence of anaemia in rural Yorkshire and in men in Cambridgeshire; also in housebound women (Morgan, 1967) and women aged 75 and over (Hallberg and Högdahl, 1971; MacLennan et al, 1973). In attempting to interpret survey findings it should be remembered that the elderly tend to co-operate in these studies less enthusiastically than the young: it may be that an appreciable number of anaemic old people are the very ones who refuse to participate.

Elwood (1971) maintains that there is no evidence that anaemia is commoner in elderly subjects than in young subjects in the community. He bases his opinion on his large-scale population surveys in Wales, including 19 000 women of all ages. He emphasizes that the WHO criteria are only meaningful if they can be correlated with impairment of function, or increase in morbidity or mortality, and he doubts if there is adequate evidence of such correlations.

Nevertheless, the high incidence of anaemia reported by the recent US studies (Htoo et al, 1979; Lipschitz et al, 1981) calls for the comments made in the previous section, although of course considerations other than definition apply. The study of Htoo et al (1979) was essentially of unselected elderly people without adequate screening for their 'normality'. Much of the 'leuco-penia' observed by Lipschitz et al (1981) lay in the range 4000–5000 white cells per ml and is of doubtful significance.

Williams and Nixon (1974) divided their 297 elderly subjects (aged 75 or over) into 3 groups according to function rather than disease. Of the anaemic subjects, 27 per cent were apparently well and functioning normally, 54 per cent were bed-fast or incapacitated to a marked degree, and 30 per cent were in an intermediate functional category. These workers showed that anaemia increased with age after 75, and was commoner in women, especially the single and widowed. In the community survey by Sheridan et al (1974) 26 per cent of anaemic subjects were iron-deficient and 9.6 per cent had folate or vitamin B_{12} deficiency. These authors found a significant correlation between serum folate and B_{12} levels and mean corpuscular volume of red cells and also polymorph lobe counts in white cells.

Mortality due to anaemia increases markedly after 60 years of age (WHO, 1969).

Table 41.2 Haemoglobin, red cell counts, and haematocrits in the elderly

Author	Subjects			Mean Hb g per dl	Mean RBC $\times 10^6$ per c mm	Mean PCV (%)	Comments
	No.	Sex	Age (years)				
Campbell	228	Male	65 to 74	15.4	—	—	Random community
et al (1968)	224	Female	65 to 74	13.6	—	—	sample
Myers et al	81	Male	65+	13.62	—	—	Fit old people at
(1968)	121	Female	65+	13.11	—	—	home★
Elwood (1971)							
(A)	132	Male	65+	14.5	—	45.5	Community surveys.
(B)	97	Male	65+	14.9	—	45.9	(A) and (B) 2 different studies
	1420	Female	65+	13.3	—	41.4	No significant difference from women aged 20 to 64 years†
	145	Female	75+	12.9	—	—	
Hodes (1971)‡	68	Male		12.88	—	—	
	130	Female	70–79	13.02	—	—	
	30	Male		12.73	—	—	
	71	Female	80+	12.14	—	—	
Earney and	200	Male	70 to 80	15.00	4.46	43.64	Residents of old
Earney (1972)		Male	81 to 94	14.80	4.38	41.65	people's home
	200	Female	70 to 80	14.43	4.35	41.19	
		Female	81 to 93	14.19	4.35	41.59	
Milne and	213	Male	62+	14.76	—	44.82	See text
Williamson (1972b)	259	Female	62+	13.53	—	41.05	
DHSS (1972)	351	Male	65+	14.9	—	—	Random community
	318	Female	65+	13.9	—	—	samples in UK
MacLennan et al	96	Male	65 to 74	14.2	—	—	
(1973)	157	Female	65 to 74	13.1	—	—	
	77	Male	75+	13.8	—	—	Small decrement
	145	Female	75+	12.9	—	—	after 75 years
Williams and Nixon	93	Male	75 to 96	14.05	—	—	
(1974)‡	193	Female	75 to 96	12.76	—	—	
Sheridan et al	155	Male	65 and	14.5	—	—	Random surveys at
(1974)	247	Female	over	13.7	—	—	home
Hill (1976)■	83	Male	65 to 74	14.63	—	—	
		Male	74 to 90+	13.82	—	—	
		Male	>65	14.38	—	—	
	137	Female	65 to 74	13.70	—	—	
		Female	74 to 90+	13.13	—	—	
		Female	>65	13.44	—	—	
Htoo et al (1979)	106	Male	65 & over	14.09	4.68	42.18	Retrospective study
	186	Female	65 & over	13.37	4.45	40.12	on ambulant geriatric centre attendees (New York)
Lipschitz et al	26	Male	>65	14.30	—	42.4	Healthy elderly
(1981)	196	Female	>65	13.02	—	38.6	attendees at US community centre

★ Housebound women had significantly lower values (mean Hb 12.48 g per dl). See also Morgan (1967).
† Variances of the distributions were significantly greater in elderly subjects, since more low levels are found in the elderly.
‡ Surveys in general practice.
■ Rural practice in island of Outer Hebrides.

Table 41.3 Anaemia in the elderly — community surveys

Author	Subjects			Criterion of anaemia Hb g per dl	% anaemic	Comments
	Total no.	Sex	Age (years)			
Williamson et al (1964)	89	Male	65+	<11.7	5.6	Edinburgh and nearby urban survey
	108	Female	65+		10.2	
Parsons et al (1965)	208	Male Female	65+	<12.5 <12	10.8 15.7	Swansea county borough. Anaemia much commoner in women 75+. Usually iron deficiency
Myers et al (1968)	81	Male	65+	<14	55	Only 14 per cent males if criterion Hb 12 g per 100 ml. Urban and rural Cambridgeshire
	121	Female	65+	<12	12.4	
Campbell et al (1968)	228	Male	65 to 74	<14	10	Part of study of adults up to 75 years in Wales
	224	Female	65 to 74	<12	10.7	
Hallberg and Högdahl (1971)	71	Female	75	<12	23	Urban Swedish (Göteborg), part of population study of ages 15 to 75
Anderson et al (1971)	879	Male Female	65+	<13.8 <12	6 to 7	Part of national nutritional survey of elderly at home, chosen at random (DHSS)
Elwood (1971)	229	Male	65+	<12	1 to 5	Several studies
	1420	Female	65+		8 to 22	
Milne and Williamson (1972b)	213	Male	62+	<12	5.6★	
	259	Female	62+		9.9	
DHSS (1972)	187	Male	65 to 74	<13	6.4	Mean % anaemic = 7.3
	178	Male	65 to 74	<12	7.9	
	164	Male	75+	<13	9.8	
	140	Female	75+	<12	5.0	
MacLennan et al (1973)	96	Male	65 to 74	<11.9	4	Random community samples in Scotland
	157	Female	65 to 74		15	
	77	Male	75+		12	
	145	Female	75+		25	
Williams and Nixon (1974)	93	Male	75 to 95	<12.7	6	General practice survey; only 30% 'healthy'
	193	Female	75 to 96		19	
Sheridan et al (1974)	155	Male	65+	<12	5.8	Hb 10 g/dl in only 1.8% of total
	247	Female	65+		9.2	
Hill (1976)	83	Male	>65	<13	13.25	General practice survey in Outer Hebrides
	137	Female	>65	<12	13.97	
Htoo et al (1979)	106	Male	65 and over	<14	42.5	80 per cent normocytic 69.2 per cent normocytic
	186	Female	65 and over	<12	14	
Campbell et al (1981)	32	Male	75–79		6.3	Community survey in New Zealand
	48	Female	75–79		12.5	
	134	Male	80+	<12	4.5	
	291	Female	80+		15.1	

★ If 14 g per dl taken as criterion for men, 25.6 per cent anaemic.

Table 41.4 Anaemia in the elderly — hospital surveys

Author	Total no.	Criterion★ Hb g per dl	% anaemic	Comments
Powell et al (1968)	333	<11.7	29	Acute geriatric wards — consecutive admissions
Evans et al (1968)	2700	<10	6.4	Consecutive admissions to geriatric wards
Griffiths et al (1970)	500	<11.7	16	Females only; low Hb associated with increased morbidity and mortality
Bose et al (1970)	229	<11	21	
DHSS (1970)	1367	<12	33	27 per cent of males; 33 per cent of females; based on questionnaires to 26 geriatricians
Banerjee (1975)	382 { 160 M / 122 F	{ <11.5	32.5 / 50.7	Macrocytic in 32.5%. 70% of these were normoblastic
Harant and Goldberger (1975)	128 { 44 M / 84 F	<13 / <12	23.2 / 45.2	Chronic diseases hospital
Bird et al (1977)	725 { 340 M / 385 F	<13.5 / <12	51.0 / 41.0	Consecutive admissions to geriatric unit
Matzer et al (1978)	104 { 55 M / 49 F }	<13	32.7	Patients aged > 60 years in a general medical ward, Israel

★ Anaemia is often considered present if Hb < 80 per cent Haldane. This is interpreted as 11.7 g per dl by some workers and 11.9 g per dl by others.

It would appear wise, on the present evidence, to seek out and treat anaemias in the elderly as far as possible.

Hospital surveys
Much of the morbidity and most of the mortality associated with anaemia are seen in hospitals.

Table 41.4 shows results from hospital surveys. There is a notably high incidence of anaemia in patients admitted to geriatric departments, with the exception of Cardiff (Evans et al, 1968). Evans (1971), in a haematological study of 886 elderly patients referred to the Cardiff Group laboratory, noted that the percentage of referrals with severe anaemias more than doubled as age increased from the seventh to the ninth decade. Severe iron-deficiency anaemia was slightly commoner in the men than the women.

Classification of anaemia in the elderly
Classification of anaemia may be morphological or aetiological (Tables 41.5 and 41.6), but in geriatric practice these must be allowed to overlap to be of most practical value. Morphology can give the physician much information and can suggest lines of investigation; but it must always be remembered that *anaemia is a symptom, not a disease*, and its cause must be discovered if effective treatment is to be appropriately instigated.

Clinical features of anaemia in the elderly
The symptoms and signs of anaemia are the same in the elderly as at younger ages, but the emphasis differs.

Table 41.5 Morphological classification of anaemias

Normocytic anaemias
Usually normochromic, occasionally mildly hypochromic, e.g. acute blood loss; 'symptomatic' anaemias.

Microcytic anaemias
(a) Usually hypochromic, e.g. iron-deficiency anaemia.
(b) Occasionally normochromic, e.g. 'symptomatic' anaemias.

Macrocytic anaemias
(a) Normoblastic, e.g. posthaemorrhagic anaemia, haemolytic anaemia, leucoerythroblastic anaemia, liver disease, scurvy.
(b) Megaloblastic, e.g. pernicious anaemia, folate deficiency.

Table 41.6 Aetiological classification of anaemias

Blood loss
    Acute or chronic
Excessive red cell destruction
    Haemolytic anaemias
Impaired red cell formation (dyshaemopoietic anaemias)
    a. *Deficiency of substances essential for erythropoiesis*
        Iron-deficiency anaemia
        Megaloblastic anaemia (vitamin B_{12} deficiency — pernicious anaemia — or folic acid deficiency)
        Scurvy
        Protein malnutrition
    b. *Other disturbance of marrow function*
        'Anaemia of chronic disorders'; 'symptomatic' anaemias'
        Infiltration
        Replacement } of bone marrow
        Aplastic anaemia

Note that more than one mechanism may operate, e.g. increased haemolysis may occur in several anaemias in the third group.

Cardiovascular and cerebral features predominate, although many anaemic patients make no complaint. Breathlessness and ankle-swelling are common presenting features, and may be due to frank congestive cardiac failure. Left ventricular failure may occur but angina is rare. Dizziness is common and mental changes are important but are non-specific. Apart from confusion there may be apathy and depression, leading to self-neglect, or agitation, possibly with delusions or hallucinations.

The tongue is often smooth and pale, and the patient may complain of 'burning' in the tongue; but a sore tongue may be due to associated nutritional deficiencies rather than to the anaemia itself (Wray et al, 1975). In such cases there may be angular stomatitis or cheilosis. However, the wearing of an upper denture may produce lesions indistinguishable from angular stomatitis, and may mislead.

Pallor, especially if recent, is important but rarely proffered as a symptom. The skin of the elderly may be very difficult to assess and attention should be paid to the colour of the buccal and lingual mucosae and the nailbeds. Changes in the nails themselves are rarely of help.

A spleen tip may be felt in severe long-standing anaemia but other causes must be excluded.

Associated features should be sought, e.g. bone tenderness, abdominal mass, lymphadenopathy, signs of neuropathy or spinal cord lesions.

The essential feature of chronic anaemias — which are the commonest seen in old age — is the insidious onset of symptoms and signs. Physiological changes can compensate to some extent for the reduction in haemoglobin, e.g. an altered oxygen-dissociation curve of haemoglobin, allowing readier availability of oxygen to the tissues (Huehns, 1971, 1974a; Brewer, 1974b; Thomas et al, 1974), which allows the anaemia to become marked before symptoms become troublesome. Furthermore, many old people are averse to seeking medical (or other) help and may suffer various symptoms without complaining. Thus, by the time an anaemia is actually diagnosed in the elderly the patient may in fact be very ill (Cantor, 1963). In milder cases untoward symptoms or failing general health may be accepted philosophically as part of 'the burden of old age'.

Investigation of anaemia

A full blood count is a valuable routine investigation in all elderly patients. If anaemia is found it must be investigated before any attempt at treatment is made. Indiscriminate use of haematinics before investigation can cause further morbidity and make accurate diagnosis extremely difficult or delayed.

It is necessary to determine the type and the cause of the anaemia. Examination of the peripheral blood film may suggest the likely cause as well as showing the type of anaemia present. The cause is finally determined by careful history and examination, the blood findings, and further investigations as required (Brunning, 1974; Israëls, 1975; Howe, 1979).

Treatment of anaemia — general principles

As well as treatment of the underlying cause, the use of haematinics and blood transfusion must be considered.

The specific haematinics are iron, vitamin B_{12} and folic acid, and perhaps ascorbic acid and pyridoxine. Non-specific haematinics include testosterone and oxymethalone.

Following an accurate diagnosis the specific haematinic required should be used alone whenever possible, and the response to full doses assessed. This helps in confirming the diagnosis and simplifies treatment.

'Blunderbuss' preparations or haematinic 'cocktails' are to be avoided; if they fail they may obscure the diagnosis.

The main indications for blood transfusion are where haematinic therapy will be ineffectual or inappropriate, or where the gravity of the patient's condition precludes undue delay, or prior to surgery.

Where transfusion does become necessary in the elderly every attempt must be made to avoid overloading the circulation, e.g. by using packed red cells in small volumes at a slow rate (e.g. 0.5 litre in 6 to 8 hours), by adding a diuretic to the transfusate, by warming the patient to open up the 'systemic capacity vessels' and so reduce the volume of blood in the pulmonary circulation, and by careful clinical observation to avoid pulmonary congestion and rise in jugular venous pressure.

IRON-DEFICIENCY AND HYPOCHROMIC ANAEMIA IN THE ELDERLY

Iron deficiency, with or without anaemia, is very common in the elderly. It is often due to chronic gastrointestinal blood loss, but inadequate dietary intake is an important factor in some cases.

Iron deficiency is not always due to a true lack of body iron but is sometimes caused by a failure of delivery of iron to the marrow from other tissues, e.g. in the anaemia of infection (Cartwright, 1966). In either case the plasma iron is low but if it is raised by treatment erythropoiesis can be increased. Occasionally the red cell fails to utilize available iron in haemoglobin synthesis (Nutrition Reviews, 1979) and hypochromic anaemia may develop ('sideraemic hypochromic anaemia') (Witts, 1969; Turnbull, 1971).

Iron metabolism

Full accounts of iron metabolism are given by Hallberg et al (1970); Dagg et al (1971), Jacobs and Worwood (1974) and Kief (1975).

Some aspects relevant to the aged follow:

Iron requirements are usually put at 10 mg per day for the elderly of both sexes (Department of Health and Social Security, 1969; World Health Organization, 1970); this figure allows a wide margin of safety.

Iron intake. A national nutritional survey of the elderly living at home (Anderson et al, 1971; Department of Health and Social Security, 1972) gave a mean iron intake of 5.2 mg per 1000 cal. In an investigation into the diet of elderly women living alone (Exton-Smith and Stanton, 1965) 60 women in two London boroughs had a mean daily iron intake of 9.9 mg (= 5.2 mg per 1000 cal). Sixteen of the women were followed up seven years later (Stanton and Exton-Smith, 1970); the mean iron intake had fallen to 8.9 mg but the mean calorie intake had also fallen, so that the mean daily iron intake per 1000 cal was 5.3 mg. The main sources of iron were meat (especially liver), flour products and eggs.

The elderly would appear to be vulnerable to dietary deficiency of iron: they often have low incomes and impaired ability to shop and cook. Women who have lived for years with diminished iron stores due to menstruation and child-bearing may reach old age with low stores; they are very vulnerable to iron-deficiency anaemia. Old men living alone are also at risk due to self-neglect.

Iron absorption depends on body iron stores and is increased in iron deficiency and decreased in iron overload, except in the case of haemochromatosis where iron absorption is increased. Increased iron requirements occur when erythropoiesis is stimulated and an increase in iron absorption then occurs (see discussion in Bothwell and Charlton, 1970).

Iron absorption may be increased by the concurrent ingestion of large doses of ascorbic acid (Brise and Hallberg, 1962; McCurdy and Dern, 1968) which acts as a reducing agent and helps to lower the pH of the gastric and duodenal contents.

There is some evidence to suggest a physiological decrease in iron absorption in old age (Vancini et al, 1967; Jacobs and Owen, 1969) but these studies are open to criticism regarding design and Marx (1979) has shown clearly that iron absorption is not decreased in elderly compared to young subjects. In iron deficiency, both young and old patients showed equal degrees of increase in iron absorption (Marx, 1979); however, it is possible that prolonged iron deficiency may lead to malabsorption of iron (reversible after iron replacement) (Kimber and Weintraub, 1968).

Recent studies of iron absorption (Callender, 1971; Layrisse, 1975), show marked variation in absorption of iron from different foodstuffs: absorption is far better from muscle and haemoglobin than from vegetable sources and eggs. Egg yolk can depress the absorption of iron from other foodstuffs in the diet. Tea and coffee reduce the absorption of iron (Disler et al, 1975; Morck et al, 1983). These observations are of considerable practical importance in considering iron balance and nutrition in the elderly.

A normal person absorbs less than 1 mg of iron daily; in iron deficiency this may rise to 3.5 mg daily (Moore, 1965). A patient with iron-deficiency anaemia absorbs about one-third of the iron in a tablet of ferrous sulphate.

Iron transport. Age changes in plasma iron, transferrin and TIBC have been outlined above.

Plasma iron may be reduced in conditions other than iron deficiency, e.g. infection, neoplasm, renal failure, or trauma. In infection there is altered iron metabolism (Cartwright, 1966) with rapid development of low plasma iron values, although anaemia may not develop for a long time. In such cases the TIBC is reduced in parallel, maintaining normal saturation. In cases of true iron deficiency the TIBC rises and saturation falls.

Plasma iron is increased in certain anaemias, notably in vitamin B_{12} and folic acid deficiency; a high saturation accompanies. If iron deficiency coexists the plasma iron level does not rise. When vitamin B_{12} and/or folic acid is given, the plasma iron falls and any coexistent iron deficiency will then become apparent. Conversely, folate (or vitamin B_{12}) deficiency may be masked by overt iron deficiency, and become apparent after iron therapy has been given for some weeks (Das et al, 1978). Masked folate deficiency may sometimes be suspected if iron deficiency is accompanied by hypersegmentation of granulocyte nuclei, but the most sensitive test for covert folate deficiency is the deoxyuridine suppression test on lymphocytes (Das et al, 1978); this test may be normal when performed on the bone marrow.

Iron utilization. Defective utilization of iron may occur in the elderly due to deficient transferrin levels leading to deposition of iron in organs instead of utilization in haemopoiesis. This leads to a refractory iron-deficiency anaemia with very low serum iron levels and has been found in intestinal and renal disease and when protein synthesis is impaired (Heilmeyer, 1966). The 'anaemia of infection' and the 'anaemia of chronic disorders' (collagenoses, neoplasms) may produce a similar haematological result (Cartwright, 1966; Turnbull, 1971). An increase in ineffective erythropoiesis is likely in old age (Marx, 1979; Nutr. Revs., 1979).

Iron kinetics have been reviewed by Finch et al (1970) and by Cavill and Ricketts (1974). Further investigation of ferrokinetics in old age will be needed (Marks, 1979).

Iron stores. The two storage forms of iron, haemosiderin and ferritin, increase in the bone marrow almost linearly with aging; at all ages, males have more storage iron than females (Burkhardt, 1975). Serum ferritin levels, where available, are superseding bone-marrow iron as an indication of body iron stores.

Serum iron is not helpful in this respect (Burkhardt, 1975) unless accompanied by measurement of the saturation of total iron-binding protein (Cape and Zirk, 1975).

In iron deficiency, storage iron is utilized before haemoglobin iron. Treatment of iron deficiency should be prolonged enough to replenish body stores after correcting the anaemia.

Iron loss. Less than 1 mg iron per day is lost by a normal man or postmenopausal woman; the loss occurs mainly in the faeces with a little in urine, sweat and bile (Jacobs P, 1971).

Causes of iron-deficiency anaemia

Chronic blood loss is a major cause of iron-deficiency anaemia at all ages, and in the elderly the loss is usually from the gastrointestinal tract (Jacobs P, 1971). Haemorrhoids and hiatus hernia are the commonest causes, but peptic ulcer, carcinoma of stomach or colon, diverticular disease and ingestion of aspirin or non-steroidal anti-inflammatory drugs are also important. Less frequent causes include coloproctitis, oesophageal varices and carcinoma of the rectum. In the tropics, hookworm infestation is a common cause. Repeated haematuria, epistaxes and haemoptyses, and postmenopausal bleeding are rarer causes of iron-deficiency anaemia.

Inadequate intake, impaired absorption and impaired utilization of iron have been considered above. Increased requirement of iron occurs in states of increased erythropoiesis such as chronic anoxia, polycythaemia, chronic haemolysis, and during treatment of other specific anaemias (e.g. vitamin B_{12} or folic acid deficiency anaemias).

There may be an hereditary factor in the development of chronic atrophic gastritis due to autoimmunity. Such patients may develop iron-deficiency anaemia followed by pernicious anaemia (Witts, 1969).

Effects of iron-deficiency on tissues (Dallman, 1974)

Buccal mucosa. Atrophic glossitis, angular stomatitis and atrophic buccal mucosa have been described. It is possible, however, that some of these changes may be attributable to concomitant pyridoxine deficiency (Jacobs and Cavill, 1968).

Nails. Nails may show brittleness and ridging and koilonychia may be seen, with or without other features of the Plummer-Vinson syndrome.

Oesophagus. An oesophageal web is rare, but may occur without overt anaemia; it is pre-malignant.

Stomach. Gastric mucosal abnormalities are common (Witts, 1966), but their extent and severity do not correlate with the degree of anaemia. A superficial

gastritis appears early and acid secretion diminishes; as atrophic gastritis develops the cellular infiltration decreases and acid secretion fails; the final picture of gastric atrophy is identical with that seen in pernicious anaemia. There is a sequential loss of ability to secrete hydrochloric acid, pepsin, and intrinsic factor, in that order (Witts, 1966). Dagg et al (1966a) found that of 22 patients with iron-deficiency anaemia and histamine-fast achlorhydria, 7 had low vitamin B_{12} absorption in the pernicious anaemia range ('latent pernicious anaemia'). These authors conclude that a patient with iron-deficiency anaemia had a 6 per cent chance of developing pernicious anaemia, and a 32 per cent chance if histamine-fast achlorhydria and gastric parietal-cell antibodies were present. Gastric mucosal changes may be secondary to iron deficiency (Jacobs A, 1971).

The relationship between gastric mucosal changes and anaemia in the elderly is further discussed by Bird et al (1977), whose findings differ in some respects from those of several other workers. For example, they found that achlorhydria was common even in the presence of normal or nearly normal gastric mucosa.

Gastric parietal-cell antibodies are commonly found in patients with iron-deficiency and histamine-fast achlorhydria (Dagg et al, 1964), and their prevalence increases with age (Wangel et al, 1968). In iron-deficiency anaemia these antibodies are associated with chronic gastritis (Coghill et al, 1965). These auto-antibodies may further damage the gastric mucosa (Anderson et al, 1967; Walder, 1968).

Clinical features

These are due to the anaemia, the tissue changes described above, and the condition producing the anaemia.

The onset is usually insidious.

The Plummer-Vinson or Kelly-Paterson syndrome consists of a postcricoid web associated with iron-deficiency anaemia and perhaps koilonychia. It is relatively uncommon, occurring mainly in women after at least 10 to 15 years of iron deficiency. Dysphagia is located by the patient at laryngeal level. Solid food cannot be swallowed, but soft food and fluids can. Malignancy must be excluded in these cases.

Haemorrhoids are easily overlooked without proctoscopy. Hiatus hernia may not give rise to the classical symptoms, and may be present in lean men as well as obese women — although the latter are particularly prone to that condition. A laparotomy scar may suggest a previous gastrectomy.

Blood picture

The blood film shows hypochromic anaemia; red cells are reduced in number and are incompletely haemoglobinized and therefore hypochromic. At first the red cells are of normal size but later they become microcytic, and may show anisocytosis and poikilocytosis. The red cell count may be reduced much less than the haemoglobin.

Red-cell absolute indices show reduced MCHC, MCH and MCV. With rapid blood-loss, the haemoglobin falls well before the MCHC becomes reduced; with more chronic blood loss the depletion of iron stores is reflected in an MCHC which is already reduced by the time the anaemia is discovered.

White cells may show a 'shift to the right' (hypersegmentation) in the nuclei of neutrophil polymorphs. This may sometimes indicate a masked folate or vitamin B_{12} deficiency which becomes apparent only after iron therapy (Das et al, 1978). A mild leucopenia (mainly neutropenia) may occur in severe cases; a neutrophil leucocytosis may follow a brisk haemorrhage.

Platelets may be somewhat increased in patients who are bleeding.

Bone marrow
Erythroid hyperplasia, with normoblastic erythropoiesis, is seen, but falls off when plasma iron drops below 12.5 μmol/l (70 μg per 100 ml). The main cells are normoblasts with only a little cytoplasm, forming a ragged border. Staining for iron shows only a trace or none at all.

Biochemical tests
Serum iron is reduced, often below 9 μmol/l (50 μg per 100 ml).

Serum TIBC is increased to 71 to 90 μmol/l (400 to 500 μg per 100 ml) or more in states of body iron deficiency but TIBC is reduced along with serum iron in the 'anaemia of chronic disorders'. Transferrin saturation is only 16 per cent or less. About half the old people in hospital have transferrin saturations of less than 16 per cent, many below 10 per cent (Thomas and Powell, 1971). These authors discuss the interpretation of these values in the light of current doubts about the normal range for the elderly. They showed that serum iron and transferrin saturation had a significant correlation with MCHC but the serum iron showed a significant correlation with haemoglobin in women only. This was due to the appreciable incidence of iron deficiency without anaemia in their patients. They emphasize that the peripheral blood picture alone is not a reliable index of iron deficiency.

Serum ferritin is below 12 μg/l unless there are certain associated conditions such as leukaemia or liver disease which may raise the levels (Jacobs and Worwood, 1975).

Radio-isotope tests
Iron absorption. ^{59}Fe and ^{55}Fe may be used, with single or double isotope techniques. The whole-body counter is a valuable tool for this purpose (Callender, 1971; Marx, 1979).

Differential ferrioxamine test (Fielding, 1965). Desferrioxamine chelates iron and is used in the treatment of acute iron poisoning, some cases of refractory anaemia with transfusional iron overload, and occasionally in haemochromatosis. This test is helpful in both latent and overt iron-deficiency states. Non-radioactive desferrioxamine is injected intramuscularly and is accompanied by an intravenous injection of ^{59}Fe-labelled ferrioxamine. The excretion of labelled ferrioxamine is compared with that of non-radioactive ferrioxamine in a 6-hour urine specimen.

Diagnosis
In most cases, a full blood count, MCHC, serum iron and TIBC will provide sufficient information.

Blood loss must be sought for assiduously. A history of drug ingestion or gastric operation is important. Rectal examination is essential but haemorrhoids may be missed if proctoscopy is omitted. Faeces should be tested repeatedly for occult blood, in sequences of three or even six consecutive daily specimens. Barium studies of the alimentary tract are often required; a barium meal (hiatus hernia, peptic ulcer or gastric operation) may be accompanied by a barium swallow (oesophageal varices or carcinoma) or may require follow-through films (small intestinal lesions, malabsorption). A barium enema (carcinoma of caecum or colon, ulcerative colitis, diverticulitis) should always be preceded by sigmoidoscopy if it is suspected that the lesion is on the left side of the colon. With the elderly, in view of the discomfort, difficulties, and risks of the procedure, it is widely held that a barium enema should only be performed if there is a definite indication for it, e.g. positive faecal occult blood tests, overt bleeding per rectum, or a mass felt per abdomen (Haggie, 1952; Exton-Smith and Osborne, 1961). Other tests of gastrointestinal structure and function may be required, such as fibreoscopy (increasingly used with advantage in elderly patients) (Gibbins et al, 1974), gastric or jejunal biopsy, the 'string' test, xylose tolerance test, faecal fat estimations, or serum gastric (parietal cell) antibodies. In suitable cases the faeces should be examined for hookworms. Liver function tests may suggest a diagnosis of cirrhosis.

The urine should be examined microscopically as well as macroscopically; the blood urea should be checked, and if necessary an IVP requested. Cystoscopy may be required.

A chest X-ray should show the source of haemoptyses and is in any case a useful routine procedure.

Where other types of anaemia may coexist, it will important to determine the serum vitamin B_{12} level, serum or red cell folate, leucocyte ascorbic acid, gastric antibodies (intrinsic factor and parietal cell), gastric acidity, and perhaps to perform a Schilling test of vitamin B_{12} absorption; a tryptophane loading test may detect pyridoxine deficiency.

In some cases where there is diagnostic difficulty due to lack of facilities or poor patient co-operation it will be necessary to resort to a therapeutic trial with iron, following the haemoglobin response. If there is intermittent or chronic bleeding there may be no apparent response at all, so this test cannot be relied upon.

Treatment

The cause must be dealt with and iron given to restore Hb to normal and to replenish body stores. The administration of iron is simple enough, yet not without problems. Relapse after treatment is common, and often due to failure to continue taking iron once the patient feels better or the blood picture is corrected. Additional problems in the elderly arise from forgetfulness: tablets may not be taken three times daily as prescribed, and a slow-release preparation may be the best remedy here (Fulcher and Hyland, 1981), although Callender (1969) and Elwood and Williams (1970) found no specific therapeutic advantage in these preparations.

Duration of oral iron therapy. Full doses should be given until the haemoglobin is normal; iron absorption decreases as the haemoglobin rises. Smaller doses should be continued for 3 to 6 months to replenish depleted tissue stores of iron. If chronic blood loss cannot be stopped, maintenance iron therapy must continue.

Adjuvant drugs. Iron preparations used for the elderly should contain no other haematinic. There is no need for a combination of iron and vitamins (except possibly vitamin C), and a combination of iron and vitamin B_{12} or folic acid is absolutely meddlesome in treating the elderly. Similarly it is unwise and unnecessary to add trace elements to iron preparations (Witts, 1969).

Vitamin C increases iron absorption but may also increase side-effects of iron. However, its use in the elderly may be justified because they may absorb iron less well and often appear deficient in vitamin C (Exton-Smith, 1971). Since large doses of vitamin C are required for this purpose it is probably best to administer it as a separate preparation but at the same time as the iron.

Failure of response to oral iron. This may be due to an error in diagnosis, to continuing blood loss, to malabsorption, or to failure to take the tablets. As indicated, this last problem is common in old people, who may forget or give up too easily if mild side-effects occur.

In the elderly, renal impairment, infection (especially chronic urinary infection) and neoplasm are common and the associated anaemia, whilst it may be hypochromic, may fail to response to oral iron ('anaemia of chronic disorders'). In some of these cases, there may be a response, for a time at least, to parenteral iron.

Parenteral iron therapy. This should be used only when specially indicated. The only absolute indication is malabsorption of oral iron, but it is also required where there is intolerance to oral iron, where oral iron is considered undesirable (peptic ulcer, colitis, functioning colostomy, unreliable or forgetful patient) or too slow (continuing bleeding, or prior to surgery), in patients refractory to oral iron ('chronic disorders') or when it is desired to replenish iron stores rapidly (continued bleeding).

A formula given by Witts (1969) for correction of the anaemia and replenishment of body iron stores is:
Iron to be injected (mg) = (15 – Hb in g per dl) × body weight (kg) × 3.
Parenteral iron preparations are taken up by the reticuloendothelial system and then slowly released.

Intramuscular iron. The two main preparations used are iron dextran injection, B.P., B.N.F., U.S.P. (Imferon) and iron sorbitol injection, B.P., B.N.F. (iron sorbitex injection, U.S.N.F) (Jectofer). Each contains 50 mg iron per ml.

Iron dextran injection is liable to stain the skin unless injected deeply, and may produce local tenderness, fever and swelling of lymph nodes. The much-publicized risk of sarcoma in rats reduced the popularity of its use for intramuscular therapy but there is no evidence that the iron-dextran complex causes such tumours in man (British Medical Journal, 1964). It seems unnecessary to withhold this treatment in later life on account of this fear. Treatment should always begin with a test dose of 1 ml; daily or twice weekly doses of 2 ml may then be given, increasing up to 5 ml daily if tolerated.

Iron sorbitol injection does not stain the skin, and rarely produces local symptoms or signs. It has not been reported to cause tumours in animals. It may produce a metallic taste in the mouth after injection, and may blacken the urine (which is of aesthetic significance only). It is more likely than iron-dextran complex to produce a systemic reaction, though it does not commonly do so. Doses should not exceed 2 ml daily. Iron sorbitol injection should not be given intravenously. Oral iron should not be given during a course of iron sorbitol injections, since most of the latter, with its small molecular size, enters the blood stream directly and may produce excessive rises in plasma iron if this is already being increased by oral iron therapy. If the plasma iron exceeds the plasma iron-binding capacity some free iron will circulate in the plasma and this will produce toxic effects.

Reactions to intramuscular iron. Local and general reactions occur; the latter resemble those seen with intravenous iron (see below) but are less common. Rees and Coles (1969) advised caution in treating uraemic patients with iron-dextran complex, since it might lead to soft-tissue calcification in such patients, who have high plasma parathyroid hormone levels.

Intravenous iron. Saccharated iron oxide (Ferrivenin) has fallen from favour because of the greater likelihood of local and general reactions and perhaps the more tedious technical aspects of its administration. Iron-dextrin injection, Dextriferron, formerly Astrafer IV, is presented similarly and is likewise suitable for intravenous use only. (Do not confuse iron-dextrin with iron-dextran! — It is perhaps best to use the proprietary names in this instance.) It is somewhat less irritant than Ferrivenin and contains 20 mg iron per ml.

Iron-dextran complex has been used as a direct intravenous injection. It provides $2\frac{1}{2}$ times as much iron per ml as Ferrivenin or Astrafer IV (Marchasin and Wallerstein, 1964). Experience with intravenous iron dextran injections (2099 injections in 471 patients and 10 volunteers) was reported by Hamstra et al (1980) who provide a useful discussion of this therapy and its adverse reactions. The iron dextran may impart a reddish-brown tinge to the serum which has caused confusion when a transfusion reaction occurred soon afterwards (Colburn and Barnes, 1982). To minimize toxic reactions, and to save time, the technique of total-dose infusion of iron (as iron dextran injection (Imferon) in saline) has superseded this and, in many cases, other forms of intravenous iron therapy also.

Total-dose infusion. By providing in a single dose the total amount of iron required to correct anaemia and replenish body stores, the saving of time and discomfort is considerable, and, although it should be regarded as potentially hazardous, with due care and attention the total-dose technique is a reasonably safe procedure. It is of particular value in certain elderly patients, as indicated by Wright (1967), in whose hands it was an easy and uneventful procedure. It has also been used with success by Andrews et al (1967). Care has to be taken over the rate of the infusion, to avoid fluid overload, and in relation to the concentration of iron. In practice, Imferon, in an amount calculated as described above, is added to 1 litre of normal saline to make a 4 to 5 per cent v/v solution, and Wright (1967) advocated adding 40 mg frusemide to ensure a diuresis. The initial rate of flow should be 10 drops per minute for 10 to 30 minutes, as a test dose, then 45 to 60 drops per minute. The whole procedure takes 4 to 6 hours and the patient should remain under observation for at least 1 hour more. Thus total-dose infusion of iron may be given in the day hospital, as advocated by Andrews et al (1967).

Patients with rheumatoid arthritis have a greater tendency to adverse reactions (Lloyd and Williams, 1970).

Reactions to intravenous iron. Local irritation, pain, venous spasm or thrombophlebitis may occur. General reactions may produce headache, nausea, vomiting, pyrexia, tachycardia and abdominal cramps. Hypersensitivity reactions may occur in allergic subjects, who should therefore not receive intravenous iron. Anaphylactoid reactions with respiratory distress and cardiovascular collapse may be fatal. Anuria has been reported.

The incidence of reactions varies according to the preparation and technique. Reactions to Ferrivenin were recorded in 5 to 35 per cent patients by Coleman et al (1955) but are less common with Dextriferron (Astrafer). Hamstra et al (1980) reported that 125 (26 per cent) of their 471 patients had reactions and three of these were life-threatening anaphylactoid reactions. Doses over 250 mg (especially in patients weighing less than 50 kg) were most likely to produce severe reactions and these were particularly common in patients with rheumatoid arthritis and other inflammatory diseases. Experience with total-dose infusion has shown severe reactions varying from 0.5 per cent to 6 per cent, with a higher incidence of less severe reactions.

Reactions are less common in severe iron deficiency, presumably due to increased plasma iron-binding capacity.

Blood transfusion. This is rarely required and the general principles already outlined apply. Iron therapy should be started at once. Blood transfusion is more appropriate in certain of the 'anaemias of chronic disorders', e.g. rheumatoid arthritis, neoplasm, chronic infection.

IRON DEFICIENCY WITHOUT ANAEMIA (SIDEROPENIA SINE ANAEMIA)

Iron deficiency without anaemia has a large bibliography (e.g. Morrow et al, 1968; Powell et al, 1968; Powell and Thomas, 1969; Lloyd, 1971; Mitchell and Pegrum, 1971). MacLennan et al (1973) found in random community samples of the elderly that this condition was commoner than iron deficiency with anaemia (9 per cent and 6 per cent respectively for men, 11 per cent and 8 per cent for women).

The investigation of iron status has been discussed above. Fielding et al (1965) used the differential ferrioxamine test to assess iron status and Dagg et al (1966b) used a desferrioxamine test to detect latent as well as overt iron deficiency.

Other helpful findings are increased iron absorption and increased red cell protoporphyrin (Dagg et al, 1966c).

Iron deficiency without anaemia is common in the elderly (Jacobs et al, 1969; Thomas and Powell, 1971). If it persists, anaemia appears within a few months; the situation is analogous to latent pernicious anaemia. Thomas and Powell (1971) found an underlying neoplasm in 7 out of 21 non-anaemic patients with a very low serum iron but they do not indicate if there was other evidence to support the diagnosis of iron deficiency. Certainly, the diagnosis of iron deficiency must lead to intensive efforts to determine the cause.

Following iron therapy, there may be general and possibly mental improvement, although the evidence from controlled trials suggests that this is unlikely if there is no increase in haemoglobin level at all (Witts, 1969).

HYPOCHROMIC ANAEMIA WITHOUT IRON DEFICIENCY

Not all hypochromic anaemias are due to iron deficiency. They may occur in several conditions in which porphyrin synthesis or globin synthesis is defective.

Defective porphyrin synthesis

Apart from lead poisoning, this group is composed of the *sideroblastic anaemias* (Bateman and Mollin, 1970; Kass and Schnitzer, 1975; Trump et al, 1975). These are characterized by refractory anaemia, hyperplastic bone marrow and signs of impaired utilization of iron. The marrow contains large numbers of erythroblasts loaded with iron (probably ferritin) granules arranged in a perinuclear ring ('ring sideroblasts').

These anaemias may be hereditary or acquired. In old age we meet acquired forms, which may be primary or secondary.

Primary acquired sideroblastic anaemia

This is commoner in the elderly than previously thought, and may at first be considered as a 'refractory' iron deficiency or megaloblastic anaemia. The blood picture shows a proportion of hypochromic cells but these may be outnumbered by normochromic cells. The anaemia is macrocytic rather than microcytic. Serum iron may be raised or normal, with increased turnover but diminished utilization of iron, leading to ineffective erythropoiesis. TIBC is often reduced and the transferrin saturation variable. Serum ferritin is high and there is excess of free erythrocyte protoprophyrin. Iron absorption may be increased.

The bone marrow shows intense erythroblastic hyperplasia. Most of the cells are ring sideroblasts. The marked increase in proportion of primitive red-cell precursors resembles the marrow picture in megaloblastic anaemia and may lead to confusion in diagnosis until an iron stain is used. In fact there may be megaloblastic change due to associated folate or (rarely) vitamin B_{12} deficiency; and this marrow change may or may not respond to treatment with the relevant nutrient. In all cases it is essential to exclude coexisting folate and B_{12} deficiency, since the 'classical' marrow appearance of the latter deficiencies may be partially or completely masked by the changes of sideroblastic anaemia.

Some cases terminate after several years in acute myeloblastic or myelomonocytic leukaemia (Cheng et al, 1979; Lewy et al, 1979); this may in fact have been their original diagnosis, or a reflection of a cytogenetic chromosomal abnormality (Krogh Jensen and Mikkelsen, 1976).

Secondary acquired sideroblastic anaemia

Sideroblastic anaemia is an uncommon feature in other diseases and may be induced by drugs. Blood and marrow findings vary, from those described for the primary form to mild changes with some hypochromic cells in the blood and a few ring sideroblasts in the marrow. Such an anaemia may be found in association with myeloproliferative disorders, myeloma, carcinoma, collagen diseases, myxoedema, malabsorption, partial gastrectomy without malabsorption, toxins such as ethyl alcohol and lead, and after drug therapy with antituberculous drugs, cytotoxic agents, phenacetin, paracetamol and chloramphenicol.

All possible secondary causes should be excluded before diagnosing primary sideroblastic anaemia, as treatment may be more effective in secondary cases.

Treatment of sideroblastic anaemias

Primary sideroblastic anaemia may respond to folic acid and/or pyridoxine, but the response is usually partial at best, and the blood and marrow do not return completely to normal. These drugs, therefore, do not correct the basic defect.

Secondary sideroblastic anaemia may improve when the primary cause is treated. Folic acid and/or pyridoxine is more often effective in the secondary forms, and may produce complete remission. Large doses are required. If giving folic acid without vitamin B_{12}, the B_{12} status *must* be reviewed at regular intervals.

Although there is often evidence of folate deficiency in these cases, there is no conclusive evidence of pyridoxine deficiency. It is not possible to predict which cases will respond, and a therapeutic trial is required. Israëls (1975) states that geriatric patients with sideroblastic anaemia do not respond to pyridoxine but quotes the successful treatment of a 72-year-old woman by Mason and Emerson (1973), who used pyridoxal-5'-phosphate. However, Datta (1975) pointed out that this success had not been repeated, and he understood that only 3 or 4 out of 80 patients so treated had shown any haematological response at all. Trump et al (1975) found decreased amino-laevulinic acid (ALA) synthetase activity in elderly patients with this disease, but very few responded to pyridoxal-5'-phosphate.

Ascorbic acid has helped some cases.

Chelating agents (e.g. desferrioxamine) have been

unsuccessful but may be more effective if used together with ascorbic acid loading (Wapnick et al, 1969).

Blood transfusions should be kept to a minimum, as they greatly increase the risk of iron overload. These patients are prone to liver damage and it is safer for them to adapt to their anaemia, whenever possible, than to be transfused very often. Should transfusion be required in severe and refractory cases, a chelating agent should be given in addition. Phlebotomy has been used to reduce body iron where the anaemia permits, in an effort to protect liver and pancreas.

Splenectomy may be dangerous and lead to severe thromboembolic phenomena. It does not improve the anaemia, nor do androgenic steroids.

Defective or unbalanced globin synthesis
This group includes the haemoglobinopathies and thalassaemias (Weatherall, 1971).

Other causes
Hume et al (1973) described a hypochromic anaemia without iron deficiency in patients with musculoskeletal pains and high ESR; these patients responded to steroid therapy.

OTHER NORMOBLASTIC ANAEMIAS

Macrocytic anaemias
These are anaemias characterized by red cells which are larger than average. Macrocytes may result from either normoblastic or megaloblastic erythropoiesis, which have totally different implications with regard to aetiology, pathogenesis, management and prognosis. The differentiation cannot be made on examination of the peripheral blood alone, and bone marrow examination is essential. Macrocytosis in the elderly is discussed by Powell (1978).

The megaloblastic anaemias are the more important and are considered separately later. Here we shall consider the normoblastic macrocytic anaemias, which are not uncommon in the elderly (Bahemuka et al, 1973; Banerjee, 1975).

Increased mean corpuscular volume (MCV) is the first evidence of the change in the blood (Chanarin, 1971) and may be detected before any anaemia becomes apparent.

Causes
Brisk marrow response to anaemia. This may occur after a haemorrhage, when there is a rapid release of reticulocytes from a normoblastic marrow: reticulocytes are larger than mature red cells, and will increase the MCV of the blood.

Associated with other disorders. These include haemolytic anaemia, leukaemia (especially acute), diseases with marrow infiltration or replacement (Hodgkin's disease, myeloma, carcinoma, myelofibrosis), aplastic anaemia, lead poisoning, liver disease, alcoholism, protein malnutrition, scurvy, myxoedema, hypopituitarism and malaria. A macrocytic anaemia occurs *sporadically* in these conditions, and is not the usual type of anaemia, which is more often normocytic. However, alcohol is very likely to lead to macrocytosis: MCV increases by about 1.7 fl for every 10 g of alcohol taken daily (Lancet, 1983).

NORMOCYTIC ANAEMIAS ('SYMPTOMATIC ANAEMIAS')

Normocytic anaemias are associated with systemic diseases such as infection, neoplasm, collagen diseases, liver disease, alcoholism, protein malnutrition, scurvy, endocrine disorders and renal failure. They are usually normocytic (and normochromic) but may occasionally be macrocytic (see above) or microcytic. They are not due to a deficiency of a basic haematinic, and the treatment is that of the primary disorder.

Infection
A mild or moderate anaemia is common in association with infections, especially chronic infections. Factors involved probably include decreased erythropoiesis; altered iron metabolism (Cartwright, 1966); reduced red-cell survival (sometimes with frank haemolysis, e.g. severe septicaemia or virus infection); and blood-loss (e.g. from an abscess or sinus).

In geriatric practice there are certain particular infections to be borne in mind in differential diagnosis: they are easily overlooked and call for a high index of suspicion, especially as they are amenable to treatment. These are:

Tuberculosis, especially the disseminated type, which may be very difficult to diagnose: a leukaemoid blood picture, raised ESR, and anaemia, possibly severe, may be the only presenting features. A marrow smear will exclude leukaemia, but granulomata are more likely to be seen if marrow is obtained by biopsy rather than by aspiration. (A liver biopsy is even better) (Cucin et al, 1973.) Proudfoot and colleagues (1969) stated that this cryptic variety was as common as the overt type in patients over 60 years old, and the peak incidence is in the eighth decade. Sideroblastic anaemia may occur after treatment with antituberculous drugs such as PAS, INAH, cycloserine or pyrazinamide.

Rarely, disseminated tuberculosis has caused pancytopenia (Mangion and Schiller, 1971; Rosenberg and

Rumans, 1978) and may on occasion be due to bone marrow necrosis (Katzen and Spagnolo, 1980).

Subacute bacterial endocarditis is being seen more often in later life than in young adults (Hughes and Gauld, 1966; Weinstein, 1972). It often presents with minimal and non-specific features in the elderly (Wedgwood, 1955, 1961), and may be overlooked even for years. One of the great problems in diagnosing this condition is that a cardiac murmur may not be present and since both temperature and ESR may be normal and the patient edentulous, the physician may be left with little to go on. However, examination of the urine for red cells is an important pointer and blood cultures should always be performed in obscure or 'refractory' anaemias. Arterial blood is said to give a greater harvest of positive blood cultures than venous blood.

Chronic pyelonephritis may be silent for a long time and yet produce anaemia. Usually, however, this is associated with impairment of renal function, and is discussed below.

Bed-sores are often associated with anaemia, which may be due to the underlying condition, chronic infection, and loss of blood and protein from the sores. Poor nutrition may contribute. The anaemia may, of course, be hypochromic in some of these cases.

Neoplasm

Anaemia is very common in malignant disease, especially with carcinomas of the alimentary tract and in cases with bony metastases. Several factors operate: blood loss (the major factor), infection, marrow infiltration by metastases, haemolysis (especially in widespread dissemination), malnutrition, malabsorption, renal impairment and bone marrow depression caused by radiotherapy or cytotoxic drugs. Bone marrow necrosis has been described recently in patients with malignant neoplasms (and some acute and chronic non-neoplastic disorders) (Norgard et al, 1979).

The anaemia is thus usually normocytic and normochromic or (if blood loss predominates) hypochromic and microcytic. It may be leucoerythroblastic if there is metastasis to the bone marrow (seen particularly in primary carcinoma of breast, prostate, lung, kidney, thyroid and stomach, and also malignant melanoma). This type of anaemia may be macrocytic, due to the presence of immature red and white cells in the blood, and the presence of large numbers of nucleated red cells is characteristic. Its pathogenesis is obscure, as there is usually adequate red marrow remaining in the affected bones.

Rarely a true autoimmune haemolytic anaemia may appear, with a positive Coombs test. It is seen mainly with malignant lymphomas, including chronic lymphatic leukaemia, but has also been recorded occasionally in carcinoma of the prostate and stomach and in secondary carcinoma in bones.

Malnutrition may interfere with red cell formation, and malabsorption may contribute.

Renal impairment and bone marrow depression are considered later.

Collagen diseases

Rheumatoid arthritis

Anaemia is very common in active rheumatoid arthritis. This disease is usually seen in a more chronic or burnt-out stage in the elderly, but an acute onset may occur for the first time in old age, and acute exacerbations are not uncommon in the elderly.

Several types of anaemia may be seen:

Normochromic or normocytic anaemia is common, and parallels activity of the disease, similar to the 'anaemia of chronic infection'.

Hypochromic, micro- or normo-cytic anaemia is due to iron-deficient erythropoiesis. As indicated above, this may be due to deficiency of body iron (e.g. bleeding due to aspirin therapy) but is often due to a block in release of iron from reticuloendothelial cells in the tissues with a consequent impairment of transport of iron to the marrow (Turnbull, 1971). Such patients have low plasma iron and TIBC and serum ferritin levels (Bentley and Williams, 1974; Blake et al, 1980), but there is plentiful haemosiderin in the reticuloendothelial cells of the marrow, although none in normoblasts. There is also a group of patients with absent marrow iron who do not respond to iron; in these it is thought that there is sequestration of iron in the joints (Senator and Muirden, 1968) so that there is not a true body iron deficiency.

A mild degree of haemolysis may contribute to the anaemia; rarely, an autoimmune acquired haemolytic anaemia supervenes.

Renal impairment associated with secondary amyloid disease or excessive phenacetin ingestion may add its effects to the anaemia.

Other drugs used in treatment of rheumatoid arthritis may depress the bone marrow (e.g. phenylbutazone, gold) and aplastic anaemia may follow as a rare complication.

Sideroblastic anaemia has been reported.

Folic acid deficiency may be present, but is usually mild, and anaemia is rare in these circumstances. There is evidence of vitamin B_{12} deficiency also (Partridge and Duthie, 1963) but this could not be confirmed by Carter and colleagues (1968).

Treatment. Iron is indicated when there is evidence of body iron deficiency; it will not help those patients with a blocked iron transport mechanism.

Corticosteroids can correct this block and permit

release of iron from the reticuloendothelial system. These drugs also correct the joint-sequestration phenomenon and allow this iron to be mobilized and delivered to the marrow. They are useful if a frank haemolytic anaemia develops.

Folic acid and vitamin B$_{12}$ are not normally used, since the mild deficiencies noted have not been thought to be of significance.

Blood transfusion leads to a temporary rise in haemoglobin; the transfused cells are destroyed more rapidly than normal. Small blood transfusions may be of help in producing a general improvement in well-being in patients with rheumatoid arthritis.

Other collagen diseases
Similar considerations apply in polyarteritis nodosa, dermatomyositis, giant-cell arteritis (including polymyalgia rheumatica) and systemic lupus erythematosus (SLE). Giant-cell arteritis is essentially a disease of old age. It was well reviewed by Paulley and Hughes (1960). It is particularly important because it may lead to blindness and this is preventable by steroid therapy; indeed, the whole condition is usually amenable to steroids, and is essentially self-limiting.

Liver disease
Haematological aspects of liver disease are considered in the chapter on The Liver.

Protein malnutrition
Protein deficiency alone does not usually cause anaemia, but may be only one factor in a situation predisposing to anaemia (e.g. cirrhosis).

Scurvy
Most scorbutic patients are anaemic. The anaemia is usually normocytic or macrocytic, and is normochromic. Hypochromic microcytic anaemia may also occur due to associated iron deficiency and blood loss.

The marrow is normoblastic and hyperplastic. Rarely it is megaloblastic (see below).

The anaemia is due to impaired erythropoiesis but shortened red cell life-span and perhaps blood loss contribute. Ascorbic acid therapy produces a reticulocytosis and corrects the anaemia, although iron may also be required.

Endocrine disorders

Myxoedema
Two out of three patients with hypothyroidism have mild or moderate anaemia. It is usually normocytic or slightly hypochromic. Significant hypochromia, with microcytosis, occurs if there is associated iron defi-

ciency. Macrocytosis may occur, but Tudhope and Wilson (1960) denied that this was seen in uncomplicated myxoedema: it should first be attributed to reticulocytosis due to recent blood loss, or to a possible associated megaloblastic anaemia — particularly pernicious anaemia, which occurs together with myxoedema in 10 per cent of cases. The degree of anaemia is often less than that suggested by the degree of pallor.

The marrow shows hypoplasia and an excess of fat.

Since treatment with L-thyroxine must begin cautiously and be built-up gradually the anaemia may take several months to disappear. Iron and vitamin B$_{12}$ should be given only if deficiency of these haematinics is proven.

Hypopituitarism
A mild or moderate anaemia of insidious onset is usual, normocytic or slightly macrocytic, and normochromic or slightly hypochromic. Disproportionately marked pallor may mislead at first.

Addison's disease
A mild normocytic normochromic anaemia is common. The red cell volume is reduced, but the plasma volume is reduced more, leading to haemoconcentration which may mask the anaemia. Correction of the haemoconcentration often reveals subnormal haemoglobin and haematocrit values. Cortisone therapy corrects the anaemia along with the other features of the disease.

Renal failure
Renal impairment is a normal accompaniment of senescence secondary to nephrosclerosis, but the blood urea does not normally become elevated (Davies and Shock, 1950). Chronic pyelonephritis or chronic glomerulonephritis may, however, accelerate the deterioration of renal function. Chronic pyelonephritis is common in the elderly and may be clinically silent for a very long time: indeed, unexplained anaemia may be its only presenting feature. Some cases may have a very high ESR with rouleaux formation, azotaemia, anaemia and possibly a palpable spleen-tip, and a mistaken diagnosis of myeloma may be made.

Anaemia develops sooner or later in all patients with chronic renal insufficiency, regardless of the underlying disease, but is more severe when renal infection is present, e.g. chronic pyelonephritis. A wide range of diseases of the kidneys or genitourinary tract may underlie the renal failure, and some of these produce anaemia in their own right.

The degree of anaemia is related to the severity of the renal failure; it may appear before the blood urea rises since this does not occur until renal reserve function falls below 50 per cent of the normal. Once azotaemia begins, anaemia is almost invariable, and the Hb may fall about

2 g per 100 ml for every rise of 50 mg per 100 ml in the blood urea over the range 50 to 250 mg per 100 ml; it then reaches a steady level. There is much variation, however.

The anaemia is normocytic and normochromic; 'burr cells' may develop later, together with other deformed shapes; in some cases fragmentation of red cells occurs and may be accompanied by haemoglobinaemia and thrombocytopenia (microangiopathic haemolytic anaemia) (Brain, 1970, 1971). It has been recorded in the elderly (Amorosi and Ultman, 1966; Jacobson and Vickery, 1968).

The marrow is normoblastic, and erythropoiesis is normal or increased until the blood urea exceeds 150 mg per ml, when some hypoplasia develops. Marrow iron is normal.

The main factors contributing to this anaemia (Fisher, 1980b) are decreased erythropoiesis (which is the major factor, of unknown causation though probably due mainly to decreased erythropoietin production and partly to inhibitors of marrow haem synthesis), increased red cell destruction, and in some cases blood loss. Blood loss is rarely significant from the renal or genitourinary lesion itself, but uraemia may be associated with a haemorrhagic tendency which can aggravate the anaemia. In the elderly it is not uncommon to find renal function impaired *secondarily* to anaemia from another cause: thus, bleeding into the intestine may cause a rise in blood urea in patients whose renal reserve has only just been coping to keep the urea normal. The sudden additional protein load (analogous to a high-protein meal), and perhaps a reduction in renal blood flow, may be enough to impair renal function further and the resulting azotaemia may be considerable and rapid. However, it can be restored to normal equally rapidly once the bleeding stops and the bowel is cleared of blood.

Treatment. The anaemia is usually refractory, but may improve if renal function can be improved with a fall in blood urea. Iron is indicated if there is a proven deficiency. The successful use of cobalt in some of these patients has been described (Geill, 1969) but its toxicity should be remembered. Androgens have a small place in the management of anaemia in chronic renal failure (BMJ, 1977; Fisher, 1980b).

Blood transfusion may be required but may cause deterioration of renal function by altering renal haemodynamics; a sharp fall in glomerular filtration rate and rise in blood urea may occur. Whole blood is better than packed cells in such cases. The transfused cells may be destroyed at an increased rate, so the treatment may be less beneficial than expected.

Potential advances in treatment are discussed briefly by Fisher (1980b).

HAEMOLYTIC ANAEMIAS

Frank haemolytic anaemias are not common in the elderly, although shortened red cell life-span is found in various types of anaemia (e.g. megaloblastic anaemias, symptomatic anaemias).

For systematic accounts of the haemolytic anaemias the reader is referred to standard haematology textbooks. Some aspects, however, pertinent to geriatric practice, may be considered here.

Hereditary spherocytosis (familial acholuric jaundice)
This is seen in the elderly very occasionally, either *de novo* or on survival of a patient affected earlier in life.

Paroxysmal nocturnal haemoglobinuria (PNH)
A rare condition, seen occasionally in old age, and due to an acquired defect of red-cell membranes (Lewis, 1967; Brain, 1971)

Autoimmune haemolytic anaemias
Autoantibodies may be warm-reacting (IgG) or cold (IgM or, more rarely, IgG).

Idiopathic autoimmune haemolytic anaemia (Dacie, 1970) may be seen at any age and is usually associated with warm antibodies. Aplastic crises may occur. A variety with cold antibodies of IgM type affects predominantly the elderly and is known as *cold haemagglutinin disease*. This presents with Raynaud's phenomenon, haemolytic anaemia and haemoglobinuria; very high titres of cold antibodies are found in the serum. It is a very chronic and persistent disorder. In both these varieties the direct Coombs test is positive.

Secondary autoimmune haemolytic anaemias. These may be associated with malignant lymphomas, myelofibrosis, paraproteinaemias, collagenoses, ulcerative colitis, or ovarian teratomata. Warm or cold antibodies may occur; the direct Coombs test is positive.

Prognosis depends on the type and titre of antibody and not on the age of the patient (Dacie, 1963); also on the aetiology. Thus warm antibody formation may eventually cease; cold antibodies may be transient (after infections) or very persistent (cold haemagglutinin disease).

Treatment. Steroids are used for warm-antibody varieties, but are of little or no value if cold antibodies are present.

Immunosuppressive drugs have been successful in some cases.

Splenectomy may be performed if steroid and immunosuppressive therapy fail but is more likely to help in warm than in cold antibody cases.

Blood transfusion is risky and its benefits transient.

Protection against cold is important in cold-antibody cases.

Haemolytic anaemia due to drugs and chemicals

Several mechanisms may operate (see Dacie and Worlledge, 1969; Worlledge, 1969; de Gruchy, 1975a).

Phenylhydrazine and sulphones, large doses of phenacetin, lead poisoning and various industrial and household chemicals may produce haemolysis directly.

Some drugs alter the antigenic properties of red cells so that an autoantibody response occurs. Haematological and serological findings are identical with those seen in 'idiopathic' autoimmune haemolytic anaemia. The most important example is methyldopa (Aldomet); 20 per cent of patients on this drug develop a positive direct Coombs test of IgG type, but anaemia occurs in only 0.15 to 0.3 per cent of treated subjects. The antibody is developed against red-cell antigens and *not* against the drug. Other drugs which may have these effects are mefanamic acid (Ponstan) and penicillin.

Thirdly, the drug may act as a hapten and thus become antigenic; on subsequent administration the red cells adsorb immune complexes or bind the drug to their surfaces and are destroyed by the reaction occurring on their membranes. The red cells are intrinsically normal. Implicated drugs include quinine, quinidine, salicylates, phenacetin and sulphasalazine.

MEGALOBLASTIC ANAEMIAS

Definition and incidence

The megaloblastic anaemias are characterized by abnormal nucleated red cell precursors (megaloblasts) in the bone marrow, which give rise to larger-than-normal red cells (macrocytes) with variable size and shape. There is an associated leucopenia with increase in hypersegmented neutrophils, and platelets may be reduced. These blood changes are in effect part of a more general disturbance in which various tissues and organs may be affected.

Megaloblastic anaemias are relatively uncommon, but their incidence increases with age. In the elderly they are often diagnosed late, so that the severest cases tend to be seen in this age group. These anaemias have a clinical significance far greater than their incidence might suggest, for they are almost all eminently treatable, with excellent results.

Pathogenesis

Megaloblastic anaemias are deficiency diseases due usually to deficiency of vitamin B_{12} or folic acid. Rare causes include other conditions in which nucleic acid synthesis is defective: deficiency of ascorbic acid or pyridoxine; and so-called 'refractory' cases.

The proximate cause of almost all megaloblastic anaemias is defective nucleic acid synthesis. Folate is the final 'antimegaloblastic' factor; vitamin B_{12} acts at an earlier stage in the metabolic processes involved in the availability of folate. Ascorbic acid may also assist in making folate available. Interrelationships between vitamin B_{12}, folic acid and ascorbic acid are discussed by Hyams and Ross (1963), Goldberg (1963), Vilter (1964) and Cox (1968). More recently it has been suggested that the ingestion of massive doses of ascorbic acid might produce a vitamin B_{12} deficiency by destroying the cobalamins during transport through the gut and possibly in the tissues (Herbert and Jacob, 1974). In addition megadoses of ascorbic acid may cause spuriously low serum B_{12} levels unless cyanide is added to the assay (Herbert et al, 1978). These suggestions have not gone uncontested, and are discussed by Hogenkamp (1980).

Vitamin B_{12} and folate metabolism

Points of special interest in geriatric medicine will be discussed here.

Vitamin B_{12} absorption

Vitamin B_{12} occurs in most animal tissues but not in plants. A normal diet contains up to 5–30 μg per day. B_{12} is stable in normal cooking and most is available for absorption, but only 2 μg can be absorbed from a single meal, as this is the limit for the ileal receptors. B_{12} loss is 1 to 12 μg per day. In fact the body loses daily about 0.1 to 0.2 per cent of its total B_{12} pool — whatever the size of the pool. Thus in B_{12} deficiency, less B_{12} is lost than in normals and correspondingly less is required to maintain the *status quo*. This may explain why latent B_{12} deficiency in patients with mild malabsorption of B_{12} (e.g. in atrophic gastritis or after partial gastrectomy) may not progress to severe B_{12} deficiency with overt megaloblastic anaemia.

Intrinsic factor (IF) is a mucoprotein which is secreted by gastric parietal cells and binds to vitamin B_{12}; the B_{12} — IF complex is absorbed in the ileum.

Absorption may also occur by simple diffusion along a steep concentration gradient from the gut lumen into intestinal mucosa (Chanarin, 1969), hence the effectiveness of massive oral doses of B_{12} alone.

An enterohepatic circulation of vitamin B_{12} occurs, of the order of 0.5 to 5 μg daily.

Vitamin B_{12} absorption and malabsorption are reviewed by Toskes and Deren (1973), Gräsbeck and Salonen (1976) and Lindenbaum (1979).

Vitamin B_{12} status in old age

A progressive fall in serum B_{12} with advancing age has been described (Cape and Shinton, 1961; Kilpatrick and Withey, 1965; Elsborg, Lund and Bastrup-Madsen,

1976). Tauber et al (1957) and Chow (1958) suggested that this implied reduction of tissue stores of B_{12} is possibly due to impaired B_{12} absorption in old age. It was postulated that such malabsorption might follow decreased IF secretion due to atrophic gastritis.

Diminished B_{12} absorption has been reported in the elderly by Glass and colleagues (1954, 1956). Others reported no significant variation of B_{12} absorption with age (Tauber et al, 1957; Droller and Dossett, 1959). Hyams (1964) studied the absorption of B_{12} in 13 elderly men and 10 younger controls, following stimulation of IF secretion by the injection of carbamylcholine (Carbachol). There was no significant difference between the two age groups. It was concluded that ileal absorption of B_{12} was as efficient in the elderly as in the younger men, and that 'normal' old men *could* produce sufficient IF, upon appropriate stimulation, to permit normal B_{12} absorption; though whether they did so under physiological conditions was not established.

More recently, McEvoy et al (1982) showed that vitamin B_{12} absorption did not correlate with age in 51 healthy subjects aged 60 to 96 years, and was no different from results obtained in younger subjects in previously reported studies (Hjelt et al, 1977).

In community surveys, Hughes et al (1970) and Elwood et al (1971) found that 15 to 20 per cent of the elderly studied had low serum vitamin B_{12} levels (<150 ng/l). Hughes et al (1970) found that treatment with injections of vitamin B_{12} produced no improvement in sense of well-being or in mental state. Morgan et al (1973) and Schepp et al (1980) found no age-related change in serum vitamin B_{12} levels.

These studies of serum B_{12} levels and B_{12} absorption should be reviewed in the context of work of Swendseid and colleagues (1957) and Halsted and colleagues (1959), who showed that the liver content of B_{12} is unaffected by age. Since the liver contains 90 per cent of the body's B_{12}, it would appear that the normal elderly do not in fact have depleted B_{12} stores. This accords well with the report by Adams and Boddy (1971) that age (and sex and iron status) had no effect on B_{12} turnover. There are conflicting opinions about the effect of iron status, however, since a low serum B_{12} level may accompany iron deficiency (Spray, 1962) and will rise after giving oral iron (Cox et al, 1959; Williams et al, 1962). There is also controversy about the effect of iron status on B_{12} absorption (Cox et al, 1959; Cook and Valberg, 1965).

Serum B_{12} levels are also subnormal in one-third of patients with nutritional megaloblastic anaemia due to folate deficiency (see below); treatment with folic acid restores the serum B_{12} level (Mollin et al, 1962).

Serum B_{12} levels are uninfluenced by time of day or proximity of food intake (Pathy and Newcombe, 1980). However, errors in serum B_{12} assay may arise if analogues of vitamin B_{12} are present in the serum — as seems to be the usual case (Kolhouse et al, 1978; Cooper and Whitehead, 1978). This is because the analogues — which do not bind to pure IF — are measured by less specific B_{12} assay methods. As a consequence, a proportion of patients with B_{12} deficiency will be overlooked.

In addition, other vitamins may interfere with the B_{12} assay and produce falsely low serum B_{12} measurements (e.g. thiamine, nicotinamide, vitamin C (see above) and vitamin E) (Herbert, 1981). Also, chloral hydrate may interfere with the B_{12} radioassay (Mitchell et al, 1981).

Thus, serum B_{12} levels do not necessarily reflect B_{12} status and are not an accurate index of B_{12} absorption.

Folate absorption

Folates occur in fresh green vegetables, nuts, yeast and liver. A mixed diet contains 500 to 800 μg folate per day, mostly in a reduced form and therefore easily destroyed by oxidation, sunlight and cooking. Reducing agents such as ascorbic acid help protect the folate but may be destroyed by the same procedures.

Minimal folate requirements (as folic acid) are 50 to 100 μg per day but up to 10 times this amount may be needed when there is increased erythropoiesis. At least 200 μg folate will be absorbed daily from an average diet.

According to Baker et al (1979) the elderly show impaired ability to utilize dietary polyglutamates (the predominant form of folate in foods) — although they can absorb synthetic monoglutamate. A more general malabsorption may occur in the elderly and increase with aging (Montgomery et al, 1978; Runcie, 1979).

Absorption of folate occurs mainly in the upper small intestine. An enterohepatic circulation of folate occurs (60 to 90 μg daily) — a significant source of loss if there is malabsorption.

Folate absorption is reviewed by Lindenbaum (1979) and by Rosenberg, Selhub & Dhar (1979).

Folate status in old age

Serum folate levels are difficult to evaluate; low levels are very common in the elderly, even the apparently normal elderly. Read and colleagues (1965) found low levels in 80 per cent of old people admitted to a residential home; in 10 subjects the folate level was below 3 ng per ml and of these, eight had normal Hb levels. Hurdle and Williams (1966) reported serum folate levels below 5 μg/l (ng per ml) in 28 of 72 elderly hospital patients; only 12 were anaemic, and only 2 had megaloblastic anaemia. Girdwood et al (1967) compared serum folate in young controls, elderly subjects at home, and elderly hospital patients. The last group showed the lowest values, but there were very low values in all groups and these authors doubted that serum folate necessarily reflected the state of the body's folate stores.

It is known that a folate-deficient diet causes the serum folate level to become very low within a few weeks, long before tissue folate stores, which last for four months, can become depleted (Herbert, 1962). Buxton and colleagues (1969) found low or very low serum folate levels (less than 1.5 μg/l (ng per ml) in 27 of 40 mentally abnormal geriatric patients and 19 of 40 mentally normal control patients matched for age and sex. Thomas and Powell (1971) consider levels above 2.5 μg/l (ng per ml) as normal, 1 to 2 μg/l (ng per ml) usually indicating deficiency and under 1.0 μg/l (ng per ml) almost invariably indicating deficiency. These authors consider that the accepted range of 6 to 21 μg/l (ng per ml) (Wintrobe, 1967) appears to be too high for the *Lactobacillus casei* method of assay.

The DHSS nutritional survey (Department of Health and Social Security, 1972) showed that about 60 per cent of 653 subjects had serum folate of less than 6 μg/l (ng/ml) and 14.6 per cent were below 3 μg/l (ng/ml), the lower limit of normal suggested by the World Health Organization (1972). Sheridan et al (1974) took 2 μg/l (ng/ml) as the lower limit of normal in their community survey; 30 of 365 subjects (8.2 per cent) had subnormal levels.

Red-cell folate turns over much more slowly than serum folate. It remains in the red cells throughout their life-span, and so indicates the folate status of the subject over the previous four months. It thus provides a better index of tissue folate stores than does serum folate (Hoffbrand et al, 1966). Normal values are 150 to 600 μg/l (ng per ml) packed red cells. Raised values are found in reticulocytosis and after blood transfusion.

In community surveys, Elwood et al (1971) found low red-cell folate (RCF) levels in 43 (8 per cent) of 533 subjects over the age of 65, and the DHSS (1972) survey reported a 16.1 per cent incidence of low RCF (below 150 μg/l (ng/ml)) in 629 subjects studied.

Webster and Leeming (1979) found that 24 per cent of 29 healthy subjects aged over 75 had RCF < 100 ng/ml (and similar proportions of low RCF values in assessment and long-stay geriatric patients in hospital). In an acute geriatric unit 156 of 400 patients had RCF < 170 ng/ml (Raper and Choudhury, 1978). Runcie (1979) reported that 115 (46 per cent) of 250 elderly persons living at home had low serum and/or red-cell folate.

CSF folate is at much higher levels than serum folate but there is a close correlation between the two; correlation with RCF is much less (Shaw, 1971). There is evidence of a blood-brain barrier mechanism for folic acid (Chanarin, Perry and Reynolds, 1974; Reynolds, 1979b).

Liver folate. The liver is the main folate store of the body, and contains 6 to 10 mg folate as 5-methyl tetra-hydrofolate (THF). Liver folate decreases as age increases (Hoppner and Lampi, 1980).

Vitamin B$_{12}$ folate interrelationships

Of the several biochemical reactions requiring either B$_{12}$ or folate, the conversion of homocysteine to methionine requires both. Folate acts as 5-methyl THF and is converted to THF in the reaction; B$_{12}$ is required as a co-enzyme. It has been postulated that in B$_{12}$ deficiency the folate is metabolically 'trapped' as 5-methyl THF, leading to a deficiency of other folate co-enzymes and consequent impairment of nucleic acid synthesis. This produces megaloblastic anaemia (Hoffbrand, 1971; Herbert, 1971; Chanarin, 1971; Shinton, 1972). The deficiencies of this hypothesis have been discussed by Chanarin (1973, 1974). More recent accounts are given by Das and Herbert (1976); Gräsback and Salonen (1976); Kass (1976); Perry et al (1976); Kass (1978); Cooper (1979).

Vitamin B$_{12}$ deficiency

Causes

Apart from vegans, in whom dietary deficiency of B$_{12}$ may be found, B$_{12}$ deficiency in adults is nearly always due to malabsorption (Table 41.7).

Table 41.7 Malabsorption of vitamin B$_{12}$

Gastric lesions
   Pernicious anaemia
   Chronic atrophic gastritis
   Gastrectomy (total or partial)
Intestinal lesions
   Gluten-sensitive enteropathy (adult coeliac disease, idiopathic malabsorption) and tropical sprue
   Anatomical abnormalities of the small gut
     — with bacterial floral (jejunal diverticula, blind loop, fistula, stricture)
     — ileal resection or disease (Crohn's disease, radiation ileitis)
   Severe pancreatic disease
   Drug-induced malabsorption (neomycin, colchicine)
   Fish tapeworm

Pernicious anaemia

Pernicious anaemia (PA) is the commonest type of megaloblastic anaemia, and is due to vitamin B$_{12}$ deficiency secondary to lack of intrinsic factor (IF) secretion as a result of gastric atrophy.

A full and recent account with a comprehensive bibliography was given by Kass (1976, 1978).

Incidence and pathogenesis

Pernicious anaemia is essentially a disease of middle and later life, occurring more frequently as age advances.

About half the patients are over 60 at the time of onset (Cantor, 1963). The overall frequency in the UK is 0.1 to 0.2 per cent, but over the age of 60 its frequency is about 1 per cent. MacLennan et al (1973) found an incidence of 2.5 per cent in 475 subjects aged 65 and over, studied in two community samples in Glasgow and Kilsyth (1.1 per cent in men, 3.3 per cent in women). It is known that PA is commoner in Scotland than in England and the incidence is higher in the north of England than in the south (Scott, 1960). In Denmark, Pedersen and Mosbech (1969) reported a prevalence of 0.9 per cent in men and 2.4 per cent in women over 80. Relatives of patients with PA show an incidence of this disease 25 times greater than in the general population; relatives also show an increased incidence of achlorhydria, chronic gastritis, parietal cell antibodies, and impaired B_{12} absorption.

In the general population the incidence of achlorhydria, chronic gastritis and circulating antibodies to gastric parietal cells rises steadily after middle age. Patients who develop PA may have a genetic predisposition to extensive atrophic gastritis resulting in gastric atrophy and failure of acid and IF secretion (see Siurala et al, 1980).

However, although Joske et al (1955) showed an increasing incidence of abnormal gastric mucosal findings with advancing age, no such realtionship was found by Bird et al (1977). These latter workers also found poor correlation between gastric mucosal changes, on the one hand, and Schilling tests and serum vitamin B_{12} levels on the other (excluding patients with pernicious anaemia).

In this connexion, it should be noted that a normal stomach can produce 2000 to 18 000 units of IF per hour (after stimulation with histamine), yet normal B_{12} absorption and normal serum levels of vitamin B_{12} can be obtained with levels as low as 200 units per hour (Chanarin, 1969).

The gastric lesion is generally considered to be an autoimmune phenomenon, as suggested by the histological features, the presence of antibodies to intrinsic factor and gastric parietal cells in blood and gastric juice, the association with other autoimmune diseases — such as thyroid disorders (thyrotoxicosis, primary myxoedema, Hashimoto's disease), idiopathic Addison's disease (adrenal atrophy), rheumatoid arthritis, and diabetes mellitus — and the response to steroids. For more details refer to Kass (1978).

There is current interest in the relationship between histocompatibility antigens (HLA) and atrophic gastritis, with or without pernicious anaemia (Chanarin et al, 1976). Different workers have shown different correlations; in two studies (Eastmond and Woodrow, 1976; Horton and Oliver, 1976) no relationships could be found. These discrepancies have been explained by the work of Ungar et al (1977, 1981), who showed a significant heterogeneity in HLA patterns in different clinical subgroups of patients with pernicious anaemia.

Clinical features

The onset is classically insidious so that the anaemia may be severe when the patient first presents. Some patients have a more rapid onset and others may develop symptoms even before anaemia appears (Rustgi and Bettigole, 1981). After partial gastrectomy, PA may appear in 5 to 6 per cent of patients over a period of 8 to 12 years; after total gastrectomy, liver B_{12} stores are depleted in 2 to 3 years, and PA follows about 9 months later.

The anaemia causes general symptoms, but in the elderly these are variable in their presence and emphasis for the usual reasons — diminished physiological reserve, multiple pathological processes, limited mobility, and in some instances the insidious onset and resistance to seeking help. Mild anaemia is all too often ignored in the elderly, yet it may be macrocytic and thus provide a clue which allows early diagnosis and the prevention of potentially severe problems (Carmel, 1979; Hall, 1981).

The skin may look slightly yellow. The hair is often white but this is not often helpful in the aged (Dawson and Ogston, 1972).

Glossitis is an important sign of B_{12} deficiency (and also of folate deficiency) (Dawson et al, 1969). It may be intermittent and may precede the the general symptoms of anaemia by a long period. Burning or soreness of the tongue should never be dismissed too readily, but is often absent. A smooth, shiny, atrophic tongue is more common, and patchy red areas of acute glossitis may be superimposed. Concomitant nutritional deficiency may coexist, e.g. iron, B vitamins (cheilosis, angular stomatitis, or 'geographical' tongue suggest the latter). Anorexia is common in PA and may well lead to secondary nutritional deficiencies.

Cardiovascular symptoms may occur, and a haemic murmur may be present.

Hepatomegaly is common, especially if there is cardiac failure. Splenomegaly occurs in 10 per cent of cases or less, and is usually mild. A laparotomy scar may suggest a previous gastrectomy.

Haemorrhagic lesions are rare; small haemorrhages may be seen in the fundi. More severe bleeding may be due to an associated thrombocytopenia, and is of serious import.

Dysphagia and postcricoid carcinoma are rare, but documented (Jacobs, 1962).

Mental changes may predominate. Some may be due specifically to B_{12} deficiency, but the evidence is conflicting. Dawson and Donald (1966) found that 26 of 100 acute medical admissions aged over 70 years had low serum B_{12} and a high incidence of psychiatric abnormalities. Droller and Dossett (1959) found that confused and demented old people often had subnormal B_{12} levels, as compared to mentally normal old people. Strachan and Henderson (1965) also emphasized the possible importance of low B_{12} status as a cause of mental changes, and suggested that screening for B_{12} deficiency might be worthwhile in psychiatric practice. This was carried out by Murphy et al (1969) who found only two cases of PA in 1004 consecutive new patients aged over 50 years admitted to a mental hospital. Since this incidence is *lower* than that expected in the general population, these authors doubted that value of such screening, at least until automated techniques for B_{12} assay were available. Schulman (1967) had taken the view that psychiatrists should be aware of the possibility of B_{12} deficiency in patients with anaemia or after gastrectomy, or where fatigue, confusion, or dementia was of unknown origin. In most patients with mental symptoms due to B_{12} deficiency it is likely that changes would be found in the blood or marrow (Lancet, 1969). Buxton et al (1969) and Thomas and Powell (1971) found no association between mental symptoms and low B_{12} levels.

Nevertheless, mental symptoms have been recorded with known B_{12} deficiency (Holmes, 1956; Roach and McLean, 1982) and a psychosis may occur (Smith, 1960). Whitehead and Chohan (1974) have described a relationship between vitamin B_{12} deficiency and paranoid delusions.

Paraesthesiae, unsteadiness, and dragging of the feet may occur and may be accompanied by signs of peripheral neuropathy (Cox-Klazinga and Endtz, 1980; Roach and McLean, 1982) and pyramidal and posterior column lesions (paraplegia and sensory ataxia). Note that extensor plantar responses may be associated with absent or increased tendon jerks in the legs. A sensory level may exist. It appears that subacute combined degeneration of the cord does not occur in severe cases of PA (Matthews and Wilson, 1971), though the serum B_{12} level is always low. Inter-relationships between the neurology of folate and vitamin B_{12} deficiency are discussed by Reynolds (1979a).

It is worth recalling the experience of Cantor (1963): heart failure, mental symptoms and walking difficulty are common in later life, and patients may be labelled 'senile' or 'arteriosclerotic', especially if the anaemia has not yet developed or is missed — as happens in many old people. Only 5 of Cantor's 13 patients with PA were referred with a diagnosis of anaemia. Atrophy of the tongue was common, but no patient complained of a sore tongue. Serious complications were common and often multiple — thus 9 patients were in heart failure on admission, and at least 2 had subacute combined degeneration of the cord. Mental changes were common. The patients tolerated sedatives and hypnotics badly — even 'normal' doses of chloral. Good responses were seen to vitamin B_{12} therapy, especially a rapid improvement in cardiac function. The cord lesion may improve, but more slowly. Four patients made a complete mental recovery. But 4 patients died, and Cantor warns that prognosis should be more guarded in the elderly than in middle age. The high mortality in megaloblastic anaemia and the danger of sudden death during treatment have recently been emphasized by Lawson, Murray and Parker (1972).

The cause of the anaemia, i.e. gastric atrophy, is usually clinically silent, but anorexia, nausea, vomiting, flatulence, dyspepsia and diarrhoea may occur. Loss of weight may ensue. The picture may suggest carcinoma of the stomach, and this may coexist since its incidence is higher in patients with PA than in the general population.

Blood picture. A macrocytic anaemia with anisocytosis, ovalocytosis and poikilocytosis suggests megaloblastic erythropoiesis.

The Hb may vary from normal levels to 3 g per dl or less, and the red cell count falls disproportionately more.

MCV is often 10 to 140 fl (μ^3) but the MCHC is normal unless there is iron deficiency. In this case, a dimorphic blood picture may occur with a population of microcytic hypochromic cells as well as the normochromic macrocytes. Israëls (1975) emphasizes that it is common for both types of anaemia to coexist in geriatric patients, quoting the data of Evans (1971) who found that, whilst 67 per cent of anaemic patients had iron deficiency, *51 per cent also had megaloblastic anaemia.* A slight reticulocytosis may be seen, together with a few nucleated red cells, possibly even a megaloblast in severe cases.

A moderate neutropenia and thrombocytopenia are usual, with a 'shift to the right' in the neutrophils, i.e. more cells with multilobed nuclei, even eight to nine lobes at times (macropolycytes).

The diagnostic value of polymorph hypersegmentation as an index of haematinic deficiency likely to cause megaloblastosis in the elderly has been stressed by Adam et al (1973) and Sheridan et al (1974). (See also Nath and Lindenbaum, 1979).

Bone marrow. The marrow is very active and the bone cortex thin. The degree of megaloblastic erythropoiesis is reflected in the severity of the anaemia. An excess of stainable iron is seen unless there is concomitant iron deficiency. A variety of abnormal processes are taking place in the marrow — ineffective erythropoiesis, haemolysis, maturation arrest, abnormal iron metabolism and abnormalities of leucocytes and megakaryocytes (Kass, 1978).

Severe iron deficiency may mask the megaloblastic changes until iron is given.

Diagnosis of pernicious anaemia

In addition to the clinical findings, blood picture and marrow film as described, the diagnosis requires the demonstration of deficiency of vitamin B_{12} and IF.

A low serum level of vitamin B_{12} is essential for the diagnosis of PA and will usually be under 100 ng/l (pg per ml). Microbiological assays may also be affected by antibiotic or cytotoxic therapy.

Various techniques have been used to demonstrate the impaired B_{12} absorption in PA. The most popular is the Schilling (1953) urinary excretion test, which may be repeated with administration of intrinsic factor together with the oral dose of vitamin B_{12} — the low result in PA will rise to normal; this will not occur in intestinal malabsorption syndromes. This test is subject to errors in the elderly due to incomplete urine collections (check with urinary creatinine estimation) or impaired renal function (Buxton et al, 1969). These disadvantages are reduced and time saved by using the 'Dicopac' test (Bell et al, 1965), a double-isotope urinary excretion test using ^{57}Co and ^{58}Co. Pathy, Pippen and Kirkman (1972) reported the use of this test in 150 elderly patients; it was of value not only in the straightforward diagnosis of PA but also in patients with suspected PA who had had prior vitamin B_{12} therapy.

Pathy et al (1979) reported on further experience with the Dicopac test: they regarded it as a useful simple screening test in patients with a megaloblastic marrow and combined low serum B_{12} and folate concentrations. However its discriminatory value was of limited diagnostic significance in one-third of their 301 elderly patients with low normal serum B_{12} concentrations. Modifications which increase diagnostic value make the test more cumbersome.

Other techniques have greater disadvantages in the elderly, e.g. the faecal excretion method (Heinle et al, 1952), the hepatic uptake method (Glass et al, 1956), and the whole body counter (Shearman et al, 1971), are all liable to error in constipated subjects and present other obvious technical difficulties. Blood radioactivity after oral radioactive B_{12} (McCurdy, 1965) is relatively insensitive.

Direct assay of IF in gastric juice (Ardeman and Chanarin, 1965) is of help in some cases, since normal amounts of IF after pentagastrin stimulation exclude PA but do not prove that the small intestine is absorbing B_{12} normally.

Histamine-fast achlorhydria has been considered an essential feature for the diagnosis of PA, but histamine has now been superseded by pentagastrin as a stimulant of gastric secretion. This does not have the side-effects of histamine and no antihistamine is necessary, so making the tests more acceptable in geriatric practice.

The 'Diagnex blue' test is a useful screening test in the elderly. The resin is taken orally and in the presence of free gastric acid it releases azure A which is excreted in the urine. This will exclude PA and avoid gastric intubation. But a negative result calls for a more accurate test, on gastric juice, in the usual way.

Antibodies

Gastric antibodies. Intrinsic factor antibodies occur in the serum of 60 per cent of patients with PA; their incidence may increase with duration of the disease (Ungar et al, 1967). They are only rarely found in thyroid disease, adrenal insufficiency, diabetes and simple atrophic gastritis.

IF antibodies occur in gastric juice (see above) but their frequency of occurrence is uncertain. They are of IgA type, as distinct from the IgG serum antibody.

Parietal cell antibodies occur in the serum of 90 per cent of patients with PA and may also be found in gastric juice. They are of less diagnostic value, since they occur often in other patients. Doniach and Roitt (1964) found them in 16 per cent of normal woman over 60 years old, and 19 per cent of women over 70. Wangel and colleagues (1968) noted an increasing incidence (together with achlorhydria) with advancing age. There is also a higher incidence in simple atrophic gastritis, relatives of PA patients, thyroid disorders. idiopathic adrenal atrophy, rheumatoid arthritis, deficiency anaemia and diabetes.

Thyroid antibodies. These are present in the serum of about 40 per cent of patients with PA, and their relatives also have an increased incidence of these antibodies. Kass (1978) discusses autoimmune aspects of pernicious anaemia.

Other tests

Deoxyuridine suppression test. Megaloblastic marrow exhibits abnormal DNA synthesis. Normal marrow readily incorporates deoxythymidine into DNA but preincubation of the marrow with deoxyuridine (du) almost completely suppresses this incorporation. Megaloblastic marrow shows less marked suppression. This forms the basis for an in vitro test for deficiency of B_{12} or folate. Addition of low concentrations of B_{12} corrects this abnormality in B_{12} deficiency; and low concentrations of folate correct this abnormality in folate deficiency (higher concentrations of folate correct the abnormality due to deficiency of either B_{12} or folate). For more details see Wickramasinghe and Longland (1974) and Wickramasinghe and Saunders (1975).

Methylmalonic acid is increased in the urine in B_{12} deficiency but not in folate deficiency; the test is more sensitive if a loading dose of L-valine is given. However, technical difficulties restrict this test to a few laboratories only.

Serum bilirubin (unconjugated) and urinary urobilinogen may be raised; so may serum uric acid and lactic dehydrogenase. Serum iron is raised unless there is concomitant iron deficiency; TIBC is normal or low, and saturation is high. Serum folate is normal or raised, and concomitant folate deficiency (common in the elderly) may be masked for a time but subnormal serum folate levels will develop later. Red-cell folate falls earlier and is a better guide. Serum alkaline phosphatase and cholesterol may be low.

The low serum alkaline phosphatase may mask the rise in alkaline phosphatase in patients with concomitant osteomalacia (e.g. after partial gastrectomy) (Hoffbrand, 1971). The low serum alkaline phosphatase rises to normal with B_{12} therapy (Van Dommelen and Klaassen, 1964).

Hepatic B_{12} may be assayed in liver biopsies (Pitney and Onesti, 1961; Bonjour, 1980).

Haematological response. An optimal response to $2 \mu g$ B_{12} injected daily confirms the diagnosis of B_{12} deficiency.

Latent pernicious anaemia
This condition is described by Callender and Denborough (1957).

Callender and Spray (1962) emphasized that IF secretion may be reduced before overt symptoms and signs of B_{12} deficiency occur. When B_{12} stores are depleted, low serum B_{12} levels are found. Overt PA will develop in a few months unless B_{12} therapy is given.

There is overlap between the normal and subnormal ranges of serum B_{12} in the region 100 to 200 ng/l (pg per ml). The DHSS survey (1972) showed that 10 per cent of the elderly subjects had serum B_{12} levels within this range. Levels of 100 to 170 ng/l (pg per ml) are comparable with B_{12} deficiency. MacLennan et al (1973) found that the prevalence of latent PA (serum $B_{12} < 140$ ng/l (pg/ml)) was 5 per cent in the elderly population they studied in two Scottish communities.

R binder deficiency. This rare condition is characterized by a deficiency of R binder (a cobalamin-binding protein ubiquitous in serum). There is a low concentration of B_{12} but megaloblastic anaemia does not occur (Carmel, 1982). The whole subject of cobalamin-binding proteins in plasma transport of vitamin B_{12} has become quite complex (see Allen, 1976 and Kass, 1978).

Treatment of pernicious anaemia
Vitamin B_{12} therapy must be continued for life. In the elderly it is especially important to give the B_{12} by injection and to avoid oral therapy except when absolutely necessary (e.g. allergy to injected B_{12}).

Hydroxocobalamin (Neo-Cytamen) is best for initial and maintenance therapy, since it is retained in the body far more efficiency than cyanocobalamin. Note that the rapid urinary excretion of cyanocobalamin makes this the form of B_{12} to be used in the Schilling and related tests.

Initial dosage should be 1000 μg on alternate days for four doses (Chalmers and Shinton, 1965). If neurological complications exist this dosage should be continued twice weekly for at least 6 months.

Maintenance dosage thereafter may be 250 to 1000 μg every two months; in the elderly 500 μg is probably adequate, but there may be advantages (e.g. in supervision) in giving monthly injections of 250 μg. Again, more generous and/or frequent dosage is advised in cases of subacute combined degeneration of the spinal cord.

A clinical response is noticeable within 48 hours. The first indication of successful treatment is a fall in serum iron, followed rapidly by a rise in reticulocytes. Peak reticulocytosis occurs on the 5th to 7th day; its level depends on the initial red cell count, but it may reach 40 to 50 per cent in severe cases. The rise in the red count and in Hb is a little slower. A delayed rise or subsequent fall in Hb may indicate concomitant iron or folate deficiency. Lack of reticulocytosis calls for review of the diagnosis.

The marrow changes begin even more rapidly, first being seen at 6 hours after B_{12} injection. Erythropoiesis changes completely from megaloblastic to normoblastic in 72 hours.

Neurological features may respond readily to B_{12} therapy if they have been present for less than 6 months. Late diagnosis may mean lesser degrees of neurological recovery. The more spastic the picture the less does it improve.

Anaphylactic reactions after B_{12} injections have occurred rarely (Ugwu and Gibbins, 1981).

Oral B_{12} therapy is possible but is very rarely indicated in the elderly. The subject is discussed by Shinton and Troughton (1971) and Thomas and Powell (1971).

Combined B_{12} intrinsic factor (IF) preparations may be effective by mouth but relapse is common due to the development of antibodies against the (hog) IF.

Iron must be given if there is evidence of deficiency (dimorphic picture, no stainable iron in marrow, slow haematological response, relapse in anaemia, serum biochemistry as described earlier). It is likely to coexist in the elderly, especially after partial gastrectomy.

Folic acid may be given as well as B_{12} in cases with evidence of folate deficiency. Folic acid alone is dangerous in PA because it may precipitate neurological complications. Other B vitamins may be required for oral changes.

Thyroxine may be indicated if there is evidence of hypothyroidism, and this should be sought for in all patients with PA who fail to respond to treatment with B_{12}.

Steroids may produce remission but have no place in the ordinary treatment of PA.

Blood transfusion is used only to tide over a crisis, but in the elderly such crises are commoner than in the young, e.g. severe cardiac failure or mental confusion. Packed cells should be used, with all precautions as outlined earlier (p. 849). Delay due to lack of reticulocyte response to B_{12}, and the consequent rethinking of the diagnosis, may make transfusion more necessary.

Failure of response to B_{12}. The commonest cause is wrong diagnosis, the anaemia being due to folate deficiency.

A coexistent deficiency must be sought (e.g. iron, folate, thyroid) and corrected. Iron deficiency is usually due to gastrointestinal blood loss, and carcinoma of the stomach in particular must be excluded in PA patients.

A coexisting disease may impair marrow response, e.g. infection, chronic renal insufficiency (common in old age).

Follow-up. Regular follow-up is essential to ensure maintenance of clinical and haematological response, and to be alert for the possible development of carcinoma of the stomach, which is said to occur in 10 per cent of patients with PA. (This association was recently denied by Hoffman (1970) but reaffirmed by von Knorre and Pechau (1975) in a 30-year follow-up study on 271 patients with PA.)

More recent Scandinavian studies have cast doubt on the importance of pernicious anemia as a risk factor for gastric cancer (Elsborg and Mosbech, 1979; Eriksson et al, 1981). Associations with gastric carcinoid tumours (Harris and Greenberg, 1978; Wilander et al, 1979) and multiple myeloma and other paraproteinemias (Perillie, 1978) have been described.

Intestinal causes of vitamin B_{12} deficiency

Gluten-sensitive enteropathy
In gluten-sensitive enteropathy, steatorrhoea and other features of the malabsorption syndrome may be apparent; but often none of these is seen, the patients presenting with a moderate anaemia, of varying morphology. The marrow contains megaloblasts. Serum B_{12} is low in 40 per cent of patients and these show impaired B_{12} absorption; when the test is repeated with IF there is no significant improvement. There may be free hydrochloric acid in the gastric juice. Evidence of folate deficiency (see below) is even commoner in these patients (90 per cent).

Diagnosis involves the standard tests for malabsorption and is clinched by a small intestinal biopsy showing villous atrophy.

Anatomical abnormalities of the small gut
With bacterial flora. Jejunal diverticula, blind loops, fistulae, strictures and disorders of motility (scleroderma, drugs) lead to the appearance of bacteria in the small gut, due to stasis. These bacteria take up most of the available B_{12} (as does the fish tapeworm), break

Inadequate dietary intake is especially likely in the elderly (Read et al, 1965; Exton-Smith and Stanton, 1965; Girdwood, 1969) and contributory factors appear to be decreased mobility interfering with shopping and cooking; poverty, apathy and depression; and mental disturbances. After gastrectomy there may be reduced intake and some malabsorption.

Vitamin C retards folate oxidation and tends to occur in the same foods as folate, but it is destroyed under those conditions which destroy folate (sunlight, cooking).

Alcoholism may lead to megaloblastic anaemia (Wu down bile salts and produce folate, which may be absorbed sufficiently to increase serum folate levels. The excess of folate predisposes to B_{12} neuropathy. Transient improvement in absorption is produced by giving a broad spectrum antibiotic.

Ileal resection or disease. Resection of little more than a metre of terminal ileum may lead to malabsorption of B_{12}.

Local diseases affecting the same area, e.g. Crohn's disease, radiation ileitis, have had a similar result.

Rare causes
Severe pancreatic disease may lower calcium ion concentration in the ileum (due to formation of calcium soaps) and may lower pH in the lumen because of bicarbonate deficiency. These changes impair the absorption of B_{12} by the ileal mucosa.

A similar change of pH may lead to B_{12} malabsorption in other conditions, e.g. Zollinger-Ellison syndrome or in patients on potassium chloride.

Other drugs may cause reversible malabsorption of B_{12}, e.g. neomycin, colchicine, anticonvulsants, PAS. The last two probably lead to folate deficiency and folic acid therapy corrects the B_{12} malabsorption.

Recent observations on vitamin B_{12} metabolism in malabsorption have been reviewed by Lindenbaum (1979).

FOLATE DEFICIENCY

Table 41.8 sets out the main causes in convenient categories, but there is much overlap, e.g. dietary inadequacy may add significantly to the effects of excessive loss or malabsorption of folate.

Inadequate intake
Nutritional deficiency is an important cause of folate deficiency, in contrast to B_{12}. Folate deficiency is second only to iron deficiency as a cause of nutritional anaemia in man (World Health Organization, 1975), and low folate status without anaemia is common in the elderly (see above).

Table 41.8 Causes of folate deficiency

Inadequate intake
  Decreased mobility
  Confusion
  Apathy
  Poverty
  After gastrectomy
Malabsorption
  Gluten-sensitive enteropathy and tropical sprue
  Dermatitis herpetiformis
  Jejunal resection
Increased utilization
  Blood disease
  Neoplasms
  Collagen disease
  Metabolic disease
Impaired effectiveness
  Scurvy
  Drugs — folic acid antagonists
          anticonvulsants
          pyrimethamine
          trimethoprim
Excessive loss
  Skin diseases
  Loss of intestinal mucosal cells
  Liver damage and biliary loss
  Dialysis

et al, 1974). Alcohol has a toxic effect on bone marrow (Sullivan and Herbert, 1964; Wu et al, 1974), and alcoholics often have diets low in folate. Folate supplementation may be inadequate to restore the marrow to normal, however, unless alcohol is withdrawn. Liver dysfunction and malabsorption of folate may play a part. The whole subject of folate deficiency in the alcoholic is reviewed by Wu and colleagues (1975) and by Bonjour (1980).

Malabsorption of folate

This has been touched on in the section on B_{12} and is discussed in some detail by Lindenbaum (1979) and Rosenberg et al (1979). Folate deficiency is common in tropical sprue, and may predispose to this condition. In gluten-induced enteropathy folate deficiency is the rule, even without megaloblastic anaemia. In some patients with these conditions absorption of food folate is worse than absorption of folic acid itself, possibly due to failure of reduction by an enzyme.

Losses of folate may contribute, as in failure to reabsorb biliary folate, and loss of folate in sloughed intestinal mucosal cells.

Malabsorption and folate deficiency are usual in dermatitis herpetiformis, and may also occur after jejunal resection.

Folic acid absorption may be affected by age (Montgomery et al, 1978); it was impaired in 19 (36 per cent) of 53 geriatric patients with nutritional deficiency, reported by Elsborg (1976). After four weeks' treatment with folic acid the absorption returned to normal. Folic acid deficiency may cause structural and functional changes in cells of the upper jejunal epithelium (Bianchi et al, 1970; Berg et al, 1972).

Increased utilization

Reutilization of folate is less efficient than that of B_{12} or iron, so that folate requirements increase when cell turnover increases, especially during production of large amounts of primitive cells.

Most varieties of chronic haemolytic anaemia may be accompanied by folate deficiency, and the folate requirements may be very high (4 to 10 times normal). Similar findings occur in many patients with myelosclerosis.

Neoplasms, including carcinoma, leukaemia, lymphoma and myeloma, may affect folic acid utilization. Megaloblastic anaemia is less common in these conditions and if it occurs it may be multifactorial in origin, giving a disappointing response to folic acid. In leukaemia and lymphomas, folic acid may accelerate tumour growth.

Infections may precipitate megaloblastic anaemia in subclinical folate deficiency states (e.g. myelosclerosis). Chronic inflammatory diseases, such as tuberculosis and Crohn's disease, may produce folate deficiency.

Folate deficiency may occur in rheumatoid arthritis and in thyrotoxicosis.

Impaired effectiveness

Vitamin C maintains folate co-enzymes, necessary for normal erythropoiesis, in their reduced (and active) states (Cox, 1968; Chanarin, 1969; Booth and Todd, 1970). In vitamin C deficiency folate metabolism may be sufficiently impaired to produce megaloblastic anaemia.

Drugs

Folic acid antagonists (methotrexate; aminopterin) rapidly inhibit DNA synthesis in the whole body. The effects are noticed mainly in haemopoietic cells and epithelial cells of the buccal and gastrointestinal mucosae, where DNA synthesis is most rapid.

Anticonvulsant drugs (diphenylhydantoin, primidone, barbiturates) may also antagonize folate metabolism, after prolonged administration. Though some folate deficiency probably occurs in over half the patients so treated, severe deficiency is rare. Macrocytosis is commoner than megaloblastic anaemia. The mechanism of this effect is unknown, but Wickramasinghe et al (1975) have produced evidence to suggest that it is by no means always due to folate deficiency. It has been shown that phenytoin interferes with DNA synthesis in incubated human marrow cells, leading to death of some of these cells. In vivo this would lead to ineffective haemopoiesis and an increased folate requirement (Reid and Chanarin, 1978).

Trimethoprim is used with sulphonamide (which itself inhibits bacterial folate synthesis) as an effective antibacterial agent (Septrin, Bactrim). Patients on this drug may have low serum folate levels because the assay is microbiological.

Excessive loss

Exfoliative dermatitis and psoriasis, with excessive turnover of skin cells, may lead to folate deficiency. Liver damage allows loss of folate from necrosing hepatic cells; the excess appears in the urine. Haemodialysis and peritoneal dialysis remove small amounts of folate from the blood. This may be significant in uraemic patients already folate-depleted because of anorexia and vomiting.

Incidence of folate-deficiency anaemias in the elderly

Megaloblastic anaemias due solely to folate deficiency do not appear to be common in the elderly. Batata et al (1967) found no such cases in their series of 100 consecutive geriatric admissions; Evans et al (1968) found only 1 case in 90 cases of megaloblastic anaemia (but 35 had both folic acid and iron deficiency). Thomas and Powell (1971) record that 7 such cases were found in a series of 100 patients presenting with anaemia (Hb < 60 per cent or 8.6 g per dl). In their department the incidence is one-third that of B_{12} deficiency but the figure can vary in either direction. In community surveys the incidence of folate-deficiency anaemia is very low or non-existent (Department of Health and Social Security, 1972; MacLennan et al, 1973).

Clinical features of folate deficiency

Mental changes may precede anaemia. They may be mild and are in any case non-specific: mild confusion, depression, apathy, intellectual loss (British Medical Journal, 1969; Botez et al, 1979; Carney, 1979; Shulman, 1979). If a low serum folate is found, folic acid may be given but the results are often disappointing. Strachan and Henderson (1967) noted a response to folate in two patients with dementia. Buxton et al (1969) found low folate levels in two-thirds of their series of mentally abnormal patients, but also in one-half of their normal controls. Shaw (1971) showed no improvement in 66 female patients with senile dementia, mean age 80.6 years, treated with large doses of folic acid and vitamin B_{12} in a double-blind crossover trial.

Sneath et al (1973) found that their 14 patients who had dementia also had a significantly lower mean red-cell folate than did their whole series of 115 consecutive geriatric admissions. For the series as a whole they also found some correlation between mental assessment scores and red-cell folate levels in those with low RCF

levels. They did not report on the effect of folic acid therapy in these patients. MacLennan et al (1973) found no evidence of any association between folate deficiency and dementia in their community study.

Peripheral neuropathy, and occasionally myelopathy, may occur and may resemble subacute combined degeneration of the cord; these may respond specifically to folic-acid therapy (Pincus et al, 1972; Manzoor and Runcie, 1976; Botez et al, 1978). Reynolds (1976a, 1979a) believes that neurological changes due to folate deficiency may sometimes be indistinguishable from those due to vitamin B_{12} deficiency because of the role of B_{12} in folate metabolism as described to explain the similar haematological changes. The subject of folate and the nervous system has been reviewed (Reynolds, 1976b; British Medical Journal, 1976a, Lancet, 1976b; Botez and Reynolds, 1979).

The anaemia is indistinguishable from that of B_{12} deficiency.

Diagnosis of folate deficiency

Serum folate is below 2 to 3 μg per ml in folate deficiency, and very often below 1 μg per ml if anaemia is present (see above).

Red-cell folate will be below 100 μg per ml packed red cells in frank folate deficiency, but should be interpreted in conjunction with serum foiate since low red cell folate occurs in PA even when serum folate is normal or raised (see above).

The value of radioassay of folate relative to microbiological assay is considered by Parry (1980).

Formininoglutamic acid excretion: folate co-enzyme converts histidine to glutamic acid by way of formiminoglutamic acid (FIGLU). Urinary FIGLU after an oral dose of L-histidine is raised in folate deficiency. This test correlates well with liver folate stores, but it is positive in some patients with pure B_{12} deficiency even after the administration of large doses of folic acid.

Folate absorption may be measured in various ways including faecal and urinary radioactivity after an oral dose of tritium-labelled folic acid and measurement of plasma folate levels after an oral dose. In this method the patient has to be 'saturated' by a dose of 15 mg folic acid 36 hours before the test (Chanarin, 1971).

Folate-clearance test measures the serum folic acid 15 minutes after an intravenous injection of folic acid. Very low levels are found in folate deficiency.

A liver biopsy may be assayed for its folate content; this gives the best indication of deficiency. Normal values are 5 to 10 μg folate per gram of wet liver (Pitney and Onesti, 1961).

Haematological response. An optimal response to 200 μg folate daily indicates folate deficiency; but where there are increased requirements it may be necessary to give 500 μg daily.

Treatment

Folic acid is given by mouth, 10 to 20 mg per day, reducing to 2.5 to 10 mg per day for maintenance. Folic acid injection (the sodium salt) may be given parenterally if there is severe anaemia or severe malabsorption. (Dosage: 15 mg per day; maintenance 5 to 10 mg per day.)

It is dangerous to give folic acid alone if a possible B_{12} deficiency has not been excluded, since neurological complications may ensue.

Control of fits in epileptics may be lost when folic acid is given. Allergic reactions are rare.

Blood transfusion: see under Pernicious Anaemia (p. 866).

Pyridoxine-responsive anaemias

These have been considered earlier in their normoblastic forms (see Sideroblastic Anaemias, p. 854). Some cases are megaloblastic, and some respond to large doses of pyridoxine or pyridoxal-5′-phosphate.

Scurvy

Megaloblastic anaemia may occur in scurvy, though rarely. It is usually due to concomitant folic acid deficiency, but occasionally seems to respond to ascorbic acid alone (Goldberg, 1963; Asquith et al, 1967; Cox, 1968).

Care should always be taken to provide folic acid or vitamin B_{12} as well as ascorbic acid, if investigations reveal associated deficiencies of these substances.

'Refractory' megaloblastic anaemia

Failure to respond to vitamin B_{12} was discussed in relation to pernicious anaemia. Some cases are sideroblastic; others may be part of a picture of developing leukaemia, myelosclerosis or di Guglielmo's syndrome.

APLASTIC ANAEMIA

Incidence

The disease is not common. It was found in 5 of 2700 hospital patients over 65 years of age by Evans and colleagues (1968).

Israëls (1975) describes a 'senile hypoplastic anaemia' characterized by underproduction of red blood cells; a few cases may recover spontaneously, but more often the platelets also become affected and haemorrhages occur.

Aetiology

Drug-induced aplasia (Lewis, 1971; de Gruchy, 1975b; Heimpel and Heit, 1980) is an important cause, and the elderly are at risk of 'polypharmacy'. Long-term effects of irradiation (especially from internal isotopes) should be kept in mind. Aplasia may ensue in other haematological disease; or, especially when drug-induced, it may itself end in leukaemia.

Clinical features and treatment

These show no peculiarities in the elderly. (See Lewis, 1971; Krantz, 1980; Najean, 1981).

Prognosis

The prognosis is said to be worse in the elderly (Lewis, 1965) but age did not influence the response of 60 patients to androgens (Pizzuto et al, 1980). Red cell aplasia is a less severe illness than aplastic anemia with pancytopenia and may remit spontaneously. The most serious effects in aplastic anemia are due to thrombocytopenia. Prognosis is reviewed in BMJ (1975) and by Najean and Pecking (1979) and Rozman et al (1981).

DISEASES OF WHITE BLOOD CELLS AND RETICULOENDOTHELIAL SYSTEM

Leucopenia and agranulocytosis

These show few differences in aetiology and presentation in old age, but certain points are worth noting in regard to geriatric medical practice.

Of infections causing leucopenia, those due to viruses are most often implicated in younger adults, but in the elderly any severe infection may cause leucopenia.

Of drugs causing leucopenia or agranulocytosis the major groups likely to be implicated in the elderly are tranquillizers, antidepressants and antibiotics. Full lists are given by de Gruchy (1975c). Agranulocytosis is apparently becoming more common particularly in the elderly (Böttiger and Böttiger, 1981). Of drugs responsible for agranulocytosis (as well as other cytopenias) sulphonamides are overtaking phenylbutazone and oxyphenbutazone. Granulocyte transfusions are now feasible in severe cases (British Medical Journal, 1976b).

Leucocytosis and 'leukaemoid reactions'

The elderly may show a typical neutrophil leucocytosis, with a 'shift to the left' in the polymorphs, in the usual clinical situations; and when the changes are very marked they may show a 'leukaemoid reaction', with some more primitive cells in the circulation. Leukaemoid reactions have been described in carcinoma of the lung (Dalal et al, 1980). On rare occasions they are eosinophilic (Varindani et al, 1982), although the latter is more commonly parasitic, allergic or due to drug reaction.

Frail and debilitated old people may show a leucopenia instead of a leucocytosis in such circumstances.

Infectious mononucleosis, essentially a disease of young adults, has been reported in the elderly. Horwitz et al (1976) review the literature and report 7 patients over the age of 40 of whom 1 was 60 and 1 was 78. A spate of reports and reviews have appeared since then (e.g. Dyer, 1979; McKendrick et al, 1979; Pickens and Murdoch, 1979; Acikalin and Akdamar, 1980). Liver dysfunction is more marked in older patients with this condition.

THE LEUKAEMIAS

Incidence

All types of leukaemia have increased in incidence in the last 50 years, and this upward trend has been very marked in the elderly (Count Brown and Doll, 1959; Videbaek, 1966; Brandt et al, 1979; Blair et al, 1980).

Chronic lymphatic leukaemia occurs mainly in old people and its incidence increases with age. Chronic myeloid leukaemia starts earlier and its peak incidence is at 50 years. Acute leukaemia, formerly considered to occur mainly in children, has now been shown to be commoner in the elderly (Thomas and Powell, 1971). Over 70 per cent of patients with acute leukaemia are said to be over the age of 50 (Richert-Boe and Bagby, 1978).

All forms are commoner in males.

Leukaemia in the elderly often shows special features with regard to morphological criteria, clinical course, and responsiveness to chemotherapy (Linman, 1970; Miescher and Farquet, 1974). The term 'myelomonocytic leukaemia' is given to a disease characterized by a mainly monocytic picture in the peripheral blood and a mainly myelocytic picture in the bone marrow. This condition is being found increasingly in the elderly. Other variants are mentioned below.

Aetiology

The cause is unknown. Gunz and Baikie (1974) review all aspects of leukaemia. One possible aetiological factor of considerable importance is that there appears to be a greater incidence of leukaemia after taking phenylbutazone than would be expected from chance (Thomas and Powell, 1971).

Acute leukaemia

In childhood this is usually lymphoblastic, but in the elderly it is usually myelomonocytic (Linman, 1970). The precise stem-line may be difficult to determine in the early primitive forms.

A 'smouldering' acute leukaemia is seen in a few patients, usually after 50 years of age. It is a variant of acute myeloid leukaemia (AML) with pancytopenia, a cellular marrow, but a tendency not to progress even if untreated. Aggressive chemotherapy rarely helps; but even in the elderly most AML is *not* of this type and in progressive cases too much procrastination may be harmful (Gunz and Baikie, 1974).

Other variants of acute leukaemia which may affect elderly patients include: hypocellular acute leukaemia (Needleman et al, 1981; Howe et al, 1982); hyperleucocytic leukaemia with possibly hyperviscosity (Lichtman and Rowe, 1982); and preleukaemia (Koeffler and Golde, 1980).

Treatment. Acute lymphoblastic leukaemia responds, at least initially, to chemotherapy, but the varieties seen in the elderly have long been thought to be much less responsive. In recent years the immediate outlook has improved with the introduction of newer agents, e.g. daunorubicin, doxorubicin (Adriamycin) cytosine arabinoside (cytarabine), vincristine and thioguanine — often used in combination (Reiffers et al, 1980; Vaughan et al, 1981). Foon et al (1981) recommend intensive chemotherapy for elderly patients with acute myelogenous leukaemia.

Crosby (1968) took a pessimistic view of treatment of acute leukaemia after the age of 50 years, and it seems that results are often worse in the aged because of their lessened tolerance to the disease and to the drugs used; remission takes longer to appear but may not be shorter in the elderly than in younger adults (Medical Research Council, 1974). Grann et al (1974) found that age after 50 had no effect on the remission rate of chemotherapy, nor on the ultimate survival; but Beard and Fairley (1974) found a falling-off in results in the seventh decade, and even poorer results in the age-group 70 to 79. They considered that age was not a bar to treatment, but that some elderly patients were too frail to withstand the inevitable period of marrow hypoplasia. They also emphasized the frequency of hypokalaemia in AML, especially the monocytic or myelomonocytic variety, correlating with increased serum and urinary lysozyme levels; lysozyme is thought to interfere with renal tubular function and lead to increased urinary loss of potassium. Some of the drugs used in therapy of leukaemia may also produce hypokalaemia.

Rosner et al (1976) obtained complete or partial remission in 20 per cent of 451 patients aged over 60 years treated with combination chemotherapy, but they noted a lower response rate and median survival than in younger adults. However, newer treatment regimes have been highly effective in patients up to 70 years of age, and complete remissions (the key to success) have been induced in patients in the ninth decade (Richert-Boe and Bagby, 1978).

Holmes et al (1979) consider the question of survival in the elderly with acute leukaemia. Initial haematological measurements were most important predictors of survival; leukaemic cell type had no predictive power.

Chronic myeloid leukaemia

Reviews are given by Stryckmans (1974) and Kardinal et al (1976).

Atypical cases may present difficulty. They may or may not show the classical features, they respond poorly to treatment, and are frequent in the older age groups. Conrad et al (1965) described some of these differences in elderly patients — hepatosplenomegaly may be minimal or absent, the white cell count may be much less, platelets may be increased and leucocyte alkaline phosphatase increased (it is usually reduced). Coexisting diseases complicate the picture. Other difficulties may arise in early stages, when the picture may be that of polycythaemia or myelofibrosis, and in late acute myeloblastic transformation. This last is common.

Detailed accounts of chronic myelomonocytic leukaemia are given by Linman (1970), Miescher and Farquet (1974), Geary et al (1975) and Zittoun (1976). It is rare before 50 and though usually of insidious onset and chronic course it may at times present as a subacute or acute illness or terminate in an acute phase. The peripheral blood shows a monocytosis but with a leucopenia and thrombocytopenia. Cells intermediate between monocyte and myeloid cell lines may appear in the blood. The marrow is hypercellular with myeloid hyperplasia and a high proportion of poorly differentiated cells. The red-cell series may be involved: the condition is then sometimes called 'erythromonocytic leukaemia' (Shaw et al, 1973). A sideroblastic anaemia may precede or accompany the leukaemic picture (Zittoun et al, 1972). Serum lysozyme is elevated.

In differential diagnosis other causes of monocytosis need to be excluded (see Maldonado and Hanlon, 1965).

Treatment. In chronic myeloid leukaemia, busulphan (Myleran) is the treatment of choice. An initial dose of up to 4 mg daily is adequate; higher doses may produce a permanently aplastic marrow and induce uric acid nephropathy and acute gout.

Details of the modern therapeutic approach are given by Spiers (1976) and by Goldman (1978). Leukapheresis may allow avoidance of chemotherapy.

In chronic myelomonocytic leukaemia, treatment is best symptomatic only; the need to avoid intensive chemotherapy is one reason why the recognition of this disease is of clinical importance in the elderly.

Splenectomy is rarely of value, but may help relieve abdominal discomfort.

Prognosis. Survival time in chronic myeloid leukaemia may be shorter in the elderly (Bodley Scott, 1957), though Kardinal et al (1976) reported that age did not affect the median survival time in Philadelphia-positive cases, which is longer than for Ph'-negative cases (Schilling and Crowley, 1979).

In chronic myelomonocytic leukaemia the course is commonly over several years; 5 of the 18 cases reported by Geary and his colleagues (1975) lived for more than 5 years without aggressive chemotherapy.

Chronic lymphatic leukaemia

This is the commonest of the lymphoproliferative disorders now regarded as monoclonal B-cell proliferations (others include myeloma, macroglobulinaemia, cold agglutinin disease and hairy cell leukaemia) (Salmon and Seligmann, 1974). Most cases have IgM and IgD on the surface of the proliferating cells; in chronic lymphatic leukaemia (CLL) the surface Ig is nearly always monoclonal IgM.

A recent review of chronic lymphocytic leukaemia in the elderly has been made by Silber (1982). Cline (1975) suggested that both B- and T-lymphocytes are increased in this disease. It is now well established that B-cells usually predominate in the peripheral blood in CLL, increasing from the normal range of 10 to 15 per cent to reach 40–99 per cent (average 70 per cent) (Silber, 1982). T-cell CLL accounts for only 1–2 per cent of all cases. However, the proportions of B- and T-cells may vary at different times in the same patient (Davis, 1976).

T-cell CLL is a more severe disease with a worse prognosis. It has atypical clinical and haematological features (Brouet et al, 1975). Unlike B-cells BLL it is not age-related. The B-cells in CLL are abnormal in several respects immunologically, metabolically and mechanically. They are relatively short-lived (Scott et al, 1973).

There is a well-recognized reduction of immunocompetence in this disease. The subject of immune responsiveness and haematological malignancy in the elderly is discussed by Fernandez and Schwartz (1976).

Clinical features. These will not be detailed here, but some particular points are worth noting.

The condition may be clinically silent, or may present as part of a spectrum extending as far as lymphosarcoma. Herpes zoster is common as in other lymphomatous conditions with immune paresis. Hypogammaglobulinaemia is common, but occasionally gamma globulins are increased and macroglobulins or cryoglobulins may be detected. The ESR may be notably low in CLL (Glass, 1971), but this may be due to an associated autoimmune haemolytic anaemia with a strongly positive Coombs test (Loeliger, 1975; Ballas, 1975; Pirofsky, 1978). In such cases the ESR becomes high in the *second* hour (Loeliger, 1976). Whole body potassium increases in proportion to the leukaemic cell mass (Silber, 1982).

Prognosis. The asymptomatic stage may last for

years, and the diagnosis is often a purely incidental one in the elderly, with death occurring from another condition. Survival for 29 years has been reported. Anaemia and haemorrhage worsen the prognosis. Staging in five tiers has been proposed by Rai et al (1975). This staging has been found to be of greater prognostic significance than factors such as age or sex. (Age, in fact, is not a significant prognostic factor if adjusted for disease stage at diagnosis and for sex [Silber, 1982]).

Factors affecting prognosis in CLL are discussed by Zippin et al (1973), Polack and Tatarski (1975, Knospe (1979) and Silber (1982).

Treatment. In many cases no treatment is required. Indications for treatment are concerned with the degree of lymphadenopathy and hepatosplenomegaly, and the haemoglobin, neutrophil and platelet levels. X-ray therapy is useful for local deposits causing symptoms.

Chlorambucil, 2 to 8 mg daily, is relatively non-toxic and easy to control. If this fails, nitrogen mustards may be tried, especially cyclophosphamide, 25 to 100 mg daily. The dose of each drug is reduced once control is achieved. Prednisone is used if anaemia persists, whether haemolytic or not. Special care over possible infection is required, especially if there is hypogammaglobulinaemia.

Splenectomy is occasionally helpful.

Other lymphoproliferative disorders which may be confused with CLL

Hairy cell leukaemia (leukaemic reticuloendotheliosis)
This accounts for 2 per cent of all leukaemias (BMJ, 1978) and affects mainly adults over 50 years. Presentation is with leucopenia, thrombocytopenia and anaemia. Splenomegaly is common. Characteristic mononuclear cells with pseudopodia and numerous short villi around the cytoplasmic membrane ('hairy cells') comprise up to 95 per cent of the circulating leucocytes. If absent from the blood they will be found in the marrow. They are probably a type of B-cell. Chemotherapy is of little benefit but splenectomy may help.

Prolymphocytic leukaemia
This is an unusual disease occurring predominantly in elderly men. It lies between CLL and lymphosarcoma-cell leukaemia (Galton et al, 1974; Bearman et al, 1978). Massive splenomegaly, little or no lymphadenopathy and a high peripheral leucocyte count consisting largely of prolymphocytes occur. Garrett and Newton (1979) report two sisters aged 75 and 82 years, one with prolymphocytic leukaemia and one with CLL. Genetic factors predisposing to lymphoproliferative disease are discussed by Conley et al (1980).

MALIGNANT LYMPHOMAS — TUMOURS OF LYMPHOID TISSUES

Classification
This is complex and is discussed by Scott and McKenna (1975) and Schnitzer (1978).

Incidence
The overall incidence approximates to that of leukaemias and has likewise risen in the last 50 years. Incidence increases with age (MacMahon, 1957; Thomas and Powell, 1971) and men are affected more often than women. Lymphosarcoma is commoner than Hodgkin's disease in older age groups.

Alderson and Nayak (1972) examined the epidemiology of Hodgkin's disease in the Manchester region and showed a bimodal age distribution with a trough at 45–49 years. The peak incidence was in the age group 65 and over.

Hodgkin's disease (lymphadenoma)
This subject is reviewed by Desforges et al (1979).

Classification
The classification suggested by Jackson and Parker (1947) has been widely used for over 20 years and consists of three sub-divisions:

1. Paragranuloma — a relatively benign form confined to cervical nodes for a long period (85 per cent of patients survive for over 10 years).
2. Granuloma — the commonest form which may be confined to liver, spleen and stomach or be more widespread.
3. Sarcoma — highly invasive, affecting mainly retroperitoneal nodes and seen mainly in older subjects.

Since most cases fell into the 'granuloma' group a new 'Rye classification' has been propounded subdividing the granuloma group (Lukes et al, 1966). This allows more accurate prognosis. The 'Rye classification' is as follows:

Lymphocytic predominance (equivalent to paragranuloma)
Lymphocyte depletion (equivalent to sarcoma)
Nodular sclerosis
Mixed cellularity

The latter two are derived from the old granuloma sub-group. Lymphocyte predominance has the best prognosis, lymphocyte depletion the worst. The 'mixed cellularity' group is the more common in old age (Desforges et al, 1979). Amyloid may develop as a complication. Older patients have a much higher incidence of infradiaphragmatic involvement and presentation and a more aggressive clinical course. There is no geographical or socioeconomic variation such as is seen in younger patients (Desforges et al, 1979).

Treatment. Treatment is planned according to the staging (see Carbone et al, 1971; Aisenberg, 1978) and the clinical features of the disease.

Intensive wide-field radiotherapy has revolutionized the treatment of localized Hodgkin's disease; the 5-year survival is 80 per cent and if there is no recurrence at that time the chance of permanent cure is 95 per cent. Accurate staging, by lymphangiography, aids treatment planning.

If there is recurrence, or if the disease is generalized, chemotherapy is used.

Combination chemotherapy has produced 90 per cent remissions (80 per cent complete) (Fairley, 1971). The subject is reviewed by Goldsmith and Carter (1974) and Desforges et al (1979).

The drugs used are of course highly toxic and greater caution than ever must be taken over their use in the elderly. In many instances the risks and discomforts attendant on their use would be considered unjustified in frail and ill old people; but the results can be so good that no old person should be denied chemotherapy if his condition and prospects warrant its use.

The course is variable and survival may occur for many years. Age itself does not influence the prognosis (Lumb, 1954) except insofar as certain types of the disease occur more often in the elderly (Keller et al, 1968).

Prognostic factors are discussed by Cline (1975), Say et al (1975) and Björkholm et al (1975).

Non-Hodgkin's lymphomas

In contrast to the general agreement on classification of Hodgkin's disease, there is ongoing controversy regarding classification and terminology of non-Hodgkin's lymphomas (see review by Schnitzer, 1978). The old Rappaport et al (1956) classification was important because of the prognostic implications of its subdivision into nodular (better prognosis) and diffuse (worse prognosis and more aggressive course) types. However, even 'good prognosis' patients usually have widespread disease when diagnosed, often with bone marrow involvement, precluding curative local therapy.

The implications of this and the value of knowing when to withhold treatment, are discussed by Chabner (1979) and by Portlock and Rosenberg (1979). Certain patients have benefited from treatment with a single alkylating agent, but accurate pathological identification is needed before instituting this regimen.

Clinical diagnosis and staging are discussed by Bloomfield (1975), the blood and marrow picture by Brunning (1975). The many and varied complications are outlined by Theologides (1975); any system may be implicated, and both humoral and cellular immunity may become impaired, with increased susceptibility to infections. Amyloid may develop. Autoimmune haemolytic anaemia

is an uncommon development: it is usually chronic, but an acute case was described in a nonagenarian by Fullerton and Phaur (1966). Presentation as primary lymphosarcoma of the breast is well documented in elderly patients and responds to local treatment (Sonnenblick and Abraham, 1976).

Treatment is discussed by Levitt (1975) (radiotherapy), Bloomfield et al (1975) (chemotherapy), and in relation to classification and staging by Canellos and Lister (1978). Despite the impressive advances in treatment during nearly two decades most patients with these diseases survive for a relatively short period. The less malignant forms of lymphosarcoma may allow survival for more than 10 years. Bloomfield et al (1976) related prognosis to cell markers of the malignant cells.

Other lymphoproliferative disorders

Angioimmunoblastic lymphadenopathy
This condition, described by Frizzera (1974) and Neiman et al (1978), is characterized by lymphadenopathy, hepatosplenomegaly, fever, weight loss, skin rash and evidence of hyperimmunity, (e.g. polyclonal hyperglobulinaemia and Coombs-positive haemolytic anaemia). Although it may mimic Hodgkin's disease or non-Hodgkin's lymphoma it is probably a non-neoplastic condition and possibly drug induced.

Other myeloproliferative disorders

The myeloproliferative diseases may be taken to include chronic myeloid leukaemia, polycythaemia vera, essential thrombocythaemia and myelofibrosis (Gunz and Baikie, 1974). Many regard these conditions as variants of a single 'myeloproliferative syndrome', but a more precise diagnosis is necessary in clinical practice.

Reviews of the myeloproliferative diseases are given by Gilbert (1973) and Wetherley-Mein (1974).

Myelofibrosis and myelosclerosis

Myelofibrosis is an increase in fibrous tissue at the expense of haemopoietic marrow.

Myelosclerosis is replacement of marrow by bone.

This disease is a major cause of leucoerythroblastic anaemia with immature red and white cells in the blood. Splenomegaly may become considerable. Bone marrow may be difficult to obtain. A biopsy is required, by trephine.

The marrow shows increased collagen and reticulin on special staining and haemopoietic marrow is reduced, with many megakaryocytes. Megaloblastic erythropoiesis is common (Hoffbrand et al, 1968), and is due to folate or B_{12} deficiency.

Treatment and prognosis. A primary (toximetabolic or infective) cause requires treatment. Blood transfusions will be necessary in most cases. Splenectomy may help if there is hypersplenism, or if a huge spleen is intolerable. (Irradiation may help in the latter case.)

Prednisone, busulphan and androgens may have a place in treatment. Folic acid, B_{12} and iron may also be needed.

Prognosis is variable, Survival may be for up to 10 years. A 'malignant', rapidly progressive form of the disease may be fatal within a few months (Bearman et al, 1979). Intercurrent infections are likely.

POLYCYTHAEMIA

Recent reviews are given by Walsh (1978) and UCLA Conference (1981). Polycythaemia is characterized by increased red cell mass. It may be primary or secondary (Modan, 1971; Lange, 1976).

Secondary polycythaemia (Balcerzak and Bromberg, 1975) may be due to hypoxia (chronic lung disease such as chronic bronchitis, emphysema, pneumoconiosis) or to excessive production of erythropoietin (renal tumours, cerebellar angioma, uterine, ovarian or adrenal cortical tumours, hepatoma). Erythropoietin titres are low in polycythaemia vera.

The red cell mass may be increased but white cells and platelets are normal. Splenomegaly is absent. The liver may be enlarged.

Red cell 2,3-diphosphoglycerate is increased in secondary (but not primary) polycythaemia (Monti, 1981). Erythrapheresis has helped patients with polycythaemia secondary to hypoxic lung disease (Wedzicha et al, 1983).

Primary polycythaemia — polycythaemia rubra vera
Lewis (1976) gives a full account of this disease of middle and late life (peak incidence 50 to 80 years). The increased cell mass has no apparent cause and is accompanied by increased leucocytes and platelets.

The symptoms are due to increased blood volume and viscosity, engorgement of capillaries and tissue hypoxia; cerebral symptoms are prominent but cardiac and peripheral vascular presentations may occur. Thromboses and haemorrhages are the commonest complications. Pruritus occurs in two-thirds of cases and gout is common. The spleen is often moderately enlarged. The ESR is low, rarely over 1 mm in the first hour; blood viscosity increases up to eight-fold. The diagnosis depends on the demonstration of an increased red cell mass (e.g. by isotope dilution technique); the packed cell volume is not an accurate measure of this (Bentley and Lewis, 1976). Red cell mass must be related to lean body mass to be meaningful (Nathan, 1966).

The treatment of choice — especially in the elderly — is radiophosphorus, ^{32}P. Busulphan or chlorambucil may be used as alternatives but with obvious disadvantages in old age. Venesection should be regarded as a temporary expedient only, as it has several disadvantages (Kiraly et al, 1976). Itching may be helped by cholestyramine (Chanarin and Szur, 1975).

The treatment and prevention of gout in chronic myeloproliferative disease is discussed by Yu et al (1976).

Prognosis is poor if untreated; survival may be over 10 years with ^{32}P, but is less in the elderly (Osgood, 1965). Note that surgery carries major risks in untreated polycythaemia vera: a 45 per cent incidence of thrombosis or haemorrhagic complications and 18 per cent mortality have been reported, but these complications decrease seven-fold in treated cases (Wasserman and Gilbert, 1963).

The inter-relationship of polycythaemia vera with other myeloproliferative disorders has been reviewed by Modan (1975).

Erythrocytosis may occur without increase in other blood elements; a few cases may progress to polycythaemia vera at a late stage (Najean et al, 1981). ^{32}P helps a majority of patients with pure erythrocytosis; if it fails other myelosuppressive therapy may be needed to reduce the risk of thrombosis from the increased blood viscosity. Venesection is a last resort in the elderly (Najean et al, 1981).

Splenomegaly and the blood
The subject of hypersplenism is considered by Jacob (1974) and Richards (1976). The functions of the spleen and its relation to anaemia are discussed by Bowdler (1970) and Holt (1970); Holt considers the indications for splenectomy in blood disorders.

PARAPROTEINAEMIAS

Recent rapid developments in immunology have led to the concept of 'immunoproliferative disorders', involving lymphocytes and plasma cells which produce abnormal amounts of immunoglobulins (Ig). They result mainly from the proliferation of *single clones* of B-cells — hence the terms *monoclonal gammopathy* and *M-protein*. Occasionally biclonal or multiband paraproteinaemia is identified. Gore et al (1979) found these pictures in 11 per cent of reports from a protein reference centre; 60 per cent of these were malignant.

Ig are classified according to their structure (World Health Organization, 1964; Martin, 1970; Sharland, 1972; Cline, 1975). Age-related alterations in plasma Ig have been discussed earlier in this chapter.

The immunoproliferative diseases include the 'immunocytomas' (myeloma — 70 to 75 per cent — macroglobulinaemia, heavy-chain and light-chain diseases, the lymphomas), 'idiopathic' and 'benign' monoclonal gammopathies, and some neoplasms. Colls and Lorier (1975) reviewed their experience of 224 cases of monoclonal gammopathy (MG) and its associated conditions; they found an immunocytoma in half the cases (myeloma in 82 and lymphoma in 30 cases) and a non-lymphoproliferative malignant tumour in 36 cases (16 per cent). In one-third of their cases the MG was apparently unrelated to the clinical state; but these authors regarded MG as possibly a significant marker of malignant disease (especially when the MG was Bence Jones protein: 91 per cent of these 65 patients had a malignant condition). Benbassat et al (1976) reviewed 154 cases.

'Benign monoclonal gammopathy' (BMG)

Waldenström (1976) has personally observed over 200 cases of MG over many years, without treatment, and is convinced of the existence of BMG as a clinical entity, perhaps to be regarded as a 'benign plasmacytoma'. Only rarely did a frankly malignant change develop in his series. Colls and Lorier (1975) found that M-protein disappeared spontaneously in five of their cases — presumably a truly BMG. Axelsson (1977) also presented evidence for the existence of a benign monoclonal gammopathy, based on an 11-year follow-up of 37 cases. Hobbs (1978) followed-up 600 cases of BMG for several years, during which time only three had changed to a malignant course.

It is clear that careful and prolonged follow-up of 'BMG' is mandatory, for it may be merely one end of the immunocytoma spectrum; myeloma, macroglobulinaemia or amyloidosis may remain in such a phase for many years before overt signs appear (Martin, 1969; Kyle, 1978).

If a diagnosis of BMG is being considered, the serum Ig should not exceed 2 g per dl and the level should remain steady or fall (but not rise); levels of other Ig in serum should not be depressed. The marrow should contain less than 9 per cent plasma cells, and there must be no Bence Jones proteinuria. Differential diagnosis of BMG and malignant monoclonal gammopathies, such as multiple myeloma, is discussed by Kyle and Greipp (1978a), Lindström and Dahlström (1978) and Morell et al (1978).

Myelomatosis

Myelomatosis is a progressive disease characterized by proliferation of a single clone of plasma cells (or, in 7 per cent of cases, two independent clones), which infiltrate the bone marrow and often other tissues. The plasma cells are abnormal and immature, and are called myeloma cells. They produce abnormal proteins as described above.

Martin (1970) states that the peak incidence is between 50 and 65, but many cases are found in the elderly. In the MRC trial (Hobbs, 1969) the peak was between 60 and 70 (mean 62 years). There is no sex difference in the incidence.

There are four types: multiple myelomatosis with multiple deposits; diffuse myelomatosis without deposits; solitary myeloma and extramedullary plasmacytoma. If the plasma cells appear in the blood in large numbers, the condition is termed 'plasma cell leukaemia'. Myelomatosis is the commonest form of immunocytoma and its incidence is probably increasing, especially in blacks in the USA (Blattner et al, 1980).

Multiple myelomatosis

This is reviewed by Kyle and Elveback (1976) and Parker and Malpas (1979).

Clinical features. Most patients present with bone pain, especially backache and pain in ribs and long bones. The bones may be tender, and tumours and pathological fractures may occur. Neurological features may be secondary to pressure from collapsed vertebrae or myeloma tissue, so that paraplegia or quadriplegia may develop. Peripheral neuropathy (mononeuritis multiplex) may be seen.

Symptoms and signs of anaemia are usual. Renal insufficiency is due to deposition of protein in the tubules; it is added to by anaemia, hypercalcaemia, plasma-cell infiltration or amyloidosis. Recurrent infections are common, associated with depressed antibody formation due to the disturbed protein metabolism ('immune paresis'), especially in the IgG variety.

Amyloidosis of atypical distribution is seen in 10 to 25 per cent of cases. It may produce a nephrotic syndrome. Visceral infiltration by plasma cells may lead to hepatosplenomegaly and lymphadenopathy.

The hyperviscosity syndrome (p. 843) may be seen with IgA or, less often, IgG myelomatosis (Preston et al, 1978) (see also Macroglobulinaemia). Bleeding is common, especially if cryoglobulinaemia or hyperviscosity occurs.

Less common presentations are given by Parker and Malpas (1979) and Fudenberg and Virella (1980). A 'smouldering' form of stable multiple myeloma, without progression, has been described by Kyle and Greipp (1980) in six patients aged 57 to 73 years followed-up for 5 years. They recommend withholding therapy if there is no anaemia or bone or kidney involvement, but stress the need for continuing follow-up.

Blood picture. Anaemia is usual sooner or later, and is normocytic and normochromic, or occasionally leucoerythroblastic and macrocytic. There may be marked rouleaux formation. The leucocyte count varies and a few atypical plasma cells may be seen; rarely, 'plasma cell leukaemia' develops, late. Platelets may be reduced. ESR is often over 100 mm in 1 hour; in rare cases with normal globulin levels the ESR is normal. Bone marrow examination usually clinches the diagnosis. Marked excess of plasma cells is seen, often abnormal and immature. Modest numbers call for other confirmation of the diagnosis. Focal changes mean that diagnostic areas could be missed. Differentiation must be made from the mild increase (10 per cent) of (mature) plasma cells in other conditions such as aplastic anaemia, secondary carcinoma, rheumatoid arthritis, hepatic cirrhosis and chronic inflammatory diseases.

Other investigations.   X-rays may show punched-out translucencies and/or pathological fractures. Intravenous urography is said to be dangerous, but the risk is small according to Cwynarski and Saxton (1969).

Bence Jones protein (BJP) is made up of light (κ or λ chains produced in excess due to imbalance during Ig synthesis in the disease. It precipitates in the kidney tubules and causes severe damage which may lead to renal failure. Bence Jones protein is found in the urine in 50 per cent of cases of myeloma by the heating test; more sensitive tests show a much higher incidence (Hobbs, 1967). It is not pathognomonic of myeloma, having been recorded in other immunocytomas, leukaemia and carcinoma. The clinical significance of BJP is discussed by Perry and Kyle (1975) and Randall et al (1976). The clinical manifestations and survival rates of patients with κ and λ light-chain diseases are described by Shustik, Bergsagel and Pruzanski (1976).

Albuminuria is common but is not usually sufficient to explain the reduced serum albumin (see above).

Blood chemistry.   Total serum protein is usually raised, sometimes greatly, but it may be normal. Globulin is often 4 to 8 g per 100 ml; albumin may be somewhat reduced.

On electrophoresis, the myeloma protein is usually in the γ-globulin band but may be in the β- or α-globulin zones, or intermediate. In 5 per cent of patients there is none. Hobbs (1969) found paraproteins as follows: IgG 53 per cent, IgA 25 per cent, Bence Jones alone 10 per cent, IgD 1 per cent, biclonal 2 per cent (of 212 patients). Very little normal γ-globulin may be present.

Occasionally myeloma protein is a cryoglobulin.

Hypercalcaemia occurs in 25 per cent of cases at some stage, but levels fluctuate. Alkaline phosphatase is usually normal. Blood urea and serum uric acid may be raised. Hyponatraemia is an occasional feature (Bloth et al, 1978).

Prognosis.   The average survival is two to three years but may be quite prolonged in some cases. Abundant immature plasma cells and Bence Jones proteinuria over 1 mg per 100 ml suggest a poor prognosis. An MRC trial (Galton, 1971) showed that serum albumin and blood urea levels at presentation were strongly and independently correlated with survival; and Kyle and Elveback (1976) found that hypercalcaemia was also important in prognosis for two-year survival.

Matzner et al (1978) emphasise that the elderly have a poorer prognosis than younger subjects. The unfavourable prognostic significance of lambda chains was reported by Bergsagel et al (1979) who found rapidly increasing risk of development of acute leukaemia over 50 months. In advanced age (80+ years), however, Kohn and Srivastava (1973) found that the disease often took a long and protracted course. Without treatment survival in these patients was little different from that of younger geriatric patients who received chemotherapeutic treatment for their myeloma. The overall mortality of such very old patients was not significantly different from unaffected individuals in the same age groups. The situation is similar to that of chronic lymphocytic leukaemia.

Rapid response to cytotoxic therapy means that the myeloma cells are rapidly dividing and the prognosis is, in fact, worse than in patients with a slower response (Peto, 1971; Hobbs, 1971; Johansson, 1971). These active myelomas appear to be the ones associated with low serum albumin; they may somehow catabolize serum albumin or inhibit its synthesis.

Other forms of myelomatosis

Plasma cell leukaemia is discussed by Woodruff et al (1978) and Toma et al (1980). In **diffuse myelomatosis** marrow changes are different and X-ray appearances resemble generalized osteoporosis.

In *solitary myeloma* a simple nodule may occur in a single bone; X-ray shows a 'cyst'.

Extramedullary plasmacytoma is rare: 75 per cent present in the submucosa of the upper air passages and are multifocal (Wiltshaw, 1971, 1976; Fu and Perzin, 1978).

Treatment of myelomatosis

Solitary bone or extramedullary lesions are usually treated by irradiation, though surgery may be required. Textbooks of haematology should be consulted for details of chemotherapy.

Symptomless elderly patients are probably best left untreated but followed clinically with particular reference to clinical changes, Hb, blood urea, serum albumin and the possible development of BJP.

The mainstays of chemotherapy in myelomatosis are melphalan and cyclophosphamide. These were compared in MRC trials by continuous administration (Galton and Peto, 1968) and by intermittent administration (Galton, 1971) and no significant differences were noted. Patients intolerant of one may be suited by the other. Prednisone is also useful if there is anaemia, uraemia or hypercalcaemia, but does not prolong survival time (Alexanian et al, 1972). Combination chemotherapy is advocated by Lee et al (1974) but its value was not confirmed by Alexanian et al (1975). No specific combination has emerged as clearly superior to single alkylating-agent therapy (Durie and Salmon, 1982). These authors also found that continuing cytotoxic therapy beyond the first year did more harm than good. This appears to be because the initial effects lead to increased growth of remaining myeloma cells so that a residual plateau of $10^{10}-10^{11}$ such cells remains; and an acute terminal phase may develop (Bergsagel, 1976).

A recent account of the current status and future prospects for treatment of multiple myelomatosis is given by Durie and Salmon (1982).

Macroglobulinaemia
Macroglobulins may occur in chronic lymphatic leukaemia, lymphosarcoma, Hodgkin's disease, immune-reaction diseases and carcinomas.

Primary (Waldenström's) macroglobulinaemia
This is a rare condition seen in the elderly (peak incidence 60 to 80 years), in males twice as often as females, in contrast to myelomatosis. It is a more benign disease than myelomatosis, often with survival for seven or more years. A recent review is by Messmore et al (1978).

Clinical features. These are due to (a) hyperplasia of cells of lymphocytic origin — producing lymphadenopathy, hepatosplenomegaly, and marrow failure with anaemia; and (b) the hyperviscosity syndrome: retinopathy with retinal venous engorgement, varicosities, haemorrhages, and exudate and sludging of blood in capillaries (leading to visual disturbances which may come on suddenly, but often regress); peripheral neuropathy, heart failure and a haemorrhagic tendency. The high plasma viscosity and anaemia cause the retinopathy, peripheral neuropathy and heart failure. It is commonest with excess IgM, but may occur with IgA (which tends to polymerize) and with IgG dyscrasias, as in some cases of myelomatosis (*British Medical Journal*, 1971; Bloch and Maki, 1973; Tuddenham et al, 1974; Virella et al, 1975; Wiederman et al 1980). Less common presentations are described by Fudenberg and Virella (1980).

Blood picture. A normochromic normocytic anaemia, below 10 g Hb per 100 ml, is common. Marked rouleaux formation is seen. Bone marrow may show a nodular lymphoid pattern or diffuse lymphoid infiltration; the former has been linked with significantly longer survival (Chelazzi et al, 1979).

Biochemical tests. Bence Jones proteinuria occurs in only 10 per cent of cases. Total serum proteins are increased markedly due to the increased globulins. Electrophoresis shows a discrete band in the γ-globulin region. IgM is identified immunologically and should be confirmed by ultracentrifugation and other special tests (Martin, 1970).

Treatment. Chlorambucil used continuously, with prednisone, is probably the best drug treatment; response may take many months, and the abnormal protein may not disappear altogether.

Cyclophosphamide may be used. Since macroglobulins are composed of globulin fractions joined by sulphydryl linkages, an attack on these linkages has been tried, using penicillamine. Though successful in vitro, the results in man have been variable (Fairley, 1971).

Weekly plasmapheresis removes macroglobulin from the body and this may be a useful emergency measure if severe cardiac failure or retinopathy develops: both may regress rapidly on this regime.

Recent advances
Heavy-chain diseases. Just as excess production of light chain (κ and λ) leads to BJP, so the imbalance in Ig-synthesis may result in excess heavy chains (γ, α or μ) (Franklin et al, 1964; Osserman and Takatsuki, 1964; Seligmann, 1972).

Gamma heavy chains show on serum electrophoresis as a broad abnormal band rather than a monoclonal peak. The patients are elderly, with a waxing and waning lymphadenopathy and hepatosplenomegaly and a tendency to recurrent infections. The palate and uvula are swollen. Bone lesions are rare. Pancytopenia with eosinophilia is common. There is no BJP.

Alpha-chain disease occurs in children and young adults and is very rare after 50 (Rambaud and Seligmann, 1976).

Mu-chain disease (Ballard et al, 1970) occurs mainly in patients who have had typical chronic lymphoid leukaemia for many years. Hypogammaglobulinaemia and BJP are likely. Immunoelectrophoresis is needed for the diagnosis.

Delta-chain disease was recently described (Vilpo et al, 1980); the clinical features were those of multiple myeloma plus the atypical paraprotein.

Amyloidosis. The modern concept of amyloid deposition is that it is an immunological process occurring in an immune system under stress and inadequately controlled — hence its striking frequency in the elderly, especially after 80 (Walford, 1969; Burnet, 1974b).

The amyloid material consists of protein fibrils (Glenner et al, 1971, 1973). The protein has been shown to be of two types (Hobbs, 1973), A and B; the B protein is composed of modified light chains κ or λ and is most likely to be deposited in paraproteinaemias; the A protein is less well defined and is more conspicuous in secondary amyloid occurring in long-standing sepsis, tuberculosis or rheumatoid arthritis. Clinical and laboratory findings in primary generalized and multiple-myeloma-related amyloidosis are reviewed by Kyle and Bayrd (1975) and Pruzanski and Katz (1976). Periorbital purpura may lead to suspicion of primary amyloidosis (Milutinovich et al, 1979; Penziner, 1982). Penziner

(1982) reviews the coagulopathy seen in amyloidosis. Treatment is unsatisfactory but may be given as for multiple myeloma (Kyle and Greipp, 1978b).

DISORDERS OF HAEMOSTASIS

Haemostasis is maintained by a mechanism involving vascular, platelet and coagulation components. A tendency to bleed may result from a disorder of one or more of these components. Purpura may occur with or without demonstrable platelet abnormalities, the chief of which is thrombocytopenia; but the commonest purpuras in the elderly are non-thrombocytopenic.

Non-thrombocytopenic purpura
This has a different significance in the elderly from that in the young. Anaphylactoid purpura is rare in old age, whereas 'senile purpura' is very common. Other causes include scurvy, drugs, and hypothermia.

Senile purpura
Senile purpura occurs mainly on the extensor surfaces of the forearms and hands, and may be seen in many otherwise normal old people. Loss of subcutaneous fat and changes in aging connective tissue allow undue mobility of the old person's thin skin and the resulting shearing forces allow rupture of small vessels. The extravasated blood tracks widely and the tissues' reaction to it is impaired (Tattersall and Seville, 1950). No history of trauma is usually obtained. Scarborough and Shuster (1960) compared senile purpura with steroid-induced purpura and discussed the mechanism. They showed (Shuster and Scarborough, 1961) that individual lesions last from one to three weeks (longer than other types of purpura) and do not undergo the typical colour changes as they resolve, due to poor phagocytic response to the extravasated blood.

Feinstein et al (1973) studied nine elderly men (mean age 78) with senile purpura and nine middle-aged men without it (mean age 48), as controls. Purpura was induced in all 18 subjects by injection of autologous red cells labelled with ^{57}Cr. The half-time ($t\frac{1}{2}$) for removal of the red cells showed no differences as between dorsal and ventral surfaces of the arms in the elderly purpuric subjects; and there were no differences in $t\frac{1}{2}$ as between the old and the younger subjects. Histological examination showed no evidence of inflammatory reaction, and no red cells in monocytes or polymorphs. By the 7th day after injection there were fewer red cells present and many had abnormal shapes. Only a few red cells remained by the 10th day. Attempts to alter the rate of removal of red cells by the use of oral bromelains (Ananase), flurandrenolide (Cordran tape), or ultraviolet light-induced erythema all failed to influence $t\frac{1}{2}$.

Clearly the structure of the red cells cannot be maintained in the extravascular milieu; they lyse and the haemoglobin released is presumably ingested by macrophages in the skin. Phagocytosis of extravasated red cells occurs when their membranes are coated with antibody; but since autologous red cells are not coated with foreign antibody they do not produce a chemotactic stimulus for inflammatory cells.

Banerjee and Etherington (1973) surveyed 533 geriatric patients (249 males and 284 females), chosen at random, for the incidence of senile purpura. Forty-seven (18.9 per cent) of the males and 29 (10.2 per cent) of the females had purpuric areas on the extensor surfaces of their limbs; there was no correlation between size or severity of the lesions and the age of the patients, nor did the underlying physical or clinical state relate to the incidence of the purpura. Platelet function studies were performed in 15 of the purpuric and 14 of the non-purpuric patients, all of whom had a leucocyte ascorbic acid level >15 μg per 10^8 WBC. Platelet aggregation in response to collagen was significantly delayed in the purpuric group and a reduction in platelet factor 3 release (which reflects platelet aggregation) was noted. After the initial delay, platelet aggregation then occurred speedily and to a normal extent. The reason for these differences was not clear. Mean leucocyte ascorbic acid levels were similar in both groups of patients.

Several attempts have been made to relate senile purpura to ascorbic acid deficiency since the suggested causal relationship by Tattersall and Seville (1950). However, no such relationship has since been demonstrated (Disselduff and Murphy, 1968; McLeod, 1972; Dymock and Brocklehurst, 1973; Banerjee and Etherington, 1973, 1974b). The relationship between sublingual petechiae and vitamin C deficiency is less clear; probably there is none (McLeod, 1972; Dymock and Brocklehurst, 1973).

Capillary fragility increases with age (Hart and Cohen, 1969; de Nicola and Morsiani, 1975), but does not correlate with leucocyte ascorbic acid levels, nor with oral vitamin C supplementation (McLeod, 1972; Dymock and Brocklehurst, 1973).

Scurvy is associated with purpura and more widespread bleeding from body surfaces, under the periosteum, or in viscera.

The haemorrhagic tendency has for long been attributed to disturbed collagen synthesis and an endothelial defect in the capillaries, but in recent years it has been demonstrated that impaired platelet function is a feature of scurvy. The findings in experimental scurvy were reported by Born and Wright (1967, 1968) and reports relating to human scurvy have come from Wilson et al (1967), Hardisty (1969) and Banerjee and Etherington (1974b).

Other causes include uraemia, steroid therapy,

Cushing's disease, dysproteinaemias, severe infections, hypothermia, neoplasia and drugs.

Many common drugs widely used in the elderly have been implicated (e.g. penicillin, sulphonamides, thiazide diuretics, salicylates, phenylbutazone, chloral, chlorpromazine and even trinitrin and insulin).

Purpura due to platelet defects

Thrombocytopenia may be primary ('idiopathic') or secondary (drug-induced, or associated with other blood diseases, infections, neoplasia and various other conditions). Occasionally thrombocythaemia, thrombasthenia or combined defects may occur (Hardisty, 1969).

Idiopathic thrombocytopenic purpura (ITP)

Though commonest in children and young adults, ITP may be seen late in life; it is commoner in females. The acute childhood form is rare in the elderly, in whom a more chronic, fluctuating course is usual. The Hess (capillary resistance) test is positive. Normally 10 to 20 petechiae appear in a 3 cm circle below the antecubital fossa after 5 minutes of venous obstruction above the elbow. In ITP there may be over 100 petechiae, due to an associated capillary fragility. The normal increase in capillary fragility seen in old age is less marked but may confuse the picture.

In ITP the platelets are reduced below $60 \times 10^9/l$ (60 000 per c mm) if bleeding occurs, though even lower counts do not necessarily lead to bleeding.

Megakaryocytes in the bone marrow are not reduced and may be increased, but show little budding-off of platelets.

Bleeding time is prolonged, up to 30 minutes or more; coagulation time is normal, but prothrombin consumption and thromboplastin generation tests are impaired. Clot retraction is impaired or lost. Platelet antibodies occur in some cases but this is not a reliable routine test. Diagnosis is easy but care must be taken to exclude a specific cause, especially drugs. Sternal puncture is not hazardous and will exclude other blood diseases.

Treatment. Corticosteroids may be tried, but if there is no satisfactory response within 3 to 12 months, splenectomy may be advisable. This is less often curative in the elderly (50 per cent) than in younger patients (80 per cent); it is more effective if platelet antibodies are present. If the operation fails, a further trial of steroids may now be successful.

Platelet transfusions, using platelet-rich plasma or platelet concentrates, are disappointing; the transfused platelets, like the endogenous platelets, have shortened life spans, and any improvement is transient.

Secondary thrombocytopenia

Drugs are a very important cause (de Gruchy, 1975d). They may be direct marrow toxins, or cause idiosyn-

crasy or hypersensitivity reactions. Any drug capable of producing aplastic anaemia may reduce platelets, either selectively or as part of the aplastic picture. In addition, some drugs are known to cause selective thrombocytopenia only. They are all low-risk drugs, and include Sedormid, quinidine, quinine, sulphonamides, penicillin, tetracycline, chloramphenicol, salicylates, paracetamol, tolbutamide, chlorpropamide, barbiturates, desipramine, chlorothiazide, digitoxin, insulin and cimetidine.

Recently awareness of heparin-induced thrombocytopenia has increased (Cimo et al, 1979; Kapsch et al, 1979). The clinical picture may resemble that of TTP (see below) or may result from disseminated intravascular coagulation (see below).

If hypersensitivity is involved, constitutional symptoms may accompany the bleeding.

Thrombocytopenia is seen in acute and in many cases of chronic leukaemias (especially terminally) but many other blood disorders may present with thrombocytopaenia including pernicious anaemia, infections and neoplasia.

Thrombotic thrombocytopenic purpura (TTP)

This condition, also known as microangiopathic haemolytic anaemia, has been much reviewed recently (e.g. Pisciotta, 1980; Ridolfi and Bell, 1981). Successful treatment of TTP with plasmipheresis with or without antiplatelet drugs has been reported (Okuno and Kosova, 1979; Myers, 1981). In some patients corticosteroids and splenectomy are also needed (Rothberg et al, 1982). Intravenous prostacyclin (Fitzgerald et al, 1981) has been successful in one patient.

Isolated unexplained thrombocytopenia in the elderly should arouse suspicion of sepsis, especially Gram-negative sepsis (Hussain, 1976). Other causes of secondary thrombocytopenia include collagenoses (especially SLE), massive or incompatible blood transfusion, various splenomegalies, paraproteinaemias, thyrotoxicosis, hepatic cirrhosis, and, rarely, food allergy.

Thrombocythaemia

An excess of platelets is usually an added feature of another blood disorder. It may occur alone in the elderly without apparently shortening life, but is rare. Bleeding, thromboses, and splenomegaly are the clinical features, with a platelet count of one or more million per c mm. The platelets show many abnormal forms and platelet function tests may be abnormal (Jamshidi and colleagues, 1973; Woodruff et al, 1980).

The bone marrow shows megakaryocytic hyperplasia (and possibly a causative blood dyscrasia and hyperploidy).

Treatment is with ^{32}P or busulphan. Splenectomy is

contraindicated: it may cause further increase in platelets and more bleeding.

Thrombasthenia

A rare qualitative platelet defect affects platelet function and leads to a haemorrhagic tendency due to impaired platelet adhesiveness and a failure of clot retraction (despite a normal platelet count). Though mostly a hereditary disease, seen in childhood, it is occasionally seen in adults where it may be idiopathic or, in the elderly, secondary to scurvy, uraemia, thrombocythaemia, or macroglobulinaemia.

Bleeding most often occurs after trauma or surgery. The Hess test is positive. Platelets may appear abnormal, but are not reduced. Other haematological tests are abnormal as in ITP, but in addition platelet aggregation and adhesion tests may be performed (see Turpie et al, 1971).

Drugs affecting platelet function

There has been much recent work on platelet function in the hope of ultimately influencing the natural history of thrombosis and atherosclerosis. Many drugs have been shown to have effects on platelet behaviour (adhesiveness, aggregation, release phenomena) and this important subject, of much potential concern in geriatric medicine, is reviewed by Hirsh (1978), Fuccella (1979), Gantmacher (1979) and Weiss (1982).

DEFECTS OF BLOOD COAGULATION

Survival into later life with congenital coagulation disorders may occur, especially in von Willebrand's disease where the defect in Factor VIII synthesis is milder than in haemophila. Successful prostatectomy in an 85-year-old haemophiliac has been reported by Wylin and Schneider (1976); this patient had no abnormality of fibrinolysis (see below).

Acquired disorders include vitamin K deficiency (Hazell and Baloch, 1970) which leads to reduction in prothrombin (Factor II), and in Factors VII, IX and X. This may occur in malabsorption syndromes, liver disease, prolonged obstructive jaundice or biliary fistula, and oral broad-spectrum antibiotic therapy.

Anticoagulant therapy reduces hepatic synthesis of the same four factors. Chronic parenchymatous liver disease may lead to reduction in the above factors and also reduced fibrinogen (Factor I) and Factor V.

Factor X deficiency occurs in amyloidosis (Greipp et al, 1981).

Circulating anticoagulants

These inhibit clotting factors, usually Factor VIII, occasionally Factor V; they are usually transient. Braverman (1966) and Denham et al (1973) have described cases of Factor VIII inhibitor in old people and have reviewed the literature. Further data on inhibitors of Factor VIII and other factors (including Factor V and fibrin polymerization) have been presented by Shapiro and Hulton (1975).

Fibrinogen deficiency

Fibrinogen deficiency may result from impaired formation (liver disease), intravascular clotting, or overactive fibrinolysis (Edson, 1974).

Disseminated intravascular coagulation (DIC)

A syndrome of diffuse intravascular coagulation may be seen in the elderly in an acute, subacute, or chronic form. There is always a serious underlying disease process which leads to thromboplastic substances (from damaged or neoplastic tissues) entering the circulation and activating the extrinsic clotting system. The intrinsic clotting system may also be involved — endothelium may be damaged by endotoxins, which also induce platelet aggregation. Antigen/antibody reactions may also lead to platelet aggregation. Platelet factor 3 is released and participates in the coagulation process. Intravascular fibrin deposition follows but fibrinolysis is activated simultaneously. The net result of these changes is bleeding, thromboses, shock, haemolysis and renal failure.

Criteria for diagnosis are not well defined; the most useful are: a low platelet count, positive plasma protamine test for fibrin, monomer-fibrinogen complexes, and levels of fibrinogen and fibrin degradation products related to the clinical condition (Feinstein, 1982). Therapy must include restoration of depleted blood components, treatment of the trigger factors and of the underlying disease (e.g. infection, neoplasia or various forms of tissue damage from trauma, burns, heatstroke, surgery, antigen/antibody reactions (drugs, incompatible transfusion, anaphylactic shock). Aortic aneurysms have been associated with extensive coagulation disorders. Liver disease, acute pancreatitis and non-bacterial thrombotic endocarditis have also given rise to DIC.

The use of heparin in treatment of DIC is controversial. It may have a place in chronic varieties with thrombotic manifestations and/or dermal necrosis. Replacement of haemostatic factors may require the 'cover' of a continuous heparin infusion, especially in complex situations such as promylocytic leukaemia. These and certain other situations where heparin may be indicated are discussed by Feinstein (1982). In the majority of cases of DIC (say 95 per cent) heparin has not been proved to be of value and may sometimes be harmful (Straub, 1975; Wintrobe et al, 1981). Heparin may itself cause thrombocytopenia and thromboses (see above).

Overactive fibrinolysis

Acute fibrinolysis may occur in acute DIC, or in severe burns or trauma. Chronic fibrinolysis may be seen with disseminated carcinoma, especially prostatic, or other neoplasia, leukaemia and liver disease.

Clotting time is usually prolonged; the clot is weak and rapidly lyses. Occasionally the blood fails to clot.

Treatment is as for DIC, but newer drugs have also helped — aminocaproic acid (EACA), and aprotinin (Trasylol). These drugs — and fibrinogen transfusion — may increase fibrin deposition and lead to intravascular coagulation with further fibrinolysis: in this case, anticoagulant therapy may be needed. Serious thrombotic complications may follow the use of EACA (Gralnick and Greipp, 1971). Dose-related orthostatic hypotension has been reported (Gardner and Helmer, 1980).

Anticoagulant therapy.   In the elderly, anticoagulant therapy is required for prevention and treatment of thromboembolic disease in a few specific instances, e.g. embolism from atrial fibrillation, pulmonary embolism and 'stuttering strokes'. It is not usual to treat all old people with atrial fibrillation or even deep vein thrombosis with anticoagulants, and individual judgement must be exercised. Sevitt and Gallagher (1959) used routine anticoagulation in association with surgery for fractured neck of femur in a controlled trial, and found excellent results although the design of their study has been criticized (Eskeland, 1962).

Although that work is about 20 years old, Morris and Mitchell (1976a) found that only 3 per cent of 411 orthopaedic surgeons who replied to a questionary asking how they attempted to prevent, and how they diagnosed, deep vein thrombosis used oral anticoagulation routinely, and 51 per cent offered no prophylaxis at all. The same authors (Morris and Mitchell, 1976b) carried out their own prospective study on 160 patients aged 60 or over who had sustained a fracture of the femoral neck. Those patients were given prophylactic warfarin sodium from the day of admission until independent mobility had been achieved, or for three months, whichever was the sooner. This management significantly reduced the frequency of deep vein thrombosis, and pulmonary embolism was eliminated in treated patients — the authors comment that maintenance of the thrombotest within the desired range of 5 to 15 per cent was difficult in the treated patients; very low levels tended to occur

in patients in poor general condition. The difference in mortality between treated and control groups was not significant, however. These findings were similar to those of Salzman et al (1966) in patients aged 75 and above.

Whereas high-dose intravenous heparin is used after an occlusive arterial embolus or a venous thrombosis has occurred, with the aim of preventing extension or recurrence, a low-dose subcutaneous regime has become widely used in recent years for the primary prevention of venous thrombosis in high-risk patients. The value of this low-dose regimen for heparin has been widely attested to (Hedlund and Blombäck, 1981; Deykin, 1982; Ockelford and Hull, 1982). Failures may be obviated by scrupulous attention to dose size and timing, and monitoring of control (Sharnoff, 1977).

For prevention of re-thrombosis, however, oral warfarin appears superior (Hull et al, 1979), although heamorrhage was significantly greater with warfarin.

Good control of oral anticoagulant therapy with warfarin is more difficult in the elderly (Eccles, 1975): both pharmacokinetic (renal and perhaps hepatic impairment, reduced protein-binding) and pharmacodynamic (increased sensitivity of the elderly to the effects of warfarin) changes appear to be involved (Hewick et al, 1975; Hayes et al, 1975). Other factors include problems with compliance and unsuspectedly high vitamin K intake in the form of liquid dietary supplements (Lee et al, 1981).

Thrombolytic therapy is difficult and hazardous and has little place in the elderly. The main indication would be major or massive pulmonary embolism (Hirsh et al, 1968; Schwartz et al, 1973). Fuller reviews are given by Bell and Meek (1979) and Marder (1979).

DISORDERS OF PIGMENT METABOLISM

Porphyrias in old age were discussed by Brocklehurst et al (1965), who review the literature and report two cases. One, a man of 72, had primary hepatocarcinoma; another such case, a woman of 72 presenting with porphyria cutanea tarda and found to have primary hepatocarcinoma, was included in the cases described by Eddleston et al (1971). Further cases of porphyria in the elderly were reported by Pearce and Payne (1981).

REFERENCES

Abengowe C U 1975 Clinical importance of grossly increased ESR. Canadian Medical Association Journal 113: 929–930
Acheson M, Jessop W J E 1962 Serum proteins in a population sample of males aged 65–85 years. Gerontologia 6: 193–205
Acikalin T, Akdamar K 1980 Infectious mononucleosis in the elderly. Journal of the Louisiana State Medical Society 132: 1–3

Adam H M, Dawson A A, Wigzell F W, Roy S K 1973 Polymorph hypersegmentation in the elderly. Age and Ageing 2: 183–188
Adams G F 1966 In: Agate J N (ed) Medicine in old age, Pitman, London, p 159–169
Adams J F, Boddy K 1971 Studies in cobalamin metabolism. In:

Arnstein H R V, Wrighton R J, The Cobalamins: A Glaxo Symposium, Churchill Livingstone, Edinburgh, p 153–168

Agarwal S S, Tuffner M, Loeb L A 1978 DNA replication in human lymphocytes during aging. Journal of Cellular Physiology 96: 235–244

Aisenberg A C 1978 The staging and treatment of Hodgkin's disease. New England Journal of Medicine 299: 1228–1232

Alderson M R, Nayak R 1972 Epidemiology of Hodgkin's disease. Journal of Chronic Diseases 25: 253–259

Alexanian R, Balcerzak S, Haut A, Hewlett J, Gehan E 1975 Remission maintenance therapy for multiple myeloma. Archives of Internal Medicine 135: 147–152

Alexanian R, Bonnet J, Gehan E, Haut A, Hewlett J, Lane M et al 1972 Combination chemotherapy for multiple myeloma. Cancer 30: 382–389

Allen R H 1976 The plasma transport of vitamin B_{12}. British Journal of Haematology 33: 161–171

Amorosi E L, Ultman J E 1966 Thrombotic thrombocytopenic purpura: report of 16 cases and review of the literature. Medicine (Baltimore) 45: 139–159

Anderson B B, Peart M B Fulford-Jones C E 1970 The measurement of serum pyridoxal by a microbiological assay using *Lactobacillus casei*. Journal of Clinical Pathology 23: 232–242

Anderson J R, Buchanan W W, Goudie R B 1967 In: Autoimmunity: clinical and experimental, C C Thomas, Springfield, Illinois

Anderson W F, Cohen C, Hyams D E, Millard P H, Plowright N M, Woodford Williams E, Berry W T C 1971 Clinical and subclinical malnutrition in old age. Symposium of the Swedish Nutrition Foundation, p 140–146

Andrew W 1971 In: The anatomy of aging in man and animals. Heinemann, London

Andrews J, Fairley A, Barker R 1967 Total dose infusion of iron dextran in the elderly. Scottish Medical Journal 12: 208–215

Andrews J, Letcher M, Brook M 1969 Vitamin C supplementation in the elderly: a 17 month trial in an old persons' home. British Medical Journal ii: 416–418

Ansell B, Bywaters E G L 1958 The 'unexplained' high ESR. British Medical Journal i: 372–374

Araki K, Rifkind J M 1980 Erythrocyte membrane cholesterol: an explanation of the aging effect on the rate of hemolysis. Life Sciences 26: 2223–2230

Ardeman S, Chanarin I 1965 Assay of gastric intrinsic factor in the diagnosis of pernicious anaemia. British Journal of Haematology 11: 305–314

Asquith P, Oelbaum M H, Dawson D W 1967 Scorbutic megaloblastic anaemia responding to ascorbic acid alone. British Medical Journal iv: 402

Axelsson U 1977 An eleven-year follow-up on 64 subjects with M-components. Acta Medica Scandinavica 201: 173–175

Bahemuka M, Denham M J, Hodkinson H M 1973 Macrocytosis. Modern Geriatrics 3: 421–422

Bahemuka M, Hodkinson H M 1976 Red-blood-cell potassium as a practical index of potassium status in elderly patients. Age and Ageing 5: 24–30

Baker H, Frank O, Thind I S, Jaslow S P, Louria D B 1979 Vitamin profiles in elderly persons living at home or in nursing homes, versus profile in healthy young subjects. Journal of the American Geriatrics Society 27: 444–450

Balcerzak S P, Bromberg P A 1975 Secondary polycythemia. Seminars in Hematology 12: 353–382

Ballard H S, Hamilton L M, Marcus A J, Illes C H 1970 A new variant of heavy-chain disease (μ-chain disease). New England Journal of Medicine 282: 1060–1062

Ballas S K 1975 ESR and Coombs-positive hemolytic anemia. New England Journal of Medicine 293: 776–777

Banerjee A K 1975 Macrocytic anaemia in the elderly. Modern Geriatrics 5: 12–16

Banerjee A K, Brocklehurst J C, Swindell R 1981 Protein status in long-stay geriatric in-patients. Gerontology 27: 161–166

Banerjee A K, Etherington M 1973 Senile purpura and platelets. Gerontologia Clinica 15: 213–220

Banerjee A K, Etherington M 1974a Platelet function in old age. Age and Ageing 3: 29–35

Banerjee A K, Etherington M 1974b Platelet function in elderly scorbutics. Age and Ageing 3: 97–105

Bankowski E, Niewiarowski S, Galasinski W 1967 Platelet aggregation by human collagen in relation to its age. Gerontologia 13: 219–226

Batata M, Spray G H, Bolton F G, Higgins G, Wollner L 1967 Blood and bone marrow changes in elderly patients, with particular reference to folic acid, vitamin B_{12}, iron and ascorbic acid. British Medical Journal ii: 667–669

Bateman C J T, Mollin D L 1970 Sideroblastic anaemia. British Journal of Hospital Medicine 4: 371–379

Beard M E J, Fairley G H 1974 Acute leukaemia in adults. Seminars in Hematology 11: 5–24

Bearman R M, Pangalis G A, Rappaport H 1978 Prolymphocytic leukemia. Clinical, histopathological and cytochemical observations. Cancer 42: 2360–2372

Bearman R M, Pangalis G A, Rappaport H 1979 Acute ('malignant') myelosclerosis. Cancer 43: 279–293

Beilin L J, Knight G J, Munro-Faure A D, Anderson J 1966 The sodium, potassium and water contents of red blood cells of healthy human adults. Journal of Clinical Investigation 45: 1817–1825

Bell G H, Lazarus S, Munro H N 1940 Capillary fragility. A critical analysis. Lancet ii: 155–157

Bell T K, Bridges J M, Nelson M G 1965 Simultaneous free and bound radioactive vitamin B_{12} urinary excretion test. Journal of Clinical Pathology 18: 611–613

Bell W R, Meek A G 1979 Guidelines for the use of thrombolytic agents. New England Journal of Medicine 301: 1266–1270

Benbassat J, Fluman N, Zlotnick A 1976 Monoclonal immunoglobulin disorders: a report of 154 cases. American Journal of Medical Sciences 271: 325–334

Bentley D P, Williams P 1974 Serum ferritin concentration as an index of storage iron in rheumatoid arthritis. Journal of Clinical Pathology 27: 786–788

Bentley S A, Lewis S M 1976 The morphological classification of red cells using an image analysing computer. British Journal of Haematology 32: 205–214

Bentzen A J, Jacobsen P A, Munch-Petersen S 1972 An investigation of the platelet adhesiveness by Hellem's method in elderly patients under long-term psychiatric care, on a controlled diet with an unsaturated fatty acid load. Gerontologia Clinica 14: 217–234

Beregi E, Biró J, Regius O 1980 Age-related morphological changes in lymphocytes as a model of aging. Mechanisms of Ageing and Development 14: 173–180

Berg N O, Dahlqvist A, Lindberg T, Lindstrand K, Nordén A 1972 Morphology, dipeptidases and disaccharidases of small intestinal mucosa in vitamin B_{12} and folic acid deficiency. Scandinavian Journal of Haematology 9: 167–173

Bergsagel D E 1976 The treatment of plasma cell myeloma. British Journal of Haematology 33: 443–449

Bersagel D E, Phil D, Bailey A J, Langley G R, MacDonald R N, White G F, Miller, A B 1979 The chemotherapy of plasma cell myeloma and the incidence of acute leukemia. New England Journal of Medicine 301: 743–748

Berlin N I, Berk P D 1975 The biological life of the red cell. In: Surgenor D N (ed) The Red Blood Cell, 2nd edn, Academic Press, New York, Vol II, p 957–1019

Bertolini A M 1969 Gerontologic Metabolism, C C Thomas, Springfield, Illinois

Bessis M, Weed R I, Leblond P F (Eds) 1973 Red Cell Shape: Physiology, Pathology, Ultrastructure. Springer Verlag, Berlin

Bianchi A, Chipman D W, Dreskin A, Rosensweig W S 1970 Nutritional folic acid deficiency with megaloblastic changes in the small bowel epithelium. New England Journal of Medicine 282: 859–861

Biggs J C, Taylor K B, Valberg L S, Witts L J 1962 Effect of iron deficiency on the absorption of vitamin B_{12} in the rat. Gastroenterology 43: 430–435

Bird T, Hall M R P, Schade R O K 1977 Gastric histology and its relation to anaemia in the elderly. Gerontology 23: 309–321

Björkholm M, Holm G, Mellstedt H, Johansson B 1975 Immunodeficiency and prognosis in Hodgkin's disease. Acta Medica Scandinavica 198: 275–279

Blair A, Fraumeni J F Jr, Mason T J 1980 Geographic patterns of leukemia in the United States. Journal of Chronic Diseases 33: 251–260

Blake D R, Scott D G I, Eastham E J, Rashid H 1980 Assessment of iron deficiency in rheumatoid arthritis. British Medical Journal 280: 527

Blattner W A, Mason T J, Blair A 1980 Changes in mortality rates from multiple myeloma. New England Journal of Medicine 302: 814–815 (letter)

Bloch K J, Maki D G 1973 Hyperviscosity syndromes associated with immunoglobulin abnormalities. Seminars in Hematology 10: 113–124

Bloomfield C D 1975 Recognizing and evaluating non-Hodgkin's lymphomas. Geriatrics 30: 56–62 (Oct)

Bloomfield C D, Kersey J H, Brunning R D, Gajl-Peczalska K J 1976 Prognostic significance of lymphocyte surface markers in adult non-Hodgkin's lymphomas. Lancet ii: 1330–1333

Bloomfield C D, Theologides A, Kennedy N J 1975 Effectiveness of chemotherapy for non-Hodgkin's lymphomas. Geriatrics 30: 105–109 (Oct)

Bloth B, Christensson T, Mellstedt H 1978 Extreme hyponatremia in patients with myelomatosis. Acta Medica Scandinavica 203: 273–275

Bock J 1948 Serum protein fractionation in normal old individuals. Journal of Gerontology 3: 119–123

Bodley-Scott R 1957 Leukaemia. Lancet i: 1053–1058, 1099–1103, 1162–1167

Bolton C H, Hampton J R, Mitchell J R A 1967 Nature of the transferable factor which causes abnormal platelet behaviour in vascular disease. Lancet ii: 1101–1105

Bonjour J P 1980 Vitamins and alcoholism. II. Folate and vitamin B_{12}. International Journal for Vitamin and Nutrition Research 50: 96–121 50: 96–121

Booth J B, Todd G B 1970 Subclinical scurvy — hypovitaminosis C. British Journal of Hospital Medicine 4: 513–526

Born G V R, Wright H P 1967 Platelet adhesiveness in experimental scurvy. Lancet i: 477–478

Born G V R, Wright H P 1968 Diminished platelet aggregation in experimental scurvy. Journal of Physiology (London) 197: 27P–28P

Bose S K, Andrews J, Roberts P D 1970 Haematological problems in a geriatric unit with special reference to anaemia. Gerontologia Clinica 12: 339–346

Botez M I, Botez T, Leveille J, Bielmann P, Cadotte M 1979 Neuropsychological correlates of folic acid deficiency: facts and hypotheses. In: Botez M I, Reynolds E H (eds) Folic acid in neurology, psychiatry and internal medicine. Raven Press, New York, p 435–461

Botez M I, Peyronnard J-M, Bachevalier J, Charron L 1978 Polyneuropathy and folate deficiency. Archives of Neurology 35: 581–584

Botez M I, Reynolds E H (eds) 1979 Folic acid in neurology, psychiatry and internal medicine. Raven Press, New York.

Bothwell T H 1966 The diagnosis of iron deficiency. New Zealand Medical Journal. Supplement 65: 880–883

Bothwell T H, Charlton R W 1970 Absorption of iron. Annual Review of Medicine 21: 145–156

Bothwell T H, Finch C A 1962. Iron Metabolism. Little, Brown, Boston.

Böttiger L E 1973 ESR and plasma lipids. Acta Medica Scandinavica 193: 53–57

Böttiger L E, Böttiger B 1981 Incidence and cause of aplastic anemia, hemolytic anemia, agranulocytosis and thrombocytopenia. Acta Medica Scandinavica 210: 475–479

Böttiger L E, Carlson L A, Eklund L G, Olsson A G 1973 Raised ESR in asymptomatic hyperlipidaemia. British Medical Journal ii: 681–684

Böttiger L E, Svedberg C A 1967 Normal erythrocyte sedimentation rate and age. British Medical Journal ii: 85–87

Bowdler A J 1970 The spleen: structure and function. British Journal of Hospital Medicine 3: 8–14

Bowdler A J, Dougherty R M, Bowdler N C 1981 Age as a factor affecting erythrocyte osmotic fragility in males. Gerontology 27: 224–231

Boyd R V, Hoffbrand B I 1966 Erythrocyte sedimentation rate in elderly hospital inpatients. British Medical Journal i: 901–902

Brain M C 1970 Microangiopathic hemolytic anemia. Annual Review of Medicine 21: 133–144

Brain M C 1971 The red cell and haemolytic anaemia. In: Goldberg A, Brain M C (eds), Recent advances in haematology. Churchill Livingstone, Edinburgh, p 146–193

Brain M C, Card R T 1972 Effect of inorganic phosphate on red cell metabolism: in vitro and in vivo studies. In: Brewer G J (ed) (Advances in Experimental and Medical Biology, vol 28) Hemoglobin and red cell structure and function. Plenum Press, New York, p 145–154

Brandt L, Nillson P G, Mitelman F 1979 Trends in incidence of acute leukaemia. Lancet ii: 1069 (letter)

Braverman A M 1966 Spontaneously-occurring anticoagulants in the elderly. Gerontologia Clinica 8: 106–110

Brewer G J 1967 Genetic and population studies of quantitative levels of adenosine triphosphate in human erythrocytes. Biochemical Genetics 1: 25–34

Brewer G J 1974a General red cell metabolism. In: Surgenor D N (ed) The red blood cell, 2nd edn. Academic Press, New York, p 387–433

Brewer G J 1974b Red cell metabolism and function. In: Surgenor D N (ed) The red blood cell, 2nd edn. Academic Press, New York, p 473–508

Brewer G J, Coan C C 1969 Interaction of red cell ATP levels and malaria, and the treatment of malaria with hyperoxia. Military Medicine 134: 1056–1067

Brise H, Hallberg L 1962 Effect of ascorbic acid on iron absorption. Acta Medica Scandinavica 171: suppl. 376, 51–58

British Medical Journal 1964 Carcinogenic risk of iron dextran. British Medical Journal i: 1583–1584

British Medical Journal 1969 Old age, nutrition and mental confusion. British Medical Journal iii: 608–609

British Medical Journal 1971 The hyperviscosity syndrome. British Medical Journal i: 184

British Medical Journal 1975 Prognosis in aplastic anaemia. British Medical Journal iv: 126–127

British Medical Journal 1976a Folate and the nervous system. British Medical Journal ii: 71

British Medical Journal 1976b Transfusing white cells. British Medical Journal ii: 662

British Medical Journal 1977 Androgens in the anaemia of chronic renal failure. British Medical Journal ii: 417–418

British Medical Journal 1978 Hairy-cell leukaemia. British Medical Journal i: 872

Britton C J C 1969a In: Disorders of the blood, 10th edn. J and A Churchill Ltd, London, p 159

Britton C J C 1969b In: Disorders of the blood. 10th edn. J and A Churchill Ltd, London, p 153

Brocklehurst J C, Humphreys G S, Gardner-Medwin D 1965 Porphyria in old age. Gerontologia Clinica 7: 83–91

Brouet J-C, Flandrin G, Sasportes M, Preud'homme J-L, Seligmann M 1975 Chronic lymphocytic leukaemia of T-cell origin. Lancet ii: 890–893

Brown I R F, Bakowska A, Millard P H 1976 Vitamin D status of patients with femoral neck fractures. Age and Ageing 5: 127–131

Brueschke G, Herrmann H, Schulz P H 1960 [Age-related changes in the white blood cell system]. Medizinische Welt 46: 2460–2464

Brueschke G, Thiele W, Schutz P H 1961 Die Abhängigkeit der Retraktion des Fibringerinnsels vom Alter. Zeitschrift Altersforschung 15: 185–190

Brunetti S, Tesi M, Caramelli L 1967 Changes in activation of the fibrinolytic system in relation to age. Rivista critica di clinica medica 67: 455–464

Brunning R 1974 Differential diagnosis of anemia. Geriatrics 29: 52–60 (Feb)

Brunning R D 1975 Bone marrow and peripheral blood involvement in non-Hodgkin's lymphomas. Geriatrics 30: 75–80 (Oct)

Buckley C E III, Dorsey F C 1970 The effect of aging on human serum Ig concentrations. Journal of Immunology 105: 964–972

Buckley C E III, Roseman J M 1976 Immunity and survival. Journal of the American Geriatrics Society 24: 241–248

Buckley C E III, Buckley E G, Dorsey F C 1974 Longitudinal changes in serum immunoglobulin levels in older humans. Federation Proceedings, Federation of American Societies for Experimental Biology 33: 2036–2039

Buckton K E, Court Brown W M, Smith P G 1967 Lymphocyte survival in men treated with X-rays for ankylosing spondylitis. Nature 214: 470–473

Bunn H E 1972 Erythrocyte destruction and hemoglobin catabolism. Seminars in Hematology 9: 3–17

Burkhardt R 1975 Iron overload of bone marrow and bone. In: Kief H (ed) Iron metabolism and its disorders. Excerpta Medica, Amsterdam, p 264–271

Burnet F M 1974a Autoimmunity and ageing. In: Brent L, Holborow J (eds) Progress in immunology II, vol 5 — Clinical Aspects, North-Holland, Amsterdam, p 27–36

Burnet, Sir M 1974b Intrinsic Mutagenesis: a genetic approach to ageing. Medical and Technical Publishing Company Limited, Lancaster

Burr M L, Elwood P C, Hole D J, Hurley R J, Hughes R E 1974 Plasma and leukocyte ascorbic acid levels in the elderly. American Journal of Clinical Nutrition 27: 144–151

Burr M L, Hurley R J, Sweetnam P M 1975 Vitamin C supplementation of old people with low blood levels. Gerontologia clinica 17: 236–243

Burr M L, Milbank J E, Gibbs D 1982 The nutritional status of the elderly. Age and Ageing 11: 89–96

Buxton P K, Davison W, Hyams D E, Irvine W J 1969 Vitamin B$_{12}$ status in mentally disturbed elderly patients. Gerontologia Clinica 11: 22–35

Bychikhin N P, Volchkova L S 1970 Thrombotest as an index of the state of the blood coagulation and anticoagulation system in aged and senile persons. Klinicheskaya meditsina 48: 105–108 (English abstract: Excerpta Medica, section XX (1971), 14 (6): Abstract No. 1148, p 207)

Caen J P, Cronberg S, Kubisz P 1977 Platelets: Physiology and Pathology. Stratton Intercontinental Medical Book Corp, New York, p 6–8

Caird F I 1973 Problems of interpretation of laboratory findings in the old. British Medical Journal iv: 348–351

Caird F I, Andrews G R, Gallie T B 1972 The leucocyte count in old age. Age and Ageing 1: 239–244

Calder E A, Irvine W J 1975 Cell-mediated immunity and immune complexes in thyroid disease. Clinical Endocrinology and Metabolism 4: 287–318

Callender S T 1971 Iron absorption from food. Gerontologia Clinica 13: 44–51

Callender S T, Denborough M A 1957 A family study of pernicious anaemia. British Journal of Haematology 3: 88–106

Callender S T, Spray G H 1962 Latent pernicious anaemia. British Journal of Haematology 8: 230–240

Campbell A J, Murphy C, Reinken J 1981 Anaemia in old age: a study of prevalence and causes. New Zealand Medical Journal 94: 209–211

Campbell H, Greene W J W, Keyser J W, Waters W E, Weddell J M, Withey J L 1968 Pilot survey of haemoglobin and plasma urea concentrations in a random sample of adults in Wales 1965–66. British Journal of Preventive and Social Medicine 22: 41–49

Canellos G P, Lister T A 1978 The staging and treatment of non-Hodgkin's lymphoma. British Journal of Haematology 39: 477–482

Cantor A M 1963 A study of pernicious anaemia in elderly patients. Gerontologia Clinica 5: 23–29

Cape R D T, Shinton N K 1961 Serum vitamin B$_{12}$ concentration in the elderly. Gerontologia Clinica 3: 163–172

Cape R D T, Zirk M H 1975 Assessment of iron stores in old people. Gerontologia Clinica 17: 101–106

Carbone P P, Kaplan H S, Musshoff K, Smithers D W, Tubiana M 1971 Report of the committee on Hodgkin's disease staging classification. Cancer Research 31: 1860–1861

Card R T, Brown G M, Valberg L S 1964 Serum iron and iron-binding capacity in normal subjects. Canadian Medical Association Journal 90: 618–622

Carlson A J 1954 Physiologic changes of normal senescence. In: Steiglitz E J, Geriatric Medicine: Medical Care of Later Maturity, 3rd edn. Pitman, London, p 64–81

Carmel R 1979 Macrocytosis, mild anemia, and delay in the diagnosis of pernicious anemia. Archives of Internal Medicine 139: 47–50

Carmel R 1982 A new case of deficiency of the R binder for cobalamin with observations on minor cobalamin-binding proteins in serum and saliva. Blood 59: 152–156

Carney M W 1979 Psychiatric aspects of folate deficiency. In: Botez M I, Reynolds E H (eds). Folic Acid in Neurology, Psychiatry and Internal Medicine, Raven Press, New York, p 475–482

Carter M E, Ardeman S, Winocour V, Perry J, Chanarin I 1968

Rheumatoid arthritis and pernicious anaemia. Annals of Rheumatic Diseases 27: 454–456

Cartwright G E 1966 The anemia of chronic disorders. Seminars in Hematology 3: 351–375

Casale G, Marinoni G L, d'Angelo R, de Nicola P 1983 Circadian rhythm of immunoglobulins in aged persons. Age and Ageing 12: 81–85

Cavill I, Ricketts C 1974 The kinetics of iron metabolism. In: Jacobs A, Worwood M (eds) Iron in Biochemistry and Medicine, Academic Press, London, p 613–647

Cerny L C, Cook F B, Valone F 1972 The erythrocyte in aging. Experimental Gerontology 7: 137–142

Chabner B A 1979 Nodular non-Hodgkin's lymphoma: the case for watchful waiting. Annals of Internal Medicine 90: 115–117

Chalmers J N M, Shinton N K 1965 Comparison of hydroxocobalamin and cyanocobalamin in the treatment of pernicious anaemia. Lancet ii: 1305–1308

Chanarin I 1969 In: The Megaloblastic Anaemias. Blackwell, Oxford

Chanarin I 1971 Macrocytic anaemias. British Journal of Hospital Medicine 6: 581–592

Chanarin I 1973 New light on pernicious anaemia. Lancet ii: 538–539

Chanarin I 1974 Vitamin B$_{12}$ — folate interrelations. In: Huntsman R G, Jenkins G C (eds), Advanced Haematology, Butterworth, London, p 87–107

Chanarin I, Knight S, O'Brien J, James D 1976 HL-A groups in pernicious anaemia, British Journal of Haematology 33: 539–541

Chanarin I, Perry J, Reynolds E H 1974 Transport of 5-methyltetrahydrofolic acid into the cerebrospinal fluid in man. Clinical Science and Molecular Medicine 46: 369–373

Chanarin I, Szur L 1975 Relief of intractable pruritus in polycythaemia rubra vera with cholestyramine. British Journal of Haematology 29: 669–670

Chelazzi G, Bettini R, Pinotti G 1979 Bone-marrow patterns and survival in Waldenström's macroglobulinaemia. Lancet ii: 965–966 (Letter)

Chen M G 1971 Age-related changes in hematopoietic stem-cell properties of a long-lived hybrid mouse. Journal of Cellular Physiology 78: 225–232

Chen M G 1974 Impaired Elkind recovery in hematopoietic colony-forming cells of aged mice. Proceedings of Society for Experimental Biology and Medicine 145: 1181–1186

Cheney K E, Walford R L 1974 Immune function and dysfunction in relation to aging. Life Sciences 14: 2075–2084

Cheng D S, Kushner J P, Wintrobe M M 1979 Idiopathic refractory sideroblastic anemia: incidence and risk factors for leukemic transformation. Cancer 44: 724–731

Chien S 1975 Biophysical behavior of red cells in suspensions. In: Surgenor D N (ed), The Red Blood Cell, 2nd edn. Academic Press, New York, Vol II, p 1031–1133

Chow B F 1958 Vitamin B$_{12}$ in relationship to aging. Gerontologia 2: 213–222

Chow B F, Gilbert J P, Okuda K, Rosenblum C 1956 The urinary excretion test for absorption of vitamin B$_{12}$: I. Reproducibility of results and agewise variation. American Journal of Clinical Nutrition 4: 142–146

Cimo P L, Moake J L, Weinger R S, Ben-Menachem Y, Khalil K G 1979 Heparin-induced thrombocytopenia: association with a platelet aggregating factor and arterial thromboses. American Journal of Hematology 6: 125–133

Clein G P 1972 The neutrophil granulocyte. British Journal of Hospital Medicine 7: 83–88

Cline M J 1975 The White Cell. Harvard University Press. Cambridge, Massachusetts

Coggle J E, Gordon M Y, Proukakis C, Bogg C E 1975 Age-related changes in the bone marrow and spleen of SAS/4 mice. Gerontologia 21: 1–9

Coghill N F, Doniach D, Roitt I M, Mollin D L, Wynn Williams A 1965 Auto-antibodies in simple atrophic gastritis. Gut 6: 48–56

Cohn J E, Shock N W 1949 Blood volume studies in middle aged and elderly males. American Journal of Medical Sciences 217: 388–391

Cohn Z A, Hirsch J G 1960 The isolation and properties of the specific cytoplasmic granules of rabbit polymorphonuclear leucocytes. Journal of Experimental Medicine 112: 983–1004

Colburn W J, Barnes A 1982 Intravenous Imferon masquerading as an acute hemolytic transfusion reaction. Transfusion 22: 163–164

Coleman D H, Stevens A R, Finch C A 1955 The treatment of iron deficiency anemia. Blood 10: 567–581

Colls B M, Lorier M A 1975 Immunocytoma, cancer and other associations of monoclonal gammopathy: a review of 224 cases. New Zealand Medical Journal 82: 221–226

Conley C L, Misiti J, Laster A J 1980 Genetic factors predisposing to chronic lymphocytic leukemia and to autoimmune disease. Medicine (Baltimore) 59: 323–324

Conrad M E, Rappaport H, Crosby W H 1965 Chronic granulocytic leukemia in the aged. Archives of Internal Medicine 116: 764–775

Cook J D, Finch C A, Smith N J 1976 Evaluation of the iron status of a population. Blood 48: 449–455

Cook J D, Lipschitz D A, Miles L E M, Finch C A 1974 Serum ferritin as a measure of iron stores in normal subjects. American Journal of Clinical Nutrition 27: 681–687

Cook J D, Valberg L S 1965 Gastrointestinal absorption, plasma transport, surface distribution and urinary and fecal excretion of radioactive vitamin B_{12} in iron deficiency. Blood 26: 335–344

Cooper B A 1979 Vitamin B_{12}-folate interrelationships in bone marrow cells. In: Botez M I, Reynolds E H (eds) Folic Acid in Neurology, Psychiatry and Internal Medicine, Raven Press, New York, p 81–87

Cooper B A, Whitehead V M 1978 Evidence that some patients with pernicious anemia are not recognized by radiodilution assay for cobalamin in serum. New England Journal of Medicine 299: 816–818

Corberand J, Ngyen F, Laharrague P, Fontanilles A M, Gleyzes B, Gyrard E, Senegas G 1981 Polymorphonuclear functions and aging in humans. Journal of the American Geriatrics Society 29: 391–397

Corless D, Beer M, Boucher B J, Gupta S P, Cohen R D 1975 Vitamin D status in long-stay geriatric patients. Lancet ii: 1404–1406

Corless D, Gupta S P, Sattar D A, Switala S, Boucher B J 1979 Vitamin D status of residents of an old people's home and long-stay patients. Gerontology 25: 350–355

Cotton R C, Shaikh M S, Dent R V 1968 Heparin resistance and plasma fibrinogen in elderly subjects with and without occlusive vascular disease. Journal of Atherosclerotic Research 8: 959–966

Court Brown W M, Doll R 1959 Adult leukaemia. Trends in mortality in relation to aetiology. British Medical Journal i: 1063–1069

Cox E V 1968 The anemia of scurvy. Vitamins and Hormones 26: 635–652

Cox E V, Meynell M J, Gaddie R, Cooke W T 1959 Interrelation of vitamin B_{12} and iron. Lancet ii: 998–1001

Cox-Klazinga M, Endtz L J 1980 Peripheral nerve involvement in pernicious anaemia. Journal of the Neurological Sciences 45: 367–371

Cream J J 1968 Prednisolone-induced granulocytosis. British Journal of Haematology 15: 259–267

Crolle G, Arturi F, Cerutti G, Del Piano G C 1968 Agglutinazione piastrinica in soggetti normali di varia età ed in arteriosclerotici (Platelet agglutination in young and elderly normal subjects and in arteriosclerotic patients). Giornale di Gerontologia 16: 89–96

Cronkite E P, Fliedner T M 1964 Granulocytopoiesis I & II. New England Journal of Medicine 270: 1347–1352, 1403–1408

Crosby W H 1968 To treat or not to treat acute granulocytic leukemia. Archives of Internal Medicine 122: 79–80

Cruickshank J M, Alexander M K 1970 The effect of age, sex, parity, haemoglobin level, and oral contraceptive preparations on the normal leucocyte count. British Journal of Haematology 18: 541–550

Cucin R L, Coleman M, Eckhardt J J, Silver R T 1973 The diagnosis of miliary tuberculosis; utility of peripheral blood abnormalities, bone marrow and liver needle biopsy. Journal of Chronic Diseases 26: 355–361

Custer R P, Ahlfeldt F E 1932 Studies on the structure and function of bone marrow. II. Variations in cellularity in various bones with advancing years of life and their relative response to stimuli. Journal of Laboratory and Clinical Medicine 17: 960–962

Cwynarski M T, Saxton H M 1969 Urography in myelomatosis. British Medical Journal i: 486

Dacie J V 1963 Prognosis in acquired haemolytic anaemia. Australasian Annals of Medicine 12: 11–15

Dacie J V 1970 Autoimmune haemolytic anaemias. British Medical Journal ii: 381–386

Dacie J V, Worlledge S M 1969 Auto-immune hemolytic anemias. Progress in Hematology VI: 82–120

Dagg J H, Cumming R L C, Goldberg A 1971 Disorders of iron metabolism In: Goldberg A, Brain M C (eds) Recent Advances in Haematology. Churchill Livingstone, Edinburgh, p 77–145

Dagg J H, Goldberg A, Anderson J R, Beck J S, Gray K G 1964 Auto-immunity in iron deficiency anaemia. British Medical Journal i: 1349–1350

Dagg J H, Goldberg A, Gibbs W N, Anderson J R 1966a Detection of latent pernicious anaemia in iron deficiency anaemia. British Medical Journal ii: 619–621

Dagg J H, Smith J A, Goldberg A 1966b Urinary excretion of iron. Clinical Science 30: 495–503

Dagg J H, Goldberg A, Lockhead A 1966c Value of erythrocyte protoporphyrin in the diagnosis of latent iron deficiency. British Journal of Haematology 12: 326–330

Dalal P R, Rosenthal R, Sarkar T K 1980 Leukemoid reaction in pulmonary carcinoma. Journal of National Medical Association 72: 683–686

Dallman P 1974 Tissue effects of iron deficiency. In: Jacobs A, Worwood M (eds) Iron in Biochemistry and Medicine, Academic Press, London, p 437–475

Danon D 1975 Biophysical aspects of red cell aging. In: Goldman R, Rockstein M (eds) The Physiology and Pathology of Human Aging, Academic Press, New York, p 47–62

Das K C, Herbert V 1976 Vitamin B_{12}-folate interrelations. Clinics in Haematology 5: 697–745

Das K C, Herbert V, Colman N, Longo D L 1978 Unmasking covert folate deficiency in iron-deficient subjects with neutrophil hypersegmentation: dU suppression tests on lymphocytes and bone marrow. British Journal of Haematology 39: 357–375

Datta S B 1975 Letter to the editor. Modern Geriatrics 5: 3

Davey F R, Huntington S 1977 Age-related variation in lymphocyte subpopulations. Gerontology 23: 381–389

Davies D F, Shock N W 1950 Age changes in glomerular filtration rate, effective renal plasma flow and tubular excretory capacity in adult males. Journal of Clinical Investigation 29: 496–507

Davis S 1976 The variable pattern of circulating lymphocyte subpopulations in chronic lymphocytic leukemia. New England Journal of Medicine 294: 1150–1153

Dawson A A, Donald D 1966 The serum vitamin B_{12} in the elderly. Gerontologia Clinica 8: 220–225

Dawson A A, Ogston D 1972 The effect of age on the diagnostic value of greying of the hair in Addisonian pernicious anaemia. Gerontologia Clinica 14: 317–320

Dawson A A, Ogston D, Fullerton H W 1969 Evaluation of diagnostic significance of certain symptoms and physical signs in anaemic patients. British Medical Journal iii: 436–439

Dawson J B 1960 The ESR in a new dress. British Medical Journal i: 1697–1704

De Gruchy G C 1975a In: Drug-induced Blood Disorders. Blackwell, Oxford, p 156–182

De Gruchy G C 1975b In: Drug-induced Blood Disorders. Blackwell, Oxford, p 39–75

De Gruchy G C 1975c In: Drug-induced Blood Disorders. Blackwell, Oxford, p 76–117

De Gruchy G C 1975d In: Drug-induced Blood Disorders. Blackwell, Oxford, p 118–155

Denham M J, Sneath P, Walford D M 1973 Treatment of a case of Factor VIII inhibitor in an elderly female. Gerontologia Clinica 15: 10–14

De Nicola P, Morsiani M 1975 Blood diseases. In: von Hahn H P (ed) Practical Geriatrics, Karger, Basel, p 210–228

Department of Health and Social Security 1969 Recommended intakes of nutrients for the UK. Reports on Public Health and Medical Subjects, No. 120. HMSO, London

Department of Health and Social Security 1970 First report by the panel on nutrition of the elderly. Reports on Public Health and Medical Subjects, No. 123. HMSO, London

Department of Health and Social Security 1972 A nutritional survey of the elderly. Reports on Health and Social Subjects, No. 3. HMSO, London

Derycke C, Fine J M, Boffa G A 1965 Dysglobulinémies 'essentielles', chez les sujets âgés. Nouvelle Revue Hematologique 5: 729–738

Desforges, J F, Rutherford C J, Piro A 1979 Hodgkin's disease. New England Journal of Medicine 301: 1212–1222

Detraglia M, Cook F B, Stasiw D M, Cerny L C 1974 Erythrocyte fragility in aging. Biochimica et Biophysica Acta 345: 213–219

Deykin D 1982 Current status of anticoagulant therapy. American Journal of Medicine 72: 659–664

Díaz-Jouanen E, Strickland R G, Williams R C Jr 1975 Studies of human lymphocytes in the newborn and the aged. American Journal of Medicine 58: 620–628

Dibble M V, Brin M, Thiele V F, Peel A, Chen N, McMullen E 1967 Evaluation of the nutritional status of elderly subjects, with a comparison between fall and spring. Journal of the American Geriatrics Society 15: 1031–1061

Dintenfass L, Julian D G, Miller G 1966 Viscosity of blood in normal subjects and in patients suffering from coronary occlusion and arterial thrombosis. American Heart Journal 71: 587–600

Dintenfass L, Lake B 1976 Beta-blockers and blood viscosity. Lancet i: 1026

Dintenfass L, Stewart J H 1974 Aggregation of red cells and plasma viscosity in renal patients treated by haemodialysis or kidney graft. Effect of proteins and ABO blood groups. Microvascular Research 7: 342–350

Disler P B, Lynch S R, Charlton R W, Torrance J D, Bothwell T H 1975 The effect of tea on iron absorption. Gut 16: 193–200

Disselduff M M, Murphy E La C 1968 Leucocyte vitamin C levels in elderly patients with reference to dietary intake and clinical findings. In: Exton-Smith A N, Scott D L (eds) Vitamins in the Elderly, John Wright & Sons Ltd, Bristol, p 60–65

Ditzel J, Kampmann J 1971 Whole-blood viscosity, hematocrit and plasma protein in normal subjects at different ages. Acta Physiologica Scandinavica 81: 264–268

Doniach D, Roitt I M 1964 An evaluation of gastric and thyroid autoimmunity in relation to hematologic disorders. Seminars in Hematology 1: 313–343

Dreyfus J C, Kahn A, Marie J, Mennecier F, Skala S, Vibert M 1979 Aging of enzyme molecules in the blood. In: Orimo H, Shimada K, Iriki M, Maeda D (eds). Recent Advances in Gerontology (Proceedings of XI International Congress of Gerontology, Tokyo, 1978), Excerpta Medica, Amsterdam, p 74–76

Droller H, Dossett J A 1959 Vitamin B₁₂ levels in senile dementia and confusional states. Gerontologia Clinica 1: 96–106

Dukes P P, Shore N A, Hammond G D, Ortega J A 1975 Prostaglandins and erythropoietin action in erythropoiesis. In: Nakao K, Fisher J W, Takaku F (eds). Erythropoiesis, University Park Press, Baltimore, p 3–14

Durie B G M, Salmon S E 1982 The current status and future prospects of treatment for multiple myeloma. Clinics in Haematology 11: 181–210

Dyer E L 1979 Epstein-Barr mononucleosis in older persons. Journal of the Indiana State Medical Association 72: 526–527

Dymock S M, Brocklehurst J C 1973 Clinical effects of water soluble vitamin supplementation in geriatric patients. Age and Ageing 2: 172–176

Earney W W, Earney A J 1972 Geriatric hematology. Journal of the American Geriatrics Society 20: 174–177

Earney W W, Earney A J, Graham J D 1975 Effects of aging on granulopoietic activity (colony-stimulating factor). Journal of the American Geriatrics Society 23: 175–179

Eastham R D 1973 ESR vs plasma viscosity readings in the old. British Medical Journal iv: 612–613

Eastmond C J, Woodrow J C 1976 Lack of association between the HL-A system and pernicious anaemia. British Journal of Haematology 33: 113–116

Eaton J W, Brewer G J 1974 Pentose phosphate metabolism In: Surgenor D N (ed) The Red Blood Cell, 2nd edn. Academic Press, New York, Vol I, p 435–471

Eccles J T 1975 Control of warfarin therapy in the elderly. Age & Ageing 4: 161–165

Eddleston A L W F, Rake M O, Pagaltsos A P, Osborn S B, Williams R 1971 ⁷⁵Se-selenomethionine in the scintiscan diagnosis of primary hepatocellular carcinoma. Gut 12: 235–249

Edelman I S, Haley H B, Schloerb P R, Sheldon D B, Friis-Hansen B J, Stoll G, Moore F D 1952 Further observations on total body water. I. Normal values throughout the life span. Surgery, Gynecology and Obstetrics 95: 1–12

Edson J R 1974 Mechanisms and dynamics of intravascular coagulation. Geriatrics 29: 65–78 (Feb)

Elsborg L 1976 Reversible malabsorption of folic acid in the elderly with nutritional folate deficiency. Acta Haematologica 55: 140–147

Elsborg L, Lund V, Bastrup-Madsen P 1976 Serum vitamin B₁₂ levels in the aged. Acta Medica Scandinavica 200: 309–314

Elsborg L, Mosbech J 1979 Pernicious anaemia as a risk factor in gastric cancer. Acta Medica Scandinavica 206: 315–318

Elwood P C 1971 Epidemiological aspects of iron deficiency in the elderly. Gerontologia Clinica 13: 2–11

Elwood P C, Williams G 1970 A comparative trial of slow-release and conventional iron preparations. Practitioner 204: 812–815

Elwood P C, Shinton N K, Wilson C I D, Sweetnam P, Frazer A C 1971 Haemoglobin, vitamin B₁₂ and folate levels in the elderly. British Journal of Haematology 21: 557–563

Englisova M, Englis M, Kyral V, Kourilek K, Dvorak K 1968 Changes of immunoglobulin synthesis in old people. Experimental Gerontology 3: 125–127

Eriksson S, Clase L, Moquist-Olsson I 1981 Pernicious anaemia as a risk factor in gastric cancer. The extent of the problem. Acta Medica Scandinavica 210: 481–484

Eskeland G 1962 Prevention of venous thrombosis and pulmonary embolism in injured patients. Lancet i: 1035–1037

Evans D M D 1971 Haematological aspects of iron deficiency in the elderly. Gerontologia Clinica 13: 12–30

Evans D M D, Pathy M S, Sanerkin N G, Deeble T J 1968 Anaemia in geriatric patients. Gerontologia Clinica 10: 228–241

Everett N B, Caffrey R W, Rieke W O 1964 Recirculation of lymphocytes. In: Symposium on leukopoiesis in health and disease. Annals of the New York Academy of Sciences 113: 887–897

Exton-Smith A N 1971 Nutrition of the elderly. British Journal of Hospital Medicine 5: 639–646

Exton-Smith A N, Osborne G 1961 Barium studies in the aged. British Medical Journal i: 1799–1802

Exton-Smith A N, Stanton B R 1965 Report of an investigation into the dietary of elderly women living alone. King Edward's Hospital Fund for London

Fagerhol M K, Abildgaard U 1970 Immunological studies on human antithrombin III. Influence of age, sex and use of oral contraceptives on serum concentration. Scandinavian Journal of Haematology 7: 10–17

Fairley G H 1971 Treatment of malignant blood diseases. In: Goldberg A, Brain M C (eds) Recent Advances in Haematology, Churchill Livingstone, Edinburgh, p 219–248

Fearnley G R, Chakrabarti R, Avis P R D 1963 Blood fibrinolytic activity in diabetes mellitus and its bearing on ischaemic heart disease and obesity. British Medical Journal i: 921–923

Feinstein D I 1982 Diagnosis and management of disseminated intravascular coagulation: the role of heparin therapy. Blood 60: 284–287

Feinstein R J, Halprin K M, Penneys N S, Taylor J R, Schenkman J 1973 Senile purpura. Archives of Dermatology and Syphilology 108: 229–232

Fernandez G, Schwartz J M 1976 Immune responsiveness and hematologic malignancy in the elderly. Medical Clinics of North America 60: 1253–1271

Fielding J 1965 Differential ferrioxamine test for measuring chelatable body iron. Journal of Clinical Pathology 18: 88–97

Fielding J, O'Shaughnessy M C, Brunström G M 1965 Iron deficiency without anaemia. Lancet ii: 9–12

Finch C A, Deubelbeiss K, Cook J D, Eschbach J W, Harker L A, Funk D D et al 1970 Ferrokinetics in man. Medicine (Baltimore) 49: 17–53

Finger H, Emmerling P, Hof H 1973 Serumimmunoglobulin — Spiegel im Senium. Deutsche medizinische Wochenschrift 98: 2455–2456

Fisher J W 1980a Prostaglandins and kidney erythropoietin production. Nephron 25: 53–56

Fisher J W 1980b Mechanisms of the anemia of chronic renal failure. Nephron 25: 106–111

Fitzgerald G A, Maas R L, Stein R, Oates J H, Roberts L U 1981 Intravenous prostacyclin in thrombotic thrombocytopenic purpura, Annals of Internal Medicine 95: 319–322

Fitzgerald P H 1975 A mechanism of X-chromosome aneuploidy in lymphocytes of aging women. Humangenetik 28: 153–158

Fixa B, Komárková O, Nožička Z 1975 Ageing and auto-immunity. Gerontologia 21: 117–123

Flanagan R J, Lewis R R, Hyams D E 1977. Unpublished observations.

Fliedner T M, Cronkite E P, Robertson J S 1964 Granulocytopoiesis: I. Senescence and random loss of neutrophilic granulocytes in human beings. Blood 24: 402–414

Foon K A, Zighelboim J, Yale C, Gale R P 1981 Intensive chemotherapy is the treatment of choice for elderly patients with acute myelogenous leukaemia. Blood 58: 467–470

Ford M J, Innes J A, Parrish F M, Allan N C, Horn D B, Munro J F 1979 The significance of gross elevations of the erythrocyte sedimentation rate in a general medical unit. European Journal of Clinical Investigation 9: 191–194

Forman J, Möller G 1973 The effector cell in antibody induced cell-mediated immunity. Transplantation Review 17: 108–149

Franklin E C, Lowenstein J, Bigelow B, Meltzer M 1964 Heavy chain disease — new disorders of serum gamma-globulins. American Journal of Medicine 37: 332–350

Freedman M L, Marcus D L 1980 Anemia and the elderly: is it physiology or pathology? American Journal of Medical Sciences 280: 81–85

Friedman G D, Siegelaub A B, Seltzer C C, Feldman R, Collen M F 1973 Smoking habits and the leukocyte count. Archives of Environmental Health 26: 137–143

Frizzera G, Moran E M, Rappaport H 1974 Angio-immunoblastic lymphadenopathy with dysproteinemia. Lancet i: 1070–1073

Fu Y S, Perzin K H 1978 Nonepithelial tumours of the nasal cavity, paranasal sinuses and nasopharynx. A clinicopathologic study. IX. Plasmacytomas. Cancer 42: 2399–2406

Fuccella L M 1979 Clinical pharmacology of inhibitors of platelet aggregation. Pharmacological Research Communications 11: 825–852

Fudenberg H H, Virella G 1980 Multiple myeloma and Waldenström macroglobulinemia: unusual presentations. Seminars in Hematology 17: 63–79

Fulcher R A, Hyland C M 1981 Effectiveness of once daily oral iron in the elderly. Age and Ageing 10: 44–46

Fullerton J M, Phaur T 1966 Unusual case of a nonagenarian with reticulum-cell sarcoma presenting as acute haemolytic anaemia. Journal of the American Geriatrics Society 14: 954–957

Galton D A G 1971 Treatment of myelomatosis — Medical Research Council trial. British Medical Journal ii: 323–324

Galton D A G, Goldman J M, Wiltshaw E, Catovsky D, Henry K, Goldenberg G J 1974 Prolymphocytic leukaemia. British Journal of Haematology 27: 7–23

Galton D A G, Peto R 1968 A progress report on the Medical Research Council's therapeutic trial in myelomatosis. British Journal of Haematology 15: 319–320

Gantmacher M L 1979 Antiplatelet agents: a review. Journal of the Royal Society of Medicine 72: 513–519

Ganzoni A M, Barras J P, Marti H R 1976 Red cell aging and death (editorial). Vox Sanguinis 30: 161–174

Gardner F H, Helmer R E III 1980 Aminocaproic acid. Use in control of hemorrhage in patients with amegakaryocytic thrombocytopenia. Journal of the American Medical Association 243: 35–37

Garrett J V, Newton R K 1979 Lymphoproliferative disease in two sisters. British Medical Journal i: 234–235

Geary C G, Catovsky D, Wiltshaw E, Milner G R, Scholes M C, Van Noorden S et al 1975 Chronic myelomonocytic leukaemia. British Journal of Haematology 30: 289–302

Geill T 1969 On the treatment of the nephrogenic anaemias with a combined cobalt-iron preparation. Gerontologia Clinica 11: 48–55

Gersovitz M, Munro H N, Udall J, Young V R 1980 Albumin synthesis in young and elderly subjects using a new stable isotope methodology: response to level of protein intake. Metabolism 29: 1075–1086

Gibbins F J, Collins H J, Hall R G P, Dellipiani A W 1974 Endoscopy in the elderly. Age and Ageing 3: 240–244

Gibson I I J M 1972 The value of the erythrocyte sedimentation rate in the aged. Gerontologia Clinica 14: 185–190

Gibson J G, Evans W A 1937 Clinical studies of the blood volume: II. The relation of plasma and total blood volume to venous pressure, blood velocity rate, physical measurements, age and sex in 90 normal humans. Journal of Clinical Investigation 16: 317–328

Gilbert H S 1973 The spectrum of myeloproliferative disorders. Medical Clinics of North America 57: 355–393

Gilbertsen V A 1965 Erythrocyte sedimentation rates in older patients: a study of 4341 cases. Postgraduate Medicine 38: A44–52

Gillette R W 1975 Change in the migration patterns of spleen and lymph node cells associated with thymectomy and aging. Journal of the Reticuloendothelial Society 18: 204–208

Girdwood R H 1969 Nutritional folate deficiency in the United Kingdom. Scottish Medical Journal 14: 296–304

Girdwood R H, Thomson A D, Williamson J 1967 Folate status in the elderly. British Medical Journal i: 670–671

Glass G B J, Boyd L J, Gellin G A, Stephanson L 1954 Uptake of radioactive vitamin B_{12} by the liver in humans: test for measurement of intestinal absorption of vitamin B_{12} and intrinsic factor activity. Archives of Biochemistry 51: 251–257

Glass G B J, Goldbloom A A, Boyd L J, Laughton R, Rosen S, Rich M 1956 Intestinal absorption and hepatic uptake of radioactive vitamin B_{12} in various age groups and the effect of intrinsic factor preparations. American Journal of Clinical Nutrition 4: 124–133

Glass R 1971 Factitiously low ESR with chronic lymphocytic leukemia. New England Journal of Medicine 285: 921

Glenner G G, Terry W D, Harada M, Isersky C, Page D 1971 Amyloid fibril proteins: proof of homology with immunoglobulin light chains by sequence analyses. Science 172: 1150–1151

Glenner G G, Terry W D, Isersky C 1973 Amyloidosis: its nature and pathogenesis. Seminars in Hematology 10: 65–86

Goldberg A 1963 The anaemia of scurvy. Quarterly Journal of Medicine 32: 51–64

Goldman J M 1978 Modern approaches to the management of chronic granulocytic leukemia. Seminars in Hematology 15: 420–430

Goldsmith M A, Carter S K 1974 Combination chemotherapy of advanced Hodgkin's disease: a review. Cancer 33: 1–8

Gore M E, Riches P G, Kohn J 1979 Indentification of the paraprotein and clinical significance of more than one paraprotein in serum of 56 patients. Journal of Clinical Pathology 32: 313–317

Gralnick H R, Greipp P 1971 Thrombosis with epsilon-aminocaproic acid therapy. American Journal of Clinical Pathology 56: 151–154

Grann V, Erichson R, Flannery J, Finch S, Clarkson B 1974 The therapy of acute granulocytic leukemia in patients more than 50 years old. Annals of Internal Medicine 80: 15–20

Grant W C, Le Grande M C 1964 The influence of age on erythropoiesis in the rat. Journal of Gerontology 19: 505–509

Gräsbeck R, Salonen E-M 1976 Vitamin B_{12}. Progress in Food and Nutrition Science 2: 193–231

Greaves M F, Owen J T, Raff M C 1973 T and B Lymphocytes. North-Holland, Amsterdam

Greipp P R, Kyle R A, Bowie E J 1981 Factor X deficiency in amyloidosis: a critical review. American Journal of Hematology 11: 443–450

Griffiths L L, Brocklehurst J C, Scott D L, Marks J, Blackley J 1967 Thiamine and ascorbic acid levels in the elderly. Gerontologia Clinica 9: 1–10

Griffiths L L, Nicholson W J, O'Gorman P (1970) A haematological study of 500 elderly females. Gerontologia Clinica 12: 18–32

Gross R T, Schroeder E A R, Brounstein S A 1963 Energy metabolism in the erythrocytes of premature infants compared to full-term newborn infants and adults. Blood 21: 755–763

Grundbacher F-J, Scheffler D C 1970 Changes in human serum immunoglobulin levels with age and sex. Zeitschrift für Immunitatsforschung, Experimentelle und Klinische Immunologie 141: 20–26

Guest M M, Bond T B 1964 Coagulation, fibrinolysis and circulation in aging organisms In: Hansen P F (ed) Age with a Future: Proceedings of the 6th International Congress of Gerontology, Munksgaard, Copenhagen, p 334–339

Gunz F, Baikie A G 1974 In: Leukemia (Dameshek & Gunz's Leukemia, 3rd edn) Grune & Stratton, New York

Hadnagy Cs 1978 Infectious mononucleosis in the case of two elderly (80 & 57 years old age) patients. Aktuelle Gerontologie 8: 153–158

Haggie M 1952 Indications for barium enema in the diagnosis of carcinoma of the colon. Lancet i: 21–23

Hall C A 1981 Vitamin B_{12} deficiency and early rise in mean corpuscular volume. Journal of the American Medical Association 245: 1144–1146

Hall D A 1968 Age changes in the water content of human plasma. Gerontologia Clinica 10: 193–200

Hallberg L, Harwerth H-G, Vannotti A (eds) 1970 Iron Deficiency: Pathogenesis, clinical aspects, therapy. Academic Press, London

Hallberg L, Högdahl A-M 1971 Anaemia and old age—observations in a population sample of women in Göteborg. Gerontologia Clinica 13: 31–43

Hallén J 1963 Frequency of 'abnormal' serum globulins (M-components) in the aged. Acta Medica Scandinavica 173: 737–744

Hallén J 1966 Discrete gamma globulin (M-) components in serum. Clinical study of 150 subjects without myelomatosis. Acta Medica Scandinavica, Suppl. 462

Hallgren H M, Buckley C E III, Gilbertsen V A, Yunis E J 1973 Lymphocyte phytohemagglutinin responsiveness, immunoglobulins and autoantibodies in aging humans. Journal of Immunology 111: 1101–1107

Halsted J A, Carroll J, Rubert S 1959 Serum and tissue concentration of vitamin B_{12} in certain pathologic states. New England Journal of Medicine 260: 575–580

Hamilton P J, Dawson A A, Ogston D, Douglas A S 1974a The effect of age on the fibrinolytic enzyme system. Journal of Clinical Pathology 27: 326–329

Hamilton P J, Allardyce M, Ogston D, Dawson A A, Douglas A S 1974b The effect of age upon the coagulation system. Journal of Clinical Pathology 27: 980–982

Hamstra R D, Block M H, Schocket A L 1980 Intravenous iron dextran in clinical medicine. Journal of the American Medical Association 243: 1726–1731

Harant Z, Goldberger J V 1975 Treatment of anemia in the aged: a common problem and challenge. Journal of the American Geriatrics Society 23: 127–131

Hardisty R M 1969 Haemorrhagic disorders due to functional abnormalities of platelets. Journal of the Royal College of Physicians (London) 3: 182–192

Hardisty R M, Weatherall D J (eds) 1974 Blood and its Disorders. Blackwell, Oxford

Harkness J 1971 The viscosity of human blood plasma; its measurement in health and disease. Biorheology 8: 171–193

Harrill I, Cervone N 1977 Vitamin status of older women. American Journal of Clinical Nutrition 30: 431–440.

Harris A I, Greenberg H 1978 Pernicious anaemia and the development of carcinoid tumours of the stomach. Journal of the American Medical Association 239: 1160–1161

Harris G J 1972 Plasma viscometry and ESR in the elderly. Medical and Laboratory Technology 29: 405–410

Harrison D E 1975 Defective erythropoietic responses of aged mice *not* improved by young marrow. Journal of Gerontology 30: 286–288

Harrison D E 1979 Proliferative capacity of erythropoietic stem cell lines and aging: an overview. Mechanisms of Ageing and Development 9: 409–426

Hart A, Cohen H 1969 Capillary fragility studies in diabetes. British Medical Journal ii: 89–91

Hartsock R J, Smith E B, Petty C S 1965 Normal variations with aging of the amount of hematopoietic tissue in bone marrow from the anterior iliac crest. American Journal of Clinical Pathology 43: 326–331

Hawkins W W, Speck E, Leonard V G 1954 Variation of the hemoglobin level with age and sex. Blood 9: 999–1007.

Hayes G S, Stinson I N 1976 Erythrocyte sedimentation rate and age. Archives of Ophthalmology (New York) 94: 939–940

Hayes M J, Langman M J S, Short A H 1975 Changes in drug metabolism with increasing age. I. Warfarin binding and plasma proteins. British Journal of Clinical Pharmacology 2: 69–72

Hazell K, Baloch K H 1970 Vitamin K deficiency in the elderly. Gerontologia Clinica 12: 10–17

Hedlund P O, Blombäck M 1981 The effects of low-dose heparin treatment on patients undergoing transvesical prostatectomy. Urology Research 9: 147–152

Heilmeyer L 1966 Die Altransferrinämien. Acta Haematologica 36: 40–49

Heimpel H, Heit W 1980 Drug-induced aplastic anaemia: clinical aspects. Clinics in Haematology 9: 641–662

Heinle R W, Welch A D, Scharf V, Meacham G C, Prusoff W H 1952 Studies of excretion (and absorption) of Co^{60} labeled vitamin B_{12} in pernicious anemia. Transactions of the Association of American Physicians 65: 214–221

Helman N, Rubinstein L S 1975 The effect of age, sex and smoking on erythrocytes and leukocytes. American Journal of Clinical Pathology 63: 35–44

Herbert V 1959 In: The Megaloblastic Anaemias. Grune & Stratton, New York, p 9

Herbert V 1962 Experimental nutritional folate deficiency in man. Transactions of the Association of American Physicians 75: 307–320

Herbert V 1971 Recent developments in cobalamin metabolism. In: Arnstein H R V, Wrighton R J (eds) The Cobalamins: a Glaxo symposium, Churchill Livingstone, Edinburgh, p 2–16

Herbert V 1981 Vitamin B_{12}. American Journal of Clinical Nutrition 34: 971–972 (Letter)

Herbert V, Jacob E 1974 Destruction of vitamin B_{12} by ascorbic acid. Journal of the American Medical Association 230: 241–242

Herbert V, Jacob E, Wong K-T J, Pfeffer R D 1978 Low serum vitamin B_{12} levels in patients receiving ascorbic acid in megadoses: studies concerning the effect of ascorbate on radioisotope vitamin B_{12} assay. American Journal of Clinical Nutrition 31: 253–258

Hewick D S, Moreland T A, Shepherd A M M, Stevenson I H 1975 The effect of age on the sensitivity to warfarin sodium. British Journal of Clinical Pharmacology 2: 189P–190P

Hilder F M, Gunz F W 1964 The effects of age on normal values of the Westergren sedimentation rate. Journal of Clinical Pathology 17: 292–293

Hill R D 1976 The prevalence of anaemia in the over 65s in a rural practice. Practitioner 217: 963–967

Hilton J G, Goodbody M F Jr, Kruesi U R 1955 The effect of prolonged administration of ammonium chloride on the blood acid-base equilibrium of geriatric subjects. Journal of the American Geriatrics Society 3: 697–703

Hirschhorn K, Weissmann G 1965 Isolation and properties of human leukocyte lysosomes in vitro. Proceedings of the Society of Experimental Biology and Medicine 119: 36–39

Hirsh J 1978 Platelet inhibitors in the treatment of thrombosis. Clinical and Investigative Medicine 1: 191–206

Hirsh J, Hale G S, McDonald I G, McCarthy R A, Pitt A 1968 Streptokinase therapy in acute major pulmonary embolism: effectiveness and problems. British Medical Journal iv: 729–734

Hjelt K, Attrup Rasmussen P, Munck O 1977 Determination of ^{58}Co-vitamin B_{12} absorption in pernicious anemia by use of whole body counting. Reproducibility and control of gut transit time. Acta Medica Scandinavica 201: 167–171

Hobbs J 1967 Paraproteins, benign or malignant? British Medical Journal iii: 699–704

Hobbs J 1969 Immunochemical classes of myelomatosis, including data from a therapeutic trial conducted by a Medical Research Council working party. British Journal of Haematology 16: 599–606

Hobbs J 1971 Myeloma workshop: modes of escape from therapeutic control in myelomatosis. British Medical Journal ii: 325

Hobbs J R 1973 An ABC of amyloid. Proceedings of the Royal Society of Medicine 66: 705–710

Hobbs J R 1978 Monitoring immunocytoma. Minerva Medica 69: 2499–2506

Hodes C 1971 Geriatric screening and care in group practice. Journal of the Royal College of General Practitioners 21: 469–472

Hodkinson H M 1973 Serum calcium in a geriatric inpatient population. Age and Ageing 2: 157–162

Hodkinson H M, Bryson E, Kelnerman L, Clarke M B, Wootton R 1979 Sex, sunlight, season, diet and the vitamin D status of elderly patients. Journal of Clinical and Experimental Gerontology 1: 13–22

Hodkinson H M, Exton-Smith A N 1976 Factors predicting mortality in the elderly in the community. Age and Ageing 5: 110–115

Hodkinson H M, Hodkinson I 1980 Range for 25-hydroxyvitamin D in elderly subjects in whom osteomalacia has been excluded on histological & biochemical criteria. Journal of Clinical and Experimental Gerontology 2: 133–139

Hoffbrand A V 1971 The megaloblastic anaemias. In: Goldberg A & Brain M C (eds) Recent Advances in Haematology, Churchill Livingstone, Edinburgh, p 1–76

Hoffbrand A V, Chanarin I, Kremenchuzky S, Szur L, Waters A H, Mollin D L 1968 Megaloblastic anaemia in myelosclerosis. Quarterly Journal of Medicine 37: 493–516

Hoffbrand A V, Newcombe B F A, Mollin D L 1966 Method of assay of red cell folate and the value of the assay as a test for folate deficiency. Journal of Clinical Pathology 19: 17–28

Hoffman N R 1970 The relationship between pernicious anemia and carcinoma of the stomach. Geriatrics 25: 90–95 (April)

Hogenkamp HPC 1980 The interaction between vitamin B_{12} and vitamin C. American Journal of Clinical Nutrition 33: 1–3

Hollander D, Morgan D 1979 Aging: its influence on vitamin A absorption in vivo by the rat. Experimental Gerontology 14: 301–305

Holmes J M 1956 Cerebral manifestations of vitamin B_{12} deficiency. British Medical Journal ii: 1394–1398

Holmes F F, Hearne E, Conant M, Garlow W 1979 Survival in the elderly with acute leukemia. Journal of the American Geriatrics Society 27: 241–243

Holt J M 1970 Splenectomy and blood disorders. British Journal of Hospital Medicine 3: 31–39

Hoorn R K J, Flikweert J P, Westerink D 1975 Vitamin B_1, B_2 and B_6 deficiencies in geriatric patients, measured by coenzyme stimulation of enzyme activities. Clinica Chimica Acta 61: 151–162

Hoppner K, Lampi B 1980 Folate levels in human liver from autopsies in Canada. American Journal of Clinical Nutrition 33: 862–864

Horton M A, Oliver R T D 1976 HL-A and pernicious anemia. New England Journal of Medicine 294: 396–397

Horwitz C A, Henle W, Henle G, Segel M, Arnold T, Lewis F B et al 1976 Clinical and laboratory evaluation of elderly patients with heterophil-antibody positive infectious mononucleosis. American Journal of Medicine 61: 333–339

Howe R B 1979 Tips on diagnosing and treating anemia in the aging. Geriatrics 34(12): 29–36 (Dec)

Howe R B Bloomfield C D, McKenna R W 1982 Hypocellular acute leukemia. American Journal of Medicine 72: 391–395

Htoo M S H, Kofkoff R L, Freedman M L 1979 Erythrocyte parameters in the elderly: An argument against new geriatric normal values. Journal of the American Geriatrics Society 27: 547–551

Huehns E 1971 Biochemical compensation in anaemia. In: Gilliland I, Francis J (eds). The Scientific Basis of Medicine Annual Review, The Athlone Press, University of London, p 216–231

Huehns E R 1974a Control of red cell oxygen affinity by 2, 3-DPG in disease. In: Huntsman R G, Jenkins G C (eds). Advanced Haematology, Butterworth, London, p 38–55

Huehns E R 1974b The structure and function of haemoglobin: clinical disorders due to abnormal haemoglobin structure. In: Hardisty R M, Weatherall D J (eds). Blood and its Disorders, Blackwell, Oxford, p 526–629e

Hughes D, Elwood P C, Shinton N K, Wrighton R J 1970 Clinical trial of the effect of vitamin B_{12} in elderly subjects with low serum B_{12} levels. British Medical Journal ii: 458–460

Hughes P, Gauld W R 1966 Bacterial endocarditis: a changing disease. Quarterly Journal of Medicine 35: 511–520

Hull R, Delmore T, Genton E, Hirsh J, Gent M, Sackett D et al 1979 Warfarin sodium versus low-dose heparin in the long-term treatment of venous thrombosis. New England Journal of Medicine 301: 855–858

Hume R, Dagg J H, Goldberg A 1973 Refractory anaemia with dysproteinemia: long-term therapy with low-dose corticosteroids. Blood 41: 27–35

Hurdle A D F, Rosin A J 1962 Red cell volume and red cell survival in normal aged people. Journal of Clinical Pathology 15: 343–345

Hurdle A D F, Williams T C P 1966 Folic acid deficiency in elderly patients admitted to hospital. British Medical Journal ii: 202–205

Hussain S 1976 Disorders of hemostasis and thrombosis in the aged. Medical Clinics of North America 60: 1273–1287

Hussein S, Prieto J, O'Shea M, Hoffbrand A V, Baillod R A, Moorhead J F 1975 Serum ferritin assay and iron status in in chronic renal failure and haemodialysis. British Medical Journal i: 546–548

Hyams D E 1964 The absorption of vitamin B_{12} in the elderly. Gerontologia Clinica 6: 193–206

Hyams D E, Ross E J 1963 Scurvy, megaloblastic anaemia and osteoporosis. British Journal of Clinical Practice 17: 332–340

Israels M C 1975 Anaemia in geriatrics. Modern Geriatrics 5: 17–22

Ivanova N I 1978 Age characteristics of the phagocytic reaction of neutrophils. Vrachebnoe Delo 5: 49

Jackson H R Jr, Parker F Jr 1947 Hodgkin's Disease and Allied Disorders. Oxford University Press, New York

Jacob H S 1974 Hypersplenism: mechanism and management. British Journal of Haematology 27: 1–5

Jacobs A 1962 Post-cricoid carcinoma in patients with pernicious anaemia. British Medical Journal ii: 91–92

Jacobs A 1971 The effect of iron deficiency on the tissues. Gerontologia Clinica 13: 61–68

Jacobs A 1975 The clinical use of serum ferritin estimation. British Journal of Haematology 31: 1–3

Jacobs A, Cavill I A J 1968 Pyridoxine and riboflavine status in the Paterson-Kelly syndrome. British Journal of Haematology 14: 153–160

Jacobs A, Cavill I A J, Hughes J N P 1968 Erythrocyte transaminase activity—effect of age, sex and vitamin B_6 supplementation. American Journal of Clinical Nutrition 21: 502–507

Jacobs A, Miller F, Worwood M, Beamish M R, Wardrop C A 1972 Ferritin in the serum of normal subjects and patients with iron deficiency and iron overload. British Medical Journal iv: 206–208

Jacobs A, Waters W E, Campbell H, Barrow A 1969 A random sample from Wales. III. Serum iron, iron binding capacity and transferrin saturation. British Journal of Haematology 17: 581–587

Jacobs A, Worwood M (eds) 1974 Iron in Biochemistry and Medicine. Academic Press, London

Jacobs A, Worwood M 1975 Ferritin: clinical aspects. In: Kief H (ed) Iron Metabolism and its Disorders, Excerpta Medica, Amsterdam, p 90–96

Jacobs A M, Owen G M 1969 The effect of age on iron absorption. Journal of Gerontology 24: 95–96

Jacobs P 1971 Body iron loss in the geriatric patient. Gerontologia Clinica 13: 207–214

Jacobs P A, Court Brown W M 1966 Age and chromosomes. Nature 212: 823–824

Jacobs P A, Court Brown W M, Doll R 1961 Distribution of human chromosome counts in relation to age. Nature 191: 1178–1180

Jacobson B M, Vickery A L Jr 1968 Case records of the Massachusetts General Hospital: (Case 1-1968). New England Journal of Medicine 278: 36–43

Jain S K, Hochstein P 1980 Polymerization of membrane components in aging red blood cells. Biochemical and Biophysical Research Communications 92: 247–254

Jamshidi K, Ansari A, Windschitl H E, Swaim W R 1973 Primary thrombocythemia. Geriatrics 28: 121–133 (Jan)

Jarvik L F, Yen F-S, Fu T-K, Matsuyama S S 1976 Chromosomes in old age: a six-year longitudinal study. Human Genetics 33: 17–22

Johansson B 1971 Myeloma workshop: prognostic factors in myelomatosis. British Medical Journal ii: 327–328

Joske R A, Finckh E S, Wood I J 1955 Gastric biopsy: a study of 1000 consecutive successful gastric biopsies. Quarterly Journal of Medicine 24: 269–294

Kalff M W 1970 A population study of serum immunoglobulin levels. Clinica Chimica Acta 28: 277–289

Kapsch D N, Adelstein E H, Rhodes G R, Silver D 1979 Heparin-induced thrombocytopenia, thrombosis, and hemorrhage. Surgery 86: 148–155

Kardinal C G, Bateman J R, Weiner J 1976 Chronic granulocytic leukemia. Archives of Internal Medicine 136: 305–313

Karpatkin S 1972 Human platelet sensescence. Annual Review of Medicine 23: 101–128

Karpatkin S, Khan Q, Freedman M 1978 Heterogeneity of platelet function: correlation with platelet volume. American Journal of Medicine 64: 542–546

Kass L 1976 Pernicious anaemia In: Major Problems in Internal Medicine, Vol II, Saunders, Philadelphia

Kass L 1978 Newer aspects of pernicious anemia. CRC Critical Reviews in Clinical and Laboratory Sciences 9: 1–47

Kass L, Schnitzer B 1975 In: Refractory Anemia, C C Thomas, Springfield, Illinois, p 113–133

Katzen H, Spagnolo S V 1980 Bone marrow necrosis from miliary tuberculosis. Journal of the American Medical Association 244: 2438–2439

Kay M M B 1976 Auto-immune disease: the consequence of deficient T-cell function? Journal of the American Geriatrics Society 24: 253–257

Kelemen E 1969 In: Physiopathology and Therapy of Human Blood Disorders, Pergamon Press, Oxford, p 80–99

Keller A R, Kaplan H S, Lukes R J, Rappaport H 1968 Correlation of histopathology with other prognostic indicators in Hodgkin's disease. Cancer (New York) 22: 487–499

Kief H (ed) 1975 Iron Metabolism and its Disorders. Excerpta Medica, Amsterdam

Kilpatrick G S, Withey J L 1965 The serum vitamin B_{12} concentration in the general population. Scandinavian Journal of Haematology 2: 220–229

Kimber C, Weintraub L R 1968 Malabsorption of iron secondary to iron deficiency. New England Journal of Medicine 279: 453–459

Kipshidze N N 1968 Quantitative changes in lipid, protein and carbohydrate metabolism in relation to age. In: Engel A, Larsson T (eds) Cancer and Aging, Thule International Symposium, Nordiska, Stockholm, p 49–57

Kiraly J F III, Feldmann J E, Wheby M S 1976 Hazards of phlebotomy in polycythemic patients with cardiovascular disease. Journal of the American Medical Association 236: 2080–2081

Kishimoto S, Takahama T, Mizumachi H 1976 In vitro immune response to the 2, 4, 6-tri-nitrophenyl determinant in aged C57 BL/65 mice: changes in the humoral immune response to, avidity for the TNP determinant and responsiveness to LPS effect with aging. Journal of Immunology 116: 294–300

Knospe W H 1979 Does therapy alter the natural history and prognosis of chronic lymphocytic leukemia? International Journal of Radiation Oncology, Biology, Physics 5: 295–298

Koeffler H P, Golde D W 1980 Human preleukemia. Annals of Internal Medicine 93: 347–353

Kohn J, Srivastava P C 1973 Paraproteinaemia in blood donors and the aged: benign and malignant. In: Peeters H (ed). Protides of the Biological Fluids — 20th Colloquium, Pergamon Press, Oxford, p 257–261

Kolhouse J F, Kondo H, Allen N C, Podell E, Allen R H 1978 Cobalamin analogues are present in human plasma and can mask cobalamin deficiency because current radio-isotope dilution assays are not specific for true cobalamin. New England Journal of Medicine 299: 785–792

Krantz S 1980 Anemia due to bone marrow failure: diagnosis and treatment. Comprehensive Therapy (Chicago) 6: 10–19

Krogh Jensen M, Mikkelsen M 1976 Cytogenetic studies in sideroblastic anaemia. Cancer 37: 271–274

Kulvin S M 1972 Erythrocyte sedimentation rates in the elderly. Archives of Ophthalmology (New York) 88: 617–618

Kyle R A 1978 Monoclonal gammopathy of underdetermined significance. Natural history in 241 cases. American Journal of Medicine 64: 814–826

Kyle R A, Bayrd E D 1975 Amyloidosis: Review of 236 cases. Medicine (Baltimore) 54: 271–300

Kyle R A, Greipp P R 1978a The laboratory investigation of monoclonal gammopathies. Mayo Clinic Proceedings 53: 719–739

Kyle R A, Greipp P R 1978b Primary systemic amyloidosis: comparison of melphalan and prednisone versus placebo. Blood 52: 818–827

Kyle R A, Greipp P R 1980 Smoldering multiple myeloma. New England Journal of Medicine 302: 1347–1349

Kyle R A, Elveback L R 1976 Management and prognosis of multiple myeloma. Mayo Clinic Proceedings 51: 751–760

La Celle P L, Kirkpatrick F H, Udkow M P, Arkin B 1973 Membrane fragmentation and Ca^{++}-membrane interaction: potential mechanisms of shape change in the senescent red cell. In: Bessis M, Weed R I, Leblond P F (eds) Red Cell Shape, Springer-Verlag, Berlin, p 69–78

Lancet 1969 Screening for vitamin B_{12} deficiency. Lancet ii: 309–310

Lancet 1976a ESR or ZSR? Lancet i: 1394–1395

Lancet 1976b Folic acid and the nervous system. Lancet ii: 836

Lancet 1983 Blood and alcohol (leading article). Lancet i: 397

Landsteiner K 1939 In: Cowdry E A (ed) Problems of Aging, 2nd edn. Williams & Wilkins, Baltimore, p 142

Lane R J M, Gill G V 1974 Standardization of the ESR. British Medical Journal iii: 577

Lange R D 1976 Erythrocytosis associated with normal blood-gas values. Advances in Internal Medicine 21: 309–333

Lawson D H, Murray R M, Parker J L W 1972 Early mortality in the megaloblastic anaemias. Quarterly Journal of Medicine 41: 1–14

Lawson I R 1960 Anaemia in a group of elderly patients. Gerontologia Clinica 2: 87–101

Layrisse M 1975 Dietary iron absorption. In: Kief H (ed) Iron Metabolism and its Disorders, Excerpta Medica, Amsterdam, p 25

Leach S 1976 What influence has immunology on ageing? Modern Geriatrics 7: 31–35

Leask R G S, Andrews G R, Caird F I 1973 Normal values for sixteen blood constituents in the elderly. Age and Ageing 2: 14–23

Lee B J, Sahakian G, Clarkson B D, Krakoff I H 1974 Combination chemotherapy of multiple myeloma with Alkeran, Cytoxan, vincristine, prednisone and BCNU. Cancer 33: 533–538

Lee M, Schwartz R N, Sharifi R 1981 Warfarin resistance and vitamin K. Annals of Internal Medicine 94: 140–141 (letter)

Lessin L S, Klug P P, Jensen W N 1976 Clinical implications of red cell shape. Advances in Internal Medicine 21: 451–500

Lester E, Skinner R K, Wills M R 1977 Seasonal variation in serum-25-hydroxyvitamin D in the elderly in Britain. Lancet i: 979–980

Levitt S H 1975 Clarifying the use of radiotherapy for non-Hodgkin's lymphomas. Geriatrics 30(10): 97–99 (October).

Lewis S M 1965 Course and prognosis of aplastic anaemia. British Medical Journal i: 1027–1031

Lewis S M 1967 Paroxysmal nocturnal haemoglobinuria. Hospital Medicine 1: 701–708

Lewis S M 1971 Aplastic anaemia. British Journal of Hospital Medicine 6: 593–604

Lewis S M 1976 Polycythaemia vera. British Journal of Hospital Medicine 16: 125–132

Lewy R I, Kansu E, Gabuzda T 1979 Leukemia in patients with acquired idiopathic sideroblastic anemia: an evaluation of prognostic indicators. American Journal of Hematology 6: 323–331

Lichtman M A, Rowe J M 1982 Hyperleukocytic leukemias: rheological, clinical and therapeutic considerations. Blood 60: 279–283

Liljestrand Å, Olhagen B 1955 I. Persistently high erythrocyte sedimentation rate: diagnostic and prognostic aspects. Acta Medica Scandinavica 151: 425–439

Lindenbaum J 1979 Aspects of vitamin B_{12} and folate metabolism in malabsorption syndromes. American Journal of Medicine 67: 1037–1048

Lindström F D, Dahlström U 1978 Multiple myeloma or benign monoclonal gammopathy? A study of differential diagnostic criteria in 44 cases. Clinical Immunology and Immunopathology 10: 168–174

Linman J W 1970 Myelomonocytic leukemia and its pre-leukemic phase. Journal of Chronic Diseases 22: 713–716

Lipinski B, Worowski K, Myśliwiec M, Farbiszewski R 1969 Erythrocyte sedimentation and soluble fibrin monomer complexes. Thrombosis et Diathesis Haemorrhagica Supplement 21:196–202

Lipschitz D A, Mitchell C O, Thompson C 1981 The anemia of senescence. American Journal of Hematology 11: 47–54

Lloyd E L 1971 Serum iron levels and haematological status in the elderly. Gerontologia Clinica 13: 246–255

Lloyd K N, Williams P 1970 Reactions to total dose infusion of iron dextran in rheumatoid arthritis. British Medical Journal ii: 323–325

Loeliger E A 1975 Unusual E S R with Coombs-positive hemolytic anemia. New England Journal of Medicine 292: 808–809

Loeliger E A 1976 Coombs-test positive hemolytic anemia. New England Journal of Medicine 294: 163

Loh H S, Wilson C W M 1971 Relationship between leucocyte and plasma ascorbic acid concentrations. British Medical Journal iii: 733–735

Lombardi V, Torzellini A, Niccolai J 1968 Considerazioni sul comportamento dell'adesività piastrinica in rapporto all'età (Platelet adhesiveness in old age). Giornale di Gerontologia 16: 295–301

Lowe G D O, Drummond M M, Forbes C D, Barbenel J C 1980 The effects of age and cigarette-smoking on blood and plasma viscosity in men. Scottish Medical Journal 25: 13–17

Lukes R J, Craver L, Hall T, Rappaport H, Rubin P 1966 Report of the nomenclature committee. In Symposium: Obstacles to the control of Hodgkin's disease. Cancer Research 26 (Part 1): 1311

Lumb G 1954 Tumours of Lymphoid Tissue. Livingstone, Edinburgh

Lyman G H, Williams C C, Preston D 1980 The use of lithium carbonate to reduce infection and leukopenia during systemic chemotherapy. New England Journal of Medicine 302: 257–260

Lyngbye J, Krøll J 1971 Quantitative immunoelectrophoresis of proteins in serum from a normal population: season-, age- and sex-related variations. Clinical Chemistry 17: 495–500

McCurdy P R 1965 The detection of intestinal absorption of Co[57] tagged vitamin B_{12} by serum counting. Annals of Internal Medicine 62: 97–102

McCurdy P R, Dern R J 1968. Some therapeutic implications of ferrous sulphate-ascorbic acid mixtures. American Journal of Clinical Nutrition 21: 284–288

McEvoy A W, Fenwick J D, Boddy K, James O F W 1982 Vitamin B_{12} absorption from the gut does not decline with age in normal elderly humans. Age and Ageing 11: 180–183

McFarlane D B, Pinkerton P H, Dagg J H, Goldberg A 1967 Incidence of iron deficiency, with and without anaemia, in women in general practice. British Journal of Haematology 13: 790–796

Mackay I R 1972 Ageing and immunological function in man. Gerontologia 18: 285–304

McKendrick M W, Geddes A M, Edwards J M 1979 Atypical infectious mononucleosis in the elderly. British Medical Journal 2: 970

MacKinney A A 1978 Effect of aging on the peripheral blood lymphocyte count. Journal of Gerontology 33: 213–216

MacLennan W J 1971 Xylose absorption and serum carotene levels in the elderly. Gerontologia Clinica 13: 370–378

MacLennan W J, Andrews G R, Macleod C, Caird F I 1973 Anaemia in the elderly. Quarterly Journal of Medicine 42: 1–13

MacLennan W J, Hamilton J C 1976 The effect of leucocytosis on leucocyte ascorbic acid levels. Age and Ageing 5: 43–48

MacLennan W J, Hamilton J C, Timothy J I 1979 25-hydroxyvitamin D concentrations in old people living at home. Journal of Clinical & Experimental Gerontology 1: 201–215

MacLennan W J, Martin P, Mason B J 1977 Protein intake & serum albumin levels in the elderly. Gerontology 23: 360–367

MacLeod R D M 1972 Abnormal tongue appearances and vitamin status of the elderly — a double blind trial. Age and Ageing 1: 99–102

MacMahon B 1957 Epidemiological evidence on the nature of Hodgkin's disease. Cancer (New York) 10: 1045–1054

Maldonado J E, Hanlon D G 1965 Monocytosis: a current appraisal. Proceedings of Mayo Clinic 40: 248–259

Mangion P B, Schiller K R F 1971 Disseminated tuberculosis complicated by pancytopenia. Proceedings of the Royal Society of Medicine 64: 42–46

Manzoor M, Runcie J 1976 Folate-responsive neuropathy: report of 10 cases. British Medical Journal i: 1176–1178

Marchasin S, Wallerstein R O 1964 The treatment of iron-deficiency anemia with intravenous iron dextran. Blood 23: 354–358

Marder V P 1979 The use of thrombolytic agents: choice of patient, drug administration, laboratory monitoring. Annals of Internal Medicine 90: 802–808

Markkanen T, Heikinheimo R, Dahl M 1969 Transketolase activity of red blood cells from infancy to old age. Acta Haematologica 42: 148–153

Markkanen T, Peltola O, Heikinheimo R 1972 Pentose phosphate metabolizing enzyme activity of leukocytes in patients of various age groups. Gerontologia Clinica 14: 149–153

Martin J M, Kellett J M, Kahn J 1980 Aneuploidy in cultured human lymphocytes: I. Age and sex differences. Age and Ageing 9: 147–153

Martin N H 1961 The incidence of myelomatosis. Lancet i: 237–239

Martin N H 1969 The immunoglobulins: a review. Journal of Clinical Pathology 22: 117–131

Martin N H 1970 The paraproteinaemias. British Journal of Hospital Medicine 3: 662–666

Marx J J M 1979 Normal iron absorption and decreased red cell iron uptake in the aged. Blood 53: 204–211

Mason D Y, Emerson P M 1973 Primary acquired sideroblastic anaemia: response to treatment with pyridoxal-5'-phosphate. British Medical Journal i: 389–390

Mattevi M S, Salzano F M 1975 Senescence and human chromosome changes. Humangenetik 27: 1–8

Matthews D M, Wilson J 1971 Cobalamins and cyanide metabolism in neurological diseases. In: Arnstein H R V, Wrighton R J (eds) Cobalamins and Cyanide Metabolism in Neurological Diseases, Churchill Livingstone, Edinburgh, p 115–136

Mattioli C A, Tomasi T B Jr 1973 The life span of IgA plasma cells from the mouse intestine. Journal of Experimental Medicine 138: 452–460

Matzner Y, Benbassat J, Polliack A 1978b Prognostic factors in multiple myeloma. A retrospective study using conventional statistical methods and a computer program. Acta Haematologica 60: 257–268

Matzner Y, Levy S, Grossowicz N, Izak G, Hershko C 1978a Prevalence and causes of anemia in the elderly. Israel Journal of Medical Sciences 14: 1165–1169

Mayer G A 1976 Blood viscosity and oral anticoagulant therapy. American Journal of Clinical Pathology 65: 402–406

Medical Research Council 1974 Working party on leukaemia in adults. British Journal of Haematology 27: 373–389

Meindok H, Franks W M 1969 Serum proteins, protein-bound iodine and T_3 uptake in the elderly. Journal of the American Geriatrics Society 17: 451–458

Messmore H L, Fareed J, Silberman S, Gawlick G M, Bermes E W Jr (1978) Macroglobulinemia of Waldenström. Diagnosis and management. Annals of Clinical and Laboratory Science 8: 310–317

Meurat G, Hoffman G 1973 Monocyte kinetic studies in normal and disease states. British Journal of Haematology 24: 275–285

Miescher P A, Farquet J J 1974 Chronic myelomonocytic leukemia in adults. Seminars in Hematology 11: 129–139

Milne J S, Lonergan M E, Williamson J, Moore F M L, McMaster R, Percy N 1971 Leucocyte ascorbic acid levels and vitamin C intake in older people. British Medical Journal iv: 383–386

Milne J S, Williamson J 1972a The ESR in older people. Gerontologia Clinica 14: 36–42

Milne J S, Williamson J 1972b Hemoglobin, hematocrit reading, leukocyte count and blood grouping in a random sample of older people. Geriatrics 27: 118–126 (Sept.)

Milutinovich J, Wu W, Savory J 1979 Periorbital purpura after renal biopsy in primary amyloidosis. Journal of the American Medical Association 242: 2555 (Letter)

Misra D P, Loudon J M, Staddon G E 1975 Albumin metabolism in elderly patients. Journal of Gerontology 30: 304–306

Mitchell C A, Tesar P J, Maynard J H, Choong S H 1981 Chloral hydrate interferes with radioassay of vitamin B_{12}. Clinical Chemistry 27: 1480–1481

Mitchell T R, Pegrum G D 1971 The diagnosis of mild iron deficiency in the elderly. Gerontologia Clinica 13: 296–306

Mitra M L 1970 Vitamin C deficiency in the elderly and its manifestations. Journal of the American Geriatrics Society 18: 67–71

Modan B 1971 In: The Polycythemia Disorders. C C Thomas, Springfield, Illinois

Modan B 1975 Inter-relationship between polycythaemia vera, leukaemia and myeloid metaplasia. Clinics in Haematology 4: 427–439

Mollin D L, Waters A H, Harriss E 1962 Clinical aspects of the metabolic interrelationships between folic acid and vitamin B_{12}. In: Heinrich H C, Vitamin B_{12} und Intrinsic Factor. 2 Europäisches Symposion, Enke, Stuttgart, p 737–755

Montgomery R D, Haeney M R, Ross I N, Sammons H G, Barford A V, Balakrishnan S et al 1978 The ageing gut: a study of intestinal absorption in relation to nutrition in the elderly. Quarterly Journal of Medicine 186: 197–211

Monti M 1981 Erythrocyte 2,3-diphosphoglycerate and adenosine triphosphate in polycythaemia vera. Scandinavian Journal of Haematology 27: 108–110

Moore C V 1965 Iron nutrition and requirements. Scandinavian Journal of Haematology Series Haematologica 6: 1–13

Morck T A, Lynch S R, Cook J D 1983 Inhibition of food iron absorption by coffee. American Journal of Clinical Nutrition 37: 416–420

Morell A, Maurer W, Skvaril F, Barandun S 1978 Differentiation between benign and malignant monoclonal gammopathies by discriminant analysis on serum and bone marrow parameters. Acta Haematologica 60: 129–136

Morgan A G, Kelleher J, Walker B E, Losowsky M S, Droller H, Middleton R S W 1973 A nutritional survey of in the elderly: haematological aspects. International Journal of Vitamin and Nutrition Research 43: 461–471

Morgan R H 1967 Anaemia in elderly housebound patients. British Medical Journal iv: 171

Moroni M, Capsoni F, Caredda F, Lazzarin H, Besaha C 1976

Demonstration of a granulocyte defect in aged persons correlated with the presence of auto-antibodies. Bollettino dell' Istituto Sieroterapico Milanese 55: 317–322

Morris G K, Mitchell J R A 1976a Prevention and diagnosis of venous thrombosis in patients with hip fractures. Lancet ii: 867–869

Morris G K, Mitchell J R A 1976b Warfarin sodium in prevention of deep venous thrombosis and pulmonary embolism in patients with fractured neck of femur. Lancet ii: 869–872

Morrow J J, Dagg J H, Goldberg A 1968 A controlled trial of iron therapy in sideropenia. Scottish Medical Journal 13: 78–83

Moser K M, Hajjar G C 1966 Age- and disease-related alterations in fibrinogen-euglobulin (fibrinolytic) behavior. American Journal of Medical Sciences 251: 536–544

Murphy F, Srivastava P C, Varadi S, Elwis A 1969 Screening of psychiatric patients for hypovitaminosis B_{12}. British Medical Journal iii: 559–560

Myers A M, Saunders C R G, Chalmers D G 1968 The haemoglobin level of fit elderly people. Lancet ii: 261–263

Myers T J 1981 Treatment of thrombotic thrombocytopenic purpura with combined exchange plasmapheresis and anti-platelet agents. Seminars in Thrombosis and Hemostasis 7: 37–42

Najean Y 1981 Long-term follow-up in patients with aplastic anemia. A study of 137 androgen-treated patients surviving more than two years. American Journal of Medicine 71: 543–551

Najean Y, Pecking A 1979 Prognostic factors in acquired aplastic anemia. A study of 352 cases. American Journal of Medicine 67: 564–571

Najean Y, Triebel F, Dresch C 1981 Pure erythrocytosis: Reappraisal of a study of 51 cases. American Journal of Hematology 10: 129–136

Nakao K, Fisher J W, Takaku F 1975 Erythropoiesis. University Park Press, Baltimore & London

Nakao M, Nakao T, Yamazoe S 1960 Adenosine triphosphate and maintenance of shape of the human red cells. Nature 187:945–946

Nakao M, Nakayama T, Fujii Y, Nakao T, Nagai F, Komatsu Y, Hara Y 1979 Comparative analysis of red cell aging in vivo and its deterioration in blood banks. In: Orimo H, Shimada K, Iriki M, Maeda D (eds) Recent Advances in Gerontology (Proceedings of the XI International Congress of Gerontology, Tokyo, 1978). Excerpta Medica, Amsterdam, p 80–81

Nath B J, Lindenbaum J 1979 Persistence of neutrophil hypersegmentation during recovery from megaloblastic granulopoiesis. Annals of Internal Medicine 90: 757–760

Nathan D G 1966 Comments on the interpretation of measurements of total red cell volume in the diagnosis of polycythemia vera. Seminars in Hematology 3: 216–219

Naylor G J 1970 The relationship between age and sodium metabolism in human erythrocytes. Gerontologia 16: 217–222

Naylor G J, Dick D A T, Worrall E P, Dick E G, Dick P, Boardman L 1977 Changes in the erythrocyte sodium pump with age. Gerontologia 23: 256–261

Needleman S W, Burns C P, Dick F R, Armitage J O 1981 Hypoplastic acute leukemia. Cancer 48: 1410–1414

Neiman R S, Dervan P, Haudenschild C, Jaffe R 1978 Angioimmunoblastic lymphadenopathy. An ultrastructural and immunologic study with review of the literature. Cancer 41: 507–518

Nilsson I M 1964 Blood coagulation studies in the aged. In: Hansen P F (ed) Age with a Future (Proceedings of the 6th International Congress of Gerontology. Copenhagen, 1963) Munksgaard, Copenhagen

Nöcker J, Bemm H 1955/6 Einwirkung von Alter und Geschlect auf die Serumglobuline. II. Mitteilung. Zeitschrift für Alternsforschung 9: 328–339

Norgard M, Carpenter J, Conrad M 1979 Bone marrow necrosis and degeneration. Archives of Internal Medicine 139: 905–911

Norman A, Sasaki M S, Ottoman R E, Fingerhut A G 1965 Lymphocyte lifetime in women. Science 147: 745

Nutrition Reviews 1979 Iron absorption and utilization in the elderly Nutrition Reviews 37: 222–224

Ockelford P A, Hull R 1982 Management of venous thrombosis and thrombophlebitis. Drugs 24: 152–162

Ødegård O R, Fagerhol M K, Lie M 1976 Heparin cofactor activity and antithrombin III concentration in plasma related to age and sex. Scandinavian Journal of Haematology 17: 258–262

Ogston C M, Ogston D 1966 Plasma fibrinogen and plasminogen levels in health and in ischaemic heart disease. Journal of Clinical Pathology 19: 352–356

Okuno T 1972 Red cell size and age. British Medical Journal i: 569–570

Okuno T, Kosova L 1979 Plasmapheresis for thrombotic thrombocytopenic purpura (TTP). Transfusion 19: 342–344

Olbrich O 1947 Blood changes in the aged. Part I. Edinburgh Medical Journal 54: 306–321

Olbrich O 1948 Blood changes in the aged. Part III. Edinburgh Medical Journal 55: 100–115

Olbrich O, Woodford Williams E, Attwood E C 1957 Distribution of body water in ageing in normal and pathological conditions. Proceedings of the 4th Congress of the International Association of Gerontology, Merano, vol 2, p 387–395

Olhagen B, Liljestrand A 1955 II. Persistently elevated erythrocyte sedimentation rate with good prognosis. Acta Medica Scandinavica 151: 441–449

Oliver J 1954 Anatomic changes of normal senescence. In: Steiglitz E J (ed) Geriatric Medicine: Medical Care of Later Maturity, 3 edn. Pitman, London, p 44–63

Ooi B S, Orlina A R, Masaitis L, First M R, Pollack V E, Ooi Y M 1974 Lymphocytotoxins in aging. Transplantation 18: 190–192

Osgood E E 1965 Polycythemia vera: age relationships and survival. Blood 26: 243–256

Osserman E F, Takatsuki K 1964 Clinical and immunochemical studies of four cases of heavy (H^{gamma2}) chain disease. American Journal of Medicine 37: 351–373

Otani T 1958 Études sur les lymphocytes. Archives françaises de pédiatrie 15: 227–237

Palmblad J, Haak A 1978 Aging does not change blood granulocyte bactericidal capacity & levels of complement factors 3 & 4. Gerontology 24: 381–385

Parker D, Malpas J S 1979 Multiple myeloma. Journal of the Royal College of Physicians (London) 13: 146–153

Parry T E 1980 The diagnosis of megaloblastic anaemia. Clinical & Laboratory Haematology 2: 89–109

Parsons P L, Withey J L, Kilpatrick G S 1965 The prevalence of anaemia in the elderly. Practitioner 195: 656–660

Partridge R E H, Duthie J J R 1963 Incidence of macrocytic anaemia in rheumatoid arthritis. British Medical Journal i: 89–91

Pathy M S, Kirkman S, Molloy M J 1979 An evaluation of simultaneously administered free and intrinsic factor bound radioactive cyanocobalamin in the diagnosis of pernicious anaemia in the elderly. Journal of Clinical Pathology 32: 244–250

Pathy M S, Newcombe R G 1980 Temporal variation of serum levels of vitamin B_{12} folate, iron and total iron-binding capacity. Gerontology 26: 34–42

Pathy M S, Pippen C A R, Kirkman S 1972 Free and intrinsic factor bound radioactive cyanocobalamin. Simultaneous administration to assess the significance of low serum vitamin B_{12} levels. Age and Ageing 1: 111–119

Paulley J W, Hughes J P 1960 Giant-cell arteritis, or arteritis of the aged. British Medical Journal ii: 1562–1567

Paulus J-M 1975 Platelet size in man. Blood 46: 321–336

Pawlotsky Y, Chales, G, Grosbois B, Louboutin Y B, Lenoir P, Bourel M 1978 Sigma SR, a new method of measuring erythrocyte sedimentation rate. Its value in studying the action and interactions of non-steroidal anti-inflammatory agents. Current Medical Research and Opinion 5: 412–417

Pearce V R, Payne B 1981 Porphyria in the elderly: case reports. Journal of the American Geriatrics Society 29: 316–318

Pedersen A B, Mosbech J 1969 Morbidity of pernicious anaemia. Incidence, prevalence and treatment in a Danish county. Acta Medica Scandinavica 185: 449–452

Penington D G 1974 The myeloproliferative syndromes. Medical Journal of Australia 2: 56–64

Penziner A S 1982 Coagulopathy in amyloidosis. Medical Grand Rounds 1: 239–244

Pepys E O, Cox M, Hodkinson H M, Pepys M B 1982 Enumeration of lymphocyte populations in whole blood of well elderly subjects. Journal of Clinical and Experimental Gerontology 4: 53–61

Perillie P E 1978 Myeloma and pernicious anemia. American Journal of the Medical Sciences 275: 93–98

Perlmann P, Perlmann H, Müller-Eberhard H J 1973 Lymphocyte mediated cytotoxicity induced by humoral antibodies: mechanism of induction and surface markers of the effector cells. International Archives of Allergy and Applied Immunology 45: 278–280

Perry J, Lumb M, Laundy M, Reynolds E H, Chanarin I 1976 Role of vitamin B_{12} in folate coenzyme synthesis. British Journal of Haematology 32: 243–248

Perry M C, Kyle R A 1975 The clinical significance of Bence Jones proteinuria. Mayo Clinic Proceedings 50: 234–238

Peto R 1971 Myeloma workshop: urea, albumin and response rates. British Medical Journal ii: 324

Phair J P, Kauffman C A, Bjornson A, Gallagher J, Adams L, Hess E V 1978 Host defences in the aged: evaluation of components of the inflammatory and immune responses. Journal of Infectious Diseases 138: 67–73

Phillips M J, Harkness J 1976 Plasma and whole blood viscosity. British Journal of Haematology 34: 347–352

Pickens S, Murdoch J M 1979 Infectious mononucleosis in the elderly. Age and Ageing 8: 93–95

Pierre R V, Hoagland H C 1972 Age-associated aneuploidy: loss of Y chromosome from human bone marrow cells with aging. Cancer 30: 889–894

Pincherle G, Shanks J 1967a Haemoglobin values in business executives. British Journal of Preventive and Social Medicine 21: 40–42

Pincherle G, Shanks L 1967b Value of the erythrocyte sedimentation rate as a screening test. British Journal of Preventive Social Medicine 21: 133–136

Pincus J H, Reynolds E H, Glaser G H 1972 Subacute combined degeneration with folic acid deficiency. Journal of the American Medical Association 221: 496–497

Pirofsky B 1978 When autoimmune hemolytic anemia complicates chronic lymphocytic leukemia. Geriatrics 33(4): 71–79 (April)

Pirrie R 1952 The influence of age upon serum iron in normal subjects. Journal of Clinical Pathology 5: 10–15

Pisciotta A V 1980 Thrombotic thrombocytopenic purpura. Annals of Internal Medicine 92: 249–250

Pitney W R, Onesti P 1961 Vitamin B_{12} and folic acid concentrations of human liver with reference to the assay of needle biopsy material. Australian Journal of Experimental Biology and Medical Sciences 39: 1–7

Pizzuto J, Conte G, Sinco A, Morales M, Aviles A, Ambriz R, Fernandez A 1980 Use of androgens in acquired aplastic anaemia. Relation of response to aetiology and severity. Acta Haematologica (Basel) 64: 18–24

Polack S, Tatarski J 1975 Factors influencing survival time in chronic lymphocytic leukaemia. Harefuah 89: 396–398 (Engl. abstr. p 444)

Portlock C S, Rosenberg S A 1979 No initial therapy for Stage III & IV non-Hodgkin's lymphomas of favorable histologic types. Annals of Internal Medicine 90: 10–13

Powell D E B 1978 Macrocytosis in the elderly. The Practitioner 221: 204–209

Powell D E B, Thomas J H 1969 The iron-binding capacity of serum in elderly hospital patients. Gerontologia Clinica 11: 36–47

Powell D E B, Thomas J H, Mills P, 1968 Serum iron in elderly hospital patients Gerontologia Clinica 10: 21–29

Preston A E, Barr A 1964 The plasma concentration of Factor VIII in the normal population. II. The effects of age, sex and blood group. British Journal of Haematology 10: 238–245

Preston F E, Cooke K B, Foster M E, Winfield D A, Lee D 1978 Myelomatosis and the hyperviscosity syndrome. British Journal of Haematology 38: 517–530

Proudfoot A T, Akhtar A J, Douglas A C, Horne N W 1969 Miliary tuberculosis in adults. British Medical Journal ii: 273–276

Pruzanski W, Katz A 1976 Clinical and laboratory findings in primary generalized and multiple-myeloma-related amyloidosis. Canadian Medical Association Journal 114: 906–909

Pryce J O, Haslam R M, Wootton I D P 1969 Extraction of normal values from a mixed hospital population. Annals of Clinical Biochemistry 6: 6–11

Radl J, Sepers J M, Skvaril F, Morell A, Hijmans W 1975 Immunoglobulin patterns in humans over 95 years of age. Clinical and Experimental Immunology 22: 84–90

Raff M C, Cantor H 1971 Subpopulations of thymus cells and thymus derived lymphocytes. In: Amos B (ed) Progress in Immunology, 1st International Congress of Endocrinology, Academic Press, New York, p 83–93

Rafsky H A, Brill A A, Stern K G, Corey H 1952 Electrophoretic studies on the serum of 'normal' aged individuals. American Journal of the Medical Sciences 224: 522–528

Rai G S 1979 Erythrocyte sedimentation rate and disease in the elderly. Journal of the American Geriatrics Society 27: 382–383

Rai K R, Sawitsky A, Cronkite E P, Chanana A D, Levy R N, Pasternack B S 1975 Clinical staging of chronic lymphocytic leukemia. Blood 46: 219–234

Rambaud J C, Seligmann M 1976 Alpha-chain disease. Clinics in Gastroenterology 5: 341–358

Randall R E, Williamson W C Jr, Mullinax F, Tung M Y, Still W J S 1976 Manifestations of systemic light chain deposition. American Journal of Medicine 60: 293–299

Ranke E, Tauber S A, Horonick A, Ranke B, Goodhart R S, Chow B F 1960 Vitamin B_6 deficiency in the aged. Journal of Gerontology 15: 41–44

Raper C G L, Choudhury M 1978 Early detection of folic acid deficiency in elderly patients. Journal of Clinical Pathology 31: 44–46

Rappaport H, Winter W J, Hicks E B 1956 Follicular lymphoma: a re-evaluation of its position in the scheme of malignant lymphoma based on a survey of 253 cases. Cancer 9: 792–821

Ray P K, Pinkerton P H 1969 Leukocyte alkaline phosphatase. The effect of age and sex. Acta Haematologica 42: 18–22

Read A E, Gough K R, Pardoe J L, Nicholas A 1965. Nutritional studies on the entrants to an old people's home with particular reference to folic acid deficiency. British Medical Journal ii: 843–848

Reading H W, Rosie R 1980 Age and sex differences related to platelet aggregation. Biochemical Society Transactions (London) 8: 180–181

Reed A H, Cannon D C, Winkelman J W, Bhasin Y P, Henry P J, Pileggi V J 1972. Estimation of normal ranges from a controlled sample survey: I. Sex- and age-related influences on the SMA 12/60 screening group of tests. Clinical Chemistry 18: 57–66

Rees J K H, Coles G A 1969 Calciphylaxis in man. British Medical Journal ii: 670–672

Reich C, Swirsky M, Smith D 1944 Sternal bone marrow in the aged. Journal of Laboratory & Clinical Medicine 29: 508–509

Reid C, Chanarin I 1978 Effect of phenytoin on DNA synthesis by human bone marrow. Scandinavian Journal of Haematology 20: 237–240

Reiffers J, Raynal F, Brousset A 1980 Acute myeloblastic leukemia in elderly patients. Treatment and prognostic factors. Cancer 45: 2816–2820

Renbourn E T, Ellison J M 1952 Some blood changes in old age. A clinical and statistical study. Human Biology 24: 57–86

Reynolds E H 1976a The neurology of vitamin B_{12} deficiency. Metabolic mechanisms. Lancet ii: 822–824

Reynolds E H 1976b Neurological aspects of folate and vitamin B_{12} metabolism. Clinics in Haematology 5: 661–696

Reynolds E H 1979a Interrelationships between the neurology of folate and vitamin B_{12} deficiency. In: Botez M I, Reynolds E H (eds) Folic Acid in Neurology, Psychiatry and Internal Medicine, Raven Press, New York, p 501–515

Reynolds E H 1979b Cerebrospinal fluid folate: clinical studies. In: Botez M I, Reynolds E H (eds) Folic Acid in Neurology, Psychiatry and Internal Medicine, Raven Press, New York, p 195–203

Richards J D M 1976 Hypersplenism. British Journal of Hospital Medicine 15: 505–511

Richards J D M, Wilding P 1973 Revised normal values for haemoglobin, red cell indices and white cells in adults. Laboratory Practice 22: 525–526

Richert-Boe K E, Bagby G C Jr 1978 Treating acute nonlymphocytic leukemia. Geriatrics 33(2): 50–55 (Feb)

Ridolfi R L, Bell W R 1981 Thrombocytopenic purpura. Report of 25 cases and review of the literature. Medicine (Baltimore) 60: 413–428

Rivnay B, Bergman S, Shinitzky M, Globerson A 1980 Correlations between membrane viscosity, serum cholesterol, lymphocyte activation and aging in man. Mechanisms of Ageing and Development 12: 119–126

Roach E S, McLean W T (1982) Neurologic disorders of vitamin B_{12} deficiency. American Family Physician 25: 111–115

Roe P F, Harkness J 1975 Plasma viscosity in the elderly. Gerontologia Clinica 17: 168–172

Rosenberg I H, Rumans L W 1978 Survival of a patient with pancytopenia and disseminated coagulation associated with miliary tuberculosis. Chest 73: 536–539

Rosenberg I H, Selhub J, Dhar G J 1979 Absorption and malabsorption of folates. In: Botez M I, Reynolds E H (eds) Folic Acid in Neurology, Psychiatry and Internal Medicine, Raven Press, New York, p 95–111

Rosner F, Sawitzky A, Grunwald H W, Rai K R 1976 Acute granulocytic leukemia in the elderly. Archives of Internal Medicine 136: 120

Rossi E C, Grogan J W 1965 Platelet clumping as an expression of platelet senescence. Blood 25: 613P

Rothberg H, Pachter I, Kosmin M, Stevens D B 1982 Thrombotic thrombocytopenic purpura: recovery after plasmapheresis, corticosteroids, splenectomy and antiplatelet agents. American Journal of Hematology 12: 281–287

Rothstein M 1975 Aging and the alteration of enzymes: a review. Mechanisms of Ageing and Development 4: 325–338

Rowlands D T Jr, Daniele R P 1975 Surface receptors in the immune response. New England Journal of Medicine 293: 26–32

Roylance P J, Hanna I R A, Tarbutt R G 1969 Changes with age in the cell proliferation of rat bone marrow. Journal of Anatomy 104: 191

Rozman C, Marin P, Granena A, Nomdedeu B, Montserrat E, Feliu E, Vives-Corrons J L 1981 Prognosis in acquired aplastic anaemia. A multivariate statistical analysis of 80 cases. Scandinavian Journal of Haematology 26: 321–329

Rubinson H, Kahn A, Boivin P, Schapira R, Gregori C, Dreyfus J-C 1976 Aging and accuracy of protein synthesis in man: search for inactive enzymatic cross-reacting material in granulocytes of aged people. Gerontology 22: 438–448

Runcie J 1979 Folate deficiency in the elderly. In: Botez M I, Reynolds E H (eds) Folic Acid in Neurology, Psychiatry & Internal Medicine, Raven Press, New York, p 493–499

Rustgi R N, Bettigole E R E 1981 Nonanemic pernicious anemia. Delay in diagnosis. New York State Journal of Medicine 81: 1739–1742

Sahi J, Stobbe H, Klatt R 1972 The azurophilic granules of lymphocytes of the aged Zietschrift für Alternsforschung 26: 49–50

Sakai H, Kato E, Matsuki S, Asano S 1968 Age and lymphocyte nucleic acids. Lancet i: 818–819

Sakuta S 1981 Blood filtrability in cerebrovascular disorders with special reference to erythrocyte deformability and ATP content. Stroke 12: 824–828

Salatka K, Kresge D, Harris L Jr, Edelstein D, Ove P 1971 Rat serum protein changes with age. Experimental Gerontology 6: 25–36

Salmon S E, Seligmann M 1974 B-cell neoplasia in man. Lancet ii, 1230–1233

Salzman E W, Harris W H, de Sanctis R W 1966 Anticoagulation for prevention of thromboembolism following fractures of the hip. New England Journal of Medicine 275: 122–130

Sanders C, Orr R G, Evans R J 1968 Blood counts on radiation, non-radiation and new-entry employees. UKAEA Research Group Report, AERE-R 5766, HMSO, London

Sass M D 1973 Adenosine triphosphate utilization by 'young' and 'old' red cells. Clinica Chimica Acta 43: 201–204

Say C, Lee Y-T N, Hori J, Spratt J S Jr 1975 Prognostic factors in Hodgkin's disease. Journal of Surgical Oncology 7: 255–267

Scarborough H, Shuster S 1960 Corticosteroid purpura. Lancet i: 93–94

Schepp W, Lindstaedt H, Miederer S E, Elster K 1980 No influence of age and gastric acid secretion on serum vitamin B_{12} concentration. Hepato-Gastroenterology 27: 294–299

Scherer R, Morarescu A, Ruhenströth-Bauer G 1976 The significance of plasma lipoproteins on erythrocyte aggregation and sedimentation. British Journal of Haematology 32: 235–241

Schilling R F 1953 Effect of gastric juice on urinary excretion of radioactive vitamin B_{12}. Journal of Laboratory and Clinical Medicine 42: 860–866

Schilling R F, Crowley J J 1979 Prognostic signs in chronic myelocytic leukemia. American Journal of Hematology 7: 1–10

Schnitzer B 1978 Classification of lymphomas. CRC Critical Reviews in Clinical Laboratory Sciences 9: 123–178

Schroder U, Tougaard L 1977 Age changes in the quantity of hematopoietic tissue. Acta Pathologica et Microbiologica Scandinavica (Sect A) 85: 559–560

Schwartz J M, Friedman S A, Schreiber Z A, Tsao L L, Richter I H 1973 Problems with streptokinase therapy in acute pulmonary embolism. Surgery 74: 727–733

Schwick H G, Becker W 1969 Humoral antibodies in older humans. In: Westphal O, Beck H E, Brundmann F (eds) Current Problems in Immunology, Springer Verlag, Berlin, p 253–257

Scott E 1960 Prevalence of pernicious anaemia in Great Britain. Journal of the College of General Practitioners 3: 80–84

Scott J L, McMillan R, Marino J V, Davidson J G 1973 Leukocyte labelling with chromium-51. IV. The kinetics of chronic lymphocytic leukemic lymphocytes. Blood 41: 155–162

Scott R E, McKenna R W 1975 Pathology of the lymphomas: past, present and future. Geriatrics 30(10): 65–71

Seligmann M 1972 Heavy chain diseases Revue Européenne d'Etudes Cliniques et Biologiques. 17: 349–355

Senator G B, Muirden K D 1968 Concentration of iron in synovial membrane, synovial fluid, and serum in rheumatoid arthritis and other joint diseases. Annals of the Rheumatic Diseases 27: 49–54

Sevitt S, Gallagher N G 1959 Prevention of venous thrombosis and pulmonary embolism in injured patients. A trial of anticoagulant prophylaxis with phenindione in middle-aged and elderly patients with fractured necks of femur. Lancet ii: 981–989

Shapiro S S, Hultin M 1975 Acquired inhibitors to the blood coagulation factors. Seminars in Thrombosis and Hemostasis 1: 336–385

Shapleigh J B, Mayes S, Moore C V 1952 Hematologic values in the aged. Journal of Gerontology 7: 207–219

Sharland D E 1972 The causes of monoclonal hypergammaglobulinaemia (gammopathy) with special reference to the older patient. Modern Geriatrics 2: 118–121

Sharland D E 1980 Erythrocyte sedimentation rate: the normal range in the elderly. Journal of the American Geriatrics Society 28: 346–348

Sharnoff J G 1977 Low-dose of small-dose heparin. Lancet ii: 1087 (letter)

Shaw D M 1971 Vitamin B_{12} and folic acid in brain metabolism. In: Arnstein H R V, Wrighton R J (eds) The Cobalamins: A Glaxo Symposium, Churchill Livingstone, Edinburgh, p 109–114

Shaw M T, Bottomley S S, Bottomley R H, Hussein K K 1973 The relationship of erythromonocytic leukemia to other myeloproliferative disorders. American Journal of Medicine 55: 542–548

Shearman D J C, Boddy K, Henderson J T, King P C, Simpson J D, Finlayson N D C 1971 Whole body monitor studies of cyanocobalamin absorption in normal patients and in patients with vitamin B_{12} malabsorption. In: Arnstein H R V, Wrighton R J (eds) The Cobalamins: A Glaxo Symposium, Churchill Livingstone, Edinburgh, p 169–181

Sheridan D J, Temperley I J, Gatenby P B B 1974 Blood indices, serum folate and vitamin B_{12} levels in the elderly. Journal of the Irish College of Physicians and Surgeons 4: 39–45

Shinton N K 1972 Vitamin B_{12} and folate metabolism. British Medical Journal i: 556–559

Shinton N K, Troughton O 1971 Therapeutic response to large oral doses of cobalamin. In: Arnstein H R V, Wrighton R J (eds) The Cobalamins: A Glaxo Symposium, Churchill Livingstone, Edinburgh, p 183–191

Shock N W 1958 The role of the kidney in electrolyte and water regulation in the aged. In: Wolstenholme G E W, O'Connor M (eds) Ciba Foundation Colloquia on Ageing, Churchill, London, vol. 4, p 229–249

Shock N W, Yiengst M J 1948 Experimental displacement of the acid-base equilibrium of the blood in aged males. Federation Proceedings 7: 114–115

Shock N W, Yiengst M J 1950 Age changes in the acid–base equilibrium of the blood of males. Journal of Gerontology 5: 1–4

Shock N W, Yiengst M J, Watkin D M 1953 Age change in body water and its relationship to basal oxygen consumption in males. Journal of Gerontology 8: 388

Shulman R 1967 Psychiatric aspects of pernicious anaemia: a prospective controlled investigation. British Medical Journal iii: 266–270

Shulman 1979 An overview of folic acid deficiency and psychiatric illness. In: Botez M I, Reynolds E H (eds) Folic Acid in Neurology, Psychiatry and Internal Medicine, Raven Press, New York, p 463–474

Shuster S, Scarborough H 1961 Senile purpura. Quarterly Journal of Medicine 30: 33–40

Shustik C, Bergsagel D E, Pruzanski W 1976 κ and λ light chain disease: survival rates and clinical manifestations. Blood 48: 41–51

Sie P, Montagut J, Blanc M, Boneu B, Caranobe C, Cazard J C, Biermé R 1981 Evaluation of some platelet parameters in a group of elderly people. Thrombosis and Haemostasis (Stuttgart) 45: 197–199

Siimes M A, Addiego J E Jr, Dallman P R 1974 Ferritin in serum: diagnosis of iron deficiency and iron overload in infants and children. Blood 43: 581–590

Silber R 1982 Chronic lymphocytic leukemia in the elderly. Hospital Practice 17: 131–141

Silini G, Andreozzi U 1974 Haematological changes in the ageing mouse. Experimental Gerontology 9: 99–108

Silini G, Andreozzi U, Briganti G 1974 Erythroid differentiation of haemopoietic progenitor cells in the course of ageing. Experimental Gerontology 9: 281–284

Siurala M, Varis K, Kekki M 1980 New aspects on epidemiology, genetics and dynamics of chronic gastritis. Frontiers of Gastrointestinal Research 6: 148–166

Silverman E M, Silverman A G 1977 Granulocyte adherence in the elderly. American Journal of Clinical Pathology 67: 49–52

Smith A D M 1960 Megaloblastic madness. British Medical Journal ii: 1840–1845

Sneath P, Chanarin I, Hodkinson H M, McPherson C K, Reynolds E H 1973. Folate status in a geriatric population and its relation to dementia. Age and Ageing 2: 177–182

Somers H, Kuhns W J 1972 Blood group antibodies in old age. Proceedings of the Society for Experimental Biology and Medicine 141: 1104–1107

Sonnenblick M, Abraham A S 1976 Primary lymphosarcoma of the breast — review of the literature on occurrence in elderly patients. Journal of the American Geriatrics Society 24: 225–227

Sparrow D, Rowe J W, Silbert J E 1981 cross-sectional and longitudinal changes in the erythrocyte sedimentation rate in men. Journal of Gerontology 36: 180–184

Sparrow D, Silbert J E, Rowe J W 1980 The influence of age on peripheral lymphocyte count in men: a cross sectional and longitudinal study. Journal of Gerontology 35: 163–166

Spiers A S 1976 The treatment of chronic granulocytic leukaemia. British Journal of Haematology 32: 291–298

Spray G H 1962 The estimation and significance of the level of vitamin B_{12} in serum. Postgraduate Medical Journal 38: 35–40

Sprent J, Basten A 1973 Circulating T and B lymphocytes of the mouse. II. Lifespan. Cell Immunology 7: 40–59

Spriggs A I, Sladden R A 1958 The influence of age on red cell diameter. Journal of Clinical Pathology 11: 53–55

Stanton B R, Exton-Smith A N 1970 A longitudinal study of the dietary habits of elderly women. King Edward's Hospital Fund for London, London

Stern K, Birmingham M, Cullen A, Richer R 1951 Peptidase activity in leucocytes, erythrocytes and plasma of young, adult and senile subjects. Journal of Clinical Investigation 30: 84–89

Stobo J D, Paul W E 1973 Functional heterogeneity of murine lymphoid cells: III. Differential responsiveness of T cells to phytohemagglutinin and concanavalin A as a probe for T cell subsets. Journal of Immunology 110: 362–375

Stoltzner G, Makinodan T 1975 Age dependent decline in proliferation of lymphocytes. Advances in Experimental Medicine and Biology 61: 21–37

Strachan R W, Henderson J G 1965 Psychiatric syndromes due to avitaminosis B_{12} with normal blood and marrow. Quarterly Journal of Medicine 34: 303–317

Strachan R W, Henderson J G 1967 Dementia and folate deficiency. Quarterly Journal of Medicine 36: 189–204

Straub P W 1975 A case against heparin therapy of intravascular coagulation. Thrombosis et Diathesis Haemorrhagica 33: 107–112

Stryckmans P A 1974 Current concepts in chronic myelogenous leukemia. Seminars in Hematology 11: 101–127

Sullivan L W, Herbert V 1964 Suppression of hematopoiesis by ethanol. Journal of Clinical Investigation 43: 2048–2062

Summers M, Worwood M, Jacobs A 1974 Ferritin in normal erythrocytes, lymphocytes, polymorphs, and monocytes. British Journal of Haematology 28: 19–26

Sunderman F W Jr 1975 Current concepts of 'normal values', 'reference values' and 'discrimination values' in clinical chemistry. Clinical Chemistry 21: 1873–1877

Suvarnakich K, Mann G V, Stare F J 1952 Riboflavine in human serum. Journal of Nutrition 47: 105–118

Swan H T 1963 Fibrinolysis related to age in men. British Journal of Haematology 9: 311–318

Swendseid M E, Hvollboll E, Schick G, Halsted J A 1957 Vitamin B_{12} content of human liver tissue and its nutritional significance. Blood 12: 24–28

Szanto S 1972 Blood platelet behaviour in primary neuronal and vascular dementia. Age and Ageing 1: 207–212

Tanaka Y, Inoue T 1976 Fatty marrow in the vertebrae. A parameter for hemopoietic activity in the aged. Journal of Gerontology 31: 527–532

Tattersall R N, Seville R 1950 Senile purpura. Quarterly Journal of Medicine 19: 151–159

Tauber S A, Goodhart R S, Hsu J M, Blumberg N, Kassab J, Chow B F 1957 Vitamin B_{12} deficiency in the aged. Geriatrics 12: 368–374

Tepper P A, Bratchik A M 1966 Blood coagulability and fibrinolysis during the natural development and uncomplicated ageing of man. Terapeyticheskii arkhiv 38: 69–75 (Eng. Abstr: Excerpta Medica (Sect. XX), 1967, 10(7): Abstr no 1140, p 188)

Theologides A 1975 The many and varied complications of non-Hodgkin's lymphomas. Geriatrics 30: 91–93 (Oct)

Thomas H, Lefrak S, Irwin R S, Fitts H W, Caldwell P R B 1974 The oxyhemoglobin dissociation curve in health and disease. American Journal of Medicine 57: 331–348

Thomas J H 1971 Values of serum iron in patients over sixty. Gerontologia Clinica 13: 52–60

Thomas J H, Powell D E B 1971 Blood Disorders in the Elderly. John Wright & Sons Ltd, Bristol

Thomson A D 1966 Thiamine absorption in old age. Gerontologia Clinica 8: 354–361

Timaffy M 1962 A comparative study of bone marrow function in young and old individuals. Gerontologia Clinica 4: 13–18

Todd M, McDevitt E, McDowell F 1973 Stroke and blood coagulation. Stroke 4: 400–405

Toh B H, Roberts-Thomson I C, Mathews J D, Whittingham S, Mackay I R 1973 Depression of cell-mediated immunity in old age and the immunopathic diseases, lupus erythematosus, chronic hepatitis and rheumatoid arthritis. Clinical and Experimental Immunology 14: 193–202

Toma V A, Retief F P, Potgeiter G M, Anderson J D 1980 Plasma cell leukaemia. Diagnostic problems in our experience with 11 cases. Acta Haematologica 63: 136–145

Toskes P P, Deren J J 1973 Vitamin B_{12} absorption and malabsorption. Gastroenterology 65: 662–683

Trump B F, Barrett L A, Valigorsky J M, Jiji R M 1975 Ultrastructural studies of sideroblastic anemia. In: Kief H (ed) Iron Metabolism and its Disorders, Excerpta Medica, Amsterdam, p 251–263

Tuddenham E G D, Whittaker J A, Bradley J, Lilleyman J S, James D R 1974 Hyperviscosity syndrome in IgA multiple myeloma. British Journal of Haematology 27: 65–76

Tudhope G R, Wilson G M 1960 Anaemia in hypothyroidism. Quarterly Journal of Medicine 29: 513–537

Turnbull A 1971 Microcytic hypochromic anaemias. British Journal of Hospital Medicine 6: 573–580

Turpie A G G, McNicol G P, Douglas A S 1971 Platelets: haemostasis and thrombosis. In: Goldberg A, Brain M C (eds) Recent Advances in Haematology, Churchill Livingstone, Edinburgh, p 249–301

Tweeddale P M, Leggett R J, Flenley D C 1976 Effect of age on oxygen-binding in normal human subjects. Clinical Science and Molecular Medicine 51: 185–188

UCLA Conference 1981 Polycythemia: mechanisms and management. Annals of Internal Medicine 95: 71–87

Ugwu C N, Gibbins F J 1981 Anaphylactic reaction to vitamin B_{12} appearing after several years of therapy. Age and Ageing 10: 196–197

Ungar B, Whittingham S, Francis C M 1967. Pernicious anaemia:

incidence and significance of circulating antibodies to intrinsic factor and to parietal cells. Australasian Annals of Medicine 16: 226–229

Ungar B, Mathews J D, Tait B D, Cowling D C 1977 HLA patterns in pernicious anaemia. British Medical Journal i: 798–800

Ungar B, Mathews J D, Tait B D, Cowling D C 1981 HLA-DR patterns in pernicious anaemia. British Medical Journal (Clinical Research) 282: 768–770

Vallance S 1979 Leucocyte ascorbic acid and the leucocyte count. British Journal of Nutrition 41: 409–411

Vancici B, Lanfranchi G A, Puddu P, Barbieri L L (1967) Studio sull' assorbimento orale del ^{59}Fe in soggetti anziani (Study on the oral absorption of ^{59}Fe in elderly subjects). Archivio di patologia e clinica medica 43: 175–184

Van Dommelen C K V, Klaassen C H L 1964 Cyanocobalamin-dependent depression of the serum alkaline phosphatase level in patients with pernicious anemia. New England Journal of Medicine 271: 541–544

Van Dyke D, Anger H O 1965 Patterns of marrow hypertrophy and atrophy in man. Journal of Nuclear Medicine 6: 109–120

Van Dyke D, Anger H, Pollycove M 1964 The effect of erythropoietic stimulation on marrow distribution in man, rabbit and rat as shown by Fe^{59} and Fe^{52}. Blood 24: 356–371

Varindani M K, Pitchumoni C S, Lucariello R J 1982 Eosinophilic leukemoid reaction in pulmonary carcinoma. New York State Journal of Medicine 82: 347–348

Vaughan W P, Karp J E, Burke P J 1981 Acute leukemia — early recognition can spell survival. Geriatrics 36(6): 32–36 (June)

Videbaek A 1966 On the pathogenesis of human leukaemia. Acta Haematologica 36: 183–197

Vilpo J A, Irjala K, Wilvanen M K, Klemi P, Kouvonen I, Ronnemaa T 1980 Delta heavy chain disease. A study of a case. Clinical Immunology and Immunopathology 17: 584–594

Vilter R W 1964 Interrelationships between folic acid and vitamin B$_{12}$ and ascorbic acid in the megaloblastic anemias. Medicine (Baltimore) 43: 727–730

Virella G, Preto R V, Graça F 1975 Polymerized monoclonal IgA in two patients with myelomatosis and hyperviscosity syndrome. British Journal of Haematology 30: 479–487

Vogel J M 1980 Hematologic problems of the aged. Mount Sinai Journal of Medicine 47: 150–165

Vogler W R, Winton E F 1975 Humoral granulopoietic inhibitors: a review. Experimental Haematology 3: 337–353

von Knorre A, Pechau K-G 1975 Spätschicksale von Perniziosakranken. Zeitschrift für die Gesamte innere Medizin und ihre Grenzgebiete 30: 701–706 (Engl. abstr.)

Waldenström J G 1976 Specific activities of immunoglobulins produced in monoclonal gammopathy — maladies of derepression. European Journal of Cancer 12: 413–418

Walder A I 1968 Experimental achlorhydria: techniques of production with parietal cell antibody. Surgery 64: 175–184

Waldorf D S, Willkens R F, Decker J L 1968 Impaired delayed hypersensitivity in an aging population. Association with antinuclear reactivity and rheumatoid factor. Journal of the American Medical Association 203: 831–834.

Walford R L 1969 The Immunologic Theory of Aging. Munksgaard, Copenhagen

Walsh J R 1978 Polycythemia vera: diagnosis, treatment and relationship to leukemia. Geriatrics 33(5): 61–69 (May)

Walsh J R 1981 Hematologic disorders in the elderly. Western Journal of Medicine 135: 446–454

Walters G O, Jacobs A, Worwood M, Trevett D, Thomson W 1975 Iron absorption in normal subjects and patients with idiopathic haemochromatosis: relationship with serum ferritin concentration. Gut 16: 188–192

Wangel A G, Callender S T, Spray G H, Wright R 1968. A family study of pernicious anaemia: I Autoantibodies, achlorhydria, serum pepsinogen and vitamin B$_{12}$. British Journal of Haematology 14: 161–181.

Wapnick A A, Lynch S R, Charlton R W, Seftel H C, Bothwell T H 1969 The effect of ascorbic acid deficiency on desferrioxamine-induced urinary iron excretion. British Journal of Haematology 17: 563–568

Wardle E N 1973 ESR in hyperlipidaemia. British Medical Journal iii: 109

Wasserman L R, Gilbert H S 1963 Surgery in polycythemia vera. New England Journal of Medicine 269: 1226–1230

Weatherall D J 1971 The abnormal haemoglobins. In: Goldberg A, Brain M C (eds) Recent Advances in Haematology, Churchill Livingstone, Edinburgh, p 194–218

Webster S G P, Leeming J T 1979 Erythrocyte folate levels in young and old. Journal of the American Geriatrics Society 27: 451–454

Wedgwood J 1955 Early diagnosis of subacute bacterial endocarditis. Lancet ii: 1058–1063

Wedgwood J 1961 Bacterial endocarditis in old age. Gerontologia Clinica 3 (suppl): 11–23

Wedzicha J A, Rudd R M, Papps M C, Cotter F E, Newland A C, Empey D W 1983 Erythrapheresis in patients with polycythaemia secondary to hypoxic lung disease. British Medical Journal 286: 511–514

Weed R I, La Celle P L, Merrill E W 1969 Metabolic dependence of red cell deformability. Journal of Clinical Investigation 48: 795–809

Weeke B, Krasilnikoff P A 1972 The concentration of 21 serum proteins in normal children and adults. Acta Medica Scandinavica 192: 149–155

Weeks B A 1979 Effects of age and nutrition on macrophage function. Journal of the Reticuloendothelial Society 26: 459–462

Weinsaft P P, Haltaufderhyde V 1965 ESR in the aged. Journal of the American Geriatrics Society 13: 738–741

Weinstein L 1972 Infective endocarditis: past, present and future. Journal of the Royal College of Physicians, London. 6: 161–174

Weinstein R S 1974 The morphology of adult red cells. In: Surgenor D N (ed) The Red Blood Cell, 2nd edn. Academic Press, New York, p 213–268

Weiss H J 1982 Platelets: Pathophysiology and antiplatelet drug therapy. Alan R Liss Inc, New York

Westergren A 1957 The ESR: range and limitations of the technique. Triangle 3: 20–25

Wetherley-Mein G 1974 The myeloproliferative disorders. In: Hardisty R M, Weatherall D J (eds) Blood and its Disorders, Blackwell, Oxford, p 1155–1206

Whitehead J A, Chohan M M 1974 Paraphrenia and pernicious anaemia. Modern Geriatrics 4: 286–289

Whitelaw D M 1966 The intravascular life span of monocytes. Blood 28: 455–464

Wickramasinghe S N, Longland J E 1974 Assessment of deoxyuridine suppression test in diagnosis of vitamin B$_{12}$ or folate deficiency. British Medical Journal iii: 148–150

Wickramasinghe S N, Saunders J E 1975 Deoxyuridine suppression test. British Medical Journal ii: 87 (letter)

Wickramasinghe S M, Williams G, Saunders J, Durston J H J 1975 Megaloblastic erythropoiesis and macrocytosis in patients on anticonvulsants. British Medical Journal iv: 136–137

Wiedermann D, Wiedermann B, Cídl K, Kodoušková V 1980 Individual serum proteins and acute phase reactants in monoclonal immunoglobulinopathies. A study in patients with macroglobulinemia. Neoplasma 27: 473–481

Wilander E, Sundström C, Grimelius L 1979 Pernicious anaemia in association with argyrophil (Sevier-Munger) gastric carcinoid. Scandinavian Journal of Haematology 23: 415–420

Wilhelm W F, Tillisch J H 1951 Relation of sedimentation rate to age. Medical Clinics of North America 35: 1209–1211

Williams E I, Nixon J V 1974 Haemoglobin levels in a group of over 75-year-old patients studied in general practice. Gerontologia Clinica 16: 210–218

Williams J A, Jones C T, Cox E V 1962 The nutritional consequences of gastric resection and the management of patients after partial gastrectomy. British Journal of Clinical Practice 16: 737–742

Williams W J 1980 The effect of aging on the blood count. Comprehensive Therapy 6: 7–9

Williamson J, Stokoe I H, Gray S, Fisher M, Smith A, McGhee A, Stephenson E 1964 Old people at home: their unreported needs. Lancet i: 1117–1120

Wilson P A, McNicol G P, Douglas A S 1967 Platelet abnormality in human scurvy. Lancet i: 975–978

Wilson P D 1973 Enzyme changes in ageing mammals. Gerontologia 19: 79–125

Wiltshaw E 1971 Myeloma workshop: extramedullary plasmacytoma. British Medical Journal ii: 327

Wiltshaw E 1976 The natural history of extramedullary plasmacytoma and its relation to solitary myeloma of bone and myelomatosis. Medicine (Baltimore) 55: 217–238

Wintrobe M M 1967 Clinical Hematology 6th edn. Lea & Febiger, Philadelphia

Wintrobe M M, Lee G R, Boggs D R, Bithell T C, Foerster J, Athens J W, Lukens J N 1981 Acquired coagulation disorders. In: Wintrobe M M (ed) Clinical Hematology 8th edn. Lea & Febiger, Philadelphia, p 1206–1246

Wiske P S, Epstein S, Bell N H, Queener S F, Edmondson J, Johnston C C Jr 1979 Increases in immunoreactive parathyroid hormone with age. New England Journal of Medicine 300: 1419–1421

Witts L J 1966 In: The Stomach and Anaemia. The Athlone Press, University of London, London, p 30–34

Witts L J 1969 Hypochromic Anaemia. Heinemann, London.

Woodford Williams E, Alvarez A S, Webster D, Landless B, Dixon M P 1964/5 Serum protein patterns in 'normal' and pathological ageing. Gerontologia 10: 86–99

Woodford Williams E, Webster D, Dixon M P, MacKenzie W 1962 Red cell longevity in old age. Gerontologia Clinica 4: 183–193

Woodruff R K, Bell W R, Castaldi P A, Streatfield K, Penington D G 1980 Essential thrombocythaemia. Haemostasis 9: 105–125

Woodruff R K, Malpas J S, Paxton A M, Lister T A 1978 Plasma cell leukemia (PCL): a report on 15 patients. Blood 52: 839–845

World Health Organization 1959 Iron deficiency anaemia. Report of a study group. WHO Technical Reports Series No 182, p 4, World Health Organization, Geneva

World Health Organization 1964 Nomenclature for human immunoglobulins. Bulletin of the World Health Organization 30: 447–450

World Health Organization 1968 Nutritional anaemias. Report of a WHO Scientific Group. WHO Technical Reports Series No 405, World Health Organization, Geneva

World Health Organization 1969 Anaemias 1922–1966. Mortality statistics. WHO Statistical Reports 22: 409–427

World Health Organization 1970 Requirements of ascorbic acid, vitamin D, vitamin B_{12}, folate and iron. Report of Joint FAO/WHO Expert Group, WHO Technical Reports Series, No 452, World Health Organization, Geneva

World Health Organization 1972 Nutritional anaemias. Report of a WHO group of experts. WHO Technical Reports Series, No 503, World Health Organization, Geneva

World Health Organization 1975 Control of nutritional anaemia with special reference to iron deficiency. Report of an IAEA/USAID/WHO Joint Meeting. WHO Technical Reports Series, No 580, World Health Organization, Geneva

Worlledge S M 1969 Immune drug-induced hemolytic anemias. Seminars in Hematology 6: 181–200

Worwood M 1982 Ferritin in human tissues and serum. Clinics in Haematology 11: 275–307

Wray D, Ferguson M M, Mason D K, Hutcheon A W, Dagg J H 1975 Recurrrent aphthae: treatment with vitamin B_{12}, folic acid and iron. British Medical Journal ii: 490–493

Wright W B 1967 Iron deficiency anaemia of the elderly treated by total dose infusion. Gerontologia Clinica 9: 107–115

Wright W B, Milner A R 1965 The serum carotene level in elderly patients. Gerontologia Clinica 7: 120–127

Wu A, Chanarin I, Levi A J 1974 Macrocytosis of chronic alcoholism. Lancet i: 829–830

Wu A, Chanarin I, Slavin G, Levi A J 1975 Folate deficiency in the alcoholic: the relationship to clinical and haematological abnormalities, liver disease and folate stores. British Journal of Haematology 29: 469–478

Wylin R, Schneider J 1976 Prostatectomy in an 85-year-old hemophiliac. Archives of Surgery (Chicago) 111: 818–821

Yan S H Y, Franks J J 1968 Albumin metabolism in healthy men and women. Journal of Laboratory and Clinical Medicine 72: 449–454

Yu T, Weinreb N, Wittman R, Wasserman L R 1976 Secondary gout associated with chronic myeloproliferative disorders. Seminars in Arthritis and Rheumatism 5: 247–256

Zacharski L R 1976 The erythrocyte sedimentation rate. British Journal of Hospital Medicine 16: 53–62

Zacharski L R, Elveback L R, Linman J W 1971 Leukocyte counts in healthy adults. American Journal of Clinical Pathology 56: 148–150

Zacharski L R, Kyle R A 1967 Significance of extreme elevation of ESR. Journal of the American Medical Association 202: 264–266

Zahavi J, Jones N A G, Leyton J, Dubiel M, Kakkar V V 1980 Enhanced in vivo platelet 'release reaction' in old healthy individuals. Thrombosis Research 17: 329–336

Zaino E C, 1981 Blood counts in the nonagenarian. New York State Journal of Medicine 81: 1199–1200

Zippin C, Cutler S J, Reeves W J Jr, Lum D 1973 Survival in chronic lymphocytic leukemia. Blood 42: 367–376

Zittoun R 1976 Subacute and chronic myelomonocytic leukaemia: a distinct haematological entity. British Journal of Haematology 32: 1–5

Zittoun R, Bilski-Pasquier G, Bonsser J 1972 Leucémie myélo-monocytaire avec anémie sidéroblastique. Semaine des Hôpitaux de Paris 48: 1977–1981

Aging and the skin

INTRODUCTION

Exposure to environmental influences occurs during normal life. Normal exposure leads to physiological aging changes in the skin except when the skin is unduly susceptible, due to genetic constitution or other body changes. A distinction between physiological and pathological aging of skin is subtle. Exposure to sunlight produces solar elastosis, then actinic keratoses, then squamous epithelioma. These changes may be complete by the fourth decade of life in otherwise healthy fair-complexioned outdoor workers in Northern Australia (Mackie and McGovern, 1958). In this example, normal exposure produces aging changes, one of which is undoubtedly pathological in that it is potentially lethal. It is more useful to divide aging changes into those which can or should be treated at an appropriate stage of their development and those which must be endured. These aging changes in skin arise from environmental influences, from genetic constitution and secondarily to other bodily changes.

Theories of aging are not discussed as we have found no evidence of an 'aging process' in the skin apart from the cumulative effects of genotype, environment, disease at other sites and disuse atrophy.

Epidermis
The thickness of the epidermis does not change with age, except for some tendency of exposed skin to increase in thickness (Whitton and Everall, 1973). There is a great increase in variability of thickness, shown as variation in cell layers of the stratum spinosum — from two to eight cells thick within one histological section (Montagna, 1965) — although the average number of cell layers does not change (Christophers and Kligman, 1965). The area of epidermis in contact with the dermis decreases due to a loss of rete ridges in both light-exposed (Andrew, 1961) and unexposed skin (Montagna, 1973).

The prickle cells forming the epidermis show greater variation in nuclear and cytoplasm size, shape and staining properties on light-exposed skin (Andrew,

1961). Also the arrangement of cells is less orderly. However, on unexposed skin very few of the changes are seen and there is no significant irregularity of the prickle cells (Nagy and Janner, 1970).

Oxygen consumption of isolated skin decreases with aging (Walter and Amersbach, 1948) and this is paralleled by a decrease in epidermal ribonucleic acid although the deoxyribonucleic acid content remains constant (Pietrzykoska and Konecki, 1967). Salsfield (1966) found a marked decrease in glycolysis and amino acid metabolism in aged skin, but his results are in direct conflict with very extensive measurements by Professor Serri's Department (Yamasawa et al, 1972) of many individual enzymes of the epidermis, which showed no decline in activity with advancing age.

The mitotic activity of prickle cells increases with advancing age in light-exposed skin (Serri and Bruni, 1967) but probably slows in unexposed skin (Baker and Blair, 1968).

Dermis
Collagen is the major component of the dermis, forming 79 per cent by weight (Sams and Smith, 1965). With increasing age the collagen content per unit area of skin decreases and the thickness of the dermis decreases (Shuster et al, 1975). This decrease is greatest on skin exposed to light (Shuster and Bottoms, 1963). The decrease in quantity of collagen is accompanied by qualitative changes which are also most marked on light-exposed skin. Solar elastosis is a change in the staining properties of dermal collagen resulting in the altered collagen taking up the staining properties of elastic tissue (Unna, 1896). The severity of the change varies widely with individual constitution and exposure to sunlight, wind and rain. The mildest changes are seen on enexposed skin such as that of the areola (Montagna, 1973). More advanced stages are macroscopically visible as the elastotic syndromes discussed later. Collagen undergoing elastotic degeneration shows a loss of striation and matrix, with an accumulation of amorphous material within the between fibres (Stevanovic, 1976). Later the collagen fibres become more disorganized and

split into microfibrils embedded in the homogeneous amorphous material (Braun-Falco, 1969).

Melanocytes in the basal layer of the epidermis decrease in number with advancing age, both on exposed and unexposed skin (Quevedo et al, 1969). The remaining melanocytes increase in size and show a more variable dopa-reaction (Fitzpatrick et al, 1965).Even on unexposed skin, melanocytes show vacuolar degeneration (Nagy and Janner, 1970). This may be due to the circulatory factor produced by exposure to light discussed later under the aetiology of malignant melanoma.

The strength and elasticity of skin is mainly due to the dermal collagen. The loss of collagen from the dermis with aging and the elastotic degeneration of remaining collagen decrease the strength of skin. This is seen in an extreme stage in the friable skin of the transparent skin syndrome described later. The collagen of aging skin shows a loss of elasticity measured in vivo, which is due to an alteration of the mechanical properties of the collagen (Grahame, 1970).

The amorphous ground substance of the dermis is composed of a variety of carbohydrate, protein and lipid materials of which the major constituent is the acid mucopolysaccharides. In man the important acid mucopolysaccharides (or glycosaminoglycans) are hyaluronic acid, dermatan sulphate and heparin sulphate. With advancing age there is a decline in dermatan sulphate and heparin sulphate per unit weight of skin, but no change in the hyaluronic acid content (Van His et al, 1973).

The cellularity of the dermis decreases with advancing age (Andrew, 1964). Fibroblasts decrease in number and show smaller, denser nuclei. There is little change in the number of macrophages. Lymphocytes are present in greater numbers as also are mast cells, although this latter has been disputed (Hellstrom and Holmgren, 1950).

Blood vessels

Andrew et al (1964) measured the vascularity of the dermis by counting endothelial cell nuclei. They found an increase with age up to 20 years of age and thereafter a decrease. This is likely to reflect the decrease in papillary capillaries described by Ryan (1966). In addition to the decline in skin blood vessels with aging, a wide range of vascular hyperplasias become very common. Venous stasis, cherry angiomas and caviar tongue are found very commonly in the elderly (Beck, 1956). Venous lakes on ears, face, lips and neck (Bean and Walsh, 1956) and palmar and finger varicosities (Clark et al, 1974) become increasingly common.

Thermoregulatory skin vascular reflexes are unchanged by age in fit persons but there is a group of the elderly who show impaired regulation of skin blood flow. This group is at risk for accidental hypothermia of the elderly (Macmillan et al, 1967). It is likely that this thermoregulatory impairment is due to degenerative neurological changes involving or affecting the autonomic nervous system (Kuntz, 1938; Andrew, 1956).

Hair

Greying of hair (canities) is normally distributed in the population (Keogh and Walsh, 1965). By the age of 50, half the population have at least 50 per cent of their body hair grey, irrespective of sex and hair colour. Greying occurs in normal individuals determined by an autosomal dominant gene (Hare, 1929). It is also seen in certain pathological states and is a feature of some rare, hereditary syndromes.

Trotter (1930) noted that hair colour tended to darken from childhood onwards. At the onset of greying, this tendency is reversed. Greying normally begins on the temples and gradually extends to the vertex of the scalp. It may not occur on axillae, presternum or pubis. Axillary hair greying is rare in females but more common in men.

The replacement of terminal hair by vellus hair is first seen in the adolescent scalp producing some frontal recession in 80 per cent of women and 100 per cent of men. Recession at the temples is often evident by the age of 20 in males and is the first manifestation of genetically determined male pattern baldness. Sixty per cent of Caucasian men by the age of 50 have some degree of vertical as well as bitemporal baldness.

Women show the same tendency but to a lesser degree, 64 per cent, aged 40 to 70, show bitemporal recession (Beck, 1950) and 20 per cent of these have obvious vertical thinning.

As well as this patterned loss of hair, there is a uniform reduction in scalp follicle density from 615 per sq cm in the third decade to under 500 per sq cm by the age of 50, after which there is little further change (Giacometti, 1965).

Silverstri (1955) found a reduction in shaft diameter with aging but there was considerable variation in degree. Wynkoop (1929) found a progressive increase in shaft diameter of scalp hair during childhood, but thereafter there was no correlation of shaft diameter with age. Trotter's work (1922, 1924, 1930) supports this and showed as well that hair shaft diameter from various regions showed a definite correlation, specific for each region, with the age of the individual, e.g. leg hairs increased in diameter throughout life, but axillary and pubic hair did not do so after 20 years.

Grey hairs have little or no pigment in the cortex. The process of greying of hair is the result of progressive replacement of fully pigmented hairs by hairs with decreasing amounts of pigment. The process is not uniform and there is usually a complete range of different pigmented hairs, until they are all white.

Light and electron microscopic studies (Montagna, 1965; Herzberg and Guseck, 1970) of hair bulbs from elderly greying people have shown normal melanocytes over the papillae of black hair with many melanin granules in the cells of their matrix and cortex. Grey hairs contained numerous normally placed melanocytes but some of them showed vacuolization and other degenerative changes in melanosomes, endoplasmic reticulum and mitochondria. The matrix and shaft contained fewer melanin granules.

In white hairs melanocytes were usually absent and there was no pigment in the matrix or cortex. The papillae of such hairs contained no pigment melanocytes or melanophores. Pigment-containing melanophores were seen outside the glassy membrane, often along blood vessels only in pigmented hairs. No Langerhans cells were seen in the bulbs of these hairs.

Body, axillary and pubic hair reaches the full terminal hair pattern by the fourth decade. Thereafter there is a progressive loss of hair in the reverse order to which it developed. Trunk hair becomes sparser first and is lost earlier in women than in men (Melick and Taft, 1959).

Pubic and axillary hair follow, and are lost earlier and more completely in women.

Axillary hair is absent in over 30 per cent of females, but only 7 per cent of males over 60. Pubic hair is rarely absent in males over 60, but is in 5 per cent of women. Thomas and Ferriman (1957) found an abrupt loss of suprapubic to umbilical hair following the menopause. Forty per cent of females have developed coarse facial hair by the age of 55. After this there is rarely any increase in the number of these hairs and the weight of hair produced daily per unit area decreases (Hamilton and Tereda, 1963).

Over the age of 60, leg hair is scanty in both sexes but arm hair is often plentiful in males (Hamilton, 1958). Eyebrow, ear and nasal hair may become coarser and longer in older men.

Nishimura and Shimuzi (1963) showed in Japanese twins that the extent and pattern of alopecia in males, the number of grey hairs and their age of onset are under genetic control.

Sweat glands

Montagna (1965) described in detail the histological aging changes of eccrine sweat glands in exposed and unexposed skin. The usual changes were unevenness of the secretory epithelium, some cells being small, others being of normal size. The clear cells tend to flow together. The lumen of the secretory coils is often large and contains homogeneous or flocculent material. The argyrophilic staining of the canaliculi is lost and there is diffusion of the argyrophilia of the dark cells.

The most striking change is a progressive accumu-

lation of lipofuscin, yellow pigmented granules in the form of rosettes, in the cytoplasm of both clear and dark cells. It fluoresces with orange light, is basophilic and argyrophilic, does not contain iron or lipid or stain with haematoxylin and is not PAS positive. Glands from exposed skin always have more granules.

In the very old the secretory coils of many glands undergo complete involution, being replaced by fibrous tissue. The duct remains intact. Remaining glands have an increase of fibrous tissue around them. There is marked reduction in the number of blood vessels and in the acetylcholine-esterase containing nerves around the glands.

Histochemically there is a marked reduction of succinic dehydrogenase and phosphorylase activities especially in clear cells. There is little or no phosphatase activity in the intercellular canaliculi compared with obvious activity in young glands.

Oberste-Lehn (1965), in a study of the effects of aging on the number and distribution of eccrine sweat glands, found that density decreases with increasing age in both sexes but between 40 and 59 there is an increase in density in both sexes. He attributed this to an absolute increase in 'free glands' as distinct from the concentrically arranged glands around hair follicles. He postulated that new sweat glands are formed. Sweat gland density is greater in girls than in boys, decreases more in women than men in the 20- to 39-year age groups, becoming greater in women of the 40- to 59-year age group. There is no difference after this age. The concentrically arranged glands decrease in density with advancing age, the overall decrease in density correlating with decrease in the number of hair follicles. There is a relative increase in single glands but an absolute decrease of significant degree compared with concentrically arranged glands.

With increasing age the thermal threshold for sweating is raised, the sweat output at a body temperature of 38°C is decreased and the maximum sweat output in response to intradermal cholinergic substances declines but the number of active glands does not change (Foster et al, 1976). There is a decreased output of sweat per sweat gland after intradermal mecholyl in the aged (Silver, 1965). Both sets of results could be explained on the basis of disuse atrophy.

Montagna (1965) was unable to confirm the earlier belief that the sebaceous glands become atrophic with age. He found little change in the histological appearance with advancing age.

The glands appear morphologically the same regardless of whether they are hypo- or hyper-active. They may become completely inactive rather than atrophic. These inactive glands (characterized histologically by their location and cords or clusters of cells similar to the cells of the malpighian layer) have a high content of glycogen and exhibit phosphorylase activity. They can even, in the very old, be reactivated by androgens. Similar inactive glands may be found in infants.

The sebaceous gland complexes (sebaceous follicles) on the face are sometimes associated with a vellus hair follicle. In the elderly, histological sections may reveal fine cords of cells sprouting from anywhere along the vellus follicle and from the neck of the sebaceous follicles. The glands extend deeply into the dermis in many cases. The sebaceous follicles also have epithelial masses of undifferentiated cells attached to them which contain glycogen but which unlike normal sebaceous glands have little reactivity for succinic dehydrogenase.

Aged sebaceous glands tend to have fewer blood vessels around them and the gland parenchyma contains more glycogen and phosphorylase than young glands. Changes in scalp glands will be considered later.

Most authors agree that sebum secretion remains constant in men until the age of 50 when there is a slight fall (Pochi and Strauss, 1965; Grasset and Brun, 1959). Kirk (1948) found a slight increase with old age. Secretion in the skin of old men falls (Rothman, 1954). In females, production is steady but less than in men until the age of 50 when there is a marked fall. The activity seems to be dependent on gonadal androgenic secretions in both men and women (Pochi and Strauss, 1963).

Apocrine glands are not reduced in number or size in old age (Way and Memmesheimer, 1938). Montagna (1965) found increased ballooning of apocrine gland tubules in elderly skin but stressed the inconsistency of this finding. Lipofuscin, the 'wear and tear pigment', accumulates in apocrine glands (Crawley et al, 1973).

Immune responses

Skin testing for immediate allergy to a battery of food allergens elicits fewer positive responses in the elderly (Tuft, 1955). Skin testing for delayed (T-lymphocyte mediated) allergy to tuberculin (Waldorf, 1968) and to a battery of antigens (Roberts-Thompson et al, 1974) also elicits fewer positive responses in the elderly. The frequency of positive delayed allergic responses to poison ivy declines with age (Smith and Kiern, 1961). But the ability to become allergic to the potent topical allergens dinitrochlorbenzene and nitrosodimethylaniline does not decline with age (Epstein and Jesser, 1959; Smith and Kiern, 1961). These findings are susceptible to so many different interpretations that they can only serve as guidelines to further research.

SOME COMMON PATHOLOGICAL CHANGES IN AGING SKIN

Aetiology

The major cause of pathological change in aging skin is sunlight. By a direct local effect sunlight causes the elastotic syndromes, keratoacanthoma, premalignant disease, basal cell epithelioma and squamous cell epithelioma. By indirect and direct effects, sunlight causes malignant melanoma. Susceptibility to this major environmental carcinogen is hereditary; exposure is related to climate, occupation and social custom. Other skin carcinogens such as topical tar, ingested arsenic and previous scarring disease are quantitatively unimportant.

The pathogenic fraction of sunlight is in the shorter ultraviolet, with a wavelength shorter than 320 nm, not transmitted by window glass. In addition to the delayed pathological effects, there wavelengths also cause the immediate sunburn erythema, the thickening of the stratum corneum, the sun tanning and increased melanin production by melanocytes. Repeated exposure has a cumulative pathological effect. In mice the induction period for skin cancer is three months (Blum, 1959). In man the induction period for skin cancers due to sunlight is 15 to 40 years. Lesser exposure produces the other long-term effects of sun damage.

In some rare hereditary dermatoses there is exceptional shortening of the induction period for sun-induced skin cancer. In severe exeroderma pigmentosum (de Sanctis Cacchione syndrome) photosensitivity appears at the age of 6 months. Freckles appear on exposed skin, then actinic keratoses, telangiectases, patchy atrophy and lesions with the histology of senile lentigo. Malignant skin tumours appear after the age of 3 and include melanoma, squamous cell epithelioma and basal cell epithelioma. Keratoacanthoma is common. There is elastotic degeneration of dermal collagen. Death from squamous cell epithelioma of exposed skin often occurs before the age of 10 and usually before 20 years of age. Thus these unfortunate children show in an exaggerated and accelerated form many of the delayed pathological effects of sunlight. They also show a biochemical defect, lack of an enzyme.

Exposure of the skin to ultraviolet light causes damage to nucleic acid (DNA), probably due to formation of pyrimidine dimers (Pathak et al, 1970). In normal individuals damaged segments of DNA chains are excised and replaced. In most patients with xeroderma pigmentosum, lack of the enzyme which excises damaged DNA prevents repair following light-induced damage to chromosomes. This defect was found in xeroderma pigmentosum skin fibroblasts in tissue culture (Cleaver, 1968, 1970) and in epidermal keratinocytes in vivo (Epstein et al, 1970) but has not been detected in neoplasms or other photodermatoses. A defect is present in both the severe de Sanctis Cacchione and in the milder varieties of xeroderma pigmentosum. In the related skin disorder, pigmented xerodermoid, a defect in DNA repair occurs at a later stage in the repair process (Jung, 1971).

As xeroderma pigmentosum so closely mimics accelerated skin aging and malignancy due to sunlight it is tempting to suppose that sunlight causes delayed skin damage by inducing somatic mutations which are not repaired. There is no good evidence that environmental influences other than ultraviolet irradiation cause aging changes in the skin.

In a healthy well-norished person covered skin usually shows little obvious diffuse change with aging. In contrast, exposed skin shows many changes. The commonest and earliest delayed sun-damage to skin is elastosis, a degeneration of dermal collagen associated with a variety of appearances of 'weather beaten' or 'tanned' skin. These changes occur particularly in those occupationally exposed such as farmers and sailors, in those of fair complexion who sun-tan with difficulty and in the white-shinned living nearer the equator. The recent changes in social custom, whereby sun-tanned skin is admired socially and sexually, has led to an enormous increase in exposure of skin to ultraviolet light. This is a wanton invitation for accelerated skin aging and increased incidence of skin cancer, after the induction period of a few decades.

There are many syndromes associated with solar elastosis, some eponymously named. One of the commonest early changes is a diffuse yellowing, thickening and wrinkling, the citrine skin of Milian. Another appears in any fair-complexioned subject and resembles X-ray atrophy with mottled yellow pigmentation and depigmentation and prominent numerous telangiectases. Another extreme stage of solar elastosis is the transparent skin syndrome. Between these extremes there are some striking clinical pictures. Linear oblique furrowing of thickened yellow skin particularly of the back of the neck is the cutis rhomboidalis nuchae of Jadassohn. Very numberous comedones, giant comedones and follicular cysts particularly around the eyes are labelled nodular elastosis or the Favre Racouchot syndrome. Discrete yellow plaques are Dubreuilh's elastoma. A related condition, solar colloid degeneration of the dermis, contributes yellow-brown papules and nodules to the appearance of elastotic syndromes.

The transparent skin syndrome is most marked on the backs of the hands and forearms. The skin is shiny, loose, inelastic, thin and transparent to the extent that underlying veins and tendons are clearly visible. Histologically the striking feature in addition to elastosis is the thinness of the dermis (McConkey et al, 1967). Transparent skin is associated with senile osteoporosis (McConkey et al, 1963) and osteoporosis is associated with prematurely-aged lax wrinkled skin (Cooke, 1955). Both have been attributed to a wasting of connective tissues with aging. Some other features of aging are particularly pronounced in transparent skin. The variations in pigmentation, depigmented areas and the

pigmented senile lentigines are common. Senile purpura occurs as the blood vessels are more fragile, being less well supported. This purpura is slow to clear as there is less active reabsorption of extravasated erythrocytes (Tattersall and Seville, 1950). Transparent skin also shows the spontaneous appearance of white pseudoscars, pseudocicatrices stellaires spontanees (Colomb et al, 1967). These appear in many bizarre shapes, the commonest is a triradiate pseudoscar. Histologically, the picture is most striking: there is the dense normal collagenous scar tissue of the pseudoscar which is abruptly demarcated at the edges where the grossly thinned elastotic dermis of the transparent skin appears. Pseudoscars are usually found with senile purpura. Iatrogenic skin atrophy from topical fluorinated steroids closely resembles transparent skin except for the changes in pigmentation.

Keratoacanthoma, basal cell epithelioma and squamous cell epithelioma are local sun-induced proliferative changes associated with elastosis. These tumours, are, more rarely, provoked by other causes, such as tar for keratoacanthoma, mineral oil for squamous cell epithelioma and chronic arsenic poisoning for basal cell epithelioma. Keratoacanthoma is a self-healing tumour occuring on hair-bearing light-exposed skin (Champion and Rook, 1962). Squamous cell epithelioma occurs on slightly different exposed sites, for instance it is often found on the thin skin of the lower lip. The incidence of keratoacanthoma and squamous cell epithelioma varies widely with exposure to sunlight but despire this variation the relative incidence is remarkably constant (Rook and Champion, 1963). Basal cell epithelioma is a tumour of exposed skin, occurring mainly on the head and neck, but the incidence is less strikingly correlated with the degree of sun exposure and the tumour tends to appear in slightly shaded skin areas such as the medial lower eyelid.

Malignant melanoma is a term describing different tumours which differ in clinical features, histology and prognosis. The Report of the Australian Committee of Pathologist (McGovern et al, 1967) and the studies of Wallance Clark in Boston (Clark et al, 1969) define the foowing divisions: lentigo maligna melanoma which occurs almost exculsively on exposed skin of fair complexioned elderly Caucasians (Wayte and Helwig, 1968; Clark and Mihm, 1969); of premalignant melanosis melanoma (synonyms pagetoid melanoma (McGovern, 1970) and superficial spreading melanoma (Clark et al, 1969)) which occurs predominantly on exposed skin; and of nodular melanoma which arises in melanocyte naevi or normal skin, but is often found on covered skin.

However, sunlight appears to be a causative factor in all three types of malignant melanoma of skin. This is supported by four sets of information. The inverse relationship between latitude of residence and melanoma incidence or mortality has been reported repeatedly (McGovern, 1952; Lancaster, 1956; Lee and Merrill, 1970; Crombie, 1979b). Incidence varies from about 20 per million in England and Wales to 250 per million in coastal regions of Queensland, Australia (Davies et al, 1966). Further immigrants to Israel from Europe loose their relatively low melanoma incidence and develop melanoma at the higher rate shown by native Israeli Jews after 20–30 years (Anaise et al, 1978). Skin colour, by a protective effect of melanin, decreases the risk of developing melanoma (Crombie, 1979a).

Two reports agree that within one region there is greater exposure to sunlight from occupation, habit or hobbies in melanoma patients than in a control group (Lancaster and Nelson, 1957; Gellin et al, 1969). Further, both these reports agree that in the melanoma patients there is an excess of subjects with fair complexion and red hair who sun-burn easily and sub-tan with difficulty.

The yearly fluctuations in melanoma incidence in Connecticut have been found to show four cycles at 8–11 year intervals from 1935 to 1975. These cycles show a sharp rise in melanoma incidence beginning at peak sunspot activity and lasting 3–5 years. A similar correlation of melanoma incidence and sunspot activity was found in data from New York and Finland (Houghton et al, 1978). In 1979 Swerdlow showed that the annual fluctuations in melanoma incidence were significantly positively correlated in men and women and a further significant correlation between the annual incidence in women and the hours of sunshine 2 years earlier. They conclude that sunshine may cause melanoma after an induction period of 2 years. Finally, in xeroderma pigmentosum, a hereditary skin disorder with greatly increased liability to skin carcinoma of exposed skin, there is an increased incidence of melanoma of exposed skin.

Melanoma causation by cumulative sunlight exposure fits with the occurence on habitually exposed skin and increase of incidence with age found for lentigo maligna melanoma. However, comparison of series of melanoma patients from Cambridge — latitude 52°N (Bakos and Macmillan, 1973); Boston — latitude 43°N (Clark et al 1969); and Sydney — latitude 34°S (McGovern, 1970), indicates that there is an increase in incidence of mela-nomas with decrease in latitude, but that this is not confined to exposed skin, nor does it selectively affect lentigo maligna melanoma. Such variation in relative frequency of the types of melanoma as is found, suggests that increasing melanoma incidence accompanying increasing ultraviolet irradiation does not affect the proportion of lentigo maligna melanoma. So Lee and Merrill (1970) postulated that there is a solar circulating factor originating in exposed skin that promotes

neoplasia in melanocytes in non-exposed skin. Both Houghton et al (1980) and Holman et al (1980) have suggested that melanoma is provoked by intermittent intense sun exposure, presumably sunbathing or rec-reational exposure. Holman et al 1980 also found a higher melanoma incidence in indoor workers rather than in outdoor workers and in residents of higher social class areas.

These and the often recorded sex difference in melanoma incidence by site, higher on the male back and female leg, suggest that sunlight causes melanoma by cumulative exposure, by exposure provoked by sun worship and by exposure dictated by fashion.

Incidence

As in other branches of geriatric medicine, most skin diseases of younger age groups are found in the elderly. For instance, psoriasis occurs in 1 per cent of older (Zakon, 1952; Tindall and Smith, 1963) and in 1 per cent of younger persons (Ingram, 1954). In addition, there are disorders largely confined to old people. Skin disease is common. Young (1965) found pathological skin conditions in 98 per cent of geriatric patients in hospital. Other geriatric hospital surveys have shown a high incidence of vascular dysplasias of the tongue and scrotum (Kocsard et al, 1958) and of palms and fingers (Clark et al, 1974). Droller (1955) found 521 dermato-logical conditions in 476 elderly persons living at home. Many conditions occur in more than half the subjects in most studies.

With increasing age a variety of skin changes become visible. Some are normal or average accompaniments of aging. Most appear earlier in life when there is environ-mental stress as from sunlight or a genetic predisposition as in xeroderma pigmentosum. Descriptions of skin disease incidence vary widely in precision of diagnosis and selection of the population sample. The incidence of many conditions varies considerably with race, complexion, climate and previous or present occupation.

Most surveys of defined elderly populations outside hospital and clinics involve only white-skinned subjects and these only in temperate climates. Very little is known of skin disease in the elderly Negro, but squa-mous carcinoma and keratoacanthoma are rare (Rook and Champion, 1963) whereas melanocyte naevi and seborrhoeic keratosis are as frequent as in Caucasians exposed to a similar environment (Tindall and Smith, 1963). The effect of climate is marked, particularly on skin neoplasms and preneoplastic conditions.

Three surveys of apparently fit elderly persons indi-cate that Caucasians living in a temperate climate may expect an incidence in excess of 50 per cent of many skin lesions once aged over 60 (Zakon et al, 1952; Droller, 1955; Tindall and Smith, 1963).

On exposed skin senile lentigo or liver spots show a

striking increase in incidence with aging, exceeding 90 per cent over 80 years of age (Hodgson, 1963). On covered skin, vascular dysplasias such as senile angiomas, cherry-red or Campbell de Morgan spots and angiokeratomas show a similar age-associated increase. These lesions of focal dermal capillary proliferation and dilatation are almost universally present after the age of 70 (Bean, 1955). The diagnosis of mild lesions of seborrhoeic keratosis demands close inspection of the surface of the lesion to differentiate it from the many other pigmented lesions found in old people. This probably accounts for variations from 30 per cent to 90 per cent in reported incidence.

Variations in diagnostic criteria and climate probably account for reported incidences from 40 per cent to 80 per cent for asteatosis or abnormally dry skin in the elderly. The wide range of elastotic syndromes describe variants of the pathological changes due to sunlight. These changes are common; the incidence, severity and age of onset vary much with climate, complexion and occupation.

Skin neoplasms are less common than these conditions and the incidence varies widely. In England the incidence of melanoma is about 0.002 per cent per year (Peterson et al, 1962). For epitheliomas the incidence is markedly age-dependent, ranging from 0.05 per cent aged 50 to 0.1 per cent in older age groups (Doll, 1968).

In contrast to the conditions of increasing incidence with aging, melanocytic naevi become progressively rarer, decreasing from an average of 30 at the age of 25 (Brown, 1943) to four at 60 years (Stegmeyer, 1959).

A different picture of incidence is obtained by analysing diseases requiring treatment in elderly patients attending a skin clinic. A variety of reports (Palmer, 1951; Noojin and Osment, 1957; Horne, 1959) agree that the commonest diagnoses are:

Pruritus, senile and anogenital
Eczema, contact and endogenous
Keratoses, actinic and seborrhoeic
Venous leg ulcer and dermatitis
Epitheliomas, basal and squamous.

Other diseases presenting special problems in the elderly are melanoma and Herpes zoster.

Keratoses

Keratoses, actinic and seborrhoeic, have little in common except occurrence in the elderly and the histological finding of increased amounts of keratin. The aetiology of *actinic keratosis* has already been described. The lesion is first detectable clinically as a small red area with a few dilated blood vessels in light-damaged skin. Clinically inapparent lesions can be demonstrated histologically and by an inflammatory response to 5-fluo-

rouracil. The initial red area is well demarcated and gradually loses the normal skin surface markings developing a rough yellow to brown keratinous surface. The lesions are often most easily identified by touch. The commonest sites are the forehead, cheeks, dorsum of hands and forearms and, in men, ears and bald scalp.

Early lesions may regress if exposure to sunlight is avoided. All actinic keratoses are potentially malignant with a latent period of usually more than 10 years. The first sign of malignant change is induration. Most squamous carcinomas developing in actinic keratoses metastasize late, unless they arise on the ear (Gretschel, 1962).

Treatment is prophylactic and (if required) by local destruction of the lesions. Incisional biopsy is necessary when there is suspicion of malignant change. Pre-malignant actinic keratoses can be destroyed by a wide range of caustics, by freezing, by cautery or by diathermy. When lesions are very extensive but not grossly indurated topical application of 5-fluorouracil is very effective treatment for the intelligent patient.

The aetiology of *seborrhoeic keratosis* is largely unknown. The very commonness of the lesions, their development late in life and at times insignificance are difficulties in obtaining an adequate survey for genetic analysis. They occur predominantly on unexposed skin in white persons. They have been reported as rare in Negroes in whom a histologically similar disorder, dermatosis papulosa niger appears on the cheeks earlier in life, but Tindall and Smith (1963) found 10 or more seborrhoeic keratoses in 61 per cent of elderly Negroes.

The first evidence of seborrhoeic keratosis is the appearance of patches of brown-grey discoloration which show loss of normal epidermal surface sheen, a fine granularity on examination with a hand lens and whose texture lacks roughness. With care these lesions can be differentiated clinically from melanocyte naevi, actinic keratoses, senile lentigo, malignant lentigo, malignant melanoma and other pigmented lesions.

Often lesions on exposed skin do not enlarge further, but those on covered skin may develop into papillomatous, greasy, friable, dark warty lesions. These lesions are benign and the ease of their removal with a curette confirms the diagnosis.

Epitheliomas

The consequences of neglect and the good results of early treatment make the early diagnosis of malignant disease of the skin important. Early diagnosis depends upon suspicion of any persistent circumscribed skin lesion.

For some skin neoplasms diagnosis and excision of the local lesion are inadequate. For instance, both Bowen's disease of unexposed skin (Graham and Helwig, 1959) and arsenic-induced superficial basal-cell epithelioma (Hill and Fanning, 1948) are associated with internal cancer. The constant association of Paget's disease of skin and carcinoma of the breast and occassionally other organs is well known.

The growth rate of a lesion is one of the most important factors in differential diagnosis. The slow relentless enlargement of basal cell epithelioma is characteristic; the diameter of lesions shows a monthly increase of 0.1 to 1.4 mm (Teloh, 1953). Squamous cell epitheliomas grow faster than this but, except for the rare highly anaplastic nodular form, much more slowly than keratoacanthoma. This benign tumour enlarges 10 to 20 mm per month during the initial growth phase (Rook and Champion, 1963).

Basal cell epithelioma is the commonest skin cancer in white races and although metastasis is rare, if left untreated it can cause gross mutilation and death by local invasion. It is most common on the face. It arises from epidermal or hair follicle cells and has a most characteristic histology.

Most commonly the initial lesion is a small, smooth, hemispherical, translucent or pearly papule covered by thinned epidermis through which dilated blood vessels and sometimes specks of brown or black pigment may be seen. At this stage it may be confused with a melanocyte naevus, nodular malignant melanoma, senile sebaceous hyperplasia which has a central pore or with non-umbilicated lesions of molluscum contagiosum. The initial papule enlarges and may form a mass of pearly nodules, a plaque composed of small papules or an ulcer surrounded by a popular rim, a rodent ulcer. The mass and the plaque may be darkly pigmented with melanin and resemble malignant melanoma. The common rodent ulcer may resemble keratoacanthoma or squamous cell epithelioma. The keratoacanthoma grows more rapidly and has a central core of keratin rather than the crust of dried blood and serum of the rodent ulcer. Squamous cell epithelioma has a less smooth rim which is a dirty yellow colour.

Another presentation is as a small persistent ulcer with an unobtrusive fine nodular border resembling an excoriation or an early squamous epithelioma. Superficial basal cell epithelioma is a red plaque with a fine nodular border which has often been misdiagnosed as eczema, psoriasis or Bowen's disease. Morphoeic basal cell carcinoma is a plaque of scar tissue, sometimes with a fine nodular border, which grows very slowly, even for a basal cell epithelioma. This form is often misdiagnosed as a scar or a scarring skin disease such as lupus vulgaris.

The most useful treatment for basal cell carcinoma is curettage and cautery under local anaesthesia. In the hands of an experienced operator this gives a cure rate equal to other techniques (Sweat, 1963; Simpson, 1966; Knox et al, 1967), a good cosmetic results, material adequate for histological confirmation of the diagnosis, is convenient for the patient and is a brief operation requiring a minimum of special equipment. At times the site, size or type of lesion may indicate treatment by excision, with or without a skin graft, or by radiotherapy. Other techniques for treatment are little used in this country.

After treatment the patient should be seen occasionally for at least 2 years to detect recurrences which occur in 5 per cent of patients after all three types of treatment.

Squamous cell epithelioma is a tumour of the epidermis and mucosae which is both locally invasive and liable to metastasize, particularly by lymphatic spread. It appears almost always on damaged skin, particularly in actinic keratoses, but also in leukoplakia, radiodermatitis, scars and sites chronically exposed to carcinogens such as oil and tar. The first sign of a squamous epithelioma is the appearance of induration with surrounding redness, the lesion being firmer than an inflammatory one. Exact appearance depends on the preceding lesion. The small, hard, red nodule enlarges in one or more of three directions, towards an ulcerated lesion with a raised, rolled, grey-yellow edge, by deep infiltration, or to form a vegetating mass resembling a giant wart — this last being least malignant.

Chronic of treatment depends on locally available skills. Initial diagnosis requires histological examination of at least a deep incisional biopsy. In regions such as Queensland and Texas (Freeman et al, 1964) where actinic keratoses and squamous carcinomas are very common, excellent results are obtained from curettage and cautery of even large lesions. Equally good results are obtained by radiotherapy and by primary excision. Prognosis depends more on duration of the lesions and site than the type of treatment provided the operator is skilled. Excluding ear carcinoma which metastasizes early (Huriez, 1962), carcinoma arising on unexposed skin, and those provoked by carcinogens such as mineral oil and arsenic, squamous carcinoma of skin has a very high overall survival rate (Knox et al, 1967).

Pigmented lesions

Many of the skin lesions which are so common in the elderly are pigmented. One group of rare pigmented tumours, the malignant melanomas, is often (in 50 per cent of patients) not diagnosed clinically until after biopsy (McMullan and Hubener, 1956). Thus it is important to be able to recognize the common pigmented lesions and always to suspect melanoma.

Pigmented lesions are conveniently considered as macular or palpable (Table 42.1). Many of the macular lesions occur on sun-damaged exposed skin. Senile purpura and senile lentigo are common on the dorsum of the hands, forearms and face. They are sharply demarcated, irregularly shaped, evenly pigmented

Table 42.1 Pigmented lesions

Macular	Palpable
Atrophic pigmentation and depigmentation — mottling	Malignant melanomas
Senile purpura	
Senile lentigo	Melanocyte naevus
Lentigo maligna	
	Keratosis
	Thrombosed virus wart
Freckle (ephelis)	Thrombosed angioma
Melanocyte naevus	Pigmented basal cell epithelioma
	Histocytoma

macules of greatly variable size. The senile purpura is transient and red-purple. The lentigo is persistent and is an even yellow-brown to black colour, darker than most freckles (ephelides) and unlike freckles does not fade when not exposed to sunlight. Lentigo maligna resembles senile lentigo except for its irregularities and in the development of invasive melanoma in about a third of cases after a latent period of 10 to 50 years. Lentigo maligna is more irregular in its border, in its extension and regression and in its pigmentation which varies patchily between areas of black, dark brown and pale brown.

These lesions can be differentiated histologically. In senile purpura there is old blood extravasated in grossly elastotic dermis with remarkably little inflammatory response. Freckles show no change in melanocytes of the epidermis except an increase in melanin production. Melanoctye naevi show characteristically arranged naevus cells in the basal layer of the epidermis and in the dermis. Senile lentigo shows accentuation of rete pegs with an increase in number and activity of individual melanocytes in the basal layer. These melanocytes may be mildly atypical. Lentigo maligna melanocytes are, in some areas, more atypical and are found in clumps in the basal layer and invading the epidermis.

Lentigo maligna is a premalignant lesion and should be excised. However, the lesion is commonly 3 to 6 cm across, on the face and in an elderly person. It is necessary in each patient to assess the life expectancy, the risk of melanoma and the effect of disfigurement from a large skin graft on the face before deciding upon treatment.

Clinical separation of palpable lesions from the macular ones may require careful palpation. Early lentigo maligna melanoma appears as a palpable thickening in lentigo maligna. Early actinic keratoses are small brown or red spots whose surface lacks normal skin markings and whose texture is rough. Early seborrhoeic keratoses are small pale brown spots whose surface is finely granular with a greasty texture.

Melanocyte naevi or moles may be confused with melanoma, particularly when they enlarge, itch and change colour due to inflammation which is often bacterial or post-traumatic.

Blood pigment may colour lesions brown or black. In thrombosed warts the spots of pigment are regularly arranged. Angiomas may be black nodules due to thrombosis or extravasated blood. Some pigmented basal cell epitheliomas show a similar jet-black colour.

The diagnosis of melanoma is difficult. Suspicious features in the history are itch or irritation of a pigmented lesion, change in colour, particularly patchy darkening, and increase in size.

Premalignant melanosis is typically a variably pigmented thickened plaque one or two centimetres across with an arciform border showing fine irregularities. The multi-coloured surface is important in differentiating this type of premalignant melanoma from fully benign lesions. The colour often found are black, brown, pale brown, pink, grey and white.

Nodular melanoma grows rapidly. The surface configuration is smooth or polypoid (like a raspberry). The epidermis typically shows at least fine scaling and often a raw surface. The colour is usually black, or pink in the amelanotic form, or a mixture of these colours. There is often a fine brown macular halo surrounding the lesion. Small pigmented skin secondary deposits are often present in the skin proximal to the nodule.

The treatment of malignant melanomas presents problems. A correct clinical diagnosis is most likely to be achieved by an experienced dermatologist. This should avoid the occasional mishap of radical mutilating removal of a benign lesion such as a seborrhoeic keratosis. Definitive treatment requires wide local removal down to deep fascia and plastic repair of the defect. Further treatment is the subject of much discussion (Edwards, 1972).

Pruritus

Generalized pruritus is a most distressing affliction; it can prevent sleep and drive a person to contemplate suicide. As a most important symptom of skin disease it deserves more respect, for often it is a sign of internal disorder and requires the same thorough diagnostic approach as haemoptysis or jaundice.

The sensation of itch comes from impulses arising in the free nerve endings in the papillary dermis and lower epidermis travelling by slowly conducting C nerve fibres to the spinothalamic tracts and thalamus. There are several qualities of itch. That from urticaria or dermographism provokes a desire to rub gently with the finger pads as more vigorous mechanical counter-irritation may be painful. Eczema-type itch where there is less acute inflammation is rubbed more vigourously often using the fingernails which become hightly polished. This repeated trauma leads to self-perpetuation of itch and eczema. This process is most obvious in lichen simplex where the prevention of trauma, by occlusion, can clear a long-standing lesion. Finally, a more severe itch, often found in generalized pruritus due to internal disorders, provokes excoriation, a form of counter-irritation achieved by excavating pieces of skin with the ends of the nail.

Examination may show the lesions of an itchy skin disease, of an infestation or of underlying internal disease (Table 42.2). Itching skin disease sufficiently severe to cause generalized pruritus usually requires the attention of a dermatologist. Infestations, however, can be diagnosed if suspected. Body lice are usually found in individuals with a poor standard of personal hygiene. The lice are 2 mm dark insects found in the seams of underclothes and the skin lesions are usually excoriations. Spots of blood may be seen in underclothes. In the elderly, scabies is often caught from younger members of the same family. However, like pubic lice, transmission is predominantly venereal. Pediculosis capitis affects the scalp and is diagnosed from the white eggs stuck onto the hairs.

Table 42.2 Causes of generalized pruritus in old age

Without rash (except excoriations)	
Systemic causes	Drug withdrawal or administration
	Liver and kidney disease
	Anaemia and polycythaemia
	Reticulosis and neoplasms
	Other
Local (dry skin) factors	Familial or hereditary
	Climatic
	Ablution
	Aging
Psychogenic	Parasitophobia (rare)
	Other (rare)
With rash	
Infestations	Scabies
	Body lice
	Crabs
	Other
Itching skin disease	Eczema
	Premphigoid
	Lichen planus
	Other

Where examination shows no sign of itchy skin disease or infestation, the presence of excoriation suggests a systemic cause for itching. In younger age groups withdrawal symptoms in drug addicts are increasingly important as a cause of generalized itch. In the elderly withdrawal of barbiturates or other drugs may provoke a similar but milder reaction. This is self-limiting, but at times it appears kinder to perpetuate an

addiction of many years' standing. Itch is a side-effect of some drugs such as morphine and curare.

Itch appears in many varieties of liver disease and is often accompanied by other skin signs of liver disease such as spider naevi and palmer erythema. Its occurrence and treatment in late obstructive jaundice as well known. More important, the itching may precede the appearance of jaundice, and evidence of liver disease may only be obtained from biochemical tests. In biliary cirrhosis itch may appear long before jaundice develops (Ahrens et al, 1950). Similarly in chronic renal failure pruritus may be the presenting symptom.

In both iron-deficiency and megaloblastic anaemia, itch is a prominent feature in a few patients, but usually occurs only when the haemoglobin concentration is below 7 g per 100 ml. There are some patients who recognize a recurrence of their anaemia by the reappearance of itching. In polycythaemia rubra vera itch may also be prominent, particularly after a bath.

Itch is one of the most important skin signs of neoplasia and may precede other symptoms by a long time. In Hodgkin's disease it is often a presenting symptom. It occurs in 30 per cent of patients (Bluefarb, 1959) and may for a long time be the sole complaint, and is characteristically resistant to treatment. The development of mycosis fungoides in a patient with premycotic dermatosis is often signalled by the appearance of itching. Itch is usually the main complaint in this skin reticulosis until the terminal stages.

Several other associations have been reported; yet there is lack of convincing evidence that they are more than coincidental. These associations link generalized pruritus with carcinoma of the stomach, breast and uterus (Cormia, 1965) and with hyperthyroidism and diabetes mellitus. If another skin sign of neoplasia in addition to pruritus is present, search for underlying malignant disease should be extensive. Other signs include acanthosis, nigricans, thrombophlebitis migrans, dermatomyositis, acquired ichthyosis, Bowen's disease occurring in unexposed skin, and arsenical pigmentation and keratoses.

The commonest cause of widespread itching in the elderly is dry skin or asteatosis, a state due to the action of several factors which combine to produce skin lacking in lipid and of increased permeability to water (Onken and Moyer, 1963). On the back such skin looks pale, dry and has attached irregular small scales; it feels rough. On the lower legs this skin has a smooth shiny surface divided into polygonal areas by fine fissures which, in more severe instances, show as red, moist cracks. On the hands the dorsum shows a similar 'crazy paving' appearance and the pulps are wrinkled and fissured. Such dry or asteatotic skin is intensely itchy, itching being exacerbated by change in temperature as in undressing, by physical irritation as from woollen garments or by chemical irritation as in using detergents or degreasing solvents.

Asteatosis appears in skin which has been subject to the influence of factors tending to degrease or to increase transpiration. Physiological greasing of the skin is largely a function of sebaceous glands whose secretion is a complex mixture of lipids. Activity of these glands is largely controlled by endogenous androgens, but responsiveness of the glands varies between individuals. This range of responsiveness is associated with a range of skin texture from greasy smooth seborrhoeic skin to dry rough skin. Individuals with dry rough skin are prone to chapping throughout life and, when sebaceous gland activity decreases further with increasing age (Strauss, 1971), are liable to asteatotic pruritus and asteatotic eczema. (The commonly used term 'senile pruritus' is no diagnosis, only a description of age and symptom).

Degreasing of the skin occurs on washing and, when frequent bathing appears to be a provocative factor, the itch may be labelled pruritus balnei. A recent cause of pruritis balnei is the use of detergent-containing bath additives to produce a foam bath or a bubble bath. Degreasing from use of detergents and lipid solvents usually only affects the hands; it is associated with the asteatotic variety of hand eczema. Other provocative factors are those encouraging transpiration of water and include a low humidity, which is common in cold weather and in centrally heated accommodation, and an increase in air movement, exposure to wind. Most of these factors are active in winter in Britain and an itch apparently provoked mainly by these may be labelled pruritus hiemalis. Thus factors which are hereditary, due to aging, due to climate and due to personal hygiene may conspire to produce the common pruritus of the elderly, that associated with asteatosis or dry skin. But this diagnosis must only be made after exclusion of itching dermatoses, infestations and systemic causes.

The principles of treatment of asteatotic pruritus are obvious. Failure is occasionally due to lack of persistent attention to sufficient factors and use of inadequate quantities of lipid. Each of the factors mentioned should be considered and, where appropriate, counteracted. Usually baths, especially using soap, should be restricted to one a week and a bath oil used. There is wide variability in individual acceptability of preparations used to apply lipid to the skin. There is a wide range of emollients containing soft or liquid paraffin with lanolin or cetomacrogols; the British National Formulary lists Aqueous Cream BP, Emulsifying Ointment BP, Hydrous Wool Fat Ointment BPC, Oily Cream BP and Wool Alcohols Ointment BP. These emollients may be dissolved in bath water to act as bath oil, used to replace soap in washing and applied thinly to the skin as a topical application — a large quantity

is required. The initial response is more rapid if a diluted topical steroid cream (such as betamethasone valerate 0.01 per cent) is applied to the whole skin surface once daily for a few days. Other measures which may be of value, are increasing environmental humidity, avoiding rapid temperature changes and avoiding woolen clothing. Continued maintenance therapy with emollients is required to prevent recurrences of the itch, particularly during winter.

Exclusively psychogenic itch is rare. Perhaps the least rare variety is parasitophobia in which the patient has a fixed delusion of infestation. This condition is most resistant to treatment except in the occasional case due to nutritional deficiency (Aleshire, 1954). A psychogenic factor in itch due to other causes is common.

Anogenital pruritus presents either acutely when a local cause is usually found or as an itch of long standing often without local cause. Itch arises from contact dermatitis, from other skin diseases and by perpetuation by rubbing and scratching.

Endogenous primary irritants are: (1) faeces which may remain in contact with skin in patients with piles, anal fissures, diarrhoea or a poor standard of hygiene, (2) urine which may remain in contact with the skin due to incontinence or poor hygiene and (3) a vaginal discharge due to trichomoniasis, candidiasis and carcinoma of the cervix or other disorder of uterus, cervix or vagina. Exogenous causes of primary irritant or allergic contact dermatitis include bath additives such as Dettol, TCP and hexachlorophene, which tend to flow along the bottom of the bath and reach the anogenital area in high concentration, and sensitizing applications such as topical antihistamines, topical anaesthetics and lanolin-containing preparations. The most common other skin diseases producing anogenital itch are infestations by crab lice, infection by dermatophytes, candida and bacteria and three endogenous dermatoses, psoriasis, seborrhoeic dermatitis and intertrigo. Itching with diabetes mellitus is almost invariably due to candidiasis. Two rarer skin conditions, lichen sclerosus and leukoplakia, often are very itchy.

In each patient the importance of each of these factors must be assessed. Local disease, parasites and skin disease must be treated. Exogenous irritants must be avoided. Lichen sclerosus requires treatment with fluorinated topical steroids and regular supervision to detect any premalignant change. Leukoplakia (carcinoma *in situ*) requires biopsy to establish the diagnosis and either excision or frequent inspection to detect any malignant change.

After local causes have been treated the skin of the anogenital area must be soothed to allow the habit of rubbing and consequently provoking itch to be broken. Unless the onset of the itch is recent, this treatment must be continued for many months. A soothing regime includes avoidance of tight clothes, wool, soap and lavatory paper, regulation of bowel habit with a high-roughage diet, use of emollients and application of the weakest effective topical steroid to control itching.

Herpes zoster

Herpes zoster (shingles) represents the reactivation of *Herpes varicellae* virus acquired during a preceding varicella infection and which has remained alive in a dorsal root ganglion. It is significantly more common in patients with Hodgkin's disease or leukaemia. The virus migrates down the senory nerve to the epidermis where is produces ballooning and reticulate degeneration of epidermal cells with vesicle formation. The first clinical feature is pain and tenderness involving one or more dermatomes, with headache, malaise and fever. After a few days the involved dermatomes show redness, then-oedema and then vesiculation. Mucosae supplied by the same sensory nerve can be affected so explaining the occasional finding of renal colic or urethritis. The vesicles rupture and the resulting erosions heal in about one month unless they become secondarily infected. In most patients treatment should be symptomatic, directed to prevent spread of chickenpox and aimed at prevention of secondary infection by the use of an antibiotic spray.

In some patients a few scattered vesicles outside the involved dermatome appear. Rarely, particularly in patients with serious disease such as a reticulosis or on immunosuppressive drugs and systemic steroids, disseminate zoster with multisystem involvement may develop. This is often fatal. In such patients there is a strong case for early vigorous treatment with soaks of 5 per cent iodoxuridine in dimethylsulphoxide (Dawber, 1974). Should this prove ineffective, a systemic anti-metabolite such as cytosine arabinoside is usually given.

In the elderly the pain and discomfort during an attack of zoster are often severe and post-herpetic neuralgia can be terrible. Topical treatment of value is 5 per cent Iodox-uridine (iodoxuridine) in Demethylsulphoxide painted over the involved skin 4-hourly for 4 days, followed by povidone iodine alcoholic paint twice daily and if crusting is persistent povidone iodine ointment applied thickly daily. Iodoxuridine often shortens the attack, but application can be very painful. Some pain relief may be obtained from non-addictive potent analgesics potentiated by chlorpromazine. The patient should be isolated sufficiently to prevent the spread of chicken pox.

The pain of both herpes zoster and of post-herpetic neuralgia can be helped by two insufficiently-used treatments. Insonation of the nerve root or the painful area with ultrasound, 1 MHz or 3 MHz, is often most helpful (Summer and Patrick, 1964; Garrett, 1981). Glucocorticoids may be given systemically or subcutaneously to the painful area. Large doses are required and

side effects are few. Systemic treatment is begun with a daily dose of 40 mg or more of prednisolone for a week and tailed off over a month giving a total dose of about 600 mg (Keczkes and Basheer, 1980; Eaglstein et al, 1970). Local treatment is by subcutaneous infiltration of triamcinolone acetonide suspension diluted with normal saline to give 2 mg/ml (Epstein, 1981). 30 ml is injected daily for up to 2 weeks, giving a similar total dose to that of systemic treatment.

Leg ulcer

The causes of leg ulcer are legion. However the only important one is trauma. The first stage of diagnosis is to exclude the rare causes of leg ulcers. The commonest rare causes are vasculitis, basal cell epithelioma, melanoma, pyoderma gangrenosum, necrobiosis lipoidica and osteomyelitis. Also it is important to exclude a pelvic cause for leg oedema and vein distension. Most leg ulcers due to vasculitis respond to systemic steroids. An alternative treatment is to use a potent steroid ointment combined with an antibacterial agent such as an imidazole cream.

Calf vein incompetence is suggested by a family and personal history of varicose veins, by a history of swollen leg following pregnancy, of a leg fracture, or of a frank deep vein thrombosis; by symptoms of aching or heaviness of the legs at the end of the day relieved by elevation or of the feet; and by signs of a venous flare at the instep or of gross varicose veins. Competence of the calf muscle pump for venous return can be assessed by examining mobility of ankle, knee and hip joints and muscle power. Pain in the ulcer is relieved by elevation of the leg and aggravated by dependency. Pain may persist on elevation where there is also arterial insufficiency or infection or dermatitis. A rare cause of calf-vein incompetence is arterio-venous anastomosis.

Arterial insufficiency shows different feature. There may be a history of intermittent claudication. The ulcer is usually painful and this pain is relieved by dependency of the leg and exacerbated by elevation. The foot is cold and the skin is pale, thin and hairless.

Vascular insufficiency may be treated by surgery to arteries or veins or injection of veins. Unfortunately, most patients are not suitable and ill-judged operation often makes the insufficiency worse. With venous incompetence the patient may be helped by compression, elevation and exercise. Compression may be continuous using elastic adhesive bandaging such as Elastoplast or Poroplast applied over a zinc oxide paste bandage or directly to the leg (Dickson Wright, 1931). Intermittent pressure may be applied using elastic web bandages or strong compression hosiery (Anonymous, 1982). These measures should increase comfort. Increase of pain raises the suspicion that the predominant vascular disorder in the leg is arterial insufficiency not venous incompetence. This applies also to elevation of the foot of the bed and of the leg while at rest out of bed. Exercise by walking when the leg is compressed and by calf muscle exercises with the leg raised promote the action of the calf-muscle pump. Standing still should be avoided. With arterial insufficiency the patient must avoid compression and elevation is unhelpful. Exercise helps.

Dermatitis on an ulcerated leg is usually due to contact with a primary irritant or an allergen and shows the changes of an acute, subacute or chronic eczema with brown pigmentation. Simple statis dermatitis is rare. The commonest causes of primary irritant dermatitis are hypochlorite solutions and desloughing agents.

To avoid delaying healing the antibacterial agents chosen should produce little irritation. If desloughing agents are to be used it must be accepted that their destructive effect on tissue on which their action depends will delay healing. Most slough can be excised using forceps and scissors without anaesthesia, or will separate without assistance. Allergic contact dermatitis is common in patients with chronic leg ulcers. Over 50 per cent of these patients have allergies to one or more topical applications. The commonest allergy is to lanolin. Other common allergies vary with local prescribing habits and include neomycin, soframycin, fucidin, gentamycin, rubber chemicals, balsam of Peru, vioform and parabens. Patch testing is an important part of treating leg ulcers. Potent allergens including topical antibiotics should be avoided. Dermatitis should be treated with hydrocortisone ointment or tar preparations.

Leg ulcers are usually infected. Some infections, mostly by streptococci, staphylocci, proteus, pseudomonas and anaerobes delay healing. Superficial infection which produces much discharge from the ulcer usually responds to topical antibacterial agents such as povidone iodine ointment or spray, polynoxylin gel, benzyl or hydrogen peroxide, chlorquinaldol ointment or imidazole preparations. A green discharge suggests proteus infection for which 0.5 per cent acetic acid soaks and helpful. An offensive smell suggests anaerobic infection, which often responds to systemic metronidazole. Even when superficial streptococcal infection identified by culture is usually treated with a systemic antibiotic.

Systemic antibiotics are the most effective treatment for deep infection (cellulitis) which is usually due to streptococci or staphylocci. The choice of systemic antibiotic depends on local patterns of bacterial resistance and on the results of bacterial culture and sensitivity testing. There is no place for topical antibiotics in the treatment of leg ulcers.

Topical applications for leg ulcers may affect healing favourably or adversely. Healing is reversed by potent topical corticosteroids unless the ulcer is due to a steroid responsive vasculitis. Delay in healing is produced by primary irritants such as hypochlorite solutions and desloughing agents. Most slough can be excised with scissors and forceps without an anaesthetic or will separate spontaneously. Topical antibacterial agents which are less irritating than hypochlorite are available and have been mentioned earlier. As over half of patients with chronic leg ulcers are allergic to some topical applications used in the treatment of ulcers, healing is often delayed by allergic contact dermatitis.

Topical applications for leg ulcers should permit healing to occur. When superficial infection is not delaying healing, bland applications such as non-adherent dressings, yellow soft paraffin, zinc and castor oil ointment and zinc oxide paste bandages are suitable. Zinc oxide paste bandages, like elastic adhesive bandages, have the advantage that they decrease un-needed disturbance of an ulcer and so increase the likelihood of healing. While resistant superficial infection can be well treated with soaks of permanganate, peroxide or acetic acid, cleansing of leg ulcers, if done, should be done with bland preparations such as tap water, saline or oil.

It would be most helpful to have topical applications which would promote healing of leg ulcers. However, leg ulcers like some other disorders such as Psoriasis have many popular treatments and new treatments are frequently marketed and published. The initial trial results showing improved healing are often not reproduced. New treatments over the last few years include sheets, moulding liquid and beads of synthetic material and sheets derived from pigskin. These treatments are usually expensive and cost is not a guide to effectiveness. Some may have a place in the treatment of a group of leg ulcers which have yet to be defined.

REFERENCES

Ahrens E H, Payne M A, Eisenmenger W S, Blonhel S H 1950 Primary biliary cirrhosis. Medicine 29: 299–364

Aleshire I D 1954 Delusion of parasitosis report of successful care with antipellagrous treatment. Journal of the American Medical Association 155: 15–17

Anaise D, Steinitz R, Ben Hur N 1978 Solar radiation: possible etcologic factor in malignant melanoma in Israel: retrospective study (1960–72). Cancer 42: 299–304

Andrew W 1956 Structural alterations with ageing in the nervous system. Journal of Chronic Diseases 3: 575

Andrew W 1961 Ageing of the skin and related structures. In: Bourne G H (ed) Structural Aspects of Ageing, Pitman, London

Anonymous 1982 Compression hosiery for stasis disorders. Drug and Therapeutics Bulletin 20: 81–84

Andrew W, Behnke R H, Sato T 1964/45 Changes with advancing age in the cell population of the human dermis. Gerontologia 10: 1–19

Baker H, Blair C P 1968 Cell replacement in the human stratum corneum in old age. British Journal of Dermatology 80: 362–372

Bakos L, MacMillan A L 1973 Malignant melanoma in East Anglia, England. British Journal of Dermatology 88: 55

Banfield W G, Brindley D C 1963 Preliminary observations on senile elastosis using the electron microscope. Journal of Investigative Dermatology 41: 9–17

Bean W B 1955 The changing incidence of certain vascular lesions of the skin with aging. In: Ciba Foundation Colloquium on Ageing, vol I, p. 80. Churchill, London

Bean W B, Walsh J R 1956 Venous lakes. Archives of Dermatology and Syphilology 74: 4 59–463

Beck C H 1950 A study of the extension and distribution of the human body hair. Dermatologica 101: 317–331

Bluefarb S M 1959 In: Cutaneous Manifestations of Malignant Lymphomas. C C Thomas, Springfield, Illinois

Blum H F 1959 In: Carcinogenesis by Ultra-violet Light: an Essay in Quantitative Biology. Princeton Univ. Press, Princeton, N.J.

Braun-Falco O 1969 Die morphogenese der senilaktinischen elastose. Eine electronenmicroskopische untersuchung. Archiv für klinische und experimentelle 235: 138–160

Brown E E 1943 Lentigines: their possible significance. Archives of Dermatology and Syphilology 47: 804–815

Champion R H, Rook A J 1962 Kerato-acanthoma. Excerpta Medica International Congress Series 55: 288–291

Christophers E, Kligman A M 1965 Percutaneous absorption in aged skin. In: Montagna W (ed) Advances in Biology of Skin, 6th edn, p. 163–174. Pergamon Press, Oxford

Clark A N G, Melcher D H, Hall-Smith P 1974 Palmar and finger varicosities of the aged. British Journal of Dermatology 91: 305–314

Clark E R 1938 Arteriovenous anastomoses. Physiological Reviews 18: 229–247

Clark W H, From L, Bernardino E A, Mihm M C 1969 The histogenesis and biologic behaviour of primary human malignant melanomas of the skin. Cancer Research 29: 705–727

Clark W H, Mihm M C 1969 Lentigo maligna and lentigo maligna melanoma. American Journal of Pathology 55: 39–67

Cleaver J E 1968 Defective repair replication of DNA in xeroderma pigmentosum. Nature, 218: 652–656

Cleaver J E 1970 DNA damage and repair in light-sensitive human skin disease. Journal of Investigative Dermatology 54: 181–195

Colomb D, Pincon J A, Lartaud J 1967 Individualisation anatomico-clinique d'une forme meconnu de la peau senile: les pseudo-cicatrices stellaires spontanees. Leur rapports avec le purpura de Bateman. Archives of Dermatology and Syphilology 94: 273–286

Cooke A M 1955 Osteoporsis. Lancet i: 929–937

Cooper Z K 1952 Aging of the skin. In: Lansing A I (ed) Cowdry's Problems of Aging, 3rd edn, p 764–790. Williams & Wilkins, Baltimore

Cormia F E 1965 Pruritus, an uncommon but important symptom of systemic carcinoma. Archives of Dermatology and Syphilology 92: 36–39

Crawley E P, Hsu Y T, Sturgill B C, Harman L E 1973 Lipofuscin ('wear and tear pigment') in human sweat glands. Journal of Investigative Dermatology 61: 105–107

Crombie I K 1979a Racial differences in melanoma incidence. British Journal of Cancer 40: 185–193

Crombie I K 1979b Variation of melanoma incidence with latitude in North America and Europe. British Journal of Cancer 40: 774–781

Davies N C, Herron J J, McLeod G R 1966 Malignant melanoma in Queensland analysis of 400 skin lesions. Lancet ii: 407–410

Dawber R 1974 Iodoxiuridine in herpes zosters: further evaluation of intermittent topical therapy. British Medical Journal 2: 526–527

Dickson Wright A 1931 Varicose ulcer. British Medical Journal 561–565

Dickson Wright A 1932 Chronic ulcers of the legs. The practitioner 77: 618–630

Doll R 1968 The age distribution of cancer in man. In: Engel A, Larsson T (eds) Cancer and Ageing, Nordaska, Bokhandelns Fonlag, Stockholm, p 15–36

Droller H 1955 Dermatologic findings in a random sample of old persons. Geriatrics 10: 421–423

Eaglstein W H, Katz R, Brown J A 1970 The effects of early corticosteroid therapy on the skin eruption and pain of herpes zoster. Journal of the American Medical Association 211: 1681–1683

Edwards J M 1972 Malignant melanoma: surgical aspects of treatment. Proceedings of the Royal Society of Medicine 65: 140–144

Epstein E 1981 Treatment of herpes zoster and postzoster neuralgia by subcutaneous injection of triamcinolone. Internal Journal of Dermatology 20: 65–68

Epstein J H, Fukuyama K, Reed W B, Epstein W L 1970 Defects in DNA synthesis in skin of patients with xeroderma pigmentosum demonstrated. In vivo. Science 168: 1477–1478

Epstein W L, Jesser R A 1959 Contact-type delayed hypersensitivity in patients with rheumatoid arthritis. Arthritis and Rheumatism 2: 178–181

FitzPatrick T B, Szabo G, Mitchell R E 1965 Age changes in the human melanocyte system. Advances in Biology of Skin 6: 35–50

Foster K G, Ellis F P, Dore C, Exton-Smith A N, Weiner J S 1976 Sweat responses in the aged. Age and Ageing 5: 91–101

Freeman R G, Knox J N, Heaton C L 1964 The treatment of skin cancer. A statistical study of 1341 tumours comprising results obtained with irradiation, surgery and curettage followed by electrodesiccation. Cancer 17: 535–538

Garrett A, Garrett M 1981 Clinical Curios. British Medical Journal 282: 372

Gellin G A, Kopf A W, Garfinkel L 1969 Malignant melanoma: a controlled study of possibly associated factors. Archives of Dermatology and Syphilology 99: 43–48

Giacometti L 1965 The anatomy of human scalp. In: Montagna W (ed) Advances in Biology of Skin, 6th edn, p 97–119. Pergamon Press, Oxford

Graham J H, Helwig E B 1959 Bowen's disease and its relationship to systemic cancer. Archives of Dermatology and Syphilology 80: 133–159

Grahame R 1970 A method for measuring human skin elasticity in vivo with observations on the effects of age, sex and pregnancy. Clincial Science 39: 223–238

Grasset N, Brun R 1959 Etude du film sebuce de sujets sains et de patients atteints d'epilepsie ou de maladie de Parkinson. Dermatologica 119: 232–237

Gretschel G E 1962 Gravite de certain epitheliomas du pavillon de l'orielle. Semaine des hộitaux de Paris 33: 1938–1941

Hamilton J B 1958 Age, sex and genetic factors in regulation of hair growth in man: A comparison of Caucasian and Japanese populations. In Biology of Hair Growth, ed. Montagna W, Ellis R H, p 399–433. New York: Academic Press

Hamilton J B, Tereda H 1963 Interdependence of genetic aging and endocrine factors in hirsutism. In: Greenblatt R B (ed) The Hirsute female, C C Thomas, Springfield, Illinois

Hare H J H 1929 Premature whitening of the skin. Journal of Heredity 20: 31–32

Harpuder K, Stein I D, Byer J 1940 The role of arteriovenous anastomosis in peripheral vascular disease. Americal Heart Journal 20: 539–545

Hellstrom B, Holmgren H J 1950 Numerical distribution of mast cells in the human skin and heart. Acta Anatomic 10: 81–107

Herzberg J, Guseck W 1970 Das Ergnaven de Kopfhaares. Ein histo fermentchemische sowie elektronenmikroskopische Studie. Archiv für klinischeund experimentelle Dermatologie 236: 368–384

Hill A B, Fanning E L 1948 Studies in the incidence of cancer in a factory handling inorganic compounds of arsenic. British Journal of Industrial Medicine 5: 1–6

Hodgson G 1963 Senile lentigo. Archives of Dermatology and Syphilology 87: 197–207

Holman C D J, Mulroney C D, Armstrong B K 1980 Epide-miology of pre-invasive and invasive malignant melanoma in Western Australia. International Journal of Cancer 25: 317–323

Horne S F 1959 Common geriatric dermatoses N Carolina Medical Journal 20: 177–181

Houghton A, Flannery J, Viola M V 1980 Malignant melanoma in Connecticut and Denmark. International Journal of Cancer 25: 95–104

Houghton A, Munster E W, Viola M V 1978 Increased incidence of malignant melanoma after peaks of sunspot activity. Lancet 1: 759–760

Huriez C, Lebeurre R, Leperre B 1962 Etude de 126 tumours auriculaires malignes observees en 9 an a la clinique dermatologique universitaire de Lille. Bulletin dela Socieété Francaise de Dermatologie et de Syphiligraphie 69: 886–892

Ingram J T 1954 The significance and management of psoriasis. British Medical Journal ii: 823–828

Izaki M 1951 Studies on senile changes in the skin. Keio Igaku 28: 59–79

Jung E G 1971 Das pigmentierte xerodermoid. Ein Defekt der Rekombinations-Erholung von UV-Schaden. Archiv für Dermatologische Forschung 241: 33–43

Keckes K, Basheer A M 1980 Do cortiscosteroids prevent post-herpetic neuralgia. British Journal of Dermatology 102: 551–555

Keogh E V, Walsh R J 1965 Rate of greying of human hair. Nature (London) 207: 877–878

Kirk E 1948 Quantitative determinations of the skin lipid secretion in middle aged and old individuals. Journal of Gerontology 3: 251–266

Knox J M, Freeman R G, Duncan W C, Heaton C L 1967 Treatment of skin cancer. Southern Medical Journal 60: 241–246

Kocsard E, Ofner F, Coles J L, Turner B 1958 Senile changes in the skin and visible mucous membranes of the Australian male. Australian Journal of Dermatology 4: 216–223

Kuntz A 1938 Histological variations in autonomic ganglia, and ganglion cells associated with age and disease. American Journal of Pathology 14: 783

Lancaster H O 1956 Some geographical aspects of the mortality from melanoma in Europeans Medical Journal of Australia. i: 1082–1087

Lancaster H O, Nelson J 1957 Sunlight as cause of melanoma: a clinical survey. Medical Journal of Australia i: 452–456

Lee J A H, Merrill J M 1970 Sunlight and the aetiology of malignant melanoma: a synthesis. Medical Journal of Australia ii: 846–851

Lee J A H, Merrill J M 1971 Sunlight and melanoma. Lancet ii: 550–551

Lee M M C 1957 Physical and structural age changes in human skin. Anatomical Record 129: 473–494

Lund H Z, Stobbe C D 1949 The natural history of the pigmented naevus; factors of age and anatomic location. American Journal of Pathology 25: 1117–1155

McConkey B, Grager M, Bligh A S, Whitley H 1963 Transparent skin and osteoporsis. Lancet i: 693–695

McConkey B, Walton K W, Carney S A, Lawrence J C, Ricketts C R 1967 Significance of the occurrence of transparent skin. Annals of the Rheumatic Disease 26: 219–225

McGovern V J 1952 Melanoblastoma. Medical Journal of Australia i: 139

McGovern V J 1970 The classification of melanoma and its relationship with prognosis. Pathology 2: 85–98

McGovern V J, Caldwell R A, Duncan C A 1967 Report of Australian Committee of Pathologists. Moles and malignant melanoma: terminology and classification. Medical Journal of Australia i: 123–125

Mackie B S, McGovern V J 1958 The mechanism of solar carcinogenesis. Archives of Dermatology and Syphilology 78: 218–244

Macmillan A L, Corbett J L, Johnson R H, Crampton Smith A, Spalding J M K, Woolner L 1967 Temperature regulation in survivors of accidental hypothermia of the elderly. Lancet ii: 165–169

McMullan F H, Hubener L F 1956 Malignant melanoma — a statistical review of clinical and histological diagnosis. Archives of Dermatology and Syphilology 74: 618–619

Meema H E, Reid D B W 1969 The relationship between the skin and cortical bone thickness in old age with special reference to osteoporosis and diabetes mellitus: A roentgenographic study. Journal of Gerontology 24: 28–32

Melick R, Taft P 1959 vations on body hair in old people. Journal of Clinical Endocrinology 19: 1597–1607

Mitchell R E 1963 The effect of prolonged solar radiation on melanocytes of the human epidermis. Journal of Investigative Dermatology 41: 199–212

Montagna W 1965 Morphology of the aging skin. The cutaneous appendages. In: Montagna W (ed) Advances in Biology of Skin, 6th end, p 1–6. Pergamon Press, Oxford

Montagna W 1973 Ageing in the nipple and areola. Minerva Dermatologica 108: 3–11

Nagy C, Janner M 1970 Senile lesions of the human epidermis. An electron microscopic investigation. Archiv für klinische und experimentelle Dermatologie 238: 70–86

Nishimura H, Shimuzi S 1963 Studies on various ageing phenomena in Japanese twins and siblings. Acta geneticae medicine et gemellologiae 12: 22–49

Noorjin R O, Osment L S 1957 Common geriatric dermatoses. Southern Medical Journal 50: 237–240

Oberste-Lehn H 1965 Effects of aging on the papillary body of the hair follicles and on the eccrine sweat glands. In: Montagna W (ed) Advances in Biology of Skin, 6th edn, p 17–34. Pergamon Press, Oxford

Onken H D, Moyer C A 1963 The water barrier in human epidermis. Archives of Dermatology and Syphilology 87: 584–590

Palmer A E 1951 Dermatologic problems of aging women. Geriatrics 6: 363–378

Pathak M A, Kramer D, Gungerick U 1970 Formation of thymine dimers in epidermis by ultraviolet (290–320 nm) radiation in vivo Journal of Investigative Dermatology 54: 351

Peterson N C, Bodenham D, Lloyd O C 1962 Malignant melanomas of the skin. A study of the origin, development, aetiology, spread, treatment and prognosis. British Journal of Plastic Surgery 15: 97–116

Pietrzykowska A, Konecki J 1967 Nucleic acids content in human epidermis in relation to age. Dermatologica 135: 472–476

Pochi P E, Strauss J S 1963 Sebaceous gland function before and after bilateral orchidectomy. Archives of Dermatology and Syphilology 88: 729–731

Pochi P E, Strauss J S 1965 The effect on aging on the activity of the sebaceous gland in man. In: Montagna W (ed) Advances in Biology of Skin, 6th edn, p 121–127. Pergamon Press. Oxford

Quevedo W C, Szabo G, Virks J 1969 Influence of age and u.v. on populations of dopa-positive melanocytes in human skin. Journal of Investigative Dermatology 52: 287–290

Roberts-Thompson I C, Whittingham S, Youngchaiyad U, MacKay I R 1974 Ageing, immune response and mortality. Lancet iii: 368–370

Rook A, Champion R H 1963 Keratoacanthoma. National Cancer Institute Monographs 10: 257–270

Rothman S 1954 In: Physiology and biochemistry of the skin. Univ. of Chicago Press, Chicago

Ryan T J 1966 The microcirculation of the skin in old age. Gerontologia Clinica 8: 327–337

Salfield K 1966 Zur Frage des energieliefernden Stoffwechsels und Aminosauremetabolisms der alternde Haut. Archiv für klinische und experimentelle Dermatologie 225: 93

Sams W M, Smith J G 1965 In: Montagna W (ed) Advances in biology of skin, vol VI, Ageing, p 199 Pergamon Press, Oxford

Serri F, Bruni I 1967 Invecchiamento e cute. Atti della Accademia Medica Lombarda: 22. Simposio su: Medicina interna et dermatologia.

Shuster S, Bottoms E 1963 Senile degeneration of skin collagen. Clinical Science 25: 487–491

Shuster S, Black M M, McVitie E 1975 Influence of age and sex on skin thickness, skin collagen and density. British Journal of Dermatology 93: 639–643

Silver A F, Montagna W, Karacan I 1865 The effect of age on human eccrine sweating. In: Montagna W (ed) Advances in biology of skin, vol VI, Ageing, p 129–150. Pergamon Press, Oxford

Silvestri U 1955 I. Faneri nella Eta Senile. Studio del capello e dei pei ambosessuali. Giornale di Gerontologia Suppl 5: 203–276

Simpson J R 1966 The treatment of rodent ulcers by curettage and cauterization. British Journal of Dermatology 78: 147–148

Smith J G, Kiern I M 1961 Allergic contact sensitivity in the aged. Journal of Gerontology 16: 118–119

Stegmeyer O C 1959 Natural regression of melanocytic naevus. Journal of Investigative Dermatology 32: 413–420

Stevanovic D V 1976 Elastotic degeneration: a light and electron microscopic study. British Journal of Dermatology 94: 23–29

Summer W, Patrick M K 1964 Ultrasonic therapy. A textbook for physiotherapists. Elsevier, Amsterdam

Sweet R D 1963 The treatment of basal cell carcinoma by curettage. British Journal of Dermatology 75: 137–148

Swerdlow A J 1979 Incidence of malignant melanoma of the skin in England and Wales and its relationship to sunshine. British Medical Journal 2: 1324–1327

Tattersall R N, Seville R 1950 Senile purpura. Quarterly Journal of Medicine 19: 151–159

Teloh H A 1953 Correlation of rate of growth with histologic characteristics of basal cell carcinoma. Archives of Dermatology and Syphilology 68: 408–416

Thomas P K, Ferriman D G 1957 Variation in facial and pubic hair growth in white women. American Journal of Physical Anthropology 15: 171–180

Thuringer J, Katzberg A 1959 The effect of age on mitosis in the human epidermis. Journal of Investigative Dermatology 33: 35–39

Tindall J P, Smith J G 1963 Skin lesions of the aged and their association with internal change. Journal of the American Medical Association 186: 1039–1042

Trotter M 1922 A study of facial hair in white and negro races. Washington University Studies 9: 273–289

Trotter M 1924 The life cycles of hair in selected regions of the body. American Journal of Physical Anthropology 7: 427–437

Trotter M 1930 The form, size and colour of head hair in American whites. American Journal of Physical Anthropology 14: 443–445

Tuft L, Heck M, Gregory D C 1955 Studies in sensitization as applied to skin test reactions. III Influence of age upon skin reactivity. Journal of Allergy 26: 359–364

Unna P G (transl. N Walker) 1896 Histopathology of the Diseases of the Skin. Macmillan, New York

Van His J M J, Kruiswick T, Mager W H, Kalsbeek G L 1973 Glycosaminoglycans in human skin. British Journal of Dermatology 88: 355–361

Van Patten H T, Drummond J A 1953 Malignant melanoma occurring in xeroderma pigmentosum. Cancer 6: 942–947

Waldorf D S, Wilkens R F, Decker J L 1968 Impaired delayed hypersensitivity in an aging population. Journal of the American Medical Association 203: 831–834

Walter E M, Amersbach J C 1948 Correlation of age and respiration of skin from the human female. Journal of Investigative Dermatology 10: 11–13

Way S C, Memmesheimer A 1938 The sudoriferous glands. II. The apocrine glands. Archives of Dermatology and Syphilology 38: 373–382

Wayte D M, Helwig E G 1968 Melanotic freckle of Hutchinson. Cancer 21: 293–911

Whitton J T, Everall J D 1973 The thickness of the epidermis. British Journal of Dermatology 89: 467–476

Wynkoop E M 1929 A study of the age correlations of the cuticular scales, medullas and shaft diameters of human head hair. American Journal of Physical Anthropology 13: 177–187

Yamasawa S, Cerimele D, Serri F 1972 The activity of metabolic enzymes of human epidermis in relation to age. British Journal of Dermatology 86: 134–140

Young A W 1965 Dermatogeriatric problem in the chronic disease hospital. New York Journal of Medicine 65: 1748–1752

Zakon S J, Goldberg A L, Forman I 1952 Geriatric dermatoses a survey of the skin of the aged. Illinois Medical Journal 101: 37–38

Aging and the skin — pressure sores

INTRODUCTION

Pressure sores, or decubitus ulcers, are one of the potent hazards facing patients who are old, ill and immobile, but they also occur in younger patients rendered bed or chair-fast by various debilitating conditions, neurological disorders or spinal injuries. Much of the literature and recent research work relates particularly to the latter, but the findings are also applicable to geriatric patients.

Pressure sores are no new phenomenon. They have been found in Egyptian mummies; in the sixteenth century Fabricius believed that nerve severance resulted in loss of blood supply and nutrients. In the eighteenth century John Hunter recognized that the cause of pressure sores was an uneven distribution of bodyweight (Lancet, 1973a). Others in the nineteenth century, like Virchow and Billroth, also blamed reduced blood supply, but some writers held that pressure sores were related to the now discredited 'trophic' changes after nerve severance (Charcot, 1868).

As the name suggests the prime cause is pressure which is not relieved as it should be, and its effects will be considered in detail below.

The incidence and cost implications of pressure sores have been variously studied. Norton et al (1962) estimated that 12.5 per cent of geriatric patients had pressure sores on admission to hospital, and sores developed in a further 20 per cent at some time in their stay. Barton and Barton (1981) suggest that geriatric assessment wards admitting patients from home might find 30 to 50 per cent had sores. Such a high incidence might however reflect delays in admission of gravely ill patients. It has been suggested nevertheless (Lancet, 1973a) that there may be 25 000 patients with bedsores in the United Kingdom at any one time, having between them 30 000 sores (Fernie, 1973). Of these 50 per cent would be under treatment in hospital, and the duration of treatment required would be 2 to 3 months. It is reckoned that once a sore has become established a 50 per cent increase in nursing time for that patient will be required. Petersen et al (1971) from Arhus in Denmark

estimated that 43.1 patients per 100 000 of the population had pressure sores. Jill David (1981) has compared several studies of incidence, amongst which the Glasgow study of Barbenel et al (1979) showed 8.8 per cent of 8685 hospital patients had significant sores, with a high prevalence in those aged 70 and above; 44.5 per cent were bedfast. Barbenel and colleagues found almost double the incidence (i.e. 85.6 per 100 000 of the population) as compared with the experience of Petersen.

Based on the figures of the Lancet leading article already quoted, the cost in 1973 for treating pressure sores at say £1000 each would have totalled £60 million. At present day prices (1984) and at a conservative estimate, such bedsore treatment might cost £130 million, plus the cost of caring at home for those not sent to hospital. However this outlay would not be entirely for treatment of pressure sores, since they occur in ill people, who will probably require extended treatment anyway. Pressure sores probably prolong the hospital stay, but this is difficult to verify.

Sores should be preventable if sufficient skill and nursing vigilance are used, but when they occur they cause great distress and danger to patients, and absorb a great deal of our resources and our nurses' invaluable time.

Besides true pressure sores there is a small minority of lesions of a less serious kind which are caused by friction of restless limbs within the sheets. They are more like burns, but cause tissue destruction like pressure sores and are commonest over prominences like heels and elbows. It has been held (Neumark, 1981) that pressure itself is not destructive, but that deformation of tissue leads to pathological changes. This concept is not helpful, since, except in the weightless state, gravity causes deformation by any firm, dense object like a bed, chair or operating table on which the body is supported.

The great risk is where a high proportion of the body weight is brought to bear through a small area, especially where a bony prominence lies close beneath the skin, e.g. the sacrum, dorsal convexity or heels when the patient is supine, or the greatest trochanter in a lateral lying position. Quantifying what is a common experience, Petersen (1976) found the anatomical distribution of 318 sores was over 20 sites, of which the commonest were sacrum (43 per cent), trochanter (12 per cent), heel (11 per cent), ischium (9 per cent) and lateral malleolus (6 per cent). Pressure effects can be seen sometimes in unexpected sites, as when severe adductor spasm leads to sores on the contiguous surfaces on the medial aspects of the thighs or knees. Most of these points become especially vulnerable with the patient lying, but the sitting position is far from safe if the patient cannot take her weight and shift herself, for after long periods pressure sores can develop beneath the ischial tuberosities, and obese old people often have sharply folded redundant skin just where they sit.

Nearly 25 years ago it was shown that high pressure for a short while is safer to skin than low pressure for long periods (Husain, 1953). Even when the patient is sitting, pressures of 300 mmHg per square centimetre can be built up (Kosiak et al, 1958), though most people do not have to sustain greater pressures than 100 mmHg per square centimetre. It has been calculated (Siegal et al, 1973) that only 17 mmHg per square centimetre would result if the entire body surface could be available to distribute the weight. Certain tissues, notably the plantar skin and subcutaneous tissues, are designed for withstanding pressure; most of the surfaces in contact with a bed are not, so recumbency itself constitutes an immediate hazard, especially in older people.

The damage done is a function of pressure multiplied by time, and Reswick and Rogers (1976) have produced a graph based on 980 observations, indicating maximum acceptable as opposed to unacceptable combinations of pressure/time applications over bony prominences. Numerous animal experiments (e.g. on rabbit ear tissue, with subsequent histological examination), have confirmed such pressure/time relationships.

The mean capillary pressure is, according to various authorities, only of the order of 20 to 30 mmHg, so the microcirculation is very easily occluded. Normally active people are restless in bed; others, who are forced to be immobile, or are in coma, or very ill, or paralysed, or too much in pain to move, are potential victims of pressure effects. Matters are all the worse if sensory stimuli, which normally cause reflex or even conscious pain-relieving movements in bed, are unable to be registered, as in a case of severe paraplegia with sensory deficit. Indeed, it is simply the unpleasant sensations from ischaemic areas which prevent normal people from getting pressure sores as they sit or lie in bed. Many old people are just as vulnerable as a young paraplegic, for many are crippled, or made stuperose by illness or sedative drugs, and many are so mentally confused during an illness as not to be able to heed warning signals from their skin when it is subjected to pressure for too long. The valuable contribution of Exton-Smith and Sherwin (1961) was to show, by placing recording apparatus under beds, how a low 'score' of nocturnal movements correlated closely with vulnerability to pressure sores. This led Exton-Smith et al (1962) to propose a *clinical* scoring system so that those geriatric patients most at risk could be quickly identified and brought under most intensive nursing care to prevent decubitus ulcers. This system has many times proved its value in practical situations. Criteria for this assessment included the patient's general condition, mental status, degree of activity and mobility, and of incontinence (Table 43.1).

Another technique for observing the movements of the body during sleep was described by Bardsley et al (1976). They placed load cells under the feet of a standard hospital bed which re?orded on a continuous pen recorder, large and small body movements being distinguished by automatic infra-red photography of the sleeping subject, triggered by the monitoring load cells.

Important observations were made by Redfern et al (1973) on the measurement of pressure between various parts of the body and various supporting surfaces, as part of an evaluation of the Low Air Loss bed system, using separation indicator pads connected to a rubber-bulb air pump and manometer. Five volunteers lay on 10 different supporting surfaces, with pressure

Table 43.1 Scoring system for evaluating the risk of pressure sores developing in an individual patient (Exton-Smith et al, 1962)

A General Physical Condition	Score	B Mental State	Score	C Activity	Score	D Mobility	Score	E Incontinence	Score
Good	4	Alert	4	Ambulant	4	Full	4	Not incontinent	4
Fair	3	Apathetic	3	Walks/help	3	Sl. limited	3	Occasional	3
Poor	2	Confused	2	Chairbound	2	Very limited	2	Usually/urine	2
Very bad	1	Stupor	1	Bed	1	Immobile	1	Doubly	1

Scores of 14 or less indicate liability to sores
Scores of <12 indicate very great risk of sores

recording from eight vulnerable anatomical sites while they were supine or in the lateral position. Compared with the generally accepted capillary pressure (20 to 30 mmHg), some disturbingly high pressure readings were observed from an interior sprung mattress on a fracture board, from lying on a lino-covered floor — which perhaps ought to have been expected — as well as from a volunteer placed on a standard operating table and an orthopaedic operating table. The pressure with the latter (i.e. 10 times the mean capillary pressure) is a highly significant finding suggesting that patients undergoing lengthy orthopaedic operations on unmodified tables might be seriously at risk and develop sores before they even returned to a bed in a ward, as had indeed been suspected on clinical grounds. The maximum pressures recorded by Redfern and colleagues for the various supporting services are given in Table 43.2. Comparisons were made between certain special preventative devices (see Support Systems below). Remarkable differences were indicated, which however cannot be taken just at face value. For example, these are maximum not mean values; furthermore, the ripple mattress (see also below) yielded high figures, but the object of that mattress is to redistribute pressure automatically every few minutes, which at such pressure levels might be satisfactory enough.

Table 43.2 Local pressures observed with supporting systems (after Redfern et al, 1973)

	Maximum pressure in mmHg
Low-Air-loss bed	26
Feather pillows	36
Simple water bed	58
Polyether foam mattress	68
Ripple mattress (Talley)	122
Operating table	140
Interior sprung mattress	164
Orthopaedic operating table with pelvic rest	260
Lino-covered floor	260

Pressure sensing devices, their suitability and limitations, have been analysed by Ferguson-Pell et al (1976). Monitoring of temperature and humidity under subjects sitting continuously for 90 minutes on 11 various seating materials is the subject for work by Brattgard et al (1976) in Sweden.

Through unrelieved pressure is the principal culprit, there are other factors — in particular, states of protein deficiency, general malnutrition and ascorbic acid deficiency, anaemia, low blood pressure, conditions causing tissue oedema or local muscle wasting, devitalization of tissue (e.g. after intramuscular injections), peripheral vascular disease, and incontinence resulting in soiled, macerated skin. Incontinence or dampness of the sheets for other reasons also increases the co-efficient of friction at that point and enhances the potential shearing stresses. Lowthian (1976) found that incontinence increased the risk of sores on the sacrum and buttocks by a factor of 5.5. Nevertheless, an *active*, demented and totally incontinent patient may be very little at risk.

In a review of the role of ascorbic acid in wound repair, Schwartz (1970) pointed out that only minimal ascorbic acid body stores are needed to promote healing, but that there are significant losses of this vitamin after surgery — a point particularly worth noting after operations on elderly patients.

Position in bed is of great significance. In particular, a patient in an upright sitting or a semirecumbent position will always be sliding down the bed and subject to skin-shearing stresses at the pressure points. If, having slid, he is dragged up the bed again instead of being lifted, contrary skin-shearing stresses will be brought in.

A patient who is sitting upright after a double mid-thigh amputation of legs (not so very uncommon a happening in older patients) will be placing her whole weight through quite a small area of buttock skin, and large sores are very likely to appear. Some very frail and cachetic patients may develop signs of skin involvement almost anywhere that touches the bed. This happens sometimes over the scapular spines and on the pinnae of the ears, whilst the pressures of the bedcovers can be enough to cause sores on the knees.

PATHOLOGY

Wounding of the skin under conditions of pressure results in two conditions which cause anoxic necrosis. First, exclusion of blood because of pressure applied higher than the mean capillary pressure; secondly, damage caused by intermittent applications of pressure or shearing forces, which damage blood vessels including capillaries and cause platelet thrombosis, occlusion of the microcirculation and anoxic necrosis of tissue. In healthy tissue the first sign would be loss of epidermal surface layers and blistering, and where there are superficial bony prominences there may be full-thickness necrosis from an early stage. Barton and Barton (1968, 1973) studied the pathogenesis of pressure sores by animal experiments and by using the electron microscope. There is no extravasation of blood, but the endothelial cells lining the capillaries are separated by trauma; the junctional complexes between contracting endothelial cells are broken, perhaps due to a loss of adhesive properties of protein polysaccharides (Barton, 1970). It is suggested further that adrenocorticotrophic hormone (ACTH) stabilizes this protein polysaccharide complex of the cell junctions, and that ACTH has value therefore in sore prevention.

This extensive separation of endothelial cells, coupled with platelet thrombosis, is said to be the root of the problem; it also occurs in an area outside that of greatest pressure, and this outer ring of tissue is highly vulnerable too. Later, if conditions are satisfactory, there is dilatation and formation of new capillaries supported by collagen deposition, and with endothelial cell proliferation. A transudate forms in the wound in which cell migration is possible. Later there is contraction of the wound and sores of up to 7.5 cm can be closed completely by this means. Finally there is re-epithelialization and remodelling of the scar tissue, much as takes place in any wound. Indeed, Constantian and Jackson (1980) hold that there is no fundamental difference between a developed sore and any other open wound, that there are no specific missing factors, and that local treatment does not therefore need to be different.

Healing will clearly be delayed or prevented if the integrity of the patient's general circulation is impaired by atheromatous or other changes. The elasticity and contraction of the wound helps to explain the tendency for sores to have overhanging edges. Where a sore is deeper than 2.5 mm epithelial remnants are destroyed and epithelialization can only take place from the edge.

It has often been pointed out that an area of skin which is indeed dead may not break down and produce an open sore for several days. During this early stage the temperature at that point may be low, but that of the skin further away may be high enough for the difference to be detectable by the plam of the hand. With skin thermometry or radiometry, which is described below, cold areas may be precisely defined. These pathological processes, the microanatomy and other aspects of this complex subject have lately been reviewed in detail by Barton and Barton (1981), and by Cruickshank (1976).

Monitoring the progress of pressure sores

It is important that the size and progression of sores, once developed, should be susceptible of measurement. Certainly this must be achieved in research work, and it may also be desirable in clinical practice. It would also be particularly valuable if the possibility of a given area of skin breaking down could be reliably predicted. Research workers now regularly record the development of ulcers at standard intervals by simple measurements, by tracing on to a transparent membrane or by photography, perhaps using polaroid pictures, under standard conditions. However Barton and Barton (1973) described observations on 200 patients by these relatively simple means and by thermography as well. Pictorial thermography is effected by recording infra-red emission at wavelengths of 3 to 10 microns, the radiation being proportional to skin temperature, which itself is affected by tissue death, by local vascular changes, and sometimes by conduction from deeper tissues or infective processes. A colour display of thermographic data with isotherms in different colours is now available. Barton opines that there is no need for insisting on uniform conditions with a patient stripped in order to come to a steady thermal state in a stable environment, because it is temperature differences between one part and another which are of importance. A rapidly responding thermograph system with an indium antimonide detector requires a bulky unmanoeuvrable expensive noisy instrument in a separate room, equipped with liquid nitrogen cooling, but a slow system for static studies does not require the latter.

Thermography of pressure sores shows the skin temperature pattern over the area in question, but may particularly involve measurements of the temperature at the edge of the decubitus ulcer as compared with normal skin some inches away. These temperature differences were found to have prognostic value. Differences of about 2.5°C (Barton, 1973) suggest active reaction and a good prognosis, but differences of less than 1°C suggest a poor response and delayed healing. Recently also, Newman and Davis in Glasgow (1981a, b), in an appraisal of a prototype of a low-cost, heat-sensitive, television camera type of thermograph for possible routine use in wards, observed 91 elderly patients with intact sacral skin, and of this group 19 had abnormal thermographic responses; 35 per cent of these developed sores later at the suspected skin sites. They concluded that this method would give a more precise prognostication than a clinical scoring system to determine risk. The instrument, the pyroelectric vidicon camera, is portable, needs no coolant, is compatible with a television screen display and costs about one-third that of a conventional thermograph. In this study a stabilizing period of 10 to 15 minutes was used at a standard ambient temperature, and each buttock had to be scanned separately, though at the patient's own bedside.

Barton and Barton (1973, 1981) also discuss the use of radiometric methods — point measurement of skin temperature without contact. It would indeed be possible to use a skin probe, thermistor, or thermocouple, but these methods are time-consuming and are affected by moisture, skin contaminants etc. Though they are much cheaper they cannot have the advantages of a method providing an instant temperature 'scan' of the area under examination, as thermography can do.

The question must be asked whether there is a case for adopting for routine use in geriatric wards these sophisticated detection devices, and if so, whether the information obtained would materially influence the management of cases. If results were reliable, those patients thought to be at greatest risk might receive special preventative treatment. The points against such instrumental methods are the high capital cost, the difficulties in interpretation of results (which may be considerable) and the need to have specially trained and experienced nurses perhaps, or if not, technicians, to take the observations, and the time factor. In places where the incidence of pressure sores is unaccountably high the method might be most valuable; in others, where admission of patients at risk is rapid and where care in prevention is practised, it would seem a strangely pessimistic provision.

CLINICAL TYPES OF DECUBITUS ULCERS

Various types and degrees of severity of sores have been described, and used in research work to quantify lesions. Thus, Bliss et al (1967) and Bliss (1981) used a grading of 0 to +++, i.e. normal skin, down to the appearance of gangrene. However, Barton and Barton (1973, 1976, 1981) consider there are basically only three types of pressure sores, and base this opinion on thermographically recorded temperature differences between the edge of the sore and an area of the skin some distance away. Thus the first type shows a temperature difference of about 2.5°, which indicates a brisk reaction, a good prognosis and a healing time of some 6 weeks. The second Barton type, with a temperature difference of less than 1° is an indolent ulcer with a poor vascular response, perhaps due to platelet thrombosis and occlusion of the microcirculation (see above): it is claimed that this type has a probable healing time of 4 months. The third type, distinguished by a nil thermal response with no temperature difference, is a totally inactive sore with a poor prognosis, usually seen in terminal states. However this classification depends on instrumentation and the interpretation of these responses, whereas artifacts due to patches of inflammation, to smoking, to various drugs and local applications etc. further complicate the matter; therefore the method and the classification do not have wide acceptance amongst clinicians who incidentally often observe that with good nursing care pressure sores will sometimes heal in patients who are known to be in a slowly progressive terminal condition. More practical gradings, based on simple observation, have been adopted by various workers when assessing the incidence of sores.

There is usually agreement on four grades (Barbenel et al, 1979; Lowthian, 1979). From the mildest, then, with skin discolouration only, these gradings proceed to superficial ulceration, to skin destruction without a cavity, and lastly to destruction of skin with cavity formation.

From the standpoint of day-to-day observation we can also recognize special types of sores which develop in particular circumstances. Superficial pressure sores, often called 'benign', occur with what is probably less pressure for less time or from excoriation, shearing stress etc., and are particularly likely when skin is macerated with urine. They are not of full-skin thickness, they are painful, but should heal rapidly if kept uncontaminated and if the causative factors are removed. When an elderly patient spontaneously complains of a sore behind, this is what is likely to be found.

Many large pressure sores apparently develop with astonishing speed, though some (see above) are already foreshadowed because the causative event, e.g. extreme pressure during an operation, took place some days previously. Under skin which is apparently intact though in fact not so, the deeper muscular layers, being very susceptible to pressure, undergo hidden necrosis, lie under the threatened skin and then burst through like an abscess. This leaves a deep cavity full of black or disintegrated slough which later may become infected and show a large area of skin loss ringed by undermined margins, the cavity sometimes penetrating down to the underlying bone. This is a deep and dangerous type of sore which bears a poor prognosis for healing and for life itself in an old person. However, with prolonged and meticulous care even these formidable ulcers may granulate from below and the patient may survive, but with hideous scarring. Such large lesions might be eradicated more quickly if the patient were fit enough for plastic surgery.

A further common type is an extensive but apparently quite superficially placed area of hard black gangrene with loss of the full skin thickness. This may, if not surgically debrided, persist for many days or even weeks without healing, but without ulcerating to form an open wound. It is often to be found over a prominence like a greater trochanter, where there is little soft tissue between the skin and the bony 'anvil' underneath. Some indolent pressure sores fail to heal completely even though the early healing stages are gone through, and a persistent sinus is observed. Such sores have usually involved the deep seated bone in low grade osteomyelitis which must be investigated by simple radiography or sinography.

Another very serious type of pressure sore results, sometimes overnight, in patients who suffer a thrombosis of the inferior vena cava, though sometimes no other evidence of the thrombosis is apparent. A hugh black area of total tissue infarction appears over the buttocks and the sacrum, 10 to 20 cm across, and the prognosis is uniformly bad.

Those geriatric patients who stay in hospital a short time, either because of death or rapid discharge, hardly have time to develop sores. However, one in three pressure sores develops within the first week, and over two-thirds appear before the first 2 weeks (Exton-Smith et al, 1962, 1975). This period usually coincides with that of greatest immobility. The earlier the sore develops and the deeper it penetrates, the worse is the outlook for the patient. Deeper sores may persist many weeks and cannot be dismissed just as a preterminal event in someone who is unable to appreciate the danger they are causing.

PREVENTION

More than anything else, the quality of nursing care and the methods used will determine whether pressure sores occur or are prevented. In the best traditions of nursing teaching, it was always emphasized that the development of a pressure sore should be an admission of failure. This may seem harsh but it is no bad tradition to maintain. As we have seen, some sores develop late, perhaps days alate, after operations or because of the patient's recumbency before admission to the ward concerned. Clearly these are not the responsibility of the nurses now caring for the patient, but there has nevertheless been unawareness of the problem, and of the principles of pressure prevention, at some stage.

The frequent occurrence of pressure sores in any ward suggests at once the likelihood of faulty nursing techniques or administration, or insufficient staff. Notwithstanding, the doctor has a vital part to play, in understanding the causation of sores, in inspecting the threatened areas and emphasizing risks, modifying his treatment to suit, and above all trying to have his patients out of bed if they can be, as active as possible and under minimum sedation, if sedation is indeed required at all. In well-run paraplegic units and geriatric hospitals, where these matters are understood, pressure sores are uncommon, but this result is achieved only by adherence to strict routines and by unremitting vigilance — and the work is hard. The time of greatest risk is at night, when there is least general activity and the natural tendency is not to disturb patients. In fact there is little risk to the patient from disturbed sleep, but great risk from unrelieved pressure effects.

The first essential in prevention is to identify the patients at greatest risk. It is helpful to group them close together to assist intensive nursing, and this is one of the strongest arguments in favour of the concept of 'progressive patient care'. Keeping the patient active and out of bed is of the greatest prophylactic value. Treatment for any illness must be prompt and vigorous, but the use of sedatives and hypnotics increases the pressure sore risk. Anaemia and malnutrition call for urgent correction. However, the main essential is regular turning of the patient, come what may, from side to side, or back to side, by careful lifting — not

dragging — and this is best done by nurses in pairs. The intervals could be 4-hourly in patients identified as at 'low risk', but 2-hourly or even hourly or half-hourly when the risks are known to be especially high. There really is no substitute for such a regimen, though special support systems for patients may reduce the risk. There is such a variety of these now available that the whole subject requires detailed consideration (see below).

All patients prone to pressure effects need a bed cradle to take the weight of the clothes, whilst a footboard to counteract forward sliding and to reduce shearing is valuable. Sheets must be clean, smooth and dry, otherwise they will be abrasive and have a high coefficient of friction.

In some inactive, heavy, incontinent patients at special risk there is a case for catheterization to help reduce the hazard, but this should not be used uncritically as a routine measure in the name of preventing sores.

Younger patients at risk can and must be taught to protect themselves from pressure effects by spontaneous movements, shifting themselves in wheelchairs etc., and keeping watch on their equipment in their own interests, not relying entirely on others. This is one principle contributing to the great success of Sir Ludwig Guttmann's unit for the treatment of paraplegia at Stoke Mandeville, where much of the pioneer work on pressure sore management was done, and which has been summarized by Guttmann (1955, 1976). Unfortunately, elderly patients frequently do not appreciate the risks and cannot protect themselves because of serious illness (major disability precluding movement) or mental deterioration. Those who can take responsibility for themselves undoubtedly should be expected to do so, however old they are. Barton and Barton (1981) believe that excessive smoking increases the risk, as suggested by thermographic studies, and that long-term steroid preparations and other anti-inflammatory drugs do so likewise and should therefore be avoided in anyone at hazard. Notwithstanding, there is some evidence (Barton and Barton, 1968, 1981) that a single dose of ACTH in a gelatine solvent administered 4 hours before a critical event like an operation, can inhibit the formation of pressure sores by stabilizing the protein polysaccharides of the endothelial cell junctions, so preventing their separation and the train of microvascular events which otherwise follow (see above). If this is true its implications for surgery in old people and for major orthopaedic procedures in particular, needs no emphasis. The dose of ACTH is 80 IU and the timing is said to be critical.

In prevention generally it is *awareness* by doctors and nurses which matters above all: awareness of what causes pressure effects and how quickly; awareness of what medical factors like low blood pressure, immobility, nutritional deficiencies, effects of drugs and sedatives in particular, contribute to additional risk; awareness particularly of which individual patients are most at hazard. It is in this respect that the scoring system to measure potential risk (Exton-Smith et al 1962, 1975) has such importance in prophylaxis (see Table 43.2).

PHYSICAL SUPPORT SYSTEMS FOR PATIENTS

The search for the best kind of supporting surface for disabled patients in bed or in chairs who cannot physiologically or by their own positive efforts protect themselves from pressure effects has accelerated in recent years. This is an appropriate time for reviewing some of the better-known systems. Their object has been to provide the 'best' support according to scientific principles, but also to relieve nurses of part of a physically exhausting, endless duty, and perhaps to reduce the risks of human error or forgetfulness. However a word of caution is necessary. Nurses trained in the best traditions acknowledge that the great majority of pressure sores can be prevented if basic nursing skills are freely available at all relevant stages in the patient's illness, including investigation and special procedures. They hold, as the writer does, that special support systems are only an adjunct, never a substitute for good nursing procedures which require constant observation, dedication and the ability to lift safely. Nor will mechanical methods significantly reduce the numbers of nurses required: all systems have to be mastered and applied intelligently with attention to technical detail. Whether with support systems or not, patients must never be left recumbent or chairfast who need not be so. Support systems must also be cost-effective, having regard to capital and maintenance costs, and to the possibility of preventive or treating pressure sores more quickly, thus saving expense. Whatever the system, it must be acceptable to elderly patients, and be comfortable. Too little attention is paid to comfort in beds and chairs, but an attempt to evaluate it has been made by Redfern (1976). Scales et al (1974) redefined the requirements of a supporting system; the desiderata include an ability to accommodate to body shape and to develop uniform thrust on the maximum surface area, minimizing shearing stresses and being contour-adjustable. The ideal system should also allow control of temperature and humidity close to the skin, and be disinfectable and capable of being made right for emergencies. Support systems are to be considered for prevention and also treatment of pressure effects. A question to be faced is how far is it possible to go in the direction of complexity and expense, and for how long, in the name of prevention, particularly if large numbers of patients are at risk.

'Local' tissue support

For many years attempts were made to minimize pressure effects by applying padding under the vunerable points, especially the buttocks, sacrum and the heels. Thus there evolved a succession of large rubber air rings, water cushions, foam rings for sitting on, and simple small padded rings in which to set the heels. The latter are now recognized as being particularly hazardous by causing shearing stresses and the risk of arterial occlusion. More satisfactory developments in recent years have been foam-padded, elasticated, sleeve-like heel protectors (e.g. Tubipad), elbow sleeves, and foam or fleece-lined bed boots (Seton Products, etc. etc.). Particularly valuable has been the wedge-shaped foam pad ('Lennard') evolved by Brocklehurst (1964), whereby the heels can be kept clear of the bed or, by wrapping the pad around one extremity and fixing, so that all risk to that heel can be avoided, whatever lying position the patient adopts. By eliminating pressure and frictional forces equally, the Lennard pad has saved many limbs but is still a surprisingly neglected preventative device.

Static support system

Beds have never been quite satisfactory places for invalids. Bedsteads have evolved from the simple pallet with straw or horsehair mattress latterly covered, perhaps, with a thick inelastic red rubber sheet, to the present sophisticated hospital bed, adjustable for height and tilt and covered with a thick interior sprung or sorbo mattress. Probably better as a mattress is the simple deep modern polyether foam variety, of some 15 centimetres thickness. A recent development of the latter is the flexible polyether foam mattress (e.g. the Clinifloat [Astec]) cut so as to form a large number of individually deformable upwards-facing truncated cones on which the body weight can, it is claimed, be more widely distributed than on a plane foam surface (Fig. 43.1). This mattress also adapts easily to contour-style bedsteads (q.v.), and is relatively cheap and so almost 'disposable'. A similar system described by Reswick and Rogers (1976), an incised block of bed-sized polyurethane foam, is called the Poly-Flotation Mattress (Talley Medical). Foam mattresses need a thin plastic waterproof cover.

Another variant is a system of padded covers for beds, chairs, operating tables etc., in which cylindrical hollow-core fibres with silicone coating make up the filling material. Such a system is Spenco Silicone Padding (Spenco Medical). The claim here is that the pads give low pressure values, provide good local temperature and humidity control, and are inert, launderable and relatively cheap.

So-called 'gel' mattresses and pads had a vogue. These are plastic envelopes containing a gel of approximately

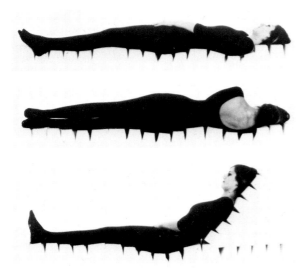

Fig. 43.1 Foam mattress with upwards-facing truncated cones to accommodate body contours in various positions. The Clinifloat Mattress (Courtesy of Astec Environmental Systems).

the same consistancy and viscosity as human fat. In some the viscosity can be varied; water is added some hours before use. It may be questionable if the body weight can be fully distributed by such means, or whether the filling material can retain a true fluid state as water beds do (q.v.).

Plain, renewable, uncovered dry sawdust had a vogue in the United States of America, but it is not always acceptable on aesthetic grounds, especially with incontinence. Sheepskin pads or their synthetic substitutes are widely used on top of mattresses: whether or not they help distribute body weight more widely is debatable, but their value probably lies in reducing temperature and humidity in the immediate vicinity of skin under pressure, and because they are comfortable (Ewing et al, 1961). Therefore they are commonly used on top of other support systems. Another notably comfortable system consists simply of eight or so feather cushions distributed randomly over a 15 cm polyether foam base. They are said to produce low pressure measurements under test, but the pillows have to be shaken and changed every 4 hours, so the work of nurses will not be much reduced.

A type of mattress or cushion pad originally evolved in Denmark has had its adherents also. It is filled with myriads of small expanded polystyrene globules like grains of sand, with a washable fabric cover. Its devotees claim that the beads quickly conform to the contour of the body pressing on them, and spread the load, redistributing it after any movement. That is eventually conforms provided the patient can move about is clear,

but whether the system usefully alters the distribution of pressure may be open to more doubt. This is the principle underlying the Cubex cushion support (Nottingham Medical Equipment), and the more comprehensive Beaufort Bead Pillow Mattress (Paraglide Limited) which employs 10 to 12 such bead-filled cushions distributed transversely on a bed over a standard mattress and kept in place with Velcro fastenings upon on impermeable under sheet. This system allows the patient to be in various positions, lying, virtually sitting up, prone, or in a chest drainage position. Lowthian (1976) makes the point that the various support systems incorporating feathers, sawdust, sand or plastic spherules utilize particulate material which can slip sideways like a viscous fluid and accommodate a load. They are grouped by Lowthian as 'viscous particulates'.

It has often been pointed out (e.g. Scales, 1976) that an inflexible substance used without soft padding, like plaster of Paris, carries no special risk of pressure effects provided it is smooth and accurately moulded to the patient's contours: so, where it is necessary for other reasons, patients are even now nursed for months in plaster beds without much risk. A similar principle governs the use of the sand tray type of bed (Stewart, 1976). A quantity of clean dry sand is laid in a tray on a rigid bedstead with containing sides, and hollowed out by hand so that the shape fits the contours of the patient, allowing pressure to be taken partly on to soft tissues, which usually barely touch a normal flat mattress. The method is well reported as being without risk, but is cumbersome in use. Certainly the basic material is cheap, abundant and could be discarded at will. It might have particular value in crisis nursing conditions, such as handling mass casualties after natural disasters.

Another static support system useful for treatment of established pressure sores is the Spinal Pack Mattress (Fig. 43.2) which was popular until more sophisticated systems became available. It consists of nine or so pieces of thick sorbo mattress piled three deep, the bottom piece being located in a wooden retaining tray. These piles of pads can be moved apart, as required, to leave

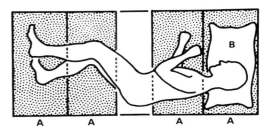

Fig. 43.2 To illustrate the principle of a 'spinal pack' set of mattresses for treatment of extensive pressure sores

an established sore free of contact with any surface, the weight being taken proximally and distally on the deep soft edges of the mattress components; or the patient may lie prone thus gently supported.

Amongst static support systems can perhaps be included the long-since discarded simple water mattress, consisting of a flat envelope of thick rubber laid on top of another mattress and filled with water. Also the Sierex simple inflatable mattress had its earlier advocates; the original design with two large longitudinal communicating air sacs was used to help in the turning of recumbent patients and keeping them in the new position once turned.

Suspension, turning and contour beds
Standard hospital beds come repeatedly under criticism (e.g. Gainsborough, 1967). Even modern types, apparently efficient, adjustable, freely movable and convenient for nursing procedures, are nevertheless thought to be only tolerable in the recumbent position. The patient who wants to sit up (as most should do), is uncomfortable, regularly slides down and her skin is subjected to shearing and frictional forces which are harmful. Hence the development of the modern adjustable 'contour' type of bed, successor perhaps to the older cardiac bed. These contouring beds, having three or four hinged sections, may be arranged so that the patient can sit or recline with trunk and thighs supported without undergoing shearing stress, and much of the discomfort is eliminated. Such beds essentially comprise an inclinable back support hinged at about hip level eliminating the need for separate backrest and piles of pillows, and a conversely hinged knee break. They are mostly mechanically operated, and patients may sometimes be able to adjust their own position unaided. Examples include the K.F. International (Hoskins), a considerable range of Profiling beds (Nesbit Evans), and the Posturcare A.P. Bed (M.S.A. Medical), the latter being power operated and designed for use in the home. These beds, though currently more expensive than the modern adjustable height (e.g. 'King's Fund') type of bed, could perhaps become the standard hospital bed of the future, and they are much used in the United States of America. This comment however does not imply that the incidence of pressure sores would necessarily be much reduced. Unless used with great circumspection, profiling or contour beds could induce flexion contractures in elderly invalids.

Special mechanical or power operated beds have been evolved to suspend and turn patients who are highly susceptible to pressure effects, and to reduce the physical workload of nurses. Some of these have been evolved from early experience with paraplegic patients, most of whom are younger but seriously disabled and perhaps more prepared to tolerate such systems than

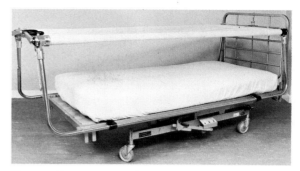

Fig. 43.3 The Mecabed, attached to a bed frame. The rotatable steel poles allow the net suspension fabric to be raised and lowered, or to be used to turn a patient from side to side. Here the handles are shown folded. (Courtesy of Mecanaids).

some aged patients might be. A simple device, the Mecabed (Mecanaids) can be made to fit upon a standard King's Fund bed, and consists of a raised frame with longitudinal rotatable steel poles with large handles operated from the foot of the bed (Fig. 43.3); from these poles stretches a net fabric on which the patient is suspended as if in a hammock, but the net can be lowered to the standard mattress or the patient can be turned from side to side by one nurse simply rotating the handles.

The Egerton Turning Net Suspension Bed (Egerton Hospital Equipment) embodies a similar deep net hammock-like suspension unit; the main frame, with the net mattress upon it, pivots on its longitudinal axis and allows an effortless tilt of 45° to either side, so that the recumbent body in effect rolls as desired, to relieve pressure. For pressure-susceptible recumbent and perhaps comatose patients net suspension systems might be an ideal solution, but for most other geriatric patients they could be alarming and unnecessarily restrictive.

The Egerton-Stoke Mandeville Turning and Tilting Bed (Egerton Hospital Equipment) has been particularly used in cases of paraplegia and severe traumatic injury etc.; the main frame can be made to adopt a longitudinal trough profile and can then be inclined from side to side or tilted as desired, by electric motors. For special cases it is clearly ideal, and will solve the problem of regular side-to-side turning, but on many counts, including cost, this apparatus would surely have few applications in geriatric work. A similar type of constant turning bed is the Mini Co-Ro (Hugh Steeper Ltd.).

Dynamic support systems embodying air and fluids
Over 20 years ago the alternating pressure air mattress for placing on top of a standard mattress was evolved (Bedford et al, 1961). The principle is simple and the result effective: the patient's weight is redistributed

every few minutes from one set of soft ridges to another, without effort, by transverse interdigitating polyvinyl chloride air sacs connected to an electric air pump which alternately inflates one set and then the other over a 7–10 minute cycle. This is the 'ripple' mattress which has been so widely adopted as a major aid to nursing the recumbent (Fig. 43.4). The first to appear had small cells about 5 cm (2 inches) across, but it was soon established (Bliss et al, 1966, 1967) that the larger-celled are more effective in preventing pressure sores, particularly on the heels. Since then several different varieties have appeared, in some of which the cells can be replaced individually if damaged. Later models permit a range of air pressures for patients of different weights, and often it proves possible to run two ripple mattresses from one pump. Currently the Frustro-Conical Alternating Pressure mattress (Talley Medical Equipment) is in widespread use; it has cells of 11.5 centimetres width and a 7-minute pumping cycle. The ripple bed is a relatively simple, quiet mechanism, and moderately priced. It is frequently used for patients at home. Running costs amount to only a few pence daily. However, testing of the integrity and proper functioning of the cells is essential, and the motor needs regular maintenance. Bliss (1978) has commented unfavourably

on later experience with alternating pressure mattresses, finding that many became defective and were not properly serviced or replaced as they should have been. The undoubted high reputation of this invaluable system clearly depends upon reliability, and it is the duty of hospital and other authorities who adopt it to organise regular inspection and servicing. The installation, testing and use of ripple mattresses has lately been reviewed again (Bliss, 1981).

Weight distribution on ripple mattresses is best when the patient is recumbent and least good for anyone sitting upright. However, equally effective ripple pads and cushions have been perfected for vunerable subjects sitting up in chairs or wheelchairs. They are almost obligatory for those who are regularly in wheelchairs by day. In some the pump is battery-operated so the patient does not have to stay within range of a power supply.

One variety of the ripple mattress is the so-called 'bubble pad' mattress (Huntleigh Medical) in which the same principle is employed, but instead of wide horizontal cells the mattress is made of a diagonally orientated set of lozenge-shaped interlocking cells which are inflated successively in the range of 30 to 80 mmHg. Yet another variant embodies interdigitating differentially-inflating air cells similar to the original ripple mattress, but the inflation cycle is arranged to produce a slow rippling wave along the length of the bed. In addition a few small perforations ·in the upper cells allow a constant flow of air against the undersite of the patient, maintaining suitable humidity and temperature close to the skin at risk. This meets another of Scales desiderata (see also below). The upper ripple element of this latter type of mattress rests on a second but permanently inflated air mattress with longitudinal cells, giving it greater depth and stability. This, the Astec A.P. Bed (Astec Environmental Systems) is gaining in popularity (Fig. 43.5). It has a remarkably silent motor and air pump. Exton-Smith et al (1982) have compared a similar but not identical system to this with the earlier large-celled type of ripple mattress. This apparatus, known as the Air Wave System (Dermalex) embodies two layers of transverse air cells held stable by polystyrene-like side moulds; it produces similar wave-like action and likewise has upwards venting from the inflatable cells. A comparison with the original ripple mattress was made on a matched-pair basis with evaluation of the severity of sores, or absence of them, after an initial assessment of risk on the Norton (1962) clinical scale (q.v.). The A.W.S. mattress proved significantly superior in preventing sores and in promoting healing of existing sores.

A simpler system of low pressure air mattress was evolved by McCubbin and Simpson (1977). It consisted of two (or sometimes three) standard box edge camping air mattresses, one upon another, in a padded wooden

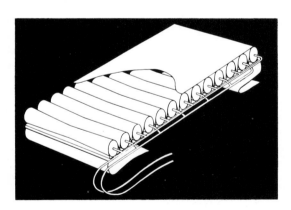

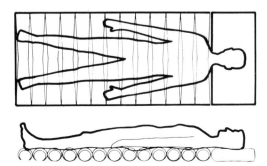

Fig. 43.4 Principle of the large-celled alternating pressure mattress for prevention of pressure sores

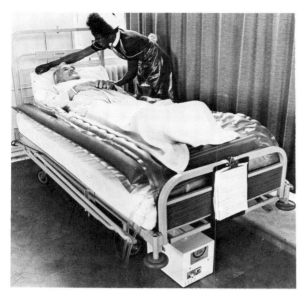

Fig. 43.5 The Astec A.P. Bed, with an alternating pressure mattress upon a second permanently inflated mattress, and allowing a flow of air upwards upon the patient's skin. The bed is shown laid on Kings Fund type of bedstead. (Courtesy of Astec Environmental Systems).

base based on a standard bedstead. The mattresses were kept inflated by an aquarium aeration pump and the pressure supply controlled by a water immersed gauge. This system has now been refined as the Alphabed L.P. Constant Low Pressure Air Bed (Flowtron Aire).

The effectiveness and practicability of both the older and newer alternating pressure mattresses has been demonstrated by trials, and confirmed by widespread usage. When appropriately used it is clear that they signifcantly reduce the incidence of sores and help to make the task of nurses lighter. Nevertheless, no-one can assume that on such a device a patient is 'safe' from pressure. General nursing attention and regular turning are still required. Care is necessary to ensure that the patient does not 'bottom out' because of excessive weight or insufficient air pressure, and that switches are not inadvertently turned off. Vigilance is needed to see that the equipment is fully operative at all times. The various air pressure devices described above are not usually suitable for use on contour beds.

Definitive water beds, other than the early rubber water mattresses, were first introduced some 15 years ago (Grant, 1967), and are much in vogue for prevention of sores in patients exceptionally at risk, and for treating the worst cases. A water bed consists of a trough some 90 cm wide and 30 to 40 cm deep on a supporting frame to allow full length lying, and containing a tough plastic (PVC) envelope filled with water, and thermostatically controlled. On this plastic membrane the patient floats, his body weight being distributed over a wide area (Fig. 43.6). There is little doubt that water beds have value; most patients find them comfortable, though some complain of motion sickness. They must lie continuously, not sit up, and nursing manoeuvres, particularly lifting the patient out, can be difficult because of the high sides. The later versions made of fibre glass (Western Medical) with contoured smooth sides, are easier for such activities. Brydon (1977) warns how important it is that the minimum temperature on the thermostat be set high enough, because a patient lying on a large envelope of cool water can become hypothermic. A water bed takes many hours to heat up to operating temperature (say 31°C) and has therefore to be kept in circuit if it is to be ready for emergencies. A disadvantage of all water beds is their bulk, weight and lack of manoeuverability when filled. Indeed, the weight is in some cases above 12 cwt (660 kg) in working order. This raises problems of structural safety in buildings if the apparatus is required on upper floors especially in old hospitals. It has been suggested that a patient suspended on a taut membrane floating on water does not have his weight distributed ideally, whereas if he were almost submerged in fluid the ideal pressure relief would be obtained. The Beaufort-Winchester Water Bed (Paraglide) adopts the principle of a deep container with thick sides and padded edges with water in an envelope, the upper surface of which is free and loose so that the patient can sink in deeply as he would

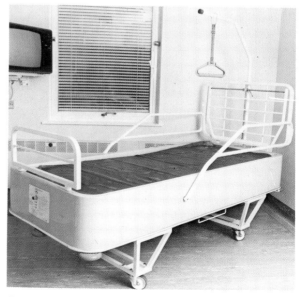

Fig. 43.6 A waterbed for prevention and treatment of pressure sores. (Courtesy of Western Medical).

do if simply immersed in fluid. This is sometimes called the 'true flotation' water bed. It requires a circulating system and water heater as a separate unit. It is bulky, heavy and difficult to manoeuvre like other water beds, and appears not altogether popular with nurses because the depth to which a patient sinks makes many nursing procedures difficult. Bliss (1981) has made a comparison of this system with a simple ripple bed, amongst other systems. No doubt for selected special cases it is of real value, but other water beds (see above) seem to be more generally used in geriatric work.

To obviate some of the disadvantages of these water beds, principally their weight and the patient-handling problems which they engender, some alternative systems have been suggested. Schatrumpf (1972) described a bed on which the weight of the patient was transmitted to a shallow, unheated water bath by a large collection of plastic balls kept in place by an upper plastic membrane; thus the patient would never be in contact with the fluid contents but the balls would conform to his contours and distribute the pressure evenly. Harper et al (1975) have described a simple non-mechanical shallow unheated flotation unit made up of several multi-compartmentalized water-filled sections with baffles, set on a bed frame with a polyfoam base and held in place by an inflatable air frame. Excellent results were claimed for this system, which has the advantage of low cost and a relatively small weight even when filled.

Great ingenuity has been shown by engineers and their colleagues in seeking to match the fullest requirements of a supporting system for patients. The low-air-loss patient-support system (L.A.L. system) was evolved from a high-air-loss system brought into use for the treatment of burns some 15 years ago. The L.A.L. bed consists of a series of some 20 to 24 air cells set vertically on edge on a hinged bed frame which can be mechanically moved into various lying and sitting positions. This is true a contour bed, and the patient can control his position if he wishes. The cells are micro-porous, polyurethane coated, and grouped in sections on the bed; each is individually inflated from a pumping system with warmed air, of which there is a steady slow loss back to the atmosphere. This ensures a 'fluid' support system for the whole body with the maintenance of correct temperature and humidity (Scales, 1972; Greenfield 1972; Scales et al, 1974). The results from the use of this bed with highly vunerable paraplegic, burns and major trauma patients are impressive, and the reduction in nursing work must be considerable. The original trials (Scales and Hopkins, 1971) were not conducted with geriatric patients however. This remarkable system does nevertheless require a nursing and maintenance team with particular expertise. It calls for the use of a suitable single room and the continuous noise level is up to 66 decibels, comparable to that of

a general ward with a vacuum cleaner in the vicinity. Jenied (1976) compared this L.A.L. bed with a King's Fund bed using a local pressure-monitoring system with volunteers adopting various positions on the bed, and found that the L.A.L. bed produced lower pressures particularly under the sacrum, buttocks and heels. Models currently available in Britain are the Mediscus Mark 5 for hospital use and the Mediscus Minor which can be used on a King's Fund bed or in domestic circumstances (Mediscus Products). The initial purchase and maintenance costs are clearly too high to allow such beds to be used widely in any geriatric department.

Another development is the Fluidized Bead Bed (Hargest, 1976,; Thomson et al, 1980). The principle adopted is that if air is blown upwards through a mass of particulate matter, i.e. glass bead microspheres 50 to 150 microns in diameter with sufficient air velocity the medium acts exactly like a fluid. On this fluidized medium the patient lies in a trough bed with its heater and compressor in the base, on a porous sheet, and floats as if on a liquid, but does not get wet. From the practical standpoint the mechanical characteristics are very like those of a water bed, but in addition the conditioned circulating air can provide the ideal milieu in respect of temperature and humidity for the threatened skin — in which regard it compares with the L.A.L. bed. In addition this system will allow patients to be turned and then maintained in the new position simply by stopping the flow of air, when the medium becomes 'solid' and conforms to the patient's exact contour — like a sand bed. No doubt this Clinitron Fluidized Bead Bed (Astec) could have great usefulness in intensive treatment units, burns units etc., but it is costly and bulky. Its advocates claim that the air system and the medium are bactericidal (Hargest, 1980) and self-cleaning. What its ultimate acceptibility would be with a doubly incontinent geriatric patient perhaps remains an open question, and its support medium consists of 100 kg of special glass beads, replacement of which would be a formidable and costly undertaking if it became necessary. Again therefore, though this system is elegant and effective, its practicability for general geriatric use is questionable. Use of the air fluidized bed was reviewed by Hargest (1976) after 7 years experience.

Following this general review, in which it is not possible to specify all the individual products, past and present, the reader must observe how many of these physical support systems have appeared: their very number may indicate that no generally applicable solution has been found. There is little doubt of the value of even the most sophisticated and costly in particular circumstances, which usually involve younger patients in desperate circumstances of burning, trauma and neurological disintegration. However, the geriatric problem is rather different. Potentially there are such large numbers of patients who could develop pressure sores, that this would raise inevitable economic and logistic questions if it were contemplated to use such equipment for even a small proportion. Difficulties of space, storage and structural reinforcement of buildings would also have to be faced. Smith (1976) has realistically presented this dilemma. One might therefore predict that good beds, perhaps a proportion being contour beds, with the various static support systems, will become almost obligatory in geriatric practice; that alternating pressure mattresses will continue to be effectively and enthusiastically used and perhaps further refined, because they are practical and cost-effective too; that water beds will find intermittent but not widespread general ward use for particularly difficult cases; but that L.A.L. and similar sophisticated support systems, the cost of which approaches £6–8000 each, will seldom be seen in geriatric departments or figure in their more realistic budgets. The relative costs of some of the support systems are shown in Table 43.3.

It is illogical, when seen from the geriatric standpoint, that so much professional and commercial time and expertise should be spent in searching for these elabor-

ate solutions when it is known that by correct and prompt handling of the cases of vunerable old people in the first place by a well trained medical and nursing team could prevent all but the minority of sores. From this it follows that the need to treat these sores should itself be uncommon. This in turn means that vunerable old people must have rapid access to geriatric departments' beds, and that other departments should acknowledge the risk and the true causation of sores, and act accordingly when they admit the elderly.

TREATMENT

General and dietary measures

The treatment of established pressure sores must first incorporate all those principles of prevention just discussed, and the same practical measures must be continued. As always vigilance is essential, for while one lesion is being treated others can appear and go unnoticed. Regular turning techniques may unavoidably cause the body weight to be thrown for longer periods on to an intact skin area and put that also at risk. Physical support systems for patients are at least as valuable for treatment as they are for prevention: ripple mattresses are used in either circumstance, while water beds and sophisticated systems like the L.A.L. bed may, because they are expensive, come to be used mainly for treatment of the worst affected victims. Regular turning by nurses at 2-hourly intervals, or more frequently when the risks are highest, is essential, and the use of special static support systems certainly does not remove the necessity of this. Indeed, with the skin broken, turning routines must be stricter, especially at night. It may be necessary to devise special supporting gear to deal with lesions in particular places, such as by suspending a limb from an overbed frame using padded canvas slings round parts which are well protected by muscle. Surgeons have sometimes resorted to suspending a patient from the frame by calipers on transpelvic Kirschner wires (Westhues, 1942). There have been advocates of prolonged prone lying, especially with gross ulceration over the sacrum and hips when all three are affected, and especially after surgical intervention (Constantian and Jones, 1980). Elderly patients can seldom tolerate much prone lying. The over-riding principle governing this background treatment is the avoidance of pressure, because any sore on which the patient's weight is allowed to rest will not heal, whatever else is done.

Dietary and other general measures must not be neglected. Blood counts must be repeated as often as necessary and anaemia must be treated. Infections of various causation may result in anaemia supervening in the course of prolonged treatment, and it may go unno-

Table 43.3 Approximate cost of some physical supporting systems for patients (1982 prices, without accessories)

System	Cost (£)
Beds: general nursing purposes	
Kings Fund bed (Nesbit Evans)	297
Profiling beds, various (Nesbit Evans)	245–460
K-F International (Hoskins)	395
Posturecare A.P. bed (M.S.A.)	450
Static Support Systems	
Poly-flotation mattress (Talley)	72
Clinifloat (Astec)	86
Spenco-Silicone padding (bed size) (Spenco)	51
Beaufort bead pillow mattress (Paraglide)	69
Suspension and Turning beds	
Mecabed (Mecanaids)	000
Egerton net suspension turning bed (Egerton)	598
Egerton Stoke Mandeville turning and tilting Mark 2 (Egerton)	1831
Mini Co-Ro turning treatment table (bed) (Hugh Steeper)	1185
Air or Fluid support systems	
Simple water mattress (Surmed)	90
'Ripple' mattress (e.g. Talley)	91
Astec A-P bed (Astec)	335
Western waterbed (Western)	675
Beaufort Winchester waterbed, 1981 model (Paraglide)	3350
Low Air Loss (L.A.L.) bed (Mediscus)	
Mediscus M.V.	6100
Mediscus Minor	3600
Clinitron fluidized-bead bed (Astec)	9500

ticed. For anaemia, transfusion, given with due caution, must be considered at the start of treatment because time is not on the side of the pressure sore sufferer. A high protein diet is necessary is most cases, sometimes supplemented by the nasogastric route, and the contra-indications are very few. Even in cases of renal failure, contrary to usual teaching, protein restriction cannot be advised because it causes the skin to break down under only mild pressure with catastrophic suddenness, producing massive cavitation and a miserable death. Guttmann (1976) reminds us that the daily loss of protein from sores can be as much as 50 g, and the patient may then become so malnourished as to appear starved. Even if anaemia is not present, plasma trans-fusion may assist if there is a suspicion of protein lack. Mulholland et al (1943) found that healing will not take place until a positive nitrogen balance is achieved, and as much as 200 g a day intake of protein may be required. It has been suggested (Findlay and Howes, 1952) that protein malnutrition is linked synergistically with the corticosteroid inhibition of wound healing which is well recognized. However it seems doubtful that steroid eyedrops would be enough to do this, as has been suggested (Barton and Barton, 1981). In any event it is not always possible with old people to omit the ster-oids which they are needing for other reasons, such as arteritic ophthalmic disorders and pemphigus vulgaris. On the other hand the same authors hold that if the blood urea is greater than 7 mmol/litre (40 mg/100 ml) epithelialization will be inhibited.

It is believed by some that anabolic steroids should be used to put the patient into positive nitrogen balance, but their effectiveness in the treatment of pressure sores is not proven. Indeed, Irvine et al (1961) demonstrated that they had no effect in the prevention of such sores.

Herman and Woodward (1972) believed that extra Vitamin A is needed for wound healing. It is well known that ascorbic deficiency inhibits healing too, and several studies have supported this view in respect of pressure sores. Thus, Taylor et al (1974), in a double-blind controlled trial, found that Vitamin C at a 1 g daily markedly accelerated sore healing and raised the ascorbic acid levels in white blood cells. Brocklehurst et al (1968) found clinical and biochemical improvement after multivitamin therapy.

Much interest has developed during recent years as to the value or otherwise of giving oral zinc salts in treat-ment, following the observation (Pories et al, 1967) that chronic skin ulcers heal more quickly by this means. In spite of various clinical studies and animal experimen-tation on wound healing, there are still many gaps in our knowledge of this subject. In a review, Carruthers (1973) agreed that the evidence of this is conflicting. It seems likely that zinc is only of value to those patients who are zinc deficient, i.e. those who have less than 100 micrograms per 100 ml, but to establish this fact in geriatric patients is as yet a difficult matter. Various authors point out moreover that there is a reduction of the serum zinc level after the long-term use of cortico-steroids, so a link between lengthy steroid dosage and special vulnerability to pressure effects might be expected in the many geriatric patients being so treated. Whatever the conflict of evidence (Lancet, 1973b), it is common practice to use zinc sulphate, 220 mg in capsules three times a day, for the treatment of pressure sores, for there might well be advantages, and the evidence of side-effects in negligible. It is also known that 15 to 20 per cent of the normal body stores of zinc are held in the skin.

Magnesium, copper and calcium are also needed for proper wound repair, but optimum levels for intake cannot be laid down.

Specific modes of treatment

Over a long period a great many forms of physical treat-ment and chemical nostra have been used against and upon pressure sores, some with a scientific principle underlying them, but many without. They have varied from James Paget's (1873) poultice of carrots, turnips, linseed oil and bread, as quoted for historical interest by various recent authors (e.g. Guttmann, 1976), through a compress of pawpaw, the fruit of Carica pepaya (Dawnay, 1982) to negative oxygen ions (Ursu, 1970), though the details of this treatment remain obscure. The medical and nursing literature abounds with references to techniques and applications, usually advocated with some enthusiasm but without much critical evaluation, it must be said. Frequently healing rates are not even measured objectively, and properly conducted controlled trials as between different prep-arations, or by measurement against a placebo, are often not attempted. Indeed, trials would never be easy to conduct because so many variables are operating, and accurate matching of patients and controls may be almost impossible. There is likely to be evidence of a placebo effect in any case, because the very fact that a trial is being conducted will heighten the interest and therefore the general pressure-conscious endeavours of nurses and others concerned, so that favourable results are produced anyway. In this respect a 'trial' by Fernie and Dornan (1976) is of particular interest. In the cases of a number of patients with established pressure sores which had not responded to various topical applications, these authors used a device built to resemble an 'elec-tromagnetic' generator in a box, with an applicator cone and switches to increase the 'power' and incidentally the noise of a fan. The staff were instructed about pressure effects and general preventative measures, but also about the supposed virtues of the apparatus, which was then directed at the sores for 30 minutes every 2 hours, day and night, during which times the pressure was of course being relieved. The sores were duly traced on cellophane and the areas monitored during the exercise. In fact the 'generator' generated nothing, but the patients and staff were unaware of this. The previously refractory sores all improved markedly, yet the only alteration in treatment was the increase in nursing activity. The ethical basis of this trial might perhaps be debated, but it shows that any trial of pressure sore treatment can hardly avoid distortion by placebo effect.

Ultraviolet light has been used over many years but evidence of its real value is hard to obtain. The aim is apparently to encourage granulations in the wound, but Barton and Barton (1981) consider this undesirable, leading as it does to tethering of the wound and to friable scar tissue instead of proper epithelialisation. But the same authors advocate a daily first degree erythema dose of UV light to the skin round a pressure sore to stimulate vascular reaction, but say that the ulcer itself must be covered at the time.

Ultrasound is also advocated, but unsupported by much evidence. Again, the above authors suggest its use for the same purposes as UV light, at a dose of 0.5 watts per square centimetre, pulsed, three times a week. Fisher (1976) suggests its general use on sores, and claims the effects are mechanical, thermal and chemical, but there is no supporting evidence. On the other hand ultrasound can, it is claimed, be specifically used for debridement, about half the ulcers healing in 6 weeks (Paul et al, 1960). The question is whether this is more rapid than other methods would achieve. In a review of the use of ultrasound in geriatric medicine Coles et al (1982) mention many diagnostic but no therapeutic uses. Thus there seems some confusion of purpose in using these radiations; nor is it clear what benefits follow from short wave diathermy, microwave, or sunlight, all of which have been used.

Hyperbaric oxygen is advocated by some of the supposition that pressure sores are anoxic (Fischer, 1966) (Rosenthal and Schurman, 1971). Treatment has to be from 2 hours to 12 hours a day at a pressure of some 45 mmHg. in a pressure cabinet, and healing is said to take 42 to 60 days. So this treatment is not likely to appeal much to elderly patients, and its particular efficacy is probably not established. The use of locally applied ice packs is suggested by Marshall (1971).

Several authors emphasize that a deep pressure sore should not be allowed to dry out as this inhibits healing (Winter, 1976, Barton and Barton, 1981). This idea thus becomes the rationale of the occlusive dressing which is the modern concept of local management, for this amongst other things stops the wound from drying (see below). However, at least one author advocated the use of chemically dried air in treatment, which fact amply illustrates the state of uncertainty in this field.

Local applications: a short review

A vast array of topical applications are known to have been used, but it is unfortunate that few have been the subject of objective studies, let alone controlled trials. In a valuable short paper Morgan (1975), in reviewing the literature from 1900 to 1974, regrets that many papers dealt with small numbers, or with ulcers of differing aetiology, and that healing times and follow-up data were not given. She groups the topical measures mentioned in the literature into 11 categories which include some of the specific remedies already mentioned above. Further, most of the reported treatments also included improved general nursing care, debridement and control of infection — which are vital and which themselves will have had effects on healing rates. The conclusion Morgan reached is that no topical agent has proved itself particularly useful for treating pressure sores, by comparison for example with the topical treatment of burns. Constantian (1980), the editor of a multi-author text on the management of pressure ulcers mainly from the surgical standpoint, has a similar opinion, and he only devotes one page out of 294 to topical agents. He also asks why full thickness pressure ulcers have to be regarded as fundamentally different from other open surgical wounds which would not be so variously treated.

Enzymes

Some chemical and biological agents are certainly used to assist debridement. Amongst these are enzymes which, when locally applied, can bring about remarkably rapid liquefaction of persistent sloughing debris. Amongst these are Collagenase ABC ointment, Trypsin cream (Hislop and Pritchard, 1962) and papain-urea-chlorophyllin ointment (Morrison and Casali, 1957). In the United Kingdom a ferment often successfully used for debridement is the mixture of streptokinase and streptodornase (Varidase) which is made from a powder with saline into a solution for application on gauze twice daily for 1–2 weeks.

Antiseptics

Clearly it is in the interests of everyone that wound infection in pressure sores should be prevented or eradicated, and at one time topical sulphonamides and antibiotics were widely used, including chlortetracycline with zinc cream (Hislop and Pritchard, 1962). Gentamicin cream is another, and so is an enzyme-neomycin cream (Spencer, 1967). More often aniline dyes like gentian violet find a topical use on infected sores, and there are few adverse effects from this treatment. Cicatrin, as cream or powder, is popular; it contains neomycin, bacitracin and various aminoacids. For major wound infections bacteriological studies will lead to proper parenteral use of the appropriate antibiotics, not local applications.

There has also been a vogue for antiseptic preparations to apply locally, such as acriflavine packs, benzalkonium chloride with cetrimide (Drapolene etc.) and silver sulphadiazine (Flamazine). Other compound preparations in frequent use are creams and solutions containing malic, benzoic and salicylic acids in propylene glycol (Aserbine, Malatex etc.), but the rationale behind them is not altogether clear. They are said to assist the cleansing of wounds and perhaps to help with the necessary debridement. In this respect hydrogen peroxide applications might assist, but are not popular because they are thought perhaps to interfere with epithelialization. Much used also are sodium hypochlorite and boric acid BPC solution (Eusol). However, Barton and Barton (1981) believe that the latter can sometimes release toxic matter from bacteria and cause acute oliguric renal failure. They also hold that any anti-inflammatory agents prevent pressure sores from healing, but they advocate the use of chlorhexidine gluconate 1.5 per cent and cetrimide 15 per cent (Savlon) or saline with Savlon added, as a lotion or soak to aid debridement. Also cetrimide 0.5 per cent in a cream base (Cetavlex) and povidone iodine spray (Betadine) are said by them to be unexceptionable for local treatment, though the evidence for this is not given.

Inert substances

There has lately been an upsurge of interest in inert substances, sometimes powders to pour into a wound, sometimes plastic substances which set after a chemical reaction to form a porous soft rubbery absorbent dressing substance conforming to the shape of the cavity. The former type, of which dextranomer (Debrisan) was the pioneer, originating in Scandinavia, consists of microscopic beads of dextran 0.1 to 0.3 mm diameter (Jacobsson et al, 1976). This substance can draw out of a wound several times its own weight of exudate, including bacteria, by direct absorption and by capillary attraction, thereby greatly assisting the debridement. This powder dressing has to be renewed once or twice daily. It is popular with nurses, and claims are made that it materially reduces the time spent in healing. If that is so this can justify its considerable expense. The same could be said of the contour-setting rubbery plastic dressing (Silastic Foam) which is more expensive still. Morgan (1975) reviews earlier developments in this field, in which pressure sores were packed with 'sponges' of fibrin foam or absorbable gelatin, but she again adds that no details were given. Debridement was also said to be added by applying dried plasma and Peruvian balsam every 3 days.

Miscellaneous applications

Morgan goes on to mention a number of preparations compounded out of many unrelated substances which, because of the impossibility of analysing their respective effects, cannot be taken too seriously. Elements and other simple remedies have been included, besides zinc, bismuth, titanium, molecules with sulphydryl groups, gold and even gold leaf (Wolf et al, 1966), alcohol and acetic aicd.

Hormones used topically have had their advocates, especially stilboesterol or diethylstilboestrol (Hislop and Pritchard, 1962) as a cream. Brine bath treatments, combined with a variety of other remedies, were reported to stimulate healing in a large series of 1400 patients (Nyquist, 1959). Much earlier (e.g. Latimer, 1934) tannic acid was much in favour, but again no supporting evidence was produced. Topical insulin was tried in the hope that it would stimulate local protein synthesis. Amongst the variety of miscellaneous substances mentioned by Morgan and others can be included formaldehyde, silicones, benzoic acid, balsam of Peru, tragacanth, pectin paste, sugar (Barnes 1973), honey (Blomfield, 1973), aluminium hydroxide together with magnesium oxide, kariya powder, not to mention cod liver oil. Anderson (1976) advised, for local application, an ointment containing cod liver oil with talc, kaolin, zinc oxide and woolfat (Thovaline) as a good general emollient, and suggests a preparation of colophony with volatile oils, thymol and phenol (Ilonium) to assist the separation of necrotic tissue. Creams containing zinc oxide have been much used locally, presumably on the theory that if zinc deficiency threatens it might be most effective when applied directly. Constantian mentions also a number of substances designed to produce a latticework for the growth of granulation tissue; these include a gelatin foam, and porcine collagen (Stoop, 1970).

It is not possible to evaluate the virtues and vices of this large assembly of possible topical applications in the absence of controlled trials. It seems best therefore to heed various warnings and eschew the use of substances which might positively inhibit healing of wounds. In that respect it would appear that saline must be satisfactory, that biological ferments are probably so, and that inert granular or deformable plastic dressings may be quite helpful because of their physical, not their chemical properties. As is the case so often in refractory medical and surgical conditions, the very multiplicity of the topical remedies suggested, and the enthusiasm with which they are advocated, indicates that none is the final solution and that few even have advantages over the others. By seeking the ideal substance to put on a sore, we are probably on the wrong tack entirely. Realistic observers like Guttmann, Constantian and others, sum up in the often-quoted phrase, attributed to Vilan of Paris: 'You can put anything you like on a pressure sore except the patient'.

Practical possibilities

In the face of bewildering array of available local applications which many experienced doctors, but fewer nurses perhaps, regard simply as 'doing more harm than good' (e.g. Bliss, 1982), the question remains: what is best advised as practical modern local treatment for the various grades of sores?

Good local treatment for an *unbroken* skin area is gentle washing, but not too often, with soap and water, drying, and the application of talc powder with gentle rubbing. Vigorous massage of pressure areas is no longer advised, and using spirit or astringents is quite outmoded. The use of water-repellant creams or sprays of silicones seems logical, especially in the incontinent; positive proof of the value of such barrier creams seems still lacking however, despite the increased risk which incontinence entails.

For minor epithelial breaks and superficial (benign) sores of less than full skin thickness, an occlusive spray or small plastic adhesive dressing which will transmit water vapour outwards are effective, and healing can normally be expected quickly, as long as further pressure and friction are avoided. Again, Bliss (1982) believes such patients should be nursed with the affected sore on a fleece, for this encourages air circulation, reduces friction, and provides comfort in what is undeniably a painful condition. Sheepskins were advocates for such reasons 20 years earlier (Ewing et al, 1961).

Larger, deeper sores of full skin thickness with or without deeper cavities must be treated as surgical wounds, with further pressure of course being eliminated. They must be kept from contamination, or if they do become infected this must be dealt with by appropriate measures (see above). This means in effect that dead tissue should be removed and the sore covered. Debridement is thought by most workers to be of fundamental importance, and some topical methods to assist have been suggested already. In practice however the best method of getting rid of gangrenous material and slough is surgical, simply with forceps and scalpel. No local or other anaesthetic is needed as at the treatment stage the dead tissue is easily recognized and the risk of haemorrhage is small indeed. Beyond this it is debatable whether regular cleansing applications are called for. Many experienced teams use saline or saline and Savlon, or even 1 : 2000 Eusol packs, especially if the odour is offensive. Despite the caveats of others, packing with saline-moistened ribbon gauze to assist drainage from lesions with undermined edges is widely practised. There are those however (e.g. Bliss 1982) who believe that packing a deep pressure sore with gauze ribbon, gauze dextranomer, Silastic Foam (q.v.) etc. is counter-productive because the sodden pad so formed impedes drainage and increases pressure — though the weight should not be on the wound in any case. At present it must be generally but not universally agreed that once the lesion is cleansed it should be covered with an occlusive dressing which protects from damage and infection, yet allows outward water vapour transmission while maintaining a local microenvironment conducive to physiological healing with epithelization rather than exuberant granulations and scar formation.

Barton and Barton (1981) make distinctions between two active types of sores detected by thermography, and have opinions about local applications for each. However some may think that this is too exclusive, even though they would agree that the use of microporous non-adhesive absorbent dressings such as Melolin (Smith and Nephew) held in place with strips of 5 cm tape such as Micropore (3M) or, where the lesion is large and and the tape produces an allergic reaction, an elastic net outer retaining dressing such as Netelast (Roussel). Others have preferred an occlusive transparent adhesive dressing applied like an additional skin layer over the lesion and for a wide area round and left for some days. Such a dressing is Op-Site (Smith and Nephew), but it does not meet with universal acceptance by nurses, and it can sometimes cause allergic skin reactions. The important principle is that dressings should embody a hydrophilic surface and a hydrophobic backing which is nevertheless able to transmit water vapour. Another such is Lyofoam (Ultra Laboratories). With further regard to the infection of the wound, many workers regard this as almost unavoidable and do not think it needs specific local or systemic treatment. They believe that it will disappear with cleansing, debridement and the healing process, except when unmistakable cellulitis is also seen in the wound or near to it, when this requires treatment. Nevertheless, surgeons contemplating reconstructive operations and grafting are understandably much concerned with the bacteriology of lesions. Sores on the heels, which are common especially in post-surgical cases, require not only dressing but also that the leg should be horizontal for most of the time, to avoid hypostasis and oedema.

Surgical treatment

Simple debridement of deep sores, which is so necessary in the opinion of the majority, has been touched on already. Surgery can be of great use in the treatment of large full-thickness skin loss, especially in younger patients with spinal cord lesions. Contributors to the surgical literature have mostly been concerned with this group of patients: thus in 1970 Bailey reviewed the whole field of pressure sore management, while more recently Constantian (1980) has edited a major multi-author text which devotes much attention to detailed surgical management of pressure ulcers, site by site, though not neglecting aetiological factors and general measures. The question is, to what extent plastic surgery can be used for the older patient. With careful pre-operative preparation of relatively fit patients whose general prognosis is good, who can co-operate with post-operative treatment, and who are not likely to run the risk of pressure effects yet again, surgery might offer much, and shorten the length of stay in hospital. However, since full-thickness sores are potentially so common, the problem may be one of logistics.

An uncomplicated open sore could be simply closed and sutured and occasionally some of the bone below the sore might be removed to prevent recurrences. A skin graft could be of great value when applied at the right time on healthy granulations. Pinch and Thiersche grafts may have a place, but for deep and extensive ulcers transposition flaps can be raised, left attached at a hinge, and swung towards the recipient area, the donor site then being grafted. Otherwise a rotation flap can be used by triangulation of the defect, undermining and rotation of the flap to fill the gap, without leaving any deficit to be covered. As with other methods of treatment, sacral and heel sores present surgery with particular difficulties, and not too much should be expected of it.

There have been advocates of specialization in the management of pressure sores, and in various places in several countries Pressure Sore Units have been set up.

These have special merits for the promotion of research into the pathology and biomechanics of this complex subject, and for mounting trials of methods of treatment and prevention. However estimates of the incidences of pressure sores and of their prognosis are sometimes unaccountably gloomy. It would surely be grossly pessimistic therefore to suggest that each district should have its own pressure sore unit. Nothing could be more damaging than to foster the idea that pressure effects are somehow mysterious, and that responsibility for managing the victims should be handed over to a team of experts.

In this field total prevention is the ideal, and prevention is everyone's business whether they be nurses, doctors, therapists, radiographers, operating theatre staff or hospital porters. Indeed, wherever possible the patient must take some personal responsibility himself. Likewise, after the disaster has occurred, treatment should be the concern of all, using sound principles and the simplest methods available. Never was this more true than in geriatric medicine. As others have said, 'no pressure, no sore; no sore, no treatment'.

Prevention and treatment must be a joint undertaking for doctors and nurses, even if it is upon the latter that the brunt of the work must fall. In this difficult and demanding task they need all the support and understanding of their problems that we can give them. Doctors should anticipate pressure problems and plan treatment accordingly. As well as nurses, too, they should examine the vunerable points frequently. A most valuable piece of equipment in a ward or at home with the patient is a simple hand mirror.

REFERENCES

Anderson W F 1976 Practical Management of the Elderly, 3rd edn. Blackwell, Oxford

Andrews J 1981 Prevention and cure of pressure sores. In: Andrews J, Von Hahn H P (eds) Geriatrics for everyday practice. Karger, Basle, p 123–133

Bailey B N 1970 Bedsores. British Journal of Hospital Medicine 3: 223–231

Barbenel J C, Jordan M M, Clark M O 1979 Incidence of pressure sores in the Greater Glasgow area. Lancet 2: 548–550

Bardsley G I, Bell F, Barbenel J C 1976 A technique for monitoring body movements during sleep. In: Kenedi R M, Cowden J M, Scales J T (eds) Bed sore biomechanics. MacMillan, London, p 225–23

Barnes J W 1973 Sugar sweetens the lot of patients with bedsores (news item). Journal of the American Medical Association 223: 122

Barton A A 1970 The pathogeneis and inhibition of pressures sores. MD thesis, University of London

Barton A A 1973 Pressure sores: an electron microscope and thermographic study. Modern Geriatrics 3: 8–14

Barton A A, Barton M 1968 The inhibition of decubitus ulceration with ACTH. Journal of Pathology and Bacteriology 96: 345–351

Barton A A, Barton M 1973 The clinical and thermographical evaluation of pressure sores. Age and Ageing 2: 60–63

Barton A A, Barton M 1976 Drug-based prevention of pressure sores. Lancet ii: 443–444

Barton A A, Barton M 1981 The management and prevention of pressure sores. Faber, London

Bedford P D, Cosin, L, McCarthy J F, Scott B O 1961 The alternating pressure mattress. Gerontologia Clinica 3: 68–82

Bliss M R 1978 The use of ripple beds. Age and Ageing 7: -25–27

Bliss M R 1981 Clinical research in patient support systems, Care Science and Practice 1: 7–36

Bliss M R 1982 Healing pressure sores. Geriatric Medicine 21: 69–73

Bliss M R McLaren R, Exton-Smith A N 1966 Department of Health and Social Security Monthly Bulletin 25: 238–268

Bliss M R McLaren R, Exton-Smith A N 1967 Preventing pressure sores in hospital: a controlled trial of a large celled ripple mattress. British Medical Journal 1: 394–397

Blomfield R 1973 Honey for decubitus ulcers. Journal of the American Medical Association 224: 905

Brattgard S O, Carlsco S, Severinsson K 1976 Temperature and humidity in the sitting area. In: Kenedi R M. Cowden J M, Scales J T (eds) Bed sore biomechanics. MacMillan, London, p 185–188

British Medical Journal Leading Article 1978 Treating pressure sores 1: 1232

Brocklehurst J C 1964 Preventing pressure sores on the heels. Nursing Times 60: 1249–1250

Brocklehurst J C, Griffiths L, Taylor G F, Marks J, Scott D L, Blackley J 1968 Clinical features of chronic vitamin deficiency: a therapeutic trial in geriatric hospital patients. Gerontologia Clinica 10: 309–344

Brydon J 1977 Making heated waterbeds work. British Journal of Hospital Equipment 2: 39

Carruthers R 1973 Oral zinc in cutaneous healing. Drugs 6: 161–164

Charcot J M 1868 Lectures on diseases of the nervous system. Translated by Sigerson G, Lea, Philadelphia

Clark A B, Rusk H 1953 Decubitus ulcers treated with dried blood plasma. Journal of the American Medical Association 153: 787–788

Coles J A, Beynon G P J, Lees W R 1982 The use of ultrasound in geriatric medicine. Age and Ageing 11: 145–152

Constantian M B 1980 (ed) Pressure ulcers. Little Brown, Boston

Constantian M B, Jackson H S 1980 Biology and care of the pressure ulcer wound. In: Constantian M B (ed) Pressure ulcers. Little Brown, Boston, ch 7, p 69–100

Constantian M B, Jones M V 1980 General nursing care of the patient with pressure ulcers. In: Constantian M B (ed) Pressure ulcers. Little Brown, Boston, ch 11, p 123–139

Cruickshank C N D 1976 The microanatomy of the epidermis in relation to trauma. In: Kenedi R M, Cowden J M, Scales J T (eds) Bed sore biomechanics. MacMillan, London, p 39–46

David J 1981 The size of the problem of pressure sores. Care Science and Practice 1: 10–13

Dawnay P 1982 Personal communication

Ewing M W, Garrow C, McHugh N 1961 Sheepskin as a nursing aid. Lancet ii: 1447–1448

Exton-Smith A N, Sherwin R W 1961 Prevention of pressure sores: significance of bodily movements. Lancet 2: 1124–1126

Exton-Smith A N, Norton D, McLaren R 1962 An investigation of geriatric nursing problems in hospital. National Corporation for the Care of Old People, London. Reprinted 1975, Churchill Livingstone, Edinburgh

Exton-Smith A N, Wedgwood J, Overstall P W, Wallace G 1982 Use of the air wave system to prevent pressure sores in hospital. Lancet i: 1288–1290

Fabricius H 1593 De gangraena set sphacelo, tractatus methodicus, Leyden. Cited by Bailey B N 1970 Bedsores: British Journal of Hospital Medicine 3: 223–231

Ferguson-Pell M W, Bell F, Evans J H 1976 Interface pressure sores In: Kenedi R M, Cowden J M, Scales J T (eds) Bed sore biomechanics. MacMillan, London, p 189–197

Fernie G R, Dornan J 1976 The problems of clinical trials with new systems of preventing or healing decubiti. In: Kenedi R M, Cowden J M, Scales J T (eds) Bed sore biomechanics. MacMillan, London, p 315–320

Findlay C W, Howes E L 1952 The combined effect of cortisone and partial protein depletion on wound healing. New England Journal of Medicine 246: 597–604

Fischer B H 1966 Low pressure hyperbaric oxygen treatment of decubiti and skin ulcers. Proceedings of the Veterans Administration Spinal Cord Injuries Conference, p 97

Fisher M V 1976 Pressure sores: treatment by ultrasound. Nursing Times 72: 302

Gainsborough H 1967 Two views of the Kings Fund bed: 2 — my second best bed. British Hospital Journal and Social Services Review 77: 859–863

Grant W Russell 1967 Weightlessness in the treatment of bedsores and burns. Proceedings of the Royal Society of Medicine 60: 711–715

Greenfield R A 1972 The L.A.L. bed system. Nursing Times 68: 1192–1194

Guttmann 1955 The problem of treatment of pressure sores. British Journal of Plastic Surgery 7: 196–213

Guttmann 1976 The prevention and treatment of pressure sores in: Kenedi R M, Cowden J M, Scales J T (eds) Bed sore biomechanics. MacMillan, London, p 153–159

Hargest T S 1976 Problems of patient support: the air fluidised bed as a solution. In: Kenedi R M, Cowden J M, Scales J T (eds) Bed sore biomechanics. MacMillan, London, p 269–275

Hargest T S 1980 Bacteriological hazards of air fluidised beds. Lancet i: 1248

Harper P J, Rocko J M, Timmes J J 1975 Flotation unit for prevention of decubitus ulcers. Journal of the Medical Society of New Jersey 72: 824–826

Herman J B, Woodward S C 1972 An experimental study of wound healing accelerators. American Surgeon 38: 26–34

Hislop H H, Pritchard J C 1962 A clinical trial of creams for the

prevention and treatment of pressure sores in geriatric patients. British Journal of Clinical Practice 16: 409–412

Husain T 1953 An experimental study of some pressure effects in tissues with reference to the bedsore problem. Journal of Pathology and Bacteriology 66: 347–358

Irvine R E, Memon A H, Schera A F 1961 Norethandrolone and the prevention of pressure sores. Lancet 2: 1333–1334

Jacobson S, Rothman U, Arturson G 1976 A new principle for the cleansing of infected wounds. Scandinavian Journal of Plastic and Reconstructive Surgery 10: 65–72

Jenied P 1976 Static and dynamic support systems: pressure differences on the body. In: Kenedi R M, Cowden J M, Scales J T (eds) Bed sore biomechanics. MacMillan, London, p 287–289

Kosiak M 1959 Etiology and pathology of ischaemic ulcers. Archives of Physical Medicine and Rehabilitation 40: 62–69

Kosiak M, Kubicek W G, Olson M, Danz J N, Kolthe F J 1958 Evaluation of pressure as a factor in the production of ulcers. Archives of Physical Medicine and Rehabilitation 39: 623–629

Lancet Leading Article 1973a The cost of pressure sores ii: 309

Lancet Leading Article 1973b Zinc deficiency in Man i: 299

Latimer E O 1934 Treatment of decubitus ulcers with tannic acid. Journal of the American Medical Association 102: 751–754

Lowthian P T 1976 Pressure sores: practical prophylaxis. Nursing Times 72: 295–298

Lowthian P T 1976 Underpads in the prevention of decubiti. Kenedi R M, Cowden J M, Scales J T (eds) Bed sore biomechanics. MacMillan, London, p 141–145

Lowthian P tT 1979 Pressure sore prevalence. Nursing Times 75: 358–360

Marshall R S 1971 Cold therapy in the treatment of pressure sores. Physiotherapy 57: 372–373

McCubbin K J Simpson D C 1977 A low pressure air bed. Journal of Medical Engineering and Technology 1: 98–99

Morgan J E 1975 Topical therapy for pressure ulcers. Surgery, Gynecology and Obstetrics 141: 945–957

Morrison J E, Casali J L 1957 Continuous proteolytic therapy for decubitus ulcers. American Journal of Surgery 93: 446–448

Mulholland J H, Tui C, Wright A M 1943 Protein metabolism and bed sores. Annals of Surgery 118: 1015–1023

Neumark O W 1981 Deformation, not pressure, is the prime cause of pressure sores. Care Science and Practice 1: 41–45

Newman P, Davis N H 1981a Thermography as a predictor of sacral pressure sores. Age and Ageing 10:14–18

Newman P, Davis M H 1981b Skin temperature measurement with respect to pressure sores and their development. Care Science and Practice 1: 46–49

Norton D, Exton-Smith A N, McLaren R 1962. An investigation of geriatric nursing problems in hospital. National Corporation for the Care of Old People, London. Reprinted 1975, Churchill Livingston, London

Nyquist R H 1959 Brine bath treatment for decubitus ulcers. Journal of the American Medical Association 169: 927–932

Paget J 1873 Clinical lecture on bedsores. Cited by Guttmann Sir Ludwig. In: Kenedi R M, Cowden R M, Scales J T (eds) Bed sore biomechanics. MacMillan, London, p 157

Paul B J, Lafratta C W, Dawson A R, Baab E, Bullock F 1960 Use of ultrasound in the treatment of pressure sores in patients with spinal cord injury. Archives of Physical Medicine and Rehabilitation 41: 438–440

Petersen N C 1976 The development of pressure sores during hospitalisation. In: Kenedi R M, Cowden J M, Scales J T (eds) Bed sore biomechanics. MacMillan, London, p 219–224

Petersen N C, Bittman S 1971 The epidemiology of pressure sores. Scandinavian Journal of Plastic and Reconstructive Surgery 5: 62–66

Pories W J, Henzel J H, Rob C G, Strain W H 1967 Acceleration of wound healing in Man with zinc sulphate given by mouth. Lancet i: 121–124

Redfern S J 1976 The comfort of the hospital bed. In: Kenedi R M, Cowden J M, Scales J T (eds) Bed Sore Biomechanics, MacMillan, London, p 211–218

Redfern S J, Jenied P A, Gillingham M E, Lunn H F 1973 Local pressures with ten types of patient support systems. Lancet ii: 277–280

Reichel S M 1958 Shearing force as a factor in decubitus ulcers in paraplegics. Journal of the American Medical Association 166: 762–763

Reswick J B, Rogers J E 1976 Experience with devices and techniques to prevent pressure sores. In: Kenedi R M, Cowden J M, Scales J T (eds) Bed sore biomechanics. MacMillan, London, p 301–10

Rosenthal A M, Schurman A 1971 Hyperbaric treatment of pressure sores. Archives of Physical Medicine and Rehabilitation 52: 413–415

Scales J T 1972 The L.A.L. patient support system. Proceedings of the Royal Society of Medicine 65: 1065–1066

Scales J T 1976 Pressure on the patient. In: Kenedi R M, Cowden J M, Scales J T, (eds) Bed Sore Biomechanics, MacMillan, London, p 11–18

Scales J T, Hopkins L A 1971 Patient support system using low pressure air. Lancet ii: 885–888

Scales J T, Lunn H F, Jenied P A, Gillingham M E, Redfern S 1974 Prevention and treatment of pressure sores using air support systems. Paraplegia 12: 118–131

Schatrumpf J R 1972 New bed for treating pressure sores. Lancet ii: 1399–1400

Schwartz P L 1970 Ascorbic acid and wound healing. Journal of the American Dietetic Association 56: 497–503

Siegal R J, Vistnes L M, Laub D R 1973 Use of water beds for the prevention of pressure sores. Plastic and Reconstructive Surgery 51: 31–57

Smith J F 1976 Economic aspects of unconventional beds and support surfaces. In: Kenedi R M, Cowden J M, Scales J T (eds) Bed sore biomechanics. MacMillan, London, p 321–325

Spencer M C 1967 Treatment of chronic skin ulcers by a proteolytic enzyme-antibiotic preparation. Journal of the American Geriatrics Society 15: 219–223

Stewart I M 1976 Sand bed nursing. In: Kenedi R M, Cowden J M, Scales J T (eds) Bed sore biomechanics. MacMillan, London p 277–285

Stoop J W F M 1970 Treatment of pressure sores in paraplegic patients with animal collagen. Paraplegia 8: 177–182

Taylor T V, Rimmer S, Day B, Butcher J, Dymock I W 1974 Ascorbic acid supplementation in the treatment of pressure sores. Lancet i: 545–546

Thomson C W, Ryan D W, Dunkin L J, Smith M, Marshall M 1980 Fluidised bead bed in the intensive-therapy unit. Lancet i: 568–570

Trumble H C 1930 Skin tolerance for pressure and pressure sores. Medical Journal of Australia 2: 724–726

Ursu G 1970 Bedsores treated with negative air-ions. Paraplegia 8: 182–185

Westhues H 1942 Half suspension of the pelvis. Chirurgia 14: 489–493

Winter G D 1976 Some factors affecting skin and wound healing. In: Kenedi R M, Cowden J M, Scales J T (eds) Bed sore biomechanics. MacMillan, London, p 47–54

Wolf M, Wheeler P C, Wolcott L 1966 Gold leaf treatment of ischaemic skin ulcers. Journal of the American Medical Association 196: 693–696

Surgery in old age

In compiling this chapter we have chosen only those
subjects which we think are pertinent to a discussion of
surgery in a textbook of geriatric medicine, the majority
of whose readers, we anticipate, will be practising
physicians. Where we have elaborated on a specific topic
we have done so not out of enthusiasm for our own sub-
specialty, but because we think it is particularly relevant
to the practice of geriatrics.

The chapter is subdivided into two sections: first, the
presentation and management of the commonly occurring surgical emergencies in this age group, and second,
a discussion of the place of elective surgery in geriatric
practice with particular reference to the treatment of
cancer and arthritis. Details of the incidence, mortality
and morbidity are included in the discussion of each
topic. Description of operative techniques has been
purposely avoided.

SURGICAL EMERGENCIES

There are several factors, commonly seen in elderly
patients, which increase the difficulty of managing
urgent surgical problems. These are (1) difficulties in
making a diagnosis, (2) the presence of coincidental
medical conditions which increase the hazard of
operation.

Diagnosis can be made difficulty by an inability to
communicate — many of these patients are deaf, others
inarticulate and some too confused to comprehend.
They can show a remarkable tolerance to pain, coupled
with a diminished ability to localize the pain accurately.
Many present in an advanced state of shock long after
the onset of symptoms, because they or their guardians
have regarded the symptoms as those of old age alone.
These difficulties are enhanced in those patients who are
receiving systemic steroid therapy.

Examination can be extremely difficult. Access to the
abdomen may be limited by kyphosis, spondylolisthesis
or an inability to co-operate and relax the abdominal
muscles. It is often very difficult to assess changes in
function due to trauma in limbs which are the site of

arthritic deformity or of previously undocumented
neurological or vascular defects.

Shock

The effects of haemorrhage and hypovolaemia are less
well tolerated in old people than in the young. Every
effort should be made to resuscitate shocked patients
prior to operation. The cause of shock may be apparent
from a history of excessive fluid loss as in cases of
persistent vomiting, diarrhoea or intestinal obstruction.
If there are clinical signs of dehydration several litres of
saline cane be infused rapidly without waiting for more
precise information. Measurement of the central venous
pressure and hourly urine output are invaluable guides
to fluid replacement. If the central venous pressure is
less than ten centimetres of water pressure then intravenous fluids can be administered very rapidly. Blood
samples for estimation of plasma electrolytes, urea,
haemoglobin packed cell volume, bicarbonate, P_{CO_2} and
P_{O_2} should be taken before and during the period of
resuscitation. The type of fluid which is necessary will
depend upon the source of fluid loss. Whole blood
should be given in cases of serious haemorrhage. Low
molecular weight dextran is an effective plasma
expander and can be given whilst blood is being cross
matched. A combination of whole blood and Ringer
lactate solution is also very effective in combating hypovolaemic shock. If the fluid loss has been from the
alimentary tract, normal saline is sufficient with, if
necessary, potassium supplements.

In patients with bacteraemic shock, adequate fluid
replacement may fail to reverse the condition. Broad
spectrum antibiotics should be given intravenously.
Acidosis may be corrected by giving bicarbonate
solution and improving oxygenation, either by respirator
or hyperbaric oxygen. Hydrocortisone in large doses
helps; its effect is thought to be through its action as a
peripheral vasoconstrictor.

If the blood pressure remains low and the central
venous pressure rises to over 12 cm of water pressure,
digitalis or isoproterenol help to increase cardiac output.
Improvement in tissue perfusion brought about by

giving low molecular weight dextran or phenoxybenza-mine may also improve the condition. Peripheral vaso-constrictors such as noradrenaline have little value in combating bacteraemic shock and are best avoided. The management of patients with refractory shock is diffi-cult, incompletely understood and merits careful atten-tion based on the physiology of the condition. The effect of coincidental diseases on surgical mortality is difficult to assess, but several important points can be stated with some certainty. First, the mortality is between two and four times higher after emergency surgery than after elective surgery. For all types of urgencies in the elderly it is between 20 per cent and 30 per cent and for ortho-paedic cases is 30 per cent. For certain conditions the mortality is very high — intestinal obstruction 45 per cent and faecal peritonitis 70 per cent.

The contribution of anaesthesia to this mortarlity is small whilst atherosclerotic heart disease increases the risk particularly in patients who have had an infarct within 3 months or have left ventricular failure. On the other hand chronic chest disease has a considerable effect on mortality and this effect is unaltered by giving prophylactic broad spectrum antiobiotics prior to operation.

Emergency surgery in the aged is commonly required for intestinal obstruction, peritonitis, appendicitis, diverticulitis, and bleeding from the gastrointestinal tract. Sudden occlusion of mesenteric arteries due to emboli, ruptured aneurysms of the abdominal aorta and mesenteric vein thrombosis occur much less frequently. The overall mortality is high — over 30 per cent. It is least for acute appendicitis and strangulated hernias and highest for ruptured abdominal aneurysms.

Haematemesis

All cases of haematemesis require investigation and patients with massive haemorrhage require immediate admission to hospital; it is with this latter group that we are concerned.

The principal causes are peptic ulcer, hiatus hernia, oesophageal varices, gastric erosions, carcinoma of the stomach and the Mallory-Weiss syndrome.

Ideally, all cases of massive gastrointestinal haemor-rhage should be managed by a team of physicians and surgeons working together from the time of admission of the patient to hospital. The first phase of treatment is to resuscitate the patient by giving blood transfusions. The volume of fluid and the rate of infusion can be determined by repeated haemoglobin and packed cell volume measurements, readings from a central venous pressure manometer, blood pressure and pulse rate charts, and repeated clinical examination. Elderly patients tolerate haemorrhage badly and to prevaricate at this stage is to invite disaster. A second haemorrhage,

without the diagnosis having been established, may make immediate operation imperative and increase the risk considerably. An attempt should be made to identify the source of the haemorrhage as soon as poss-ible. Haemoptysis and regurgitation of swallowed blood can be eliminated by clinical examination in most cases. Patients usually fall into one of three categories:

— those with a previously proven or suspected peptic ulcer,
— those with signs of portal hypertension
— the remainder, in whom the source of bleeding is obscure.

In this latter group, a barium meal and/or endoscopy should be performed as soon as the patient has been resuscitated.

A barium meal examination is very effective in estab-lishing the diagnosis and is not detrimental to the patient if an operation is to be undertaken. The exclusion of oesophageal varices as the source of bleeding is most helpful in that the management is complicated and needs careful planning prior to laparotomy. If the bleeding does come from oesophageal varices, control can be achieved initially by Sengstaken tube. Continued bleeding after removal of the tube, which can be left for 24 hours or so, can be controlled by transoesophageal sclerosis, transoesophageal ligation or transection of the cardia (Either Tanner's operation or using a stapling device). Immediate porto-systemic shunt is indicated in appropriate patients.

Massive haemorrhage is in itself an indication for surgery in elderly patients; urgent surgery is required in those who have successive haemorrhages or respond poorly to adequate resuscitation. About one-quarter to one-third of all patients with a peptic ulcer have a haemorrhage from the ulcer. The mortality rises with age being 69 per cent in patients over 75 years old. The mortality after operation for bleeding peptic ulcer has fallen considerably, since vagotomy and pyloroplasty, with ligation of the bleeding point, became the standard operation. It varies from 15 per cent to 28 per cent and is higher in patients over the age of 70 years. The mortality is highest when the bleeding comes from a car-cinoma of the stomach, followed in descending order by oesophageal varices, hiatus hernia and peptic ulcer.

In those patients in whom haemorrhage follows prolonged vomiting the Mallory-Weiss syndrome should be borne in mind. The tear may extend through the muscular coat of the oesophagus as well, resulting in a spontaneous rupture of the oesophagus. These patients present with severe chest pain and shock; surgical emphysema may be detectable in the neck and can be seen in the mediastinum on chest X-ray. Immediate operative repair offers some hope of survival.

Rectal bleeding

In elderly patients, massive rectal bleeding is usually due to diverticular disease, about one-fifth of patients with diverticular disease have rectal bleeding at some time. In patients under 60 years of age, the source of bleeding is more often due to carcinoma of the colon or ulcerative colitis.

Treatment is to rest the patient in bed and give blood transfusions; the haemorrhage almost invariably ceases spontaneously. All patients should be investigated to identify the site of the haemorrhage. This can be done by sigmoidoscopy, colonoscopy, barium enema and angiography is necessary. In those who continue to bleed, emergency operation and a near-total colectomy is the procedure of choice, since the source of bleeding and extent of diverticular disease are difficult to ascertain at operation.

Intestinal obstruction

Complete intestinal obstruction may present with a combination of symptoms and signs — pain, vomiting and distension. The diagnosis and differentiation from other causes of these symptoms can be arrived at clinically. Treatment is by operation but before considering this, the site of the obstruction and its cause should be ascertained. Clues to the site of the obstruction can be obtained from the history and examination. In small bowel obstruction, colicky pain occurs frequently and vomiting follows the onset of pain after only a short interval. In large bowel obstruction, pain is less frequent, about every 30 minutes, the pain is felt in the lower abdomen and distension is a prominent feature. A previous history of alteration in bowel habit suggests that obstruction occurred as the culmination of a progressively stenosing lesion, the syndrome commonly seen in carcinoma of the descending colon.

Examination should begin with a careful search of both groins for hernia and the abdominal wall for the signs of previous operations. Adhesions, inguinal and femoral hernias are the commonest causes of acute small bowel obstruction, whilst carcinoma of the left side of the colon is the commonest cause of large bowel obstruction.

If an area of localized peritonitis is found on clinical examination of a case of obstruction, a mesenteric vascular occlusion should be suspected. The presence of atrial fibrillation makes the diagnosis certain.

Confirmation of the site of obstruction can be obtained by radiological examination of the abdomen. Films are taken both in the upright and supine positions. Certain unusual types of obstruction can be diagnosed from the X-ray plates — (volvulus of the sigmoid colon or caecum, and Spigelian hernia).

The timing of operation is dependent upon the patient's general condition and the need for resuscitation but should not be unduly delayed. Before operation, a Ryles tube is passed and an intravenous infusion commenced. Many of these patients are grossly dehydrated and require rapid re-hydration. In seriously ill elderly patients, operations for obstructed femoral and inguinal hernias can be carried out under local anaesthesia.

The mortality of operations for obstruction depends upon the site of the obstruction. The overall mortality from strangulated hernia is low, but it rises steeply if resection of gangrenous bowel is required. The mortality from large bowel obstructions is approximately 10 per cent to 16.5 per cent for sigmoid colon and 4 per cent to 18 per cent for ascending colon.

Surgical opinion varies as to whether an immediate resection or a three stage resection should be performed for acute obstruction of the left side of the colon. If the cases are carefully selected primary resection and a guarding transverse colostomy is a safe procedure with a low mortality. It is now standard practice to perform an immediate resection and end to end anastomosis for obstruction in the caecum, hepatic flexure and the right side of the transverse colon.

Peritonitis

Peritonitis can be described as primary or secondary according to the aetiology. It is with the seondary type that surgeons are principally concerned.

Secondary peritonitis

The term localized peritonitis applies to the condition in which inflammation is limited to a specific area of the peritoneum. Acute cholecystitis, appendix abscess, subphrenic abscess and peri-diverticular abscess are all examples of this. Clinically the pain and signs of peritoneal irritation are localized to the area round the source of the inflammation, complete localization to the site of primary pathology is much less usual in elderly patients than in young ones and, unless patient's general condition precludes it, early operation is the safest course.

Generalized peritonitis

In this group the entire peritoneal cavity is inflamed and early surgery is mandatory. The common causes are perforated duodenal ulcer, appendicitis, acute diverticulitis, strangulation of the small bowel due to hernia or infarct, and occasionally trauma.

The diagnosis is made after finding guarding, rigidity, or rebound tenderness over the whole of the peritoneal cavity. The diagnosis is notoriously difficult in elderly patients receiving systemic steroids. The white cell count and paracentesis of the abdominal cavity are both unreliable if confirmation of the diagnosis is sought.

Perforation of a duodenal ulcer. This occurs frequently in elderly patients and often does so without antecedent symptoms. The diagnosis is not difficult, and finding gas under the diaphragm on clinical or X-ray examination confirms the diagnosis. Intra-peritoneal rupture of the colon seldom gives rise to this sign. After initial resuscitation the patient should be operated on without delay, and the operation should be a simple repair of the perforation. This can be done expeditiously and the possibility of recurrent ulcer has less influence on the choice of operation than it has in younger patients.

The mortality in those patients admitted in a moribund condition, is almost 100 per cent. In less seriously ill patients there is virtually no motrality under the age of 50 years; after this the rate rises rapidly and is particularly high in the over 80-year-old patients.

In patients with peritonitis from a ruptured gastric ulcer the mortality is higher than for a perforated duodenal ulcer. The mortality for both rises if there is any delay between perforation and the commencement of treatment.

Acute diverticulitis. This is a common complication of diverticular disease. The inflammation may remain localized, in which case the signs are those of a localized peritonitis in the left iliac fossa. About half the cases of acute diverticulitis come into this category and the majority settle with bed rest, analgesics and systemic broad spectrum antibiotics. In those who develop signs of generalized peritonitis, accompanied by toxaemia, an operation should be undertaken. Approximately one-fifth of such cases are so ill that resuscitation fails to reverse the circulatory collapse and virtually all these patients die. In those who come to operation it is impossible to be dogmatic about the operative procedure to be undertaken. The general condition of the patient, peritoneal soiling, the state of the bowel and the operators' experience of colonic surgery are all factors to be considered when selecting the type and extent of operation.

Drainage of the left iliac fossa coupled with right transverse colostomy is the usual operation but it is said to give results no better than drainage alone.

A Paul-Mikulicz resection or a primary resection and immediate anastomosis give good results when performed by experienced surgeons. The mortality of these operations is between 10 and 30 per cent.

Severe shock on admission, faecal peritonitis and increasing age all make the prognosis much worse. The mortality is doubled in the over sixties.

Acute appendicitis. Acute appendicitis is a serious illness in old people. Diffuse peritonitis occurs early and its mortality in the over sixties is 4 per cent. This figure rises to 20 per cent in the over seventies. Prompts surgery and adequate resuscitation are imperative.

Other causes. A high proportion of patients with acute abdominal pain have biliary tract pathology (approximately 47.5 per cent). All patients presenting with epigastric pain and signs of localized peritonitis should have a serum amylase estimation prior to operation. In 75 per cent of cases of acute pancreatitis there are stones in the biliary tree. Surgery is best avoided in the acute phase of pancreatitis but may be required for complications such as pseudo cyst and abscess formation.

Mesenteric infarction is relatively uncommon — 8.8 in 10 000 cases — but is present to some degree in 2 per cent of all hospital autopsies. It deserves consideration because of the high mortality — 90 per cent. It may occur during periods of low cardiac output or secondary to an arterial embolus; occasionally it complicates a dissecting aneurysm of the aorta. The patient complains of severe abdominal pain and vomiting. The signs are those of small bowel obstruction with localized peritonitis and severe shock.

The treatment is prompt resuscitation and early operation. Completely gangrenous bowel should be resected. Patients can survive remarkably well on only short remanants of jejunum. In certain circumstances it may be possible to remove the arterial embolus, or to do a limited endarterectomy and vein patch reconstruction when an arteriosclerotic occlusion is found.

Peritonitis is not always due to bacterial inflammation; bilary peritonitis, intraperitoneal haemorrhage and intraperitoneal rupture of the bladder can give rise to difficulties in diagnosis. Bile peritonitis may occur spontaneously in the presence of stones in the common bile duct or as a complication of acute gangrenous cholecystitis.

Urinary retention

Approximately one-fifth of surgical emergencies in patients over 70 years of age are cases of acute retention of urine. The commonest causes are bladder neck obstruction, posterior urethral stricture and neurological abnormalities. Distortion of the bladder due to masses in the pelvis, including impacted faeces, is common and should be excluded by rectal and pelvic examination. The majority of cases of acute retention occur in men and are a result of bladder neck obstruction due to prostatic hypertrophy. A previous history of hesitancy, poor stream, nocturia and dribbling, in association with a palpably enlarged prostate make this diagnosis fairly certain.

When the cause of obstruction has been diagnosed the retention should be relieved as soon as possible. Occasionally morphia and a hot bath or small doses of carbachol will help to overcome the obstruction. If these methods do not work the bladder should be emptied by passing a catheter *per urethram*. A narrow Gibbon catheter with closed drainage into a plastic bag is ideal. If a catheter cannot be passed even when attempted under anaesthetic by an experienced surgeon, supra-pubic drainage is indicated.

The neurogenic bladder

In acute paraplegia a plastic catheter can be left in for up to six weeks. Antibiotics should be given continuously during this time and bladder washouts avoided if possible. In special centres intermittent catheterization gives excellent results. Recovery of function may follow relief of the spinal cord compression. In some patients an automatic bladder develops, obviating the need for continuous catheterization. In patients with permanent neurological damage division of the external urethral sphincter may remove the necessity for permanent catheterization.

Urethral stricture

Patients with a stricture of the posterior urethra should be investigated by urethrography. Those who have stricture following prostatectomy usually fare better with intermittent bouginage. Reconstruction of the posterior urethra can be undertaken in suitable cases with excellent results.

Hypertrophy of the prostate

This may cause compression of the prostatic urethra or disrupt the mechanism of the bladder neck sphincter, the so-called trapped prostate or median lobe syndrome. This subject is considered in detail in chapter 31.

Gangrene

Gangrene of a limb in an elderly patient is not necessarily the prelude to an amputation nor the initiator of a series of events inevitably leading to death. In old age most cases of gangrene are caused by a block in the circulation; gas gangrene occurs occasionally as a complication of amputation. Gangrene may be the result of obstruction to either arteries or veins, it may occur acutely after an arterial embolus or be the culmination of a progressive arteriosclerotic obliteration of the limb vessels. Rarely, it may be a feature of a dissecting aneurysm, or may be caused by trauma or poisons. It is vital to diagnose the cause as soon as possible in order to treat the condition adequately.

The diagnosis can be made from a history of claudication in chronic ischaemia or atrial fibrillation in embolic occlusion. A history of sudden onset of pain and paralysis, in conjunction with signs of a mottled cold pulseless limb, is sufficient to diagnose embolic occlusion. Finding the irregular pulse of atrial fibrillation or a history of coronary thrombosis would confirm the diagnosis and explain the source of the embolus.

Signs of potentially reversible gangrene are important in that if the condition is recognized and treatment initiated promptly the limb can be saved. It is this type of case that we shall consider more fully. When gangrene is established and necrosis has taken place, the only course is to amputate at the most suitable level.

Peripheral arterial embolus

In the majority of patients the source of the embolus is the left side of the heart and the patient has artrial fibrillation. Reversal of this to a normal rhythm with digitalis often precipitates embolism.

Signs of swelling and tenderness in the calf muscle with apparent shortening of the tendo achilles indicate muscle necrosis and irreversible damage. About 60 per cent of emboli lodge in the femoral, popliteal, or iliac arteries; of the remainder the aortic bifurcation accounts for between 10 per cent and 20 per cent and the axillary artery 12 per cent.

If the diagnosis of embolic occulsion at one of these sites is made and muscle necrosis is not present, an embolectomy should be carried out without delay. The introduction of the Fogarty catheter has completely altered the management of this condition. The operation can be performed under local anaesthesia in the groin, or in the upper arm in cases of axillary artery occlusion. Whilst waiting for operation the limb should remain exposed but not artificially cooled. The introduction of the balloon catheter has improved the prognosis for the limbs but has not reduced the mortality which varies between 20 per cent and 40 per cent. This high mortality is due to the cardiac condition rather than the embolus. Following embolectomy the patient should receive long-term anti-coagulant therapy.

Ischaemia due to diffuse arteriosclerosis may culminate in gangrene. This is often preceded by a period of rest pain and the foot appears swollen, red and cold. Irrespective of the patient's general condition an operation to save the leg and alleviate the pain is preferable to an amputation. In our experience elderly patients seldom manage to walk on a prosthesis nor do they manage well on crutches.

The mortality from mid thigh amputation approaches 50 per cent in the over 70's.

Gangrene is usually preceeded by a period in which the patients complain of pain in the feet at rest.

Patients who have pregangrene should be investigated by arteriography. The new technique of intravenous arteriography makes this easier to do in frail old patients. Symptoms are due to obstruction of the major arteries, aorta, iliac and femoral usually at two sites. A variety of reconstructions is available, aortic and iliac bypass, ilio-profundaplasty and femoro-popliteal bypass. Recently the range has been extended and it is now possible to carry out successfully combined reconstruction of aorta-iliac and femoral arteries and bypass from common femoral to tibial arteries at the ankle.

Endarterectomy and sympathectomy have only a limited application in selected patients.

Diabetic gangrene

This differs from the preceding types in that there are several factors involved. These are, ischaemia due to occlusion in both major and peripheral arteries, neuropathy and a predisposition to infection. They may be found in combination.

Patients with diabetes are particularly prone to infection; pus spreads subcutaneously and along the tissue planes involving tendons and bones. Treatment includes control of the infection by local dressings, drainage and the administration of appropriate antibiotics. The diabetes is controlled medically. Surgery is indicated when drainage of pus is required, to excise infected bone, or to amputate gangrenous toes. In those patients in whom the main vessels remain patent, sympathectomy helps to demarcate non-viable areas. Direct arterial surgery is indicated in cases with main vessel occlusion when the entire limb is threatened. The amputation rate is much higher in diabetics with lower limb ischaemia than in non-diabetics.

Amputation for arterial disease in the lower limb

Arteriosclerotic vascular occlusions and diabetic gangrene are the most frequent indications for amputation of the leg (71 per cent of cases). Infection, trauma or tumour is the indication for amputation in only 22 per cent of all cases. The incidence of amputation in patients with arteriosclerosis is almost trebled if they have diabetes as well.

In diabetic gangrene amputation of the toes or through the tarsal bones is often followed by healing which remains satisfactory for years. Below knee amputation has previously been condemned in artherosclerosis, on the grounds that re-amputation above the knee is necessary in a large number of patients but good results have been reported for below knee amputation in selected patients. Patients with a below knee amputation walk more readily than those with a mid-thigh amputation. It is our impression that many of our patients with above knee amputations wear their prostheses only for visits to the clinic. Only half of the male patients and less than half of female patients with above knee amputations can walk on a prosthesis.

In elderly patients with concurrent disease, and in non-ambulatory patients a mid-thigh amputation remains the operation of choice. The percentage of these healing without serious complications is high.

We cannot stress too much the fact that reconstruction of the major abdominal arteries carries a much lower mortality than amputation; it is well worth doing aortograms on every patient with pre-gangrene with a view to carrying out some form of revascularization. When direct arterial surgery is out of the question because of local or general conditions, lumbar sympathectomy helps to relieve pain in a substantial number of patients.

After amputation for ischaemia of the lower limb the average life expectancy is three years. Only half the patients who are fitted with a prosthesis wear it, and half the survivors will lose the other leg.

EXTRACRANIAL VASCULAR DISEASE

Extracranial vascular disease, predominantly at the origins of the internal carotid and vertebral arteries, is the cause of approximately 40 per cent of all cerebrovascular accidents. In almost one-quarter of patients who develop a stroke there are no prodromal symptoms, but usually a stroke is preceded by 'transient ischaemic attacks' (T.I.A.), and a bruit can be heard over the carotid bifurcation. If the clinical features of the T.I.A. suggest cerebral rather than cerebellar dysfunction and the patient is otherwise well it is worth considering investigation with a view to carotid endarterectomy. The risk of a permanent stroke is much higher than the risk of complications from operation, and anticoagulants have little or no value in preventing strokes in these circumstances.

When the symptoms and signs suggest cerebellar dysfunction it is usual to treat patients with anticoagulants, the risk of a stroke is fairly low and anticoagulants seem to reduce the number of T.I.A.s. If such patients have evidence of subclavian steal, arch aortography should be carried out because the condition is eminently remediable.

Whilst a number of new non-invasive techniques are under evaluation the mainstay of investigation remains arteriography. Arch aortography has superseded carotid angiography, principally because a knowledge of all four arteries to the brain is essential if surgery is contemplated.

The incidence of a stroke following a successful carotid endarterectomy is almost nil.

ELECTIVE SURGERY

It is the established practice in surgery to divide the indications for an operation into two groups, absolute indications and relative indications. The tendency, when considering elderly patients, is to avoid operation when the indications are relative. Considerable symptomatic benefit can be derived from non-operative measures, spinal and abdominal supports, elastic stockings, walking aids, hearing aids and spectacles.

Simple surgery may be of inestimable value in removing a long standing source of pain and irritation; and a well planned elective operation is the treatment of choice in certain circumstances. A Keller's operation for a painful hallux valgus can be of comparable value to one patient as a replacement arthroplasty of the hip to another. Repair of an inguino-scrotal hernia may increase the mobility of an elderly man considerably, improving the quality of his life and avoiding the possibility of an emergency operation for strangulation.

Treatment should be suited to the patient's general condition and his ability to co-operate in rehabilitation. Attention should be paid to the specific requirements of each individual; a bedridden man of 90 will make less demand on his legs than an ambulant 70 year old.

The principal surgical problems in geriatric patients are those of cancer and degenerative diseases of the joints.

Carcinoma of the breast

This is the commonest carcinoma in women, although the incidence falls beyond 70 years of age. Metastatic cancer of the breast may present in this age group after a long cancer-free interval. The diagnosis is made by clinical examination; in those clinics where examination by mammography, is undertaken the diagnostic accuracy and detection rate is increased. Confirmation of the diagnosis by histological examination of biopsy material should always be obtained. The extent of the disease is assessed by clinical staging based on the TNM system (Fig. 44.1).

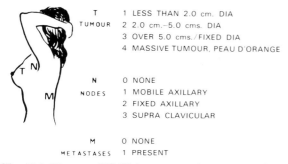

T		
TUMOUR	1	LESS THAN 2.0 cm. DIA
	2	2.0 cm.–5.0 cms. DIA
	3	OVER 5.0 cms./FIXED DIA
	4	MASSIVE TUMOUR, PEAU D'ORANGE
N	0	NONE
NODES	1	MOBILE AXILLARY
	2	FIXED AXILLARY
	3	SUPRA CLAVICULAR
M	0	NONE
METASTASES	1	PRESENT

Fig. 44.1 Diagram of TNM (tumours, nodes, metastases) system of staging breast cancer

The survival of the patient is influenced principally by the extent of the disease when first treated. Early breast cancer is usually treated by local mastectomy, or 'lampectomy', and the prognosis is good. Comparison of local and radical mastectomy, shows no significant difference and the former operation is usually preferred.

Where the primary growth is extensive or fungating, and spread beyond the confines of the breast has occurred, a toilet mastectomy has little advantage over local X-ray therapy. Radiotherapy to local lymph node metastases is equally effective if reserved until the metastases become clinically apparent, as when given prophylactically.

Advanced breast cancer should be treated by some form of hormone therapy, if necessary supplemented by local X-ray treatment of painful skeletal metastases. A trial of hormone therapy can be carried out without prejudice to the results of any subsequent surgical procedure. A long latent interval, metastases in skin and bones, a previous good response to oophorectomy are factors favouring a good result. The fact that tumour growth is generally slower in the elderly also supports hormone therapy.

Both oestrogens and androgens have frequent side-effects, some of which are serious, and should only be given under close supervision. The virilizing effects of the androgens can be reduced by using fluoxymesterone or methyldihydrotestosterone.

Those patients who have an initial good response to hormone therapy also do well after endocrine surgery. Bilateral adrenalectomy produces a worthwhile remission in one-third of the patients who have passed the menopause. The results of bilateral adrenalectomy and hypophysectomy are comparable, varying slightly from centre to centre.

So far it has not been possible to predict which patients are likely to respond to hormone or chemotherapy. Discriminants based on the ratio of the levels of various hormones in blood and urine, and on the oestrogen receptor status of the tumour have so far failed to provide information on the basis of which an accurate prediction of the patient's response can be made.

Cytotoxic drugs used singly have little effect on survival whilst combinations of cytotoxics often produce side effects the severity of which outweigh any increase in longevity.

Cancer of the stomach

The high incidence of this type of cancer makes it a frequent cause of death in geriatric patients despite its maximum incidence being between 50 and 70 years. Factors affecting its occurrence are social class (commonest in classes IV and V), atrophic gastritis and pernicious anaemia. It is three times more common in patients who have had a partial gastrectomy for duodenal ulcer but there is an impression that the incidence is falling.

The symptoms are variable depending upon the size and the site of the lesion. Antral lesions are the commonest and give rise to anorexia, weight loss, anaemia and eventually to symptoms of pyloric obstruction. Growths in the body of the stomach, in particular those on the lesser curve, need to be differentiated from benign gastric ulcer. Adenocarcinoma of the stomach arising near the cardia presents with symptoms of dysphagia. The clinical rule, that all cases of indigestion arising *de novo* in a person over 50 years of age are due to malignancy until proved otherwise, is a safe one.

Radiology will confirm the diagnosis in most cases but two other diagnostic aids are of help — fibreoptic gastroscopy and exfoliative cytology. A negative result in the latter case is good confirmation that carcinoma is not present.

Every effort should be made to obtain an early diagnosis: in cases treated early the cure rate is high. Screening programmes using a gastro camera have proved valuable in Japan where the incidence is extremely high. In Europe and America, where the incidence is lower, patients with pernicious anaemia should be gastroscoped at regular intervals.

Between 25 per cent and 40 per cent of patients submitted to laporatomy for carcinoma of the stomach have the lesion resected. The overall 5 year survival is approximately 5 per cent. Worthwhile palliation can be achieved by gastrectomy; (we prefer to do a total gastrectomy in patients with carcinoma of the body and fundus if possible removing the spleen and greater omentum *en masse*. The duodenum can be anastomosed to the oesophagus without difficulty and the palliation is surprisingly good). The more common method of reconstruction is by oesophagojejunostomy in the from of a Roux-en-Y anastomosis. When this operation is performed as a curative measure rather than as a palliative one there is a 25 per cent 5 year survival.

Tumours with lymphocyte infiltration have been found to have a better prognosis, and the presence of tumour in local lymph nodes is not necessarily associated with a poor prognosis.

Carcinoma of the large bowel

Carcinoma of the large bowel is the cause of death in approximately 15 000 people every year (Registrar General's figures for 1962 and 1963) and of these about half have carcinoma of the rectum. Carcinomas of the rectum and sigmoid colon account for over 70 per cent of all large bowel growths. The distribution is equal between the sexes and the incidence rises with age, over half the cases occurring patients over 60 years old.

Presenting symptoms vary according to the site of the growth. Tumours in the ascending colon give rise to anaemia and often there is a palpable mass. Tumours in the transverse colon may mimic gastric or biliary symptoms in addition to causing anaemia and weight loss. Tumours in the descending and sigmoid colon present with a history of change in bowel habit, increasing constipation, and frequently, complete intes-

tinal obstruction. Carcinoma of the rectum is often the cause of rectal bleeding and the patient may complain of tenesmus.

Examination of patients with any of the above symptoms should include a double contrast barium enema, sigmoidoscopy and rectal examination. The distal sigmoid colon, previously difficult to visualize by either of these methods, can now be fully examined by the flexible colonoscope.

A high proportion of all cases of rectal carcinoma is initially treated for haemorrhoids. Sigmoidoscopy is mandatory in all patients presenting with symptoms attributable to piles, before treatment is given.

With few exceptions all patients with cancer of the large bowel are best treated by resection of the tumour. Even in those with metastases, worthwhile palliation can be achieved by surgery.

Pre-operative preparation of the bowel is vital and should include thorough mechanical cleaning combined with a course of oral antibiotics. Which antibiotic regime to employ is a matter of opinion. Various combinations of antibiotics in routine use provide comparable protection against infection at the site of the operation.

The basis of all operations for carcinoma of the large bowel is resection of the growth and as much of the extramural lymphatic drainage of the affected segment as possible. Continuity of the bowel is restored by end to end anastomosis in the majority of cases. It is now possible, using stapling devices, to resect and re-anastomose tumours at a lower level in the pelvis than was previously possible and by this means abdomino perineal resections with the associated colostomy can be avoided.

In the case of cancer of the colon the resection rate is about 90 per cent and the operative mortality 5 per cent. The operative mortality after resection of the left side of the colon is approximately twice as high as that after resection on the right side. Of those patients surviving the operation about half are alive after 5 years. The absolute 5 year survival rate for all cases of carcinoma of the colon is 33 per cent. The 5 year corrected survival rate for patients with localized tumours treated surgically is 56 per cent. The mortality after abdomino-perineal resection for carcinoma of the rectum is slightly less than for colonic resections. The mortality after anterior resection of the rectum is slightly lower than that of abdomino-perineal resections; again palliative resections fare rather worse. The survival rate, after operations for large bowel cancer, depends on the extent of the growth when first treated. Dukes' method of staging into three groups, A, B and C according to the extent of the spread of the tumour judged histologically, is now universally accepted. The corrected 5 year survival for patients with group A tumours is 97 per cent, for group B 79 per cent and for group C 32 per cent.

Survival is marginally better if the growth is above 11 cm from anal margin. This is probably the reason for the marginally better survival figures for anterior resection when compared with abdomino-perineal resections.

Most surgeons agree that, in cases of advanced rectal or sigmoid cancer, resection is the best method of palliation. In elderly patients permanent colostomy should be avoided whenever possible. Arthritis, failing eyesight and failure to adapt to changed circumstances makes a colostomy an unbearable burden to some of these patients.

In elderly infirm patients with an advanced rectal growth, diathermy fulguration is an alternative to a colostomy.

DEEP VEIN THROMBOSIS

This common post-operative complication in the elderly also occurs after fractures of the neck of the femur and in patients confined to bed. The incidence is approximately 30 to 35 per cent of all patients operated on and is much more frequent in the over seventies.

The thrombosis occurs silently and is clinically difficult to detect. Swelling of the ankles or a combination of swelling with pain in the calf and tenderness can be detected in 60 per cent of cases. Early diagnosis may be assisted by ancillary techniques. To incorporation of radio-iodine labelled fibrinogen into the thrombus can be detected with a Geiger counter, or an obstruction to transmitted pressure waves detected by ultrasound.

The extent of the thrombosis varies; it may involve the veins of the soleal sinus only or extend to involve the common iliac veins. In the latter case the whole leg becomes oedematous and painful. This condition is termed plegmasia alba dolens. When the condition occurs spontaneously it is often associated with the presence of a pelvic neoplasm and not infrequently leads to peripheral gangrene (phlegmasia caerulea dolens).

Deep vein thrombosis gives rise to two principal sequalae, pulmonary embolism and permanent obstruction to the venous drainage from the leg. Pulmonary embolism is common and a deep vein thrombosis is present in all cases of pulmonary embolism. Pulmonary emboli may be massive and rapidly fatal or they may be multiple and result in impaired pulmonary function. Iliofemoral vein thrombosis results in a permanently swollen leg and pain on exercise in the majority of cases. Thrombosis in the peripheral veins produces superficial varices, pigmentation and stasis ulcers.

The initial treatment of this condition is by elevation of the limb and anti-coagulant therapy. Phenylbutazone is helpful in relieving pain and its anti-inflammatory action may help with resolution of the thrombosis.

The place of surgery in iliofemoral vein thrombosis is not yet established. Venous thrombectomy requires a general anaesthetic and image intensification for X-ray control of the proceedings. Thrombectomy should be considered in those cases which are seen early in their course and fail to respond to medical treatment over a period of 48 hours. Venous bypass using the contralateral saphenous vein and a temporary a-v fistula is being tried for patients with iliac vein thrombosis but the long term effects and success rate are as yet uncertain.

In the management of the embolic complications, pulmonary embolectomy is indicated in patients who show signs of right heart failure, have recovered from a cardiac arrest, have a systolic blood pressure less than 100 mmHg or have arterial desaturation in the presence of tachypnoea.

If recurrent small emboli occur despite anticoagulant therapy a plication clip can be placed across the inferior vena cava. Caval filters may be extrinsic (De Weese clip) or intrinsic (Mobin-Udin, Greenfield filter) complications are few with extrinsic clips but the Greenfield filter can be inserted through the groin under local anaesthetic. This operation has reduced the incidence of fatal pulmonary embolism when performed prophylactically in elderly patients undergoing abdominal surgery.

Several methods of promoting venous return from the veins in the calf of the leg have been tried, including physiotherapy, elevation, elastic stockings and muscle stimulation. Some have been partially successful in preventing thrombosis but no completely reliable method has emerged so far.

RECOMMENDED FURTHER READING

Selections from:

Bailey H 1977 Emergency surgery, 10th edn. John Wright and Sons, Bristol
Davis L E, Christopher F 1981 Textbook of surgery: The biological basis of modern surgical practice, 12th edn. W B Saunders, Philadelphia
Eastcott H H G 1973 Arterial surgery, 2nd edn. Pitman Medical, London

Goligher J C 1980 Surgery of the anus, rectum and colon 4th edn. Ballière-Tindall and Cassell, London
Ledingham I, McKay C 1978 Jamieson & Kay's Textbook of Surgical Physiology, 3rd edn. Churchill Livingstone, Edinburgh
Rhoads J E, Allen J G, Harkins H N, Moyer C A 1970 Principles and practice of surgery, 4th edn. J B Lippincott, Philadelphia
Tindall V R (ed) 1981 Essential sciences for clinicians. Blackwell Scientific, Oxford

Anaesthesia in old age

INTRODUCTION

The purpose of anaesthesia is to enable surgery to be performed. There is never any justification for refusing to give an anaesthetic on grounds of age alone; the important questions are the appropriateness of operating, the urgency of surgery and the potential benefits to be gained in relation to the various possible risks. The right decision will not invariably be made, and one recalls Osler's remark that 'Errors of judgement must occur in the practice of an art which consists largely of balancing probabilities'.

Whether or not surgery is the appropriate course is largely a matter for the surgeon himself to decide. The question of the optimum timing of the operation is something to be discussed jointly by the surgeon and the anaesthetist. The extent to which anaesthesia itself may contribute either to improvement of the patient's condition or to morbidity and mortality is a question on which the expert opinion of the anaesthetist himself is needed. There are doubtless many cases in which the benefits of surgery are not so much due to the actual operative correction of a minor abnormality as to the opportunity which this gives for intravenous infusion, aspiration of the trachea and bronchi and controlled oxygen therapy, together with the fact that the iminence of an operation may focus attention upon other ways in which the patient's condition might be improved. Proper preparation for an anaesthetic is no bad preparation for continued life itself.

SURGICAL AND ANAESTHETIC MORTALITY AND MORBIDITY

In 1979, 21 per cent of 6754 operations carried out at the Royal Liverpool Hospital were on patients over 65 years of age. It is probable that this figure is fairly typical of the developed countries, but it is a common impression that this figure may be increasing. Statistical studies over the next few years will show whether this is so. The problems and risks of geriatric anaesthesia are

thus part, and possibly an increasing part, of the experience of all anaesthetists. Although the problems are to some extent common to all age groups, there are special considerations.

It is known that long-term exposure to anaesthetics may have toxic effects. Indeed, work on the effects of anaesthetics on cells and cell constituents dates back to the early part of the century (Hamburger, 1916; Heilbrunn, 1920). Interaction of anaesthetics with proteins, which may be relevant to antigen–antibody reactions (Moudgil and Wade, 1976) has been demonstrated, for example, by Schoenborn et al (1965). There are also reports of the effects of anaesthetics on cell motility (Nunn et al, 1968) including lymphocyte motility (Nunn et al, 1970) and possibly phagocytosis (Cullen, 1974). Interference with cell division has been studied experimentally (Ostergren, 1944; Nunn et al, 1971; Bruce and Taurig, 1969; Sturrock and Nunn, 1975); clinically, bone marrow depression from the administration of nitrous oxide over a period of several days was reported from Scandinavia (Lassen et al, 1956). Teratogenic effects of most anaesthetic agents have been reported (e.g. Fink, 1966).

The relationship between anaesthesia and immunology has been reviewed by Duncan and Cullen (1976) who consider that anaesthetic agents may modify the total immunosuppressive response. The anaesthetist can also prevent or reduce other stress factors including hypoxia, hypercarbia and hypotension which will theoretically enhance immunosuppression. It is doubtful whether any of these reported or alleged toxic effects of anaesthetics have any practical significance for the geriatric patient undergoing an anaesthetic of normal duration.

Since the latter part of the nineteenth century anaesthesia has been cited from time to time as a possible cause of dementia in old people (for earlier references see Simpson et al, 1961). There has not, however, been good supporting evidence. Bedford (1955) drew attention to the allegedly oft-heard remark 'He's never been the same since his operation', and reviewed 18 cases of extreme dementia after surgery, all of which were in his own care. Some histories of these cases, in fact, revealed possible causes of cerebral ischaemia, for example precipitous fall of blood pressure under anaesthesia or delayed recovery for unexplained reasons. Bedford commented on this and stressed the dangers of untreated hypotension and of nursing in the head-up position when compensatory reflexes are impaired. He referred to similar cases of dementia in his experience following massive haemorrhage, cardiac infarction and pneumonia, in which no anaesthetic had been given. Nevertheless, he concluded that there must be a 'rare and unpredictable' idiosyncrasy to some factor concerned in operations under general anaesthesia which accounted for otherwise inexplicable dementia in some elderly patients.

The importance of this kind of unsubstantiated suspicion is not so much that it may influence the anaesthetist's choice of technique, which is unlikely, but that it may seriously affect the judgement of those who have the responsibility of advising for or against surgery in the elderly. It is far better to repair a hernia under optimal conditions than to be presented with an emergency case of strangulation at a later date; and the patient who is denied surgery because of a groundless fear of some strange 'toxic' effect of anaesthesia in old age may pay a high price for this over-cautious advice.

In response to the views of Bedford (1955) and the Lancet (1955) Simpson et al (1961) reviewed all elective surgical admissions over the age of 65 to the Radcliffe Infirmary, Oxford, for a whole year. Careful pre- and postoperative psychological tests were done on the most susceptible cases; all patients, and in most cases their relatives, were interviewed at home after discharge from hospital. This study showed, as would be expected, that relief of disability or discomfort, for example by repair of a large hernia, was if anything followed by improvement in social integration whereas the creation of disability, for instance by amputation or colostomy, carried a risk of deterioration. The study included 472 general anaesthetics, 206 local, regional and spinal anaesthetics and 63 patients who had no anaesthetic or operation. In the last 'control' group there was a general tendency towards deterioration, but not in the other groups. There was no evidence that change in mental performance or in the results of psychological testing could be attributed to any form of anaesthesia. The authors made the further point that they had met with six patients who had had more than 20 anaesthetics after the age of 65, with no signs of ill-effect. A single study of this kind, however meticulous and comprehensive, can never hope to prove a negative. It nevertheless remains true that there is, to date, no evidence of any specific deleterious effect of anaesthetic drugs in themselves on old people subjected to clinical anaesthesia. The most potentially

dangerous aspect of any anaesthetic is the anaesthetist himself. Powell (1976) referred to the desirability of further work on intellectual impairment in the elderly, and preliminary studies have been carried out by Gordon and Tomlinson (personal communication).

Surgical mortality

A number of studies of surgical mortality in patients over the age of 70 have been reported in the literature (including Brander et al, 1970; Andersen and Otberg 1972; Santos and Gelperin, 1975; Djokovic and Hedley-White, 1979; Palmberg and Hirsjavi, 1979; Symour and Pringle, 1982). The reported overall mortality figures have varied from 5 to 23 per cent, and from these studies, several important factors emerge which contribute to the mortality. Palmberg and Hirsjavi (1979) in their study of 590 patients age 70 and over found that the mortality after emergency surgery was four times that after elective surgery, 36.8 per cent as opposed to 7.8 per cent. Similar figures are reported by Seymour and Pringle (1982). The latter authors also found increasing mortality with increasing age, the rate being 9.9 per cent in patients age 65–74, rising to 20.9 per cent in patients over 75. However, Andersen and Østberg (1972) followed up 7922 elderly patients for up to 17 years, and concluded that the long-term prognosis in geriatric surgery was reasonably good compared to that of the population as a whole. They considered that this was partly due to careful selection of the most suitable cases for surgery.

The figures of mortality following different operations show large variations. A consistently high mortality is recorded after operations on the gastrointestinal tract, approximately 20 per cent by Santos and Gelperin (1975) and Djokovic and Hedley-White (1979), and 15 per cent by Palmberg and Hirsjävi (1979). In contrast, a mortality rate of 1–3 per cent has been found after transurethral resection of the prostate.

Santos and Gelperin made a further important point, that in older patients, even minor surgical procedures are associated with a higher mortality than than which would be found in younger patients. This view is supported by the finding of Seymour and Pringle (1982) of a mortality rate of 6.1 per cent after procedures such as endoscopy, removal of small cutaneous lesions ,and arteriography. This is highly relevant to anaesthesia. It serves to illustrate the old adage that although there may be minor operations there are no minor anaesthetics. Indeed, the more trivial the operation, the more important, relatively speaking, the anaesthetic becomes, and this is never more true than in the elderly patient.

Santos and Gelperin also expressed the view, with which many surgeons would agree, that the operation should be performed as quickly as possible. Palmberg and Hirsjävi (1979) found that the mortality of operations lasting over 2 hours was 36 per cent, whereas that of operations lasting less than this time was only 7.5 per cent. Multiple procedures should probably also be discouraged. Lorhan's 1967 figures show that although the mortality after first and second operations in octogenarians was very similar, that after third and fourth procedures was almost doubled to 42 per cent.

Anaesthetic mortality

There are several studies of the risks and deaths associated with anaesthesia itself (e.g. Edwards et al, 1956; Dinnick, 1964; Goldstein and Keats, 1970; Clifton and Hotten, 1963; Memery, 1965; Holland et al, 1970; McIntyre, 1973; Bodlander, 1975; Wylie, 1975). The increased risk in older age groups is referred to (Goldstein and Keats, 1970) and is attributed largely to decreased physiological reserve and multiple intercurrent pathology (Stevens and Aldrete, 1969; Lorhan, 1967). As Simpson et al (1961) observed, the reduction of reserves in old people 'not only decreases the margin of error permissible to the anaesthetist but also increases the penalties for even minor shortcomings in patient care'.

The Australian special committee, investigating deaths under anaesthesia from 1960 to 1968 (Holland et al, 1970) documented the steep climb in incidence of anaesthetic-related mortality in the later decades of life from about 0.4 deaths per 100 000 of population in young adults to 6 per 100 000 over the age of 80. By looking at the figures in this way the authors were able to make the point that as an overall cause of mortality in the community, anaesthesia was ahead of influenza, although kidney disease accounted for 10 times as many deaths, diabetes 20 times as many and bronchitis 30 times as many. In this study, no causes of anaesthetic death were unique to the elderly, but the commonest problems associated with anaesthetic mortality were intestinal obstruction and laparotomy for peritonitis. Inadequate preparation for surgery and anaesthesia was one of the five commonest causes of death. This most useful review related to clinical practice 9 to 17 years ago, and standards have improved. Bodlander (1975), for example, reported that at the Royal Prince Alfred Hospital, Sydney, in the period 1963 to 1972 there were 15 deaths as a result of anaesthesia alone out of a total of 408 deaths associated with surgery. This incidence of 3.7 per cent contrasted with a figure of 20.9 per cent for the previous decade. Full age details for the 15 anaesthetic deaths were not given, but the three reported cases of cardiovascular collapse due to anaesthesia were aged 79, 80 and 83, and a case of inhalation of gastric contents occurred in an 81-year-old woman with a strangulated femoral hernia. Although such traditional causes remain, no deaths directly attributable to anaesthesia

were found in the series of 500 patients over 80 years reported by Djokovic and Hedley-White in 1979. They considered that the main potential dangers of anaesthesia in the elderly are myocardial depression and hypotension, especially following thiopentone; hypertension and tachycardia associated with laryngoscopy and endotracheal intubation; and postoperative respiratory inadequacy.

Differences in anaesthetic technique may contribute to mortality. Two studies have compared two different anaesthetics in patients having surgical repair of fractured femur. In both studies, one group of patients was paralysed and ventilation was controlled (IPPV). McLaren and his colleagues (1978) compared this technique with spinal analgesia and found a greatly reduced mortality in the latter group (1 died out of 81) compared with IPPV (18 died out of 83). Similarly, the use of ketamine anaesthesia was followed by a reduced mortality (1 out of 30) compared with IPPV (6 out of 30) (Spreadbury, 1980). The reasons for these differences are not clear.

Causes of death

The tendency for postoperative chest complications to occur more frequently in old people, especially after upper abdominal surgery, has been known for many years (Dripps and Van N Deming, 1964). Despite advances in antibiotic therapy and anaesthetic techniques, the mortality from postoperative pneumonia is still considerable, being 33 per cent in 1967 (Lorhan), and around 20 per cent in 1979 (Djokovic and Hedley-White, 1979; Palmberg and Hirsjävi, 1979).

Deaths from pulmonary embolism may be decreasing. Palmberg and Hirsjävi, looking at patients operated upon during the decade 1964–74, found that 33 per cent of deaths were due to this cause, whereas the figure was only 3 per cent in a study relating to more recent operations (Djokovic and Hedley-White, 1979). Such a decrease would be expected in view of the increasing use of prophylactic measures such as low-dose heparin to prevent deep vein thrombosis.

Postoperative myocardial infarction continues an important cause of death, especially in patients who are operated upon within 3 months of a previous infarct. Steen et al (1978) in a study of 587 surgical patients who had had a myocardial infarct before operation, found that 36 (6.1 per cent) developed a new infarct. In this study, and also that of Arkins et al (1964) the postoperative infarct rate in patients whose preoperative infarct had occurred within 3 months of surgery rose to 27 per cent (4 out of 11) and 40 per cent (11 out of 17) respectively. The mortality rate of all patients in whom an infarct had occurred during the 6 months preceding surgery was 6 out of 33, 18 per cent.

PREANAESTHETIC ASSESSMENT AND PREMEDICATION

General assessment

Recent work suggests that although life-span is not increasing, more people are approaching this span with little disability due to physiological or pathological changes. Thus the period of increasing disability preceding death is shortening, and the degree of disability will increase rapidly during this time. This fact, together with the likelihood of multiple coexisting disease, (Wilder and Fishbein, 1961), make it essential for all patients over the age of 65 to be seen preoperatively by an anaesthetist.

Most elderly patients are easy to talk to. They can give a clear account of their problem, and have a philosophical acceptance of this new crisis in their lives. However, history taking may be more difficult in some patients for three reasons. Firstly, slower speech, mental processes and movement mean that more time must be allowed. Secondly, the fit elderly patient, proud of independence and maintained activity, may not admit to any disability! Thirdly, memory is often impaired to some extent, and even episodes of serious illness may be forgotten. Good relations will not be established by patronising old people and talking down to them. The anaesthetist should introduce himself, address the patient by name (not christian name), and sit down to talk. While the history is being taken, important observations can be made of dyspnoea, cough, mobility, colour, tremor, oedema and anxiety.

Apart from the usual clinical history, questions must be asked about activity, both medical and physical, and occupation. Glenn (1973) stressed the importance of these in elderly patients, as the man who becomes completely sedentary after retirement is likely to have lower cardiac and respiratory reserves than the man who continues to be physically active. Volpitto (1967) quotes the case of a man of 109 who was successfully anaesthetized for operation on a fractured hip, sustained while running across a field from his illicit still in fear of pursuit from the law.

Another important point in general assessment, as mentioned above is the probable outcome of surgery. Glenn (1973) suggests that operations in the elderly may be classified broadly into those expected to result in complete restoration of health, those aimed at diminishing disability and those aimed at achieving a limited postponement of inevitable death. The attitude of the anaesthetist will clearly be influenced by this.

Other useful pointers to potential problems include a history of falls or postural hypotension, paroxsymal nocturnal dyspnoea, angina at rest, and recent onset of unexplained tiredness or mental confusion.

When enquiring about drugs, it must be remembered that a prescribed drug is often not taken.

It would be helpful to be able to predict the risks of surgery and anaesthesia, and some recent studies have attempted to do this (Goldman et al, 1977; Schneider et al, 1979; Djokovic and Hedley-White, 1979; Klidjian et al, 1980). Goldman and his colleagues clearly showed that an age greater than 70 increased the risk of postoperative life-threatening or fatal cardiac complications. They also showed that in patients of any age, risk was increased by evidence of congestive cardiac failure; myocardial infarction in the preceding 6 months; rhythm other than sinus or premature atrial contractions; more than five premature ventricular contractions per minute at any time before operation; intraperitoneal, intrathoracic or aortic operations; important valvular aortic stenosis; emergency operation; and poor general condition.

Any obvious abnormalities of fluid and electrolyte balance must be corrected before operation, and medical management, for example, of arrhythmias, initiated. As the adaptive mechanisms of the elderly react more slowly, any corrective measures should be instituted gradually whenever possible, taking days rather than hours.

The details of physiological changes with aging in the body as a whole, and its various systems, are discussed in detail in other chapters of this book. The present discussion will therefore be confined to the main points of concern to the anaesthetist.

Cardiovascular system

The most dramatically sudden and potentially lethal complications during anaesthesia are likely to be those related to the circulatory system. A precipitous fall in blood pressure may be due either to a sudden drop in cardiac output or to sudden loss of peripheral resistance. The elderly heart has a reduced reserve, and the elasticity of the cardiovascular system is lost with degenerative arterial disease. The lack of circulatory compensation which results is exacerbated by autonomic disturbances which occur in old age and in diabetes (British Medical Journal, 1973; Collins et al, 1977; Wollner et al, 1979). Rapid changes in posture or in intrathoracic pressure during vigorous artificial ventilation of the lungs will be poorly tolerated, particularly under the influence of intravenous barbiturates and other drugs, and if potent inhalation agents such as halothane are being used. Dehydration due to illness and to diuretic therapy may also contribute to hypotension.

24-hour ambulant monitoring of fit elderly subjects has shown, that arrhythmias are quite common (Clee et al, 1979). Although Kuner (1967) found some arrhythmia during anaesthesia in almost 62 per cent of his patients, he did not find a higher incidence in older patients. Regional and general anaesthesia showed a comparable incidence of arrhythmias. In fact, it is the general experience that ectopic beats and even coupling occur fairly frequently during anaesthesia in the elderly, and rarely require treatment. However, if such a new arrhythmia appears, a cause must be sought, such as hypokalaemia (especially in the presence of a digitalis) and acidosis. The increased risk of surgery in patients with preoperative ventricular contractions has been emphasized by Goldman et al (1977).

Conduction defects may be intensified during surgery and anaesthesia so that any preoperative evidence of heart block (other than bundle branch block) should be regarded with suspicion and prophylactic arrangements made for cardiac pacing during surgery should it be required. When a pacemaker is already in situ, care should be taken to avoid interference from any other equipment in the operating theatres, especially diathermy.

Rodstein and Zeman (1967) noted the occurrence of loud systolic murmurs in over 60 per cent of old patients and commented on the difficulty that often exists in clinically defining the underlying lesion. This is of importance since any condition which fixes or severely limits the cardiac output, and especially aortic stenosis, may lead to sudden death, especially if there is loss of peripheral resistance or acute rhythm disturbance. The presence of congestive failure, narrow pulse pressure, systolic aortic thrill and a faint or absent aortic second sound are valuable clinical guides to the diagnosis of stenosis.

Myocardial infarct.   As has been mentioned, there is an increased risk of myocardial infarct during or after operation especially in patients who have had a recent preoperative infarct. The literature has been recently reviewed by Portal (1982). Steen et al (1978) in their study of patients with a history of an infarct, also noted that a perioperative infarct is more likely in patients who have hypertension (17 out of 181) whereas only 19 patients reinfarcted out of 406 normotensive patients. Their study suggested that other possible contributory factors are length of operation; site of operation, the risk being greater in operations on the great vessels and thoracic and upper abdominal surgery; and intraoperative hypotension.

Carotid sinus syndrome.   Attention should be paid to any preoperative history of syncope that may suggest hypersensitivity of the carotid sinus. The carotid sinus syndrome occurs in a number of elderly patients, especially those with hypertension and arteriosclerosis (Heron et al, 1965).

Hypertension.   Hypertension in the elderly patient is always a difficult problem. Many studies have shown that when falls in blood pressure occur during anaes-

thesia, they are usually greater in hypertensive than normotensive patients. However, a steady blood pressure may be observed in both treated and untreated hypertensives. Since even transient falls in blood pressure, if severe, can readily lead to cerebral and myocardial ischaemia in older patients, there is need for extreme caution in the use of any drugs which may cause hypotension, and for gentleness in handling at all times. The preoperative placement of an intravenous infusion is an invaluable safety precaution.

There is also a potential risk associated with rises in blood pressure during anaesthesia. Prys-Roberts and his colleagues (1971b) noted that peaks of hypertension in response to laryngoscopy and endotracheal intubation were more likely to occur in hypertensives, especially those not on any therapy. As such changes are mediated via the sympathetic nervous system, these authors argued the case, on logical grounds, for prior administration of beta adrenergic blocking drugs. Although there are occasional patients in whom it is considered particularly advisable to obtund sympathetic responses with a small dose of one of these drugs given before operation, their routine use is not recommended.

There are still some differences of opinion concerning anaesthesia in the patient receiving antihypertensive drugs, but the most common view, following the work of Papper (1965), Prys-Roberts et al (1971) and others, is that patients well controlled on antihypertensive treatment should not have drugs withdrawn in the immediate preoperative period, and that untreated hypertension carries more risk. The question of whether to start antihypertensive therapy in the elderly is still being debated, but there is little place for such therapy to be commenced in the immediate preoperative period on the basis of a casual high blood pressure reading.

Preoperative digitalization.   The question of preoperative digitalization will often arise: it may well be helpful to the patient with little cardiac reserve who requires major surgery and prolonged anaesthesia, provided no contraindication exists. Rapid digitalization, however, is not without risk (Liu and Callis, 1964). Two articles in the early 1960s suggested care in the use of suxamethonium in digitalized patients (Galindo and Davis, 1962; Dowdy and Fabian, 1963). However, no further evidence has appeared to support the view that this combination of drugs is particularly likely to cause dangerous cardiac arrhythmias. A factor which clearly does increase the toxicity of digitalis is hypokalaemia, and this must be corrected preoperatively, and sought intraoperatively if necessary (see above).

It will be clear that a preoperative ECG in the elderly patient will provide useful evidence of any conduction defect or other pre-existing arrhythmia, of previous myocardial infarction, which may not be obvious from the clinical history, and of other abnormalities such as left ventricular hypertrophy and strain. It will also provide a baseline for reference during the course of anaesthesia and the early postoperative period, so that further evidence of myocardial ischaemia, pulmonary embolism or conduction disturbance can be more precisely evaluated. ST segment and T wave changes are, however, so common in elderly patients, without notable physical findings or clinical history, that in a predictive sense the ECG may be unhelpful in relation to anaesthesia and surgery (Liu and Callis, 1964).

Respiratory system

The physiological changes which occur with increasing age result in relative overinflation of the lungs and rigidity of the chest wall. In addition, chronic bronchitis is extremely common in Britain among elderly patients, and this is often accompanied by obstructive airways disease of varying degrees of severity. This requires careful assessment from the history, using simple bedside tests, by clinical examination, and from measurement of the forced expiratory volume in one second (FEV_1) and the forced vital capacity, and of arterial blood gases. McFadden and his colleagues (1982) have drawn attention recently to the value of a raised respiratory rate in the diagnosis of acute lower respiratory tract infection in the elderly. This overall assessment allows treatment of some problems before operation, such as bronchospasm, antibiotics for infection and physiotherapy for sputum reduction. Smoking can be discouraged. In addition, an estimate can be made of the ability to maintain spontaneous ventilation during recovery from anaesthesia, and to cough and avoid postoperative pulmonary complications. This is especially important when upper abdominal surgery is required. Patients with an FEV_1 of less than 1 litre are likely to require special care, although such a test alone is not a very reliable guide (Nunn 1976). When Pa_{CO_2} is raised, plans should be made to continue artificial ventilation of the lungs after operation as further carbon dioxide retention can be caused by residual effects of premedicant, anaesthetic and muscle relaxant drugs, and by postoperative pain and strong analgesics.

Some degree of arterial hypoxaemia is usually observed in older patients, even when apparently healthy. Conway et al (1965) found a mean arterial Po_2 of 11.5 kPa (86 mmHg) in a group of hospital patients over the age of 60, compared to a mean of 12.9 kPa (96.8 mmHg) in patients below the age of 30. The patients were clinically free from cardiovascular or respiratory disease and had not been premedicated. A severe degree of preoperative hypoxaemia is seen in some patients with disabling obstructive airways disease. Such patients may be considered unsuitable for a general anaesthetic, and the required procedure carried out under local or conduction block. It must be remembered that respiratory failure may be precipitated in such patients by the injudicious use of a high inspired oxygen concentration. One such patient was recently seen by one author (M.E.D.) — his normal arterial oxygen tension was only 5.1 kPa (37 mmHg) and he became comatose when oxygen was administered via nasal spectacles after his femoral embolectomy under local anaesthesia.

Renal and hepatic systems

Renal function deteriorates with age, due largely to a decrease in functioning nephrons and decreased blood flow causing a reduction in glomerular filtration rate (GFR). Thus the additional stress of any sudden change in blood volume or blood pressure during surgery and the early postoperative period may lead to failure of compensation. One of the main concerns of the anaesthetist in relation to impaired renal function is electrolyte imbalance with its potential effect on the actions of a number of drugs. Knowledge of preoperative electrolyte, haemoglobin and haematocrit values is essential for preoperative preparation and the planning of fluid therapy during and after surgery. When there is pathological impairment of renal function, care must be taken with drugs which are primarily excreted by the kidney, for example, gallamine triethiodide, or those which are potentially nephrotoxic, such as methoxyflurane or enflurane. There is no evidence, however, that any of these drugs should not be administered to the elderly subject whose renal function is impaired as a result of normal aging processes.

For major surgery, the insertion of an indwelling bladder catheter is desirable, particularly if there is the possibility of incontinence. Secretion of urine is a useful clinical guide to the adequacy of renal perfusion and the measurement of urine output is, of course, an important guide to fluid therapy. The development of acute-on-chronic failure is always a danger in elderly patients, and may readily be precipitated by inadequate fluid replacement or incautious use of drugs, especially tetracyclines and steroids.

With increasing age, the efficiency of some functions of the liver diminishes. For example, bromsulphthalein retention increases, and protein synthesis is reduced. The liver is less able to metabolize some drugs, for example, lignocaine and diazepam. On the other hand, there seems to be little impairment of glucuronidation. These facts, together with other alterations of pharmacokinetics and pharmacodynamics in the elderly, pose many problems concerning drug administration particularly in relation to preoperative therapy and analgesics. Liver blood flow decreases with age; this may have advantages as well as disadvantages. Although the delivery of nutrients and oxygen will be reduced, there will also be a decrease in the delivery to the liver of potentially toxic substances which have been absorbed from the intestine.

There is controversy concerning the role of anaesthesia as a cause of postoperative jaundice and liver failure; halothane does not generally appear to be contraindicated for biliary surgery (Dawson et al, 1963; Jones et al, 1965; Bunker et al, 1969) although it should be noted that Lippmann and Lorhan (1968), in a series of 53 portacaval shunt operations for oesophageal varices (not predominantly geriatric) abandoned the use of halothane after all of the first 10 cases died in hepatic failure postoperatively, the mortality in the remainder of the series, from all causes, being 56 per cent. If a previous halothane anaesthetic has recently been given, further halothane is better avoided unless it is considered to be the best anaesthetic. Suitable alternatives may be found in enflurane, or the use of repeat injections of intravenous agents.

Oral hygiene and dentition. It is important to check for the presence of loose teeth or precarious dental artifacts which may become dislodged during anaesthesia, and even lost, without the anaesthetist's knowledge, into the respiratory tract. Oral sepsis should be corrected as well as possible since it predisposes to postoperative parotitis which carries a high mortality in this age group. Lorhan et al (1962) reported 28 cases of postoperative parotitis with an average age of 73 and pointed out that at that time the condition was by no means a mere problem of the past. Drying agents such as atropine, which will exert their effect for a considerable number of hours, should be avoided if possible when oral hygiene is poor.

DRUG REACTIONS AND INTERACTIONS

The profusion of drugs that are nowadays prescribed makes it essential to ask every patient, and if need be his relatives, about the details of medication. Older patients often become confused about the drugs that have been prescribed for them, or bought from the pharmacist. They will not infrequently confess, on questioning, that they have a bathroom cupboard full of bottles which they are afraid to use because they have forgotten what most of them are for. A number of reports have shown the high proportion of old patients who fail to take drugs, make errors in self-administration and endanger their health through drug misuse (Wandless and Davie, 1977). It is no surprise that the incidence of drug reactions is reported to be considerably greater in the geriatric age group (Roberts, 1976) and the multiplicity of drugs which are taken increases the possibility of drug interactions. It would be no exaggeration to say that drug reactions and interactions as causes of unexpected anxiety, and occasionally

fatality, during anaesthesia have become more frequent in recent years. There are clear indications for the avoidance of any more than the minimum number of welltried drugs during the anaesthetic (Bethune, 1964).

Special preoperative enquiry should always be made about use of steroids, antihypertensive drugs, digitalis, anticoagulants, beta adrenergic blockers, monoamineoxidase inhibitors, tricyclic antidepressants and drugs to control diabetes. Useful reviews of drug reactions in relation to anaesthesia are given by Lorhan (1971) and Dodson (1975, 1982a), and the 'Danger Lists for the Anaesthetist' of Grogono and Jones (1968) are a useful source of ready reference.

Premedication

There are very few indications for premedication in geriatric practice; in co-operative patients it is unnecessary and in confused or unco-operative patients it is often ineffective even when pushed to the point of becoming dangerous, or it may actually increase the confusion and lack of co-operation. There is little indication for an opiate, unless the patient is in pain. The routine use of antisialogogues is unnecessary — the dryness of the mouth may predispose to monilial infections or parotitis, and interference with visual accommodation may persist for some hours. If an anticholinergic drug is needed, atropine should be used rather than hyoscine because of the appreciable incidence of disorientation with the latter drug in the elderly. Benzodiazepine tranquillisers may occasionally be needed, but the amnesia which they can cause may be prolonged in the elderly (Kortilla et al, 1981). Barbiturates should also be avoided in patients with a tendency to become agitated; their use may lead to restlessness and lack of co-operation (Lorhan, 1971). Reassurance of the patient and explanation by the anaesthetist are perhaps more important than any sedative or tranquilliser drug.

ANAESTHESIA

General considerations

In general, smaller doses of drugs are required in the elderly who are much more sensitive to both the therapeutic and the side-effects of many drugs, especially those acting on the central nervous system. A discussion of pharmacology in relation to anaesthesia in the elderly is found in Dodson (1983). Apprehension and physical resistance are not to be expected in this age group, and serious autonomic reflex disturbances under light anaesthesia, such as hypotension, bradycardia and sweating as a result of vagal traction or pelvic manipulation, are less often seen than in young patients. Relatively mild degrees of hypoxaemia, CO_2 retention or acidosis will, on the other hand, precipitate cardiac irregularities more readily and this may be a useful warning sign that meticulous standards of administration have not been maintained. The particular problem of the carotid sinus syndrome has already been referred to.

As a general principle, simple methods of anaesthesia are the best, with a minimum of interference and instrumentation. For many procedures not requiring muscle relaxation very light anaesthesia is sufficient and will be found to be most rewarding. If the surgeon can be reassured that there is nothing inherently wrong with operating on a gently moving patient, so much the better. Rapid recovery of consciousness and orientation, and of protective reflexes is especially important in the elderly.

During venepuncture, the skin is often penetrated surprisingly easily and since the veins themselves may be fragile great care must be taken to avoid haematoma formation or extra-venous injection. In other cases the veins are tortuous and sclerotic and should be held firmly in relation to the surrounding tissues and entered with a relatively small needle. Mucous membranes are also fragile and every care must be taken to avoid damage during endotracheal intubation and other procedures. Hollowing of the cheeks and prominence of the chin often produce a 'man in the moon' type of facial configuration which makes it difficult to achieve an airtight fit with a face mask; the Everseal mask, with the lower rim below the point of the jaw, is often useful. By contrast, loss of teeth and generally reduced muscle tone tend to make intubation easy except where one or two sentinel teeth obstruct vision or passage of the tube towards the larynx.

Osteoporosis and stiffening of the joints easily result in trauma, so that movement and positioning of the patient must always be carried out with great care. The temptation to stretch joints beyond what has become their normal range of movement, under the influence of anaesthesia, must be resisted. The bodily configuration of many old people is such that when lying supine the occiput will remain in mid-air unless at least one pillow is used. Adequate support for the neck and head must therefore be ensured throughout anaesthesia.

Heat loss occurs readily in the elderly who have diminished thermoregulatory control. This is, of course, particularly true if the viscera are exposed for any length of time and if substantial quantities of blood are transfused. The theatre should always be warm when major surgery is undertaken in old patients, and a heated mattress is also desirable. A blood warmer should be used when anything but a minimal transfusion is required of either blood or clear fluids. During any major or prolonged procedure, it is valuable to be able to measure the skin and the rectal, or preferably oeso-

phageal, temperature. The converse danger of heat gain, which can also occur, should be kept in mind.

In summary, in anaesthetizing old people everything should be done slowly, gradually and gently. There should be no sudden changes, of position, depth of anaesthesia, pulmonary ventilation or circulating fluid volume.

Deep venous thrombosis (DVT), and its main complication, pulmonary embolus is a common problem in the elderly, particularly in malignant disease and orthopaedic surgery. It is the commonest complication of hip fracture surgery (Ring, 1976) and therefore a suitable method of prophylaxis should be considered. There are several effective methods for the prevention of DVT, and these are reviewed by Hirsch (1981). For high risk patients, he recommends the use of low dose heparin, starting before operation, and continuing until the patient is ambulant.

ANAESTHETIC DRUGS AND TECHNIQUES

All methods have been used in old patients, and all have their advocates. A number of publications, particularly from the United States, show that spinal anaesthesia is still well favoured in some centres for geriatric work, and a successful spinal anaesthetic has been reported in a patient of 102 (Milliken, 1972). On the other hand, unless the administrator has very great skill and experience, the injection of a predetermined volume of solution into the subarachnoid space is likely to be an imprecise means of achieving the desired end; loss of vasomotor compensation and the prevalence of respiratory problems must invite complications from all but the most limited low spinal unless great care is exercised. Saddle block for transurethral resection is an excellent technique.

Local and regional methods are useful, and the anaesthetist who deals with large numbers of geriatric patients will find it worth while acquiring skill with intravenous local anaesthesia for the limbs, caudal block and the simpler nerve blocks. Epidural anaesthesia can be very successful in the older age group, and its use has been widely reported in a number of countries including the USSR (Schelkunov, 1973). As with spinal anaesthesia, considerable care and skill are needed as the complications are similar; the higher the block the greater the degree of hypotension, which may be more difficult to control and correct in the elderly.

Bromage (1962) studied epidural analgesia, and documented the strong negative correlation of age with volume of local anaesthetic required for a given extent of analgesia, and described a useful regression formula for calculation of dose (Bromage, 1969). He made the further observation in 1962 that marked arteriosclerosis

A reduced dose of local anaesthetic will probably be needed wherever it is injected. This increased sensitivity is partly due to decreased thickness of myelin sheaths in the elderly. Other factors include a longer half-life and reduced volume of distribution and rate of metabolism of lignocaine (lidocaine hydrochloride) which has been shown in older subjects (Nation et al, 1977). There is probably also increased sensitivity of the central nervous system and the heart to the effects of lignocaine.

When *general anaesthesia* is used the emphasis should be on simplicity. For major abdominal procedures and in other circumstances where muscular relaxation is necessary, endotracheal intubation and controlled ventilation will be required. In many other cases intubation is unnecessary and spontaneous respiration can well be allowed to continue. The MAC (minimum alveolar concentration) of halothane has been shown to decrease with age and it is probable that the MAC for other inhalation agents will show the same trend. Thus lower inspired concentrations will produce adequate anaesthesia as shown by Haldeman et al, (1975) for enflurane. Halothane is widely used, but there has been favourable comment on enflurane in geriatric anaesthesia (Dobkin et al, 1969; Santos and Gelperin, 1975; Wahling, personal communication). This agent is much safer in the presence of raised blood catecholamines (Johnstone et al, 1976) but there is some suggestion that it may cause a greater fall in cardiac output than halothane (Haldeman et al, 1975).

Ketamine is the only intravenous induction agent which does not cause a drop in blood pressure and may in fact cause a rise. It thus has potential usefulness for procedures such as amputation for gangrene in poor risk patients. Disturbing hallucinations unfortunately occur frequently with this drug (Lorhan, 1971) but these can be reduced or prevented by the concomitant use of a benzodiazepine.

The use of neurolept analgesia has been enthusiastically reported from a number of centres (Gemperle et al, 1973; Ward, 1972). A good account of a technique is given by Gemperle et al (1973), who also give figures purporting to demonstrate a reduction in geriatric surgical mortality in their unit with the increasing use is an indication for reduced dosage. It might be expected that the intervertebral foramina of elderly subjects would be more likely to be occluded by fibrosis, calcification of ligaments and osteophyte formation, which would theoretically cause a given volume of solution to spread higher in the epidural space. However, Burn et al (1973) were unable to show a correlation between age (up to 70 years) and vertical spread of solution in the epidural space. They considered the marked reduction in volume of anaesthetic solutions required by the elderly to be due to much greater degree of neuraxial spread and greater permeability of the perineurium.

of this technique. In regard to this and all other anaesthetic methods, however, it may confidently be reaffirmed that the skill of the anaesthetist is the most important factor in good patient care and reduction of morbidity. A good anaesthetist who is familiar with a drug or technique, and has used it on many thousands of occasions, will always be able to produce results as good as those of another skilful and experienced anaesthetist using a totally different method. In 1948 Mushin writing on 'Anaesthesia for the Poor Risk' referred to the catch-phrase of Marie Lloyd: 'a little of what you fancy does you good' and this principle is as true today as it was in 1948, or indeed 1848.

Induced hypotension. The deliberate use of induced hypotension during anaesthesia in the elderly is, naturally enough, controversial. The main sources of anxiety are the adequacy of cerebral perfusion and the risk of vascular occlusion with reduced flow, the possible effect on cardiac oxygenation and performance, and the danger of renal failure. Deliberate hypotension during anaesthesia in elderly patients has been reported by Robinson (1967), and by Rollason and Hough (1960) who referred to other studies in which, as with their own, no significant increases in morbidity or mortality were observed. Rollason et al (1971) studied elderly patients who were anaesthetized and given spinal anesthesia for prostatectomy; some patients received vasopressors and in others the systolic pressure was allowed to fall by a mean of 56 per cent. Psychometric tests failed to distinguish between these two groups; mental function five days postoperatively was below the preoperative level in both groups and appeared to be restored after 6 weeks. This was a small series (14 hypotensive cases), but as with the studies of Eckenhoff et al (1963, 1964) in much younger patients subjected to hypotensive anaesthesia, there was no evidence of adverse cerebral effects. In a study of ECG changes, Rollason and Hough (1969) observed that the rate of fall of blood pressure was important and concluded that very rapid falls were liable to be associated with clinically significant ischaemic changes. They also pointed out that the development of ECG changes suggestive of myocardial ischaemia, during carefully induced hypotension, should be taken as an indication for raising the blood pressure. However, lack of ECG evidence of hypoxia cannot be taken as evidence of good cerebral or renal oxygenation. Robinson (1967) illustrated this with a record of a patient with a normal ECG pattern at a systolic pressure of 2 kPa (15 mmHg) at a time when there was EEG evidence of cerebral hypoxia. The actual method used to lower the blood pressure is probably of less importance than attention to such factors as perfect oxygenation (FIO_2 not less than 50 per cent), constant observation of even the smallest changes in blood pressure, maintenance of good tissue perfusion, and easy controllability of the blood pressure. Applying general knowledge of physiology and pharmacology in the elderly, it would be expected that smaller doses of drug will be effective in producing hypotension and this has been shown by Lawson and his colleagues (1976) for sodium nitroprusside. As the complications of hypotension in the elderly are unpredictable and often undetectable until damage has been done, the indications for the use of a hypotensive technique must be very strong.

Hypertension and tachycardia. The danger of hypertension and tachycardia is less obvious, but Loeb and his colleagues (1978) demonstrated that increased blood pressure and heart rate can cause ischaemic changes and angina, the mechanism being an increase in myocardial oxygen requirement. Cokkinos and Voridis (1976) found that, in any individual subject, there was a constant product of heart rate × systolic pressure at which angina would occur. It would be useful to be able to determine this value preoperatively, but this would rarely be possible. Thus any high pulse rate, especially if combined with a high systolic blood pressure must be regarded as potentially dangerous especially in the patient with a history of myocardial ischaemia.

EMERGENCY ANAESTHESIA

Emergency anaesthesia should be avoided in old people whever possible. Although this principle is obvious enough, there are still, regrettably, patients who have been advised against elective surgery with the result that they are later admitted with urgent, life-threatening complications.

For the anaesthetist, emergency anaesthesia in old people presents all the usual problems of the unprepared patient, plus the additional difficulty of obtaining a good history about preoperative drug therapy and other relevant matters. When presented with an old patient at short notice it may be extremely difficult to assess the degree of dehydration, the state of nutrition, the amount of blood loss, the respiratory reserve, the resilience of the cardiovascular system, and it will usually be possible to discover very little about the state of the liver and kidneys. The anaesthetist will often have to feel his way cautiously with regard to blood and fluid replacement and the use of drugs, particularly as errors will be poorly tolerated. It is for reasons of this kind that emergency surgery in the elderly carries a relatively high mortality.

In any case of bowel obstruction, haematemesis or where the stomach is not known to be empty, there is a major risk of regurgitation. Apart from the need for the usual precautions such as Sellick's (1961) manoeuvre during the induction of general anaesthesia it is important to remember that many old patients, particularly those who are severely ill, have poor laryngeal

protective reflexes even without the administration of additional anaesthetic drugs (Pontoppidan and Beecher, 1960). Howard Jones as long ago as 1933 warned against aspiration of intestinal contents into the lungs during spinal anaesthesia. Few anaesthetists would choose spinal anaesthesia in these circumstances today, but the same danger exists when local and regional techniques are used and, of course, with epidural block. It is worth remembering that in the old, edentulous patient endotracheal intubation can often be performed very easily after spraying of the mouth, pharynx and larynx with local anaesthetic solution.

POSTOPERATIVE CARE

Recovery of consciousness

Recovery of consciousness is a relative term. Most patients who are awake enough to respond to the anaesthetist before leaving the operating theatre have no memory of the event and, indeed, often remember nothing for several hours after return to the ward (Lambrechts and Parkhouse, 1961). This is particularly true of older people, and the need to repeat postoperative reassurance and instructions must be remembered. It is also important to remember that protective reflexes may be sluggish and return only slowly. The patient must never be left unattended until he is fully able to protect his airway; nurses should not be allowed to remove artificial airways prematurely and, whenever serious arthritis or other disability does not provide an absolute contraindication, the patient should be in the lateral or semi-prone position until recovery of consciousness is complete.

Simpson et al (1976) studied short-term recovery of mental efficiency after two forms of general anaesthesia for herniorrhaphy. They concluded that if a minimum of 60 per cent of normal mental efficiency were to be required before discharge, this being comparable to the level of efficiency recorded after a totally sleepless night, then a stay in hospital of 7 to 9 hours would be required after premedication and anaesthesia averaging 35 minutes in duration. The study was carried out on men aged 29 to 68 (average age 50 years) and the implications for day surgery in the elderly, where general anaesthesia is required, are clear. Fully adequate recovery facilities should be available and no anaesthetic should be given unless the anaesthetist has personally satisfied himself that the patient will be accompanied home by a responsible person and will not be allowed to drive or manipulate any potentially dangerous device for at least 24 hours.

Whenever the patient does not awaken as expected at the termination of anaesthesia, relative overdosage of premedication or anaesthetic drugs should be suspected.

In addition to the causes of delayed recovery of consciousness which are common to all age groups, the possibility of hypothermia, hypoglycaemia, myxoedema, or non-ketotic hyperosmolar coma should always be considered in the elderly.

Adequacy of respiration

This is particularly likely to be impaired if either competitive muscle relaxants or narcotic analgesics have been used, especially if the patient also has some disease of the respiratory tract.

All the competitive muscle relaxants at present widely used are to some extent excreted in the urine, and so repeat doses are cumulative. As GFR is decreased in the elderly, smaller repeat doses should be used to reduce the possibility of difficulty in reversal. Two new competitive neuromuscular blocking drugs are now being studied, atracrurium and Org NC 45, which seem to be devoid of cumulation, and may be particularly useful in the elderly (Hunt et al, 1980; Marshall et al, 1980). Another problem was shown in a study of recovery of twitch height after reversal of pancuronium by neostigmine. Marsh and his colleagues (1980) demonstrated a slower recovery in older patients of up to 29 minutes, which cannot be explained by reduced renal excretion of the muscle relaxant. While the older muscle relaxants are still in use, adequate time must be allowed after reversal for the return of good respiration. It may often by advisable to continue IPPV in the early postoperative period, or to leave an endotracheal tube in situ until adequacy of respiration and competence of reflexes are confirmed. The possibility of interaction of competitive relaxants with intraperitoneally or systematically administered streptomycin and other aminoglycosides antibiotics should be remembered. The use of atropine with neostigmine to reverse the competitive muscle relaxants may be accompanied by arrhythmias, and there is some evidence to suggest that these may be reduced by the use of glycopyrrholate instead of atropine, and pyridostigmine instead of neostigmine (Owens et al, 1978; Muravchick et al, 1979).

The elderly are more sensitive to the analgesic effect of the narcotics (Karko, 1980) and it is probable that they are also more sensitive to their respiratory depressant effects. Naloxone may be needed to overcome this, but the administration of 0.4 mg intravenously has been followed by severe hypertension (Azar and Turndorf, 1979). It is essential therefore to use doses of only 0.1 mg intravenously.

Other factors which may contribute to decreased oxygen availability in the elderly are the physiological changes of increased functional residual capacity and closing volume, decreased ventilation-perfusion ratios which frequently follow anaesthesia, and postoperative pain especially from thoracic or upper abdominal wounds. Supplementary oxygen should be given routinely in an appropriate concentration to all elderly patients except perhaps those having very minor procedures. The duration of this therapy will vary. Other important considerations are good positioning, effective physiotherapy and avoidance of abdominal constriction, and adequate pain relief.

Monitoring

Apart from the observations noted above, there should be regular monitoring of pulse, blood pressure and skin colour at frequent intervals during the period of recovery from anaesthesia. The wound and any drainage tubes should also be kept under observation. In certain operations, particularly prostatectomy, it is not uncommon for the anaesthetist to take great pains to maintain the circulating blood volume during anaesthesia, only to find that within the first half hour after leaving the theatre further blood loss has occurred without adequate replacement. This is a dangerous period for the elderly patient, particularly if he is to be moved or changed in position; hypotension, with serious consequences, can occur unless fully adequate fluid replacement is maintained.

Restlessness and confusion

Some degree of disorientation and restlessness is common in old people during emergence from anaesthesia. It is usually transient but when it continues an adequate explanation must be sought. Hypoxaemia is, of course, the first and most important possibility to consider. Possible drug effects should be borne in mind, as any central nervous system depressant drug may cause confusion in the elderly. Other causes include hyponatraemia or incomplete reversal of the muscle relaxants. Older patients frequently find it difficult to express themselves adequately at this early stage of recovery and may not be fully aware of what is disturbing them. Apart from the likelihood of pain from the operation site, it must therefore be remembered that restlessness may be due to a full bladder, to dislodgement of an infusion into the tissues, or to the fact that the patient's position is putting strain on an arthritic joint. When confusion persists and simple causes have been excluded, the possibility of a cerebral vacular accident or embolism will need to be considered. Myocardial infarction and cerebral vascular accidents can cause hypotension and delayed awakening in the elderly; ECG changes or inequality of the pupils, will be valuable clues to diagnosis. Fat embolism is estimated to occur in about one per cent of geriatric orthopaedic cases (Lorhan, 1971).

Pain relief

As a general rule, old patients are more tolerant of pain

than younger people. This rather sweeping statement should certainly not mean, however, that they are allowed or expected to endure more or for longer without relief. As has already been mentioned, they are more sensitive to narcotic analgesic drugs which can produce a greater degree of pain relief for a longer period of time. A small dose of a postoperative analgesic given early, and preferably in anticipation of pain, is far better than a larger dose given too late. There is much to be said for the practice of giving very small doses intravenously, for example 10 to 15 mg pethidine, immediately before the conclusion of anaesthesia and supplementing this, if need be, with a further small intramuscular or intravenous dose as soon as the patient gives any indications of being aware of discomfort. It is most important to be cautious with dosage; a frail and elderly patient whose blood pressure and general condition have been carefully maintained during a prolonged, major operation can very easily be reduced to a hypotensive state or coma by the administration of a 'normal' dose of postoperative morphine, or perhaps of an antiemetic such as promethazine given for the relief of narcotic-induced nausea or vomiting. It is by single, thoughtless acts of this kind that much of the good achieved by surgeon and anaesthetist can readily be undone in old patients.

Newer approaches to the relief of postoperative pain are discussed by Dodson (1982b). Their place in the elderly has not yet been fully evaluated. The most widely investigated has been the use of intraspinal (subarachnoid or epidural) opiates, which seem to be able to produce prolonged analgesia. However, the increased sensitivity of the elderly to opiates renders them more likely to develop the worrying complication of respiratory depression which is sometimes delayed for several hours after the original injection. There is a place for the use of continuous intravenous infusions of morphine for 24 hours or so after major surgery, but it is usually advisable to control ventilation during this time to ensure oxygenation and carbon dioxide elemination.

Shivering

Postoperative shivering is common after halothane and enflurane anaesthesia, and also after prolonged operations in cold operating theatres. Shivering increases postoperative stress in two ways. The oxygen consumption of the body increases 2- or 3-fold and although patients can compensate for this by increasing ventilation and cardiac output (Bay et al, 1968), these mechanisms are less likely to be effective in the elderly, if they come into play at all. In addition, shivering is accompanied by increased activity of the sympathoadrenal system, with increases of pulse rate and blood pressure. The deleterious effect of such increases which raise myocardial oxygen consumption, has already been mentioned.

Shivering can thus cause a marked decrease in oxygen delivery to many tissues, which is especially important in relation to myocardium, brain and kidney. There is a clear argument for keeping the cold elderly patient paralysed and ventilated during the time that there is a likelihood of shivering, especially after prolonged surgery. This also has the advantage of allowing the administration of doses of narcotics which will provide good analgesia (see above).

REFERENCES

Andersen B, Østberg J 1973 Long-term prognosis in geriatric surgery: 2–17 year follow-up of 7922 patients. Journal of the American Geriatric Society 20: 255–258

Arkins R, Smessaert A A, Hicks R G 1964 Morality and morbidity in surgical patients with coronary artery disease. Journal of the American Medical Association 190: 485–488

Azar I, Turndorf H 1979 Severe hypertension and multiple atrial premature contractions following naloxone administration Anesthesia and Analgesia (Cleveland OH) 58: 524–525

Bay J, Nunn J F, Prys-Roberts C 1968 Factors influencing arterial pO$_2$ during recovery from anaesthesia. British Journal of Anaesthesia 40: 398–407

Bedford P D 1955 Adverse cerebral effects of anaesthesia on old people. Lancet ii: 259–263

Bethune R W M 1964 Inhalation anaesthesia in the aged. International Anesthesiology Clinics 3: 51–76

British Medical Journal 1973 Postural hypotension in the elderly (Editorial). 4: 246–247

Bodlander F M S 1975 Deaths associated with anaesthesia. British Journal of Anaesthesia 47: 36–40

Brander P, Kjellberg M, Tammisto T 1970 The effects of anaesthesia and general surgery on geriatric patients. Annales Chirurgiae et Gynaecologiae (Helsinki)

Bromage P R 1962 Spread of analgesic solutions in the epidural space

and their site of action: a statistical study. British Journal of Anaesthesia 34: 161–178

Bromage P R 1969 Aging and epidural requirements. British Journal of Anaesthesia 41: 1016–1022

Bruce D L, Taurig H H 1969 The effect of halothane on the cell cycle in rat small intestine. Anesthesiology 30: 401–405

Bunker J P, Forrest W H Jr, Mosteller F, Vandam L D (eds) 1969 National Halothane Study: a study of the possible association between halothane anaesthesia and postoperative hepatic necrosis. US Government Printing Office, Bethesda

Burn J M, Guyer P B, Langdon L 1973 The spread of solutions injected into the epidural space. British Journal of Anaesthesia 45: 338–345

Clee M D, Smith N, McNeill G P, Wright D S 1979 Dysrhythmias in apparently healthy elderly subjects. Age and Ageing 8: 173–176

Clifton B S, Hotten W I T 1963 Deaths associated with anaesthesia. British Journal of Anaesthesia 35: 250–259

Cokkinos D V, Voridis E M 1976 Constancy of pressure rate product in pacing-induced angina pectoris. British Heart Journal 38: 39–42

Collins K J, Dore C, Exton-Smith A N, Fox R H, McDonald I C, Woodward P M 1977 Accidental hypothermia and impaired homeostasis in the elderly. British Medical Journal 1: 353–356

Conway C M, Payne J P, Tomlin P J 1965 Arterial oxygen tensions of patients awaiting surgery. British Journal of Anaesthesia 37: 405–408

Cullen B F 1974 The effect of halothane and nitrous oxide on phagocytosis and human leukocyte metabolism. Anesthesia and Analgesia (Cleveland OH) 531–536

Dawson B, Jones R R, Schnelle N, Hartridge V B, Paulson J A, Adson M A, Summerskill W H J 1963 Halothane and ether anesthesia in gall bladder and bile duct surgery: a retrospective study into mortality and hepatobiliary complications. Anesthesia and Analgesia (Cleveland OH) 42: 759–770

Dinnick O P 1964 Deaths associated with anaesthesia. Anaesthesia 19: 536–556

Djokovic J L, Hedey-White J 1979 Prediction of outcome of surgery and anesthesia in patients over 80. Journal of the American Medical Association 242: 2301–2306

Dobkin A B, Nishioka K, Gengaje D B, Kim D A, Evers W, Israel J S 1969 Ethrane (compound 347) Anesthesia: a clinical and laboratory review of 700 cases. Anesthesia and Analgesia (Cleveland OH) 48: 477–494

Dodson M E 1975 Mechanisms of Drug Interactions. In: Anaesthesia Rounds 8, ICI, Macclesfield

Dodson M E 1982a Adverse drug reactions and anaesthesia. 'Adverse Drug Reaction Bulletin No 96

Dodson M E 1982b A review of methods of postoperative analgesia. Annals of the Royal College of Surgeons (London) 64: 324–327

Dodson M E 1984 Anaesthesia in the Elderly. In: O'Malley K (ed) Clinical Pharmacology and Drug Treatment Churchill Livingstone, Edinburgh, p 196

Dowdy E G, Favian L W 1963 Ventricular arrhythmias induced by succinylcholine in digitalized patients: a preliminary report. Anesthesia and Analgesia (Cleveland OH) 42: 501–513

Dripps R D, Van N Deming M 1946 Postoperative atelectasis and pneumonia. Annals of Surgery 124: 94–110

Duncan P G, Cullen B F 1976 Anesthesia and Immunology. Anesthesiology 45: 522–538

Eckenhoff J E, Enderby G E H, Larson A, Davies R, Judevine D E 1963 Human cerebral circulation during deliberate hypotension and head-up tilt. Journal of Applied Physiology 18: 1130–1138

Eckenhoff J E, Compton J R, Larson A, Davies R M 1964 Assessment of cerebral effects of deliberate hypotension by psychological measurements. Lancet 2: 711–714

Edwards G, Morton H J V, Pask E A, Wylie W D 1956 Deaths associated with anaesthesia: a report on 100 cases. Asaesthesia 2: 194–220

Fink B R 1966 Symposium: Clinical Evaluation of Analgesic Drugs. Acta Anaesthesiologica Scandinavica Supplementum XXV: 335–336

Galindo A H, Davis T B 1962 Succinylcholine and cardiac excitability. Anesthesiology 23: 32–40

Gemperle M, Szappanyos G, Rifat K 1973 Neuroleptanesthesia in gerontosurgery. International Anesthesiology Clinics 2: 125–138

Glenn F 1973 Pre and postoperative management of elderly surgical patients. Journal of the American Geriatrics Society 21: 385–393

Goldman L, Caldera D L, Nussbaum S R, Southwick F S, Krogstad D, Murray B et al 1977 Multifactorial index of cardiac risk in noncardiac surgical procedures. New England Journal of Medicine 297: 845–850

Goldstein A Jr, Keats A S 1970 The Risk of Anesthesia. Anesthesiology 33: 130–142

Grogono A W, Jones A E P 1968 Danger lists for the anaesthetist. Anaesthesia 23: 215–219

Haldeman G, Schmid E, Frey P, Hossli G, Schaer H 1975 Wirking von Ethrane auf die Kreislauf grössen geriatrischer Patienten. Anaesthetist 24: 343–346

Hamburger H J 1916 Researches on phagocytosis. British Medical Journal 1: 37–41

Heilbrunn L V 1920 The physical effect of anaesthetics upon living protoplasm (i). Biological Bulletin 39: 307–315

Heron J R, Anderson E G, Noble I M 1965 Cardiac abnormalities associated with carotid-sinus syndrome. Lancet 2: 214–216

Hirsch J 1981 Prevention of deep vein thrombosis. British Journal of Hospital Medicine 26: 143–147

Holland R (Secretary) 1970 Special Committee investigating deaths under anaesthesia: Report on 745 classified cases. Medical Journal of Australia 1: 573–594

Hunt T M Hughes R, Payne J P 1980 Preliminary studies with atracrurium in anaesthetised man. British Journal of Anaesthesia 52: 238–239

Johnstone R R, Eger E I II, Wilson C 1976 A comparative interaction of epinephrine with enfluane isoflurane and halothane in man. Anesthesia and Analgesia (Cleveland OH) 55: 709–712

Jones R R, Dawson B, Adson M A, Summerskill W J J 1965 Halothane and non-halogenated anesthetic agents in patients with cirrhosis of the liver: mortality and morbidity following portal-systemic venous anastomoses. Surgical Clinics of North America 45: 983–990

Jones W, Howard 1933 Death under spinal anaesthesia. British Medical Journal 1: 119

Karko R 1980 Age and morphine analgesia in cancer patients with post-operative pain. Clinical Pharmacology and Therapeutics 28: 823–826

Klidjian A M, Foster K J, Kammerling R M, Cooper A, Karran 1980 Relation of anthropometric and dynamometric valuables to serious post-operative complications. British Medical Journal 281: 899–902

Kortlla K, Saarnivaara L, Tarkkanen J, Humberg J J, Hýtonen M 1978 Effect of age on amnesia and sedation induced by flunitrazepam during local anaesthesia for bronchoscopy. British Journal of Anaesthesia 50: 1211–1218

Kuner J, Enescu V, Utsu F, Boszormenyi E, Bernstein H, Corday E 1967 Cardiac arrhythmias during Anesthesia. Diseases of the Chest 52: 580–587

Lambrechts W, Parkhouse J 1961 Postoperative amnesia. British Journal of Anaesthesia 33: 397–404

Lancet 1955 Anaesthesia in the elderly (Editorial) 2: 279

Lassen H C A, Henriksen E, Neukirch F, Kristensen H S 1956 Treatment of tetanus: severe bone-marrow depression after prolonged mitrous oxide anaesthesia. Lancet 1: 527–530

Lawson N W, Thompson D S, Nelson C L, Flacke J W, Seifen A B 1976 A dosage nomogram for sodium nitroprusside-induced hypotension under anesthesia. Anesthesia and Analgesia (Cleveland OH) 55: 574–580

Lippmann M, Lorhan P H 1968 Anesthetic management of the patient with portacaval shunts. American Journal of Surgery 116: 49–53

Liu S, Callis G 1964 Preoperative evaluation and preparation of the aged patient with cardiovascular disease. International Anesthesiology Clinics 3: 31–37

Loeb H S, Saudye A, Croke R, Talano J V, Kodnycky M L, Gunnar R M 1978 Effects of pharmacologically induced hypertension on myocardial ischemia and coronary hemodynamics in patients with fixed coronary obstruction. Circulation 57: 41–46

Lorhan P H 1967 Anesthesia experiences with the octogenarian. Anesthesia and Analgesia (Cleveland OH) 46: 601–607

Lorhan P H 1971 Anesthesia for the Aged. C C Thomas, Springfield Illinois

Lorhan P H, Lewis G, Bearden C R, Averbook B D 1962 Postoperative parotitis. Anesthesiology 23: 659–661

McFadden J P, Price R C, Eastwood H D, Briggs R S 1982 Raised repiratory rate in elderly patients: a valuable clinical sign. British Medical Journal 284: 626–627

McIntyre J W R 1973 Evolution of a Provincial Committee on anaesthetic and operative deaths, Alberta 1957–1972. Canadian Anaesthetists Society Journal 20: 578–585

McLaren A D, Stockwell M C, Reid V J 1978 Anaesthetic techniques for surgical correction of fractured neck of femur. A comparative study of spinal and general anaesthesia. Anaesthesia 33: 10–14

Marsh R H L, Chimielewski A T, Goat V A 1980 Recovery from pancuronium. A comparison between old and young patients. Anaesthesia 35: 1193–1196

Marshall I G, Agoston S, Booij L H D, Divrant N N, Foldes F F 1980 Pharmacology of ORG NC45 compared with other non-depolarizing neuromuscular blocking drugs. British Journal of Anaesthesia 52: 115–195

Memery H N 1965 Anesthesia mortality in private practice. Journal of the American Medical Association 194: 1185–1188

Milliken R A 1972 Geriatric spinal anesthesia in a 102 year old man. Anesthesia and Analgesia (Cleveland OH) 51: 400–401

Moudgil G C, Wade A G 1976 Anaesthesia and immunocompetence. British Journal of Anaesthesia 48: 31–39

Murauchick S, Owens W D, Felts J A 1979 Glycopyrrholate and

cardiac arrhythmias in geriatric patients after reversal of neuromuscular blockade. Canadian Anaesthetists Society Journal 26: 22–25

Mushin W W 1948 Anaesthesia for the Poor Risk. Blackwell, Oxford

Nation R L, Triggs J, Selig M 1977 Lignocaine kinetics in cardiac patients and aged subjects. British Journal of Clinical Pharmacology 4: 439–448

Nunn J F 1976 In Symposium on 'An Appraisal of Current Practice in Anaesthesia' 4–5 November

Nunn J F, Dixon K L, Moore J R 1968 Effect of halothane on tetrahymena pyriformis. British Journal of Anaesthesia 40: 145

Nunn J F, Lovis J D, Kimball K L 1971 Arrest of mitosis by halothane. British Journal of Anaesthesia 43: 524–530

Nunn J F, Sharp J A, Kimball K L 1970 Reversible effect of an inhalation anaesthetic on lymphocyte motility. Nature (London) 226: 85–86

Ostergren G 1944 Colchicine mitosis chromosone contraction, narcosis and protein chain folding. Hereditas 30: 429–467

Owens W D, Waldbaum L S, Stephen C R 1978 Cardiac arrhythmias following reveal of neuromuscular blocking agents in geriatric patients. Anaesthesia and Analgesia (Cleveland OH) 57: 186–190

Palmberg S, Hirsjavi E 1979 Mortality in geriatric surgery. Gerontology 25: 103–112

Papper E M 1965 Selection and management of anaesthesia in those suffering from diseases and disorders of the heart. Canadian Anaesthetists society Journal 12: 245–254

Pontoppidan H, Beecher H K 1960 Progressive loss of protective reflexes in the airway with the advance of age. Journal of the American Medical Association 174: 2209–2213

Portal R W 1982 Ectivesurgery after myocardial infarct (Editorial) British Medical Journal 284: 843–844

Powell K J 1976 Anaesthesia for the Aged. Annals of the Royal College of Surgeons, England 58: 21–24

Prys-Roberts C, Meloche R, Foëx P 1971a Studies of anaesthesia in relation to hypertension I. Cardiovascular responses of treated and untreated patients. British Journal of Anaesthesia 43: 122–137

Prys-Roberts C, Greene L T, Meloche R, Foëx P 1971b Studies of anaesthesia in relation to hypertension II. Haemodynamic consequences of induction and endotracheal intubation. British Journal of Anaesthesia 43: 531–547

Ring P A 1976 Hip fractures up to date. British Medical Journal 2: 1429–1431

Roberts M T S 1976 Anaesthesia for the geriatric patient. Drugs II: 220–228

Robinson J S 1967 Hypotension without hypoxia. International Anesthesiology Clinics 5: 467–480

Rodstein M, Zeman F D 1967 Aortic stenosis in the aged. American Journal of Medical Science 254: 577–584

Rollason W N, Hough J M 1960 A study of hypotensive anaesthesia in the elderly. British Journal of Anaesthesia 32: 276–285

Rollason W N, Hough J M 1969 A re-examination of some electrocardiographic studies during hypotensive anaesthesia. British Journal of Anaesthesia 41: 985–986

Rollason W N, Robertson G S, Cordiner C M, Hall D J 1971 A comparison of mental function in relation to hypotensive and normotensive anaesthesia in the elderly. British Journal of Anaesthesia 43: 561–566

Santos A L, Gelperin A 1975 Surgical mortality in the elderly. Journal of the American Geriatrics Society 23: 42–46

Schelkunov V S 1973 Peridural anaesthesia in aged patients. Vestnik Khirurghil 3: 118–121

Schneider A J L, Knoke J D, Zollinger R M, McLaren C E, Baetz W R 1979 Morbidity prediction using pre- and intraoperative data. Anesthesiology 51: 4–10

Schoenborn B P, Watson H C, Kendrew J C 1965 Binding of xenon to sperm whale myoglobin. Nature (London) 207: 28–30

Sellick B A 1961 Cricoid pressure to control regurgitation of stomach contents during induction of anaesthesia. Lancet 2: 404–406

Seymour D G, Pringle R 1982 A new method of auditing surgical mortality rates: application to a group of elderly general surgical patients. British Medical Journal 284: 1539–1542

Simpson B R, Williams M, Scott J F, Crampton Smith A 1961 The effects of anaesthesia and elective surgery on old people. Lancet 2: 887–893

Simpson J E P, Glynn C J, Cox A G, Folkard S 1976 Comparative study of short-term recovery of mental efficiency after anaesthesia. British Medical Journal 1: 1560–1562

Spreadbury T H 1980 Anaesthetic techniques for surgical correction of fractured neck of femur. A comparative study of ketamine and relaxant anaesthesia in elderly women. Anaesthesia 35: 208–214

Steen P A, Tinker J H, Tarhan S 1978 Myocardial re-infarction after anaesthesia and surgery. Journal of the American Medical Association 239: 2566–2570

Stevens K M, Aldrete J A 1969 Anesthesia factors affecting surgical morbidity and mortality in the elderly male. Journal of the American Geriatrics Society 17: 659–667

Sturrock J E, Nunn J F 1975 Mitosis in mammalian cells during exposure to anesthetics. Anesthesiology 43: 21–33

Volpitto P P 1967 Discussion: Anesthesia and experiences with the octogenarian. Anesthesia and Analgesia (Cleveland OH) 46: 606–607

Wandless I, Davie J W 1977 Can drug compliance in the elderly be improved? British Medical Journal I: 359–361

Ward P A 1972 Anesthesia in centenarians. Journal of the American Medical Association 219: 1476–1477

Wilder R J, Fishbein R H 1961 Operative experience with patients over 80 years of age. Surgery, Gynecology and Obstetrics 113: 205–212

Wollner L, McCarthy S T, Soper N D W, Macy D J 1979 Failure of cerebral autoregulation as a cause of brain dysfunction in the elderly. British Medical Journal 1: 1117–1118

Wylie W D 1975 'There, but for the grace of God . . .' Annals of the Royal College of Surgeons, England 56: 171–180

PART THREE

Medical and Community Care

The elderly in society

INTRODUCTION

This chapter is concerned with old people, not as physical beings liable to suffer from various pathological conditions as a result of their biological aging, but as members of very complex societies, the functioning of which they influence and which in turn influence their lives and their health. Indeed, it is the first thesis of this chapter that the well-being of all old people, as individuals and collectively, is as much if not more a function of their social status as it is of their physical state: the second proposition of the chapter flows from the first, namely, that measures which tackle the social status of elderly people are likely to be as effective as, if not more effective than, clinical practices, however advanced, in improving the quality of their lives.

The arrangement of the chapter flows from these two points. It is useful at the outset to be reminded that chronological age itself has a different significance in different societies. There is a degree of apparent arbitrariness in the designation of a particular age in any single national state as that at which an individual can be identified as entitled to certain privileges, or as excluded from certain positions. Arbitrariness is not necessarily dysfunctional from the point of view of the collectivity; for example, it may help society, including the majority of those over a certain age, to know that that age confers certain automatic benefits and withdraws others: but the 'institutionalization' of the rule and its universal application can also create difficulties for individuals or groups.

The chapter then describes the basic demographic characteristics of that part of the population designated elderly, including its age, sex, geographical and marital status distributions. It looks at the kind of households and institutions in which that population is accommodated, how far it is gainfully occupied and its sources and levels of income. It then proceeds to consider what services and other facilities are made available to meet the needs of this part of the population. Finally, it considers the extent to which society through a complex network of statutory and voluntary organizations,

commercial enterprises and informal activities carried out by kin, can take pride and satisfaction in the lives of its old people.

WHO DOES SOCIETY CALL OLD?

Aging as defined by biologists is a continuing process which starts with the conception of the new unique organism and continues to its death. In humans there are certain landmarks in the process which help us to mark it out into various stages. Birth itself, although not the beginning, is the most dramatic, marking as it does the transition from biological dependence on another organism to viable separate existence. It is more difficult to say when full puberty, signifying the maturation of the reproductive organs to a level where they are capable of fulfilling that function, is reached. The physiological changes involved in the transition from the pre- to post-pubertal state take place gradually and at different paces in different individuals. In women, the final cessation of the menses provides a biological landmark, although this event — or rather non-event — has been preceded by a continuous decline, sometimes of many years' duration, in fecundity. In men, there is no such definite landmark with which to break senescence into stages. Yet, it indisputably takes place in all individuals smoothly or erratically and at a fast or slow pace.

The absence of clear physiological markers in the life span of humans after puberty has made gerontologists reluctant to use such labels as 'old', 'elderly' or 'aged'. Women can be labelled 'premenopausal' or 'postmenopausal'; but no biologist would use the latter category interchangeably with the terms 'old', 'elderly' or 'aged'. Yet these latter terms are applied to some individuals in every society and it is important to ask first, to whom the terms are applied and second, what the effects of labelling individuals in such terms are.

A century ago, the term 'old' was probably applied to any individual whose physical appearance — white locks, toothlessness, sunken cheeks, lacklustre eyes, wrinkles, shrivelled skin, bent back, shambling gait —

denoted advanced age. It is probable, although not proven, that the chronological age at which a person was likely to have such an appearance was earlier then than it is in the last decades of the twentieth century. Some such historical change is generally assumed on the basis of cross-national comparisons made by contemporary observers. Badly nourished men and women of 30 or 40 years of age in parts of Africa or the Indian subcontinent have only too often much the same physical appearance as men and women of over 70 in Europe and North America.

With the changes which have occurred in the economic and demographic structure of advanced industrial societies, the term 'old' began to be applied not so much to individuals with particular characteristics as to those who had lived a certain numbers of years. Naturally enough, those who did not feel that they could be categorized as old in terms of their physique resented the blanket application of a label which they perceived as stigmatizing. Various ways of diminishing the sense of stigma while retaining the classification of individuals by age have since been adopted. In Britain the term 'elderly' was once thought to be more dignified than the term 'old', perhaps because it was associated with the word 'elder' which usually denoted a person of importance in religious or civic hierarchies. In the United States in an effort to avoid the word 'old' or its synonyms, people of 65 or more have been called 'senior citizens', 'senior' being a word designed to suggest respect. In the UK this term has been regarded as somewhat folksy and too obviously euphemistic for general acceptance. A deliberate effort has been made, however, through the wording of legislation to induce the population at large to call men over 65 'retirement pensioners' or 'persons of pensionable age', and not 'old age pensioners', but the latter term is still widely used.

The choice of a particular number of years of life to classify individuals as old, elderly or aged then is a product of social history rather than the result of validated epidemiological studies of physical and mental capacity. In Britain, public concern with the fate of people of advanced age led in 1908 to legislation which entitled those of 70 or over who could show themselves to be without means to a small weekly pension. The earlier surveys of Booth in London (1884) and Rowntree in York (1902), the investigations set in train by the Royal Commission on the Aged Poor in 1895, together with evidence to the Royal Commission on the Poor Laws between 1805–1809, had convinced the Government and Parliament that substantial numbers of people of 70 or more could not expect to obtain or keep employment and would therefore inevitably become dependent on poor relief. Trade Unions welcomed the move because it reduced the competition for work from older people. After the First World War, with high levels of unemployment among all age groups, trade union pressure was exerted on the Government and in 1925 a compulsory form of insurance covering most manual workers was instituted which entitled the insured worker to a retirement pension at the age of 65 for a man, and at 60 for a woman (Widows', Orphans' and Old Age Contributory Pension Act, 1925).

Sex differences

The sex difference in the age of eligiblity for retirement pensions then established still persists in Britain. It was not founded on any scientifically conducted enquiries into the relative capacity of men and women to continue to work productively, but on contemporary views about the appropriate place of women in society and the fear of the trade unions dominated by men that women's cheaper labour would depress still further the wages which could be earned by their members. It was advantageous, therefore, for them to perpetuate the belief (belied at least by life-expectancy statistics) that women were frailer than men and should consequently be retired earlier. For other reasons the Government of the day was only too ready to concur. It was resisting substantial pressure from the trade unions to make 60 years the age at which all manual workers could draw a pension. Such pressures were only too understandable at a time when unemployment among much younger men was high and rising, and conditions of work in many industries could by no stretch of the imagination be described as likely to invite continued participation in the labour force if a reasonable pension could be secured instead. The Government's reluctance to cede to the request for earlier retirement pensions was also understandable: yielding would have involved a substantial increase in the Exchequer contribution to the National Insurance Fund from which pensions were paid. A desire to keep public expenditure down, then as now, was a greater determinant of who should be labelled old or elderly than any consideration of data based on scientific enquiry into the relationship between working capacity and age.

Since 1924 the rationale for this sex distinction in eligibility for retirement pensions has only once been seriously considered. This was done by a Committee which considered the Economic and Financial Problems of the Provision for Old Age (Phillips Committee) (Ministry of Pensions and National Insurance (MPNI), 1954). It pointed to the lack of biological justification for the difference in the age of eligibility but suggested that there would be substantial political and economic difficulties in eliminating it by reducing the age at which men could draw the pension or increasing that at which women would be entitled to it.

Since that time a new mood is discernible about the

differential treatment of the sexes in public and private life. Important legislative measures have been taken to eliminate practices which discriminated against women and an Equal Opportunities Commission has been set up to maintain a watching brief on matters pertaining to sex equality in employment, ownership, the family, and in general matters of citizenship such as access to places of public entertainment. In this light, fresh looks have been taken (Equal Opportunities Commission, 1977; Department of Health and Social Security (DHSS), 1977) at the sex differences in the age of eligibility for retirement pensions. Once again arbitrariness of the age differences was underlined. There is no strong lobby from women to end the differences. Indeed, there appears to be some reluctance on the part of women's organizations to make public pronouncements on the issues, perhaps because they are not clear whether the present position may not be one of the few measures which discriminate in their favour! Indeed, the tendency is for trade unions, particularly but not exclusively in the public sector of the economy, to try to secure earlier retirement and increased occupationally-related pensions for their members.

Further proof, if further proof were needed, that social rather than biological considerations determine the age at which individuals are at one and the same time able to draw a state-facilitated retirement pension and enjoy the doubtful benefit of being considered part of an elderly or old-age group is to be found in cross-national comparisons. For example in Norway, the requisite age is 70, in Denmark 67; in the United States, 65 for men and women; and in France 60 for both sexes. The arbitrariness of any general cut-off point in years, and the knowledge that there is a great diversity of physical and mental states among those of any given chronological age should serve as an additional reminder, if reminder is needed, that whatever age is chosen to distinguish a group of old, elderly or aged in any society, it will always include individuals of widely differing physical and mental capacities.

In this chapter, which seeks primarily to describe the social situation, broadly interpreted, of the elderly in contemporary Britain, many of the readily ascertainable facts refer to all those of statutory pensionable age (i.e. to men of 65 and over and women of 60 and over). This is merely a consequence of the availability of officially collected data much of which is only available for age groups categorized in this way. Where possible, a finer tooth comb is used, since evidence suggests that for many reasons distinctions should be made between those over and under 75 or 80, rather than those of over or under 65. Indeed, those between pensionable age and 75 are now often referred to as the 'young elderly' and those over 75 as the 'old elderly'. And as we shall see there is now good reason for making this distinction.

THE DEMOGRAPHIC PICTURE — CHANGING AGE PATTERNS

In developing countries of Africa and Asia, the proportion of the population over the age of 60 is typically still not more than 5 per cent, and life expectancy at birth for both men and women does not always reach 40 years of age. In contrast, Britain, in common with other industrialized societies, has seen a dramatic growth in the relative as well as the absolute numbers of individuals of advanced age in the course of the twentieth century.

In the nineteenth century the population increased rapidly, the growth being most marked in the younger age groups. High infant mortality rates and death rates in young adults from tuberculosis and diseases associated with poverty meant a smaller relative growth in the numbers in the older age groups. However, since 1901, the rate of growth of the elderly population (defined as those of present retirement age, i.e. 60 for women and 65 for men) has been greater than that of other age groups with the result that it now accounts for a larger proportion of the population. In 1901, the 2.4 million elderly constituted 6.3 per cent of the population of Great Britain: by 1980 the total numbers had more than trebled (9.7 million) and the proportion increased to 17.6 per cent or approximately one in six.

Even more spectacular than the growth in the numbers of elderly people as a whole has been the growth in the number and proportion among them of those aged 75 to 84 and of those 85 and over. Table 46.1 illustrates the growth which has already taken place since 1951 in these advanced age groups and the projections which are currently being made by Government actuaries for 1991 and 2001.

Population projections are notoriously difficult to make due to the difficulty of predicting birth rates. Hence it is dangerous to forecast with certainty what proportion the elderly and in particular the over 75s will form of the total population in 1991 or 2001. However, those who will become elderly in these years are now alive and predictions of how many of them will survive can be made with some confidence, assuming that there are no startling changes in current death rates at more advanced ages or man-made disasters of world-shaking dimensions. As Table 46.1 indicates we can expect an actual decline in the numbers of 'young elderly' during the 1980s and 1990s as the cohort born in the low birth rate years from 1920 to 1940 reach this age. There will be an initial expansion in those aged 75 to 84 but a slight decline in their numbers at the end of the century. The 1980s, however, will see an increase of well over a half in the over 85s, and a continuing but more modest increase in the 1990s.

In short, there has already been in the last 30 years

Table 46.1 Numbers in three age groups of the elderly population (United Kingdom 1951–2001) and percentage change between dates

| | 65–74 | | 75–84 | | 85 and over | | All over 65 | |
	millions	+ or – (%)	millions	+ or – (%)	millions	+ or – (%)	millions	+ or – (%)
1951	3.7	—	1.6	—	0.2	—	5.5	
1980	5.2	41	2.6	63	0.5	150	8.3	49
1991	4.9	–6	2.9	12	0.8	60	8.6	4
2001	4.5	–8	2.8	–3	0.9	13	8.2	–5

* Source — Social Trends No. 12, 1982 Central Statistical Office

a dramatic change in the age pattern of those who have already reached pensionable age: by the beginning of the twenty-first century the total numbers over 65 are likely to be much the same as they are in the early 1980s; but they will be a much older group with all that that implies for medical and social services.

These figures of absolute and proportionate growth are not unusual in Western Europe and North America. These countries, like Britain, have experienced similar increases in their elderly populations; the differences which remain reflect past trends in birth and death rates and in migration patterns. For example, Britain's elderly population in relative terms is rather greater than that of the United States of America for three reasons. In the USA in 1979 only 11.7 per cent were over 65 compared to 15.0 per cent in Britain. First, the USA population grew rapidly through the early years of the twentieth century through immigration as well as by natural growth, the two growth rates being related to one another since the immigrants were preponderantly young adults likely to contribute more to the birth than the death rates of the native population. Second, the United States experienced a more pronounced 'baby boom' in the 1940s and 1950s than did Britain. Third, the sex ratio in Britain throughout the first half of the twentieth century was much more uneven than it was in the United States. This was a consequence of sex differences in Britain in emigration rates in the late nineteenth and early twentieth century and, during the 1914–18 war, of even greater than usual young adult male mortality. The USA also experienced the latter but not to the same extent. In short, differences in the experiences of the two countries some 60 to 80 years ago help to explain differences in the demographic structure of their populations in the 1980s and 1990s.

Sex ratios among the pensionable

The trend in industrialized society to the survival into their sixties, seventies and eighties of greater proportions of each succeeding birth cohort has not been exactly the same for the sexes. In the mid-nineteenth century in Britain women over 65 outnumbered men of the same age by roughly five to four. The female superiority in numbers at advanced ages was not then due so much to differences in early mortality (the greater vulnerability of prepubescent males being somewhat offset by the greater vulnerability of young adult females) as to differential emigration rates. Many more men than women emigrated during the nineteenth and early twentieth century. In 1981, women of 65 and over outnumbered men by rather over three to two, a difference which was almost entirely due to differences in mortality rates in late middle age. While life expectancy at birth for both sexes improved over the past century and males in 1980 outnumbered females in every 5-year age group from birth to 45, after that latter age male mortality rates greatly exceeded those for females. Women survivors at age 50 in 1978 could expect to live to 78.8 years while men could only expect to live to 73.6. Even at age 80 British women on average live more than one year longer (7.1 as against 5.6) than their male contemporaries. Actuarial projections suggest that there will be a slight modification in these comparative expectations if recent indications of a slight decrease in middle-aged mortality among men are sustained. In 2001 the gross disparities in the sex ratio in all but the most aged groups may have been somewhat reduced.

In other industrial countries, elderly females also invariably outnumber their male counterparts, but to varying extents. In the United States, for example, the male and female ratio among the 65s and over in 1979 was about two to three, as it was in Britain: but among those aged 85 and over just under 70 per cent compared with nearly 80 per cent in Britain, were female. In France women of 85 and over outnumbered men to about the same extent as in Britain: but in the Netherlands and Sweden the female superiority in survival was less marked.

Geographical variation

The demographic pictures drawn here are national composite ones. However, a feature of the second half of the twentieth century is the unevenness in the geographical distribution of the elderly population within national states. These differences are the result of two factors; differential mortality at all ages in different geographical areas and internal migration, the latter being the more weighty. A phenomenon of recent times has been the tendency of retired people to migrate from heavily industrialized conurbations in which they once worked to more salubrious towns and villages near the sea coast or in rural areas. There has also been a tendency on the part of the elderly to move from colder to warmer climes. In the northern hemisphere this has meant a move from north to south — for example, in England, from the north and midlands to the south coast, and, in the United States, from the northern states to Florida and the south west.

The effect of intra-country migration has been that the demographic maps of most industrialized countries show considerable variations in age structure. Generally speaking, the expanding suburban and semi-rural areas including, in Britain, the New Towns of the 1950s and 1960s have a low proportion of elderly people (low defined as less than 10 per cent). Those with a high proportion (that is, with 20 per cent or more) and especially those with a very high proportion (over 30 per cent) are overwhelmingly in coastal areas, largely in the south.

Not only does the proportion of elderly in the total population vary from area to area but within the elderly group there are varying proportions of very old in different areas. Generally speaking, the areas with high proportions of elderly also have high proportions of the old elderly, suggesting that these areas either enjoy lower death rates among the young elderly (65 to 74) or that there is continued migration from other areas into them from people over 75. The former is quite possible if the age group in this area is already distinguished by physical and social characteristics favourable to survival, for example, by higher social class status whose standard mortality ratios compare favourably with those of lower social class status.

Attention has been drawn to the existence of substantial differences in the proportion of elderly people in the population of particular areas because of the implications for resource allocation, a point which will be considered later.

FAMILY AND KIN

Most children in contemporary society live until they become adults with a group of people to whom they are related by blood. This group constitutes their family, the family of origin, and they will generally continue to think of its members as *their* family, even when they no longer share the same roof and have established through marriage or cohabitation another nuclear family unit, their family of procreation. This second family, in its turn, will transmogrify from a unit characterized for a time by the sharing of a common roof, board and child-rearing functions as well as mutually sustaining affectional relationships into one which persists only through the fulfilment of mutually acceptable obligations usually based on continuing affectional ties. Such ties usually serve to bond adult brothers and sisters as well as parents and children and to create a network of supportive kin around successive nuclear families. Few will dispute that the quality of ties of this kind are likely to be a major determinant of the way in which individuals cope with life at any time including their old age.

By the time individuals reach pensionable age they are likely to have created a nuclear family and seen it disintegrate as a living unit as their children in turn form new ones. How far they still see themselves as part of a nuclear family and how far they have meaningful associations with individuals from their family of origin, their family of procreation and their wider kinship will depend upon many things, including the extent to which they have surviving relatives. It will also depend upon the size, composition and stability of nuclear families and in this respect the twentieth century has seen great changes. Yet another factor of significance is whether the work of younger women is primarily centred around family-maintenance tasks which constitutes the greater part of the 'hidden' or unpaid labour of all national economies or whether it is carried on in the 'open market place' of remunerated labour. This too has changed considerably especially since the second world war and will affect the resources which a kinship network can muster for the care of its old members as they become increasingly frail and reliant upon help from others for coping with the mundane activities of daily life.

Let us review, therefore some of the salient trends in marriage, the family, fertility and women's work as they are likely to affect old people.

Marital status

Disparities in the survival of the sexes into their 60s and beyond are paralleled by disparities in their marital status. For example, of those aged 65 and over in 1980, nearly three-quarters of the men (73.6 per cent) were married compared to only just over one-third of the women (36.8 per cent). There were almost identical proportions of divorced who numbered less than 2 per cent of the population. Women were rather more likely to have never married (12.0 per cent compared to 7.5 per cent of the men); but they were considerably more likely to be widowed. Just under a half of them were compared to only one in six of the surviving men.

The marital status of survivors into old age has changed over the century because there has been a secular trend for both more men and more women to marry. Hence there are relatively fewer never-married old men and women now than at any time in the past 100 years. Reciprocally the proportion of once married of both sexes (this includes of course widowed, divorced and separated as well as still married) has increased. The trend is likely to continue and it can safely be predicted that there will be fewer never-married elderly people for the remainder of the twentieth century.

Family support

The significance of information about the marital status of the elderly population lies in the capacity it gives to make certain inferences concerning the potential for familial support available to them. For example, it seems legitimate to infer that those who have never married are most unlikely to have surviving offspring and hence, on balance, fewer potential sources of familial support than those who married. Among the latter, however, there will be at the one extreme some who have no surviving children and at the other those who have many. The Census itself does not provide this important information for the elderly population at large; but a sample survey carried out in 1977 by Age Concern in four representative areas found that 35 per cent of those aged 75 or over had either been childless or had outlived their children; among those aged 65 to 74 there were 33 per cent without children (Abrams, 1980). These figures exclude those living in institutions, who are even more likely to have been childless. The present generation of elderly people, indeed, belong to a cohort distinguished by the relatively small number of children they had had compared to previous generations. The cohorts which will succeed them between the 1970s and the end of the twentieth century less frequently remained childless and more commonly had medium sized (two or three children) compared to large (four or more) or small (one only) families. This points to a situation in the next two decades in which fewer old people will be childless but there will be fewer who have many direct descendants.

It is one thing to have children; it is another for those children to be in a position to provide the kind of support which their parents may need with advancing age. Among the many factors which will determine how much and what kind of help elderly people obtain from their younger kin are, importantly, the sex and marital status, family and work commitments of the latter, how close they live to one another, and how strong the affectional ties between them are.

It is clear that in the past, especially among the middle class, the task of daily care and companionship for elderly people often fell to an unmarried, usually non-gainfully employed, daughter where she existed. Generally speaking, she shared the parental home. Another not uncommon arrangement, particularly where a working-class woman had been widowed relatively young, was for a son to remain single and live with his mother who would housekeep for him. Shanas and others found in the 1960s that nearly a quarter (23 per cent) of widowed men and women lived with one or more unmarried children. The same proportion were found in that study to be living with a married offspring, the chances being about three to one that it would be a daughter rather than a son. In 1979–80, however, only 4 per cent of elderly men and 10 per cent of elderly women were living with children or children-in-law (General Household Survey, 1980). Among the 85 and over age group, however, 27 per cent of both sexes did live with offspring.

Other studies have drawn attention to the marked tendency in modern industrialized societies for daughters rather than sons to be the main source of kin support for elderly people (Townsend, 1957). This applies not only to those instances where the elderly person lives with a younger relative; it is equally true of the support provided by kin who do not share the same accommodation. Studies based on sample surveys in various parts of Britain and other industrialized societies have the same tale to tell. It is that since the Second World War many elderly people who live alone are visited often on a day-to-day basis by their children, and most commonly by daughters who are more likely to live close to their parents than are sons (Sheldon, 1948; Townsend, 1957; Shanas et al, 1968; Isaacs, 1971; Tunstall, 1973; OPCS, 1978; Abrams, 1980). The predominant role of daughters as compared with sons is even to be seen when, as happens to an increasing extent, employment or housing exigencies increase the distance between generations beyond daily visiting feasibility. Willmott and Young (1960) found that contact between parents and daughters by telephone, letter and visit was more frequent than that between parents and sons. The predominant supportive role played by women is not new. It was justified in the past on the grounds that women were usually unwaged and hence would not lose income by taking on nursing or domestic tasks for the frail and dependent. Perhaps it was their universal assignment to such work which led to the widespread but untested assumption that women to a greater extent than men possess the appropriate personal characteristics to comfort and care for the old.

Employment of younger kin

Since the Second World War, however, there has been a great change in the employment of women, especially of those who are married. In some parts of industrialized Britain such as the cotton-manufacturing districts of Lancashire, it has long been common for working-class women, irrespective of their marital and parental status, to work in the mills. Elsewhere and more generally during the first four decades of this century women of all classes were expected, except during the two world wars, to give up gainful employment on marriage. Since the Second World War, for a variety of reasons, it is rare for women to retire from gainful employment until they are several months pregnant with their first child, and relatively common for them to return to gainful employment on a full- or part-time basis when the youngest of their two- or three-child family reaches school age. These tendencies are reflected in data from the Central Statistical Office which show that the proportion of married women who were economically active increased considerably between 1951 and 1979, particularly in the age groups over 45 (Table 46.2). This trend has led to a sharp increase in the numbers of women in the age groups most likely to have an elderly parent who would have to forgo a source of personal income were they to care on an intensive daily basis for such a person. Taken together with the decline in the numbers of single women and hence a diminution in the numbers of those traditionally assigned to fulfil the kinship obligation of caring for aged parents, these statistics may lead to the legitimate inference that the part which kin played in previous generations in solving problems encountered in the care of the elderly is no longer so feasible. Much emphasis is given to the desirability of community care for the frail elderly as compared to hospital or institutional care. Insufficient attention appears to have been paid to the implications of such a policy for the employment prospects of younger women or for family income.

Table 46.2 Percentage of married women economically active in age groups — 1961, 1971 and 1979*

Age group	1961	1971	1979
20–24	41.3	45.7	57.8
25–44	33.1	46.4	58.7
45–59	32.6	53.4	61.0
60 and over	7.3	14.2	10.1

* Source — Central Statistical Office. Social Trends No. 12. HMSO

It is not legitimate to infer from these trends that there has been a loosening of the affectional ties which bind younger kin to their elderly relatives. Observers of the contemporary scene who allege such a tendency forget that poverty in Victorian times prevented many families from caring for their old people and that many of the latter were abandoned or left to finish their days in workhouses. While instances of apparent ingratitude and denial of obligation can always be found, the evidence points to the continuing efforts made by most kin, often at considerable personal sacrifice of income and convenience, to care for their elderly relatives (Cartwright et al, 1973; Sanford, 1975).

That these efforts are not unsuccessful at least in helping elderly people to continue to live in their own homes and not in a hospital or other institutional setting is suggested by the evidence of where and how the elderly live.

ACCOMMODATION

Institutional care

It is commonly believed, especially it seems by health service personnel, that a majority of the elderly live permanently in hospitals or old people's homes and not in ordinary houses or flats which they or their relatives rent or own. The truth is very different and often very surprising to those working in hospitals. They have in their permanent care only a tiny minority of the elderly, although a substantial number come and go for care in an acute period of illness or to give respite to their kinsfolk who care for them in their usual home.

At the time of writing, information concerning the housing of the British population from the 1981 Census is not available. Ten years earlier, only 3 per cent of the total population of Great Britain were staying on the Census night in other than private households, that is, in hotels, boarding houses and schools, prisons, hospitals and other residential institutions, and among those of pensionable age the proportion was only marginally greater — 4.9 per cent; but within that age group it rose in each progressive age group from 1 per cent of the women aged 60–64 to over a third (34.7 per cent) of the men and women of 95 and over.

The 1971 Census figures included individuals who were only temporary residents of the establishments in which they were enumerated and were normally domiciled in private dwellings. Those whose usual residence was the hospital or old people's home constituted therefore an even smaller proportion of the elderly population. This was particularly likely to be so in the case of those enumerated in general hospitals which included those in acute as well as longer-stay wards.

As the percentages in Table 46.3 indicate, about equal proportions of the pensionable age group (two out of five in each case) were in general hospitals and old people's homes and half that proportion (one in five) in psychiatric hospitals; but these proportions were not the same for all ages. With increasing age the proportion in old age homes increased dramatically and the proportion in psychiatric hospitals declined equally dramatically. There was also a slight decline with increasing age in the proportion in general hospitals.

It is likely that there are few people of any age who would choose voluntarily to live in an institutional setting in preference to a home which they shared with kith or kin, or, if alone, could call their own. There are

Table 46.3 Numbers and percentages of each age group enumerated in general hospitals, psychiatric hospitals and Old People's Homes* (Great Britain, 1971)

Institution	Age 60–74F 65–74M		Age 75–84 Both sexes		Age 85+ Both sexes		All pensionable ages	
	No.	%	No.	%	No.	%	No.	%
General hospitals	55975	42.6	53335	37.1	31725	34.6	141045	38.5
Psychiatric hospitals	42525	32.3	23075	16.0	8105	8.9	73705	20.1
Old people's homes	32990	25.1	67390	46.9	51655	56.5	152045	41.4
All institutions	131490	100.0	143800	100.0	91485	100.0	366775	100.0

* Census 1971. Non-private households. Office of Population Censuses and Surveys. HMSO 1974

no satisfactory statistics which show us whether old people of manual working-class origin are more likely than those of other social classes to live in institutions, although there are many indications that this is the case. There are, however, signs that earlier life experience in relation to marriage does influence the likelihood of entering an institution in old age. For example, the single, divorced and widowed of both sexes in that descending order of frequency were more likely than currently married people to be enumerated in insti-

tutions in the 1971 Census (Figs. 46.1 and 46.2). The single of both sexes, and particularly the single men, were very likely to be in an institution compared with the ever-married. Among the older group (Fig. 46.2) the distinction between divorced and widowed almost disappeared, while the discrepancy between them (the no longer married) and the currently married increased. These statistics provide strong inferential evidence to suggest that marriage and its perpetuation into old age are protective against the risk of long-term

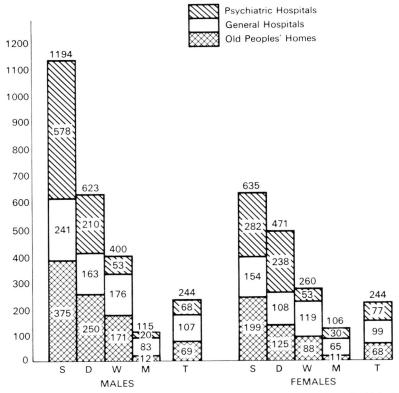

Fig. 46.1 Males and females aged 65–74 of different marital statuses in institutions in 1971 (per 10 000 in the age group) (Great Britain). S = single, D = divorced, W = widowed, M = married, T = total statuses. Source: Census 1971 Non-private households. Office of Population Censuses and Surveys. HMSO, 1974

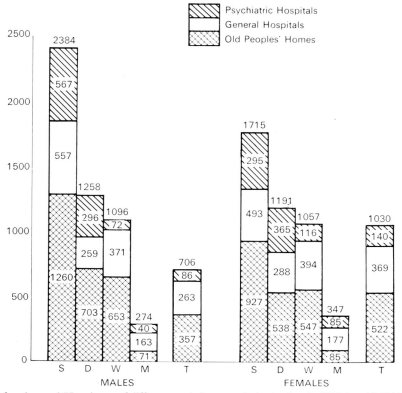

Fig. 46.2 Males and females aged 75 and over of different marital statuses in institutions in 1971 (per 10 000 in age group) (Great Britain). S = single, D = divorced, W = widowed, M = married, T = total statuses. Source: Census 1971. Non-private households. Office of Population Censuses and Surveys. HMSO, 1974

institutional care in both old people's home and hospitals.

Information about the living conditions of those who reside in non-private dwellings is not as comprehensive as is information about the domestic amenities enjoyed by those in private households. It often comes from such sources as reports from the Hospital Advisory Service and the occasional reports made by official Committees of Enquiry into allegations of cruelty and neglect, or by independent investigators. Some such reports (South East Thames Regional Health Authority, 1976) have suggested that poor living arrangements are not uncommon. Certainly, although many of the old Victorian work-houses, which used to shelter the poor whether old or young, sick or well, have now been demolished, many of the old poor law infirmaries, as well as fever hospitals and lunatic asylums, still exist and, where they do, they are most often in use as long-stay geriatric or psychiatric hospitals. These are often grim, forbidding structures. They have proved difficult to modernize and are subject to high cost of repairs and maintenance which, in times of severe restriction on

expenditure in the public sector, can lead to structural and decorative deterioration. They contribute to the depressing image of work with the elderly in institutions which is apparently held by many members of the caring professions who can perhaps be forgiven for not wishing to work in the depressing atmosphere of a large, impersonal building if they can find more salubrious settings for their work. Until recently, when rising unemployment reduced the number of unfilled vacancies in psychiatric and long-stay geriatric hospitals, these institutions had the greatest difficulties in finding trained staff of all kinds.

Residential homes

The situation of the elderly in residential homes run by local authorities and voluntary associations has improved more radically since the 1960s than has that of the elderly in the hospital sector. A Census of Residential Accommodation undertaken in 1970 (DHSS, 1975) indicated that few homes then had as many as 100 beds, a commonplace in 1960 (Townsend, 1962). Most housed from 20 to 50 old people. Within the homes, too, steps have been taken to ensure greater privacy by increasing the number of single bedrooms and reducing the number of rooms housing two or more unrelated people. More attention has also been paid to improving the physical appearance of communal dining and sitting rooms, to installing lifts and ramps and other aids to greater mobility and to providing adequate fire precautions.

The provision of places in residential homes for those who can no longer manage to look after themselves in their own home, or in the home of relatives or friends, is not evenly distributed throughout the country. Much of the accommodation is owned by voluntary associations; it owes its existence to the charitable impulses of past benefactors and bears little relationship to the current geographical distribution of needs for such accommodation. The result is that some parts of the country have sufficient to meet all locally generated demands as well as a surplus to offer, while others have a dire shortage which raises real problems for the elderly who, although no longer in their own homes, wish to remain close to kith and kin and their familiar environment.

Another problem for elderly people in some residential homes is that they may not have security of tenure. Some local authorities and voluntary associations have felt compelled, on grounds of both sound finance and equity, to admit someone else from their waiting lists when a place has become vacant through the admission of a resident to hospital, following, for example, a stroke or a fractured femur. This action is understandable since the patient may not recover sufficient independence in self-care to be able to return to a home where there is no provision for nursing care; but many patients do recover their functional capacity, and the knowledge that they have no place to which, by right, they can return after a spell in hospital can hardly reduce anxiety or speed recovery. This dilemma is primarily the outcome of a shortage of accommodation in residential homes for the frail who do not need continuing nursing care but cannot manage entirely on their own, and it will not cease until that shortage is overcome. Indeed, it is likely to grow with the increase in residential homes in the proportion of the very old and very frail.

Since 1960 statutory authorities at central and local government level as well as many voluntary associations have committed themselves in principle to a policy of seeking to reduce the numbers of individuals of every age, including the elderly, who have to live permanently in institutions and particularly in hospitals. The task has proved difficult for many reasons, not least because of the relative increase in the numbers of the very old and very frail who need constant supervision. In the past such survivors would have been more likely than present-day 80- and 90-year-olds to have had middle-aged non-employed female kin to see to their needs. For these and other reasons it is unreasonable to think that in the foreseeable future there will be any substantial reduction in the number or proportion of elderly people needing institutional care.

For this reason, if for no other, the aim must be to improve the quality of life of those who now and in the future will be domiciled permanently in long-stay hospitals or local authority and voluntary association homes. This means, in addition to improving the physical surroundings, attempting to eliminate the negative aspects of the psychosocial environment. Residents are too often subjected to routines which can be impersonal, humiliating and in the last resort alienating. Some of the restrictions are justified by staff on the grounds that they are for the protection of the old people themselves: but restrictions can violate the rights of individuals to determine for themselves the degree of risk they should run. (Norman, 1980; Muir Gray, 1980). When there are staffing shortages it is possible to see why an authoritarian approach to residents comes to be used; in the short run it is easier to keep to a routine by ignoring the individualities of patients. In the long run, however, such an approach is dangerous because it can too easily slip into cruelty, apathy and the consequent demoralization of staff and residents alike. One safeguard against such a thing happening is to open hospitals and homes to the members of the community in which they are situated and to encourage them to forge links with local people individually and through local organizations which seek to enrich the lives of their members.

The elderly in private households

While the conditions of the elderly people who live in various kind of institutions must be a matter of concern to all those involved in health services, it must be remembered that, at most, they constitute less than one-twentieth of the pensionable age population. The living conditions of the remainder are more significant whether we consider them in economic, social or physical terms.

Table 46.4 shows that nearly a half (45 per cent) of all the women over 65 in the UK lived alone. Among those over 75 the proportion was well over a half. Among the men, on the other hand, only 17 per cent or about one in six lived alone. The major reason for the differences in the living situations of men and women is also revealed by Table 46.4. No less than four out of five of the men aged 65 to 74 were married and living with a spouse which was only true for less than half the women of that age. At subsequent ages the differences increased. Moreover, it is permissible to infer that widowhood for women in the over 85s more commonly than widowhood for men of the same age meant living alone rather than living with children.

Table 46.4 Percentage of elderly by age groups in different living situations in 1979–80★ (Great Britain)

Living situation	65–74		75–84		85+		All	
	M %	F %	M %	F %	M %	F %	M %	F %
With spouse								
Spouse only	66	42	54	19	30	6	61	32
Spouse and others	14	7	9	3	9	1	13	5
Total	80	49	63	22	39	7	74	37
Without spouse								
Children plus in laws	2	7	6	15	27	27	4	10
Siblings and other relatives	3	4	2	7	6	9	3	6
Non-relatives	1	1	2	2	2	2	1	2
Total	6	12	10	24	35	38	8	18
Alone	13	39	27	56	27	54	17	45
Total	99	100	100	100	100	99	100	100

★ General Household Survey. Office of Population Censuses and Surveys 1982 HMSO

In Britain as a whole standards of housing amenity have improved throughout the twentieth century. Considerably less overcrowding was recorded in the Census in 1971 than in the early years of the century and a substantial reduction in the number of households which either had no such domestic facilities as a fixed bath, indoor toilet or running hot water or had to share them with other households.

Elderly people have shared in this overall improvement in living standards. Because they so frequently live alone they are less likely to live in overcrowded households. Indeed, because they often stay on in houses and flats which once housed their spouses and children, they are more likely than younger households to have too much rather than too little space to occupy. By the same token, however, they are more likely than people in younger households to occupy accommodation which lacks modern domestic facilities. For example, a Government social survey of the elderly at home in 1977 (OPCS, 1978) found that the greater the age the greater the proportion without amenities which most younger people would consider essential for satisfactory daily living (Table 46.5). Such figures reflect the fact that elderly people were more likely than the population at large to live both in remote country areas and in decaying city centres where housing conditions have seen least improvement. They were more likely too, when they occupied rented accommodation to depend on private landlords for it rather than on local authorities, than were younger householders. For example, in 1980 30 per cent of the tenanted households where the head was 70 or more were privately rented compared with only 20 per cent of those where the household head was between 45 and 59. By and large, and perhaps understandably, the latter have not given as high

Table 46.5 Percentage of elderly households without selected amenities in England 1977.

Amenity	Age of household head				All ages
	60–64	65–74	75–84	85 and over	
Bathroom	2	10	11	20	10
Hot water supply	2	8	8	15	8
Inside lavatory	6	11	14	15	12
Vacuum cleaner	6	10	16	22	13
Refrigerator	2	21	32	47	25
Television	13	9	12	19	11
Washing machine	26	47	41	59	67
Telephone	41	57	62	65	59
Car	61	65	83	87	72

★ Source. Office of Population Censuses and Surveys (1978) The Elderly at Home

priority to the housing needs of the elderly as to those of couples with young children.

There is little doubt that improving the standards of accommodation and amenities would enable many elderly people to maintain their social independence for longer. It is often the difficulty of coping with daily living activities in inconvenient, insanitary and hypothermia-inducing circumstances which provides the straw which eventually breaks the camel's back and induces elderly people or their relatives to seek institutional accommodation. Such circumstances may also make it impossible to welcome back into their own home those who have been admitted to hospital during an episode of acute illness and have since recovered but may not be able to face the rigours of life alone in a house which even able-bodied young adults might find daunting.

Special housing

A contribution has been made to easing the housing problems of elderly people in the form of specially designed flatlets or small bungalows which are grouped together and where a warden is available to keep a watchful eye open for anyone in distress. The Department of Health and Social Security (Central Statistical Office, 1982) puts the number of elderly people accommodated in sheltered units of this kind in 1979 at about 237 000 or between 2 and 3 per cent of the total pensionable aged population of England and Wales. Both local authorities and housing associations are being encouraged to build more sheltered housing especially but not exclusively for their elderly populations. In other countries such as the United States the major contribution comes from speculative builders who have developed estates especially for those sections of the elderly population which can afford to move to southern states and invest their life savings in securing sheltered housing and services for themselves until their death. In Britain, the economic difficulties in which the middle-class has found itself has restricted private enterprise development of this kind, and more emphasis is placed on the role of central and local government in facilitating this kind of solution to the basic problem of finding suitable living surroundings in which to enjoy to the greatest extent possible the remaining years of life.

EMPLOYMENT AND RETIREMENT

There has been a long-term, and quite dramatic, fall in the proportion of men over 65 in the work force in Britain since the early years of the twentieth century. This has been attributed by some to the increasing use of mechanization and the speed of innovation, the theory being that older workers are less likely to adjust to change (Le Gros Clark, 1966). However, this argument is somewhat weakened because, amongst women, the trend has been in the opposite direction. More women over pensionable age but under 70 were economically active in 1971 than in the previous two decennial census years. It is possible that the Census figures as a whole underestimate somewhat the numbers who continue to earn, perhaps erratically, in part-time, casual employment, especially among the under 70-year-olds. The latter may not draw their full retirement pension if they earn more than a small sum weekly. Some of them may find it convenient therefore to 'forget' about the activities which bring in some earned income when they complete census forms. Inaccuracies in the figures for reasons such as this are not great enough, however, to upset the general conclusion to be drawn, namely that there has been a secular trend towards retirement from gainful employment for men who have reached the statutory pensionable age of 65. Fewer than a third of the 65- and 69-year-olds are working and scarcely more than a tenth of those over 70. While the proportion of women who are gainfully employed has risen, it is still much smaller than the comparable proportion among men.

For many men, retirement from work may mean release from a job which has brought them little intrinsic satisfaction and has perhaps helped to undermine their physical health. Consequently trade union pressure to reduce the age at which a reasonable statutory retirement pension may be drawn as of right is likely to be welcomed by some. For many other people, however, retirement is not the peaceful, welcome retreat to pleasant pastures from the hurly-burly of unmitigated, burdensome toil. Work provides most people with a source of legitimate income and hence with self-respect. It may also provide companionship and a routinized structure to daily activities which are welcome in themselves. For many, their customary work continues to offer intrinsic interest and challenge. Finally, many would like to continue to contribute to the national income while they are able rather than simply draw upon it.

Compulsory retirement can therefore be an unwelcome change for several reasons. It is likely to reduce substantially the individual's income. A married man, whose status in his own family has been derived from his role of breadwinner, may feel that he has lost some of the authority and respect that this role gave him (Townsend, 1957). Besides an earned income he has also lost the companionship and the security associated with the daily performance of a routine of activities. The self-confidence which he derived from knowing how to cope with work in which he had acquired skills through experience may be undermined. To these real problems for the individual we must add the cost to the community at large in the form of the resources required for pensions for the compulsory retirement of the unwilling.

It has been suggested that some of the depression and anxiety which manifests itself among men in their late 60s and early 70s is a result of the sense of loss of status and function which enforced retirement may bring. Hence many doctors as well as those reaching pensionable age have felt that employers should not automatically require the retirement of their workers when the latter reach the age at which they are entitled to draw a statutory pension. In the decade and a half immediately following the end of the Second World War, labour shortages in most forms of employment led many to hope that those elderly men and women who did not wish to retire would continue to work in their customary employment as long as they felt able to do so. Furthermore, it seemed reasonable to hope that the abrupt transition from full-time work to full retirement from gainful employment could be mediated through a gradual reduction in the hours worked by the individual person, a reduction phased to meet his particular needs.

These hopes, if not finally dashed, have not been realized to any great extent. The rate of expansion in the economy of Great Britain and other industrial countries began to slow down in the 1960s and levels of unemployment among young workers to increase. When the labour market is unable to absorb all the men and women of 16 to 65 who seek work, the prospect for the elderly worker who is at least entitled to draw a retirement pension is bleak. Indeed, in such circumstances the energies of the trade unions of non-manual as well as ·manual employees are increasingly devoted to securing greater opportunities for earlier retirement with the right to draw a pension at a level which will enable the individuals concerned to enjoy their new-found leisure. There is still comparatively little emphasis given by either employers or trade unions to helping those nearing retirement to prepare themselves for it, although there is a growing awareness by general practitioners, priests and bartenders among others that the process of adjusting to a new role and self-image is a difficult one for many men. Marris (1974) has likened it to other forms of loss experienced by individuals (for example, through the death of a spouse, the amputation of a limb, the failure of a business or expulsion from the homeland). Individuals must be allowed to grieve if they are successfully to reconstruct their lives around the performance of a new role. In practice, the newly retired can feel themselves to be ignored if not ostracized by those still at work and not allowed by their kin to express their sense of loss. It is still an open question whether the potential psychological trauma of retirement can be reduced by systematic pre-retirement preparation conducted either on a do-it-yourself or a collective basis. Claims for the beneficial effects of courses run by further education colleges and voluntary organizations have seldom been based on the kind of evidence required to validate them in the eyes of the behavioural scientist.

Before leaving the question of work it is interesting to note that a 1972 study (OPCS, 1975) showed that the over 65s were much more likely than younger workers to express great satisfaction with their work: 70 per cent of them did so compared with only 46 per cent of workers of all ages. This statistic does not of course tell us whether liking for work increases with age or whether those who remain at work after the usual retirement age are drawn predominantly from those who have always liked work. It is legitimate, however, to conclude that few men and women over retirement age who remain economically active find their work dissatisfying.

In an ideal world, therefore, it would seem desirable that older workers should have a genuine choice of continuing to remain economically active or of retiring on a pension sufficient to allow them to pursue a reasonable range of favoured leisure pursuits as well as a standard of living not too different from that which they enjoyed in their last working years. As it is, that genuine choice does not exist for many people, and since giving men and women that choice may appear to conflict with the interests of younger people seeking employment and career advancement, the problem is unlikely to be resolved except in periods of full employment.

THE FINANCIAL CIRCUMSTANCES OF THE ELDERLY

The comparatively small proportion of elderly people in gainful employment is the reason why they have both quite different sources and different levels of income from those of the adult population generally.

In 1980 an average of 73 per cent of the mean income of all households included in the annual Family Expenditure Survey (Department of Employment, 1982) came from wages, salaries or self-employment, while only 28 per cent of the much smaller mean income of households with heads aged 65 or more came from this source. Social security benefits, which for the elderly meant predominantly national insurance retirement and supplementary pensions, constituted 42 per cent of the average household income of the 65s and over, but made up only 9 per cent of the average income of all households. Investments, including annuities and occupational pensions, a category which accounted for only 6 per cent of the average income of all households, provided 24 per cent of the income of households with a head of 65 or over (Central Statistical Office, 1982).

These figures indicate the extent to which those of pensionable age are dependent on the fiscal policies of governments. Even if they were effectively organized as a collective pressure group, which they are not, elderly retired people cannot use the threat of strike action to support a claim for a larger share of national resources. Moreover, when national policies seek to establish the principle that an increase in an individual's or in an occupational group's share of resources in real terms must only be based on greater productivity, elderly people, who are denied the opportunity to contribute to the creation of the gross national product, are at a great disadvantage. Furthermore, since social security benefits are seen as an item of public expenditure on which the prevailing political economy theories propose an absolute ceiling, there is an ever-present threat to the income level of pensioners, a threat which is exacerbated by continuous inflation.

The claim which elderly retired people have on society has therefore to be expressed in terms of social justice or of charity, and not in terms of economic good sense. During the nineteenth century, the prevailing free enterprise ethos emphasized the need for the growing number of middle-class men to save and invest to secure an income when it was no longer possible for them to work. Skilled craftsmen and technicians, on the other hand, began to make provision through trade unions or non-profit-making mutual benefit friendly societies for annuities on retirement. Most workers, however, were unable to accumulate the capital sums required to live on investments during their working lives and were dependent on relief under the poor law or on charity from a voluntary organization. Apart from the fact that the amount of relief given was usually insufficient to allow for anything other than a spartan existence, there was increasing awareness that the manner in which it was given, as well as what was felt to be the underlying indignity imposed on those who had to beg for it, could not be tolerated in a society which claimed that it would use its increasing wealth in the cause of human welfare.

Retirement pensions

The device chosen to signify acceptance of the individual's moral claim on society for a regular income once he had reached a certain age was the compulsory insurance. contribution. Taxed weekly throughout their working lives, employees could feel that they had established a legitimate claim to benefit from the national fund on their retirement. Commercial insurance relates premiums or contributions to relative risk as well as to benefits. National insurance deliberately did not. Its base in actuarial terms is unsound. In political terms, however, it has proved an acceptable way of transferring resources from current to past contributors to the national income. Elderly people do not feel demeaned by this method of securing them an income and the electorate as a whole is content to transfer considerable resources from current producers to past producers in this manner.

In this respect it is important to note that the *real* value of the national insurance retirement pension of a married couple more than doubled between 1948 and 1974 (105 per cent increase) while the real value of average gross earnings of manual workers only increased by 91 per cent (DHSS, 1975). After 1974 and until 1981, as Figure 46.3 indicates, the retirement pension has just maintained its real value although inflation tends annually to reduce that value until it is re-established through its statutory link to the retail price index. Those on unemployment benefit did not fare as well. In other words, the political process has succeeded in the post Second World War years in transferring a slightly larger share of the nation's purchasing power from current producers to its retirement pensioners.

Nevertheless, an individual or couple solely dependent on the statutory national insurance retirement pension

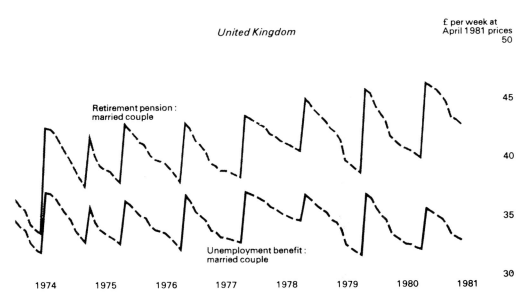

Fig. 46.3 Real value of retirement pensions and unemployment benefit, 1974 to 1981. Reproduced from Social Trends (1982) with permission of the Controller of Her Majesty's Stationery Office.

would subsist at below what has now become a nationally accepted bench mark — a kind of poverty line. In 1948, a scheme, originally called National Assistance, and since 1966 Supplementary Benefits, was established to provide a subsistence level income for all those not in employment whose other resources fell below what was deemed to be a minimally acceptable level given their unavoidable expenses including rent or mortgage repayment commitments. An elderly person who feels that her income is insufficient to enable her to meet her subsistence needs and unavoidable expenses can apply to the local office of the Supplementary Benefits Commission for a supplementary pension. Her needs will be assessed including any expenses she may have to meet for a special diet, extra heating or domestic assistance, and if her income (disregarding small savings) is insufficient to meet them she will be able to draw a supplementary pension.

Supplementary pensions

In 1980, 18 per cent of those drawing national insurance retirement pensions were also receiving supplementary pensions. However, studies undertaken by independent investigators in the 1960s (Townsend and Wedderburn, 1965; Wedderburn, 1967; Atkinson, 1969), to some extent confirmed by official investigations in the 1970s (DHSS, 1975) showed there were still many whose income was less than the Supplementary Benefit poverty line bench mark. Estimates vary but the figures suggest that in the mid-1970s they may have been between 5 and 15 per cent of the eligible. The proportion was probably greater in the decade and a half following the Second World War when Supplementary Benefit (then called National Assistance) appeared to many to be little more than Poor Law relief given under another guise. Memories of the ignominy associated with seeking financial assistance in the early years of the century die hard. A change in the name of the benefit in 1966 and a deliberate attempt to persuade elderly people that they had a right to it and would receive sympathetic consideration led to an immediate and substantial increase in the numbers who applied; but pride and ignorance continue, it appears, to play a part in restricting the numbers who would be eligible from receiving the help which they need. The ignorance, it should be stressed, is not merely on the part of the retired people themselves. Some share of the blame must fall on those in touch with elderly people who fail to inform them of their rights and help set aside their fears of what may be in store for them if they do apply for assistance. The medical profession bears a particularly heavy responsibility in this regard because entitlement to Supplementary Benefits is often based on medically assessed needs for special diets, laundry facilities or domestic assistance. It is also true that the procedures and instructions which need to be followed are often complex and sometimes unnecessarily obfuscating.

Other benefits

Many other benefits, for example, in the way of waived or reduced charges for services are linked to Supplementary Benefit. Everyone over the age of 65 is automatically exempt from prescription charges; and Supplementary Benefit recipients do not have to pay for dental treatment or ophthalmic services under the NHS. In many areas bus services are free to all those over retirement age at off-peak hours and British Rail provides half-price fares for them if they have purchased a rail card now costing £10 per annum. Rate rebates from local authorities are available to those with low incomes and most retirement pensioners qualify. The problem is that many of these financial benefits are not fully utilized. Pride based on the mistaken assumption that to take up the benefit would imply an acceptance of charity may be a reason for the reluctance of some eligible people to profit by the schemes. It is more probable that they are deterred from applying by ignorance or by the complexity of the regulations. The latter often appear to have been designed to deter all but the most persistent and intrepid from seeking help.

Nevertheless, in total the effect of various benefits and of fiscal policy more generally is to transfer some disposable income from younger groups in the community to the retired as illustrated in Figure 46.4, which shows the effect of cash benefits less taxation of the original income of various kinds of household.

WELFARE NEEDS AND THE PROVISION TO MEET THEM

In 1942, Lord (then Sir William) Beveridge produced a visionary document in parabolic terms (Beveridge, 1942). Industrial societies by the very nature of their social organization and economic activities exposed their citizens to various unavoidable hazards. It was therefore both morally right and economically propitious for the collectivity to accept responsibility for the victims of its own malfunctioning. Beveridge advocated also the provision of health services and education facilities on a universal scale, that is, freely available to individuals on the basis of an assessment of their needs or intellectual potential rather than on that of their capacity to pay. He believed, moreover, that the universality of the provision and its manifest objective of meeting fundamental human needs for social, economic, physical and psychological security would reduce class and sectional strife.

The British people, engaged in a war which seemed

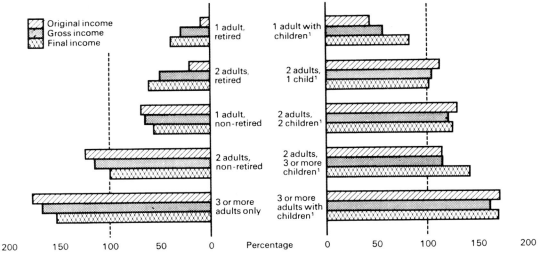

Fig. 46.4 Original, gross, and final income: by household type, 1979. Reproduced from Social Trends (1982) with permission of the Controller of Her Majesty's Stationery Office.

to underline the futility of the social divisions of their pre-war society and the injustices of its political economy, were fired by Beveridge's vision of a welfare society; by their votes in the first post-war election they put into power the political party which they considered most likely to implement this blueprint for a more secure and equitable society.

Amongst the phrases used in the parliamentary debates preceding the legislative measures, 1944 to 1948, which caught the collective imagination was one which set as an objective of social legislation, the achievement for all citizens of security 'from the cradle to the grave' or in another version 'from the womb to the tomb'. In latter years adherence to this principle has been held by some to lie behind the stagnation of the British economy!

In the nature of things it was inevitable that an open-ended national commitment of this kind could not be met. Resources of manpower and capital were insufficient to provide goods and services on a scale which could satisfy at an optimal level the self-defined needs of the entire citizenry for food, clothing, shelter, education and health. Originally, the inability to do so was largely blamed on the destruction of resources during the war and the backlog of unfilled need which it, and previous decades of neglect and squalor, had created. As these immediate shortages were overcome, however, it became clear that the policy of meeting needs was based on a false conception. As soon as some needs were met others which had not been foreseen appeared. Moreover, it was becoming apparent that the demand for services and the supply of them were not independent of each other. Additional supply stimulated

a demand which had not been foreseen. In these circumstances, it has become, as it has always been, a matter of controversy first as to which and whose needs should be given priority when resources were limited, and second as to the best mechanism of financing and delivering services whether these latter were of cash or kind. The policy decisions taken inevitably reflected the political process in the society of which it was a part, which takes many factors into account including the level of current economic prosperity, the voting strength of special interest groups, the state of the art or technology in various fields and the climate of opinion as to the moral worth of individuals who have a claim to make on the public purse.

By and large, the extent to which public authorities at central or local government level should seek to meet the particular service needs of retired people and the way in which it should be done have not been matters of acute party political controversy in post-war Britain. There have been differences of opinion on the extent to which the national insurance scheme itself should seek to provide graduated pensions for the retired which would reflect the relative differences in remuneration among the working population. Conservative policies have tended to favour occupational pension schemes run by employers to supplement a minimally differentiated national insurance pension as the preferred strategy. Labour has wanted the statutory scheme itself through differential contributions to incorporate differential benefits; but both political parties share, in principle, certain common assumptions about the extent and nature of the service needs of retired people and how they should be met.

Who is to blame?

That as a society we have not been able in practice to meet the acknowledged needs of elderly people tends to be ascribed by politicians, administrators and those providing services on a one-to-one basis to three different kinds of factor. First, there have been *financial constraints*, which have led to an absolute shortage of physical facilities such as sheltered housing, hospital beds, day hospital provision, telephones and radios or of such caring personnel as home nurses, physiotherapists and home helps. Second, there is held to have been *poor deployment* of existing resources of manpower stemming from faulty communication between different agencies and workers and a failure to co-ordinate plans for services generally and for the management of individual cases in particular (DHSS, 1974). Third, failure of kin and community to accept moral responsibility to ease the difficulties which elderly people may have in carrying out the normal activities of daily living and hence in maintaining the preferred norm of independence has often been seen as the reason for the intractable nature of the problem of caring for retired people.

Assignment of responsibility for what is frequently seen as an unforgiveable blot on the escutcheon of a society which should be both affluent and knowledgeable enough to solve preventable problems of ill-health as well as those of poverty and distress amongst its elderly citizens tends to vary depending upon the nature of the commentator's personal involvement with the issues. Moreover, since the cause of the elderly is often an issue highly charged with emotion, if not with feelings of guilt, attempts to stand back and view the problems with some regard for evidence are noticeable for their sparseness.

For example, sweeping statements amplified by the media alleging wholesale neglect of elderly people by kin, neighbours or social workers are apt to follow the reporting of a case of an elderly, perhaps eccentric, recluse found dead. In the face of some such event, doctors and nurses may forget the well-authenticated evidence of studies such as that of Isaacs et al (1972) which show the devotion and self-sacrifice to which most adult children are prepared to go to make an elderly parent's life tolerable. They are apt only to remember a recent instance of apparent neglect or callous disregard which they themselves have witnessed.

From another viewpoint, kin who have been caring continuously for a severely disabled elderly relative may well seek scapegoats from among health or social service workers for their own inability to secure help when they are at the end of their tether. Mutual accusations also fly only too readily between social service departments of local authorities, responsible for a wide range of domestic and amenity services to people in their own homes and for residential accommodation for those needing more help and surveillance than they can obtain in their own home or in that of a relative, and health service workers providing both domiciliary and hospital-based services. It is natural that each agency, unable to meet all the pressures on its own services, may like to believe that these pressures might be reduced if other agencies were 'doing their job' humanely and efficiently.

The truth is, of course, that the elderly age group, and in particular the 'old elderly', includes more seriously disadvantaged people than does any other, and consequently is likely to require more in the way of care than any other. In addition to the relative inferiority of their domestic amenities, their lower income per head and their greater propensity to live alone, which have already been detailed in this chapter, elderly people are much more likely than younger adults to suffer from long-standing incapacitating illnesses or disabilities. Some recent statistics are enough to illustrate these points. In 1977, only 20 per cent of the men and 14 per cent of the women of 75 and over who were interviewed in the General Household Survey said they had either no health problem or a short-term problem only. All the rest (80 per cent and 86 per cent respectively) had chronic health problems. The percentages for the sample of all ages was 56 for men and 70 for women (Table 46.6).

Table 46.6 Health problems reported by age and sex in 1977 per cent*

Age group	None or short term		Chronic problems	
	Men %	Women %	Men %	Women %
16–44	55	38	45	62
45–64	35	25	65	75
65–74	26	18	74	82
75 and over	20	14	80	86
All age groups	44	30	56	70

* Office of Population Censuses and Surveys 1979. General Household Survey 1977. HMSO

SERVICE PROVISION

With the major exception of social security benefits people over statutory retirement age were not, until the 1960s, formally distinguished administratively from younger people when it came to securing access to or paying for the use of most forms of health and personal social services. They, like everyone else in Great Britain, were entitled to the free service of a general practitioner under contract to the National Health Service and to specialist attention as an in-patient, out-patient or day patient in a NHS hospital. The Health Authority was also responsible for their dental treatment, optical services, chiropody and home nursing.

Like younger people who are disabled or chronically ill they are entitled, on the establishment of proof of physical rather than financial need, to a range of services provided through the local authority social service department. These include home-help and meals-on-wheels services, adaptations to housing and the advice of a social worker. The range of services which these departments were empowered to provide was considerably extended by the Chronically Sick and Disabled Persons Act, 1970. It enabled social service departments to meet a wide range of needs for continuing contact with the outside world and in particular with local educational and cultural activities. The Act made it mandatory for these departments to identify the severely disabled and ascertain their needs. The volume of services most of which go to old people expanded considerably during the 1970s. (Table 46.7).

Table 46.7 Numbers of meals provided and of cases attended by home helps in 1972 and 1980 (England and Wales)*

Service	1972	1980	Increase (%)
Meals			
At home (millions)	16.7	29.0	74
Elsewhere (millions)	9.3	15.2	63
Home help			
Cases attended (thousands)	432	704	63

* Social Trends No. 12 1982 Central Statistical Office HMSO

Since the 1960s, however, one or two important distinctions have been made between those over statutory pensionable age and the rest of the population. These are embedded in the legislation in the form of statutory regulations. Their purpose is generally to eliminate or reduce the cost of a service to retired people in order to ensure that individuals on small incomes who, if left to themselves, might be unable or reluctant to use a service are not deterred from doing so. Thus, for example, and perhaps of most importance everyone over statutory retirement age is entitled to free doctor-prescribed drugs, while the rest of the community pays for them, albeit only a fixed sum representing a fraction of the drugs' cost. In another field public transport authorities are empowered to reduce the fares they charge to retired people or waive them altogether at certain times.

For elderly people whose incomes are so low that they receive a regular Supplementary Pension in addition to their National Insurance Pension, a number of benefits for which normally a charge is made after a means test,

Table 46.8 Percentage of young elderly and old elderly receiving various services in their homes in 1979 (Great Britain)*

Service	Young elderly 65–74			Old elderly 75 and over		
	Men %	Women %	Total %	Men %	Women %	Total %
Chiropodist	5	10	8	10	17	15
District Nurse	2	3	3	6	11	9
Health Visitor	1	1	1	2	3	3

* Social Trends. No. 12 1982 Central Statistical Office. HMSO

are usually provided free of charge. These include, for example, meals on wheels, home help and chiropody. The 'old elderly' are the greatest users, although these services are only available to a small minority of the age group. (Table 46.8). Rebates on rates, the local government tax on property, are also available to householders receiving supplementary benefits. There is also provision for reviewing the charges made for a variety of services such as dental treatment, hearing aids and spectacles for retired people who are not receiving supplementary pensions but whose income is only a little above the level established by the Commission as the one at which they would be entitled to assistance.

Some care has been taken in designing these benefits to remove any suggestion that those who apply for them would be receiving charity or possibly making fraudulent claims for help when they should be self-supporting. In the past, surveys among old people showed that many of them were deterred from seeking help to which they were entitled for such reasons (Townsend and Wedderburn, 1965; Shanas et al, 1968). That this objective has not been fully achieved is evidenced by the fact that there are still eligible individuals who fail to apply for the various benefits available.

The services which elderly people may require while they remain in their own homes are of course extremely varied. Organizations concerned with old people's welfare have campaigned continuously for an extensive range of services to meet directly the needs of the elderly for companionship as well as practical assistance and indirectly those of the relatives who still provide most of the day-to-day support of old people. Cartwright and colleagues (1973), in their study of the final year of the lives of a representative sample of individuals who died in 1969, were able to show that near relatives received comparatively little help in that last year and, subsequently, in overcoming their own grief after bereavement. More recent studies by Hunt in 1976 (1978) and

Abrams in 1977 (1980) confirmed the Cartwright findings. They also indicated that substantial proportions of the 'old elderly', especially if living alone, were lonely and received no help with some activities of daily living or of personal hygiene maintenance that they found difficult.

Local disparities in service provision

Even more important is it to note that the services available to old people through their district health authority and social service department are not uniform throughout the country and that the level of utilization of services also varies regionally. Wright (1977), in an analysis undertaken for the Disability Alliance, illustrated the range in services given in different local authority areas. She showed that, in March 1976, Manchester had registered 44.4 per 1000 of its population as handicapped compared with Cambridge which had registered only 7.4. There may be, indeed probably are, great local disparities in the proportion of elderly and handicapped in the population, but they are hardly likely to be of the order of one to six. The disparities are also apparent in the services provided. For example, in the year ended 31st March, 1975, Manchester provided over eight times as many meals on wheels per head of its population of 65 and over as did Leeds. On the other hand, Leeds provided 50 per cent more hours of home help than did Manchester (Chartered Institute of Public Finance, 1976).

Provision of health services in the form both of facilities and personnel has also been uneven and, as the Report of the Resource Allocation Working Party (DHSS, 1976) indicated, the allocation of revenue from central government to the regions which prevailed until then could scarcely be justified on the grounds of differential health needs or of social justice. Indeed, if anything, it tended to favour regions which had inherited the most generous provision of hospital facilities when the NHS began in 1948 rather than those with the poorest facilities and the greatest indications of health need. It can only be concluded that central government has found it difficult politically to change customary differentials and that custom plays a part in determining the levels of local government commitment to welfare programmes.

VOLUNTARY ORGANIZATIONS

While the last 30 years have seen a substantial growth in the statutory provision of services for the benefit entirely or mainly of those over retirement age, this expansion has not been at the expense of services provided by voluntary agencies working usually in collaboration with social service departments. Many religious and social organizations call on their members to help those in need of companionship, transport, holidays, recreation and redecoration in their homes.

Much of the effort for stimulating and co-ordinating the work of local volunteers and of encouraging research into the extent and nature of unmet needs is undertaken by local Age Concern (Old People's Welfare) Committees. These are now co-ordinated and vigorously led by Age Concern from its four national centres in England, Scotland, Wales and Northern Ireland. In addition to stimulating volunteers to work effectively, Age Concern publishes many useful guides to assist elderly people themselves to make as much use as they can of existing services. Another body, the Centre for Policy on Ageing, financed largely by the Nuffield Foundation, has also made a major contribution through its research and development work to improving services, particularly perhaps to the quality of the residential provision offered by voluntary organizations to old people.

There has over the years inevitably been a change in the volunteer force. There are fewer non-gainfully-employed middle-class women available than there once were to give almost whole-term service in a voluntary capacity. Although such women still provide the mainstay of much voluntary effort in local communities (Aves 1969), there is now more emphasis on drawing in men, young people of both sexes and retired people. Since 1975, a new source of quasi-volunteer labour has become available. In suitable cases, offenders can volunteer to undertake community service as an alternative to other forms of expiating their guilt. Much of their work is devoted to assisting elderly people by such activities as helping in the garden or in house repairs.

THE BALANCE SHEET

What conclusions is it permissible to draw from this review of the social circumstances of elderly people and of the services provided to meet their needs?

Both the anecdotal and the statistical evidence reviewed suggest that since the Second World War there has been a considerable if geographically uneven extension in the scope and quantity of services available in cash and kind through the medium of public expenditure to meet the needs of elderly people. Moreover, this extension does not merely reflect the increase in the *per capita* real income of the total population over the same period. It represents a shift in resource allocation from the current to the past work force, from those of working age to the retired population. It is difficult in these circumstances to paint a picture of increasing callousness. The shift owes something to the advocacy of professional people involved with old people, but it also reflects a general consensus of opinion in society as a whole that sympathizes with old people and sees them as deserving consideration.

It is of course more difficult to conclude with the same certainty that the additional resources have had the effect of improving the quality of life of today's elderly people compared with those of an earlier period. It has been frequently pointed out, for example, that while life expectancy at birth has increased dramatically in the twentieth century, those who survive into their sixties cannot expect to live much longer than the survivors of a previous generation (McKeown, 1976).

Secondly, while the proportion of those aged 60 to 74 who live permanently in old people's homes and hospitals has declined, the numbers of individuals of 75 and over in institutional care have increased considerably. Few can regard such a trend as indicating an improvement in the quality of life of very old people, although it is possible that life for those who have entered some form of institutional care in the 1970s and 1980s is richer in both economic and social terms than it was for those in a comparable position in the 1950s.

Thirdly, it can scarcely be taken as evidence of success for social service policy that the proportion of elderly men and women who live alone has increased considerably since the war. While many live alone because they prefer it to any other choice open to them, others do so because they do not have offspring able and willing to offer them a home. On the other hand, a simple statistic of this kind cannot be taken to infer failure of policies for the care of the elderly. In some respects it could be considered something of a triumph that more than a half of those women aged 85 and over still living in private households managed to maintain sufficient independence of others to be able to live alone.

These points are sufficient to indicate how difficult and possibly dangerous it is from global statistics, first to make inferences about the quality of life of any group of individuals, and second to judge the success of particular programmes and policies from them.

The difficulty is itself a reflection of the complexity of the task of defining and measuring needs and the extent to which they are met, as well as the problem of determining how they can be met. As Bradshaw (1972) pointed out the word 'need' is often used loosely without a clear definition of what is meant by it. Welfare agencies are likely to define need as eligibility for their services and to consider that it is met when the service has been given (Blaxter, 1976). Professional workers are apt to define it in relation to their own specialty or skills and to see it as being met if they are able to exercise those skills. A patient or client may see his own needs in a different light. He will tend to perceive the service offered him by the agency or the professional worker as instrumental or not in helping him achieve his own objective. He will regard his need as met only if that objective is fulfilled. A still further element of confusion may result when there is potential conflict between the objective of a client and that of his kin or family. Such differences in perception of what need is and how it can be satisfied may lead to misunderstanding, mutual non-comprehension and accusations of indifference or ingratitude.

It is not possible, therefore, to end this chapter on a note of unqualified optimism about the future position of elderly people in modern highly industrialized societies. However, there is a great deal of sympathy for them from younger people and evidence of a willingness to redistribute resources in their favour. The redistribution probably needs to go much further than it has so far done if any substantial change relative to other groups in the community is to occur. For instance, a massive increase in the number of units of sheltered accommodation provided by local authorities and housing associations might allay the anxieties of those who live alone and their relatives as well as provide some safeguards against loneliness. Equally, an increase in the income of people over retirement age by encouraging those who wish to remain at work to do so and by raising pensions of those who retire would help to turn old age into a state less resented for its economic consequences, including the insecurity engendered by the fact that the cost of maintaining life-long standards in a situation of mounting handicap may outstrip the capacity to pay.

It can be argued, indeed, from the evidence of the history of elderly people in our own society as well as in the orient, that when old people are rich in material goods, in wisdom or in the capacity to form loving relationships, they are very likely to live contented lives. Their eccentricities if they possess them are tolerated and, as their dependency on others increases, they are still able by virtue of their capacity to give as well as receive, to retain the devoted attention of others. On the other hand, those who are poor in these qualities have seldom enjoyed their lives to the full.

It may be utopian to envisage a vast redistribution of material goods in the last two decades of the twentieth century through changes in employment, fiscal and housing policies. It is difficult too to redistribute wisdom, although there is evidence of neglect of the store already possessed by old people from many walks of life. It is perhaps most difficult of all to develop in old age a capacity to form loving human relationships with others if it atrophied in childhood.

If it is not possible to transform the situation overnight, however, it is still possible to do something in a much shorter-term sense to ease the emotional suffering and physical hardship endured by many old people and their kinsfolk. The medical profession, the occupational group most likely to come into contact with old people and well placed to gain their confidence, bears in particular a major responsibility for the way in which a community helps its elderly population. By listening to patients and their relatives, by appropriate referral to social service departments or voluntary organizations, by campaigning for greater resources for social services for the care of the elderly, doctors can be instrumental in helping to improve the quality of life of the elderly.

REFERENCES

Abrams M 1980 Beyond three score and ten. A 2nd Report on a Survey of the Elderly. Age Concern, London
Atkinson A B 1969 Poverty in Britain and the reform of social security. Cambridge University Press, Cambridge
Aves G 1969 The voluntary worker in the social services. Report of a committee of the National Council of Social Service and the National Institute for Social Work Training. Allen & Unwin, London
Beveridge W 1942 Social insurance and allied services. HMSO, London
Blaxter M 1976 The meaning of disability. Heinemann, London
Booth C 1894 The aged poor in England and Wales. Macmillan, London
Bradshaw J 1972 A taxonomy of social need. In: McLachlan G (ed) Problems and progress in medical care 7. Oxford University Press for Nuffield Provincial Hospitals Trust, London
Cartwright A, Hockey L, Anderson J L 1973 Life before death. Routledge and Kegan Paul, London
Central Statistical Office 1982 Social Trends 12
Department of Employment 1982 Family expenditure survey. HMSO, London
Department of Health & Social Security 1974 Social work support for the health service. Report of a working party. HMSO, London
Department of Health & Social Security 1975 Census of residential accommodation 1970. HMSO, London
Department of Health & Social Security 1976 Sharing resources for health in England. Report of the Resource Allocation Working Party. HMSO, London
Department of Health & Social Security 1977 Equal status for men and women in occupational pension schemes. Cmnd 6599. HMSO, London
Equal Opportunities Commission 1977 Sex equality and the pension age: a choice of routes. Limited mimeo edition. London
Isaacs B 1971 Studies of illness and death in the elderly in Glasgow. Scottish Home and Health Department, Edinburgh
Isaacs B, Livingstone M, Neville Y 1972 Survival of the unfittest. Routledge and Kegan Paul, London
Le Gros Clark F 1966 Work age and leisure. Michael Joseph, London
McKeown T 1976 The modern rise of population. Arnold, London
Marris P 1974 Loss and change. Routledge and Kegan Paul, London
Ministry of Pensions and National Insurance 1954 Report of the committee on the economic and financial problems of the provision for old age (Phillips Committee). Cmnd 9333. HMSO, London

Muir Gray J A 1980 Do we care too much for our elders? Lancet i: 1289–1291
Norman A J 1980 Rights and risks. National Corporation for the Care of Old People, London
Office of Population Censuses and Surveys 1974 Census 1971. Non-private households. HMSO, London
Office of Population Censuses and Surveys 1975 General household survey 1972. HMSO, London
Office of Population Censuses and Surveys 1978 The elderly at home. Hunt A, Government social survey. HMSO, London
Office of Population Censuses and Surveys 1979 General household survey 1977. HMSO, London
Office of Population Censuses and Surveys 1982 General household survey 1980. HMSO, London
Rowntree B S 1902 Poverty: a study of town life. Nelson, London
Royal Commission on the Aged Poor 1895 Report. Eyre and Spottiswoode for HMSO, London
Royal Commission on the Poor Laws 1809 Report. 2 vols. Cmnd 4499. HMSO, London
Sanford J R A 1975 Tolerance of debility in elderly dependants by supporters at home: its significance for hospital practice. British Medical Journal iii: 471–473
Shanas E, Townsend P, Wedderburn D, Friis H, Stenhouwer J, Milhj P 1968 Old people in three industrial societies. Routledge and Kegan Paul, London
Sheldon J H 1948 The social medicine of old age. Oxford University Press, London
South East Thames Regional Health Authority 1976 Report of a committee of inquiry into St Augustine's Hospital, Chartham, Canterbury. Limited mimeo edition. Croydon
Townsend P 1957 The family life of old people. Routledge and Kegan Paul, London
Townsend P 1962 The last refuge. Routledge and Kegan Paul, London
Townsend P, Wedderburn D 1965 The aged in the welfare state. Bell, London
Tunstall J 1966 Old and alone. Routledge and Kegan Paul, London
Wedderburn D 1967 Social security survey. New Society 263: 514
Widows Orphans and Old Age Contributory Pensions Act 1925
Willmott P, Young M 1960 Family and class in a London suburb. Routledge and Kegan Paul, London
Wright F 1977 Public expenditure cuts affecting services for disabled people. Disability Alliance, London

The geriatric service and the day hospital

INTRODUCTION

In this chapter it is intended to trace the general development of special medical services for elderly people, and then to examine the structure of these services in the United Kingdom. The effectiveness of geriatric services depends, of course, not only on the work which is done in hospitals but also on the way in which this work interlocks with that carried out by community and voluntary services. Care of old people can be seen first on a national scale, but the true picture is likely to be reflected in the care that is offered within a geographical community of from one to three hundred thousand people. Such care will depend on the effectiveness, the adequacy of provision and the degree of co-ordination of the services concerned.

Geriatric services have grown to a common pattern in the United Kingdom although there is still a good deal of regional variation in the expression of this pattern. It is interesting that in most of the European countries and in other developed societies similar forces have been at work moulding the shape of medical and social services for old people. The problems are basically the same and although some very differing ideologies underlie the way they are met, nevertheless, the structure of the services in the end emerges in many such countries with very great similarities (Brocklehurst, 1975). The geriatrician or physician in geriatric medicine has been an accepted specialist in the British National Health Service since the day of its inception. In many other countries the acceptability of such a specialty is still a matter for argument. Although the nomenclature used may vary nevertheless some countries such as Sweden, Holland and Denmark have accepted a specialist geriatric service as a normal branch of hospital medicine. Others such as France, Belgium and Australia show a great variation in different localities. In some areas there are practising geriatricians and in others the concept of such a specialty is still unacceptable.

HISTORY

In Great Britain the first generally accepted landmark, of community care for old people, is the Poor Relief Act of 1601, which established the responsibility of the local community (the Parish) for care of the poor, the chronic sick and the aged, and authorized it to raise money for this purpose, by the levying of a rate on all owners of property. The fact that the old were included with the chronic sick ('the lame, the blind, the halt and the impotent') and the poor, set a precedent which has continued ever since. The fortunes and misfortunes of the old throughout successive waves of legislation were identified with those of the poor. This became a matter of great misfortune during the mid-nineteenth century when, in the rigours of post-industrial revolution England, it seemed that the lot of the pauper was not hard enough in the face of the miseries of life outside the workhouse. A Royal Commission on the Poor Law was set up in 1832 under the Chairmanship of the Bishop of London and their report in 1834 embodied the principle of 'less eligibility'. This was described in the words of Chadwick, its secretary, as follows:

His situation on the whole shall not be made really or apparently so eligible as the situation of the independent labourer of the lowest class . . . every penny bestowed that tends to render the condition of the pauper more eligible than that of the independent labourer is a bounty on indolence and vice.

The measures that were intended to discourage the poor from seeking refuge in the workhouse also affected the old, and while it was realized that for 'the aged poor of good conduct', there should be some special provision, this was very often not made. Infirmaries attached to the workhouses gradually accumulated the aged and chronic sick. Their lot stirred the consciences of some citizens from time to time as in the *Lancet* report on conditions in workhouses and infirmaries in 1866, but throughout the nineteenth and first half of the twentieth centuries the workhouse remained a dreaded institution which was also, *faux de mieux*, the last refuge of many old people.

It was on this basis that geriatric medicine had its foundations. The burden of undiagnosed and untreated illness which Marjorie Warren found in such an institution in 1935 (see Warren, 1943, 1946, 1960) was subsequently discovered in other workhouse infirmaries by the pioneers of geriatric medicine. They showed that if proper medical management was applied to the unfortunate aged and chronic sick (patients who for the most part were permanently bedfast), then most were able to get up, the majority to become partially independent and many to leave the infirmary altogether. The importance of a proper assessment and some attempt at rehabilitative therapy for patients in these institutions slowly became established throughout the 1940s. Similar attention was given to those on the long waiting lists for many of these institutions. By seeing such old people in their homes it often became possible to initiate treatment and eliminate the necessity for admission to hospital at all. In many case home assessment allowed the rapid admission of those in urgent need and the later admission of those whose need was less urgent, and so the principle of assessment visiting of patients in their homes became established. More detailed accounts of this development may be found in the papers by Sheldon (1971) and Andrews (1971).

Thompson (1949) described in detail the condition of such infirmaries before they were transformed to geriatric departments. Writing of the Western Road Infirmary, Birmingham, a hospital with 1083 patients, of whom 983 were bedfast and 49 per cent incontinent, he noted that there were six doctors who in addition to looking after over a thousand patients had responsibility for 300 others in another place, and a venereal disease clinic. There were 226 nurses on the staff and the average staffing was two nurses at a time for 70 patients, but nevertheless there were only nine pressure sores. The mean length of stay for males was 34 months and for females 37 months. Thompson's touching description of the devotion of the nurses has become a classic of medical writing:

In their quiet endurance and their efficiency, as in their triumph over discouraging circumstances and lack of proper equipment, the nurses recalled the virtues of their fathers in the rank and file of the county regiments who held the trenches in Flanders in the campaigns of 1914–1918 and saved Europe.

Since then over 500 consultant geriatricians have been appointed to area geriatric services. There is now a specialist geriatric department in the majority of areas in the United Kingdom.

DEFINITION OF GERIATRICS

A question often asked is 'who is a geriatric patient?'

Regrettably at the present time there is no easy answer. Analogy with the specialty of paediatrics might suggest that any, and indeed all, patients aged 65 or 70 and over requiring admission to hospital are the concern of the geriatrician. Although many geriatricians see such a clearly age-defined specialty as the ultimate objective, this is hardly an acceptable definition at the present time, since one-third of all patients occupying hospital beds are aged 65 and over. These patients are distributed now as follows:

Geriatric wards	32 per cent
General medical wards	10 per cent
Other general hospital departments	21 per cent
Psychiatric hospitals and wards	37 per cent

Evans et al (1971) have suggested that geriatrics should be defined as the comprehensive care of the sick over the age of 75, the service being organized by a geriatrician whose role should involve both hospital and community care. They take 75 as a cut-off age following their survey, carried out in London, sampling the ages of patients admitted to different types of hospital accommodation. They found that in the 65 to 74 age group, two-thirds of the patients were admitted to a general hospital department and only one-fifth to geriatric departments, whereas beyond the age of 75, over half the patients were admitted to the geriatric department.

There are some good arguments in support of a hospital-based specialty for all patients beyond such an age as 70 or 75. (See Hodkinson and Jeffreys, 1972; O'Brien et al, 1973; Bagnall et al, 1977). This would involve a considerable expansion of the specialty. In 1981 there were 486 Consultant Geriatricians in post and a Department of Health and Social Security projection suggests a target of 800 by 1990 (DHSS, 1981).

In contrast to an age-based specialty is the concept of a geriatric department in which neither an upper nor a lower age limit is thought of, but where the specialty is defined according to the nature of the care which it has to offer. It would be neither age-related nor a system, organ, or instrument based specialty, but rather an organizational specialty in which the geriatrician provides a care complex whose primary objective is to meet and overcome breakdown in independent living among old people. Such breakdown is complex and is unique to the old. Ingredients tending to cause breakdown include:

— the decremental effects of aging, making the old person more susceptible to external events,
— the accumulation of pathologies, again leading to decrease in function,
— the untoward effects of many drugs which all too often contribute to breakdown
— underlying social deprivation.

Many old people live precariously in the community balancing these factors tending to cause breakdown by others which help them to maintain an equilibrium (Fig. 47.1). These include networks of support from neighbours, family and social services, such physical and mental competence as the old person has and in particular the innate desire present in most old people to retain independence as long as they possibly can. It is against this precarious equilibrium that breakdown occurs either by the addition of an acute or subacute medical problem to one side of the balance or the removal of a social support from the other. Thus medical conditions which in younger people could be reasonably combated at home, in the old may lead to gradual or sudden breakdown requiring action from the geriatric service. Similarly, loss of social support such as death of a spouse (or even increasingly commonly, the effects of burglary and vandalism, (Coakley and Woodford-Williams, 1979)) may tilt the balance.

Breakdown may occur suddenly, presenting with incontinence or confusion, or it may occur a number of days. The ultimate objective of the geriatric service, of course, is to prevent this breakdown but at the present time most of its efforts are directed towards dealing with it. To do this an organization has been evolved which provides for assessment (medical, nursing, social and functional), rehabilitation, continuing support in the community by day hospitals, planned short-term admissions etc and when independence cannot be restored, long-term hospital care.

Most geriatricians in the United Kingdom would probably see their work in the following terms:

1. The immediate admission of elderly patients from the community presenting with problems of extreme urgency, which may stem partly from a social element and partly from the breakdown of an unstable equilibrium in health, contributed to by more than one pathological process.

2. The assessment of patients with similar but less urgent problems either in their own homes or at an outpatient consultative clinic.

3. The continuing management of physically disabling disease in old age, through stages of rehabilitation both in hospital and in a day hospital, and perhaps indefinite support in the community thereafter.

4. The long-term care of old people who are so physically disabled as to be unable to maintain an independent life in the community.

5. The short-term admission of elderly patients for 'holiday' purposes which is basically for the relief of relatives' strain.

6. The transfer of patients from other hospitals' departments, either for rehabilitation or long-term care.

7. Participation in co-operative medical care with one or more of the following departments — psychiatry, younger disabled, orthopaedics, stroke rehabilitation.

These terms include patients aged less than 65, but the majority of such patients are certainly likely to be in the 75 and over age group.

Sanford (1975) showed that 12 per cent of geriatric admissions were for people whose relatives could no longer cope with them at home. He categorized the main reasons for this, and the extent to which these different reasons could be tolerated by relatives. Sleep disturbance headed the list — occurring in 62 per cent of cases and being tolerated in only 16 per cent, while incontinence of urine occurring in 54 per cent had a tolerance rate of 81 per cent. Personality conflicts and social restrictions were also important reasons for admission. For instance, inability to leave the dependant for one hour occurred in 28 per cent but had a high tolerance rate (71 per cent).

As an all-embracing, general definition of geriatric medicine, that of the British Geriatrics Society cannot be improved upon. It is as follows:

Geriatrics is the branch of general medicine concerned with the clinical, preventative, remedial and social aspects of illness in the elderly.

Geriatric and general medicine

The common ground lying between the clinical content of geriatric medicine and general internal medicine has

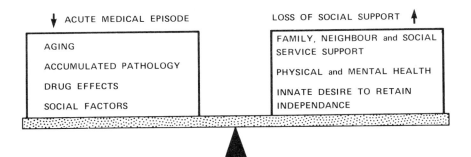

Fig. 47.1 The precarious equilibrium maintained by many old people in the community — and some causes of breakdown

over recent years led to much thought and discussion as to the boundaries. Geriatric medicine has moved from a state of waiting lists to one of responding immediately to breakdown and so to providing an emergency service. General medicine on the other hand has become increasingly specialized on a system and organ basis, many specialists retaining their only basis in general medicine in dealing with medical emergencies. The main area of overlap, therefore, has been in relation to emergencies and in many districts this is now solved by the two departments agreeing on an age related policy for emergency admissions. This has led to the proposal made by a working party of the Royal College of Physicians (1977), that geriatricians and general physicians should share one group of acute wards. The logical outcome of this would be that while the general physicians have their specialist interests the geriatrician would be a general physician with special responsibility for the elderly. This means that while sharing medical emergencies, the geriatrician is the specialist in the management of complex breakdown in old age, rehabilitation, day care and long term care. Burley et al (1979) showed that the attachment of a geriatrician to a group of general physicians was very quickly followed by an improved turnover among elderly people admitted to such a unit.

Isaacs (1969) has defined differences between geriatric and general medical referrals and notes that patients referred to geriatric wards were on the whole much older, more of them were widowed, more lived alone, more were in poor housing and more were in social class V.

He also found that strokes were equally common in both departments but that, in geriatric referrals, falls were three times more common, immobility five times, incontinence six times and mental abnormality 10 times more common.

Isaacs (1971) categorizes the reasons for admission of patients to a geriatric ward into four groups:

therapeutic optimism
medical urgency
basic care
relief of strain

He envisages the geriatrician faced with a request to admit a patient to hospital asking himself four questions — as follows:

1. 'Is it likely that if this patient is admitted to hospital and treated, he can be sent home again within a period of about three months?' If the answer to this is 'yes', then the patient is admitted under the category 'therapeutic optimism'.

2. 'Does the patient require to enter hospital as a matter of medical urgency, even if it is unlikely he will return home again?' If the answer is 'yes', then this is the group of 'medical urgency'.

3. 'Does the patient need hospital admission because he fails to receive sufficient basic care?' If 'yes', he is admitted for 'basic care'.

4. 'Does the patient require admission in order to relieve intolerable strain on relatives — this is a burden of care arising from the patient's illness, threatening the physical and or mental well being of the relatives?' If the answer to this is 'yes', then the patient is admitted for 'relief of strain'.

PROBLEMS OF HOSPITALIZATION AND DISCHARGE

Admission to hospital is not without its hazards for elderly people. This was well demonstrated by Rosin and Boyd (1964) who examined complications arising in geriatric patients after they had been admitted to hospital. They found that in 70 per cent of cases some complication arose. While half of these were a direct consequence of the illness causing admission, the other half were incidental, not related to the illness, but were rather occasioned by the stay in hospital itself. These included respiratory infection developing in 16 per cent of patients, falls in 15 per cent (most of these being associated with the illness causing admission), untoward drug reactions in 8 per cent and pressure sores in 12 per cent.

These complications depend on two main factors. One is that when old people are admitted to hospital either on a short-term or longer-term basis they are at that very time deteriorating in their health, and complications arising after admission must be expected. The other concerns the real hazards present in a hospital environment, particularly for an old person who has been isolated from contact with other people for many years and lived in a very limited and protected environment. The environmental change involved in such a move is fraught with problems of re-adjustment and likely to produce mental confusion. The hospital ward may be a hot-bed of infection compared to the isolated room in which the patient may have lived for many years; in addition the beds may be more difficult to get out of, furniture less sturdy to get hold of and so falls more likely. For these reasons special furniture and equipment are needed in geriatric wards.

A great deal of thought and research has been directed towards the problems which arise when elderly patients are discharged from hospital. This is perhaps the most critical time in the patient's progress through the geriatric department. Many emotional and social factors conflict with each other, some tending to prevent discharge, others to facilitate it and others related to the need for close continuing care when the patient goes home. Nisbet (1970) examined the attitudes of 50 female patients discharged home from a geriatric ward. She found that only 15 were really happy to be leaving hospital and that 16 were positively reluctant to leave. Twelve were returning to live alone, and four previously alone were going to live with relatives. In only nine cases could it be said that the relatives were genuinely pleased to have the old people back. The fact that many elderly people leave hospital with very mixed feelings, venturing out of a situation of security back to one which had previously been disastrous, indicates the need for very much greater provision of residential hostel accommodation for such patients where they may retain the security which they cling to but at the same time leave the hospital environment.

Brocklehurst and Shergold (1968) followed up 200 patients, consecutive discharges from two geriatric departments. They found that 93 per cent of the patients went back to the same type of accommodation (i.e. private household or residential home) as they were admitted from. Of those who returned to live with relatives this return was judged unwelcome in 21 per cent. This applied to only 5 per cent of those going to live with spouse alone, but rose to 25 per cent of those going to live with a married child, and 39 per cent of those going to live with an unmarried child. These attitudes were no doubt the result of long continued strain and stress prior to admission, the stress in turn being due to illness, physical disability, incontinence and mental confusion.

In view of these problems arising at the time of discharge it is remarkable that so few relatives positively refuse to receive their elderly parent or aunt back to their homes (see Isaacs, 1971).

These stressful situations, which may well be largely unique to elderly people leaving hospital, increase the importance of a careful discharge policy. All services which are likely to be needed for the patient's return home must be firmly arranged with the individuals concerned, and both the general practitioner and the patient's family know exactly what to expect and what has to be done. The fact that a great deal of the benefit of hospital treatment is lost because of neglect of these discharge arrangements has been well documented. Skeet's book *Home from Hospital* (1971) surveys arrangements made for patients leaving hospital in the United Kingdom. Only a minority of these were coming from geriatric wards and there is little doubt that more adequate arrangements are made within the geriatric department than in other departments discharging elderly people. Skeet found that less than one-third of discharged patients aged 65 and over were asked by the hospital about their domestic arrangements, that over half the home helps arranged for old people either failed to come back after the first morning, or came infrequently. The same problem has been investigated in

Liverpool and the appointment of after-care co-ordinators recommended as the best way of overcoming the serious deficiencies in care which were uncovered (Age Concern, Liverpool, 1975). Brocklehurst and Shergold (1969) found that 37 per cent of patients discharged from two geriatric units had no contact with their general practitioner during the first month after leaving hospital.

It seems beyond doubt that many patients are discharged home by geriatricians only because there is no alternative residential hostel accommodation to which they can go, and because they must leave hospital to make way for the even more ill and suffering elderly people waiting to come in. This shortage of resources in the United Kingdom is emphasized in studies such as that by Shanas and colleagues ('Old people in three industrial societies', 1968). This shows among other things that the proportion of elderly people in institutions in England and Wales is lower than in both America and Denmark. It is well known that the same applies in relation to Sweden and many other European countries.

Discharge arrangements

What attempts have been made to overcome these problems arising on discharge? One of the most important is the provision of geriatric day hospitals (see below). There is little doubt that where a day hospital is available the old person feels more security at the time of discharge — particularly if the day hospital has also served as the rehabilitation inpatient unit and the patient knows she will come back to the same place and to the same therapists in whom she already has confidence.

Another important method is to hold regular case conferences involving doctors, hospital and domiciliary nurses and hospital and community social workers in which the needs of all patients about to leave hospital may be discussed. To be successful these need to be held once weekly; it is essential that each inpatient is discussed and clear agreement is arrived at as to who will be responsible for taking action on decisions made. Such case conferences bring the community and hospital workers together, allow a feed-back of information about patients who have been discharged and altogether offer perhaps the most useful *milieu* for fruitful liaison.

A third method is to have community nurses or health visitors attached to the geriatric department who will personally follow up each patient discharged from that department. This may involve visiting the patient's home before discharge and then keeping in touch until the situation appears stable, particularly with regard to provision of domiciliary services. The extent to which geriatric patients leaving home require such services has been emphasized by Wilson and Wilson (1971) who found that 98 per cent needed one or more social services, the heaviest demand being for home nursing, and also by Brocklehurst and Shergold (1969). Reference has already been made to the proposal to appoint after-care co-ordinators in all hospitals from which patients aged 60 and above are discharged (Age Concern, Liverpool, 1975).

Variations of these methods which attempt to secure a smooth passage of the elderly person home from hospital are becoming generally implemented in the Kingdom. Looking to the future, however, it may well be that this kind of work could be more successfully supervised by a worker based within the community health centre. Again this might be a health visitor who would take over the patient before she actually left hospital.

Re-admission

Inevitably there will be a high re-admission rate among geriatric patients leaving hospital. They are old and their illnesses are likely to have a continuing basis so that even with the best of follow-up services relapse requiring re-admission will occur. It is indeed a feature of hospital geriatric practice that the clinician gets to know a number of his patients very well throughout a series of admissions and their day-hospital attendance in between these times. Nisbet (1970) showed a re-admission rate of 48 per cent within the first year of patients discharged from her department. Silver and Zuberi (1965) gave a figure of 44 per cent and Rosin and Eddison (1964) found 33 per cent re-admitted within 6 months. None of these geriatric departments had a day hospital at the time of the various surveys. The usefulness of a day hospital in preventing re-admission is therefore well demonstrated by comparing these figures with those of Brocklehurst and Shergold (1969) who found that a total of only 26 per cent of their discharged patients were readmitted within a year. Thirty-seven per cent of patients in this series attended a day hospital after discharge and very many fewer of these patients required re-admission.

Intermittent admissions

The idea of intermittent admissions was first described by Delargy in his paper on 'Six weeks in, six weeks out' (1960). The effect of this was also examined by Isaacs and Thompson (1960) who indicated a risk in such hospital admission — one in five under age 74 and one in three over that age deteriorated or died in hospital. They stressed, however, the beneficial effects in the majority of patients.

Since that time the policy of planned intermittent admissions has been widely developed both in geriatric practice and in residential old peoples' homes. The programme in Oxford was reviewed in detail by Robertson et al (1977). They divided intermittent admissions into three types — a) 'the floating bed' for a three day–two night admission, usually every two weeks, b) intermittent readmission for longer periods (e.g. seven days each three months) and c) holiday admissions, usually for two weeks pre-arranged to coincide with the timing of the carer's holidays. They reviewed 50 patients in one or other of these programmes. The major diagnosis and cause of disability was stroke and while their study was uncontrolled and therefore was limited in its usefulness, it was clear that the primary care teams and the patient's carers in particular were very satisfied with the arrangements.

THE STRUCTURE OF A GERIATRIC SERVICE

While each geriatric department in the United Kingdom differs from others in minor particulars there is a common pattern found throughout most of them; a similar pattern is found in many geriatric departments in other European countries. This pattern follows a form of progressive patient care (see Exton-Smith (1962) and Brocklehurst (1975). The admission of the patient to hospital is very often preceded by a pre-admission assessment carried out by the consultant or a senior member of his medical staff either in the patient's home or at an outpatients' consultative clinic. Such pre-admission assessment visits to patients at home allow not only an appraisal of the urgency of admission (which is particularly relevant if the department has a waiting list) but also it gives the clinician an opportunity of getting a good history from relatives or neighbours which is frequently not available (because of deafness, dysphasia or confusion) once the patient is in hospital. The geriatrician sees the type of accommodation that the patient comes from and is thus assisted in planning future care. It also allows him to discuss the likely pattern of care with the patient's relatives, so that they may be informed of the probability of discharge home in due course. This helps to avoid misunderstanding later on. The assessment visit also allows the consultant to suggest other types of care (such as attending the day hospital or the outpatient department) which may obviate the need for admission.

The inpatient beds themselves may be divided into three stages — assessment, rehabilitation and long-stay care. It is the custom to admit all patients to the assessment wards in the first place (with the exception of patients transferred from other hospital departments who have already been fully medically investigated). In the assessment ward a complete medical investigation is carried out and the treatment of acute conditions initiated. Social factors are examined and a programme mapped out for the patient's further treatment. Many patients are able to go home or to community accommodation directly from assessment wards. A few clearly need long-term care and can be transferred to the long-stay wards. Others will be transferred to the rehabilitation wards. Patients are likely to remain in assessment wards for an average of 14 days. The whole accent of care here is medical. The ward rounds are essentially medical procedures carried out in the traditional pattern.

Rehabilitation

Rehabilitation wards receive patients who need more prolonged physical treatment. It is a great advantage if the rehabilitation department is linked with the day hospital. Patients from the rehabilitation wards can then go to the rehabilitation department and day hospital complex early in the morning, can have their midday meal there and remain until the late afternoon. Their treatment programmes can then be scheduled along with those of patients coming from their own homes.

The length of stay in a rehabilitation ward is likely to be in the region of 8 to 12 weeks — although the range is wide. From rehabilitation wards, patients will go back home and to other forms of care in the community, including sheltered housing and residential homes. Others, despite some improvement, will not achieve sufficient independence to live in the community either with relatives or in a residential home, and these often then must move on to the third stage of progressive care, that of long-term or continuing care.

The subject of rehabilitation is considered in detail in chapter 24.

Continuing or long-term care

It is the usual practice for long-stay hospital beds to be in separate wards and sometimes in separate hospitals from the assessment and rehabilitation beds, and this is generally accepted as the right policy. There are some geriatricians, however, who take the view that patients requiring long-term care should be looked after in small numbers in all geriatric wards and indeed some would say in all hospital wards (see Adams, 1968).

The requirements of long-stay hospital patients are so basically different from those of patients undergoing medical assessment and rehabilitation that their distribution among all types of hospital wards can only be for the convenience of nurses and certainly not in the interests of continuing care patients themselves. Elderly people who are going to spend the last two or three years of their lives in hospital require special accommodation and specially motivated staff every bit as much as those who are looked after in residential homes. In fact continuing care wards have much more in common with residential homes thna they have with the more acute hospital wards, and it has been regretted that recent legislation in the United Kingdom should have continued the separate management of residential care in and outside hospital.

It must be realized that long-term care geriatric patients are not necessarily dying patients. They are people who require the constant attendance of nurses because of their disability, and for whom such assistance is available only in hospital. Nisbet (1967) has analysed the length of time spent in hospital by such patients and found that the percentage survival at the end of one, two and three years for females was 52 per cent, 41 per cent and 34 per cent respectively, while for males the figures were 31 per cent, 18 per cent and 9 per cent. Thus for one-third of the female patients continuing care means a period of more than three years. Experience elsewhere suggests that long term care may now be a good deal shorter than that. Hodkinson and Hodkinson (1981) reported on all patients who remained in their geriatric unit for more than 6 months and who comprised 5.6 per cent of total geriatric admissions. At the end of 2 years only 20 per cent of this original cohort remained in hospital. The great majority of the remainder (88 per cent) had died. In the majority of these cases, the process of dying will only occupy the last week or two of this period. This simply emphasizes the need to provide proper facilities for continuing care patients, so that they may be sat out of bed, that they may be dressed, and that where possible they should be independent in wheelchairs. The accommodation they live in should provide therefore separate places for sleeping, for dining and for recreation together with access to a garden.

Nursing in long-term care wards is a special vocation for which little specific training is at present available. The responsibility of the nurse was emphasized in a joint publication between the British Geriatrics Society and the Royal College of Nursing — Improving Geriatric Care in Hospital (Royal College of Nursing, 1975). Specific measures which had been successfully used in implementing these proposals in Exeter were described by Cruise et al (1978).

It is clear, however, that the quality of life in long term care wards is not the sole responsibility of the nurses. Increasingly, Activities Organizers are being appointed to develop recreational services both within the wards and in special recreational centres. These include concerts, tea parties, films and opportunities to leave the hospital in visits to local shops or to the homes of local citizens. Adult education classes are also being set up increasingly in hospitals — patients enrolling just as they would in a separate institution. Painting, modelling, craft work and music are all popular (see Poulden, 1975; Bright, 1972, 1981). Other activities include group psychotherapy (Cordiner and Wilson, 1982) and reality orientation programmes (Woods and Holden, 1982).

The particular needs of long term geriatric patients have been reviewed by Elliot (1975), Central Health Services Council (1976), Brocklehurst (1977a, b) and by several contributors in Denham (1983).

An experiment is being carried out by the Department of Health and Social Security at the present time with so called 'National Health Nursing Homes'. These are to be purposely designed or adapted buildings for long term care of patients where the role of the geriatrician will be largely confined to assessment and to selection of patients requiring long-term care and the management of patients in the nursing home will be entirely in the hands of of nurses.

Other developments include an experiment in Oxford where two community hospitals providing intermittent and long term care are managed entirely by general practitioners who are responsible for their own patients (Griffiths and Willcock, 1981).The crux of the matter, here, as with the National Health Service Nursing Home is that selection of patients for admission is carried out by the geriatrician. Patients thus have every opportunity of full medical, functional and social assessment and rehabilitation before moving into long term care.

The relatives' conference
A realization of the profound physical and emotional problems confronting relatives of elderly people who have become disabled and particularly those suffering from stroke has led to the development of a form of group therapy for such relatives which is usually called 'The relatives' conference'. Hawker (1964) described the shape of such a conference at Edgware General Hospital in London and this can probably be claimed as the pioneer experiment. The conference is chaired by a member of the medical staff; it includes various therapists and patients' relatives. Patients themselves may be present throughout the whole or part of the conference, and others involved, particularly community nursing and social workers, may also attend. The conference is held regularly and it allows both instruction in methods of assisting handicapped elderly people, given by the therapists, and also mutual discussion among the relatives with a mutual sharing of their problems. The subject is reviewed by Leeming and Luke (1977).

Special units within the geriatric service
Over the last 15 to 20 years a gradual specialization within rehabilitation has become evident and in departments of geriatric medicine this has been reflected, particularly in the development of orthopaedic geriatric and stroke rehabilitation units. Both of these may be associated with involvement of the geriatrician at a very early stage in fracture of the femur, amputation and stroke. Their particular advantage is that all staff

involved (physician, nurse, therapists, social worker) may accept and develop similar techniques and approaches and so the whole of a patient's treatment throughout 24 hours a day is consistent. Such units achieve special enthusiasm among their staff members and promote better understanding and communication with patients. Their effectiveness is still being studied. The subject is considered further in Chapter 51.

The younger disabled
The problems of younger disabled people, particularly those needing long-term care in hospital, have been the cause of a great deal of concern and political action in the United Kingdom in the past 15 years. The problems were explored in detail by a working party set up under the auspices of 'The National Fund for Crippling Diseases', whose findings were published in two major reports (Bradley, 1967; and 'At home or in hospital', 1968). This working party also undertook a fact-finding survey in Edinburgh and Exeter (Pearson et al, 1970) and at the same time a major survey of the prevalence of disability was undertaken on behalf of the Department of Health and Social Security (Harris, 1971). Harris's report showed that out of a total population of 54 million, 1 129 000 people were handicapped to such a degree that they needed some support, and 157 000 of these were so severely handicapped that they needed special care. Harris showed that the great majority of these handicapped people were aged 75 years and over (73 per cent of the very severely handicapped and 64 per cent of the total number of disabled people). However, appreciable numbers were younger and some of them much younger.

There had been no special provision made under the National Health Service for the care of these patients. As mentioned in the historical introduction to this chapter, most of them shared their fate with the poor and the aged and so found their homes in workhouse infirmaries and in the chronic sick wards of general hospitals. They thus gradually became the responsibility of physicians appointed as consultant geriatricians and in many cases physical facilities in the wards did not allow separate accommodation for them. A major piece of legislation (the Chronically Sick and Disabled Persons' Act, 1970) has now mandated the provision of special units for younger long term patients and these are slowly being built, generally on the campus of district general hospitals. In some cases these are likely to be under the general supervision of the geriatrician but they are not truly part of the geriatric service.

THE DAY HOSPITAL

The development of day hospitals as adjuncts to inpatient

care has been a striking feature of British geriatric practice in the last decade. The first purpose-built day hospital was opened at Cowley Road, Oxford, in 1958; it had been preceded by the reception of day patients within hospital geriatric departments in that hospital and in a number of others. Day hospitals are now found associated with the majority of geriatric departments. The development of the day hospital movement in Great Britain, including psychiatric and geriatric day hospitals, together with· day centres was reviewed by Ferndale in 1961, Brocklehurst (1970, 1973) and Brocklehurst and Tucker (1980). The wider issues of adult day care (including day hospitals and social day centres) have been reviewed by Carter (1981). The position in the United States is considered in the report *Adult Day Care* (National Centre for Health Services Research, 1975).

There are several reasons why day hospitals have been developed and have proved so popular in such a short period of time. In the first place they are an attempt to dissociate the investigational and therapeutic aspect of hospital treatment from the hotel aspect which so often requires patients to be looked after at night time and throughout weekend, when no investigation or treatment is being carried out. This is a desirable change from many patients' point of view and also is economically worthwhile. Further, since the day hospital maintains 'office hours' it appeals to many nurses who might otherwise be lost to the profession. The day hospital allows a close and prolonged supervision of patients suffering from chronic disease who if cut off completely from hospital care would almost certainly deteriorate and require re-admission.

Although it is hard to prove that a day hospital saves inpatient beds, there seems on the face of it little doubt that this is the case and there is some evidence to confirm it in Brocklehurst and Shergold's (1969) study of geriatric patients leaving hospital, some of whom were day hospital attenders and others not. Woodford-Williams and her colleagues (1962) and Brocklehurst (1964) give further evidence that the presence of a day hospital diminished the number of inpatient days and allowed earlier discharge from hospital.

In defining a geriatric day hospital it is necessary in the first place to distinguish it from a day centre for old people (see Anderson, 1972; Morley, 1974; Central Council for Education and Training in Social Work report, 1975; Eastman, 1976; Carter, 1981); the latter provides social facilities, a midday meal and a variety of amenities such as hairdressing, bathing and chiropody, but it is not part of the hospital service, its staff does not include doctors, nurses and therapists and it does not provide medical investigation or treatment. A geriatric day hospital on the other hand is essentially a place that provides therapy, most prominently rehabilitation and physical maintenance treatment. It also provides for the medical investigation and nursing treatment of elderly people. Where it does undertake the function of social care this is for the physically disabled or mentally disordered for whom such care involves the services of nurses. One feature common to both the geriatric day hospital and day centre is that both require transport facilities for bringing patients to them. Neither can exist without adequate and regular transport services. The geriatric day hospital is generally situated alongside the inpatient rehabilitation department and in many day hospitals in the United Kingdom, the facilities provided are shared between both day patients coming from their homes and inpatients coming from the geriatric rehabilitation wards. This is obviously a pattern providing for the greatest economy in use of both facilities and therapists. It is also a great advantage for inpatients to know when they are being discharged that they will be able to continue coming on a day basis to the same department and meeting the same therapists whom they already know. This is an important feature in bridging the very vulnerable gap between hospital and home and it may require attendance at the day hospital for only a few weeks to ensure that this bridge has been successfully crossed.

The functions of a geriatric day hospital

The functions of a geriatric day hospital are listed in Table 47.1 which also illustrates the relative value which geriatricians subjectively alloted to each of the categories in 1970. Since that time the development of psychogeriatric day hospitals providing social care for the mentally confused has emphasized the 'somatic' function of the geriatric day hospital. The proportion of patients attending for these different purposes is shown in Table 47.2 and this indicates, as might be expected, that the reason for attendance at the time of referral may be very different to that at a later time. In general, the main functions may be briefly described as follows:

Table 47.1 Opinions of 90 consultant geriatricians in the UK as to the relative importance of various activities in their day hospitals (Brocklehurst, 1970)

	Very important %	Little or no importance %
Physical rehabilitation	89	3
Physical maintenance	78	2
Social care of physically disa disabled	50	13
Medical or nursing procedures	36	26
Social care of mentally confused	21	35

Table 47.2 Reason for day hospital attendance. First column — Reason for referral by consultant (Brocklehurst and Tucker, 1980) (456 new patients). Second column — Reason for attendance of a random selection of patients at 30 day hospitals (233 patients). Third column — from Brocklehurst 1970.

	Reason for referral	Reason for attendance	1970 survey
Rehabilitation	53	43	27
Assessment	20	0	0
Maintenance	11	21	42
Social and relatives' relief	5	17	26
Medical and nursing supervision	8	19	5

(All figures %)

Rehabilitation. This may be continued from a period of in patient admission or may be provided from an early stage at the day hospital (for instance in patients with mild moderate strokes who may be treated at the day hospital without previous hospital admission).

Assessment. Assessment of function (physical, psychological, social) is an integral and continuing part of geriatric practice. Such assessments may form a periodic component of rehabilitation. However, numbers of patients are referred to day hospitals specifically for functional assessment usually by an occupational therapist, in relation to their ability to cope in their domiciliary environment Assessment and rehabilitation are therefore closely related and in a recent survey accounted between them for almost three quarters of day hospital referrals (see Table 47.2).

Maintenance. Since rehabilitation anticipates improvement there must come a time when patients reach their optimum level of functioning and so rehabilitation is at an end. Some old people will manage to maintain the level of functioning they have achieved by their own efforts aided sometimes by their relatives. Others, however, will continue to deteriorate if all contact with physical therapy is withdrawn and this may be because they lack confidence at home or because their carers are over protective. Maintenance treatment at the day hospital involves attendance once or more often a week to 'top up' with physical therapy and maintain an optimal level of physical functioning.

Social reasons. These are usually attendances arranged to relieve the carers and to maintain the stability of the patient and his carers at home. Old people who are not disabled should receive this type of care at a social day centre. However the most demanding patients are those who need assistance with personal care and hygiene and who may have problems with continence and balance. For them the facilities of a day hospital are required.

Medical and nursing procedures. These include medical and nursing observations and the management of therapy. Patients, of course, should not attend day hospitals primarily for such procedures if they can equally well be carried out at home and if there is no other reason for the patient's attendance. Some medical/social emergencies may be dealt with at the day hospital obviating the need for inpatient admission (see Pathy, 1969).

Number of places required
The Department of Health and Social Security (DHSS) allows two geriatric day hospital places and two psychogeriatric day places for every 1000 people aged 65 and over in the catchment area served by these services (DHSS, 1972). It may be that these figures are over generous (Pathy, 1969; Brocklehurst and Tucker 1980). It is generally agreed that geriatric and psychogeriatric day hospitals should be separate although they may share some services.

Characteristics of patients attending day hospitals
The diagnostic categories, age groups, social features and duration of attendance of geriatric day hospital patients have been analysed by Brocklehurst (1970). About one-third suffer from stroke and a further third from disease of the locomotor system (principally arthritis but also a small number of patients with fracture of the femur). The larger number of the remainder suffered from the chronic brain syndrome in one or other of its manifestations.

Among the younger patients, stroke is the principal diagnosis and is indeed the commonest reason for attendance in those under 80 years. Over that age the chronic brain syndrome and arthritis become the more frequent diagnoses and these patients attend mainly for maintenance or social reasons. Very often they continue attending until they are either admitted to hospital or become ill and die at home. Much larger numbers of the stroke patients on the other hand are able to be discharged at the completion of a successful course of treatment. The patients are of course very dependent. In one survey reported by Brocklehurst (1970) 13 per cent were wheelchair patients.

The great majority of geriatric day patients come on 1 or 2 days a week (47 per cent 1 day and 41 per cent 2 days — Brocklehurst and Tucker, 1980). A very small proportion attend 4 or 5 days a week and these mainly for rehabilitation. The duration of attendance varies considerably between different day hospitals and many elderly patients have more than one period of attendance. Brocklehurst and Tucker's survey (1980) showed that 39 per cent had attended for up to 3 months, 17 per cent between 3 and 6 months and 43 per cent for longer than 6 months. Therefore, for many patients the day hospital provides a moderately long-term solution to their management.

Transport

Adequate transport is a *sine qua non* of geriatric day care. Ideally day hospital patients should come in well-heated vehicles with comfortable individual seats to which they can be safely strapped and from which they can have a good view of the passing scene. These matters are important because some of the patients are likely to spend upward of an hour in the vehicle on each journey and in any case for most patients this will represent their only excursion from the enclosure of their homes and so the journey itself is likely to be of great interest to them. A vehicle may carry six to ten passengers and requires to be equipped with a lift which will take both disabled people and patients in wheelchairs. Unfortunately the majority of vehicles used are 'multipurpose' — that is they are equipped with stretchers etc. to cope with emergencies, have frosted windows and are unsuitable for transporting day patients (Brocklehurst and Tucker, 1980).

Transport schedules should be regular so that patients arrive at times when the therapists expect them and so that they leave on time at the end of the day. The driver and other crew members are important people in the day hospital team; their attitude towards the patients will colour the success of the day hospital. They must be tolerant and encouraging and also able to report reasons for non-attendance of individual patients to the day hospital staff. Ambulance crews are divided equally between those who enjoy this work and those who do not, (Brocklehurst and Tucker, 1980).

Problems posed for the ambulance service by the mushrooming demands of geriatric and psychogeriatric day hospitals are discussed by Buckley (1978). Transport provided by relatives is exceptional.

The dependence of the whole enterprise on transport has been well illustrated by Prinsley (1971) who showed that when the ambulance service was disrupted as a result of industrial action for a period of five weeks, 39 per cent of the geriatric day patients whose attendance was thus interrupted deteriorated appreciably and many extra hospital admissions resulted.

Medical supervision

The importance of medical supervision cannot be overemphasized. The day hospital is in all respects similar to an inpatient ward and requires the daily attendance of medical staff, together with regular review of all patients by the consultant geriatrician. This is often best carried out as a case conference in which therapists, nurses and social workers participate. To maintain a dynamic function the day hospital must discharge patients in the same way as assessment and rehabilitation wards must do. This therefore requires the closest regular medical surveillance. Discharge is greatly facilitated if adequate social day centres are available in the area to which patients may be transferred. If these are not available then discharge will often amount to banishment of the patient back to his social isolation which he will regard even more bitterly than before, having become used to the companionship and support of the day hospital.

Cost

Day hospitals do not necessarily provide a cheaper alternative to inpatient care although this is so in the majority of cases. Account has to be taken of the number of days per week the patient visits the day hospital and the various services and other costs resulting from his spending the other days at home, including those involved in maintaining the home. Many of these are directly financed by the state — for instance meals-on-wheels, home helps, home nursing, heating allowance, rent allowance and many other possible payments. The cost of maintaining an older person at home was described by Opit (1977) who showed that even without day hospital attendance there may be little financial advantage. A mean daily cost and range of costs for eleven day hospitals were calculated by Brocklehurst and Tucker (1980). They showed that including the cost of transport this was £13.57, a figure which approached closely that of an independent study in Glasgow (MacFarlane et al, 1981) where a figure of £13.70 was arrived at. Both of these studies were carried out in 1978 when the average cost of long term care in a geriatric bed was £13.77 per day (Health Service Costing Returns, 1977/78). The day hospital may obviate the need for admission and in some circumstances may prevent long term care. In many of these cases money will be saved to the state. Even when this is not so many patients will welcome the opportunity of retaining their independence at home rather than being institutionalied.

The training of a physician in geriatric medicine

In the United Kingdom the Royal Colleges of Physicians and the British Geriatrics Society agree that training for the specialist geriatrician (as for other medical specialists) should fall into two stages. The first, to be undertaken for three or four years immediately after registration, should be spent principally in internal medicine with some experience in related specialties, such as neurology, psychiatry, physical medicine, pathology and general practice. This period of training would culminate in the passing of the membership examination of a Royal College of Physicians. The second period of training which would also last for three to four years would be in geriatric medicine itself with opportunities for travel and research.

Training programmes have been laid down in other countries where the specialties of geriatrics or long-term care have been recognized: thus in Sweden, after registration, training would consist of 2 years in internal medicine, 2 years in geriatrics and 6 months in psychiatry. The subject is reviewed by Isaacs (1964) and Brocklehurst (1974 and 1977c).

Geriatric nursing

To say that sufficient numbers of well-trained nurses are an essential part of a geriatric department is to state the obvious. The Society of Clinical Psychiatrists report (1971) states clearly this important principle:

the number of inpatients should be geared to the staff available rather than the beds available.

The work of the nurses in hospital geriatric departments has been the subject of a considerable amount of analysis (Norton et al, 1962; Adams and McIlwraith, 1963; the report, 'Development of Services for the Elderly and Elderly Confused', South East Met. Regional Hospital Board, 1971; and the British Medical Association working party report, 1976). All are agreed that nursing in geriatric wards equals and often exceeds in quantity that required in general wards, and the recommended norms of staff are that there should be one nurse to 1.25 patients in geriatric wards (with reduction in the time of the working week this should now be 1 : 1.15). This allows for 24-hour cover including sickness and holidays and includes the ward sister, staff nurses, enrolled nurses and nursing aides but excludes domestic staff. Nevertheless many hospitals continue to admit and attempt to care for more patients than their nursing resources can possibly cope with. This policy can only lead to disaster in the end, and is to be resisted.

Special post-basic courses in geriatric nursing should lead to better understanding and practice, once sufficient geriatric nurses have experienced these courses (Joint Board of Clinical Nursing Studies, 1972 and 1976).

Co-ordination of care for old people

Medical and community care for old people in developed societies is now so complex that inevitably it must involve the work of different agencies and is likely to be financed from different sources. In the United Kingdom there are three main bodies concerned, the local authority through its department of social work, the health service through its general practitioner and hospital services, and voluntary services. These are likely to be more or less organized together in different areas.

Each health service district now has a Health Care Planning Team for the Elderly and planning and co-ordination are its responsibilities.

Voluntary work is channelled by Age Concern through more than 1100 committees in England and Wales. These groups offer a further forum for co-ordination (Roberts, 1970; Age Concern, England, 1977).

One area in which difficulty often arises is in distinguishing between a long-stay geriatric patient needing hospital care and an elderly person who could be looked after in a residential home.

Over the past 25 years the level of disability of residents in old people homes has increased to such extent that there is now a considerable overlap between such homes and geriatric long stay wards, (McLauchlan and Wilkins, 1982). A study was carried out in Leicestershire which is broadly representative of UK, to compare the status of old people in different types of institutions. The authors (Clarke et al, 1979) surveyed every person 65 and over in Leicestershire who was in any form of institutional care during one night in 1976. This comprised 4 per cent of the over 65's. 42 per cent were in National Health Service establishments (17 per cent geriatric, 16 per cent psychiatric, 9 per cent general wards), 50 per cent were in residential homes (statutory, voluntary and private) and 8 per cent in hostels for the mentally ill. Those assessed as heavily dependent on other people were 43 per cent of the hospitalized patients and 14 per cent of the residents in old peoples' homes. However, the staff of these homes only regarded half of this 14 per cent as being inappropriately placed (and the staff's attitude is clearly based on the feeling that people who have lived in a home for some years should be allowed to continue there even when they become dependent). This degree of dependency of old people in residential homes suggests either that more of them should be transferred to geriatric accommodation or that nursing units are provided within old peoples' homes. This is a dilemma which has not yet been solved. The subject was reviewed in a report from the National Corporation for Care of Old People and Age Concern England (1977).

REFERENCES

Adams G F 1964 Clinical Undertaking? Lancet i: 1055–1058
Adams G F 1968 Tomorrow's hospital. British Journal of Hospital Medicine Nov. 211–212
Adams G F, McIlwraith P O 1963 Geriatric nursing — A study of the work of geriatric ward staff. University Press, Oxford
Age Concern, England 1977 Focus on the future

Age Concern, Liverpool 1975 Report on the continuing care project
Anderson, D C 1972 Report on leisure and day care facilities for the old. Age Concern, London
Andrews C T 1971 Early days in rural England. Modern Geriatrics, 1: 117–122
At Home or in Hospital 1968 The report of a working party

established to consider the problems of enabling the young chronic sick to live at home. London: National Fund for Research into Crippling Diseases

Beales D L 1982 A new form of community hospital service for the elderly. British Medical Journal 284: 840–841

Bagnall W E, Datta S R, Knox J, Horrocks P 1977 Geriatric medicine in Hull: a comprehensive service. British Medical Journal iii: 102–104

Bhowmick B K, Arnold J P 1976 Halfway House in Geriatric Practice. British Medical Journal ii: 293–294

Bradley W H 1967 (ed) Proc. of a symposium on the disabled young adult. London: Nat. Fund for Research into Crippling Diseases

Bright R 1972 Music in geriatric care. Angus and Robertson

Bright R 1981 Practical planning in music therapy for the aged. Musicgraphics, New York

British Medical Association 1976 Care of the elderly, p 36–37. London: B.M.J.

Brocklehurst J C 1964 The work of a geriatric day hospital. Gerontologia Clinica 6: 151–166

Brocklehurst J C 1970 The geriatric day hospital. London: King Edward's Memorial Hospital Fund for London

Brocklehurst J C 1973 Role of Day Hospital Care. British Medical Journal iv: 223–225

Brocklehurst J C 1974 Educational Opportunities in Geriatrics. Age and ageing, 3: 3–11

Brocklehurst J C 1977a Geriatric care in advanced societies. MTP Publishers, Lancaster

Brocklehurst J C 1977b The quality of life in long stay geriatric wards. In: The quality of life in residential homes and hospitals. Bill Johnson Foundation Publications, Stoke-on-Trent

Brocklehurst J C 1977c Education and Training Inculcation of appropriate Attitudes and Skills. In: Exton-Smith A N (ed) Care of the elderly — Meeting the challenge of dependence. Academic Press

Brocklehurst J C, Shergold M 1968 What happens when geriatric patients leave hospital? Lancet, ii: 1133–1135

Brocklehurst J C, Shergold M 1969 Old people leaving hospital. Gerontologia Clinica II: 115–126

Brocklehurst J C, Tucker J S 1980 Progress in geriatric day care. King Edwards Hospital Fund for London

Burley L E, Smith R G, Williamson J 1979 Contribution from geriatric medicine within acute medical wards British Medical Journal 2: 90–92

Carter J 1981 Day services for adults. Nat. Inst. Soc. Services Library No 40. Allen and Unwin, London

Clarke M, Hughes A O, Dodd K J, Palmer R L, Brandon S, Holdon A M, Pearce D 1979 The elderly in residential care: Patterns of disability. Health Trends 11: 17–20

Coatsley D, Woodford Williams E 1979 Effects of burglary and vandalism on the health of old people. Lancet ii: 1066–1067

Central Health Services Council 1976 The organization of the in-patient's day. London: H.M.S.O.

Cordiner C M, Wilson L A 1982 Group psychotherapy for hospital patients with chronic physical illness. Hospital Bulletin 40: 16–19

Cruise J, Gledhill F E, Wright W B 1978 Better geriatric care — making it happen. Health Trends 10: 92–95

Davison W, Coni N K 1971 Psychogeriatric services. British Medical Journal iii: 531–553

Denham M J 1983 Care of the long stay elderly patient. Croom Helm, London

DHSS 1981 The respective roles of the general acute and geriatric sectors in care of the elderly hospital patient

Eastman M L 1976 Whatever happened to casework with the elderly? Age Concern Today, 18: 9–12

Elliot J R 1975 Living in hospital. King Edward's Memorial Hospital Fund for London

Enoch M D, Howells J G 1971 The organization of psycho-geriatrics. Report of the Society of Clinical Psychiatrists

Evans G J, Hodkinson H M, Mezey A G 1971 The elderly sick — who looks after them? Lancet, ii: 539–541

Exton-Smith A N 1962 Progressive Patient Care in Geriatrics. Lancet, 1: 260–262

Farndale J 1961 The day hospital movement in Great Britain. Pergamon Press, London

Griffiths R A, Wilcock G K 1981 Geriatric medicine in two community hospitals — the Oxford Experience. Journal of Clinical and Experimental Gerontology 00: 399–409

Halliburton P M, Wright W B 1973 Variations in standard of hospital geriatric care. Lancet, i: 1300–1302

Harris A I 1971 Handicapped and impaired in Great Britain. HMSO, London

Hawker M B 1964 The Relatives' Conference. Lancet, i: 1098

Hodkinson I, Hodkinson M 1981 The long stay patient. Gerontology 27: 167–172

Isaacs B 1964 The training of a geriatric physician. Lancet, i: 1339–1342

Isaacs B 1969 Some characteristics of geriatric patients. Scottish Medical Journal 14: 243–251

Isaacs B, Thompson J 1960 Holiday admissions to a geriatric unit. Lancet, i: 969–971

Isaacs B 1971 Studies of illness and death in the elderly in Glasgow. Scotland: Scottish Home and Health Dept.

Isaacs B 1971 Geriatric patients — Do their families care? Br. med. J. iv: 282–286

Isaacs B, Livingstone M, Neville Y 1972 Survival of the unfittest. Routledge and Kegan Paul, London

Joint Board of clinical Nursing Studies 1976 Outline curriculum in geriatric nursing for state registered and state enrolled nurses. Course No 297

Joint Board of Clinical Nursing Studies 1982 Short course on the care of the elderly and the principles of geriatric nursing. Course No 941

Leeming J T, Luke A 1977 Multi-disciplinary meetings with relatives of elderly hospital patients in continuing-care wards. Age and ageing, 6: 1–5

Lowther C P, Williamson J 1966 Old People and Their Relatives. Lancet, ii: 145–149

MacFarlane J P R, Collings T, Graham K, MacIntosh J C 1979 Day hospitals in modern clinical practice — Cost benefit. Age and Ageing 8 suppl: 80–86

McLauchlan S, Wilkins D 1982 Levels of provision and of dependency in residential homes for the elderly — Implications for planning. Health Trends 14: 63–65

Morley D 1974 Day care and leisure provision for the elderly. Age Concern, England

National Centre for Health Services Research 1975 Adult care in the U.S. A comparative study. Trans Century Corporation, Washington D.C.

National Corp. for Care of Old People and Age Concern England 1977 Extra care?

Nisbet N H 1967 How long is long term? Scottish Medical Journal 12: 223–227

Nisbet N H 1970 'Who Benefits?' Lancet, i: 133–134

Norton D, McLaren R, Exton-Smith A N 1962 An investigation of geriatric nursing problems in hospital. Nat. Corp. Care of Old People

O'Brien T D, Joshi D M, Warren E W 1973 No apology for Geriatrics. British Medical Journal iv: 245–308

Opit L J 1977 Domiciliary care for the elderly sick — Economy or neglect? British Medical Journal 1: 30–38

Patel A R 1971 Modes of Admission to Hospital. A survey of emergency admissions to a general medical unit. British Medical Journal i: 281–283

Pathy M S 1969 Day hospitals for geriatric patients. Lancet, ii: 533–535

Pearson N G, Ashford J R, Lowther C P, MacAlpine D, Seiler H E, Sowden R R 1970 Report on studies of disability in Exeter and Edinburgh. Exeter Univ. Inst. of Biometry and Comm. Medicine

Poulden S M 1971 Art in the geriatric ward British Hospital Journal and Social Service Review. May

Pouldon S 1977 Education and stimulation for the elderly in residential homes and hospitals. Beth Johnson Foundation

Prinsley D N 1971 Effects of industrial action by the ambulance service on the day hospital patients. British Medical Journal ii: 170–171

Roberts N 1970 Our future selves George Allen & Unwin Ltd, London

Robertson D, Griffiths A, Cosin L Z 1977 A community based continuency care program for the elderly disabled. Journal of Geronotology 32: 334–339

Rosin A J, Boyd R V 1966 Complications of illness in geriatric hospital patients. J. Chron. Dis. 19: 307–313

Royal College of Physicians of London 1972 Report of the College Committee on Geriatric Medicine R.C.P.L., London

Royal College of Physicians of London 1977 Working Party Report on Care of the Elderly

Royal College of Nursing 1975 Improving geriatric care in hospital. Royal College of Nursing, London

Sanford J R A 1975 Tolerance of Debility in Elderly Dependants by Supporters at Home. British Medical Journal ii: 471–473

Shanas E, Townsend P, Weddburn D, Friis H, Milhoj P, Stenhouwer J 1968 Old people in three industrial societies. Routeledge and Kegan Paul, London

Sheldon J H 1971 A history of British geriatrics. Modern Geriatrics, 1: 457–464

Silver C P, Zuberi S J 1965 Prognosis of patients admitted to a geriatric unit. Gerontologia Clinica 7: 348–357

Skeet M 1971 Home from hospital. Dan. Mason Nursing Res. Cttee., London

South-East Metropolitan Regional Hospital Board 1971 Development of services for the elderly and elderly confused. London

Thompson A P 1949 Problems of aging and chronic sickness. British Medical Journal ii: 243–250, 300–305

Voluntary Help in the Care of the Elderly 1971 London: King's Fund Hospital Centre

Warren M W 1943 A case for treating chronic sick in blocks in a general hospital. Lancet i: 822–823

Warren M W 1946 Care of the Chronic Aged Sick. Lancet, i: 841–843

Warren M W 1960 The Evolution of Geriatric Medicine. Gerontologia Clinica 2: 1–7

Whitehead J A 1971a In the service of old age. Penguin, London

Whitehead J A 1971b Boarding out since St. Dymphona. Nursing Times, 67: 1555–1558

Wigley G 1968 Community services for mentally infirm old people. Lancet, ii: 962–966

Wilson E H, Wilson B O 1971 Integration of hospital and local-authority services in the discharge of patients from a geriatric unit. Lancet, ii: 864–866

Woodford-Williams E, McKeon J A, Trotter I S, Watson D, Bushby C 1962 The Day Hospital in the community care of the elderly. Gerontologia Clinica 4: 241–256

Woods R, Holden U P 1982 In: Isaacs B (ed) Recent advances in geriatric medicine, 2, Churchill Livingstone, Edinburgh, p 181

Care of the aged in the United States of America

INTRODUCTION

The elderly population of the United States has been growing steadily for many decades both in absolute numbers and relative to the total population. But the nation's health and social care services have not kept pace. They have neither been well tailored nor oriented to the needs of an older population (Butler, 1975). Some scattered pockets of well organized geriatric care exist, but the mainstream of American medicine has only recently begun to accept geriatric medicine as a priority. It is encouraging that a small but growing number of medical schools have begun to develop classes in and even programs of geriatric medicine. The volume of geriatric and gerontologic research has also slowly increased.

There is an increasing awareness by the public that while enormous sums are spent on social and medical services for the elderly, these services are often ill-suited to older patients and are not comprehensive. Most physicians are still untrained in the principles of geriatric care and most hospitals are designed to provide care for acute rather than chronic illness. Insurance arrangements in the private sector do little to support long-term care and the main public-sector program, Medicaid, is only for the poor. This fact, in turn, leads to the pauperization of the middle class so that Medicaid coverage can be obtained. The predominant method of payment for physician services, fee-for-service, underpays for primary geriatric care and inhibits the development of geriatrics. No formally recognized specialty of geriatric medicine exists in the United States.

In the 1980's geriatric medicine in the USA is in transition. The medical care establishment is beginning to reassess its relationship to long-term care, including social and other supportive services. Pressure for this reassessment comes in part from public uneasiness with the soaring costs of health care and questions about its thrift and effectiveness, especially in meeting the needs of a graying society.

The USA spent about $287 billion in 1981 for personal health care, about 10 per cent of the gross national product. Its population of 26.6 million elderly, one-ninth of the total population, accounts for 30 per cent of this cost. The older population will expand to 55 million people in the year 2030. Within this group, the fastest growing segment is that of the 'old old' — those over 85 years of age, which today numbers 2.3 million and is expected to reach 3.8 million by the year 2000 and 5.7 million by 2030. This increased longevity may bring heavier burdens of illness or disability. At present, one person in five of this very old group lives in an institution and many of the rest need, or would benefit from, social and medical support in order to maintain an independent status in the community (Brotman, 1982).

Because change in the profession of medicine proceeds slowly, there appears to be little time to spare in preparing for an ever-graying society. American medicine, so heavily focused on acute care for so long, must begin to foster the development of a variety of long-term care services and not rely solely on the nursing home. The history of nursing home care has had some regrettable episodes and by and large these institutions have remained outside the mainstream of American medicine. Poor medical surveillance and the resulting neglect of patients in the 18 000 American skilled-nursing and intermediate-care facilities have been documented repeatedly (Solon, 1974).

There are reasons why long-term care has been repeatedly underemphasized. Physicians are trained in medical schools which are usually associated with teaching hospitals but are rarely connected with long-term care facilities. In this training, age-related changes in the body are not stressed, and often a prejudice exists against the chronically ill patient who cannot be 'cured'. Finally, negative attitudes are allowed to persist which depersonalize older patients; thus too often they may be referred to in a derogatory manner such as 'crocks' or through other demeaning epithets.

Private health insurance has emphasized reimbursement for acute-care services. This model was also used to develop the Medicare program, established in 1965, which provides government health insurance for the old.

The issues that dominated the preparation of this federal program hinged on questions of what was 'insurable', rather than on the blend of services needed for sound geriatric care. Medicare today lacks both long-term care and preventive care benefits and promotes the separation of chronic from acute-care services (The Commonwealth Fund, 1952).

There are other reasons for the imbalance in the American health care system. Historically, research and training pertinent to the needs of the elderly have been underfinanced. Research receives only the equivalent of 0.2 per cent of government spending on health care services for the elderly. An investment on such a small order is not likely to speed acquisition of new knowledge about processes of aging and the problems of elderly patients.

The number of USA physicians who lay claim to some expertise in geriatrics is extremely low. A 1977 survey by the American Medical Association disclosed that of those responding, fewer than 0.2 USA doctors listed geriatrics as a major focus in their practice (Freeman, 1971). Thus in a time of increasing specialization, elderly patients and their families have great difficulty in finding physicians who are interested in geriatric problems and have expertise in this area.

According to a report by the Rand Corporation (Kane et al, 1981) the USA needs 1600 academic geriatricians just to staff each of the 125 USA medical schools and residency programs. The Rand group estimates that if one wanted geriatricians to deliver consultative service and some primary care to those over 65 and provide a cadre of academic geriatricians, over 16 000 physicians would be needed. But if a cadre of trained geriatric nurse-practitioners, physician-assistants and social workers could be developed and utilized well, the number could be cut by a third. Unfortunately, even when viewing the increased interest in gerontology in the most positive light, it is unlikely that even a mid-range estimate of 8000 physicians can be trained in geriatrics by the year 1990.

While some might debate the numbers presented by the Rand group, this report does suggest the distance that American medicine has to go in order to meet the demographic imperatives of a rapidly increasing older population. In addition to increased numbers, the USA needs a fair geographical distribution of physicians who are versed in geriatric principles. But at this time many sections of the country are short of physicians, particularly the rural regions and inner-city areas with high concentrations of poverty. Private medical care available to minority groups tends to be scarce. Hence, in the USA generally these individuals who are poor, black, and live in a rural area are least likely to have access to professional medical care.

Critics of American medicine often have difficulty in appreciating the geographical, economic, demographic, and political diversity of the country, especially in comparison to European countries. In this chapter we will consider some of the socioeconomic characteristics of the American population who are over age 65, describe the major social welfare programs, highlights of the historical development of geriatric medicine, and provide a summary of current geriatric services. All of this should be viewed in the context of a nation with over 240 million persons of diverse ethnic, religious, and cultural background — a nation spanning a 2500 miles continent with 50 states which include many counties and local regions.

DEMOGRAPHY

There were 26.6 million Americans over age 65 in the USA in 1982, or 11 per cent of the total population. This elderly population has been growing at a faster rate than the younger population. Barring major changes in patterns of fertility and immigration, the USA population will be 12.2 per cent elderly by the year 2000, 15.6 per cent by 2020, and 18.3 per cent by 2030. The accelerated growth reates expected in the second decade of the 21st Century reflect the aging of the enormous 'baby boom' generation of post-World War II.

Today's elderly have about half the annual income of their younger counterparts. About half of the 9.2 million families headed by an older person in 1980 had incomes below $12 881. For the 8 million living alone or with unrelated persons, the median income was $5095. Over one-sixth of the elderly population was poor by the official U.S. definition of poverty ($4954 for an older couple and $3941 for an older person living alone).

Women and persons who are black, Hispanic, or from other minority groups are more likely to be among the aged poor. Although recent census counts have shown an increase in the numbers of poor elderly there has been marked improvement since 1970. This improved status is largely due to Social Security payments to many older Americans.

In the last 30 years older men have been a diminishing proportion of the labour force, declining from nearly 46 per cent in 1950 to 19.1 per cent in 1980. Much less change in labour force participation has occurred among older women (from 9.7 per cent in 1950 to 2.1 per cent today). Social Security payments are a mainstay for 19.8 million retired workers, 3 million spouses, and 4.4 million widows and widowers. In mid-1981 the average monthly benefit check for a retired worker was $383. Many of the USA elderly become poor upon retirement when their incomes drop from between two-thirds to one-half of their working levels.

About half of the 16.4 million households headed by

an elderly person were considered poor in a 1978 survey. 'Poor' in this context was defined as having family income at half or less of the median for families of all ages (after adjustment for family size). About half of these lived in poor housing units classed as inadequate, adequate but crowded, or relatively costly for the dwellers (for example, with gross housing expense at 40 per cent of income for homeowners with mortgages or 30 per cent for renters). Compared to younger persons, the elderly tend to occupy older structures (30 years or older).

Some 83 per cent of older men and 57 per cent of older women live in families. The others live along or with persons not related to them. Four out of 10 older women live alone or with a non-relative, which reflects the longer life expectancy of women.

The longer life expectancy of women produced a sex ratio of 148:100 in the elderly population (15.2 million women and 10.3 million men) in 1970. By age 85, the ratio reaches 229:100. Most older men are married (78 per cent) while most older women are widowed (51 per cent). And in the 75+ female population, almost 70 per cent are widowed.

According to the National Household Interview survey*, about 68 per cent of those elderly living outside of institutions[†] report their health as good or excellent when compared to others of their age. The other 22 per cent report fair health and 9 per cent in poor health. In the last group disproportionate numbers of individuals are poor, live in 'rural areas' and belong to ethnic or racial minorities. While half the elderly report having a chronic condition which limits activity, only 17 per cent are unable to carry out everyday activities.

A 1977 study on disability, a supplement to the National Household Interview survey, showed that the number of elderly confined to bed was 2.1 per cent; those needing help to move about in their homes 2.6, per cent; those needing assistance about the neighbourhood, 6 per cent; and those needing help outside the neighbourhood, 8.4 per cent. Those needing help in performing activities of daily living included 3.8 per cent for bathing, 2.6 per cent for dressing, 1.4 per cent for toilet, and 0.8 per cent for eating.

The most frequently reported chronic conditions among the elderly who live in communities (as opposed to institutions) were arthritis (44.3 per cent), hypertension (38.5), hearing impairment (28.2), heart disease (27.4), arteriosclerosis (12), visual impairment (11.9, and diabetes (8). An estimated 10–15 per cent have mental illness.

Compared to younger adults, older Americans have twice as much disability and four times the limitation in activity. And their use of health services is proportionately greater. They visit physicians more often (42 per cent), have longer periods of hospitalization (10.7 versus 7.3 days), and are the primary users of nursing homes. Of the 11 million older people occupying nursing-home beds, 80 per cent are over age 75.

Nearly 30 per cent of all spending for personal health care in USA is for persons over 65. They account for 27.8 per cent of the total expense of hospital care, 25.2 per cent of physicians' services, 21.2 per cent of drugs, 10.5 per cent of dental services, and 80.2 per cent of the nation's nursing-home bill of $22 billion a year.

Public payments (constituting 63 per cent of all payments for the elderly) came primarily from Medicare (69.8 per cent) and Medicaid (21.2 per cent). Public sources pay 87.5 per cent for hospital physicians, 59.4 for private physicians, 15.6 for drugs, 3.3 for dentists, and 46.2 for nursing homes (Brotman, 1982).

SOCIAL WELFARE LEGISLATION

The federal nature of the American government must be understood to appreciate the complexity of its social welfare legislation. For most of its 205-year history, the USA regarded programs of health and social services to be the responsibility of its states or private organizations. Major government involvement has occurred only in the last 50 years.

The year 1935 stands out in American social and medical history because of the enactment of the Social Security Law. The federal government, leaning on the experience of various states and abroad, began this program of social insurance which made available cash benefits to persons upon retirement at age 65. This was to be in proportion to the amount of ones taxed earnings. At the same time, the government was authorized to make financial grants to the states for the support of their programs to aid the poor and handicapped.

Out of this legislation, a generation later, came Medicare and Medicaid. Medicare belongs to a family of social insurance benefits. It provides payment for hospital and medical services in the manner of private health insurance, and eligibility is based on whether or not one receives Social Security benefits. Medicaid, on the other hand, is not an insurance program. Individuals who are poor (as defined by federal and state laws) receive care at no charge to themselves.

While many of the same types of benefits are provided for under both Medicare and Medicaid, only Medicaid supports long-term care — and only on a grudging basis. For example, Medicare provides for care in a skilled nursing home as part of convalescence from an acute illness. But once the patient's condition is stabilized to the point of no longer requiring skilled nursing care to bring improvement, Medicare stops paying for the nursing-home services. Medicaid pays for maintenance care provided the individual is too poor to cover the expenses. The official definition of poverty, however, is so stringent that even an allowance of 125 per cent of the official poverty level leaves many poor individuals without coverage. Thus many older people are exposed to poverty by the expenses of long-term care. The objective of preventing poverty — specifically attached to the 1935 law and repeated by the enactment of Medicare in 1965 — is frustrated. Given the association of poverty and disease and of both conditions with old age, perhaps the mildest conclusion one may draw from gaps in these systems is that the evolution into thorough 'old-age security' is still incomplete.

Medicare is Title 18 of the Social Security Act. Medicaid is Title 19. Two other titles are of major consequence to the elderly. Title 20, enacted in 1974, assists states in funding social services for the poor. To receive federal aid, (which totaled $2.5 billion in 1980) states must design a program covering social-service needs. These must include measures for promoting self support, the protection of vulnerable persons, institutional care when appropriate, and community-based services to avoid institutionalization.

Title 16 of the Social Security Act established a program of Supplemental Security Income for the elderly, blind, and disabled who are poor — even when they receive Social Security retirement benefits. Some states add to the federal payment. (Many individuals who qualify under this program are eligible for the food stamps, provided by the Department of Agriculture to low-income families and individuals, so they may buy food at markets or pay for home-delivered or group meals.)

There are several programs outside of the Social Security legislation that benefit the elderly. For example, The Older Americans Act has a system of state and local programs of social services specifically for persons over age 60. The Act supports senior centres, nutritional sites (places where older persons may obtain a hot meal regularly), home-delivered meals, demonstrations on innovations in the delivery of social services, research on needs of the elderly, training for caregivers, training for faculty leadership in geriatrics, development of gerontology centers for the chronically disabled elderly, and demonstrations of case-management where an individual's circumstances are assessed and a plan drawn recommending medical and social care. A variety of federal programs in the housing field assist the elderly in buying, renting, and renovating dwellings. A 'Section 8' program provides rent subsidies for low and moderate-income families. Section 202 of the Housing Act provides for loans to finance housing construction for the elderly and handicapped. And a public housing program provides for services in complexes occupied by elderly citizens, which may include communal dining, in-home, and basic health services.

Because some 500 000 military veterans reach age 65 each year, the Veterans Administration has developed a number of programs for the elderly. Giving priority to veterans having service-connected disabilities, the VA offers in- and outpatient care in its own hospitals, domiciliaries, and nursing homes; it also purchases services and provides for home care.

The Public Health Service Act supports a spectrum of research activities, notably through the National Institute on Aging, one of the 11 of the National Institutes of Health. Started in 1974, the National Institute on Aging conducts and supports biomedical and psychosocial research; it also funds the training of investigators in aging research and the development of medical school curricula in geriatrics. The training of professionals for geriatric services — physicians, nurses, and allied health personnel — is assisted under various parts of the Public Health Service Act.

This short survey of major elements of national programs for the elderly shows some of the complexity and even confusion that confront the individual, family, and practitioner in locating and organizing support. Eligibility for a program may depend on income, resources, disability, military service, and age. Since services are not uniformly distributed throughout the nation, distance may be a barrier to receiving care. Reimbursement rates may make it difficult for a poor patient to find a willing practitioner. Hospitals may limit their 'load' of patients whose care is paid for by public programs, such as Medicare and Medicaid. Some individuals may have to 'spend down' their resources until they qualify for programs serving the poor.

HISTORY OF GERIATRICS IN THE UNITED STATES

An American pathologist, Ignatz Nascher, is credited with coining the term 'geriatrics'. He incorporated it in his 1914 textbook, *Geriatrics: The Diseases of Old Age and Their Treatment*. More than a half century later, geriatric medicine remains a stranger to formal USA medical education, although it has gained recognition in Great Britain under the 1946 National Health Service Act. Texts on aging written even after Nascher's pioneering effort bore only occasional fruit in the formal training of physicians. Such early texts did, however, become part of a growing literature on a graying society.

The development of research, training, and services relevant to geriatric medicine in the USA must be credited to a variety of public and private actions. Among the early landmark activities was a symposium of scholars supported by the Josiah Macy Jr. Foundation in the late 1930's. The group's work was published under the editorship of E. V. Cowdry as *Problems of Ageing* in 1938 (Shock, 1981).

The Macy Foundation's seminal activities extended to a grant which was given to the U.S. Public Health Service, a government agency, to establish a gerontology research unit in 1940. This unit, placed within the National Institutes of Health, was physically located at the Baltimore (Maryland) City Hospitals, a clinical facility which NIH lacked at the time. First led by Dr Edward J. Stieglitz, the research unit was turned over to Dr Nathan J. Shock in 1941. Dr Shock continued as its director for the next 35 years while its name and NIH affiliations changed. It is today the Gerontology Research Center, part of the National Institute on Aging — with a staff of over 300, an unusual colony of aging research animals, and one of the oldest longitudinal studies of human aging.

Stieglitz went on to produce in 1943 the textbook, *Geriatric Medicine: Diagnosis and Management of Disease in the Aging*. The volume covered the biology of aging, clinical issues, and socioeconomic problems. By differentiating the normal aging process from disease, the text presented a more positive view of old age than previous USA texts.

The mid-1940's were marked by the following events which encouraged the development of geriatrics in the USA: an interdisciplinary Gerontological Society was founded, an American Geriatrics Society, a few state agencies on aging, and several university teaching and research centers on aging.

While Great Britain was inaugurating its National Health Service, the drive for a similar national health insurance in the USA failed since it was opposed by organized medicine. Much of the fervour for improving the accessibility and effectiveness of medical and hospital services was channeled into support of hospital construction, biomedical research, and training of physicians and other health professionals. Some of this energy also went into the protracted effort for national health insurance for the elderly, or Medicare.

The 1950's witnessed many activities by the government to raise public consciousness of the aging population. With presidential support, a national conference on aging was convened in 1950, the first of a series of White House Conferences on Aging which occur every 10 years. These conferences sought to identify issues, propose remedies, and stimulate business, labour, religious, state and local government, philanthropic, and other organizations to define positions and roles.

In the mid-1950's an Inter-University Council on Social Gerontology was formed to stimulate professional training in the field. Its efforts produced two landmark handbooks in gerontology: the *Individual: Psychological and Biological Aspects* (Birren, 1959) and the *Handbook of Social Gerontology: Societal Aspects of Aging* (Tibbitts, 1960)*.

AGING AND MEDICAL EDUCATION

Following the 1961 White House Conference, a branch on aging was established within the National Institute of Child Health and Human Development (National Institutes of Health) to support gerontological research and training at universities. Five university centers of aging research as well as individual investigations were supported by this special aging program. Ultimately, however, the combination of aging with child health interests did not yield a budget distribution satisfactory to groups in aging research. The 1971 White House Conference recommended that a separate institute on aging be created; hence, in 1974 the Research on Aging Act was passed authorizing the National Institute on Aging.

Almost immediately after it was organized, the institute began to stimulate the interest of medical educators throughout the country toward geriatric medicine through a variety of programs. A number of these programs are described in the following items:

1. The support of conferences which collect and disseminate information on the care of the elderly, such as the 1976 Anglo-American Conference that led the publication of *Care of the Elderly: Meeting the Challenge of Dependency* (Exton-Smith and Evans, 1977).

2. Meetings and studies which explore ways of incorporating geriatric medicine into undergraduate and graduate medical education. For example, the Institute of Medicine, of the National Academy of Sciences, was commissioned to prepare a report on *Aging and Medical Education* (Institute of Medicine, 1978). The report called for recognition of gerontology and geriatrics as academic disciplines within medical specialties, rather than the designation of geriatrics as its own separate speciality. It recommended the development of a cadre of faculty to teach gerontology and geriatrics in addition to changes in undergraduate medical courses, clinical

---

* The handbooks have been revised in recent years to include the following three volumes:
Finch C E and Hayflick L (eds) 1977 Handbook of the biology of aging. Van Nostrand Reinhold, New York
Birren J E and Schaie K W (eds) 1977 Handbook of the psychology of aging. Van Nostrand Reinhold, New York
Binstock R H and Shanas E (eds) Handbook of aging and the social sciences. Van Nostrand Reinhold, New York

clerkships, in-house staff training, and licensure examinations.

3. Co-operation with other federal agencies to promote the training of health professionals. As a result of these co-operative efforts for example, the Veterans Administration established a fellowship program in geriatric medicine in 1978 in which physicians are trained to be teachers, clinicians, administrators, and policy makers.

4. Grants to support the development of geriatric curricula in medical schools and foster the training of researchers in the field of aging (National Institute on Aging, 1978).

5. Financial aid to academic health centers and nursing homes to collaborate in teaching and research programs (Butler, 1981).

The climate for incorporating geriatrics within the mainstream of medical education has been shaped by both public and private organizations. The U.S. Senate Special Committee on Aging sponsored a debate in 1977 on the need for geriatric medicine in medical school curricula. And the American Association of Retired Persons (a non-profit organization with 14 million members) sponsored a 1979 meeting on the role of medical schools and teaching hospitals in developing geriatric medicine.

The American Medical Student Association organised a Task Force on Aging and years later published a *Directory of Clinical Geriatrics Training Sites* for undergraduate and graduate medical students (Coccaro, 1979).

The Administration on Aging, another federal agency, supported geriatric fellowships for physicians and funded links between academic and community services. This included several long-term care gerontology centers operated by university or private nonprofit organizations. A formal geriatric residency program was established at the Mount Sinai-City Hospital Center in New York in 1972, which generated a second program at the Long Island (New York) Jewish-Hillside Medical Center.

The Mount Sinai School of Medicine and the Mount Sinai Hospital in New York City, the first department of geriatrics in the USA, is attempting to provide comprehensive in-and outpatient services, multidisciplinary training for health and social service practitioners, and research on topics relating to biomedical, psychosocial, and health delivery issues. Organized in 1982, the Gerald and May Ellen Ritter Department of Geriatrics and Adult Development is attached to the Jewish Home For Aged, a sophisticated nursing home for the elderly which has a specialized hospital as well as services for in-home care. The department will offer or co-ordinate hospice, home-care assessment, and referral services.

OPTIONS IN GERIATRIC CARE

The growth in expense of nursing-home care — now 22 billion dollars a year — has begun to alarm those in government, business, professional unions, and others. For example, health planners have recently warned of a financial crisis for the State of Connecticut unless alternatives to nursing-home care could be provided. In projecting current utilization patterns, the planners expect a 22 per cent rise in the state's institutional population, within one decade, which would require an additional 6000 beds at a construction cost of $240 million, plus $578 million in additional operating costs. Urging the development of community-based services, the planners cautioned that these might not necessarily reduce current spending but they would allow more control over future costs. In addition, they recommended further development of activities to help older people stay healthy.

Triage, a non-profit organization in several Connecticut counties, recently completed one phase in a demonstration of community-based services. When usual Medicare and Medicaid restrictions on services were waivered, Triage reported it had been able to provide a broader range of comparable services for its population at about the same cost. Moreover, vulnerable persons were able to remain at home and presumably with greater life satisfaction than in a nursing home.

An ideal system

Different options in long-term care have been demonstrated in the last 5 years and have provided a practical basis for comprehensive planning. The various services for geriatric patients might best be realized by imagining an ideal system. The major elements of this ideal system would include preventive health care services — so that the individual arrives at old age in good health, information about self-care and monitoring (or health screening) for these healthy older persons and the system would also seek out the elderly who are widowed, poor, or isolated in order to monitor their status through daily telephone checks and be ready to call for emergency medical or other services when necessary.

The physical, mental, and social assessment of the individual is another element in an ideal system. Caregivers would study an individual's health and social history, style of life, and aspirations. Practitioners would have the capacity to discern the pace of progressive dependency and arrange for counselling so the individual and family can make appropriate housing, service, lifestyle, and other adjustments.

To assist those family members who are able to care for their infirm at home, sociomedical services would be available through a coordinating agency which would, in turn, be linked to the private physician. The various services that would be brought to the home include visiting nurses, home-health aides, homemakers, chore workers, and social workers. Transportation would be available to the family for bringing a patient regularly to a day-care center or to a hospital or a nursing home's outpatient services (such as physical therapy, occupational therapy, and speech therapy). Respite care for an older patient would also be made available, permiting the family time for vacations.

The patient's status would be evaluated periodically to determine whether or not the patient's health goals were being achieved or required adjustment. Particular attention would be given to the older patient's psychosocial needs by professionals trained in principles of geriatic psychiatry. And for dying patients and their families, hospice services would be available in the home or an institution.

Underlying the entire system would be the concept of later life as a natural part of the life cycle. Practitioners would encourage and capitalize on the individual's ability to make compensations or to use alternative resources — thus maximizing the gains while minimizing the losses. Cure might be unlikely in many cases, yet patients would receive help in order to maintain their health and protect their autonomy to the greatest extent possible.

The system also would integrate new knowledge gained from advances in research and training, recognizing that efficient systems of geriatric health care are important in stretching resources to cover an enormous variety and volume of demands. The design of an effective system would incorporate self- and outside appraisal. Participation in policy and program planning by the elderly as well as other members of the public would be provided for. Finally, the system would encourage the public to gain the broadest understanding of its goals and activities.

The foregoing ideal exists in the USA, although the elements are not integrated within one system. The most comprehensive systems that exist currently are probably those of church-sponsored institutions; some homes for the aging are part of housing and health-care complexes arranged in a campus format. Another comprehensive system is the multipurpose senior centre, which offers education, leisure activities, and health and social services (health screening, family counselling, job finding, and legal assistance). Day care for individuals living with their families and for nursing-home patients is offered in a few advanced centers. Such centers also may be sites for medical and social work training.

Day care

There is a growing movement to develop adult day care

facilities. In a recent directory as many as 600 programs were listed, serving 13 500 older persons in 46 states. One big advantage to day care is the cost is usually less than for care in a nursing home. And while it provides treatment for the patient, the families are also assisted in making adjustments and finding aid. A day care facility can often make it possible to avoid or delay institutionalization.

Hospice services

Hospice services, which focus on support for dying patients and their families, have appeared relatively recently in the USA and under various sponsors. Perhaps 700 or more hospice programs exist, and the care is covered by a few private insurers. Some measure of Medicare coverage was added in 1982. It is generally understood that a hospice is not an institution but a service that may be rendered in various settings. Criticism of conventional care for dying patients — such as inadequate pain-control regimens and the use of prolonged or heroic procedures despite patients' wishes — led to the establishment of the first U.S. hospice program in 1974. The quality of care in hospices, is now being studied as well as identifying what services would be provided and the cost differences between providing care in institutions versus providing it at home.

Recent innovations

The search for options in long-term care is reflected by the wide variety of the following recent innovations:

1. Social and health maintenance organizations for the elderly operate under government funding. In addition to regular services, they incorporate care for the well elderly — testing the theory that preventive services, primary care, and early intervention reduce illness and the need for inpatient care.

2. San Pedro (California) Peninsula Hospital operates a round-the-clock centre responding to emergency telephone calls from frail individuals at home.

3. The Pima County (Arizona) Community Services System wants to prevent institutionalization. It pools county resources for the aging population, then draws on a general fund to supply individual needs. This way the country avoids the administrative burden of determining which need fits which funding source's requirements (such as those of Medicare, Title 20, or the Older Americans Act). Each client is assigned a case co-ordinator at no charge. Clients ineligible for categorical services but who still require aid to maintain independence are paid for by the county when the clients cannot pay.

4. The University of Tennessee at Baptist Memorial Hospital in Memphis operates a geriatric assessment and rehabilitation unit with 10 beds. They found that only one in seven of the first 150 patients required immediate

nursing-home care, while one in five required admission within 6 months.

5. In Pittsburgh (Pennsylvania) a hospital-based home health agency operates a hospice program for six hospitals. A hospice nurse serves as a co-ordinator for these services; patients retain their own physicians, and other professionals provide counselling to patients and their families.

6. In Rochester (New York) a comprehensive program of psychogeriatric care includes both in- and outpatient and services, nursing-home consultations and outreach activities (home visits for evaluation or family support), and workshops for community agencies and professionals.

7. In Anchorage (Alaska) a community mental health agency sponsors classes for elderly persons and family members. Topics include coping with stress, depression, brain damage, and retirement.

8. In Howard County (Maryland) a program for the homebound uses 25 volunteers to provide practical aid (such as shopping, meal preparation, and respite care), information on community services, and emotional support for the elderly and their families.

The search for alternatives to nursing home care has revealed both possibilities for financial assistance and for community services to be brought to the home. A few states provide money, tax relief, or subsidized loans to families in order to help them maintain an elderly member at home. However, the extent to which cash strategies or community-based services produce savings in long-term care is in doubt. It still remains unclear whether these strategies prevent or deter institutionalization or whether they benefit just those individuals whose circumstances would not otherwise require institutionalization.

Estimates vary on the extent to which placement in a nursing home can be prevented. Based on medical criteria alone some guess from 10 to 40 per cent of people who go into nursing homes could receive alternative types of support — presuming such services exist in the community and families are willing to receive the patients.

Developing a reliable method of assessing the social and medical status of patients would be necessary before a true estimate could be made of the population for which community-based services are a practical substitute for placement in a nursing home. However, methodologies that would do this appear to be incomplete at present. They still reflect gaps in knowledge about processes of aging, diseases in old age, and evaluation of intervention strategies.

Experiments are being conducted to link organized referral arrangements with social and medical evaluations. The government is supporting 10 'channeling' demonstrations which reflect the ability of local organizations to manage various types of services which are used in the home, the community, or the institution. Each organization searches for and screens cases, as well as evaluates their need and management. The program allows for the waiver of Medicare and Medicaid restrictions so that services can be flexibly arranged and paid.

CONCLUSION

About 80 billion dollars each year are spent on personal health services for the 26.6 million Americans who are over 65. Immense as this sum is, it has not produced an organized spectrum of services. Indeed, those services supplied often seem to fulfil geriatric purposes only inadvertently. Yet while the USA is getting a late start on meeting the needs for long-term care in accord with sound principles of geriatric medicine, it is embarked. The National Institute on Aging is well into its first decade. Programs to train physicians in geriatric medicine have been started. A few chairs in geriatric medicine have been established. And the first department of geriatrics at a medical school is evolving. Each step makes another step possible. The demographic imperatives will supply the needed political impetus; basic research has begun; and, hopefully, rapid progress will follow in meeting the needs of the elderly.

REFERENCES

Birren J E (ed) 1959 Handbook of aging and the individual: psychological and biological aspects. University of Chicago Press, Chicago

Brotman H B 1982 Every ninth American (unpublished report). Falls Church, Virginia

Butler R N 1981 The teaching nursing home. Journal of the American Medical Association 245: 1435–1437

Butler R N 1975 Why Survive? Being Old in America. Harper and Row, New York

Coccaro E F (ed) 1979 Clinical geriatrics training sites directory:
training opportunities in clinical geriatrics/research in aging. American Medical Student Association, Chantilly, Virginia

The Commonwealth Fund 1952 Chronic Illness in the United States. Harvard Press, Boston

Exton-Smith A N Evans (eds) 1977 Care of the Elderly: Meeting the Challenge of Dependency. Academic Press, London

Freeman J T 1971 A survey of geriatric education: catalogues of United States medical schools. Journal of the American Geriatrics Society 19: 746–762.

Institute of Medicine 1978 Aging and Medical Education. National
    Academy of Sciences, Washington, D C
Kane R L, Solomon D H, Beck J C, Keeler E B, Kane R A 1981
    Geriatrics in the United States. Lexington Books D C Heath,
    Massachusetts
National Institute on Aging 1978 Geriatric medicine academic award.
    NIH Guide for Grants and Contracts 7: 29–32

Shock N W 1981 Historical perspectives of aging. In: Horvath S M,
    Yousef M K (eds) Environmental Physiology, Elsevier North
    Holland, New York, p 383–398
Solon J A, Greenawalt L F 1974 Physicians' participation in nursing
    homes. Medical Care 12: 486–497
Tibbitts C (ed) 1960 Handbook of Social Gerontology: Societal Aspects
    of Aging. University of Chicago Press, Chicago

Psychogeriatric services

Psychogeriatrics has developed in little more than a decade into a new sub-specialty of psychiatry. The extent and pace of progress has varied from one country to another, but in many developed countries there are now psychiatrists and associated workers in the other health professions who specialise in the psychiatry of old age. This short account is based chiefly on the British scene, where development is probably more advanced, and better documented, than elsewhere. The models of services developed in the United Kingdom have often guided progress in other countries, but most already have much that is new and original.

ORIGINS OF PSYCHOGERIATRIC SERVICES

Until the 1960's the main activity in old age psychiatry was research — epidemiological, genetic and clinical; and even these fields were cultivated by relatively few workers. In the 1960's, and accelerating during the 1970's, a new preoccupation became evident with planning, delivery, and monitoring of services. This derived from the growing pressure of the aging of populations, and particularly the rapid increase in the numbers of the very aged which was everywhere pressing upon services. The development of geriatric medicine, together with progress in epidemiology, evaluation and organisation in health services generally, and particularly in psychiatry, were to hand for the new 'psychogeriaticians'; achievements in clinical psychiatry exceeded by far the extent to which the aged were benefiting from them.

Governments too were becoming aware of the need to give priority to these developments within health services, though the direction which they should take and the degree of differentiation from other services which was appropriate were still subjects of controversy. The history of these trends in Britain has been described by Arie and Isaacs (1978), and the state of development at the end of 1980 was reported following a national survey of psychogeriatricians and their services by Wattis et al (1981).

By the end of 1980, Wattis et al reported, specialized psychiatric services for the elderly existed in some 90 British health districts, and over one-tenth of all general psychiatrists were specialising in the care of the elderly. These developments had accelerated rapidly in the previous 5 years, during which more than half of the 120 psychiatrists working in this field had taken up the work. Despite much local variation, it is possible now to define a 'typical' psychogeriatric service, in terms of its sphere of responsibility, its facilities, the nature and ratios of the different staff involved, and their patterns of working together. Emphasis has been given also to the 'style' of such services — those attributes, over and above types and levels of resources, which determine whether services are effective or not. The organization and 'style' of psychogeriatric services, together with the many relevant policy statements from government, from the Royal College of Psychiatrists, and from individuals, which have both led and reflected these developments, have been reviewed by Arie and Jolley (1982), and Hemsi (1982) has described in detail the functioning of these services in the community.

A TYPICAL PSYCHOGERIATRIC SERVICES

A psychogeriatric service takes all psychiatriac referrals of persons aged above about 65 years ('organic' and 'functional' alike) within a geographical catchment area. 'About' 65 years is important, for here as everywhere flexibility is appropriate. Generally the catchment area is the size of a typical British health district — some 200 000 people, of whom in Britain some 15 per cent will be aged over 65, making 30 000 over-65's, of whom just over a third or 11 000 will be over 75. How far the service is able to cope with those younger people who have organic mental disorders (presenile dementias, brain trauma, etc.) which may need services similar to those provided for the elderly will depend on the extent of its resources, and on what is available elsewhere locally. The service will accept all referrals of elderly people with psychiatric problems, although those long-stay in-patients who, after often decades of residence, have reached old age within the mental hospital, are usually not held to be the responsibility of the psychogeriatric service; were it otherwise, the psychogeriatrician's load would often be impossible, for over-65's now occupy one half of all psychiatric beds. But if individual such elderly 'graduates' need specific services best provided within the psychogeriatric arrangements, they too should have access to them. Of the under-75's referred to a comprehensive service the majority will suffer from functional disorders, of the over-75's from organic. Referral rates vary widely but are likely to run between 1 and 2 per cent of over-65's per annum.

A few services confine themselves, or are confined by colleagues, to seeing only patients with organic disorders, or patients whose disorders appear to the referrers to be organic. Often this is so in the early stages of a service, and when it becomes established the range of its clientele grows (or shrinks) with its reputation. All services deploy to greater or lesser extent a similar range of facilities and staff, though the extent to which different services rely on particular facilities varies greatly. Some, for instance, claim to depend heavily on day hospital care (Baker and Byrne, 1977) others on domiciliary support by community nurses (Black and Simons, 1980). Most services expect to take responsibility for their patients from the first point of referral, whilst others act as a 'secondary' resource to other psychiatrist colleagues who make the initial contact and select those who seem likely to benefit by specialized psychogeriatric services — or, alas, often those whom they simply do not wish to look after themselves. A systematic review of different models of services has yet to be made, though a recent excellent personal review of a wide range of visits and reports goes some way towards this objective (Norman, 1982). In regard to dementia, it is the ambulant severely behaviourly disturbed patient that is the responsibility of psychiatrists; the immobile physically disabled dement falls in the province of geriatric services (DHSS, 1972).

The facilities

As well as the network of extramural staff and facilities, three basic *hospital* facilities are essential: an acute admission or assessment unit; a longer stay unit; and facilities for day patients.

Admission unit

Whenever possible this should be in a general hospital, for elderly patients even when appropriately referred to psychiatrists often have serious physical disorders, or require access to a wide range of investigative resources. If such a unit is to receive all in-patients from a comprehensive district service, then it will need about one bed per 1000 old people — a 30-bed ward will

usually be appropriate for a typical health district. Whether organic and functional patients are admitted to separate wards, or to sub-areas of the same ward, must depend on the nature of local facilities — though scope for some segregation is essential. Plenty of day space is desirable, and this also makes such segregation easier. The pros and cons of mixing such patients have only recently begun to be studied (Wilkin et al, 1982); important as it is, this issue is not unique to psychogeriatrics, but arises also in other settings where heterogeneous sick or deviant people are looked after.

Where such a unit is in a general hospital, access to other medical specialties and especially geriatric, should be easy; where the admission ward is in a psychiatric hospital, often remote, and sometimes ill provided with investigative resources, then there is merit in a small *joint unit* run either in a general hospital or in the acute geriatric unit (if that is not in the general hospital) by staff of both services together. Such a unit ensures that patients who need joint care and investigation by physicians and psychiatrists can receive it, and it can be a fruitful focus for collaboration between the services, giving the confidence that comes from working side-by-side. Such joint units may be purpose-planned and built, or established by rearrangement of existing facilities (Arie and Dunn, 1973; Pitt and Silver, 1980).

Longer stay unit

This will usually be either in a psychiatric hospital or more appropriately in small 'community hospitals' serving particular neighbourhoods. At least three beds per 1000 old people will be needed (DHSS, 1972), often more (Jolley, 1977); but the bed ration is better expressed in relation to the main users of these long stay beds — the over-75's or over-80's; *at least* nine beds per 1000 aged 75 or over may be about right — but obviously the need for beds depends on style of practice, social characteristics of the locality, and on what is available elsewhere in the long-stay sector, statutory and private. Problems of morale of staff and of monitoring of standards loom large — the long-stay sector is the Achilles' heel of services for the elderly. The Health Advisory Service (Crossman, 1977), which is responsible for visiting and reporting on units for the elderly and the mentally ill, as well as for other groups for which long-term care is needed, has rightly given special emphasis to psychogeriatrics (HAS, 1983), where breakdowns of care have lead in recent years to several 'scandals'. Paramount is the need to provide stimulation and activity, and to maintain the highest level of function of which the resident is capable, together with the maximum of dignity and choice (Brody, 1977).

Day hospitals

These are an essential arm of psychogeriatric services.

The government target of three places per 1000 elderly (DHSS, 1972) is very rarely attained, but a facility to admit day patients, whether to a separate unit, or to the ward areas, is essential. Day care, which has been described as 'one of psychiatry's gifts to medicine' (Arie, 1975) is only a generation or two old, and is one of the few really good new ideas in this field. But the original hope that day hospitals would chiefly be useful as savers of inpatient beds has been only partly fulfilled, such saving as there is being by deferring the stage at which inpatient care is necessary rather than by avoiding it altogether (Green and Timbury, 1979). In this and other respects there are important differences in the function of a day hospital between psychogeriatrics and medical geriatrics (Arie, 1975, and see Chapter 47).

The main function of a day hospital in psychogeriatrics is to extend treatment and care to a wider range of patients and to give relief to a wider range of families, rather than merely to be a substitute for inpatient care. In psychogeriatrics there are few patients (though there are some) that come only for specific treatment or investigations, by contrast with medical geriatrics; the majority have continuing disabilities, functional or organic. The main groups of attenders are:

1. Patients from the inpatient unit, for whom the day hospital acts as a stepping stone to full independence.

2. Patients otherwise coping fairly satisfactorily in the community, for whom attendance perhaps one day a week is an 'umbilical cord' which, if severed, promptly results in breakdown.

3. Patients who need a short period of observation, investigation, or treatment — ranging occasionally from electroplexy to, more commonly, treatment of some intercurrent minor derangement which disturbs an otherwise adequate equilibrium.

4. A large group of dependent patients, the great majority of whom suffer from dementias, whose family are enabled to continue to care for them at home provided they are able to spend several days (often every day and just occasionally, when this is feasible, also at the weekend) at a day hospital.

There are also a few demented patients who live alone, and who are not too deteriorated, who can be supported through the day hospital, but the otherwise unsupported dement living alone at home has both a high likelihood of breaking down rapidly to the point of needing institutional care, and a very high mortality (Bergmann et al, 1978; Peace, 1982).

The cause of severance from the day hospital for the great bulk of dependant attenders is through deterioration to the point of needing inpatient treatment, or through death. It detracts in no way from the value of the day hospital to emphasize that, unlike other hospitals, most patients are discharged because they get worse rather than because they improve; a day hospital that

does not show this pattern should be suspected of 'geriatric spivvery' (Adams, 1974) for it must be excluding the most needy. The long term demented attenders at a psychogeriatric hospital will overlap with those at non-medical day centres and to some extent, at geriatric day hospitals. Behaviourally disturbed ambulant demented patients often require the tolerance of a psychiatric setting, but tolerance is variable, and is hardly to be determined merely by specialty labels.

Staff

Teamwork, so much a feature of geriatric services, is equally central in psychogeriatrics. This concept is more hardworked than clearly defined, but its essence is that people work together across professional boundaries, and that save where there are legal or sapiential constraints, roles overlap and members of the team derive their duties from the assessed needs of the patients, rather than merely from their professional labels or from the prescription of the 'leader' of the team.

The members of the team are the same as in geriatrics, though with differences of emphasis. Medical input is from psychiatrists and their trainees, sometimes assisted by family doctors on a sessional basis. The main educational function in regard to doctors is the training of psychiatrists, who should rotate through the unit, but cross-training with geriatric physicians and general (internal) physicians, and family doctors, is part and parcel of its role. In teaching centres medical student teaching is a central role. Arie (1981) has described the teaching role of a university department for the elderly in which psychiatric and medical services, along with orthopaedic, are combined together.

The bedrock of staffing is *nurses*, and senior nurses should be doubly qualified in both psychiatric and general nursing if they are to cope properly with the high prevalence of physical disabilities in the mentally ill aged. *Community nurses*, either working outwards from the hospital team in the support of patients at home, or based in the community and liaising with the hospital team, are a crucial arm of the service. Community nursing is one of the most fruitful recent developments in psychiatry (Royal College of Psychiatrists, 1980) and psychogeriatric services generally appear to have had less than their share of this important new resource.

Within the hospital, but operating beyond its confines in assessment of patients at home either initially or in preparation for re-settlement, are *remedial therapists* of whom occupational therapists have the longest history in psychiatry, but physiotherapists are increasingly necessary and valuable (Varley, 1982). Access to speech therapy is important too, though few services will need the unshared services of a speech therapist. Staff must be enabled to become a team in a real sense — mere 'sessions' of multiple individuals whose centre of gravity is elsewhere, even if they add up to approximately enough 'whole-time equivalents', are unlikely to be capable of forming a real team in which members have confidence in each other.

Social work provision in Britain is complicated by its separation from the Health Service, and the social work support of psychogeriatric as of other medical teams has to be negotiated with the local social services department; it ranges from excellent in style and quantity to grossly deficient. But social services departments increasingly are finding it worth their while to invest in supporting psychogeriatric units, which can greatly ease the pressure on overstretched social services.

Psychologists

Clinical psychologists have been slower to move into psychogeriatric work in Britain than in some other countries, perhaps because it features even more thinly in their professional education than in that of other health workers. The nature and the level of their training makes them potentially rich contributors, and their work may embrace psychological techniques of behaviour modification in individuals or groups, for instance by planning token economies, or 'reality orientation' (Holden and Woods, 1982), conducting staff and relative groups and more formal psychotherapeutic work. Psychometric testing is a relatively small, though sometimes essential part of their work; but above all they are highly trained colleagues who have yet to fulfill their potential in this field.

'Untrained' staff

Many services, through lack of resources or recruitment difficulties, depend largely on untrained staff — who for practical purposes are local housewives, sometimes working part-time. In nursing they are nursing auxiliaries, but occupational and physiotherapy helpers, psychologists' assistants, even untrained speech therapy helpers, may play a valuable part. Often the unprofessionalized outlook of such people is an invigorating asset, complementing that of professional staff.

Volunteers

The issues here are no different than in other related forms of work. Suffice it to say that volunteers can fulfil a multitude of useful roles, though their full potential is unlikely to be achieved unless there exists a Volunteers Organizer to recruit and deploy, and to support and encourage them. The quality and availability of volunteers will differ widely from area to area; in an age likely to see a continuing high level of unemployment, they may become increasingly available.

Staff ratios

Quality of care depends on many factors, but adequate staff ratios are essential. Without them there will either be neglect, or substitutes for staff in the form of restraints and coercions. Staff shortage is the enemy of dignity and choice, and tends to restrictive, regimented care and 'playing safe'.

There are no firm guidelines on staff levels, though the Royal College of Psychiatrists has issued tentative ones (Royal College of Psychiatrists, 1978, 1981). It is unlikely that there will be adequate care on a 30-bed psychogeriatric ward if there are fewer than five nurses, at least two of them trained, on duty at any time of the day, and there should be two to three at night. Lower levels are seen often, and far higher levels occasionally, though rarely in Britain.

The primary care team

The specialized service is interdependent with the team around the family doctor. The care of elderly mentally ill people is central to good family practice and collaboration and mutual support with the psychogeriatric service is essential. Identification of those of special risk, case-finding and surveillance, aimed where possible at prevention and early intervention (where the health visitor has a growing new role) is where psychogeriatrics begins, and that task largely depends on the primary care team (Williamson, 1981).

'Style' of services

The object of psychogeriatric services, as indeed of all services, is that what users of services receive should match their assessed needs, rather than it should be constrained merely by what is available in that compartment of services into which they happen to have fallen. It follows that assessment must be meticulous and openminded and collaboration between services must be easy and comfortable. This is easier said than done, but it needs to be said.

The components of 'style' have been discussed in detail by Arie and Jolley, (1982); suffice it here to say that a service must seek to be available without fuss or defensiveness (and since demand always threatens to outrun resources by far, defensiveness comes all too easily). It must be willing to try new ways of helping; sometimes the users of services themselves come up with the best ideas. It must capitalize on its assets of personality (and to set great store by this in selection of staff) rather than merely limiting roles to those defined by professional credentials. It must above all strive to win the confidence of those who use the service, and of potential users. The interests of the various groups of users may often point in different directions: thus, families and neighbours may press for relief by admission — but resources are likely to be short, and these pressures will compete with those from hospital colleagues for transfer of patients who are 'blocking' their acute beds; whilst the staff of one's own service may press for protection against a pressure of admissions which outruns their capacity to cope, or against frank overcrowding. Yet winning the confidence of all three groups — the public, colleagues, and one's own staff — is essential if one is to keep the show successfully on the road.

These principles may sound general, but they are of intense practical importance. Two features of the *modus operandi* of services need special emphasis: domiciliary assessment, and collaboration between services.

Domiciliary assessment

In psychogeriatrics all referrals, however urgent, should first be seen at home. This is not so in medical geriatrics, where many patients will be acutely and life-threateningly ill and need to be got into hospital fast. There is no psychogeriatric crisis so urgent that it will not benefit by the patient being first assessed (preferably by a senior psychiatrist) in her normal setting; but such assessment must be prompt.

The case for universal domiciliary assessment in psychogeriatrics has been argued elsewhere (Arie and Jolley, 1982). In brief it rests on points such as the following: psychiatric problems in old people comprise derangements of function, and this is best assessed in the normal setting; moves to unfamiliar surroundings may grossly distort it. In the home the characteristics of the setting can be observed, its amenities, its warmth, its supply of food (and whether it is being eaten), whether the bed is slept in, whether there are accumulations of empty bottles.

It is often difficult for family doctors to communicate all the information that the specialist needs. The picture, therefore, may look quite different when seen at home from what was described in the referral message. The essential sources of collateral information — neighbours, shopkeepers, visiting friends — may often be brought to the scene only by the crisis that has occurred. They may subsequently 'disappear', or be unable to come up to the hospital, yet to have their information available at the time of decision-making following a first contact is invaluable.

The very process of moving an old person may exac-erbate the disorder especially if the patient is already confused. Moreover, hospitalization, the most crucial of all decisions, may pre-empt more appropriate solutions, and above all may undermine the essential aim of maintaining an old person wherever possible in her own home. The 'hole' in the community left by a person who is removed even temporarily has a way of closing rapidly, and it may be very difficult to resettle that person however good the eventual recovery. Last, the initial visit may establish what are the likely resources, material and human, which may assist in eventual resettlement.

Collaboration

This is the lynchpin of good practice, a point underlined by the close relevance to mentally ill old people of much of the contents of the present book, and by the presence of psychiatrists among the contributors. Collaboration means being ready to support each other, and each other's patients. At the centre of collaboration is that between psychiatrists and geriatric physicians, and it is likely that this will communicate itself to other colleagues and set the local style. A happy feature of the growth of psychogeriatrics in Britain has been the ease with which professional bodies representing psychiatry and geriatrics have reached agreement on every issue that has come to them, and the Standing Joint Committee of the British Geriatrics Society and the Royal College of Psychiatrists have agreed a series of Guidelines for Collaboration (Royal College of Psychiatrists, 1979). Their essence is goodwill and good sense and the aim to provide a dependable service in which patients, having made contact with one part of the service, have ready access to all other parts. Emphasized too is the importance of keeping an open mind — patients with a psychiatric history who develop physical illness need to be re-assessed *de novo* rather than merely being automatically labelled 'psychiatric'; and *vice versa*.

Conclusion

This short account is a mere outline, with emphasis on ideas. The reader will find ample reference, and further numerical data, in the bibliography provided; given a basic adequacy of skill and resources, and a rational scheme of organization, it is ideas and 'style' that determine whether or not things work.

REFERENCES

Adams G F 1974 Eld health. British Medical Journal ii: 789–791
Arie T 1975 Day care in geriatric psychiatry. Gerontologia Clinica 17: 31–39
Arie T 1981 In: Arie T (ed) Health care of the elderly. Croom Helm, London and Johns Hopkins Press, Baltimore
Arie T, Dunn T B 1973 A do-it-yourself psychiatric-geriatric joint patient unit. Lancet ii: 313–316

Arie T, Isaacs A D 1978 The development of psychiatric services for the elderly in Britain. In: Post F, Isaacs A D (eds) Studies in geriatric psychiatry. John Wiley, New York
Arie T, Jolley D J 1982 Making services work: Organisation and style of psychogeriatric services. In: Levy R, Post F (eds) The psychiatry of late life. Blackwell Scientific Publications, Oxford
Black S, Simons R 1980 The specialist nurse, support care and the

elderly mentally infirm. Nursing Times (Community Outlook), February 14th, 45–46

Baker A A, Byrne R J F 1977 Another style of psychogeriatric service. British Journal of Psychiatry 130: 123–126

Bergmann K, Foster E M, Justice A W et al 1978 Management of the demented elderly patient in the community. British Journal of Psychiatry 132: 441–447

Brody E 1977 Long-term care of older people. Human Sciences Press, New York

Crossman R H S 1977 Diaries of a Cabinet Minister. Vol II. Hamish Hamilton, London

DHSS 1972 Services for mental illness related to old age. Circular HM(72)71. Dept. of Health and Social Security, London

Greene J G, Timbury G C 1979 A geriatric psychiatry day hospital service. Age and Ageing 8: 49–53

HAS 1983 The rising tide. Developing services for mental illness in old age. NHS Health Advisory Service, Sutherland House, Sutton, Surrey

Hemsi L 1982 Psychogeriatric care in the community. In: Levy R, Post F (eds) The psychiatry of late life. Blackwell Scientific Publications, Oxford

Holden U P, Woods R T 1982 Reality orientation: Psychological approaches to the confused elderly. Churchill Livingstone, Edinburgh

Jolley D J 1977 Hospital in-patient provision for patients with dementia. British Medical Journal i: 1335–1336

Norman A 1982 Mental illness in old age: Meeting the challenge.

Policy Studies in Ageing No 1. Centre for Policy on Ageing, London

Peace S M 1982 Review of day hospital provision in psychogeriatrics. Health Trends 14: 92–95

Pitt B, Silver C P 1980 The combined approach to geriatrics and psychiatry. Age and Ageing 9: 33–37

Royal College of Psychiatrists 1978 Nursing needs for the elderly mentally infirm. Bulletin of the Royal College of Psychiatrists, January, 4–5

Royal College of Psychiatrists 1979 Guidelines for collaboration between geriatric physicians and psychiatrists in the care of the elderly. Bulletin, November, 168–169. Reprinted in Arie and Jolley, Norman, 1982

Royal College of Psychiatrists 1980 Community psychiatric nursing. Bulletin, August, 114–118

Royal College of Psychiatrists 1981 Interim guidelines on consultant posts in psychiatry of old age. Bulletin, June, 110–111. Reprinted in Norman, 1982

Wattis J, Wattis L, Arie T 1981 Psychogeriatrics: A national survey of a new branch of psychiatry. British Medical Journal 282: 1529–1533

Wilkin D, Evans G, Hughes B, Jolley D 1982 The implications of managing confused and disabled people in non-specialist residential homes for the elderly. Health Trends 14: 98–100

Williamson J 1981 Screening surveillance and case-finding. In: Arie T (ed) Health care of the elderly. Croom Helm, London and Johns Hopkins Press, Baltimore

Preventive medicine and old age

The late nineteenth and early twentieth centuries witnessed the most spectacular advances that medicine is ever likely to achieve. These were associated with the discovery of the infectious nature of communicable disease which led to rational policies of isolation of infectious cases and the elimination of common sources of infection such as contaminated water supplies. These measures together with vaccination and immunization programmes led to control of many epidemic and pandemic diseases such as smallpox, typhoid, typhus, plague and cholera. These advances benefitted mainly the younger members of society and led incidentally to the ensuing remarkable aging of populations through securing the survival into old age of many who, in previous generations, would have succumbed in youth or early adulthood.

In those heroic days of preventive medicine the Medical Officer of Health was a person of great importance in the community and wielded great influence within the medical profession. This era of great change was overtaken by the spectacular advances in clinical science, pharmaceuticals and medical technology. Preventive medicine was rapidly overshadowed by these dramatic advances, which, although of great benefit to individual patients have had little effect upon community or public health. Prevention was either totally neglected in medical education or relegated to a lowly status. The Medical Officer of Health was progressively divested of his power and authority and was finally ignominiously abolished in the United Kingdom in 1974.

If prevention has become unfashionable and 'unglamorous' in medicine in general, this has been even more so in relation to old age where the commonly held negative steretype has been that little or nothing can usefully be done to mitigate the disabilities of late life. This negative stereotype has tended to be particularly strongly held within the medical and allied professions largely because until very recently medical education has been centred exclusively in teaching hospitals which, by their very nature, tend to afford students a very biased view of old age. It is strange that even the majority of

doctors who were destined for General Practice continued until recently to obtain all their training in a settling in which none of them would ever practice!

There are, however, welcome signs that the fundamental importance of prevention is being rediscovered and great significance must be attached to the striking decline in deaths from ischaemic heart disease since the mid-60's in the United States which appears to be of the order of 15 per cent to 30 per cent and has benefited all age groups from 35–44 to 85+. This has been attributed to declines in per capita consumption of tobacco and animal fats and perhaps also to adoption of healthier and less sedentary life styles. Similar reductions in deaths from cerebrovascular disease have also been recorded (20 to 30 per cent) once again involving all ages. This is rather more difficult to explain since it started much earlier (1952) than the preventive campaigns of the Surgeon General and the American Heart Association (Walker, 1977; Stern 1979). It is not clear what effect the development of antihypertensive therapy has had on these incidences and even less clear is the role of coronary and intensive care units. Interest in prevention has been fostered in the United Kingdom by such publications as 'Prevention and Health' (1976). This report, however excellent it may be in many ways, makes scant mention of prevention in old age. Geriatric services in the United Kingdom have tended to reflect these changes in medical opinion over the last few decades. While the geriatric services were initially exclusively hospital orientated, movement towards the community soon took place and thereafter interest proceeded towards preventive care (Williamson, 1977, 1979).

For success in old age preventive measures must be applied in a variety of ways and at different levels of care. This involves prevention of disease, earlier detection of disabling conditions and better and more appropriate treatment and rehabilitation of chronic conditons. It is also necessary to widen the scope to include family members and other carers so that they may be helped to continue their supportive roles for as long as possible. Paediatricians have taught for decades that only a healthy mother (in a healthy family setting) can ensure healthy children. When confronted with a sickly child the paediatrician looks to the family to see if therein lies the cause of the child's poor health. The aged are in this respect (as in many others) akin to the young child in that their well-being may readily be prejudiced by adverse environmental factors among which family circumstances are often paramount.

CLASSIFICATION OF PREVENTION

Morris (1975) has suggested a simple classification into primary, secondary and tertiary prevention. As will become apparent, these three phases are less sharply defined and demarcated in later life but the classification nevertheless possesses merit.

Primary prevention
This implies 'genuine prevention' through the eradication of disease by removal of causative factors, or by rendering subjects resistant to disease, both influences often operating simultaneously. Examples are the eradication of smallpox through world wide vigilance in isolation of infectious cases and policies of vaccination. Diseases related to poverty or malnutrition may be prevented by action directed towards relief of poverty and the provision of suitable nutrition. Such prevention is very largely dependent upon appropriate economic and political action. It will be obvious that these remedies become more difficult to apply in old age, e.g. in relation to the problems of changing eating habits of a lifetime. Primary malnutrition is rare in old people in the United Kingdom (DHSS, 1972) and persons who have low energy, low protein intakes generally are malnourished because of some specific illness or frequently due to apathy and depression following upon loneliness, isolation and widowhood. Problems arise much more commonly in old age due to the imbalance between calorie intake and energy expenditure with resultant obesity (DHSS, 1979).

Immunization and vaccination in old age
Immunization and vaccination have produced spectacular results in the control of such conditions as smallpox, poliomyelitis, typhoid and (to a lesser extent) influenza. In chapter 5 it has been shown that immune competence declines in old age thus rendering the aged more liable to infection. This also tends to result in more severe and prolonged illness, which may lead to serious sequelae or prove fatal. What, therefore, are the practical implications for the elderly? Each year in the United Kingdom, Health Departments circulate information relating to expected influenza outbreaks and list the groups in the population for whom influenza immunization may be indicated. Among these groups are the

'institutionalized elderly'. The final decision as to whether to immunize or not is always left to the 'individual doctor'. In the past influenza vaccines were often of dubious potency and purity and so protection was uncertain and reactions common (Ruben, 1982). In addition most controlled studies of influenza vaccination have been carried out in younger populations (e.g. members of the Armed Forces) and it was not certain that similar protection would be bestowed upon older subjects. It was known that influenza vaccines were effective in raising antibody titres in the elderly (Douglas et al, 1977) but this would not of necessity confer effective protection. Barker and Mullooly (1980), however, showed that, using an appropriate vaccine, it is possible to achieve about 70 per cent reduction in hospitalization rates and almost 90 per cent reduction in mortality in influenza and pneumonia in elderly subjects. These authors maintain that the degree of protection achieved in the elderly was of a level similar to that in younger groups.

What, therefore, ought to be our policy towards the use of influenza vaccines in the elderly? For the healthy elderly living in the community, the policy to be adopted should be identical to that for the rest of the community, i.e. if an epidemic due to a virulent strain is threatening, then appropriate vaccination should be offered. For the institutionalized elderly similar policies should be pursued but there is little logic in yearly dosing in the rather vain hope that should influenza strike it will be due to a strain for which protection has been provided. What is perhaps equally necessary (although often overlooked) is the desirability of offering protection to nursing and other caring staff in institutions for the elderly in the face of a threatening epidemic of influenza. Whatever doubts one may harbour about the desirability of banishing the 'old man's friend' (pneumonia resulting in a short, sharp terminal illness in a deteriorated, unhappy and pain-wracked old person) there can be no doubt about the baneful effects upon elderly residents in institutions when the staff is decimated by the depredations of influenza.

Morbidity and deaths from pneumonia are common in old age and recently there have been suggestions that polyvalent pneumococcal vaccines should be offered to protect the elderly especially those in institutions. The Food and Drug Administration of the United States has recommended that persons over 50, especially those in institutions, should receive pneumonococcal vaccine (FDA, 1978). The validity of this recommendation is by no means certain, however, and Bently et al (1981) concluded that it would be unlikely to reduce total cases of pneumonia or even of pneumococcal pneumonia. It seems likely that polyvalent pneumococcal vaccines may boost resistancee to the strains they contain but this may merely offer an opportunity to other strains to invade and cause pneumonia. At present, therefore, it seems there is no good evidence to support the use of available pneumococcal vaccines in old age (see also pp 96–97).

Maintenance and promotion of health in old age

The importance of promoting healthy lifestyles and of avoiding unhealthy behaviour is now well recognized in young and middle-aged subjects. Elaborate programmes of health education have been conducted with the intention of encouraging people to take adequate exercise, to eat well balanced diets and avoid obesity. There is little doubt that, where successful, these measures have resulted in higher levels of fitness and enhanced well-being. Their impact upon health in old age, on longevity and patterns of mortality are, however, still uncertain.

Healthy exercise undoubtedly improves fitness even in old age. Tanner (1964) showed that the body composition of elderly subjects who continued to exercise tended to be closer to 'normality'. Olympic athletes, however, even in old age are likely to be much more 'health conscious' in other important respects, e.g. in avoiding hazards of tobacco and alcohol abuse (Shepherd, 1977). Encouraging and hopeful results have recently been reported from Sweden in relation to the potential benefits of regular physical training in old age. A group of 70 year old subjects in Gothenburg undertook thrice weekly physical training and showed a 26 per cent increase in maximum oxygen consumption and marked increase in muscle strength compared to a control group of the same age. This improvement was also reflected in lower heart rates after submaximal exercise and muscle biopsy showed significant increase in the proportion of type II muscle fibres. It seems likely therefore that for many old persons (perhaps a considerable majority) some proportion of observed losses in physical, mental and social competence are at least partly attributable to a degree of 'disuse atrophy' and are only partly related to the changes of age or disease. It is clear that much more research is needed to confirm these findings and, if substantiated, means must be found of communicating these findings and changing attitudes both in society in general and in the elderly in particular.

Screening for risk factors (precursors of disease)

Primary prevention also includes the process of screening or the planned detection of risk factors in asymptomatic subjects. This form of screening has been described in the following terms: 'Screening differs from ordinary clinical practice in that it involves seeking out people with no overt symptoms of disease and asking them to undergo examination and tests to see whether the condition to be identified is present' (DHSS, 1976). Precursors commonly sought are asymptomatic hyper-

tension, raised plasma cholesterol and triglyceride levels, increased intraocular pressure and cervical metaplasia (by taking cervical smears). These procedures seem sensible and rational and have appealed strongly to the modern medical mind since complex technology could be widely applied. Having proposed that various risk factors should be sought a natural development seemed to be multiple screening, i.e. the individual should be subjected to a battery of tests rather than the search for a single factor. The development of automated techniques for electrocardiographic interpretation and of multichannel autoanalysers for assays of blood samples seemed to offer great opportunities for this variant of primary prevention. Multiphasic screening centres were established and individuals encouraged to participate. Multiple investigations included anthropometry, respiratory function tests, electrocardiography, chest X-ray, and samples of blood and urine were collected for multiple assays. Cervical smears and mammograms were done in women and in some centres sigmoidoscopy was performed. Results were then collated and sent to the subject's primary physician. It was anticipated that in cases with significant 'risk factors' suitable steps would be taken to counteract their harmful effects and thus prevent or delay onset of the disease to which the subject was at risk.

Because of the complexity and multiplicity of factors involved, evaluation of such screening has proved to be very difficult and requires properly conducted controlled trials. Such trials have been few, partly because of the difficulty in conducting them but also because the medical profession (and substantial numbers of the public) accept that the rationale for screening is self-evident and hence scientific validation scarcely necessary. However, even the most enthusiastic proponents of multiphasic screening have been hard pressed to show any positive value (Cutler et al 1973) and a well conducted controlled study in London showed no difference between screened subjects and controls in terms of mortality, morbidity or use of services. (South East London Screening Study Group, 1977).

This study was specifically designed to answer the question as to whether multiphasic screening should be promoted within the National Health Service. Its negative result led to a firm decision that scarce and finite resources should not be diverted into this unrewarding activity. Not surprisingly a degree of backlash followed claiming that failure to show benefits from screening simply indicated an inefficient 'follow-through' after detection of disease precursors. This argument is difficult to sustain since the subjects screened were all patients of general practitioners who collaborated enthusiastically in the scheme; it is highly improbable that 'ordinary' or 'average' GPs would have performed more effectively. The London Study was concerned with persons aged 45 to 64 years and it may be assumed that similar activity in older age groups would be no more successful. Indeed, there exists the danger that a screening process which identifies several precursor states but which cannot offer any hope of preventing disease merely converts an 'elderly person' into an 'elderly patient'?

Screening for hypertension in old age

A special problem exists in relation to hypertension in old age since its detection and effective control in younger people has been shown conclusively to reduce morbidity and mortality from ischaemic heart disease and stroke. The Framingham Study (Kannel et al, 1976) appears to show that the adverse effects of raised systolic and diastolic pressures persist into ages 64 to 75. It may be argued that if the aim of detecting and reducing raised blood pressure is the prevention of 'target tissue damage' then it is too late to start at age 75 or 80 years. It may also be argued that the significance of raised blood pressure (especially systolic pressure) is quite different in an aged person compared to a younger one. For example, raised systolic waves of pressure may simply reflect a relatively inelastic arterial tree. It must also be emphasized that in younger subjects any reduction in blood pressure will be immediately compensated for by cerebral arterial dilatation which effectively safeguards cerebral perfusion. This cerebral autoregulation may be impaired or lost in elderly subjects (Wollner et al, 1979). These authors state that since some elderly patients are unable to compensate normally for falls in blood pressure this 'may explain . . . the varying effects of hypotensive drugs in the elderly'. Indeed it could be postulated that for a patient who has very poor auto-regulation a drop in blood pressure may be accomplished by a parallel drop in cerebral perfusion. This, of course, would explain those cases which all experienced physicians have seen of strokes developing within days or weeks of starting hypotensive therapy.

Two recent longitudinal population studies of elderly subjects (Milne, 1981; Evans et al, 1980) have failed to show significant relationships between raised blood pressure and the incidence of stroke or heart disease. Both these studies confirmed the finding of 'regression towards the mean' whereby subjects who had raised blood pressure on entering tended to show a downward pressure drift over the ensuing 5 years while those who had lower pressures initially tended to show increases with the passage of the years.

In the light of these considerations what, therefore, ought to be our attitude towards the discovery and possible lowering of 'high' blood pressure in the elderly? The best advice is 'extreme caution' and many would subscribe to the view that blood pressure should only be lowered if it is indeed shown to be persistently increased and there are manifest signs of its direct effects, e.g. left ventricular strain as evidenced by pulmonary oedema or persistent and and disabling angina. An ever present danger of tampering with blood pressure in old age is that of provoking or aggravating postural hypotension. Whatever arguments there may be about the dangers of raised blood pressure there can be none about the dangers of this important side effect of hypotensive therapy in the old.

Recently the whole concept of the significance of risk factors in production of disease has been questioned by Oliver (1982) who debated the dangers of using drugs to correct risk factors for coronary disease and stroke. He pointed out that only a minority of subjects shown to have risk factors will actually develop the disease. Hence if all those identified as possessing the risk factor are treated with drugs the majority will unavoidably be exposed to the dangers of adverse, unwanted drug reactions without any possibility of benefit to individuals. Oliver also argues that 'aggressiveness in the use of these drugs should be inversely proportional to age' and to this view most experienced Geriatricians would add a heartfelt 'Amen'.

Secondary prevention

By this is meant earlier diagnosis, mostly of conditions with reversible pathology. Hence the condition is usually at an early stage and in younger subjects may be subclinical, although in older subjects with their diminished functional reserves it may be symptomatic. Such symptoms are generally non-specific (confusion, falls, general ill health etc.) and hence misleading.

Although it may reasonably be argued that early diagnosis is merely a reiteration of classical medical teaching throughout history, its importance is even greater in old age since the affected system may already be affected by age changes and hence reduction of functional reserves. If effective and prompt treatment is not carried out immediately there are multiple dangers — of organ failure, of 'knock-on' multisystem failure and of incomplete recovery.

Other problems, however, exist in old age since it may often be difficult to separate the effects of aging from those of disease and only better education and training of doctors and other health professionals can help towards better understanding of these matters. It has now become a matter of extreme urgency that medical schools should react appropriately to the changes in medical practice occasioned by the aging of populations. Suitable teaching and training in Gerontology and Geriatric Medicine is required (Svanborg and Williamson, 1980).

Tertiary prevention

This phase of prevention implies the detection of established and incapacitating chronic disease in the elderly thus offering the chance of earlier and more effective management. It differs from screening as already defined in that the conditions sought are not precursors of disease nor are they being sought in persons 'with no overt symptoms of disease'. Rather they are being sought in patients who are already experiencing discomfort, pain or other distress. The earlier detection of these conditions offers the prospect of more effective treatment, of successful rehabilitation and also appropriate support for patient and family so that the patient remains as comfortable and independent as possible (with minimal stress upon the family) and with reduced chance of secondary consequences of disability such as loneliness etc. It will be immediately apparent that tertiary prevention has the most immediate and obvious relevance to persons who are already old. It will also be apparent that in this age group the dividing line between secondary and tertiary prevention is distinctly unclear.

The pioneers of geriatric medicine showed that even in elderly and aged subjects such apparently unpromising conditions as stroke, arthropathy and Parkinsonism could often be effectively treated and a high proportion of sufferers could be restored to higher levels of independence by appropriate treatment and rehabilitation. Prior to this the almost universal view of such conditions in old age was that they warranted only custodial care since they were classified as 'incurable' both upon the nature of the condition had their occurrence in old age. The horrifying description of the plight of old people in the 'chronic wards' of a previous era are movingly described by Thomson (1949). It should be noted that these descriptions refer to the state of affairs which widely prevailed in the United Kingdom less than 40 years ago and which persist in some degree today in many other parts of the world where the negative stereotype of old age still results in custodial care rather than active therapy and rehabilitation.

Soon after the specialty of Geriatric Medicine was established in the United Kingdom, some physicians began to realise the need for earlier detection of chronic and disabling conditions and threatening social deprivation. Anderson and Cowan (1955) described the potential benefits of consultative clinics for the elderly at which medical, psychological and social assessments could be made. In 1964 the results of a study in Edinburgh were published. A sample of old people was investigated in detail and the findings compared to the information possessed by their general practitioners (Williamson et al, 1964). This study showed that old people often failed to report certain conditions to their general practitioners even though the conditions were unpleasant, painful and incapacitating. They suffered these disabilities in silence until a crisis occured. The report began as follows:

One of the most striking and distressing features of work in a geriatric unit is that patients are so often admitted in a very advanced stage of disease. Many have pressure sores or permanent joint contractures, and show signs of prolonged neglect and subnutrition. Yet the family doctor may write: 'I saw this patient for the first time yesterday', or 'the last time I saw this old lady was two years ago when her husband died'. Careful history taking will establish that timely medical or social intervention might have prevented much of the disability. Why then was it not forthcoming?

This phenomenon of non-reporting by older patients of serious, progressive, disabling and unpleasant conditions is of considerable importance. There are probably several reasons for it. In younger people several factors operate to encourage them to seek medical help. There is the threat from disability to the male's employability and hence his income; then there is the recognition that disability involves significant restriction of life-style; for females there is the additional threat to the ability to fulfil roles as mother, wife and household manager. In addition the young have generally been brought up in a society where medical help is readily sought. It is useful to contrast this with old age where these incentives are either absent or operate much less strongly. Thus for the retired male there is no threat to employment from disability since his pension comes in whether he is fit or unfit. For the female, earlier roles are often diminished or absent through widowhood and family dispersal. In addition many old people subscribe to the common stereotype of old age that these losses are merely inescapable accompaniments of old age. Thus, it is common for old people to say 'What else can I expect at my age?' or 'We just have to put up with aches and pains when we get old'. Unfortunately many doctors have also shared this negative view and so confirm the patient's pessimistic impression. Some old people also fear the consequences of divulging their disabilities to medical authorities in case this may lead to their admission to hospital (or other institution). They fear greatly the threat of loss of independence and reduced control over their own lives which medical intervention may bring about. The past record of the medical profession in this field and the tendency to think in terms of 'disposal' rather than 'treatment and rehabilitation' makes it easy to understand why some old people behave in this apparently irrational fashion.

There appear to be two distinct sets of conditions in the context of Reporting/Non-Reporting. Conditions related to the respiratory system, to the cardiovascular system and to the central nervous system seem to be, on the whole, well reported. The old lady who is breathless, wheezy and has cough and sputum is easily convinced that she needs a doctor. For his part, the doctor is trained to diagnose and treat such conditions and obtains professional satisfaction from doing so. This is shared territory — patients and doctors are in agreement about what has to be done. There is, however, another range of conditions which are much less likely to be well reported and these are illustrated in Figure 50.1.

This shows that locomotor problems (especially those relating to foot trouble), bladder disturbance and both dementia and depression tend to be unreported and hence unknown to medical attendants. These important conditions are not only unpleasant and distressing but may lead to significant secondary effects. Thus, locomotor problems impair mobility, narrowing social horizons and increasing the chance of loneliness and dependence. Bladder dysfunction (whether it be the post-micturition dribbling of prostatism or the frequent stress incontinence in old women) may readily become socially inhibiting and eventually lead to reduced social competence. The dangers of unrecognized dementia or depression are easily understood. All these poorly reported conditions lower morale and self esteem — particularly dangerous at a time when other socio-economic pressures may be tending to produce similar effects.

Case finding in old age
The planned search for poorly reported conditions in old age may be described as case finding. This has now become an important function of primary medical care (backed up by efficient geriatric services).

The exact method and effectiveness of case finding still require evaluation. Furthermore, there is considerable individual variation in the effect of specific pathological states. These facts cause doubts about the scientific validity of case finding. This may be illustrated by citing the example of two elderly females with identical degrees of osteoarthrosis of knee joints. Clinically, radiologically and pathologically their knee joints are equally abnormal and yet one old lady is still independent, going up and down stairs and regularly visiting her family, her church and her friends. The other is housebound, moves with great difficulty about the house and needs much help from her family, the home help service and the community nurses to keep her going at a low level of independence. Chamberlain (1973) found this paradox so perplexing and scientifically discouraging that she thought case finding in old age was so inaccurate and misleading as to be scarcely worthwhile. It is necessary therefore to 'think beyond the pathology' in this context and, instead of concentrating upon the detection of pathology, to assess instead, *functional loss*. The case finding process then becomes a search for significant loss of function (physical, mental and social). Since the well-being of the elderly person is often closely dependent upon the effectiveness and goodwill of family members, case finding must also be extended to include family carers.

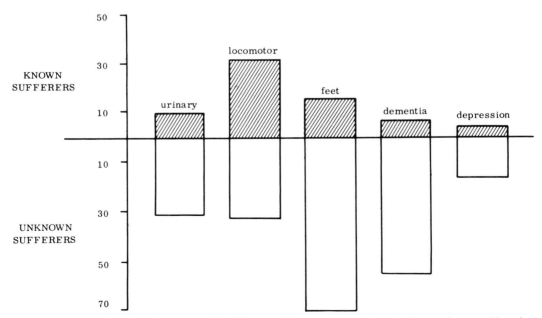

Fig. 50.1 Unknown disabilities in older persons. Disabilities in which most of the iceberg is submerged — practitioner's awareness is low. (Reproduced from Arie T, Essays in Health Care of the Elderly, Croom Helm, London)

Who should carry out case finding?

Case finding must be a function of the primary health care team and the obvious person to do it is the Health Visitor (or Public Health Nurse); her training in social and preventive aspects of health is appropriate to this task. If health visitors are not available for this work it is quite possible to train other registered nurses to carry it out (Milne et al, 1972).

The scope of the case finding process

While it might reasonably be arugued that if the screening is for the detection of disease or its precursors then the patient should be seen in the general practitioner's office or surgery, this argument loses much of its force when the search is for loss of significant function. What matters is the ability of the individual to function in her usual environment and this may be most appropriately assessed in her home. Additionally, patients invited to the surgery for screening often decline to come. For instance Pike

(1976) found that less than 40 per cent of those invited to such sessions actually attended. Case finding therefore should be carried out in the patient's home. Arcand and Williamson (1981) have shown that a home visit paid by an experienced observer may yield a very large amount of extremely valuable information. This includes the suitability of premises, furnishings and equipment (heights of beds, chairs and toilet seats etc.) as well as assessment of adequacy of heating and cooking facilities. Most important is to observe medications available and those that are actually being taken. Relatives and other carers may also demonstrate the causes of their anxiety such as dangerous stairs, evidence of poor catering and inadequate housekeeping etc.

Information sought at the case finding home visit should be based upon questions and observations. It may conveniently be divided into (1) items which the nurse observer uncovers and acts upon herself and (2) items which, when detected lead to referral to the general practitioner (Table 50.1).

Table 50.1 Items for detection and action by nurse observer

Observation	Action
Expressed loneliness	Counselling patient and family, invoking voluntary agencies
Isolation, poor and few social contacts	Counselling patient and family, invoking voluntary agencies
Effects of rehousing (or other relocation)	Counselling, help with introduction to local shopping, social and other agencies. Contact housing authority
Family ineffectiveness	Determine cause, counsel family members, put patient in touch with sources of help, e.g. help towards telephone installation
Signs of family stress, demoralization, resentment, hostility, exhaustion	Counsel family, indicating sources of help, especially day care and respite admission. Contact appropriate services.
Fear and uncertainty in patient (fear of falls and lying on floor, fear of robbery or vandalism)	Reassurance, remove hazards (including help from occupational therapist). Arrange for patient to be instructed in rising from floor. Instal radio alarm device.
Danger of hypothermia. Check ambient temperatures in livingroom, bedroom and bathroom. Check heaters	Advice on how to keep warm — clothing, heating, insulation. Financial assistance for payment of heating bills etc.
Vision — Simple test of visual capacity. Inspection of spectacles.	Refer to Optician

Observation	Action
Hearing — Simple hearing assessment. Inspection of any existing aids.	Refer to Hearing Aid Centre
Medication — Inspection of medication in the home and patient's understanding of its purpose, dosage etc.	Patient should know what is being taken and why. Refer to GP for review and simplification.
Nutrition — Assessment of diet, dentition, cooking appliances in regular use, food store	Advice on diet, low cost nutritious foods. If obese reduce calorie intake. Refer to dietitian.
The following may be detected and referred to the general practioner:	
Cardiac and respiratory problems.	Cough, sputum, dyspnoea, orthopnoea. Look for cyanosis, oedema, cardiac dysrhythmia.
Locomotor problems	Pain and stiffness, swelling of joints. Examine gait. Look at feet and footwear. Refer to GP or chiropodist.
Bladder dysfunction	Frequency, nocturia, dysuria, incontinence, prostatism. Need for commode etc.
Bowel dysfunction	Constipation, alteration in bowel habit, blood in stool. Overuse of laxatives.
History of falls or blackouts. Examine gait and general stability.	Search for environmental hazards. Exclude postural hypotension. Seek help from GP and/or occupational therapist (walking aids, hand rails etc).

How widely should the case finding net be cast?
It would be inappropriate and impracticable to attempt case finding among all people aged over, say, 65 years, since it would offer no benefit to the large majority. It is therefore useful to attempt to specify certain high risk groups and the following suggestions are offered:

1. The very old. Akhtar et al (1973) showed that 80 per cent of the 85+ group were unable to exist at home without some help. Case finding among this age group would therefore be directed towards those who needed help and seeing that it was supplied.

2. Those who appear isolated and receive few visitors or have few social contacts. These may or may not be among patients who express loneliness since the latter is a very subjective state. Some isolated old people are genuine 'loners' and hence ought not to be interfered with since this is their chosen way of life.

3. The bereaved, most commonly the elderly widow. Those already identified as having special needs through being in receipt of extra services such as social security, home help, community nursing care etc.

4. Those recently discharged from hospital. This is especially important when, at time of admission, there was evidence of recent or more prolonged self neglect (bodily and foot uncleanliness, uncut toenails, dirty clothing plus any suggestion of poor nutrition).

5. Those recently relocated. This may mean persons rehoused or even persons admitted to some form of institutional care. Any relocation in old age may constitute a profound stress and create a need for help.

6. Those liable to special stress associated with local factors eg in inner city areas of multiple deprivation.

An interesting way of detecting high risk groups within general practice has been described by Barber et al (1980). They sent a postal questionnaire to elderly persons on a practice list asking them to answer 'Yes' or 'No' to nine simple questions as below:

— Do you live on your own?
— Are you without a relative you could call on for help?
— Do you depend on someone for help?
— Are there many days when you are unable to have a hot meal?
— Are you confined to your home through ill health?
— Is there anything about your health causing you concern or difficulty?
— Do you have difficulty with vision?
— Do you have difficulty with hearing?
— Have you been in hospital during the past year?

They had a response of 81 per cent with high accuracy of responses. This simple approach could be used to identify the old people in a practice who would justify a more detailed case finding enquiry.

Evaluation of case finding
It has been extremely difficult to determine the value of case finding of the type outlined above for a wide variety of reasons. Lowther et al (1970) reported the findings among 300 elderly subjects who had been involved in a case finding study. At 18 to 30 months after their involvement, 29 per cent were still judged to be deriving benefit from the process. Williams (1974) reached a very similar figure of 27 per cent showing benefit after one year. Pike (1976) showed that in his practice where screening had been in operation there were lower mean consultation rates than for the rest of the practices involved in the National Morbidity Study. These studies were all uncontrolled and so it is very difficult to know what significance to attach to their findings. Tulloch and Moore (1979) conducted a controlled trial of 'screening and surveillance' in patients aged 70+ in Dr Tulloch's practice. Over a two year period the only significant difference between test subjects and controls was that the test group had significantly shorter duration of hospitalization. The numbers involved were small and a larger sample might have shown other differences of statistical significance.

All of these studies have involved combinations of screening (as previously defined) and case finding and the actual scope and nature of the enquiry have generally been unclear and unspecified. A clear statement upon the actual process of 'functional screening' and a thorough appraisal of its value are required.

Screening for cancer in old age
The rationale of screening for cancer is to detect the disease at a stage when it may be cured. This, of course, implies early diagnosis but the problem is complicated by the fact that the staging of the disease is by no means always related to its duration. Thus a small cancerous lump recently occurring in a woman's breast may be accompanied by widespread metastases while it is not at all uncommon to find a breast cancer in an old lady which remains apparently unchanged for years, the patient dying in due course from a totally unrelated condition. Chamberlain (1982) has recently reviewed the field of cancer screening and has given a useful list of advantages and disadvantages (Table 51.2).

Table 51.2 indicates that the older the subject, the more likely it is that disadvantages will outweigh advantages both for patient and health services. For the very old who are often the victims of multiple diseases treatment of any cancer found by screening may well be precluded by the patient's poor general condition and unfitness for surgery or cytotoxic therapy. Cancer in old age is in many cases only slowly progressive and in some cases it may scarcely affect the patient's life and manner of dying.

Table 51.2 Advantages, and Disadvantages of Cancer Screening (adapted with permission from Chamberlain, 1982)

Advantages	Disadvantages
Improved prognosis for some	Longer period of morbidity and 'patient status' for those whose prognosis is unaltered
Less radical treatment for 'earlier cases'	More 'aggressive' treatment required. Danger of 'overtreatment'.
Reassurance for those with negative results	False reassurance for 'false negatives'. Unnecessary anxiety and distress for 'false positives'.
Resource savings from less extensive treatment and greater chance of independent existence	Costs of screening programme. Costs arising from treatment of 'positives'. Waste of resources in dealing with 'false positives'.

There seems therefore to be little justification for embarking upon cancer screening programmes among the elderly. This, of course, does not absolve the physician from the obligation of making resolute efforts to diagnose cancer in patients who come to him for help. The presentation of malignant disease in old age is often atypical and non-specific and only the alert physician will realize that the condition underlying a vague loss of well-being may be a cancer of lower bowel — many of which may be diagnosed by a simple rectal examination.

THE PREVENTIVE ROLE OF NON-MEDICAL SERVICES

The declared objective of geriatric services is to help old people to remain as independent as possible for as long as possible and to offer them as much control over their lives as possible. They must therefore be helped to retain significant family and community roles and thus retain their sense of self esteem.

A civilized society ought to be able to ensure safety and security for all its citizens including the elderly but even once this has been achieved there will remain the fear of medical crises — especially falls and the inability to get up from the floor. The use of small portable and relatively cheap radio alarms offers the possibility of countering these fears and dealing with the resulting crises. This is a new field in which modern electronic technology may offer considerable help to old people but, as with other aspects of technology, the matter is much more complex than is initially apparent. It is important to ensure that old people who are given these alarms are genuinely in need of such provision and that the alarm is not used as a cheap substitute for some other more personal service. They must be capable of using the device sensibly (in one study 23 per cent of patients failed to operate their alarms when the crisis occurred).

Lastly the actual appliance must be suitably designed and reasonably priced. As with some other services it is necessary to emphasize that alarms must not be used merely to assuage the rest of society's anxieties about old people 'at risk'; instead they should be used to meet needs in a way acceptable to the individual old person (Butler and Oldman, 1981). Voluntary organizations have traditionally been concerned with the elderly. Nowadays they increasingly see their role as offering opportunities for the fit elderly to continue to contribute to the life of their communities not least through helping their less fit contemporaries.

REFERENCES

Akhtar A J, Broe G A, Crombie A, McLean W M R, Andrews G R, Caird F I 1973 Disability and dependency in the elderly at home. Age and Ageing 2: 102–111

Anderson W F, Cowan N R 1955 A consultative health centre for older people: The Rutherglen experiment. Lancet 2: 239

Aniansson A, Grinby G, Rundgren A, Svanborg A, Orlander J 1980 Physical training in old men. Age and Ageing 9: 186–187

Arcand M, Williamson J 1981 An evaluation of home visiting of patients by physicians in Geriatric Medicine. British Medical Journal 283: 718–720

Barber J H, Wallis J B, McKeating E 1980 Postal screening questionnaire in preventive geriatric care. Journal of Royal College of General Practitioners 30: 49–51

Barker W H, Mullooly J P 1980 Influenza vaccination of elderly persons. Reduction in pneumonia and influenza hospitalizations and deaths. Journal of the American Medical Association 244: 2547–2549

Bently D W, Ha K, Mamot K, Moon D, Moore L, Poletto P, Springett A 1981 Pneumococcal vaccine in the institutionalized elderly: design of a non-randomized trial and preliminary results. Review of Infectious Diseases 3 (supplement): 71–81

Butler A, Oldman C 1981 Alarm systems for the elderly: report of workshop held at the University of Leeds, September 1980, Department of Social Policy and Administration, University of Leeds

Chamberlain J 1982 Screening for cancer. British Journal of Hospital Medicine 27(6): 583–591

Chamberlain J O P 1973 Screening elderly people. Proceedings of Royal Society of Medicine 66: 888

Cutler J, Ramcharan S, Feldman R, Siegelaub A B, Campbell C, Friedman G D et al 1973 Multiphasic check-up evaluation study, 1–3. Preventive Medicine 2: 197–246

Department of Health and Social Security (3) 1972 A Nutrition survey of the elderly. HMSO, London

Department of Health and Social Security 1976 Prevention and health: everybody's business. HMSO, London

Department of Health and Social Security (16) 1979 Nutrition and health in old age. HMSO, London

Douglas R G, Bently D W, Brandriss M W 1977 Responses of elderly and chronically ill subjects to bivalent influenza A/New Jersey/8/76 (HSW INT) — A/Victoria 3/75 (H3N2) vaccine. Journal of Infectious Diseases 136 (supplement): 526–533

Evans J G, Prudham D, Wandless I 1980 Risk factors for stroke in the elderly. In: Barbagallo-Sangiorgi G, Exton-Smith A N (eds) The Ageing Brain, Plenum Press, London, p 113–126

FDA Drug Bulletin 1978 Pneumococcal vaccine, polyvalent licensed. Jan–Feb 8: 4–5

Fries J F, Crapo L M 1981 Vitality and aging. W H Freeman & Co, San Francisco

Kannel W B, McGhee D, Gordon T 1976 A General cardiovascular risk profile: The Framingham Study. American Journal of Cardiology 38: 46–51

Langer E J, Rodin J 1976 The effects of choice and enhanced personal responsibility: A field experiment in an institutional setting. Journal of Personality and Social Psychology 34: 191–198

Langer E J, Rodin J, Beck P, Weinman C, Spitzer L 1978 Environmental determinants of memory improvement in late adulthood. Journal of Personality and Social Psychology 37: 2003–2013

Lowther C P, MacLeod R D M, Williamson J 1970 Evaluation of early diagnostic services for the elderly. British Medical Journal 3: 275–277

Milne J S 1981 A longitudinal study of blood pressure and stroke in older people. Journal of Clinical and Experimental Gerontology 3: 135–159

Milne J S, Maule M M, Cormack S, Williamson J 1972 The design and testing of a questionnaire and examination to assess physical and mental health in older people using a staff nurse as the observer. Journal of Chronic Diseases 25: 385–405

Morris J N 1975 The uses of epidemiology. Churchill Livingstone, Edinburgh

Oliver M F 1982 Risks of correcting the risks of coronary disease and stroke with drugs. New England Journal of Medicine 306: 297–298

Pike L A 1976 Screening the elderly in general practice. Journal of Royal College of General Practitioners 26: 698–703

Plemons J K, Willis S L, Baltes P B 1978 Modifiability of fluid intelligence in aging: short-term longitudinal training approach. Journal of Gerontology 33: 224–231

Ruben F L 1982 Prevention of influenza in the elderly. Journal of the American Geriatrics Society 30, 9: 577–580

Shepherd R J 1977 Physical activity and aging. Croom Helm, London

South-East London Screening Study Group 1977. International Journal of Epidemiology 6: 357–363

Svanborg A, Williamson J 1980 Health care of the elderly: Implications for education and training of physicians and other health care professionals. World Health Organization Discussion Paper EUR/HCE/80/1

Tanner J M 1964 The physique of the olympic athlete. Allen and Unwin, London

Thomson A P 1949 Problems of aging and chronic sickness. British Medical Journal 2: 244–250 and 300–305

Tulloch A J, Moore V 1979 A Randomised controlled trial of geriatric screening and surveillance in general practice. Journal of Royal College of General Practitioners 29: 733–742

Williams I 1974 A follow-up of geriatric patients after sociomedical assessment. Journal of Royal College of General Practitioners 24: 341–346

Williamson J 1977 Geriatric medicine: whose specialty? Annals of Internal Medicine 91: 774–777

Williamson J 1979 Three views on Geriatric Medicine: 3. Notes on the historical development of Geriatric Medicine as a specialty. Age and Ageing 8: 144–148

Williamson J, Stokoe I H, Gray S, Fisher M, Smith A, McGhee A, Stephenson E 1964 Old people at home: Their unreported needs. Lancet i: 1119–1120

Wollner L, McCarthy S T, Soper N W, Macy D J 1979 Failure of cerebral autoregulation as a cause of brain dysfunction in the elderly. British Medical Journal 1: 1117–1118

Rehabilitation

INTRODUCTION

Rehabilitation is often thought of in terms of organized activities carried out by remedial therapists using complicated equipment and techniques. This concept must be widened to include the coordinated support of the patient and his family to enable the optimal level of independence to be achieved. As such, rehabilitation involves not only the physiotherapist, occupational therapist and speech therapist but also doctors, nurses, social workers, chiropodists, dieticians, technicians, volunteers, neighbours and community support. Where so many people are involved it may be difficult to move from the medical-surgical model of care, where professionals take responsibility for the patient, i.e. by doing things for the patient, to the educational model where professionals help the patient and family to cope for themselves (Anderson, 1978). It was with this in mind that Hyams (1969) defined rehabilitation as 'the planned withdrawal of support'.

Planning is the basis of good rehabilitation management. This requires effective team work — which may be difficult to achieve. Rothberg (1981) defined a health care team as 'a group of persons, each possessing particular expertise, who have a common purpose and goal . . . . The members meet together to communicate, collaborate and consolidate knowledge from which plans are made, action determined, future decisions influenced and the accomplishment of goals evaluated'.

It is important to differentiate between 'interdisciplinary' and 'multidisciplinary' management (Melvin, 1980). In the latter the patient obtains the benefit of the expertise of a number of professionals, each providing what they feel is the most appropriate form of treatment. In the case of 'interdisciplinary' approach the members of the team have agreed a common policy of management and use of specific techniques. This can be difficult to achieve and requires staff who are prepared to modify strongly held views in the interest of the team approach. This is essential if the patient is not to be confused by different advice from each member of the team.

It is interesting that the popular concept of the importance of each member of the team is inversely proportional to the time he spends with the patient. Kushlick (1975) described four groups of direct care (DC):

DC 24 — those who give care throughout the 24 hours — these are usually relatives.

DC 12 — those who provide continuing care on a shift basis, e.g. nurses and staff in residential homes.

DC 2–6 — those who provide treatment for shorter periods of 2 to 6 hours, e.g. therapists.

DC 10 (minutes) — those 'hit and run' carers who provide very short periods of intervention, e.g. doctors.

In view of this all those involved should appreciate their real importance and in successful teams there is overlap of the specific roles of each group of professionals. The large amount of time spent in direct care by relatives and nurses emphasises the importance of these groups being fully aware of the rehabilitation approach and goals.

Terminology

Dysfunction in rehabilitation can be defined as follows (Harris 1971):

Impairment — lacking part or all of a limb, or having a defective limb, organ or mechanism of the body.

Disability — loss or reduction of functional ability.

Handicap — the disadvantage or restriction of activity caused by disability.

Wood (1980) has suggested that there is a difference between 'disability' and 'disablement'. He regards 'disability' as a restriction or lack of ability to perform an activity in the manner, or within the range, considered normal. It therefore represents objectification of impairment and is a disturbance at the level of the person. 'Disablement', on the other hand, is a collective description referring to any experience identified variously by the terms impairment, disability and handicap.

The difference between these terms can be seen as follows:

Impairment	Disability	Handicap
Amputation of lower limb	Walking difficulties	Inability to climb stairs
Dementia	Forgetful	Unable to live alone
Dysphasia	Communication difficulties	Unable to shop

It will be noted that handicap varies markedly between individuals with the same degree of impairment. For instance a patient with a below knee amputation who lives in a house with rooms on different levels is more handicapped than a person with an identical impairment who lives in a ground floor flat. Knight and Warren (1978) have also suggested that 'need' is as relative a concept as is handicap. This involves a question of values and there may be major differences between the needs as perceived by the patient and those perceived by the professionals.

PLANNING A REHABILITATION PROGRAMME

There are four processes in the planning of a rehabilitation programme:

1. Determination of the level of activity prior to the episode which resulted in the need for rehabilitation.
2. Determination of the present physical, mental and emotional state of the patient.
3. Setting of short- and long-term goals.
4. Determination of the techniques necessary to achieve the goals.

Determination of previous disability

Rehabilitation may be required for an acute episode in the life of an otherwise healthy person but more often there has been long-term limitation of activities. In addition many elderly people have more than one type of disability (Wilson et al, 1962). For instance, of 184 consecutive patients admitted to the author's unit, 13 disorders which complicate rehabilitation were common (Table 51.1) with considerable overlap between them — 35 per cent having a combination of four or more present.

Chronic conditions occur with increasing frequency with advancing age (Harris, 1971 — Table 51.2) as does the prevalance and severity of handicap (Table 51.3). Some restriction of personal activity is present in 18 per cent of patients over the age of 65 years with nearly all finding difficulty with activities such as cutting toe nails (Henrard, 1980).

Multiple pathology is important since even single

Table 51.1 Conditions present in 184 consecutive patients admitted to a geriatric unit

Condition	Percentage of patients
Disorders of balance	63.6
Arthritis	35.3
Symptomatic heart disease	30.4
Incontinence of urine	27.7
Confusion	25.0
Chronic lung disease	22.3
Stroke	21.7
Hearing difficulties (severe)	19.6
Fracture of femur	12.0
Depression	10.9
Peripheral vasculae disease (excluding amputation)	9.2
Severe visual problems	7.6
Parkinsonism	4.9

Table 51.2 Estimated severely disabled in a population of 250 000 people (after Harris 1971)

	Total	(Per 1000 population)	Number 65+	Percentage 65+
Rheumatoid arthritis	323	(1.29)	173	54
Other arthritis	751	(3.0)	583	78
Stroke	427	(1.7)	316	74
Multiple sclerosis	96	(0.38)	12	13
Parkinsonism	72	(0.29)	34	47
Amputation	52	(0.21)	24	46
Paraplegia	45	(0.18)	23	51
Circulatory disorder	309	(1.24)	244	79
Respiratory disorder	144	(0.58)	90	63
Blind	66	(0.26)	58	88

Table 51.3 Prevalence of handcap by age and severity (After Harris 1971)

Age	Number/1000 population	Number severely affected	Percentage severely affected
16–29	8.9	0.9	10
30–49	27.9	3.2	11
50–64	85.0	12.2	14
65–74	220.7	33.0	15
75+	378.0	89.4	24

disabilities produce marked increase in energy requirements. Energy expenditure on normal walking is in the range of 3.19–3.486 J/m/kg body weight (McDonald, 1961; Corcoran and Brengelman, 1970; Waters et al, 1976). Patients with a below knee amputation using a prosthesis consume 4.242–5.25 J/m/kg body weight (Waters et al, 1976; Ganguli et al, 1973; Gonzalez et al, 1974) whilst hemiplegic patients expend 4.452–6.258 J/m/kg body weight (Bard, 1963; Concoran et al, 1970). Fisher and Patterson (1981a) have shown that even in young healthy subjects the energy requirement when using crutches was about twice that of normal walking. Walking with crutches acts as an upper extremity in terms of cardiovascular stress (Fisher and Patterson, 1981b) and it is known (Vokac et al, 1975) that arm work requires significantly more coronary blood flow than an equal amount of lower limb work. This has obvious implications for the elderly person who needs to use walking aids or an arm propelled wheelchair, especially in the presence of a decline in the working capacity associated with increasing age (Böttiger, 1973).

Disabilities are not always physical. Confusion, a long-standing adynamic personality, social isolation and environmental difficulties may create dependence in the absence of physical problems.

Assessment of present problems
Assessment for rehabilitation requirements depends on an understanding of the following:

1. What problems does the patient have which can be corrected?
2. What problems which, though not correctable, are able to be modified?
3. What complications can be prevented?
4. What are the likely barriers to recovery?

Each member of the team assesses for different aspects of disability: the doctor assesses for medical problems; the physiotherapist assesses muscle strength and tone and for joint deformities and range of movement; the occupational therapist assesses the ability to carry out activities of daily living; nurses asses for bowel and bladder function, for pressure sores and the patient's general approach; and the social worker will investigate the social resources of the patient including the relationship and support of relatives, friends and neighbours.

There is a major role for counselling in the early stages especially when the disability is new. Here the patient and family have to develop new concepts of 'self'. It is not unusual for there to be a major change in roles with the dominant partner having to adjust to some degree of dependency whilst the non-dominant partner has to learn the role of decision maker.

Disabled people are at risk of developing complications such as pressure sores, contractures, postural imbalance and, in the hemiplegic patient, a painful shoulder — all of which are preventable by good early care. Since most of the responsibility for this falls to the

nursing staff it is essential that they are conversant with the rehabilitation approach — this includes night staff.

Rehabilitation time can be wasted if the barriers to recovery are not recognised. Intellectual impairment is generally associated with poor functional prognosis (Wilson et al, 1973; Feldman et al, 1962; Cain 1969). Not only do mentally alert patients benefit more from rehabilitation but demented patients may be made worse by a rehabilitation programme (Schuman et al, 1981). It is recognized, however, that some patients with mental impairment do functionally improve following rehabilitation (Wilson et al, 1973; Feigenson et al, 1977a; Lehmann et al, 1975a). Demented patients require a different rehabilitation approach (Fowler and Fordyce, 1972; Miller, 1977) based on behaviour modification and learning techniques requiring a great degree of patient-therapist interaction (Belmont et al, 1969).

Other factors also play a part. Haber (1973) noted that women, older people, the under-educated and unskilled had less adaptive capacity or faced more demanding requirements. The patient's previous personality is also likely to influence the outcome (Wolff, 1966). The inadequate, unstable, compulsive or paranoid personality, as well as the passive dependent type who allows others to do things for him, all have a poor outcome. It must also be recognized that some patients have much to gain from being dependent — being allowed to withdraw from unpleasant or difficult life styles for an acceptable reason.

Dependency can also be produced by those around the patient. For instance half the stroke patients attending a Day Hospital did not continue their activities at home, usually because their relatives, for one reason or another, helped the patient unnecessarily (Andrews and Stewart, 1979). Lincoln (1981) found similar discrepancies in patients with multiple sclerosis and disabilities not involving the brain. She also noted that those with brain damage often overestimated their own rating.

Setting goals
Rehabilitation does not end with discharge from hospital. The aim is to train the patient to cope within his own unique situation. Trieschmann (1974) has suggested that one of the key determinants of coping with disability is the number of rewards that are available. Rehabilitation which improves the patient so that he is fit to be lonely is less likely to be successful than that which returns him to a constructive or productive lifestyle.

Becker et al (1974) involved the patient and the family in rehabilitation planning. They set up a list of 30 items of activity which were discussed with the patient and the relatives separately. Where there were discrepancies between the expected goals of the patient, relatives and staff, compromise goals were negotiated and agreed on. They concluded that this system helped to identify early conflicts of interest, improved planning of individual treatment whilst encouraging patient–staff–relative interaction.

This involvement of patient and family is important since the concepts of reality and hope can differ markedly between staff, patient and relatives (New et al, 1969). The staff have an understanding of what is possible given a set of physical disabilities, whilst the relative bases expectations on the knowledge of the patient's premorbid attitude to life. The patient's attitude to disability is paramount: when the expectations are in line with the reality then the outcome is good; when expectations are low, potential for recovery is limited; when hope is greater than reality the patient becomes frustrated, depressed and wants to prolong treatment in the hope of some further improvement. A lack of awareness of these problems results in inappropriate planning. Goals must be both realistic and achievable (Hunt, 1980; Hyams, 1969)

Techniques and methods
The methods used depend on the underlying condition and will be discussed under individual headings. There are, however, a number of considerations common to all rehabilitation problems.

Many elderly patients develop temporary confusional states and others become insecure and agitated when admitted to hospital. Sedation should be avoided and the security of the patient maintained by providing a constant environment in that the patient is allowed to wear his own clothes and is not moved around the ward unneccesarily. There should be easy access to a toilet or commode to encourage normal toileting.

It is assumed that the patient is at risk of developing pressure sore, contractures, joint deformities, constipation and infectious and thus the appropriate preventive measures taken.

Rehabilitation is concerned with four types of disability (Partridge, 1980):

1. Those due to soft tissue injuries which are localized and are mainly treated by physiotherapists. The main aim is to relieve symptoms, increase range of movement, restore muscle strength and prevent complications. Full recovery is anticipated.

2. Conditions in which recovery can be expected but which require a multidisciplinary approach. Fractured femur and other postoperative conditions fall into this group. Speed of recovery depends more on medical and surgical complications than the rehabilitation programme.

3. Conditions which involve irreversible damage and where some lasting disability is expected, e.g. stroke,

paraplegia and amputation. The aims are to achieve optimal levels of function and maintenance at home. A multidisciplinary approach is essential in this group.

4. Conditions where deterioration is expected, e.g. motor neurone disease, rheumatoid arthritis and malignant disease. The aim is to maintain optimal ability. Regular review is essential to modify goals as the patient deteriorates. Much of the emphasis will be in maintaining the emotional, social and environmental factors rather than the use of specific rehabilitation techniques.

NEUROLOGICAL DISORDERS

Stroke
It has been argued by Birch et al (1960) that since neurological deficits result from death of brain cells which cannot regenerate, then recovery cannot occur due to retraining. Hurwitz and Adams (1972) suggested that, although there are no positive ways or restoring function in a paralyzed limb, rehabilitation can enable the most to be made from spontaneous recovery. Evidence that rehabilitation improves recovery is lacking though uncontrolled trials (Feigenson et al, 1977a; Feigenson, 1977b; Lehmann et al, 1975a; Lehmann et al, 1975b; Anderson et al, 1974; Lowenthal et al, 1959) suggest that it has a positive effect. Those who start rehabilitation early do better than those who start late (Stern et al, 1971; Adams and Merrett, 1961; Geltner and Lupo, 1964) though the groups are not comparable. Indeed rehabilitation has been shown to be effective even when started long after spontaneous recovery was completed (Hoberman and Springer, 1958).

In a controlled trial (Smith et al, 1981) of different intensities of outpatient rehabilitation for patients with a moderate stroke, intensive therapy (four whole days a week) was found to be more effective than three half days which in turn was more effective than no rehabilitation. Decreasing intensity of treatment was associated with increase in the proportion of patients who deteriorated. In the Manchester study (Andrews et al, 1981) those with moderate disability all made a good recovery and over half of those with severe deficits at the onset recovered to mild or no deficit levels.

Attempts to compare formal rehabilitation with simple functional help (Feldman et al, 1962; Waylonis et al, 1973) suggest that both are successful. Those with impaired intellectual function benefitted more from the simple functional approach and those with a clear mental state from the formal programme. This fits in with clinical experience which suggests that those who are confused, anxious or have perceptual disorders improve more in a stable environment where the pressure to carry out unfamiliar activities are not too intense.

There are several rehabilitation programmes based on neurophysiological principles. Bobath (1978) emphasizes the development of normal postural motor patterns and the inhibition of abnormal reflex patterns. On the other hand Brunnstrom (1970) utilises the abnormal reflexes and automatic responses occurring in stroke. The patient is encouraged to establish voluntary control of the synergies by repetition, at first by stimulation and then without. Functional movement is then obtained by combining the voluntary control of synergies with antagonistic synergic movement. The Rood approach (Stockmeyer, 1967) encourages the use of stimuli to produce normal reactions whereas proprioceptive neuromuscular facilitation (Knott and Voss, 1968) uses positioning of joints to facilitate voluntary mass muscle contraction. Flanagan (1967) reviewing these different techniques points out that they have much in common: they all emphasize the importance of neurophysiological sequencing of human motor development; they attempt to modify motor activity by inhibition and facilitation of reflex activity; they stress the importance of sensation on function; and all use repetition. These approaches are important in their concern for the total patient rather than local disability. More important they all involve close personal contact between the patient and the therapist.

The value of these techniques is difficult to determine. Stern et al (1969) in a randomly controlled trial, were unable to show any significant difference between one group treated by a neurophysiological approach and another by traditional methods. Chin (1982) examining walking competence could not find changes in recovery pattern over a 7-year period during which different approaches had been tried.

The early stage of stroke

Apart from the lifesaving measures required for any acutely ill patient, the early stage of stroke is important for preparing the patient and family for the rehabilitation programme. Prevention of pressure sores, spasticity and the painful shoulder all require correct positioning with regular turning: the limbs are placed in a position which unravels the spastic pose. The shoulder is protracted and externally rotated, the forearm extended with the fingers extended and abducted, whilst the hip is protracted with internal rotation of the leg and the hip, knee and ankle held in flexion.

Shoulder pain, which may be due to subluxation of the humerus, post hemiplegic reflex sympathetic dystrophy, disuse, capsulitis or the thalamic syndrome, is troublesome in 70 per cent of stroke patients (Caldwell et al, 1969; Najenson et al, 1971) though Brocklehurst et al (1978) found it to be present in only 30 per cent of cases.

Some (Miglietta et al, 1959; Najenson and Pikieiny,

1965; Najenson et al, 1971) regard subluxation as the main cause of shoulder pain. Contrast arthrography of the painful shoulder (Nepomuceno and Miller, 1974) suggests that that one-third have tears of the rotator cuff or biceps tendon, especially in those with left hemiplegia.

Although subluxation is associated with the flaccid limb it is the patient with spasticity who is more likely to complain of shoulder pain (Caldwell et al, 1969; Dardier and Reid, 1972). This is probably because a cycle of stretch-pain-protective spasm and anxiety is produced. Cailliet (1980) has pointed out that for abduction of the glenohumeral joint to take place without compression of the surrounding soft tissue it is necessary for the scapula to rotate upwards and the humeral head to depress and rotate externally. If this does not happen then there will be damage to the capsule, bursa or tendons. This is important since the scapula tends to be tied down by spasticity and therefore injudicious handling may produce damage. Similarly the use of an overhead pulley to move the paralyzed arm abducts the glenohumeral joint without rotating the scapula (Najenson et al, 1971; Voss, 1969).

Weiss et al (1974) suggest that those who have abnormal arthrographic changes respond better to drug therapy whereas those with no pathological change improve with physical measures. The role of physiotherapy in treating the painful shoulder is uncertain: Hazelman (1972) could find little difference in the outcome between local steroid injection, physiotherapy or manipulation under anaesthesia whereas McLaughin (1961) found that rotator cuff tears sometimes occurred after manipulation. Sheldon (1972) however found that physiotherapy could reduce the time to recovery. Ultrasound decreases the period of pain and allows a greater range of movement than acieved by exercise alone (Munting, 1978) and ice or heat may relax the painful spasticity.

The value of slings for the arm is debatable. Tobis (1957) suggested that a sling was important to support the subluxed shoulder but Hurd et al (1974) could not find any difference in the range of movement, shoulder pain, subluxation of the shoulder or peripheral nerve injury when a sling was worn. This could be because many slings do not prevent subluxation. They may also aggravate the spastic flexion pattern, encourage shoulder contracture, make balance difficult, interfere with sensation and body image whilst preventing use of the arm. There are a few slings (DeVore and Denny, 1970; Cohen, 1978; Moskowitz, 1969; Cailliet, 1980) which do produce good humeral head positioning though those with an axillary pad may produce axillary artery thrombosis (Wilson and Caldwell, 1978).

It is important that staff and relatives are aware of the dangers of sudden and abnormal movement of the shoulder and this includes avoiding lifting the patient under the axilla.

Intensive rehabilitation phase

The greatest potential for recovery takes place in the first 3 months (Caroll, 1962; Katz et al, 1966; Cassvan et al, 1976; Andrews et al, 1981). During this phase the aims are to improve muscle strength, gain a good walking gait and functional ability by improving balance, spasticity and sensation.

There are two approaches: one compensates for unilateral disability by concentrating on the function of the non-affected side; the other uses a bilateral approach to gain maximum use of both sides. Recovery of the affected side depends on many factors. There may be delayed processing of information between the damaged and intact brain which results in inhibition of activities of the affected side (Birch et al, 1967). Thus the patient may find it easier not to use the affected side. Ostendorf and Wolf (1981) forced a patient to use the affected side by strapping the intact arm and found that the frequency of purposful action improved and did not completely return to the pre-restraint level on releasing the normal limb.

Biofeedback techniques will correct foot drop (Johnson, 1973; Basmajian et al, 1975; Brudny et al, 1976) but the legs respond better to EMG biofeedback than do the arms (Wolf et al, 1979). The peroneal nerve can be stimulated by an electrical orthosis (Vodovnik et al, 1978) which is switched on when the heel is lifted from the ground. More complex multichannel stimulation is now possible (Teng et al, 1976) to control more than one group of paralyzed muscles.

How biofeedback works is uncertain but some (Shapiro and Swartz, 1972; Huffman, 1978) believe that it acts as operant conditioning which reinforces the learning process. Awareness of the result of an action is essential to successful performance and biofeedback may provide the necessary information (Welford, 1976).

In general sitting balance is obtained before the patient is expected to stand; and standing balance achieved before the patient is encouraged to walk. The policy of 'walking' the patient supported by two helpers before the patient has standing balance produces anxiety, abnormal gait patterns and damage to unprotected joints.

Balance training techniques aim to improve proprioceptive awareness. Vincelli (1978) described a simple biofeedback method using electronically controlled bathroom scales to provide auditory and visual signals when too much pressure was placed on one foot; and Triptree and Harrison (1980) used a simple pressure sensor pad to improve balance where there was proprioceptive loss.

Some patients will require orthoses and there are different indications for their use on the arm than on the leg (McCollough, 1978).

The indications for leg orthoses (Waters and Montgomery, 1974) include inadequate dorsiflexion, ankle instability, knee instability, proprioceptive deficit and post surgical protection.

The trend has been to move away from foot drop calipers, for several reasons. First the stretching of the Achilles tendon, especially by toe springs, results in a reflex spasticity of the calf muscles further exacerbating the tendency to foot drop. Secondly, most calipers are heavy and produce extra work for the already weakened leg to perform. In addition the difficulty in bringing the foot forward on walking encourages 'hitching' of the hip which the modern therapy approach attempts to prevent. The present physiotherapy technique encourages bending of the knee with the pelvis level and allows sliding through of the foot. This is not always easy to perform where carpets do not allow the sliding action and some form of ankle support may be necessary for a small number of patients.

There are several types of ankle support. The caliper with metal uprights and T-strap has the advantage that it is adaptable and adjustable but is heavy, conspicious and limits the shoe choice. The plastic splint which is shaped to the leg and foot can be used in different shoes is light but it is not adjustable.

Knee orthoses support the knee and prevent hyperextension of the knee joint. It is preferable to have one that is light but also allows the knee to bend when not weight bearing.

During this intensive phase the occupational therapist will teach the patient techniques for carrying out every day activities. The provision of aids plays only a small part in the rehabilitation programme. Aids should be simple and as normal looking as is possible. Non-slip mats, plates with raised edges (to prevent food being pushed off) and cutlery with thickened handles are normally all that is required — multipurpose cutlery is difficult to use and emphasizes the disability.

Dysphasia is another major problem requiring attention during this phase. Dysphasia, because of associated learning defects (Katz, 1958; Tikofsky and Reynolds, 1962; Rosenberg and Edwards, 1964) is associated with poor functional recovery (Baker et al, 1968; Marquardsen, 1969) though it may not necessarily interfere with the rehabilitation programme (Cain, 1969; Peszczynski, 1961).

The speech therapy techniques include those based on learning theory, similar to that used for learning a foreign language (Sarno and Sands, 1970); those using melodic intonation as in singing (Albert et al, 1973); and those using non-verbal clues, such as pictures to stimulate word finding (Velletri-Glass et al, 1973; Hall, 1981).

The value of speech therapy is uncertain. Some (Butfield and Zangwill, 1946; Godfrey and Douglass, 1959; Marks et al, 1957) claim a positive benefit but others (Vignolo, 1964; Lenneberg, 1967; Sarno et al, 1970) have been unable to confirm this. Rusk (1977) has commented that although many patients do receive benefit from speech therapy this improvement is not carried over into the home situation. Possibly one of the reasons for speech therapy being ineffective is the lack of available therapy time for each patient (Brocklehurst et al, 1978).

The experience of Griffith (1970) in her work with a famous actress who became dysphasic, and later followed up by volunteer schemes throughout the country (Griffith, 1975; Griffith and Miller, 1980), suggests that volunteers may be as effective as speech therapists in supporting the dysphasic patient and this is supported by other studies (Lesser and Watt, 1978; Meikle et al, 1979; David et al, 1979).

Late stage of rehabilitation

Long-term management depends on many factors. Labi et al (1980) described patients who although they had made a good physical recovery had marked social disability. This psychosocial effect produces marked disability (Gresham et al, 1979) and may be due to the stigma the patient attaches to having had a stroke, the feeling of isolation and dissatisfaction with the new life style (Hyman, 1971; Hyman, 1972; Folstein et al, 1977). The type of adjustment the patient and his family make determines whether the patient will return home (Hyman, 1975) and functional levels are maintained as much through education of relatives as through professional techniques (Anderson et al, 1977). Although good family support is essential (Litman, 1966), Labi et al (1980) record that patients living alone were more likely to have outside activities following a stroke. Family involvement is important even if the patient is treated in hospital (Overs and Belknap, 1967) so that relatives can learn how to help and to aid adjustment to the stroke (Oradei and Waite, 1974).

Social isolation can be overcome by attendance at a Stroke Club. Most offer social outlets for both the patient and his family and encourage the disabled patient to become part of the local community.

Spasticity and contracture

Methods of preventing spasticity were discussed earlier but special techniques are required when spasticity or contracture are present. Physical measures such as vibration (Carr and Shepherd, 1980), ice (Lee and Warren, 1978; Hartviksen, 1962; Chambers, 1969; Kelly, 1969) or heat (Lehmann et al, 1961, 1974) help to decrease spasticity. Heat increases the extensibility of collagen (Lehmann et al, 1970) and animal experiments suggest that gentle stretching over a long period of time produces greater residual elongation than short duration high load stretching in the heated tendon (Warren et al, 1971).

Rhythmical stretching is more effective when it is slow, regular and of low amplitude and the limb can be maintained in the anti-spastic position by an inflatable splint (Johnstone, 1978).

When a contracture is present serial stretching with plaster of Paris splinting may help through may result in difficulty in mobilization and produce fixation of the joint. An alternative method is to use pneumatic intermittent compression with splinting only at night.

Parkinsonism

There have been very few studies assessing the value of rehabilitation in the treatment of Parkinson's disease. One controlled trial (Gibberd et al, 1981) on a small number of outpatients compared a neurophysiological approach with non-specific techniques and was unable to show significant benefit from the specialized techniques. However Beattie and Caird (1980) found that a large number of parkinsonian patients did benefit from occupational therapy and this is in keeping with clinical experience. Speech disorders, especially the rhythm and clarity of speech, can also be improved by speech therapy (Scott and Caird, 1981).

The aims of rehabilitation are to improve muscle weakness, movement and breathing patterns whilst correcting faulty positioning. The patient should not be hurried since this results in an increase in muscle tone, whilst warming the stiff muscles before exercise aids mobilisation.

The walking gait can be improved by encouraging extension of the back and rotation of the hips when walking. The aim is to lengthen the stride and this can be achieved by stepping on pieces of paper, or over lines drawn on the floor, placed at the required step length. A rhythmical gait can be encouraged by walking to the sound of a metronome, music or verbal commands. Swinging of the arms aids the gait and this can be reinforced by moving sticks which are held by the patient and controlled by the therapist.

Patients with Parkinson's disease often find difficulty in initiating action. This can be overcome by rocking and rolling movements or taking a step backwards before walking.

For those whose feet seem to stick to the floor (stammering gait) Wright (1979) has described the technique of achieving a stepping gait. This includes encouraging the patient to step over the attendants foot or over flexible strips attached to the rear legs of a walking frame.

Clothing should have wide openings and easy fastenings whilst elastic shoe laces help dressing. Chairs, bed and toilet or commode need to be adapted to an appropriate height for ease of transfer.

Vascular disorders

Peripheral vascular disease

Drug therapy for peripheral vascular disease has been disappointing (Gillespie, 1959; Coffman and Mannick, 1972; Mashiah et al, 1978) and the long-term effects of surgery are poor (Denck, 1975; Hammarsten et al, 1976). There have been numerous physical approaches to the treatment of vascular disease including heat, electrical stimulation, alternating vacuum and compression and either active or passive exercises.

Personal experience suggests that pneumatic intermittent compression of the legs improves some of the symptoms of peripheral vascular disease. This may be partly due to improved blood flow (Calnan et al, 1970; Sabri et al, 1972; Roberts et al, 1972) and partly due to increased fibrinolysis (Allenby et al, 1973).

Passive (Buerger's) exercises of raising the foot until it is blanched and then lowering it until red are commonly used but have not been shown to be effective (Wisham et al, 1953).

Animal experiments (Sanne and Silvertsson, 1968) suggest that exercise improves the collateral circulation though not necessarily the distal blood flow. In man active exercises can improve walking distance (Pernow and Zetterquist, 1968; Zetterquist, 1970; Ekroth et al, 1978; Clifford et al, 1980) especially in the absence of coronary insufficiency (Jonason et al, 1979). Larsen and Lassen (1966) found that although exercise improved the exercise tolerance they were unable to show the improvement in blood flow described by others (Skinner and Strandness, 1967; Alpert et al, 1969; Ericsson et al, 1970; Hayne, 1980). This improvement may also have been due in part to improved muscle metabolism (Dahllöf et al, 1974; Sorlie and Myhre, 1978).

Home exercises are possibly not as effective as those supervised in hospital. Blood flow seems to be increased more by exercises on a treadmill than an exercise bicycle (Kitamura et al, 1976) though a pedalator, which produces reciprocal dorsal and plantar ankle flexion, may be more effective (Lee et al, 1980) and produces less rise in blood pressure.

The patient should be advised in methods of protecting the feet from trauma including wearing comfortable shoes with the laces not tied too tightly. Situations which result in obstruction of the circulation, such as wearing tight garments and crossing the legs at rest, should be avoided.

Amputation

The rehabilitation potential of the amputee is limited by the associated high incidence of cardiovascular disease (Kavanagh and Shepherd, 1973), the compromized blood flow in the 'sound' limb (Susak et al, 1980) and other medical complications which occur in the early postoperative days (Thompson et al, 1965).

These complications result in many amputees being unable to return home (Chilvers and Browse, 1971; Weaver and Marshall, 1973; Harris et al, 1974). Although a long period of rehabilitation may be required (Weaver and Marshall, 1973) a high level of independence can be achieved. Half of the elderly patients with at least one knee joint may walk sufficiently for self care activities and rehabilitation can also benefit those who will remain confined to a wheelchair (Sakuma et al, 1974; Clarke-Williams, 1969).

Many patients develop a sense of numbness and deny the loss of the limb (Parkes, 1975) and they may be left with a psychological trauma worse than the amputation (Kessler, 1951). This requires preoperative counselling and preparation for the rehabilitation programme.

Joint contractures are prevented by lying the patient on a firm bed with periods in the prone position. Pillows are not placed under the knees and special care is taken to protect the good foot.

Standing on one leg aids balance training and Vitali and Readhead (1967) have used a pre-amputation prosthesis to give the sensation of 'kneeling' on an artificial stump.

In the post-amputation phase the aims are to reduce oedema, promote wound healing and a good shaped stump whilst preventing contractures and training a good walking gait. Badly fitting or tight bandages encourage oedema (Callen, 1981) and even pressure graded bandages may not mould the tissues satisfactorily (Manella, 1981). The stump stocking may slip and produce local pressure unless it is anchored to the vertical bars of the prosthesis (Hamilton, 1978).

Good results are claimed for early mobilization on a temporary prosthesis (Golbranson et al, 1967; Burgess and Romano, 1968; Mooney et al, 1971) and reduces the morbidity and mortality (Hutton and Rothnie, 1977). The early temporary prosthesis (Devas, 1971) was basically a sawn off crutch attached to a polyethylene socket but rigid sockets require a thermoplastic insertion (McPoil et al, 1980) to avoid shearing stress at the stump-socket interface. One modern temporary prosthesis is an inflatable cuff supported by a metal frame which does not need to be measured for individual patients and has even been used for bilateral amputees (White, 1979).

Some patients will only be fit for wheelchair independence. It must be recognized that wheelchair mobility is very stressful to the cardiovascular system (Glaser et al, 1980; Hildebrandt et al, 1970) and that simple daily use of a wheelchair is insufficient in itself to improve the cardiac response (Hildebrandt et al, 1970). However Glaser et al (1981) have shown that additional arm exercises can improve the potential for rehabilitation.

Phantom limb awareness occurs in about one-third of amputees and severe pain in about 5 per cent (Melzack, 1971). Over a period of time the phantom appears to shorten, especially in the proximal part. The cause of pain is uncertain though there does seem to be a large psychological element. Parkes (1973) found that persistent phantom limb pain was associated with a rigid or compulsively self-reliant personality, living with more than one person, a long pre-amputation illness or persisting illness.

Apart from drug therapy such as carbamazepine (Elliot et al, 1976) there have been a number of physical measures used to relieve the stump or phantom pain. As far back as 1947 Russell described benefit from tapping the stump and since then vibrators, ultrasound (Kobak, 1954; Schwartz, 1954; Anderson, 1958), and transcutaneous electrical stimulation (Long, 1974) have been described as being effective. In more severe cases implanted electrodes into the dorsal column (Miles et al, 1974) or the brain (Mazaras et al, 1974) have been tried. Other techniques such as relaxation therapy (Sherman et al, 1979), hypnotherapy (Solomon and Schmidt, 1978) and acupuncture (Monga and Jaksic, 1981) also have their advocates.

PRESSURE SORES AND WOUNDS

Ideally good rehabilitation techniques will prevent pressure sores from developing. Where present certain physical measures may help healing. Ultrasound stimulates new tissue growth (Dyson and Pond, 1970), possibly by increasing fibroblast protein synthesis. Ultrasound is effective in healing varicose ulceration (Dyson and Suckling, 1978), pressure sores (Paul et al, 1960) and trophic ulcers (Galitsky and Levina, 1964).

Ozone irradiation, a gaseous mixture of ionized water vapour, ozone and oxygen, gives pain relief (Church, 1980) and seems to increase the rate of ulcer healing. It may cause a gentle increase in blood flow, but its main action is probably a batericidal effect due to the decomposition of the ozone resulting in local ultraviolet irradiation. (See also chapter 43.)

ORTHOPAEDICS

In orthopaedic rehabilitation the emphasis is on treating pain, stiffness, maintaining the range of joint movement and correcting or preventing of deformities.

Pain

Joint pain often responds to physical treatment, especially changes in temperature. Heat can be provided superficially (hot water bottle, wax, infra-red irradiation) or to deep tissues (shortwave, microwave or ultrasound). Superficial forms of heat are more appropriate for temperature changes to a depth of 1.2 cm (Borrell et al, 1980) but beyond this they may have a cooling effect (Horvath and Hollander, 1949). Temperature changes not only depend on the intensity of the heat provided but also its form — wax baths, for instance, provide a gentle but prolonged effect since the first layer acts as an insulating agent to further layers (Abramson et al, 1964).

The mechanism of pain relief due to heat is uncertain. It may act by raising the pain threshold due to its action on free nerve endings, by increasing collagen extensibility or by decreasing muscle spasm.

There are contraindications to the use of heat and these include impaired sensation, haemorrhage, trauma, malignancy, thrombophlebitis, acute inflammation and oedema. Joint destruction may be produced from long-term use of heat (Harris and McCroskery, 1974) due to an increase in enzymatic lysis of cartilage collagen. This may also be aggravated by urate deposites in joints (Dowart et al, 1974) though short term superficial heat cools the joint by reflex action (Horvath and Hollander, 1949).

Heat produced in deep tissues by microwave is limited if there is a large amount of soft tissue overlying the joint (Lehmann et al, 1968). Difficulties arise with microwave in the presence of metal implants (Scott, 1965) or over boney prominences or fluid since excess temperatures may be produced.

Ultrasound can also produce heat in deeper tissues by producing oscillation of particles. Vasodilatation can be produced (Shroeder, 1962; Stuhlfauth, 1952) due to the effect of ultrasound waves on the sympathetic nervous system and there may be an associated increase in blood flow (Abramson et al, 1960) though others (Paaske et al, 1973; Wyper et al, 1978) have been unable to confirm this. It seems that blood flow is increased more by microwave diathermy than by ultrasound (Wyper and McNiven, 1976; Hovind and Nielsen, 1974).

The contraindications to the use of ultrasound (Oakley, 1978) include arterial disease, thrombophlebitis, acute sepsis or inflammation or tumours. The electromagnetic irradiation may also interfere with cardiac pacemaker action (Bryan et al, 1969). It is generally felt that ultrasound should not be used in the presence of a metal implant though Lehmann (1965) reports that the temperature rise in metal joints is quickly conducted away and does not produce clinical problems unless the metal is near to the skin surface.

Transcutaneous electrical stimulation (TENS) can relieve joint pain in rheumatoid arthritis (Mannheimer et al, 1978) though some patients reported that the pain returned with greater intensity when the effect wore off. The side effects of TENS are skin irritation (Loesser et al, 1975), cardiac dysrhythmia (Richardson et al, 1979), interference with cardiac pacemakers (Eriksson et al, 1978) and paraesthesia with vasodilatation (Griffin and McClure, 1981).

Cold, provided by frozen gel packs, ice in towels or ethyl chloride spray, relieves pain and reduces the tissue response to injury (Janssen and Waaler, 1967). It can therefore be used in the presence of inflammation. Cold is more effective than heat in raising the pain threshold (Benson and Copp, 1974) and also relieves muscle spasm (Grant, 1964; Lane, 1971).

Cryotherapy is contraindicated in the presence of ischaemia, slowly healing wounds, anaesthetic areas, Raynaud's phenomena and cryoglobulinaemia.

Arthritis

In rehabilitation of arthritis the underlying pathology is less important than the degree of inflammation present.

Acute arthritis

The aim in acute arthritis is to relieve pain, decrease inflammation, prevent deformities and control the systemic manifestations of the disease. Bed rest in the acute phase is well recognized as being effective (Ropes, 1961; Mills et al, 1971; Curtiss, 1969) but the positioning of the patient is crucial to the prevention of deformities. Pillows should not be placed under the knees and the elevated and abducted arms should be supported on pillows or slings.

The degree of immobility required is uncertain. Some (Harris and Copp, 1962; Partridge and Duthie, 1963) recommend total immobilization in plaster but there is evidence that the articular cartilage decreases in thickness during rest with a lower flow of nutritional solutes to bone (Ekholm, 1953). It is however of note that rheumatoid deformities do not seem to occur in the presence of paralysis (Bland and Eddy, 1968; Glick, 1967). Splinting produces a decrease in joint inflammation (Gault and Spyker, 1969; Convery and Minteer, 1974) though incorrect splinting will produce deformities (Convery et al, 1967).

Chronic arthritis

In chronic arthritis the aims are to maintain pain control, strengthen muscles, relieve stiffness, mobilize the patient and prevent or treat deformities.

Limitation of joint movement may be due to tightness of the skin, muscle spasm or spasticity, adhesions or destruction of tendon, cartilage or bone. In rheumatoid arthritis the stiffness is associated with poor extensibility of collagen (Backlund and Tiselius, 1967) and this can be improved by heat treatment prior to mobilization (Ross and Clawson, 1970).

Splinting in the chronic phase provides symptomatic relief though most patients wear splints for support during activities requiring strength rather than for the relief of pain (Nicholas et al, 1982) though few will wear a splint unless it does give some pain relief (Zoeckler and Nicholas, 1969).

Joint protection is an essential part of the rehabilitation programme (Brattström, 1973) and consists of providing aids, and training the patient techniques of avoiding joint strain.

Mobility can be helped by weight loss since one kilogram of weight is equivalent to about 3 kg of load on the knee joint (Chamberlain and Buchann, 1978). Shoes should be comfortable and larger than normal to allow for foot deformity (Smidt and Dixon, 1980). Difficulty in rising from a chair may need spring assisted seats though most problems can be overcome by a chair of the appropriate height and shape (Munton, 1981).

Backache

Backache is a notoriously difficult problem to treat even in young people and there is very little research information about the rehabilitation of the elderly person with back problems.

Bedrest substantially decreases the amount of discomfort (Wiesel et al, 1980) though there is little to be gained by the use of traction (Matthews and Hickling, 1975) and most patients will benefit from lying on a firm mattress. A bead bed can give more complete support and is especially of value in those patients at risk of developing pressure sores. Many patients have a poor posture when sitting in a chair and this can be corrected by the use of a vacuum posture controller — a bag of small beads which conforms to a rigid shell around the patient when the air is extracted from the bag.

Lumbar supports relieve pain probably by correcting excessive lumbar lordosis and taking the load off the lumber spine when tha abdominal muscles are weak. Although it decreases movement at the intervertebral joints (Norton and Brown, 1957) it does not seem to prevent rotation of the lumbar spine (Lumsden and Morris, 1968). For a lumbar support to be effective it should extend from the sacrum to the lower thoracic spine; it should have metal ribs posteriorly to prevent excessive lordosis; and the anterior abdominal support must compress and elevate the lower portion of the abdominal wall. This splinting will transform the abdominal contents into a semi-rigid cylinder (Morris, 1974) which transmits some of the stress normally taken by the vertebral column.

There have been many trials (Rohinger, 1963; Glover

et al, 1974; Kane et al, 1974; Doran and Newill, 1975; Zylbergold and Piper, 1981) which have cast doubt on the value of physiotherapy in the treatment of backache. These have mainly been concerned with young patients and it is unlikely that the elderly would respond any better. As far as the elderly are concerned the rehabilitation efforts concentrate on correcting abnormal postures whilst sitting and walking, building up the spinal muscles to splint the back (Kendall and Jenkins, 1968; Lidstrom and Zachrisson, 1970) and relieving pain by heat, vibrators, splinting or transcutaneous electrical stimulation (Lampe, 1978; Wyke, 1979).

Femoral neck fractures

The prognosis following fracture of the neck of the femur has improved dramatically since the introduction of surgical internal fixation of the fracture which allows early mobilization. Non-union of the fracture site can be prevented by good surgical reduction, accurately placed internal fixation and carefully supervised postoperative care (Banks, 1962). Surgical treatment is mainly of value to those who will benefit from early mobilization and Lyon and Nevins (1977) have pointed out that a patient not only has to survive the operation but also be fit enough to undergo a rigorous rehabilitation programme. In their experience, surgery was not necessary to survival in the demented patient and once pain had settled mobilization could begin without prolonged traction. Where the patient is unfit for surgery Patrick (1981) has described the use of an inflatable hip spica to aid early mobilization. Most patients will however undergo surgery though Bossingham et al (1980) found that as many as 28 per cent of patients referred for elective orthopaedic surgery were unfit for an operation.

Passive movement can start within 48 hours of surgery without too much risk of further bleeding and during this time an abductor pillow between the legs is helpful in preventing gross hip movement. Partial weight bearing can start after the first three days with full standing by the end of the first week. Banks (1962) has suggested that even 3–5 months post operation is too early to weight bear and that there should be radiological evidence of union before normal walking is allowed. This view is not widely held and there have been several studies (Abrami and Stevens, 1964; Häggqvist, 1969; Graham, 1968; Ainsworth, 1971; Nieminen, 1975) which have shown that early weight bearing does not increase the risk of complications and in fact prolonged non-weight bearing was often associated with a higher morbidity and mortality with a slower rate of healing of the fracture. Early weight bearing is not so suitable for those where reduction is poor or if the femoral head is fragmented.

Pain in the hip on weight bearing should always be taken seriously and investigated for bending or slipping of the prosthesis, refracture, aseptic necrosis or infection.

Shortening of the fractured leg is not uncommon and can be corrected simply with a raise on the sole of the shoe. As with other orthopaedic disabilities chairs, toilets, commodes and beds should have raised seats to prevent further damage to the joint.

Fracture of long bones

A non-operative approach to fractures of the tibia and long shaft of femur allows immediate weight bearing (Dehne, 1974) in a plaster cast. This is preferable to traction which has an adverse effect on muscle strength (Imms et al, 1980), produces decreased function of the knee (Nichols, 1963; Stryker et al, 1970) and a prolonged hospital stay (Thomas and Meggitt, 1981). Functional bracing is based on the principle that pressure applied to a rigid container of fluid is equally transmitted in all directions which in the case of the leg cast splints the bones and supports the weight. This technique has been shown to be effective for fractures of the femoral shaft (Pearson, 1980; Mooney et al, 1970; Connoly and King, 1973; Lesin et al, 1977) and for tibial fractures (Sarmiento, 1967; Bassett et al, 1981). Provided this produces good fixation of the bones the fracture should heal (Weber and Brunner, 1981) and the use of bone grafts are only necessary in the case of a vascular or infected non-union.

There is a large literature on the use of electric currents to aid the healing process in non-union of fractures. The early machines (Brighton et al, 1977; Friedenberg et al, 1970, 1974; Lavine et al, 1971) required constant direct current to be provided by implanted electrodes but the modern approach using pulsing electromagnetic currents (Bassett et al, 1981; Sutcliffe et al, 1980; Heckman et al, 1981) is equally effective and are non-invasive. Failure to respond to this technique (Brighton et al, 1981) is usually due to inadequate current, the presence of synovial pseudoarthrosis or infection.

ORGANIZATION

The aim of rehabilitation is to return the patient to independent living within his or her own environment. Much will depend on the correct goals being set early in the rehabilitation programme. A 'feeling' for what is possible is experienced at the pre-admission home visit. This depends not only on the degree of neglect or physical environmental problems found but also on the attitude of relatives and neighbours. This may take the form of expressions of 'having had enough' or evidence of an overprotective attitude. The decision of the form of rehabilitation required will take place at this visit and may consist of admission to hospital, to a Day Hospital or referral for domiciliary physiotherapy.

Hospital rehabilitation

Admission to hospital for rehabilitation has the advantage that the patient can receive professional support throughout the whole 24 hour period. It is therefore especially of value for those patients who require the skills of several professional groups or who are at risk of injuring themselves. There are however some disadvantages to admission. These include the tendency to become confused when moving to a new environment. Anxious, confused, depressed patients, and those with perceptual disorders, may be inhibited by the intensive approach of the rehabilitation unit and often benefit more from a gentler functional approach to recovery. The hospital ward is an artificial environment in which to assess patients' capabilities and may give the wrong impression of their ability to manage at home. This can be minimized by assessing the patient's ability to cope in an assessment flat independently for several days. The patient is expected to carry out activities such as getting up in the morning, dressing, making meals, carry out small domestic duties and take his own medication, all without the encouragement or stimulation of the staff. Inability to cope in the flat raises great doubts about the ability to manage at home and will require a readjustment of goals.

A home visit by the patient and team members along with relatives, neighbours, district nurse and community services, where applicable, will reveal additional problems. The advice given may be either corrective (removing loose carpets, fixing loose floor boards or rearranging furniture) or adaptive (raising the height of the bed or chair, providing aids, handrails or ramps). It is wise to arrange this visit several weeks before the discharge date since it takes time to carry out the recommended changes and new goals may have to be set. However a further assessment visit may be required immediately before discharge.

Some patients will benefit from a trial discharge home for one or more days. Weekend discharges, unless for a specific reason, are usually avoided because the necessary staff for assessment and support are not available.

Discharge planning requires good communication between hospital and community services. This can be achieved by the social worker and district nurse attending the consultant's ward round (Wilson and Wilson, 1971). The author's policy is to discuss the progress of each patient in the weekly case conference with the nurses, remedial therapists and social worker. This is then followed up in another meeting with the hospital and community social workers, district nurse

liason officer, health visitor liason officer, home help organiser and welfare rights officer to discuss imminent discharge of patients and to review the progress of those already discharged.

Day hospitals

The organization of Day Hospitals is discussed elsewhere (p. 990). Transport problems (Beer et al, 1974; Frazer, 1979) and cancellation of appointments by patients (Tyndall, 1978; Peach and Pathy, 1981) complicates the rehabilitation in the Day Hospital. Patients have to be fit to attend since they must be dressed early and able to withstand an ambulance journey. Patients with backache, acute arthritis, a tendency to travel nausea, marked balance difficulties and spasticity benefit the least.

The Day Hospital is of benefit to those who need specific therapeutic skills or equipment but who do not need admission to hospital. It may also be of value in helping the patient recently discharge from hospital to resettle into the community.

Domiciliary rehabilitation

Domiciliary rehabilitation is practical in dealing with the patient in his own environment. It also is a great advantage in rural areas (Lamont and Langford, 1980) where journeys to hospital may be too exhausting. Home therapy is particularly of value in training relatives in the correct approach to disability. There are additional advantages (Glossop and Smith, 1981) in that flexible hours can be used to the advantage of patient, relatives and staff; and student remedial therapists can be trained in the community needs of patients.

Domiciliary therapy is of particular value in acute painful conditions, acute chest problems and where daily treatment is required. The confused patient is more likely to benefit from rehabilitation in familiar surroundings.

Specialized rehabilitation units

There are advantages in grouping patients with specific problems in units where the staff have expertise in that disorder.

Stroke units may decrease the morbidity and mortality following a stroke (Taylor, 1970; Cooper et al, 1972; Truscott, 1972; Drake et al, 1973) though this has not been confirmed in other studies (Kennedy et al, 1970; Pitner and Mance, 1973). The patient most likely to benefit from a stroke unit is possibly the one who has a severe (rather than profound) stroke (Blower and Ali, 1979; McCann and Culbertson, 1976).

In a controlled trial (Garraway et al, 1980a) a stroke unit was shown to improve patients with a moderate stroke quicker and in less therapeutic time than treatment on a general medical ward though there was no difference between the two groups for the outcome at one year (Garraway et al, 1980b).

The major advantage of the stroke unit is that all the staff understand the methods of preventing spasticity and painful shoulders whilst appreciating the complex problems of dysphasia and perceptual difficulties. There is however a danger that the unit becomes occupied by patients who are not progressing with the resulting under-use of the available expertise.

Geriatric-Orthopaedic units (Devas 1964, 1974, 1976, 1977; Clarke and Wainwright, 1966) have been set up to deal with the multiple medical and social complications often present in the elderly. Most elderly patients admitted to an orthopaedic unit following trauma have underlying medical problems requiring the attention of

a physician. The combined care by orthopaedic surgeon and physician in geriatric medicine provides the optimal care of the elderly patient.

CONCLUSION

Rehabilitation of the elderly requires a complex management system of hospital and home care involving a large number of professional groups. The close liason between hospital and community services is essential in maintaining the elderly handicapped person at an optimal level of independence. Within this framework much can be achieved in supporting patients and their families through a well planned rehabilitation programme.

REFERENCES

Abrami G, Stevens J 1964 Early weightbearing after internal fixation of transcervical fracture of the femur. Journal of Bone and Joint Surgery 46B: 204–205

Abramson D I, Burnett C, Bell Y, Tuck S, Rejal H, Fleischer C J 1960 Changes in blood flow, oxygen uptake and tissue temperature produced by therapeutic physical agents. 1 Effect of ultrasound. American Journal of Physical Medicine 39: 51–86

Abramson D I, Tusk S Jr, Chu L S W 1964 Effect of paraffin bath and hot fomentations on local tissue temperature. Archives of Physical Medicine and Rehabilitation 45: 87–94

Adams G F, Merrett J D 1961 Prognosis and survival in the aftermath of hemiplegia. British Medical Journal 1: 309–314

Ainsworth T H 1971 Immediate full weight-bearing in the treatment of hip fractures. Journal of Trauma 11: 1031–1040

Albert M, Sparks R, Helm N 1973 Melodic intonation therapy for aphasia. Archives of Neurology 29: 130–131

Allenby F, Boardman L, Pflug J J, Calnan J S 1973 Effects of external pneumatic intermittent compression on fibrinolysis in man. Lancet ii: 1412–1414

Alpert J S, Larsen O A, Lassen N A 1969 Exercise and intermittent claudication blood flow in calf muscles during walking studied by Xenon 133 clearance method. Circulation 39: 353–359

Anderson E, Anderson T P, Kottke F J 1977 Stroke rehabilitation: maintenance of achieved gains. Archives of Physical Medicine and Rehabilitation 58: 345–352

Anderson M 1958 Four cases of phantom limb treated with ultrasound. Physical Therapy Review 38: 419–420

Anderson T P 1978 Educational frame of reference: An additional model for rehabilitation medicine. Archives of Physical Medicine and Rehabilitation 59: 203–206

Anderson T P, Bourstom N, Greenberg F R, Hilyard V G 1974 Predictive factors in stroke rehabilitation. Archives of Physical Medicine and Rehabilitation 55: 545–553

Andrews K, Brocklehurst J C, Richards B, Laycock P J 1981 The rate of recovery from stroke and its measurement. International Rehabilitation Medicine 3: 155–161

Andrews K, Stewart J 1979 Stroke recovery: He can but does he? Rheumatology and Rehabilitation 18: 43–48

Backlund L, Tiselius P 1967 Objective measurement of joint stiffness in rheumatoid arthritis. Acta Rheumatologia Scandinavica 13: 275–288

Baker R N, Schwartz W S, Ramseyer J C 1968 Prognosis among survivors of ischaemic stroke. Neurology 18: 933–941

Banks H H 1962 Factors influencing the result in fractures of the femoral neck. Journal of Bone and Joint Surgery 44A: 931–964

Bard B 1963 Energy expenditure of hemiplegic subjects during walking. Archives of Physical Medicine and Rehabilitation 44: 368–370

Basmajian J V, Kukulla C G, Narayan M G, Takebe K 1975

Biofeedback treatment of footdrop after stroke compared with standard rehabilitation techniques: Effect on voluntary control and strength. Archives of Physical Medicine and Rehabilitation 56: 231–236

Bassett C A L, Mitchell S N, Gaston S R 1981 Treatment of ununited tibial diaphyseal fracture with pulsing electromagnetic fields. Journal of Bone and Joint Surgery 63A: 511–523

Beattie A, Caird F I 1980 The occupational therapist and the patient with Parkinson's disease. British Medical Journal 280: 1354–1355

Becker M C, Abrams K S, Onder J 1974 Goal setting: A joint patient staff method. Archives of Physical Medicine and Rehabilitation 55: 87–89

Beer T C, Goldberg E, Smith D S, Mason A S 1974 Can I have an ambulance doctor? British Medical Journal 1: 226–228

Belmont I, Benjamin H, Ambrose J, Resticcia R D 1969 Effect of cerebral damage on motivation in rehabilitation. Archives of Physical Medicine and Rehabilitation 50: 507–511

Benson T P, Copp E P 1974 Effects of therapeutic forms of heat and ice on pain threshold of the normal shoulder. Rheumatology and Rehabilitation 13: 101–104

Birch H G, Belmont I, Karp E 1967 Delayed information processing and extinction following cerebral damage. Brain 90: 118–130

Birch H G, Proctor F, Bortner M, Lowenthal M 1960 Perception in hemiplegia I Judgement of vertical and horizontal by hemiplegic patients. Archives of Physical Medicine and Rehabilitation 41: 19–27

Bland J H, Eddy W M 1968 Hemiplegia and rheumatoid hemiparesis. Arthritis and Rheumatism 2: 72

Blower P, Ali S 1979 A stroke unit in a district general hospital: The Greenwich experience. British Medical Journal 2: 644–646

Bobath B 1978 Adult Hemiplegia: Evaluation and treatment. 2nd edn, William Heinemann, London

Borrell R M, Parker R, Henley E J, Masley D, Repinecz M 1980 Comparison of in vivo temperatures produced by hydrotherapy paraffin wax treatment and fluidotherapy. Physical Therapy 60: 1273–1276

Bossingham D H, Mattingly P C, Mowat A G 1980 Medicine in orthopaedics: A role for the rheumatologist? Rheumatology and Rehabilitation 19: 1–7

Böttiger L E 1973 Regular decline in physical working capacity with age. British Medical Journal 3: 270–271

Brattström M 1973 Principles of joint protection in chronic rheumatoid diease. Wolfe, London

Brighton C T, Black J, Friedenberg Z B, Esterhai J L, Day L J, Connolly J F 1981 Multicentre study of treatment of non union with constant direct current. Journal of Bone and Joint Surgery 63A: 2–13

Brighton C T, Friedenberg Z B, Mitchell E I, Booth R E 1977

Treatment of non-union with constant direct current. Clinical Orthopaedics and Related Research 124: 106–123

Brocklehurst J C, Andrews K, Richards B, Laycock P J 1978 How much therapy for patients with stroke? British Medical Journal i: 1307–1310

Brudny J, Korein J, Grynbaum B B, Friedmann L W, Weinstein S, Sachs-Frankel G, Belandres P V 1976 EMG feedback therapy: review of treatment of 114 patients. Archives of Physical Medicine and Rehabilitation 57: 55–61

Brunnstrom S 1970 Movement therapy in hemiplegia: A neurophysiological approach. Harper and Row, London

Bryan P, Furman S, Escher D J 1969 Input signal to pacemakers in a hospital environment. Annals of the New York Academy of Science 167: 823–824

Burgess E M, Romano R L 1968 The management of lower extremity amputees using immediate post surgical prosthesis. Clinical Orthopaedics and Related Research 57: 137–146

Butfield E, Zangwill O L 1946 Re-education in aphasia. Journal of Neurology, Neurosurgery and Psychiatry 9: 75–79

Cailliet R 1980 The shoulder in hemiplegia. Davis, Philadelphia

Cain L S 1969 Determining the factors that affect rehabilitation. Journal of the American Geriatrics Society 17: 595–604

Caldwell C B, Wilson D J, Braun R M 1969 Evaluation and treatment of the upper extremity in the hemiplegic stroke patient. Clinical Orthopaedics 63: 69–93

Callen S 1981 A modern method of stump bandaging. Physiotherapy 67: 137–138

Calnan J S, Pflug J J, Mills C 1970 Pneumatic intermittent compression legging simulating calf muscle pump. Lancet ii: 505–503

Carr J H, Shepherd R 1980 Physiotherapy in disorders of the brain. Heinmann, London

Carroll D 1962 The disability in hemiplegia caused by cerebrovascular disease. Journal of Chronic Disease 15: 179–189

Cassvan A, Ross A L, Dyer P R, Zane L 1976 Lateralisation in stroke syndrome. A factor in ambulation. Archives of Physical Medicine and Rehabilitation 57: 583–587

Chamberlain M A, Buchanan J 1978 Mobility in arthritis. Reports on Rheumatic Disease No 66. Arthritis and Rheumatism Council

Chambers R 1969 Clinical use of cryotherapy. Physical Therapy 49: 245–249

Chilvers A S, Browse N L 1971 The social fate of amputees. Lancet 2: 1192–1193

Chin P L 1982 Physical techniques in stroke rehabilitation. Journal of the Royal College of Physicians of London 16: 165–169

Church L 1980 Ionozone therapy for skin lesions in elderly patients. Physiotherapy 66: 50–51

Clarke A N G, Wainwright D 1966 Management of the fractured neck of femur in the elderly female. A joint approach of orthopaedic surgery and geriatric medicine. Gerontologia Clinica 8: 321–326

Clarke-Williams M J 1969 The elderly double amputee. Gerontologia Clinica 11: 183–189

Clifford P C, Davies P W, Haynes J A, Baird R N 1980 Intermittent claudication. Is a supervised exercise class worthwhile? British Medical Journal 280: 1503–1505

Coffman J D, Mannick J A 1972 Failure of vasodilator drugs in arteriosclerosis obliterans. Annals of Internal Medicine 76: 35–39

Cohen B A 1978 A new shoulder-elbow-wrist sling for hemiplegic patients. Journal of Clinical Engineering 3: 389–392

Connolly J F, King P 1973 Closed reduction and early cast-brace ambulation in the treatment of femoral fracture. Journal of Bone and Joint Surgery 55A: 1559–1580

Convery F R, Conaty J P, Nickel V L 1967 Dynamic splinting of the rheumatoid hand. Orthosis and Prosthetics 21: 249–254

Convery F R, Minteer M A 1974 The use of orthoses in the management of rheumatoid arthritis. Clinical Orthopaedics 102: 118–125

Cooper S W, Olivet J A, Woolsey F M 1972 Establishment and operation of combined intensive care units. New York State Journal of Medicine 72: 2215–2220

Corcoran P J, Brengelmann G L 1970 Oxygen uptake in normal and handicapped subjects in relation to speed of walking beside velocity controlled cart. Archives of Physical Medicine and Rehabilitation 51: 78–87

Corcoran P J, Jebsen R H, Brengelmann G L, Simons B C 1970

Effects of plastic and metal leg braces on speed and energy cost of hemiparetic ambulation. Archives of Physical Medicine and Rehabilitation 51: 69–77

Curtiss P H Jr 1969 Cartilage damage in septic arthritis. Clinical Orthopaedics 64: 87–90

Dahllöf A G, Bjorntorp P, Holm J, Schesten T 1974 Metabolic activity of skeletal muscle in patients with peripheral arterial insufficiency: Effect of physical training. European Journal of Clinical Investigation 4: 9–15

Dardier E, Reid C 1972 Hemiplegia and the painful shoulder. Physical Therapy 52: 1208

David R M, Enderby P, Bainton D 1979 Progress report on evaluation of speech therapy for dysphasia. British Journal of Communication 14: 85–88

Dehne E 1974 Ambulatory treatment of the fractured tibia. Clinical Orthopaedics 105: 192–201

Denck H 1975 Reocclusion rate after arterial reconstructive surgery. Journal of Cardiovascular Surgery 16: 352

Devas M B 1964 Fracture in the elderly. Gerontologia Clinica 6: 347–359

Devas M B 1971 Early walking of geriatric amputees. British Medical Journal 1: 394–396

Devas M B 1974 Geriatric orthopaedics. British Medical Journal 1: 190–192

Devas M B 1976 Geriatric Orthopaedics. Annals of the Royal College of Surgeons of England 58: 15–21

Devas M B 1977 Geriatric orthopaedics. Academic Press, London

De Vore G L, Denny E 1970 A sling to prevent subluxation of the shoulder. American Journal of Occupational Therapy 24: 580–581

Doran D M L, Newell D J 1975 Manipulation in the treatment of low back pain: A multicentre study. British Medical Journal 2: 161–164

Dorwart B B, Hansell J R, Schumacher H R Jr 1974 Effects of cold and heat on urate crystal induced synovitis in dogs. Arthritis and Rheumatism 17: 563–571

Drake W E, Hamilton M J, Carlsson M, Blumenkrantz J 1973 Acute stroke management and patient outcome. The value of a neurovascular care unit. Stroke 4: 933–945

Dyson M, Pond J B 1970 The effect of pulsed ultrasound on tissue regeneration. Physiotherapy 56: 136–142

Dyson M, Suckling J 1978 Stimulation of tissue repair by ultrasound: A survey of the mechanisms involved. Physiotherapy 64: 105–108

Ekholm R 1953 Nutrition of cartilage: A radio-autographic study Acta Anatomy 24: 329–337

Ekroth R, Dahllöf A, Gunderall B, Holm J 1978 Physical training of patients with intermittent claudication: indications, methods and results. Surgery 84: 640–643

Elliot F, Little A, Milbrandt W 1976 Carbamazepine for phantom limb phenomena. New England Journal of Medicine 295: 678

Ericsson B, Haeger K, Lindell S E 1970 Effect of physical training on intermittent claudication. Angiology 21: 188–192

Eriksson M, Schuller H, Sjolund B 1978 Hazard from transcutaneous nerve stimulation in patients with pacemaker. Lancet i: 1319

Feigenson J S, McCarthy M L, Greenberg S D, Feigenson W D 1977a Factors influencing outcome and length of stay in a stroke rehabilitation unit II Comparison of 318 screened and 248 unscreened patients. Stroke 8: 657–662

Feigenson J S, McCarthy M L, Meese P D, Feigenson W D, Greenberg S D, Rubin E, McDowell F H 1977b Stroke rehabilitation: Factors predicting outcome and length of stay — an overview. New York State Journal of Medicine 77: 1426–1430

Feldman D J, Lee P R, Unterecker M D, Lloyd K, Rusk H A, Toole A 1962 A comparison of functionally oriented medical care and formal rehabilitation in the management of patients with hemiplegia due to cerebrosvascular disease. Journal of Chronic Disease 15: 297–310

Fisher S V, Patterson R P 1981a Energy cost of ambulation with crutches. Archives of Physical Medicine and Rehabilitation 62: 250–256

Fisher S V, Patterson R P 1981b Cardiovascular stress of crutch walking. Archives of Physical Medicine and Rehabilitation 62: 257–260

Flanagan E M 1967 Methods of facilitation and inhibition of motor activity. American Journal of Physical Medicine 46: 1006–1011

Folstein M F, Mailberger R, McHugh P R 1977 Mood disorder as a specific complication of stroke. Journal of Neurology, Neurosurgery and Psychiatry 40: 1018–1020

Fowler R S Jr, Fordyce W 1972 Adapting care for the brain damaged patient. American Journal of Nursing 72: 2056–2059

Frazer W F 1979 Evaluation of a domiciliary physiotherapy source to the elderly. M. Phil Thesis. University of Aston and Brimingham

Friedenberg Z B, Andrews E T, Smolenski B I, Pearl B W, Brighton C T 1970 Bone reaction to varying amounts of direct current. Surgery, Gynecology and Obstetrics 131: 894–899

Friedenberg Z B, Zeinsky L M, Pollis R P, Brighton C T 1974 The response of non-traumatised bone to direct current. Journal of Bone and Joint Surgery 56A: 1023–1030

Galitsky A B, Levina S I 1964 Vascular origins of trophic ulcers and applications of ultrasound on pre-operative treatment to plastic surgery. Acta Chirurgica Plastica 6: 271–278

Ganguli S, Datta S R, Chatterjee B B 1973 Performance evaluation of amputee-prosthesis system in below knee amputees. Ergonomics 16: 797–810

Garraway W M, Akhtar A J, Prescott R J, Hockey L 1980a Management of acute stroke in the elderly: Preliminary results of a controlled trial. British Medical Journal 280: 1040–1043

Garraway W M, Akhtar A J, Hockey L, Prescott R J 1980b Management of acute stroke in elderly: Follow up of a controlled trial. British Medical Journal 281: 827–829

Gault S J, Spyker J M, 1969 Beneficial effect of immobilization of joints in rheumatoid arthritis and related arthritides: Splint study using sequential analysis. Arthritis and Rheumatism 12: 34–44

Geltner L, Lupo G 1964 Clinical problems in cerebrosvascular accidents. Israel Medical Journal 23: 241–248

Gibberd F B, Page N G R, Spencer K M, Kinnear E, Hawksworth J B 1981 Controlled trial of physiotherapy and occupational therapy for Parkinson's disease. British Medical Journal 282: 1196

Gillespie J A 1959 The case against vasodilator drugs in occlusive vascular disease of the legs. Lancet 2: 995–997

Glaser R M, Barr S A, Laubach L L, Sawka M N, Suryaprasad A G 1980 Relative stress of Wheelchair activity. Human Factors 22: 177–181

Glaser R M, Sawka M N, Durbin R J, Foley D M, Suryaprasad A G 1981 Exercise programme for wheelchair activity. American Journal Physical Medicine 60: 67–75

Glick E N 1967 Asymptomatic rheumatoid arthritis after poliomyelitis. British Medical Journal 3: 26–28

Glossop E S, Smith D S 1981 Domiciliary physiotherapy research project 1976–1978. Physiotherapy 67: 79

Glover J R, Morris J G, Khosla T 1974 Back pain, a randomised clinical trial of rotational manipulation of the trunk. British Journal of Industrial Medicine 31: 59–64

Godfrey C M, Douglass E 1959 The recovery process in aphasia. Canadian Medical Association Journal 80: 618–624

Golbranson F L, Asbelle C, Stand D 1967 Immediate post surgical fitting and early ambulation. A new concept in amputee rehabilitation. Clinical Orthopaedics 56: 119–131

Gonzalez E G, Cocoran P J, Reyes R L 1974 Energy expenditure in below-knee amputees. Correlation with stump lenth. Archives of Physical Medicine and Rehabilitation 55: 111–119

Graham J 1968 Early or delayed weight-bearing after internal fixation of trans-cervical fracture of the femur. Journal of Bone and Joint Surgery 50B: 166–171

Grant A E 1964 Massage with ice (cryokinetics) in the treatment of painful conditions of the musculoskeletal system. Archives of Physical Medicine and Rehabilitation 45: 233–238

Gresham G E, Phillips T F, Wolf P A, McNamara P M, Kannel W B, Dawber T R 1979 Epidemiology profile of long term stroke disability Framingham study. Archives of Physical Medicine and Rehabilitation 60: 487–491

Griffin J W, McClure M 1981 Adverse response to transcutaneous electrical nerve stimulation in patients with rheumatoid arthritis. Physical Therapy 61: 354–355

Griffith V E 1970 A stroke in the family. Penguin, London

Griffith V E 1975 Volunteer scheme for dysphasia and allied problems in stroke patients. British Medical Journal 3: 633–635

Griffith V E, Miller C L 1980 Volunteer stroke scheme for dysphasia patients with stroke. British Medical Journal 2: 1605–1607

Haber L D 1973 Disabling effects of chronic disease and impairment

II Functional capacity limitations. Journal of Chronic Disease 26: 127–151

Häggqvist S O 1969 Results of early weight bearing in cases of operated subcapital femoral neck fractures. Acta Orthopaedica Scandinavica 40: 684–685

Hall P 1981 Speech therapy. In: Evans C D (ed) Rehabilitation after severe head injury, Churchill Livingstone, Edinburgh, p 51–75

Hamilton A 1978 Sock care for amputees. Physiotherapy 64: 267–268

Hammarsten J, Holm J, Schersten T 1976 Peripheral arterial insufficiency experience for 229 operated limbs. Journal of Cardiovascular Surgery 17: 503–508

Harris A I 1971 Handicapped and impaired in Great Britain. HMSO, London

Harris E D Jr, McCroskey P A 1974 Influence of temperature and fibril stability on degradation of cartilage collagen by rheumatoid synovial collagenase. New England Journal of Medicine 290: 1–6

Harris P L, Read F, Eardley A, Charleworth D, Wakefield J, Sellwood R A 1974 The fate of elderly amputees. British Journal of Surgery 61: 665–668

Harris R, Copp E P 1962 Immobilization of the knee joint in rheumatoid arthritis. Annals of Rheumatic Disease 21: 353–359

Hartviksen K 1962 Ice therapy in spasticity. Acta Neurologica Scandinavica 38 Supplement 3: 79–84

Hayne J A 1980 The effect of exercise with early claudication. Physiotherapy 66: 260–261

Hazelman B L 1972 The painful stiff shoulder. Rheumatology and Physical Medicine 11: 413–421

Heckman J D, Ingram A J, Loyd R O, Luck J V, Mayer P W 1981 Non union treatment with pulsed electromagnetic field. Clinical Orthopaedics 161: 58–66

Henrard J C 1980 Epidemiology of disablement in the elderly. International Rehabilitation Medicine 2: 167–171

Hildebrandt G, Voigt E D, Bahn D, Berended B, Kröger J 1970 Energy cost of propelling wheelchairs at various speeds: cardiac response and effect on steering accuracy. Archives of Physical Medicine and Rehabilitation 51: 131–136

Hoberman M, Springer C F 1958 Rehabilitation of the 'permanently and totally disabled' patient. Archives of Physical Medicine and Rehabilitation 39: 235–340

Horvath S M, Hollander J L 1949 Intra-articular temperatures as a measure of joint reaction. Journal of Clinical Investigation 28: 469–473

Hovind H, Nielsen S L 1974 Local blood flow after short-wave diathermy: preliminary report. Archives of Physical Medicine 55: 217–221

Huffman A 1978 Biofeedback treatment of orofacial dysfunction a preliminary study. American Journal of Occupational Therapy 32: 149–154

Hunt T E 1980 Practical considerations in the rehabilitation of the aged. Journal of American Geriatric Society 28: 59–64

Hurd M M, Farrell K H, Waylonis G W 1974 Shoulder sling for hemiplegia: Friend or foe? Archives of Physical Medicine and Rehabilitation 55: 519–522

Hurwitz L J, Adams G F 1972 Rehabilitation of hemiplegia: Indices of assessment and prognosis. British Medical Journal 1: 94–98

Hutton I M, Rothnie N G 1977 The early mobilization of the elderly amputee. British Journal of Surgery 64: 267–270

Hyams D E 1969 Psychological factors in rehabilitation of the elderly. Gerontologia Clinica 11: 129–136

Hyman M D 1971 Stigma of stroke: Its effects on performance during and after rehabilitation. Geriatrics 26: 132–141

Hyman M D 1972 Social psychological determinants of patient's performance in stroke rehabilitation. Archives of Physical Medicine and Rehabilitation 53: 217–226

Hyman M D 1975 Some psychological factors affecting disability among ambulatory patients. Journal of Chronic Disease 28: 199–216

Imms F J, Pretidge S P, Mayers F B 1980 The decline of aerobic capacity and muscle strength following fracture of the lower limb. Injury 11: 219–224

Janssen C W, Waaler E 1967 Body temperature, antibody formation and the inflammatory response. Archives of Physical Medicine and Rehabilitation 69: 557–566

Johnson H E 1973 Muscle re-education in hemiplegia by use of an EMG device. Archives of Physical Medicine and Rehabilitation 54: 320–322

Johnstone M 1978 Restoration of motor function in the stroke patient. Churchill Livingstone, Edinburgh

Jonason T, Jonzon B, Ringrist I, Oman-Rydberg A 1979 Effects of physical training on different categories of patient with intermittent claudication. Acta Medica Scandivanica 206: 253–258

Kane R L, Olsen D, Leymaster C, Wooley F R, Fisher F D 1974 Manipulating the patient. A comparison of the effectiveness of physician and chiropractor care. Lancet i: 1333–1336

Katz L 1958 Learning in aphasia patients. Journal of Consulting and Clinical Psychology 22: 143–146

Katz S, Ford A B, Chinn A B, Newill V A 1966 Prognosis after stroke. II Long term course of 159 patients. Medicine (Baltimore) 45: 236–246

Kavanagh T, Shepherd R J 1973 The application of exercise testing in the elderly amputee. Canadian Medical Association Journal 108: 314–317

Kelly M 1969 Effectiveness of a cryotherapy technique on spasticity. Physical Therapy 49: 349–353

Kendall P H, Jenkins J M 1968 Exercise for backache. A double blind controlled trial. Physiotherapy 54: 154–157

Kennedy F B, Pozen T J, Gabelman E H, Tuthill J E, Zaentz S D 1970 Stroke Intensive care — an appraisal. American Heart Journal 80: 188–196

Kessler H H 1951 Psychological preparation of the amputee. Industrial Medicine and Surgery 20: 107–108

Kitamura K, Miyamura M, Matsui H 1976 Blood flow of the lower limb in maximal treadmill and bicycle exercise. Journal of the Physiological Society of Japan 38: 457–459

Knight R, Warren M D 1978 Physically disabled people living at home: A study of number and needs. Report on Health and Social Services 13, HMSO, London

Knott M, Voss D E 1968 Prorioceptive neuromuscular facilitation. Harper and Row, New York

Kobak D 1954 Some physiologic considerations of the therapeutic action of ultrasonics. American Journal of Physical Medicine 33: 21–30

Kushlick A 1975 Health care evaluation research team report. Report No 116

Labi M L C, Phillips T F, Gresham G E 1980 Psychosocial disability in physically restored long-term stroke survivors. Archives of Physical Medicine and Rehabilitation 61: 561–565

Lamont P, Langford R 1980 Community physiotherapy in a rural area. Physiotherapy 66: 8–10

Lampe G N 1978 Introduction to the use of transcutaneous electrical nerve stimulation. Physical Therapy 58: 1455–1462

Lane L E 1971 Localised hypothermia for the relief of pain in musculoskeletal injuries. Physical Therapy 51: 182–183

Larsen O A, Lassen N A 1966 Effect of daily muscular exercise in patients with intermittent claudication. Lancet ii: 1093–1096

Lavine L S, Lustrin I, Shamos M H, Moss H L 1971 The influence of electric current on bone regeneration in vivo. Acta Orthopaedica Scandivanica 42: 305–314

Lee K H, Gutierrez I, Smiehorowski T 1980 Pedalator assessment of occlusive vascular disease of the lower extremities. Archives of Physical Medicine and Rehabilitation 61: 265–269

Lee J M, Warren M P 1978 Cold therapy in rehabilitation. Bell and Hyman, London

Lehmann J F 1965 Ultrasonic therapy. In: Licht S (ed) Therapeutic Heat, Waverly Press, Baltimore, p 321–386

Lehmann J F, DeLateur B, Fowler R S, Warren M P A, Arnold R, Schertzer G 1975a Stroke rehabilitation: outcome and prediction. Archives of Physical Medicine and Rehabilitation 56: 383–389

Lehmann J F, DeLateur B J, Fowler R S, Warren M P A, Arnhold R, Schertzer G 1975b Stroke: Does rehabilitation affect outcome? Archives of Physical Medicine and Rehabilitation 56: 375–382

Lehmann J F, Fordyce W E, Rathbun L A, Larson R E, Wood D H 1961 Clinical evaluation of a new approach in the treatment of contracture associated with hip fractures after internal fixation. Archives of Physical Medicine and Rehabilitation 42: 95–102

Lehmann J F, Guy A W, DeLateur B J, Stonebridge J B, Warren C G 1968 Heating patterns produced by shortwave using helical induction coil applicators. Archives of Physical Medicine and Rehabilitation 49: 193–198

Lehmann J F, Masock A J, Warren C G 1970 Effects of therapeutic temperature on tendon extensibility. Archives of Physical Medicine and Rehabilitation 51: 481–488

Lehmann J F, Warren C G, Schain S M 1974 Therapeutic heat and cold. Clinical Orthopaedics 99: 207–247

Lenneberg E H 1967 Biological foundations of language. Wiley, New York

Lesin B E, Mooney V, Asby M 1977 Cast bracing for fracture of the femur, a preliminary report of a modified device. Journal of Bone and Joint Surgery 59A: 917–923

Lesser R, Watt M 1978 Untrained community help in the rehabilitation of stroke sufferers with language disorders. British Medical Journal 2: 1045–1048

Lidstrom A, Zachrisson M 1970 Physical therapy for low back pain and sciatica. Scandinavian Journal of Rehabilitation Medicine 2: 37–42

Lincoln N B 1981 Discrepancies between capabilities and performance of activities of daily living in multiple sclerosis patients. International Rehabilitation Medicine 3: 84–88

Litman T J 1966 Family and physical rehabilitation. Journal of Chronic Disease 19: 211–217

Loesser J D, Black R G, Chritmas A 1975 Relief of pain by transcutaneous stimulation. Journal of Neurosurgery 42: 308–314

Long D 1974 Cutaneous afferent stimulation for relief of chronic pain. Clinical Neurosurgery 21: 257–268

Lowenthal M, Tobis J S, Howard I R 1959 An analysis of rehabilitation needs and prognosis of 232 cases of cerebrovascular accident. Archives of Physical Medicine and Rehabilitation 40: 183–186

Lumsden R M, Morris J M 1968 An in vivo study of axial rotation and immobilization at the lumbosacral joint. Journal of Bone and Joint Surgery 50A: 1591–1602

Lyon L J, Nevins M A 1977 Non-treatment of hip fractures in senile patients. Journal of American Medical Association 238: 1175–1176

Manella K J 1981 Comparing the effectiveness of elastic bandages and shrinker socks for lower extremity amputees. Physical Therapy 61: 334–337

Mannheimer C, Lund S, Carlsson C 1978 The effect of transcutaneous stimulation (TENS) on joint pain in patients with rheumatoid arthritis. Scandivanian Journal of Rheumatology 7: 13–16

Marks M M, Taylor M L, Rusk L A 1957 Rehabilitation of the aphasic patient. Neurology (Minneapolis) 7: 837–843

Marquardsen J 1969 The natural history of acute cerebrosvascular disease. Acta Neurologica Scandinavica 45 Supplement 38

Mashiah A, Patel P, Schraibman I, Carlesworth D 1978 Drug therapy in intermittent claudication: an assessment of the effects of three drugs on patients with intermittent claudication. British Journal of Surgery 65: 342–345

Matthews J A, Hickling J 1975 Lumbar traction: A double blind controlled trial for sciatica. Rheumatology and Rehabilitation 14: 222–225

Mazaras G, Merienne L, Cioloca C 1974 Implantable thalamic stimulation for the management of some types of intractable pain. Neurochirurgie 20: 117–124

McCann R C, Culbertson R A 1976 Comparison of two systems for stroke rehabilitation in a general hospital. Journal of the American Geriatrics Society 24: 211–216

McCollough III N C 1978 Orthotic management in adult hemiplegia. Clinical Orthopaedics 131: 38–46

McDonald I 1961 Statistical studies or recorded energy expenditure in man Part II expenditure on walking related to weight, sex, age, height, speed and gradient. Nutrition Abstracts and Reviews 31: 739–762

McLaughlin H 1961 The frozen shoulder. Clinical Orthopaedics 20: 126–130

McPoil T G, Bergtholdt H T, Hunt G C 1980 Modification of temporary below knee sockets for amputees with absent or diminished sensation. Physical Therapy 60: 437–438

Meikle M, Wechsler E, Tupper A, Benenson M, Butler J, Mulhall D, Stern G 1979 Comparative trial of volunteer and professional treatment of dysphasia after stroke. British Medical Journal 2: 87–89

Melvin J L 1980 Interdisciplinary and Multidisciplinary activities and ACRM. Archives of Physical Medicine and Rehabilitation 61: 379–382

Melzack R 1971 Phantom limb pain: implications for treatment of pathological pain. Anaesthesiology 33: 505–519

Miglietta O, Lewitan A, Rogoff J B 1959 Subluxation of the shoulder in hemiplegic subjects. New York State Journal of Medicine 59: 457–460

Miles J, Lipton S, Hayward M, Bowsher D, Mumford J, Molony V 1974 Pain relief by implanted electrical stimulation. Lancet i: 777–779

Miller E 1977 Management of dementia: review of some possibilities. British Journal of Social and Clinical Psychology 16: 77–83

Mills J A, Pinals R S, Ropes M W, Short C C, Sutcliffe J 1971 Value of bed rest in patients with rheumatoid arthritis. New England Journal of Medicine 284: 453–458

Monga T N, Jaksic T 1981 Acupuncture in phantom limb pain. Archives of Physical Medicine and Rehabilitation 62: 229–231

Mooney V, Harvey J P Jr, McBride E, Snelson R 1971 Comparison of postoperative stump management: Plaster v soft dressing. Journal of Bone and Joint Surgery 53A: 241–249

Mooney V, Nickel V L, Harvey J P Jr, Snelson R 1970 Cast bracing treatment for fracture of the distal part of the femur. Journal of Bone and Joint Surgery 52A: 1563–1578

Morris J M 1974 Low back bracing. Clinical Orthopaedics 102: 126–132

Moskowitz E 1969 Complications in rehabilitation of hemiplegic patients. Medical Clinics of North America 53: 541–559

Munting E 1978 Ultrasonic therapy for the painful shoulder. Physiotherapy 64: 180–181

Munton J 1981 Seating for the arthritic. Reports on Rheumatic Disease No 78. Arthritis and Rheumatism Council

Najenson T, Pikieiny S 1965 Malignment of the glenohumeral joint following hemiplegia: A review of 500 cases. Annals of Physical Medicine 8: 96–99

Najenson T, Yacubovich E, Pikieiny S 1971 Rotator cuff injury in shoulder joints of hemiplegic patients. Scandinavian Journal of Rehabilitation Medicine 3: 131–137

Nepomuceno C S, Miller J M 1974 Shoulder arthrography in hemiplegic patients. Archives of Physical Medicine and Rehabilitation 55: 49–51

New P K, Ruscio A T, George L A 1969 Towards an understanding of the rehabilitation system. Rehabilitation Literature 30: 130–139

Nicholas J J, Green H, Weiner G, Crawshaw C, Taylor F 1982 Splinting in rheumatoid arthritis, I Factors affecting patient. Compliance. Archives of Physical Medicine and Rehabilitation 63: 92–94

Nichols P J R 1963 Rehabilitation after fracture of the shaft of femur. Journal of Bone and Joint Surgery 45B: 96–102

Nieminen S 1975 Early weight-bearing after classical internal fixation of medial fractures of the femoral neck. Acta Orthopaedica Scandinavica 46: 782–794

Norton P L, Brown T 1957 The immobilizing efficiency of back braces. Journal of Bone and Joint Surgery 39A: 111–139

Oakley E M 1978 Danger and contraindications of therapeutic ultrasound. Physiotherapy 64: 173–174

Oradei D M, Waite N 1974 Group psychotherapy with stroke patients during the moderate recovery phase. American Journal of Orthopsychiatry 44: 386–395

Ostendorf C G, Wolf S L 1981 Effect of forced use of the upper extremity of a hemiplegic patient on change in function. Physical Therapy 61: 1022–1028

Overs R P, Belknap E L 1967 Educating stroke patients families. Journal of Chronic Disease 20: 45–51

Paaske W B, Horind H, Sejersen P 1973 Influence of therapeutic ultrasound irradiation on blood low in human cutaneous, subcutaneous and muscular tissue. Scandinavian Journal of Clinical and Laboratory Investigation 31: 389–394

Parkes C M 1973 Factors determining persistence of phantom pain in the amputee. Journal of Psychosomatic Research 17: 97–108

Parkes C M 1975 Psychosocial transitions: Comparison between reaction to loss of limb and loss of a spouse. Britaih Journal of Psychiatry 127: 204–210

Partridge C J 1980 The effectiveness of physiotherapy: A classification for evaluation. Physiotherapy 66: 153–155

Partridge R E H, Duthie J J R 1963 Controlled trial of the effect of complete immobilization of the joints in rheumatoid arthritis. Annals of Rheumatic Disease 22: 91–99

Patrick J H 1981 Intertrochanteric hip fracture treated by immediate mobilization in a splint. Lancet 1: 301–303

Paul B J, LaPratta C W, Dawson A R, Barr E, Bullock P 1960 Use of ultrasound in the treatment of pressure sores in patients with spinal cord injury. Archives of Physical Medicine and Rehabilitation 41: 438–440

Peach H, Pathy M S 1981 Role of non-attendance statistics in assessing the efficiency of geriatric day hospitals. Community Medicine 3: 123–130

Pearson M 1980 Functional bracing of fractures. Physiotherapy 66: 186–188

Pernow B, Zetterquist S 1968 Metabolic evaluation of the leg blood flow in claudicating patients with arterial obstruction at different levels. Scandinavian Journal of Clinical and Laboratory Investigations 21: 277–287

Peszczynski M 1961 Prognosis for rehabilitation of the adult and aged hemiplegic patient. American Journal of Cardiology 7: 365–369

Pitner S E, Mance C J 1973 An evaluation of stroke intensive care. Results in a municipal hospital. Stroke 4: 737–741

Richardson R R, Meyer P R, Raimondi A J 1979 Transabdominal neurostimulation in acute spinal cord injuries. Spine 4: 47–51

Roberts V C, Sabri S, Beeley A H, Cotton L T 1972 The effect of intermittently applied external pressure on the haemodynamics of the lower limb in man. British Journal of Surgery 59: 223–226

Rohinger C 1963 Pilot study on low back pain. Journal of Canadian Physiotherapy Association 15: 16–18

Ropes M W 1961 Conservative treatment of rheumatoid arthritis. Medical Clinics of North American 45: 1197–1207

Rosenberg B, Edwards A 1964 The performance of aphasia in three automated perceptual discrimination programs. Journal of Speech and Hearing Research 7: 295–298

Ross C, Clawson D K 1970 Introduction to the muskuloskeletal system. Harper and Row, New York

Rothberg J S 1981 The rehabilitation team: Future directions. Archives of Physical Medicine and Rehabilitation 62: 407–410

Rusk H A 1977 Principles in management of communication impairment. In: Rehabilitation Medicine 4th edn. Mosby, St Louis, p 259–269

Russell W 1947 painful amputation stump and phantom limb treated by repeated percussion of the stump neuroma. British Medical Journal 1: 2024–2026

Sabri S, Roberts V C, Cotton L T 1972 The effects of intermittently applied external pressure on the haemodynamics of the hind limb in greyhound dogs. British Journal of Surgery 59: 219–222

Sakuma J, Hinterbuchner C, Green R F, Silber M 1974 Rehabilitation of geriatric patients having bilateral lower extremity amputation. Archives of Physical Medicine and Rehabilitation 55: 101–111

Sanne H, Sivertsson R 1968 The effect of exercise on the development of collateral circulation after experimental occlusion of the femoral artery in the cat. Acta Physiologica Scandinavica 73: 257–263

Sarmiento A 1967 A functional below knee cast for tibial function. Journal of Bone and Joint Surgery 49A: 855–875

Sarno M T, Sands E 1970 An objective method of evaluation of speech therapy in aphasia. Archives of Physical Medicine and Rehabilitation 51: 49–54

Sarno M T, Silverman M, Sands E 1970 Speech therapy and language recovery in severe aphasia. Journal of Speech and Hearing Research 13: 607–613

Schuman J E, Beattie E J, Steed D A, Merry G M, Kraus A S 1981 Geriatric patients with and without intellectual dysfunction. Effectiveness of a standard rehabilitation program. Archives of Physical Medicine and Rehabilitation 12: 612–618

Schwartz F 1954 The value of ultrasonics in physical medicine. American Journal of Physical Medicine 33: 38–40

Scott B O 1965 Shortwave diathermy. In: Licht (ed) Therapeutic Heat and Cold, Waverly Press, New Haven

Scott S, Caird F I 1981 Speech therapy for patients with Parkinson's disease. British Medical Journal 283: 1088

Shapiro D, Swartz G E 1972 Biofeedback and visceral learning: clinical applications. Seminars in Psychiatry 4: 171–184

Sheldon P J H 1972 A retrospective survey of 102 cases of shoulder pain. Rheumatology and Physical Medicine 11: 422–427

Sherman R, Gall N, Gormly J 1979 Treatment of phantom limb pain with muscular relaxation to disrupt the pain-anxiety-tension cycle. Pain 6: 47–55

Shroeder K P 1962 Effect of ultrasound on lumbar sympathetic nerves. Archives Physical Medicine 43: 182–185

Skinner J S, Strandness D E 1967 Exercise and intermittent claudication effect of physical training. Circulation 36: 23–29

Smidt L A, Dixon A StJ 1980 Chiropody and the painful foot. Report on Rheumatic Disease No 74, Arthritis and Rheumatism Council

Smith D S, Goldenberg E, Ashburn A, Kinsella G, Sheikh K, Brennan P J et al 1981 Remedial therapy after stroke: a randomized controlled trial. British Medical Journal 282: 517–520

Solomon G F, Schmidt M 1978 A burning issue. Archives of Surgery 113: 185–186

Sorlie D, Myhre K 1978 Effects of physical training in intermittent claudication. Scandinavian Journal of Clinical and Laboratory Investigation 38: 217–222

Stern P H, McDowell F, Miller J M, Robinson M 1969 Effects of facilitation exercise techniques in stroke rehabilitation. Archives of Physical Medicine and Rehabilitation 51: 526–531

Stern P H, McDowell F, Miller J M, Robinson M 1971 Factors influencing rehabilitation. Stroke 2: 213–215

Stockmeyer S A 1967 An interpretation of the approach of Rood to the treatment of neuromuscular dysfunction. American Journal of Physical Medicine 46: 900–961

Stryker W S, Fussell M E, West H D 1970 Comparison of the result of operative and non operative treatment of diaphyseal fracture of the femur at the Naval Hospital San Diego over a five year period. Journal of Bone and Joint Surgery 52A: 815

Stuhlfauth K 1952 Neural effects of ultrasonic waves. British Journal of Physical Medicine 15: 10–14

Susak Z, Gaspar A, Najenson T 1980 Arterial occlusive disease in amputee patients. Assessment with Doppler ultrasound flowmeter and correlation with rehabilitation. Archives of Physical Medicine and Rehabilitation 61: 269–271

Sutcliffe M L, Sharrard W J W, MacEachern A G 1980 The treatment of fracture non-union by electomagnetic induction. Journal of Bone and Joint Surgery 63B: 123–127

Taylor R R 1970 Acute stroke demonstration project in a community hospital. Journal of South Carolina Medical Association 66: 225–227

Teng E L, McNeal D R, Kralj A, Waters R L 1976 Electrical stimulation and feedback tracing: Effect on the voluntary control of paretic muscle. Archives of Physical Medicine and Rehabilitation 57: 228–233

Thomas T L, Meggitt B F 1981 A comparative study of methods for treating fractures of the distal half of the femur. Journal of Bone and Joint Surgery 63B: 3–6

Thompson R C Jr, Delbanco T L, McAllister F F 1965 Complications following lower extremity amputation. Surgery Gynaecology and Obstetrics 120: 301–304

Tikofsky R S, Reynolds G 1962 Preliminary study: Non verbal learning and aphasia. Journal of Speech and Hearing Research 5: 133–143

Tobis J S 1957 Post hemiplegic shoulder pain. New York Journal Medicine 57: 1377–1380

Trieschman R B 1974 Coping with disability: a sliding scale of goals. Archives of Physical Medicine and Rehabilitation 55: 556–560

Triptree V J, Harrison M A 1980 The use of sensor pads in the treatment of adult hemiplegia. Physiotherapy 66: 299

Truscott B L 1972 Health care delivery in the community: use of available resources. Journal of the American Medical Association 221: 289–291

Tyndall R M Day hospital dilemma: when patients refuse. Modern Geriatrics 8: 34–37

Velletri-Glass A, Gassaniga M, Premack D 1973 Artificial language training in global aphasics. Neuropsychologia 11: 95–103

Vignolo L A 1964 Evolution of aphaisa and language rehabilitation: A retrospective study. Cortex 1: 344–367

Vincelli S 1978 A biofeedback aid for hemiplegia. Canadian Journal of Occupational Therapy 45: 181–187

Vitali M, Readhead R G 1967 The modern concept of the general

management of amputee rehabilitation. Annals of the Royal College of Surgeons of England 40: 251–260

Vodovnik L, Kralj A, Stanic U, Acimovic R, Gros N 1978 Recent applications of functional electrical stimulation to stroke patients in Ljubljana. Clinical Orthopaedics 131: 64–70

Vokac Z, Bell H, Bautz-Holter, Rodahl K 1975 Oxygen uptake/heart rate relationship in leg and arm exercises, sitting and standing. Journal of Applied Physiology 39: 54–59

Voss D 1969 Should patients with hemiplegia wear a sling. Physical Therapy 49: 1030

Warren C G, Lehmann J F, Koblanski J N 1971 Elongation of rat tail tendon: Effect of load and temperature. Archives of Physical Medicine and Rehabilitation 52: 465–474

Waters R, Montgomery J 1974 Lower extremity management of hemiparesis. Clinical Orthopaedics 102: 133–143

Waters R L, Perry J, Antonelli D, Hislop H 1976 Energy cost of walking of amputees: Influence of the level of amputation. Journal of Bone and Joint Surgery 58A: 42–46

Waylonis G W, Keith M W, Aseff J N 1973 Stroke rehabilitation in a Mid Western County. Archives of Physical Medicine and Rehabilitation 54: 151–155

Weaver P C, Marshall S A 1973 A functional and social review of lower limb amputees. British Journal of Surgery 60: 732–737

Weber B G, Brunner C 1981 The treatment of non union without electrical stimulation. Clinical Orthopaedics 161: 24–32

Weiss J J, Thompson G R, Doust V, Burgener F A 1974 Arthrography in the diagnosis of shoulder pain and immobility. Archives of Physical Medicine and Rehabilitation 55: 205–209

Welford A T 1976 Skilled Performance: perceptual and motor skills. Scott, Foresman and Co, Illnois

White S A 1979 Treatment of a bilateral amputee using pneumatic mobility aids. Physiotherapy 65: 15

Wiesal S W, Cuckler J M, Deluca F, Jones F, Zeide M S, Rothman R H 1980 Acute low back pain. An objective analysis of conservative therapy. Spine 5: 324–330

Wilson D, Caldwell C B 1978 Central control insufficiency disturbed motor control and sensation: A treatment approach emphasising upper extremity orthoses. Physical Therapy 58: 313–320

Wilson E H, Wilson B O 1971 Integration of hospital and local authority services in the discharge of patients from a geriatric unit. Lancet ii: 864–866

Wilson L A, Grant K, Witney P M, Kerridge D F 1973 Mental status of elderly hospital patients related to occupational therapist's assessment of activities of daily living. Gerontologia Clinica 15: 197–202

Wilson L A, Lawson I R, Brass W 1962 Multiple disorders in the elderly — a clinical and statistical study. Lancet ii: 841–843

Wisham L H, Abramson A S, Ebel A 1953 Value of exercise in peripheral vascular disease. Journal of American Medical Association 153: 10–12

Wolf S L, Baker M P, Kelly J L 1979 EMG biofeedback in stroke. Archives of Physical Medicine and Rehabilitation 60: 960102

Wolff K 1966 Personality type and reaction toward ageing and death. Geriatrics 21: 189–192

Wood P H N 1980 The language of disablement: a glossary relating to disease and its consequences. International Rehabilitation Medicine 2: 86–92

Wright W B 1979 Stammering gait. Age and Ageing 8: 8–12

Wyke B 1979 Neurology of the cervical spine joints. Physiotherapy 65: 72–76

Wyper D J, McNiven D R 1976 The effect of microwave therapy upon blood flow in man. British Journal of Sports Medicine 10: 19

Wyper D J, McNiven D R, Donnolly T J 1978 Therapeutic ultrasound and muscle blood flow. Physiotherapy 64: 321–322

Zetterquist S 1970 The effect of active training on the nutritional blood flow in exercising ischaemic legs. Scandinavian Journal of Clinical and Laboratory Investigation 25: 101–111

Zoeckler A A, Nicholas J J 1969 Prenyl hand splint in rheumatoid arthritis. Physical Therapy 49: 377–379

Zylbergold R S, Piper M C 1981 Lumbar disc disease: comparative analysis of physical therapy treatments. Archives of Physical Medicine and Rehabilitation 62: 176–179

The psychology of long-term and terminal illness in old age

INTRODUCTION

In this chapter, the experience of human aging as it relates to older persons who are chronically and/or terminally ill will be discussed from a psychosocial life cycle perspective rather than from a medical perspective. Firstly, a section is presented on aging and the individual, emphasizing diagnostic assessment, treatment, and management of these individuals based upon a life cycle perspective. Next, it will be shown that in caring for them it is often best to augment a purely medical model with a multi-functional psychosocial health care model. While still not a fully developed and established part of clinical practice, both in the United States of America and in Europe, this model has already shown to have some characteristics which promise a very different approach to the health care of chronically and/or the terminally ill older persons than that exemplified by the acute disease, short-term care and treatment oriented medical model. These characteristics include an emphasis on the use of a multi-disciplinary geriatric team approach and a joint focus on both physical and psychosocial health care needs of patients and their families or 'significant' others in the institution or community-based caring environment. Finally, some other major concerns of the provision of care to the chronically and/or terminally ill will also be referred to. These concerns include alternatives in long-term care and psychological aspects of such care in old age as they affect the patients themselves and their families. Continuity in long-term whole-patient-care will be stressed.

AGING AND THE INDIVIDUAL

One basic assumption commonly made in the study of human aging is that it can best be understood as a developmental process within the context of the human life span as a whole (Anderson, 1957; Bloom, 1964; Bromley, 1974; Buhler and Massarik, 1968; Goulet and Baltes, 1970; Hurlock, 1968; Pressey and Kuhlen, 1957). Viewed within this context, while aging is undoubtedly a continuous process of change throughout life until death, its course in individuals remains largely unpredictable.

While certain biological, social, and psychological developmental changes are known to occur in most individuals during the course of life, and are known to have some systematic influence in the ordering of human behaviour, the chronological age level of their occurrence, and the rate of progress in these changes over time, vary from individual to individual (Atchley, 1980; Binstock and Shanas, 1976; Birren, 1964; Birren and Schaie, 1977; Bromley, 1974; Finch and Hayflick, 1976; Hendricks and Hendricks, 1981). Moreover, similar changes associated with aging or growing older affect people differently at various times in their lives, e.g. biologically, in terms of their ability to function within their social environment; psychologically, in terms of their capacity to adapt to the demands of that environment (Lawton, 1980); and sociologically, in terms of their ability to perform the roles permitted to them in line with societal expectations (George, 1980). In turn, people respond differently in terms of their behaviour during the course of life.

Behavioural aspects in human aging continue to be especially complex as amply demonstrated in recent handbooks on the Psychology of Aging (Birren and Schaie, 1977; Poon, 1980). Thus, whereas the significance of behavioural change is relatively easy to demonstrate during childhood and adolescence, it becomes progressively more difficult to do this successfully in later years, unless the individual's past behaviour and experience, his hopes, expectations and, possibly, anxieties regarding the future are taken into account.

An individual's changing behaviour with increasing age results from the interaction of biological changes (e.g. the gradual and cumulative deterioration in body structure and function, including the brain) with social and psychological changes which are also related to aging.

During the life course, his behaviour may furthermore have become affected by the impact of historical events (e.g. a war or a period of severe economic depression), and by the effects of environmental variables (e.g. the level of formal education available and that received in youth, and such factors as race and social class). Historical events and environmental variables are likely to have a differential impact upon the behaviour of individuals born at different points in historical time (inter-cohort differential effects), but may also have this kind of impact upon the behaviour of individuals born at roughly the same point in historical time (intra-cohort differential effects) (Bengtson, 1973; Bengtson and Cutler, 1976; Bigot, 1971, Laufer and Bengtson, 1974).

Finally, concomitant with the effects of changes related to aging and those of historical events and environmental variables, his behaviour is also likely to be affected by societal expectations and value orientations. Value orientations do not only influence a society's attributes towards aging as a process and the individual's attitudes towards his own personal aging (Bengtson et al, 1975; Hickey et al, 1975), but also those towards the aged as a target group defined in terms of chronological age (Rubin and Brown, 1975; Seltzer and Atchley, 1971; Thomas and Yamamoto, 1975; Thorson, 1975; Weinberger and Milham, 1975). Regarding the latter it is significant that, while few would deny the importance of positive attitudes towards the aged among professional and paraprofessional care givers in the physical/mental health and social welfare services, there is overwhelming evidence that these workers often hold negative attitudes towards the aged in general, and towards their elderly clients or patients in particular, regardless of whether they are being served in institutional or in community settings (Kosberg, 1973; Kosberg et al, 1972; Thorson et al, 1974; Troll and Schossberg, 1970; Vicker, 1974; Wolk and Wolk, 1971).

AGING AND OLD AGE

The study of human aging differs from that of the problems of old age or of the aged, unless old age is viewed as that period of the individual's life span in which the expectation of change associated with distance from death, or possibly from psychosocial breakdown is substantially different from that in earlier life periods. Some support for this expectation is provided by life tables and epidemiological studies of distributions of diseases and physical/mental impairments, which clearly demonstrate the relationship between chronological age and illness. Many, although not all, older persons are at considerably higher risk for disease impairment and death than younger persons (Fries and Crapo, 1981; Hickey, 1980; Libow and Sherman, 1981).

However, while chronological age is undoubtedly the most useful actuarial predictor to date of morbidity (as shown in an age-related incidence and prevalence of

disease and disability), and of mortality (as indicated by death rates), it is a relatively weak predictor of age-related psychological and social behaviour (Neugarten and Hagestad, 1976; Wohlwill, 1970). For example, it is now recognized that to a large extent: '. . . the observed decline in intellectual functioning among the aged is attributable to poor health, social isolation, economic plight, limited education, lowered motivation, or other variables not intrinsically related to the aging process,' and that in so far as intelligence scores do decline with increasing age: '. . . such change is associated primarily with tasks where speed of response is critical' (Eisdorfer and Lawton, 1973). Alternative age concepts, e.g. biological age, psychological age, and social age substantiate empirical observation that an individual who is chronologically old, is not necessarily also biologically, psychologically and/or socially old. For example, a terminally ill patient may be considered very old from a biological/physiological point of view regardless of that patient's chronological age; he should also be considered much older than another individual of the same chronological age who does not suffer from terminal illness. Potentially highly useful, both in practice with individuals of all age levels including the aged, and in gerontological research, is the concept of functional age (Schaie, 1977). This concept, which attempts to provide an indicator of age based on performance capacity, has been used mainly in industrial gerontological research in job skills — including cognitive abilities and sense perception — and worker performance (Clark and Anderson, 1967; McFarland, 1973). The usefulness of this concept might be expanded by using it in relation to the entire range of the older person's functioning, including, for example, the individual's capacity to perform the essential activities of daily living. The measurement of functional age in contrast to chronological age allows for more sensitive decision-making in relation to issues such as, for example, when someone should retire, should or could remain in the community, or should be encouraged to enter a skilled nursing facility. In such decisions, functional rather than chronological age should be the primary determinant.

THE MULTI-DISCIPLINARY TEAM APPROACH IN GERONTOLOGY AND GERIATRIC MEDICINE

Given the complex nature of human aging, whether 'normal' or 'pathological', it is now well recognized that gerontological research benefits most from a multi-disciplinary problem-centred team approach. In this approach, investigators from several disciplines, e.g. the biological, social, and behavioural sciences, as well as workers representing applied medicine and the helping professions work together as a group on a common topic, for example, the treatment and rehabilitation of the elderly stroke patient (Bigot, 1974), mental illness in later life (Busse and Pfeiffer, 1977), and long-term care of the chronically ill (Sherwood, 1975; Somers and Fabian, 1981).

Similarly, in geriatric health care, especially for most if not all older persons who are chronically and/or terminally ill, a multi-disciplinary team approach is increasingly being preferred over a purely clinical one (Libow and Sherman, 1981; NIH, 1980; Besdine, 1979). Although teams may vary in scope and focus, they usually are comprised of a combination of health and social services professionals. As a team, their diagnosis and patient management tends to reflect a life span perspective thus complementing a purely clinical assessment and treatment plan. An assessment based upon a life cycle perspective takes account of the patient's past behaviour and experience, his hopes, expectations, and possibly anxieties. Regarding the future, it considers the values, feelings, social and psychological needs and personal desires of individual patients. Most importantly, this assessment allows a deeper understanding of those aspects of the patient's current behaviour which while not always directly related to clinical observations are nevertheless likely to influence the patient's response to receiving care, treatment and rehabilitation.

Jointly, the clinical diagnosis and the assessment based upon a life cycle perspective form the beginning of what may be termed a multi-functional, psychosocial health care model. In instances where variations of this model are applied, e.g. at the Hebrew Rehabilitation Center for Aged in Boston (Besdine, 1979), the Jewish Institute for Geriatric Care in New York (Libow, 1976), it has become evident that this approach to geriatric health care is especially appropriate for older persons requiring long-term rather than acute care. A purely medical model which emphasizes disease oriented, acute, and short-term care and treatment is clearly inappropriate in the long-term care of the chronologically and/or terminally ill.

THE DEFINITION OF CHRONIC ILLNESS, CHRONIC DISEASE AND LONG-TERM CARE OF THE CHRONICALLY AND TERMINALLY ILL

Undoubtedly, problems related to chronic and terminal illness loom largest in the more developed countries of the world (in fact, the subject is hardly discussed elsewhere). In these countries, the existing literature usually offers many definitions of what typically constitutes a chronically and/or terminally ill patient, rather than of chronic or terminal illness *per se*. Moreover, these definitions tend to attach more weight to the duration of the illness than to its type. Thus, for example, as early as 1964, Wessen considered a patient to be chronically ill if he stayed in a hospital for more than 30 days (Wessen, 1964). The reasons for choosing this particular period were firstly, that most acute illnesses can be remedied within this period; and secondly, that a distinction between younger and older patients is facilitated since the latter usually require a longer recovery period largely because of a combination of somatic, psychological, and social factors.

While this is as it may be even today, current definitions of chronic illness *per se* often refer to aspects of care, especially long term care. Thus, for example, a well-known article on 'Problems in Chronic Illness Care' (Gerson and Strauss, 1975) identified three major problems in the health field which, according to the authors, were beginning to merge in the mid-1970's into a larger and more complex series of problems for public policy. These were: (1) the increasingly chronic character of the illness load suffered by the total population; (2) the increasing emphasis, both within the medical profession and in general public discussion, on problems of quality of life; and, (3) the increasing attention being given to the organization of health care focusing both on reducing costs and on improving the quality of care, and (recognizing) that:

1. Chronic illnesses are long-term.
2. Chronic illnesses are uncertain in a variety of ways.
3. Chronic diseases require proportionately large efforts at palliation.
4. Chronic diseases are multiple diseases.
5. Chronic diseases are disproportionately intrusive upon the lives of patients.
6. Chronic diseases require a wide variety of ancillary services if they are to be properly cared for.
7. Chronic diseases imply conflicts of authority among patients, medical workers and funding agencies.
8. Chronic illnesses are expensive.
9. Chronic disease care is primary care.

The observation that definitions of chronic illness do not usually include references to specific disease is important, for it points to a medical problem area. Clearly, chronic illness is not exclusively a medical problem requiring medical treatment.

For the patients, chronic illness also has its social and psychological implications which are likely to impede care and rehabilitation, unless they are properly taken account of. For example, it is a fair assumption that if long-term care services (whether provided in an institutional or in a community setting) are tailored to help the patient only with those daily tasks of living which he is unable to accomplish by himself, leaving it to him to carry out the tasks which he is able to accomplish, there will be minimal loss in such personal aspects of his self-integrity, control, feelings of independence and confidence.

It should be noted that while chronic illness *per se* and the various chronic diseases are considered 'long-term', no specific duration is indicated. It is currently increasingly being recognized that definitions of chronic illness *per se* and of chronic diseases in terms of time has about as much value as chronological age has in predicting when someone is 'old', i.e. little or none. Thus, for example, in their consideration of what constitutes a chronic disease, Fries and Carpo recently suggested that instead of emphasizing a particular duration — one would do better to define chronic diseases in terms of the fact that 'these diseases tend to (1) be incremental, (2) be universal, (3) have a clinical threshold, and (4) be characterized by a progressive loss of organ reserve' (Fries and Crapo, 1981).

Even although the duration of chronic illness or chronic disease does not appear to offer important insights into their nature the fact remains that chronically and/or terminally ill patients usually require long-term care, whether in institutions or in the family and community. There are numerous definitions of long term care but perhaps the most comprehensive one to date reads as follows: 'Long-term care refers to one or more services provided on a sustained basis to enable individuals whose functional capacities are chronically impaired to be maintained at their maximum levels of health and well being' (Brody, 1977). Paraphrasing this definition, it implies that for chronically and/or terminally ill patients 'one or more services' should not only promote their health but also their social and psychological well being. The care may be continuous or intermittent but is virtually always required for an extended period of time.

From a medical perspective, the above suggests that diagnostically oriented procedures, treatment, and patient management should not only cope with clinical aspects of individually often very different patients, but also with the psychological and social consequences of their chronic or terminal illness over the long-term. In this regard, it is particularly important that a number of factors relating to the patient himself are recognized for their potential to influence effective treatment and rehabilitation and the likelihood of his eventual discharge from one institution (e.g. a community hospital) to another (e.g. a skilled nursing home) or to the community (i.e. home). These include his past medical and social history; the impact of the transfer from the community (i.e. his private home, or a residential home) to a hospital based geriatric unit; the impact of hospitalization; and various aspects of his psychological make-up (e.g. cognitive functioning, personality, health and body orientation, time perspec-

tive and expectations regarding the future, and self-concept). The factors which do not operate in a mutually exclusive fashion, affect his social relationships during the disease process, with the medical, nursing and rehabilitation staff concerned, as well as with 'significant others', e.g. relatives and friends. The combination of factors and the social relationships which they affect in turn influence his social and psychological behavioural response to treatment and rehabilitation and ultimately may affect his chance of discharge.

In addition, within this context and from the standpoint that being a chronically or terminally ill patient almost inevitably implies some form of institutionalization at one time or another during the disease process, it is equally important that some of the phases are recognized and understood which many a chronically or terminally ill patient may have to pass through following his admission to, for example, a geriatric unit of a local community hospital. Thus, upon his admission there is first an incubation period, during which (1) he has to accustom himself to some extent to the idea of staying in the unit and to the kind of treatment and rehabilitation he is given; (2) he has to establish social relationships with the medical, nursing and rehabilitation staff concerned, as well as with his fellow patients; and (3) he will have to review, and he may attempt to preserve, his contacts with relatives and friends. If the treatment leads to his improvement, he is likely to be discharged either to his own private home or to some other institution, e.g. a residential home for the aged, or a nursing home. If the treatment has, however, not been successful he will stay in the geriatric unit, probably being transferred to a long-stay ward or hospital and herewith enter into a period of crisis during which (4) he will have to reconcile himself with the idea that rehabilitation and eventual recovery may necessitate a much longer stay in hospital, or may even be unlikely. From this point onwards, he may be regarded as a truly hospitalized patient, who sooner or later is likely to pass through the terminal phase of his life during which (5) he may enter into a period of crisis in which he must come to grips with the prospects of death and dying.

THE CHRONICALLY AND/OR TERMINALLY ILL POPULATION AT RISK AND IMPLICATIONS FOR ITS GERIATRIC CARE

In the United States, currently almost 25 million people or a little over 11 per cent of the country's total population are 65 years of age or older. It has been projected, (1) that this overall population will grow to almost 32 million by the year 2000 and to some 55 million by the year 2030; and (2) that the group aged 85 years or older

— the so called 'old old' — will increase from its present 2 million to over 1.5 times as much by the year 2000 and by some 2.5 times as much by the year 2030 (Federal Council of Aging, 1981). The prevalence of chronic conditions, limited mobility, and the need for assistance in basic activities of daily living, e.g. bathing, dressing, eating, and going to the toilet, (Katz et al, 1963, 1970, 1972) one finds especially among the 'old old'. In other words, while recognizing the difficulties in accurately estimating the proportions of elderly persons involved (Nagi, 1976), there is little doubt that the 'old old' are at greatest risk of requiring long-term care, whether formally through compensated long-term services or informally through assistance by relatives of friends without pay. Moreover, these older persons often face problems related to low income (Social Security Administration, 1980), and inadequate housing (U.S. Department of Housing and Urban Development, 1979). Finally, since women have a longer life expectancy than men, the problems of the 'old old' are increasingly those of women. In view of the fact that in the United States some 41 per cent of elderly women live alone in contrast to 15 per cent of the elderly men (Federal Council on Aging, 1981), it should not be surprising that — in addition to all other problems faced by them — elderly women tend to be more vulnerable to social isolation, depression, and institutionalization.

These demographic projections and hard data on the elderly at greater risk, while applying in the United States, reflect trends also found to varying degrees in other parts of Western civilization, notably in Europe (Shanas, 1971). In essence, previously unimagined numbers of people are or will be surviving into extreme old age. Many of these people, especially the 'old old' will suffer one or more chronic conditions, social disadvantages (e.g. living alone, limited mobility), emotional vulnerability (e.g. isolation, depression, suicidal tendencies) and poverty. To meet these people's demands on the prevailing health care and social services system or — as Isaacs put it — to promote 'the survival of the unfittest' (Isaacs et al, 1972), two issues in geriatric care appear to be particularly deserving of increasing attention presently and in the years ahead: (1) the further development of education in geriatric medicine and gerontology for health professions students, practicing physicians and other health care professionals, e.g. nurses, therapists, social workers, and (2) the need for a holistic approach to geriatric care based on the concept of wholepatient care.

Education in geriatric medicine and gerontology

Currently, there exist several overlapping definitions of what constitutes geriatric medicine or 'geriatrics' for short. The general consensus, however, appears to be that it is that field of general medicine which concerns itself with the promotion of *health* and, thus, with the preventive, clinical, remedial, and psychosocial aspects of *illness* and *disability* in the elderly (see, for example, Anderson, 1976; Besdine, 1979; Libow and Sherman, 1981).

In Europe, notably Britain has chairs in geriatric medicine at many medical schools and the subject has been taught and practiced as a formal discipline with specialty status for more than a quarter of this century. In the United States, there is still only a beginning of educational development in this field. Its first chair in geriatric medicine was established in 1978 at the New York Hospital Cornell Medical Center, and most recently, another one was established at the Mt Sinai Medical Center in New York City. In addition, most medical school curricula now incorporate at least some geriatric content. Overall, it is increasingly recognized that geriatrics cannot but become a dominant force in medical thought, research, training, and practice within the next 25 to 50 years (Butler, 1976; Dans and Kerr, 1979; Institute of Medicine, 1978; Libow, 1980). Accordingly, in order to equip medical students as well as health care professionals (e.g. primary care physicians, nurses, therapists, and social workers) with the appropriate knowledge and understanding not only of clinical aspects but also of social and psychological aspects of aging, of chronic illness, and functional disability, it is now considered imperative that a core geriatrics and gerontology curriculum be established and fully integrated into the overall basic, clinical, and applied curricula of all medical schools (see, for example, Begala, 1980; Somers and Fabian, 1981; White House Conference on Aging Reports, 1981). Preferably, this core curriculum will concern itself in depth with (1) *Geriatrics*, i.e. clinical medicine about disease in old age, presented in this textbook and several others in recent years (including Anderson, 1976; Rossman, 1971, 1979); (2) *Gerontology*, i.e. the study of normal aging, including the biomedical, behavioural psychosocial, cultural and sociological aspects of aging; and (3) *the organization and delivery of health and health-related services to the elderly*. Regarding the latter, medical education must also include courses in geriatrics which provide a 'detailed understanding of community services, how they operate and how they influence patient's and family's ability to function . . .' (Eisdorfer, 1981).

The overall objective of the geriatrics and gerontology curriculum is 'to produce special medical leaders of geriatric medicine, i.e. geriatricians' (Libow, 1980). Paraphrasing Besdine (1979), geriatricians are highly competent clinicians, who are particularly knowledgeable in the biology of aging, familiar with clinical research methods and data, and aware that 'common diseases present themselves in uncommon ways in old people'. They will act as advocates in gaining comprehensive health care for the aged and they will be able to teach geriatric medicine to other health professionals (e.g. primary care physicians, nurses, physical therapists, social workers). They will feel comfortable with the management of the irremediable chronically and/or terminally ill older person, and — above all else — they will provide a leadership role in holistic geriatric care based on the concept of whole-patient care.

Holistic geriatric care

The holistic approach to geriatric care acknowledges the fact that — in actual practice — 'the ill elderly often need much more than any one health practitioner can provide' (Libow, 1980), and that 'most problems of the elderly do not require the services of geriatricians (physicians), but rather a multidisciplinary team approach in concert with patients, their families and community groups' (Institute of Medicine, 1977). Undoubtedly, this applies particularly to the chronically and terminally ill among them. Essentially, the approach advocates the use of a multidisciplinary health care team in which the skills of the geriatrician (or, as the case may be, the primary care physician) and registered nurses are complemented by those of other health care and social services professionals. These additional professionals may include but are not limited to physician assistants and geriatric nurse practitioners, nurses'aides and orderlies, physical/occupational/speech/ and hearing therapists, social workers, applied social and clinical behavioural scientists. The multi-functional psychosocial health care model, referred to earlier, exemplifies such an approach to holistic geriatric care. In it's delivery of geriatric care, it is characterized by an interactive process which focuses on co-operation and co-ordination among diverse health professionals, older recipients of care, the immediate community (including the patients' informal networks), and society at large. The leadership role of the geriatrician (primary care physician) is usually recognized: while this individual is not and cannot be directly responsible for the delivery of all services needed by the individual older patient, he/she must be aware and take account — through the co-operative efforts of team members, of the social and psychological implications of the illness for that patient and of the multiple factors that may contribute to his overall well-being. These factors often include but are not limited to biological, physiological, psychological, and spiritual changes in the course of the illness, social interactions, education, economics, community services, and environmental conditions (Liss and McPherson-Turner, 1980; Bigot, 1982).

The team concept in multidisciplinary holistic geriatric care, its ability to bring together diverse skills and expertise enabling the provision of more effective, better co-ordinated and higher quality services for patients; and, its implications for the training of health professionals in multidisciplinary team participation and management skills, have been the subjects of a number of recent publications (Dans and Kerr, 1979; Dube and Mather, 1981; Hudson and Norse, 1975; McCally et al, 1977; Portnoi, 1979; Williamson, 1979). Regarding the latter, multi-disciplinary team training must provide knowledge, skills, and attitudes leading to effective team action in holistic team care. Put differently — beside a thorough grounding in the basic principles of gerontology/geriatrics — shared meetings and clinical experiences using common resources and facilities should create the multidisciplinary context of holistic geriatric team care. In this regard, it may be suggested that the multidisciplinary team training should highlight and practice a number of common, ideal basic competencies that team members can and will share as they provide holistic geriatric team care. These suggested competencies, translated into behavioural objectives, are indicated in Table 52.1.

A note of caution is appropriate at this point. Holistic geriatric team care as an approach to (1) the education of, and (2) service delivery by health professionals involved in geriatrics/gerontology, is a very recent development. Initiated in the United States by this country's Veterans Administration (Beard, 1981; Calkins, 1981; Mather and Dube, 1981), the approach, as applied to chronically and/or terminally ill long-term patients, is still subject to constant review and scrutiny to assure that it is more efficient and effective than traditional health professions' collaboration. For the moment, it would appear that where as holistic geriatric team care may be particularly appropriate for long-term patients in institutional settings, it may be less feasible to activate for patients living at home or with other individuals, (e.g. relatives, friends) in the community.

MAJOR CONCERNS IN LONG-TERM CARE

In this section, brief reference is made to some important issues in long-term patient care of chronically and/or terminally ill older persons. These include: (1) Alternatives in long-term care; (2) Non-medical and psychological aspects in the treatment and rehabilitation process of the chronically ill older person; and (3) That of the terminally ill older person.

Long-term care: alternatives

Long-term care, i.e. '. . . the sustained and prolonged health, social, and personal care given to individuals who are chronically ill and/or disabled' (Hammerman et al, 1975) is a type of care given to those older persons whose chronic conditions (e.g. physical and cognitive

Table 52.1 Common, ideal basic competencies of health professionals in the delivery of holistic geriatric team care (HGTC)*

Objectives	Cognitive knowledge and skill acquisition	Skills practice	Affective health including attitudes
To describe and implement the roles of the HGTC	The ability to explain the structure of the program within the sponsoring human service facility (e.g. a hospital, a medical school)	The ability to demonstrate the ability to work as a professional within the inter-professional structure	The ability to develop appreciation of how team structure relates to individual skills of the various team members
To describe the organizational structure of the geriatric facility	The ability to define the management techniques, strategy development and organizational planning: 1. To describe the mechanics of multi-disciplinary geriatric care for the elderly — skill, functions, and roles of professionals in other disciplines. 2. To relate to principles of group dynamics: team skills, management skills	The ability to develop an organizational structure that will facilitate team management: 1. To demonstrate effective communication skills for relating to patients and colleagues. 2. To demonstrate effective professional skills within HGTC. 3. To formulate an interdisciplinary treatment plan. 4. Perform triage with the geriatric patient. 5. To facilitate group interaction through competent application of the principles of group dynamics.	The ability to develop awareness of the relationship of theory to practice: 1. To develop appreciation of and respect for interdisciplinary competencies. 2. To appreciate the necessity and value of interdisciplinary geriatric care for the elderly.
To describe the basic principles of gerontology/geriatrics	1. To state governmental and private resources available to older persons. 2. To define social, economic, psychological and physiological factors which influence the behaviour of the older persons. 3. To describe the political and economic environment and its implications for geriatric medicine. 4. To describe the demography and epidemiology of the older population.	To engage community services as appropriate; and facilitate interaction among all of these services	1. To develop positive attitudes toward older persons. 2. To develop a sensitivity to the social, economic, physiological and psychological factors which affect the elderly person.

* Adapted from ideas and suggestions expressed by Marion (1979, 1980, 1981); Rapoport and Cahn (1981).

impairments) and accompanying problems (which may include an inability to deal with medical crises, carry out prescribed regimens, fight social isolation, loneliness, and depression) have affected their daily functioning. It is important to be aware that there are many older persons with chronic conditions who are not restricted in activities of daily living or in their performance of social roles (Commission of Chronic Illness, 1957; U.S. Department of Health and Human Services Health Care Financing Administration, 1981) and who therefore do not require long-term care.

The provision of long-term care is not limited to older persons living in institutional settings (e.g. long-stay hospitals, nursing homes, home for the aged). Increasingly, it is also provided to older persons living in the community, for example, through mechanisms of co-ordinated services in day care, sheltered and/or public housing, and home health care programmes. Regardless of the environmental setting in which an older person receives long-term care, individualized supportive services and specialized programmes are usually required. Their provision always involves a physician and, more often than not, also the combined efforts of a team which may include a nurse, a social worker, a physical therapist, and other workers, most notable among them: members of the immediate and/or extended family of the patients. On the part of all these involved individuals, caring for the patient calls for knowledge, understanding, and acceptance of that patient's condition, an awareness of his problems concomitant with the condition, and a considerable degree of appreciation of the ways in which his condition and problems affect him in his physical, social and emotional well-being as well as in his behaviour.

One of the most persistently debated issues in the provision of long-term care is that of community-based service program alternatives to institutional care (see, for example, The Gerontologist, February, 1974; February, 1976). Undoubtedly, this debate and the active attempt to develop alternatives to institutional care has been heavily influenced by the 'considerable outcry about the detrimental effects of institutional life' (Bennett and Eisdorfer, 1975), as well as by evidence regarding the 'inappropriate' placement of certain proportions of older persons in institutions (Pfeiffer, 1973). While one obviously does not wish to discourage the development of programmatic community-based service programmes for the elderly, the prevalent motivating cast of mind behind their development which views these programmes in opposition to institutional care (Solon, 1974), is unfortunate as well as unrealistic. It is unfortunate in the sense that it has tended to inhibit efforts to develop a more positive stance toward institutions and institutional care as well as constructive advocacy to improve institutional life, especially in relation to social and psychological quality of life supports for the residents. Realistically, both community-based services and institutional care services are needed, now and in the future. The provision of the former may be able to slow down, but cannot prevent the gradual continued deterioration in the older person's state of health and in his ability to cope with the tasks of daily living; eventually, that person is likely to enter an institution (if he lives long enough). One of the tasks of community-based service providers should appropriately be to prepare the older person for that eventuality.

It may be suggested that the debate on community alternatives of care *to* institutional care would greatly benefit if increased attention were focused on the concept of continuity *in* long-term care. From this perspective one is more concerned with life supports in long-term care making up a comprehensive health and welfare delivery system. The point of entry into such a system varies in accordance with the older person's needs, and there is no orderly progression from one life support to another; thus, the individual may need to enter a hospital several times, may benefit from services rendered at home intermittently, may enter a nursing home, and may return to the community. Yet, there appear to be transition points, beginning when that person can no longer manage for himself. For a time he

can usually continue living at home with various levels of support (from the immediate and/or extended family, the neighbourhood and/or the larger community), before his transition to a semi-protective environment (e.g. sheltered or public housing with support services), then may need to move to an environment that provides complete protection (e.g. a home for the aged, a nursing home, a mental health institution). From this perspective, the question regarding the most appropriate supportive living environment for the older person is not concerned with alternatives but rather with the function the institution will serve 'within a continuum of optimally developed, linked and supported services for long-term care' (Hammerman, 1974; Brody, 1977).

It is clear that while a considerable amount of research has been concerned with the process of aging, through a framework implying changed social, psychological and physical conditions, within which the aged individual must operate, as regards the chronically and terminally ill, more research is certainly required into the separation of aspects of radical environmental change and subsequent hospitalization or institutionalization which are likely to be stressful for the patient, from those which do not have these negative effects or only marginally so. Clarity of information regarding the impact of hospitalization and institutional care upon the patient is required, and could lead to the augmentation of medical services with greater responsiveness to the social and psychological needs as well as the personal desires of the long-term care patient. Furthermore, such information regarding the impact of hospitalization or institutionalization could contribute towards the development of methods of treatment and rehabilitation with a greater likelihood of the patient's eventual discharge and resettlement into the community.

Medical and non-medical aspects in the treatment and rehabilitation of the chronically ill older person

The problems involved in the development of viable strategies for the successful treatment and rehabilitation of physically and/or mentally impaired older persons in institutions as well as those living in the community, have been discussed both in conceptual and practical contexts (see for example, Brocklehurst and Hanley, 1976; Busse and Pfeiffer, 1973, 1977; Eisdorfer and Cohen, 1978). On the one hand, there appears to be a consensus that while the diagnosis and treatment of *physical* impairments do not usually pose problems for the physician and other health care professionals, impaired *mental* functioning — e.g. confusion, forgetfulness, and depression — may easily go undetected or, worse, is often and mistakenly assumed to be an inevitable and irreversible part of growing older and thus not worth bothering about. On the other hand, it is increasingly emphasized that the early detection, diagnosis, and subsequent treatment of impaired mental functioning, especially at the time 'when the disease process is in its incipient stages and the symptomatology is very mild or subtle' (Cohen, 1979), is not only possible but absolutely essential to maintain and improve the mentally (and often physically) impaired older person's quality of life 'even in the face of irremediable decline' (Gaitz et al, 1977). From this perspective, physical and psychosocial treatment and rehabilitation techniques should always be intended to restore or to arrest further decline in functional capacity of physically and/or mentally impaired individuals, among them older persons.

As referred to earlier, these techniques, if deemed appropriate, should be applied within a pattern of whole-patient care, involving consideration not only of the multifactoral causes of illness and disability in the older person, but also of that older person's personal, past and present perspectives on social and psychological quality of life components in terms of, for example, his values, feelings, desires, and perceptions. Put differently, whole-patient care in this connection suggests that these treatment and rehabilitation techniques 'should capitalize upon already-existing expertise in such areas as life span development, clinical psychology, and community psychology' (Smyer and Gatz, 1978). Further, and especially if the older person is presently hospitalized/institutionalized but with the distinct possibility of his eventual discharge to his own home, the treatment and rehabilitation techniques should involve community support mechanisms as well as members of his family (e.g. the spouse, a daughter).

The spouse. The role of the spouse in the patient's treatment and rehabilitation process deserves special attention. For example, if the husband is the patient, then the spouse herself an older person, may be willing yet feel apprehensive about her *ability to cope* with her husband at home, given her expectations regarding his as well as her own residual physical disabilities, emotional well-being and mood tone upon his discharge from the hospital (Lazarus, 1978; Mechanic, 1974; Moos, 1976; Pearlin and Schooler, 1978; White, 1974). The psychological or affective state in which she finds herself concomitant with socio-biological and socio-economical consequences following her husband's illness requires careful assessment, and may necessitate a rehabilitative effort distinguishable from that made on behalf of her husband. She and possibly other members of the family may have to be taught (e.g. in the rehabilitation ward, or the day hospital) nursing skills, and the use and care of remedial equipment, including wheelchairs and other home aids. She must be made aware of her husband's current physical skills which require daily exercise, developing physical abilities which need to be encouraged, and residual physical disabilities for which she as well as her husband must compensate. Given that

many chronically ill and/or disabled older persons can remain in their own homes, or be resettled in their homes following hospitalization, one does well to recognize that '. . . the biggest nursing service in the world is the family . . .', and that therefore, in addition to the rehabilitative efforts of physicians and other qualified workers, '. . . the properly learned rehabilitative techniques used by the *family* are also of considerable importance' (Cosin, 1973).

Regarding the older person who either remains hospitalized or is admitted into a skilled nursing home or a home for the aged providing intermediate care, the family's most important role is that of maintaining social relationships with him. In particular, regular visits to this older person may to an appreciable extent enable him to compensate for an apparent inability to control significant life events outside the institution as well as to counter possible feelings of helplessness, hopelessness, and — ultimately — depression (Seligman, 1975, 1976). In the effort to promote — through social relationships — the institutionalized older person's psychological well-being, there is no doubt that his family represents the major support system. A healthy psychological well-being not only adds to the older person's quality of life but is also likely to contribute positively to his response in treatment and rehabilitation. Overall then, recognizing the complex nature of an holistic approach to the physical and mental well-being of older persons living in the community and those living in institutions, it may be suggested that while quality of care does not necessarily lead to quality of life, the approach if properly executed, would come close to achieving the latter, particularly for these older persons who are chronically and/or terminally ill.

Types of rehabilitation. Depending on which programmatic outcomes of rehabilitation are deemed desirable in the patient, it is possible to distinguish between two general types of approach. On the one hand, there are various techniques whose chief aim is individual rehabilitation, e.g. occupational therapy, physical therapy, medical therapies including symptomatic drug treatment (Busse and Pfeiffer, 1969, 1973) relational and supportive psychotherapy (Rechtschaffen, 1959), behaviour therapy (Gendlin and Rychlak, 1970; Krasner, 1971), and the sheltered environment or workshop approach (e.g. Nathanson and Reingold, 1969). On the other hand, there are techniques which are mainly intended to promote the patient's social functioning, group psycho-therapy and counselling (Linden, 1953; Liederman et al, 1967; Saul and Saul, 1974), milieu therapy and reality orientation (Barnes, 1974; Bok, 1971; Gottesman et al, 1971, 1973; Letcher et al, 1974; Rechtschaffen et al, 1958), group process (Brudno and Seltzer, 1968), sensory training (Pijnenborg, 1970), and role playing.

Non-medical techniques may be expected to assume increasing importance in the case of long-term patients, especially when these patients have no prospect of recovery, and/or are mentally impaired. In this connection, any rehabilitation programme for older persons must take account of the extent to which they suffer from various effects of brain syndrome, e.g. memory impairment, poor concentration, limited span of attention, repetitive behaviour, and affective liability, in addition to functional incapacity due to serious physical disability.

For them, the objective of rehabilitation is remotivation in terms of (1) resocialization, i.e. stimulation of verbalization and interaction between patients, and between patients and hospital staff or nursing home staff; (2) facilitation of activities within the institution, i.e., the provision of opportunities for activities which correspond with the patient's wishes; and (3) independent actions, i.e. the promotion of a sense of worth enabling the patients to move towards some degree of independent action within the framework of the communal life in the institution (Toepfer et al, 1974). While for some long-term patients, for example, those with prospects of partial recovery, the rehabilitation program may accelerate their discharge, from the institution to the community, for other patients, especially the chronic mentally ill, it may not. These latter patients may still be capable of learning, provided the level of teaching is adapted to them and developed step by step; provided also that this happens in a therapeutic milieu which encourages them to create their own humane environment and which considers their preferences within the course of treatment (Kahana, 1973). However, they are also likely to remain institutionalized in which case the following suggestions from Paul (1969) are particularly relevant:

1. It is advisable to emphasize the status of 'resident' rather than 'patient' through informal dress for the staff, open channels of communication in all directions and a broad but clear structure of authority.

2. It is advisable to make clear, through rules and staff members' attitudes, that the residents are responsible human beings; that they are expected to comply with the minimum rules of group life and to participate in self-care, work, recreation and social activities.

3. It is advisable to use a system in which the expectations with regard to the residents (in terms of their degrees of independence, levels of responsibility) are raised progressively.

4. It is advisable to stimulate social interaction and skills, and the availability of a wide range of activities should be ensured; regular meetings in large and small groups should be arranged.

5. It is advisable to stress clarity in communication, with concrete instructions of appropriate conduct, and to pay more attention to demonstrating the usefulness of any action rather than to explaining it to the patient.

6. It is advisable to provide practical opportunities for practicing professional and domestic skills, with feedback and specialized training for those skills for which there is a demand.

7. It is advisable to encourage residents to come into contact with the outside world by exposing them to society and by bringing in volunteers from society for discussion.

8. It is advisable to identify special areas for alteration and support for each individual in concrete terms.

9. It is advisable to prepare residents and 'significant others' for a life of mutual support and assistance in society through training both before discharge and by programmed aftercare.

10. If there are no 'significant others' it is advisable to train and discharge residents in small groups of two or three as 'families' who can act as 'significant others' for each other.

The terminally ill older person

Old people in this group are often, though not always, admitted to a hospital shortly before their death. They, and chronically ill patients in the terminal phase of their lives, are confronted with the last phase of life — dying and death. An important question is whether they should be informed of their condition, and also whether their relatives should be told.

The advantage to the patient of his knowing about the condition is that it enables him to talk about death and dying to relatives, close friends, and possibly, fellow patients and hospital staff. Some patients may, of course, have come to know about their condition without being told; yet, they may be in need of confirmation by their physician. The manner in which the news is broken to the patient by the physician depends on that physician's 'own attitude and ability to face terminal illness and death' (Kübler-Ross, 1969; Glaser and Strauss, 1965).

No matter how the patient becomes informed about his condition, upon the awareness that for him life may shortly come to an end, he will have to adjust himself to this fact. It may be suggested that the adjustment assumes the characteristics of a developmental psychological process, which may include a number of phases. For example, Kübler-Ross (1969) distinguished the following phases: denial and isolation (see also Weisman, 1972); anger; bargaining (e.g. with the hereafter); acceptance. It may furthermore be suggested that whatever the real nature of the process of adjustment, the patient's initial fear of death will tend to decrease rather than to increase with the passage of time. Finally, a number of determining variables are likely to play a role in the process of adjustment, including: the patient's life cycle; his environment; the quality of the attitude towards the experience that life is coming to an end; the intensity of this experience and the time of experience; and the patient's philosophy of life — especially the significance of this to the patient (Munnichs, 1966).

Perhaps the most pressing need of the terminally ill patient is concerned with communication. Those who are responsible for his care in hospital, as well as his relatives and close friends, must let him know that they are ready and willing to share his concerns. These concerns may include: the meaning of death and dying for the patient; the manner in which he will die; and what will happen to his dependants or next of kin, and to himself after death. As regards the first concern, the patient will rarely be able to disengage himself fully from life while he is still alive. Sometimes, however, death may be interpreted as release from further suffering, especially by chronically ill patients.

Regarding the manner of dying, many patients may feel afraid of pain or oppression, and especially of solitude. These fears can, however, be ameliorated in practice by discussion. Through discussion between patient and physician, a relationship of trust can develop, which should help the physician to decide on the appropriate treatment and guidance. It is worth noting in this connection that much of the literature on the dying person is concerned more with the discovery of psychopathology and psychological deterioration than with the exploration of the dying patient's ability to cope adequately, i.e. to grow 'positively' in the event (Zinker, 1966). Regarding the latter, also the role of the nursing staff in caring for the patient is extremely important (Earle et al, 1976).

By talking openly to the next of kin about the approaching death, it is possible to ascertain important issues and to make the required arrangements. The knowledge of these interactions to the patient may give him peace of mind. One important issue for the next of kin, which may not be of direct relevance to the patient, is the extent to which they feel 'anticipatory' bereavement or grief (Schoenberg et al, 1974). Bereavement from a psychological viewpoint, refers to the emotional state and behaviour of the survivor(s) following the death of a relative or friend. It is a temporary condition from which the bereaved person is expected to recover, but little if anything is known about the duration of bereavement after death, and the likelihood of 'antici-

patory' bereavement prior to the death. It would appear that research into 'anticipatory' bereavement may throw light on the ways in which this condition influences the behaviour of the next of kin, including older persons such as the patient's spouse, in relation to the dying person (Heyman and Gianturco, 1973; Kastenbaum and Aisenberg, 1972; Parkes, 1972; Schoenberg et al, 1975).

What will happen to the patient himself after his death is predominantly a philosophical problem. If the patient's evaluation of his own life is favourable, he may be able to surrender to death easily; if unfavourable, however, feelings of insecurity may be dominant. In the latter case, support from the environment in the tradition of Cicely Saunders (1972) would seem appropriate. At St Christopher's Hospice in London, she has been able to produce results in relation to a satisfactory death through the careful management of pain in conjunction with the maintenance of maximal social and psychological support.

In the United States the hospice movement, aiming at providing compassionate holistic care to the terminally ill, has mushroomed from a handful of programmes in the mid-1970's to approximately 500 such programmes currently operating or being planned. The complex medical, psychological, and social needs of the terminally ill, their consequent need for flexible and individualized care (in the hospital, the hospice, or at home through family or social supports) are of increasing interest (Clark, 1982; Crandall and Tobin, 1974; Earle et al, 1976; Oalighill, 1976; Schoenberg et al, 1972; Stoddard, 1978).

Conclusion

This chapter began with a section on aging and the individual and attempted to show that a multi-functional medical and psychosocial health model for the diagnostic assessment, treatment and rehabilitation of chronically ill and/or disabled older patients, based upon a life span strategy, is an essential requirement for the development of optimal methods of clinical, social, and psychological care. Whole-patient care as well as continuity in long-term care was emphasized. In the final section, some major concerns in the provision of care for the chronically ill and/or disabled older person were summarized. These concerns were (1) alternatives in long-term care; (2) medical and non-medical aspects in the treatment and rehabilitation process of the chronic mentally ill patient; and (3) that of the terminally ill patient.

REFERENCES

Anderson J E 1957 Dynamics of development: systems in process. In: Harris D B (ed) The Concept of Development. University of Minnesota Press, Minneapolis, p 25–46
Anderson F 1976 Practical Management of the Elderly. 3rd edn.

Blackwell Scientific Publications, Oxford
Atchley R C 1980 The Social Forces in Later Life: An Introduction to Social Gerontology. 3rd edn. Wadsworth Publishing Company, Inc., Belmont, California

Barnes J 1974 Effects of reality orientation classroom on memory loss, confusion and disorientation in geriatric patients. Gerontologist 14: 138–144

Beard O W 1981 The veterans administration hospitals and resources for geriatric education — the experience at the University of Arkansas. In: Steel K (ed) Geriatric education, p 49–51. The Collamore Press, Lexington, Massachusetts

Begala J A 1980 Geriatric education in Ohio: A model for change. Gerontologist 20: 547–551

Bengtson V L 1973 The Social Psychology of Aging. The Bobbs-Merrill Company Inc, New York

Bengtson V L, Cutler N E 1976 Generations and intergenerational relations: perspectives on age groups and social change. In: Binstock R N, Shanas E (ed) Handbook of Aging and the Social Sciences, p 130–159. Van Nostrand Reinhold Company, New York

Bengtson V L, Dowd J J, Inkeles A 1975 Modernization, modernity, and perceptions of aging: a cross-cultural study. Journal of Gerontology 30: 688–695

Bennett R, Eisdorfer C 1975 The institutional environment and behavior change. In: Sherwood S (ed) Long-term Care: A Handbook for Researchers, Planners and Providers, p 391–453. Spectrum Publications Inc, New York

Besdine R W 1979 Observations on geriatric medicine. U.S. Department of Health, Education and Welfare, Public Health Service, National Institutes of Health

Bigot A 1971 Patterns of aging: A pilot study, final research and summary report. Social Science Research Council, London

Bigot A 1974 Medical, social, and psychological aspects of stroke in elderly patients. Progress Report No 1. Manchester: Department of Geriatric Medicine, University Hospital of South Manchester

Bigot A 1982 Gerontological issues: Long term and terminal illness in old age. Paper presented at the Dayton Chapter of the Association for Women in Science, The University of Dayton, November, Dayton, Ohio

Binstock R N, Shanas E 1976 Handbook of Aging and the Social Sciences. Van Nostrand Reinhold Company, New York

Birren J E 1964 The Psychology of Aging. Prentice-Hall, Englewood Cliffs, New Jersey

Birren J E, Schaie K W 1976 Handbook of the Psychology of Aging. Van Nostrand Reinhold Company, New York

Bloom M 1964 Life-span analysis: a theoretical framework for behavioral science research. Human Relations 12: 538–554

Bok M 1971 Some problems in milieu treatment of the chronic older mental patient. Gerontologist 2: 141–147

Brocklehurst J C, Hanley T 1976 Geriatric Medicine for Students. Churchill Livingstone, Edinburgh

Brody E M 1977 Long-term Care of Older People: A Practical Guide, p 14. Human Sciences Press, New York

Bromley D B 1974 The Psychology of Human Aging. 2nd edn. Penguin Books, Middlesex, England

Brudno J J, Seltzer H 1968 Re-socialization therapy through group process with senile patients in a geriatric hospital. Gerontologist 8: 211–214

Buhler C, Massarik F 1968 The Course of Human Life. Springer, New York

Busse E W, Pfeiffer E 1973 Mental Illness in Later Life. American Psychiatric Association, Washington, D.C.

Busse E W, Pfeiffer E 1977 Behavior and Adaptation in Late Life. 2nd edn. Little, Brown and Company, Boston

Butler R N 1976 Medicine and aging: An assessment of opportunities and neglect. Testimony before the U.S. Senate Special Committee on Aging, October 13

Calkins E 1981 Role of veterans administration hospitals as bases for academic units in geriatric medicine — A historical perspective. Steel K (ed), Geriatric education, p 53–58. The Collamore Press, Lexington, Massachusetts

Clark M D 1982 Hospice of Columbus, Ohio: An alternative way of caring for the dying. Ohio's Health 34: 32–35

Clark M, Anderson B G 1967 Culture and Aging: An Anthropological Study of Older Americans. C C Thomas, Springfield, Illinois

Cohen S 1979 Mental impairment in the aged: Fable and Fact, p 14. American Psychiatric Association, 132nd Annual Meeting, Chicago, Illinois

Commission on Chronic Illness 1957 Chronic illness in the United States, vol 4. Chronic illness in a large city: The Baltimore Study. Harvard University Press, Cambridge, Mass

Cosin L Z 1973 Rehabilitation of the older patient. World Hospitals, ix 4: 199–202

Crandall W, Tobin S 1974 Facilitating a satisfactory death. Paper presented at 27th Annual Gerontological Society Meeting, October, Portland, Oregon

Dans P E, Kerr M R 1979 Gerontology and geriatrics in medical education. New England Journal of Medicine 300: 228

Dube W F, Mather J H 1981 Health professions education in geriatrics and gerontology: In the VA and Other Federal Agencies. Health Values: Achieving High Level Wellness 5: 1

Earle A, Argondizzo N, Kutscher A H, Goldberg I K 1976 The Role of the Nurse in the Care of the Dying Patients and Bereaved. Columbia University Press

Eisdorfer C, Cohen D 1978 In: Storandt M, Siegler I C, Elias M F (eds.) The Clinical Psychology of Aging, p 7–42. Plenum Publishing Corporation, New York

Eisdorfer C, Lawton M P 1973 Recommendations to the White House Conference on Aging, APA Task Force on Aging. In: Eisdorfer C, Lawton M P (ed) The psychology of adult development and aging ix. American Psychological Association, Washington, D.C.

Federal Council of Aging, U.S. Department of Health and Human Services 1981 The need for long-term care: Information and issues. DHHS Pub. No. (OHDS) 81-20704. U.S. Govt. Printing Office, Washington, D.C.

Finch C E, Hayflick L 1976 Handbook of the Biology of Aging. Van Nostrand Reinhold Company, New York

Fries J F, Crapo L M 1981 Vitality and Aging. W H Freeman and Company, San Francisco, Ca.

Gaitz C M, Varner R V, Calvert W, Linden M E 1977 Realistic expectations and treatment goals in caring for the impaired elderly. American Medical Association, 126th Annual Convention, San Francisco, June 18–22

Gendlin E, Rychlak S 1970 Psychotherapeutic processes. Ann. Rev. Psychol.: 21

George L K 1980 Role Transitions in Later Life. Brooks/Cole Publishing Company, Monterey, Ca.

Gerson E M, Strauss A L 1975 Time for living: problems in chronic illness care. Social Policy, November/December, 12–18

Glaser B G, Strauss A C 1965 Awareness of Dying. Aldine Publishing Co., Chicago

Gottesman L E, Bourestom N, Donahue W, Coons D 1971 The technology of milieu treatment of the aged mental patient. Institute of Gerontology, Ann Arbor, Michigan

Gottesman L E, Quarterman C E, Cohn G M 1973 Psychosocial treatment of the aged. In: Eisdorfer C, Lawton M P (eds) The Psychology of Adult Development and Aging. American Psychological Association, Washington, D.C.

Goulet L R, Baltes P B 1970 Life-span Developmental Psychology. Academic Press, New York

Hammerman J 1974 The role of the institution and the concept of parallel services. Gerontologist 14: 11–14

Hammerman J, Friedsam H H, Shore H 1975 Management perspectives in long-term-care facilities. In: Sherwood S (ed), Long-term Care: A Handbook for Researchers, Planners and Providers, p 179–212. Spectrum Publications, Inc, New York

Hendricks J, Hendricks C D 1981 Aging in Mass Society: Myths and Realities. Winthrop Publishers, Inc, Cambridge, Massachusetts

Heyman D H, Gianturco D T 1973 Long-term adaptation by the elderly to bereavement. Journal of Gerontology 28: 359–363

Hickey 1980 Health and Aging. Brooks/Cole Publishing Company, Monterey, Ca.

Hickey T, Hultsch D F, Fatula B J, Rakowski W 1975 Age effects in practitioner training for attitude change. Paper presented at 28th Annual Meeting of the Gerontological Society, October, Louisville, Kentucky

Hudson J I, Norse E S 1975 Perspectives in primary care education. Journal of Medical Education 50, No 12, December, Part 2

Hurlock E B 1968 Developmental Psychology. McGraw-Hill, New York

Institute of Medicine, National Academy of Sciences 1977 A policy statement: The elderly and functional dependency, Washington, D.C.

Institute of Medicine, National Academy of Sciences 1978 Aging and medical education, Washington, D.C.

Isaacs B, Livingstone M, Neville Y 1972 Survival of the Unfittest. Routledge & Kegan Paul, London

Kahana E 1973 The humane treatment of old people in institutions. Gerontologist 13: 282–289

Kastenbaum R, Aisenberg R 1972 The Psychology of Death. Springer Publishing Company, New York

Katz S, Ford A B, Moskowitz R W, Jackson B A, Jaffe M W 1963 Studies of illness in the aged: The index of ADL — A standardized measure of biological and psychosocial function. Journal of American Medical Association 185: 914–919

Katz S, Downs T D, Cask H R, Gratz R C 1970 Progress in development of the indicator of ADL. Gerontologist 10 (1, Part 1): 20–30

Katz S, Ford A B, Downs T D, Adams M, Rusby D 1972 Effects of continued care: A study of chronic illness in the home. DHHS, National Center for Health Services Research and Development, Publication No. (HSM) 73-3010

Kosberg J I 1973 Nursing homes: a social work paradox. Social Work 18, 2: 104–110

Kosberg J I, Cohen S Z, Mendlowitz A 1972 Comparison of supervisors' attitudes in a home for the aged. Gerontologist 12: 241–245

Krasner L 1971 Behavior therapy. Annual Review of Psychology 22: 483–532

Kubler-Ross E 1970 On Death and Dying, p 28, 34–121. Tavistock Publications, London

Laufer R, Bengtson V L 1974 Generations, aging, and social stratification: on the development of generational units. Journal of Social Issues 30: 181–205

Lawton M P 1980 Environment and Aging. Brooks/Cole Publishing Company, Monterey, Ca.

Lazarus R S 1978 The stress and coping paradigm. Paper presented at a conference entitled 'The critical evaluation of behavioral paradigms for psychiatric science'. Gleneden Beach, Oregon, November

Letcher P, Peterson L, Scarborough D 1974 Reality orientation: a historical study of patient progress. Journal of Hospital and Community Psychiatry 25: 801–803

Libow L S 1980 Physician manpower needs in care of the elderly in the next 25 years: future needs in geriatric medicine. In: Future directions for aging policy: A human service model, p 136–140. Select Committee on Aging: U.S. House of Representatives, Community Publications No 96-226, U.S. Govt. Printing Office, Washington, D.C.

Libow L S 1976 A geriatric medical residency program: A four year experience. Annals of Internal Medicine 85: 641–647

Libow L S, Sherman F T 1981 The Core of Geriatric Medicine: A Guide for Students and Practitioners. The C V Mosby Company, St. Louis, Missouri

Liederman P, Green R, Liederman V 1967 Outpatient group therapy with geriatric patients. Geriatrics 22: 148–153

Linden M 1953 Group psychotherapy with institutionalized senile women: Study in gerontologic human relations. International Journal of Group Psychotherapy 3: 150–170

Liss L, McPherson-Turner C 1980 Interdisciplinary health care for the aged: A curriculum development project. Progress report from The Ohio State University College of Medicine to the U.S. Department of Health, Education, and Welfare, Public Health Service, Health Resources Administration

Marion R 1979 Group effectiveness scale. Strategies for evaluation, monograph No 2, Center for Interdisciplinary Education in Allied Health, College of Allied Health Professions, University of Kentucky, Lexington

Marion R 1980 Team interaction analysis. Strategies for evaluation, monograph No 5, Center for Interdisciplinary Education in Allied Health, College of Allied Health Professions, University of Kentucky, Lexington

Marion R 1981 Tests of health professions skills. Strategies for evaluation, monograph No 6, Center for Interdisciplinary Education in Allied Health, College of Allied Health Professions, University of Kentucky, Lexington

Mather J H, Dube W F 1981 Veterans administration's development of health professions education programs in geriatrics and

gerontology. In: Somers A R, Fabian D R (eds) The Geriatric Imperative: an Introduction to gerontology and Clinical Geriatrics, p 329–335. Appleton-Century-Crofts, New York

McCally E, Sorem M K, Silverman M 1977 Interprofessional education of new health practitioners. Journal of Medical Education 52: 177–182

McFarland R A 1973 The need for functional age measurements in industrial gerontology. Journal of Industrial Gerontology 1–19

Mechanic D 1974 Social structure and personal adaptation: some neglected dimensions. In: Coelho G V, Hamburg D A, Adams J E (eds) Coping and Adaptation. Basic Books, New York

Moos R H 1976 Human Adaptation: Coping with Life Crises. D C Heath and Company, Lexington, Massachusetts

Munnichs J M A 1966 Old age and finitude. S Kargen, Basel, Switzerland

Nagi S Z 1976 An epidemiology of disability among adults in the United States. Milbank Memorial Fund Quarterly 54 (4), Fall

Nathanson B F, Reingold J 1969 A workshop for mentally impaired aged. Gerontologist 9: 293–295

National Institutes of Health, U.S. Department of Health and Human Services, Public Health Service 1981 Progress report on geriatric medicine. U.S. Govt. Printing Office, Publication No. 81-2307, Washington, D.C.

Neugarten B L, Hagestad G O 1976 Age and the life course. In: Binstock R H, Shanas E (eds) Handbook of Aging and the Social Sciences, p 35–55. Van Nostrand Reinhold Company, New York

Oaughill R E 1976 The Dying Patient: A Supportive Approach. Little, Brown and Company, Boston

Parkes C 1872 Bereavement. International University Press, London

Paul G L 1969 Chronic mental patient: current status, future directions. Psychiatric Bulletin 71: 81–94

Pearlin L I, Schooler C 1978 The structure of coping. Journal of Health and Social Behavior 19: 2–21

Pfeiffer E 1973 Introduction to the conference report. In: Pfeiffer E, Durham N C (ed) Alternatives to Institutional Care for Older Americans: Practice and Planning — conference report, Duke University Center for the Study of Aging and Human Development

Pijnenborg Fr J B 1970 Sensory training in the USA. Ned. Tijdschrift voor Geron 1: 68–70

Poon L W 1980 Aging in the 1980s. American Psychological Association, Washington, D.C.

Portnoi V A 1979 A health-care system for the elderly. New England Journal of Medicine 300: 1387–1390

Pressey S L, Kuhlen R G 1957 Psychological Development through the life Span. Harper and Row, New York

Rapoport M, Cahn B 1981 The geriatric AHEC at the University of Maryland: A model for geriatric education. In: Steel K (ed) Geriatric Education, p 201–207. The Collamore Press, Lexington, Massachusetts

Rechtschaffen A 1959 Psychotherapy with geriatric patients: A review of the literature. Gerontology 14: 73–84

Rechtschaffen A, Atkinson S, Freedman J G 1958 An intensive treatment program for state hospital geriatric patients. Geriatrics 9: 28–34

Rossman I 1971, 2nd edn. 1979 Clinical Geriatrics. Lippincott, Philadelphia

Rubin K H, Brown I D R 1975 A life-span look at person perception and its relationship to communicative interaction. Journal of Gerontology 30: 461–468

Saul S R, Saul S 1974 Group psychotherapy in a proprietary nursing home. Gerontologist 14: 446–450

Saunders C 1972 A therapeutic community: St. Christopher's Hospice. Psychosocial Aspects of Terminal Care, 3–15, Columbia University Press

Schaie K W 1977 Functional age and retirement. In U Lehr (Chair), Social and biological aspects of retirement age. Symposium presented at the 4th Biennial Congress of the International Society for the Study of Behavioral Development, Pavio, Italy, September 21

Schoenberg B, Carr A C, Peretz D, Kutscher A H 1972 Psychological Aspects of Terminal Care. Columbia University Press

Schoenberg B, Carr A C, Peretz D, Kutscher A H, Goldberg K 1974 Anticipatory Grief. Columbia University Press

Schoenberg B, Gerber I, Wiener A, Kutscher A H, Peretz D, Carr

A C 1975 Bereavement: Its Psychosocial Aspects. Columbia University Press

Seligman M 1975 Helplessness on Depression, Development, and Death. W H Freeman, San Francisco

Seligman M 1976 Learned helplessness and depression in animals and men. In: Spence J T (ed) Behavioral Approaches to Therapy. General Learning Press, Morristown, New York

Seltzer M, Atchley R C 1971 The concept of old: changing attitudes and stereotypes. Gerontologist 15: 226–230

Shanas E 1971 Measuring the home health needs of the aged in five countries. Journal of Gerontology 26: 37–40

Sherwood S 1975 Long-term Care: A handbook for Researchers, Planners and Providers. Spectrum Publications, Inc, New York

Smyer M A, Gatz M 1978 Aging and mental health: Business as usual? Paper presented at the 31st Annual Meeting of the Gerontological Society, Dallas, Texas, November

Social Security Administration, U.S. Department of Health and Human Services 1980 Income and resources of the aged. SSA Pub. No 13 — 11727, U.S. Govt Printing Office, Washington, D.C.

Solon R 1974 The evaluation of a service delivery system. Paper presented at the 27th Annual Meeting of the Gerontological Society, Portland, Oregon, October

Somers A R, Fabian D R 1981 The Geriatric Imperative: An Introduction to Gerontology and Clinical Geriatrics. Appleton-Century-Crofts, New York

Thomas E C, Yamamoto K 1975 Attitudes toward age: an exploration in school-age children. International Journal of Aging and Human Development 6: 117–129

Thorson J A 1975 Attitudes toward the aged as a function of race and social class. Gerontologist 15: 343–344

Thorson J A, Whatley L, Hancock K 1974 Attitudes toward the aged as a function of age and education. Gerontologist 14: 316–318

Toepfer C T, Bicknell A T, Shaw D O 1974 Remotivation as behavior therapy. Gerontologist 14: 451–453

Troll L E, Schossberg N 1970 A preliminary investigation of 'age bias' in the helping professions. Paper presented at 23rd Annual Meeting of the Gerontological Society, Toronto, Ontario, October

U.S. Department of Health and Human Services, Health Care Financing Administration 1981 Long term care: Background and future directions. HCFA 81-20047, U.S. Govt Printing Office, Washington, D.C.

U.S. Department of Housing and Urban Development 1979 How well are we housed? The elderly. U.S. Govt Printing Office, Washington, D.C.

Vicker R L 1974 Factors among nursing home personnel which relate to their attitudes toward aging, with implications for in-service training programs. Paper presented at 27th Annual Meeting of the Gerontological Society, Portland, Oregon, October

Weinberger L E, Millham J 1975 Multidimensional, multiple method analysis of attitudes toward the elderly. Journal of Gerontology 30: 343–348

Weisman A 1972 On dying and denying. Behavioral Publications

Wessen A F 1961 Some sociological characteristics of long-term care, symposium on research in long-term care, St. Louis, Missouri, Gerontologist 4: 7–14

White R W 1974 Strategies of adaptation: An attempt as systematic description. In: Coelho G V, Hamburg D A, Adams J E (eds.) Coping and Adaptation. Basic Books, New York

White House Conference on Aging 1981 Report of the technical committee on social and health aspects of long-term care. U.S. Govt Printing Office, Washington, D.C.

White House Conference on Aging 1981 Report of the mini-conference on long-term care. U.S. Govt Printing Office, Washington, D.C.

Williamson J 1979 Geriatric medicine: Whose speciality? Annals of Internal Medicine 91: 774

Wohlwill J F 1970 Methodology and research strategy in the study of developmental change. In: Goulet L R, Baltes P B (ed) Life-span Developmental Psychology, p 149–191. Academic Press, New York

Wolk R L, Wolk R B 1971 Professional workers' attitudes toward the aged. Journal of the American Geriatrics Society 19: 624–639

Zinker J C 1966 Rosa Lee, motivation and the crisis of dying, p 5–21. Lake Erie College Studies, Painsville, Ohio

Index

(Note: Entries in *italics* indicate illustrations or tables; those in **bold** indicate main treatment of a subject)